O'CONNOR'S
CRIMINAL CODES PLUS

AUTHOR
GEORGE MCCALL SECREST, JR.

JONES MCCLURE PUBLISHING
HOUSTON, TEXAS

O'CONNOR'S ANNOTATED CODES SERIES

Suggested cite form: *O'Connor's Criminal Codes Plus* (2008-09)

Jones McClure Publishing
Product List

To order: Call 1-800-OCONNOR or visit www.JonesMcClure.com

Texas Litigation Series
O'Connor's Texas Rules ★ Civil Trials
O'Connor's Texas Civil Forms (with CD)
O'Connor's Texas Civil Appeals (with CD)

Texas Expert Series
O'Connor's Texas Causes of Action
O'Connor's Texas Causes of Action Pleadings (with CD)
Texas Rules of Evidence Handbook
O'Connor's Texas Family Law Handbook

Texas Annotated Codes Series
O'Connor's Civil Practice & Remedies Code Plus
O'Connor's Family Code Plus
O'Connor's Probate Code Plus
O'Connor's Criminal Codes Plus
O'Connor's Texas Crimes & Consequences
O'Connor's Texas Employment Codes Plus
O'Connor's Business & Commerce Code Plus
O'Connor's Business Organizations Code Plus
O'Connor's Property Code Plus

Federal Litigation Series
O'Connor's Federal Rules ★ Civil Trials
O'Connor's Federal Civil Forms (with CD)

Federal Annotated Codes Series
O'Connor's Federal Employment Codes Plus
O'Connor's Federal Intellectual Property Codes Plus

JONES McCLURE
PUBLISHING

Mailing address:
P.O. Box 3348
Houston, TX 77253-3348

Shipping address:
2160 Taylor St.
Houston, TX 77007

Phone: (713) 335-8200
(800) OCONNOR (626-6667)
Fax: (713) 335-8201

www.JonesMcClure.com

This book is intended to provide attorneys with current information about selected Texas codes, rules, and statutes. The information in this book, however, may not be sufficient in dealing with a client's particular legal problem, and Jones McClure Publishing, Michol O'Connor, and George McCall Secrest, Jr., do not warrant or represent its suitability for this purpose. Attorneys using this book do so with the understanding that the information published in it should not be relied on as a substitute for independent research using original sources of authority.

Subscription Notice: By ordering this book, you are enrolled in our subscription program, which entitles you to a lower annual price. Before we send you an updated book, we send you a letter and reply card confirming that you want the new edition. You have the option at that time to change or cancel your order. If you do not change or cancel your order, the book will be shipped to you. If you decide to return the book, the return postage is your responsibility. You can change your subscription status at any time in writing. If you want to order a product but do not wish to enroll in the subscription program, please call 1-800-OCONNOR for pricing details.

CONVENTIONS & LEGISLATIVE CONFLICTS

The Legislature met in 2007 and made a number of changes important to Texas attorneys. In this book, the 2007 legislative changes are marked with Ⓐ, Ⓔ, or Ⓒ, depending on whether the section was amended, enacted, or codified. Former sections that remain in effect before the effective dates of the amendments are shaded in gray. Rule changes that have been made in 2008 are marked with ⑧.

Occasionally, the Legislature enacts multiple code sections with the same number. The identically numbered sections are marked with ⚍ and accompanied by an editor's note describing the duplicate numbering. Each section is also labeled with a bracketed letter (e.g., [A*]) to help distinguish it.

Likewise, when the Legislature passes a bill that amends a section or subsection without reference to another bill's conflicting amendment to the same section or subsection, both versions of the section or subsection are presented. Each version is marked with ⚍ and is accompanied by an editor's note describing the conflict.

When multiple amendments to the same section or subsection are enacted during the same legislative session, the amendments should be harmonized unless they are irreconcilable. Tex. Gov't Code §311.025(b); *Burke v. Union Pac. Res.*, 138 S.W.3d 46, 75 (Tex.App.—Texarkana 2004, pet. denied). Conflicting amendments are irreconcilable only if both provisions cannot be complied with at the same time. *State v. Jackson*, 370 S.W.2d 797, 800 (Tex. App.—Houston [1st Dist.] 1963), *aff'd*, 376 S.W.2d 341 (Tex.1964). In that circumstance, the amendment enacted last will prevail. Tex. Gov't Code §311.025(b). For this reason, the editor's note accompanying each conflict includes the date each bill was enacted, which in most cases is the date of the last vote on the bill (not the bill's effective date). *See* Tex. Gov't Code §311.025(d), (e).

To determine whether conflicting statutory provisions can be harmonized, you should review the text carefully and consult the Code Construction Act (Government Code ch. 311), the canons of statutory construction, and the legislative history for those provisions. Legislative history for recent bills can be found on the Texas Legislature Online (TLO) website at www.capitol.state.tx.us. To find a bill analysis on TLO, select the correct legislative session in the drop-down box under "Search Legislation," enter the bill number (e.g., HB 387) in the box below that, select "Go," click on the "Text" tab, and then select the latest document under the "Bill Analysis" column. Other legislative history, such as passed and rejected amendments, floor journals, fiscal notes, and audio or video recordings of hearings, can also be found on the TLO website.

Because some conflicting versions of sections and subsections persist beyond the following legislative session, editor's notes may contain references to session laws (e.g., Acts 2003, 78th Leg., ch. 213 ...) rather than bill numbers. To find a bill number from past session laws, use the "Bill-chapter cross reference" function on the Legislative Reference Library website at www.lrl.state.tx.us.

2007 LEGISLATIVE SUMMARY

The Legislature made a number of significant changes to the Code of Criminal Procedure, Penal Code, and other codes affecting criminal law. The important 2007 amendments and enactments include the following:

Jessica's Law

Jessica's Law, H.B. 8, is the most significant piece of criminal-law legislation passed by the 80th Legislature. Jessica's Law creates tougher penalties for sexual predators who target children and affects many criminal-law statutes. For example, Penal Code §21.02 was enacted to impose a 25-year minimum sentence for defendants who commit sexually violent offenses against children under 14. Government Code §508.145 was amended to eliminate parole eligibility for certain sex offenders. Penal Code §12.42 was amended and CCP art. 37.072 was enacted to make a second conviction of a sexually violent offense against a child under 14 a capital felony. CCP art. 12.01 was amended to extend the statute of limitations for sexually violent offenses against children under 14.

Concealed-Handgun Licenses

Disarming licensed holders. Government Code §411.207 was amended to authorize peace officers to temporarily disarm a licensed holder of a concealed handgun who enters a nonpublic, secure portion of a law-enforcement facility if the facility has gun lockers to secure handguns.

Judges & attorneys. Government Code §411.179 was amended to direct the Department of Public Safety to indicate on a concealed-handgun license issued to a judge, justice, district attorney, criminal district attorney, or county attorney the title held by that individual. Penal Code §46.15 was amended to increase the number of places these individuals are permitted to carry a concealed weapon. Government Code §411.1882 was enacted to exempt these individuals from handgun-proficiency requirements.

Controlled Substances

Child present during manufacture. H&SC §481.1122 was enacted to increase the penalty for manufacturing a Schedule I drug if a child is present.

Prescription abuse. To prevent substance abusers from using several different prescriptions to obtain drugs, H&SC §§481.074 and 481.076 were amended to extend monitoring of prescriptions to Schedule III through V drugs. H&SC chapter 481, subchapter H, was amended to establish administrative penalties for noncompliance with prescription monitoring.

Summary forfeiture & destruction. H&SC §§481.152 and 481.153 were amended to provide that controlled-substance property or plants seized as evidence may be destroyed without a court order after analysis.

Criminal Procedure

Appeals by State. CCP art. 44.01 was amended to give prosecutors 30 days (instead of 15) to appeal an order, ruling, or sentence in a criminal case.

Attorney fees in indigent defense. CCP arts. 26.05 and 26.051 were amended to encourage prompt rulings on fee vouchers issued to an attorney representing an indigent defendant and to allow an attorney to appeal a decision reducing or denying a requested fee. An attorney can now appeal a judge's refusal to act if the judge does not respond to requests for payment for more than 60 days.

Attorney General jurisdiction. Penal Code §§1.09 and 39.015 were enacted to authorize the Attorney General to seek concurrent jurisdiction with the consent of the local prosecutor in cases involving the use, unlawful appropriation, or misapplication of state property, cases in which an element of the offense occurred on state property, and cases dealing with abuse of office.

Capias pro fine. Several CCP articles, including arts. 15.18, 17.19, 23.01, and 43.015, were amended to authorize district courts and county courts to issue a capias pro fine, which is a writ ordering the arrest of a criminal defendant who has failed to pay court-ordered fines or fees. The amendments clarified the differences among the capias issued before trial, the capias relating to the execution of judgment, the capias pro fine currently provided for under CCP chapter 45, and the arrest warrant issued by a magistrate.

Community supervision. CCP arts. 42.03, §15 and 42.12, §23 were amended to require that a defendant receive credit on the defendant's sentence for time spent in a substance-abuse treatment facility as a condition of regular or deferred-adjudication community supervision if the defendant successfully completes the treatment program. • CCP art. 42.12, §3 was amended to provide that in a felony case, the minimum period of community supervision is the same as the minimum term of imprisonment for the offense. The maximum period of community supervision is also specified in §3, subject to the extensions provided by CCP art. 42.12, §22. • CCP art. 42.12, §3g was amended to provide that a defendant cannot be placed on judge-ordered community supervision if the defendant is found guilty of injury to a child and the offense is punishable as a first-degree felony. • CCP art. 42.12, §4 was amended to provide that a defendant found guilty of murder is not eligible for jury-recommended community supervision. • CCP art. 42.12, §5 was amended to add "driving while intoxicated with a child passenger" and "assembling or operating an amusement ride while intoxicated" to the list of offenses for which a judge cannot order deferred adjudication. • CCP art. 42.12, §15 was amended to require a judge sentencing a defendant for certain drug-related state-jail felonies whose penalties have been reduced to a Class A misdemeanor to suspend the sentence and place the offender on community supervision. • CCP art. 42.12, §16 was amended to provide that community service as a requirement of community supervision is permissive rather than mandatory. • CCP art. 42.12, §20 was amended to require the judge to review a defendant's record and consider whether to reduce or terminate the period of community supervision after the defendant completes half of the original community-supervision period or two years of community supervision, whichever is more. Community supervision cannot be reduced or terminated if the defendant is delinquent in paying required restitution, fines, costs, or fees that the defendant has the ability to pay or if the defendant has not completed court-ordered counseling or treatment. • CCP art. 42.12, §21 was amended to provide that during a community-supervision-revocation hearing, the State must prove by a preponderance of the evidence that the defendant was able to pay restitution, fees, or costs but did not pay as ordered by the judge. • CCP art. 42.12, §22 was amended to require a showing of good cause to extend a period of community supervision.

Execution of defendant. CCP art. 46.05 was amended to allow an inmate to appeal a court's ruling that the defendant is competent to be executed. The article was also amended to allow a court to grant a stay of execution at its discretion.

Expunction. CCP art. 55.02 was amended to require that each official, agency, or nongovernmental entity named in an expunction petition or order be given reasonable notice of the hearing or order. The requirement that the petitioner request the notice in writing in order for it to be sent by a secure e-mail or fax transmission has been eliminated.

Family violence. CCP chapter 56, subchapter C, and chapter 57B were added to protect the identity of victims of family violence, sexual assault, and stalking by providing them with a confidential mailing address.

Forensic testing. CCP arts. 11.07, 64.02, and 64.03 were amended to authorize judges to order postconviction forensic testing and to specify who will pay for a forensic test.

Jurors. CCP arts. 33.011 and 36.29 were amended to delay the discharge of alternate jurors until the jury renders a verdict.

Protective orders. CCP arts. 7A.01 and 7A.03 were amended and 7A.07 was enacted to allow a victim of sexual assault or aggravated sexual assault to obtain a lifetime protective order against the offender. • CCP art. 17.292 was amended to authorize a magistrate to issue an order for emergency protection against a defendant accused of sexual assault.

Search warrants. CCP art. 18.01 was amended to allow non-law-licensed magistrates to issue evidentiary search warrants. • CCP art. 18.011 was amended to authorize a district or appellate court to seal an affidavit for a specified time period when there is a compelling state interest. • CCP arts. 18.20 and 18.21 were amended to expedite the process to apply for an electronic-eavesdropping warrant by giving local law enforcement in cities with populations of 500,000 or more the ability to operate a pen register, an ESN reader, or similar equipment, and by expanding the list of persons able to file an application for their installation and use.

Waiver of right to counsel. CCP art. 1.051 was amended to clarify the circumstances in which a court can obtain a waiver of the right to counsel and to clarify when an attorney representing the State can communicate with a defendant who is not represented by counsel.

Witnesses. CCP arts. 56.11 and 56.12 were amended to allow witnesses to be added to the victim-notification-release program.

INTRODUCTION

Offenses

Aircraft. Penal Code §42.14 was added to make it an offense to illuminate an aircraft with an intense light.

Animal cruelty. Penal Code §42.09 was amended to apply to livestock animals and §42.092 was enacted to apply to nonlivestock animals. These sections seek to address violent acts toward animals while preserving longstanding protections against prosecution for persons who fear bodily injury from a dangerous wild animal or who engage in bona fide scientific experimentation, hunting, fishing, trapping, regulated wildlife control, farming, animal husbandry, and certain acts against animals caught in the act of injuring or killing livestock.

Assault. Penal Code §22.01 was amended to make it a third-degree felony to assault emergency-services personnel.

Children. Penal Code §22.041 was amended to make it an offense to possess methamphetamine or introduce methamphetamine into the body of any person in the presence of a child or to engage in any conduct that would cause methamphetamine to be near or accessible to a child. • Penal Code §25.03 was amended to make it an offense to violate a temporary child-custody order. • Penal Code §33.021 was amended to add the use of text messages or other electronic-message services to the list of ways in which online solicitation of a minor may be committed.

Habitual sex offender. Penal Code §12.42 was amended to eliminate any chronological prerequisite for previous offenses so that any two offenses in any order, including offenses committed simultaneously, will qualify the offender for the habitual-sex-offender penalty.

Identifying information. Penal Code §32.51 was amended to make it an offense if a person, with the intent to harm or defraud another, obtains, possesses, transfers, or uses information about a deceased person that would be identifying information if the person were alive.

Improper photography. Penal Code §21.15 was amended to make it an offense to broadcast or transmit the visual image of another person without that person's consent for the purpose of sexual arousal or gratification of the sexual desire of any person.

Intoxication offenses. Penal Code §§49.07, 49.08, and 49.09 were amended to increase the penalty for an intoxication assault from a third-degree felony to a second-degree felony. The amendments increase the penalty for intoxication manslaughter of a peace officer, a firefighter, or emergency-medical-services personnel from a second-degree felony to a first-degree felony.

Metals. Penal Code §28.03 was amended to make any act of criminal mischief on transportation communications equipment or devices composed of copper, aluminum, or bronze, with a pecuniary loss of less than $100,000, a third-degree felony. • Penal Code §31.03 was amended to make the theft of wiring or cable that consists of at least 50 percent aluminum, bronze, or copper and has a value of less than $20,000 a state-jail felony.

Retail theft. Penal Code §31.16 was enacted to crack down on organized criminal activity that involves many thieves organized by a central "fence" who collects the stolen merchandise and then resells it to the general public.

Self-defense & deadly force. Penal Code §§9.31 and 9.32 were amended to state explicitly that a person has no duty to retreat if the person is attacked in a place where the person has a right to be present, the person has not provoked the attacker, and the person using force is not engaged in criminal activity at the time the force is used.

Tampering with evidence. Penal Code §37.09 was amended to make the crime of altering, destroying, or concealing physical evidence a second-degree felony if the evidence is a human corpse.

Weapons. Penal Code §46.02 was amended to clarify that a person has a right to carry a handgun, a club, or certain knives on the person's own premises or premises under the person's control, or inside of or en route to a motor vehicle under the person's control.

INTRODUCTION

ABOUT THE AUTHOR

George McCall Secrest, Jr., was admitted to the State Bar of Texas in 1977. "Mac" received his Juris Doctorate with distinction from St. Mary's University School of Law in 1977, and was a briefing attorney for the Honorable Wendell Odom of the Texas Court of Criminal Appeals from 1977 to 1978. He served as an Assistant District Attorney for Harris County from 1978 to 1981 in both the trial and appellate bureaus. In 1981, he was appointed as an Assistant Federal Public Defender for the Southern District of Texas and served in that capacity for two years. He has been in the private practice of law since 1984.

He is a member of the U.S. District Courts for the Southern, Northern, Eastern, and Western Districts of Texas; the U.S. Courts of Appeals for the Fifth, Sixth, and Eleventh Circuits; and the U.S. Supreme Court. He has been board-certified in criminal law by the Texas Board of Legal Specialization since 1982 and has served the Board as an examination commissioner, assisting in the drafting of questions for the certification exam in criminal law.

Mac is an adjunct professor of law, teaching Texas criminal procedure at the University of Houston Law Center; he has also taught criminal-trial advocacy, appellate advocacy, and criminal procedure. He has authored numerous articles on criminal procedure, including "Jury Selection and Criminal Law" and "Texas Criminal Jury Practice," published in *Texas Practice Guide* (2d ed. 1983) and "Criminal Law Survey" in 26 Tex. Tech L.Rev. 517 (1995).

Mac was selected as a member of the Ad Hoc Committee to Revise the Texas Code of Criminal Procedure for the Office of the Governor from 1995 to 1996. He was honored by the Criminal Justice Section of the State Bar of Texas as the 1998 Criminal Defense Lawyer of the Year and was selected 2007 Lawyer of the Year by the Harris County Criminal Lawyers Association. He has also been listed in *Best Lawyers in America* from 1997 to 2007. Mac is a partner at the law firm of Bennett & Secrest, L.L.P.

SPECIAL THANKS

The author would like to dedicate this edition to Dianna Greer—my new mom and boss who keeps me on the straight and narrow (or at least tries to), and the dearest of friends.

ACKNOWLEDGMENT

We thank Lexis Law Publishing for allowing us to use the information for the charts on penalties, felony and misdemeanor punishment ranges, and enhancement.

CURRENCY

The statutes in this book are current through the 80th Legislature, Regular Session (2007).

CAVEAT

This book provides citations to important opinions that interpret the Code of Criminal Procedure, Penal Code, and related statutes, as well as charts that summarize information from the codes, statutes, and cases. You may disagree with the choice of cases for the various statutes or with the summarized information in the charts. You should therefore use this book only as a research guide. Read the codes, statutes, and cases yourself and make your own evaluation of them.

YOUR SUGGESTIONS

We welcome your comments. If you think we should have included (or excluded) something, or if you see anything that needs to be corrected, please let us know. Send your comments to the mailing address or fax number shown on the copyright page, or by e-mail to Carlos Goenaga, Managing Editor, at carlos@JonesMcClure.com.

INTRODUCTION

EDITORIAL & PRODUCTION STAFF

As always, the staff of Jones McClure worked hard to prepare this publication, both in its substance and in its layout. The people who worked on this edition of *O'Connor's Criminal Codes Plus* are listed below.

EXECUTIVE EDITOR
Jeffrey C. Hunter, J.D.

MANAGING LEGAL EDITOR
Carlos Goenaga, J.D.

ASSISTANT MANAGING LEGAL EDITOR
Brian Tees, J.D.

LEGAL EDITORIAL ASSISTANTS
Zach Bowman
Mike Bradford
Christopher Burt
Erin Kutinac Craig, J.D.
Heather Daniels, J.D.
Patrick W. Fogarty
Rebecca L. Grohmann, J.D.
Eunice B. Kuo
Raymond Kutch
Christina Richardson
Leslie Melissa Schulman
A. Ashley Stanley
Venkat Thiagarajan
Hillary K. Valderrama
Holly R. Veselka
Robert A. Vuong
Crystal M. Wright

PRODUCTION MANAGER
Donna E. Vass

PRODUCTION STAFF
Fiona K. Adams
Jack Arthur
Beverly B. Bellot
Adam J. Dyer
Michael P. Dyer
Julie Fitzgerald
Trevor Pittinger
Jenny Rees
Sara C. Rolater
Tiffany M. Satterfield
Jessica P. Schunke
Camille Walker

PROOFREADERS
Jenny Rees
Tiffany M. Satterfield
Jessica P. Schunke

JONES McCLURE PUBLISHING
Houston, Texas

MASTER TABLE OF CONTENTS

CODE OF CRIMINAL PROCEDURE

TABLE OF CONTENTS

★

⭐

CCP

★

TITLE 1

ART. 1.01. SHORT TITLE

This Act shall be known, and may be cited, as the "Code of Criminal Procedure."

History of CCP art. 1.01: Acts 1965, 59th Leg., vol. 2, ch. 722.

ART. 1.02. EFFECTIVE DATE

This Code shall take effect and be in force on and after January 1, 1966. The procedure herein prescribed shall govern all criminal proceedings instituted after the effective date of this Act and all proceedings pending upon the effective date hereof insofar as are applicable.

History of CCP art. 1.02: Acts 1965, 59th Leg., vol. 2, ch. 722.

ANNOTATIONS

Baxter v. Texas Dept. of H.R., 678 S.W.2d 265, 267 (Tex.App.—Austin 1984, no writ) (civil case). "The exclusionary rule codified in [CCP] art. 38.23 is inapplicable to [civil actions] because the [CCP] applies only to criminal actions...."

ART. 1.03. OBJECTS OF THIS CODE

This Code is intended to embrace rules applicable to the prevention and prosecution of offenses against the laws of this State, and to make the rules of procedure in respect to the prevention and punishment of offenses intelligible to the officers who are to act under them, and to all persons whose rights are to be affected by them. It seeks:

1. To adopt measures for preventing the commission of crime;

2. To exclude the offender from all hope of escape;

3. To insure a trial with as little delay as is consistent with the ends of justice;

4. To bring to the investigation of each offense on the trial all the evidence tending to produce conviction or acquittal;

5. To insure a fair and impartial trial; and

6. The certain execution of the sentence of the law when declared.

History of CCP art. 1.03: Acts 1965, 59th Leg., vol. 2, ch. 722.

ANNOTATIONS

Reese v. State, 772 S.W.2d 288, 290 (Tex.App.—Waco 1989, pet. ref'd). "Procedural rules have the same force and effect as statutes. [T]hey should be interpreted and construed under the rules applicable to legislative enactments. Criminal rules should be liberally construed to accomplish their objective of insuring a fair and impartial trial. The ultimate goal of interpretation and construction is to determine what the enacting authority intended when it adopted the rule. [¶] A court cannot enact a procedural rule which conflicts with a constitutional provision. Therefore, when a rule may be fairly given two interpretations, one of which results in its validity, a court must presume that the enacting authority did not intend to adopt an invalid rule, and shall interpret it so that it will be valid and constitutional."

Parker v. State, 745 S.W.2d 934, 937 (Tex.App.—Houston [1st Dist.] 1988, pet. ref'd). "'No one, under any circumstances, should be deprived of any right given him by the laws of this state, and, if any provision of our [CCP] has been overlooked or disregarded, if, in the remotest degree, it could have been hurtful or harmful to the person on trial, the verdict should be set aside. He has a right to be tried in accordance with the rules and form of law, and if this sort of a trial is not accorded him he has a right to complain, and to this complaint we will always give an attentive ear.'"

ART. 1.04. DUE COURSE OF LAW

No citizen of this State shall be deprived of life, liberty, property, privileges or immunities, or in any manner disfranchised, except by the due course of the law of the land.

History of CCP art. 1.04: Acts 1965, 59th Leg., vol. 2, ch. 722.
See also Tex. Const. art. 1, §§13, 19.

ANNOTATIONS

McCambridge v. State, 725 S.W.2d 418, 422 (Tex. App.—Houston [1st Dist.] 1987), *aff'd*, 778 S.W.2d 70 (Tex.Crim.App.1989). "The wording of the state due course of law provisions closely corresponds to the language of the fourteenth amendment of the U.S. Constitution. Although we may not automatically assume that the state protections correspond to the federal ones, ... we have found no independent historical or policy basis to conclude that the state provisions were intended to offer greater protection than the federal ones."

ART. 1.05. RIGHTS OF ACCUSED

In all criminal prosecutions the accused shall have a speedy public trial by an impartial jury. He shall have the right to demand the nature and cause of the accusation against him, and to have a copy thereof. He shall not be compelled to give evidence against himself. He shall have the right of being heard by himself, or counsel, or both; shall be confronted with the witnesses against him, and shall have compulsory process for obtaining witnesses in his favor. No person shall be held to answer for a felony unless on indictment of a grand jury.

History of CCP art. 1.05: Acts 1965, 59th Leg., vol. 2, ch. 722.
See also Tex. Const. art. 1, §10, art. 5, §13.

ANNOTATIONS

Speedy Trial

Cantu v. State, 253 S.W.3d 273, ___ (Tex.Crim.App. 2008). "The right [to a speedy trial] attaches once a person becomes an 'accused'—that is, once he is arrested or charged. Supreme Court precedent requires state courts to analyze federal constitutional speedy-trial claims 'on an ad hoc basis' by weighing and then balancing the four ***Barker v. Wingo*** factors: 1) length

of the delay, 2) reason for the delay, 3) assertion of the right, and 4) prejudice to the accused. While the State has the burden of justifying the length of delay, the defendant has the burden of proving the assertion of the right and showing prejudice. The defendant's burden of proof on the latter two factors 'varies inversely' with the State's degree of culpability for the delay. Thus, the greater the State's bad faith or official negligence and the longer its actions delay a trial, the less a defendant must show actual prejudice or prove diligence in asserting his right to a speedy trial. [¶] The ***Barker*** test is triggered by a delay that is unreasonable enough to be 'presumptively prejudicial.' There is no set time element that triggers the analysis, but we have held that a delay of four months is not sufficient while a seventeen-month delay is. Once the ***Barker*** test is triggered, courts must analyze the speedy-trial claim by first weighing the strength of each of the ***Barker*** factors and then balancing their relative weights in light of 'the conduct of both the prosecution and the defendant.' No one factor is 'either a necessary or sufficient condition to the finding of a deprivation of the right of speedy trial.' Instead, the four factors are related and must be considered together along with any other relevant circumstances. As no factor possesses 'talismanic qualities,' courts must engage 'in a difficult and sensitive balancing process' in each individual case. [¶] Dismissal of the charging instrument with prejudice is mandated only upon a finding that an accused's Sixth Amendment speedy-trial right was actually violated. [C]ourts must apply the ***Barker*** balancing test with common sense and sensitivity to ensure that charges are dismissed only when the evidence shows that a defendant's actual and asserted interest in a speedy trial has been infringed. The constitutional right is that of a speedy trial, not dismissal of the charges. [¶] 'In reviewing the trial court's ruling on appellant's federal constitutional speedy trial claim, we apply a bifurcated standard of review: an abuse of discretion standard for the factual components, and a *de novo* standard for the legal components.' Review of the individual ***Barker*** factors necessarily involves fact determinations and legal conclusions, but '[t]he balancing test as a whole ... is a purely legal question.' [¶] Under the abuse of discretion standard, appellate courts defer not only to a trial judge's resolution of disputed facts, but also to his right to draw reasonable inferences from those facts. In assessing the evidence at a speedy-trial hearing, the trial judge may completely disregard a witness's testimony, based on credibility and demeanor evaluations, even if that testimony is uncontroverted. The trial judge may disbelieve any evidence so long as there is a reasonable and articulable basis for doing so. And all of the evidence must be viewed in the light most favorable to his ultimate ruling."

State v. Empak, Inc., 889 S.W.2d 618, 623 (Tex. App.—Houston [14th Dist.] 1994, pet. ref'd). "Corporations have a speedy trial right under federal and Texas constitutions. In Texas, a speedy trial right is also assured by ... art. 1.05, and the [CCP] expressly applies to corporations."

Right to Trial by Jury

Yarborough v. State, 981 S.W.2d 846, 848 (Tex. App.—Houston [1st Dist.] 1998, pet. ref'd). "By constitution and statute, Texas has firmly established a right to jury trial in all criminal proceedings, regardless of punishment."

Right to Remain Silent

Johnson v. State, 83 S.W.3d 229, 232 (Tex.App.—Waco 2002, pet. ref'd). "Although not specifically adopted as definitive or exhaustive, the courts have looked to several factors to determine whether an instruction to disregard cured the prejudicial effect [of comment on a defendant's constitutionally protected silence]. They are as follows: 1) the nature of the error; 2) the persistence of the prosecution in committing the error; 3) the flagrancy of the violation; 4) the particular instruction given; 5) the weight of the incriminating evidence; and 6) the harm to the accused as measured by the severity of sentence."

Right to Counsel

Herron v. State, 86 S.W.3d 621, 628-29 (Tex.Crim. App.2002). "One officer's knowledge that a defendant has requested counsel is imputed to every other state agent. The failure to convey such knowledge cannot justify the State's failure to suspend interrogations until counsel has been provided. [¶] However, ... '[a]n accused, ... having expressed his desire to deal with the police only through counsel, is not subject to further interrogation by the authorities until counsel has been made available to him, *unless the accused himself initiates further communication, exchanges, or conversations with the police.*'"

Garcia v. State, 57 S.W.3d 436, 440 (Tex.Crim.App. 2001). "[T]o obtain a reversal of a conviction on the ground of ineffective assistance, an appellant must demonstrate that (1) defense counsel's performance fell below an objective standard of reasonableness and (2) there is a reasonable probability that, but for counsel's unprofessional error(s), the result of the proceeding would have been different. [A]n appellate court 'must indulge a strong presumption that counsel's conduct [fell] within the wide range of reasonable professional assistance; that is, the [appellant] must overcome the presumption that, under the circumstances, the challenged action might be considered sound trial strategy.' Also, in the absence of evidence of counsel's reasons for the challenged conduct, an appellate court 'commonly will assume a strategic motivation if any can possibly be imagined,' and will not conclude the challenged conduct constituted deficient performance unless the conduct was so outrageous that no competent attorney would have engaged in it. Finally, an appellant's failure to satisfy one prong ... negates a court's need to consider the other prong." *See also Bates v. State*, 88 S.W.3d 724, 728-29 (Tex.App.—Tyler 2002, pet. ref'd).

Jennings v. State, 890 S.W.2d 809, 810 (Tex.Crim. App.1995). "[R]emand by this Court to a court of appeals reinstate[s] the status of the case to the first level of appeal and a defendant [stands] in the same position as when the initial appeal was filed. Thus, a defendant should be provided counsel in the court of appeals if indigent at the time of the remand to the court of appeals. The total absence of any assistance of counsel at this point constitutes complete denial of counsel and is not subject to a harm analysis."

Garcia v. State, 787 S.W.2d 957, 958 (Tex.Crim. App.1990). The question "is when the right to counsel attaches to the proceedings. [I]n *McCambridge v. State*[,] we determined that for purposes of [Tex. Const. art.] I, §10 ... the right to counsel attaches at the critical stage in the proceedings, that is, at the time formal charges are brought against a suspect. We also determined that [Tex. Const. art.] I, §19 and [a]rts. 1.04 and 1.05 ... do not include a right to counsel other than that encompassed by Art. I, §10. Further we found that [CCP arts.] 15.17 and 38.22 do not 'provide a right to counsel prior to the administration of a chemical breath test.'"

Samudio v. State, 648 S.W.2d 312, 314 (Tex.Crim. App.1983). "[T]he U.S. Supreme Court applies the same rule to the waiver of the right to trial by jury that it does to the waiver of the right to counsel in that such waiver cannot be presumed from a silent record."

Cormier v. State, 85 S.W.3d 496, 497 (Tex.App.— Houston [1st Dist.] 2002, pet. ref'd). "We ... consider whether a criminal appellant has a right to appellate self-representation. We conclude that there is no such right." *But see Fewins v. State*, 170 S.W.3d 293, 294-95 (Tex.App.—Waco 2005, order) (Article 1.05 allows self-representation).

State v. Frye, 846 S.W.2d 443, 448 (Tex.App.— Houston [14th Dist.] 1992), *aff'd*, 897 S.W.2d 324 (Tex. Crim.App.1995). "The U.S. Supreme Court has defined the Sixth amendment right to counsel to include not only the actual trial, but to certain pretrial critical stages of criminal cases. Accordingly, the Sixth amendment right to counsel attaches at the point in which the state initiates adversary judicial proceedings. Such proceedings include formal charge, preliminary hearing, indictment, information or arraignment. Similarly the Texas Court of Criminal Appeals has held that the filing of a criminal complaint constitutes the initiation of formal judicial criminal proceedings in Texas."

Right to Grand Jury Indictment

Sledge v. State, 903 S.W.2d 105, 108 (Tex.App.— Fort Worth 1995), *aff'd*, 953 S.W.2d 253 (Tex.Crim.App. 1997). Tex. Const. art. I, §10, CCP art. 105, "and the 5th Amendment to the U.S. Constitution prohibit trying a defendant for a felony without first presenting the accusation to the grand jury. The grand jury must inquire into the offense and, if nine jurors vote a true bill, return an indictment, which is the written statement of a grand jury accusing the person named in the indictment of some act or omission constituting an offense. If the State is permitted to wait until trial or until a pretrial hearing to choose the transaction to proceed upon, it is difficult to understand how this procedure complies with the requirements of grand jury oversight."

ART. 1.051. RIGHT TO REPRESENTATION BY COUNSEL

(a) A defendant in a criminal matter is entitled to be represented by counsel in an adversarial judicial proceeding. The right to be represented by counsel includes the right to consult in private with counsel sufficiently in advance of a proceeding to allow adequate preparation for the proceeding.

(b) For the purposes of this article and Articles 26.04 and 26.05 of this code, "indigent" means a person who is not financially able to employ counsel.

(c) An indigent defendant is entitled to have an attorney appointed to represent him in any adversary judicial proceeding that may result in punishment by confinement and in any other criminal proceeding if the court concludes that the interests of justice require representation. Except as otherwise provided by this subsection, if an indigent defendant is entitled to and requests appointed counsel and if adversarial judicial proceedings have been initiated against the defendant, a court or the courts' designee authorized under Article 26.04 to appoint counsel for indigent defendants in the county shall appoint counsel as soon as possible, but not later than the end of the third working day after the date on which the court or the courts' designee receives the defendant's request for appointment of counsel. In a county with a population of 250,000 or more, the court or the courts' designee shall appoint counsel as required by this subsection as soon as possible, but not later than the end of the first working day after the date on which the court or the courts' designee receives the defendant's request for appointment of counsel.

(d) An eligible indigent defendant is entitled to have the trial court appoint an attorney to represent him in the following appellate and postconviction habeas corpus matters:

(1) an appeal to a court of appeals;

(2) an appeal to the Court of Criminal Appeals if the appeal is made directly from the trial court or if a petition for discretionary review has been granted;

(3) a habeas corpus proceeding if the court concludes that the interests of justice require representation; and

(4) any other appellate proceeding if the court concludes that the interests of justice require representation.

🅐 *Subsection (e) below is effective for proceedings at which an indigent defendant appears without counsel after having refused appointed counsel if the proceedings occur on or after Sept. 1, 2007.*

(e) An appointed counsel is entitled to 10 days to prepare for a proceeding but may waive the preparation time with the consent of the defendant in writing or on the record in open court. If a nonindigent defendant appears without counsel at a proceeding after having been given a reasonable opportunity to retain counsel, the court, on 10 days' notice to the defendant of a dispositive setting, may proceed with the matter without securing a written waiver or appointing counsel. If an indigent defendant who has refused appointed counsel in order to retain private counsel appears without counsel after having been given an opportunity to retain counsel, the court, after giving the defendant a reasonable opportunity to request appointment of counsel or, if the defendant elects not to request appointment of counsel, after obtaining a waiver of the right to counsel pursuant to Subsections (f) and (g), may proceed with the matter on 10 days' notice to the defendant of a dispositive setting.

Subsection (e) below is effective for proceedings at which an indigent defendant appears without counsel after having refused appointed counsel if the proceedings occur before Sept. 1, 2007.

(e) An appointed counsel is entitled to 10 days to prepare for a proceeding but may waive the preparation time with the consent of the defendant in writing or on the record in open court. If a nonindigent defendant or an indigent defendant who has refused appointed counsel in order to retain private counsel appears without counsel at a proceeding after having been given a reasonable opportunity to retain counsel, the court, on 10 days' notice to the defendant of a dispositive setting, may proceed with the matter without securing a written waiver or appointing counsel.

 Subsection (f) below is effective for waivers of counsel or communications with a defendant that occur on or after Sept. 1, 2007.

(f) A defendant may voluntarily and intelligently waive in writing the right to counsel. A waiver obtained in violation of Subsection (f-1) or (f-2) is presumed invalid.

Subsection (f) below is effective for waivers of counsel or communications with a defendant that occur before Sept. 1, 2007.

(f) A defendant may voluntarily and intelligently waive in writing the right to counsel.

 (f-1) In any adversary judicial proceeding that may result in punishment by confinement, the attorney representing the state may not:

(1) initiate or encourage an attempt to obtain from a defendant who is not represented by counsel a waiver of the right to counsel; or

(2) communicate with a defendant who has requested the appointment of counsel, unless the court or the court's designee authorized under Article 26.04 to appoint counsel for indigent defendants in the county has denied the request and, subsequent to the denial, the defendant:

(A) has been given a reasonable opportunity to retain and has failed to retain private counsel; or

(B) waives or has waived the opportunity to retain private counsel.

 (f-2) In any adversary judicial proceeding that may result in punishment by confinement, the court may not direct or encourage the defendant to communicate with the attorney representing the state until the court advises the defendant of the right to counsel and the procedure for requesting appointed counsel and the defendant has been given a reasonable opportunity to request appointed counsel. If the defendant has requested appointed counsel, the court may not direct or encourage the defendant to communicate with the attorney representing the state unless the court or the court's designee authorized under Article 26.04 to appoint counsel for indigent defendants in the county has denied the request and, subsequent to the denial, the defendant:

(1) has been given a reasonable opportunity to retain and has failed to retain private counsel; or

(2) waives or has waived the opportunity to retain private counsel.

 (g) If a defendant wishes to waive the right to counsel for purposes of entering a guilty plea or proceeding to trial, the court shall advise the defendant of the nature of the charges against the defendant and, if the defendant is proceeding to trial, the dangers and disadvantages of self-representation. If the court determines that the waiver is voluntarily and intelligently made, the court shall provide the defendant with a statement substantially in the following form, which, if signed by the defendant, shall be filed with and become part of the record of the proceedings:

"I have been advised this _____ day of _____, 2 ____, by the (name of court) Court of my right to representation by counsel in the case pending against me. I have been further advised that if I am

unable to afford counsel, one will be appointed for me free of charge. Understanding my right to have counsel appointed for me free of charge if I am not financially able to employ counsel, I wish to waive that right and request the court to proceed with my case without an attorney being appointed for me. I hereby waive my right to counsel. (signature of defendant)"

(h) A defendant may withdraw a waiver of the right to counsel at any time but is not entitled to repeat a proceeding previously held or waived solely on the grounds of the subsequent appointment or retention of counsel. If the defendant withdraws a waiver, the trial court, in its discretion, may provide the appointed counsel 10 days to prepare.

(i) Except as otherwise provided by this subsection, if an indigent defendant is entitled to and requests appointed counsel and if adversarial judicial proceedings have not been initiated against the defendant, a court or the courts' designee authorized under Article 26.04 to appoint counsel for indigent defendants in the county shall appoint counsel immediately following the expiration of three working days after the date on which the court or the courts' designee receives the defendant's request for appointment of counsel. If adversarial judicial proceedings are initiated against the defendant before the expiration of the three working days, the court or the courts' designee shall appoint counsel as provided by Subsection (c). In a county with a population of 250,000 or more, the court or the courts' designee shall appoint counsel as required by this subsection immediately following the expiration of one working day after the date on which the court or the courts' designee receives the defendant's request for appointment of counsel. If adversarial judicial proceedings are initiated against the defendant before the expiration of the one working day, the court or the courts' designee shall appoint counsel as provided by Subsection (c).

(j) Notwithstanding any other provision of this section, if an indigent defendant is released from custody prior to the appointment of counsel under this section, appointment of counsel is not required until the defendant's first court appearance or when adversarial judicial proceedings are initiated, whichever comes first.

(k) A court or the courts' designee may without unnecessary delay appoint new counsel to represent an indigent defendant for whom counsel is appointed under Subsection (c) or (i) if:

(1) the defendant is subsequently charged in the case with an offense different from the offense with which the defendant was initially charged; and

(2) good cause to appoint new counsel is stated on the record as required by Article 26.04(j)(2).

History of CCP art. 1.051: Acts 1987, 70th Leg., ch. 979, §1, eff. Sept. 1, 1987. Amended by Acts 2001, 77th Leg., ch. 906, §2, eff. Jan. 1, 2002; Acts 2007, 80th Leg., ch. 463, §1, eff. Sept. 1, 2007.

ANNOTATIONS

Collier v. State, 959 S.W.2d 621, 625-26 (Tex.Crim. App.1997). The decision to waive counsel, "to be constitutionally effective, must be made (1) competently, (2) knowingly and intelligently, and (3) voluntarily. The decision to … proceed *pro se* is made 'knowingly and intelligently' if it is made with a full understanding of the right to counsel, which is being abandoned, as well as the dangers and disadvantages of self-representation. The decision is made 'voluntarily' if it is uncoerced."

Ex parte Gonzales, 945 S.W.2d 830, 836 (Tex.Crim. App.1997). "[A] contemnor is entitled to representation, either by retained or appointed counsel, in a contempt proceeding."

Marin v. State, 891 S.W.2d 267, 272 (Tex.Crim.App. 1994). "The primary goal of art. 1.051(e) is to ensure the indigent defendant receives appointed counsel who is prepared for the proceeding. For this reason we have focused on the actual preparation time afforded counsel. … If the defendant was represented by more than one attorney, we found compliance where at least *one* of the defendant's attorneys was afforded the statutory preparation time. However, when the defendant was represented by only one attorney and that attorney was not afforded the statutory preparation time, we have always found no compliance because the minimum statutory preparation time is mandatory."

Green v. State, 872 S.W.2d 717, 721 (Tex.Crim.App. 1994). "[A]n examining trial in Texas serves as an adversarial proceeding designed to inquire into the probable cause of the State to justify detention of an accused pending formal prosecution, and state law permits the examining magistrate to appoint counsel for the indigent accused."

Barnes v. State, 921 S.W.2d 881, 884 (Tex.App.— Austin 1996, pet. ref'd). "According to the plain language of article 1.051(h), an attorney who is appointed to represent a defendant who has withdrawn a previous waiver of counsel is not automatically entitled to ten days to prepare for trial. Instead, the decision to give counsel the ten-day preparation period is left to the discretion of the trial court. Of course, the discretion to provide the ten-day preparation period necessarily includes the discretion to refuse it. Thus, article 1.051(h) creates an exception to the general rule of article 1.051(e) in those cases to which it applies."

Barcroft v. State, 881 S.W.2d 838, 842 (Tex.App.— Tyler 1994, no pet.). "[C]ounsel need not be appointed to represent an indigent defendant in a class C misdemeanor case unless 'the court concludes that the interests of justice require such representation.'"

ART. 1.052. SIGNED PLEADINGS OF DEFENDANT

(a) A pleading, motion, and other paper filed for or on behalf of a defendant represented by an attorney must be signed by at least one attorney of record in the attorney's name and state the attorney's address. A defendant who is not represented by an attorney must sign any pleading, motion, or other paper filed for or on the defendant's behalf and state the defendant's address.

(b) The signature of an attorney or a defendant constitutes a certificate by the attorney or defendant that the person has read the pleading, motion, or other paper and that to the best of the person's knowledge, information, and belief formed after reasonable inquiry that the instrument is not groundless and brought in bad faith or groundless and brought for harassment, unnecessary delay, or other improper purpose.

(c) If a pleading, motion, or other paper is not signed, the court shall strike it unless it is signed promptly after the omission is called to the attention of the attorney or defendant.

(d) An attorney or defendant who files a fictitious pleading in a cause for an improper purpose described by Subsection (b) or who makes a statement in a pleading that the attorney or defendant knows to be groundless and false to obtain a delay of the trial of the cause or for the purpose of harassment shall be held guilty of contempt.

(e) If a pleading, motion, or other paper is signed in violation of this article, the court, on motion or on its own initiative, after notice and hearing, shall impose an appropriate sanction, which may include an order to pay to the other party or parties to the prosecution or to the general fund of the county in which the pleading, motion, or other paper was filed the amount of reasonable expenses incurred because of the filing of the pleading, motion, or other paper, including reasonable attorney's fees.

(f) A court shall presume that a pleading, motion, or other paper is filed in good faith. Sanctions under this article may not be imposed except for good cause stated in the sanction order.

(g) A plea of "not guilty" or "no contest" or "nolo contendere" does not constitute a violation of this article. An allegation that an event took place or occurred on or about a particular date does not constitute a violation of this article.

(h) In this article, "groundless" means without basis in law or fact and not warranted by a good faith argument for the extension, modification, or reversal of existing law.

History of CCP art. 1.052: Acts 1997, 75th Leg., ch. 189, §11, eff. May 21, 1997.

ART. 1.06. SEARCHES & SEIZURES

The people shall be secure in their persons, houses, papers and possessions from all unreasonable seizures or searches. No warrant to search any place or to seize any person or thing shall issue without describing them as near as may be, nor without probable cause supported by oath or affirmation.

History of CCP art. 1.06: Acts 1965, 59th Leg., vol. 2, ch. 722.
See also Tex. Const. art. 1, §9.

ANNOTATIONS

Corbin v. State, 85 S.W.3d 272, 276-77 (Tex.Crim. App.2002). "[T]he Supreme Court has characterized a police officer's job as encompassing a community caretaking function. [A] police officer may not properly invoke his community caretaking function if he is primarily motivated by a non-community caretaking purpose. [¶] Once it is determined that an officer is primarily motivated by his community caretaking function, it must then be determined whether the officer's belief that the defendant needs help is reasonable. In evaluating whether an officer reasonably believes that a person needs help, courts may look to a list of four non-exclusive factors: (1) the nature and level of the distress exhibited by the individual; (2) the location of the individual; (3) whether or not the individual was alone and/or had access to assistance other than that offered by the officer; and (4) to what extent the individual, if not assisted, presented a danger to himself or others. [¶] [T]he first factor is entitled to the greatest weight. ... This is not to say that the weight of the first factor alone will always be dispositive. In fact, the remaining three factors help to give more definition to the first factor." Held: The officer's exercise of his community-caretaking function was not reasonable. *See also Laney v. State*, 117 S.W.3d 854, 862-63 (Tex.Crim.App.2003).

State v. Cantwell, 85 S.W.3d 849, 852 (Tex.App.—Waco 2002, pet. ref'd). "A defendant who seeks to suppress evidence because of an illegal search that violates the federal or state constitution bears the initial burden to rebut the presumption of proper police conduct. The burden is met by proving that the police seized him or performed a search without a warrant. Once the defendant establishes (1) that a search or seizure occurred and (2) that no warrant was obtained, the burden shifts to the State to produce either evidence of a warrant or to prove the reasonableness of the search or seizure pursuant to one of the recognized exceptions to the warrant requirement."

Morris v. State, 50 S.W.3d 89, 94 (Tex.App.—Fort Worth 2001, no pet.). "An investigative detention ... may be founded upon a reasonable, articulable suspicion while an arrest ... must be supported by probable cause. [¶] An arrest occurs when a person's liberty of movement is restricted or restrained. *At 95:* An investigative stop ... occurs when an officer lacks probable cause to arrest but nonetheless possesses a reasonable suspicion; that is, the officer is able to point to specific, articulable facts that, taken together with rational inferences from those facts, reasonably warrants the detention. [¶] When officers possess reasonable suspicion justifying a temporary investigative detention, they may use such force as is reasonably necessary to effect the goal of the stop: investigation, maintenance of the status quo, or officer safety. ... However, if the force utilized exceeds that reasonably necessary to effect the goal of the stop, such force may transform an investigative stop into a full blown arrest."

Rios v. State, 901 S.W.2d 704, 706 (Tex.App.—San Antonio 1995, no pet.). "The Fourth Amendment states that 'no Warrants shall issue, but upon probable cause, supported by Oath or affirmation, and particularly describing the place to be searched, and the persons or things to be seized.' Both the Texas Constitution and the [CCP] provide that a search warrant describe the place to be searched 'as near as may be.' A valid search warrant must contain a description of the place to be searched. [¶] [T]he description contained in the affidavit limits and controls the description contained in the warrant."

Jimenez v. State, 750 S.W.2d 798, 804 (Tex.App.—El Paso 1988, pet. ref'd). "Standing is a function of the citizen's reasonable expectation of privacy, and as such has application in assessing challenges predicated solely upon [CCP] arts. 1.06 and 38.23...." *See also Maysonet v. State*, 91 S.W.3d 365, 375 (Tex.App.—Texarkana 2002, pet. ref'd); *Head v. State*, 82 S.W.3d 735, 738 (Tex.App.—Corpus Christi 2002, pet. ref'd).

ART. 1.07. RIGHT TO BAIL

All prisoners shall be bailable unless for capital offenses when the proof is evident. This provision shall not be so construed as to prevent bail after indictment found upon examination of the evidence, in such manner as may be prescribed by law.

History of CCP art. 1.07: Acts 1965, 59th Leg., vol. 2, ch. 722.
See also Tex. Const. art. 1, §§11, 11A; CCP arts. 11.41, 16.15.

ANNOTATIONS

Ex parte Wilson, 527 S.W.2d 310, 311 (Tex.Crim. App.1975). "The term 'proof is evident' means that the evidence is clear and strong, leading a well-guarded and dispassionate judgment to the conclusion that the offense of capital murder has been committed; that the accused is the guilty party; and that the accused will not only be convicted but that the jury will return findings which will require a sentence of death. The burden of proof is on the State to establish that the proof is evident."

ART. 1.08. HABEAS CORPUS

The writ of habeas corpus is a writ of right and shall never be suspended.

History of CCP art. 1.08: Acts 1965, 59th Leg., vol. 2, ch. 722.
See also Tex. Const. art. 1, §12.

ART. 1.09. CRUELTY FORBIDDEN

Excessive bail shall not be required, nor excessive fines imposed, nor cruel or unusual punishment inflicted.

History of CCP art. 1.09: Acts 1965, 59th Leg., vol. 2, ch. 722.
See also Tex. Const. art. 1, §13.

Robertson v. State, 245 S.W.3d 545, 549 (Tex. App.—Tyler 2007, pet. ref'd). "Appellant ... contends [his punishment] is grossly disproportionate to the facts in violation of the constitutional prohibition against cruel and unusual punishment. The proportionality of a sentence is evaluated by considering (1) the gravity of the offense and the harshness of the penalty, (2) the sentences imposed on other criminals in the same jurisdiction, and (3) the sentences imposed for commission of the same crime in other jurisdictions." Held: The sentence was not cruel or unusual.

Ex parte Prelow, 929 S.W.2d 54, 55 (Tex. App.—San Antonio 1996, no pet.). "Article 1.09 ... proscribes excessive bail. The primary purpose of an appearance bond is to secure the presence of the defendant in court for the trial of the offense charged. Bail should be set sufficiently high to give reasonable assurance that the defendant will appear at trial, but it should not be used as an instrument of oppression."

ART. 1.10. JEOPARDY

No person for the same offense shall be twice put in jeopardy of life or liberty; nor shall a person be again put upon trial for the same offense, after a verdict of not guilty in a court of competent jurisdiction.

History of CCP art. 1.10: Acts 1965, 59th Leg., vol. 2, ch. 722. See also Tex. Const. art. 1, §14.

Ex parte Lewis, 219 S.W.3d 335, 336-37 (Tex.Crim. App.2007). "In ***Oregon v. Kennedy***, the U.S. Supreme Court held that the 5th Amendment's Double Jeopardy Clause barred retrial after a defendant successfully moved for mistrial *only* when it was shown that the prosecutor engaged in conduct that was 'intended to provoke the defendant into moving for a mistrial.' In ***Bauder v. State***, we interpreted the Double Jeopardy provision of the Texas Constitution more expansively, to cover 'reckless' conduct, holding that retrial would also be barred 'when the prosecutor was aware but consciously disregarded the risk that an objectionable event for which he was responsible would require a mistrial at the defendant's request.' ... We conclude that ***Bauder*** should be overruled and that the proper rule under the Texas Constitution is the rule articulated by the U.S. Supreme Court in ***Oregon v. Kennedy***."

Ex parte Cavazos, 203 S.W.3d 333, 337 (Tex.Crim. App.2006). "When a defendant is convicted of two offenses that are the 'same' for double-jeopardy purposes, our case law tells us that the conviction for the 'most serious' offense is retained and the other conviction is set aside. [T]he 'most serious' offense is determined by the degree of the felony, range of punishment and sentence imposed, with rules of parole eligibility and good-conduct time as a tie-breaker."

Langs v. State, 183 S.W.3d 680, 682 (Tex.Crim.App. 2006). "[T]he face of the trial record must clearly show a double jeopardy violation before a defendant may successfully raise a 'multiple punishment' double jeopardy claim for the first time on appeal. *At 685:* There are three distinct types of double jeopardy claims: (1) a second prosecution for the same offense after acquittal; (2) a second prosecution for the same offense after conviction; and (3) multiple punishments for the same offense. A multiple punishments claim can arise in two contexts: (1) the lesser-included offense context, in which the same conduct is punished twice; once for the basic conduct, and a second time for that same conduct plus more (for example, attempted assault of Y and assault of Y; assault of X and aggravated assault of X); and (2) punishing the same criminal act twice under two distinct statutes when the legislature intended the conduct to be punished only once (for example, causing a single death by committing both intoxication manslaughter and involuntary manslaughter). The 'same elements' test first articulated by the U.S. Supreme Court in ***Blockburger v. United States***[, 284 U.S. 299 (1932)] is used to determine if two convictions constitute 'multiple punishment' under the Double Jeopardy Clause: 'The applicable rule is that where the same act or transaction constitutes a violation of two distinct statutory provisions the test to be applied to determine whether there are two offenses or only one, is whether each provision requires proof of a fact which the other does not.'"

Ex parte Fierro, 79 S.W.3d 54, 57 (Tex.Crim.App. 2002). "[A]fter erroneously discharging [the] juror, the trial court immediately declared a mistrial. ... Without evidence that the trial court considered [less drastic] alternatives, as it was required to do, a mistrial was not 'necessary,' manifestly or otherwise. We therefore conclude that the trial court abused its discretion in declaring a mistrial. [¶] Appellant's pretrial applications to preclude retrial of the charges against him under the instant indictments should have been granted."

Ex parte Watkins, 73 S.W.3d 264, 267-68 (Tex. Crim.App.2002). "The doctrine of collateral estoppel is embodied within the constitutional bar against double jeopardy. But the two are not identical. Double jeopardy bars any retrial of a criminal offense, while collateral estoppel bars any retrial of specific and discrete facts that have been fully and fairly adjudicated. Double jeopardy applies only to criminal cases, while collateral estoppel applies in both criminal and civil proceedings. Thus, cases hinging on the doctrine of double jeopardy do not necessarily apply to a collateral estoppel claim and those hinging on the doctrine of collateral estoppel do not necessarily apply to a claim of double jeopardy. The two doctrines are treated similarly, however, when a collateral estoppel claim is based on the constitutional rule set out in *Ashe v. Swenson*. [¶] Under this constitutionally based doctrine of collateral estoppel, 'when an issue of ultimate fact has once been determined by a valid and final judgment, that issue cannot again be litigated between the same parties in any future lawsuit.' That is, once a jury determines a discrete fact in favor of a criminal defendant, the State cannot contest the jury's finding in a subsequent proceeding."

Ex parte Granger, 850 S.W.2d 513, 518 (Tex.Crim. App.1993). "[T]he [U.S.] Supreme Court has ... held that reprosecution for the same offense is *not* barred after *conviction* where the defendant has managed through appeal or some other procedure to have his conviction set aside because of reversible error."

Moore v. State, 749 S.W.2d 54, 58 (Tex.Crim.App. 1988), *overruled on other grounds, Awadelkariem v. State*, 974 S.W.2d 721 (Tex.Crim.App.1998). "[T]he Double Jeopardy Clause ... bars any retrial of a case once a judge grants a motion for new trial based solely on insufficiency of the evidence. [O]nce the trial judge grants a motion for new trial based solely on insufficiency of the evidence, the only further action permitted by the Double Jeopardy Clause is the entry of a judgment of acquittal. To allow a trial judge to change his ruling and deny the motion having once granted it is, in our view, just as violative of the Double Jeopardy Clause as allowing a trial judge to change his ruling and find a defendant guilty having once found him not guilty."

McGee v. State, 909 S.W.2d 516, 519 (Tex.App.— Tyler 1995, pet. ref'd). "[E]ngaging in organized criminal activity is to be treated like conspiracy for double jeopardy purposes, and the 'Double Jeopardy Clause does not bar successive prosecutions for a substantive offense and for conspiracy to commit that offense, even where the State proves the same conduct in both prosecutions, and even where the previously prosecuted conduct constitutes an overt act in the conspiracy prosecution.'"

Ex parte May, 852 S.W.2d 3, 5 (Tex.App.—Dallas 1993, pet. ref'd). "A defendant has the burden to go forward with evidence in support of an allegation of former jeopardy. The trial court, as the fact finder, determines the witnesses' credibility and the weight given their testimony. The fact finder may believe or disbelieve all or part of any witness's testimony."

Smithwick v. State, 732 S.W.2d 768, 769 (Tex. App.—Fort Worth 1987, pet. ref'd). "In a jury trial, jeopardy attaches when the jury panel is impaneled and sworn to try the case. Once jeopardy attaches, the defendant possesses a valued right to have his guilt or innocence determined by the jury impaneled."

Zuniga v. State, 717 S.W.2d 484, 485 (Tex. App.—San Antonio 1986, no pet.). "[T]he fact that the jury [is] hung, and the court declare[s] a mistrial does not constitute a bar to retrial."

Reseburg v. State, 656 S.W.2d 84, 86 (Tex.App.— Tyler 1983, pet. ref'd). "[T]he State may in a single indictment allege two or more separate offenses arising out of the same incident or transaction, and ... the State is *not required* to elect between the counts for jury submission. [¶] The State may elect during the trial at any time before submission to the jury or it may refuse to elect and the court, instead of compelling election, may submit each of the counts and instruct the jury that it may return a verdict of guilty on one count only. No double jeopardy problems exist with this type of submission because the jury returns either an acquittal on all counts or a verdict of guilty on only one count."

State v. Marshall, 503 S.W.2d 875, 876 (Tex. App.—Houston [1st Dist.] 1973, no pet.). "Our constitutional guarantee against twice being put in jeopardy for the same offense ... extends to juveniles in delinquency proceedings."

ART. 1.11. ACQUITTAL A BAR

An acquittal of the defendant exempts him from a second trial or a second prosecution for the same offense, however irregular the proceedings may have been; but if the defendant shall have been acquitted upon trial in a court having no jurisdiction of the offense, he may be prosecuted again in a court having jurisdiction.

History of CCP art. 1.11: Acts 1965, 59th Leg., vol. 2, ch. 722.

ANNOTATIONS

Ex parte George, 913 S.W.2d 523, 526 (Tex.Crim. App.1995). "[T]he judgment in a criminal case merely documents the fact of ... the process leading to conviction or acquittal. It is not the conviction or acquittal itself. Consequently, if the judgment reflects that an accused was acquitted, and it is later made to appear that he was not acquitted in fact, the judgment may be reformed accordingly. [¶] In an ordinary case, [there is] a presumption of regularity in support of the judgment, finding that its recitation of acquittal is sufficient to establish an acquittal in fact. *At 527:* [T]he word 'acquittal' ... means a finding that the accused is not guilty of the criminal offense with which he is charged."

Ex parte Aviles, 78 S.W.2d 677, 681 (Tex.App.— Austin 2002, orig. proceeding). CCP art. 1.11 "bars retrial of a defendant after an acquittal, 'however irregular the proceedings may have been.'"

Boulos v. State, 775 S.W.2d 8, 10 (Tex.App.— Houston [1st Dist.] 1989, pet. ref'd). "The statute protects a defendant not just from a second conviction, but from a second trial or prosecution. [¶] The 'exemption' language of art. 1.11 indicates that the trial court lacked power to adjudicate. When a court lacks power to adjudicate, its judgment can be attacked even without a trial objection, even upon a collateral attack, and even after a guilty plea."

ART. 1.12. RIGHT TO JURY

The right of trial by jury shall remain inviolate.

History of CCP art. 1.12: Acts 1965, 59th Leg., vol. 2, ch. 722.
See also Tex. Const. art. 1, §§10, 15, art. 5, §13.

ANNOTATIONS

Marquez v. State, 921 S.W.2d 217, 220 (Tex.Crim. App.1996). "[A] jury trial is 'fundamental to the American scheme of justice....'"

Bearden v. State, 648 S.W.2d 688, 693 (Tex.Crim. App.1983). "The right to trial by jury is no less protected because the trial is for a misdemeanor."

Ex parte York, 899 S.W.2d 47, 48-49 (Tex.App.— Waco 1995, orig. proceeding). "The nature of a case is traditionally determined by the pleadings. Here, the former spouse plead for a $500 fine and/or 6 months jail confinement *for each violation* of 43 alleged failures to pay child support, thereby placing [r]elator in jeopardy of receiving fines totaling $21,500 and/or jail time of 21½ years. [¶] [W]e find that this was a 'serious' case in which the court should have admonished [r]elator concerning his right to trial by jury and his right not to be compelled to give testimony against himself. [¶] We will follow the ruling in *Sproull* which instructs us that if 'confinement *may* exceed six months' that the case is 'serious' and that the constitutional safeguards should be given." *But see In re Brown*, 114 S.W.3d 7, 11-12 (Tex.App.—Amarillo 2003, no pet.) ("serious" case determined by punishment actually imposed, not possible punishment).

ART. 1.13. WAIVER OF TRIAL BY JURY

(a) The defendant in a criminal prosecution for any offense other than a capital felony case in which the State notifies the court and the defendant that it will seek the death penalty shall have the right, upon entering a plea, to waive the right of trial by jury, conditioned, however, that such waiver must be made in person by the defendant in writing in open court with the consent and approval of the court, and the attorney representing the State. The consent and approval by the court shall be entered of record on the minutes of the court, and the consent and approval of the attorney representing the State shall be in writing, signed by him, and filed in the papers of the cause before the defendant enters his plea.

(b) In a capital felony case in which the attorney representing the State notifies the court and the defendant that it will not seek the death penalty, the defendant may waive the right to trial by jury but only if the attorney representing the State, in writing and in open court, consents to the waiver.

(c) A defendant may agree to waive a jury trial regardless of whether the defendant is represented by an attorney at the time of making the waiver, but before a defendant charged with a felony who has no attorney can agree to waive the jury, the court must appoint an attorney to represent him.

History of CCP art. 1.13: Acts 1965, 59th Leg., vol. 2, ch. 722. Amended by Acts 1991, 72nd Leg., ch. 652, §1, eff. Sept. 1, 1991; Acts 1997, 75th Leg., ch. 285, §1, eff. Sept. 1, 1997.

See also CCP art. 45.025.

ANNOTATIONS

Johnson v. State, 72 S.W.3d 346, 347 (Tex.Crim. App.2002). "This issue in this case is whether the failure to obtain a written jury waiver is harmful. We conclude that the lack of a written jury waiver is not harmful when the record reflects that the defendant waived his right to a jury trial."

Ex parte Tovar, 901 S.W.2d 484, 485 (Tex.Crim. App.1995). "[A] conviction secured without a jury and without a written jury waiver under ... Article 1.13 was invalid, and no showing of harm was required. However, the same cannot be said for cases raising the issue on post-conviction collateral attack."

Ex parte Sadberry, 864 S.W.2d 541, 543 (Tex.Crim. App.1993). "[W]here the applicant does not claim he desired and was deprived of his constitutional right to a trial by jury, that he did not intend to waive a jury trial or that he was otherwise harmed, and the record reflects that the applicant agreed to the waiver, we will not set aside a conviction by habeas corpus or collateral attack due to the applicant's failure to sign a written jury form pursuant to article 1.13."

Taylor v. State, ___ S.W.3d ___ (Tex.App.— Texarkana 2008, pet. filed 6-6-08) (No. 06-07-00142-CR; 5-06-08). "A defendant may withdraw his waiver of jury trial if the motion to withdraw is made sufficiently in advance of trial that the granting of the motion will not produce adverse consequences. Adverse consequences that may authorize a court to deny a motion to withdraw a jury waiver are (1) interference with the orderly administration of the business of the court; (2) unnecessary delay or inconvenience to witnesses; or (3) prejudice to the State. If any of these adverse consequences would occur, the court does not err in overruling the motion to withdraw. Because a motion to withdraw a jury waiver is a request to change the status quo, the movant has the burden to show facts entitling him to relief, i.e., that no adverse consequence will follow from granting the motion to withdraw."

Hanley v. State, 909 S.W.2d 117, 119 (Tex.App.— Houston [14th Dist.] 1995, no pet.). "The statutory authority for waiver of a trial by jury carries with it the concomitant 'right to agree to a trial by jury composed of less than six men.' If article 1.13(a) dictates that the waiver of a jury trial must be in writing, then ... waiver of a jury composed of less than six jurors must also be executed according to the same procedures."

Garner v. State, 864 S.W.2d 92, 102 (Tex.App.— Houston [1st Dist.] 1993, pet. ref'd). "Appellant had no right to a bench trial, except as conferred by statute, and subject to any procedural conditions placed upon it. Under [CCP] art. 1.13, the consent of the attorney representing the State is a prerequisite to trial without a jury in a felony case. The term 'consent' inherently implies the idea that consent may be withheld, and the terms of article 1.13 place no limitations upon the discretion of the attorney representing the State to do so. Trial counsel was not ineffective for failing to secure a bench trial for appellant because, in the face of prosecutorial insistence on a jury trial, no defense lawyer could have done so."

ART. 1.14. WAIVER OF RIGHTS

(a) The defendant in a criminal prosecution for any offense may waive any rights secured him by law except that a defendant in a capital felony case may waive the right of trial by jury only in the manner permitted by Article 1.13(b) of this code.

(b) If the defendant does not object to a defect, error, or irregularity of form or substance in an indictment or information before the date on which the trial on the merits commences, he waives and forfeits the right to object to the defect, error, or irregularity and he may not raise the objection on appeal or in any other postconviction proceeding. Nothing in this article prohibits a trial court from requiring that an objection to an indictment or information be made at an earlier time in compliance with Article 28.01 of this code.

History of CCP art. 1.14: Acts 1965, 59th Leg., vol. 2, ch. 722. Amended by Acts 1967, 60th Leg., ch. 659, §1, eff. Aug. 28, 1967; Acts 1973, 63rd Leg., ch. 426, art. 3, §5, eff. June 14, 1973; Acts 1985, 69th Leg., ch. 577, §1, eff. Dec. 1, 1985; Acts 1991, 72nd Leg., ch. 652, §2, eff. Sept. 1, 1991.

See also Tex. Const. art. 5, §12(b).

ANNOTATIONS

Teal v. State, 230 S.W.3d 172, 181 (Tex.Crim.App. 2007). "Implicit within both *Studer* [*v. State*, 799 S.W.2d 263 (Tex.Crim.App.1990)] and *Cook* [*v. State*,

902 S.W.2d 471 (Tex.Crim.App.1995)] is that 'the offense' charged must be one for which the trial court has subject-matter jurisdiction. Although the 'indictment' provision of the constitution explicitly speaks only of the two requirements of 'a person' and 'an offense,' the constitution also sets out the subject-matter jurisdiction of Texas courts. An indictment must also satisfy the constitutional requirement of subject-matter jurisdiction over 'an offense.' [¶] Thus, the complete test for the constitutional sufficiency of a particular charging instrument goes slightly further than that expressly set out in **Studer** and **Cook**: Can the district court and the defendant determine, from the face of the indictment, that the indictment intends to charge a felony or other offense for which a district court has jurisdiction?"

Sanchez v. State, 120 S.W.3d 359, 367 (Tex.Crim. App.2003). "The right to be charged by an instrument that is free of defects, errors, and omissions is neither a 'systemic' requirement nor a 'waivable' right. By the requirement of an act of the legislature under specific authority granted by an amendment of the Constitution, any error in the charging instrument [including the failure to allege a culpable mental state] must be objected to in a timely … and specific manner, and any unobjected-to error in the instrument is not 'fundamental.'" *See also* **Fisher v. State**, 887 S.W.2d 49, 54-55 (Tex.Crim.App.1994).

Monreal v. State, 99 S.W.3d 615, 616 (Tex.Crim. App.2003). "This case presents the question of whether a valid, non-negotiated waiver of appeal prevents a defendant from appealing any issue without the consent of the trial court. We hold that it does."

Blanco v. State, 18 S.W.3d 218, 220 (Tex.Crim.App. 2000). "Where … there has been no unfairness 'in securing agreement between an accused and a prosecutor,' there is no reason why this rule [that a party is entitled to insist on the benefit of his bargain] should not apply to defendants. Appellant was 'fully aware of the likely consequences' when he waived his right to appeal, and it is 'not unfair to expect him to live with those consequences now.'"

Ieppert v. State, 908 S.W.2d 217, 218 (Tex.Crim. App.1995). "This statute was enacted to avoid original postconviction attacks, either by direct appeal or by habeas corpus, upon the sufficiency of charging instruments containing one or more defects of substance listed in [CCP art.] 27.08…. *At 219:* [A]n *ex post facto*

complaint about the improper retroactive application of a penal statute is not really a complaint about errors or defects in an accusatory pleading or a jury charge. … Accordingly, the default provisions of [CCP art.] 1.14(b) and the forfeiture/harmless error provisions of [CCP art.] 36.19 do not purport to bar full appellate review of such complaints, at least when they are not expressly directed to the sufficiency of an accusatory pleading or a jury charge."

Huynh v. State, 901 S.W.2d 480, 481 (Tex.Crim.App. 1995). "Article 1.14 specifically addresses 'indictments and informations' and does not mention 'complaints'…. While numerous other provisions in the Code expressly refer to all three types of charging instruments, article 1.14 does not. … Were article 1.14 to refer to 'charging instruments' in place of 'indictments and informations,' we would be compelled to agree with the Court of Appeals that as a charging instrument in the municipal court context, a complaint would be covered thereunder. However, we are without authority to project such an intention in the face of the statute's specific and plain language."

State v. Vasquez, 140 S.W.3d 758, 759-60 (Tex. App.—Houston [14th Dist.] 2004, no pet.). "It is established that an indictment contains a cognizable defect when it relies on a void judgment to enhance. Accordingly, appellee insists that he met his burden under article 1.14 by objecting at the beginning of the present trial. While we agree that an involuntary waiver of the right to a jury trial will render a judgment void, we consider appellee's collateral attack of the judgment … untimely considering the procedural history of this case. [¶] [A]ppellee cannot attack a conviction two and three-times removed from the present case. Prior convictions are elements of a felony DWI charge. Accordingly, the [allegedly void judgment] was listed in the indictment for [a later, valid judgment]. Assuming that [there is a void judgment], the indictment in [the later, valid judgment] would contain a cognizable defect. However, [the allegedly void judgment] is not named in the present indictment or directly used to enhance his punishment. Thus, in order to avoid waiver, appellee should have asserted his objections when [allegedly void judgment] was an element of the indictment in [the later, valid judgment]."

Crittendon v. State, 923 S.W.2d 632, 634 (Tex. App.—Houston [1st Dist.] 1995, no pet.). "A motion in arrest of judgment is essentially a post-trial motion to quash the indictment. With the advent of ... art. 1.14(b), requiring that objections to the indictment be raised prior to the date of trial or be waived, ... a motion in arrest of judgment now appears to be confined to reurging complaints about indictments made by timely objection prior to trial. An exception appears to have been carved, however, where an indictment fails to allege the name of the defendant."

Anderson v. State, 905 S.W.2d 367, 369-70 (Tex. App.—Fort Worth 1995, pet. ref'd). "The Court of Criminal Appeals has ... addressed the applicability of article 1.14(b) to offenses apparently barred by the statute of limitations. The court held that article 1.14(b) does mandate a motion to quash when complaining an offense is so barred. [¶] We hold that article 1.14(b) now requires objection to preserve the error of misjoinder. Failure to object prior to trial waives the error."

ART. 1.141. WAIVER OF INDICTMENT FOR NONCAPITAL FELONY

A person represented by legal counsel may in open court or by written instrument voluntarily waive the right to be accused by indictment of any offense other than a capital felony. On waiver as provided in this article, the accused shall be charged by information.

History of CCP art. 1.141: Acts 1971, 62nd Leg., ch. 260, §1, eff. May 19, 1971.

ANNOTATIONS

Ex parte Hyett, 610 S.W.2d 787, 788 (Tex.Crim.App. 1981). "Under this statute when a defendant waives the right to be tried upon an indictment and agrees to be tried upon an information, the prosecution is not required to also file a complaint."

Garrett v. State, 625 S.W.2d 809, 810 (Tex.App.— Houston [14th Dist.] 1981, no pet.). "For a waiver of an indictment to be effective, it must be intelligently, voluntarily and knowingly given by the accused while represented by counsel. The waiver signed by appellant, specifically stated, 'My attorney has explained to me my right to be prosecuted by grand jury indictment, which I hereby waive....' The waiver form also included a signed statement by the trial judge, specifically stating that the appellant was advised by the court of the right to be prosecuted by indictment and that appellant '*knowingly*' and '*voluntarily*' waived that right. This written form for waiver of indictment signed by appellant, indicates that the requirements of Art. 1.141

were met in full. It is not necessary that the waiver, on its face, specifically enumerate every possible advantage of going through the grand jury system."

ART. 1.15. JURY IN FELONY

No person can be convicted of a felony except upon the verdict of a jury duly rendered and recorded, unless the defendant, upon entering a plea, has in open court in person waived his right of trial by jury in writing in accordance with Articles 1.13 and 1.14; provided, however, that it shall be necessary for the state to introduce evidence into the record showing the guilt of the defendant and said evidence shall be accepted by the court as the basis for its judgment and in no event shall a person charged be convicted upon his plea without sufficient evidence to support the same. The evidence may be stipulated if the defendant in such case consents in writing, in open court, to waive the appearance, confrontation, and cross-examination of witnesses, and further consents either to an oral stipulation of the evidence and testimony or to the introduction of testimony by affidavits, written statements of witnesses, and any other documentary evidence in support of the judgment of the court. Such waiver and consent must be approved by the court in writing, and be filed in the file of the papers of the cause.

History of CCP art. 1.15: Acts 1965, 59th Leg., vol. 2, ch. 722. Amended by Acts 1967, 60th Leg., ch. 659, §2, eff. Aug. 28, 1967; Acts 1971, 62nd Leg., ch. 996, §1, eff. June 15, 1971; Acts 1973, 63rd Leg., ch. 426, art. 3, §5, eff. June 14, 1973; Acts 1991, 72nd Leg., ch. 652, §3, eff. Sept. 1, 1991.

ANNOTATIONS

Stringer v. State, 241 S.W.3d 52, 59 (Tex.Crim.App. 2007). "Because Article 1.15 applies only to the guilt stage, we hold that Stringer's written waiver of his right to confrontation and cross-examination applied only to the guilt stage. Therefore, contrary to the determination of the court of appeals, Stringer did not knowingly, voluntarily, and intelligently waive his right to confront and cross-examine witnesses at sentencing."

Stone v. State, 919 S.W.2d 424, 426 (Tex.Crim.App. 1996). "This Court has routinely found that a stipulation as to what witnesses would testify had they been present at trial is sufficient to support a conviction in the context of Art. 1.15.... Art. applies whether the stipulation relates to what a witness would testify or to the truth of the allegations in the indictment."

Messer v. State, 729 S.W.2d 694, 698 (Tex.Crim. App.1986). "[I]t is not the stipulation itself that must be approved in writing by the trial court but the defendant's waiver of his rights and consent to stipulate."

Chindaphone v. State, 241 S.W.3d 217, 219-20 (Tex.App.—Fort Worth 2007, pet. ref'd). "An appellate court will affirm the trial court's judgment under article 1.15 if the State introduced evidence that embraces every essential element of the offense charged and that is sufficient to establish the defendant's guilt. A judicial confession, standing alone, is sufficient to sustain a conviction upon a guilty plea and to satisfy the requirements of article 1.15. [¶] When a trial court takes judicial notice of adjudicative facts, it authorizes the factfinder to accept the facts as true without requiring formal proof. Thus, as here, when the trial court takes judicial notice of a judicial confession, the State is not required to introduce the judicial confession into evidence. And when the accused specifically states in the judicial confession, 'I have read the indictment or information filed in this case and I committed each and every act alleged therein,' the judicial confession standing alone is sufficient to support a guilty plea under article 1.15...."

Burger v. State, 920 S.W.2d 433, 435 (Tex.App.—Houston [1st Dist.] 1996, pet. ref'd). "As used in article 1.15 ..., the term 'stipulation' includes agreements about what particular evidence or testimony would be, if presented in full in open court, without conceding the truthfulness of that evidence or otherwise waiving the need for proof. In reviewing the sufficiency of stipulated evidence to support the trial court's finding of guilt, we view stipulations as if they were actual witness testimony. The relevant inquiry is whether, after viewing the evidence in the light most favorable to the verdict, the trial judge as a rational trier of fact could have found the essential elements of the crime beyond a reasonable doubt."

Martin v. State, 745 S.W.2d 411, 412 (Tex.App.—Dallas 1988, pet. ref'd). "[A]rticle 1.15 ... does not apply to misdemeanor cases. We find no statutory or common law authority requiring consent to a stipulation in a misdemeanor case to be in writing."

Carrizales v. State, 737 S.W.2d 116, 117 (Tex. App.—Corpus Christi 1987, no pet.). "The plain language requirements of Article 1.15 do not apply to probation revocation hearings. The result of a revocation hearing is neither a conviction nor an acquittal. Nor does the probationer have the right to a jury. The hearing is not even a criminal prosecution; it is in the nature of an administrative proceeding in which the trial court sits in its capacity as supervisor of the probationer."

Harmes v. State, 636 S.W.2d 513, 515 (Tex. App.—San Antonio 1982, pet. ref'd). "[A]rticle 1.15 [is] inapplicable to a plea entered at the punishment stage of the trial."

ART. 1.16. LIBERTY OF SPEECH & PRESS

Every person shall be at liberty to speak, write or publish his opinion on any subject, being liable for the abuse of that privilege; and no law shall ever be passed curtailing the liberty of speech or of the press. In prosecutions for the publication of papers investigating the conduct of officers or men in public capacity, or when the matter published is proper for public information, the truth thereof may be given in evidence. In all indictments for libels, the jury shall have the right to determine the law and the facts, under the direction of the court, as in other cases.

History of CCP art. 1.16: Acts 1965, 59th Leg., vol. 2, ch. 722.

ART. 1.17. RELIGIOUS BELIEF

No person shall be disqualified to give evidence in any court of this State on account of his religious opinions, or for the want of any religious belief; but all oaths or affirmations shall be administered in the mode most binding upon the conscience, and shall be taken subject to the pains and penalties of perjury.

History of CCP art. 1.17: Acts 1965, 59th Leg., vol. 2, ch. 722.

ANNOTATIONS

Bisby v. State, 907 S.W.2d 949, 954-55 (Tex.App.—Fort Worth 1995, pet. ref'd). "[A]n '[a]ffirmation is simply a solemn undertaking to tell the truth; no special verbal formula is required.' [¶] When a trial judge is confronted by a witness who refuses on religious grounds to take an oath or an affirmation, the trial judge 'should take reasonable steps to accommodate the witness's beliefs.' Faced with such a situation, the trial judge should 'strive to devise, in consultation with the witness if necessary, some alternative form of serious public commitment to answer truthfully that does not transgress the prospect's sincerely held beliefs.'"

ART. 1.18. OUTLAWRY & TRANSPORTATION

No citizen shall be outlawed, nor shall any person be transported out of the State for any offense committed within the same.

History of CCP art. 1.18: Acts 1965, 59th Leg., vol. 2, ch. 722.
See also Tex. Const. art. 1, §20.

ANNOTATIONS

Brewer v. Taylor, 737 S.W.2d 421, 423 n.2 (Tex. App.—Dallas 1987, no writ). "Although the question has never been answered directly in Texas as far as we know, Texas courts appear to assume that an incarcerated felon has the right to initiate a civil action unrelated to his conviction or imprisonment. Such assumption is properly based upon the constitutional prohibition of outlawry."

ART. 1.19. CORRUPTION OF BLOOD, ETC.

No conviction shall work corruption of blood or forfeiture of estate.

History of CCP art. 1.19: Acts 1965, 59th Leg., vol. 2, ch. 722.
See also Tex. Const. art. 1, §21.

ART. 1.20. CONVICTION OF TREASON

No person shall be convicted of treason except on the testimony of two witnesses to the same overt act, or on confession in open court.

History of CCP art. 1.20: Acts 1965, 59th Leg., vol. 2, ch. 722.
See also Tex. Const. art. 1, §22.

ART. 1.21. PRIVILEGE OF LEGISLATORS

Senators and Representatives shall, except in cases of treason, felony or breach of the peace, be privileged from arrest during the session of the Legislature, and in going to and returning from the same, allowing one day for every twenty miles such member may reside from the place at which the Legislature is convened.

History of CCP art. 1.21: Acts 1965, 59th Leg., vol. 2, ch. 722.

ART. 1.22. REPEALED

Repealed by Acts 1985, 69th Leg., ch. 211, §9(a)(6), eff. Jan. 1, 1986.

ART. 1.23. DIGNITY OF STATE

All justices of the Supreme Court, judges of the Court of Criminal Appeals, justices of the Courts of Appeals and judges of the District Courts, shall, by virtue of their offices, be conservators of the peace throughout the State. The style of all writs and process shall be "The State of Texas." All prosecutions shall be carried on "in the name and by authority of The State of Texas", and conclude, "against the peace and dignity of the State."

History of CCP art. 1.23: Acts 1965, 59th Leg., vol. 2, ch. 722. Amended by Acts 1981, 67th Leg., ch. 291, §97, eff. Sept. 1, 1981.

ART. 1.24. PUBLIC TRIAL

The proceedings and trials in all courts shall be public.

History of CCP art. 1.24: Acts 1965, 59th Leg., vol. 2, ch. 722.

ANNOTATIONS

In re Thoma, 873 S.W.2d 477, 499 (Tex.Rev.Trib. 1994). "A modification of probation, although administrative in nature, is nonetheless a facet of a criminal proceeding in which society has an interest. It is a proceeding to which a probationer and the District Attorney are entitled to notice and, if desired, an opportunity to be present and heard, if a hearing is not otherwise waived or required."

San Antonio Express-News v. Roman, 861 S.W.2d 265, 267 n.1 (Tex.App.—San Antonio 1993, no writ). "This broad grant of access [in Article 1.24] to the public has certain limitations. For example, the public has no right to, and may not be present during grand jury proceedings; *in camera* hearings, as in the case of a bill of exceptions; appellate court deliberations; or jury deliberations."

Guillry v. State, 856 S.W.2d 477, 477-78 (Tex. App.—Houston [1st Dist.] 1993, pet. ref'd). "An accused's right to a public trial is not absolute. [L]imitations on public attendance may be imposed so long as they are no more restrictive than necessary to protect a state interest that outweighs the accused's interest in public scrutiny of the proceedings. The protection of witnesses from embarrassment or intimidation so extreme that it would traumatize them or render them unable to testify is a state interest sufficiently weighty to justify partial or complete exclusion of the public. [¶] A public trial protects the right of the accused to have the public know what happened in court; to let the citizenry weigh his guilt or innocence for itself, whatever the jury verdict; to assure that the procedures employed are fair. ... It is 'a check on judicial conduct and tends to improve the performance of both the parties and of the judiciary.' Even absent a showing of prejudice, infringement of the right to public trial exacts reversal as the remedy."

ART. 1.25. CONFRONTED BY WITNESSES

The defendant, upon a trial, shall be confronted with the witnesses, except in certain cases provided for in this Code where depositions have been taken.

History of CCP art. 1.25: Acts 1965, 59th Leg., vol. 2, ch. 722.

ART. 1.26. CONSTRUCTION OF THIS CODE

The provisions of this Code shall be liberally construed, so as to attain the objects intended by the Legislature: The prevention, suppression and punishment of crime.

History of CCP art. 1.26: Acts 1965, 59th Leg., vol. 2, ch. 722.
See also Gov't Code ch. 311.

ANNOTATIONS

State v. Morse, 903 S.W.2d 100, 103-04 (Tex. App.—El Paso 1995, no pet.). "When interpreting a statute, an appellate court should necessarily focus on the literal text of the statute in question and attempt to discern the fair, objective meaning of that text at the time of its enactment. When the literal text of a statute is clear, an appellate court must give effect to the statute's plain language and purposely eschew reliance on its legislative history. It is only when the literal text of the statute is either unclear or would lead to results so absurd that the Legislature could not *possibly* have intended them, that the courts should then resort to legislative history or other extraneous means to assist them in their interpretation of a statute."

ART. 1.27. COMMON LAW GOVERNS

If this Code fails to provide a rule of procedure in any particular state of case which may arise, the rules of the common law shall be applied and govern.

History of CCP art. 1.27: Acts 1965, 59th Leg., vol. 2, ch. 722.

ANNOTATIONS

Enos v. State, 889 S.W.2d 303, 305 (Tex.Crim.App. 1994). "[A]statute must not be interpreted as abrogating a principle of the common law unless such overruling is clearly indicated, either by the express terms of the statute or by necessary implication from the language used. This ... canon is based on the reasonable supposition that if the Legislature intended to overrule a principle of the common law, then it would have made its intent clear."

CHAPTER 2. GENERAL DUTIES OF OFFICERS

ART. 2.01. DUTIES OF DISTRICT ATTORNEYS

Each district attorney shall represent the State in all criminal cases in the district courts of his district and in appeals therefrom, except in cases where he has been, before his election, employed adversely. When any criminal proceeding is had before an examining court in his district or before a judge upon habeas corpus, and he is notified of the same, and is at the time within his district, he shall represent the State therein, unless prevented by other official duties. It shall be the primary duty of all prosecuting attorneys, including any special prosecutors, not to convict, but to see that justice is done. They shall not suppress facts or secrete witnesses capable of establishing the innocence of the accused.

History of CCP art. 2.01: Acts 1965, 59th Leg., vol. 2, ch. 722. Amended by Acts 1981, 67th Leg., ch. 291, §98, eff. Sept. 1, 1981.

ANNOTATIONS

Landers v. State, ___ S.W.3d ___ (Tex.Crim.App. 2008) (No. PD-1065-07; 6-18-08). "For a prosecuting attorney to 'switch sides' in the same criminal case is an actual conflict of interest and constitutes a due-process violation, even without a specific showing of prejudice. This has been called a 'hard and fast rule of disqualification.' [¶] But in the context of a conflict-of-interest claim that does not involve prior representation in the same criminal matter, the rule is somewhat different. A district attorney is not automatically disqualified from prosecuting a person whom he had previously represented, even when it is for the same type of offense. In that context, a due-process violation occurs only when the defendant can establish 'actual prejudice,' not just the threat of possible prejudice to his rights by virtue of the district attorney's prior representation. Actual prejudice would occur, for example, if: 1. The prosecuting attorney has previously personally represented the defendant in 'a substantially related matter'; and 2. The prosecuting attorney obtained 'confidential' information by virtue of that prior representation which was used to the defendant's disadvantage. [¶] '[T]wo matters are 'substantially related' ... when a genuine threat exists that a lawyer may divulge in one matter confidential information obtained in the other because the facts and issues involved in both are so similar.' [¶] The question is whether the same or inextricably related facts, circumstances or legal questions are at issue in both proceedings, not whether both charges are for the same criminal offense, or both offenses involve guns, drugs, or other specific facts. [¶] The second prong, 'confidential communications,' includes both privileged and unprivileged client information which the prosecutor learned by virtue of the former attorney-client relationship, but it excludes information that is generally known."

Duggan v. State, 778 S.W.2d 465, 468 (Tex.Crim. App.1989). "The prosecutor's constitutional duty to correct known false evidence is well established both in law and in the professional regulations which govern prosecutorial conduct. ... As a trustee of the State's interest in providing fair trials, the prosecutor is obliged to illuminate the court with the truth of the cause, so that the judge and jury may properly render justice. Thus the prosecutor is more than a mere advocate, but a fiduciary to fundamental principles of fairness. [¶] It does not matter whether the prosecutor actually knows that the evidence is false; it is enough that he or she should have recognized the misleading nature of the evidence. *At 469:* The purpose of imposing this paramount constitutional duty is 'not to punish the prosecutor or the trial court for the error committed, but rather to avoid an unfair trial to the accused.'" *See also Rougeau v. State*, 738 S.W.2d 651, 657 (Tex.Crim.App. 1987), *overruled on other grounds*, *Harris v. State*, 784 S.W.2d 5 (Tex.Crim.App.1989).

State ex rel. Turner v. McDonald, 676 S.W.2d 371, 373 (Tex.Crim.App.1984). "As a matter of 'right,' the State technically has none to trial by jury, and Respondent is correct that due process and due course of law are guarantees to citizens and not governments or their agents. But ... if the prosecutor believes that it is essential to the interest of doing justice that a particular accused be tried by a fair and impartial jury of his peers, our Legislature has provided the means for vindicating that interest...."

Canady v. State, 100 S.W.3d 28, 29 (Tex.App.—Waco 2002, no pet.). "When a district attorney prosecutes someone whom he previously represented in the same case, the conflict of interest is obvious and the integrity of the prosecutor's office suffers. ... The movant has the burden to prove the district attorney is disqualified. If an elected district attorney is lawfully disqualified from prosecution of a certain cause, his assistants will also be disqualified."

Franks v. State, 90 S.W.3d 771, 796 (Tex.App.—Fort Worth 2002, no pet.). "A due process violation [i.e., a violation of a prosecutor's duty to disclose exculpatory material information] occurs if: (1) the prosecutor fails to disclose evidence; (2) the evidence is favorable to the defendant; and (3) the evidence is material. Favorable evidence is 'material' if there is a reasonable probability that, had the evidence been disclosed to the defense, the result of the proceeding would have been different. Therefore, the essential issue is whether there is a reasonable probability that, had the suppressed evidence been disclosed to the defense, the outcome of the proceeding would have been different." *See also Johnson v. State*, 810 S.W.2d 785, 786 (Tex. App.—Waco 1991, pet. ref'd).

Gaitan v. State, 905 S.W.2d 703, 707 (Tex.App.—Houston [14th Dist.] 1995, pet. ref'd). "[A]ppellant maintains the trial court erred in permitting an assistant attorney general to act as counsel for the State in violation of [CCP art.] 2.01 ... and [Tex. Const. art.] V, §21.... [¶] A district attorney may employ any assistant prosecuting attorney, including an assistant attorney general, he deems necessary to carry out the constitutional duties of his office."

Tex. Atty. Gen. Op. JM-266 (12-21-84). "[T]he office of the district attorney is not within the judiciary exception [to the Open Records Act]. This office is not a court, nor is it directly controlled or supervised by a court. Its functions, moreover, are primarily executive, in the sense that its primary duty is to enforce the law."

ART. 2.02. DUTIES OF COUNTY ATTORNEYS

The county attorney shall attend the terms of court in his county below the grade of district court, and shall represent the State in all criminal cases under examination or prosecution in said county; and in the absence of the district attorney he shall represent the State alone and, when requested, shall aid the district attorney in the prosecution of any case in behalf of the State in the district court. He shall represent the State in cases he has prosecuted which are appealed.

History of CCP art. 2.02: Acts 1965, 59th Leg., vol. 2, ch. 722. Amended by Acts 1981, 67th Leg., ch. 291, §99, eff. Sept. 1, 1981.

ANNOTATIONS

Hartsfield v. State, 200 S.W.3d 813, 816 (Tex. App.—Texarkana 2006, pet. ref'd). "The first issue before this Court is whether the election of a different County Attorney invalidated [Assistant Attorney General's] authority to prosecute this matter. [¶] [W]e do not believe error is present. There is no question that [previous County Attorney] deputized [Assistant Attorney General] to prosecute this case. ... When [previous County Attorney] left office, [Assistant Attorney General] began serving at the will and pleasure of [newly elected County Attorney]. [¶] Instead of being a deputy, as in the [previous County Attorney's] tenure, [Assistant Attorney General] could have remained on the case under [newly elected County Attorney's] direction in the capacity of a special prosecutor. On request, a special prosecutor assists a county attorney in the investigation and prosecution of a particular case. A special prosecutor differs from a deputy because a special prosecutor is not required to take a constitutional oath of office, unless the elected district attorney is absent or disqualified. *At 817:* Further, with a special prosecutor, the county attorney must retain control and responsibility for the prosecution. 'Control of the prosecution' means control of crucial prosecutorial decisions, including, but not limited to, decisions regarding whether to prosecute, what investigative powers to utilize, and what plea bargains to strike. Control of the prosecution is not determined according to quantitative analysis or by simply looking at who was lead counsel at trial; in fact, for tactical reasons, a county attorney can give substantial portions of the conduct at trial to a particularly skilled assistant without relinquishing control."

Prado v. State, 822 S.W.2d 819, 821 (Tex.App.—Eastland 1992, pet. ref'd). "[T]he failure of a county attorney to perform his official duties, as directed in Article 2.02, does not render a judgment of conviction void."

ART. 2.021. DUTIES OF ATTORNEY GENERAL

 Article 2.021 below is effective for offenses committed on or after Sept. 1, 2007.

The attorney general may offer to a county or district attorney the assistance of the attorney general's office in the prosecution of an offense described by Article 60.051(g) the victim of which is younger than 17 years of age at the time the offense is committed. On request of a county or district attorney, the attorney general shall assist in the prosecution of an offense described by Article 60.051(g) the victim of which is younger than 17 years of age at the time the offense is committed. For purposes of this article, assistance includes investigative, technical, and litigation assistance of the attorney general's office.

History of CCP art. 2.021: Acts 2007, 80th Leg., ch. 593, §1.02, eff. Sept. 1, 2007.

ART. 2.025. SPECIAL DUTY OF DISTRICT OR COUNTY ATTORNEY RELATING TO CHILD SUPPORT

If a district or county attorney receives money from a person who is required by a court order to pay child support through a local registry or the Title IV-D agency and the money is presented to the attorney as payment for the court-ordered child support, the attorney shall transfer the money to the local registry or Title IV-D agency designated as the place of payment in the child support order.

History of CCP art. 2.025: Acts 1999, 76th Leg., ch. 40, §1, eff. Sept. 1, 1999.

ART. 2.03. NEGLECT OF DUTY

(a) It shall be the duty of the attorney representing the State to present by information to the court having jurisdiction, any officer for neglect or failure of any duty enjoined upon such officer, when such neglect or failure can be presented by information, whenever it shall come to the knowledge of said attorney that there has been a neglect or failure of duty upon the part of said officer; and he shall bring to the notice of the grand jury any act of violation of law or neglect or failure of duty upon the part of any officer, when such violation, neglect or failure is not presented by information, and whenever the same may come to his knowledge.

(b) It is the duty of the trial court, the attorney representing the accused, the attorney representing the state and all peace officers to so conduct themselves as to insure a fair trial for both the state and the defendant, not impair the presumption of innocence, and at the same time afford the public the benefits of a free press.

History of CCP art. 2.03: Acts 1965, 59th Leg., vol. 2, ch. 722. Amended by Acts 1967, 60th Leg., ch. 659, §3, eff. Aug. 28, 1967.

Randle v. State, 826 S.W.2d 943, 946 (Tex.Crim. App.1992). "By virtue of ... Art. 2.03(b), the officers of the court have a duty to ensure a fair trial and a duty not to impair the presumption of innocence. Appellant's attorney fulfilled his duty by objecting, in a timely fashion, to his client being placed before the jury in jail clothing. [¶] By forcing [appellant] to trial in jail clothes, the court and its officers failed in their duty to preserve his presumption of innocence."

Miller v. State, 874 S.W.2d 908, 916 (Tex.App.— Houston [1st Dist.] 1994, pet. ref'd). "[T]he district attorney has a duty to present to the grand jury any information of official misconduct by an officer."

ART. 2.04. SHALL DRAW COMPLAINTS

Upon complaint being made before a district or county attorney that an offense has been committed in his district or county, he shall reduce the complaint to writing and cause the same to be signed and sworn to by the complainant, and it shall be duly attested by said attorney.

History of CCP art. 2.04: Acts 1965, 59th Leg., vol. 2, ch. 722.
See also CCP art. 21.22.

Shackelford v. State, 516 S.W.2d 180, 180 (Tex. Crim.App.1974). "The complaint upon which this conviction was founded contains a fundamental defect. The jurat on the complaint is defective because it was undated. [¶] An undated jurat vitiates the complaint. Since there can be no valid information in the absence of a valid complaint, a complaint without a proper jurat will not support an information." *But see Studer v. State*, 799 S.W.2d 263 (Tex.Crim.App.1990).

Taylor v. Gately, 870 S.W.2d 204, 204 (Tex.App.— Waco 1994, writ dism'd). Appellant "asserts that [CCP arts.] 2.04, 2.05, 2.12, and 2.13 ... impose a 'ministerial duty' upon the District Attorney to accept and file his complaint. [¶] We have been directed to no case, nor has our research revealed any case, in which mandamus has issued against a prosecuting attorney for failure to institute a criminal case."

ART. 2.05. WHEN COMPLAINT IS MADE

If the offense be a misdemeanor, the attorney shall forthwith prepare an information based upon such complaint and file the same in the court having jurisdiction; provided, that in counties having no county attorney, misdemeanor cases may be tried upon complaint alone, without an information, provided, however, in counties having one or more criminal district courts an information must be filed in each misdemeanor case. If the offense be a felony, he shall forthwith file the complaint with a magistrate of the county.

History of CCP art. 2.05: Acts 1965, 59th Leg., vol. 2, ch. 722.

ANNOTATIONS

Ex parte Thomas, 234 S.W.3d 656, 661 (Tex. App.—Beaumont 2007, no pet.). "In counties where the county attorney is responsible for misdemeanor prosecution, the county attorney generally prosecutes a misdemeanor offense by filing an information. The county attorney prepares the information based upon a complaint, and files the information in the court having jurisdiction. An information may not be presented until an affidavit has been made by some credible person charging the defendant with an offense. If an information is required, the failure to file an information deprives the trial court of jurisdiction to try the case."

ART. 2.06. MAY ADMINISTER OATHS

For the purpose mentioned in the two preceding Articles, district and county attorneys are authorized to administer oaths.

History of CCP art. 2.06: Acts 1965, 59th Leg., vol. 2, ch. 722.

ART. 2.07. ATTORNEY PRO TEM

(a) Whenever an attorney for the state is disqualified to act in any case or proceeding, is absent from the county or district, or is otherwise unable to perform the duties of his office, or in any instance where there is no attorney for the state, the judge of the court in which he represents the state may appoint any competent attorney to perform the duties of the office during the absence or disqualification of the attorney for the state.

(b) Except as otherwise provided by this subsection, if the appointed attorney is also an attorney for the state, the duties of the appointed office are additional duties of his present office, and he is not entitled to additional compensation. Nothing herein shall prevent a commissioners court of a county from contracting with another commissioners court to pay expenses and reimburse compensation paid by a county to an attorney for the state who is appointed to perform additional duties.

(b-1) An attorney for the state who is not disqualified to act may request the court to permit him to recuse himself in a case for good cause and upon approval by the court is disqualified.

(c) If the appointed attorney is not an attorney for the state, he is qualified to perform the duties of the office for the period of absence or disqualification of the attorney for the state on filing an oath with the clerk of the court. He shall receive compensation in the same amount and manner as an attorney appointed to represent an indigent person.

(d) In this article, "attorney for the state" means a county attorney, a district attorney, or a criminal district attorney.

(e) In Subsections (b) and (c) of this article, "attorney for the state" includes an assistant attorney general.

(f) In Subsection (a) of this article, "competent attorney" includes an assistant attorney general.

(g) An attorney appointed under Subsection (a) of this article to perform the duties of the office of an attorney for the state in a justice or municipal court may be paid a reasonable fee for performing those duties.

History of CCP art. 2.07: Acts 1965, 59th Leg., vol. 2, ch. 722. Amended by Acts 1967, 60th Leg., ch. 659, §4, eff. Aug. 28, 1967; Acts 1973, 63rd Leg., ch. 154, §1, eff. May 23, 1973; Acts 1987, 70th Leg., ch. 918, §1, eff. Aug. 31, 1987; Acts 1995, 74th Leg., ch. 785, §1, eff. Sept. 1, 1995; Acts 1999, 76th Leg., ch. 1545, §1, eff. Sept. 1, 1999.

ANNOTATIONS

Coleman v. State, 246 S.W.3d 76, 84 (Tex.Crim. App.2008). "Appellant claims that the court of appeals erred by not following the plain language of Article 2.07. He argues that the statute limits an attorney pro tem to serving only 'during' the disqualification of the district attorney, and that the disqualification in this case ended the moment that the newly elected district attorney took office. *At 85:* Because (1) the new and non-disqualified district attorney had taken office only nine days prior to the start of trial; (2) the new district attorney did not object to allowing the attorneys pro tem to continue; (3) the two attorneys pro tem had spent over 21 months researching, investigating, and preparing this case for a trial that was then imminent; and (4) the trial would have occurred months earlier (during [disqualified DA's] tenure) but for the defense-requested continuances, we agree that the trial court did not err in allowing the trial to proceed with the attorneys pro tem representing the State."

State v. Rosenbaum, 852 S.W.2d 525, 527 (Tex. Crim.App.1993). "Upon approval of the recusal request by the judge, the district attorney is considered disqualified. *At 528:* [A]n attorney *pro tem* or special prosecutor *takes the place of* the disqualified district attorney assuming all the district attorney's powers and duties in the case. Therefore, the special prosecutor is not subject to the direction of the disqualified district attorney as is a subordinate, but, for that case, he *is* the district attorney."

In re Guerra, 235 S.W.3d 392, 414-15 (Tex.App.— Corpus Christi 2007, orig. proceeding). "A judge has the authority, as well as an obligation, to appoint an attorney pro tem to assist a grand jury that intends to criminally investigate the district attorney. In such a situation, the district attorney is deemed 'disqualified to act' for purposes of article 2.07(a) ..., and disqualification need not solely arise from the attorney's own motion to recuse under subsection (b-1). [¶] While we find that respondent's appointment of an attorney pro tem was explicitly authorized by article 2.07, we further find that such appointment was implicitly authorized by a court's inherent power. *At 420-21:* We hold that article 2.07 implicitly affords a district attorney the right to notice and a hearing before he is deemed disqualified to act in any case or proceeding. We further hold, however, that this right ceases to exist in situations like the one now before us, where: (1) a grand jury, on its own initiative, sought to investigate the district attorney for possible criminal wrongdoing; (2) the judge, upon being confronted with the grand jury's desire to investigate the district attorney, disqualified the district attorney from participating in the grand jury's investigation; and (3) the judge subsequently appointed an attorney pro tem to assist the grand jury with its investigation."

State v. Newton, 158 S.W.3d 582, 590 (Tex. App.—San Antonio 2005, pet. dism'd). "Although the trial court's order of appointment used the term 'special prosecutor,' [prosecuting attorney] is, in substance, an attorney pro tem. And, [D's attorneys'] failure to timely object to [prosecuting attorney's] qualifications as an attorney pro tem under article 2.07 made [prosecuting

attorney] a de facto attorney pro tem capable of invoking the jurisdiction of this court. Therefore, the notice of appeal signed by [prosecuting attorney] invoiced our jurisdiction over this appeal."

Evans v. State, 769 S.W.2d 319, 322 (Tex.App.— Dallas 1989, no pet.). Appellant "claims that his conviction is void since the special prosecutor failed to execute an oath as required by article 2.07(c).... We disagree. [¶] Unless there is something in the appellate record to show that the State's attorney *pro tem* was not duly and legally appointed, we must presume that he was duly and legally appointed and that he rightfully exercised the office."

ART. 2.08. DISQUALIFIED

District and county attorneys shall not be of counsel adversely to the State in any case, in any court, nor shall they, after they cease to be such officers, be of counsel adversely to the State in any case in which they have been of counsel for the State.

History of CCP art. 2.08: Acts 1965, 59th Leg., vol. 2, ch. 722.

ANNOTATIONS

Holland v. State, 729 S.W.2d 366, 368 (Tex.App.— Beaumont 1987, no pet.). Article 2.08 "disqualifies former prosecuting attorneys from switching sides in cases where they have been of counsel for the state. This conflict of interest is not present when the former representation involves an enhancing offense because that previous conviction is not part of the same case as the one to be tried."

Ⓐ ART. 2.09. WHO ARE MAGISTRATES

Each of the following officers is a magistrate within the meaning of this Code: The justices of the Supreme Court, the judges of the Court of Criminal Appeals, the justices of the Courts of Appeals, the judges of the District Court, the magistrates appointed by the judges of the district courts of Bexar County, Dallas County, or Tarrant County that give preference to criminal cases, the criminal law hearing officers for Harris County appointed under Subchapter L, Chapter 54, Government Code, the criminal law hearing officers for Cameron County appointed under Subchapter BB, Chapter 54, Government Code, the magistrates appointed by the judges of the district courts of Lubbock County, Nolan County, or Webb County, the magistrates appointed by the judges of the criminal district courts of Dallas County or Tarrant County, the masters appointed by the judges of the district courts and the county courts at law that give preference to criminal cases in Jefferson County, the magistrates appointed by the judges of the district courts and the statutory county courts of Brazos County, Nueces County, or Williamson County, the magistrates appointed by the judges of the district courts and statutory county courts that give preference to criminal cases in Travis County, the county judges, the judges of the county courts at law, judges of the county criminal courts, the judges of statutory probate courts, the associate judges appointed by the judges of the statutory probate courts under Subchapter G, Chapter 54, Government Code, the justices of the peace, and the mayors and recorders and the judges of the municipal courts of incorporated cities or towns.

History of CCP art. 2.09: Acts 1965, 59th Leg., vol. 2, ch. 722. Amended by Acts 1981, 67th Leg., ch. 291, §100, eff. Sept. 1, 1981; Acts 1983, 68th Leg., ch. 204, §1, eff. Aug. 29, 1983; Acts 1989, 71st Leg., ch. 25, §2 (eff. Aug. 28, 1989), ch. 79, §1 (eff. May 15, 1989), ch. 916, §1 (eff. Sept. 1, 1989), ch. 1068, §2 (eff. Aug. 28, 1989); Acts 1991, 72nd Leg., ch. 16, §4.01, eff. Aug. 26, 1991; Acts 1993, 73rd Leg., ch. 224, §2 (eff. Aug. 30, 1993), ch. 413, §1 (eff. Sept. 1, 1993), ch. 468, §1 (eff. June 9, 1993), ch. 577, §2 (eff. Aug. 30, 1993); Acts 1999, 76th Leg., ch. 586, §2 (eff. June 18, 1999), ch. 1503, §2 (eff. Sept. 1, 1999); Acts 2003, 78th Leg., ch. 979, §1 (eff. Sept. 1, 2003), ch. 1066, §9 (eff. Sept. 1, 2003); Acts 2005, 79th Leg., ch. 109, §2, (eff. May 20, 2005), ch. 767, §2 (eff. Sept. 1, 2005), ch. 1331, §1 (eff. Sept. 1, 2005); Acts 2007, 80th Leg., ch. 1141, §1, eff. Sept. 1, 2007.

ANNOTATIONS

Rabb v. State, 730 S.W.2d 751, 754 (Tex.Crim.App. 1987). The 1983 "amendments to [CCP arts.] 2.09 and 4.01 ... vis-a-vis the Magistrate's Act do not alter the function of Dallas County magistrates or the powers available to them so as to remove them from the supervision of district court judges. [¶] Since the magistrates' actions continue to be subject to the approval of the referring district courts, the magistrates do not exercise power and authority which is equal to that of district court judges."

O'Quinn v. State, 462 S.W.2d 583, 588 (Tex.Crim. App.1970). "That it was not the intent of the legislature to limit the authority of the judge, recorder or mayor to administering the oath to complaints charging offenses which the corporation court has jurisdiction to try is made clear by Art. 2.09 ..., making the mayors and recorders and the judges of the city courts of incorporated cities or towns magistrates...."

ART. 2.10. DUTY OF MAGISTRATES

It is the duty of every magistrate to preserve the peace within his jurisdiction by the use of all lawful means; to issue all process intended to aid in preventing and suppressing crime; to cause the arrest of offenders by the use of lawful means in order that they may be brought to punishment.

History of CCP art. 2.10: Acts 1965, 59th Leg., vol. 2, ch. 722.

ANNOTATIONS

Bitner v. State, 135 S.W.3d 906, 906 (Tex.App.— Fort Worth 2004, pet. ref'd). "The issue before us is whether a justice of the peace who is physically outside her geographical jurisdiction may sign a search warrant for property located within her geographical jurisdiction. We conclude the answer is yes...."

ART. 2.11. EXAMINING COURT

When the magistrate sits for the purpose of inquiring into a criminal accusation against any person, this is called an examining court.

History of CCP art. 2.11: Acts 1965, 59th Leg., vol. 2, ch. 722.

ART. 2.12. WHO ARE PEACE OFFICERS

The following are peace officers:

(1) sheriffs, their deputies, and those reserve deputies who hold a permanent peace officer license issued under Chapter 1701, Occupations Code;

(2) constables, deputy constables, and those reserve deputy constables who hold a permanent peace officer license issued under Chapter 1701, Occupations Code;

(3) marshals or police officers of an incorporated city, town, or village, and those reserve municipal police officers who hold a permanent peace officer license issued under Chapter 1701, Occupations Code;

(4) rangers and officers commissioned by the Public Safety Commission and the Director of the Department of Public Safety;

(5) investigators of the district attorneys', criminal district attorneys', and county attorneys' offices;

(6) law enforcement agents of the Texas Alcoholic Beverage Commission;

(7) each member of an arson investigating unit commissioned by a city, a county, or the state;

(8) officers commissioned under Section 37.081, Education Code, or Subchapter E, Chapter 51, Education Code;

(9) officers commissioned by the General Services Commission;

(10) law enforcement officers commissioned by the Parks and Wildlife Commission;

(11) airport police officers commissioned by a city with a population of more than 1.18 million that operates an airport that serves commercial air carriers;

(12) airport security personnel commissioned as peace officers by the governing body of any political subdivision of this state, other than a city described by Subdivision (11), that operates an airport that serves commercial air carriers;

(13) municipal park and recreational patrolmen and security officers;

(14) security officers and investigators commissioned as peace officers by the comptroller;

(15) officers commissioned by a water control and improvement district under Section 49.216, Water Code;

(16) officers commissioned by a board of trustees under Chapter 54, Transportation Code;

(17) investigators commissioned by the Texas Medical Board;

(18) officers commissioned by the board of managers of the Dallas County Hospital District, the Tarrant County Hospital District, or the Bexar County Hospital District under Section 281.057, Health and Safety Code;

(19) county park rangers commissioned under Subchapter E, Chapter 351, Local Government Code;

(20) investigators employed by the Texas Racing Commission;

(21) officers commissioned under Chapter 554, Occupations Code;

(22) officers commissioned by the governing body of a metropolitan rapid transit authority under Section 451.108, Transportation Code, or by a regional transportation authority under Section 452.110, Transportation Code;

(23) investigators commissioned by the attorney general under Section 402.009, Government Code;

(24) security officers and investigators commissioned as peace officers under Chapter 466, Government Code;

(25) an officer employed by the Department of State Health Services under Section 431.2471, Health and Safety Code;

(26) officers appointed by an appellate court under Subchapter F, Chapter 53, Government Code;

(27) officers commissioned by the state fire marshal under Chapter 417, Government Code;

(28) an investigator commissioned by the commissioner of insurance under Section 701.104, Insurance Code;

(29) apprehension specialists and inspectors general commissioned by the Texas Youth Commission as officers under Sections 61.0451 and 61.0931, Human Resources Code;

(30) officers appointed by the inspector general of the Texas Department of Criminal Justice under Section 493.019, Government Code;

(31) investigators commissioned by the Commission on Law Enforcement Officer Standards and Education under Section 1701.160, Occupations Code;

(32) commission investigators commissioned by the Texas Private Security Board under Section 1702.061(f), Occupations Code;

(33) the fire marshal and any officers, inspectors, or investigators commissioned by an emergency services district under Chapter 775, Health and Safety Code;

(34) officers commissioned by the State Board of Dental Examiners under Section 254.013, Occupations Code, subject to the limitations imposed by that section; and

(35) investigators commissioned by the Texas Juvenile Probation Commission as officers under Section 141.055, Human Resources Code.

History of CCP art. 2.12: Acts 1965, 59th Leg., vol. 2, ch. 722. Amended by Acts 1967, 60th Leg., ch. 659, §5, eff. Aug. 28, 1967; Acts 1971, 62nd Leg., ch. 246, §3, eff. May 17, 1971; Acts 1973, 63rd Leg., ch. 7, §2 (eff. Aug. 27, 1973), ch. 459, §1 (eff. Aug. 27, 1973); Acts 1975, 64th Leg., ch. 204, §1, eff. Sept. 1, 1975; Acts 1977, 65th Leg., ch. 227, §2 (eff. May 24, 1977), ch. 396, §1 (eff. Aug. 29, 1977); Acts 1983, 68th Leg., ch. 114, §1 (eff. May 17, 1983), ch. 699, §11 (eff. June 19, 1983), ch. 867, §2 (eff. June 19, 1983), ch. 974, §11 (eff. Aug. 29, 1983); Acts 1985, 69th Leg., ch. 384, §2 (eff. Aug. 26, 1985), ch. 907, §6 (eff. Sept. 1, 1985); Acts 1986, 69th Leg., 2nd C.S., ch. 19, §4, eff. Dec. 4, 1986; Acts 1987, 70th Leg., ch. 262, §20 (eff. Sept. 1, 1987), ch. 350, §1 (eff. Aug. 31, 1987); Acts 1989, 71st Leg., ch. 277, §4 (eff. June 14, 1989), ch. 794, §1 (eff. Aug. 28, 1989), ch. 1104, §4 (eff. June 16, 1989); Acts 1991, 72nd Leg., ch. 16, §4.02 (eff. Aug. 26, 1991), ch. 228, §1 (eff. Sept. 1, 1991), ch. 287, §24 (eff. Sept. 1, 1991), ch. 386, §70 (eff. Aug. 26, 1991), ch. 446, §1 (eff. June 11, 1991), ch. 544, §1 (eff. Aug. 26, 1991), ch. 545, §2 (eff. Aug. 26, 1991), ch. 597, §57 (eff. Sept. 1, 1991), ch. 853, §2 (eff. Sept. 1, 1991), 1st C.S., ch. 6, §6, ch. 14, §3.01 (eff. Nov. 12, 1991); Acts 1993, 73rd Leg., ch. 107, §4.07 (eff. Aug. 30, 1993), ch. 116, §1 (eff. Aug. 30, 1993), ch. 339, §2 (eff. Sept. 1, 1993), ch. 695, §2 (eff. Sept. 1, 1993), ch. 912, §25 (eff. Sept. 1, 1993); Acts 1995, 74th Leg., ch. 260, §10 (eff. May 30, 1995), ch. 621, §2 (eff. Sept. 1, 1995), ch. 729, §1 (eff. Aug. 28, 1995); Acts 1997, 75th Leg., ch. 1423, §4.01, eff. Sept. 1, 1997; Acts 1999, 76th Leg., ch. 90, §1 (eff. Sept. 1, 1999), ch. 322, §2 (eff. May 29, 1999), ch. 882, §2 (eff. June 18, 1999), ch. 974, §37 (eff. Sept. 1, 1999); Acts 2001, 77th Leg., ch. 272, §7 (eff. Sept. 1, 2001), ch. 442, §1 (eff. Sept. 1, 2001), ch. 669, §8 (eff. Sept. 1, 2001), ch. 1420, §3.001 (eff. Sept. 1, 2001); Acts 2003, 78th Leg., ch. 235, §16 (eff. Sept. 1, 2003), ch. 474, §1 (eff. June 20, 2003), ch. 930, §12 (eff. Sept. 1, 2003); Acts 2005, 79th Leg., ch. 728, §4.001, eff. Sept. 1, 2005; Acts 2007, 80th Leg., ch. 263, §1 (eff. June 8, 2007), ch. 838, §1 (eff. June 15, 2007), ch. 908, §1 (eff. Sept. 1, 2007), ch. 1172, §1 (eff. June 15, 2007).

ANNOTATIONS

Deltenre v. State, 808 S.W.2d 97, 99 (Tex.Crim.App. 1991). "[A] jailer who is not a deputy sheriff is not a 'peace officer'…. [T]he legislature did not intend for jailers to be considered peace officers because of the distinctive statutory treatment given these terms. *At 101:* [T]he term 'peace officer' has acquired a technical meaning by legislative definition."

Irvin v. State, 563 S.W.2d 920, 923 n.5 (Tex.Crim. App.1978). "We note that a private security guard is not a peace officer…."

State v. Garza, 783 S.W.2d 198, 199 (Tex.1989). "The [CCP] defines 'peace officers' to include sheriffs and their deputies but not DEA officers."

Blackwell v. Harris Cty., 909 S.W.2d 135, 138 (Tex. App.—Houston [14th Dist.] 1995, writ denied). "Unless elected to a law enforcement office, a peace officer must hold a license from the Texas Commission on Law Enforcement Standards certifying his qualifications, and be commissioned by a governmental agency named in Article 2.12…."

State v. Carroll, 855 S.W.2d 128, 129 (Tex.App.— Austin 1993, no pet.). "Campus police officers are peace officers."

ART. 2.121. RAILROAD PEACE OFFICERS

(a) The director of the Department of Public Safety may appoint up to 250 railroad peace officers who are employed by a railroad company to aid law enforcement agencies in the protection of railroad property and the protection of the persons and property of railroad passengers and employees.

(b) Except as provided by Subsection (c) of this article, a railroad peace officer may make arrests and exercise all authority given peace officers under this code when necessary to prevent or abate the commission of an offense involving injury to passengers and employees of the railroad or damage to railroad property or to protect railroad property or property in the custody or control of the railroad.

(c) A railroad peace officer may not issue a traffic citation for a violation of Chapter 521, Transportation Code, or Subtitle C, Title 7, Transportation Code.

(d) A railroad peace officer is not entitled to state benefits normally provided by the state to a peace officer.

(e) A person may not serve as a railroad peace officer for a railroad company unless:

(1) the Texas Railroad Association submits the person's application for appointment and certification as a railroad peace officer to the director of the Department of Public Safety and to the executive director of the Commission on Law Enforcement Officer Standards and Education;

(2) the director of the department issues the person a certificate of authority to act as a railroad peace officer; and

(3) the executive director of the commission determines that the person meets minimum standards required of peace officers by the commission relating to competence, reliability, education, training, morality, and physical and mental health and issues the person a license as a railroad peace officer; and

(4) the person has met all standards for certification as a peace officer by the Commission on Law Enforcement Officer Standards and Education.

(f) For good cause, the director of the department may revoke a certificate of authority issued under this article and the executive director of the commission may revoke a license issued under this article. Termination of employment with a railroad company, or the revocation of a railroad peace officer license, shall constitute an automatic revocation of a certificate of authority to act as a railroad peace officer.

(g) A railroad company is liable for any act or omission by a person serving as a railroad peace officer for the company that is within the person's scope of employment. Neither the state nor any political subdivision or agency of the state shall be liable for any act or omission by a person appointed as a railroad peace officer. All expenses incurred by the granting or revocation of a certificate of authority to act as a railroad peace officer shall be paid by the employing railroad company.

(h) A railroad peace officer who is a member of a railroad craft may not perform the duties of a member of any other railroad craft during a strike or labor dispute.

(i) The director of the department and the executive director of the commission shall have the authority to promulgate rules necessary for the effective administration and performance of the duties and responsibilities delegated to them by this article.

History of CCP art. 2.121: Acts 1985, 69th Leg., ch. 531, §1, eff. June 12, 1985. Amended by Acts 1999, 76th Leg., ch. 62, §3.01, eff. Sept. 1, 1999.

ART. 2.122. SPECIAL INVESTIGATORS

(a) The following named criminal investigators of the United States shall not be deemed peace officers, but shall have the powers of arrest, search and seizure as to felony offenses only under the laws of the State of Texas:

(1) Special Agents of the Federal Bureau of Investigation;

(2) Special Agents of the Secret Service;

(3) Special Agents of the United States Customs Service;

(4) Special Agents of Alcohol, Tobacco and Firearms;

(5) Special Agents of Federal Drug Enforcement Agency;

(6) Inspectors of the United States Postal Service;

(7) Special Agents of the Criminal Investigation Division and Inspectors of the Internal Security Division of the Internal Revenue Service;

(8) Civilian Special Agents of the United States Naval Investigative Service;

(9) Marshals and Deputy Marshals of the United States Marshals Service;

(10) Special Agents of the United States Immigration and Naturalization Service; and

(11) Special Agents of the United States Department of State, Bureau of Diplomatic Security.

(b) A person designated as a special policeman by the Federal Protective Services division of the General Services Administration under 40 U.S.C. Section 318 or 318d is not a peace officer but has the powers of arrest and search and seizure as to any offense under the laws of this state.

(c) A customs inspector of the United States Customs Service or a border patrolman or immigration officer of the United States Department of Justice is not a peace officer under the laws of this state but, on the premises of a port facility designated by the commissioner of the United States Immigration and Naturalization Service as a port of entry for arrival in the United States by land transportation from the United Mexican States into the State of Texas or at a permanent established border patrol traffic check point, has the authority to detain a person pending transfer without unnecessary delay to a peace officer if the inspector, patrolman, or officer has probable cause to believe that the person has engaged in conduct that is a violation of Section 49.02, 49.04, 49.07, or 49.08, Penal Code, regardless of whether the violation may be disposed of in a criminal proceeding or a juvenile justice proceeding.

(d) A commissioned law enforcement officer of the National Park Service is not a peace officer under the laws of this state, except that the officer has the powers of arrest, search, and seizure as to any offense under the laws of this state committed within the boundaries of a national park or national recreation area. In this subsection, "national park or national recreation area" means a national park or national recreation area included in the National Park System as defined by 16 U.S.C. Section 1c(a).

(e) A Special Agent or Law Enforcement Officer of the United States Forest Service is not a peace officer under the laws of this state, except that the agent or officer has the powers of arrest, search, and seizure as to any offense under the laws of this state committed within the National Forest System. In this subsection, "National Forest System" has the meaning assigned by 16 U.S.C. Section 1609.

(f) Security personnel working at a commercial nuclear power plant, including contract security personnel, trained and qualified under a security plan approved by the United States Nuclear Regulatory Commission, are not peace officers under the laws of this state, except that such personnel have the powers of arrest, search, and seizure, including the powers under Section 9.51, Penal Code, while in the performance of their duties on the premises of a commercial nuclear power plant site or under agreements entered into with local law enforcement regarding areas surrounding the plant site.

(g) In addition to the powers of arrest, search, and seizure under Subsection (a), a Special Agent of the Secret Service protecting a person described by 18 U.S.C. Section 3056(a) or investigating a threat against a person described by 18 U.S.C. Section 3056(a) has the powers of arrest, search, and seizure as to:

(1) misdemeanor offenses under the laws of this state; and

(2) any criminal offense under federal law.

History of CCP art. 2.122: Acts 1977, 65th Leg., ch. 396, §2. Designated as Art. 2.121 and amended by Acts 1985, 69th Leg., ch. 543, §1, eff. Sept. 1, 1985. Renumbered from Art. 2.121 and amended by Acts 1987, 70th Leg., ch. 503, §1 (eff. Aug. 31, 1987), ch. 854, §1 (eff. Aug. 31, 1987). Amended by Acts 1989, 71st Leg., ch. 841, §1, eff. June 14, 1989; Acts 1993, 73rd Leg., ch. 927, §1, eff. June 19, 1993; Acts 1997, 75th Leg., ch. 290, §1 (eff. May 26, 1997), ch. 717, §1 (eff. June 17, 1997); Acts 1999, 76th Leg., ch. 197, §1 (eff. May 24, 1999), ch. 628, §1 (eff. June 18, 1999), ch. 863, §1 (eff. June 18, 1999); Acts 2001, 77th Leg., ch. 1420, §21.001(7), eff. Sept. 1, 2001; Acts 2003, 78th Leg., ch. 1237, §1, eff. June 20, 2003; Acts 2005, 79th Leg., ch. 1337, §5, eff. June 18, 2005.

ART. 2.123. ADJUNCT POLICE OFFICERS

(a) Within counties under 200,000 population, the chief of police of a municipality or the sheriff of the county, if the institution is outside the corporate limits of a municipality, that has jurisdiction over the geographical area of a private institution of higher education, provided the governing board of such institution consents, may appoint up to 50 peace officers who are commissioned under Section 51.212, Education Code, and who are employed by a private institution of higher education located in the municipality or county, to serve as adjunct police officers of the municipality or county. Officers appointed under this article shall aid law enforcement agencies in the protection of the municipality or county in a geographical area that is designated by agreement on an annual basis between the appointing chief of police or sheriff and the private institution.

(b) The geographical area that is subject to designation under Subsection (a) of this article may include only the private institution's campus area and an area that:

(1) is adjacent to the campus of the private institution;

(2) does not extend further than a distance of one mile from the perimeter of the campus of the private institution; and

(3) is inhabited primarily by students or employees of the private institution.

(c) A peace officer serving as an adjunct police officer may make arrests and exercise all authority given peace officers under this code only within the geographical area designated by agreement between the appointing chief of police or sheriff and the private institution.

(d) A peace officer serving as an adjunct police officer has all the rights, privileges, and immunities of a peace officer but is not entitled to state compensation and retirement benefits normally provided by the state to a peace officer.

(e) A person may not serve as an adjunct police officer for a municipality or county unless:

(1) the institution of higher education submits the person's application for appointment and certification as an adjunct police officer to the chief of police of the municipality or, if outside a municipality, the sheriff of the county that has jurisdiction over the geographical area of the institution;

(2) the chief of police of the municipality or sheriff of the county to whom the application was made issues the person a certificate of authority to act as an adjunct police officer; and

(3) the person undergoes any additional training required for that person to meet the training standards of the municipality or county for peace officers employed by the municipality or county.

(f) For good cause, the chief of police or sheriff may revoke a certificate of authority issued under this article.

(g) A private institution of higher education is liable for any act or omission by a person while serving as an adjunct police officer outside of the campus of the institution in the same manner as the municipality or county governing that geographical area is liable for any act or omission of a peace officer employed by the municipality or county. This subsection shall not be construed to act as a limitation on the liability of a municipality or county for the acts or omissions of a person serving as an adjunct police officer.

(h) The employing institution shall pay all expenses incurred by the municipality or county in granting or revoking a certificate of authority to act as an adjunct police officer under this article.

(i) This article does not affect any duty of the municipality or county to provide law enforcement services to a geographical area designated under Subsection (a) of this article.

History of CCP art. 2.123: Acts 1987, 70th Leg., ch. 1128, §1, eff. Aug. 31, 1987.

ART. 2.124. PEACE OFFICERS FROM ADJOINING STATES

(a) A commissioned peace officer of a state of the United States of America adjoining this state, while the officer is in this state, has under this subsection the same powers, duties, and immunities as a peace officer of this state who is acting in the discharge of an official duty, but only:

(1) during a time in which:

(A) the peace officer from the adjoining state has physical custody of an inmate or criminal defendant and is transporting the inmate or defendant from a county in the adjoining state that is on the border between the two states to a hospital or other medical facility in a county in this state that is on the border between the two states; or

(B) the peace officer has physical custody of the inmate or defendant and is returning the inmate or defendant from the hospital or facility to the county in the adjoining state; and

(2) to the extent necessary to:

(A) maintain physical custody of the inmate or defendant while transporting the inmate or defendant; or

(B) regain physical custody of the inmate or defendant if the inmate or defendant escapes while being transported.

(b) A commissioned peace officer of a state of the United States of America adjoining this state, while the officer is in this state, has under this subsection the same powers, duties, and immunities as a peace officer of this state who is acting in the discharge of an official duty, but only in a municipality some part of the municipal limits of which are within one mile of the boundary between this state and the adjoining state and only at a time the peace officer is regularly assigned to duty in a county, parish, or municipality that adjoins this state. A peace officer described by this subsection may also as part of the officer's powers in this state enforce the ordinances of a Texas municipality described by this subsection but only after the governing body of the municipality authorizes that enforcement by majority vote at an open meeting.

History of CCP art. 2.124: Acts 1995, 74th Leg., ch. 156, §1, eff. May 19, 1995. Amended by Acts 1999, 76th Leg., ch. 107, §1, eff. Sept. 1, 1999.

ART. 2.125. SPECIAL RANGERS OF TEXAS & SOUTHWESTERN CATTLE RAISERS ASSOCIATION

(a) The director of the Department of Public Safety may appoint up to 50 special rangers who are employed by the Texas and Southwestern Cattle Raisers Association to aid law enforcement agencies in the investigation of the theft of livestock or related property.

(b) Except as provided by Subsection (c) of this article, a special ranger may make arrests and exercise all authority given peace officers under this code when necessary to prevent or abate the commission of an offense involving livestock or related property.

(c) A special ranger may not issue a traffic citation for a violation of Chapter 521, Transportation Code, or Subtitle C, Title 7, Transportation Code.

(d) A special ranger is not entitled to state benefits normally provided by the state to a peace officer.

(e) A person may not serve as a special ranger unless:

(1) the Texas and Southwestern Cattle Raisers Association submits the person's application for appointment and certification as a special ranger to the director of the Department of Public Safety and to the executive director of the Commission on Law Enforcement Officer Standards and Education;

(2) the director of the department issues the person a certificate of authority to act as a special ranger;

(3) the executive director of the commission determines that the person meets minimum standards required of peace officers by the commission relating to competence, reliability, education, training, morality, and physical and mental health and issues the person a license as a special ranger; and

(4) the person has met all standards for certification as a peace officer by the Commission on Law Enforcement Officer Standards and Education.

(f) For good cause, the director of the department may revoke a certificate of authority issued under this article and the executive director of the commission may revoke a license issued under this article. Termination of employment with the association, or the revocation of a special ranger license, shall constitute an automatic revocation of a certificate of authority to act as a special ranger.

(g) The Texas and Southwestern Cattle Raisers Association is liable for any act or omission by a person serving as a special ranger for the association that is within the person's scope of employment. Neither the state nor any political subdivision or agency of the state shall be liable for any act or omission by a person appointed as a special ranger. All expenses incurred by the granting or revocation of a certificate of authority to act as a special ranger shall be paid by the association.

(h) The director of the department and the executive director of the commission shall have the authority to promulgate rules necessary for the effective administration and performance of the duties and responsibilities delegated to them by this article.

History of CCP art. 2.125: Acts 2005, 79th Leg., ch. 209, §1, eff. Sept. 1, 2005.

ART. 2.13. DUTIES & POWERS

(a) It is the duty of every peace officer to preserve the peace within the officer's jurisdiction. To effect this purpose, the officer shall use all lawful means.

(b) The officer shall:

(1) in every case authorized by the provisions of this Code, interfere without warrant to prevent or suppress crime;

(2) execute all lawful process issued to the officer by any magistrate or court;

(3) give notice to some magistrate of all offenses committed within the officer's jurisdiction, where the officer has good reason to believe there has been a violation of the penal law; and

(4) arrest offenders without warrant in every case where the officer is authorized by law, in order that they may be taken before the proper magistrate or court and be tried.

(c) It is the duty of every officer to take possession of a child under Article 63.009(g).

History of CCP art. 2.13: Acts 1965, 59th Leg., vol. 2, ch. 722. Amended by Acts 1999, 76th Leg., ch. 685, §1, eff. Sept. 1, 1999; Acts 2003, 78th Leg., ch. 1276, §5.0005, eff. Sept. 1, 2003.

ANNOTATIONS

McCain v. State, 995 S.W.2d 229, 234-35 (Tex. App.—Houston [14th Dist.] 1999, pet. ref'd). "A peace officer cannot make warrantless arrests anywhere in the State. Common law and statutory law limit a peace officer's authority to his own geographic jurisdiction. 'Generally, a peace officer is a peace officer only while in his jurisdiction and *when the officer leaves that jurisdiction, he can not perform the functions of his office.*' The officers who searched the property and recovered the pistol were officers in the Fort Bend County Sheriff's Department, and they were unable to perform the functions of their office while they were in Wharton County."

City of Dallas v. Half Price Books, Inc., 883 S.W.2d 374, 377 (Tex.App.—Dallas 1994, no writ). "Police officers have a duty to prevent crime and arrest offenders. An off-duty police officer who observes a crime immediately becomes an on-duty police officer."

ART. 2.131. RACIAL PROFILING PROHIBITED

A peace officer may not engage in racial profiling.

History of CCP art. 2.131: Acts 2001, 77th Leg., ch. 947, §1, eff. Sept. 1, 2001.

ART. 2.132. LAW ENFORCEMENT POLICY ON RACIAL PROFILING

(a) In this article:

(1) "Law enforcement agency" means an agency of the state, or of a county, municipality, or other political subdivision of the state, that employs peace officers who make traffic stops in the routine performance of the officers' official duties.

(2) "Race or ethnicity" means of a particular descent, including Caucasian, African, Hispanic, Asian, or Native American descent.

(b) Each law enforcement agency in this state shall adopt a detailed written policy on racial profiling. The policy must:

(1) clearly define acts constituting racial profiling;

(2) strictly prohibit peace officers employed by the agency from engaging in racial profiling;

(3) implement a process by which an individual may file a complaint with the agency if the individual believes that a peace officer employed by the agency has engaged in racial profiling with respect to the individual;

(4) provide public education relating to the agency's complaint process;

(5) require appropriate corrective action to be taken against a peace officer employed by the agency who, after an investigation, is shown to have engaged in racial profiling in violation of the agency's policy adopted under this article;

(6) require collection of information relating to traffic stops in which a citation is issued and to arrests resulting from those traffic stops, including information relating to:

(A) the race or ethnicity of the individual detained; and

(B) whether a search was conducted and, if so, whether the person detained consented to the search; and

(7) require the agency to submit to the governing body of each county or municipality served by the agency an annual report of the information collected under Subdivision (6) if the agency is an agency of a county, municipality, or other political subdivision of the state.

(c) The data collected as a result of the reporting requirements of this article shall not constitute prima facie evidence of racial profiling.

(d) On adoption of a policy under Subsection (b), a law enforcement agency shall examine the feasibility of installing video camera and transmitter-activated equipment in each agency law enforcement motor vehicle regularly used to make traffic stops and transmitter-activated equipment in each agency law enforcement motorcycle regularly used to make traffic stops. If a law enforcement agency installs video or audio equipment as provided by this subsection, the policy adopted by the agency under Subsection (b) must include standards for reviewing video and audio documentation.

(e) A report required under Subsection (b)(7) may not include identifying information about a peace officer who makes a traffic stop or about an individual who is stopped or arrested by a peace officer. This subsection does not affect the collection of information as required by a policy under Subsection (b)(6).

(f) On the commencement of an investigation by a law enforcement agency of a complaint described by Subsection (b)(3) in which a video or audio recording of the occurrence on which the complaint is based was made, the agency shall promptly provide a copy of the recording to the peace officer who is the subject of the complaint on written request by the officer.

History of CCP art. 2.132: Acts 2001, 77th Leg., ch. 947, §1, eff. Sept. 1, 2001.

ANNOTATIONS

Ex parte Brooks, 97 S.W.3d 639, 640 (Tex.App.— Waco 2002, orig. proceeding). Held: D's pretrial application for writ of habeas corpus is denied because he has an adequate remedy at law. His racial-profiling claims may be asserted in a motion to suppress.

ART. 2.133. REPORTS REQUIRED FOR TRAFFIC & PEDESTRIAN STOPS

(a) In this article:

(1) "Race or ethnicity" has the meaning assigned by Article 2.132(a).

(2) "Pedestrian stop" means an interaction between a peace officer and an individual who is being

detained for the purpose of a criminal investigation in which the individual is not under arrest.

(b) A peace officer who stops a motor vehicle for an alleged violation of a law or ordinance regulating traffic or who stops a pedestrian for any suspected offense shall report to the law enforcement agency that employs the officer information relating to the stop, including:

(1) a physical description of each person detained as a result of the stop, including:

(A) the person's gender; and

(B) the person's race or ethnicity, as stated by the person or, if the person does not state the person's race or ethnicity, as determined by the officer to the best of the officer's ability;

(2) the traffic law or ordinance alleged to have been violated or the suspected offense;

(3) whether the officer conducted a search as a result of the stop and, if so, whether the person detained consented to the search;

(4) whether any contraband was discovered in the course of the search and the type of contraband discovered;

(5) whether probable cause to search existed and the facts supporting the existence of that probable cause;

(6) whether the officer made an arrest as a result of the stop or the search, including a statement of the offense charged;

(7) the street address or approximate location of the stop; and

(8) whether the officer issued a warning or a citation as a result of the stop, including a description of the warning or a statement of the violation charged.

History of CCP art. 2.133: Acts 2001, 77th Leg., ch. 947, §1, eff. Sept. 1, 2001.

ART. 2.134. COMPILATION & ANALYSIS OF INFORMATION COLLECTED

(a) In this article, "pedestrian stop" means an interaction between a peace officer and an individual who is being detained for the purpose of a criminal investigation in which the individual is not under arrest.

(b) A law enforcement agency shall compile and analyze the information contained in each report received by the agency under Article 2.133. Not later than March 1 of each year, each local law enforcement agency shall submit a report containing the information compiled during the previous calendar year to the governing body of each county or municipality served by the agency in a manner approved by the agency.

(c) A report required under Subsection (b) must include:

(1) a comparative analysis of the information compiled under Article 2.133 to:

(A) determine the prevalence of racial profiling by peace officers employed by the agency; and

(B) examine the disposition of traffic and pedestrian stops made by officers employed by the agency, including searches resulting from the stops; and

(2) information relating to each complaint filed with the agency alleging that a peace officer employed by the agency has engaged in racial profiling.

(d) A report required under Subsection (b) may not include identifying information about a peace officer who makes a traffic or pedestrian stop or about an individual who is stopped or arrested by a peace officer. This subsection does not affect the reporting of information required under Article 2.133(b)(1).

(e) The Commission on Law Enforcement Officer Standards and Education shall develop guidelines for compiling and reporting information as required by this article.

(f) The data collected as a result of the reporting requirements of this article shall not constitute prima facie evidence of racial profiling.

History of CCP art. 2.134: Acts 2001, 77th Leg., ch. 947, §1, eff. Sept. 1, 2001.

ART. 2.135. EXEMPTION FOR AGENCIES USING VIDEO & AUDIO EQUIPMENT

(a) A peace officer is exempt from the reporting requirement under Article 2.133 and a law enforcement agency is exempt from the compilation, analysis, and reporting requirements under Article 2.134 if:

(1) during the calendar year preceding the date that a report under Article 2.134 is required to be submitted:

(A) each law enforcement motor vehicle regularly used by an officer employed by the agency to make traffic and pedestrian stops is equipped with video camera and transmitter-activated equipment and each law enforcement motorcycle regularly used to make traffic and pedestrian stops is equipped with transmitter-activated equipment; and

(B) each traffic and pedestrian stop made by an officer employed by the agency that is capable of being recorded by video and audio or audio equipment, as appropriate, is recorded by using the equipment; or

(2) the governing body of the county or municipality served by the law enforcement agency, in conjunction with the law enforcement agency, certifies to the Department of Public Safety, not later than the date specified by rule by the department, that the law enforcement agency needs funds or video and audio equipment for the purpose of installing video and audio equipment as described by Subsection (a)(1)(A) and the agency does not receive from the state funds or video and audio equipment sufficient, as determined by the department, for the agency to accomplish that purpose.

(b) Except as otherwise provided by this subsection, a law enforcement agency that is exempt from the requirements under Article 2.134 shall retain the video and audio or audio documentation of each traffic and pedestrian stop for at least 90 days after the date of the stop. If a complaint is filed with the law enforcement agency alleging that a peace officer employed by the agency has engaged in racial profiling with respect to a traffic or pedestrian stop, the agency shall retain the video and audio or audio record of the stop until final disposition of the complaint.

(c) This article does not affect the collection or reporting requirements under Article 2.132.

History of CCP art. 2.135: Acts 2001, 77th Leg., ch. 947, §1, eff. Sept. 1, 2001.

ART. 2.136. LIABILITY

A peace officer is not liable for damages arising from an act relating to the collection or reporting of information as required by Article 2.133 or under a policy adopted under Article 2.132.

History of CCP art. 2.136: Acts 2001, 77th Leg., ch. 947, §1, eff. Sept. 1, 2001.

ART. 2.137. PROVISION OF FUNDING OR EQUIPMENT

(a) The Department of Public Safety shall adopt rules for providing funds or video and audio equipment to law enforcement agencies for the purpose of installing video and audio equipment as described by Article 2.135(a)(1)(A), including specifying criteria to prioritize funding or equipment provided to law enforcement agencies. The criteria may include consideration of tax effort, financial hardship, available revenue, and budget surpluses. The criteria must give priority to:

(1) law enforcement agencies that employ peace officers whose primary duty is traffic enforcement;

(2) smaller jurisdictions; and

(3) municipal and county law enforcement agencies.

(b) The Department of Public Safety shall collaborate with an institution of higher education to identify law enforcement agencies that need funds or video and audio equipment for the purpose of installing video and audio equipment as described by Article 2.135(a)(1)(A). The collaboration may include the use of a survey to assist in developing criteria to prioritize funding or equipment provided to law enforcement agencies.

(c) To receive funds or video and audio equipment from the state for the purpose of installing video and audio equipment as described by Article 2.135(a)(1)(A), the governing body of a county or municipality, in conjunction with the law enforcement agency serving the county or municipality, shall certify to the Department of Public Safety that the law enforcement agency needs funds or video and audio equipment for that purpose.

(d) On receipt of funds or video and audio equipment from the state for the purpose of installing video and audio equipment as described by Article 2.135(a)(1)(A), the governing body of a county or municipality, in conjunction with the law enforcement agency serving the county or municipality, shall certify to the Department of Public Safety that the law enforcement agency has installed video and audio equipment as described by Article 2.135(a)(1)(A) and is using the equipment as required by Article 2.135(a)(1).

History of CCP art. 2.137: Acts 2001, 77th Leg., ch. 947, §1, eff. Sept. 1, 2001.

ART. 2.138. RULES

The Department of Public Safety may adopt rules to implement Articles 2.131-2.137.

History of CCP art. 2.138: Acts 2001, 77th Leg., ch. 947, §1, eff. Sept. 1, 2001.

ART. 2.14. MAY SUMMON AID

Whenever a peace officer meets with resistance in discharging any duty imposed upon him by law, he shall summon a sufficient number of citizens of his county to overcome the resistance; and all persons summoned are bound to obey.

History of CCP art. 2.14: Acts 1965, 59th Leg., vol. 2, ch. 722.

ART. 2.15. PERSON REFUSING TO AID

The peace officer who has summoned any person to assist him in performing any duty shall report such person, if he refuse to obey, to the proper district or county attorney, in order that he may be prosecuted for the offense.

History of CCP art. 2.15: Acts 1965, 59th Leg., vol. 2, ch. 722.

ANNOTATIONS

Polke v. State, 118 S.W.2d 793, 794-95 (Tex.Crim. App.1938). "[A] citizen called to the aid of an officer certainly should not be expected to respond without arms for his own protection."

ART. 2.16. NEGLECTING TO EXECUTE PROCESS

If any sheriff or other officer shall wilfully refuse or fail from neglect to execute any summons, subpoena or attachment for a witness, or any other legal process which it is made his duty by law to execute, he shall be liable to a fine for contempt not less than ten nor more than two hundred dollars, at the discretion of the court. The payment of such fine shall be enforced in the same manner as fines for contempt in civil cases.

History of CCP art. 2.16: Acts 1965, 59th Leg., vol. 2, ch. 722.

ART. 2.17. CONSERVATOR OF THE PEACE

Each sheriff shall be a conservator of the peace in his county, and shall arrest all offenders against the laws of the State, in his view or hearing, and take them before the proper court for examination or trial. He shall quell and suppress all assaults and batteries, affrays, insurrections and unlawful assemblies. He shall apprehend and commit to jail all offenders, until an examination or trial can be had.

History of CCP art. 2.17: Acts 1965, 59th Leg., vol. 2, ch. 722.

ANNOTATIONS

Angel v. State, 740 S.W.2d 727, 733 (Tex.Crim.App. 1987). "A sheriff's jurisdiction ... is county-wide."

ART. 2.18. CUSTODY OF PRISONERS

When a prisoner is committed to jail by warrant from a magistrate or court, he shall be placed in jail by the sheriff. It is a violation of duty on the part of any sheriff to permit a defendant so committed to remain out of jail, except that he may, when a defendant is committed for want of bail, or when he arrests in a bailable case, give the person arrested a reasonable time to procure bail; but he shall so guard the accused as to prevent escape.

History of CCP art. 2.18: Acts 1965, 59th Leg., vol. 2, ch. 722.

ART. 2.19. REPORT AS TO PRISONERS

On the first day of each month, the sheriff shall give notice, in writing, to the district or county attorney, where there be one, as to all prisoners in his custody, naming them, and of the authority under which he detains them.

History of CCP art. 2.19: Acts 1965, 59th Leg., vol. 2, ch. 722.

ART. 2.20. DEPUTY

Wherever a duty is imposed by this Code upon the sheriff, the same duty may lawfully be performed by his deputy. When there is no sheriff in a county, the duties of that office, as to all proceedings under the criminal law, devolve upon the officer who, under the law, is empowered to discharge the duties of sheriff, in case of vacancy in the office.

History of CCP art. 2.20: Acts 1965, 59th Leg., vol. 2, ch. 722.

ART. 2.21. DUTY OF CLERKS

(a) In a criminal proceeding, a clerk of the district or county court shall:

(1) receive and file all papers;

(2) receive all exhibits at the conclusion of the proceeding;

(3) issue all process; and

(4) perform all other duties imposed on the clerk by law.

(b) At any time during or after a criminal proceeding, the court reporter shall release for safekeeping any firearm or contraband received as an exhibit in that proceeding to:

(1) the sheriff; or

(2) in a county with a population of 500,000 or more, the law enforcement agency that collected, seized, or took possession of the firearm or contraband or produced the firearm or contraband at the proceeding.

(c) The sheriff or the law enforcement agency, as applicable, shall receive and hold the exhibits consisting of firearms or contraband and release them only to the person or persons authorized by the court in which such exhibits have been received or dispose of them as provided by Chapter 18.

(d) In this article, "eligible exhibit" means an exhibit filed with the clerk that:

(1) is not a firearm or contraband;

(2) has not been ordered by the court to be returned to its owner; and

(3) is not an exhibit in another pending criminal action.

(e) An eligible exhibit may be disposed of as provided by this article:

(1) on or after the first anniversary of the date on which a conviction becomes final in the case, if the case is a misdemeanor or a felony for which the sentence imposed by the court is five years or less; or

(2) on or after the second anniversary of the date on which a conviction becomes final in the case, if the case is a non-capital felony for which the sentence imposed by the court is greater than five years.

(f) A clerk in a county with a population of 1.7 million or more may dispose of an eligible exhibit on the date provided by Subsection (e) of this article if on that date the clerk has not received a request for the exhibit from either the attorney representing the state in the case or the attorney representing the defendant.

(g) A clerk in a county with a population of less than 1.7 million must provide written notice by mail to the attorney representing the state in the case and the attorney representing the defendant before disposing of an eligible exhibit.

(h) The notice under Subsection (g) of this article must:

(1) describe the eligible exhibit;

(2) give the name and address of the court holding the exhibit; and

(3) state that the eligible exhibit will be disposed of unless a written request is received by the clerk before the 31st day after the date of notice.

(i) If a request is not received by a clerk covered by Subsection (g) of this article before the 31st day after the date of notice, the clerk may dispose of the eligible exhibit.

(j) If a request is timely received, the clerk shall deliver the eligible exhibit to the person making the request if the court determines the requestor is the owner of the eligible exhibit.

History of CCP art. 2.21: Acts 1965, 59th Leg., vol. 2, ch. 722. Amended by Acts 1979, 66th Leg., ch. 119, §1, eff. Aug. 27, 1979; Acts 1993, 73rd Leg., ch. 967, §1, eff. Sept. 1, 1993; Acts 1999, 76th Leg., ch. 580, §1, eff. Sept. 1, 1999; Acts 2005, 79th Leg., ch. 1026, §1, eff. Sept. 1, 2005.

ANNOTATIONS

Todd v. State, 598 S.W.2d 286, 292 (Tex.Crim.App. 1980). "Appellant contends ... that State's Exhibits ... are inadmissible because, assuming that the record clerk has attested the authenticity of the judgments and sentences, ... that responsibility [is] imposed solely upon the State's district clerks. [¶] [T]he attestation of a district clerk of a county of this State, upon a copy of a judgment or sentence received and filed by that district clerk, is alone sufficient to render such documents admissible into evidence for the truth of the matters stated therein. [¶] The [exhibits] bear the proper certification of the Dallas County District Clerk.... *At 293:* [B]ecause the judgments and sentences are not 'official writings' or 'official instruments' made *BY* an officer of *the Texas Department of Corrections* ..., the [Official Records] Act requires that the record clerk's attestation be accompanied by a certificate that he is in fact a legal custodian of such 'official writings,' made by the officer of the Dallas County District Clerk...."

ART. 2.211. HATE CRIME REPORTING

In addition to performing duties required by Article 2.21, a clerk of a district or county court in which an affirmative finding under Article 42.014 is requested shall report that request to the Texas Judicial Council, along with a statement as to whether the request was granted by the court and, if so, whether the affirmative finding was entered in the judgment in the case. The clerk shall make the report required by this article not later than the 30th day after the date the judgment is entered in the case.

History of CCP art. 2.211: Acts 2001, 77th Leg., ch. 85, §4.01, eff. Sept. 1, 2001.

ART. 2.22. POWER OF DEPUTY CLERKS

Whenever a duty is imposed upon the clerk of the district or county court, the same may be lawfully performed by his deputy.

History of CCP art. 2.22: Acts 1965, 59th Leg., vol. 2, ch. 722.

ART. 2.23. REPORT TO ATTORNEY GENERAL

(a) The clerks of the district and county courts shall, when requested in writing by the Attorney General, report to the Attorney General not later than the 10th day after the date the request is received, and in the form prescribed by the Attorney General, information in court records that relates to a criminal matter, including information requested by the Attorney General for purposes of federal habeas review.

(b) A state agency or the office of an attorney representing the state shall, when requested in writing by the Attorney General, provide to the Attorney General any record that is needed for purposes of federal habeas review. The agency or office must provide the record not later than the 10th day after the date the request is received and in the form prescribed by the Attorney General.

(c) A district court, county court, state agency, or office of an attorney representing the state may not restrict or delay the reproduction or delivery of a record requested by the Attorney General under this article.

History of CCP art. 2.23: Acts 1965, 59th Leg., vol. 2, ch. 722. Amended by Acts 2005, 79th Leg., ch. 933, §1, Sept. 1, 2005.

ART. 2.24. AUTHENTICATING OFFICER

(a) The governor may appoint an authenticating officer, in accordance with Subsection (b) of this article, and delegate to that officer the power to sign for the governor or to use the governor's facsimile signature for signing any document that does not have legal effect under this code unless it is signed by the governor.

(b) To appoint an authenticating officer under this article, the governor shall file with the secretary of state a document that contains:

(1) the name of the person to be appointed as authenticating officer and a copy of the person's signature;

(2) the types of documents the authenticating officer is authorized to sign for the governor; and

(3) the types of documents on which the authenticating officer is authorized to use the governor's facsimile signature.

(c) The governor may revoke an appointment made under this article by filing with the secretary of state a document that expressly revokes the appointment of the authenticating agent.

(d) If an authenticating officer signs a document described in Subsection (a) of this article, the officer shall sign in the following manner: "_____, Authenticating Officer for Governor _____."

(e) If a provision of this code requires the governor's signature on a document before that document has legal effect, the authorized signature of the authenticating officer or an authorized facsimile signature of the governor gives the document the same legal effect as if it had been signed manually by the governor.

History of CCP art. 2.24: Acts 1983, 68th Leg., ch. 684, §1, eff. June 19, 1983.

ART. 2.25. REPORTING CERTAIN ALIENS TO FEDERAL GOVERNMENT

A judge shall report to the United States Immigration and Naturalization Service a person who has been convicted in the judge's court of a crime or has been placed on deferred adjudication for a felony and is an illegal criminal alien as defined by Section 493.015(a), Government Code.

History of CCP art. 2.25: Acts 1995, 74th Leg., ch. 85, §2, eff. May 16, 1995.

ART. 2.26. DIGITAL SIGNATURE & ELECTRONIC DOCUMENTS

(a) In this section, "digital signature" means an electronic identifier intended by the person using it to have the same force and effect as the use of a manual signature.

(b) An electronically transmitted document issued or received by a court or a clerk of the court in a criminal matter is considered signed if a digital signature is transmitted with the document.

(b-1) An electronically transmitted document is a written document for all purposes and exempt from any additional writing requirement under this code or any other law of this state.

(c) This section does not preclude any symbol from being valid as a signature under other applicable law, including Section 1.201(39), Business & Commerce Code.

(d) The use of a digital signature under this section is subject to criminal laws pertaining to fraud and computer crimes, including Chapters 32 and 33, Penal Code.

History of CCP art. 2.26: Acts 1999, 76th Leg., ch. 701, §1, eff. Aug. 30, 1999. Amended by Acts 2005, 79th Leg., 312, §§1, 2, eff. June 17, 2005.

History of Former CCP art. 2.26: Repealed by Acts 1989, 71st Leg., ch. 1248, §85(1), eff. Sept. 1, 1989.

ART. 2.27. INVESTIGATION OF CERTAIN REPORTS ALLEGING ABUSE

(a) On receipt of a report that is assigned the highest priority in accordance with rules adopted by the Department of Protective and Regulatory Services under Section 261.301(d), Family Code, and that alleges an immediate risk of physical or sexual abuse of a child that could result in the death of or serious harm to the child by a person responsible for the care, custody, or welfare of the child, a peace officer from the appropriate local law enforcement agency shall investigate the report jointly with the department or with the agency responsible for conducting an investigation under Subchapter E, Chapter 261, Family Code. As soon as possible after being notified by the department of the report, but not later than 24 hours after being notified, the peace officer shall accompany the department investigator in initially responding to the report.

(b) On receipt of a report of abuse or neglect or other complaint of a resident of a nursing home, convalescent home, or other related institution under Section 242.126(c)(1), Health and Safety Code, the appropriate local law enforcement agency shall investigate the report as required by Section 242.135, Health and Safety Code.

History of CCP art. 2.27: Acts 2001, 77th Leg., ch. 492, §1, eff. Sept. 1, 2001. Amended by Acts 2003, 78th Leg., ch. 867, §2 (eff. Sept. 1, 2003), ch. 1210, §5 (eff. Sept. 1, 2003).

ART. 2.28. DUTIES REGARDING MISUSED IDENTITY

On receipt of information to the effect that a person's identifying information was falsely given by a person arrested as the arrested person's identifying information, the local law enforcement agency responsible for collecting identifying information on arrested persons in the county in which the arrest was made shall:

(1) notify the person that:

(A) the person's identifying information was misused by another person arrested in the county;

(B) the person may file a declaration with the Department of Public Safety under Section 411.0421, Government Code; and

(C) the person is entitled to expunction of information contained in criminal records and files under Chapter 55 of this code; and

(2) notify the Department of Public Safety regarding:

(A) the misuse of the identifying information;

(B) the actual identity of the person arrested, if known by the agency; and

(C) whether the agency was able to notify the person whose identifying information was misused.

History of CCP art. 2.28: Acts 2003, 78th Leg., ch. 339, §1, eff. Sept. 1, 2003.

ART. 2.29. REPORT REQUIRED IN CONNECTION WITH FRAUDULENT USE OR POSSESSION OF IDENTIFYING INFORMATION

(a) A peace officer to whom an alleged violation of Section 32.51, Penal Code, is reported shall make a written report to the law enforcement agency that employs the peace officer that includes the following information:

(1) the name of the victim;

(2) the name of the suspect, if known;

(3) the type of identifying information obtained, possessed, transferred, or used in violation of Section 32.51, Penal Code; and

(4) the results of any investigation.

(b) On the victim's request, the law enforcement agency shall provide the report created under Subsection (a) to the victim. In providing the report, the law enforcement agency shall redact any otherwise confidential information that is included in the report, other than the information described by Subsection (a).

History of CCP art. 2.29: Acts 2005, 79th Leg., ch. 294, §1(a), eff. Sept. 1, 2005.

Ⓔ ART. 2.30. REPORT CONCERNING CERTAIN ASSAULTIVE OR TERRORISTIC OFFENSES

(a) This article applies only to the following offenses:

(1) assault under Section 22.01, Penal Code;

(2) aggravated assault under Section 22.02, Penal Code;

(3) sexual assault under Section 22.011, Penal Code;

(4) aggravated sexual assault under Section 22.021, Penal Code; and

(5) terroristic threat under Section 22.07, Penal Code.

(b) A peace officer who investigates the alleged commission of an offense listed under Subsection (a) shall prepare a written report that includes the information required under Article 5.05(a).

(c) On request of a victim of an offense listed under Subsection (a), the local law enforcement agency responsible for investigating the commission of the offense shall provide the victim, at no cost to the victim, with any information that is:

(1) contained in the written report prepared under Subsection (b);

(2) described by Article 5.05(a)(1) or (2); and

(3) not exempt from disclosure under Chapter 552, Government Code, or other law.

History of CCP art. 2.30: Acts 2007, 80th Leg., ch. 1057, §1, eff. Sept. 1, 2007.

CHAPTER 3. DEFINITIONS

ART. 3.01. WORDS & PHRASES

All words, phrases and terms used in this Code are to be taken and understood in their usual acceptation in common language, except where specially defined.

History of CCP art. 3.01: Acts 1965, 59th Leg., vol. 2, ch. 722. Amended by Acts 1975, 64th Leg., ch. 341, §1, eff. June 19, 1975.

See also Gov't Code ch. 311.

ANNOTATIONS

Bingham v. State, 913 S.W.2d 208, 210 (Tex.Crim. App.1995). "While common acceptation of an unspecialized word is certainly critical, it is the common acceptation of the word in the context in which it appears that is determinative."

Lackey v. State, 819 S.W.2d 111, 118 (Tex.Crim. App.1989). If "the term has not been defined by statute, the term is to be understood in its usual acceptance in common language and need not be defined in the charge to the jury." *See also Clark v. State*, 190 S.W.3d 59, 64 (Tex.App.—Amarillo 2005, no pet.).

ART. 3.02. CRIMINAL ACTION

A criminal action is prosecuted in the name of the State of Texas against the accused, and is conducted by some person acting under the authority of the State, in accordance with its laws.

History of CCP art. 3.02: Acts 1965, 59th Leg., vol. 2, ch. 722.

Burks v. State, 795 S.W.2d 913, 915 (Tex.App.—Amarillo 1990, pet. ref'd). "A crime constitutes an offense against the sovereign. For that reason, a criminal action is pursued under the authority and in the name of the State."

ART. 3.03. OFFICERS

The general term "officers" includes both magistrates and peace officers.

History of CCP art. 3.03: Acts 1965, 59th Leg., vol. 2, ch. 722.

ART. 3.04. OFFICIAL MISCONDUCT

In this code:

(1) "Official misconduct" means an offense that is an intentional or knowing violation of a law committed by a public servant while acting in an official capacity as a public servant.

(2) "Public servant" has the meaning assigned by Section 1.07, Penal Code.

History of CCP art. 3.04: Acts 1993, 73rd Leg., ch. 900, §1.03, eff. Sept. 1, 1994.

State v. Denton, 893 S.W.2d 125, 126 (Tex.App.—Austin 1995, pet. ref'd). "For a criminal act to constitute 'official misconduct' as used in [CCP art.] 4.05, 'it must be both wilful and related to the duties of the defendant's office.'"

ART. 3.05. RACIAL PROFILING

In this code, "racial profiling" means a law enforcement-initiated action based on an individual's race, ethnicity, or national origin rather than on the individual's behavior or on information identifying the individual as having engaged in criminal activity.

History of CCP art. 3.05: Acts 2001, 77th Leg., ch. 947, §2, eff. Sept. 1, 2001.

CHAPTER 4. COURTS & CRIMINAL JURISDICTION

ART. 4.01. WHAT COURTS HAVE CRIMINAL JURISDICTION

The following courts have jurisdiction in criminal actions:

1. The Court of Criminal Appeals;

2. Courts of appeals;

3. The district courts;

4. The criminal district courts;

5. The magistrates appointed by the judges of the district courts of Bexar County, Dallas County, Tarrant County, or Travis County that give preference to criminal cases and the magistrates appointed by the judges of the criminal district courts of Dallas County or Tarrant County;

6. The county courts;

7. All county courts at law with criminal jurisdiction;

8. County criminal courts;

9. Justice courts;

10. Municipal courts; and

11. The magistrates appointed by the judges of the district courts of Lubbock County.

History of CCP art. 4.01: Acts 1965, 59th Leg., vol. 2, ch. 722. Amended by Acts 1981, 67th Leg., ch. 291, §101, eff. Sept. 1, 1981; Acts 1983, 68th Leg., ch. 204, §2, eff. Aug. 29, 1983; Acts 1989, 71st Leg., ch. 25, §3 (eff. Aug. 28, 1989), ch. 79, §2 (eff. May 15, 1989), ch. 1068, §3 (eff. Aug. 28, 1989); Acts 1991, 72nd Leg., ch. 16, §4.03, eff. Aug. 26, 1991; Acts 1993, 73rd Leg., ch. 413, §2, eff. Sept. 1, 1993.

Ex parte George, 913 S.W.2d 523, 526 (Tex.Crim. App.1995). "[J]urisdiction ... is something possessed by courts, not by judges. The judge is merely an officer of the court, like the lawyers, the bailiff and the court reporter. He is not the court itself."

Rabb v. State, 730 S.W.2d 751, 754 (Tex.Crim.App. 1987). The 1983 "amendments to [CCP arts.] 2.09 and 4.01 ... vis-a-vis the Magistrate's Act do not alter the function of Dallas County magistrates or the powers available to them so as to remove them from the supervision of district court judges."

Fairfield v. State, 610 S.W.2d 771, 779 (Tex.Crim. App.1981). "'[J]urisdiction' is comprised not of the 'place' of the prosecution, but of the power of the court over the 'subject matter' of the case, conveyed by statute or constitutional provision, coupled with 'personal' jurisdiction over the accused, which is invoked in felony prosecutions, by the filing of a sufficient indictment or information if indictment is waived."

ART. 4.02. EXISTING COURTS CONTINUED

No existing courts shall be abolished by this Code and shall continue with the jurisdiction, organization, terms and powers currently existing unless otherwise provided by law.

History of CCP art. 4.02: Acts 1965, 59th Leg., vol. 2, ch. 722.

ART. 4.03. COURTS OF APPEALS

The Courts of Appeals shall have appellate jurisdiction coextensive with the limits of their respective districts in all criminal cases except those in which the death penalty has been assessed. This Article shall not be so construed as to embrace any case which has been appealed from any inferior court to the county court, the county criminal court, or county court at law, in which the fine imposed by the county court, the county criminal court or county court at law does not exceed one hundred dollars, unless the sole issue is the constitutionality of the statute or ordinance on which the conviction is based.

History of CCP art. 4.03: Acts 1965, 59th Leg., vol. 2, ch. 722. Amended by Acts 1981, 67th Leg., ch. 291, §102, eff. Sept. 1, 1981.

See also CCP art. 11.05.

ANNOTATIONS

Thompson v. State, 85 S.W.3d 415, 417 (Tex. App.—Fort Worth 2002), *aff'd*, 108 S.W.3d 287 (Tex. Crim.App.2003). "[B]ecause the trial court did not pronounce sentence for the indecency offense, we lack jurisdiction to hear Appellant's appeal from this conviction." Held: The appellate court retained jurisdiction over the offense for which sentence was pronounced.

Meisner v. State, 907 S.W.2d 664, 666 (Tex.App.— Waco 1995, no pet.). "[T]he courts of appeals shall not have criminal jurisdiction in those cases appealed from any inferior court to the county court of law in which

the fine imposed by the county court of law does not exceed $100 dollars, unless the sole issue is the constitutionality of the statute or ordinance upon which the conviction is based."

Owens v. State, 851 S.W.2d 398, 401 (Tex.App.— Fort Worth 1993, no pet.). "[T]his court [of appeal does not have] the power to reform [a] prior conviction in a post-conviction collateral attack. [O]nly the court of criminal appeals has such power."

Norris v. State, 630 S.W.2d 362, 364 (Tex.App.— Houston [1st Dist.] 1982, no pet.). "The 1981 amendments ... that gave the Courts of Appeals criminal jurisdiction, did not invest this court with original habeas corpus jurisdiction in criminal matters."

ART. 4.04. COURT OF CRIMINAL APPEALS

Sec. 1. The Court of Criminal Appeals and each judge thereof shall have, and is hereby given, the power and authority to grant and issue and cause the issuance of writs of habeas corpus, and, in criminal law matters, the writs of mandamus, procedendo, prohibition, and certiorari. The court and each judge thereof shall have, and is hereby given, the power and authority to grant and issue and cause the issuance of such other writs as may be necessary to protect its jurisdiction or enforce its judgments.

Sec. 2. The Court of Criminal Appeals shall have, and is hereby given, final appellate and review jurisdiction in criminal cases coextensive with the limits of the state, and its determinations shall be final. The appeal of all cases in which the death penalty has been assessed shall be to the Court of Criminal Appeals. In addition, the Court of Criminal Appeals may, on its own motion, with or without a petition for such discretionary review being filed by one of the parties, review any decision of a court of appeals in a criminal case. Discretionary review by the Court of Criminal Appeals is not a matter of right, but of sound judicial discretion.

History of CCP art. 4.04: Acts 1965, 59th Leg., vol. 2, ch. 722. Amended by Acts 1971, 62nd Leg., §6, eff. Aug. 30, 1971; Acts 1981, 67th Leg., ch. 291, §103, eff. Sept. 1, 1981.

ANNOTATIONS

Ex parte Brand, 822 S.W.2d 636, 639 (Tex.Crim. App.1992). "[W]e now decide that the writ [of common-law certiorari] shall not issue in any case in which there is a right to appeal."

Callins v. State, 726 S.W.2d 555, 557 (Tex.Crim. App.1986). "A 'case,' for appellate purposes, is that aggregate of facts that resulted in a conviction for a single offense. A 'case' in which the death penalty has been assessed only refers to those facts that resulted in a conviction for the offense of capital murder and a sentence of death. Consequently, under Article 4.04, §2, ... only the direct appeal of a capital murder conviction 'in which the death penalty has been assessed shall be to the Court of Criminal Appeals.'"

Homan v. Hughes, 708 S.W.2d 449, 452 (Tex.Crim. App.1986). "This Court has jurisdiction to issue writs of mandamus...." *See also State ex rel. Curry v. Davis*, 689 S.W.2d 214, 215 (Tex.Crim.App.1984).

ART. 4.05. JURISDICTION OF DISTRICT COURTS

District courts and criminal district courts shall have original jurisdiction in criminal cases of the grade of felony, of all misdemeanors involving official misconduct, and of misdemeanor cases transferred to the district court under Article 4.17 of this code.

History of CCP art. 4.05: Acts 1965, 59th Leg., vol. 2, ch. 722. Amended by Acts 1983, 68th Leg., ch. 303, §5, eff. Jan. 1, 1984.

ANNOTATIONS

State v. Smith, 957 S.W.2d 163, 164 (Tex.App.— Austin 1997, no pet.). "The problem presented in this appeal arises because what appears to be a Runnels County indictment was filed and tried in Tom Green County, and because the State produced evidence that the offense was committed in Tom Green County rather than in Runnels County as alleged. *At 165:* The presentment of a constitutionally sufficient indictment to a court invests the court with jurisdiction of the cause. A Texas district court has jurisdiction to try any criminal offense committed in this State. The filing of the indictment in the 119th District Court of Tom Green County invested that court with jurisdiction to try this cause...."

State v. Meyer, 953 S.W.2d 822, 824-25 (Tex. App.—Corpus Christi 1997, no pet.). "After declaration of mistrial, a case reverts to the posture it had before trial. Although a declaration of mistrial renders a pending trial a nugatory proceeding, the trial court does not lose jurisdiction over the matter. If an indictment still exists, giving the trial court subject-matter and personal jurisdiction, then the trial court has authority to

withdraw or rescind the order of mistrial. However, the circumstances of the proceedings must be considered to determine whether rescission of the mistrial order is a viable option. [¶] Because we believe that withdrawing an order of mistrial and granting an instructed verdict more than 6 months after the jury has been discharged exceeds the boundaries of judicial propriety, we hold that withdrawing the mistrial order was not a viable option for the trial court."

Campos v. State, 783 S.W.2d 7, 8 (Tex.App.— Houston [14th Dist.] 1989, pet. ref'd). "[T]he Court of Criminal Appeals dictated that original jurisdiction in the context of [art. 4.05] is the functional equivalent of exclusive jurisdiction."

ART. 4.06. WHEN FELONY INCLUDES MISDEMEANOR

Upon the trial of a felony case, the court shall hear and determine the case as to any grade of offense included in the indictment, whether the proof shows a felony or a misdemeanor.

History of CCP art. 4.06: Acts 1965, 59th Leg., vol. 2, ch. 722.

ART. 4.07. JURISDICTION OF COUNTY COURTS

The county courts shall have original jurisdiction of all misdemeanors of which exclusive original jurisdiction is not given to the justice court, and when the fine to be imposed shall exceed five hundred dollars.

History of CCP art. 4.07: Acts 1965, 59th Leg., vol. 2, ch. 722. Amended by Acts 1991, 72nd Leg., ch. 108, §3, eff. Sept. 1, 1991.

ART. 4.08. APPELLATE JURISDICTION OF COUNTY COURTS

The county courts shall have appellate jurisdiction in criminal cases of which justice courts and other inferior courts have original jurisdiction.

History of CCP art. 4.08: Acts 1965, 59th Leg., vol. 2, ch. 722.

ART. 4.09. APPEALS FROM INFERIOR COURT

If the jurisdiction of any county court has been transferred to the district court or to a county court at law, then an appeal from a justice or other inferior court will lie to the court to which such appellate jurisdiction has been transferred.

History of CCP art. 4.09: Acts 1965, 59th Leg., vol. 2, ch. 722.

ART. 4.10. TO FORFEIT BAIL BONDS

County courts and county courts at law shall have jurisdiction in the forfeiture and final judgment of all bail bonds and personal bonds taken in criminal cases of which said courts have jurisdiction.

History of CCP art. 4.10: Acts 1965, 59th Leg., vol. 2, ch. 722.

ART. 4.11. JURISDICTION OF JUSTICE COURTS

(a) Justices of the peace shall have original jurisdiction in criminal cases:

(1) punishable by fine only or punishable by:

(A) a fine; and

(B) as authorized by statute, a sanction not consisting of confinement or imprisonment; or

(2) arising under Chapter 106, Alcoholic Beverage Code, that do not include confinement as an authorized sanction.

(b) The fact that a conviction in a justice court has as a consequence the imposition of a penalty or sanction by an agency or entity other than the court, such as a denial, suspension, or revocation of a privilege, does not affect the original jurisdiction of the justice court.

E (c) A justice court has concurrent jurisdiction with a municipal court in criminal cases that arise in the municipality's extraterritorial jurisdiction and that arise under an ordinance of the municipality applicable to the extraterritorial jurisdiction under Section 216.902, Local Government Code.

History of CCP art. 4.11: Acts 1965, 59th Leg., vol. 2, ch. 722. Amended by Acts 1991, 72nd Leg., ch. 108, §4, eff. Sept. 1, 1991; Acts 1995, 74th Leg., ch. 449, §1, eff. Sept. 1, 1995; Acts 1997, 75th Leg., ch. 533, §1 (eff. Sept. 1, 1997), ch. 1013, §38 (eff. Sept. 1, 1997); Acts 2007, 80th Leg., ch. 612, §13, eff. Sept. 1, 2007.

ANNOTATIONS

Ex parte Knight, 904 S.W.2d 722, 726 (Tex.App.— Houston [1st Dist.] 1995, pet. ref'd). "[T]he justice court has authority to take a felony complaint and issue a warrant of arrest, but does not have jurisdiction of a felony case."

ART. 4.12. MISDEMEANOR CASES; PRECINCT IN WHICH DEFENDANT TO BE TRIED IN JUSTICE COURT

(a) Except as otherwise provided by this article, a misdemeanor case to be tried in justice court shall be tried:

(1) in the precinct in which the offense was committed;

(2) in the precinct in which the defendant or any of the defendants reside; or

(3) with the written consent of the state and each defendant or the defendant's attorney, in any other precinct within the county.

(b) In any misdemeanor case in which the offense was committed in a precinct where there is no qualified justice court, then trial shall be held:

(1) in the next adjacent precinct in the same county which has a duly qualified justice court; or

(2) in the precinct in which the defendant may reside.

(c) In any misdemeanor case in which each justice of the peace in the precinct where the offense was committed is disqualified for any reason, such case may be tried in the next adjoining precinct in the same county having a duly qualified justice of the peace.

(d) A defendant who is taken before a magistrate in accordance with Article 15.18 may waive trial by jury and enter a written plea of guilty or nolo contendere.

History of CCP art. 4.12: Acts 1965, 59th Leg., vol. 2, ch. 722. Amended by Acts 1999, 76th Leg., ch. 1545, §2, eff. Sept. 1, 1999; Acts 2001, 77th Leg., ch. 145, §1, eff. Sept. 1, 2001.

ART. 4.13. JUSTICE MAY FORFEIT BOND

A justice of the peace shall have the power to take forfeitures of all bonds given for the appearance of any party at his court, regardless of the amount.

History of CCP art. 4.13: Acts 1965, 59th Leg., vol. 2, ch. 722.

ART. 4.14. JURISDICTION OF MUNICIPAL COURT

(a) A municipal court, including a municipal court of record, shall have exclusive original jurisdiction within the territorial limits of the municipality in all criminal cases that:

(1) arise under the ordinances of the municipality; and

(2) are punishable by a fine not to exceed:

(A) $2,000 in all cases arising under municipal ordinances that govern fire safety, zoning, or public health and sanitation, including dumping of refuse; or

(B) $500 in all other cases arising under a municipal ordinance.

(b) The municipal court shall have concurrent jurisdiction with the justice court of a precinct in which the municipality is located in all criminal cases arising under state law that:

(1) arise within the territorial limits of the municipality and are punishable by fine only, as defined in Subsection (c) of this article; or

(2) arise under Chapter 106, Alcoholic Beverage Code, and do not include confinement as an authorized sanction.

(c) In this article, an offense which is punishable by "fine only" is defined as an offense that is punishable by fine and such sanctions, if any, as authorized by statute not consisting of confinement in jail or imprisonment.

(d) The fact that a conviction in a municipal court has as a consequence the imposition of a penalty or sanction by an agency or entity other than the court, such as a denial, suspension, or revocation of a privilege, does not affect the original jurisdiction of the municipal court.

(e) The municipal court has jurisdiction in the forfeiture and final judgment of all bail bonds and personal bonds taken in criminal cases of which the court has jurisdiction.

History of CCP art. 4.14: Acts 1965, 59th Leg., vol. 2, ch. 722. Amended by Acts 1983, 68th Leg., ch. 601, §3, eff. Sept. 1, 1983; Acts 1985, 69th Leg., ch. 329, §3, eff. Sept. 1, 1985; Acts 1987, 70th Leg., ch. 641, §2 (eff. Sept. 1, 1987), ch. 680, §1 (eff. Sept. 1, 1987); Acts 1995, 74th Leg., ch. 449, §3, eff. Sept. 1, 1995; Acts 1997, 75th Leg., ch. 533, §2 (eff. Sept. 1, 1997), ch. 1013, §39 (eff. Sept. 1, 1997).

ANNOTATIONS

State v. Church, 882 S.W.2d 47, 48 (Tex.App.—Waco 1994, pet. ref'd). "[T]he trial court interpreted [CCP art.] 4.14 as barring prosecution of the complaint in a state justice court because the offense alleged arose from the violation of a speed limit set by city ordinance. [¶] The trial court's interpretation of Article 4.14 was erroneous.... [¶] [B]ecause the offense alleged in the complaint was a state law violation, the provisions of Article 4.14 pertaining to state law violations applied, granting *concurrent* jurisdiction for prosecution of state law offenses to both the municipal court *and* the state justice courts."

Rose v. State, 799 S.W.2d 381, 383 (Tex.App.—Dallas 1990, no pet.). "Although justice of the peace court precincts always lie within a single county, municipal boundaries may encompass more than one county. ... For this reason an obvious need exists for different requirements for a complaint in a municipal court than in a justice of the peace court."

ART. 4.15. MAY SIT AT ANY TIME

Justice courts and corporation courts may sit at any time to try criminal cases over which they have jurisdiction. Any case in which a fine may be assessed shall be tried in accordance with the rules of evidence and this Code.

History of CCP art. 4.15: Acts 1965, 59th Leg., vol. 2, ch. 722.

ART. 4.16. CONCURRENT JURISDICTION

When two or more courts have concurrent jurisdiction of any criminal offense, the court in which an indictment or a complaint shall first be filed shall retain jurisdiction except as provided in Article 4.12.

History of CCP art. 4.16: Acts 1965, 59th Leg., vol. 2, ch. 722.

ANNOTATIONS

State v. Johnson, 821 S.W.2d 609, 611 (Tex.Crim. App.1991). "The court of appeals held that Article 4.16 gives the first court legally taking jurisdiction exclusive jurisdiction. That jurisdiction, however, may be voluntarily surrendered by dismissal of the charge."

Ex parte Clear, 573 S.W.2d 224, 228 (Tex.Crim.App. 1978). "As far as this statute is concerned, a criminal 'offense' is the equivalent of a criminal 'case,' which this Court has defined to be 'an action, suit, or cause instituted to secure a conviction and punishment for crime, or to punish an infraction of the criminal law.'"

Mills v. State, 742 S.W.2d 831, 835 (Tex.App.—Dallas 1987, no pet.). "A defendant who does not interpose a plea to the jurisdiction may waive the right to question jurisdiction under article 4.16."

Conner v. State, 725 S.W.2d 454, 456 (Tex.App.—Beaumont 1987, no pet.). Appellant "alleges the verdict is void because appellant was indicted in the 9th District Court and was tried in the 221st District Court. Appellant's contentions are without merit.... [W]hile [Article] 4.16 ... provides that the first court in which an indictment is filed retains jurisdiction, this does not preclude or oust jurisdiction of other courts with concurrent jurisdiction."

ART. 4.17. TRANSFER OF CERTAIN MISDEMEANORS

On a plea of not guilty to a misdemeanor offense punishable by confinement in jail, entered in a county court of a judge who is not a licensed attorney, on the motion of the state or the defendant, the judge may transfer the case to a district court having jurisdiction in the county or to a county court at law in the county presided over by a judge who is a licensed attorney. The judge may make the transfer on his own motion. The attorney representing the state in the case in county court shall continue the prosecution in the court to which the case is transferred. Provided, in no case may any such case be transferred to a district court except with the written consent of the judge of the district court to which the transfer is sought.

History of CCP art. 4.17: Acts 1983, 68th Leg., ch. 303, §6, eff. Jan. 1, 1984. Amended by Acts 1989, 71st Leg., ch. 295, §1, eff. Sept. 1, 1989.

ANNOTATIONS

Wolff v. Thornton, 670 S.W.2d 764, 766 (Tex. App.—Houston [1st Dist.] 1984, orig. proceeding). "There is no language in [Article 4.17] indicating an intent on the part of the legislature to create an absolute right of transfer, and to the contrary, the legislature's use of the word 'may' reflects an intent to leave the question of transfer to the discretion of the county court judge. [¶] [T]here is no mandatory requirement that relator's trial be conducted by a judge who is a licensed attorney."

ART. 4.18. CLAIM OF UNDERAGE

(a) A claim that a district court or criminal district court does not have jurisdiction over a person because jurisdiction is exclusively in the juvenile court and that the juvenile court could not waive jurisdiction under Section 8.07(a), Penal Code, or did not waive jurisdiction under Section 8.07(b), Penal Code, must be made by written motion in bar of prosecution filed with the court in which criminal charges against the person are filed.

(b) The motion must be filed and presented to the presiding judge of the court:

(1) if the defendant enters a plea of guilty or no contest, before the plea;

(2) if the defendant's guilt or punishment is tried or determined by a jury, before selection of the jury begins; or

(3) if the defendant's guilt is tried by the court, before the first witness is sworn.

(c) Unless the motion is not contested, the presiding judge shall promptly conduct a hearing without a jury and rule on the motion. The party making the motion has the burden of establishing by a preponderance of the evidence those facts necessary for the motion to prevail.

(d) A person may not contest the jurisdiction of the court on the ground that the juvenile court has exclusive jurisdiction if:

(1) the person does not file a motion within the time requirements of this article; or

(2) the presiding judge finds under Subsection (c) that a motion made under this article does not prevail.

(e) An appellate court may review a trial court's determination under this article, if otherwise authorized by law, only after conviction in the trial court.

(f) A court that finds that it lacks jurisdiction over a case because exclusive jurisdiction is in the juvenile court shall transfer the case to the juvenile court as provided by Section 51.08, Family Code.

(g) This article does not apply to a claim of a defect or error in a discretionary transfer proceeding in juvenile court. A defendant may appeal a defect or error only as provided by Article 44.47.

History of CCP art. 4.18: Acts 1995, 74th Leg., ch. 262, §80, eff. Jan. 1, 1996. Amended by Acts 1999, 76th Leg., ch. 1477, §§27, 28, eff. Sept. 1, 1999.

ANNOTATIONS

Rushing v. State, 85 S.W.3d 283, 286 (Tex.Crim. App.2002). Article 4.18 "prevents a claim [of underage] from being raised in *any* context if the statute's preservation requirements are not met. If a written objection is not timely filed before trial, the trial judge is deprived of the ability to decide the claim. Likewise, a failure to comply with Article 4.18's requirements would prevent consideration of the claim on habeas corpus." *See also* ***Adams v. State***, 161 S.W.3d 113, 113-14 (Tex.App.— Houston [14th Dist.] 2004, pet. ref'd).

CHAPTER 5. FAMILY VIOLENCE PREVENTION

ART. 5.01. LEGISLATIVE STATEMENT

(a) Family violence is a serious danger and threat to society and its members. Victims of family violence are entitled to the maximum protection from harm or abuse or the threat of harm or abuse as is permitted by law.

(b) In any law enforcement, prosecutorial, or judicial response to allegations of family violence, the responding law enforcement or judicial officers shall protect the victim, without regard to the relationship between the alleged offender and victim.

History of CCP art. 5.01: Acts 1985, 69th Leg., ch. 583, §1, eff. Sept. 1, 1985.

ART. 5.02. DEFINITIONS

In this chapter, "family violence," "family," "household," and "member of a household" have the meanings assigned by Chapter 71, Family Code.

History of CCP art. 5.02: Acts 1985, 69th Leg., ch. 583, §1, eff. Sept. 1, 1985. Amended by Acts 2003, 78th Leg., ch. 1276, §7.002 (c), eff. Sept. 1, 2003.

ART. 5.03. FAMILY OR HOUSEHOLD RELATIONSHIP DOES NOT CREATE AN EXCEPTION TO OFFICIAL DUTIES

A general duty prescribed for an officer by Chapter 2 of this code is not waived or excepted in any family violence case or investigation because of a family or household relationship between an alleged violator and the victim of family violence. A peace officer's or a magistrate's duty to prevent the commission of criminal offenses, including acts of family violence, is not waived or excepted because of a family or household relationship between the potential violator and victim.

History of CCP art. 5.03: Acts 1985, 69th Leg., ch. 583, §1, eff. Sept. 1, 1985.

ART. 5.04. DUTIES OF PEACE OFFICERS

(a) The primary duties of a peace officer who investigates a family violence allegation or who responds to a disturbance call that may involve family violence are to protect any potential victim of family violence, enforce the law of this state, enforce a protective order from another jurisdiction as provided by Chapter 88, Family Code, and make lawful arrests of violators.

E (a-1) A peace officer who investigates a family violence allegation or who responds to a disturbance call that may involve family violence shall determine whether the address of the persons involved in the allegation or call matches the address of a current licensed foster home or verified agency foster home listed in the Texas Crime Information Center.

(b) A peace officer who investigates a family violence allegation or who responds to a disturbance call that may involve family violence shall advise any possible adult victim of all reasonable means to prevent further family violence, including giving written notice of a victim's legal rights and remedies and of the availability of shelter or other community services for family violence victims.

(c) A written notice required by Subsection (b) of this article is sufficient if it is in substantially the following form with the required information in English and in Spanish inserted in the notice:

"NOTICE TO ADULT VICTIMS OF FAMILY VIOLENCE

"It is a crime for any person to cause you any physical injury or harm EVEN IF THAT PERSON IS A MEMBER OR FORMER MEMBER OF YOUR FAMILY OR HOUSEHOLD.

"Please tell the investigating peace officer:

"IF you, your child, or any other household resident has been injured; or

"IF you feel you are going to be in danger when the officer leaves or later.

"You have the right to:

"ASK the local prosecutor to file a criminal complaint against the person committing family violence; and

"APPLY to a court for an order to protect you (you should consult a legal aid office, a prosecuting attorney, or a private attorney). If a family or household member assaults you and is arrested, you may request that a magistrate's order for emergency protection be issued. Please inform the investigating officer if you want an order for emergency protection. You need not be present when the order is issued. You cannot be charged a fee by a court in connection with filing, serving, or entering a protective order. For example, the court can enter an order that:

"(1) the abuser not commit further acts of violence;

"(2) the abuser not threaten, harass, or contact you at home;

"(3) directs the abuser to leave your household; and

"(4) establishes temporary custody of the children and directs the abuser not to interfere with the children or any property.

"A VIOLATION OF CERTAIN PROVISIONS OF COURT-ORDERED PROTECTION (such as (1) and (2) above) MAY BE A FELONY.

"CALL THE FOLLOWING VIOLENCE SHELTERS OR SOCIAL ORGANIZATIONS IF YOU NEED PROTECTION:

"_____

"_____."

History of CCP art. 5.04: Acts 1985, 69th Leg., ch. 583, §1, eff. Sept. 1, 1985. Amended by Acts 1991, 72nd Leg., ch. 366, §4, eff. Sept. 1, 1991; Acts 1995, 74th Leg., ch. 1024, §24, eff. Sept. 1, 1995; Acts 1997, 75th Leg., ch. 610, §2 (eff. Sept. 1, 1997), ch. 1193, §23 (eff. Sept. 1, 1997); Acts 2007, 80th Leg., ch. 524, §2, eff. June 16, 2007.

See also *O'Connor's Family Law Handbook*, "Duties of Law Enforcement," ch. 6-E.

ANNOTATIONS

Atkins v. State, 919 S.W.2d 770, 776 (Tex.App.— Houston [14th Dist.] 1996, no pet.). "[A]ppellant maintains that the trial court erred by including in the jury charge [a] provision from article 5.04.... Appellant contends the instruction ... calls for the jury to assume an officer makes a lawful arrest each and every time he responds to a disturbance call. We disagree. [¶] [T]he trial court specifically instructed the jury to look at the totality of the circumstances to determine whether the officer had probable cause to arrest appellant. The trial court further instructed the jury that they must find beyond a reasonable doubt that the officer had probable cause to believe appellant assaulted his wife before considering the evidence obtained in the search of appellant. [A]n objective consideration of the totality of the circumstances is necessary to determine whether the officer's actions were justified by probable cause. By instructing the jury as to the duties of a peace officer and the necessity of finding probable cause, the trial court afforded the jury the opportunity to objectively consider whether the officer had probable cause to arrest appellant."

ART. 5.045. STANDBY ASSISTANCE; LIABILITY

(a) In the discretion of a peace officer, the officer may stay with a victim of family violence to protect the victim and allow the victim to take the personal property of the victim or of a child in the care of the victim to a place of safety in an orderly manner.

(b) A peace officer who provides assistance under Subsection (a) of this article is not:

(1) civilly liable for an act or omission of the officer that arises in connection with providing the assistance or determining whether to provide the assistance; or

(2) civilly or criminally liable for the wrongful appropriation of any personal property by the victim.

History of CCP art. 5.045: Acts 1995, 74th Leg., ch. 565, §1, eff. June 14, 1995.

See also *O'Connor's Family Law Handbook*, "Duties of Law Enforcement," ch. 6-E.

ART. 5.05. REPORTS & RECORDS

(a) A peace officer who investigates a family violence incident or who responds to a disturbance call that may involve family violence shall make a written report, including but not limited to:

(1) the names of the suspect and complainant;

(2) the date, time, and location of the incident;

(3) any visible or reported injuries; and

(4) a description of the incident and a statement of its disposition.

E (a-1) In addition to the written report required under Subsection (a), a peace officer who investigates a family violence incident or who responds to a disturbance call that may involve family violence shall make a report to the Department of Family and Protective Services if the location of the incident or call, or the known address of a person involved in the incident or call, matches the address of a current licensed foster home or a verified agency foster home as listed in the Texas Crime Information Center. The report under this subsection may be made orally or electronically and must:

(1) include the information required by Subsection (a); and

(2) be filed with the Department of Family and Protective Services within 24 hours of the beginning of the investigation or receipt of the disturbance call.

A (b) Each local law enforcement agency shall establish a departmental code for identifying and retrieving family violence reports as outlined in Subsection (a) of this section. A district or county attorney or an assistant district or county attorney exercising authority in the county where the law enforcement agency maintains records under this section is entitled to access to the records. The Department of Family and Protective

Services is entitled to access the records relating to any person who is 14 years of age or older and who resides in a licensed foster home or a verified agency foster home.

(c) In order to ensure that officers responding to calls are aware of the existence and terms of protective orders, each municipal police department and sheriff shall establish procedures within the department or office to provide adequate information or access to information for law enforcement officers of the names of persons protected by a protective order and of persons to whom protective orders are directed.

(d) Each law enforcement officer shall accept a certified copy of an original or modified protective order as proof of the validity of the order and it is presumed the order remains valid unless:

(1) the order contains a termination date that has passed;

(2) it is more than one year after the date the order was issued; or

(3) the law enforcement officer has been notified by the clerk of the court vacating the order that the order has been vacated.

(e) A peace officer who makes a report under Subsection (a) of this article shall provide information concerning the incident or disturbance to the bureau of identification and records of the Department of Public Safety for its recordkeeping function under Section 411.042, Government Code. The bureau shall prescribe the form and nature of the information required to be reported to the bureau by this article.

(f) On request of a victim of an incident of family violence, the local law enforcement agency responsible for investigating the incident shall provide the victim, at no cost to the victim, with any information that is:

(1) contained in the written report prepared under Subsection (a);

(2) described by Subsection (a)(1) or (2); and

(3) not exempt from disclosure under Chapter 552, Government Code, or other law.

History of CCP art. 5.05: Acts 1985, 69th Leg., ch. 583, §1, eff. Sept. 1, 1985. Amended by Acts 1989, 71st Leg., ch. 614, §27 (eff. Sept. 1, 1989), ch. 739, §8 (eff. Sept. 1, 1989); Acts 1993, 73rd Leg., ch. 900, §8.01, eff. Sept. 1, 1993; Acts 2007, 80th Leg., ch. 524, §3 (eff. June 16, 2007), ch. 1057, §2 (eff. Sept. 1, 2007).

See also *O'Connor's Family Law Handbook*, "Duties of Law Enforcement," ch. 6-E.

ART. 5.06. DUTIES OF PROSECUTING ATTORNEYS & COURTS

(a) Neither a prosecuting attorney nor a court may:

(1) dismiss or delay any criminal proceeding that involves a prosecution for an offense that constitutes family violence because a civil proceeding is pending or not pending; or

(2) require proof that a complaining witness, victim, or defendant is a party to a suit for the dissolution of a marriage or a suit affecting the parent-child relationship before presenting a criminal allegation to a grand jury, filing an information, or otherwise proceeding with the prosecution of a criminal case.

(b) A prosecuting attorney's decision to file an application for a protective order under Chapter 71, Family Code, should be made without regard to whether a criminal complaint has been filed by the applicant. A prosecuting attorney may require the applicant to provide information for an offense report, relating to the facts alleged in the application, with a local law enforcement agency.

(c) The prosecuting attorney having responsibility under Section 71.04(c), Family Code, for filing applications for protective orders under Chapter 71, Family Code, shall provide notice of those responsibilities to all law enforcement agencies within the jurisdiction of the prosecuting attorney for the prosecuting attorney.

History of CCP art. 5.06: Acts 1985, 69th Leg., ch. 583, §1, eff. Sept. 1, 1985. Amended by Acts 1989, 71st Leg., ch. 614, §28 (eff. Sept. 1, 1989), ch. 739, §9 (eff. Sept. 1, 1989); Acts 1995, 74th Leg., ch. 564, §2 (eff. Sept. 1, 1995), ch. 1024, §25 (eff. Sept. 1, 1995).

ART. 5.07. VENUE FOR PROTECTIVE ORDER OFFENSES

The venue for an offense under Section 25.07, Penal Code, is in the county in which the order was issued or, without regard to the identity or location of the court that issued the protective order, in the county in which the offense was committed.

History of CCP art. 5.07: Acts 1989, 71st Leg., ch. 614, §29 (eff. Sept. 1, 1989), ch. 739, §10 (eff. Sept. 1, 1989). Amended by Acts 1995, 74th Leg., ch. 76, §14.16, eff. Sept. 1, 1995.

ART. 5.08. MEDIATION IN FAMILY VIOLENCE CASES

Notwithstanding Article 26.13(g) or Section 11(a)(16), Article 42.12, of this code, in a criminal prosecution arising from family violence, as that term is defined by Section 71.004, Family Code, a court shall not refer or order the victim or the defendant involved to mediation, dispute resolution, arbitration, or other similar procedures.

History of CCP art. 5.08: Acts 1999, 76th Leg., ch. 389, §1, eff. Aug. 30, 1999.

CHAPTER 6. PREVENTING OFFENSES BY THE ACT OF MAGISTRATES & OTHER OFFICERS

Art. 6.01   When magistrate hears threat
Art. 6.02   Threat to take life
Art. 6.03   On attempt to injure
Art. 6.04   May compel offender to give security
Art. 6.05   Duty of peace officer as to threats
Art. 6.06   Peace officer to prevent injury
Art. 6.07   Conduct of peace officer
Art. 6.08   Protective order prohibiting offense caused by bias or prejudice

ART. 6.01. WHEN MAGISTRATE HEARS THREAT

It is the duty of every magistrate, when he may have heard, in any manner, that a threat has been made by one person to do some injury to himself or the person or property of another, including the person or property of his spouse, immediately to give notice to some peace officer, in order that such peace officer may use lawful means to prevent the injury.

History of CCP art. 6.01: Acts 1965, 59th Leg., vol. 2, ch. 722. Amended by Acts 1979, 66th Leg., ch. 164, §1, eff. Sept. 1, 1979.

ART. 6.02. THREAT TO TAKE LIFE

If, within the hearing of a magistrate, one person shall threaten to take the life of another, including that of his spouse, or himself, the magistrate shall issue a warrant for the arrest of the person making the threat, or in case of emergency, he may himself immediately arrest such person.

History of CCP art. 6.02: Acts 1965, 59th Leg., vol. 2, ch. 722. Amended by Acts 1979, 66th Leg., ch. 164, §1, eff. Sept. 1, 1979.

ART. 6.03. ON ATTEMPT TO INJURE

Whenever, in the presence or within the observation of a magistrate, an attempt is made by one person to inflict an injury upon himself or to the person or property of another, including the person or property of his spouse, it is his duty to use all lawful means to prevent the injury. This may be done, either by verbal order to a peace officer to interfere and prevent the injury, or by the issuance of an order of arrest against the offender, or by arresting the offender; for which purpose he may call upon all persons present to assist in making the arrest.

History of CCP art. 6.03: Acts 1965, 59th Leg., vol. 2, ch. 722. Amended by Acts 1979, 66th Leg., ch. 164, §1, eff. Sept. 1, 1979.

ART. 6.04. MAY COMPEL OFFENDER TO GIVE SECURITY

When the person making such threat is brought before a magistrate, he may compel him to give security to keep the peace, or commit him to custody.

History of CCP art. 6.04: Acts 1965, 59th Leg., vol. 2, ch. 722.

ART. 6.05. DUTY OF PEACE OFFICER AS TO THREATS

It is the duty of every peace officer, when he may have been informed in any manner that a threat has been made by one person to do some injury to himself or to the person or property of another, including the person or property of his spouse, to prevent the threatened injury, if within his power; and, in order to do this, he may call in aid any number of citizens in his county. He may take such measures as the person about to be injured might for the prevention of the offense.

History of CCP art. 6.05: Acts 1965, 59th Leg., vol. 2, ch. 722. Amended by Acts 1979, 66th Leg., ch. 164, §1, eff. Sept. 1, 1979.

ANNOTATIONS

Pope v. State, 695 S.W.2d 341, 343 (Tex.App.—Houston [1st Dist.] 1985, pet. ref'd). "Article 6.05 ... authorizes a peace officer only to prevent a wrong from being committed or attempted and does not otherwise confer authority to arrest without a warrant."

ART. 6.06. PEACE OFFICER TO PREVENT INJURY

Whenever, in the presence of a peace officer, or within his view, one person is about to commit an offense against the person or property of another, including the person or property of his spouse, or injure himself, it is his duty to prevent it; and, for this purpose the peace officer may summon any number of the citizens of his county to his aid. The peace officer must use the amount of force necessary to prevent the commission of the offense, and no greater.

History of CCP art. 6.06: Acts 1965, 59th Leg., vol. 2, ch. 722. Amended by Acts 1979, 66th Leg., ch. 164, §1, eff. Sept. 1, 1979.

ANNOTATIONS

Blackwell v. Harris Cty., 909 S.W.2d 135, 139 (Tex. App.—Houston [14th Dist.] 1995, writ denied). "Peace officers are not relieved of this responsibility [to prevent injury] simply because they are 'off-duty.'"

ART. 6.07. CONDUCT OF PEACE OFFICER

The conduct of peace officers, in preventing offenses about to be committed in their presence, or within their view, is to be regulated by the same rules as are prescribed to the action of the person about to be injured. They may use all force necessary to repel the aggression.

History of CCP art. 6.07: Acts 1965, 59th Leg., vol. 2, ch. 722.

ART. 6.08. PROTECTIVE ORDER PROHIBITING OFFENSE CAUSED BY BIAS OR PREJUDICE

(a) At any proceeding in which the defendant appears in constitutional county court, statutory county court, or district court that is related to an offense under Title 5, Penal Code, or Section 28.02, 28.03, or 28.08, Penal Code, in which it is alleged that the defendant committed the offense because of bias or prejudice as described by Article 42.014, a person may request the court to render a protective order under Title 4, Family Code, for the protection of the person.

(b) The court shall render a protective order in the manner provided by Title 4, Family Code, if, in lieu of the finding that family violence occurred and is likely to occur in the future as required by Section 85.001, Family Code, the court finds that probable cause exists to believe that an offense under Title 5, Penal Code, or Section 28.02, 28.03, or 28.08, Penal Code, occurred, that the defendant committed the offense because of bias or prejudice, and that the nature of the scheme or course of conduct engaged in by the defendant in the commission of the offense indicates that the defendant is likely to engage in the future in conduct prohibited by Title 5, Penal Code, or Section 28.02, 28.03, or 28.08, Penal Code, and committed because of bias or prejudice.

(c) The procedure for the enforcement of a protective order under Title 4, Family Code, applies to the fullest extent practicable to the enforcement of a protective order under this article, including provisions relating to findings, contents, duration, warning, delivery, law enforcement duties, and modification, except that:

(1) the printed statement on the warning must refer to the prosecution of subsequent offenses committed because of bias or prejudice;

(2) the court shall require a constable to serve a protective order issued under this article; and

(3) the clerk of the court shall forward a copy of a protective order issued under this article to the Department of Public Safety with a designation indicating that the order was issued to prevent offenses committed because of bias or prejudice.

(d) For an original or modified protective order rendered under this article, on receipt of the order from the clerk of the court, a law enforcement agency shall immediately, but not later than the 10th day after the date the order is received, enter the information required by Section 411.042(b)(6), Government Code, into the statewide law enforcement information system maintained by the Department of Public Safety.

History of CCP art. 6.08: Acts 2001, 77th Leg., ch. 85, §3.01, eff. Sept. 1, 2001.

CHAPTER 7. PROCEEDINGS BEFORE MAGISTRATES TO PREVENT OFFENSES

ART. 7.01. SHALL ISSUE WARRANT

Whenever a magistrate is informed upon oath that an offense is about to be committed against the person or property of the informant, or of another, or that any person has threatened to commit an offense, the magistrate shall immediately issue a warrant for the arrest of the accused; that he may be brought before such magistrate or before some other named in the warrant.

History of CCP art. 7.01: Acts 1965, 59th Leg., vol. 2, ch. 722.

ART. 7.02. APPEARANCE BOND PENDING PEACE BOND HEARING

In proceedings under this Chapter, the accused shall have the right to make an appearance bond; such bond shall be conditioned as appearance bonds in other cases, and shall be further conditioned that the accused, pending the hearing, will not commit such offense and that he will keep the peace toward the person threatened or about to be injured, and toward all others, pending the hearing. Should the accused enter into such appearance bond, such fact shall not constitute any evidence of the accusation brought against him at the hearing on the merits before the magistrate.

History of CCP art. 7.02: Acts 1965, 59th Leg., vol. 2, ch. 722.

ART. 7.03. ACCUSED BROUGHT BEFORE MAGISTRATE

When the accused has been brought before the magistrate, he shall hear proof as to the accusation, and if he be satisfied that there is just reason to apprehend that the offense was intended to be committed, or that the threat was seriously made, he shall make an order that the accused enter into bond in such sum as he may in his discretion require, conditioned that he will not commit such offense, and that he will keep the peace toward the person threatened or about to be injured, and toward all others named in the bond for any period of time, not to exceed one year from the date of the bond. The magistrate shall admonish the accused that if the accused violates a condition of the bond, the court, in addition to ordering forfeiture of the bond, may punish the accused for contempt under Section 21.002(c), Government Code.

History of CCP art. 7.03: Acts 1965, 59th Leg., vol. 2, ch. 722. Amended by Acts 1997, 75th Leg., ch. 773, §1, eff. Sept. 1, 1997.

ART. 7.04. FORM OF PEACE BOND

Such bond shall be sufficient if it be payable to the State of Texas, conditioned as required in said order of the magistrate, be for some certain sum, and be signed by the defendant and his surety or sureties and dated, and the provisions of Article 17.02 permitting the deposit of current United States money in lieu of sureties is applicable to this bond. No error of form shall vitiate such bond, and no error in the proceedings prior to the execution of the bond shall be a defense in a suit thereon.

History of CCP art. 7.04: Acts 1965, 59th Leg., vol. 2, ch. 722.

ART. 7.05. OATH OF SURETY; BOND FILED

The officer taking such bond shall require the sureties of the accused to make oath as to the value of their property as pointed out with regard to bail bonds. Such officer shall forthwith deposit such bond and oaths in the office of the clerk of the county where such bond is taken.

History of CCP art. 7.05: Acts 1965, 59th Leg., vol. 2, ch. 722.

ART. 7.06. AMOUNT OF BAIL

The magistrate, in fixing the amount of such bonds, shall be governed by the pecuniary circumstances of the accused and the nature of the offense threatened or about to be committed.

History of CCP art. 7.06: Acts 1965, 59th Leg., vol. 2, ch. 722.

ART. 7.07. SURETY MAY EXONERATE HIMSELF

A surety upon any such bond may, at any time before a breach thereof, exonerate himself from the obligations of the same by delivering to any magistrate of the county where such bond was taken, the person of the defendant; and such magistrate shall in that case again require of the defendant bond, with other security in the same amount as the first bond; and the same proceeding shall be had as in the first instance, but the one year's time shall commence to run from the date of the first order.

History of CCP art. 7.07: Acts 1965, 59th Leg., vol. 2, ch. 722.

ART. 7.08. FAILURE TO GIVE BOND

If the defendant fail to give bond, he shall be committed to jail for one year from the date of the first order requiring such bond.

History of CCP art. 7.08: Acts 1965, 59th Leg., vol. 2, ch. 722.

ART. 7.09. DISCHARGE OF DEFENDANT

A defendant committed for failing to give bond shall be discharged by the officer having him in custody, upon giving the required bond, or at the expiration of the time for which he has been committed.

History of CCP art. 7.09: Acts 1965, 59th Leg., vol. 2, ch. 722.

ART. 7.10. MAY DISCHARGE DEFENDANT

If the magistrate believes from the evidence that there is no good reason to apprehend that the offense was intended or will be committed, or that no serious threat was made by the defendant, he shall discharge the accused, and may, in his discretion, tax the cost of the proceeding against the party making the complaint.

History of CCP art. 7.10: Acts 1965, 59th Leg., vol. 2, ch. 722.

ARTS. 7.11, 7.12. REPEALED

Repealed by Acts 1973, 63rd Leg., ch. 399, §3(b), eff. Jan. 1, 1974.

ART. 7.13. WHEN THE DEFENDANT HAS COMMITTED A CRIME

If it appears from the evidence before the magistrate that the defendant has committed a criminal offense, the same proceedings shall be had as in other cases where parties are charged with crime.

History of CCP art. 7.13: Acts 1965, 59th Leg., vol. 2, ch. 722.

ART. 7.14. COSTS

If the accused is found subject to the charge and required to give bond, the costs of the proceedings shall be adjudged against him.

History of CCP art. 7.14: Acts 1965, 59th Leg., vol. 2, ch. 722.

ART. 7.15. MAY ORDER PROTECTION

When, from the nature of the case and the proof offered to the magistrate, it may appear necessary and proper, he shall have a right to order any peace officer to protect the person or property of any individual threatened; and such peace officer shall have the right to summon aid by requiring any number of citizens of his county to assist in giving the protection.

History of CCP art. 7.15: Acts 1965, 59th Leg., vol. 2, ch. 722.

ART. 7.16. SUIT ON BOND

A suit to forfeit any bond taken under the provisions of this Chapter shall be brought in the name of the State by the district or county attorney in the county where the bond was taken.

History of CCP art. 7.16: Acts 1965, 59th Leg., vol. 2, ch. 722.

ART. 7.17. LIMITATION & PROCEDURE

Suits upon such bonds shall be commenced within two years from the breach of the same, and not thereafter, and shall be governed by the same rules as civil actions, except that the sureties may be sued without joining the principal. To entitle the State to recover, it shall only be necessary to prove that the accused violated any condition of said bond. The full amount of such bond may be recovered of the accused and the sureties.

History of CCP art. 7.17: Acts 1965, 59th Leg., vol. 2, ch. 722.

ART. 7.18. CONTEMPT

Violation of a condition of bond imposed under this chapter is punishable by:

(1) forfeiture of the bond;

(2) imposition of the fine and confinement for contempt under Section 21.002(c), Government Code; or

(3) both forfeiture of the bond and imposition of the fine and confinement.

History of CCP art. 7.18: Acts 1997, 75th Leg., ch. 773, §2, eff. Sept. 1, 1997.

CHAPTER 7A. PROTECTIVE ORDER FOR VICTIM OF SEXUAL ASSAULT

ART. 7A.01. APPLICATION FOR PROTECTIVE ORDER

A *Subsection (a) below is effective for offenses committed on or after Sept. 1, 2007. Subsection (a) below is effective for protective orders issued on or after Sept. 1, 2007.*

(a) A person who is the victim of an offense under Section 21.02, 21.11, 22.011, or 22.021, Penal Code, a parent or guardian acting on behalf of a person younger than 17 years of age who is the victim of such an offense, or a prosecuting attorney acting on behalf of the person may file an application for a protective order under this chapter without regard to the relationship between the applicant and the alleged offender.

Subsection (a) below is effective for offenses in which any element of the offense was committed before Sept. 1, 2007. Subsection (a) below is effective for protective orders issued before Sept. 1, 2007.

(a) A person who is the victim of an offense under Section 22.011 or 22.021, Penal Code, or a prosecuting attorney acting on behalf of the person, may file an application for a protective order under this chapter without regard to the relationship between the applicant and the alleged offender.

(b) An application for a protective order under this chapter may be filed in a district court, juvenile court having the jurisdiction of a district court, statutory county court, or constitutional county court in:

(1) the county in which the applicant resides; or

(2) the county in which the alleged offender resides.

History of CCP art. 7A.01: Acts 2003, 78th Leg., ch. 836, §1, eff. Sept. 1, 2003. Amended by Acts 2007, 80th Leg., ch. 593, §3.05 (eff. Sept. 1, 2007), ch. 882, §1 (eff. Sept. 1, 2007).

ART. 7A.02. TEMPORARY EX PARTE ORDER

If the court finds from the information contained in an application for a protective order that there is a clear and present danger of a sexual assault or other harm to the applicant, the court, without further notice to the alleged offender and without a hearing, may enter a temporary ex parte order for the protection of the applicant or any other member of the applicant's family or household.

History of CCP art. 7A.02: Acts 2003, 78th Leg., ch. 836, §1, eff. Sept. 1, 2003.

ART. 7A.03. REQUIRED FINDINGS; ISSUANCE OF PROTECTIVE ORDER

A *Article 7A.03 below is effective for protective orders issued on or after Sept. 1, 2007.*

(a) At the close of a hearing on an application for a protective order under this chapter, the court shall find whether there are reasonable grounds to believe that the applicant is the victim of a sexual assault and:

(1) is younger than 18 years of age; or

(2) regardless of age, is the subject of a threat that reasonably places the applicant in fear of further harm from the alleged offender.

(b) If the court finds reasonable grounds to believe that the applicant is the victim of a sexual assault and is younger than 18 years of age, or regardless of age, the subject of a threat that reasonably places the applicant in fear of further harm from the alleged offender, the court shall issue a protective order that includes a statement of the required findings.

History of CCP art. 7A.03: Acts 2003, 78th Leg., ch. 836, §1, eff. Sept. 1, 2003. Amended by Acts 2007, 80th Leg., ch. 882, §2, eff. Sept. 1, 2007.

ART. 7A.03. REQUIRED FINDINGS; ISSUANCE OF PROTECTIVE ORDER

Article 7A.03 below is effective for protective orders issued before Sept. 1, 2007.

(a) At the close of a hearing on an application for a protective order under this chapter, the court shall find whether there are reasonable grounds to believe that the applicant is:

(1) the victim of a sexual assault; and

(2) the subject of a threat that reasonably places the applicant in fear of further harm from the alleged offender.

(b) If the court finds reasonable grounds to believe that the applicant is the victim of a sexual assault and

is the subject of a threat that reasonably places the applicant in fear of further harm from the alleged offender, the court shall issue a protective order that includes a statement of the required findings.

ART. 7A.04. APPLICATION OF OTHER LAW

To the extent applicable, except as otherwise provided by this chapter, Title 4, Family Code, applies to a protective order issued under this chapter.

History of CCP art. 7A.04: Acts 2003, 78th Leg., ch. 836, §1, eff. Sept. 1, 2003.

ART. 7A.05. CONDITIONS SPECIFIED BY ORDER

(a) In a protective order issued under this chapter, the court may:

(1) order the alleged offender to take action as specified by the court that the court determines is necessary or appropriate to prevent or reduce the likelihood of future harm to the applicant or a member of the applicant's family or household; or

(2) prohibit the alleged offender from:

(A) communicating directly or indirectly with the applicant or any member of the applicant's family or household in a threatening or harassing manner;

(B) going to or near the residence, place of employment or business, or child-care facility or school of the applicant or any member of the applicant's family or household;

(C) engaging in conduct directed specifically toward the applicant or any member of the applicant's family or household, including following the person, that is reasonably likely to harass, annoy, alarm, abuse, torment, or embarrass the person; and

(D) possessing a firearm, unless the alleged offender is a peace officer, as defined by Section 1.07, Penal Code, actively engaged in employment as a sworn, full-time paid employee of a state agency or political subdivision.

(b) In an order under Subsection (a)(2)(B), the court shall specifically describe each prohibited location and the minimum distance from the location, if any, that the alleged offender must maintain. This subsection does not apply to an order with respect to which the court has received a request to maintain confidentiality of information revealing the locations.

(c) In a protective order, the court may suspend a license to carry a concealed handgun issued under Section 411.177, Government Code, that is held by the alleged offender.

History of CCP art. 7A.05: Acts 2003, 78th Leg., ch. 836, §1, eff. Sept. 1, 2003.

ART. 7A.06. WARNING ON PROTECTIVE ORDER

(a) Each protective order issued under this chapter, including a temporary ex parte order, must contain the following prominently displayed statements in bold-faced type, capital letters, or underlined:

"A PERSON WHO VIOLATES THIS ORDER MAY BE PUNISHED FOR CONTEMPT OF COURT BY A FINE OF AS MUCH AS $500 OR BY CONFINEMENT IN JAIL FOR AS LONG AS SIX MONTHS, OR BOTH."

"NO PERSON, INCLUDING A PERSON WHO IS PROTECTED BY THIS ORDER, MAY GIVE PERMISSION TO ANYONE TO IGNORE OR VIOLATE ANY PROVISION OF THIS ORDER. DURING THE TIME IN WHICH THIS ORDER IS VALID, EVERY PROVISION OF THIS ORDER IS IN FULL FORCE AND EFFECT UNLESS A COURT CHANGES THE ORDER."

"IT IS UNLAWFUL FOR ANY PERSON, OTHER THAN A PEACE OFFICER, AS DEFINED BY SECTION 1.07, PENAL CODE, ACTIVELY ENGAGED IN EMPLOYMENT AS A SWORN, FULL-TIME PAID EMPLOYEE OF A STATE AGENCY OR POLITICAL SUBDIVISION, WHO IS SUBJECT TO A PROTECTIVE ORDER TO POSSESS A FIREARM OR AMMUNITION."

(b) Each protective order issued under this chapter, except for a temporary ex parte order, must contain the following prominently displayed statement in bold-faced type, capital letters, or underlined:

"A VIOLATION OF THIS ORDER BY COMMISSION OF AN ACT PROHIBITED BY THE ORDER MAY BE PUNISHABLE BY A FINE OF AS MUCH AS $4,000 OR BY CONFINEMENT IN JAIL FOR AS LONG AS ONE YEAR, OR BOTH. AN ACT THAT RESULTS IN A SEPARATE OFFENSE MAY BE PROSECUTED AS A SEPARATE OFFENSE IN ADDITION TO A VIOLATION OF THIS ORDER."

History of CCP art. 7A.06: Acts 2003, 78th Leg., ch. 836, §1, eff. Sept. 1, 2003.

ART. 7A.07. DURATION OF PROTECTIVE ORDER

 Article 7A.07 below is effective for protective orders issued on or after Sept. 1, 2007.

(a) A protective order issued under Article 7A.03 may be effective for the duration of the lives of the offender and victim as provided by Subsection (b), or for any shorter period stated in the order. If a period is not stated in the order, the order is effective until the second anniversary of the date the order was issued.

(b) A protective order issued under Article 7A.03 may be effective for the duration of the lives of the offender and victim only if the court finds reasonable cause to believe that the victim is the subject of a threat that reasonably places the victim in fear of further harm from the alleged offender.

(c) A victim who is 17 years of age or older or a parent or guardian acting on behalf of a victim who is younger than 17 years of age may file at any time an application with the court to rescind the protective order.

(d) If a person who is the subject of a protective order issued under Article 7A.03 is confined or imprisoned on the date the protective order is due to expire under Subsection (a), the period for which the order is effective is extended, and the order expires on the first anniversary of the date the person is released from confinement or imprisonment.

(e) To the extent of any conflict with Section 85.025, Family Code, this article prevails.

History of CCP art. 7A.07: Acts 2007, 80th Leg., ch. 882, §3, eff. Sept. 1, 2007.

CHAPTER 8. SUPPRESSION OF RIOTS & OTHER DISTURBANCES

ART. 8.01. OFFICER MAY REQUIRE AID

When any officer authorized to execute process is resisted, or when he has sufficient reason to believe that he will meet with resistance in executing the same, he may command as many of the citizens of his county as he may think proper; and the sheriff may call any military company in the county to aid him in overcoming the resistance, and if necessary, in seizing and arresting the persons engaged in such resistance.

History of CCP art. 8.01: Acts 1965, 59th Leg., vol. 2, ch. 722.

ART. 8.02. MILITARY AID IN EXECUTING PROCESS

If it be represented to the Governor in such manner as to satisfy him that the power of the county is not sufficient to enable the sheriff to execute process, he may, on application, order any military company of volunteers or militia company from another county to aid in overcoming such resistance.

History of CCP art. 8.02: Acts 1965, 59th Leg., vol. 2, ch. 722.

ART. 8.03. MILITARY AID IN SUPPRESSING RIOTS

Whenever, for the purpose of suppressing riots or unlawful assemblies, the aid of military or militia companies is called, they shall obey the orders of the civil officer who is engaged in suppressing the same.

History of CCP art. 8.03: Acts 1965, 59th Leg., vol. 2, ch. 722.

ART. 8.04. DISPERSING RIOT

Whenever a number of persons are assembled together in such a manner as to constitute a riot, according to the penal law of the State, it is the duty of every magistrate or peace officer to cause such persons to disperse. This may either be done by commanding them to disperse or by arresting the persons engaged, if necessary, either with or without warrant.

History of CCP art. 8.04: Acts 1965, 59th Leg., vol. 2, ch. 722.

ART. 8.05. OFFICER MAY CALL AID

In order to enable the officer to disperse a riot, he may call to his aid the power of the county in the same manner as is provided where it is necessary for the execution of process.

History of CCP art. 8.05: Acts 1965, 59th Leg., vol. 2, ch. 722.

ART. 8.06. MEANS ADOPTED TO SUPPRESS

The officer engaged in suppressing a riot, and those who aid him are authorized and justified in adopting such measures as are necessary to suppress the riot, but are not authorized to use any greater degree of force than is requisite to accomplish that object.

History of CCP art. 8.06: Acts 1965, 59th Leg., vol. 2, ch. 722.

ART. 8.07. UNLAWFUL ASSEMBLY

The Articles of this Chapter relating to the suppression of riots apply equally to an unlawful assembly and other unlawful disturbances, as defined by the Penal Code.

History of CCP art. 8.07: Acts 1965, 59th Leg., vol. 2, ch. 722.

ART. 8.08. SUPPRESSION AT ELECTION

To suppress riots, unlawful assemblies and other disturbances at elections, any magistrate may appoint a sufficient number of special constables. Such appointments shall be made to each special constable, shall be in writing, dated and signed by the magistrate, and shall recite the purposes for which such appointment is made, and the length of time it is to continue. Before the same is delivered to such special constable, he shall take an oath before the magistrate to suppress, by lawful means, all riots, unlawful assemblies and breaches of the peace of which he may receive information, and to act impartially between all parties and persons interested in the result of the election.

History of CCP art. 8.08: Acts 1965, 59th Leg., vol. 2, ch. 722.

ART. 8.09. POWER OF SPECIAL CONSTABLE

Special constables so appointed shall, during the time for which they are appointed, exercise the powers and perform the duties properly belonging to peace officers.

History of CCP art. 8.09: Acts 1965, 59th Leg., vol. 2, ch. 722.

CHAPTER 9. OFFENSES INJURIOUS TO PUBLIC HEALTH

ART. 9.01. TRADE INJURIOUS TO HEALTH

After an indictment or information has been presented against any person for carrying on a trade, business or occupation injurious to the health of those in the neighborhood, the court shall have power, on the application of anyone interested, and after hearing proof both for and against the accused, to restrain the defendant, in such penalty as may be deemed proper, from carrying on such trade, business or occupation, or may make such order respecting the manner and place of carrying on the same as may be deemed advisable; and if upon trial, the defendant be convicted, the restraint shall be made perpetual, and the party shall be required to enter into bond, with security, not to continue such trade, business or occupation to the detriment of the health of such neighborhood, or of any other neighborhood within the county.

History of CCP art. 9.01: Acts 1965, 59th Leg., vol. 2, ch. 722.

ART. 9.02. REFUSAL TO GIVE BOND

If the party refuses to give bond when required under the provisions of the preceding Article, the court may either commit him to jail, or make an order requiring the sheriff to seize upon the implements of such trade, business or occupation, or the goods and property used in conducting such trade, business or occupation, and destroy the same.

History of CCP art. 9.02: Acts 1965, 59th Leg., vol. 2, ch. 722.

ART. 9.03. REQUISITES OF BOND

Such bond shall be payable to the State of Texas, in a reasonable amount to be fixed by the court, conditioned that the defendant will not carry on such trade, business or occupation, naming the same, at such place, naming the place, or at any other place in the county, to the detriment of the health of the neighborhood. The bond shall be signed by the defendant and his sureties and dated, and shall be approved by the court taking the same, and filed in such court.

History of CCP art. 9.03: Acts 1965, 59th Leg., vol. 2, ch. 722.

ART. 9.04. SUIT UPON BOND

Any such bond, upon the breach thereof, may be sued upon by the district or county attorney, in the name of the State of Texas, within two years after such breach, and not afterwards; and such suits shall be governed by the same rules as civil actions.

History of CCP art. 9.04: Acts 1965, 59th Leg., vol. 2, ch. 722.

ART. 9.05. PROOF

It shall be sufficient proof of the breach of any such bond to show that the party continued after executing the same, to carry on the trade, business or occupation which he bound himself to discontinue; and the full amount of such bond may be recovered of the defendant and his sureties.

History of CCP art. 9.05: Acts 1965, 59th Leg., vol. 2, ch. 722.

ART. 9.06. UNWHOLESOME FOOD

After conviction for selling unwholesome food or adulterated medicine, the court shall enter and issue an order to the sheriff or other proper officer to seize and destroy such as remains in the hands of the defendant.

History of CCP art. 9.06: Acts 1965, 59th Leg., vol. 2, ch. 722.

CHAPTER 10. OBSTRUCTIONS OF PUBLIC HIGHWAYS

ART. 10.01. ORDER TO REMOVE

After prosecution begun against any person for obstructing any highway, any one, in behalf of the public, may apply to the county judge of the county in which such highway is situated; and upon hearing proof, such judge, either in term time or in vacation, may issue his written order to the sheriff or other proper officer of the county, directing him to remove the obstruction. Before the issuance of such order, the applicant therefor shall give bond with security in an amount to be fixed by the judge, to indemnify the accused, in case of his acquittal, for the loss he sustains. Such bond shall be approved by the county judge and filed with the papers in the cause.

History of CCP art. 10.01: Acts 1965, 59th Leg., vol. 2, ch. 722.

ART. 10.02. BOND OF APPLICANT

If the defendant be acquitted after a trial upon the merits of the case, he may maintain a civil action against the applicant and his sureties upon such bond, and may recover the full amount of the bond, or such damages, less than the full amount thereof, as may be assessed by a court or jury; provided, he shows on the trial that the place was not in fact, at the time he placed the obstruction or impediment thereupon, a public highway established by proper authority, but was in fact his own property or in his lawful possession.

History of CCP art. 10.02: Acts 1965, 59th Leg., vol. 2, ch. 722.

ART. 10.03. REMOVAL

Upon the conviction of a defendant for obstructing a public highway, if such obstruction still exists, the court shall order the sheriff or other proper officer to forthwith remove the same at the cost of the defendant, to be taxed and collected as other costs in the case.

History of CCP art. 10.03: Acts 1965, 59th Leg., vol. 2, ch. 722.

CHAPTER 11. HABEAS CORPUS

ART. 11.01. WHAT WRIT IS

The writ of habeas corpus is the remedy to be used when any person is restrained in his liberty. It is an order issued by a court or judge of competent jurisdiction, directed to any one having a person in his custody, or under his restraint, commanding him to produce such person, at a time and place named in the writ, and show why he is held in custody or under restraint.

History of CCP art. 11.01: Acts 1965, 59th Leg., vol. 2, ch. 722.
See also Tex. Const. art. 1, §12.

ANNOTATIONS

Ex parte Rich, 194 S.W.3d 508, 510 (Tex.Crim.App. 2006). "The issue we decide today is whether Applicant should be allowed to raise a claim of illegal sentence based on an improper enhancement for the first time on a writ of habeas corpus, or whether such claim is forfeited by: (1) Applicant's failure to raise it on direct appeal; or (2) Applicant's plea of true to such enhancements during the plea proceedings. We conclude that Applicant may raise such a claim and that, in this case, he is entitled to relief."

Ex parte Cathcart, 13 S.W.3d 414, 417 (Tex.Crim. App.2000). "[D] cannot be said to have been 'restrained' in her liberty, even within this broad construction of that term. The pending DWI case against defendant was dismissed and her bond closed. She was then no longer restrained in her liberty as to the charge of [DWI]. The state's notation that it would 'refile as intoxication assault' cannot, of itself, be said to have restrained [D] in her liberty; until such a charge was actually filed against [D], this was, at best, a statement of intent on the part of the state."

Ex parte Robinson, 641 S.W.2d 552, 553 (Tex.Crim. App.1982). "A person who is subject to the conditions of a bond is restrained in his liberty within the meaning of Article 11.01."

Ex parte Mangrum, 564 S.W.2d 751, 752 (Tex. Crim.App.1978). "The general rule is that when there is a valid statute or ordinance under which a prosecution may be brought, habeas corpus is not available to test the sufficiency of the complaint, information, or indictment."

Jaime v. State, 81 S.W.3d 920, 924-25 (Tex. App.—El Paso 2002, pet. ref'd). "A defendant may raise by pretrial habeas corpus claims concerning double jeopardy, collateral estoppel, and bail, because if he were not allowed to do so, those protections would be undermined if review were not permitted until after conviction. The applicant must establish his entitlement to habeas corpus relief. The writ of habeas corpus is not available where judicial determination of the question presented, even if resolved in favor of the applicant, would not result in immediate release."

Gibson v. State, 921 S.W.2d 747, 753 (Tex.App.—El Paso 1996, writ denied). "Article 11.01 describes the writ as the remedy to be used when 'any person,' not just a person accused or convicted of a crime, is restrained in his liberty. [¶] An applicant for habeas corpus relief has the burden of proving facts which would entitle the applicant to the relief sought. The applicant must establish that he is either 'confined' or 'restrained.'"

ART. 11.02. TO WHOM DIRECTED

The writ runs in the name of "The State of Texas." It is addressed to a person having another under restraint, or in his custody, describing, as near as may be, the name of the office, if any, of the person to whom it is directed, and the name of the person said to be detained. It shall fix the time and place of return, and be signed by the judge, or by the clerk with his seal, where issued by a court.

History of CCP art. 11.02: Acts 1965, 59th Leg., vol. 2, ch. 722.

ART. 11.03. WANT OF FORM

The writ of habeas corpus is not invalid, nor shall it be disobeyed for any want of form, if it substantially appear that it is issued by competent authority, and the writ sufficiently show the object of its issuance.

History of CCP art. 11.03: Acts 1965, 59th Leg., vol. 2, ch. 722.

ART. 11.04. CONSTRUCTION

Every provision relating to the writ of habeas corpus shall be most favorably construed in order to give effect to the remedy, and protect the rights of the person seeking relief under it.

History of CCP art. 11.04: Acts 1965, 59th Leg., vol. 2, ch. 722.

ART. 11.05. BY WHOM WRIT MAY BE GRANTED

The Court of Criminal Appeals, the District Courts, the County Courts, or any Judge of said Courts, have power to issue the writ of habeas corpus; and it is their duty, upon proper motion, to grant the writ under the rules prescribed by law.

History of CCP art. 11.05: Acts 1965, 59th Leg., vol. 2, ch. 722.
See also CCP art. 4.03.

ANNOTATIONS

Greenville v. State, 798 S.W.2d 361, 362 (Tex. App.—Beaumont 1990, no pet.). Article 11.05 "specifically omits the various Texas Courts of Appeals from the list of courts empowered to issue or grant a writ of habeas corpus."

Ex parte Williams, 786 S.W.2d 781, 782 (Tex. App.—Houston [1st Dist.] 1990, pet. ref'd). "[A] district judge may hear a writ of habeas corpus and *grant relief* even though an indictment for the offense is pending in the county court."

ART. 11.051. FILING FEE PROHIBITED

Notwithstanding any other law, a clerk of a court may not require a filing fee from an individual who files an application or petition for a writ of habeas corpus.

History of CCP art. 11.051: Acts 1999, 76th Leg., ch. 392, §1, eff. Aug. 30, 1999.

ART. 11.06. RETURNABLE TO ANY COUNTY

Before indictment found, the writ may be made returnable to any county in the State.

History of CCP art. 11.06: Acts 1965, 59th Leg., vol. 2, ch. 722.

ART. 11.07. PROCEDURE AFTER CONVICTION WITHOUT DEATH PENALTY

Sec. 1. This article establishes the procedures for an application for writ of habeas corpus in which the applicant seeks relief from a felony judgment imposing a penalty other than death.

Sec. 2. After indictment found in any felony case, other than a case in which the death penalty is imposed, and before conviction, the writ must be made returnable in the county where the offense has been committed.

Sec. 3. (a) After final conviction in any felony case, the writ must be made returnable to the Court of Criminal Appeals of Texas at Austin, Texas.

(b) An application for writ of habeas corpus filed after final conviction in a felony case, other than a case in which the death penalty is imposed, must be filed with the clerk of the court in which the conviction being challenged was obtained, and the clerk shall assign the application to that court. When the application is received by that court, a writ of habeas corpus, returnable to the Court of Criminal Appeals, shall issue by operation of law. The clerk of that court shall make appropriate notation thereof, assign to the case a file number (ancillary to that of the conviction being challenged), and forward a copy of the application by certified mail, return receipt requested, or by personal service to the attorney representing the state in that court, who shall answer the application not later than the 15th day after the date the copy of the application is received. Matters alleged in the application not admitted by the state are deemed denied.

(c) Within 20 days of the expiration of the time in which the state is allowed to answer, it shall be the duty of the convicting court to decide whether there are controverted, previously unresolved facts material to the legality of the applicant's confinement. Confinement means confinement for any offense or any collateral consequence resulting from the conviction that is the basis of the instant habeas corpus. If the convicting court decides that there are no such issues, the clerk shall immediately transmit to the Court of Criminal Appeals a copy of the application, any answers filed, and a certificate reciting the date upon which that finding was made. Failure of the court to act within the allowed 20 days shall constitute such a finding.

Ⓐ *Subsection (d) below is effective for applications for writs of habeas corpus filed on or after Sept. 1, 2007.*

(d) If the convicting court decides that there are controverted, previously unresolved facts which are material to the legality of the applicant's confinement, it shall enter an order within 20 days of the expiration of the time allowed for the state to reply, designating the issues of fact to be resolved. To resolve those issues the court may order affidavits, depositions, interrogatories, additional forensic testing, and hearings, as well as using personal recollection. The state shall pay the cost of additional forensic testing ordered under this subsection, except that the applicant shall pay the cost

of the testing if the applicant retains counsel for purposes of filing an application under this article. The convicting court may appoint an attorney or a magistrate to hold a hearing and make findings of fact. An attorney so appointed shall be compensated as provided in Article 26.05 of this code. It shall be the duty of the reporter who is designated to transcribe a hearing held pursuant to this article to prepare a transcript within 15 days of its conclusion. After the convicting court makes findings of fact or approves the findings of the person designated to make them, the clerk of the convicting court shall immediately transmit to the Court of Criminal Appeals, under one cover, the application, any answers filed, any motions filed, transcripts of all depositions and hearings, any affidavits, and any other matters such as official records used by the court in resolving issues of fact.

Subsection (d) below is effective for applications for writs of habeas corpus filed before Sept. 1, 2007.

(d) If the convicting court decides that there are controverted, previously unresolved facts which are material to the legality of the applicant's confinement, it shall enter an order within 20 days of the expiration of the time allowed for the state to reply, designating the issues of fact to be resolved. To resolve those issues the court may order affidavits, depositions, interrogatories, and hearings, as well as using personal recollection. Also, the convicting court may appoint an attorney or a magistrate to hold a hearing and make findings of fact. An attorney so appointed shall be compensated as provided in Article 26.05 of this code. It shall be the duty of the reporter who is designated to transcribe a hearing held pursuant to this article to prepare a transcript within 15 days of its conclusion. After the convicting court makes findings of fact or approves the findings of the person designated to make them, the clerk of the convicting court shall immediately transmit to the Court of Criminal Appeals, under one cover, the application, any answers filed, any motions filed, transcripts of all depositions and hearings, any affidavits, and any other matters such as official records used by the court in resolving issues of fact.

Ⓔ **(e)** For the purposes of Subsection (d), "additional forensic testing" does not include forensic DNA testing as provided for in Chapter 64.

Sec. 4. (a) If a subsequent application for writ of habeas corpus is filed after final disposition of an initial application challenging the same conviction, a court may not consider the merits of or grant relief based on the subsequent application unless the application contains sufficient specific facts establishing that:

(1) the current claims and issues have not been and could not have been presented previously in an original application or in a previously considered application filed under this article because the factual or legal basis for the claim was unavailable on the date the applicant filed the previous application; or

(2) by a preponderance of the evidence, but for a violation of the United States Constitution no rational juror could have found the applicant guilty beyond a reasonable doubt.

(b) For purposes of Subsection (a)(1), a legal basis of a claim is unavailable on or before a date described by Subsection (a)(1) if the legal basis was not recognized by and could not have been reasonably formulated from a final decision of the United States Supreme Court, a court of appeals of the United States, or a court of appellate jurisdiction of this state on or before that date.

(c) For purposes of Subsection (a)(1), a factual basis of a claim is unavailable on or before a date described by Subsection (a)(1) if the factual basis was not ascertainable through the exercise of reasonable diligence on or before that date.

Sec. 5. The Court of Criminal Appeals may deny relief upon the findings and conclusions of the hearing judge without docketing the cause, or may direct that the cause be docketed and heard as though originally presented to said court or as an appeal. Upon reviewing the record the court shall enter its judgment remanding the applicant to custody or ordering his release, as the law and facts may justify. The mandate of the court shall issue to the court issuing the writ, as in other criminal cases. After conviction the procedure outlined in this Act shall be exclusive and any other proceeding shall be void and of no force and effect in discharging the prisoner.

Sec. 6. Upon any hearing by a district judge by virtue of this Act, the attorney for applicant, and the state, shall be given at least seven full days' notice before such hearing is held.

Sec. 7. When the attorney for the state files an answer, motion, or other pleading relating to an application for a writ of habeas corpus or the court issues an order relating to an application for a writ of habeas corpus, the clerk of the court shall mail or deliver to the applicant a copy of the answer, motion, pleading, or order.

History of CCP art. 11.07: Acts 1965, 59th Leg., vol. 2, ch. 722. Amended by Acts 1967, 60th Leg., ch. 659, §7, eff. Aug. 28, 1967; Acts 1973, 63rd Leg., ch. 465, §2, eff. June 14, 1973; Acts 1977, 65th Leg., ch. 789, §1, eff. Aug. 29, 1977; Acts 1979, 66th Leg., ch. 451, §1, eff. Sept. 1, 1979; Acts 1995, 74th Leg., ch. 319, §5, eff. Sept. 1, 1995; Acts 1999, 76th Leg., ch. 580, §2, eff. Sept. 1, 1999; Acts 2007, 80th Leg., ch. 1006, §1, eff. Sept. 1, 2007.

See also timetable, "Postconviction Non-Death-Penalty Felony Writ of Habeas Corpus," p. 1285.

ANNOTATIONS

Generally

Ex parte Douthit, 232 S.W.3d 69, 74 (Tex.Crim.App. 2007). "[W]e hold that we will not grant habeas relief where there is no federal constitutional right and the defendant waived a right in a manner inconsistent with the procedures outlined only by statute, but the record reflects that [D] did so knowingly and voluntarily." *See also **Ex parte McCain***, 67 S.W.3d 204, 206 (Tex.Crim. App.2002).

Ex parte Thompson, 153 S.W.3d 416, 417 (Tex. Crim.App.2005). "[B]are claims of actual innocence are cognizable in a habeas proceeding, even in noncapital cases. To merit relief, the applicant bears the burden of showing that the newly discovered evidence unquestionably establishes his or her innocence. The court reviewing the habeas claim must examine the new evidence in light of the evidence presented at trial...." *See also **State ex rel. Holmes v. Third Ct. of Appeals***, 885 S.W.2d 389, 399 (Tex.Crim.App.1994).

Ex parte Rieck, 144 S.W.3d 510, 521 (Tex.Crim.App. 2004). "We hold that [Gov't Code] §498.0045 [concerning the forfeiture of good-conduct time for frivolous lawsuits] does not apply to [CCP art.] 11.07 habeas corpus proceedings."

Ex parte Valle, 104 S.W.3d 888, 890 (Tex.Crim.App. 2003). "Because all juvenile adjudications—including appeals—remain on the civil side of our judicial system unless transferred to a criminal court, [CCP art.] 11.07 should not be used to transport juvenile cases to the criminal side for the single, specific proceeding of an application for writ of habeas corpus. [¶] We have held that [Tex. Const. art. 5, §8] gives the district court plenary power to issue the writ of habeas corpus."

Ex parte Geiken, 28 S.W.3d 553, 556 (Tex.Crim. App.2000). "[A]pplicant's habeas corpus claims alleging illegal confinement arising after his felony conviction, but not contesting the validity of the judgment, may be raised under [Article 11.07]."

Ex parte Chappell, 959 S.W.2d 627, 627-28 n.1 (Tex.Crim.App.1998). "[A] double jeopardy claim is a proper subject for a writ of habeas corpus under Article 11.07, despite the applicant's failure ... to raise the issue in the trial court."

Ex parte Sanchez, 918 S.W.2d 526, 527 (Tex.Crim. App.1996). "Habeas corpus is reserved for those instances in which there is a jurisdictional defect in the trial court which renders the judgment void, or for denials of fundamental or constitutional rights. [¶] The requirement in the IAD [Interstate Agreement on Detainers] that trial occur within 180 days of a defendant's request is statutory and not based on either the federal or state constitution. ... In order to present a cognizable claim on habeas, we conclude that an applicant must establish not just a violation of the IAD, but also a jurisdictional defect or the denial of a fundamental or a constitutional right." *See also Ex parte Carmona*, 185 S.W.3d 492, 494-95 (Tex.Crim.App.2006).

Board of Pardons & Paroles ex rel. Keene v. Eighth Ct. of Appeals, 910 S.W.2d 481, 483 (Tex.Crim. App.1995). "Article 11.07 provides the exclusive means to challenge a final felony conviction. Jurisdiction to grant post conviction habeas corpus relief on a final felony conviction rests exclusively with this Court. Any other proceeding shall be void and of no force and effect in discharging the prisoner. [¶] Parole is a form of restraint which allows an applicant to pursue the remedies afforded under Article 11.07."

Ex parte Bartmess, 739 S.W.2d 51, 52 (Tex.Crim. App.1987). "A claimed deprivation of adequate notice cannot be raised for the first time in an Article 11.07 action."

Art. 11.07, §3

Ex parte Chavez, 213 S.W.3d 320, 321 (Tex.Crim. App.2006). "We filed and set this post-conviction application for writ of habeas corpus ... in order to consider the recommendation of the convicting court that the applicant receive a new punishment proceeding on the basis of evidence of actual innocence. The convicting court did *not* recommend that the applicant be granted a new guilt-phase proceeding. We hold that, at least on the facts presented in this application, a new punishment proceeding is not warranted under the guise of actual innocence, or any other due-process principle, and we deny relief."

Ex parte Deeringer, 210 S.W.3d 616, 618 (Tex. Crim.App.2006). "We ... hold that when a habeas applicant files an initial post-conviction application for writ of habeas corpus raising *both* claims challenging the conviction *and* a claim of the denial of pre-sentence jail-time credit, we will dispose of the claims challenging the conviction on the merits, either granting or denying relief as appropriate, and then dismiss the jail-time credit claim unless that claim is rendered moot by a disposition granting relief on the merits of a claim challenging the conviction."

Ex parte Burgess, 152 S.W.3d 123, 123-24 (Tex. Crim.App.2004). "We filed and set this case to address the procedure to follow when, as here, an applicant files an Article 11.07 habeas corpus application with the district clerk of a county other than the county of conviction. We will dismiss applicant's writ of habeas corpus. [¶] A 'plain reading' of §3(b) bespeaks a legislative intent to no longer require a district clerk to *transfer* an Article 11.07 habeas corpus application 'to the court in which the challenged conviction was obtained' when the application 'is presented to a district clerk in a county in which the challenged conviction was not entered.' Section 3(b) left intact the other holding in [*Ex parte*] *Alexander* [861 S.W.2d 921 (Tex.Crim.App. 1993)] that 'when an application is presented to the district clerk of the county in which the challenged conviction was entered, the clerk shall *assign* the application to the appropriate court.'"

Martin v. Hamlin, 25 S.W.3d 718, 719 (Tex.Crim. App.2000). "Upon receipt of an application for writ of habeas corpus challenging a final felony conviction, the attorney representing the State is allowed 15 days in which to respond. After the expiration of the time for the State to answer, the trial court is allowed 20 days in which to determine whether the application contains allegations of controverted, previously unresolved facts material to the legality of the applicant's confinement. If the trial court determines an application for writ of habeas corpus does present such issues, it is the duty of the trial court to enter an order within the 20 day period after expiration of the time allowed for the State to reply, designating the issues of fact to be resolved. The statute does not supply authority to the trial court to extend the time limitations imposed by the statute, other than by timely entry of an order designating issues to be resolved. Without the timely entry of an order designating issues, Article 11.07 imposes a duty upon the clerk of the trial court to immediately transmit to this Court the record from the application for writ of habeas corpus, deeming the trial court's inaction a finding that no issues of fact require further resolution."

Ex parte Stokes, 15 S.W.3d 532, 533 (Tex.Crim.App. 2000). "All persons seeking time credit relief in an application filed pursuant to Art. 11.07, §3, filed in the district clerk's office on or after January 1, 2000, must show that a written decision has been obtained or that he is within 180 days of release according to current department records, or must allege that he sought resolution of his credit complaint more than 180 days before the application was filed."

Johnson v. State, 12 S.W.3d 472, 473 (Tex.Crim. App.2000). The Court of Criminal Appeals "does not have jurisdiction to consider an application for writ of habeas corpus pursuant to Art. 11.07 until the felony judgment from which relief is sought becomes final. A direct appeal is final when the mandate from the court of appeals issues. Prior to mandate, a judgment is not final."

Ex parte Carrio, 992 S.W.2d 486, 488 (Tex.Crim. App.1999). "We agree with the State that the doctrine of laches is a theory which we may, and should, employ in our determination of whether to grant relief in any given 11.07 case. *At 488 n.3:* The doctrine of laches concerns prejudice, not mere passage of time. In this opinion, we do not impose any time limits on habeas claims."

Rodriguez v. Court of Appeals, 769 S.W.2d 554, 557 (Tex.Crim.App.1989). "Where a habeas corpus petitioner has been granted probation and it has not been revoked, the defendant is not confined and the conviction is not final for purposes of Art. 11.07. Thus, [an applicant in this situation,] having been placed on probation which has not been revoked, cannot seek habeas corpus relief from this Court under Art. 11.07."

Ex parte Brown, 662 S.W.2d 3, 4 (Tex.Crim.App. 1983). "A conviction which has been affirmed by this Court but which is the subject of a stay of execution issued by the Supreme Court of the United States is not a final felony conviction for habeas corpus purposes."

Art. 11.07, §4

Ex parte Santana, 227 S.W.3d 700, 703-04 (Tex. Crim.App.2007). "In two prior cases—*Ex parte Evans*[, 964 S.W.2d 643 (Tex.Crim.App.1998)] and *Ex parte McPherson*[, 32 S.W.3d 860 (Tex.Crim.

App.2000)]—we identified two claims that do not constitute a challenge to a conviction when raised on an initial application for purposes of §4. In *Ex parte Evans*, we held that the applicant's initial application, which challenged only the revocation of parole, did not qualify as an application that challenged the conviction within the meaning of Article 11.07, §4. A claim that attacks a parole revocation is not addressed to the validity of the underlying conviction. In *Ex parte McPherson*, we held that the applicant's initial application that sought only an out-of-time appeal due to counsel's failure to file a notice of appeal did not challenge the conviction under §4. We concluded that an allegation directed at an attorney's failure to preserve an applicant's right or opportunity to appeal does not pertain to the validity of the prosecution or the judgment of guilt. Similarly, when an initial application presents claims challenging the validity of the prosecution or the judgment of guilt and presents a claim concerning the denial of the right to appeal and this Court grants an out-of-time appeal while dismissing the remaining grounds for relief, the initial application does not qualify as an application that challenged the conviction for purposes of §4(a). Granting an out-of-time appeal restores the pendency of the direct appeal, thereby making any substantive claims challenging the conviction premature. [¶] Now we must determine whether Santana's first application, which advanced only a claim concerning appellate counsel's failure to challenge the indictment on appeal, constitutes an initial application that challenged his conviction for aggravated robbery under §4. In making this determination, we must consider whether Santana's first application should be treated like those that fall under the holding of *Ex parte McPherson*. The State argues that it should not. According to the State, Santana challenged the validity of the prosecution by alleging that the indictment was defective and that his appellate counsel was ineffective for failing to raise this claim. We agree." (Internal quotes omitted.)

Ex parte Brooks, 219 S.W.3d 396, 401 (Tex.Crim. App.2007). "Under §4, we may not consider the merits of an application unless it includes sufficient specific facts establishing by a preponderance of the evidence that, but for a constitutional violation, no rational juror would have found the Applicant guilty. We have determined that this necessarily includes a prima facie showing of actual innocence in order for the applicant to demonstrate that the constitutional violation at his trial resulted in a miscarriage of justice. This showing allows us to consider a constitutional claim which otherwise would have been barred by §4."

Ex parte Lemke, 13 S.W.3d 791, 793 (Tex.Crim.App. 2000). "On August 17, 1994, applicant filed in the district court an Application for Writ of Habeas Corpus (the 'initial application'), alleging he was deprived of effective assistance of counsel.... The initial application was denied by this Court on May 17, 1995. Applicant filed in the district court a second application for writ of habeas corpus (the 'instant application') on November 28, 1995. In the instant application, applicant alleges he was denied effective assistance of counsel on [a different ground]. [¶] We initially address whether the instant application is barred as a 'subsequent application' under §4, or whether it falls within an exception to such bar. *At 794-95:* Given that applicant had previously asked his attorney about the existence of plea bargain offers, was told that none were made, and applicant otherwise did not doubt his attorney's representations, applicant satisfied §4's requirement of 'reasonable diligence.'"

Ex parte Whiteside, 12 S.W.3d 819, 821 (Tex.Crim. App.2000). "[O]nce an applicant files an application challenging the conviction, all subsequent applications regarding the same conviction must meet one of the two conditions set forth in §4(a)(1) & (2). The Legislature modified 'initial application' with the phrase 'challenging the same conviction' but did not so modify 'subsequent application.' The lack of any language modifying 'subsequent application' plainly indicates the Legislature's intent that 'subsequent applications' include *all* subsequent habeas corpus applications regarding the same conviction, rather than only those that 'challenge' the conviction."

Ex parte Torres, 943 S.W.2d 469, 474 (Tex.Crim. App.1997). "[W]e believe that a 'final disposition' of an initial writ [of habeas corpus] must entail a disposition relating to the merits of all the claims raised. Dispositions relating to the merits should be labeled 'denials' while dispositions unrelated to the merits should be labeled 'dismissals,' but, regardless of the label given to a previous disposition, we will look to the substance of that disposition to determine whether a subsequent writ is barred by §4. A disposition is related to the merits if it decides the merits or makes a determination that the merits of the applicant's claims can never be decided."

Art. 11.07, §5

Ex parte Adams, 768 S.W.2d 281, 288 (Tex.Crim. App.1989). "It is a fundamental principle of our habeas corpus law ... that under the procedure authorized by Article 11.07, if the trial court convenes a hearing, elicits testimony and thereby develops facts, the Court of Criminal Appeals is not bound by the trial court's findings and conclusions of law. Accordingly, this Court is obligated to determine if the record developed supports the trial judge's findings."

Ex parte Mendenhall, 209 S.W.3d 260, 261 (Tex. App.—Waco 2006, no pet.). "Because an article 11.07 habeas is the exclusive means to set aside a prior felony conviction in a collateral proceeding, the writ of audita querela is not available in Texas to accomplish this purpose."

ART. 11.071. PROCEDURE IN DEATH PENALTY CASE

§1. Application to Death Penalty Case

Notwithstanding any other provision of this chapter, this article establishes the procedures for an application for a writ of habeas corpus in which the applicant seeks relief from a judgment imposing a penalty of death.

§2. Representation by Counsel

(a) An applicant shall be represented by competent counsel unless the applicant has elected to proceed pro se and the convicting trial court finds, after a hearing on the record, that the applicant's election is intelligent and voluntary.

(b) If a defendant is sentenced to death the convicting court, immediately after judgment is entered under Article 42.01, shall determine if the defendant is indigent and, if so, whether the defendant desires appointment of counsel for the purpose of a writ of habeas corpus.

(c) At the earliest practical time, but in no event later than 30 days, after the convicting court makes the findings required under Subsections (a) and (b), the convicting court shall appoint competent counsel, unless the applicant elects to proceed pro se or is represented by retained counsel. On appointing counsel under this section, the convicting court shall immediately notify the court of criminal appeals of the appointment, including in the notice a copy of the judgment and the name, address, and telephone number of the appointed counsel.

(d) The court of criminal appeals shall adopt rules for the appointment of attorneys as counsel under this section and the convicting court may appoint an attorney as counsel under this section only if the appointment is approved by the court of criminal appeals in any manner provided by those rules. The rules must require that an attorney appointed as lead counsel under this section not have been found by a federal or state court to have rendered ineffective assistance of counsel during the trial or appeal of any capital case.

(e) If the court of criminal appeals denies an applicant relief under this article, an attorney appointed under this section to represent the applicant shall, not later than the 15th day after the date the court of criminal appeals denies relief or, if the case is filed and set for submission, the 15th day after the date the court of criminal appeals issues a mandate on the initial application for a writ of habeas corpus under this article, move to be appointed as counsel in federal habeas review under 21 U.S.C. Section 848(q) or equivalent provision or, if necessary, move for the appointment of other counsel under 21 U.S.C. Section 848(q) or equivalent provision. The attorney shall immediately file a copy of the motion with the court of criminal appeals, and if the attorney fails to do so, the court may take any action to ensure that the applicant's right to federal habeas review is protected, including initiating contempt proceedings against the attorney.

(f) The convicting court shall reasonably compensate as provided by Section 2A an attorney appointed under this section, regardless of whether the attorney is appointed by the convicting court or was appointed by the court of criminal appeals under prior law.

§2A. State Reimbursement; County Obligation

(a) The state shall reimburse a county for compensation of counsel under Section 2 and payment of expenses under Section 3. The total amount of reimbursement to which a county is entitled under this section for an application under this article may not exceed $25,000. Compensation and expenses in excess of the $25,000 reimbursement provided by the state are the obligation of the county.

(b) A convicting court seeking reimbursement for a county shall certify to the comptroller of public accounts the amount of compensation that the county is entitled to receive under this section. The comptroller

of public accounts shall issue a warrant to the county in the amount certified by the convicting court, not to exceed $25,000.

(c) The limitation imposed by this section on the reimbursement by the state to a county for compensation of counsel and payment of reasonable expenses does not prohibit a county from compensating counsel and reimbursing expenses in an amount that is in excess of the amount the county receives from the state as reimbursement, and a county is specifically granted discretion by this subsection to make payments in excess of the state reimbursement.

(d) The comptroller shall reimburse a county for the compensation and payment of expenses of an attorney appointed by the court of criminal appeals under prior law. A convicting court seeking reimbursement for a county as permitted by this subsection shall certify the amount the county is entitled to receive under this subsection for an application filed under this article, not to exceed a total amount of $25,000.

§3. Investigation of Grounds for Application

(a) On appointment, counsel shall investigate expeditiously, before and after the appellate record is filed in the court of criminal appeals, the factual and legal grounds for the filing of an application for a writ of habeas corpus.

(b) Not later than the 30th day before the date the application for a writ of habeas corpus is filed with the convicting court, counsel may file with the convicting court an ex parte, verified, and confidential request for prepayment of expenses, including expert fees, to investigate and present potential habeas corpus claims. The request for expenses must state:

(1) the claims of the application to be investigated;

(2) specific facts that suggest that a claim of possible merit may exist; and

(3) an itemized list of anticipated expenses for each claim.

(c) The court shall grant a request for expenses in whole or in part if the request for expenses is timely and reasonable. If the court denies in whole or in part the request for expenses, the court shall briefly state the reasons for the denial in a written order provided to the applicant.

(d) Counsel may incur expenses for habeas corpus investigation, including expenses for experts, without prior approval by the convicting court or the court of criminal appeals. On presentation of a claim for reimbursement, which may be presented ex parte, the convicting court shall order reimbursement of counsel for expenses, if the expenses are reasonably necessary and reasonably incurred. If the convicting court denies in whole or in part the request for expenses, the court shall briefly state the reasons for the denial in a written order provided to the applicant. The applicant may request reconsideration of the denial for reimbursement by the convicting court.

(e) Materials submitted to the court under this section are a part of the court's record.

§4. Filing of Application

(a) An application for a writ of habeas corpus, returnable to the court of criminal appeals, must be filed in the convicting court not later than the 180th day after the date the convicting court appoints counsel under Section 2 or not later than the 45th day after the date the state's original brief is filed on direct appeal with the court of criminal appeals, whichever date is later.

(b) The convicting court, before the filing date that is applicable to the applicant under Subsection (a), may for good cause shown and after notice and an opportunity to be heard by the attorney representing the state grant one 90-day extension that begins on the filing date applicable to the defendant under Subsection (a). Either party may request that the court hold a hearing on the request. If the convicting court finds that the applicant cannot establish good cause justifying the requested extension, the court shall make a finding stating that fact and deny the request for the extension.

(c) An application filed after the filing date that is applicable to the applicant under Subsection (a) or (b) is untimely.

(d) If the convicting court receives an untimely application or determines that after the filing date that is applicable to the applicant under Subsection (a) or (b) no application has been filed, the convicting court immediately, but in any event within 10 days, shall send to the court of criminal appeals and to the attorney representing the state:

(1) a copy of the untimely application, with a statement of the convicting court that the application is untimely, or a statement of the convicting court that no application has been filed within the time periods required by Subsections (a) and (b); and

(2) any order the judge of the convicting court determines should be attached to an untimely application or statement under Subdivision (1).

(e) A failure to file an application before the filing date applicable to the applicant under Subsection (a) or (b) constitutes a waiver of all grounds for relief that were available to the applicant before the last date on which an application could be timely filed, except as provided by Section 4A.

§4A. Untimely Application; Application Not Filed

(a) On command of the court of criminal appeals, a counsel who files an untimely application or fails to file an application before the filing date applicable under Section 4(a) or (b) shall show cause as to why the application was untimely filed or not filed before the filing date.

(b) At the conclusion of the counsel's presentation to the court of criminal appeals, the court may:

(1) find that good cause has not been shown and dismiss the application;

(2) permit the counsel to continue representation of the applicant and establish a new filing date for the application, which may be not more than 180 days from the date the court permits the counsel to continue representation; or

(3) appoint new counsel to represent the applicant and establish a new filing date for the application, which may be not more than 270 days after the date the court appoints new counsel.

(c) The court of criminal appeals may hold in contempt counsel who files an untimely application or fails to file an application before the date required by Section 4(a) or (b). The court of criminal appeals may punish as a separate instance of contempt each day after the first day on which the counsel fails to timely file the application. In addition to or in lieu of holding counsel in contempt, the court of criminal appeals may enter an order denying counsel compensation under Section 2A.

(d) If the court of criminal appeals establishes a new filing date for the application, the court of criminal appeals shall notify the convicting court of that fact and the convicting court shall proceed under this article.

(e) Sections 2A and 3 apply to compensation and reimbursement of counsel appointed under Subsection (b)(3) in the same manner as if counsel had been appointed by the convicting court.

(f) Notwithstanding any other provision of this article, the court of criminal appeals shall appoint counsel and establish a new filing date for application, which may be no later than the 270th day after the date on which counsel is appointed, for each applicant who before September 1, 1999, filed an untimely application or failed to file an application before the date required by Section 4(a) or (b). Section 2A applies to the compensation and payment of expenses of counsel appointed by the court of criminal appeals under this subsection.

§5. Subsequent Application

(a) If a subsequent application for a writ of habeas corpus is filed after filing an initial application, a court may not consider the merits of or grant relief based on the subsequent application unless the application contains sufficient specific facts establishing that:

(1) the current claims and issues have not been and could not have been presented previously in a timely initial application or in a previously considered application filed under this article or Article 11.07 because the factual or legal basis for the claim was unavailable on the date the applicant filed the previous application;

(2) by a preponderance of the evidence, but for a violation of the United States Constitution no rational juror could have found the applicant guilty beyond a reasonable doubt; or

A *Subsection (3) below is effective for offenses committed on or after Sept. 1, 2007.*

(3) by clear and convincing evidence, but for a violation of the United States Constitution no rational juror would have answered in the state's favor one or more of the special issues that were submitted to the jury in the applicant's trial under Article 37.071, 37.0711, or 37.072.

Subsection (3) below is effective for offenses in which any element of the offense was committed before Sept. 1, 2007.

(3) by clear and convincing evidence, but for a violation of the United States Constitution no rational juror would have answered in the state's favor one or more of the special issues that were submitted to the jury in the applicant's trial under Article 37.071 or 37.0711.

(b) If the convicting court receives a subsequent application, the clerk of the court shall:

(1) attach a notation that the application is a subsequent application;

(2) assign to the case a file number that is ancillary to that of the conviction being challenged; and

(3) immediately send to the court of criminal appeals a copy of:

(A) the application;

(B) the notation;

(C) the order scheduling the applicant's execution, if scheduled; and

(D) any order the judge of the convicting court directs to be attached to the application.

(c) On receipt of the copies of the documents from the clerk, the court of criminal appeals shall determine whether the requirements of Subsection (a) have been satisfied. The convicting court may not take further action on the application before the court of criminal appeals issues an order finding that the requirements have been satisfied. If the court of criminal appeals determines that the requirements have not been satisfied, the court shall issue an order dismissing the application as an abuse of the writ under this section.

(d) For purposes of Subsection (a)(1), a legal basis of a claim is unavailable on or before a date described by Subsection (a)(1) if the legal basis was not recognized by or could not have been reasonably formulated from a final decision of the United States Supreme Court, a court of appeals of the United States, or a court of appellate jurisdiction of this state on or before that date.

(e) For purposes of Subsection (a)(1), a factual basis of a claim is unavailable on or before a date described by Subsection (a)(1) if the factual basis was not ascertainable through the exercise of reasonable diligence on or before that date.

(f) If an amended or supplemental application is not filed within the time specified under Section 4(a) or (b), the court shall treat the application as a subsequent application under this section.

§6. Issuance of Writ

(a) If a timely application for a writ of habeas corpus is filed in the convicting court, a writ of habeas corpus, returnable to the court of criminal appeals, shall issue by operation of law.

(b) If the convicting court receives notice that the requirements of Section 5 for consideration of a subsequent application have been met, a writ of habeas corpus, returnable to the court of criminal appeals, shall issue by operation of law.

(c) The clerk of the convicting court shall:

(1) make an appropriate notation that a writ of habeas corpus was issued;

(2) assign to the case a file number that is ancillary to that of the conviction being challenged; and

(3) send a copy of the application by certified mail, return receipt requested, to the attorney representing the state in that court.

(d) The clerk of the convicting court shall promptly deliver copies of documents submitted to the clerk under this article to the applicant and the attorney representing the state.

§7. Answer to Application

(a) The state shall file an answer to the application for a writ of habeas corpus not later than the 120th day after the date the state receives notice of issuance of the writ. The state shall serve the answer on counsel for the applicant or, if the applicant is proceeding pro se, on the applicant. The state may request from the convicting court an extension of time in which to answer the application by showing particularized justifying circumstances for the extension, but in no event may the court permit the state to file an answer later than the 180th day after the date the state receives notice of issuance of the writ.

(b) Matters alleged in the application not admitted by the state are deemed denied.

§8. Findings of Fact Without Evidentiary Hearing

(a) Not later than the 20th day after the last date the state answers the application, the convicting court shall determine whether controverted, previously unresolved factual issues material to the legality of the applicant's confinement exist and shall issue a written order of the determination.

(b) If the convicting court determines the issues do not exist, the parties shall file proposed findings of fact and conclusions of law for the court to consider on or before a date set by the court that is not later than the 30th day after the date the order is issued.

(c) After argument of counsel, if requested by the court, the convicting court shall make appropriate written findings of fact and conclusions of law not later than the 15th day after the date the parties filed proposed findings or not later than the 45th day after the date the court's determination is made under Subsection (a), whichever occurs first.

(d) The clerk of the court shall immediately send to:

(1) the court of criminal appeals a copy of the:

(A) application;

(B) answer;

(C) orders entered by the convicting court;

(D) proposed findings of fact and conclusions of law; and

(E) findings of fact and conclusions of law entered by the court; and

(2) counsel for the applicant or, if the applicant is proceeding pro se, to the applicant, a copy of:

(A) orders entered by the convicting court;

(B) proposed findings of fact and conclusions of law; and

(C) findings of fact and conclusions of law entered by the court.

§9. Hearing

(a) If the convicting court determines that controverted, previously unresolved factual issues material to the legality of the applicant's confinement exist, the court shall enter an order, not later than the 20th day after the last date the state answers the application, designating the issues of fact to be resolved and the manner in which the issues shall be resolved. To resolve the issues, the court may require affidavits, depositions, interrogatories, and evidentiary hearings and may use personal recollection.

(b) The convicting court shall hold the evidentiary hearing not later than the 30th day after the date on which the court enters the order designating issues under Subsection (a). The convicting court may grant a motion to postpone the hearing, but not for more than 30 days, and only if the court states, on the record, good cause for delay.

(c) The presiding judge of the convicting court shall conduct a hearing held under this section unless another judge presided over the original capital felony trial, in which event that judge, if qualified for assignment under Section 74.054 or 74.055, Government Code, may preside over the hearing.

(d) The court reporter shall prepare a transcript of the hearing not later than the 30th day after the date the hearing ends and file the transcript with the clerk of the convicting court.

(e) The parties shall file proposed findings of fact and conclusions of law for the convicting court to consider on or before a date set by the court that is not later than the 30th day after the date the transcript is filed. If the court requests argument of counsel, after argument the court shall make written findings of fact that are necessary to resolve the previously unresolved facts and make conclusions of law not later than the 15th day after the date the parties file proposed findings or not later than the 45th day after the date the court reporter files the transcript, whichever occurs first.

(f) The clerk of the convicting court shall immediately transmit to:

(1) the court of criminal appeals a copy of:

(A) the application;

(B) the answers and motions filed;

(C) the court reporter's transcript;

(D) the documentary exhibits introduced into evidence;

(E) the proposed findings of fact and conclusions of law;

(F) the findings of fact and conclusions of law entered by the court;

(G) the sealed materials such as a confidential request for investigative expenses; and

(H) any other matters used by the convicting court in resolving issues of fact; and

(2) counsel for the applicant or, if the applicant is proceeding pro se, to the applicant, a copy of:

(A) orders entered by the convicting court;

(B) proposed findings of fact and conclusions of law; and

(C) findings of fact and conclusions of law entered by the court.

(g) The clerk of the convicting court shall forward an exhibit that is not documentary to the court of criminal appeals on request of the court.

§10. Rules of Evidence

The Texas Rules of Criminal Evidence apply to a hearing held under this article.

§11. Review by Court of Criminal Appeals

The court of criminal appeals shall expeditiously review all applications for a writ of habeas corpus submitted under this article. The court may set the cause for oral argument and may request further briefing of the issues by the applicant or the state. After reviewing the record, the court shall enter its judgment remanding the applicant to custody or ordering the applicant's release, as the law and facts may justify.

History of CCP art. 11.071: Acts 1995, 74th Leg., ch. 319, §1, eff. Sept. 1, 1995; Acts 1997, 75th Leg., ch. 1336, §§1-5, eff. Sept. 1, 1997. Amended by Acts 1999, 76th Leg., ch. 803, §§1-10, eff. Sept. 1, 1999; Acts 2003, 78th Leg., ch. 315, §§1-3, eff. June 18, 2003; Acts 2005, 79th Leg., ch. 787, §13 (eff. Sept. 1, 2005) ch. 965, §5 (eff. Sept. 1, 2005); Acts 2007, 80th Leg., ch. 593, §3.06, eff. Sept. 1, 2007.

ANNOTATIONS

Ex parte Reynoso, ___ S.W.3d ___ (Tex.Crim.App. 2008) (No. AP-75,963; 7-2-08). "[W]e hold that [Govt Code] §311.014 and [TRAP] 4.1 do not apply to the calculation of an original due date under Article 11.071 §4(b) when an extension has been granted under that provision."

Ex parte Alba, ___ S.W.3d ___ (Tex.Crim.App. 2008) (No. AP-75,510; 6-9-08). "A writ application filed pursuant to Article 11.071 must seek 'relief from a judgment imposing a penalty of death.' A death-penalty writ application that does not challenge the validity of the underlying judgment and which, even if meritorious, would not result in immediate relief from a capital-murder conviction or death sentence, is not a proper application for purposes of Article 11.071. [¶] Habeas corpus serves to remedy existing constitutional violations; it is not for claims that a statute may potentially be applied in a way that may possibly be determined to be unconstitutional in the future. We do not grant habeas corpus relief on an abstract proposition." *See also Ex parte Kerr*, 64 S.W.3d 414, 419 (Tex.Crim.App. 2002).

Ex parte Blue, 230 S.W.3d 151, 154 (Tex.Crim.App. 2007). "We hold that, having afforded the applicant one opportunity to raise his *Atkins* claim in a post-conviction setting, the Texas Legislature may legitimately limit any second chance it may afford him to raise it again, notwithstanding the absolute nature of the prohibition against executing the mentally retarded. We conclude that through Article 11.071, §5(a)(3), the Legislature has provided a mechanism whereby a subsequent habeas applicant may proceed with an *Atkins* claim if he is able to demonstrate to this Court that there is evidence that could reasonably show, to a level of confidence by clear and convincing evidence, that no rational finder of fact would fail to find he is mentally retarded. However, because we find that the applicant in this case has failed to satisfy this heightened-threshold burden, we deny him leave to proceed."

Ex parte Hood, 211 S.W.3d 767, 774 (Tex.Crim.App. 2007). "[T]he [unavailability] exception requires that the claim in question be unavailable not only for the first habeas application but *also* for any 'previously considered application.' *At 775:* Thus, to satisfy the exception, applicant's claim must have been unavailable as to *both* of his previous applications. [¶] [T]he structure of the statutory provision requires that availability be negated for all the types of courts listed. For a legal basis to be unavailable, then, it must be true that no decision from any of these types of courts makes the claim available (either by explicit recognition or reasonable formulation). Stated another way, if the legal basis for the claim was recognized by or could have been reasonably formulated from a Supreme Court decision, any federal court of appeals decision, or any state appellate court decision, then the applicant has failed to meet the unavailability exception. It is not enough, for example, for an applicant to show that the legal basis could not have been derived from any Texas state court decision if there existed a federal appellate decision from which the legal basis could be derived. [¶] Another point that deserves emphasis is that lack of recognition is not enough to render a legal basis unavailable. If the legal basis *could have been reasonably formulated* from a decision issued by a requisite court, then the exception is not met."

Ex parte Medellín, 223 S.W.3d 315, 321 (Tex.Crim. App.2006), *aff'd*, 128 S.Ct. 1346 (2008). Applicant "filed this subsequent application, alleging that the International Court of Justice *Avena* decision and the President's memorandum directing state courts to give effect to *Avena*, require this Court to reconsider his Article 36 Vienna Convention claim because they (1) constitute binding federal law that preempt [CCP] §5, [art.] 11.071 and (2) were previously unavailable factual and legal bases under §5(a)(1). We hold that *Avena* and the President's memorandum do not preempt §5 and do not qualify as previously unavailable factual or legal bases."

Ex parte Briseno, 135 S.W.3d 1, 5 (Tex.Crim.App. 2004). "[W]e set out the following judicial standards for courts considering [*Atkins* mental-retardation habeas corpus] claims under [CCP art.] 11.071. *At 7:* Under the [American Association on Mental Retardation] definition, mental retardation is a disability characterized by: (1) significantly subaverage general intellectual functioning; (2) accompanied by related limitations in adaptive functioning; (3) the onset of which occurs prior to the age of 18. [T]he definition under [H&SC §591.003(13)] is similar: mental retardation means significantly subaverage general intellectual functioning that is concurrent with deficits in adaptive behavior and originates during the developmental period. *At 8:* Until the Texas Legislature provides an alternate statutory definition of mental retardation for use in capital sentencing, we will follow the AAMR or §591.003(13) criteria in addressing *Atkins* mental retardation claims. *At 11:* [W]e hold that, when an inmate sentenced to death files a habeas corpus application raising a cognizable *Atkins* claim, the factual merit of that claim should be determined by the judge of the convicting court. His findings of fact and conclusions of law shall be reviewed by this Court in accordance with article 11.071, §11." Held: The applicant has the burden of proof to establish mental retardation by a preponderance of the evidence.

Ex parte Graves, 70 S.W.3d 103, 105 (Tex.Crim. App.2002). "Because we find that competency of prior habeas counsel is not a cognizable issue on habeas corpus review, applicant's allegation cannot fulfill the requirements of article 11.071 §5 for a subsequent writ. Therefore, we dismiss applicant's writ under article 11.071 §5(c) as an abuse of the writ."

Ex parte Mines, 26 S.W.3d 910, 915 (Tex.Crim.App. 2000). There is "no justification in inferring a statutory requirement that the applicant be mentally competent for habeas corpus proceedings in the way that a defendant must be mentally competent for trial."

Ex parte Ramos, 977 S.W.2d 616, 617 (Tex.Crim. App.1998). Notwithstanding the fact that the writ of habeas corpus was filed two days late, the writ will be considered on its merits. Applicant "met an incorrectly-calculated deadline that the court had entered and, on which he relied in good faith.... [¶] [W]e hold that, on these specific facts, the regulatory statute cannot be constitutionally applied to require the dismissal of the application."

Graham v. Board of Pardons & Paroles, 913 S.W.2d 745, 751 (Tex.App.—Austin 1996, writ dism'd). "Upon a showing of new evidence that undermines confidence in the jury verdict, Graham will be entitled to an evidentiary hearing in accordance with statutory post-conviction habeas corpus procedures. A post-conviction habeas hearing affords the essential requisites of due process: an evidentiary hearing before a district-court judge, the right to counsel, time to prepare for the hearing, transcription of the hearing by a court reporter, and written findings of fact and conclusions of law by the court."

ART. 11.072. PROCEDURE IN COMMUNITY SUPERVISION CASE

Sec. 1. This article establishes the procedures for an application for a writ of habeas corpus in a felony or misdemeanor case in which the applicant seeks relief from an order or a judgment of conviction ordering community supervision.

Sec. 2. (a) An application for a writ of habeas corpus under this article must be filed with the clerk of the court in which community supervision was imposed.

(b) At the time the application is filed, the applicant must be, or have been, on community supervision, and the application must challenge the legal validity of:

(1) the conviction for which or order in which community supervision was imposed; or

(2) the conditions of community supervision.

Sec. 3. (a) An application may not be filed under this article if the applicant could obtain the requested relief by means of an appeal under Article 44.02 and Rule 25.2, Texas Rules of Appellate Procedure.

(b) An applicant seeking to challenge a particular condition of community supervision but not the legality of the conviction for which or the order in which community supervision was imposed must first attempt to gain relief by filing a motion to amend the conditions of community supervision.

(c) An applicant may challenge a condition of community supervision under this article only on constitutional grounds.

Sec. 4. (a) When an application is filed under this article, a writ of habeas corpus issues by operation of law.

(b) At the time the application is filed, the clerk of the court shall assign the case a file number ancillary to that of the judgment of conviction or order being challenged.

Sec. 5. (a) Immediately on filing an application, the applicant shall serve a copy of the application on the attorney representing the state, by either certified mail, return receipt requested, or personal service.

(b) The state may file an answer within the period established by Subsection (c), but is not required to file an answer.

(c) The state may not file an answer after the 30th day after the date of service, except that for good cause the convicting court may grant the state one 30-day extension.

(d) Any answer, motion, or other document filed by the state must be served on the applicant by certified mail, return receipt requested, or by personal service.

(e) Matters alleged in the application not admitted by the state are considered to have been denied.

Sec. 6. (a) Not later than the 60th day after the day on which the state's answer is filed, the trial court shall enter a written order granting or denying the relief sought in the application.

(b) In making its determination, the court may order affidavits, depositions, interrogatories, or a hearing, and may rely on the court's personal recollection.

(c) If a hearing is ordered, the hearing may not be held before the eighth day after the day on which the applicant and the state are provided notice of the hearing.

(d) The court may appoint an attorney or magistrate to hold a hearing ordered under this section and make findings of fact. An attorney appointed under this subsection is entitled to compensation as provided by Article 26.05.

Sec. 7. (a) If the court determines from the face of an application or documents attached to the application that the applicant is manifestly entitled to no relief, the court shall enter a written order denying the application as frivolous. In any other case, the court shall enter a written order including findings of fact and conclusions of law. The court may require the prevailing party to submit a proposed order.

(b) At the time an order is entered under this section, the clerk of the court shall immediately, by certified mail, return receipt requested, send a copy of the order to the applicant and to the state.

Sec. 8. If the application is denied in whole or part, the applicant may appeal under Article 44.02 and Rule 31, Texas Rules of Appellate Procedure. If the application is granted in whole or part, the state may appeal under Article 44.01 and Rule 31, Texas Rules of Appellate Procedure.

Sec. 9. (a) If a subsequent application for a writ of habeas corpus is filed after final disposition of an initial application under this article, a court may not consider the merits of or grant relief based on the subsequent application unless the application contains sufficient specific facts establishing that the current claims and issues have not been and could not have been presented previously in an original application or in a previously considered application filed under this article because the factual or legal basis for the claim was unavailable on the date the applicant filed the previous application.

(b) For purposes of Subsection (a), a legal basis of a claim is unavailable on or before a date described by that subsection if the legal basis was not recognized by and could not have been reasonably formulated from a final decision of the United States Supreme Court, a court of appeals of the United States, or a court of appellate jurisdiction of this state on or before that date.

(c) For purposes of Subsection (a), a factual basis of a claim is unavailable on or before a date described by that subsection if the factual basis was not ascertainable through the exercise of reasonable diligence on or before that date.

History of CCP art. 11.072: Acts 2003, 78th Leg., ch. 587, §1, eff. June 20, 2003.

ANNOTATIONS

Ex parte Villanueva, 252 S.W.3d 391, 397 (Tex. Crim.App.2008). "By enacting [CCP art.] 11.072, it is clear that the Legislature intended Article 11.072 to provide the exclusive means by which the district courts may exercise their original habeas jurisdiction under [Tex. Const. art.] V, §8 ... in cases involving an individual who is either serving a term of community supervision or who has completed a term of community supervision. [Article 11.072,] §4, which states that the writ issues by operation of law, represents a significant departure from prior writ law that allowed a judge, in his or her discretion, to refuse to issue a writ. [U]nder the rule discussed in [*Ex parte*] *Hargett* [819 S.W.2d 866, 868-79 (Tex.Crim.App.1991)], when the trial judge refused to issue a writ, an applicant had no right to appeal. In providing for automatic issuance, it is evident that §4 was enacted with the specific purpose of eliminating a trial judge's discretion to refuse to issue a writ. ... Accordingly, the rule discussed in *Hargett*—to the extent that it applies to an appeal from the disposal of an 11.072 application for a writ of habeas corpus filed by a person on community supervision or who has completed a term of community supervision—has been superceded by §§4 and 8 of Article 11.072. Against this backdrop, we are compelled to conclude that §8 ... plainly regulates an applicant's right to appeal. Therefore, the appealability of an application for writ of habeas corpus filed under Article 11.072 following a disposition by the district court is controlled by §8...."

ART. 11.08. APPLICANT CHARGED WITH FELONY

If a person is confined after indictment on a charge of felony, he may apply to the judge of the court in which he is indicted; or if there be no judge within the district, then to the judge of any district whose residence is nearest to the court house of the county in which the applicant is held in custody.

History of CCP art. 11.08: Acts 1965, 59th Leg., vol. 2, ch. 722.

ANNOTATIONS

Kniatt v. State, 206 S.W.3d 657, 663-64 (Tex.Crim. App.2006). "At the time appellant filed his application for writ of habeas corpus, it was a pre-conviction application [because appellant was under deferred adjudication], and, pursuant to Article 11.08, the trial court had jurisdiction to hear it. Did the trial court lose jurisdiction to hear appellant's application once that court adjudicated him guilty? [¶] [T]he jurisdiction of a court to consider an application for writ of habeas corpus is determined at the time the application is filed. [T]he trial court in this case did not lose jurisdiction to hear appellant's pre-conviction application once that court adjudicated him guilty."

In re Piper, 105 S.W.3d 107, 108 (Tex.App.—Waco 2003, orig. proceeding). Petitioner "petitions the Court for a writ of mandamus to compel the [judge of the 18th district] to issue a writ of habeas corpus. We deny the petition. *At 110:* [A]fter an indictment is returned against a defendant 'he may apply to the judge of the court in which he is indicted.' But this language is 'advisory or permissive, not mandatory.' [Petitioner's] remedy is to file a petition for writ of habeas corpus in the Texas Court of Criminal Appeals, in any Texas district court other than the 18th, or in any Texas county court."

ART. 11.09. APPLICANT CHARGED WITH MISDEMEANOR

If a person is confined on a charge of misdemeanor, he may apply to the county judge of the county in which the misdemeanor is charged to have been committed, or if there be no county judge in said county, then to the county judge whose residence is nearest to the courthouse of the county in which the applicant is held in custody.

History of CCP art. 11.09: Acts 1965, 59th Leg., vol. 2, ch. 722.

ANNOTATIONS

Ex parte Schmidt, 109 S.W.3d 480, 481 (Tex.Crim. App.2003). "We are asked in this case to decide whether Article 11.09 ... limits the jurisdiction of the county court to issue the writ of habeas corpus to cases in which the applicant is confined. We hold that it does not."

State ex rel. Rodriguez v. Onion, 741 S.W.2d 433, 434 (Tex.Crim.App.1987). "An examination of the language of Article 11.09 ... reveals that it is permissive, not mandatory, and is therefore merely advisory in nature. Article 11.09 is not sufficient to deprive the District Court of its jurisdiction to hear post conviction habeas corpus petitions in cases involving misdemeanors."

ART. 11.10. PROCEEDINGS UNDER THE WRIT

When motion has been made to a judge under the circumstances set forth in the two preceding Articles, he shall appoint a time when he will examine the cause of the applicant, and issue the writ returnable at that time, in the county where the offense is charged in the indictment or information to have been committed. He shall also specify some place in the county where he will hear the motion.

History of CCP art. 11.10: Acts 1965, 59th Leg., vol. 2, ch. 722.

ANNOTATIONS

LeBlanc v. State, 826 S.W.2d 640, 642-43 (Tex. App.—Houston [14th Dist.] 1992, pet. ref'd). "[I]t is important to recognize the difference between issuing

a writ of habeas corpus and granting the relief requested in the writ. The writ itself is merely the process by which all persons involved are noticed that the court is considering the issue, parties are physically attached, if necessary and the response (or the return) is made. Issuance of the writ without delay is required unless 'it be manifest ... that a party is entitled to no relief whatever.' Once the writ issues, the court considers the return, all attached documents, any testimony, and then either grants or denies the requested relief."

ART. 11.11. EARLY HEARING

The time so appointed shall be the earliest day which the judge can devote to hearing the cause of the applicant.

History of CCP art. 11.11: Acts 1965, 59th Leg., vol. 2, ch. 722.

ART. 11.12. WHO MAY PRESENT PETITION

Either the party for whose relief the writ is intended, or any person for him, may present a petition to the proper authority for the purpose of obtaining relief.

History of CCP art. 11.12: Acts 1965, 59th Leg., vol. 2, ch. 722.

ART. 11.13. APPLICANT

The word applicant, as used in this Chapter, refers to the person for whose relief the writ is asked, though the petition may be signed and presented by any other person.

History of CCP art. 11.13: Acts 1965, 59th Leg., vol. 2, ch. 722.

ANNOTATIONS

Hoang v. State, 872 S.W.2d 694, 699 n.9 (Tex.Crim. App.1993). "Our statutes governing the writ of habeas corpus provide that 'any person' may petition for the writ on behalf of someone unlawfully restrained of his liberty."

ART. 11.14. REQUISITES OF PETITION

The petition must state substantially:

1. That the person for whose benefit the application is made is illegally restrained in his liberty, and by whom, naming both parties, if their names are known, or if unknown, designating and describing them;

2. When the party is confined or restrained by virtue of any writ, order or process, or under color of either, a copy shall be annexed to the petition, or it shall be stated that a copy cannot be obtained;

3. When the confinement or restraint is not by virtue of any writ, order or process, the petition may state only that the party is illegally confined or restrained in his liberty;

4. There must be a prayer in the petition for the writ of habeas corpus; and

5. Oath must be made that the allegations of the petition are true, according to the belief of the petitioner.

History of CCP art. 11.14: Acts 1965, 59th Leg., vol. 2, ch. 722.

ANNOTATIONS

Ex parte Emmons, 660 S.W.2d 106, 107 (Tex.Crim. App.1983). CCP art. 11.14 "requires that an application contain sworn allegations of fact rather than mere conclusions. [A]n application for writ of habeas corpus pursuant to [CCP art.] 11.07 must be properly verified."

ART. 11.15. WRIT GRANTED WITHOUT DELAY

The writ of habeas corpus shall be granted without delay by the judge or court receiving the petition, unless it be manifest from the petition itself, or some documents annexed to it, that the party is entitled to no relief whatever.

History of CCP art. 11.15: Acts 1965, 59th Leg., vol. 2, ch. 722.

ART. 11.16. WRIT MAY ISSUE WITHOUT MOTION

A judge of the district or county court who has knowledge that any person is illegally confined or restrained in his liberty within his district or county may, if the case be one within his jurisdiction, issue the writ of habeas corpus, without any motion being made for the same.

History of CCP art. 11.16: Acts 1965, 59th Leg., vol. 2, ch. 722.

ANNOTATIONS

Ex parte Chapman, 601 S.W.2d 380, 383 n.6 (Tex. Crim.App.1980). "[A] motion for writ of habeas corpus is not always required to activate the constitutional and statutory power of a district or county court judge to issue the writ. For example, [CCP arts.] 11.16 and 11.17 authorize a judge, if within his jurisdictional power, to issue the writ on his own motion, to take the initiative in order to examine situations in which he 'has knowledge' of illegal confinement or restraint or either is made to 'appear by satisfactory evidence' along with certain specified other factors."

ART. 11.17. JUDGE MAY ISSUE WARRANT OF ARREST

Whenever it appears by satisfactory evidence to any judge authorized to issue such writ that any one is held in illegal confinement or custody, and there is good reason to believe that he will be carried out of the State, or suffer some irreparable injury before he can obtain relief in the usual course of law, or whenever the writ of habeas corpus has been issued and disregarded, the said judge may issue a warrant to any peace officer, or to any person specially named by said judge, directing him to take and bring such person before such judge, to be dealt with according to law.

History of CCP art. 11.17: Acts 1965, 59th Leg., vol. 2, ch. 722.

ART. 11.18. MAY ARREST DETAINER

Where it appears by the proof offered, under circumstances mentioned in the preceding Article, that the person charged with having illegal custody of the prisoner is, by such act, guilty of an offense against the law, the judge may, in the warrant, order that he be arrested and brought before him; and upon examination, he may be committed, discharged, or held to bail, as the law and the nature of the case may require.

History of CCP art. 11.18: Acts 1965, 59th, Leg., vol. 2, ch. 722.

ART. 11.19. PROCEEDINGS UNDER THE WARRANT

The officer charged with the execution of the warrant shall bring the persons therein mentioned before the judge or court issuing the same, who shall inquire into the cause of the imprisonment or restraint, and make an order thereon, as in cases of habeas corpus, either remanding into custody, discharging or admitting to bail the party so imprisoned or restrained.

History of CCP art. 11.19: Acts 1965, 59th Leg., vol. 2, ch. 722.

ART. 11.20. OFFICER EXECUTING WARRANT

The same power may be exercised by the officer executing the warrant in cases arising under the foregoing Articles as is exercised in the execution of warrants of arrest.

History of CCP art. 11.20: Acts 1965, 59th Leg., vol. 2, ch. 722.

ART. 11.21. CONSTRUCTIVE CUSTODY

The words "confined," "imprisoned," "in custody," "confinement," "imprisonment," refer not only to the actual, corporeal and forcible detention of a person, but

✦

likewise to any coercive measures by threats, menaces or the fear of injury, whereby one person exercises a control over the person of another, and detains him within certain limits.

History of CCP art. 11.21: Acts 1965, 59th Leg., vol. 2, ch. 722.

ANNOTATIONS

Ex parte Canada, 754 S.W.2d 660, 666 (Tex.Crim. App.1988). "[A] parolee, although no longer in physical custody is nevertheless in legal constructive custody of the State. However, when [a] pre-revocation warrant is executed his practical status is obviously altered—he is again in the physical custody of the State. Thus, although the parolee's parole status has not changed (he is still on parole), he no longer enjoys the primary benefit of parole, the release from confinement."

ART. 11.22. RESTRAINT

By "restraint" is meant the kind of control which one person exercises over another, not to confine him within certain limits, but to subject him to the general authority and power of the person claiming such right.

History of CCP art. 11.22: Acts 1965, 59th Leg., vol. 2, ch. 722.

ART. 11.23. SCOPE OF WRIT

The writ of habeas corpus is intended to be applicable to all such cases of confinement and restraint, where there is no lawful right in the person exercising the power, or where, though the power in fact exists, it is exercised in a manner or degree not sanctioned by law.

History of CCP art. 11.23: Acts 1965, 59th Leg., vol. 2, ch. 722.

ART. 11.24. ONE COMMITTED IN DEFAULT OF BAIL

Where a person has been committed to custody for failing to enter into bond, he is entitled to the writ of habeas corpus, if it be stated in the petition that there was no sufficient cause for requiring bail, or that the bail required is excessive. If the proof sustains the petition, it will entitle the party to be discharged, or have the bail reduced.

History of CCP art. 11.24: Acts 1965, 59th Leg., vol. 2, ch. 722.

ART. 11.25. PERSON AFFLICTED WITH DISEASE

When a judge or court authorized to grant writs of habeas corpus shall be satisfied, upon investigation, that a person in legal custody is afflicted with a disease which will render a removal necessary for the preservation of life, an order may be made for the removal of the prisoner to some other place where his health will not be likely to suffer; or he may be admitted to bail when it appears that any species of confinement will endanger his life.

History of CCP art. 11.25: Acts 1965, 59th Leg., vol. 2, ch. 722.

ANNOTATIONS

Ex parte Baltimore, 616 S.W.2d 205, 206-07 (Tex. Crim.App.1981). "[T]he phrase 'legal custody' ... does not contemplate a release after conviction of a felony. [¶] 'Where the confinement is after conviction, it must be shown that *any* confinement would endanger the life of the prisoner before he is entitled to release.'"

ART. 11.26. WHO MAY SERVE WRIT

The service of the writ may be made by any person competent to testify.

History of CCP art. 11.26: Acts 1965, 59th Leg., vol. 2, ch. 722.

ART. 11.27. HOW WRIT MAY BE SERVED & RETURNED

The writ may be served by delivering a copy of the original to the person who is charged with having the party under restraint or in custody, and exhibiting the original, if demanded; if he refuse to receive it, he shall be informed verbally of the purport of the writ. If he refuses admittance to the person wishing to make the service, or conceals himself, a copy of the writ may be fixed upon some conspicuous part of the house where such person resides or conceals himself, or of the place where the prisoner is confined; and the person serving the writ of habeas corpus shall, in all cases, state fully, in his return, the manner and the time of the service of the writ.

History of CCP art. 11.27: Acts 1965, 59th Leg., vol. 2, ch. 722.

ART. 11.28. RETURN UNDER OATH

The return of a writ of habeas corpus, under the provisions of the preceding Article, if made by any person other than an officer, shall be under oath.

History of CCP art. 11.28: Acts 1965, 59th Leg., vol. 2, ch. 722.

ART. 11.29. MUST MAKE RETURN

The person on whom the writ of habeas corpus is served shall immediately obey the same, and make the return required by law upon the copy of the original writ served on him, and this, whether the writ be directed to him or not.

History of CCP art. 11.29: Acts 1965, 59th Leg., vol. 2, ch. 722.

ART. 11.30. HOW RETURN IS MADE

The return is made by stating in plain language upon the copy of the writ or some paper connected with it:

1.   Whether it is true or not, according to the statement of the petition, that he has in his custody, or under his restraint, the person named or described in such petition;

2.   By virtue of what authority, or for what cause, he took and detains such person;

3.   If he had such person in his custody or under restraint at any time before the service of the writ, and has transferred him to the custody of another, he shall state particularly to whom, at what time, for what reason or by what authority he made such transfer;

4.   He shall annex to his return the writ or warrant, if any, by virtue of which he holds the person in custody; and

5.   The return must be signed and sworn to by the person making it.

History of CCP art. 11.30: Acts 1965, 59th Leg., vol. 2, ch. 722.

ART. 11.31. APPLICANT BROUGHT BEFORE JUDGE

The person on whom the writ is served shall bring before the judge the person in his custody, or under his restraint, unless it be made to appear that by reason of sickness he cannot be removed; in which case, another day may be appointed by the judge or court for hearing the cause, and for the production of the person confined; or the application may be heard and decided without the production of the person detained, by the consent of his counsel.

History of CCP art. 11.31: Acts 1965, 59th Leg., vol. 2, ch. 722.

ART. 11.32. CUSTODY PENDING EXAMINATION

When the return of the writ has been made, and the applicant brought before the court, he is no longer detained on the original warrant or process, but under the authority of the habeas corpus. The safekeeping of the prisoner, pending the examination or hearing, is entirely under the direction and authority of the judge or court issuing the writ, or to which the return is made. He may be bailed from day to day, or be remanded to the same jail whence he came, or to any other place of safekeeping under the control of the judge or court, till the case is finally determined.

History of CCP art. 11.32: Acts 1965, 59th Leg., vol. 2, ch. 722.

ART. 11.33. COURT SHALL ALLOW TIME

The court or judge granting the writ of habeas corpus shall allow reasonable time for the production of the person detained in custody.

History of CCP art. 11.33: Acts 1965, 59th Leg., vol. 2, ch. 722.

ART. 11.34. DISOBEYING WRIT

When service has been made upon a person charged with the illegal custody of another, if he refuses to obey the writ and make the return required by law, or, if he refuses to receive the writ, or conceals himself, the court or judge issuing the writ shall issue a warrant directed to any officer or other suitable person willing to execute the same, commanding him to arrest the person charged with the illegal custody or detention of another, and bring him before such court or judge. When such person has been arrested and brought before the court or judge, if he still refuses to return the writ, or does not produce the person in his custody, he shall be committed to jail and remain there until he is willing to obey the writ of habeas corpus, and until he pays all the costs of the proceeding.

History of CCP art. 11.34: Acts 1965, 59th Leg., vol. 2, ch. 722.

ART. 11.35. FURTHER PENALTY FOR DISOBEYING WRIT

Any person disobeying the writ of habeas corpus shall also be liable to a civil action at the suit of the party detained, and shall pay in such suit fifty dollars for each day of illegal detention and restraint, after service of the writ. It shall be deemed that a person has disobeyed the writ who detains a prisoner a longer time than three days after service thereof, unless where further time is allowed in the writ for making the return thereto.

History of CCP art. 11.35: Acts 1965, 59th Leg., vol. 2, ch. 722.

ART. 11.36. APPLICANT MAY BE BROUGHT BEFORE COURT

In case of disobedience of the writ of habeas corpus, the person for whose relief it is intended may also be brought before the court or judge having competent authority, by an order for that purpose, issued to any peace officer or other proper person specially named.

History of CCP art. 11.36: Acts 1965, 59th Leg., vol. 2, ch. 722.

ART. 11.37. DEATH, ETC., SUFFICIENT RETURN OF WRIT

It is a sufficient return of the writ of habeas corpus that the person, once detained, has died or escaped, or that by some superior force he has been taken from the custody of the person making the return; but where any such cause shall be assigned, the court or judge shall proceed to hear testimony; and the facts stated in the return shall be proved by satisfactory evidence.

History of CCP art. 11.37: Acts 1965, 59th Leg., vol. 2, ch. 722.

ART. 11.38. WHEN A PRISONER DIES

When a prisoner confined in jail, or who is in legal custody, shall die, the officer having charge of him shall forthwith report the same to a justice of the peace of the county, who shall hold an inquest to ascertain the cause of his death. All the proceedings had in such cases shall be reduced to writing, certified and returned as in other cases of inquest; a certified copy of which shall be sufficient proof of the death of the prisoner at the hearing of a motion under habeas corpus.

History of CCP art. 11.38: Acts 1965, 59th Leg., vol. 2, ch. 722.

ART. 11.39. WHO SHALL REPRESENT THE STATE

If neither the county nor the district attorney be present, the judge may appoint some qualified practicing attorney to represent the State, who shall be paid the same fee allowed district attorneys for like services.

History of CCP art. 11.39: Acts 1965, 59th Leg., vol. 2, ch. 722.

ART. 11.40. PRISONER DISCHARGED

The judge or court before whom a person is brought by writ of habeas corpus shall examine the writ and the papers attached to it; and if no legal cause be shown for the imprisonment or restraint, or if it appear that the imprisonment or restraint, though at first legal, cannot for any cause be lawfully prolonged, the applicant shall be discharged.

History of CCP art. 11.40: Acts 1965, 59th Leg., vol. 2, ch. 722.

ART. 11.41. WHERE PARTY IS INDICTED FOR CAPITAL OFFENSE

If it appears by the return and papers attached that the party stands indicted for a capital offense, the judge or court having jurisdiction of the case shall, nevertheless, proceed to hear such testimony as may be offered on the part of the State and the applicant, and may either remand or admit him to bail, as the law and the facts may justify.

History of CCP art. 11.41: Acts 1965, 59th Leg., vol. 2, ch. 722.
See also CCP art. 1.07.

ART. 11.42. IF COURT HAS NO JURISDICTION

If it appear by the return and papers attached that the judge or court has no jurisdiction, such court or judge shall at once remand the applicant to the person from whose custody he has been taken.

History of CCP art. 11.42: Acts 1965, 59th Leg., vol. 2, ch. 722.

ART. 11.43. PRESUMPTION OF INNOCENCE

No presumption of guilt arises from the mere fact that a criminal accusation has been made before a competent authority.

History of CCP art. 11.43: Acts 1965, 59th Leg., vol. 2, ch. 722.

ART. 11.44. ACTION OF COURT UPON EXAMINATION

The judge or court, after having examined the return and all documents attached, and heard the testimony offered on both sides, shall, according to the facts and circumstances of the case, proceed either to remand the party into custody, admit him to bail or discharge him; provided, that no defendant shall be discharged after indictment without bail.

History of CCP art. 11.44: Acts 1965, 59th Leg., vol. 2, ch. 722.

ART. 11.45. VOID OR INFORMAL

If it appears that the applicant is detained or held under a warrant of commitment which is informal, or void; yet, if from the document on which the warrant was based, or from the proof on the hearing of the habeas corpus, it appears that there is probable cause to believe that an offense has been committed by the prisoner, he shall not be discharged, but shall be committed or held to bail.

History of CCP art. 11.45: Acts 1965, 59th Leg., vol. 2, ch. 722.

ART. 11.46. IF PROOF SHOWS OFFENSE

Where, upon an examination under habeas corpus, it appears to the court or judge that there is probable cause to believe that an offense has been committed by the prisoner, he shall not be discharged, but shall be committed or admitted to bail.

History of CCP art. 11.46: Acts 1965, 59th Leg., vol. 2, ch. 722.

ART. 11.47. MAY SUMMON MAGISTRATE

To ascertain the grounds on which an informal or void warrant has been issued, the judge or court may cause to be summoned the magistrate who issued the warrant, and may, by an order, require him to bring with him all the papers and proceedings touching the matter. The attendance of such magistrate and the production of such papers may be enforced by warrant of arrest.

History of CCP art. 11.47: Acts 1965, 59th Leg., vol. 2, ch. 722.

ART. 11.48. WRITTEN ISSUE NOT NECESSARY

It shall not be necessary, on the trial of any cause arising under habeas corpus, to make up a written issue, though it may be done by the applicant for the writ. He may except to the sufficiency of, or controvert the return or any part thereof, or allege any new matter in avoidance. If written denial on his part be not made, it shall be considered, for the purpose of investigation, that the statements of said return are contested by a denial of the same; and the proof shall be heard accordingly, both for and against the applicant for relief.

History of CCP art. 11.48: Acts 1965, 59th Leg., vol. 2, ch. 722.

ART. 11.49. ORDER OF ARGUMENT

The applicant shall have the right by himself or counsel to open and conclude the argument upon the trial under habeas corpus.

History of CCP art. 11.49: Acts 1965, 59th Leg., vol. 2, ch. 722.

ART. 11.50. COSTS

The judge trying the cause under habeas corpus may make such order as is deemed right concerning the cost of bringing the defendant before him, and all other costs of the proceeding, awarding the same either against the person to whom the writ was directed, the person seeking relief, or may award no costs at all.

History of CCP art. 11.50: Acts 1965, 59th Leg., vol. 2, ch. 722.

ART. 11.51. RECORD OF PROCEEDINGS

If a writ of habeas corpus be made returnable before a court in session, all the proceedings had shall be entered of record by the clerk thereof, as in any other case in such court. When the motion is heard out of the county where the offense was committed, or in the Court of Criminal Appeals, the clerk shall transmit a certified copy of all the proceedings upon the motion to the clerk of the court which has jurisdiction of the offense.

History of CCP art. 11.51: Acts 1965, 59th Leg., vol. 2, ch. 722.

ART. 11.52. PROCEEDINGS HAD IN VACATION

If the return is made and the proceedings had before a judge of a court in vacation, he shall cause all of the proceedings to be written, shall certify to the same, and cause them to be filed with the clerk of the court which has jurisdiction of the offense, who shall keep them safely.

History of CCP art. 11.52: Acts 1965, 59th Leg., vol. 2, ch. 722.

ART. 11.53. CONSTRUING THE TWO PRECEDING ARTICLES

The two preceding Articles refer only to cases where an applicant is held under accusation for some offense; in all other cases the proceedings had before the judge shall be filed and kept by the clerk of the court hearing the case.

History of CCP art. 11.53: Acts 1965, 59th Leg., vol. 2, ch. 722.

ART. 11.54. COURT MAY GRANT NECESSARY ORDERS

The court or judge granting a writ of habeas corpus may grant all necessary orders to bring before him the testimony taken before the examining court, and may issue process to enforce the attendance of witnesses.

History of CCP art. 11.54: Acts 1965, 59th Leg., vol. 2, ch. 722.

ART. 11.55. MEANING OF "RETURN"

The word "return," as used in this Chapter, means the report made by the officer or person charged with serving the writ of habeas corpus, and also the answer made by the person served with such writ.

History of CCP art. 11.55: Acts 1965, 59th Leg., vol. 2, ch. 722.

ART. 11.56. EFFECT OF DISCHARGE BEFORE INDICTMENT

Where a person, before indictment found against him, has been discharged or held to bail on habeas corpus by order of a court or judge of competent jurisdiction, he shall not be again imprisoned or detained in custody on an accusation for the same offense, until after he shall have been indicted, unless surrendered by his bail.

History of CCP art. 11.56: Acts 1965, 59th Leg., vol. 2, ch. 722.

ART. 11.57. WRIT AFTER INDICTMENT

Where a person once discharged or admitted to bail is afterward indicted for the same offense for which he has been once arrested, he may be committed on the indictment, but shall be again entitled to the writ of habeas corpus, and may be admitted to bail, if the facts of the case render it proper; but in cases where, after indictment is found, the cause of the defendant has been investigated on habeas corpus, and an order made, either remanding him to custody, or admitting him to bail, he shall neither be subject to be again placed in custody, unless when surrendered by his bail, nor shall he be again entitled to the writ of habeas corpus, except in the special cases mentioned in this Chapter.

History of CCP art. 11.57: Acts 1965, 59th Leg., vol. 2, ch. 722.

ART. 11.58. PERSON COMMITTED FOR A CAPITAL OFFENSE

If the accusation against the defendant for a capital offense has been heard on habeas corpus before indictment found, and he shall have been committed after such examination, he shall not be entitled to the writ, unless in the special cases mentioned in Articles 11.25 and 11.59.

History of CCP art. 11.58: Acts 1965, 59th Leg., vol. 2, ch. 722.

ART. 11.59. OBTAINING WRIT A SECOND TIME

A party may obtain the writ of habeas corpus a second time by stating in a motion therefor that since the hearing of his first motion important testimony has been obtained which it was not in his power to produce at the former hearing. He shall also set forth the testimony so newly discovered; and if it be that of a witness, the affidavit of the witness shall also accompany such motion.

History of CCP art. 11.59: Acts 1965, 59th Leg., vol. 2, ch. 722.

ART. 11.60. REFUSING TO EXECUTE WRIT

Any officer to whom a writ of habeas corpus, or other writ, warrant or process authorized by this Chapter shall be directed, delivered or tendered, who refuses to execute the same according to his directions, or who wantonly delays the service or execution of the same, shall be liable to fine as for contempt of court.

History of CCP art. 11.60: Acts 1965, 59th Leg., vol. 2, ch. 722.

ART. 11.61. REFUSAL TO OBEY WRIT

Any one having another in his custody, or under his power, control or restraint who refuses to obey a writ of habeas corpus, or who evades the service of the same, or places the person illegally detained under the control

of another, removes him, or in any other manner attempts to evade the operation of the writ, shall be dealt with as provided in Article 11.34 of this Code.

History of CCP art. 11.61: Acts 1965, 59th Leg., vol. 2, ch. 722.

ART. 11.62. REFUSAL TO GIVE COPY OF PROCESS

Any jailer, sheriff or other officer who has a prisoner in his custody and refuses, upon demand, to furnish a copy of the process under which he holds the person, is guilty of an offense, and shall be dealt with as provided in Article 11.34 of this Code for refusal to return the writ therein required.

History of CCP art. 11.62: Acts 1965, 59th Leg., vol. 2, ch. 722.

ART. 11.63. HELD UNDER FEDERAL AUTHORITY

No person shall be discharged under the writ of habeas corpus who is in custody by virtue of a commitment for any offense exclusively cognizable by the courts of the United States, or by order or process issuing out of such courts in cases where they have jurisdiction, or who is held by virtue of any legal engagement or enlistment in the army, or who, being rightfully subject to the rules and articles of war, is confined by any one legally acting under the authority thereof, or who is held as a prisoner of war under the authority of the United States.

History of CCP art. 11.63: Acts 1965, 59th Leg., vol. 2, ch. 722.

ART. 11.64. APPLICATION OF CHAPTER

This Chapter applies to all cases of habeas corpus for the enlargement of persons illegally held in custody or in any manner restrained in their personal liberty, for the admission of prisoners to bail, and for the discharge of prisoners before indictment upon a hearing of the testimony. Instead of a writ of habeas corpus in other cases heretofore used, a simple order shall be substituted.

History of CCP art. 11.64: Acts 1965, 59th Leg., vol. 2, ch. 722.

ART. 11.65. BOND FOR CERTAIN APPLICANTS

(a) This article applies to an applicant for a writ of habeas corpus seeking relief from the judgment in a criminal case, other than an applicant seeking relief from a judgment imposing a penalty of death.

(b) On making proposed findings of fact and conclusions of law jointly stipulated to by the applicant and the state, or on approving proposed findings of fact and conclusions of law made by an attorney or magistrate appointed by the court to perform that duty and jointly stipulated to by the applicant and the state, the convicting court may order the release of the applicant on bond, subject to conditions imposed by the convicting court, until the applicant is denied relief, remanded to custody, or ordered released.

(c) For the purposes of this chapter, an applicant released on bond under this article remains restrained in his liberty.

(d) Article 44.04(b) does not apply to the release of an applicant on bond under this article.

History of CCP art. 11.65: Acts 2003, 78th Leg., ch. 197, §1, eff. June 2, 2003.

CHAPTER 12. LIMITATION

ART. 12.01. FELONIES

Except as provided in Article 12.03, felony indictments may be presented within these limits, and not afterward:

Ⓐ **(1)** no limitation:

(A) murder and manslaughter;

Ⓔ *Subsection (B) below is effective for the prosecution of offenses that were not barred by limitations before Sept. 1, 2007.*

(B) sexual assault under Section 22.011(a)(2), Penal Code, or aggravated sexual assault under Section 22.021(a)(1)(B), Penal Code;

(C) sexual assault, if during the investigation of the offense biological matter is collected and subjected to forensic DNA testing and the testing results show that the matter does not match the victim or any other person whose identity is readily ascertained; or

Ⓔ *Subsections (D) & (E) below are effective for the prosecution of offenses that were not barred by limitations before Sept. 1, 2007.*

(D) continuous sexual abuse of young child or children under Section 21.02, Penal Code;

(E) indecency with a child under Section 21.11, Penal Code; or

(F) an offense involving leaving the scene of an accident under Section 550.021, Transportation Code, if the accident resulted in the death of a person;

(2) ten years from the date of the commission of the offense:

(A) theft of any estate, real, personal or mixed, by an executor, administrator, guardian or trustee, with intent to defraud any creditor, heir, legatee, ward, distributee, beneficiary or settlor of a trust interested in such estate;

(B) theft by a public servant of government property over which he exercises control in his official capacity;

(C) forgery or the uttering, using or passing of forged instruments;

Ⓐ *Subsection (D) below is effective for the prosecution of offenses that were not barred by limitations before Sept. 1, 2007.*

(D) injury to an elderly or disabled individual punishable as a felony of the first degree under Section 22.04, Penal Code;

Subsection (D) below is effective for the prosecution of offenses that were barred by limitations before Sept. 1, 2007.

(D) injury to a child, elderly individual, or disabled individual punishable as a felony of the first degree under Section 22.04, Penal Code;

(E) sexual assault, except as provided by Subdivision (1) or (5); or

(F) arson;

(3) seven years from the date of the commission of the offense:

(A) misapplication of fiduciary property or property of a financial institution;

(B) securing execution of document by deception; or

(C) a violation under Sections 162.403(22)-(39), Tax Code;

☠Ⓔ *Subsections (D) & (E) below were enacted by Acts 2007, 80th Leg., ch. 285, §6, effective Sept. 1, 2007, without reference to the conflicting enactment made by Acts 2007, 80th Leg., ch. 640, §1, effective Sept. 1, 2007. For resolving conflicts, see p. V. Subsections (D) & (E) below are effective for the prosecution of offenses that were not barred by limitations before Sept. 1, 2007.*

(D) false statement to obtain property or credit; or

(E) money laundering;

Subsections (D) & (E) below were enacted by Acts 2007, 80th Leg., ch. 640, §1, effective Sept. 1, 2007, without reference to the conflicting enactment made by Acts 2007, 80th Leg., ch. 285, §6, effective Sept. 1, 2007. For resolving conflicts, see p. V. Subsections (D)-(F) below are effective for the prosecution of offenses that were not barred by limitations before Sept. 1, 2007.

(D) credit card or debit card abuse under Section 32.31, Penal Code;

(E) false statement to obtain property or credit under Section 32.32, Penal Code; or

(F) fraudulent use or possession of identifying information under Section 32.51, Penal Code;

Subsections (4) & (5) below were amended by Acts 2007, 80th Leg., ch. 593, §1.03, enacted May 18, 2007, effective Sept. 1, 2007, without reference to the conflicting amendment made by Acts 2007, 80th Leg., ch. 841, §1, enacted May 23, 2007, effective Sept. 1, 2007. For resolving conflicts, see p. V. Subsections (4) & (5) below are effective for the prosecution of offenses that were not barred by limitations before Sept. 1, 2007.

(4) five years from the date of the commission of the offense:

(A) theft or robbery;

(B) except as provided by Subdivision (5), kidnapping or burglary;

(C) injury to a child, elderly individual, or disabled individual that is not punishable as a felony of the first degree under Section 22.04, Penal Code;

(D) abandoning or endangering a child; or

(E) insurance fraud;

(5) if the investigation of the offense shows that the victim is younger than 17 years of age at the time the offense is committed, 20 years from the 18th birthday of the victim of one of the following offenses:

(A) sexual performance by a child under Section 43.25, Penal Code;

(B) aggravated kidnapping under Section 20.04(a)(4), Penal Code, if the defendant committed the offense with the intent to violate or abuse the victim sexually;

(C) burglary under Section 30.02, Penal Code, if the offense is punishable under Subsection (d) of that section and the defendant committed the offense with the intent to commit an offense described by Subdivision (1)(B) or (D) of this article or Paragraph (B) of this subdivision; or

Subsections (4) & (5) below were amended by Acts 2007, 80th Leg., ch. 841, §1, enacted May 23, 2007, effective Sept. 1, 2007, without reference to the conflicting amendment made by Acts 2007, 80th Leg., ch. 593, §1.03, enacted May 18, 2007, effective Sept. 1, 2007. For resolving conflicts, see p. V. Subsections (4) & (5) below are effective for the prosecution of offenses that were not barred by limitations before Sept. 1, 2007.

(4) five years from the date of the commission of the offense:

(A) theft, burglary, robbery;

(B) kidnapping;

(C) injury to an elderly or disabled individual that is not punishable as a felony of the first degree under Section 22.04, Penal Code;

(D) abandoning or endangering a child; or

(E) insurance fraud;

(5) ten years from the 18th birthday of the victim of the offense:

(A) indecency with a child under Section 21.11(a)(1) or (2), Penal Code;

(B) except as provided by Subdivision (1), sexual assault under Section 22.011(a)(2), Penal Code, or aggravated sexual assault under Section 22.021(a)(1)(B), Penal Code; or

(C) injury to a child under Section 22.04, Penal Code; or

Subsections (4) & (5) below are effective for the prosecution of offenses that were barred by limitations before Sept. 1, 2007.

(4) five years from the date of the commission of the offense:

(A) theft, burglary, robbery;

(B) kidnapping;

(C) injury to a child, elderly individual, or disabled individual that is not punishable as a felony of the first degree under Section 22.04, Penal Code;

(D) abandoning or endangering a child; or

(E) insurance fraud;

(5) ten years from the 18th birthday of the victim of the offense:

(A) indecency with a child under Section 21.11(a)(1) or (2), Penal Code; or

(B) except as provided by Subdivision (1), sexual assault under Section 22.011(a)(2), Penal Code, or aggravated sexual assault under Section 22.021(a)(1)(B), Penal Code; or

(6) three years from the date of the commission of the offense: all other felonies.

History of CCP art. 12.01: Acts 1965, 59th Leg., vol. 2, ch. 722. Amended by Acts 1973, 63rd Leg., ch. 399, §2(B), eff. Jan. 1, 1974; Acts 1975, 64th Leg., ch. 203, §5, eff. Sept. 1, 1975; Acts 1983, 68th Leg., ch. 85, §1 (eff. Sept. 1, 1983), ch. 977, §7 (eff. Sept. 1, 1983); Acts 1985, 69th Leg., ch. 330, §1, eff. Aug. 26, 1985; Acts 1987, 70th Leg., ch. 716, §1, eff. Sept. 1, 1987; Acts 1991, 72nd Leg., ch. 565, §6, eff. Sept. 1, 1991; Acts 1995, 74th Leg., ch. 476, §1, eff. Sept. 1, 1995; Acts 1997, 75th Leg., ch. 740, §1, eff. Sept. 1, 1997; Acts 1999, 76th Leg., ch. 39, §1 (eff. Sept. 1, 1999), ch. 1285, §33 (eff. Sept. 1, 2000); Acts 2001, 77th Leg., ch. 12, §1 (eff. Sept. 1, 2001), ch. 1479, §1 (eff. Sept. 1, 2001), ch. 1482, §1 (eff. Sept. 1, 2001); Acts 2003, 78th Leg., ch. 371, §6 (eff. Sept. 1, 2003), ch. 1276, §5.001 (eff. Sept. 1, 2003); Acts 2005, 79th Leg., ch. 1162, §6, eff. Sept. 1, 2005; Acts 2007, 80th Leg., ch. 285, §6 (eff. Sept. 1, 2007), ch. 593, §1.03 (eff. Sept. 1, 2007), ch. 640, §1 (eff. Sept. 1, 2007), ch. 841, §1 (eff. Sept. 1, 2007).

See also CCP art. 27.08.

ANNOTATIONS

Proctor v. State, 967 S.W.2d 840, 844 (Tex.Crim. App.1998). The defense of limitations "is forfeited if not asserted at or before the guilt/innocence stage of trial. Before trial, a defendant may assert the statute of limitations defense by filing a motion to dismiss under [CCP art.] 27.08(2).... At trial, the defendant may assert the defense by requesting a jury instruction on limitations if there is some evidence before the jury, from any source, that the prosecution is limitations-barred. If there is some such evidence and the defendant requests a jury instruction on the limitations defense, then the State must prove beyond a reasonable doubt that the prosecution is not limitations-barred. Finally, the defendant may, either before trial or at trial, waive the statute of limitations defense. ... Anything in our prior decisions to the contrary is overruled."

Ex parte Matthews, 873 S.W.2d 40, 42 (Tex.Crim. App.1994). Held: A claim that an indictment is barred by limitations may be raised by pretrial writ of habeas corpus. *But see **Ex parte Gutierrez***, 989 S.W.2d 55, 56 (Tex.App.—San Antonio 1998, no pet.).

Ex parte Martin, 159 S.W.3d 262, 263 (Tex.App.— Beaumont 2005, pet. ref'd). "The indictment on bail jumping is clearly outside the three-year statute of limitations for that offense. *At 265-66:* The aggravated robbery alleged to have occurred sometime before September 30, 1998, is obviously not the same conduct as jumping bail; the factual basis is clearly not the same for the two indictments. Therefore, the indictment for aggravated robbery did not toll the statute of limitations. [¶] Accordingly, the order denying habeas corpus relief is reversed and the indictment ... is dismissed."

Garcia v. State, 907 S.W.2d 635, 636 (Tex.App.— Corpus Christi 1995), *aff'd*, 981 S.W.2d 683 (Tex.Crim. App.1998). "When an indictment alleges that some relevant event transpired 'on or about' a particular date, the accused is put on notice to prepare for proof that the event happened at any time within the statutory period of limitations. ... When an indictment alleges an 'on or about' date for the commission of the offense of indecency with a child, the statutory period of limitations encompasses the ten year period prior to the presentment of the indictment. [¶] The alleged 'on or about' dates ... sufficiently put appellant on notice to prepare for proof that the offenses happened at any time between April 27, 1983 and April 27, 1993."

Monroe v. State, 871 S.W.2d 801, 805 (Tex.App.— Houston [14th Dist.] 1994, no pet.), *overruled on other grounds, **State v. Hight***, 907 S.W.2d 845 (Tex.Crim.App. 1995). "Generally, a criminal action commences when an indictment, information, or complaint against the defendant is filed in court. However, if a defendant is to be retried following a mistrial, a criminal action commences on the date of the mistrial."

ART. 12.02. MISDEMEANORS

An indictment or information for any misdemeanor may be presented within two years from the date of the commission of the offense, and not afterward.

History of CCP art. 12.02: Acts 1965, 59th Leg., vol. 2, ch. 722. Amended by Acts 1973, 63rd Leg., ch. 399, §2(B), eff. Jan. 1, 1974.

ANNOTATIONS

State v. Yount, 853 S.W.2d 6, 7-9 (Tex.Crim.App. 1993). D, who was charged with three separate offenses of involuntary manslaughter, requested lesser included offense of DWI, which was submitted to jury. The jury returned a verdict of guilty as to the lesser included offense. Although the statute of limitations had run for the lesser included offense, D "cannot benefit from the lesser included offense instruction and then attack his conviction to the lesser included offense on limitations grounds. Since [D] requested that the jury be instructed on the lesser included offense, he is now estopped from complaining that his conviction of that offense is barred by limitations."

State v. Empak, Inc., 889 S.W.2d 618, 623 (Tex. App.—Houston [14th Dist.] 1994, pet. ref'd). "Delay beyond the limitations period is prejudicial. The filing of an information tolls the statute of limitations."

ART. 12.03. AGGRAVATED OFFENSES, ATTEMPT, CONSPIRACY, SOLICITATION, ORGANIZED CRIMINAL ACTIVITY

(a) The limitation period for criminal attempt is the same as that of the offense attempted.

(b) The limitation period for criminal conspiracy or organized criminal activity is the same as that of the most serious offense that is the object of the conspiracy or the organized criminal activity.

(c) The limitation period for criminal solicitation is the same as that of the felony solicited.

(d) Except as otherwise provided by this chapter, any offense that bears the title "aggravated" shall carry the same limitation period as the primary crime.

History of CCP art. 12.03: Acts 1965, 59th Leg., vol. 2, ch. 722. Amended by Acts 1973, 63rd Leg., ch. 399, §2(B), eff. Jan. 1, 1974; Acts 1987, 70th Leg., ch. 1133, §1, eff. Sept. 1, 1987; Acts 1997, 75th Leg., ch. 740, §2, eff. Sept. 1, 1997.

ART. 12.04. COMPUTATION

The day on which the offense was committed and the day on which the indictment or information is presented shall be excluded from the computation of time.

History of CCP art. 12.04: Acts 1965, 59th Leg., vol. 2, ch. 722. Amended by Acts 1973, 63rd Leg., ch. 399, §2(B), eff. Jan. 1, 1974.

ANNOTATIONS

Al Haj v. State, 916 S.W.2d 660, 662 n.3 (Tex. App.—Houston [14th Dist.] 1996), *pet. dism'd*, 932 S.W.2d 519 (Tex.Crim.App.1996). "The period of time beginning with the day the indictment is filed in a court of competent jurisdiction, and ending with the day such accusation is, by an order of a trial court having jurisdiction thereof, determined to be invalid for any reason, shall not be computed in the period of limitation."

ART. 12.05. ABSENCE FROM STATE & TIME OF PENDENCY OF INDICTMENT, ETC., NOT COMPUTED

(a) The time during which the accused is absent from the state shall not be computed in the period of limitation.

(b) The time during the pendency of an indictment, information, or complaint shall not be computed in the period of limitation.

(c) The term "during the pendency," as used herein, means that period of time beginning with the day the indictment, information, or complaint is filed in a court of competent jurisdiction, and ending with the day such accusation is, by an order of a trial court having jurisdiction thereof, determined to be invalid for any reason.

History of CCP art. 12.05: Acts 1965, 59th Leg., vol. 2, ch. 722. Amended by Acts 1973, 63rd Leg., ch. 399, §2(B), eff. Jan. 1, 1974.

ANNOTATIONS

Hernandez v. State, 127 S.W.3d 768, 768-69 (Tex. Crim.App.2004). "The question ... is whether ... Article 12.05(b) permits an earlier indictment for a violation of one law to toll the statute of limitations in the prosecution of a later indictment of the same defendant for violating a different law. We conclude that the first indictment tolls the statute of limitations if both indictments allege the same conduct, same act, or same transaction, even if the offenses charged do not fall within the same statute." *See also Ex parte Martin*, 159 S.W.3d 262, 264-65 (Tex.App.—Beaumont 2005, pet. ref'd); *Prince v. State*, 914 S.W.2d 672, 674-75 (Tex.App.—Eastland 1996, pet. ref'd) (amended law).

Ex parte Matthews, 933 S.W.2d 134, 138 (Tex. Crim.App.1996), *overruled on other grounds*, *Proctor v. State*, 967 S.W.2d 840 (Tex.Crim.App.1998). "[A] person is 'accused' from the time any 'criminal action' is commenced against him, and 'a legal arrest without a warrant; a complaint to a magistrate; and a warrant legally issued' among others are examples of 'accusation,' under any one of such proceeding a person is said to be 'accused.'" Held: Applicant was not an "accused" during her absence from the state, and therefore statute of limitations was not tolled in light of prosecution's failure to file any accusatory pleading.

Ex parte Ward, 560 S.W.2d 660, 662 (Tex.Crim.App. 1978). "While the justice court had authority to take a complaint and issue a warrant of arrest, we find that such court did not have jurisdiction of the felony offense charged herein so as to come within the ambit of Art. 12.05. To hold to the contrary would be to allow a 'credible person' to file a complaint in the justice court charging an accused with a felony offense without inquiry being made about the nature of the knowledge upon which an affiant bases his factual statements, and thereby toll the statute of limitations forever. [¶] We hold that the indictment shows on its face that it is barred by limitation. The indictment is thus void...."

ART. 12.06. AN INDICTMENT IS "PRESENTED," WHEN

An indictment is considered as "presented" when it has been duly acted upon by the grand jury and received by the court.

History of CCP art. 12.06: Acts 1965, 59th Leg., vol. 2, ch. 722. Amended by Acts 1973, 63rd Leg., ch. 399, §2(B), eff. Jan. 1, 1974.

ART. 12.07. AN INFORMATION IS "PRESENTED," WHEN

An information is considered as "presented," when it has been filed by the proper officer in the proper court.

History of CCP art. 12.07: Acts 1965, 59th Leg., vol. 2, ch. 722. Amended by Acts 1973, 63rd Leg., ch. 399, §2(B), eff. Jan. 1, 1974.

ANNOTATIONS

Queen v. State, 701 S.W.2d 314, 315-16 (Tex. App.—Austin 1985, pet. ref'd). "[P]resentment of an information may be accomplished by the prosecuting attorney delivering the information to the clerk's office. [A]lso ... when there is more than one district court in the county, an indictment need not show on its face in which district court it was presented. The rules applicable to indictments are also applicable to informations. [¶] Therefore, when the information in the present cause was delivered by the county attorney to the county clerk's office, it was properly presented. The fact that the information did not specify in which numbered county court at law the case was to be heard did not affect the validity of the presentment."

CHAPTER 13. VENUE

ART. 13.01. OFFENSES COMMITTED OUTSIDE THIS STATE

Offenses committed wholly or in part outside this State, under circumstances that give this State jurisdiction to prosecute the offender, may be prosecuted in any county in which the offender is found or in any county in which an element of the offense occurs.

History of CCP art. 13.01: Acts 1965, 59th Leg., vol. 2, ch. 722. Amended by Acts 1973, 63rd Leg., ch. 399, §2(C), eff. Jan. 1, 1974.

ART. 13.02. FORGERY

Forgery may be prosecuted in any county where the writing was forged, or where the same was used or passed, or attempted to be used or passed, or deposited or placed with another person, firm, association, or corporation either for collection or credit for the account of any person, firm, association or corporation. In addition, a forging and uttering, using or passing of forged instruments in writing which concern or affect the title to land in this State may be prosecuted in the county in which such land, or any part thereof, is situated.

History of CCP art. 13.02: Acts 1965, 59th Leg., vol. 2, ch. 722. Amended by Acts 1973, 63rd Leg., ch. 399, §2(C), eff. Jan. 1, 1974.

ART. 13.03. PERJURY

Perjury and aggravated perjury may be prosecuted in the county where committed, or in the county where the false statement is used or attempted to be used.

History of CCP art. 13.03: Acts 1965, 59th Leg., vol. 2, ch. 722. Amended by Acts 1973, 63rd Leg., ch. 399, §2(C), eff. Jan. 1, 1974.

ANNOTATIONS

Soliz v. State, 97 S.W.3d 137, 138 (Tex.Crim.App. 2003). "[V]enue for a perjury prosecution, that is based on a false statement made in a party's deposition, lies both in the county in which the deposition was taken and in the county in which the underlying lawsuit is pending. For purposes of [Article 13.03], deposition testimony by a party in a civil lawsuit is 'used or attempted to be used' in the county in which the underlying lawsuit is pending as soon as that party makes a false statement in his sworn deposition with the intent to deceive and with knowledge of the statement's meaning."

ART. 13.04. ON THE BOUNDARIES OF COUNTIES

An offense committed on the boundaries of two or more counties, or within four hundred yards thereof, may be prosecuted and punished in any one of such counties and any offense committed on the premises of any airport operated jointly by two municipalities and situated in two counties may be prosecuted and punished in either county.

History of CCP art. 13.04: Acts 1965, 59th Leg., vol. 2, ch. 722. Amended by Acts 1973, 63rd Leg., ch. 399, §2(C) (eff. Jan. 1, 1974), ch. 454, art. 2, §1 (eff. Jan. 1, 1974); Acts 1981, 67th Leg., ch. 534, §1, eff. Aug. 31, 1981.

ANNOTATIONS

Wilson v. State, 825 S.W.2d 155, 160 (Tex.App.— Dallas 1992, pet. ref'd). "Venue was proper in Dallas County in this case because the offense allegedly occurred within 400 yards of Dallas County. Venue is a place where the case may be tried. Venue is not a constituent element of the offense."

ART. 13.05. CRIMINAL HOMICIDE COMMITTED OUTSIDE THIS STATE

The offense of criminal homicide committed wholly or in part outside this State, under circumstances that give this State jurisdiction to prosecute the offender, may be prosecuted in the county where the injury was inflicted, or in the county where the offender was located when he inflicted the injury, or in the county where the victim died or the body was found.

History of CCP art. 13.05: Acts 1965, 59th Leg., vol. 2, ch. 722. Amended by Acts 1973, 63rd Leg., ch. 399, §2(C), eff. Jan. 1, 1974.

ART. 13.06. COMMITTED ON A BOUNDARY STREAM

If an offense be committed upon any river or stream, the boundary of this State, it may be prosecuted in the county the boundary of which is upon such stream or river, and the county seat of which is nearest the place where the offense was committed.

History of CCP art. 13.06: Acts 1965, 59th Leg., vol. 2, ch. 722. Amended by Acts 1973, 63rd Leg., ch. 399, §2(C), eff. Jan. 1, 1974.

ART. 13.07. INJURED IN ONE COUNTY & DYING IN ANOTHER

If a person receives an injury in one county and dies in another by reason of such injury, the offender may be prosecuted in the county where the injury was received or where the death occurred, or in the county where the dead body is found.

History of CCP art. 13.07: Acts 1965, 59th Leg., vol. 2, ch. 722. Amended by Acts 1973, 63rd Leg., ch. 399, §2(C), eff. Jan. 1, 1974.

Ⓐ ART. 13.08. THEFT; ORGANIZED RETAIL THEFT

(a) Where property is stolen in one county and removed by the offender to another county, the offender may be prosecuted either in the county where he took the property or in any other county through or into which he may have removed the same.

Ⓔ *Subsection (b) below is effective for offenses committed on or after Sept. 1, 2007.*

(b) An offense under Section 31.16, Penal Code, may be prosecuted in any county in which an underlying theft could have been prosecuted as a separate offense.

History of CCP art. 13.08: Acts 1965, 59th Leg., vol. 2, ch. 722. Amended by Acts 1973, 63rd Leg., ch. 399, §2(C), eff. Jan. 1, 1974; Acts 2007, 80th Leg., ch. 1274, §2, eff. Sept. 1, 2007.
See also Pen. Code ch. 31.

ANNOTATIONS

Stewart v. State, 44 S.W.3d 582, 589 (Tex.Crim. App.2001). "Appellant 'exercise[d] control' over the property and committed theft when, by his threats, he caused the complainant to release the money to the police in Montgomery County. Further, because appellant directed the removal of the money from Montgomery County to Harris County, he is responsible for that removal. Article 13.08, the theft-specific venue statute, is appropriate here and venue is proper in Montgomery County."

ART. 13.09. HINDERING SECURED CREDITORS

If secured property is taken from one county and unlawfully disposed of in another county or state, the offender may be prosecuted either in the county in which such property was disposed of, or in the county from which it was removed, or in the county in which the security agreement is filed.

History of CCP art. 13.09: Acts 1965, 59th Leg., vol. 2, ch. 722. Amended by Acts 1973, 63rd Leg., ch. 399, §2(C), eff. Jan. 1, 1974.

ART. 13.10. PERSONS ACTING UNDER AUTHORITY OF THIS STATE

An offense committed outside this State by any officer acting under the authority of this State, under circumstances that give this state jurisdiction to prosecute the offender, may be prosecuted in the county of his residence or, if a nonresident of this State, in Travis County.

History of CCP art. 13.10: Acts 1965, 59th Leg., vol. 2, ch. 722. Amended by Acts 1973, 63rd Leg., ch. 399, §2(C), eff. Jan. 1, 1974.

ART. 13.11. ON VESSELS

An offense committed on board a vessel which is at the time upon any navigable water within the boundaries of this State, may be prosecuted in any county through which the vessel is navigated in the course of her voyage, or in the county where the voyage commences or terminates.

History of CCP art. 13.11: Acts 1965, 59th Leg., vol. 2, ch. 722. Amended by Acts 1973, 63rd Leg., ch. 399, §2(C), eff. Jan. 1, 1974.

ART. 13.12. FALSE IMPRISONMENT & KIDNAPPING

Venue for false imprisonment and kidnapping is in either the county in which the offense was committed, or in any county through, into or out of which the person falsely imprisoned or kidnapped may have been taken.

History of CCP art. 13.12: Acts 1965, 59th Leg., vol. 2, ch. 722. Amended by Acts 1973, 63rd Leg., ch. 399, §2(C), eff. Jan. 1, 1974.

ART. 13.13. CONSPIRACY

Criminal conspiracy may be prosecuted in the county where the conspiracy was entered into, in the county where the conspiracy was agreed to be executed, or in any county in which one or more of the conspirators does any act to effect an object of the conspiracy. If a conspiracy was entered into outside this State under circumstances that give this State jurisdiction to prosecute the offender, the offender may be prosecuted in the county where the conspiracy was agreed to be executed, or in the county where any one of the conspirators was found, or in Travis County.

History of CCP art. 13.13: Acts 1965, 59th Leg., vol. 2, ch. 722. Amended by Acts 1973, 63rd Leg., ch. 399, §2(C), eff. Jan. 1, 1974.

ART. 13.14. BIGAMY

Bigamy may be prosecuted:

(1) in the county where the bigamous marriage occurred;

(2) in any county in this State in which the parties to such bigamous marriage may live or cohabit together as man and wife; or

(3) in any county in this State in which a party to the bigamous marriage not charged with the offense resides.

History of CCP art. 13.14: Acts 1965, 59th Leg., vol. 2, ch. 722. Amended by Acts 1973, 63rd Leg., ch. 399, §2(C), eff. Jan. 1, 1974; Acts 1989, 71st Leg., ch. 1112, §1, eff. Aug. 28, 1989.

ART. 13.15. SEXUAL ASSAULT

Sexual assault may be prosecuted in the county in which it is committed, in the county in which the victim is abducted, or in any county through or into which the victim is transported in the course of the abduction and sexual assault. When it shall come to the knowledge of any district judge whose court has jurisdiction under this Article that sexual assault has probably been committed, he shall immediately, if his court be in session, and if not in session, then, at the first term thereafter in any county of the district, call the attention of the grand jury thereto; and if the court be in session, but the grand jury has been discharged, he shall immediately recall the grand jury to investigate the accusation. The district courts are authorized and directed to change the venue in such cases whenever it shall be necessary to secure a speedy trial.

History of CCP art. 13.15: Acts 1965, 59th Leg., vol. 2, ch. 722. Amended by Acts 1973, 63rd Leg., ch. 399, §2(C), eff. Jan. 1, 1974; Acts 1977, 65th Leg., ch. 262, §1, eff. May 25, 1977; Acts 1981, 67th Leg., ch. 707, §4(17), eff. Aug. 31, 1981; Acts 1983, 68th Leg., ch. 977, §7, eff. Sept. 1, 1983.

ANNOTATIONS

Cavazos v. State, 668 S.W.2d 435, 438-39 (Tex. App.—Austin 1984, pet. ref'd). "'Abduct,' as it is used in article 13.15, has no technical meaning. While the ordinary meaning of the term generally connotes the use of force, such a connotation is not 'invariable.' A widely used dictionary of the English language defines 'abduct' as 'to take (a person) away unlawfully and by force *or fraud.*' [F]or the purpose of prosecution under [Pen. Code ch.] 20 ..., one may abduct another by use of deception and without the use or threatened use of force."

ART. 13.16. CRIMINAL NONSUPPORT

Criminal nonsupport may be prosecuted in the county where the offended spouse or child is residing at the time the information or indictment is presented.

History of CCP art. 13.16: Acts 1965, 59th Leg., vol. 2, ch. 722. Amended by Acts 1973, 63rd Leg., ch. 399, §2(C), eff. Jan. 1, 1974.

ART. 13.17. PROOF OF VENUE

In all cases mentioned in this Chapter, the indictment or information, or any pleading in the case, may allege that the offense was committed in the county where the prosecution is carried on. To sustain the allegation of venue, it shall only be necessary to prove by the preponderance of the evidence that by reason of the facts in the case, the county where such prosecution is carried on has venue.

History of CCP art. 13.17: Acts 1965, 59th Leg., vol. 2, ch. 722. Amended by Acts 1973, 63rd Leg., ch. 399, §2(C), eff. Jan. 1, 1974.

ANNOTATIONS

Black v. State, 645 S.W.2d 789, 790 (Tex.Crim.App. 1983). "A plea of not guilty puts in issue the allegations of venue, and the State must prove such allegations or a conviction will not be warranted. It is unnecessary for the defendant to put venue in issue by either special plea or negation of the allegation: venue must be proved as alleged. [¶] Generally it is noted that in criminal cases venue need only be proven by a preponderance of the evidence. Proof of venue must be demonstrated by either direct or circumstantial evidence."

Edwards v. State, 97 S.W.3d 279, 286 (Tex.App.—Houston [14th Dist.] 2003, pet. ref'd). "Where venue is sought to be established by someone in a moving vehicle, specific points of reference and measurable passages of time can establish the offense occurred in the State's proffered county."

Braddy v. State, 908 S.W.2d 465, 467 (Tex.App.—Dallas 1995, no pet.). "'Venue,' as applied to criminal cases, means the place in which the prosecution is to begin. Venue is not synonymous with 'jurisdiction,' which is the power of the court to hear and determine the case. [¶] Additionally, a trial court may take judicial notice of the location of a certain city or town, and of the fact that the county or town is the county seat of a particular county. [¶] It is presumed that venue is proved in the trial, unless the record affirmatively shows otherwise or venue is made an issue at trial. A motion for an instructed verdict of acquittal, specifically challenging the proof of venue, timely raises the issue of venue."

Cunningham v. State, 848 S.W.2d 898, 902 (Tex. App.—Corpus Christi 1993, pet. ref'd). "Although appellant made no motion for instructed verdict raising the issue [of venue], nor did he at any time prior to closing argument challenge the sufficiency of the evidence to sustain the allegation of venue in Brazos County, he did 'make an issue' regarding venue [during final argument] at a time when the state could have re-opened its evidence.... [W]e find that the appellate presumption does not apply...."

Granados v. State, 843 S.W.2d 736, 737 (Tex. App.—Corpus Christi 1992, no pet.). "By announcing 'ready' we conclude that appellant consented to the case being tried in Kleberg County [even though offense occurred in Kenedy County]."

Mosley v. State, 643 S.W.2d 212, 216 (Tex.App.—Fort Worth 1982, no pet.). A specific objection in a motion for new trial that venue was not proved is untimely for purposes of preserving issue for appellate review.

ART. 13.18. OTHER OFFENSES

If venue is not specifically stated, the proper county for the prosecution of offenses is that in which the offense was committed.

History of CCP art. 13.18: Acts 1965, 59th Leg., vol. 2, ch. 722. Amended by Acts 1973, 63rd Leg., ch. 399, §2(C), eff. Jan. 1, 1974.

ART. 13.19. WHERE VENUE CANNOT BE DETERMINED

If an offense has been committed within the state and it cannot readily be determined within which county or counties the commission took place, trial may be held in the county in which the defendant resides, in the county in which he is apprehended, or in the county to which he is extradited.

History of CCP art. 13.19: Acts 1965, 59th Leg., vol. 2, ch. 722. Amended by Acts 1973, 63rd Leg., ch. 399, §2(C), eff. Jan. 1, 1974.

ANNOTATIONS

Murphy v. State, 112 S.W.3d 592, 604-05 (Tex. Crim.App.2003). "There is no special venue statute expressly applicable to the prosecution of a capital murder. Nor is there any statute providing that in capital murder cases, venue occurs only where the homicide takes place. Any number of the special venue provisions may apply to a given capital murder case, depending upon its facts. [¶] Venue will stand if it is sufficient under any one of the venue provisions the jury was instructed upon."

ART. 13.20. VENUE BY CONSENT

The trial of all felony cases, without a jury, may, with the consent of the defendant in writing, his attorney, and the attorney for the state, be held in any county within the judicial district or districts for the county where venue is otherwise authorized by law.

History of CCP art. 13.20: Acts 1975, 64th Leg., ch. 91, §1, eff. Sept. 1, 1975.

ART. 13.21. ORGANIZED CRIMINAL ACTIVITY

The offense of engaging in organized criminal activity may be prosecuted in any county in which any act is committed to effect an objective of the combination.

History of CCP art. 13.21: Acts 1977, 65th Leg., ch. 346, §2, eff. June 10, 1977.

ART. 13.22. POSSESSION & DELIVERY OF MARIHUANA

An offense of possession or delivery of marihuana may be prosecuted in the county where the offense was committed or with the consent of the defendant in a county that is adjacent to and in the same judicial district as the county where the offense was committed.

History of CCP art. 13.22: Acts 1979, 66th Leg., ch. 10, §1, eff. March 7, 1979.

ART. 13.23. UNAUTHORIZED USE OF A VEHICLE

An offense of unauthorized use of a vehicle may be prosecuted in any county where the unauthorized use of the vehicle occurred or in the county in which the vehicle was originally reported stolen.

History of CCP art. 13.23: Acts 1985, 69th Leg., ch. 719, §1, eff. Aug. 26, 1985.

ANNOTATIONS

Gonzales v. State, 784 S.W.2d 140, 142 (Tex. App.—Austin 1990, no pet.). "In most cases the unauthorized use occurs in the same county where the vehicle is originally reported stolen leaving no question about where venue lies. Under article 13.23 the State may, however, allege venue in the county where the vehicle is originally reported stolen and prove unauthorized use in another county. [T]he offense of unauthorized use of a motor-propelled vehicle may be a continuing offense. There may be unauthorized use by a person in the county where the vehicle is originally reported stolen as well as unauthorized use in another county by the same person."

ART. 13.24. ILLEGAL RECRUITMENT OF ATHLETES

An offense of illegal recruitment of an athlete may be prosecuted in any county in which the offense was committed or in the county in which is located the institution of higher education in which the athlete agreed to enroll or was influenced to enroll.

History of CCP art. 13.24: Acts 1989, 71st Leg., ch. 125, §2, eff. Sept. 1, 1989.

ART. 13.25. COMPUTER CRIMES

(a) In this section "access," "computer," "computer network," "computer program," "computer system," and "owner" have the meanings assigned to those terms by Section 33.01, Penal Code.

(b) An offense under Chapter 33, Penal Code, may be prosecuted in:

(1) the county of the principal place of business of the owner or lessee of a computer, computer network, or computer system involved in the offense;

(2) any county in which a defendant had control or possession of:

(A) any proceeds of the offense; or

(B) any books, records, documents, property, negotiable instruments, computer programs, or other material used in furtherance of the offense; or

(3) any county from which, to which, or through which access to a computer, computer network, computer program, or computer system was made in violation of Chapter 33, whether by wires, electromagnetic waves, microwaves, or any other means of communication.

History of CCP art. 13.25: Acts 1989, 71st Leg., ch. 306, §4, eff. Sept. 1, 1989. Renumbered from Art. 13.24 by Acts 1991, 72nd Leg., ch. 16, §19.01(1), eff. Aug. 26, 1991. Amended by Acts 1993, 73rd Leg., ch. 900, §3.01, eff. Sept. 1, 1994; Acts 1997, 75th Leg., ch. 306, §4, eff. Sept. 1, 1997.

ART. 13.26. TELECOMMUNICATIONS CRIMES

An offense under Chapter 33A, Penal Code, may be prosecuted in the county in which the telecommunications service originated or terminated or in the county to which the bill for the telecommunications service was or would have been delivered.

History of CCP art. 13.26: Acts 1997, 75th Leg., ch. 306, §5, eff. Sept. 1, 1997.

ART. 13.27. SIMULATING LEGAL PROCESS

An offense under Section 32.46, 32.48, 32.49, or 37.13, Penal Code, may be prosecuted either in the county from which any material document was sent or in the county in which it was delivered.

History of CCP art. 13.27: Acts 1997, 75th Leg., ch. 189, §12, eff. May 21, 1997. Renumbered from Art. 13.26 by Acts 1999, 76th Leg., ch. 62, §19.01(6), eff. Sept. 1, 1999.

ART. 13.28. ESCAPE; UNAUTHORIZED ABSENCE

An offense of escape under Section 38.06, Penal Code, or unauthorized absence under Section 38.113, Penal Code, may be prosecuted in:

(1) the county in which the offense of escape or unauthorized absence was committed; or

(2) the county in which the defendant committed the offense for which the defendant was placed in custody, detained, or required to submit to treatment.

History of CCP art. 13.28: Acts 2003, 78th Leg., ch. 392, §1, eff. Sept. 1, 2003.

ART. 13.29. FRAUDULENT USE OR POSSESSION OF IDENTIFYING INFORMATION

An offense under Section 32.51, Penal Code, may be prosecuted in any county in which the offense was committed or in the county of residence for the person whose identifying information was fraudulently obtained, possessed, transferred, or used.

History of CCP art. 13.29: Acts 2003, 78th Leg., ch. 415, §1, eff. Sept. 1, 2003. Renumbered from Art. 13.28 by Acts 2005, 79th Leg., ch. 728, §23.001(7), eff. Sept. 1, 2005.

ART. 13.30. FRAUDULENT, SUBSTANDARD, OR FICTITIOUS DEGREE

An offense under Section 32.52, Penal Code, may be prosecuted in the county in which an element of the offense occurs or in Travis County.

History of CCP art. 13.30: Acts 2005, 79th Leg., ch. 1039, §9, eff. Sept. 1, 2005.

Ⓐ ART. 13.31. FAILURE TO COMPLY WITH SEX OFFENDER REGISTRATION STATUTE

An offense under Chapter 62 may be prosecuted in:

(1) any county in which an element of the offense occurs;

(2) the county in which the person subject to Chapter 62 last registered, verified registration, or otherwise complied with a requirement of Chapter 62;

(3) the county in which the person required to register under Chapter 62 has indicated that the person intends to reside; or

(4) any county in which the person required to register under Chapter 62 is placed under custodial arrest for an offense subsequent to the person's most recent reportable conviction or adjudication under Chapter 62.

History of CCP art. 13.31: Acts 2005, 79th Leg., ch. 1008, §1.02, eff. Sept. 1, 2005. Renumbered from 13.30 by Acts 2007, 80th Leg., ch. 921, §17.001(8), eff. Sept. 1, 2007.

Ⓔ ART. 13.315. FAILURE TO COMPLY WITH SEXUALLY VIOLENT PREDATOR CIVIL COMMITMENT REQUIREMENT

An offense under Section 841.085, Health and Safety Code, may be prosecuted in the county in which any element of the offense occurs or in Montgomery County.

History of CCP art. 13.315: Acts 2007, 80th Leg., ch. 1219, §10, eff. Sept. 1, 2007.

Ⓐ ART. 13.32. MISAPPLICATION OF CERTAIN PROPERTY

(a) An offender who misapplies property held as a fiduciary or property of a financial institution in one county and removes the property to another county may be prosecuted in the county where the offender misapplied the property, in any other county through or into which the offender removed the property, or, as applicable, in the county in which the fiduciary was appointed to serve.

(b) An offense related to misapplication of construction trust funds under Chapter 162, Property Code, must be prosecuted in the county where the construction project is located.

History of CCP art. 13.32: Acts 2005, 79th Leg., ch. 1275, §1, eff. Sept. 1, 2005. Renumbered from 13.30 by Acts 2007, 80th Leg., ch. 921, §17.001(9), eff. Sept. 1, 2007.

CHAPTER 14. ARREST WITHOUT WARRANT

ART. 14.01. OFFENSE WITHIN VIEW

(a) A peace officer or any other person, may, without a warrant, arrest an offender when the offense is committed in his presence or within his view, if the offense is one classed as a felony or as an offense against the public peace.

(b) A peace officer may arrest an offender without a warrant for any offense committed in his presence or within his view.

History of CCP art. 14.01: Acts 1965, 59th Leg., vol. 2, ch. 722. Amended by Acts 1967, 60th Leg., ch. 659, §8, eff. Aug. 28, 1967.

ANNOTATIONS

Miles v. State, 241 S.W.3d 28, 42 (Tex.Crim.App. 2007). "[A] citizen may make a warrantless arrest of a person who commits a misdemeanor within the citizen's presence or view if the evidence shows that the person's conduct poses a threat of continuing violence or harm to himself or the public. It is the exigency of the situation, not the title of the offense, that gives both officer and citizen statutory authorization to protect the public from an ongoing threat of violence, harm, or danger by making a warrantless arrest." Held: Citizen's arrest of D for DWI was legal. *See also **Sanchez v. State***, 582 S.W.2d 813, 815 (Tex.Crim.App.1979); ***Heck v. State***, 507 S.W.2d 737, 740 (Tex.Crim.App.1974) (citizen may make an arrest without a warrant for a misdemeanor offense when it is a breach of peace).

State v. Steelman, 93 S.W.3d 102, 107 (Tex.Crim. App.2002). "An offense is deemed to have occurred within the presence or view of an officer when any of his senses afford him an awareness of its occurrence. However, the information afforded to the officer by his senses must give the officer reason to believe that *a particular suspect* committed the offense. *At 108:* The odor of marijuana, standing alone, does not authorize a warrantless search and seizure in a home."

Woods v. State, 956 S.W.2d 33, 38 (Tex.Crim.App. 1997). "[T]he 'as consistent with innocent activity as with criminal activity' construct is no longer a viable test for determining reasonable suspicion. ... We hold that the reasonableness of a temporary detention must be examined in terms of the totality of the circumstances and will be justified when the detaining officer has specific articulable facts, which taken together with rational inferences from those facts, lead him to conclude that the person detained actually is, has been, or soon will be engaged in criminal activity."

Woodward v. State, 668 S.W.2d 337, 344 (Tex. Crim.App.1982). "[W]hen there has been some cooperation between law enforcement agencies or between members of the same agency, the sum of the information known to the cooperating agencies or officers at the time of an arrest or search by any of the officers involved is to be considered in determining whether there was sufficient probable cause...."

Akins v. State, 202 S.W.3d 879, 889 (Tex.App.— Fort Worth 2006, pet. ref'd). "The test for probable cause for a warrantless arrest under this provision is '[w]hether at that moment the facts and circumstances within the officer's knowledge and of which he had reasonably trustworthy information were sufficient to warrant a prudent man in believing that the arrested person *had committed or was committing* an offense.' In other words, although the statute states that the offense must be one that is committed within the officer's presence or view, an officer can make a warrantless arrest based on an offense that was committed at an earlier time and further, the officer does not even have to personally see the offense committed before the warrantless arrest is justified under article 14.01(b). [¶] This means that in determining whether probable cause exists to believe an offense was committed within a officer's presence or view, an officer's knowledge and trustworthy information may come from facts and circumstances obtained from lay citizens." *See also **Torres v. State***, 182 S.W.3d 899, 902 (Tex.Crim.App. 2005); ***Cornejo v. State***, 917 S.W.2d 480, 482-83 (Tex. App.—Houston [14th Dist.] 1996, pet. ref'd).

Arnold v. State, 971 S.W.2d 588, 589 (Tex.App.— Dallas 1998, no pet.). "The general rule is that a warrantless arrest for DWI will be upheld even if the officer did not see the person driving, if the person committed the offense of public intoxication in the officer's view and there is no proof of sham or fraud."

Givens v. State, 949 S.W.2d 449, 451 (Tex.App.— Fort Worth 1997, pet. ref'd). "The burden of proof is on the State to prove the existence of probable cause to justify a warrantless arrest." *See also **Reichaert v. State***, 830 S.W.2d 348, 349 (Tex.App.—San Antonio 1992, pet. ref'd).

Dominguez v. State, 924 S.W.2d 950, 954 (Tex. App.—El Paso 1996, no pet.). "While [this provision seems] to grant peace officers unlimited geographic jurisdiction for making warrantless arrests committed in their presence or within their view, ... a peace officer can make a warrantless arrest only within his geographic or territorial jurisdiction. If a statute granting authority to act does not define the geographic scope within which a peace officer may act, then that geographic scope must find its source in some other statute or be controlled by the common law."

Owens v. State, 861 S.W.2d 419, 420 (Tex.App.—Dallas 1993, no pet.). "Except for a speeding offense, an officer may arrest and take into custody a person seen committing a traffic offense."

ART. 14.02. WITHIN VIEW OF MAGISTRATE

A peace officer may arrest, without warrant, when a felony or breach of the peace has been committed in the presence or within the view of a magistrate, and such magistrate verbally orders the arrest of the offender.

History of CCP art. 14.02: Acts 1965, 59th Leg., vol. 2, ch. 722.

ANNOTATIONS

Henderson v. State, 600 S.W.2d 788, 790-91 (Tex. Crim.App.1979). "The term breach of the peace is generic, and includes all violations of the public peace or order, or decorum; in other words, it signifies the offense of disturbing the public peace or tranquility enjoyed by the citizens of a community; a disturbance of the public tranquility by any act or conduct inciting to violence or tending to provoke or excite others to break the peace; a disturbance of the public order by an act of violence, or by any act likely to produce violence, or which, by causing consternation and alarm disturbs the peace and quiet of the community." (Internal quotes omitted.)

ART. 14.03. AUTHORITY OF PEACE OFFICERS

(a) Any peace officer may arrest, without warrant:

(1) persons found in suspicious places and under circumstances which reasonably show that such persons have been guilty of some felony, violation of Title 9, Chapter 42, Penal Code, breach of the peace, or offense under Section 49.02, Penal Code, or threaten, or are about to commit some offense against the laws;

(2) persons who the peace officer has probable cause to believe have committed an assault resulting in bodily injury to another person and the peace officer has probable cause to believe that there is danger of further bodily injury to that person;

(3) persons who the peace officer has probable cause to believe have committed an offense defined by Section 25.07, Penal Code (violation of Protective Order), or by Section 38.112, Penal Code (violation of Protective Order issued on basis of sexual assault), if the offense is not committed in the presence of the peace officer;

(4) persons who the peace officer has probable cause to believe have committed an offense involving family violence;

(5) persons who the peace officer has probable cause to believe have prevented or interfered with an individual's ability to place a telephone call in an emergency, as defined by Section 42.062(d), Penal Code, if the offense is not committed in the presence of the peace officer; or

(6) a person who makes a statement to the peace officer that would be admissible against the person under Article 38.21 and establishes probable cause to believe that the person has committed a felony.

(b) A peace officer shall arrest, without a warrant, a person the peace officer has probable cause to believe has committed an offense under Section 25.07, Penal Code (violation of Protective Order), or Section 38.112, Penal Code (violation of Protective Order issued on basis of sexual assault), if the offense is committed in the presence of the peace officer.

(c) If reasonably necessary to verify an allegation of a violation of a protective order or of the commission of an offense involving family violence, a peace officer shall remain at the scene of the investigation to verify the allegation and to prevent the further commission of the violation or of family violence.

(d) A peace officer who is outside his jurisdiction may arrest, without warrant, a person who commits an offense within the officer's presence or view, if the offense is a felony, a violation of Chapter 42 or 49, Penal Code, or a breach of the peace. A peace officer making an arrest under this subsection shall, as soon as practicable after making the arrest, notify a law enforcement agency having jurisdiction where the arrest was made. The law enforcement agency shall then take custody of the person committing the offense and take the person before a magistrate in compliance with Article 14.06 of this code.

(e) The justification for conduct provided under Section 9.21, Penal Code, applies to a peace officer when the peace officer is performing a duty required by this article.

(f) In this article, "family violence" has the meaning assigned by Section 71.004, Family Code.

(g)(1) A peace officer listed in Subdivision (1), (2), or (5), Article 2.12, who is licensed under Chapter 1701, Occupations Code, and is outside of the officer's jurisdiction may arrest without a warrant a person who commits any offense within the officer's presence or view, other than a violation of Subtitle C, Title 7, Transportation Code.

(2) A peace officer listed in Subdivision (3), Article 2.12, who is licensed under Chapter 1701, Occupations Code, and is outside of the officer's jurisdiction may arrest without a warrant a person who commits any offense within the officer's presence or view, except that an officer described in this subdivision who is outside of that officer's jurisdiction may arrest a person for a violation of Subtitle C, Title 7, Transportation Code, only if the offense is committed in the county or counties in which the municipality employing the peace officer is located.

(3) A peace officer making an arrest under this subsection shall as soon as practicable after making the arrest notify a law enforcement agency having jurisdiction where the arrest was made. The law enforcement agency shall then take custody of:

(A) the person committing the offense and take the person before a magistrate in compliance with Article 14.06; and

(B) any property seized during or after the arrest as if the property had been seized by a peace officer of that law enforcement agency.

History of CCP art. 14.03: Acts 1965, 59th Leg., vol. 2, ch. 722. Amended by Acts 1967, 60th Leg., ch. 659, §9, eff. Aug. 28, 1967; Acts 1981, 67th Leg., ch. 442, §1, eff. Aug. 31, 1981; Acts 1985, 69th Leg., ch. 583, §2, eff. Sept. 1, 1985; Acts 1987, 70th Leg., ch. 68, §1, eff. Sept. 1, 1987; Acts 1989, 71st Leg., ch. 740, §1, eff. Aug. 28, 1989; Acts 1991, 72nd Leg., ch. 542, §9, eff. Sept. 1, 1991; Acts 1993, 73rd Leg., ch. 900, §3.02, eff. Sept. 1, 1994; Acts 1995, 74th Leg., ch. 76, §14.17 (eff. Sept. 1, 1995), ch. 829, §1 (eff. Aug. 28, 1995); Acts 1999, 76th Leg., ch. 62, §3.02 (eff. Sept. 1, 1999), ch. 210, §2 (eff. May 24, 1999); Acts 2003, 78th Leg., ch. 460, §2 (eff. Sept. 1, 2003), ch. 836, §2 (eff. Sept. 1, 2003), ch. 897, §1 (eff. Sept. 1, 2003), ch. 989, §1 (eff. Sept. 1, 2003), ch. 1164, §2 (eff. Sept. 1, 2003), ch. 1276, §7.002(d) (eff. Sept. 1, 2003); Acts 2005, 79th Leg., ch. 1015, §1 (eff. Sept. 1, 2005), ch. 728, §4.002 (eff. Sept. 1, 2005), ch. 788, §§4, 5 (eff. Sept. 1, 2005), ch. 847, §1 (eff. Sept. 1, 2005).

See also *O'Connor's Family Law Handbook*, "Duties of Law Enforcement," ch. 6-E.

ANNOTATIONS

Gallups v. State, 151 S.W.3d 196, 201 (Tex.Crim. App.2004). "We have held that driving while intoxicated is a breach of the peace. And ... we held that a hospital, where the defendant was arrested for driving while intoxicated soon after he was transported there after an accident, was a 'suspicious place' under Article 14.03(a)(1). Similarly, under the facts of this case, appellant's home, where he was arrested for driving while intoxicated soon after he walked there after abandoning his wrecked truck at the scene of an accident, was a 'suspicious place' under Article 14.03(a)(1)...."

Dyar v. State, 125 S.W.3d 460, 468 (Tex.Crim.App. 2003). "[T]he test under Article 14.03(a)(1) is a totality of the circumstances test. First, probable cause that the defendant committed a crime must be found and second, the defendant must be found in a 'suspicious place.'" *See also **Sandoval v. State***, 35 S.W.3d 763, 768 (Tex.App.—El Paso 2000, pet. ref'd).

Yeager v. State, 104 S.W.3d 103, 106 (Tex.Crim.App. 2003). "[T]he 'hot pursuit' [of a suspect outside a peace officer's jurisdiction] doctrine [does not apply] only 'where a police officer has the right to arrest'.... *At 107:* Under the 'hot pursuit' doctrine, the relevant consideration [can be] whether the initial 'pursuit' was 'lawfully initiated on the ground of suspicion.'"

State v. Purdy, 244 S.W.3d 591, 594 (Tex.App.—Dallas 2008, pet. filed 6-2-08). "An 'arrest' under article 14.03 is not limited to a formal, custodial arrest. Thus, the provisions of article 14.03 also apply when an officer temporarily detains a person based on reasonable suspicion."

Buchanan v. State, 175 S.W.3d 868, 875-76 (Tex. App.—Texarkana 2005), *rev'd on other grounds*, 207 S.W.3d 772 (Tex.Crim.App.2006). "To hold that a dwelling is a suspicious place solely because it is in poor condition would be tantamount to holding that a car is a suspicious place simply because it needs a tune-up. Admittedly, there is no bright-line rule for determining whether a place is suspicious. Any determination is necessarily fact-specific. [¶] While there are no specific time limits, the Texas Court of Criminal Appeals has said, '[T]he time between the crime and the apprehension of the suspect in a suspicious place is an important factor.' In finding a place as suspicious, 'one factor seems to be constant throughout the case law.

The time frame between the crime and the apprehension of a suspect in a suspicious place is short.' Buchanan was arrested four weeks after the robbery took place. A span of nearly a month between an alleged crime and the arrest of a suspect in a particular place is far from short and does not lead to the conclusion that the place is suspicious."

Dogay v. State, 101 S.W.3d 614, 617 (Tex.App.—Houston [1st Dist.] 2003, no pet.). "[M]unicipal and county officers are authorized to arrest a person for a felony or misdemeanor offense, other than traffic violations, committed in his presence, anywhere in Texas, and are authorized to arrest for traffic violations occurring within the county where the officer is employed." *See also Taylor v. State*, 152 S.W.3d 749, 752 (Tex. App.—Houston [1st Dist.] 2004, pet. ref'd); *Preston v. State*, 983 S.W.2d 24, 26-27 (Tex.App.—Tyler 1998, no pet.).

ART. 14.031. PUBLIC INTOXICATION

(a) In lieu of arresting an individual who commits an offense under Section 49.02, Penal Code, a peace officer may release an individual if:

(1) the officer believes detention in a penal facility is unnecessary for the protection of the individual or others; and

(2) the individual:

(A) is released to the care of an adult who agrees to assume responsibility for the individual; or

(B) verbally consents to voluntary treatment for chemical dependency in a program in a treatment facility licensed and approved by the Texas Commission on Alcohol and Drug Abuse, and the program admits the individual for treatment.

(b) A magistrate may release from custody an individual arrested under Section 49.02, Penal Code, if the magistrate determines the individual meets the conditions required for release in lieu of arrest under Subsection (a) of this article.

(c) The release of an individual under Subsection (a) or (b) of this article to an alcohol or drug treatment program may not be considered by a peace officer or magistrate in determining whether the individual should be released to such a program for a subsequent incident or arrest under Section 49.02, Penal Code.

(d) A peace officer and the agency or political subdivision that employs the peace officer may not be held liable for damage to persons or property that results from the actions of an individual released under Subsection (a) or (b) of this article.

History of CCP art. 14.031: Acts 1993, 73rd Leg., ch. 900, §1.04, eff. Sept. 1, 1994.

ART. 14.04. WHEN FELONY HAS BEEN COMMITTED

Where it is shown by satisfactory proof to a peace officer, upon the representation of a credible person, that a felony has been committed, and that the offender is about to escape, so that there is no time to procure a warrant, such peace officer may, without warrant, pursue and arrest the accused.

History of CCP art. 14.04: Acts 1965, 59th Leg., vol. 2, ch. 722.

ANNOTATIONS

Florida v. J.L., 529 U.S. 266, 271, 120 S.Ct. 1375, 1379 (2000). "The tip ... lacked the moderate indicia of reliability present in [*Alabama v.*] *White*, [496 U.S. 325, 332, 110 S.Ct. 2412, 2417 (1990)] and essential to the Court's decision in that case. The anonymous call concerning J.L. provided no predictive information and therefore left the police without means to test the informant's knowledge or credibility. That the allegation about the gun turned out to be correct does not suggest that the officers, prior to the frisks, had a reasonable basis for suspecting J.L. of engaging in unlawful conduct: The reasonableness of official suspicion must be measured by what the officers knew before they conducted their search. All the police had to go on in this case was the bare report of an unknown, unaccountable informant who neither explained how he knew about the gun nor supplied any basis for believing he had inside information about J.L."

Dowthitt v. State, 931 S.W.2d 244, 259 (Tex.Crim. App.1996). "The only potentially applicable warrantless arrest exception is the felony/escape rule found in Article 14.04. [A]rticle 14.04 must be strictly construed in the suspect's favor. [T]he law enforcement officer must have some evidence amounting to satisfactory proof ... that the defendant was about to escape. ... In interpreting ambiguous behavior by a suspect, it is important to keep in mind the temporal proximity of the actions of [the] suspect both to the commission of the crime, and to the suspect's discovery of the police investigation of him. [S]atisfactory proof of escape is not established by the mere fact that a suspect travels from one place to another." (Internal quotes omitted.)

Crane v. State, 786 S.W.2d 338, 346 (Tex.Crim.App. 1990). "Police broadcasts, based on probable cause, reporting a felony and a description of the suspect satisfy the requirements for arrest under Article 14.04. *At 347:* Article 14.04 does not require a showing that the offender was in fact about to escape, nor does it require a showing that there was in fact no time to procure a warrant. The statute merely requires a showing that there is *satisfactory proof from representations by a credible person* that the felony offender 'is about to escape, so that there is no time to procure a warrant.' The police officers themselves may observe conduct which indicates that the offender is about to escape."

Pyles v. State, 755 S.W.2d 98, 109 (Tex.Crim.App. 1988). "There are several factors which can help to indicate that a suspect may be committing, or have just committed, an offense, or that the suspect may be attempting to escape from the commission of the offense. These factors include furtive movements and gestures, flight at the approach of strangers or law officers, the place where a suspect is found and the direction in which he is traveling, and being on a public street instead of in a private residence. These factors are strong indicia of mens rea, and when coupled with specific knowledge on the part of the officer relating the suspect to the evidence of the crime, are properly considered in the decision to make an arrest. When taken alone and by themselves, these factors may be as insufficient for this purpose as an inarticulate hunch on the part of the arresting officer."

Brick v. State, 738 S.W.2d 676, 681 (Tex.Crim.App. 1987). Appellant contends that "there were no grounds for the officers to believe he was about to escape [and that] his warrantless arrest was ... perpetrated in violation of Article 14.04.... Though this ... illegality would stem from a violation of statute rather than constitution, in either event a taint analysis would be required."

McGee v. State, 23 S.W.3d 156, 164 (Tex.App.— Houston [14th Dist.] 2000), *rev'd on other grounds*, 105 S.W.3d 609 (Tex.Crim.App.2003). "[T]here is ... no showing that appellant was about to escape. ... Appellant was found exactly where the citizen told officers he would be found. Further, when the officers approached the appellant and asked him to place his hands on the patrol car, he complied. [¶] The State argues that we

should infer escape since appellant was found on a public street.... We cannot agree. [T]he suspect's presence on a public street is yet another factor to consider when analyzing escape...."

Laca v. State, 893 S.W.2d 171, 178 (Tex.App.—El Paso 1995, pet. ref'd). "[A]n identified private citizen whose only contact with the police results from witnessing a criminal act is inherently credible."

ART. 14.05. RIGHTS OF OFFICER

In each case enumerated where arrests may be lawfully made without warrant, the officer or person making the arrest is justified in adopting all the measures which he might adopt in cases of arrest under warrant, except that an officer making an arrest without a warrant may not enter a residence to make the arrest unless:

(1) a person who resides in the residence consents to the entry; or

(2) exigent circumstances require that the officer making the arrest enter the residence without the consent of a resident or without a warrant.

History of CCP art. 14.05: Acts 1965, 59th Leg., vol. 2, ch. 722. Amended by Acts 1987, 70th Leg., ch. 532, §1, eff. Aug. 31, 1987.

ANNOTATIONS

Gouldsby v. State, 202 S.W.3d 329, 337 (Tex. App.—Texarkana 2006, pet. ref'd). "Exigent circumstances are those which justify an immediate need to enter a residence without first obtaining a search warrant. A variety of such circumstances may place a police officer in situations in which a warrantless entry is viewed as a reasonable reaction by the officer. Situations creating exigent circumstances usually include factors pointing to some danger to the officer or victims, an increased likelihood of apprehending a suspect, or the possible destruction of evidence. [¶] [T]he determination of whether an officer has probable cause and exigent circumstances is a factual one based on the sum of all the information known to the officer at the time of entry."

Odom v. State, 200 S.W.3d 333, 335 (Tex.App.— Corpus Christi 2006, no pet.). "The three exceptions under which a warrantless search can be justified are (1) the plain view doctrine, (2) consent, and (3) exigent circumstances. *At 336:* To the Fourth Amendment rule ordinarily prohibiting the warrantless entry of a person's house as unreasonable *per se*, one jealously and carefully drawn exception recognizes the validity of searches with the voluntary consent of an individual possessing authority. The exception for consent extends even to entries made with the permission of one whom the police reasonably, but mistakenly, believe to possess such authority. *At 337:* The burden is on the State to prove exigency." (Internal quotes omitted.)

ART. 14.051. ARREST BY PEACE OFFICER FROM OTHER JURISDICTION

(a) A peace officer commissioned and authorized by another state to make arrests for felonies who is in fresh pursuit of a person for the purpose of arresting that person for a felony may continue the pursuit into this state and arrest the person.

(b) In this article, "fresh pursuit" means a pursuit without unreasonable delay by a peace officer of a person the officer reasonably suspects has committed a felony.

History of CCP art. 14.051: Acts 1989, 71st Leg., ch. 997, §2, eff. Aug. 28, 1989.

ART. 14.06. MUST TAKE OFFENDER BEFORE MAGISTRATE

Ⓐ *Subsection (a) below is effective for offenses committed on or after Sept. 1, 2007.*

(a) Except as otherwise provided by this article, in each case enumerated in this Code, the person making the arrest or the person having custody of the person arrested shall take the person arrested or have him taken without unnecessary delay, but not later than 48 hours after the person is arrested, before the magistrate who may have ordered the arrest, before some magistrate of the county where the arrest was made without an order, or, to provide more expeditiously to the person arrested the warnings described by Article 15.17 of this Code, before a magistrate in any other county of this state. The magistrate shall immediately perform the duties described in Article 15.17 of this Code.

Subsection (a) below is effective for offenses in which any element of the offense was committed before Sept. 1, 2007.

(a) Except as provided by Subsection (b), in each case enumerated in this Code, the person making the arrest or the person having custody of the person arrested shall take the person arrested or have him

taken without unnecessary delay, but not later than 48 hours after the person is arrested, before the magistrate who may have ordered the arrest, before some magistrate of the county where the arrest was made without an order, or, to provide more expeditiously to the person arrested the warnings described by Article 15.17 of this Code, before a magistrate in any other county of this state. The magistrate shall immediately perform the duties described in Article 15.17 of this Code.

(b) A peace officer who is charging a person, including a child, with committing an offense that is a Class C misdemeanor, other than an offense under Section 49.02, Penal Code, may, instead of taking the person before a magistrate, issue a citation to the person that contains written notice of the time and place the person must appear before a magistrate, the name and address of the person charged, and the offense charged.

Ⓔ *Subsections (c) & (d) below are effective for offenses committed on or after Sept. 1, 2007.*

(c) If the person resides in the county where the offense occurred, a peace officer who is charging a person with committing an offense that is a Class A or B misdemeanor may, instead of taking the person before a magistrate, issue a citation to the person that contains written notice of the time and place the person must appear before a magistrate of this state as described by Subsection (a), the name and address of the person charged, and the offense charged.

(d) Subsection (c) applies only to a person charged with committing an offense under:

(1) Section 481.121, Health and Safety Code, if the offense is punishable under Subsection (b)(1) or (2) of that section;

(2) Section 28.03, Penal Code, if the offense is punishable under Subsection (b)(2) of that section;

(3) Section 28.08, Penal Code, if the offense is punishable under Subsection (b)(1) of that section;

(4) Section 31.03, Penal Code, if the offense is punishable under Subsection (e)(2)(A) of that section;

(5) Section 31.04, Penal Code, if the offense is punishable under Subsection (e)(2) of that section;

(6) Section 38.114, Penal Code, if the offense is punishable as a Class B misdemeanor; or

(7) Section 521.457, Transportation Code.

History of CCP art. 14.06: Acts 1965, 59th Leg., vol. 2, ch. 722. Amended by Acts 1967, 60th Leg., ch. 659, §10, eff. Aug. 28, 1967; Acts 1987, 70th Leg., ch. 455, §1, eff. Aug. 31, 1987; Acts 1991, 72nd Leg., ch. 84, §1, eff. Sept. 1, 1991; Acts 1993, 73rd Leg., ch. 900, §1.05, eff. Sept. 1, 1994; Acts 1995, 74th Leg., ch. 262, §81, eff. Jan. 1, 1996; Acts 2001, 77th Leg., ch. 906, §3, eff. Jan. 1, 2002; Acts 2005, 79th Leg., ch. 1094, §1, eff. Sept. 1, 2005; Acts 2007, 80th Leg., ch. 320, §1, eff. Sept. 1, 2007.

See also CCP art. 15.07.

ANNOTATIONS

Jones v. State, 944 S.W.2d 642, 649 n.10 (Tex.Crim. App.1996). "[F]ailure to take an arrestee before a magistrate in a timely manner will not invalidate a confession unless there is proof of a causal connection between the delay and the confession. ... Further, even if we held a ... delay unreasonable, the delay will not vitiate an otherwise voluntary confession if the arrestee was properly advised of his Miranda rights."

Corbin v. State, 426 S.W.2d 238, 240 (Tex.Crim. App.1968). "[T]he purpose of taking an accused before a magistrate is for the magistrate to give him the warnings and discharge the duties required by [CCP art.] 15.17.... Such warnings are not prerequisite to the search of the person of the accused."

CHAPTER 15. ARREST UNDER WARRANT

ART. 15.01. WARRANT OF ARREST

A "warrant of arrest" is a written order from a magistrate, directed to a peace officer or some other person specially named, commanding him to take the body of the person accused of an offense, to be dealt with according to law.

History of CCP art. 15.01: Acts 1965, 59th Leg., vol. 2, ch. 722.

ART. 15.02. REQUISITES OF WARRANT

It issues in the name of "The State of Texas," and shall be sufficient, without regard to form, if it have these substantial requisites:

1. It must specify the name of the person whose arrest is ordered, if it be known, if unknown, then some reasonably definite description must be given of him.

2. It must state that the person is accused of some offense against the laws of the State, naming the offense.

3. It must be signed by the magistrate, and his office be named in the body of the warrant, or in connection with his signature.

History of CCP art. 15.02: Acts 1965, 59th Leg., vol. 2, ch. 722.

ANNOTATIONS

Ex parte Medina, 417 S.W.2d 409, 410 (Tex.Crim. App.1967). "'The law with reference to executive warrants does not seem to make any exception to matters required in the general definition of warrants of arrest given in said article. The warrant of arrest is the legal authority by virtue of which the officer takes the person accused of an offense into custody and retains him. If the warrant shows that the person named ... is not accused of an offense, the arrest, detention, and removal from the state would appear to be illegal.'"

Belton v. State, 900 S.W.2d 886, 893 (Tex.App.—El Paso 1995, pet. ref'd). An arrest "warrant is sufficient without regard to form, if it specifies the name of the person whose arrest is ordered, it states that the person is accused of some offense against the laws of the State and names the offense, and is signed by the magistrate and names his office in the body of the warrant. ... Article 15.02 [does not] require that the time of the issuance of the warrant appear on the document."

ART. 15.03. MAGISTRATE MAY ISSUE WARRANT OR SUMMONS

(a) A magistrate may issue a warrant of arrest or a summons:

1. In any case in which he is by law authorized to order verbally the arrest of an offender;

2. When any person shall make oath before the magistrate that another has committed some offense against the laws of the State; and

3. In any case named in this Code where he is specially authorized to issue warrants of arrest.

(b) A summons may be issued in any case where a warrant may be issued, and shall be in the same form as the warrant except that it shall summon the defendant to appear before a magistrate at a stated time and place. The summons shall be served upon a defendant by delivering a copy to him personally, or by leaving it at his dwelling house or usual place of abode with some person of suitable age and discretion then residing therein or by mailing it to the defendant's last known address. If a defendant fails to appear in response to the summons a warrant shall be issued.

History of CCP art. 15.03: Acts 1965, 59th Leg., vol. 2, ch. 722.

ANNOTATIONS

Gonzales v. State, 577 S.W.2d 226, 231 (Tex.Crim. App.1979). Appellant "asserts that one affiant's swearing to the facts in the affidavit is an untruth because the affiant never actually conversed with the informer, but signed the affidavit on the basis of information received from the other affiant. The affidavit is not rendered invalid because the other affiant also swore to the facts, as evidenced by his signature. One signature under oath is sufficient to comply with the requirement that the affidavit be sworn to before the magistrate."

ART. 15.04. COMPLAINT

The affidavit made before the magistrate or district or county attorney is called a "complaint" if it charges the commission of an offense.

History of CCP art. 15.04: Acts 1965, 59th Leg., vol. 2, ch. 722.

ANNOTATIONS

State v. Martin, 833 S.W.2d 129, 132 (Tex.Crim. App.1992). "In order to issue a valid warrant ..., the underlying affidavit must contain, viewed in the totality of the circumstances, information sufficient to justify a neutral and detached magistrate issuing it. [H]earsay-upon-hearsay will support issuance of a warrant 'as long as the underlying circumstances indicate that there is a substantial basis for crediting the hearsay at each level.' *At 133:* [If] the underlying affidavit [is] not patently conclusory, we defer to the judgment of the issuing magistrate."

Peterson v. State, 781 S.W.2d 933, 935 (Tex.Crim. App.1989). "[T]he Legislature precluded a prosecutor from presenting an information 'until affidavit has been made by some credible person charging the defendant with an offense,' and also mandated, 'The affidavit shall be filed with the information.' Such an affidavit is ... a complaint within the meaning of Article 15.04.... 'In other words, a prosecuting attorney is not authorized to institute prosecutions in the county court upon his independent act or of his own volition.' One may not be 'both the accuser and the prosecutor in misdemeanor cases.'"

Rios v. State, 718 S.W.2d 730, 732 (Tex.Crim.App. 1986). A complaint "has at least two discrete functions. One is to supply a basis for a magistrate to issue warrant for arrest pursuant to Article 15.03.... Another is to serve as a charging instrument for trial in municipal court ... and in justice court...."

Porter v. State, 93 S.W.3d 342, 345 (Tex.App.— Houston [14th Dist.] 2002, pet. ref'd). "Appellant ... challenges the validity of the affidavit on the ground that information reflected in it and necessary to establish probable cause was illegally obtained by officers' entry onto appellant's property ... through a closed gate in the fence surrounding it. *At 346:* [P]ushing the [remote-controlled] gate open to approach the front door was reasonably within the scope of what the conditions allowed the officers to do."

Hess v. State, 953 S.W.2d 837, 840 (Tex.App.—Fort Worth 1997, pet. ref'd). "The correction of a defendant's name in a complaint and information vitiates the complaint because the correction is not that which was sworn to by the affiant. [¶] A valid complaint is a prerequisite to a valid information."

ART. 15.05. REQUISITES OF COMPLAINT

The complaint shall be sufficient, without regard to form, if it have these substantial requisites:

1. It must state the name of the accused, if known, and if not known, must give some reasonably definite description of him.

2. It must show that the accused has committed some offense against the laws of the State, either directly or that the affiant has good reason to believe, and does believe, that the accused has committed such offense.

3. It must state the time and place of the commission of the offense, as definitely as can be done by the affiant.

4. It must be signed by the affiant by writing his name or affixing his mark.

History of CCP art. 15.05: Acts 1965, 59th Leg., vol. 2, ch. 722.

ANNOTATIONS

Hess v. State, 953 S.W.2d 837, 840 (Tex.App.—Fort Worth 1997, pet. ref'd). "The rule is well settled that the name of the defendant as stated in the complaint may not be changed by amendment, nor may it be added by amendment if omitted. [¶] The correction of a defendant's name in a complaint and information vitiates the complaint because the correction is not that which was sworn to by the affiant. [¶] A valid complaint is a prerequisite to a valid information."

Brent v. State, 916 S.W.2d 34, 37 (Tex.App.—Houston [1st Dist.] 1995, pet. ref'd). "Article 15.05(4) … does not allow for a verbal oath…. It is clear … that the legislature, by utilizing words like 'signed' and 'writing,' intended an arrest warrant affidavit to carry, not just the oath of the affiant, but specifically the oath of the affiant as represented by his *signature*."

Kindley v. State, 879 S.W.2d 261, 263 (Tex.App.—Houston [14th Dist.] 1994, no pet.). "The particularity in pleading that is required for an indictment or an information is not required for a complaint, and a complaint will not be dismissed due to a mere informality. A complaint is sufficient if it 'meets the substantial requisites' of … art. 15.05."

Young v. State, 776 S.W.2d 673, 677 (Tex.App.—Amarillo 1989, no pet.). "[T]he requirement that an affiant state that he or she 'does believe' that an accused committed an offense is a statutory requirement and its absence vitiates a complaint."

State v. Barron, 760 S.W.2d 763, 764 (Tex.App.—Beaumont 1988, no pet.). "An indictment, information, or complaint is fatally defective if it alleges an offense to have been committed on an impossible date. [¶] Logically, the court [can assume] the offense alleged in the complaint did not occur [on the impossible date],

however, in the case of a charging instrument, where notice to the defendant is so crucial, the court [will] not make this assumption."

ART. 15.051. REQUIRING POLYGRAPH EXAMINATION OF COMPLAINANT PROHIBITED

Ⓐ *Subsection (a) below is effective for offenses committed on or after Sept. 1, 2007.*

(a) A peace officer or an attorney representing the state may not require a polygraph examination of a person who charges or seeks to charge in a complaint the commission of an offense under Section 21.02, 21.11, 22.011, 22.021, or 25.02, Penal Code.

Subsection (a) below is effective for offenses in which any element of the offense was committed before Sept. 1, 2007.

(a) A peace officer or an attorney representing the state may not require a polygraph examination of a person who charges or seeks to charge in a complaint the commission of an offense under Section 21.11, 22.011, 22.021, or 25.02, Penal Code.

(b) If a peace officer or an attorney representing the state requests a polygraph examination of a person who charges or seeks to charge in a complaint the commission of an offense listed in Subsection (a), the officer or attorney must inform the complainant that the examination is not required and that a complaint may not be dismissed solely:

(1) because a complainant did not take a polygraph examination; or

(2) on the basis of the results of a polygraph examination taken by the complainant.

(c) A peace officer or an attorney representing the state may not take a polygraph examination of a person who charges or seeks to charge the commission of an offense listed in Subsection (a) unless the officer or attorney provides the information in Subsection (b) to the person and the person signs a statement indicating the person understands the information.

(d) A complaint may not be dismissed solely:

(1) because a complainant did not take a polygraph examination; or

(2) on the basis of the results of a polygraph examination taken by the complainant.

History of CCP art. 15.051: Acts 1995, 74th Leg., ch. 24, §1, eff. Sept. 1, 1995; Acts 1997, 75th Leg., ch. 608, §1, eff. Sept. 1, 1997. Amended by Acts 2007, 80th Leg., ch. 593, §3.07, eff. Sept. 1, 2007.

ART. 15.06. WARRANT EXTENDS TO EVERY PART OF THE STATE

A warrant of arrest, issued by any county or district clerk, or by any magistrate (except mayors of an incorporated city or town), shall extend to any part of the State; and any peace officer to whom said warrant is directed, or into whose hands the same has been transferred, shall be authorized to execute the same in any county in this State.

History of CCP art. 15.06: Acts 1965, 59th Leg., vol. 2, ch. 722. Amended by Acts 1985, 69th Leg., ch. 666, §1, eff. June 14, 1985.

ART. 15.07. WARRANT ISSUED BY OTHER MAGISTRATE

When a warrant of arrest is issued by any mayor of an incorporated city or town, it cannot be executed in another county than the one in which it issues, except:

1. It be endorsed by a judge of a court of record, in which case it may be executed anywhere in the State; or

2. If it be endorsed by any magistrate in the county in which the accused is found, it may be executed in such county. The endorsement may be: "Let this warrant be executed in the county of _____." Or, if the endorsement is made by a judge of a court of record, then the endorsement may be: "Let this warrant be executed in any county of the State of Texas." Any other words of the same meaning will be sufficient. The endorsement shall be dated, and signed officially by the magistrate making it.

History of CCP art. 15.07: Acts 1965, 59th Leg., vol. 2, ch. 722. Amended by Acts 1985, 69th Leg., ch. 666, §2, eff. June 14, 1985.

See also CCP art. 14.06.

ART. 15.08. WARRANT MAY BE TELEGRAPHED

A warrant of arrest may be forwarded by telegraph from any telegraph office to another in this State. If issued by any magistrate named in Article 15.06, the peace officer receiving the same shall execute it without delay. If it be issued by any other magistrate than is named in Article 15.06, the peace officer receiving the same shall proceed with it to the nearest magistrate of his county, who shall endorse thereon, in substance, these words:

"Let this warrant be executed in the county of _____," which endorsement shall be dated and signed officially by the magistrate making the same.

History of CCP art. 15.08: Acts 1965, 59th Leg., vol. 2, ch. 722.

ART. 15.09. COMPLAINT BY TELEGRAPH

A complaint in accordance with Article 15.05, may be telegraphed, as provided in the preceding Article, to any magistrate in the State; and the magistrate who receives the same shall forthwith issue a warrant for the arrest of the accused; and the accused, when arrested, shall be dealt with as provided in this Chapter in similar cases.

History of CCP art. 15.09: Acts 1965, 59th Leg., vol. 2, ch. 722.

ART. 15.10. COPY TO BE DEPOSITED

A certified copy of the original warrant or complaint, certified to by the magistrate issuing or taking the same, shall be deposited with the manager of the telegraph office from which the same is to be forwarded, taking precedence over other business, to the place of its destination or to the telegraph office nearest thereto, precisely as it is written, including the certificate of the seal attached.

History of CCP art. 15.10: Acts 1965, 59th Leg., vol. 2, ch. 722.

ART. 15.11. DUTY OF TELEGRAPH MANAGER

When a warrant or complaint is received at a telegraph office for delivery, it shall be delivered to the party to whom it is addressed as soon as practicable, written on the proper blanks of the telegraph company and certified to by the manager of the telegraph office as being a true and correct copy of the warrant or complaint received at his office.

History of CCP art. 15.11: Acts 1965, 59th Leg., vol. 2, ch. 722.

ART. 15.12. WARRANT OR COMPLAINT MUST BE UNDER SEAL

No manager of a telegraph office shall receive and forward a warrant or complaint unless the same shall be certified to under the seal of a court of record or by a justice of the peace, with the certificate under seal of the district or county clerk of his county that he is a legally qualified justice of the peace of such county; nor shall it be lawful for any magistrate to endorse a warrant received by telegraph, or issue a warrant upon a complaint received by telegraph, unless all the requirements of the law in relation thereto have been fully complied with.

History of CCP art. 15.12: Acts 1965, 59th Leg., vol. 2, ch. 722.

ART. 15.13. TELEGRAM PREPAID

Whoever presents a warrant or complaint to the manager of a telegraph office to be forwarded by telegraph, shall pay for the same in advance, unless, by the rules of the company, it may be sent collect.

History of CCP art. 15.13: Acts 1965, 59th Leg., vol. 2, ch. 722.

ART. 15.14. ARREST AFTER DISMISSAL BECAUSE OF DELAY

If a prosecution of a defendant is dismissed under Article 32.01, the defendant may be rearrested for the same criminal conduct alleged in the dismissed prosecution only upon presentation of indictment or information for the offense and the issuance of a capias subsequent to the indictment or information.

History of CCP art. 15.14: Acts 1997, 75th Leg., ch. 289, §3, eff. May 26, 1997.

History of Former CCP art. 15.14: Repealed by Acts 1991, 72nd Leg., ch. 446, §2, eff. June 11, 1991.

See also CCP art. 32.01.

ART. 15.15. REPEALED

Repealed by Acts 1991, 72nd Leg., ch. 446, §2, eff. June 11, 1991.

ART. 15.16. HOW WARRANT IS EXECUTED

(a) The officer or person executing a warrant of arrest shall without unnecessary delay take the person or have him taken before the magistrate who issued the warrant or before the magistrate named in the warrant, if the magistrate is in the same county where the person is arrested. If the issuing or named magistrate is in another county, the person arrested shall without unnecessary delay be taken before some magistrate in the county in which he was arrested.

(b) Notwithstanding Subsection (a), to provide more expeditiously to the person arrested the warnings described by Article 15.17, the officer or person executing the arrest warrant may as permitted by that article take the person arrested before a magistrate in a county other than the county of arrest.

History of CCP art. 15.16: Acts 1965, 59th Leg., vol. 2, ch. 722. Amended by Acts 1967, 60th Leg., ch. 659, §11, eff. Aug. 28, 1967; Acts 2005, 79th Leg., ch. 1094, §2, eff. Sept. 1, 2005.

ANNOTATIONS

Ex parte Garcia, 547 S.W.2d 271, 274 (Tex.Crim. App.1977). "The peace officer has some discretion, but the primary and ultimate decision to restrict the citizen's liberty must be made by a neutral and detached magistrate. This fact is fundamental to our system of criminal justice. Whether the arrest is made with or without warrant, one of the arresting officer's first duties after arrest is to have the arrested person taken before a magistrate, and the magistrate must then inform the accused of his right to an examining trial."

ART. 15.17. DUTIES OF ARRESTING OFFICER & MAGISTRATE

(a) In each case enumerated in this Code, the person making the arrest or the person having custody of the person arrested shall without unnecessary delay, but not later than 48 hours after the person is arrested, take the person arrested or have him taken before some magistrate of the county where the accused was arrested or, to provide more expeditiously to the person arrested the warnings described by this article, before a magistrate in any other county of this state. The arrested person may be taken before the magistrate in person or the image of the arrested person may be presented to the magistrate by means of an electronic broadcast system. The magistrate shall inform in clear language the person arrested, either in person or through the electronic broadcast system, of the accusation against him and of any affidavit filed therewith, of his right to retain counsel, of his right to remain silent, of his right to have an attorney present during any interview with peace officers or attorneys representing the state, of his right to terminate the interview at any time, and of his right to have an examining trial. The magistrate shall also inform the person arrested of the person's right to request the appointment of counsel if the person cannot afford counsel. The magistrate shall inform the person arrested of the procedures for requesting appointment of counsel. If the person does not speak and understand the English language or is deaf, the magistrate shall inform the person in a manner consistent with Articles 38.30 and 38.31, as appropriate. The magistrate shall ensure that reasonable assistance in completing the necessary forms for requesting appointment of counsel is provided to the person at the same time. If the person arrested is indigent and requests appointment of counsel and if the magistrate is authorized under Article 26.04 to appoint counsel for indigent defendants in the county, the magistrate shall appoint counsel in accordance with Article 1.051. If the magistrate is not authorized to appoint counsel, the magistrate shall without unnecessary delay, but not later than 24 hours after the person arrested requests appointment of counsel, transmit, or cause to be transmitted to the court or to the courts' designee authorized under Article 26.04 to appoint counsel in the county, the forms requesting the appointment of counsel. The magistrate shall also inform the person arrested that he is not required to make a statement and that any statement made by him may be used against him. The magistrate shall allow the person arrested reasonable time and opportunity to consult counsel and shall, after determining whether the person is currently on bail for a separate criminal offense, admit the person arrested to bail if allowed by law. A recording of the communication between the arrested person and the magistrate shall be made. The recording shall be preserved until the earlier of the following dates: (1) the date on which the pretrial hearing ends; or (2) the 91st day after the date on which the recording is made if the person is charged with a misdemeanor or the 120th day after the date on which the recording is made if the person is charged with a felony. The counsel for the defendant may obtain a copy of the recording on payment of a reasonable amount to cover costs of reproduction. For purposes of this subsection, "electronic broadcast system" means a two-way electronic communication of image and sound between the arrested person and the magistrate and includes secure Internet videoconferencing.

(b) After an accused charged with a misdemeanor punishable by fine only is taken before a magistrate under Subsection (a) of this article and the magistrate has identified the accused with certainty, the magistrate may release the accused without bond and order the accused to appear at a later date for arraignment in the county court or statutory county court. The order must state in writing the time, date, and place of the arraignment, and the magistrate must sign the order. The accused shall receive a copy of the order on release. If an accused fails to appear as required by the order, the judge of the court in which the accused is required to appear shall issue a warrant for the arrest of the accused. If the accused is arrested and brought before the judge, the judge may admit the accused to bail, and in admitting the accused to bail, the judge should set as the amount of bail an amount double that generally set for the offense for which the accused was arrested. This subsection does not apply to an accused who has previously been convicted of a felony or a misdemeanor other than a misdemeanor punishable by fine only.

(c) When a deaf accused is taken before a magistrate under this article or Article 14.06 of this Code, an interpreter appointed by the magistrate qualified and sworn as provided in Article 38.31 of this Code shall interpret the warning required by those articles in a language that the accused can understand, including but not limited to sign language.

(d) If a magistrate determines that a person brought before the magistrate after an arrest authorized by Article 14.051 of this code was arrested unlawfully, the magistrate shall release the person from custody. If the magistrate determines that the arrest was lawful, the person arrested is considered a fugitive from justice for the purposes of Article 51.13 of this code, and the disposition of the person is controlled by that article.

(e) In each case in which a person arrested is taken before a magistrate as required by Subsection (a), a record shall be made of:

(1) the magistrate informing the person of the person's right to request appointment of counsel;

(2) the magistrate asking the person whether the person wants to request appointment of counsel; and

(3) whether the person requested appointment of counsel.

(f) A record required under Subsection (e) may consist of written forms, electronic recordings, or other documentation as authorized by procedures adopted in the county under Article 26.04(a).

E *Subsection (g) below is effective for offenses committed on or after Sept. 1, 2007.*

(g) If a person charged with an offense punishable as a misdemeanor appears before a magistrate in compliance with a citation issued under Article 14.06(b) or (c), the magistrate shall perform the duties imposed by this article in the same manner as if the person had been arrested and brought before the magistrate by a peace officer. After the magistrate performs the duties imposed by this article, the magistrate except for good cause shown may release the person on personal bond. If a person who was issued a citation under Article 14.06(c) fails to appear as required by that citation, the magistrate before which the person is required to appear shall issue a warrant for the arrest of the accused.

History of CCP art. 15.17: Acts 1965, 59th Leg., vol. 2, ch. 722. Amended by Acts 1967, 60th Leg., ch. 659, §12, eff. Aug. 28, 1967; Acts 1979, 66th Leg., ch. 186, §3, eff. May 15, 1979; Acts 1987, 70th Leg., ch. 455, §2, eff. Aug. 31, 1987; Acts 1989, 71st Leg., ch. 467, §1 (eff. Aug. 28, 1989), ch. 977, §1 (eff. Aug. 28,

1989), ch. 997, §3 (eff. Aug. 28, 1989); Acts 1991, 72nd Leg., ch. 16, §19.01(2), eff. Aug. 26, 1991; Acts 2001, 77th Leg., ch. 906, §4 (eff. Jan. 1, 2002), ch. 1281, §1 (eff. Sept. 1, 2001); Acts 2005, 79th Leg., ch. 1094, §3, eff. Sept. 1, 2005; Acts 2007, 80th Leg., ch. 320, §2, eff. Sept. 1, 2007.

ANNOTATIONS

Maestas v. State, 987 S.W.2d 59, 62 (Tex.Crim.App. 1999). "[T]he following factors [are] important to [the] analysis [of whether police scrupulously honored a suspect's right to cut off questioning]: (1) whether the suspect was informed of his right to remain silent prior to the initial questioning; (2) whether the suspect was informed of his right to remain silent prior to the subsequent questioning; (3) the length of time between initial questioning and subsequent questioning; (4) whether the subsequent questioning focused on a different crime; and (5) whether police honored the suspect's initial invocation of the right to remain silent. *At 63:* The third ... factor was meant to guard against abuses in subsequent questioning. *At 64:* [W]e also consider other facts and circumstances in determining whether Appellant's right to remain silent was 'scrupulously honored.' Appellant was not coerced, threatened, or promised anything for talking with officers. Officers testified Appellant had access to necessities such as food, water, and restroom facilities. Finally, although officers initiated the questioning that resulted in Appellant's statement, ongoing investigations provided them with additional information which tended to show that Appellant was present at the scene of the murder. These additional considerations tend to support the conclusion that police 'scrupulously honored' Appellant's right to remain silent."

Jones v. State, 944 S.W.2d 642, 649 n.10 (Tex.Crim. App.1996). "[E]ven if we held a ... delay unreasonable, the delay will not vitiate an otherwise voluntary confession if the arrestee was properly advised of his *Miranda* rights."

Ontiveros v. State, 890 S.W.2d 919, 928-29 (Tex. App.—El Paso 1994, no pet.). "The defendant has the burden to show the delay was unreasonable, and to show the causal connection between the confession and the failure to take him before a magistrate without unreasonable delay. [¶] What constitutes a reasonable time depends upon the facts of each case and varies with the circumstances of that particular case, but the Texas courts have approved detentions spanning a wide range of durations."

ART. 15.18. ARREST FOR OUT-OF-COUNTY OFFENSE

(a) A person arrested under a warrant issued in a county other than the one in which the person is arrested shall be taken before a magistrate of the county where the arrest takes place or, to provide more expeditiously to the arrested person the warnings described by Article 15.17, before a magistrate in any other county of this state, including the county where the warrant was issued. The magistrate shall:

(1) take bail, if allowed by law, and, if without jurisdiction, immediately transmit the bond taken to the court having jurisdiction of the offense; or

(2) in the case of a person arrested under warrant for an offense punishable by fine only, accept a written plea of guilty or nolo contendere, set a fine, determine costs, accept payment of the fine and costs, give credit for time served, determine indigency, or, on satisfaction of the judgment, discharge the defendant, as the case may indicate.

(b) Before the 11th business day after the date a magistrate accepts a written plea of guilty or nolo contendere in a case under Subsection (a)(2), the magistrate shall, if without jurisdiction, transmit to the court having jurisdiction of the offense:

(1) the written plea;

(2) any orders entered in the case; and

(3) any fine or costs collected in the case.

(c) The arrested person may be taken before a magistrate by means of an electronic broadcast system as provided by and subject to the requirements of Article 15.17.

E *Subsection (d) below is effective for fees imposed for a warrant or capias issued for offenses committed on or after Sept. 1, 2007.*

(d) This article does not apply to an arrest made pursuant to a capias pro fine issued under Chapter 43 or Article 45.045.

History of CCP art. 15.18: Acts 1965, 59th Leg., vol. 2, ch. 722. Amended by Acts 2001, 77th Leg., ch. 145, §2, eff. Sept. 1, 2001; Acts 2005, 79th Leg., ch. 1094, §4, eff. Sept. 1, 2005; Acts 2007, 80th Leg., ch. 1263, §1, eff. Sept. 1, 2007.

A ## ART. 15.19. NOTICE OF ARREST

A **(a)** If the arrested person fails or refuses to give bail, as provided in Article 15.18, the arrested person shall be committed to the jail of the county where the person was arrested; and the magistrate committing the arrested person shall immediately provide notice to the sheriff of the county in which the offense is alleged to have been committed regarding:

(1) the arrest and commitment, which notice may be given by telegraph, mail, or other written means; and

E *Subsection (2) below is effective for persons arrested under a warrant on or after June 15, 2007.*

(2) whether the person was also arrested under a warrant issued under Section 508.251, Government Code.

(b) If a person is arrested and taken before a magistrate in a county other than the county in which the arrest is made and if the person is remanded to custody, the person may be confined in a jail in the county in which the magistrate serves for a period of not more than 72 hours after the arrest before being transferred to the county jail of the county in which the arrest occurred.

History of CCP art. 15.19: Acts 1965, 59th Leg., vol. 2, ch. 722. Amended by Acts 1987, 70th Leg., 2nd C.S., ch. 40, §1, eff. Oct. 20, 1987; Acts 2005, 79th Leg., ch. 1094, §5, eff. Sept. 1, 2005; Acts 2007, 80th Leg., ch. 1308, §1, eff. June 15, 2007.

ART. 15.20. DUTY OF SHERIFF RECEIVING NOTICE

A **(a)** Subject to Subsection (b), the sheriff receiving the notice of arrest and commitment under Article 15.19 shall forthwith go or send for the arrested person and have the arrested person brought before the proper court or magistrate.

E *Subsection (b) below is effective for persons arrested under a warrant on or after June 15, 2007.*

(b) A sheriff who receives notice under Article 15.19(a)(2) of a warrant issued under Section 508.251, Government Code, shall have the arrested person brought before the proper magistrate or court before the 11th day after the date the person is committed to the jail of the county in which the person was arrested.

History of CCP art. 15.20: Acts 1965, 59th Leg., vol. 2, ch. 722. Amended by Acts 2007, 80th Leg., ch. 1308, §2, eff. June 15, 2007.

A ART. 15.21. PRISONER DISCHARGED IF NOT TIMELY DEMANDED

If the proper office of the county where the offense is alleged to have been committed does not demand the arrested person and take charge of the arrested person before the 11th day after the date the person is committed to the jail of the county in which the person is arrested, the arrested person shall be discharged from custody.

History of CCP art. 15.21: Acts 1965, 59th Leg., vol. 2, ch. 722; Amended by Acts 2007, 80th Leg., ch. 1308, §3, eff. June 15, 2007.

ART. 15.22. WHEN A PERSON IS ARRESTED

A person is arrested when he has been actually placed under restraint or taken into custody by an officer or person executing a warrant of arrest, or by an officer or person arresting without a warrant.

History of CCP art. 15.22: Acts 1965, 59th Leg., vol. 2, ch. 722.

ANNOTATIONS

Rhodes v. State, 945 S.W.2d 115, 117 (Tex.Crim. App.1997). "At the suppression hearing, [arresting officer] testified he was not arresting appellant when he handcuffed him. The officer's testimony is a factor to be considered, along with the other facts and circumstances of the detention, in determining whether an arrest has taken place. [¶] [Arresting officer] also testified he placed handcuffs on appellant primarily out of concern for his safety, based on the circumstances: it was dark; the area was a high-crime location; the officers had just concluded a car chase which was initiated due to commission of a traffic violation and during which a bag was dropped from the car; and, his partner was chasing the driver, leaving [arresting officer] alone with the suspect. *At 118:* The court of appeals' conclusion that [arresting officer] made a temporary investigative detention of appellant under ***Terry*** [*v. Ohio*] that was reasonable and justified under the circumstances surrounding the detention is soundly based on applicable case law."

Washburn v. State, 235 S.W.3d 346, 350 (Tex. App.—Texarkana 2007, no pet.). "'A person is in 'custody' only if, under the circumstances, a reasonable person would believe that his freedom of movement was restrained to the degree associated with a formal arrest.' At least four general situations may constitute custody: (1) the suspect is physically deprived of his or her freedom of action in any significant way, (2) a law enforcement officer tells the suspect that he or she cannot leave, (3) law enforcement officers create a situation that would lead a reasonable person to believe that his or her freedom of movement has been significantly restricted, and (4) there is probable cause to arrest and law enforcement officers do not tell the suspect that he or she is free to leave." *See also **Nottingham v. State**,* 908 S.W.3d 585, 588 (Tex.App.—Austin 1995, no pet.).

McCraw v. State, 117 S.W.3d 47, 52 (Tex.App.—Fort Worth 2003, pet. ref'd). "Although the term ['arrest'] implies an element of detention, custody, or control of the accused, it is not the actual, physical taking into custody that will constitute an arrest. A suspect's submission to an officer's show of authority will also constitute an arrest."

Zone v. State, 84 S.W.3d 733, 740 (Tex.App.—Houston [1st Dist.] 2002), *aff'd*, 118 S.W.3d 776 (Tex. Crim.App.2003). "'[T]he article 15.22 arrest definition is inadequate, *by itself*, to be used as the standard for distinguishing arrests from investigative detentions.' … First, the article 15.22 arrest definition was enacted prior to the emergence of the concept of a temporary investigative detention. Second, [we consider] the officer's opinion and 'other facts and circumstances of the detention, in determining whether an arrest has taken place.'" *See also Francis v. State*, 896 S.W.2d 406, 410 (Tex.App.—Houston [1st Dist.] 1995), *pet. ref'd*, 922 S.W.2d 176 (Tex.Crim.App.1996).

ART. 15.23. TIME OF ARREST

An arrest may be made on any day or at any time of the day or night.

History of CCP art. 15.23: Acts 1965, 59th Leg., vol. 2, ch. 722.

ART. 15.24. WHAT FORCE MAY BE USED

In making an arrest, all reasonable means are permitted to be used to effect it. No greater force, however, shall be resorted to than is necessary to secure the arrest and detention of the accused.

History of CCP art. 15.24: Acts 1965, 59th Leg., vol. 2, ch. 722.

ART. 15.25. MAY BREAK DOOR

In case of felony, the officer may break down the door of any house for the purpose of making an arrest, if he be refused admittance after giving notice of his authority and purpose.

History of CCP art. 15.25: Acts 1965, 59th Leg., vol. 2, ch. 722.

ANNOTATIONS

Reno v. State, 882 S.W.2d 106, 109 (Tex.App.—Fort Worth 1994, pet. ref'd). "[A] violation of the notice of authority and purpose provision of §15.25 is not a basis to suppress evidence."

ART. 15.26. AUTHORITY TO ARREST MUST BE MADE KNOWN

In executing a warrant of arrest, it shall always be made known to the accused under what authority the arrest is made. The warrant shall be executed by the arrest of the defendant. The officer need not have the warrant in his possession at the time of the arrest, provided the warrant was issued under the provisions of this Code, but upon request he shall show the warrant to the defendant as soon as possible. If the officer does not have the warrant in his possession at the time of arrest he shall then inform the defendant of the offense charged and of the fact that a warrant has been issued. The arrest warrant, and any affidavit presented to the magistrate in support of the issuance of the warrant, is public information, and beginning immediately when the warrant is executed the magistrate's clerk shall make a copy of the warrant and the affidavit available for public inspection in the clerk's office during normal business hours. A person may request the clerk to provide copies of the warrant and affidavit on payment of the cost of providing the copies.

History of CCP art. 15.26: Acts 1965, 59th Leg., vol. 2, ch. 722. Amended by Acts 1967, 60th Leg., ch. 659, §13, eff. Aug. 28, 1967; Acts 2003, 78th Leg., ch. 390, §1, eff. Sept. 1, 2003.

ANNOTATIONS

Bradley v. State, 478 S.W.2d 527, 530 (Tex.Crim. App.1972). "The arresting officers, knowing that an arrest warrant had been issued, did not need to have the arrest warrant in their possession when they made the arrest."

Vasquez v. State, 682 S.W.2d 407, 414 (Tex.App.—Houston [1st Dist.] 1984, no pet.). "[W]hen an accused objects to admission of evidence on the ground it is tainted by a warrantless arrest, and the State relies on an arrest warrant, in the absence of waiver, error results unless the arrest warrant is exhibited to the trial judge for a ruling."

ART. 15.27. NOTIFICATION TO SCHOOLS REQUIRED

(a) A law enforcement agency that arrests any person or refers a child to the office or official designated by the juvenile board who the agency believes is enrolled as a student in a public primary or secondary school, for an offense listed in Subsection (h), shall attempt to ascertain whether the person is so enrolled. If the law enforcement agency ascertains that the individual is enrolled as a student in a public primary or secondary school, the agency shall orally notify the superintendent or a person designated by the superintendent in the school district in which the student is enrolled of that arrest or referral within 24 hours after the arrest or referral is made, or on the next school day. If the law enforcement agency cannot ascertain whether the individual is enrolled as a student, the agency shall orally notify the superintendent or a person designated by the superintendent in the school district in which the student is believed to be enrolled of that arrest or detention within 24 hours after the arrest or detention, or on the next school day. If the individual is a student, the superintendent shall promptly notify all instructional and support personnel who have responsibility for supervision of the student. All personnel shall keep the information received in this subsection confidential. The State Board for Educator Certification may revoke or suspend the certification of personnel who intentionally violate this subsection. Within seven days after the date the oral notice is given, the law enforcement agency shall mail written notification, marked "PERSONAL and CONFIDENTIAL" on the mailing envelope, to the superintendent or the person designated by the superintendent. Both the oral and written notice shall contain sufficient details of the arrest or referral and the acts allegedly committed by the student to enable the superintendent or the superintendent's designee to determine whether there is a reasonable belief that the student has engaged in conduct defined as a felony offense by the Penal Code. The information contained in the notice may be considered by the superintendent or the superintendent's designee in making such a determination.

(a-1) The superintendent or a person designated by the superintendent in the school district may send to a school district employee having direct supervisory responsibility over the student the information contained in the confidential notice under Subsection (a) if the superintendent or the person designated by the superintendent determines that the employee needs the information for educational purposes or for the protection of the person informed or others.

(b) On conviction, deferred prosecution, or deferred adjudication or an adjudication of delinquent conduct of an individual enrolled as a student in a public primary or secondary school, for an offense or for any conduct listed in Subsection (h) of this article, the office of the prosecuting attorney acting in the case shall orally notify the superintendent or a person designated by the superintendent in the school district in which the student is enrolled of the conviction or adjudication and whether the student is required to register as a sex offender under Chapter 62. Oral notification must be given within 24 hours of the time of the order or on the next school day. The superintendent shall, within 24 hours of receiving notification from the office of the prosecuting attorney, notify all instructional and support personnel who have regular contact with the student. Within seven days after the date the oral notice is given, the office of the prosecuting attorney shall mail written notice, which must contain a statement of the offense of which the individual is convicted or on which the adjudication, deferred adjudication, or deferred prosecution is grounded and a statement of whether the student is required to register as a sex offender under Chapter 62.

(c) A parole, probation, or community supervision office, including a community supervision and corrections department, a juvenile probation department, the pardons and paroles division of the Texas Department of Criminal Justice, and the Texas Youth Commission, having jurisdiction over a student described by Subsection (a), (b), or (e) who transfers from a school or is subsequently removed from a school and later returned to a school or school district other than the one the student was enrolled in when the arrest, referral to a juvenile court, conviction, or adjudication occurred shall within 24 hours of learning of the student's transfer or reenrollment notify the superintendent or a person designated by the superintendent of the school district to which the student transfers or is returned or, in the case of a private school, the principal or a school employee designated by the principal of the school to which the student transfers or is returned of the arrest or referral in a manner similar to that provided for by Subsection (a) or (e)(1), or of the conviction or delinquent adjudication in a manner similar to that provided for by Subsection (b) or (e)(2). The superintendent of the school district to which the student transfers or is returned or, in the case of a private school, the principal of the school to which the student transfers or is returned shall, within 24 hours of receiving notification under this subsection, notify all instructional and support personnel who have regular contact with the student.

(d) Repealed by Acts 2007, 80th Leg., ch. 1240, §5, eff. June 15, 2007; Acts 2007, 80th Leg., ch. 1291, §8, eff. Sept. 1, 2007.

(e)(1) A law enforcement agency that arrests, or refers to a juvenile court under Chapter 52, Family Code, an individual who the law enforcement agency knows or believes is enrolled as a student in a private primary or secondary school shall make the oral and written notifications described by Subsection (a) to the principal or a school employee designated by the principal of the school in which the student is enrolled.

(2) On conviction, deferred prosecution, or deferred adjudication or an adjudication of delinquent conduct of an individual enrolled as a student in a private primary or secondary school, the office of prosecuting attorney shall make the oral and written notifications described by Subsection (b) of this article to the principal or a school employee designated by the principal of the school in which the student is enrolled.

(3) The principal of a private school in which the student is enrolled or a school employee designated by the principal may send to a school employee having direct supervisory responsibility over the student the information contained in the confidential notice, for the same purposes as described by Subsection (d) of this article.

(f) A person who receives information under this article may not disclose the information except as specifically authorized by this article. A person who intentionally violates this article commits an offense. An offense under this subsection is a Class C misdemeanor.

(g) The office of the prosecuting attorney or the office or official designated by the juvenile board shall, within two working days, notify the school district that removed a student to a disciplinary alternative education program under Section 37.006, Education Code, if:

(1) prosecution of the student's case was refused for lack of prosecutorial merit or insufficient evidence and no formal proceedings, deferred adjudication, or deferred prosecution will be initiated; or

(2) the court or jury found the student not guilty or made a finding the child did not engage in delinquent conduct or conduct indicating a need for supervision and the case was dismissed with prejudice.

(h) This article applies to any felony offense and the following misdemeanors:

(1) an offense under Section 20.02, 21.08, 22.01, 22.05, 22.07, or 71.02, Penal Code;

(2) the unlawful use, sale, or possession of a controlled substance, drug paraphernalia, or marihuana, as defined by Chapter 481, Health and Safety Code; or

(3) the unlawful possession of any of the weapons or devices listed in Sections 46.01(1)-(14) or (16), Penal Code, or a weapon listed as a prohibited weapon under Section 46.05, Penal Code.

(i) A person may substitute electronic notification for oral notification where oral notification is required by this article. If electronic notification is substituted for oral notification, any written notification required by this article is not required.

E (j) The notification provisions of this section concerning a person who is required to register as a sex offender under Chapter 62 do not lessen the requirement of a person to provide any additional notification prescribed by that chapter.

History of CCP art. 15.27: Acts 1993, 73rd Leg., ch. 461, §1, eff. Sept. 1, 1993. Amended by Acts 1995, 74th Leg., ch. 76, §14.18 (eff. Sept. 1, 1995), ch. 626, §1 (eff. Aug. 28, 1995); Acts 1997, 75th Leg., ch. 1233, §1 (eff. on beginning of 1997-1998 school year), ch. 1015, §§12-14 (eff. on beginning of 1997-1998 school year), ch. 165, §12.02 (eff. Sept. 1, 1997); Acts 2001, 77th Leg., ch. 1297, §§48, 49, eff. Sept. 1, 2001; Acts 2003, 78th Leg., ch. 1055, §§25-27, eff. June 20, 2003; Acts 2005, 79th Leg., ch. 949, §31, eff. Sept. 1, 2005; Acts 2007, 80th Leg., ch. 492, §1 (eff. June 16, 2007), ch. 1240, §§4, 5 (eff. June 15, 2007), ch. 1291, §§1, 8 (eff. Sept. 1, 2007).

CHAPTER 16. THE COMMITMENT OR DISCHARGE OF THE ACCUSED

ART. 16.01. EXAMINING TRIAL

When the accused has been brought before a magistrate for an examining trial that officer shall proceed to examine into the truth of the accusation made, allowing the accused, however, sufficient time to procure counsel. In a proper case, the magistrate may appoint counsel to represent an accused in such examining trial only, to be compensated as otherwise provided in this Code. The accused in any felony case shall have the right to an examining trial before indictment in the county having jurisdiction of the offense, whether he be in custody or on bail, at which time the magistrate at the hearing shall determine the amount or sufficiency of bail, if a bailable case. If the accused has been transferred for criminal prosecution after a hearing under Section 54.02, Family Code, the accused may be granted an examining trial at the discretion of the court.

History of CCP art. 16.01: Acts 1965, 59th Leg., vol. 2, ch. 722. Amended by Acts 1987, 70th Leg., ch. 140, §4, eff. Sept. 1, 1987.

ANNOTATIONS

Green v. State, 872 S.W.2d 717, 721 (Tex.Crim.App. 1994). "[A]n examining trial … serves as an adversarial proceeding designed to inquire into the probable cause of the State to justify detention of an accused pending formal prosecution, and state law permits the examining magistrate to appoint counsel for the indigent accused. [A]n examining trial in large measure affords an accused the opportunity to discover the State's case against him. Given its adversarial character, and the potential it presents for the preparation of a trial defense, an examining trial is arguably a critical stage for purposes of Sixth Amendment analysis."

State ex rel. Holmes v. Salinas, 784 S.W.2d 421, 427 (Tex.Crim.App.1990). It is not "the law in this state that an adult accused is entitled to an examining trial before the case may be presented to a grand jury. Due process considerations are not implicated since the primary purpose for the examining trial, a determination of probable cause, is at least as timely accomplished by presenting evidence directly to the grand jury."

ART. 16.02. EXAMINATION POSTPONED

The magistrate may at the request of either party postpone the examination to procure testimony; but the accused shall in the meanwhile be detained in custody unless he give bail to be present from day to day before the magistrate until the examination is concluded, which he may do in all cases except murder and treason.

History of CCP art. 16.02: Acts 1965, 59th Leg., vol. 2, ch. 722.

ART. 16.03. WARNING TO ACCUSED

Before the examination of the witnesses, the magistrate shall inform the accused that it is his right to make a statement relative to the accusation brought against him, but at the same time shall also inform him that he cannot be compelled to make any statement whatever, and that if he does make such statement, it may be used in evidence against him.

History of CCP art. 16.03: Acts 1965, 59th Leg., vol. 2, ch. 722.

ART. 16.04. VOLUNTARY STATEMENT

If the accused desires to make a voluntary statement, he may do so before the examination of any witness, but not afterward. His statement shall be reduced to writing by or under the direction of the magistrate, or by the accused or his counsel, and shall be signed by the accused by affixing his name or mark, but shall not be sworn to by him. The magistrate shall attest by his own certificate and signature to the execution and signing of the statement.

History of CCP art. 16.04: Acts 1965, 59th Leg., vol. 2, ch. 722.

ART. 16.05. REPEALED

Repealed by the Texas Court of Criminal Appeals' adoption of the Texas Rules of Criminal Evidence on Dec. 18, 1985, eff. Sept. 1, 1986. 701 S.W.2d xxix, lxvi-lxvii.

ART. 16.06. COUNSEL MAY EXAMINE WITNESS

The counsel for the State, and the accused or his counsel may question the witnesses on direct or cross examination. If no counsel appears for the State the magistrate may examine the witnesses.

History of CCP art. 16.06: Acts 1965, 59th Leg., vol. 2, ch. 722.

ART. 16.07. SAME RULES OF EVIDENCE AS ON FINAL TRIAL

The same rules of evidence shall apply to and govern a trial before an examining court that apply to and govern a final trial.

History of CCP art. 16.07: Acts 1965, 59th Leg., vol. 2, ch. 722.

ART. 16.08. PRESENCE OF THE ACCUSED

The examination of each witness shall be in the presence of the accused.

History of CCP art. 16.08: Acts 1965, 59th Leg., vol. 2, ch. 722.

ART. 16.09. TESTIMONY REDUCED TO WRITING

The testimony of each witness shall be reduced to writing by or under the direction of the magistrate, and shall then be read over to the witness, or he may read it over himself. Such corrections shall be made in the same as the witness may direct; and he shall then sign the same by affixing thereto his name or mark. All the testimony thus taken shall be certified to by the magistrate. In lieu of the above provision, a statement of facts authenticated by State and defense counsel and approved by the presiding magistrate may be used to preserve the testimony of witnesses.

History of CCP art. 16.09: Acts 1965, 59th Leg., vol. 2, ch. 722.

ANNOTATIONS

Russell v. State, 604 S.W.2d 914, 926 (Tex.Crim. App.1980). "[A] purported statement of facts containing testimony given by one or more witnesses presented by the State at an examining trial may not be considered as reproduced testimony in determining the confrontation issue unless it has been authenticated in the manner prescribed by Article 16.09, without a convincing showing of some extraordinary circumstance that prevented full authentication by the magistrate and counsel for the State and for the accused. None is shown here; to the contrary the attempt was never made."

ART. 16.10. ATTACHMENT FOR WITNESS

The magistrate has the power in all cases, where a witness resides or is in the county where the prosecution is pending, to issue an attachment for the purpose of enforcing the attendance of such witness; this he may do without having previously issued a subpoena for that purpose.

History of CCP art. 16.10: Acts 1965, 59th Leg., vol. 2, ch. 722.

ART. 16.11. ATTACHMENT TO ANOTHER COUNTY

The magistrate may issue an attachment for a witness to any county in the State, when affidavit is made by the party applying therefor that the testimony of the witness is material to the prosecution, or the defense, as the case may be; and the affidavit shall further state the facts which it is expected will be proved by the witness; and if the facts set forth are not considered material by the magistrate, or if they be admitted to be true by the adverse party, the attachment shall not issue.

History of CCP art. 16.11: Acts 1965, 59th Leg., vol. 2, ch. 722.

ART. 16.12. WITNESS NEED NOT BE TENDERED HIS WITNESS FEES OR EXPENSES

A witness attached need not be tendered his witness fees or expenses.

History of CCP art. 16.12: Acts 1965, 59th Leg., vol. 2, ch. 722.

ART. 16.13. ATTACHMENT EXECUTED FORTHWITH

The officer receiving the attachment shall execute it forthwith by bringing before the magistrate the witness named therein, unless such witness shall give bail for his appearance before the magistrate at the time and place required by the writ.

History of CCP art. 16.13: Acts 1965, 59th Leg., vol. 2, ch. 722.

ART. 16.14. POSTPONING EXAMINATION

After examining the witness in attendance, if it appear to the magistrate that there is other important testimony which may be had by a postponement, he shall, at the request of the prosecutor or of the defendant, postpone the hearing for a reasonable time to enable such testimony to be procured; but in such case the accused shall remain in the custody of the proper officer until the day fixed for such further examination. No postponement shall take place, unless a sworn statement be made by the defendant, or the prosecutor, setting forth the name and residence of the witness, and the facts which it is expected will be proved. If it be testimony other than that of a witness, the statement made shall set forth the nature of the evidence. If the magistrate is satisfied that the testimony is not material, or if the same be admitted to be true by the adverse party, the postponement shall be refused.

History of CCP art. 16.14: Acts 1965, 59th Leg., vol. 2, ch. 722.

ART. 16.15. WHO MAY DISCHARGE CAPITAL OFFENSE

The examination of one accused of a capital offense shall be conducted by a justice of the peace, county judge, county court at law, or county criminal court. The judge may admit to bail, except in capital cases where the proof is evident.

History of CCP art. 16.15: Acts 1965, 59th Leg., vol. 2, ch. 722.
See also CCP art. 1.07.

Angleton v. State, 955 S.W.2d 655, 657 (Tex.App.—Houston [14th Dist.] 1997), *rev'd on other grounds*, 971 S.W.2d 65 (Tex.Crim.App.1998). "The term 'proof is evident' means the evidence is clear and strong, leading a well-guarded and dispassionate judgment to the conclusions that 1) the offense of capital murder has been committed; 2) the accused is the guilty party; and 3) the jury will both convict the accused and will return findings requiring a death sentence. [¶] The burden of proof is on the State to show the proof evident."

ART. 16.16. IF INSUFFICIENT BAIL HAS BEEN TAKEN

Where it is made to appear by affidavit to a judge of the Court of Criminal Appeals, a justice of a court of appeals, or to a judge of the district or county court, that the bail taken in any case is insufficient in amount, or that the sureties are not good for the amount, or that the bond is for any reason defective or insufficient, such judge shall issue a warrant of arrest, and require of the defendant sufficient bond and security, according to the nature of the case.

History of CCP art. 16.16: Acts 1965, 59th Leg., vol. 2, ch. 722. Amended by Acts 1981, 67th Leg., ch. 291, §104, eff. Sept. 1, 1981.

ART. 16.17. DECISION OF JUDGE

After the examining trial has been had, the judge shall make an order committing the defendant to the jail of the proper county, discharging him or admitting him to bail, as the law and facts of the case may require. Failure of the judge to make or enter an order within 48 hours after the examining trial has been completed operates as a finding of no probable cause and the accused shall be discharged.

History of CCP art. 16.17: Acts 1965, 59th Leg., vol. 2, ch. 722.

ART. 16.18. WHEN NO SAFE JAIL

If there is no safe jail in the county in which the prosecution is carried on, the magistrate may commit defendant to the nearest safe jail in any other county.

History of CCP art. 16.18: Acts 1965, 59th Leg., vol. 2, ch. 722.

ART. 16.19. WARRANT IN SUCH CASE

The commitment in the case mentioned in the preceding Article shall be directed to the sheriff of the county to which the defendant is sent, but the sheriff of the county from which the defendant is taken shall be required to deliver the prisoner into the hands of the sheriff to whom he is sent.

History of CCP art. 16.19: Acts 1965, 59th Leg., vol. 2, ch. 722.

ART. 16.20. "COMMITMENT"

A "commitment" is an order signed by the proper magistrate directing a sheriff to receive and place in jail the person so committed. It will be sufficient if it have the following requisites:

1. That it run in the name of "The State of Texas";

2. That it be addressed to the sheriff of the county to the jail of which the defendant is committed;

3. That it state in plain language the offense for which the defendant is committed, and give his name, if it be known, or if unknown, contain an accurate description of the defendant;

4. That it state to what court and at what time the defendant is to be held to answer;

5. When the prisoner is sent out of the county where the prosecution arose, the warrant of commitment shall state that there is no safe jail in the proper county; and

6. If bail has been granted, the amount of bail shall be stated in the warrant of commitment.

History of CCP art. 16.20: Acts 1965, 59th Leg., vol. 2, ch. 722.

Ex parte Culp, 816 S.W.2d 564, 565 (Tex.App.—Houston [14th Dist.] 1991, orig. proceeding). "[T]here is no particular form for an order of commitment, and it 'may be contained in an authenticated copy of the court's judgment or in a separate order signed by the judge or by the clerk of the court at the judge's direction.'"

ART. 16.21. DUTY OF SHERIFF AS TO PRISONERS

Every sheriff shall keep safely a person committed to his custody. He shall use no cruel or unusual means to secure this end, but shall adopt all necessary measures to prevent the escape of a prisoner. He may summon a guard of sufficient number, in case it becomes necessary to prevent an escape from jail, or the rescue of a prisoner.

History of CCP art. 16.21: Acts 1965, 59th Leg., vol. 2, ch. 722.

ART. 16.22. EXAMINATION & TRANSFER OF DEFENDANT SUSPECTED OF HAVING MENTAL ILLNESS OR MENTAL RETARDATION

(a)(1) Not later than 72 hours after receiving evidence or a statement that may establish reasonable cause to believe that a defendant committed to the sheriff's custody has a mental illness or is a person with mental retardation, the sheriff shall notify a magistrate of that fact. A defendant's behavior or the result of a prior evaluation indicating a need for referral for further mental health or mental retardation assessment must be considered in determining whether reasonable cause exists to believe the defendant has a mental illness or is a person with mental retardation. On a determination that there is reasonable cause to believe that the defendant has a mental illness or is a person with mental retardation, the magistrate, except as provided by Subdivision (2), shall order an examination of the defendant by the local mental health or mental retardation authority or another qualified mental health or mental retardation expert to determine whether the defendant has a mental illness as defined by Section 571.003, Health and Safety Code, or is a person with mental retardation as defined by Section 591.003, Health and Safety Code.

Ⓔ (2) The magistrate is not required to order an examination described by Subdivision (1) if the defendant in the year preceding the defendant's applicable date of arrest has been evaluated and determined to have a mental illness or to be a person with mental retardation by the local mental health or mental retardation authority or another mental health or mental retardation expert described by Subdivision (1). A court that elects to use the results of that evaluation may proceed under Subsection (c).

(3) If the defendant fails or refuses to submit to an examination required under Subdivision (1), the magistrate may order the defendant to submit to an examination in a mental health facility determined to be appropriate by the local mental health or mental retardation authority for a reasonable period not to exceed 21 days. The magistrate may order a defendant to a facility operated by the Department of State Health Services or the Department of Aging and Disability Services for examination only on request of the local mental health or mental retardation authority and with the consent of the head of the facility. If a defendant who has been ordered to a facility operated by the Department of State Health Services or the Department of Aging and Disability Services for examination remains in the facility for a period exceeding 21 days, the head of that facility shall cause the defendant to be immediately transported to the committing court and placed in

the custody of the sheriff of the county in which the committing court is located. That county shall reimburse the facility for the mileage and per diem expenses of the personnel required to transport the defendant calculated in accordance with the state travel regulations in effect at the time.

(b) A written report of the examination shall be submitted to the magistrate not later than the 30th day after the date of any order of examination issued in a felony case and not later than the 10th day after the date of any order of examination issued in a misdemeanor case, and the magistrate shall provide copies of the report to the defense counsel and the prosecuting attorney. The report must include a description of the procedures used in the examination and the examiner's observations and findings pertaining to:

(1) whether the defendant is a person who has a mental illness or is a person with mental retardation;

(2) whether there is clinical evidence to support a belief that the defendant may be incompetent to stand trial and should undergo a complete competency examination under Subchapter B, Chapter 46B; and

(3) recommended treatment.

(c) After the court receives the examining expert's report relating to the defendant under Subsection (b) or elects to use the results of an evaluation described by Subsection (a)(2), the court may, as applicable:

(1) resume criminal proceedings against the defendant, including any appropriate proceedings related to the defendant's release on personal bond under Article 17.032; or

(2) resume or initiate competency proceedings, if required, as provided by Chapter 46B or other proceedings affecting the defendant's receipt of appropriate court-ordered mental health or mental retardation services, including proceedings related to the defendant's receipt of outpatient mental health services under Section 574.034, Health and Safety Code.

Ⓔ (d) Nothing in this article prevents the court from, pending an evaluation of the defendant as described by this article:

(1) releasing a mentally ill or mentally retarded defendant from custody on personal or surety bond; or

(2) ordering an examination regarding the defendant's competency to stand trial.

History of CCP art. 16.22: Acts 1993, 73rd Leg., ch. 900, §3.05, eff. Sept. 1, 1994. Amended by Acts 1997, 75th Leg., ch. 312, §1, eff. Sept. 1, 1997; Acts 2001, 77th Leg., ch. 828, §1, eff. Sept 1, 2001; Acts 2003, 78th Leg., ch. 35, §2, eff. Jan. 1, 2004; Acts 2007, 80th Leg., ch. 1307, §1, eff. Sept. 1, 2007.

CHAPTER 17. BAIL

ART. 17.01. DEFINITION OF "BAIL"

"Bail" is the security given by the accused that he will appear and answer before the proper court the accusation brought against him, and includes a bail bond or a personal bond.

History of CCP art. 17.01: Acts 1965, 59th Leg., vol. 2, ch. 722. See also Tex. Const. art. 1, §§11, 11A.

ANNOTATIONS

Ex parte Davis, 574 S.W.2d 166, 168 (Tex.Crim.App. 1978). "The general rule favors the allowance of bail. 'Thus, presumptions are not to be indulged against the applicant, and the power to deny or require bail will not be used as an instrument of oppression.'"

Trammel v. State, 529 S.W.2d 528, 529-30 (Tex. Crim.App.1975). The "'purpose of bail is to secure the presence of an accused upon trial of an accusation against him. It is not a revenue measure intended to be a substitution for a fine, but is intended to secure the trial of the alleged offender rather than turn his securities or those of his bondsman into a penalty.'"

ART. 17.02. DEFINITION OF "BAIL BOND"

A "bail bond" is a written undertaking entered into by the defendant and his sureties for the appearance of the principal therein before some court or magistrate to answer a criminal accusation; provided, however, that the defendant upon execution of such bail bond may deposit with the custodian of funds of the court in which the prosecution is pending current money of the United States in the amount of the bond in lieu of having sureties signing the same. Any cash funds deposited under this Article shall be receipted for by the officer receiving the same and shall be refunded to the defendant if and when the defendant complies with the conditions of his bond, and upon order of the court.

History of CCP art. 17.02: Acts 1965, 59th Leg., vol. 2, ch. 722.

ANNOTATIONS

Ex parte Deaton, 582 S.W.2d 151, 153 (Tex.Crim. App.1979). "[T]he Legislature intended that a defendant be given the option ... of posting cash in lieu of having sureties sign the bond. It does not grant to the court the authority to deny a defendant the right of posting a surety bond in a bailable case."

ART. 17.03. PERSONAL BOND

(a) Except as provided by Subsection (b) of this article, a magistrate may, in the magistrate's discretion, release the defendant on his personal bond without sureties or other security.

(b) Only the court before whom the case is pending may release on personal bond a defendant who:

(1) is charged with an offense under the following sections of the Penal Code:

(A) Section 19.03 (Capital Murder);

(B) Section 20.04 (Aggravated Kidnapping);

(C) Section 22.021 (Aggravated Sexual Assault);

(D) Section 22.03 (Deadly Assault on Law Enforcement or Corrections Officer, Member or Employee of Board of Pardons and Paroles, or Court Participant);

(E) Section 22.04 (Injury to a Child, Elderly Individual, or Disabled Individual);

(F) Section 29.03 (Aggravated Robbery);

(G) Section 30.02 (Burglary);

(H) Section 71.02 (Engaging in Organized Criminal Activity); or

 Subsection (1) below is effective for offenses committed on or after Sept. 1, 2007.

(I) Section 21.02 (Continuous Sexual Abuse of Young Child or Children);

(2) is charged with a felony under Chapter 481, Health and Safety Code, or Section 485.033, Health and Safety Code, punishable by imprisonment for a minimum term or by a maximum fine that is more than a minimum term or maximum fine for a first degree felony; or

(3) does not submit to testing for the presence of a controlled substance in the defendant's body as requested by the court or magistrate under Subsection (c) of this article or submits to testing and the test shows evidence of the presence of a controlled substance in the defendant's body.

(c) When setting a personal bond under this chapter, on reasonable belief by the investigating or arresting law enforcement agent or magistrate of the presence of a controlled substance in the defendant's body or on the finding of drug or alcohol abuse related to the offense for which the defendant is charged, the court or a magistrate shall require as a condition of personal bond that the defendant submit to testing for alcohol or a controlled substance in the defendant's body and participate in an alcohol or drug abuse treatment or education program if such a condition will serve to reasonably assure the appearance of the defendant for trial.

(d) The state may not use the results of any test conducted under this chapter in any criminal proceeding arising out of the offense for which the defendant is charged.

(e) Costs of testing may be assessed as court costs or ordered paid directly by the defendant as a condition of bond.

(f) In this article, "controlled substance" has the meaning assigned by Section 481.002, Health and Safety Code.

(g) The court may order that a personal bond fee assessed under Section 17.42 be:

(1) paid before the defendant is released;

(2) paid as a condition of bond;

(3) paid as court costs;

(4) reduced as otherwise provided for by statute; or

(5) waived.

History of CCP art. 17.03: Acts 1965, 59th Leg., vol. 2, ch. 722. Amended by Acts 1989, 71st Leg., ch. 374, §1, eff. Sept. 1, 1989; Acts 1991, 72nd Leg., ch. 14, §§284(45), (57) (eff. Sept. 1, 1991); Acts 1995, 74th Leg., ch. 76, §14.19, eff. Sept. 1, 1995; Acts 2007, 80th Leg., ch. 593, §3.08, eff. Sept. 1, 2007.

ANNOTATIONS

Guerra v. Garza, 987 S.W.2d 593, 593-94 (Tex. Crim.App.1999). County judge "conducted 'bail review' hearings at the jail for inmates awaiting formal charges. Although a municipal judge, acting as a magistrate, had already set bonds for these individuals, [county judge] changed their status from surety to personal bonds. The prisoners had not filed writs of habeas corpus. The District Attorney applied to this Court for writs of mandamus and prohibition, contending that, [county judge] lacked jurisdiction to grant personal bonds in these cases. We agree. [¶] [I]n order to change the bonds already properly set by a magistrate with jurisdiction to set them, [county judge] must first have jurisdiction over the cases. [I]n *Ex parte Clear*[, w]e held that since the justice of the peace had properly assumed jurisdiction over the case, and nothing had been done to invoke the district court's jurisdiction, the district judge had 'exceeded his authority by usurping the lawful jurisdiction of the justice court.'"

ART. 17.031. RELEASE ON PERSONAL BOND

(a) Any magistrate in this state may release a defendant eligible for release on personal bond under Article 17.03 of this code on his personal bond where the complaint and warrant for arrest does not originate in the county wherein the accused is arrested if the magistrate would have had jurisdiction over the matter had the complaint arisen within the county wherein the magistrate presides. The personal bond may not be revoked by the judge of the court issuing the warrant for arrest except for good cause shown.

(b) If there is a personal bond office in the county from which the warrant for arrest was issued, the court releasing a defendant on his personal bond will forward a copy of the personal bond to the personal bond office in that county.

History of CCP art. 17.031: Acts 1971, 62nd Leg., ch. 787, §1, eff. June 8, 1971. Amended by Acts 1989, 71st Leg., ch. 374, §2, eff. Sept. 1, 1989.
See also Tex. Const. art. 1, §§11, 11A.

ART. 17.032. RELEASE ON PERSONAL BOND OF CERTAIN MENTALLY ILL DEFENDANTS

(a) In this article, "violent offense" means an offense under the following sections of the Penal Code:

(1) Section 19.02 (murder);

(2) Section 19.03 (capital murder);

(3) Section 20.03 (kidnapping);

(4) Section 20.04 (aggravated kidnapping);

(5) Section 21.11 (indecency with a child);

(6) Section 22.01(a)(1) (assault);

(7) Section 22.011 (sexual assault);

(8) Section 22.02 (aggravated assault);

(9) Section 22.021 (aggravated sexual assault);

(10) Section 22.04 (injury to a child, elderly individual, or disabled individual);

(11) Section 29.03 (aggravated robbery); or

 Subsection (12) below is effective for offenses committed on or after Sept. 1, 2007.

(12) Section 21.02 (continuous sexual abuse of young child or children).

(b) A magistrate shall release a defendant on personal bond unless good cause is shown otherwise if the:

(1) defendant is not charged with and has not been previously convicted of a violent offense;

(2) defendant is examined by the local mental health or mental retardation authority or another mental health expert under Article 16.22 of this code;

(3) examining expert, in a report submitted to the magistrate under Article 16.22:

(A) concludes that the defendant has a mental illness or is a person with mental retardation and is nonetheless competent to stand trial; and

(B) recommends mental health treatment for the defendant; and

(4) magistrate determines, in consultation with the local mental health or mental retardation authority, that appropriate community-based mental health or mental retardation services for the defendant are available through the Texas Department of Mental Health and Mental Retardation under Section 534.053, Health and Safety Code, or through another mental health or mental retardation services provider.

(c) The magistrate, unless good cause is shown for not requiring treatment, shall require as a condition of release on personal bond under this article that the defendant submit to outpatient or inpatient mental health or mental retardation treatment as recommended by the local mental health or mental retardation authority if the defendant's:

(1) mental illness or mental retardation is chronic in nature; or

(2) ability to function independently will continue to deteriorate if the defendant is not treated.

(d) In addition to a condition of release imposed under Subsection (c) of this article, the magistrate may require the defendant to comply with other conditions that are reasonably necessary to protect the community.

(e) In this article, a person is considered to have been convicted of an offense if:

(1) a sentence is imposed;

(2) the person is placed on community supervision or receives deferred adjudication; or

(3) the court defers final disposition of the case.

History of CCP art. 17.032: Acts 1993, 73rd Leg., ch. 900, §3.06, eff. Sept. 1, 1994. Amended by Acts 1995, 74th Leg., ch. 76, §14.20, eff. Sept. 1, 1995; Acts 1997, 75th Leg., ch. 312, §2, eff. Sept. 1, 1997; Acts 2001, 77th Leg., ch. 828, §2, eff. Sept. 1, 2001; Acts 2007, 80th Leg., ch. 593, §3.09, eff. Sept. 1, 2007.

ART. 17.033. RELEASE ON BOND OF CERTAIN PERSONS ARRESTED WITHOUT A WARRANT

(a) Except as provided by Subsection (c), a person who is arrested without a warrant and who is detained in jail must be released on bond, in an amount not to exceed $5,000, not later than the 24th hour after the person's arrest if the person was arrested for a misdemeanor and a magistrate has not determined whether probable cause exists to believe that the person committed the offense. If the person is unable to obtain a surety for the bond or unable to deposit money in the amount of the bond, the person must be released on personal bond.

(b) Except as provided by Subsection (c), a person who is arrested without a warrant and who is detained in jail must be released on bond, in an amount not to exceed $10,000, not later than the 48th hour after the person's arrest if the person was arrested for a felony and a magistrate has not determined whether probable cause exists to believe that the person committed the offense. If the person is unable to obtain a surety for the bond or unable to deposit money in the amount of the bond, the person must be released on personal bond.

(c) On the filing of an application by the attorney representing the state, a magistrate may postpone the release of a person under Subsection (a) or (b) for not more than 72 hours after the person's arrest. An application filed under this subsection must state the reason a magistrate has not determined whether probable cause exists to believe that the person committed the offense for which the person was arrested.

(d) The time limits imposed by Subsections (a) and (b) do not apply to a person arrested without a warrant who is taken to a hospital, clinic, or other medical facility before being taken before a magistrate under Article 15.17. For a person described by this subsection, the time limits imposed by Subsections (a) and (b) begin to run at the time, as documented in the records of the hospital, clinic, or other medical facility, that a physician or other medical professional releases the person from the hospital, clinic, or other medical facility.

History of CCP art. 17.033: Acts 2001, 77th Leg., ch. 906, §5(a), eff. Jan. 1, 2002. Amended by Acts 2003, 78th Leg., ch. 298, §1, eff. June 18, 2003.

ART. 17.04. REQUISITES OF A PERSONAL BOND

A personal bond is sufficient if it includes the requisites of a bail bond as set out in Article 17.08, except that no sureties are required. In addition, a personal bond shall contain:

(1) the defendant's name, address, and place of employment;

(2) identification information, including the defendant's:

(A) date and place of birth;

(B) height, weight, and color of hair and eyes;

(C) driver's license number and state of issuance, if any; and

(D) nearest relative's name and address, if any; and

(3) the following oath sworn and signed by the defendant:

"I swear that I will appear before (the court or magistrate) at (address, city, county) Texas, on the (date), at the hour of (time, a.m. or p.m.) or upon notice by the court, or pay to the court the principal sum of (amount) plus all necessary and reasonable expenses incurred in any arrest for failure to appear."

History of CCP art. 17.04: Acts 1965, 59th Leg., vol. 2, ch. 722. Amended by Acts 1987, 70th Leg., ch. 623, §1, eff. Sept. 1, 1987.

ART. 17.045. BAIL BOND CERTIFICATES

A bail bond certificate with respect to which a fidelity and surety company has become surety as provided in the Automobile Club Services Act, or for any truck and bus association incorporated in this state, when posted by the person whose signature appears thereon, shall be accepted as bail bond in an amount not to exceed $200 to guarantee the appearance of such person in any court in this state when the person is arrested for violation of any motor vehicle law of this state or ordinance of any municipality in this state, except for the offense of driving while intoxicated or for any felony, and the alleged violation was committed prior to the date of expiration shown on such bail bond certificate.

History of CCP art. 17.045: Acts 1969, 61st Leg., ch. 697, §2, eff. Sept. 1, 1969.

ART. 17.05. WHEN A BAIL BOND IS GIVEN

A bail bond is entered into either before a magistrate, upon an examination of a criminal accusation, or before a judge upon an application under habeas corpus; or it is taken from the defendant by a peace officer if authorized by Article 17.20, 17.21, or 17.22.

History of CCP art. 17.05: Acts 1965, 59th Leg., vol. 2, ch. 722. Amended by Acts 1971, 62nd Leg., ch. 1006, §1, eff. Aug. 30, 1971.

ART. 17.06. CORPORATION AS SURETY

Wherever in this Chapter, any person is required or authorized to give or execute any bail bond, such bail bond may be given or executed by such principal and any corporation authorized by law to act as surety, subject to all the provisions of this Chapter regulating and governing the giving of bail bonds by personal surety insofar as the same is applicable.

History of CCP art. 17.06: Acts 1965, 59th Leg., vol. 2, ch. 722.

ANNOTATIONS

Freedom, Inc. v. State, 569 S.W.2d 48, 48 (Tex. App.—Austin 1978, no pet.). "A corporation may qualify to write bail bonds provided the corporation is empowered to act as a surety. A corporation acting as a professional surety is engaged in the insurance business, and is therefore required to obtain a certificate of authority from the State Board of Insurance."

ART. 17.07. CORPORATION TO FILE WITH COUNTY CLERK POWER OF ATTORNEY DESIGNATING AGENT

Any corporation authorized by the law of this State to act as a surety, shall before executing any bail bond as authorized in the preceding Article, first file in the office of the county clerk of the county where such bail bond is given, a power of attorney designating and authorizing the named agent, agents or attorney of such corporation to execute such bail bonds and thereafter the execution of such bail bonds by such agent, agents or attorney, shall be a valid and binding obligation of such corporation.

History of CCP art. 17.07: Acts 1965, 59th Leg., vol. 2, ch. 722.

ART. 17.08. REQUISITES OF A BAIL BOND

A bail bond must contain the following requisites:

1.   That it be made payable to "The State of Texas";

2.   That the defendant and his sureties, if any, bind themselves that the defendant will appear before the proper court or magistrate to answer the accusation against him;

3.   If the defendant is charged with a felony, that it state that he is charged with a felony. If the defendant is charged with a misdemeanor, that it state that he is charged with a misdemeanor;

4.   That the bond be signed by name or mark by the principal and sureties, if any, each of whom shall write thereon his mailing address;

5.   That the bond state the time and place, when and where the accused binds himself to appear, and the court or magistrate before whom he is to appear. The bond shall also bind the defendant to appear before any court or magistrate before whom the cause may thereafter be pending at any time when, and place where, his presence may be required under this Code or by any court or magistrate, but in no event shall the sureties be bound after such time as the defendant receives an order of deferred adjudication or is acquitted, sentenced, placed on community supervision, or dismissed from the charge;

6.   The bond shall also be conditioned that the principal and sureties, if any, will pay all necessary and reasonable expenses incurred by any and all sheriffs or other peace officers in rearresting the principal in the event he fails to appear before the court or magistrate named in the bond at the time stated therein. The amount of such expense shall be in addition to the principal amount specified in the bond. The failure of any bail bond to contain the conditions specified in this paragraph shall in no manner affect the legality of any such bond, but it is intended that the sheriff or other peace officer shall look to the defendant and his sureties, if any, for expenses incurred by him, and not to the State for any fees earned by him in connection with the rearresting of an accused who has violated the conditions of his bond.

History of CCP art. 17.08: Acts 1965, 59th Leg., vol. 2, ch. 722. Amended by Acts 1999, 76th Leg., ch. 1506, §1, eff. Sept. 1, 1999.

ANNOTATIONS

Scott v. State, 617 S.W.2d 691, 692 (Tex.Crim.App. 1981). "[T]he requirement that the bond state the court in which the defendant must appear [is] for the benefit of the principal and the sureties and [can] be waived by them. Omission of this item from the bond [can] not be the basis for complaint after the forfeiture."

Serrano v. State, 804 S.W.2d 543, 545 (Tex.App.—Houston [14th Dist.] 1991, no pet.). "A condition of the bond was that the principal was required to personally appear before the 338th District Court 'instanter.' Such wording of the bond provided the principal with sufficient and proper notice of when he was to appear in the trial court."

Tietz v. State, 744 S.W.2d 353, 354 (Tex.App.—Austin 1988, no pet.). Article 17.08(4) "requires that the surety sign the bond personally, rather than permitting an attorney-in-fact for the surety to sign the bond."

ART. 17.085. NOTICE OF APPEARANCE DATE

E *Article 17.085 below is effective for bonds issued on or after Sept. 1, 2007.*

The clerk of a court that does not provide online Internet access to that court's criminal case records shall post in a designated public place in the courthouse notice of a criminal court docket setting not less than 48 hours before the docket setting.

History of CCP art. 17.085: Acts 2007, 80th Leg., ch. 1038, §1, eff. Sept. 1, 2007.

ART. 17.09. DURATION; ORIGINAL & SUBSEQUENT PROCEEDINGS; NEW BAIL

Sec. 1. Where a defendant, in the course of a criminal action, gives bail before any court or person authorized by law to take same, for his personal appearance before a court or magistrate, to answer a charge against him, the said bond shall be valid and binding upon the defendant and his sureties, if any, thereon, for the defendant's personal appearance before the court or magistrate designated therein, as well as before any other court to which same may be transferred, and for any and all subsequent proceedings had relative to the charge, and each such bond shall be so conditioned except as hereinafter provided.

Sec. 2. When a defendant has once given bail for his appearance in answer to a criminal charge, he shall not be required to give another bond in the course of the same criminal action except as herein provided.

Sec. 3. Provided that whenever, during the course of the action, the judge or magistrate in whose court such action is pending finds that the bond is defective,

excessive or insufficient in amount, or that the sureties, if any, are not acceptable, or for any other good and sufficient cause, such judge or magistrate may, either in term-time or in vacation, order the accused to be rearrested, and require the accused to give another bond in such amount as the judge or magistrate may deem proper. When such bond is so given and approved, the defendant shall be released from custody.

E **Sec. 4.** Notwithstanding any other provision of this article, the judge or magistrate in whose court a criminal action is pending may not order the accused to be rearrested or require the accused to give another bond in a higher amount because the accused:

(1) withdraws a waiver of the right to counsel; or

(2) requests the assistance of counsel, appointed or retained.

History of CCP art. 17.09: Acts 1965, 59th Leg., vol. 2, ch. 722. Amended by Acts 2007, 80th Leg., ch. 463, §2, eff. Sept. 1, 2007.

See also Tex. Const. art. 1, §§11, 11A.

ANNOTATIONS

Harris v. State, 891 S.W.2d 730, 731 (Tex.App.—San Antonio 1994, pet. ref'd). "[S]ince the purpose of article 17.09 ... is to ensure the presence of the defendant for trial on the offenses charged, the article contemplates that principals and sureties will remain liable on the appearance bonds for all subsequent proceedings and until disposition of the criminal cases."

Miller v. State, 855 S.W.2d 92, 93-94 (Tex.App.—Houston [14th Dist.] 1993, pet. ref'd). "It is within the trial court's discretion to increase the bail set. ... No precise standard exists for determining what constitutes 'good and sufficient cause' under Article 17.09. Therefore, each case must be reviewed on a fact-by-fact basis."

ART. 17.091. NOTICE OF CERTAIN BAIL REDUCTIONS REQUIRED

A *Article 17.091 below is effective for offenses committed on or after Sept. 1, 2007.*

Before a judge or magistrate reduces the amount of bail set for a defendant charged with an offense listed in Section 3g, Article 42.12, or an offense described by Article 62.001(5), the judge or magistrate shall provide:

(1) to the attorney representing the state, reasonable notice of the proposed bail reduction; and

(2) on request of the attorney representing the state or the defendant or the defendant's counsel, an opportunity for a hearing concerning the proposed bail reduction.

History of CCP art. 17.091: Acts 2005, 79th Leg., ch. 671, §1, eff. Sept. 1, 2005. Amended by Acts 2007, 80th Leg., ch. 593, §3.10, eff. Sept. 1, 2007.

ART. 17.091. NOTICE OF CERTAIN BAIL REDUCTIONS REQUIRED

Article 17.091 below is effective for offenses in which any element of the offense was committed before Sept. 1, 2007.

Before a judge or magistrate reduces the amount of bail set for a defendant charged with an offense listed in Section 3g, Article 42.12, or an offense described by Article 62.01(5), the judge or magistrate shall provide:

(1) to the attorney representing the state, reasonable notice of the proposed bail reduction; and

(2) on request of the attorney representing the state or the defendant or the defendant's counsel, an opportunity for a hearing concerning the proposed bail reduction.

ART. 17.10. DISQUALIFIED SURETIES

(a) A minor may not be surety on a bail bond, but the accused party may sign as principal.

(b) A person, for compensation, may not be a surety on a bail bond written in a county in which a county bail bond board regulated under Chapter 1704, Occupations Code, does not exist unless the person, within two years before the bail bond is given, completed in person at least eight hours of continuing legal education in criminal law courses or bail bond law courses that are:

(1) approved by the State Bar of Texas; and

(2) offered by an accredited institution of higher education in this state.

History of CCP art. 17.10: Acts 1965, 59th Leg., vol. 2, ch. 722. Amended by Acts 2005, 79th Leg., ch. 743, §1, eff. Sept. 1, 2005.

ART. 17.11. HOW BAIL BOND IS TAKEN

Sec. 1. Every court, judge, magistrate or other officer taking a bail bond shall require evidence of the sufficiency of the security offered; but in every case, one surety shall be sufficient, if it be made to appear that such surety is worth at least double the amount of the sum for which he is bound, exclusive of all property exempted by law from execution, and of debts or other encumbrances; and that he is a resident of this state, and has property therein liable to execution worth the sum for which he is bound.

Sec. 2. Provided, however, any person who has signed as a surety on a bail bond and is in default thereon shall thereafter be disqualified to sign as a surety so long as he is in default on said bond. It shall be the duty of the clerk of the court wherein such surety is in default on a bail bond, to notify in writing the sheriff, chief of police, or other peace officer, of such default. A surety shall be deemed in default from the time execution may be issued on a final judgment in a bond forfeiture proceeding under the Texas Rules of Civil Procedure, unless the final judgment is superseded by the posting of a supersedeas bond.

History of CCP art. 17.11: Acts 1965, 59th Leg., vol. 2, ch. 722. Amended by Acts 1967, 60th Leg., ch. 659, §14, eff. Aug. 28, 1967; Acts 1999, 76th Leg., ch. 1506, §2, eff. Sept. 1, 1999.

ANNOTATIONS

Burns v. Harris Cty. Bail Bond Bd., 663 S.W.2d 615, 616 (Tex.App.—Houston [1st Dist.] 1983, no pet.). "The test of when default occurs is set out in ... art. 17.11, §2.... Since appellant was in default, he was disqualified to sign as a surety...."

ART. 17.12. EXEMPT PROPERTY

The property secured by the Constitution and laws from forced sale shall not, in any case, be held liable for the satisfaction of bail, either as to principal or sureties, if any.

History of CCP art. 17.12: Acts 1965, 59th Leg., vol. 2, ch. 722.

ART. 17.13. SUFFICIENCY OF SURETIES ASCERTAINED

To test the sufficiency of the security offered to any bail bond, unless the court or officer taking the same is fully satisfied as to its sufficiency, the following oath shall be made in writing and subscribed by the sureties: "I, do swear that I am worth, in my own right, at least the sum of (here insert the amount in which the surety is bound), after deducting from my property all that which is exempt by the Constitution and Laws of the State from forced sale, and after the payment of all my debts of every description, whether individual or security debts, and after satisfying all encumbrances upon my property which are known to me; that I reside in _____ County, and have property in this State liable to execution worth said amount or more.

(Dated _____, and attested by the judge of the court, clerk, magistrate or sheriff.)"

Such affidavit shall be filed with the papers of the proceedings.

History of CCP art. 17.13: Acts 1965, 59th Leg., vol. 2, ch. 722.

ART. 17.14. AFFIDAVIT NOT CONCLUSIVE

Such affidavit shall not be conclusive as to the sufficiency of the security; and if the court or officer taking the bail bond is not fully satisfied as to the sufficiency of the security offered, further evidence shall be required before approving the same.

History of CCP art. 17.14: Acts 1965, 59th Leg., vol. 2, ch. 722.

ANNOTATIONS

Font v. Carr, 867 S.W.2d 873, 874 (Tex.App.— Houston [1st Dist.] 1993, writ dism'd). "[T]he prosecutor's reliance on [CCP] art. 17.14 is not conclusive evidence that he acted in good faith because that article does not apply in Harris County or in any county that has a bail bond board under [TRCS] art. 2372p-3. *At 881:* [T]hus, the sheriff has no authority to question the solvency of a bail bondsman licensed in Harris County. [¶] If article 17.14 gives the sheriff of a county in which article 2372p-3 applies the authority to question solvency even though the bondsman meets the financial requirements of article 2372p-3, then the Act is meaningless for that bondsman."

ART. 17.141. ELIGIBLE BAIL BOND SURETIES IN CERTAIN COUNTIES

In a county in which a county bail bond board regulated under Chapter 1704, Occupations Code, does not exist, the sheriff may post a list of eligible bail bond sureties whose security has been determined to be sufficient. Each surety listed under this article must file annually a sworn financial statement with the sheriff.

History of CCP art. 17.141: Acts 2005, 79th Leg., ch. 743, §2, eff. Sept. 1, 2005.

ART. 17.15. RULES FOR FIXING AMOUNT OF BAIL

The amount of bail to be required in any case is to be regulated by the court, judge, magistrate or officer taking the bail; they are to be governed in the exercise of this discretion by the Constitution and by the following rules:

1. The bail shall be sufficiently high to give reasonable assurance that the undertaking will be complied with.

2. The power to require bail is not to be so used as to make it an instrument of oppression.

3. The nature of the offense and the circumstances under which it was committed are to be considered.

4. The ability to make bail is to be regarded, and proof may be taken upon this point.

5. The future safety of a victim of the alleged offense and the community shall be considered.

History of CCP art. 17.15: Acts 1965, 59th Leg., vol. 2, ch. 722. Amended by Acts 1985, 69th Leg., ch. 588, §2, eff. Sept. 1, 1985; Acts 1993, 73rd Leg., ch. 396, §1, eff. Sept. 1, 1993.

See also Tex. Const. art. 1, §13.

ANNOTATIONS

Ludwig v. State, 812 S.W.2d 323, 325 (Tex.Crim. App.1991). "We are not inclined to read 'victim' in [art. 17.15(5)] to cover anyone not actually a complainant in the charged offense."

Clemons v. State, 220 S.W.3d 176, 178 (Tex.App.— Eastland 2007, no pet.). "In addition to the rules listed in Article 17.15, the following factors may also be considered: possible punishment, the accused's work record, his ties to the community, the length of his residency, his prior criminal record, his conformity with any prior bail bond conditions, his ability or inability to make a bail bond, and the existence of any outstanding bail bonds."

Perez v. State, 897 S.W.2d 893, 898 (Tex.App.— San Antonio 1995, no pet.). "[T]he court of criminal appeals has considered the nonviolent aspect of an offense as a factor favorable to a bond reduction."

ART. 17.151. RELEASE BECAUSE OF DELAY

Sec. 1. A defendant who is detained in jail pending trial of an accusation against him must be released either on personal bond or by reducing the amount of bail required, if the state is not ready for trial of the criminal action for which he is being detained within:

(1) 90 days from the commencement of his detention if he is accused of a felony;

(2) 30 days from the commencement of his detention if he is accused of a misdemeanor punishable by a sentence of imprisonment in jail for more than 180 days;

(3) 15 days from the commencement of his detention if he is accused of a misdemeanor punishable by a sentence of imprisonment for 180 days or less; or

(4) five days from the commencement of his detention if he is accused of a misdemeanor punishable by a fine only.

Sec. 2. The provisions of this article do not apply to a defendant who is:

(1) serving a sentence of imprisonment for another offense while the defendant is serving that sentence;

(2) being detained pending trial of another accusation against the defendant as to which the applicable period has not yet elapsed;

(3) incompetent to stand trial, during the period of the defendant's incompetence; or

(4) being detained for a violation of the conditions of a previous release related to the safety of a victim of the alleged offense or to the safety of the community under this article.

Sec. 3. Repealed by Acts 2005, 79th Leg., ch. 110, §2, eff. Sept. 1, 2005.

History of CCP art. 17.151: Acts 1977, 65th Leg., ch. 787, §2, eff. July 1, 1978. Amended by Acts 2005, 79th Leg., ch. 110, §§1, 2, eff. Sept. 1, 2005. See also CCP art. 29.12.

ANNOTATIONS

Rowe v. State, 853 S.W.2d 581, 582 (Tex.Crim.App. 1993). "Article 17.151 provides that if the State is not ready for trial within 90 days after commencement of detention for a felony, the accused 'must be released either on personal bond or by reducing the amount of bail required[.]' Thus the trial court has two options: release upon personal bond or reduce the bail amount. However, there is nothing in the statute indicating that the provisions do not apply if the delay was based upon the accused's request to testify before the grand jury. Article 17.151 contains no provisions excluding certain periods from the statutory time limit to accommodate exceptional circumstances."

Vargas v. State, 109 S.W.3d 26, 29 (Tex.App.—Amarillo 2003, no pet.). "The courts of appeals have split over whether appellate jurisdiction exists in regard to direct appeals from pretrial bail rulings such as the one before us. [¶] We lack a statutory grant of jurisdiction over this appeal. And, although TRAP 31 addresses, in part, appeals from bail proceedings, we note that the [TRAPs] do not establish jurisdiction of courts of appeals, and cannot create jurisdiction where none exists. [¶] We lack jurisdiction over this direct appeal from interlocutory pretrial orders refusing to lower bail

pursuant to CCP 17.151." *See also **Benford v. State**, 994 S.W.2d 404, 409 (Tex.App.—Waco 1999, no pet.) (no appellate jurisdiction); **Ex parte Shumake**, 953 S.W.2d 842, 846-47 (Tex.App.—Austin 1997, no pet.) (same). *But see **Ramos v. State**, 89 S.W.3d 122, 124-26 (Tex.App.—Corpus Christi 2002, no pet.) (TRAP 31.1 contemplates appeals of orders in bail proceedings).

Ramos v. State, 89 S.W.3d 122, 128 (Tex.App.—Corpus Christi 2002, no pet.). "Article 17.151 does not require the State to 'announce ready.' The question of the State's 'readiness' within the statutory limits refers to the preparedness of the prosecution for trial. We hold that the State made a *prima facie* showing that it was ready for trial within the statutory period. Accordingly, it became appellant's burden to rebut the State's showing of readiness."

Ex parte McNeil, 772 S.W.2d 488, 489 (Tex.App.—Houston [1st Dist.] 1989, orig. proceeding). "Readiness for trial should be determined [by] the existence of a charging instrument [as] an element of preparedness. Where there is no indictment, the State cannot announce ready for trial." *See also **Ex parte Avila**, 201 S.W.3d 824, 826-27 (Tex.App.—Waco 2006, no pet.).

ⓔ ART. 17.152. DENIAL OF BAIL FOR VIOLATION OF CERTAIN COURT ORDERS OR CONDITIONS OF BOND IN A FAMILY VIOLENCE CASE

(a) In this article, "family violence" has the meaning assigned by Section 71.004, Family Code.

(b) Except as otherwise provided by Subsection (d), a person who commits an offense under Section 25.07, Penal Code, related to a violation of a condition of bond set in a family violence case and whose bail in the case under Section 25.07, Penal Code, or in the family violence case is revoked or forfeited for a violation of a condition of bond may be taken into custody and, pending trial or other court proceedings, denied release on bail if following a hearing a judge or magistrate determines by a preponderance of the evidence that the person violated a condition of bond related to:

(1) the safety of the victim of the offense under Section 25.07, Penal Code, or the family violence case, as applicable; or

(2) the safety of the community.

(c) Except as otherwise provided by Subsection (d), a person who commits an offense under Section 25.07, Penal Code, other than an offense related to a violation of a condition of bond set in a family violence case, may be taken into custody and, pending trial or other court proceedings, denied release on bail if following a hearing a judge or magistrate determines by a preponderance of the evidence that the person committed the offense.

(d) A person who commits an offense under Section 25.07(a)(3), Penal Code, may be held without bail under Subsection (b) or (c), as applicable, only if following a hearing the judge or magistrate determines by a preponderance of the evidence that the person went to or near the place described in the order or condition of bond with the intent to commit or threaten to commit:

(1) family violence; or

(2) an act in furtherance of an offense under Section 42.072, Penal Code.

(e) In determining whether to deny release on bail under this article, the judge or magistrate may consider:

(1) the order or condition of bond;

(2) the nature and circumstances of the alleged offense;

(3) the relationship between the accused and the victim, including the history of that relationship;

(4) any criminal history of the accused; and

(5) any other facts or circumstances relevant to a determination of whether the accused poses an imminent threat of future family violence.

(f) A person arrested for committing an offense under Section 25.07, Penal Code, shall without unnecessary delay and after reasonable notice is given to the attorney representing the state, but not later than 48 hours after the person is arrested, be taken before a magistrate in accordance with Article 15.17. At that time, the magistrate shall conduct the hearing and make the determination required by this article.

History of CCP art. 17.152: Acts 2007, 80th Leg., ch. 1113, §3, eff. Jan. 1, 2008.

ART. 17.16. DISCHARGE OF LIABILITY; SURRENDER OR INCARCERATION OF PRINCIPAL BEFORE FORFEITURE

(a) A surety may before forfeiture relieve himself of his undertaking by:

(1) surrendering the accused into the custody of the sheriff of the county where the prosecution is pending; or

(2) delivering to the sheriff of the county where the prosecution is pending an affidavit stating that the accused is incarcerated in federal custody, in the custody of any state, or in any county of this state.

(b) For the purposes of Subsection (a)(2) of this article, the bond is discharged and the surety is absolved of liability on the bond on the sheriff's verification of the incarceration of the accused.

History of CCP art. 17.16: Acts 1965, 59th Leg., vol. 2, ch. 722. Amended by Acts 1987, 70th Leg., ch. 1047, §1, eff. June 20, 1987.

ANNOTATIONS

Austin v. State, 541 S.W.2d 162, 165 (Tex.Crim.App. 1976). "We conclude that where the surety proposes to surrender his principal, he may do so without a warrant under the provisions of [CCP art.] 17.16 if the principal will surrender willingly and without the use of force. Otherwise, the surety must comply with the requirements of [CCP art.] 17.19, and secure a warrant of arrest for the principal."

ART. 17.17. WHEN SURRENDER IS MADE DURING TERM

If a surrender of the accused be made during a term of the court to which he has bound himself to appear, the sheriff shall take him before the court; and if he is willing to give other bail, the court shall forthwith require him to do so. If he fails or refuses to give bail, the court shall make an order that he be committed to jail until the bail is given, and this shall be a sufficient commitment without any written order to the sheriff.

History of CCP art. 17.17: Acts 1965, 59th Leg., vol. 2, ch. 722.

ART. 17.18. SURRENDER IN VACATION

When the surrender is made at any other time than during the session of the court, the sheriff may take the necessary bail bond, but if the defendant fails or refuses to give other bail, the sheriff shall take him before the nearest magistrate; and such magistrate shall issue a warrant of commitment, reciting the fact that the accused has been once admitted to bail, has been surrendered, and now fails or refuses to give other bail.

History of CCP art. 17.18: Acts 1965, 59th Leg., vol. 2, ch. 722.

ART. 17.19. SURETY MAY OBTAIN A WARRANT

(a) Any surety, desiring to surrender his principal and after notifying the principal's attorney, if the principal is represented by an attorney, in a manner provided by Rule 21a, Texas Rules of Civil Procedure, of the surety's intention to surrender the principal, may file an affidavit of such intention before the court or magistrate before which the prosecution is pending. The affidavit must state:

(1) the court and cause number of the case;

(2) the name of the defendant;

(3) the offense with which the defendant is charged;

(4) the date of the bond;

(5) the cause for the surrender; and

(6) that notice of the surety's intention to surrender the principal has been given as required by this subsection.

 Subsections (b) & (c) below are effective for fees imposed for a warrant or capias issued for offenses committed on or after Sept. 1, 2007.

(b) In a prosecution pending before a court, if the court finds that there is cause for the surety to surrender the surety's principal, the court shall issue a capias for the principal. In a prosecution pending before a magistrate, if the magistrate finds that there is cause for the surety to surrender the surety's principal, the magistrate shall issue a warrant of arrest for the principal. It is an affirmative defense to any liability on the bond that:

(1) the court or magistrate refused to issue a capias or warrant of arrest for the principal; and

(2) after the refusal to issue the capias or warrant of arrest, the principal failed to appear.

(c) If the court or magistrate before whom the prosecution is pending is not available, the surety may deliver the affidavit to any other magistrate in the county and that magistrate, on a finding of cause for the surety to surrender the surety's principal, shall issue a warrant of arrest for the principal.

Subsections (b) & (c) below are effective for fees imposed for a warrant or capias issued for offenses committed before Sept. 1, 2007.

(b) If the court or magistrate finds that there is cause for the surety to surrender his principal, the court shall issue a warrant of arrest or capias for the principal. It is an affirmative defense to any liability on the bond that:

(1) the court or magistrate refused to issue a warrant of arrest or capias for the principal; and

(2) after the refusal to issue the warrant or capias the principal failed to appear.

(c) If the court or magistrate before whom the prosecution is pending is not available, the surety may deliver the affidavit to any other magistrate in the county and that magistrate, on a finding of cause for the surety to surrender his principal, shall issue a warrant of arrest or capias for the principal.

(d) An arrest warrant or capias issued under this article shall be issued to the sheriff of the county in which the case is pending, and a copy of the warrant or capias shall be issued to the surety or his agent.

(e) An arrest warrant or capias issued under this article may be executed by a peace officer, a security officer, or a private investigator licensed in this state.

History of CCP art. 17.19: Acts 1965, 59th Leg., vol. 2, ch. 722. Amended by Acts 1987, 70th Leg., ch. 1047, §2, eff. June 20, 1987; Acts 1989, 71st Leg., ch. 374, §3, eff. Sept. 1, 1989; Acts 1999, 76th Leg., ch. 1506, §3, eff. Sept. 1, 1999; Acts 2003, 78th Leg., ch. 942, §4, eff. June 20, 2003; Acts 2007, 80th Leg., ch. 1263, §2, eff. Sept. 1, 2007.

ANNOTATIONS

McConathy v. State, 545 S.W.2d 166, 168-69 (Tex. Crim.App.1977). "We find no authority for the trial judge to refuse the issuance of the arrest warrant after the requisite affidavit. If the trial judge considered the attempt to surrender without reasonable cause, the remedy is [to require the surety to return all bonding fees]."

Maya v. State, 126 S.W.3d 581, 583 (Tex.App.— Texarkana 2004, no pet.). "[F]or refusal to occur under Article 17.19, the thing being refused (in this case an affidavit to go off bond) must first be offered by the party requesting approval and in some manner called to the attention of the magistrate."

ART. 17.20. BAIL IN MISDEMEANOR

The sheriff, or other peace officer, in cases of misdemeanor, may, whether during the term of the court or in vacation, where he has a defendant in custody, take of the defendant a bail bond.

History of CCP art. 17.20: Acts 1965, 59th Leg., vol. 2, ch. 722. Amended by Acts 1971, 62nd Leg., ch. 1006, §1, eff. Aug. 30, 1971.

ART. 17.21. BAIL IN FELONY

In cases of felony, when the accused is in custody of the sheriff or other peace officer, and the court before which the prosecution is pending is in session in the county where the accused is in custody, the court shall fix the amount of bail, if it is a bailable case and determine if the accused is eligible for a personal bond; and the sheriff, or other peace officer, unless it be the police of a city, is authorized to take a bail bond of the accused in the amount as fixed by the court, to be approved by such officer taking the same, and will thereupon discharge the accused from custody. It shall not be necessary for the defendant or his sureties to appear in court.

History of CCP art. 17.21: Acts 1965, 59th Leg., vol. 2, ch. 722.
See also Tex. Const. art. 1, §11A.

ART. 17.22. MAY TAKE BAIL IN FELONY

In a felony case, if the court before which the same is pending is not in session in the county where the defendant is in custody, the sheriff, or other peace officer having him in custody, may take his bail bond in such amount as may have been fixed by the court or magistrate, or if no amount has been fixed, then in such amount as such officer may consider reasonable.

History of CCP art. 17.22: Acts 1965, 59th Leg., vol. 2, ch. 722.
See also Tex. Const. art. 1, §11A.

ART. 17.23. SURETIES SEVERALLY BOUND

In all bail bonds taken under any provision of this Code, the sureties shall be severally bound. Where a surrender of the principal is made by one or more of them, all the sureties shall be considered discharged.

History of CCP art. 17.23: Acts 1965, 59th Leg., vol. 2, ch. 722.

ART. 17.24. GENERAL RULES APPLICABLE

All general rules in the Chapter are applicable to bail defendant before an examining court.

History of CCP art. 17.24: Acts 1965, 59th Leg., vol. 2, ch. 722.

ART. 17.25. PROCEEDINGS WHEN BAIL IS GRANTED

After a full examination of the testimony, the magistrate shall, if the case be one where bail may properly be granted and ought to be required, proceed to make an order that the accused execute a bail bond with sufficient security, conditioned for his appearance before the proper court.

History of CCP art. 17.25: Acts 1965, 59th Leg., vol. 2, ch. 722.

ART. 17.26. TIME GIVEN TO PROCURE BAIL

Reasonable time shall be given the accused to procure security.

History of CCP art. 17.26: Acts 1965, 59th Leg., vol. 2, ch. 722.

ART. 17.27. WHEN BAIL IS NOT GIVEN

If, after the allowance of a reasonable time, the security be not given, the magistrate shall make an order committing the accused to jail to be kept safely until legally discharged; and he shall issue a commitment accordingly.

History of CCP art. 17.27: Acts 1965, 59th Leg., vol. 2, ch. 722.

ART. 17.28. WHEN READY TO GIVE BAIL

If the party be ready to give bail, the magistrate shall cause to be prepared a bond, which shall be signed by the accused and his surety or sureties, if any.

History of CCP art. 17.28: Acts 1965, 59th Leg., vol. 2, ch. 722.

ART. 17.29. ACCUSED LIBERATED

(a) When the accused has given the required bond, either to the magistrate or the officer having him in custody, he shall at once be set at liberty.

(b) Before releasing on bail a person arrested for an offense under Section 42.072, Penal Code, or a person arrested or held without warrant in the prevention of family violence, the law enforcement agency holding the person shall make a reasonable attempt to give personal notice of the imminent release to the victim of the alleged offense or to another person designated by the victim to receive the notice. An attempt by an agency to give notice to the victim or the person designated by the victim at the victim's or person's last known telephone number or address, as shown on the records of the agency, constitutes a reasonable attempt to give notice under this subsection. If possible, the arresting officer shall collect the address and telephone number of the victim at the time the arrest is made and shall communicate that information to the agency holding the person.

(c) A law enforcement agency or an employee of a law enforcement agency is not liable for damages arising from complying or failing to comply with Subsection (b) of this article.

(d) In this article, "family violence" has the meaning assigned by Section 71.004, Family Code.

History of CCP art. 17.29: Acts 1965, 59th Leg., vol. 2, ch. 722. Amended by Acts 1995, 74th Leg., ch. 656, §1 (eff. June 14, 1995), ch. 661, §1 (eff. Aug. 28, 1995); Acts 1997, 75th Leg., ch. 1, §3, eff. Jan. 28, 1997; Acts 2003, 78th Leg., ch. 1276, §7.002(e), eff. Sept. 1, 2003.

See also *O'Connor's Family Law Handbook*, "Duties of Law Enforcement," ch. 6-E.

ART. 17.291. FURTHER DETENTION OF CERTAIN PERSONS

(a) In this article:

(1) "family violence" has the meaning assigned to that phrase by Section 71.004, Family Code; and

(2) "magistrate" has the meaning assigned to it by Article 2.09 of this code.

(b) Article 17.29 does not apply when a person has been arrested or held without a warrant in the prevention of family violence if there is probable cause to believe the violence will continue if the person is immediately released. The head of the agency arresting or holding such a person may hold the person for a period of not more than four hours after bond has been posted. This detention period may be extended for an additional period not to exceed 48 hours, but only if authorized in a writing directed to the person having custody of the detained person by a magistrate who concludes that:

(1) the violence would continue if the person is released; and

(2) if the additional period exceeds 24 hours, probable cause exists to believe that the person committed the instant offense and that, during the 10-year period preceding the date of the instant offense, the person has been arrested:

(A) on more than one occasion for an offense involving family violence; or

(B) for any other offense, if a deadly weapon, as defined by Section 1.07, Penal Code, was used or exhibited during commission of the offense or during immediate flight after commission of the offense.

History of CCP art. 17.291: Acts 1991, 72nd Leg., ch. 552, §2, eff. June 16, 1991. Amended by Acts 1999, 76th Leg., ch. 1341, §1, eff. Sept. 1, 1999; Acts 2003, 78th Leg., ch. 1276, §7.002(f), eff. Sept. 1, 2003.

See also *O'Connor's Family Law Handbook*, "Duties of Law Enforcement," ch. 6-E, p. 604.

ART. 17.292. MAGISTRATE'S ORDER FOR EMERGENCY PROTECTION

 The introductory paragraph of subsection (a) below is effective for defendants arrested on or after May 11, 2007.

(a) At a defendant's appearance before a magistrate after arrest for an offense involving family violence or an offense under Section 22.011, 22.021, or 42.072, Penal Code, the magistrate may issue an order for emergency protection on the magistrate's own motion or on the request of:

The introductory paragraph of subsection (a) below is effective for defendants arrested before May 11, 2007.

(a) At a defendant's appearance before a magistrate after arrest for an offense involving family violence or an offense under Section 42.072, Penal Code, the magistrate may issue an order for emergency protection on the magistrate's own motion or on the request of:

(1) the victim of the offense;

(2) the guardian of the victim;

(3) a peace officer; or

(4) the attorney representing the state.

(b) At a defendant's appearance before a magistrate after arrest for an offense involving family violence, the magistrate shall issue an order for emergency protection if the arrest is for an offense that also involves:

(1) serious bodily injury to the victim; or

(2) the use or exhibition of a deadly weapon during the commission of an assault.

(c) The magistrate in the order for emergency protection may prohibit the arrested party from:

(1) committing:

(A) family violence or an assault on the person protected under the order; or

(B) an act in furtherance of an offense under Section 42.072, Penal Code;

(2) communicating:

(A) directly with a member of the family or household or with the person protected under the order in a threatening or harassing manner; or

(B) a threat through any person to a member of the family or household or to the person protected under the order;

(3) going to or near:

(A) the residence, place of employment, or business of a member of the family or household or of the person protected under the order; or

(B) the residence, child care facility, or school where a child protected under the order resides or attends; or

(4) possessing a firearm, unless the person is a peace officer, as defined by Section 1.07, Penal Code, actively engaged in employment as a sworn, full-time paid employee of a state agency or political subdivision.

(d) The victim of the offense need not be present in court when the order for emergency protection is issued.

(e) In the order for emergency protection the magistrate shall specifically describe the prohibited locations and the minimum distances, if any, that the party must maintain, unless the magistrate determines for the safety of the person or persons protected by the order that specific descriptions of the locations should be omitted.

(f) To the extent that a condition imposed by an order for emergency protection issued under this article conflicts with an existing court order granting possession of or access to a child, the condition imposed under this article prevails for the duration of the order for emergency protection.

(f-1) To the extent that a condition imposed by an order issued under this article conflicts with a condition imposed by an order subsequently issued under Chapter 85, Subtitle B, Title 4, Family Code, or under Title 1 or Title 5, Family Code, the condition imposed by the order issued under the Family Code prevails.

(f-2) To the extent that a condition imposed by an order issued under this article conflicts with a condition imposed by an order subsequently issued under Chapter 83, Subtitle B, Title 4, Family Code, the condition imposed by the order issued under this article prevails unless the court issuing the order under Chapter 83, Family Code:

(1) is informed of the existence of the order issued under this article; and

(2) makes a finding in the order issued under Chapter 83, Family Code, that the court is superseding the order issued under this article.

(g) An order for emergency protection issued under this article must contain the following statements printed in bold-face type or in capital letters:

"A VIOLATION OF THIS ORDER BY COMMISSION OF AN ACT PROHIBITED BY THE ORDER MAY BE PUNISHABLE BY A FINE OF AS MUCH AS $4,000 OR BY CONFINEMENT IN JAIL FOR AS LONG AS ONE YEAR OR BY BOTH. AN ACT THAT RESULTS IN FAMILY VIOLENCE OR A STALKING OFFENSE MAY BE PROSECUTED AS A SEPARATE MISDEMEANOR OR FELONY OFFENSE. IF THE ACT IS PROSECUTED AS A SEPARATE FELONY OFFENSE, IT IS PUNISHABLE BY CONFINEMENT IN PRISON FOR AT LEAST TWO YEARS.

THE POSSESSION OF A FIREARM BY A PERSON, OTHER THAN A PEACE OFFICER, AS DEFINED BY SECTION 1.07, PENAL CODE, ACTIVELY ENGAGED IN EMPLOYMENT AS A SWORN, FULL-TIME PAID EMPLOYEE OF A STATE AGENCY OR POLITICAL SUBDIVISION, WHO IS SUBJECT TO THIS ORDER MAY BE PROSECUTED AS A SEPARATE OFFENSE PUNISHABLE BY CONFINEMENT OR IMPRISONMENT.

"NO PERSON, INCLUDING A PERSON WHO IS PROTECTED BY THIS ORDER, MAY GIVE PERMISSION TO ANYONE TO IGNORE OR VIOLATE ANY PROVISION OF THIS ORDER. DURING THE TIME IN WHICH THIS ORDER IS VALID, EVERY PROVISION OF THIS ORDER IS IN FULL FORCE AND EFFECT UNLESS A COURT CHANGES THE ORDER."

(h) The magistrate issuing an order for emergency protection under this article shall send a copy of the order to the chief of police in the municipality where the member of the family or household or individual protected by the order resides, if the person resides in a municipality, or to the sheriff of the county where the person resides, if the person does not reside in a municipality. If the victim of the offense is not present when the order is issued, the magistrate issuing the order shall order an appropriate peace officer to make a good faith effort to notify, within 24 hours, the victim that the order has been issued by calling the victim's residence and place of employment. The clerk of the court shall send a copy of the order to the victim.

(i) If an order for emergency protection issued under this article prohibits a person from going to or near a child care facility or school, the magistrate shall send a copy of the order to the child care facility or school.

(j) An order for emergency protection issued under this article is effective on issuance, and the defendant shall be served a copy of the order in open court. An order for emergency protection issued under Subsection (a) or (b)(1) of this article remains in effect up to the 61st day but not less than 31 days after the date of issuance. An order for emergency protection issued under Subsection (b)(2) of this article remains in effect up to the 91st day but not less than 61 days after the date of issuance. After notice to each affected party and a hearing, the issuing court may modify all or part of an order issued under this article if the court finds that:

(1) the order as originally issued is unworkable;

(2) the modification will not place the victim of the offense at greater risk than did the original order; and

(3) the modification will not in any way endanger a person protected under the order.

(k) To ensure that an officer responding to a call is aware of the existence and terms of an order for emergency protection issued under this article, each municipal police department and sheriff shall establish a procedure within the department or office to provide adequate information or access to information for peace officers of the names of persons protected by an order for emergency protection issued under this article and of persons to whom the order is directed. The police department or sheriff may enter an order for emergency protection issued under this article in the department's or office's record of outstanding warrants as notice that the order has been issued and is in effect.

(l) In the order for emergency protection, the magistrate may suspend a license to carry a concealed handgun issued under Section 411.177, Government Code, that is held by the defendant.

(m) In this article:

(1) "Family," "family violence," and "household" have the meanings assigned by Chapter 71, Family Code.

(2) "Firearm" has the meaning assigned by Chapter 46, Penal Code.

(n) On motion, notice, and hearing, or on agreement of the parties, an order for emergency protection issued under this article may be transferred to the court assuming jurisdiction over the criminal act giving rise to the issuance of the emergency order for protection. On transfer, the criminal court may modify all or part of an order issued under this subsection in the same manner and under the same standards as the issuing court under Subsection (j).

History of CCP art. 17.292: Acts 1995, 74th Leg., ch. 658, §1, eff. June 14, 1995. Amended by Acts 1997, 75th Leg., ch. 1, §4 (eff. Jan. 28, 1997), ch. 610, §1 (eff. Sept. 1, 1997); Acts 1999, 76th Leg., ch. 514, §1, (eff. Sept. 1, 1999), ch. 1412, §1, (eff. Sept. 1, 1999); Acts 2001, 77th Leg., ch. 23, §4, eff. Sept. 1, 2001; Acts 2003, 78th Leg., ch. 424, §1, eff. Sept. 1, 2003; Acts 2005, 79th Leg., ch. 361, §1, eff. June 17, 2005; Acts 2007, 80th Leg., ch. 66, §1, eff. May 11, 2007.

See also *O'Connor's Family Law Handbook*, "Duties of Law Enforcement," ch. 6-E.

ART. 17.293. DELIVERY OF ORDER FOR EMERGENCY PROTECTION TO OTHER PERSONS

The magistrate or the clerk of the magistrate's court issuing an order for emergency protection under Article 17.292 that suspends a license to carry a concealed handgun shall immediately send a copy of the order to the appropriate division of the Department of Public Safety at its Austin headquarters. On receipt of the order suspending the license, the department shall:

(1) record the suspension of the license in the records of the department;

(2) report the suspension to local law enforcement agencies, as appropriate; and

(3) demand surrender of the suspended license from the license holder.

History of CCP art. 17.293: Acts 1999, 76th Leg., ch. 1412, §1, eff. Sept. 1, 1999.

ART. 17.30. SHALL CERTIFY PROCEEDINGS

The magistrate, before whom an examination has taken place upon a criminal accusation, shall certify to all the proceedings had before him, as well as where he discharges, holds to bail or commits, and transmit them, sealed up, to the court before which the defendant may be tried, writing his name across the seals of the envelope. The voluntary statement of the defendant, the testimony, bail bonds, and every other proceeding in the case, shall be thus delivered to the clerk of the proper court, without delay.

History of CCP art. 17.30: Acts 1965, 59th Leg., vol. 2, ch. 722.

ART. 17.31. DUTY OF CLERKS WHO RECEIVE SUCH PROCEEDINGS

If the proceedings be delivered to a district clerk, he shall keep them safely and deliver the same to the next grand jury. If the proceedings are delivered to a county clerk, he shall without delay deliver them to the district or county attorney of his county.

History of CCP art. 17.31: Acts 1965, 59th Leg., vol. 2, ch. 722.

ART. 17.32. IN CASE OF NO ARREST

Upon failure from any cause to arrest the accused the magistrate shall file with the proper clerk the complaint, warrant of arrest, and a list of the witnesses.

History of CCP art. 17.32: Acts 1965, 59th Leg., vol. 2, ch. 722.

ART. 17.33. REQUEST SETTING OF BAIL

The accused may at any time after being confined request a magistrate to review the written statements of the witnesses for the State as well as all other evidence available at that time in determining the amount of bail. This setting of the amount of bail does not waive the defendant's right to an examining trial as provided in Article 16.01.

History of CCP art. 17.33: Acts 1965, 59th Leg., vol. 2, ch. 722.

ART. 17.34. WITNESSES TO GIVE BOND

Witnesses for the State or defendant may be required by the magistrate, upon the examination of any criminal accusation before him, to give bail for their appearance to testify before the proper court. A personal bond may be taken of a witness by the court before whom the case is pending.

History of CCP art. 17.34: Acts 1965, 59th Leg., vol. 2, ch. 722.

ART. 17.35. SECURITY OF WITNESS

The amount of security to be required of a witness is to be regulated by his pecuniary condition, character and the nature of the offense with respect to which he is a witness.

History of CCP art. 17.35: Acts 1965, 59th Leg., vol. 2, ch. 722.

ART. 17.36. EFFECT OF WITNESS BOND

The bond given by a witness for his appearance has the same effect as a bond of the accused and may be forfeited and recovered upon in the same manner.

History of CCP art. 17.36: Acts 1965, 59th Leg., vol. 2, ch. 722.

ART. 17.37. WITNESS MAY BE COMMITTED

A witness required to give bail who fails or refuses to do so shall be committed to jail as in other cases of a failure to give bail when required, but shall be released from custody upon giving such bail.

History of CCP art. 17.37: Acts 1965, 59th Leg., vol. 2, ch. 722.

ART. 17.38. RULES APPLICABLE TO ALL CASES OF BAIL

The rules in this Chapter respecting bail are applicable to all such undertakings when entered into in the course of a criminal action, whether before or after an indictment, in every case where authority is given to any court, judge, magistrate, or other officer, to require bail of a person accused of an offense, or of a witness in a criminal action.

History of CCP art. 17.38: Acts 1965, 59th Leg., vol. 2, ch. 722.

ANNOTATIONS

Ex parte Johnston, 533 S.W.2d 349, 352 (Tex.Crim. App.1976). "[T]he return of the indictment has no effect whatsoever upon the rules respecting the determination of the proper amount of bail."

ART. 17.39. RECORDS OF BAIL

A magistrate or other officer who sets the amount of bail or who takes bail shall record in a well-bound book the name of the person whose appearance the bail secures, the amount of bail, the date bail is set, the magistrate or officer who sets bail, the offense or other cause for which the appearance is secured, the magistrate or other officer who takes bail, the date the person is released, and the name of the bondsman, if any.

History of CCP art. 17.39: Acts 1977, 65th Leg., ch. 618, §1, eff. Aug. 29, 1977.

ART. 17.40. CONDITIONS RELATED TO VICTIM OR COMMUNITY SAFETY

(a) To secure a defendant's attendance at trial, a magistrate may impose any reasonable condition of bond related to the safety of a victim of the alleged offense or to the safety of the community.

 Subsection (b) below is effective for offenses committed on or after Jan. 1, 2008.

(b) At a hearing limited to determining whether the defendant violated a condition of bond imposed under Subsection (a), the magistrate may revoke the defendant's bond only if the magistrate finds by a preponderance of the evidence that the violation occurred. If the magistrate finds that the violation occurred, the magistrate shall revoke the defendant's bond and order that the defendant be immediately returned to custody. Once the defendant is placed in custody, the revocation of the defendant's bond discharges the sureties on the bond, if any, from any future liability on the bond. A discharge under this subsection from any future liability on the bond does not discharge any surety from liability for previous forfeitures on the bond.

History of CCP art. 17.40: Acts 1999, 76th Leg., ch. 768, §1, eff. Sept. 1, 1999. Amended by Acts 2007, 80th Leg., ch. 1113, §4, eff. Jan. 1, 2008.

History of Former CCP art. 17.40: Repealed by Acts 1989, 71st Leg., ch. 374, §5, eff. Sept. 1, 1989.

ANNOTATIONS

Burson v. State, 202 S.W.3d 423, 425 (Tex.App.— Tyler 2006, no pet.). "Section 17.40(a) is confusing in that it can be read to require that conditions for pretrial bail must relate to all three criteria—reasonableness, securing the defendant's appearance at trial, and protecting the safety of others. [***Ex parte Anderer***, 61 S.W.3d 398 (Tex.Crim.App.2001)] suggests that a condition required for the protection of the victim or the community must also be related to securing the defendant's trial appearance. However, conditions related to the safety of others are not always related to insuring the defendant's appearance at trial. The issue in *Anderer* was the reasonableness of a bail condition pending appeal, not a pretrial bail condition. *At 426: Anderer* did not address whether, under §17.40(a), a condition might be required that is solely related to the safety of the victim or the community. We believe that §17.40(a) should be interpreted as 'authorizing conditions that are reasonably related to securing the accused's presence at trial, the safety of the victim, *or* the safety of the community.'"

ART. 17.41. CONDITION WHERE CHILD ALLEGED VICTIM

(a) This article applies to a defendant charged with an offense under any of the following provisions of the Penal Code, if committed against a child 12 years of age or younger:

(1) Chapter 21 (Sexual Offenses) or 22 (Assaultive Offenses);

(2) Section 25.02 (Prohibited Sexual Conduct); or

(3) Section 43.25 (Sexual Performance by a Child).

(b) A magistrate may require as a condition of bond for a defendant charged with an offense described by Subsection (a) of this article that the defendant not directly communicate with the alleged victim of the offense or go near a residence, school, or other location, as specifically described in the bond, frequented by the alleged victim.

(c) A magistrate who imposes a condition of bond under this article may grant the defendant supervised access to the alleged victim.

(d) To the extent that a condition imposed under this article conflicts with an existing court order granting possession of or access to a child, the condition imposed under this article prevails for a period specified by the magistrate, not to exceed 90 days.

History of CCP art. 17.41: Acts 1985, 69th Leg., ch. 595, §1, eff. Sept. 1, 1985. Amended by Acts 1995, 74th Leg., ch. 76, §14.21, eff. Sept. 1, 1995.

ANNOTATIONS

Ex parte Tucker, 977 S.W.2d 713, 717 (Tex.App.— Fort Worth 1998), *pet. dism'd*, 3 S.W.3d 576 (Tex.Crim. App.1999). "[W]e hold that the trial court does not have inherent authority to impose conditions on a defendant's pre-trial bond that are not authorized by statute and further, that [CCP art.] 17.15 does not implicitly authorize other conditions not expressly stated. The

trial court thus erred in setting conditions on [appellant's] bond at the conclusion of the habeas hearing that restricted him from having unsupervised contact or living with children under age 18."

ART. 17.42. PERSONAL BOND OFFICE

Sec. 1. Any county, or any judicial district with jurisdiction in more than one county, with the approval of the commissioners court of each county in the district, may establish a personal bond office to gather and review information about an accused that may have a bearing on whether he will comply with the conditions of a personal bond and report its findings to the court before which the case is pending.

Sec. 2. (a) The commissioners court of a county that establishes the office or the district and county judges of a judicial district that establishes the office may employ a director of the office.

(b) The director may employ the staff authorized by the commissioners court of the county or the commissioners court of each county in the judicial district.

Sec. 3. If a judicial district establishes an office, each county in the district shall pay its pro rata share of the costs of administering the office according to its population.

Sec. 4. (a) If a court releases an accused on personal bond on the recommendation of a personal bond office, the court shall assess a personal bond fee of $20 or three percent of the amount of the bail fixed for the accused, whichever is greater. The court may waive the fee or assess a lesser fee if good cause is shown.

(b) Fees collected under this article may be used solely to defray expenses of the personal bond office, including defraying the expenses of extradition.

(c) Fees collected under this article shall be deposited in the county treasury, or if the office serves more than one county, the fees shall be apportioned to each county in the district according to each county's pro rata share of the costs of the office.

Sec. 5. (a) A personal bond pretrial release office established under this article shall:

(1) prepare a record containing information about any accused person identified by case number only who, after review by the office, is released by a court on personal bond;

(2) update the record on a monthly basis; and

(3) post a copy of the record in the office of the clerk of the county court in any county served by the office.

(b) In preparing a record under Subsection (a), the office shall include in the record a statement of:

(1) the offense with which the person is charged;

(2) the dates of any court appearances scheduled in the matter that were previously unattended by the person;

(3) whether a warrant has been issued for the person's arrest for failure to appear in accordance with the terms of the person's release;

(4) whether the person has failed to comply with conditions of release on personal bond; and

(5) the presiding judge or magistrate who authorized the personal bond.

(c) This section does not apply to a personal bond pretrial release office that on January 1, 1995, was operated by a community corrections and supervision department.

Sec. 6. (a) Not later than April 1 of each year, a personal bond office established under this article shall submit to the commissioners court or district and county judges that established the office an annual report containing information about the operations of the office during the preceding year.

(b) In preparing an annual report under Subsection (a), the office shall include in the report a statement of:

(1) the office's operating budget;

(2) the number of positions maintained for office staff;

(3) the number of accused persons who, after review by the office, were released by a court on personal bond; and

(4) the number of persons described by Subdivision (3):

(A) who were convicted of the same offense or of any felony within the six years preceding the date on which charges were filed in the matter pending during the person's release;

(B) who failed to attend a scheduled court appearance;

(C) for whom a warrant was issued for the person's arrest for failure to appear in accordance with the terms of the person's release; or

(D) who were arrested for any other offense while on the personal bond.

(c) This section does not apply to a personal bond pretrial release office that on January 1, 1995, was operated by a community corrections and supervision department.

History of CCP art. 17.42: Acts 1989, 71st Leg., ch. 2, §5.01(a) (eff. Aug. 28, 1989), ch. 1080, §1 (eff. Sept. 1, 1989). Amended by Acts 1995, 74th Leg., ch. 318, §44, eff. Sept. 1, 1995.

ART. 17.43. HOME CURFEW & ELECTRONIC MONITORING AS CONDITION

(a) A magistrate may require as a condition of release on personal bond that the defendant submit to home curfew and electronic monitoring under the supervision of an agency designated by the magistrate.

(b) Cost of monitoring may be assessed as court costs or ordered paid directly by the defendant as a condition of bond.

History of CCP art. 17.43: Acts 1989, 71st Leg., ch. 374, §4, eff. Sept. 1, 1989.

ART. 17.44. HOME CONFINEMENT, ELECTRONIC MONITORING, & DRUG TESTING AS CONDITION

(a) A magistrate may require as a condition of release on bond that the defendant submit to:

(1) home confinement and electronic monitoring under the supervision of an agency designated by the magistrate; or

(2) testing on a weekly basis for the presence of a controlled substance in the defendant's body.

(b) In this article, "controlled substance" has the meaning assigned by Section 481.002, Health and Safety Code.

(c) If a defendant violates a condition of home confinement and electronic monitoring, refuses to submit to a test for controlled substances, or submits to a test for controlled substances and the test indicates the presence of a controlled substance in the defendant's body, the magistrate may revoke the bond and order the defendant arrested.

(d) The community justice assistance division of the Texas Department of Criminal Justice may provide grants to counties to implement electronic monitoring programs authorized by this article.

History of CCP art. 17.44: Acts 1989, 71st Leg., ch. 785, §4.03, eff. Sept. 1, 1989. Renumbered from Art. 17.42 and amended by Acts 1991, 72nd Leg., ch. 14, §284(46) (eff. Sept. 1, 1991), ch. 16, §19.01(3) (eff. Aug. 26, 1991).

Speth v. State, 939 S.W.2d 769, 771 (Tex.App.— Houston [14th Dist.] 1997, no pet.). "[E]lectronic monitoring is a reasonable appeal bond condition because it furthers the paramount purpose of ensuring appellant's appearance if and when his conviction becomes final and non-appealable." *But see Ex parte Anderer*, 61 S.W.3d 398, 404-05 (Tex.Crim.App.2001).

ART. 17.441. CONDITIONS REQUIRING MOTOR VEHICLE IGNITION INTERLOCK

(a) Except as provided by Subsection (b), a magistrate shall require on release that a defendant charged with a subsequent offense under Sections 49.04-49.06, Penal Code, or an offense under Section 49.07 or 49.08 of that code:

(1) have installed on the motor vehicle owned by the defendant or on the vehicle most regularly driven by the defendant, a device that uses a deep-lung breath analysis mechanism to make impractical the operation of a motor vehicle if ethyl alcohol is detected in the breath of the operator; and

(2) not operate any motor vehicle unless the vehicle is equipped with that device.

(b) The magistrate may not require the installation of the device if the magistrate finds that to require the device would not be in the best interest of justice.

(c) If the defendant is required to have the device installed, the magistrate shall require that the defendant have the device installed on the appropriate motor vehicle, at the defendant's expense, before the 30th day after the date the defendant is released on bond.

(d) The magistrate may designate an appropriate agency to verify the installation of the device and to monitor the device. If the magistrate designates an agency under this subsection, in each month during which the agency verifies the installation of the device or provides a monitoring service the defendant shall pay a fee to the designated agency in the amount set by the magistrate. The defendant shall pay the initial fee at the time the agency verifies the installation of the device. In each subsequent month during which the defendant is required to pay a fee the defendant shall pay the fee on the first occasion in that month that the agency provides a monitoring service. The magistrate shall set the fee in an amount not to exceed $10 as determined by the county auditor, or by the commissioners court of the county if the county does not have a county auditor, to be sufficient to cover the cost incurred by the designated agency in conducting the verification or providing the monitoring service, as applicable in that county.

History of CCP art. 17.441: Acts 1995, 74th Leg., ch. 318, §45, eff. Sept. 1, 1995. Amended by Acts 1999, 76th Leg., ch. 537, §1, eff. Sept. 1, 1999.

ART. 17.45. CONDITIONS REQUIRING AIDS & HIV INSTRUCTION

A magistrate may require as a condition of bond that a defendant charged with an offense under Section 43.02, Penal Code, receive counseling or education, or both, relating to acquired immune deficiency syndrome or human immunodeficiency virus.

History of CCP art. 17.45: Acts 1989, 71st Leg., ch. 1195, §8, eff. Sept. 1, 1989. Renumbered from Art. 17.42 by Acts 1991, 72nd Leg., ch. 16, §19.01(4), eff. Aug. 26, 1991.

ART. 17.46. CONDITIONS FOR A DEFENDANT CHARGED WITH STALKING

(a) A magistrate may require as a condition of release on bond that a defendant charged with an offense under Section 42.072, Penal Code, may not:

(1) communicate directly or indirectly with the victim; or

(2) go to or near the residence, place of employment, or business of the victim or to or near a school, day-care facility, or similar facility where a dependent child of the victim is in attendance.

(b) If the magistrate requires the prohibition contained in Subsection (a)(2) of this article as a condition of release on bond, the magistrate shall specifically describe the prohibited locations and the minimum distances, if any, that the defendant must maintain from the locations.

History of CCP art. 17.46: Acts 1993, 73rd Leg., ch. 10, §2, eff. Mar. 19, 1993. Amended by Acts 1995, 74th Leg., ch. 657, §3, eff. June 14, 1995; Acts 1997, 75th Leg., ch. 1, §5, eff. Jan. 28, 1997.

ART. 17.47. CONDITIONS REQUIRING SUBMISSION OF SPECIMEN

(a) A magistrate may require as a condition of release on bail or bond of a defendant that the defendant provide to a local law enforcement agency one or more specimens for the purpose of creating a DNA record under Subchapter G, Chapter 411, Government Code.

(b) A magistrate shall require as a condition of release on bail or bond of a defendant described by Section 411.1471(a), Government Code, that the defendant provide to a local law enforcement agency one or more specimens for the purpose of creating a DNA record under Subchapter G, Chapter 411, Government Code.

History of CCP art. 17.47: Acts 2001, 77th Leg., ch. 1490, §5, eff. Sept. 1, 2001. Amended by Acts 2005, 79th Leg., ch. 1224, §17, eff. Sept. 1, 2005.

See also *O'Connor's Crimes & Consequences* (2008-09), chart 2-K, "DNA Records of Persons Charged or Convicted of Certain Offenses."

ART. 17.48. POSTTRIAL ACTIONS

A convicting court on entering a finding favorable to a convicted person under Article 64.04, after a hearing at which the attorney representing the state and the counsel for the defendant are entitled to appear, may release the convicted person on bail under this chapter pending the conclusion of court proceedings or proceedings under Section 11, Article IV, Texas Constitution, and Article 48.01.

History of CCP art. 17.48: Acts 2001, 77th Leg., ch. 2, §3, eff. Apr. 5, 2001. Renumbered from Art. 17.47 by Acts 2003, 78th Leg., ch. 1275, §2(6), eff. Sept. 1, 2003.

CHAPTER 17A. CORPORATIONS & ASSOCIATIONS

ART. 17A.01. APPLICATION & DEFINITIONS

(a) This chapter sets out some of the procedural rules applicable to the criminal responsibility of corporations and associations. Where not in conflict with this chapter, the other chapters of this code apply to corporations and associations.

(b) In this code, unless the context requires a different definition:

(1) "Agent" means a director, officer, employee, or other person authorized to act in behalf of a corporation or association.

(2) "Association" means a government or governmental subdivision or agency, trust, partnership, or two or more persons having a joint or common economic interest.

(3) "High managerial agent" means:

(A) an officer of a corporation or association;

(B) a partner in a partnership; or

(C) an agent of a corporation or association who has duties of such responsibility that his conduct may reasonably be assumed to represent the policy of the corporation or association.

(4) "Person," "he," and "him" include corporation and association.

History of CCP art. 17A.01: Acts 1973, 63rd Leg., ch. 399, §2(D), eff. Jan. 1, 1974.

ART. 17A.02. ALLEGATION OF NAME

(a) In alleging the name of a defendant corporation, it is sufficient to state in the complaint, indictment, or information the corporate name, or to state any name or designation by which the corporation is known or may be identified. It is not necessary to allege that the defendant was lawfully incorporated.

(b) In alleging the name of a defendant association it is sufficient to state in the complaint, indictment, or information the association's name, or to state any name or designation by which the association is known or may be identified, or to state the name or names of one or more members of the association, referring to the unnamed members as "others." It is not necessary to allege the legal form of the association.

History of CCP art. 17A.02: Acts 1973, 63rd Leg., ch. 399, §2(D), eff. Jan. 1, 1974.

ART. 17A.03. SUMMONING CORPORATION OR ASSOCIATION

(a) When a complaint is filed or an indictment or information presented against a corporation or association, the court or clerk shall issue a summons to the corporation or association. The summons shall be in the same form as a capias except that:

(1) it shall summon the corporation or association to appear before the court named at the place stated in the summons; and

(2) it shall be accompanied by a certified copy of the complaint, indictment, or information; and

(3) it shall provide that the corporation or association appear before the court named at or before 10 a.m. of the Monday next after the expiration of 20 days after it is served with summons, except when service is made upon the secretary of state or the Commissioner of Insurance, in which instance the summons shall provide that the corporation or association appear before the court named at or before 10 a.m. of the Monday next after the expiration of 30 days after the secretary of state or the Commissioner of Insurance is served with summons.

(b) No individual may be arrested upon a complaint, indictment, information, judgment, or sentence against a corporation or association.

History of CCP art. 17A.03: Acts 1973, 63rd Leg., ch. 399, §2(D), eff. Jan. 1, 1974. Amended by Acts 1987, 70th Leg., ch. 46, §10, eff. Sept. 1, 1987.

ART. 17A.04. SERVICE ON CORPORATION

(a) Except as provided in Paragraph (d) of this article, a peace officer shall serve a summons on a corporation by personally delivering a copy of it to the corporation's registered agent. However, if a registered agent has not been designated, or cannot with reasonable diligence be found at the registered office, then the peace officer shall serve the summons by personally delivering a copy of it to the president or a vice-president of the corporation.

(b) If the peace officer certifies on the return that he diligently but unsuccessfully attempted to effect service under Paragraph (a) of this article, or if the corporation is a foreign corporation that has no certificate of authority, then he shall serve the summons on the secretary of state by personally delivering a copy of it to him, or to the deputy secretary of state, or to any clerk in charge of the corporation department of his office. On receipt of the summons copy, the secretary of state shall immediately forward it by certified or registered mail, return receipt requested, addressed to the defendant corporation at its registered or principal office in the state or country under whose law it was incorporated.

(c) The secretary of state shall keep a permanent record of the date and time of receipt and his disposition of each summons served under Paragraph (b) of this article together with the return receipt.

(d) The method of service on a corporation regulated under the Insurance Code is governed by that code.

History of CCP art. 17A.04: Acts 1973, 63rd Leg., ch. 399, §2(D), eff. Jan. 1, 1974. Amended by Acts 2005, 79th Leg., ch. 41, §15, eff. Sept. 1, 2005.

ART. 17A.05. SERVICE ON ASSOCIATION

(a) Except as provided in Paragraph (b) of this article, a peace officer shall serve a summons on an association by personally delivering a copy of it:

(1) to a high managerial agent at any place where business of the association is regularly conducted; or

(2) if the peace officer certifies on the return that he diligently but unsuccessfully attempted to serve a high managerial agent, to any employee of suitable age and discretion at any place where business of the association is regularly conducted; or

(3) if the peace officer certifies on the return that he diligently but unsuccessfully attempted to serve a high managerial agent, or employee of suitable age and discretion, to any member of the association.

(b) The method of service on an association regulated under the Insurance Code is governed by that code.

History of CCP art. 17A.05: Acts 1973, 63rd Leg., ch. 399, §2(D), eff. Jan. 1, 1974.

ART. 17A.06. APPEARANCE

(a) In all criminal actions instituted against a corporation or association, in which original jurisdiction is in a district or county-level court:

(1) appearance is for the purpose of arraignment;

(2) the corporation or association has 10 full days after the day the arraignment takes place and before the day the trial begins to file written pleadings.

(b) In all criminal actions instituted against a corporation or association, in which original jurisdiction is in a justice court or corporation court:

(1) appearance is for the purpose of entering a plea; and

(2) 10 full days must elapse after the day of appearance before the corporation or association may be tried.

History of CCP art. 17A.06: Acts 1973, 63rd Leg., ch. 399, §2(D), eff. Jan. 1, 1974.

ART. 17A.07. PRESENCE OF CORPORATION OR ASSOCIATION

(a) A defendant corporation or association appears through counsel.

(b) If a corporation or association does not appear in response to summons, or appears but fails or refuses to plead:

(1) it is deemed to be present in person for all purposes; and

(2) the court shall enter a plea of not guilty in its behalf; and

(3) the court may proceed with trial, judgment, and sentencing.

(c) If, having appeared and entered a plea in response to summons, a corporation or association is absent without good cause at any time during later proceedings:

(1) it is deemed to be present in person for all purposes; and

(2) the court may proceed with trial, judgment, or sentencing.

History of CCP art. 17A.07: Acts 1973, 63rd Leg., ch. 399, §2(D), eff. Jan. 1, 1974.

ART. 17A.08. PROBATION

The benefits of the adult probation laws shall not be available to corporations and associations.

History of CCP art. 17A.08: Acts 1973, 63rd Leg., ch. 399, §2(D), eff. Jan. 1, 1974.

ART. 17A.09. NOTIFYING ATTORNEY GENERAL OF CORPORATION'S CONVICTION

If a corporation is convicted of an offense, or if a high managerial agent is convicted of an offense committed in the conduct of the affairs of the corporation, the court shall notify the attorney general in writing of the conviction when it becomes final and unappealable. The notice shall include:

(1) the corporation's name, and the name of the corporation's registered agent and the address of the registered office, or the high managerial agent's name and address, or both; and

(2) certified copies of the judgment and sentence and of the complaint, information, or indictment on which the judgment and sentence were based.

History of CCP art. 17A.09: Acts 1973, 63rd Leg., ch. 399, §2(D), eff. Jan. 1, 1974.

ART. 18.01. SEARCH WARRANT

(a) A "search warrant" is a written order, issued by a magistrate and directed to a peace officer, commanding him to search for any property or thing and to seize the same and bring it before such magistrate or commanding him to search for and photograph a child and to deliver to the magistrate any of the film exposed pursuant to the order.

 Subsection (b) below is effective for affidavits presented on or after Sept. 1, 2007.

(b) No search warrant shall issue for any purpose in this state unless sufficient facts are first presented to satisfy the issuing magistrate that probable cause does in fact exist for its issuance. A sworn affidavit setting forth substantial facts establishing probable cause shall be filed in every instance in which a search warrant is requested. Except as provided by Article 18.011, the affidavit is public information if executed, and the magistrate's clerk shall make a copy of the affidavit available for public inspection in the clerk's office during normal business hours.

Subsection (b) below is effective for affidavits presented before Sept. 1, 2007.

(b) No search warrant shall issue for any purpose in this state unless sufficient facts are first presented to satisfy the issuing magistrate that probable cause does in fact exist for its issuance. A sworn affidavit setting forth substantial facts establishing probable cause shall be filed in every instance in which a search warrant is requested. The affidavit is public information if executed, and the magistrate's clerk shall make a copy of the affidavit available for public inspection in the clerk's office during normal business hours.

(c) A search warrant may not be issued pursuant to Subdivision (10) of Article 18.02 of this code unless the sworn affidavit required by Subsection (b) of this article sets forth sufficient facts to establish probable cause: (1) that a specific offense has been committed, (2) that the specifically described property or items that are to be searched for or seized constitute evidence of that offense or evidence that a particular person committed that offense, and (3) that the property or items constituting evidence to be searched for or seized are located at or on the particular person, place, or thing to be searched. Except as provided by Subsections (d) and (i) of this article, only a judge of a municipal court of record or county court who is an attorney licensed by the State of Texas, statutory county court, district court, the Court of Criminal Appeals, or the Supreme Court may issue warrants pursuant to Subdivision (10), Article 18.02 of this code.

(d) Only the specifically described property or items set forth in a search warrant issued under Subdivision (10) of Article 18.02 of this code or property, items or contraband enumerated in Subdivisions (1) through (9) or in Subdivision (12) of Article 18.02 of this code may be seized. A subsequent search warrant may be issued pursuant to Subdivision (10) of Article 18.02 of this code to search the same person, place, or thing subjected to a prior search under Subdivision (10) of Article 18.02 of this code only if the subsequent search warrant is issued by a judge of a district court, a court of appeals, the court of criminal appeals, or the supreme court.

(e) A search warrant may not be issued under Subdivision (10) of Article 18.02 of this code to search for and seize property or items that are not described in Subdivisions (1) through (9) of that article and that are located in an office of a newspaper, news magazine, television station, or radio station, and in no event may property or items not described in Subdivisions (1) through (9) of that article be legally seized in any search pursuant to a search warrant of an office of a newspaper, news magazine, television station, or radio station.

(f) A search warrant may not be issued pursuant to Article 18.021 of this code unless the sworn affidavit required by Subsection (b) of this article sets forth sufficient facts to establish probable cause:

(1) that a specific offense has been committed;

(2) that a specifically described person has been a victim of the offense;

(3) that evidence of the offense or evidence that a particular person committed the offense can be detected by photographic means; and

(4) that the person to be searched for and photographed is located at the particular place to be searched.

(g) A search warrant may not be issued under Subdivision (12), Article 18.02, of this code unless the sworn affidavit required by Subsection (b) of this article sets forth sufficient facts to establish probable cause that a specific felony offense has been committed and that the specifically described property or items that are to be searched for or seized constitute contraband as defined in Article 59.01 of this code and are located at or on the particular person, place, or thing to be searched.

(h) Except as provided by Subsection (i) of this article, a warrant under Subdivision (12), Article 18.02 of this code may only be issued by:

(1) a judge of a municipal court of record who is an attorney licensed by the state;

(2) a judge of a county court who is an attorney licensed by the state; or

(3) a judge of a statutory county court, district court, the court of criminal appeals, or the supreme court.

Ⓐ *Subsection (i) below is effective for warrants issued on or after Sept. 1, 2007.*

(i) In a county that does not have a judge of a municipal court of record who is an attorney licensed by the state, a county court judge who is an attorney licensed by the state, or a statutory county court judge, any magistrate may issue a search warrant under Subdivision (10) or Subdivision (12) of Article 18.02 of this code. This subsection is not applicable to a subsequent search warrant under Subdivision (10) of Article 18.02 of this code.

Subsection (i) below is effective for warrants issued before Sept. 1, 2007.

(i) In a county in which the only judge serving the county who is a licensed attorney is a district judge whose district includes more than one county or in which the only judges serving the county who are licensed attorneys are two or more district judges each of whose district includes more than one county, any magistrate may issue a search warrant under Subdivision

(10) or Subdivision (12) of Article 18.02 of this code. This section is not applicable to a subsequent search warrant under Subdivision (10) of Article 18.02 of this code.

History of CCP art. 18.01: Acts 1965, 59th Leg., vol. 2, ch. 722. Amended by Acts 1973, 63rd Leg., ch. 399, §2(E), eff. Jan. 1, 1974; Acts 1977, 65th Leg., ch. 237, §1, eff. May 25, 1977; Acts 1979, 66th Leg., ch. 505, §1 (eff. Sept. 1, 1979), ch. 536, §1 (eff. June 11, 1979); Acts 1981, 67th Leg., ch. 289, §§3, 4 (eff. Sept. 1, 1981), ch. 755, §1 (eff. Sept. 1, 1981); Acts 1987, 70th Leg., ch. 686, §1, eff. Sept. 1, 1987; Acts 1989, 71st Leg., 1st C.S., ch. 12, §2, eff. Oct. 18, 1989; Acts 1991, 72nd Leg., ch. 73, §1, eff. May 9, 1991; Acts 1995, 74th Leg., ch. 670, §1, eff. Sept. 1, 1995; Acts 1997, 75th Leg., ch. 604, §1, eff. Sept. 1, 1997; Acts 1999, 76th Leg., ch. 167, §1 (eff. Aug. 30, 1999), ch. 1469, §1 (eff. June 19, 1999); Acts 2001, 77th Leg., ch. 1395, §1, eff. June 16, 2001; Acts 2007, 80th Leg., ch. 355, §1 (eff. Sept. 1, 2007), ch. 748, §1 (eff. Sept. 1, 2007).

ANNOTATIONS

Smith v. State, 207 S.W.3d 787, 788 (Tex.Crim.App. 2006). "[W]e address whether a search warrant is defective if the affiant swore before the magistrate that the facts within the affidavit were true, but he failed to sign the affidavit. [¶] We ... hold that the failure to sign a search warrant affidavit does not, by itself, invalidate the warrant if other evidence proves that the affiant personally swore to the truth of the facts in the affidavit before the issuing magistrate."

Swearingen v. State, 143 S.W.3d 808, 811 (Tex. Crim.App.2004). "[A] magistrate's determination to issue a warrant is subject to the deferential standard of review...." *See also Guzman v. State*, 955 S.W.2d 85, 87-89 (Tex.Crim.App.1997) (standard of review for warrantless search).

Arrick v. State, 107 S.W.3d 710, 715 (Tex.App.— Austin 2003, pet. ref'd). "Probable cause to support the issuance of a search warrant exists when the facts submitted to the magistrate are sufficient to justify a conclusion that the object of the search is probably on the premises at the time the warrant is issued. The sufficiency of a search warrant affidavit is determined by use of 'totality of the circumstances' analysis. Only the facts found within the four corners of the affidavit may be considered. Reasonable inferences may be drawn from the affidavit, however, and the affidavit must be interpreted in a common-sense and realistic manner." *See also Lowery v. State*, 98 S.W.3d 398 (Tex.App.— Amarillo 2003, no pet.); *Borsari v. State*, 919 S.W.2d 913, 917-18 (Tex.App.—Houston [14th Dist.] 1996, pet. ref'd).

State v. Young, 8 S.W.3d 695, 698 (Tex.App.—Fort Worth 1999, no pet.). "Appellee contends that the warrant in this case was a 'mere evidentiary' warrant governed by [CCP art.] 18.02(10), and not a warrant for an implement or instrument of a crime under article 18.02(9). As such, appellee argues the warrant did not authorize the seizure of the unspecified items because the warrant did not specifically identify them. The trial court suppressed the seized items, stating that [CCP art.] 18.01(d) plainly limits what can be ceased [sic] under 18.02(10).' However, we disagree with the trial court's classification of the warrant under 18.02(10).... [¶] [T]he police were searching for evidence. [¶] However, the documents also reflect an intent to search for an instrument of the crime."

State v. Anderson, 917 S.W.2d 92, 95 (Tex.App.— Houston [14th Dist.] 1996, pet. ref'd). "The affidavit must be more than a mere conclusory statement that gives the magistrate virtually no basis at all for making a judgment regarding probable cause. The magistrate must be presented with 'sufficient information' to allow that individual to determine probable cause[, which must be established by 'sufficient' and 'substantial' facts]. *At 96:* The reliability of the affiant and his sources of information are part of the totality of the circumstances that the magistrate should evaluate in making his probable cause determination. A magistrate, however, is entitled to rely on source information supplied by an average citizen, since, unlike many police informants, they are much less likely to produce false or untrustworthy information. The same rule applies to law enforcement officers. The magistrate may rely on the affidavit of a police officer based on his knowledge or the knowledge of other officers." (Internal quotes omitted.)

ART. 18.011. SEALING OF AFFIDAVIT

ⓔ *Article 18.011 below is effective for affidavits presented under article 18.01(b) on or after Sept. 1, 2007.*

(a) An attorney representing the state in the prosecution of felonies may request a district judge or the judge of an appellate court to seal an affidavit presented under Article 18.01(b). The judge may order the affidavit sealed if the attorney establishes a compelling state interest in that:

(1) public disclosure of the affidavit would jeopardize the safety of a victim, witness, or confidential informant or cause the destruction of evidence; or

(2) the affidavit contains information obtained from a court-ordered wiretap that has not expired at the time the attorney representing the state requests the sealing of the affidavit.

(b) An order sealing an affidavit under this section expires on the 31st day after the date on which the search warrant for which the affidavit was presented is executed. After an original order sealing an affidavit is issued under this article, an attorney representing the state in the prosecution of felonies may request, and a judge may grant, before the 31st day after the date on which the search warrant for which the affidavit was presented is executed, on a new finding of compelling state interest, one 30-day extension of the original order.

(c) On the expiration of an order issued under Subsection (b) and any extension, the affidavit must be unsealed.

(d) An order issued under this section may not:

(1) prohibit the disclosure of information relating to the contents of a search warrant, the return of a search warrant, or the inventory of property taken pursuant to a search warrant; or

(2) affect the right of a defendant to discover the contents of an affidavit.

History of CCP art. 18.011: Acts 2007, 80th Leg., ch. 355, §2, eff. Sept. 1, 2007.

ART. 18.02. GROUNDS FOR ISSUANCE

A search warrant may be issued to search for and seize:

(1) property acquired by theft or in any other manner which makes its acquisition a penal offense;

(2) property specially designed, made, or adapted for or commonly used in the commission of an offense;

(3) arms and munitions kept or prepared for the purposes of insurrection or riot;

(4) weapons prohibited by the Penal Code;

(5) gambling devices or equipment, altered gambling equipment, or gambling paraphernalia;

(6) obscene materials kept or prepared for commercial distribution or exhibition, subject to the additional rules set forth by law;

(7) a drug, controlled substance, immediate precursor, chemical precursor, or other controlled substance property, including an apparatus or paraphernalia kept, prepared, or manufactured in violation of the laws of this state;

(8) any property the possession of which is prohibited by law;

(9) implements or instruments used in the commission of a crime;

(10) property or items, except the personal writings by the accused, constituting evidence of an offense or constituting evidence tending to show that a particular person committed an offense;

(11) persons; or

(12) contraband subject to forfeiture under Chapter 59 of this code.

History of CCP art. 18.02: Acts 1965, 59th Leg., vol. 2, ch. 722. Amended by Acts 1973, 63rd Leg., ch. 399, §2(E), eff. Jan. 1, 1974; Acts 1977, 65th Leg., ch. 237, §2, eff. May 25, 1977; Acts 1981, 67th Leg., ch. 755, §5, eff. Sept. 1, 1981; Acts 1989, 71st Leg., 1st C.S., ch. 12, §3, eff. Oct. 18, 1989; Acts 2003, 78th Leg., ch. 1099, §16, eff. Sept. 1, 2003.

ANNOTATIONS

Ramos v. State, 934 S.W.2d 358, 365 (Tex.Crim. App.1996). "[T]he term 'persons' in Article 18.02(11) refers to both the living and the dead."

Gentry v. State, 640 S.W.2d 899, 902-03 (Tex.Crim. App.1982). "[T]hough 'blood' is not specifically itemized in Article 18.02, it is nonetheless an item of evidence to search for and to seize which a search warrant may issue in accordance with other applicable provisions of Chapter Eighteen."

Mullican v. State, 157 S.W.3d 870, 873 (Tex.App.— Fort Worth 2005, pet. ref'd). "Personal writings refers to writings like diaries, memos, and journals that were not intended by the writer to be published to third parties, and personal, nonbusiness letters. These forms of personal written expression do not include pornographic photographs of children." *See also **Reeves v. State***, 969 S.W.2d 471, 486 (Tex.App.—Waco 1998, pet. ref'd).

Reeves v. State, 969 S.W.2d 471, 486 (Tex.App.— Waco 1998, pet. ref'd). "[T]he evidence [appellant] objected to was properly seized, although it was not listed in the warrant issued under [CCP art.] 18.02(10) and although the items were 'mere evidence' rather than fruits, instrumentalities, or contraband. There is no dispute that the evidence was discovered and seized in the course of a good faith search conducted within the parameters of a valid search warrant. Further, the evidence was reasonably related to the offense under investigation, and the officer seizing the evidence had a reasonable basis for drawing the connection between the evidence observed and the crime. [¶] [W]e are not convinced that a 'form letter' or an advertisement to be placed in a magazine are 'personal writings.' ... Second, we would find that, because the warrant did not authorize their seizure, Article 18.02(10) was not violated. If under ***Bower*** undescribed items constituting 'mere evidence' can be seized notwithstanding the provisions of [CCP art.] 18.01(d), we see no reason why these items could not also be seized."

Scott v. State, 868 S.W.2d 430, 432-33 (Tex.App.—Waco 1994, pet. ref'd). "Specific items not listed in [art. 18.02(1)-(9)] may be sought in a search warrant under the catch-all language of subsection (10). A search warrant issued under article 18.02(10) is referred to as an 'evidentiary warrant.' Only judges of municipal courts of record licensed as attorneys, statutory county or district judges, or judges from the Court of Criminal Appeals or Supreme Court may issue evidentiary warrants under article 18.02(10). However, if the item sought to be seized is listed in article 18.02 then any magistrate may issue the warrant." *See also* ***State v. Acosta***, 99 S.W.3d 301, 304 (Tex.App.—Corpus Christi 2003, pet. ref'd).

Davis v. State, 831 S.W.2d 426, 440 (Tex.App.—Austin 1992, pet. ref'd). "To justify the issuance of a search warrant under article 18.02(10), there must be a supporting affidavit setting out sufficient facts to establish probable cause that a specific offense has been committed, that the specifically described property or items that are to be searched for or seized constitute either evidence of that offense or evidence that a particular person committed that offense, and that the property or items constituting evidence to be searched for or seized are located at or on the particular person, place, or thing to be searched."

ART. 18.021. ISSUANCE OF SEARCH WARRANT TO PHOTOGRAPH INJURED CHILD

 Subsection (a) below is effective for offenses committed on or after Sept. 1, 2007.

(a) A search warrant may be issued to search for and photograph a child who is alleged to be the victim of the offenses of injury to a child as prohibited by Section 22.04, Penal Code; sexual assault of a child as prohibited by Section 22.011(a), Penal Code; aggravated sexual assault of a child as prohibited by Section 22.021, Penal Code; or continuous sexual abuse of young child or children as prohibited by Section 21.02, Penal Code.

Subsection (a) below is effective for offenses in which any element of the offense was committed before Sept. 1, 2007.

(a) A search warrant may be issued to search for and photograph a child who is alleged to be the victim of the offenses of injury to a child as defined by Section 22.04, Penal Code, as amended; sexual assault of a child as defined by Section 22.011(a), Penal Code, as amended; or aggravated sexual assault of a child as defined by Section 22.021, Penal Code.

(b) The officer executing the warrant may be accompanied by a photographer who is employed by a law enforcement agency and who acts under the direction of the officer executing the warrant. The photographer is entitled to access to the child in the same manner as the officer executing the warrant.

(c) In addition to the requirements of Subdivisions (1) and (4) of Article 18.04 of this code, a warrant issued under this article shall identify, as near as may be, the child to be located and photographed, shall name or describe, as near as may be, the place or thing to be searched, and shall command any peace officer of the proper county to search for and cause the child to be photographed.

(d) After having located and photographed the child, the peace officer executing the warrant shall take possession of the exposed film and deliver it forthwith to the magistrate. The child may not be removed from the premises on which he or she is located except under Subchapters A and B, Chapter 262, Family Code.

(e) A search warrant under this section shall be executed by a peace officer of the same sex as the alleged victim or, if the officer is not of the same sex as the alleged victim, the peace officer must be assisted by a person of the same sex as the alleged victim. The person assisting an officer under this subsection must be acting under the direction of the officer and must be with the alleged victim during the taking of the photographs.

History of CCP art. 18.021: Acts 1981, 67th Leg., ch. 289, §2, eff. Sept. 1, 1981. Amended by Acts 1983, 68th Leg., ch. 977, §8, eff. Sept. 1, 1983; Acts 1997, 75th Leg., ch. 165, §7.01, eff. Sept. 1, 1997; Acts 2007, 80th Leg., ch. 593, §3.11, eff. Sept. 1, 2007.

ART. 18.03. SEARCH WARRANT MAY ORDER ARREST

If the facts presented to the magistrate under Article 18.02 of this chapter also establish the existence of probable cause that a person has committed some offense under the laws of this state, the search warrant may, in addition, order the arrest of such person.

★

History of CCP art. 18.03: Acts 1965, 59th Leg., vol. 2, ch. 722. Amended by Acts 1973, 63rd Leg., ch. 399, §2(E), eff. Jan. 1, 1974.

ANNOTATIONS

Montez v. State, 608 S.W.2d 211, 215 n.10 (Tex. Crim.App.1980). "'[A]n arrest warrant incorporated within a search warrant is no different than an arrest warrant issued separate and independent of a search warrant' so that 'the authority to arrest under an arrest warrant incorporated in a search warrant is *not* limited to the premises described in the search warrant.'"

ART. 18.04. CONTENTS OF WARRANT

A search warrant issued under this chapter shall be sufficient if it contains the following requisites:

(1) that it run in the name of "The State of Texas";

(2) that it identify, as near as may be, that which is to be seized and name or describe, as near as may be, the person, place, or thing to be searched;

(3) that it command any peace officer of the proper county to search forthwith the person, place, or thing named; and

(4) that it be dated and signed by the magistrate.

History of CCP art. 18.04: Acts 1965, 59th Leg., vol. 2, ch. 722. Amended by Acts 1973, 63rd Leg., ch. 399, §2(E), eff. Jan. 1, 1974.

ANNOTATIONS

State v. Chavarria, 992 S.W.2d 22, 24-25 (Tex. App.—Houston [1st Dist.] 1997, pet. ref'd). "When testing the sufficiency of a warrant, the court uses a two prong test. First, the warrant must be sufficient to enable the executing officer to locate and distinguish the property from others in the community. Second, it must protect innocent parties from a reasonable probability of a mistaken execution of a defective warrant. However, technical discrepancies in the descriptive portions of a search warrant will not automatically void a warrant. [¶] Where a warrant describes a multi-unit dwelling, the description must contain sufficient guidelines to apprise the officers executing the warrant of the particular unit to be searched."

Rios v. State, 901 S.W.2d 704, 706 (Tex.App.—San Antonio 1995, no pet.). "A valid search warrant must contain a description of the place to be searched. [¶] [T]he description contained in the affidavit limits and controls the description contained in the warrant."

Lindley v. State, 773 S.W.2d 579, 581 (Tex.App.—Tyler 1989, pet. ref'd). "[T]he warrant must describe as nearly as possible the items to be seized. The requirement that the search be specific prohibits general searches and prevents the vesting of complete discretion in the officer who executes the warrant. [¶] The requirement for a sufficiently particular description can vary according to what is being described. In a search for property which by reason of its character is illegal, a specific description is unnecessary and ordinarily impossible."

ART. 18.05. WARRANTS FOR FIRE, HEALTH, & CODE INSPECTIONS

 (a) Except as provided by Subsection (e) of this article, a search warrant may be issued to a fire marshal, health officer, or code enforcement official of the state or of any county, city, or other political subdivision for the purpose of allowing the inspection of any specified premises to determine the presence of a fire or health hazard or unsafe building condition or a violation of any fire, health, or building regulation, statute, or ordinance.

(b) A search warrant may not be issued under this article except upon the presentation of evidence of probable cause to believe that a fire or health hazard or violation or unsafe building condition is present in the premises sought to be inspected.

(c) In determining probable cause, the magistrate is not limited to evidence of specific knowledge, but may consider any of the following:

(1) the age and general condition of the premises;

(2) previous violations or hazards found present in the premises;

(3) the type of premises;

(4) the purposes for which the premises are used; and

(5) the presence of hazards or violations in and the general condition of premises near the premises sought to be inspected.

 Subsection (d) below is effective for warrants issued on or after Sept. 1, 2007.

(d) Each city or county may designate one or more code enforcement officials for the purpose of being issued a search warrant as authorized by Subsection (a) of this article. A political subdivision other than a city or county may designate not more than one code enforcement official for the purpose of being issued a search warrant as authorized by Subsection (a) of this article only if the political subdivision routinely inspects premises to determine whether there is a fire or health hazard or unsafe building condition or a violation of fire, health, or building regulation, statute, or ordinance.

Subsection (d) below is effective for warrants issued before Sept. 1, 2007.

(d) Each city or county may designate one code enforcement official for the purpose of being issued a search warrant as authorized by Subsection (a) of this article. A political subdivision other than a city or county may designate one code enforcement official for the purpose of being issued a search warrant as authorized by Subsection (a) of this article only if the political subdivision routinely inspects premises to determine whether there is a fire or health hazard or unsafe building condition or a violation of fire, health, or building regulation, statute, or ordinance.

(e) A search warrant may not be issued under this article to a code enforcement official of a county with a population of 2.4 million or more for the purpose of allowing the inspection of specified premises to determine the presence of an unsafe building condition or a violation of a building regulation, statute, or ordinance.

History of CCP art. 18.05: Added as Art. 18.011 by Acts 1969, 61st Leg., ch. 502, §1, eff. Sept. 1, 1969. Amended by Acts 1973, 63rd Leg., ch. 399, §2(E), eff. Jan. 1, 1974; Acts 1989, 71st Leg., ch. 382, §1, eff. Aug. 28, 1989; Acts 2007, 80th Leg., ch. 769, §1, eff. Sept. 1, 2007.

ART. 18.06. EXECUTION OF WARRANTS

(a) A peace officer to whom a search warrant is delivered shall execute it without delay and forthwith return it to the proper magistrate. It must be executed within three days from the time of its issuance, and shall be executed within a shorter period if so directed in the warrant by the magistrate.

(b) On searching the place ordered to be searched, the officer executing the warrant shall present a copy of the warrant to the owner of the place, if he is present. If the owner of the place is not present but a person who is present is in possession of the place, the officer shall present a copy of the warrant to the person. Before the officer takes property from the place, he shall prepare a written inventory of the property to be taken. He shall legibly endorse his name on the inventory and present

a copy of the inventory to the owner or other person in possession of the property. If neither the owner nor a person in possession of the property is present when the officer executes the warrant, the officer shall leave a copy of the warrant and the inventory at the place.

History of CCP art. 18.06: Acts 1965, 59th Leg., vol. 2, ch. 722. Amended by Acts 1973, 63rd Leg., ch. 399, §2(E), eff. Jan. 1, 1974; Acts 1981, 67th Leg., ch. 755, §2, eff. Sept. 1, 1981.

ANNOTATIONS

Green v. State, 799 S.W.2d 756, 759 (Tex.Crim.App. 1990). "When a search warrant is not executed within the time period provided by [CCP arts.] 18.06 and 18.07, ... it [has] no further official force or effect. It follows that any search whose legality depends on the warrant is unauthorized. However, ... purely *technical* discrepancies in dates or times do not automatically vitiate the validity of search or arrest warrants. The issue then becomes whether a warrant containing a discrepancy in time of issuance and execution so as to make the warrant apparently invalid under Art. 18.06 and 18.07, may nevertheless be held to be a valid instrument under which a proper search or seizure can be conducted.... [¶] [C]ases dealing with the issue have all apparently decided a particular document's validity by pointing to the existence of testimony in the record which explains the discrepancy in light of the circumstances surrounding issuance and execution."

Robles v. State, 711 S.W.2d 752, 753 (Tex. App.—San Antonio 1986, pet. ref'd). "[T]he Court of Criminal Appeals has consistently held that ministerial violations of the search warrant statutes do not vitiate the search warrant in the absence of a showing of prejudice. We hold that the failure of the officers to deliver a copy of the search warrant and an itemized copy of the return to the defendant in the absence of a showing of injury reveals no error."

ART. 18.07. DAYS ALLOWED FOR WARRANT TO RUN

The time allowed for the execution of a search warrant shall be three whole days, exclusive of the day of its issuance and of the day of its execution. The magistrate issuing a search warrant under the provisions of this chapter shall endorse on such search warrant the date and hour of the issuance of the same.

History of CCP art. 18.07: Acts 1965, 59th Leg., vol. 2, ch. 722. Amended by Acts 1973, 63rd Leg., ch. 399, §2(E), eff. Jan. 1, 1974.

Gonzalez v. State, 768 S.W.2d 436, 437 (Tex. App.—Houston [1st Dist.] 1989, no pet.). "When a search warrant is not executed within the time period provided for by [CCP arts.] 18.06 and 18.07, ... any search whose legality depends on the warrant is unauthorized. [¶] Appellant argues that the period within which a search warrant must be executed is computed from the *time* it is issued; that it must be executed 'within the 24 hours ending one day after the three days in which the warrant was good.' We disagree. *At 438:* We do not believe the intent of the statute ... was to calculate 'days' as 24-hour periods starting from the time of issuance, since the warrant would not have the hour of issuance endorsed thereon; therefore, ... it is our opinion that a search warrant had to be executed by midnight of the fourth day after the day of its issuance. [¶] [T]here is no requirement that the hour of execution of a search warrant be included in the officer's return."

ART. 18.08. POWER OF OFFICER EXECUTING WARRANT

In the execution of a search warrant, the officer may call to his aid any number of citizens in this county, who shall be bound to aid in the execution of the same.

History of CCP art. 18.08: Acts 1965, 59th Leg., vol. 2, ch. 722. Amended by Acts 1973, 63rd Leg., ch. 399, §2(E), eff. Jan. 1, 1974.

Schalk v. State, 767 S.W.2d 441, 453 (Tex.App.— Dallas 1988), *aff'd*, 823 S.W.2d 633 (Tex.Crim.App. 1991). "A literal reading of [art. 18.08] would suggest that any citizen called upon to aid an officer is bound to aid the officer and has little or no choice to do otherwise. [Art. 18.08] gives the option to call for aid to the officer and it is not necessary that the officer get his authority to request aid from the warrant...."

ART. 18.09. SHALL SEIZE ACCUSED & PROPERTY

When the property which the officer is directed to search for and seize is found he shall take possession of the same and carry it before the magistrate. He shall also arrest any person whom he is directed to arrest by the warrant and immediately take such person before the magistrate. For purposes of this chapter, "seizure,"

in the context of property, means the restraint of property, whether by physical force or by a display of an officer's authority, and includes the collection of property or the act of taking possession of property.

History of CCP art. 18.09: Acts 1965, 59th Leg., vol. 2, ch. 722. Amended by Acts 1973, 63rd Leg., ch. 399, §2(E), eff. Jan. 1, 1974; Acts 2005, 79th Leg., ch. 1026, §2, eff. Sept. 1, 2005.

ART. 18.10. HOW RETURN MADE

Upon returning the search warrant, the officer shall state on the back of the same, or on some paper attached to it, the manner in which it has been executed and shall likewise deliver to the magistrate a copy of the inventory of the property taken into his possession under the warrant. The officer who seized the property shall retain custody of it until the magistrate issues an order directing the manner of safekeeping the property. The property may not be removed from the county in which it was seized without an order approving the removal, issued by a magistrate in the county in which the warrant was issued; provided, however, nothing herein shall prevent the officer, or his department, from forwarding any item or items seized to a laboratory for scientific analysis.

History of CCP art. 18.10: Acts 1965, 59th Leg., vol. 2, ch. 722. Amended by Acts 1973, 63rd Leg., ch. 399, §2(E), eff. Jan. 1, 1974; Acts 1981, 67th Leg., ch. 755, §3, eff. Sept. 1, 1981.

Kutzner v. State, 994 S.W.2d 180, 186-87 (Tex. Crim.App.1999). "[A]ppellant alleges the trial court erred in admitting evidence over his objection which was seized in Harris County, but later removed to Montgomery County without order and for use in a criminal proceeding against Appellant, in violation of [CCP arts.] 18.10 and 38.23. [¶] Appellant points to five State's Exhibits [all of which were photographs of seized property]. [¶] The photographs complained-of are the work product of the officers investigating the instant offense and are not items which were seized pursuant to a search warrant. Hence, Articles 18.10 and 38.23 do not apply."

ART. 18.11. CUSTODY OF PROPERTY FOUND

Property seized pursuant to a search warrant shall be kept as provided by the order of a magistrate issued in accordance with Article 18.10 of this code.

History of CCP art. 18.11: Acts 1965, 59th Leg., vol. 2, ch. 722. Amended by Acts 1973, 63rd Leg., ch. 399, §2(E), eff. Jan. 1, 1974; Acts 1981, 67th Leg., ch. 755, §4, eff. Sept. 1, 1981.

ART. 18.12. MAGISTRATE SHALL INVESTIGATE

The magistrate, upon the return of a search warrant, shall proceed to try the questions arising upon the same, and shall take testimony as in other examinations before him.

History of CCP art. 18.12: Acts 1965, 59th Leg., vol. 2, ch. 722. Amended by Acts 1973, 63rd Leg., ch. 399, §2(E), eff. Jan. 1, 1974.

ART. 18.13. SHALL DISCHARGE DEFENDANT

If the magistrate be not satisfied, upon investigation, that there was good ground for the issuance of the warrant, he shall discharge the defendant and order restitution of the property taken from him, except for criminal instruments. In such case, the criminal instruments shall be kept by the sheriff subject to the order of the proper court.

History of CCP art. 18.13: Acts 1965, 59th Leg., vol. 2, ch. 722. Amended by Acts 1973, 63rd Leg., ch. 399, §2(E), eff. Jan. 1, 1974.

ART. 18.14. EXAMINING TRIAL

The magistrate shall proceed to deal with the accused as in other cases before an examining court if he is satisfied there was good ground for issuing the warrant.

History of CCP art. 18.14: Acts 1965, 59th Leg., vol. 2, ch. 722. Amended by Acts 1973, 63rd Leg., ch. 399, §2(E), eff. Jan. 1, 1974.

ART. 18.15. CERTIFY RECORD TO PROPER COURT

The magistrate shall keep a record of all the proceedings had before him in cases of search warrants, and shall certify the same and deliver them to the clerk of the court having jurisdiction of the case, before the next term of said court, and accompany the same with all the original papers relating thereto, including the certified schedule of the property seized.

History of CCP art. 18.15: Acts 1965, 59th Leg., vol. 2, ch. 722. Amended by Acts 1973, 63rd Leg., ch. 399, §2(E), eff. Jan. 1, 1974.

ART. 18.16. PREVENTING CONSEQUENCES OF THEFT

Any person has a right to prevent the consequences of theft by seizing any personal property that has been stolen and bringing it, with the person suspected of committing the theft, if that person can be taken, before a magistrate for examination, or delivering the property and the person suspected of committing the theft to a peace officer for that purpose. To justify a seizure under this article, there must be reasonable ground to believe the property is stolen, and the seizure must be openly made and the proceedings had without delay.

History of CCP art. 18.16: Acts 1965, 59th Leg., vol. 2, ch. 722. Amended by Acts 1973, 63rd Leg., ch. 399, §2(E), eff. Jan. 1, 1974; Acts 2001, 77th Leg., ch. 109, §2, eff. Sept. 1, 2001.

ANNOTATIONS

Aitch v. State, 879 S.W.2d 167, 172 (Tex.App.—Houston [14th Dist.] 1994, pet. ref'd). "[A]rticle 18.16 'may not restrict an individual's right to be free from unreasonable searches and seizures.' [T]he applicability of Article 18.16 must be determined in light of a Fourth Amendment analysis. The 'reasonable grounds' required by article 18.16 equate to 'probable cause' under the Fourth Amendment."

Simpson v. State, 815 S.W.2d 900, 902 (Tex.App.—Fort Worth 1991, no pet.). "A store employee who witnesses someone commit the offense of theft of property from the store has the lawful right to arrest the offender under the authority of [CCP art.] 18.16.... [¶] We hold that the force authorized by article 18.16 is the same as that provided in [CCP art.] 15.24, which provides that all reasonable means are permitted to be used to effect an arrest, but that no greater force shall be used than is necessary."

ART. 18.17. DISPOSITION OF ABANDONED OR UNCLAIMED PROPERTY

(a) All unclaimed or abandoned personal property of every kind, other than contraband subject to forfeiture under Chapter 59 of this code and whiskey, wine and beer, seized by any peace officer in the State of Texas which is not held as evidence to be used in any pending case and has not been ordered destroyed or returned to the person entitled to possession of the same by a magistrate, which shall remain unclaimed for a period of 30 days shall be delivered for disposition to a person designated by the municipality or the purchasing agent of the county in which the property was seized. If a peace officer of a municipality seizes the property, the peace officer shall deliver the property to a person designated by the municipality. If any other peace officer seizes the property, the peace officer shall deliver the property to the purchasing agent of the county. If the county has no purchasing agent, then such property shall be disposed of by the sheriff of the county.

(b) The county purchasing agent, the person designated by the municipality, or the sheriff of the county, as the case may be, shall mail a notice to the last known address of the owner of such property by certified mail. Such notice shall describe the property being held, give the name and address of the officer holding such property, and shall state that if the owner does not claim such property within 90 days from the date of the notice such property will be disposed of and the proceeds, after deducting the reasonable expense of keeping such property and the costs of the disposition, placed in the treasury of the municipality or county giving the notice.

(c) If the property has a fair market value of $500 or more and the owner or the address of the owner is unknown, the person designated by the municipality, the county purchasing agent, or the sheriff, as the case may be, shall cause to be published once in a paper of general circulation in the municipality or county a notice containing a general description of the property held, the name of the owner if known, the name and address of the officer holding such property, and a statement that if the owner does not claim such property within 90 days from the date of the publication such property will be disposed of and the proceeds, after deducting the reasonable expense of keeping such property and the costs of the disposition, placed in the treasury of the municipality or county disposing of the property. If the property has a fair market value of less than $500 and the owner or the address of the owner is unknown, the person designated by the municipality, the county purchasing agent, or the sheriff may sell or donate the property. The person designated by the municipality, the purchasing agent, or the sheriff shall deposit the sale proceeds, after deducting the reasonable expense of keeping the property and costs of the sale, in the treasury of the municipality or county selling or donating the property.

(d) The sale under this article of any property that has a fair market value of $500 or more shall be preceded by a notice published once at least 14 days prior to the date of such sale in a newspaper of general circulation in the municipality or county where the sale is to take place, stating the general description of the property, the names of the owner if known, and the date and place that such sale will occur. This article does not require disposition by sale.

(e) The real owner of any property disposed of shall have the right to file a claim to the proceeds with the commissioners court of the county or with the governing body of the municipality in which the disposition took place. A claim by the real owner must be filed not later than the 30th day after the date of disposition. If the claim is allowed by the commissioners court or the governing body of the municipality, the municipal or county treasurer shall pay the owner such funds as were paid into the treasury of the municipality or county as proceeds of the disposition. If the claim is denied by the commissioners court or the governing body or if said court or body fails to act upon such claim within 90 days, the claimant may sue the municipal or county treasurer in a court of competent jurisdiction in the county, and upon sufficient proof of ownership, recover judgment against such municipality or county for the recovery of the proceeds of the disposition.

(f) For the purposes of this article:

(1) "Person designated by a municipality" means an officer or employee of a municipality who is designated by the municipality to be primarily responsible for the disposition of property under this article.

(2) "Property held as evidence" means property related to a charge that has been filed or to a matter that is being investigated for the filing of a charge.

(g) If the provisions of this section have been met and the property is scheduled for disposition, the municipal or county law enforcement agency that originally seized the property may request and have the property converted to agency use. The agency at any time may transfer the property to another municipal or county law enforcement agency for the use of that agency. The agency last using the property shall return the property to the person designated by the municipality, county purchasing agent, or sheriff, as the case may be, for disposition when the agency has completed the intended use of the property.

(h) If the abandoned or unclaimed personal property is money, the person designated by the municipality, the county purchasing agent, or the sheriff of the county, as appropriate, may, after giving notice under Subsection (b) or (c) of this article, deposit the money in the treasury of the municipality or county giving notice without conducting the sale as required by Subsection (d) of this article.

(i) While offering the property for sale under this article, if a person designated by a municipality, county purchasing agent, or sheriff considers any bid as insufficient, the person, agent, or sheriff may decline the bid and reoffer the property for sale.

(j) Chapters 72, 74, 75, and 76, Property Code, do not apply to unclaimed or abandoned property to which this article applies.

History of CCP art. 18.17: Acts 1965, 59th Leg., vol. 2, ch. 722. Amended by Acts 1967, 60th Leg., ch. 659, §15, eff. Aug. 27, 1967; Acts 1973, 63rd Leg., ch. 399, §2(E), eff. Jan. 1, 1974; Acts 1987, 70th Leg., ch. 1002, §1, eff. Sept. 1, 1987; Acts 1989, 71st Leg., 1st C.S., ch. 12, §4, eff. Oct. 18, 1989; Acts 1991, 72nd Leg., ch. 254, §1, eff. June 5, 1991; Acts 1993, 73rd Leg., ch. 157, §1 (eff. Sept. 1, 1993), ch. 321, §§1-4 (eff. May 28, 1993); Acts 1995, 74th Leg., ch. 76, §§3.01-3.05, eff. Sept. 1, 1995; Acts 2001, 77th Leg., ch. 402, §18, eff. Sept. 1, 2001.

ART. 18.18. DISPOSITION OF GAMBLING PARAPHERNALIA, PROHIBITED WEAPON, CRIMINAL INSTRUMENT, & OTHER CONTRABAND

(a) Following the final conviction of a person for possession of a gambling device or equipment, altered gambling equipment, or gambling paraphernalia, for an offense involving a criminal instrument, for an offense involving an obscene device or material, for an offense involving child pornography, or for an offense involving a scanning device or re-encoder, the court entering the judgment of conviction shall order that the machine, device, gambling equipment or gambling paraphernalia, instrument, obscene device or material, child pornography, or scanning device or re-encoder be destroyed or forfeited to the state. Not later than the 30th day after the final conviction of a person for an offense involving a prohibited weapon, the court entering the judgment of conviction on its own motion, on the motion of the prosecuting attorney in the case, or on the motion of the law enforcement agency initiating the complaint on notice to the prosecuting attorney in the case if the prosecutor fails to move for the order shall order that the prohibited weapon be destroyed or forfeited to the law enforcement agency that initiated the complaint. If the court fails to enter the order within the time required by this subsection, any magistrate in the county in which the offense occurred may enter the order. Following the final conviction of a person for an offense involving dog fighting, the court entering the judgment of conviction shall order that any dog-fighting equipment be destroyed or forfeited to the state. Destruction of dogs, if necessary, must be carried out by a veterinarian licensed in this state or, if one is not available, by trained personnel of a humane society or an animal shelter. If forfeited, the court shall order the

contraband delivered to the state, any political subdivision of the state, or to any state institution or agency. If gambling proceeds were seized, the court shall order them forfeited to the state and shall transmit them to the grand jury of the county in which they were seized for use in investigating alleged violations of the Penal Code, or to the state, any political subdivision of the state, or to any state institution or agency.

(b) If there is no prosecution or conviction following seizure, the magistrate to whom the return was made shall notify in writing the person found in possession of the alleged gambling device or equipment, altered gambling equipment or gambling paraphernalia, gambling proceeds, prohibited weapon, obscene device or material, child pornography, scanning device or re-encoder, criminal instrument, or dog-fighting equipment to show cause why the property seized should not be destroyed or the proceeds forfeited. The magistrate, on the motion of the law enforcement agency seizing a prohibited weapon, shall order the weapon destroyed or forfeited to the law enforcement agency seizing the weapon, unless a person shows cause as to why the prohibited weapon should not be destroyed or forfeited. A law enforcement agency shall make a motion under this section in a timely manner after the time at which the agency is informed in writing by the attorney representing the state that no prosecution will arise from the seizure.

(c) The magistrate shall include in the notice a detailed description of the property seized and the total amount of alleged gambling proceeds; the name of the person found in possession; the address where the property or proceeds were seized; and the date and time of the seizure.

(d) The magistrate shall send the notice by registered or certified mail, return receipt requested, to the person found in possession at the address where the property or proceeds were seized. If no one was found in possession, or the possessor's address is unknown, the magistrate shall post the notice on the courthouse door.

(e) Any person interested in the alleged gambling device or equipment, altered gambling equipment or gambling paraphernalia, gambling proceeds, prohibited weapon, obscene device or material, child pornography, scanning device or re-encoder, criminal instrument, or dog-fighting equipment seized must appear before the magistrate on the 20th day following the date the notice was mailed or posted. Failure to timely appear forfeits any interest the person may have in the property or proceeds seized, and no person after failing to timely appear may contest destruction or forfeiture.

(f) If a person timely appears to show cause why the property or proceeds should not be destroyed or forfeited, the magistrate shall conduct a hearing on the issue and determine the nature of property or proceeds and the person's interest therein. Unless the person proves by a preponderance of the evidence that the property or proceeds is not gambling equipment, altered gambling equipment, gambling paraphernalia, gambling device, gambling proceeds, prohibited weapon, obscene device or material, child pornography, criminal instrument, scanning device or re-encoder, or dog-fighting equipment and that he is entitled to possession, the magistrate shall dispose of the property or proceeds in accordance with Paragraph (a) of this article.

(g) For purposes of this article:

(1) "criminal instrument" has the meaning defined in the Penal Code;

(2) "gambling device or equipment, altered gambling equipment or gambling paraphernalia" has the meaning defined in the Penal Code;

(3) "prohibited weapon" has the meaning defined in the Penal Code;

(4) "dog-fighting equipment" means:

(A) equipment used for training or handling a fighting dog, including a harness, treadmill, cage, decoy, pen, house for keeping a fighting dog, feeding apparatus, or training pen;

(B) equipment used for transporting a fighting dog, including any automobile, or other vehicle, and its appurtenances which are intended to be used as a vehicle for transporting a fighting dog;

(C) equipment used to promote or advertise an exhibition of dog fighting, including a printing press or similar equipment, paper, ink, or photography equipment; or

(D) a dog trained, being trained, or intended to be used to fight with another dog;

(5) "obscene device" and "obscene" have the meanings assigned by Section 43.21, Penal Code;

Subsections (6) & (7) below are effective until Apr. 1, 2009.

(6) "re-encoder" has the meaning assigned by Section 35.60, Business & Commerce Code;

(7) "scanning device" has the meaning assigned by Section 35.60, Business & Commerce Code; and

 Subsections (6) & (7) below are effective on or after Apr. 1, 2009.

(6) "re-encoder" has the meaning assigned by Section 522.001, Business & Commerce Code;

(7) "scanning device" has the meaning assigned by Section 522.001, Business & Commerce Code; and

(8) "obscene material" and "child pornography" include digital images and the media and equipment on which those images are stored.

(h) No provider of an electronic communication service or of a remote computing service to the public shall be held liable for an offense involving obscene material or child pornography under this section on account of any action taken in good faith in providing that service.

History of CCP art. 18.18: Acts 1965, 59th Leg., vol. 2, ch. 722. Amended by Acts 1973, 63rd Leg., ch. 399, §2(E), eff. Jan. 1, 1974; Acts 1983, 68th Leg., ch. 305, §§2, 3 (eff. Sept. 1, 1983), ch. 351, §1 (eff. Sept. 1, 1983); Acts 1987, 70th Leg., ch. 167, §5.01(a)(6) (eff. Sept. 1, 1987), ch. 980, §1 (eff. Sept. 1, 1987); Acts 1993, 73rd Leg., ch. 157, §2, eff. Sept. 1, 1993; Acts 2003, 78th Leg., ch. 441, §1 (eff. Sept. 1, 2003), ch. 649, §2 (eff. Sept. 1, 2003); Acts 2005, 79th Leg., ch. 522, §§1, 2 (eff. Sept. 1, 2005), ch. 728, §23.002(1), (eff. Sept. 1, 2005); Acts 2007, 80th Leg., ch. 885, §2.13 (eff. Apr. 1, 2009), ch. 921, §17.002(1) (eff. Sept. 1, 2009).

See also Pen. Code §§16.01, 42.10, 46.05, ch. 47.

ANNOTATIONS

Hardy v. State, 102 S.W.3d 123, 125 (Tex.2003). "We hold that the State must establish probable cause before initiating a forfeiture proceeding under article 18.18.... The person found in possession of the seized property must then appear at a show cause hearing and prove, by a preponderance of the evidence, that those machines are not gambling devices."

State v. Rumfolo, 545 S.W.2d 752, 754 (Tex.1976), *overruled on other grounds*, ***Hardy v. State***, 102 S.W.3d 123 (Tex.2003). "A statutory proceeding for the forfeiture of personal property is one in rem, not against the owner but against the property itself, and is a proceeding of a civil nature in that it does not involve the conviction of the owner or possessor of the property seized."

Craig v. State, 707 S.W.2d 164, 165 (Tex.App.— Houston [1st Dist.] 1986, no pet.). "Although the State, under Article 18.18, has the right to initiate forfeiture proceedings against gambling proceeds and gambling paraphernalia, it may do so only under certain circumstances: (1) following the conviction of a person for possession of gambling paraphernalia or other items listed in the statute, and (2) if there is no prosecution or conviction following seizure. [¶] Although Article 18.18 requires the person claiming ownership of the property to show cause why the property should not be forfeited, the State initiated the forfeiture proceeding and therefore, has the burden of proving that it is entitled to forfeiture. Thus, it must prove all the elements set forth in Article 18.18."

ART. 18.181. DISPOSITION OF EXPLOSIVE WEAPONS & CHEMICAL DISPENSING DEVICES

(a) After seizure of an explosive weapon or chemical dispensing device, as these terms are defined in Section 46.01, Penal Code, a peace officer or a person acting at the direction of a peace officer shall:

(1) photograph the weapon in the position where it is recovered before touching or moving it;

(2) record the identification designations printed on a weapon if the markings are intact;

(3) if the weapon can be moved, move it to an isolated area in order to lessen the danger to the public;

(4) if possible, retain a portion of a wrapper or other packaging materials connected to the weapon;

(5) retain a small portion of the explosive material and submit the material to a laboratory for chemical analysis;

(6) separate and retain components associated with the weapon such as fusing and triggering mechanisms if those mechanisms are not hazardous in themselves;

(7) destroy the remainder of the weapon in a safe manner;

(8) at the time of destruction, photograph the destruction process and make careful observations of the characteristics of the destruction;

(9) after destruction, inspect the disposal site and photograph the site to record the destructive characteristics of the weapon; and

(10) retain components of the weapon and records of the destruction for use as evidence in court proceedings.

(b) Representative samples, photographs, and records made pursuant to this article are admissible in civil or criminal proceedings in the same manner and

to the same extent as if the explosive weapon were offered in evidence, regardless of whether or not the remainder of the weapon has been destroyed. No inference or presumption of spoliation applies to weapons destroyed pursuant to this article.

History of CCP art. 18.181: Acts 1983, 68th Leg., ch. 852, §5, eff. Sept. 1, 1983.

ART. 18.182. REPEALED

Repealed by Acts 1991, 72nd Leg., ch. 916, §3, eff. Sept. 1, 1991.

ART. 18.183. DEPOSIT OF MONEY PENDING DISPOSITION

(a) If money is seized by a law enforcement agency in connection with a violation of Chapter 47, Penal Code, the state or the political subdivision of the state that employs the law enforcement agency may deposit the money in an interest-bearing bank account in the jurisdiction of the agency that made seizure or in the county in which the money was seized until a final judgment is rendered concerning the violation.

(b) If a final judgment is rendered concerning a violation of Chapter 47, Penal Code, money seized in connection with the violation that has been placed in an interest-bearing bank account shall be distributed according to this chapter, with any interest being distributed in the same manner and used for the same purpose as the principal.

History of CCP art. 18.183: Acts 1987, 70th Leg., ch. 167, §4.02(a), eff. Sept. 1, 1987. Renumbered from Art. 18.182 by Acts 1989, 71st Leg., ch. 2, §16.01(6), eff. Aug. 28, 1989.

ART. 18.19. DISPOSITION OF SEIZED WEAPONS

(a) Weapons seized in connection with an offense involving the use of a weapon or an offense under Penal Code Chapter 46 shall be held by the law enforcement agency making the seizure, subject to the following provisions, unless:

(1) the weapon is a prohibited weapon identified in Penal Code Chapter 46, in which event Article of this code applies; or

(2) the weapon is alleged to be stolen property, in which event Chapter 47 of this code applies.

(b) When a weapon described in Paragraph (a) of this article is seized, and the seizure is not made pursuant to a search or arrest warrant, the person seizing the same shall prepare and deliver to a magistrate a written inventory of each weapon seized.

(c) If there is no prosecution or conviction for an offense involving the weapon seized, the magistrate to whom the seizure was reported shall, before the 61st day after the date the magistrate determines that there will be no prosecution or conviction, notify in writing the person found in possession of the weapon that the person is entitled to the weapon upon written request to the magistrate. The magistrate shall order the weapon returned to the person found in possession before the 61st day after the date the magistrate receives a request from the person. If the weapon is not requested before the 61st day after the date of notification, the magistrate shall, before the 121st day after the date of notification, order the weapon destroyed or forfeited to the state for use by the law enforcement agency holding the weapon or by a county forensic laboratory designated by the magistrate. If the magistrate does not order the return, destruction, or forfeiture of the weapon within the applicable period prescribed by this subsection, the law enforcement agency holding the weapon may request an order of destruction or forfeiture of the weapon from the magistrate.

(d) A person either convicted or receiving deferred adjudication under Chapter 46, Penal Code, is entitled to the weapon seized upon request to the court in which the person was convicted or placed on deferred adjudication. However, the court entering the judgment shall order the weapon destroyed or forfeited to the state for use by the law enforcement agency holding the weapon or by a county forensic laboratory designated by the court if:

(1) the person does not request the weapon before the 61st day after the date of the judgment of conviction or the order placing the person on deferred adjudication;

(2) the person has been previously convicted under Chapter 46, Penal Code;

(3) the weapon is one defined as a prohibited weapon under Chapter 46, Penal Code;

(4) the offense for which the person is convicted or receives deferred adjudication was committed in or on the premises of a playground, school, video arcade facility, or youth center, as those terms are defined by Section 481.134, Health and Safety Code; or

(5) the court determines based on the prior criminal history of the defendant or based on the circumstances surrounding the commission of the offense that possession of the seized weapon would pose a threat to the community or one or more individuals.

(e) If the person found in possession of a weapon is convicted of an offense involving the use of the weapon, before the 61st day after the date of conviction the court entering judgment of conviction shall order destruction of the weapon or forfeiture to the state for use by the law enforcement agency holding the weapon or by a county forensic laboratory designated by the court. If the court entering judgment of conviction does not order the destruction or forfeiture of the weapon within the period prescribed by this subsection, the law enforcement agency holding the weapon may request an order of destruction or forfeiture of the weapon from a magistrate.

History of CCP art. 18.19: Acts 1965, 59th Leg., vol. 2, ch. 722. Amended by Acts 1973, 63rd Leg., ch. 399, §2(E), eff. Jan. 1, 1974; Acts 1987, 70th Leg., ch. 980, §2, eff. Sept. 1, 1987; Acts 1993, 73rd Leg., ch. 157, §3, eff. Sept. 1, 1993; Acts 1995, 74th Leg., ch. 318, §46(a), eff. Sept. 1, 1995; Acts 2001, 77th Leg., ch. 1083, §1, eff. Sept. 1, 2001; Acts 2005, 79th Leg., ch. 509, §1, eff. Sept. 1, 2005.

ANNOTATIONS

Nickens v. State, 965 S.W.2d 603, 604 (Tex.App.—Houston [1st Dist.] 1998, no pet.). "If a person found in possession of a weapon is subsequently convicted or received deferred adjudication, he is entitled to return of the weapon seized, upon request. The court entering judgment can order the weapon destroyed or forfeited, however, if it determines that possession of the weapon would pose a threat to the community. [¶] There is no factual evidence in the forfeiture hearing record upon which the trial court could rationally base its finding of threat to the community. If we examine the record of appellant's criminal conviction, the most we see is a conviction for possession of an illegal weapon. There are no additional facts which would suggest danger, such as use or threatened use of the weapon. We do not believe that conviction of possession of an illegal weapon, standing alone, suffices to support a finding that possession of the weapon poses a threat to the community."

Martin v. State, 873 S.W.2d 457, 459 (Tex.App.—Waco 1994, no pet.). Appellant "argues that he was never 'found in possession' of the [rifle and silencer] because they were 'found' on or near a dirt country road near the vehicle that his companions had abandoned. [¶] One attorney general opinion summarizes article 18.19(e) as 'appl[ying] to the forfeiture or destruction of a weapon *belonging* to someone convicted of an offense involving the use of a deadly weapon.' [¶] [Appellant] admitted owning and possessing the gun and silencer and using them to illegally hunt deer. … Mindful of the object sought to be attained by article 18.19(e), we believe the evidence is sufficient to support the court's implied finding that [appellant] was 'found in possession' of the rifle and silencer."

ART. 18.20. INTERCEPTION & USE OF WIRE, ORAL, OR ELECTRONIC COMMUNICATIONS

§1. Definitions

In this article:

(1) "Wire communication" means an aural transfer made in whole or in part through the use of facilities for the transmission of communications by the aid of wire, cable, or other like connection between the point of origin and the point of reception, including the use of such a connection in a switching station, furnished or operated by a person authorized to engage in providing or operating the facilities for the transmission of communications as a communications common carrier. The term includes the electronic storage of a wire communication.

(2) "Oral communication" means an oral communication uttered by a person exhibiting an expectation that the communication is not subject to interception under circumstances justifying that expectation. The term does not include an electronic communication.

(3) "Intercept" means the aural or other acquisition of the contents of a wire, oral, or electronic communication through the use of an electronic, mechanical, or other device.

(4) "Electronic, mechanical, or other device" means a device that may be used for the nonconsensual interception of wire, oral, or electronic communications. The term does not include a telephone or telegraph instrument, the equipment or a facility used for the transmission of electronic communications, or a component of the equipment or a facility used for the transmission of electronic communications if the instrument, equipment, facility, or component is:

(A) furnished to the subscriber or user by a provider of wire or electronic communications service in the ordinary course of the provider's business and being used by the subscriber or user in the ordinary course of its business;

(B) furnished by a subscriber or user for connection to the facilities of a wire or electronic communications service for use in the ordinary course of the subscriber's or user's business;

(C) being used by a communications common carrier in the ordinary course of its business; or

(D) being used by an investigative or law enforcement officer in the ordinary course of the officer's duties.

(5) "Investigative or law enforcement officer" means an officer of this state or of a political subdivision of this state who is empowered by law to conduct investigations of or to make arrests for offenses enumerated in Section 4 of this article or an attorney authorized by law to prosecute or participate in the prosecution of the enumerated offenses.

(6) "Contents," when used with respect to a wire, oral, or electronic communication, includes any information concerning the substance, purport, or meaning of that communication.

(7) "Judge of competent jurisdiction" means a judge from the panel of nine active district judges with criminal jurisdiction appointed by the presiding judge of the court of criminal appeals as provided by Section 3 of this article.

(8) "Prosecutor" means a district attorney, criminal district attorney, or county attorney performing the duties of a district attorney, with jurisdiction in the county within an administrative judicial district described by Section 3(b).

(9) "Director" means the director of the Department of Public Safety or, if the director is absent or unable to serve, the assistant director of the Department of Public Safety.

(10) "Communication common carrier" means a person engaged as a common carrier for hire in the transmission of wire or electronic communications.

(11) "Aggrieved person" means a person who was a party to an intercepted wire, oral, or electronic communication or a person against whom the interception was directed.

(12) "Covert entry" means any entry into or onto premises which if made without a court order allowing such an entry under this Act, would be a violation of the Penal Code.

(13) "Residence" means a structure or the portion of a structure used as a person's home or fixed place of habitation to which the person indicates an intent to return after any temporary absence.

(14) "Pen register," "ESN reader," "trap and trace device," and "mobile tracking device" have the meanings assigned by Article 18.21.

(15) "Electronic communication" means a transfer of signs, signals, writing, images, sounds, data, or intelligence of any nature transmitted in whole or in part by a wire, radio, electromagnetic, photoelectronic, or photo-optical system. The term does not include:

(A) a wire or oral communication;

(B) a communication made through a tone-only paging device; or

(C) a communication from a tracking device.

(16) "User" means a person who uses an electronic communications service and is authorized by the provider of the service to use the service.

(17) "Electronic communications system" means a wire, radio, electromagnetic, photo-optical or photoelectronic facility for the transmission of wire or electronic communications, and any computer facility or related electronic equipment for the electronic storage of those communications.

(18) "Electronic communications service" means a service that provides to users of the service the ability to send or receive wire or electronic communications.

(19) "Readily accessible to the general public" means, with respect to a radio communication, a communication that is not:

(A) scrambled or encrypted;

(B) transmitted using modulation techniques whose essential parameters have been withheld from the public with the intention of preserving the privacy of the communication;

(C) carried on a subcarrier or other signal subsidiary to a radio transmission;

(D) transmitted over a communication system provided by a common carrier, unless the communication is a tone-only paging system communication;

(E) transmitted on frequencies allocated under Part 25, Subpart D, E, or F of Part 74, or Part 94 of the rules of the Federal Communications Commission, unless, in the case of a communication transmitted on a frequency allocated under Part 74 that is not exclusively allocated to broadcast auxiliary services, the communication is a two-way voice communication by radio; or

(F) an electronic communication.

(20) "Electronic storage" means:

(A) a temporary, intermediate storage of a wire or electronic communication that is incidental to the electronic transmission of the communication; or

(B) storage of a wire or electronic communication by an electronic communications service for purposes of backup protection of the communication.

(21) "Aural transfer" means a transfer containing the human voice at any point between and including the point of origin and the point of reception.

(22) "Immediate life-threatening situation" means a hostage, barricade, or other emergency situation in which a person unlawfully and directly:

(A) threatens another with death; or

(B) exposes another to a substantial risk of serious bodily injury.

A (23) "Member of a law enforcement unit specially trained to respond to and deal with life-threatening situations" means a peace officer who, as evidenced by the submission of appropriate documentation to the Commission on Law Enforcement Officer Standards and Education:

(A) receives a minimum of 40 hours a year of training in hostage and barricade suspect situations; or

E (B) has received a minimum of 24 hours of training on kidnapping investigations and is:

(i) the sheriff of a county with a population of 3.3 million or more or the sheriff's designee; or

(ii) the police chief of a police department in a municipality with a population of 500,000 or more or the police chief's designee.

(24) "Access," "computer," "computer network," "computer system," and "effective consent" have the meanings assigned by Section 33.01, Penal Code.

(25) "Computer trespasser" means a person who:

(A) is accessing a protected computer without effective consent of the owner; and

(B) has no reasonable expectation of privacy in any communication transmitted to, through, or from the protected computer. The term does not include a person who accesses the computer under an existing contractual relationship with the owner or operator of the protected computer.

(26) "Protected computer" means a computer, computer network, or computer system that is:

(A) owned by a financial institution or governmental entity; or

(B) used by or for a financial institution or governmental entity and conduct constituting an offense affects that use.

§2. Prohibition of Use as Evidence of Intercepted Communications

(a) The contents of an intercepted communication and evidence derived from an intercepted communication may be received in evidence in any trial, hearing, or other proceeding in or before any court, grand jury, department, officer, agency, regulatory body, legislative committee, or other authority of the United States or of this state or a political subdivision of this state unless:

(1) the communication was intercepted in violation of this article, Section 16.02, Penal Code, or federal law; or

(2) the disclosure of the contents of the intercepted communication or evidence derived from the communication would be in violation of this article, Section 16.02, Penal Code, or federal law.

(b) The contents of an intercepted communication and evidence derived from an intercepted communication may be received in a civil trial, hearing, or other proceeding only if the civil trial, hearing, or other proceeding arises out of a violation of a penal law.

(c) This section does not prohibit the use or admissibility of the contents of a communication or evidence derived from the communication if the communication was intercepted in a jurisdiction outside this state in compliance with the law of that jurisdiction.

§3. Judges Authorized to Consider Interception Applications

(a) The presiding judge of the court of criminal appeals, by order filed with the clerk of that court, shall appoint one district judge from each of the administrative judicial districts of this state to serve at his pleasure as the judge of competent jurisdiction within that administrative judicial district. The presiding judge shall fill vacancies, as they occur, in the same manner.

(b) Except as provided by Subsection (c), a judge appointed under Subsection (a) may act on an application for authorization to intercept wire, oral, or electronic communications if the judge is appointed as the judge of competent jurisdiction within the administrative judicial district in which the following is located:

(1) the site of:

(A) the proposed interception; or

(B) the interception device to be installed or monitored;

(2) the communication device to be intercepted;

(3) the billing, residential, or business address of the subscriber to the electronic communications service to be intercepted;

(4) the headquarters of the law enforcement agency that makes a request for or executes an order authorizing an interception; or

(5) the headquarters of the service provider.

(c) If the judge of competent jurisdiction for an administrative judicial district is absent or unable to serve or if exigent circumstances exist, the application may be made to the judge of competent jurisdiction in an adjacent administrative judicial district. Exigent circumstances does not include a denial of a previous application on the same facts and circumstances. To be valid, the application must fully explain the circumstances justifying application under this subsection.

§4. Offenses for Which Interceptions May Be Authorized

A judge of competent jurisdiction may issue an order authorizing interception of wire, oral, or electronic communications only if the prosecutor applying for the order shows probable cause to believe that the interception will provide evidence of the commission of:

(1) a felony under Section 19.02, 19.03, or 43.26, Penal Code;

(2) a felony under:

(A) Chapter 481, Health and Safety Code, other than felony possession of marihuana;

(B) Section 485.033, Health and Safety Code; or

(C) Chapter 483, Health and Safety Code;

(3) an offense under Section 20.03 or 20.04, Penal Code;

(4) an offense under Chapter 20A, Penal Code;

(5) an offense under Chapter 34, Penal Code, if the criminal activity giving rise to the proceeds involves the commission of an offense under Title 5, Penal Code, or an offense under federal law or the laws of another state containing elements that are substantially similar to the elements of an offense under Title 5; or

(6) an attempt, conspiracy, or solicitation to commit an offense listed in this section.

§5. Control of Intercepting Devices

(a) Except as provided by Section 8A, only the Department of Public Safety is authorized by this article to own, possess, install, operate, or monitor an electronic, mechanical, or other device. The Department of Public Safety may be assisted by an investigative or law enforcement officer or other person in the operation and monitoring of an interception of wire, oral, or electronic communications, provided that the officer or other person:

(1) is designated by the director for that purpose; and

(2) acts in the presence and under the direction of a commissioned officer of the Department of Public Safety.

(b) The director shall designate in writing the commissioned officers of the Department of Public Safety who are responsible for the possession, installation, operation, and monitoring of electronic, mechanical, or other devices for the department.

§6. Request for Application for Interception

(a) The director may, based on written affidavits, request in writing that a prosecutor apply for an order authorizing interception of wire, oral, or electronic communications.

(b) The head of a local law enforcement agency or, if the head of the local law enforcement agency is absent or unable to serve, the acting head of the local law enforcement agency may, based on written affidavits, request in writing that a prosecutor apply for an order authorizing interception of wire, oral, or electronic communications. Prior to the requesting of an application under this subsection, the head of a local law enforcement agency must submit the request and supporting affidavits to the director, who shall make a finding in writing whether the request and supporting affidavits establish that other investigative procedures have been tried and failed or they reasonably appear unlikely to succeed or to be too dangerous if tried, is feasible, is justifiable, and whether the Department of Public Safety has the necessary resources available. The prosecutor may file the application only after a written positive finding on all the above requirements by the director.

§7. Authorization for Disclosure & Use of Intercepted Communications

(a) An investigative or law enforcement officer who, by any means authorized by this article, obtains knowledge of the contents of a wire, oral, or electronic communication or evidence derived from the communication may disclose the contents or evidence to another investigative or law enforcement officer, including a federal law enforcement officer or agent or a law enforcement officer or agent of another state, to the extent that the disclosure is appropriate to the proper performance of the official duties of the officer making or receiving the disclosure.

(b) An investigative or law enforcement officer who, by any means authorized by this article, obtains knowledge of the contents of a wire, oral, or electronic communication or evidence derived from the communication may use the contents or evidence to the extent the use is appropriate to the proper performance of his official duties.

(c) A person who receives, by any means authorized by this article, information concerning a wire, oral, or electronic communication or evidence derived from a communication intercepted in accordance with the provisions of this article may disclose the contents of that communication or the derivative evidence while giving testimony under oath in any proceeding held under the authority of the United States, of this state, or of a political subdivision of this state.

(d) An otherwise privileged wire, oral, or electronic communication intercepted in accordance with, or in violation of, the provisions of this article does not lose its privileged character and any evidence derived from such privileged communication against the party to the privileged communication shall be considered privileged also.

(e) When an investigative or law enforcement officer, while engaged in intercepting wire, oral, or electronic communications in a manner authorized by this article, intercepts wire, oral, or electronic communications relating to offenses other than those specified in the order of authorization, the contents of and evidence derived from the communication may be disclosed or used as provided by Subsections (a) and (b) of this section. Such contents and any evidence derived therefrom may be used under Subsection (c) of this section when authorized by a judge of competent jurisdiction where the judge finds, on subsequent application, that the contents were otherwise intercepted in accordance with the provisions of this article. The application shall be made as soon as practicable.

§8. Application for Interception Authorization

(a) To be valid, an application for an order authorizing the interception of a wire, oral, or electronic communication must be made in writing under oath to a judge of competent jurisdiction and must state the applicant's authority to make the application. An applicant must include the following information in the application:

(1) the identity of the prosecutor making the application and of the officer requesting the application;

(2) a full and complete statement of the facts and circumstances relied on by the applicant to justify his belief that an order should be issued, including:

(A) details about the particular offense that has been, is being, or is about to be committed;

(B) a particular description of the nature and location of the facilities from which or the place where the communication is to be intercepted;

(C) a particular description of the type of communication sought to be intercepted; and

(D) the identity of the person, if known, committing the offense and whose communications are to be intercepted;

(3) a full and complete statement as to whether or not other investigative procedures have been tried and failed or why they reasonably appear to be unlikely to succeed or to be too dangerous if tried;

(4) a statement of the period of time for which the interception is required to be maintained and, if the nature of the investigation is such that the authorization for interception should not automatically terminate when the described type of communication is first obtained, a particular description of facts establishing probable cause to believe that additional communications of the same type will occur after the described type of communication is obtained;

(5) a statement whether a covert entry will be necessary to properly and safely install the wiretapping or electronic surveillance or eavesdropping equipment and, if a covert entry is requested, a statement as to why such an entry is necessary and proper under the facts of the particular investigation, including a full and complete statement as to whether other investigative techniques have been tried and have failed or why they reasonably appear to be unlikely to succeed or to be too dangerous if tried or are not feasible under the circumstances or exigencies of time;

(6) a full and complete statement of the facts concerning all applications known to the prosecutor making the application that have been previously made to a judge for authorization to intercept wire, oral, or electronic communications involving any of the persons, facilities, or places specified in the application and of the action taken by the judge on each application; and

(7) if the application is for the extension of an order, a statement setting forth the results already obtained from the interception or a reasonable explanation of the failure to obtain results.

(b) The judge may, in an ex parte hearing in chambers, require additional testimony or documentary evidence in support of the application, and such testimony or documentary evidence shall be preserved as part of the application.

§8A. Emergency Installation & Use of Intercepting Device

(a) The prosecutor in a county in which an electronic, mechanical, or other device is to be installed or used to intercept wire, oral, or electronic communications shall designate in writing each peace officer in the county, other than a commissioned officer of the Department of Public Safety, who:

(1) is a member of a law enforcement unit specially trained to respond to and deal with life-threatening situations; and

(2) is authorized to possess such a device and responsible for the installation, operation, and monitoring of the device in an immediate life-threatening situation.

(b) A peace officer designated under Subsection (a) or under Section 5(b) may possess, install, operate, or monitor an electronic, mechanical, or other device to intercept wire, oral, or electronic communications if the officer:

(1) reasonably believes an immediate life-threatening situation exists that:

(A) is within the territorial jurisdiction of the officer or another officer the officer is assisting; and

(B) requires interception of communications before an order authorizing the interception can, with due diligence, be obtained under this section;

(2) reasonably believes there are sufficient grounds under this section on which to obtain an order authorizing the interception; and

(3) obtains oral or written consent to the interception before beginning the interception from:

(A) a district judge for the county in which the device will be installed or used; or

(B) a judge or justice of a court of appeals or of a higher court.

(c) An official described in Subsection (b)(3) may give oral or written consent to the interception of communications under this section to provide evidence of the commission of a felony, or of a threat, attempt, or conspiracy to commit a felony, in an immediate life-threatening situation. Oral or written consent given under this section expires 48 hours after the grant of consent or at the conclusion of the emergency justifying the interception, whichever occurs first.

(d) If an officer installs or uses a device under Subsection (b), the officer shall:

(1) promptly report the installation or use to the prosecutor in the county in which the device is installed or used; and

(2) within 48 hours after the installation is complete or the interception begins, whichever occurs first, obtain a written order from a judge of competent jurisdiction authorizing the interception.

(e) A judge of competent jurisdiction under Section 3 or under Subsection (b) may issue a written order authorizing interception of communications under this section during the 48-hour period prescribed by Subsection (d)(2). A written order under this section expires on the 30th day after execution of the order or at the conclusion of the emergency that initially justified the interception, whichever occurs first. If an order is denied or is not issued within the 48-hour period, the officer shall terminate use of and remove the device promptly on the earlier of:

(1) the denial;

(2) the end of the emergency that initially justified the interception; or

(3) the expiration of 48 hours.

(f) The state may not use as evidence in a criminal proceeding any information gained through the use of a device installed under this section if authorization for the device is not sought or is sought but not obtained.

(g) A peace officer may certify to a communications common carrier that the officer is acting lawfully under this section.

§9. Action on Application for Interception Order

(a) On receipt of an application, the judge may enter an ex parte order, as requested or as modified, authorizing interception of wire, oral, or electronic communications if the judge determines from the evidence submitted by the applicant that:

(1) there is probable cause to believe that a person is committing, has committed, or is about to commit a particular offense enumerated in Section 4 of this article;

(2) there is probable cause to believe that particular communications concerning that offense will be obtained through the interception;

(3) normal investigative procedures have been tried and have failed or reasonably appear to be unlikely to succeed or to be too dangerous if tried;

(4) there is probable cause to believe that the facilities from which or the place where the wire, oral, or electronic communications are to be intercepted are being used or are about to be used in connection with the commission of an offense or are leased to, listed in the name of, or commonly used by the person; and

(5) a covert entry is or is not necessary to properly and safely install the wiretapping or electronic surveillance or eavesdropping equipment.

(b) An order authorizing the interception of a wire, oral, or electronic communication must specify:

(1) the identity of the person, if known, whose communications are to be intercepted;

(2) the nature and location of the communications facilities as to which or the place where authority to intercept is granted;

(3) a particular description of the type of communication sought to be intercepted and a statement of the particular offense to which it relates;

(4) the identity of the officer making the request and the identity of the prosecutor;

(5) the time during which the interception is authorized, including a statement of whether or not the interception will automatically terminate when the described communication is first obtained; and

(6) whether or not a covert entry or surreptitious entry is necessary to properly and safely install wiretapping, electronic surveillance, or eavesdropping equipment.

(c) On request of the applicant for an order authorizing the interception of a wire, oral, or electronic communication, the judge may issue a separate order directing that a provider of wire or electronic communications service, a communication common carrier, landlord, custodian, or other person furnish the applicant all information, facilities, and technical assistance necessary to accomplish the interception unobtrusively and with a minimum of interference with the services that the provider, carrier, landlord, custodian, or other person is providing the person whose communications are to be intercepted. Any provider of wire or electronic communications service, communication common carrier, landlord, custodian, or other person furnishing facilities or technical assistance is entitled to compensation by the applicant for reasonable expenses incurred in providing the facilities or assistance at the prevailing rates. The interception order may include an order to:

(1) install or use a pen register, ESN reader, trap and trace device, or mobile tracking device, or similar equipment that combines the function of a pen register and trap and trace device;

(2) disclose a stored communication, information subject to an administrative subpoena, or information subject to access under Article 18.21, Code of Criminal Procedure.

(d) An order entered pursuant to this section may not authorize the interception of a wire, oral, or electronic communication for longer than is necessary to achieve the objective of the authorization and in no event may it authorize interception for more than 30 days. The issuing judge may grant extensions of an order, but only on application for an extension made in accordance with Section 8 and the court making the findings required by Subsection (a). The period of extension may not be longer than the authorizing judge deems necessary to achieve the purposes for which it is granted and in no event may the extension be for more than 30 days. To be valid, each order and extension of an order must provide that the authorization to intercept be executed as soon as practicable, be conducted in a way that minimizes the interception of communications not otherwise subject to interception under this article, and terminate on obtaining the authorized objective or within 30 days, whichever occurs sooner. If the intercepted communication is in code or a foreign language and an expert in that code or language is not reasonably available during the period of interception, minimization may be accomplished as soon as practicable after the interception.

(e) An order entered pursuant to this section may not authorize a covert entry into a residence solely for the purpose of intercepting a wire or electronic communication.

(f) An order entered pursuant to this section may not authorize a covert entry into or onto a premises for the purpose of intercepting an oral communication unless:

(1) the judge, in addition to making the determinations required under Subsection (a) of this section, determines that:

(A)(i) the premises into or onto which the covert entry is authorized or the person whose communications are to be obtained has been the subject of a pen register previously authorized in connection with the same investigation;

(ii) the premises into or onto which the covert entry is authorized or the person whose communications are to be obtained has been the subject of an interception of wire or electronic communications previously authorized in connection with the same investigation; and

(iii) that such procedures have failed; or

(B) that the procedures enumerated in Paragraph (A) reasonably appear to be unlikely to succeed or to be too dangerous if tried or are not feasible under the circumstances or exigencies of time; and

(2) the order, in addition to the matters required to be specified under Subsection (b) of this section, specifies that the covert entry is for the purpose of intercepting oral communications of two or more persons and that there is probable cause to believe they are committing, have committed, or are about to commit a particular offense enumerated in Section 4 of this article.

(g) Whenever an order authorizing interception is entered pursuant to this article, the order may require reports to the judge who issued the order showing what progress has been made toward achievement of the authorized objective and the need for continued interception. Reports shall be made at any interval the judge requires.

(h) A judge who issues an order authorizing the interception of a wire, oral, or electronic communication may not hear a criminal prosecution in which evidence derived from the interception may be used or in which the order may be an issue.

§10. Procedure for Preserving Intercepted Communications

(a) The contents of a wire, oral, or electronic communication intercepted by means authorized by this article shall be recorded on tape, wire, or other comparable device. The recording of the contents of a wire, oral, or electronic communication under this subsection shall be done in a way that protects the recording from editing or other alterations.

(b) Immediately on the expiration of the period of the order and all extensions, if any, the recordings shall be made available to the judge issuing the order and sealed under his directions. Custody of the recordings shall be wherever the judge orders. The recordings may not be destroyed until at least 10 years after the date of expiration of the order and the last extension, if any. A recording may be destroyed only by order of the judge of competent jurisdiction for the administrative judicial district in which the interception was authorized.

(c) Duplicate recordings may be made for use or disclosure pursuant to Subsections (a) and (b), Section 7, of this article for investigations.

(d) The presence of the seal required by Subsection (b) of this section or a satisfactory explanation of its absence is a prerequisite for the use or disclosure of the contents of a wire, oral, or electronic communication or evidence derived from the communication under Subsection (c), Section 7, of this article.

§11. Sealing of Orders & Applications

The judge shall seal each application made and order granted under this article. Custody of the applications and orders shall be wherever the judge directs. An application or order may be disclosed only on a showing of good cause before a judge of competent jurisdiction and may not be destroyed until at least 10 years after the date it is sealed. An application or order may be destroyed only by order of the judge of competent jurisdiction for the administrative judicial district in which it was made or granted.

§12. Contempt

A violation of Section 10 or 11 of this article may be punished as contempt of court.

§13. Notice & Disclosure of Interception to a Party

(a) Within a reasonable time but not later than 90 days after the date an application for an order is denied or after the date an order or the last extension, if any, expires, the judge who granted or denied the application shall cause to be served on the persons named in the order or the application and any other parties to intercepted communications, if any, an inventory, which must include notice:

(1) of the entry of the order or the application;

(2) of the date of the entry and the period of authorized interception or the date of denial of the application; and

(3) that during the authorized period wire, oral, or electronic communications were or were not intercepted.

(b) The judge, on motion, may in his discretion make available to a person or his counsel for inspection any portion of an intercepted communication, application, or order that the judge determines, in the interest of justice, to disclose to that person.

(c) On an ex parte showing of good cause to the judge, the serving of the inventory required by this section may be postponed, but in no event may any evidence derived from an order under this article be disclosed in any trial, until after such inventory has been served.

§14. Preconditions to Use as Evidence

(a) The contents of an intercepted wire, oral, or electronic communication or evidence derived from the communication may not be received in evidence or otherwise disclosed in a trial, hearing, or other proceeding in a federal or state court unless each party, not later than the 10th day before the date of the trial, hearing, or other proceeding, has been furnished with a copy of the court order and application under which the interception was authorized or approved. This 10-day period may be waived by the judge if he finds that it is not possible to furnish the party with the information 10 days before the trial, hearing, or proceeding and that the party will not be prejudiced by the delay in receiving the information.

(b) An aggrieved person charged with an offense in a trial, hearing, or proceeding in or before a court, department, officer, agency, regulatory body, or other authority of the United States or of this state or a political subdivision of this state may move to suppress the contents of an intercepted wire, oral, or electronic

★

communication or evidence derived from the communication on the ground that:

(1) the communication was unlawfully intercepted;

(2) the order authorizing the interception is insufficient on its face; or

(3) the interception was not made in conformity with the order.

(c) A person identified by a party to an intercepted wire, oral, or electronic communication during the course of that communication may move to suppress the contents of the communication on the grounds provided in Subsection (b) of this section or on the ground that the harm to the person resulting from his identification in court exceeds the value to the prosecution of the disclosure of the contents.

(d) The motion to suppress must be made before the trial, hearing, or proceeding unless there was no opportunity to make the motion or the person was not aware of the grounds of the motion. The hearing on the motion shall be held in camera upon the written request of the aggrieved person. If the motion is granted, the contents of the intercepted wire, oral, or electronic communication and evidence derived from the communication shall be treated as having been obtained in violation of this article. The judge, on the filing of the motion by the aggrieved person, shall make available to the aggrieved person or his counsel for inspection any portion of the intercepted communication or evidence derived from the communication that the judge determines, in the interest of justice, to make available.

(e) Any judge of this state, upon hearing a pretrial motion regarding conversations intercepted by wire pursuant to this article, or who otherwise becomes informed that there exists on such intercepted wire, oral, or electronic communication identification of a specific individual who is not a party or suspect to the subject of interception:

(1) shall give notice and an opportunity to be heard on the matter of suppression of references to that person if identification is sufficient so as to give notice; or

(2) shall suppress references to that person if identification is sufficient to potentially cause embarrassment or harm which outweighs the probative value, if any, of the mention of such person, but insufficient to require the notice provided for in Subdivision (1), above.

§15. Reports Concerning Intercepted Wire, Oral, or Electronic Communications

(a) Within 30 days after the date an order or the last extension, if any, expires or after the denial of an order, the issuing or denying judge shall report to the Administrative Office of the United States Courts:

(1) the fact that an order or extension was applied for;

(2) the kind of order or extension applied for;

(3) the fact that the order or extension was granted as applied for, was modified, or was denied;

(4) the period of interceptions authorized by the order and the number and duration of any extensions of the order;

(5) the offense specified in the order or application or extension;

(6) the identity of the officer making the request and the prosecutor; and

(7) the nature of the facilities from which or the place where communications were to be intercepted.

(b) In January of each year each prosecutor shall report to the Administrative Office of the United States Courts the following information for the preceding calendar year:

(1) the information required by Subsection (a) of this section with respect to each application for an order or extension made;

(2) a general description of the interceptions made under each order or extension, including the approximate nature and frequency of incriminating communications intercepted, the approximate nature and frequency of other communications intercepted, the approximate number of persons whose communications were intercepted, and the approximate nature, amount, and cost of the manpower and other resources used in the interceptions;

(3) the number of arrests resulting from interceptions made under each order or extension and the offenses for which arrests were made;

(4) the number of trials resulting from interceptions;

(5) the number of motions to suppress made with respect to interceptions and the number granted or denied;

(6) the number of convictions resulting from interceptions, the offenses for which the convictions were obtained, and a general assessment of the importance of the interceptions; and

---

★

---

(7) the information required by Subdivisions (2) through (6) of this subsection with respect to orders or extensions obtained.

(c) Any judge or prosecutor required to file a report with the Administrative Office of the United States Courts shall forward a copy of such report to the director of the Department of Public Safety. On or before March 1 of each year, the director shall submit to the governor; lieutenant governor; speaker of the house of representatives; chairman, senate jurisprudence committee; and chairman, house of representatives criminal jurisprudence committee a report of all intercepts as defined herein conducted pursuant to this article and terminated during the preceding calendar year. Such report shall include:

(1) the reports of judges and prosecuting attorneys forwarded to the director as required in this section;

(2) the number of Department of Public Safety personnel authorized to possess, install, or operate electronic, mechanical, or other devices;

(3) the number of Department of Public Safety and other law enforcement personnel who participated or engaged in the seizure of intercepts pursuant to this article during the preceding calendar year; and

(4) the total cost to the Department of Public Safety of all activities and procedures relating to the seizure of intercepts during the preceding calendar year, including costs of equipment, manpower, and expenses incurred as compensation for use of facilities or technical assistance provided to the department.

§16. Recovery of Civil Damages Authorized

(a) A person whose wire, oral, or electronic communication is intercepted, disclosed, or used in violation of this article, or in violation of Chapter 16, Penal Code, has a civil cause of action against any person who intercepts, discloses, or uses or solicits another person to intercept, disclose, or use the communication and is entitled to recover from the person:

(1) actual damages but not less than liquidated damages computed at a rate of $100 a day for each day of violation or $1,000, whichever is higher;

(2) punitive damages; and

(3) a reasonable attorney's fee and other litigation costs reasonably incurred.

(b) A good faith reliance on a court order or legislative authorization constitutes a complete defense to an action brought under this section.

(c) A person is subject to suit by the federal or state government in a court of competent jurisdiction for appropriate injunctive relief if the person engages in conduct that:

(1) constitutes an offense under Section 16.05, Penal Code, but is not for a tortious or illegal purpose or for the purpose of direct or indirect commercial advantage or private commercial gain; and

(2) involves a radio communication that is:

(A) transmitted on frequencies allocated under Subpart D of Part 74 of the rules of the Federal Communications Commission; and

(B) not scrambled or encrypted.

(d) A defendant is liable for a civil penalty of $500 if it is shown at the trial of the civil suit brought under Subsection (c) that the defendant:

(1) has been convicted of an offense under Section 16.05, Penal Code; or

(2) is found liable in a civil action brought under Subsection (a).

(e) Each violation of an injunction ordered under Subsection (c) is punishable by a fine of $500.

(f) The attorney general, or the county or district attorney of the county in which the conduct, as described by Subsection (c), is occurring, may file suit under Subsection (c) on behalf of the state.

(g) A computer trespasser or a user, aggrieved person, subscriber, or customer of a communications common carrier or electronic communications service does not have a cause of action against the carrier or service, its officers, employees, or agents, or other specified persons for providing information, facilities, or assistance as required by a good faith reliance on:

(1) legislative authority; or

(2) a court order, warrant, subpoena, or certification under this article.

§17. Nonapplicability

This article does not apply to conduct described as an affirmative defense under Section 16.02(c), Penal Code.

§18. Repealed

Repealed by Acts 2005, 79th Leg., ch. 889, §2, eff. June 17, 2005.

History of CCP art. 18.20: Acts 1981, 67th Leg., ch. 275, §1, eff. Aug. 31, 1981. Amended by Acts 1983, 68th Leg., ch. 864, §4, eff. June 19, 1983; Acts 1985, 69th Leg., ch. 587, §§2-4, eff. Aug. 26, 1985; Acts 1989, 71st Leg., ch. 1166, §§1-15, eff. Sept. 1, 1989; Acts 1991, 72nd Leg., ch. 14, §284(38), (57), eff. Sept. 1, 1991; Acts 1993, 73rd Leg., ch. 790, §15 (eff. Sept. 1, 1993), ch. 900, §1.06 (eff.

Sept. 1, 1994); Acts 1997, 75th Leg., ch. 1051, §§1-4, eff. Sept. 1, 1997; Acts 2001, 77th Leg., ch. 1270, §§1-6, eff. Sept. 1, 2001; Acts 2003, 78th Leg., ch. 678, §§2-7, eff. Sept. 1, 2003; Acts 2005, 79th Leg., ch. 390, §1 (eff. Sept. 1, 2005), ch. 889, §2 (eff. June 17, 2005); Acts 2007, 80th Leg., ch. 186, §1 (eff. May 23, 2007), ch. 258, §6.01 (eff. Sept. 1, 2007).

ANNOTATIONS

Moseley v. State, 252 S.W.3d 398, ___ (Tex.Crim. App.2008). "At the homicide division of the police department, detectives questioned appellant in an interview room. That interrogation and the periods of time during which appellant was left alone and allowed to make telephone calls were recorded on a digital video disc (DVD). Appellant unsuccessfully sought to prevent admission of that DVD into evidence at trial. Held: Because (1) only appellant's half of the conversation was recorded, (2) there was no expectation of privacy, and (3) the conversation could be overheard without resort to a wiretap, the admission of the DVD was not error. *See also Ex parte Graves*, 853 S.W.2d 701, 705-06 (Tex. App.—Houston [1st Dist.] 1993, pet. ref'd).

Castillo v. State, 818 S.W.2d 803, 805 (Tex.Crim. App.1991), *overruled on other grounds, Torres v. State*, 182 S.W.3d 899 (Tex.Crim.App.2005). "[T]he inclusion of tainted allegations in an affidavit does not necessarily render a resulting search warrant invalid. Rather, the relevant inquiry on a motion to suppress evidence seized pursuant to such a warrant is whether, putting aside all tainted allegations, the independently acquired and lawful information stated in the affidavit nevertheless clearly established probable cause. The rationale for the rule is obvious: if the tainted information was *clearly* unnecessary to establish probable cause for the search warrant, then the defendant could not have been harmed by the inclusion of the tainted information in the affidavit. This rule is plainly applicable to Article 18.20 wiretap orders, which are simply a particular type of search warrant."

Castillo v. State, 810 S.W.2d 180, 181 (Tex.Crim. App.1990). "[A]ppellants argued that under Article 18.20, §3(b), [judge] had no power to authorize the Ellis County wiretaps because that county is not in [judge's] administrative judicial district; that all information derived from the Ellis County was therefore tainted; and that all information from the Navarro County wiretap was also tainted because that wiretap was authorized in part based on information obtained from the Ellis County wiretaps. *At 184:* [T]he language of §3(b) plainly contemplates territorial *restriction.* [¶] [W]e hold that, for the purposes of Article 18.20,

§3(b), a communication is 'intercepted' where the wiretap device is physically placed." Held: Intercepted communications should have been excluded from evidence.

Hall v. State, 862 S.W.2d 710, 713 (Tex.App.— Beaumont 1993, no pet.). "[T]he restrictions of the wiretap statute do not apply when a private individual consents to the taping of conversation with a defendant, even without the knowledge or consent of the defendant."

ART. 18.21. PEN REGISTERS & TRAP & TRACE DEVICES; ACCESS TO STORED COMMUNICATIONS; MOBILE TRACKING DEVICES

§1. Definitions

In this article:

(1) "Aural transfer," "communication common carrier," "computer trespasser," "electronic communication," "electronic communications service," "electronic communications system," "electronic storage," "immediate life-threatening situation," "member of a law enforcement unit specially trained to respond to and deal with life-threatening situations," "readily accessible to the general public," "user," and "wire communication" have the meanings assigned by Article 18.20.

(2) "Authorized peace officer" means:

(A) a sheriff or a sheriff's deputy;

(B) a constable or deputy constable;

(C) a marshal or police officer of an incorporated city;

(D) a ranger or officer commissioned by the Public Safety Commission or the director of the Department of Public Safety;

(E) an investigator of a prosecutor's office;

(F) a law enforcement agent of the Alcoholic Beverage Commission;

(G) a law enforcement officer commissioned by the Parks and Wildlife Commission; or

(H) an enforcement officer appointed by the executive director of the Texas Department of Criminal Justice under Section 493.019, Government Code.

(3) "Department" means the Department of Public Safety.

E (3-a) "Designated law enforcement agency" means:

(A) the sheriff's department of a county with a population of 3.3 million or more; or

(B) a police department in a municipality with a population of 500,000 or more.

(4) "ESN reader" means a device that records the electronic serial number from the data track of a wireless telephone, cellular telephone, or similar communication device that transmits its operational status to a base site, if the device does not intercept the contents of a communication.

(5) "Mobile tracking device" means an electronic or mechanical device that permits tracking the movement of a person, vehicle, container, item, or object. The term does not include a device designed, made, adapted, or capable of:

(A) intercepting the content of a communication; or

(B) functioning as a pen register, ESN reader, trap and trace device, or similar equipment.

(6) "Pen register" means a device or process that records or decodes dialing, routing, addressing, or signaling information transmitted by an instrument or facility from which a wire or electronic communication is transmitted, if the information does not include the contents of the communication. The term does not include a device used by a provider or customer of a wire or electronic communication service in the ordinary course of the provider's or customer's business for purposes of:

(A) billing or recording as an incident to billing for communications services; or

(B) cost accounting, security control, or other ordinary business purposes.

(7) "Prosecutor" means a district attorney, criminal district attorney, or county attorney performing the duties of a district attorney.

(8) "Remote computing service" means the provision to the public of computer storage or processing services by means of an electronic communications system.

(9) "Supervisory official" means:

(A) an investigative agent or an assistant investigative agent who is in charge of an investigation;

(B) an equivalent person at an investigating agency's headquarters or regional office; and

(C) the principal prosecuting attorney of the state or of a political subdivision of the state or the first assistant or chief assistant prosecuting attorney in the office of either.

(10) "Trap and trace device" means a device or process that records an incoming electronic or other impulse that identifies the originating number or other dialing, routing, addressing, or signaling information reasonably likely to identify the source of a wire or electronic communication, if the information does not include the contents of the communication. The term does not include a device or telecommunications network used in providing:

(A) a caller identification service authorized by the Public Utility Commission of Texas under Subchapter E, Chapter 55, Utilities Code;

(B) the services referenced in Section 55.102(b), Utilities Code; or

(C) a caller identification service provided by a commercial mobile radio service provider licensed by the Federal Communications Commission.

§2. Application & Order

(a) A prosecutor with jurisdiction in a county within a judicial district described by this subsection may file an application for the installation and use of a pen register, ESN reader, trap and trace device, or similar equipment that combines the function of a pen register and a trap and trace device with a district judge in the judicial district. The judicial district must be a district in which is located:

(1) the site of the proposed installation or use of the device or equipment;

(2) the site of the communication device on which the device or equipment is proposed to be installed or used;

(3) the billing, residential, or business address of the subscriber to the electronic communications service on which the device or equipment is proposed to be installed or used;

(4) the headquarters of:

(A) the office of the prosecutor filing an application under this section; or

(B) a law enforcement agency that requests the prosecutor to file an application under this section or that proposes to execute an order authorizing installation and use of the device or equipment; or

(5) the headquarters of a service provider ordered to install the device or equipment.

A *Subsection (b) below is effective for applications for the installation and use of a pen register, ESN reader, or similar equipment filed on or after May 23, 2007.*

(b) A prosecutor may file an application under this section or under federal law on the prosecutor's own motion or on the request of an authorized peace officer, regardless of whether the officer is commissioned by the department. A prosecutor who files an application on the prosecutor's own motion or who files an application for the installation and use of a pen register, ESN reader, or similar equipment on the request of an authorized peace officer not commissioned by the department, other than an authorized peace officer employed by a designated law enforcement agency, must make the application personally and may not do so through an assistant or some other person acting on the prosecutor's behalf. A prosecutor may make an application through an assistant or other person acting on the prosecutor's behalf if the prosecutor files an application for the installation and use of:

(1) a pen register, ESN reader, or similar equipment on the request of:

(A) an authorized peace officer who is commissioned by the department; or

(B) an authorized peace officer of a designated law enforcement agency; or

(2) a trap and trace device or similar equipment on the request of an authorized peace officer, regardless of whether the officer is commissioned by the department.

Subsection (b) below is effective for applications for the installation and use of a pen register, ESN reader, or similar equipment filed before May 23, 2007.

(b) A prosecutor may file an application under this section or under federal law on the prosecutor's own motion or on the request of an authorized peace officer, regardless of whether the officer is commissioned by the department. A prosecutor who files an application on the prosecutor's own motion or who files an application for the installation and use of a pen register, ESN reader, or similar equipment on the request of an authorized peace officer not commissioned by the department must make the application personally and may not do so through an assistant or some other person acting on the prosecutor's behalf. A prosecutor may

make an application through an assistant or other person acting on the prosecutor's behalf if the prosecutor files an application for the installation and use of:

(1) a pen register, ESN reader, or similar equipment on the request of an authorized peace officer who is commissioned by the department; or

(2) a trap and trace device or similar equipment on the request of an authorized peace officer, regardless of whether the officer is commissioned by the department.

(c) The application must:

(1) be made in writing under oath;

(2) include the name of the subscriber and the telephone number and location of the communication device on which the pen register, ESN reader, trap and trace device, or similar equipment will be used, to the extent that information is known or is reasonably ascertainable; and

(3) state that the installation and use of the device or equipment will likely produce information that is material to an ongoing criminal investigation.

A *Subsection (d) below is effective for applications for the installation and use of a pen register, ESN reader, or similar equipment filed on or after May 23, 2007.*

(d) On presentation of the application, the judge may order the installation and use of the pen register, ESN reader, or similar equipment by an authorized peace officer commissioned by the department or an authorized peace officer of a designated law enforcement agency, and, on request of the applicant, the judge shall direct in the order that a communication common carrier or a provider of electronic communications service furnish all information, facilities, and technical assistance necessary to facilitate the installation and use of the device or equipment by the department or designated law enforcement agency unobtrusively and with a minimum of interference to the services provided by the carrier or service. The carrier or service is entitled to compensation at the prevailing rates for the facilities and assistance provided to the department or a designated law enforcement agency.

Subsection (d) below is effective for applications for the installation and use of a pen register, ESN reader, or similar equipment filed before May 23, 2007.

(d) On presentation of the application, the judge may order the installation and use of the pen register,

ESN reader, or similar equipment by an authorized peace officer commissioned by the department, and, on request of the applicant, the judge shall direct in the order that a communication common carrier or a provider of electronic communications service furnish all information, facilities, and technical assistance necessary to facilitate the installation and use of the device or equipment by the department unobtrusively and with a minimum of interference to the services provided by the carrier or service. The carrier or service is entitled to compensation at the prevailing rates for the facilities and assistance provided to the department.

(e) On presentation of the application, the judge may order the installation and use of the trap and trace device or similar equipment by the communication common carrier or other person on the appropriate line. The judge may direct the communication common carrier or other person, including any landlord or other custodian of equipment, to furnish all information, facilities, and technical assistance necessary to install or use the device or equipment unobtrusively and with a minimum of interference to the services provided by the communication common carrier, landlord, custodian, or other person. Unless otherwise ordered by the court, the results of the trap and trace device or similar equipment shall be furnished to the applicant, designated by the court, at reasonable intervals during regular business hours, for the duration of the order. The carrier is entitled to compensation at the prevailing rates for the facilities and assistance provided to the law enforcement agency.

(f) Except as otherwise provided by this subsection, an order for the installation and use of a device or equipment under this section is valid for not more than 60 days after the earlier of the date the device or equipment is installed or the 10th day after the date the order is entered, unless the prosecutor applies for and obtains from the court an extension of the order before the order expires. The period of extension may not exceed 60 days for each extension granted, except that with the consent of the subscriber or customer of the service on which the device or equipment is used, the court may extend an order for a period not to exceed one year.

(g) The district court shall seal an application and order granted under this article.

(h) A peace officer is not required to file an application or obtain an order under this section before the officer makes an otherwise lawful search, with or without a warrant, to determine the contents of a caller identification message, pager message, or voice message that is contained within the memory of an end-user's identification, paging, or answering device.

(i) A peace officer of a designated law enforcement agency is authorized to possess, install, operate, or monitor a pen register, ESN reader, or similar equipment if the officer's name is on the list submitted to the director of the department under Subsection (k).

(j) Each designated law enforcement agency shall:

(1) adopt a written policy governing the application of this article to the agency; and

(2) submit the policy to the director of the department, or the director's designee, for approval.

(k) If the director of the department or the director's designee approves the policy submitted under Subsection (j), the sheriff or chief of a designated law enforcement agency, as applicable, or the sheriff's or chief's designee, shall submit to the director a written list of all officers in the agency who are authorized to possess, install, monitor, or operate pen registers, ESN readers, or similar equipment.

(l) The department may conduct an audit of a designated law enforcement agency to ensure compliance with this article. If the department determines from the audit that the designated law enforcement agency is not in compliance with the policy adopted by the agency under Subsection (j), the department shall notify the agency in writing that it is not in compliance. If the department determines that the agency still is not in compliance with the policy 90 days after the date the agency receives written notice under this subsection, the agency loses the authority granted by this article until:

(1) the agency adopts a new written policy governing the application of this article to the agency; and

(2) the department approves the written policy.

(m) The sheriff or chief of a designated law enforcement agency shall submit to the director of the department a written report of expenditures made by the designated law enforcement agency for the purchase and maintenance of a pen register, ESN reader, or similar equipment, authorized pursuant to Subsection (i). The director of the department shall report such expenditures publicly on an annual basis via the department's website, or other comparable means.

§3. Emergency Installation & Use of Pen Register or Trap & Trace Device

(a) A peace officer authorized to possess, install, operate, or monitor a device under Section 8A, Article 18.20, may install and use a pen register or trap and trace device if the officer:

(1) reasonably believes an immediate life-threatening situation exists that:

(A) is within the territorial jurisdiction of the officer or another officer the officer is assisting; and

(B) requires the installation of a pen register or trap and trace device before an order authorizing the installation and use can, with due diligence, be obtained under this article; and

(2) reasonably believes there are sufficient grounds under this article on which to obtain an order authorizing the installation and use of a pen register or trap and trace device.

(b) If an officer installs or uses a pen register or trap and trace device under Subsection (a), the officer shall:

(1) promptly report the installation or use to the prosecutor in the county in which the device is installed or used; and

(2) within 48 hours after the installation is complete or the use of the device begins, whichever occurs first, obtain an order under Section 2 authorizing the installation and use.

(c) A judge may issue an order authorizing the installation and use of a device under this section during the 48-hour period prescribed by Subsection (b)(2). If an order is denied or is not issued within the 48-hour period, the officer shall terminate use of and remove the pen register or the trap and trace device promptly on the earlier of the denial or the expiration of 48 hours.

(d) The state may not use as evidence in a criminal proceeding any information gained through the use of a pen register or trap and trace device installed under this section if an authorized peace officer does not apply for or applies for but does not obtain authorization for the pen register or trap and trace device.

§4. Requirements for Government Access to Stored Communications

(a) An authorized peace officer may require a provider of electronic communications service to disclose the contents of an electronic communication that has been in electronic storage for not longer than 180 days by obtaining a warrant.

(b) An authorized peace officer may require a provider of electronic communications service to disclose the contents of an electronic communication that has been in electronic storage for longer than 180 days:

(1) if notice is not being given to the subscriber or customer, by obtaining a warrant;

(2) if notice is being given to the subscriber or customer, by obtaining:

(A) an administrative subpoena authorized by statute;

(B) a grand jury subpoena; or

(C) a court order issued under Section 5 of this article; or

(3) as otherwise permitted by applicable federal law.

(c)(1) An authorized peace officer may require a provider of a remote computing service to disclose the contents of an electronic communication as described in Subdivision (2) of this subsection:

(A) if notice is not being given to the subscriber or customer, by obtaining a warrant issued under this code;

(B) if notice is being given to the subscriber or customer, by:

(i) an administrative subpoena authorized by statute;

(ii) a grand jury subpoena; or

(iii) a court order issued under Section 5 of this article; or

(C) as otherwise permitted by applicable federal law.

(2) Subdivision (1) of this subsection applies only to an electronic communication that is in electronic storage:

(A) on behalf of a subscriber or customer of the service and is received by means of electronic transmission from or created by means of computer processing of communications received by means of electronic transmission from the subscriber or customer; and

(B) solely for the purpose of providing storage or computer processing services to the subscriber or customer if the provider of the service is not authorized to obtain access to the contents of those communications for purposes of providing any service other than storage or computer processing.

(d) An authorized peace officer may require a provider of remote computing service to disclose records or other information pertaining to a subscriber or customer of the service, other than communications described in Subsection (c) of this section, without giving the subscriber or customer notice:

(1) by obtaining an administrative subpoena authorized by statute;

(2) by obtaining a grand jury subpoena;

(3) by obtaining a warrant;

(4) by obtaining the consent of the subscriber or customer to the disclosure of the records or information;

(5) by obtaining a court order under Section 5 of this article; or

(6) as otherwise permitted by applicable federal law.

(e) A provider of telephonic communications service shall disclose to an authorized peace officer, without any form of legal process, subscriber listing information, including name, address, and telephone number or similar access code that:

(1) the service provides to others in the course of providing publicly available directory or similar assistance; or

(2) is solely for use in the dispatch of emergency vehicles and personnel responding to a distress call directed to an emergency dispatch system or when the information is reasonably necessary to aid in the dispatching of emergency vehicles and personnel for the immediate prevention of death, personal injury, or destruction of property.

(f) A provider of telephonic communications service shall provide an authorized peace officer with the name of the subscriber of record whose published telephone number is provided to the service by an authorized peace officer.

§5. Court Order to Obtain Access to Stored Communications

(a) A court shall issue an order authorizing disclosure of contents, records, or other information of a wire or electronic communication held in electronic storage if the court determines that there is reasonable belief that the information sought is relevant to a legitimate law enforcement inquiry.

(b) A court may grant a motion by the service provider to quash or modify the order issued under Subsection (a) of this section if the court determines that the information or records requested are unusually voluminous in nature or that compliance with the order would cause an undue burden on the provider.

§6. Backup Preservation

(a) A subpoena or court order for disclosure of the contents of an electronic communication in a remote computing service under Section 4(c) of this article may require that the service provider to whom the request is directed create a copy of the contents of the electronic communications sought by the subpoena or court order for the purpose of preserving those contents. The service provider may not inform the subscriber or customer whose communications are being sought that the subpoena or court order has been issued. The service provider shall create the copy not later than two business days after the date of the receipt by the service provider of the subpoena or court order.

(b) The service provider shall immediately notify the authorized peace officer who presented the subpoena or court order requesting the copy when the copy has been created.

(c) Except as provided by Section 7 of this article, the authorized peace officer shall notify the subscriber or customer whose communications are the subject of the subpoena or court order of the creation of the copy not later than three days after the date of the receipt of the notification from the service provider that the copy was created.

(d) The service provider shall release the copy to the requesting authorized peace officer not earlier than the 14th day after the date of the peace officer's notice to the subscriber or customer if the service provider has not:

(1) initiated proceedings to challenge the request of the peace officer for the copy; or

(2) received notice from the subscriber or customer that the subscriber or customer has initiated proceedings to challenge the request.

(e) The service provider may not destroy or permit the destruction of the copy until the information has been delivered to the law enforcement agency or until the resolution of any court proceedings, including appeals of any proceedings, relating to the subpoena or court order requesting the creation of the copy, whichever occurs last.

(f) An authorized peace officer who reasonably believes that notification to the subscriber or customer of the subpoena or court order would result in the destruction of or tampering with information sought may request the creation of a copy of the information. The peace officer's belief is not subject to challenge by the subscriber or customer or service provider.

(g)(1) A subscriber or customer who receives notification as described in Subsection (c) of this section may file a written motion to quash the subpoena or vacate the court order in the court that issued the subpoena or court order not later than the 14th day after the date of the receipt of the notice. The motion must contain an affidavit or sworn statement stating that:

(A) the applicant is a subscriber or customer of the service from which the contents of electronic communications stored for the subscriber or customer have been sought; and

(D) the applicant's reasons for believing that the information sought is not relevant to a legitimate law enforcement inquiry or that there has not been substantial compliance with the provisions of this article in some other respect.

(2) The subscriber or customer shall give written notice to the service provider of the challenge to the subpoena or court order. The authorized peace officer or law enforcement agency requesting the subpoena or court order shall be served a copy of the papers filed by personal delivery or by registered or certified mail.

(h)(1) The court shall order the authorized peace officer to file a sworn response to the motion filed by the subscriber or customer if the court determines that the subscriber or customer has complied with the requirements of Subsection (g) of this section. On request of the peace officer, the court may permit the response to be filed in camera. The court may conduct any additional proceedings the court considers appropriate if the court is unable to make a determination on the motion on the basis of the parties' initial allegations and response.

(2) The court shall rule on the motion as soon after the filing of the officer's response as practicable. The court shall deny the motion if the court finds that the applicant is not the subscriber or customer whose

stored communications are the subject of the subpoena or court order or that there is reason to believe that the peace officer's inquiry is legitimate and that the communications sought are relevant to that inquiry. The court shall quash the subpoena or vacate the order if the court finds that the applicant is the subscriber or customer whose stored communications are the subject of the subpoena or court order and that there is not a reason to believe that the communications sought are relevant to a legitimate law enforcement inquiry or that there has not been substantial compliance with the provisions of this article.

(3) A court order denying a motion or application under this section is not a final order and no interlocutory appeal may be taken from the denial.

§7. Delay of Notification

(a) An authorized peace officer seeking a court order to obtain information under Section 4(c) of this article may include a request for an order delaying the notification required under Section 4(c) of this article for a period not to exceed 90 days. The court shall grant the request if the court determines that there is reason to believe that notification of the existence of the court order may have an adverse result, as described in Subsection (c) of this section.

(b) An authorized peace officer who has obtained a subpoena authorized by statute or a grand jury subpoena to seek information under Section 4(c) of this article may delay the notification required under that section for a period not to exceed 90 days on the execution of a written certification of a supervisory official that there is reason to believe that notification of the existence of the subpoena may have an adverse result as described in Subsection (c) of this section. The peace officer shall maintain a true copy of the certification.

(c) In this section an "adverse result" means:

(1) endangering the life or physical safety of an individual;

(2) flight from prosecution;

(3) destruction of or tampering with evidence;

(4) intimidation of a potential witness; or

(5) otherwise seriously jeopardizing an investigation or unduly delaying a trial.

(d) A court may grant one or more extensions of the delay of notification provided by this section of up to 90 days on request or by certification by a supervisory official if the original requirements under Subsection (a) or (b) of this section are met for each extension.

(e) When the delay of notification under this section expires, the authorized peace officer shall serve, by personal delivery or registered or certified mail, the subscriber or customer a copy of the process or request together with notice that:

(1) states with reasonable specificity the nature of the law enforcement inquiry; and

(2) informs the subscriber or customer:

(A) that information stored for the subscriber or customer by the service provider named in the process or request was supplied to or requested by the peace officer and the date on which the information was supplied or requested;

(B) that notification to the subscriber or customer was delayed;

(C) of the name of the supervisory official who made the certification or the court that granted the request for the delay of notification; and

(D) of which provision of this article permitted the delay of notification.

§8. Preclusion of Notification

When an authorized peace officer seeking information under Section 4 of this article is not required to give notice to the subscriber or customer or is delaying notification under Section 7 of this article, the peace officer may apply to the court for an order commanding the service provider to whom a warrant, subpoena, or court order is directed not to disclose to any other person the existence of the warrant, subpoena, or court order. The order is effective for the period the court considers appropriate. The court shall enter the order if the court determines that there is reason to believe that notification of the existence of the warrant, subpoena, or court order will have an adverse result as described in Section 7(c) of this article.

§9. Reimbursement of Costs

(a) Except as provided by Subsection (c) of this section, an authorized peace officer who obtains information under this article shall reimburse the person assembling or providing the information for all costs that are reasonably necessary and that have been directly incurred in searching for, assembling, reproducing, or otherwise providing the information. These costs include costs arising from necessary disruption of normal operations of an electronic communications service or remote computing service in which the information may be stored.

(b) The authorized peace officer and the person providing the information may agree on the amount of reimbursement. If there is no agreement, the court that issued the order for production of the information shall determine the amount. If no court order was issued for production of the information, the court before which the criminal prosecution relating to the information would be brought shall determine the amount.

(c) Subsection (a) of this section does not apply to records or other information maintained by a communications common carrier that relate to telephone toll records or telephone listings obtained under Section 4(e) of this article unless the court determines that the amount of information required was unusually voluminous or that an undue burden was imposed on the provider.

§10. No Cause of Action

A subscriber or customer of a wire or electronic communications or remote computing service does not have a cause of action against a wire or electronic communications or remote computing service, its officers, employees, agents, or other specified persons for providing information, facilities, or assistance as required by a court order, warrant, subpoena, or certification under this article.

§11. Disclosure of Stored Communications

(a) Except as provided by Subsection (c) of this section, a provider of an electronic communications service may not knowingly divulge the contents of a communication that is in electronic storage.

(b) Except as provided by Subsection (c) of this section, a provider of remote computing service may not knowingly divulge the contents of any communication that is:

(1) in electronic storage;

(2) stored on behalf of a subscriber or customer of the service and is received by means of electronic transmission from or created by means of computer processing of communications received by means of electronic transmission from the subscriber or customer; and

(3) solely for the purpose of providing storage or computer processing services to the subscriber or

customer if the provider of the service is not authorized to obtain access to the contents of those communications for purposes of providing any service other than storage or computer processing.

(c) A provider of an electronic communications or remote computing service may divulge the contents of an electronically stored communication:

(1) to an intended recipient of the communication or that person's agent;

(2) to the addressee or that person's agent;

(3) with the consent of the originator, to the addressee or the intended recipient of the communication, or the subscriber of a remote computing service;

(4) to a person whose facilities are used to transmit the communication to its destination or the person's employee or authorized representative;

(5) as may be necessary to provide the service or to protect the property or rights of the provider of the service;

(6) to a law enforcement agency if the contents were obtained inadvertently by the service provider and the contents appear to pertain to the commission of a crime; or

(7) as authorized under federal or other state law.

§12. Cause of Action

(a) Except as provided by Section 10 of this article, a provider of electronic communications service or subscriber or customer of an electronic communications service aggrieved by a violation of this article has a civil cause of action if the conduct constituting the violation was committed knowingly or intentionally and is entitled to:

(1) injunctive relief;

(2) a reasonable attorney's fee and other litigation costs reasonably incurred; and

(3) the sum of the actual damages suffered and any profits made by the violator as a result of the violation or $1,000, whichever is more.

(b) The reliance in good faith on a court order, warrant, subpoena, or legislative authorization is a complete defense to any civil action brought under this article.

(c) A civil action under this section may be presented within two years after the date the claimant first discovered or had reasonable opportunity to discover the violation, and not afterward.

§13. Exclusivity of Remedies

The remedies and sanctions described in this article are the exclusive judicial remedies and sanctions for a violation of this article other than a violation that infringes on a right of a party guaranteed by a state or federal constitution.

§14. Mobile Tracking Devices

(a) A district judge may issue an order for the installation and use within the judge's judicial district of a mobile tracking device.

(b) The order may authorize the use of a mobile tracking device outside the judicial district but within the state, if the device is installed within the district.

(c) A district judge may issue the order only on the application of an authorized peace officer. An application must be written and signed and sworn to or affirmed before the judge. The affidavit must:

(1) state the name, department, agency, and address of the applicant;

(2) identify the vehicle, container, or item to which, in which, or on which the mobile tracking device is to be attached, placed, or otherwise installed;

(3) state the name of the owner or possessor of the vehicle, container, or item described in Subdivision (2);

(4) state the judicial jurisdictional area in which the vehicle, container, or item described in Subdivision (2) is expected to be found; and

(5) state the facts and circumstances that provide the applicant with a reasonable suspicion that:

(A) criminal activity has been, is, or will be committed; and

(B) the installation and use of a mobile tracking device is likely to produce information that is material to an ongoing criminal investigation of the criminal activity described in Paragraph (A).

(d) Within 72 hours after the time the mobile tracking device was activated in place on or within the vehicle, container, or item, the applicant shall notify in writing the judge who issued an order under this section.

(e) An order under this section expires not later than the 90th day after the date that the device has been activated in place on or within the vehicle, container, or item. For good cause shown, the judge may grant an extension for an additional 90-day period.

(f) The applicant shall remove or cause to be removed a mobile tracking device as soon as is practicable after the authorization period expires. If removal is not practicable, monitoring of the device shall cease on expiration of the authorization order.

(g) This section does not apply to a global positioning or similar device installed in or on an item of property by the owner or with the consent of the owner of the property. A device described by this subsection may be monitored by a private entity in an emergency.

§15. Subpoena Authority

(a) The director of the department, the director's designee, or the sheriff or chief of a designated law enforcement agency, or the sheriff's or chief's designee, may issue an administrative subpoena to a communications common carrier or an electronic communications service to compel the production of the carrier's or service's business records that:

(1) disclose information about:

(A) the carrier's or service's customers; or

(B) users of the services offered by the carrier or service; and

(2) are material to a criminal investigation.

(b) Not later than the 30th day after the date on which the administrative subpoena is issued under Subsection (a), the sheriff or chief of a designated law enforcement agency shall report the issuance of the subpoena to the department.

(c) If, based on reports received under Subsection (b), the department determines that a designated law enforcement agency is not in compliance with the policy adopted by the agency under Section 2(j), the department shall notify the agency in writing that it is not in compliance. If the department determines that the agency still is not in compliance with the policy 90 days after the date the agency receives written notice under this subsection, the agency loses the authority granted by this article until:

(1) the agency adopts a new written policy governing the application of this article to the agency; and

(2) the department approves the written policy.

§16. Limitation

A governmental agency authorized to install and use a pen register under this article or other law must use reasonably available technology to only record and decode electronic or other impulses used to identify the numbers dialed, routed, addressed, or otherwise processed or transmitted by a wire or electronic communication so as to not include the contents of the communication.

History of CCP art. 18.21: Acts 1985, 69th Leg., ch. 587, §5, eff. Aug. 26, 1985. Amended by Acts 1989, 71st Leg., ch. 958, §1, eff. Sept. 1, 1989; Acts 1993, 73rd Leg., ch. 659, §2, eff. Sept. 1, 1993; Acts 1995, 74th Leg., ch. 170, §1 (eff. Aug. 28, 1995), ch. 318, §47 (eff. Sept. 1, 1995); Acts 1997, 75th Leg., ch. 165, §31.01(40) (eff. Sept. 1, 1997), ch. 1051, §§5-8 (eff. Sept. 1, 1997); Acts 1999, 76th Leg., ch. 62, §18.20, eff. Sept. 1, 1999; Acts 2001, 77th Leg., ch. 1270, §§7-10, eff. Sept. 1, 2001; Acts 2003, 78th Leg., ch. 678, §§8-11, eff. Sept. 1, 2003; Acts 2007, 80th Leg., ch. 186, §§2-4, eff. May 23, 2007.

ANNOTATIONS

Richardson v. State, 865 S.W.2d 944, 953-54 (Tex. Crim.App.1993). "[S]ociety recognizes as objectively reasonable the expectation of the telephone customer that the numbers he dials as a necessary incident of his use of the telephone will not be published to the rest of the world. [¶] It follows that the use of a pen register may well constitute a 'search' under [Tex. Const. art.] I, §9.... The question remaining is whether such a search would be 'unreasonable' in the absence of probable cause. If so, then to the extent it authorizes a court ordered pen register without a showing of probable cause, [CCP art.] 18.21 violates Article I, §9."

Uresti v. State, 98 S.W.3d 321, 333 (Tex.App.—Houston [1st Dist.] 2003, no pet.). "[A] trap and trace device [records] the numbers assigned to those calling one's telephone. [¶] We hold that the use of a trap and trace device does not constitute a search under [Tex. Const. art.] I, §9...." *Contra* **McArthur v. State**, 1 S.W.3d 323, 329 n.3 (Tex.App.—Fort Worth 1999, pet. ref'd).

ART. 18.22. TESTING FOR COMMUNICABLE DISEASES FOLLOWING CERTAIN ARRESTS

(a) A person who is arrested for a misdemeanor or felony and who during the commission of that offense or an arrest following the commission of that offense causes a peace officer to come into contact with the person's bodily fluids shall, at the direction of the court having jurisdiction over the arrested person, undergo a medical procedure or test designed to show or help show whether the person has a communicable disease. The court may direct the person to undergo the procedure or test on its own motion or on the request of the peace officer. If the person refuses to submit voluntarily to the procedure or test, the court shall require the person to submit to the procedure or test. Notwithstanding any other law, the person performing the procedure or test shall make the test results available to the local health authority, and the local health authority shall notify the peace officer of the test result. The state may not use the fact that a medical procedure or test was performed on a person under this article, or use the results of the procedure or test, in any criminal proceeding arising out of the alleged offense.

(b) Testing under this article shall be conducted in accordance with written infectious disease control protocols adopted by the Texas Board of Health that clearly establish procedural guidelines that provide criteria for testing and that respect the rights of the arrested person and the peace officer.

(c) Nothing in this article authorizes a court to release a test result to a person other than a person specifically authorized by this article, and Section 81.103(d), Health and Safety Code, does not authorize that disclosure.

History of CCP art. 18.22: Acts 2001, 77th Leg., ch. 1480, §2, eff. Sept. 1, 2001. Amended by Acts 2003, 78th Leg., ch. 1250, §1, eff. Sept. 1, 2003.

ART. 18.23. EXPENSES FOR MOTOR VEHICLE TOWED & STORED FOR CERTAIN PURPOSES

(a) A law enforcement agency that directs the towing and storage of a motor vehicle for an evidentiary or examination purpose shall pay the cost of the towing and storage.

(b) Subsection (a) applies whether the motor vehicle is taken to or stored on property that is:

(1) owned or operated by the law enforcement agency; or

(2) owned or operated by another person who provides storage services to the law enforcement agency, including:

(A) a governmental entity; and

(B) a vehicle storage facility, as defined by Section 2303.002, Occupations Code.

(c) Subsection (a) does not require a law enforcement agency to pay the cost of:

(1) towing or storing a motor vehicle for a purpose that is not an evidentiary or examination purpose, including towing or storing a vehicle that has been abandoned, illegally parked, in an accident, or recovered after being stolen; or

(2) storing a motor vehicle after the date the law enforcement agency authorizes the owner or operator of the property to which the vehicle was taken or on which the vehicle is stored to release the vehicle to the vehicle's owner.

(d) This subsection applies only to a motor vehicle taken to or stored on property described by Subsection (b)(2). After a law enforcement agency authorizes the release of a motor vehicle held for an evidentiary or examination purpose, the owner or operator of the storage property may not refuse to release the vehicle to the vehicle's owner because the law enforcement agency has not paid the cost of the towing and storage.

 (e) Subchapter J, Chapter 2308, Occupations Code, does not apply to a motor vehicle directed by a law enforcement agency to be towed and stored for an evidentiary or examination purpose.

History of CCP art. 18.23: Acts 2005, 79th Leg., ch. 1197, §1, eff. Sept. 1, 2005; Amended by Acts 2007, 80th Leg., ch. 1046, §3.01, eff. Sept. 1, 2007.

CHAPTER 19. ORGANIZATION OF THE GRAND JURY

ART. 19.01. APPOINTMENT OF JURY COMMISSIONERS; SELECTION WITHOUT JURY COMMISSION

(a) The district judge, at or during any term of court, shall appoint not less than three, nor more than five persons to perform the duties of jury commissioners, and shall cause the sheriff to notify them of their appointment, and when and where they are to appear. The district judge shall, in the order appointing such commissioners, designate whether such commissioners shall serve during the term at which selected or for the next succeeding term. Such commissioners shall receive as compensation for each day or part thereof they may serve the sum of Ten Dollars, and they shall possess the following qualifications:

1.   Be intelligent citizens of the county and able to read and write the English language;

2.   Be qualified jurors in the county;

3.   Have no suit in said court which requires intervention of a jury;

4.   Be residents of different portions of the county; and

5.   The same person shall not act as jury commissioner more than once in any 12-month period.

(b) In lieu of the selection of prospective jurors by means of a jury commission, the district judge may direct that 20 to 125 prospective grand jurors be selected and summoned, with return on summons, in the same manner as for the selection and summons of panels for the trial of civil cases in the district courts. The judge shall try the qualifications for and excuses from service as a grand juror and impanel the completed grand jury in the same manner as provided for grand jurors selected by a jury commission.

History of CCP art. 19.01: Acts 1965, 59th Leg., vol. 2, ch. 722. Amended by Acts 1971, 62nd Leg., ch. 131, §1, eff. May 10, 1971; Acts 1979, 66th Leg., ch. 184, §1, eff. Sept. 1, 1979; Acts 1983, 68th Leg., ch. 514, §1, eff. June 19, 1983; Acts 1991, 72nd Leg., ch. 67, §1, eff. Sept. 1, 1991; Acts 2001, 77th Leg., ch. 344, §1, eff. Sept. 1, 2001.

Gentry v. State, 770 S.W.2d 780, 794 (Tex.Crim. App.1988). "Regardless of the 'shall' wording, the statutes relating to the organization of grand juries are directory and not mandatory. Courts are required to follow the 'means and methods provided by the legislature in selecting grand juries,' and 'an arbitrary disregard of those statutes in the selection and organization of the grand jury vitiates and renders such grand jury without authority.'"

De La Garza v. State, 650 S.W.2d 870, 874 (Tex. App.—San Antonio 1983, pet. ref'd). "The Court of Criminal Appeals upheld the jury wheel method of selecting Texas petit jury panels in criminal cases.... Because article 19.01(b) utilizes the same method when grand jurors are selected, we ... hold that no constitutional violation in the method of selection of grand jurors in this case has been shown."

ART. 19.02. NOTIFIED OF APPOINTMENT

The judge shall cause the proper officer to notify such appointees of such appointment, and when and where they are to appear.

History of CCP art. 19.02: Acts 1965, 59th Leg., vol. 2, ch. 722.

ART. 19.03. OATH OF COMMISSIONERS

When the appointees appear before the judge, he shall administer to them the following oath: "You do swear faithfully to discharge the duties required of you as jury commissioners; that you will not knowingly elect any man as juryman whom you believe to be unfit and not qualified; that you will not make known to any one the name of any juryman selected by you and reported to the court; that you will not, directly or indirectly, converse with any one selected by you as a juryman concerning the merits of any case to be tried at the next term of this court, until after said cause may be tried or continued, or the jury discharged."

History of CCP art. 19.03: Acts 1965, 59th Leg., vol. 2, ch. 722.

ART. 19.04. INSTRUCTED

The jury commissioners, after they have been organized and sworn, shall be instructed by the judge in their duties and shall then retire in charge of the sheriff to a suitable room to be secured by the sheriff for that purpose. The clerk shall furnish them the necessary stationery, the names of those appearing from the records of the court to be exempt or disqualified from serving on the jury at each term, and the last assessment roll of the county.

History of CCP art. 19.04: Acts 1965, 59th Leg., vol. 2, ch. 722.

ART. 19.05. KEPT FREE FROM INTRUSION

The jury commissioners shall be kept free from the intrusion of any person during their session, and shall not separate without leave of the court until they complete their duties.

History of CCP art. 19.05: Acts 1965, 59th Leg., vol. 2, ch. 722.

ANNOTATIONS

San Antonio Express-News v. Roman, 861 S.W.2d 265, 267 n.1 (Tex.App.—San Antonio 1993, no writ). "[T]he public has no right to, and may not be present during grand jury proceedings...."

ART. 19.06. SHALL SELECT GRAND JURORS

The jury commissioners shall select not less than 15 nor more than 40 persons from the citizens of the county to be summoned as grand jurors for the next term of court, or the term of court for which said commissioners were selected to serve, as directed in the order of the court selecting the commissioners. The commissioners shall, to the extent possible, select grand jurors who the commissioners determine represent a broad cross-section of the population of the county, considering the factors of race, sex, and age. A commissioner is not qualified to be selected for or to serve as a grand juror during the term of court for which the commissioner is serving as a commissioner.

History of CCP art. 19.06: Acts 1965, 59th Leg., vol. 2, ch. 722. Amended by Acts 1967, 60th Leg., ch. 515, §1, eff. Aug. 28, 1967; Acts 1979, 66th Leg., ch. 184, §4, eff. Sept. 1, 1979; Acts 2001, 77th Leg., ch. 344, §2, eff. Sept. 1, 2001; Acts 2005, 79th Leg., ch. 801, §1, eff. Sept. 1, 2005.

ART. 19.07. EXTENSION BEYOND TERM OF PERIOD FOR WHICH GRAND JURORS SHALL SIT

If prior to the expiration of the term for which the grand jury was impaneled, it is made to appear by a declaration of the foreman or of a majority of the grand jurors in open court, that the investigation by the grand jury of the matters before it cannot be concluded before the expiration of the term, the judge of the district court in which said grand jury was impaneled may, by the entry of an order on the minutes of said court, extend, from time to time, for the purpose of concluding the investigation of matters then before it, the period during which said grand jury shall sit, for not to exceed a total of ninety days after the expiration of the term for which it was impaneled, and all indictments pertaining thereto returned by the grand jury within said extended period shall be as valid as if returned before the expiration of the term. The extension of the term of a grand jury under this article does not affect the provisions of Article 19.06 relating to the selection and summoning of grand jurors for each regularly scheduled term.

History of CCP art. 19.07: Acts 1965, 59th Leg., vol. 2, ch. 722.

ANNOTATIONS

Land v. State, 695 S.W.2d 712, 714 (Tex.App.—Austin 1985, pet. ref'd). "The term of a grand jury ordinarily coincides with the term of the district court, but can be extended by the court to enable the grand jury to conclude its investigation of the matters before it."

ART. 19.08. QUALIFICATIONS

No person shall be selected or serve as a grand juror who does not possess the following qualifications:

1. The person must be a citizen of the state, and of the county in which the person is to serve, and be qualified under the Constitution and laws to vote in said county, provided that the person's failure to register to vote shall not be held to disqualify the person in this instance;

2. The person must be of sound mind and good moral character;

3. The person must be able to read and write;

4. The person must not have been convicted of misdemeanor theft or a felony;

5. The person must not be under indictment or other legal accusation for misdemeanor theft or a felony;

6. The person must not be related within the third degree of consanguinity or second degree of affinity, as determined under Chapter 573, Government Code, to any person selected to serve or serving on the same grand jury;

7. The person must not have served as grand juror or jury commissioner in the year before the date on which the term of court for which the person has been selected as grand juror begins;

8.   The person must not be a complainant in any matter to be heard by the grand jury during the term of court for which the person has been selected as a grand juror.

History of CCP art. 19.08: Acts 1965, 59th Leg., vol. 2, ch. 722. Amended by Acts 1969, 61st Leg., ch. 412, §5, eff. Sept. 1, 1969; Acts 1981, 67th Leg., ch. 827, §5, eff. Aug. 31, 1981; Acts 1989, 71st Leg., ch. 1065, §1, eff. Sept. 1, 1989; Acts 1991, 72nd Leg., ch. 561, §8, eff. Aug. 26, 1991; Acts 1995, 74th Leg., ch. 76, §5.95(27), eff. Sept. 1, 1995; Acts 1999, 76th Leg., ch. 1177, §1, eff. Sept. 1, 1999; Acts 2005, 79th Leg., ch. 801, §2, eff. Sept. 1, 2005.

ANNOTATIONS

Cantu v. State, 842 S.W.2d 667, 677-78 (Tex.Crim. App.1992). "[A] grand jury commissioner is not an 'officer' as that term is used in the Nepotism Statute. Rather, commissioners are citizens appointed by district judges and paid a nominal fee. [¶] In 1989 ... the Legislature added subsection 6 to Article 19.08 and prohibited persons from serving on grand juries with close relatives. ... At no time ... has Article 19.08 ever contained a substantive nepotism provision. Nor has any other portion of the Code contained a substantive nepotism provision concerning grand jurors."

ART. 19.09. NAMES RETURNED

The names of those selected as grand jurors by the commissioners shall be written upon a paper; and the fact that they were so selected shall be certified and signed by the jury commissioners, who shall place said paper, so certified and signed, in an envelope, and seal the same, and endorse thereon the words, "The list of grand jurors selected at ... term of the district court," the blank being for the month and year in which the term of the court began its session. The commissioners shall write their names across the seal of said envelope, direct the same to the district judge and deliver it to him in open court.

History of CCP art. 19.09: Acts 1965, 59th Leg., vol. 2, ch. 722.

ART. 19.10. LIST TO CLERK

The judge shall deliver the envelope containing the list of grand jurors to the clerk or one of his deputies in open court without opening the same.

History of CCP art. 19.10: Acts 1965, 59th Leg., vol. 2, ch. 722.

ART. 19.11. OATH TO CLERK

Before the list of grand jurors is delivered to the clerk, the judge shall administer to the clerk and each of his deputies in open court the following oath: "You do swear that you will not open the jury lists now delivered you, nor permit them to be opened until the time prescribed by law; that you will not, directly or indirectly, converse with any one selected as a juror concerning any case or proceeding which may come before such juror for trial in this court at its next term."

History of CCP art. 19.11: Acts 1965, 59th Leg., vol. 2, ch. 722.

ANNOTATIONS

Gentry v. State, 770 S.W.2d 780, 795 (Tex.Crim. App.1988). Judge "testified that he 'administered the required oath to all of the *deputy district clerks* immediately upon receiving the envelope from the *grand jury* [sic].' ... The grand jury for the July, 1983 term was not yet impaneled when the envelope was handed to the judge. If there was any harm caused by the failure of the judge to recollect whether he gave the oath to the clerk and deputies in open court or in the clerk's office, such harm could hardly be considered egregious. This is especially true in light of the judge's testimony that the *normal* procedure is to deliver the oath in open court. A one time deviation from this practice does not amount to a pattern of statutory violations, nor does it reflect an 'arbitrary disregard of those statutes'.... We find that the required oath was given to the 'clerk and each of his deputies'...."

ART. 19.12. DEPUTY CLERK SWORN

Should the clerk subsequently appoint a deputy, such clerk shall administer to him the same oath, at the time of such appointment.

History of CCP art. 19.12: Acts 1965, 59th Leg., vol. 2, ch. 722.

ART. 19.13. CLERK SHALL OPEN LISTS

The grand jury may be convened on the first or any subsequent day of the term. The judge shall designate the day on which the grand jury is to be impaneled and notify the clerk of such date; and within thirty days of such date, and not before, the clerk shall open the envelope containing the list of grand jurors, make out a copy of the names of those selected as grand jurors, certify to it under his official seal, note thereon the day for which they are to be summoned, and deliver it to the sheriff.

History of CCP art. 19.13: Acts 1965, 59th Leg., vol. 2, ch. 722.

ANNOTATIONS

Gentry v. State, 770 S.W.2d 780, 795 (Tex.Crim. App.1988). "Appellant grounds his complaint on the absence of an 'official seal' and a notation for the day for which the grand jurors were to be summoned. However, [judge] testified that the envelope was 'sealed' and 'signed by the members of the grand jury commission' when it was delivered to him. Moreover, despite the absence of a date, the grand jurors somehow managed to respond to their summons and appear as directed for the July, 1983 term."

ART. 19.14. SUMMONING

The sheriff shall summon the persons named in the list at least three days, exclusive of the day of service, prior to the day on which the grand jury is to be impaneled, by giving personal notice to each juror of the time and place when and where he is to attend as a grand juror, or by leaving at his place of residence with a member of his family over sixteen years old, a written notice to such juror that he has been selected as a grand juror, and the time and place when and where he is to attend; or the judge, at his election, may direct the sheriff to summon the grand jurors by registered or certified mail.

History of CCP art. 19.14: Acts 1965, 59th Leg., vol. 2, ch. 722. Amended by Acts 1993, 73rd Leg., ch. 268, §5, eff. Sept. 1, 1993.

ART. 19.15. RETURN OF OFFICER

The officer executing such summons shall return the list on the day on which the grand jury is to be impaneled, with a certificate thereon of the date and manner of service upon each juror. If any of said jurors have not been summoned, he shall also state in his certificate the reason why they have not been summoned.

History of CCP art. 19.15: Acts 1965, 59th Leg., vol. 2, ch. 722.

ART. 19.16. ABSENT JUROR FINED

A juror legally summoned, failing to attend without a reasonable excuse, may, by order of the court entered on the record, be fined not less than ten dollars nor more than one hundred dollars.

History of CCP art. 19.16: Acts 1965, 59th Leg., vol. 2, ch. 722.

ART. 19.17. FAILURE TO SELECT

If for any reason a grand jury shall not be selected or summoned prior to the commencement of any term of court, or when none of those summoned shall attend, the district judge may at any time after the commencement of the term, in his discretion, direct a writ to be issued to the sheriff commanding him to summon a jury commission, selected by the court, which commission shall select not more than 40 persons, as provided by law, who shall serve as grand jurors.

History of CCP art. 19.17: Acts 1965, 59th Leg., vol. 2, ch. 722. Amended by Acts 2001, 77th Leg., ch. 344, §3, eff. Sept. 1, 2001.

ART. 19.18. IF LESS THAN FOURTEEN ATTEND

When less than fourteen of those summoned to serve as grand jurors are found to be in attendance and qualified to so serve, the court shall order the sheriff to summon such additional number of persons as may be deemed necessary to constitute a grand jury of twelve persons and two alternates.

History of CCP art. 19.18: Acts 1965, 59th Leg., vol. 2, ch. 722. Amended by Acts 1999, 76th Leg., ch. 1065, §1, Sept. 1, 1999.

ART. 19.19. JURORS TO ATTEND FORTHWITH

The jurors provided for in the two preceding Articles shall be summoned in person to attend before the court forthwith.

History of CCP art. 19.19: Acts 1965, 59th Leg., vol. 2, ch. 722.

ART. 19.20. TO SUMMON QUALIFIED PERSONS

Upon directing the sheriff to summon grand jurors not selected by the jury commissioners, the court shall instruct him that he must summon no person to serve as a grand juror who does not possess the qualifications prescribed by law.

History of CCP art. 19.20: Acts 1965, 59th Leg., vol. 2, ch. 722.

ART. 19.21. TO TEST QUALIFICATIONS

When as many as fourteen persons summoned to serve as grand jurors are in attendance upon the court, it shall proceed to test their qualifications as such.

History of CCP art. 19.21: Acts 1965, 59th Leg., vol. 2, ch. 722. Amended by Acts 1999, 76th Leg., ch. 1065, §2, eff. Sept. 1, 1999.

ART. 19.22. INTERROGATED

Each person who is presented to serve as a grand juror shall, before being impaneled, be interrogated on oath by the court or under his direction, touching his qualifications.

History of CCP art. 19.22: Acts 1965, 59th Leg., vol. 2, ch. 722.

ART. 19.23. MODE OF TEST

In trying the qualifications of any person to serve as a grand juror, he shall be asked:

1.   Are you a citizen of this state and county, and qualified to vote in this county, under the Constitution and laws of this state?

2.   Are you able to read and write?

3.   Have you ever been convicted of a felony?

4.   Are you under indictment or other legal accusation for theft or for any felony?

History of CCP art. 19.23: Acts 1965, 59th Leg., vol. 2, ch. 722. Amended by Acts 1969, 61st Leg., ch. 412, §6, eff. Sept. 1, 1969.

ART. 19.24. QUALIFIED JUROR ACCEPTED

When, by the answer of the person, it appears to the court that he is a qualified juror, he shall be accepted as such, unless it be shown that he is not of sound mind or of good moral character, or unless it be shown that he is in fact not qualified to serve as a grand juror.

History of CCP art. 19.24: Acts 1965, 59th Leg., vol. 2, ch. 722.

ANNOTATIONS

Howard v. State, 704 S.W.2d 575, 578 (Tex.App.— Beaumont 1986, no pet.). "[W]hen construed harmoniously, [CCP arts. 19.08 and 19.21-19.24] mean that the qualifications of a grand juror are to be set, fixed and determined by the court as of the time of impaneling the grand jurors."

ART. 19.25. EXCUSES FROM SERVICE

Any person summoned who does not possess the requisite qualifications shall be excused by the court from serving. The following qualified persons may be excused from grand jury service:

(1) a person older than 70 years;

(2) a person responsible for the care of a child younger than 18 years;

(3) a student of a public or private secondary school;

(4) a person enrolled and in actual attendance at an institution of higher education; and

(5) any other person that the court determines has a reasonable excuse from service.

History of CCP art. 19.25: Acts 1965, 59th Leg., vol. 2, ch. 722. Amended by Acts 1979, 66th Leg., ch. 184, §2, eff. Sept. 1, 1979; Acts 1999, 76th Leg., ch. 1177, §2, eff. Sept. 1, 1999.

ART. 19.26. JURY IMPANELED

(a) When fourteen qualified jurors are found to be present, the court shall proceed to impanel the grand jury, unless a challenge is made, which may be to the array or to any particular person presented to serve as a grand juror or an alternate.

(b) The grand jury is composed of not more than twelve qualified jurors. In addition, the court shall qualify and impanel not more than two alternates to serve on disqualification or unavailability of a juror during the term of the grand jury. On learning that a grand juror has become disqualified or unavailable during the term of the grand jury, the attorney representing the state shall prepare an order for the court identifying the disqualified or unavailable juror, stating the basis for the disqualification or unavailability, dismissing the disqualified or unavailable juror from the grand jury, and naming one of the alternates as a member of the grand jury. The procedure established by this subsection may be used on disqualification or unavailability of a second grand juror during the term of the grand jury. For purposes of this subsection, a juror is unavailable if the juror is unable to participate fully in the duties of the grand jury because of the death of the juror or a physical or mental illness of the juror.

History of CCP art. 19.26: Acts 1965, 59th Leg., vol. 2, ch. 722. Amended by Acts 1999, 76th Leg., ch. 1065, §3, eff. Sept. 1, 1999; Acts 2003, 78th Leg., ch. 889, §1, eff. Sept. 1, 2003.

ART. 19.27. ANY PERSON MAY CHALLENGE

Before the grand jury has been impaneled, any person may challenge the array of jurors or any person presented as a grand juror. In no other way shall objections to the qualifications and legality of the grand jury be heard. Any person confined in jail in the county shall upon his request be brought into court to make such challenge.

History of CCP art. 19.27: Acts 1965, 59th Leg., vol. 2, ch. 722.

ANNOTATIONS

Rogers v. State, 774 S.W.2d 247, 261 (Tex.Crim. App.1989), *overruled in part on other grounds*, *Peek v. State*, 106 S.W.3d 72 (Tex.Crim.App.2003). "Unless it can be demonstrated that selection of the grand jurors was in fact made with a view to securing the indictment of particular persons, or in such other manner as effectively to defeat the grand jury's impartiality or independence, due process of law is not offended merely because a personal or professional relationship exists between certain grand jurors and the commissioners who appointed them."

Muniz v. State, 672 S.W.2d 804, 807 (Tex.Crim.App. 1984). We interpret Article 19.27 "to mean that the array must be challenged at the first opportunity which ordinarily means when the grand jury is impaneled. If challenge at this early date is impossible, as when the offense occurs after the grand jury is impaneled, the array can be attacked in a motion to quash the indictment before trial commences."

ART. 19.28. "ARRAY"

By the "array" of grand jurors is meant the whole body of persons summoned to serve as such before they have been impaneled.

History of CCP art. 19.28: Acts 1965, 59th Leg., vol. 2, ch. 722.

ART. 19.29. "IMPANELED" & "PANEL"

A grand juror is said to be "impaneled" after his qualifications have been tried and he has been sworn. By "panel" is meant the whole body of grand jurors.

History of CCP art. 19.29: Acts 1965, 59th Leg., vol. 2, ch. 722.

ART. 19.30. CHALLENGE TO "ARRAY"

A challenge to the "array" shall be made in writing for these causes only:

1. That those summoned as grand jurors are not in fact those selected by the method provided by Article 19.01(b) of this chapter or by the jury commissioners; and

2. In case of grand jurors summoned by order of the court, that the officer who summoned them had acted corruptly in summoning any one or more of them.

History of CCP art. 19.30: Acts 1965, 59th Leg., vol. 2, ch. 722. Amended by Acts 1979, 66th Leg., ch. 184, §3, eff. Sept. 1, 1979.

ART. 19.31. CHALLENGE TO JUROR

A challenge to a particular grand juror may be made orally for the following causes only:

1. That he is not a qualified juror; and

2. That he is the prosecutor upon an accusation against the person making the challenge.

History of CCP art. 19.31: Acts 1965, 59th Leg., vol. 2, ch. 722.

ART. 19.32. SUMMARILY DECIDED

When a challenge to the array or to any individual has been made, the court shall hear proof and decide in a summary manner whether the challenge be well-founded or not.

History of CCP art. 19.32: Acts 1965, 59th Leg., vol. 2, ch. 722.

ART. 19.33. OTHER JURORS SUMMONED

The court shall order another grand jury to be summoned if the challenge to the array be sustained, or order the panel to be completed if by challenge to any particular grand juror their number be reduced below twelve.

History of CCP art. 19.33: Acts 1965, 59th Leg., vol. 2, ch. 722.

ART. 19.34. OATH OF GRAND JURORS

When the grand jury is completed, the court shall appoint one of the number foreman; and the following oath shall be administered by the court, or under its direction, to the jurors: "You solemnly swear that you will diligently inquire into, and true presentment make, of all such matters and things as shall be given you in charge; the State's counsel, your fellows and your own, you shall keep secret, unless required to disclose the same in the course of a judicial proceeding in which the truth or falsity of evidence given in the grand jury room, in a criminal case, shall be under investigation. You shall present no person from envy, hatred or malice; neither shall you leave any person unpresented for love, fear, favor, affection or hope of reward; but you shall present things truly as they come to your knowledge, according to the best of your understanding, so help you God."

History of CCP art. 19.34: Acts 1965, 59th Leg., vol. 2, ch. 722.

ANNOTATIONS

Stern v. State ex rel. Ansel, 869 S.W.2d 614, 620 (Tex.App.—Houston [14th Dist.] 1994, writ denied). "Article 19.34 swears grand jurors to secrecy."

ART. 19.35. TO INSTRUCT JURY

The court shall instruct the grand jury as to their duty.

History of CCP art. 19.35: Acts 1965, 59th Leg., vol. 2, ch. 722.

ART. 19.36. BAILIFFS APPOINTED

The court and the district attorney may each appoint one or more bailiffs to attend upon the grand jury, and at the time of appointment, the following oath shall be administered to each of them by the court, or under its direction: "You solemnly swear that you will faithfully and impartially perform all the duties of bailiff of the grand jury, and that you will keep secret the proceedings of the grand jury, so help you God." Such bailiffs shall be compensated in a sum to be set by the commissioners court of said county.

History of CCP art. 19.36: Acts 1965, 59th Leg., vol. 2, ch. 722.

ART. 19.37. BAILIFF'S DUTIES

A bailiff is to obey the instructions of the foreman, to summon all witnesses, and generally, to perform all such duties as the foreman may require of him. One bailiff shall be always with the grand jury, if two or more are appointed.

History of CCP art. 19.37: Acts 1965, 59th Leg., vol. 2, ch. 722.

ART. 19.38. BAILIFF VIOLATING DUTY

No bailiff shall take part in the discussions or deliberations of the grand jury nor be present when they are discussing or voting upon a question. The grand jury shall report to the court any violation of duty by a bailiff and the court may punish him for such violation as for contempt.

History of CCP art. 19.38: Acts 1965, 59th Leg., vol. 2, ch. 722.

ART. 19.39. ANOTHER FOREMAN APPOINTED

If the foreman of the grand jury is from any cause absent or unable or disqualified to act, the court shall appoint in his place some other member of the body.

History of CCP art. 19.39: Acts 1965, 59th Leg., vol. 2, ch. 722.

ART. 19.40. QUORUM

Nine members shall be a quorum for the purpose of discharging any duty or exercising any right properly belonging to the grand jury.

History of CCP art. 19.40: Acts 1965, 59th Leg., vol. 2, ch. 722.

ART. 19.41. REASSEMBLED

A grand jury discharged by the court for the term may be reassembled by the court at any time during the term.

History of CCP art. 19.41: Acts 1965, 59th Leg., vol. 2, ch. 722. Amended by Acts 1999, 76th Leg., ch. 1065, §4, eff. Sept. 1, 1999.

ART. 19.42. PERSONAL INFORMATION ABOUT GRAND JURORS

(a) Except as provided by Subsection (b), information collected by the court, court personnel, or prosecuting attorney during the grand jury selection process about a person who serves as a grand juror, including the person's home address, home telephone number, social security number, driver's license number, and other personal information, is confidential and may not be disclosed by the court, court personnel, or prosecuting attorney.

(b) On a showing of good cause, the court shall permit disclosure of the information sought to a party to the proceeding.

History of CCP art. 19.42: Acts 1999, 76th Leg., ch. 1177, §3, eff. Sept. 1, 1999.

CHAPTER 20. DUTIES & POWERS OF THE GRAND JURY

ART. 20.01. GRAND JURY ROOM

After the grand jury is organized they shall proceed to the discharge of their duties in a suitable place which the sheriff shall prepare for their sessions.

History of CCP art. 20.01: Acts 1965, 59th Leg., vol. 2, ch. 722.

ART. 20.011. WHO MAY BE PRESENT IN GRAND JURY ROOM

(a) Only the following persons may be present in a grand jury room while the grand jury is conducting proceedings:

(1) grand jurors;

(2) bailiffs;

(3) the attorney representing the state;

(4) witnesses while being examined or when necessary to assist the attorney representing the state in examining other witnesses or presenting evidence to the grand jury;

(5) interpreters, if necessary; and

(6) a stenographer or person operating an electronic recording device, as provided by Article 20.012.

(b) Only a grand juror may be in a grand jury room while the grand jury is deliberating.

History of CCP art. 20.011: Acts 1995, 74th Leg., ch. 1011, §1, eff. Sept. 1, 1995.

Walter v. State, 209 S.W.3d 722, 740 (Tex.App.—Texarkana 2006, pet. granted 5-2-07). "Article 20.011 does not authorize the setting aside of the indictment on the basis that unauthorized persons were present during grand jury testimony."

ART. 20.012. RECORDING OF CERTAIN TESTIMONY

(a) Questions propounded by the grand jury or the attorney representing the state to a person accused or suspected and the testimony of that person to the grand jury shall be recorded either by a stenographer or by use of an electronic device capable of recording sound.

(b) The validity of a grand jury proceeding is not affected by an unintentional failure to record all or part of questions propounded or testimony made under Subsection (a).

(c) The attorney representing the state shall maintain possession of all records other than stenographer's notes made under this article and any typewritten transcription of those records, except as provided by Article 20.02.

History of CCP art. 20.012: Acts 1995, 74th Leg., ch. 1011, §1, eff. Sept. 1, 1995.

ART. 20.02. PROCEEDINGS SECRET

(a) The proceedings of the grand jury shall be secret.

(b) A grand juror, bailiff, interpreter, stenographer or person operating an electronic recording device, or person preparing a typewritten transcription of a stenographic or electronic recording who discloses anything transpiring before the grand jury, regardless of whether the thing transpiring is recorded, in the course of the official duties of the grand jury shall be liable to a fine as for contempt of the court, not exceeding five hundred dollars, imprisonment not exceeding thirty days, or both such fine and imprisonment.

(c) A disclosure of a record made under Article 20.012, a disclosure of a typewritten transcription of that record, or a disclosure otherwise prohibited by Subsection (b) or Article 20.16 may be made by the attorney representing the state in performing the attorney's duties to a grand juror serving on the grand jury before whom the record was made, another grand jury, a law enforcement agency, or a prosecuting attorney, as permitted by the attorney representing the state and determined by the attorney as necessary to assist the attorney in the performance of the attorney's duties. The attorney representing the state shall warn any person the attorney authorizes to receive information under this subsection of the person's duty to maintain the secrecy of the information. Any person who receives information under this subsection and discloses the information for purposes other than those permitted by this subsection is subject to punishment for contempt in the same manner as persons who violate Subsection (b).

(d) The defendant may petition a court to order the disclosure of information otherwise made secret by this article or the disclosure of a recording or typewritten transcription under Article 20.012 as a matter preliminary to or in connection with a judicial proceeding. The court may order disclosure of the information, recording, or transcription on a showing by the defendant of a particularized need.

(e) A petition for disclosure under Subsection (d) must be filed in the district court in which the case is pending. The defendant must also file a copy of the petition with the attorney representing the state, the parties to the judicial proceeding, and any other persons required by the court to receive a copy of the petition. All persons receiving a petition under this subsection are entitled to appear before the court. The court shall provide interested parties with an opportunity to appear and present arguments for the continuation of or end to the requirement of secrecy.

(f) A person who receives information under Subsection (d) or (e) and discloses that information is subject to punishment for contempt in the same manner as a person who violates Subsection (b).

CCP ART. 20.02

(g) The attorney representing the state may not disclose anything transpiring before the grand jury except as permitted by Subsections (c), (d), and (e).

(h) A subpoena or summons relating to a grand jury proceeding or investigation must be kept secret to the extent and for as long as necessary to prevent the unauthorized disclosure of a matter before the grand jury. This subsection may not be construed to limit a disclosure permitted by Subsection (c), (d), or (e).

History of CCP art. 20.02: Acts 1965, 59th Leg., vol. 2, ch. 722. Amended by Acts 1995, 74th Leg., ch. 1011, §2, eff. Sept. 1, 1995; Acts 2007, 80th Leg., ch. 628, §1, eff. Sept. 1, 2007.

ANNOTATIONS

Ray v. State, 561 S.W.2d 480, 481 (Tex.Crim.App. 1977). "[W]hen the evidence shows that unauthorized persons were present during the deliberations of the grand jury the indictment must be invalidated and a new trial ordered."

Kelly v. State, 151 S.W.3d 683, 686-87 (Tex.App.—Waco 2004, no pet.). "[A] post-dismissal motion for disclosure of grand jury proceedings under article 20.02 is a criminal law matter. [¶] This Court has jurisdiction in a criminal case only when expressly provided by law. No statute authorizes an appeal from the denial of a post-dismissal motion for disclosure of grand jury proceedings."

Stern v. State ex rel. Ansel, 869 S.W.2d 614, 619 (Tex.App.—Houston [14th Dist.] 1994, writ denied). "The goal of [Article 20.02] is not to limit the prohibition against disclosure to grand jurors and bailiffs alone [but] to penalize a grand juror or bailiff for making such a disclosure. Nothing in the article suggests that individuals such as witnesses, counsel for the accused, court reporters or state attorneys can publicly divulge events that take place before a grand jury. *At 621:* Not only 'deliberations' are included within the ambit of the rule of secrecy, but *anything* that takes place before the bailiffs and grand jurors, including testimony. ... *Any* communication made to the grand jury in the regular performance of its duties is secret."

Carter v. State, 691 S.W.2d 112, 116 (Tex.App.—Fort Worth 1985, no pet.). "It is well settled that unauthorized persons are not allowed in the grand jury room during deliberations. However, there is no rule prohibiting persons from appearing before the grand jury at other times."

ART. 20.03. ATTORNEY REPRESENTING STATE ENTITLED TO APPEAR

"The attorney representing the State" means the Attorney General, district attorney, criminal district attorney, or county attorney. The attorney representing the State, is entitled to go before the grand jury and inform them of offenses liable to indictment at any time except when they are discussing the propriety of finding an indictment or voting upon the same.

History of CCP art. 20.03: Acts 1965, 59th Leg., vol. 2, ch. 722.

ANNOTATIONS

State ex rel. Holmes v. Salinas, 784 S.W.2d 421, 426 (Tex.Crim.App.1990). "[A] district attorney has ... the authority ... to bring matters 'liable to indictment' to the attention of the grand jury. This responsibility does not begin after an examining trial; the district attorney is charged with informing the grand jury of alleged offenses '*at any time*' other than the time the panel is engaged in discussion or deliberation. Moreover, the statute speaks in terms of the district attorney's *right* to seek an indictment at any such time...."

ART. 20.04. ATTORNEY MAY EXAMINE WITNESSES

The attorney representing the State may examine the witnesses before the grand jury and shall advise as to the proper mode of interrogating them. No person other than the attorney representing the State or a grand juror may question a witness before the grand jury. No person may address the grand jury about a matter before the grand jury other than the attorney representing the State, a witness, or the accused or suspected person or the attorney for the accused or suspected person if approved by the State's attorney.

History of CCP art. 20.04: Acts 1965, 59th Leg., vol. 2, ch. 722. Amended by Acts 1989, 71st Leg., ch. 1065, §2, eff. Sept. 1, 1989.

ANNOTATIONS

Smith v. State, 36 S.W.3d 134, 137 (Tex.App.—Houston [14th Dist.] 2000, pet. ref'd). "[A] violation of [Article 20.04] affects substantial rights of the defendant and is subject to a harm analysis. The questions complained of appear in the record and may be analyzed in relation to the rest of the witness testimony before the grand jury, thereby allowing this court to meaningfully gauge or quantify the effect of the error." (Internal quotes omitted.)

ART. 20.05. MAY SEND FOR ATTORNEY

The grand jury may send for the attorney representing the state and ask his advice upon any matter of law or upon any question arising respecting the proper discharge of their duties.

History of CCP art. 20.05: Acts 1965, 59th Leg., vol. 2, ch. 722. Amended by Acts 1989, 71st Leg., ch. 1065, §3, eff. Sept. 1, 1989.

ART. 20.06. ADVICE FROM COURT

The grand jury may also seek and receive advice from the court touching any matter before them, and for this purpose, shall go into court in a body; but they shall so guard the manner of propounding their questions as not to divulge the particular accusation that is pending before them; or they may propound their questions in writing, upon which the court may give them the desired information in writing.

History of CCP art. 20.06: Acts 1965, 59th Leg., vol. 2, ch. 722.

ANNOTATIONS

Bean v. State, 691 S.W.2d 773, 777 (Tex.App.—El Paso 1985, pet. ref'd). "Due to the inquiries raised by Appellant's witnesses, [judge] was in the posture of a witness and could not refuse to answer the grand jurors' questions. He did, however, divest himself of his consulting authority as convening judge. From that point on[, judge] functioned as a witness only, answered only those questions posed by the grand jurors and presented testimony not atypical of other grand jury witnesses."

ART. 20.07. FOREMAN SHALL PRESIDE

The foreman shall preside over the sessions of the grand jury, and conduct its business and proceedings in an orderly manner. He may appoint one or more members of the body to act as clerks for the grand jury.

History of CCP art. 20.07: Acts 1965, 59th Leg., vol. 2, ch. 722.

ART. 20.08. ADJOURNMENTS

The grand jury shall meet and adjourn at times agreed upon by a majority of the body; but they shall not adjourn, at any one time, for more than three days, unless by consent of the court. With the consent of the court, they may adjourn for a longer time, and shall as near as may be, conform their adjournments to those of the court.

History of CCP art. 20.08: Acts 1965, 59th Leg., vol. 2, ch. 722.

ANNOTATIONS

Smith v. State, 907 S.W.2d 522, 526 (Tex.Crim.App. 1995). "[T]he requirements of Article 20.08 are mandatory.... [A]rticle 20.08 requires only the court's consent to adjourn for more than three days and no formal order is required."

ART. 20.09. DUTIES OF GRAND JURY

The grand jury shall inquire into all offenses liable to indictment of which any member may have knowledge, or of which they shall be informed by the attorney representing the State, or any other credible person.

History of CCP art. 20.09: Acts 1965, 59th Leg., vol. 2, ch. 722.

ANNOTATIONS

Taylor v. State, 735 S.W.2d 930, 946 (Tex.App.— Dallas 1987), *aff'd*, 786 S.W.2d 295 (Tex.Crim.App. 1990). "[T]he grand jury has the authority to conduct their own investigations, to subpoena evidence and witnesses, to fail to return indictments sought by the district attorney, and to indict on matters as to which the district attorney has presented no evidence and sought no indictment. They summon witnesses and the like *and determine for themselves whether there are sufficient facts to justify an indictment.*"

ART. 20.10. ATTORNEY OR FOREMAN MAY ISSUE PROCESS

The attorney representing the state, or the foreman, in term time or vacation, may issue a summons or attachment for any witness in the county where they are sitting; which summons or attachment may require the witness to appear before them at a time fixed, or forthwith, without stating the matter under investigation.

History of CCP art. 20.10: Acts 1965, 59th Leg., vol. 2, ch. 722.

ART. 20.11. OUT-OF-COUNTY WITNESSES

Sec. 1. The foreman or the attorney representing the State may, upon written application to the district court stating the name and residence of the witness and that his testimony is believed to be material, cause a subpoena or an attachment to be issued to any county in the State for such witness, returnable to the grand jury then in session, or to the next grand jury for the county from whence the same issued, as such foreman or attorney may desire. The subpoena may require the witness to appear and produce records and documents. An attachment shall command the sheriff or any constable of the county where the witness resides to serve the witness, and have him before the grand jury at the time and place specified in the writ.

Sec. 2. A subpoena or attachment issued pursuant to this article shall be served and returned in the manner prescribed in Chapter 24 of this code.

A witness subpoenaed pursuant to this article shall be compensated as provided in this code.

History of CCP art. 20.11: Acts 1965, 59th Leg., vol. 2, ch. 722. Amended by Acts 1973, 63rd Leg., ch. 350, §1, eff. June 12, 1973.

ART. 20.12. ATTACHMENT IN VACATION

The attorney representing the state may cause an attachment for a witness to be issued, as provided in the preceding Article, either in term time or in vacation.

History of CCP art. 20.12: Acts 1965, 59th Leg., vol. 2, ch. 722.

ART. 20.13. EXECUTION OF PROCESS

The bailiff or other officer who receives process to be served from a grand jury shall forthwith execute the same and return it to the foreman, if the grand jury be in session; and if the grand jury be not in session, the process shall be returned to the district clerk. If the process is returned not executed, the return shall state why it was not executed.

History of CCP art. 20.13: Acts 1965, 59th Leg., vol. 2, ch. 722.

ART. 20.14. EVASION OF PROCESS

If it be made to appear satisfactorily to the court that a witness for whom an attachment has been issued to go before the grand jury is in any manner wilfully evading the service of such summons or attachment, the court may fine such witness, as for contempt, not exceeding five hundred dollars.

History of CCP art. 20.14: Acts 1965, 59th Leg., vol. 2, ch. 722.

ART. 20.15. WHEN WITNESS REFUSES TO TESTIFY

When a witness, brought in any manner before a grand jury, refuses to testify, such fact shall be made known to the attorney representing the State or to the court; and the court may compel the witness to answer the question, if it appear to be a proper one, by imposing a fine not exceeding five hundred dollars, and by committing the party to jail until he is willing to testify.

History of CCP art. 20.15: Acts 1965, 59th Leg., vol. 2, ch. 722.

ANNOTATIONS

Ex parte Edone, 740 S.W.2d 446, 448 (Tex.Crim. App.1987). Article 20.15 "gives the district court jurisdiction, power and authority over one not otherwise subject to the power of the court. ... The court thus aids the investigation of the grand jury under the authority of Art. 20.15. However, the court also exerts some 'control' or supervision over the grand jury under Art. 20.15. ... Without the action of the court the grand jury is powerless to enforce its investigative duty to gain testimony from a witness and decide on the presentment of an indictment. *At 449:* [O]nce the *court orders* the witness to answer before the grand jury, then a violation of such order constitutes contempt of the *court*. While the act of refusal—the violation of the specific order—occurs before the grand jury, the contempt is the violation of the *court's order*, and is, thus, contempt of the court."

Ex parte Marek, 653 S.W.2d 35, 37-38 (Tex.Crim. App.1983). "Given the specific procedures provided by [CCP ch.] 24 for penalizing one who refuses to produce before a grand jury material sought by a subpoena duces tecum, we are unwilling to extend terms of [CCP art.] 20.15 to cover the same default."

ART. 20.16. OATHS TO WITNESSES

Ⓐ *Article 20.16 below is effective for grand-jury proceedings that begin on or after Sept. 1, 2007.*

(a) The following oath shall be administered by the foreman, or under the foreman's direction, to each witness before being interrogated: "You solemnly swear that you will not reveal, by your words or conduct, and will keep secret any matter about which you may be interrogated or that you have observed during the proceedings of the grand jury, and that you will answer truthfully the questions asked of you by the grand jury, or under its direction, so help you God."

(b) A witness who reveals any matter about which the witness is interrogated or that the witness has observed during the proceedings of the grand jury, other than when required to give evidence thereof in due course, shall be liable to a fine as for contempt of court, not exceeding $500, and to imprisonment not exceeding six months.

History of CCP art. 20.16: Acts 1965, 59th Leg., vol. 2, ch. 722. Amended by Acts 1973, 63rd Leg., ch. 399, §2(A), eff. Jan. 1, 1974; Acts 2007, 80th Leg., ch. 28, §1, eff. Sept. 1, 2007.

ART. 20.16. OATHS TO WITNESSES

Article 20.16 below is effective for grand-jury proceedings that begin before Sept. 1, 2007.

The following oath shall be administered by the foreman, or under his direction, to each witness before being interrogated: "You solemnly swear that you will not divulge, either by words or signs, any matter about which you may be interrogated, and that you will keep secret all proceedings of the grand jury which may be had in your presence, and that you will true answers make to such questions as may be propounded to you by the grand jury, or under its direction, so help you God." Any witness who divulges any matter about which he is interrogated, or any proceedings of the grand jury had in his presence, other than when required to give evidence thereof in due course, shall be liable to a fine as for contempt of court, not exceeding $500, and to imprisonment not exceeding six months.

ART. 20.17. HOW SUSPECT OR ACCUSED QUESTIONED

(a) The grand jury, in propounding questions to the person accused or suspected, shall first state the offense with which he is suspected or accused, the county where the offense is said to have been committed and as nearly as may be, the time of commission of the offense, and shall direct the examination to the offense under investigation.

(b) Prior to any questioning of an accused or suspected person who is subpoenaed to appear before the grand jury, the accused or suspected person shall be furnished a written copy of the warnings contained in Subsection (c) of this section and shall be given a reasonable opportunity to retain counsel or apply to the court for an appointed attorney and to consult with counsel prior to appearing before the grand jury.

(c) If an accused or suspected person is subpoenaed to appear before a grand jury prior to any questions before the grand jury, the person accused or suspected shall be orally warned as follows:

(1) "Your testimony before this grand jury is under oath";

(2) "Any material question that is answered falsely before this grand jury subjects you to being prosecuted for aggravated perjury";

(3) "You have the right to refuse to make answers to any question, the answer to which would incriminate you in any manner";

(4) "You have the right to have a lawyer present outside this chamber to advise you before making answers to questions you feel might incriminate you";

(5) "Any testimony you give may be used against you at any subsequent proceeding";

(6) "If you are unable to employ a lawyer, you have the right to have a lawyer appointed to advise you before making an answer to a question, the answer to which you feel might incriminate you."

History of CCP art. 20.17: Acts 1965, 59th Leg., vol. 2, ch. 722. Amended by Acts 1989, 71st Leg., ch. 1065, §4, eff. Sept. 1, 1989.

ANNOTATIONS

Martinez v. State, 91 S.W.3d 331, 337 (Tex.Crim. App.2002). "Is a person who allegedly commits perjury in making a statement to the grand jury entitled to suppress that sworn statement because he was not fully advised of his rights to remain silent and make no statement at all? No."

Andino v. State, 645 S.W.2d 615, 623 (Tex.App.— Austin 1983, no pet.). "[T]he essential purpose of art. 20.17 is to establish with some definiteness the setting wherein the presiding judge may, on an application for an order of contempt, evaluate the putative defendant's claim that a particular question posed to him before the grand jury cannot be answered, or his assertion of his Fifth Amendment privilege be explained, because his response may tend to incriminate him. The nature of the offense of which a putative defendant is suspected, and the time and place of its commission, having been established as a frame of reference, the presiding judge may … evaluate … the putative defendant['s] invocation of the privilege against self-incrimination, the sufficiency of any grant of immunity contemplated by the judge, and other matters relating to the propriety of the question which the putative defendant has refused to answer."

ART. 20.18. HOW WITNESS QUESTIONED

When a felony has been committed in any county within the jurisdiction of the grand jury, and the name of the offender is known or unknown or where it is uncertain when or how the felony was committed, the grand jury shall first state to the witness called the subject matter under investigation, then may ask pertinent questions relative to the transaction in general terms and in such a manner as to determine whether he has knowledge of the violation of any particular law by any person, and if so, by what person.

History of CCP art. 20.18: Acts 1965, 59th Leg., vol. 2, ch. 722.

ART. 20.19. GRAND JURY SHALL VOTE

After all the testimony which is accessible to the grand jury shall have been given in respect to any criminal accusation, the vote shall be taken as to the presentment of an indictment, and if nine members concur in finding the bill, the foreman shall make a memorandum of the same with such data as will enable the attorney who represents the State to write the indictment.

History of CCP art. 20.19: Acts 1965, 59th Leg., vol. 2, ch. 722.

ANNOTATIONS

Bruns v. State, 924 S.W.2d 176, 179 (Tex. App.—San Antonio 1996, no pet.). "[T]he requirements in [CCP arts.] 20.19 and 20.20 relating to the preparation of a memorandum by the grand jury foreman and the indorsement of witnesses are merely directory despite the use of the word 'shall' therein."

Sledge v. State, 903 S.W.2d 105, 108 (Tex.App.— Fort Worth 1995), *aff'd*, 953 S.W.2d 253 (Tex.Crim.App. 1997). "[A] true bill … is the written statement of a grand jury accusing the person named in the indictment of some act or omission constituting an offense. If the State is permitted to wait until trial or until a pretrial hearing to choose the transaction to proceed upon, it is difficult to understand how this procedure complies with the requirements of grand jury oversight."

McCoy v. State, 773 S.W.2d 777, 779 (Tex.App.— Corpus Christi 1989, pet. ref'd). "The grand jury is impaneled to inquire into offenses liable to indictment and, after reviewing all relevant evidence, to vote on the presentment of an indictment. Although the evidence presented need not take any particular form, the grand jury will ultimately determine the competency and sufficiency of the evidence for the return of an indictment. [T]he courts will not go behind the actions of a grand jury to determine whether sufficient evidence existed to justify the return of an indictment; rather, an indictment, valid on its face, is sufficient to mandate trial on the merits."

ART. 20.20. INDICTMENT PREPARED

The attorney representing the State shall prepare all indictments which have been found, with as little delay as possible, and deliver them to the foreman, who shall sign the same officially, and said attorney shall endorse thereon the names of the witnesses upon whose testimony the same was found.

History of CCP art. 20.20: Acts 1965, 59th Leg., vol. 2, ch. 722.

ANNOTATIONS

Nichols v. State, 494 S.W.2d 830, 835 (Tex.Crim. App.1973). "[I]n the absence of a proper motion, the failure to comply with [Art. 20.20] is not a ground for excluding the testimony of a State's witness whose name was not placed on the indictment."

ART. 20.21. INDICTMENT PRESENTED

When the indictment is ready to be presented, the grand jury shall through their foreman, deliver the indictment to the judge or clerk of the court. At least nine members of the grand jury must be present on such occasion.

History of CCP art. 20.21: Acts 1965, 59th Leg., vol. 2, ch. 722. Amended by Acts 1979, 66th Leg., ch. 463, §1, eff. June 7, 1979.

ANNOTATIONS

State v. Dotson, 224 S.W.3d 199, 204 (Tex.Crim. App.2007). "Once an indictment is presented, jurisdiction vests with the trial court. The fact that an indictment is later lost, mislaid or destroyed does not divest the trial court of jurisdiction. [¶] The fact that a signed indictment features an original file stamp of the district clerk's office is strong evidence that a returned indictment was 'presented' to the court clerk within the meaning of Article 20.21."

Ⓐ ART. 20.22. PRESENTMENT ENTERED OF RECORD

The fact of a presentment of indictment by a grand jury shall be entered upon the record of the court, if the defendant is in custody or under bond, noting briefly the style of the criminal action and the file number of the indictment and the defendant's name. If the defendant is not in custody or under bond at the time of the presentment of indictment, the entry in the record of the court relating to said indictment shall be delayed until such time as the capias is served and the defendant is placed in custody or under bond.

History of CCP art. 20.22: Acts 1965, 59th Leg., vol. 2, ch. 722. Amended by Acts 1979, 66th Leg., ch. 463, §2, eff. June 7, 1979; Acts 1999, 76th Leg., ch. 580, §3, eff. Sept. 1, 1999; Acts 2007, 80th Leg., ch. 628, §2, eff. Sept. 1, 2007.

ANNOTATIONS

Hawkins v. State, 792 S.W.2d 491, 493-94 (Tex. App.—Houston [1st Dist.] 1990, no pet.). "The purpose of [Article 20.20] is to ensure that persons are tried only under true bills."

CHAPTER 21. INDICTMENT & INFORMATION

ART. 21.01. "INDICTMENT"

An "indictment" is the written statement of a grand jury accusing a person therein named of some act or omission which, by law, is declared to be an offense.

History of CCP art. 21.01: Acts 1965, 59th Leg., ch. 722, §1, eff. Jan. 1, 1966. See also Tex. Const. art. 5, §12(b).

ANNOTATIONS

Ex parte Patterson, 740 S.W.2d 766, 775 (Tex. Crim.App.1987), *overruled on other grounds*, *Ex parte Beck*, 769 S.W.2d 525 (Tex.Crim.App.1989). CCP art. 21.01 "gives statutory substance to the right conferred in [Tex. Const. art.] I, §10 ... to have a grand jury screening before a person may 'be held to answer for a criminal offense' of the magnitude of felony."

ART. 21.011. FILING OF CHARGING INSTRUMENT OR RELATED DOCUMENT IN ELECTRONIC FORM

(a) An indictment, information, complaint, or other charging instrument or a related document in a criminal case may be filed in electronic form with a judge or clerk of the court authorized to receive the document.

(b) A judge or clerk of the court is authorized to receive for filing purposes an information, indictment, complaint, or other charging instrument or a related document in electronic form in accordance with Subchapter I, Chapter 51, Government Code, if:

(1) the document complies with the requirements that would apply if the document were filed in hardcopy form;

(2) the clerk of the court has the means to electronically store the document for the statutory period of record retention;

(3) the judge or clerk of the court is able to reproduce the document in hard-copy form on demand; and

(4) the clerk of the court is able to display or otherwise make the document available in electronic form to the public at no charge.

(c) The person filing the document and the person receiving the document must complete the electronic filing as provided by Section 51.804, Government Code.

(d) Notwithstanding Section 51.806, Government Code, an indictment, information, complaint, or other charging instrument or a related document transmitted in electronic form is exempt from a requirement under this code that the pleading be endorsed by a natural person. The requirement of an oath under this code is satisfied if:

(1) all or part of the document was sworn to; and

(2) the electronic form states which parts of the document were sworn to and the name of the officer administering the oath.

(e) An electronically filed document described by this section may be amended or modified in compliance with Chapter 28 or other applicable law. The amended or modified document must reflect that the original document has been superseded.

(f) This section does not affect the application of Section 51.318, Government Code, Section 118.052(3), Local Government Code, or any other law permitting the collection of fees for the provision of services related to court documents.

History of CCP art. 21.011: Acts 2005, 79th Leg., ch. 312, §3, eff. June 17, 2005.

ART. 21.02. REQUISITES OF AN INDICTMENT

An indictment shall be deemed sufficient if it has the following requisites:

1. It shall commence, "In the name and by authority of The State of Texas."

2. It must appear that the same was presented in the district court of the county where the grand jury is in session.

3. It must appear to be the act of a grand jury of the proper county.

4. It must contain the name of the accused, or state that his name is unknown and give a reasonably accurate description of him.

5. It must show that the place where the offense was committed is within the jurisdiction of the court in which the indictment is presented.

6. The time mentioned must be some date anterior to the presentment of the indictment, and not so remote that the prosecution of the offense is barred by limitation.

7. The offense must be set forth in plain and intelligible words.

8. The indictment must conclude, "Against the peace and dignity of the State."

9. It shall be signed officially by the foreman of the grand jury.

History of CCP art. 21.02: Acts 1965, 59th Leg., ch. 722, §1, eff. Jan. 1, 1966.

ANNOTATIONS

Generally

Brooks v. State, 957 S.W.2d 30, 34 (Tex.Crim.App. 1997). "As with deadly weapon findings, prior convictions used as enhancements must be pled in some form, but they need not be pled in the indictment—

although it is permissible and perhaps preferable to do so." *See also **Cochran v. State**,* 107 S.W.3d 96, 98-99 (Tex.App.—Texarkana 2003, no pet.).

Duron v. State, 956 S.W.2d 547, 549 (Tex.Crim.App. 1997). "'[T]o comprise an indictment within the meaning provided by the constitution, an instrument must charge: (1) a person; (2) with the commission of an offense.' *At 550:* [A] written instrument is an indictment or information under the Constitution if it accuses someone of a crime with enough clarity and specificity to identify the penal statute under which the State intends to prosecute, even if the instrument is otherwise defective."

Art. 21.02(1)

Ex parte Cooper, 589 S.W.2d 130, 131 (Tex.Crim.App.1979). "It has long been held that an indictment or an information must commence 'In the name and by authority of The State of Texas' and these words have been held to be indispensable. This constitutional requirement is a matter of substance rather than of form. [¶] Although minor variations in the wording of the required constitutional and statutory language, such as adding the word 'the' before the word 'authority', have been held to be immaterial, the complete omission of the required constitutional statutory wording ... is controlled by long-standing precedent."

Art. 21.02(4)

London v. State, 739 S.W.2d 842, 844 (Tex.Crim.App.1987). "The term 'defendant' is usually defined to mean the following: 'The person defending or denying; the party against whom relief or recovery is sought in an action or suit or the accused in a criminal case.' [W]hen used in an indictment, the term 'the defendant' is merely a shorthand rendition for the name of the accused person which must ... be stated in the indictment."

Art. 21.02(5)

Skillern v. State, 890 S.W.2d 849, 859 (Tex.App.—Austin 1994, pet. ref'd). "Article 21.02(5) must be read with the understanding that there is a distinct difference between 'jurisdiction' and 'venue.' Jurisdiction concerns the authority or the power of the court to try a case. District courts have the authority to try felony cases in this State. Venue means the place where the case may be tried. The fact that venue does not lie in a particular district court does not mean that the court has no jurisdiction of the offense. Venue, proper or not, does not affect the power of a district court to hear and determine a felony case."

Art. 21.02(6)

Wright v. State, 28 S.W.3d 526, 532 (Tex.Crim.App. 2000). "[T]he 'on or about' language of an indictment allows the state to prove a date other than the one alleged as long as the date proven is anterior to the presentment of the indictment and within the statutory limitation period. There is no statute of limitations period for murder. Hence, when appellant was indicted for murder, he was put on notice to prepare for proof that the crime happened any time before the presentment of the indictment. Because both the original date and the date of the attempted amendment, which differed by two days, were prior to the presentment of the indictment, the indictment provided adequate notice for proof of either date."

Mireles v. State, 901 S.W.2d 458, 465 (Tex.Crim. App.1995). "[T]he allegation of a specific date in an indictment or information is not an element of the charged offense, nor even a fact which the State must prove to sustain a conviction, but is set forth only to provide a point of reference for the State's averment that its criminal action is not barred by limitation. It does not follow ... that the phrase 'on or about' actually means 'anterior to the presentment of the indictment, and not so remote that the prosecution of the offense is barred by limitation.' [T]he popular imagination of lawyers and judges has come to embrace the myth that pleading 'on or about' magically avoids the necessity of proving a specific date. But no such incantation [is] necessary. Pleading that the offense was committed 'on' a particular date will perform exactly the same magic."

Art. 21.02(9)

Stigers v. State, 702 S.W.2d 301, 302 (Tex.App.— Houston [1st Dist.] 1985, no pet.). "[T]he purpose of the [CCP's] requirement that each indictment be signed by the foreman is to insure that the indictment presented is in fact the one voted on and returned by the grand jury and that this purpose is fulfilled as well by a stamped facsimile as by the personal signature of the foreman."

ART. 21.03. WHAT SHOULD BE STATED

Everything should be stated in an indictment which is necessary to be proved.

History of CCP art. 21.03: Acts 1965, 59th Leg., ch. 722, §1, eff. Jan. 1, 1966.

Teal v. State, 230 S.W.3d 172, 181 (Tex.Crim.App. 2007). "[T]he complete test for the constitutional sufficiency of a particular charging instrument [is]: Can the district court and the defendant determine, from the face of the indictment, that the indictment intends to charge a felony or other offense for which a district court has jurisdiction? Suppose, for example, that a named person is indicted for the offense of speeding. The constitutional requirements of an indictment are met—a named person and an offense—but district courts do not have subject-matter jurisdiction over speeding offenses, regardless of how 'perfect' the wording of the charging instrument might be. Thus, the indictment, despite whatever substantive defects it contains, must be capable of being construed as intending to charge a felony (or a misdemeanor for which the district court has jurisdiction)."

Flenteroy v. State, 187 S.W.3d 406, 411 (Tex.Crim. App.2005). "The issue ... comes down to whether the variance between the named instrument in the indictment (a 'screwdriver') and the proof at trial (a 'hard metal-like object') was material. Where ... the evidence is sufficient to support the jury's finding that appellant used a 'hard metal-like object' as a deadly weapon but the State did not prove exactly what it alleged (*i.e.*, a 'screwdriver'), the issue is whether the indictment 'informed appellant of the charge against him sufficiently to allow him to prepare an adequate defense at trial.' [¶] Appellant's defense did not depend on whether any particular type of weapon was used. On the contrary, appellant denied that any weapon was used. The variance between the indictment's allegation of a 'screwdriver' and the State's proof at trial of 'a hard metal-like object' was, therefore, immaterial."

Olurebi v. State, 870 S.W.2d 58, 62 (Tex.Crim.App. 1994). "Generally, an indictment which tracks the statutory language will survive a motion to quash, and when a term is defined by statute, it need not also be defined in the indictment. However, if 'the statutory language is not completely descriptive of the offense, then additional specificity will be required in the face of a timely motion to quash.'"

ART. 21.04. THE CERTAINTY REQUIRED

The certainty required in an indictment is such as will enable the accused to plead the judgment that may be given upon it in bar of any prosecution for the same offense.

History of CCP art. 21.04: Acts 1965, 59th Leg., ch. 722, §1, eff. Jan. 1, 1966.

ANNOTATIONS

Livingston v. State, 739 S.W.2d 311, 321 (Tex.Crim. App.1987). "When a challenge to an accusation for failure to provide adequate notice on which to prepare a defense is properly and timely asserted with adequate statement of the manner in which notice is deficient, 'fundamental constitutional protections are invoked.' [Tex. Const.] art. I, §10 … mandates that the notice petitioned for must come from the face of the charging instrument. [¶] If additional information requested in a motion to quash is evidentiary in nature and not required for notice or plea in bar, the indictment is sufficient. The important question is whether a defendant has notice adequate to prepare his defense."

Hodge v. State, 527 S.W.2d 289, 290 (Tex.Crim.App. 1975). "The seldom challenged and almost universal practice in preparing indictments is to describe the place where the criminal offense was committed by merely alleging that it was committed in a certain county."

Ansley v. State, 468 S.W.2d 862, 864 (Tex.Crim.App. 1971). "The omission of a word or words, in an indictment, is not fatal if that part omitted is not essential to the certainty necessary in the description of the offense and does not affect the meaning."

Rose v. State, 807 S.W.2d 626, 629 (Tex.App.— Houston [14th Dist.] 1991, no pet.). "An indictment must allege on its face facts necessary to show that an offense was committed, bar a subsequent prosecution for the same offense and give defendant notice of precisely what he is charged with."

ART. 21.05. PARTICULAR INTENT; INTENT TO DEFRAUD

Where a particular intent is a material fact in the description of the offense, it must be stated in the indictment; but in any case where an intent to defraud is required to constitute an offense, it shall be sufficient to allege an intent to defraud, without naming therein the particular person intended to be defrauded.

History of CCP art. 21.05: Acts 1965, 59th Leg., ch. 722, §1, eff. Jan. 1, 1966.

ANNOTATIONS

Telfair v. State, 565 S.W.2d 522, 523 (Tex.Crim. App.1977). "[T]he 'specific intent to commit an offense' is both a particular intent and a material fact in the description of the offense of criminal attempt; therefore, it *must* be alleged in any indictment charging criminal attempt."

Baldwin v. State, 538 S.W.2d 109, 112 (Tex.Crim. App.1976). "This provision … has a counterpart in [Pen. Code ch. 6, which] provides for four 'culpable mental states' which are to be used in the Penal Code in defining the various offenses. These culpable mental states … set forth the various degrees of guilty knowledge which are requisite before culpability attaches. [¶] Unless the definition of an offense clearly dispenses with the requirement of a culpable mental state (a strict liability offense), one of the four above-mentioned 'intents' is mandatory. [I]f the definition does not prescribe a culpable mental state but one is required, intent, knowledge or recklessness suffice to establish criminal responsibility."

ART. 21.06. ALLEGATION OF VENUE

When the offense may be prosecuted in either of two or more counties, the indictment may allege the offense to have been committed in the county where the same is prosecuted, or in any county or place where the offense was actually committed.

History of CCP art. 21.06: Acts 1965, 59th Leg., ch. 722, §1, eff. Jan. 1, 1966. See also CCP art. 13.22

ANNOTATIONS

Rodriguez v. State, 918 S.W.2d 34, 37 (Tex.App.— Corpus Christi 1996, pet. ref'd). "The Texas legislature has provided that proper venue for trying a criminal case for possession of marihuana lies either in the county where the crime took place or in an adjacent county in the same district, provided the defendant consents."

Skillern v. State, 890 S.W.2d 849, 860 (Tex.App.— Austin 1994, pet. ref'd). "Venue is not a 'criminative fact' and it is not a constituent element of the offense."

ART. 21.07. ALLEGATION OF NAME

In alleging the name of the defendant, or of any other person necessary to be stated in the indictment, it shall be sufficient to state one or more of the initials of the given name and the surname. When a person is known by two or more names, it shall be sufficient to state either name. When the name of the person is unknown to the grand jury, that fact shall be stated, and if it be the accused, a reasonably accurate description of him shall be given in the indictment.

History of CCP art. 21.07: Acts 1965, 59th Leg., ch. 722, §1, eff. Jan. 1, 1966. Amended by Acts 1995, 74th Leg., ch. 830, §1, eff. Sept. 1, 1995.
See also CCP art. 57.02.

ANNOTATIONS

Grant v. State, 970 S.W.2d 22, 22-23 (Tex.Crim.App. 1998). "The information charging the offense stated … that appellant did: 'then and there unlawfully and intentionally flee from Officer Lawson, a peace officer, who Bobbie Grant knew to be a peace officer, who was attempting to arrest or detain Bobbie Grant.' The evidence at trial identified the peace officer as 'Lt. Craig Lawson.' Appellant contends that the evidence at trial was insufficient to support his conviction because the State pled, but failed to prove, that Lawson's first name was 'Officer.' Appellant thus alleged a fatal variance between the charging instrument allegation and the proof of the complainant's name at trial. [¶] This case does not involve a 'variance' of any type; it simply involves a missing allegation that is required by statute to be in the charging instrument. 'Officer' is clearly Lawson's title, rather than his first name; hence, his first name is missing from the information in violation of [CCP art.] 21.07. This missing first name is a defect that was waived … when appellant failed to object. Because 'Officer' was not an allegation of Lawson's first name, the State was not required to prove that it was Lawson's first name."

Cuba v. State, 905 S.W.2d 729, 732 (Tex.App.—Texarkana 1995, no pet.). "A variance between the allegation and the proof of a middle name is neither material nor fatal. And the suffix 'Jr.' is not part of a name. Its inclusion or omission with a name is immaterial in criminal proceedings. … Failure to order a defendant's name changed in an indictment to that suggested by the defendant is not improper where the defendant uses different names, one of which is used in the indictment."

Brown v. State, 843 S.W.2d 709, 712 (Tex.App.—Dallas 1992, pet. ref'd). "If the question is one of *idem sonans*, sound, not spelling of a name, controls in determining similarity of names. The rule of *idem sonans* does not permit the State to amend the name of the complainant in the indictment. When the question of *idem sonans* arises at the trial, it is a fact for the jury to decide under instructions from the court."

Chambless v. State, 776 S.W.2d 718, 720-21 (Tex. App.—Corpus Christi 1989, no pet.). "[T]he owner of the vehicle in question testified that his name is 'Paul A. Goike.' The indictment alleges the owner of the vehicle in question as 'P. Goike.' The initial 'P.' is the first initial of the complainant's Christian name, Paul. We hold that the variance between 'Paul A. Goike' and 'P. Goike' is not material and that the alleged variance was not prejudicial or misleading to appellant."

ART. 21.08. ALLEGATION OF OWNERSHIP

Where one person owns the property, and another person has the possession of the same, the ownership thereof may be alleged to be in either. Where property is owned in common, or jointly, by two or more persons, the ownership may be alleged to be in all or either of them. When the property belongs to the estate of a deceased person, the ownership may be alleged to be in the executor, administrator or heirs of such deceased person, or in any one of such heirs. Where the ownership of the property is unknown to the grand jury, it shall be sufficient to allege that fact.

History of CCP art. 21.08: Acts 1965, 59th Leg., ch. 722, §1, eff. Jan. 1, 1966. Amended by Acts 1967, 60th Leg., ch. 659, §16, eff. Aug. 28, 1967.

ANNOTATIONS

Harrell v. State, 852 S.W.2d 521, 523 (Tex.Crim. App.1993). "To show corporate ownership, it is sufficient to allege ownership in the employee who has care, custody, and control of the property, the 'special owner.'"

Freeman v. State, 707 S.W.2d 597, 603 (Tex.Crim. App.1986). "[T]he State … has the burden of proving beyond a reasonable doubt the ownership allegation. [¶] The issue of 'ownership' goes to the scope of the property interest protected by the law and is intended to protect all ownership interests in property from criminal behavior. When there are equal competing possessory interests in property allegedly stolen, we believe that the key to answering the question of which person has the greater right to possession of the property is who, *at the time of the commission of the offense*, had the greater right to possession of the property."

Araiza v. State, 555 S.W.2d 746, 747 (Tex.Crim.App. 1977). "[E]ven if the proof showed that A was the title owner of the property, an allegation that B was the owner with proof that B had possession of the property at the time of the offense would present no variance and would be sufficient under the law."

Gerhardt v. State, 965 S.W.2d 55, 58 (Tex.App.—Houston [1st Dist.] 1998, pet. ref'd). "Article 21.08 ... provides that when property belongs to the estate of a deceased person, ownership of the property 'may be alleged to be in the executor, administrator or heirs of such deceased person, or in any one of such heirs.' Article 21.08 is a rule of pleading; it is not part of the definition of the offense of theft."

ART. 21.09. DESCRIPTION OF PROPERTY

If known, personal property alleged in an indictment shall be identified by name, kind, number, and ownership. When such is unknown, that fact shall be stated, and a general classification, describing and identifying the property as near as may be, shall suffice. If the property be real estate, its general locality in the county, and the name of the owner, occupant or claimant thereof, shall be a sufficient description of the same.

History of CCP art. 21.09: Acts 1965, 59th Leg., ch. 722, §1, eff. Jan. 1, 1966. Amended by Acts 1975, 64th Leg., ch. 341, §2, eff. June 19, 1975.

ANNOTATIONS

Wood v. State, 632 S.W.2d 734, 736 (Tex.Crim.App. 1982). "[A] descriptive averment of personal property is adequate if it alleges (1) quantity; (2) the general type of property, as long as it is more specific than merely stating 'property' or 'merchandise'; (3) 'ownership' of the property; and (4) if necessary, the jurisdictional value of the property."

Reed v. State, 762 S.W.2d 640, 645 (Tex.App.—Texarkana 1988, pet. ref'd). "[U]nless the property is the *object* of the offense rather than the *situs*, merely naming the county where the property is located is sufficient if (1) the offense may be committed anywhere in the county, (2) the place where it is committed is not an element of the offense, and (3) the court in which the offense is tried has countywide jurisdiction."

Roberson v. State, 741 S.W.2d 563, 565 (Tex. App.—Texarkana 1987, no pet.). "Although the term 'merchandise' alone is so insufficient as to amount to no description, ... it is a sufficient description where name, kind, number and ownership of stolen property are unknown and that fact is stated in the indictment."

ART. 21.10. "FELONIOUS" & "FELONIOUSLY"

It is not necessary to use the words "felonious" or "feloniously" in any indictment.

History of CCP art. 21.10: Acts 1965, 59th Leg., ch. 722, §1, eff. Jan. 1, 1966.

ART. 21.11. CERTAINTY; WHAT SUFFICIENT

An indictment shall be deemed sufficient which charges the commission of the offense in ordinary and concise language in such a manner as to enable a person of common understanding to know what is meant, and with that degree of certainty that will give the defendant notice of the particular offense with which he is charged, and enable the court, on conviction, to pronounce the proper judgment; and in no case are the words "force and arms" or "contrary to the form of the statute" necessary.

History of CCP art. 21.11: Acts 1965, 59th Leg., ch. 722, §1, eff. Jan. 1, 1966.

ANNOTATIONS

Gollihar v. State, 46 S.W.3d 243, 246 (Tex.Crim. App.2001). "A 'variance' occurs when there is a discrepancy between the allegations in the charging instrument and the proof at trial. In a variance situation, the State has proven the defendant guilty of a crime, but has proven its commission in a manner that varies from the allegations in the charging instrument. *At 247-48:* The widely-accepted rule ... is that a variance that is not prejudicial to a defendant's 'substantial rights' is immaterial. *At 249-50:* Surplusage may often be responsible for a variance between the pleading and the proof. The general rule regarding surplusage is that 'allegations which are not essential to constitute the offense, and which might be entirely omitted without affecting the charge against the defendant, and without detriment to the indictment, are treated as surplusage' and may be disregarded. [¶] The exception to the general surplusage rule ... may run counter to the fatal variance doctrine [and] provides that where an extra or unnecessary allegation 'is descriptive of that which is legally essential to charge a crime, the State must prove it as alleged though needlessly pleaded.' *At 256-57:* [W]e hold that a hypothetically correct charge need not incorporate allegations that give rise to immaterial variances. [W]e reaffirm the fatal variance doctrine and overrule surplusage law and [its] exception. ... We adopt the materiality test applied by many other courts.... [W]hen faced with a sufficiency of the evidence claim based upon a variance between the indictment and the proof, only a 'material' variance will render the evidence insufficient."

State v. Edmond, 933 S.W.2d 120, 130 (Tex.Crim. App.1996). "[W]hen a statute defines the manner or means of committing an offense, an indictment based upon that statute need not allege anything beyond that definition."

Olurebi v. State, 870 S.W.2d 58, 62 (Tex.Crim.App. 1994). "Generally, an indictment which tracks the statutory language will survive a motion to quash, and when a term is defined by statute, it need not also be defined in the indictment. However, if 'the statutory language is not completely descriptive of the offense, then additional specificity will be required in the face of a timely motion to quash.'"

Lehman v. State, 792 S.W.2d 82, 84-85 (Tex.Crim. App.1990). "The State is allowed to anticipate variances in the proof by pleading alternative 'manner and means' in the conjunctive when proof of any one 'manner or means' will support a guilty verdict. Likewise, the State should be allowed to plead all property which the evidence may ultimately prove stolen without thereby being required to prove theft of any larger quantum of property than the statute at issue requires."

ART. 21.12. SPECIAL & GENERAL TERMS

When a statute defining any offense uses special or particular terms, indictment on it may use the general term which, in common language, embraces the special term. To charge an unlawful sale, it is necessary to name the purchaser.

History of CCP art. 21.12: Acts 1965, 59th Leg., ch. 722, §1, eff. Jan. 1, 1966.

ANNOTATIONS

Coleman v. State, 643 S.W.2d 124, 125 (Tex.Crim. App.1982). "Generally, if the word or term is defined by statute, it need not be further clarified in the charging instrument, even where a motion to quash is the mechanism used to challenge the word or term in the charging instrument. However, if a word or term in a charging instrument goes to an *act or omission* of the defendant, and the defendant files and presents to the trial court a motion to quash, the word or term, even though statutorily defined, must be further clarified by the State because the 'lack of notice of acts or omissions is by definition a denial of fair notice' to an accused."

ART. 21.13. ACT WITH INTENT TO COMMIT AN OFFENSE

An indictment for an act done with intent to commit some other offense may charge in general terms the commission of such act with intent to commit such other offense.

History of CCP art. 21.13: Acts 1965, 59th Leg., ch. 722, §1, eff. Jan. 1, 1966.

ART. 21.14. PERJURY & AGGRAVATED PERJURY

(a) An indictment for perjury or aggravated perjury need not charge the precise language of the false statement, but may state the substance of the same, and no such indictment shall be held insufficient on account of any variance which does not affect the subject matter or general import of such false statement; and it is not necessary in such indictment to set forth the pleadings, records or proceeding with which the false statement is connected, nor the commission or authority of the court or person before whom the false statement was made; but it is sufficient to state the name of the court or public servant by whom the oath was administered with the allegation of the falsity of the matter on which the perjury or aggravated perjury is assigned.

(b) If an individual is charged with aggravated perjury before a grand jury, the indictment may not be entered by the grand jury before which the false statement was alleged to have been made.

History of CCP art. 21.14: Acts 1965, 59th Leg., ch. 722, §1, eff. Jan. 1, 1966. Amended by Acts 1973, 63rd Leg., ch. 399, §2(A), eff. Jan. 1, 1974; Acts 1989, 71st Leg., ch. 1065, §5, eff. Sept. 1, 1989.

ANNOTATIONS

McCullar v. State, 696 S.W.2d 579, 581-82 (Tex. Crim.App.1985). "Naming the court or person who administered the oath is not an element and is not essential to an element of the offense. [I]ts omission ... does not render the indictment fundamentally defective."

ART. 21.15. MUST ALLEGE ACTS OF RECKLESSNESS OR CRIMINAL NEGLIGENCE

Whenever recklessness or criminal negligence enters into or is a part or element of any offense, or it is charged that the accused acted recklessly or with criminal negligence in the commission of an offense, the complaint, information, or indictment in order to be sufficient in any such case must allege, with reasonable certainty, the act or acts relied upon to constitute recklessness or criminal negligence, and in no event shall it be sufficient to allege merely that the accused, in committing the offense, acted recklessly or with criminal negligence.

History of CCP art. 21.15: Acts 1965, 59th Leg., ch. 722, §1, eff. Jan. 1, 1966. Amended by Acts 1973, 63rd Leg., ch. 399, §2(A), eff. Jan. 1, 1974.

ANNOTATIONS

Reed v. State, 117 S.W.3d 260, 265 (Tex.Crim.App. 2003). "Article 21.15 does not keep the parties from submitting a lesser included offense with a reckless culpable mental state to the jury. However, when recklessness is left out of the indictment for the charged offense, and no lesser included offense is submitted to the jury ... then Article 21.15 precludes the inclusion of recklessness or criminal negligence in the jury instructions for the charged offense."

Rodriguez v. State, 799 S.W.2d 301, 302 (Tex.Crim. App.1990). "[A]lthough the information failed to allege the acts constituting recklessness, which we recognized was a substance defect, the appellant's failure to object to this defect pre-trial waived the error on appeal...."

Hankins v. State, 85 S.W.3d 433, 436 (Tex.App.— Corpus Christi 2002, no pet.). "Article 21.15 imposes two requirements on a charging instrument alleging reckless misconduct. First, the indictment must allege the act or acts relied on to constitute the forbidden conduct committed with recklessness. Second, the indictment must allege the acts or circumstances relied on to demonstrate that the forbidden conduct was committed in a reckless manner." *But see Boyd v. State*, 217 S.W.3d 37, 41-42 (Tex.App.—Eastland 2006, pet. ref'd).

ART. 21.16. CERTAIN FORMS OF INDICTMENTS

The following form of indictments is sufficient:

"In the name and by authority of the State of Texas: The grand jury of _____ County, State of Texas, duly organized at the _____ term, A.D. _____, of the district court of said county, in said court at said term, do present that _____ (defendant) on the _____ day of _____ A.D. _____, in said county and State, did _____ (description of offense) against the peace and dignity of the State.

_____, Foreman of the grand jury."

History of CCP art. 21.16: Acts 1965, 59th Leg., ch. 722, §1, eff. Jan. 1, 1966.

ART. 21.17. FOLLOWING STATUTORY WORDS

Words used in a statute to define an offense need not be strictly pursued in the indictment; it is sufficient to use other words conveying the same meaning, or which include the sense of the statutory words.

History of CCP art. 21.17: Acts 1965, 59th Leg., ch. 722, §1, eff. Jan. 1, 1966.

ANNOTATIONS

State v. Kinsey, 861 S.W.2d 383, 384 (Tex.Crim.App. 1993). "[I]f the words equivalent to the 'common everyday usage' of the technical term were equivalent to the technical definition found in the Penal Code, substitution would be allowed."

Murphy v. State, 665 S.W.2d 116, 118 (Tex.Crim. App.1983). "If a charging instrument omits specific reference to a word, term, or phrase that is a constituent element of the offense but, from reading the indictment as a whole, that element is supplied by *necessary* inclusion within an expressed word, term, or phrase, then the failure to specifically plead the word, term, or phrase will not render the charging instrument fundamentally defective."

ART. 21.18. MATTERS OF JUDICIAL NOTICE

Presumptions of law and matters of which judicial notice is taken (among which are included the authority and duties of all officers elected or appointed under the General Laws of this State) need not be stated in an indictment.

History of CCP art. 21.18: Acts 1965, 59th Leg., ch. 722, §1, eff. Jan. 1, 1966. See also TRE 201.

ANNOTATIONS

Gonzales v. State, 723 S.W.2d 746, 751 (Tex.Crim. App.1987). "'The theory [of judicial notice] is that, where a fact is well known by all reasonably intelligent people in the community or *its existence is so easily determinable with certainty from sources considered reliable*, it would not be good sense to require formal proof.' *At 752:* [F]or purposes of determining the adequacy of an indictment, we deem it sufficient that a fact is *susceptible* to establishment by judicial notice in the trial court, to obviate the need to allege that fact, under Art. 21.18...."

ART. 21.19. DEFECTS OF FORM

An indictment shall not be held insufficient, nor shall the trial, judgment or other proceedings thereon be affected, by reason of any defect of form which does not prejudice the substantial rights of the defendant.

History of CCP art. 21.19: Acts 1965, 59th Leg., ch. 722, §1, eff. Jan. 1, 1966.

Adams v. State, 707 S.W.2d 900, 903 (Tex.Crim. App.1986). "The important question is whether a defendant had notice adequate to prepare his defense. The first step in answering this question is to decide whether the charging instrument failed to convey some requisite item of 'notice.' If sufficient notice is given, this ends our inquiry. If not, the next step is to decide whether, in the context of the case, this had an impact on the defendant's ability to prepare a defense, and, finally, how great an impact."

State v. Goodman, 221 S.W.3d 116, 120 (Tex. App.—Fort Worth 2006, no pet.). "If an indictment or information contains allegations regarding all the necessary elements of the offense, so that it is not fundamentally defective and void, and if a defendant requests additional factual information upon which to prepare a defense, a defect of form has been raised and the State may properly amend the indictment to reflect the requested information. [¶] [T]he issue becomes whether the amended information on its face fails to convey some requisite item of notice. The notice provided by the information in question must be examined from the perspective of the accused in light of his constitutional presumption of innocence. A motion to quash should only be granted when the language regarding the accused's conduct is so vague or indefinite that it fails to give the accused adequate notice of the acts he allegedly committed."

ART. 21.20. "INFORMATION"

An "information" is a written statement filed and presented in behalf of the State by the district or county attorney, charging the defendant with an offense which may by law be so prosecuted.

History of CCP art. 21.20: Acts 1965, 59th Leg., ch. 722, §1, eff. Jan. 1, 1966. See also Tex. Const. art. 5, §17.

Ex parte Garcia, 547 S.W.2d 271, 273 (Tex.Crim. App.1977). "If the complaint alone is insufficient, ... then the prosecutorial act of filing an information upon that complaint adds nothing in the way of evidence of probable cause to believe the accused to be guilty of a criminal act."

ART. 21.21. REQUISITES OF AN INFORMATION

An information is sufficient if it has the following requisites:

1. It shall commence, "In the name and by authority of the State of Texas";

2. That it appear to have been presented in a court having jurisdiction of the offense set forth;

3. That it appear to have been presented by the proper officer;

4. That it contain the name of the accused, or state that his name is unknown and give a reasonably accurate description of him;

5. It must appear that the place where the offense is charged to have been committed is within the jurisdiction of the court where the information is filed;

6. That the time mentioned be some date anterior to the filing of the information, and that the offense does not appear to be barred by limitation;

7. That the offense be set forth in plain and intelligible words;

8. That it conclude, "Against the peace and dignity of the State"; and

9. It must be signed by the district or county attorney, officially.

History of CCP art. 21.21: Acts 1965, 59th Leg., ch. 722, §1, eff. Jan. 1, 1966.

Hopkins v. State, 46 S.W.3d 896, 897 (Tex.Crim. App.2001). "Appellant was arrested for driving while intoxicated ... on ... December 20, 1997. The State charged appellant by complaint and information filed on that same date, alleging he committed the offense of driving while intoxicated 'on or about' that date. *At 899:* [T]he State's use of the phrase, 'on or about,' in conjunction with past tense language, sufficiently alleged the offense occurred prior to the filing of the information. The trial court committed no error in refusing to quash the information."

Adams v. State, 707 S.W.2d 900, 901 (Tex.Crim. App.1986). "'When the defendant petitions for sufficient notice of the state's charge by motion to quash adequately setting out the manner in which notice is deficient, the presumption of innocence coupled with his right to notice requires that he be given such notice.' [¶] [Tex. Const.] art. I, §10 ... mandates that the notice petitioned for—information on which to prepare a defense—must come from the face of the charging instrument. ... It is improper to look to the record of the case in order to determine whether the allegation in the charging instrument constitutes adequate notice...."

Ex parte Thomas, 234 S.W.3d 656, 663 (Tex. App.—Beaumont 2007, no pet.). "Although the statute does not expressly prohibit combining a complaint and an information in one document, the different requirements indicate the documents are to be separate. Cases decided before and after the 1985 amendments treat a complaint and information as having separate filing requirements. Nevertheless, [appellant] was required to object before trial to the combination of the complaint and information into one document. He waived his objection to this alleged defect."

ART. 21.22. INFORMATION BASED UPON COMPLAINT

No information shall be presented until affidavit has been made by some credible person charging the defendant with an offense. The affidavit shall be filed with the information. It may be sworn to before the district or county attorney who, for that purpose, shall have power to administer the oath, or it may be made before any officer authorized by law to administer oaths.

History of CCP art. 21.22: Acts 1965, 59th Leg., ch. 722, §1, eff. Jan 1., 1966. See also CCP art. 2.04.

ANNOTATIONS

Ramirez v. State, 105 S.W.3d 628, 629 (Tex.Crim. App.2003). "[T]he mere presentment of an information to a trial court invests that court with jurisdiction over the person of the defendant, regardless of any defect that might exist in the underlying complaint. Defects in complaints are no longer jurisdictional in the traditional sense. *At 630:* By not ... objecting to the information prior to trial, the appellant waived any contention that the information was defective because it was based upon a defective underlying complaint." *See also* ***Holland v. State***, 623 S.W.2d 651, 652 (Tex.Crim. App.1981).

Chapple v. State, 521 S.W.2d 280, 282 (Tex.Crim. App.1975). "[W]hen an accused waives the right to be tried upon an indictment and elects to be tried upon an information, no complaint is required."

Wells v. State, 516 S.W.2d 663, 664 (Tex.Crim.App. 1974). "A person authorized to present informations and conduct prosecutions cannot be the affiant to the complaint supporting an information."

Le v. State, 963 S.W.2d 838, 842 (Tex.App.—Corpus Christi 1998, pet. ref'd). "[A] 'complaint' in county court has a different meaning than a 'complaint' in justice or municipal court. In the latter, if a defendant pleads not guilty, the complaint itself serves as the charging instrument. In county court, however, the information is the charging instrument. While the information does need to be accompanied by a complaint, the 'complaint' referenced in the county court proceedings is an affidavit made by a particular credible person which supports the charging instrument. Although this complaint accompanies the information, it is not a charging instrument in and of itself, but is merely a component of the instrument."

ART. 21.23. RULES AS TO INDICTMENT APPLY TO INFORMATION

The rules with respect to allegations in an indictment and the certainty required apply also to an information.

History of CCP art. 21.23: Acts 1965, 59th Leg., ch. 722, §1, eff. Jan. 1, 1966.

ART. 21.24. JOINDER OF CERTAIN OFFENSES

(a) Two or more offenses may be joined in a single indictment, information, or complaint, with each offense stated in a separate count, if the offenses arise out of the same criminal episode, as defined in Chapter 3 of the Penal Code.

(b) A count may contain as many separate paragraphs charging the same offense as necessary, but no paragraph may charge more than one offense.

(c) A count is sufficient if any one of its paragraphs is sufficient. An indictment, information, or complaint is sufficient if any one of its counts is sufficient.

History of CCP art. 21.24: Acts 1965, 59th Leg., ch. 722, §1, eff. Jan. 1, 1966. Amended by Acts 1973, 63rd Leg., ch. 399, §2(A), eff. Jan. 1, 1974. See also Pen. Code §3.02.

ANNOTATIONS

Martinez v. State, 225 S.W.3d 550, 554 (Tex.Crim. App.2007). "When the State wishes to charge multiple offenses in a single indictment, it is required by statute to set out each separate offense in a separate 'count.' Then separate 'paragraphs' within a single count may allege different methods of committing the same offense. But since each 'count' alleges a single offense, an indictment cannot authorize more convictions than there are counts. [T]he indictment [here] authorized only three convictions (and only one conviction per count). [¶] Permitting more convictions than authorized by the indictment implicates a defendant's due-process right to notice. [¶] Permitting more convictions than the indictment authorizes performs the function of an implied amendment to that indictment and thus also implicates the defendant's constitutional right to a grand jury screening of the charges. *At 555:* The trial judge committed no error in submitting the various paragraphs in six separate verdict forms. These paragraphs were all pled in the indictment, so the State was entitled to prosecute all of them. [¶] But even though the State was entitled to submit all of the allegations included in the indictment to the jury, the State was not entitled to mix what were really separate offenses into a single general-verdict submission, because that would violate [D's] constitutional right to a unanimous verdict. When confronted with a single count that contains multiple allegations that are really separate offenses, the trial judge should protect the rights of both parties by submitting the separate allegations to the jury, but in such a way as to ensure that each allegation is decided unanimously. Perhaps the simplest way to do that is to submit separate verdict forms.... [¶] The mistake the trial judge made here was in rendering judgment on all of those counts. ... Once the judge receives the jury's verdicts, he should perform the task of deciding what judgment is authorized by those verdicts in light of the controlling law, the indictment, and the evidence presented at trial. In this case, the trial judge did not perform that task." Held: The CCA amended the verdict by striking the inappropriate conviction.

Hathorn v. State, 848 S.W.2d 101, 113 (Tex.Crim. App.1992). "[T]he indictment may and should be comprised of as many counts (paragraphs) as necessary to meet the contingencies of the evidence."

Sifford v. State, 741 S.W.2d 440, 441 (Tex.Crim. App.1987). "When the State violates the misjoinder rule, the defendant has two options at trial. He may object to the charging instrument on the ground that the State has misjoined offenses. The trial court should

then grant the motion to quash, or it may force the State to elect the offense upon which it will proceed. The defendant may, instead, forgo the motion to quash and file a motion requesting the State elect the count in the charging instrument upon which it will proceed. The trial court should grant the motion if the State has misjoined offenses. The State must make this election by the end of the State's case and before the defense begins to present evidence. Once the State has been forced to make an election, any misjoinder error is cured."

Saenz v. State, 131 S.W.3d 43, 52-53 (Tex. App.—San Antonio 2003), *aff'd*, 166 S.W.3d 270 (Tex. Crim.App.2005). "Unlike other assault-type offenses that require only one victim, [Pen. Code] §19.03(a)(7)(A) states that in committing capital murder, a person must murder more than one victim. As such, §19.03(a)(7)(A) necessarily requires the murder of more than one victim. Therefore, we hold that the allowable unit of prosecution for §19.03(a)(7)(A) is more than one victim. [¶] Here, Saenz was accused in three separate counts of the capital murder of three victims. ... All three counts contain the same victims, the same allowable unit of prosecution. All three counts, therefore, constitute only one offense of capital murder. Because the indictment states only one allowable unit of prosecution, Saenz can be convicted of only one offense. As such, Saenz's double jeopardy rights were violated. Moreover, because the three counts of capital murder constitute a single offense, the indictment did not comply with article 21.24(a)...."

Sperling v. State, 924 S.W.2d 722, 727 (Tex.App.— Amarillo 1996, pet. ref'd). When "the statute sets out several ways the offense may be committed, each of which embrace the same definition, are punishable in the same manner, and are not repugnant to each other, the various methods of commission are not distinct offenses, and may be charged in the same indictment. Consequently, the State need not elect between the various theories alleged; rather, the jury may consider all theories and return a general verdict of guilty."

ART. 21.25. WHEN INDICTMENT HAS BEEN LOST, ETC.

When an indictment or information has been lost, mislaid, mutilated or obliterated, the district or county attorney may suggest the fact to the court; and the same shall be entered upon the minutes of the court. In such case, another indictment or information may be substituted, upon the written statement of such attorney that it is substantially the same as that which has been lost, mislaid, mutilated, or obliterated. Or another indictment may be presented, as in the first instance; and in such case, the period for the commencement of the prosecution shall be dated from the time of making such entry.

History of CCP art. 21.25: Acts 1965, 59th Leg., ch. 722, §1, eff. Jan. 1, 1966.

ANNOTATIONS

State v. Dotson, 224 S.W.3d 199, 203 (Tex.Crim. App.2007). "We are faced with what we hope is an unusual factual scenario in which the district clerk's file contains identical indictments in separately numbered causes charging the appellant with the same offense. The State alleges that the court of appeals erred when it determined Article 21.25 was inapplicable to this case. The State contends that if the indictment returned by the grand jury in cause number 113 is not the indictment presently located in the clerk's file, then the original indictment has either been lost or mislaid. The appellant counters that Article 21.25 is not applicable because the original indictment in cause number 113 is the filed indictment, and, thus, has never been lost or mislaid. *At 204-05:* [W]e conclude Article 21.25 is applicable. The statute allows for substitution when an indictment has been lost, mislaid, mutilated or obliterated. The State contends that the purported original indictment was lost or mislaid because at some point after it was duly presented to the district clerk, it was inexplicably omitted from the clerk's file due to a clerical error. We agree."

Carrillo v. State, 2 S.W.3d 275, 278 (Tex.Crim.App. 1999). "The procedural requirements of article 21.25 were not satisfied, and thus a duplicate indictment was not properly substituted. But the jurisdiction of the court, already vested, was not affected. Upon presentment of the indictment against appellant, jurisdiction vested. Nothing in the constitution or statutes suggests that continued presence of the indictment in the file or courtroom is necessary *in order to maintain already vested jurisdiction*. The fact that the indictment was later lost did not divest the court of jurisdiction; the fact that the procedural requirements of article 21.25 were not met did not cause the court to lose its jurisdiction. While prior caselaw held to the contrary, in light of the

unequivocal language in the constitutional amendment to [Tex. Const. art.] 5, §12, this body of law is no longer valid."

Glover v. State, 740 S.W.2d 94, 97-98 (Tex.App.— Dallas 1987, no pet.). CCP art. 21.25 "controls over [TRAP 34.5(e)]. Article 21.25 exclusively concerns lost indictments, while [TRAP 34.5(e)] applies to any lost portions of the record."

ART. 21.26. ORDER TRANSFERRING CASES

Upon the filing of an indictment in the district court which charges an offense over which such court has no jurisdiction, the judge of such court shall make an order transferring the same to such inferior court as may have jurisdiction, stating in such order the cause transferred and to what court transferred.

History of CCP art. 21.26: Acts 1965, 59th Leg., ch. 722, §1, eff. Jan. 1, 1966.

ANNOTATIONS

Martinez v. State, 632 S.W.2d 783, 786 (Tex. App.—Houston [14th Dist.] 1982, no pet.). Article 21.26 "confers authority on a court otherwise lacking jurisdiction over a cause of action to transfer an indictment to a court of appropriate jurisdiction."

ART. 21.27. CAUSES TRANSFERRED TO JUSTICE COURT

Causes over which justices of the peace have jurisdiction may be transferred to a justice of the peace at the county seat, or in the discretion of the judge, to a justice of the precinct in which the same can be most conveniently tried, as may appear by memorandum endorsed by the grand jury on the indictment or otherwise. If it appears to the judge that the offense has been committed in any incorporated town or city, the cause shall be transferred to a justice in said town or city, if there be one therein; and any justice to whom such cause may be transferred shall have jurisdiction to try the same.

History of CCP art. 21.27: Acts 1965, 59th Leg., ch. 722, §1, eff. Jan. 1, 1966.

ART. 21.28. DUTY ON TRANSFER

The clerk of the court, without delay, shall deliver the indictments in all cases transferred, together with all the papers relating to each case, to the proper court or justice, as directed in the order of transfer; and shall accompany each case with a certified copy of all the proceedings taken therein in the district court, and with a bill of the costs that have accrued therein in the district court. The said costs shall be taxed in the court in which said cause is tried, in the event of a conviction.

History of CCP art. 21.28: Acts 1965, 59th Leg., ch. 722, §1, eff. Jan. 1, 1966.

ART. 21.29. PROCEEDINGS OF INFERIOR COURT

Any case so transferred shall be entered on the docket of the court to which it is transferred. All process thereon shall be issued and the defendant tried as if the case had originated in the court to which it was transferred.

History of CCP art. 21.29: Acts 1965, 59th Leg., ch. 722, §1, eff. Jan. 1, 1966.

ART. 21.30. CAUSE IMPROVIDENTLY TRANSFERRED

When a cause has been improvidently transferred to a court which has no jurisdiction of the same, the court to which it has been transferred shall order it to be re-transferred to the proper court; and the same proceedings shall be had as in the case of the original transfer. In such case, the defendant and the witnesses shall be held bound to appear before the court to which the case has been re-transferred, the same as they were bound to appear before the court so transferring the same.

History of CCP art. 21.30: Acts 1965, 59th Leg., ch. 722, §1, eff. Jan. 1, 1966.

ART. 21.31. TESTING FOR AIDS & CERTAIN OTHER DISEASES

 Subsection (a) below is effective for offenses committed on or after Sept. 1, 2007.

(a) A person who is indicted for or who waives indictment for an offense under Section 21.02, 21.11(a)(1), 22.011, or 22.021, Penal Code, shall, at the direction of the court, undergo a medical procedure or test designed to show or help show whether the person has a sexually transmitted disease or has acquired immune deficiency syndrome (AIDS) or human immunodeficiency virus (HIV) infection, antibodies to HIV, or infection with any other probable causative agent of AIDS. The court may direct the person to undergo the procedure or test on its own motion or on the request of the victim of the alleged offense. If the person refuses to submit voluntarily to the procedure or test, the court shall require the person to submit to the procedure or test. The court may require a defendant previously required under this article to undergo a medical procedure or test on indictment for an offense to undergo a

subsequent medical procedure or test following conviction of the offense. The person performing the procedure or test shall make the test results available to the local health authority, and the local health authority shall be required to make the notification of the test result to the victim of the alleged offense and to the defendant.

Subsection (a) below is effective for offenses in which any element of the offense was committed before Sept. 1, 2007.

(a) A person who is indicted for or who waives indictment for an offense under Section 21.11(a)(1), 22.011, or 22.021, Penal Code, shall, at the direction of the court, undergo a medical procedure or test designed to show or help show whether the person has a sexually transmitted disease or has acquired immune deficiency syndrome (AIDS) or human immunodeficiency virus (HIV) infection, antibodies to HIV, or infection with any other probable causative agent of AIDS. The court may direct the person to undergo the procedure or test on its own motion or on the request of the victim of the alleged offense. If the person refuses to submit voluntarily to the procedure or test, the court shall require the person to submit to the procedure or test. The court may require a defendant previously required under this article to undergo a medical procedure or test on indictment for an offense to undergo a subsequent medical procedure or test following conviction of the offense. The person performing the procedure or test shall make the test results available to the local health authority, and the local health authority shall be required to make the notification of the test result to the victim of the alleged offense and to the defendant.

(b) The court shall order a person who is charged with an offense under Section 22.11, Penal Code, to undergo in the manner provided by Subsection (a) a medical procedure or test designed to show or help show whether the person has HIV, hepatitis A, hepatitis B, tuberculosis, or any other disease designated as a reportable disease under Section 81.048, Health and Safety Code. The person charged with the offense shall pay the costs of testing under this subsection.

(c) The state may not use the fact that a medical procedure or test was performed on a person under Subsection (a) or use the results of a procedure or test conducted under Subsection (a) in any criminal proceeding arising out of the alleged offense.

⭐

(d) Testing under this article shall be conducted in accordance with written infectious disease control protocols adopted by the Texas Board of Health that clearly establish procedural guidelines that provide criteria for testing and that respect the rights of the person accused and any victim of the alleged offense.

(e) This article does not permit a court to release a test result to anyone other than those authorized by law, and the provisions of Section 81.103(d), Health and Safety Code, may not be construed to allow that disclosure.

History of CCP art. 21.31: Acts 1987, 70th Leg., 2nd C.S., ch. 55, §3, eff. Oct. 20, 1987. Amended by Acts 1991, 72nd Leg., ch. 14, §284(7), eff. Sept. 1, 1991; Acts 1993, 73rd Leg., ch. 811, §1, eff. Sept. 1, 1993; Acts 2005, 79th Leg., ch. 543, §3, eff. Sept. 1, 2005; Acts 2007, 80th Leg., ch. 593, §3.12, eff. Sept. 1, 2007.

ANNOTATIONS

State ex rel. Hilbig v. McDonald, 839 S.W.2d 854, 856 (Tex.App.—San Antonio 1992, no pet.). "[W]e conclude that a crime victim does not have a constitutional or statutory right to discover evidence regarding the pending criminal case that is contained within the prosecutor's file. *At 859:* The Legislature intended to give victims access to the prosecutor—not to the prosecutor's file. [¶] [O]ur disposition of this case does not affect the victim's ability to petition the trial court to have [D] tested for AIDS or HIV infection...."

CHAPTER 22. FORFEITURE OF BAIL

ART. 22.01. BAIL FORFEITED, WHEN

When a defendant is bound by bail to appear and fails to appear in any court in which such case may be pending and at any time when his personal appearance is required under this Code, or by any court or magistrate, a forfeiture of his bail and a judicial declaration of such forfeiture shall be taken in the manner provided in Article 22.02 of this Code and entered by such court.

History of CCP art. 22.01: Acts 1965, 59th Leg., ch. 722, §1, eff. Jan. 1, 1966. Amended by Acts 1981, 67th Leg., ch. 312, §2, eff. Aug. 31, 1981.

ANNOTATIONS

Moore v. State, 828 S.W.2d 497, 498 (Tex.App.—Dallas 1992, pet. ref'd). CCP arts. 22.01-22.17 "recognize the differences between court costs and interest, and treat them differently. While the code places specific restrictions on the assessment of prejudgment and postjudgment interest, it does not impose the same restrictions on the assessment of court costs. *At 499:* The code ... demonstrates a legislative scheme that assesses civil court costs against the surety in all bond-forfeiture proceedings."

ART. 22.01A. REPEALED

Repealed by Acts 1973, 63rd Leg., ch. 399, §3(b), eff. Jan. 1, 1974.

ART. 22.02. MANNER OF TAKING A FORFEITURE

Bail bonds and personal bonds are forfeited in the following manner: The name of the defendant shall be called distinctly at the courthouse door, and if the defendant does not appear within a reasonable time after such call is made, judgment shall be entered that the State of Texas recover of the defendant the amount of money in which he is bound, and of his sureties, if any, the amount of money in which they are respectively bound, which judgment shall state that the same will be made final, unless good cause be shown why the defendant did not appear.

History of CCP art. 22.02: Acts 1965, 59th Leg., ch. 722, §1, eff. Jan. 1, 1966.

ANNOTATIONS

Tocher v. State, 517 S.W.2d 299, 301 (Tex.Crim. App.1975). "[T]he State's case in a bond forfeiture proceeding consists of the bond and the judicial declaration of the forfeiture of the bond, which is the judgment nisi. Once this has been established, the defendant must then prove that one of the elements has not been complied with." *See also Cervantes v. State*, 980 S.W.2d 220, 222 (Tex.App.—Corpus Christi 1998, no pet.).

ART. 22.021. REPEALED

History of CCP art. 22.021: Repealed by Acts 2007, 80th Leg., ch. 1113, §6, eff. Jan. 1, 2008.

ART. 22.03. CITATION TO SURETIES

(a) Upon entry of judgment, a citation shall issue forthwith notifying the sureties of the defendant, if any, that the bond has been forfeited, and requiring them to appear and show cause why the judgment of forfeiture should not be made final.

Ⓐ *Subsection (b) below is effective for citations of forfeiture issued on or after Sept. 1, 2007.*

(b) A citation to a surety who is an individual shall be served to the individual at the address shown on the face of the bond or the last known address of the individual.

Subsection (b) below is effective for citations of forfeiture issued before Sept. 1, 2007.

(b) A citation to a surety who is an individual shall be served to the individual at the address shown on the face of the bond.

(c) A citation to a surety that is a corporation or other entity shall be served to the attorney designated for service of process by the corporation or entity under Chapter 804, Insurance Code.

(d) By filing the waiver or designation in writing with the clerk of the court, a surety may waive service of citation or may designate a person other than the surety or the surety's attorney to receive service of citation under this article. The waiver or designation is effective until a written revocation is filed with the clerk.

History of CCP art. 22.03: Acts 1965, 59th Leg., ch. 722, §1, eff. Jan. 1, 1966. Amended by Acts 2005, 79th Leg., ch. 743, §3, eff. Sept. 1, 2005; Acts 2007, 80th Leg., ch. 657, §1, eff. Sept. 1, 2007.

ART. 22.035. CITATION TO DEFENDANT POSTING CASH BOND

Ⓔ *Article 22.035 below is effective for citations of forfeiture issued on or after Sept. 1, 2007.*

A citation to a defendant who posted a cash bond shall be served to the defendant at the address shown on the face of the bond or the last known address of the defendant.

History of CCP art. 22.035: Acts 2007, 80th Leg., ch. 657, §2, eff. Sept. 1, 2007.

ART. 22.04. REQUISITES OF CITATION

A citation shall be sufficient if it be in the form provided for citations in civil cases in such court; provided, however, that a copy of the judgment of forfeiture entered by the court, a copy of the forfeited bond, and a copy of any power of attorney attached to the forfeited bond shall be attached to the citation and the citation shall notify the parties cited to appear and show cause why the judgment of forfeiture should not be made final.

History of CCP art. 22.04: Acts 1965, 59th Leg., ch. 722, §1, eff. Jan. 1, 1966. Amended by Acts 2005, 79th Leg., ch. 743, §4, eff. Sept. 1, 2005.

ANNOTATIONS

Hubbard v. State, 814 S.W.2d 402, 404 (Tex.App.—Waco 1991, no pet.). "[T]he language in Art. 22.04 is mandatory. [A]ttaching a copy of the judgment nisi, which includes the statutorily required language, to the citation is insufficient to meet the mandatory requirement that the citation notify the parties to appear and show cause."

ART. 22.05. CITATION AS IN CIVIL ACTIONS

Ⓐ *Article 22.05 below is effective for citations of forfeiture issued on or after Sept. 1, 2007.*

If service of citation is not waived under Article 22.03, a surety is entitled to notice by service of citation, the length of time and in the manner required in civil actions; and the officer executing the citation shall return the same as in civil actions. It shall not be necessary to give notice to the defendant unless he has furnished his address on the bond, in which event notice to the defendant shall be deposited in the United States mail directed to the defendant at the address shown on the bond or the last known address of the defendant.

History of CCP art. 22.05: Acts 1965, 59th Leg., ch. 722, §1, eff. Jan. 1, 1966. Amended by Acts 2005, 79th Leg., ch. 743, §5, eff. Sept. 1, 2005; Acts 2007, 80th Leg., ch. 657, §3, eff. Sept. 1, 2007.

ANNOTATIONS

Escobar v. State, 587 S.W.2d 714, 715 (Tex.Crim. App.1979). "This citation must be properly served on the surety and, if the principal's address is on the bond, the citation must be mailed to that address. *At 716:* A silent record does not necessarily mean that no mailing occurred. ... Absent such an indication in the record, compliance with Art. 22.05 will be presumed."

ART. 22.05. CITATION AS IN CIVIL ACTIONS

Article 22.05 below is effective for citations of forfeiture issued before Sept. 1, 2007.

If service of citation is not waived under Article 22.03, a surety is entitled to notice by service of citation, the length of time and in the manner required in civil actions; and the officer executing the citation shall return the same as in civil actions. It shall not be necessary to give notice to the defendant unless he has furnished his address on the bond, in which event notice to the defendant shall be deposited in the United States mail directed to the defendant at the address shown on the bond.

ART. 22.06. CITATION BY PUBLICATION

Where the surety is a nonresident of the State, or where he is a transient person, or where his residence is unknown, the district or county attorney may, upon application in writing to the county clerk, stating the facts, obtain a citation to be served by publication; and the same shall be served by a publication and returned as in civil actions.

History of CCP art. 22.06: Acts 1965, 59th Leg., ch. 722, §1, eff. Jan. 1, 1966.

ART. 22.07. COST OF PUBLICATION

When service of citation is made by publication, the county in which the forfeiture has been taken shall pay the costs thereof, to be taxed as costs in the case.

History of CCP art. 22.07: Acts 1965, 59th Leg., ch. 722, §1, eff. Jan. 1, 1966.

ART. 22.08. SERVICE OUT OF THE STATE

Service of a certified copy of the citation upon any absent or non-resident surety may be made outside of the limits of this State by any person competent to make oath of the fact; and the affidavit of such person, stating the facts of such service, shall be a sufficient return.

History of CCP art. 22.08: Acts 1965, 59th Leg., ch. 722, §1, eff. Jan. 1, 1966.

ART. 22.09. WHEN SURETY IS DEAD

If the surety is dead at the time the forfeiture is taken, the forfeiture shall nevertheless be valid. The final judgment shall not be rendered where a surety has died, either before or after the forfeiture has been taken, unless his executor, administrator or heirs, as the case may be, have been cited to appear and show cause why the judgment should not be made final, in the same manner as provided in the case of the surety.

History of CCP art. 22.09: Acts 1965, 59th Leg., ch. 722, §1, eff. Jan. 1, 1966.

ART. 22.10. SCIRE FACIAS DOCKET

When a forfeiture has been declared upon a bond, the court or clerk shall docket the case upon the scire facias or upon the civil docket, in the name of the State of Texas, as plaintiff, and the principal and his sureties, if any, as defendants; and, except as otherwise provided by this chapter, the proceedings had therein shall be governed by the same rules governing other civil suits.

History of CCP art. 22.10: Acts 1965, 59th Leg., ch. 722, §1, eff. Jan. 1, 1966. Amended by Acts 1981, 67th Leg., ch. 312, §3, eff. Aug. 31, 1981; Acts 1999, 76th Leg., ch. 1506, §4, eff. Sept. 1, 1999.

ANNOTATIONS

State v. Sellers, 790 S.W.2d 316, 321 (Tex.Crim. App.1990). The State contends "'it has a right of appeal independent of the criminal rules.' We disagree. [¶] [B]ond forfeiture is a criminal matter. Article 22.10 ... simply prescribes that civil rules shall govern all proceedings in the trial court following judgment nisi. It does not transform a bond forfeiture proceeding from a criminal into 'a civil case'...."

ART. 22.11. SURETIES MAY ANSWER

After the forfeiture of the bond, if the sureties, if any, have been duly notified, the sureties, if any, may answer in writing and show cause why the defendant did not appear, which answer may be filed within the time limited for answering in other civil actions.

History of CCP art. 22.11: Acts 1965, 59th Leg., ch. 722, §1, eff. Jan. 1, 1966.

ART. 22.12. PROCEEDINGS NOT SET ASIDE FOR DEFECT OF FORM

The bond, the judgment declaring the forfeiture, the citation and the return thereupon, shall not be set aside because of any defect of form; but such defect of form may, at any time, be amended under the direction of the court.

History of CCP art. 22.12: Acts 1965, 59th Leg., ch. 722, §1, eff. Jan. 1, 1966.

ART. 22.12A. RENUMBERED

Renumbered as Art. 22.125 by Acts 1987, 69th Leg., ch. 167, §5.02(1), eff. Sept. 1, 1987.

ART. 22.125. POWERS OF THE COURT

After a judicial declaration of forfeiture is entered, the court may proceed with the trial required by Article 22.14 of this code. The court may exonerate the defendant and his sureties, if any, from liability on the forfeiture, remit the amount of the forfeiture, or set aside the forfeiture only as expressly provided by this chapter. The court may approve any proposed settlement of the liability on the forfeiture that is agreed to by the state and by the defendant or the defendant's sureties, if any.

History of CCP art. 22.125: Acts 1981, 67th Leg., ch. 312, §4, eff. Aug. 31, 1981. Renumbered from Art. 22.12a by Acts 1987, 70th Leg., ch. 167, §5.02(1), eff. Sept. 1, 1987. Amended by Acts 1999, 76th Leg., ch. 1506, §5, eff. Sept. 1, 1999.

ANNOTATIONS

Williams v. State, 707 S.W.2d 40, 43 (Tex.Crim.App. 1986). "Reading [CCP art.] 22.12a [now 22.125] with [CCP art.] 22.16 shows that after a judicial declaration of forfeiture is entered and before a final judgment is entered, the court has discretionary remittitur power. *At 44·* After a final judgment has been rendered and within two years of a judgment nisi, [TRCS art.] 2372p-3, §13(b) applies and the trial court must remit at least 95 percent of the bond amount when the statutory requirements are met."

ART. 22.13. CAUSES WHICH WILL EXONERATE

(a) The following causes, and no other, will exonerate the defendant and his sureties, if any, from liability upon the forfeiture taken:

1.   That the bond is, for any cause, not a valid and binding undertaking in law. If it be valid and binding as to the principal, and one or more of his sureties, if any, they shall not be exonerated from liability because of its being invalid and not binding as to another surety or sureties, if any. If it be invalid and not binding as to the principal, each of the sureties, if any, shall be exonerated from liability. If it be valid and binding as to the principal, but not so as to the sureties, if any, the principal shall not be exonerated, but the sureties, if any, shall be.

2.   The death of the principal before the forfeiture was taken.

3.   The sickness of the principal or some uncontrollable circumstance which prevented his appearance at court, and it must, in every such case, be shown that his failure to appear arose from no fault on his part. The causes mentioned in this subdivision shall not be deemed sufficient to exonerate the principal and his sureties, if any, unless such principal appear before final judgment on the bond to answer the accusation against him, or show sufficient cause for not so appearing.

4.   Failure to present an indictment or information at the first term of the court which may be held after the principal has been admitted to bail, in case where the party was bound over before indictment or information, and the prosecution has not been continued by order of the court.

5.   The incarceration of the principal in any jurisdiction in the United States:

(A) in the case of a misdemeanor, at the time of or not later than the 180th day after the date of the principal's failure to appear in court; or

(B) in the case of a felony, at the time of or not later than the 270th day after the date of the principal's failure to appear in court.

(b) A surety exonerated under Subdivision 5, Subsection (a), remains obligated to pay costs of court, any reasonable and necessary costs incurred by a county to secure the return of the principal, and interest accrued on the bond amount from the date of the judgment nisi to the date of the principal's incarceration.

History of CCP art. 22.13: Acts 1965, 59th Leg., ch. 722, §1, eff. Jan. 1, 1966. Amended by Acts 2003, 78th Leg., ch. 942, §1, eff. June 20, 2003.

ANNOTATIONS

Hill v. State, 955 S.W.2d 96, 100 (Tex.Crim.App. 1997). "[I]ncarceration in another country can be an 'uncontrollable circumstance' under Art. 22.13 [that 'will exonerate the defendant and his sureties, if any, from liability upon a forfeiture taken']."

Hernden v. State, 505 S.W.2d 546, 547 (Tex.Crim. App.1974). "[D]oes the death of the principal after judgment nisi but before final judgment relieve the surety under Art. 22.13(2)? Appellant [surety] contends that a forfeiture cannot be taken until final judgment, and that a judgment nisi is, in effect, only a summons to appear. [¶] Under appellant's reasoning, the terms forfeiture and final judgment would be used interchangeably. The terms are not and have never been so used in the statute. *At 548:* [T]he term forfeiture [is] equated with a judgment nisi."

Safety Nat'l Cas. Corp. v. State, ___ S.W.3d ___ (Tex.App.—Houston [1st Dist.] 2008, n.p.h.) (No. 01-07-00122-CV; 4-17-08). "Appellant argues that it owes interest only from the date of the judgment nisi to the date of the principal's incarceration *in any jurisdiction in the U.S.* The State argues that the surety is liable for interest from the date of the judgment nisi until the date of the principal's incarceration in the county from which the judgment nisi was issued. This statute is not ambiguous. By its plain language, the statute requires the surety to pay interest on the bond only until the date of the principal's incarceration. It does not require that the principal be incarcerated in the county from which the judgment nisi issued."

Gonzales Bail Bonds v. State, 147 S.W.3d 557, 558 (Tex.App.—Waco 2004, no pet.). "The elements of [bail bondsman's] affirmative defense [of bail-bond exoneration] are: (1) '[f]ailure to present an indictment or information at the first term of the court which may be held after the principal has been admitted to bail,' (2) the principal 'was bound over before indictment or information,' and (3) the prosecution was not 'continued by order of the court.'"

ART. 22.14. JUDGMENT FINAL

When, upon a trial of the issues presented, no sufficient cause is shown for the failure of the principal to appear, the judgment shall be made final against him and his sureties, if any, for the amount in which they are respectively bound; and the same shall be collected by execution as in civil actions. Separate executions shall issue against each party for the amount adjudged against him. The costs shall be equally divided between the sureties, if there be more than one.

History of CCP art. 22.14: Acts 1965, 59th Leg., ch. 722, §1, eff. Jan. 1, 1966.

ANNOTATIONS

State v. Sellers, 790 S.W.2d 316, 320-21 (Tex.Crim. App.1990). "If the bond and judgment nisi are sufficient, then it is incumbent upon the defendant to show 'sufficient cause ... for the failure of the principal to appear,' and if he cannot, 'the judgment shall be made final.'"

ART. 22.15. JUDGMENT FINAL BY DEFAULT

When the sureties have been duly cited and fail to answer, and the principal also fails to answer within the time limited for answering in other civil actions, the court shall enter judgment final by default.

History of CCP art. 22.15: Acts 1965, 59th Leg., ch. 722, §1, eff. Jan. 1, 1966.

ANNOTATIONS

Schnitzius v. Koons, 813 S.W.2d 213, 216 (Tex. App.—Dallas 1991, no pet.). "[A] judgment of forfeiture against the surety is considered a final judgment. That certainly is the rule in criminal cases, even when the surety on the appearance bond suffers a default judgment."

ART. 22.16. REMITTITUR AFTER FORFEITURE

(a) After forfeiture of a bond and before entry of a final judgment, the court shall, on written motion, remit to the surety the amount of the bond, after deducting the costs of court and any reasonable and necessary costs to the county for the return of the principal, and the interest accrued on the bond amount as provided by Subsection (c) if the principal is released on new bail in the case or the case for which bond was given is dismissed.

(b) For other good cause shown and before the entry of a final judgment against the bond, the court in its discretion may remit to the surety all or part of the amount of the bond after deducting the costs of court and any reasonable and necessary costs to the county for the return of the principal, and the interest accrued on the bond amount as provided by Subsection (c).

(c) For the purposes of this article, interest accrues on the bond amount from the date of forfeiture in the same manner and at the same rate as provided for the accrual of prejudgment interest in civil cases.

History of CCP art. 22.16: Acts 1965, 59th Leg., ch. 722, §1, eff. Jan. 1, 1966. Amended by Acts 1981, 67th Leg., ch. 312, §5, eff. Aug. 31, 1981; Acts 1987, 70th Leg., ch. 1047, §3, eff. June 20, 1987; Acts 2003, 78th Leg., ch. 942, §2, eff. June 20, 2003.

ANNOTATIONS

Safety Nat'l Cas. Corp. v. State, 225 S.W.3d 684, 689 (Tex.App.—El Paso 2006), *rev'd on other grounds*, ___ S.W.3d ___ (Tex.Crim.App.2008) (No. PD-0413-07; 5-14-08). Surety "did not file a separate written motion but included its request for remittitur in a trial brief filed after the final hearing but before judgment. ... While the better practice is to request remittitur in a separate motion, we conclude that [surety's] request for remittitur constitutes a written motion as required by the statute. *At 692:* An abuse of discretion [under Article 22.16(b)] may exist when there is a showing of sufficient cause for the accused's failure to appear. However, the mere subsequent appearance by the accused is not sufficient cause for complete remission of the forfeiture. If it were, the defendant would not really be bound to appear as required by the terms of his recognizance, but would be able to create continuances at will. Generally, sufficient cause is a showing that the party did not break his recognizance intentionally with the design of evading justice, or without a sufficient cause or reasonable excuse, such as an unavoidable accident or inevitable necessity preventing his appearance. Although resulting extreme hardship on the surety may be considered, a balancing consideration may be whether compensation was received by the surety for taking the risk. While not seeking to punish the surety for the principal's failure to appear, the law does contemplate that such noncompliance will result in forfeiture of the bond amount."

ART. 22.17. SPECIAL BILL OF REVIEW

(a) Not later than two years after the date a final judgment is entered in a bond forfeiture proceeding, the surety on the bond may file with the court a special bill of review. A special bill of review may include a request, on equitable grounds, that the final judgment be reformed and that all or part of the bond amount be remitted to the surety, after deducting the costs of court, any reasonable costs to the county for the return of the principal, and the interest accrued on the bond amount from the date of forfeiture. The court in its discretion may grant or deny the bill in whole or in part.

(b) For the purposes of this article, interest accrues on the bond amount from the date of:

(1) forfeiture to the date of final judgment in the same manner and at the same rate as provided for the accrual of prejudgment interest in civil cases; and

(2) final judgment to the date of the order for remittitur at the same rate as provided for the accrual of postjudgment interest in civil cases.

History of CCP art. 22.17: Acts 1987, 70th Leg., ch. 1047, §4, eff. June 20, 1987.

ANNOTATIONS

McKenna v. State, 247 S.W.3d 716, 719 (Tex.Crim. App.2008). "Although the statute does not state that the surety has the burden of proof with respect to the existence of such equitable grounds [for remittitur], we are

of the view that the surety does indeed have that burden, since the surety is the party attempting to change the status quo. [¶] In making its decision, the trial court must keep in mind that, since the purpose of bail is to secure the accused's appearance in court, the law contemplates that the accused's nonappearance will normally result in total forfeiture of the bond amount. While keeping that fact in mind, the trial court may consider any factor bearing upon the equity of the situation, including, but not necessarily limited to, the following: (1) whether the accused's failure to appear in court was willful; (2) whether the delay caused by the accused's failure to appear in court prejudiced the State or harmed the public interest; (3) whether the surety participated in the re-arrest of the accused; (4) whether the State incurred costs or suffered inconvenience in the re-arrest of the accused; (5) whether the surety received compensation for the risk of executing the bail bond; and (6) whether the surety will suffer extreme hardship in the absence of a remittitur." *See also Gramercy Ins. Co. v. State*, 834 S.W.2d 379, 381-82 (Tex.App.—San Antonio 1992, pet. ref'd).

ART. 22.18. LIMITATION

An action by the state to forfeit a bail bond under this chapter must be brought not later than the fourth anniversary of the date the principal fails to appear in court.

History of CCP art. 22.18: Acts 1999, 76th Leg., ch. 1506, §6, eff. Sept. 1, 1999.

CHAPTER 23. THE CAPIAS

ART. 23.01. DEFINITION OF A "CAPIAS"

 Article 23.01 below is effective for a capias issued for offenses committed on or after Sept. 1, 2007.

In this chapter, a "capias" is a writ that is:

(1) issued by a judge of the court having jurisdiction of a case after commitment or bail and before trial, or by a clerk at the direction of the judge; and

(2) directed "To any peace officer of the State of Texas," commanding the officer to arrest a person accused of an offense and bring the arrested person before that court immediately or on a day or at a term stated in the writ.

History of CCP art. 23.01: Acts 1965, 59th Leg., ch. 722, §1, eff. Jan. 1, 1966. Amended by Acts 2007, 80th Leg., ch. 1263, §3, eff. Sept. 1, 2007.

ART. 23.01. DEFINITION OF A "CAPIAS"

Article 23.01 below is effective for a capias issued for offenses committed before Sept. 1, 2007.

A "capias" is a writ issued by the court or clerk, and directed "To any peace officer of the State of Texas," commanding him to arrest a person accused of an offense and bring him before that court immediately, or on a day or at a term stated in the writ.

ART. 23.02. ITS REQUISITES

A capias shall be held sufficient if it have the following requisites:

1.   That it run in the name of "The State of Texas";

2.   That it name the person whose arrest is ordered, or if unknown, describe him;

3.   That it specify the offense of which the defendant is accused, and it appear thereby that he is accused of some offense against the penal laws of the State;

4.   That it name the court to which and the time when it is returnable; and

5.   That it be dated and attested officially by the authority issuing the same.

History of CCP art. 23.02: Acts 1965, 59th Leg., ch. 722, §1, eff. Jan. 1, 1966.

ART. 23.03. CAPIAS OR SUMMONS IN FELONY

(a) A capias shall be issued by the district clerk upon each indictment for felony presented, after bail has been set or denied by the judge of the court. Upon the request of the attorney representing the State, a summons shall be issued by the district clerk. The capias or summons shall be delivered by the clerk or mailed to the sheriff of the county where the defendant resides or is to be found. A capias or summons need not issue for a defendant in custody or under bond.

(b) Upon the request of the attorney representing the State a summons instead of a capias shall issue. If a defendant fails to appear in response to the summons a capias shall issue.

(c) Summons. The summons shall be in the same form as the capias except that it shall summon the defendant to appear before the proper court at a stated time and place. The summons shall be served upon a defendant by delivering a copy to him personally, or by leaving it at his dwelling house or usual place of abode with some person of suitable age and discretion then residing therein or by mailing it to the defendant's last known address.

(d) A summons issued to any person must clearly and prominently state in English and in Spanish the following:

"It is an offense for a person to intentionally influence or coerce a witness to testify falsely or to elude legal process. It is also a felony offense to harm or threaten to harm a witness or prospective witness in retaliation for or on account of the service of the person as a witness or to prevent or delay the person's service as a witness to a crime."

History of CCP art. 23.03: Acts 1965, 59th Leg., ch. 722, §1, eff. Jan. 1, 1966. Amended by Acts 1979, 66th Leg., ch. 463, §3, eff. June 7, 1979; Acts 1995, 74th Leg., ch. 67, §1, eff. Sept. 1, 1995.

ANNOTATIONS

Green v. State, 839 S.W.2d 935, 942 (Tex.App.—Waco 1992, pet. ref'd). "Green contends his arrest was illegal because the district clerk could issue the capias only after the court had set or denied bail. We interpret the phrase, 'after bail has been set or denied by the judge of the court,' as being a directory requirement only and not a mandatory requirement that, if not strictly followed, would make the capias void or defective."

ART. 23.031. ISSUANCE OF CAPIAS IN ELECTRONIC FORM

 Article 23.031 below is effective for a capias issued for offenses committed on or after Sept. 1, 2007.

A district clerk, county clerk, or court may issue in electronic form a capias for the failure of a person to appear before a court or comply with a court order.

History of CCP art. 23.031: Acts 2005, 79th Leg., ch. 312, §4, eff. June 17, 2005. Amended by Acts 2007, 80th Leg., ch. 1263, §4, eff. Sept. 1, 2007.

ART. 23.031. ISSUANCE OF CAPIAS IN ELECTRONIC FORM

Article 23.031 below is effective for a capias issued for offenses committed before Sept. 1, 2007.

A district clerk, county clerk, or court may issue in electronic form a capias for the failure of a person to appear before a court, pay a fine, or comply with a court order.

ART. 23.04. IN MISDEMEANOR CASE

Ⓐ *Article 23.04 below is effective for a capias issued for offenses committed on or after Sept. 1, 2007.*

In misdemeanor cases, the capias or summons shall issue from a court having jurisdiction of the case on the filing of an information or complaint. The summons shall be issued only upon request of the attorney representing the State and on the determination of probable cause by the judge, and shall follow the same form and procedure as in a felony case.

History of CCP art. 23.04: Acts 1965, 59th Leg., ch. 722, §1, eff. Jan. 1, 1966. Amended by Acts 2007, 80th Leg., ch. 1263, §5, eff. Sept. 1, 2007.

ART. 23.04. IN MISDEMEANOR CASE

Article 23.04 below is effective for a capias issued for offenses committed before Sept. 1, 2007.

In misdemeanor cases the capias or summons shall issue from a court having jurisdiction of the case. The summons shall be issued only upon request of the attorney representing the State and shall follow the same form and procedure as in a felony case.

ART. 23.05. CAPIAS AFTER SURRENDER OR FORFEITURE

Ⓐ *Subsection (a) below is effective for a capias issued for offenses committed on or after Sept. 1, 2007.*

(a) If a forfeiture of bail is declared by a court or a surety surrenders a defendant under Article 17.19, a capias shall be immediately issued for the arrest of the defendant, and when arrested, in its discretion, the court may require the defendant, in order to be released from custody, to deposit with the custodian of funds of the court in which the prosecution is pending current money of the United States in the amount of the new bond as set by the court, in lieu of a surety bond, unless a forfeiture is taken and set aside under the third subdivision of Article 22.13, in which case the defendant and the defendant's sureties shall remain bound under the same bail.

Subsection (a) below is effective for a capias issued for offenses committed before Sept. 1, 2007.

(a) If a forfeiture of bail is declared or a surety surrenders a defendant under Article 17.19, a capias shall be immediately issued for the arrest of the defendant, and when arrested, in its discretion, the court may require the defendant, in order to be released from custody, to deposit with the custodian of funds of the court in which the prosecution is pending current money of the United States in the amount of the new bond as set by the court, in lieu of a surety bond, unless a forfeiture is taken and set aside under the third subdivision of Article 22.13 of this code, in which case the defendant and his sureties shall remain bound under the same bail.

(b) A capias issued under this article may be executed by a peace officer or by a private investigator licensed under Chapter 1702, Occupations Code.

(c) A capias under this article must be issued not later than the 10th business day after the date of the court's issuance of the order of forfeiture or order permitting surrender of the bond.

(d) The sheriff of each county shall enter a capias issued under this article into a local warrant system not later than the 10th business day after the date of issuance of the capias by the clerk of court.

History of CCP art. 23.05: Acts 1965, 59th Leg., ch. 722, §1, eff. Jan. 1, 1966. Amended by Acts 1971, 62nd Leg., ch. 740, §1, eff. Aug. 30, 1971; Acts 1999, 76th Leg., ch. 1506, §7, eff. Sept. 1, 1999; Acts 2001, 77th Leg., ch. 1420, §14.733, eff. Sept. 1, 2001; Acts 2003, 78th Leg., ch. 942, §5, eff. June 20, 2003; Acts 2007, 80th Leg., ch. 1263, §6, eff. Sept. 1, 2007.

ART. 23.06. NEW BAIL IN FELONY CASE

When a defendant who has been arrested for a felony under a capias has previously given bail to answer said charge, his sureties, if any, shall be released by such arrest, and he shall be required to give new bail.

History of CCP art. 23.06: Acts 1965, 59th Leg., ch. 722, §1, eff. Jan. 1, 1966.

ART. 23.07. CAPIAS DOES NOT LOSE ITS FORCE

A capias shall not lose its force if not executed and returned at the time fixed in the writ, but may be executed at any time afterward, and return made. All proceedings under such capias shall be as valid as if the same had been executed and returned within the time specified in the writ.

History of CCP art. 23.07: Acts 1965, 59th Leg., ch. 722, §1, eff. Jan. 1, 1966.

ART. 23.08. REASONS FOR RETAINING CAPIAS

When the capias is not returned at the time fixed in the writ, the officer holding it shall notify the court from whence it was issued, in writing, of his reasons for retaining it.

History of CCP art. 23.08: Acts 1965, 59th Leg., ch. 722, §1, eff. Jan. 1, 1966.

ART. 23.09. CAPIAS TO SEVERAL COUNTIES

Capiases for a defendant may be issued to as many counties as the district or county attorney may direct.

History of CCP art. 23.09: Acts 1965, 59th Leg., ch. 722, §1, eff. Jan. 1, 1966.

ART. 23.10. BAIL IN FELONY

In cases of arrest for felony in the county where the prosecution is pending, during a term of court, the officer making the arrest may take bail as provided in Article 17.21.

History of CCP art. 23.10: Acts 1965, 59th Leg., ch. 722, §1, eff. Jan. 1, 1966.

ART. 23.11. SHERIFF MAY TAKE BAIL IN FELONY

In cases of arrest for felony less than capital, made during vacation or made in another county than the one in which the prosecution is pending, the sheriff may take bail; in such cases the amount of the bail bond shall be the same as is endorsed upon the capias; and if no amount be endorsed on the capias, the sheriff shall require a reasonable amount of bail. If it be made to appear by affidavit, made by any district attorney, county attorney, or the sheriff approving the bail bond, to a judge of the Court of Criminal Appeals, a justice of a court of appeals, or to a judge of the district or county court, that the bail taken in any case after indictment is insufficient in amount, or that the sureties are not good for the amount, or that the bond is for any reason defective or insufficient, such judge shall issue a warrant of arrest and require of the defendant sufficient bond, according to the nature of the case.

History of CCP art. 23.11: Acts 1965, 59th Leg., ch. 722, §1, eff. Jan. 1, 1966. Amended by Acts 1981, 67th Leg., ch. 291, §105, eff. Sept. 1, 1981.

ART. 23.12. COURT SHALL FIX BAIL IN FELONY

In felony cases which are bailable, the court shall, before adjourning, fix and enter upon the minutes the amount of the bail to be required in each case. The clerk shall endorse upon the capias the amount of bail required. In case of neglect to so comply with this Article, the arrest of the defendant, and the bail taken by the sheriff, shall be as legal as if there had been no such omission.

History of CCP art. 23.12: Acts 1965, 59th Leg., ch. 722, §1, eff. Jan. 1, 1966.

ART. 23.13. WHO MAY ARREST UNDER CAPIAS

A capias may be executed by any peace officer. In felony cases, the defendant must be delivered immediately to the sheriff of the county where the arrest is made together, with the writ under which he was taken.

History of CCP art. 23.13: Acts 1965, 59th Leg., ch. 722, §1, eff. Jan. 1, 1966.

ART. 23.14. BAIL IN MISDEMEANOR

Any officer making an arrest under a capias in a misdemeanor may in term time or vacation take a bail bond of the defendant.

History of CCP art. 23.14: Acts 1965, 59th Leg., ch. 722, §1, eff. Jan. 1, 1966.

ART. 23.15. ARREST IN CAPITAL CASES

Where an arrest is made under a capias in a capital case, the sheriff shall confine the defendant in jail, and the capias shall, for that purpose, be a sufficient commitment. This Article is applicable when the arrest is made in the county where the prosecution is pending.

History of CCP art. 23.15: Acts 1965, 59th Leg., ch. 722, §1, eff. Jan. 1, 1966.

ART. 23.16. ARREST IN CAPITAL CASE IN ANOTHER COUNTY

In each capital case where a defendant is arrested under a capias in a county other than that in which the case is pending, the sheriff who arrests or to whom the defendant is delivered, shall convey him immediately to the county from which the capias issued and deliver him to the sheriff of such county.

History of CCP art. 23.16: Acts 1965, 59th Leg., ch. 722, §1, eff. Jan. 1, 1966.

ART. 23.17. RETURN OF BAIL & CAPIAS

When an arrest has been made and a bail taken, such bond, together with the capias, shall be returned forthwith to the proper court.

History of CCP art. 23.17: Acts 1965, 59th Leg., ch. 722, §1, eff. Jan. 1, 1966.

ART. 23.18. RETURN OF CAPIAS

The return of the capias shall be made to the court from which it is issued. If it has been executed, the return shall state what disposition has been made of the defendant. If it has not been executed, the cause of the failure to execute it shall be fully stated. If the defendant has not been found, the return shall further show what efforts have been made by the officer to find him, and what information he has as to the defendant's whereabouts.

History of CCP art. 23.18: Acts 1965, 59th Leg., ch. 722, §1, eff. Jan. 1, 1966.

CHAPTER 24. SUBPOENA & ATTACHMENT

ART. 24.01. ISSUANCE OF SUBPOENAS

(a) A subpoena may summon one or more persons to appear:

(1) before a court to testify in a criminal action at a specified term of the court or on a specified day; or

(2) on a specified day:

(A) before an examining court;

(B) at a coroner's inquest;

(C) before a grand jury;

(D) at a habeas corpus hearing; or

(E) in any other proceeding in which the person's testimony may be required in accordance with this code.

(b) The person named in the subpoena to summon the person whose appearance is sought must be:

(1) a peace officer; or

(2) at least 18 years old and, at the time the subpoena is issued, not a participant in the proceeding for which the appearance is sought.

(c) A person who is not a peace officer may not be compelled to accept the duty to execute a subpoena, but if he agrees in writing to accept that duty and neglects or refuses to serve or return the subpoena, he may be punished in accordance with Article 2.16 of this code.

(d) A court or clerk issuing a subpoena shall sign the subpoena and indicate on it the date it was issued, but the subpoena need not be under seal.

History of CCP art. 24.01: Acts 1965, 59th Leg., ch. 722, §1, eff. Jan. 1, 1966. Amended by Acts 1981, 67th Leg., ch. 200, §1, eff. Sept. 1, 1981.

ART. 24.011. SUBPOENAS; CHILD WITNESSES

(a) If a witness is younger than 18 years, the court may issue a subpoena directing a person having custody, care, or control of the child to produce the child in court.

(b) If a person, without legal cause, fails to produce the child in court as directed by a subpoena issued under this article, the court may impose on the person penalties for contempt provided by this chapter. The court may also issue a writ of attachment for the person and the child, in the same manner as other writs of attachment are issued under this chapter.

(c) If the witness is in a placement in the custody of the Texas Youth Commission, a juvenile secure detention facility, or a juvenile secure correctional facility, the court may issue a bench warrant or direct that an attachment issue to require a peace officer or probation officer to secure custody of the person at the placement and produce the person in court. When the person is no longer needed as a witness, the court shall order the peace officer or probation officer to return the person to the placement from which the person was released.

(d) The court may order that the person who is the witness be detained in a certified juvenile detention facility if the person is younger than 17 years of age. If

---

★

---

the person is at least 17 years of age, the court may order that the person be detained without bond in an appropriate county facility for the detention of adults accused of criminal offenses.

(e) In this article, "secure detention facility" and "secure correctional facility" have the meanings assigned by Section 51.02, Family Code.

History of CCP art. 24.011: Acts 1987, 70th Leg., ch. 520, §1, eff. June 17, 1987. Amended by Acts 2005, 79th Leg., ch. 949, §32, eff. Sept. 1, 2005.

ART. 24.02. SUBPOENA DUCES TECUM

If a witness have in his possession any instrument of writing or other thing desired as evidence, the subpoena may specify such evidence and direct that the witness bring the same with him and produce it in court.

History of CCP art. 24.02: Acts 1965, 59th Leg., ch. 722, §1, eff. Jan. 1, 1966.

ART. 24.03. SUBPOENA & APPLICATION THEREFOR

(a) Before the clerk or his deputy shall be required or permitted to issue a subpoena in any felony case pending in any district or criminal district court of this State of which he is clerk or deputy, the defendant or his attorney or the State's attorney shall make an application in writing or by electronic means to such clerk for each witness desired. Such application shall state the name of each witness desired, the location and vocation, if known, and that the testimony of said witness is material to the State or to the defense. The application must be filed with the clerk and placed with the papers in the cause or, if the application is filed electronically, placed with any other electronic information linked to the number of the cause. The application must also be made available to both the State and the defendant. Except as provided by Subsection (b), as far as is practical such clerk shall include in one subpoena the names of all witnesses for the State and for defendant, and such process shall show that the witnesses are summoned for the State or for the defendant. When a witness has been served with a subpoena, attached or placed under bail at the instance of either party in a particular case, such execution of process shall inure to the benefit of the opposite party in such case in the event such opposite party desires to use such witness on the trial of the case, provided that when a witness has once been served with a subpoena, no further subpoena shall be issued for said witness.

(b) If the defendant is a member of a combination as defined by Section 71.01, Penal Code, the clerk shall issue for each witness a subpoena that does not include a list of the names of all other witnesses for the State or the defendant.

History of CCP art. 24.03: Acts 1965, 59th Leg., ch. 722, §1, eff. Jan. 1, 1966. Amended by Acts 1993, 73rd Leg., ch. 900, §10.01, eff. Sept. 1, 1993; Acts 1999, 76th Leg., ch. 580, §4 (eff. Sept. 1, 1999), ch. 614, §2 (eff. June 18, 1999).

ANNOTATIONS

Coleman v. State, 966 S.W.2d 525, 527-28 (Tex. Crim.App.1998). "The 6th Amendment right to compulsory process 'is in plain terms the right to present a defense, the right to present the defendant's version of the facts as well as the prosecution's to the jury so it may decide where the truth lies.' The 6th Amendment does not guarantee, however, the right to secure the attendance and testimony of any and all witnesses; rather, it guarantees only compulsory process for obtaining witnesses whose testimony would be both material and favorable to the defense. To exercise the federal constitutional compulsory process right, the defendant must make a plausible showing to the trial court, by sworn evidence or agreed facts, that the witness's testimony would be both material and favorable to the defense. A defendant who has not had an opportunity to interview a witness may make the necessary showing by establishing the matters to which the witness might testify and the relevance and importance of those matters to the success of the defense. [¶] On the record before us, it is clear that appellant did not make the necessary showing ... that the reporters' testimony would actually be *material* and *favorable* to either of his defensive theories. Absent such a showing, the 6th Amendment did not require the District Court to compel the reporters to testify."

ART. 24.04. SERVICE & RETURN OF SUBPOENA

(a) A subpoena is served by:

(1) reading the subpoena in the hearing of the witness;

(2) delivering a copy of the subpoena to the witness;

(3) electronically transmitting a copy of the subpoena, acknowledgment of receipt requested, to the last known electronic address of the witness; or

(4) mailing a copy of the subpoena by certified mail, return receipt requested, to the last known address of the witness unless:

(A) the applicant for the subpoena requests in writing that the subpoena not be served by certified mail; or

(B) the proceeding for which the witness is being subpoenaed is set to begin within seven business days after the date the subpoena would be mailed.

(b) The officer having the subpoena shall make due return thereof, showing the time and manner of service, if served under Subsection (a)(1) or (2) of this article, the acknowledgment of receipt, if served under Subsection (a)(3) of this article, or the return receipt, if served under Subsection (a)(4) of this article. If the subpoena is not served, the officer shall show in his return the cause of his failure to serve it. If receipt of an electronically transmitted subpoena is not acknowledged within a reasonable time or a mailed subpoena is returned undelivered, the officer shall use due diligence to locate and serve the witness. If the witness could not be found, the officer shall state the diligence he has used to find him, and what information he has as to the whereabouts of the witness.

(c) A subpoena served under Subsection (a)(3) of this article must be accompanied by notice that an acknowledgment of receipt of the subpoena must be made in a manner enabling verification of the person acknowledging receipt.

History of CCP art. 24.04: Acts 1965, 59th Leg., ch. 722, §1, eff. Jan. 1, 1966. Amended by Acts 1979, 66th Leg., ch. 336, §1, eff. Aug. 27, 1979; Acts 1995, 74th Leg., ch. 374, §1, eff. June 8, 1995; Acts 1999, 76th Leg., ch. 580, §5, eff. Sept. 1, 1999.

ART. 24.05. REFUSING TO OBEY

If a witness refuses to obey a subpoena, he may be fined at the discretion of the court, as follows: In a felony case, not exceeding five hundred dollars; in a misdemeanor case, not exceeding one hundred dollars.

History of CCP art. 24.05: Acts 1965, 59th Leg., ch. 722, §1, eff. Jan. 1, 1966.

ANNOTATIONS

Ex parte Dotson, 76 S.W.3d 393, 396 (Tex.Crim. App.2002). "Because applicant's refusal to answer [and testify after being served with a subpoena] was in the context of a criminal prosecution, we apply the statute which is specific to such failure, [CCP art.] 24.05, and hold that such failure does not fall under the provisions of [TRCP] 176.8. The penalty for failure to answer a subpoena in a criminal case is limited to the provisions of Art. 24.05. … The punishment assessed by the trial court[, 180 days confinement and a $500 fine,] exceeded that permitted by law, and the trial court did not act within its authority."

ART. 24.06. WHAT IS DISOBEDIENCE OF A SUBPOENA

It shall be held that a witness refuses to obey a subpoena:

1. If he is not in attendance on the court on the day set apart for taking up the criminal docket or on any day subsequent thereto and before the final disposition or continuance of the particular case in which he is a witness;

2. If he is not in attendance at any other time named in a writ; and

3. If he refuses without legal cause to produce evidence in his possession which he has been summoned to bring with him and produce.

History of CCP art. 24.06: Acts 1965, 59th Leg., ch. 722, §1, eff. Jan. 1, 1966.

ANNOTATIONS

Gentry v. State, 770 S.W.2d 780, 785-86 (Tex.Crim. App.1988). "It would be illogical and unreasonable to require a subpoenaed witness to appear on a certain date, at a certain time and remain there *ad infinitum*. Accordingly, Article 24.06(1) … demands the presence of a subpoenaed witness only so long as the case is not finally disposed of or the case is continued. In the event the case is concluded or continued the witness is no longer subject to the subpoena."

ART. 24.07. FINE AGAINST WITNESS CONDITIONAL

When a fine is entered against a witness for failure to appear and testify, the judgment shall be conditional; and a citation shall issue to him to show cause, at the term of the court at which said fine is entered, or at the first term thereafter, at the discretion of the judge of said court, why the same should not be final; provided, citation shall be served upon said witness in the manner and for the length of time prescribed for citations in civil cases.

History of CCP art. 24.07: Acts 1965, 59th Leg., ch. 722, §1, eff. Jan. 1, 1966.

ART. 24.08. WITNESS MAY SHOW CAUSE

A witness cited to show cause, as provided in the preceding Article, may do so under oath, in writing or verbally, at any time before judgment final is entered against him; but if he fails to show cause within the time limited for answering in civil actions, a judgment final by default shall be entered against him.

History of CCP art. 24.08: Acts 1965, 59th Leg., ch. 722, §1, eff. Jan. 1, 1966.

ART. 24.09. COURT MAY REMIT FINE

It shall be within the discretion of the court to judge of the sufficiency of an excuse rendered by a witness, and upon the hearing the court shall render judgment against the witness for the whole or any part of the fine, or shall remit the fine altogether, as to the court may appear proper and right. Said fine shall be collected as fines in misdemeanor cases.

History of CCP art. 24.09: Acts 1965, 59th Leg., ch. 722, §1, eff. Jan. 1, 1966.

ART. 24.10. WHEN WITNESS APPEARS & TESTIFIES

When a fine has been entered against a witness, but no trial of the cause takes place, and such witness afterward appears and testifies upon the trial thereof, it shall be discretionary with the judge, though no good excuse be rendered, to reduce the fine or remit it altogether; but the witness, in such case, shall, nevertheless, be adjudged to pay all the costs accruing in the proceeding against him by reason of his failure to attend.

History of CCP art. 24.10: Acts 1965, 59th Leg., ch. 722, §1, eff. Jan. 1, 1966.

ART. 24.11. REQUISITES OF AN "ATTACHMENT"

An "attachment" is a writ issued by a clerk of a court under seal, or by any magistrate, or by the foreman of a grand jury, in any criminal action or proceeding authorized by law, commanding some peace officer to take the body of a witness and bring him before such court, magistrate or grand jury on a day named, or forthwith, to testify in behalf of the State or of the defendant, as the case may be. It shall be dated and signed officially by the officer issuing it.

History of CCP art. 24.11: Acts 1965, 59th Leg., ch. 722, §1, eff. Jan. 1, 1966.

ANNOTATIONS

Boyle v. State, 820 S.W.2d 122, 128 (Tex.Crim.App. 1989). "[A]n attachment for a witness is not authorized until the witness fails to obey a properly served subpoena."

ART. 24.12. WHEN ATTACHMENT MAY ISSUE

When a witness who resides in the county of the prosecution has been duly served with a subpoena to appear and testify in any criminal action or proceeding fails to so appear, the State or the defendant shall be entitled to have an attachment issued forthwith for such witness.

History of CCP art. 24.12: Acts 1965, 59th Leg., ch. 722, §1, eff. Jan. 1, 1966.

ANNOTATIONS

Sturgeon v. State, 106 S.W.3d 81, 90 (Tex.Crim. App.2003). "[A]ttachment of a witness who has been duly served with a subpoena *is a matter of right.* Article 24.12 does not contain any language requiring sworn testimony or affidavits. We do not believe that more should be required of counsel than to assert, on the record, the grounds for his motion or objection to the trial court's ruling, and to articulate sufficient information about the expected testimony to show materiality."

ART. 24.13. ATTACHMENT FOR CONVICT WITNESSES

All persons who have been or may be convicted in this State, and who are confined in an institution operated by the Department of Corrections or any jail in this State, shall be permitted to testify in person in any court for the State and the defendant when the presiding judge finds, after hearing, that the ends of justice require their attendance, and directs that an attachment issue to accomplish the purpose, notwithstanding any other provision of this Code. Nothing in this Article shall be construed as limiting the power of the courts of this State to issue bench warrants.

History of CCP art. 24.13: Acts 1965, 59th Leg., ch. 722, §1, eff. Jan. 1, 1966.

ART. 24.131. NOTIFICATION TO DEPARTMENT OF CRIMINAL JUSTICE

If after the Texas Department of Criminal Justice transfers a defendant or inmate to a county under Article 24.13 and before that person is returned to the department the person is released on bail or the charges on which the person was convicted and for which the person was transferred to the department are dismissed, the county shall immediately notify an officer designated by the department of the release on bail or the dismissal.

History of CCP art. 24.131: Acts 2001, 77th Leg., ch. 857, §1, eff. June 14, 2001.

ART. 24.14. ATTACHMENT FOR RESIDENT WITNESS

When a witness resides in the county of the prosecution, whether he has disobeyed a subpoena or not, either in term-time or vacation, upon the filing of an affidavit with the clerk by the defendant or State's counsel, that he has good reason to believe, and does believe, that such witness is a material witness, and is about to move out of the county, the clerk shall forthwith issue an attachment for such witness; provided, that in misdemeanor cases, when the witness makes oath that he cannot give surety, the officer executing the attachment shall take his personal bond.

History of CCP art. 24.14: Acts 1965, 59th Leg., ch. 722, §1, eff. Jan. 1, 1966.

ANNOTATIONS

Gentry v. State, 770 S.W.2d 780, 786 (Tex.Crim. App.1988). Article 24.14 "authorizes the issuance of an attachment for a resident witness prior to the disobedience of a subpoena."

ART. 24.15. TO SECURE ATTENDANCE BEFORE GRAND JURY

At any time before the first day of any term of the district court, the clerk, upon application of the State's attorney, shall issue a subpoena for any witness who resides in the county. If at the time such application is made, such attorney files a sworn application that he has good reason to believe and does believe that such witness is about to move out of the county, then said clerk shall issue an attachment for such witness to be and appear before said district court on the first day thereof to testify as a witness before the grand jury. Any witness so summoned, or attached, who shall fail or refuse to obey a subpoena or attachment, shall be punished by the court by a fine not exceeding five hundred dollars, to be collected as fines and costs in other criminal cases.

History of CCP art. 24.15: Acts 1965, 59th Leg., ch. 722, §1, eff. Jan. 1, 1966.

ANNOTATIONS

Boyle v. State, 820 S.W.2d 122, 128 (Tex.Crim.App. 1989). "First, Article 24.15 is restricted to 'any witness who resides in the county....' [¶] Second, before an attachment for a resident witness can issue under Article 24.15 the State's attorney must file a sworn application stating 'that he has good reason to believe and does believe that such witness is about to move out of the

county.' It is apparent that such a sworn claim must be made before an attachment can issue.... [¶] Third, Article 24.15 does not authorize the issuing magistrate to set a bond to insure a witnesses appearance. It only authorizes the imposition of a fine if the witness fails or refuses to obey the subpoena."

ART. 24.16. APPLICATION FOR OUT-COUNTY WITNESS

Where, in misdemeanor cases in which confinement in jail is a permissible punishment, or in felony cases, a witness resides out of the county in which the prosecution is pending, the State or the defendant shall be entitled, either in term-time or in vacation, to a subpoena to compel the attendance of such witness on application to the proper clerk or magistrate. Such application shall be in the manner and form as provided in Article 24.03. Witnesses in such misdemeanor cases shall be compensated in the same manner as in felony cases. This Article shall not apply to more than one character witness in a misdemeanor case.

History of CCP art. 24.16: Acts 1965, 59th Leg., ch. 722, §1, eff. Jan. 1, 1966.

ART. 24.17. DUTY OF OFFICER RECEIVING SAID SUBPOENA

The officer receiving said subpoena shall execute the same by delivering a copy thereof to each witness therein named. He shall make due return of said subpoena, showing therein the time and manner of executing the same, and if not executed, such return shall show why not executed, the diligence used to find said witness, and such information as the officer has as to the whereabouts of said witness.

History of CCP art. 24.17: Acts 1965, 59th Leg., ch. 722, §1, eff. Jan. 1, 1966.

ART. 24.18. SUBPOENA RETURNABLE FORTHWITH

When a subpoena is returnable forthwith, the officer shall immediately serve the witness with a copy of the same; and it shall be the duty of said witness to immediately make his appearance before the court, magistrate or other authority issuing the same. If said witness makes affidavit of his inability from lack of funds to appear in obedience to said subpoena, the officer executing the same shall provide said witness, if said subpoena be issued as provided in Article 24.16, with the necessary funds or means to appear in obedience to said subpoena, taking his receipt therefor, and showing in his return on said subpoena, under oath, the amount furnished to said witness, together with the amount of his fees for executing said subpoena.

History of CCP art. 24.18: Acts 1965, 59th Leg., ch. 722, §1, eff. Jan. 1, 1966.

ART. 24.19. CERTIFICATE TO OFFICER

The clerk, magistrate, or foreman of the grand jury issuing said process, immediately upon the return of said subpoena, if issued as provided in Article 24.16, shall issue to such officer a certificate for the amount furnished such witness, together with the amount of his fees for executing the same, showing the amount of each item; which certificate shall be approved by the district judge and recorded by the district clerk in a book kept for that purpose; and said certificate transmitted to the officer executing such subpoena, which amount shall be paid by the State, as costs are paid in other criminal matters.

History of CCP art. 24.19: Acts 1965, 59th Leg., ch. 722, §1, eff. Jan. 1, 1966.

ART. 24.20. SUBPOENA RETURNABLE AT FUTURE DATE

If the subpoena be returnable at some future date, the officer shall have authority to take bail of such witness for his appearance under said subpoena, which bond shall be returned with such subpoena, and shall be made payable to the State of Texas, in the amount in which the witness and his surety, if any, shall be bound and conditioned for the appearance of the witness at the time and before the court, magistrate or grand jury named in said subpoena, and shall be signed by the witness and his sureties. If the witness refuses to give bond, he shall be kept in custody until such time as he starts in obedience to said subpoena, when he shall be, upon affidavit being made, provided with funds necessary to appear in obedience to said subpoena.

History of CCP art. 24.20: Acts 1965, 59th Leg., ch. 722, §1, eff. Jan. 1, 1966.

ART. 24.21. STATING BAIL IN SUBPOENA

The court or magistrate issuing said subpoena may direct therein the amount of the bail to be required. The officer may fix the amount if not specified, and in either case, shall require sufficient security, to be approved by himself.

History of CCP art. 24.21: Acts 1965, 59th Leg., ch. 722, §1, eff. Jan. 1, 1966.

ART. 24.22. WITNESS FINED & ATTACHED

If a witness summoned from without the county refuses to obey a subpoena, he shall be fined by the court or magistrate not exceeding five hundred dollars, which fine and judgment shall be final, unless set aside after due notice to show cause why it should not be final, which notice may immediately issue, requiring the defaulting witness to appear at once or at the next term of said court, in the discretion of the judge, to answer for such default. The court may cause to be issued at the same time an attachment for said witness, directed to the proper county, commanding the officer to whom said writ is directed to take said witness into custody and have him before said court at the time named in said writ; in which case such witness shall receive no fees, unless it appears to the court that such disobedience is excusable, when the witness may receive the same pay as if he had not been attached. Said fine when made final and all costs thereon shall be collected as in other criminal cases. Said fine and judgment may be set aside in vacation or at the time or any subsequent term of the court for good cause shown, after the witness testifies or has been discharged. The following words shall be written or printed on the face of such subpoena for out-county witnesses: "A disobedience of this subpoena is punishable by fine not exceeding five hundred dollars, to be collected as fines and costs in other criminal cases."

History of CCP art. 24.22: Acts 1965, 59th Leg., ch. 722, §1, eff. Jan. 1, 1966.

ART. 24.23. WITNESS RELEASED

A witness who is in custody for failing to give bail shall be at once released upon giving bail required.

History of CCP art. 24.23: Acts 1965, 59th Leg., ch. 722, §1, eff. Jan. 1, 1966.

ART. 24.24. BAIL FOR WITNESS

Witnesses on behalf of the State or defendant may, at the request of either party, be required to enter into bail in an amount to be fixed by the court to appear and testify in a criminal action; but if it shall appear to the court that any witness is unable to give security upon such bail, he shall be released without security.

History of CCP art. 24.24: Acts 1965, 59th Leg., ch. 722, §1, eff. Jan. 1, 1966.

ART. 24.25. PERSONAL BOND OF WITNESS

When it appears to the satisfaction of the court that personal bond of the witness will insure his attendance, no security need be required of him; but no bond without security shall be taken by any officer.

History of CCP art. 24.25: Acts 1965, 59th Leg., ch. 722, §1, eff. Jan. 1, 1966.

ART. 24.26. ENFORCING FORFEITURE

The bond of a witness may be enforced against him and his sureties, if any, in the manner pointed out in this Code for enforcing the bond of a defendant in a criminal case.

History of CCP art. 24.26: Acts 1965, 59th Leg., ch. 722, §1, eff. Jan. 1, 1966.

ART. 24.27. NO SURRENDER AFTER FORFEITURE

The sureties of a witness have no right to discharge themselves by the surrender of the witness after the forfeiture of their bond.

History of CCP art. 24.27: Acts 1965, 59th Leg., ch. 722, §1, eff. Jan. 1, 1966.

ART. 24.28. UNIFORM ACT TO SECURE ATTENDANCE OF WITNESSES FROM WITHOUT STATE

§1. Short Title

This Act may be cited as the "Uniform Act to Secure the Attendance of Witnesses from Without the State in Criminal Proceedings."

§2. Definitions

"Witness" as used in this Act shall include a person whose testimony is desired in any proceeding or investigation by a grand jury or in a criminal action, prosecution or proceeding.

The word "State" shall include any territory of the United States and the District of Columbia.

The word "summons" shall include a subpoena, order or other notice requiring the appearance of a witness.

§3. Summoning Witness in This State to Testify in Another State

(a) If a judge of a court of record in any State which by its laws has made provision for commanding persons within that State to attend and testify in this State certifies under the seal of such court that there is a criminal prosecution pending in such court, or that a grand jury investigation has commenced or is about to commence, that a person being within this State is a material witness in such prosecution, or grand jury investigation, and that his presence will be required for a specified number of days, upon presentation of such certificate to any judge of a court of record in the county in which such person is, such judge shall fix a time and place for a hearing, and shall make an order directing the witness to appear at a time and place certain for the hearing.

(b) If at a hearing the judge determines that the witness is material and necessary, that it will not cause undue hardship to the witness to be compelled to attend and testify in the prosecution or a grand jury investigation in the other State, and that the laws of the State in which the prosecution is pending, or grand jury investigation has commenced or is about to commence, (and of any other State through which the witness may be required to pass by ordinary course of travel), will give to him protection from arrest and the service of civil and criminal process, he shall issue a summons, with a copy of the certificate attached, directing the witness to attend and testify in the court where the prosecution is pending, or where a grand jury investigation has commenced or is about to commence at a time and place specified in the summons. In any such hearing the certificate shall be prima facie evidence of all the facts stated therein.

(c) If said certificate recommends that the witness be taken into immediate custody and delivered to an officer of the requesting State to assure his attendance in the requesting State, such judge may, in lieu of notification of the hearing, direct that such witness be forthwith brought before him for said hearing; and the judge at the hearing being satisfied of the desirability of such custody and delivery, for which determination the certificate shall be prima facie proof of such desirability may, in lieu of issuing subpoena or summons, order that said witness be forthwith taken into custody and delivered to an officer of the requesting State.

(d) If the witness, who is summoned as above provided, after being paid or tendered by some properly authorized person the compensation for nonresident witnesses authorized and provided for by Article 35.27 of this Code, fails without good cause to attend and testify as directed in the summons, he shall be punished in the manner provided for the punishment of any witness who disobeys a summons issued from a court of record in this State.

§4. Witness from Another State Summoned to Testify in This State

(a) If a person in any State, which by its laws has made provision for commanding persons within its borders to attend and testify in criminal prosecutions, or grand jury investigations commenced or about to commence, in this State, is a material witness in a prosecution pending in a court of record in this State, or in a grand jury investigation which has commenced or is about to commence, a judge of such court may issue a certificate under the seal of the court stating these facts and specifying the number of days the witness will be required. Said certificate may include a recommendation that the witness be taken into immediate custody and delivered to an officer of this State to assure his attendance in this State. This certificate shall be presented to a judge of a court of record in the county in which the witness is found.

(b) If the witness is summoned to attend and testify in this State he shall be tendered the compensation for nonresident witnesses authorized by Article 35.27 of this Code, together with such additional compensation, if any, required by the other State for compliance. A witness who has appeared in accordance with the provisions of the summons shall not be required to remain within this State a longer period of time than the period mentioned in the certificate, unless otherwise ordered by the court. If such witness, after coming into this State, fails without good cause to attend and testify as directed in the summons, he shall be punished in the manner provided for the punishment of any witness who disobeys a summons issued from a court of record in this State.

§5. Exemption from Arrest & Service of Process

If a person comes into this State in obedience to a summons directing him to attend and testify in this State he shall not while in this State pursuant to such summons be subject to arrest or the service of process, civil or criminal, in connection with matters which arose before his entrance into this State under the summons.

If a person passes through this State while going to another State in obedience to a summons to attend and testify in that State or while returning therefrom, he shall not while so passing through this State be subject to arrest or the service of process, civil or criminal, in connection with matters which arose before his entrance into this State under the summons.

History of CCP art. 24.28: Acts 1965, 59th Leg., ch. 722, §1, eff. Jan. 1, 1966. Amended by Acts 1973, 63rd Leg., ch. 477, §1, eff. Aug. 27, 1973.

ART. 24.29. UNIFORM ACT TO SECURE RENDITION OF PRISONERS IN CRIMINAL PROCEEDINGS

§1. Short Title

This article may be cited as the "Uniform Act to Secure Rendition of Prisoners in Criminal Proceedings."

§2. Definitions

In this Act:

(1) "Penal institution" means a jail, prison, penitentiary, house of correction, or other place of penal detention.

(2) "State" means a state of the United States, the District of Columbia, the Commonwealth of Puerto Rico, and any territory of the United States.

(3) "Witness" means a person who is confined in a penal institution in a state and whose testimony is desired in another state in a criminal proceeding or investigation by a grand jury or in any criminal action before a court.

§3. Summoning Witness in This State to Testify in Another State

(a) A judge of a state court of record in another state, which by its laws has made provision for commanding persons confined in penal institutions within that state to attend and testify in this state, may certify that:

(1) there is a criminal proceeding or investigation by a grand jury or a criminal action pending in the court;

(2) a person who is confined in a penal institution in this state may be a material witness in the proceeding, investigation, or action; and

(3) his presence will be required during a specified time.

(b) On presentation of the certificate to any judge having jurisdiction over the person confined and on notice to the attorney general, the judge in this state shall fix a time and place for a hearing and shall make an order directed to the person having custody of the prisoner requiring that the prisoner be produced before him at the hearing.

§4. Court Order

(a) A judge may issue a transfer order if at the hearing the judge determines that:

(1) the witness may be material and necessary;

(2) his attending and testifying are not adverse to the interest of this state or to the health or legal rights of the witness;

(3) the laws of the state in which he is requested to testify will give him protection from arrest and the service of civil and criminal process because of any act committed prior to his arrival in the state under the order; and

(4) as a practical matter the possibility is negligible that the witness may be subject to arrest or to the service of civil or criminal process in any state through which he will be required to pass.

(b) If a judge issues an order under Subsection (a) of this section, the judge shall attach to the order a copy of a certificate presented under Section 3 of this Act. The order shall:

(1) direct the witness to attend and testify;

(2) except as provided by Subsection (c) of this section, direct the person having custody of the witness to produce him in the court where the criminal action is pending or where the grand jury investigation is pending at a time and place specified in the order; and

(3) prescribe such conditions as the judge shall determine.

(c) The judge, in lieu of directing the person having custody of the witness to produce him in the requesting jurisdiction's court, may direct and require in his order that:

(1) an officer of the requesting jurisdiction come to the Texas penal institution in which the witness is confined to accept custody of the witness for physical transfer to the requesting jurisdiction;

(2) the requesting jurisdiction provide proper safeguards on his custody while in transit;

(3) the requesting jurisdiction be liable for and pay all expenses incurred in producing and returning the witness, including but not limited to food, lodging, clothing, and medical care; and

(4) the requesting jurisdiction promptly deliver the witness back to the same or another Texas penal institution as specified by the Texas Department of Corrections at the conclusion of his testimony.

§5. Terms & Conditions

An order to a witness and to a person having custody of the witness shall provide for the return of the witness at the conclusion of his testimony, proper safeguards on his custody, and proper financial reimbursement or prepayment by the requesting jurisdiction for all expenses incurred in the production and return of the witness. The order may prescribe any other condition the judge thinks proper or necessary. The judge shall not require prepayment of expenses if the judge directs and requires the requesting jurisdiction to accept custody of the witness at the Texas penal institution in which the witness is confined and to deliver the

witness back to the same or another Texas penal institution at the conclusion of his testimony. An order does not become effective until the judge of the state requesting the witness enters an order directing compliance with the conditions prescribed.

§6. Exceptions

This Act does not apply to a person in this state who is confined as mentally ill or who is under sentence of death.

§7. Prisoner from Another State Summoned to Testify in This State

(a) If a person confined in a penal institution in any other state may be a material witness in a criminal action pending in a court of record or in a grand jury investigation in this state, a judge of the court may certify that:

(1) there is a criminal proceeding or investigation by a grand jury or a criminal action pending in the court;

(2) a person who is confined in a penal institution in the other state may be a material witness in the proceeding, investigation, or action; and

(3) his presence will be required during a specified time.

(b) The judge of the court in this state shall:

(1) present the certificate to a judge of a court of record in the other state having jurisdiction over the prisoner confined; and

(2) give notice that the prisoner's presence will be required to the attorney general of the state in which the prisoner is confined.

§8. Compliance

A judge of the court in this state may enter an order directing compliance with the terms and conditions of an order specified in a certificate under Section 3 of this Act and entered by the judge of the state in which the witness is confined.

§9. Exemption from Arrest & Service of Process

If a witness from another state comes into or passes through this state under an order directing him to attend and testify in this or another state, while in this state pursuant to the order he is not subject to arrest or the service of civil or criminal process because of any act committed prior to his arrival in this state under the order.

§10. Uniformity of Interpretation

This Act shall be so construed as to effect its general purpose to make uniform the laws of those states which enact it.

History of CCP art. 24.29: Acts 1983, 68th Leg., ch. 240, §1, eff. Aug. 29, 1983.

CHAPTER 24A. RESPONDING TO SUBPOENAS & CERTAIN OTHER COURT ORDERS; PRESERVING CERTAIN INFORMATION

SUBCHAPTER A. RESPONDING TO SUBPOENAS & CERTAIN OTHER COURT ORDERS

ART. 24A.001. APPLICABILITY OF SUBCHAPTER

This subchapter applies only to a subpoena, search warrant, or other court order that:

(1) relates to the investigation or prosecution of a criminal offense under Section 33.021, Penal Code; and

(2) is served on or issued with respect to an Internet service provider that provides service in this state.

History of CCP art. 24A.001: Acts 2007, 80th Leg., ch. 1291, §2, eff. Sept. 1, 2007.

ART. 24A.002. RESPONSE REQUIRED; DEADLINE FOR RESPONSE

(a) Except as provided by Subsection (b), not later than the 10th day after the date on which an Internet service provider is served with or otherwise receives a subpoena, search warrant, or other court order described by Article 24A.001, the Internet service provider shall:

(1) fully comply with the subpoena, warrant, or order; or

(2) petition a court to excuse the Internet service provider from complying with the subpoena, warrant, or order.

(b) As soon as is practicable, and in no event later than the second business day after the date the Internet service provider is served with or otherwise receives a subpoena, search warrant, or other court order described by Article 24A.001, the Internet service provider shall fully comply with the subpoena, search warrant, or order if the subpoena, search warrant, or order indicates that full compliance is necessary to address a situation that threatens a person with death or other serious bodily injury.

(c) For the purposes of Subsection (a)(1), full compliance with the subpoena, warrant, or order includes:

(1) producing or providing, to the extent permitted under federal law, all documents or information requested under the subpoena, warrant, or order; or

(2) providing, to the extent permitted under federal law, electronic access to all documents or information requested under the subpoena, warrant, or order.

History of CCP art. 24A.002: Acts 2007, 80th Leg., ch. 1291, §2, eff. Sept. 1, 2007.

ART. 24A.003. DISOBEYING SUBPOENA, WARRANT, OR ORDER

An Internet service provider that disobeys a subpoena, search warrant, or other court order described by Article 24A.001 and that was not excused from complying with the subpoena, warrant, or order under Article 24A.002(a)(2) may be punished in any manner provided by law.

History of CCP art. 24A.003: Acts 2007, 80th Leg., ch. 1291, §2, eff. Sept. 1, 2007.

Articles 24A.004-24A.050 reserved for expansion

SUBCHAPTER B. PRESERVING CERTAIN INFORMATION

ART. 24A.051. PRESERVING INFORMATION

(a) On written request of a law enforcement agency in this state or a federal law enforcement agency and pending the issuance of a subpoena or other court order described by Article 24A.001, an Internet service provider that provides service in this state shall take all steps necessary to preserve all records or other potential evidence in a criminal trial that is in the possession of the Internet service provider.

(b) Subject to Subsection (c), an Internet service provider shall preserve information under Subsection (a) for a period of 90 days after the date the Internet service provider receives the written request described by Subsection (a).

(c) An Internet service provider shall preserve information under Subsection (a) for the 90-day period immediately following the 90-day period described by Subsection (b) if the requesting law enforcement agency in writing requests an extension of the preservation period.

History of CCP art. 24A.051: Acts 2007, 80th Leg., ch. 1291, §2, eff. Sept. 1, 2007.

CHAPTER 25. SERVICE OF A COPY OF THE INDICTMENT

Art. 25.01 In felony
Art. 25.02 Service & return
Art. 25.03 If on bail in felony
Art. 25.04 In misdemeanor

ART. 25.01. IN FELONY

In every case of felony, when the accused is in custody, or as soon as he may be arrested, the clerk of the court where an indictment has been presented shall immediately make a certified copy of the same, and deliver such copy to the sheriff, together with a writ directed to such sheriff, commanding him forthwith to deliver such certified copy to the accused.

History of CCP art. 25.01: Acts 1965, 59th Leg., ch. 722, §1, eff. Jan. 1, 1966.

ANNOTATIONS

Johnson v. State, 567 S.W.2d 214, 215 (Tex.Crim. App.1978). "Appellant's right to be served with a copy of the indictment is not affected by the fact that it was a reindictment. [¶] The State contends that no error was committed because appellant was given a 'copy' of the indictment before it was returned by the grand jury. *At 216:* While the proposed indictment ... is identical with the one actually returned by the grand jury, there was no way of knowing what action the grand jury would take before they were presented with the case. The grand jury could have made substantial changes in the indictment or refused to return an indictment at all."

Young v. State, 806 S.W.2d 340, 344 (Tex.App.— Austin 1991, pet. ref'd). "No objection was voiced by appellant at trial, complaint of failure to be served with a copy of the indictment being urged for the first time on appeal. The record is silent regarding service. *At 345:* We hold that a complaint made for the first time on appeal is too late to preserve error."

ART. 25.02. SERVICE & RETURN

Upon receipt of such writ and copy, the sheriff shall immediately deliver such certified copy of the indictment to the accused and return the writ to the clerk issuing the same, with his return thereon, showing when and how the same was executed.

History of CCP art. 25.02: Acts 1965, 59th Leg., ch. 722, §1, eff. Jan. 1, 1966.

ART. 25.03. IF ON BAIL IN FELONY

When the accused, in case of felony, is on bail at the time the indictment is presented, it is not necessary to serve him with a copy, but the clerk shall on request deliver a copy of the same to the accused or his counsel, at the earliest possible time.

History of CCP art. 25.03: Acts 1965, 59th Leg., ch. 722, §1, eff. Jan. 1, 1966.

ART. 25.04. IN MISDEMEANOR

In misdemeanors, it shall not be necessary before trial to furnish the accused with a copy of the indictment or information; but he or his counsel may demand a copy, which shall be given as early as possible.

History of CCP art. 25.04: Acts 1965, 59th Leg., ch. 722, §1, eff. Jan. 1, 1966.

CHAPTER 26. ARRAIGNMENT

Art. 26.01   Arraignment
Art. 26.011 Waiver of arraignment
Art. 26.02   Purpose of arraignment
Art. 26.03   Time of arraignment
Art. 26.04   Procedures for appointing counsel
Art. 26.044 Public defender
Art. 26.05   Compensation of counsel appointed to defend
Art. 26.051 Indigent inmate defense
Art. 26.052 Appointment of counsel in death penalty case; reimbursement of investigative expenses
Art. 26.053 Public defender in Randall County
Art. 26.056 Contribution from state in certain counties
Art. 26.057 Cost of employment of counsel for certain minors
Art. 26.06   Elected officials not to be appointed
Art. 26.07   Name as stated in indictment
Art. 26.08   If defendant suggests different name
Art. 26.09   If accused refuses to give his real name
Art. 26.10   Where name is unknown
Art. 26.11   Indictment read
Art. 26.12   Plea of not guilty entered
Art. 26.13   Plea of guilty
Art. 26.14   Jury on plea of guilty
Art. 26.15   Correcting name

ART. 26.01. ARRAIGNMENT

In all felony cases, after indictment, and all misdemeanor cases punishable by imprisonment, there shall be an arraignment.

History of CCP art. 26.01: Acts 1965, 59th Leg., ch. 722, §1, eff. Jan. 1, 1966.

ANNOTATIONS

Price v. State, 866 S.W.2d 606, 611 (Tex.Crim.App. 1993). "[T]he legislative purpose was to provide a final opportunity for an indigent accused to obtain appointed counsel. ... However, the constitutional requirement for appointment of counsel at arraignment or for trial does not apply where from a measure of the seriousness and gravity of the misdemeanor offense the trial judge is satisfied the court will not assess punishment of imprisonment."

Minafee v. State, 482 S.W.2d 273, 277 (Tex.Crim. App.1972). "The practice of delaying arraignment and conducting such proceedings in the jury's presence should not be condoned. Trial judges should be careful to avoid such practice."

Adkison v. State, 762 S.W.2d 255, 259 (Tex.App.— Beaumont 1988, pet. ref'd). "[S]ince there was no objection made ... concerning any alleged lack of proper arraignment prior to the time of this appeal, any ... error ... was waived."

ART. 26.011. WAIVER OF ARRAIGNMENT

An attorney representing a defendant may present a waiver of arraignment, and the clerk of the court may not require the presence of the defendant as a condition of accepting the waiver.

History of CCP art. 26.011: Acts 2001, 77th Leg., ch. 818, §1, eff. June 14, 2001.

ART. 26.02. PURPOSE OF ARRAIGNMENT

An arraignment takes place for the purpose of fixing his identity and hearing his plea.

History of CCP art. 26.02: Acts 1965, 59th Leg., ch. 722, §1, eff. Jan. 1, 1966.

ANNOTATIONS

Hinojosa v. State, 788 S.W.2d 594, 599 (Tex.App.— Corpus Christi 1990, pet. ref'd). "After the impanelment of the jury, the charging instrument is read to the jury by the prosecuting attorney ... to inform both the accused and the jury of the charge being brought against the accused. [¶] An arraignment, on the other hand, is a procedure to determine the identity and the plea of the person charged."

ART. 26.03. TIME OF ARRAIGNMENT

No arraignment shall take place until the expiration of at least two entire days after the day on which a copy of the indictment was served on the defendant, unless the right to such copy or to such delay be waived, or unless the defendant is on bail.

History of CCP art. 26.03: Acts 1965, 59th Leg., ch. 722, §1, eff. Jan. 1, 1966.

ART. 26.04. PROCEDURES FOR APPOINTING COUNSEL

(a) The judges of the county courts, statutory county courts, and district courts trying criminal cases in each county, by local rule, shall adopt and publish written countywide procedures for timely and fairly appointing counsel for an indigent defendant in the county arrested for or charged with a misdemeanor punishable by confinement or a felony. The procedures must be consistent with this article and Articles 1.051, 15.17, 26.05, and 26.052. A court shall appoint an attorney from a public appointment list using a system of rotation, unless the court appoints an attorney under Subsection (f), (h), or (i). The court shall appoint attorneys from among the next five names on the appointment list in the order in which the attorneys' names appear on the list, unless the court makes a finding of good cause on the record for appointing an attorney out of order. An attorney who is not appointed in the order in which the attorney's name appears on the list shall remain next in order on the list.

(b) Procedures adopted under Subsection (a) shall:

(1) authorize only the judges of the county courts, statutory county courts, and district courts trying criminal cases in the county, or the judges' designee, to appoint counsel for indigent defendants in the county;

(2) apply to each appointment of counsel made by a judge or the judges' designee in the county;

(3) ensure that each indigent defendant in the county who is charged with a misdemeanor punishable by confinement or with a felony and who appears in court without counsel has an opportunity to confer with appointed counsel before the commencement of judicial proceedings;

(4) require appointments for defendants in capital cases in which the death penalty is sought to comply with the requirements under Article 26.052;

(5) ensure that each attorney appointed from a public appointment list to represent an indigent defendant perform the attorney's duty owed to the defendant in accordance with the adopted procedures, the requirements of this code, and applicable rules of ethics; and

(6) ensure that appointments are allocated among qualified attorneys in a manner that is fair, neutral, and nondiscriminatory.

(c) Whenever a court or the courts' designee authorized under Subsection (b) to appoint counsel for indigent defendants in the county determines that a defendant charged with a felony or a misdemeanor punishable by confinement is indigent or that the interests of justice require representation of a defendant in a criminal proceeding, the court or the courts' designee shall appoint one or more practicing attorneys to defend the defendant in accordance with this subsection and the procedures adopted under Subsection (a). If the court or the courts' designee determines that the defendant does not speak and understand the English language or that the defendant is deaf, the court or the courts' designee shall make an effort to appoint an attorney who is capable of communicating in a language understood by the defendant.

(d) A public appointment list from which an attorney is appointed as required by Subsection (a) shall contain the names of qualified attorneys, each of whom:

(1) applies to be included on the list;

(2) meets the objective qualifications specified by the judges under Subsection (e);

(3) meets any applicable qualifications specified by the Task Force on Indigent Defense; and

(4) is approved by a majority of the judges who established the appointment list under Subsection (e).

(e) In a county in which a court is required under Subsection (a) to appoint an attorney from a public appointment list:

(1) the judges of the county courts and statutory county courts trying misdemeanor cases in the county, by formal action:

(A) shall:

(i) establish a public appointment list of attorneys qualified to provide representation in the county in misdemeanor cases punishable by confinement; and

(ii) specify the objective qualifications necessary for an attorney to be included on the list; and

(B) may establish, if determined by the judges to be appropriate, more than one appointment list graduated according to the degree of seriousness of the offense and the attorneys' qualifications; and

(2) the judges of the district courts trying felony cases in the county, by formal action:

(A) shall:

(i) establish a public appointment list of attorneys qualified to provide representation in felony cases in the county; and

(ii) specify the objective qualifications necessary for an attorney to be included on the list; and

(B) may establish, if determined by the judges to be appropriate, more than one appointment list graduated according to the degree of seriousness of the offense and the attorneys' qualifications.

(f) In a county in which a public defender is appointed under Article 26.044, the court or the courts' designee may appoint the public defender to represent the defendant in accordance with guidelines established for the public defender.

(g) A countywide alternative program for appointing counsel for indigent defendants in criminal cases is established by a formal action in which two-thirds of the judges of the courts designated under this subsection vote to establish the alternative program. An alternative program for appointing counsel in misdemeanor and felony cases may be established in the manner provided by this subsection by the judges of the county courts, statutory county courts, and district courts trying criminal cases in the county. An alternative program for appointing counsel in misdemeanor cases may be established in the manner provided by this subsection by the judges of the county courts and statutory county courts trying criminal cases in the county. An alternative program for appointing counsel in felony cases may be established in the manner provided by this subsection by the judges of the district courts trying criminal cases in the county. In a county in which an alternative program is established:

(1) the alternative program may:

(A) use a single method for appointing counsel or a combination of methods; and

(B) use a multicounty appointment list using a system of rotation; and

(2) the procedures adopted under Subsection (a) must ensure that:

(A) attorneys appointed using the alternative program to represent defendants in misdemeanor cases punishable by confinement:

(i) meet specified objective qualifications, which may be graduated according to the degree of seriousness of the offense, for providing representation in misdemeanor cases punishable by confinement; and

(ii) are approved by a majority of the judges of the county courts and statutory county courts trying misdemeanor cases in the county;

(B) attorneys appointed using the alternative program to represent defendants in felony cases:

(i) meet specified objective qualifications, which may be graduated according to the degree of seriousness of the offense, for providing representation in felony cases; and

(ii) are approved by a majority of the judges of the district courts trying felony cases in the county;

(C) appointments for defendants in capital cases in which the death penalty is sought comply with the requirements of Article 26.052; and

(D) appointments are reasonably and impartially allocated among qualified attorneys.

(h) In a county in which an alternative program for appointing counsel is established as provided by Subsection (g) and is approved by the presiding judge of the administrative judicial region, a court or the courts' designee may appoint an attorney to represent an indigent defendant by using the alternative program. In establishing an alternative program under Subsection (g), the judges of the courts establishing the program may not, without the approval of the commissioners court, obligate the county by contract or by the creation of new positions that cause an increase in expenditure of county funds.

(i) A court or the courts' designee required under Subsection (c) to appoint an attorney to represent a defendant accused of a felony may appoint an attorney from any county located in the court's administrative judicial region.

(j) An attorney appointed under this article shall:

(1) make every reasonable effort to contact the defendant not later than the end of the first working day after the date on which the attorney is appointed and to interview the defendant as soon as practicable after the attorney is appointed; and

(2) represent the defendant until charges are dismissed, the defendant is acquitted, appeals are exhausted, or the attorney is relieved of his duties by the court or replaced by other counsel after a finding of good cause is entered on the record.

(k) A court may replace an attorney who violates Subsection (j)(1) with other counsel. A majority of the judges of the county courts and statutory county courts or the district courts, as appropriate, trying criminal cases in the county may remove from consideration for appointment an attorney who intentionally or repeatedly violates Subsection (j)(1).

(*l*) Procedures adopted under Subsection (a) must include procedures and financial standards for determining whether a defendant is indigent. The procedures and standards shall apply to each defendant in the county equally, regardless of whether the defendant is in custody or has been released on bail.

(m) In determining whether a defendant is indigent, the court or the courts' designee may consider the defendant's income, source of income, assets, property owned, outstanding obligations, necessary expenses, the number and ages of dependents, and spousal income that is available to the defendant. The court or the courts' designee may not consider whether the defendant has posted or is capable of posting bail, except to the extent that it reflects the defendant's financial circumstances as measured by the considerations listed in this subsection.

(n) A defendant who requests a determination of indigency and appointment of counsel shall:

(1) complete under oath a questionnaire concerning his financial resources;

(2) respond under oath to an examination regarding his financial resources by the judge or magistrate responsible for determining whether the defendant is indigent; or

(3) complete the questionnaire and respond to examination by the judge or magistrate.

(o) Before making a determination of whether a defendant is indigent, the court shall request the defendant to sign under oath a statement substantially in the following form:

"On this _____ day of _____, 20___, I have been advised by the (name of the court) Court of my right to representation by counsel in the trial of the charge pending against me. I certify that I am without means to employ counsel of my own choosing and I hereby request the court to appoint counsel for me. (signature of the defendant)"

(p) A defendant who is determined by the court to be indigent is presumed to remain indigent for the remainder of the proceedings in the case unless a material change in the defendant's financial circumstances occurs. If there is a material change in financial circumstances after a determination of indigency or non-indigency is made, the defendant, the defendant's counsel, or the attorney representing the state may move for reconsideration of the determination.

(q) A written or oral statement elicited under this article or evidence derived from the statement may not be used for any purpose, except to determine the defendant's indigency or to impeach the direct testimony of the defendant. This subsection does not prohibit prosecution of the defendant under Chapter 37, Penal Code.

(r) A court may not threaten to arrest or incarcerate a person solely because the person requests the assistance of counsel.

History of CCP art. 26.04: Acts 1965, 59th Leg., ch. 722, §1, eff. Jan. 1, 1966. Amended by Acts 1987, 70th Leg., ch. 979, §2, eff. Sept. 1, 1987; Acts 2001, 77th Leg., ch. 906, §6, eff. Jan. 1, 2002.

See also TRAP 20.2.

ANNOTATIONS

Roe v. Flores-Ortega, 528 U.S. 470, 478, 120 S.Ct. 1029, 1035 (2000). "In those cases where the defendant neither instructs counsel to file an appeal nor asks that an appeal not be taken, we believe the question whether counsel has performed deficiently by not filing a notice of appeal is best answered by first asking a separate, but antecedent, question: whether counsel in fact consulted with the defendant about an appeal. We employ the term 'consult' to convey a specific meaning—advising the defendant about the advantages and disadvantages of taking an appeal, and making a reasonable effort to discover the defendant's wishes. If counsel has consulted with the defendant, the question of deficient performance is easily answered: Counsel performs in a professionally unreasonable manner only by failing to follow the defendant's express instructions with respect to an appeal. If counsel has not consulted with the defendant, the court must in turn ask a second, and subsidiary question: whether counsel's failure to consult with the defendant itself constitutes deficient performance. *At 480, 1036:* We ... hold that counsel has a constitutionally-imposed duty to consult with the defendant about an appeal when there is reason to think either (1) that a rational defendant would want to appeal ..., or (2) that this particular defendant reasonably demonstrated to counsel that he was interested in appealing. [C]ourts must take into account all the information counsel knew or should have known."

In re Schulman, 252 S.W.3d 403, ___ (Tex.Crim. App.2008). "Although the defense attorney is required to *file* a motion to withdraw at the same time that he files an *Anders* brief, the court of appeals will not *grant* that motion until: (1) the attorney has sent a copy of his *Anders* brief to his client along with a letter explaining that the defendant has the right to file a *pro se* brief within 30 days, and he has ensured that his client has, at some point, been informed of his right to file a *pro se* PDR; (2) the attorney has informed the court of appeals that he has performed the above duties; (3) the defendant has had time in which to file a *pro se* response; and (4) the court of appeals has itself reviewed the record, the *Anders* brief, and any *pro se* brief. After the completion of these four steps, the court of appeals will either agree that the appeal is wholly frivolous, grant the attorney's motion to withdraw, and dismiss the appeal, or it will determine that there may be plausible grounds for appeal. If the court of appeals decides that there are any colorable claims for appeal, it will: (1) grant the original attorney's motion to withdraw; and (2) abate the case and send it back to the trial court to appoint a new attorney with directions to file a merits brief."

Whitehead v. State, 130 S.W.3d 866, 876 (Tex. Crim.App.2004). "The trial court is not completely free to disbelieve the defendant's allegations concerning his own financial status, but the trial court may disbelieve an allegation if there is a reasonable, articulable basis for doing so, either because there is conflicting evidence or because the evidence submitted is in some manner suspect or determined by the court to be inadequate. *At 877:* Appellant submitted 'an income and expense summary' and a 'net worth statement,' along with a signed affidavit swearing that the information contained in these financial documents was true. [T]he documents served the same purpose as answering a written questionnaire and thus sufficed to meet the requirements of Article 26.04(n)(1)."

Jones v. State, 98 S.W.3d 700, 703-04 (Tex.Crim. App.2003). "[T]he appellant's trial attorney failed to perform his responsibilities under [*Ex parte*] ***Axel***, [757 S.W.2d 369 (Tex.Crim.App.1988)] when he did not contemporaneously file a pro se written notice of appeal with the motion to withdraw [and appellant's affidavit of inability to afford counsel]. However, we should not penalize the appellant for this mistake; nor should the trial court be relieved of its independent duties under ***Axel*** ... to ensure that an indigent defendant is not left without representation when he clearly desires to appeal his case." Held: Appellant was granted an out-of-time appeal.

Ex parte Wilson, 956 S.W.2d 25, 27 (Tex.Crim.App. 1997). "Counsel may not deny a defendant the right or opportunity to avail himself of discretionary review, but counsel need not discuss the merits of such review because a defendant has no right to counsel for discretionary review. [¶] The scope of the duty attached to counsel is governed by the right to which that duty attaches. The right to counsel on an appeal of right, under Art. 26.04, ends with the conclusion of the direct appeal. [¶] We overrule *Jarrett* to the extent it held that an appellate attorney has an obligation to inform a defendant of anything other than the fact that his conviction has been affirmed and he can pursue discretionary review on his own. This information sufficiently protects the defendant's right to file a petition for discretionary review."

Stotts v. Wisser, 894 S.W.2d 366, 367 (Tex.Crim. App.1995). "[A] trial judge does not have discretion to replace appointed trial counsel over the objection of both counsel and the defendant when the only justification for such replacement is the trial judge's personal practice, experience, feelings or preference. Rather, there must be some principled reason, apparent from the record, to justify the trial judge's *sua sponte* replacement of appointed counsel. [¶] [A]n attorney is appointed to represent a defendant rather than as an aid or assistant to other appointed counsel."

Harville v. State, 591 S.W.2d 864, 869 (Tex.Crim. App.1979). Article 26.04 "is not applicable when the defendant is represented by retained counsel."

Empy v. State, 571 S.W.2d 526, 528 (Tex.Crim.App. 1978). We construe Article 26.04 "to require the appointment of counsel only when the court knows it will assess punishment including imprisonment or when the trial is before a jury where the possible punishment authorized includes imprisonment. A defendant is not *punishable* by imprisonment if he is unrepresented by counsel unless he waives counsel."

Ex parte Bain, 568 S.W.2d 356, 361 (Tex.Crim.App. 1978). "[A] trial court may not force an accused to accept an attorney if he wishes to waive representation and defend himself. [I]f an accused is solvent, he should be given an opportunity to and be required to employ his own attorney or attorneys for the trial...."

Ex parte King, 550 S.W.2d 691, 694 (Tex.Crim.App. 1977). Relatives "are not legally bound to pay for the expenses of an accused in hiring counsel. Even though they assist him in putting up a bond for his appearance, further obligation is not incurred. Even though ... relatives of an accused have money, this does not mean a defendant is not indigent."

Griffin v. State, 489 S.W.2d 290, 291-92 (Tex.Crim. App.1973). "[W]here there is a showing that there has been a failure to comply with the mandatory provisions of this article, reversal is ordinarily called for without any question of harm or prejudice."

Massingill v. State, 8 S.W.3d 733, 737 (Tex.App.—Austin 1999, pet. ref'd). "'[A]ppointment of counsel for an indigent is required at every stage of a criminal proceeding where substantial rights of a criminal accused may be affected.' Once the trial court determines that the defendant is indigent and entitled to appointed counsel, there is a presumption that the defendant remains indigent unless shown otherwise. Because the 30-day period following sentencing was a critical stage of the proceedings, the district court should have appointed substitute counsel when it permitted trial counsel to withdraw."

In re Behee, 987 S.W.2d 903, 905 (Tex.App.—Waco 1999, orig. proceeding). "The statute allows [judge] to reconsider the determination of [appellant's] indigency upon a motion that there has been a material change in his circumstances. Here, however, there was no hearing to reconsider that determination. The sole reason for [judge's] action that is apparent in the record is that [appellant] had posted bond—a situation specifically prohibited under the statute. [¶] Under these circumstances, [judge] acted outside his statutory authority and abused his discretion in terminating the appointment of counsel."

Johnson v. State, 894 S.W.2d 529, 533 (Tex.App.—Austin 1995, no pet.). "The sole purpose of an indigency hearing is to determine the purely factual matter of whether a defendant can afford to employ counsel. [A]ppellant was not entitled to have the trial court appoint counsel for her at the indigency hearing."

ARTS. 26.041 TO 26.043. REPEALED
Repealed by Acts 2001, 77th Leg., ch. 906, §15, eff. Jan. 1, 2002.

ART. 26.044. PUBLIC DEFENDER

(a) In this chapter:

(1) "Governmental entity" includes a county, a group of counties, a branch or agency of a county, an administrative judicial region created by Section 74.042, Government Code, and any entity created under the Interlocal Cooperation Act as permitted by Chapter 791, Government Code.

(2) "Public defender" means a governmental entity or nonprofit corporation:

(A) operating under a written agreement with a governmental entity, other than an individual judge or court;

(B) using public funds; and

(C) providing legal representation and services to indigent defendants accused of a crime or juvenile offense, as those terms are defined by Section 71.001, Government Code.

(b) The commissioners court of any county, on written approval of a judge of a county court, statutory county court, or district court trying criminal cases in the county, may appoint a governmental entity or non-profit corporation to serve as a public defender. The commissioners courts of two or more counties may enter into a written agreement to jointly appoint and fund a regional public defender. In appointing a public defender under this subsection, the commissioners court shall specify or the commissioners courts shall jointly specify, if appointing a regional public defender:

(1) the duties of the public defender;

(2) the types of cases to which the public defender may be appointed under Article 26.04(f) and the courts in which the public defender may be required to appear;

(3) whether the public defender is appointed to serve a term or serve at the pleasure of the commissioners court or the commissioners courts; and

(4) if the public defender is appointed to serve a term, the term of appointment and the procedures for removing the public defender.

(c) Before appointing a public defender under Subsection (b), the commissioners court or commissioners courts shall solicit proposals for the public defender. A proposal must include:

(1) a budget for the public defender, including salaries;

(2) a description of each personnel position, including the chief public defender position;

(3) the maximum allowable caseloads for each attorney employed by the proponent;

(4) provisions for personnel training;

(5) a description of anticipated overhead costs for the public defender; and

(6) policies regarding the use of licensed investigators and expert witnesses by the proponent.

(d) After considering each proposal for the public defender submitted by a governmental entity or non-profit corporation, the commissioners court or commissioners courts shall select a proposal that reasonably demonstrates that the proponent will provide adequate quality representation for indigent defendants in the county or counties.

(e) The total cost of the proposal may not be the sole consideration in selecting a proposal.

(f) To be eligible for appointment as a public defender, the governmental entity or nonprofit corporation must be directed by a chief public defender who:

(1) is a member of the State Bar of Texas;

(2) has practiced law for at least three years; and

(3) has substantial experience in the practice of criminal law.

(g) A public defender is entitled to receive funds for personnel costs and expenses incurred in operating as a public defender in amounts fixed by the commissioners court and paid out of the appropriate county fund, or jointly fixed by the commissioners courts and proportionately paid out of each appropriate county fund if the public defender serves more than one county.

(h) A public defender may employ attorneys, licensed investigators, and other personnel necessary to perform the duties of the public defender as specified by the commissioners court or commissioners courts under Subsection (b)(1).

(i) Except as authorized by this article, the chief public defender or an attorney employed by a public defender may not:

(1) engage in the private practice of criminal law; or

(2) accept anything of value not authorized by this article for services rendered under this article.

(j) A public defender may refuse an appointment under Article 26.04(f) if:

(1) a conflict of interest exists;

(2) the public defender has insufficient resources to provide adequate representation for the defendant;

(3) the public defender is incapable of providing representation for the defendant in accordance with the rules of professional conduct; or

(4) the public defender shows other good cause for refusing the appointment.

CCP ART. 26.044

(**k**) The judge may remove a public defender who violates a provision of Subsection (i).

(*l*) A public defender may investigate the financial condition of any person the public defender is appointed to represent. The defender shall report the results of the investigation to the appointing judge. The judge may hold a hearing to determine if the person is indigent and entitled to representation under this article.

(**m**) If it is necessary that an attorney other than a public defender be appointed, the attorney is entitled to the compensation provided by Article 26.05 of this code.

History of CCP art. 26.044: Acts 1985, 69th Leg., ch. 480, §17, eff. Sept. 1, 1985. Amended by Acts 1987, 70th Leg., ch. 167, §4.03(a), eff. Sept. 1, 1987; Acts 2001, 77th Leg., ch. 906, §7, eff. Jan. 1, 2002; Acts 2005, 79th Leg., ch. 965, §6, eff. Sept. 1, 2005.

ARTS. 26.045 TO 26.049. REPEALED

Repealed by Acts 2001, 77th Leg., ch. 906, §15, eff. Jan. 1, 2002.

ART. 26.05. COMPENSATION OF COUNSEL APPOINTED TO DEFEND

(**a**) A counsel, other than an attorney with a public defender, appointed to represent a defendant in a criminal proceeding, including a habeas corpus hearing, shall be paid a reasonable attorney's fee for performing the following services, based on the time and labor required, the complexity of the case, and the experience and ability of the appointed counsel:

(**1**) time spent in court making an appearance on behalf of the defendant as evidenced by a docket entry, time spent in trial, and time spent in a proceeding in which sworn oral testimony is elicited;

(**2**) reasonable and necessary time spent out of court on the case, supported by any documentation that the court requires;

(**3**) preparation of an appellate brief and preparation and presentation of oral argument to a court of appeals or the Court of Criminal Appeals; and

(**4**) preparation of a motion for rehearing.

(**b**) All payments made under this article shall be paid in accordance with a schedule of fees adopted by formal action of the judges of the county courts, statutory county courts, and district courts trying criminal cases in each county. On adoption of a schedule of fees as provided by this subsection, a copy of the schedule shall be sent to the commissioners court of the county.

🅐 (**c**) Each fee schedule adopted shall state reasonable fixed rates or minimum and maximum hourly rates, taking into consideration reasonable and necessary overhead costs and the availability of qualified attorneys willing to accept the stated rates, and shall provide a form for the appointed counsel to itemize the types of services performed. No payment shall be made under this article until the form for itemizing the services performed is submitted to the judge presiding over the proceedings and the judge approves the payment. If the judge disapproves the requested amount of payment, the judge shall make written findings stating the amount of payment that the judge approves and each reason for approving an amount different from the requested amount. An attorney whose request for payment is disapproved or is not otherwise acted on by the 60th day after the date the request for payment is submitted may appeal the disapproval or failure to act by filing a motion with the presiding judge of the administrative judicial region. On the filing of a motion, the presiding judge of the administrative judicial region shall review the disapproval of payment or failure to act and determine the appropriate amount of payment. In reviewing the disapproval or failure to act, the presiding judge of the administrative judicial region may conduct a hearing. Not later than the 45th day after the date an application for payment of a fee is submitted under this article, the commissioners court shall pay to the appointed counsel the amount that is approved by the presiding judge of the administrative judicial region and that is in accordance with the fee schedule for that county.

(**d**) A counsel in a noncapital case, other than an attorney with a public defender, appointed to represent a defendant under this code shall be reimbursed for reasonable and necessary expenses, including expenses for investigation and for mental health and other experts. Expenses incurred with prior court approval shall be reimbursed in the same manner provided for capital cases by Articles 26.052(f) and (g), and expenses incurred without prior court approval shall be reimbursed in the manner provided for capital cases by Article 26.052(h).

(**e**) A majority of the judges of the county courts and statutory county courts or the district courts, as appropriate, trying criminal cases in the county may remove an attorney from consideration for appointment if, after a hearing, it is shown that the attorney submitted a claim for legal services not performed by the attorney.

★

(f) All payments made under this article shall be paid from the general fund of the county in which the prosecution was instituted or habeas corpus hearing held and may be included as costs of court.

(g) If the court determines that a defendant has financial resources that enable him to offset in part or in whole the costs of the legal services provided, including any expenses and costs, the court shall order the defendant to pay during the pendency of the charges or, if convicted, as court costs the amount that it finds the defendant is able to pay.

(h) Reimbursement of expenses incurred for purposes of investigation or expert testimony may be paid directly to a private investigator licensed under Chapter 1702, Occupations Code, or to an expert witness in the manner designated by appointed counsel and approved by the court.

 (i) The indigent defense representation fund is a separate account in the general revenue fund. The fund:

(1) consists of criminal fees collected under Section 133.107, Local Government Code; and

(2) may be used only for the purposes for which the fair defense account established under Section 71.058, Government Code, may be used, including compensating appointed counsel in accordance with this code.

History of CCP art. 26.05: Acts 1965, 59th Leg., ch. 722, §1, eff. Jan. 1, 1966. Amended by Acts 1969, 61st Leg., ch. 347, §1, eff. May 27, 1969; Acts 1971, 62nd Leg., ch. 520, §1, eff. Aug. 30, 1971; Acts 1973, 63rd Leg., ch. 426, art. 3, §3, eff. June 14, 1973; Acts 1981, 67th Leg., ch. 291, §106, eff. Sept. 1, 1981; Acts 1987, 70th Leg., ch. 979, §3, eff. Sept. 1, 1987; Acts 1999, 76th Leg., ch. 837, §1, eff. Sept. 1, 1999; Acts 2001, 77th Leg., ch. 906, §8 (eff. Jan. 1, 2002), ch. 1420, §14.734 (eff. Sept. 1, 2001); Acts 2007, 80th Leg., ch. 1014, §1, eff. Sept. 1, 2007.

ANNOTATIONS

Williams v. State, 958 S.W.2d 186, 194 (Tex.Crim. App.1997). "[A]n indigent defendant is entitled, upon proper request, to make his *Ake (v. Oklahoma)* motion [for an expert] *ex parte*. The trial judge erred in overruling appellant's request to make his *Ake* motion *ex parte*. *At 195:* The state has failed to meet its burden of proving that the disclosure did not contribute to the jury's verdict at punishment."

Ex parte Gonzales, 945 S.W.2d 830, 832-33 (Tex. Crim.App.1997). "The issue … is whether a defendant can be held in contempt and confined for violating an order made pursuant to [CCP] art. 26.05(e) [now 26.05(g)]. *At 834:* [W]e hold that, at a minimum, a trial court may not order a defendant confined for failure to repay the costs of his legal defense pursuant to art. 26.05(e) [now 26.05(g)] unless the court considers the defendant's ability to make the payment. The trial court's power to order reimbursement should be limited to the extent a defendant is reasonably able to do so. If that requirement is followed, there is no reason a defendant could not be held in contempt and confined for failure to satisfy a court's order under art. 26.05."

Curry v. Wilson, 853 S.W.2d 40, 45 (Tex.Crim.App. 1993). "It is true that, when it ordered applicant to repay the county, the trial court no longer had authority to determine the issues presented in the indictment against applicant because the jury had already returned a verdict of not guilty. However, [CCP art. 26.05(e), now 26.05(g)] provided it with continuing authority to order repayment of the county funds expended for applicant's appointed legal defense…. *At 46:* [I]t is not an inherent violation of due process for the State to take reasonable steps to collect on expenditures made on behalf of those who have the ability to off-set the state's expenses."

De Freece v. State, 848 S.W.2d 150, 159 (Tex.Crim. App.1993). "Once it is shown that insanity will be a significant factor at trial, the trial court abuses its discretion in failing to appoint, or to give 'prior … approval' to 'reasonable expenses incurred' by counsel for the accused to obtain, a competent psychiatrist to assist in the evaluation, preparation and presentation of his insanity defense."

Mullings v. Morgan, 891 S.W.2d 15, 16-17 (Tex. App.—Eastland 1994, no pet.). CCP art. 26.05(e), now 26.05(g) "does not authorize the sale of a specific asset to offset costs and does not provide that a defendant can be ordered to deliver an asset for a forced sale to offset costs."

Coleman v. State, 860 S.W.2d 496, 498 (Tex.App.— Dallas 1993, no pet.). "The trial court has discretion in determining the proper value of the legal fees it orders a defendant to pay under article 26.05. However, due process considerations require evidence in the record to provide a factual basis for the *amount* set by the trial court."

Sampson v. State, 854 S.W.2d 659, 662 (Tex. App.—Dallas 1992, no pet.). "The trial court has no authority to order payment of attorney fees accumulated prior to formal appointment."

Johnson v. State, 746 S.W.2d 791, 793 (Tex.App.—Corpus Christi 1987, pet. ref'd). "[A]n appellant complaining of improper action under [CCP] art. 26.05 … must present and preserve evidence of harm or injury."

ART. 26.05-1. RENUMBERED

Renumbered as Art. 26.056 by Acts 1987, 70th Leg., ch. 167, §5.02(2), eff. Sept. 1, 1987.

ART. 26.050. REPEALED

Repealed by Acts 2001, 77th Leg., ch. 906, §15, eff. Jan. 1, 2002.

ART. 26.051. INDIGENT INMATE DEFENSE

(a) In this article:

(1) "Board" means the Texas Board of Criminal Justice.

A (2) "Correctional institutions division" means the correctional institutions division of the Texas Department of Criminal Justice.

(b), (c) Repealed by Acts 2007, 80th Leg., ch. 1014, §7, eff. Sept. 1, 2007.

A (d) A court shall:

(1) notify the board if it determines that a defendant before the court is indigent and is an inmate charged with an offense committed while in the custody of the correctional institutions division or a correctional facility authorized by Section 495.001, Government Code; and

(2) request that the board provide legal representation for the inmate.

(e) The board shall provide legal representation for inmates described by Subsection (d) of this section. The board may employ attorneys, support staff, and any other personnel required to provide legal representation for those inmates. All personnel employed under this article are directly responsible to the board in the performance of their duties. The board shall pay all fees and costs associated with providing legal representation for those inmates.

(f) Repealed by Acts 1993, 73rd Leg., ch. 988, §7.02, eff. Sept. 1, 1993.

(g) The court shall appoint an attorney other than an attorney provided by the board if the court determines for any of the following reasons that a conflict of interest could arise from the use of an attorney provided by the board under Subsection (e) of this article:

(1) the case involves more than one inmate and the representation of more than one inmate could impair the attorney's effectiveness;

(2) the case is appealed and the court is satisfied that conflict of interest would prevent the presentation of a good faith allegation of ineffective assistance of counsel by a trial attorney provided by the board; or

(3) any conflict of interest exists under the Texas Disciplinary Rules of Professional Conduct of the State Bar of Texas that precludes representation by an attorney appointed by the board.

A (h) When the court appoints an attorney other than an attorney provided by the board:

(1) except as otherwise provided by this article, the inmate's legal defense is subject to Articles 1.051, 26.04, 26.05, and 26.052, as applicable; and

(2) the county in which a facility of the correctional institutions division or a correctional facility authorized by Section 495.001, Government Code, is located shall pay from its general fund the total costs of the aggregate amount allowed and awarded by the court for attorney compensation and expenses under Article 26.05 or 26.052, as applicable.

E (i) The state shall reimburse a county for attorney compensation and expenses awarded under Subsection (h). A court seeking reimbursement for a county shall certify to the comptroller of public accounts the amount of compensation and expenses for which the county is entitled to be reimbursed under this article. Not later than the 60th day after the date the comptroller receives from the court the request for reimbursement, the comptroller shall issue a warrant to the county in the amount certified by the court.

History of CCP art. 26.051: Acts 1990, 71st Leg., 6th C.S., ch. 15, §2, eff. June 14, 1990. Amended by Acts 1991, 72nd Leg., ch. 719, §1, eff. Sept. 1, 1991; Acts 1993, 73rd Leg., ch. 988, §§7.01, 7.02, eff. Sept. 1, 1993; Acts 2007, 80th Leg., ch. 1014, §§2, 3, 7, eff. Sept. 1, 2007.

ART. 26.052. APPOINTMENT OF COUNSEL IN DEATH PENALTY CASE; REIMBURSEMENT OF INVESTIGATIVE EXPENSES

(a) Notwithstanding any other provision of this chapter, this article establishes procedures in death penalty cases for appointment and payment of counsel to represent indigent defendants at trial and on direct appeal and to apply for writ of certiorari in the United States Supreme Court.

(b) If a county is served by a public defender's office, trial counsel and counsel for direct appeal or to apply for a writ of certiorari may be appointed as provided by the guidelines established by the public defender's

✦

office. In all other cases in which the death penalty is sought, counsel shall be appointed as provided by this article.

(c) A local selection committee is created in each administrative judicial region created under Section 74.042, Government Code. The administrative judge of the judicial region shall appoint the members of the committee. A committee shall have not less than four members, including:

(1) the administrative judge of the judicial region;

(2) at least one district judge;

(3) a representative from the local bar association; and

(4) at least one practitioner who is board certified by the State Bar of Texas in criminal law.

(d)(1) The committee shall adopt standards for the qualification of attorneys to be appointed to represent indigent defendants in capital cases in which the death penalty is sought.

☠ *Subsection (2) below was amended by Acts 2005, 79th Leg., ch. 787, §14, enacted May 28, 2005, effective Sept. 1, 2005, without reference to the conflicting amendment made by Acts 2005, 79th Leg., ch. 965, §7, enacted May 28, 2005, effective Sept. 1, 2005. For resolving conflicts, see p. V.*

(2) The standards must require that a trial attorney appointed as lead counsel to a capital case or an attorney appointed as lead counsel in the direct appeal of a death penalty case:

☠ *Subsection (2) below was amended by Acts 2005, 79th Leg., ch. 965, §7, enacted May 28, 2005, effective Sept. 1, 2005, without reference to the conflicting amendment made by Acts 2005, 79th Leg., ch. 787, §14, enacted May 28, 2005, effective Sept. 1, 2005. For resolving conflicts, see p. V.*

(2) The standards must require that a trial attorney appointed as lead counsel to a capital case or an attorney appointed as lead appellate counsel in the direct appeal of a capital case:

(A) be a member of the State Bar of Texas;

(B) exhibit proficiency and commitment to providing quality representation to defendants in death penalty cases;

(C) have not been found by a federal or state court to have rendered ineffective assistance of counsel during the trial or appeal of any capital case;

(D) have at least five years of experience in criminal litigation;

(E) have tried to a verdict as lead defense counsel a significant number of felony cases, including homicide trials and other trials for offenses punishable as second or first degree felonies or capital felonies;

(F) have trial experience in:

(i) the use of and challenges to mental health or forensic expert witnesses; and

(ii) investigating and presenting mitigating evidence at the penalty phase of a death penalty trial; and

(G) have participated in continuing legal education courses or other training relating to criminal defense in death penalty cases.

(3) The committee shall prominently post the standards in each district clerk's office in the region with a list of attorneys qualified for appointment.

(4) Not later than the second anniversary of the date an attorney is placed on the list of attorneys qualified for appointment in death penalty cases and each year following the second anniversary, the attorney must present proof to the committee that the attorney has successfully completed the minimum continuing legal education requirements of the State Bar of Texas, including a course or other form of training relating to the defense of death penalty cases. The committee shall remove the attorney's name from the list of qualified attorneys if the attorney fails to provide the committee with proof of completion of the continuing legal education requirements.

(e) The presiding judge of the district court in which a capital felony case is filed shall appoint two attorneys, at least one of whom must be qualified under this chapter, to represent an indigent defendant as soon as practicable after charges are filed, unless the state gives notice in writing that the state will not seek the death penalty.

(f) Appointed counsel may file with the trial court a pretrial ex parte confidential request for advance payment of expenses to investigate potential defenses. The request for expenses must state:

(1) the type of investigation to be conducted;

(2) specific facts that suggest the investigation will result in admissible evidence; and

(3) an itemized list of anticipated expenses for each investigation.

(g) The court shall grant the request for advance payment of expenses in whole or in part if the request is reasonable. If the court denies in whole or in part the request for expenses, the court shall:

(1) state the reasons for the denial in writing;

(2) attach the denial to the confidential request; and

(3) submit the request and denial as a sealed exhibit to the record.

(h) Counsel may incur expenses without prior approval of the court. On presentation of a claim for reimbursement, the court shall order reimbursement of counsel for the expenses, if the expenses are reasonably necessary and reasonably incurred.

(i) If the indigent defendant is convicted of a capital felony and sentenced to death, the defendant is entitled to be represented by competent counsel on appeal and to apply for a writ of certiorari to the United States Supreme Court.

(j) As soon as practicable after a death sentence is imposed in a capital felony case, the presiding judge of the convicting court shall appoint counsel to represent an indigent defendant on appeal and to apply for a writ of certiorari, if appropriate.

(k) The court may not appoint an attorney as counsel on appeal if the attorney represented the defendant at trial, unless:

(1) the defendant and the attorney request the appointment on the record; and

(2) the court finds good cause to make the appointment.

(*l*) An attorney appointed under this article to represent a defendant at trial or on direct appeal is compensated as provided by Article 26.05 from county funds. Advance payment of expenses anticipated or reimbursement of expenses incurred for purposes of investigation or expert testimony may be paid directly to a private investigator licensed under Chapter 1702, Occupations Code, or to an expert witness in the manner designated by appointed counsel and approved by the court.

(m) The local selection committee shall annually review the list of attorneys posted under Subsection (d) to ensure that each listed attorney satisfies the requirements under this chapter.

History of CCP art. 26.052: Acts 1995, 74th Leg., ch. 319, §2, eff. Sept. 1, 1995. Amended by Acts 1999, 76th Leg., ch. 837, §2, eff. Sept. 1, 1999; Acts 2001, 77th Leg., ch. 906, §9 (eff. Jan. 1, 2002), ch. 1420, §14.735 (eff. Sept. 1, 2001); Acts 2005, 79th Leg., ch. 787, §14 (eff. Sept. 1, 2005), ch. 965, §7 (eff. Sept. 1, 2005).

Kirk v. State, 199 S.W.3d 467, 473 (Tex.App.—Fort Worth 2006, pet. ref'd). "A failure to comply with [CCP art.] 26.052 is susceptible to a harmless error analysis under [TRAP] 44.2(b)."

ART. 26.053. PUBLIC DEFENDER IN RANDALL COUNTY[1]

(a) The Commissioners Court of Randall County may appoint an attorney to serve as a public defender. The public defender serves at the pleasure of the commissioners court.

(b) To be eligible for appointment as a public defender, a person must be a member of the State Bar of Texas.

(c) With the approval of the commissioners court, the public defender may employ assistant public defenders, investigators, secretaries, and other necessary personnel. An assistant public defender must be a licensed attorney and may perform the duties of a public defender under this article.

(d) A public defender's office consists of the public defender and the personnel employed by the public defender under Subsection (c).

(e) A public defender is entitled to receive an annual salary in an amount set by the commissioners court. Subchapter B, Chapter 152, Local Government Code, applies to the compensation of personnel and the payment of office expenses in the public defender's office.

(f) Except as authorized by this article, a public defender or an assistant public defender may not:

(1) engage in the private practice of law; or

(2) accept anything of value not authorized by this article for services rendered under this article.

(g) The commissioners court may remove a public defender or an assistant public defender who violates Subsection (f).

(h) The public defender or an assistant public defender shall represent each indigent person who is:

(1) charged with a criminal offense in Randall County punishable by confinement or imprisonment;

(2) a minor who is a party to a juvenile delinquency proceeding in the county; or

(3) entitled to representation under:

(A) Chapter 462, Health and Safety Code; or

(B) Subtitle C or D, Title 7, Health and Safety Code.

(i) If at any stage of the proceeding the judge determines that a conflict of interest exists between the public defender and the indigent person, the judge may appoint another attorney to represent the person. The attorney must be licensed to practice law in this state and is entitled to the compensation provided by Article 26.05.

(j) The public defender's office shall investigate the financial condition of any person the public defender is appointed to represent. The public defender's office shall report the results of the investigation to the appointing judge. The judge may hold a hearing to determine if the person is indigent and entitled to representation under this article.

(k) Except for the provisions relating to daily appearance fees, Article 26.05 applies to the public defender and an assistant public defender.

(l) The commissioners court may accept gifts and grants from any source to finance an adequate and effective public defender program.

1. **Editor's note:** Acts 2001, 77th Leg., ch. 906, §15, eff. Jan. 1, 2002, repealed Art. 26.053 "as added by S.B. 1781, 77th Leg." The repealer probably should have read "as added by S.B. 1789, 77th Leg."

History of CCP art. 26.053: Acts 2001, 77th Leg., ch. 184, §1, eff. May 21, 2001.

ART. 26.054. REPEALED

Repealed by Acts 2001, 77th Leg., ch. 906, §15, eff. Jan. 1, 2002.

ART. 26.055. REPEALED

Repealed by Acts 2007, 80th Leg., ch. 1014, §7, eff. Sept. 1, 2007.

ART. 26.056. CONTRIBUTION FROM STATE IN CERTAIN COUNTIES

Sec. 1. A county in which a state training school for delinquent children is located shall pay from its general fund the first $250 of fees awarded for court-appointed counsel under Article 26.05 toward defending a child committed to the school from another county who is being prosecuted for a felony or misdemeanor in the county where the training school is located.

Sec. 2. If the fees awarded for counsel compensation are in excess of $250, the court shall certify the amount in excess of $250 to the Comptroller of Public Accounts of the State of Texas. The Comptroller shall issue a warrant to the court-appointed counsel in the amount certified to the comptroller by the court.

History of CCP art. 26.056: Acts 1967, 60th Leg., ch. 307, §1, eff. Aug. 28, 1967. Renumbered from Art. 26.05-1 by Acts 1987, 70th Leg., ch. 167, §5.02(2), eff. Sept. 1, 1987.

ART. 26.057. COST OF EMPLOYMENT OF COUNSEL FOR CERTAIN MINORS

If a juvenile has been transferred to a criminal court under Section 54.02, Family Code, and if a court appoints counsel for the juvenile under Article 26.04 of this code, the county that pays for the counsel has a cause of action against a parent or other person who is responsible for the support of the juvenile and is financially able to employ counsel for the juvenile but refuses to do so. The county may recover its cost of payment to the appointed counsel and may recover attorney's fees necessary to prosecute the cause of action against the parent or other person.

History of CCP art. 26.057: Acts 1987, 70th Leg., ch. 979, §4, eff. Sept. 1, 1987. Renumbered from Art. 26.056 by Acts 1989, 71st Leg., ch. 2, §16.01(8), eff. Aug. 28, 1989.

ART. 26.058. REPEALED

Repealed by Acts 2001, 77th Leg., ch. 906, §15, eff. Jan. 1, 2002.

ART. 26.06. ELECTED OFFICIALS NOT TO BE APPOINTED

No court may appoint an elected county, district or state official to represent a person accused of crime, unless the official has notified the court of his availability for appointment. If an official has notified the court of his availability and is appointed as counsel, he may decline the appointment if he determines that it is in the best interest of his office to do so. Nothing in this Code shall modify any statutory provision for legislative continuance.

History of CCP art. 26.06: Acts 1965, 59th Leg., ch. 722, §1, eff. Jan. 1, 1966.

ART. 26.07. NAME AS STATED IN INDICTMENT

When the defendant is arraigned, his name, as stated in the indictment, shall be distinctly called; and unless he suggest by himself or counsel that he is not indicted by his true name, it shall be taken that his name is truly set forth, and he shall not thereafter be allowed to deny the same by way of defense.

History of CCP art. 26.07: Acts 1965, 59th Leg., ch. 722, §1, eff. Jan. 1, 1966.

ANNOTATIONS

Wynn v. State, 864 S.W.2d 539, 540 (Tex.Crim.App. 1993). "[T]he correction of a defendant's name in the indictment is governed by [CCP] arts. 26.07 and 26.08."

London v. State, 739 S.W.2d 842, 844 (Tex.Crim. App.1987). "Although count one of the indictment was dismissed, it could still be looked to in order to satisfy the requirement of naming [D]."

ART. 26.08. IF DEFENDANT SUGGESTS DIFFERENT NAME

If the defendant, or his counsel for him, suggests that he bears some name different from that stated in the indictment, the same shall be noted upon the minutes of the court, the indictment corrected by inserting therein the name of the defendant as suggested by himself or his counsel for him, the style of the case changed so as to give his true name, and the cause proceed as if the true name had been first recited in the indictment.

History of CCP art. 26.08: Acts 1965, 59th Leg., ch. 722, §1, eff. Jan. 1, 1966.

ANNOTATIONS

Kelley v. State, 823 S.W.2d 300, 302 (Tex.Crim.App. 1992). "The name change of [D] does not constitute an amendment as that term is perceived by [CCP art.] 28.10.... [¶] [CCP art.] 26.08 ... controls. The act of changing the name of the defendant is a ministerial act."

ART. 26.09. IF ACCUSED REFUSES TO GIVE HIS REAL NAME

If the defendant alleges that he is not indicted by his true name, and refuses to say what his real name is, the cause shall proceed as if the name stated in the indictment were true; and the defendant shall not be allowed to contradict the same by way of defense.

History of CCP art. 26.09: Acts 1965, 59th Leg., ch. 722, §1, eff. Jan. 1, 1966.

ART. 26.10. WHERE NAME IS UNKNOWN

A defendant described as a person whose name is unknown may have the indictment so corrected as to give therein his true name.

History of CCP art. 26.10: Acts 1965, 59th Leg., ch. 722, §1, eff. Jan. 1, 1966.

ART. 26.11. INDICTMENT READ

The name of the accused having been called, if no suggestion, such as is spoken of in the four preceding Articles, be made, or being made is disposed of as before directed, the indictment shall be read, and the defendant asked whether he is guilty or not, as therein charged.

History of CCP art. 26.11: Acts 1965, 59th Leg., ch. 722, §1, eff. Jan. 1, 1966.

ANNOTATIONS

Decker v. State, 734 S.W.2d 393, 394 (Tex.App.—Houston [1st Dist.] 1987, pet. ref'd). "Though the State may elect to proceed to trial on a lesser included offense, the right of election belongs to the State, not the defendant."

ART. 26.12. PLEA OF NOT GUILTY ENTERED

If the defendant answers that he is not guilty, such plea shall be entered upon the minutes of the court; if he refuses to answer, the plea of not guilty shall in like manner be entered.

History of CCP art. 26.12: Acts 1965, 59th Leg., ch. 722, §1, eff. Jan. 1, 1966.

ART. 26.13. PLEA OF GUILTY

(a) Prior to accepting a plea of guilty or a plea of nolo contendere, the court shall admonish the defendant of:

(1) the range of the punishment attached to the offense;

(2) the fact that the recommendation of the prosecuting attorney as to punishment is not binding on the court. Provided that the court shall inquire as to the existence of any plea bargaining agreements between the state and the defendant and, in the event that such an agreement exists, the court shall inform the defendant whether it will follow or reject such agreement in open court and before any finding on the plea. Should the court reject any such agreement, the defendant shall be permitted to withdraw his plea of guilty or nolo contendere;

(3) the fact that if the punishment assessed does not exceed the punishment recommended by the prosecutor and agreed to by the defendant and his attorney, the trial court must give its permission to the defendant before he may prosecute an appeal on any matter in the case except for those matters raised by written motions filed prior to trial;

(4) the fact that if the defendant is not a citizen of the United States of America, a plea of guilty or nolo contendere for the offense charged may result in deportation, the exclusion from admission to this country, or the denial of naturalization under federal law;

(5) the fact that the defendant will be required to meet the registration requirements of Chapter 62, if the defendant is convicted of or placed on deferred adjudication for an offense for which a person is subject to registration under that chapter; and

E (6) the fact that it is unlawful for the defendant to possess or transfer a firearm or ammunition if the defendant is convicted of a misdemeanor involving family violence, as defined by Section 71.004, Family Code.

(b) No plea of guilty or plea of nolo contendere shall be accepted by the court unless it appears that the defendant is mentally competent and the plea is free and voluntary.

(c) In admonishing the defendant as herein provided, substantial compliance by the court is sufficient, unless the defendant affirmatively shows that he was not aware of the consequences of his plea and that he was misled or harmed by the admonishment of the court.

(d) The court may make the admonitions required by this article either orally or in writing. If the court makes the admonitions in writing, it must receive a statement signed by the defendant and the defendant's attorney that he understands the admonitions and is aware of the consequences of his plea. If the defendant is unable or refuses to sign the statement, the court shall make the admonitions orally.

(e) Before accepting a plea of guilty or a plea of nolo contendere, the court shall inquire as to whether a victim impact statement has been returned to the attorney representing the state and ask for a copy of the statement if one has been returned.

(f) The court must substantially comply with Subsection (e) of this article. The failure of the court to comply with Subsection (e) of this article is not grounds for the defendant to set aside the conviction, sentence, or plea.

(g) Before accepting a plea of guilty or a plea of nolo contendere and on the request of a victim of the offense, the court may assist the victim and the defendant in participating in a victim-offender mediation program.

(h) The court must substantially comply with Subsection (a)(5). The failure of the court to comply with Subsection (a)(5) is not a ground for the defendant to set aside the conviction, sentence, or plea.

(i) Notwithstanding this article, a court shall not order the state or any of its prosecuting attorneys to participate in mediation, dispute resolution, arbitration, or other similar procedures in relation to a criminal prosecution unless upon written consent of the state.

History of CCP art. 26.13: Acts 1965, 59th Leg., ch. 722, §1, eff. Jan. 1, 1966. Amended by Acts 1973, 63rd Leg., ch. 399, §2(A), eff. Jan. 1, 1974; Acts 1975, 64th Leg., ch. 341, §3, eff. June 19, 1975; Acts 1977, 65th Leg., ch. 280, §1, eff. Aug. 29, 1977; Acts 1979, 66th Leg., ch. 524, §1 (eff. Sept. 1, 1979), ch. 561, §1 (eff. Sept. 1, 1979); Acts 1985, 69th Leg., ch. 671, §1 (eff. June 14, 1985), ch. 685, §8(a) (eff. Aug. 26, 1985); Acts 1987, 70th Leg., ch. 443, §1, eff. Aug. 1,

1987; Acts 1991, 72nd Leg., ch. 202, §1, eff. Sept. 1, 1991; Acts 1997, 75th Leg., ch. 670, §4, eff. Sept. 1, 1997; Acts 1999, 76th., ch. 425, §1 (eff. Aug. 30, 1999), ch. 1415, §1 (eff. Sept. 1, 1999); Acts 2001, 77th Leg., ch. 1420, §21.001(8), eff. Sept. 1, 2001; Acts 2005, 79th Leg., ch. 1008, §1.03, eff. Sept. 1, 2005; Acts 2007, 80th Leg., ch. 125, §1, eff. Sept. 1, 2007.

ANNOTATIONS

Generally
Bitterman v. State, 180 S.W.3d 139, 141-42 (Tex. Crim.App.2005). "[I]t is a defendant's right to have the State honor a plea bargain entered into by the defendant in exchange for a guilty plea, after the judge has accepted the plea bargain in open court. ... When a defendant enters into a plea bargain, he waives a number of fundamental constitutional rights, including a trial by jury, the right to confront one's accusers, the right to present witnesses in one's defense, the right to remain silent, and the right to be convicted only by proof beyond a reasonable doubt. [I]f a defendant's plea is made based on a promise given by the State, the State must keep up its part of the agreement or the plea will be rendered involuntary. When the prosecution breaches its promise with respect to an executed plea agreement, the defendant pleads guilty on a false premise, and hence his conviction cannot stand. *At 144:* [W]e hold that Appellant properly preserved the issue of the plea bargain breach by bringing it to the trial court's attention as soon as the error could be cured, in a motion for a new trial."

Gutierrez v. State, 108 S.W.3d 304, 309-10 (Tex. Crim.App.2003). "[I]n the context of revocation proceedings, the legislature has not authorized binding plea agreements, has not required the court to inquire as to the existence of a plea agreement or admonish the defendant pursuant to [Article] 26.13, and has not provided for withdrawal of a plea after sentencing."

Ortiz v. State, 933 S.W.2d 102, 104 (Tex.Crim.App. 1996). "[T]he trial judge 'accepted' the guilty plea to robbery, but did not make any finding on this plea and did not accept or reject the plea agreement. The trial judge would have more accurately followed Art. 26.13 had he not stated that he accepted the plea without *also* making a finding on the plea agreement. [T]he trial judge accepted the plea conditionally while he deferred a final decision until the pre-sentence investigation was complete. He did not adjudicate guilt or accept the plea agreement. [¶] A plea agreement is a contractual arrangement. Until all of the necessary parties agree to the terms of the contract, the agreement is not binding. [T]he trial judge never accepted the plea agreement.

[T]he contract of the plea agreement was never binding on the parties." *See also* ***Ex parte Spicuzza***, 903 S.W.2d 381, 384 (Tex.App.—Houston [1st Dist.] 1995, pet. ref'd).

Ex parte Sims, 868 S.W.2d 803, 804 (Tex.Crim.App. 1993), *overruled on other grounds*, ***Ex parte McJunkins***, 954 S.W.2d 39 (Tex.Crim.App.1997). "When a defendant successfully challenges a conviction obtained through a negotiated plea of guilty, the appropriate remedy is specific performance of the plea agreement, if possible. If specific performance is not possible, the plea must be withdrawn and the parties must be returned to their original positions." *See also* ***Wright v. State***, 158 S.W.3d 590, 593-94 (Tex. App.—San Antonio 2005, pet. ref'd).

DeVary v. State, 615 S.W.2d 739, 740 (Tex.Crim. App.1981). "'[A] defendant may withdraw his guilty plea as a matter of right without assigning reason until … judgment has been pronounced or the case has been taken under advisement. However, where the defendant decides to withdraw his guilty plea after the trial judge takes the case under advisement or pronounces judgment, the withdrawal of such plea is within the sound discretion of the trial court.'"

McGill v. State, 200 S.W.3d 325, 330 (Tex.App.— Dallas 2006, no pet.). "The entry of a valid guilty plea 'has the effect of admitting all material facts alleged in the formal criminal charge.' In a trial before the court, once a defendant enters a valid guilty plea, no constitutional 'fact questions' remain for the purposes of his constitutional right to a factual sufficiency review of the evidence used to convict him. The State is no longer required to prove his guilt beyond a reasonable doubt. In fact, for the purposes of federal due process, a plea of guilty is itself a conviction awaiting only determination of punishment. In Texas, however, the State is also bound by [CCP art. 1.15] to support the plea with sufficient evidence. [¶] In a guilty plea case where the defendant has waived his right to a jury trial, the State must 'introduce evidence into the record showing the guilt of the defendant.' Under this 'procedural safeguard,' there is no requirement that the supporting evidence prove the defendant's guilt beyond a reasonable doubt. Instead, the supporting evidence must simply embrace every essential element of the offense charged. Our review of the record to determine whether the State complied with article 1.15 is not a factual sufficiency review. [¶] We note that in a trial before the court, when evidence is introduced that either makes the defendant's innocence evident or reasonably and fairly raises an issue as to his guilt, the trial court has the authority to consider the facts of the case and decide that the 'evidence did not create a reasonable doubt as to guilt' or, alternatively, acquit the defendant or find him guilty of a lesser included offense. In such circumstances, the trial court is not required to affirmatively withdraw the defendant's plea before choosing to evaluate the State's evidence under a reasonable doubt standard. The court may simply proceed as though it has withdrawn the guilty plea and entered a not guilty plea in its place. There is no duty placed upon the trial court to inform the parties of this change; indeed the court of criminal appeals describes the process as the court just 'consider[ing] the evidence that is before it.'"

Art. 26.13(a)

Vannortrick v. State, 227 S.W.3d 706, 714 (Tex. Crim.App.2007). "[W]e hold that, when the trial court fails to admonish a defendant about the immigration consequences of his guilty plea, a silent record on citizenship, or a record such as here that is insufficient to determine citizenship, establishes harm by the standard of [TRAP] 44.2(b)."

Burnett v. State, 88 S.W.3d 633, 638 (Tex.Crim. App.2002). "[A] reviewing court must independently examine the record for indications that a defendant was or was not aware of the consequences of his plea and whether he was misled or harmed by the trial court's failure to admonish him of the punishment range."

Aguirre-Mata v. State, 992 S.W.2d 495, 499 (Tex. Crim.App.1999). "[A]dmonishments embodied in [CCP art.] 26.13(a) are not constitutionally required because their purpose and function is to assist the trial court in making the determination that a guilty plea is knowingly and voluntarily entered. Hence … error should be reviewed under [TRAP] 44.2(b). [¶] Appellant did not claim on direct appeal that the trial court's failure to admonish him of the range of punishment caused his plea to be obtained in violation of the Due Process Clause of the Fifth Amendment made applicable to the States through the Fourteenth Amendment." *See also* ***State v. Jimenez***, 987 S.W.2d 886, 888-89 (Tex.Crim.App.1999) (deportation); ***Ex parte Williams***, 704 S.W.2d 773, 775 (Tex.Crim.App.1986) (probation eligibility).

Talbott v. State, 93 S.W.3d 521, 524 (Tex.App.—Houston [14th Dist.] 2002, no pet.). "[A]ppellant reached a plea agreement only as to the number of indictments that would be presented to the court. There were four indictments; the State agreed to dismiss two. No agreement was made as to punishment. Thus, here, the protection afforded by article 26.13(a)(2)—which requires the trial judge to tell the defendant if the judge will follow the plea agreement—is insufficient. [¶] [A]ppellant's waiver of her right to appeal was ineffective because it was made before trial and without an agreement as to punishment. [A]ppellant did not waive her right to appeal knowingly and voluntarily...." *See also **Blanco v. State***, 18 S.W.3d 218, 219-20 (Tex.Crim. App.2000).

High v. State, 998 S.W.2d 642, 644-45 (Tex.App.—Houston [1st Dist.] 1999, pet. ref'd). "[A]ppellant told the psychologist he was 'unsure' of the maximum sentence, but he had been told the punishment range was five years to life. ... However, almost six months later, the appellant pled true to the enhancement paragraph, raising the minimum sentence to 15 years. The psychologist's statement is evidence that the appellant did not have full knowledge of the applicable punishment range before entry of his guilty plea. [T]he trial court's error had a substantial and injurious effect or influence on the appellant's decision to pled (sic) guilty."

Gorham v. State, 981 S.W.2d 315, 318 (Tex.App.—Houston [14th Dist.] 1998, pet. ref'd). "[W]e have not found any case in which the court of criminal appeals has held that pre-printed, boilerplate recitals signed only by the trial judge overcome a reporter's record which affirmatively shows the judge did not admonish a defendant as to the deportation consequences of his plea. Therefore, given the record before us, we cannot conclude the trial judge complied with article 26.13(a). The judge's failure to fully admonish appellant violates the mandatory language of article 26.13 and constitutes error."

Papillion v. State, 908 S.W.2d 621, 624 (Tex. App.—Beaumont 1995, no pet.). "[W]here a defendant pleads guilty or nolo contendere to the trial court with the benefit of a negotiated punishment recommendation, the trial court commits reversible error by making any finding on [the] guilty or nolo plea without *first* informing the defendant whether the court accepts or rejects the ... negotiated punishment recommendation *and then* affirmatively inquiring as to whether or not the defendant wishes to withdraw his plea of guilty or nolo contendere if the trial court rejects [the] punishment recommendation. [The] error is reversible and not subject to a harm analysis." *But see **Medina v. State***, 985 S.W.2d 192, 194 (Tex.App.—San Antonio 1998, no pet.).

Art. 26.13(b)

Boykin v. Alabama, 395 U.S. 238, 242, 89 S.Ct. 1709, 1711-12 (1969). "It was error, plain on the face of the record, for the trial judge to accept petitioner's guilty plea without an affirmative showing that it was intelligent and voluntary. [¶] A plea of guilty is more than a confession which admits that the accused did various acts; it is itself a conviction; nothing remains but to give judgment and determine punishment. Admissibility of a confession must be based on a 'reliable determination on the voluntariness issue which satisfies the constitutional rights of the defendant.' ... We think that the [defendant's guilty plea must be made understandingly and intelligently] to determin[e] whether a guilty plea is voluntarily made. *At 243:* Several federal constitutional rights are involved in a waiver that takes place when a plea of guilty is entered in a state criminal trial. First, is the privilege against compulsory self-incrimination guaranteed by the Fifth Amendment and applicable to the States by reason of the Fourteenth. Second, is the right to trial by jury. Third, is the right to confront one's accusers. We cannot presume a waiver of these three important federal rights from a silent record." *See also **Kniatt v. State***, 206 S.W.3d 657, 664 (Tex.Crim.App.2006).

Ex parte Morrow, 952 S.W.2d 530, 534-35 (Tex. Crim.App.1997). "[A] plea of guilty entered by one fully aware of the direct consequences, including the actual value of any commitments made to him by the court, prosecutor, or his own counsel, must stand unless induced by threats (or promises to discontinue improper harassment), misrepresentation (including unfulfilled or unfulfillable promises), or perhaps by promises that are by their nature improper as having no proper relationship to the prosecutor's business (e.g. bribes). [¶] [T]he plea papers show ... that one of the provisions of the plea bargain stated that all funds seized ... would be returned to applicant. However, the *mere inclusion* of such a provision in the plea bargain does not render applicant's pleas 'involuntary.'"

Ex parte Williams, 704 S.W.2d 773, 776-77 (Tex. Crim.App.1986). "[A] plea is involuntarily induced: 1) when a defendant shows that the trial court volunteered an admonishment that included information on the availability of probation, thereby creating an affirmative duty on the part of the trial judge to provide accurate information on the availability of probation, 2) when a defendant shows that the trial court provided him with inaccurate information on the availability of probation, thereby leaving the defendant unaware of the consequences of his plea, and 3) when a defendant makes an objective showing that he was misled or harmed by the inaccurate admonishment."

Melton v. State, 987 S.W.2d 72, 75 n.2 (Tex.App.— Dallas 1998, no pet.). "Although an open plea of guilty waives all nonjurisdictional defects that occur prior to entry of plea, the waiver rule is predicated on a knowing and voluntary plea [and thus] does not apply to bar appeals in open plea cases when a defendant claims plea was involuntary."

Abu-Ein v. State, 921 S.W.2d 807, 808 (Tex.App.— Houston [14th Dist.] 1996, pet. ref'd). "A defendant's election to plead guilty when based upon erroneous advice of counsel is not made voluntarily and knowingly."

Gillum v. State, 959 S.W.2d 642, 644 (Tex.App.— Houston [1st Dist.] 1995, pet. ref'd). "If a defendant pleads guilty or no contest on the false understanding that the merits of a pretrial motion would be preserved for appeal, the defendant's plea is not voluntarily and understandingly made."

Art. 26.13(c)

Martinez v. State, 981 S.W.2d 195, 197 (Tex.Crim. App.1998). "When a record shows that the trial court delivered an incorrect admonishment regarding the range of punishment, and the actual sentence lies within both the actual and misstated maximum, substantial compliance is attained."

Ray v. State, 919 S.W.2d 125, 127 (Tex.Crim.App. 1996). CCP art. 42.12, §5(a), "does not require, either in felonies or misdemeanors, that the defendant entering an open plea of guilty or nolo contendere be informed prior to his plea of the possible consequences under §5(b) of a probation violation. [T]he failure to provide the information does not render such a plea involuntary. [¶] Although §5(a) does not require in an open plea of guilty or nolo contendere that the information in §5(b) be provided to the defendant prior to his plea, the statute does require that it be provided at some time."

Eubanks v. State, 599 S.W.2d 815, 816 (Tex.Crim. App.1980). "This Court has interpreted 'the consequences of the [accused's] plea,' as used in Art. 26.13 to mean 'the punishment provided by law for the offense and the punishment which could be inflicted under his plea.' ... We have rejected arguments that Art. 26.13 requires the trial court to admonish a defendant ... that the court has the discretion to cumulate sentences, or that a conviction on a guilty plea may be used for enhancement of punishment of a subsequent felony conviction. [W]e hold that the provisions of Art. 26.13 [do] not require the trial court ... to inform [appellant] of the possible effect on his right to appeal under Art. 44.02."

Cano v. State, 4 S.W.3d 356, 358 (Tex.App.— Houston [1st Dist.] 1999, pet. ref'd). "[T]he loss of voting rights, like possible immigration consequences, is a collateral consequence that, as a matter of constitutional law, does not require admonishment."

Art. 26.13(d)

Edwards v. State, 921 S.W.2d 477, 481 (Tex.App.— Houston [1st Dist.] 1996, no pet.). "[W]ritten admonitions were given to appellant and ... he signed a statement attesting that he understood the admonitions. The trial court was not required by statute to further question appellant about voluntariness of his plea. The evidence actually exceeds the requirements [of Article 26.13(d)] by showing that the trial court examined the written plea papers and questioned both appellant and his attorney to determine that appellant was knowingly and voluntarily entering his plea."

ART. 26.14. JURY ON PLEA OF GUILTY

Where a defendant in a case of felony persists in pleading guilty or in entering a plea of nolo contendere, if the punishment is not absolutely fixed by law, a jury shall be impaneled to assess the punishment and evidence may be heard to enable them to decide thereupon, unless the defendant in accordance with Articles 1.13 or 37.07 shall have waived his right to trial by jury.

History of CCP art. 26.14: Acts 1965, 59th Leg., ch. 722, §1, eff. Jan. 1, 1966.

Wilkerson v. State, 736 S.W.2d 656, 659 (Tex.Crim. App.1987). "A plea of guilty to a felony offense before a jury … is a unitary trial, not a bifurcated one. A plea of guilty to a felony before a jury admits the existence of all incriminating facts necessary to establish guilt. [W]here such guilty plea is before the jury the presumption of innocence does not obtain under the plea and there is no issue of justification under it. [¶] Introduction of evidence by the State in a felony case involving a plea of guilty before the jury is to enable the jury to [assess the penalty]. [T]he State's right to introduce evidence is not restricted by the entry of a plea of guilty, or by his admission of facts sought to be proved; relevant facts admissible under a plea of not guilty are also admissible under a plea of guilty. An application for probation does not limit the State's right to offer evidence."

Garza v. State, 878 S.W.2d 213, 216 (Tex.App.— Corpus Christi 1994, pet. ref'd). "[A] plea of guilty is not evidence. [A] plea of guilty to a felony charge before a jury amounts to an admission of all facts necessary to establish guilt, and any introduction of evidence by the State is made to enable the jury to assess punishment."

ART. 26.15. CORRECTING NAME

In any case, the same proceedings shall be had with respect to the name of the defendant and the correction of the indictment or information as provided with respect to the same in capital cases.

History of CCP art. 26.15: Acts 1965, 59th Leg., ch. 722, §1, eff. Jan. 1, 1966.

Bowden v. State, 628 S.W.2d 782, 786 (Tex.Crim. App.1982). "[I]f a defendant timely suggest[s] his true name, the court [is] authorized to correct the indictment to reflect the true name. *At 787:* [T]o be timely[, the correction] must be made at the time of the arraignment or it comes too late."

CHAPTER 27. THE PLEADING IN CRIMINAL ACTIONS

ART. 27.01. INDICTMENT OR INFORMATION

The primary pleading in a criminal action on the part of the State is the indictment or information.

History of CCP art. 27.01: Acts 1965, 59th Leg., ch. 722, §1, eff. Jan. 1, 1966.

Peterson v. State, 781 S.W.2d 933, 935 (Tex.Crim. App.1989). "An information is … a written pleading in behalf of the State drawn, filed and presented by a prosecuting attorney charging an accused with an offense that may be prosecuted under the law. [¶] [A]n information must be based on a complaint, and the offense stated in the former 'must be characterized by and correspond with that stated in the affidavit….'"

Ex parte Patterson, 740 S.W.2d 766, 775 (Tex. Crim.App.1987), *overruled on other grounds*, *Ex parte Beck*, 769 S.W.2d 525 (Tex.Crim.App.1989). "An indictment serves a dual function. On the one hand it 'is the written statement of a grand jury accusing a person therein named of some act or omission which, by law, is declared to be an offense.' … On the other hand, the indictment is '[t]he primary pleading in a [felony] criminal action on the part of the State[.]' Thus the indictment serves interests of both the State and the accused."

ART. 27.02. DEFENDANT'S PLEADINGS

The pleadings and motions of the defendant shall be:

(1) A motion to set aside or an exception to an indictment or information for some matter of form or substance;

(2) A special plea as provided in Article 27.05 of this code;

(3) A plea of guilty;

(4) A plea of not guilty;

(5) A plea of nolo contendere, the legal effect of which shall be the same as that of a plea of guilty, except that such plea may not be used against the defendant as an admission in any civil suit based upon or growing out of the act upon which the criminal prosecution is based;

(6) An application for probation, if any;

(7) An election, if any, to have the jury assess the punishment if he is found guilty; and

(8) Any other motions or pleadings that are by law permitted to be filed.

History of CCP art. 27.02: Acts 1965, 59th Leg., ch. 722, §1, eff. Jan. 1, 1966. Amended by Acts 1967, 60th Leg., ch. 659, §17, eff. Aug. 28, 1967; Acts 1973, 63rd Leg., ch. 399, §2(A), eff. Jan. 1, 1974.

ANNOTATIONS

State v. Rosenbaum, 910 S.W.2d 934, 941 (Tex. Crim.App.1994). "[A] motion to quash is a 'pleading of the defendant' as defined in Article 27.02. [¶] [T]he Motion for Pretrial Determination [is] a 'pleading of the defendant,' defined by Article 27.02(8)...."

Ex parte Walker, 794 S.W.2d 36, 36 (Tex.Crim.App. 1990). "After voir dire of the venire began, applicant's attorney realized that he had not filed the [motion electing to have the jury assess punishment]. He attempted to file the jury election, but the trial court rejected it as untimely."

Dees v. State, 676 S.W.2d 403, 404 (Tex.Crim.App. 1984). "[W]hen a defendant, who is charged with committing a misdemeanor offense, pleads guilty or nolo contendere to the charge, such plea constitutes an admission to every element of the charged offense."

Ellerbe v. State, 80 S.W.3d 721, 723 (Tex.App.— Houston [1st Dist.] 2002, pet. ref'd). "A plea of nolo contendere does not relieve a defendant from having to admit to the commission of an offense so as to fully participate in a treatment program as a condition of community supervision."

ART. 27.03. MOTION TO SET ASIDE INDICTMENT

In addition to any other grounds authorized by law, a motion to set aside an indictment or information may be based on the following:

1. That it appears by the records of the court that the indictment was not found by at least nine grand jurors, or that the information was not based upon a valid complaint;

2. That some person not authorized by law was present when the grand jury was deliberating upon the accusation against the defendant, or was voting upon the same; and

3. That the grand jury was illegally impaneled; provided, however, in order to raise such question on motion to set aside the indictment, the defendant must show that he did not have an opportunity to challenge the array at the time the grand jury was impaneled.

History of CCP art. 27.03: Acts 1965, 59th Leg., ch. 722, §1, eff. Jan. 1, 1966.

ANNOTATIONS

Smith v. Gohmert, 962 S.W.2d 590, 593 (Tex.Crim. App.1998). "[A] defendant seeking to compel a dismissal of an indictment on speedy trial grounds has an adequate remedy at law, and therefore, has no need for the drastic remedy of mandamus."

State v. Terrazas, 962 S.W.2d 38, 41 (Tex.Crim.App. 1998). "[E]ven though a particular constitutional violation was not among those set out as an authorized basis for a trial court's dismissal of a charging instrument ..., that did not preclude the trial court from having the authority to dismiss on that ground."

Aguilar v. State, 846 S.W.2d 318, 320 (Tex.Crim. App.1993). "Defects in complaints ... must ... be raised before trial...."

Miller v. State, 909 S.W.2d 586, 591-92 (Tex.App.— Austin 1995, no pet.). "An order quashing or setting aside a charging instrument effectively terminates or dismisses a prosecution whenever the order requires an alteration of the charging instrument or the filing of a new charging instrument. The fact that an order quashing the indictment may have been based upon an erroneous interpretation of the applicable law in no way affects the validity of the order to quash. A trial court lacks the jurisdiction to rescind the order quashing the indictment."

ART. 27.04. MOTION TRIED BY JUDGE

An issue of fact arising upon a motion to set aside an indictment or information shall be tried by the judge without a jury.

History of CCP art. 27.04: Acts 1965, 59th Leg., ch. 722, §1, eff. Jan. 1, 1966.

ART. 27.05. DEFENDANT'S SPECIAL PLEA

A defendant's only special plea is that he has already been prosecuted for the same or a different offense arising out of the same criminal episode that was or should have been consolidated into one trial, and that the former prosecution:

(1) resulted in acquittal;

(2) resulted in conviction;

(3) was improperly terminated; or

(4) was terminated by a final order or judgment for the defendant that has not been reversed, set aside, or vacated and that necessarily required a determination inconsistent with a fact that must be established to secure conviction in the subsequent prosecution.

History of CCP art. 27.05: Acts 1965, 59th Leg., ch. 722, §1, eff. Jan. 1, 1966. Amended by Acts 1973, 63rd Leg., ch. 399, §2(A), eff. Jan. 1, 1974.

ANNOTATIONS

Ex parte Apolinar, 820 S.W.2d 792, 793-94 (Tex. Crim.App.1991). "A defendant may file a special plea in order to assert a former jeopardy claim. However, all issues of fact presented in the special plea are to be tried by the trier of fact on the trial on the merits. [¶] The statutorily prescribed procedure utilized on a special plea mandates that the defendant's claim in the special plea shall not be determined before the trial on the merits. Trial courts are required to submit the special plea to the trier of fact unless, assuming all the facts alleged in the plea to be true, the special plea does not present a legally sufficient former jeopardy claim. If the trial court determines that the special plea presents a legally sufficient claim to submit it to the trier of fact then it must be submitted and tried by the trier of fact together with the plea of not guilty. [¶] There is no statutory provision which grants the courts of appeals jurisdiction over a special plea before a final judgment has been entered. Thus, the procedure authorized for a special plea requires the defendant to be twice put to trial before the merits of his former jeopardy claim may be reached."

Ex parte Siller, 686 S.W.2d 617, 618 n.1 (Tex.Crim. App.1985). "Though [CCP art.] 27.05 ... uses the term 'criminal episode,' it is not defined in the procedural code. In the penal code 'criminal episode' is defined only in ... [Pen. Code] §3.01 ... and that definition is expressly just for purposes of Chapter 3. [U]nless Chapter 3 is implicated, ... practitioners and courts would be well advised to avoid loosely using the term."

ART. 27.06. SPECIAL PLEA VERIFIED

Every special plea shall be verified by the affidavit of the defendant.

History of CCP art. 27.06: Acts 1965, 59th Leg., ch. 722, §1, eff. Jan. 1, 1966.

ANNOTATIONS

State v. Neff, 841 S.W.2d 68, 69 n.3 (Tex.App.—El Paso 1992, no pet.). "Ordinarily, when a defendant fails to raise a double jeopardy claim by filing the requisite *verified* special plea, no error is presented to the trial court or preserved for appellate review. [However, we] find that the prosecutor in the instant case wholly failed to object to the obvious defect in the pleading and consequently has waived any such error on review."

ART. 27.07. SPECIAL PLEA TRIED

All issues of fact presented by a special plea shall be tried by the trier of the facts on the trial on the merits.

History of CCP art. 27.07: Acts 1965, 59th Leg., ch. 722, §1, eff. Jan. 1, 1966.

ANNOTATIONS

Goins v. State, 841 S.W.2d 527, 529 (Tex.App.—Houston [1st Dist.] 1992, pet. ref'd). "[A] defendant must present evidence in support of his claim of double jeopardy. Submitting a plea of double jeopardy constitutes only pleading, and does not establish as true issues of fact alleged in the plea. ... 'Where no evidence has been introduced in support of such plea, the court is neither required, nor is it its duty, to submit such plea to the jury.'"

ART. 27.08. EXCEPTION TO SUBSTANCE OF INDICTMENT

There is no exception to the substance of an indictment or information except:

1. That it does not appear therefrom that an offense against the law was committed by the defendant;

2. That it appears from the face thereof that a prosecution for the offense is barred by a lapse of time, or that the offense was committed after the finding of the indictment;

3. That it contains matter which is a legal defense or bar to the prosecution; and

4.   That it shows upon its face that the court trying the case has no jurisdiction thereof.

History of CCP art. 27.08: Acts 1965, 59th Leg., ch. 722, §1, eff. Jan. 1, 1966.

Proctor v. State, 967 S.W.2d 840, 844 (Tex.Crim. App.1998). "The defense [the statute of limitations] creates is forfeited if not asserted at or before the guilt/innocence stage of trial. Before trial, a defendant may assert the statute of limitations defense by filing a motion to dismiss under [CCP art.] 27.08(2).... At trial, the defendant may assert the defense by requesting a jury instruction on limitations if there is some evidence before the jury, from any source, that the prosecution is limitations-barred. If there is some such evidence and the defendant requests a jury instruction on the limitations defense, then the State must prove beyond a reasonable doubt that the prosecution is not limitations-barred. Finally, the defendant may, either before trial or at trial, waive the statute of limitations defense."

Studer v. State, 799 S.W.2d 263, 267 (Tex.Crim. App.1990). "A substance defect [is] considered 'fundamental error' since a charging instrument with such a defect failed to confer jurisdiction upon the trial court, and any conviction had upon that instrument was therefore void. [T]his Court has used the terms 'substance defect', 'fundamental error', and 'fatally defective' interchangeably when addressing errors in charging instruments which led to void convictions. *At 268:* [A] substance defect is, among other things, a failure to allege an element of an offense in the charging instrument."

ART. 27.09. EXCEPTION TO FORM OF INDICTMENT

Exceptions to the form of an indictment or information may be taken for the following causes only:

1.   That it does not appear to have been presented in the proper court as required by law;

2.   The want of any requisite prescribed by Articles 21.02 and 21.21.

3.   That it was not returned by a lawfully chosen or empaneled grand jury.

History of CCP art. 27.09: Acts 1965, 59th Leg., ch. 722, §1, eff. Jan. 1, 1966.
See also CCP art. 12.01.

Janecka v. State, 739 S.W.2d 813, 819 (Tex.Crim. App.1987). "[I]f an indictment is found to allege all of the elements necessary to show commission of an offense and is therefore not fundamentally defective and void, and if a defendant requests additional factual information upon which to prepare his defense, a defect of form has been raised and the State may properly amend the indictment to reflect the requested information. *At 818 n.4:* [A]ll notice defects are exceptions to form...."

State v. Salinas, 982 S.W.2d 9, 10 n.1 (Tex.App.—Houston [1st Dist.] 1997, pet. ref'd). "The [CCP] uses the terminology 'motion to set aside' rather than 'motion to quash' and 'motion to dismiss,' even though these designations are common in practice. A motion to quash may contend that the indictment is too vague to give adequate notice of the defendant's alleged conduct. This is an exception to the form of an indictment. A motion to dismiss, however, is generally directed at a defect of substance that precludes prosecution altogether."

ART. 27.10. WRITTEN PLEADINGS

All motions to set aside an indictment or information and all special pleas and exceptions shall be in writing.

History of CCP art. 27.10: Acts 1965, 59th Leg., ch. 722, §1, eff. Jan. 1, 1966.

State v. Abrego, 974 S.W.2d 177, 179 (Tex. App.—San Antonio 1998, no pet.). "Article 27.10 ... states in unambiguous terms that 'all motions to set aside an indictment or information and all special pleas and exceptions *shall be in writing*.' ... Because the trial court entertained an oral motion to quash in derogation of article 27.10, we reverse the order of the trial court quashing the information and remand the cause to the trial court with instructions to reinstate the information against [D]."

Peden v. State, 917 S.W.2d 941, 955 (Tex.App.—Fort Worth 1996, pet. ref'd). "We construe article 27.10 as not imposing any requirement on the State's objections to a special plea by which a defendant has challenged an indictment or information. We hold that article 27.10 did not require the State to present a written exception ..., and the State's oral objection [is] sufficient."

ART. 27.11. TEN DAYS ALLOWED FOR FILING PLEADINGS

In all cases the defendant shall be allowed ten entire days, exclusive of all fractions of a day after his arrest, and during the term of the court, to file written pleadings.

History of CCP art. 27.11: Acts 1965, 59th Leg., ch. 722, §1, eff. Jan. 1, 1966.

ANNOTATIONS

Ashcraft v. State, 900 S.W.2d 817, 830 (Tex.App.—Corpus Christi 1995, pet. ref'd). "When timely and properly invoked, the statutory 10 days must be afforded the accused. Refusal to grant such time will result in reversible error, and the defendant need not show harm."

Trevino v. State, 900 S.W.2d 815, 817 (Tex.App.—Corpus Christi 1995, no pet.). "[W]hen a reindictment is filed more than 10 days before trial, defendants' reliance upon article 27.11 for a 10 day 'filings' period is inappropriate. [¶] [I]n non-arrest cases the date that the new charging instrument is filed is used as the starting point. ... When a new indictment is filed, the new indictment is new in fact and not an amendment of the first indictment, and therefore, the defendant is entitled to 10 entire days after the new indictment is filed to respond to the new indictment with written pleadings."

ART. 27.12. TIME AFTER SERVICE

In cases where the defendant is entitled to be served with a copy of the indictment, he shall be allowed the ten days time mentioned in the preceding Article to file written pleadings after such service.

History of CCP art. 27.12: Acts 1965, 59th Leg., ch. 722, §1, eff. Jan. 1, 1966.

ANNOTATIONS

Moreno v. State, 659 S.W.2d 395, 398 n.8 (Tex.Crim.App.1983). "[T]ime allowed under Article 27.12 must be properly requested and refused in order to show reversible error."

Roberts v. State, 93 S.W.3d 528, 532 (Tex.App.—Houston [14th Dist.] 2002, pet. ref'd). "When an accused timely and properly invokes his rights under the statute, the court must afford him the statutory ten days. However, the right to time statutes [CCP arts. 27.01, 27.11, and 27.12] are not properly invoked when the objectives of the statute have been achieved. *At 533:* [A]ppellant's counsel acknowledged that she had informed appellant of the charges against him and that

he was aware of these charges. More importantly, she acknowledged that she had received the indictment at or near the time it was issued and had had sufficient time to prepare for trial. [¶] Under these circumstances, appellant's complaint under article 27.12 ... has no merit, and the trial court did not err in denying appellant's motion for continuance."

ART. 27.13. PLEA OF GUILTY OR NOLO CONTENDERE IN FELONY

A plea of "guilty" or a plea of "nolo contendere" in a felony case must be made in open court by the defendant in person; and the proceedings shall be as provided in Articles 26.13, 26.14 and 27.02. If the plea is before the judge alone, same may be made in the same manner as is provided for by Articles 1.13 and 1.15.

History of CCP art. 27.13: Acts 1965, 59th Leg., ch. 722, §1, eff. Jan. 1, 1966.

ANNOTATIONS

Costilla v. State, 146 S.W.3d 213, 217 (Tex.Crim.App.2004). Held: Although D's guilty plea was made orally by his attorney after his attorney translated the admonishment, statement, and waiver forms into Spanish, the plea was voluntary. However, the better practice is to ask the defendant personally what his plea is.

Tindel v. State, 830 S.W.2d 135, 136 (Tex.Crim.App. 1992). Article 27.13 "does not apply to a hearing on punishment.... [¶] [T]he personal plea requirement ... does not apply to pleas of 'true' to enhancement paragraphs."

White v. State, 932 S.W.2d 593, 596-97 (Tex.App.—Tyler 1995, pet. ref'd). "[A]fter White announced his guilty plea ..., the attorney for the State asserted that he had misspoken when he said the State was abandoning count two of the indictment. He averred that the State intended to convict White on both the cocaine and marijuana charges. The trial court did not thereafter secure White's guilty plea to the marijuana charge but proceeded to find White guilty on both counts. White's trial counsel did not object to the omission or to the judge's pronouncement of guilt. [¶] [T]he effect of this chain of events was to convict White on the marijuana count without a guilty plea or a trial. This omission violated the express language of Article 27.13 as well as White's right to due process not withstanding the fact that the Stipulation of Evidence signed by White reflects that he fully intended to plead guilty to the second count of the indictment...."

ART. 27.14. PLEA OF GUILTY OR NOLO CONTENDERE IN MISDEMEANOR

(a) A plea of "guilty" or a plea of "nolo contendere" in a misdemeanor case may be made either by the defendant or his counsel in open court; in such case, the defendant or his counsel may waive a jury, and the punishment may be assessed by the court either upon or without evidence, at the discretion of the court.

(b) A defendant charged with a misdemeanor for which the maximum possible punishment is by fine only may, in lieu of the method provided in Subsection (a) of this article, mail or deliver in person to the court a plea of "guilty" or a plea of "nolo contendere" and a waiver of jury trial. The defendant may also request in writing that the court notify the defendant, at the address stated in the request, of the amount of an appeal bond that the court will approve. If the court receives a plea and waiver before the time the defendant is scheduled to appear in court, the court shall dispose of the case without requiring a court appearance by the defendant. The court shall notify the defendant either in person or by certified mail, return receipt requested, of the amount of any fine assessed in the case and, if requested by the defendant, the amount of an appeal bond that the court will approve. The defendant shall pay any fine assessed or give an appeal bond in the amount stated in the notice before the 31st day after receiving the notice.

(c) In a misdemeanor case for which the maximum possible punishment is by fine only, payment of a fine or an amount accepted by the court constitutes a finding of guilty in open court as though a plea of nolo contendere had been entered by the defendant and constitutes a waiver of a jury trial in writing.

(d) If written notice of an offense for which maximum possible punishment is by fine only or of a violation relating to the manner, time, and place of parking has been prepared, delivered, and filed with the court and a legible duplicate copy has been given to the defendant, the written notice serves as a complaint to which the defendant may plead "guilty," "not guilty," or "nolo contendere." If the defendant pleads "not guilty" to the offense, a complaint shall be filed that conforms to the requirements of Chapter 45 of this code, and that complaint serves as an original complaint. A defendant may waive the filing of a sworn complaint and elect that the prosecution proceed on the written notice of the charged offense if the defendant agrees in writing with the prosecution, signs the agreement, and files it with the court.

History of CCP art. 27.14: Acts 1965, 59th Leg., ch. 722, §1, eff. Jan. 1, 1966. Amended by Acts 1967, 60th Leg., ch. 659, §18, eff. Aug. 28, 1967; Acts 1977, 65th Leg., ch. 858, §1, eff. June 16, 1977; Acts 1979, 66th Leg., ch. 207, §1, eff. Sept. 1, 1979; Acts 1983, 68th Leg., ch. 273, §1, eff. Sept. 1, 1983; Acts 1985, 69th Leg., ch. 87, §1, eff. Sept. 1, 1985; Acts 1993, 73rd Leg., ch. 76, §1, eff. Sept. 1, 1993; Acts 2001, 77th Leg., ch. 285, §1, eff. Sept. 1, 2001.

ANNOTATIONS

Price v. State, 866 S.W.2d 606, 611 (Tex.Crim.App. 1993). "[W]hen represented by counsel the accused need not to be present at any stage of a misdemeanor plea proceeding...."

Ex parte Martin, 747 S.W.2d 789, 792 (Tex.Crim. App.1988). "[I]n pleas of guilty or nolo contendere in a misdemeanor case before the court punishment may be assessed by the court with or without evidence.... Thus, normally on appeal from a misdemeanor conviction based on a plea of guilty or nolo contendere there can be no question of the sufficiency of the evidence. [A] collateral attack of the sufficiency of the evidence to support a misdemeanor conviction by habeas corpus is not permitted."

State v. Shaw, 822 S.W.2d 807, 809 (Tex.App.— Austin 1992, no pet.). "If the defendant pleads guilty or no contest, no formal complaint is required and there is nothing for the defendant to waive. Because appellee pleaded no contest, the requirement that a formal complaint be filed was never triggered and, as a logical consequence, no waiver was necessary."

ART. 27.15. CHANGE OF VENUE TO PLEAD GUILTY

When in any county which is located in a judicial district composed of more than one county, a party is charged with a felony and the maximum punishment therefor shall not exceed fifteen years, and the district court of said county is not in session, such party may, if he desires to plead guilty, or enter a plea of nolo contendere, make application to the district judge of such district for a change of venue to the county in which said court is in session, and said district judge may enter an order changing the venue of said cause to the county in which the court is then in session, and the defendant may plead guilty or enter a plea of nolo contendere to said charge in said court to which the venue has been changed.

History of CCP art. 27.15: Acts 1965, 59th Leg., ch. 722, §1, eff. Jan. 1, 1966.

ART. 27.16. PLEA OF NOT GUILTY, HOW MADE

(a) The plea of not guilty may be made orally by the defendant or by his counsel in open court. If the defendant refuses to plead, the plea of not guilty shall be entered for him by the court.

(b) A defendant charged with a misdemeanor for which the maximum possible punishment is by fine only may, in lieu of the method provided in Subsection (a) of this article, mail to the court a plea of not guilty.

History of CCP art. 27.16: Acts 1965, 59th Leg., ch. 722, §1, eff. Jan. 1, 1966. Amended by Acts 1977, 65th Leg., ch. 858, §2, eff. June 16, 1977.

ART. 27.17. PLEA OF NOT GUILTY CONSTRUED

The plea of not guilty shall be construed to be a denial of every material allegation in the indictment or information. Under this plea, evidence to establish the insanity of defendant, and every fact whatever tending to acquit him of the accusation may be introduced, except such facts as are proper for a special plea under Article 27.05.

History of CCP art. 27.17: Acts 1965, 59th Leg., ch. 722, §1, eff. Jan. 1, 1966.

ART. 27.18. PLEA OR WAIVER OF RIGHTS BY CLOSED CIRCUIT VIDEO TELECONFERENCING

(a) Notwithstanding any provision of this code requiring that a plea or a waiver of a defendant's right be made in open court, a court may accept the plea or waiver by broadcast by closed circuit video teleconferencing to the court if:

(1) the defendant and the attorney representing the state file with the court written consent to the use of closed circuit video teleconferencing;

(2) the closed circuit video teleconferencing system provides for a simultaneous, compressed full motion video, and interactive communication of image and sound between the judge, the attorney representing the state, the defendant, and the defendant's attorney; and

(3) on request of the defendant, the defendant and the defendant's attorney are able to communicate privately without being recorded or heard by the judge or the attorney representing the state.

(b) On motion of the defendant or the attorney representing the state or in the court's discretion, the court may terminate an appearance by closed circuit video teleconferencing at any time during the appearance and require an appearance by the defendant in open court.

(c) A recording of the communication shall be made and preserved until all appellate proceedings have been disposed of. The defendant may obtain a copy of the recording on payment of a reasonable amount to cover the costs of reproduction or, if the defendant is indigent, the court shall provide a copy to the defendant without charging a cost for the copy.

(d) A defendant who is confined in a county other than the county in which charges against the defendant are pending may use the teleconferencing method provided by this article or the electronic broadcast system authorized in Article 15.17 to enter a plea or waive a right in the court with jurisdiction over the case.

(e) A defendant who enters a plea or waiver under Subsection (d):

(1) consents to venue in the county in which the court receiving the plea or waiver is located; and

(2) waives any claim of error related to venue.

(f) Subsection (e) does not prohibit a court from granting a defendant's motion for a change of venue during the trial of the defendant.

(g) If a defendant enters a plea of guilty or nolo contendere under Subsection (d), the attorney representing the state may request at the time the plea is entered that the defendant submit a fingerprint of the defendant suitable for attachment to the judgment. On request for a fingerprint under this subsection, the county in which the defendant is confined shall obtain a fingerprint of the defendant and use first-class mail or other means acceptable to the attorney representing the state and the county to forward the fingerprint to the court accepting the plea.

History of CCP art. 27.18: Acts 1997, 75th Leg., ch. 1014, §1, eff. Sept. 1, 1997. Amended by Acts 2005, 79th Leg., ch. 1094, §6, eff. Sept. 1, 2005.

ANNOTATIONS

East v. State, 48 S.W.3d 412, 414 (Tex.App.— Houston [14th Dist.] 2001, no pet.). "[W]e hold that absent appellant's written consent to video teleconferencing, the ***Faretta*** [*v. California*, 422 U.S. 806 (1976)] hearing must be conducted in open court."

CHAPTER 28. MOTIONS, PLEADINGS & EXCEPTIONS

ART. 28.01. PRE-TRIAL

Sec. 1. The court may set any criminal case for a pre-trial hearing before it is set for trial upon its merits, and direct the defendant and his attorney, if any of record, and the State's attorney, to appear before the court at the time and place stated in the court's order for a conference and hearing. The defendant must be present at the arraignment, and his presence is required during any pre-trial proceeding. The pre-trial hearing shall be to determine any of the following matters:

(1) Arraignment of the defendant, if such be necessary; and appointment of counsel to represent the defendant, if such be necessary;

(2) Pleadings of the defendant;

(3) Special pleas, if any;

(4) Exceptions to the form or substance of the indictment or information;

(5) Motions for continuance either by the State or defendant; provided that grounds for continuance not existing or not known at the time may be presented and considered at any time before the defendant announces ready for trial;

(6) Motions to suppress evidence—When a hearing on the motion to suppress evidence is granted, the court may determine the merits of said motion on the motions themselves, or upon opposing affidavits, or upon oral testimony, subject to the discretion of the court;

(7) Motions for change of venue by the State or the defendant; provided, however, that such motions for change of venue, if overruled at the pre-trial hearing, may be renewed by the State or the defendant during the voir dire examination of the jury;

(8) Discovery;

(9) Entrapment; and

(10) Motion for appointment of interpreter.

Sec. 2. When a criminal case is set for such pre-trial hearing, any such preliminary matters not raised or filed seven days before the hearing will not thereafter be allowed to be raised or filed, except by permission of the court for good cause shown; provided that the defendant shall have sufficient notice of such hearing to allow him not less than 10 days in which to raise or file such preliminary matters. The record made at such pre-trial hearing, the rulings of the court and the exceptions and objections thereto shall become a part of the trial record of the case upon its merits.

Sec. 3. The notice mentioned in Section 2 above shall be sufficient if given in any one of the following ways:

(1) By announcement made by the court in open court in the presence of the defendant or his attorney of record;

(2) By personal service upon the defendant or his attorney of record;

(3) By mail to either the defendant or his attorney of record deposited by the clerk in the mail at least six days prior to the date set for hearing. If the defendant has no attorney of record such notice shall be addressed to defendant at the address shown on his bond, if the bond shows such an address, and if not, it may be addressed to one of the sureties on his bond. If the envelope containing the notice is properly addressed, stamped and mailed, the state will not be required to show that it was received.

History of CCP art. 28.01: Acts 1965, 59th Leg., ch. 722, §1, eff. Jan. 1, 1966. Amended by Acts 1967, 60th Leg., ch. 659, §19, eff. Aug. 28, 1967; Acts 1973, 63rd Leg., ch. 399, §2(A), eff. Jan. 1, 1974; Acts 1979, 66th Leg., ch. 113, §1 (eff. Aug. 27, 1979), ch. 209, §2 (eff. Aug. 27, 1979).

ANNOTATIONS

Generally

Warren v. State, 804 S.W.2d 597, 598 (Tex.App.—Houston [1st Dist.] 1991, no pet.). Appellant "contends he can waive his 'right,' under article 28.01, to attend his pretrial hearing. We disagree. Article 28.01 imposes a requirement on defendants, not a 'right.' There is a right to be present at one's trial, but not a right to be absent."

Art. 28.01, §1(4)

Cates v. State, 120 S.W.3d 352, 359 (Tex.Crim.App. 2003). "[A] person who has made a substantial preliminary showing of falsity in the affidavit is entitled to an 'evidentiary hearing.' That phrase, 'evidentiary hearing,' normally means a live hearing in court with witnesses on the witness stand. But we need not today decide whether a *Franks* [*v. Delaware*, 438 U.S. 154, 156 (1978)] evidentiary hearing must always be conducted with live witnesses because, in this case, the trial judge did not allow appellant the opportunity to offer evidence to prove his *Franks* claim in any of the ways set out in article 28.01, §1(6). Accordingly, by denying the defendant the opportunity to present testimony or any other evidence to prove his specific allegations of falsity, the trial court denied appellant his right to a full *Franks* hearing."

Art. 28.01, §1(6)

State v. Cullen, 195 S.W.3d 696, 699 (Tex.Crim.App. 2006). "[U]pon the request of the losing party on a motion to suppress evidence, the trial court shall state its essential findings. By 'essential findings,' we mean that the trial court must make findings of fact and conclusions of law adequate to provide an appellate court with a basis upon which to review the trial court's application of the law to the facts."

Bishop v. State, 85 S.W.3d 819, 822 (Tex.Crim.App. 2002). "[T]he court of appeals noted that, while appellant did claim that she was the subject of a warrantless arrest in her suppression motion, her affidavit did not make such a claim. It then affirmed the conviction, saying that appellant had alleged the lack of a warrant only in her unsworn motion to suppress and not in her affidavit and that she had therefore not alleged lack of a warrant. [¶] We conclude that ... the court of appeals should have considered both appellant's motion to suppress and the affidavits in addressing appellant's complaint about the trial court's ruling on that motion."

Granados v. State, 85 S.W.3d 217, 227 (Tex.Crim. App.2002). "Because suppression hearings involve the determination of preliminary questions concerning the admissibility of evidence, the language of the current rules indicates that the rules of evidence (except privileges) no longer apply to suppression hearings. This conclusion is consistent with the U.S. Supreme Court's interpretation of the [FRE], which has a counterpart to [TRE] 104(a)...."

Beall v. State, 237 S.W.3d 841, 845-46 (Tex.App.— Fort Worth 2007, no pet.). "We review a trial court's ruling on a motion to suppress evidence under a bifurcated standard of review. In reviewing the trial court's decision, we do not engage in our own factual review. The trial judge is the sole trier of fact and judge of the credibility of the witnesses and the weight to be given

their testimony. Therefore, we give almost total deference to the trial court's rulings on (1) questions of historical fact, even if the trial court's determination of those facts was not based on an evaluation of credibility and demeanor, and (2) application-of-law-to-fact questions that turn on an evaluation of credibility and demeanor. But when the trial court's rulings do not turn on the credibility and demeanor of the witnesses, we review de novo a trial court's rulings on mixed questions of law and fact. [¶] When the record is silent on the reasons for the trial court's ruling, or when ... there are no explicit fact findings and neither party timely requested findings and conclusions from the trial court, we imply the necessary fact findings that would support the trial court's ruling if the evidence, viewed in the light most favorable to the trial court's ruling, supports those findings. We then review the trial court's legal ruling de novo unless the implied fact findings supported by the record are also dispositive of the legal ruling. [¶] In determining whether a trial court's decision is supported by the record, we generally only consider evidence adduced at the suppression hearing only because the ruling was based on it rather than on evidence introduced later. But this general rule is inapplicable where the suppression issue has been consensually relitigated by the parties during the trial on the merits. Where the State raises the issue at trial either without objection or with subsequent participation in the inquiry by the defense, the defendant has made an election to re-open the evidence, and consideration of the relevant trial testimony is appropriate in our review." *See also* **Guzman v. State**, 955 S.W.2d 85, 87 (Tex.Crim.App.1997).

Vasquez v. State, 101 S.W.3d 794, 796 (Tex.App.— Houston [1st Dist.] 2003, pet. ref'd). "When faced with a [motion to suppress] challenge to an out-of-court identification, a trial court must look to the totality of the circumstances surrounding the identification to determine if a procedure was so unnecessarily suggestive and conducive to irreparable mistaken identification that the defendant was denied due process of law. In the first step in this analysis, the trial court determines whether the identification procedure was impermissibly suggestive. If the trial court determines the identification is impermissibly suggestive, the court must then consider [factors] to determine whether the suggestive procedure gave rise to a substantial likelihood of irreparable misidentification. *At n.1:* These factors are:

(1) the witness's opportunity to view the criminal act, (2) the witness's degree of attention, (3) the accuracy of the suspect's description, (4) the level of certainty at the time of confrontation, and (5) the time between the crime and confrontation. [T]he burden is on the movant to show impermissible suggestion and substantial likelihood of misidentification by clear and convincing evidence."

State v. Brunner, 917 S.W.2d 103, 105 (Tex. App.—San Antonio 1996, pet. ref'd). "[I]t is evident that a trial judge, in conducting a hearing on a motion to suppress, may determine the merits of the motion by considering the motion standing alone, or it may consider the motion plus affidavits, or it may consider the motion plus oral testimony. These three methods of consideration exist independently of one another." *See also* **State v. Miller**, 116 S.W.3d 912, 915 (Tex.App.—Austin 2003, no pet.).

Art. 28.01, §1(7)

Foster v. State, 779 S.W.2d 845, 852 (Tex.Crim.App. 1989). "When a defendant files a motion for change of venue, he may present evidence in support of that motion at a pre-trial hearing. Because a question of a change of venue is a question of constitutional dimensions, a defendant's failure to comply with the time limitations of [Article 28.01] does not waive the defendant's right to a hearing to consider evidence on his motion. It is not necessary that a motion to change venue be filed 10 days before a pre-trial hearing or 10 days prior to jury selection. A hearing is called for when the issue of venue has been joined by a defendant filing his affidavits in support of his motion and by the State filing controverting affidavits."

Art. 28.01, §1(8)

Johnson v. State, 233 S.W.3d 109, 115 (Tex.App.—Houston [14th Dist.] 2007, no pet.). The "test [to exclude a defendant's expert witness after the defendant failed to disclose the expert's identity] encompasses two factors: (1) whether the party's action in failing to timely disclose the expert witness constituted bad faith; and (2) whether the opposing party could have reasonably anticipated that the undisclosed witness would testify."

Art. 28.01, §1(9)

Taylor v. State, 886 S.W.2d 262, 265 (Tex.Crim.App. 1994). "The entrapment defense is unique in that the Legislature deliberately provided it may be tested and determined at a pretrial hearing. *At 266:* [W]e conclude that because a pretrial determination of defense of entrapment favorable to an accused does not impact the charging instrument, but is, instead, a finding in the nature of an acquittal, the appropriate order is one dismissing the prosecution with prejudice...."

Art. 28.01, §2

Saathoff v. State, 908 S.W.2d 523, 525 (Tex. App.—San Antonio 1995, no pet.). "[T]he State initially claims the motion [to quash] was untimely filed under article 28.01 ..., which requires all preliminary matters to be raised or filed seven days before a pretrial hearing. Article 28.01, however, is not a mandatory provision, but is merely directed to the court's discretion." *See also* **Saenz v. State**, 840 S.W.2d 96, 99 (Tex. App.—El Paso 1992, pet. ref'd).

ART. 28.02. ORDER OF ARGUMENT

The counsel of the defendant has the right to open and conclude the argument upon all pleadings of the defendant presented for the decision of the judge.

History of CCP art. 28.02: Acts 1965, 59th Leg., ch. 722, §1, eff. Jan. 1, 1966.

ART. 28.03. PROCESS FOR TESTIMONY ON PLEADINGS

When the matters involved in any written pleading depend in whole or in part upon testimony, and not altogether upon the record of the court, every process known to the law may be obtained on behalf of either party to procure such testimony; but there shall be no delay on account of the want of the testimony, unless it be shown to the satisfaction of the court that all the means given by the law have been used to procure the same.

History of CCP art. 28.03: Acts 1965, 59th Leg., ch. 722, §1, eff. Jan. 1, 1966.

ART. 28.04. QUASHING CHARGE IN MISDEMEANOR

If the motion to set aside or the exception to an indictment or information is sustained, the defendant in a misdemeanor case shall be discharged, but may be again prosecuted within the time allowed by law.

History of CCP art. 28.04: Acts 1965, 59th Leg., ch. 722, §1, eff. Jan. 1, 1966.

ANNOTATIONS

Wilson v. State, 792 S.W.2d 477, 481 (Tex.App.—Dallas 1990, no pet.). "When a trial court empowered with jurisdiction over a criminal case sustains a motion to dismiss the indictment or information, the accused is discharged and there is no case pending against him; accordingly, no jurisdiction remains in the dismissing court."

ART. 28.05. QUASHING INDICTMENT IN FELONY

If the motion to set aside or the exception to the indictment in cases of felony be sustained, the defendant shall not therefor be discharged, but may immediately be recommitted by order of the court, upon motion of the State's attorney or without motion; and proceedings may afterward be had against him as if no prosecution had ever been commenced.

History of CCP art. 28.05: Acts 1965, 59th Leg., ch. 722, §1, eff. Jan. 1, 1966.

State v. Bragg, 920 S.W.2d 407, 408 (Tex.App.—Houston [1st Dist.] 1996, pet. ref'd). "[A] trial court lacks the express or implied authority to dismiss an indictment with prejudice for failure to amend. The [CCP] only authorizes a trial court to quash an indictment for exceptions thereto, but disallows the defendant's discharge, unless the offense will be barred by limitation before another indictment can be presented."

ART. 28.06. SHALL BE FULLY DISCHARGED, WHEN

Where, after the motion or exception is sustained, it is made known to the court by sufficient testimony that the offense of which the defendant is accused will be barred by limitation before another indictment can be presented, he shall be fully discharged.

History of CCP art. 28.06: Acts 1965, 59th Leg., ch. 722, §1, eff. Jan. 1, 1966.

ART. 28.061. DISCHARGE FOR DELAY

Article 28.061 below was declared unconstitutional on grounds of separation of powers in **Meshell v. State**, *739 S.W.2d 246 (Tex.Crim.App.1987), below.*

If a motion to set aside an indictment, information, or complaint for failure to provide a speedy trial is sustained, the court shall discharge the defendant. A discharge under this article is a bar to any further prosecution for the offense discharged and for any other offense arising out of the same transaction, other than an offense of a higher grade that the attorney representing the state and prosecuting the offense that was discharged does not have the primary duty to prosecute.

History of CCP art. 28.061: Acts 1977, 65th Leg., ch. 787, §4, eff. July 1, 1978. Amended by Acts 1987, 70th Leg., ch. 383, §1, eff. Sept. 1, 1987; Acts 1997, 75th Leg., ch. 289, §1, eff. May 26, 1997.

See also Tex. Const. art. 1, §10; CCP art. 1.05.

Meshell v. State, 739 S.W.2d 246, 257 (Tex.Crim.App.1987). "Because we are not aware of any other constitutional provision expressly granting the Legislature the power to control a prosecutor's preparation for trial, we must conclude that the Legislature, by providing for such a right in the instant case, violated the separation of powers doctrine, [Tex. Const. art.] 2, §1. [¶] Therefore, we hold that Chapter 32A.02, in its entirety, and Article 28.061 … are rendered void."

ART. 28.07. IF EXCEPTION IS THAT NO OFFENSE IS CHARGED

If an exception to an indictment or information is taken and sustained upon the ground that there is no offense against the law charged therein, the defendant shall be discharged, unless an affidavit be filed accusing him of the commission of a penal offense.

History of CCP art. 28.07: Acts 1965, 59th Leg., ch. 722, §1, eff. Jan. 1, 1966.

ART. 28.08. WHEN DEFENDANT IS HELD BY ORDER OF COURT

If the motion to set aside the indictment or any exception thereto is sustained, but the court refuses to discharge the defendant, then at the expiration of ten days from the order sustaining such motions or exceptions, the defendant shall be discharged, unless in the meanwhile complaint has been made before a magistrate charging him with an offense, or unless another indictment has been presented against him for such offense.

History of CCP art. 28.08: Acts 1965, 59th Leg., ch. 722, §1, eff. Jan. 1, 1966.

ART. 28.09. EXCEPTION ON ACCOUNT OF FORM OR SUBSTANCE

If the exception to an indictment or information is sustained, the information or indictment may be amended if permitted by Article 28.10 of this code, and the cause may proceed upon the amended indictment or information.

History of CCP art. 28.09: Acts 1965, 59th Leg., ch. 722, §1, eff. Jan. 1, 1966. Amended by Acts 1985, 69th Leg., ch. 577, §1, eff. Dec. 1, 1985.

ANNOTATIONS

Rodriguez v. State, 899 S.W.2d 658, 668 (Tex.Crim.App.1995). The "omissions in the indictments were matters of form and could have been amended prior to trial or during trial if appellant did not object."

ART. 28.10. AMENDMENT OF INDICTMENT OR INFORMATION

(a) After notice to the defendant, a matter of form or substance in an indictment or information may be amended at any time before the date the trial on the merits commences. On the request of the defendant, the court shall allow the defendant not less than 10 days, or a shorter period if requested by the defendant, to respond to the amended indictment or information.

(b) A matter of form or substance in an indictment or information may also be amended after the trial on the merits commences if the defendant does not object.

(c) An indictment or information may not be amended over the defendant's objection as to form or substance if the amended indictment or information charges the defendant with an additional or different offense or if the substantial rights of the defendant are prejudiced.

History of CCP art. 28.10: Acts 1965, 59th Leg., ch. 722, §1, eff. Jan. 1, 1966. Amended by Acts 1985, 69th Leg., ch. 577, §1, eff. Dec. 1, 1985.

ANNOTATIONS

Eastep v. State, 941 S.W.2d 130, 132-33 (Tex.Crim.App.1997), *overruled on other grounds*, *Riney v. State*, 28 S.W.3d 561 (Tex.Crim.App.2000). "[N]ot every alteration to the face of the charging instrument is an amendment. In certain situations such an alteration is an abandonment. [¶] An amendment is an alteration to the face of the charging instrument which affects the substance of the charging instrument. For example, ... we found the alteration of a cause number in an enhancement paragraph was an amendment[,] the alteration of a weapon in an aggravated assault indictment was an amendment[,] the addition of the manner and means of committing an offense was an amendment[,] the alteration of the alleged date was an amendment[, and] the addition of a complainant was an amendment. [¶] [A]n abandonment, even though accomplished by an actual physical alteration to the face of the charging instrument, does not affect its substance."

Kelley v. State, 823 S.W.2d 300, 302 (Tex.Crim.App.1992). "The name change of the defendant [in an indictment] does not constitute an amendment [under] article 28.10...."

Flores v. State, 139 S.W.3d 61, 65 (Tex.App.—Texarkana 2004, pet. ref'd). Appellant "cites *Sodipo v. State*, 815 S.W.2d 551 (Tex.Crim.App.1990) (op. on reh'g), for the proposition that the trial court's error is not subject to harm analysis and requires automatic reversal. In *Sodipo*, the trial court permitted the state to amend the indictment, over the defendant's objection, before jury selection. The Texas Court of Criminal Appeals reversed Sodipo's conviction, explaining that the absolute provisions of Article 28.10 cannot be subject to a harmless error analysis in a meaningful manner. [¶] The Texas Court of Criminal Appeals has not overruled *Sodipo* in the specific context of Article 28.10. Nonetheless, the court's more recent jurisprudence suggests harm analysis is required."

Lebo v. State, 100 S.W.3d 417, 421 (Tex.App.—San Antonio 2002, pet. ref'd). "A different offense means a different statutory offense. Adding an additional mental culpable state does not allege a separate statutory offense. Therefore, the addition of the word 'recklessly' did not violate article 28.10."

Nichols v. State, 52 S.W.3d 501, 503 (Tex.App.—Dallas 2001, no pet.). Held: Amendment of indictment alleging possession of cocaine to possession of methamphetamine, over objection, violated Article 28.10(c) because "possession of *each* individual substance within the same penalty group constitutes a different statutory offense."

Curry v. State, 1 S.W.3d 175, 177 (Tex.App.—El Paso 1999), *aff'd*, 30 S.W.3d 394 (Tex.Crim.App.2000). "Amendment of the indictment over objection after start of trial is error because Article 28.10(b) inferentially prohibits trial amendments over objection. [¶] [T]he State may abandon alternative allegations where two or more ways of committing the charged offense are alleged conjunctively in the same count. [T]he State may abandon surplusage. 'Surplusage' means allegations that are neither essential to the validity of the indictment nor descriptive of that which is essential."

Sanders v. State, 978 S.W.2d 597, 599 (Tex.App.—Tyler 1997, pet. ref'd). "[T]he State may not amend an indictment on the day trial on the merits commences even if the amendment is requested before the actual trial begins. In a similar case, this court held that trial on the merits had commenced on the day when the jury was sworn although the actual trial did not begin until 14 days later." *See also Westfall v. State*, 970 S.W.2d 590, 592-93 (Tex.App.—Waco 1998, pet. ref'd).

Collins v. State, 890 S.W.2d 893, 896 (Tex.App.—El Paso 1994, no pet.). "In the absence of an effective amendment, the original indictment controls."

ART. 28.11. HOW AMENDED

All amendments of an indictment or information shall be made with the leave of the court and under its direction.

History of CCP art. 28.11: Acts 1965, 59th Leg., ch. 722, §1, eff. Jan. 1, 1966.

ANNOTATIONS

Riney v. State, 28 S.W.3d 561, 565-66 (Tex.Crim. App.2000). "Physical interlineation of the original indictment is an acceptable but not the exclusive means of effecting an amendment to the indictment. ... It is acceptable for the State to proffer, for the trial court's approval, its amended version of a photocopy of the original indictment. If approved, the amended photocopy of the original indictment need only be incorporated into the record under the direction of the court ... with the knowledge and affirmative assent of the defense. This version of the indictment would then become the 'official' indictment in the case...."

Brown v. State, 900 S.W.2d 805, 807 (Tex. App.—San Antonio 1995, pet. ref'd). While "the State may orally waive, abandon or dismiss a charge or portion of the indictment, such waiver is only effective to preserve the count for further prosecution *if the State obtains the trial judge's permission to waive the count, on the record, before jeopardy attaches.*"

ART. 28.12. EXCEPTION & TRIAL OF SPECIAL PLEAS

When a special plea is filed by the defendant, the State may except to it for substantial defects. If the exception be sustained, the plea may be amended. If the plea be not excepted to, it shall be considered that issue has been taken upon the same. Such special pleas as set forth matter of fact proper to be tried by a jury shall be submitted and tried with a plea of not guilty.

History of CCP art. 28.12: Acts 1965, 59th Leg., ch. 722, §1, eff. Jan. 1, 1966.

ANNOTATIONS

Peden v. State, 917 S.W.2d 941, 955 (Tex.App.—Fort Worth 1996, pet. ref'd). Article 28.12 imposes "no requirement of a written exception by the State to

Peden's amended special plea. We hold that the State's oral objection was sufficient."

ART. 28.13. FORMER ACQUITTAL OR CONVICTION

A former judgment of acquittal or conviction in a court of competent jurisdiction shall be a bar to any further prosecution for the same offense, but shall not bar a prosecution for any higher grade of offense over which said court had not jurisdiction, unless such judgment was had upon indictment or information, in which case the prosecution shall be barred for all grades of the offense.

History of CCP art. 28.13: Acts 1965, 59th Leg., ch. 722, §1, eff. Jan. 1, 1966.

ANNOTATIONS

State v. Engelking, 817 S.W.2d 64, 67 (Tex.Crim. App.1991). The State is "attempting to reprosecute appellees for lesser included offenses after a finding on appeal of insufficient evidence to support the greater, aggravated offenses for which they were prosecuted at an earlier trial. Under both state and federal constitutions, ... all such issues must be resolved in a single trial, and may not be made the subject of successive prosecutions."

Benard v. State, 481 S.W.2d 427, 429 (Tex.Crim. App.1972). "[T]he statute provides that a conviction or acquittal in a lower court is not a bar to a subsequent prosecution in a higher court unless the first prosecution was had upon indictment or information. A conviction or acquittal had upon a complaint only is not a bar to a subsequent prosecution for a higher grade of offense if the court which tried the first case lacked jurisdiction to try the higher offense."

ART. 28.14. PLEA ALLOWED

Judgment shall, in no case, be given against the defendant where his motion, exception or plea is overruled; but in all cases the plea of not guilty may be made by or for him.

History of CCP art. 28.14: Acts 1965, 59th Leg., ch. 722, §1, eff. Jan. 1, 1966.

CHAPTER 29. CONTINUANCE

ART. 29.01. BY OPERATION OF LAW

Criminal actions are continued by operation of law if:

(1) The individual defendant has not been arrested;

(2) A defendant corporation or association has not been served with summons; or

(3) There is not sufficient time for trial at that term of court.

History of CCP art. 29.01: Acts 1965, 59th Leg., ch. 722, §1, eff. Jan. 1, 1966. Amended by Acts 1973, 63rd Leg., ch. 399, §2(A), eff. Jan. 1, 1974.

ANNOTATIONS

Freeman v. State, 556 S.W.2d 287, 307 (Tex.Crim. App.1977), *overruled on other grounds*, *Cuevas v. State*, 641 S.W.2d 558, 560 (Tex.Crim.App.1982). "[T]he disposition of a motion for continuance based on equitable grounds lies in the sound discretion of the trial court."

ART. 29.011. RELIGIOUS HOLY DAY

(a) In this article:

(1) "Religious organization" means an organization that meets the standards for qualifying as a religious organization under Section 11.20, Tax Code.

(2) "Religious holy day" means a day on which the tenets of a religious organization prohibit its members from participating in secular activities, such as court proceedings.

(b) If a defendant, an attorney representing the defendant, or an attorney representing the state in a criminal action is required to appear at a court proceeding on a religious holy day observed by the person, the court shall continue the action.

(c) A defendant or attorney seeking a continuance must file with the court an affidavit stating:

(1) the grounds for the continuance; and

(2) that the person holds religious beliefs that prohibit him from taking part in a court proceeding on the day for which the continuance is sought.

(d) An affidavit filed under Subsection (c) of this article is proof of the facts stated and need not be corroborated.

History of CCP art. 29.011: Acts 1987, 70th Leg., ch. 825, §1, eff. Sept. 1, 1987. Amended by Acts 1991, 72nd Leg., ch. 815, §1, eff. Sept. 1, 1991.

ART. 29.012. RELIGIOUS HOLY DAY

(a) In this article:

(1) "Religious organization" means an organization that meets the standards for qualification as a religious organization under Section 11.20, Tax Code.

(2) "Religious holy day" means a day on which the tenets of a religious organization prohibit its members from participating in secular activities, such as court proceedings.

(b) If a juror in a criminal action is required to appear at a court proceeding on a religious holy day observed by the juror, the court or the court's designee shall recess the criminal action until the next day the court is in session after the conclusion of the holy day.

(c) A juror seeking a recess must file with the court before the final selection of the jury an affidavit stating:

(1) the grounds for the recess; and

(2) that the juror holds religious beliefs that prohibit him from taking part in a court proceeding on the day for which the recess is sought.

(d) An affidavit filed under Subsection (c) of this section is proof of the facts stated and need not be corroborated.

History of CCP art. 29.012: Acts 1987, 70th Leg., ch. 589, §1 (eff. Aug. 31, 1987), ch. 825, §4 (eff. Sept. 1, 1987).

ART. 29.02. BY AGREEMENT

A criminal action may be continued by consent of the parties thereto, in open court, at any time on a showing of good cause, but a continuance may be only for as long as is necessary.

History of CCP art. 29.02: Acts 1965, 59th Leg., ch. 722, §1, eff. Jan. 1, 1966. Amended by Acts 1977, 65th Leg., ch. 787, §3, eff. July 1, 1978.

ANNOTATIONS

Fisher v. State, 832 S.W.2d 641, 643-44 (Tex. App.—Corpus Christi 1992, pet. ref'd). "A pre-trial diversion agreement ... refers to a written agreement the defendant and State enter into [in which the] State agrees to dismiss the case if the defendant performs certain conditions within a specified period of time. Both the State and the defendant request that the trial court continue the present trial setting to a certain date in the future to give the defendant time to comply with the agreed conditions. The agreement is then presented to the trial court for its approval. If the trial court does not approve the agreement, the case proceeds to trial as scheduled on the docket. If the trial court approves the agreement, it grants the joint request for continuance and resets the trial to a certain date in the future. On that date, the defendant must appear before the trial court. If the defendant has complied with the conditions of the agreement, the trial court grants the State's motion to dismiss the pending criminal charges. If the defendant has not complied with the conditions of the agreement, the case proceeds to trial as scheduled."

ART. 29.03. FOR SUFFICIENT CAUSE SHOWN

A criminal action may be continued on the written motion of the State or of the defendant, upon sufficient cause shown; which cause shall be fully set forth in the motion. A continuance may be only for as long as is necessary.

History of CCP art. 29.03: Acts 1965, 59th Leg., ch. 722, §1, eff. Jan. 1, 1966. Amended by Acts 1977, 65th Leg., ch. 787, §3, eff. July 1, 1978.

ANNOTATIONS

Heiselbetz v. State, 906 S.W.2d 500, 511 (Tex.Crim. App.1995). "Where denial of a continuance has resulted in representation by counsel who was not prepared, we have not hesitated to declare an abuse of discretion. Nevertheless, the granting or denial of a motion for continuance is within the sound discretion of the trial court. *At 512:* [T]he assertion that counsel did not have time to adequately investigate medical records for potential mitigating evidence without any showing of harm likewise fails to establish an abuse of discretion."

ART. 29.04. FIRST MOTION BY STATE

It shall be sufficient, upon the first motion by the State for a continuance, if the same be for the want of a witness, to state:

1. The name of the witness and his residence, if known, or that his residence is unknown;

2. The diligence which has been used to procure his attendance; and it shall not be considered sufficient diligence to have caused to be issued, or to have applied for, a subpoena, in cases where the law authorized an attachment to issue; and

3. That the testimony of the witness is believed by the applicant to be material for the State.

History of CCP art. 29.04: Acts 1965, 59th Leg., ch. 722, §1, eff. Jan. 1, 1966.

ART. 29.05. SUBSEQUENT MOTION BY STATE

On any subsequent motion for a continuance by the State, for the want of a witness, the motion, in addition to the requisites in the preceding Article, must show:

1. The facts which the applicant expects to establish by the witness, and it must appear to the court that they are material;

2. That the applicant expects to be able to procure the attendance of the witness at the next term of the court; and

3. That the testimony cannot be procured from any other source during the present term of the court.

History of CCP art. 29.05: Acts 1965, 59th Leg., ch. 722, §1, eff. Jan. 1, 1966.

ANNOTATIONS

State v. Bacon, 751 S.W.2d 713, 716 (Tex.App.— Tyler 1988, no pet.). "[W]here no diligence issue is involved, and the motion meets the statutory requirements and is based on the absence of a material witness, the trial judge has a duty to grant the motion."

ART. 29.06. FIRST MOTION BY DEFENDANT

In the first motion by the defendant for a continuance, it shall be necessary, if the same be on account of the absence of a witness, to state:

1. The name of the witness and his residence, if known, or that his residence is not known.

2. The diligence which has been used to procure his attendance; and it shall not be considered sufficient diligence to have caused to be issued, or to have applied for, a subpoena, in cases where the law authorized an attachment to issue.

3. The facts which are expected to be proved by the witness, and it must appear to the court that they are material.

4. That the witness is not absent by the procurement or consent of the defendant.

5. That the motion is not made for delay.

6. That there is no reasonable expectation that attendance of the witness can be secured during the present term of court by a postponement of the trial to some future day of said term. The truth of the first, or

any subsequent motion, as well as the merit of the ground set forth therein and its sufficiency shall be addressed to the sound discretion of the court called to pass upon the same, and shall not be granted as a matter of right. If a motion for continuance be overruled, and the defendant convicted, if it appear upon the trial that the evidence of the witness or witnesses named in the motion was of a material character, and that the facts set forth in said motion were probably true, a new trial should be granted, and the cause continued or postponed to a future day of the same term.

History of CCP art. 29.06: Acts 1965, 59th Leg., ch. 722, §1, eff. Jan. 1, 1966.

ANNOTATIONS

Harrison v. State, 187 S.W.3d 429, 433 (Tex.Crim. App.2005). "Today we expressly disavow the holding in *Benoit* [*v. State*, 561 S.W.2d 810 (Tex.Crim.App.1977)] that to preserve error for the denial of a motion for continuance a defendant must file a motion for new trial. [¶] We hold that, to preserve for review a claim that the trial court erred in denying a motion for continuance, the defendant must timely file a motion that sufficiently advises the trial court of the defendant's request and the grounds therefor."

Franklin v. State, 858 S.W.2d 537, 539-40 (Tex. App.—Beaumont 1993, pet. ref'd). "[A] trial court does not abuse its discretion in denying a motion for continuance where the evidence does not indicate a probability that the missing witness can be located with the help of a postponement of the trial."

ART. 29.07. SUBSEQUENT MOTION BY DEFENDANT

Subsequent motions for continuance on the part of the defendant shall, in addition to the requisites in the preceding Article, state also:

1. That the testimony cannot be procured from any other source known to the defendant; and

2. That the defendant has reasonable expectation of procuring the same at the next term of the court.

History of CCP art. 29.07: Acts 1965, 59th Leg., ch. 722, §1, eff. Jan. 1, 1966.

ANNOTATIONS

Seals v. State, 634 S.W.2d 899, 903 (Tex.App.—San Antonio 1982, no pet.). "[I]t is not error to deny a second application for continuance on the basis of absent testimony where the motion is made to secure cumulative testimony."

ART. 29.08. MOTION SWORN TO

All motions for continuance must be sworn to by a person having personal knowledge of the facts relied on for the continuance.

History of CCP art. 29.08: Acts 1965, 59th Leg., ch. 722, §1, eff. Jan. 1, 1966. Amended by Acts 1981, 67th Leg., ch. 210, §1, eff. Sept. 1, 1981.

ANNOTATIONS

Dewberry v. State, 4 S.W.3d 735, 755 (Tex.Crim. App.1999). "A motion for continuance not in writing and not sworn preserves nothing for review."

Cuellar v. State, 521 S.W.2d 277, 279 (Tex.Crim. App.1975). TRCS art. 2168a, now CPRC §30.003, which provides for a legislative continuance, "is a special statute, with a special and limited purpose. [CCP art.] 29.08 is a general statute. ... Where the special statute is complete within itself, it controls, even though other statutes concerning the same subject matter contain requirements not enumerated in the special statute."

ART. 29.09. CONTROVERTING MOTION

Any material fact stated, affecting diligence, in a motion for a continuance, may be denied in writing by the adverse party. The denial shall be supported by the oath of some credible person, and filed as soon as practicable after the filing of such motion.

History of CCP art. 29.09: Acts 1965, 59th Leg., ch. 722, §1, eff. Jan. 1, 1966.

ART. 29.10. WHEN DENIAL IS FILED

When such denial is filed, the issue shall be tried by the judge; and he shall hear testimony by affidavits, and grant or refuse continuance, according to the law and facts of the case.

History of CCP art. 29.10: Acts 1965, 59th Leg., ch. 722, §1, eff. Jan. 1, 1966.

ART. 29.11. ARGUMENT

No argument shall be heard on a motion for a continuance, unless requested by the judge; and when argument is heard, the applicant shall have the right to open and conclude it.

History of CCP art. 29.11: Acts 1965, 59th Leg., ch. 722, §1, eff. Jan. 1, 1966.

ART. 29.12. BAIL RESULTING FROM CONTINUANCE

If a defendant in a capital case demand a trial, and it appears that more than one continuance has been granted to the State, and that the defendant has not before applied for a continuance, he shall be entitled to be admitted to bail, unless it be made to appear to the satisfaction of the court that a material witness of the State had been prevented from attendance by the procurement of the defendant or some person acting in his behalf.

History of CCP art. 29.12: Acts 1965, 59th Leg., ch. 722, §1, eff. Jan. 1, 1966. See also CCP art. 17.151.

ANNOTATIONS

Walker v. State, 629 S.W.2d 199, 201 (Tex.App.—Corpus Christi 1982, pet. dism'd). "The fact that the continuances were granted in the Travis County trial, which was subsequently dismissed, [and that appellant is now being tried in Hidalgo County] does not change the fact that the appellant has been held in jail without bail throughout two continuances by the State. We hold that art. 29.12 applies to the appellant, and therefore appellant is entitled to be admitted to bail."

ART. 29.13. CONTINUANCE AFTER TRIAL IS BEGUN

A continuance or postponement may be granted on the motion of the State or defendant after the trial has begun, when it is made to appear to the satisfaction of the court that by some unexpected occurrence since the trial began, which no reasonable diligence could have anticipated, the applicant is so taken by surprise that a fair trial cannot be had.

History of CCP art. 29.13: Acts 1965, 59th Leg., ch. 722, §1, eff. Jan. 1, 1966.

ANNOTATIONS

Gentry v. State, 770 S.W.2d 780, 786 (Tex.Crim. App.1988). "[T]o be entitled to [the] continuance a defendant must comply with each of the statutory prerequisites. Initially, the request for a continuance must be in writing and sworn to by the defendant. [T]he written motion must allege facts sufficient to constitute surprise and diligence. [T]he record must contain an affidavit or otherwise reflect what the absent witness would have testified to. And, the expected testimony has to be material to the defendant."

Vega v. State, 898 S.W.2d 359, 361 (Tex.App.—San Antonio 1995, pet. ref'd). It is "an abuse of discretion for the trial court to deny [D's] oral motion for continuance made during trial after [D] discovered on the first day of trial that the State possessed exculpatory evidence which it failed to disclose prior to trial."

CHAPTER 30. DISQUALIFICATION OF THE JUDGE

ART. 30.01. CAUSES WHICH DISQUALIFY

No judge or justice of the peace shall sit in any case where he may be the party injured, or where he has been of counsel for the State or the accused, or where the accused or the party injured may be connected with him by consanguinity or affinity within the third degree, as determined under Chapter 573, Government Code.

History of CCP art. 30.01: Acts 1965, 59th Leg., ch. 722, §1, eff. Jan. 1, 1966. Amended by Acts 1991, 72nd Leg., ch. 561, §9, eff. Aug. 26, 1991; Acts 1995, 74th Leg., ch. 76, §5.95(27), eff. Sept. 1, 1995.

See also Gov't Code §21.005, ch. 573; chart, "Relatives by Degrees," p. 261.

ANNOTATIONS

Whitehead v. State, ___ S.W.3d ___ (Tex.Crim. App.2008) (No. PD-0713-07; 6-25-08). "[W]e interpret the opening clause of Article 30.01 to mean that a trial court judge, in any particular criminal prosecution, 'may be the party injured,' and is therefore disqualified from presiding, if the evidence shows that he was among the defendant's victims in the criminal transaction or episode at issue, such that a reasonable person would harbor doubts as to the judge's impartiality. At ___ n.3: [I]f a trial court judge is disqualified under Article 30.01 from presiding at a trial, then any resulting judgment is a nullity and may be challenged for the first time on appeal." See also **Ex parte Vivier**, 699 S.W.2d 862, 863 (Tex.Crim.App.1985).

Ex parte Richardson, 201 S.W.3d 712, 712 (Tex. Crim.App.2006). "Applicant asks us to overturn his probation revocation because the judge who presided over the revocation proceeding was the prosecutor in the original prosecution. The question is whether he may obtain relief on this claim by way of postconviction habeas corpus—even though applicant had this information before pleading true and he chose not to complain. We hold that he may not."

Lyon v. State, 872 S.W.2d 732, 736-37 (Tex.Crim. App.1994). "'Affinity is the tie which exists between one of the spouses with the kindred of the other....' [T]he victim is not part of the kindred of the trial judge's wife; therefore, no affinity exists between the

CCP ART. 30.01

trial judge and the victim even though the trial 'judge's daughter was related by affinity to the victim.'"

Gamez v. State, 737 S.W.2d 315, 318 (Tex.Crim. App.1987). Article 30.01 has "been held to be mandatory. [¶] It is not necessary that an objection be made. The disqualification of a judge may not be waived even by consent of the parties. The issue may be raised at any time. *At 319:* '[T]he mere fact that a judge was district attorney at the time of the offense or at the time that the accused was examined or indicted does not work a disqualification if, when district attorney, he had nothing to do with the prosecution.'"

State ex rel. Millsap v. Lozano, 692 S.W.2d 470, 475 (Tex.Crim.App.1985). "'It is not necessary ... that the judge, claimed to be disqualified, seek an independent determination of his impartiality in the cause by another judge.' [¶] [A] judge is presumed to be qualified until the contrary is shown."

Hathorne v. State, 459 S.W.2d 826, 829 (Tex.Crim. App.1970). "[T]he mere fact that the trial judge personally prosecuted the appellant in past cases does not disqualify him from presiding over a trial where a new offense is charged. [¶] [T]he same rule would have application where the trial judge had defended the accused at the time of the prior conviction."

Burkett v. State, 196 S.W.3d 892, 895 (Tex.App.— Texarkana 2006, no pet.). "Any discretionary act performed by a disqualified judge is void. On the other hand, a disqualified judge may perform purely ministerial tasks. [¶] An act is ministerial when the law requires that a duty be performed and leaves nothing to the exercise of discretion or judgment. Discretionary acts are those in which one has the right to determine between two or more courses of action. *At 896:* A judge shall recuse in any proceeding in which the judge's impartiality might reasonably be questioned. In determining whether a judge's impartiality might be reasonably questioned so as to require recusal, the proper inquiry is whether a reasonable member of the public at large, knowing all the facts in the public domain concerning the judge and the case, would have a reasonable doubt that the judge is actually impartial." Held: The act of deciding who may serve on a jury is discretionary and intimately associated with, and capable of a potent influence on, the trial of a case. Even if the disqualified judge's involvement in a case was harmless, that involvement still requires reversal of the case.

Stafford v. State, 948 S.W.2d 921, 924 (Tex.App.— Texarkana 1997, pet. ref'd). "Before an alleged bias becomes sufficient to warrant the disqualification of a judge, it 'must stem from an extrajudicial source and result in an opinion on the merits on some basis other than what the judge learned from his participation in the case.'"

ART. 30.02. DISTRICT JUDGE DISQUALIFIED

Whenever any case is pending in which the district judge or criminal district judge is disqualified from trying the case, no change of venue shall be made necessary thereby; but the judge presiding shall certify that fact to the presiding judge of the administrative judicial district in which the case is pending and the presiding judge of such administrative judicial district shall assign a judge to try such case in accordance with the provisions of Article 200a, V.A.C.S.[1]

1. **Editor's note:** Now Gov't Code §74.042 et seq.

History of CCP art. 30.02: Acts 1965, 59th Leg., ch. 722, §14, eff. Jan. 1, 1966.

See also TRCP 18a, 18b.

ANNOTATIONS

DeLeon v. Aguilar, 127 S.W.3d 1, 5 (Tex.Crim.App. 2004). "The procedures for recusal of judges set out in [TRCP] Rule 18a ... apply in criminal cases."

ARTS. 30.03 TO 30.06. REPEALED

Repealed by Acts 1999, 76th Leg., ch. 1388, §1, eff. Sept. 1, 1999.

ART. 30.07. JUSTICE DISQUALIFIED

If a justice of the peace be disqualified from sitting in any criminal action pending before him, he shall transfer the same to any justice of the peace in the county who is not disqualified to try the case.

History of CCP art. 30.07: Acts 1965, 59th Leg., ch. 722, §1, eff. Jan. 1, 1966.
See also TRCP 18a, 18b.

ART. 30.08. ORDER OF TRANSFER

In cases provided for in the preceding Article, the order of transfer shall state the cause of the transfer, and name the court to which the transfer is made, and the time and place, when and where, the parties and witnesses shall appear before such court. The rules governing the transfer of cases from the district to inferior courts shall govern in the transfer of cases under the preceding Article.

History of CCP art. 30.08: Acts 1965, 59th Leg., ch. 722, §1, eff. Jan. 1, 1966.
See also TRCP 18a, 18b.

RELATIVES BY DEGREES

1ST DEGREE	2ND DEGREE	3RD DEGREE
Spouse	Granddaughter & spouse	Great-grandmother & spouse
Mother & spouse	Grandson & spouse	Great-grandfather & spouse
Father & spouse	Grandmother & spouse	Great-granddaughter & spouse
Daughter & spouse	Grandfather & spouse	Great-grandson & spouse
Son & spouse	Sister & spouse	Niece & spouse
Mother-in-law	Brother & spouse	Nephew & spouse
Father-in-law	Sister-in-law	Aunt & spouse
Stepdaughter	Brother-in-law	Uncle & spouse
Stepson	Grandmother-in-law	Half-aunt & spouse
	Grandfather-in-law	Half-uncle & spouse
	Step-granddaughter	Great-grandmother-in-law
	Step-grandson	Great-grandfather-in-law
	Half-sister & spouse	Aunt-in-law
	Half-brother & spouse	Uncle-in-law
	Stepsister & spouse	Niece-in-law
	Stepbrother & spouse	Nephew-in-law
		Step-great-granddaughter
		Step-great-grandson
		Step-niece & spouse
		Step-nephew & spouse

CHAPTER 31. CHANGE OF VENUE

ART. 31.01. ON COURT'S OWN MOTION

Whenever in any case of felony or misdemeanor punishable by confinement, the judge presiding shall be satisfied that a trial, alike fair and impartial to the accused and to the State, cannot, from any cause, be had in the county in which the case is pending, he may, upon his own motion, after due notice to accused and the State, and after hearing evidence thereon, order a change of venue to any county in the judicial district in which such county is located or in an adjoining district, stating in his order the grounds for such change of venue. The judge, upon his own motion, after ten days notice to the parties or their counsel, may order a change of venue to any county beyond an adjoining district; provided, however, an order changing venue to a county beyond an adjoining district shall be grounds for reversal if, upon timely contest by the defendant, the record of the contest affirmatively shows that any county in his own and the adjoining district is not subject to the same conditions which required the transfer.

History of CCP art. 31.01: Acts 1965, 59th Leg., ch. 722, §1, eff. Jan. 1, 1966.

Brimage v. State, 918 S.W.2d 466, 508 (Tex.Crim. App.1996). "'When the Legislature enact[ed] Art. 31.01, its purpose was evidently to require a court, once satisfied that a fair trial cannot be had, to give notice to both parties of its intention to change venue and to hold a hearing allowing either party to offer evidence either in support of or against the court's proposed change in venue. The statute does not require the court to offer evidence in support of its own motion, but rather merely offers the parties a chance to be heard on the matter. The court is only required to state in its order the grounds for its decision to change venue.'"

Smith v. State, 850 S.W.2d 275, 279 (Tex.App.— Fort Worth 1993, pet. ref'd). CCP arts. 31.01-31.03 provide "only for a requested change of venue hearing to be held before the trial is completed. [T]he Court of Criminal Appeals has stated that a trial court does not commit error by holding in abeyance a ruling on a motion to change venue until after jury selection."

ART. 31.02. STATE MAY HAVE

Whenever the district or county attorney shall represent in writing to the court before which any felony or misdemeanor case punishable by confinement, is pending, that, by reason of existing combinations or influences in favor of the accused, or on account of the lawless condition of affairs in the county, a fair and impartial trial as between the accused and the State cannot be safely and speedily had; or whenever he shall represent that the life of the prisoner, or of any witness, would be jeopardized by a trial in the county in which the case is pending, the judge shall hear proof in relation thereto, and if satisfied that such representation is well-founded and that the ends of public justice will be subserved thereby, he shall order a change of venue to any county in the judicial district in which such county is located or in an adjoining district.

History of CCP art. 31.02: Acts 1965, 59th Leg., ch. 722, §1, eff. Jan. 1, 1966.

ART. 31.03. GRANTED ON MOTION OF DEFENDANT

(a) A change of venue may be granted in any felony or misdemeanor case punishable by confinement on the written motion of the defendant, supported by his own affidavit and the affidavit of at least two credible persons, residents of the county where the prosecution is instituted, for either of the following causes, the truth and sufficiency of which the court shall determine:

1.   That there exists in the county where the prosecution is commenced so great a prejudice against him that he cannot obtain a fair and impartial trial; and

2.   That there is a dangerous combination against him instigated by influential persons, by reason of which he cannot expect a fair trial.

An order changing venue to a county beyond an adjoining district shall be grounds for reversal, if upon timely contest by defendant, the record of the contest affirmatively shows that any county in his own and the adjoining district is not subject to the same conditions which required the transfer.

(b) For the convenience of parties and witnesses, and in the interest of justice, the court upon motion of the defendant and with the consent of the attorney for the state may transfer the proceeding as to him to another district.

(c) The court upon motion of the defendant and with the consent of the attorney for the state may transfer the proceedings to another district in those cases wherein the defendant stipulates that a plea of guilty will be entered.

History of CCP art. 31.03: Acts 1965, 59th Leg., ch. 722, §1, eff. Jan. 1, 1966. Amended by Acts 1979, 66th Leg., ch. 140, §1, eff. Aug. 27, 1979.

ANNOTATIONS

Gonzalez v. State, 222 S.W.3d 446, 449 (Tex.Crim. App.2007). "To justify a change of venue based upon media attention, a defendant must show that the publicity was pervasive, prejudicial, and inflammatory. Widespread publicity by itself is not considered inherently prejudicial. Indeed, even extensive knowledge of the case or defendant in the community as a result of pretrial publicity is not sufficient if there is not also some showing of prejudicial or inflammatory coverage. The mere existence of media attention or publicity is not enough, by itself, to merit a change of venue. [¶] The standard of review on appeal from a ruling on a motion for change of venue is 'abuse of discretion.' [¶] The two primary means of discerning whether publicity is pervasive are a hearing on the motion to change venue and the voir dire process. *At 451:* In examining whether the pretrial publicity is prejudicial and inflammatory, a trial court may take three matters into consideration: 1) the nature of the publicity, 2) any evidence presented at a change of venue hearing, and 3) testimony received from veniremembers at voir dire. News stories, be it from print, radio, or television, that are accurate and objective in their coverage, are generally considered by this Court not to be prejudicial or inflammatory." *See also* **Rule v. State**, 890 S.W.2d 158, 168-69 (Tex.App.—Texarkana 1994, pet. ref'd).

ART. 31.04. MOTION MAY BE CONTROVERTED

The credibility of the persons making affidavit for change of venue, or their means of knowledge, may be attacked by the affidavit of a credible person. The issue thus formed shall be tried by the judge, and the motion granted or refused, as the law and facts shall warrant.

History of CCP art. 31.04: Acts 1965, 59th Leg., ch. 722, §1, eff. Jan. 1, 1966.

ANNOTATIONS

Burks v. State, 876 S.W.2d 877, 890 (Tex.Crim.App. 1994). "A controverting affidavit ... is a notarized statement of the opinion of the compurgator [county resident] that the opposing affiant is not credible, and/or that opposing affiant's means of knowledge are not sufficient."

Clarke v. State, 928 S.W.2d 709, 718 (Tex.App.—Fort Worth 1996, pet. ref'd). "Although [Article 31.04] does not specify that the State must file controverting affidavits, ... until this is done, there is no issue between the parties to argue at a hearing. If the State files no controverting affidavits, the defendant is entitled to a change of venue as a matter of law."

Alvarado v. State, 709 S.W.2d 339, 341 (Tex. App.—Houston [14th Dist.] 1986, pet. ref'd). "Once the controverting affidavit to the defendant's motion for change of venue is filed, the burden is then upon the accused to prove he cannot receive a fair and impartial trial."

ART. 31.05. CLERK'S DUTIES ON CHANGE OF VENUE

Where an order for a change of venue of any court in any criminal cause in this State has been made the clerk of the court where the prosecution is pending shall make out a certified copy of the court's order directing such change of venue, together with a certified copy of the defendant's bail bond or personal bond, together with all the original papers in said cause and also a certificate of the said clerk under his official seal that such papers are the papers and all the papers on file in said court in said cause; and he shall transmit the same to the clerk of the court to which the venue has been changed.

History of CCP art. 31.05: Acts 1965, 59th Leg., ch. 722, §1, eff. Jan. 1, 1966.

ART. 31.06. IF DEFENDANT BE IN CUSTODY

When the venue is changed in any criminal action if the defendant be in custody, an order shall be made for his removal to the proper county, and his delivery to the sheriff thereof before the next succeeding term of the court of the county to which the case is to be taken, and he shall be delivered by the sheriff as directed in the order.

History of CCP art. 31.06: Acts 1965, 59th Leg., ch. 722, §1, eff. Jan. 1, 1966.

ART. 31.07. WITNESS NEED NOT AGAIN BE SUMMONED

When the venue in a criminal action has been changed, it shall not be necessary to have the witnesses therein again subpoenaed, attached or bailed, but all the witnesses who have been subpoenaed, attached or bailed to appear and testify in the cause shall be held bound to appear before the court to which the cause has been transferred, as if there had been no such transfer.

History of CCP art. 31.07: Acts 1965, 59th Leg., ch. 722, §1, eff. Jan. 1, 1966.

ART. 31.08. RETURN TO COUNTY OF ORIGINAL VENUE

Sec. 1. (a) On the completion of a trial in which a change of venue has been ordered and after the jury has been discharged, the court, with the consent of counsel for the state and the defendant, may return the cause to the original county in which the indictment or information was filed. Except as provided by Subsection (b) of this section, all subsequent and ancillary proceedings, including the pronouncement of sentence after appeals have been exhausted, must be heard in the county in which the indictment or information was filed.

(b) A motion for new trial alleging jury misconduct must be heard in the county in which the cause was tried. The county in which the indictment or information was filed must pay the costs of the prosecution of the motion for new trial.

Sec. 2. (a) Except as provided by Subsection (b), on an order returning venue to the original county in which the indictment or information was filed, the clerk of the county in which the cause was tried shall:

(1) make a certified copy of the court's order directing the return to the original county;

(2) make a certified copy of the defendant's bail bond, personal bond, or appeal bond;

(3) gather all the original papers in the cause and certify under official seal that the papers are all the original papers on file in the court; and

(4) transmit the items listed in this section to the clerk of the court of original venue.

(b) This article does not apply to a proceeding in which the clerk of the court of original venue was present and performed the duties as clerk for the court under Article 31.09.

 Section 3 below is effective for offenses committed on or after Sept. 1, 2007.

Sec. 3. Except for the review of a death sentence under Section 2(h), Article 37.071, or under Section 2(h), Article 37.072, an appeal taken in a cause returned to the original county under this article must be docketed in the appellate district in which the county of original venue is located.

Section 3 below is effective for offenses in which any element of the offense was committed before Sept. 1, 2007.

Sec. 3. Except for the review of a death sentence under Article 37.071(h) of this code, an appeal taken in a cause returned to the original county under this article must be docketed in the appellate district in which the county of original venue is located.

History of CCP art. 31.08: Acts 1989, 71st Leg., ch. 824, §1, eff. Sept. 1, 1989. Amended by Acts 1995, 74th Leg., ch. 651, §1, eff. Sept. 1, 1995; Acts 2007, 80th Leg., ch. 593, §3.13, eff. Sept. 1, 2007.

ART. 31.09. CHANGE OF VENUE; USE OF EXISTING SERVICES

(a) If a change of venue in a criminal case is ordered under this chapter, the judge ordering the change of venue may, with the written consent of the prosecuting attorney, the defense attorney, and the defendant, maintain the original case number on its own docket, preside over the case, and use the services of the court reporter, the court coordinator, and the clerk of the court of original venue. The court shall use the courtroom facilities and any other services or facilities of the district or county to which venue is changed. A jury, if required, must consist of residents of the district or county to which venue is changed.

(b) Notwithstanding Article 31.05, the clerk of the court of original venue shall:

(1) maintain the original papers of the case, including the defendant's bail bond or personal bond;

(2) make the papers available for trial; and

(3) act as the clerk in the case.

History of CCP art. 31.09: Acts 1995, 74th Leg., ch. 651, §2, eff. Sept. 1, 1995.

CHAPTER 32. DISMISSING PROSECUTIONS

Art. 32.01   Defendant in custody & no indictment presented
Art. 32.02   Dismissal by State's attorney

ART. 32.01. DEFENDANT IN CUSTODY & NO INDICTMENT PRESENTED

When a defendant has been detained in custody or held to bail for his appearance to answer any criminal accusation, the prosecution, unless otherwise ordered by the court, for good cause shown, supported by affidavit, shall be dismissed and the bail discharged, if indictment or information be not presented against such defendant on or before the last day of the next term of the court which is held after his commitment or admission to bail or on or before the 180th day after the date of commitment or admission to bail, whichever date is later.

History of CCP art. 32.01: Acts 1965, 59th Leg., ch. 722, §1, eff. Jan. 1, 1966. Amended by Acts 1997, 75th Leg., ch. 289, §2, eff. May 26, 1997; Acts 2005, 79th Leg., ch. 743, §6, eff. Sept. 1, 2005.

See also CCP art. 15.14.

Ex parte Countryman, 226 S.W.3d 435 436 (Tex. Crim.App.2007). "Because the State had not obtained an indictment by the next term of court, Appellant filed an application for writ of habeas corpus to have the case dismissed. After Appellant filed the application, but before the trial court held a hearing, the grand jury returned an indictment. The trial court denied the application and Appellant appealed. The court of appeals reversed the trial court's order denying habeas relief and ordered that the indictment be dismissed. We granted the State's petition for discretionary review to determine whether a speedy-indictment claim is moot when it is filed before the indictment, but not heard until after the indictment is returned." Held: The court of appeals erred. The claim was moot because even a determination that the State did not show good cause would not provide a remedy to appellant.

Ex parte Seidel, 39 S.W.3d 221, 223-24 (Tex.Crim. App.2001). "[A] district court lacks jurisdiction over a case when an information or indictment has not yet been filed in that court. In this case, an information or indictment had not yet been filed when the trial judge dismissed the bail and prosecution against appellee. The district court, however, had proper jurisdiction to act under the Speedy Trial Act because appellee was 'held to bail for his appearance to answer any criminal accusation before the district court.' [¶] Generally, a trial court does not have the power to dismiss a case unless the prosecutor so requests. A trial court does, however, have the power to dismiss a case without the State's consent under [CCP art.] 32.01. [CCP art.] 28.061, which bars further prosecution for a discharged offense … no longer applies to a discharge under Article 32.01. Therefore, even if a defendant is entitled to discharge from custody under Article 32.01, that defendant is not free from subsequent prosecution." *Author's note:* The dismissal cannot be with prejudice.

Ex parte Martin, 6 S.W.3d 524, 528 (Tex.Crim.App. 1999). "In *Barker v. Wingo*, the [U.S.] Supreme Court set out a balancing test with four factors to determine when pretrial delay denies an accused of his right to a speedy trial…. Today we adopt a *Barker*-like, totality-of-circumstances test for the determination of good cause under article 32.01. The habeas court should consider, among other things, the length of the delay, the State's reason for delay, whether the delay was due to lack of diligence on the part of the State, and whether the delay caused harm to the accused. [¶] Another relevant inquiry is whether the grand jury has voted not to pre-sent an indictment. *At 529:* By adopting this test, we are not adding constitutional, speedy-trial rights to article 32.01. We are adopting a test for a fact-based situation."

Cameron v. State, 988 S.W.2d 835, 843 (Tex. App.—San Antonio 1999, pet. ref'd). "[A] defendant cannot complain of the timeliness of a second or other indictment under article 32.01 once a valid and timely indictment is secured by the State. For timeliness purposes, we hold that article 32.01 is satisfied once the State secures a timely indictment arising out of the same criminal transaction or occurrence. The defendant suffers no due process violation if he continues under a valid indictment, although it is not the indictment he is ultimately prosecuted and convicted for, so long as the indictment arises out of the same criminal transaction or occurrence. ... Article 32.01 should not be read to preclude the State from advancing alternative theories or charges arising out of the same criminal transaction once the State has acted within the timetable prescribed by article 32.01 for initially securing a timely indictment. If the State is dilatory in prosecuting the case, the defendant may invoke his speedy trial right."

Soderman v. State, 915 S.W.2d 605, 608 (Tex. App.—Houston [14th Dist.] 1996, pet. ref'd). "[T]his provision applies only to district courts. Absent any language in the statute or case law to support applying this provision to county courts, we are without authority to do so."

Uptergrove v. State, 881 S.W.2d 529, 531 (Tex. App.—Texarkana 1994, pet. ref'd). Article 32.01 "does not apply to a juvenile proceeding to determine whether a juvenile is to be transferred to district court to be tried as an adult."

ART. 32.02. DISMISSAL BY STATE'S ATTORNEY

The attorney representing the State may, by permission of the court, dismiss a criminal action at any time upon filing a written statement with the papers in the case setting out his reasons for such dismissal, which shall be incorporated in the judgment of dismissal. No case shall be dismissed without the consent of the presiding judge.

History of CCP art. 32.02: Acts 1965, 59th Leg., ch. 722, §1, eff. Jan. 1, 1966.

Smith v. State, 70 S.W.3d 848, 850-51 (Tex.Crim. App.2002). "The authority to grant immunity derives from the authority of a prosecutor to dismiss prosecutions. The authority to dismiss a case is governed by [Article] 32.02. A grant of immunity from prosecution is, conceptually, a prosecutorial promise to dismiss a case. Article 32.02 directs that a dismissal made by the prosecutor must be approved by the trial court. Therefore, a District Attorney has no authority to grant immunity without court approval, for the approval of the court is 'essential' to establish immunity. *At 855:* Provided the judge approves the dismissal that results from an immunity agreement, and is aware that the dismissal is pursuant to an immunity agreement, the judge does not have to be aware of the specific terms of that immunity agreement for it to be enforceable."

CHAPTER 32A. SPEEDY TRIAL
Art. 32A.01   Trial priorities

ART. 32A.01. TRIAL PRIORITIES

Insofar as is practicable, the trial of a criminal action shall be given preference over trials of civil cases, and the trial of a criminal action against a defendant who is detained in jail pending trial of the action shall be given preference over trials of other criminal actions.

History of CCP art. 32A.01: Acts 1977, 65th Leg., ch. 787, §1, eff. July 1, 1978.

ART. 32A.02. REPEALED
Repealed by Acts 2005, 79th Leg., ch. 1019, §2, eff. June 18, 2005.

CHAPTER 33. THE MODE OF TRIAL
Art. 33.01   Jury size
Art. 33.011   Alternate jurors
Art. 33.02   Failure to register
Art. 33.03   Presence of defendant
Art. 33.04   May appear by counsel
Art. 33.05   On bail during trial
Art. 33.06   Sureties bound in case of mistrial
Art. 33.07   Record of criminal actions
Art. 33.08   To fix day for criminal docket
Art. 33.09   Jury drawn

ART. 33.01. JURY SIZE

(a) Except as provided by Subsection (b), in the district court, the jury shall consist of twelve qualified jurors. In the county court and inferior courts, the jury shall consist of six qualified jurors.

(b) In a trial involving a misdemeanor offense, a district court jury shall consist of six qualified jurors.

History of CCP art. 33.01: Acts 1965, 59th Leg., ch. 722, §1, eff. Jan. 1, 1966. Amended by Acts 2003, 78th Leg., ch. 466, §1, eff. Jan. 1, 2004.

See also Tex. Const. art. 5, §13; Gov't Code §62.201.

ANNOTATIONS

Roberts v. State, 957 S.W.2d 80, 81 (Tex.Crim.App. 1997). "[A] defendant may waive his statutory right to a jury of twelve members."

ART. 33.011. ALTERNATE JURORS

(a) In district courts, the judge may direct that not more than four jurors in addition to the regular jury be called and impaneled to sit as alternate jurors. In county courts, the judge may direct that not more than two jurors in addition to the regular jury be called and impaneled to sit as alternate jurors.

 Subsection (b) below is effective for trials commenced on or after Sept. 1, 2007.

(b) Alternate jurors in the order in which they are called shall replace jurors who, prior to the time the jury renders a verdict on the guilt or innocence of the defendant and, if applicable, the amount of punishment, become or are found to be unable or disqualified to perform their duties or are found by the court on agreement of the parties to have good cause for not performing their duties. Alternate jurors shall be drawn and selected in the same manner, shall have the same qualifications, shall be subject to the same examination and challenges, shall take the same oath, and shall have the same functions, powers, facilities, security, and privileges as regular jurors. An alternate juror who does not replace a regular juror shall be discharged after the jury has rendered a verdict on the guilt or innocence of the defendant and, if applicable, the amount of punishment.

Subsection (b) below is effective for trials commenced before Sept. 1, 2007.

(b) Alternate jurors in the order in which they are called shall replace jurors who, prior to the time the jury retires to consider its verdict, become or are found to be unable or disqualified to perform their duties. Alternate jurors shall be drawn and selected in the same manner, shall have the same qualifications, shall be subject to the same examination and challenges, shall take the same oath, and shall have the same functions, powers, facilities, security, and privileges as regular jurors. An alternate juror who does not replace a regular juror shall be discharged after the jury retires to consider its verdict.

History of CCP art. 33.011: Acts 1983, 68th Leg., ch. 775, §2, eff. Aug. 29, 1983. Amended by Acts 2007, 80th Leg., ch. 846, §1, eff. Sept. 1, 2007.

ART. 33.02. FAILURE TO REGISTER

Failure to register to vote shall not disqualify any person from jury service.

History of CCP art. 33.02: Acts 1965, 59th Leg., ch. 722, §1, eff. Jan. 1, 1966. Amended by Acts 1981, 67th Leg., ch. 827, §6, eff. Aug. 31, 1981.

ART. 33.03. PRESENCE OF DEFENDANT

In all prosecutions for felonies, the defendant must be personally present at the trial, and he must likewise be present in all cases of misdemeanor when the punishment or any part thereof is imprisonment in jail; provided, however, that in all cases, when the defendant voluntarily absents himself after pleading to the indictment or information, or after the jury has been selected when trial is before a jury, the trial may proceed to its conclusion. When the record in the appellate court shows that the defendant was present at the commencement, or any portion of the trial, it shall be presumed in the absence of all evidence in the record to the contrary that he was present during the whole trial. Provided, however, that the presence of the defendant shall not be required at the hearing on the motion for new trial in any misdemeanor case.

History of CCP art. 33.03: Acts 1965, 59th Leg., ch. 722, §1, eff. Jan. 1, 1966. Amended by Acts 1979, 66th Leg., ch. 745, §1, eff. Aug. 27, 1979.

ANNOTATIONS

Garcia v. State, 919 S.W.2d 370, 393-94 (Tex.Crim. App.1996). Appellant "affirmatively waived his right to be present at the ... proceedings, a confrontation clause-based right granted under [art. 33.03]. We have held that this right, even if denied, is subject to harmless error analysis."

Miller v. State, 692 S.W.2d 88, 93 (Tex.Crim.App. 1985). "[T]he jury had been 'selected' for purposes of [art. 33.03] 'when the parties handed in their respective jury lists, with the [peremptory] challenges noted thereon.'" *See also Chambers v. State*, 903 S.W.2d 21, 31 (Tex.Crim.App.1995).

Moore v. State, 670 S.W.2d 259, 261 (Tex.Crim.App. 1984). "Since the trial court could have reasonably inferred from the information before it that appellant voluntarily absented himself, the court did not abuse its discretion in denying appellant's motion for continuance and proceeding with trial as authorized by Art. 33.03.... [¶] [T]he Court of Appeals was incorrect in holding that in reviewing the validity of a court's decision to proceed with trial under Art. 33.03, an appellate court can only consider the evidence which was before the trial court at the time it made its ruling, and must ignore evidence which develops subsequent to the ruling, even if such evidence substantiates the trial court's finding that the defendant's absence was voluntary."

Kerr v. State, 83 S.W.3d 832, 834 (Tex.App.—Texarkana 2002, no pet.). "Although Kerr appeared before the court before his trial began, the record clearly reflects that, at the time he voluntarily left the courtroom, jury selection had not begun and Kerr had not personally, or by his counsel, entered a plea before the jury. The State directs us to a docket sheet entry for evidence that Kerr had entered a plea before trial began. However, the docket sheet is not part of the record...." Held: D's conviction was reversed because of his absence.

Valadez v. State, 979 S.W.2d 18, 20 (Tex.App.—Houston [14th Dist.] 1998, pet. ref'd). "Valadez contends the trial court erred in conducting hearings upon the State's motion in limine outside his presence. ... [¶] Valadez's complaint has two fundamental problems: his counsel did not object to his absence and, more importantly, he has not shown any harm by the court's actions. In this regard, under the case law, before we can reverse the trial court for violating the requirement that the defendant must be personally present at trial, Valadez must make an actual showing of injury or a showing of facts which can be inferred in order to require reversal." *See also Mares v. State*, 571 S.W.2d 303, 307 (Tex.Crim.App.1978).

ART. 33.04. MAY APPEAR BY COUNSEL

In other misdemeanor cases, the defendant may, by consent of the State's attorney, appear by counsel, and the trial may proceed without his personal presence.

History of CCP art. 33.04: Acts 1965, 59th Leg., ch. 722, §1, eff. Jan. 1, 1966.

ART. 33.05. ON BAIL DURING TRIAL

If the defendant is on bail when the trial commences, such bail shall be considered as discharged if he is acquitted. If a verdict of guilty is returned against him, the discharge of his bail shall be governed by other provisions of this Code.

History of CCP art. 33.05: Acts 1965, 59th Leg., ch. 722, §1, eff. Jan. 1, 1966.

ART. 33.06. SURETIES BOUND IN CASE OF MISTRIAL

If there be a mistrial in a felony case, the original sureties, if any, of the defendant shall be still held bound for his appearance until they surrender him in accordance with the provisions of this Code.

History of CCP art. 33.06: Acts 1965, 59th Leg., ch. 722, §1, eff. Jan. 1, 1966.

ART. 33.07. RECORD OF CRIMINAL ACTIONS

Each clerk of a court of record having criminal jurisdiction shall keep a record in which shall be set down the style and file number of each criminal action, the nature of the offense, the names of counsel, the proceedings had therein, and the date of each proceeding.

History of CCP art. 33.07: Acts 1965, 59th Leg., ch. 722, §1, eff. Jan. 1, 1966. Amended by Acts 2007, 80th Leg., ch. 628, §3, eff. Sept. 1, 2007.

ANNOTATIONS

Flores v. State, 888 S.W.2d 193, 195 (Tex.App.—Houston [1st Dist.] 1994, pet. ref'd). "[D]ocket sheet entries and other instruments found in the appellate record will not constitute substantial compliance with [TRAP] 40(b)(1) [now 25.2(b)(3)]. The reason for this is that, in most cases, the docket sheet is merely a record kept by the clerk showing the order and nature of the proceedings for each criminal action."

ART. 33.08. TO FIX DAY FOR CRIMINAL DOCKET

The district courts and county courts shall have control of their respective dockets as to the settings of criminal cases.

History of CCP art. 33.08: Acts 1965, 59th Leg., ch. 722, §1, eff. Jan. 1, 1966.

ART. 33.09. JURY DRAWN

Jury panels, including special venires, for the trial of criminal cases shall be selected and summoned (with return on summons) in the same manner as the selection of panels for the trial of civil cases except as otherwise provided in this Code.

History of CCP art. 33.09: Acts 1965, 59th Leg., ch. 722, §1, eff. Jan. 1, 1966.

ANNOTATIONS

Wyle v. State, 777 S.W.2d 709, 714 (Tex.Crim.App. 1989). "Appellant argues Art. 33.09 ... was violated because the same one hundred and fifty veniremen who were called for his competency trial were also called for the trial on the merits in this cause. ... Ninety of those persons were not qualified for jury service for various reasons, and the twelve persons who served as jurors in the competency hearing were excused by the trial judge from the panel in the trial on the merits without objection from either the State or appellant. Appellant presents no authority to support his contention that the trial judge erred in denying his motion to quash or that the jury panels were improperly impaneled."

CHAPTER 34. SPECIAL VENIRE IN CAPITAL CASES

ART. 34.01. SPECIAL VENIRE

A "special venire" is a writ issued in a capital case by order of the district court, commanding the sheriff to summon either verbally or by mail such a number of persons, not less than 50, as the court may order, to appear before the court on a day named in the writ from whom the jury for the trial of such case is to be selected. Where as many as one hundred jurors have been summoned in such county for regular service for the week in which such capital case is set for trial, the judge of the court having jurisdiction of a capital case in which a motion for a special venire has been made, shall grant or refuse such motion for a special venire, and upon such refusal require the case to be tried by regular jurors summoned for service in such county for the week in which such capital case is set for trial and such additional talesmen as may be summoned by the sheriff upon order of the court as provided in Article 34.02 of this Code, but the clerk of such court shall furnish the defendant or his counsel a list of the persons summoned as provided in Article 34.04.

History of CCP art. 34.01: Acts 1965, 59th Leg., ch. 722, §1, eff. Jan. 1, 1966.

ANNOTATIONS

Barnes v. State, 876 S.W.2d 316, 324 (Tex.Crim. App.1994). "Because more than 100 jurors were called for service the week of appellant's trial, the decision to grant a special venire was within the discretion of the trial court."

Esquivel v. State, 595 S.W.2d 516, 520 (Tex.Crim. App.1980). "Upon refusal [of a special venire], the court shall require the case to be tried by the regular jurors summoned for the week."

ART. 34.02. ADDITIONAL NAMES DRAWN

In any criminal case in which the court deems that the veniremen theretofore drawn will be insufficient for the trial of the case, or in any criminal case in which the venire has been exhausted by challenge or otherwise, the court shall order additional veniremen in such numbers as the court may deem advisable, to be summoned as follows:

(a) In a jury wheel county, the names of those to be summoned shall be drawn from the jury wheel.

(b) In counties not using the jury wheel, the veniremen shall be summoned by the sheriff.

History of CCP art. 34.02: Acts 1965, 59th Leg., ch. 722, §1, eff. Jan. 1, 1966.

ART. 34.03. INSTRUCTIONS TO SHERIFF

When the sheriff is ordered by the court to summon persons upon a special venire whose names have not been selected under the Jury Wheel Law, the court shall, in every case, caution and direct the sheriff to summon such persons as have legal qualifications to serve on juries, informing him of what those qualifications are, and shall direct him, as far as he may be able to summon persons of good character who can read and write, and such as are not prejudiced against the defendant or biased in his favor, if he knows of such bias or prejudice.

History of CCP art. 34.03: Acts 1965, 59th Leg., ch. 722, §1, eff. Jan. 1, 1966.

ART. 34.04. NOTICE OF LIST

No defendant in a capital case in which the state seeks the death penalty shall be brought to trial until he shall have had at least two days (including holidays) a copy of the names of the persons summoned as veniremen, for the week for which his case is set for trial except where he waives the right or is on bail. When such defendant is on bail, the clerk of the court in which the case is pending shall furnish such a list to the defendant or his counsel at least two days prior to the trial (including holidays) upon timely motion by the defendant or his counsel therefor at the office of such clerk, and the defendant shall not be brought to trial until such list has been furnished defendant or his counsel for at least two days (including holidays). Where the venire is exhausted, by challenges or otherwise, and additional names are drawn, the defendant shall not be entitled to two days service of the names additionally drawn, but the clerk shall compile a list of such names promptly after they are drawn and if the defendant is not on bail, the sheriff shall serve a copy of such list promptly upon the defendant, and if on bail, the clerk shall furnish a copy of such list to the defendant or his counsel upon request, but the proceedings shall not be delayed thereby.

History of CCP art. 34.04: Acts 1965, 59th Leg., ch. 722, §1, eff. Jan. 1, 1966. Amended by Acts 1991, 72nd Leg., ch. 652, §4, eff. Sept. 1, 1991.

ANNOTATIONS

Wyle v. State, 777 S.W.2d 709, 714 (Tex.Crim.App. 1989). Article 34.04 "'does not require personal service of the list upon an accused, and that sufficient compliance is evinced by delivery to the accused's counsel in sufficient time to prepare for trial.'"

Smith v. State, 744 S.W.2d 86, 96 (Tex.Crim.App. 1987). "The terms of Article 34.04 ... and its predecessors have been construed to be mandatory so that an accused may be assured of the opportunity to examine the prospective juror list prior to the voir dire examination. Complete failure timely to provide such a list to an accused has been grounds for reversal of the accused's conviction. [¶] [I]n situations where Article 34.04 ... has been complied with, this Court has found no error when an accused has requested additional time in which to examine the jury list."

Esquivel v. State, 595 S.W.2d 516, 520-21 (Tex. Crim.App.1980). "[A]fter denying the request for a special venire, appellant was furnished with a list of the persons summoned as provided in [CCP art.] 34.04. This action was in lieu of a special venire and in compliance with [CCP art.] 34.01. We conclude that the trial court's action ... did not constitute an abuse of discretion."

ART. 34.05. MECHANICAL OR ELECTRONIC SELECTION METHOD

A mechanical or electronic method of jury selection as provided by Chapter 62, Government Code, may be used under this chapter.

History of CCP art. 34.05: Acts 1995, 74th Leg., ch. 694, §1, eff. Sept. 1, 1995.

CHAPTER 35. FORMATION OF THE JURY

ART. 35.01. JURORS CALLED

When a case is called for trial and the parties have announced ready for trial, the names of those summoned as jurors in the case shall be called. Those not present may be fined not exceeding fifty dollars. An attachment may issue on request of either party for any absent summoned juror, to have him brought forthwith before the court. A person who is summoned but not present, may upon an appearance, before the jury is qualified, be tried as to his qualifications and impaneled as a juror unless challenged, but no cause shall be unreasonably delayed on account of his absence.

History of CCP art. 35.01: Acts 1965, 59th Leg., ch. 722, §1, eff. Jan. 1, 1966.

ANNOTATIONS

Dowthitt v. State, 931 S.W.2d 244, 251-52 (Tex. Crim.App.1996). "To preserve error concerning the denial of a challenge for cause, the appellant must exhaust all peremptory challenges, ask for more, be refused, and point out an objectionable juror who was seated. [¶] The statute for attaching veniremen, Article 35.01, is directory, not mandatory, and in the absence of governmental misconduct in summoning the venire, the failure to grant attachments is not reversible error unless appellant shows injury. [¶] While there is a constitutional right to a 'cross-section' of the community in the venire, this right relates to the relative composition of the panel, not the number of veniremen who show up. The complaining party must show an 'identifiable class' excluded from the venire."

Coleman v. State, 881 S.W.2d 344, 351-52 (Tex. Crim.App.1994). "[A]ppellant failed to seek process to require the absent veniremembers to appear before the trial court. Appellant has preserved nothing for appeal...."

ART. 35.02. SWORN TO ANSWER QUESTIONS

To those present the court shall cause to be administered this oath: "You, and each of you, solemnly swear that you will make true answers to such questions as may be propounded to you by the court, or under its directions, touching your service and qualifications as a juror, so help you God."

History of CCP art. 35.02: Acts 1965, 59th Leg., ch. 722, §1, eff. Jan. 1, 1966.

ANNOTATIONS

Harris v. State, 738 S.W.2d 207, 226 (Tex.Crim.App. 1986). "[A]ppellant contends that the trial court erred in excusing two prospective jurors who were never sworn by the trial court prior to voir dire examination. [¶] There is nothing in the record to show affirmatively that they were not sworn. Rather, the record shows that the jury panel was sworn as a group, and is silent as to whether the two specific prospective jurors were sworn. [¶] [W]e find that the presumption that the jurors were sworn applies to the instant case."

Craig v. State, 480 S.W.2d 680, 683 (Tex.Crim.App. 1972). Appellant "urges that the ... oaths required of grand and petit jurors ... 'systematically exclude non-believers from said juries and that appellant, an atheist, was therefore deprived of judgments of his peers.' [¶] There is no ... requirement [to declare a belief in God] under either the Constitution or statutes of this state."

ART. 35.03. EXCUSES

Sec. 1. Except as provided by Sections 2 and 3 of this article, the court shall then hear and determine excuses offered for not serving as a juror, including any claim of an exemption or a lack of qualification, and if the court considers the excuse sufficient, the court shall discharge the prospective juror or postpone the prospective juror's service to a date specified by the court, as appropriate.

Sec. 2. Under a plan approved by the commissioners court of the county in the same manner as a plan is approved for jury selection under Section 62.011, Government Code, in a case other than a capital felony case, the court's designee may hear and determine an excuse offered for not serving as a juror, including any claim of an exemption or a lack of qualification. The court's designee may discharge the prospective juror or postpone the prospective juror's service to a date specified by the court's designee, as appropriate, if:

(1) the court's designee considers the excuse sufficient; and

(2) the juror submits to the court's designee a statement of the ground of the exemption or lack of qualification or other excuse.

Sec. 3. A court or a court's designee may discharge a juror or postpone the juror's service on the basis of the juror's observation of a religious holy day or religious beliefs only if the juror provides an affidavit as required by Article 29.012(c) of this code.

History of CCP art. 35.03: Acts 1965, 59th Leg., ch. 722, §1, eff. Jan. 1, 1966. Amended by Acts 1987, 70th Leg., ch. 589, §2 (eff. Aug. 31, 1987), 2nd C.S., ch. 43, §2 (eff. Oct. 20, 1987); Acts 2005, 79th Leg., ch. 905, §1, eff. Sept. 1, 2005.

ANNOTATIONS

Crutsinger v. State, 206 S.W.3d 607, 608 (Tex. Crim.App.2006). "This Court has consistently held that Article 35.03 gives a trial court broad discretion to excuse prospective jurors for good reason. ... Unless the excuse given is economic in nature, neither appellant nor his attorney is required to be present. The postponement or cancellation of jury service because of a pre-existing scheduling conflict is a legitimate exercise of the trial court's discretion under Article 35.03."

Wright v. State, 28 S.W.3d 526, 533 (Tex.Crim.App. 2000). "[B]efore the entire jury has been empaneled and sworn, the trial court may excuse a juror with or without the consent of the parties." *See also Rousseau v. State*, 855 S.W.2d 666, 676-77 (Tex.Crim.App.1993).

Chambers v. State, 903 S.W.2d 21, 29 (Tex.Crim. App.1995). "[A]ppellant claims the trial court erred ... on the ground that the trial judge before whom the case was tried did not personally determine the excuses and disqualifications of those summoned initially to the central jury room. [¶] Appellant ... contends [art. 35.03 is] mandatory and violation thereof is harmful per se. *At 30:* Nothing in the plain language of the provisions cited by appellant requires his trial judge to make rulings with respect to venirepersons *summoned to the central jury room that have not yet been assigned to appellant's case.* [¶] [W]e ... cannot conclude that [art. 35.03] would prohibit the general assembly judge from designating personnel to make such decisions. ... In the case of a special venire called in a capital case, the trial judge cannot designate others to make decisions with respect to excuses."

Sayyadi v. State, 40 S.W.3d 722, 724 (Tex.App.— Austin 2001, no pet.). "Even if we were to agree with appellant that it is a violation of the Equal Protection Clause to *disqualify* a potential juror who is not literate in English, a court retains the discretion under article 35.03 to grant a venire member's request to be *excused* from jury service because of limited English skills."

Leberta v. State, 770 S.W.2d 828, 830 (Tex.App.— Fort Worth 1988, pet. ref'd). "It is not sufficient ... for the appellant to show harm by the fact that the State exhausted all of its peremptory challenges; instead, the appellant must show the trial judge abused his discretion by excusing the venireperson."

ART. 35.04. CLAIMING EXEMPTION

Any person summoned as a juror who is exempt by law from jury service may establish his exemption without appearing in person by filing a signed statement of the ground of his exemption with the clerk of the court at any time before the date upon which he is summoned to appear.

History of CCP art. 35.04: Acts 1965, 59th Leg., ch. 722, §1, eff. Jan. 1, 1966. Amended by Acts 1971, 62nd Leg., ch. 421, §3, eff. May 26, 1971.

ART. 35.05. EXCUSED BY CONSENT

One summoned upon a special venire may by consent of both parties be excused from attendance by the court at any time before he is impaneled.

History of CCP art. 35.05: Acts 1965, 59th Leg., ch. 722, §1, eff. Jan. 1, 1966.

ART. 35.06. CHALLENGE TO ARRAY FIRST HEARD

The court shall hear and determine a challenge to the array before interrogating those summoned as to their qualifications.

History of CCP art. 35.06: Acts 1965, 59th Leg., ch. 722, §1, eff. Jan. 1, 1966.

ART. 35.07. CHALLENGE TO THE ARRAY

Each party may challenge the array only on the ground that the officer summoning the jury has wilfully summoned jurors with a view to securing a conviction or an acquittal. All such challenges must be in writing setting forth distinctly the grounds of such challenge. When made by the defendant, it must be supported by his affidavit or the affidavit of any credible person. When such challenge is made, the judge shall hear evidence and decide without delay whether or not the challenge shall be sustained.

History of CCP art. 35.07: Acts 1965, 59th Leg., ch. 722, §1, eff. Jan. 1, 1966.

ANNOTATIONS

Pondexter v. State, 942 S.W.2d 577, 580 (Tex.Crim. App.1996). "[I]n order to establish a prima facie violation of the requirement that there be a fair cross section of the community represented, appellant must show: 1) that the group alleged to be excluded is a 'distinctive' group in the community; 2) that the representation of this group in venires from which juries are selected is not fair and reasonable in relation to the number of such persons in the community; and 3) that this underrepresentation is due to systematic exclusion of the group in the jury selection process. *At 581:* '[D]isproportionate representation in a single panel does not demonstrate the systematic exclusion of distinctive groups in violation of appellant's rights under the 6th Amendment.'"

Garcia v. State, 919 S.W.2d 370, 392 (Tex.Crim. App.1996). "Appellant's challenge to the first array and his motion to quash the array are both in writing, but neither are sworn to. An instrument that is not sworn to is not supported by affidavit. As neither of appellant's motions are supported by affidavit, nothing is preserved for review."

Wallace v. State, 707 S.W.2d 928, 938 (Tex.App.— Texarkana 1986), *aff'd*, 782 S.W.2d 854 (Tex.Crim.App. 1989). "Wallace challenged the array on the ground that ... there had been a systematic exclusion of a significant number of qualified jurors merely because they had not registered to vote. [¶] The constitutionality of the use of voter registration rolls from which to compile federal and state jury lists has been affirmed."

ART. 35.08. WHEN CHALLENGE IS SUSTAINED

The array of jurors summoned shall be discharged if the challenge be sustained, and the court shall order other jurors to be summoned in their stead, and direct that the officer who summoned those so discharged, and on account of whose misconduct the challenge has been sustained shall not summon any other jurors in the case.

History of CCP art. 35.08: Acts 1965, 59th Leg., ch. 722, §1, eff. Jan. 1, 1966.

ART. 35.09. LIST OF NEW VENIRE

When a challenge to the array has been sustained, the defendant shall be entitled, as in the first instance, to service of a copy of the list of names of those summoned by order of the court.

History of CCP art. 35.09: Acts 1965, 59th Leg., ch. 722, §1, eff. Jan. 1, 1996.

ART. 35.10. COURT TO TRY QUALIFICATIONS

When no challenge to the array has been made, or if made, has been over-ruled, the court shall proceed to try the qualifications of those present who have been summoned to serve as jurors.

History of CCP art. 35.10: Acts 1965, 59th Leg., ch. 722, §1, eff. Jan. 1, 1966.

ART. 35.11. PREPARATION OF LIST

The trial judge, on the demand of the defendant or his attorney, or of the State's counsel, shall cause a sufficient number of jurors from which a jury may be selected to try the case to be randomly selected from the members of the general panel drawn or assigned as jurors in the case. The clerk shall randomly select the jurors by a computer or other process of random selection and shall write or print the names, in the order selected, on the jury list from which the jury is to be selected to try the case. The clerk shall deliver a copy of the list to the State's counsel and to the defendant or his attorney.

History of CCP art. 35.11: Acts 1965, 59th Leg., ch. 722, §1, eff. Jan. 1, 1966. Amended by Acts 1991, 72nd Leg., ch. 337, §1, eff. Sept. 1, 1991.

ANNOTATIONS

Ford v. State, 73 S.W.3d 923, 926 (Tex.Crim.App. 2002). "Because the law requires that venire panels be assembled in random order, a trial judge's failure to order a shuffle does not, by itself, indicate a nonrandom listing of the venire. Nothing in the record of this trial indicates that the procedures outlined in the applicable statutes and rules were disregarded, that the panel was reordered after being assembled, or that the process of assembling a jury panel was subverted in some fashion to achieve a nonrandom listing of the venire. [T]he error in refusing to allow a jury shuffle has been shown to be harmless under [TRAP] 44.2(b)."

Garza v. State, 7 S.W.3d 164, 166 (Tex.Crim.App. 1999). "We hold that a trial court is neither required to allow nor prohibited from allowing a party to review written questionnaires before deciding whether to request a shuffle. It is within the court's discretion to allow it or disallow it. And we hold that voir dire does not commence simply because a party has read the answers to written jury questionnaires."

Chappell v. State, 850 S.W.2d 508, 511 (Tex.Crim. App.1993). "[A]bsent a showing of misconduct, only one shuffle is authorized under art. 35.11. *At 513:* As a violation of art. 35.11 is not subject to a meaningful harm analysis ..., a violation of art. 35.11 necessarily requires reversal." *But see Richardson v. State*, 981 S.W.2d 453, 457 (Tex.App.—El Paso 1998, pet. ref'd).

Davis v. State, 782 S.W.2d 211, 214 (Tex.Crim.App. 1989). "We have never interpreted ... Article [35.11] as requiring the trial court to afford the defendant anything more than being able to view the outward appearance of the venire members. [¶] A motion to shuffle the names of the venire must be timely presented to the trial court. We have determined that a motion to shuffle is untimely if presented after the voir dire has commenced. [F]or purposes of Article 35.11, voir dire in a non-capital murder case commences when the State begins its examination of the prospective jurors; it does not begin when the judge begins his or her initial instructions." *See also Railsback v. State*, 95 S.W.3d 473, 483 (Tex.App.—Houston [1st Dist.] 2002, pet. ref'd).

Urbano v. State, 808 S.W.2d 519, 520 (Tex.App.—Houston [14th Dist.] 1991, no pet.). "Although ... it is a better practice to conduct the shuffle in the courtroom, ... it is not a requirement of the [CCP]."

ART. 35.12. MODE OF TESTING

(a) In testing the qualification of a prospective juror after the juror has been sworn, the juror shall be asked by the court, or under its direction:

1. Except for failure to register, are you a qualified voter in this county and state under the Constitution and laws of this state?

2. Have you ever been convicted of theft or any felony?

3. Are you under indictment or legal accusation for theft or any felony?

(b) In testing the qualifications of a prospective juror, with respect to whether the juror has been the subject of an order of nondisclosure or has a criminal history that includes information subject to that order, the juror may state only that the matter in question has been sealed.

History of CCP art. 35.12: Acts 1965, 59th Leg., ch. 722, §1, eff. Jan. 1, 1966. Amended by Acts 1969, 61st Leg., ch. 412, §2, eff. Sept. 1, 1969; Acts 1981, 67th Leg., ch. 827, §7, eff. Aug. 31, 1981; Acts 2005, 79th Leg., ch. 1309, §4, eff. Sept. 1, 2005.

ANNOTATIONS

Smith v. State, 742 S.W.2d 847, 851 (Tex.App.— Austin 1987, no pet.). "The trial court apparently did fail to [ask the jury panel whether any member had ever been convicted of theft], but the oversight was not brought to the court's attention. [¶] Although the district court erred and this error may not be waived, [appellant] has failed to demonstrate harm...."

Matthias v. State, 695 S.W.2d 736, 740 (Tex. App.—Houston [14th Dist.] 1985, pet. ref'd). "The mandatory language of Article 35.12 merely requires the court to accurately prescribe the test upon which the parties may base their challenges for cause."

ART. 35.13. PASSING JUROR FOR CHALLENGE

A juror in a capital case in which the state has made it known it will seek the death penalty, held to be qualified, shall be passed for acceptance or challenge first to the state and then to the defendant. Challenges to jurors are either peremptory or for cause.

History of CCP art. 35.13: Acts 1965, 59th Leg., ch. 722, §1, eff. Jan. 1, 1966. Amended by Acts 1967, 60th Leg., ch. 659, §20, eff. Aug. 28, 1967.

ANNOTATIONS

Hughes v. State, 24 S.W.3d 833, 840 (Tex.Crim.App. 2000). "[A] trial court has the discretion to decide (1) whether the State must voice both a challenge for cause or a peremptory challenge before the defendant, or (2) that both sides issue any challenges for cause before the State first lodges a peremptory challenge."

Ransom v. State, 920 S.W.2d 288, 292-93 (Tex. Crim.App.1994). "[P]eremptory challenges remaining at the end of the voir dire would not remove the harm of an erroneous grant of a State's challenge for cause. ... 'The statute would give the benefit to the defendant in instances where both sides might desire to strike the same venireman. Allowing the State to wait until the end of the selection process would transfer that benefit to the State.'"

Bigby v. State, 892 S.W.2d 864, 879-80 (Tex.Crim. App.1994). "[T]he legislature intended that defendant's challenges for cause could be made after the State has made its decision to accept a veniremember. [¶] When [CCP art. 35.20 is] read in conjunction with [CCP art.] 35.13, the clear import of the statute is to provide that in capital cases, the jurors shall be called individually. Upon completion of voir dire by both parties of that potential juror, the State must choose to accept the veniremember or challenge him for cause or peremptorily, and then the defendant or his counsel may exercise its peremptory or causal challenge."

Janecka v. State, 739 S.W.2d 813, 834 (Tex.Crim. App.1987). "Capital defendants do not have to exercise a peremptory strike against a particular venireman until the State has first decided whether to do so. Thus, if the State and the defendant do not want a given venireman, and he cannot be excluded for cause, the defendant will benefit by saving one of his peremptory challenges."

Campbell v. State, 742 S.W.2d 759, 761 (Tex. App.—San Antonio 1987, pet. ref'd). "Having requested that art. 35.13 not be applied to the jury selection process ... and the trial court granting appellant's request prior to the initiation of jury selection, appellant cannot ... claim error in the trial court's refusal of his request on the second day of jury selection that art. 35.13 be made applicable to the remainder of the jury selection proceedings. Any error ... was invited by appellant's written motion requesting such action and appellant cannot now complain of the very error he invited."

ART. 35.14. A PEREMPTORY CHALLENGE

A peremptory challenge is made to a juror without assigning any reason therefor.

History of CCP art. 35.14: Acts 1965, 59th Leg., ch. 722, §1, eff. Jan. 1, 1966.

ANNOTATIONS

Barnes v. State, 876 S.W.2d 316, 325 (Tex.Crim. App.1994). CCP art. 35.14 "provides a vehicle with which to exclude potential jurors that an advocate believes are prejudiced against his cause. ... Subject to the constraints of [CCP art.] 35.261, we have held that a party need not assign a reason for exercising his peremptory strikes, even where the discernible purpose of the strike is to exclude a prospective juror who is not in favor of the death penalty."

ART. 35.15. NUMBER OF CHALLENGES

(a) In capital cases in which the State seeks the death penalty both the State and defendant shall be entitled to fifteen peremptory challenges. Where two or more defendants are tried together, the State shall be entitled to eight peremptory challenges for each defendant; and each defendant shall be entitled to eight peremptory challenges.

(b) In non-capital felony cases and in capital cases in which the State does not seek the death penalty, the State and defendant shall each be entitled to ten peremptory challenges. If two or more defendants are tried together each defendant shall be entitled to six peremptory challenges and the State to six for each defendant.

(c) The State and the defendant shall each be entitled to five peremptory challenges in a misdemeanor tried in the district court and to three in the county court, or county court at law. If two or more defendants are tried together, each defendant shall be entitled to three such challenges and the State to three for each defendant in either court.

(d) The State and the defendant shall each be entitled to one peremptory challenge in addition to those otherwise allowed by law if one or two alternate jurors are to be impaneled and two peremptory challenges if three or four alternate jurors are to be impaneled. The additional peremptory challenges provided by this subsection may be used against an alternate juror only, and the other peremptory challenges allowed by law may not be used against an alternate juror.

History of CCP art. 35.15: Acts 1965, 59th Leg., ch. 722, §1, eff. Jan. 1, 1966. Amended by Acts 1973, 63rd Leg., ch. 426, art. 3, §4, eff. June 14, 1973; Acts 1983, 68th Leg., ch. 775, §3, eff. Aug. 29, 1983; Acts 1991, 72nd Leg., ch. 652, §5, eff. Sept. 1, 1991.

ANNOTATIONS

Green v. State, 934 S.W.2d 92, 105 (Tex.Crim.App. 1996). "To preserve error for a trial court's denial of a valid challenge for cause, it must be demonstrated on the record that appellant asserted a clear and specific challenge for cause, that he used a peremptory challenge on that juror, that all his peremptory challenges were exhausted, that his request for additional strikes was denied, and that an objectionable juror sat on the jury."

Cooks v. State, 844 S.W.2d 697, 721 (Tex.Crim.App. 1992). "Selection of alternate jurors is treated as distinct ... from selection of the primary panel. Following selection of the required number of jurors for the panel, the parties' unused peremptory strikes are essentially wiped out and each party is given the designated number of strikes for use in selecting one or more alternate jurors. [T]he rules for preserving error on challenges for cause during selection of an alternate juror should [not] differ from those applicable during the primary panel selection."

Goode v. State, 740 S.W.2d 453, 459 (Tex.Crim.App. 1987), *overruled on other grounds*, ***Qualley v. State***, 206 S.W.3d 624 (Tex.Crim.App.2006). "There is no rational basis for holding ... that appellant was 'tried together' with a [co-D], and so she alone of all the [co-Ds] could be limited to eight peremptory strikes, merely because she and [co-D] proceeded jointly through a portion of her trial." (Emphasis omitted.)

Truong v. State, 782 S.W.2d 904, 905 (Tex.App.— Houston [14th Dist.] 1989, pet. ref'd). "[T]he trial court abuses its discretion by refusing to allow the defense to correct a mistake in peremptory strikes."

ART. 35.16. REASONS FOR CHALLENGE FOR CAUSE

(a) A challenge for cause is an objection made to a particular juror, alleging some fact which renders the juror incapable or unfit to serve on the jury. A challenge for cause may be made by either the state or the defense for any one of the following reasons:

1. That the juror is not a qualified voter in the state and county under the Constitution and laws of the state; provided, however, the failure to register to vote shall not be a disqualification;

2. That the juror has been convicted of misdemeanor theft or a felony;

3. That the juror is under indictment or other legal accusation for misdemeanor theft or a felony;

4. That the juror is insane;

5. That the juror has such defect in the organs of feeling or hearing, or such bodily or mental defect or disease as to render the juror unfit for jury service, or that the juror is legally blind and the court in its discretion is not satisfied that the juror is fit for jury service in that particular case;

6. That the juror is a witness in the case;

7. That the juror served on the grand jury which found the indictment;

8. That the juror served on a petit jury in a former trial of the same case;

9. That the juror has a bias or prejudice in favor of or against the defendant;

10. That from hearsay, or otherwise, there is established in the mind of the juror such a conclusion as to the guilt or innocence of the defendant as would influence the juror in finding a verdict. To ascertain whether this cause of challenge exists, the juror shall first be asked whether, in the juror's opinion, the conclusion so established will influence the juror's verdict. If the juror answers in the affirmative, the juror shall be discharged without further interrogation by either party or the court. If the juror answers in the negative, the juror shall be further examined as to how the juror's conclusion was formed, and the extent to which it will affect the juror's action; and, if it appears to have been formed from reading newspaper accounts, communications, statements or reports or mere rumor or hearsay, and if the juror states that the juror feels able, notwithstanding such opinion, to render an impartial verdict upon the law and the evidence, the court, if satisfied that the juror is impartial and will render such verdict, may, in its discretion, admit the juror as competent to serve in such case. If the court, in its discretion, is not satisfied that the juror is impartial, the juror shall be discharged;

11. That the juror cannot read or write.

No juror shall be impaneled when it appears that the juror is subject to the second, third or fourth grounds of challenge for cause set forth above, although both parties may consent. All other grounds for challenge may be waived by the party or parties in whose favor such grounds of challenge exist.

In this subsection "legally blind" shall mean having not more than 20/200 of visual acuity in the better eye with correcting lenses, or visual acuity greater than 20/200 but with a limitation in the field of vision such that the widest diameter of the visual field subtends an angle no greater than 20 degrees.

(b) A challenge for cause may be made by the State for any of the following reasons:

1. That the juror has conscientious scruples in regard to the infliction of the punishment of death for crime, in a capital case, where the State is seeking the death penalty;

2. That he is related within the third degree of consanguinity or affinity, as determined under Chapter 573, Government Code, to the defendant; and

3. That he has a bias or prejudice against any phase of the law upon which the State is entitled to rely for conviction or punishment.

(c) A challenge for cause may be made by the defense for any of the following reasons:

1. That he is related within the third degree of consanguinity or affinity, as determined under Chapter 573, Government Code, to the person injured by the commission of the offense, or to any prosecutor in the case; and

2. That he has a bias or prejudice against any of the law applicable to the case upon which the defense is entitled to rely, either as a defense to some phase of the offense for which the defendant is being prosecuted or as a mitigation thereof or of the punishment therefor.

History of CCP art. 35.16: Acts 1965, 59th Leg., ch. 722, §1, eff. Jan. 1, 1966. Amended by Acts 1969, 61st Leg., ch. 412, §3, eff. Sept. 1, 1969; Acts 1975, 64th Leg., ch. 202, §2, eff. Sept. 1, 1975; Acts 1981, 67th Leg., ch. 827, §8, eff. Aug. 31, 1981; Acts 1983, 68th Leg., ch. 134, §2, eff. Sept. 1, 1983; Acts 1991, 72nd Leg., ch. 561, §10, eff. Aug. 26, 1991; Acts 1995, 74th Leg., ch. 76, §5.95(27), eff. Sept. 1, 1995; Acts 2005, 79th Leg., ch. 801, §3, eff. Sept. 1, 2005.

See also CCP art. 44.46; chart, "Relatives by Degrees," p. 261.

ANNOTATIONS

Generally

Webb v. State, 232 S.W.3d 109, 112 (Tex.Crim.App. 2007). "All grounds for challenge for cause may be forfeited. Therefore, the challenge for cause is forfeited if not made. Failure to question the jurors on that subject constitutes a forfeiture of the right to complain thereafter."

Sells v. State, 121 S.W.3d 748, 758 (Tex.Crim.App. 2003). "To preserve error on denied challenges for cause, an appellant must demonstrate on the record that: 1) he asserted a clear and specific challenge for cause; 2) he used a peremptory challenge on the complained-of venireperson; 3) all his peremptory challenges were exhausted; 4) his request for additional strikes was denied; and 5) an objectionable juror sat on the jury."

Jones v. State, 982 S.W.2d 386, 394 (Tex.Crim.App. 1998). "We overrule the holding of ***Payton v. State***[, 572 S.W.2d 677 (Tex.Crim.App.1978)] that a conviction will be reversed when a juror was erroneously excused and the State used all its peremptory challenges. We return to our previous rule, that the erroneous excusing of a veniremember will call for reversal only if the record shows that the error deprived the defendant of a lawfully constituted jury."

Mason v. State, 905 S.W.2d 570, 577-78 (Tex.Crim. App.1995). "A challenge for cause can be properly asserted on grounds which are not specifically enumerated in Article 35.16 where such a challenge is based on facts that show that the prospective juror would be 'incapable or unfit to serve on the jury.' Challenges which are not based upon any ground specifically enumerated in the statutes are ordinarily addressed to the sound discretion of the trial judge."

Cooks v. State, 844 S.W.2d 697, 718 (Tex.Crim.App. 1992). "[W]here the reason that the juror is incapable or unfit to serve is obvious to the court and opposing counsel and there is no indication that the parties were unaware of the grounds for the challenge, we hold that facts need not be alleged in making the challenge."

Contreras v. State, 56 S.W.3d 274, 277 (Tex.App.— Houston [14th Dist.] 2001, pet. ref'd). "It is clear from the record that the parties agreed to make all challenges for cause as soon as such challenges became apparent. During its voir dire, the State adhered to this agreement. Appellant, however, did not adhere to this agreement. *At 278:* Where … it is abundantly clear that the parties knew and understood when challenges for cause must be made, because they had agreed to make them at a certain time, the court does not abuse its discretion by refusing to entertain untimely challenges."

Art. 35.16(a)(1)

Mayo v. State, 4 S.W.3d 9, 11 (Tex.Crim.App.1999). "[C]ounty citizenship is a part of the Art. 35.16 requirement that a person be a qualified voter in the county under the constitution and laws of this state in order to be fit to serve as a juror. *At 12:* Because the [CCP] specifically provides for waiver of certain qualifications in criminal cases, we hold that those qualifications found in the Government Code that are also contained in Art. 35.16 and are waivable under Art. 35.16, are waivable in a criminal case. [¶] The requirement that a juror be a county citizen is not an absolute requirement that cannot be waived."

Art. 35.16(a)(2)

State v. Read, 965 S.W.2d 74, 76 (Tex.App.—Austin 1998, no pet.). "After trial and sentencing, Read discovered that a juror had not disclosed information about her criminal history even though the trial court asked for this information at voir dire and on the jury questionnaire. [¶] After trial and sentencing, but within the time permitted for a motion for new trial, Read discovered that this juror had been convicted of misdemeanor theft…." Held: The trial court did not err in granting a new trial.

Art. 35.16(a)(3)

Ristoff v. State, 985 S.W.2d 623, 623-24 (Tex. App.—Houston [1st Dist.] 1999, no pet.). Juror "was unaware of [her] indictment until after the appellant's trial ended, apparently due to both a change of address and administrative processing time. [¶] [B]ecause the disqualification was not discovered, and thus not brought to the attention of the trial court, until after the verdict was entered, appellant may be granted a new trial only if the juror's service caused 'significant harm.' [¶] Appellant filed a motion for new trial in each case, asserting the jury was absolutely disqualified from jury service by virtue of her indictment. However, at the hearing on appellant's motions, appellant made no attempt to show significant harm, nor is any apparent. Appellant failed to meet his burden."

Art. 35.16(a)(5)

Matamoros v. State, 901 S.W.2d 470, 476-77 (Tex. Crim.App.1995). "A venireman's inability to comprehend the limited function of a juror at the punishment phase of a capital case may constitute 'such … mental defect … as to render him unfit for jury service….' [A] mental defect may be present where a venireman's responses show an inability to understand the jury's role in capital proceedings. One sign of this condition may be the court's inability to determine the venireman's views for the purpose of deciding other possible grounds of disqualification."

Art. 35.16(a)(7)

Graham v. State, ___ S.W.3d ___ (Tex.App.— Waco 2008, n.p.h.) (No. 10-06-00357-CR; 2-27-08). "It is error for a trial court to overrule a challenge for cause to a panelist who was a member of the grand jury that returned the indictment being tried. But a claim that a juror served on the indicting grand jury is a ground for a challenge for cause, not an absolute disqualification. The failure to question a juror about whether the juror was a member of the grand jury that returned the indictment constitutes a waiver of the right to thereafter complain that the juror was disqualified on that basis."

Art. 35.16(a)(9)

Penry v. State, 903 S.W.2d 715, 728 (Tex.Crim.App. 1995). "There is no requirement in our law that jurors be completely ignorant of the facts of a case. The sole question is whether a juror can put aside prior knowledge and opinion and render an impartial verdict."

Hernandez v. State, 563 S.W.2d 947, 950 (Tex.Crim.App.1978). Appellant "contends that [the] venireman['s] inability to believe that a police officer would tell a wilful falsehood disqualified her.... [¶] [T]here is no doubt that [the] venireman['s] attitude toward police officers constituted a bias against the appellant."

Lopez v. State, ___ S.W.3d ___ (Tex.App.—San Antonio 2008, n.p.h.) (No. 04-06-00655-CR; 3-19-08). "Initially, the burden is on the parties to be diligent during voir dire and ask all pertinent questions to reveal potential bias. When, notwithstanding the complaining party's diligence during voir dire, a juror later discloses his knowledge of or relationship with a witness, the juror is considered to have withheld information during voir dire. When the withheld information is material, it is constitutional error to deny a motion for mistrial. When the withheld information is not material and the record does not show the appellant has been deprived of an impartial jury or denied a fair trial, the trial court's denial of a motion for mistrial is not error. [¶] 'To determine materiality, we evaluate whether the withheld information would likely reveal the juror harbored a bias or prejudice to such a degree that the juror should have been excused from jury service.' '[M]ere familiarity with a witness is not necessarily material information.' A potential juror's acquaintance with a witness is material only if the nature of the relationship reveals a potential for bias or prejudice on the part of the juror. The fact the juror did not intentionally withhold the information is 'largely irrelevant when considering the materiality of the information withheld.'"

Morales v. State, 217 S.W.3d 731, 735 (Tex.App.—El Paso 2007), *rev'd on other grounds*, ___ S.W.3d ___ (Tex.Crim.App.2008) (No. PD-0462-07; 5-14-08). "Whether a juror's partiality may be presumed from the circumstances is a question of law. ... In *Smith v. Phillips*, 455 U.S. 209, 102 S.Ct. 940 (1982), Justice O'Connor writing in a concurring opinion, provided examples of extreme situations that would justify a finding of implied bias to avoid a miscarriage of justice: Some examples might include a revelation that the juror is an actual employee of the prosecuting agency.... Justice O'Connor further stated, [w]hether or not the state proceedings result in a finding of no bias, the Sixth Amendment right to an impartial jury should not allow a verdict to stand under such circumstances. We are now presented with the very extreme situation which gave Justice O'Connor such grave concern. *At 736:* While venireperson ... may have believed she could set aside her status as an employee of the prosecuting agency, even a well-meaning person would find it difficult to remain impartial under such circumstances and most likely would be unconsciously blinded by otherwise good intentions. It is fair to say that venireperson ... may believe herself to be fair and impartial, but nevertheless she should have been disqualified in the interest of justice." (Internal quotes omitted.)

Art. 35.16(a)(10)

Curry v. State, 910 S.W.2d 490, 493 (Tex.Crim.App. 1995). "In order for error to be preserved under Art. 35.16(a)(10), there must be a showing that the venire member has stated that his conclusions on the defendant's guilt or innocence would indeed affect his decision during deliberation."

Art. 35.16(a)(11)

Rodriguez v. State, 919 S.W.2d 136, 139 (Tex.App.—San Antonio 1995, no pet.). "In assessing a juror's ability to read and write, courts have traditionally focused on the juror's ability to complete the juror questionnaire and the juror's ability to understand the special issues and instructions likely to be presented. *At 140:* It is within the trial court's discretion to control or restrict voir dire examination. An abuse of discretion may be shown where a defendant is prevented from asking a proper question. ... If a proper question is not allowed, harm is presumed."

Art. 35.16(b)(1)

Clark v. State, 929 S.W.2d 5, 8-9 (Tex.Crim.App. 1996). "It is the burden of the challenging party to establish the venireman he has challenged for cause will be substantially impaired in his ability to follow the law. Demonstrating that the venireman has conscientious scruples against the death penalty is not alone sufficient to meet the State's burden to show he will be substantially impaired from honestly answering the special issues of former Article 37.071(b) in accordance with the evidence. In order to meet that burden, the State should directly ask the question of the venireman whether his opposition to the death penalty is such as to cause him to answer one of the special issues in such a way as to assure a life sentence will be imposed, irrespective of what the evidence may be. Once that question is asked, the trial court's task is clear. If the venireman steadfastly maintains he will not consciously distort his answer to the special issues, he has shown no inability to follow the law, and may not be excused on State's challenge for cause. A venireman who steadfastly maintains he *will* consciously distort his answers *must* be excused on challenge for cause. ... On the other hand, once the question is asked, the venireman who genuinely equivocates or vacillates in his answer may be excused for cause or not, depending on demeanor, intonation, or expression. Here the trial court's discretion comes fully into play. However the trial court exercises its discretion under these circumstances, it will be upheld on appeal."

Wolfe v. State, 917 S.W.2d 270, 275-76 (Tex.Crim.App.1996). "The U.S. Constitution prohibits excusing a prospective juror for holding conscientious scruples against the death penalty unless his views would 'prevent or substantially impair the performance of his duties as a juror in accordance with his instructions and his oath.' It is not enough that the prospective juror's views would 'affect' his deliberations."

Art. 35.16(b)(2)

Ex parte Fierro, 79 S.W.3d 54, 55 (Tex.Crim.App.2002). "The day after a petit jury of twelve persons was selected and sworn for trial of both causes, one of the jurors informed the trial court that she was appellant's cousin. The state then challenged that juror for cause pursuant to [CCP art.] 35.16(b)(2).... *At 56:* The juror ... was not ... related to appellant within the third degree of consanguinity. [A] cousin is not included among such relatives [named in Gov't Code §573.023]."

Art. 35.16(b)(3)

Howard v. State, 941 S.W.2d 102, 107 (Tex.Crim.App.1996). "When a potential juror vacillates on the question of his or her ability to follow the law as it pertains to the juror's legal role in a criminal proceeding, this Court defers to the findings of the trial court. A vacillating veniremember is one who gives contradictory responses to those voir dire questions which test the veniremember's ability to follow the legal mandates set by the Legislature and by the holdings of this Court." *See also* **Brown v. State**, 913 S.W.2d 577, 580 (Tex.Crim.App.1996).

Zinger v. State, 932 S.W.2d 511, 514 (Tex.Crim.App.1996). "'[A] venireman who categorically refuses to render a guilty verdict on the basis of only one eyewitness is not challengeable for cause on that account so long as his refusal is predicated on his reasonable understanding of what constitutes proof beyond a reasonable doubt.'" *See also* **Castillo v. State**, 913 S.W.2d 529, 534 (Tex.Crim.App.1995).

Garcia v. State, 919 S.W.2d 370, 389 (Tex.Crim.App.1996). "A prospective juror who is unable to consider the full range of punishment may be challenged for cause.... *At 390:* [A]rt. 35.16(b)(3) allows the State to challenge for cause a venireperson who indicates he or she is biased against the defendant." *See also* **Fuller v. State**, 829 S.W.2d 191, 200 (Tex.Crim.App.1992).

Morrow v. State, 910 S.W.2d 471, 473 (Tex.Crim.App.1995). "Veniremembers are not challengeable for their particular views about particular evidence. *At 474:* Appellant contends that he should be able to challenge a potential juror for cause because he would hold the State to a greater burden of proof than 'beyond a reasonable doubt.' ... Were we to grant appellant's argument ..., then we would essentially be permitting defense attorneys to challenge veniremembers to the detriment of their clients. Therefore, defendants may not challenge potential jurors for cause who are biased against the law which the State is entitled to rely under art. 35.16(b)(3)."

Art. 35.16(c)

Sells v. State, 121 S.W.3d 748, 759 (Tex.Crim.App.2003). "The test [for dismissing a juror for cause because of bias or prejudice] is whether the bias or prejudice would substantially impair the prospective juror's ability to carry out his oath and instructions in accordance with the law. Before a prospective juror can be excused for cause on this basis, however, the law must be explained to him and he must be asked whether he can follow that law regardless of his personal views. Finally, the proponent of a challenge for cause has the burden of establishing his challenge is proper. The proponent does not meet his burden until he has shown that the venireman understood the requirements of the law and could not overcome his prejudice well enough to follow it."

Courtney v. State, 115 S.W.3d 640, 642 (Tex. App.—Waco 2003, no pet.) (memo op.). "[W]e hold that the challenged juror was not subject to a challenge for cause [under art. 35.16(c)(1)] merely because her husband served on the grand jury which returned Courtney's indictment."

ART. 35.17. VOIR DIRE EXAMINATION

1. When the court in its discretion so directs, except as provided in Section 2, the state and defendant shall conduct the voir dire examination of prospective jurors in the presence of the entire panel.

2. In a capital felony case in which the State seeks the death penalty, the court shall propound to the entire panel of prospective jurors questions concerning the principles, as applicable to the case on trial, of reasonable doubt, burden of proof, return of indictment by grand jury, presumption of innocence, and opinion. Then, on demand of the State or defendant, either is entitled to examine each juror on voir dire individually and apart from the entire panel, and may further question the juror on the principles propounded by the court.

History of CCP art. 35.17: Acts 1965, 59th Leg., ch. 722, §1, eff. Jan. 1, 1966. Amended by Acts 1973, 63rd Leg., ch. 426, art. 3, §5, eff. June 14, 1973; Acts 1991, 72nd Leg., ch. 652, §6, eff. Sept. 1, 1991.

ANNOTATIONS

Generally

Jones v. State, 223 S.W.3d 379, 381 (Tex.Crim.App. 2007). "A long line of cases has held that the 'right to counsel' under [Tex. Const. art. 1, §10] includes the right to pose proper questions during voir dire examination." Held: The trial court's denial of the defense attorney's asking a proper question of the venire to determine use of a peremptory challenge was a constitutional error.

Simpson v. State, 119 S.W.3d 262, 265 (Tex.Crim. App.2003). "[A]ppellant claims the trial court erred in sustaining the State's challenge for cause against venire member ... without allowing the appellant's counsel an opportunity to question her. *At 266:* The trial court, upon demand of either party, is required to permit that party to individually question a venire member on the principles already discussed by the trial court. As a result, a trial court that denies a party's request has erred." Held: The error was nonconstitutional and harmless under TRAP 44.2(b).

Franklin v. State, 12 S.W.3d 473, 475 (Tex.Crim. App.2000). "During voir dire, the State asked if any of the venire-members knew of [alleged victim of aggravated sexual assault]. No one in the venire mentioned that they knew [alleged victim]. *At 476:* After the State's opening statement, [alleged victim] came into the courtroom. Juror Spradlin then passed a note to the trial court judge stating that she knew [alleged victim]. *At 478-79:* [B]ecause appellant acted in voir dire on the answers given to him, he was deprived of the opportunity to either challenge Juror Spradlin for cause or peremptorily strike her. [A]ppellant was never permitted to question Juror Spradlin concerning her relationship with the victim to determine the extent of prejudice that might have existed. Under these circumstances, we cannot conclude that Juror Spradlin's relationship with the victim was immaterial to the appellant's questioning of Juror Spradlin or appellant's use of peremptory strikes. The trial court erred in denying appellant the opportunity to ask questions of Juror Spradlin."

Chambers v. State, 903 S.W.2d 21, 31 (Tex.Crim. App.1995). "'Panels' are ... the group of prospective jurors that are assigned to the trial court from the central jury assembly. Under the [CCP,] 'voir dire examination' refers to the examination of prospective jurors *after* they have been assigned to a particular court and case from the general assembly. We cannot conclude the trial court abused its discretion in failing to direct its court reporter to record the questioning of prospective jurors in the general assembly."

Staley v. State, 887 S.W.2d 885, 897 (Tex.Crim.App. 1994). "[N]othing in Article 35.17 *requires* a trial court to define terms for the venire. [A] trial court does not abuse its discretion in refusing to instruct the venire upon a definition of a legal term at the request of either party."

Capital-Punishment Case

Wainwright v. Witt, 469 U.S. 412, 424-26, 105 S.Ct. 844, 852 (1985). "[T]he proper standard for determining when a prospective juror may be excluded for cause because of his or her views on capital punishment ... is whether the juror's views would 'prevent or substantially impair the performance of his duties as a juror in accordance with his instructions and his oath.' [T]his standard likewise does not require that a juror's bias be proved with 'unmistakable clarity.' This is because determinations of juror bias cannot be reduced to question-and-answer sessions which obtain results in the manner of a catechism. [D]eference must be paid to the trial judge who sees and hears the juror."

Lagrone v. State, 942 S.W.2d 602, 609 (Tex.Crim. App.1997). In a capital case, "a trial court does not abuse its discretion by refusing to permit counsel to question a veniremember regarding his definition of the term 'probability.'"

Garcia v. State, 919 S.W.2d 370, 391-92 (Tex.Crim. App.1996). "Appellant fails to cite any authority to support his position that the trial court's action with respect to use of an intermediate and additional step in the voir dire process constitutes reversible error. This court has ... upheld the use of sub-panels prior to one-on-one individual voir dire."

Woolridge v. State, 827 S.W.2d 900, 905-06 (Tex. Crim.App.1992). "In capital murder cases, ... we have allowed trial judges to limit the voir dire examination when it appeared to be taking an 'unreasonable' length of time. [¶] [I]t is improper for a trial judge to impose restrictions based on the mere possibility that the otherwise proper question might lengthen the process. The trial judge must first allow the question, and may later curtail similar questions if the voir dire process proves to be unduly lengthy. [T]rial judges may prohibit an otherwise proper question which substantially repeats others posed by the same party, or when the prospective juror has stated his position clearly, unequivocally, and without reservation." *See also Beets v. State*, 767 S.W.2d 711, 744-45 (Tex.Crim.App.1987).

Commitment Questions

Sanchez v. State, 165 S.W.3d 707, 713 (Tex.Crim. App.2005). "Under [TRAP] 44.2(b), reviewing courts should assess the potential harm of the State's improper commitment questioning by focusing upon whether a biased juror—one who had explicitly or implicitly promised to prejudge some aspect of the case because of the State's improper questioning—actually sat on the jury. The ultimate harm question is: was the defendant tried by an impartial jury, or, conversely, was the jury or any specific juror 'poisoned' by the State's improper commitment questions on a legal issue or fact that was important to the determination of the verdict or sentence? *At 714:* There is no single, specific rule by which reviewing courts should assess this question of harm. But factors to consider in determining whether a trial court's error in permitting the State to ask improper commitment questions to an entire jury panel

over the defendant's objection is harmful might include: whether the questions were unambiguously improper and attempted to commit one or more veniremen to a specific verdict or course of action; how many, if any, veniremen agreed to commit themselves to a specific verdict or course of action if the State produced certain evidence; whether the veniremen who agreed to commit themselves actually served on the jury; whether the defendant used peremptory challenges to eliminate any or all of those veniremen who had committed themselves; whether the defendant exhausted all of his peremptory challenges upon those veniremen and requested additional peremptory challenges to compensate for their use on improperly committed veniremen; whether the defendant timely asserted that a named objectionable veniremen actually served on the jury because he had to waste strikes on the improperly committed jurors; and whether there is a reasonable likelihood that the jury's verdict or course of action in reaching a verdict or sentence was substantially affected by the State's improper commitment questioning during voir dire. [¶] This is not ... an exhaustive or exclusive list of factors that reviewing courts might consider." *See also Wingo v. State*, 189 S.W.3d 270, 271-72 (Tex.Crim.App.2006) (listing commitment questions); *Tijerina v. State*, 202 S.W.3d 299, 300 (Tex.App.—Fort Worth 2006, pet. ref'd) ("Is there anybody here who feels that you would automatically disbelieve somebody simply because they are a convicted felon, be they a witness, a police officer, a defendant, anybody?" is a commitment question).

Standefer v. State, 59 S.W.3d 177, 179 (Tex.Crim. App.2001). "'[A]n attorney cannot attempt to bind or commit a prospective juror to a verdict based on a hypothetical set of facts.' ... Commitment questions are those that commit a prospective juror to resolve, or to refrain from resolving, an issue a certain way after learning a particular fact. Often, such questions ask for a 'yes' or 'no' answer, in which one or both of the possible answers commits the jury to resolving an issue a certain way. ... A commitment question can also be a question that asks a prospective juror to *refrain* from resolving an issue on the basis of a fact that might be used to resolve the issue. *At 180:* [A]n open-ended question can be a commitment question if the question asks the prospective juror to set the hypothetical parameters for his decision-making. *At 181-83:* Not all commitment questions are improper. [¶] When the law requires a certain type of commitment from jurors, the attorneys may ask the prospective jurors whether they can follow the law in that regard. [¶] However, where the law does not require the commitment, a commitment question is invariably improper. [¶] [T]he inquiry for improper commitment questions has two steps: (1) Is the question a commitment question, and (2) Does the question include facts—and only those facts—that lead to a valid challenge for cause? If the answer to (1) is 'yes' and the answer to (2) is 'no,' then the question is an improper commitment question, and the trial court should not allow the question." *See also Lee v. State*, 206 S.W.3d 620, 623-24 (Tex. Crim.App.2006); *Barajas v. State*, 93 S.W.3d 36, 38-39 (Tex.Crim.App.2002); *Atkins v. State*, 951 S.W.2d 787, 789 (Tex.Crim.App.1997).

ART. 35.18. OTHER EVIDENCE ON CHALLENGE

Upon a challenge for cause, the examination is not confined to the answers of the juror, but other evidence may be heard for or against the challenge.

History of CCP art. 35.18: Acts 1965, 59th Leg., ch. 722, §1, eff. Jan. 1, 1966.

ART. 35.19. ABSOLUTE DISQUALIFICATION

No juror shall be impaneled when it appears that he is subject to the second, third or fourth cause of challenge in Article 35.16, though both parties may consent.

History of CCP art. 35.19: Acts 1965, 59th Leg., ch. 722, §1, eff. Jan. 1, 1966. Amended by Acts 1969, 61st Leg., ch. 412, §4, eff. Sept. 1, 1969.

See also CCP art. 44.46.

ANNOTATIONS

Chambers v. State, 903 S.W.2d 21, 27 (Tex.Crim. App.1995). "We apply an abuse of discretion standard when reviewing a trial court's ruling on an absolute disqualification. [A] trial court's ruling on an absolute disqualification is a question of fact."

Green v. State, 764 S.W.2d 242, 246 (Tex.Crim.App. 1989). "[T]he primary factor that dictates the legal propriety of a *sua sponte* excusal is the inherent statutory qualifications of the venireperson. ... Should a prospective juror be plagued with any [art. 35.19] deficiency then the trial court has the authority to excuse the juror *sua sponte*. [¶] If, however, the prospective juror is otherwise qualified to serve the trial court has no authority to *sua sponte* excuse the juror."

State v. Read, 965 S.W.2d 74, 76 (Tex.App.—Austin 1998, no pet.). "After trial and sentencing, Read discovered that a juror had not disclosed information about her criminal history even though the trial court asked for this information at voir dire and on the jury questionnaire. [¶] After trial and sentencing, but within the time permitted for a motion for new trial, Read discovered that this juror had been convicted of misdemeanor theft.... A conviction of theft constitutes an absolute disqualification from jury service and a person who has been so convicted may not be impaneled as a juror even though both parties may consent to it."

Matthews v. State, 960 S.W.2d 750, 753 (Tex. App.—Tyler 1997, no pet.). "The list of enumerated reasons in the statute are not exclusive ... and a prospective juror may be successfully challenged if the facts show that the juror is 'incapable or unfit to serve on the jury.' A juror's failure to truthfully answer questions put to him by the court may support a challenge for cause. The trial court may determine that a prospective juror's failure to truthfully answer a question reflects a lack of credibility which might prevent him from obeying his oath and following his instructions."

ART. 35.20. NAMES CALLED IN ORDER

In selecting the jury from the persons summoned, the names of such persons shall be called in the order in which they appear upon the list furnished the defendant. Each juror shall be tried and passed upon separately. A person who has been summoned, but who is not present, may, upon his appearance before the jury is completed, be tried as to his qualifications and impaneled as a juror, unless challenged, but no cause shall be unreasonably delayed on account of such absence.

History of CCP art. 35.20: Acts 1965, 59th Leg., ch. 722, §1, eff. Jan. 1, 1966.

ANNOTATIONS

Ferguson v. State, 573 S.W.2d 516, 520 (Tex.Crim. App.1978). Article 35.20 "does not require that voir dire be postponed whenever a prospective juror is not present at the time his name is called. The court did not err in continuing with voir dire after [venireperson] failed to timely appear in court."

ART. 35.21. JUDGE TO DECIDE QUALIFICATIONS

The court is the judge, after proper examination, of the qualifications of a juror, and shall decide all challenges without delay and without argument thereupon.

History of CCP art. 35.21: Acts 1965, 59th Leg., ch. 722, §1, eff. Jan. 1, 1966.

ANNOTATIONS

Winfrey v. State, 104 S.W.3d 282, 283 (Tex.App.—Eastland 2003, pet. ref'd). "After the jury was selected, but not sworn, and the panel had been dismissed, it was discovered that one of the members of the jury was disqualified. After discussing the problem with the parties, the trial court elected to dismiss the disqualified juror and replace that juror with the next venireperson from the original venire panel who had not been struck or challenged by either party. [¶] [W]e hold that the trial court did not err in replacing the disqualified juror." *See also Williams v. State*, 631 S.W.2d 955, 957 (Tex.App.—Austin 1982, no pet.).

Earls v. State, 650 S.W.2d 858, 860 (Tex.App.—Houston [14th Dist.] 1982), *aff'd*, 707 S.W.2d 82 (Tex.Crim.App.1986). "In order for this court to hold that a trial court has abused its discretion, an appellant must show on appeal that he was injured by such action."

Brown v. State, 639 S.W.2d 505, 507 (Tex.App.—Fort Worth 1982, pet. ref'd). "Reading [CCP arts.] 35.21 and 35.12 together, it readily appears that 'proper examination' includes a trial court's asking questions as to the qualifications of the prospective jurors."

ART. 35.22. OATH TO JURY

When the jury has been selected, the following oath shall be administered them by the court or under its direction: "You and each of you do solemnly swear that in the case of the State of Texas against the defendant, you will a true verdict render according to the law and the evidence, so help you God."

History of CCP art. 35.22: Acts 1965, 59th Leg., ch. 722, §1, eff. Jan. 1, 1966.

ANNOTATIONS

Smith v. State, 744 S.W.2d 86, 91 (Tex.Crim.App. 1987). "[A] juror who will ultimately be guided by his or her personal beliefs rather than the law is not qualified to sit on a jury in the State of Texas. Clearly [this] was such a juror. He repeatedly stated that because of his personal beliefs he could not take the oath mandated by Article 35.22 ..., and thereby render a verdict solely based on the evidence and the law."

Brown v. State, 220 S.W.3d 552, 554 (Tex.App.—Texarkana 2007, no pet.). "This jury had begun its deliberation before having been sworn in as jurors. ... Texas has not addressed the validity of the actions of a jury which is administered its oath after it has already begun its deliberations. *At 555:* It was error not to have sworn the jury at the proper stage of the trial but the error was rendered harmless by the actions of the court in causing the oath to be administered when it was; it seems most unlikely that any different result would have been forthcoming in the trial if the proper procedure had been followed. We accordingly find that the trial court did not abuse its discretion in swearing in the jury, readmitting all of the evidence it had already heard, and referring the jury to the previously-given charge after the jury had begun deliberation."

ART. 35.23. JURORS MAY SEPARATE

The court may adjourn veniremen to any day of the term. When jurors have been sworn in a felony case, the court may, at its discretion, permit the jurors to separate until the court has given its charge to the jury. The court on its own motion may and on the motion of either party shall, after having given its charge to the jury, order that the jury not be allowed to separate, after which the jury shall be kept together, and not permitted to separate except to the extent of housing female jurors separate and apart from male jurors, until a verdict has been rendered or the jury finally discharged. Any person who makes known to the jury which party made the motion not to allow separation of the jury shall be punished for contempt of court. If such jurors are kept overnight, facilities shall be provided for female jurors separate and apart from the facilities provided for male jurors. In misdemeanor cases the court may, at its discretion, permit the jurors to separate at any time before the verdict. In any case in which the jury is permitted to separate, the court shall first give the jurors proper instructions with regard to their conduct as jurors when so separated.

History of CCP art. 35.23: Acts 1965, 59th Leg., ch. 722, §1, eff. Jan. 1, 1966. Amended by Acts 1989, 71st Leg., ch. 825, §1, eff. Sept. 1, 1989.

ANNOTATIONS

Garner v. State, 957 S.W.2d 112, 113 (Tex.App.—Amarillo 1997, no pet.). "The court had prepared a written charge to the jury, a copy of which was handed to each member. The judge began reading the charge to the jury, and as he did so noticed an error in the charge. The necessary correction could not be made that day so the judge, over appellant's objection, dismissed the jury until the following day. [¶] Thus, the question presented by this point is whether the charge was 'given' to the jury when the judge partially read the imperfect charge, as well as physically handed the jurors an imperfect charge. *At 114:* [W]e hold the charge was not 'given' to the jury until the trial judge had completed the oral presentation which did not take place until the day following the discovery of the error in the charge. Because of that holding, the court did not err in allowing the jury to separate...."

Sanchez v. State, 906 S.W.2d 176, 178 (Tex.App.—Fort Worth 1995, pet. ref'd). Article 35.23 "allows separation unless the court or a party makes a motion to sequester the jury or a party timely objects to a request to separate. [T]he defendant must either timely file a motion to sequester or timely object to a request to separate to preserve for appeal a complaint that the trial court deprived the defendant of the right to have the jury sequestered."

ART. 35.24. REPEALED
Repealed by Acts 1975, 64th Leg., ch. 510, §2, eff. Sept. 1, 1975.

ART. 35.25. MAKING PEREMPTORY CHALLENGE

In non-capital cases and in capital cases in which the State's attorney has announced that he will not qualify the jury for, or seek the death penalty, the party desiring to challenge any juror peremptorily shall strike the name of such juror from the list furnished him by the clerk.

History of CCP art. 35.25: Acts 1965, 59th Leg., ch. 722, §1, eff. Jan. 1, 1966.

ANNOTATIONS

Linnell v. State, 935 S.W.2d 426, 430 (Tex.Crim. App.1996). "[I]f the trial judge intends to select more than one jury from a single venire, the veniremembers selected to serve as jurors must be excluded from the venire from which the other jurors will be selected. [¶] In the instant case this process was not followed and eight members of appellant's jury served on the interim jury. Consequently, appellant was denied the intelligent use of his peremptory challenges. In these situations harm is presumed."

Grijalva v. State, 614 S.W.2d 420, 424 (Tex.Crim. App.1980). "The manner of exercising peremptory challenges is explicitly differentiated in [CCP arts.] 35.13 and 35.25. [¶] [I]t is clear that in capital cases each party must exercise any peremptory challenge at the

time the particular prospective juror has been qualified. The parties may not wait until all prospective jurors have been examined before exercising peremptory challenges as is allowed in non-capital cases."

ART. 35.26. LISTS RETURNED TO CLERK

(a) When the parties have made or declined to make their peremptory challenges, they shall deliver their lists to the clerk. Except as provided in Subsection (b) of this section, the clerk shall, if the case be in the district court, call off the first twelve names on the lists that have not been stricken. If the case be in the county court, he shall call off the first six names on the lists that have not been stricken. Those whose names are called shall be the jury.

(b) In a capital case in which the state seeks the death penalty, the court may direct that two alternate jurors be selected and that the first fourteen names not stricken be called off by the clerk. The last two names to be called are the alternate jurors.

History of CCP art. 35.26: Acts 1965, 59th Leg., ch. 722, §1, eff. Jan. 1, 1966. Amended by Acts 1981, 67th Leg., ch. 545, §1, eff. June 12, 1981; Acts 1991, 72nd Leg., ch. 652, §7, eff. Sept. 1, 1991.

ANNOTATIONS

Saur v. State, 918 S.W.2d 64, 66-67 (Tex. App.—San Antonio 1996, no pet.). "A distinction exists ... between a 'jury list,' which only contains the names of the jurors, and the 'juror information sheets,' which contain background information on each juror. [¶] [CCP] art. 35.26 only requires a party to deliver the jury lists, not the juror information sheets. [CCP] art. 35.29 prohibits the court and litigants from disclosing personal information about jurors ... in the information sheets; however, it does not authorize the court to order the delivery of the sheets to the clerk. [¶] In some cases, ... collecting both the jury list and the information sheets, without warning counsel not to annotate them or without allowing counsel to transcribe them, could be reversible error."

Brossette v. State, 885 S.W.2d 841, 842 (Tex. App.—Dallas 1994, pet. ref'd). "A violation of article 35.26 per se does not constitute reversible error."

ART. 35.261. PEREMPTORY CHALLENGES BASED ON RACE PROHIBITED

(a) After the parties have delivered their lists to the clerk under Article 35.26 of this code and before the court has impanelled the jury, the defendant may request the court to dismiss the array and call a new array in the case. The court shall grant the motion of a defendant for dismissal of the array if the court determines that the defendant is a member of an identifiable racial group, that the attorney representing the state exercised peremptory challenges for the purpose of excluding persons from the jury on the basis of their race, and that the defendant has offered evidence of relevant facts that tend to show that challenges made by the attorney representing the state were made for reasons based on race. If the defendant establishes a prima facie case, the burden then shifts to the attorney representing the state to give a racially neutral explanation for the challenges. The burden of persuasion remains with the defendant to establish purposeful discrimination.

(b) If the court determines that the attorney representing the state challenged prospective jurors on the basis of race, the court shall call a new array in the case.

History of CCP art. 35.261: Acts 1987, 70th Leg., ch. 751, §1, eff. Aug. 31, 1987.

ANNOTATIONS

J.E.B. v. Alabama, 511 U.S. 127, 130, 114 S.Ct. 1419, 1422 (1994). "Intentional discrimination on the basis of gender by state actors violates the Equal Protection Clause.... *At 143, 1429:* Our conclusion [is] that litigants may not strike potential jurors solely on the basis of gender.... *At 144, 1429:* As with race-based *Batson* claims, a party alleging gender discrimination must make a prima facie showing of intentional discrimination before the party exercising the challenge is required to explain the basis for the strike. When an explanation is required, it need not rise to the level of a 'for cause' challenge; rather, it merely must be based on a juror characteristic other than gender, and the proffered explanation may not be pretextual." *See also Fritz v. State*, 946 S.W.2d 844, 844 (Tex.Crim.App.1997).

Batson v. Kentucky, 476 U.S. 79, 89, 106 S.Ct. 1712, 1719 (1986). "Although a prosecutor ordinarily is entitled to exercise ... peremptory challenges 'for any reason at all, as long as that reason is related to his view concerning the outcome' of the case to be tried, the Equal Protection Clause forbids the prosecutor to challenge potential jurors solely on account of their race or on the assumption that black jurors ... will be unable impartially to consider the State's case against a

black defendant. *At 96, 1723:* [A] defendant may establish a prima facie case of purposeful discrimination ... on evidence concerning the prosecutor's exercise of peremptory challenges.... [T]he defendant first must show that he is a member of a cognizable racial group, and that the prosecutor has exercised peremptory challenges to remove ... members of the defendant's race. Second, the defendant is entitled to rely on the fact ... that peremptory challenges constitute a jury selection practice that permits 'those to discriminate who are of a mind to discriminate.' Finally, the defendant must show that [the] circumstances raise an inference that the prosecutor used that practice to exclude the veniremen ... on account of their race. *At 97:* Once the defendant makes a prima facie showing, the burden shifts to the State to come forward with a neutral explanation for challenging black jurors." *See also Powers v. Ohio*, 499 U.S. 400, 405-06, 111 S.Ct. 1364, 1370 (1991).

Watkins v. State, 245 S.W.3d 444, 448 (Tex.Crim. App.2008). "In assaying the record for clear error, *vel non*, the reviewing court should consider the entire record of voir dire; it need not limit itself to arguments or considerations that the parties specifically called to the trial court's attention so long as those arguments or considerations are manifestly grounded in the appellate record. But a reviewing court should examine a trial court's conclusion that a facially race-neutral explanation for a peremptory challenge is genuine, rather than a pretext, with great deference, reversing only when that conclusion is, in view of the record as a whole, clearly erroneous."

Hutchinson v. State, 86 S.W.3d 636, 639-40 (Tex. Crim.App.2002). "[W]hen there has been a *prima facie* showing of discriminatory use of peremptory strikes but no *Batson* hearing, the supplemented record represents material omitted from the record. The trial court here held a *Batson* hearing, but only as to the first four venire members. There was no hearing as to the fifth venire member. [T]he court of appeals was authorized to abate the appeal and order the trial court to supplement the record by making findings and conclusions regarding appellant's *Batson* challenge as to the fifth venire member."

Guzman v. State, 85 S.W.3d 242, 244 (Tex.Crim. App.2002). "[W]hen the motives behind a challenged peremptory strike are 'mixed,' i.e., both impermissible (race or gender-based) and permissible (race and gender-neutral), if the striking party shows that he would have struck the juror based solely on the neutral reasons, then the strike does not violate the juror's 14th Amendment right to equal protection of the law."

Yarborough v. State, 947 S.W.2d 892, 896 (Tex. Crim.App.1997). "[S]ubjective evaluations of venire members could be used to disguise violations of the Equal Protection Clause. [T]his does not mean that such evaluations must always be held to have no weight. Trial judges are not without ability to detect pretexts. '[I]mplausible or fantastic justifications may (and probably will) be found to be pretexts for purposeful discrimination.' [A]ppellate courts are not bound by the rule of deference to accept every ruling of a trial court, especially when there is no specific finding of fact."

Morris v. State, 940 S.W.2d 610, 612 (Tex.Crim. App.1996). "We will not disturb a trial court's ruling on a *Batson* issue unless it is clearly erroneous. [¶] A ruling on a *Batson* objection is a credibility determination. Because the trial judge determines the issue of the prosecutor's credibility, it is not error for the court to consider its past experiences with a prosecutor in determining his credibility." *See also Gibson v. State*, 144 S.W.3d 530, 534 (Tex.Crim.App.2004); *Kemp v. State*, 846 S.W.2d 289, 304 (Tex.Crim.App.1992).

Staley v. State, 887 S.W.2d 885, 891 (Tex.Crim.App. 1994). "[T]he *prima facie* showing at the trial court was *only* that the State struck a member of an identifiable racial group. This is not sufficient to meet a defendant's *prima facie* burden for purposes of *Batson*."

State ex rel. Curry v. Bowman, 885 S.W.2d 421, 425 (Tex.Crim.App.1993). "[W]here a *Batson* claim is sustained the court may fashion a remedy in its discretion consistent with *Batson* and its progeny. Therefore, respondent's decision to reinstate the excluded veniremembers to the jury is consistent with our decision today...." *See also Peetz v. State*, 180 S.W.3d 755, 760 (Tex.App.—Houston [14th Dist.] 2005, no pet.).

Cook v. State, 858 S.W.2d 467, 472 (Tex.Crim.App. 1993). "Just as it is not necessary ... to show that the defendant is a member of a cognizable racial group, it is also not necessary under art. 35.261(a) that the veniremember be of a particular racial group."

Moore v. State, ___ S.W.3d ___ (Tex.App.— Houston [1st Dist.] 2008, n.p.h.) (No. 01-06-00656-CR; 5-01-08). "A defendant's *Batson* challenge to a peremptory strike is a three-step process. The defendant must first make a prima facie case of racial discrimination, based on the totality of relevant facts about the prosecutor's conduct during the trial. If the defendant makes a prima facie case, the burden of production shifts to the State to present a race-neutral reason for its challenged strike, a reason that is 'a clear and reasonably specific explanation of [the] legitimate reasons' for exercising its strike. A reason is deemed race neutral if no discriminatory intent is inherent in the prosecutor's explanation. [¶] When the prosecutor responds by offering a race-neutral explanation, the inquiry whether the defendant has made a prima facie case becomes moot, and the defendant may rebut the State's explanation. In the third and final step, the trial court must decide whether the defendant carried the burden to establish purposeful discrimination. The trial court's inquiry addresses whether the neutral reasons provided by the prosecutor for the peremptory challenge were contrived in order to conceal racially discriminatory intent. [¶] Throughout the challenge, the burden of persuasion remains with the defendant, ... who may continue to rebut the prosecutor's explanations before the trial court decides the *Batson* challenge."

Green v. State, 839 S.W.2d 935, 939 (Tex.App.— Waco 1992, pet. ref'd). "The reason behind a peremptory strike does not have to rise to the level of a challenge for cause to be considered legitimately race-neutral."

ART. 35.27. REIMBURSEMENT OF NONRESIDENT WITNESSES

§1. Expenses for Nonresident Witnesses

(a) Every person subpoenaed by either party or otherwise required or requested in writing by the prosecuting attorney or the court to appear for the purpose of giving testimony in a criminal proceeding who resides outside the state or the county in which the prosecution is pending shall be reimbursed by the state for the reasonable and necessary transportation, meal, and lodging expenses he incurs by reason of his attendance as a witness at such proceeding.

(b) The state may reimburse a witness for transportation only if the transportation is provided by a commercial transportation company or the witness uses the witness's personally owned or leased motor vehicle. In this article, "commercial transportation company" means an entity that offers transportation of people or goods to the public in exchange for compensation.

(c) The state may reimburse a witness for lodging only if the lodging is provided by a commercial lodging establishment. In this article, "commercial lodging establishment" means a motel, hotel, inn, apartment, or similar entity that offers lodging to the public in exchange for compensation.

§2. Amount of Reimbursement for Expenses

Any person seeking reimbursement as a witness shall make an affidavit setting out the transportation, meal, and lodging expenses necessitated by his travel to and from and attendance at the place he appeared to give testimony, together with the number of days that such travel and attendance made him absent from his place of residence. A reimbursement paid by the state to a witness for transportation, meal, or lodging expenses may not be paid at a rate that exceeds the maximum rates provided by law for state employees.

§2A. Direct Payment of Transportation or Lodging Expenses

If this article requires the state to reimburse a witness for transportation or lodging expenses, the state may instead directly pay a commercial transportation company or commercial lodging establishment for those expenses.

§3. Other Expenses

In addition to reimbursement or payment for transportation, meal, and lodging expenses, the comptroller, upon proper application by the attorney for the state, shall reimburse or pay the other expenses required by the laws of this state or the state from which the attendance of the witness is sought.

§4. Application & Approval by Judge

A reimbursement to a witness as provided by this article shall be paid by the state to the witness or his assignee. Claim shall be made by sworn application to the comptroller, a copy of which shall be filed with the clerk of the court, setting out the facts showing entitlement as provided in this article to the reimbursement, which application shall be presented for approval by the judge who presided over the court or empaneled the grand jury before whom the criminal proceeding was pending. No fee shall be required of any witness for the processing of his claim for reimbursement.

§5. Payment by State

The Comptroller of Public Accounts, upon receipt of a claim approved by the judge, shall examine it and, if he deems the claim in compliance with and authorized by this Article, draw his warrant on the State Treasury for the amount due the witness, or to any person to which the certificate has been assigned by the witness, but no warrant may issue to any assignee of a witness claim unless the assignment is made under oath and acknowledged before some person authorized to administer oaths, certified to by the officer, and under seal. If the appropriation for paying the account is exhausted, the Comptroller of Public Accounts shall file it away and issue a certificate in the name of the witness entitled to it, stating therein the amount of the claim. Each claim not filed in the office of the Comptroller of Public Accounts within twelve months from the date it became due and payable shall be forever barred.

§6. Advance by State

Funds required to be tendered to an out-of-state witness pursuant to Article 24.28 of this Code shall be paid by the Comptroller of Public Accounts into the registry of the Court in which the case is to be tried upon certification by the Court such funds are necessary to obtain attendance of said witness. The court shall then cause to be issued checks drawn upon the registry of the Court to secure the attendance of such witness. In the event that such funds are not used pursuant to this Act, the Court shall return the funds to the Comptroller of Public Accounts.

§7. Advance by County

The county in which a criminal proceeding is pending, upon request of the district attorney or other prosecutor charged with the duty of prosecution in the proceeding, may advance funds from its treasury to any witness who will be entitled to reimbursement under this article. The amount advanced may not exceed the amount that is reasonably necessary to enable the witness to attend as required or requested. However, the amount advanced may include sums in excess of the reimbursement provided for by this article if the excess is required for compliance with Section 4 of Article 24.28 in securing the attendance of a witness from another state under the Uniform Act. A county that advances funds to a witness under this section is entitled to reimbursement by the state as an assignee of the witness.

§8. Advance for Expenses for Witnesses of Indigent Defendant

Upon application by a defendant shown to be indigent and a showing to the court of reasonable necessity

⭐

and materiality for the testimony of a witness residing outside the State, the court shall act pursuant to Section 6 hereof to secure advance of funds necessary for the attendance of such witness.

§9. Limitations

A witness, when attached and conveyed by a sheriff or other officer, is not eligible to receive reimbursement of transportation, meal, or lodging expenses incurred while in the custody of the officer. A court, in its discretion, may limit the number of character witnesses allowed reimbursement under this article to not fewer than two for each defendant and two per defendant for the state.

History of CCP art. 35.27: Acts 1965, 59th Leg., ch. 722, §1, eff. Jan. 1, 1966. Amended by Acts 1973, 63rd Leg., ch. 477, §2, eff. Aug. 27, 1973; Acts 1979, 66th Leg., ch. 469, §1, eff. Sept. 1, 1979; Acts 1993, 73rd Leg., ch. 449, §18, eff. Sept. 1, 1993.

ANNOTATIONS

Johnson v. State, 746 S.W.2d 791, 794 (Tex.App.—Corpus Christi 1987, pet. ref'd). CCP arts. 24.28 and 35.27 "provide the methods by which out-of-state witnesses will be obtained and funds secured for their appearance. [U]nder those Articles, it is incumbent upon the appellant to establish that the expected testimony of the witnesses would be material and necessary to the criminal proceeding in order to have them subpoenaed."

ART. 35.28. WHEN NO CLERK

In each instance in Article 35.27 in which the clerk of the court is authorized or directed to perform any act, the judge of such court shall perform the same if there is no clerk of the court.

History of CCP art. 35.28: Acts 1965, 59th Leg., ch. 722, §1, eff. Jan. 1, 1966.

ART. 35.29. PERSONAL INFORMATION ABOUT JURORS

Information collected by the court or by a prosecuting attorney during the jury selection process about a person who serves as a juror, including the juror's home address, home telephone number, social security number, driver's license number, and other personal information, is confidential and may not be disclosed by the court, the prosecuting attorney, the defense counsel, or any court personnel except on application by a party in the trial or on application by a bona fide member of the news media acting in such capacity to the court in which the person is serving or did serve as a juror. On a showing of good cause, the court shall permit disclosure of the information sought.

History of CCP art. 35.29: Acts 1993, 73rd Leg., ch. 371, §1, eff. Sept. 1, 1993.

ANNOTATIONS

Saur v. State, 918 S.W.2d 64, 67 (Tex.App.—San Antonio 1996, no pet.). "Article 35.29 prohibits the court and litigants from disclosing personal information about jurors ... in the information sheets; however, it does not authorize the court to order the delivery of the sheets to the clerk. [¶] In some cases, ... collecting both the jury list and the information sheets, without warning counsel not to annotate them or without allowing counsel to transcribe them, could be reversible error."

ART. 36.01. ORDER OF PROCEEDING IN TRIAL

(a) A jury being impaneled in any criminal action, except as provided by Subsection (b) of this article, the cause shall proceed in the following order:

1. The indictment or information shall be read to the jury by the attorney prosecuting. When prior convictions are alleged for purposes of enhancement only and are not jurisdictional, that portion of the indictment or information reciting such convictions shall not be read until the hearing on punishment is held as provided in Article 37.07.

2. The special pleas, if any, shall be read by the defendant's counsel, and if the plea of not guilty is also relied upon, it shall also be stated.

3. The State's attorney shall state to the jury the nature of the accusation and the facts which are expected to be proved by the State in support thereof.

4. The testimony on the part of the State shall be offered.

5. The nature of the defenses relied upon and the facts expected to be proved in their support shall be stated by defendant's counsel.

6. The testimony on the part of the defendant shall be offered.

7. Rebutting testimony may be offered on the part of each party.

8. In the event of a finding of guilty, the trial shall then proceed as set forth in Article 37.07.

(b) The defendant's counsel may make the opening statement for the defendant immediately after the attorney representing the State makes the opening statement for the State. After the defendant's attorney concludes the defendant's opening statement, the State's testimony shall be offered. At the conclusion of the presentation of the State's testimony, the defendant's testimony shall be offered, and the order of proceedings shall continue in the manner described by Subsection (a) of this article.

History of CCP art. 36.01: Acts 1965, 59th Leg., vol. 2, ch. 722. Amended by Acts 1987, 70th Leg., ch. 519, §1, eff. Sept. 1, 1987.

ANNOTATIONS

Generally

Penry v. State, 903 S.W.2d 715, 760 (Tex.Crim.App. 1995). "[A]rticle 36.01 does not apply to the punishment phase of trial."

Stratman v. State, 436 S.W.2d 144, 146 (Tex.Crim.App.1969). Art. 36.01 "relate[s] to jury trials, and there is no statute requiring a separate hearing on punishment in a trial before the court."

Art. 36.01(a)

Farr v. State, 193 S.W.3d 904, 912 (Tex.Crim.App. 2006). "[O]nce the State rests its case in chief, on the timely request of a defendant the trial court must order the State to make its election [of the offenses it would use to convict on each count], regardless of the lack of erroneous evidentiary rulings and jury instructions. It is at this juncture that the defense needs notice so that it can put forward a vigorous defense and argue to the jury the evidence that challenges some or all of the elements of the State's case. Additionally, an election allows a defendant to tailor a request for a limiting instruction and the trial judge to craft that instruction on the basis of the State's theory of proving its case. [¶] [D] did not request election at the close of the State's case. [D] did not move for election until the close of all evidence. The question, then, is whether his request for election was timely.... Undoubtedly, if [D] had petitioned for election at the close of the State's evidence, the trial court would have been obligated to require the State to elect at that time. Because [D] did not move for election until the close of all evidence, [D] was not entitled to an election at the close of the State's evidence. However, [D] was still entitled to an unanimous verdict. He preserved his right to an unanimous verdict by calling for an election at the close of the all evidence. Therefore, [D's] request was timely insofar as he was entitled to a unanimous jury verdict, and the trial court had an obligation to require the State to elect at that juncture."

Turner v. State, 897 S.W.2d 786, 789 (Tex.Crim.App.1995). "Because of the double jeopardy implications of failing to comply with Article 36.01, and the potential for harm to a defendant's right to a fair punishment hearing and wasted judicial resources in future cases, it is not unreasonable ... to require the State to strictly comply with [Art. 36.01(a)(1) and (2)]." *But see* **Linton v. State**, 15 S.W.3d 615, 620 (Tex.App.—Houston [14th Dist.] 2000, pet. ref'd).

Warren v. State, 693 S.W.2d 414, 415 (Tex.Crim.App.1985). "The reading of the indictment [is] mandatory. The rationale for the rule is to inform the accused of the charges against him and to inform the jury of the precise terms of the particular charge against the accused. Without the reading of the indictment and the entering of a plea, no issue is joined upon which to try. This mandatory provision of Art. 36.01 is applicable to the penalty stage of a bifurcated trial. *At 416:* Error which results from not reading the indictment (or enhancement allegations) and not entering a plea can be cured at trial. The procedure to be followed [is] upon learning of the error, the indictment is read to the jury, the accused enters a plea and the State reintroduces the evidence; or the parties may stipulate to the evidence. When this is done, the issue is joined and a trial on the issue may be held. [¶] However, when the error is discovered *after* the trial, the above-mentioned procedure will not cure the error. Rather, the error can be preserved by means of a motion for new trial, bill of exception or motion to arrest judgment." *See also **Hernandez v. State**,* 190 S.W.3d 856, 866-67 (Tex.App.—Corpus Christi 2006, no pet.) (failure to read enhancement counts at punishment phase).

***Johnson v. State**,* 901 S.W.2d 525, 532 (Tex. App.—El Paso 1995, pet ref'd). "Article 36.01 is designed to prevent the prejudice that would inevitably result from 'an announcement at the outset of proceedings that the State believes that the defendant was previously convicted of a **particular offense at a particular time and in a particular court**.' [A]rticle 36.01 proscribes informing the jury 'of any of the **specific allegations** contained in the enhancement paragraph' of the indictment. It does not, however, prevent the trial court or the prosecutor from informing the jury in hypothetical terms of the applicable range of punishment if the State proves any prior convictions for enhancement purposes." *See also **McIlroy v. State**,* 188 S.W.3d 789, 791 (Tex.App.—Fort Worth 2006, no pet.).

***Vasquez v. State**,* 653 S.W.2d 492, 494-95 (Tex. App.—Corpus Christi 1983), *aff'd,* 665 S.W.2d 484 (Tex. Crim.App.1984). "The record ... fails to show that the appellant entered his plea of 'not guilty' in the presence of the jury as required by Art. 36.01.... [G]enerally the failure to comply with this statute would constitute reversible error. However, ... there was no objection made at the trial and the issue was not raised in a motion for new trial. [¶] No reversible error is shown."

Art. 36.01(b)

***Penry v. State**,* 903 S.W.2d 715, 760 (Tex.Crim.App. 1995). "Article 36.01 allows a defendant to make an opening statement prior to presentation of the State's case only when the State first makes one." *See also **Sanders v. State**,* 688 S.W.2d 676, 678 (Tex.App.—Dallas 1985, pet. ref'd).

***Norton v. State**,* 564 S.W.2d 714, 718 (Tex.Crim. App.1978). "While the right of a defendant to have his counsel make an opening statement is 'a valuable right, and the denial of a timely request by the defendant to make an opening statement constitutes reversible error, the character and extent of such statement[s] are subject to the control of the trial court....' [¶] [S]ince the appellant called no witnesses, did not testify himself nor otherwise offer any evidence in his defense, the trial court did not err in [denying appellant an opening statement]." *See also **McGowen v. State**,* 25 S.W.3d 741, 745 (Tex.App.—Houston [14th Dist.] 2000, pet. ref'd).

***Robles v. State**,* 104 S.W.3d 649, 652 (Tex.App.—Houston [1st Dist.] 2003, no pet.). The right to make an opening statement "may be waived for failure to make a timely request to present an opening statement."

***Twine v. State**,* 929 S.W.2d 685, 686 (Tex.App.—Eastland 1996), *pet. dism'd,* 970 S.W.2d 18 (Tex.Crim. App.1998). "[A]ppellant contends that the trial court committed reversible error in denying defense counsel's request to make an opening statement immediately following the State's opening statement. *At 687:* The record reflects that appellant made an opening statement after the State's case-in-chief. ... The nature of appellant's defense was apparent from her counsel's voir dire and from the cross-examination of the State's witnesses. ... Appellant's ... point of error is overruled."

ART. 36.02. TESTIMONY AT ANY TIME

The court shall allow testimony to be introduced at any time before the argument of a cause is concluded, if it appears that it is necessary to a due administration of justice.

History of CCP art. 36.02: Acts 1965, 59th Leg., vol. 2, ch. 722.

ANNOTATIONS

***Peek v. State**,* 106 S.W.3d 72, 79 (Tex.Crim.App. 2003). "[A] 'due administration of justice' means a judge should reopen the case if the evidence would materially change the case in the proponent's favor." *See also **Reeves v. State**,* 113 S.W.3d 791, 794 (Tex.App.—Dallas 2003, no pet.).

Love v. State, 861 S.W.2d 899, 902 n.4 (Tex.Crim. App.1993). "Although not expressly limited, [CCP art. 36.02] has generally been applied in those cases where a party has moved to 'reopen' the evidence after he has *rested* or *closed* at trial. The application of this article is necessarily limited by the [TRE]." *But see Allman*, below.

Lackey v. State, 638 S.W.2d 439, 457 (Tex.Crim. App.1982). "This Court has often held that [Art. 36.02] mean[s] that testimony may be introduced in the rebuttal portion of a trial whether it specifically rebuts other testimony or not."

Allman v. State, 164 S.W.3d 717, 721 (Tex.App.— Austin 2005, no pet.). "Article 36.02 makes it clear that the court had no discretion or authority to admit evidence after the close of argument. [¶] Nor are we persuaded by the State's argument that no error is presented because both parties were permitted further argument after the new testimony was adduced. [¶] The trial court in this cause permitted the State to introduce further evidence after both parties had concluded argument in clear violation of article 36.02. As the State itself argues in its brief, the additional testimony was such as to materially change the case in the State's favor. We conclude that the court's error affected Allman's substantial rights and cannot be disregarded." *But see Love*, above.

Cantu v. State, 662 S.W.2d 455, 458 (Tex.App.— Corpus Christi 1983, no pet.). "Although Art. 36.02 … applies only to trials before the jury, the same general rule should be no less applicable to probation hearings, which by their very nature are administrative in nature."

ART. 36.03. INVOCATION OF RULE

(a) Notwithstanding Rule 614, Texas Rules of Evidence, a court at the request of a party may order the exclusion of a witness who for the purposes of the prosecution is a victim, close relative of a deceased victim, or guardian of a victim only if the witness is to testify and the court determines that the testimony of the witness would be materially affected if the witness hears other testimony at the trial.

(b) On the objection of the opposing party, the court may require the party requesting exclusion of a witness under Subsection (a) to make an offer of proof to justify the exclusion.

(c) Subsection (a) does not limit the authority of the court on its own motion to exclude a witness or other person to maintain decorum in the courtroom.

(d) In this article:

(1) "Close relative of a deceased victim" and "guardian of a victim" have the meanings assigned by Article 56.01.

(2) "Victim" means a victim of any criminal offense.

(e) At the commencement of a trial, the court shall admonish each witness who is to testify as to those persons whom the court determines the witness may talk to about the case before the trial ends and those persons whom the witness may not talk to about the case. The court may punish as contempt a witness who violates the admonishment provided by the court.

History of CCP art. 36.03: Acts 2001, 77th Leg., ch. 1034, §1, eff. Sept. 1, 2001.

ART. 36.04. REPEALED

Repealed by the Texas Court of Criminal Appeals' adoption of the Texas Rules of Criminal Evidence on Dec. 18, 1985, eff. Sept. 1, 1986. 701 S.W.2d xxix, lxvi-lxvii.

ART. 36.05. NOT TO HEAR TESTIMONY

Witnesses under rule shall be attended by an officer, and all their reasonable wants provided for, unless the court, in its discretion, directs that they be allowed to go at large; but in no case where the witnesses are under rule shall they be allowed to hear any testimony in the case.

History of CCP art. 36.05: Acts 1965, 59th Leg., vol. 2, ch. 722.
See also TRE 614.

ANNOTATIONS

Webb v. State, 766 S.W.2d 236, 239-40 (Tex.Crim. App.1989). "Issues concerning this evidentiary rule arise in two basic contexts: (1) where a party complains of the *admission* into evidence of certain testimony due to violation of the invoked rule by an adverse witness; and (2) the more rare case where the complaint is founded upon the party's *own* witness being excluded due to violation of the rule. In the former situation we have said that a violation of the rule is not in itself reversible error, but only becomes so where the objected-to testimony is admitted and the complaining party is harmed thereby. In turn, injury or prejudice to the party in a criminal trial is dependent upon a showing of two criteria: (a) did the witness actually confer with or hear the testimony of the other witness; and (b) did the witness's testimony contradict the testimony of a witness from the opposing side or corroborate the testimony of another witness he had conferred with or had otherwise actually heard. Analysis of applicable decisions of this Court reflects that witnesses, usually those called by the State, who are technically disqualified but allowed to testify in the discretion of the trial court fall into two main categories: witnesses who have been sworn or listed as witnesses in the case and either hear facts or discuss another's testimony; and persons who were not intended to be witnesses and who are not connected with the case-in-chief but who have, due to events during trial, become necessary witnesses. This Court has usually held there to be no abuse of discretion in allowing the witness to testify. [¶] In the second type of case involving the rule, the focus is on testimony excluded by the trial court. [T]he issue revolves around the disqualification of a witness called by the defense. In such a case, state statutory law is juxtaposed with a criminal defendant's constitutional right to the compulsory attendance of witnesses. *At 241:* [A]n accused has the right to call and have his witness testify, albeit that witness's credibility may be properly challenged due to his violation of the rule, subject only to the exercise of sound discretion by the trial court to exclude the testimony based upon the particular circumstances in the case."

Upton v. State, 894 S.W.2d 426, 428 (Tex.App.— Amarillo 1995, pet. ref'd). "[T]he manner of enforcing [the Rule] lies within the trial court's discretion.... [¶] [T]he reviewing court must consider the witness, the nature of his testimony, and its relationship to the case in chief. For instance, those who were not originally anticipated to be called due to their lack of personal knowledge about the offense may subsequently testify with little risk of error; this is especially so when the testimony neither corroborates or contradicts that of another witness. Similarly, the admission of testimony related to something other than guilt or innocence is unlikely to result in the violation of ... article 36.05."

ART. 36.06. INSTRUCTED BY THE COURT

Witnesses, when placed under rule, shall be instructed by the court that they are not to converse with each other or with any other person about the case, except by permission of the court, and that they are not to read any report of or comment upon the testimony in the case while under rule. The officer who attends the witnesses shall report to the court at once any violation of its instructions, and the party violating the same shall be punished for contempt of court.

History of CCP art. 36.06: Acts 1965, 59th Leg., vol. 2, ch. 722.
See also TRE 614.

ART. 36.07. ORDER OF ARGUMENT

The order of argument may be regulated by the presiding judge; but the State's counsel shall have the right to make the concluding address to the jury.

History of CCP art. 36.07: Acts 1965, 59th Leg., vol. 2, ch. 722.

ANNOTATIONS

Gallo v. State, 239 S.W.3d 757, 767 (Tex.Crim.App. 2007). "Permissible jury argument falls into one of four areas: (1) summation of the evidence; (2) reasonable deduction from the evidence; (3) an answer to the argument of opposing counsel; or (4) a plea for law enforcement. We have consistently held that argument that strikes at a defendant over the shoulders of defense counsel is improper. [¶] Assuming, as the trial court did, that the prosecutor's comment was inappropriate, we next turn to the question of harm. We conduct a harm analysis using the following three-factor test: (1) the severity of the misconduct (the magnitude of the prejudicial effect of the prosecutor's remarks); (2) the measures adopted to cure the misconduct (the efficacy of any cautionary instruction by the judge); and, (3) the certainty of conviction absent the misconduct (the strength of the evidence supporting the conviction)."

Cruz v. State, 225 S.W.3d 546, 549 (Tex.Crim.App. 2007). "There is ... no particular 'trigger' word or phrase that makes any jury argument automatically improper. Rather, any objectionable argument should be evaluated on a case-by-case basis for what it would 'necessarily and naturally' mean to a jury when taken in the full context of its utterance. What determines the impermissibility of a reference to the defendant's failure to testify is not the use of 'I' or 'he' or 'she' or any other word, but rather the entirety of the prosecutor's statements, taken in the context in which the words were used and heard by the jury."

Dang v. State, 154 S.W.3d 616, 620 (Tex.Crim.App. 2005). "Because the legislature addressed the order in which arguments should be presented, we can assume that an implicit right to closing argument exists."

Jimenez v. State, 240 S.W.3d 384, 410 (Tex.App.—Austin 2007, pet. ref'd). "Improper jury argument is reversible error when it (1) violates a statute, (2) injects new and harmful facts into the case, or (3) is manifestly improper, harmful, and prejudicial to the rights of the accused. However, 'a defendant's failure to object to a jury argument or a defendant's failure to pursue to an adverse ruling his objection to a jury argument *forfeits* his right to complain about the argument on appeal.'"

Webster v. State, 627 S.W.2d 818, 821 (Tex.App.—Fort Worth 1982), *pet. ref'd*, 634 S.W.2d 322 (Tex.Crim. App.1982). "[T]he matter of permitting the State to waive its first closing statement of the punishment phase was discretionary with the court...."

ART. 36.08. NUMBER OF ARGUMENTS

The court shall never restrict the argument in felony cases to a number of addresses less than two on each side.

History of CCP art. 36.08: Acts 1965, 59th Leg., vol. 2, ch. 722.

ANNOTATIONS

Dang v. State, 154 S.W.3d 616, 621 (Tex.Crim.App. 2005). "We conclude that [in] reviewing [what is a reasonable amount of time for argument,] courts should consider, but are not limited to considering, the following non-exclusive list of factors on a case-by-case basis: (1) the quantity of the evidence, (2) the duration of the trial (3) conflicts in the testimony, (4) the seriousness of the offense, (5) the complexity of the case, (6) whether counsel used the time allotted efficiently, and (7) whether counsel set out what issues were not discussed because of the time limitation."

Varela v. State, 561 S.W.2d 186, 192 (Tex.Crim.App. 1978). "[W]here the accused has only one attorney it is within the court's discretion whether defense counsel may make more than one argument to the jury. Article 36.08 does not give the accused the right to rebut the closing argument of the State."

ART. 36.09. SEVERANCE ON SEPARATE INDICTMENTS

Two or more defendants who are jointly or separately indicted or complained against for the same offense or any offense growing out of the same transaction may be, in the discretion of the court, tried jointly or separately as to one or more defendants; provided that in any event either defendant may testify for the other or on behalf of the state; and provided further, that in cases in which, upon timely motion to sever, and evidence introduced thereon, it is made known to the court that there is a previous admissible conviction against one defendant or that a joint trial would be prejudicial to any defendant, the court shall order a severance as to the defendant whose joint trial would prejudice the other defendant or defendants.

History of CCP art. 36.09: Acts 1965, 59th Leg., vol. 2, ch. 722. Amended by Acts 1967, 60th Leg., ch. 659, §21, eff. Aug. 28, 1967.

ANNOTATIONS

Qualley v. State, 206 S.W.3d 624, 636 (Tex.Crim. App.2006). "To establish prejudice, the defendant must show a serious risk that a specific trial right would be compromised by a joint trial, or that a joint trial would prevent the jury from making a reliable judgment about guilt or innocence, and that the problem could not be adequately addressed by lesser curative measures, such as a limiting instruction. *At 637:* In connection with this holding, we observe that prejudice must be analyzed with regard to each defendant. Prejudice may be shown for one defendant but not another. This fact becomes clearer in a case involving more than two defendants, in which some defendants can be severed while others cannot. Even in a two-defendant case, however, the principle applies for purposes of reviewing the case on appeal. One defendant may be entitled to a severance while the other is not. While a severance at trial in that situation would in essence grant both defendants a separate trial, only the defendant entitled to the severance can obtain relief on appeal. [¶] [A]ntagonistic defenses are not prejudicial *per se*...."

Aguilar v. State, 26 S.W.3d 901, 909 (Tex.Crim.App. 2000). "[T]he trial court has a continuing duty to order a severance after trial begins upon a showing of sufficient prejudice. *At 910:* When unduly-prejudicial evidence first emerges during trial, it is neither logical nor reasonable to mandate that a motion to sever based on prejudicial grounds be presented pre-trial, a time when the prejudice is neither known or demonstrable. [A] motion to sever on the grounds of unfair prejudice under Art. 36.09 is 'timely' if made at the first opportunity or as soon as the grounds for prejudice become apparent or should have become apparent...."

Webb v. State, 763 S.W.2d 773, 775 (Tex.Crim.App. 1989). "Separate trials are required ... only when one codefendant is entitled to comment on the silence of another *and* the other is entitled to be tried free of such comment—where it would be an error against one co-defendant to let the evidence in and an error against another to keep it out."

Latham v. State, 656 S.W.2d 478, 480 (Tex.Crim. App.1983). "[T]he right to a severance is an extremely limited one. The general rule … is that except in the instance where one defendant does not have any admissible prior convictions, and the other defendant does, there is no absolute right to a severance prior to trial."

Lacy v. State, 901 S.W.2d 518, 519-20 (Tex.App.— Tyler 1995, no pet.). "Although the right to a severance is not absolute, the denial of a motion to sever constitutes an abuse of discretion when the movant can show that a joint trial was clearly prejudicial to his case. To establish prejudice on the basis of the right to have a co-defendant testify as a witness, the moving party must demonstrate: (1) a bona fide need for the testimony; (2) the substance of the desired testimony; (3) its exculpatory nature and effect; and (4) evidence that the designated co-defendant will in fact testify at a separate trial."

ART. 36.10. ORDER OF TRIAL

If a severance is granted, the defendants may agree upon the order in which they are to be tried, but if they fail to agree, the court shall direct the order of the trial.

History of CCP art. 36.10: Acts 1965, 59th Leg., vol. 2, ch. 722.

ANNOTATIONS

Mitchell v. State, 649 S.W.2d 715, 718 (Tex.App.— Fort Worth 1983, no pet.). "The order in which cases are called for trial … rests largely within the discretion of the trial court; and unless it is made to appear that the court has abused his discretion [and harmed] the appellant, [the reviewing] court would not be authorized to reverse the case…."

ART. 36.11. DISCHARGE BEFORE VERDICT

If it appears during a trial that the court has no jurisdiction of the offense, or that the facts charged in the indictment do not constitute an offense, the jury shall be discharged. The accused shall also be discharged, but such discharge shall be no bar in any case to a prosecution before the proper court for any offense unless termination of the former prosecution was improper.

History of CCP art. 36.11: Acts 1965, 59th Leg., vol. 2, ch. 722. Amended by Acts 1973, 63rd Leg., ch. 399, §2(A), eff. Jan. 1, 1974.

ART. 36.12. COURT MAY COMMIT

If the want of jurisdiction arises from the fact that the defendant is not liable to prosecution in the county where the indictment was presented, the court may in felony cases order the accused into custody for a reasonable length of time to await a warrant for his arrest from the proper county; or if the offense be bailable, may require him to enter into recognizance to answer before the proper court; in which case a certified copy of the recognizance shall be sent forthwith to the clerk of the proper court, to be enforced by that court in case of forfeiture.

History of CCP art. 36.12: Acts 1965, 59th Leg., vol. 2, ch. 722.

ART. 36.13. JURY IS JUDGE OF FACTS

Unless otherwise provided in this Code, the jury is the exclusive judge of the facts, but it is bound to receive the law from the court and be governed thereby.

History of CCP art. 36.13: Acts 1965, 59th Leg., vol. 2, ch. 722. See also CCP art. 38.04.

ANNOTATIONS

Pickens v. State, 921 S.W.2d 774, 776-77 (Tex. App.—El Paso 1996, no pet.). "In a jury trial, the issue of whether a deadly weapon was used or exhibited during the commission of the offense is an issue of fact which must be submitted to the jury for its exclusive determination. Since Appellant was tried by a jury, the trial court had no authority to make an affirmative finding that Appellant used a deadly weapon."

Powers v. State, 737 S.W.2d 53, 54 (Tex.App.—San Antonio 1987, pet. ref'd). "[T]he court should instruct the jury on the law, and not anyone else. Therefore, the trial court erred in permitting the prosecutor to read the law. [¶] A correct statement of the law by the trial court, even during the trial, is not reversible error."

Hargett v. State, 718 S.W.2d 923, 924 n.2 (Tex. App.—Tyler 1986), *pet. ref'd*, 729 S.W.2d 748 (Tex. Crim.App.1987). "[A] jury cannot convict a defendant of an offense not submitted to it by the court."

Rhodes v. State, 624 S.W.2d 770, 771 (Tex.App.— Houston [14th Dist.] 1981, no pet.). "An appellate court may not review the credibility of witnesses and the weight given their testimony, for these duties are within the exclusive province of the trier of fact."

ART. 36.14. CHARGE OF COURT

Subject to the provisions of Article 36.07 in each felony case and in each misdemeanor case tried in a court of record, the judge shall, before the argument begins, deliver to the jury, except in pleas of guilty, where a jury has been waived, a written charge distinctly setting forth the law applicable to the case; not expressing any opinion as to the weight of the evidence, not summing up the testimony, discussing the facts or using any argument in his charge calculated to arouse the sympathy or excite the passions of the jury. Before said charge is read to the jury, the defendant or his counsel shall have a reasonable time to examine the same and he shall present his objections thereto in writing, distinctly specifying each ground of objection. Said objections may embody errors claimed to have been committed in the charge, as well as errors claimed to have been committed by omissions therefrom or in failing to charge upon issues arising from the facts, and in no event shall it be necessary for the defendant or his counsel to present special requested charges to preserve or maintain any error assigned to the charge, as herein provided. The requirement that the objections to the court's charge be in writing will be complied with if the objections are dictated to the court reporter in the presence of the court and the state's counsel, before the reading of the court's charge to the jury. Compliance with the provisions of this Article is all that is necessary to preserve, for review, the exceptions and objections presented to the charge and any amendment or modification thereof. In no event shall it be necessary for the defendant to except to the action of the court in overruling defendant's exceptions or objections to the charge.

History of CCP art. 36.14: Acts 1965, 59th Leg., vol. 2, ch. 722. Amended by Acts 1975, 64th Leg., ch. 253, §1, eff. Sept. 1, 1975; Acts 1981, 67th Leg., ch. 537, §1, eff. June 12, 1981.

ANNOTATIONS

Warner v. State, 245 S.W.3d 458, 464 (Tex.Crim. App.2008). "To dispel any lack of clarity in our cases, we affirm that burdens of proof or persuasion have no place in a harm analysis conducted under *Almanza* [*v. State*, 686 S.W.2d 157 (Tex.Crim.App.1984)]. Because the Court of Appeals placed a burden of proof on the appellant, we shall remand the case to the Court of Appeals for a review of the record, giving consideration to the fact that neither party has a burden to show harm."

Delgado v. State, 235 S.W.3d 244, 246 (Tex.Crim. App.2007). "We granted appellant's petition for discretionary review to resolve a conflict between various courts of appeals. Some courts of appeals have held that a trial court must, *sua sponte*, include a reasonable-doubt instruction in the jury charge when the State offers evidence of an extraneous offense at the guilt stage of a criminal trial. Others, including the Second Court of Appeals in this case, have held that a trial judge must include such an instruction only when requested by the defendant. We agree with the latter position, and thus we affirm the court of appeals."

Brown v. State, 122 S.W.3d 794, 802-03 (Tex.Crim. App.2003). "We hold that [the] instruction ['intent or knowledge may be inferred by acts done or words spoken'] marginally falls on the wrong side of the 'improper-judicial-comment' scale because it is simply unnecessary and fails to clarify the law for the jury. It is not a statutory presumption, but it is a judicial review device for assessing the sufficiency of evidence to support a jury's finding of culpable intent. It is a common-sense tool for a trial judge to use in gauging the sufficiency of the evidence at a motion for directed verdict or motion for new trial and for sufficiency review by appellate courts, but it is not an explicit legal tool for the jury. Thus, the trial court erred in giving this instruction to the jury." Held: The error was harmless.

Paulson v. State, 28 S.W.3d 570, 573 (Tex.Crim. App.2000). "We specifically overrule that portion of *Geesa* which requires trial courts to instruct juries on the definition of 'beyond a reasonable doubt.' [T]he better practice is to give no definition of reasonable doubt at all to the jury. On the other hand, if both the State and the defense were to agree to give the *Geesa* instruction to the jury, it would not constitute reversible error for the trial court to acquiesce to their agreement."

Posey v. State, 966 S.W.2d 57, 59 (Tex.Crim.App. 1998). "On direct appeal to the Court of Appeals, appellant complained for the first time that the trial court reversibly erred by not *sua sponte* instructing the jury on the defense of mistake of fact. It is undisputed that at trial appellant did not request this instruction and he did not object to the absence of this instruction to the jury charge. *At 61:* Consistent with general rules of procedural default, the 'plain' language of Article 36.14 mandates that a defendant must object in writing to claimed 'errors' of *commission and omission* in the charge. *At 62:* Article 36.14 also mandates that a trial court submit a charge setting for the law 'applicable to the case.' The question in this case is whether this imposes a duty on trial courts to *sua sponte* instruct the jury on unrequested defensive issues. We hold Article 36.14 imposes no such duty."

Atkinson v. State, 923 S.W.2d 21, 25 (Tex.Crim. App.1996). "[A] jury instruction which identifies evidence requiring special jury consideration under the law, and which sets out the law governing such consideration, does not violate the article 36.14 prohibition against judicial comment so long as it does not intimate that the jury should resolve any fact question in a certain way or that any of the evidence bearing upon such a fact question should be given greater weight or credibility than other evidence bearing on the same question." *But see Matamoros v. State*, 901 S.W.2d 470, 477 (Tex.Crim.App.1995).

Chapman v. State, 921 S.W.2d 694, 695 (Tex.Crim. App.1996). "'[T]he requested charge must only be sufficient to call the trial court's attention to the omission in the court's charge.'"

Wilder v. State, 111 S.W.3d 249, 258 (Tex.App.— Texarkana 2003, pet. ref'd). "A jury instruction from the court that a witness lied or committed perjury would violate the prohibition against judicial comment and would express the trial judge's personal estimation of the credibility of evidence."

Lindsay v. State, 102 S.W.3d 223, 230 (Tex.App.— Houston [14th Dist.] 2003, pet. ref'd). Held: Because the term "criminal responsibility," which is defined by Pen. Code §7.02, was not defined in the jury charge, there was harmful error.

ART. 36.15. REQUESTED SPECIAL CHARGES

Before the court reads his charge to the jury, counsel on both sides shall have a reasonable time to present written instructions and ask that they be given to the jury. The requirement that the instructions be in writing is complied with if the instructions are dictated to the court reporter in the presence of the court and the state's counsel, before the reading of the court's charge to the jury. The court shall give or refuse these charges. The defendant may, by a special requested instruction, call the trial court's attention to error in the charge, as well as omissions therefrom, and no other exception or objection to the court's charge shall be necessary to preserve any error reflected by any special requested instruction which the trial court refuses.

Any special requested charge which is granted shall be incorporated in the main charge and shall be treated as a part thereof, and the jury shall not be advised that it is a special requested charge of either party. The judge shall read to the jury only such special charges as he gives.

When the defendant has leveled objections to the charge or has requested instructions or both, and the court thereafter modifies his charge and rewrites the same and in so doing does not respond to objections or requested charges, or any of them, then the objections or requested charges shall not be deemed to have been waived by the party making or requesting the same, but shall be deemed to continue to have been urged by the party making or requesting the same unless the contrary is shown by the record; no exception by the defendant to the action of the court shall be necessary or required in order to preserve for review the error claimed in the charge.

History of CCP art. 36.15: Acts 1965, 59th Leg., vol. 2, ch. 722. Amended by Acts 1979, 36th Leg., ch. 525, §1, eff. Sept. 1, 1979; Acts 1981, 67th Leg., ch. 537, §1, eff. June 12, 1981.

ANNOTATIONS

Walters v. State, 247 S.W.3d 204, 212 (Tex.Crim. App.2007). "[W]e hold that, generally speaking, neither the defendant nor the State is entitled to a special jury instruction relating to a statutory offense or defense if that instruction (1) is not grounded in the Penal Code, (2) is covered by the general charge to the jury, and (3) focuses the jury's attention on a specific type of evidence that may support an element of an offense or a defense. In such a case, the non-statutory instruction would constitute a prohibited comment on the weight of the evidence. [¶] In this case, the 'prior verbal threats' instruction meets all three criteria."

Vasquez v. State, 919 S.W.2d 433, 435 (Tex.Crim. App.1996). "[U]nder art. 36.15, if the defendant requests a special charge no objection is required to preserve error. All that is necessary ... is that the requested charge be in writing or dictated to the court reporter." *See also Stone v. State*, 703 S.W.2d 652, 655 (Tex.Crim.App.1986).

Perkins v. State, 528 S.W.2d 598, 600 (Tex.Crim. App.1975). "[A]rticle 36.15 is mandatory in all respects; it follows that the trial court in this case erred by failing to incorporate the requested charges and, second, by advising the jury that the charges were the requested charges of the appellant."

Rojas v. State, 662 S.W.2d 466, 469 (Tex.App.—Corpus Christi 1983, pet. ref'd). "Appellant's objection to the charge was made after the court read the charge to the jury and the jury retired to the deliberation room. The objection, having not been made before the charge was read to the jury, is not timely made and cannot be considered on appeal."

ART. 36.16. FINAL CHARGE

After the judge shall have received the objections to his main charge, together with any special charges offered, he may make such changes in his main charge as he may deem proper, and the defendant or his counsel shall have the opportunity to present their objections thereto and in the same manner as is provided in Article 36.15, and thereupon the judge shall read his charge to the jury as finally written, together with any special charges given, and no further exception or objection shall be required of the defendant in order to preserve any objections or exceptions theretofore made. After the argument begins no further charge shall be given to the jury unless required by the improper argument of counsel or the request of the jury, or unless the judge shall, in his discretion, permit the introduction of other testimony, and in the event of such further charge, the defendant or his counsel shall have the right to present objections in the same manner as is prescribed in Article 36.15. The failure of the court to give the defendant or his counsel a reasonable time to examine the charge and specify the ground of objection shall be subject to review either in the trial court or in the appellate court.

History of CCP art. 36.16: Acts 1965, 56th Leg., vol. 2, ch. 722.

ANNOTATIONS

Ngo v. State, 175 S.W.3d 738, 748 (Tex.Crim.App. 2005). "The State posits that jury unanimity is required only if the defendant requests an election between separate offenses. A request for an election, however, is not a prerequisite for implementing Texas' constitutional and statutory requirement of jury unanimity. An election simply limits the number of specific offenses that the jury may consider during its deliberations. Appellant's failure to request an election means that the jury may be instructed on several different criminal

acts in the disjunctive, but it will still be instructed that it must unanimously agree on one specific criminal act. *At 749:* The error here is not in submitting the three separate offenses 'in the disjunctive.' The error is in failing to instruct the jury that it must be unanimous in deciding which one (or more) of the three disjunctively submitted offenses it found appellant committed."

Garza v. State, 55 S.W.3d 74, 77 (Tex.App.—Corpus Christi 2001, pet. ref'd). "We conclude the submission of the supplemental charge was error under article 36.16. None of the prerequisites of the article was met in this case; the jury did not request further instructions, and there had been neither improper argument nor any new testimony adduced after the original charge was given. We further conclude that the erroneous submission of the lesser included offense of kidnapping, after the jury had begun to deliberate, egregiously harmed appellant by depriving him of a valuable right—his right to representation by counsel."

Morlett v. State, 656 S.W.2d 603, 606 (Tex.App.—Corpus Christi 1983, no pet.). "[T]he court [can], *before verdict*, withdraw and correct its charge if convinced that a erroneous charge had been given." *See also* ***Roberson v. State***, 113 S.W.3d 381, 384 (Tex.App.—Fort Worth 2003, pet. ref'd); ***Seals v. State***, 90 S.W.3d 422, 424 (Tex.App.—Eastland 2002, pet. ref'd) (trial court did not err when it corrected an erroneous charge during jury's deliberations; supplemental instruction was given in response to request from jury).

Smith v. State, 635 S.W.2d 591, 593 (Tex.App.—Dallas 1982, no pet.). "[T]he failure to supply the omitted definitions was ... invited by action of appellant. When the court offered to correct the charge, and the State assented, the option to correct then lay solely with appellant. His objection, or refusal to assent, was tantamount to a request that the charge be given as originally submitted. His objection tells us that he received the charge he wanted. He is therefore in no position to benefit from error in the charge."

ART. 36.17. CHARGE CERTIFIED BY JUDGE

The general charge given by the court and all special charges given or refused shall be certified by the judge and filed among the papers in the cause.

History of CCP art. 36.17: Acts 1965, 59th Leg., vol. 2, ch. 722.

Nolan v. State, 39 S.W.3d 697, 698 (Tex.App.—Houston [1st Dist.] 2001, no pet.). "There is no evidence that the lack of the judge's signature [on the jury charge] influenced the jury in assessing appellant's punishment. Accordingly, the error was harmless."

ART. 36.18. JURY MAY TAKE CHARGE

The jury may take to their jury room the charges given by the court after the same have been filed. They shall not be permitted to take with them any charge or part thereof which the court has refused to give.

History of CCP art. 36.18: Acts 1965, 59th Leg., vol. 2, ch. 722.

ART. 36.19. REVIEW OF CHARGE ON APPEAL

Whenever it appears by the record in any criminal action upon appeal that any requirement of Articles 36.14, 36.15, 36.16, 36.17 and 36.18 has been disregarded, the judgment shall not be reversed unless the error appearing from the record was calculated to injure the rights of defendant, or unless it appears from the record that the defendant has not had a fair and impartial trial. All objections to the charge and to the refusal of special charges shall be made at the time of the trial.

History of CCP art. 36.19: Acts 1965, 59th Leg., vol. 2, ch. 722.

ANNOTATIONS

Wooley v. State, ___ S.W.3d ___ (Tex.Crim.App. 2008) (No. PD-0861-07; 6-25-08). "We decide that *Malik*'s rule of measuring evidentiary sufficiency 'by the elements of the offense as defined by a hypothetically correct jury charge' applies when the evidence is reviewed for factual sufficiency."

Olivas v. State, 202 S.W.3d 137, 143-44 (Tex.Crim. App.2006). "This Court uses the same rule as the Supreme Court regarding erroneous jury instructions relating to reasonable doubt, except that Texas courts apply the specialized harmless-error analysis set out in *Almanza v. State*[, 686 S.W.2d 157 (Tex.Crim.App. 1984)] for 'partial' reasonable-doubt errors: 'if there is a total omission of the instruction on reasonable doubt, such error defies meaningful analysis by harmless-error standards. However, if the jury is given a partial or substantially correct charge on reasonable doubt, then

any error therein is subject to a harm analysis under *Abdnor* [*v. State*, 871 S.W.2d 726, 731 (Tex.Crim. App.1994)], *Almanza*, and [CCP] art. 36.19.'"

Jimenez v. State, 32 S.W.3d 233, 233 (Tex.Crim. App.2000). The "standard of harmless error [that] applies to error in a court's charge that was not objected to, and that is claimed to violate a constitutional provision … is that provided by article 36.19…: 'the judgment shall not be reversed … unless it appears from the record that the defendant has not had a fair and impartial trial." *See also* *Guevara v. State*, 152 S.W.3d 45, 47 (Tex.Crim.App.2004).

Malik v. State, 953 S.W.2d 234, 239-40 (Tex.Crim. App.1997). "No longer shall sufficiency of the evidence be measured by the jury charge actually given. [M]easuring sufficiency by the indictment is an inadequate substitute because some important issues relating to sufficiency—e.g. the law of parties and the law of transferred intent—are not contained in the indictment. [S]ufficiency of the evidence should be measured by the elements of the offense as defined by the hypothetically correct jury charge for the case. Such a charge would be one that accurately sets out the law, is authorized by the indictment, does not unnecessarily increase the State's burden of proof or unnecessarily restrict the State's theories of liability, and adequately describes the particular offense for which the defendant was tried. [T]he standard we formulate today ensures that a judgment of acquittal is reserved for those situations in which there is an actual failure in the State's proof of the crime rather than a mere error in the jury charge submitted." *See also* *Midence v. State*, 108 S.W.3d 564, 565 (Tex.App.—Houston [14th Dist.] 2003, no pet.).

Atkinson v. State, 923 S.W.2d 21, 27 (Tex.Crim. App.1996). "[W]e … hold that the harmless error rule of [CCP art.] 36.19 applies to the appellate review of errors predicated upon a disregard of the [CCP art.] 38.23 requirement of a jury instruction concerning evidence allegedly obtained in violation of the law."

Hutch v. State, 922 S.W.2d 166, 170-71 (Tex.Crim. App.1996). Article 36.19 "prescribe[s] the manner in which jury charge error is reviewed on appeal. First, an appellate court must determine whether error exists in the jury charge. Second, the appellate court must determine whether sufficient harm was caused by the error to require reversal. The degree of harm necessary for reversal depends upon whether the error was preserved. Error properly preserved by an objection to the charge will require reversal 'as long as the error is not harmless.' We have interpreted this to mean *any* harm, regardless of degree, is sufficient to require reversal. However, when the charging error is not preserved a greater degree of harm is required. This standard of harm is described as 'egregious harm.' [E]rrors which result in egregious harm are those which affect 'the very basis of the case,' deprive the defendant of a 'valuable right,' or 'vitally affect a defensive theory.' [¶] In either event, when conducting a harm analysis the reviewing court may consider the following four factors: 1) the charge itself; 2) the state of the evidence including contested issues and the weight of the probative evidence; 3) arguments of counsel; and, 4) any other relevant information revealed by the record of the trial as a whole." *See also* **Simmons v. State**, 106 S.W.3d 756, 764 (Tex.App.—Texarkana 2003, no pet.).

Almanza v. State, 686 S.W.2d 157, 171 (Tex.Crim. App.1984). Article 36.19 "separately contains the standards for *both* fundamental error and ordinary reversible error."

ART. 36.20. REPEALED

Repealed by the Texas Court of Criminal Appeals' adoption of the Texas Rules of Appellate Procedure on Apr. 10, 1986. 707 S.W.2d xxx, xxxv.

ART. 36.21. TO PROVIDE JURY ROOM

The sheriff shall provide a suitable room for the deliberation of the jury and supply them with such necessary food and lodging as he can obtain. No intoxicating liquor shall be furnished them. In all cases wherein a jury consists partly of male jurors and partly of female jurors, the sheriff shall provide facilities for the female jurors separate and apart from the facilities provided for the male jurors.

History of CCP art. 36.21: Acts 1965, 59th Leg., vol. 2, ch. 722.

ANNOTATIONS

McDuff v. State, 431 S.W.2d 547, 550 (Tex.Crim. App.1968). "'The mere drinking of liquor by a juror shall not be sufficient ground for new trial.'"

ART. 36.215. RECORDING OF JURY DELIBERATIONS

A person may not use any device to produce or make an audio, visual, or audio-visual broadcast, recording, or photograph of a jury while the jury is deliberating.

History of CCP art. 36.215: Acts 2003, 78th Leg., ch. 54, §1, eff. Sept. 1, 2003.

ART. 36.22. CONVERSING WITH JURY

No person shall be permitted to be with a jury while it is deliberating. No person shall be permitted to converse with a juror about the case on trial except in the presence and by the permission of the court.

History of CCP art. 36.22: Acts 1965, 59th Leg., vol. 2, ch. 722.

ANNOTATIONS

Quinn v. State, 958 S.W.2d 395, 401 (Tex.Crim.App. 1997). "When a juror converses with an unauthorized person about the case, 'injury to the accused is presumed' and new trial may be warranted. [T]he state may rebut this presumption of harm. In determining whether the state rebutted the presumption of harm, appellate courts should defer to the trial court's resolution of the historical facts and its determinations concerning credibility and demeanor."

Alba v. State, 905 S.W.2d 581, 587 (Tex.Crim.App. 1995). "When a juror converses with an unauthorized person, injury is presumed. However, the presumption is rebuttable if it is shown that the case was not discussed or that nothing prejudicial to the accused was said, then appellant has not been injured and the verdict will be upheld."

Norman v. State, 588 S.W.2d 340, 347 (Tex.Crim. App.1979). "Since the court believed its own instructions had been violated, it was perfectly proper for the court itself to make inquiries into possible jury misconduct. Determinations as to jury misbehavior are up to the discretion of the court."

Saunders v. State, 49 S.W.3d 536, 540 (Tex.App.— Eastland 2001, pet. ref'd). CPRC §§21.002(a) and 21.009 governing interpreters for the deaf "are specific provisions and will prevail over [CCP art.] 36.22."

Franks v. State, 961 S.W.2d 253, 255 (Tex.App.— Houston [1st Dist.] 1997, pet. ref'd). "[N]o Texas case has addressed the situation ... involving a defendant who initiates unauthorized conversation with jurors. [¶] The difficulty with treating a defendant initiating jury contact like other instances of unauthorized conversation with the jury is that it gives a defendant the power to create a mistrial by his own actions. [¶] It is a well-settled principle of law that an accused cannot invite error and then complain of it. The rule applies when a defendant is the 'moving factor' creating the error. [¶] There is no question that [D] was the moving factor creating the error in this case."

ART. 36.23. VIOLATION OF PRECEDING ARTICLE

Any juror or other person violating the preceding Article shall be punished for contempt of court by confinement in jail not to exceed three days or by fine not to exceed one hundred dollars, or by both such fine and imprisonment.

History of CCP art. 36.23: Acts 1965, 59th Leg., vol. 2, ch. 722.

ART. 36.24. OFFICER SHALL ATTEND JURY

The sheriff of the county shall furnish the court with a bailiff during the trial of any case to attend the wants of the jury and to act under the direction of the court. If the person furnished by the sheriff is to be called as a witness in the case he may not serve as bailiff.

History of CCP art. 36.24: Acts 1965, 59th Leg., vol. 2, ch. 722.

ANNOTATIONS

Silva v. State, 499 S.W.2d 147, 151 (Tex.Crim.App. 1973). "[T]he failure of the sheriff to furnish the court with a bailiff who was not to be called as a witness would not ordinarily call for reversal unless harm or prejudice was shown."

ART. 36.25. WRITTEN EVIDENCE

There shall be furnished to the jury upon its request any exhibits admitted as evidence in the case.

History of CCP art. 36.25: Acts 1965, 59th Leg., vol. 2, ch. 722.

ANNOTATIONS

Lopez v. State, 628 S.W.2d 82, 85 (Tex.Crim.App. 1982). "[A] refusal or failure to allow the jury to have such exhibits is not error unless the jury requests the exhibits."

Lewis v. State, 529 S.W.2d 533, 535 n.1 (Tex.Crim. App.1975). "We do not approve the State's offer of its transcribed version of the taped conversation. ... Technical imperfections in the reproduction of the conversation did not authorize the State to submit its version in written form and thereby make the written transcript available to the jury during its deliberations."

ART. 36.26. FOREMAN OF JURY

Each jury shall appoint one of its members foreman.

History of CCP art. 36.26: Acts 1965, 59th Leg., vol. 2, ch. 722.

ANNOTATIONS

Elizaldi v. State, 519 S.W.2d 881, 883 (Tex.Crim. App.1975). "[S]hould the foreman resign or refuse to serve, certainly the jury could choose another member of its choice."

ART. 36.27. JURY MAY COMMUNICATE WITH COURT

When the jury wishes to communicate with the court, it shall so notify the sheriff, who shall inform the court thereof. Any communication relative to the cause must be written, prepared by the foreman and shall be submitted to the court through the bailiff. The court shall answer any such communication in writing, and before giving such answer to the jury shall use reasonable diligence to secure the presence of the defendant and his counsel, and shall first submit the question and also submit his answer to the same to the defendant or his counsel or objections and exceptions, in the same manner as any other written instructions are submitted to such counsel, before the court gives such answer to the jury, but if he is unable to secure the presence of the defendant and his counsel, then he shall proceed to answer the same as he deems proper. The written instruction or answer to the communication shall be read in open court unless expressly waived by the defendant.

All such proceedings in felony cases shall be a part of the record and recorded by the court reporter.

History of CCP art. 36.27: Acts 1965, 59th Leg., vol. 2, ch. 722.

ANNOTATIONS

Word v. State, 206 S.W.3d 646, 651 (Tex.Crim.App. 2006). "[W]e understand appellant to claim that 'waiver' of Article 36.27 requirements (including 'waiver' of a defendant's opportunity to object to a trial court's answers to jury questions) must affirmatively appear in the record and cannot be presumed on a silent record. [¶] Appellant cites no authority to support this claim. Our research indicates that the Supreme Court has never decided that federal constitutional due process principles prohibit an appellate court from presuming on a silent record a trial court's compliance with Article 36.27...." *See also Green v. State*, 912 S.W.2d 189, 192 (Tex.Crim.App.1995).

Moreno v. State, 587 S.W.2d 405, 412 (Tex.Crim. App.1979). "The giving of additional instructions on the law without complying with [Article 36.27] constitutes reversible error. [H]owever, communication between court and jury which does not amount to additional instructions, although not in compliance with [Article 36.27], does not constitute reversible error."

Brooks v. State, 967 S.W.2d 946, 949-50 (Tex. App.—Austin 1998, no pet.). "In general, article 36.27 is mandatory, and noncompliance is reversible error. When the trial judge responds substantively to a jury question during deliberations, that communication essentially amounts to an additional or supplemental jury instruction. [¶] Our review of the record, however, reveals that appellant made no objection to the court's oral statements to the jury. Because appellant failed to object at trial, her point of error may be sustained only if she can show egregious harm, i.e., harm so great that she was denied a fair and impartial trial. Errors that result in egregious harm are those which affect the essential dispute in a case or disturb the basis of the defensive theory. [¶] The court's error affected the very basis of the case, vitally affecting appellant's primary defensive theory, i.e., that the strike and resulting injury were accidental. Considering the record as a whole, we conclude that appellant has demonstrated egregious harm." *See also McGowan v. State*, 664 S.W.2d 355, 358 (Tex.Crim.App.1984); *Talley v. State*, 909 S.W.2d 233, 235 (Tex.App.—Texarkana 1995, pet. ref'd).

ART. 36.28. JURY MAY HAVE WITNESS RE-EXAMINED OR TESTIMONY READ

In the trial of a criminal case in a court of record, if the jury disagree as to the statement of any witness they may, upon applying to the court, have read to them from the court reporter's notes that part of such witness testimony or the particular point in dispute, and no other; but if there be no such reporter, or if his notes cannot be read to the jury, the court may cause such witness to be again brought upon the stand and the judge shall direct him to repeat his testimony as to the point in dispute, and no other, as nearly as he can in the language used on the trial.

History of CCP art. 36.28: Acts 1965, 59th Leg., vol. 2, ch. 722.

ANNOTATIONS

DeGraff v. State, 962 S.W.2d 596, 598 (Tex.Crim. App.1998). "[T]he jurors must disagree as to the testimony of a witness before the testimony may be read

back to them. However, a simple request for testimony does not by itself reflect disagreement, implicit or explicit, and is not a proper request under Art. 36.28." *See also Howell v. State*, 175 S.W.3d 786, 792 (Tex.Crim. App.2005) (judge may infer a dispute among the jurors).

Neal v. State, 108 S.W.3d 577, 579 (Tex.App.—Amarillo 2003, no pet.). "[T]he trial court must interpret the communication, decide what portion of the testimony best answers the question, and limit the testimony accordingly. *At 580:* [A] trial court may consider a progression of notes from the jury when attempting to fulfill the mandate of art. 36.28. [¶] [T]here must be a logical nexus between the prior and ultimate notes for the former to be properly contextual of the latter. And, all this is done on a case by case manner to avoid commenting upon the evidence and to give the jury that needed to resolve factual disputes."

Walker v. State, 994 S.W.2d 199, 206 (Tex.App.—Houston [1st Dist.] 1999, pet. ref'd). "Considering the testimony that was read back to the jury in the context of the evidence as a whole, we cannot say that the trial court's error [of reading back testimony without a jury disagreement about the testimony] had a 'substantial and injurious effect' on the jury's verdict."

ART. 36.29. IF A JUROR DIES OR BECOMES DISABLED

(a) Not less than twelve jurors can render and return a verdict in a felony case. It must be concurred in by each juror and signed by the foreman. Except as provided in Subsection (b), however, after the trial of any felony case begins and a juror dies or, as determined by the judge, becomes disabled from sitting at any time before the charge of the court is read to the jury, the remainder of the jury shall have the power to render the verdict; but when the verdict shall be rendered by less than the whole number, it shall be signed by every member of the jury concurring in it.

(b) If alternate jurors have been selected in a capital case in which the state seeks the death penalty and a juror dies or becomes disabled from sitting at any time before the charge of the court is read to the jury, the alternate juror whose name was called first under Article 35.26 of this code shall replace the dead or disabled juror. Likewise, if another juror dies or becomes disabled from sitting before the charge of the court is read to the jury, the other alternate juror shall replace the second juror to die or become disabled.

(c) After the charge of the court is read to the jury, if any one of them becomes so sick as to prevent the continuance of his duty, or any accident of circumstance occurs to prevent their being kept together under circumstances under which the law or the instructions of the court requires that they be kept together, the jury shall be discharged, except that on agreement on the record by the defendant, the defendant's counsel, and the attorney representing the state 11 members of a jury may render a verdict and, if punishment is to be assessed by the jury, assess punishment. If a verdict is rendered by less than the whole number of the jury, each member of the jury shall sign the verdict.

Ⓐ *Subsection (d) below is effective for trials commenced on or after Sept. 1, 2007.*

(d) After the jury has rendered a verdict on the guilt or innocence of the defendant and, if applicable, the amount of punishment, the court shall discharge an alternate juror who has not replaced a juror.

Subsection (d) below is effective for trials commenced before Sept. 1, 2007.

(d) After the charge of the court is read to the jury, the court shall discharge an alternate juror who has not replaced a juror.

History of CCP art. 36.29: Acts 1965, 59th Leg., vol. 2, ch. 722. Amended by Acts 1981, 67th Leg., ch. 545, §2, eff. June 12, 1981; Acts 1991, 72nd Leg., ch. 652, §8, eff. Sept. 1, 1991; Acts 1997, 75th Leg., ch. 866, §1, eff. Sept. 1, 1997; Acts 2001, 77th Leg., ch. 1000, §§1, 2, eff. Sept. 1, 2001; Acts 2007, 80th Leg., ch. 846, §2, eff. Sept. 1, 2007.

See also Tex. Const. art. 5, §13.

ANNOTATIONS

Generally

Hatch v. State, 958 S.W.2d 813, 816 (Tex.Crim.App. 1997). "[A] defendant may waive Art. 36.29(a)'s requirement that not less than twelve jurors can return a verdict in a non-capital felony case."

Juror Disability

Chavez v. State, 91 S.W.3d 797, 801 (Tex.Crim.App. 2002). "[B]ecause the decision to proceed with the trial [after a juror dies] over appellant's objection is a violation of a purely statutory right, we hold that the error is subject to a harm analysis under [TRAP] 44.2(b)."

Hill v. State, 90 S.W.3d 308, 315 (Tex.Crim.App. 2002). "We conclude that proceeding to trial with eleven jurors was not just an available alternative [when a juror became disabled]. It was a mandatory alternative under our constitutional, statutory, and case

law. Regardless of [D's] consent, the judge was required to proceed to trial with eleven jurors."

Reyes v. State, 30 S.W.3d 409, 411 (Tex.Crim.App. 2000). "[A] disability is not limited to physical disease, but also includes 'any condition that inhibits a juror from fully and fairly performing the functions of a juror.' *At 412:* [A] juror's bias or prejudice for or against a defendant does not render a juror 'disabled.' However, ... a juror [may be] 'disabled' ... through knowledge of a defendant when such knowledge 'inhibits [him] from fully and fairly performing the functions of a juror.' [T]he court of appeals erred in determining that ... fear of retaliation due to a juror's knowledge of a defendant can never result in rendering the juror 'disabled'...."

Broussard v. State, 910 S.W.2d 952, 957 (Tex.Crim. App.1995). Article 36.29 "is not applicable until the jury is sworn. *At 958:* [B]ecause an alternate juror was available, the trial court had the ... possible option of using the alternate to replace the disabled venireman. Faced with the need to complete the jury ... the trial court chose an acceptable option by replacing the disabled venireman with a venireman who had already been qualified and accepted by both parties." *See also* **Bermea v. State**, 188 S.W.3d 337, 340 (Tex.App.—Tyler 2006, no pet.); **McClellan v. State**, 143 S.W.3d 395, 399-400 (Tex.App.—Austin 2004, no pet.).

Carrillo v. State, 597 S.W.2d 769, 770 (Tex.Crim. App.1980). "[D]ischarges because of a disability based upon the following have been upheld: a juror was arrested for driving under the influence of intoxicating liquors during a noon recess; a juror was emotionally upset over the death of his father-in-law and needed to go out of the state to be with his wife and none of the parties objected to proceeding with the remaining jurors; a juror became ill after some sort of attack and was taken to the hospital; a juror was struck by an automobile and taken to a hospital; a juror was ill with influenza." *See also* **Owens v. State**, 202 S.W.3d 276, 277 (Tex.App.— Amarillo 2006, pet. ref'd) (juror was single parent of special-needs child).

Jury Unanimity

Jefferson v. State, 189 S.W.3d 305, 311 (Tex.Crim. App.2006). "'[W]hile jury unanimity is required on the essential elements of the offense, when the statute in question establishes different modes or means by which the offense may be committed, unanimity is generally not required on the alternate modes or means of commission. [¶] [T]he first step in a unanimity challenge is an examination of the language of the statute in order to determine the elements of the crime and whether the legislature has created a single offense with multiple or alternate modes of commission. 'The point is to determine legislative intent: did the legislature intend to create multiple, separate offenses, or a single offense capable of being committed in several different ways?' For example, where the legislature has specified that any of several different mental states will satisfy the intent or mens rea element of a particular crime, unanimity is not required on the specific alternate mental state as long as the jury unanimously agrees that the state has proven the intent element beyond a reasonable doubt. *At 312:* Federal constitutional due process considerations, however, limit the state's ability to define a crime so as to dispense with the requirement of jury unanimity on the alternate means or modes of committing it. So the second step in the analysis is an evaluation of whether the lack of jury unanimity on the alternate means or modes of commission violates due process. This involves an inquiry into the fundamental fairness and rationality of the legislative choice, starting, however, with a presumption that the legislature has made its determination fairly and rationally. [T]he due process fundamental fairness and rationality test for unanimity challenges was established by the Supreme Court in *Schad* [*v. Arizona*, 501 U.S. 624, 111 S.Ct. 2491 (1991)] and focuses on historical practice and the relative moral and conceptual equivalence of the alternate modes or means of committing the crime.'"

ART. 36.30. DISCHARGING JURY IN MISDEMEANOR

If nine of the jury can be kept together in a misdemeanor case in the district court, they shall not be discharged. If more than three of the twelve are discharged, the entire jury shall be discharged.

History of CCP art. 36.30: Acts 1965, 59th Leg., vol. 2, ch. 722.
See also CCP art. 37.02.

ART. 36.31. DISAGREEMENT OF JURY

After the cause is submitted to the jury, it may be discharged when it cannot agree and both parties consent to its discharge; or the court may in its discretion discharge it where it has been kept together for such time as to render it altogether improbable that it can agree.

History of CCP art. 36.31: Acts 1965, 59th Leg., vol. 2, ch. 722.

ANNOTATIONS

Andrade v. State, 700 S.W.2d 585, 589 (Tex.Crim. App.1985). "Length of time that the jury may be held for deliberation rests ... in the discretion of the court...."

Bowles v. State, 606 S.W.2d 875, 876 (Tex.Crim. App.1980). A discharge under Article 36.31 "requires the personal consent of the defendant, and that counsel's consent is not sufficient.... [I]n this case, the decision to discharge the jury was not initiated by the court, but was at the *request* of defense counsel. Since the court did not initiate the action to discharge, but simply acted on counsel's request, we hold it was not necessary for the court to secure appellant's personal consent."

Zavala v. State, 956 S.W.2d 715, 719-20 (Tex. App.—Corpus Christi 1997, no pet.). "There can be no manifest necessity, and consequently no mistrial without the trial judge first reviewing the alternative courses of action and choosing the one, which, in light of all the circumstances, best preserves the defendant's 'right to have his trial completed before a particular tribunal.' Where a trial judge grants a mistrial despite the available option of less drastic alternatives there is no manifest necessity and we will find an abuse of discretion."

ART. 36.32. RECEIPT OF VERDICT & FINAL ADJOURNMENT

During the trial of any case, the term shall be deemed to have been extended until such time as the jury has rendered its verdict or been discharged according to law.

History of CCP art. 36.32: Acts 1965, 59th Leg., vol. 2, ch. 722.

ART. 36.33. DISCHARGE WITHOUT VERDICT

When a jury has been discharged, as provided in the four preceding Articles, without having rendered a verdict, the cause may be again tried at the same or another term.

History of CCP art. 36.33: Acts 1965, 59th Leg., vol. 2, ch. 722.

CHAPTER 37. THE VERDICT

ART. 37.01. VERDICT

A "verdict" is a written declaration by a jury of its decision of the issue submitted to it in the case.

History of CCP art. 37.01: Acts 1965, 59th Leg., vol. 2, ch. 722.
See also CCP art. 37.10.

ANNOTATIONS

Fairfield v. State, 610 S.W.2d 771, 780 n.15 (Tex. Crim.App.1981). "[A] 'verdict' is an indispensable prerequisite to the entry of a valid judgment in *every* case, irrespective of the plea, unless the right to trial by jury has been waived."

Cardona v. State, 957 S.W.2d 674, 676 (Tex.App.—Waco 1997, no pet.). "A jury, instructed on a charged offense and a lesser included offense, has not decided the issue submitted until it declares the accused guilty of one offense or not guilty of all offenses."

State v. Davenport, 866 S.W.2d 767, 769 n.2 (Tex. App.—San Antonio 1993, no pet.). "'Verdict' by definition does not apply to a trial court's decision. The word, however, is used loosely in the statutes and case law."

ART. 37.02. VERDICT BY NINE JURORS

In misdemeanor cases in the district court, where one or more jurors have been discharged from serving after the cause has been submitted to them, if all the alternate jurors selected under Article 33.011 of this code have either been seated or discharged, and there be as many as nine of the jurors remaining, those remaining may render and return a verdict; but in such case, the verdict must be signed by each juror rendering it.

History of CCP art. 37.02: Acts 1965, 59th Leg., vol. 2, ch. 722. Amended by Acts 1983, 68th Leg., ch. 775, §4, eff. Aug. 29, 1983.

See also CCP art. 36.30.

ART. 37.03. IN COUNTY COURT

In the county court the verdict must be concurred in by each juror.

History of CCP art. 37.03: Acts 1965, 59th Leg., vol. 2, ch. 722.

ART. 37.04. WHEN JURY HAS AGREED

When the jury agrees upon a verdict, it shall be brought into court by the proper officer; and if it states that it has agreed, the verdict shall be read aloud by the judge, the foreman, or the clerk. If in proper form and no juror dissents therefrom, and neither party requests a poll of the jury, the verdict shall be entered upon the minutes of the court.

History of CCP art. 37.04: Acts 1965, 59th Leg., vol. 2, ch. 722. Amended by Acts 1981, 67th Leg., ch. 78, §1, eff. April 30, 1981.

ANNOTATIONS

Jones v. State, 795 S.W.2d 199, 201-02 (Tex.Crim. App.1990). "[A] defendant has been adjudged guilty *when the verdict convicting him has been received and accepted by the trial judge*. No further ritual or special incantation from the bench is necessary ... beyond the pronouncement of sentence as required by law. Such pronouncement by the trial judge is sufficient ... if it 'orders that the punishment be carried into execution in the manner prescribed by law.'"

ART. 37.05. POLLING THE JURY

The State or the defendant shall have the right to have the jury polled, which is done by calling separately the name of each juror and asking him if the verdict is his. If all, when asked, answer in the affirmative, the verdict shall be entered upon the minutes; but if any juror answer in the negative, the jury shall retire again to consider its verdict.

History of CCP art. 37.05: Acts 1965, 59th Leg., vol. 2, ch. 722.

ANNOTATIONS

Barnett v. State, 189 S.W.3d 272, 273 (Tex.Crim. App.2006). "In this case we must decide whether a defendant forfeits his complaint on appeal that the trial court gave the jury a coercive oral '*Allen* charge' if he failed to object to the court's earlier improper polling of the jury. We hold that the failure to object to unauthorized polling of the jury does not forfeit the separate issue of the propriety of the trial judge's later [coercive] oral statement to the two hold-out jurors...."

Batten v. State, 549 S.W.2d 718, 721 n.5 (Tex.Crim. App.1977). "[I]n polling a jury it was not intended that the jurors shall be interrogated further than to ask each of them the direct question: 'Is that your verdict?' If the juror answers in the affirmative, his answer is conclusive, and further inquiry is not permissible."

ART. 37.06. PRESENCE OF DEFENDANT

In felony cases the defendant must be present when the verdict is read unless his absence is wilful or voluntary. A verdict in a misdemeanor case may be received and read in the absence of the defendant.

History of CCP art. 37.06: Acts 1965, 59th Leg., vol. 2, ch. 722.

ART. 37.07. VERDICT MUST BE GENERAL; SEPARATE HEARING ON PROPER PUNISHMENT

Sec. 1. (a) The verdict in every criminal action must be general. When there are special pleas on which a jury is to find they must say in their verdict that the allegations in such pleas are true or untrue.

(b) If the plea is not guilty, they must find that the defendant is either guilty or not guilty, and, except as provided in Section 2, they shall assess the punishment in all cases where the same is not absolutely fixed by law to some particular penalty.

(c) If the charging instrument contains more than one count or if two or more offenses are consolidated for trial pursuant to Chapter 3 of the Penal Code, the jury shall be instructed to return a finding of guilty or not guilty in a separate verdict as to each count and offense submitted to them.

Sec. 2. (a) In all criminal cases, other than misdemeanor cases of which the justice court or municipal court has jurisdiction, which are tried before a jury on a plea of not guilty, the judge shall, before argument begins, first submit to the jury the issue of guilt or innocence of the defendant of the offense or offenses charged, without authorizing the jury to pass upon the punishment to be imposed. If the jury fails to agree on the issue of guilt or innocence, the judge shall declare a mistrial and discharge the jury, and jeopardy does not attach in the case.

Ⓐ *Subsection (b) below is effective for offenses committed on or after Sept. 1, 2007.*

(b) Except as provided by Article 37.071 or 37.072, if a finding of guilty is returned, it shall then be the responsibility of the judge to assess the punishment applicable to the offense; provided, however, that (1) in any criminal action where the jury may recommend community supervision and the defendant filed his sworn motion for community supervision before the trial began, and (2) in other cases where the defendant so elects in writing before the commencement of the voir dire examination of the jury panel, the punishment shall be assessed by the same jury, except as provided in Section 3(c) of this article and in Article 44.29. If a finding of guilty is returned, the defendant may, with the consent of the attorney for the state, change his election of one who assesses the punishment.

Subsection (b) below is effective for offenses in which any element of the offense was committed before Sept. 1, 2007.

(b) Except as provided in Article 37.071, if a finding of guilty is returned, it shall then be the responsibility of the judge to assess the punishment applicable to the offense; provided, however, that (1) in any criminal action where the jury may recommend community supervision and the defendant filed his sworn motion for community supervision before the trial began, and (2) in other cases where the defendant so elects in writing before the commencement of the voir dire examination of the jury panel, the punishment shall be assessed by the same jury, except as provided in Section 3(c) of this article and in Article 44.29. If a finding of guilty is returned, the defendant may, with the consent of the attorney for the state, change his election of one who assesses the punishment.

(c) Punishment shall be assessed on each count on which a finding of guilty has been returned.

Sec. 3. Evidence of prior criminal record in all criminal cases after a finding of guilty.

(a)(1) Regardless of the plea and whether the punishment be assessed by the judge or the jury, evidence may be offered by the state and the defendant as to any matter the court deems relevant to sentencing, including but not limited to the prior criminal record of the defendant, his general reputation, his character, an opinion regarding his character, the circumstances of the offense for which he is being tried, and, notwithstanding Rules 404 and 405, Texas Rules of Evidence, any other evidence of an extraneous crime or bad act that is shown beyond a reasonable doubt by evidence to have been committed by the defendant or for which he could be held criminally responsible, regardless of

★

whether he has previously been charged with or finally convicted of the crime or act. A court may consider as a factor in mitigating punishment the conduct of a defendant while participating in a program under Chapter 17 as a condition of release on bail. Additionally, notwithstanding Rule 609(d), Texas Rules of Evidence, and subject to Subsection (h), evidence may be offered by the state and the defendant of an adjudication of delinquency based on a violation by the defendant of a penal law of the grade of:

(A) a felony; or

(B) a misdemeanor punishable by confinement in jail.

(2) Notwithstanding Subdivision (1), evidence may not be offered by the state to establish that the race or ethnicity of the defendant makes it likely that the defendant will engage in future criminal conduct.

(b) After the introduction of such evidence has been concluded, and if the jury has the responsibility of assessing the punishment, the court shall give such additional written instructions as may be necessary and the order of procedure and the rules governing the conduct of the trial shall be the same as are applicable on the issue of guilt or innocence.

(c) If the jury finds the defendant guilty and the matter of punishment is referred to the jury, the verdict shall not be complete until a jury verdict has been rendered on both the guilt or innocence of the defendant and the amount of punishment. In the event the jury shall fail to agree on the issue of punishment, a mistrial shall be declared only in the punishment phase of the trial, the jury shall be discharged, and no jeopardy shall attach. The court shall impanel another jury as soon as practicable to determine the issue of punishment.

(d) When the judge assesses the punishment, he may order an investigative report as contemplated in Section 9 of Article 42.12 of this code and after considering the report, and after the hearing of the evidence hereinabove provided for, he shall forthwith announce his decision in open court as to the punishment to be assessed.

(e) Nothing herein contained shall be construed as affecting the admissibility of extraneous offenses on the question of guilt or innocence.

(f) In cases in which the matter of punishment is referred to a jury, either party may offer into evidence the availability of community corrections facilities serving the jurisdiction in which the offense was committed.

(g) On timely request of the defendant, notice of intent to introduce evidence under this article shall be given in the same manner required by Rule 404(b), Texas Rules of Evidence. If the attorney representing the state intends to introduce an extraneous crime or bad act that has not resulted in a final conviction in a court of record or a probated or suspended sentence, notice of that intent is reasonable only if the notice includes the date on which and the county in which the alleged crime or bad act occurred and the name of the alleged victim of the crime or bad act. The requirement under this subsection that the attorney representing the state give notice applies only if the defendant makes a timely request to the attorney representing the state for the notice.

(h) Regardless of whether the punishment will be assessed by the judge or the jury, neither the state nor the defendant may offer before sentencing evidence that the defendant plans to undergo an orchiectomy.

(i) Evidence of an adjudication for conduct that is a violation of a penal law of the grade of misdemeanor punishable by confinement in jail is admissible only if the conduct upon which the adjudication is based occurred on or after January 1, 1996.

 Subsections (a) & (b) below are effective for offenses committed on or after Sept. 1, 2007.

Sec. 4. (a) In the penalty phase of the trial of a felony case in which the punishment is to be assessed by the jury rather than the court, if the offense of which the jury has found the defendant guilty is listed in Section 3g(a)(1), Article 42.12, of this code or if the judgment contains an affirmative finding under Section 3g(a)(2), Article 42.12, of this code, unless the defendant has been convicted of an offense under Section 21.02, Penal Code, an offense under Section 22.021, Penal Code, that is punishable under Subsection (f) of that section, or a capital felony, the court shall charge the jury in writing as follows:

"Under the law applicable in this case, the defendant, if sentenced to a term of imprisonment, may earn time off the period of incarceration imposed through the award of good conduct time. Prison authorities may award good conduct time to a prisoner who exhibits good behavior, diligence in carrying out prison work assignments, and attempts at rehabilitation. If a prisoner

engages in misconduct, prison authorities may also take away all or part of any good conduct time earned by the prisoner.

"It is also possible that the length of time for which the defendant will be imprisoned might be reduced by the award of parole.

"Under the law applicable in this case, if the defendant is sentenced to a term of imprisonment, he will not become eligible for parole until the actual time served equals one-half of the sentence imposed or 30 years, whichever is less, without consideration of any good conduct time he may earn. If the defendant is sentenced to a term of less than four years, he must serve at least two years before he is eligible for parole. Eligibility for parole does not guarantee that parole will be granted.

"It cannot accurately be predicted how the parole law and good conduct time might be applied to this defendant if he is sentenced to a term of imprisonment, because the application of these laws will depend on decisions made by prison and parole authorities.

"You may consider the existence of the parole law and good conduct time. However, you are not to consider the extent to which good conduct time may be awarded to or forfeited by this particular defendant. You are not to consider the manner in which the parole law may be applied to this particular defendant."

(b) In the penalty phase of the trial of a felony case in which the punishment is to be assessed by the jury rather than the court, if the offense is punishable as a felony of the first degree, if a prior conviction has been alleged for enhancement of punishment as provided by Section 12.42(b), (c)(1) or (2), or (d), Penal Code, or if the offense is a felony not designated as a capital felony or a felony of the first, second, or third degree and the maximum term of imprisonment that may be imposed for the offense is longer than 60 years, unless the offense of which the jury has found the defendant guilty is an offense that is punishable under Section 21.02(h), Penal Code, or is listed in Section 3g(a)(1), Article 42.12, of this code or the judgment contains an affirmative finding under Section 3g(a)(2), Article 42.12, of this code, the court shall charge the jury in writing as follows:

"Under the law applicable in this case, the defendant, if sentenced to a term of imprisonment, may earn time off the period of incarceration imposed through the award of good conduct time. Prison authorities may

award good conduct time to a prisoner who exhibits good behavior, diligence in carrying out prison work assignments, and attempts at rehabilitation. If a prisoner engages in misconduct, prison authorities may also take away all or part of any good conduct time earned by the prisoner.

"It is also possible that the length of time for which the defendant will be imprisoned might be reduced by the award of parole.

"Under the law applicable in this case, if the defendant is sentenced to a term of imprisonment, he will not become eligible for parole until the actual time served plus any good conduct time earned equals one-fourth of the sentence imposed or 15 years, whichever is less. Eligibility for parole does not guarantee that parole will be granted.

"It cannot accurately be predicted how the parole law and good conduct time might be applied to this defendant if he is sentenced to a term of imprisonment, because the application of these laws will depend on decisions made by prison and parole authorities.

"You may consider the existence of the parole law and good conduct time. However, you are not to consider the extent to which good conduct time may be awarded to or forfeited by this particular defendant. You are not to consider the manner in which the parole law may be applied to this particular defendant."

Subsections (a) & (b) below are effective for offenses in which any element of the offense was committed before Sept. 1, 2007.

Sec. 4 (a) In the penalty phase of the trial of a felony case in which the punishment is to be assessed by the jury rather than the court, if the offense of which the jury has found the defendant guilty is listed in Section 3g(a)(1), Article 42.12, of this code or if the judgment contains an affirmative finding under Section 3g(a)(2), Article 42.12, of this code, unless the defendant has been convicted of a capital felony the court shall charge the jury in writing as follows:

"Under the law applicable in this case, the defendant, if sentenced to a term of imprisonment, may earn time off the period of incarceration imposed through the award of good conduct time. Prison authorities may award good conduct time to a prisoner who exhibits good behavior, diligence in carrying out prison work assignments, and attempts at rehabilitation. If a prisoner

engages in misconduct, prison authorities may also take away all or part of any good conduct time earned by the prisoner.

"It is also possible that the length of time for which the defendant will be imprisoned might be reduced by the award of parole.

"Under the law applicable in this case, if the defendant is sentenced to a term of imprisonment, he will not become eligible for parole until the actual time served equals one-half of the sentence imposed or 30 years, whichever is less, without consideration of any good conduct time he may earn. If the defendant is sentenced to a term of less than four years, he must serve at least two years before he is eligible for parole. Eligibility for parole does not guarantee that parole will be granted.

"It cannot accurately be predicted how the parole law and good conduct time might be applied to this defendant if he is sentenced to a term of imprisonment, because the application of these laws will depend on decisions made by prison and parole authorities.

"You may consider the existence of the parole law and good conduct time. However, you are not to consider the extent to which good conduct time may be awarded to or forfeited by this particular defendant. You are not to consider the manner in which the parole law may be applied to this particular defendant."

(b) In the penalty phase of the trial of a felony case in which the punishment is to be assessed by the jury rather than the court, if the offense is punishable as a felony of the first degree, if a prior conviction has been alleged for enhancement of punishment as provided by Section 12.42(b), (c), or (d), Penal Code, or if the offense is a felony not designated as a capital felony or a felony of the first, second, or third degree and the maximum term of imprisonment that may be imposed for the offense is longer than 60 years, unless the offense of which the jury has found the defendant guilty is listed in Section 3g(a)(1), Article 42.12, of this code or the judgment contains an affirmative finding under Section 3g(a)(2), Article 42.12, of this code, the court shall charge the jury in writing as follows:

"Under the law applicable in this case, the defendant, if sentenced to a term of imprisonment, may earn time off the period of incarceration imposed through the award of good conduct time. Prison authorities may award good conduct time to a prisoner who exhibits

good behavior, diligence in carrying out prison work assignments, and attempts at rehabilitation. If a prisoner engages in misconduct, prison authorities may also take away all or part of any good conduct time earned by the prisoner.

"It is also possible that the length of time for which the defendant will be imprisoned might be reduced by the award of parole.

"Under the law applicable in this case, if the defendant is sentenced to a term of imprisonment, he will not become eligible for parole until the actual time served plus any good conduct time earned equals one-fourth of the sentence imposed or 15 years, whichever is less. Eligibility for parole does not guarantee that parole will be granted.

"It cannot accurately be predicted how the parole law and good conduct time might be applied to this defendant if he is sentenced to a term of imprisonment, because the application of these laws will depend on decisions made by prison and parole authorities.

"You may consider the existence of the parole law and good conduct time. However, you are not to consider the extent to which good conduct time may be awarded to or forfeited by this particular defendant. You are not to consider the manner in which the parole law may be applied to this particular defendant."

(c) In the penalty phase of the trial of a felony case in which the punishment is to be assessed by the jury rather than the court, if the offense is punishable as a felony of the second or third degree, if a prior conviction has been alleged for enhancement as provided by Section 12.42(a), Penal Code, or if the offense is a felony not designated as a capital felony or a felony of the first, second, or third degree and the maximum term of imprisonment that may be imposed for the offense is 60 years or less, unless the offense of which the jury has found the defendant guilty is listed in Section 3g(a)(1), Article 42.12, of this code or the judgment contains an affirmative finding under Section 3g(a)(2), Article 42.12, of this code, the court shall charge the jury in writing as follows:

"Under the law applicable in this case, the defendant, if sentenced to a term of imprisonment, may earn time off the period of incarceration imposed through the award of good conduct time. Prison authorities may award good conduct time to a prisoner who exhibits good behavior, diligence in carrying out prison work assignments, and attempts at rehabilitation. If a prisoner

engages in misconduct, prison authorities may also take away all or part of any good conduct time earned by the prisoner.

"It is also possible that the length of time for which the defendant will be imprisoned might be reduced by the award of parole.

"Under the law applicable in this case, if the defendant is sentenced to a term of imprisonment, he will not become eligible for parole until the actual time served plus any good conduct time earned equals one-fourth of the sentence imposed. Eligibility for parole does not guarantee that parole will be granted.

"It cannot accurately be predicted how the parole law and good conduct time might be applied to this defendant if he is sentenced to a term of imprisonment, because the application of these laws will depend on decisions made by prison and parole authorities.

"You may consider the existence of the parole law and good conduct time. However, you are not to consider the extent to which good conduct time may be awarded to or forfeited by this particular defendant. You are not to consider the manner in which the parole law may be applied to this particular defendant."

(d) This section does not permit the introduction of evidence on the operation of parole and good conduct time laws.

History of CCP art. 37.07: Acts 1965, 59th Leg., vol. 2, ch. 722. Amended by Acts 1967, 60th Leg., ch. 659, §22, eff. Aug. 28, 1967; Acts 1973, 63rd Leg., ch. 399, §2(A) (eff. Jan. 1, 1974), ch. 426, art. 3, §2 (eff. June 14, 1973); Acts 1981, 67th Leg., ch. 639, §1, eff. Sept. 1, 1981; Acts 1985, 69th Leg., ch. 291, §1 (eff. Sept. 1, 1985), ch. 576, §1 (eff. Sept. 1, 1985), ch. 685, §8(b) (eff. Aug. 26, 1985); Acts 1987, 70th Leg., ch. 66, §1 (eff. May 6, 1987), ch. 179, §2 (eff. Aug. 31, 1987), ch. 385, §19 (eff. Sept. 1, 1987), ch. 386, §1 (eff. Sept. 1, 1987), ch. 1101, §15 (eff. Sept. 1, 1987); Acts 1989, 71st Leg., ch. 103, ch. 785, §4.04, eff. Sept. 1, 1989; Acts 1990, 71st Leg., 6th C.S., ch. 25, §30, eff. June 18, 1990; Acts 1993, 73rd Leg., ch. 900, §§5.01, 5.02, 5.05, 5.06, eff. Sept. 1, 1993; Acts 1995, 74th Leg., ch. 262, §82, eff. Jan. 1, 1996; Acts 1997, 75th Leg., ch. 144, §2 (eff. May 20, 1997), ch. 1086, §31 (eff. Sept. 1, 1997); Acts 1999, 76th Leg., ch. 62, §19.01(7), eff. Sept. 1, 1999; Acts 2001, 77th Leg., ch. 585, §1, eff. Sept. 1, 2001; Acts 2005, 79th Leg., ch. 660, §§1, 2 (eff. Sept. 1, 2005), ch. 728, §4.003 (eff. Sept. 1, 2005); Acts 2007, 80th Leg., ch. 593, §§3.14, 3.15, eff. Sept. 1, 2007.

See also CCP art. 42.12.

ANNOTATIONS

Generally

Leday v. State, 983 S.W.2d 713, 720 (Tex.Crim.App. 1998). "[T]he Court of Appeals erred in deeming the appellant's point of error waived by his testimony at the guilt stage under an extension of the '*DeGarmo* doctrine.' [¶] [This doctrine] arose only after the enactment of [CCP art.] 37.07.... This article was the first authority for criminal trials to be held in two parts, the first concerned only with the guilt of the defendant, and the second only with the punishment. [¶] Because the defendant's testimony comes after the verdict of guilt, the *DeGarmo* doctrine is conceptually different from the doctrine of harmless error.... [¶] Under the traditional doctrine of harmless error (or waiver), such testimony might very well 'cure' the harm of evidence erroneously received from other witnesses. [¶] [H]armful effects of the introduction of inadmissible testimony were on the jury's decision of guilt[, and not] ameliorated by the defendant's testimony which follows that decision. [¶] [T]he *DeGarmo* doctrine is more like estoppel than waiver...."

Art. 37.07, §1

Ngo v. State, 175 S.W.3d 738, 744 (Tex.Crim.App. 2005). "When the State charges different criminal acts, regardless of whether those acts constitute violations of the same or different statutory provisions, the jury must be instructed that it cannot return a guilty verdict unless it unanimously agrees upon the commission of any one of these criminal acts."

Zuniga v. State, 144 S.W.3d 477, 487 (Tex.Crim. App.2004), *overruled in part on other grounds*, ***Watson v. State***, 204 S.W.3d 404 (Tex.Crim.App.2006). "'It is appropriate where the alternate theories of committing the same offense are submitted to the jury in the disjunctive for the jury to return a general verdict if the evidence is sufficient to support a finding under any of the theories submitted.'"

Art. 37.07, §2

Sterry v. State, 959 S.W.2d 249, 257-58 (Tex. App.—Dallas 1997, no pet.). "A defendant in a criminal case has no constitutional right to have a jury assess punishment. He does, however, have a statutory right to have a jury assess punishment. This valuable statutory right may not be taken away without due process of law. [¶] Appellant waived his valuable statutory right to have the jury assess punishment based on the trial judge's misstatement that the applicable sentencing range for his offense was that of a state jail felony with mandatory probation. When the trial judge later stated that the applicable sentencing range was not a state jail felony but rather a third-degree felony, the jury had been discharged. The trial judge could not order a new jury to assess punishment. Fundamental fairness does not allow a judge's misstatements of the law to mislead a defendant into waiving his valuable right to a jury. We conclude appellant was denied a fair trial in the punishment phase of the trial because of the particular circumstances under which he waived his right to a jury for assessment of punishment."

Hamlin v. State, 902 S.W.2d 613, 617 n.3 (Tex. App.—Houston [1st Dist.] 1995, no pet.). "[A] defendant is required to file a written pleading to raise a legal issue [when] an application for probation [is made]."

Pine v. State, 889 S.W.2d 625, 634 (Tex.App.—Houston [14th Dist.] 1994, pet. ref'd). "Where the defendant files no election [to have the jury assess punishment], the trial court has the duty to assess punishment."

Art. 37.07, §3

Sims v. State, ___ S.W.3d ___ (Tex.Crim.App. 2008) (No. PD-1575-07; 7-2-08). "We granted the appellant's petition for discretionary review to determine whether the State, during the punishment phase of trial, may introduce character evidence in the form of opinion testimony when that opinion is based on no more than a single encounter with law enforcement that constitutes an extraneous offense. [W]e hold that the evidence presented at the punishment phase of trial was proper and that the trial court committed no error in allowing its admission."

Smith v. State, 227 S.W.3d 753, 763 (Tex.Crim.App. 2007). CCP art. 37.07, §3(a)(1) "does not prohibit a trial court, as a sentencing entity, from considering extraneous misconduct evidence in assessing punishment just because the extraneous misconduct has not been shown to have been committed by the defendant beyond a reasonable doubt, if that extraneous misconduct is contained in a PSI [ordered under CCP art. 42.12, §9]."

Flowers v. State, 220 S.W.3d 919, 921-22 (Tex. Crim.App.2007). "To establish that a defendant has been convicted of a prior offense, the State must prove beyond a reasonable doubt that (1) a prior conviction exists, and (2) the defendant is linked to that conviction. No specific document or mode of proof is required to prove these two elements. There is no 'best evidence' rule in Texas that requires that the fact of a prior conviction be proven with any document, much less any specific document. While evidence of a certified copy of a final judgment and sentence may be a preferred and convenient means, the State may prove both of these

elements in a number of different ways, including (1) the defendant's admission or stipulation, (2) testimony by a person who was present when the person was convicted of the specified crime and can identify the defendant as that person, or (3) documentary proof (such as a judgment) that contains sufficient information to establish both the existence of a prior conviction and the defendant's identity as the person convicted."

Ellison v. State, 201 S.W.3d 714, 717 (Tex.Crim. App.2006). "[W]e hold that suitability [for probation] is a matter 'relevant to sentencing' under the current version of [CCP art.] 37.07, §3(a) when a defendant seeks placement on community supervision under [CCP art.] 42.12, §4...."

Haley v. State, 173 S.W.3d 510, 514-15 (Tex.Crim. App.2005). Section 3(a) "does not contemplate any significant distinction between the terms 'bad act' or 'extraneous offense.' ... Under this statute, it is irrelevant whether the conduct the offering party is attempting to prove is, or can be characterized, as an offense under the Texas Penal Code. The inclusion of acts rising to the level of criminal responsibility and acts appropriately labeled 'bad' in the statute's language make it clear that the act's nomenclature does not place each on a separate path towards admissibility. [¶] [T]he statutorily imposed burden of proof beyond a reasonable doubt does not require the offering party to necessarily prove that the act was a criminal act or that the defendant committed a crime. Before the jury can consider this evidence in assessing punishment, it must be satisfied beyond a reasonable doubt that the acts are attributable to the defendant. We interpret the statute to require the burden of proof to be applied to a defendant's involvement in the act itself, instead of the elements of a crime necessary for a finding of guilt. [¶] Unlike the guilt-innocence phase, the question at punishment is not whether the defendant has committed a crime, but instead what sentence should be assessed. Whereas the guilt-innocence stage requires the jury to find the defendant guilty beyond a reasonable doubt of each element of the offense, the punishment phase requires the jury only find that these prior acts are attributable to the defendant beyond a reasonable doubt." *See also Lamb v. State*, 186 S.W.3d 136, 141-42 (Tex. App.—Houston [1st Dist.] 2005, no pet.).

Bluitt v. State, 137 S.W.3d 51, 54 (Tex.Crim.App. 2004). "In any final conviction, the evidence was subjected to judicial testing of guilt with a standard of proof of beyond a reasonable doubt, and the burden of proof was met. In any probation, the defendant has plead guilty or been found guilty by a judge or jury. In any deferred adjudication, the defendant has plead guilty, and the court has found sufficient evidence to support a finding of guilty. In all these circumstances, the burden of proof has been met. Thus, in all such cases no further proof of guilt is required. [¶] The trial court did not err in refusing to give the requested instruction [that extraneous offenses must be proved beyond a reasonable doubt] when, as here, all of the evidence as to appellant's criminal behavior was in the form of prior offenses which had been subjected to judicial testing under the proper burden and the burden had been met." *See also Willover v. State*, 84 S.W.3d 751, 753 (Tex.App.—Houston [1st Dist.] 2002, pet. ref'd).

Sunbury v. State, 88 S.W.3d 229, 235 (Tex.Crim. App.2002). "[T]he punishment assessed for non-final convictions is relevant evidence during the punishment phase of a trial." *See also Davis v. State*, 968 S.W.2d 368, 373 (Tex.Crim.App.1998) (evidence of deferred adjudication).

Jaubert v. State, 74 S.W.3d 1, 4 (Tex.Crim.App. 2002). "The extraneous offense evidence in this case was introduced during cross-examination and rebuttal testimony, not in the State's case-in-chief. Therefore, appellant was not entitled to notice of the extraneous offenses."

Huizar v. State, 12 S.W.3d 479, 484 (Tex.Crim.App. 2000). "While §3(a) says nothing about the submission of [instructions that the jury may not consider extraneous bad acts and offenses in assessing punishment until the jury is satisfied beyond a reasonable doubt that the acts and offenses are attributable to the defendant], the jury might apply a standard of proof less than reasonable doubt in its determination of the defendant's connection to such offenses and bad acts, contrary to §3(a). ... As this was 'law applicable to the case' appellant was not required to make an objection or request under §3(a) in order for the trial court to instruct the jury thereunder. For this reason, the Court of Appeals was correct to conclude the trial judge erroneously failed to instruct the jury under §3(a)."

Coffel v. State, 242 S.W.3d 907, 911 (Tex.App.— Texarkana 2007, no pet.). "[T]o the extent Coffel now seeks to characterize 'technical' violations of community supervision [under CCP art. 42.12, §11] as new offenses, and thereby require the State to provide pretrial notice of its intent to introduce evidence regarding technical community supervision violations in a future prosecution pursuant to [CCP art.] 37.07 or [TRE] 404(b), Coffel's argument finds no support in our statutes or caselaw."

Ford v. State, 106 S.W.3d 765, 766-67 (Tex.App.— Texarkana 2003, no pet.). "The obligation of the State to give the notice required by §3(g) is not triggered unless and until the defense requests such notice. [¶] When a motion requests trial court action, even if it also asks the State to provide notice, it is insufficient to trigger the duty to provide notice under Article 37.07, §3(g). Moreover, if the defendant files a motion for the trial court to order the State to give such notice, the motion does not trigger the duty unless the trial court orders the State to give such notice."

Minor v. State, 91 S.W.3d 824, 830 (Tex.App.—Fort Worth 2002, pet. ref'd). "Evidence is relevant to the assessment of punishment if it provides information about the defendant's life and characteristics." *See also Rogers v. State*, 991 S.W.2d 263, 265 (Tex.Crim.App. 1999).

James v. State, 47 S.W.3d 710, 714 (Tex.App.— Texarkana 2001, no pet.). "The lack of even an approximate date for the [extraneous] acts is [a] serious defect. Lacking even a general statement about the time the acts occurred, the notice was not adequate for James to identify and investigate them. We further note that James is not required to complain about the adequacy of the notice, but that the State is required by statute to provide specific information. The State did not do so here. We therefore conclude that in these circumstances, the notices were inadequate to give James the full notice required by the statute."

Peters v. State, 31 S.W.3d 704, 722 (Tex.App.— Houston [1st Dist.] 2000, pet. ref'd). "[W]e find no basis on this record for excluding [doctor's] testimony on recidivism rates for treated incest offenders, especially when the State itself put recidivism in issue. [¶] We point out to the bench and bar that the important changes in article 37.07, §3(a) may make evidence like this admissible, despite much case law holding similar evidence per se inadmissible under the prior and more restrictive version of that statute. [¶] We hold the trial judge abused her discretion in excluding [doctor's] testimony...."

Williamson v. State, 990 S.W.2d 404, 406 (Tex. App.—Dallas 1999, no pet.). "The law is clear that exonerating evidence is not admissible under article 37.07, §3(a) because it is not relevant to the assessment of punishment."

Stevenson v. State, 963 S.W.2d 801, 803 (Tex. App.—Fort Worth 1998, pet. ref'd). "[S]ection 3(a) does not require a showing of the county where the extraneous crimes or bad acts occurred."

Art. 37.07, §4

Luquis v. State, 72 S.W.3d 355, 365 (Tex.Crim.App. 2002). "The constitutional issue before us ... is this: Does a statute which informs the jury of the existence of good conduct time, briefly describes that concept, and explicitly tells the jury not to apply that concept to the particular defendant, violate due process if the defendant's eligibility for parole or release on mandatory supervision will not be affected by good conduct time? We conclude that it does not."

Hill v. State, 913 S.W.2d 581, 586 (Tex.Crim.App. 1996). "[A]rticle 37.07 'implicitly requires the deadly weapon issue to be submitted at the guilt—innocence stage so that the trial court will know which parole law instruction to give the jury during the punishment phase.' [T]he *better* practice is to submit the deadly weapons special issue charge at the guilt/innocence phase of the trial."

Villareal v. State, 205 S.W.3d 103, 107 (Tex.App.—Texarkana 2006, pet. dism'd). "In light of the generally accepted effect of the parole instruction, and the absence of any objection by [D], the initial omission of the parole instruction was not egregious error. However, when it became apparent the jury was concerned with application of the parole law, the trial court was required to give the mandatory parole instruction pursuant to Article 37.07. The trial court's deviation from Article 37.07 under these circumstances caused egregious harm."

ART. 37.071. PROCEDURE IN CAPITAL CASE

Sec. 1. If a defendant is found guilty in a capital felony case in which the state does not seek the death penalty, the judge shall sentence the defendant to life imprisonment without parole.

Sec. 2. (a)(1) If a defendant is tried for a capital offense in which the state seeks the death penalty, on a finding that the defendant is guilty of a capital offense, the court shall conduct a separate sentencing proceeding to determine whether the defendant shall be sentenced to death or life imprisonment without parole. The proceeding shall be conducted in the trial court and, except as provided by Article 44.29(c) of this code, before the trial jury as soon as practicable. In the proceeding, evidence may be presented by the state and the defendant or the defendant's counsel as to any matter that the court deems relevant to sentence, including evidence of the defendant's background or character or the circumstances of the offense that mitigates against the imposition of the death penalty. This subdivision shall not be construed to authorize the introduction of any evidence secured in violation of the Constitution of the United States or of the State of Texas. The state and the defendant or the defendant's counsel shall be permitted to present argument for or against sentence of death. The introduction of evidence of extraneous conduct is governed by the notice requirements of Section 3(g), Article 37.07. The court, the attorney representing the state, the defendant, or the defendant's counsel may not inform a juror or a prospective juror of the effect of a failure of a jury to agree on issues submitted under Subsection (c) or (e).

(2) Notwithstanding Subdivision (1), evidence may not be offered by the state to establish that the race or ethnicity of the defendant makes it likely that the defendant will engage in future criminal conduct.

(b) On conclusion of the presentation of the evidence, the court shall submit the following issues to the jury:

(1) whether there is a probability that the defendant would commit criminal acts of violence that would constitute a continuing threat to society; and

(2) in cases in which the jury charge at the guilt or innocence stage permitted the jury to find the defendant guilty as a party under Sections 7.01 and 7.02, Penal Code, whether the defendant actually caused the death of the deceased or did not actually cause the death of the deceased but intended to kill the deceased or another or anticipated that a human life would be taken.

(c) The state must prove each issue submitted under Subsection (b) of this article beyond a reasonable doubt, and the jury shall return a special verdict of "yes" or "no" on each issue submitted under Subsection (b) of this Article.

(d) The court shall charge the jury that:

(1) in deliberating on the issues submitted under Subsection (b) of this article, it shall consider all evidence admitted at the guilt or innocence stage and the punishment stage, including evidence of the defendant's background or character or the circumstances of the offense that militates for or mitigates against the imposition of the death penalty;

(2) it may not answer any issue submitted under Subsection (b) of this article "yes" unless it agrees unanimously and it may not answer any issue "no" unless 10 or more jurors agree; and

(3) members of the jury need not agree on what particular evidence supports a negative answer to any issue submitted under Subsection (b) of this article.

(e)(1) The court shall instruct the jury that if the jury returns an affirmative finding to each issue submitted under Subsection (b), it shall answer the following issue:

Whether, taking into consideration all of the evidence, including the circumstances of the offense, the defendant's character and background, and the personal moral culpability of the defendant, there is a sufficient mitigating circumstance or circumstances to warrant that a sentence of life imprisonment without parole rather than a death sentence be imposed.

(2) The court shall:

(A) instruct the jury that if the jury answers that a circumstance or circumstances warrant that a sentence of life imprisonment without parole rather than a death sentence be imposed, the court will sentence the defendant to imprisonment in the institutional division of the Texas Department of Criminal Justice for life without parole; and

(B) charge the jury that a defendant sentenced to confinement for life without parole under this article is ineligible for release from the department on parole.

(f) The court shall charge the jury that in answering the issue submitted under Subsection (e) of this article, the jury:

(1) shall answer the issue "yes" or "no";

(2) may not answer the issue "no" unless it agrees unanimously and may not answer the issue "yes" unless 10 or more jurors agree;

(3) need not agree on what particular evidence supports an affirmative finding on the issue; and

(4) shall consider mitigating evidence to be evidence that a juror might regard as reducing the defendant's moral blameworthiness.

(g) If the jury returns an affirmative finding on each issue submitted under Subsection (b) and a negative finding on an issue submitted under Subsection (e)(1), the court shall sentence the defendant to death. If the jury returns a negative finding on any issue submitted under Subsection (b) or an affirmative finding on an issue submitted under Subsection (e)(1) or is unable to answer any issue submitted under Subsection (b) or (e), the court shall sentence the defendant to confinement in the institutional division of the Texas Department of Criminal Justice for life imprisonment without parole.

(h) The judgment of conviction and sentence of death shall be subject to automatic review by the Court of Criminal Appeals.

(i) This article applies to the sentencing procedure in a capital case for an offense that is committed on or after September 1, 1991. For the purposes of this section, an offense is committed on or after September 1, 1991, if any element of that offense occurs on or after that date.

History of CCP art. 37.071: Acts 1973, 63rd Leg., ch. 426, art. 3, §1, eff. June 14, 1973. Amended by Acts 1981, 67th Leg., ch. 725, §1, eff. Aug. 31, 1981; Acts 1985, 69th Leg., ch. 44, §2, eff. Sept. 1, 1985; Acts 1991, 72nd Leg., ch. 652, §9 (eff. Sept. 1, 1991), ch. 838, §1 (eff. Sept. 1, 1991); Acts 1993, 73rd Leg., ch. 781, §1, eff. Aug. 30, 1993; Acts 1999, 76th Leg., ch. 140, §1, eff. Sept. 1, 1999; Acts 2001, 77th Leg., ch. 585, §2, eff. Sept. 1, 2001; Acts 2005, 79th Leg., ch. 399, §1 (eff. Sept. 1, 2005), ch. 787, §§6-9 (eff. Sept. 1, 2005).

ANNOTATIONS

Generally

Jurek v. Texas, 428 U.S. 262, 276, 96 S.Ct. 2950, 2958 (1976). "[T]exas' capital-sentencing procedures ... do not violate the Eighth and Fourteenth Amendments. By narrowing its definition of capital murder, Texas has essentially said that there must be at least one statutory aggravating circumstance in a first-degree murder case before a death sentence may even be considered. By authorizing the defense to bring before the jury at the separate sentencing hearing whatever mitigating circumstances relating to the individual defendant can be adduced, Texas has ensured that the sentencing jury will have adequate guidance to enable it to perform its sentencing function. By providing prompt judicial review of the jury's decision in a court with statewide jurisdiction, Texas has provided a means to promote the evenhanded, rational, and consistent imposition of death sentences under law."

Art. 37.071, §2(a)

Tong v. State, 25 S.W.3d 707, 713 (Tex.Crim.App. 2000). "Impact testimony from the victims of an extraneous offense is not the type of 'victim impact evidence' contemplated by **Mosley** and **Payne v. Tennessee**, and therefore, was arguably objectionable. *At 713 n.9:* [Although the] testimony was arguably objectionable, we are not deciding that the evidence was necessarily *inadmissible*. Instead, we only mean to suggest that, given the fact that the evidence was offered during the State's case-in-chief on punishment rather than as rebuttal to any defensive mitigation evidence, the testimony provided defense counsel with a ripe opportunity to litigate the issue."

Jackson v. State, 992 S.W.2d 469, 477 (Tex.Crim. App.1999). "[I]n capital cases, '[w]here the charge to the jury properly requires the State to prove each of the special punishment issues beyond a reasonable doubt, no burden of proof instruction concerning extraneous offenses is required.'"

Art. 37.071, §2(b)

Druery v. State, 225 S.W.3d 491, 507 (Tex.Crim. App.2007). "[W]hen determining whether a defendant will pose a continuing threat to society, a jury may consider a variety of factors. As we have said, these factors include, but are not limited to, the circumstances of the capital offense, including: the defendant's state of mind and whether he was working alone or with other parties; the calculated nature of the defendant's acts; the forethought and deliberateness exhibited by the crime's execution; the existence and severity of prior crimes; the defendant's age and personal circumstances at the time of the offense; whether the defendant was acting under duress or the domination of another at the time of the commission of the offense; psychiatric evidence; and character evidence. But the circumstances of the offense itself 'can be among the most revealing evidence of future dangerousness and alone may be sufficient to support an affirmative answer to that special issue.'"

Hankins v. State, 132 S.W.3d 380, 385-86 (Tex. Crim.App.2004). "The future-dangerousness issue asks the jury to consider all the evidence and determine whether there are certain aggravating factors beyond a reasonable doubt. Although consideration of aggravating circumstances in deliberating on the mitigation issue is permitted, it is not required. Even when aggravating circumstances are considered in the context of the mitigation issue, the fact finder's purpose differs when considering those same circumstances on the question of future dangerousness. In the context of future dangerousness, aggravating circumstances are considered in determining whether to impose the death penalty; in the context of the mitigation issue, aggravating circumstances [are] used to determine whether the jury should decline to impose the death penalty. Thus, an affirmative finding on the first does not necessarily compel a negative answer on the latter." (Internal quotes omitted.)

McFarland v. State, 928 S.W.2d 482, 519 (Tex. Crim.App.1996), *overruled on other grounds*, **Mosely v. State**, 983 S.W.2d 249, 272 n.18 (Tex.Crim.App.1998). "[T]here is no constitutional inhibition to concealing from jurors the consequences of their deliberations, so long as they are not misled into believing that ultimate responsibility for the verdict rests elsewhere."

Penry v. State, 903 S.W.2d 715, 764 (Tex.Crim.App. 1995). "The matter of parole or a defendant's release thereon is not a proper consideration for a jury's deliberations in the punishment phase of a capital murder trial. A jury's only task at the punishment phase is to answer the special issues as required in Article 37.071."

Smith v. State, 898 S.W.2d 838, 846 (Tex.Crim.App. 1995). "[T]he term 'society' includes *both* the prison and non-prison populations."

Ex parte Broxton, 888 S.W.2d 23, 28 (Tex.Crim. App.1994). "Extraneous offenses serve a purely evidentiary function at the punishment phase of a capital case. They are admissible to the extent they are relevant to prove the special issues. In most cases they will be admitted to facilitate the prediction whether the defendant will constitute a future danger to society. But in making the prediction regarding 'future dangerousness,' the jury is permitted to consider many different factors. Evidence of extraneous offenses is certainly not necessary for the jury to make an affirmative finding of 'future dangerousness' and for the defendant to receive the death penalty."

Art. 37.071, §2(e)

Williams v. State, ___ S.W.3d ___ (Tex.Crim.App. 2008) (No. AP-74,391; 6-11-08). "We conclude that the mitigation special issue is a defensive issue that cannot be forfeited by inaction but can be waived, and because it is a defensive issue, the defendant has a right to insist upon its waiver."

Penry v. State, 178 S.W.3d 782, 787 (Tex.Crim.App. 2005). "Because there is a reasonable likelihood that the jury believed that it could not give effect to mental impairment, outside of tending to show that the appellant is mentally retarded, the trial court erred in instructing the jury to 'consider whether any other mitigating circumstance or circumstances exist as defined herein.'" Held: A jury may consider a defendant's mental impairment as a mitigating circumstance.

Skinner v. State, 956 S.W.2d 532, 542 (Tex.Crim. App.1997). "The issue of mitigating evidence is ... applicable to capital cases in which the death penalty is sought as jurors are asked to determine whether a sufficient mitigating circumstance or circumstances exist to warrant that a sentence of life be imposed rather than death. However, jurors are also instructed that 'mitigating evidence' is 'evidence that a juror might regard as reducing the defendant's moral blameworthiness.' Hence, the wording of appellant's desired question, whether jurors could consider evidence not related to appellant's blameworthiness to be mitigating, was, in fact, contrary to the law."

Rhoades v. State, 934 S.W.2d 113, 128 (Tex.Crim. App.1996). "In cases where mitigating evidence is presented, all that is constitutionally required is a vehicle by which the jury may give mitigating effect to appellant's evidence. [¶] There is no evidence that must be viewed by a juror as having a definitive mitigating effect, per se."

Green v. State, 934 S.W.2d 92, 106 (Tex.Crim.App. 1996). "[T]his Court has stated that it will not review the jury's finding under §2(e) for sufficiency of the evidence because the determination as to whether mitigating evidence calls for a life sentence is a value judgment left to the discretion of the factfinder. *At 107:* Each juror individually determines what evidence, if any, mitigates against the just imposition of the death sentence."

Cockrell v. State, 933 S.W.2d 73, 92-93 (Tex.Crim. App.1996). "Appellant claims the mitigation special issue contained in Article 37.071, §2(e) ... allows untrammeled discretion in imposing the death sentence.

However, appellant also claims the definition of mitigating evidence contained in Article 37.071, §2(f)(4), ... is unconstitutionally too narrow. [¶] With one notable exception, Texas' death penalty scheme ... is the same as the one the United States Supreme Court upheld. ... The exception involves Texas' legislative response to ... *Penry* mandat[ing] the mitigating evidence instruction contained in Article 37.071, §2(e). [E]ven with this legislative response to *Penry*, Texas' death penalty scheme continues to narrow the class of 'death-eligible' defendants while also providing a jury with more discretion than it had under Texas' prior statutory scheme 'to decline to impose one death penalty.' [¶] [A] majority of the Supreme Court would hold Texas is not constitutionally prohibited from mandating the submission of the mitigation special issue contained in Article 37.071 §2(e). [¶] [A]t least a plurality of the Supreme Court would hold the giving of the definition of mitigating evidence contained in Article 37.071, §2(f)(4), in conjunction with the giving of one mitigating evidence special issue contained in Article 37.071, §2(e), provides more protection to a defendant than what the Federal Constitution now requires."

Goff v. State, 931 S.W.2d 537, 556 (Tex.Crim.App. 1996). "We have previously required that evidence proffered by a defendant must tend to demonstrate that this defendant is less morally culpable for a crime than a similarly-situated defendant without this evidence. In other words, in order for mitigating evidence to have relevance beyond the scope of the special issues, there must be relevance between the mitigating evidence and the circumstances surrounding the crime that tends to excuse or explain the criminal act, so as to make that particular defendant less deathworthy. [¶] Applying the relevancy requirement ..., it cannot be said that the evidence of the victim's homosexuality is relevant to [D's] background, character, or the circumstances of the crime."

Art. 37.071, §2(f)

Lawton v. State, 913 S.W.2d 542, 556 (Tex.Crim. App.1995), *overruled on other grounds*, ***Mosley v. State***, 983 S.W.2d 249, 272 n.18 (Tex.Crim.App.1998). "[A]n appellate sufficiency review of a negative verdict regarding the mitigation special issue is neither constitutionally required nor possible under our current law. [¶] Evidence is not *per se* mitigating; each juror individually determines what evidence, if any, mitigates against the just imposition of the death sentence."

Hughes v. State, 897 S.W.2d 285, 299 (Tex.Crim. App.1994). "[T]he evidence of appellant's mental and emotional instability could be considered within the scope of the submitted issues...."

Art. 37.071, §2(h)

Ex parte Jackson, 187 S.W.3d 416, 416 (Tex.Crim. App.2005). "Chapter 48 [Pardon & Parole] does not alter [the Court of Criminal Appeals'] appellate jurisdiction when the Governor grants commutation of punishment."

ART. 37.0711. PROCEDURE IN CAPITAL CASE FOR OFFENSE COMMITTED BEFORE SEPTEMBER 1, 1991

Sec. 1. This article applies to the sentencing procedure in a capital case for an offense that is committed before September 1, 1991, whether the sentencing procedure is part of the original trial of the offense, an award of a new trial for both the guilt or innocence stage and the punishment stage of the trial, or an award of a new trial only for the punishment stage of the trial. For the purposes of this section, an offense is committed before September 1, 1991, if every element of the offense occurs before that date.

Sec. 2. If a defendant is found guilty in a case in which the state does not seek the death penalty, the judge shall sentence the defendant to life imprisonment.

Sec. 3. (a) (1) If a defendant is tried for a capital offense in which the state seeks the death penalty, on a finding that the defendant is guilty of a capital offense, the court shall conduct a separate sentencing proceeding to determine whether the defendant shall be sentenced to death or life imprisonment. The proceeding shall be conducted in the trial court and, except as provided by Article 44.29(c) of this code, before the trial jury as soon as practicable. In the proceeding, evidence may be presented as to any matter that the court deems relevant to sentence. This subdivision shall not be construed to authorize the introduction of any evidence secured in violation of the Constitution of the United States or of this state. The state and the defendant or the defendant's counsel shall be permitted to present argument for or against sentence of death.

(2) Notwithstanding Subdivision (1), evidence may not be offered by the state to establish that the race or ethnicity of the defendant makes it likely that the defendant will engage in future criminal conduct.

(b) On conclusion of the presentation of the evidence, the court shall submit the following three issues to the jury:

(1) whether the conduct of the defendant that caused the death of the deceased was committed deliberately and with the reasonable expectation that the death of the deceased or another would result;

(2) whether there is a probability that the defendant would commit criminal acts of violence that would constitute a continuing threat to society; and

(3) if raised by the evidence, whether the conduct of the defendant in killing the deceased was unreasonable in response to the provocation, if any, by the deceased.

(c) The state must prove each issue submitted under Subsection (b) of this section beyond a reasonable doubt, and the jury shall return a special verdict of "yes" or "no" on each issue submitted.

(d) The court shall charge the jury that:

(1) it may not answer any issue submitted under Subsection (b) of this section "yes" unless it agrees unanimously; and

(2) it may not answer any issue submitted under Subsection (b) of this section "no" unless 10 or more jurors agree.

(e) The court shall instruct the jury that if the jury returns an affirmative finding on each issue submitted under Subsection (b) of this section, it shall answer the following issue:

Whether, taking into consideration all of the evidence, including the circumstances of the offense, the defendant's character and background, and the personal moral culpability of the defendant, there is a sufficient mitigating circumstance or circumstances to warrant that a sentence of life imprisonment rather than a death sentence be imposed.

(f) The court shall charge the jury that, in answering the issue submitted under Subsection (e) of this section, the jury:

(1) shall answer the issue "yes" or "no";

(2) may not answer the issue "no" unless it agrees unanimously and may not answer the issue "yes" unless 10 or more jurors agree; and

CCP ART. 37.0711

(3) shall consider mitigating evidence that a juror might regard as reducing the defendant's moral blameworthiness.

(g) If the jury returns an affirmative finding on each issue submitted under Subsection (b) of this section and a negative finding on the issue submitted under Subsection (e) of this section, the court shall sentence the defendant to death. If the jury returns a negative finding on any issue submitted under Subsection (b) of this section or an affirmative finding on the issue submitted under Subsection (e) of this section or is unable to answer any issue submitted under Subsection (b) or (e) of this section, the court shall sentence the defendant to confinement in the institutional division of the Texas Department of Criminal Justice for life.

(h) If a defendant is convicted of an offense under Section 19.03(a)(7), Penal Code, the court shall submit the issues under Subsections (b) and (e) of this section only with regard to the conduct of the defendant in murdering the deceased individual first named in the indictment.

(i) The court, the attorney for the state, or the attorney for the defendant may not inform a juror or prospective juror of the effect of failure of the jury to agree on an issue submitted under this article.

(j) The Court of Criminal Appeals shall automatically review a judgment of conviction and sentence of death not later than the 60th day after the date of certification by the sentencing court of the entire record, unless the Court of Criminal Appeals extends the time for an additional period not to exceed 30 days for good cause shown. Automatic review under this subsection has priority over all other cases before the Court of Criminal Appeals, and the court shall hear automatic reviews under rules adopted by the court for that purpose.

History of CCP art. 37.0711: Acts 1993, 73rd Leg., ch. 781, §2, eff. Aug. 30, 1993. Amended by Acts 1995, 74th Leg., ch. 76, §14.22, eff. Sept. 1, 1995; Acts 2001, 77th Leg., ch. 585, §3, eff. Sept. 1, 2001.

ANNOTATIONS

Martinez v. State, 924 S.W.2d 693, 696 n.6 (Tex. Crim.App.1996). "The jury is permitted to look at several factors in its review of future dangerousness including, but not limited to: 1. the circumstances of the capital offense, including the defendant's state of mind and whether he was working alone or with other parties; 2. the calculated nature of the defendant's acts; 3. the forethought and deliberateness exhibited by the crime's execution; 4. the existence of a prior criminal record, and the severity of the prior crimes; 5. the defendant's age and personal circumstances at the time of the offense; 6. whether the defendant was acting under duress or the domination of another at the time of the offense; 7. psychiatric evidence; and 8. character evidence."

ART. 37.072. PROCEDURE IN REPEAT SEX OFFENDER CAPITAL CASE

 Article 37.072 below is effective for offenses committed on or after Sept. 1, 2007.

Sec. 1. If a defendant is found guilty in a capital felony case punishable under Section 12.42(c)(3), Penal Code, in which the state does not seek the death penalty, the judge shall sentence the defendant to life imprisonment without parole.

Sec. 2. (a)(1) If a defendant is tried for an offense punishable under Section 12.42(c)(3), Penal Code, in which the state seeks the death penalty, on a finding that the defendant is guilty of a capital offense, the court shall conduct a separate sentencing proceeding to determine whether the defendant shall be sentenced to death or life imprisonment without parole. The proceeding shall be conducted in the trial court and, except as provided by Article 44.29(d) of this code, before the trial jury as soon as practicable. In the proceeding, evidence may be presented by the state and the defendant or the defendant's counsel as to any matter that the court considers relevant to sentence, including evidence of the defendant's background or character or the circumstances of the offense that mitigates against the imposition of the death penalty. This subdivision may not be construed to authorize the introduction of any evidence secured in violation of the Constitution of the United States or of the State of Texas. The state and the defendant or the defendant's counsel shall be permitted to present argument for or against sentence of death. The introduction of evidence of extraneous conduct is governed by the notice requirements of Section 3(g), Article 37.07. The court, the attorney representing the state, the defendant, or the defendant's counsel may not inform a juror or a prospective juror of the effect of a failure of a jury to agree on issues submitted under Subsection (b) or (e).

(2) Notwithstanding Subdivision (1), evidence may not be offered by the state to establish that the race or ethnicity of the defendant makes it likely that the defendant will engage in future criminal conduct.

(b) On conclusion of the presentation of the evidence, the court shall submit the following issues to the jury:

(1) whether there is a probability that the defendant would commit criminal acts of violence that would constitute a continuing threat to society; and

(2) in cases in which the jury charge at the guilt or innocence stage permitted the jury to find the defendant guilty as a party under Sections 7.01 and 7.02, Penal Code, whether the defendant actually engaged in the conduct prohibited by Section 22.021, Penal Code, or did not actually engage in the conduct prohibited by Section 22.021, Penal Code, but intended that the offense be committed against the victim or another intended victim.

(c) The state must prove beyond a reasonable doubt each issue submitted under Subsection (b) of this section, and the jury shall return a special verdict of "yes" or "no" on each issue submitted under Subsection (b) of this section.

(d) The court shall charge the jury that:

(1) in deliberating on the issues submitted under Subsection (b) of this section, it shall consider all evidence admitted at the guilt or innocence stage and the punishment stage, including evidence of the defendant's background or character or the circumstances of the offense that militates for or mitigates against the imposition of the death penalty;

(2) it may not answer any issue submitted under Subsection (b) of this section "yes" unless it agrees unanimously and it may not answer any issue "no" unless 10 or more jurors agree; and

(3) members of the jury need not agree on what particular evidence supports a negative answer to any issue submitted under Subsection (b) of this section.

(e)(1) The court shall instruct the jury that if the jury returns an affirmative finding to each issue submitted under Subsection (b), it shall answer the following issue:

Whether, taking into consideration all of the evidence, including the circumstances of the offense, the defendant's character and background, and the personal moral culpability of the defendant, there is a sufficient mitigating circumstance or circumstances to warrant that a sentence of life imprisonment without parole rather than a death sentence be imposed.

(2) The court shall:

(A) instruct the jury that if the jury answers that a circumstance or circumstances warrant that a sentence of life imprisonment without parole rather than a death sentence be imposed, the court will sentence the defendant to imprisonment in the Texas Department of Criminal Justice for life without parole; and

(B) charge the jury that a defendant sentenced to confinement for life without parole under this article is ineligible for release from the department on parole.

(f) The court shall charge the jury that in answering the issue submitted under Subsection (e) of this section, the jury:

(1) shall answer the issue "yes" or "no";

(2) may not answer the issue "no" unless it agrees unanimously and may not answer the issue "yes" unless 10 or more jurors agree;

(3) need not agree on what particular evidence supports an affirmative finding on the issue; and

(4) shall consider mitigating evidence to be evidence that a juror might regard as reducing the defendant's moral blameworthiness.

(g) If the jury returns an affirmative finding on each issue submitted under Subsection (b) and a negative finding on an issue submitted under Subsection (e)(1), the court shall sentence the defendant to death. If the jury returns a negative finding on any issue submitted under Subsection (b) or an affirmative finding on an issue submitted under Subsection (e)(1) or is unable to answer any issue submitted under Subsection (b) or (e), the court shall sentence the defendant to imprisonment in the Texas Department of Criminal Justice for life without parole.

(h) The judgment of conviction and sentence of death shall be subject to automatic review by the Court of Criminal Appeals.

History of CCP art. 37.072: Acts 2007, 80th Leg., ch. 593, §1.04, eff. Sept. 1, 2007.

ART. 37.073. REPAYMENT OF REWARDS

(a) After a defendant has been convicted of a felony offense, the judge may order a defendant to repay all or part of a reward paid by a crime stoppers organization.

(b) In determining whether the defendant must repay the reward or part of the reward, the court shall consider:

(1) the ability of the defendant to make the payment and the financial hardship on the defendant to make the required payment; and

(2) the importance of the information to the prosecution of the defendant as provided by the arresting officer or the attorney for the state with due regard for the confidentiality of the crime stoppers organization records.

(c) In this article, "crime stoppers organization" means a crime stoppers organization, as defined by Subdivision (2), Section 414.001, Government Code, that is approved by the Crime Stoppers Advisory Council to receive payments of rewards under this article and Article 42.152 of this code.

History of CCP art. 37.073: Acts 1989, 71st Leg., ch. 611, §1, eff. Sept. 1, 1989. Renumbered from Art. 37.072 by Acts 1991, 72nd Leg., ch. 16, §19.01(5), eff. Aug. 26, 1991; Acts 1997, 75th Leg., ch. 700, §10, eff. Sept. 1, 1997.

ART. 37.08. CONVICTION OF LESSER INCLUDED OFFENSE

In a prosecution for an offense with lesser included offenses, the jury may find the defendant not guilty of the greater offense, but guilty of any lesser included offense.

History of CCP art. 37.08: Acts 1965, 59th Leg., vol. 2, ch. 722. Amended by Acts 1973, 63rd Leg., ch. 399, §2(A), eff. Jan. 1, 1974.

See also chart, "Lesser Included Offenses," p. 692.

ANNOTATIONS

Arevalo v. State, 943 S.W.2d 887, 889 (Tex.Crim. App.1997). "[T]he jury is instructed as to a lesser included offense only when that offense constitutes a valid, rational alternative to the charged offense. If a jury were instructed on a lesser included offense even though the evidence did not raise it, then the instruction 'would constitute an invitation to the jury to return a compromise or otherwise unwarranted verdict.'"

Stephens v. State, 806 S.W.2d 812, 817 (Tex.Crim. App.1990). "[T]exas law provides for consolidating greater and lesser included offenses by including both in the charge to the jury on the trial of the greater offense."

Bell v. State, 693 S.W.2d 434, 442 (Tex.Crim.App. 1985). "If evidence from any source raises the issue of a lesser included offense, the charge must be given. A defendant's testimony alone is sufficient to raise the issue."

Sanders v. State, 664 S.W.2d 705, 706 (Tex.Crim. App.1982). "While it is true 'An indictment or information should allege every fact which may affect the degree or kind of punishment,' …, this rule of law does not prohibit conviction for an offense included in the offense properly alleged merely because the elements of the included offense are not all set out in the indictment."

ART. 37.09. LESSER INCLUDED OFFENSE

An offense is a lesser included offense if:

(1) it is established by proof of the same or less than all the facts required to establish the commission of the offense charged;

(2) it differs from the offense charged only in the respect that a less serious injury or risk of injury to the same person, property, or public interest suffices to establish its commission;

(3) it differs from the offense charged only in the respect that a less culpable mental state suffices to establish its commission; or

(4) it consists of an attempt to commit the offense charged or an otherwise included offense.

History of CCP art. 37.09: Acts 1965, 59th Leg., vol. 2, ch. 722. Amended by Acts 1973, 63rd Leg., ch. 399, §2(A), eff. Jan. 1, 1974.

See also chart, "Lesser Included Offenses," p. 692.

ANNOTATIONS

Hall v. State, 225 S.W.3d 524, 535-36 (Tex.Crim. App.2007). "We now hold that the pleadings approach is the sole test for determining in the first step whether a party may be entitled to a lesser-included-offense instruction. The availability of a lesser-included instruction in a given case still would depend on the second step, whether there is some evidence adduced at trial to support such an instruction. [¶] The first step in the lesser-included-offense analysis, determining whether an offense is a lesser-included offense of the alleged offense, is a question of law. It does not depend on the evidence to be produced at the trial. It may be, and to provide notice to the defendant must be, capable of being performed before trial by comparing the elements of the offense as they are alleged in the indictment or information with the elements of the potential lesser-included offense. [¶] The evidence adduced at trial should remain an important part of the court's decision whether to charge the jury on lesser-included offenses.

The second step in the analysis should ask whether there is evidence that supports giving the instruction to the jury. 'A defendant is entitled to an instruction on a lesser-included offense where the proof for the offense charged includes the proof necessary to establish the lesser-included offense and there is some evidence in the record that would permit a jury rationally to find that if the defendant is guilty, he is guilty only of the lesser-included offense.' In this step of the analysis, anything more than a scintilla of evidence may be sufficient to entitle a defendant to a lesser charge. In other words, the evidence must establish the lesser-included offense as 'a valid, rational alternative to the charged offense.'"

ART. 37.10. INFORMAL VERDICT

(a) If the verdict of the jury is informal, its attention shall be called to it, and with its consent the verdict may, under the direction of the court, be reduced to the proper form. If the jury refuses to have the verdict altered, it shall again retire to its room to deliberate, unless it manifestly appear that the verdict is intended as an acquittal; and in that case, the judgment shall be rendered accordingly, discharging the defendant.

(b) If the jury assesses punishment in a case and in the verdict assesses both punishment that is authorized by law for the offense and punishment that is not authorized by law for the offense, the court shall reform the verdict to show the punishment authorized by law and to omit the punishment not authorized by law. If the trial court is required to reform a verdict under this subsection and fails to do so, the appellate court shall reform the verdict as provided by this subsection.

History of CCP art. 37.10: Acts 1965, 59th Leg., vol. 2, ch. 722. Amended by Acts 1985, 69th Leg., ch. 442, §1, eff. June 11, 1985.

See also CCP art. 37.01.

ANNOTATIONS

Eads v. State, 598 S.W.2d 304, 307 (Tex.Crim.App. 1980). "While a trial court may correct an informal or contradictory verdict with the jury's consent, the court cannot substitute its judgment for the jury's verdict."

Cranford v. State, 124 S.W.3d 811, 812 (Tex. App.—Dallas 2003, pet. ref'd). Held: Article 37.10(b) authorizes appellate court to reform sentence by deleting an unauthorized punishment assessed by the jury, but it does not authorize reformation when punishment was assessed by court.

Land v. State, 890 S.W.2d 229, 234 (Tex.App.—Beaumont 1994, no pet.). "[T]he power granted courts to reform judgments under ... art. 37.10(b) does not include the power to *add* punishment to incomplete verdicts, even if the addition is de minimis."

ART. 37.11. DEFENDANTS TRIED JOINTLY

Where several defendants are tried together, the jury may convict each defendant it finds guilty and acquit others. If it agrees to a verdict as to one or more, it may find a verdict in accordance with such agreement, and if it cannot agree as to others, a mistrial may be entered as to them.

History of CCP art. 37.11: Acts 1965, 59th Leg., vol. 2, ch. 722.

ART. 37.12. JUDGMENT ON VERDICT

On each verdict of acquittal or conviction, the proper judgment shall be entered immediately. If acquitted, the defendant shall be at once discharged from all further liability upon the charge for which he was tried; provided that, in misdemeanor cases where there is returned a verdict, or a plea of guilty is entered and the punishment assessed is by fine only, the court may, on written request of the defendant and for good cause shown, defer judgment until some other day fixed by order of the court; but in no event shall the judgment be deferred for a longer period of time than six months. On expiration of the time fixed by the order of the court, the court or judge thereof, shall enter judgment on the verdict or plea and the same shall be executed as provided by Chapter 43 of this Code. Provided further, that the court or judge thereof, in the exercise of sound discretion may permit the defendant where judgment is deferred, to remain at large on his personal bond, or may require him to enter into bail bond in a sum at least double the amount of the assessed fine and costs, conditioned that the defendant and sureties, jointly and severally, will pay such fine and costs unless the defendant personally appears on the day, set in the order and discharges the judgment in the manner provided by Chapter 43 of this Code; and for the enforcement of any judgment entered, all writs, processes and remedies of this Code are made applicable so far as necessary to carry out the provisions of this Article.

History of CCP art. 37.12: Acts 1965, 59th Leg., vol. 2, ch. 722.

Curry v. Wilson, 853 S.W.2d 40, 45 n.3 (Tex.Crim. App.1993). Article 37.12 "serves only to discharge a defendant from any further criminal liability for the offense for which he was tried. ... Art. 37.12 does not indicate a defendant is also to be discharged from any civil liability for repayment of attorney's fees upon the event of an acquittal."

Scott v. State, 988 S.W.2d 947, 948 (Tex.App.—Houston [1st Dist.] 1999, no pet.). "The trial judge erred by not assessing the fine. We cannot reform the judgment by adding punishment of any amount, as the State suggests. Nor has appellant waived his complaint by not raising it below. A void sentence cannot be waived. Thus, the sole remedy is a new punishment hearing. [¶] [CCP art. 37.10] does not apply ... because it allows courts to 'omit' punishment, not to add it."

ART. 37.13. IF JURY BELIEVES ACCUSED INSANE

When a jury has been impaneled to assess the punishment upon a plea of guilty, it shall say in its verdict what the punishment is which it assesses; but if it is of the opinion that a person pleading guilty is insane, it shall so report to the court, and an issue as to that fact shall be tried before another jury; and if, upon such trial, it be found that the defendant is insane, such proceedings shall be had as directed in cases where a defendant becomes insane after conviction.

History of CCP art. 37.13: Acts 1965, 59th Leg., vol. 2, ch. 722.

ART. 37.14. ACQUITTAL OF HIGHER OFFENSE AS JEOPARDY

If a defendant, prosecuted for an offense which includes within it lesser offenses, be convicted of an offense lower than that for which he is indicted, and a new trial be granted him, or the judgment be arrested for any cause other than the want of jurisdiction, the verdict upon the first trial shall be considered an acquittal of the higher offense; but he may, upon a second trial, be convicted of the same offense of which he was before convicted, or any other inferior thereto.

History of CCP art. 37.14: Acts 1965, 59th Leg., vol. 2, ch. 722.

Windom v. State, 968 S.W.2d 360, 363 (Tex.Crim. App.1998). "[B]oth appellant and the State exchanged benefits to obtain a plea agreement: the State agreed to reduce the charge from aggravated robbery to robbery in exchange for appellant's plea of no contest to the lesser offense; appellant, in turn, offered to plead no contest in exchange for the benefit of having the charge reduced from aggravated robbery to robbery. When the trial judge granted appellant's motion for new trial, that agreement was voided. The law is clear ... that if appellant withdraws his negotiated plea, the remedy is to return the parties to their original positions. Therefore, the Court of Appeals erred in holding that subsequent prosecution for aggravated robbery was barred...."

State v. Restrepo, 878 S.W.2d 327, 328 (Tex.App.—Waco 1994, pet. dism'd). "When the jury is given the option of convicting on either a greater or lesser-included offense, a guilty verdict on the lesser offense is an implied acquittal of the greater offense. [T]he verdict can be treated as though the jury had returned a verdict which expressly read: We find the defendant not guilty of [the greater offense] but guilty of [the lesser included offense]." (Internal quotes omitted.)

ART. 37.15. EXPIRED

CHAPTER 38. EVIDENCE IN CRIMINAL ACTIONS

Art. 38.01	Texas Forensic Science Commission
Art. 38.03	Presumption of innocence
Art. 38.04	Jury are judges of facts
Art. 38.05	Judge shall not discuss evidence
Art. 38.07	Testimony in corroboration of victim of sexual offense
Art. 38.071	Testimony of child who is victim of offense
Art. 38.072	Hearsay statement of child abuse victim
Art. 38.073	Testimony of inmate witnesses
Art. 38.08	Defendant may testify
Art. 38.10	Exceptions to the spousal adverse testimony privilege
Art. 38.101	Communications by drug abusers
Art. 38.12	Religious opinion
Art. 38.14	Testimony of accomplice
Art. 38.141	Testimony of undercover peace officer or special investigator
Art. 38.15	Two witnesses in treason
Art. 38.16	Evidence in treason
Art. 38.17	Two witnesses required
Art. 38.18	Perjury & aggravated perjury
Art. 38.19	Intent to defraud in forgery
Art. 38.21	Statement
Art. 38.22	When statements may be used
Art. 38.23	Evidence not to be used
Art. 38.25	Written part of instrument controls
Art. 38.27	Evidence of handwriting

ART. 38.01. TEXAS FORENSIC SCIENCE COMMISSION

§1. Creation

The Texas Forensic Science Commission is created.

§2. Definition

In this article, "forensic analysis" has the meaning assigned by Article 38.35(a).

§3. Composition

(a) The commission is composed of the following nine members:

(1) four members appointed by the governor:

(A) two of whom must have expertise in the field of forensic science;

(B) one of whom must be a prosecuting attorney that the governor selects from a list of 10 names submitted by the Texas District and County Attorneys Association; and

(C) one of whom must be a defense attorney that the governor selects from a list of 10 names submitted by the Texas Criminal Defense Lawyers Association;

(2) three members appointed by the lieutenant governor:

(A) one of whom must be a faculty member or staff member of The University of Texas who specializes in clinical laboratory medicine selected from a list of 10 names submitted to the lieutenant governor by the chancellor of The University of Texas System;

(B) one of whom must be a faculty member or staff member of Texas A&M University who specializes in clinical laboratory medicine selected from a list of 10 names submitted to the lieutenant governor by the chancellor of The Texas A&M University System;

(C) one of whom must be a faculty member or staff member of Texas Southern University who has expertise in pharmaceutical laboratory research selected from a list of 10 names submitted to the lieutenant governor by the chancellor of Texas Southern University; and

(3) two members appointed by the attorney general:

(A) one of whom must be a director or division head of the University of North Texas Health Science Center at Fort Worth Missing Persons DNA Database; and

(B) one of whom must be a faculty or staff member of the Sam Houston State University College of Criminal Justice and have expertise in the field of forensic science or statistical analyses selected from a list of 10 names submitted to the lieutenant governor by the chancellor of Texas State University System.

(b) Each member of the commission serves a two year term. The term of the members appointed under Subsections (a)(1) and (2) expires on September 1 of each odd-numbered year. The term of the members appointed under Subsection (a)(3) expires on September 1 of each even-numbered year.

(c) The governor shall designate a member of the commission to serve as the presiding officer.

§4. Duties

(a) The commission shall:

(1) develop and implement a reporting system through which accredited laboratories, facilities, or entities report professional negligence or misconduct;

(2) require all laboratories, facilities, or entities that conduct forensic analyses to report professional negligence or misconduct to the commission; and

(3) investigate, in a timely manner, any allegation of professional negligence or misconduct that would substantially affect the integrity of the results of a forensic analysis conducted by an accredited laboratory, facility, or entity.

(b) An investigation under Subsection (a)(3):

(1) must include the preparation of a written report that identifies and also describes the methods and procedures used to identify:

(A) the alleged negligence or misconduct;

(B) whether negligence or misconduct occurred; and

(C) any corrective action required of the laboratory, facility, or entity; and

(2) may include one or more:

(A) retrospective reexaminations of other forensic analyses conducted by the laboratory, facility, or entity that may involve the same kind of negligence or misconduct; and

(B) follow-up evaluations of the laboratory, facility, or entity to review:

(i) the implementation of any corrective action required under Subdivision (1)(C); or

(ii) the conclusion of any retrospective reexamination under Paragraph (A).

(c) The commission by contract may delegate the duties described by Subsections (a)(1) and (3) to any person the commission determines to be qualified to assume those duties.

(d) The commission may require that a laboratory, facility, or entity investigated under this section pay any costs incurred to ensure compliance with Subsection (b)(1).

(e) The commission shall make all investigation reports completed under Subsection (b)(1) available to the public. A report completed under Subsection (b)(1), in a subsequent civil or criminal proceeding, is not prima facie evidence of the information or findings contained in the report.

§5. Reimbursement

A member of the commission may not receive compensation but is entitled to reimbursement for the member's travel expenses as provided by Chapter 660, Government Code, and the General Appropriations Act.

§6. Assistance

The Texas Legislative Council, the Legislative Budget Board, and The University of Texas at Austin shall assist the commission in performing the commission's duties.

§7. Submission

The commission shall submit any report received under Section 4(a)(2) and any report prepared under Section 4(b)(1) to the governor, the lieutenant governor, and the speaker of the house of representatives not later than December 1 of each even-numbered year.

History of CCP art. 38.01: Acts 2005, 79th Leg., ch. 1224, §1, eff. Sept. 1, 2005.

History of Former CCP art. 38.01: Repealed by the Texas Court of Criminal Appeals' adoption of the Texas Rules of Criminal Evidence on Dec. 18, 1985, eff. Sept. 1, 1986. 701 S.W.2d xxix, lxvi-lxvii.

ART. 38.02. REPEALED

Repealed by the Texas Court of Criminal Appeals' adoption of the Texas Rules of Criminal Evidence on Dec. 18, 1985, eff. Sept. 1, 1986. 701 S.W.2d xxix, lxvi-lxvii.

ART. 38.03. PRESUMPTION OF INNOCENCE

All persons are presumed to be innocent and no person may be convicted of an offense unless each element of the offense is proved beyond a reasonable doubt. The fact that he has been arrested, confined, or indicted for, or otherwise charged with, the offense gives rise to no inference of guilt at his trial.

History of CCP art. 38.03: Acts 1965, 59th Leg., vol. 2, ch. 722. Amended by Acts 1981, 67th Leg., ch. 539, §1, eff. June 12, 1981.

ANNOTATIONS

Alvarado v. State, 912 S.W.2d 199, 206-07 (Tex. Crim.App.1995). "[N]o person may be convicted of a criminal offense and denied his liberty unless his criminal responsibility for the offense is proved beyond a reasonable doubt."

ART. 38.04. JURY ARE JUDGES OF FACTS

The jury, in all cases, is the exclusive judge of the facts proved, and of the weight to be given to the testimony, except where it is provided by law that proof of any particular fact is to be taken as either conclusive or presumptive proof of the existence of another fact, or where the law directs that a certain degree of weight is to be attached to a certain species of evidence.

History of CCP art. 38.04: Acts 1965, 59th Leg., vol. 2, ch. 722. See also CCP art. 36.13.

ANNOTATIONS

Maestas v. State, 963 S.W.2d 151, 156 (Tex.App.— Corpus Christi 1998), *aff'd*, 987 S.W.2d 59 (Tex.Crim. App.1999). "The trier of fact is the exclusive judge of the facts, credibility of witnesses, and weight to be afforded their testimony. The jury is free to accept one version of the facts, reject another, or reject all or any of a witness's testimony. Simply because the defendant presents a different version of the facts does not render the State's evidence insufficient."

ART. 38.05. JUDGE SHALL NOT DISCUSS EVIDENCE

In ruling upon the admissibility of evidence, the judge shall not discuss or comment upon the weight of the same or its bearing in the case, but shall simply decide whether or not it is admissible; nor shall he, at any stage of the proceeding previous to the return of the verdict, make any remark calculated to convey to the jury his opinion of the case.

History of CCP art. 38.05: Acts 1965, 59th Leg., vol. 2, ch. 722.

ANNOTATIONS

Moore v. State, 907 S.W.2d 918, 923 (Tex.App.—Houston [1st Dist.] 1995, pet. ref'd). "[T]he article 38.05 right to prohibit the judge from commenting on the weight of the evidence or conveying his opinion of the case ... is ... forfeitable by inaction. We base this conclusion on the absence of a waiver clause in article 38.05. Errors of this type can be readily cured with a proper jury instruction." *See also Hoang v. State*, 997 S.W.2d 678, 680-81 (Tex.App.—Texarkana 1999, no pet.).

Clark v. State, 878 S.W.2d 224, 226 (Tex.App.—Dallas 1994, no pet.). "To determine whether the comment is either reasonably calculated to benefit the State or to prejudice the defendant, we must first examine whether the trial court's statement was material to the case. An issue is material if the jury had the same issue before it. [¶] A trial court improperly comments on the weight of the evidence if it makes a statement that: (1) implies approval of the State's argument, (2) indicates any disbelief in the defense's position, (3) diminishes the credibility of the defense's approach to its case. [¶] We consider the consequences that probably resulted from the trial court's comments to determine whether the comments prejudiced the defendant's rights. If we 'determine beyond a reasonable doubt that the court's error made no contribution to the conviction,' we hold the error harmless." *See also Simon v. State*, 203 S.W.3d 581, 590 (Tex.App.—Houston [14th Dist.] 2006, no pet.).

ART. 38.06. REPEALED

Repealed by the Texas Court of Criminal Appeals' adoption of the Texas Rules of Criminal Evidence on Dec. 18, 1985, eff. Sept. 1, 1986. 701 S.W.2d xxix, lxvi-lxvii.

ART. 38.07. TESTIMONY IN CORROBORATION OF VICTIM OF SEXUAL OFFENSE

(a) A conviction under Chapter 21, Section 22.011, or Section 22.021, Penal Code, is supportable on the uncorroborated testimony of the victim of the sexual offense if the victim informed any person, other than the defendant, of the alleged offense within one year after the date on which the offense is alleged to have occurred.

(b) The requirement that the victim inform another person of an alleged offense does not apply if at the time of the alleged offense the victim was a person:

(1) 17 years of age or younger;

(2) 65 years of age or older; or

(3) 18 years of age or older who by reason of age or physical or mental disease, defect, or injury was substantially unable to satisfy the person's need for food, shelter, medical care, or protection from harm.

History of CCP art. 38.07: Acts 1975, 64th Leg., ch. 203, §6, eff. Sept. 1, 1975. Amended by Acts 1983, 68th Leg., ch. 382, §1 (eff. Sept. 1, 1983), ch. 977, §7 (eff. Sept. 1, 1983); Acts 1993, 73rd Leg., ch. 200, §1 (eff. May 19, 1993), ch. 900, §12.01 (eff. Sept. 1, 1993); Acts 2001, 77th Leg., ch. 1018, §1, eff. Sept. 1, 2001.

ANNOTATIONS

Carmell v. Texas, 529 U.S. 513, 529, 120 S.Ct. 1620, 1631 (2000). "Article 38.07 is unquestionably a law 'that alters the legal rules of evidence, and receives less, or different, testimony, than the law required at the time of the commission of the offence, in order to convict the offender.' Under the law in effect at the time the acts were committed, the prosecution's case was legally insufficient and petitioner was entitled to a judgment of acquittal, unless the State could produce both the victim's testimony *and* corroborative evidence. The amended law, however, changed the quantum of evidence necessary to sustain a conviction; under the new law, petitioner could be (and was) convicted on the victim's testimony alone, without any corroborating evidence. Under any commonsense understanding of *Calder*'s [*v. Bull*, 3 U.S. (3 Dall.) 386, 390 (1798)] fourth category, Article 38.07 plainly fits. Requiring only the victim's testimony to convict, rather than the victim's testimony plus other corroborating evidence is surely 'less testimony required to convict' in any straightforward sense of those words. *At 552, 1643:* [W]e hold that the petitioner's convictions ... insofar as they are not corroborated by other evidence, cannot be sustained under the *Ex Post Facto* Clause, because Texas' amendment to Article 38.07 falls within *Calder*'s fourth category."

Martinez v. State, 178 S.W.3d 806, 812 (Tex.Crim. App.2005). "While [CCP art.] 38.072 assists the prosecution by making certain hearsay outcry statements admissible, [CCP art.] 38.07 protects the accused by creating a statutory corroboration requirement. *At 813-14:* Article 38.07 requires the State to offer *some* corroborative evidence, such as eyewitness testimony, a defendant's admissions, medical testimony, or other circumstantial proof, if the competent adult complainant in a sexual assault prosecution has not informed any adult, other than the defendant, of the alleged offense within a year of its commission. Of course, if the victim's statements to that witness are otherwise admissible under the hearsay rule, then the witness may recount the victim's outcry. But Article 38.07 is not itself an exception to the hearsay rule. [¶] In sum, Article 38.07 deals with the *sufficiency* of evidence required to sustain a conviction for sexual assault but does not act as a hearsay exception, while Article 38.072 deals with the *admissibility* of evidence that would otherwise be barred by the hearsay rule."

ART. 38.071. TESTIMONY OF CHILD WHO IS VICTIM OF OFFENSE

Sec. 1. This article applies only to a hearing or proceeding in which the court determines that a child younger than 13 years of age would be unavailable to testify in the presence of the defendant about an offense defined by any of the following sections of the Penal Code:

(1) Section 19.02 (Murder);

(2) Section 19.03 (Capital Murder);

(3) Section 19.04 (Manslaughter);

(4) Section 20.04 (Aggravated Kidnapping);

(5) Section 21.11 (Indecency with a Child);

(6) Section 22.011 (Sexual Assault);

(7) Section 22.02 (Aggravated Assault);

(8) Section 22.021 (Aggravated Sexual Assault);

(9) Section 22.04(e) (Injury to a Child, Elderly Individual, or Disabled Individual);

(10) Section 22.04(f) (Injury to a Child, Elderly Individual, or Disabled Individual), if the conduct is committed intentionally or knowingly;

(11) Section 25.02 (Prohibited Sexual Conduct);

(12) Section 29.03 (Aggravated Robbery);

(13) Section 43.25 (Sexual Performance by a Child); or

 Subsection (14) below is effective for offenses committed on or after Sept. 1, 2007.

(14) Section 21.02 (Continuous Sexual Abuse of Young Child or Children).

Sec. 2. (a) The recording of an oral statement of the child made before the indictment is returned or the complaint has been filed is admissible into evidence if the court makes a determination that the factual issues of identity or actual occurrence were fully and fairly inquired into in a detached manner by a neutral individual experienced in child abuse cases that seeks to find the truth of the matter.

(b) If a recording is made under Subsection (a) of this section and after an indictment is returned or a complaint has been filed, by motion of the attorney representing the state or the attorney representing the defendant and on the approval of the court, both attorneys may propound written interrogatories that shall be presented by the same neutral individual who made the initial inquiries, if possible, and recorded under the same or similar circumstances of the original recording with the time and date of the inquiry clearly indicated in the recording.

(c) A recording made under Subsection (a) of this section is not admissible into evidence unless a recording made under Subsection (b) is admitted at the same time if a recording under Subsection (b) was requested prior to the time of the hearing or proceeding.

Sec. 3. (a) On its own motion or on the motion of the attorney representing the state or the attorney representing the defendant, the court may order that the testimony of the child be taken in a room other than the courtroom and be televised by closed circuit equipment in the courtroom to be viewed by the court and the finder of fact. To the extent practicable, only the judge, the court reporter, the attorneys for the defendant and for the state, persons necessary to operate the equipment, and any person whose presence would contribute to the welfare and well-being of the child may be present in the room with the child during his testimony. Only the attorneys and the judge may question the child. To the extent practicable, the persons necessary to operate the equipment shall be confined to an adjacent room or behind a screen or mirror that permits them to see and hear the child during his testimony, but does not permit the child to see or hear them. The court shall permit the defendant to observe and hear the testimony of the child and to communicate contemporaneously with his attorney during periods of recess or by audio contact, but the court shall attempt to ensure that the child cannot hear or see the defendant. The court shall permit the attorney for the defendant adequate opportunity to confer with the defendant during cross-examination of the child. On application of the attorney for the defendant, the court may recess the proceeding before or during cross-examination of the child for a reasonable time to allow the attorney for the defendant to confer with defendant.

(b) The court may set any other conditions and limitations on the taking of the testimony that it finds just and appropriate, taking into consideration the interests of the child, the rights of the defendant, and any other relevant factors.

Sec. 4. (a) After an indictment has been returned or a complaint filed, on its own motion or on the motion of the attorney representing the state or the attorney representing the defendant, the court may order that the testimony of the child be taken outside the courtroom and be recorded for showing in the courtroom before the court and the finder of fact. To the extent practicable, only those persons permitted to be present at the taking of testimony under Section 3 of this article may be present during the taking of the child's testimony, and the persons operating the equipment shall be confined from the child's sight and hearing as provided by Section 3. The court shall permit the defendant to observe and hear the testimony of the child and to communicate contemporaneously with his attorney during periods of recess or by audio contact but shall attempt to ensure that the child cannot hear or see the defendant.

(b) The court may set any other conditions and limitations on the taking of the testimony that it finds just and appropriate, taking into consideration the interests of the child, the rights of the defendant, and any other relevant factors. The court shall also ensure that:

(1) the recording is both visual and aural and is recorded on film or videotape or by other electronic means;

(2) the recording equipment was capable of making an accurate recording, the operator was competent, the quality of the recording is sufficient to allow the court and the finder of fact to assess the demeanor of the child and the interviewer, and the recording is accurate and is not altered;

(3) each voice on the recording is identified;

(4) the defendant, the attorneys for each party, and the expert witnesses for each party are afforded an opportunity to view the recording before it is shown in the courtroom;

(5) before giving his testimony, the child was placed under oath or was otherwise admonished in a manner appropriate to the child's age and maturity to testify truthfully;

(6) the court finds from the recording or through an in camera examination of the child that the child was competent to testify at the time the recording was made; and

(7) only one continuous recording of the child was made or the necessity for pauses in the recordings or for multiple recordings is established at the hearing or proceeding.

(c) After a complaint has been filed or an indictment returned charging the defendant, on the motion of the attorney representing the state, the court may order that the deposition of the child be taken outside of the courtroom in the same manner as a deposition may be taken in a civil matter. A deposition taken under this subsection is admissible into evidence.

Sec. 5. (a) On the motion of the attorney representing the state or the attorney representing the defendant and on a finding by the court that the following requirements have been substantially satisfied, the recording of an oral statement of the child made before a complaint has been filed or an indictment returned is admissible into evidence if:

(1) no attorney or peace officer was present when the statement was made;

(2) the recording is both visual and aural and is recorded on film or videotape or by other electronic means;

(3) the recording equipment was capable of making an accurate recording, the operator of the equipment was competent, the quality of the recording is sufficient to allow the court and the finder of fact to assess the demeanor of the child and the interviewer, and the recording is accurate and has not been altered;

(4) the statement was not made in response to questioning calculated to lead the child to make a particular statement;

(5) every voice on the recording is identified;

(6) the person conducting the interview of the child in the recording is expert in the handling, treatment, and investigation of child abuse cases, present at the hearing or proceeding, called by the state, and subject to cross-examination;

(7) immediately after a complaint was filed or an indictment returned, the attorney representing the state notified the court, the defendant, and the attorney representing the defendant of the existence of the recording;

(8) the defendant, the attorney for the defendant, and the expert witnesses for the defendant were afforded an opportunity to view the recording before it is offered into evidence and, if a proceeding was requested as provided by Subsection (b) of this section, in a proceeding conducted before a district court judge but outside the presence of the jury were afforded an opportunity to cross-examine the child as provided by Subsection (b) of this section from any time immediately following the filing of the complaint or the returning of an indictment charging the defendant until the date the hearing or proceeding begins;

(9) the recording of the cross-examination, if there is one, is admissible under Subsection (b) of this section;

(10) before giving his testimony, the child was placed under oath or was otherwise admonished in a manner appropriate to the child's age and maturity to testify truthfully;

(11) the court finds from the recording or through an in camera examination of the child that the child was competent to testify at the time that the recording was made; and

(12) only one continuous recording of the child was made or the necessity for pauses in the recordings or for multiple recordings has been established at the hearing or proceeding.

(b) On the motion of the attorney representing the defendant, a district court may order that the cross-examination of the child be taken and be recorded before the judge of that court at any time until a recording made in accordance with Subsection (a) of this section has been introduced into evidence at the hearing or proceeding. On a finding by the court that the following requirements were satisfied, the recording of the cross-examination of the child is admissible into evidence and shall be viewed by the finder of fact only after the finder of fact has viewed the recording authorized by Subsection (a) of this section if:

(1) the recording is both visual and aural and is recorded on film or videotape or by other electronic means;

(2) the recording equipment was capable of making an accurate recording, the operator of the equipment was competent, the quality of the recording is sufficient to allow the court and the finder of fact to assess the demeanor of the child and the attorney representing the defendant, and the recording is accurate and has not been altered;

(3) every voice on the recording is identified;

(4) the defendant, the attorney representing the defendant, the attorney representing the state, and the expert witnesses for the defendant and the state were afforded an opportunity to view the recording before the hearing or proceeding began;

(5) the child was placed under oath before the cross-examination began or was otherwise admonished in a manner appropriate to the child's age and maturity to testify truthfully; and

(6) only one continuous recording of the child was made or the necessity for pauses in the recordings or for multiple recordings was established at the hearing or proceeding.

(c) During cross-examination under Subsection (b) of this section, to the extent practicable, only a district court judge, the attorney representing the defendant, the attorney representing the state, persons necessary to operate the equipment, and any other person whose presence would contribute to the welfare and well-being of the child may be present in the room with the child during his testimony. Only the attorneys and the judge may question the child. To the extent practicable, the persons operating the equipment shall be confined to an adjacent room or behind a screen or mirror that permits them to see and hear the child during his testimony but does not permit the child to see or hear them. The court shall permit the defendant to observe and hear the testimony of the child and to communicate contemporaneously with his attorney during periods of recess or by audio contact, but shall attempt to ensure that the child cannot hear or see the defendant.

(d) Under Subsection (b) of this section the district court may set any other conditions and limitations on the taking of the cross-examination of a child that it finds just and appropriate, taking into consideration the interests of the child, the rights of the defendant, and any other relevant factors.

Sec. 6. If the court orders the testimony of a child to be taken under Section 3 or 4 of this article or if the court finds the testimony of the child taken under Section 2 or 5 of this article is admissible into evidence, the child may not be required to testify in court at the proceeding for which the testimony was taken, unless the court finds there is good cause.

Sec. 7. In making any determination of good cause under this article, the court shall consider the rights of the defendant, the interests of the child, the relationship of the defendant to the child, the character and duration of the alleged offense, any court finding related to the availability of the child to testify, the age, maturity, and emotional stability of the child, the time elapsed since the alleged offense, and any other relevant factors.

Sec. 8. (a) In making a determination of unavailability under this article, the court shall consider relevant factors including the relationship of the defendant to the child, the character and duration of the alleged offense, the age, maturity, and emotional stability of the child, and the time elapsed since the alleged offense, and whether the child is more likely than not to be unavailable to testify because:

(1) of emotional or physical causes, including the confrontation with the defendant; or

(2) the child would suffer undue psychological or physical harm through his involvement at the hearing or proceeding.

(b) A determination of unavailability under this article can be made after an earlier determination of availability. A determination of availability under this article can be made after an earlier determination of unavailability.

Sec. 9. If the court finds the testimony taken under Section 2 or 5 of this article is admissible into evidence or if the court orders the testimony to be taken under Section 3 or 4 of this article and if the identity of the perpetrator is a contested issue, the child additionally must make an in-person identification of the defendant either at or before the hearing or proceeding.

Sec. 10. In ordering a child to testify under this article, the court shall take all reasonable steps necessary and available to minimize undue psychological trauma to the child and to minimize the emotional and physical stress to the child caused by relevant factors, including the confrontation with the defendant and the ordinary participation of the witness in the courtroom.

Sec. 11. In a proceeding under Section 2, 3, or 4 or Subsection (b) of Section 5 of this article, if the defendant is not represented by counsel and the court finds that the defendant is not able to obtain counsel for the purposes of the proceeding, the court shall appoint counsel to represent the defendant at the proceeding.

Sec. 12. In this article, "cross-examination" has the same meaning as in other legal proceedings in the state.

Sec. 13. The attorney representing the state shall determine whether to use the procedure provided in Section 2 of this article or the procedure provided in Section 5 of this article.

History of CCP art. 38.071: Acts 1983, 68th Leg., ch. 599, §1, eff. Aug. 29, 1983. Amended by Acts 1987, 70th Leg., ch. 998, §1 (eff. Aug. 31, 1987), 2nd C.S., ch. 55, §1 (eff. Oct. 20, 1987); Acts 1991, 72nd Leg., ch. 266, §1, eff. Sept. 1, 1991; Acts 1995, 74th Leg., ch. 76, §14.24, eff. Sept. 1, 1995; Acts 2001, 77th Leg., ch. 338, §§1-8, eff. Sept. 1, 2001; Acts 2007, 80th Leg., ch. 593, §3.16, eff. Sept. 1, 2007.

ANNOTATIONS

Smith v. State, 61 S.W.3d 409, 412-13 (Tex.Crim. App.2001). When the testimony of a child victim of sexual assault is introduced not by in-court testimony but by closed circuit or videotape, the trial court should consider whether there are sufficient indicia of reliability. "This can be shown either by demonstrating that the tapes fall within a 'firmly rooted' hearsay exception or that they are supported by 'particularized guarantees of trustworthiness.' [¶] Particularized guarantees of trustworthiness must be shown from the totality of the circumstances surrounding the making of the statement, without considering other evidence admitted at trial. Some factors which may be considered in this analysis include the following: (a) the spontaneity of the statement; (b) whether the statement is consistently repeated; (c) the mental state of the declarant; (d) the use of terminology unexpected of a child of similar age; (e) a lack of motive to fabricate; (f) the giving of an age-appropriate oath before the statement is made; (g) the presence of the defendant during the interview; (h) the presence of the child's parent during the interview; (i) the relationship of the declarant to the interviewer; (j) the length of time between the child's first outcry and the making of the statement; (k) the quality of the tape; and (*l*) the method by which the interview is conducted, including whether the questions are leading, whether the child is given a break when needed, and whether written interrogatories from the defendant are submitted and answered." *See also* **Smith v. State**, 88 S.W.3d 652, 664 (Tex.App.—Tyler 2002, pet. ref'd); **Moon v. State**, 856 S.W.2d 276, 278 (Tex.App.—Fort Worth 1993, pet. ref'd).

Torres v. State, 33 S.W.3d 252, 253 (Tex.Crim.App. 2000). "At appellant's trial for indecency with a child by contact, the State sought to admit into evidence a videotaped interview with the alleged child victim. Appellant objected to the admission of the tape ... because the child was not placed under oath or admonished prior to the questioning. *At 257:* The Court of Appeals erred in holding that the discussion with the child at the end of her interview substantially satisfied the requirement that she be sworn or admonished before giving testimony, under §5(a)(10). Accordingly, the videotaped interview was not admissible into evidence."

Matz v. State, 14 S.W.3d 746, 747 (Tex.Crim.App. 2000). "We ... determine whether 'the trial court erred in allowing the state to play for the jury a videotaped interview of the complaining party after the child testified live, in that such evidence is hearsay.' [¶] In holding that appellant had not preserved error, the Court of Appeals misunderstood the basis for appellant's complaint about admission of the videotaped testimony. Appellant did not object to the *substance* of that testimony, but to the *form*, i.e., that it was hearsay...."

Lively v. State, 968 S.W.2d 363, 367 (Tex.Crim.App. 1998). "Appellant complains that the necessity for using a special procedure for [child witness's] testimony at his trial was not shown because the trial court did not *explicitly* make the three findings spelled out in *Maryland v. Craig* [110 S.Ct. 3157 (1990)]. We are unpersuaded by appellant's argument. Nothing in *Maryland v. Craig* requires that a trial court make explicit, as opposed to implicit, findings regarding the necessity of a special procedure to protect a child witness in a child abuse case. [T]he three findings required by *Maryland v. Craig* were implicit in the trial court's single explicit finding. That is, it was implicit in the trial court's explicit finding that the special procedure was necessary to prevent substantial harm to [child

witness] caused by appellant's presence in the courtroom." *See also* **Edwards v. State**, 107 S.W.3d 107, 109-11 (Tex.App.—Texarkana 2003, pet. ref'd).

Hightower v. State, 822 S.W.2d 48, 51 (Tex.Crim. App.1991). "[B]efore a trial court is allowed to utilize a closed-circuit system of transmitting a child's testimony into the courtroom, the court must hear evidence and make a case-specific determination that: *First,* ... use of the one-way closed-circuit procedure is necessary to protect the welfare of the particular child witness who seeks to testify. *Second,* ... the child witness would be traumatized ... by the presence of the defendant. *Third,* ... the emotional distress suffered by the child witness in the presence of the defendant is more than ... mere nervousness or excitement or some reluctance to testify." (Internal quotes omitted.) *See also* **Gonzales v. State**, 818 S.W.2d 756 (Tex.Crim.App. 1991); **Bousquet v. State**, 47 S.W.3d 131, 136 (Tex. App.—Houston [1st Dist.] 2001, pet. ref'd).

Ozuna v. State, 199 S.W.3d 601, 606 (Tex.App.—Corpus Christi 2006, no pet.). "Courts give wide latitude to testimony given by child victims of sexual abuse. The victim's description of what happened to him need not be precise, and he is not expected to express himself at the same level of sophistication as an adult. A child victim need not testify to penetration, which the State may prove through circumstantial evidence. However, the testimony of a child victim alone is sufficient evidence of penetration to support a conviction. There is no requirement that the victim's testimony be corroborated by medical or physical evidence. Further, outcry testimony alone can be sufficient to sustain a conviction for aggravated sexual assault."

Rangel v. State, 199 S.W.3d 523, 537 (Tex.App.—Fort Worth 2006, pet. dism'd). "We hold that in this case, the Confrontation Clause [of the U.S. Constitution] was not violated because article 38.071 allowed appellant an opportunity to submit written interrogatories to [child victim] after the trial court determined that [child victim] was unavailable. Further, by submitting interrogatories, appellant would have had the opportunity to test the reliability of [child victim's] statements from the prior interview."

Laredo v. State, 194 S.W.3d 637, 639 (Tex.App.—Houston [14th Dist.] 2006, pet. ref'd). "Appellant's sole argument on appeal is that the complainant was 'per se' available to testify because she did, in fact, testify;

thus, the trial court erred in finding that she was unavailable under article 38.071. This characterization is inaccurate. Section 1 of the article limits the inquiry regarding the child's availability to testify to 'in the presence of the defendant.' The State unsuccessfully attempted to have the complainant testify remotely, outside of appellant's presence. ... Additionally, it is clear that unavailability under article 38.071[, §8] is not strictly a matter of physical unavailability. ... Accordingly, the trial court did not abuse its discretion in ruling that the complainant was unavailable to testify." *Editor's note*: On appeal, appellant did *not* raise confrontation objections. *See also **Crawford v. Washington***, 541 U.S. 36, 124 (2004).

Neal v. State, 862 S.W.2d 203, 204-05 (Tex.App.—Houston [1st Dist.] 1993, no pet.). Article 38.071 "'denotes a general legislative intent to protect the youth of this state from the trauma associated with testifying in a courtroom....' Our youth deserve that protection regardless of whether the proceeding is a jury trial or a motion to revoke probation."

ART. 38.072. HEARSAY STATEMENT OF CHILD ABUSE VICTIM

Sec. 1. This article applies to a proceeding in the prosecution of an offense under any of the following provisions of the Penal Code, if committed against a child 12 years of age or younger:

(1) Chapter 21 (Sexual Offenses) or 22 (Assaultive Offenses);

(2) Section 25.02 (Prohibited Sexual Conduct); or

(3) Section 43.25 (Sexual Performance by a Child).

Sec. 2. (a) This article applies only to statements that describe the alleged offense that:

(1) were made by the child against whom the offense was allegedly committed; and

(2) were made to the first person, 18 years of age or older, other than the defendant, to whom the child made a statement about the offense.

(b) A statement that meets the requirements of Subsection (a) of this article is not inadmissible because of the hearsay rule if:

(1) on or before the 14th day before the date the proceeding begins, the party intending to offer the statement:

(A) notifies the adverse party of its intention to do so;

(B) provides the adverse party with the name of the witness through whom it intends to offer the statement; and

(C) provides the adverse party with a written summary of the statement;

(2) the trial court finds, in a hearing conducted outside the presence of the jury, that the statement is reliable based on the time, content, and circumstances of the statement; and

(3) the child testifies or is available to testify at the proceeding in court or in any other manner provided by law.

History of CCP art. 38.072: Acts 1985, 69th Leg., ch. 590, §1, eff. Sept. 1, 1985. Amended by Acts 1995, 74th Leg., ch. 76, §14.25, eff. Sept. 1, 1995.

ANNOTATIONS

Nino v. State, 223 S.W.3d 749, 752-53 (Tex.App.—Houston [14th Dist.] 2007, no pet.). "Appellant contends the trial court should have designated [mother] rather than [forensic investigator] as the outcry witness because, based on [child's] statements in the shower and later in the living room, [mother] was the first adult to whom [child] made a statement that in some discernible manner described the alleged offense. We agree with appellant. The evidence before the trial court was sufficient to show that [child] had described the offense in a discernible manner to his mother before he talked to the forensic interviewer. [¶] Therefore, the trial court abused its discretion in designating [forensic investigator], rather than [mother], as the outcry witness under §38.072 ...." *See also **Brown v. State***, 189 S.W.3d 382, 385 (Tex.App.—Texarkana 2006, pet. ref'd).

Dunn v. State, 125 S.W.3d 610, 612 (Tex.App.—Texarkana 2003, no pet.). "Dunn contends the trial court abused its discretion by admitting a videotape of interviews with the victims as the 'outcry' because a video recorder is not a person and cannot be cross-examined as would a witness. *At 614:* The videotape [was] admissible only if some [hearsay] exception applied. The only suggested authority for such admission lies in Article 38.072. We cannot agree that the article contemplates that a videotape of the 'outcry' will be introduced. It clearly contemplates that a person, subject to confrontation and cross-examination, will testify about what was said."

Josey v. State, 97 S.W.3d 687, 693 (Tex.App.—Texarkana 2003, no pet.). "Multiple outcry witnesses can testify about separate instances of abuse committed by the defendant if each witness is the first person to whom the child victim relayed information about the separate incidents. 'If the child victim first described one type of abuse to one outcry witness, and first described a different type of abuse to a second outcry witness, the second witness could testify about the different issue of abuse.'" *See also Jones v. State*, 92 S.W.3d 619, 621 (Tex.App.—Austin 2002, no pet.); *Hollinger v. State*, 911 S.W.2d 35, 39 (Tex.App.—Tyler 1995, pet. ref'd).

Duncan v. State, 95 S.W.3d 669, 672 (Tex.App.—Houston [1st Dist.] 2002, pet. ref'd). "[W]e apply [TRAP] 44.2(b) to determine whether the trial court's error [in refusing appellant's demand for a CCP art. 38.072 hearing] constitutes reversible error."

Broderick v. State, 89 S.W.3d 696, 699 (Tex.App.—Houston [1st Dist.] 2002, pet. ref'd). "The line of questioning appellant sought to introduce on cross-examination during the preliminary hearing focused on the circumstances of the abuse itself, not the circumstances of [child's] statement to her father. Because the questions were outside the narrow scope of the inquiry into the time, circumstances, or content of the outcry statement, the trial court did not abuse its discretion by limiting the questions."

Gallegos v. State, 918 S.W.2d 50, 54 (Tex.App.—Corpus Christi 1996, pet. ref'd). "[W]e cannot expect child victims to testify with the same clarity and ability as is expected of mature and capable adults. Where the child has sufficiently communicated that the touching occurred to a part of the body within the definition of the statute, the evidence will be sufficient to support a conviction regardless of the unsophisticated language that the child uses. *At 56:* Article 38.072 expressly applies only to statements that describe the alleged offense."

ART. 38.073. TESTIMONY OF INMATE WITNESSES

In a proceeding in the prosecution of a criminal offense in which an inmate in the custody of the Texas Department of Criminal Justice is required to testify as a witness, any deposition or testimony of the inmate witness may be conducted by electronic means, in the same manner as permitted in civil cases under Section 30.012, Civil Practice and Remedies Code.

History of CCP art. 38.073: Acts 2001, 77th Leg., ch. 778, §2, eff. June 14, 2001.

ART. 38.08. DEFENDANT MAY TESTIFY

Any defendant in a criminal action shall be permitted to testify in his own behalf therein, but the failure of any defendant to so testify shall not be taken as a circumstance against him, nor shall the same be alluded to or commented on by counsel in the cause.

History of CCP art. 38.08: Acts 1965, 59th Leg., vol. 2, ch. 722.

ANNOTATIONS

Archie v. State, 221 S.W.3d 695, 700 (Tex.Crim.App. 2007). "In determining whether improper jury argument [about a defendant's lack of testimony] warrants a mistrial, [three factors are used]: 1) severity of the misconduct (the magnitude of the prejudicial effect of the prosecutor's remarks); 2) measures adopted to cure the misconduct (the efficacy of any cautionary instruction by the judge); and 3) the certainty of conviction absent the misconduct (the strength of the evidence supporting the conviction). [¶] [If] this argument occurred at punishment, we analyze the third factor with regard to the certainty of the punishment assessed."

Moore v. State, 849 S.W.2d 350, 352 (Tex.Crim.App. 1993). "Argument will constitute a comment upon the defendant's failure to testify if 'the language used [is] manifestly intended or [is] of such character that the jury would naturally and necessarily take it to be a comment on the accused's failure to testify.' [¶] [T]he argument is improper if it directs the jury's attention to an absence of testimony only the defendant could supply. When there is no testimony suggesting the defendant's lack of remorse, a comment upon the lack of remorse would naturally and necessarily be one upon the defendant's failure to testify because only a defendant can testify as to his own remorse. [¶] However, when there is evidence in the record indicating a lack of remorse, a comment upon the defendant's lack of remorse does not naturally and necessarily lead the jury to understand it to be a comment upon the defendant's failure to testify. [T]he comment need not be specifically connected to the evidence indicating lack of remorse so long as the jury could reasonably construe the comment to refer to such evidence." *See also Villareal v. State*, 79 S.W.3d 806, 813-14 (Tex.App.—Corpus Christi 2002, pet. ref'd).

ART. 38.09. REPEALED

Repealed by the Texas Court of Criminal Appeals' adoption of the Texas Rules of Criminal Evidence on Dec. 18, 1985, eff. Sept. 1, 1986. 701 S.W.2d xxix, lxvi-lxvii.

ART. 38.10. EXCEPTIONS TO THE SPOUSAL ADVERSE TESTIMONY PRIVILEGE

The privilege of a person's spouse not to be called as a witness for the state does not apply in any proceeding in which the person is charged with:

(1) a crime committed against the person's spouse, a minor child, or a member of the household of either spouse; or

(2) an offense under Section 25.01, Penal Code (Bigamy).

History of CCP art. 38.10: Acts 1995, 74th Leg., ch. 67, §2, eff. Sept. 1, 1995. Amended by Acts 2005, 79th Leg., ch. 268, §4.01, eff. Sept. 1, 2005.

See also TRE 504.

ANNOTATIONS

Huddleston v. State, 997 S.W.2d 319, 321 (Tex. App.—Houston [1st Dist.] 1999, no pet.). "Article 38.10 makes it clear that the exception to the [spousal] privilege applies when a crime is committed against *any* minor child even if the defendant or spouse is not the parent of the child."

ART. 38.101. COMMUNICATIONS BY DRUG ABUSERS

A communication to any person involved in the treatment or examination of drug abusers by a person being treated voluntarily or being examined for admission to voluntary treatment for drug abuse is not admissible. However, information derived from the treatment or examination of drug abusers may be used for statistical and research purposes if the names of the patients are not revealed.

History of CCP art. 38.101: Acts 1971, 62nd Leg., ch. 983, §2, eff. June 15, 1971.

See also TRE 510.

ANNOTATIONS

Lovorn v. State, 536 S.W.2d 356, 356 n.1 (Tex.Crim. App.1976). "The witness ... stated he knew appellant had a drug problem and he was able to get appellant into a federal drug program in Arizona. Thus, statements made by appellant to [witness] might have been inadmissible under Article 38.101.... However, failure to object on this basis waived the privilege."

ARTS. 38.11, 38.111. REPEALED

Repealed by the Texas Court of Criminal Appeals' adoption of the Texas Rules of Criminal Evidence on Dec. 18, 1985, eff. Sept. 1, 1986. 701 S.W.2d xxix, lxvi-lxvii.

ART. 38.12. RELIGIOUS OPINION

No person is incompetent to testify on account of his religious opinion or for the want of any religious belief.

History of CCP art. 38.12: Acts 1965, 59th Leg., vol. 2, ch. 722.

ART. 38.13. REPEALED

Repealed by the Texas Court of Criminal Appeals' adoption of the Texas Rules of Criminal Evidence on Dec. 18, 1985, eff. Sept. 1, 1986. 701 S.W.2d xxix, lxvi-lxvii.

ART. 38.14. TESTIMONY OF ACCOMPLICE

A conviction cannot be had upon the testimony of an accomplice unless corroborated by other evidence tending to connect the defendant with the offense committed; and the corroboration is not sufficient if it merely shows the commission of the offense.

History of CCP art. 38.14: Acts 1965, 59th Leg., vol. 2, ch. 722.
See also Pen. Code §§15.03(b), 43.06(b).

ANNOTATIONS

Generally

Cocke v. State, 201 S.W.3d 744, 747-48 (Tex.Crim. App.2006). "A witness may be an accomplice either as a matter of law or as a matter of fact; the evidence in a case determines what jury instruction, if any, needs to be given. Unless the evidence clearly shows that the witness is an accomplice as a matter of law, e.g., the witness has been, or could have been, indicted for the same offense, a question about whether a particular witness is an accomplice is properly left to the jury with an instruction defining the term 'accomplice.' If a witness is an accomplice as a matter of law, the trial court is required to provide an accomplice-witness instruction to the jury. If, however, the parties present conflicting or unclear evidence as to whether a witness is an accomplice, the jury must first determine whether the witness is an accomplice as a matter of fact. The trial court is not required to give the jury an accomplice-witness instruction when the evidence is clear that the witness is neither an accomplice as a matter of law nor as a matter of fact."

Accomplice Status

Cocke v. State, 201 S.W.3d 744, 748 (Tex.Crim.App. 2006). "[P]roof that a witness purchased stolen property will not transform his testimony into that of an accomplice when there is no evidence of facts that would put the witness on notice that the property was stolen. Payment of below-market price for stolen items, by itself, is also insufficient to make the purchaser an accomplice as a matter of law."

Rodriguez v. State, 104 S.W.3d 87, 88 (Tex.Crim. App.2003). "[C]an a minor be an accomplice to a defendant's delivery of cocaine to her? No. *At 91-92:* [Minor] is not a party to the delivery offense that appellant committed even though appellant could not have committed this offense without [minor's] participation. [T]here is an exception to the law of criminal responsibility 'where the crime is so defined that participation by another is inevitably incident to its commission.' *Delivery* is such an offense."

Medina v. State, 7 S.W.3d 633, 641-42 (Tex.Crim. App.1999). "The question is whether gang membership, combined with presence at and/or concealment of a crime often associated with gang activity, is sufficient evidence to support a finding of accomplice status. ... While the issue is close in this case, we hold that the following combined evidence was sufficient to permit a rational jury to infer that [accomplice witness] was a party to the crime, and hence, raises a fact issue to [witness's] accomplice status: (1) [witness's] presence in the car with appellant when the crime occurred, (2) evidence that the crime was a gang-motivated crime, (3) [witness's] membership in the same gang as appellant, and (4) [witness's] efforts to cover up the crime."

McFarland v. State, 928 S.W.2d 482, 514 (Tex. Crim.App.1996), *overruled on other grounds*, *Mosley v. State*, 983 S.W.2d 249 (Tex.Crim.App.1998). "An accomplice witness is one who participates with a defendant before, during, or after the commission of a crime. The participation must involve some form of an affirmative act committed by the witness to promote the commission of that offense. In order to be an accomplice as a matter of law, the witness must be susceptible to prosecution for the offense with which the accused is charged. [¶] A witness is not an accomplice witness merely because he may have known of the offense and did not disclose it or even concealed it. Furthermore, complicity with an accused in the commission of another offense does not make that witness an accomplice in the offense for which the accused is on trial if there is no showing of the witness' complicity in that particular offense." *See also* **Paredes v. State**, 129 S.W.3d 530, 536 (Tex.Crim.App.2004).

Badillo v. State, 963 S.W.2d 854, 857 (Tex. App.—San Antonio 1998, pet. ref'd). "If a witness has been indicted for the crime, he or she is an accomplice as a matter of law."

Tran v. State, 870 S.W.2d 654, 657 (Tex.App.— Houston [1st Dist.] 1994, pet. ref'd). "Concealing or failing to disclose the commission of an offense will not make a witness an accomplice, nor will mere presence at the scene of a crime. ... Flight may also be considered in determining whether the evidence raises an issue on whether a witness is an accomplice."

Corroboration

Castillo v. State, 221 S.W.3d 689, 691 (Tex.Crim. App.2007). "Under this rule, the reviewing court eliminates all of the accomplice testimony from consideration and then examines the remaining portions of the record to see if there is any evidence that tends to connect the accused with the commission of the crime. The corroborating evidence need not be sufficient by itself to establish guilt; there simply needs to be other evidence tending to connect the defendant to the offense. We have noted that unlike extra-judicial confessions, testimony of an accomplice need be corroborated only as to facts tending to connect the defendant with the offense committed and not as to the corpus delicti itself. And [t]he non-accomplice evidence does not have to directly link appellant to the crime, nor does it alone have to establish his guilt beyond a reasonable doubt. There must simply be *some* non-accomplice evidence which *tends* to connect appellant to the commission of the offense alleged in the indictment." (Internal quotes omitted.)

Vasquez v. State, 56 S.W.3d 46, 48 (Tex.Crim.App. 2001). "The Court of Appeals erred to expand the scope of Art. 38.14 and hold that it requires corroboration of accomplice witness testimony regarding a deadly weapon finding. The statute is not so broad. It requires corroboration for a conviction only."

Dowthitt v. State, 931 S.W.2d 244, 249 (Tex.Crim. App.1996). "Because [appellant's son] was clearly an accomplice as a matter of law, his testimony must be corroborated by other evidence tending to connect appellant to the offense. ... While the accused's mere presence in the company of the accomplice before, during, and after the commission of the offense is insufficient by itself to corroborate accomplice testimony, evidence of such presence, coupled with other suspicious circumstances, may tend to connect the accused to the offense. Even apparently insignificant incriminating circumstances may sometimes afford satisfactory evidence of corroboration." *See also McAfee v. State*, 204 S.W.3d 868, 871 (Tex.App.—Corpus Christi 2006, pet. ref'd); *Rios v. State*, 982 S.W.2d 558, 561 (Tex. App.—San Antonio 1998, pet. ref'd).

Bingham v. State, 913 S.W.2d 208, 210 (Tex.Crim. App.1995). "[I]n the context of Article 38.14, the 'testimony' that must be corroborated is the legally understood kind…: 'Evidence given by a competent witness under oath or affirmation; as distinguished from evidence derived from writings, and other sources. Testimony is a particular kind of evidence that comes to tribunal through live witnesses speaking under oath or affirmation in presence of tribunal, judicial, or quasi-judicial.' [¶] Clearly, in context, the 'other evidence' referred to in Article 38.14 is 'evidence' adduced 'in presence of tribunal.' [W]e construe the 'testimony' contemplated by Article 38.14 to be of the narrower, evidentiary kind, the kind adduced in open court by live witnesses under oath."

Badillo v. State, 963 S.W.2d 854, 857 (Tex. App.—San Antonio 1998, pet. ref'd). "One accomplice witness's testimony may not corroborate the testimony of another accomplice witness."

Juvenile Exception

Taylor v. State, 10 S.W.3d 673, 676 (Tex.Crim.App. 2000). The "abolition of the juvenile exception to the accomplice witness rule, announced in *Blake v. State*, applies retroactively to cases currently pending on direct review or not yet final."

Blake v. State, 971 S.W.2d 451, 461 (Tex.Crim.App. 1998). "The Court-created unilateral juvenile exception to the accomplice witness rule is abolished. The testimony of juvenile participants potentially subject to state sanctioned punishment falls within the milieu of the accomplice witness rule. We emphasize that the determination of whether a particular juvenile is an accomplice for purposes of the accomplice witness rule should be made in the same manner as the determination of whether a particular adult is an accomplice for purposes of the rule. Juveniles against whom criminal proceedings or juvenile adjudications have been instituted for the same offense as the defendant or a lesser included offense are accomplices as a matter of law. If no proceedings have been instituted, the juvenile is an accomplice as a matter of fact if the jury finds the record contains sufficient evidence linking the juvenile

to the criminal offense as a blameworthy participant. Each case must be considered on its own facts."

ART. 38.141. TESTIMONY OF UNDERCOVER PEACE OFFICER OR SPECIAL INVESTIGATOR

(a) A defendant may not be convicted of an offense under Chapter 481, Health and Safety Code, on the testimony of a person who is not a licensed peace officer or a special investigator but who is acting covertly on behalf of a law enforcement agency or under the color of law enforcement unless the testimony is corroborated by other evidence tending to connect the defendant with the offense committed.

(b) Corroboration is not sufficient for the purposes of this article if the corroboration only shows the commission of the offense.

(c) In this article, "peace officer" means a person listed in Article 2.12, and "special investigator" means a person listed in Article 2.122.

History of CCP art. 38.141: Acts 2001, 77th Leg., ch. 1102, §1, eff. Sept. 1, 2001.

ANNOTATIONS

Malone v. State, 253 S.W.3d 253, ___ (Tex.Crim. App.2008). "[W]e hold that the standard for evaluating sufficiency of the evidence for corroboration under the accomplice-witness rule applies when evaluating sufficiency of the evidence for corroboration under the covert-agent rule. Accordingly, when weighing the sufficiency of corroborating evidence under Article 38.141(a), a reviewing court must exclude the testimony of the covert agent from consideration and examine the remaining evidence (i.e., non-covert agent evidence) to determine whether there is evidence that tends to connect the defendant to the commission of the offense."

Jefferson v. State, 99 S.W.3d 790, 793 (Tex.App.— Eastland 2003, pet. ref'd). "The [surreptitious] recording [of the drug buy] is also 'other evidence tending to connect' appellant with the offense which was committed."

ART. 38.15. TWO WITNESSES IN TREASON

No person can be convicted of treason except upon the testimony of at least two witnesses to the same overt act, or upon his own confession in open court.

History of CCP art. 38.15: Acts 1965, 59th Leg., vol. 2, ch. 722.

ART. 38.16. EVIDENCE IN TREASON

Evidence shall not be admitted in a prosecution for treason as to an overt act not expressly charged in the indictment; nor shall any person be convicted under an indictment for treason unless one or more overt acts are expressly charged therein.

History of CCP art. 38.16: Acts 1965, 59th Leg., vol. 2, ch. 722.

ART. 38.17. TWO WITNESSES REQUIRED

In all cases where, by law, two witnesses, or one with corroborating circumstances, are required to authorize a conviction, if the requirement be not fulfilled, the court shall instruct the jury to render a verdict of acquittal, and they are bound by the instruction.

History of CCP art. 38.17: Acts 1965, 59th Leg., vol. 2, ch. 722.

ANNOTATIONS

Ex parte Reynolds, 588 S.W.2d 900, 902 (Tex.Crim. App.1979). "[W]hen the evidence is insufficient to corroborate an accomplice witness, the jury cannot properly return any verdict except an acquittal."

ART. 38.18. PERJURY & AGGRAVATED PERJURY

(a) No person may be convicted of perjury or aggravated perjury if proof that his statement is false rests solely upon the testimony of one witness other than the defendant.

(b) Paragraph (a) of this article does not apply to prosecutions for perjury or aggravated perjury involving inconsistent statements.

History of CCP art. 38.18: Acts 1965, 59th Leg., vol. 2, ch. 722. Amended by Acts 1973, 63rd Leg., ch. 399, §2(A), eff. Jan. 1, 1974.

See also Pen. Code §§37.02, 37.03.

ART. 38.19. INTENT TO DEFRAUD IN FORGERY

In trials of forgery, it need not be proved that the defendant committed the act with intent to defraud any particular person. It shall be sufficient to prove that the forgery was, in its nature, calculated to injure or defraud any of the sovereignties, bodies corporate or politic, officers or persons, named in the definition of forgery in the Penal Code.

History of CCP art. 38.19: Acts 1965, 59th Leg., vol. 2, ch. 722.

ART. 38.20. REPEALED

Repealed by the Texas Court of Criminal Appeals' adoption of the Texas Rules of Criminal Evidence on Dec. 18, 1985, eff. Sept. 1, 1986. 701 S.W.2d xxix, lxvi-lxvii.

ART. 38.21. STATEMENT

A statement of an accused may be used in evidence against him if it appears that the same was freely and voluntarily made without compulsion or persuasion, under the rules hereafter prescribed.

History of CCP art. 38.21: Acts 1965, 59th Leg., vol. 2, ch. 722. Amended by Acts 1977, 65th Leg., ch. 348, §1, eff. Aug. 29, 1977.

ANNOTATIONS

Delao v. State, 235 S.W.3d 235, 236 (Tex.Crim.App. 2007). "Appellant asks us to determine whether the voluntariness of a confession given by a mentally retarded and mentally ill person can be assessed under the same standard as that used for a person of normal mentality. We hold that the totality of the circumstances standard of review applied by the court of appeals is appropriate for persons of all mentalities and that the court of appeals properly evaluated the voluntariness of Appellant's confession."

Henderson v. State, 962 S.W.2d 544, 564 (Tex. Crim.App.1997). "For a promise to render a confession invalid under Article 38.21, it must be (1) positive, (2) made or sanctioned by someone in authority, and (3) of such an influential nature that it would cause a defendant to speak untruthfully." *See also Martinez v. State*, 127 S.W.3d 792, 794 (Tex.Crim.App.2004).

Creager v. State, 952 S.W.2d 852, 856 (Tex.Crim. App.1997). "[S]tatements must not have been 'obtained by the influence of hope or fear, applied by a third person to the prisoner's mind.' The ultimate question is whether the suspect's will was overborne. [¶] Trickery or deception does not make a statement involuntary unless the method was calculated to produce an untruthful confession or was offensive to due process."

Samuel v. State, 688 S.W.2d 492, 495-96 (Tex.Crim. App.1985). "[T]he proper objection [to a violation of this statute] would be that at the time the question was asked, that the appellant was under arrest and that such a question is in violation of the appellant's rights against self-incrimination and of the confession statute."

ART. 38.22. WHEN STATEMENTS MAY BE USED

Sec. 1. In this article, a written statement of an accused means a statement signed by the accused or a statement made by the accused in his own handwriting or, if the accused is unable to write, a statement bearing his mark, when the mark has been witnessed by a person other than a peace officer.

Sec. 2. No written statement made by an accused as a result of custodial interrogation is admissible as evidence against him in any criminal proceeding unless it is shown on the face of the statement that:

(a) the accused, prior to making the statement, either received from a magistrate the warning provided in Article 15.17 of this code or received from the person to whom the statement is made a warning that:

(1) he has the right to remain silent and not make any statement at all and that any statement he makes may be used against him at his trial;

(2) any statement he makes may be used as evidence against him in court;

(3) he has the right to have a lawyer present to advise him prior to and during any questioning;

(4) if he is unable to employ a lawyer, he has the right to have a lawyer appointed to advise him prior to and during any questioning; and

(5) he has the right to terminate the interview at any time; and

(b) the accused, prior to and during the making of the statement, knowingly, intelligently, and voluntarily waived the rights set out in the warning prescribed by Subsection (a) of this section.

Sec. 3. (a) No oral or sign language statement of an accused made as a result of custodial interrogation shall be admissible against the accused in a criminal proceeding unless:

(1) an electronic recording, which may include motion picture, video tape, or other visual recording, is made of the statement;

(2) prior to the statement but during the recording the accused is given the warning in Subsection (a) of Section 2 above and the accused knowingly, intelligently, and voluntarily waives any rights set out in the warning;

(3) the recording device was capable of making an accurate recording, the operator was competent, and the recording is accurate and has not been altered;

(4) all voices on the recording are identified; and

(5) not later than the 20th day before the date of the proceeding, the attorney representing the defendant is provided with a true, complete, and accurate copy of all recordings of the defendant made under this article.

(b) Every electronic recording of any statement made by an accused during a custodial interrogation must be preserved until such time as the defendant's conviction for any offense relating thereto is final, all direct appeals therefrom are exhausted, or the prosecution of such offenses is barred by law.

(c) Subsection (a) of this section shall not apply to any statement which contains assertions of facts or circumstances that are found to be true and which conduce to establish the guilt of the accused, such as the finding of secreted or stolen property or the instrument with which he states the offense was committed.

(d) If the accused is a deaf person, the accused's statement under Section 2 or Section 3(a) of this article is not admissible against the accused unless the warning in Section 2 of this article is interpreted to the deaf person by an interpreter who is qualified and sworn as provided in Article 38.31 of this code.

(e) The courts of this state shall strictly construe Subsection (a) of this section and may not interpret Subsection (a) as making admissible a statement unless all requirements of the subsection have been satisfied by the state, except that:

(1) only voices that are material are identified; and

(2) the accused was given the warning in Subsection (a) of Section 2 above or its fully effective equivalent.

Sec. 4. When any statement, the admissibility of which is covered by this article, is sought to be used in connection with an official proceeding, any person who swears falsely to facts and circumstances which, if true, would render the statement admissible under this article is presumed to have acted with intent to deceive and with knowledge of the statement's meaning for the purpose of prosecution for aggravated perjury under Section 37.03 of the Penal Code. No person prosecuted under this subsection shall be eligible for probation.

Sec. 5. Nothing in this article precludes the admission of a statement made by the accused in open court at his trial, before a grand jury, or at an examining trial in compliance with Articles 16.03 and 16.04 of this code, or of a statement that is the res gestae of the arrest or of the offense, or of a statement that does not stem from custodial interrogation, or of a voluntary statement, whether or not the result of custodial interrogation, that has a bearing upon the credibility of the accused as a witness, or of any other statement that may be admissible under law.

Sec. 6. In all cases where a question is raised as to the voluntariness of a statement of an accused, the court must make an independent finding in the absence of the jury as to whether the statement was made under voluntary conditions. If the statement has been found to have been voluntarily made and held admissible as a matter of law and fact by the court in a hearing in the absence of the jury, the court must enter an order stating its conclusion as to whether or not the statement was voluntarily made, along with the specific finding of facts upon which the conclusion was based, which order shall be filed among the papers of the cause. Such order shall not be exhibited to the jury nor the finding thereof made known to the jury in any manner. Upon the finding by the judge as a matter of law and fact that the statement was voluntarily made, evidence pertaining to such matter may be submitted to the jury and it shall be instructed that unless the jury believes beyond a reasonable doubt that the statement was voluntarily made, the jury shall not consider such statement for any purpose nor any evidence obtained as a result thereof. In any case where a motion to suppress the statement has been filed and evidence has been submitted to the court on this issue, the court within its discretion may reconsider such evidence in his finding that the statement was voluntarily made and the same evidence submitted to the court at the hearing on the motion to suppress shall be made a part of the record the same as if it were being presented at the time of trial. However, the state or the defendant shall be entitled to present any new evidence on the issue of the voluntariness of the statement prior to the court's final ruling and order stating its findings.

Sec. 7. When the issue is raised by the evidence, the trial judge shall appropriately instruct the jury, generally, on the law pertaining to such statement.

Sec. 8. Notwithstanding any other provision of this article, a written, oral, or sign language statement of an accused made as a result of a custodial interrogation is admissible against the accused in a criminal proceeding in this state if:

(1) the statement was obtained in another state and was obtained in compliance with the laws of that state or this state; or

(2) the statement was obtained by a federal law enforcement officer in this state or another state and was obtained in compliance with the laws of the United States.

History of CCP art. 38.22: Acts 1965, 59th Leg., vol. 2, ch. 722. Amended by Acts 1967, 60th Leg., ch. 659, §23, eff. Aug. 28, 1967; Acts 1977, 65th Leg., ch. 348, §2, eff. Aug. 29, 1977; Acts 1979, 66th Leg., ch. 186, §§4, 5, eff. May 15, 1979; Acts 1981, 67th Leg., ch. 271, §1, eff. Sept. 1, 1981; Acts 1989, 71st Leg., ch. 777, §§1, 2, eff. Sept. 1, 1989; Acts 2001, 77th Leg., ch. 990, §1, eff. Sept. 1, 2001.

See also U.S. Const. 6th amend.

ANNOTATIONS

Generally

Wilkerson v. State, 173 S.W.3d 521, 523-24 (Tex. Crim.App.2005). "We hold that only when a CPS investigator (or other non-law enforcement state agent) is acting in tandem with police to investigate and gather evidence for a criminal prosecution are [CCP art. 38.22 and *Miranda*] warnings required. Here there was no evidence that the CPS worker was acting in tandem with police officers when she interviewed appellant. Thus, the trial court did not abuse its discretion in admitting appellant's statements."

Murphy v. State, 112 S.W.3d 592, 601 (Tex.Crim. App.2003). "A trial court satisfies the requirements of Article 38.22 when it dictates its findings and conclusions to the court reporter, and they are transcribed and made a part of the statement of facts, filed with the district clerk and made a part of the appellate record."

Dowthitt v. State, 931 S.W.2d 244, 255 (Tex.Crim. App.1996). There are "at least four general situations which may constitute custody: (1) when the suspect is physically deprived of his freedom of action in any significant way, (2) when a law enforcement officer tells the suspect that he cannot leave, (3) when law enforcement officers create a situation that would lead a reasonable person to believe that his freedom of movement has been significantly restricted, and (4) when there is probable cause to arrest and law enforcement officers do not tell the suspect that he is free to leave." *See also* **Rodgers v. State**, 111 S.W.3d 236, 241 (Tex. App.—Texarkana 2003, no pet.); **State v. Lacy**, 80 S.W.3d 207, 210 (Tex.App.—Austin 2002, no pet.).

Zavala v. State, 956 S.W.2d 715, 724 (Tex.App.— Corpus Christi 1997, no pet.). "If circumstances show that the person brought to a police station is acting only upon the request or urging of police, and there are no threats, express or implied, that he will be taken forcibly, the accompaniment is voluntary and such person is not then in custody."

Art. 38.22, §2

Herrera v. State, 241 S.W.3d 520, 526 (Tex.Crim. App.2007). "The warnings provided in §2(a) are virtually identical to the *Miranda* warnings, with one exception—the warning that an accused 'has the right to terminate the interview at any time' as set out in §2(a)(5) is not required by *Miranda*. As with the *Miranda* warnings, the warnings in §2(a) of Article 38.22 are required only when there is custodial interrogation. Our construction of 'custody' for purposes of Article 38.22 is consistent with the meaning of 'custody' for purposes of *Miranda*. *At 532:* Because we refuse to equate incarceration with 'custody' for purposes of *Miranda* when an inmate is questioned by a state agent about an offense unrelated to the inmate's incarceration, we turn to our traditional 'custody' analytical framework. We evaluate 'custody' 'on an ad hoc basis, after considering all of the (objective) circumstances' and apply the 'reasonable person' standard. 'Two discrete inquiries are essential to the determination [of 'custody']: first, what were the circumstances surrounding the interrogation; and second, given those circumstances, would a reasonable person have felt he or she was not at liberty to terminate the interrogation and leave.' [¶] [A]n evaluation of the circumstances surrounding an interrogation in this context should include an examination of [these] factors: the language used to summon the inmate; the physical surroundings of the interrogation; the extent to which the inmate is confronted with evidence of his or her guilt; the additional pressure exerted to detain the inmate or the change in the surroundings of the inmate which results in an added imposition on the inmate's freedom of movement; and the inmate's freedom to leave the scene and the purpose, place, and length of the questioning."

Nonn v. State, 117 S.W.3d 874, 882-83 (Tex.Crim. App.2003). "Although appellant's Chicago statement did not conform to the requirements of Article 38.22, it did meet the criteria of *Miranda*, and appellant produced no evidence that the statement was not voluntary. Although appellant was not aware that the Chicago statement could not be used against him, there is no indication that the making of that statement influenced appellant's decision to make further statements to Texas law enforcement authorities a month later. The Texas statements, which *did* conform to the requirements of Article 38.22, bear no indicia of having been coerced. Therefore, the Texas statements would, in all

likelihood, have been admissible at trial even if the Chicago statement had been ruled inadmissible. [¶] Because the Texas statements contained much of the same information as the Chicago statement, the erroneous admission of the Chicago statement may not have had any significantly adverse effect on the jury's verdict."

Cockrell v. State, 933 S.W.2d 73, 90 (Tex.Crim.App. 1996). Appellant claims "the trial court erred in charging the jury that 'so long as the language of the warning used was the substantial equivalent of the language [of the applicable statute] and conveyed the same meaning' the warnings on the face of his confession need not be in the literal language of Article 38.22, §2(a). Appellant argues the court's instruction was a comment on the weight of the evidence. The State claims the instruction was a proper statement of law relating to an issue before the jury. [¶] Once the question of facial compliance with Article 38.22, §2(a), was placed before the jury, the instruction complained of was a necessary clarification of the law, and not a comment on the weight of the evidence."

Dinkins v. State, 894 S.W.2d 330, 348 (Tex.Crim. App.1995). "A confession resulting from a person's statement that it can be used 'for or against' the defendant is inadmissible as a matter of law because it constitutes an improper inducement and because it does not comply with the statutory warnings in art. 38.22. However, where there is a factual discrepancy as to whether such a representation was made, the trial judge is responsible for determining whether the confession is admissible."

Garcia v. State, 919 S.W.2d 370, 379 (Tex.Crim. App.1994). "[A]ppellant, by initialing each warning reflected on the written statement form, did not affirmatively *waive* the rights contained within the warnings. At best, appellant's initials only indicated he read and understood those warnings. *At 387:* The clearly preferable practice [for complying with Article 38.22] is for a written statement, to meet unambiguously the requirements of §2(b), to contain the following language, near or adjacent to the signature of the individual giving the statement: 'I knowingly, voluntarily and intelligently waived the rights described above before and during the making of this statement.'"

Franks v. State, 90 S.W.3d 771, 785 (Tex.App.— Fort Worth 2002, no pet.). "An inquiry into the waiver of *Miranda* rights has two distinct dimensions. First, the waiver must be voluntary in the sense that it was the product of free and deliberate choice rather than intimidation, coercion, or deception. Second, the waiver must be made with a full awareness both of the nature of the right being abandoned and the consequences of the decision to abandon it."

Ramos v. State, 961 S.W.2d 637, 638-39 (Tex. App.—San Antonio 1998, no pet.). "Although Ramos was 17 at the time of the arrest, he was under 17 when the first murder was committed, and police accordingly arrested him on a juvenile warrant. He claims that, because he was arrested as a juvenile, he should have been given the admonishments required for juveniles by the [Fam.] Code. ... Ramos was admonished under the [CCP], and he made and signed his statement [about a homicide committed when Ramos was 18] in the presence of a Bexar County detective. [¶] We believe the admonishments under the [CCP] were appropriate. [I]n order for the Family Code to be applicable, the statement must concern the acts that were committed when the defendant was a juvenile."

Mestiza v. State, 923 S.W.2d 720, 724 (Tex.App.—Corpus Christi 1996, no pet.). Appellant "argues that the face of the confession fails to reflect the warnings required by [Art. 38.22]. Appellant admits that the record contains a Spanish document bearing his signature which shows he was warned of his rights. Appellant asserts, however, that there is no English translation of this document and, therefore, no evidence that he was warned as required. ... Appellant's signed statement contains, in English, all of the required warnings. Furthermore, the officer who obtained appellant's statement testified that the warnings were translated for appellant before the statement was obtained. Appellant's initials appear by each warning on the face of the English language confession. Thus, the record plainly contains the matter which appellant asserts is missing."

Art. 38.22, §3

Woods v. State, 152 S.W.3d 105, 116-17 (Tex.Crim. App.2004). "Strict compliance with all portions of §3(a) is required. [¶] Under the exception set out in §3(c), oral statements asserting facts or circumstances establishing the guilt of the accused are admissible if, at the time they were made, they contained assertions unknown by law enforcement but later corroborated. Such oral statements need only circumstantially demonstrate the defendant's guilt. Furthermore, if such an oral statement contains even a single assertion of fact found to be true and conducive to establishing the defendant's guilt, then the statement is admissible in its entirety." *See also Dansby v. State*, 931 S.W.2d 297, 298-99 (Tex.Crim.App.1996).

Sells v. State, 121 S.W.3d 748, 764 (Tex.Crim.App. 2003). "We conclude that §3(a)(5) applies to pretrial hearings."

Davidson v. State, 25 S.W.3d 183, 186 (Tex.Crim. App.2000). "Art. 38.22, §3(a)(1) makes no distinction between in-state and out-of-state oral statements, made as a result of custodial interrogation, which are not in compliance with its dictates. Thus, we are similarly required to advance the Legislature's purpose to declare inadmissible all such statements unless an electronic recording is made of them. Therefore, we hold that the Court of Appeals erred in concluding that the testimony regarding oral statements made by the appellant as a result of custodial interrogation was admissible [under the Full Faith & Credit Clause of U.S. Const. art. 4, §1] against appellant."

Rocha v. State, 16 S.W.3d 1, 12 (Tex.Crim.App. 2000). "[T]he record shows that no express waiver of his rights appears on the recording. However, the law does not require that the recording reflect an express waiver of the rights."

Lane v. State, 933 S.W.2d 504, 516 (Tex.Crim.App. 1996). "So long as defense counsel is informed of the existence of the [surreptitious] recording and permitted reasonable access to a copy, the purpose of §3(a)(5) has been met. Requiring actual delivery would have the adverse consequence of excluding evidence that is both relevant and legally obtained where the defense has suffered no harm but has had the opportunity to evaluate and test the evidence. If the legislature had intended to require actual delivery, they could have used the word 'served,' 'given,' or 'delivered' instead of 'provide.' [T]he word 'provide' in §3(a)(5) means to 'make available or furnish.'"

Dowthitt v. State, 931 S.W.2d 244, 258 (Tex.Crim. App.1996). "[T]he language in Article 38.22 §2(a), requiring warnings to be given by the person 'to whom the statement is made,' does not apply to oral statements but applies only to written statements. [¶] Oral statements are governed by §3 of the Article, and §3 does not contain the language in question. [Section] 3 contains its own unique safeguards for an accused.

Most significantly, the oral statement must be electronically recorded and the warnings must be contained in the recording." *See also* ***Cloer v. State***, 88 S.W.3d 285, 289 (Tex.App.—San Antonio 2002, no pet.).

Tigner v. State, 928 S.W.2d 540, 543 (Tex.Crim.App. 1996). "In subsection (5), the statute dictates that the State provide defense counsel with a 'copy of all recordings.' By 'recording,' it is plain that the legislature meant 'electronic recording.' [¶] 'What is provided to defense counsel *must be recordings constituting copies*—presumably, accurate ones—of the recordings covered. [A] transcription of the recording is not sufficient. *Such a transcription, even if accurate, might not fully reflect matters bearing on admissibility and credibility.*' Hence, we hold that a 'transcript' is not a 'copy' for the purpose of Article 38.22 §3(a)(5). *At 546:* We [further] conclude that the term 'proceeding,' as used in Article 38.22 §3(a)(5), encompasses voir dire."

Heiselbetz v. State, 906 S.W.2d 500, 512 (Tex.Crim. App.1995). "As long as the confession is voluntary, law officers are ... permitted to reduce defendants' oral statements into writing; they are even allowed to paraphrase the statements. And as long as the warnings appear on the written statement, it is admissible."

Pina v. State, 38 S.W.3d 730, 734 (Tex.App.— Texarkana 2001, pet. ref'd). Detective "testified to oral statements Pina made in response to questions [detective] posed to him about his written statement, and the fact that Pina made no response or gave no satisfactory answer to questions posed by [detective] about alleged inconsistencies or improbabilities in Pina's written statement. *At 735:* Pina's responses or lack of responses to [detective's] questions were 'statements' as contemplated in Article 38.22, §3(a)(1), whose admissibility required that they be electronically recorded and that copies be timely provided to defense counsel before trial."

Flemming v. State, 949 S.W.2d 876, 878 (Tex. App.—Houston [14th Dist.] 1997, no pet.). "[A]n officer's intentional concealment of a recording device to 'trick' a suspect into making a recorded statement does not render the suspect's oral confession inadmissible. *At 879:* Criminal defendants ... are constitutionally protected only from *compulsory* self-incrimination. Police, therefore, may not exert physical or mental compulsion to obtain a statement. ... While a suspect may knowingly, voluntarily, and intelligently waive a constitutional right, physical or mental compulsion may remove the element of voluntariness from a defendant's decision to incriminate himself. The waiver, therefore, must be voluntary in the sense that it is the product of a free and deliberate choice rather than intimidation, coercion or deception."

Art. 38.22, §6

Osbourn v. State, ___ S.W.3d ___ (Tex.Crim.App. 2008) (No. PD-1687-06; 6-4-08). "We granted review in this case to clarify when a trial court has the duty to instruct the jury on the voluntariness of a defendant's statement in the absence of any request for such instructions. We hold that when the evidence raises an issue of the 'voluntariness' of a defendant's statement under Article 38.22, the trial judge must give a general voluntariness instruction under §§6 and 7 of that article because it is the 'law applicable to the case.' But when the defendant does not request this statutorily mandated instruction, the trial court's failure to include it is reviewed only for 'egregious harm' under *Almanza*."

Vasquez v. State, 225 S.W.3d 541, 545-46 (Tex. Crim.App.2007). "[T]he jury's role under [CCP art.] 38.22 is different from its role under [CCP art.] 38.23. Under article 38.22, §6, even when there is no dispute about the historical facts of the accused's statement, there can still be an issue of the voluntariness of the statement—which may be an issue for the jury. [¶] '[T]he application of the legal standard for voluntariness to agreed facts should be a jury issue, *if* those facts are ones from which a reasonable jury could conclude that the statement at issue was involuntary. Voluntariness is not a strictly factual question, but it similarly is not a mechanical application of historical facts to a purely objective legal standard.' [¶] Under this standard, the defense is still required to introduce evidence at trial from which a reasonable jury could conclude that the statement was not voluntary. Under article 38.22, there is no error in refusing to include a jury instruction where there is no evidence before the jury to raise the issue. Some evidence must have been presented to the jury that the defendant's confession was not given voluntarily. However, when, as in this case, the defense introduces evidence at trial from which a reasonable jury could find that the confession was not voluntarily made, a voluntariness instruction should be given."

Garcia v. State, 15 S.W.3d 533, 536 (Tex.Crim.App. 2000). "The legislature has specifically authorized 'paper hearings' in a limited number of contexts. That the legislature has used language which specifically authorizes such a procedure in one specific setting (e.g., habeas hearings pursuant to [CCP art.] 11.07), but has omitted such language in another (e.g., hearings pursuant to [CCP art.] 38.22), suggests that the legislature did not intend for such a procedure to be used in the latter setting.... The legislature did not use language permitting use of affidavits in [CCP art.] 38.22, and, therefore, we must assume that 'paper hearings' are not approved in that setting."

Garza v. State, 915 S.W.2d 204, 211 (Tex.App.—Corpus Christi 1996, pet. ref'd). "The making and filing of findings concerning the voluntariness of a confession are mandatory, and if findings are not made, an appeal will be abated for the trial court to perform its mandatory duty. However, no findings of fact or conclusions of law are required when a statement does not stem from custodial interrogation. This is because 'voluntariness' is only an issue if the confession was obtained when the speaker was in custody." *See also Urias v. State*, 155 S.W.3d 141, 143 (Tex.Crim.App. 2004).

Art. 38.22, §7

Mendoza v. State, 88 S.W.3d 236, 240 (Tex.Crim. App.2002). "What is 'appropriate' is largely left to the discretion of the trial court, within the mandates of [CCP] arts. 38.22 and 38.23...."

Butler v. State, 872 S.W.2d 227, 236 (Tex.Crim.App. 1994). Article 38.22, §7, "provides that where the issue of voluntariness of a confession is raised by the evidence, the trial judge shall appropriately instruct the jury ... on the law pertaining to such statement. However, before the requested instruction is required, some evidence must be presented to the jury which raises the issue of voluntariness. The trial judge is sole judge of credibility of witnesses in a pretrial hearing and, absent a showing of abuse of discretion, a trial court's finding on the voluntariness of a confession will not be disturbed."

ART. 38.23. EVIDENCE NOT TO BE USED

(a) No evidence obtained by an officer or other person in violation of any provisions of the Constitution or laws of the State of Texas, or of the Constitution or laws of the United States of America, shall be admitted in evidence against the accused on the trial of any criminal case.

In any case where the legal evidence raises an issue hereunder, the jury shall be instructed that if it believes, or has a reasonable doubt, that the evidence was obtained in violation of the provisions of this Article, then and in such event, the jury shall disregard any such evidence so obtained.

(b) It is an exception to the provisions of Subsection (a) of this Article that the evidence was obtained by a law enforcement officer acting in objective good faith reliance upon a warrant issued by a neutral magistrate based on probable cause.

History of CCP art. 38.23: Acts 1965, 59th Leg., vol. 2, ch. 722. Amended by Acts 1987, 70th Leg., ch. 546, §1, eff. Sept. 1, 1987.

ANNOTATIONS

Generally

Pierce v. State, 32 S.W.3d 247, 253 (Tex.Crim.App. 2000). "When a trial court has denied a motion to suppress evidence, the verdict of guilty from a jury that was charged to disregard illegally obtained evidence does not prevent the defendant from appealing the court's ruling. [¶] Even when a jury's verdict of guilty necessarily means that it found that essential evidence was not obtained in violation of the constitutions and laws of the U.S. and of this state, such a finding cannot supplant the trial court's ruling on a motion to suppress evidence."

State v. Callaghan, 222 S.W.3d 610, 615-16 (Tex. App.—Houston [14th Dist.] 2007, pet. ref'd). "Before evidence can be suppressed under Article 38.23, there must be a *causal connection* between a police officer's violation of a law and his collection of evidence. Further, the burden is on the defendant, as the moving party, to produce evidence showing the causal connection. The burden then shifts to the State to either disprove the defendant's evidence or raise an attenuation-of-taint argument to demonstrate that the causal chain asserted by the defendant was broken. Therefore, not only must there be a causal connection between the violation and the collection of evidence, the defendant must also prove that the causal connection exists."

Appellate Review

Johnson v. State, 95 S.W.3d 568, 573 (Tex.App.—Houston [1st Dist.] 2002, pet. ref'd). "[A]n appellate court may not engage in a factual sufficiency review of suppression issues submitted to juries pursuant to article 38.23(b)...."

Jury Instruction

Holmes v. State, 248 S.W.3d 194, 196 (Tex.Crim. App.2008). "A defendant who affirmatively states, 'No objection,' when evidence is offered, waives his right to complain on appeal that the evidence was, as a matter of law, illegally obtained under Article 38.23. But that same defendant may still request and receive a jury instruction under Article 38.23 if the evidence raises a contested factual issue that is material to the lawfulness of obtaining the evidence. These are two distinct issues: one is a legal question of admissibility for the judge and the other is a question of disputed fact for the jury's consideration and resolution."

Madden v. State, 242 S.W.3d 504, 509-11 (Tex. Crim.App.2007). "A defendant's right to the submission of jury instructions under Article 38.23(a) is limited to disputed issues of fact that are material to his claim of a constitutional or statutory violation that would render evidence inadmissible. We have previously explained: 'The terms of the statute are mandatory, and when an issue of fact is raised, a defendant has a statutory right to have the jury charged accordingly. The only question is whether under the facts of a particular case an issue has been raised by the evidence so as to require a jury instruction. Where no issue is raised by the evidence, the trial court acts properly in refusing a request to charge the jury.' There are three requirements that a defendant must meet before he is entitled to the submission of a jury instruction under Article 38.23(a): '(1) The evidence heard by the jury must raise an issue of fact; (2) The evidence on that fact must be affirmatively contested; and (3) That contested factual issue must be material to the lawfulness of the challenged conduct in obtaining the evidence.' There must be a genuine dispute about a material fact. If there is no disputed factual issue, the legality of the conduct is determined by the trial judge alone, as a question of law. And if other facts, not in dispute, are sufficient to support the lawfulness of the challenged conduct, then the disputed fact issue is not submitted to the jury because it is not material to the ultimate admissibility of the evidence. The disputed fact must be an essential one in deciding the lawfulness of the challenged conduct." *See also Mendoza v. State*, 88 S.W.3d 236, 239 (Tex.Crim. App.2002); *Maldonado v. State*, 998 S.W.2d 239, 246 (Tex.Crim.App.1999).

Hanks v. State, 137 S.W.3d 668, 672 (Tex.Crim.App. 2004). "We hold that factual-sufficiency review [by a court of appeals] is appropriate only as to the sufficiency of the state's proof as to elements of the offense. Such a review is not appropriate as to the admissibility of evidence when such a question is submitted to the jury pursuant to Article 38.23(a)."

Middleton v. State, 125 S.W.3d 450, 454 (Tex.Crim. App.2003). "[E]ven if 'probable cause' has acquired a technical legal meaning, that does not necessarily mean that it had to be defined. [T]here was no risk that the jurors would arbitrarily apply their own personal definition, nor was a definition of the term required to assure a fair understanding of the evidence."

Atkinson v. State, 923 S.W.2d 21, 23 (Tex.Crim. App.1996). "Evidence obtained in violation of the law must be excluded from jury consideration in criminal cases on request of the defendant. The judge should withhold such evidence from the jury altogether when it is inadmissible purely as a matter of law. But, when there are disputed issues of fact affecting the legality of its seizure, the question of exclusion may be tried to the jury. In such event, the judge must include in his final charge an instruction that, if the jury 'believes, or has a reasonable doubt, that the evidence was obtained in violation of ... any provisions of the Constitution or laws of the State of Texas, or of the Constitution or laws of the U.S., ... then and in such event, the jury shall disregard any such evidence so obtained.'"

Muniz v. State, 851 S.W.2d 238, 254 (Tex.Crim.App. 1993). "The evidence which raises the issue [of whether the evidence was obtained illegally] may be either strong, weak, contradicted, unimpeached, or unbelievable."

Objective Good Faith

Dunn v. State, 951 S.W.2d 478, 479 (Tex.Crim.App. 1997). "The record establishes that appellant was arrested by officers acting in objective good faith reliance upon a warrant based on probable cause and issued by a neutral magistrate. Appellant argues that [CCP art.] 38.23(b) is inapplicable because a warrant cannot *issue* without the signature of the magistrate as required by [CCP art.] 15.02(3). The record reflects that the magistrate found probable cause to issue the warrant, signed the accompanying warrants, and intended but inadvertently failed to sign appellant's arrest warrant. This appears to be exactly the type of situation intended to be covered by article 38.23(b)." *See also Hunter v. State*, 92 S.W.3d 596, 604 (Tex.App.—Waco 2002, pet. ref'd).

Curry v. State, 808 S.W.2d 481, 482 (Tex.Crim.App. 1991). An affidavit under "*Art. 38.23(b) requires a finding of probable cause*, while [the federal good-faith exception is] more flexible in allowing [an] officer's belief in probable cause [to be] reasonable."

Other Person

Miles v. State, 241 S.W.3d 28, 39 (Tex.Crim.App. 2007). "[A] private person can do what a police officer standing in his shoes can legitimately do, but cannot do what a police officer cannot do…. We conclude that the historical rationale for including unlawful conduct by an 'other person' under the Texas exclusionary statute is best explained and implemented by this rule."

Violation of Laws

Jenschke v. State, 147 S.W.3d 398, 399 (Tex.Crim. App.2004). "The question in this case is whether Article 38.23(a) … permits the admission, against the accused in the trial of a criminal case, of evidence that private persons acquired by conduct that violated a criminal law. We hold that Article 38.23(a) may permit the admission of such evidence when private persons turn over such evidence to an officer, but that the article does not permit it in this case…." *See also McCuller v. State*, 999 S.W.2d 801, 804-05 (Tex.App.— Tyler 1999, pet. ref'd); *State v. Johnson*, 939 S.W.2d 586, 587 (Tex.Crim.App.1996).

Gonzales v. State, 67 S.W.3d 910, 911 (Tex.Crim. App.2002). "[A]ppellant argued that his confession must be suppressed [under Fam. Code §52.02(b)] because the police did not promptly notify his parents that he was in custody. *At 912:* In order for a juvenile's written statement to be suppressed because of a violation of §52.02(b), there must be some exclusionary mechanism. Unlike [Fam. Code] §51.095(a), §52.02(b) is not an independent exclusionary statute. [Fam.] Code §51.17, however, provides that '[CCP ch.] 38, appl[ies] in a judicial proceeding under this title.' Thus, if evidence is to be excluded because of a §52.02(b) violation, it must be excluded through the operation of [CCP art.] 38.23(a). [¶] In light of Article 38.23(a), … before a juvenile's written statement can be excluded, there must be a causal connection between the Family Code violation and the making of the statement."

Rocha v. State, 16 S.W.3d 1, 13 (Tex.Crim.App. 2000). "The Vienna Convention on Consular Relations [art. 36] grants a foreign national who has been arrested, imprisoned or taken into custody a right to contact his consulate and requires the arresting government authorities to inform the individual of this right without delay. *At 19:* Given the language of [CCP art.] 38.23, the purpose and function that treaties provide, and the uniquely federal aspect involved in enforcing international agreements, we hold that treaties do not constitute laws for Article 38.23 purposes." (Internal quotes omitted.) *See also* Vienna Convention on Consular Relations art. 36, p. 665; *Sierra v. State*, 218 S.W.3d 85, 87-88 (Tex.Crim.App.2007).

Chavez v. State, 9 S.W.3d 817, 818 (Tex.Crim.App. 2000). "The issue in this case is whether … Article 38.23(a), requires the exclusion of evidence that [an] undercover police officer obtains outside the geographical boundaries set out in an Interlocal Assistance Agreement…. *At 820:* Any causal relationship between [officer's] alleged breach of the Agreement and his acquisition of the cocaine is too remote for Article 38.23(a) to consider the cocaine to have been 'obtained' by the 'illegality' of [officer's] alleged contractual breach of the Agreement."

Henderson v. State, 962 S.W.2d 544, 557 (Tex. Crim.App.1997). Whether "evidence [that] is the fruit of a revealed privileged communication … must be suppressed under Art. 38.23 depends upon whether the privileged communication leading to that evidence was validly disclosed or compelled pursuant to strong public policy interests requiring the privilege to yield. If the privilege was legitimately required to yield then no law violation exists, and fruits of the privileged communication are not barred from evidence by Art. 38.23."

Baker v. State, 956 S.W.2d 19, 24 (Tex.Crim.App. 1997). "[M]ere violations of the *Miranda* rule are not covered by the state exclusionary rule contained in Article 38.23." *But see Alvarado v. State*, 853 S.W.2d 17, 21 (Tex.Crim.App.1993).

Villareal v. State, 935 S.W.2d 134, 137 (Tex.Crim. App.1996). "We have found no precedent that would impute an expectation of privacy for the purposes of standing to an invited guest who is not an overnight guest. *At 138:* The following … are relevant to the court's determination of whether the accused's subjective expectation was one that society was prepared to recognize as objectively reasonable: (1) whether the accused had a property or possessory interest in the place invaded; (2) whether he was legitimately in the place invaded; (3) whether he had complete dominion or control and the right to exclude others; (4) whether, before the intrusion, he took normal precautions customarily taken by those seeking privacy; (5) whether he put the place to some private use; and (6) whether his claim of privacy is consistent with historical notions of privacy."

State v. Daugherty, 931 S.W.2d 268, 270 (Tex.Crim. App.1996). "[T]he language of Article 38.23 plainly does not accommodate a doctrine of inevitable discovery. The inevitable discovery doctrine *assumes* a causal relationship between the illegality and the evidence. It *assumes* that the evidence was actually 'obtained' illegally. The doctrine then asks whether the evidence would have been 'obtained' eventually in any event by lawful means. [T]he fact that evidence could have been 'obtained' lawfully anyway does not negate the fact that it was in fact 'obtained' illegally. Under Article 38.23 the inquiry regarding the possible legal attainment of the evidence should never be reached. Once the illegality and its causal connection to the evidence have been established, the evidence must be excluded." *See also Henderson v. State*, 82 S.W.3d 750, 753 (Tex.App.— Corpus Christi 2002, pet. ref'd).

Johnson v. State, 871 S.W.2d 744, 750-51 (Tex. Crim.App.1994). "[T]he attenuation doctrine is applicable to Art. 38.23's prohibition against evidence 'obtained' in violation of the law because evidence sufficiently attenuated from the violation of the law is not considered to be 'obtained' therefrom. [T]he attenuation doctrine is not an exception to Art. 38.23, but rather is a method of determining whether evidence was 'obtained' in violation of the law, with 'obtained' being included in the plain language of the statute."

Fuller v. State, 829 S.W.2d 191, 202 (Tex.Crim.App. 1992). "[W]e do not interpret the sweeping language of article 38.23(a) to confer automatic third party standing upon all persons accused of crimes, such that they may complain about the receipt of evidence which was obtained by violation of the rights of others...."

Pitonyak v. State, ___ S.W.3d ___ (Tex.App.— Austin 2008, n.p.h.) (No. 03-07-00131-CR; 3-27-08). "A search warrant may not be procured lawfully by the use of unlawfully obtained information. When a search warrant is issued on the basis of an affidavit containing unlawfully obtained information, the evidence seized under the warrant is admissible only if the warrant 'clearly could have been issued on the basis of the untainted information in the affidavit.' If the tainted information was clearly unnecessary to establish probable cause for the search warrant, then the defendant could not have been harmed by the inclusion of the tainted information in the affidavit. This rule has been held to apply under article 38.23(a) when a search warrant contains information obtained by the unlawful act of a private person."

Davidson v. State, 249 S.W.3d 709, 722 (Tex. App.—Austin 2008, n.p.h.). "[E]vidence obtained by federal agents acting lawfully and in conformity with federal authority is admissible in state criminal proceedings. But appellant is correct when she argues that federal agents may not act as agents of the state police to circumvent the requirements of state law. If military personnel are not acting pursuant to the special powers granted them under federal law to pursue their independent military purpose and are instead acting as agents for the state police, they are subject to the same statutes and constitutional standards as state officers. Where an operation involves actors from various jurisdictions then ... the relationship must be examined to determine whether federal agents are acting so as to circumvent the requirements of state law."

Rodriguez v. State, 106 S.W.3d 224, 230 (Tex. App.—Houston [1st Dist.] 2003, pet. ref'd). "We hold that the use of a drug-dog to sniff for narcotics outside appellant's house was not a 'search,' and therefore there was no need for a previously-issued warrant for the sniff.... Because neither the sniff nor its use to obtain a warrant violated the federal or state constitution, the sniff did not violate Article 38.23...."

Reeves v. State, 969 S.W.2d 471, 486 (Tex.App.— Waco 1998, pet. ref'd). Appellant "complains that the court erred in admitting evidence seized under a Tarrant County warrant, when the transfer of that evidence to Bosque County was not authorized by [CCP art.] 18.10[.] Because no order was issued in Tarrant County, Reeves maintains that the evidence should have been excluded under [CCP art.] 38.23.... *At 487:* The violation of just any law does not invoke the provisions of Article 38.23. Article 38.23(a) may not be invoked for statutory violations unrelated to the purpose of the exclusionary rule. [¶] We hold that the evidence taken from Tarrant County to Bosque County for court proceedings was not 'obtained' in violation of any law within the meaning of Article 38.23."

Vicarious-Consent Doctrine

Alameda v. State, 181 S.W.3d 772, 778 (Tex.App.— Fort Worth 2005), *aff'd*, 235 S.W.3d 218 (Tex.Crim. App.2007). "We agree with the federal and state courts that have adopted the vicarious consent doctrine. We hereby adopt the standard set forth in ***Pollock*** [***v. Pollock***, 154 F.3d 601 (6th Cir. 1998)], and hold that as long as a parent has a good faith, objectively reasonable basis for believing that the taping of telephone conversations is in the best interest of the parent's minor child, the parent may vicariously consent to the recording on behalf of the child."

ART. 38.24. REPEALED

Repealed by the Texas Court of Criminal Appeals' adoption of the Texas Rules of Criminal Evidence on Dec. 18, 1985, eff. Sept. 1, 1986. 701 S.W.2d xxix, lxvi-lxvii.

ART. 38.25. WRITTEN PART OF INSTRUMENT CONTROLS

When an instrument is partly written and partly printed, the written shall control the printed portion when the two are inconsistent.

History of CCP art. 38.25: Acts 1965, 59th Leg., vol. 2, ch. 722.

ART. 38.26. REPEALED

Repealed by the Texas Court of Criminal Appeals' adoption of the Texas Rules of Criminal Evidence on Dec. 18, 1985, eff. Sept. 1, 1986. 701 S.W.2d xxix, lxvi-lxvii.

ART. 38.27. EVIDENCE OF HANDWRITING

It is competent to give evidence of handwriting by comparison, made by experts or by the jury. Proof by comparison only shall not be sufficient to establish the handwriting of a witness who denies his signature under oath.

History of CCP art. 38.27: Acts 1965, 59th Leg., vol. 2, ch. 722.

ANNOTATIONS

Camacho v. State, 765 S.W.2d 431, 434 (Tex.Crim. App.1989). "[I]f a defendant denies either his signature or his handwriting under oath then the State must present other evidence tending to connect the defendant to the authorship of the disputed document."

Moore v. State, 700 S.W.2d 193, 203 (Tex.Crim.App. 1985). CCP art. 38.27 "becomes applicable … only when proof of a signature is done by comparison only. When the State … relies upon the testimony of a witness who observed the signing, then this statute is inapplicable."

ARTS. 38.28, 38.29. REPEALED

Repealed by the Texas Court of Criminal Appeals' adoption of the Texas Rules of Criminal Evidence on Dec. 18, 1985, eff. Sept. 1, 1986. 701 S.W.2d xxix, lxvi-lxvii.

ART. 38.30. INTERPRETER

(a) When a motion for appointment of an interpreter is filed by any party or on motion of the court, in any criminal proceeding, it is determined that a person charged or a witness does not understand and speak the English language, an interpreter must be sworn to interpret for the person charged or the witness. Any person may be subpoenaed, attached or recognized in any criminal action or proceeding, to appear before the proper judge or court to act as interpreter therein, under the same rules and penalties as are provided for witnesses. In the event that the only available interpreter is not considered to possess adequate interpreting skills for the particular situation or the interpreter is not familiar with use of slang, the person charged or witness may be permitted by the court to nominate another person to act as intermediary between the person charged or witness and the appointed interpreter during the proceedings.

(a-1) A qualified telephone interpreter may be sworn to interpret for the person in the trial of a Class C misdemeanor or a proceeding before a magistrate if an interpreter is not available to appear in person before the court or if the only available interpreter is not considered to possess adequate interpreting skills for the particular situation or is unfamiliar with the use of slang. In this subsection, "qualified telephone interpreter" means a telephone service that employs:

(1) licensed court interpreters as defined by Section 57.001, Government Code; or

(2) federally certified court interpreters.

(b) Except as provided by Subsection (c) of this article, interpreters appointed under the terms of this article will receive from the general fund of the county for their services a sum not to exceed $100 a day as follows: interpreters shall be paid not less than $15 nor more than $100 a day at the discretion of the judge presiding, and when travel of the interpreter is involved all the actual expenses of travel, lodging, and meals incurred by the interpreter pertaining to the case the interpreter is appointed to serve shall be paid at the same rate applicable to state employees.

(c) A county commissioners court may set a payment schedule and expend funds for the services of interpreters in excess of the daily amount of not less than $15 or more than $100 established by Subsection (b) of this article.

History of CCP art. 38.30: Acts 1965, 59th Leg., vol. 2, ch. 722. Amended by Acts 1979, 66th Leg., ch. 209, §1, eff. Aug. 27, 1979; Acts 1991, 72nd Leg., ch. 700, §1, eff. June 16, 1991; Acts 2005, 79th Leg., ch. 956, §1, eff. Sept. 1, 2005.

See also Gov't Code §57.002.

ANNOTATIONS

Garcia v. State, 149 S.W.3d 135, 145 (Tex.Crim. App.2004). "[W]hen a trial judge is aware that the defendant has a problem understanding the English language, the defendant's right to have an interpreter translate the trial proceedings into a language which the defendant understands is a ... right. In these circumstances, the judge has an independent duty to implement this right in the absence of a knowing and voluntary waiver by the defendant. The judge may become aware of the defendant's language problem either by being informed of it by one or both parties or by noticing the problem *sua sponte.*" *See also* ***Ridge v. State***, 205 S.W.3d 591, 597 (Tex.App.—Waco 2006, pet. ref'd).

Garcia v. State, 887 S.W.2d 862, 875 (Tex.Crim. App.1994), *overruled on other grounds*, ***Hammock v. State***, 46 S.W.3d 889 (Tex.Crim.App.2001). "We, as an appellate court, can no more determine whether a translation is accurate or which of two translations is more accurate, than we can determine which of two witnesses is telling the truth, or which of the two is more truthful; these are questions for the factfinder. ... Similarly, just as appellant may not preserve error by objecting at trial that a witness is lying, he may not preserve error objecting that a translation is inaccurate; there is simply no reviewable question to preserve. [A] defendant must impeach the inaccurate or incomplete translation to cure it."

Leal v. State, 782 S.W.2d 844, 849 (Tex.Crim.App. 1989). "The admissibility of a tape recording of a conversation in a foreign language [is a] situation ... analogous to one where a non-English speaking witness testifies, and the safeguards of Art. 38.30 apply. In the face of a proper motion or objection an interpreter must be sworn to translate the conversation.... [¶] [T]he trial court erred when it admitted the tape recording into evidence without it being translated from Spanish to English by a sworn interpreter."

Abdygapparova v. State, 243 S.W.3d 191, 201 (Tex.App.—San Antonio 2007, pet. ref'd). There is a two-prong test for providing an interpreter: "(1) the defendant must show an inability to understand English; and (2) the defendant must make a timely request for an interpreter. [¶] '[T]he mere fact that an accused may be more fluent in [another language] does not, in and of itself, make it incumbent upon a trial court to appoint an interpreter for an accused who speaks and understands the English language.'"

ART. 38.31. INTERPRETERS FOR DEAF PERSONS

(a) If the court is notified by a party that the defendant is deaf and will be present at an arraignment, hearing, examining trial, or trial, or that a witness is deaf and will be called at a hearing, examining trial, or trial, the court shall appoint a qualified interpreter to interpret the proceedings in any language that the deaf person can understand, including but not limited to sign language. On the court's motion or the motion of a party, the court may order testimony of a deaf witness and the interpretation of that testimony by the interpreter visually, electronically recorded for use in verification of the transcription of the reporter's notes. The clerk of the court shall include that recording in the appellate record if requested by a party under Article 40.09 of this Code.

(b) Following the filing of an indictment, information, or complaint against a deaf defendant, the court on the motion of the defendant shall appoint a qualified interpreter to interpret in a language that the defendant can understand, including but not limited to sign language, communications concerning the case between the defendant and defense counsel. The interpreter may not disclose a communication between the defendant and defense counsel or a fact that came to the attention of the interpreter while interpreting those communications if defense counsel may not disclose that communication or fact.

(c) In all cases where the mental condition of a person is being considered and where such person may be committed to a mental institution, and where such person is deaf, all of the court proceedings pertaining to him shall be interpreted by a qualified interpreter appointed by the court.

(d) A proceeding for which an interpreter is required to be appointed under this Article may not commence until the appointed interpreter is in a position not exceeding ten feet from and in full view of the deaf person.

(e) The interpreter appointed under the terms of this Article shall be required to take an oath that he will make a true interpretation to the person accused or being examined, which person is deaf, of all the proceedings of his case in a language that he understands; and that he will repeat said deaf person's answer to questions to counsel, court, or jury, in the English language, in his best skill and judgment.

(f) Interpreters appointed under this Article are entitled to a reasonable fee determined by the court after considering the recommendations of the Texas Commission for the Deaf and Hard of Hearing. When travel of the interpreter is involved all the actual expenses of travel, lodging, and meals incurred by the interpreter pertaining to the case he is appointed to serve shall be paid at the same rate applicable to state employees.

(g) In this Code:

(1) "Deaf person" means a person who has a hearing impairment, regardless of whether the person also has a speech impairment, that inhibits the person's comprehension of the proceedings or communication with others.

(2) "Qualified interpreter" means an interpreter for the deaf who holds a current legal certificate issued by the National Registry of Interpreters for the Deaf or a current court interpreter certificate issued by the Board for Evaluation of Interpreters at the Department of Assistive or Rehabilitative Services.

History of CCP art. 38.31: Acts 1965, 59th Leg., vol. 2, ch. 722. Amended by Acts 1967, 60th Leg., ch. 105, §2, eff. Aug. 28, 1967; Acts 1979, 66th Leg., ch. 186, §1, eff. May 15, 1979; Acts 1987, 70th Leg., ch. 434, §1, eff. June 17, 1987; Acts 1995, 74th Leg., ch. 835, §14, eff. Sept. 1, 1995; Acts 2005, 79th Leg., ch. 614, §11, eff. Sept. 1, 2006.

ANNOTATIONS

Salazar v. State, 93 S.W.3d 339, 341 (Tex.App.—Texarkana 2002, pet. dism'd). "If a hearing-impaired defendant is unable to understand sign language, the court has an obligation to fashion a remedy suitable to overcome the defendant's disability. A defendant's failure to object or request relief does not waive his confrontation right if it is otherwise apparent he cannot hear or understand the proceedings."

Minor v. State, 659 S.W.2d 161, 164 (Tex.App.—Fort Worth 1983, no pet.). "Although the use of a partisan interpreter should be avoided, the appointment of an interpreter is a matter to be left to the [discretion of the] trial court.... [T]here [is] no requirement that an interpreter should be unbiased as far as the accused is concerned, only that he should interpret correctly and

fairly. ... A complaining witness has even been allowed to act as interpreter without an abuse of discretion being shown."

ART. 38.32. PRESUMPTION OF DEATH

(a) Upon introduction and admission into evidence of a valid certificate of death wherein the time of death of the decedent has been entered by a licensed physician, a presumption exists that death occurred at the time stated in the certificate of death.

(b) A presumption existing pursuant to Section (a) of this Article is sufficient to support a finding as to time of death but may be rebutted through a showing by a preponderance of the evidence that death occurred at some other time.

History of CCP art. 38.32: Acts 1969, 61st Leg., ch. 337, §1, eff. May 27, 1969.

ART. 38.33. PRESERVATION & USE OF EVIDENCE OF CERTAIN MISDEMEANOR CONVICTIONS

Sec. 1. The court shall order that a defendant who is convicted of a felony or a misdemeanor offense that is punishable by confinement in jail have a thumbprint of the defendant's right thumb rolled legibly on the judgment or the docket sheet in the case. The court shall order a defendant who is placed on probation under Section 5 of Article 42.12, Code of Criminal Procedure, for an offense described by this section to have a thumbprint of the defendant's right thumb rolled legibly on the order placing the defendant on probation. If the defendant does not have a right thumb, the defendant must have a thumbprint of the defendant's left thumb rolled legibly on the judgment, order, or docket sheet. The defendant must have a fingerprint of the defendant's index finger rolled legibly on the judgment, order, or docket sheet if the defendant does not have a right thumb or a left thumb. The judgment, order, or docket sheet must contain a statement that describes from which thumb or finger the print was taken, unless a rolled 10-finger print set was taken. A clerk or bailiff of the court or other person qualified to take fingerprints shall take the thumbprint or fingerprint, either by use of the ink-rolled print method or by use of a live-scanning device that prints the thumbprint or fingerprint image on the judgment, order, or docket sheet.

Sec. 2. This article does not prohibit a court from including in the records of the case additional information to identify the defendant.

History of CCP art. 38.33: Acts 1979, 66th Leg., ch. 751, §1, eff. Sept. 1, 1979. Amended by Acts 1983, 68th Leg., ch. 303, §7, eff. Jan. 1, 1984; Acts 1987, 70th Leg., ch. 721, §1, eff. Sept. 1, 1987; Acts 1989, 71st Leg., ch. 603, §1, eff. Sept. 1, 1989; Acts 1991, 72nd Leg., 2nd C.S., ch. 10, §7.01, eff. Dec. 1, 1991.

ART. 38.34. PHOTOGRAPHIC EVIDENCE IN THEFT CASES

(a) As used herein, the term "property" means tangible personal property offered for sale or lease by a person engaged in the business of selling goods or services to buyers.

(b) A photograph of property which a person is alleged to have unlawfully appropriated with the intent to deprive the owner of such property is admissible into evidence under rules of law governing the admissibility of photographs and such photograph is as admissible in evidence as the property itself.

(c) The provisions of Article 18.16 of this code concerning the bringing of stolen property before a magistrate for examination are complied with if a photograph of the stolen property is brought before the magistrate.

(d) The defendant's rights of discovery and inspection of tangible physical evidence are satisfied if a photograph of the tangible property is made available to the defendant by the state upon order of any court having jurisdiction over the cause.

History of CCP art. 38.34: Acts 1985, 69th Leg., ch. 144, §1, eff. Sept. 1, 1985.

ART. 38.35. FORENSIC ANALYSIS OF EVIDENCE; ADMISSIBILITY

(a) In this article:

(1) "Crime laboratory" includes a public or private laboratory or other entity that conducts a forensic analysis subject to this article.

(2) "Criminal action" includes an investigation, complaint, arrest, bail, bond, trial, appeal, punishment, or other matter related to conduct proscribed by a criminal offense.

(3) "Director" means the public safety director of the Department of Public Safety.

(4) "Forensic analysis" means a medical, chemical, toxicologic, ballistic, or other expert examination or test performed on physical evidence, including DNA evidence, for the purpose of determining the connection of the evidence to a criminal action. The term includes an examination or test requested by a law enforcement agency, prosecutor, criminal suspect or defendant, or court. The term does not include:

(A) latent print examination;

(B) a test of a specimen of breath under Chapter 724, Transportation Code;

(C) digital evidence;

(D) an examination or test excluded by rule under Section 411.0205(c), Government Code;

(E) a presumptive test performed for the purpose of determining compliance with a term or condition of community supervision or parole and conducted by or under contract with a community supervision and corrections department, the parole division of the Texas Department of Criminal Justice, or the Board of Pardons and Paroles; or

(F) an expert examination or test conducted principally for the purpose of scientific research, medical practice, civil or administrative litigation, or other purpose unrelated to determining the connection of physical evidence to a criminal action.

(5) "Physical evidence" means any tangible object, thing, or substance relating to a criminal action.

(b) A law enforcement agency, prosecutor, or court may request a forensic analysis by a crime laboratory of physical evidence if the evidence was obtained in connection with the requesting entity's investigation or disposition of a criminal action and the requesting entity:

(1) controls the evidence;

(2) submits the evidence to the laboratory; or

(3) consents to the analysis.

(c) A law enforcement agency, other governmental agency, or private entity performing a forensic analysis of physical evidence may require the requesting law enforcement agency to pay a fee for such analysis.

(d)(1) Except as provided by Subsection (e), a forensic analysis of physical evidence under this article and expert testimony relating to the evidence are not admissible in a criminal action if, at the time of the analysis, the crime laboratory conducting the analysis was not accredited by the director under Section 411.0205, Government Code.

(2) If before the date of the analysis the director issues a certificate of accreditation under Section 411.0205, Government Code, to a crime laboratory conducting the analysis, the certificate is prima facie evidence that the laboratory was accredited by the director at the time of the analysis.

(e) A forensic analysis of physical evidence under this article and expert testimony relating to the evidence are not inadmissible in a criminal action based solely on the accreditation status of the crime laboratory conducting the analysis if the laboratory:

(A) except for making proper application, was eligible for accreditation by the director at the time of the examination or test; and

(B) obtains accreditation from the director before the time of testimony about the examination or test.

(f) This article does not apply to the portion of an autopsy conducted by a medical examiner or other forensic pathologist who is a licensed physician.

History of CCP art. 38.35: Acts 1991, 72nd Leg., ch. 298, §1, eff. Sept. 1, 1991. Amended by Acts 2003, 78th Leg., ch. 698, §§1-3, eff. June 20, 2003; Acts 2005, 79th Leg., ch. 1224, §2, eff. Sept. 1, 2005.

ART. 38.36. EVIDENCE IN PROSECUTIONS FOR MURDER

(a) In all prosecutions for murder, the state or the defendant shall be permitted to offer testimony as to all relevant facts and circumstances surrounding the killing and the previous relationship existing between the accused and the deceased, together with all relevant facts and circumstances going to show the condition of the mind of the accused at the time of the offense.

(b) In a prosecution for murder, if a defendant raises as a defense a justification provided by Section 9.31, 9.32, or 9.33, Penal Code, the defendant, in order to establish the defendant's reasonable belief that use of force or deadly force was immediately necessary, shall be permitted to offer:

(1) relevant evidence that the defendant had been the victim of acts of family violence committed by the deceased, as family violence is defined by Section 71.004, Family Code; and

(2) relevant expert testimony regarding the condition of the mind of the defendant at the time of the offense, including those relevant facts and circumstances relating to family violence that are the basis of the expert's opinion.

History of CCP art. 38.36: Acts 1993, 73rd Leg., ch. 900, §7.03, eff. Sept. 1, 1994. Amended by Acts 2003, 78th Leg., ch. 1276, §7.002(g), eff. Sept. 1, 2003. See also TRE 404(b).

ANNOTATIONS

Garcia v. State, 201 S.W.3d 695, 702-03 (Tex.Crim. App.2006). "The nature of the relationship—such as whether the victim and the accused were friends, were co-workers, were married, estranged, separated, or divorcing—is clearly admissible under this Article. However, in some situations, prior acts of violence between the victim and the accused may be offered to illustrate the nature of the relationship. These specific acts of violence must meet the requirements of the [TRE] in order to be admissible. [TRE] 404(b) deals with prior acts of violence and specifically instructs courts regarding the admissibility of such evidence. [CCP art.] 38.36(a) and [TREs] 403 and 404(b) can be applied congruously. The fact that [CCP art.] 38.37 lists the specific offenses for which evidence of extraneous offenses or acts are admissible without having to meet the requirements of Rule 404 indicates that other offenses, such as the murder in the case before us, *are* subject to the requirements of Rule 404. [¶] [I]t is clear that there are additional other purposes for which evidence of prior acts may be admitted. For example, in cases in which the prior relationship between the victim and the accused is a material issue, illustrating the nature of the relationship may be the purpose for which evidence of prior bad acts will be admissible. [E]vidence will be relevant to a material issue if the purpose for which the party seeks to have it submitted tends to make the existence of any fact that is of consequence to the determination of the action more probable or less probable than it would be without the evidence. What issues are material will depend on the theories of the prosecution and the defense." (Internal quotes omitted.)

Jackson v. State, 160 S.W.3d 568, 574-75 (Tex. Crim.App.2005). "Even if evidence is relevant to an element of the offense, the trial court still must determine whether the evidence is admissible. Therefore, the trial judge has discretion to determine whether evidence of mental illness may be presented to negate the element of *mens rea*, or whether the evidence should be excluded on special grounds. If such evidence is admitted, the trial judge additionally has the discretion to determine whether the evidence supports a lesser-included-offense instruction. In cases where such evidence was not admitted, it may be presented in the punishment phase in order to reduce the sentence assessed by the jury. [¶] The only thing Appellant was prevented from doing is arguing that the jury should find that he did not have the capacity to make the decision to intentionally and knowingly cause bodily injury and thus should find him not guilty. However, presenting evidence of mental illness does not then allow the defense to argue that the defendant is absolutely incapable i.e., does not have the capacity to intentionally or knowingly perform an act. There is simply no defense recognized by Texas law stating that, due to the defendant's mental illness, he did not have the requisite *mens rea* at the time of the offense because he does not have the capacity, or is absolutely incapable of ever forming that frame of mind. There is no indication of an abuse of discretion in this case." *See also* **Ruffin v. State**, 234 S.W.3d 224, 227 (Tex.App.—Waco 2007, pet. granted 3-19-08); **Mays v. State**, 223 S.W.3d 651, 653-55 (Tex.App.—Texarkana 2007, pet. granted 10-03-07).

Ex parte Varelas, 45 S.W.3d 627, 631 (Tex.Crim. App.2001). "[W]hen the State is permitted to introduce evidence of defendant's extraneous acts for a limited purpose, the defendant also has the burden of requesting an instruction limiting consideration of those acts. When a defendant so requests this instruction, the trial court errs in not giving the instruction."

Soto v. State, 156 S.W.3d 131, 134 (Tex.App.—Fort Worth 2005, pet. ref'd). "[W]e hold that article 38.36(a) applies to attempted capital murder prosecutions."

Bisby v. State, 907 S.W.2d 949, 957 (Tex.App.—Fort Worth 1995, pet. ref'd). "Article 38.36 does not allow a showing of the relationship between the deceased and third parties, but it does allow the showing of the relationship between the accused and the deceased."

Henderson v. State, 906 S.W.2d 589, 597 (Tex. App.—El Paso 1995, pet. ref'd), *overruled on other grounds*, **Potier v. State**, 68 S.W.3d 657 (Tex.Crim. App.2002). Article 38.36 "appears to be limited on its face to evidence showing prior acts of violence by the deceased. However … the Court of Criminal Appeals [has] held that … the defendant is permitted to show prior acts of violence toward third parties by the 'intended victim' in order to show the reasonableness of the defendant's claim of apprehension of danger."

ART. 38.37. EVIDENCE OF EXTRANEOUS OFFENSES OR ACTS

Sec. 1. This article applies to a proceeding in the prosecution of a defendant for an offense under the following provisions of the Penal Code, if committed against a child under 17 years of age:

(1) Chapter 21 (Sexual Offenses);

(2) Chapter 22 (Assaultive Offenses);

(3) Section 25.02 (Prohibited Sexual Conduct);

(4) Section 43.25 (Sexual Performance by a Child); or

(5) an attempt or conspiracy to commit an offense listed in this section.

Sec. 2. Notwithstanding Rules 404 and 405, Texas Rules of Evidence, evidence of other crimes, wrongs, or acts committed by the defendant against the child who is the victim of the alleged offense shall be admitted for its bearing on relevant matters, including:

(1) the state of mind of the defendant and the child; and

(2) the previous and subsequent relationship between the defendant and the child.

Sec. 3. On timely request by the defendant, the state shall give the defendant notice of the state's intent to introduce in the case in chief evidence described by Section 2 in the same manner as the state is required to give notice under Rule 404(b), Texas Rules of Evidence.

Sec. 4. This article does not limit the admissibility of evidence of extraneous crimes, wrongs, or acts under any other applicable law.

1. **Editor's note:** Even if admissible under CCP art. 38.37, the evidence may still be excluded under TRE 403 if its probative value is substantially outweighed by the danger of unfair prejudice. See **Wheeler v. State**, 67 S.W.3d 879, 888 (Tex.Crim.App.2002).

History of CCP art. 38.37: Acts 1995, 74th Leg., ch. 318, §48(a), eff. Sept. 1, 1995. Amended by Acts 2005, 79th Leg., ch. 728, §4.004, eff. Sept. 1, 2005.

ANNOTATIONS

Phillips v. State, 193 S.W.3d 904, 911 (Tex.Crim. App.2006). "Article 38.37 does allow for the admission of other crimes, wrongs or acts to be admitted when relevant. However, it does not restrict a defendant's right to have the State elect the incident for which it will seek a conviction by forcing the defendant to request a limiting instruction when the evidence is admitted. The requirement of an election [of offenses the State would use to convict on each count] upon timely request is well-settled and distinct from a limiting instruction. The purpose of a limiting instruction is to 'restrict evidence to its proper scope and instruct the jury accordingly.' An election partly serves this purpose; but it serves other salutary purposes as well, providing explicit notice to the defendant, and promoting unanimous jury verdicts. A limiting instruction alone does not adequately serve all these purposes. Nor does a defendant somehow waive or forfeit his right to an election, with all of its attendant advantages, by his failure to request a limiting instruction at the absolute earliest opportunity."

Ex parte Varelas, 45 S.W.3d 627, 631 (Tex.Crim. App.2001). "[W]hen the State is permitted to introduce evidence of defendant's extraneous acts for a limited purpose, the defendant also has the burden of requesting an instruction limiting consideration of those acts. When a defendant so requests this instruction, the trial court errs in not giving the instruction."

Howland v. State, 990 S.W.2d 274, 277 (Tex.Crim. App.1999). "[B]y making article 38.37 applicable to a proceeding in a prosecution, the rule itself expressly distinguishes between a proceeding and a prosecution in a way that implies there can be more than one proceeding in a given case. [W]e hold that article 38.37 is applicable to any one of the many isolated proceedings within a prosecution...."

Rivera v. State, 233 S.W.3d 403, 406 (Tex.App.— Waco 2007, pet. ref'd). "[I]n a case such as this where the extraneous offenses are the unelected offenses that were admissible under §2 of article 38.37 and the defendant merely testifies that he did not commit the elected offenses and the now-extraneous (*i.e.*, unelected) offenses, a limiting instruction to the jury that it may use those extraneous offenses to pass on the credibility of the defendant's testimony is erroneous." *See also Crawford v. State*, 696 S.W.2d 903, 907-08 (Tex.Crim.App.1985).

Hitt v. State, 53 S.W.3d 697, 705 (Tex.App.—Austin 2001, pet. ref'd). "Appellant ... contends that [witnesses'] testimony should have been excluded under [CCP art.] 38.37 because he was not given timely notice that the State intended to use the testimony in its case-in-chief. Appellant concedes that he did not make a timely request for such evidence under §3 of article 38.37, but relies upon his timely request for evidence of extraneous matters expressly made under [TRE] 404(b). *At 706:* Article 38.37 put appellant's counsel on notice of the evidentiary procedure required '[n]otwithstanding Rule 404.' Appellant argues that article 38.37, §3 refers to Rule 404(b). Indeed it does, but the reference is to the nature of the State's response to a timely request made under article 38.37. The reference is not to the required request. No timely request for notice under article 38.37 having been made, the evidence was admissible."

ART. 38.38. EVIDENCE RELATING TO RETAINING ATTORNEY

Evidence that a person has contacted or retained an attorney is not admissible on the issue of whether the person committed a criminal offense. In a criminal case, neither the judge nor the attorney representing the state may comment on the fact that the defendant has contacted or retained an attorney in the case.

History of CCP art. 38.38: Acts 1995, 74th Leg., ch. 318, §49, eff. Sept. 1, 1995.

ANNOTATIONS

Kalisz v. State, 32 S.W.3d 718, 723 (Tex.App.— Houston [14th Dist.] 2000, pet. ref'd). "Because evidence of an accused invoking his constitutional right to counsel may be construed adversely to a defendant and may improperly be considered as an inference of guilt, the trial court erred in admitting [officer's] query concerning the right to counsel and everything that followed."

ART. 38.39. EVIDENCE IN AN AGGREGATION PROSECUTION WITH NUMEROUS VICTIMS

In trials involving an allegation of a continuing scheme of fraud or theft alleged to have been committed against a large class of victims in an aggregate amount or value, it need not be proved by direct evidence that each alleged victim did not consent or did not effectively consent to the transaction in question. It shall be sufficient if the lack of consent or effective consent to a particular transaction or transactions is proven by either direct or circumstantial evidence.

History of CCP art. 38.39: Acts 2001, 77th Leg., ch. 1411, §2, eff. Sept. 1, 2001. Amended by Acts 2003, 78th Leg., ch. 1275, §2(7), eff. Sept. 1, 2003.

ART. 38.40. EVIDENCE OF PREGNANCY

(a) In a prosecution for the death of or injury to an individual who is an unborn child, the prosecution shall provide medical or other evidence that the mother of the individual was pregnant at the time of the alleged offense.

(b) For the purpose of this section, "individual" has the meaning assigned by Section 1.07, Penal Code.

History of CCP art. 38.40: Acts 2003, 78th Leg., ch. 822, §2.06, eff. Sept. 1, 2003.

ART. 38.41. CERTIFICATE OF ANALYSIS

Sec. 1. A certificate of analysis that complies with this article is admissible in evidence on behalf of the state or the defendant to establish the results of a laboratory analysis of physical evidence conducted by or for a law enforcement agency without the necessity of the analyst personally appearing in court.

Sec. 2. This article does not limit the right of a party to summon a witness or to introduce admissible evidence relevant to the results of the analysis.

Sec. 3. A certificate of analysis under this article must contain the following information certified under oath:

(1) the names of the analyst and the laboratory employing the analyst;

(2) a statement that the laboratory employing the analyst is accredited by a nationally recognized board or association that accredits crime laboratories;

(3) a description of the analyst's educational background, training, and experience;

(4) a statement that the analyst's duties of employment included the analysis of physical evidence for one or more law enforcement agencies;

(5) a description of the tests or procedures conducted by the analyst;

(6) a statement that the tests or procedures used were reliable and approved by the laboratory employing the analyst; and

(7) the results of the analysis.

Sec. 4. Not later than the 20th day before the trial begins in a proceeding in which a certificate of analysis under this article is to be introduced, the certificate must be filed with the clerk of the court and a copy must be provided by fax, hand delivery, or certified mail, return receipt requested, to the opposing party. The certificate is not admissible under Section 1 if, not later than the 10th day before the trial begins, the opposing party files a written objection to the use of the certificate with the clerk of the court and provides a copy of the objection by fax, hand delivery, or certified mail, return receipt requested, to the offering party.

Sec. 5. A certificate of analysis is sufficient for purposes of this article if it uses the following form or if it otherwise substantially complies with this article:

CERTIFICATE OF ANALYSIS

BEFORE ME, the undersigned authority, personally appeared _____, who being duly sworn, stated as follows:

My name is _____. I am of sound mind, over the age of 18 years, capable of making this affidavit, and personally acquainted with the facts stated in this affidavit.

I am employed by the _____, which was authorized to conduct the analysis referenced in this affidavit. Part of my duties for this laboratory involved the analysis of physical evidence for one or more law enforcement agencies. This laboratory is accredited by _____.

My educational background is as follows: (description of educational background)

My training and experience that qualify me to perform the tests or procedures referred to in this affidavit and determine the results of those tests or procedures are as follows: (description of training and experience)

I received the physical evidence listed on laboratory report no. _____ (attached) on the _____ day of _____, 20___. On the date indicated in the laboratory report, I conducted the following tests or procedures on the physical evidence: (description of tests and procedures)

The tests and procedures used were reliable and approved by the laboratory. The results are as indicated on the lab report.

_____

Affiant

SWORN TO AND SUBSCRIBED before me on the ___ day of _____, 20___.

_____

Notary Public, State of Texas

History of CCP art. 38.41: Acts 2003, 78th Leg., ch. 923, §1, eff. Sept. 1, 2003.

ANNOTATIONS

Deener v. State, 214 S.W.3d 522, 526-28 (Tex. App.—Dallas 2006, pet. ref'd). Held: Affidavits and certificates authorized under CCP arts. 38.41, §4, and 38.42, §4, are "testimonial" within the meaning of ***Crawford v. Washington***, 541 U.S. 36 (2004), but failure to object results in forfeiture of the right to confrontation.

ART. 38.42. CHAIN OF CUSTODY AFFIDAVIT

Sec. 1. A chain of custody affidavit that complies with this article is admissible in evidence on behalf of the state or the defendant to establish the chain of custody of physical evidence without the necessity of any person in the chain of custody personally appearing in court.

Sec. 2. This article does not limit the right of a party to summon a witness or to introduce admissible evidence relevant to the chain of custody.

Sec. 3. A chain of custody affidavit under this article must contain the following information stated under oath:

(1) the affiant's name and address;

(2) a description of the item of evidence and its container, if any, obtained by the affiant;

(3) the name of the affiant's employer on the date the affiant obtained custody of the physical evidence;

(4) the date and method of receipt and the name of the person from whom or location from which the item of physical evidence was received;

(5) the date and method of transfer and the name of the person to whom or location to which the item of physical evidence was transferred; and

(6) a statement that the item of evidence was transferred in essentially the same condition as received except for any minor change resulting from field or laboratory testing procedures.

Sec. 4. Not later than the 20th day before the trial begins in a proceeding in which a chain of custody affidavit under this article is to be introduced, the affidavit must be filed with the clerk of the court and a copy must be provided by fax, hand delivery, or certified mail, return receipt requested, to the opposing party. The affidavit is not admissible under Section 1 if, not later than the 10th day before the trial begins, the opposing party files a written objection to the use of the affidavit with the clerk of the court and provides a copy of the objection by fax, hand delivery, or certified mail, return receipt requested, to the offering party.

Sec. 5. A chain of custody affidavit is sufficient for purposes of this article if it uses the following form or if it otherwise substantially complies with this article:

CHAIN OF CUSTODY AFFIDAVIT

BEFORE ME, the undersigned authority, personally appeared _____, who being by me duly sworn, stated as follows:

My name is _____. I am of sound mind, over the age of 18 years, capable of making this affidavit, and personally acquainted with the facts stated in this affidavit.

My address is _____.

On the ____ day of _____, 20___, I was employed by _____.

On that date, I came into possession of the physical evidence described as follows: (description of evidence)

I received the physical evidence from _____ _____ (name of person or description of location) on the _____ day of _____, 20___, by _____ (method of receipt).

This physical evidence was in a container described and marked as follows: (description of container)

I transferred the physical evidence to _____ _____ (name of person or description of location) on the _____ day of _____, 20___, by _____ _____ (method of delivery).

During the time that the physical evidence was in my custody, I did not make any changes or alterations to the condition of the physical evidence except for those resulting from field or laboratory testing procedures, and the physical evidence or a representative sample of the physical evidence was transferred in essentially the same condition as received.

_____
Affiant

SWORN TO AND SUBSCRIBED before me on the _____ day of _____, 20___.

_____
Notary Public, State of Texas

History of CCP art. 38.42: Acts 2003, 78th Leg., ch. 923, §1, eff. Sept. 1, 2003.

<hr>

ANNOTATIONS

Deener v. State, 214 S.W.3d 522, 526-28 (Tex. App.—Dallas 2006, pet. ref'd). Held: Affidavits and certificates authorized under CCP arts. 38.41, §4, and 38.42, §4, are "testimonial" within the meaning of ***Crawford v. Washington***, 541 U.S. 36 (2004), but failure to object results in forfeiture of the right to confrontation.

ART. 38.43. PRESERVATION OF EVIDENCE CONTAINING BIOLOGICAL MATERIAL

(a) In a criminal case in which a defendant is convicted, the attorney representing the state, a clerk, or any other officer in possession of evidence described by Subsection (b) shall ensure the preservation of the evidence.

(b) This article applies to evidence that:

(1) was in the possession of the state during the prosecution of the case; and

(2) at the time of conviction was known to contain biological material that if subjected to scientific testing would more likely than not:

(A) establish the identity of the person committing the offense; or

(B) exclude a person from the group of persons who could have committed the offense.

(c) Except as provided by Subsection (d), material required to be preserved under this article must be preserved:

(1) until the inmate is executed, dies, or is released on parole, if the defendant was convicted of a capital felony; or

(2) until the defendant dies, completes the defendant's sentence, or is released on parole or mandatory supervision, if the defendant is sentenced to a term of confinement or imprisonment.

(d) The attorney representing the state, clerk, or other officer in possession of evidence described by Subsection (b) may destroy the evidence, but only if the attorney, clerk, or officer by mail notifies the defendant, the last attorney of record for the defendant, and the convicting court of the decision to destroy the evidence and a written objection is not received by the attorney, clerk, or officer from the defendant, attorney of record, or court before the 91st day after the later of the following dates:

(1) the date on which the attorney representing the state, clerk, or other officer receives proof that the defendant received notice of the planned destruction of evidence; or

(2) the date on which notice of the planned destruction of evidence is mailed to the last attorney of record for the defendant.

(e) To the extent of any conflict, this article controls over Article 2.21.

History of CCP art. 38.43: Acts 2001, 77th Leg., ch. 2, §1, eff. Apr. 5, 2001. Renumbered from art. 38.39 by Acts 2005, 79th Leg., ch. 728, §23.001(8), eff. Sept. 1, 2005.

See also Gov't Code §§411.141-411.154.

ART. 38.44. ADMISSIBILITY OF ELECTRONICALLY PRESERVED DOCUMENT

An electronically preserved document has the same legal significance and admissibility as if the document had been maintained in hard-copy form. If a party opposes admission of the document on the grounds that the document has been materially altered, the proponent of the document must disprove the allegation by a preponderance of the evidence.

History of CCP art. 38.44: Acts 2005, 79th Leg., ch. 312, §5, eff. June 17, 2005.

CHAPTER 39. DEPOSITIONS & DISCOVERY

ART. 39.01. IN EXAMINING TRIAL

When an examination takes place in a criminal action before a magistrate, the State or the defendant may have the deposition of any witness taken by any officer authorized by this chapter. The State or the defendant may not use the deposition for any purpose unless that party first acknowledges that the entire evidence or statement of the witness may be used for or against the defendant on the trial of the case, subject to all legal objections. The deposition of a witness duly taken before an examining trial or a jury of inquest and reduced to writing and certified according to law where the defendant was present when that testimony was taken, and had the privilege afforded of cross-examining the witness, or taken at any prior trial of the defendant for the same offense, may be used by either the State or the defendant in the trial of the defendant's criminal case under the following circumstances:

When oath is made by the party using the deposition that the witness resides outside the State; or that since the witness's testimony was taken, the witness has died, or has removed beyond the limits of the State, or has been prevented from attending the court through the act or agency of the other party, or by the act or agency of any person whose object was to deprive the State or the defendant of the benefit of the testimony; or that by reason of age or bodily infirmity, that witness cannot attend. When the testimony is sought to be used by the State, the oath may be made by any credible person. When sought to be used by the defendant, the oath must be made by the defendant in person.

History of CCP art. 39.01: Acts 1965, 59th Leg., vol. 2, ch. 722. Amended by Acts 2005, 79th Leg., ch. 1021, §1, eff. Sept. 1, 2005.

ANNOTATIONS

Porier v. State, 662 S.W.2d 602, 604 (Tex.Crim.App. 1984). "Though it is not clear from the language of the statute that Art. 39.01 should cover the admission of testimony taken at former trials, our cases have so held. [¶] It has … been held that unavailability for purposes of Art. 39.01 cannot be established by hearsay testimony."

Russell v. State, 604 S.W.2d 914, 920 (Tex.Crim. App.1980). "In seeking to reproduce testimony of a deceased witness given at a prior examining trial, the State has the burden of establishing clearly and satisfactorily that the testimony was given under oath, that it was competent, that the accused on trial is the same accused who was present, as an accused, at the examining trial and that the accused had adequate opportunity through counsel to cross-examine the deceased witness. *At 921:* Bearing on the issue [of opportunity to cross-examine] are such factors as matters that are material to the ultimate finding concerning probable cause, limitations generally imposed by the magistrate as to scope and depth of permitted cross-examination, constraints deterring defense counsel from extending cross-examination into explorations of details, reflections of a properly authenticated record of cross-examination as actually conducted, intimations of ineffective assistance of counsel and others that may appear from time to time to be significantly weighty."

ART. 39.02. WITNESS DEPOSITIONS

Depositions of witnesses may be taken by either the state or the defendant. When a party desires to take the deposition of a witness, the party shall file with the clerk of the court in which the case is pending an affidavit stating the facts necessary to constitute a good reason for taking the witness's deposition and an application to take the deposition. On the filing of the affidavit and application, and after notice to the opposing party, the court shall hear the application and determine if good reason exists for taking the deposition.

The court shall base its determination and shall grant or deny the application on the facts made known at the hearing. This provision is limited to the purposes stated in Article 39.01.

History of CCP art. 39.02: Acts 1965, 59th Leg., vol. 2, ch. 722. Amended by Acts 1967, 60th Leg., ch. 659, §24, eff. Aug. 28, 1967; Acts 2005, 79th Leg., ch. 1021, §1, eff. Sept. 1, 2005.

ANNOTATIONS

Cooks v. State, 844 S.W.2d 697, 729 (Tex.Crim.App. 1992). "The trial court has broad discretion in ruling on an application to take a deposition…. [T]here is not an abuse of discretion for the denial of a motion to take a deposition where the witness testifies at trial and is subject to cross-examination by the defense."

ART. 39.03. OFFICERS WHO MAY TAKE THE DEPOSITION

Upon the filing of such an affidavit and application, the court shall appoint, order or designate one of the following persons before whom such deposition shall be taken:

1. A district judge.
2. A county judge.
3. A notary public.
4. A district clerk.
5. A county clerk.

Such order shall specifically name such person and the time when and place where such deposition shall be taken. Failure of a witness to respond thereto, shall be punishable by contempt by the court. Such deposition shall be oral or written, as the court shall direct.

History of CCP art. 39.03: Acts 1965, 59th Leg., vol. 2, ch. 722. Amended by Acts 1967, 60th Leg., ch. 659, §25, eff. Aug. 28, 1967.

ART. 39.04. APPLICABILITY OF CIVIL RULES

The rules prescribed in civil cases for issuance of commissions, subpoenaing witnesses, taking the depositions of witnesses and all other formalities governing depositions shall, as to the manner and form of taking and returning the same and other formalities to the taking of the same, govern in criminal actions, when not in conflict with this Code.

History of CCP art. 39.04: Acts 1965, 59th Leg., vol. 2, ch. 722.

ART. 39.05. OBJECTIONS

The rules of procedure as to objections in depositions in civil actions shall govern in criminal actions when not in conflict with this Code.

History of CCP art. 39.05: Acts 1965, 59th Leg., vol. 2, ch. 722.

ART. 39.06. WRITTEN INTERROGATORIES

When any such deposition is to be taken by written interrogatories, such written interrogatories shall be filed with the clerk of the court, and a copy of the same served on all other parties or their counsel for the length of time and in the manner required for service of interrogatories in civil action, and the same procedure shall also be followed with reference to cross-interrogatories as that prescribed in civil actions.

History of CCP art. 39.06: Acts 1965, 59th Leg., vol. 2, ch. 722.

ART. 39.07. CERTIFICATE

Where depositions are taken under commission in criminal actions, the officer or officers taking the same shall certify that the person deposing is the identical person named in the commission; or, if they cannot certify to the identity of the witness, there shall be an affidavit of some person attached to the deposition proving the identity of such witness, and the officer or officers shall certify that the person making the affidavit is known to them.

History of CCP art. 39.07: Acts 1965, 59th Leg., vol. 2, ch. 722. Amended by Acts 1967, 60th Leg., ch. 659, §26, eff. Aug. 28, 1967.

ART. 39.08. AUTHENTICATING THE DEPOSITION

The official seal and signature of the officer taking the deposition shall be attached to the certificate authenticating the deposition.

History of CCP art. 39.08: Acts 1965, 59th Leg., vol. 2, ch. 722.

ART. 39.09. NON-RESIDENT WITNESSES

Depositions of a witness residing out of the State may be taken before a judge or before a commissioner of deeds and depositions for this State, who resides within the State where the deposition is to be taken, or before a notary public of the place where such deposition is to be taken, or before any commissioned officer of the armed services or before any diplomatic or consular officer. The deposition of a non-resident witness who may be temporarily within the State, may be taken under the same rules which apply to the taking of depositions of other witnesses in the State.

History of CCP art. 39.09: Acts 1965, 59th Leg., vol. 2, ch. 722.

ART. 39.10. RETURN

In all cases the return of depositions may be made as provided in civil actions.

History of CCP art. 39.10: Acts 1965, 59th Leg., vol. 2, ch. 722.

ART. 39.11. WAIVER

The State and defense may agree upon a waiver of any formalities in the taking of a deposition other than that the taking of such deposition must be under oath.

History of CCP art. 39.11: Acts 1965, 59th Leg., vol. 2, ch. 722.

ART. 39.12. PREDICATE TO READ

Depositions taken in criminal actions shall not be read unless oath be made that the witness resides out of the State; or that since his deposition was taken, the witness has died; or that he has removed beyond the limits of the State; or that he has been prevented from attending the court through the act or agency of the defendant; or by the act or agency of any person whose object was to deprive the defendant of the benefit of the testimony; or that by reason of age or bodily infirmity, such witness cannot attend. When the deposition is sought to be used by the State, the oath may be made by any credible person. When sought to be used by the defendant, the oath shall be made by him in person.

History of CCP art. 39.12: Acts 1965, 59th Leg., vol. 2, ch. 722.

ART. 39.13. IMPEACHMENT

Nothing contained in the preceding Articles shall be construed as prohibiting the use of any such evidence for impeachment purposes under the rules of evidence heretofore existing at common law.

History of CCP art. 39.13: Acts 1965, 59th Leg., vol. 2, ch. 722.

ART. 39.14. DISCOVERY

(a) Upon motion of the defendant showing good cause therefor and upon notice to the other parties, the court in which an action is pending shall order the State before or during trial of a criminal action therein pending or on trial to produce and permit the inspection and copying or photographing by or on behalf of the defendant of any designated documents, papers, written statement of the defendant, (except written statements of witnesses and except the work product of counsel in the case and their investigators and their notes or report), books, accounts, letters, photographs, objects or tangible things not privileged, which constitute or contain evidence material to any matter involved in the action and which are in the possession, custody or control of the State or any of its agencies. The order shall specify the time, place and manner of making the inspection and taking the copies and photographs of any of the aforementioned documents or tangible evidence; provided, however, that the rights herein granted shall not extend to written communications between the State or any of its agents or representatives or employees. Nothing in this Act shall authorize the removal of such evidence from the possession of the State, and any inspection shall be in the presence of a representative of the State.

(b) On motion of a party and on notice to the other parties, the court in which an action is pending may order one or more of the other parties to disclose to the party making the motion the name and address of each person the other party may use at trial to present evidence under Rules 702, 703, and 705, Texas Rules of Evidence. The court shall specify in the order the time and manner in which the other party must make the disclosure to the moving party, but in specifying the time in which the other party shall make disclosure the court shall require the other party to make the disclosure not later than the 20th day before the date the trial begins.

History of CCP art. 39.14: Acts 1965, 59th Leg., vol. 2, ch. 722. Amended by Acts 1999, 76th Leg., ch. 578, §1, eff. Sept. 1, 1999; Acts 2005, 79th Leg., ch. 1019, §1, eff. June 18, 2005.

See also Gov't Code §§552.021, 552.108.

ANNOTATIONS

Pope v. State, 207 S.W.3d 352, 360 (Tex.Crim.App. 2006). "[O]nce a party designates a particular person as an expert that he may use as a witness at trial, that person is no longer a 'consulting' expert, he is a 'testifying' expert, and the opposing party, whether the State or the defendant, may seek further information from or about him for use at trial."

Etheridge v. State, 903 S.W.2d 1, 7 (Tex.Crim.App. 1994). "'[T]he State has no obligation to furnish counsel for the accused with information he has in regard to prospective jurors.'"

McBride v. State, 838 S.W.2d 248, 250 (Tex.Crim. App.1992). "[T]he trial judge is required 'to permit discovery if the evidence sought is material to the *defense* of the accused.' *At 251:* [A] criminal defendant has a right to inspect evidence indispensable to the State's case because that evidence is necessarily material to the defense of the accused."

Kinnamon v. State, 791 S.W.2d 84, 91 (Tex.Crim. App.1990), *overruled on other grounds*, *Cook v. State*, 884 S.W.2d 485 (Tex.Crim.App.1994). "[A] defendant does not have a general right to discovery of evidence in possession of the State. Decisions involving pretrial discovery of evidence which is not exculpatory, mitigating, or privileged are within the discretion of the trial court."

Whitchurch v. State, 650 S.W.2d 422, 425 (Tex. Crim.App.1983). "In determining materiality, the omission must be evaluated in the context of the entire record and constitutional error is committed only if the omitted evidence creates a reasonable doubt that did not otherwise exist."

In re State, 116 S.W.3d 376, 382 (Tex.App.—El Paso 2003, orig. proceeding). "[A] defendant's right to discover exculpatory evidence ... does not include a post-conviction search of the police department's property room for DNA evidence."

Thornton v. State, 37 S.W.3d 490, 493 (Tex.App.— Texarkana 2000, pet. ref'd). Article 39.14(b) "was intended to establish a limited exception to the general rule that the State cannot obtain discovery of the witnesses the defendant intends to call at trial. [T]he trial court generally cannot order discovery of the defendant's witnesses...."

CHAPTER 40. NEW TRIALS

Art. 40.001   New trial on material evidence

ART. 40.001. NEW TRIAL ON MATERIAL EVIDENCE

A new trial shall be granted an accused where material evidence favorable to the accused has been discovered since trial.

History of CCP art. 40.001: Acts 1993, 73rd Leg., ch. 900, §11.01, eff. Sept. 1, 1993.

ANNOTATIONS

Keeter v. State, 74 S.W.3d 31, 38 (Tex.Crim.App. 2002). With respect to evidence of recantation, in denying a motion for new trial based on newly discovered evidence, "the trial court acts within its discretion so long as the record provides some basis for disbelieving the testimony. Such bases include, but are not limited to: evidence that the recanting witness was subject to pressure by family members or to threats from co-conspirators, evidence showing part of the recantation to be false, circumstances showing that the complainant recanted after moving in with family members of the defendant, and where an accomplice recants after being convicted."

ARTS. 40.01 TO 40.11. REPEALED

Repealed by the Texas Court of Criminal Appeals' adoption of the Texas Rules of Appellate Procedure on Apr. 10, 1986. 707 S.W.2d xxx, xxxv.

CHAPTER 41. ARREST OF JUDGMENT

ARTS. 41.01 TO 41.05. REPEALED

Repealed by the Texas Court of Criminal Appeals' adoption of the Texas Rules of Appellate Procedure on Apr. 10, 1986. 707 S.W.2d xxx, xxxv.

CHAPTER 42. JUDGMENT & SENTENCE

ART. 42.01. JUDGMENT

Sec. 1. A judgment is the written declaration of the court signed by the trial judge and entered of record showing the conviction or acquittal of the defendant. The sentence served shall be based on the information contained in the judgment. The judgment shall reflect:

1.   The title and number of the case;

2.   That the case was called and the parties appeared, naming the attorney for the state, the defendant, and the attorney for the defendant, or, where a defendant is not represented by counsel, that the defendant knowingly, intelligently, and voluntarily waived the right to representation by counsel;

3.   The plea or pleas of the defendant to the offense charged;

4.   Whether the case was tried before a jury or a jury was waived;

5.   The submission of the evidence, if any;

6.   In cases tried before a jury that the jury was charged by the court;

7.   The verdict or verdicts of the jury or the finding or findings of the court;

8.   In the event of a conviction that the defendant is adjudged guilty of the offense as found by the verdict of the jury or the finding of the court, and that the defendant be punished in accordance with the jury's verdict or the court's finding as to the proper punishment;

9.   In the event of conviction where death or any punishment is assessed that the defendant be sentenced to death, a term of confinement or community supervision, or to pay a fine, as the case may be;

10.   In the event of conviction where the imposition of sentence is suspended and the defendant is placed on community supervision, setting forth the punishment assessed, the length of community supervision, and the conditions of community supervision;

11. In the event of acquittal that the defendant be discharged;

12. The county and court in which the case was tried and, if there was a change of venue in the case, the name of the county in which the prosecution was originated;

13. The offense or offenses for which the defendant was convicted;

14. The date of the offense or offenses and degree of offense for which the defendant was convicted;

15. The term of sentence;

16. The date judgment is entered;

17. The date sentence is imposed;

18. The date sentence is to commence and any credit for time served;

19. The terms of any order entered pursuant to Article 42.08 of this code that the defendant's sentence is to run cumulatively or concurrently with another sentence or sentences;

20. The terms of any plea bargain;

21. Affirmative findings entered pursuant to Subdivision (2) of Subsection (a) of Section 3g of Article 42.12 of this code;

22. The terms of any fee payment ordered under Article 42.151 of this code;

23. The defendant's thumbprint taken in accordance with Article 38.33 of this code;

24. In the event that the judge orders the defendant to repay a reward or part of a reward under Articles 37.073 and 42.152 of this code, a statement of the amount of the payment or payments required to be made;

25. In the event that the court orders restitution to be paid to the victim, a statement of the amount of restitution ordered and:

(A) the name of the victim and the permanent mailing address of the victim at the time of the judgment; or

(B) if the court determines that the inclusion of the victim's name and address in the judgment is not in the best interest of the victim, the name and address of a person or agency that will accept and forward restitution payments to the victim;

26. In the event that a presentence investigation is required by Section 9(a), (b), (h), or (i), Article 42.12 of this code, a statement that the presentence investigation was done according to the applicable provision;

27. In the event of conviction of an offense for which registration as a sex offender is required under Chapter 62, a statement that the registration requirement of that chapter applies to the defendant and a statement of the age of the victim of the offense;

28. The defendant's state identification number required by Section 60.052(a)(2), if that number has been assigned at the time of the judgment; and

29. The incident number required by Section 60.052(a)(4), if that number has been assigned at the time of the judgment.

Sec. 2. The judge may order the prosecuting attorney, or the attorney or attorneys representing any defendant, or the court clerk under the supervision of an attorney, to prepare the judgment, or the court may prepare the same.

Sec. 3. The provisions of this article shall apply to both felony and misdemeanor cases.

Sec. 4. The Office of Court Administration of the Texas Judicial System shall promulgate a standardized felony judgment form that conforms to the requirements of Section 1 of this article. A court entering a felony judgement shall use the form promulgated under this section.

Sec. 5. In addition to the information described by Section 1 of this article, the judgment should reflect affirmative findings entered pursuant to Article 42.013 of this code.

Sec. 6. In addition to the information described by Section 1 of this article, the judgment should reflect affirmative findings entered pursuant to Article 42.014 of this code.

Sec. 7. In addition to the information described by Section 1, the judgment should reflect affirmative findings entered pursuant to Article 42.015.

Sec. 8. In addition to the information described by Section 1, the judgment should reflect affirmative findings entered pursuant to Article 42.017.

History of CCP art. 42.01: Acts 1965, 59th Leg., vol. 2, ch. 722. Amended by Acts 1975, 64th Leg., ch. 95, §1, eff. Sept. 1, 1975; Acts 1981, 67th Leg., ch. 291, §111, eff. Sept. 1, 1981; Acts 1985, 69th Leg., ch. 344, §1 (eff. Jan. 1, 1986), ch. 344, §2 (eff. June 10, 1985); Acts 1987, 70th Leg., ch. 110, §2, eff. Aug. 31, 1987; Acts 1989, 71st Leg., ch. 360, §2 (eff. Sept. 1, 1989), ch. 603, §2 (eff. Sept. 1, 1989), ch. 611, §2 (eff. Sept. 1, 1989), ch. 806, §1 (eff. Sept. 1, 1989); Acts 1991, 72nd Leg., ch. 16, §4.04 (eff. Aug. 26, 1991), 2nd C.S., ch. 10, §7.02 (eff. Dec. 1, 1991); Acts 1993, 73rd Leg., ch. 900, §§5.03, 9.02 (eff. Sept. 1, 1993), ch. 987, §4 (eff. Sept. 1, 1993); Acts 1995, 74th Leg., ch. 258, §9, eff. Sept. 1, 1995; Acts 1997, 75th Leg., ch. 668, §2, eff. Sept. 1, 1997; Acts 1999, 76th Leg., ch. 580, §6 (eff. Sept. 1, 1999), ch. 1415, §§1, 2 (eff. Sept. 1, 1999), ch. 1193, §1 (eff. Sept. 1, 1999); Acts 2001, 77th Leg., ch. 1159, §1, eff. Sept. 1, 2001; Acts 2005, 79th Leg., ch. 1218, §1, eff. Sept. 1, 2005.

Rhodes v. State, 240 S.W.3d 882, 888 (Tex.Crim. App.2007). "[W]e point out that there is a difference between an entire judgment being 'void' and a *portion* of a judgment being 'void.' For example, a judgment may contain two or more sentencing elements (e.g. imprisonment and fine), one of which may be valid while the other is void. When only one of the sentencing elements is void, the *judgment* is rendered void only if the judgment cannot be reformed to cure the infirmity (i.e. the infirmity cannot be cured without resort to resentencing). Some cases addressing other types of judgment defects have likewise indicated that the judgment is not void if the defect could have been reformed on the direct appeal of the judgment in question or in a nunc pro tunc order."

State v. Cullen, 195 S.W.3d 696, 700 (Tex.Crim.App. 2006). "Because an appellate court's review of a trial court's ruling is restricted by an inadequate record of the basis for the trial court's ruling, we find it necessary to require a trial court to express its findings of fact and conclusions of law when requested by the losing party."

State v. Savage, 933 S.W.2d 497, 499 (Tex.Crim. App.1996). "[T]he trial court does not have the authority to grant a different judgment—a judgment non obstante verdicto—than that rendered by the jury. [I]n criminal trials the court 'may not receive a verdict ... and enter another and different judgment from that called for by the verdict.' [¶] [T]rial courts do maintain the authority to order new trials for evidentiary insufficiency in criminal cases; a power which is the functional equivalent of granting a JNOV in a civil case. [¶] [T]he State [has] the right to appeal the trial court's JNOV ruling as the functional equivalent of an order granting a new trial for insufficient evidence." *See also* ***Ex parte McIver***, 586 S.W.2d 851, 854 (Tex. Crim.App.1979).

Ex parte George, 913 S.W.2d 523, 526 (Tex.Crim. App.1995). "[E]ntry of a judgment of acquittal is ... a ministerial duty, not a matter of discretion. [T]he judgment in a criminal case merely documents the fact of, and certain important events associated with, the process leading to conviction or acquittal. It is not the conviction or acquittal itself. [I]f the judgment reflects that an accused was acquitted, and it is later made to appear that he was not acquitted in fact, the judgment may be reformed accordingly."

Rodarte v. State, 860 S.W.2d 108, 109 n.1 (Tex. Crim.App.1993). "'The written judgment is not itself the conviction but evidence, among other things, that a conviction has occurred.' [W]hile it is true that appeal 'may not be taken' until the written judgment has been entered, it is not the signing of the judgment that constitutes the appealable event."

Ex parte Kopecky, 821 S.W.2d 957, 960 (Tex.Crim. App.1992). "A conviction is meaningless without a *judgment* of conviction.... Punishment and sentence are incorporated in the judgment. [S]entence is a necessary component of a judgment of conviction." (Internal quotes omitted.)

Weir v. State, 252 S.W.3d 85, ___ (Tex.App.— Austin 2008, pet. filed 6-12-08). "A trial court's pronouncement of sentence is oral, while the judgment, including the sentence assessed, is the written declaration and embodiment of that oral pronouncement. When the court's written judgment diverges from the court's oral pronouncement of sentence, the oral pronouncement controls. [¶] This appeal centers on whether restitution, attorney's fees, and court costs are part of the sentence such that the oral pronouncement (or the absence of an oral pronouncement regarding them) determines whether they may be properly included in the written judgment. [B]ecause restitution is punishment, it must be included in the oral pronouncement of sentence in order to be properly included in the written judgment. [¶] In contrast, the assessment of fees for an appointed attorney is not punishment. [W]e determine that appointed attorney's fees are not a sentencing issue and need not be pronounced orally in order to be properly included in the written judgment. [¶] Because court costs are assessed ... only against convicted defendants, we conclude that the award of court costs other than attorney's fees is, at least in part, punishment and must be orally pronounced in order to be properly included in the written judgment."

ART. 42.011. JUDGMENT AFFECTING AN OFFICER OR JAILER

If a person licensed under Chapter 415, Government Code, is charged with the commission of a felony and a court that knows the person is licensed under that chapter convicts the person or places the person on community supervision, the clerk of the court shall send the Commission on Law Enforcement Officer

Standards and Education, by mail or electronically, the license number of the person and a certified copy of the court's judgment reflecting that the person has been convicted or placed on community supervision.

History of CCP art. 42.011: Acts 1995, 74th Leg., ch. 538, §10, eff. Sept. 1, 1995.

ART. 42.012. FINDING THAT CONTROLLED SUBSTANCE USED TO COMMIT OFFENSE

In the punishment phase of the trial of an offense under Chapter 29, Chapter 31, or Title 5, Penal Code, if the court determines beyond a reasonable doubt that the defendant administered or provided a controlled substance to the victim of the offense with the intent of facilitating the commission of the offense, the court shall make an affirmative finding of that fact and enter the affirmative finding in the judgment of that case.

History of CCP art. 42.012: Acts 1999, 76th Leg., ch. 417, §2(b), eff. Sept. 1, 1999. Renumbered from art. 42.015 by Acts 2001, 77th Leg., ch. 1420, §21.001(9), eff. Sept. 1, 2001.

ART. 42.013. FINDING OF FAMILY VIOLENCE

In the trial of an offense under Title 5, Penal Code, if the court determines that the offense involved family violence, as defined by Section 71.004, Family Code, the court shall make an affirmative finding of that fact and enter the affirmative finding in the judgment of the case.

History of CCP art. 42.013: Acts 1993, 73rd Leg., ch. 900, §9.01, eff. Sept. 1, 1993. Amended by Acts 2003, 78th Leg., ch. 1276, §7.002(h), eff. Sept. 1, 2003.

ANNOTATIONS

Goodwin v. State, 91 S.W.3d 912, 919 (Tex.App.—Fort Worth 2002, no pet.). "There is no language in either [CCP art.] 42.013 or [Pen. Code] §22.01(b)(2) that would exclude the use of extrinsic evidence to prove that a previous assault was against a family member when the trial court failed to make an affirmative finding in the case. There is nothing to suggest that the Texas Legislature intended, by adopting article 42.013, to exclude the introduction of extrinsic evidence to prove a prior assault was against a family member."

Ⓔ ART. 42.0131. REQUIRED NOTICE FOR PERSONS CONVICTED OF MISDEMEANORS INVOLVING FAMILY VIOLENCE

If a person is convicted of a misdemeanor involving family violence, as defined by Section 71.004, Family Code, the court shall notify the person of the fact that it is unlawful for the person to possess or transfer a firearm or ammunition.

Hist. of art. 42.0131: Acts 2007, 80th Leg., ch. 125, §2, eff. Sept. 1, 2007.

ART. 42.014. FINDING THAT OFFENSE WAS COMMITTED BECAUSE OF BIAS OR PREJUDICE

(a) In the trial of an offense under Title 5, Penal Code, or Section 28.02, 28.03, or 28.08, Penal Code, the judge shall make an affirmative finding of fact and enter the affirmative finding in the judgment of the case if at the guilt or innocence phase of the trial, the judge or the jury, whichever is the trier of fact, determines beyond a reasonable doubt that the defendant intentionally selected the person against whom the offense was committed or intentionally selected property damaged or affected as a result of the offense because of the defendant's bias or prejudice against a group identified by race, color, disability, religion, national origin or ancestry, age, gender, or sexual preference.

(b) The sentencing judge may, as a condition of punishment, require attendance in an educational program to further tolerance and acceptance of others.

(c) In this article, "sexual preference" has the following meaning only: a preference for heterosexuality, homosexuality, or bisexuality.

History of CCP art. 42.014: Acts 1993, 73rd Leg., ch. 987, §5, eff. Sept. 1, 1993. Amended by Acts 1995, 74th Leg., ch. 318, §50, eff. Sept. 1, 1995; Acts 2001, 77th Leg., ch. 85, §1.02, eff. Sept. 1, 2001.

ANNOTATIONS

Jaynes v. State, 216 S.W.3d 839, 846 (Tex.App.—Corpus Christi 2006, no pet.). "Punishment enhancement under the Texas Hate Crimes Act may be based on circumstantial evidence of the defendant's bias or prejudicial motive, including previous racial epithets directed at the victim, provided, however, the circumstantial evidence must be relevant and reliable to prevent enhancement of punishment for crimes committed by a person who entertains a bias or prejudice, but whose bias was not the primary motivation for the criminal conduct. [¶] State must prove a causal link between the crime and the proven bias or prejudice. By requiring the State to prove a causal link, the statutes prevent prosecution of offenses committed by a person who entertains bias or prejudice but whose bias or prejudice was not a primary motivating factor in the offense charged."

ART. 42.015. FINDING OF AGE OF VICTIM

In the trial of an offense under Section 20.02, 20.03, or 20.04, Penal Code, or an attempt, conspiracy, or solicitation to commit one of those offenses, the judge shall make an affirmative finding of fact and enter the affirmative finding in the judgment in the case if the judge determines that the victim or intended victim was younger than 17 years of age at the time of the offense.

History of CCP art. 42.015: Acts 1999, 76th Leg., ch. 1193, §2 (eff. Sept. 1, 1999), ch. 1415, §3 (eff. Sept. 1, 1999).

ART. 42.016. SPECIAL DRIVER'S LICENSE OR IDENTIFICATION REQUIREMENTS FOR CERTAIN SEX OFFENDERS

If a person is convicted of, receives a grant of deferred adjudication for, or is adjudicated as having engaged in delinquent conduct based on a violation of an offense for which a conviction or adjudication requires registration as a sex offender under Chapter 62, the court shall:

(1) issue an order requiring the Texas Department of Public Safety to include in any driver's license record or personal identification certificate record maintained by the department for the person an indication that the person is subject to the registration requirements of Chapter 62;

(2) require the person to apply to the Texas Department of Public Safety in person for an original or renewal driver's license or personal identification certificate not later than the 30th day after the date the person is released or the date the department sends written notice to the person of the requirements of Article 62.060, as applicable, and to annually renew the license or certificate;

(3) notify the person of the consequence of the conviction or order of deferred adjudication as it relates to the order issued under this article; and

(4) send to the Texas Department of Public Safety a copy of the record of conviction, a copy of the order granting deferred adjudication, or a copy of the juvenile adjudication, as applicable, and a copy of the order issued under this article.

History of CCP art. 42.016: Acts 1999, 76th Leg., ch. 1401, §1, eff. Sept. 1, 2000. Amended by Acts 2005, 79th Leg., ch. 1008, §2.01, eff. Sept. 1, 2005.

ART. 42.017. FINDING REGARDING AGE-BASED OFFENSE

 Article 42.017 below is effective for offenses committed on or after Sept. 1, 2007.

In the trial of an offense under Section 21.02, 21.11, 22.011, 22.021, or 43.25, Penal Code, the judge shall make an affirmative finding of fact and enter the affirmative finding in the judgment in the case if the judge determines that:

(1) at the time of the offense, the defendant was younger than 19 years of age and the victim was at least 13 years of age; and

(2) the conviction is based solely on the ages of the defendant and the victim or intended victim at the time of the offense.

History of CCP art. 42.017: Acts 2001, 77th Leg., ch. 1159, §2, eff. Sept. 1, 2001. Amended by Acts 2007, 80th Leg., ch. 593, §3.17, eff. Sept. 1, 2007.

ART. 42.017. FINDING REGARDING AGE-BASED OFFENSE

Article 42.017 below is effective for offenses in which any element of the offense was committed before Sept. 1, 2007.

In the trial of an offense under Section 21.11, 22.011, 22.021, or 43.25, Penal Code, the judge shall make an affirmative finding of fact and enter the affirmative finding in the judgment in the case if the judge determines that:

(1) at the time of the offense, the defendant was younger than 19 years of age and the victim was at least 13 years of age; and

(2) the conviction is based solely on the ages of the defendant and the victim or intended victim at the time of the offense.

ART. 42.018. NOTICE PROVIDED BY CLERK OF COURT

(a) This article applies only:

(1) to conviction or deferred adjudication granted on the basis of:

(A) an offense under Title 5, Penal Code; or

(B) an offense on conviction of which a defendant is required to register as a sex offender under Chapter 62; and

(2) if the victim of the offense is under 18 years of age.

(b) Not later than the fifth day after the date a person who holds a certificate issued under Subchapter B, Chapter 21, Education Code, is convicted or granted deferred adjudication on the basis of an offense, the clerk of the court in which the conviction or deferred adjudication is entered shall provide to the State Board for Educator Certification written notice of the person's conviction or deferred adjudication, including the offense on which the conviction or deferred adjudication was based.

History of CCP art. 42.018: Acts 2003, 78th Leg., ch. 920, §2, eff. June 20, 2003.

ART. 42.0181. NOTICE OF THEFT, FRAUD, MONEY LAUNDERING, OR INSURANCE FRAUD PROVIDED BY CLERK OF COURT

Not later than the fifth day after the date a person who holds a certificate of authority, license, or other authority issued by the Texas Department of Insurance is convicted of or granted deferred adjudication for an offense under Chapter 31, 32, 34, or 35, Penal Code, the clerk of the court in which the conviction or order of deferred adjudication is entered shall provide to the Texas Department of Insurance written notice of the person's conviction or deferred adjudication, including the offense on which the conviction or deferred adjudication was based.

History of CCP art. 42.0181: Acts 2005, 79th Leg., ch. 1162, §7, eff. Sept. 1, 2005.

ART. 42.019. MOTOR FUEL THEFT

(a) A judge shall enter an affirmative finding in the judgment in a case if the judge or jury, whichever is the finder of fact, determines beyond a reasonable doubt in the guilt or innocence phase of the trial of an offense under Section 31.03, Penal Code, that the defendant, in committing the offense:

(1) dispensed motor fuel into the fuel tank of a motor vehicle on the premises of an establishment at which motor fuel is offered for retail sale; and

(2) after dispensing the motor fuel, left the premises of the establishment without paying the establishment for the motor fuel.

(b) If a judge enters an affirmative finding as required by Subsection (a) and determines that the defendant has previously been convicted of an offense the judgment for which contains an affirmative finding under Subsection (a), the judge shall enter a special affirmative finding in the judgment in the case.

History of CCP art. 42.019: Acts 2001, 77th Leg., ch. 359, §1, eff. Sept. 1, 2001.

ART. 42.0191. FINDING REGARDING VICTIMS OF TRAFFICKING OR OTHER ABUSE

 Article 42.0191 below is effective for judgments of conviction entered or grants of deferred adjudication or dispositions of delinquent conduct made on or after June 15, 2007.

(a) In the trial of an offense, on the motion of the attorney representing the state the judge shall make an affirmative finding of fact and enter the affirmative finding in the papers in the case if the judge determines that, regardless of whether the conduct at issue is the subject of the prosecution or part of the same criminal episode as the conduct that is the subject of the prosecution, a victim in the trial:

(1) is or has been a victim of a severe form of trafficking in persons, as defined by 22 U.S.C. Section 7102(8); or

(2) has suffered substantial physical or mental abuse as a result of having been a victim of criminal activity described by 8 U.S.C. Section 1101(a)(15)(U)(iii).

(b) That part of the papers in the case containing an affirmative finding under this article:

(1) must include specific information identifying the victim, as available;

(2) may not include information identifying the victim's location; and

(3) is confidential, unless written consent for the release of the affirmative finding is obtained from the victim or, if the victim is younger than 18 years of age, the victim's parent or guardian.

History of CCP art. 42.0191: Acts 2007, 80th Leg., ch. 849, §1, eff. June 15, 2007.

ART. 42.02. SENTENCE

The sentence is that part of the judgment, or order revoking a suspension of the imposition of a sentence, that orders that the punishment be carried into execution in the manner prescribed by law.

History of CCP art. 42.02: Acts 1965, 59th Leg., vol. 2, ch. 722. Amended by Acts 1981, 67th Leg., ch. 291, §112, eff. Sept. 1, 1981; Acts 1993, 73rd Leg., ch. 900, §5.03, eff. Sept. 1, 1993.

ANNOTATIONS

State v. Kersh, 127 S.W.3d 775, 776 (Tex.Crim.App. 2004). "[T]he meaning of 'sentence' under [CCP arts. 42.02 and 44.01(b)] includes enhancement allegations.... *At 777:* [A] deadly-weapon finding is not part of the sentence, and ... the State is not entitled to appeal an omission of one from a trial court's judgment." *See also State v. Ross*, 953 S.W.2d 748, 750 (Tex.Crim. App.1997).

Carroll v. State, 42 S.W.3d 129, 133 (Tex.Crim.App. 2001). "[A]fter *Mitchell* [*v. United States*, 119 S.Ct. 1307 (1999)], [we cannot conclude] that the trial court may consider invocation by appellant of her federal constitutional right to silence as a circumstance against her when determining her punishment."

Ex parte Renier, 734 S.W.2d 349, 369 n.25 (Tex. Crim.App.1987). "'A sentence ... is required to be pronounced in all cases before an appeal is taken, except in death penalty cases and in probation cases where imposition of sentence is suspended.' [¶] [T]he date of sentence is the point from which the time for giving notice of appeal begins to run. But, because the pronouncement of sentence is not a prerequisite to appeal in cases where sentence is suspended and the defendant placed on probation, it follows that the judgment of conviction is complete in such cases without the necessity of a sentence."

ART. 42.023. JUDGE MAY CONSIDER ALTERNATIVE SENTENCING

Before pronouncing sentence on a defendant convicted of a criminal offense, the judge may consider whether the defendant should be committed for care and treatment under Section 462.081, Health and Safety Code.

History of CCP art. 42.023: Acts 1993, 73rd Leg., ch. 900, §5.03, eff. Sept. 1, 1993.

ART. 42.03. PRONOUNCING SENTENCE; TIME; CREDIT FOR TIME SPENT IN JAIL BETWEEN ARREST & SENTENCE OR PENDING APPEAL

Sec. 1. (a) Except as provided in Article 42.14, sentence shall be pronounced in the defendant's presence.

(b) The court shall permit a victim, close relative of a deceased victim, or guardian of a victim, as defined by Article 56.01 of this code, to appear in person to present to the court and to the defendant a statement of the person's views about the offense, the defendant, and the effect of the offense on the victim. The victim, relative, or guardian may not direct questions to the defendant while making the statement. The court reporter may not transcribe the statement. The statement must be made:

(1) after punishment has been assessed and the court has determined whether or not to grant community supervision in the case;

(2) after the court has announced the terms and conditions of the sentence; and

(3) after sentence is pronounced.

🅐 **Sec. 2. (a)** In all criminal cases the judge of the court in which the defendant is convicted shall give the defendant credit on the defendant's sentence for the time that the defendant has spent:

(1) in jail for the case, other than confinement served as a condition of community supervision, from the time of his arrest and confinement until his sentence by the trial court; or

🅔 *Subsection (2) below is effective for defendants initially placed on community supervision on or after Sept. 1, 2007.*

(2) in a substance abuse treatment facility operated by the Texas Department of Criminal Justice under Section 493.009, Government Code, or another court-ordered residential program or facility as a condition of deferred adjudication community supervision granted in the case if the defendant successfully completes the treatment program at that facility.

(b) In all revocations of a suspension of the imposition of a sentence the judge shall enter the restitution or reparation due and owing on the date of the revocation.

Sec. 3. If a defendant appeals his conviction, is not released on bail, and is retained in a jail as provided in Section 7, Article 42.09, pending his appeal, the judge of the court in which the defendant was convicted shall give the defendant credit on his sentence for the time that the defendant has spent in jail pending disposition of his appeal. The court shall endorse on both the commitment and the mandate from the appellate court all credit given the defendant under this section, and the institutional division of the Texas Department of Criminal Justice shall grant the credit in computing the defendant's eligibility for parole and discharge.

Sec. 4. When a defendant who has been sentenced to imprisonment in the institutional division of the Texas Department of Criminal Justice has spent time in jail pending trial and sentence or pending appeal, the judge of the sentencing court shall direct the sheriff to attach to the commitment papers a statement assessing the defendant's conduct while in jail.

Secs. 5, 6. Repealed by Acts 1989, 71st Leg., ch. 785, §4.24, eff. Sept. 1, 1989.

Secs. 7, 8. Deleted by Acts 1993, 73rd Leg., ch. 900, §5.03, eff. Sept. 1, 1993.

(g) Repealed by Acts 2003, 78th Leg., ch. 406, §2, eff. Sept. 1, 2003.

History of CCP art. 42.03: Acts 1965, 59th Leg., vol. 2, ch. 722. Amended by Acts 1967, 60th Leg., ch. 659, §28, eff. Aug. 28, 1967; Acts 1973, 63rd Leg., ch. 91, §1, eff. Aug. 27, 1973; Acts 1977, 65th Leg., ch. 382, §1 (eff. Aug. 29, 1977),

★

ch. 827, §1 (eff. Aug. 29, 1977); Acts 1981, 67th Leg., ch. 141, §1 (eff. Sept. 1, 1981), ch. 291, §113 (eff. Sept. 1, 1981), ch. 616, §1 (eff. Aug. 31, 1981); Acts 1983, 68th Leg., ch. 586, §4 (eff. Aug. 29, 1983), ch. 809, §1 (eff. Aug. 29, 1983); Acts 1985, 69th Leg., ch. 232, §13, eff. Sept. 1, 1985; Acts 1989, 71st Leg., ch. 785, §4.06 (eff. June 15, 1989), ch. 848, §1 (eff. June 14, 1989), ch. 1040, §§1, 2 (eff. Aug. 28, 1989); Acts 1991, 72nd Leg., ch. 16, §4.05 (eff. Aug. 26, 1991), ch. 278, §1 (eff. June 5, 1991), 2nd C.S., ch. 10, §§14.01-14.04, 15.03 (eff. Oct. 1, 1991), ch. 10, §8.02 (eff. Dec. 1, 1991); Acts 1993, 73rd Leg., ch. 201, §1 (eff. Aug. 30, 1993), ch. 900, §5.03 (eff. Sept. 1, 1993); Acts 1995, 74th Leg., ch. 556, §1, eff. Sept. 1, 1995; Acts 2003, 78th Leg., ch. 406, §2, eff. Sept. 1, 2003; Acts 2007, 80th Leg., ch. 1205, §1, eff. Sept. 1, 2007.

ANNOTATIONS

Ex parte Rodriguez, 195 S.W.3d 700, 703 (Tex. Crim.App.2006). "[A]pplicant is permitted to show that he was detained in this cause by some means other than formal detainer. We conclude that the letter from the U.S. Department of Justice asserting that applicant was arrested by Mexican authorities based upon the provisional arrest request that it had previously filed on behalf of TDCJ is such other means of showing that he was detained in this cause when held by Mexican authorities. *At 704:* [A]pplicant is entitled to receive jail-time credit for the time between his arrest in Mexico and his return to the custody of TDCJ authorities."

Taylor v. State, 131 S.W.3d 497, 502 (Tex.Crim.App. 2004). "[T]he order granting Taylor deferred adjudication was set aside. Taylor was not sentenced until his guilt was adjudicated. At that time, the judge did not orally pronounce a fine, but included a fine within the written judgment. When there is a conflict between the two, the oral pronouncement controls. Since the judge did not orally assess a fine as part of Taylor's sentence when guilt was adjudicated, the Court of Appeals was correct to delete the fine from the judgment." *See also Coffey v. State*, 979 S.W.2d 326, 329 (Tex.Crim.App. 1998) (oral pronouncement unnecessary in probation revocation).

Ex parte Hale, 117 S.W.3d 866, 867 (Tex.Crim.App. 2003). "The issue in this case is whether the applicant should be given credit on a subsequent sentence for the time during which he was erroneously released on mandatory supervision when he should have continued to be imprisoned under the previous sentence." Held: No credit should be given.

Ex parte Harvey, 846 S.W.2d 328, 329 (Tex.Crim. App.1993). "No requirement exists for the trial court to detail the reasons for the award of credits for time spent in jail prior to sentencing other than the documentation required in [CCP art.] 42.09, §8, ... provided that such credit does not exceed the time between date of commission of the offense and the imposition of sentence."

Ex parte Green, 688 S.W.2d 555, 557 (Tex.Crim. App.1985). "We do not think that in enacting Article 42.03, §2(a) the Legislature intended that an individual initially detained as a juvenile and later certified an adult, then prosecuted and sentenced accordingly, should be treated any differently than one who is initially detained as an adult."

Abbott v. State, 245 S.W.3d 19, 22-23 (Tex.App.— Waco 2007, pet. granted 3-12-08). "We held that Abbott's original 20-year sentence was erroneous.... Abbott served 740 days of that 20-year sentence, and he has now served almost two-thirds of the 180-day confinement as a condition of community supervision. Abbott is entitled to credit on the 180-day confinement for his time in prison pending the appeal of his erroneous sentence."

Johnson v. State, 240 S.W.3d 76, 79 (Tex.App.— Austin 2007, pet. granted 1-16-08). CCP art. 42.12 §12(c) "permits the trial court to impose confinement in jail as a condition of supervision when placing the defendant on supervision or 'at any time during the supervision period.' Thus, even if the conditions of supervision must generally be determined and announced before any victim statement is made [according to CCP art. 42.03 §1(b)], §12(c) of the community supervision statute creates an exception to this rule. The court below was and remains authorized to impose jail time as a condition of appellant's community supervision at any time during the five-year supervision period. Under the circumstances, if the court's determination to impose the jail time condition was made after the victim statements were made, it was at most harmless error."

In re Risley, 190 S.W.3d 853, 854, n.2 (Tex.App.— Fort Worth 2006, orig. proceeding). "A felony defendant may not waive the right to be present at sentencing. Thus, relator cannot be deemed to have waived the requirement of article 42.03, §1(a) by voluntarily absenting himself from trial."

Tagorda v. State, 977 S.W.2d 632, 634 (Tex.App.— Fort Worth 1998, no pet.). "[A] criminal defendant is not entitled to receive credit on his sentence for time spent on electronic monitoring as a condition of bond before sentencing."

Mayo v. State, 861 S.W.2d 953, 954-55 (Tex.App.— Houston [1st Dist.] 1993, pet. ref'd). "[T]he trial court permitted the victim ... to testify before punishment had been assessed and before the trial court determined whether or not to grant probation. ... The appellant did not object to the substance of [victim's] testimony or that he should only be permitted to testify after punishment was assessed. Thus, the appellant waived any error in admitting [victim's] testimony."

ART. 42.031. WORK RELEASE PROGRAM

Sec. 1. (a) The sheriff of each county may attempt to secure employment for each defendant sentenced to the county jail work release program under Article 42.034 of this code and each defendant confined in the county jail awaiting transfer to the institutional division of the Texas Department of Criminal Justice.

(b) The employer of a defendant participating in a program under this article shall pay the defendant's salary to the sheriff. The sheriff shall deposit the salary into a special fund to be given to the defendant on his release after deducting:

(1) the cost to the county for the defendant's confinement during the pay period based on the average daily cost of confining defendants in the county jail, as determined by the commissioners court of the county;

(2) support of the defendant's dependents; and

(3) restitution to the victims of an offense committed by the defendant.

(c) At the time of sentencing or at a later date, the court sentencing a defendant may direct the sheriff not to deduct the cost described under Subdivision (1) of Subsection (b) of this section or to deduct only a specified portion of the cost if the court determines that the full deduction would cause a significant financial hardship to the defendant's dependents.

(d) If the sheriff does not find employment for a defendant who would otherwise be sentenced to imprisonment in the institutional division, the sheriff shall:

(1) transfer the defendant to the sheriff of a county who agrees to accept the defendant as a participant in the county jail work release program; or

(2) retain the defendant in the county jail for employment as soon as possible in a jail work release program.

Sec. 2. A defendant participating in a program under this article shall be confined in the county jail or in another facility designated by the sheriff at all times except for:

(1) time spent at work and traveling to or from work; and

(2) time spent attending or traveling to or from an education or rehabilitation program approved by the sheriff.

Sec. 3. (a) The sheriff of each county shall classify each felon serving a sentence in the county jail work release program for the purpose of awarding good conduct time credit in the same manner as inmates of the institutional division of the Texas Department of Criminal Justice are classified under Chapter 498, Government Code, and shall award good conduct time in the same manner as the director of the department does in that chapter.

(b) If the sheriff determines that the defendant is conducting himself in a manner that is dangerous to inmates in the county jail or to society as a whole, the sheriff may remove the defendant from participation in the program pending a hearing before the sentencing court. At the hearing, if the court determines that the sheriff's assessment of the defendant's conduct is correct, the court may terminate the defendant's participation in the program and order the defendant to the term of imprisonment that the defendant would have received had he not entered the program. If the court determines that the sheriff's assessment is incorrect, the court shall order the sheriff to readmit the defendant to the program. A defendant shall receive as credit toward his sentence any time served as a participant in the program.

History of CCP art. 42.031: Acts 1989, 71st Leg., ch. 2, §5.03(a), eff. Aug. 28, 1989. Amended by Acts 1991, 72nd Leg., 2nd C.S., ch. 10, §§14.10, 14.11 (eff. Oct. 1, 1991); Acts 1993, 73rd Leg., ch. 900, §5.03, eff. Sept. 1, 1993.

ART. 42.032. GOOD CONDUCT

Sec. 1. To encourage county jail discipline, a distinction may be made to give orderly, industrious, and obedient defendants the comforts and privileges they deserve. The reward for good conduct may consist of a relaxation of strict county jail rules and extension of social privileges consistent with proper discipline.

Sec. 2. The sheriff in charge of each county jail may grant commutation of time for good conduct, industry, and obedience. A deduction not to exceed one day for each day of the original sentence actually served may be made for the term or terms of sentences if a charge of misconduct has not been sustained against the defendant.

Sec. 3. This article applies whether or not the judgment of conviction is a fine or jail sentence or both, but the deduction in time may not exceed one-third of the original sentence as to fines and court costs assessed in the judgment of conviction.

Sec. 4. A defendant serving two or more cumulative sentences shall be allowed commutation as if the sentences were one sentence.

Sec. 5. Any part or all of the commutation accrued under this article may be forfeited and taken away by the sheriff:

(1) for a sustained charge of misconduct in violation of any rule known to the defendant, including escape or attempt to escape, if the sheriff has complied with discipline proceedings as approved by the Commission on Jail Standards; or

(2) on receipt by the sheriff of a certified copy of a final order of a state or federal court that dismisses as frivolous or malicious a lawsuit brought by a defendant while the defendant was in the custody of the sheriff.

Sec. 6. Except for credit earned by a defendant under Article 43.10, no other time allowance or credits in addition to the commutation of time under this article may be deducted from the term or terms of sentences.

Sec. 7. The sheriff shall keep a conduct record in card or ledger form and a calendar card on each defendant showing all forfeitures of commutation time and the reasons for the forfeitures.

History of CCP art. 42.032: Acts 1989, 71st Leg., ch. 2, §5.04(a), eff. Aug. 28, 1989. Amended by Acts 1991, 72nd Leg., 2nd C.S., ch. 10, §14.05, eff. Oct. 1, 1991; Acts 1993, 73rd Leg., ch. 900, §5.03, eff. Sept. 1, 1993; Acts 1999, 76th Leg., ch. 655, §2(a), eff. June 18, 1999.

ANNOTATIONS

Hencey v. State, 904 S.W.2d 160, 161 n.1 (Tex. App.—San Antonio 1995, no pet.). "The judgment … purports to order that appellant's sentence be served 'day for day.' This command improperly conflicts with the statutory authority granted to the sheriff to award 'good time' credits and is beyond the authority of the trial court." *See also **In re Cortez***, 143 S.W.3d 265, 268 (Tex.App.—San Antonio 2004, no pet.).

ART. 42.033. SENTENCE TO SERVE TIME DURING OFF-WORK HOURS

(a) Where jail time has been awarded to a person sentenced for a misdemeanor or sentenced to confinement in the county jail for a felony or when a defendant is serving a period of confinement as a condition of community supervision, the trial judge, at the time of the pronouncement of sentence or at any time while the defendant is serving the sentence or period of confinement, when in the judge's discretion the ends of justice would best be served, may permit the defendant to serve the defendant's sentence or period of confinement intermittently during his off-work hours or on weekends. The judge may require bail of the defendant to ensure the faithful performance of the sentence or period of confinement. The judge may attach conditions regarding the employment, travel, and other conduct of the defendant during the performance of such a sentence or period of confinement.

(b) The court may impose as a condition to permitting a defendant to serve the jail time assessed or period of confinement intermittently an additional requirement that the defendant make any of the following payments to the court, agencies, or persons, or that the defendant execute a letter and direct it to the defendant's employer directing the employer to deduct from the defendant's salary an amount directed by the court, which is to be sent by the employer to the clerk of the court. The money received by the court under this section may be used to pay the following expenses as directed by the court:

(1) the support of the defendant's dependents, if necessary;

(2) the defendant's documented personal, business, and travel expenses;

(3) reimbursement of the general fund of the county for the maintenance of the defendant in jail; and

(4) installment payments on restitution, fines, and court costs ordered by the court.

(c) The condition imposed under Subsection (b) of this article is not binding on an employer, except that income withheld for child support is governed by Chapter 158, Family Code.

(d) The court may permit the defendant to serve the defendant's sentence or period of confinement intermittently in order for the defendant to continue employment if the court imposes confinement for failure to pay a fine or court costs, as punishment for criminal nonsupport under Section 25.05, Penal Code, or for contempt of a court order for periodic payments for the support of a child.

(e) The court may permit the defendant to seek employment or obtain medical, psychological, or substance abuse treatment or counseling or obtain training or needed education under the same terms and conditions that apply to employment under this article.

History of CCP art. 42.033: Acts 1989, 71st Leg., ch. 785, §4.07, eff. Sept. 1, 1989. Amended by Acts 1991, 72nd Leg., 2nd C.S., ch. 10, §14.06, eff. Oct. 1, 1991; Acts 1993, 73rd Leg., ch. 900, §5.03, eff. Sept. 1, 1993; Acts 1997, 75th Leg., ch. 165, §7.03, eff. Sept. 1, 1997.

ART. 42.034. COUNTY JAIL WORK RELEASE PROGRAM

(a) If jail time has been awarded to a person sentenced for a misdemeanor or sentenced to confinement in the county jail for a felony, the trial judge at the time of pronouncement of sentence or at any time while the defendant is serving the sentence, when in the judge's discretion the ends of justice would best be served, may require the defendant to serve an alternate term for the same period of time in the county jail work release program of the county in which the offense occurred, if the person is classified by the sheriff as a low-risk offender under the classification system developed by the Commission on Jail Standards under Section 511.009, Government Code.

(b) The sheriff shall provide a classification report for a defendant to a judge as necessary so that the judge can determine whether to require the defendant to participate in the work release program under this article.

(c) A defendant sentenced under this article who would otherwise be sentenced to confinement in jail may earn good conduct credit in the same manner as provided by Article 42.032 of this code, but only while actually confined.

History of CCP art. 42.034: Acts 1989, 71st Leg., ch. 785, §4.08, eff. Sept. 1, 1989. Amended by Acts 1991, 72nd Leg., 2nd C.S., ch. 10, §14.07, eff. Oct. 1, 1991; Acts 1993, 73rd Leg., ch. 900, §5.03, eff. Sept. 1, 1993; Acts 1995, 74th Leg., ch. 722, §1, eff. Sept. 1, 1995.

ART. 42.035. ELECTRONIC MONITORING; HOUSE ARREST

(a) A court in a county served by a community supervision and corrections department that has an electronic monitoring program approved by the community justice assistance division of the Texas Department of Criminal Justice may require a defendant to serve all or part of a sentence of confinement in county jail by submitting to electronic monitoring rather than being confined in the county jail.

(b) A judge, at the time of the pronouncement of a sentence of confinement or at any time while the defendant is serving the sentence, on the judge's own motion or on the written motion of the defendant, may permit the defendant to serve the sentence under house arrest, including electronic monitoring and any other conditions the court chooses to impose, during the person's off-work hours. The judge may require bail of the defendant to ensure the faithful performance of the sentence.

(c) The court may require the defendant to pay to the community supervision and corrections department or the county any reasonable cost incurred because of the defendant's participation in the house arrest program, including the cost of electronic monitoring.

(d) A defendant who submits to electronic monitoring or participates in the house arrest program under this section discharges a sentence of confinement without deductions, good conduct time credits, or commutations.

History of CCP art. 42.035: Acts 1989, 71st Leg., ch. 785, §4.09, eff. Sept. 1, 1989. Amended by Acts 1993, 73rd Leg., ch. 900, §5.03, eff. Sept. 1, 1993.

ART. 42.036. COMMUNITY SERVICE

(a) A court may require a defendant, other than a defendant convicted of an offense under Sections 49.04-49.08, Penal Code, to serve all or part of a sentence of confinement or period of confinement required as a condition of community supervision in county jail by performing community service rather than by being confined in county jail unless the sentence of confinement was imposed by the jury in the case.

(b) In its order requiring a defendant to participate in community service work, the court must specify:

(1) the number of hours the defendant is required to work; and

(2) the entity or organization for which the defendant is required to work.

(c) The court may order the defendant to perform community service work under this article only for a governmental entity or a nonprofit organization that provides services to the general public that enhance social welfare and the general well-being of the community. A governmental entity or nonprofit organization that accepts a defendant under this section to perform community service must agree to supervise the defendant in the performance of the defendant's work and report on the defendant's work to the community supervision and corrections department or court-related services office.

(d) The court may require bail of a defendant to ensure the defendant's faithful performance of community service and may attach conditions to the bail as it determines are proper.

(e) A court may not order a defendant who is employed to perform more than 16 hours per week of community service under this article unless the court determines that requiring the defendant to work additional hours does not work a hardship on the defendant or the defendant's dependents. A court may not order a defendant who is unemployed to perform more than 32 hours per week of community service under this article, but may direct the defendant to use the remaining hours of the week to seek employment.

(f) A defendant is considered to have served one day in jail for each eight hours of community service performed under this article.

(g) Deleted by Acts 1993, 73rd Leg., ch. 900, §5.03, eff. Sept. 1, 1993.

(h) Repealed by Acts 1995, 74th Leg., ch. 76, §3.14, eff. Sept. 1, 1995.

History of CCP art. 42.036: Acts 1989, 71st Leg., ch. 785, §4.10, eff. Sept. 1, 1989. Amended by Acts 1990, 71st Leg., 6th C.S., ch. 25, §27, eff. June 18, 1990; Acts 1991, 72nd Leg., 2nd C.S., ch. 10, §§14.08, 15.01 (eff. Oct. 1, 1991); Acts 1993, 73rd Leg., ch. 201, §2 (eff. Aug. 30, 1993), ch. 900, §5.03 (eff. Sept. 1, 1993); Acts 1995, 74th Leg., ch. 76, §3.14, eff. Sept. 1, 1995.

ART. 42.037. RESTITUTION

(a) In addition to any fine authorized by law, the court that sentences a defendant convicted of an offense may order the defendant to make restitution to any victim of the offense or to the compensation to victims of crime fund established under Subchapter B, Chapter 56, to the extent that fund has paid compensation to or on behalf of the victim. If the court does not order restitution or orders partial restitution under this subsection, the court shall state on the record the reasons for not making the order or for the limited order.

(b)(1) If the offense results in damage to or loss or destruction of property of a victim of the offense, the court may order the defendant:

(A) to return the property to the owner of the property or someone designated by the owner; or

(B) if return of the property is impossible or impractical or is an inadequate remedy, to pay an amount equal to the greater of:

(i) the value of the property on the date of the damage, loss, or destruction; or

(ii) the value of the property on the date of sentencing, less the value of any part of the property that is returned on the date the property is returned.

(2) If the offense results in personal injury to a victim, the court may order the defendant to make restitution to:

(A) the victim for any expenses incurred by the victim as a result of the offense; or

(B) the compensation to victims of crime fund to the extent that fund has paid compensation to or on behalf of the victim.

(3) If the victim or the victim's estate consents, the court may, in addition to an order under Subdivision (2), order the defendant to make restitution by performing services instead of by paying money or make restitution to a person or organization, other than the compensation to victims of crime fund, designated by the victim or the estate.

(c) The court, in determining whether to order restitution and the amount of restitution, shall consider:

(1) the amount of the loss sustained by any victim and the amount paid to or on behalf of the victim by the compensation to victims of crime fund as a result of the offense; and

(2) other factors the court deems appropriate.

(d) If the court orders restitution under this article and the victim is deceased the court shall order the defendant to make restitution to the victim's estate.

(e) The court shall impose an order of restitution that is as fair as possible to the victim or to the compensation to victims of crime fund, as applicable. The imposition of the order may not unduly complicate or prolong the sentencing process.

(f)(1) The court may not order restitution for a loss for which the victim has received or will receive compensation only from a source other than the compensation to victims of crime fund. The court may, in the interest of justice, order restitution to any person who has compensated the victim for the loss to the extent the person paid compensation. An order of restitution shall require that all restitution to a victim or to the compensation to victims of crime fund be made before any restitution to any other person is made under the order.

(2) Any amount recovered by a victim from a person ordered to pay restitution in a federal or state civil proceeding is reduced by any amount previously paid to the victim by the person under an order of restitution.

(g)(1) The court may require a defendant to make restitution under this article within a specified period or in specified installments. If the court requires the defendant to make restitution in specified installments, in addition to the installment payments, the court may require the defendant to pay a one-time restitution fee of $12, $6 of which the court shall retain for costs incurred in collecting the specified installments and $6 of which the court shall order to be paid to the compensation to victims of crime fund.

(2) The end of the period or the last installment may not be later than:

(A) the end of the period of probation, if probation is ordered;

(B) five years after the end of the term of imprisonment imposed, if the court does not order probation; or

(C) five years after the date of sentencing in any other case.

(3) If the court does not provide otherwise, the defendant shall make restitution immediately.

(4) Except as provided by Subsection (n), the order of restitution must require the defendant to make restitution directly to the victim or other person eligible for restitution under this article, including the compensation to victims of crime fund, or to deliver the amount or property due as restitution to a community supervision and corrections department for transfer to the victim or person.

(h) If a defendant is placed on community supervision or is paroled or released on mandatory supervision, the court or the parole panel shall order the payment of restitution ordered under this article as a condition of community supervision, parole, or mandatory supervision. The court may revoke community supervision and the parole panel may revoke parole or mandatory supervision if the defendant fails to comply with the order. In determining whether to revoke community supervision, parole, or mandatory supervision, the court or parole panel shall consider:

(1) the defendant's employment status;

(2) the defendant's current and future earning ability;

(3) the defendant's current and future financial resources;

(4) the willfulness of the defendant's failure to pay;

(5) any other special circumstances that may affect the defendant's ability to pay; and

(6) the victim's financial resources or ability to pay expenses incurred by the victim as a result of the offense.

(i) In addition to any other terms and conditions of probation imposed under Article 42.12, the court may require a probationer to reimburse the compensation to victims of crime fund created under Subchapter B, Chapter 56, for any amounts paid from that fund to or on behalf of a victim of the probationer's offense. In this subsection, "victim" has the meaning assigned by Article 56.32.

(j) The court may order a community supervision and corrections department to obtain information pertaining to the factors listed in Subsection (c) of this article. The probation officer shall include the information in the report required under Section 9(a), Article 42.12, of this code or a separate report, as the court directs. The court shall permit the defendant and the prosecuting attorney to read the report.

(k) The court shall resolve any dispute relating to the proper amount or type of restitution. The standard of proof is a preponderance of the evidence. The burden of demonstrating the amount of the loss sustained by a victim as a result of the offense is on the prosecuting attorney. The burden of demonstrating the financial resources of the defendant and the financial needs of the defendant and the defendant's dependents is on the defendant. The burden of demonstrating other matters as the court deems appropriate is on the party designated by the court as justice requires.

(*l*) Conviction of a defendant for an offense involving the act giving rise to restitution under this article estops the defendant from denying the essential allegations of that offense in any subsequent federal civil proceeding or state civil proceeding brought by the victim, to the extent consistent with state law.

(m) An order of restitution may be enforced by the state or a victim named in the order to receive the restitution in the same manner as a judgment in a civil action.

(n) If a defendant is convicted of or receives deferred adjudication for an offense under Section 25.05, Penal Code, if the child support order on which prosecution of the offense was based required the defendant to pay the support to a local registry or the Title IV-D agency, and if the court orders restitution under this article, the order of restitution must require the defendant to pay the child support in the following manner:

(1) during any period in which the defendant is under the supervision of a community supervision and corrections department, to the department for transfer to the local registry or Title IV-D agency designated as the place of payment in the child support order; and

(2) during any period in which the defendant is not under the supervision of a department, directly to the registry or agency described by Subdivision (1).

(o) The pardons and paroles division may waive a supervision fee or an administrative fee imposed on an inmate under Section 508.182, Government Code, during any period in which the inmate is required to pay restitution under this article.

(p)(1) A court shall order a defendant convicted of an offense under Section 28.03(f), Penal Code, involving damage or destruction inflicted on a place of human burial or under Section 42.08, Penal Code, to make restitution in the amount described by Subsection (b)(1)(B) to a cemetery organization operating a cemetery affected by the commission of the offense.

(2) If a court orders an unemancipated minor to make restitution under Subsection (a) and the minor is financially unable to make the restitution, the court may order:

(A) the minor to perform a specific number of hours of community service to satisfy the restitution; or

(B) the parents or other person responsible for the minor's support to make the restitution in the amount described by Subsection (b)(1)(B).

(3) In this subsection, "cemetery" and "cemetery organization" have the meanings assigned by Section 711.001, Health and Safety Code.

A **(q)** The court shall order a defendant convicted of an offense under Section 22.11, Penal Code, to make restitution to the victim of the offense or the victim's employer in an amount equal to the sum of any expenses incurred by the victim or employer to:

(1) test the victim for HIV, hepatitis A, hepatitis B, tuberculosis, or any other disease designated as a reportable disease under Section 81.048, Health and Safety Code; or

(2) treat the victim for HIV, hepatitis A, hepatitis B, tuberculosis, or any other disease designated as a reportable disease under Section 81.048, Health and Safety Code, the victim contracts as a result of the offense.

E *Subsection (s) below is effective for offenses committed or conduct engaged in on or after Sept. 1, 2007.*

(s)(1) If a court orders a defendant convicted of an offense under Section 28.08, Penal Code, to make restitution to the victim of the offense, the court may order the defendant to make restitution as provided by Subsection (b)(1)(B) or by personally restoring the property by removing or painting over any markings the defendant made.

(2) A court shall order a defendant convicted of an offense under Section 28.08, Penal Code, to make restitution to a political subdivision that owns public property or erects a street sign or official traffic-control device on which the defendant makes markings in violation of Section 28.08, Penal Code. The amount of the restitution ordered must be equal to the lesser of the amount of restitution authorized by Subsection (b)(1)(B) or the cost to the political subdivision of restoring the public property, street sign, or official traffic-control device. If the court orders a defendant to make restitution under this subdivision and the defendant is financially unable to make the restitution, the court may order the defendant to perform a specific number of hours of community service, including service restoring the property by removing or painting over any markings the defendant made, to satisfy the restitution. For purposes of this subdivision, "official traffic-control device" has the meaning assigned by Section 541.304, Transportation Code.

History of CCP art. 42.037: Acts 1993, 73rd Leg., ch. 806, §1, eff. Sept. 1, 1993. Amended by Acts 1995, 74th Leg., ch. 76, §5.95(111) (eff. Sept. 1, 1995), ch. 318, §51 (eff. Sept. 1, 1995); Acts 1999, 76th Leg., ch. 40, §§2, 3, eff. Sept. 1, 1999; Acts 2001, 77th Leg., ch. 856, §10 (eff. Sept. 1, 2001), ch. 1034, §2 (eff. Sept. 1, 2001); Acts 2005, 79th Leg., ch. 543, §4 (eff. Sept. 1, 2005), ch. 969, §1 (eff. Sept. 1, 2005), ch. 1025, §2 (eff. June 18, 2005); Acts 2007, 80th Leg., ch. 921, §17.001(10) (eff. Sept. 1, 2007), ch. 1053, §2 (eff. Sept. 1, 2007).
See also CCP art. 42.12.

ANNOTATIONS

Idowu v. State, 73 S.W.3d 918, 921 (Tex.Crim.App. 2002). "If a defendant wishes to complain about the appropriateness of (as opposed to the factual basis for) a trial court's restitution order, he must do so in the trial court, and he must do so explicitly. *At 922:* We ordinarily allow defendants to raise sufficiency of the evidence questions for the first time on appeal. Whether the record provides a sufficient factual basis for a particular restitution order could be considered an evidentiary sufficiency question that need not be preserved by objection at the trial level." *See also In re J.R.*, 907 S.W.2d 107, 109 (Tex.App.—Austin 1995, no writ).

Martin v. State, 874 S.W.2d 674, 676 n.5 (Tex.Crim. App.1994). CCP art. 42.037 "addresses matters related to an order of restitution in cases of probation, parole or mandatory supervision, but does not repeal the restitution provisions contained in [CCP art.] 42.12."

Tyler v. State, 137 S.W.3d 261, 267 (Tex.App.— Houston [1st Dist.] 2004, no pet.). "Although Article 42.037 serves as a vehicle by which the victim's heirs may ultimately receive funds paid as restitution, the trial court [has] no authority to determine the beneficiaries of the estate [and order restitution to be paid directly to the heirs]."

Quisenberry v. State, 88 S.W.3d 745, 754-55 (Tex. App.—Waco 2002, pet. ref'd). "The factors [in art. 42.037(h)] should be viewed on a case-by-case basis. No factor is necessary to justify revocation; no factor alone is sufficient to justify revocation. The first four must be considered together, along with such special circumstances as may be relevant. Addressing the first factor, ... if a defendant is unemployed but has the ability to work, that factor weighs in favor of revocation. If the evidence shows that the defendant is deliberately underemployed, the second factor ... will favor revocation; the amount and frequency of his earnings compared to the amount and frequency of court-ordered restitution payments should also be considered in connection with the second factor. If a defendant has financial resources separate and apart from employment and unreasonably fails to use them, or has the ability to borrow money but unreasonably fails to employ that option, then the third factor will weigh in favor of revocation when he fails to pay. If a defendant willfully fails to pay restitution while possessing the ability to pay, the fourth factor will weigh in favor of revocation. The final factor ... may weigh in favor of or against revocation, depending on what the evidence shows."

Narvaez v. State, 40 S.W.3d 729, 730 (Tex. App.—San Antonio 2001, pet. dism'd). There "is no evidence the $20,000 payment was intended as full compensation for [victim]'s injuries or as compensation for his medical bills. [W]e hold the trial court did not abuse its discretion in ordering [D] to pay restitution to [medical provider] in the amount of $27,476.87, representing the amount due for [victim]'s medical services and, in effect, advanced by [medical provider] and the federal government to [victim]."

ART. 42.0371. MANDATORY RESTITUTION FOR KIDNAPPED OR ABDUCTED CHILDREN

(a) The court shall order a defendant convicted of an offense under Chapter 20, Penal Code, or Section 25.03, 25.031, or 25.04, Penal Code, to pay restitution in an amount equal to the cost of necessary rehabilitation, including medical, psychiatric, and psychological care and treatment, for the victim of the offense if the victim is younger than 17 years of age.

(b) The court shall, after considering the financial circumstances of the defendant, specify in a restitution order issued under Subsection (a) the manner in which the defendant must pay the restitution.

(c) A restitution order issued under Subsection (a) may be enforced by the state or a victim named in the order to receive the restitution in the same manner as a judgment in a civil action.

(d) The court may hold a hearing, make findings of fact, and amend a restitution order issued under Subsection (a) if the defendant fails to pay the victim named in the order in the manner specified by the court.

History of CCP art. 42.0371: Acts 1999, 76th Leg., ch. 657, §1, eff. Sept. 1, 1999.

ART. 42.038. REIMBURSEMENT FOR CONFINEMENT EXPENSES

(a) In addition to any fine, cost, or fee authorized by law, a court that sentences a defendant convicted of a misdemeanor to serve a term of confinement in county jail and orders execution of the sentence may require the defendant to reimburse the county for the defendant's confinement at a rate of $25 a day.

(b) A court that requires a defendant convicted of a misdemeanor or placed on deferred adjudication for a misdemeanor to submit to a period of confinement in county jail as a condition of community supervision may also require as a condition of community supervision that the defendant reimburse the county for the defendant's confinement, with the amount of reimbursement determined as if the defendant were serving an executed sentence.

(c) A judge may not require reimbursement under this article if the judge determines the defendant is indigent based on the defendant's sworn statement or affidavit filed with the court. A court that requires reimbursement under this article may require the defendant to reimburse the county only for those days the defendant is confined after the date of conviction or on which a plea of guilty or nolo contendere was entered. The court may not require a defendant to reimburse the county for those days the defendant was confined after arrest and before the date of conviction or on which the plea of guilty or nolo contendere was entered.

(d) The court, in determining whether to order reimbursement under this article, shall consider:

(1) the defendant's employment status, earning ability, and financial resources; and

(2) any other special circumstances that may affect the defendant's ability to pay, including child support obligations and including any financial responsibilities owed by the defendant to dependents or restitution payments owed by the defendant to a victim.

(e) On the day on which a defendant who is required to reimburse the county under this article discharges an executed sentence of confinement or completes the period of confinement required as a condition of community supervision, the sheriff shall present to the defendant a bill computed by multiplying the daily rate of $25 times the number of days the defendant was confined in the county jail, not counting the day on which the execution of the sentence or the period of confinement began. For purposes of this subsection, a defendant who is confined in county jail for only a portion of a day is nonetheless considered to have been confined for the whole day.

(f) The court may require a defendant to reimburse the county under this article by paying to the sheriff the bill presented by the sheriff within a specified period or in specified installments. The end of the period or the last installment may not be later than:

(1) the end of the period of community supervision, if community supervision is ordered; or

(2) the fifth anniversary of the last day of the term of confinement, if the court does not order community supervision.

History of CCP art. 42.038: Acts 1999, 76th Leg., ch. 295, §1, eff. Sept. 1, 1999.

ART. 42.04. SENTENCE WHEN APPEAL IS TAKEN

When a defendant is sentenced to death, no date shall be set for the execution of sentence until after the receipt by the clerk of the trial court of the mandate of affirmance of the court of criminal appeals.

History of CCP art. 42.04: Acts 1965, 59th Leg., vol. 2, ch. 722. Amended by Acts 1981, 67th Leg., ch. 291, §114, eff. Sept. 1, 1981.

ANNOTATIONS

Dunn v. State, 733 S.W.2d 212, 214 n.5 (Tex.Crim. App.1987). "Until … review is complete, execution of appellant's [death] sentence is 'suspended.'"

ART. 42.04A. REPEALED

Repealed by the Texas Court of Criminal Appeals' adoption of the Texas Rules of Appellate Procedure on April 10, 1986. 707 S.W.2d xxx, xxxv.

ART. 42.045. ISSUANCE OF MANDATE; JUDGMENTS FINAL

☠ *Article 42.045 below was renumbered from article 42.04a by Acts 1987, 70th Leg., ch. 167, §5.02(3), effective Sept. 1, 1987, without reference to the repeal of former article 42.04a by the Texas Court of Criminal Appeals' adoption of the Texas Rules of Appellate Procedure on April 10, 1986. 707 S.W.2d xxx, xxxv.*

(a) When a decision of a court of appeals or the Court of Criminal Appeals becomes final, the clerk of such court shall issue a mandate in the case to the trial court.

(b) A decision of a court of appeals shall be final:

(1) at the expiration of 45 days after the final ruling of the court, unless:

(A) a petition for review has been filed within 30 days after the final ruling of the court of appeals; or

(B) the Court of Criminal Appeals has filed an order for review of the decision on its own motion; or

(2) at the expiration of 15 days from the date of refusal of the Court of Criminal Appeals to grant a petition for review.

(c) A decision of the Court of Criminal Appeals shall be final at the expiration of 15 days from the ruling on the final motion for rehearing or from the rendition of the decision if no motion for rehearing is filed.

History of CCP art. 42.045: Former art. 42.04a repealed by the Texas Court of Criminal Appeals' adoption of the Texas Rules of Appellate Procedure on April 10, 1986. 707 S.W.2d xxx, xxxv. Renumbered from art. 42.04a by Acts 1987, 70th Leg., ch. 167, §5.02(3) eff. Sept. 1, 1987.

ART. 42.05. IF COURT IS ABOUT TO ADJOURN

The time limit within which any act is to be done within the meaning of this Code shall not be affected by the expiration of the term of the court.

History of CCP art. 42.05: Acts 1965, 59th Leg., vol. 2, ch. 722.

ANNOTATIONS

Ex parte Brown, 477 S.W.2d 552, 554 n.3 (Tex. Crim.App.1972). Article 42.05 "allow[s] trial courts to make amendments, and correct clerical errors, in the judgments and sentences after the term of court expires."

ART. 42.06. REPEALED

Repealed by the Texas Court of Criminal Appeals' adoption of the Texas Rules of Appellate Procedure on April 10, 1986. 707 S.W.2d xxx, xxxv.

ART. 42.07. REASONS TO PREVENT SENTENCE

Before pronouncing sentence, the defendant shall be asked whether he has anything to say why the sentence should not be pronounced against him. The only reasons which can be shown, on account of which sentence cannot be pronounced, are:

1. That the defendant has received a pardon from the proper authority, on the presentation of which, legally authenticated, he shall be discharged.

2. That the defendant is incompetent to stand trial; and if evidence be shown to support a finding of incompetency to stand trial, no sentence shall be pronounced, and the court shall proceed under Chapter 46B; and

3. When a person who has been convicted escapes after conviction and before sentence and an individual supposed to be the same has been arrested he may before sentence is pronounced, deny that he is the person convicted, and an issue be accordingly tried before a jury, or before the court if a jury is waived, as to his identity.

History of CCP art. 42.07: Acts 1965, 59th Leg., vol. 2, ch. 722. Amended by Acts 1975, 64th Leg., ch. 415, §3, eff. June 19, 1975; Acts 1981, 67th Leg., ch. 291, §115, eff. Sept. 1, 1981; Acts 2003, 78th Leg., ch. 35, §3, eff. Jan. 1, 2004.

ANNOTATIONS

Casey v. State, 924 S.W.2d 946, 949 (Tex.Crim.App. 1996). CCP art. 42.07(2), "which states that a reason to prevent sentence is '[t]hat the defendant is incompetent to stand trial,' includes competency at the time of sentencing because sentencing is 'during trial' for purposes of [CCP arts.] 42.07(2) and 42.06."

Tenon v. State, 563 S.W.2d 622, 623 (Tex.Crim.App. 1978). "[W]here there [is] no objection in the trial court that defendant [has] been denied the right of allocution, no error [is] shown on claim that recitation in formal sentence that defendant was asked by the court whether he had anything to say why sentence should not be pronounced against him and he answered nothing in bar thereof was not supported in the transcription of the court reporter's notes."

ART. 42.08. CUMULATIVE OR CONCURRENT SENTENCE

(a) When the same defendant has been convicted in two or more cases, judgment and sentence shall be pronounced in each case in the same manner as if there had been but one conviction. Except as provided by Sections (b) and (c) of this article, in the discretion of the court, the judgment in the second and subsequent convictions may either be that the sentence imposed or suspended shall begin when the judgment and the sentence imposed or suspended in the preceding conviction has ceased to operate, or that the sentence imposed or suspended shall run concurrently with the other case or cases, and sentence and execution shall be accordingly; provided, however, that the cumulative total of suspended sentences in felony cases shall not exceed 10 years, and the cumulative total of suspended sentences in misdemeanor cases shall not exceed the maximum period of confinement in jail applicable to the misdemeanor offenses, though in no event more than three years, including extensions of periods of community supervision under Section 22, Article 42.12, of this code, if none of the offenses are offenses under Chapter 49, Penal Code, or four years, including extensions, if any of the offenses are offenses under Chapter 49, Penal Code.

(b) If a defendant is sentenced for an offense committed while the defendant was an inmate in the institutional division of the Texas Department of Criminal Justice and the defendant has not completed the sentence he was serving at the time of the offense, the judge shall order the sentence for the subsequent offense to commence immediately on completion of the sentence for the original offense.

(c) If a defendant has been convicted in two or more cases and the court suspends the imposition of the sentence in one of the cases, the court may not order a sentence of confinement to commence on the completion of a suspended sentence for an offense.

History of CCP art. 42.08: Acts 1965, 59th Leg., vol. 2, ch. 722. Amended by Acts 1985, 69th Leg., ch. 29, §1, eff. Sept. 1, 1985; Acts 1987, 70th Leg., ch. 513, §1, eff. Aug. 31, 1987; Acts 1989, 71st Leg., ch. 785, §4.11, eff. Sept. 1, 1989; Acts 1993, 73rd Leg., ch. 900, §5.03, eff. Sept. 1, 1993.

ANNOTATIONS

Beedy v. State, 250 S.W.3d 107, 110 (Tex.Crim.App. 2008). "[W]hen a trial judge lawfully exercises the option to cumulate [under CCP art. 42.08(a)], that decision is unassailable on appeal. But when a trial judge unlawfully enters a cumulation order in a case that did not involve a negotiated plea agreement, the appellate court, according to our precedent, will reform the judgment by deleting the order. [¶] By questioning this well-established remedy, the State's ground for review requires us to decide whether an unlawful cumulation order can be remedied by a reversal. To resolve this question, we turn to [CCP art.] 44.29…. Although we have never discussed the role of Article 44.29 when setting aside an unlawful cumulation order, our precedent applying this remedy makes clear that we have never interpreted 'reversible error' under Article 44.29 to encompass an unlawful cumulation order."

Mungaray v. State, 188 S.W.3d 178, 183 (Tex.Crim. App.2006). "1. When reviewing the sufficiency of the evidence to support an order cumulating sentences entered pursuant to [art.] 42.08(a), may the court of appeals disregard in-court statements made by the prosecutor as evidence of the existence of the prior sentence? 2. When reviewing the sufficiency of the evidence to support an order cumulating sentences entered pursuant to [art.] 42.08(a), may the court of appeals disregard partial admissions by the defendant and his attorney that support the challenged order? 3. Must the State prove the offense name, date, court, and cause number of the prior sentence before a trial judge may exercise its discretion to cumulate sentences under [art.] 42.08(a)?" Held: The answer to each question is no.

Barela v. State, 180 S.W.3d 145, 148 (Tex.Crim.App. 2005). "At the time of sentencing [under art. 42.08(a)], there must be before the court both evidence of the former conviction and evidence that the defendant was the same person previously convicted. *At 148 n.6:* [T]his Court has recommended five requirements for a proper cumulation order: (1) the trial court number of

the prior conviction; (2) the correct name of the court where the prior conviction was had; (3) the date of the prior conviction; (4) the term of years of the prior conviction; and (5) the nature of the prior conviction. However, we also note that orders containing fewer than the recommended number of elements have been upheld. *At 148:* The relevant version of the statute contains no language that limits cumulation of multiple sentences to only defendants who are confined by the [TDCJ] in all the cases identified in the cumulation order. The deletion in 1987 of such limiting language effectively authorized cumulation with sentences from other jurisdictions. *At 149:* It is the order of conviction, rather than the order of sentencing, that is important when contemplating the propriety of a cumulation order. There is no requirement that a sentence must be imposed in the first conviction before a stacked sentence can be imposed in any subsequent sentence. A defendant cannot begin to serve the sentence in the subsequent conviction until the sentence in the preceding conviction is completed if the sentences are to run consecutively, but there is no language in Article 42.08(a) that indicates when the sentence in the preceding conviction must occur." *See also* *Townsend v. State*, 187 S.W.3d 131, 133-34 (Tex.App.—Texarkana 2006, pet. ref'd).

Ex parte Wrigley, 178 S.W.3d 828, 829 (Tex.Crim. App.2005). "This case presents the novel issue of whether an original sentence is completed and a stacked sentence begins to run at the time the defendant makes parole on the original offense, if his parole is revoked before the trial court sentences the defendant for the stacked offense. We hold that [under art. 42.08(b)] it does not."

Ex parte Madding, 70 S.W.3d 131, 136 (Tex.Crim. App.2002). "Once applicant was removed from the courtroom and began serving his sentence, it was too late [for trial court] to cumulate the sentence just imposed with an earlier one. A trial court does not have the statutory authority or discretion to orally pronounce one sentence in front of the defendant, but enter a different sentence in his written judgment, outside the defendant's presence. [¶] A defendant has a due process 'legitimate expectation' that the sentence he heard orally pronounced in the courtroom is the same sentence that he will be required to serve."

Pettigrew v. State, 48 S.W.3d 769, 771 (Tex.Crim. App.2001). "[F]or the purpose of stacking, a case [can] be treated as a 'conviction' at the time sentence is suspended *or* at the time sentence is imposed. [W]hen community supervision is revoked, the trial court would have the discretion to treat the case as a conviction at the time of community supervision and stack a subsequently committed offense onto the revoked offense, or the trial court could treat the case as a conviction upon revocation and stack the revocation sentence onto the sentence for the new offense, if the revocation occurred after the conviction for the new offense." *See also Moore v. State*, 109 S.W.3d 537, 540 (Tex.App.—Tyler 2001, no pet.).

Bell v. State, 994 S.W.2d 173, 174 (Tex.Crim.App. 1999). "Article 42.08(b) clearly and plainly does not require 'record evidence of the prior conviction and that [appellant] was the person convicted.'"

Ex parte Nickerson, 893 S.W.2d 546, 548 (Tex. Crim.App.1995). "Because no conviction remains when the judgment has been reversed and remanded for a new trial, the sentence … has ceased to operate because it no longer exists. Therefore, in accord with the cumulation order, the sentence in the second or subsequent conviction should begin to operate when the reversal in the preceding conviction is final."

Ex parte Applewhite, 729 S.W.2d 706, 708 (Tex. Crim.App.1987). "'[U]nless the trial court, by order, expressly makes cumulative the several punishments, they run concurrently.'"

Morris v. State, 214 S.W.3d 159, 188 (Tex.App.— Beaumont 2007, pet. granted). "The jury convicted Morris of three counts of intoxication manslaughter and sentenced him to eighteen years on each conviction. When a defendant is convicted on multiple counts of intoxication manslaughter, the trial court has authority to cumulate the sentences or have them run concurrently. [¶] Instead of making Morris's sentence concurrent or consecutive, the trial court ordered Morris's sentences to run partially concurrent and partially consecutive…. *At 189:* Article 42.08 … prohibits trial courts from partially cumulating criminal sentences."

Hurley v. State, 130 S.W.3d 501, 503 (Tex.App.— Dallas 2004, no pet.). "Because a deferred adjudication order does not involve a 'conviction,' we conclude it cannot be the subject of cumulative sentencing under Texas law." *See also Beedy v. State*, 194 S.W.3d 595, 601 (Tex.App.—Houston [1st Dist.] 2006), *aff'd*, 250 S.W.3d 107 (Tex.Crim.App.2008).

Baker v. State, 107 S.W.3d 671, 672 (Tex. App.—San Antonio 2003, no pet.). "The trial court's general authority under … article 42.08 to order consecutive sentences is statutorily limited by [Pen. Code] §3.03."

ART. 42.09. COMMENCEMENT OF SENTENCE; STATUS DURING APPEAL; PEN PACKET

Sec. 1. Except as provided in Sections 2 and 3, a defendant shall be delivered to a jail or to the institutional division of the Texas Department of Criminal Justice when his sentence is pronounced, or his sentence to death is announced, by the court. The defendant's sentence begins to run on the day it is pronounced, but with all credits, if any, allowed by Article 42.03.

Sec. 2. If a defendant appeals his conviction and is released on bail pending disposition of his appeal, when his conviction is affirmed, the clerk of the trial court, on receipt of the mandate from the appellate court, shall issue a commitment against the defendant. The officer executing the commitment shall endorse thereon the date he takes the defendant into custody and the defendant's sentence begins to run from the date endorsed on the commitment. The institutional division of the Texas Department of Criminal Justice shall admit the defendant named in the commitment on the basis of the commitment.

Sec. 3. If a defendant is convicted of a felony and sentenced to death, life, or a term of more than ten years in the institutional division of the Texas Department of Criminal Justice and he gives notice of appeal, he shall be transferred to the institutional division on a commitment pending a mandate from the court of appeals or the Court of Criminal Appeals.

Sec. 4. If a defendant is convicted of a felony, is eligible for release on bail pending appeal under Article 44.04(b), and gives notice of appeal, he shall be transferred to the institutional division of the Texas Department of Criminal Justice on a commitment pending a mandate from the court of appeals or the Court of Criminal Appeals upon request in open court or upon written request to the sentencing court. Upon a valid transfer to the institutional division under this section, the defendant may not thereafter be released on bail pending his appeal.

Sec. 5. If a defendant is transferred to the institutional division of the Texas Department of Criminal

Justice pending appeal under Section 3 or 4, his sentence shall be computed as if no appeal had been taken if the appeal is affirmed.

Sec. 6. All defendants who have been transferred to the institutional division of the Texas Department of Criminal Justice pending the appeal of their convictions under this article shall be under the control and authority of the institutional division for all purposes as if no appeal were pending.

Sec. 7. If a defendant is sentenced to a term of imprisonment in the institutional division of the Texas Department of Criminal Justice but is not transferred to the institutional division under Section 3 or 4 of this article, the court, before the date on which it would lose jurisdiction under Section 6(a), Article 42.12, of this code, shall send to the department a document containing a statement of the date on which the defendant's sentence was pronounced and credits earned by the defendant under Article 42.03 of this code as of the date of the statement.

Sec. 8. (a) A county that transfers a defendant to the Texas Department of Criminal Justice under this article shall deliver to an officer designated by the department:

(1) a copy of the judgment entered pursuant to Article 42.01 of this code, completed on a standardized felony judgment form described by Section 4 of that article;

(2) a copy of any order revoking community supervision and imposing sentence pursuant to Section 23, Article 42.12, of this code, including:

(A) any amounts owed for restitution, fines, and court costs, completed on a standardized felony judgment form described by Section 4, Article 42.01, of this code; and

(B) a copy of the client supervision plan prepared for the defendant by the community supervision and corrections department supervising the defendant, if such a plan was prepared;

(3) a written report that states the nature and the seriousness of each offense and that states the citation to the provision or provisions of the Penal Code or other law under which the defendant was convicted;

(4) a copy of the victim impact statement, if one has been prepared in the case under Article 56.03 of this code;

(5) a statement as to whether there was a change in venue in the case and, if so, the names of the county prosecuting the offense and the county in which the case was tried;

(6) a copy of the record of arrest for each offense;

(7) if requested, information regarding the criminal history of the defendant, including the defendant's state identification number if the number has been issued;

(8) a copy of the indictment or information for each offense;

(9) a checklist sent by the department to the county and completed by the county in a manner indicating that the documents required by this subsection and Subsection (c) of this section accompany the defendant;

(10) if prepared, a copy of a presentence or postsentence investigation report prepared under Section 9, Article 42.12 of this code;

(11) a copy of any detainer, issued by an agency of the federal government, that is in the possession of the county and that has been placed on the defendant;

ⓔ *Subsection (12) below is effective for defendants transferred to the TDCJ on or after June 15, 2007.*

(12) if prepared, a copy of the defendant's Texas Uniform Health Status Update Form; and

(13) a written description of a hold or warrant, issued by any other jurisdiction, that the county is aware of and that has been placed on or issued for the defendant.

(b) The Texas Department of Criminal Justice shall not take a defendant into custody under this article until the designated officer receives the documents required by Subsections (a) and (c) of this section. The designated officer shall certify under the seal of the department the documents received under Subsections (a) and (c) of this section. A document certified under this subsection is self-authenticated for the purposes of Rules 901 and 902, Texas Rules of Evidence.

(c) A county that transfers a defendant to the Texas Department of Criminal Justice under this article shall also deliver to the designated officer any presentence or postsentence investigation report, revocation report, psychological or psychiatric evaluation of the defendant, including an evaluation prepared for the juvenile court before transferring the defendant to criminal court and contained in the criminal prosecutor's file, and available social or psychological background information relating to the defendant and may deliver to the designated officer any additional information upon which the judge or jury bases the punishment decision.

(d) The institutional division of the Texas Department of Criminal Justice shall make documents received under Subsections (a) and (c) available to the pardons and paroles division on the request of the pardons and paroles division and shall, on release of a defendant on parole or to mandatory supervision, immediately provide the pardons and paroles division with copies of documents received under Subsection (a). The pardons and paroles division shall provide to the parole officer appointed to supervise the defendant a comprehensive summary of the information contained in the documents referenced in this section not later than the 14th day after the date of the defendant's release. The summary shall include a current photograph of the defendant and a complete set of the defendant's fingerprints. Upon written request from the county sheriff, the photograph and fingerprints shall be filed with the sheriff of the county to which the parolee is assigned if that county is not the county from which the parolee was sentenced.

(e) A county is not required to deliver separate documents containing information relating to citations to provisions of the Penal Code or other law and to changes of venue, as otherwise required by Subsections (a)(3) and (a)(5) of this article, if the standardized felony judgment form described by Section 4, Article 42.01, of this code is modified to require that information.

(f) Except as provided by Subsection (g) of this section, the county sheriff is responsible for ensuring that documents and information required by this section accompany defendants sentenced by district courts in the county to the Texas Department of Criminal Justice.

(g) If the presiding judge of the administrative judicial region in which the county is located determines that the county sheriff is unable to perform the duties required by Subsection (f) of this section, the presiding judge may impose those duties on:

(1) the district clerk; or

(2) the prosecutor of each district court in the county.

(h) If a parole panel releases on parole a person who is confined in a jail in this state, a federal correctional institution, or a correctional institution in another state, the Texas Department of Criminal Justice shall request the sheriff who would otherwise be required to transfer the person to the department to forward to the department the information described by Subsections (a) and (c) of this section. The sheriff shall comply with the request of the department. The department shall determine whether the information forwarded by the sheriff under this subsection contains a thumbprint taken from the person in the manner provided by Article 38.33 of this code and, if not, the department shall obtain a thumbprint taken in the manner provided by that article and shall forward the thumbprint to the department for inclusion with the information sent by the sheriff.

(i) A county may deliver the documents required under Subsections (a) and (c) of this section to the Texas Department of Criminal Justice by electronic means. For purposes of this subsection, "electronic means" means the transmission of data between word processors, data processors, or similar automated information equipment over dedicated cables, commercial lines, or other similar methods of transmission.

(j) If after a county transfers a defendant or inmate to the Texas Department of Criminal Justice the charges on which the defendant or inmate was convicted and for which the defendant or inmate was transferred are dismissed, the county shall immediately notify an officer designated by the department of the dismissal.

Sec. 9. A county that transfers a defendant to the Texas Department of Criminal Justice under this article may deliver to an officer designated by the department a certified copy of a final order of a state or federal court that dismisses as frivolous or malicious a lawsuit brought by the inmate while the inmate was confined in the county jail awaiting transfer to the department following conviction of a felony or revocation of community supervision, parole, or mandatory supervision. The county may deliver the copy to the department at the time of the transfer of the inmate or at any time after the transfer of the inmate.

History of CCP art. 42.09: Acts 1965, 59th Leg., vol. 2, ch. 722. Amended by Acts 1973, 63rd Leg., ch. 91, §2, eff. Aug. 27, 1973; Acts 1977, 65th Leg., ch. 806, §1, eff. Aug. 29, 1977; Acts 1981, 67th Leg., ch. 291, §117, eff. Sept. 1, 1981; Acts 1983, 68th Leg., ch. 40, §1 (eff. April 26, 1983), p. 4668, ch. 810, §1 (eff. Sept. 1, 1983); Acts 1985, 69th Leg., ch. 344, §3, eff. Jan. 1, 1986; Acts 1987, 70th Leg., ch. 1049, §53, eff. Sept. 1, 1987; Acts 1989, 71st Leg., ch. 33, §2 (eff. April 26,

1989), ch. 785, §4.12 (eff. Sept. 1, 1989); Acts 1991, 72nd Leg., 2nd C.S., ch. 10, §11.05, eff. Aug. 29, 1991; Acts 1993, 73rd Leg., ch. 900, §5.03, eff. Sept. 1, 1993; Acts 1995, 74th Leg., ch. 321, §3.001 (eff. Sept. 1, 1995), ch. 723, §1 (eff. Sept. 1, 1995); Acts 1999, 76th Leg., ch. 655, §1 (eff. June 18, 1999), ch. 1188, §1.42 (eff. Sept. 1, 1999), ch. 1477, §29 (eff. Sept. 1, 1999); Acts 2001, 77th Leg., ch. 214, §1 (eff. May 23, 2001), ch. 453, §1 (eff. June 8, 2001); Acts 2003, 78th Leg., ch. 14, §1, eff. Sept. 1, 2003; Acts 2005, 79th Leg., ch. 728, §4.005, eff. Sept. 1, 2005; Acts 2007, 80th Leg., ch. 1308, §4, eff. June 15, 2007.

ANNOTATIONS

State v. Aguilera, 165 S.W.3d 695, 697-98 (Tex. Crim.App.2005). "At a minimum, a trial court retains plenary power to modify its sentence if a motion for new trial or motion in arrest of judgment is filed within 30 days of sentencing. We hold that a trial court also retains plenary power to modify its sentence if … the modification is made on the same day as the assessment of the initial sentence and before the court adjourns for the day. The re-sentencing must be done in the presence of the defendant, his attorney, and counsel for the state. Such modifications comport with the provisions of [CCP art.] 42.09, §1, that a defendant's sentence begins to run on the day that it is pronounced, and the provisions of [CCP art.] 42.03, §1(a), that a felony sentence shall be pronounced in the defendant's presence. In such circumstances, a trial court has the authority to re-sentence a defendant after assessing an initial sentence if the modified sentence is authorized by statute."

Ex parte Hernandez, 758 S.W.2d 594, 596 (Tex. Crim.App.1988). "Frequently trial courts try to 'back date' the sentence or order the sentence to commence on a date earlier than imposed to give credit for jail time. This is not proper. The sentence is never dated back, but the defendant is merely given credit from the date of confinement to the date of the sentence, or for actual jail time where applicable. The date of the imposition of the sentence always remains the same."

ART. 42.10. SATISFACTION OF JUDGMENT AS IN MISDEMEANOR CONVICTIONS

When a person is convicted of a felony, and the punishment assessed is only a fine or a term in jail, or both, the judgment may be satisfied in the same manner as a conviction for a misdemeanor is by law satisfied.

History of CCP art. 42.10: Acts 1965, 59th Leg., vol. 2, ch. 722.

ART. 42.11. REPEALED

Repealed by Acts 2001, 77th Leg., ch. 543, §2, eff. June 11, 2002.

ART. 42.111. DEFERRAL OF PROCEEDINGS IN CASES APPEALED TO COUNTY COURT

If a defendant convicted of a misdemeanor punishable by fine only appeals the conviction to a county court, on the trial in county court the defendant may enter a plea of guilty or nolo contendere to the offense. If the defendant enters a plea of guilty or nolo contendere, the court may defer further proceedings without entering an adjudication of guilt in the same manner as provided for the deferral of proceedings in justice court or municipal court under Article 45.051 of this code. This article does not apply to a misdemeanor case disposed of under Subchapter B, Chapter 543, Transportation Code, or a serious traffic violation as defined by Section 522.003, Transportation Code.

History of CCP art. 42.111: Acts 1989, 71st Leg., ch. 399, §2, eff. June 14, 1989. Amended by Acts 1991, 72nd Leg., ch. 775, §18, eff. Sept. 1, 1991; Acts 1999, 76th Leg., ch. 62, §3.03 (eff. Sept. 1, 1999), ch. 1545, §62 (eff. Sept. 1, 1999).

ART. 42.12. COMMUNITY SUPERVISION
§1. Purpose

It is the purpose of this article to place wholly within the state courts the responsibility for determining when the imposition of sentence in certain cases shall be suspended, the conditions of community supervision, and the supervision of defendants placed on community supervision, in consonance with the powers assigned to the judicial branch of this government by the Constitution of Texas. It is the purpose of this article to remove from existing statutes the limitations, other than questions of constitutionality, that have acted as barriers to effective systems of community supervision in the public interest.

§2. Definitions

In this article:

(1) "Court" means a court of record having original criminal jurisdiction.

(2) "Community supervision" means the placement of a defendant by a court under a continuum of programs and sanctions, with conditions imposed by the court for a specified period during which:

(A) criminal proceedings are deferred without an adjudication of guilt; or

(B) a sentence of imprisonment or confinement, imprisonment and fine, or confinement and fine, is probated and the imposition of sentence is suspended in whole or in part.

★

(3) "Supervision officer" means a person appointed or employed under Section 76.004, Government Code, to supervise defendants placed on community supervision.

(4) "Electronic monitoring" includes voice tracking systems, position tracking systems, position location systems, biometric tracking systems, and any other electronic or telecommunications system that may be used to assist in the supervision of individuals under this article.

§3. Judge Ordered Community Supervision

(a) A judge, in the best interest of justice, the public, and the defendant, after conviction or a plea of guilty or nolo contendere, may suspend the imposition of the sentence and place the defendant on community supervision or impose a fine applicable to the offense and place the defendant on community supervision.

 Subsection (b) below is effective for defendants initially placed on community supervision on or after Sept. 1, 2007.

(b) In a felony case the minimum period of community supervision is the same as the minimum term of imprisonment applicable to the offense and the maximum period of community supervision is, subject to the extensions provided by Section 22:

(1) 10 years, for a felony other than a third degree felony described by Subdivision (2); and

(2) five years, for the following third degree felonies:

(A) a third degree felony under Title 7, Penal Code, other than an offense under Section 33.021(c), Penal Code; and

(B) a third degree felony under Chapter 481, Health and Safety Code.

Subsection (b) below is effective for defendants initially placed on community supervision before Sept. 1, 2007.

(b) Except as provided by Subsection (f), in a felony case the minimum period of community supervision is the same as the minimum term of imprisonment applicable to the offense and the maximum period of community supervision is 10 years.

(c) The maximum period of community supervision in a misdemeanor case is two years.

(d) A judge may increase the maximum period of community supervision in the manner provided by Section 22(c) or 22A of this article.

(e) A defendant is not eligible for community supervision under this section if the defendant:

(1) is sentenced to a term of imprisonment that exceeds 10 years; or

(2) is sentenced to serve a term of confinement under Section 12.35, Penal Code.

(f) The minimum period of community supervision for a felony described by Section 13B(b) is five years and the maximum period of supervision is 10 years.

(g) A judge shall not deny community supervision to a defendant based solely on the defendant's inability to speak, read, write, hear, or understand English.

E *Subsection (h) below is effective for offenses committed on or after Sept. 1, 2007.*

(h) The minimum period of community supervision under this section for an offense under Section 30.04, Penal Code, punishable as a Class A misdemeanor with a minimum term of confinement of six months is one year.

See also *O'Connor's Crimes & Consequences* (2008-09), chart 4-A, "Community Supervision—Felony," 4-B, "Community Supervision—Misdemeanor."

Sections 3a to 3f. [Blank]
§3g. Limitation on Judge Ordered Community Supervision

(a) The provisions of Section 3 of this article do not apply:

(1) to a defendant adjudged guilty of an offense under:

(A) Section 19.02, Penal Code (Murder);

(B) Section 19.03, Penal Code (Capital murder);

(C) Section 21.11(a)(1), Penal Code (Indecency with a child);

(D) Section 20.04, Penal Code (Aggravated kidnapping);

(E) Section 22.021, Penal Code (Aggravated sexual assault);

(F) Section 29.03, Penal Code (Aggravated robbery);

(G) Chapter 481, Health and Safety Code, for which punishment is increased under:

(i) Section 481.140, Health and Safety Code; or

(ii) Section 481.134(c), (d), (e), or (f), Health and Safety Code, if it is shown that the defendant has been previously convicted of an offense for which punishment was increased under any of those subsections; or

★

(H) Section 22.011, Penal Code (Sexual assault); or

☠ **E** *Subsection (I) below was enacted by Acts 2007, 80th Leg., ch. 405, §1, effective Sept. 1, 2007, without reference to the conflicting enactment made by Acts 2007, 80th Leg., ch. 593, §1.05, effective Sept. 1, 2007. Subsection (I) below is effective for offenses committed on or after Sept. 1, 2007.*

(I) Section 22.04(a)(1), Penal Code (Injury to a child, elderly individual, or disabled individual), if the offense is punishable as a felony of the first degree and the victim of the offense is a child; or

☠ **E** *Subsection (I) below was enacted by Acts 2007, 80th Leg., ch. 593, §1.05, effective Sept. 1, 2007, without reference to the conflicting enactment made by Acts 2007, 80th Leg., ch. 405, §1, effective Sept. 1, 2007. Subsection (I) below is effective for offenses committed on or after Sept. 1, 2007.*

(I) Section 43.25, Penal Code (Sexual performance by a child); or

(2) to a defendant when it is shown that a deadly weapon as defined in Section 1.07, Penal Code, was used or exhibited during the commission of a felony offense or during immediate flight therefrom, and that the defendant used or exhibited the deadly weapon or was a party to the offense and knew that a deadly weapon would be used or exhibited. On an affirmative finding under this subdivision, the trial court shall enter the finding in the judgment of the court. On an affirmative finding that the deadly weapon was a firearm, the court shall enter that finding in its judgment.

(b) If there is an affirmative finding under Subsection (a)(2) in the trial of a felony of the second degree or higher that the deadly weapon used or exhibited was a firearm and the defendant is granted community supervision, the court may order the defendant confined in the institutional division of the Texas Department of Criminal Justice for not less than 60 and not more than 120 days. At any time after the defendant has served 60 days in the custody of the institutional division, the sentencing judge, on his own motion or on motion of the defendant, may order the defendant released to community supervision. The institutional division shall release the defendant to community supervision after he has served 120 days.

See also *O'Connor's Crimes & Consequences* (2008-09), chart 4-A, "Community Supervision—Felony," 4-D, "Community-Supervision Limitations."

§4. Jury Recommended Community Supervision

(a) A jury that imposes confinement as punishment for an offense may recommend to the judge that the judge suspend the imposition of the sentence and place the defendant on community supervision. A judge shall suspend the imposition of the sentence and place the defendant on community supervision if the jury makes that recommendation in the verdict.

(b) If the jury recommends to the judge that the judge place the defendant on community supervision, the judge shall place the defendant on community supervision for any period permitted under Section 3(b) or 3(c) of this article, as appropriate.

(c) A judge may increase the maximum period of community supervision in the manner provided by Section 22(c) or Section 22A of this article.

(d) A defendant is not eligible for community supervision under this section if the defendant:

(1) is sentenced to a term of imprisonment that exceeds 10 years;

(2) is convicted of a state jail felony for which suspension of the imposition of the sentence occurs automatically under Section 15(a);

(3) does not file a sworn motion under Subsection (e) of this section or for whom the jury does not enter in the verdict a finding that the information contained in the motion is true;

A *Subsection (4) below is effective for offenses committed on or after Sept. 1, 2007.*

(4) is convicted of an offense for which punishment is increased under Section 481.134(c), (d), (e), or (f), Health and Safety Code, if it is shown that the defendant has been previously convicted of an offense for which punishment was increased under any one of those subsections;

Subsection (4) below is effective for offenses in which any element of the offense was committed before Sept. 1, 2007.

(4) is adjudged guilty of an offense for which punishment is increased under Section 481.134(c), (d), (e), or (f), Health and Safety Code, if it is shown that the defendant has been previously convicted of an offense for which punishment was increased under any one of those subsections; or

☠ **E** *Subsection (5) below was enacted by Acts 2007, 80th Leg., ch. 1205, §3, effective Sept. 1, 2007, without* *reference to the conflicting enactment made by Acts 2007, 80th Leg., ch. 593, §1.06, effective Sept. 1, 2007. Subsection (5) below is effective for defendants initially placed on community supervision on or after Sept. 1, 2007.*

(5) is adjudged guilty of an offense under Section 19.02, Penal Code.

 Subsection (5) below was enacted by Acts 2007, 80th Leg., ch. 593, §1.06, effective Sept. 1, 2007, without reference to the conflicting enactment made by Acts 2007, 80th Leg., ch. 1205, §3, effective Sept. 1, 2007. Subsection (5) below is effective for offenses committed on or after Sept. 1, 2007.

(5) is convicted of an offense listed in Section 3g(a)(1)(C), (E), or (H), if the victim of the offense was younger than 14 years of age at the time the offense was committed;

E *Subsections (6) & (7) below are effective for offenses committed on or after Sept. 1, 2007.*

(6) is convicted of an offense listed in Section 3g(a)(1)(D), if the victim of the offense was younger than 14 years of age at the time the offense was committed and the actor committed the offense with the intent to violate or abuse the victim sexually; or

(7) is convicted of an offense listed in Section 3g(a)(1)(I).

(e) A defendant is eligible for community supervision under this section only if before the trial begins the defendant files a written sworn motion with the judge that the defendant has not previously been convicted of a felony in this or any other state, and the jury enters in the verdict a finding that the information in the defendant's motion is true.

E *Subsection (f) below is effective for offenses committed on or after Sept. 1, 2007.*

(f) The minimum period of community supervision under this section for an offense under Section 30.04, Penal Code, punishable as a Class A misdemeanor with a minimum term of confinement of six months is one year.

See also *O'Connor's Crimes & Consequences* (2008-09), chart 4-A, "Community Supervision—Felony," 4-D, "Community-Supervision Limitations."

§5. Deferred Adjudication; Community Supervision

(a) Except as provided by Subsection (d) of this section, when in the judge's opinion the best interest of society and the defendant will be served, the judge may, after receiving a plea of guilty or plea of nolo contendere, hearing the evidence, and finding that it substantiates the defendant's guilt, defer further proceedings without entering an adjudication of guilt, and place the defendant on community supervision. A judge may place on community supervision under this section a defendant charged with an offense under Section 21.11, 22.011, or 22.021, Penal Code, regardless of the age of the victim, or a defendant charged with a felony described by Section 13B(b) of this article, only if the judge makes a finding in open court that placing the defendant on community supervision is in the best interest of the victim. The failure of the judge to find that deferred adjudication is in the best interest of the victim is not grounds for the defendant to set aside the plea, deferred adjudication, or any subsequent conviction or sentence. After placing the defendant on community supervision under this section, the judge shall inform the defendant orally or in writing of the possible consequences under Subsection (b) of this section of a violation of community supervision. If the information is provided orally, the judge must record and maintain the judge's statement to the defendant. The failure of a judge to inform a defendant of possible consequences under Subsection (b) of this section is not a ground for reversal unless the defendant shows that he was harmed by the failure of the judge to provide the information. In a felony case, the period of community supervision may not exceed 10 years. For a defendant charged with a felony under Section 21.11, 22.011, or 22.021, Penal Code, regardless of the age of the victim, and for a defendant charged with a felony described by Section 13B(b) of this article, the period of community supervision may not be less than five years. In a misdemeanor case, the period of community supervision may not exceed two years. A judge may increase the maximum period of community supervision in the manner provided by Section 22(c) or 22A of this article. The judge may impose a fine applicable to the offense and require any reasonable conditions of community supervision, including mental health treatment under Section 11(d) of this article, that a judge could impose on a defendant placed on community supervision for a conviction that was probated and suspended, including confinement. The provisions of Section 15 of this article specifying whether a defendant convicted of a state jail felony is to be confined in a county jail or state jail felony facility and establishing the minimum and maximum terms of confinement as a condition of community supervision apply in the same manner to a defendant placed on community supervision after pleading guilty or nolo contendere to a state jail felony. However, upon written motion of the defendant requesting final adjudication filed within 30 days after entering such plea and the deferment of adjudication, the judge shall proceed to final adjudication as in all other cases.

🅐 **(b)** On violation of a condition of community supervision imposed under Subsection (a) of this section, the defendant may be arrested and detained as provided in Section 21 of this article. The defendant is entitled to a hearing limited to the determination by the court of whether it proceeds with an adjudication of guilt on the original charge. This determination is reviewable in the same manner as a revocation hearing conducted under Section 21 of this article in a case in which an adjudication of guilt had not been deferred. After an adjudication of guilt, all proceedings, including assessment of punishment, pronouncement of sentence, granting of community supervision, and defendant's appeal continue as if the adjudication of guilt had not been deferred. A court assessing punishment after an adjudication of guilt of a defendant charged with a state jail felony may suspend the imposition of the sentence and place the defendant on community supervision or may order the sentence to be executed, regardless of whether the defendant has previously been convicted of a felony.

(c) On expiration of a community supervision period imposed under Subsection (a) of this section, if the judge has not proceeded to adjudication of guilt, the judge shall dismiss the proceedings against the defendant and discharge him. The judge may dismiss the proceedings and discharge a defendant, other than a defendant charged with an offense requiring the defendant to register as a sex offender under Chapter 62, as added by Chapter 668, Acts of the 75th Legislature, Regular Session, 1997, prior to the expiration of the term of community supervision if in the judge's opinion the best interest of society and the defendant will be served. The judge may not dismiss the proceedings and discharge a defendant charged with an offense requiring the defendant to register under Chapter 62, as added by Chapter 668, Acts of the 75th Legislature, Regular Session, 1997. Except as provided by Section

12.42(g), Penal Code, a dismissal and discharge under this section may not be deemed a conviction for the purposes of disqualifications or disabilities imposed by law for conviction of an offense. For any defendant who receives a dismissal and discharge under this section:

(1) upon conviction of a subsequent offense, the fact that the defendant had previously received community supervision with a deferred adjudication of guilt shall be admissible before the court or jury to be considered on the issue of penalty;

(2) if the defendant is an applicant for a license or is a licensee under Chapter 42, Human Resources Code, the Texas Department of Human Services may consider the fact that the defendant previously has received community supervision with a deferred adjudication of guilt under this section in issuing, renewing, denying, or revoking a license under that chapter; and

(3) if the defendant is a person who has applied for registration to provide mental health or medical services for the rehabilitation of sex offenders, the Interagency Council on Sex Offender Treatment may consider the fact that the defendant has received community supervision under this section in issuing, renewing, denying, or revoking a license or registration issued by that council.

(d) In all other cases the judge may grant deferred adjudication unless:

(1) the defendant is charged with an offense:

🅐 *Subsection (A) below is effective for offenses committed on or after Sept. 1, 2007.*

(A) under Sections 49.04-49.08, Penal Code; or

Subsection (A) below is effective for offenses in which any element of the offense was committed before Sept. 1, 2007.

(A) under Section 49.04, 49.05, 49.06, 49.07, or 49.08, Penal Code; or

(B) for which punishment may be increased under Section 481.134(c), (d), (e), or (f), Health and Safety Code, if it is shown that the defendant has been previously convicted of an offense for which punishment was increased under any one of those subsections; or

(2) the defendant:

(A) is charged with an offense under Section 21.11, 22.011, or 22.021, Penal Code, regardless of the age of the victim, or a felony described by Section 13B(b) of this article; and

---

★

(B) has previously been placed on community supervision for any offense under Paragraph (A) of this subdivision; or

 Subsection (3) below is effective for offenses committed on or after Sept. 1, 2007.

(3) the defendant is charged with an offense under:

(A) Section 21.02, Penal Code; or

(B) Section 22.021, Penal Code, that is punishable under Subsection (f) of that section or under Section 12.42(c)(3), Penal Code.

(e) If a judge places on community supervision under this section a defendant charged with an offense under Section 20.02, 20.03, or 20.04, Penal Code, or an attempt, conspiracy, or solicitation to commit one of those offenses, the judge shall make an affirmative finding of fact and file a statement of that affirmative finding with the papers in the case if the judge determines that the victim or intended victim was younger than 17 years of age at the time of the offense.

(f) A record in the custody of the court clerk regarding a case in which a person is granted deferred adjudication is not confidential.

(g) If a judge places on community supervision under this section a defendant charged with an offense under Section 21.11, 22.011, 22.021, or 43.25, Penal Code, the judge shall make an affirmative finding of fact and file a statement of that affirmative finding with the papers in the case if the judge determines that:

(1) at the time of the offense, the defendant was younger than 19 years of age and the victim or intended victim was at least 13 years of age; and

(2) the charge to which the plea is entered under this section is based solely on the ages of the defendant and the victim or intended victim at the time of the offense.

(h) A court retains jurisdiction to hold a hearing under Subsection (b) and to proceed with an adjudication of guilt, regardless of whether the period of community supervision imposed on the defendant has expired, if before the expiration the attorney representing the state files a motion to proceed with the adjudication and a capias is issued for the arrest of the defendant.

 Subsections (i) & (j) below are effective for judgments of conviction entered or grants of deferred adjudication or dispositions of delinquent conduct made on or after June 15, 2007.

(i) If a judge places on community supervision under this section a defendant charged with an offense, on the motion of the attorney representing the state the judge shall make an affirmative finding of fact and file a statement of that affirmative finding in the papers in the case if the judge determines that, regardless of whether the conduct at issue is the subject of the prosecution or part of the same criminal episode as the conduct that is the subject of the prosecution, a victim in the trial:

(1) is or has been a victim of a severe form of trafficking in persons, as defined by 22 U.S.C. Section 7102(8); or

(2) has suffered substantial physical or mental abuse as a result of having been a victim of criminal activity described by 8 U.S.C. Section 1101(a)(15)(U)(iii).

(j) That part of the papers in the case containing an affirmative finding under Subsection (i):

(1) must include specific information identifying the victim, as available;

(2) may not include information identifying the victim's location; and

(3) is confidential, unless written consent for the release of the affirmative finding is obtained from the victim or, if the victim is younger than 18 years of age, the victim's parent or guardian.

See also *O'Connor's Crimes & Consequences* (2008-09), chart 4-A, "Community Supervision—Felony," 4-B, "Community Supervision—Misdemeanor," 4-D, "Community-Supervision Limitations," 4-G, "Early Termination."

§6. Continuing Court Jurisdiction in Felony Cases

(a) For the purposes of this section, the jurisdiction of a court in which a sentence requiring imprisonment in the institutional division of the Texas Department of Criminal Justice is imposed by the judge of the court shall continue for 180 days from the date the execution of the sentence actually begins. Before the expiration of 180 days from the date the execution of the sentence actually begins, the judge of the court that imposed such sentence may on his own motion, on the motion of the attorney representing the state, or on the written motion of the defendant, suspend further execution of the sentence and place the defendant on community supervision under the terms and conditions of this article, if in the opinion of the judge the defendant would not benefit from further imprisonment and:

(1) the defendant is otherwise eligible for community supervision under this article; and

(2) the defendant had never before been incarcerated in a penitentiary serving a sentence for a felony.

(b) When the defendant or the attorney representing the state files a written motion requesting suspension by the judge of further execution of the sentence and placement of the defendant on community supervision, and when requested to do so by the judge, the clerk of the court shall request a copy of the defendant's record while imprisoned from the institutional division of the Texas Department of Criminal Justice or, if the defendant is confined in county jail, from the sheriff. Upon receipt of such request, the institutional division of the Texas Department of Criminal Justice or the sheriff shall forward to the judge, as soon as possible, a full and complete copy of the defendant's record while imprisoned or confined. When the defendant files a written motion requesting suspension of further execution of the sentence and placement on community supervision, he shall immediately deliver or cause to be delivered a true and correct copy of the motion to the office of the attorney representing the state.

(c) The judge may deny the motion without a hearing but may not grant the motion without holding a hearing and providing the attorney representing the state and the defendant the opportunity to present evidence on the motion.

See also *O'Connor's Crimes & Consequences* (2008-09), chart 4-F, "Shock Probation."

§7. Continuing Court Jurisdiction in Misdemeanor Cases

(a) For the purposes of this section, the jurisdiction of the courts in this state in which a sentence requiring confinement in a jail is imposed for conviction of a misdemeanor shall continue for 180 days from the date the execution of the sentence actually begins. The judge of the court that imposed such sentence may on his own motion, on the motion of the attorney representing the state, or on the written motion of the defendant suspend further execution of the sentence and place the defendant on community supervision under the terms and conditions of this article, if in the opinion of the judge the defendant would not benefit from further confinement.

(b) When the defendant files a written motion with the court requesting suspension of further execution of the sentence and placement on community supervision or when requested to do so by the judge, the clerk of the court shall request a copy of the defendant's record while confined from the agency operating the jail where the defendant is confined. Upon receipt of such

request, the agency operating the jail where the defendant is confined shall forward to the court as soon as possible a full and complete copy of the defendant's record while confined.

(c) The judge may deny the motion without a hearing but may not grant a motion without holding a hearing and allowing the attorney representing the state and the defendant to present evidence in the case.

See also *O'Connor's Crimes & Consequences* (2008-09), chart 4-F, "Shock Probation."

§8. State Boot Camp Program

(a) For the purposes of this section, the jurisdiction of a court in which a sentence requiring imprisonment in the institutional division of the Texas Department of Criminal Justice is imposed for conviction of a felony shall continue for 180 days from the date on which the convicted person is received into custody by the institutional division. After the expiration of 75 days but prior to the expiration of 180 days from the date on which the convicted person is received into custody by the institutional division, the judge of the court that imposed the sentence may suspend further execution of the sentence imposed and place the person on community supervision under the terms and conditions of this article, if in the opinion of the judge the person would not benefit from further imprisonment. The court shall clearly indicate in its order recommending the placement of the person in the state boot camp program that the court is not retaining jurisdiction over the person for the purposes of Section 6 of this article. A court may recommend a person for placement in the state boot camp program only if:

(1) the person is otherwise eligible for community supervision under this article;

(2) the person is 17 years of age or older but younger than 26 years and is physically and mentally capable of participating in a program that requires strenuous physical activity; and

(3) the person is not convicted of an offense punishable as a state jail felony.

(b) On the 76th day after the day on which the convicted person is received into custody by the institutional division, the institutional division shall send the convicting court the record of the person's progress, conduct, and conformity to institutional division rules.

(c) The judge's recommendation that a person be placed in the state boot camp program created under

Section 499.052, Government Code, does not give the court the power to hold the Texas Department of Criminal Justice or any officer or employee of the department in contempt of court for failure to adhere to that recommendation.

§9. Presentence Investigations

(a) Except as provided by Subsection (g) of this section, before the imposition of sentence by a judge in a felony case, and except as provided by Subsection (b) of this section, before the imposition of sentence by a judge in a misdemeanor case the judge shall direct a supervision officer to report to the judge in writing on the circumstances of the offense with which the defendant is charged, the amount of restitution necessary to adequately compensate a victim of the offense, the criminal and social history of the defendant, and any other information relating to the defendant or the offense requested by the judge. It is not necessary that the report contain a sentencing recommendation, but the report must contain a proposed client supervision plan describing programs and sanctions that the community supervision and corrections department would provide the defendant if the judge suspended the imposition of the sentence or granted deferred adjudication.

(b) The judge is not required to direct a supervision officer to prepare a report in a misdemeanor case if:

(1) the defendant requests that a report not be made and the judge agrees to the request; or

(2) the judge finds that there is sufficient information in the record to permit the meaningful exercise of sentencing discretion and the judge explains this finding on the record.

(c) The judge may not inspect a report and the contents of the report may not be disclosed to any person unless:

(1) the defendant pleads guilty or nolo contendere or is convicted of the offense; or

(2) the defendant, in writing, authorizes the judge to inspect the report.

(d) Unless waived by the defendant, at least 48 hours before sentencing a defendant, the judge shall permit the defendant or his counsel to read the presentence report.

(e) The judge shall allow the defendant or his attorney to comment on a presentence investigation or a postsentence report and, with the approval of the judge, introduce testimony or other information alleging a factual inaccuracy in the investigation or report.

(f) The judge shall allow the attorney representing the state access to any information made available to the defendant under this section.

(g) A judge is not required to direct an officer to prepare a presentence report in a felony case under this section if:

(1) punishment is to be assessed by a jury;

(2) the defendant is convicted of or enters a plea of guilty or nolo contendere to capital murder;

(3) the only available punishment is imprisonment; or

(4) the judge is informed that a plea bargain agreement exists, under which the defendant agrees to a punishment of imprisonment, and the judge intends to follow the agreement.

(h) On a determination by the judge that alcohol or drug abuse may have contributed to the commission of the offense, or in any case involving a second or subsequent offense under Section 49.04, Penal Code, committed within five years of the date on which the most recent preceding offense was committed, or a second or subsequent offense under Section 49.07 or 49.08 of that code that involves the operation of a motor vehicle, committed within five years of the date on which the most recent preceding offense was committed, the judge shall direct a supervision officer approved by the community supervision and corrections department or the judge or a person, program, or other agency approved by the Texas Commission on Alcohol and Drug Abuse, to conduct an evaluation to determine the appropriateness of, and a course of conduct necessary for, alcohol or drug rehabilitation for a defendant and to report that evaluation to the judge. The evaluation shall be made:

(1) after arrest and before conviction, if requested by the defendant;

(2) after conviction and before sentencing, if the judge assesses punishment in the case;

(3) after sentencing and before the entry of a final judgment, if the jury assesses punishment in the case; or

(4) after community supervision is granted, if the evaluation is required as a condition of community supervision under Section 13 of this article.

(i) A presentence investigation conducted on any defendant convicted of a felony offense who appears to the judge through its own observation or on suggestion of a party to have a mental impairment shall include a psychological evaluation which determines, at a minimum, the defendant's IQ and adaptive behavior score. The results of the evaluation shall be included in the report to the judge as required by Subsection (a) of this section.

(j) The judge by order may direct that any information and records that are not privileged and that are relevant to a report required by Subsection (a) or Subsection (k) of this section be released to an officer conducting a presentence investigation under Subsection (i) of this section or a postsentence report under Subsection (k) of this section. The judge may also issue a subpoena to obtain that information. A report and all information obtained in connection with a presentence investigation or postsentence report are confidential and may be released only:

(1) to those persons and under those circumstances authorized under Subsections (d), (e), (f), (h), (k), and (*l*) of this section;

(2) pursuant to Section 614.017, Health and Safety Code; or

(3) as directed by the judge for the effective supervision of the defendant.

(k) If a presentence report in a felony case is not required under this section, the judge may direct the officer to prepare a postsentence report containing the same information that would have been required for the presentence report, other than a proposed client supervision plan and any information that is reflected in the judgment. If the postsentence report is ordered, the officer shall send the report to the clerk of the court not later than the 30th day after the date on which sentence is pronounced or deferred adjudication is granted, and the clerk shall deliver the postsentence report with the papers in the case to a designated officer of the Texas Department of Criminal Justice, as described by Section 8(a), Article 42.09.

(*l*), (m) Repealed by Acts 2003, 78th Leg., ch. 353, §5, eff. Sept. 1, 2003.

§9A. Sex Offenders: Presentence Investigation & Postsentence Treatment & Supervision

(a) In this section:

(1) "Council" means the Council on Sex Offender Treatment.

(2) "Sex offender" means a person who has been convicted or has entered a plea of guilty or nolo contendere for an offense under any one of the following provisions of the Penal Code:

(A) Section 20.04(a)(4) (Aggravated Kidnapping), if the person committed the offense with the intent to violate or abuse the victim sexually;

(B) Section 21.08 (Indecent Exposure);

(C) Section 21.11 (Indecency with a Child);

(D) Section 22.011 (Sexual Assault);

(E) Section 22.021 (Aggravated Sexual Assault);

(F) Section 25.02 (Prohibited Sexual Conduct);

(G) Section 30.02 (Burglary), if:

(i) the offense is punishable under Subsection (d) of that section; and

(ii) the person committed the offense with the intent to commit a felony listed in this subsection;

(H) Section 43.25 (Sexual Performance by a Child); or

(I) Section 43.26 (Possession or Promotion of Child Pornography).

(b) If the defendant is a sex offender, a supervision officer may release information in a presentence or postsentence report concerning the social and criminal history of the defendant to a person who:

(1) is licensed or certified in this state to provide mental health or medical services, including a:

(A) physician;

(B) psychiatrist;

(C) psychologist;

(D) licensed professional counselor;

(E) licensed marriage and family therapist; or

(F) certified social worker; and

(2) provides mental health or medical services for the rehabilitation of the defendant.

(c) If the defendant is a sex offender, the judge shall direct a supervision officer approved by the community supervision and corrections department or the judge or a person, program, or other agency approved by the council to evaluate the appropriateness of, and a course of conduct necessary for, treatment, specialized supervision, or rehabilitation of the defendant and to report the results of the evaluation to the judge. The judge may require the evaluation to use offense-specific standards of practice adopted by the council and may require the report to reflect those standards. The evaluation shall be made after conviction and before the entry of a final judgment or, if requested by the defendant, after arrest and before conviction.

§10. Authority to Impose, Modify, or Revoke Community Supervision

(a) Only the court in which the defendant was tried may grant community supervision, impose conditions, revoke the community supervision, or discharge the defendant, unless the judge has transferred jurisdiction of the case to another court with the latter's consent. Except as provided by Subsection (d) of this section, only the judge may alter conditions of community supervision. In a felony case, only the judge who originally sentenced the defendant may suspend execution thereof and place the defendant under community supervision pursuant to Section 6 of this article. If the judge who originally sentenced the defendant is deceased or disabled or if the office is vacant and the judge who originally sentenced the defendant is deceased or disabled or if the office is vacant and a motion is filed in accordance with Section 6 of this article, the clerk of the court shall promptly forward a copy of the motion to the presiding judge of the administrative judicial district for that court, who may deny the motion without a hearing or appoint a judge to hold a hearing on the motion.

(b) After a defendant has been placed on community supervision, jurisdiction of the case may be transferred to a court of the same rank in this state having geographical jurisdiction where the defendant is residing or where a violation of the conditions of community supervision occurs. Upon transfer, the clerk of the court of original jurisdiction shall forward a transcript of such portions of the record as the transferring judge shall direct to the court accepting jurisdiction, which latter court shall thereafter proceed as if the trial and conviction had occurred in that court.

(c) Any judge of a court having geographical jurisdiction where the defendant is residing or where a violation of the conditions of community supervision occurs may issue a warrant for his arrest, but the determination of action to be taken after arrest shall be only by the judge of the court having jurisdiction of the case at the time the action is taken.

(d) A judge that places a defendant on community supervision may authorize the supervision officer supervising the defendant or a magistrate appointed by the district courts in the county that give preference to criminal cases to modify the conditions of community supervision for the limited purpose of transferring the defendant to different programs within the community supervision continuum of programs and sanctions.

(e) If a supervision officer or magistrate modifies the conditions of community supervision, the officer or magistrate shall deliver a copy of the modified conditions to the defendant, shall file a copy of the modified conditions with the sentencing court, and shall note the date of delivery of the copy in the defendant's file. If the defendant agrees to the modification in writing, the officer or magistrate shall file a copy of the modified conditions with the district clerk and the conditions shall be enforced as modified. If the defendant does not agree to the modification in writing, the supervision officer or magistrate shall refer the case to the judge of the court for modification in the manner provided by Section 22 of this article.

(j-3) Deleted by Acts 1993, 73rd Leg., ch. 900, §4.01, eff. Sept. 1, 1993.

§11. Basic Conditions of Community Supervision

(a) The judge of the court having jurisdiction of the case shall determine the conditions of community supervision and may, at any time, during the period of community supervision alter or modify the conditions. The judge may impose any reasonable condition that is designed to protect or restore the community, protect or restore the victim, or punish, rehabilitate, or reform the defendant. Conditions of community supervision may include, but shall not be limited to, the conditions that the defendant shall:

(1) Commit no offense against the laws of this State or of any other State or of the United States;

(2) Avoid injurious or vicious habits;

(3) Avoid persons or places of disreputable or harmful character;

(4) Report to the supervision officer as directed by the judge or supervision officer and obey all rules and regulations of the community supervision and corrections department;

(5) Permit the supervision officer to visit the defendant at the defendant's home or elsewhere;

(6) Work faithfully at suitable employment as far as possible;

(7) Remain within a specified place;

(8) Pay the defendant's fine, if one be assessed, and all court costs whether a fine be assessed or not, in one or several sums;

(9) Support the defendant's dependents;

(10) Participate, for a time specified by the judge in any community-based program, including a community-service work program under Section 16 of this article;

(11) Reimburse the county in which the prosecution was instituted for compensation paid to appointed counsel for defending the defendant in the case, if counsel was appointed, or if the defendant was represented by a county-paid public defender, in an amount that would have been paid to an appointed attorney had the county not had a public defender;

(12) Remain under custodial supervision in a community corrections facility, obey all rules and regulations of such facility, and pay a percentage of the defendant's income to the facility for room and board;

(13) Pay a percentage of the defendant's income to the defendant's dependents for their support while under custodial supervision in a community corrections facility;

(14) Submit to testing for alcohol or controlled substances;

(15) Attend counseling sessions for substance abusers or participate in substance abuse treatment services in a program or facility approved or licensed by the Texas Commission on Alcohol and Drug Abuse;

(16) With the consent of the victim of a misdemeanor offense or of any offense under Title 7, Penal Code, participate in victim-defendant mediation;

(17) Submit to electronic monitoring;

(18) Reimburse the compensation to victims of crime fund for any amounts paid from that fund to or on behalf of a victim, as defined by Article 56.32, of the defendant's offense, or if no reimbursement is required, make one payment to the compensation to victims of crime fund in an amount not to exceed $50 if the offense is a misdemeanor or not to exceed $100 if the offense is a felony;

(19) Reimburse a law enforcement agency for the analysis, storage, or disposal of raw materials, controlled substances, chemical precursors, drug paraphernalia, or other materials seized in connection with the offense;

(20) Pay all or part of the reasonable and necessary costs incurred by the victim for psychological counseling made necessary by the offense or for counseling and education relating to acquired immune deficiency syndrome or human immunodeficiency virus made necessary by the offense;

(21) Make one payment in an amount not to exceed $50 to a crime stoppers organization as defined by Section 414.001, Government Code, and as certified by the Crime Stoppers Advisory Council;

(22) Submit a DNA sample to the Department of Public Safety under Subchapter G, Chapter 411, Government Code, for the purpose of creating a DNA record of the defendant;

(23) In any manner required by the judge, provide public notice of the offense for which the defendant was placed on community supervision in the county in which the offense was committed; and

(24) Reimburse the county in which the prosecution was instituted for compensation paid to any interpreter in the case.

(b) A judge may not order a defendant to make any payments as a term or condition of community supervision, except for fines, court costs, restitution to the victim, and other conditions related personally to the rehabilitation of the defendant or otherwise expressly authorized by law. The court shall consider the ability of the defendant to make payments in ordering the defendant to make payments under this article.

(c) If the judge or jury places a defendant on community supervision, the judge shall require the defendant to demonstrate to the court whether the defendant has an educational skill level that is equal to or greater than the average skill level of students who have completed the sixth grade in public schools in this state. If the judge determines that the defendant has not attained that skill level, the judge shall require as a condition of community supervision that the defendant attain that level of educational skill, unless the judge determines that the defendant lacks the intellectual capacity or the learning ability to ever achieve that level of skill.

(d) If the judge places a defendant on community supervision and the defendant is determined to have a mental illness or be a person with mental retardation by an examining expert under Article 16.22 or Chapter 46B or in a psychological evaluation conducted under

Section 9(i) of this article, the judge may require the defendant as a condition of community supervision to submit to outpatient or inpatient mental health or mental retardation treatment if the:

(1) defendant's:

(A) mental impairment is chronic in nature; or

(B) ability to function independently will continue to deteriorate if the defendant does not receive mental health or mental retardation services; and

(2) judge determines, in consultation with a local mental health or mental retardation services provider, that appropriate mental health or mental retardation services for the defendant are available through the Texas Department of Mental Health and Mental Retardation under Section 534.053, Health and Safety Code, or through another mental health or mental retardation services provider.

(e) A judge granting community supervision to a defendant required to register as a sex offender under Chapter 62 shall require that the defendant, as a condition of community supervision:

(1) register under that chapter; and

(2) submit a DNA sample to the Department of Public Safety under Subchapter G, Chapter 411, Government Code, for the purpose of creating a DNA record of the defendant, unless the defendant has already submitted the required sample under other state law.

(f) A judge may not require a defendant to undergo an orchiectomy as a condition of community supervision.

(g) A judge who grants community supervision to a person may require the person to make one payment in an amount not to exceed $50 to a children's advocacy center established under Subchapter E, Chapter 264, Family Code, if the person is charged with or convicted of an offense under Section 21.11 or 22.011(a)(2), Penal Code.

(h) If a judge grants community supervision to a person convicted of an offense under Title 5, Penal Code, that the court determines involves family violence, the judge may require the person to make one payment in an amount not to exceed $100 to a family violence shelter center that receives state or federal funds and that serves the county in which the court is located. In this subsection, "family violence" has the meaning assigned by Section 71.004, Family Code, and "family violence shelter center" has the meaning assigned by Section 51.002, Human Resources Code.

(i) A judge who grants community supervision to a sex offender evaluated under Section 9A may require the sex offender as a condition of community supervision to submit to treatment, specialized supervision, or rehabilitation according to offense-specific standards of practice adopted by the Council on Sex Offender Treatment. On a finding that the defendant is financially able to make payment, the judge shall require the defendant to pay all or part of the reasonable and necessary costs of the treatment, supervision, or rehabilitation.

(j), (k) [Blank].

(*l*)(1) If the court grants community supervision to a person convicted of an offense under Section 42.072, Penal Code, the court may require as a condition of community supervision that the person may not:

(A) communicate directly or indirectly with the victim; or

(B) go to or near the residence, place of employment, or business of the victim or to or near a school, day-care facility, or similar facility where a dependent child of the victim is in attendance.

(2) If the court requires the prohibition contained in Subdivision (1)(B) of this subsection as a condition of community supervision, the court shall specifically describe the prohibited locations and the minimum distances, if any, that the person must maintain from the locations.

§12. Confinement as a Condition of Community Supervision

(a) If a judge having jurisdiction of a misdemeanor case requires as a condition of community supervision that the defendant submit to a period of confinement in a county jail, the period of confinement may not exceed 30 days. If a judge having jurisdiction of a felony case requires as a condition of community supervision that the defendant submit to a period of confinement in a county jail, the period of confinement may not exceed 180 days.

(b) A judge that requires as a condition of community supervision that the defendant serve a term in a community corrections facility under Section 18 of this article may not impose a term of confinement under this section that, when added to the term imposed under Section 18, exceeds 24 months.

(c) A judge may impose confinement as a condition of community supervision under Subsection (a) of this section on placing the defendant on supervision or at any time during the supervision period. The judge may impose periods of confinement as a condition of community supervision in increments smaller than the maximum periods provided by Subsection (a) of this section but may not impose periods of confinement that if added together exceed the maximum periods provided by Subsection (a).

See also *O'Connor's Crimes & Consequences* (2008-09), chart 4-A, "Community Supervision—Felony," 4-B, "Community Supervision—Misdemeanor."

§13. DWI Community Supervision

(a) A judge granting community supervision to a defendant convicted of an offense under Chapter 49, Penal Code, shall require as a condition of community supervision that the defendant submit to:

(1) not less than 72 hours of continuous confinement in county jail if the defendant was punished under Section 49.09(a); not less than five days of confinement in county jail if the defendant was punished under Section 49.09(a) and was subject to Section 49.09(h); not less than 10 days of confinement in county jail if the defendant was punished under Section 49.09(b) or (c); or not less than 30 days of confinement in county jail if the defendant was convicted under Section 49.07; and

(2) an evaluation by a supervision officer or by a person, program, or facility approved by the Texas Commission on Alcohol and Drug Abuse for the purpose of having the facility prescribe and carry out a course of conduct necessary for the rehabilitation of the defendant's drug or alcohol dependence condition.

(b) A judge granting community supervision to a defendant convicted of an offense under Section 49.08, Penal Code, shall require as a condition of community supervision that the defendant submit to a period of confinement of not less than 120 days.

(c) If the director of a facility to which a defendant is referred under Subdivision (2) of Subsection (a) of this section determines that the defendant is not making a good faith effort to participate in a program of rehabilitation, the director shall notify the judge that referred the defendant of that fact.

(d) If a judge requires as a condition of community supervision that the defendant participate in a prescribed course of conduct necessary for the rehabilitation of the defendant's drug or alcohol dependence condition, the judge shall require that the defendant pay for all or part of the cost of such rehabilitation based on

the defendant's ability to pay. The judge may, in its discretion, credit such cost paid by the defendant against the fine assessed. In making a determination of a defendant's ability to pay the cost of rehabilitation under this subsection, the judge shall consider whether the defendant has insurance coverage that will pay for rehabilitation.

(e) The confinement imposed shall be treated as a condition of community supervision, and in the event of a sentence of confinement upon the revocation of community supervision, the term of confinement served may not be credited toward service of such subsequent confinement.

(f) If a judge grants community supervision to a defendant convicted of an offense under Sections 49.04-49.08, Penal Code, and if before receiving community supervision the defendant has not submitted to an evaluation under Section 9 of this article, the judge shall require the defendant to submit to the evaluation as a condition of community supervision. If the evaluation indicates to the judge that the defendant is in need of treatment for drug or alcohol dependency, the judge shall require the defendant to submit to that treatment as a condition of community supervision in a program or facility approved or licensed by the Texas Commission on Alcohol and Drug Abuse or in a program or facility that complies with standards established by the community justice assistance division of the Texas Department of Criminal Justice, after consultation by the division with the commission.

(g) A jury that recommends community supervision for a person convicted of an offense under Sections 49.04-49.08, Penal Code, may recommend that any driver's license issued to the defendant under Chapter 521, Transportation Code, not be suspended. This subsection does not apply to a person punished under Section 49.09(a) or (b), Penal Code, and subject to Section 49.09(h) of that code.

(h) If a person convicted of an offense under Sections 49.04-49.08, Penal Code, is placed on community supervision, the judge shall require, as a condition of the community supervision, that the defendant attend and successfully complete before the 181st day after the day community supervision is granted an educational program jointly approved by the Texas Commission on Alcohol and Drug Abuse, the Department of Public

Safety, the Traffic Safety Section of the Texas Department of Transportation, and the community justice assistance division of the Texas Department of Criminal Justice designed to rehabilitate persons who have driven while intoxicated. The Texas Commission on Alcohol and Drug Abuse shall publish the jointly approved rules and shall monitor, coordinate, and provide training to persons providing the educational programs. The Texas Commission on Alcohol and Drug Abuse is responsible for the administration of the certification of approved educational programs and may charge a nonrefundable application fee for the initial certification of approval and for renewal of a certificate. The judge may waive the educational program requirement or may grant an extension of time to successfully complete the program that expires not later than one year after the beginning date of the person's community supervision, however, if the defendant by a motion in writing shows good cause. In determining good cause, the judge may consider but is not limited to: the defendant's school and work schedule, the defendant's health, the distance that the defendant must travel to attend an educational program, and the fact that the defendant resides out of state, has no valid driver's license, or does not have access to transportation. The judge shall set out the finding of good cause for waiver in the judgment. If a defendant is required, as a condition of community supervision, to attend an educational program or if the court waives the educational program requirement, the court clerk shall immediately report that fact to the Department of Public Safety, on a form prescribed by the department, for inclusion in the person's driving record. If the court grants an extension of time in which the person may complete the program, the court clerk shall immediately report that fact to the Department of Public Safety on a form prescribed by the department. The report must include the beginning date of the person's community supervision. Upon the person's successful completion of the educational program, the person's instructor shall give notice to the Department of Public Safety for inclusion in the person's driving record and to the community supervision and corrections department. The community supervision and corrections department shall then forward the notice to the court clerk for filing. If the Department of Public Safety does not receive notice that a defendant required to complete an educational program has successfully completed the program within the period required by this section, as shown on department records,

the department shall revoke the defendant's driver's license, permit, or privilege or prohibit the person from obtaining a license or permit, as provided by Sections 521.344(e) and (f), Transportation Code. The Department of Public Safety may not reinstate a license suspended under this subsection unless the person whose license was suspended makes application to the department for reinstatement of the person's license and pays to the department a reinstatement fee of $50. The Department of Public Safety shall remit all fees collected under this subsection to the comptroller for deposit in the general revenue fund. This subsection does not apply to a defendant if a jury recommends community supervision for the defendant and also recommends that the defendant's driver's license not be suspended.

(i) If a person convicted of an offense under Sections 49.04-49.08, Penal Code, is placed on community supervision, the court may require as a condition of community supervision that the defendant have a device installed, on the motor vehicle owned by the defendant or on the vehicle most regularly driven by the defendant, that uses a deep-lung breath analysis mechanism to make impractical the operation of the motor vehicle if ethyl alcohol is detected in the breath of the operator and that the defendant not operate any motor vehicle that is not equipped with that device. If it is shown on the trial of the offense that an analysis of a specimen of the person's blood, breath, or urine showed an alcohol concentration level of 0.15 or more at the time the analysis was performed, or if the person is convicted of an offense under Sections 49.04-49.06, Penal Code, and punished under Section 49.09(a) or (b), Penal Code, or of a second or subsequent offense under Section 49.07 or 49.08, Penal Code, and the person after conviction of either offense is placed on community supervision, the court shall require as a condition of community supervision that the defendant have the device installed on the appropriate vehicle and that the defendant not operate any motor vehicle unless the vehicle is equipped with that device. Before placing on community supervision a person convicted of an offense under Sections 49.04-49.08, Penal Code, the court shall determine from criminal history record information maintained by the Department of Public Safety whether the person has one or more previous convictions under Sections 49.04-49.08, Penal Code, or has one previous conviction under Sections 49.04-49.07, Penal Code, or one previous conviction under Section

49.08, Penal Code. If it is shown on the trial of the offense that an analysis of a specimen of the person's blood, breath, or urine showed an alcohol concentration level of 0.15 or more at the time the analysis was performed, or if the court determines that the person has one or more such previous convictions, the court shall require as a condition of community supervision that the defendant have that device installed on the motor vehicle owned by the defendant or on the vehicle most regularly driven by the defendant and that the defendant not operate any motor vehicle unless the vehicle is equipped with the device described in this subsection. The court shall require the defendant to obtain the device at the defendant's own cost before the 30th day after the date of conviction unless the court finds that to do so would not be in the best interest of justice and enters its findings on record. The court shall require the defendant to provide evidence to the court within the 30-day period that the device has been installed on the appropriate vehicle and order the device to remain installed on that vehicle for a period not less than 50 percent of the supervision period. If the court determines the offender is unable to pay for the device, the court may impose a reasonable payment schedule not to exceed twice the period of the court's order. The Department of Public Safety shall approve devices for use under this subsection. Section 521.247, Transportation Code, applies to the approval of a device under this subsection and the consequences of that approval. Notwithstanding the provisions of this section, if a person is required to operate a motor vehicle in the course and scope of the person's employment and if the vehicle is owned by the employer, the person may operate that vehicle without installation of an approved ignition interlock device if the employer has been notified of that driving privilege restriction and if proof of that notification is with the vehicle. This employment exemption does not apply, however, if the business entity that owns the vehicle is owned or controlled by the person whose driving privilege has been restricted. A previous conviction may not be used for purposes of restricting a person to the operation of a motor vehicle equipped with an interlock ignition device under this subsection if:

(1) the previous conviction was a final conviction under Section 49.04, 49.045, 49.05, 49.06, 49.07, or 49.08, Penal Code, and was for an offense committed more than 10 years before the instant offense for which the person was convicted and placed on community supervision; and

(2) the person has not been convicted of an offense under Section 49.04, 49.045, 49.05, 49.06, 49.07, or 49.08 of that code, committed within 10 years before the date on which the instant offense for which the person was convicted and placed on community supervision.

(j) The judge shall require a defendant who is punished under Section 49.09, Penal Code, as a condition of community supervision, to attend and successfully complete an educational program for repeat offenders approved by the Texas Commission on Alcohol and Drug Abuse. The Texas Commission on Alcohol and Drug Abuse shall adopt rules and shall monitor, coordinate, and provide training to persons providing the educational programs. The Texas Commission on Alcohol and Drug Abuse is responsible for the administration of the certification of approved educational programs and may charge a nonrefundable application fee for initial certification of approval or for renewal of the certification. The judge may waive the educational program requirement only if the defendant by a motion in writing shows good cause. In determining good cause, the judge may consider the defendant's school and work schedule, the defendant's health, the distance that the defendant must travel to attend an educational program, and whether the defendant resides out of state or does not have access to transportation. The judge shall set out the finding of good cause in the judgment. If a defendant is required, as a condition of community supervision, to attend an educational program, the court clerk shall immediately report that fact to the Department of Public Safety, on a form prescribed by the department, for inclusion in the defendant's driving record. The report must include the beginning date of the defendant's community supervision. On the defendant's successful completion of the educational program for repeat offenders, the defendant's instructor shall give notice to the Department of Public Safety for inclusion in the defendant's driving record and to the community supervision and corrections department. The community supervision and corrections department shall then forward the notice to the court clerk for filing. If the Department of Public Safety does not receive notice that a defendant required to complete an educational program has successfully completed the program for repeat offenders within the period required by the judge, as shown on department records, the department shall revoke the defendant's driver's license, permit, or privilege or prohibit the defendant from obtaining a license or permit, as provided by Sections 521.344(e) and (f), Transportation Code.

(k) Notwithstanding Sections 521.344(d)-(i), Transportation Code, if the judge, under Subsection (h) or (j) of this section, permits or requires a defendant punished under Section 49.09, Penal Code, to attend an educational program as a condition of community supervision, or waives the required attendance for such a program, and the defendant has previously been required to attend such a program, or the required attendance at the program had been waived, the judge nonetheless shall order the suspension of the driver's license, permit, or operating privilege of that person for a period determined by the judge according to the following schedule:

(1) not less than 90 days or more than 365 days, if the defendant is convicted under Sections 49.04-49.08, Penal Code;

(2) not less than 180 days or more than two years, if the defendant is punished under Section 49.09(a) or (b), Penal Code; or

(3) not less than one year or more than two years, if the person is convicted of a second or subsequent offense under Sections 49.04-49.08, Penal Code, committed within five years of the date on which the most recent preceding offense was committed.

(*l*) If the Department of Public Safety receives notice that a defendant has been required or permitted to attend a subsequent educational program under Subsection (h), (j), or (k) of this section, although the previously required attendance had been waived, but the judge has not ordered a period of suspension, the department shall suspend the defendant's driver's license, permit, or operating privilege, or shall issue an order prohibiting the defendant from obtaining a license or permit for a period of 365 days.

(m) If a judge revokes the community supervision of a defendant for an offense under Section 49.04, Penal Code, or an offense involving the operation of a motor vehicle under Section 49.07, Penal Code, and the driver's license or privilege to operate a motor vehicle has not previously been ordered by the judge to be suspended, or if the suspension was previously probated, the judge shall suspend the license or privilege for a period provided under Subchapter O, Chapter 521, Transportation Code. The suspension shall be reported to the Department of Public Safety as provided under Section 521.347, Transportation Code.

(n) Notwithstanding any other provision of this section or other law, the judge who places on community supervision a defendant who is younger than 21 years of age and convicted for an offense under Sections 49.04-49.08, Penal Code, shall:

(1) order that the defendant's driver's license be suspended for 90 days beginning on the date that the person is placed on community supervision; and

(2) require as a condition of community supervision that the defendant not operate a motor vehicle unless the vehicle is equipped with the device described by Subsection (i) of this section.

See also H&SC §469.008; *O'Connor's Crimes & Consequences* (2008 09), chart 4-E, "Minimum Confinements for Intoxication Offenses."

§13A. Community Supervision for Offense Committed Because of Bias or Prejudice

(a) A court granting community supervision to a defendant convicted of an offense for which the court has made an affirmative finding under Article 42.014 of this code shall require as a term of community supervision that the defendant:

(1) serve a term of not more than one year imprisonment in the institutional division of the Texas Department of Criminal Justice if the offense is a felony other than an offense under Section 19.02, Penal Code; or

(2) serve a term of not more than 90 days confinement in jail if the offense is a misdemeanor.

(b) The court may not grant community supervision on its own motion or on the recommendation of the jury to a defendant convicted of an offense for which the court has made an affirmative finding under Article 42.014 of this code if:

(1) the offense is murder under Section 19.02, Penal Code; or

(2) the defendant has been previously convicted of an offense for which the court made an affirmative finding under Article 42.014 of this code.

§13B. Defendants Placed on Community Supervision for Sexual Offenses Against Children

(a) If a judge grants community supervision to a defendant described by Subsection (b) and the judge determines that a child as defined by Section 22.011(c), Penal Code, was the victim of the offense, the judge shall establish a child safety zone applicable to the defendant by requiring as a condition of community supervision that the defendant:

(1) not:

(A) supervise or participate in any program that includes as participants or recipients persons who are 17 years of age or younger and that regularly provides athletic, civic, or cultural activities; or

(B) go in, on, or within 1,000 feet of a premises where children commonly gather, including a school, day-care facility, playground, public or private youth center, public swimming pool, or video arcade facility; and

(2) attend psychological counseling sessions for sex offenders with an individual or organization which provides sex offender treatment or counseling as specified by or approved by the judge or the community supervision and corrections department officer supervising the defendant.

(b) This section applies to a defendant placed on community supervision for an offense:

(1) under Section 43.25 or 43.26, Penal Code;

(2) under Section 21.08, 21.11, 22.011, 22.021, or 25.02, Penal Code;

(3) under Section 20.04(a)(4), Penal Code, if the defendant committed the offense with the intent to violate or abuse the victim sexually; or

(4) under Section 30.02, Penal Code, punishable under Subsection (d) of that section, if the defendant committed the offense with the intent to commit a felony listed in Subdivision (2) or (3) of this subsection.

(c) A community supervision and corrections department officer who under Subsection (a)(2) specifies a sex offender treatment provider to provide counseling to a defendant shall contact the provider before the defendant is released, establish the date, time, and place of the first session between the defendant and the provider, and request the provider to immediately notify the officer if the defendant fails to attend the first session or any subsequent scheduled session.

(d) Notwithstanding Subsection (a)(1), a judge is not required to impose the conditions described by Subsection (a)(1) if the defendant is a student at a primary or secondary school.

(e) At any time after the imposition of a condition under Subsection (a)(1), the defendant may request the court to modify the child safety zone applicable to the defendant because the zone as created by the court:

(1) interferes with the ability of the defendant to attend school or hold a job and consequently constitutes an undue hardship for the defendant; or

(2) is broader than is necessary to protect the public, given the nature and circumstances of the offense.

(f) A community supervision and corrections department officer supervising a defendant described by Subsection (b) may permit the defendant to enter on an event-by-event basis into the child safety zone from which the defendant is otherwise prohibited from entering if:

(1) the defendant has served at least two years of the period of community supervision;

(2) the defendant enters the zone as part of a program to reunite with the defendant's family;

(3) the defendant presents to the officer a written proposal specifying where the defendant intends to go within the zone, why and with whom the defendant is going, and how the defendant intends to cope with any stressful situations that occur;

(4) the sex offender treatment provider treating the defendant agrees with the officer that the defendant should be allowed to attend the event; and

(5) the officer and the treatment provider agree on a chaperon to accompany the defendant and the chaperon agrees to perform that duty.

(g) Section 10(a) does not prohibit a community supervision and corrections department officer from altering a condition of community supervision by permitting a defendant to enter a child safety zone under Subsection (f).

(h) In this section, "playground," "premises," "school," "video arcade facility," and "youth center" have the meanings assigned by Section 481.134, Health and Safety Code.

(i) Notwithstanding Subsection (a)(1)(B), a requirement that a defendant not go in, on, or within 1,000 feet of certain premises does not apply to a defendant while the defendant is in or going immediately to or from a:

(1) community supervision and corrections department office;

(2) premises at which the defendant is participating in a program or activity required as a condition of community supervision;

(3) residential facility in which the defendant is required to reside as a condition of community supervision, if the facility was in operation as a residence for defendants on community supervision on June 1, 2003; or

(4) private residence at which the defendant is required to reside as a condition of community supervision.

See also *O'Connor's Crimes & Consequences* (2008-09), chart 4-A, "Community Supervision—Felony."

§13C. Community Supervision for Making a Firearm Accessible to a Child

(a) A court granting community supervision to a defendant convicted of an offense under Section 46.13, Penal Code, may require as a condition of community supervision that the defendant:

(1) provide an appropriate public service activity designated by the court; or

(2) attend a firearms safety course which meets or exceeds the requirements set by the National Rifle Association as of January 1, 1995, for a firearms safety course that requires not more than 17 hours of instruction.

(b) The court shall require the defendant to pay the cost of attending the firearms safety course under Subsection (a)(2).

§13D. Defendants Placed on Community Supervision for Violent Offenses; Protecting Children

(a) If a judge grants community supervision to a defendant convicted of an offense listed in Section 3g(a)(1) or for which the judgment contains an affirmative finding under Section 3g(a)(2), the judge, if the nature of the offense for which the defendant is convicted warrants the establishment of a child safety zone, may establish a child safety zone applicable to the defendant by requiring as a condition of community supervision that the defendant not:

(1) supervise or participate in any program that includes as participants or recipients persons who are 17 years of age or younger and that regularly provides athletic, civic, or cultural activities; or

(2) go in or on, or within a distance specified by the judge of, a premises where children commonly gather, including a school, day-care facility, playground, public or private youth center, public swimming pool, or video arcade facility.

(b) At any time after the imposition of a condition under Subsection (a), the defendant may request the judge to modify the child safety zone applicable to the defendant because the zone as created by the judge:

(1) interferes with the ability of the defendant to attend school or hold a job and consequently constitutes an undue hardship for the defendant; or

(2) is broader than is necessary to protect the public, given the nature and circumstances of the offense.

(c) This section does not apply to a defendant described by Section 13B.

(d) In this section, "playground," "premises," "school," "video arcade facility," and "youth center" have the meanings assigned by Section 481.134, Health and Safety Code.

§14. Child Abusers & Family Violence Offenders; Special Conditions

(a) If the court grants probation to a person convicted of an offense described by Article 17.41(a) of this code, the court may require as a condition of probation that the defendant not directly communicate with the victim of the offense or go near a residence, school, or other location, as specifically described in the copy of terms and conditions, frequented by the victim. In imposing the condition, the court may grant the defendant supervised access to the victim. To the extent that a condition imposed under this subsection conflicts with an existing court order granting possession of or access to a child, the condition imposed under this subsection prevails for a period specified by the court granting probation, not to exceed 90 days.

(b) Repealed by Acts 2003, 78th Leg., ch. 353, §6, eff. Sept. 1, 2003.

 Subsection (c) below is effective for court orders granting community supervision or protective orders or modifications of orders rendered on or after Sept. 1, 2007.

(c) If the court grants community supervision to a person convicted of an offense involving family violence, as defined by Section 71.004, Family Code, the court may require the defendant, at the direction of the community supervision and corrections department officer, to:

(1) attend a battering intervention and prevention program as defined by Article 42.141;

(2) beginning on September 1, 2008, if the referral option under Subdivision (1) is not available, attend a program or counsel with a provider that has begun the accreditation process described by Subsection (c-1); or

(3) if the referral option under Subdivision (1) or, beginning on September 1, 2008, the referral option under Subdivision (2) is not available, attend counseling sessions for the elimination of violent behavior with a licensed counselor, social worker, or other professional who has completed family violence intervention training that the community justice assistance division of the Texas Department of Criminal Justice has approved, after consultation with the licensing authorities described by Chapters 152, 501, 502, 503, and 505, Occupations Code, and experts in the field of family violence.

Subsection (c) below is effective for court orders granting community supervision or protective orders or modifications of orders rendered before Sept. 1, 2007

(c) If the court grants community supervision to a person convicted of an offense involving family violence, as defined by Section 71.004, Family Code, the court may require the defendant to attend, at the direction of the community supervision and corrections department officer, counseling sessions for the elimination of violent behavior with a licensed counselor, social worker, or other professional who has been trained in family violence intervention or to attend a battering intervention and prevention program if available that meets guidelines adopted by the community justice assistance division of the Texas Department of Criminal Justice. If the court requires the defendant to attend counseling or a program, the court shall require the defendant to begin attendance not later than the 60th day after the date the court grants community supervision, notify the community supervision and corrections department officer of the name, address, and phone number of the counselor or program, and report the defendant's attendance to the officer. The court shall require the defendant to pay all the reasonable costs of the counseling sessions or attendance in the program on a finding that the defendant is financially able to make payment. If the court finds the defendant is unable to make payment, the court shall make the counseling sessions or enrollment in the program available without cost to the defendant. The court may

also require the defendant to pay all or a part of the reasonable costs incurred by the victim for counseling made necessary by the offense, on a finding that the defendant is financially able to make payment. The court may order the defendant to make payments under this subsection for a period not to exceed one year after the date on which the order is entered.

E *Subsection (c-1) below is effective for court orders granting community supervision or protective orders or modifications of orders rendered on or after Sept. 1, 2007.*

(c-1) Beginning on September 1, 2009, a program or provider serving as a referral option for the courts under Subsection (c)(1) or (2) must be accredited under Section 4A, Article 42.141, as conforming to program guidelines under that article.

(c-2) If the court requires the defendant to attend counseling or a program, the court shall require the defendant to begin attendance not later than the 60th day after the date the court grants community supervision, notify the community supervision and corrections department officer of the name, address, and phone number of the counselor or program, and report the defendant's attendance to the officer. The court shall require the defendant to pay all the reasonable costs of the counseling sessions or attendance in the program on a finding that the defendant is financially able to make payment. If the court finds the defendant is unable to make payment, the court shall make the counseling sessions or enrollment in the program available without cost to the defendant. The court may also require the defendant to pay all or a part of the reasonable costs incurred by the victim for counseling made necessary by the offense, on a finding that the defendant is financially able to make payment. The court may order the defendant to make payments under this subsection for a period not to exceed one year after the date on which the order is entered.

§14. Substance Abuse Felony Program

☠ *Section 14 below was added by Acts 1993, 73rd Leg., ch. 900, §4.01, effective Sept. 1, 1994, without reference to the conflicting enactment made by Acts 1993, 73rd Leg., ch. 165, §1, effective Sept. 1, 1993.*

(a) If a court places a defendant on community supervision under any provision of this article as an alternative to imprisonment, the judge may require as a condition of community supervision that the defendant

⎯⎯⎯⎯⎯⎯⎯⎯⎯⎯ ★ ⎯⎯⎯⎯⎯⎯⎯⎯⎯⎯

serve a term of confinement and treatment in a substance abuse treatment facility operated by the Texas Department of Criminal Justice under Section 493.009, Government Code. A term of confinement and treatment imposed under this section must be an indeterminate term of not more than one year or less than 90 days.

(b) A judge may impose the condition of community supervision created under this section if:

(1) the judge places the defendant on community supervision under this article;

(2) the defendant is charged with or convicted of a felony other than:

(A) a felony under Section 21.11, 22.011, or 22.021, Penal Code; or

(B) criminal attempt of a felony under Section 21.11, 22.011, or 22.021, Penal Code; and

(3) the judge makes an affirmative finding that:

(A) drug or alcohol abuse significantly contributed to the commission of the crime or violation of community supervision; and

(B) the defendant is a suitable candidate for treatment, as determined by the suitability criteria established by the Texas Board of Criminal Justice under Section 493.009(b), Government Code.

(c) If a judge requires as a condition of community supervision that the defendant serve a term of confinement and treatment in a substance abuse treatment facility under this section, the judge shall also require as a condition of community supervision that on release from the facility the defendant:

(1) participate in a drug or alcohol abuse continuum of care treatment plan; and

(2) pay a fee in an amount established by the judge for residential aftercare required as part of the treatment plan.

(d) The Texas Commission on Alcohol and Drug Abuse shall develop the continuum of care treatment plan.

(e) The clerk of a court that collects a fee imposed under Subsection (c)(2) shall not later than the last day of the month following the end of the calendar quarter in which the fee is collected deposit the fee to be sent to the comptroller as provided by subchapter B, Chapter 133, Local Government Code, and the comptroller shall deposit the fee into the general revenue fund.

If the clerk does not collect a fee imposed under Subsection (c)(2), the clerk is not required to file any report required by the comptroller relating to the collection of the fee. In requiring the payment of a fee under Subsection (c)(2), the judge shall consider fines, fees, and other necessary expenses for which the defendant is obligated in establishing the amount of the fee. The judge may not:

(1) establish the fee in an amount that is greater than 25 percent of the defendant's gross income while the defendant is a participant in residential aftercare; or

(2) require the defendant to pay the fee at any time other than a time at which the defendant is both employed and a participant in residential aftercare.

§15. Procedures Relating to State Jail Felony Community Supervision

 Subsection (1) below is effective for defendants convicted of state jail felonies on or after Sept. 1, 2007. Subsection (1) below is effective for defendants placed on deferred adjudication community supervision for offenses committed on or after June 15, 2007.

(a)(1) On conviction of a state jail felony under Section 481.115(b), 481.1151(b)(1), 481.116(b), 481.121(b)(3), or 481.129(g)(1), Health and Safety Code, that is punished under Section 12.35(a), Penal Code, the judge shall suspend the imposition of the sentence and place the defendant on community supervision, unless the defendant has previously been convicted of a felony, other than a felony punished under Section 12.44(a), Penal Code, or unless the conviction resulted from an adjudication of the guilt of a defendant previously placed on deferred adjudication community supervision for the offense, in which event the judge may suspend the imposition of the sentence and place the defendant on community supervision or may order the sentence to be executed. The provisions of this subdivision requiring the judge to suspend the imposition of the sentence and place the defendant on community supervision do not apply to a defendant who under Section 481.1151(b)(1), Health and Safety Code, possessed more than five abuse units of the controlled substance or under Section 481.121(b)(3), Health and Safety Code, possessed more than one pound of marihuana.

Subsection (1) below is effective for defendants convicted of state jail felonies before Sept. 1, 2007. Subsection (1) below is effective for defendants placed on deferred adjudication community supervision for offenses in which any element of the offense was committed before June 15, 2007.

(a)(1) On conviction of a state jail felony under Section 481.115(b), 481.1151(b)(1), 481.116(b), 481.121(b)(3), or 481.129(g)(1), Health and Safety Code, that is punished under Section 12.35(a), Penal Code, the judge shall suspend the imposition of the sentence and place the defendant on community supervision, unless the defendant has previously been convicted of a felony, in which event the judge may suspend the imposition of the sentence and place the defendant on community supervision or may order the sentence to be executed. The provisions of this subdivision requiring the judge to suspend the imposition of the sentence and place the defendant on community supervision do not apply to a defendant who under Section 481.1151(b)(1), Health and Safety Code, possessed more than five abuse units of the controlled substance or under Section 481.121(b)(3), Health and Safety Code, possessed more than one pound of marihuana.

(2) On conviction of a state jail felony punished under Section 12.35(a), Penal Code, other than a state jail felony listed in Subdivision (1), the judge may suspend the imposition of the sentence and place the defendant on community supervision or may order the sentence to be executed.

(3) The judge may suspend in whole or in part the imposition of any fine imposed on conviction.

(b) The minimum period of community supervision a judge may impose under this section is two years. The maximum period of community supervision a judge may impose under this section is five years, except that the judge may extend the maximum period of community supervision under this section to not more than 10 years. A judge may extend a period of community supervision under this section at any time during the period of community supervision, or if a motion for revocation of community supervision is filed before the period of community supervision ends, before the first anniversary of the expiration of the period of community supervision.

(c)(1) A judge may impose any condition of community supervision on a defendant that the judge could impose on a defendant placed on supervision for an offense other than a state jail felony.

(2) Except as otherwise provided by Subdivision (3), a judge who places a defendant on community supervision for an offense listed in Subsection (a)(1) shall require the defendant to comply with substance abuse treatment conditions that are consistent with standards adopted by the Texas Board of Criminal Justice under Section 509.015, Government Code.

(3) A judge is not required to impose conditions described by Subdivision (2) if the judge makes an affirmative finding that the defendant does not require imposition of the conditions to successfully complete the period of community supervision.

(d) A judge may impose as a condition of community supervision that a defendant submit at the beginning of the period of community supervision to a term of confinement in a state jail felony facility for a term of not less than 90 days or more than 180 days, or a term of not less than 90 days or more than one year if the defendant is convicted of an offense punishable as a state jail felony under Section 481.112, 481.1121, 481.113, or 481.120, Health and Safety Code. A judge may not require a defendant to submit to both the term of confinement authorized by this subsection and a term of confinement under Section 5 or 12 of this article. For the purposes of this subsection, a defendant previously has been convicted of a felony regardless of whether the sentence for the previous conviction was actually imposed or was probated and suspended.

(e) If a defendant violates a condition of community supervision imposed on the defendant under this article and after a hearing under Section 21 of this article the judge modifies the defendant's community supervision, the judge may impose any sanction permitted by Section 22 of this article, except that if the judge requires a defendant to serve a period of confinement in a state jail felony facility as a modification of the defendant's community supervision, the minimum term of confinement is 90 days and the maximum term of confinement is 180 days.

(f)(1) If a defendant violates a condition of community supervision imposed on the defendant under this article and after a hearing under Section 21 of this article the judge revokes the defendant's community supervision, the judge shall dispose of the case in the manner provided by Section 23 of this article.

(2) The court retains jurisdiction over the defendant for the period during which the defendant is confined in a state jail. At any time after the 75th day after the date the defendant is received into the custody of a state jail, the judge on the judge's own motion, on the motion of the attorney representing the state, or on the motion of the defendant may suspend further execution of the sentence and place the defendant on community supervision under the conditions of this section.

(3) When the defendant or the attorney representing the state files a written motion requesting suspension by the judge of further execution of the sentence and placement of the defendant on community supervision, the clerk of the court, if requested to do so by the judge, shall request a copy of the defendant's record while confined from the facility director of the state jail felony facility in which the defendant is confined or, if the defendant is confined in county jail, from the sheriff. On receipt of the request, the facility director or the sheriff shall forward to the judge, as soon as possible, a full and complete copy of the defendant's record while confined. When the defendant files a written motion requesting suspension of further execution of the sentence and placement on community supervision, he shall immediately deliver or cause to be delivered a true and correct copy of the motion to the office of the attorney representing the state. The judge may deny the motion without a hearing but may not grant the motion without holding a hearing and providing the attorney representing the state and the defendant the opportunity to present evidence on the motion.

(g) The facility director of a state jail felony facility shall report to a judge who orders a defendant confined in the facility as a condition of community supervision or as sanction imposed as a modification of community supervision under Subsection (e) not less than every 90 days on the defendant's programmatic progress, conduct, and conformity to the rules of the facility.

(h)(1) A defendant confined in a state jail felony facility does not earn good conduct time for time served in the facility.

A *Subsections (2) & (3) below are effective for defendants initially placed on community supervision on or after Sept. 1, 2007.*

(2) A judge:

(A) may credit against any time a defendant is required to serve in a state jail felony facility time served by the defendant in a county jail from the time of the defendant's arrest and confinement until sentencing by the trial court; and

(B) shall credit against any time a defendant is required to serve in a state jail felony facility time served by the defendant in a substance abuse treatment facility operated by the Texas Department of Criminal Justice under Section 493.009, Government Code, or other court-ordered residential program or facility as a condition of deferred adjudication community supervision before sentencing, but only if the defendant successfully completes the treatment program in that facility.

(3) A judge shall credit against any time a defendant is subsequently required to serve in a state jail felony facility after revocation of community supervision any time served after sentencing by the defendant:

(A) in a state jail felony facility; or

(B) in a substance abuse treatment facility operated by the Texas Department of Criminal Justice under Section 493.009, Government Code, or another court-ordered residential program or facility if the defendant successfully completes the treatment program in that facility.

Subsections (2) & (3) below are effective for defendants initially placed on community supervision before Sept. 1, 2007.

(2) A judge may credit against any time a defendant is required to serve in a state jail felony facility time served by the defendant in county jail from the time of the defendant's arrest and confinement until sentencing by the trial court.

(3) A judge shall credit against any time a defendant is subsequently required to serve in a state jail felony facility after revocation of community supervision any time served by the defendant in a state jail felony facility after sentencing.

E (i) If a defendant is convicted of a state jail felony and the sentence is executed, the judge sentencing the defendant may release the defendant to a medically suitable placement if the judge determines that the defendant does not constitute a threat to public safety and the Texas Correctional Office on Offenders with Medical or Mental Impairments:

(1) in coordination with the Correctional Managed Health Care Committee prepares a case summary and medical report that identifies the defendant as being elderly, physically disabled, mentally ill, terminally ill, or mentally retarded or having a condition requiring long-term care; and

(2) in cooperation with the community supervision and corrections department serving the sentencing court, prepares for the defendant a medically recommended intensive supervision and continuity of care plan that:

(A) ensures appropriate supervision of the defendant by the community supervision and corrections department; and

(B) requires the defendant to remain under the care of a physician at and reside in a medically suitable placement.

☠ Ⓔ *Subsection (j) below was enacted by Acts 2007, 80th Leg., ch. 1308, §7, effective June 15, 2007, without reference to the conflicting enactment made by Acts 2007, 80th Leg., ch. 617, §1, effective Sept. 1, 2007.*

(j) The Texas Correctional Office on Offenders with Medical or Mental Impairments shall submit to a judge who releases a defendant to an appropriate medical care facility under Subsection (i) a quarterly status report concerning the defendant's medical and treatment status.

☠ Ⓔ *Subsection (j) below was enacted by Acts 2007, 80th Leg., ch. 617, §1, effective Sept. 1, 2007, without reference to the conflicting enactment made by Acts 2007, 80th Leg., ch. 1308, §7, effective June 15, 2007.*

(j) If a defendant released to a medical care facility or medical treatment program under Subsection (i) violates the terms of that release, the judge may dispose of the matter as provided by Subsections (e) and (f)(1).

Ⓔ (k) If a defendant released to a medically suitable placement under Subsection (i) violates the terms of that release, the judge may dispose of the matter as provided by Subsections (e) and (f)(1).

See also *O'Connor's Crimes & Consequences* (2008-09), chart 4-A, "Community Supervision—Felony," 4-C, "Mandatory Community Supervision," 4-F, "Shock Probation."

§15A. Enhanced Disorderly Conduct & Public Intoxication Offenses

On conviction of an offense for which punishment is enhanced under Section 12.43(c), Penal Code, the court may suspend the imposition of the sentence and place the defendant on community supervision if the court finds that the defendant would benefit from community supervision and enters its finding on the record. The judge may suspend in whole or in part the imposition of any fine imposed on conviction. All provisions of this article applying to a defendant placed on community supervision for a misdemeanor apply to a defendant placed on community supervision under this section, except that the court shall require the defendant as a condition of community supervision to:

(1) submit to diagnostic testing for addiction to alcohol or a controlled substance or drug;

(2) submit to a psychological assessment;

(3) if indicated as necessary by testing and assessment, participate in an alcohol or drug abuse treatment or education program; and

(4) pay the costs of testing, assessment, and treatment or education, either directly or as a court cost.

§16. Community Service

Ⓐ *Subsections (a) & (b) below are effective for defendants initially placed on community supervision on or after Sept. 1, 2007.*

(a) A judge may require as a condition of community supervision that the defendant work a specified number of hours at a community service project or projects for an organization or organizations approved by the judge and designated by the department. The judge may not require that a defendant work at a community service project if the judge determines and notes on the order placing the defendant on community supervision that:

(1) the defendant is physically or mentally incapable of participating in the project;

(2) participating in the project will work a hardship on the defendant or the defendant's dependents;

(3) the defendant is to be confined in a substance abuse punishment facility as a condition of community supervision; or

(4) there is other good cause shown.

(b) The amount of community service work ordered by the judge:

(1) may not exceed 1,000 hours for an offense classified as a first degree felony;

(2) may not exceed 800 hours for an offense classified as a second degree felony;

(3) may not exceed 600 hours for an offense classified as a third degree felony;

(4) may not exceed 400 hours for an offense classified as a state jail felony;

(5) may not:

(A) exceed 600 hours for an offense under Section 30.04, Penal Code, classified as a Class A misdemeanor; or

(B) exceed 200 hours for any other offense classified as a Class A misdemeanor or for any other misdemeanor for which the maximum permissible confinement, if any, exceeds six months or the maximum permissible fine, if any, exceeds $4,000; and

(6) may not exceed 100 hours for an offense classified as a Class B misdemeanor or for any other misdemeanor for which the maximum permissible confinement, if any, does not exceed six months and the maximum permissible fine, if any, does not exceed $4,000.

Subsections (a) & (b) below are effective for defendants initially placed on community supervision before Sept. 1, 2007.

(a) A judge shall require as a condition of community supervision, that the defendant work a specified number of hours at a community service project or projects for an organization or organizations approved by the judge and designated by the department, unless the judge determines and notes on the order placing the defendant on community supervision that:

(1) the defendant is physically or mentally incapable of participating in the project;

(2) participating in the project will work a hardship on the defendant or the defendant's dependents;

(3) the defendant is to be confined in a substance abuse punishment facility as a condition of community supervision; or

(4) there is other good cause shown.

(b) The amount of community service work ordered by the judge:

(1) may not exceed 1,000 hours and may not be less than 320 hours for an offense classified as a first degree felony;

(2) may not exceed 800 hours and may not be less than 240 hours for an offense classified as a second degree felony;

(3) may not exceed 600 hours and may not be less than 160 hours for an offense classified as a third degree felony;

(4) may not exceed 400 hours and may not be less than 120 hours for an offense classified as a state jail felony;

(5) may not:

(A) exceed 600 hours or be less than 160 hours for an offense under Section 30.04, Penal Code, classified as a Class A misdemeanor; or

(B) exceed 200 hours or be less than 80 hours for any other offense classified as a Class A misdemeanor or for any other misdemeanor for which the maximum permissible confinement, if any, exceeds six months or the maximum permissible fine, if any, exceeds $4,000; and

(6) may not exceed 100 hours and may not be less than 24 hours for an offense classified as a Class B misdemeanor or for any other misdemeanor for which the maximum permissible confinement, if any, does not exceed six months and the maximum permissible fine, if any, does not exceed $4,000.

(c) A defendant required to perform community service under this section is not a state employee for the purposes of Article 8309g or 8309h, Revised Statutes.

(d) If the court makes an affirmative finding under Article 42.014 of this code, the judge may order the defendant to perform community service under this section at a project designated by the judge that primarily serves the person or group who was the target of the defendant. If the judge orders community service under this subsection the judge shall order the defendant to perform not less than:

(1) 100 hours of service if the offense is a misdemeanor; or

(2) 300 hours of service if the offense is a felony.

(e) A defendant required to perform community service under this section after conviction of an offense under Section 352.082, Local Government Code, shall perform 60 hours of service. The community service must consist of picking up litter in the county in which the defendant resides or working at a recycling facility if a program for performing that type of service is available in the community in which the court is located.

❸ (f) In lieu of requiring a defendant to work a specified number of hours at a community service project or projects under Subsection (a), the judge may order a defendant to make a specified donation to a nonprofit food bank or food pantry in the community in which the defendant resides.

See also H&SC §469.008; *O'Connor's Crimes & Consequences* (2008-09), chart 9, "Community-Service-Hours Range."

§17. Change of Residence; Leaving the State

(a) If, for good and sufficient reasons, a defendant desires to change his residence within the state, the change may be effected by application to the supervising supervision officer, which change shall be subject to the judge's consent and subject to such regulations as the judge may require in the absence of an officer in the locality to which the defendant is transferred.

(b) Any defendant who removes himself from the state without permission of the judge having jurisdiction of the case shall be considered a fugitive from justice and shall be subject to extradition as provided by law.

§18. Community Corrections Facilities

(a) In this section, "community corrections facility" has the meaning assigned by Section 509.001, Government Code.

(b) If a judge requires as a condition of community supervision or participation in a drug court program established under Chapter 469, Health and Safety Code, that the defendant serve a term in a community corrections facility, the term may not be more than 24 months.

(c) A defendant granted community supervision under this section may not earn good conduct credit for time spent in a community corrections facility or apply time spent in the facility toward completion of a prison sentence if the community supervision is revoked.

(d) As directed by the judge, the community corrections facility director shall file with the community supervision and corrections department director or administrator of a drug court program, as applicable, a copy of an evaluation made by the facility director of the defendant's behavior and attitude at the facility. The community supervision and corrections department director or program administrator shall examine the evaluation, make written comments on the evaluation that the director or administrator considers relevant, and file the evaluation and comments with the judge who granted community supervision to the defendant or placed the defendant in a drug court program. If the evaluation indicates that the defendant has made significant progress toward compliance with court-ordered conditions of community supervision or objectives of placement in the drug court program, as applicable, the court may release the defendant from the community corrections facility. A defendant who served a term in the facility as a condition of community supervision shall serve the remainder of the defendant's community supervision under any terms and conditions the court imposes under this article.

(e) No later than 18 months after the date on which a defendant is granted community supervision under this section, the community corrections facility director shall file with the community supervision and corrections department director a copy of an evaluation made by the director of the defendant's behavior and attitude at the center. The director shall examine the evaluation, make written comments on the evaluation that he considers relevant, and file the evaluation and comments with the judge who granted community supervision to the defendant. If the report indicates that the defendant has made significant progress toward court-ordered conditions of community supervision, the judge shall modify the judge's sentence and release the defendant in the same manner as provided by Subsection (d) of this section. If the report indicates that the defendant would benefit from continued participation in the community corrections facility program, the judge may order the defendant to remain at the community corrections facility for a period determined by the judge. If the report indicates that the defendant has not made significant progress toward rehabilitation, the judge may revoke community supervision and order the defendant to the term of confinement specified in the defendant's sentence.

(f) If ordered by the judge who placed the defendant on community supervision, a community corrections facility director shall attempt to place a defendant as a worker in a community-service project of a type described by Section 16 of this article.

(g) A defendant participating in a program under this article shall be confined in the community corrections facility at all times except for:

(1) time spent attending and traveling to and from an education or rehabilitation program as ordered by the court;

(2) time spent attending and traveling to and from a community-service project;

(3) time spent away from the facility for purposes described by this section; and

(4) time spent traveling to and from work, if applicable.

(h) A judge that requires as a condition of community supervision that the defendant serve a term in a community corrections facility may not impose a subsequent term in a community corrections facility or jail during the same supervision period that, when added to the terms previously imposed, exceeds 36 months.

(i) If a judge who places a defendant on community supervision under this section does not require the

defendant to deliver the defendant's salary to the restitution center director, the employer of the defendant
shall deliver the salary to the director. The director shall
deposit the salary into a fund to be given to the defendant on release after deducting:

(1) the cost to the center for the defendant's food,
housing, and supervision;

(2) necessary travel expense to and from work and
community-service projects and other incidental expenses of the defendant;

(3) support of the defendant's dependents; and

(4) restitution to the victims of an offense committed by the defendant.

§19. Fees

(a) Except as otherwise provided by this subsection, a judge granting community supervision shall fix
a fee of not less than $25 and not more than $60 per
month to be paid during the period of community supervision by the defendant to the court of original jurisdiction or, in the case of an intrastate transfer described by Section 10(b) of this article, to the court to
which jurisdiction of the defendant's case is transferred. The judge may make payment of the fee a condition of granting or continuing the community supervision. The judge may waive or reduce the fee or suspend
a monthly payment of the fee if the judge determines
that payment of the fee would cause the defendant a
significant financial hardship.

(b) A judge shall deposit any fee received under
Subsection (a) of this section in the special fund of the
county treasury, to be used for the same purposes for
which state aid may be used under Chapter 76, Government Code.

(c) A judge receiving a defendant for supervision
as authorized by Article 42.11 of this code may impose
on the defendant any term of community supervision
authorized by this article and may require the defendant to pay the fee authorized by Subsection (a) of this
section. Fees received under this section shall be deposited in the same manner as required by Subsection
(b) of this section.

(d) For the purpose of determining when fees due
on conviction are to be paid to any officer or officers,
the placing of the defendant on community supervision
shall be considered a final disposition of the case, without the necessity of waiting for the termination of the
period of community supervision.

(e) If the judge grants community supervision to a
defendant convicted of an offense under Section 21.08,
21.11, 22.011, 22.021, 25.02, 43.25, or 43.26, Penal Code,
the judge shall require as a condition of community supervision that the defendant pay to the community corrections and supervision department officer supervising the defendant a community supervision fee of $5
each month during the period of community supervision. The fee is in addition to court costs or any other
fee imposed on the defendant.

☙ *Subsection (f) below was amended by Acts 2003,
78th Leg., ch. 1310, §3, enacted June 2, 2003, effective
Sept. 1, 2003, without reference to the conflicting
amendment made by Acts 2003, 78th Leg., ch. 209,
§64(a), enacted June 2, 2003, effective Jan. 1, 2004. For
resolving conflicts, see p. V.*

(f) A community corrections and supervision department shall remit fees collected under Subsection
(e) of this section to the comptroller not later than the
last day of the month following the end of the calendar
quarter in which the fee is collected. The comptroller
shall deposit the fee in the special revenue fund to the
credit of the sexual assault program fund established
under Section 44.0061, Health and Safety Code. If the
department does not collect a fee imposed under Subsection (e), the department is not required to file any report required by the comptroller relating to the collection of the fee.

☙ *Subsection (f) below was amended by Acts 2003,
78th Leg., ch. 209, §64(a), enacted June 2, 2003, effective Jan. 1, 2004, without reference to the conflicting
amendment made by Acts 2003, 78th Leg., ch. 1310, §3,
enacted June 2, 2003, effective Sept. 1, 2003. For resolving conflicts, see p. V.*

(f) A community corrections and supervision department shall deposit the fees collected under Subsection (e) of this section to be sent to the comptroller as
provided by Subchapter B, Chapter 133, Local Government Code. The comptroller shall deposit the fee in the
sexual assault program fund under Section 420.008,
Government Code.

(g) A court to which jurisdiction of a defendant's
case is transferred under Section 10(b) of this article
shall enter an order directing the defendant to pay the
monthly fee described by Subsection (a) of this section
to that court in lieu of paying the monthly fee to the
court of original jurisdiction. To the extent of any conflict between an order issued under this subsection and

an order issued by a court of original jurisdiction, the order entered under this subsection prevails.

(h) Repealed by Acts 2005, 79th Leg., ch. 1008, §4.07, eff. Sept. 1, 2005.

§20. Reduction or Termination of Community Supervision

A *Section 20 below is effective for defendants initially placed on community supervision on or after Sept. 1, 2007.*

(a) At any time after the defendant has satisfactorily completed one-third of the original community supervision period or two years of community supervision, whichever is less, the period of community supervision may be reduced or terminated by the judge. On completion of one-half of the original community supervision period or two years of community supervision, whichever is more, the judge shall review the defendant's record and consider whether to reduce or terminate the period of community supervision, unless the defendant is delinquent in paying required restitution, fines, costs, or fees that the defendant has the ability to pay or the defendant has not completed court-ordered counseling or treatment. Before conducting the review, the judge shall notify the attorney representing the state and the defendant. If the judge determines that the defendant has failed to satisfactorily fulfill the conditions of community supervision, the judge shall advise the defendant in writing of the requirements for satisfactorily fulfilling those conditions. Upon the satisfactory fulfillment of the conditions of community supervision, and the expiration of the period of community supervision, the judge, by order duly entered, shall amend or modify the original sentence imposed, if necessary, to conform to the community supervision period and shall discharge the defendant. If the judge discharges the defendant under this section, the judge may set aside the verdict or permit the defendant to withdraw the defendant's plea, and shall dismiss the accusation, complaint, information or indictment against the defendant, who shall thereafter be released from all penalties and disabilities resulting from the offense or crime of which the defendant has been convicted or to which the defendant has pleaded guilty, except that:

(1) proof of the conviction or plea of guilty shall be made known to the judge should the defendant again be convicted of any criminal offense; and

(2) if the defendant is an applicant for a license or is a licensee under Chapter 42, Human Resources Code, the Health and Human Services Commission may consider the fact that the defendant previously has received community supervision under this article in issuing, renewing, denying, or revoking a license under that chapter.

(b) This section does not apply to a defendant convicted of an offense under Sections 49.04-49.08, Penal Code, a defendant convicted of an offense for which on conviction registration as a sex offender is required under Chapter 62, or a defendant convicted of a felony described by Section 3g.

See also *O'Connor's Crimes & Consequences* (2008-09), chart 4-G, "Early Termination."

§20. Reduction or Termination of Community Supervision

Section 20 below is effective for defendants initially placed on community supervision before Sept. 1, 2007.

(a) At any time, after the defendant has satisfactorily completed one-third of the original community supervision period or two years of community supervision, whichever is less, the period of community supervision may be reduced or terminated by the judge. Upon the satisfactory fulfillment of the conditions of community supervision, and the expiration of the period of community supervision, the judge, by order duly entered, shall amend or modify the original sentence imposed, if necessary, to conform to the community supervision period and shall discharge the defendant. If the judge discharges the defendant under this section, the judge may set aside the verdict or permit the defendant to withdraw his plea, and shall dismiss the accusation, complaint, information or indictment against the defendant, who shall thereafter be released from all penalties and disabilities resulting from the offense or crime of which he has been convicted or to which he has pleaded guilty, except that:

(1) proof of the conviction or plea of guilty shall be made known to the judge should the defendant again be convicted of any criminal offense; and

(2) if the defendant is an applicant for a license or is a licensee under Chapter 42, Human Resources Code, the Texas Department of Human Services may consider the fact that the defendant previously has received community supervision under this article in issuing, renewing, denying, or revoking a license under that chapter.

★

(b) This section does not apply to a defendant convicted of an offense under Sections 49.04-49.08, Penal Code, a defendant convicted of an offense for which on conviction registration as a sex offender is required under Chapter 62, as added by Chapter 668, Acts of the 75th Legislature, Regular Session, 1997, or a defendant convicted of an offense punishable as a state jail felony.

§21. Violation of Community Supervision: Detention & Hearing

(a) At any time during the period of community supervision the judge may issue a warrant for violation of any of the conditions of the community supervision and cause a defendant convicted under Section 43.02, Penal Code, or under Chapter 481, Health and Safety Code, or Sections 485.031 through 485.035, Health and Safety Code, or placed on deferred adjudication after being charged with one of those offenses, to be subject to the control measures of Section 81.083, Health and Safety Code, and to the court-ordered-management provisions of Subchapter G, Chapter 81, Health and Safety Code.

(b) At any time during the period of community supervision the judge may issue a warrant for violation of any of the conditions of the community supervision and cause the defendant to be arrested. Any supervision officer, police officer or other officer with power of arrest may arrest such defendant with or without a warrant upon the order of the judge to be noted on the docket of the court. A defendant so arrested may be detained in the county jail or other appropriate place of confinement until he can be taken before the judge. Such officer shall forthwith report such arrest and detention to such judge. If the defendant has not been released on bail, on motion by the defendant the judge shall cause the defendant to be brought before the judge for a hearing within 20 days of filing of said motion, and after a hearing without a jury, may either continue, extend, modify, or revoke the community supervision. A judge may revoke the community supervision of a defendant who is imprisoned in a penal institution without a hearing if the defendant in writing before a court of record in the jurisdiction where imprisoned waives his right to a hearing and to counsel, affirms that he has nothing to say as to why sentence should not be pronounced against him, and requests the judge to revoke community supervision and to pronounce sentence. In a felony case, the state may amend the motion to revoke community supervision any time up to seven days before the date of the revocation hearing, after which

time the motion may not be amended except for good cause shown, and in no event may the state amend the motion after the commencement of taking evidence at the hearing. The judge may continue the hearing for good cause shown by either the defendant or the state.

 (c) In a community supervision revocation hearing at which it is alleged only that the defendant violated the conditions of community supervision by failing to pay compensation paid to appointed counsel, community supervision fees, or court costs, the state must prove by a preponderance of the evidence that the defendant was able to pay and did not pay as ordered by the judge. The court may order a community supervision and corrections department to obtain information pertaining to the factors listed under Article 42.037(h) of this code and include that information in the report required under Section 9(a) of this article or a separate report, as the court directs.

(d) A defendant has a right to counsel at a hearing under this section.

(e) A court retains jurisdiction to hold a hearing under Subsection (b) and to revoke, continue, or modify community supervision, regardless of whether the period of community supervision imposed on the defendant has expired, if before the expiration the attorney representing the state files a motion to revoke, continue, or modify community supervision and a capias is issued for the arrest of the defendant.

§22. Continuation or Modification

(a) If after a hearing under Section 21 of this article a judge continues or modifies community supervision after determining that the defendant violated a condition of community supervision, the judge may impose any other conditions the judge determines are appropriate, including:

(1) a requirement that the defendant perform community service for a number of hours specified by the court under Section 16 of this article, or an increase in the number of hours that the defendant has previously been required to perform under those sections in an amount not to exceed double the number of hours permitted by Section 16;

(2) an increase in the period of community supervision, in the manner described by Subsection (b) of this section;

(3) an increase in the defendant's fine, in the manner described by Subsection (d) of this section; or

★

(4) the placement of the defendant in a substance abuse felony punishment program operated under Section 493.009, Government Code, if:

(A) the defendant is convicted of a felony other than:

(i) a felony under Section 21.11, 22.011, or 22.021, Penal Code; or

(ii) criminal attempt of a felony under Section 21.11, 22.011, or 22.021, Penal Code; and

(B) the judge makes an affirmative finding that:

(i) drug or alcohol abuse significantly contributed to the commission of the crime or violation of community supervision; and

(ii) the defendant is a suitable candidate for treatment, as determined by the suitability criteria established by the Texas Board of Criminal Justice under Section 493.009(b), Government Code.

(b) If the judge imposes a sanction under Subsection (a)(4) of this section, the judge shall also impose a condition requiring the defendant on successful completion of the program to participate in a drug or alcohol abuse continuum of care program.

A *Subsection (c) below is effective for defendants initially placed on community supervision on or after Sept. 1, 2007.*

(c) The judge may extend a period of community supervision on a showing of good cause under this section as often as the judge determines is necessary, but the period of community supervision in a first, second, or third degree felony case may not exceed 10 years and, except as otherwise provided by this subsection, the period of community supervision in a misdemeanor case may not exceed three years. The judge may extend the period of community supervision in a misdemeanor case for any period the judge determines is necessary, not to exceed an additional two years beyond the three-year limit, if the defendant fails to pay a previously assessed fine, costs, or restitution and the judge determines that extending the period of supervision increases the likelihood that the defendant will fully pay the fine, costs, or restitution. A court may extend a period of community supervision under this section at any time during the period of supervision or, if a motion for revocation of community supervision is filed before the period of supervision ends, before the first anniversary of the date on which the period of supervision expires.

Subsection (c) below is effective for defendants initially placed on community supervision before Sept. 1, 2007.

(c) The judge may extend a period of community supervision under this section as often as the judge determines is necessary, but the period of community supervision in a first, second, or third degree felony case may not exceed 10 years and, except as otherwise provided by this subsection, the period of community supervision in a misdemeanor case may not exceed three years. The judge may extend the period of community supervision in a misdemeanor case for any period the judge determines is necessary, not to exceed an additional two years beyond the three-year limit, if the defendant fails to pay a previously assessed fine, costs, or restitution and the judge determines that extending the period of supervision increases the likelihood that the defendant will fully pay the fine, costs, or restitution. A court may extend a period of community supervision under this section at any time during the period of supervision or, if a motion for revocation of community supervision is filed before the period of supervision ends, before the first anniversary of the date on which the period of supervision expires.

(d) A judge may impose a sanction on a defendant described by Subsection (a)(3) of this section by increasing the fine imposed on the defendant. The original fine imposed on the defendant and an increase in the fine imposed under this subsection may not exceed the maximum fine for the offense for which the defendant was sentenced. The judge shall deposit money received from an increase in the defendant's fine under this subsection in the special fund of the county treasury to be used for the same purposes for which state aid may be used under Chapter 76, Government Code.

See also *O'Connor's Crimes & Consequences* (2008-09), chart 4-B, "Community Supervision—Misdemeanor."

§22A. Extending Supervision Period for Sex Offenders

(a) If a defendant is placed on community supervision after receiving a grant of deferred adjudication for or being convicted of an offense under Section 21.11, 22.011, or 22.021, Penal Code, at any time during the period of community supervision, the judge may extend the period of community supervision as provided by this section.

(b) If at a hearing at which the defendant is provided the same rights as are provided a defendant at a

✦

hearing under Section 21 the judge determines that the defendant has not sufficiently demonstrated a commitment to avoid future criminal behavior and that the release of the defendant from supervision would endanger the public, the judge may extend the period of supervision for a period not to exceed 10 additional years.

(c) A judge may extend a period of community supervision under this section only once; however, the judge may extend a period of community supervision for a defendant under both Section 22(c) and this section, and the prohibition in Section 22(c) against a period of community supervision in a felony case exceeding 10 years does not apply to a defendant for whom community supervision is increased under this section or under both Section 22(c) and this section.

§23. Revocation

(a) If community supervision is revoked after a hearing under Section 21 of this article, the judge may proceed to dispose of the case as if there had been no community supervision, or if the judge determines that the best interests of society and the defendant would be served by a shorter term of confinement, reduce the term of confinement originally assessed to any term of confinement not less than the minimum prescribed for the offense of which the defendant was convicted. The judge shall enter the amount of restitution or reparation owed by the defendant on the date of revocation in the judgment in the case.

 Subsection (b) below is effective for defendants initially placed on community supervision on or after Sept. 1, 2007.

(b) No part of the time that the defendant is on community supervision shall be considered as any part of the time that he shall be sentenced to serve, except that on revocation, the judge shall credit to the defendant time served by the defendant as a condition of community supervision in a substance abuse treatment facility operated by the Texas Department of Criminal Justice under Section 493.009, Government Code, or another court-ordered residential program or facility, but only if the defendant successfully completes the treatment program in that facility. The right of the defendant to appeal for a review of the conviction and punishment, as provided by law, shall be accorded the defendant at the time he is placed on community supervision. When he is notified that his community supervision is revoked for violation of the conditions of community supervision and he is called on to serve a sentence in a jail or in the institutional division of the Texas Department of Criminal Justice, he may appeal the revocation.

Subsection (b) below is effective for defendants initially placed on community supervision before Sept. 1, 2007.

(b) No part of the time that the defendant is on community supervision shall be considered as any part of the time that he shall be sentenced to serve. The right of the defendant to appeal for a review of the conviction and punishment, as provided by law, shall be accorded the defendant at the time he is placed on community supervision. When he is notified that his community supervision is revoked for violation of the conditions of community supervision and he is called on to serve a sentence in a jail or in the institutional division of the Texas Department of Criminal Justice, he may appeal the revocation.

§24. Due Diligence Defense

For the purposes of a hearing under Section 5(b) or 21(b), it is an affirmative defense to revocation for an alleged failure to report to a supervision officer as directed or to remain within a specified place that a supervision officer, peace officer, or other officer with the power of arrest under a warrant issued by a judge for that alleged violation failed to contact or attempt to contact the defendant in person at the defendant's last known residence address or last known employment address, as reflected in the files of the department serving the county in which the order of community supervision was entered.

Sections 25 to 28. [Blank]
§29. Repealed by Acts 1995, ch. 76, §3.15, eff. Sept. 1, 1995.

History of art. 42.12: Acts 1965, 59th Leg., vol. 2, ch. 722. Amended by Acts 1967, 60th Leg., ch. 659, §29, eff. Aug. 28, 1967; Acts 1973, 63rd Leg., ch. 241, §1 (eff. Aug. 27, 1973), ch. 447, §1 (eff. June 14, 1973), ch. 464, §1 (eff. June 14, 1973); Acts 1975, 64th Leg., ch. 110, §1 (eff. Sept. 1, 1975), ch. 231, §1 (eff. Sept. 1, 1975), ch. 341, §4 (eff. June 19, 1975), ch. 467, §1 (eff. June 19, 1975), ch. 468, §1 (eff. Sept. 1, 1975), ch. 692, §1 (eff. Sept. 1, 1975); Acts 1977, 65th Leg., ch. 22, §1 (eff. Aug. 29, 1977), ch. 47, §1 (eff. Apr. 5, 1977), ch. 306, §§1, 2 (eff. Aug. 29, 1977), ch. 342, §§1, 2 (eff. Aug. 29, 1977), ch. 343, §2 (eff. Sept. 1, 1978), ch. 347, §§1, 2, (eff. Aug. 29, 1977), ch. 388, §§1, 2 (eff. Aug. 29, 1977), ch. 735, §2.133 (eff. Aug. 29, 1977); Acts 1979, 66th Leg., ch. 139, §1 (eff. Aug. 27, 1979), ch. 605, §§1, 2, 4 (eff. Aug. 27, 1979); Acts 1981, 67th Leg., ch. 69, §§1-4 (eff. Sept. 1, 1981), ch. 141, §§2-9 (eff. Sept. 1, 1981), ch. 268, §16 (eff. Sept. 1, 1981), ch. 276, §3 (eff. Sept. 1, 1981), ch. 291, §118 (eff. Sept. 1, 1981), ch. 538, §§1, 2 (eff. June 12, 1981), ch. 544, §1 (eff. Sept. 1, 1981), ch. 638, §1 (eff. Sept. 1, 1981), ch. 639, §2 (eff. Sept. 1, 1981); Acts 1983, 68th Leg., ch. 40, §§2, 3 (eff. Apr. 26, 1983), ch. 232, §§1-5 (eff. Nov. 8, 1983); ch. 548, §2 (eff. June 19, 1983), ch. 237, §§1, 2, 4 (eff. Aug. 29, 1983), ch. 303, §§8-13 (eff. Jan. 1, 1984), ch. 325, §2 (eff. Sept. 1, 1983), ch. 343, §1 (eff. Aug. 29, 1983), ch. 372,

CCP ART. 42.12

§1 (eff. Aug. 29, 1983), ch. 425, §25 (eff. Aug. 29, 1983), ch. 548, §3 (eff. June 19, 1983); ch. 747, §1 (eff. June 19, 1983), ch. 762, §1 (eff. Aug. 29, 1983), ch. 811, §1 (eff. Aug. 29, 1983), ch. 863, §§1, 2 (eff. Aug. 29, 1983), ch. 897, §1 (eff. Aug. 29, 1983), ch. 977, §§9, 10 (eff. Sept. 1, 1983), Acts 1985, 69th Leg., ch. 239, §§24, 80(a) (eff. Sept. 1, 1985), ch. 255, §1 (eff. June 4, 1985), ch. 427, §1 (eff. Sept. 1, 1985), ch. 479, §163 (eff. Sept. 1, 1985), ch. 481, §1 (eff. Aug. 26, 1985), ch. 508, §1 (eff. Aug. 26, 1985), ch. 554, §§1, 2 (eff. Aug. 26, 1985), ch. 588, §3 (eff. Sept. 1, 1985), ch. 595, §§2, 3 (eff. Sept. 1, 1985), ch. 632, §13 (eff. Sept. 1, 1985), ch. 714, §§1, 2 (eff. Aug. 26, 1985), ch. 727, §1 (eff. Jan. 1, 1986), ch. 729, §5 (eff. Sept. 1, 1985), ch. 801, §1 (eff. Aug. 26, 1985), ch. 956, §1 (eff. June 16, 1985); Acts 1987, 70th Leg., ch. 1, §§4-6 (eff. Feb. 20, 1987), ch. 167, §5.01(a)(8) (eff. Sept. 1, 1987), ch. 441, §1 (eff. Sept. 1, 1987), ch. 473, §3 (eff. Sept. 1, 1987), ch. 507, §§1, 2 (eff. Sept. 1, 1987), ch. 922, §4 (eff. Sept. 1, 1987), ch. 928, §1 (eff. Sept. 1, 1987), ch. 939, §§2-9 (eff. Sept. 1, 1987), ch. 1049, §54 (eff. Sept. 1, 1987), ch. 1101, §16 (eff. Sept. 1, 1987); Acts 1989, 71st Leg., ch. 2, §§5.02(a), 8.11(c), 16.01(9), (10) (eff. Aug. 28, 1989), ch. 86, §1 (eff. Sept. 1, 1989), ch. 111, §1 (eff. Sept. 1, 1989), ch. 191, §1 (eff. May 26, 1989), ch. 236, §11 (eff. Apr. 1, 1990), ch. 260, §1 (eff. Sept. 1, 1989), ch. 679, §§1-3 (eff. Sept. 1, 1989), ch. 785, §4.17 (eff. Sept. 1, 1989), ch. 1040, §5 (eff. Aug. 28, 1989), ch. 1074, §8 (eff. Sept. 1, 1989), ch. 1135, §5 (eff. Aug. 28, 1989), ch. 1195, §§9, 10 (eff. Sept. 1, 1989), 1st C.S., ch. 6, §1 (eff. Jan. 1, 1990), 1st C.S., ch. 8, §1 (eff. Oct. 18, 1989), 6th C.S., ch. 25, §§8-12, 31 (eff. June 18, 1990); Acts 1991, 72nd Leg., ch. 541, §1 (eff. Sept. 1, 1991), ch. 14, §284(52) (eff. Sept. 1, 1991), 2nd C.S., ch. 10, §§15.02, 19.02 (eff. Oct. 1, 1991), ch. 343, §1 (eff. Aug. 26, 1991), 2nd C.S., ch. 10, §§6.01, 8.01, 16.01 (eff. Dec. 1, 1991), ch. 572, §2 (eff. Sept. 1, 1991), ch. 202, §2 (eff. Sept. 1, 1991), ch. 285, §1 (eff. Sept. 1, 1991), ch. 555, §3 (eff. Sept. 1, 1991), ch. 784, §9 (eff. Sept. 1, 1991), ch. 900, §3 (eff. Aug. 26, 1991), ch. 14, §284(8), (9), (60) (eff. Sept. 1, 1991), ch. 344, §1 (eff. June 5, 1991); Acts 1993, 73rd Leg., ch. 10, §3 (eff. Mar. 19, 1993), ch. 107, §10.01(1) (eff. Aug. 30, 1993), ch. 165, §1 (eff. Sept. 1, 1993), ch. 201, §§3, 4 (eff. Aug. 30, 1993), ch. 470, §2 (eff. Sept. 1, 1993), ch. 662, §§1, 8 (eff. Sept. 1, 1993), ch. 790, §§30, 36 (eff. Sept. 1, 1993), ch. 796, §§1, 2 (eff. Sept. 1, 1993), ch. 805, §7 (eff. Aug. 30, 1993), ch. 806, §§2, 3 (eff. Sept. 1, 1993), ch. 886, §15 (eff. Jan. 1, 1995), ch. 889, §1 (eff. Sept. 1, 1993), ch. 900, §4.01 (eff. Sept. 1, 1993), ch. 987, §§2, 3 (eff. Sept. 1, 1993); Acts 1995, 74th Leg., ch. 18, §§60, 61 (eff. Jan. 1, 1996), ch. 76, §§3.06, 3.07(a), (b), 3.08-3.12(a), (b), 3.15-3.18, 7.02, 7.13-7.15 (eff. Sept. 1, 1995), ch. 83, §2 (eff. Sept. 1, 1995), ch. 256, §§1-3 (eff. Sept. 1, 1995), ch. 257, §1 (eff. Sept. 1, 1995), ch. 258, §10 (eff. Sept. 1, 1995), ch. 260, §§14-16 (eff. May 30, 1995), ch. 318, §§52, 54-59 (eff. Sept. 1, 1995), ch. 318, §53 (eff. Jan. 1, 1996), ch. 321, §§3.003-3.008, 3.020(a) (eff. Sept. 1, 1995), ch. 595, §2 (eff. Sept. 1, 1995), ch. 657, §4 (eff. June 14, 1995); Acts 1997, 75th Leg., ch. 1, §6 (eff. Jan. 28, 1997), ch. 144, §3 (eff. May 20, 1997), ch. 165, §§12.03, 31.01(10), (11) (eff. Sept. 1, 1997), ch. 312, §3 (eff. Sept. 1, 1997), ch. 488, §§1-4 (eff. Sept. 1, 1997), ch. 577, §18 (eff. Sept. 1, 1997), ch. 667, §1 (eff. Sept. 1, 1997), ch. 668, §§3, 4 (eff. Sept. 1, 1997), ch. 700, §11 (eff. Sept. 1, 1997), ch. 706, §1 (eff. Sept. 1, 1997), ch. 745, §34 (eff. Jan. 1, 1998), ch. 754, §1 (eff. Sept. 1, 1997), ch. 1430, §§1-5 (eff. Sept. 1, 1997); Acts 1999, 76th Leg., ch. 27, §1 (eff. Sept. 1, 1999), ch. 56, §1 (eff. Sept. 1, 1999), ch. 62, §3.04 (eff. Sept. 1, 1999), ch. 323, §1 (eff. Sept. 1, 1999), ch. 564, §2 (eff. Sept. 1, 1999), ch. 580, §§7, 8 (eff. Sept. 1, 1999), ch. 806, §1 (eff. Sept. 1, 1999), ch. 910, §1 (eff. Sept. 1, 1999), ch. 1005, §3 (eff. Sept. 1, 1999), ch. 1188, §§1.43, 1.44 (eff. Sept. 1, 1999), ch. 1193, §3 (eff. Sept. 1, 1999), ch. 1263, §1 (eff. Sept. 1, 1999), ch. 1415, §§4, 5(a), (b), 6(a) (eff. Sept. 1, 1999); Acts 2001, 77th Leg., ch. 211, §1 (eff. Sept. 1, 2001), ch. 786, §2 (eff. June 14, 2001), ch. 969, §§8, 9 (eff. Sept. 1, 2001), ch. 970, §1 (eff. Sept. 1, 2001), ch. 992, §1 (eff. Sept. 1, 2001), ch. 1159, §3 (eff. Sept. 1, 2001), ch. 1351, §1 (eff. Sept. 1, 2001), ch. 1420, §21.001(10), (11) (eff. Sept. 1, 2001); Acts 2003, 78th Leg., ch. 35, §4 (eff. Jan. 1, 2004), ch. 209, §§63(a), 64(a) (eff. Jan. 1, 2004), ch. 239, §1 (eff. Sept. 1, 2003), ch. 250, §§1-3 (eff. June 18, 2003), ch. 353, §§1-6 (eff. Sept. 1, 2003), ch. 892, §20 (eff. Sept. 1, 2003), ch. 1122, §1 (eff. Sept. 1, 2003), ch. 1275, §3(3) (eff. Sept. 1, 2003), ch. 1300, §1 (eff. Sept. 1, 2003), ch. 1310, §§2, 3 (eff. Sept. 1, 2003); Acts 2005, 79th Leg., ch. 210, §§1, 2 (eff. Sept. 1, 2005), ch. 500, §1 (eff. Sept. 1, 2005), ch. 904, §3 (eff. Sept. 1, 2005), ch. 956, §2 (eff. Sept. 1, 2005), ch. 969, §2 (eff. Sept. 1, 2005), ch. 996, §2 (eff. Sept. 1, 2005), ch. 1008, §4.07 (eff. Sept. 1, 2005), ch. 1139, §4 (eff. June 18, 2005), ch. 1188, §1 (eff. Sept. 1, 2005), ch. 1224, §18 (eff. Sept. 1, 2005); Acts 2007, 80th Leg., ch. 113, §1 (eff. Sept. 1, 2007), ch. 308, §§2, 3 (eff. Sept. 1, 2007), ch. 405, §1 (eff. Sept. 1, 2007), ch. 593, §§1.05-1.07 (eff. Sept. 1, 2007), ch. 604, §1 (eff. Sept. 1, 2007), ch. 617, §1 (eff. Sept. 1, 2007), ch. 849, §2 (eff. June. 15, 2007), ch. 1025, §1 (eff. Sept. 1, 2007), ch. 1050, §1 (eff. Sept. 1, 2007), ch. 1205, §§2-8 (eff. Sept. 1, 2007), ch. 1308, §§5-9 (eff. June 15, 2007).

See also CCP arts. 37.07, 42.037; Pen. Code §§21.11, 22.011, 22.021.

ANNOTATIONS

Art. 42.12, §2

Ex parte Spicuzza, 903 S.W.2d 381, 382 n.1 (Tex. App.—Houston [1st Dist.] 1995, pet. ref'd). The Legislature "replaced references to 'probation' in the [CCP] with the term 'community supervision.' A defendant who was placed on probation or who received deferred adjudication probation before September 1, 1993, is nevertheless considered to have previously been placed on community supervision."

Art. 42.12, §3

Nesbit v. State, 227 S.W.3d 64, 69 (Tex.Crim.App. 2007). "[T]he duration of a time period during which a person suffers specified restrictions upon his freedom by virtue of either a sentence of imprisonment or community supervision includes the first day in which such restrictions upon freedom operate and excludes the anniversary date. The same day cannot be double counted. [¶] In this case, appellant was placed on 'regular' community supervision on April 29, 1994. The court of appeals held that his term of probation ended ten years later on April 28, 2004. Because the term of community supervision began on the very day of 'sentencing,' appellant suffered some restrictions upon his freedom on that day. We necessarily reject the State's argument that appellant is required to serve ten years and a day when he was placed on community supervision for exactly ten years, no more, no less."

Chauncey v. State, 877 S.W.2d 305, 308 (Tex.Crim. App.1994). "We see nothing in the plain language of §3 which limits the trial court, in assessing the term of probation, to a term that does not exceed the maximum sentence of imprisonment statutorily allowable for the offense."

Ex parte Langley, 833 S.W.2d 141, 143 (Tex.Crim. App.1992). "It is well-settled that a probated sentence is not a final conviction for enhancement purposes unless it is revoked. When a defendant receives 'regular' probation pursuant to Article 42.12, … he is convicted and punishment is assessed. However, the imposition of that sentence is suspended, and the conviction does not become final for purposes of enhancement unless the probation is revoked. A successfully served probation is not available for enhancement purposes."

Thomas v. State, 54 S.W.3d 907, 908 (Tex.App.— Corpus Christi 2001, no pet.). In 1988, "appellant [was placed on deferred adjudication] for eight years. [¶] In

1993, the trial court adjudicated appellant guilty, revoked his probation, and sentenced him to confinement for ten years. Appellant applied for probation, and [in] 1994, the trial court suspended appellant's sentence and placed him on probation for a period of ten years. [¶] Thereafter, the State filed a motion to revoke probation, and the trial court held a hearing on the motion.... The trial court revoked appellant's probation and sentenced him to eight years confinement on April 20, 2000. *At 909-10:* [T]he trial court was entitled to revoke appellant's adjudicated probation in 2000, as this date was within the authorized ten year sentence."

Visosky v. State, 953 S.W.2d 819, 821 (Tex.App.—Corpus Christi 1997, no pet.). "The very essence of deferred adjudication is that a defendant is not found guilty and is not convicted of any offense. [¶] There is a technical, but important distinction between §§3(a) and 5(a) of article 42.12. Section 3(a) ... provides that the trial court, '*after conviction* or a plea of guilty or nolo contendere, may suspend the imposition *of the sentence* and place the defendant on community supervision....' On the other hand, §5(a) ... provides that the court may 'defer further proceedings *without entering an adjudication of guilt*, and place the defendant on community supervision.' [¶] The phrase 'without entering an adjudication of guilt' is omitted from §3(a), just as the phrase 'after conviction' is not contained in §5(a). Thus, while §3(a) permits the court to place a defendant on community supervision and may do so after the defendant has been convicted or enters a plea, a plain reading of §5(a) indicates the legislature did not intend for a defendant to be eligible for deferred adjudication if he (1) has been convicted or (2) did not plea guilty or *nolo contendere*."

Art. 42.12, §3g

Ex parte Nelson, 137 S.W.3d 666, 668 (Tex.Crim. App.2004). "[W]e hold that persons ... who could have complained of [deadly weapon findings] in their judgments by appeal[] may not raise such complaints for the first time on habeas corpus."

Lafleur v. State, 106 S.W.3d 91, 92 (Tex.Crim.App. 2003). "[W]e hold that courts may look to the application paragraph of a lesser-included offense to determine if the express deadly weapon allegation in that portion of the jury charge matches the deadly weapon allegation in the indictment for the charged offense. If so, the trial court may enter a deadly weapon finding in

the judgment based upon the jury's verdict of guilt on the lesser-included offense."

Ex parte Jones, 957 S.W.2d 849, 851 (Tex.Crim. App.1997). "Art. 42.12, §3g(a)(2), requires the use of the deadly weapon to be during the transaction from which a conviction for a felony offense is obtained in order to trigger the entry of an affirmative finding of use or exhibition of that weapon." *See also **Cates v. State***, 102 S.W.3d 735, 739 (Tex.Crim.App.2003); ***Gale v. State***, 998 S.W.2d 221, 225-26 (Tex.Crim.App.1999).

Hill v. State, 913 S.W.2d 581, 584 (Tex.Crim.App. 1996). "[A]n affirmative finding [of use or exhibition of a deadly weapon during the commission of the charged offense] may be made if, during the punishment phase, the jury is presented with and responds in the affirmative to a special issue regarding the defendant's use or exhibition...." *See also **Grant v. State***, 33 S.W.3d 875, 880 (Tex.App.—Houston [14th Dist.] 2000, pet. ref'd).

Patterson v. State, 769 S.W.2d 938, 941 (Tex.Crim. App.1989). "'[U]sed ... a deadly weapon' during the commission of the offense means that the deadly weapon was employed or utilized in order to achieve its purpose. Whereas 'exhibited a deadly weapon' means that the weapon was consciously shown or displayed during the commission of the offense. Therefore, the court of appeals was correct when it stated that 'used ... during the commission of a felony offense' refers certainly to the wielding of a firearm with effect, but it extends as well to *any* employment of a deadly weapon, even its simple possession, if such possession facilitates the associated felony.' However, to 'exhibit' a deadly weapon it need only be consciously displayed during the commission of the required felony offense. Thus, one can 'use' a deadly weapon without exhibiting it, but it is doubtful one can exhibit a deadly weapon during the commission of a felony without using it." *See also **Whatley v. State***, 946 S.W.2d 73, 76 (Tex.Crim. App.1997); ***Tyra v. State***, 897 S.W.2d 796, 797 (Tex. Crim.App.1995); ***Coleman v. State***, 145 S.W.3d 649, 655 (Tex.Crim.App.2004).

Ex parte Beck, 769 S.W.2d 525, 527 (Tex.Crim.App. 1989). "[N]otice ... remains necessary in cases where there is no allegation of death or serious bodily injury being caused by a weapon, and there is no use of the nomenclature 'deadly weapon' in the indictment, but there will be evidence at trial that the defendant used or exhibited a weapon in the commission of the offense. In this instance, where there is no allegation in the indictment which comports with the definition of deadly weapon as set out in [Pen. Code §1.07] the defendant is clearly *not* put on notice that there will be an issue in the case concerning use or exhibition of a deadly weapon." *See also **Blount v. State**,* ___ S.W.3d ___ (Tex.Crim.App.2008) (No. PD-1645-06; 7-2-08) (allegation of assault gives notice of deadly weapon).

Johnson v. State, 233 S.W.3d 420, 425 (Tex.App.— Fort Worth 2007, pet. ref'd). "Where the trial court is the finder of fact, it is discretionary with the court whether to make an affirmative deadly weapon finding in the first instance even when such a finding would be supported by the evidence. [¶] And even where the trial court, as trier of fact, has made an affirmative deadly weapon finding either expressly or as a matter of law, it nevertheless retains the discretion not to enter the deadly weapon finding in the judgment. *At 428:* We hold that the nunc pro tunc orders amending the judgment by deleting 'NONE' and substituting an affirmative finding that Appellant did use or exhibit a deadly weapon are not a correction of a clerical error in the original judgment but are an improper modification of a product of judicial reasoning and are, as a matter of law, void."

Rivers v. State, 99 S.W.3d 659, 660 (Tex.App.— Waco 2003, no pet.). "In his sole issue, Rivers contends that the trial court erred by entering an affirmative deadly weapon finding in the order revoking Rivers's community supervision. The trial court had not entered a deadly weapon finding in its earlier judgment. Rivers is correct. [¶] [W]hen a trial court forgoes an affirmative finding regarding a deadly weapon at the time of the judgment and suspends the sentence, it has no authority to enter such finding in connection with the subsequent revocation of community supervision. The trial court had no authority to enter the deadly weapon finding in the order revoking Rivers's community supervision." *But see **Sampson**, below.*

Sampson v. State, 983 S.W.2d 842, 843-44 (Tex. App.—Houston [1st Dist.] 1998, pet. ref'd). "We address whether the trial court could make an affirmative finding of a deadly weapon in the order adjudicating appellant's guilt when the trial court had not made the affirmative finding in its order deferring adjudication. [¶] An affirmative finding of a deadly weapon is not applicable to an order of deferred adjudication because

parole eligibility only applies to persons who are imprisoned. When a defendant's adjudication of guilt is deferred, the defendant is not imprisoned; instead, the defendant is placed on community supervision. [¶] If a trial court determines that a defendant has violated the terms of his deferred adjudication and assesses imprisonment as punishment, the trial court is required to enter any affirmative finding of a deadly weapon in its order adjudicating guilt. It is at this point that the affirmative finding of a deadly weapon becomes applicable." *But see **Rivers**, above.*

Mulanax v. State, 882 S.W.2d 68, 71 (Tex.App.— Houston [14th Dist.] 1994, no pet.). "[S]ince a party may now receive an affirmative finding of a deadly weapon when he knew that a deadly weapon would be used or exhibited, the affirmative finding must state that [defendant] knew that a deadly weapon would be used or exhibited. A finding that a deadly weapon 'was used' is not proper and should be deleted. Without the deletion, the judgment implies that [defendant] used or exhibited a deadly weapon. In order for an affirmative finding to stand on the law of parties, there must have been a specific finding that appellant knew a deadly weapon would be used or exhibited." *See also **Sarmiento v. State**,* 93 S.W.3d 566, 569-70 (Tex. App.—Houston [14th Dist.] 2002, pet. ref'd) (when use of a deadly weapon is an element of the offense, the trial court may imply the affirmative finding by a guilty verdict); ***Howard v. State**,* 966 S.W.2d 821, 829 (Tex. App.—Austin 1998, pet. ref'd). *But see **Johnson v. State**,* 6 S.W.3d 709, 714-15 (Tex.App.—Houston [1st Dist.] 1999, pet. ref'd).

Mapps v. State, 880 S.W.2d 144, 147 n.1 (Tex. App.—Tyler 1994, no pet.). Article 42.12, §8 "appears to create an exception to the limitations of the court to grant probation under Article 42.12 §3g(a)(2) to deal with young offenders who have no prior convictions."

Dellinger v. State, 872 S.W.2d 49, 50 (Tex.App.— Fort Worth 1994, pet. ref'd). "[O]nly a jury can grant probation when there is a finding that a defendant used a deadly weapon during the commission of a felony offense."

Art. 42.12, §4

Milburn v. State, 201 S.W.3d 749, 750 (Tex.Crim. App.2006). "Appellant was convicted of a felony and placed on community supervision. Before the time had expired for filing a notice of appeal from that conviction, he was convicted of the present offense. The question here is whether he was entitled to a jury instruction on community supervision in this case, in spite of his previous conviction. The answer to this question is 'yes.'"

McDowell v. State, 235 S.W.3d 294, 298 (Tex. App.—Texarkana 2007, no pet.). "Unless there has been an express finding by the trial court that the defendant was exonerated from the previous finding of guilt, the defendant is still ineligible for community supervision [under §4(e)] even though she has been discharged from community supervision and the conviction is set aside or even if she has been pardoned."

Beyince v. State, 954 S.W.2d 878, 880 (Tex.App.—Houston [14th Dist.] 1997, no pet.). "Without evidence in the record showing [appellant] was actually eligible for probation, he can not prove his counsel was ineffective based solely on his failure to file a motion for probation."

Art. 42.12, §5

Durgan v. State, 240 S.W.3d 875, 878 (Tex.Crim. App.2007). "An assertion that a defendant was not competent at the time of the adjudication hearing is such a complaint [that may be appealed after a decision to adjudicate]; it raises a preliminary due-process issue that must be resolved before the adjudication process may begin. The adjudication process begins when the state files a motion to adjudicate, a motion that is based on an alleged violation of the terms or conditions of the deferred adjudication. The status of being incompetent is not a violation of a term or condition of community supervision and cannot, therefore, be the basis for a motion to adjudicate. If incompetence cannot be the basis for a motion to adjudicate, it cannot be the basis for a decision to adjudicate. It is thus separate and distinct from the decision to adjudicate. Because it is a separate and distinct inquiry, the court of appeals has jurisdiction to resolve the issue. [¶] With respect to its decision regarding its lack of jurisdiction over appellant's competence claim, we reverse the judgment of the court of appeals and remand to that court to consider the merits of appellant's competence claim."

State v. Juvrud, 187 S.W.3d 492, 493 (Tex.Crim. App.2006). "The question in this case is whether §20 of Article 42.12 ... mandates that a defendant on deferred-adjudication community supervision must complete 'one-third of the original community supervision period or two years of community supervision, whichever is less,' or whether §5(c) of Article 42.12 permits a trial court to terminate a defendant's deferred-adjudication community supervision at any time. [¶] [T]he trial court had authority to terminate Juvrud's community supervision under Article 42.12, §5(c)."

Hogans v. State, 176 S.W.3d 829, 830-31 (Tex.Crim. App.2005). "In this case we hold that a court of appeals has jurisdiction to consider the merits of a claim that temporally arises before the act of adjudication if the claim directly and distinctly relates to punishment rather than to the decision to adjudicate. However, because appellant raised a claim of ineffective assistance of counsel that relates to the decision to adjudicate, it was properly dismissed on jurisdictional grounds by the court of appeals."

Donovan v. State, 68 S.W.3d 633, 636 (Tex.Crim. App.2002). "A defendant on deferred adjudication has not been found guilty. *At 637-38:* [To challenge a plea's voluntariness after a defendant has been placed on deferred adjudication,] a defendant can move for adjudication within 30 days.... [¶] If the trial judge refuses to permit withdrawal of the plea and refuses to hear evidence on the matter, proceedings will continue normally, through judgment and sentence. ... A motion for new trial may be filed, in accordance with the rules as in any other case in which a defendant is convicted and sentenced. The defendant will then have the opportunity to raise in that motion any alleged errors in the proceedings, including questions about the voluntariness of the plea, and procure a hearing.... If relief is not granted by the trial court, the appeal from final adjudication will be the first and only appeal of the defendant's conviction.... [¶] If a defendant fails to move for final adjudication within 30 days, he has another available avenue for relief: an application for writ of habeas corpus under [CCP art.] 11.08 or 11.09. A claim that the plea was involuntary is cognizable in such a proceeding. [¶] The trial court correctly concluded that it had no authority to consider a motion for new trial before adjudication."

Nix v. State, 65 S.W.3d 664, 667-68 (Tex.Crim.App. 2001). There are "two exceptions to the general rule [that a defendant placed on deferred adjudication community supervision may raise issues relating to the original plea proceeding only in appeals taken when deferred adjudication community supervision is first imposed] ... (1) the 'void judgment' exception, and (2) the 'habeas corpus' exception. The void judgment exception recognizes that there are some rare situations in which a trial court's judgment is accorded no respect due to a complete lack of power to render the judgment in question. A void judgment is a 'nullity' and can be attacked at any time. *At 669-70:* The habeas corpus exception essentially involves the litigation of a writ of habeas corpus at the probation revocation proceedings. Because probation is not considered to be a 'final' conviction, an application for writ of habeas corpus filed during the pendency of revocation proceedings would be returnable to the trial court, whose ruling would be reviewable by a court of appeals and, ultimately, subject to a petition for discretionary review from this court. Had the application been filed separately, then, the same trial court would be responsible for resolving both the habeas application and the revocation proceedings, and these two proceedings would follow the same appellate path. We have held that, in the interest of judicial economy, the probationer need not file a separate writ application but may mount his attack during the revocation hearing. To invoke the habeas corpus exception on appeal, the defendant must show: (a) that the claim is cognizable on a writ of habeas corpus and (b) that the defendant attempted to litigate the claim at the revocation proceeding."

Von Schounmacher v. State, 5 S.W.3d 221, 223 (Tex.Crim.App.1999). "[R]egardless of whether the deferred adjudication was part of a plea bargain, recommended by the prosecution, imposed by the trial court without objection by the appellant, or granted under other circumstances, once the trial court proceeds to adjudication, it is restricted in the sentence it imposes only by the relevant statutory limits." *See also McCoy v. State*, 81 S.W.3d 917, 919 (Tex.App.—Dallas 2002, pet. ref'd).

Brown v. State, 943 S.W.3d 35, 42 (Tex.Crim.App. 1997). "[A] defendant who receives deferred adjudication as part of a plea agreement may raise an involuntariness claim based upon the trial judge's failure to give the required information."

Chandler v. State, 165 S.W.3d 63, 66-67 (Tex. App.—Austin 2005, pet. ref'd). "[W]e find nothing preventing courts from imposing different terms of imprisonment at different times on separate convictions for which identical terms of deferred-adjudication community supervision were originally imposed. ... Although the court in this case initially imposed identical community supervision terms for the aggravated assault and deadly conduct offenses, they remain separate offenses."

Salinas v. State, 920 S.W.2d 431, 432 (Tex.App.—Houston [1st Dist.] 1996, pet. ref'd). "'[U]ntil the court decides to defer further proceedings and place a defendant on probation without entering an adjudication of guilt, the duty to inform a defendant of the possible consequences of a violation of probation while on deferred adjudication does not arise.'"

Taylor v. State, 911 S.W.2d 906, 909 (Tex.App.—Fort Worth 1995, pet. ref'd). "[I]f a defendant is placed on deferred adjudication and successfully lives out the conditions of his probation, then evidence of that deferred adjudication would be admissible in a subsequent trial for another offense. Likewise, a defendant unsuccessful in living out the conditions of deferred adjudication status would be vulnerable to a revelation of that fact at a subsequent trial."

Art. 42.12, §6

Chauncey v. State, 877 S.W.2d 305, 307 n.5 (Tex. Crim.App.1994). In the case of shock probation, "a defendant is not placed on probation as an alternative to imprisonment but is placed on probation *in addition to* the service of a portion of the sentence of imprisonment."

State v. Dean, 895 S.W.2d 814, 816 (Tex.App.—Houston [14th Dist.] 1995, pet. ref'd). Article 42.12, §6 "indicates an intent to allow shock probation after *incarceration*, whether it be in the Institutional Division of the Texas Department of Criminal Justice or in county jail."

Art. 42.12, §8

In re Hall, 989 S.W.2d 786, 789 (Tex.App.—Waco 1999, no pet.). "[D] argues that Respondent's orders suspending his sentence [and placing him into boot-camp program] are void because they were entered outside the 75- to 90-day [now 75- to 180-day] statutory window. [¶] The boot camp statute provides a 75- to 90-day [now 75- to 180-day] window. The Court of Criminal Appeals has interpreted a similar window under the former shock probation statute to require the sentencing court to act solely within that window. We believe that the boot camp statute should be similarly applied."

Art. 42.12, §9

Griffith v. State, 166 S.W.3d 261, 262 (Tex.Crim. App.2005). "[B]ased on the plain meaning of the language in Article 42.12, the appellant could waive his right to the PSI report during the initial plea proceedings and the waiver was effective for the sentencing proceedings. *At 265:* We want to make clear that we are not holding that the trial court was unauthorized to have a PSI report prepared in this case. We are holding that the plain meaning of the language of §9, when read in the context of the entirety of Article 42.12, does not require that the trial court have a report prepared under the circumstances of this case." *See also **Alberto v. State***, 100 S.W.3d 528, 529 (Tex.App.—Texarkana 2003, no pet.).

Fryer v. State, 68 S.W.3d 628, 633 (Tex.Crim.App. 2002). "Because a victim's opinion regarding a defendant's suitability for probation falls within the scope and plain language of 'any other information relating to the defendant or the offense,' the PSI was authorized to contain that information...." *See also **Wilson v. State***, 108 S.W.3d 328, 331-32 (Tex.App.—Fort Worth 2003, pet. ref'd).

Bradford v. State, 89 S.W.3d 143, 144-45 (Tex. App.—Texarkana 2002, no pet.). "A substance abuse evaluation ... was ordered in 1997 as a condition of Bradford's community supervision. ... The issue [is] whether Article 42.12, §9(h)(3) requires a second evaluation before sentencing Bradford after the trial court had determined it would revoke Bradford's community supervision." Held: A second substance-abuse evaluation is discretionary.

Watson v. State, 919 S.W.2d 845, 846 (Tex.App.—Austin 1996, no pet.). "[T]he trial court's failure to afford Watson an opportunity to present evidence or argument, relating to the presentence investigation or to punishment in general, resulted in an improper punishment under [CCP art. 37.07,] §3 ... and [CCP art. 42.12,] §9.... Watson's failure to object ... does not preclude our review of the error claimed." *But see **Baxter v. State***, 936 S.W.2d 469, 472 (Tex.App.—Fort Worth 1996), *pet. dism'd*, 960 S.W.2d 82 (Tex.Crim. App.1998).

Glivens v. State, 918 S.W.2d 30, 33 (Tex.App.—Houston [1st Dist.] 1996, pet. ref'd). CCP art. 37.07 "is the more specific statute concerning the admissibility of evidence at the punishment stage of trial. [A]rticle 37.07 controls over article [CCP art.] 42.12[, §9] in the event of a conflict."

Pady v. State, 908 S.W.2d 65, 67 (Tex.App.—Houston [1st Dist.] 1995, no pet.). "[A]pproval of the court is required before the defendant may introduce evidence challenging the accuracy of the report. Nothing in this statute abridges the appellant's right to take the stand and present additional evidence to mitigate punishment."

Art. 42.12, §10

Rickels v. State, 108 S.W.3d 900, 902 (Tex.Crim. App.2003). "We have held that a defendant 'must complain at trial to the conditions he finds objectionable.' ... A distinction must be made, however, for those instances when a condition is imposed by way of an amendment to the probation order. ... Under these circumstances, the relevant inquiry is whether the probationer was given an opportunity to object to the modification. In this case, the court modified the terms of Rickels's probation without a hearing, and Rickels had no opportunity to object. We therefore address the merits of his argument."

Gutierrez v. State, 108 S.W.3d 304, 309-10 (Tex. Crim.App.2003). "The statutes governing probation do not make reference to [CCP art.] 26.13 or to any right of a plea-bargainer to withdraw a plea. Therefore, it follows that, in the context of revocation proceedings, the legislature has not authorized binding plea agreements, has not required the court to inquire as to the existence of a plea agreement or admonish the defendant pursuant to 26.13, and has not provided for withdrawal of a plea after sentencing."

Pino v. State, 189 S.W.3d 911, 912-13 (Tex.App.—Texarkana 2006, pet. ref'd). Held: The trial court lacked jurisdiction to revoke D's deferred adjudication community supervision because the State filed its motion to revoke community supervision and to proceed to adjudication of guilt one day after D's term of supervision had expired. *See also **Nesbit v. State***, 227 S.W.3d 64, 65 (Tex.Crim.App.2007) ("regular" community supervision).

Anthony v. State, 962 S.W.2d 242, 246 (Tex.App.—Fort Worth 1998, no pet.). "[A] defendant's admission of a violation to a probation officer, by itself, is sufficient to support a revocation [of community supervision]."

Bailey v. State, 888 S.W.2d 600, 603 (Tex.App.—Beaumont 1994, no pet.). "[N]owhere in this jurisdictional provision does the statute make a motion to revoke[ ] a jurisdictional prerequisite to the court's extension of probation as long as that action is taken prior to the expiration of the probationary period."

Art. 42.12, §11

Barton v. State, 21 S.W.3d 287, 290 (Tex.Crim.App. 2000). An "error regarding a condition of community supervision [is not] considered reversible error requiring a new punishment trial."

Cabla v. State, 6 S.W.3d 543, 550 (Tex.Crim.App. 1999). "[A]ppellant's previous Chapter 7 bankruptcy did not discharge the trial court's restitution orders in appellant's conditions of probation."

Speth v. State, 6 S.W.3d 530, 535 (Tex.Crim.App. 1999). "Appellant did not object at trial to the imposition of the conditions. The Court of Appeals erred in holding appellant could complain about the community supervision conditions for the first time on appeal."

Humphries v. State, ___ S.W.3d ___ (Tex.App.—San Antonio 2008, n.p.h.) (No. 04-07-00857-CR; 4-9-08). "[W]hen an appeal is taken from a criminal judgment assessing a probated sentence, the terms of community supervision do not commence until the judgment is final and the appellate mandate has issued."

Croft v. State, 148 S.W.3d 533, 539-40 (Tex.App.—Houston [14th Dist.] 2004, no pet.). "[A]ppellant contends the trial court erred by failing to include all of the requirements of sex offender registration in the jury charge during punishment. Appellant alleges that simply listing the requirement that sex offenders register as a possible condition of community supervision was incorrect and incomplete. [¶] Because the [CCP ch.] 62 registration requirement is a condition of community supervision, all other applicable terms of that chapter need not be listed in the jury charge at the punishment stage."

Ex parte Renfro, 999 S.W.2d 557, 559 (Tex.App.—Houston [14th Dist.] 1999, pet. ref'd). "Approximately five years into the term of his community supervision, the conditions of Appellant's community supervision were amended to require Appellant submit to a polygraph examination to assist with treatment, planning, and case monitoring. *At 560:* [W]e find that the polygraph condition is valid. Appellant pled guilty to a sex crime committed upon minor females. One condition of community supervision is that Appellant not have any contact with any minor under the age of 17 unless specifically permitted by the court. ... The polygraph condition helps to monitor compliance and is therefore reasonably related to Appellant's criminal offense [and] is reasonably related to future criminality. *At 561:* Appellant also contends that the polygraph condition violates his privilege against self-incrimination. [U]nless he invokes the privilege, shows a realistic threat of self-incrimination and nevertheless is required to answer, no violation of his right against self-incrimination is suffered."

Carroll v. State, 915 S.W.2d 246, 247 (Tex.App.—Beaumont 1996, no pet.). "Whether to order any restitution is within the discretion of the trial court. [¶] [T]here must be a factual basis in the record supporting the amount of restitution ordered.... There is ... no authority that non-economic damages, i.e., mental anguish, disfigurement, loss of consortium, etc., should be included as restitution or reparation...."

Pennington v. State, 902 S.W.2d 752, 754 (Tex.App.—Fort Worth 1995, pet. ref'd). Section 11(b) "requires the trial court to 'consider' the probationer's ability to make the payments ordered by the court. The language does not mandate that the payments be within the financial means of the probationers." *See also Keith v. State*, 916 S.W.2d 602, 608 (Tex.App.—Amarillo 1996, no pet.).

Saenz v. State, 879 S.W.2d 301, 306 (Tex.App.—Corpus Christi 1994, pet. ref'd). "A trial court need not inform the jury of any conditions of probation."

Art. 42.12, §12

Kesaria v. State, 189 S.W.3d 279, 279 (Tex.Crim.App.2006). "The principal issue in these cases is whether, after a court suspends the imposition of two sentences that would be served concurrently because they arose from the same criminal episode, the law permits a judge to impose conditions of probation that a defendant be confined in jail for two, consecutive periods of 180 days. We hold that it does."

Ballard v. State, 126 S.W.3d 919, 919 (Tex.Crim.App.2004). "In the community supervision revocation context, we must determine whether the due diligence requirement applies when the capias is issued and the defendant is apprehended within the community supervision period but the revocation hearing is held outside of that period. We hold that the due diligence requirement does not apply under those circumstances."

Chauncey v. State, 877 S.W.2d 305, 307 n.5 (Tex. Crim.App.1994). "[I]n the case of shock probation, ... a defendant is not placed on probation as an alternative to imprisonment but is placed on probation *in addition to* the service of a portion of the sentence of imprisonment. This differs from the case where, [provided for in §12], the execution of the sentence of imprisonment is suspended, but imprisonment is imposed as a condition of probation."

Art. 42.12, §13

Chauncey v. State, 877 S.W.2d 305, 306 n.3 (Tex. Crim.App.1994). "[W]hile §13 does deal with DWI probation conditions, it does not purport to provide an exhaustive list of options for the trial court."

State v. Lucero, 979 S.W.2d 400, 403 (Tex.App.— Amarillo 1998, no pet.). "[W]e hold that a trial court may waive (as a condition of probation) installation of the deep-lung device under article 42.12, §13(i), upon making the finding described therein."

Art. 42.12, §13B

Ex parte Alakayi, 102 S.W.3d 426, 435 (Tex.App.— Houston [14th Dist.] 2003, pet. ref'd). "Section 13B cannot mean that a trial court has authority to impose a child-safety zone only if the victim was a child, because §13D of article 42.12 permits a trial court to impose a child-safety zone for defendants placed on community supervision for violent offenses, regardless of the victim's age."

Art. 42.12, §14

Ex parte Wilson, 171 S.W.3d 925, 927 (Tex.App.— Dallas 2005, no pet.). "[W]e must determine whether the provisions for the Substance Abuse Felony Program (SAFP) contained in article 42.12, §14 ... exclude state jail felonies." Held: No; therefore, Article 42.12, §14, applies to state jail felonies.

Art. 42.12, §15

Jordan v. State, 36 S.W.3d 871, 875 (Tex.Crim.App. 2001). "[A] 'conviction' must be a final conviction for purposes of §15. [¶] [S]o long as any appeal of the imposition of probation has been resolved, a probated conviction does constitute a final conviction for the purpose of determining a defendant's eligibility for probation in a new case.... A conviction in which a probated sentence is imposed is considered final for this purpose even if probation is never revoked or the revocation of probation is on appeal. Only an appeal of the original conviction proceedings (in which probation was granted) can render the conviction nonfinal. *At 876:* A motion for new trial ... may likewise render a conviction nonfinal. [H]owever, for the purpose of determining probation eligibility in a new prosecution, a motion for new trial could affect the finality of a judgment granting probation only if the motion pertained to the original proceedings. [¶] Unlike regular probation, a deferred adjudication does not constitute a final conviction for the purpose of determining eligibility for probation in a subsequent prosecution. Only upon revocation (i.c. adjudication of guilt) does a deferred adjudication become a conviction. ... Even after revocation of his deferred adjudication probation, however, such a defendant can file a motion for new trial, and if a new trial is granted, the conviction itself would be undone. *At 877:* At the time the trial judge sentenced appellant to state jail in connection with the primary offense, appellant still had time to file a motion for new trial in the proceedings involving the prior conviction. The prior conviction was, therefore, not final and could not be used to deny appellant community supervision in the primary offense."

Ex parte Harris, 946 S.W.2d 79, 80 (Tex.Crim.App. 1997). "It is discretionary with the trial court whether to grant Applicant credit for this time. However, ... the equal protection clause of the 14th Amendment requires that inmates receive credit for their pretrial jail time if they had been unable to post bond due to their indigence, even though the relevant statute provided that the award of such credit was discretionary with the trial court. The record reflects that [applicant] was unable to post bond due to his indigence and he was sentenced to the maximum sentence. Thus, he is entitled to credit for this time period."

Jimerson v. State, 957 S.W.2d 875, 878 (Tex. App.—Texarkana 1997, no pet.). "We hold that the statute[, which gives trial court discretion to decide whether to grant credit for time served between arrest under prerevocation warrant and date community supervision for state jail felony is revoked,] is unconstitutional ... and we will direct the trial court to provide [appellant] with credit for the time spent in the penal institution between his arrest on the revocation warrant and the hearing on revocation."

State v. Hudson, 915 S.W.2d 879, 882 (Tex.App.—Houston [1st Dist.] 1995, pet. ref'd). "The ... application of ... §15(d) to require up-front confinement of one year as a condition of community supervision [is] discretionary and entirely proper."

Art. 42.12, §16

Cotten v. State, 893 S.W.2d 200, 204 (Tex.App.—Fort Worth 1995, no pet.). "[T]he current version of article 42.12[, §16] omits the language ... that require[s] a trial court to name a specific community services project or organization."

Art. 42.12, §18

Chauncey v. State, 877 S.W.2d 305, 307 (Tex.Crim. App.1994). "[S]ection 18[] does not preclude the imposition of time in a [community corrections facility], together with jail time which was imposed as a condition of [community supervision]."

Art. 42.12, §20

Cuellar v. State, 70 S.W.2d 815, 820 (Tex.Crim.App. 2002). "[A] person who successfully completes all of the terms and conditions of community supervision must be discharged from community supervision. This is not a discretionary matter. [A] person whose conviction is set aside pursuant to [a CCP art.] 42.12, §20, order *is not a convicted felon*. [¶] Penal Code §46.04(a) requires a felony conviction as an element of the offense. Here, appellant's prior felony conviction was set aside pursuant to an Article 42.12, §20, order. Accordingly, there was no predicate felony conviction to support a conviction under §46.04(a)."

Wolfe v. State, 917 S.W.2d 270, 277 (Tex.Crim.App. 1996). "Article 42.12, §20 ... provides a mechanism to release a convicted person of all legal disabilities upon successful completion of probation. ... Appellant claims that the statute is mandatory, and therefore, a person who successfully completes his probation is discharged from his legal disabilities even in the absence of an order from the trial judge. [¶] We disagree with appellant's contention.... The plain language of Article 44.12, §20(a) clearly contemplates the entry of an order before releasing a defendant from legal disabilities resulting from conviction...."

R.R.E. v. Glenn, 884 S.W.2d 189, 193 (Tex.App.—Fort Worth 1994, writ denied). "[A]rticle 42.12, §20 does not have the effect of removing all disabilities imposed by the Constitution. ... Nothing in the Constitution contemplates the full restoration of the rights of felons other than by executive pardon. [¶] [The] statute is not absolute and fails to do what it says it is doing in that there are stated exceptions to the restoration of rights: the prior conviction shall be made known on a subsequent conviction of any offense; it may be considered if the person convicted holds a license or applies for a license to operate a child-care facility; and the restoration of rights does not apply to state jail felonies." *But see* ***Hoffman v. State***, 922 S.W.2d 663, 687 (Tex. App.—Waco 1996, pet. ref'd) (Fort Worth court is alone in holding statute is not absolute).

Art. 42.12, §21

Bawcom v. State, 78 S.W.3d 360, 361 (Tex.Crim. App.2002). "This is a probation revocation case in which the probationer failed to report as required. The State made numerous efforts to contact the probationer before filing a motion to revoke probation and made a few efforts to contact him after the capias issued, but the probationer was not apprehended until after his probationary period had expired. The question presented is whether the trial court may consider actions taken by the State before the motion to revoke is filed in determining whether the State has exercised due diligence in apprehending the probationer. We hold that the trial court may consider such evidence."

Pierce v. State, 113 S.W.3d 431, 436 (Tex.App.—Texarkana 2003, pet. ref'd). "Considering the unique nature of the revocation hearing and the trial court's broad discretion in the proceedings, the general standards for reviewing factual sufficiency do not apply. If the greater weight of credible evidence creates a reasonable belief a defendant has violated a condition of his or her probation, the trial court's order of revocation did not abuse its discretion and must be upheld."

Jackson v. State, 915 S.W.2d 104, 106 (Tex. App.—San Antonio 1996, no pet.). "In a proceeding to revoke probation where the grounds for revocation are the probationer's failure to pay fees assessed as a condition of probation, the inability of the probationer to pay the enumerated fees is an affirmative defense. [T]he probationer must prove his inability to pay by a preponderance of the evidence."

Lugaro v. State, 904 S.W.2d 842, 843-44 (Tex. App.—Corpus Christi 1995, no pet.). "A defendant has the right to counsel at a revocation hearing unless it is affirmatively waived. [C]ourts indulge every reasonable presumption against waiver. On direct appeal, the State bears the burden of establishing that the record affirmatively shows a valid waiver of counsel. The waiver of counsel must be made voluntarily, knowingly, and intelligently. [¶] [T]he trial judge has an obligation to determine whether a defendant understands the importance of legal counsel...."

Art. 42.12, §23

Lyons v. State, 222 S.W.3d 658, 660 (Tex.App.—Houston [14th Dist.] 2007, no pet.). "When a defendant is indicted for an offense, the indictment necessarily includes all lesser included offenses. When an indictment alleges an offense that includes lesser offenses, the accused may be tried and convicted of a lesser offense. We discern no reason why this rule is inapplicable to the context of a motion to adjudicate guilt. Thus, appellant cannot expect some different or greater level of notice not provided to criminal defendants through an indictment."

Flores v. State, 102 S.W.3d 336, 337 (Tex.App.—Eastland 2003, pet. ref'd). "If the revocation order is based alone on a conviction that was not final at the time of revocation, the order cannot stand."

Dureso v. State, 988 S.W.2d 448, 450 (Tex.App.—Houston [1st Dist.] 1999, pet. ref'd). "We find the trial court abused its discretion in finding a violation of [community-supervision] condition ... when appellant was arrested and the State filed its motion to revoke [for allegedly not performing community service] before the expiration of the term in which appellant could perform the community service required for the month."

Amado v. State, 983 S.W.2d 330, 332 (Tex.App.—Houston [1st Dist.] 1998, pet. ref'd). "[A]ppellant's probation was revoked and the trial court, as permitted by §23 of article 42.12, reduced appellant's term of confinement to two years and imposed a two year sentence, which appellant began to serve. The trial court then granted appellant 'shock probation.' When the second probation was revoked, the sentence to be reinstated was the two year sentence, and the trial court abused its discretion in imposing a sentence that was greater than the reduced sentence of two years."

Holiday v. State, 983 S.W.2d 326, 327-28 (Tex.App.—Houston [14th Dist.] 1998, pet. ref'd). "It is well settled that a defendant whose community supervision is revoked may only appeal from the revocation. The underlying adjudication may only be appealed at the time probation was given. Appellant did not appeal his adjudication of guilt when he was adjudicated guilty and given community supervision. Therefore, we have no jurisdiction to consider appellant's sole point of error attacking the underlying adjudication. [¶] In the present case, appellant appeals not from his adjudication of guilt; instead, he appeals from a subsequent revocation of 'ordinary' probation, i.e., 'community supervision,' where his sentence had been suspended after being adjudicated guilty."

Weed v. State, 891 S.W.2d 22, 24 (Tex.App.—Fort Worth 1995, no pet.). "Probation revocation proceedings are not criminal trials in the constitutional sense; rather, they are administrative in nature. [¶] A probationer must be afforded minimum due process rights in a revocation hearing."

ART. 42.121. REPEALED

Repealed by Acts 1989, 71st Leg., ch. 785, §3.10, eff. Sept. 1, 1989; Acts 1995, 74th Leg., ch. 321, §3.020(b), (c), eff. Sept. 1, 1995.

ART. 42.122. ADULT PROBATION OFFICERS OF THE 222ND JUDICIAL DISTRICT[1]

The adult probation officer of the 222nd Judicial District receives a salary of not less than $15,000 per annum. Also, the probation officer receives allowances, not to exceed the amount allowed by the federal government for traveling the most practical route to and from the place where the duties are discharged, for his necessary travel and hotel expenses. Upon the sworn statement of the officer, approved by the judge, the respective counties of the judicial district pay the expenses incurred for their regular or special term of court out of the general county fund. In lieu of travel allowances the commissioners court of each county, by agreement, may provide transportation under the same terms and conditions as provided for sheriffs.

1. **Editor's note:** Heading supplied by editor.

History of CCP art. 42.122: Acts 1985, 69th Leg., ch. 480, §18, eff. Sept. 1, 1985.

ART. 42.13. REPEALED

CCP art. 42.13, was partially repealed and transferred to Gov't Code ch. 76 by Acts 1995, 74th Leg., ch. 509, §7.10, eff. Sept. 1, 1995. The remaining portions were repealed and transferred to Gov't Code ch. 76 by Acts 1997, 75th Leg., ch. 165, §§12.23-12.29, eff. Sept. 1, 1997.

ART. 42.131. REPEALED

CCP art. 42.131, was partially repealed and transferred to Gov't Code ch. 76 by Acts 1995, 74th Leg., ch. 76, §7.16, eff. Sept. 1, 1995. The remaining portions were repealed and transferred to Gov't Code ch. 509 by Acts 1997, 75th Leg., ch. 165, §§9.02-9.06, eff. Sept. 1, 1997.

ART. 42.14. IN ABSENCE OF DEFENDANT

The judgment and sentence in a misdemeanor case may be rendered in the absence of the defendant.

History of CCP art. 42.14: Acts 1965, 59th Leg., vol. 2, ch. 722.

ART. 42.141. BATTERING INTERVENTION & PREVENTION PROGRAM

§1. Definitions

In this article:

(1) "Batterer" means a person who commits repeated acts of violence or who repeatedly threatens violence against another who is:

(A) related to the actor by affinity or consanguinity, as determined under Chapter 573, Government Code;

(B) is a former spouse of the actor; or

(C) resides or has resided in the same household with the actor.

(2) "Division" means the community justice assistance division of the Texas Department of Criminal Justice.

(3) "Family" has the meaning assigned by Section 71.003, Family Code.

(4) "Family violence" has the meaning assigned by Section 71.004, Family Code.

(5) "Shelter center" has the meaning assigned by Section 51.002, Human Resources Code.

(6) "Household" has the meaning assigned by Section 71.005, Family Code.

(7) "Program" means a battering intervention and prevention program that:

(A) meets:

(i) the guidelines adopted by the community justice assistance division of the Texas Department of Criminal Justice with the assistance of the statewide nonprofit organization described by Section 3(1); and

(ii) any other eligibility requirements adopted by the Texas Department of Criminal Justice; and

(B) provides, on a local basis to batterers referred by the courts for intervention, educational services and intervention designed to help the batterers stop their abusive behavior.

(8) "Project" means the statewide activities for the funding of battering intervention and prevention programs, the related community educational campaign, and education and research regarding such programs.

(9) "Responsive law enforcement climate" means an area where, in cases of family violence:

(A) the local law enforcement agency has a policy or record of arresting batterers; and

(B) the local criminal justice system:

(i) cooperates with the victim in filing protective orders; and

(ii) takes appropriate action against a person who violates protective orders.

§2. Establishment

The battering intervention and prevention program is established in the division.

§3. Duties of the Division

The division shall:

(1) contract with a nonprofit organization that for the five-year period before the date on which a contract is to be signed has been involved in providing to shelter centers, law enforcement agencies, and the legal community statewide advocacy and technical assistance relating to family violence, with the contract requiring the nonprofit organization to perform the duties described in Section (4) of this article;

(2) seek the input of the statewide nonprofit organization described in Subdivision (1) in the development of standards for selection of programs for inclusion in the project and the review of proposals submitted by programs;

(3) issue requests for proposals for the programs and an educational campaign not later than January 1, 1990;

(4) award contracts for programs that are operated by nonprofit organizations and that take into consideration:

(A) a balanced geographical distribution of urban, rural, and suburban models; and

(B) the presence of a responsive law enforcement climate in the community;

(5) develop and monitor the project in cooperation with the nonprofit organization described by Subdivision (1);

(6) monitor the development of a community educational campaign in cooperation with the nonprofit organization described by Subdivision (1);

(7) assist the nonprofit organization described by Subdivision (1) in designing program evaluations and research activities;

(8) facilitate training of probation officers and other criminal justice professionals by the nonprofit organization described by Subdivision (1) and by programs;

(9) seek the assistance of the nonprofit organization described by Subdivision (1) in developing program guidelines and in accrediting programs and providers providing battering intervention and prevention services as conforming to those guidelines; and

(10) before adopting program guidelines under Section 4A:

(A) notify the licensing authorities described by Chapters 152, 501, 502, 503, and 505, Occupations Code, that the division is considering adopting program guidelines; and

(B) invite the licensing authorities to comment on the program guidelines.

§4. Duties of the Nonprofit Organization

The nonprofit organization with which the division contracts under Section 3(1) shall:

(1) assist the division in developing and issuing requests for proposals for the programs and the educational campaign;

(2) assist the division in reviewing the submitted proposals and making recommendations for proposals to be selected for funding;

(3) develop and monitor the project in cooperation with the division;

(4) provide technical assistance to programs to:

(A) develop appropriate services for batterers;

(B) train staff;

(C) improve coordination with shelter centers, the criminal justice system, the judiciary, law enforcement agencies, prosecutors, and other appropriate officials and support services;

(D) implement the community educational campaign; and

(E) participate in project administered program evaluation and research activities;

(5) provide technical assistance to the division to:

(A) develop and implement standards for selection of programs for inclusion in the project; and

(B) develop standards for selection of the community educational campaign described in Section 6 of this article;

(6) submit an annual written report to the division and to the legislature with recommendations for continuation, elimination, or changes in the project;

(7) evaluate the programs and the community educational campaign, including an analysis of the effectiveness of the project and the level of public awareness relating to family violence; and

(8) assist the division in developing program guidelines and in accrediting programs and providers providing battering intervention and prevention services as conforming to those guidelines.

§4A. Adoption of Program Guidelines; Accreditation Process

With the assistance of the statewide nonprofit organization described by Section 3(1) and after notifying the licensing authorities described by Section 3(10), the division shall adopt guidelines for programs and shall accredit programs and providers providing battering intervention and prevention services as conforming to those guidelines. The division shall collect from each program or provider that applies for accreditation under this section a one-time application fee in an amount set by the Texas Department of Criminal Justice.

§5. Programs

(a) A program proposal must:

(1) describe the counseling or treatment the program will offer;

(2) include letters from a local law enforcement agency or agencies, courts, probation officers, and other community resources describing the community's commitment to improve the criminal justice system's response to victims and batterers and to cooperate with and interact in the programs' activities;

(3) include a letter from the local shelter center describing the support services available to victims of family violence in the community and the shelter's commitment to cooperate and work with the program; and

(4) describe the public education and local community outreach activities relating to family violence currently available in the community and a statement of commitment to participate on the local level in the public educational campaign described in Section 6 of this article.

(b) A program must:

(2) offer counseling or treatment in which the primary approach is direct intervention with the batterer,

on an individual or group basis, but that does not require the victim of the family violence to participate in the counseling or treatment;

(3) offer training to law enforcement prosecutors, judges, probation officers, and others on the dynamics of family violence, treatment options, and program activities; and

(4) have a system for receiving referrals from the courts and for reporting to the court regarding batterers' compliance with the treatment program.

(c) This section does not preclude a program from serving a batterer other than one who was ordered by a court to participate in the program established under this subchapter.

§6. Community Educational Campaign

(a) The division, with assistance from the nonprofit organization, shall select the community educational campaign relating to family violence after the commission has selected the programs. The campaign is to be implemented in the areas covered by the programs.

(b) The campaign shall use a variety of media, including newspapers, radio, television, and billboards, and shall focus on:

(1) the criminality of acts of violence toward family members;

(2) the consequences of family violence crimes to the batterer; and

(3) eradicating public misconceptions of family violence.

§7. Use of Legislative Appropriation

Of a legislative appropriation for the project established under this article:

(1) not more than six percent may be used by the division for management and administration of the project;

(2) not more than 14 percent may be applied to the contract between the division and the nonprofit organization; and

(3) not more than three percent may be applied to the contract for the community educational campaign.

§8. Contract Date

The contract required under Section 3(a) of this article shall be signed not later than November 1, 1989.

History of CCP art. 42.141: Acts 1989, 71st Leg., ch. 785, §3.05, eff. Sept. 1, 1989. Amended by Acts 1991, 72nd Leg., ch. 561, §11, eff. Aug. 26, 1991; Acts 1995, 74th Leg., ch. 76, §5.95(27), eff. Sept. 1, 1995; Acts 2003, 78th Leg., ch. 1276, §7.002(i), eff. Sept. 1, 2003; Acts 2007, 80th Leg., ch. 113, §§2, 3, eff. Sept. 1, 2007.

ART. 42.15. FINES

(a) When the defendant is fined, the judgment shall be that the defendant pay the amount of the fine and all costs to the state.

(b) When imposing a fine and costs a court may direct a defendant:

(1) to pay the entire fine and costs when sentence is pronounced; or

(2) to pay the entire fine and costs at some later date; or

(3) to pay a specified portion of the fine and costs at designated intervals.

History of CCP art. 42.15: Acts 1965, 59th Leg., vol. 2, ch. 722. Amended by Acts 1971, 62nd Leg., ch. 987, §1, eff. June 15, 1971.

ANNOTATIONS

Ex parte Sanchez, 489 S.W.2d 295, 297-98 (Tex. Crim.App.1972). It is "a denial of equal protection to convert a fine to imprisonment for those who are unable to pay a fine."

ART. 42.151. FEES FOR ABUSED CHILDREN'S COUNSELING

If a court orders a defendant to pay a fee under Article 37.072 of this code, the court shall assess the fee against the defendant in the same manner as other costs of prosecution are assessed against a defendant. The court may direct a defendant:

(1) to pay the entire fee when sentence is pronounced;

(2) to pay the entire fee at some later date; or

(3) to pay a specified portion of the fee at designated intervals.

History of CCP art. 42.151: Acts 1989, 71st Leg., ch. 360, §3, eff. Sept. 1, 1989.

ART. 42.152. REPAYMENT OF REWARD

(a) If a judge orders a defendant to repay a reward or part of a reward under Article 37.073 of this code, the court shall assess this cost against the defendant in the same manner as other costs of prosecution are assessed against a defendant. The court may order the defendant to:

(1) pay the entire amount required when sentence is pronounced;

(2) pay the entire amount required at a later date specified by the court; or

(3) pay specified portions of the required amount at designated intervals.

(b) After receiving a payment from a person ordered to make the payment under this article, the clerk of the court or fee officer shall:

(1) make a record of the payment;

(2) deduct a one-time $7 processing fee from the reward repayment;

(3) forward the payment to the designated crime stoppers organization; and

(4) make a record of the forwarding of the payment.

History of CCP art. 42.152: Acts 1989, 71st Leg., ch. 611, §3, eff. Sept. 1, 1989. Renumbered from art. 42.151 by Acts 1991, 72nd Leg., ch. 16, §19.01(6), eff. Aug. 26, 1991; Acts 1997, 75th Leg., ch. 700, §12, eff. Sept. 1, 1997.

ART. 42.16. ON OTHER JUDGMENT

If the punishment is any other than a fine, the judgment shall specify it, and order it enforced by the proper process. It shall also adjudge the costs against the defendant, and order the collection thereof as in other cases.

History of CCP art. 42.16: Acts 1965, 59th Leg., vol. 2, ch. 722.

ART. 42.17. TRANSFER UNDER TREATY

When a treaty is in effect between the United States and a foreign country providing for the transfer of convicted offenders who are citizens or nationals of foreign countries to the foreign countries of which they are citizens or nationals, the governor is authorized, subject to the terms of such treaty, to act on behalf of the State of Texas and to consent to the transfer of such convicted offenders under the provisions of Article IV, Section 11 of the Constitution of the State of Texas.

History of CCP art. 42.17: Acts 1977, 65th Leg., ch. 489, §1, eff. June 15, 1977.

ART. 42.18. REPEALED

Repealed by Acts 1997, 75th Leg., ch. 165, §12.22, eff. Sept. 1, 1997.

ART. 42.19. INTERSTATE CORRECTIONS COMPACT

Article I. Purpose & Policy

The party states, desiring by common action to fully utilize and improve their institutional facilities and provide adequate programs for the confinement, treatment, and rehabilitation of various types of offenders, declare that it is the policy of each of the party states to provide such facilities and programs on a basis of cooperation with one another, thereby serving the best interests of such offenders and of society and effecting economies in capital expenditures and operational costs. The purpose of this compact is to provide for the mutual development and execution of such programs of cooperation for the confinement, treatment, and rehabilitation of offenders with the most economical use of human and material resources.

Article II. Definitions

As used in this compact, unless the context clearly requires otherwise:

(a) "State" means a state of the United States; the United States of America; a territory or possession of the United States; the District of Columbia; the commonwealth of Puerto Rico.

(b) "Sending state" means a state party to this compact in which conviction or court commitment was had.

(c) "Receiving state" means a state party to this compact to which an inmate is sent for confinement other than a state in which conviction or court commitment was had.

(d) "Inmate" means a male or female offender who is committed, under sentence to or confined in a penal or correctional institution.

(e) "Institution" means any penal or correctional facility, including but not limited to a facility for the mentally ill or mentally defective, in which inmates as defined in (d) above may lawfully be confined.

Article III. Contracts

(a) Each party state may make one or more contracts with any one or more of the other party states for the confinement of inmates on behalf of a sending state in institutions situated within receiving states. Any such contract shall provide for:

1. Its duration.

2. Payments to be made to the receiving state by the sending state for inmate maintenance, extraordinary medical and dental expenses, and any participation in or receipt by inmates of rehabilitative or correctional services, facilities, programs, or treatment not reasonably included as part of normal maintenance.

3. Participation in programs of inmate employment, if any; the disposition or crediting of any payments received by inmates on account thereof; and the crediting of proceeds from or disposal of any products resulting therefrom.

4. Delivery and retaking of inmates.

5. Such other matters as may be necessary and appropriate to fix the obligations, responsibilities, and rights of the sending and receiving states.

(b) The terms and provisions of this compact shall be a part of any contract entered into by the authority of or pursuant thereto, and nothing in any such contract shall be inconsistent therewith.

Article IV. Procedures & Rights

(a) Whenever the duly constituted authorities in a state party to this compact, and which has entered into a contract pursuant to Article III, shall decide that confinement in, or transfer of an inmate to, an institution within the territory of another party state is necessary or desirable in order to provide adequate quarters and care or an appropriate program of rehabilitation or treatment, such official may direct that the confinement be within an institution within the territory of such other party state, the receiving state to act in that regard solely as agent for the sending state.

(b) The appropriate officials of any state party to this compact shall have access, at all reasonable times, to any institution in which it has a contractual right to confine inmates for the purpose of inspecting the facilities thereof and visiting such of its inmates as may be confined in the institution.

(c) Inmates confined in an institution pursuant to this compact shall at all times be subject to the jurisdiction of the sending state and may at any time be removed therefrom for transfer to a prison or other institution within the sending state, for transfer to another institution in which the sending state may have a contractual or other right to confine inmates, for release on probation or parole, for discharge, or for any other purpose permitted by the laws of the sending state. However, the sending state shall continue to be obligated to such payments as may be required pursuant to the terms of any contract entered into under the terms of Article III.

(d) Each receiving state shall provide regular reports to each sending state on the inmates of that sending state who are in institutions pursuant to this compact including a conduct record of each inmate and shall certify such record to the official designated by the sending state, in order that each inmate may have official review of his or her record in determining and altering the disposition of the inmate in accordance with the law which may obtain in the sending state and in order that the same may be a source of information for the sending state.

(e) All inmates who may be confined in an institution pursuant to this compact shall be treated in a reasonable and humane manner and shall be treated equally with such similar inmates of the receiving state as may be confined in the same institution. The fact of confinement in a receiving state shall not deprive any inmate so confined of any legal rights which the inmate would have had if confined in an appropriate institution of the sending state.

(f) Any hearing or hearings to which an inmate confined pursuant to this compact may be entitled by the laws of the sending state may be had before the appropriate authorities of the sending state, or of the receiving state if authorized by the sending state. The receiving state shall provide adequate facilities for such hearing as may be conducted by the appropriate officials of a sending state. In the event such hearing or hearings are had before officials of the receiving state, the governing law shall be that of the sending state and a record of the hearing or hearings as prescribed by the sending state shall be made. The record together with any recommendations of the hearing officials shall be transmitted forthwith to the official or officials before whom the hearing would have been had if it had taken place in the sending state. In any and all proceedings had pursuant to the provisions of this paragraph (f), the officials of the receiving state shall act solely as agents of the sending state and no final determination shall be made in any matter except by the appropriate officials of the sending state.

(g) Any inmate confined pursuant to this compact shall be released within the territory of the sending state unless the inmate and the sending and receiving states shall agree upon release in some other place. The sending state shall bear the cost of such return to its territory.

(h) Any inmate confined pursuant to this compact shall have any rights and all rights to participate in and derive any benefits or incur or be relieved of any obligations or have such obligations modified or his status changed on account of any action or proceeding in which he could have participated if confined in any appropriate institution of the sending state located within such state.

(i) The parent, guardian, trustee, or other person or persons entitled under the laws of the sending state to act for, advise, or otherwise function with respect to any inmate shall not be deprived of or restricted in his exercise of any power in respect of any inmate confined pursuant to the terms of this compact.

Article V. Act Not Reviewable in Receiving State: Extradition

(a) Any decision of the sending state in respect of any matter over which it retains jurisdiction pursuant to this compact shall be conclusive upon and not reviewable within the receiving state, but if at the time the sending state seeks to remove an inmate from an institution in the receiving state there is pending against the inmate within such state any criminal charge or if the inmate is formally accused of having committed within such state a criminal offense, the inmate shall not be returned without the consent of the receiving state until discharged from prosecution or other form of proceeding, imprisonment, or detention for such offense. The duly accredited officer of the sending state shall be permitted to transport inmates pursuant to this compact through any and all states party to this compact without interference.

(b) An inmate who escapes from an institution in which he is confined pursuant to this compact shall be deemed a fugitive from the sending state and from the state in which the institution escaped from is situated. In the case of an escape to a jurisdiction other than the sending or receiving state, the responsibility for institution of extradition or rendition proceedings shall be that of the sending state, but nothing contained herein shall be construed to prevent or affect the activities of officers and agencies of any jurisdiction directed toward the apprehension and return of an escapee.

Article VI. Federal Aid

Any state party to this compact may accept federal aid for use in connection with any institution or program, the use of which is or may be affected by this compact or any contract pursuant thereto. Any inmate in a receiving state pursuant to this compact may participate in any such federally aided program or activity for which the sending and receiving states have made

contractual provision. However, if such program or activity is not part of the customary correctional regimen, the express consent of the appropriate official of the sending state shall be required therefor.

Article VII. Entry Into Force

This compact shall enter into force and become effective and binding upon the states so acting when it has been enacted into law by any two states. Thereafter, this compact shall enter into force and become effective and binding as to any other of such states upon similar action by such state.

Article VIII. Withdrawal & Termination

This compact shall continue in force and remain binding upon a party state until it shall have enacted a statute repealing the compact and providing for the sending of formal written notice of withdrawal from the compact to the appropriate officials of all other party states. An actual withdrawal shall not take effect until one year after the notices provided in the statute have been sent. Such withdrawal shall not relieve the withdrawing state from its obligations assumed hereunder prior to the effective date of withdrawal. Before the effective date of withdrawal, a withdrawal state shall remove to its territory, at its own expense, such inmates as it may have confined pursuant to the provisions of this compact.

Article IX. Other Arrangements Unaffected

Nothing contained in this compact shall be construed to abrogate or impair an agreement or other arrangement which a party state may have with a nonparty state for the confinement, rehabilitation, or treatment of inmates, nor to repeal any other laws of a party state authorizing the making of cooperative institutional arrangements.

Article X. Construction & Severability

(a) The provisions of this compact shall be liberally construed and shall be severable. If any phrase, clause, sentence, or provision of this compact is declared to be contrary to the constitution of any participating state or of the United States or the applicability thereof to any government, agency, person, or circumstance is held invalid, the validity of the remainder of this compact and the applicability thereof to any government, agency, person, or circumstance shall not be affected thereby. If this compact shall be held contrary to the constitution of any state participating therein, the compact shall remain in full force and effect as to the remaining states and in full force and effect as to the state affected as to all severable matters.

(b) Powers. The director of the Texas Department of Corrections is authorized and directed to do all things necessary or incidental to the carrying out of the compact in every particular.

History of CCP art. 42.19: Acts 1985, 69th Leg., ch. 24, §1, eff. Jan. 1, 1986. Renumbered from art. 42.18 by Acts 1987, 70th Leg., ch. 167, §5.01(a)(9), eff. Sept. 1, 1987.

ART. 42.20. IMMUNITIES

(a) An individual listed in Subsection (c) of this article and the governmental entity that the individual serves as an officer or employee are not liable for damages arising from an act or failure to act by the individual or governmental entity in connection with a community service program or work program established under this chapter or in connection with an inmate, offender, or releasee programmatic or nonprogrammatic activity, including work, educational, and treatment activities, if the act or failure to act:

(1) was performed pursuant to a court order or was otherwise performed in an official capacity; and

(2) was not performed with conscious indifference for the safety of others.

(b) Chapter 101, Civil Practice and Remedies Code, does not apply to a claim based on an act or a failure to act of an individual listed in Subsection (c) of this article or a governmental entity the officer serves as an officer or employee if the act or failure to act is in connection with a program described by Subsection (a) of this article.

(c) This article applies to:

(1) a director or employee of a community supervision and corrections department or a community corrections facility;

(2) a sheriff or employee of a sheriff's department;

(3) a county judge, county attorney, county commissioner, or county employee;

(4) a district judge, district attorney, or criminal district attorney;

(5) an officer or employee of a state agency; or

(6) an officer or employee of a political subdivision other than a county.

History of CCP art. 42.20: Acts 1993, 73rd Leg., ch. 900, §5.03, eff. Sept. 1, 1993. Amended by Acts 1995, 74th Leg., ch. 76, §3.13, eff. Sept. 1, 1995; Acts 2003, 78th Leg., ch. 406, §1, eff. Sept. 1, 2003.

ANNOTATIONS

Tarrant Cty. v. Morales, 207 S.W.3d 870, 874 (Tex. App.—Fort Worth 2006, no pet.). "The term 'conscious indifference' is not defined in article 42.20. The Supreme Court of Texas has held that conscious indifference is an element of gross negligence. Gross negligence consists of two elements: (1) the actor has actual, subjective awareness of the risk involved but nonetheless proceeds with conscious indifference to the rights and safety or welfare of others and (2) the conduct at issue is an act or omission involving an extreme degree of risk, considering the probability and magnitude of the potential harm to others. The test for 'conscious indifference' focuses on the actor's mental state. To establish conscious indifference, it is only necessary to show that the actor proceeded with knowledge that the harm was a 'highly probable' consequence of the act or failure to act; it is not necessary to show that the actor actually intended to cause harm."

ART. 42.21. NOTICE OF RELEASE OF FAMILY VIOLENCE OFFENDERS

(a) Before releasing a person convicted of a family violence offense, the entity holding the person shall make a reasonable attempt to give personal notice of the imminent release to the victim of the offense or to another person designated by the victim to receive the notice. An attempt by an entity to give notice to the victim or person designated by the victim at the victim's or person's last known telephone number or address, as shown on the records of the entity, constitutes a reasonable attempt to give notice under this subsection.

(b) An entity or an employee of an entity is not liable for damages arising from complying or failing to comply with Subsection (a) of this article.

(c) In this article, "family violence" has the meaning assigned by Section 71.004, Family Code.

History of CCP art. 42.21: Acts 1995, 74th Leg., ch. 661, §2, eff. Aug. 28, 1995. Amended by Acts 2003, 78th Leg., ch. 1276, §7.002(j), eff. Sept. 1, 2003.

ART. 42.22. RESTITUTION LIENS
§1. Definitions

In this article:

(1) "Department" means the Texas Department of Transportation.

(2) "Motor vehicle" has the meaning assigned by Chapter 501, Transportation Code.

(3) "State" means the State of Texas and all political subdivisions thereof.

(4) "Victim" means:

(A) a "close relative of a deceased victim," "guardian of a victim," or "victim," as those terms are defined by Article 56.01 of this code; or

(B) an individual who suffers damages as a result of another committing an offense under Section 38.04, Penal Code, in which the defendant used a motor vehicle while the defendant was in flight.

(5) "Personal property" means any property other than real property including all tangible and intangible types of property and including but not limited to copyrights, book rights, movie rights, patents, and trademarks acquired by the defendant prior to, during, and after conviction.

§2. Lien Established

(a) The victim of a criminal offense has a restitution lien to secure the amount of restitution to which the victim is entitled under the order of a court in a criminal case.

(b) The state also has a restitution lien to secure the:

(1) amount of fines or costs entered against a defendant in the judgment in a felony criminal case;

(2) amount of reimbursement for costs of:

(A) confinement ordered under Article 42.038; or

(B) notice provided under Article 62.056 or 62.201; and

(3) amount of damages incurred by the state as a result of the commission of an offense under Section 38.04, Penal Code, in which the defendant used a motor vehicle while the defendant was in flight.

§3. Perfection

(a) Except as provided by this section, a restitution lien attaches and is perfected when an affidavit to perfect the lien is filed in accordance with this article.

(b) If a lien established under this article is attached to a motor vehicle, the lien must be perfected in the manner provided by Chapter 501, Transportation Code, and the court that entered the order of restitution giving rise to the lien shall include in the order a requirement that the defendant surrender to the court evidence of current legal ownership of the motor vehicle and the title, if applicable, against which the lien attaches. A lien against a motor vehicle as provided by this article is not perfected until the defendant's title to the vehicle has been surrendered to the court and the department has issued a subsequent title that discloses on its face the fact that the vehicle is subject to a restitution lien established as provided by this article.

§4. Judgment Required

An affidavit to perfect a restitution lien may not be filed under this article until a court has ordered restitution or entered a judgment requiring the defendant to pay a fine or costs.

§5. Persons Who May File

The following persons may file an affidavit to perfect a restitution lien:

(1) the attorney representing the state in a criminal case in which a victim is determined by the court to be entitled to restitution or in which a defendant is ordered to pay fines or costs; or

(2) a victim in a criminal case determined by the court to be entitled to restitution.

§6. Affidavit

An affidavit to perfect a restitution lien must be signed by the attorney representing the state or a magistrate and must contain:

(1) the name and date of birth of the defendant whose property or other interests are subject to the lien;

(2) the residence or principal place of business of the person named in the lien, if known;

(3) the criminal proceeding giving rise to the lien, including the name of the court, the name of the case, and the court's file number for the case;

(4) the name and address of the attorney representing the state and the name of the person entitled to restitution;

(5) a statement that the notice is being filed under this article;

(6) the amount of restitution and the amount of fines and costs the defendant has been ordered to pay by the court;

(7) a statement that the amount of restitution owed at any one time may be less than the original balance and that the outstanding balance is reflected in the records of the clerk of the court hearing the criminal proceeding giving rise to the lien; and

(8) the vehicle description and vehicle identification number.

§7. Filing

(a) An affidavit to perfect a restitution lien may be filed with:

(1) the secretary of state;

(2) the department in the manner provided by Chapter 501, Transportation Code; or

(3) the county clerk of the county in which:

(A) the crime was committed;

(B) the defendant resides; or

(C) the property is located.

(b) The uniform fee for filing and indexing and for stamping a copy furnished by the state or victim to show the date and place of filing is $5.

(c) The secretary of state shall deposit the filing fee in the state treasury to the credit of the statutory filing fund solely to defray the costs of administration of this section. The department shall deposit the filing fee in the state treasury to the credit of the state highway fund to be used solely to defray the costs of administering this section.

(d) The county clerk shall immediately record the restitution lien in the judgment records of the county. The clerk shall note in the records the date and hour the lien is received.

(e) The secretary of state shall immediately file the restitution lien in the security interest and financing statement records of the secretary of state. The secretary of state shall note in the records the date and hour the lien is received.

(f) The department shall immediately file the restitution lien in the motor vehicle records of the department. The department shall note in the records the date and hour the lien is received.

(g) When a restitution lien is filed, the county clerk or secretary of state shall enter the restitution lien in an alphabetical index to the records in which the lien is filed showing:

(1) the name of the person entitled to restitution;

(2) the name of the defendant obligated to pay restitution, fines, or costs;

(3) the amount of the lien; and

(4) the name of the court that ordered restitution.

(h) A person who files an affidavit to perfect a restitution lien under this article shall notify in writing the clerk of the court entering the judgment creating the lien of all officers or entities with which the affidavit was filed.

§8. Subject Property

A restitution lien extends to:

(1) any interest of the defendant in real property whether then owned or after-acquired located in a county in which the lien is perfected by the filing of an affidavit with the county clerk;

(2) any interest of the defendant in tangible or intangible personal property whether then owned or after-acquired other than a motor vehicle if the lien is perfected by the filing of the affidavit with the secretary of state; or

(3) any interest of the defendant in a motor vehicle whether then owned or after-acquired if the lien is perfected by the filing of the affidavit with the department.

§9. Priority

The perfection of a restitution lien under this article is notice of the claim to all persons dealing with the defendant or the property identified in the affidavit perfecting the lien. Without regard to whether perfected before or after the perfection of a restitution lien filed and perfected under this article, a perfected real estate mortgage lien, a vendor's lien, a purchase money security interest, a chattel paper security interest, a lien on a motor vehicle perfected as provided by Chapter 501, Transportation Code, or a worker's lien perfected in the manner provided by law is superior and prior to a restitution lien filed and perfected under this article. Except as provided by this article, a perfected lien in favor of a victim is superior and prior to a lien perfected by the state under this article, and the perfected lien in favor of the state is superior and prior to the claim or interest of any other person, other than:

(1) a person who acquires a valid lien or security interest perfected before the perfection of the restitution lien;

(2) a bona fide purchaser who acquires an interest in the property, if personal property, before the filing of the restitution lien, to the extent that the purchaser gives value; or

(3) a bona fide purchaser for value who acquires and files for record an interest in the property, if real property, before the perfection of the restitution lien.

§10. Payment

The clerk receiving a payment from a defendant ordered to pay restitution shall make payments to the person having an interest in the restitution lien on a schedule of not less than quarterly payments as determined by the clerk or agency.

§11. Foreclosure

If a defendant fails to timely make a payment required by the order of the court entering the judgment creating the restitution lien, the person having an interest in the lien may file suit in a court of competent jurisdiction to foreclose the lien. If the defendant cures the default on or before the 20th day after the date the suit is filed and pays the person who files the suit costs of court and reasonable attorney's fees, the court may dismiss the suit without prejudice to the person. The person may refile the suit against the defendant if the defendant subsequently defaults.

§12. Expiration; Records

(a) A restitution lien expires on the 10th anniversary of the date the lien was filed or on the date the defendant satisfies the judgment creating the lien, whichever occurs first. The person having an interest in the lien may refile the lien before the date the lien expires. A lien that is refiled expires on the 10th anniversary of the date the lien was refiled or the date the defendant satisfies the judgment creating the lien, whichever occurs first.

(b) Failure to execute or foreclose the restitution lien does not cause dormancy of the lien.

(c) The clerk of the court entering the judgment creating the restitution lien shall maintain a record of the outstanding balance of restitution, fines, or costs owed. If the defendant satisfies the judgment, the clerk shall immediately execute and file for record a release of the restitution lien with all officers or entities with which the affidavit perfecting the lien was filed, as indicated by the notice received by the clerk under Section 7(h) of this article, unless a release was executed and filed by the person who filed the affidavit to perfect the lien.

(d) A partial release of a lien as to specific property may be executed by the attorney representing the state or a magistrate who signs an affidavit described by Section 6 of this article on payment of a sum determined to represent the defendant's interest in any property to which the lien may attach.

History of CCP art. 42.22: Acts 1995, 74th Leg., ch. 997, §1, eff. Sept. 1, 1996. Amended by Acts 1997, 75th Leg., ch. 1118, §1, eff. Sept. 1, 1997. Renumbered from art. 42.21 by Acts 1997, 75th Leg., ch. 165, §31.01(12), eff. Sept. 1, 1997. Amended by Acts 1999, 76th Leg., ch. 295, §2, eff. Sept. 1, 1999; Acts 2001, 77th Leg., ch. 1334, §§1, 2, eff. Sept. 1, 2001; Acts 2003, 78th Leg., ch. 1300, §2, eff. Sept. 1, 2003; Acts 2005, 79th Leg., ch. 1008, §2.02, eff. Sept. 1, 2005.

ART. 42.23. NOTIFICATION OF COURT OF FAMILY VIOLENCE CONVICTION

(a) In this article, "family violence" has the meaning assigned by Section 71.004, Family Code.

(b) If the attorney representing the state in a criminal case involving family violence learns that the defendant is subject to the jurisdiction of another court relating to an order that provides for the appointment of a conservator or that sets the terms and conditions of conservatorship or for possession of or access to a child, the attorney representing the state shall notify the court in which the defendant is being tried of the existence of the order and the identity of the court of continuing jurisdiction.

(c) On the conviction or entry of an order deferring adjudication of a defendant for an offense involving family violence, the convicting court or the court entering the order shall notify the court of continuing jurisdiction of the conviction or deferred adjudication.

History of CCP art. 42.23: Acts 2001, 77th Leg., ch. 1289, §11, eff. Sept. 1, 2001.

ART. 43.01. DISCHARGING JUDGMENT FOR FINE

(a) When the sentence against an individual defendant is for fine and costs, he shall be discharged from the same:

(1) when the amount thereof has been fully paid;

(2) when remitted by the proper authority;

(3) when he has remained in custody for the time required by law to satisfy the amount thereof; or

(4) when the defendant has discharged the amount of fines and costs in any other manner permitted by this code.

(b) When the sentence against a defendant corporation or association is for fine and costs, it shall be discharged from same:

(1) when the amount thereof has been fully paid;

(2) when the execution against the corporation or association has been fully satisfied; or

(3) when the judgment has been fully satisfied in any other manner.

History of CCP art. 43.01: Acts 1965, 59th Leg., vol. 2, ch. 722. Amended by Acts 1973, 63rd Leg., ch. 399, §2(A), eff. Jan. 1, 1974; Acts 1993, 73rd Leg., ch. 900, §5.04, eff. Sept. 1, 1993.

ART. 43.015. DEFINITIONS

E *Article 43.015 below is effective for fees imposed for the execution or processing of a warrant or capias issued for offenses committed on or after Sept. 1, 2007.*

In this chapter:

(1) "Capias" means a writ that is:

(A) issued by a court having jurisdiction of a case after judgment and sentence; and

(B) directed "To any peace officer of the State of Texas" and commanding the officer to arrest a person convicted of an offense and bring the arrested person before that court immediately or on a day or at a term stated in the writ.

(2) "Capias pro fine" means a writ that is:

(A) issued by a court having jurisdiction of a case after judgment and sentence for unpaid fines and costs; and

(B) directed "To any peace officer of the State of Texas" and commanding the officer to arrest a person convicted of an offense and bring the arrested person before that court immediately.

History of CCP art. 43.015: Acts 2007, 80th Leg., ch. 1263, §7, eff. Sept. 1, 2007.

ART. 43.02. PAYABLE IN MONEY

All recognizances, bail bonds, and undertakings of any kind, whereby a party becomes bound to pay money to the State, and all fines and forfeitures of a pecuniary character, shall be collected in the lawful money of the United States only.

History of CCP art. 43.02: Acts 1965, 59th Leg., vol. 2, ch. 722.

ART. 43.021. CAPIAS OR CAPIAS PRO FINE IN ELECTRONIC FORM

E *Article 43.021 below is effective for fees imposed for the execution or processing of a warrant or capias issued for offenses committed on or after Sept. 1, 2007.*

A capias or capias pro fine may be issued in electronic form.

History of CCP art. 43.021: Acts 2007, 80th Leg., ch. 1263, §8, eff. Sept. 1, 2007.

ART. 43.03. PAYMENT OF FINE

(a) If a defendant is sentenced to pay a fine or costs or both and the defendant defaults in payment, the court after a hearing under Subsection (d) of this article may order the defendant confined in jail until discharged as provided by law, may order the defendant to discharge the fines and costs in any other manner provided by Article 43.09 of this code, or may waive payment of the fines and costs as provided by Article 43.091. A certified copy of the judgment, sentence, and order is sufficient to authorize confinement under this subsection.

(b) A term of confinement for default in payment of fine or costs or both may not exceed the maximum term of confinement authorized for the offense for which the defendant was sentenced to pay the fine or costs or both. If a court orders a term of confinement for default in payment of fines or costs under this article at a time during which a defendant is serving another term of confinement for default or is serving a term of confinement for conviction of an offense, the term of confinement for default runs concurrently with the other term of confinement, unless the court orders the terms to run consecutively under Article 42.08 of this code.

(c) If a defendant is sentenced both to confinement and to pay a fine or costs or both, and he defaults in payment of either, a term of confinement for the default, when combined with the term of confinement already assessed, may not exceed the maximum term of confinement authorized for the offense for which the defendant was sentenced.

Ⓐ *Subsection (d) below is effective for fees imposed for the execution or processing of a warrant or capias issued for offenses committed on or after Sept. 1, 2007.*

(d) A court may not order a defendant confined under Subsection (a) of this article unless the court at a hearing makes a written determination that:

(1) the defendant is not indigent and has failed to make a good faith effort to discharge the fines and costs; or

(2) the defendant is indigent and:

(A) has failed to make a good faith effort to discharge the fines and costs under Article 43.09(f); and

(B) could have discharged the fines and costs under Article 43.09 without experiencing any undue hardship.

Subsection (d) below is effective for fees imposed for the execution or processing of a warrant or capias issued for offenses in which any element of the offense was committed before Sept. 1, 2007.

(d) A court may not order a defendant confined under Subsection (a) of this article unless the court at a hearing:

(1) determines that the defendant is not indigent or determines that the defendant wilfully refused to pay or failed to make sufficient bona fide efforts legally to acquire the resources to pay and enters that determination in writing in the court docket; and

(2) determines that no alternative method of discharging fines and costs provided by Article 43.09 of this code is appropriate for the defendant.

Ⓔ *Subsection (e) below is effective for fees imposed for the execution or processing of a warrant or capias issued for offenses committed on or after Sept. 1, 2007.*

(e) This article does not apply to a court governed by Chapter 45.

History of CCP art. 43.03: Acts 1965, 59th Leg., vol. 2, ch. 722. Amended by Acts 1971, 62nd Leg., ch. 987, §2, eff. June 15, 1971; Acts 1973, 63rd Leg., ch. 399, §2(A), eff. Jan. 1, 1974; Acts 1993, 73rd Leg., ch. 900, §5.04, eff. Sept. 1, 1993; Acts 2001, 77th Leg., ch. 1111, §1, eff. Sept. 1, 2001; Acts 2007, 80th Leg., ch. 1263, §9, eff. Sept. 1, 2007.

Ex parte Minjares, 582 S.W.2d 105, 109 (Tex.Crim. App.1978). "[A] defendant 'may not be imprisoned because he is too poor to pay his accumulated traffic fines.'"

ART. 43.04. IF DEFENDANT IS ABSENT

Ⓐ *Article 43.04 below is effective for fees imposed for the execution or processing of a warrant or capias issued for offenses committed on or after Sept. 1, 2007.*

When a judgment and sentence have been rendered against a defendant in the defendant's absence, the court may order a capias issued for the defendant's arrest. The sheriff shall execute the capias by bringing the defendant before the court or by placing the defendant in jail until the defendant can be brought before the court.

History of CCP art. 43.04: Acts 1965, 59th Leg., vol. 2, ch. 722. Amended by Acts 1971, 62nd Leg., ch. 987, §3, eff. June 15, 1971; Acts 2007, 80th Leg., ch. 1263, §10, eff. Sept. 1, 2007.

ART. 43.04. IF DEFENDANT IS ABSENT

Article 43.04 below is effective for fees imposed for the execution or processing of a warrant or capias issued for offenses in which any element of the offense was committed before Sept. 1, 2007.

When a judgment and sentence have been rendered against a defendant for a fine in his absence, the court may order a capias issued for his arrest. The sheriff shall execute the capias by bringing the defendant before the court or by placing the defendant in jail until he can be brought before the court.

ART. 43.05. CAPIAS PRO FINE SHALL RECITE

Ⓐ *Article 43.05 below is effective for fees imposed for the execution or processing of a warrant or capias issued for offenses committed on or after Sept. 1, 2007.*

(a) A capias pro fine issued for the arrest and commitment of a defendant convicted of a misdemeanor or felony, or found in contempt, the penalty for which includes a fine, shall recite the judgment and sentence and command a peace officer to immediately bring the defendant before the court.

(b) A capias pro fine authorizes a peace officer to place the defendant in jail until the business day following the date of the defendant's arrest if the defendant cannot be brought before the court immediately.

History of CCP art. 43.05: Acts 1965, 59th Leg., vol. 2, ch. 722. Amended by Acts 1971, 62nd Leg., ch. 987, §4, eff. June 15, 1971; Acts 2007, 80th Leg., ch. 1263, §11, eff. Sept. 1, 2007.

ART. 43.05. CAPIAS SHALL RECITE WHAT

Article 43.05 below is effective for fees imposed for the execution or processing of a warrant or capias issued for offenses in which any element of the offense was committed before Sept. 1, 2007.

Where such capias issues, it shall state the rendition and amount of the judgment and sentence, and command the sheriff to bring the defendant before the court or place him in jail until he can be brought before the court.

ART. 43.06. CAPIAS OR CAPIAS PRO FINE MAY ISSUE TO ANY COUNTY

A *Article 43.06 below is effective for fees imposed for the execution or processing of a warrant or capias issued for offenses committed on or after Sept. 1, 2007.*

A capias or capias pro fine may be issued to any county in the State, and shall be executed and returned as in other cases, but no bail shall be taken in such cases.

History of CCP art. 43.06: Acts 1965, 59th Leg., vol. 2, ch. 722. Amended by Acts 2007, 80th Leg., ch. 1263, §12, eff. Sept. 1, 2007.

ART. 43.06. CAPIAS MAY ISSUE TO ANY COUNTY

Article 43.06 below is effective for fees imposed for the execution or processing of a warrant or capias issued for offenses in which any element of the offense was committed before Sept. 1, 2007.

The capias provided for in this Chapter may be issued to any county in the State, and shall be executed and returned as in other cases, but no bail shall be taken in such cases.

ART. 43.07. EXECUTION FOR FINE & COSTS

A *Article 43.07 below is effective for fees imposed for the execution or processing of a warrant or capias issued for offenses committed on or after Sept. 1, 2007.*

In each case of pecuniary fine, an execution may issue for the fine and costs, though a capias pro fine was

issued for the defendant; and a capias pro fine may issue for the defendant though an execution was issued against the defendant's property. The execution shall be collected and returned as in civil actions. When the execution has been collected, the defendant shall be at once discharged; and whenever the fine and costs have been legally discharged in any way, the execution shall be returned satisfied.

History of CCP art. 43.07: Acts 1965, 59th Leg., vol. 2, ch. 722. Amended by Acts 2007, 80th Leg., ch. 1263, §13, eff. Sept. 1, 2007.

ART. 43.07. EXECUTION FOR FINE & COSTS

Article 43.07 below is effective for fees imposed for the execution or processing of a warrant or capias issued for offenses in which any element of the offense was committed before Sept. 1, 2007.

In each case of pecuniary fine, an execution may issue for the fine and costs, though a capias was issued for the defendant; and a capias may issue for the defendant though an execution was issued against his property. The execution shall be collected and returned as in civil actions. When the execution has been collected, the defendant shall be at once discharged; and whenever the fine and costs have been legally discharged in any way, the execution shall be returned satisfied.

ART. 43.08. FURTHER ENFORCEMENT OF JUDGMENT

When a defendant has been committed to jail in default of the fine and costs adjudged against him, the further enforcement of such judgment and sentence shall be in accordance with the provisions of this Code.

History of CCP art. 43.08: Acts 1965, 59th Leg., vol. 2, ch. 722.

ART. 43.09. FINE DISCHARGED

(a) When a defendant is convicted of a misdemeanor and his punishment is assessed at a pecuniary fine or is confined in a jail after conviction of a felony for which a fine is imposed, if he is unable to pay the fine and costs adjudged against him, he may for such time as will satisfy the judgment be put to work in the county jail industries program, in the workhouse, or on the county farm, or public improvements and maintenance projects of the county or a political subdivision located in whole or in part in the county, as provided in the succeeding article; or if there be no such county jail industries program, workhouse, farm, or improvements and maintenance projects, he shall be confined in jail for a sufficient length of time to discharge the full amount of fine and costs adjudged against him; rating such confinement at $50 for each day and rating such labor at $50 for each day; provided, however, that the defendant may pay the pecuniary fine assessed against him at any time while he is serving at work in the county jail industries program, in the workhouse, or on the county farm, or on the public improvements and maintenance projects of the county or a political subdivision located in whole or in part in the county, or while he is serving his jail sentence, and in such instances he shall be entitled to the credit he has earned under this subsection during the time that he has served and he shall only be required to pay his balance of the pecuniary fine assessed against him. A defendant who performs labor under this article during a day in which he is confined is entitled to both the credit for confinement and the credit for labor provided by this article.

(b) In its discretion, the court may order that for each day's confinement served by a defendant under this article, the defendant receive credit toward payment of the pecuniary fine and credit toward payment of costs adjudged against the defendant. Additionally, the court may order that the defendant receive credit under this article for each day's confinement served by the defendant as punishment for the offense.

(c) In its discretion, the court may order that a defendant serving concurrent, but not consecutive, sentences for two or more misdemeanors may, for each day served, receive credit toward the satisfaction of costs and fines imposed for each separate offense.

(d) Notwithstanding any other provision of this article, in its discretion, the court or the sheriff of the county may grant an additional two days credit for each day served to any inmate participating in an approved work program under this article or a rehabilitation, restitution, or education program.

(e) A court in a county served by a community supervision and corrections department that has an electronic monitoring program approved by the community justice assistance division of the Texas Department of Criminal Justice may require a defendant who is unable to pay a fine or costs to discharge all or part of the fine or costs by submitting to electronic monitoring. A defendant that submits to electronic monitoring under this subsection discharges fines and costs in the same manner as if the defendant were confined in county jail.

(f) A court may require a defendant who is unable to pay a fine or costs to discharge all or part of the fine or costs by performing community service.

(g) In its order requiring a defendant to participate in community service work under Subsection (f) of this article, the court must specify:

(1) the number of hours the defendant is required to work; and

(2) whether the community supervision and corrections department or a court-related services office will perform the administrative duties required by the placement of the defendant in the community service program.

(h) The court may order the defendant to perform community service work under Subsection (f) of this article only for a governmental entity or a nonprofit organization that provides services to the general public that enhance social welfare and the general well-being of the community. A governmental entity or nonprofit organization that accepts a defendant under Subsection (f) of this article to perform community service must agree to supervise the defendant in the performance of the defendant's work and report on the defendant's work to the district probation department or court-related services office.

(i) The court may require bail of a defendant to ensure the defendant's faithful performance of community service under Subsection (f) of this article and may attach conditions to the bail as it determines are proper.

(j) A court may not order a defendant to perform more than 16 hours per week of community service under Subsection (f) of this article unless the court determines that requiring the defendant to work additional hours does not work a hardship on the defendant or the defendant's dependents.

(k) A defendant is considered to have discharged $100 of fines or costs for each eight hours of community service performed under Subsection (f) of this article.

☠ *Subsection (l) below was amended by Acts 1993, 73rd Leg., ch. 578, §2, enacted May 30, 1993, eff. June 11, 1993, without reference to the conflicting deletion made by Acts 1993, 73rd Leg., ch. 900, §5.04, enacted May 31, 1993, eff. Sept. 1, 1993. For resolving conflicts, see p. V.*

(*l*) A sheriff, employee of a sheriff's department, county commissioner, county employee, county judge, an employee of a community corrections and supervision department, restitution center, or officer or employee of a political subdivision other than a county is not liable for damages arising from an act or failure to act in connection with manual labor performed by an inmate pursuant to this article if the act or failure to act:

(1) was performed pursuant to confinement or other court order; and

(2) was not intentional, wilfully or wantonly negligent, or performed with conscious indifference or reckless disregard for the safety of others.

(m) Repealed by Acts 2007, 80th Leg., ch. 1263, §22, eff. Sept. 1, 2007.

Subsection (m) below is effective for fees imposed for the execution or processing of a warrant or capias issued for offenses in which any element of the offense was committed before Sept. 1, 2007.

(m) Fines and costs imposed by a municipal court, regardless of whether the court is a court of record, may be discharged in the manner provided by Subsection (f) of this article. A community supervision and corrections department or a court-related services office may provide the administrative duties and other services necessary for the placement in programs under this article of a defendant convicted in a municipal court, regardless of whether the municipal court is a court of record.

E *Subsection (n) below is effective for fees imposed for the execution or processing of a warrant or capias issued for offenses committed on or after Sept. 1, 2007.*

(n) This article does not apply to a court governed by Chapter 45.

History of CCP art. 43.09: Acts 1965, 59th Leg., vol. 2, ch. 722. Amended by Acts 1981, 67th Leg., ch. 143, §1, eff. May 14, 1981; Acts 1987, 70th Leg., ch. 347, §1, eff. Sept. 1, 1987; Acts 1989, 71st Leg., ch. 753, §1 (eff. Sept. 1, 1989), ch. 785, §4.13 (eff. Sept. 1, 1989), ch. 1040, §§3, 4 (eff. Aug. 28, 1989); Acts 1991, 72nd Leg., ch. 16, §4.06 (eff. Aug. 26, 1991), ch. 900, §1 (eff. Aug. 26, 1991); Acts 1993, 73rd Leg., ch. 414, §1 (eff. June 6, 1993), ch. 578, §2 (eff. June 11, 1993), ch. 900, §5.04 (eff. Sept. 1, 1993); Acts 1999, 76th Leg., ch. 1545, §3, eff. Sept. 1, 1999; Acts 2007, 80th Leg., ch. 1263, §§14, 22, eff. Sept. 1, 2007.

ART. 43.091. WAIVER OF PAYMENT OF FINES & COSTS FOR INDIGENT DEFENDANTS

A *Article 43.091 below is effective for fees imposed for the execution or processing of a warrant or capias issued for offenses committed on or after Sept. 1, 2007.*

A court may waive payment of a fine or cost imposed on a defendant who defaults in payment if the court determines that:

(1) the defendant is indigent; and

(2) each alternative method of discharging the fine or cost under Article 43.09 would impose an undue hardship on the defendant.

History of CCP art. 43.091: Acts 2001, 77th Leg., ch. 1111, §2, eff. Sept. 1, 2001. Amended by Acts 2007, 80th Leg., ch. 1263, §15, eff. Sept. 1, 2007.

ART. 43.091. WAIVER OF PAYMENT OF FINES & COSTS FOR INDIGENT DEFENDANTS IN JUSTICE OR MUNICIPAL COURT

Article 43.091 below is effective for fees imposed for the execution or processing of a warrant or capias issued for offenses in which any element of the offense was committed before Sept. 1, 2007.

A municipal court, regardless of whether the court is a court of record, or a justice court may waive payment of a fine or cost imposed on a defendant who defaults in payment if the court determines that:

(1) the defendant is indigent; and

(2) each alternative method of discharging the fine or cost under Article 43.09 would impose an undue hardship on the defendant.

ART. 43.10. MANUAL LABOR

Where the punishment assessed in a conviction for misdemeanor is confinement in jail for more than one day, or where in such conviction the punishment is assessed only at a pecuniary fine and the party so convicted is unable to pay the fine and costs adjudged against him, or where the party is sentenced to jail for a felony or is confined in jail after conviction of a felony, the party convicted shall be required to work in the county jail industries program or shall be required to do manual labor in accordance with the provisions of this article under the following rules and regulations:

1. Each commissioners court may provide for the erection of a workhouse and the establishment of a county farm in connection therewith for the purpose of utilizing the labor of said parties so convicted;

2. Such farms and workhouses shall be under the control and management of the sheriff, and the sheriff may adopt such rules and regulations not inconsistent with the rules and regulations of the Commission on Jail Standards and with the laws as the sheriff deems necessary;

3. Such overseers and guards may be employed by the sheriff under the authority of the commissioners

court as may be necessary to prevent escapes and to enforce such labor, and they shall be paid out of the county treasury such compensation as the commissioners court may prescribe;

4. They shall be put to labor upon public works and maintenance projects, including public works and maintenance projects for a political subdivision located in whole or in part in the county. They may also be put to labor upon maintenance projects for a cemetery that the commissioners court uses public funds, county employees, or county equipment to maintain under Section 713.028, Health and Safety Code. They may also be put to labor providing maintenance and related services to a nonprofit organization that qualifies for a tax exemption under Section 501(a), Internal Revenue Code of 1986, as an organization described by Section 501(c)(3) of that code, and is organized as a nonprofit corporation under the Texas Non-Profit Corporation Act (Article 1396-1.01 et seq., Vernon's Texas Civil Statutes), provided that, at the sheriff's request, the commissioners court determines that the nonprofit organization provides a public service to the county or to a political subdivision located in whole or in part in the county;

5. One who from age, disease, or other physical or mental disability is unable to do manual labor shall not be required to work. His inability to do manual labor may be determined by a physician appointed for that purpose by the county judge or the commissioners court, who shall be paid for such service such compensation as said court may allow; and

6. For each day of manual labor, in addition to any other credits allowed by law, a defendant is entitled to have one day deducted from each sentence he is serving. The deduction authorized by this article, when combined with the deduction required by Article 42.10 of this code, may not exceed two-thirds (2/3) of the sentence.

History of CCP art. 43.10: Acts 1965, 59th Leg., vol. 2, ch. 722. Amended by Acts 1981, 67th Leg., ch. 708, §1, eff. Aug. 31, 1981; Acts 1989, 71st Leg., ch. 753, §2 (eff. Sept. 1, 1989), ch. 785, §4.14 (eff. Sept. 1, 1989); Acts 1991, 72nd Leg., ch. 900, §2 (eff. Aug. 26, 1991), 2nd C.S., ch. 10, §14.09 (eff. Oct. 1, 1991); Acts 1993, 73rd Leg., ch. 578, §3 (eff. June 11, 1993), ch. 900, §5.04 (eff. Sept. 1, 1993); Acts 1995, 74th Leg., ch. 76, §3.19 (eff. Sept. 1, 1995), ch. 321, §3.015 (eff. Sept. 1, 1995); Acts 2005, 79th Leg., ch. 853, §2 (eff. Sept. 1, 2005), ch. 1187, §1, (eff. June 18, 2005).

ANNOTATIONS

Kopeski v. Martin, 629 S.W.2d 743, 745 (Tex.Crim. App.1982). Article 43.10(6) "creates an entitlement to credits against a misdemeanor sentence to jail...."

ART. 43.101. VOLUNTARY WORK

(a) A defendant confined in county jail awaiting trial or a defendant confined in county jail after conviction of a felony or revocation of community supervision, parole, or mandatory supervision and awaiting transfer to the institutional division of the Texas Department of Criminal Justice may volunteer to participate in any work program operated by the sheriff that uses the labor of convicted defendants.

(b) The sheriff may accept a defendant as a volunteer under Subsection (a) of this section if the defendant is not awaiting trial for an offense involving violence or is not awaiting transfer to the institutional division of the Texas Department of Criminal Justice after conviction of a felony involving violence, and if the sheriff determines that the inmate has not engaged previously in violent conduct and does not pose a security risk to the general public if allowed to participate in the work program.

(c) A defendant participating in a work program under this section is not an employee for the purposes of Chapter 501 or 504, Labor Code.

History of CCP art. 43.101: Acts 1989, 71st Leg., ch. 753, §3, eff. Sept. 1, 1989. Amended by Acts 1993, 73rd Leg., ch. 86, §1 (eff. Aug. 30, 1993), ch. 900, §5.04 (eff. Sept. 1, 1993); Acts 1995, 74th Leg., ch. 76, §3.20, eff. Sept. 1, 1995.

ART. 43.11. AUTHORITY FOR CONFINEMENT

When, by the judgment and sentence of the court, a defendant is to be confined in jail, a certified copy of such judgment and sentence shall be sufficient authority for the sheriff to place such defendant in jail.

History of CCP art. 43.11: Acts 1965, 59th Leg., vol. 2, ch. 722. Amended by Acts 1993, 73rd Leg., ch. 900, §5.04, eff. Sept. 1, 1993.

ART. 43.12. REPEALED
Repealed by Acts 2007, 80th Leg., ch. 1263, §22, eff. Sept. 1, 2007.

ART. 43.12. CAPIAS FOR CONFINEMENT

Article 43.12 below is effective for fees imposed for the execution or processing of a warrant or capias issued for offenses in which any element of the offense was committed before Sept. 1, 2007.

A capias issued for the arrest and commitment of one convicted of a misdemeanor, the penalty of which or any part thereof is a fine, shall recite the judgment and sentence and command the sheriff to immediately bring the defendant before the court; and this writ shall be sufficient to authorize the sheriff to place the defendant in jail until the defendant appears before the court.

History of CCP art. 43.12: Acts 1965, 59th Leg., vol. 2, ch. 722. Amended by Acts 1993, 73rd Leg., ch. 900, §5.04, eff. Sept. 1, 1993.

ART. 43.13. DISCHARGE OF DEFENDANT

(a) A defendant who has remained in jail the length of time required by the judgment and sentence shall be discharged. The sheriff shall return the copy of the judgment and sentence, or the capias under which the defendant was imprisoned, to the proper court, stating how it was executed.

(b) A defendant convicted of a misdemeanor and sentenced to a term of confinement of more than 30 days discharges the defendant's sentence at any time between the hours of 6 a.m. and 7 p.m. on the day of discharge.

History of CCP art. 43.13: Acts 1965, 59th Leg., vol. 2, ch. 722. Amended by Acts 1997, 75th Leg., ch. 714, §1, eff. Sept. 1, 1997.

ART. 43.131. IMMUNITIES

(a) An individual listed in Subsection (c) of this article and the governmental entity that the individual serves as an officer or employee are not liable for damages arising from an act or failure to act by the individual or governmental entity in connection with a community service program or work program established under this chapter if the act or failure to act:

(1) was performed pursuant to a court order or was otherwise performed in an official capacity; and

(2) was not performed with conscious indifference for the safety of others.

(b) Chapter 101, Civil Practice and Remedies Code, does not apply to a claim based on an act or a failure to act of an individual listed in Subsection (c) of this article or a governmental entity the officer serves as an officer or employee if the act or failure to act is in connection with a program described by Subsection (a) of this article.

(c) This article applies to:

(1) a director or employee of a community supervision and corrections department or a community corrections facility;

(2) a sheriff or employee of a sheriff's department;

(3) a county judge, county commissioner, or county employee;

(4) an officer or employee of a state agency; or

(5) an officer or employee of a political subdivision other than a county.

History of CCP art. 43.131: Acts 1993, 73rd Leg., ch. 900, §5.04, eff. Sept. 1, 1993.

ART. 43.14. EXECUTION OF CONVICT

Whenever the sentence of death is pronounced against a convict, the sentence shall be executed at any time after the hour of 6 p.m. on the day set for the execution, by intravenous injection of a substance or substances in a lethal quantity sufficient to cause death and until such convict is dead, such execution procedure to be determined and supervised by the Director of the institutional division of the Texas Department of Criminal Justice.

History of CCP art. 43.14: Acts 1965, 59th Leg., vol. 2, ch. 722. Amended by Acts 1977, 65th Leg., ch. 138, §1, eff. Aug. 29, 1977; Acts 1981, 67th Leg., ch. 291, §120, eff. Sept. 1, 1981; Acts 1991, 72nd Leg., ch. 652, §11, eff. Sept. 1, 1991; Acts 1995, 74th Leg., ch. 319, §3, eff. Sept. 1, 1995.

ANNOTATIONS

Ex parte Granviel, 561 S.W.2d 503, 513 (Tex.Crim. App.1978). "[W]e cannot conclude that failure to specify the exact substances and the procedures to be used render the statute unconstitutionally vague. The statute here, unlike penal statutes, was not intended to give fair notice of what specific behavior or elements constitutes a criminal offense. ... The context of the statute is a public statement of the general manner of execution. In this sense the statute is sufficiently definite."

ART. 43.141. SCHEDULING OF EXECUTION DATE; WITHDRAWAL; MODIFICATION

(a) If an initial application under Article 11.071 is timely filed, the convicting court may not set an execution date before:

(1) the court of criminal appeals denies relief; or

(2) if the case is filed and set for submission, the court of criminal appeals issues a mandate.

(b) If an original application is not timely filed under Article 11.071 or good cause is not shown for an untimely application under Article 11.071, the convicting court may set an execution date.

(c) The first execution date may not be earlier than the 91st day after the date the convicting court enters the order setting the execution date. A subsequent execution date may not be earlier than the 31st day after the date the convicting court enters the order setting the execution date.

(d) The convicting court may modify or withdraw the order of the court setting a date for execution in a death penalty case if the court determines that additional proceedings are necessary on:

(1) a subsequent or untimely application for a writ of habeas corpus filed under Article 11.071; or

(2) a motion for forensic testing of DNA evidence submitted under Chapter 64.

(e) If the convicting court withdraws the order of the court setting the execution date, the court shall recall the warrant of execution. If the court modifies the order of the court setting the execution date, the court shall recall the previous warrant of execution, and the clerk of the court shall issue a new warrant.

History of CCP art. 43.141: Acts 1995, 74th Leg., ch. 319, §4, eff. Sept. 1, 1995. Amended by Acts 2003, 78th Leg., ch. 13, §6, eff. Sept. 1, 2003.

ART. 43.15. WARRANT OF EXECUTION

Whenever any person is sentenced to death, the clerk of the court in which the sentence is pronounced, shall within ten days after the court enters its order setting the date for execution, issue a warrant under the seal of the court for the execution of the sentence of death, which shall recite the fact of conviction, setting forth specifically the offense, the judgment of the court, the time fixed for his execution, and directed to the Director of the Department of Corrections at Huntsville, Texas, commanding him to proceed, at the time and place named in the order of execution, to carry the same into execution, as provided in the preceding Article, and shall deliver such warrant to the sheriff of the county in which such judgment of conviction was had, to be by him delivered to the said Director of the Department of Corrections, together with the condemned person if he has not previously been so delivered.

History of CCP art. 43.15: Acts 1965, 59th Leg., vol. 2, ch. 722. Amended by Acts 1981, 67th Leg., ch. 291, §121, eff. Sept. 1, 1981.

ART. 43.16. TAKEN TO DEPARTMENT OF CORRECTIONS

Immediately upon the receipt of such warrant, the sheriff shall transport such condemned person to the Director of the Department of Corrections, if he has not already been so delivered, and shall deliver him and the warrant aforesaid into the hands of the Director of the

Department of Corrections and shall take from the Director of the Department of Corrections his receipt for such person and such warrant, which receipt the sheriff shall return to the office of the clerk of the court where the judgment of death was rendered. For his services, the sheriff shall be entitled to the same compensation as is now allowed by law to sheriffs for removing or conveying prisoners under the provisions of Section 4 of Article 1029 or 1030 of the Code of Criminal Procedure of 1925, as amended.

History of CCP art. 43.16: Acts 1965, 59th Leg., vol. 2, ch. 722. Amended by Acts 1981, 67th Leg., ch. 291, §122, eff. Sept. 1, 1981.

ART. 43.17. VISITORS

Upon the receipt of such condemned person by the Director of the Department of Corrections, the condemned person shall be confined therein until the time for his or her execution arrives, and while so confined, all persons outside of said prison shall be denied access to him or her, except his or her physician, lawyer, and clergyperson, who shall be admitted to see him or her when necessary for his or her health or for the transaction of business, and the relatives and friends of the condemned person, who shall be admitted to see and converse with him or her at all proper times, under such reasonable rules and regulations as may be made by the Board of Directors of the Department of Corrections.

History of CCP art. 43.17: Acts 1965, 59th Leg., vol. 2, ch. 722. Amended by Acts 1979, 66th Leg., p. 1181; ch. 572, §1, eff. Aug. 27, 1979.

ART. 43.18. EXECUTIONER

The Director of the Texas Department of Corrections, shall designate an executioner to carry out the death penalty provided by law.

History of CCP art. 43.18: Acts 1965, 59th Leg., vol. 2, ch. 722. Amended by Acts 1975, 64th Leg., ch. 341, §6, eff. June 19, 1975; Acts 1977, 65th Leg., ch. 138, §2, eff. Aug. 29, 1977.

ART. 43.19. PLACE OF EXECUTION

The execution shall take place at a location designated by the Texas Department of Corrections in a room arranged for that purpose.

History of CCP art. 43.19: Acts 1965, 59th Leg., vol. 2, ch. 722. Amended by Acts 1985, 69th Leg., ch. 250, §1, eff. Aug. 26, 1985.

ART. 43.20. PRESENT AT EXECUTION

The following persons may be present at the execution: the executioner, and such persons as may be necessary to assist him in conducting the execution; the

Board of Directors of the Department of Corrections, two physicians, including the prison physician, the spiritual advisor of the condemned, the chaplains of the Department of Corrections, the county judge and sheriff of the county in which the Department of Corrections is situated, and any of the relatives or friends of the condemned person that he may request, not exceeding five in number, shall be admitted. No convict shall be permitted by the prison authorities to witness the execution.

History of CCP art. 43.20: Acts 1965, 59th Leg., vol. 2, ch. 722.

ART. 43.21. ESCAPE AFTER SENTENCE

If the condemned escape after sentence and before his delivery to the Director of the Department of Corrections, and be not rearrested until after the time fixed for execution, any person may arrest and commit him to the jail of the county in which he was sentenced; and thereupon the court by whom the condemned was sentenced; either in term-time or vacation, on notice of such arrest being given by the sheriff, shall again appoint a time for the execution, not less than thirty days from such appointment, which appointment shall be by the clerk of said court immediately certified to the Director of the Department of Corrections and such clerk shall place such certificate in the hands of the sheriff, who shall deliver the same, together with the warrant aforesaid and the condemned person to the Director of the Department of Corrections, who shall receipt to the sheriff for the same and proceed at the appointed time to carry the sentence of death into execution as hereinabove provided.

History of CCP art. 43.21: Acts 1965, 59th Leg., vol. 2, ch. 722.

ART. 43.22. ESCAPE FROM DEPARTMENT OF CORRECTIONS

If the condemned person escapes after his delivery to the Director of the Department of Corrections, and is not retaken before the time appointed for his execution, any person may arrest and commit him to the Director of the Department of Corrections whereupon the Director of the Department of Corrections shall certify the fact of his escape and recapture to the court in which sentence was passed; and the court, either in term-time or vacation, shall again appoint a time for the execution which shall not be less than thirty days from the date of such appointment; and thereupon the clerk of such court shall certify such appointment to the

Director of the Department of Corrections, who shall proceed at the time so appointed to execute the condemned, as hereinabove provided. The sheriff or other officer or other person performing any service under this and the preceding Article shall receive the same compensation as is provided for similar services under the provisions of Articles 1029 or 1030 of the Code of Criminal Procedure of 1925, as amended. If for any reason execution is delayed beyond the date set, then the court which originally sentenced the defendant may set a later date for execution.

History of CCP art. 43.22: Acts 1965, 59th Leg., vol. 2, ch. 722.

ART. 43.23. RETURN OF DIRECTOR

When the execution of sentence is suspended or respited to another date, same shall be noted on the warrant and on the arrival of such date, the Director of the Department of Corrections shall proceed with such execution; and in case of death of any condemned person before the time for his execution arrives, or if he should be pardoned or his sentence commuted by the Governor, no execution shall be had; but in such cases, as well as when the sentence is executed, the Director of the Department of Corrections shall return the warrant and certificate with a statement of any such act and his proceedings endorsed thereon, together with a statement showing what disposition was made of the dead body of the convict, to the clerk of the court in which the sentence was passed, who shall record the warrant and return in the minutes of the court.

History of CCP art. 43.23: Acts 1965, 59th Leg., vol. 2, ch. 722.

ART. 43.24. TREATMENT OF CONDEMNED

No torture, or ill treatment, or unnecessary pain, shall be inflicted upon a prisoner to be executed under the sentence of the law.

History of CCP art. 43.24: Acts 1965, 59th Leg., vol. 2, ch. 722.

ART. 43.25. BODY OF CONVICT

The body of a convict who has been legally executed shall be embalmed immediately and so directed by the Director of the Department of Corrections. If the body is not demanded or requested by a relative or bona fide friend within forty-eight hours after execution then it shall be delivered to the Anatomical Board of the State of Texas, if requested by the Board. If the body is requested by a relative, bona fide friend, or the Anatomical Board of the State of Texas, such recipient shall pay a fee of not to exceed twenty-five dollars to the mortician for his services in embalming the body for which the mortician shall issue to the recipient a written receipt. When such receipt is delivered to the Director of the Department of Corrections, the body of the deceased shall be delivered to the party named in the receipt or his authorized agent. If the body is not delivered to a relative, bona fide friend, or the Anatomical Board of the State of Texas, the Director of the Department of Corrections shall cause the body to be decently buried, and the fee for embalming shall be paid by the county in which the indictment which resulted in conviction was found.

History of CCP art. 43.25: Acts 1965, 59th Leg., vol. 2, ch. 722.

ART. 43.26. PREVENTING RESCUE

The sheriff may, when he supposes there will be a necessity, order such number of citizens of his county, or request any military or militia company, to aid in preventing the rescue of a prisoner.

History of CCP art. 43.26: Acts 1965, 59th Leg., vol. 2, ch. 722.

CHAPTER 44. APPEAL & WRIT OF ERROR

ART. 44.01. APPEAL BY STATE

(a) The state is entitled to appeal an order of a court in a criminal case if the order:

(1) dismisses an indictment, information, or complaint or any portion of an indictment, information, or complaint;

(2) arrests or modifies a judgment;

(3) grants a new trial;

(4) sustains a claim of former jeopardy;

(5) grants a motion to suppress evidence, a confession, or an admission, if jeopardy has not attached in the case and if the prosecuting attorney certifies to the trial court that the appeal is not taken for the purpose of delay and that the evidence, confession, or admission is of substantial importance in the case; or

(6) is issued under Chapter 64.

(b) The state is entitled to appeal a sentence in a case on the ground that the sentence is illegal.

(c) The state is entitled to appeal a ruling on a question of law if the defendant is convicted in the case and appeals the judgment.

 Subsection (d) below is effective for appeals of orders, rulings, or sentences entered on or after Sept. 1, 2007.

(d) The prosecuting attorney may not make an appeal under Subsection (a) or (b) of this article later than the 20th day after the date on which the order, ruling, or sentence to be appealed is entered by the court.

Subsection (d) below is effective for appeals of orders, rulings, or sentences entered before Sept. 1, 2007.

(d) The prosecuting attorney may not make an appeal under Subsection (a) or (b) of this article later than the 15th day after the date on which the order, ruling, or sentence to be appealed is entered by the court.

(e) The state is entitled to a stay in the proceedings pending the disposition of an appeal under Subsection (a) or (b) of this article.

(f) The court of appeals shall give precedence in its docket to an appeal filed under Subsection (a) or (b) of this article. The state shall pay all costs of appeal under Subsection (a) or (b) of this article, other than the cost of attorney's fees for the defendant.

(g) If the state appeals pursuant to this article and the defendant is on bail, he shall be permitted to remain at large on the existing bail. If the defendant is in custody, he is entitled to reasonable bail, as provided by law, unless the appeal is from an order which would terminate the prosecution, in which event the defendant is entitled to release on personal bond.

(h) The Texas Rules of Appellate Procedure apply to a petition by the state to the Court of Criminal Appeals for review of a decision of a court of appeals in a criminal case.

(i) In this article, "prosecuting attorney" means the county attorney, district attorney, or criminal district attorney who has the primary responsibility of prosecuting cases in the court hearing the case and does not include an assistant prosecuting attorney.

(j) Nothing in this article is to interfere with the defendant's right to appeal under the procedures of Article 44.02 of this code. The defendant's right to appeal under Article 44.02 may be prosecuted by the defendant where the punishment assessed is in accordance with Subsection (a), Section 3d, Article 42.12 of this code, as well as any other punishment assessed in compliance with Article 44.02 of this code.

(k) The state is entitled to appeal an order granting relief to an applicant for a writ of habeas corpus under Article 11.072.

(l) The state is entitled to appeal an order entered under:

(1) Subchapter G or H, Chapter 62, that exempts a person from complying with the requirements of Chapter 62; and

(2) Subchapter I, Chapter 62, that terminates a person's obligation to register under Chapter 62.

History of CCP art. 44.01: Acts 1965, 59th Leg., vol. 2, ch. 722. Amended by Acts 1981, 67th Leg., ch. 291, §123, eff. Sept. 1, 1981; Acts 1987, 70th Leg., ch. 382, §1, eff. Nov. 3, 1987; Acts 2003, 78th Leg., ch. 13, §7 (eff. Sept. 1, 2003), ch. 587, §2 (eff. June 20, 2003); Acts 2005, 79th Leg., ch. 1008, §1.04, eff. Sept. 1, 2005; Acts 2007, 80th Leg., ch. 1038, §2, eff. Sept. 1, 2007.

ANNOTATIONS

Generally

State v. Blankenship, 146 S.W.3d 218, 220 (Tex. Crim.App.2004). "[W]e decide that the timely-made assertion in the City's amended notice of appeal that the 'County Attorney has consented to the City Attorney prosecuting this appeal' is 'in some fashion' a written express personal authorization by the County Attorney of this specific notice of appeal in this particular case." Held: Although City Attorney prosecuted appeal, County Attorney "made" appeal, and appeal was timely filed.

State ex rel. Healey v. McMeans, 884 S.W.2d 772, 774 (Tex.Crim.App.1994). "[M]andamus may not be used to give the State a right to appeal that was not granted by the Legislature in [Art. 44.01]. But the limitations in Article 44.01 on the State's right to appeal are no impediment to the State's use of mandamus to correct judicial action *that is clearly contrary to well-settled law*, whether that law is derived from a statute, rule, or opinion of a court."

State v. Cox, 235 S.W.3d 283, 285 (Tex.App.—Fort Worth 2007, no pet.). "[W]e … hold that a docket sheet entry does not constitute a written order for the purpose of appealing the granting of a motion to suppress under article 44.01."

Art. 44.01(a)

Collins v. State, 240 S.W.3d 925, 928 (Tex.Crim. App.2007). "[A]n order that modifies the amount of back-time received by a defendant via an improperly granted judgment nunc pro tunc may be appealed by the State."

State v. Stanley, 201 S.W.3d 754, 755 (Tex.Crim. App.2006). "These consolidated cases present the question whether the State may appeal an order dismissing a prosecution on the grounds that it proceeds upon an unconstitutional ordinance if the trial court delays its ruling until after both parties have submitted their evidence at the trial on the merits, but before the issue of guilt or innocence has been resolved. We conclude that the State may appeal such an order. *At 758:* [Article 44.01(a)(1)] entitles the State to appeal any order, short of an acquittal, which has the effect of terminating the prosecution, regardless of how the trial court characterizes its order. [¶] We also reject the implicit assumption of the court of appeals majority that, in order to be appealable, an order dismissing must come before the attachment of jeopardy." *See also* **State v. Garrett**, 824 S.W.2d 181, 183 (Tex.Crim.App.1992); *State v. Eaves*, 800 S.W.2d 220, 220 (Tex.Crim.App. 1990).

State v. Johnson, 175 S.W.3d 766, 767 (Tex. Crim.App.2005). "The issue … is whether Article 44.01(a)(5) requires the certification to be in the notice of appeal. Article 44.01(a)(5) does not require this."

State v. Morgan, 160 S.W.3d 1, 5 (Tex.Crim.App. 2004). "Subsection (a)(5) allows the State to file an interlocutory appeal from a trial court's order granting a motion to suppress evidence. But the statute specifies conditions to such an appeal. The prosecutor must include a certification that the appeal is not taken for purposes of delay. [¶] There is no certification requirement under any of the other subsections, including subsection (a)(1). So an appeal under subsection (a)(1) is not to be utilized as an interlocutory appeal. It is supposed to be used only if the prosecution is terminated."

State v. Gutierrez, 129 S.W.3d 113, 114 (Tex.Crim. App.2004). "Article 44.01(a)(2) ... allows the State to appeal from ... an order that reduces a defendant's sentence, and that is signed after the trial court's plenary jurisdiction has expired."

State v. Medrano, 67 S.W.3d 892, 903 (Tex.Crim. App.2002). "[A]rticle 44.01(a)(5) is not limited solely to pretrial rulings that suppress 'illegally obtained' evidence. The State may appeal an adverse ruling on *any* pretrial motion to suppress evidence as long as the other requirements of the statute are met." *See also State v. Cowsert*, 207 S.W.3d 347, 350-51 (Tex.Crim. App.2006).

State v. Riewe, 13 S.W.3d 408, 409 (Tex.Crim.App. 2000). "We must consider whether the lack of timely certifications deprived the court of appeals of jurisdiction over the case, and if so, whether the amended notice of appeal was sufficient to retroactively confer jurisdiction on the appellate court. We conclude that the certification requirement is jurisdictional, and that jurisdiction cannot be retroactively obtained."

State v. Gonzalez, 855 S.W.2d 692, 695 (Tex.Crim. App.1993). "When the State acquired the right to appeal under [CCP] art. 44.01(a)(3), the State acquired the corresponding duty to provide the appellate court a record subject to meaningful appellate review. *At 696:* [A]buse of discretion is the proper standard of appellate review under art. 44.01(a)(3)."

State v. Doyle, 140 S.W.3d 890, 892 (Tex.App.— Corpus Christi 2004, pet. ref'd). "We conclude that the trial court's order granting a mistrial is functionally indistinguishable from a grant of a new trial. Accordingly, the State has the right of appeal." *See also State v. Boyd*, 202 S.W.3d 393, 400 (Tex.App.—Dallas 2006, pet. ref'd).

State v. Fowler, 97 S.W.3d 721, 721-22 (Tex.App.— Waco 2003, no pet.). "The State may bring an interlocutory appeal from an adverse probable cause determination [in a habeas proceeding] only when that decision is made in an order granting a motion to suppress evidence."

Art. 44.01(b)

State v. Kersh, 127 S.W.3d 775, 776 (Tex.Crim.App. 2004). "Because the meaning of 'sentence' under [CCP arts. 42.02 and 44.01(b)] includes enhancement allegations, we hold that the State may appeal a trial court's failure to consider them and that the court of appeals did not err in taking jurisdiction of the State's appeal in this case. *At 777:* [A] deadly-weapon finding is not part of the sentence, and ... the State is not entitled to appeal an omission of one from a trial court's judgment."

Mizell v. State, 119 S.W.3d 804, 805 (Tex.Crim.App. 2003). "We ... address the question of whether the State may bring a cross-point in its appellate brief arguing that the defendant's sentence is illegal when the defendant appeals his conviction but the State does not file its own notice of appeal. Because we hold that any court—trial or appellate—may notice, on its own, an illegal sentence and rectify that error, the State was not obligated to file a notice of appeal before the court of appeals could address that issue. *At 806:* A sentence that is outside the maximum or minimum range of punishment is unauthorized by law and therefore illegal."

State v. Ross, 953 S.W.2d 748, 750 (Tex.Crim.App. 1997). "[O]nce the court of appeals determines that the State is appealing a sentence and not something else, jurisdiction is properly invoked and questions of legality can be addressed on their merits. This, [is] because art. 44.01(b) provides for the appeal of a sentence not *when* a sentence is illegal, but *on the ground* that it is illegal. [¶] [A] sentence is nothing more than the portion of the judgment setting out the terms of punishment. *At 752:* [A] deadly weapon finding is not part of a sentence. [¶] The court of appeals therefore did not err in dismissing this appeal for want of jurisdiction...." *See also State v. Baize*, 981 S.W.2d 204, 206 (Tex.Crim.App.1998).

State v. Wilcox, 993 S.W.2d 848, 850 (Tex.App.— Austin 1999), *pet. dism'd*, 18 S.W.3d 636 (Tex.Crim.App. 2000). "Because an order deferring adjudication does not constitute or contain a sentence, Art. 44.01(b) does not apply. As a consequence, the State is not entitled to appeal, and we are without jurisdiction."

Art. 44.01(c)

Strong v. State, 87 S.W.3d 206, 212-13 (Tex.App.—Dallas 2002, pet. ref'd). Held: The State must file a TRAP 25.2(a) notice of appeal when it appeals under CCP art. 44.01(c).

Art. 44.01(d)

State v. Muller, 829 S.W.2d 805, 811-12 (Tex.Crim. App.1992). "Article 44.01 requires the elected 'prosecuting attorney' (and not his assistant) to 'make' the State's notice of appeal, within the prescribed fifteen-day time period, either through the physical act of signing the notice or by personally and expressly authorizing an assistant to file a specific notice of appeal on his behalf."

State v. Shaw, 4 S.W.3d 875, 878 (Tex.App.—Dallas 1999, no pet.). "[A] docket sheet entry does not constitute a written order for purposes of a State's appeal under Article 44.01."

State v. Rollins, 4 S.W.3d 453, 455 (Tex.App.—Austin 1999, no pet.). "Although the district attorney was proceeding in the good faith belief that no orders of dismissal had been signed, we may not disregard the clear terms of Article 44.01(d) and extend the time for perfecting appeal. The State's motions for extensions of time to file notice of appeal were overruled. Because the State did not file its notices of appeal within 15 days following the signing of the dismissal orders, we have no alternative but to dismiss the appeals for want of jurisdiction."

State v. Gobel, 988 S.W.2d 852, 854 (Tex.App.—Tyler 1999, no pet.). "Although on Dec. 2, 1998, the trial court signed a Nunc Pro Tunc Order, that order made no substantive change in the original Order of Dismissal of Nov. 5, 1998, and thus created no new, separate right to appeal under Art. 44.01(a). Consequently, ... the State was required to perfect an appeal on or before Nov. 20, 1998."

State v. Acosta, 948 S.W.2d 555, 556 (Tex.App.—Waco 1997, no pet.). "[T]he timetable for [the State's] notice of appeal begins on the day of the signing of the appealable order, e.g., the order ... suppressing evidence...."

Art. 44.01(f)

State v. Alley, 158 S.W.3d 485, 488 (Tex.Crim.App. 2005). CCP art. 44.01(a) "allows the State to appeal certain orders. [CCP arts.] 4.08 and 45.042 establish that appeals from a justice court must be taken to the county court. [CCP arts.] 44.17 and 45.042 specify that an appeal to county court shall be conducted *de novo*. If the State takes an appeal after such a *de novo* proceeding in the county court, Article 44.01(f) means that that appeal shall be given precedence by the court of appeals." Held: The State must initially appeal disposition in the justice courts to the county courts, before proceeding to the court of appeals.

ART. 44.02. DEFENDANT MAY APPEAL

A defendant in any criminal action has the right of appeal under the rules hereinafter prescribed, provided, however, before the defendant who has been convicted upon either his plea of guilty or plea of nolo contendere before the court and the court, upon the election of the defendant, assesses punishment and the punishment does not exceed the punishment recommended by the prosecutor and agreed to by the defendant and his attorney may prosecute his appeal, he must have permission of the trial court, except on those matters which have been raised by written motion filed prior to trial. This article in no way affects appeals pursuant to Article 44.17 of this chapter.

History of CCP art. 44.02: Acts 1965, 59th Leg., vol. 2, ch. 722. Amended by Acts 1977, 65th Leg., ch. 351, §1, eff. Aug. 29, 1977.

Proviso repealed by the Texas Court of Criminal Appeals' adoption of the Texas Rules of Appellate Procedure on Apr. 10, 1986. 707 S.W.2d xxx, xxxv. *See also* TRAP 25.2(a)(2)(B).

ANNOTATIONS

Robinson v. State, 240 S.W.3d 919, 920 (Tex.Crim. App.2007). "The issue in this case is whether an appeal may be taken from a ruling on a *pro se* motion made by a defendant who has counsel. We hold that it may."

Ex parte Delaney, 207 S.W.3d 794, 799 (Tex.Crim. App.2006). "To remove the confusion that has arisen related to pretrial waivers of appeal, we hold that, in order for a pretrial or presentencing waiver of the right to appeal to be binding at the punishment phase of trial, the waiver must be voluntary, knowing, and intelligent. One way to indicate that the waiver was knowing and intelligent is for the actual punishment or maximum punishment to have been determined by a plea agreement when the waiver was made. However, simply knowing the range of punishment for the offense is not enough to make the consequences of a waiver known with certainty, because it still does not allay the concern that unanticipated errors may occur at the punishment phase of trial."

Young v. State, 8 S.W.3d 656, 667 (Tex.Crim.App. 2000). "[A] valid plea of guilty or nolo contendere 'waives' or forfeits the right to appeal a claim of error only when the judgment of guilt was rendered independent of, and is not supported by, the error. In addition, if the appeal is from a judgment rendered on the defendant's plea of guilty or nolo contendere under [CCP art.] 1.15, and the punishment assessed did not exceed the punishment recommended by the prosecutor and agreed to by the defendant, the substance of the appeal must have been raised by written motion and ruled on before trial (unless the appeal is for a jurisdictional defect or the trial court granted permission to appeal)."

Manuel v. State, 994 S.W.2d 658, 661 (Tex.Crim. App.1999). "We have long held that a defendant placed on 'regular' community supervision may raise issues relating to the conviction, such as evidentiary sufficiency, only in appeals taken when community supervision is originally imposed. That is, such issues may not be raised in appeals filed after 'regular' community supervision is revoked. Given the legislative intent behind [CCP art.] 44.01(j), we now hold that this rule also applies in the deferred adjudication context. In other words, a defendant placed on deferred adjudication community supervision may raise issues relating to the original plea proceeding, such as evidentiary sufficiency, only in appeals taken when deferred adjudication community supervision is first imposed. Certainly, it was not the Legislature's intent, in enacting Article 44.01(j), to permit *two* reviews of the legality of a deferred adjudication order, one at the time deferred adjudication community supervision is first imposed and another when, and if, it is later revoked."

Everett v. State, 91 S.W.3d 386, 386 (Tex.App.— Waco 2002, no pet.). "A defendant in a criminal case should perfect a separate appeal when a trial court denies his request for a free appellate record. However, no statute vests this Court with jurisdiction over an appeal from an order denying a request for a free copy of the trial record when such a request is not presented in conjunction with a timely-filed appeal. [W]e dismiss this appeal for want of jurisdiction."

ART. 44.03. REPEALED

Repealed by the Texas Court of Criminal Appeals' adoption of the Texas Rules of Appellate Procedure on Apr. 10, 1986, eff. Sept. 1, 1986. 707 S.W.2d xxx, xxxv.

ART. 44.04. BOND PENDING APPEAL

(a) Pending the determination of any motion for new trial or the appeal from any misdemeanor conviction, the defendant is entitled to be released on reasonable bail.

(b) The defendant may not be released on bail pending the appeal from any felony conviction where the punishment equals or exceeds 10 years confinement or where the defendant has been convicted of an offense listed under Section 3g(a)(1), Article 42.12, but shall immediately be placed in custody and the bail discharged.

(c) Pending the appeal from any felony conviction other than a conviction described in Subsection (b) of this section, the trial court may deny bail and commit the defendant to custody if there then exists good cause to believe that the defendant would not appear when his conviction became final or is likely to commit another offense while on bail, permit the defendant to remain at large on the existing bail, or, if not then on bail, admit him to reasonable bail until his conviction becomes final. The court may impose reasonable conditions on bail pending the finality of his conviction. On a finding by the court on a preponderance of the evidence of a violation of a condition, the court may revoke the bail.

(d) After conviction, either pending determination of any motion for new trial or pending final determination of the appeal, the court in which trial was had may increase or decrease the amount of bail, as it deems proper, either upon its own motion or the motion of the State or of the defendant.

(e) Any bail entered into after conviction and the sureties on the bail must be approved by the court where trial was had. Bail is sufficient if it substantially meets the requirements of this code and may be entered into and given at any term of court.

(f) In no event shall the defendant and the sureties on his bond be released from their liability on such bond or bonds until the defendant is placed in the custody of the sheriff.

(g) The right of appeal to the Court of Appeals of this state is expressly accorded the defendant for a review of any judgment or order made hereunder, and said appeal shall be given preference by the appellate court.

(h) If a conviction is reversed by a decision of a Court of Appeals, the defendant, if in custody, is entitled to release on reasonable bail, regardless of the length of term of imprisonment, pending final determination of an appeal by the state or the defendant on a motion for discretionary review. If the defendant requests bail before a petition for discretionary review has been filed, the Court of Appeals shall determine the amount of bail. If the defendant requests bail after a petition for discretionary review has been filed, the Court of Criminal Appeals shall determine the amount of bail. The sureties on the bail must be approved by the court where the trial was had. The defendant's right to release under this subsection attaches immediately on the issuance of the Court of Appeals' final ruling as defined by Tex.Cr. App.R. 209(c).

History of CCP art. 44.04: Acts 1965, 59th Leg., vol. 2, ch. 722. Amended by Acts 1977, 65th Leg., ch. 234, §1, eff. Aug. 29, 1977; Acts 1981, 67th Leg., ch. 268, §17 (eff. Sept. 1, 1981), ch. 291, §125 (eff. Sept. 1, 1981); Acts 1983, 68th Leg., ch. 249, §2 (eff. Aug. 29, 1983), ch. 425, §26 (eff. Aug. 29, 1983); Acts 1985, 69th Leg., ch. 968, §1, eff. Aug. 26, 1985; Sept. 1, 1991; Acts 1999, 76th Leg., ch. 546, §1, eff. Sept. 1, 1999; Acts 2003, 78th Leg., ch. 942, §3, eff. June 20, 2003.

ANNOTATIONS

Art. 44.04(a)

Hill v. State, 902 S.W.2d 57, 60 (Tex.App.— Houston [1st Dist.] 1995, pet. ref'd). "[A]ppellant contends the trial court erred in setting no appeal bond.... [¶] [A]ppellant did not object to the trial court's action, did not develop a record, and did not obtain an adverse ruling. Therefore, he has waived review of this issue...."

Art. 44.04(b)

Lebo v. State, 90 S.W.3d 324, 326 (Tex.Crim.App. 2002). "We granted review to determine whether a person who is sentenced to ten years' imprisonment, but who is placed under community supervision, is entitled to bond pending appeal. [¶] We conclude that article 44.04(b) prohibits the setting of bail pending appeal only when the sentence of imprisonment is actually imposed and the defendant would, had he not appealed, be immediately incarcerated to serve his term of imprisonment."

Art. 44.04(c)

Ex parte Anderer, 61 S.W.3d 398, 406 (Tex.Crim. App.2001). "The only interest that is furthered by a defendant's right to remain free during appeal is the interest in protecting the defendant from an erroneous judgment. The issue is ... while [bail-eligible appellants] are free on appeal, what conditions on their freedom are reasonable? [¶] Against the interest of such appellants must be balanced the interest of society in enforcing the penal laws. Chief among these, in the cases of those who have been convicted of felonies, is 'to insure the public safety through: (A) the deterrent influence of the penalties ... provided; (B) the rehabilitation of those convicted of violations...; and (C) such punishment as may be necessary to prevent likely recurrence of criminal behavior.' If the public policy of this state permits a magistrate to consider the public safety in imposing a condition on pre-trial bail, surely it must be reasonable for a condition on bail pending appeal to have the purpose of protecting the public safety."

Speth v. State, 939 S.W.2d 769, 770 (Tex.App.— Houston [14th Dist.] 1997, no pet.). "When an appeal bond condition does not take effect until the appellant's probation begins, it is unenforceable until the mandate from the appellate court, effecting final disposition of the appeal, is issued."

Art. 44.04(g)

Faerman v. State, 966 S.W.2d 843, 848 (Tex.App.— Houston [14th Dist.] 1998, no pet.). "In regard to bail pending appeal, the issue should be resolved at the *inception* of the appeal when the defendant can still derive some benefit from a bond. The legislature has, therefore, expressly accorded the defendant a preferential right of review in the court of appeals from any order or judgment entered by the trial court regarding his right to bail pending appeal. To provide meaningful review, an accelerated appeal under Article 44.04(g) from an order denying bail is separate and distinct from a defendant's general appeal from a judgment of conviction."

Art. 44.04(h)

Aviles v. State, 26 S.W.3d 696, 699 (Tex.App.— Houston [14th Dist.] 2000, pet. ref'd). "Once a conviction is reversed, we hold the primary factors that should be considered by the court of appeals [in setting bail] are: (1) the fact that the conviction has been overturned; (2) the State's ability, if any, to retry the appellant; and (3) the likelihood that the decision of the court of appeals will be overturned."

ART. 44.041. CONDITIONS IN LIEU OF BOND

(a) If a defendant is confined in county jail pending appeal and is eligible for release on bond pending appeal but is financially unable to make bond, the court may release the defendant without bond pending the conclusion of the appeal only if the court determines that release under this article is reasonable given the circumstances of the defendant's offense and the sentence imposed.

(b) A court that releases a defendant under this article must require the defendant to participate in a program under Article 42.033, 42.034, 42.035, or 42.036 of this code during the pendency of the appeal. The defendant may not receive credit toward completion of the defendant's sentence while participating in a program required by this subsection.

History of CCP art. 44.041: Acts 1989, 71st Leg., ch. 785, §4.15, eff. Sept. 1, 1989.

ARTS. 44.05, 44.06. REPEALED

Repealed by the Texas Court of Criminal Appeals' adoption of the Texas Rules of Appellate Procedure on Apr. 10, 1986, eff. Sept. 1, 1986. 707 S.W.2d xxx, xxxv.

ART. 44.07. RIGHT OF APPEAL NOT ABRIDGED

The right of appeal, as otherwise provided by law, shall in no wise be abridged by any provision of this Chapter.

History of CCP art. 44.07: Acts 1965, 59th Leg., vol. 2, ch. 722.

Jack v. State, 871 S.W.2d 741, 744 (Tex.Crim.App. 1994). "[C]ourts of appeals lack jurisdiction to entertain appellate claims of alleged error occurring at or after the entry of a negotiated guilty plea unless the notice of appeal reflects, as required by Rule 40(b)(1) [now TRAP 25.2], that the trial court gave permission to appeal that alleged error. There is no such jurisdictional bar to appealing matters following a nonnegotiated guilty plea. ... It is true that by virtue of his nonnegotiated plea a defendant may waive nonjurisdictional defects occurring prior to the entry of the plea. This only means the defendant will not ultimately prevail in his appeal of such matters, not that an appellate court lacks jurisdiction to entertain it."

ARTS. 44.08, 44.09. REPEALED

Repealed by the Texas Court of Criminal Appeals' adoption of the Texas Rules of Appellate Procedure on Apr. 10, 1986, eff. Sept. 1, 1986. 707 S.W.2d xxx, xxxv.

ART. 44.10. SHERIFF TO REPORT ESCAPE

When any such escape occurs, the sheriff who had the prisoner in custody shall immediately report the fact under oath to the district or county attorney of the county in which the conviction was had, who shall forthwith forward such report to the State prosecuting attorney. Such report shall be sufficient evidence of the fact of such escape to authorize the dismissal of the appeal.

History of CCP art. 44.10: Acts 1965, 59th Leg., vol. 2, ch. 722.

ART. 44.11. REPEALED

Repealed by the Texas Court of Criminal Appeals' adoption of the Texas Rules of Appellate Procedure on Apr. 10, 1986, eff. Sept. 1, 1986. 707 S.W.2d xxx, xxxv.

ART. 44.12. PROCEDURE AS TO BAIL PENDING APPEAL

The amount of any bail given in any felony or misdemeanor case to perfect an appeal from any court to the Court of Appeals shall be fixed by the court in which the judgment or order appealed from was rendered. The sufficiency of the security thereon shall be tested, and the same proceedings had in case of forfeiture, as in other cases regarding bail.

History of CCP art. 44.12: Acts 1965, 59th Leg., vol. 2, ch. 722. Amended by Acts 1981, 67th Leg., ch. 291, §130, eff. Sept. 1, 1981.

ART. 44.13. REPEALED

Repealed by Acts 1999, 76th Leg., ch. 1545, §75(a), eff. Sept. 1, 1999.

ART. 44.14. RENUMBERED

Renumbered to art. 45.0426 by Acts 1999, 76th Leg., ch. 1545, §42, eff. Sept. 1, 1999.

ART. 44.15. APPELLATE COURT MAY ALLOW NEW BOND

When an appeal is taken from any court of this State, by filing a bond within the time prescribed by law in such cases, and the court to which appeal is taken determines that such bond is defective in form or substance, such appellate court may allow the appellant to amend such bond by filing a new bond, on such terms as the court may prescribe.

History of CCP art. 44.15: Acts 1965, 59th Leg., vol. 2, ch. 722.

ART. 44.16. APPEAL BOND GIVEN WITHIN WHAT TIME

If the defendant is not in custody, a notice of appeal as provided in Article 44.13 shall have no effect whatever until the required appeal bond has been given and approved. The appeal bond shall be given within ten days after the sentence of the court has been rendered, except as provided in Article 27.14 of this code.

History of CCP art. 44.16: Acts 1965, 59th Leg., vol. 2, ch. 722. Amended by Acts 1979, 66th Leg., ch. 207, §3, eff. Sept. 1, 1979.

ART. 44.17. APPEAL TO COUNTY COURT, HOW CONDUCTED

In all appeals to a county court from justice courts and municipal courts other than municipal courts of record, the trial shall be de novo in the trial in the county court, the same as if the prosecution had been originally commenced in that court. An appeal to the county court from a municipal court of record may be based only on errors reflected in the record.

History of CCP art. 44.17: Acts 1965, 59th Leg., vol. 2, ch. 722. Amended by Acts 1987, 70th Leg., ch. 641, §3, eff. Sept. 1, 1987.

ANNOTATIONS

Zulauf v. State, 591 S.W.2d 869, 871 n.3 (Tex.Crim. App.1979). "The action in County Court at Law ... being a trial de novo on appeal from justice court, the original complaint in justice court served as the functional equivalent of an information in county court at law."

ART. 44.18. ORIGINAL PAPERS SENT UP

In appeals from justice and corporation courts, all the original papers in the case, together with the appeal bond, if any, and together, with a certified transcript of all the proceedings had in the case before such court shall be delivered without delay to the clerk of the court to which the appeal was taken, who shall file the same and docket the case.

History of CCP art. 44.18: Acts 1965, 59th Leg., vol. 2, ch. 722.

ART. 44.181. DEFECT IN COMPLAINT

(a) A court conducting a trial de novo based on an appeal from a justice or municipal court may dismiss the case because of a defect in the complaint only if the defendant objected to the defect before the trial began in the justice or municipal court.

(b) The attorney representing the state may move to amend a defective complaint before the trial de novo begins.

History of CCP art. 44.181: Acts 1995, 74th Leg., ch. 478, §2, eff. Sept. 1, 1995. Amended by Acts 1999, 76th Leg., ch. 1545, §4, eff. Sept. 1, 1999.

ART. 44.19. WITNESSES NOT AGAIN SUMMONED

In the cases mentioned in the preceding Article, the witnesses who have been summoned or attached to appear in the case before the court below, shall appear before the court to which the appeal is taken without further process. In case of their failure to do so, the same proceedings may be had as if they had been originally summoned or attached to appear before such court.

History of CCP art. 44.19: Acts 1965, 59th Leg., vol. 2, ch. 722.

ART. 44.20. RULES GOVERNING APPEAL BONDS

The rules governing the taking and forfeiture of bail shall govern appeal bonds, and the forfeiture and collection of such appeal bonds shall be in the court to which such appeal is taken.

History of CCP art. 44.20: Acts 1965, 59th Leg., vol. 2, ch. 722.

ARTS. 44.21 TO 44.24. REPEALED

Repealed by the Texas Court of Criminal Appeals' adoption of the Texas Rules of Appellate Procedure on Apr. 10, 1986, eff. Sept. 1, 1986. 707 S.W.2d xxx, xxxv.

ART. 44.25. CASES REMANDED

The courts of appeals or the Court of Criminal Appeals may reverse the judgment in a criminal action, as well upon the law as upon the facts.

History of CCP art. 44.25: Acts 1965, 59th Leg., vol. 2, ch. 722. Amended by Acts 1981, 67th Leg., ch. 291, §134, eff. Sept. 1, 1981.

ANNOTATIONS

Grotti v. State, ___ S.W.3d ___ (Tex.Crim.App. 2008) (No. PD-134-07; 6-25-08). "In a factual-sufficiency review, the evidence is reviewed in a neutral light. Only one question is to be answered in a factual-sufficiency review: Considering all of the evidence in a neutral light, was a jury rationally justified in finding guilt beyond a reasonable doubt? Evidence can be factually insufficient in one of two ways: (1) when the evidence supporting the verdict is so weak that the verdict seems clearly wrong and manifestly unjust; and (2) when the supporting evidence is outweighed by the great weight and preponderance of the contrary evidence so as to render the verdict clearly wrong and manifestly unjust. '[A]n appellate court must first be able to say, with some objective basis in the record, that the great weight and preponderance of the ... evidence contradicts the jury's verdict before it is justified in exercising its appellate fact jurisdiction to order a new

⋆

trial.' A reversal for factual insufficiency cannot occur when 'the greater weight and preponderance of the evidence actually favors conviction.' Although an appellate court has the ability to second-guess the jury to a limited degree, the factual-sufficiency review should still be deferential, with a high level of skepticism about the jury's verdict required before a reversal can occur. It is not within this Court's authority to conduct our own factual-sufficiency analysis. We are permitted to evaluate only whether the court of appeals applied the correct rule of law."

Wooley v. State, ___ S.W.3d ___ (Tex.Crim.App. 2008) (No. PD-0861-07; 6-25-08). "We decide that *Malik*'s rule of measuring evidentiary sufficiency 'by the elements of the offense as defined by a hypothetically correct jury charge' applies when the evidence is reviewed for factual sufficiency."

Watson v. State, 204 S.W.3d 404, 417 (Tex.Crim. App.2006). "We ... disavow ... *Zuniga* and reiterate that it is not enough that the appellate court harbor a subjective level of reasonable doubt to overturn a conviction that is founded on legally sufficient evidence. An appellate court judge cannot conclude that a conviction is 'clearly wrong' or 'manifestly unjust' simply because, on the quantum of evidence admitted, he would have voted to acquit had he been on the jury. Nor can an appellate court judge declare that a conflict in the evidence justifies a new trial simply because he disagrees with the jury's resolution of that conflict. We have always held that an appellate court must first be able to say, with some objective basis in the record, that the *great weight and preponderance* of the (albeit legally sufficient) evidence contradicts the jury's verdict before it is justified in exercising its appellate fact jurisdiction to order a new trial. We have never, at least until *Zuniga*, interpreted the factual review jurisdiction of criminal appellate courts to include the ability to overturn a jury verdict and remand for a new trial when the greater weight and preponderance of the evidence actually favors *conviction*!" *See also Clewis v. State*, 922 S.W.2d 126, 130 (Tex.Crim.App.1996).

ART. 44.251. REFORMATION OF SENTENCE IN CAPITAL CASE

 Subsection (a) below is effective for offenses committed on or after Sept. 1, 2007.

(a) The court of criminal appeals shall reform a sentence of death to a sentence of confinement in the

Texas Department of Criminal Justice for life without parole if the court finds that there is legally insufficient evidence to support an affirmative answer to an issue submitted to the jury under Section 2(b), Article 37.071, or Section 2(b), Article 37.072.

Subsection (a) below is effective for offenses in which any element of the offense was committed before Sept. 1, 2007.

(a) The court of criminal appeals shall reform a sentence of death to a sentence of confinement in the institutional division of the Texas Department of Criminal Justice for life without parole if the court finds that there is legally insufficient evidence to support an affirmative answer to an issue submitted to the jury under Section 2(b), Article 37.071.

(b) The court of criminal appeals shall reform a sentence of death to a sentence of confinement in the institutional division of the Texas Department of Criminal Justice for life without parole if:

(1) the court finds reversible error that affects the punishment stage of the trial other than a finding of insufficient evidence under Subsection (a) of this article; and

(2) within 30 days after the date on which the opinion is handed down, the date the court disposes of a timely request for rehearing, or the date that the United States Supreme Court disposes of a timely filed petition for writ of certiorari, whichever date is later, the prosecuting attorney files a motion requesting that the sentence be reformed to confinement for life without parole.

 Subsection (c) below is effective for offenses committed on or after Sept. 1, 2007.

(c) If the court of criminal appeals finds reversible error that affects the punishment stage of the trial only, as described by Subsection (b) of this article, and the prosecuting attorney does not file a motion for reformation of sentence in the period described by that subsection, the defendant shall receive a new sentencing trial in the manner required by Article 44.29(c) or (d), as applicable.

Subsection (c) below is effective for offenses in which any element of the offense was committed before Sept. 1, 2007.

(c) If the court of criminal appeals finds reversible error that affects the punishment stage of the trial only, as described by Subsection (b) of this article, and the prosecuting attorney does not file a motion for reformation of sentence in the period described by that subsection, the defendant shall receive a new sentencing trial in the manner required by Article 44.29(c) of this code.

E *Subsection (d) below is effective for offenses committed on or after Sept. 1, 2007.*

(d) The court of criminal appeals shall reform a sentence of death imposed under Section 12.42(c)(3), Penal Code, to a sentence of imprisonment in the Texas Department of Criminal Justice for life without parole if the United States Supreme Court:

(1) finds that the imposition of the death penalty under Section 12.42(c)(3), Penal Code, violates the United States Constitution; and

(2) issues an order that is not inconsistent with this article.

History of CCP art. 44.251: Acts 1981, 67th Leg., ch. 725, §2, eff. Aug. 31, 1981. Amended by Acts 1991, 72nd Leg., ch. 838, §3, eff. Sept. 1, 1991; Acts 1993, 73rd Leg., ch. 781, §3, eff. Aug. 30, 1993; Acts 2005, 79th Leg., ch. 787, §10, eff. Sept. 1, 2005; Acts 2007, 80th Leg., ch. 593, §3.18, eff. Sept. 1, 2007.

ART. 44.2511. REFORMATION OF SENTENCE IN CAPITAL CASE FOR OFFENSE COMMITTED BEFORE SEPTEMBER 1, 1991

(a) This article applies to the reformation of a sentence of death in a capital case for an offense committed before September 1, 1991. For purposes of this subsection, an offense is committed before September 1, 1991, if every element of the offense occurred before that date.

(b) The court of criminal appeals shall reform a sentence of death to a sentence of confinement in the institutional division of the Texas Department of Criminal Justice for life if the court finds that there is legally insufficient evidence to support an affirmative answer to an issue submitted to the jury under Section 3(b), Article 37.0711.

(c) The court of criminal appeals shall reform a sentence of death to a sentence of confinement in the institutional division of the Texas Department of Criminal Justice for life if:

(1) the court finds reversible error that affects the punishment stage of the trial other than a finding of insufficient evidence under Subsection (b); and

(2) within 30 days after the date on which the opinion is handed down, the date the court disposes of a timely request for rehearing, or the date that the

United States Supreme Court disposes of a timely filed petition for writ of certiorari, whichever date is later, the prosecuting attorney files a motion requesting that the sentence be reformed to confinement for life.

(d) If the court of criminal appeals finds reversible error that affects the punishment stage of the trial only, as described by Subsection (c), and the prosecuting attorney does not file a motion for reformation of sentence in the period described by that subsection, the defendant shall receive a new sentencing trial in the manner required by Article 44.29(c).

History of CCP art. 44.2511: Acts 2005, 79th Leg., ch. 787, §11, eff. Sept. 1, 2005.

ARTS. 44.26, 44.27. REPEALED

Repealed by the Texas Court of Criminal Appeals' adoption of the Texas Rules of Appellate Procedure on Apr. 10, 1986, eff. Sept. 1, 1986. 707 S.W.2d xxx, xxxv.

ART. 44.28. WHEN MISDEMEANOR IS AFFIRMED

In misdemeanor cases where there has been an affirmance, no proceedings need be had after filing the mandate, except to forfeit the bond of the defendant, or to issue a capias for the defendant, or an execution against his property, to enforce the judgment of the court, as if no appeal had been taken.

History of CCP art. 44.28: Acts 1965, 59th Leg., vol. 2, ch. 722.

ART. 44.281. DISPOSITION OF FINES & COSTS WHEN MISDEMEANOR AFFIRMED

In misdemeanor cases affirmed on appeal from a municipal court, the fine imposed on appeal and the costs imposed on appeal shall be collected from the defendant, and the fine of the municipal court when collected shall be paid into the municipal treasury.

History of CCP art. 44.281: Acts 1965, 59th Leg., vol. 2, ch. 722. Renumbered from art. 45.11 and amended by Acts 1999, 76th Leg., ch. 1545, §65, eff. Sept. 1, 1999.

ART. 44.29. EFFECT OF REVERSAL

(a) Where the court of appeals or the Court of Criminal Appeals awards a new trial to the defendant on the basis of an error in the guilt or innocence stage of the trial or on the basis of errors in both the guilt or innocence stage of the trial and the punishment stage of the trial, the cause shall stand as it would have stood in case the new trial had been granted by the court below.

(b) If the court of appeals or the Court of Criminal Appeals awards a new trial to a defendant other than a defendant convicted of an offense under Section 19.03, Penal Code, only on the basis of an error or errors made in the punishment stage of the trial, the cause shall stand as it would have stood in case the new trial had been granted by the court below, except that the court shall commence the new trial as if a finding of guilt had been returned and proceed to the punishment stage of the trial under Subsection (b), Section 2, Article 37.07, of this code. If the defendant elects, the court shall empanel a jury for the sentencing stage of the trial in the same manner as a jury is empaneled by the court for other trials before the court. At the new trial, the court shall allow both the state and the defendant to introduce evidence to show the circumstances of the offense and other evidence as permitted by Section 3 of Article 37.07 of this code.

(c) If any court sets aside or invalidates the sentence of a defendant convicted of an offense under Section 19.03, Penal Code, and sentenced to death on the basis of any error affecting punishment only, the court shall not set the conviction aside but rather shall commence a new punishment hearing under Article 37.071 or Article 37.0711 of this code, as appropriate, as if a finding of guilt had been returned. The court shall empanel a jury for the sentencing stage of the trial in the same manner as a jury is to be empaneled by the court in other trials before the court for offenses under Section 19.03, Penal Code. At the new punishment hearing, the court shall permit both the state and the defendant to introduce evidence as permitted by Article 37.071 or Article 37.0711 of this code.

 Subsection (d) below is effective for offenses committed on or after Sept. 1, 2007.

(d) If any court sets aside or invalidates the sentence of a defendant convicted of an offense punishable as a capital felony under Section 12.42(c)(3), Penal Code, and sentenced to death on the basis of any error affecting punishment only, the court shall not set the conviction aside but rather shall commence a new punishment hearing under Article 37.072, as if a finding of guilt had been returned. The court shall empanel a jury for the sentencing stage of the trial in the same manner as a jury is to be empaneled by the court in other trials before the court for the offense of which the defendant was convicted. At the new punishment hearing, the court shall permit both the state and the defendant to introduce evidence as permitted by Article 37.072.

History of CCP art. 44.29: Acts 1965, 59th Leg., vol. 2, ch. 722. Amended by Acts 1981, 67th Leg., ch. 291, §137, eff. Sept. 1, 1981; Acts 1987, 70th Leg., ch. 179, §1, eff. Aug. 31, 1987; Acts 1991, 72nd Leg., ch. 838, §2, eff. Sept. 1, 1991; Acts 1993, 73rd Leg., ch. 781, §4, eff. Aug. 30, 1993; Acts 2007, 80th Leg., ch. 593, §3.19, eff. Sept. 1, 2007.

ANNOTATIONS

McNatt v. State, 188 S.W.3d 198, 204 (Tex.Crim. App.2006). "We conclude that the Court of Appeals erred in holding that the untimeliness of an enhancement allegation carries over to any retrial of the punishment proceedings. As long as the enhancement is not barred by other considerations (e.g. prosecutorial vindictiveness), the State is free to use a prior conviction for enhancement if proper notice of its intent to do so is conveyed with respect to the new punishment hearing."

Barton v. State, 21 S.W.3d 287, 290 (Tex.Crim.App. 2000). "The proper procedure where the amount of restitution ordered as a condition of community supervision is not supported by the record is to abate the appeal, set aside the amount of restitution, and remand the case for a hearing to determine a just amount of restitution."

Carson v. State, 6 S.W.3d 536, 539 (Tex.Crim.App. 1999). "[A]rticle 44.29(b) permits retrials limited to assessment of punishment only for errors that were, literally, made *in* the punishment stage of the trial. Voir dire errors are not in that category." *See also* ***Lopez v. State***, 18 S.W.3d 637, 640 (Tex.Crim.App.2000).

Clark v. State, 994 S.W.2d 166, 168 (Tex.Crim.App. 1999). "Article 44.29(c) [is] applicable to offenses regardless of when they occurred."

State v. Hight, 907 S.W.2d 845, 846 (Tex.Crim.App. 1995). "[A] trial court does not have authority to grant a new trial as to punishment only. [O]nly *appellate* courts may grant new trials as to punishment only."

Saldana v. State, 826 S.W.2d 948, 950 (Tex.Crim. App.1992). "[T]he reference in [CCP art.] 44.29 to [CCP art.] 37.07 does not apply where the defendant pleads guilty before the judge. [¶] [T]he enactment of Art. 44.29(b) has created a right to choose either jury or court assessment of punishment after such a remand, notwithstanding such choice at the original trial."

Levy v. State, 818 S.W.2d 801, 803 (Tex.Crim.App. 1991). "In cases where a defendant enters a plea of guilty or nolo contendere without the benefit of a plea bargain agreement with the State and the trial judge

⸻ ★ ⸻

assesses a punishment not authorized by law, the appropriate remedy is to allow the finding of guilt to remain and to remand the case to the trial court for the proper assessment of punishment."

ARTS. 44.30 TO 44.32. REPEALED

Repealed by the Texas Court of Criminal Appeals' adoption of the Texas Rules of Appellate Procedure on Apr. 10, 1986, eff. Sept. 1, 1986. 707 S.W.2d xxx, xxxv.

ART. 44.33. HEARING IN APPELLATE COURT

(a) The Court of Criminal Appeals shall make rules of posttrial and appellate procedure as to the hearing of criminal actions not inconsistent with this Code.

(b) Appellant's failure to file his brief in the time prescribed shall not authorize a dismissal of the appeal by the Court of Appeals or the Court of Criminal Appeals, nor shall the Court of Appeals or the Court of Criminal Appeals, for such reason, refuse to consider appellant's case on appeal.

History of CCP art. 44.33: Acts 1965, 59th Leg., vol. 2, ch. 722. Amended by Acts 1981, 67th Leg., ch. 291, §139, eff. Sept. 1, 1981. On Apr. 10, 1986, by the Texas Court of Criminal Appeals' adoption of the Texas Rules of Appellate Procedure, all of CCP art. 44.33 was repealed with the exception of the first sentence and subsection (b). *See also* TRAPs 38, 39. 707 S.W.2d xxx, xxxv.

ART. 44.34. REPEALED

Repealed by the Texas Court of Criminal Appeals' adoption of the Texas Rules of Appellate Procedure on Apr. 10, 1986, eff. Sept. 1, 1986. 707 S.W.2d xxx, xxxv.

ART. 44.35. BAIL PENDING HABEAS CORPUS APPEAL

In any habeas corpus proceeding in any court or before any judge in this State where the defendant is remanded to the custody of an officer and an appeal is taken to an appellate court, the defendant shall be allowed bail by the court or judge so remanding the defendant, except in capital cases where the proof is evident. The fact that such defendant is released on bail shall not be grounds for a dismissal of the appeal except in capital cases where the proof is evident.

History of CCP art. 44.35: Acts 1965, 59th Leg., vol. 2, ch. 722.

ANNOTATIONS

Luciano v. State, 906 S.W.2d 523, 528 (Tex.Crim. App.1995). "When the habeas court denied relief, effectively remanding [applicant] to custody, applicant was then also entitled to be enlarged on bail pending decision on appeal. ... The applicable rule in such habeas cases is that in the absence of a showing applicant was

in custody or released from custody on bail pending appeal the appellate court is without jurisdiction to entertain the appeal."

ARTS. 44.36 TO 44.38. REPEALED

Repealed by the Texas Court of Criminal Appeals' adoption of the Texas Rules of Appellate Procedure on Apr. 10, 1986, eff. Sept. 1, 1986. 707 S.W.2d xxx, xxxv.

ART. 44.39. APPELLANT DETAINED BY OTHER THAN OFFICER

If the appellant in a case of habeas corpus be detained by any person other than an officer, the sheriff receiving the mandate of the appellate court, shall immediately cause the person so held to be discharged; and the mandate shall be sufficient authority therefor.

History of CCP art. 44.39: Acts 1965, 59th Leg., vol. 2, ch. 722. Amended by Acts 1981, 67th Leg., ch. 291, §144, eff. Sept. 1, 1981.

ART. 44.40. REPEALED

Repealed by the Texas Court of Criminal Appeals' adoption of the Texas Rules of Appellate Procedure on Apr. 10, 1986, eff. Sept. 1, 1986. 707 S.W.2d xxx, xxxv.

ART. 44.41. WHO SHALL TAKE BAIL BOND

When, by the judgment of the appellate court upon cases of habeas corpus, the applicant is ordered to give bail, such judgment shall be certified to the officer holding him in custody; and if such officer be the sheriff, the bail bond may be executed before him; if any other officer, he shall take the person detained before some magistrate, who may receive a bail bond, and shall file the same in the proper court of the proper county; and such bond may be forfeited and enforced as provided by law.

History of CCP art. 44.41: Acts 1965, 59th Leg., vol. 2, ch. 722. Amended by Acts 1981, 67th Leg., ch. 291, §146, eff. Sept. 1, 1981.

ART. 44.42. APPEAL ON FORFEITURES

An appeal may be taken by the defendant from every final judgment rendered upon a personal bond, bail bond or bond taken for the prevention or suppression of offenses, where such judgment is for twenty dollars or more, exclusive of costs, but not otherwise.

History of CCP art. 44.42: Acts 1965, 59th Leg., vol. 2, ch. 722.

ANNOTATIONS

State v. Sellers, 790 S.W.2d 316, 318 (Tex.Crim. App.1990). "Article 44.42 [does not] *preclude* a State's appeal in bond forfeiture cases...."

ART. 44.43. WRIT OF ERROR

The defendant may also have any such judgment as is mentioned in the preceding Article, and which may have been rendered in courts other than the justice and corporation courts, reviewed upon writ of error.

History of CCP art. 44.43: Acts 1965, 59th Leg., vol. 2, ch. 722.

ART. 44.44. RULES IN FORFEITURES

In the cases provided for in the two preceding Articles, the proceeding shall be regulated by the same rules that govern civil actions where an appeal is taken or a writ of error sued out.

History of CCP art. 44.44: Acts 1965, 59th Leg., vol. 2, ch. 722.

ANNOTATIONS

Surety Ins. Co. v. State, 514 S.W.2d 454, 455 (Tex. Crim.App.1974). "The proceedings for the review of bond forfeiture cases are controlled by the law and the rules applicable for the review of civil actions."

ART. 44.45. REVIEW BY COURT OF CRIMINAL APPEALS

☠ *Subsection (a) below was amended by the Texas Court of Criminal Appeals' adoption of the Texas Rules of Appellate Procedure on Apr. 10, 1986, by repealing the second sentence of the subsection.*

(a) The Court of Criminal Appeals may review decisions of the court of appeals on its own motion.

☠ *The second sentence of subsection (a) below was amended by Acts 1987, 70th Leg., ch. 167, §5.02(3), effective Sept. 1, 1987, without reference to the repeal of that sentence by the Texas Court of Criminal Appeals' adoption of the Texas Rules of Appellate Procedure on Apr. 10, 1986.*

The Court of Criminal Appeals may review decisions of the court of appeals on its own motion. An order for review must be filed before the decision of the court of appeals becomes final as determined by Article 42.045.

(c) The Court of Criminal Appeals may promulgate rules pursuant to this article.

History of CCP art. 44.45: Acts 1981, 67th Leg., ch. 291, §147, eff. Sept. 1, 1981. Amended by Acts 1983, 68th Leg., ch. 249, §1, eff. Aug. 29, 1983; Acts 1987, 70th Leg., ch. 167, §5.02(3), eff. Sept. 1, 1987. On Apr. 10, 1986, by the Texas Court of Criminal Appeals' adoption of the Texas Rules of Appellate Procedure, the second sentence of subsection (a), subsection (b)(1)-(7), and subsection (d) were repealed, eff. Sept. 1, 1986. *See also* TRAPs 9, 25.2, 26.2. 707 S.W.2d xxx, xxxv.

ART. 44.46. REVERSAL OF CONVICTION ON THE BASIS OF SERVICE ON JURY BY A DISQUALIFIED JUROR

A conviction in a criminal case may be reversed on appeal on the ground that a juror in the case was absolutely disqualified from service under Article 35.19 of this code only if:

(1) the defendant raises the disqualification before the verdict is entered; or

(2) the disqualification was not discovered or brought to the attention of the trial court until after the verdict was entered and the defendant makes a showing of significant harm by the service of the disqualified juror.

History of CCP art. 44.46: Acts 1993, 73rd Leg., ch. 372, §1, eff. Sept. 1, 1993.

See also CCP art. 35.16; Gov't Code §62.102.

ANNOTATIONS

White v. State, 225 S.W.3d 571, 574-75 (Tex.Crim. App.2007). "Although appellant argues that the presence of the two 'absolutely disqualified' jurors participating in the deliberations was itself such an 'outside influence,' we are unconvinced. ... The plain language of [TRE] 606(b) indicates that an outside influence is something outside of both the jury room and the juror. [¶] We are ... unconvinced by appellant's contention that the challenged jurors' mere presence was 'significant harm' and that holding otherwise, coupled with the prohibitions in Rule 606(b), would preclude any possible avenue for discovering whether these jurors caused substantial harm.... The U.S. Supreme Court has held that, while juror testimony is barred under [FRE] 606(b), 'a party may seek to impeach the verdict by non-juror evidence of misconduct.' Likewise, [TRE] 606(b) does not prevent appellant from demonstrating such 'significant harm' by use of non-juror evidence. Appellant has failed to carry her burden under [CCP art.] 44.46(2)."

Nelson v. State, 129 S.W.3d 108, 112 (Tex.Crim. App.2004). "Clause (2) puts a burden on the defendant to meet a new standard of harm ... when the disqualification is raised after the entry of the verdict. In this clause it makes no difference who discovers the disqualification or how it is brought to the attention of the trial court; that portion of the clause is in the passive voice. A duty on the defendant arises in an appeal to make a showing of significant harm. A defendant may have his conviction reversed on appeal, even though he did nothing before the verdict was entered, but only if he meets a high standard that Article 44.46(2) raises on appeal. *At 113:* Clause (1), which is in the active voice, puts a duty on the defendant to raise a disqualification before the verdict is entered. If a defendant takes that action, he may obtain a reversal on appeal without carrying a high burden to show harm." *See also Ristoff v. State*, 985 S.W.2d 623, 624 (Tex.App.—Houston [1st Dist.] 1999, no pet.); *State v. Read*, 965 S.W.2d 74, 76 (Tex.App.—Austin 1998, no pet.).

Perez v. State, 11 S.W.3d 218, 220 (Tex.Crim.App. 2000). "In its determination that, as applied to appellant, [CCP] art. 44.46 conflicted with [Tex. Const.] art. 16, §2, the Court of Appeals first determined that the phrase 'high crimes,' as it appears in art. 16, §2, refers to felonies. *At 221:* [T]he complained-of juror was convicted of felony driving while intoxicated. This offense, which does not even require a culpable mental state, cannot reasonably be characterized as a 'high crime.' Thus, even under the broadest reading of Tex. Const. art. 16, §2, the juror was not constitutionally disqualified from serving; rather, the disqualification was statutory. As such, there is no conflict in the instant case between art. 16, §2, and art. 44.46, the latter is not unconstitutional as applied to appellant."

White v. State, 181 S.W.3d 514, 517 (Tex.App.—Texarkana 2005), *aff'd*, 225 S.W.3d 571 (Tex.Crim. App.2007) (No. PD-0118-06; 6-6-07). "[T]he record from the post-trial hearing must demonstrate the defendant's alleged substantial harm is directly attributable to the service of the objectionable jurors."

ART. 44.47. APPEAL OF TRANSFER FROM JUVENILE COURT

(a) A defendant may appeal an order of a juvenile court certifying the defendant to stand trial as an adult and transferring the defendant to a criminal court under Section 54.02, Family Code.

(b) A defendant may appeal a transfer under Subsection (a) only in conjunction with the appeal of a conviction of or an order of deferred adjudication for the offense for which the defendant was transferred to criminal court.

(c) An appeal under this section is a criminal matter and is governed by this code and the Texas Rules of Appellate Procedure that apply to a criminal case.

(d) An appeal under this article may include any claims under the law that existed before January 1, 1996, that could have been raised on direct appeal of a transfer under Section 54.02, Family Code.

History of CCP art. 44.47: Acts 1995, 74th Leg., ch. 262, §85, eff. Jan. 1, 1996. Amended by Acts 2003, 78th Leg., ch. 283, §30, eff. Sept. 1, 2003.
See also Fam. Code §54.02.

CHAPTER 45. JUSTICE & MUNICIPAL COURTS

ARTS. 45.01, 45.02. REPEALED

Repealed by Acts 1999, 76th Leg., ch. 1545, §75(a), eff. Sept. 1, 1999.

ART. 45.021. RENUMBERED

Renumbered to art. 45.012 by Acts 1999, 76th Leg., ch. 1545, §9, eff. Sept. 1, 1999.

ART. 45.03. RENUMBERED

Renumbered to art. 45.201 by Acts 1999, 76th Leg., ch. 1545, §75(a), eff. Sept. 1, 1999.

ART. 45.031. RENUMBERED

Renumbered to art. 45.032 by Acts 1999, 76th Leg., ch. 1545, §30, eff. Sept. 1, 1999.

ART. 45.04. RENUMBERED

Renumbered to art. 45.202 by Acts 1999, 76th Leg., ch. 1545, §60, eff. Sept. 1, 1999.

ART. 45.05. REPEALED

Repealed by Acts 1999, 76th Leg., ch. 1545, §75(a), eff. Sept. 1, 1999.

ART. 45.06. RENUMBERED

Renumbered to art. 45.203 by Acts 1999, 76th Leg., ch. 1545, §61, eff. Sept. 1, 1999.

ARTS. 45.07 TO 45.09. REPEALED

Repealed by Acts 1999, 76th Leg., ch. 1545, §75(a), eff. Sept. 1, 1999.

ART. 45.10. RENUMBERED

Renumbered to art. 45.042 by Acts 1999, 76th Leg., ch. 1545, §40, eff. Sept. 1, 1999.

ART. 45.11. RENUMBERED

Renumbered to art. 44.281 by Acts 1999, 76th Leg., ch. 1545, §65, eff. Sept. 1, 1999.

ART. 45.12. REPEALED

Repealed by Acts 1999, 76th Leg., ch. 1545, §75(a), eff. Sept. 1, 1999.

ART. 45.13. RENUMBERED

Renumbered to art. 45.017 by Acts 1999, 76th Leg., ch. 1545, §14, eff. Sept. 1, 1999.

ART. 45.14. REPEALED

Repealed by Acts 1989, 71st Leg., ch. 499, §2, eff. Aug. 28, 1989.

ART. 45.15. RENUMBERED

Renumbered to art. 45.103 by Acts 1999, 76th Leg., ch. 1545, §57, eff. Sept. 1, 1999.

ART. 45.16. REPEALED

Repealed by Acts 1999, 76th Leg., ch. 1545, §75(a), eff. Sept. 1, 1999.

ART. 45.17. RENUMBERED

Renumbered to art. 45.019 by Acts 1999, 76th Leg., ch. 1545, §16, eff. Sept. 1, 1999.

ART. 45.18. RENUMBERED

Renumbered to art. 45.014 by Acts 1999, 76th Leg., ch. 1545, §11, eff. Sept. 1, 1999.

ART. 45.19. REPEALED

Repealed by Acts 1999, 76th Leg., ch. 1545, §75(a), eff. Sept. 1, 1999.

ART. 45.20. REPEALED

Repealed by Acts 1991, 72nd Leg., ch. 446, §2, eff. June 11, 1991.

ART. 45.21. RENUMBERED

Renumbered to art. 45.102 by Acts 1999, 76th Leg., ch. 1545, §56, eff. Sept. 1, 1999.

ARTS. 45.22, 45.23. REPEALED

Repealed by Acts 1999, 76th Leg., ch. 1545, §75(a), eff. Sept. 1, 1999.

ART. 45.231. RENUMBERED

Renumbered to art. 45.044 by Acts 1999, 76th Leg., ch. 1545, §44, eff. Sept. 1, 1999.

ART. 45.24. RENUMBERED

Renumbered to art. 45.025 by Acts 1999, 76th Leg., ch. 1545, §23, eff. Sept. 1, 1999.

ART. 45.25. RENUMBERED

Renumbered to art. 45.027 by Acts 1999, 76th Leg., ch. 1545, §25, eff. Sept. 1, 1999.

ART. 45.251. RENUMBERED

Renumbered to art. 45.026 by Acts 1999, 76th Leg., ch. 1545, §24, eff. Sept. 1, 1999.

ARTS. 45.26, 45.27. REPEALED

Repealed by Acts 1999, 76th Leg., ch. 1545, §75(a), eff. Sept. 1, 1999.

ART. 45.28. RENUMBERED

Renumbered to art. 45.029 by Acts 1999, 76th Leg., ch. 1545, §27, eff. Sept. 1, 1999.

ART. 45.29. RENUMBERED

Renumbered to art. 45.028 by Acts 1999, 76th Leg., ch. 1545, §26, eff. Sept. 1, 1999.

ART. 45.30. RENUMBERED

Renumbered to art. 45.030 by Acts 1999, 76th Leg., ch. 1545, §28, eff. Sept. 1, 1999.

ART. 45.31. RENUMBERED

Renumbered to art. 45.023 by Acts 1999, 76th Leg., ch. 1545, §21, eff. Sept. 1, 1999.

ART. 45.32. REPEALED

Repealed by Acts 1999, 76th Leg., ch. 1545, §75(a), eff. Sept. 1, 1999.

ART. 45.34. RENUMBERED

Renumbered to art. 45.022 by Acts 1999, 76th Leg., ch. 1545, §20, eff. Sept. 1, 1999.

ART. 45.35. RENUMBERED

Renumbered to art. 43.024 by Acts 1999, 76th Leg., ch. 1545, §22, eff. Sept. 1, 1999.

ART. 45.36. RENUMBERED

Renumbered to art. 45.031 by Acts 1999, 76th Leg., ch. 1545, §29, eff. Sept. 1, 1999.

ART. 45.37. RENUMBERED

Renumbered to art. 45.020 by Acts 1999, 76th Leg., ch. 1545, §17, eff. Sept. 1, 1999.

ART. 45.38. RENUMBERED

Renumbered to art. 45.011 by Acts 1999, 76th Leg., ch. 1545, §8, eff. Sept. 1, 1999.

ART. 45.39. RENUMBERED

Renumbered to art. 45.034 by Acts 1999, 76th Leg., ch. 1545, §32, eff. Sept. 1, 1999.

ART. 45.40. RENUMBERED

Renumbered to art. 45.035 by Acts 1999, 76th Leg., ch. 1545, §33, eff. Sept. 1, 1999.

ART. 45.41. RENUMBERED

Renumbered to art. 45.016 by Acts 1999, 76th Leg., ch. 1545, §13, eff. Sept. 1, 1999.

ART. 45.42. RENUMBERED

Renumbered to art. 45.036 by Acts 1999, 76th Leg., ch. 1545, §34, eff. Sept. 1, 1999.

ART. 45.43. RENUMBERED

Renumbered to art. 45.015 by Acts 1999, 76th Leg., ch. 1545, §12, eff. Sept. 1, 1999.

ART. 45.44. RENUMBERED

Renumbered to art. 45.038 by Acts 1999, 76th Leg., ch. 1545, §36, eff. Sept. 1, 1999.

ART. 45.45. RENUMBERED

Renumbered to art. 45.037 by Acts 1999, 76th Leg., ch. 1545, §35, eff. Sept. 1, 1999.

ART. 45.46. RENUMBERED

Renumbered to art. 45.039 by Acts 1999, 76th Leg., ch. 1545, §37, eff. Sept. 1, 1999.

ART. 45.47. RENUMBERED

Renumbered to art. 45.040 by Acts 1999, 76th Leg., ch. 1545, §38, eff. Sept. 1, 1999.

ART. 45.48. RENUMBERED

Renumbered to art. 45.043 by Acts 1999, 76th Leg., ch. 1545, §43, eff. Sept. 1, 1999.

ART. 45.49. REPEALED

Repealed by Acts 1999, 76th Leg., ch. 1545, §75(a), eff. Sept. 1, 1999.

ART. 45.50. RENUMBERED

Renumbered to art. 45.041 by Acts 1999, 76th Leg., ch. 1545, §39, eff. Sept. 1, 1999.

ART. 45.51. RENUMBERED

Renumbered to art. 45.045 by Acts 1999, 76th Leg., ch. 1545, §45, eff. Sept. 1, 1999.

ART. 45.52. RENUMBERED

Renumbered to art. 45.046 by Acts 1999, 76th Leg., ch. 1545, §46, eff. Sept. 1, 1999.

ART. 45.521. RENUMBERED

Renumbered to art. 45.049 by Acts 1999, 76th Leg., ch. 1545, §49, eff. Sept. 1, 1999.

ART. 45.522. RENUMBERED

Renumbered to art. 45.050 by Acts 1999, 76th Leg., ch. 1545, §49, eff. Sept. 1, 1999.

ART. 45.53. RENUMBERED

Renumbered to art. 45.048 by Acts 1999, 76th Leg., ch. 1545, §48, eff. Sept. 1, 1999.

ART. 45.54. RENUMBERED

Renumbered to art. 45.051 by Acts 1999, 76th Leg., ch. 1545, §50, eff. Sept. 1, 1999.

ART. 45.55. RENUMBERED

Renumbered to art. 45.052 by Acts 1999, 76th Leg., ch. 1545, §52, eff. Sept. 1, 1999.

ART. 45.56. RENUMBERED

Renumbered to art. 45.053 by Acts 1999, 76th Leg., ch. 1545, §53, eff. Sept. 1, 1999.

SUBCHAPTER A. GENERAL PROVISIONS

ART. 45.001. OBJECTIVES OF CHAPTER

The purpose of this chapter is to establish procedures for processing cases that come within the criminal jurisdiction of the justice courts and municipal courts. This chapter is intended and shall be construed to achieve the following objectives:

(1) to provide fair notice to a person appearing in a criminal proceeding before a justice or municipal court and a meaningful opportunity for that person to be heard;

(2) to ensure appropriate dignity in court procedure without undue formalism;

(3) to promote adherence to rules with sufficient flexibility to serve the ends of justice; and

(4) to process cases without unnecessary expense or delay.

History of CCP art. 45.001: Acts 1999, 76th Leg., ch. 1545, §6, eff. Sept. 1, 1999.

ART. 45.002. APPLICATION OF CHAPTER

Criminal proceedings in the justice and municipal courts shall be conducted in accordance with this chapter, including any other rules of procedure specifically made applicable to those proceedings by this chapter. If this chapter does not provide a rule of procedure governing any aspect of a case, the justice or judge shall apply the other general provisions of this code to the extent necessary to achieve the objectives of this chapter.

History of CCP art. 45.002: Acts 1999, 76th Leg., ch. 1545, §6, eff. Sept. 1, 1999.

ART. 45.003. DEFINITION FOR CERTAIN PROSECUTIONS

For purposes of dismissing a charge under Section 502.407 or 548.605, Transportation Code, "day" does not include Saturday, Sunday, or a legal holiday.

History of CCP art. 45.003: Acts 1999, 76th Leg., ch. 1545, §6, eff. Sept. 1, 1999.

SUBCHAPTER B. PROCEDURES FOR JUSTICE & MUNICIPAL COURTS

ART. 45.011. RULES OF EVIDENCE

The rules of evidence that govern the trials of criminal actions in the district court apply to a criminal proceeding in a justice or municipal court.

History of CCP art. 45.011: Acts 1965, 59th Leg., vol. 2, ch. 722. Renumbered from art. 45.38 and amended by Acts 1999, 76th Leg., ch. 1545, §§7, 8, eff. Sept. 1, 1999.

ART. 45.012. ELECTRONICALLY CREATED RECORDS

(a) Notwithstanding any other provision of law, a document that is issued or maintained by a justice or municipal court or a notice or a citation issued by a law enforcement officer may be created by electronic means, including optical imaging, optical disk, digital imaging, or other electronic reproduction technique that does not permit changes, additions, or deletions to the originally created document.

(b) The court may use electronic means to:

(1) produce a document required by law to be written;

(2) record an instrument, paper, or notice that is permitted or required by law to be recorded or filed; or

(3) maintain a docket.

(c) The court shall maintain original documents as provided by law.

(d) An electronically recorded judgment has the same force and effect as a written signed judgment.

(e) A record created by electronic means is an original record or a certification of the original record.

(f) A printed copy of an optical image of the original record printed from an optical disk system is an accurate copy of the original record.

(g) A justice or municipal court shall have a court seal, the impression of which must be attached to all papers issued out of the court except subpoenas, and which must be used to authenticate the official acts of the clerk and of the recorder. A court seal may be created by electronic means, including optical imaging, optical disk, or other electronic reproduction technique that does not permit changes, additions, or deletions to an original document created by the same type of system.

(h) A statutory requirement that a document contain the signature of any person, including a judge, clerk of the court, or defendant, is satisfied if the document contains that signature as captured on an electronic device.

History of CCP art. 45.012: Acts 1995, 74th Leg., ch. 735, §2, eff. Sept. 1, 1995. Renumbered from art. 45.021 and amended by Acts 1999, 76th Leg., ch. 1545, §9, eff. Sept. 1, 1999. Amended by Acts 1999, 76th Leg., ch. 701, §2, eff. Aug. 30, 1999; Acts 2001, 77th Leg., ch. 1420, §21.001(12), eff. Sept. 1, 2001.

ART. 45.013. FILING WITH CLERK BY MAIL

(a) Notwithstanding any other law, for the purposes of this chapter a document is considered timely filed with the clerk of a court if:

(1) the document is deposited with the United States Postal Service in a first class postage prepaid envelope properly addressed to the clerk on or before the date the document is required to be filed with the clerk; and

(2) the clerk receives the document not later than the 10th day after the date the document is required to be filed with the clerk.

(b) A legible postmark affixed by the United States Postal Service is prima facie evidence of the date the document is deposited with the United States Postal Service.

(c) In this article, "day" does not include Saturday, Sunday, or a legal holiday.

History of CCP art. 45.013: Acts 1999, 76th Leg., ch. 1545, §10, eff. Sept. 1, 1999.

ART. 45.014. WARRANT OF ARREST

(a) When a sworn complaint or affidavit based on probable cause has been filed before the justice or municipal court, the justice or judge may issue a warrant for the arrest of the accused and deliver the same to the proper officer to be executed.

(b) The warrant is sufficient if:

(1) it is issued in the name of "The State of Texas";

(2) it is directed to the proper peace officer or some other person specifically named in the warrant;

(3) it includes a command that the body of the accused be taken, and brought before the authority issuing the warrant, at the time and place stated in the warrant;

(4) it states the name of the person whose arrest is ordered, if known, or if not known, it describes the person as in the complaint;

(5) it states that the person is accused of some offense against the laws of this state, naming the offense; and

(6) it is signed by the justice or judge, naming the office of the justice or judge in the body of the warrant or in connection with the signature of the justice or judge.

(c) Chapter 15 applies to a warrant of arrest issued under this article, except as inconsistent or in conflict with this chapter.

(d) In a county with a population of more than two million that does not have a county attorney, a justice or judge may not issue a warrant under this section for an offense under Section 32.41, Penal Code, unless the district attorney has approved the complaint or affidavit on which the warrant is based.

History of CCP art. 45.014: Acts 1965, 59th Leg., vol. 2, ch. 722. Renumbered from art. 45.18 and amended by Acts 1999, 76th Leg., ch. 1545, §11, eff. Sept. 1, 1999. Amended by Acts 2005, 79th Leg., ch. 644, §1, eff. Sept. 1, 2005.

ART. 45.015. DEFENDANT PLACED IN JAIL

Whenever, by the provisions of this title, the peace officer is authorized to retain a defendant in custody, the peace officer may place the defendant in jail in accordance with this code or other law.

History of CCP art. 45.015: Acts 1965, 59th Leg., vol. 2, ch. 722. Renumbered from art. 45.43 and amended by Acts 1999, 76th Leg., ch. 1545, §12, eff. Sept. 1, 1999.

ART. 45.016. BAIL

The justice or judge may require the defendant to give bail to secure the defendant's appearance in accordance with this code. If the defendant fails to give bail, the defendant may be held in custody.

History of CCP art. 45.016: Acts 1965, 59th Leg., vol. 2, ch. 722. Renumbered from art. 45.41 and amended by Acts 1999, 76th Leg., ch. 1545, §13, eff. Sept. 1, 1999.

ART. 45.017. CRIMINAL DOCKET

(a) The justice or judge of each court, or, if directed by the justice or judge, the clerk of the court, shall keep a docket containing the following information:

(1) the style and file number of each criminal action;

(2) the nature of the offense charged;

(3) the plea offered by the defendant and the date the plea was entered;

(4) the date the warrant, if any, was issued and the return made thereon;

(5) the date the examination or trial was held, and if a trial was held, whether it was by a jury or by the justice or judge;

(6) the verdict of the jury, if any, and the date of the verdict;

(7) the judgment and sentence of the court, and the date each was given;

(8) the motion for new trial, if any, and the decision thereon; and

(9) whether an appeal was taken and the date of that action.

(b) The information in the docket may be processed and stored by the use of electronic data processing equipment, at the discretion of the justice of the peace or the municipal court judge.

History of CCP art. 45.017: Acts 1965, 59th Leg., vol. 2, ch. 722. Amended by Acts 1989, 71st Leg., ch. 499, §1, eff. Aug. 28, 1989. Renumbered from art. 45.13 and amended by Acts 1999, 76th Leg., ch. 1545, §14, eff. Sept. 1, 1999.

ART. 45.018. COMPLAINT

(a) For purposes of this chapter, a complaint is a sworn allegation charging the accused with the commission of an offense.

(b) A defendant is entitled to notice of a complaint against the defendant not later than the day before the date of any proceeding in the prosecution of the defendant under the complaint. The defendant may waive the right to notice granted by this subsection.

History of CCP art. 45.018: Acts 1999, 76th Leg., ch. 1545, §15, eff. Sept. 1, 1999.

ANNOTATIONS

Kindley v. State, 879 S.W.2d 261, 262 (Tex.App.— Houston [14th Dist.] 1994, no pet.). "The purpose of ... a 'complaint' is to apprise the accused of the facts surrounding the offense with which he is charged so that he may prepare a defense."

ART. 45.019. REQUISITES OF COMPLAINT

(a) A complaint is sufficient, without regard to its form, if it substantially satisfies the following requisites:

(1) it must be in writing;

(2) it must commence "In the name and by the authority of the State of Texas";

(3) it must state the name of the accused, if known, or if unknown, must include a reasonably definite description of the accused;

(4) it must show that the accused has committed an offense against the law of this state, or state that the affiant has good reason to believe and does believe that the accused has committed an offense against the law of this state;

(5) it must state the date the offense was committed as definitely as the affiant is able to provide;

(6) it must bear the signature or mark of the affiant; and

(7) it must conclude with the words "Against the peace and dignity of the State" and, if the offense charged is an offense only under a municipal ordinance, it may also conclude with the words "Contrary to the said ordinance."

(b) A complaint filed in justice court must allege that the offense was committed in the county in which the complaint is made.

(c) A complaint filed in municipal court must allege that the offense was committed in the territorial limits of the municipality in which the complaint is made.

(d) A complaint may be sworn to before any officer authorized to administer oaths.

(e) A complaint in municipal court may be sworn to before:

(1) the municipal judge;

(2) the clerk of the court or a deputy clerk;

(3) the city secretary; or

(4) the city attorney or a deputy city attorney.

(f) If the defendant does not object to a defect, error, or irregularity of form or substance in a charging instrument before the date on which the trial on the merits commences, the defendant waives and forfeits the right to object to the defect, error, or irregularity. Nothing in this article prohibits a trial court from requiring that an objection to a charging instrument be made at an earlier time.

(g) In a county with a population of more than two million that does not have a county attorney, a complaint for an offense under Section 32.41, Penal Code, must be approved by the district attorney, regardless of whether a collection proceeding is initiated by the district attorney under Section 32.41(e), Penal Code.

History of CCP art. 45.019: Acts 1965, 59th Leg., vol. 2, ch. 722. Renumbered from art. 45.17 and amended by Acts 1999, 76th Leg., ch. 1545, §16, eff. Sept. 1, 1999. Amended by Acts 2005, 79th Leg., ch. 644, §2, eff. Sept. 1, 2005.

ANNOTATIONS

Sanchez v. State, 138 S.W.3d 324, 330 (Tex.Crim. App.2004). "Article 45.019(f) means what it says, that a party can move to quash a charging instrument at any time prior to the day on which the trial on the merits commences."

Zulauf v. State, 591 S.W.2d 869, 871 (Tex.Crim. App.1979). "The complaint facially follows the letter and tenor of [CCP art.] 45.17 [now art. 45.019], notwithstanding its failure to state precisely the justice precinct in which the offense was committed or in which appellant resided."

Schmitz v. State, 952 S.W.2d 922, 924 (Tex.App.— Fort Worth 1997, pet. ref'd). "Although a complaint in justice court must state facts sufficient to show the commission of an offense charged, it need not show the same particularity or specificity as is necessary in an indictment or information. [¶] The State argues that the complaint sufficiently complies with [CCP art.] 45.17 [now art. 45.019]. Appellant contends that article 45.17 addresses the form of a complaint rather than the substantive requirements for pleading the offense itself. We agree."

ART. 45.020. APPEARANCE BY COUNSEL

(a) The defendant has a right to appear by counsel as in all other cases.

(b) Not more than one counsel shall conduct either the prosecution or defense. State's counsel may open and conclude the argument.

History of CCP art. 45.020: Acts 1965, 59th Leg., vol. 2, ch. 722. Renumbered from art. 45.37 and amended by Acts 1999, 76th Leg., ch. 1545, §17, eff. Sept. 1, 1999.

ART. 45.021. PLEADINGS

All pleading of the defendant in justice or municipal court may be oral or in writing as the court may direct.

History of CCP art. 45.021: Acts 1965, 59th Leg., vol. 2, ch. 722. Renumbered from art. 45.33 and amended by Acts 1999, 76th Leg., ch. 1545, §18, eff. Sept. 1, 1999.

ART. 45.0215. PLEA BY MINOR & APPEARANCE OF PARENT

(a) If a defendant is younger than 17 years of age and has not had the disabilities of minority removed, the judge or justice:

(1) must take the defendant's plea in open court; and

(2) shall issue a summons to compel the defendant's parent, guardian, or managing conservator to be present during:

(A) the taking of the defendant's plea; and

(B) all other proceedings relating to the case.

(b) If the court is unable to secure the appearance of the defendant's parent, guardian, or managing conservator by issuance of a summons, the court may, without the defendant's parent, guardian, or managing conservator present, take the defendant's plea and proceed against the defendant.

(c) If the defendant resides in a county other than the county in which the alleged offense occurred, the defendant may, with leave of the judge of the court of original jurisdiction, enter the plea, including a plea under Article 45.052, before a judge in the county in which the defendant resides.

(d) A justice or municipal court shall endorse on the summons issued to a parent an order to appear personally at a hearing with the child. The summons must include a warning that the failure of the parent to appear may result in arrest and is a Class C misdemeanor.

History of CCP art. 45.0215: Acts 1997, 75th Leg., ch. 193, §1, eff. Sept. 1, 1997. Renumbered from art. 45.331 and amended by Acts 1999, 76th Leg., ch. 1545, §19, eff. Sept. 1, 1999. Amended by Acts 2005, 79th Leg., ch. 949, §33, eff. Sept. 1, 2005.

ART. 45.0216. EXPUNCTION OF CERTAIN CONVICTION RECORDS OF CHILDREN

(a) In this article, "child" has the meaning assigned by Section 51.02, Family Code.

(b) A person convicted of not more than one offense described by Section 8.07(a)(4) or (5), Penal Code, while the person was a child may, on or after the person's 17th birthday, apply to the court in which the child was convicted to have the conviction expunged as provided by this article.

(c) The person must make a written request to have the records expunged. The request must be under oath.

(d) The request must contain the person's statement that the person was not convicted while the person was a child of any offense described by Section 8.07(a)(4) or (5), Penal Code, other than the offense the person seeks to have expunged.

(e) The judge shall inform the person and any parent in open court of the person's expunction rights and provide them with a copy of this article.

(f) If the court finds that the person was not convicted of any other offense described by Section 8.07(a)(4) or (5), Penal Code, while the person was a child, the court shall order the conviction, together with all complaints, verdicts, sentences, and prosecutorial and law enforcement records, and any other documents relating to the offense, expunged from the person's record. After entry of the order, the person is released from all disabilities resulting from the conviction and the conviction may not be shown or made known for any purpose.

(g) This article does not apply to any offense otherwise covered by:

(1) Chapter 106, Alcoholic Beverage Code;

(2) Chapter 161, Health and Safety Code; or

(3) Section 25.094, Education Code.

(h) Records of a person under 17 years of age relating to a complaint dismissed as provided by Article 45.051 or 45.052 may be expunged under this article.

(i) The justice or municipal court shall require a person who requests expungement under this article to pay a fee in the amount of $30 to defray the cost of notifying state agencies of orders of expungement under this article.

(j) The procedures for expunction provided under this article are separate and distinct from the expunction procedures under Chapter 55.

History of CCP art. 45.0216: Acts 2001, 77th Leg., ch. 1297, §50, eff. Sept. 1, 2001. Amended by Acts 2005, 79th Leg., ch. 886, §2, eff. Sept. 1, 2005.

ART. 45.022. PLEA OF GUILTY OR NOLO CONTENDERE

Proof as to the offense may be heard upon a plea of guilty or a plea of nolo contendere and the punishment assessed by the court.

History of CCP art. 45.022: Acts 1965, 59th Leg., vol. 2, ch. 722. Renumbered from art. 45.34 and amended by Acts 1999, 76th Leg., ch. 1545, §20, eff. Sept. 1, 1999.

ART. 45.023. DEFENDANT'S PLEA

After the jury is impaneled, or after the defendant has waived trial by jury, the defendant may:

(1) plead guilty or not guilty;

(2) enter a plea of nolo contendere; or

(3) enter the special plea of double jeopardy as described by Article 27.05.

History of CCP art. 45.023: Acts 1965, 59th Leg., vol. 2, ch. 722. Renumbered from art. 45.31 and amended by Acts 1999, 76th Leg., ch. 1545, §21, eff. Sept. 1, 1999.

ART. 45.024. DEFENDANT'S REFUSAL TO PLEAD

The justice or judge shall enter a plea of not guilty if the defendant refuses to plead.

History of CCP art. 45.024: Acts 1965, 59th Leg., vol. 2, ch. 722. Renumbered from art. 45.35 and amended by Acts 1999, 76th Leg., ch. 1545, §22, eff. Sept. 1, 1999.

ART. 45.025. DEFENDANT MAY WAIVE JURY

The accused may waive a trial by jury in writing. If the defendant waives a trial by jury, the justice or judge shall hear and determine the cause without a jury.

History of CCP art. 45.025: Acts 1965, 59th Leg., vol. 2, ch. 722. Renumbered from art. 45.24 and amended by Acts 1999, 76th Leg., ch. 1545, §23, eff. Sept. 1, 1999.

See also CCP art. 1.13.

ANNOTATIONS

Huynh v. State, 901 S.W.2d 480, 482-83 (Tex.Crim. App.1995). "This article does not require that the waiver be in writing. [CCP art.] 45.24 [now art. 45.025] ... is controlling, to the preclusion of [CCP art.] 1.13."

ART. 45.026. JURY TRIAL; FAILURE TO APPEAR

(a) A justice or municipal court may order a party who does not waive a jury trial in a justice or municipal court and who fails to appear for the trial to pay the costs incurred for impaneling the jury.

(b) The justice or municipal court may release a party from the obligation to pay costs under this section for good cause.

(c) An order issued by a justice or municipal court under this section may be enforced by contempt as prescribed by Section 21.002(c), Government Code.

History of CCP art. 45.026: Acts 1995, 74th Leg., ch. 122, §1, eff. Sept. 1, 1995. Renumbered from art. 45.251 and amended by Acts 1999, 76th Leg., ch. 1545, §24, eff. Sept. 1, 1999.

ART. 45.027. JURY SUMMONED

(a) If the accused does not waive a trial by jury, the justice or judge shall issue a writ commanding the proper officer to summon a venire from which six qualified persons shall be selected to serve as jurors in the case.

(b) The jurors when so summoned shall remain in attendance as jurors in all cases that may come up for hearing until discharged by the court.

(c) Any person so summoned who fails to attend may be fined an amount not to exceed $100 for contempt.

History of CCP art. 45.027: Acts 1965, 59th Leg., vol. 2, ch. 722. Amended by Acts 1995, 74th Leg., ch. 802, §1, eff. Sept. 1, 1995. Renumbered from art. 45.25 and amended by Acts 1999, 76th Leg., ch. 1545, §25, eff. Sept. 1, 1999.

ART. 45.028. OTHER JURORS SUMMONED

If, from challenges or any other cause, a sufficient number of jurors are not in attendance, the justice or judge shall order the proper officer to summon a sufficient number of qualified persons to form the jury.

History of CCP art. 45.028: Acts 1965, 59th Leg., vol. 2, ch. 722. Renumbered from art. 45.29 and amended by Acts 1999, 76th Leg., ch. 1545, §26, eff. Sept. 1, 1999.

ART. 45.029. PEREMPTORY CHALLENGES

In all jury trials in a justice or municipal court, the state and each defendant in the case is entitled to three peremptory challenges.

History of CCP art. 45.029: Acts 1965, 59th Leg., vol. 2, ch. 722. Renumbered from art. 45.28 and amended by Acts 1999, 76th Leg., ch. 1545, §27, eff. Sept. 1, 1999.

ART. 45.030. FORMATION OF JURY

The justice or judge shall form the jury and administer the appropriate oath in accordance with Chapter 35.

History of CCP art. 45.030: Acts 1965, 59th Leg., vol. 2, ch. 722. Renumbered from art. 45.30 and amended by Acts 1999, 76th Leg., ch. 1545, §28, eff. Sept. 1, 1999.

ART. 45.031. COUNSEL FOR STATE NOT PRESENT

If the state is not represented by counsel when the case is called for trial, the justice or judge may:

(1) postpone the trial to a date certain;

(2) appoint an attorney pro tem as provided by this code to represent the state; or

(3) proceed to trial.

History of CCP art. 45.031: Acts 1965, 59th Leg., vol. 2, ch. 722. Renumbered from art. 45.36 and amended by Acts 1999, 76th Leg., ch. 1545, §29, eff. Sept. 1, 1999.

ART. 45.032. DIRECTED VERDICT

If, upon the trial of a case in a justice or municipal court, the state fails to prove a prima facie case of the offense alleged in the complaint, the defendant is entitled to a directed verdict of "not guilty."

History of CCP art. 45.032: Acts 1969, 61st Leg., ch. 520, §2, eff. June 10, 1969. Renumbered from art. 45.031 and amended by Acts 1999, 76th Leg., ch. 1545, §30, eff. Sept. 1, 1999.

ART. 45.033. JURY CHARGE

The judge shall charge the jury. The charge may be made orally or in writing, except that the charge shall be made in writing if required by law.

History of CCP art. 45.033: Acts 1999, 76th Leg., ch. 1545, §31, eff. Sept. 1, 1999.

ART. 45.034. JURY KEPT TOGETHER

The jury shall retire in charge of an officer when the cause is submitted to them, and be kept together until they agree to a verdict, are discharged, or the court recesses.

History of CCP art. 45.034: Acts 1965, 59th Leg., vol. 2, ch. 722. Renumbered from art. 45.39 and amended by Acts 1999, 76th Leg., ch. 1545, §32, eff. Sept. 1, 1999.

ART. 45.035. MISTRIAL

A jury shall be discharged if it fails to agree to a verdict after being kept together a reasonable time. If a jury is discharged because it fails to agree to a verdict, the justice or judge may impanel another jury as soon as practicable to try such cause.

History of CCP art. 45.035: Acts 1965, 59th Leg., vol. 2, ch. 722. Amended by Acts 1995, 74th Leg., ch. 1005, §1, eff. Sept. 1, 1995. Renumbered from art. 45.40 and amended by Acts 1999, 76th Leg., ch. 1545, §33, eff. Sept. 1, 1999.

ART. 45.036. VERDICT

(a) When the jury has agreed on a verdict, the jury shall bring the verdict into court.

(b) The justice or judge shall see that the verdict is in proper form and shall render the proper judgment and sentence on the verdict.

History of CCP art. 45.036: Acts 1965, 59th Leg., vol. 2, ch. 722. Renumbered from art. 45.42 and amended by Acts 1999, 76th Leg., ch. 1545, §34, eff. Sept. 1, 1999.

ART. 45.037. MOTION FOR NEW TRIAL

A motion for a new trial must be made within one day after the rendition of judgment and sentence, and not afterward.

History of CCP art. 45.037: Acts 1965, 59th Leg., vol. 2, ch. 722. Renumbered from art. 45.45 and amended by Acts 1999, 76th Leg., ch. 1545, §35, eff. Sept. 1, 1999.

ART. 45.038. NEW TRIAL GRANTED

(a) Not later than the 10th day after the date that the judgment is entered, a justice or judge may, for good cause shown, grant the defendant a new trial, whenever the justice or judge considers that justice has not been done the defendant in the trial of the case.

(b) If a motion for a new trial is not granted before the 11th day after the date that the judgment is entered, the motion shall be considered denied.

History of CCP art. 45.038: Acts 1965, 59th Leg., vol. 2, ch. 722. Renumbered from art. 45.44 and amended by Acts 1999, 76th Leg., ch. 1545, §36, eff. Sept. 1, 1999.

ART. 45.039. ONLY ONE NEW TRIAL GRANTED

Not more than one new trial shall be granted the defendant in the same case. When a new trial has been granted, the justice or judge shall proceed, as soon as practicable, to try the case again.

History of CCP art. 45.039: Acts 1965, 59th Leg., vol. 2, ch. 722. Renumbered from art. 45.46 and amended by Acts 1999, 76th Leg., ch. 1545, §37, eff. Sept. 1, 1999.

ART. 45.040. STATE NOT ENTITLED TO NEW TRIAL

In no case shall the state be entitled to a new trial.

History of CCP art. 45.040: Acts 1965, 59th Leg., vol. 2, ch. 722. Renumbered from art. 45.47 and amended by Acts 1999, 76th Leg., ch. 1545, §38, eff. Sept. 1, 1999.

ART. 45.041. JUDGMENT

(a) The judgment and sentence, in case of conviction in a criminal action before a justice of the peace or municipal court judge, shall be that the defendant pay the amount of the fine and costs to the state.

(b) The justice or judge may direct the defendant:

(1) to pay:

(A) the entire fine and costs when sentence is pronounced;

(B) the entire fine and costs at some later date; or

(C) a specified portion of the fine and costs at designated intervals;

Ⓐ *Subsection (2) below is effective for sentences pronounced on or after Sept. 1, 2007.*

(2) if applicable, to make restitution to any victim of the offense; and

Subsection (2) below is effective for sentences pronounced before Sept. 1, 2007.

(2) if applicable, to make restitution to any victim of the offense in an amount not to exceed $500; and

(3) to satisfy any other sanction authorized by law.

Ⓔ *Subsection (b-1) below is effective for sentences pronounced on or after Sept. 1, 2007.*

(b-1) Restitution made under Subsection (b)(2) may not exceed $5,000 for an offense under Section 32.41, Penal Code.

(c) The justice or judge shall credit the defendant for time served in jail as provided by Article 42.03. The credit shall be applied to the amount of the fine and costs at the rate provided by Article 45.048.

(d) All judgments, sentences, and final orders of the justice or judge shall be rendered in open court.

History of CCP art. 45.041: Acts 1965, 59th Leg., vol. 2, ch. 722. Amended by Acts 1971, 62nd Leg., ch. 987, §5, eff. June 15, 1971. Renumbered from art. 45.50 and amended by Acts 1999, 76th Leg., ch. 1545, §39, eff. Sept. 1, 1999. Amended by Acts 2007, 80th Leg., ch. 1393, §2, eff. Sept. 1, 2007.

ART. 45.042. APPEAL

(a) Appeals from a justice or municipal court, including appeals from final judgments in bond forfeiture proceedings, shall be heard by the county court except in cases where the county court has no jurisdiction, in which counties such appeals shall be heard by the proper court.

(b) Unless the appeal is taken from a municipal court of record and the appeal is based on error reflected in the record, the trial shall be de novo.

(c) In an appeal from the judgment and sentence of a justice or municipal court, if the defendant is in custody, the defendant is to be committed to jail unless the defendant gives bail.

History of CCP art. 45.042: Acts 1965, 59th Leg., vol. 2, ch. 722. Amended by Acts 1987, 70th Leg., ch. 641, §4, eff. Sept. 1, 1987. Renumbered from art. 45.10 and amended by Acts 1999, 76th Leg., ch. 1545, §40, eff. Sept. 1, 1999.

ART. 45.0425. APPEAL BOND

(a) If the court from whose judgment and sentence the appeal is taken is in session, the court must approve the bail. The amount of a bail bond may not be less than two times the amount of the fine and costs adjudged against the defendant, payable to the State of Texas. The bail may not in any case be for a sum less than $50. If the appeal bond otherwise meets the requirements of this code, the court without requiring a court appearance by the defendant shall approve the appeal bond in the amount the court under Article 27.14(b) notified the defendant would be approved.

(b) An appeal bond shall recite that in the cause the defendant was convicted and has appealed and be conditioned that the defendant shall make the defendant's personal appearance before the court to which the appeal is taken instanter, if the court is in session, or, if the court is not in session, at its next regular term, stating the time and place of that session, and there remain from day to day and term to term, and answer in the cause in the court.

History of CCP art. 45.0425: Acts 1999, 76th Leg., ch. 1545, §41, eff. Sept. 1, 1999.

ART. 45.0426. FILING BOND PERFECTS APPEAL

(a) When the appeal bond has been filed with the justice or judge who tried the case not later than the 10th day after the date the judgment was entered, the appeal in such case shall be held to be perfected.

(b) If an appeal bond is not timely filed, the appellate court does not have jurisdiction over the case and shall remand the case to the justice or municipal court for execution of the sentence.

(c) An appeal may not be dismissed because the defendant failed to give notice of appeal in open court. An appeal by the defendant or the state may not be dismissed on account of any defect in the transcript.

History of CCP art. 45.0426: Acts 1965, 59th Leg., vol. 2, ch. 722. Amended by Acts 1995, 74th Leg., ch. 478, §1, eff. Sept. 1, 1995. Renumbered from art. 44.14 and amended by Acts 1999, 76th Leg., ch. 1545, §42, eff. Sept. 1, 1999.

ANNOTATIONS

Crawford v. Campbell, 124 S.W.3d 778, 780-81 (Tex.App.—Houston [1st Dist.] 2003, no pet.). "By voluntarily paying the fine and costs assessed against

---

him, appellant rendered his appeal moot: his election to satisfy the judgment left him nothing from which to appeal. [¶] [T]he fact that appellant had complied with the statutory requirements for filing an appeal from the municipal court judgment did not entitle appellant to an appeal after he had voluntarily satisfied the judgment."

ART. 45.043. EFFECT OF APPEAL

When a defendant files the appeal bond required by law with the justice or municipal court, all further proceedings in the case in the justice or municipal court shall cease.

History of CCP art. 45.043: Acts 1965, 59th Leg., vol. 2, ch. 722. Renumbered from art. 45.48 and amended by Acts 1999, 76th Leg., ch. 1545, §43, eff. Sept. 1, 1999.

ART. 45.044. FORFEITURE OF CASH BOND IN SATISFACTION OF FINE

(a) A justice or judge may enter a judgment of conviction and forfeit a cash bond posted by the defendant in satisfaction of the defendant's fine and cost if the defendant:

(1) has entered a written and signed plea of nolo contendere and a waiver of jury trial; and

(2) fails to appear according to the terms of the defendant's release.

(b) A justice or judge who enters a judgment of conviction and forfeiture under Subsection (a) of this article shall immediately notify the defendant in writing, by regular mail addressed to the defendant at the defendant's last known address, that:

(1) a judgment of conviction and forfeiture of bond was entered against the defendant on a date certain and the forfeiture satisfies the defendant's fine and costs in the case; and

(2) the defendant has a right to a new trial in the case if the defendant applies for the new trial not later than the 10th day after the date of judgment and forfeiture.

(c) Notwithstanding Article 45.037 of this code, the defendant may file a motion for a new trial within the period provided by Subsection (b) of this article, and the court shall grant the motion if the motion is made within that period. On the new trial, the court shall permit the defendant to withdraw the previously entered plea of nolo contendere and waiver of jury trial.

History of CCP art. 45.044: Acts 1993, 73rd Leg., ch. 109, §1, eff. May 9, 1993. Renumbered from art. 45.231 and amended by Acts 1999, 76th Leg., ch. 1545, §44, eff. Sept. 1, 1999.

ART. 45.045. CAPIAS PRO FINE

 Subsection (a) below is effective for fees imposed for the execution or processing of a warrant or capias issued for offenses committed on or after Sept. 1, 2007.

(a) If the defendant is not in custody when the judgment is rendered or if the defendant fails to satisfy the judgment according to its terms, the court may order a capias pro fine, as defined by Article 43.015, issued for the defendant's arrest. The capias pro fine shall state the amount of the judgment and sentence, and command the appropriate peace officer to bring the defendant before the court immediately or place the defendant in jail until the business day following the date of the defendant's arrest if the defendant cannot be brought before the court immediately.

Subsection (a) below is effective for fees imposed for the execution or processing of a warrant or capias issued for offenses in which any element of the offense was committed before Sept. 1, 2007.

(a) If the defendant is not in custody when the judgment is rendered or if the defendant fails to satisfy the judgment according to its terms, the court may order a capias pro fine issued for the defendant's arrest. The capias pro fine shall state the amount of the judgment and sentence, and command the appropriate peace officer to bring the defendant before the court or place the defendant in jail until the defendant can be brought before the court.

(b) A capias pro fine may not be issued for an individual convicted for an offense committed before the individual's 17th birthday unless:

(1) the individual is 17 years of age or older;

(2) the court finds that the issuance of the capias pro fine is justified after considering:

(A) the sophistication and maturity of the individual;

(B) the criminal record and history of the individual; and

(C) the reasonable likelihood of bringing about the discharge of the judgment through the use of procedures and services currently available to the court; and

(3) the court has proceeded under Article 45.050 to compel the individual to discharge the judgment.

(c) This article does not limit the authority of a court to order a child taken into custody under Article 45.058 or 45.059.

✦

History of CCP art. 45.045: Acts 1965, 59th Leg., vol. 2, ch. 722. Amended by Acts 1971, 62nd Leg., ch. 987, §6, eff. June 15, 1971. Renumbered from art. 45.51 and amended by Acts 1999, 76th Leg., ch. 1545, §45, eff. Sept. 1, 1999. Amended by Acts 2003, 78th Leg., ch. 283, §31, eff. Sept. 1, 2003; Acts 2007, 80th Leg., ch. 1263, §16, eff. Sept. 1, 2007.

ANNOTATIONS

Jones v. State, 119 S.W.3d 766, 786 (Tex.Crim.App. 2003). "While a capias is issued after a judgment has been rendered against the defendant, it must still be supported by probable cause. But because a judgment against a defendant signifies a finding beyond a reasonable doubt that he has committed the charged offense, we have held in the context of a parole violation that a judgment coupled with a finding by the court that there is a 'reason to believe' that the defendant has violated the conditions of his parole will constitute sufficient probable cause to support the issuance of a parole violation warrant. [A] judgment for a traffic violation, together with a finding by the court that the defendant has failed to satisfy its terms, will comprise sufficient probable cause to support issuance of the capias pro finc."

ART. 45.046. COMMITMENT

Ⓐ *Subsection (a) below is effective for fees imposed for the execution or processing of a warrant or capias issued for offenses committed on or after Sept. 1, 2007.*

(a) When a judgment and sentence have been entered against a defendant and the defendant defaults in the discharge of the judgment, the judge may order the defendant confined in jail until discharged by law if the judge at a hearing makes a written determination that:

(1) the defendant is not indigent and has failed to make a good faith effort to discharge the fine and costs; or

(2) the defendant is indigent and:

Ⓔ **(A)** has failed to make a good faith effort to discharge the fines and costs under Article 45.049; and

Ⓔ **(B)** could have discharged the fines and costs under Article 45.049 without experiencing any undue hardship.

Subsection (a) below is effective for fees imposed for the execution or processing of a warrant or capias issued for offenses in which any element of the offense was committed before Sept. 1, 2007.

(a) When a judgment and sentence have been entered against a defendant and the defendant defaults in the discharge of the judgment, the judge may order the defendant confined in jail until discharged by law if the judge determines that:

(1) the defendant intentionally failed to make a good faith effort to discharge the judgment; or

(2) the defendant is not indigent.

(b) A certified copy of the judgment, sentence, and order is sufficient to authorize such confinement.

History of CCP art. 45.046: Acts 1965, 59th Leg., vol. 2, ch. 722. Amended by Acts 1971, 62nd Leg., ch. 987, §7, eff. June 15, 1971. Renumbered from art. 45.52 and amended by Acts 1999, 76th Leg., ch. 1545, §46, eff. Sept. 1, 1999. Amended by Acts 2007, 80th Leg., ch. 1263, §19, eff. Sept. 1, 2007.

ART. 45.047. CIVIL COLLECTION OF FINES AFTER JUDGMENT

If after a judgment and sentence is entered the defendant defaults in payment of a fine, the justice or judge may order the fine and costs collected by execution against the defendant's property in the same manner as a judgment in a civil suit.

History of CCP art. 45.047: Acts 1999, 76th Leg., ch. 1545, §47., eff. Sept. 1, 1999.

ART. 45.048. DISCHARGED FROM JAIL

(a) A defendant placed in jail on account of failure to pay the fine and costs shall be discharged on habeas corpus by showing that the defendant:

(1) is too poor to pay the fine and costs; or

(2) has remained in jail a sufficient length of time to satisfy the fine and costs, at the rate of not less than $50 for each period of time served, as specified by the convicting court in the judgment in the case.

(b) A convicting court may specify a period of time that is not less than eight hours or more than 24 hours as the period for which a defendant who fails to pay the fines and costs in the case must remain in jail to satisfy $50 of the fine and costs.

History of CCP art. 45.048: Acts 1965, 59th Leg., vol. 2, ch. 722. Amended by Acts 1981, 67th Leg., ch. 708, §3, eff. Aug. 31, 1981. Renumbered from art. 45.53 and amended by Acts 1999, 76th Leg., ch. 1545, §48, eff. Sept. 1, 1999; Acts 2001, 77th Leg., ch. 872, §1, eff. Sept. 1, 2001; Acts 2003, 78th Leg., ch. 209, §65(a), eff. Jan. 1, 2004.

ART. 45.049. COMMUNITY SERVICE IN SATISFACTION OF FINE OR COSTS

(a) A justice or judge may require a defendant who fails to pay a previously assessed fine or costs, or who is determined by the court to have insufficient resources or income to pay a fine or costs, to discharge all or part of the fine or costs by performing community service. A defendant may discharge an obligation to perform community service under this article by paying at any time the fine and costs assessed.

(b) In the justice's or judge's order requiring a defendant to participate in community service work under this article, the justice or judge must specify the number of hours the defendant is required to work.

(c) The justice or judge may order the defendant to perform community service work under this article only for a governmental entity or a nonprofit organization that provides services to the general public that enhance social welfare and the general well-being of the community. A governmental entity or nonprofit organization that accepts a defendant under this article to perform community service must agree to supervise the defendant in the performance of the defendant's work and report on the defendant's work to the justice or judge who ordered the community service.

(d) A justice or judge may not order a defendant to perform more than 16 hours per week of community service under this article unless the justice or judge determines that requiring the defendant to work additional hours does not work a hardship on the defendant or the defendant's dependents.

(e) A defendant is considered to have discharged not less than $50 of fines or costs for each eight hours of community service performed under this article.

(f) A sheriff, employee of a sheriff's department, county commissioner, county employee, county judge, justice of the peace, municipal court judge, or officer or employee of a political subdivision other than a county is not liable for damages arising from an act or failure to act in connection with manual labor performed by a defendant under this article if the act or failure to act:

(1) was performed pursuant to court order; and

(2) was not intentional, wilfully or wantonly negligent, or performed with conscious indifference or reckless disregard for the safety of others.

Subsection (g) below was enacted by Acts 2007, 80th Leg., ch. 1263, §17, effective Sept. 1, 2007, without reference to the conflicting enactment made by Acts 2007, 80th Leg., ch. 1113, §5, effective Sept. 1, 2007. Subsection (g) below is effective for fees imposed for the execution or processing of a warrant or capias issued for offenses committed on or after Sept. 1, 2007.

(g) A community supervision and corrections department or a court-related services office may provide the administrative and other services necessary for supervision of a defendant required to perform community service under this article.

Subsection (g) below was enacted by Acts 2007, 80th Leg., ch. 1113, §5, effective Sept. 1, 2007, without reference to the conflicting enactment made by Acts 2007, 80th Leg., ch. 1263, §17, effective Sept. 1, 2007. Subsection (g) below is effective for offenses committed on or after Sept. 1, 2007.

(g) This subsection applies only to a defendant who is charged with a traffic offense or an offense under Section 106.05, Alcoholic Beverage Code, and is a resident of this state. If under Article 45.051(b)(10), Code of Criminal Procedure, the judge requires the defendant to perform community service as a condition of the deferral, the defendant is entitled to elect whether to perform the required governmental entity or nonprofit organization community service in:

(1) the county in which the court is located; or

(2) the county in which the defendant resides, but only if the entity or organization agrees to:

(A) supervise the defendant in the performance of the defendant's community service work; and

(B) report to the court on the defendant's community service work.

Subsection (h) below is effective for offenses committed on or after Sept. 1, 2007.

(h) This subsection applies only to a defendant charged with an offense under Section 106.05, Alcoholic Beverage Code, who, under Subsection (g), elects to perform the required community service in the county in which the defendant resides. The community service must comply with Sections 106.071(d) and (e), Alcoholic Beverage Code, except that if the educational programs or services described by Section 106.071(e) are not available in the county of the defendant's residence, the court may order community service that it considers appropriate for rehabilitative purposes.

History of CCP art. 45.049: Acts 1993, 73rd Leg., ch. 298, §1, eff. May 27, 1993. Renumbered from art. 45.521 and amended by Acts 1999, 76th Leg., ch. 1545, §49, eff. Sept. 1, 1999. Amended by Acts 2003, 78th Leg., ch. 209, §66(a), eff. Jan. 1, 2004; Acts 2007, 80th Leg., ch. 1113, §5 (eff. Sept. 1, 2007), ch. 1263, §17 (eff. Sept. 1, 2007).

ART. 45.0491. WAIVER OF PAYMENT OF FINES FOR INDIGENT DEFENDANTS

Article 45.0491 below is effective for fees imposed for the execution or processing of a warrant or capias issued for offenses committed on or after Sept. 1, 2007.

A municipal court, regardless of whether the court is a court of record, or a justice court may waive payment of a fine or costs imposed on a defendant who defaults in payment if the court determines that:

(1) the defendant is indigent; and

(2) discharging the fine and costs under Article 45.049 would impose an undue hardship on the defendant.

History of CCP art. 45.0491: Acts 2007, 80th Leg., ch. 1263, §18, eff. Sept. 1, 2007.

ART. 45.050. FAILURE TO PAY FINE; CONTEMPT: JUVENILES

(a) In this article, "child" has the meaning assigned by Article 45.058(h).

(b) A justice or municipal court may not order the confinement of a child for:

(1) the failure to pay all or any part of a fine or costs imposed for the conviction of an offense punishable by fine only; or

(2) contempt of another order of a justice or municipal court.

(c) If a child fails to obey an order of a justice or municipal court under circumstances that would constitute contempt of court, the justice or municipal court, after providing notice and an opportunity to be heard, may:

(1) refer the child to the appropriate juvenile court for delinquent conduct for contempt of the justice or municipal court order; or

(2) retain jurisdiction of the case, hold the child in contempt of the justice or municipal court, and order either or both of the following:

(A) that the contemnor pay a fine not to exceed $500; or

(B) that the Department of Public Safety suspend the contemnor's driver's license or permit or, if the contemnor does not have a license or permit, to deny the issuance of a license or permit to the contemnor until the contemnor fully complies with the orders of the court.

(d) A justice or municipal court may hold a person in contempt and impose a remedy authorized by Subsection (c)(2) if:

(1) the person was convicted for an offense committed before the person's 17th birthday;

(2) the person failed to obey the order while the person was 17 years of age or older; and

(3) the failure to obey occurred under circumstances that constitute contempt of court.

(e) A justice or municipal court may hold a person in contempt and impose a remedy authorized by Subsection (c)(2) if the person, while younger than 17 years of age, engaged in conduct in contempt of an order issued by the justice or municipal court, but contempt proceedings could not be held before the person's 17th birthday.

(f) A court that orders suspension or denial of a driver's license or permit under Subsection (c)(2)(B) shall notify the Department of Public Safety on receiving proof of compliance with the orders of the court.

(g) A justice or municipal court may not refer a child who violates a court order while 17 years of age or older to a juvenile court for delinquency proceedings for contempt of court.

History of CCP art. 45.050: Acts 1995, 74th Leg., ch. 262, §86, eff. Jan. 1, 1996. Renumbered from art. 45.522 and amended by Acts 1999, 76th Leg., ch. 1545, §49, eff. Sept. 1, 1999. Amended by Acts 1999, 76th Leg., ch. 76, §7, eff. Sept. 1, 1999; Acts 2001, 77th Leg., ch. 1297, §51 (eff. Sept. 1, 2001), ch. 1514, §8 (eff. Sept. 1, 2001); Acts 2003, 78th Leg., ch. 283, §32 (eff. Sept. 1, 2003), ch. 1276, §5.002 (eff. Sept. 1, 2003).

ART. 45.051. SUSPENSION OF SENTENCE & DEFERRAL OF FINAL DISPOSITION

(a) On a plea of guilty or nolo contendere by a defendant or on a finding of guilt in a misdemeanor case punishable by fine only and payment of all court costs, the judge may, at the judge's discretion, defer further proceedings without entering an adjudication of guilt and place the defendant on probation for a period not to exceed 180 days. An order of deferral under this subsection terminates any liability under a bail bond or an appearance bond given for the charge.

 (a-1) Notwithstanding any other provision of law, as an alternative to requiring a defendant charged with one or more offenses to make payment of all court costs as required by Subsection (a), the judge, in the judge's discretion, may:

(1) allow the defendant to enter into an agreement for payment of those costs in installments during the defendant's period of probation;

(2) require an eligible defendant to discharge all or part of those costs by performing community service under Article 45.049; or

(3) take any combination of actions authorized by Subdivision (1) or (2).

(b) During the deferral period, the judge may, at the judge's discretion, require the defendant to:

(1) post a bond in the amount of the fine assessed to secure payment of the fine;

(2) pay restitution to the victim of the offense in an amount not to exceed the fine assessed;

(3) submit to professional counseling;

(4) submit to diagnostic testing for alcohol or a controlled substance or drug;

(5) submit to a psychosocial assessment;

(6) participate in an alcohol or drug abuse treatment or education program;

(7) pay the costs of any diagnostic testing, psychosocial assessment, or participation in a treatment or education program either directly or through the court as court costs;

(8) complete a driving safety course approved under Chapter 1001, Education Code, or another course as directed by the judge;

(9) present to the court satisfactory evidence that the defendant has complied with each requirement imposed by the judge under this article; and

(10) comply with any other reasonable condition.

(b-1) If the defendant is younger than 25 years of age and the offense committed by the defendant is a traffic offense classified as a moving violation:

(1) Subsection (b)(8) does not apply;

(2) during the deferral period, the judge shall require the defendant to complete a driving safety course approved under Chapter 1001, Education Code; and

(3) if the defendant holds a provisional license, during the deferral period the judge shall require that the defendant be examined by the Department of Public Safety as required by Section 521.161(b)(2), Transportation Code; a defendant is not exempt from the examination regardless of whether the defendant was examined previously.

(b-2) A person examined as required by Subsection (b-1)(3) must pay a $10 examination fee.

(b-3) The fee collected under Subsection (b-2) must be deposited to the credit of a special account in the general revenue fund and may be used only by the Department of Public Safety for the administration of Chapter 521, Transportation Code.

(c) On determining that the defendant has complied with the requirements imposed by the judge under this article, the judge shall dismiss the complaint, and it shall be clearly noted in the docket that the complaint is dismissed and that there is not a final conviction. If the complaint is dismissed, a special expense not to exceed the amount of the fine assessed may be imposed.

 Subsections (c-1) & (c-2) below are effective for offenses committed on or after Sept. 1, 2007.

(c-1) If the defendant fails to present within the deferral period satisfactory evidence of compliance with the requirements imposed by the judge under this article, the court shall:

(1) notify the defendant in writing, mailed to the address on file with the court or appearing on the notice to appear, of that failure; and

(2) require the defendant to appear at the time and place stated in the notice to show cause why the order of deferral should not be revoked.

(c-2) On the defendant's showing of good cause for failure to present satisfactory evidence of compliance with the requirements imposed by the judge under this article, the court may allow an additional period during which the defendant may present evidence of the defendant's compliance with the requirements.

Ⓐ *Subsections (d) & (d-1) below are effective for offenses committed on or after Sept. 1, 2007.*

(d) If on the date of a show cause hearing under Subsection (c-1) or, if applicable, by the conclusion of an additional period provided under Subsection (c-2) the defendant does not present satisfactory evidence that the defendant complied with the requirements imposed, the judge may impose the fine assessed or impose a lesser fine. The imposition of the fine or lesser fine constitutes a final conviction of the defendant. This subsection does not apply to a defendant required under Subsection (b-1) to complete a driving safety course approved under Chapter 1001, Education Code, or an examination under Section 521.161(b)(2), Transportation Code.

(d-1) If the defendant was required to complete a driving safety course or an examination under Subsection (b-1) and on the date of a show cause hearing under Subsection (c-1) or, if applicable, by the conclusion of an additional period provided under Subsection (c-2) the defendant does not present satisfactory evidence that the defendant completed that course or examination, the judge shall impose the fine assessed. The imposition of the fine constitutes a final conviction of the defendant.

Subsections (d) & (d-1) below are effective for offenses in which any element of the offense was committed before Sept. 1, 2007.

(d) If by the conclusion of the deferral period the defendant does not present satisfactory evidence that the defendant complied with the requirements imposed, the judge may impose the fine assessed or impose a lesser fine. The imposition of the fine or lesser fine constitutes a final conviction of the defendant. This subsection does not apply to a defendant required under Subsection (b-1) to complete a driving safety course approved under Chapter 1001, Education Code, or an examination under Section 521.161(b)(2), Transportation Code.

(d-1) If the defendant was required to complete a driving safety course or an examination under Subsection (b-1) and by the conclusion of the deferral period the defendant does not present satisfactory evidence that the defendant completed that course or examination, the judge shall impose the fine assessed. The imposition of the fine constitutes a final conviction of the defendant.

(e) Records relating to a complaint dismissed as provided by this article may be expunged under Article 55.01. If a complaint is dismissed under this article, there is not a final conviction and the complaint may not be used against the person for any purpose.

(f) This article does not apply to:

 (1) an offense to which Section 542.404, Transportation Code, applies; or

(2) a violation of a state law or local ordinance relating to motor vehicle control, other than a parking violation, committed by a person who:

(A) holds a commercial driver's license; or

(B) held a commercial driver's license when the offense was committed.

History of CCP art. 45.051: Acts 1981, 67th Leg., ch. 318, §1, eff. Sept. 1, 1981. Amended by Acts 1987, 70th Leg., ch. 226, §1, eff. Sept. 1, 1987; Acts 1989, 71st Leg., ch. 399, §1, eff. June 14, 1989; Acts 1991, 72nd Leg., ch. 775, §19 (eff. Sept. 1, 1991), ch. 835, §4 (eff. Sept. 1, 1991); Acts 1993, 73rd Leg., ch. 900, §5.07, eff. Sept. 1, 1993. Renumbered from art. 45.54 and amended by Acts 1999, 76th Leg., ch. 1545, §50, eff. Sept. 1, 1999. Amended by Acts 1999, 76th Leg., ch. 62, §3.06 (eff. Sept. 1, 1999), ch. 532, §1 (eff. Sept. 1, 1999), ch. 1387, §1 (eff. Sept. 1, 1999); Acts 2001, 77th Leg., ch. 1420, §3.002, eff. Sept. 1, 2001; Acts 2003, 78th Leg., ch. 991, §12 (eff. Sept. 1, 2003), ch. 1182, §1 (eff. Sept. 1, 2003), 3rd C.S., ch. 8, §§4.01, 4.03 (eff. Jan. 11, 2004); Acts 2005, 79th Leg., ch. 90, §1 (eff. Sept. 1, 2005), ch. 281, §3.01(a) (eff. June 14, 2005), ch. 357, §6 (eff. Sept. 1, 2005); Acts 2007, 80th Leg., ch. 508, §1 (eff. Sept. 1, 2007), ch. 714, §1 (eff. Sept. 1, 2007), ch. 921, §3.001 (eff. Sept. 1, 2007).

ART. 45.0511. DRIVING SAFETY COURSE OR MOTORCYCLE OPERATOR COURSE DISMISSAL PROCEDURES

(a) Except as provided by Subsection (a-1), this article applies only to an alleged offense that:

(1) is within the jurisdiction of a justice court or a municipal court;

(2) involves the operation of a motor vehicle; and

(3) is defined by:

(A) Section 472.022, Transportation Code;

(B) Subtitle C, Title 7, Transportation Code; or

(C) Section 729.001(a)(3), Transportation Code.

(a-1) If the defendant is younger than 25 years of age, this article applies to any alleged offense that:

(1) is within the jurisdiction of a justice court or a municipal court;

(2) involves the operation of a motor vehicle; and

(3) is classified as a moving violation.

 Subsection (b) below is effective for offenses committed on or after Sept. 1, 2007.

(b) The judge shall require the defendant to successfully complete a driving safety course approved by the Texas Education Agency or a course under the motorcycle operator training and safety program approved by the designated state agency under Chapter 662, Transportation Code, if:

(1) the defendant elects driving safety course or motorcycle operator training course dismissal under this article;

(2) the defendant:

(A) has not completed an approved driving safety course or motorcycle operator training course, as appropriate, within the 12 months preceding the date of the offense; or

(B) does not have a valid Texas driver's license or permit, is a member, or the spouse or dependent child of a member, of the United States military forces serving on active duty, and has not completed a driving safety course or motorcycle operator training course, as appropriate, in another state within the 12 months preceding the date of the offense;

(3) the defendant enters a plea under Article 45.021 in person or in writing of no contest or guilty on or before the answer date on the notice to appear and:

(A) presents in person or by counsel to the court a request to take a course; or

(B) sends to the court by certified mail, return receipt requested, postmarked on or before the answer date on the notice to appear, a written request to take a course;

(4) the defendant:

(A) has a valid Texas driver's license or permit; or

(B) is a member, or the spouse or dependent child of a member, of the United States military forces serving on active duty;

(5) the defendant is charged with an offense to which this article applies, other than speeding at a speed of:

(A) 95 miles per hour or more; or

(B) 25 miles per hour or more over the posted speed limit; and

(6) the defendant provides evidence of financial responsibility as required by Chapter 601, Transportation Code.

Subsection (b) below is effective for offenses in which any element of the offense was committed before Sept. 1, 2007.

(b) The judge shall require the defendant to successfully complete a driving safety course approved by the Texas Education Agency or a course under the motorcycle operator training and safety program approved by the designated state agency under Chapter 662, Transportation Code, if:

(1) the defendant elects driving safety course or motorcycle operator training course dismissal under this article;

(2) the defendant:

(A) has not completed an approved driving safety course or motorcycle operator training course, as appropriate, within the 12 months preceding the date of the offense; or

(B) does not have a valid Texas driver's license or permit, is a member of the United States military forces serving on active duty, and has not completed a driving safety course or motorcycle operator training course, as appropriate, in another state within the 12 months preceding the date of the offense;

(3) the defendant enters a plea under Article 45.021 in person or in writing of no contest or guilty on or before the answer date on the notice to appear and:

(A) presents in person or by counsel to the court a request to take a course; or

(B) sends to the court by certified mail, return receipt requested, postmarked on or before the answer date on the notice to appear, a written request to take a course;

(4) the defendant:

(A) has a valid Texas driver's license or permit; or

(B) is a member of the United States military forces serving on active duty;

(5) the defendant is charged with an offense to which this article applies, other than speeding 25 miles per hour or more over the posted speed limit; and

(6) the defendant provides evidence of financial responsibility as required by Chapter 601, Transportation Code.

(c) The court shall enter judgment on the defendant's plea of no contest or guilty at the time the plea is made, defer imposition of the judgment, and allow the defendant 90 days to successfully complete the approved driving safety course or motorcycle operator training course and present to the court:

(1) a uniform certificate of completion of the driving safety course or a verification of completion of the motorcycle operator training course;

(2) unless the judge proceeds under Subsection (c-1), the defendant's driving record as maintained by the Department of Public Safety, if any, showing that the defendant had not completed an approved driving safety course or motorcycle operator training course, as applicable, within the 12 months preceding the date of the offense;

(3) an affidavit stating that the defendant was not taking a driving safety course or motorcycle operator training course, as applicable, under this article on the date the request to take the course was made and had not completed such a course that is not shown on the defendant's driving record within the 12 months preceding the date of the offense; and

A *Subsection (4) below is effective for offenses committed on or after Sept. 1, 2007.*

(4) if the defendant does not have a valid Texas driver's license or permit and is a member, or the spouse or dependent child of a member, of the United States military forces serving on active duty, an affidavit stating that the defendant was not taking a driving safety course or motorcycle operator training course, as

---

★

appropriate, in another state on the date the request to take the course was made and had not completed such a course within the 12 months preceding the date of the offense.

Subsection (4) below is effective for offenses in which any element of the offense was committed before Sept. 1, 2007.

(4) if the defendant does not have a valid Texas driver's license or permit and is a member of the United States military forces serving on active duty, an affidavit stating that the defendant was not taking a driving safety course or motorcycle operator training course, as appropriate, in another state on the date the request to take the course was made and had not completed such a course within the 12 months preceding the date of the offense.

 Subsection (c-1) below is effective for offenses committed on or after Sept. 1, 2007.

(c-1) In this subsection, "TexasOnline" has the meaning assigned by Section 2054.003, Government Code. As an alternative to receiving the defendant's driving record under Subsection (c)(2), the judge, at the time the defendant requests a driving safety course or motorcycle operator training course dismissal under this article, may require the defendant to pay a fee in an amount equal to the sum of the amount of the fee established by Section 521.048, Transportation Code, and the TexasOnline fee and, using TexasOnline, may request the Texas Department of Public Safety to provide the judge with a copy of the defendant's driving record that shows the information described by Section 521.047(b), Transportation Code. As soon as practicable and using TexasOnline, the Texas Department of Public Safety shall provide the judge with the requested copy of the defendant's driving record. The fee authorized by this subsection is in addition to any other fee required under this article. If the copy of the defendant's driving record provided to the judge under this subsection shows that the defendant has not completed an approved driving safety course or motorcycle operator training course, as appropriate, within the 12 months preceding the date of the offense, the judge shall allow the defendant to complete the appropriate course as provided by this article. The custodian of a municipal or county treasury who receives fees collected under this subsection shall keep a record of the fees and, without deduction or proration, forward the

fees to the comptroller, with and in the manner required for other fees and costs received in connection with criminal cases. The comptroller shall credit fees received under this subsection to the Texas Department of Public Safety.

Subsection (c-1) below is effective for offenses in which any element of the offense was committed before Sept. 1, 2007.

(c-1) As an alternative to presenting the defendant's driving record to the court under Subsection (c)(2), the judge, at the time the defendant requests a driving safety course or motorcycle operator training course dismissal under this article, may require the defendant to pay a fee of $10 for a copy of the driving record and the judge may obtain a copy of the driving record from the Texas Department of Public Safety. The $10 fee under this subsection is in addition to any other fee required under this article. If the defendant's driving record shows that the defendant has not completed an approved driving safety course or motorcycle operator training course, as appropriate, within the 12 months preceding the date of the offense, the judge shall allow the defendant to complete the appropriate course as provided by this article. The custodian of a municipal or county treasury who receives fees collected under this subsection shall keep a record of the fees and, without deduction, forward the fees to the comptroller, with and in the manner required for other fees and costs received in connection with criminal cases. The comptroller shall credit fees received under this subsection to the Texas Department of Public Safety.

(d) Notwithstanding Subsections (b)(2) and (3), before the final disposition of the case, the court may grant a request to take a driving safety course or a motorcycle operator training course under this article.

(e) A request to take a driving safety course or motorcycle operator training course made at or before the time and at the place at which a defendant is required to appear in court is an appearance in compliance with the defendant's promise to appear.

(f) In addition to court costs and fees authorized or imposed by a law of this state and applicable to the offense, the court may:

(1) require a defendant requesting a course under Subsection (b) to pay an administrative fee set by the court to cover the cost of administering this article at an amount of not more than $10; or

(2) require a defendant requesting a course under Subsection (d) to pay a fee set by the court at an amount not to exceed the maximum amount of the fine for the offense committed by the defendant.

(g) A defendant who requests but does not take a course is not entitled to a refund of the fee.

(h) Fees collected by a municipal court shall be deposited in the municipal treasury. Fees collected by another court shall be deposited in the county treasury of the county in which the court is located.

(i) If a defendant requesting a course under this article fails to comply with Subsection (c), the court shall:

(1) notify the defendant in writing, mailed to the address on file with the court or appearing on the notice to appear, of that failure; and

(2) require the defendant to appear at the time and place stated in the notice to show cause why the evidence was not timely submitted to the court.

(j) If the defendant fails to appear at the time and place stated in the notice under Subsection (i), or appears at the time and place stated in the notice but does not show good cause for the defendant's failure to comply with Subsection (c), the court shall enter an adjudication of guilt and impose sentence.

(k) On a defendant's showing of good cause for failure to furnish evidence to the court, the court may allow an extension of time during which the defendant may present:

(1) a uniform certificate of course completion as evidence that the defendant successfully completed the driving safety course; or

(2) a verification of course completion as evidence that the defendant successfully completed the motorcycle operator training course.

(l) When a defendant complies with Subsection (c), the court shall:

(1) remove the judgment and dismiss the charge;

(2) report the fact that the defendant successfully completed a driving safety course or a motorcycle operator training course and the date of completion to the Texas Department of Public Safety for inclusion in the person's driving record; and

(3) state in that report whether the course was taken under this article to provide information necessary to determine eligibility to take a subsequent course under Subsection (b).

(m) The court may dismiss only one charge for each completion of a course.

(n) A charge that is dismissed under this article may not be part of a person's driving record or used for any purpose.

(o) An insurer delivering or issuing for delivery a motor vehicle insurance policy in this state may not cancel or increase the premium charged an insured under the policy because the insured completed a driving safety course or a motorcycle operator training course, or had a charge dismissed under this article.

(p) The court shall advise a defendant charged with a misdemeanor under Section 472.022, Transportation Code, Subtitle C, Title 7, Transportation Code, or Section 729.001(a)(3), Transportation Code, committed while operating a motor vehicle of the defendant's right under this article to successfully complete a driving safety course or, if the offense was committed while operating a motorcycle, a motorcycle operator training course. The right to complete a course does not apply to a defendant charged with:

(1) a violation of Section 545.066, 550.022, or 550.023, Transportation Code;

(2) a serious traffic violation; or

(3) an offense to which Section 542.404 or 729.004(b), Transportation Code, applies.

(q) A notice to appear issued for an offense to which this article applies must inform a defendant charged with an offense under Section 472.022, Transportation Code, an offense under Subtitle C, Title 7, Transportation Code, or an offense under Section 729.001(a)(3), Transportation Code, committed while operating a motor vehicle of the defendant's right to complete a driving safety course or, if the offense was committed while operating a motorcycle, of the defendant's right to complete a motorcycle operator training course. The notice required by this subsection must read substantially as follows:

"You may be able to require that this charge be dismissed by successfully completing a driving safety course or a motorcycle operator training course. You will lose that right if, on or before your appearance date, you do not provide the court with notice of your request to take the course."

(r) If the notice required by Subsection (q) is not provided to the defendant charged with the offense, the defendant may continue to exercise the defendant's right to take a driving safety course or a motorcycle operator training course until the notice required by Subsection (q) is provided to the defendant or there is a final disposition of the case.

(s) This article does not apply to an offense committed by a person who:

(1) holds a commercial driver's license; or

(2) held a commercial driver's license when the offense was committed.

(t) An order of deferral under Subsection (c) terminates any liability under a bail bond or appearance bond given for the charge.

(u) The requirement of Subsection (b)(2) does not apply to a defendant charged with an offense under Section 545.412, Transportation Code, if the judge requires the defendant to attend and present proof that the defendant has successfully completed a specialized driving safety course that includes four hours of instruction that encourages the use of child passenger safety seat systems, and any driving safety course taken by the defendant under this section within the 12 months preceding the date of the offense did not include that training. The person's driving record under Subsection (c)(2) and the affidavit of the defendant under Subsection (c)(3) is required to include only previous or concurrent courses that included that training.

History of CCP art. 45.0511: Acts 1999, 76th Leg., ch. 1545, §51, eff. Sept. 1, 1999. Amended by Acts 2001, 77th Leg., ch. 1420, §3.0021(a), eff. Sept. 1, 2001; Acts 2003, 78th Leg., ch. 991, §13 (eff. Sept. 1, 2003), ch. 1182, §2 (eff. Sept. 1, 2003), 3rd C.S., ch. 8, §4.02 (eff. Jan. 11, 2004); Acts 2005, 79th Leg., ch. 90, §2 (eff. Sept. 1, 2005), ch. 357, §7 (eff. Sept. 1, 2005), ch. 913, §6, (eff. Sept. 1, 2005), ch. 1194, §1 (eff. Sept. 1, 2005), ch. 1209, §1 (eff. Sept. 1, 2005); Acts 2007, 80th Leg., ch. 805, §1 (eff. Sept. 1, 2007), ch. 829, §1 (eff. Sept. 1, 2007).

ART. 45.052. DISMISSAL OF MISDEMEANOR CHARGE ON COMPLETION OF TEEN COURT PROGRAM

(a) A justice or municipal court may defer proceedings against a defendant who is under the age of 18 or enrolled full time in an accredited secondary school in a program leading toward a high school diploma for not more than 180 days if the defendant:

(1) is charged with an offense that the court has jurisdiction of under Article 4.11 or 4.14, Code of Criminal Procedure;

(2) pleads nolo contendere or guilty to the offense in open court with the defendant's parent, guardian, or managing conservator present;

(3) presents to the court an oral or written request to attend a teen court program; and

(4) has not successfully completed a teen court program in the two years preceding the date that the alleged offense occurred.

(b) The teen court program must be approved by the court.

(c) A defendant for whom proceedings are deferred under Subsection (a) shall complete the teen court program not later than the 90th day after the date the teen court hearing to determine punishment is held or the last day of the deferral period, whichever date is earlier. The justice or municipal court shall dismiss the charge at the time the defendant presents satisfactory evidence that the defendant has successfully completed the teen court program.

(d) A charge dismissed under this article may not be part of the defendant's criminal record or driving record or used for any purpose. However, if the charge was for a traffic offense, the court shall report to the Department of Public Safety that the defendant successfully completed the teen court program and the date of completion for inclusion in the defendant's driving record.

(e) The justice or municipal court may require a person who requests a teen court program to pay a fee not to exceed $10 that is set by the court to cover the costs of administering this article. Fees collected by a municipal court shall be deposited in the municipal treasury. Fees collected by a justice court shall be deposited in the county treasury of the county in which the court is located. A person who requests a teen court program and fails to complete the program is not entitled to a refund of the fee.

(f) A court may transfer a case in which proceedings have been deferred under this section to a court in another county if the court to which the case is transferred consents. A case may not be transferred unless it is within the jurisdiction of the court to which it is transferred.

(g) In addition to the fee authorized by Subsection (e) of this article, the court may require a child who requests a teen court program to pay a $10 fee to cover the cost to the teen court for performing its duties under this article. The court shall pay the fee to the teen court program, and the teen court program must account to the court for the receipt and disbursal of the fee. A child who pays a fee under this subsection is not entitled to a refund of the fee, regardless of whether the child successfully completes the teen court program.

(h) A justice or municipal court may exempt a defendant for whom proceedings are deferred under this article from the requirement to pay a court cost or fee that is imposed by another statute.

 Subsection (i) below is effective for fees relating to a request for a teen court program made on or after Sept. 1, 2007.

(i) Notwithstanding Subsection (e) or (g), a justice or municipal court that is located in the Texas-Louisiana border region, as defined by Section 2056.002, Government Code, may charge a fee of $20 under those subsections.

History of CCP art. 45.052: Acts 1989, 71st Leg., ch. 1031, §1, eff. Sept. 1, 1989; Acts 1995, 74th Leg., ch. 598, §1 (eff. Sept. 1, 1995), ch. 748, §2 (eff. Sept. 1, 1995); Acts 1997, 75th Leg., ch. 165, §31.01(13), eff. Sept. 1, 1997. Renumbered from art. 45.55 by Acts 1999, 76th Leg., ch. 1545, §52, eff. Sept. 1, 1999. Amended by Acts 1999, 76th Leg., ch. 76, §6, eff. Sept. 1, 1999; Acts 2001, 77th Leg., ch. 216, §1, eff. Sept. 1, 2001; Acts 2007, 80th Leg., ch. 910, §1, eff. Sept. 1, 2007.

ART. 45.053. DISMISSAL OF MISDEMEANOR CHARGE ON COMMITMENT OF CHEMICALLY DEPENDENT PERSON

(a) On a plea of guilty or nolo contendere by a defendant or on a finding of guilt in a misdemeanor case punishable by a fine only, a justice or municipal court may defer further proceedings for 90 days without entering an adjudication of guilt if:

(1) the court finds that the offense resulted from or was related to the defendant's chemical dependency; and

(2) an application for court-ordered treatment of the defendant is filed in accordance with Chapter 462, Health and Safety Code.

(b) At the end of the deferral period, the justice or municipal court shall dismiss the charge if satisfactory evidence is presented that the defendant was committed for and completed court-ordered treatment in accordance with Chapter 462, Health and Safety Code, and it shall be clearly noted in the docket that the complaint is dismissed and that there is not a final conviction.

(c) If at the conclusion of the deferral period satisfactory evidence that the defendant was committed for and completed court-ordered treatment in accordance with Chapter 462, Health and Safety Code, is not presented, the justice or municipal court may impose the fine assessed or impose a lesser fine. The imposition of a fine constitutes a final conviction of the defendant.

(d) Records relating to a complaint dismissed under this article may be expunged under Article 55.01 of this code. If a complaint is dismissed under this article, there is not a final conviction and the complaint may not be used against the person for any purpose.

History of CCP art. 45.053: Acts 1991, 72nd Leg., ch. 198, §1, eff. Sept. 1, 1991. Renumbered from art. 45.56 by Acts 1999, 76th Leg., ch. 1545, §53, eff. Sept. 1, 1999.

ART. 45.054. FAILURE TO ATTEND SCHOOL PROCEEDINGS

(a) On a finding by a county, justice, or municipal court that an individual has committed an offense under Section 25.094, Education Code, the court has jurisdiction to enter an order that includes one or more of the following provisions requiring that:

(1) the individual:

(A) attend school without unexcused absences;

(B) attend a preparatory class for the high school equivalency examination administered under Section 7.111, Education Code, if the court determines that the individual is too old to do well in a formal classroom environment; or

(C) if the individual is at least 16 years of age, take the high school equivalency examination administered under Section 7.111, Education Code;

(2) the individual attend a special program that the court determines to be in the best interest of the individual, including:

(A) an alcohol and drug abuse program;

(B) a rehabilitation program;

(C) a counseling program, including self-improvement counseling;

(D) a program that provides training in self-esteem and leadership;

(E) a work and job skills training program;

(F) a program that provides training in parenting, including parental responsibility;

(G) a program that provides training in manners;

(H) a program that provides training in violence avoidance;

(I) a program that provides sensitivity training; and

(J) a program that provides training in advocacy and mentoring;

(3) the individual and the individual's parent attend a class for students at risk of dropping out of school designed for both the individual and the individual's parent;

(4) the individual complete reasonable community service requirements; or

(5) for the total number of hours ordered by the court, the individual participate in a tutorial program covering the academic subjects in which the student is enrolled provided by the school the individual attends.

(a-1) On a finding by a juvenile court in a county with a population of less than 100,000 that the individual has engaged in conduct that violates Section 25.094, Education Code, the court has jurisdiction to enter an order that includes one or more of the provisions listed under Subsection (a).

 Subsection (a-2) below is effective for conduct occurring on or after Sept. 1, 2007, for orders rendered by a juvenile court on or after Sept. 1, 2007, and for information and documents relating to juvenile cases before, on, or after Sept. 1, 2007. Conduct violating penal law occurs on or after Sept. 1, 2007, if any element of the violation occurs on or after that date. In all other instances, the law is effective on Sept. 1, 2007.

(a-2) An order under Subsection (a) may not require a student to attend a juvenile justice alternative education program.

(b) An order under Subsection (a)(3) that requires the parent of an individual to attend a class for students at risk of dropping out of school is enforceable in the justice, municipal, or juvenile court by contempt.

(c) A court having jurisdiction under this article shall endorse on the summons issued to the parent of the individual who is the subject of the hearing an order directing the parent to appear personally at the hearing and directing the person having custody of the individual to bring the individual to the hearing.

(d) An individual commits an offense if the individual is a parent who fails to attend a hearing under this article after receiving notice under Subsection (c) that the individual's attendance is required. An offense under this subsection is a Class C misdemeanor.

(e) On the commencement of proceedings under this article, the court shall inform the individual who is the subject of the hearing and the individual's parent in open court of the individual's expunction rights and provide the individual and the individual's parent with a written copy of Article 45.055.

(f) In addition to any other order authorized by this article, the court may order the Department of Public Safety to suspend the driver's license or permit of the individual who is the subject of the hearing or, if the individual does not have a license or permit, to deny the issuance of a license or permit to the individual for a period specified by the court not to exceed 365 days.

(g) A dispositional order under this article is effective for the period specified by the court in the order but may not extend beyond the 180th day after the date of the order or beyond the end of the school year in which the order was entered, whichever period is longer.

(h) In this article, "parent" includes a person standing in parental relation.

History of CCP art. 45.054: Acts 2001, 77th Leg., ch. 1514, §9, eff. Sept. 1, 2001. Amended by Acts 2003, 78th Leg., ch. 137, §14 (eff. Sept. 1, 2003), ch. 180, §1 (eff. Sept. 1, 2003); Acts 2007, 80th Leg., ch. 908, §2, eff. Sept. 1, 2007.

History of Former CCP art. 45.054: Repealed by Acts 2003, 78th Leg., ch. 283, §61(4), eff. Sept. 1, 2003.

ART. 45.055. EXPUNCTION OF CONVICTION & RECORDS IN FAILURE TO ATTEND SCHOOL CASES

(a) An individual convicted of not more than one violation of Section 25.094, Education Code, may, on or after the individual's 18th birthday, apply to the court in which the individual was convicted to have the conviction and records relating to the conviction expunged.

(b) To apply for an expunction, the applicant must submit a written request that:

(1) is made under oath;

(2) states that the applicant has not been convicted of more than one violation of Section 25.094, Education Code; and

(3) is in the form determined by the applicant.

(c) The court may expunge the conviction and records relating to the conviction without a hearing or, if facts are in doubt, may order a hearing on the application. If the court finds that the applicant has not been convicted of more than one violation of Section 25.094, Education Code, the court shall order the conviction, together with all complaints, verdicts, sentences, and other documents relating to the offense, including any documents in the possession of a school district or law enforcement agency, to be expunged from the applicant's record. After entry of the order, the applicant is released from all disabilities resulting from the conviction, and the conviction may not be shown or made known for any purpose. The court shall inform the applicant of the court's decision on the application.

(d) The court shall require an individual who files an application under this article to pay a fee in the amount of $30 to defray the cost of notifying state agencies of orders of expunction under this article.

History of CCP art. 45.055: Acts 2001, 77th Leg., ch. 1514, §9, eff. Sept. 1, 2001. Amended by Acts 2003, 78th Leg., ch. 137, §15, eff. Sept. 1, 2003; Acts 2005, 79th Leg., ch. 886, §3, eff. Sept. 1, 2005.

ART. 45.056. AUTHORITY TO EMPLOY JUVENILE CASE MANAGERS; REIMBURSEMENT

(a) On approval of the commissioners court, city council, school district board of trustees, juvenile board, or other appropriate authority, a county court, justice court, municipal court, school district, juvenile probation department, or other appropriate governmental entity may:

(1) employ a case manager to provide services in cases involving juvenile offenders before a court consistent with the court's statutory powers; or

(2) agree in accordance with Chapter 791, Government Code, to jointly employ a case manager.

(b) A local entity may apply or more than one local entity may jointly apply to the criminal justice division of the governor's office for reimbursement of all or part of the costs of employing one or more juvenile case managers from funds appropriated to the governor's office or otherwise available for that purpose. To be eligible for reimbursement, the entity applying must present to the governor's office a comprehensive plan to reduce juvenile crimes in the entity's jurisdiction that addresses the role of the case manager in that effort.

(c) A county or justice court on approval of the commissioners court or a municipal court on approval of the city council may employ one or more full-time juvenile case managers to assist the court in administering the court's juvenile docket and in supervising its court orders in juvenile cases.

(d) Pursuant to Article 102.0174, the court may pay the salary and benefits of the juvenile case manager from the juvenile case manager fund.

(e) A juvenile case manager employed under Subsection (c) shall work primarily on cases brought under Sections 25.093 and 25.094, Education Code.

History of CCP art. 45.056: Acts 2001, 77th Leg., ch. 1514, §9, eff. Sept. 1, 2001. Amended by Acts 2003, 78th Leg., ch. 283, §33, eff. Sept. 1, 2003; Acts 2005, 79th Leg., ch. 949, §34, eff. Sept. 1, 2005.

ART. 45.057. OFFENSES COMMITTED BY JUVENILES

(a) In this article:

(1) "Child" has the meaning assigned by Article 45.058(h).

(2) "Residence" means any place where the child lives or resides for a period of at least 30 days.

(3) "Parent" includes a person standing in parental relation, a managing conservator, or a custodian.

(b) On a finding by a justice or municipal court that a child committed an offense that the court has jurisdiction of under Article 4.11 or 4.14, the court has jurisdiction to enter an order:

(1) referring the child or the child's parent for services under Section 264.302, Family Code;

(2) requiring that the child attend a special program that the court determines to be in the best interest of the child and, if the program involves the expenditure of county funds, that is approved by the county commissioners court, including a rehabilitation, counseling, self-esteem and leadership, work and job skills training, job interviewing and work preparation, self-improvement, parenting, manners, violence avoidance, tutoring, sensitivity training, parental responsibility, community service, restitution, advocacy, or mentoring program; or

(3) requiring that the child's parent do any act or refrain from doing any act that the court determines will increase the likelihood that the child will comply with the orders of the court and that is reasonable and necessary for the welfare of the child, including:

(A) attend a parenting class or parental responsibility program; and

(B) attend the child's school classes or functions.

(c) The justice or municipal court may order the parent, managing conservator, or guardian of a child required to attend a program under Subsection (b) to pay an amount not greater than $100 to pay for the costs of the program.

(d) A justice or municipal court may require a child, parent, managing conservator, or guardian required to attend a program, class, or function under this article to submit proof of attendance to the court.

(e) A justice or municipal court shall endorse on the summons issued to a parent an order to appear personally at the hearing with the child. The summons must include a warning that the failure of the parent to appear may result in arrest and is a Class C misdemeanor.

(f) An order under this article involving a child is enforceable under Article 45.050.

(g) A person commits an offense if the person is a parent, managing conservator, or guardian who fails to attend a hearing under this article after receiving an order under Subsection (e). An offense under this subsection is a Class C misdemeanor.

(h) A child and parent required to appear before the court have an obligation to provide the court in writing with the current address and residence of the child. The obligation does not end when the child reaches age 17. On or before the seventh day after the date the child or parent changes residence, the child or parent shall notify the court of the current address in the manner directed by the court. A violation of this subsection may result in arrest and is a Class C misdemeanor. The obligation to provide notice terminates on discharge and satisfaction of the judgment or final disposition not requiring a finding of guilt.

(i) If an appellate court accepts an appeal for a trial de novo, the child and parent shall provide the notice under Subsection (h) to the appellate court.

(j) The child and parent are entitled to written notice of their obligation under Subsections (h) and (i), which may be satisfied by being given a copy of those subsections by:

(1) the court during their initial appearance before the court;

(2) a peace officer arresting and releasing a child under Article 45.058(a) on release; and

(3) a peace officer that issues a citation under Section 543.003, Transportation Code, or Article 14.06(b) of this code.

(k) It is an affirmative defense to prosecution under Subsection (h) that the child and parent were not informed of their obligation under this article.

(l) Any order under this article is enforceable by the justice or municipal court by contempt.

History of CCP art. 45.057: Acts 2001, 77th Leg., ch. 1514, §9, eff. Sept. 1, 2001. Amended by Acts 2003, 78th Leg., ch. 283, §34, eff. Sept. 1, 2003.

ART. 45.058. CHILDREN TAKEN INTO CUSTODY

(a) A child may be released to the child's parent, guardian, custodian, or other responsible adult as provided by Section 52.02(a)(1), Family Code, if the child is taken into custody for an offense that a justice or municipal court has jurisdiction of under Article 4.11 or 4.14, other than public intoxication.

(b) A child described by Subsection (a) must be taken only to a place previously designated by the head of the law enforcement agency with custody of the child as an appropriate place of nonsecure custody for children unless the child:

(1) is released under Section 52.02(a)(1), Family Code; or

(2) is taken before a justice or municipal court.

(c) A place of nonsecure custody for children must be an unlocked, multipurpose area. A lobby, office, or interrogation room is suitable if the area is not designated, set aside, or used as a secure detention area and is not part of a secure detention area. A place of nonsecure custody may be a juvenile processing office designated under Section 52.025, Family Code, if the area is not locked when it is used as a place of nonsecure custody.

(d) The following procedures shall be followed in a place of nonsecure custody for children:

(1) a child may not be secured physically to a cuffing rail, chair, desk, or other stationary object;

(2) the child may be held in the nonsecure facility only long enough to accomplish the purpose of identification, investigation, processing, release to parents, or the arranging of transportation to the appropriate juvenile court, juvenile detention facility, secure detention facility, justice court, or municipal court;

(3) residential use of the area is prohibited; and

(4) the child shall be under continuous visual supervision by a law enforcement officer or facility staff person during the time the child is in nonsecure custody.

(e) Notwithstanding any other provision of this article, a child may not, under any circumstances, be detained in a place of nonsecure custody for more than six hours.

(f) A child taken into custody for an offense that a justice or municipal court has jurisdiction of under Article 4.11 or 4.14, other than public intoxication, may be presented or detained in a detention facility designated by the juvenile court under Section 52.02(a)(3), Family Code, only if:

(1) the child's non-traffic case is transferred to the juvenile court by a justice or municipal court under Section 51.08(b), Family Code; or

(2) the child is referred to the juvenile court by a justice or municipal court for contempt of court under Article 45.050.

(g) A law enforcement officer may issue a field release citation as provided by Article 14.06 in place of taking a child into custody for a traffic offense or an offense, other than public intoxication, punishable by fine only.

(h) In this article, "child" means a person who is:

(1) at least 10 years of age and younger than 17 years of age; and

(2) charged with or convicted of an offense that a justice or municipal court has jurisdiction of under Article 4.11 or 4.14.

History of CCP art. 45.058: Acts 2001, 77th Leg., ch. 1514, §9, eff. Sept. 1, 2001.

ART. 45.059. CHILDREN TAKEN INTO CUSTODY FOR VIOLATION OF JUVENILE CURFEW OR ORDER

(a) A peace officer taking into custody a person younger than 17 years of age for violation of a juvenile curfew ordinance of a municipality or order of the commissioners court of a county shall, without unnecessary delay:

(1) release the person to the person's parent, guardian, or custodian;

(2) take the person before a justice or municipal court to answer the charge; or

(3) take the person to a place designated as a juvenile curfew processing office by the head of the law enforcement agency having custody of the person.

(b) A juvenile curfew processing office must observe the following procedures:

(1) the office must be an unlocked, multipurpose area that is not designated, set aside, or used as a secure detention area or part of a secure detention area;

(2) the person may not be secured physically to a cuffing rail, chair, desk, or stationary object;

(3) the person may not be held longer than necessary to accomplish the purposes of identification, investigation, processing, release to a parent, guardian, or custodian, or arrangement of transportation to school or court;

(4) a juvenile curfew processing office may not be designated or intended for residential purposes;

(5) the person must be under continuous visual supervision by a peace officer or other person during the time the person is in the juvenile curfew processing office; and

(6) a person may not be held in a juvenile curfew processing office for more than six hours.

(c) A place designated under this article as a juvenile curfew processing office is not subject to the approval of the juvenile board having jurisdiction where the governmental entity is located.

History of 45.059: Acts 2001, 77th Leg., ch. 1514, §9, eff. Sept. 1, 2001.

ART. 45.060. UNADJUDICATED CHILDREN, NOW ADULTS; NOTICE ON REACHING AGE OF MAJORITY; OFFENSE

(a) Except as provided by Articles 45.058 and 45.059, an individual may not be taken into secured custody for offenses alleged to have occurred before the individual's 17th birthday.

(b) On or after an individual's 17th birthday, if the court has used all available procedures under this chapter to secure the individual's appearance to answer allegations made before the individual's 17th birthday, the court may issue a notice of continuing obligation to appear by personal service or by mail to the last known address and residence of the individual. The notice must order the individual to appear at a designated time, place, and date to answer the allegations detailed in the notice.

(c) Failure to appear as ordered by the notice under Subsection (b) is a Class C misdemeanor independent of Section 38.10, Penal Code, and Section 543.003, Transportation Code.

(d) It is an affirmative defense to prosecution under Subsection (c) that the individual was not informed of the individual's obligation under Articles 45.057(h) and (i) or did not receive notice as required by Subsection (b).

(e) A notice of continuing obligation to appear issued under this article must contain the following statement provided in boldfaced type or capital letters:

"WARNING: COURT RECORDS REVEAL THAT BEFORE YOUR 17TH BIRTHDAY YOU WERE ACCUSED OF A CRIMINAL OFFENSE AND HAVE FAILED TO MAKE AN APPEARANCE OR ENTER A PLEA IN THIS MATTER. AS AN ADULT, YOU ARE NOTIFIED THAT YOU HAVE A CONTINUING OBLIGATION TO APPEAR IN THIS CASE. FAILURE TO APPEAR AS REQUIRED BY THIS NOTICE MAY BE AN ADDITIONAL CRIMINAL OFFENSE AND RESULT IN A WARRANT BEING ISSUED FOR YOUR ARREST."

History of CCP art. 45.060: Acts 2003, 78th Leg., ch. 283, §35, eff. Sept. 1, 2003.

SUBCHAPTER C. PROCEDURES IN JUSTICE COURT

ART. 45.101. JUSTICE COURT PROSECUTIONS

(a) All prosecutions in a justice court shall be conducted by the county or district attorney or a deputy county or district attorney.

(b) Except as otherwise provided by law, appeals from justice court may be prosecuted by the district attorney or a deputy district attorney with the consent of the county attorney.

History of CCP art. 45.101: Acts 1999, 76th Leg., ch. 1545, §§54, 55, eff. Sept. 1, 1999.

ART. 45.102. OFFENSES COMMITTED IN ANOTHER COUNTY

Whenever complaint is made before any justice of the peace that a felony has been committed in any other than a county in which the complaint is made, the justice shall issue a warrant for the arrest of the accused, directed as in other cases, commanding that the accused be arrested and taken before any magistrate of the county where such felony is alleged to have been committed, forthwith, for examination as in other cases.

History of CCP art. 45.102: Acts 1965, 59th Leg., vol. 2, ch. 722. Renumbered from art. 45.21 and amended by Acts 1999, 76th Leg., ch. 1545, §56, eff. Sept. 1, 1999.

ART. 45.103. WARRANT WITHOUT COMPLAINT

If a criminal offense that a justice of the peace has jurisdiction to try is committed within the view of the justice, the justice may issue a warrant for the arrest of the offender.

History of CCP art. 45.103: Acts 1965, 59th Leg., vol. 2, ch. 722. Renumbered from art. 45.15 and amended by Acts 1999, 76th Leg., ch. 1545, §57, eff. Sept. 1, 1999.

SUBCHAPTER D. PROCEDURES IN MUNICIPAL COURT

ART. 45.201. MUNICIPAL PROSECUTIONS

(a) All prosecutions in a municipal court shall be conducted by the city attorney of the municipality or by a deputy city attorney.

(b) The county attorney of the county in which the municipality is situated may, if the county attorney so desires, also represent the state in such prosecutions.

In such cases, the county attorney is not entitled to receive any fees or other compensation for those services.

(c) With the consent of the county attorney, appeals from municipal court to a county court, county court at law, or any appellate court may be prosecuted by the city attorney or a deputy city attorney.

(d) It is the primary duty of a municipal prosecutor not to convict, but to see that justice is done.

History of CCP art. 45.201: Acts 1965, 59th Leg., vol. 2, ch. 722; Acts 1987, 70th Leg., ch. 923, §1, eff. Aug. 31, 1987. Renumbered from art. 45.03 and amended by Acts 1999, 76th Leg., ch. 1545, §§58, 59, eff. Sept. 1, 1999.

ANNOTATIONS

State v. Blankenship, 146 S.W.3d 218, 220 (Tex. Crim.App.2004). "[W]e decide that the timely-made assertion in the City's amended notice of appeal that the 'County Attorney has consented to the City Attorney prosecuting this appeal' is 'in some fashion' a written express personal authorization by the County Attorney of this specific notice of appeal in this particular case." Held: Although City Attorney prosecuted appeal, County Attorney "made" appeal, and appeal was timely filed.

ART. 45.202. SERVICE OF PROCESS

(a) All process issuing out of a municipal court may be served and shall be served when directed by the court, by a peace officer or marshal of the municipality within which it is situated, under the same rules as are provided by law for the service by sheriffs and constables of process issuing out of the justice court, so far as applicable.

(b) The peace officer or marshal may serve all process issuing out of a municipal court anywhere in the county in which the municipality is situated. If the municipality is situated in more than one county, the peace officer or marshal may serve the process throughout those counties.

History of CCP art. 45.202: Acts 1965, 59th Leg., vol. 2, ch. 722. Amended by Acts 1967, 60th Leg., ch. 523, §1, eff. Aug. 28, 1967. Renumbered from art. 45.04 and amended by Acts 1999, 76th Leg., ch. 1545, §60, eff. Sept. 1, 1999.

ART. 45.203. COLLECTION OF FINES, COSTS, & SPECIAL EXPENSES

(a) The governing body of each municipality shall by ordinance prescribe rules, not inconsistent with any law of this state, as may be proper to enforce the collection of fines imposed by a municipal court. In addition to any other method of enforcement, the municipality may enforce the collection of fines by:

(1) execution against the property of the defendant; or

(2) imprisonment of the defendant.

(b) The governing body of a municipality may adopt such rules and regulations, not inconsistent with any law of this state, concerning the practice and procedure in the municipal court as the governing body may consider proper.

(c) The governing body of each municipality may prescribe by ordinance the collection, after due notice, of a special expense, not to exceed $25 for the issuance and service of a warrant of arrest for an offense under Section 38.10, Penal Code, or Section 543.009, Transportation Code. Money collected from the special expense shall be paid into the municipal treasury for the use and benefit of the municipality.

(d) Costs may not be imposed or collected in criminal cases in municipal court by municipal ordinance.

History of CCP art. 45.203: Acts 1965, 59th Leg., vol. 2, ch. 722. Amended by Acts 1983, 68th Leg., ch. 389, §1, eff. Sept. 1, 1983; Acts 1987, 70th Leg., ch. 124, §1, eff. Sept. 1, 1987; Acts 1995, 74th Leg., ch. 76, §14.26, eff. Sept. 1, 1995. Renumbered from art. 45.06 and amended by Acts 1999, 76th Leg., ch. 1545, §61, eff. Sept. 1, 1999. Amended by Acts 1999, 76th Leg., ch. 62, §3.05, eff. Sept. 1, 1999.

ART. 45.541. REPEALED

Repealed by Acts 2001, 77th Leg., ch. 1420, §3.0021(b), eff. Sept. 1, 2001.

CHAPTER 46. INSANITY AS DEFENSE

Art. 46.04   Transportation to a mental health facility or residential care facility

Art. 46.05   Competency to be executed

ART. 46.01. REPEALED

Repealed by Acts 1999, 76th Leg., ch. 561, §8, eff. Sept. 1, 1999.

ART. 46.02. REPEALED

Repealed by Acts 2003, 78th Leg., ch. 35, §15, eff. Jan. 1, 2004.

ART. 46.03. REPEALED

Repealed by Acts 2005, 79th Leg., ch. 831, §1, eff. Sept. 1, 2005.

ART. 46.03. INSANITY DEFENSE

☠ *In 2005, the 79th Legislature repealed CCP art. 46.03 §§1-3 and 4(a)-(d)(7) with Acts 2005, 79th Leg., ch. 831, §1, enacted May 27, 2005, effective Sept. 1, 2005, and recodified its substance in CCP ch. 46C. However, the 79th Legislature also added §4(8) to CCP art. 46.03 with Acts 2005, 79th Leg., ch. 485, §1, enacted May 24, 2005, effective Sept. 1, 2005, which is included here and marked accordingly. For resolving conflicts, see p. V.*

§§1-3. Repealed by Acts 2005, 79th Leg., ch. 831, §1, eff. Sept. 1, 2005.

§4(a)-(d)(7) Repealed by Acts 2005, 79th Leg., ch. 831, §1, eff. Sept. 1, 2005.

☠ *Subsection (8) below was enacted by Acts 2005, 79th Leg., ch. 485, §1, enacted May 24, 2005, effective Sept. 1, 2005, without reference to the conflicting repeal of CCP art. 46.03 made by Acts 2005, 79th Leg., ch. 831, §1, enacted May 27, 2005, effective Sept. 1, 2005. For resolving conflicts, see p. V.*

(8) Victim Notification of Release. If the court issues an order under Subdivision (4) or (5) that requires the release of an acquitted person on discharge or on a regimen of outpatient care, the clerk of the court issuing the order, using the information provided on any victim impact statement received by the court under Article 56.03 or other information made available to the court, shall provide name, address, and phone number information to the Texas Department of Criminal Justice victim services division to enable the division to notify the victim or the victim's guardian or close relative of the release. The victim services division shall notify any victim or guardian or close relative named in the victim impact statement or other information. Notwithstanding Article 56.03(f), the clerk of the court may inspect a victim impact statement for the purpose of notification under this subdivision.

History of CCP art. 46.03: Acts 1975, 64th Leg., ch. 415, §2, eff. June 19, 1975. Amended by Acts 1977, 65th Leg., ch. 596, §2, eff. Sept. 1, 1977; Acts 1983, 68th Leg., ch. 454, §§2, 3, eff. Aug. 29, 1983; Acts 1989, 71st Leg., ch. 393, §§7-9, eff. June 14, 1989; Acts 2001, 77th Leg., ch. 985, §1, eff. Sept. 1, 2001; Acts 2003, 78th Leg., ch. 35, §5, eff. Jan. 1, 2004. Repealed by Acts 2005, 79th Leg., ch. 831, §1, eff. Sept. 1, 2005. Amended by Acts 2005, 79th Leg., ch. 485, §1, eff. Sept. 1, 2005.

See also H&SC §574.023; Pen. Code §8.01.

ART. 46.04. TRANSPORTATION TO A MENTAL HEALTH FACILITY OR RESIDENTIAL CARE FACILITY

§1. Persons Accompanying Transport

(a) A patient transported from a jail or detention facility to a mental health facility or a residential care facility shall be transported by a special officer for mental health assignment certified under Section 1701.404, Occupations Code, or by a sheriff or constable.

(b) The court ordering the transport shall require appropriate medical personnel to accompany the person transporting the patient, at the expense of the county from which the patient is transported, if there is reasonable cause to believe the patient will require medical assistance or will require the administration of medication during the transportation.

★

(c) A female patient must be accompanied by a female attendant.

§2. Requirements for Transport

The transportation of a patient from a jail or detention facility to a mental health facility or residential care facility must meet the following requirements:

(1) the patient must be transported directly to the facility within a reasonable amount of time and without undue delay;

(2) a vehicle used to transport the patient must be adequately heated in cold weather and adequately ventilated in warm weather;

(3) a special diet or other medical precautions recommended by the patient's physician must be followed;

(4) the person transporting the patient shall give the patient reasonable opportunities to get food and water and to use a bathroom; and

(5) the patient may not be transported with a state prisoner.

History of CCP art. 46.04: Acts 1999, 76th Leg., ch 1512, §6, eff. Sept. 1, 1999. Amended by Acts 2001, 77th Leg., ch. 1420, §14.736, eff. Sept. 1, 2001.

ART. 46.05. COMPETENCY TO BE EXECUTED

(a) A person who is incompetent to be executed may not be executed.

(b) The trial court retains jurisdiction over motions filed by or for a defendant under this article.

(c) A motion filed under this article must identify the proceeding in which the defendant was convicted, give the date of the final judgment, set forth the fact that an execution date has been set if the date has been set, and clearly set forth alleged facts in support of the assertion that the defendant is presently incompetent to be executed. The defendant shall attach affidavits, records, or other evidence supporting the defendant's allegations or shall state why those items are not attached. The defendant shall identify any previous proceedings in which the defendant challenged the defendant's competency in relation to the conviction and sentence in question, including any challenge to the defendant's competency to be executed, competency to stand trial, or sanity at the time of the offense. The motion must be verified by the oath of some person on the defendant's behalf.

(d) On receipt of a motion filed under this article, the trial court shall determine whether the defendant has raised a substantial doubt of the defendant's competency to be executed on the basis of:

(1) the motion, any attached documents, and any responsive pleadings; and

(2) if applicable, the presumption of competency under Subsection (e).

(e) If a defendant is determined to have previously filed a motion under this article, and has previously been determined to be competent to be executed, the previous adjudication creates a presumption of competency and the defendant is not entitled to a hearing on the subsequent motion filed under this article, unless the defendant makes a prima facie showing of a substantial change in circumstances sufficient to raise a significant question as to the defendant's competency to be executed at the time of filing the subsequent motion under this article.

(f) If the trial court determines that the defendant has made a substantial showing of incompetency, the court shall order at least two mental health experts to examine the defendant using the standard described by Subsection (h) to determine whether the defendant is incompetent to be executed.

 Subsection (g) below is effective for motions filed on or after Sept. 1, 2007.

(g) If the trial court does not determine that the defendant has made a substantial showing of incompetency, the court shall deny the motion and may set an execution date as otherwise provided by law.

Subsection (g) below is effective for motions filed before Sept. 1, 2007.

(g) If the trial court does not determine that the defendant has made a substantial showing of incompetency, the court shall deny the motion.

(h) A defendant is incompetent to be executed if the defendant does not understand:

(1) that he or she is to be executed and that the execution is imminent; and

(2) the reason he or she is being executed.

(i) Mental health experts who examine a defendant under this article shall provide within a time ordered by the trial court copies of their reports to the attorney representing the state, the attorney representing the defendant, and the court.

(j) By filing a motion under this article, the defendant waives any claim of privilege with respect to, and consents to the release of, all mental health and medical records relevant to whether the defendant is incompetent to be executed.

 Subsections (k) & (l) below are effective for motions filed on or after Sept. 1, 2007.

(k) The trial court shall determine whether, on the basis of reports provided under Subsection (i), the motion, any attached documents, any responsive pleadings, and any evidence introduced in the final competency hearing, the defendant has established by a preponderance of the evidence that the defendant is incompetent to be executed. If the court makes a finding that the defendant is not incompetent to be executed, the court may set an execution date as otherwise provided by law.

(*l*) Following the trial court's determination under Subsection (k) and on motion of a party, the clerk shall send immediately to the court of criminal appeals in accordance with Section 8(d), Article 11.071, the appropriate documents for that court's review and entry of a judgment of whether to adopt the trial court's order, findings, or recommendations issued under Subsection (g) or (k). The court of criminal appeals also shall determine whether any existing execution date should be withdrawn and a stay of execution issued while that court is conducting its review or, if a stay is not issued during the review, after entry of its judgment.

Subsections (k) & (l) below are effective for motions filed before Sept. 1, 2007.

(k) If, on the basis of reports provided under Subsection (i), the motion, any attached documents, any responsive pleadings, and any evidence introduced in the final competency hearing, the trial court makes a finding by a preponderance of the evidence that the defendant is incompetent to be executed, the clerk shall send immediately to the court of criminal appeals in accordance with Section 8(d), Article 11.071, the appropriate documents for that court's determination of whether any existing execution date should be withdrawn and a stay of execution issued. If a stay of execution is issued by the court of criminal appeals, the trial court periodically shall order that the defendant be reexamined by mental health experts to determine whether the defendant is no longer incompetent to be executed.

(*l*) If the trial court does not make the finding as described by Subsection (k), the court may set an execution date as otherwise provided by law.

 Subsections (l-1)-(n) below are effective for motions filed on or after Sept. 1, 2007.

(*l*-1) Notwithstanding Subsection (*l*), the court of criminal appeals may not review any finding of the defendant's competency made by a trial court as a result of a motion filed under this article if the motion is filed on or after the 20th day before the defendant's scheduled execution date.

(m) If a stay of execution is issued by the court of criminal appeals, the trial court periodically shall order that the defendant be reexamined by mental health experts to determine whether the defendant is no longer incompetent to be executed.

(n) If the court of criminal appeals enters a judgment that a defendant is not incompetent to be executed, the court may withdraw any stay of execution issued under Subsection (*l*), and the trial court may set an execution date as otherwise provided by law.

History of CCP art. 46.05: Acts 1999, 76th Leg., ch. 654, §1, eff. Sept. 1, 1999. Renumbered from art. 46.04 by Acts 2001, 77th Leg., ch. 1420, §21.001(13), eff. Sept. 1, 2001. Amended by Acts 2007, 80th Leg., ch. 677, §1, eff. Sept. 1, 2007.

CHAPTER 46A. AIDS & HIV TESTING IN COUNTY & MUNICIPAL JAILS

Art. 46A.01   Testing; segregation; disclosure

ART. 46A.01. TESTING; SEGREGATION; DISCLOSURE

(a) In this article "AIDS" and "HIV" have the meanings assigned those terms by Section 81.101, Health and Safety Code.

(b) A county or municipality may test an inmate confined in the county or municipal jail or in a contract facility authorized by Article 5115d, Revised Statutes, or Article 5115e, Revised Statutes, to determine the proper medical treatment of the inmate or the proper social management of the inmate or other inmates in the jail or facility.

(c) If the county or municipality determines that an inmate has a positive test result for AIDS or HIV, the county or municipality may segregate the inmate from other inmates in the jail or facility.

(d) This article does not provide a duty to test for AIDS or HIV, and a cause of action does not arise under this article from a failure to test for AIDS or HIV.

History of CCP art. 46A.01: Acts 1989, 71st Leg., ch. 1195, §13, eff. Sept. 1, 1989. Amended by Acts 1991, 72nd Leg., ch. 14, §284(10), eff. Sept. 1, 1991.

CHAPTER 46B. INCOMPETENCY TO STAND TRIAL

SUBCHAPTER A. GENERAL PROVISIONS

ART. 46B.001. DEFINITIONS

In this chapter:

(1) "Department" means the Department of State Health Services.

(2) "Inpatient mental health facility" has the meaning assigned by Section 571.003, Health and Safety Code.

(3) "Local mental health authority" has the meaning assigned by Section 571.003, Health and Safety Code.

(4) "Local mental retardation authority" has the meaning assigned by Section 531.002, Health and Safety Code.

(5) "Mental health facility" has the meaning assigned by Section 571.003, Health and Safety Code.

(6) "Mental illness" has the meaning assigned by Section 571.003, Health and Safety Code.

(7) "Mental retardation" has the meaning assigned by Section 591.003, Health and Safety Code.

(8) "Residential care facility" has the meaning assigned by Section 591.003, Health and Safety Code.

(9) "Electronic broadcast system" means a two-way electronic communication of image and sound between the defendant and the court and includes secure Internet videoconferencing.

History of CCP art. 46B.001: Acts 2003, 78th Leg., ch. 35, §1, eff. Jan. 1, 2004. Amended by Acts 2005, 79th Leg., ch. 324, §1, eff. Sept. 1, 2005.

ART. 46B.002. APPLICABILITY

This chapter applies to a defendant charged with a felony or with a misdemeanor punishable by confinement.

History of CCP art. 46B.002: Acts 2003, 78th Leg., ch. 35, §1, eff. Jan. 1, 2004.

ART. 46B.003. INCOMPETENCY; PRESUMPTIONS

(a) A person is incompetent to stand trial if the person does not have:

(1) sufficient present ability to consult with the person's lawyer with a reasonable degree of rational understanding; or

(2) a rational as well as factual understanding of the proceedings against the person.

(b) A defendant is presumed competent to stand trial and shall be found competent to stand trial unless proved incompetent by a preponderance of the evidence.

History of CCP art. 46B.003: Acts 2003, 78th Leg., ch. 35, §1, eff. Jan. 1, 2004.

ANNOTATIONS

Morris v. State, 214 S.W.3d 159, 168-69 (Tex. App.—Beaumont 2007, pet. granted 9-12-07). "For Morris to have a rational and factual understanding of the proceedings, Texas law requires that he understand the proceeding against him.... Pursuant to the statute, the relevant time frame for the defendant's understanding is at the time of the proceeding. The statute does not require that the defendant remember or recall the event in order for the defendant to understand the nature of the proceeding or the factual basis of the State's claims against him."

ART. 46B.004. RAISING ISSUE OF INCOMPETENCY TO STAND TRIAL

(a) Either party may suggest by motion, or the trial court may suggest on its own motion, that the defendant may be incompetent to stand trial. A motion suggesting that the defendant may be incompetent to stand trial may be supported by affidavits setting out the facts on which the suggestion is made.

(b) If evidence suggesting the defendant may be incompetent to stand trial comes to the attention of the court, the court on its own motion shall suggest that the defendant may be incompetent to stand trial.

(c) On suggestion that the defendant may be incompetent to stand trial, the court shall determine by informal inquiry whether there is some evidence from any source that would support a finding that the defendant may be incompetent to stand trial.

(d) If the court determines there is evidence to support a finding of incompetency, the court, except as provided by Subsection (e) and Article 46B.005(d), shall stay all other proceedings in the case.

(e) At any time during the proceedings under this chapter after the issue of the defendant's incompetency to stand trial is first raised, the court on the motion of the attorney representing the state may dismiss all charges pending against the defendant, regardless of whether there is any evidence to support a finding of the defendant's incompetency under Subsection (d) or whether the court has made a finding of incompetency under this chapter. If the court dismisses the charges against the defendant, the court may not continue the proceedings under this chapter, except that, if there is evidence to support a finding of the defendant's incompetency under Subsection (d), the court may proceed under Subchapter F. If the court does not elect to proceed under Subchapter F, the court shall discharge the defendant.

History of CCP art. 46B.004: Acts 2003, 78th Leg., ch. 35, §1, eff. Jan. 1, 2004. Amended by Acts 2005, 79th Leg., ch. 324, §2, eff. Sept. 1, 2005.

ANNOTATIONS

Rojas v. State, 228 S.W.3d 770, 771 (Tex.App.—Amarillo 2007, no pet.). "A competency inquiry is not required ... unless the evidence is sufficient to create a bona fide doubt in the mind of the judge whether the defendant is legally competent. Evidence is usually sufficient to create a bona fide doubt regarding competency if it shows 'recent severe mental illness, at least moderate mental retardation, or truly bizarre acts by the defendant.'"

Greene v. State, 225 S.W.3d 324, 328 (Tex. App.—San Antonio 2007, pet. filed 5-30-08). "We review a trial court's decision not to conduct a competency inquiry for an abuse of discretion."

ART. 46B.005. DETERMINING INCOMPETENCY TO STAND TRIAL

(a) If after an informal inquiry the court determines that evidence exists to support a finding of incompetency, the court shall order an examination under Subchapter B to determine whether the defendant is incompetent to stand trial in a criminal case.

(b) Except as provided by Subsection (c), the court shall hold a trial under Subchapter C before determining whether the defendant is incompetent to stand trial on the merits.

(c) A trial under this chapter is not required if:

(1) neither party's counsel requests a trial on the issue of incompetency;

(2) neither party's counsel opposes a finding of incompetency; and

(3) the court does not, on its own motion, determine that a trial is necessary to determine incompetency.

(d) If the issue of the defendant's incompetency to stand trial is raised after the trial on the merits begins, the court may determine the issue at any time before the sentence is pronounced. If the determination is delayed until after the return of a verdict, the court shall make the determination as soon as reasonably possible after the return. If a verdict of not guilty is returned, the court may not determine the issue of incompetency.

History of CCP art. 46B.005: Acts 2003, 78th Leg., ch. 35, §1, eff. Jan. 1, 2004. Amended by Acts 2005, 79th Leg., ch. 324, §3, eff. Sept. 1, 2005.

ART. 46B.006. APPOINTMENT OF & REPRESENTATION BY COUNSEL

(a) A defendant is entitled to representation by counsel before any court-ordered competency evaluation and during any proceeding at which it is suggested that the defendant may be incompetent to stand trial.

(b) If the defendant is indigent and the court has not appointed counsel to represent the defendant, the court shall appoint counsel as necessary to comply with Subsection (a).

History of CCP art. 46B.006: Acts 2003, 78th Leg., ch. 35, §1, eff. Jan. 1, 2004.

ART. 46B.007. ADMISSIBILITY OF STATEMENTS & CERTAIN OTHER EVIDENCE

A statement made by a defendant during an examination or trial on the defendant's incompetency, the testimony of an expert based on that statement, and evidence obtained as a result of that statement may not be admitted in evidence against the defendant in any criminal proceeding, other than at:

(1) a trial on the defendant's incompetency; or

(2) any proceeding at which the defendant first introduces into evidence a statement, testimony, or evidence described by this article.

History of CCP art. 46B.007: Acts 2003, 78th Leg., ch. 35, §1, eff. Jan. 1, 2004. Amended by Acts 2005, 79th Leg., ch. 324, §3, eff. Sept. 1, 2005.

ART. 46B.008. RULES OF EVIDENCE

Notwithstanding Rule 101, Texas Rules of Evidence, the Texas Rules of Evidence apply to a trial under Subchapter C or other proceeding under this chapter whether the proceeding is before a jury or before the court.

History of CCP art. 46B.008: Acts 2003, 78th Leg., ch. 35, §1, eff. Jan. 1, 2004. Amended by Acts 2005, 79th Leg., ch. 324, §3, eff. Sept. 1, 2005.

Ⓐ ART. 46B.009. TIME CREDITS

A court sentencing a person convicted of a criminal offense shall credit to the term of the person's sentence the time the person is confined in a mental health facility, residential care facility, or jail pending trial under Subchapter C.

History of CCP art. 46B.009: Acts 2003, 78th Leg., ch. 35, §1, eff. Jan. 1, 2004. Amended by Acts 2005, 79th Leg., ch. 324, §3, eff. Sept. 1, 2005; Acts 2007, 80th Leg., ch. 1307, §2, eff. Sept. 1, 2007.

ART. 46B.0095. MAXIMUM PERIOD OF FACILITY COMMITMENT OR OUTPATIENT TREATMENT PROGRAM PARTICIPATION DETERMINED BY MAXIMUM TERM FOR OFFENSE

Ⓔ *Article 46B.0095 below is effective for proceedings conducted on or after Sept. 1, 2007.*

(a) A defendant may not, under this chapter, be committed to a mental hospital or other inpatient or residential facility, ordered to participate in an outpatient treatment program, or subjected to both inpatient and outpatient treatment for a cumulative period that exceeds the maximum term provided by law for the offense for which the defendant was to be tried, except that if the defendant is charged with a misdemeanor and has been ordered only to participate in an outpatient treatment program under Subchapter D or E, the maximum period of restoration is two years beginning on the date of the initial order for outpatient treatment program participation was entered.

(b) On expiration of the maximum restoration period under Subsection (a), the defendant may be confined for an additional period in a mental hospital or other inpatient or residential facility or ordered to participate for an additional period in an outpatient treatment program, as appropriate, only pursuant to civil commitment proceedings.

History of CCP art. 46B.0095: Acts 2007, 80th Leg., ch. 1307, §2, eff. Sept. 1, 2007.

Ⓐ
ART. 46B.010. MANDATORY DISMISSAL OF MISDEMEANOR CHARGES

If a court orders the commitment of or participation in an outpatient treatment program by a defendant who is charged with a misdemeanor punishable by confinement and the defendant is not tried before the date of expiration of the maximum period of restoration under this chapter as described by Article 46B.0095, the court on the motion of the attorney representing the state shall dismiss the charge.

History of CCP art. 46B.010: Acts 2003, 78th Leg., ch. 35, §1, eff. Jan. 1, 2004. Amended by Acts 2007, 80th Leg., ch. 1307, §2, eff. Sept. 1, 2007.

ART. 46B.011. APPEALS

Neither the state nor the defendant is entitled to make an interlocutory appeal relating to a determination or ruling under Article 46B.005.

History of CCP art. 46B.011: Acts 2003, 78th Leg., ch. 35, §1, eff. Jan. 1, 2004. Amended by Acts 2005, 79th Leg., ch. 324, §3, eff. Sept. 1, 2005.

ART. 46B.012. COMPLIANCE WITH CHAPTER

The failure of a person to comply with this chapter does not provide a defendant with a right to dismissal of charges.

History of CCP art. 46B.012: Acts 2003, 78th Leg., ch. 35, §1, eff. Jan. 1, 2004.

ART. 46B.013. USE OF ELECTRONIC BROADCAST SYSTEM IN CERTAIN PROCEEDINGS UNDER THIS CHAPTER

(a) A hearing may be conducted using an electronic broadcast system as permitted by this chapter and in accordance with the other provisions of this code if:

(1) written consent to the use of an electronic broadcast system is filed with the court by:

(A) the defendant or the attorney representing the defendant; and

(B) the attorney representing the state;

(2) the electronic broadcast system provides for a simultaneous, compressed full motion video, and interactive communication of image and sound between the judge, the attorney representing the state, the attorney representing the defendant, and the defendant; and

(3) on request of the defendant or the attorney representing the defendant, the defendant and the attorney representing the defendant are able to communicate privately without being recorded or heard by the judge or the attorney representing the state.

(b) On the motion of the defendant, the attorney representing the defendant, or the attorney representing the state or on the court's own motion, the court may terminate an appearance made through an electronic broadcast system at any time during the appearance and require an appearance by the defendant in open court.

(c) A recording of the communication shall be made and preserved until any appellate proceedings have been concluded. The defendant may obtain a copy of the recording on payment of a reasonable amount to cover the costs of reproduction or, if the defendant is indigent, the court shall provide a copy to the defendant without charging a cost for the copy.

History of CCP art. 46B.013: Acts 2005, 79th Leg., ch. 324, §4, eff. Sept. 1, 2005.

SUBCHAPTER B. EXAMINATION
ART. 46B.021. APPOINTMENT OF EXPERTS

(a) On a suggestion that the defendant may be incompetent to stand trial, the court may appoint one or more disinterested experts to:

(1) examine the defendant and report to the court on the competency or incompetency of the defendant; and

(2) testify as to the issue of competency or incompetency of the defendant at any trial or hearing involving that issue.

(b) On a determination that evidence exists to support a finding of incompetency to stand trial, the court shall appoint one or more experts to perform the duties described by Subsection (a).

(c) An expert involved in the treatment of the defendant may not be appointed to examine the defendant under this article.

(d) The movant or other party as directed by the court shall provide to experts appointed under this article information relevant to a determination of the defendant's competency, including copies of the indictment or information, any supporting documents used to establish probable cause in the case, and previous mental health evaluation and treatment records.

(e) The court may appoint as experts under this chapter qualified psychiatrists or psychologists employed by the local mental health authority or local mental retardation authority. The local mental health authority or local mental retardation authority is entitled to compensation and reimbursement as provided by Article 46B.027.

(f) If a defendant wishes to be examined by an expert of the defendant's own choice, the court on timely request shall provide the expert with reasonable opportunity to examine the defendant.

History of CCP art. 46B.021: Acts 2003, 78th Leg., ch. 35, §1, eff. Jan. 1, 2004.

Sosa v. State, 201 S.W.3d 831, 832 (Tex.App.—Fort Worth 2006, pet. ref'd). "Here, no evidence of incompetency exists; Sosa's motion for an examination was not supported by an affidavit or other evidence, and the trial court's careful questioning of Sosa at the adjudication hearing did not produce any evidence of incompetence. Therefore, the trial court was not required to appoint an expert to examine Sosa to determine if he was competent."

ART. 46B.022. EXPERTS: QUALIFICATIONS

(a) To qualify for appointment under this subchapter as an expert, a psychiatrist or psychologist must:

(1) as appropriate, be a physician licensed in this state or be a psychologist licensed in this state who has a doctoral degree in psychology; and

(2) have the following certification or experience or training:

(A) as appropriate, certification by:

(i) the American Board of Psychiatry and Neurology with added or special qualifications in forensic psychiatry; or

(ii) the American Board of Professional Psychology in forensic psychology; or

(B) experience or training consisting of:

(i) at least 24 hours of specialized forensic training relating to incompetency or insanity evaluations;

(ii) for an appointment made before January 1, 2005, at least five years of experience before January 1, 2004, in performing criminal forensic evaluations for courts; or

(iii) for an appointment made on or after January 1, 2005, at least five years of experience before January 1, 2004, in performing criminal forensic evaluations for courts and eight or more hours of continuing education relating to forensic evaluations, completed in the 12 months preceding the appointment and documented with the court.

(b) In addition to meeting qualifications required by Subsection (a), to be appointed as an expert a psychiatrist or psychologist must have completed six hours of required continuing education in courses in forensic psychiatry or psychology, as appropriate, in either of the reporting periods in the 24 months preceding the appointment.

(c) A court may appoint as an expert a psychiatrist or psychologist who does not meet the requirements of Subsections (a) and (b) only if exigent circumstances require the court to base the appointment on professional training or experience of the expert that directly provides the expert with a specialized expertise to examine the defendant that would not ordinarily be possessed by a psychiatrist or psychologist who meets the requirements of Subsections (a) and (b).

History of CCP art. 46B.022: Acts 2003, 78th Leg., ch. 35, §1, eff. Jan. 1, 2004.

ART. 46B.023. CUSTODY STATUS

During an examination under this subchapter, except as otherwise ordered by the court, the defendant shall be maintained under the same custody or status as the defendant was maintained under immediately before the examination began.

History of CCP art. 46B.023: Acts 2003, 78th Leg., ch. 35, §1, eff. Jan. 1, 2004.

ART. 46B.024. FACTORS CONSIDERED IN EXAMINATION

During an examination under this subchapter and in any report based on that examination, an expert shall consider, in addition to other issues determined relevant by the expert, the following:

(1) the capacity of the defendant during criminal proceedings to:

(A) rationally understand the charges against the defendant and the potential consequences of the pending criminal proceedings;

(B) disclose to counsel pertinent facts, events, and states of mind;

(C) engage in a reasoned choice of legal strategies and options;

(D) understand the adversarial nature of criminal proceedings;

(E) exhibit appropriate courtroom behavior; and

(F) testify;

(2) whether the defendant has a diagnosable mental illness or is a person with mental retardation;

(3) the impact of the mental illness or mental retardation, if existent, on the defendant's capacity to engage with counsel in a reasonable and rational manner; and

(4) if the defendant is taking psychoactive or other medication:

(A) whether the medication is necessary to maintain the defendant's competency; and

(B) the effect, if any, of the medication on the defendant's appearance, demeanor, or ability to participate in the proceedings.

History of CCP art. 46B.024: Acts 2003, 78th Leg., ch. 35, §1, eff. Jan. 1, 2004.

ART. 46B.025. EXPERT'S REPORT

(a) An expert's report to the court must state an opinion on a defendant's competency or incompetency to stand trial or explain why the expert is unable to state such an opinion and must also:

(1) identify and address specific issues referred to the expert for evaluation;

(2) document that the expert explained to the defendant the purpose of the evaluation, the persons to whom a report on the evaluation is provided, and the limits on rules of confidentiality applying to the relationship between the expert and the defendant;

(3) in general terms, describe procedures, techniques, and tests used in the examination and the purpose of each procedure, technique, or test; and

(4) state the expert's clinical observations, findings, and opinions on each specific issue referred to the expert by the court, and state specifically any issues on which the expert could not provide an opinion.

(b) If in the opinion of an expert appointed under Article 46B.021 the defendant is incompetent to proceed, the expert shall state in the report:

(1) the exact nature of the deficits resulting from the defendant's mental illness or mental retardation, if any, that impact the factors listed in Article 46B.024, contributing to the defendant's incompetency; and

(2) prospective treatment options, if any, appropriate for the defendant.

(c) An expert's report may not state the expert's opinion on the defendant's sanity at the time of the alleged offense, if in the opinion of the expert the defendant is incompetent to proceed.

(d) The court shall direct an expert to provide the expert's report to the court and the appropriate parties in the form approved by the Texas Correctional Office on Offenders with Medical or Mental Impairments under Section 614.0032(b), Health and Safety Code.

History of CCP art. 46B.025: Acts 2003, 78th Leg., ch. 35, §1, eff. Jan. 1, 2004. Amended by Acts 2005, 79th Leg., ch. 1269, §1, eff. June 18, 2005.

ART. 46B.026. REPORT DEADLINE

(a) Except as provided by Subsection (b), an expert examining the defendant shall provide the report on the defendant's competency or incompetency to stand trial to the court, the attorney representing the state, and the attorney representing the defendant not later than the 30th day after the date on which the expert was ordered to examine the defendant and prepare the report.

(b) For good cause shown, the court may permit an expert to complete the examination and report and provide the report to the court and attorneys at a date later than the date required by Subsection (a).

(c) As soon as practicable after the court receives a report under this article, the court shall forward the report to the Texas Correctional Office on Offenders with Medical or Mental Impairments to enable that office to discharge its duties under Section 614.0032(b), Health and Safety Code.

History of CCP art. 46B.026: Acts 2003, 78th Leg., ch. 35, §1, eff. Jan. 1, 2004. Amended by Acts 2005, 79th Leg., ch. 1269, §2, eff. June 18, 2005.

ART. 46B.027. COMPENSATION OF EXPERTS; REIMBURSEMENT OF FACILITIES

(a) For any appointment under this chapter, the county in which the indictment was returned or information was filed shall pay for services described by Articles 46B.021(a)(1) and (2). If those services are provided by an expert who is an employee of the local mental health authority or local mental retardation authority, the county shall pay the authority for the services.

(b) The county in which the indictment was returned or information was filed shall reimburse a facility that accepts a defendant for examination under this chapter for expenses incurred that are determined by the department to be reasonably necessary and incidental to the proper examination of the defendant.

History of CCP art. 46B.027: Acts 2003, 78th Leg., ch. 35, §1, eff. Jan. 1, 2004.

SUBCHAPTER C. INCOMPETENCY TRIAL

ART. 46B.051. TRIAL BEFORE JUDGE OR JURY

(a) If a court holds a trial to determine whether the defendant is incompetent to stand trial, on the request of either party or the motion of the court, a jury shall make the determination.

(b) The court shall make the determination of incompetency if a jury determination is not required by Subsection (a).

(c) If a jury determination is required by Subsection (a), a jury that has not been selected to determine the guilt or innocence of the defendant must determine the issue of incompetency.

History of CCP art. 46B.051: Acts 2003, 78th Leg., ch. 35, §1, eff. Jan. 1, 2004. Amended by Acts 2005, 79th Leg., ch. 324, §§5, 6, eff. Sept. 1, 2005.

ART. 46B.052. JURY VERDICT

(a) If a jury determination of the issue of incompetency to stand trial is required by Article 46B.051(a), the court shall require the jury to state in its verdict whether the defendant is incompetent to stand trial.

(b) The verdict must be concurred in by each juror.

History of CCP art. 46B.052: Acts 2003, 78th Leg., ch. 35, §1, eff. Jan. 1, 2004.

ART. 46B.053. PROCEDURE AFTER FINDING OF COMPETENCY

If the court or jury determines that the defendant is competent to stand trial, the court shall continue the trial on the merits. If a jury determines that the defendant is competent and the trial on the merits is to be held before a jury, the court shall continue the trial with another jury selected for that purpose.

History of CCP art. 46B.053: Acts 2003, 78th Leg., ch. 35, §1, eff. Jan. 1, 2004. Amended by Acts 2005, 79th Leg., ch. 324, §7, eff. Sept. 1, 2005.

ART. 46B.054. UNCONTESTED INCOMPETENCY

If the court finds that evidence exists to support a finding of incompetency to stand trial and the court and the counsel for each party agree that the defendant is incompetent to stand trial, the court shall proceed in the same manner as if a jury had been impaneled and had found the defendant incompetent to stand trial.

History of CCP art. 46B.054: Acts 2003, 78th Leg., ch. 35, §1, eff. Jan. 1, 2004. Amended by Acts 2005, 79th Leg., ch. 324, §7, eff. Sept. 1, 2005.

ART. 46B.055. PROCEDURE AFTER FINDING OF INCOMPETENCY

If the defendant is found incompetent to stand trial, the court shall proceed under Subchapter D.

History of CCP art. 46B.055: Acts 2003, 78th Leg., ch. 35, §1, eff. Jan. 1, 2004.

SUBCHAPTER D. PROCEDURES AFTER DETERMINATION OF INCOMPETENCY

ART. 46B.071. OPTIONS ON DETERMINATION OF INCOMPETENCY

On a determination that a defendant is incompetent to stand trial, the court shall:

(1) commit the defendant to a facility under Article 46B.073; or

(2) release the defendant on bail under Article 46B.072.

History of CCP art. 46B.071: Acts 2003, 78th Leg., ch. 35, §1, eff. Jan. 1, 2004. Amended by Acts 2005, 79th Leg., ch. 324, §8, eff. Sept. 1, 2005.

ART. 46B.072. RELEASE ON BAIL

 (a) Subject to conditions reasonably related to assuring public safety and the effectiveness of the defendant's treatment, if the court determines that a defendant found incompetent to stand trial is not a danger to others and may be safely treated on an outpatient basis with the specific objective of attaining competency to stand trial and if an appropriate outpatient treatment program is available for the defendant, the court:

(1) may release on bail a defendant found incompetent to stand trial with respect to a felony or may continue the defendant's release on bail; and

(2) shall release on bail a defendant found incompetent to stand trial with respect to a misdemeanor or shall continue the defendant's release on bail.

E *Subsections (b)-(d) below are effective for proceedings conducted on or after Sept. 1, 2007.*

(b) The court shall order a defendant released on bail under Subsection (a) to participate in an outpatient treatment program for a period not to exceed 120 days.

(c) Notwithstanding Subsection (a), the court may order a defendant to participate in an outpatient treatment program under this article only if:

(1) the court receives and approves a comprehensive plan that:

(A) provides for the treatment of the defendant for purposes of competency restoration; and

(B) identifies the person who will be responsible for providing that treatment to the defendant; and

(2) the court finds that the treatment proposed by the plan will be available to and will be provided to the defendant.

(d) An order issued under this article may require the defendant to participate in:

(1) as appropriate, an outpatient treatment program administered by a community center or an outpatient treatment program administered by any other entity that provides outpatient competency restoration services; and

(2) an appropriate prescribed regimen of medical, psychiatric, or psychological care or treatment, including care or treatment involving the administration of psychoactive medication, including those required under Article 46B.086.

History of CCP art. 46B.072: Acts 2003, 78th Leg., ch. 35, §1, eff. Jan. 1, 2004. Amended by Acts 2007, 80th Leg., ch. 1307, §3, eff. Sept. 1, 2007.

ART. 46B.073. COMMITMENT FOR RESTORATION TO COMPETENCY

(a) This article applies only to a defendant not released on bail.

(b) The court shall commit a defendant described by Subsection (a) to a mental health facility or residential care facility for a period not to exceed 120 days for

further examination and treatment toward the specific objective of attaining competency to stand trial.

A (c) If the defendant is charged with an offense listed in Article 17.032(a), other than an offense listed in Article 17.032(a)(6), or the indictment alleges an affirmative finding under Section 3g(a)(2), Article 42.12, the court shall enter an order committing the defendant to the maximum security unit of any facility designated by the department, to an agency of the United States operating a mental hospital, or to a Department of Veterans Affairs hospital.

A (d) If the defendant is not charged with an offense described by Subsection (c) and the indictment does not allege an affirmative finding under Section 3g(a)(2), Article 42.12, the court shall enter an order committing the defendant to a mental health facility or residential care facility determined to be appropriate by the local mental health authority or local mental retardation authority.

History of CCP art. 46B.073: Acts 2003, 78th Leg., ch. 35, §1, eff. Jan. 1, 2004. Amended by Acts 2005, 79th Leg., ch. 324, §9, eff. Sept. 1, 2005; Acts 2007, 80th Leg., ch. 1307, §4, eff. Sept. 1, 2007.

ART. 46B.074. COMPETENT TESTIMONY REQUIRED

(a) A defendant may be committed to a mental health facility or residential care facility under this subchapter only on competent medical or psychiatric testimony provided by an expert qualified under Article 46B.022.

(b) The court may allow an expert to substitute the expert's report under Article 46B.025 for any testimony by the expert that may be required under this article.

History of CCP art. 46B.074: Acts 2003, 78th Leg., ch. 35, §1, eff. Jan. 1, 2004. Amended by Acts 2005, 79th Leg., ch. 324, §10, eff. Sept. 1, 2005.

A ART. 46B.075. TRANSFER OF DEFENDANT TO FACILITY OR OUTPATIENT TREATMENT PROGRAM

An order issued under Article 46B.072 or 46B.073 must place the defendant in the custody of the sheriff for transportation to the facility or outpatient treatment program, as applicable, in which the defendant is to receive treatment for purposes of competency restoration.

History of CCP art. 46B.075: Acts 2003, 78th Leg., ch. 35, §1, eff. Jan. 1, 2004. Amended by Acts 2007, 80th Leg., ch. 1307, §5, eff. Sept. 1, 2007.

A ART. 46B.076. COURT'S ORDER

(a) If the defendant is found incompetent to stand trial, not later than the date of the order of commitment or of release on bail, as applicable, the court shall send a copy of the order to the facility of the department to which the defendant is committed or the outpatient treatment program to which the defendant is released. The court shall also provide to the facility or outpatient treatment program copies of the following made available to the court during the incompetency trial:

(1) reports of each expert;

(2) psychiatric, psychological, or social work reports that relate to the mental condition of the defendant;

(3) documents provided by the attorney representing the state or the attorney representing the defendant that relate to the defendant's current or past mental condition;

(4) copies of the indictment or information and any supporting documents used to establish probable cause in the case;

(5) the defendant's criminal history record; and

(6) the addresses of the attorney representing the state and the attorney representing the defendant.

(b) The court shall order that the transcript of all medical testimony received by the jury or court be promptly prepared by the court reporter and forwarded to the proper facility or outpatient treatment program.

History of CCP art. 46B.076: Acts 2003, 78th Leg., ch. 35, §1, eff. Jan. 1, 2004. Amended by Acts 2005, 79th Leg., ch. 324, §11, eff. Sept. 1, 2005; Acts 2007, 80th Leg., ch. 1307, §5, eff. Sept. 1, 2007.

ANNOTATIONS

Queen v. State, 212 S.W.3d 619, 622-23 (Tex. App.—Austin 2006, no pet.). "The legislature has not … provided for appeal, interlocutory or otherwise, from a temporary commitment under subchapter D, which is preliminary to a more permanent commitment under subchapter E. The provisions of the [H&SC] which allow for appeals from orders of commitment or in-patient mental health services are not applicable to criminal defendants until a subchapter E proceeding has occurred. By the absence of any similar provisions allowing for appeal and the legislature's explicit bar of appeals from a determination under article 46B.005, a determination that is an essential part of the competency process and that starts the process of evaluation and commitment, we conclude that the legislature did not intend to allow interlocutory appeals from orders of temporary commitment made after a determination of incompetence but before a subchapter E proceeding."

ART. 46B.077. INDIVIDUAL TREATMENT PROGRAM

 (a) The facility to which the defendant is committed or the outpatient treatment program to which the defendant is released on bail shall:

(1) develop an individual program of treatment;

(2) assess and evaluate whether the defendant will obtain competency in the foreseeable future; and

(3) report to the court and to the local mental health authority or to the local mental retardation authority on the defendant's progress toward achieving competency.

(b) If the defendant is committed to an inpatient mental health facility or to a residential care facility, the facility shall report to the court at least once during the commitment period. If the defendant is released to a treatment program not provided by an inpatient mental health facility or a residential care facility, the treatment program shall report to the court:

(1) not later than the 14th day after the date on which the defendant's treatment begins; and

(2) until the defendant is no longer released to the treatment program, at least once during each 30-day period following the date of the report required by Subdivision (1).

History of CCP art. 46B.077: Acts 2003, 78th Leg., ch. 35, §1, eff. Jan. 1, 2004. Amended by Acts 2007, 80th Leg., ch. 1307, §6, eff. Sept. 1, 2007.

ART. 46B.078. CHARGES SUBSEQUENTLY DISMISSED

If the charges pending against a defendant are dismissed, the court that issued the order under Article 46B.072 or 46B.073 shall send a copy of the order of dismissal to the sheriff of the county in which the court is located and to the head of the facility or the provider of the outpatient treatment program, as appropriate. On receipt of the copy of the order, the facility or outpatient treatment program shall discharge the defendant into the care of the sheriff for transportation in the manner described by Article 46B.082.

History of CCP art. 46B.078: Acts 2003, 78th Leg., ch. 35, §1, eff. Jan. 1, 2004. Amended by Acts 2007, 80th Leg., ch. 1307, §7, eff. Sept. 1, 2007.

ART. 46B.079. NOTICE & REPORT TO COURT

(a) The head of the facility or the provider of the outpatient treatment program, as appropriate, not later than the 15th day before the date on which a restoration period is to expire, shall notify the applicable court that the restoration period is about to expire.

(b) The head of the facility or outpatient treatment program provider shall promptly notify the court when the head of the facility or outpatient treatment program provider believes that:

(1) the defendant has attained competency to stand trial; or

(2) the defendant will not attain competency in the foreseeable future.

(c) When the head of the facility or outpatient treatment program provider gives notice to the court under Subsection (a) or (b), the head of the facility or outpatient treatment program provider also shall file a final report with the court stating the reason for the proposed discharge under this chapter and including a list of the types and dosages of medications with which the defendant was treated for mental illness while in the facility or participating in the outpatient treatment program. To enable any objection to the findings of the report to be made in a timely manner under Article 46B.084(a), the court shall provide copies of the report to the attorney representing the defendant and the attorney representing the state.

(d) If the head of the facility or outpatient treatment program provider notifies the court that the initial restoration period is about to expire, the notice may contain a request for an extension of the period for an additional period of 60 days and an explanation for the basis of the request.

History of CCP art. 46B.079: Acts 2003, 78th Leg., ch. 35, §1, eff. Jan. 1, 2004. Amended by Acts 2005, 79th Leg., ch. 324, §12, eff. Sept. 1, 2005; Acts 2007, 80th Leg., ch. 1307, §7, eff. Sept. 1, 2007.

A ART. 46B.080. EXTENSION OF ORDER

(a) On a request of the head of a facility or a treatment program provider that is made under Article 46B.079(d) and notwithstanding any other provision of this subchapter, the court may enter an order extending the initial restoration period for an additional period of 60 days.

(b) The court may enter an order under Subsection (a) only if the court determines that, on the basis of information provided by the head of the facility or the treatment program provider:

(1) the defendant has not attained competency; and

(2) an extension of the restoration period will likely enable the facility or program to restore the defendant to competency.

(c) The court may grant only one extension under this article for a period of restoration ordered under this subchapter.

History of CCP art. 46B.080: Acts 2003, 78th Leg., ch. 35, §1, eff. Jan. 1, 2004. Amended by Acts 2005, 79th Leg., ch. 324, §12, eff. Sept. 1, 2005; Acts 2007, 80th Leg., ch. 1307, §7, eff. Sept. 1, 2007.

A ART. 46B.081. RETURN TO COURT

Subject to Article 46B.082(b), a defendant committed or released on bail under this subchapter shall be returned to the applicable court as soon as practicable after notice to the court is provided under Article 46B.079, but not later than the date of expiration of the period for restoration specified by the court under Article 46B.072 or 46B.073.

History of CCP art. 46B.081: Acts 2003, 78th Leg., ch. 35, §1, eff. Jan. 1, 2004. Amended by Acts 2005, 79th Leg., ch. 324, §13, eff. Sept. 1, 2005; Acts 2007, 80th Leg., ch. 1307, §7, eff. Sept. 1, 2007.

A ART. 46B.082. TRANSPORTATION OF DEFENDANT

(a) On notification from the court under Article 46B.078, the sheriff of the county in which the court is located or the sheriff's designee shall transport the defendant to the court.

(b) If before the 15th day after the date on which the court received notification under Article 46B.079 a defendant committed to a facility of the department or ordered to participate in an outpatient treatment program has not been transported to the court that issued the order under Article 46B.072 or 46B.073, as applicable, the head of the facility to which the defendant is committed or the provider of the outpatient treatment program in which the defendant is participating shall cause the defendant to be promptly transported to the court and placed in the custody of the sheriff of the county in which the court is located. The county in which the court is located shall reimburse the department for the mileage and per diem expenses of the personnel required to transport the defendant, calculated in accordance with rates provided in the General Appropriations Act for state employees.

History of CCP art. 46B.082: Acts 2003, 78th Leg., ch. 35, §1, eff. Jan. 1, 2004. Amended by Acts 2007, 80th Leg., ch. 1307, §7, eff. Sept. 1, 2007.

A ART. 46B.083. SUPPORTING COMMITMENT INFORMATION PROVIDED BY FACILITY HEAD OR OUTPATIENT TREATMENT PROGRAM PROVIDER

(a) If the head of the facility or outpatient treatment program provider believes that the defendant is a person with mental illness and meets the criteria for court-ordered mental health services under Subtitle C, Title 7, Health and Safety Code, the head of the facility or the outpatient treatment program provider shall have submitted to the court a certificate of medical examination for mental illness.

(b) If the head of the facility or the outpatient treatment program provider believes that the defendant is a person with mental retardation, the head of the facility or the outpatient treatment program provider shall have submitted to the court an affidavit stating the conclusions reached as a result of the examination.

History of CCP art. 46B.083: Acts 2003, 78th Leg., ch. 35, §1, eff. Jan. 1, 2004. Amended by Acts 2005, 79th Leg., ch. 324, §14, eff. Sept. 1, 2005; Acts 2007, 80th Leg., ch. 1307, §7, eff. Sept. 1, 2007.

ART. 46B.084. PROCEEDINGS ON RETURN OF DEFENDANT TO COURT

Ⓐ **(a)** On the return of a defendant to the court, the court shall make a determination with regard to the defendant's competency to stand trial. The court may make the determination based solely on the report filed under Article 46B.079(c), unless any party objects in writing or in open court to the findings of the report not later than the 15th day after the date on which the court received notification under Article 46B.079. The court shall make the determination not later than the 20th day after the date on which the court received notification under Article 46B.079, regardless of whether a party objects to the report as described by this subsection and the issue is set for hearing under Subsection (b).

(b) If a party objects under Subsection (a), the issue shall be set for a hearing. The hearing is before the court, except that on motion by the defendant, the defense counsel, the prosecuting attorney, or the court, the hearing shall be held before a jury.

Ⓐ **(b-1)** If the hearing is before the court, the hearing may be conducted by means of an electronic broadcast system as provided by Article 46B.013. Notwithstanding any other provision of this chapter, the defendant is not required to be returned to the court with respect to any hearing that is conducted under this article in the manner described by this subsection.

(c) Repealed by Acts 2007, 80th Leg., ch. 1307, §21, eff. Sept. 1, 2007.

(d) If the defendant is found competent to stand trial, criminal proceedings against the defendant may be resumed.

(e) If the defendant is found incompetent to stand trial and if all charges pending against the defendant are not dismissed, the court shall proceed under Subchapter E.

(f) If the defendant is found incompetent to stand trial and if all charges pending against the defendant are dismissed, the court shall proceed under Subchapter F.

History of CCP art. 46B.084: Acts 2003, 78th Leg., ch. 35, §1, eff. Jan. 1, 2004. Amended by Acts 2005, 79th Leg., ch. 324, §15, eff. Sept. 1, 2005; Acts 2007, 80th Leg., ch. 1307, §§8, 21, eff. Sept. 1, 2007.

Ⓐ ART. 46B.085. SUBSEQUENT RESTORATION PERIODS & EXTENSIONS OF THOSE PERIODS PROHIBITED

(a) The court may order only one initial period of restoration and one extension under this subchapter in connection with the same offense.

(b) After an initial restoration period and an extension are ordered as described by Subsection (a), any subsequent court orders for treatment must be issued under Subchapter E or F.

History of CCP art. 46B.085: Acts 2003, 78th Leg., ch. 35, §1, eff. Jan. 1, 2004. Amended by Acts 2005, 79th Leg., ch. 324, §16, eff. Sept. 1, 2005; Acts 2007, 80th Leg., ch. 1307, §9, eff. Sept. 1, 2007.

Ⓐ ART. 46B.086. COURT-ORDERED MEDICATIONS

(a) This article applies only to a defendant:

(1) who is determined under this chapter to be incompetent to stand trial;

(2) for whom an inpatient mental health facility, residential care facility, or outpatient treatment program provider has prepared a continuity of care plan that requires the defendant to take psychoactive medications; and

(3) who, after a hearing held under Section 574.106, Health and Safety Code, has been found not to meet the criteria prescribed by Sections 574.106(a) and (a-1), Health and Safety Code, for court-ordered administration of psychoactive medications; or

(4) who is subject to Article 46B.072.

(b) If a defendant described by Subsection (a) refuses to take psychoactive medications as required by the defendant's continuity of care plan, the director of the correctional facility or outpatient treatment provider shall notify the court in which the criminal proceedings are pending of that fact not later than the end of the next business day following the refusal. The court shall promptly notify the attorney representing the state and the attorney representing the defendant of the defendant's refusal. The attorney representing the state may file a written motion to compel medication. The motion to compel medication must be filed not later than the 15th day after the date a judge issues an order stating that the defendant does not meet the criteria for court-ordered administration of psychoactive medications under Section 574.106, Health and Safety Code. The motion to compel medication for a defendant in an outpatient treatment program may be filed at any time.

(c) The court, after notice and after a hearing held not later than the fifth day after the defendant is returned to the committing court, may authorize the director of a correctional facility or the program provider, as applicable, to have the medication administered to the defendant, by reasonable force if necessary.

(d) The court may issue an order under this article only if the order is supported by the testimony of two physicians, one of whom is the physician at or with the applicable correctional facility or outpatient treatment program who is prescribing the medication as a component of the defendant's continuity of care plan and another who is not otherwise involved in proceedings against the defendant. The court may require either or both physicians to examine the defendant and report on the examination to the court.

(e) The court may issue an order under this article if the court finds by clear and convincing evidence that:

(1) the prescribed medication is medically appropriate, is in the best medical interest of the defendant, and does not present side effects that cause harm to the defendant that is greater than the medical benefit to the defendant;

(2) the state has a clear and compelling interest in the defendant obtaining and maintaining competency to stand trial;

(3) no other less invasive means of obtaining and maintaining the defendant's competency exists; and

(4) the prescribed medication will not unduly prejudice the defendant's rights or use of defensive theories at trial.

(f) A statement made by a defendant to a physician during an examination under Subsection (d) may not be admitted against the defendant in any criminal proceeding, other than at:

(1) a hearing on the defendant's incompetency; or

(2) any proceeding at which the defendant first introduces into evidence the contents of the statement.

History of CCP art. 46B.086: Acts 2003, 78th Leg., ch. 35, §1, eff. Jan. 1, 2004. Amended by Acts 2005, 79th Leg., ch. 717, §8, eff. June 17, 2005; Acts 2007, 80th Leg., ch. 1307, §9, eff. Sept. 1, 2007.

SUBCHAPTER E. CIVIL COMMITMENT: CHARGES PENDING

ART. 46B.101. APPLICABILITY

This subchapter applies to a defendant against whom a court is required to proceed under Article 46B.084(e).

History of CCP art. 46B.101: Acts 2003, 78th Leg., ch. 35, §1, eff. Jan. 1, 2004. Amended by Acts 2005, 79th Leg., ch. 324, §17, eff. Sept. 1, 2005.

ART. 46B.102. CIVIL COMMITMENT HEARING: MENTAL ILLNESS

Ⓐ (a) If it appears to the court that the defendant may be a person with mental illness, the court shall hold a hearing to determine whether the defendant should be court-ordered to mental health services under Subtitle C, Title 7, Health and Safety Code.

Ⓐ (b) Proceedings for commitment of the defendant to court-ordered mental health services are governed by Subtitle C, Title 7, Health and Safety Code, to the extent that Subtitle C applies and does not conflict with this chapter, except that the criminal court shall conduct the proceedings whether or not the criminal court is also the county court.

(c) If the court enters an order committing the defendant to a mental health facility, the defendant shall be:

(1) treated in conformity with Subtitle C, Title 7, Health and Safety Code, except as otherwise provided by this chapter; and

(2) released in conformity with Article 46B.107.

Ⓔ *Subsection (d) below is effective for proceedings conducted on or after Sept. 1, 2007.*

(d) In proceedings conducted under this subchapter for a defendant described by Subsection (a):

(1) an application for court-ordered temporary or extended mental health services may not be required;

(2) the provisions of Subtitle C, Title 7, Health and Safety Code, relating to notice of hearing do not apply; and

(3) appeals from the criminal court proceedings are to the court of appeals as in the proceedings for court-ordered inpatient mental health services under Subtitle C, Title 7, Health and Safety Code.

History of CCP art. 46B.102: Acts 2003, 78th Leg., ch. 35, §1, eff. Jan. 1, 2004. Amended by Acts 2005, 79th Leg., ch. 324, §18, eff. Sept. 1, 2005; Acts 2007, 80th Leg., ch. 1307, §10, eff. Sept. 1, 2007.

ART. 46B.103. CIVIL COMMITMENT HEARING: MENTAL RETARDATION

(a) If it appears to the court that the defendant may be a person with mental retardation, the court shall hold a hearing to determine whether the defendant is a person with mental retardation.

(b) Proceedings for commitment of the defendant to a residential care facility are governed by Subtitle D, Title 7, Health and Safety Code, to the extent that Subtitle D applies and does not conflict with this chapter, except that the criminal court shall conduct the proceedings whether or not the criminal court is also a county court.

(c) If the court enters an order committing the defendant to a residential care facility, the defendant shall be:

(1) treated and released in accordance with Subtitle D, Title 7, Health and Safety Code, except as otherwise provided by this chapter; and

(2) released in conformity with Article 46B.107.

(d) In the proceedings conducted under this subchapter for a defendant described by Subsection (a):

(1) an application to have the defendant declared a person with mental retardation may not be required;

(2) the provisions of Subtitle D, Title 7, Health and Safety Code, relating to notice of hearing do not apply; and

(3) appeals from the criminal court proceedings are to the court of appeals as in the proceedings for commitment to a residential care facility under Subtitle D, Title 7, Health and Safety Code.

History of CCP art. 46B.103: Acts 2003, 78th Leg., ch. 35, §1, eff. Jan. 1, 2004. Amended by Acts 2005, 79th Leg., ch. 324, §19, eff. Sept. 1, 2005; Acts 2007, 80th Leg., ch. 1307, §11, eff. Sept. 1, 2007.

ART. 46B.104. CIVIL COMMITMENT PLACEMENT: FINDING OF VIOLENCE

A defendant committed to a facility as a result of proceedings initiated under this chapter shall be committed to the maximum security unit of any facility designated by the department if:

(1) the defendant is charged with an offense listed in Article 17.032(a), other than an offense listed in Article 17.032(a)(6); or

(2) the indictment charging the offense alleges an affirmative finding under Section 3g(a)(2), Article 42.12.

History of CCP art. 46B.104: Acts 2003, 78th Leg., ch. 35, §1, eff. Jan. 1, 2004. Amended by Acts 2005, 79th Leg., ch. 324, §20, eff. Sept. 1, 2005; Acts 2007, 80th Leg., ch. 1307, §12, eff. Sept. 1, 2007.

ART. 46B.105. TRANSFER FOLLOWING CIVIL COMMITMENT PLACEMENT

(a) Unless a defendant is determined to be manifestly dangerous by a department review board, not later than the 60th day after the date the defendant arrives at the maximum security unit, the defendant shall be transferred to:

(1) a unit of an inpatient mental health facility other than a maximum security unit;

(2) a residential care facility; or

(3) a program designated by a local mental health authority or a local mental retardation authority.

(b) The commissioner of mental health and mental retardation shall appoint a review board of five members, including one psychiatrist licensed to practice medicine in this state and two persons who work directly with persons with mental illness or mental retardation, to determine whether the defendant is manifestly dangerous and, as a result of the danger the defendant presents, requires continued placement in a maximum security unit.

(c) The review board may not make a determination as to the defendant's need for treatment.

(d) A finding that the defendant is not manifestly dangerous is not a medical determination that the defendant no longer meets the criteria for involuntary civil commitment under Subtitle C or D, Title 7, Health and Safety Code.

(e) If the superintendent of the facility at which the maximum security unit is located disagrees with the determination, the matter shall be referred to the commissioner of mental health and mental retardation. The commissioner shall decide whether the defendant is manifestly dangerous.

History of CCP art. 46B.105: Acts 2003, 78th Leg., ch. 35, §1, eff. Jan. 1, 2004. Amended by Acts 2005, 79th Leg., ch. 324, §21, eff. Sept. 1, 2005.

ART. 46B.106. CIVIL COMMITMENT PLACEMENT: NO FINDING OF VIOLENCE

(a) A defendant committed to a facility as a result of the proceedings initiated under this chapter, other than a defendant described by Article 46B.104, shall be committed to:

(1) a facility designated by the department; or

(2) an outpatient treatment program.

(b) A facility or outpatient treatment program may not refuse to accept a placement ordered under this article on the grounds that criminal charges against the defendant are pending.

History of CCP art. 46B.106: Acts 2003, 78th Leg., ch. 35, §1, eff. Jan. 1, 2004. Amended by Acts 2005, 79th Leg., ch. 324, §22, eff. Sept. 1, 2005; Acts 2007, 80th Leg., ch. 1307, §13, eff. Sept. 1, 2007.

Ⓐ ART. 46B.107. RELEASE OF DEFENDANT AFTER CIVIL COMMITMENT

(a) The release from the department, an outpatient treatment program, or a facility of a defendant committed under this chapter is subject to disapproval by the committing court if the court or the attorney representing the state has notified the head of the facility or outpatient treatment provider, as applicable, to which the defendant has been committed that a criminal charge remains pending against the defendant.

(b) If the head of the facility or outpatient treatment provider to which a defendant has been committed under this chapter determines that the defendant should be released from the facility, the head of the facility or outpatient treatment provider shall notify the committing court and the sheriff of the county from which the defendant was committed in writing of the release not later than the 14th day before the date on which the facility or outpatient treatment provider intends to release the defendant.

(c) The head of the facility or outpatient treatment provider shall provide with the notice a written statement that states an opinion as to whether the defendant to be released has attained competency to stand trial.

(d) The court may, on motion of the attorney representing the state or on its own motion, hold a hearing to determine whether release is appropriate under the applicable criteria in Subtitle C or D, Title 7, Health and Safety Code. The court may conduct the hearing:

(1) at the facility; or

(2) by means of an electronic broadcast system as provided by Article 46B.013.

(e) If the court determines that release is not appropriate, the court shall enter an order directing the head of the facility or the outpatient treatment provider to not release the defendant.

(f) If an order is entered under Subsection (e), any subsequent proceeding to release the defendant is subject to this article.

History of CCP art. 46B.107: Acts 2003, 78th Leg., ch. 35, §1, eff. Jan. 1, 2004. Amended by Acts 2005, 79th Leg., ch. 324, §§23, 24, eff. Sept. 1, 2005; Acts 2007, 80th Leg., ch. 1307, §14, eff. Sept. 1, 2007.

ART. 46B.108. REDETERMINATION OF COMPETENCY

(a) If criminal charges against a defendant found incompetent to stand trial have not been dismissed, the trial court at any time may determine whether the defendant has been restored to competency.

Ⓐ **(b)** An inquiry into restoration of competency under this subchapter may be made at the request of the head of the mental health facility, outpatient treatment provider, or residential care facility to which the defendant has been committed, the defendant, the attorney representing the defendant, or the attorney representing the state, or may be made on the court's own motion.

History of CCP art. 46B.108: Acts 2003, 78th Leg., ch. 35, §1, eff. Jan. 1, 2004. Amended by Acts 2005, 79th Leg., ch. 324, §25, eff. Sept. 1, 2005; Acts 2007, 80th Leg., ch. 1307, §15, eff. Sept. 1, 2007.

Ⓐ ART. 46B.109. REQUEST BY HEAD OF FACILITY OR OUTPATIENT TREATMENT PROVIDER

(a) The head of a facility or outpatient treatment provider to which a defendant has been committed as a result of a finding of incompetency to stand trial may request the court to determine that the defendant has been restored to competency.

(b) The head of the facility or outpatient treatment provider shall provide with the request a written statement that in their opinion the defendant is competent to stand trial.

History of CCP art. 46B.109: Acts 2003, 78th Leg., ch. 35, §1, eff. Jan. 1, 2004. Amended by Acts 2007, 80th Leg., ch. 1307, §16, eff. Sept. 1, 2007.

ART. 46B.110. MOTION BY DEFENDANT, ATTORNEY REPRESENTING DEFENDANT, OR ATTORNEY REPRESENTING STATE

(a) The defendant, the attorney representing the defendant, or the attorney representing the state may move that the court determine that the defendant has been restored to competency.

(b) A motion for a determination of competency may be accompanied by affidavits supporting the moving party's assertion that the defendant is competent.

History of CCP art. 46B.110: Acts 2003, 78th Leg., ch. 35, §1, eff. Jan. 1, 2004. Amended by Acts 2005, 79th Leg., ch. 324, §26, eff. Sept. 1, 2005.

ART. 46B.111. APPOINTMENT OF EXAMINERS

On the filing of a request or motion to determine that the defendant has been restored to competency or on the court's decision on its own motion to inquire into restoration of competency, the court may appoint disinterested experts to examine the defendant in accordance with Subchapter B.

History of CCP art. 46B.111: Acts 2003, 78th Leg., ch. 35, §1, eff. Jan. 1, 2004.

ART. 46B.112. DETERMINATION OF RESTORATION WITH AGREEMENT

On the filing of a request or motion to determine that the defendant has been restored to competency or on the court's decision on its own motion to inquire into restoration of competency, the court shall find the defendant competent to stand trial and proceed in the same manner as if the defendant had been found restored to competency at a hearing if:

(1) both parties agree that the defendant is competent to stand trial; and

(2) the court concurs.

History of CCP art. 46B.112: Acts 2003, 78th Leg., ch. 35, §1, eff. Jan. 1, 2004.

Ⓐ ART. 46B.113. DETERMINATION OF RESTORATION WITHOUT AGREEMENT

(a) The court shall hold a hearing on a request by the head of a facility or outpatient treatment provider to which a defendant has been committed as a result of a finding of incompetency to stand trial to determine whether the defendant has been restored to competency.

(b) The court may hold a hearing on a motion to determine whether the defendant has been restored to competency or on the court's decision on its own motion to inquire into restoration of competency, and shall hold a hearing if a motion and any supporting material establish good reason to believe the defendant may have been restored to competency.

(c) If a court holds a hearing under this article, on the request of the counsel for either party or the motion of the court, a jury shall make the competency determination. If the competency determination will be made by the court rather than a jury, the court may conduct the hearing:

(1) at the facility; or

(2) by means of an electronic broadcast system as provided by Article 46B.013.

(d) If the head of a facility or outpatient treatment provider to which the defendant was committed as a result of a finding of incompetency to stand trial has provided an opinion that the defendant has regained competency, competency is presumed at a hearing under this subchapter and continuing incompetency must be proved by a preponderance of the evidence.

(e) If the head of a facility or outpatient treatment provider has not provided an opinion described by Subsection (d), incompetency is presumed at a hearing under this subchapter and the defendant's competency must be proved by a preponderance of the evidence.

History of CCP art. 46B.113: Acts 2003, 78th Leg., ch. 35, §1, eff. Jan. 1, 2004. Amended by Acts 2005, 79th Leg., ch. 324, §27, eff. Sept. 1, 2005; Acts 2007, 80th Leg., ch. 1307, §17, eff. Sept. 1, 2007.

ART. 46B.114. TRANSPORTATION OF DEFENDANT TO COURT

If the hearing is not conducted at the facility to which the defendant has been committed under this chapter or conducted by means of an electronic broadcast system as described by this subchapter, an order setting a hearing to determine whether the defendant has been restored to competency shall direct that, as soon as practicable but not earlier than 72 hours before the date the hearing is scheduled, the defendant be placed in the custody of the sheriff of the county in which the committing court is located or the sheriff's designee for transportation to the court. The sheriff or the sheriff's designee may not take custody of the defendant under this article until 72 hours before the date the hearing is scheduled.

History of CCP art. 46B.114: Acts 2003, 78th Leg., ch. 35, §1, eff. Jan. 1, 2004. Amended by Acts 2005, 79th Leg., ch. 324, §28, eff. Sept. 1, 2005.

ART. 46B.115. SUBSEQUENT REDETERMINATIONS OF COMPETENCY

(a) If the court has made a determination that a defendant has not been restored to competency under this subchapter, a subsequent request or motion for a redetermination of competency filed before the 91st day after the date of that determination must:

(1) explain why the person making the request or motion believes another inquiry into restoration is appropriate; and

(2) provide support for the belief.

(b) The court may hold a hearing on a request or motion under this article only if the court first finds reason to believe the defendant's condition has materially changed since the prior determination that the defendant was not restored to competency.

(c) If the competency determination will be made by the court, the court may conduct the hearing at the facility to which the defendant has been committed under this chapter or may conduct the hearing by means of an electronic broadcast system as provided by Article 46B.013.

History of CCP art. 46B.115: Acts 2003, 78th Leg., ch. 35, §1, eff. Jan. 1, 2004. Amended by Acts 2005, 79th Leg., ch. 324, §29, eff. Sept. 1, 2005.

ART. 46B.116. DISPOSITION ON DETERMINATION OF COMPETENCY

If the defendant is found competent to stand trial, the proceedings on the criminal charge may proceed.

History of CCP art. 46B.116: Acts 2003, 78th Leg., ch. 35, §1, eff. Jan. 1, 2004.

ART. 46B.117. DISPOSITION ON DETERMINATION OF INCOMPETENCY

If a defendant under order of commitment to a facility or outpatient treatment program is found to not have been restored to competency to stand trial, the court shall remand the defendant pursuant to that order of commitment, and, if applicable, order the defendant placed in the custody of the sheriff or the sheriff's designee for transportation back to the facility or outpatient treatment program.

History of CCP art. 46B.117: Acts 2003, 78th Leg., ch. 35, §1, eff. Jan. 1, 2004. Amended by Acts 2005, 79th Leg., ch. 324, §30, eff. Sept. 1, 2005; Acts 2007, 80th Leg., ch. 1307, §18, eff. Sept. 1, 2007.

SUBCHAPTER F. CIVIL COMMITMENT: CHARGES DISMISSED

ART. 46B.151. COURT DETERMINATION RELATED TO CIVIL COMMITMENT

(a) If a court is required by Article 46B.084(f) or permitted by Article 46B.004(e) to proceed under this subchapter, the court shall determine whether there is evidence to support a finding that the defendant is either a person with mental illness or a person with mental retardation.

(b) If it appears to the court that there is evidence to support a finding of mental illness or mental retardation, the court shall enter an order transferring the defendant to the appropriate court for civil commitment proceedings and stating that all charges pending against the defendant in that court have been dismissed. The court may order the defendant:

(1) detained in jail or any other suitable place pending the prompt initiation and prosecution by the attorney for the state or other person designated by the court of appropriate civil proceedings to determine whether the defendant will be committed to a mental health facility or residential care facility; or

(2) placed in the care of a responsible person on satisfactory security being given for the defendant's proper care and protection.

(c) Notwithstanding Subsection (b), a defendant placed in a facility of the department pending civil hearing under this article may be detained in that facility only with the consent of the head of the facility and pursuant to an order of protective custody issued under Subtitle C, Title 7, Health and Safety Code.

(d) If the court does not detain or place the defendant under Subsection (b), the court shall release the defendant.

History of CCP art. 46B.151: Acts 2003, 78th Leg., ch. 35, §1, eff. Jan. 1, 2004. Amended by Acts 2005, 79th Leg., ch. 324, §§31-33, eff. Sept. 1, 2005.

SUBCHAPTER G. PROVISIONS APPLICABLE TO SUBCHAPTERS E & F

ART. 46B.171. TRANSCRIPTS & OTHER RECORDS

(a) The court shall order that:

(1) a transcript of all medical testimony received in both the criminal proceedings and the civil commitment proceedings under Subchapter E or F be prepared as soon as possible by the court reporters; and

(2) copies of documents listed in Article 46B.076 accompany the defendant to the mental health facility, outpatient treatment program, or residential care facility.

(b) On the request of the defendant or the attorney representing the defendant, a mental health facility, an outpatient treatment program, or a residential care facility shall provide to the defendant or the attorney copies of the facility's records regarding the defendant.

History of CCP art. 46B.171: Acts 2003, 78th Leg., ch. 35, §1, eff. Jan. 1, 2004. Amended by Acts 2005, 79th Leg., ch. 324, §34, eff. Sept. 1, 2005; Acts 2007, 80th Leg., ch. 1307, §19, eff. Sept. 1, 2007.

CHAPTER 46C. INSANITY DEFENSE

SUBCHAPTER A. GENERAL PROVISIONS

ART. 46C.001. DEFINITIONS

In this chapter:

(1) "Commissioner" means the commissioner of state health services.

(2) "Department" means the Department of State Health Services.

(3) "Mental illness" has the meaning assigned by Section 571.003, Health and Safety Code.

(4) "Mental retardation" has the meaning assigned by Section 591.003, Health and Safety Code.

(5) "Residential care facility" has the meaning assigned by Section 591.003, Health and Safety Code.

History of CCP art. 46C.001: Acts 2005, 79th Leg., ch. 831, §2, eff. Sept. 1, 2005.

ART. 46C.002. MAXIMUM PERIOD OF COMMITMENT DETERMINED BY MAXIMUM TERM FOR OFFENSE

(a) A person acquitted by reason of insanity may not be committed to a mental hospital or other inpatient or residential care facility or ordered to receive outpatient or community-based treatment and supervision under Subchapter F for a cumulative period that exceeds the maximum term provided by law for the offense for which the acquitted person was tried.

(b) On expiration of that maximum term, the acquitted person may be further confined in a mental hospital or other inpatient or residential care facility or ordered to receive outpatient or community-based treatment and supervision only under civil commitment proceedings.

History of CCP art. 46C.002: Acts 2005, 79th Leg., ch. 831, §2, eff. Sept. 1, 2005.

Articles 46C.003-46C.050 reserved for expansion

SUBCHAPTER B. RAISING THE INSANITY DEFENSE

ART. 46C.051. NOTICE OF INTENT TO RAISE INSANITY DEFENSE

(a) A defendant planning to offer evidence of the insanity defense must file with the court a notice of the defendant's intention to offer that evidence.

(b) The notice must:

(1) contain a certification that a copy of the notice has been served on the attorney representing the state; and

(2) be filed at least 20 days before the date the case is set for trial, except as described by Subsection (c).

(c) If before the 20-day period the court sets a pretrial hearing, the defendant shall give notice at the hearing.

History of CCP art. 46C.051: Acts 2005, 79th Leg., ch. 831, §2, eff. Sept. 1, 2005.

ART. 46C.052. EFFECT OF FAILURE TO GIVE NOTICE

Unless notice is timely filed under Article 46C.051, evidence on the insanity defense is not admissible unless the court finds that good cause exists for failure to give notice.

History of CCP art. 46C.052: Acts 2005, 79th Leg., ch. 831, §2, eff. Sept. 1, 2005.

Articles 46C.053-46C.100 reserved for expansion

SUBCHAPTER C. COURT-ORDERED EXAMINATION & REPORT

ART. 46C.101. APPOINTMENT OF EXPERTS

(a) If notice of intention to raise the insanity defense is filed under Article 46C.051, the court may, on its own motion or motion by the defendant, the defendant's counsel, or the attorney representing the state, appoint one or more disinterested experts to:

(1) examine the defendant with regard to the insanity defense; and

(2) testify as to the issue of insanity at any trial or hearing involving that issue.

(b) The court shall advise an expert appointed under this article of the facts and circumstances of the offense with which the defendant is charged and the elements of the insanity defense.

History of CCP art. 46C.101: Acts 2005, 79th Leg., ch. 831, §2, eff. Sept. 1, 2005.

ART. 46C.102. EXPERTS: QUALIFICATIONS

(a) The court may appoint qualified psychiatrists or psychologists as experts under this chapter. To qualify for appointment under this subchapter as an expert, a psychiatrist or psychologist must:

(1) as appropriate, be a physician licensed in this state or be a psychologist licensed in this state who has a doctoral degree in psychology; and

(2) have the following certification or experience or training:

(A) as appropriate, certification by:

(i) the American Board of Psychiatry and Neurology with added or special qualifications in forensic psychiatry; or

(ii) the American Board of Professional Psychology in forensic psychology; or

(B) experience or training consisting of:

(i) at least 24 hours of specialized forensic training relating to incompetency or insanity evaluations;

(ii) at least five years of experience in performing criminal forensic evaluations for courts; and

(iii) eight or more hours of continuing education relating to forensic evaluations, completed in the 12 months preceding the appointment and documented with the court.

(b) In addition to meeting qualifications required by Subsection (a), to be appointed as an expert a psychiatrist or psychologist must have completed six hours of required continuing education in courses in forensic psychiatry or psychology, as appropriate, in the 24 months preceding the appointment.

(c) A court may appoint as an expert a psychiatrist or psychologist who does not meet the requirements of Subsections (a) and (b) only if exigent circumstances require the court to base the appointment on professional training or experience of the expert that directly provides the expert with a specialized expertise to examine the defendant that would not ordinarily be possessed by a psychiatrist or psychologist who meets the requirements of Subsections (a) and (b).

History of CCP art. 46C.102: Acts 2005, 79th Leg., ch. 831, §2, eff. Sept. 1, 2005.

ART. 46C.103. COMPETENCY TO STAND TRIAL: CONCURRENT APPOINTMENT

(a) An expert appointed under this subchapter to examine the defendant with regard to the insanity defense also may be appointed by the court to examine the defendant with regard to the defendant's competency to stand trial under Chapter 46B, if the expert files with the court separate written reports concerning the defendant's competency to stand trial and the insanity defense.

(b) Notwithstanding Subsection (a), an expert may not examine the defendant for purposes of determining the defendant's sanity and may not file a report regarding the defendant's sanity if in the opinion of the expert the defendant is incompetent to proceed.

History of CCP art. 46C.103: Acts 2005, 79th Leg., ch. 831, §2, eff. Sept. 1, 2005.

ART. 46C.104. ORDER COMPELLING DEFENDANT TO SUBMIT TO EXAMINATION

(a) For the purposes described by this chapter, the court may order any defendant to submit to examination, including a defendant who is free on bail. If the defendant fails or refuses to submit to examination, the court may order the defendant to custody for examination for a reasonable period not to exceed 21 days. Custody ordered by the court under this subsection may include custody at a facility operated by the department.

(b) If a defendant who has been ordered to a facility operated by the department for examination remains in the facility for a period that exceeds 21 days, the head of that facility shall cause the defendant to be immediately transported to the committing court and placed in the custody of the sheriff of the county in which the committing court is located. That county shall reimburse the facility for the mileage and per diem expenses of the personnel required to transport the defendant, calculated in accordance with the state travel rules in effect at that time.

(c) The court may not order a defendant to a facility operated by the department for examination without the consent of the head of that facility.

History of CCP art. 46C.104: Acts 2005, 79th Leg., ch. 831, §2, eff. Sept. 1, 2005.

ART. 46C.105. REPORTS SUBMITTED BY EXPERTS

(a) A written report of the examination shall be submitted to the court not later than the 30th day after the date of the order of examination. The court shall provide copies of the report to the defense counsel and the attorney representing the state.

(b) The report must include a description of the procedures used in the examination and the examiner's observations and findings pertaining to the insanity defense.

(c) The examiner shall submit a separate report stating the examiner's observations and findings concerning:

(1) whether the defendant is presently a person with a mental illness and requires court-ordered mental health services under Subtitle C, Title 7, Health and Safety Code; or

(2) whether the defendant is presently a person with mental retardation.

History of CCP art. 46C.105: Acts 2005, 79th Leg., ch. 831, §2, eff. Sept. 1, 2005.

ART. 46C.106. COMPENSATION OF EXPERTS

(a) The appointed experts shall be paid by the county in which the indictment was returned or information was filed.

(b) The county in which the indictment was returned or information was filed shall reimburse a facility operated by the department that accepts a defendant for examination under this subchapter for expenses incurred that are determined by the department to be reasonably necessary and incidental to the proper examination of the defendant.

History of CCP art. 46C.106: Acts 2005, 79th Leg., ch. 831, §2, eff. Sept. 1, 2005.

ART. 46C.107. EXAMINATION BY EXPERT OF DEFENDANT'S CHOICE

If a defendant wishes to be examined by an expert of the defendant's own choice, the court on timely request shall provide the examiner with reasonable opportunity to examine the defendant.

History of CCP art. 46C.107: Acts 2005, 79th Leg., ch. 831, §2, eff. Sept. 1, 2005.

Articles 46C.108-46C.150 reserved for expansion

SUBCHAPTER D. DETERMINATION OF ISSUE OF DEFENDANT'S SANITY

ART. 46C.151. DETERMINATION OF SANITY ISSUE BY JURY

(a) In a case tried to a jury, the issue of the defendant's sanity shall be submitted to the jury only if the issue is supported by competent evidence. The jury shall determine the issue.

(b) If the issue of the defendant's sanity is submitted to the jury, the jury shall determine and specify in the verdict whether the defendant is guilty, not guilty, or not guilty by reason of insanity.

History of CCP art. 46C.151: Acts 2005, 79th Leg., ch. 831, §2, eff. Sept. 1, 2005.

ART. 46C.152. DETERMINATION OF SANITY ISSUE BY JUDGE

(a) If a jury trial is waived and if the issue is supported by competent evidence, the judge as trier of fact shall determine the issue of the defendant's sanity.

(b) The parties may, with the consent of the judge, agree to have the judge determine the issue of the defendant's sanity on the basis of introduced or stipulated competent evidence, or both.

(c) If the judge determines the issue of the defendant's sanity, the judge shall enter a finding of guilty, not guilty, or not guilty by reason of insanity.

History of CCP art. 46C.152: Acts 2005, 79th Leg., ch. 831, §2, eff. Sept. 1, 2005.

ART. 46C.153. GENERAL PROVISIONS RELATING TO DETERMINATION OF SANITY ISSUE BY JUDGE OR JURY

(a) The judge or jury shall determine that a defendant is not guilty by reason of insanity if:

(1) the prosecution has established beyond a reasonable doubt that the alleged conduct constituting the offense was committed; and

(2) the defense has established by a preponderance of the evidence that the defendant was insane at the time of the alleged conduct.

(b) The parties may, with the consent of the judge, agree to both:

(1) dismissal of the indictment or information on the ground that the defendant was insane; and

(2) entry of a judgment of dismissal due to the defendant's insanity.

(c) An entry of judgment under Subsection (b)(2) has the same effect as a judgment stating that the defendant has been found not guilty by reason of insanity.

History of CCP art. 46C.153: Acts 2005, 79th Leg., ch. 831, §2, eff. Sept. 1, 2005.

ART. 46C.154. INFORMING JURY REGARDING CONSEQUENCES OF ACQUITTAL

The court, the attorney representing the state, or the attorney for the defendant may not inform a juror or a prospective juror of the consequences to the defendant if a verdict of not guilty by reason of insanity is returned.

History of CCP art. 46C.154: Acts 2005, 79th Leg., ch. 831, §2, eff. Sept. 1, 2005.

ART. 46C.155. FINDING OF NOT GUILTY BY REASON OF INSANITY CONSIDERED ACQUITTAL

(a) Except as provided by Subsection (b), a defendant who is found not guilty by reason of insanity stands acquitted of the offense charged and may not be considered a person charged with an offense.

(b) A defendant who is found not guilty by reason of insanity is not considered to be acquitted for purposes of Chapter 55.

History of CCP art. 46C.155: Acts 2005, 79th Leg., ch. 831, §2, eff. Sept. 1, 2005.

ART. 46C.156. JUDGMENT

(a) In each case in which the insanity defense is raised, the judgment must reflect whether the defendant was found guilty, not guilty, or not guilty by reason of insanity.

(b) If the defendant was found not guilty by reason of insanity, the judgment must specify the offense of which the defendant was found not guilty.

(c) If the defendant was found not guilty by reason of insanity, the judgment must reflect the finding made under Article 46C.157.

History of CCP art. 46C.156: Acts 2005, 79th Leg., ch. 831, §2, eff. Sept. 1, 2005.

ART. 46C.157. DETERMINATION REGARDING DANGEROUS CONDUCT OF ACQUITTED PERSON

If a defendant is found not guilty by reason of insanity, the court immediately shall determine whether the offense of which the person was acquitted involved conduct that:

(1) caused serious bodily injury to another person;

(2) placed another person in imminent danger of serious bodily injury; or

(3) consisted of a threat of serious bodily injury to another person through the use of a deadly weapon.

History of CCP art. 46C.157: Acts 2005, 79th Leg., ch. 831, §2, eff. Sept. 1, 2005.

ART. 46C.158. CONTINUING JURISDICTION OF DANGEROUS ACQUITTED PERSON

If the court finds that the offense of which the person was acquitted involved conduct that caused serious bodily injury to another person, placed another person in imminent danger of serious bodily injury, or consisted of a threat of serious bodily injury to another person through the use of a deadly weapon, the court retains jurisdiction over the acquitted person until either:

(1) the court discharges the person and terminates its jurisdiction under Article 46C.268; or

(2) the cumulative total period of institutionalization and outpatient or community-based treatment and supervision under the court's jurisdiction equals the maximum term provided by law for the offense of which the person was acquitted by reason of insanity and the court's jurisdiction is automatically terminated under Article 46C.269.

History of CCP art. 46C.158: Acts 2005, 79th Leg., ch. 831, §2, eff. Sept. 1, 2005.

ART. 46C.159. PROCEEDINGS REGARDING NONDANGEROUS ACQUITTED PERSON

If the court finds that the offense of which the person was acquitted did not involve conduct that caused serious bodily injury to another person, placed another person in imminent danger of serious bodily injury, or consisted of a threat of serious bodily injury to another person through the use of a deadly weapon, the court shall proceed under Subchapter E.

History of CCP art. 46C.159: Acts 2005, 79th Leg., ch. 831, §2, eff. Sept. 1, 2005.

ART. 46C.160. DETENTION PENDING FURTHER PROCEEDINGS

(a) On a determination by the judge or jury that the defendant is not guilty by reason of insanity, pending further proceedings under this chapter, the court may order the defendant detained in jail or any other suitable place for a period not to exceed 14 days.

(b) The court may order a defendant detained in a facility of the department or a facility of the Department of Aging and Disability Services under this article only with the consent of the head of the facility.

History of CCP art. 46C.160: Acts 2005, 79th Leg., ch. 831, §2, eff. Sept. 1, 2005.

Articles 46C.161-46C.200 reserved for expansion

SUBCHAPTER E. DISPOSITION FOLLOWING ACQUITTAL BY REASON OF INSANITY: NO FINDING OF DANGEROUS CONDUCT

ART. 46C.201. DISPOSITION: NONDANGEROUS CONDUCT

(a) If the court determines that the offense of which the person was acquitted did not involve conduct that caused serious bodily injury to another person, placed another person in imminent danger of serious bodily injury, or consisted of a threat of serious bodily injury to another person through the use of a deadly weapon, the court shall determine whether there is evidence to support a finding that the person is a person with a mental illness or with mental retardation.

(b) If the court determines that there is evidence to support a finding of mental illness or mental retardation, the court shall enter an order transferring the person to the appropriate court for civil commitment proceedings to determine whether the person should receive court-ordered mental health services under Subtitle C, Title 7, Health and Safety Code, or be committed to a residential care facility to receive mental retardation services under Subtitle D, Title 7, Health and Safety Code. The court may also order the person:

(1) detained in jail or any other suitable place pending the prompt initiation and prosecution of appropriate civil proceedings by the attorney representing the state or other person designated by the court; or

(2) placed in the care of a responsible person on satisfactory security being given for the acquitted person's proper care and protection.

History of CCP art. 46C.201: Acts 2005, 79th Leg., ch. 831, §2, eff. Sept. 1, 2005.

ART. 46C.202. DETENTION OR RELEASE

(a) Notwithstanding Article 46C.201(b), a person placed in a department facility or a facility of the Department of Aging and Disability Services pending civil hearing as described by that subsection may be detained only with the consent of the head of the facility and under an Order of Protective Custody issued under Subtitle C or D, Title 7, Health and Safety Code.

(b) If the court does not detain or place the person under Article 46C.201(b), the court shall release the person.

History of CCP art. 46C.202: Acts 2005, 79th Leg., ch. 831, §2, eff. Sept. 1, 2005.

Articles 46C.203-46C.250 reserved for expansion

SUBCHAPTER F. DISPOSITION FOLLOWING ACQUITTAL BY REASON OF INSANITY: FINDING OF DANGEROUS CONDUCT

ART. 46C.251. COMMITMENT FOR EVALUATION & TREATMENT; REPORT

(a) The court shall order the acquitted person to be committed for evaluation of the person's present mental condition and for treatment to the maximum security unit of any facility designated by the department. The period of commitment under this article may not exceed 30 days.

(b) The court shall order that:

(1) a transcript of all medical testimony received in the criminal proceeding be prepared as soon as possible by the court reporter and the transcript be forwarded to the facility to which the acquitted person is committed; and

(2) the following information be forwarded to the facility and, as applicable, to the department or the Department of Aging and Disability Services:

(A) the complete name, race, and gender of the person;

(B) any known identifying number of the person, including social security number, driver's license number, or state identification number;

(C) the person's date of birth; and

(D) the offense of which the person was found not guilty by reason of insanity and a statement of the facts and circumstances surrounding the alleged offense.

(c) The court shall order that a report be filed with the court under Article 46C.252.

(d) To determine the proper disposition of the acquitted person, the court shall hold a hearing on disposition not later than the 30th day after the date of acquittal.

History of CCP art. 46C.251: Acts 2005, 79th Leg., ch. 831, §2, eff. Sept. 1, 2005.

ART. 46C.252. REPORT AFTER EVALUATION

(a) The report ordered under Article 46C.251 must be filed with the court as soon as practicable before the hearing on disposition but not later than the fourth day before that hearing.

(b) The report in general terms must describe and explain the procedure, techniques, and tests used in the examination of the person.

(c) The report must address:

(1) whether the acquitted person has a mental illness or mental retardation and, if so, whether the mental illness or mental retardation is severe;

(2) whether as a result of any severe mental illness or mental retardation the acquitted person is likely to cause serious harm to another;

(3) whether as a result of any impairment the acquitted person is subject to commitment under Subtitle C or D, Title 7, Health and Safety Code;

(4) prospective treatment and supervision options, if any, appropriate for the acquitted person; and

(5) whether any required treatment and supervision can be safely and effectively provided as outpatient or community-based treatment and supervision.

History of CCP art. 46C.252: Acts 2005, 79th Leg., ch. 831, §2, eff. Sept. 1, 2005.

ART. 46C.253. HEARING ON DISPOSITION

(a) The hearing on disposition shall be conducted in the same manner as a hearing on an application for involuntary commitment under Subtitle C or D, Title 7, Health and Safety Code, except that the use of a jury is governed by Article 46C.255.

(b) At the hearing, the court shall address:

(1) whether the person acquitted by reason of insanity has a severe mental illness or mental retardation;

(2) whether as a result of any mental illness or mental retardation the person is likely to cause serious harm to another; and

(3) whether appropriate treatment and supervision for any mental illness or mental retardation rendering the person dangerous to another can be safely and effectively provided as outpatient or community-based treatment and supervision.

(c) The court shall order the acquitted person committed for inpatient treatment or residential care under Article 46C.256 if the grounds required for that order are established.

(d) The court shall order the acquitted person to receive outpatient or community-based treatment and supervision under Article 46C.257 if the grounds required for that order are established.

(e) The court shall order the acquitted person transferred to an appropriate court for proceedings under Subtitle C or D, Title 7, Health and Safety Code, if the state fails to establish the grounds required for an order under Article 46C.256 or 46C.257 but the evidence provides a reasonable basis for believing the acquitted person is a proper subject for those proceedings.

(f) The court shall order the acquitted person discharged and immediately released if the evidence fails to establish that disposition under Subsection (c), (d), or (e) is appropriate.

History of CCP art. 46C.253: Acts 2005, 79th Leg., ch. 831, §2, eff. Sept. 1, 2005.

ART. 46C.254. EFFECT OF STABILIZATION ON TREATMENT REGIMEN

If an acquitted person is stabilized on a treatment regimen, including medication and other treatment modalities, rendering the person no longer likely to cause serious harm to another, inpatient treatment or residential care may be found necessary to protect the safety of others only if:

(1) the person would become likely to cause serious harm to another if the person fails to follow the treatment regimen on an Order to Receive Outpatient or Community-Based Treatment and Supervision; and

(2) under an Order to Receive Outpatient or Community-Based Treatment and Supervision either:

(A) the person is likely to fail to comply with an available regimen of outpatient or community-based treatment, as determined by the person's insight into the need for medication, the number, severity, and controllability of side effects, the availability of support and treatment programs for the person from community members, and other appropriate considerations; or

(B) a regimen of outpatient or community-based treatment will not be available to the person.

History of CCP art. 46C.254: Acts 2005, 79th Leg., ch. 831, §2, eff. Sept. 1, 2005.

ART. 46C.255. TRIAL BY JURY

(a) The following proceedings under this chapter must be before the court, and the underlying matter determined by the court, unless the acquitted person or the state requests a jury trial or the court on its own motion sets the matter for jury trial:

(1) a hearing under Article 46C.253;

(2) a proceeding for renewal of an order under Article 46C.261;

(3) a proceeding on a request for modification or revocation of an order under Article 46C.266; and

(4) a proceeding seeking discharge of an acquitted person under Article 46C.268.

(b) The following proceedings may not be held before a jury:

(1) a proceeding to determine outpatient or community-based treatment and supervision under Article 46C.262; or

(2) a proceeding to determine modification or revocation of outpatient or community-based treatment and supervision under Article 46C.267.

(c) If a hearing is held before a jury and the jury determines that the person has a mental illness or mental retardation and is likely to cause serious harm to another, the court shall determine whether inpatient treatment or residential care is necessary to protect the safety of others.

History of CCP art. 46C.255: Acts 2005, 79th Leg., ch. 831, §2, eff. Sept. 1, 2005.

ART. 46C.256. ORDER OF COMMITMENT TO INPATIENT TREATMENT OR RESIDENTIAL CARE

(a) The court shall order the acquitted person committed to a mental hospital or other appropriate facility for inpatient treatment or residential care if the state establishes by clear and convincing evidence that:

(1) the person has a severe mental illness or mental retardation;

(2) the person, as a result of that mental illness or mental retardation, is likely to cause serious bodily injury to another if the person is not provided with treatment and supervision; and

(3) inpatient treatment or residential care is necessary to protect the safety of others.

(b) In determining whether inpatient treatment or residential care has been proved necessary, the court shall consider whether the evidence shows both that:

(1) an adequate regimen of outpatient or community-based treatment will be available to the person; and

(2) the person will follow that regimen.

(c) The order of commitment to inpatient treatment or residential care expires on the 181st day following the date the order is issued but is subject to renewal as provided by Article 46C.261.

History of CCP art. 46C.256: Acts 2005, 79th Leg., ch. 831, §2, eff. Sept. 1, 2005.

ART. 46C.257. ORDER TO RECEIVE OUTPATIENT OR COMMUNITY-BASED TREATMENT & SUPERVISION

(a) The court shall order the acquitted person to receive outpatient or community-based treatment and supervision if:

(1) the state establishes by clear and convincing evidence that the person:

(A) has a severe mental illness or mental retardation; and

(B) as a result of that mental illness or mental retardation is likely to cause serious bodily injury to another if the person is not provided with treatment and supervision; and

(2) the state fails to establish by clear and convincing evidence that inpatient treatment or residential care is necessary to protect the safety of others.

(b) The order of commitment to outpatient or community-based treatment and supervision expires on the first anniversary of the date the order is issued but is subject to renewal as provided by Article 46C.261.

History of CCP art. 46C.257: Acts 2005, 79th Leg., ch. 831, §2, eff. Sept. 1, 2005.

ART. 46C.258. RESPONSIBILITY OF INPATIENT OR RESIDENTIAL CARE FACILITY

(a) The head of the facility to which an acquitted person is committed has, during the commitment period, a continuing responsibility to determine:

(1) whether the acquitted person continues to have a severe mental illness or mental retardation and is likely to cause serious harm to another because of any severe mental illness or mental retardation; and

(2) if so, whether treatment and supervision cannot be safely and effectively provided as outpatient or community-based treatment and supervision.

(b) The head of the facility must notify the committing court and seek modification of the order of commitment if the head of the facility determines that an acquitted person no longer has a severe mental illness or mental retardation, is no longer likely to cause serious harm to another, or that treatment and supervision can be safely and effectively provided as outpatient or community-based treatment and supervision.

(c) Not later than the 60th day before the date of expiration of the order, the head of the facility shall transmit to the committing court a psychological evaluation of the acquitted person, a certificate of medical examination of the person, and any recommendation for further treatment of the person. The committing court shall make the documents available to the attorneys representing the state and the acquitted person.

History of CCP art. 46C.258: Acts 2005, 79th Leg., ch. 831, §2, eff. Sept. 1, 2005.

ART. 46C.259. STATUS OF COMMITTED PERSON

If an acquitted person is committed under this subchapter, the person's status as a patient or resident is governed by Subtitle C or D, Title 7, Health and Safety Code, except that:

(1) transfer to a nonsecure unit is governed by Article 46C.260;

(2) modification of the order to direct outpatient or community-based treatment and supervision is governed by Article 46C.262; and

(3) discharge is governed by Article 46C.268.

History of CCP art. 46C.259: Acts 2005, 79th Leg., ch. 831, §2, eff. Sept. 1, 2005.

ART. 46C.260. TRANSFER OF COMMITTED PERSON TO NONSECURE FACILITY

(a) A person committed to a facility under this subchapter shall be committed to the maximum security unit of any facility designated by the department.

(b) A person committed under this subchapter shall be transferred to the maximum security unit immediately on the entry of the order of commitment.

(c) Unless the person is determined to be manifestly dangerous by a review board within the department, not later than the 60th day following the date of the person's arrival at the maximum security unit the person shall be transferred to a nonsecure unit of a facility designated by the department or the Department of Aging and Disability Services, as appropriate.

(d) The commissioner shall appoint a review board of five members, including one psychiatrist licensed to practice medicine in this state and two persons who work directly with persons with mental illnesses or with mental retardation, to determine whether the person is manifestly dangerous and, as a result of the danger the person presents, requires continued placement in a maximum security unit.

(e) If the head of the facility at which the maximum security unit is located disagrees with the determination, then the matter shall be referred to the commissioner. The commissioner shall decide whether the person is manifestly dangerous.

History of CCP art. 46C.260: Acts 2005, 79th Leg., ch. 831, §2, eff. Sept. 1, 2005.

ART. 46C.261. RENEWAL OF ORDERS FOR INPATIENT COMMITMENT OR OUTPATIENT OR COMMUNITY-BASED TREATMENT & SUPERVISION

(a) A court that orders an acquitted person committed to inpatient treatment or orders outpatient or community-based treatment and supervision annually shall determine whether to renew the order.

(b) Not later than the 30th day before the date an order is scheduled to expire, the institution to which a person is committed, the person responsible for providing outpatient or community-based treatment and supervision, or the attorney representing the state may file a request that the order be renewed. The request must explain in detail the reasons why the person requests renewal under this article. A request to renew an order committing the person to inpatient treatment must also explain in detail why outpatient or community-based treatment and supervision is not appropriate.

(c) The request for renewal must be accompanied by a certificate of medical examination for mental illness signed by a physician who examined the person during the 30-day period preceding the date on which the request is filed.

(d) On the filing of a request for renewal under this article, the court shall:

(1) set the matter for a hearing; and

(2) appoint an attorney to represent the person.

(e) The court shall act on the request for renewal before the order expires.

(f) If a hearing is held, the person may be transferred from the facility to which the acquitted person was committed to a jail for purposes of participating in the hearing only if necessary but not earlier than 72 hours before the hearing begins. If the order is renewed, the person shall be transferred back to the facility immediately on renewal of the order.

(g) If no objection is made, the court may admit into evidence the certificate of medical examination for mental illness. Admitted certificates constitute competent medical or psychiatric testimony, and the court may make its findings solely from the certificate and the detailed request for renewal.

(h) A court shall renew the order only if the court finds that the party who requested the renewal has established by clear and convincing evidence that continued mandatory supervision and treatment are appropriate. A renewed order authorizes continued inpatient commitment or outpatient or community-based treatment and supervision for not more than one year.

(i) The court, on application for renewal of an order for inpatient or residential care services, may modify the order to provide for outpatient or community-based treatment and supervision if the court finds the acquitted person has established by a preponderance of the evidence that treatment and supervision can be safely and effectively provided as outpatient or community-based treatment and supervision.

History of CCP art. 46C.261: Acts 2005, 79th Leg., ch. 831, §2, eff. Sept. 1, 2005.

ART. 46C.262. COURT-ORDERED OUTPATIENT OR COMMUNITY-BASED TREATMENT & SUPERVISION AFTER INPATIENT COMMITMENT

(a) An acquitted person, the head of the facility to which the acquitted person is committed, or the attorney representing the state may request that the court modify an order for inpatient treatment or residential care to order outpatient or community-based treatment and supervision.

(b) The court shall hold a hearing on a request made by the head of the facility to which the acquitted person is committed. A hearing under this subsection must be held not later than the 14th day after the date of the request.

(c) If a request is made by an acquitted person or the attorney representing the state, the court must act on the request not later than the 14th day after the date of the request. A hearing under this subsection is at the discretion of the court, except that the court shall hold a hearing if the request and any accompanying material provide a basis for believing modification of the order may be appropriate.

(d) If a request is made by an acquitted person not later than the 90th day after the date of a hearing on a previous request, the court is not required to act on the request except on the expiration of the order or on the expiration of the 90-day period following the date of the hearing on the previous request.

(e) The court shall rule on the request during or as soon as practicable after any hearing on the request but not later than the 14th day after the date of the request.

(f) The court shall modify the commitment order to direct outpatient or community-based treatment and supervision if at the hearing the acquitted person establishes by a preponderance of the evidence that treatment and supervision can be safely and effectively provided as outpatient or community-based treatment and supervision.

History of CCP art. 46C.262: Acts 2005, 79th Leg., ch. 831, §2, eff. Sept. 1, 2005.

ART. 46C.263. COURT-ORDERED OUTPATIENT OR COMMUNITY-BASED TREATMENT & SUPERVISION

(a) The court may order an acquitted person to participate in an outpatient or community-based regimen of treatment and supervision:

(1) as an initial matter under Article 46C.253;

(2) on renewal of an order of commitment under Article 46C.261; or

(3) after a period of inpatient treatment or residential care under Article 46C.262.

(b) An acquitted person may be ordered to participate in an outpatient or community-based regimen of treatment and supervision only if:

(1) the court receives and approves an outpatient or community-based treatment plan that comprehensively provides for the outpatient or community-based treatment and supervision; and

(2) the court finds that the outpatient or community-based treatment and supervision provided for by the plan will be available to and provided to the acquitted person.

(c) The order may require the person to participate in a prescribed regimen of medical, psychiatric, or psychological care or treatment, and the regimen may include treatment with psychoactive medication.

(d) The court may order that supervision of the acquitted person be provided by the appropriate community supervision and corrections department or the facility administrator of a community center that provides mental health or mental retardation services.

(e) The court may order the acquitted person to participate in a supervision program funded by the Texas Correctional Office on Offenders with Medical or Mental Impairments.

(f) An order under this article must identify the person responsible for administering an ordered regimen of outpatient or community-based treatment and supervision.

(g) In determining whether an acquitted person should be ordered to receive outpatient or community-based treatment and supervision rather than inpatient care or residential treatment, the court shall have as its primary concern the protection of society.

History of CCP art. 46C.263: Acts 2005, 79th Leg., ch. 831, §2, eff. Sept. 1, 2005.

ART. 46C.264. LOCATION OF COURT-ORDERED OUTPATIENT OR COMMUNITY-BASED TREATMENT & SUPERVISION

(a) The court may order the outpatient or community-based treatment and supervision to be provided in any appropriate county where the necessary resources are available.

(b) This article does not supersede any requirement under the other provisions of this subchapter to obtain the consent of a treatment and supervision provider to administer the court-ordered outpatient or community-based treatment and supervision.

History of CCP art. 46C.264: Acts 2005, 79th Leg., ch. 831, §2, eff. Sept. 1, 2005.

ART. 46C.265. SUPERVISORY RESPONSIBILITY FOR OUTPATIENT OR COMMUNITY-BASED TREATMENT & SUPERVISION

(a) The person responsible for administering a regimen of outpatient or community-based treatment and supervision shall:

(1) monitor the condition of the acquitted person; and

(2) determine whether the acquitted person is complying with the regimen of treatment and supervision.

(b) The person responsible for administering a regimen of outpatient or community-based treatment and supervision shall notify the court ordering that treatment and supervision and the attorney representing the state if the person:

(1) fails to comply with the regimen; and

(2) becomes likely to cause serious harm to another.

History of CCP art. 46C.265: Acts 2005, 79th Leg., ch. 831, §2, eff. Sept. 1, 2005.

ART. 46C.266. MODIFICATION OR REVOCATION OF ORDER FOR OUTPATIENT OR COMMUNITY-BASED TREATMENT & SUPERVISION

(a) The court, on its own motion or the motion of any interested person and after notice to the acquitted person and a hearing, may modify or revoke court-ordered outpatient or community-based treatment and supervision.

(b) At the hearing, the court without a jury shall determine whether the state has established clear and convincing evidence that:

(1) the acquitted person failed to comply with the regimen in a manner or under circumstances indicating the person will become likely to cause serious harm to another if the person is provided continued outpatient or community-based treatment and supervision; or

(2) the acquitted person has become likely to cause serious harm to another if provided continued outpatient or community-based treatment and supervision.

(c) On a determination under Subsection (b), the court may take any appropriate action, including:

(1) revoking court-ordered outpatient or community-based treatment and supervision and ordering the person committed for inpatient or residential care; or

(2) imposing additional or more stringent terms on continued outpatient or community-based treatment.

(d) An acquitted person who is the subject of a proceeding under this article is entitled to representation by counsel in the proceeding.

(e) The court shall set a date for a hearing under this article that is not later than the seventh day after the applicable motion was filed. The court may grant one or more continuances of the hearing on the motion of a party or of the court and for good cause shown.

History of CCP art. 46C.266: Acts 2005, 79th Leg., ch. 831, §2, eff. Sept. 1, 2005.

ART. 46C.267. DETENTION PENDING PROCEEDINGS TO MODIFY OR REVOKE ORDER FOR OUTPATIENT OR COMMUNITY-BASED TREATMENT & SUPERVISION

(a) The state or the head of the facility or other person responsible for administering a regimen of outpatient or community-based treatment and supervision may file a sworn application with the court for the detention of an acquitted person receiving court-ordered outpatient or community-based treatment and supervision. The application must state that the person meets the criteria of Article 46C.266 and provide a detailed explanation of that statement.

(b) If the court determines that the application establishes probable cause to believe the order for outpatient or community-based treatment and supervision should be revoked, the court shall issue an order to an on-duty peace officer authorizing the acquitted person to be taken into custody and brought before the court.

(c) An acquitted person taken into custody under an order of detention shall be brought before the court without unnecessary delay.

(d) When an acquitted person is brought before the court, the court shall determine whether there is probable cause to believe that the order for outpatient or community-based treatment and supervision should be revoked. On a finding that probable cause for revocation exists, the court shall order the person held in protective custody pending a determination of whether the order should be revoked.

(e) An acquitted person may be detained under an order for protective custody for a period not to exceed 72 hours, excluding Saturdays, Sundays, legal holidays, and the period prescribed by Section 574.025(b), Health and Safety Code, for an extreme emergency.

(f) This subchapter does not affect the power of a peace officer to take an acquitted person into custody under Section 573.001, Health and Safety Code.

History of CCP art. 46C.267: Acts 2005, 79th Leg., ch. 831, §2, eff. Sept. 1, 2005.

ART. 46C.268. ADVANCE DISCHARGE OF ACQUITTED PERSON & TERMINATION OF JURISDICTION

(a) An acquitted person, the head of the facility to which the acquitted person is committed, the person responsible for providing the outpatient or community-based treatment and supervision, or the state may request that the court discharge an acquitted person from inpatient commitment or outpatient or community-based treatment and supervision.

(b) Not later than the 14th day after the date of the request, the court shall hold a hearing on a request made by the head of the facility to which the acquitted person is committed or the person responsible for providing the outpatient or community-based treatment and supervision.

(c) If a request is made by an acquitted person, the court must act on the request not later than the 14th day after the date of the request. A hearing under this subsection is at the discretion of the court, except that the court shall hold a hearing if the request and any accompanying material indicate that modification of the order may be appropriate.

(d) If a request is made by an acquitted person not later than the 90th day after the date of a hearing on a previous request, the court is not required to act on the request except on the expiration of the order or on the expiration of the 90-day period following the date of the hearing on the previous request.

(e) The court shall rule on the request during or shortly after any hearing that is held and in any case not later than the 14th day after the date of the request.

(f) The court shall discharge the acquitted person from all court-ordered commitment and treatment and supervision and terminate the court's jurisdiction over the person if the court finds that the acquitted person has established by a preponderance of the evidence that:

(1) the acquitted person does not have a severe mental illness or mental retardation; or

(2) the acquitted person is not likely to cause serious harm to another because of any severe mental illness or mental retardation.

History of CCP art. 46C.268: Acts 2005, 79th Leg., ch. 831, §2, eff. Sept. 1, 2005.

ART. 46C.269. TERMINATION OF COURT'S JURISDICTION

(a) The jurisdiction of the court over a person covered by this subchapter automatically terminates on the date when the cumulative total period of institutionalization and outpatient or community-based treatment and supervision imposed under this subchapter equals the maximum term of imprisonment provided by law for the offense of which the person was acquitted by reason of insanity.

(b) On the termination of the court's jurisdiction under this article, the person must be discharged from any inpatient treatment or residential care or outpatient or community-based treatment and supervision ordered under this subchapter.

(c) An inpatient or residential care facility to which a person has been committed under this subchapter or a person responsible for administering a regimen of outpatient or community-based treatment and supervision under this subchapter must notify the court not later than the 30th day before the court's jurisdiction over the person ends under this article.

(d) This subchapter does not affect whether a person may be ordered to receive care or treatment under Subtitle C or D, Title 7, Health and Safety Code.

History of CCP art. 46C.269: Acts 2005, 79th Leg., ch. 831, §2, eff. Sept. 1, 2005.

ART. 46C.270. APPEALS

(a) An acquitted person may appeal a judgment reflecting an acquittal by reason of insanity on the basis of the following:

(1) a finding that the acquitted person committed the offense; or

(2) a finding that the offense on which the prosecution was based involved conduct that:

(A) caused serious bodily injury to another person;

(B) placed another person in imminent danger of serious bodily injury; or

(C) consisted of a threat of serious bodily injury to another person through the use of a deadly weapon.

(b) Either the acquitted person or the state may appeal from:

(1) an Order of Commitment to Inpatient Treatment or Residential Care entered under Article 46C.256;

(2) an Order to Receive Outpatient or Community-Based Treatment and Supervision entered under Article 46C.257 or 46C.262;

(3) an order renewing or refusing to renew an Order for Inpatient Commitment or Outpatient or Community-Based Treatment and Supervision entered under Article 46C.261;

(4) an order modifying or revoking an Order for Outpatient or Community-Based Treatment and Supervision entered under Article 46C.266 or refusing a request to modify or revoke that order; or

(5) an order discharging an acquitted person under Article 46C.268 or denying a request for discharge of an acquitted person.

(c) An appeal under this subchapter may not be considered moot solely due to the expiration of an order on which the appeal is based.

History of CCP art. 46C.270: Acts 2005, 79th Leg., ch. 831, §2, eff. Sept. 1, 2005.

CHAPTER 47. DISPOSITION OF STOLEN PROPERTY

ART. 47.01. SUBJECT TO ORDER OF COURT

(a) Except as provided by Subsection (b), an officer who comes into custody of property alleged to have been stolen shall hold it subject to the order of the proper court only if the ownership of the property is contested or disputed.

(b) An officer who comes into custody of property governed by Chapter 371, Finance Code, that is alleged to have been stolen shall hold the property subject to the order of the proper court regardless of whether the ownership of the property is contested or disputed.

History of CCP art. 47.01: Acts 1965, 59th Leg., vol. 2, ch. 722. Amended by Acts 1993, 73rd Leg., ch. 860, §1, eff. Aug. 30, 1993; Acts 1999, 76th Leg., ch. 62, §3.07, eff. Sept. 1, 1999; Acts 2001, 77th Leg., ch. 752, §1, eff. Sept. 1, 2001.

ART. 47.01a. RESTORATION WHEN NO TRIAL IS PENDING

(a) If a criminal action relating to allegedly stolen property is not pending, a district judge, county court judge, statutory county court judge, or justice of the peace having jurisdiction as a magistrate in the county in which the property is held or a municipal judge having jurisdiction as a magistrate in the municipality in which the property is being held may hold a hearing to determine the right to possession of the property, upon the petition of an interested person, a county, a city, or the state. Jurisdiction under this section is based solely on jurisdiction as a criminal magistrate under this code and not jurisdiction as a civil court. The court shall:

(1) order the property delivered to whoever has the superior right to possession, without conditions; or

(2) on the filing of a written motion before trial by an attorney representing the state, order the property delivered to whoever has the superior right to possession, subject to the condition that the property be made available to the prosecuting authority should it be needed in future prosecutions; or

(3) order the property awarded to the custody of the peace officer, pending resolution of criminal investigations regarding the property.

(b) If it is shown in a hearing that probable cause exists to believe that the property was acquired by theft or by another manner that makes its acquisition an offense and that the identity of the actual owner of the property cannot be determined, the court shall order the peace officer to:

(1) deliver the property to a government agency for official purposes;

(2) deliver the property to a person authorized by Article 18.17 of this code to receive and dispose of the property; or

(3) destroy the property.

(c) At a hearing under Subsection (a) of this article, any interested person may present evidence showing that the property was not acquired by theft or another offense or that the person is entitled to possess the property. At the hearing, hearsay evidence is admissible.

(d) Venue for a hearing under this article is in any justice, county, statutory county, or district court in the county in which the property is seized or in any municipal court in any municipality in which the property is seized, except that the court may transfer venue to a court in another county on the motion of any interested party.

History of CCP art. 47.01a: Acts 1977, 65th Leg., ch. 813, §1, eff. Aug. 29, 1977. Amended by Acts 1987, 70th Leg., ch. 548, §1, eff. Aug. 31, 1987; Acts 1993, 73rd Leg., ch. 860, §1, eff. Aug. 30, 1993; Acts 1995, 74th Leg., ch. 184, §3, eff. May 23, 1995.

ART. 47.02. RESTORED ON TRIAL

Upon the trial of any criminal action for theft, or for any other illegal acquisition of property which is by law a penal offense, the court trying the case shall order the property to be restored to the person appearing by the proof to be the owner of the same.

Likewise, the judge of any court in which the trial of any criminal action for theft or any other illegal acquisition of property which is by law a penal offense is pending may, upon hearing, if it is proved to the satisfaction of the judge of said court that any person is a true owner of the property alleged to have been stolen, and which is in possession of a peace officer, by written order, direct the property to be restored to such owner.

As to property subject to the Certificate of Title Act (Chapter 501, Transportation Code), any magistrate having jurisdiction in the county in which the criminal action is pending may hold a hearing to determine the right to possession of the property, even if a criminal action is pending, upon written consent of the prosecuting attorney.

History of CCP art. 47.02: Acts 1965, 59th Leg., vol. 2, ch. 722. Amended by Acts 1997, 75th Leg., ch. 1415, §1, eff. Sept. 1, 1997.

ANNOTATIONS

Four B's Inc. v. State, 902 S.W.2d 683, 684 (Tex. App.—Austin 1995, writ denied). "[A] proceeding to restore property is a civil case."

ART. 47.03. SCHEDULE

When an officer seizes property alleged to have been stolen, he shall immediately file a schedule of the same, and its value, with the court having jurisdiction of the case, certifying that the property has been seized by him, and the reason therefor. The officer shall notify the court of the names and addresses of each party known to the officer who has a claim to possession of the seized property.

History of CCP art. 47.03: Acts 1965, 59th Leg., vol. 2, ch. 722. Amended by Acts 1993, 73rd Leg., ch. 860, §1, eff. Aug. 30, 1993.

ART. 47.04. RESTORED TO OWNER

Upon an examining trial, if it is proven to the satisfaction of the court that any person is the true owner of property alleged to have been stolen, and which is in possession of a peace officer, the court may upon motion by the state, by written order direct the property to be restored to such owner subject to the conditions that such property shall be made available to the state or by order of any court having jurisdiction over the offense to be used for evidentiary purposes.

History of CCP art. 47.04: Acts 1965, 59th Leg., vol. 2, ch. 722. Amended by Acts 1993, 73rd Leg., ch. 860, §1, eff. Aug. 30, 1993.

ART. 47.05. BOND REQUIRED

If the court has any doubt as to the ownership of the property, the court may require a bond of the claimant for its re-delivery in case it should thereafter be shown not to belong to such claimant; or the court may, in its discretion, direct the property to be retained by the sheriff until further orders as to its possession. Such bond shall be in a sum equal to the value of the property, with sufficient security, payable to and approved by the county judge of the county in which the property is in custody. Such bond shall be filed in the office of the county clerk of such county, and in case of a breach thereof may be sued upon in such county by any claimant of the property; or by the county treasurer of such county.

History of CCP art. 47.05: Acts 1965, 59th Leg., vol. 2, ch. 722. Amended by Acts 1993, 73rd Leg., ch. 860, §1, eff. Aug. 30, 1993.

ART. 47.06. PROPERTY SOLD

If the property is not claimed within 30 days from the conviction of the person accused of illegally acquiring it, the same procedure for its disposition as set out in Article 18.17 of this Code shall be followed.

History of CCP art. 47.06: Acts 1965, 59th Leg., vol. 2, ch. 722. Amended by Acts 1987, 70th Leg., ch. 66, §2, eff. May 6, 1987.

ART. 47.07. OWNER MAY RECOVER

The real owner of the property sold under the provisions of Article 47.06 may recover such property under the same terms as prescribed in Subsection (e) of Article 18.17 of this Code.

History of CCP art. 47.07: Acts 1965, 59th Leg., vol. 2, ch. 722. Amended by Acts 1987, 70th Leg., ch. 66, §2, eff. May 6, 1987.

ART. 47.08. WRITTEN INSTRUMENT

If the property is a written instrument, it shall be deposited with the county clerk of the county where the proceedings are had, subject to the claim of any person who may establish his right thereto. The claimant of any such written instrument shall file his written sworn claim thereto with the county judge. If such judge be satisfied that such claimant is the real owner of the written instrument, the same shall be delivered to him. The county judge may, in his discretion, require a bond of such claimant, as in other cases of property claimed under any provision of this Chapter, and may also before such delivery require the written instrument to be recorded in the minutes of his court.

History of CCP art. 47.08: Acts 1965, 59th Leg., vol. 2, ch. 722.

ART. 47.09. CLAIMANT TO PAY CHARGES

The claimant of the property, before he shall be entitled to have the same delivered to him, shall pay all reasonable charges for the safekeeping of the same while in the custody of the law, which charges shall be verified by the affidavit of the officer claiming the same, and determined by the court having jurisdiction thereof. If said charges are not paid, the property shall be sold as under execution; and the proceeds of sale, after the payment of said charges and costs of sale, paid to the owner of such property.

History of CCP art. 47.09: Acts 1965, 59th Leg., vol. 2, ch. 722. Amended by Acts 1993, 73rd Leg., ch. 860, §1, eff. Aug. 30, 1993.

ART. 47.10. CHARGES OF OFFICER

When property is sold, and the proceeds of sale are ready to be paid into the county treasury, the amount of expenses for keeping the same and the costs of sale shall be determined by the county judge. The account thereof shall be in writing and verified by the officer claiming the same, with the approval of the county judge thereto for the amount allowed and shall be filed in the office of the county treasurer at the time of paying into his hands the balance of the proceeds of such sale.

History of CCP art. 47.10: Acts 1965, 59th Leg., vol. 2, ch. 722.

ART. 47.11. SCOPE OF CHAPTER

Each provision of this Chapter relating to stolen property applies as well to property acquired in any manner which makes the acquisition a penal offense.

History of CCP art. 47.11: Acts 1965, 59th Leg., vol. 2, ch. 722.

ART. 47.12. APPEAL

(a) Appeals from a hearing in a district court, county court, or statutory county court under Article 47.01a of this code shall be heard by a court of appeals. The appeal is governed by the applicable rules of procedure for appeals of civil cases to a court of appeals.

(b) Appeals from a hearing in a municipal court or justice court under Article 47.01a of this code shall be heard by a county court or statutory county court. The appeal is governed by the applicable rules of procedure for appeals for civil cases in justice courts to a county court or statutory county court.

(c) Only an interested person who appears at a hearing under this article may appeal, and such person must give an oral notice of appeal at the conclusion of the hearing and must post an appeal bond by the end of the next business day, exclusive of Saturdays, Sundays, and legal holidays.

(d) The court may require an appeal bond, in an amount determined appropriate by the court, but not to exceed twice the value of the property. The bond shall be made payable to the party who was awarded possession at the hearing, with sufficient sureties approved by the court, and conditioned that appellant will prosecute his appeal to conclusion.

History of CCP art. 47.12: Acts 1993, 73rd Leg., ch. 860, §2, eff. Aug. 30, 1993.

ART. 48.01. GOVERNOR MAY PARDON

In all criminal cases, except treason and impeachment, the Governor shall have power, after conviction, on the written signed recommendation and advice of the Board of Pardons and Paroles, or a majority thereof, to grant reprieves and commutations of punishments and pardons; and upon the written recommendation and advice of a majority of the Board of Pardons and Paroles, he shall have the power to remit fines and forfeitures. The Governor shall have the power to grant one reprieve in any capital case for a period not to exceed 30 days; and he shall have power to revoke conditional pardons. With the advice and consent of the Legislature, the Governor may grant reprieves, commutations of punishment and pardons in cases of treason.

History of CCP art. 48.01: Acts 1965, 59th Leg., vol. 2, ch. 722. Amended by Acts 1995, 74th Leg., ch. 321, §2.019, eff. Sept. 1, 1995.

ANNOTATIONS

Ex parte May, 717 S.W.2d 84, 86 (Tex.Crim.App. 1986), *overruled in part*, ***Ex parte Elizondo***, 947 S.W.2d 202 (Tex.Crim.App.1996). "[T]he inclusion of mistaken information in a letter [on which the Board based its decision] from the District Attorney to the Board of Pardons and Paroles was harmless. *At 87:* [T]hat the commutation of sentence was imposed without the consent of the applicant or against his will, and at a proceeding at which he was not represented by counsel, does not render the commutation invalid."

ART. 48.02. SHALL FILE REASONS

When the Governor remits fines or forfeitures, or grants reprieves, commutation of punishment or pardons, he shall file in the office of Secretary of State his reasons therefor.

History of CCP art. 48.02: Acts 1965, 59th Leg., vol. 2, ch. 722.

ART. 48.03. GOVERNOR'S ACTS UNDER SEAL

All remissions of fines and forfeitures, and all reprieves, commutations of punishment and pardons, shall be signed by the Governor, and certified by the Secretary of State, under the state seal, and shall be forthwith obeyed by any officer to whom the same may be presented.

History of CCP art. 48.03: Acts 1965, 59th Leg., vol. 2, ch. 722. Amended by Acts 1993, 73rd Leg., ch. 300, §26, eff. Aug. 30, 1993.

ART. 48.04. POWER TO REMIT FINES & FORFEITURES

The Governor shall have the power to remit forfeitures of bail bonds.

History of CCP art. 48.04: Acts 1965, 59th Leg., vol. 2, ch. 722.

ART. 48.05. RESTORATION OF CIVIL RIGHTS

(a)(1) An individual convicted of an offense described by Subdivision (2) of this subsection may, except as provided by Subsection (b) of this article, submit an application for restoration of any civil rights forfeited under the laws of this state as a result of the conviction.

(2) This article applies to:

(A) a federal offense, other than an offense involving:

(i) violence or the threat of violence;

(ii) drugs; or

(iii) firearms; and

(B) an offense under the laws of another country, other than an offense involving:

(i) violence or the threat of violence;

(ii) drugs; or

(iii) firearms, if the elements of the offense are substantially similar to elements of an offense under the laws of this state punishable as a felony.

(b) An individual may not apply for restoration of civil rights under this article unless:

(1) the individual has completed the sentence for the offense;

(2) the conviction occurred:

(A) three or more years before the date of application, if the offense is a federal offense; or

(B) two or more years before the date of application, if the offense is an offense under the laws of another country; and

(3) the individual has not been convicted at any other time of an offense under the laws of this state, another state, or the United States.

(c) An application for restoration of civil rights must contain:

(1) a completed application on a form adopted by the Board of Pardons and Paroles;

(2) three or more affidavits attesting to the good character of the applicant; and

(3) proof that the applicant has completed the sentence for the offense.

(d) The applicant must submit the application to:

(1) the sheriff of the county in which the applicant resides at the time of application or resided at the time of conviction of the offense, if the individual resided in this state at that time; or

(2) the Board of Pardons and Paroles.

(e) If an application is submitted to a sheriff, the sheriff shall review the application and recommend to the Board of Pardons and Paroles whether the individual's civil rights should be restored. If the sheriff recommends restoration of the individual's civil rights, the board may either:

(1) concur in the recommendation and forward the recommendation to the governor; or

(2) independently review the application to determine whether to recommend to the governor the restoration of the individual's civil rights.

(f) If the sheriff does not recommend the restoration of the individual's civil rights, the individual may apply directly to the Board of Pardons and Paroles.

(g) If an application is submitted to the Board of Pardons and Paroles without first being submitted to a sheriff, the board shall review the application and recommend to the governor as to whether the individual's civil rights should be restored.

(h) The Board of Pardons and Paroles may require or obtain additional information as necessary to perform a review under Subsection (e)(2) or Subsection (g) of this article.

(i) On receipt from the Board of Pardons and Paroles of a recommendation to restore the civil rights of an individual, the governor may either grant or deny the restoration of civil rights to the individual. If the governor grants the restoration of civil rights to the individual, the governor shall issue a certificate of restoration of civil rights.

(j) If an application under this article is denied by the Board of Pardons and Paroles or the governor, the individual may not file another application under this article before the first anniversary of the date of the denial.

(k) A restoration of civil rights under this article is a form of pardon that restores all civil rights under the laws of this state that an individual forfeits as a result of the individual's conviction of an offense, except as specifically provided in the certificate of restoration.

History of CCP art. 48.05: Acts 1993, 73rd Leg., ch. 900, §7.01(a), eff. Sept. 1, 1993. Amended by Acts 2001, 77th Leg., ch. 150, §1, eff. May 16, 2001.

CHAPTER 49. INQUESTS UPON DEAD BODIES

SUBCHAPTER A. DUTIES PERFORMED BY JUSTICES OF THE PEACE

ART. 49.01. DEFINITIONS

In this article:

(1) "Autopsy" means a post mortem examination of the body of a person, including X-rays and an examination of the internal organs and structures after dissection, to determine the cause of death or the nature of any pathological changes that may have contributed to the death.

(2) "Inquest" means an investigation into the cause and circumstances of the death of a person, and a determination, made with or without a formal court hearing, as to whether the death was caused by an unlawful act or omission.

(3) "Inquest hearing" means a formal court hearing held to determine whether the death of a person was caused by an unlawful act or omission and, if the death was caused by an unlawful act or omission, to obtain evidence to form the basis of a criminal prosecution.

(4) "Institution" means any place where health care services are rendered, including a hospital, clinic, health facility, nursing home, extended-care facility, out-patient facility, foster-care facility, and retirement home.

(5) "Physician" means a practicing doctor of medicine or doctor of osteopathic medicine who is licensed by the Texas State Board of Medical Examiners under Subtitle B, Title 3, Occupations Code.

History of CCP art. 49.01: Acts 1965, 59th Leg., vol. 2, ch. 722. Amended by Acts 1969, 61st Leg., ch. 727, §1, eff. Sept. 1, 1969; Acts 1987, 70th Leg., ch. 529, §1, eff. Sept. 1, 1987; Acts 1989, 71st Leg., ch. 72, §1, eff. May 9, 1989; Acts 2001, 77th Leg., ch. 1420, §14.737, eff. Sept. 1, 2001.

ART. 49.02. APPLICABILITY

This subchapter applies to the inquest into a death occurring in a county that does not have a medical examiner's office or that is not part of a medical examiner's district.

History of CCP art. 49.02: Acts 1965, 59th Leg., vol. 2, ch. 722. Amended by Acts 1987, 70th Leg., ch. 529, §1, eff. Sept. 1, 1987.

ART. 49.03. POWERS & DUTIES

The powers granted and duties imposed on a justice of the peace under this article are independent of the powers and duties of a law enforcement agency investigating a death.

History of CCP art. 49.03: Acts 1965, 59th Leg., vol. 2, ch. 722. Amended by Acts 1969, 61st Leg., ch. 618, §1, eff. June 11, 1969; Acts 1977, 65th Leg., ch. 261, §1, eff. Aug. 29, 1977; Acts 1987, 70th Leg., ch. 529, §1, eff. Sept. 1, 1987.

ART. 49.04. DEATHS REQUIRING AN INQUEST

(a) A justice of the peace shall conduct an inquest into the death of a person who dies in the county served by the justice if:

(1) the person dies in prison under circumstances other than those described by Section 501.055(b), Government Code, or in jail;

(2) the person dies an unnatural death from a cause other than a legal execution;

(3) the body or a body part of a person is found, the cause or circumstances of death are unknown, and:

(A) the person is identified; or

(B) the person is unidentified;

(4) the circumstances of the death indicate that the death may have been caused by unlawful means;

(5) the person commits suicide or the circumstances of the death indicate that the death may have been caused by suicide;

(6) the person dies without having been attended by a physician;

(7) the person dies while attended by a physician who is unable to certify the cause of death and who requests the justice of the peace to conduct an inquest; or

(8) the person is a child younger than six years of age and an inquest is required by Chapter 264, Family Code.

(b) Except as provided by Subsection (c) of this section, a physician who attends the death of a person and who is unable to certify the cause of death shall report the death to the justice of the peace of the precinct where the death occurred and request that the justice conduct an inquest.

(c) If a person dies in a hospital or other institution and an attending physician is unable to certify the cause of death, the superintendent or general manager of the hospital or institution shall report the death to the justice of the peace of the precinct where the hospital or institution is located.

(d) A justice of the peace investigating a death described by Subsection (a)(3)(B) shall report the death to the missing children and missing persons information clearinghouse of the Department of Public Safety and the national crime information center not later than the 10th working day after the date the investigation began.

History of CCP art. 49.04: Acts 1965, 59th Leg., vol. 2, ch. 722. Amended by Acts 1987, 70th Leg., ch. 529, §1, eff. Sept. 1, 1987; Acts 1995, 74th Leg., ch. 255, §3 (eff. Sept. 1, 1995), ch. 321, §1.105 (eff. Sept. 1, 1995), ch. 878, §2 (eff. Sept. 1, 1995); Acts 1997, 75th Leg., ch. 656, §1, eff. Sept. 1, 1997; Acts 1999, 76th Leg., ch. 785, §2, eff. Sept. 1, 1999; Acts 2003, 78th Leg., ch. 826, §1 (eff. Sept. 1, 2003), ch. 1295, §1 (eff. Sept. 1, 2003).

ART. 49.041. REOPENING AN INQUEST

A justice of the peace may reopen an inquest if, based on information provided by a credible person or facts within the knowledge of the justice of the peace, the justice of the peace determines that reopening the inquest may reveal a different cause or different circumstances of death.

History of CCP art. 49.041: Acts 1997, 75th Leg., ch. 897, §1, eff. Sept. 1, 1997.

ART. 49.05. TIME & PLACE OF INQUEST; REMOVAL OF PROPERTY & BODY FROM PLACE OF DEATH

(a) A justice of the peace shall conduct an inquest immediately or as soon as practicable after the justice receives notification of the death.

(b) A justice of the peace may conduct an inquest:

(1) at the place where the death occurred;

(2) where the body was found; or

(3) at any other place determined to be reasonable by the justice.

(c) A justice of the peace may direct the removal of a body from the scene of death or move any part of the physical surroundings of a body only after a law enforcement agency is notified of the death and a peace officer has conducted an investigation or, if a law enforcement agency has not begun an investigation, a reasonable time has elapsed from the time the law enforcement agency was notified.

(d) A law enforcement agency that is notified of a death requiring an inquest under Article 49.04 of this code shall begin its investigation immediately or as soon as practicable after the law enforcement agency receives notification of the death.

(e) Except in emergency circumstances, a peace officer or other person conducting a death investigation for a law enforcement agency may not move the body or any part of the physical surroundings of the place of death without authorization from a justice of the peace.

(f) A person not authorized by law to move the body of a decedent or any part of the physical surroundings of the body commits an offense if the person tampers with a body that is subject to an inquest under Article 49.04 of this code or any part of the physical surroundings of the body. An offense under this section is punishable by a fine in an amount not to exceed $500.

History of CCP art. 49.05: Acts 1965, 59th Leg., vol. 2, ch. 722. Amended by Acts 1977, 65th Leg., ch. 407, §1, eff. Aug. 29, 1977; Acts 1987, 70th Leg., ch. 529, §1, eff. Sept. 1, 1987.

ANNOTATIONS

Eddowes v. Oswald, 621 S.W.2d 843, 846 (Tex. App.—Fort Worth 1981, no writ). "[A] surviving brother of a deceased does not have the right to control the remains of his deceased brother's body so long as there is a surviving wife, children, or parents of the deceased."

ART. 49.06. HINDERING AN INQUEST

(a) A person commits an offense if the person intentionally or knowingly hinders the entrance of a justice of the peace to a premises where a death occurred or a body is found.

(b) An offense under this article is a Class B misdemeanor.

History of CCP art. 49.06: Acts 1965, 59th Leg., vol. 2, ch. 722. Amended by Acts 1969, 61st Leg., ch. 618, §2, eff. June 11, 1969; Acts 1987, 70th Leg., ch. 529, §1, eff. Sept. 1, 1987.

ART. 49.07. NOTIFICATION OF INVESTIGATING OFFICIAL

(a) A physician or other person who has possession of a body or body part of a person whose death requires an inquest under Article 49.04 of this code shall immediately notify the justice of the peace who serves the precinct in which the body or body part was found.

(b) A peace officer who has been notified of the death of a person whose death requires an inquest under Article 49.04 of this code shall immediately notify the justice of the peace who serves the precinct in which the body or body part was found.

(c)(1) If the justice of the peace who serves the precinct in which the body or body part was found is not available to conduct an inquest, a person required to give notice under this article shall notify the nearest available justice of the peace serving the county in which the body or body part was found, and that justice of the peace shall conduct the inquest.

(2) If no justice of the peace serving the county in which the body or body part was found is available to conduct an inquest, a person required to give notice under this article shall notify the county judge, and the county judge shall initiate the inquest. The county judge may exercise any power and perform any duty otherwise granted to or imposed under this subchapter on the justice of the peace serving the county in which the body or body part was found, except that not later than the fifth day after the day on which the inquest is initiated, the county judge shall transfer all information obtained by the judge to the justice of the peace in whose precinct the body or body part was found for final disposition of the matter.

(d) A person commits an offense if the person is required by this article to give notice and intentionally or knowingly fails to give the notice. An offense under this subsection is a Class C misdemeanor.

History of CCP art. 49.07: Acts 1965, 59th Leg., vol. 2, ch. 722. Amended by Acts 1987, 70th Leg., ch. 529, §1, eff. Sept. 1, 1987; Acts 1997, 75th Leg., ch. 656, §2, eff. Sept. 1, 1997; Acts 2001, 77th Leg., ch. 229, §1, eff. May 22, 2001; Acts 2003, 78th Leg., ch. 1295, §2, eff. Sept. 1, 2003; Acts 2003, 78th Leg., ch. 826, §2, eff. Sept. 1, 2003.

ART. 49.08. INFORMATION LEADING TO AN INQUEST

A justice of the peace conducting an inquest may act on information the justice receives from any credible person or on facts within his knowledge.

History of CCP art. 49.08: Acts 1965, 59th Leg., vol. 2, ch. 722. Amended by Acts 1987, 70th Leg., ch. 529, §1, eff. Sept. 1, 1987.

ART. 49.09. BODY DISINTERRED OR CREMATED

(a) If a body or body part subject to investigation under Article 49.04 of this code is interred and an authorized person has not conducted an inquest required under this subchapter, a justice of the peace may direct the disinterment of the body or body part in order to conduct an inquest.

(b) A person may not cremate or direct the cremation of a body subject to investigation under Article 49.04 unless the body is identified and the person has received from the justice of the peace a certificate signed by the justice stating that:

(1) an autopsy was performed on the body under Article 49.10 of this code; or

(2) no autopsy was necessary.

(c) An owner or operator of a crematory shall retain a certificate received under Subsection (b) of this article for a period of 10 years from the date of cremation of the body named on the certificate.

(d) A person commits an offense if the person cremates or directs the cremation of a body without obtaining a certificate from a justice of the peace as required by Subsection (b) of this article. An offense under this section is a Class B misdemeanor.

(e) If the body of a deceased person is unidentified, a person may not cremate or direct the cremation of the body under this article. If the body is buried, the justice of the peace shall record and maintain for not less than 10 years all information pertaining to the body and the location of burial.

History of CCP art. 49.09: Acts 1965, 59th Leg., vol. 2, ch. 722. Amended by Acts 1987, 70th Leg., ch. 529, §1, eff. Sept. 1, 1987; Acts 1997, 75th Leg., ch. 656, §3, eff. Sept. 1, 1997; Acts 2003, 78th Leg., ch. 826, §3 (eff. Sept. 1, 2003), ch. 1295, §3 (eff. Sept. 1, 2003).

ART. 49.10. AUTOPSIES & TESTS

(a) At his discretion, a justice of the peace may obtain the opinion of a county health officer or a physician concerning the necessity of obtaining an autopsy in order to determine or confirm the nature and cause of a death.

(b) The commissioners court of the county shall pay a reasonable fee for a consultation obtained by a justice of the peace under Subsection (a) of this article.

(c) Except as required by Section 264.514, Family Code, for each body that is the subject of an inquest by a justice of the peace, the justice, in the justice's discretion, shall:

(1) direct a physician to perform an autopsy; or

(2) certify that no autopsy is necessary.

(d) A justice of the peace may not order a person to perform an autopsy on the body of a deceased person whose death was caused by Asiatic cholera, bubonic plague, typhus fever, or smallpox. A justice of the peace may not order a person to perform an autopsy on the body of a deceased person whose death was caused by a communicable disease during a public health disaster.

(e) A justice of the peace shall order an autopsy performed on a body if:

(1) the justice determines that an autopsy is necessary to determine or confirm the nature and cause of death;

(2) the deceased was a child younger than six years of age and the death is determined under Section 264.514, Family Code, to be unexpected or the result of abuse or neglect; or

(3) directed to do so by the district attorney, criminal district attorney, or, if there is no district or criminal district attorney, the county attorney.

(f) A justice of the peace shall request a physician to perform the autopsy.

(g) The commissioners court shall pay a reasonable fee to a physician performing an autopsy on the order of a justice of the peace, if a fee is assessed.

(h) The commissioners court shall pay a reasonable fee for the transportation of a body to a place where an autopsy can be performed under this article if a justice of the peace orders the body to be transported to the place.

(i) If a justice of the peace determines that a complete autopsy is unnecessary to confirm or determine the cause of death, the justice may order a physician to take or remove from a body a sample of body fluids, tissues, or organs in order to determine the nature and cause of death. Except as provided by Subsection (j) of this article, a justice may not order any person other than a physician to take samples from the body of a deceased person.

(j) A justice of the peace may order a physician, qualified technician, paramedic, chemist, registered professional nurse, or licensed vocational nurse to take a specimen of blood from the body of a person who died as the result of a motor vehicle accident if the justice determines that circumstances indicate that the person may have been driving while intoxicated.

(k) A justice of the peace may order an investigative or laboratory test to determine the identity of a deceased person. After proper removal of a sample from a body, a justice may order any person specially trained in identification work to complete any tests necessary to determine the identity of the deceased person.

(*l*) A medical examination on an unidentified person shall include the following information to enable a timely and accurate identification of the person:

(1) all available fingerprints and palm prints;

(2) dental charts and radiographs (X-rays) of the person's teeth;

(3) frontal and lateral facial photographs with scale indicated;

(4) notation and photographs, with scale indicated, of a significant scar, mark, tattoo, or item of clothing or other personal effect found with or near the body;

(5) notation of antemortem medical conditions;

(6) notation of observations pertinent to the estimation of time of death; and

(7) precise documentation of the location of burial of the remains.

(m) A medical examination on an unidentified person may include the following information to enable a timely and accurate identification of the person:

(1) full body radiographs (X-rays); and

(2) hair specimens with roots.

(n) On discovering the body or a body part of a deceased person in the circumstances described by Article 49.04(a)(3)(B), the justice of the peace may request the aid of a forensic anthropologist in the examination of the body or body part. The forensic anthropologist must hold a doctoral degree in anthropology with an emphasis in physical anthropology. The forensic anthropologist shall attempt to establish whether the body or body part is of a human or animal, whether evidence of childbirth, injury, or disease exists, and the sex, race, age, stature, and physical anomalies of the body or body part. The forensic anthropologist may also attempt to establish the cause, manner, and time of death.

(o) If a person is injured in one county and dies as a result of those injuries, with the death occurring in another county, the attorney representing the state in the prosecution of felonies in the county in which the injury occurred may request a justice of the peace in the county in which the death occurred to order an autopsy be performed on the body of the deceased person. If the justice of the peace orders that the autopsy be performed, the county in which the injury occurred shall reimburse the county in which the death occurred.

History of CCP art. 49.10: Acts 1965, 59th Leg., vol. 2, ch. 722. Amended by Acts 1987, 70th Leg., ch. 529, §1, eff. Sept. 1, 1987; Acts 1995, 74th Leg., ch. 255, §4 (eff. Sept. 1, 1995), ch. 878, §3 (eff. Sept. 1, 1995); Acts 1997, 75th Leg., ch. 656, §4 (eff. Sept. 1, 1997), ch. 1022, §102 (eff. Sept. 1, 1997), ch. 1301, §1 (eff. Sept. 1, 1997); Acts 1999, 76th Leg., ch. 1071, §1 (eff. Aug. 30, 1999), ch. 1132, §1 (eff. Sept. 1, 1999; Acts 2001, 77th Leg., ch. 237, §1 (eff. May 23, 2001), ch. 240, §1 (eff. Sept. 1, 2001); Acts 2003, 78th Leg., ch. 198, §2.190 (eff. Sept. 1, 2003), ch. 826, §4 (eff. Sept. 1, 2003), ch. 1295, §4 (eff. Sept. 1, 2003).

ART. 49.11. CHEMICAL ANALYSIS

(a) A justice of the peace may obtain a chemical analysis of a sample taken from a body in order to determine whether death was caused, in whole or in part, by the ingestion, injection, or introduction into the body of a poison or other chemical substance. A justice may obtain a chemical analysis under this article from a chemist, toxicologist, pathologist, or other medical expert.

(b) A justice of the peace shall obtain a chemical analysis under Subsection (a) of this article if requested to do so by the physician who performed an autopsy on the body.

(c) The commissioners court shall pay a reasonable fee to a person who conducts a chemical analysis at the request of a justice of the peace.

History of CCP art. 49.11: Acts 1965, 59th Leg., vol. 2, ch. 722. Amended by Acts 1987, 70th Leg., ch. 529, §1, eff. Sept. 1, 1987.

ART. 49.12. LIABILITY OF PERSON PERFORMING AUTOPSY OR TEST

A person who performs an autopsy or makes a test on a body on the order of a justice of the peace in the good faith belief that the order is valid is not liable for damages if the order is invalid.

History of CCP art. 49.12: Acts 1965, 59th Leg., vol. 2, ch. 722. Amended by Acts 1987, 70th Leg., ch. 529, §1, eff. Sept. 1, 1987.

ART. 49.13. CONSENT TO AUTOPSY

(a) Consent for a physician to conduct an autopsy is sufficient if given by the following:

(1) if the deceased was married, the surviving spouse;

(2) if the deceased was married but not survived by a spouse, an adult child of the deceased;

(3) if the deceased was married but not survived by a spouse, and a child of the deceased is under the care of a guardian or a court, the guardian or court having care of the child; or

(4) if the deceased person was unmarried or is not survived by a spouse or a child, the following persons in the order stated:

(A) a parent;

(B) a guardian;

(C) the next of kin; or

(D) any person who assumes custody of and responsibility for the burial of the body.

(b) Notwithstanding Subsection (a), consent for a physician to conduct an autopsy is sufficient if given by the Texas Department of Criminal Justice or an authorized official of the department in accordance with Section 501.055, Government Code.

History of CCP art. 49.13: Acts 1965, 59th Leg., vol. 2, ch. 722. Amended by Acts 1987, 70th Leg., ch. 529, §1, eff. Sept. 1, 1987; Acts 1997, 75th Leg., ch. 1422, §4, eff. June 20, 1997.

ART. 49.14. INQUEST HEARING

(a) A justice of the peace conducting an inquest may hold an inquest hearing if the justice determines that the circumstances warrant the hearing. The justice shall hold an inquest hearing if requested to do so by a district attorney or a criminal district attorney who serves the county in which the body was found.

(b) An inquest hearing may be held with or without a jury unless the district attorney or criminal district attorney requests that the hearing be held with a jury.

(c) A jury in an inquest hearing is composed of six persons. Jurors shall be summoned in the same manner as are jurors for county court. A juror who is properly summoned and fails to appear, other than a juror exempted by law, commits an offense. An offense under this subsection is punishable by a fine not to exceed $100.

(d) A justice of the peace may hold a public or a private inquest hearing. If a person has been arrested and charged with causing the death of the deceased, the defendant and the defendant's counsel are entitled to be present at the inquest hearing, examine witnesses, and introduce evidence.

(e) A justice of the peace may issue a subpoena to enforce the attendance of a witness at an inquest hearing and may issue an attachment for a person who is subpoenaed and fails to appear at the time and place cited on the subpoena.

(f) A justice of the peace may require bail of a witness to secure the appearance of the witness at an inquest hearing or before a grand jury, examining court, or other court investigating a death.

(g) The justice of the peace shall swear witnesses appearing at an inquest hearing. The justice and an attorney representing the state may examine witnesses at an inquest hearing. The justice shall direct that all sworn testimony be reduced to writing and the justice shall subscribe the transcription.

(h) Only the justice of the peace, a person charged in the death under investigation, the counsel for the person charged, and an attorney representing the state may question a witness at an inquest hearing.

(i) A justice of the peace may hold a person who disrupts the proceedings of an inquest hearing in contempt of court. A person who is found in contempt of court under this subsection may be fined in an amount not to exceed $100 and removed from court by a peace officer.

History of CCP art. 49.14: Acts 1965, 59th Leg., vol. 2, ch. 722. Amended by Acts 1987, 70th Leg., ch. 529, §1, eff. Sept. 1, 1987.

ART. 49.15. INQUEST RECORD

(a) A justice of the peace or other person authorized under this subchapter to conduct an inquest shall make an inquest record for each inquest he conducts. The inquest record must include a report of the events, proceedings, findings, and conclusions of the inquest. The record must also include any autopsy prepared in the case and all other papers of the case. All papers of the inquest record must be marked with the case number and be clearly indexed and be maintained in the office of the justice of the peace and be made available to the appropriate officials upon request.

(b) As part of the inquest record, the justice of the peace shall make and keep complete and permanent records of all inquest hearings. The inquest hearing records must include:

(1) the name of the deceased person or, if the person is unidentified, a description of the body;

(2) the time, date, and place where the body was found;

(3) the time, date, and place where the inquest was held;

(4) the name of every witness who testified at the inquest;

(5) the name of every person who provided to the justice information pertinent to the inquest;

(6) the amount of bail set for each witness and person charged in the death;

(7) a transcript of the testimony given by each witness at the inquest hearing;

(8) the autopsy report, if an autopsy was performed; and

(9) the name of every person arrested as a suspect in the death who appeared at the inquest and the details of that person's arrest.

(c) The commissioners court shall pay a reasonable fee to a person who records or transcribes sworn testimony during an inquest hearing.

(d) The justice of the peace shall certify a copy of the inquest summary report and deliver the certified copy in a sealed envelope to the clerk of the district court. The clerk of the district court shall retain the summary report subject to an order by the district court.

History of CCP art. 49.15: Acts 1965, 59th Leg., vol. 2, ch. 722. Amended by Acts 1987, 70th Leg., ch. 529, §1, eff. Sept. 1, 1987.

ART. 49.16. ORDERS & DEATH CERTIFICATES

The justice of the peace or other person who conducts an inquest under this subchapter shall sign the death certificate and all orders made as a necessary part of the inquest.

History of CCP art. 49.16: Acts 1965, 59th Leg., vol. 2, ch. 722. Amended by Acts 1973, 63rd Leg., ch. 399, §2(A), eff. Jan. 1, 1974; Acts 1987, 70th Leg., ch. 529, §1, eff. Sept. 1, 1987.

ART. 49.17. EVIDENCE

A justice of the peace shall preserve all tangible evidence that the justice accumulates in the course of an inquest that tends to show the real cause of death or identify the person who caused the death. The justice shall:

(1) deposit the evidence with the appropriate law enforcement agency to be stored in the agency's property room for safekeeping; or

(2) deliver the evidence to the district clerk for safekeeping subject to the order of the court.

History of CCP art. 49.17: Acts 1965, 59th Leg., vol. 2, ch. 722. Amended by Acts 1987, 70th Leg., ch. 529, §1, eff. Sept. 1, 1987.

ART. 49.18. DEATH IN CUSTODY

(a) If a person confined in a penal institution dies, the sheriff or other person in charge of the penal institution shall as soon as practicable inform the justice of the peace of the precinct where the penal institution is located of the death.

(b) If a person dies while in the custody of a peace officer or as a result of a peace officer's use of force or if a person incarcerated in a jail, correctional facility, or state juvenile facility dies, the director of the law enforcement agency of which the officer is a member or of the facility in which the person was incarcerated shall investigate the death and file a written report of the cause of death with the attorney general no later than the 30th day after the date on which the person in custody or the incarcerated person died. The director shall make a good faith effort to obtain all facts relevant to the death and include those facts in the report. The attorney general shall make the report, with the exception of any portion of the report that the attorney general determines is privileged, available to any interested person.

(c) Subsection (a) does not apply to a death that occurs in a facility operated by or under contract with the Texas Department of Criminal Justice. Subsection (b) does not apply to a death that occurs in a facility operated by or under contract with the Texas Department of Criminal Justice if the death occurs under circumstances described by Section 501.055(b)(2), Government Code.

(d) In this article:

(1) "Correctional facility" means a confinement facility or halfway house operated by or under contract with any division of the Texas Department of Criminal Justice.

(2) "In the custody of a peace officer" means:

(A) under arrest by a peace officer; or

(B) under the physical control or restraint of a peace officer.

(3) "State juvenile facility" means any facility or halfway house:

(A) operated by or under contract with the Texas Youth Commission; or

(B) described by Section 51.02(13) or (14), Family Code.

History of CCP art. 49.18: Acts 1965, 59th Leg., vol. 2, ch. 722. Amended by Acts 1973, 63rd Leg., ch. 399, §2(A), eff. Jan. 1, 1974; Acts 1987, 70th Leg., ch. 529, §1, eff. Sept. 1, 1987; Acts 1995, 74th Leg., ch. 321, §1.106, eff. Sept. 1, 1995; Acts 1997, 75th Leg., ch. 1422, §1, eff. June 20, 1997; Acts 2003, 78th Leg., ch. 894, §1, eff. Sept. 1, 2003.

ART. 49.19. WARRANT OF ARREST

(a) A justice of the peace who is conducting an inquest of a death under this subchapter may issue a warrant for the arrest of a person suspected of causing the death if:

(1) the justice has knowledge that the person caused the death of the deceased;

(2) the justice receives an affidavit stating that the person caused the death; or

(3) evidence is adduced at an inquest hearing that shows probable cause to believe the person caused the death.

(b) A peace officer who receives an arrest warrant issued by a justice of the peace shall:

(1) execute the warrant without delay; and

(2) detain the person arrested until the person's discharge is ordered by the justice of the peace or other proper authority.

(c) A person who is charged in a death and arrested under a warrant of a justice of the peace shall remain in the custody of the arresting peace officer and may not be removed from the peace officer's custody on the authority of a warrant from another magistrate. A person charged in a death who has not been arrested under a warrant of a justice of the peace may be arrested on the order of a magistrate other than the justice of the peace and examined by that magistrate while an inquest is pending.

History of CCP art. 49.19: Acts 1965, 59th Leg., vol. 2, ch. 722. Amended by Acts 1987, 70th Leg., ch. 529, §1, eff. Sept. 1, 1987.

ART. 49.20. REQUISITES OF WARRANT

A warrant of arrest issued under Article 49.19 of this code is sufficient if it:

(1) is issued in the name of "The State of Texas";

(2) specifies the name of the person whose arrest is ordered or, if the person's name is unknown, reasonably describes the person;

(3) recites in plain language the offense with which the person is charged; and

(4) is signed and dated by a justice of the peace.

History of CCP art. 49.20: Acts 1965, 59th Leg., vol. 2, ch. 722. Amended by Acts 1987, 70th Leg., ch. 529, §1, eff. Sept. 1, 1987.

ART. 49.21. COMMITMENT OF HOMICIDE SUSPECT

At the conclusion of an inquest, if a justice of the peace finds that a person who has been arrested in the case caused or contributed to the death of the deceased, the justice may:

(1) commit the person to jail; or

(2) require the person to execute a bail bond with security for the person's appearance before the proper court to answer for the offense.

History of CCP art. 49.21: Acts 1965, 59th Leg., vol. 2, ch. 722. Amended by Acts 1987, 70th Leg., ch. 529, §1, eff. Sept. 1, 1987.

ART. 49.22. SEALING PREMISES OF DECEASED

(a) If a body or body part that is subject to an inquest under Article 49.04 of this code is found on premises that were under the sole control of the deceased, a justice of the peace or other person authorized under this subchapter to conduct an inquest may direct that the premises be locked and sealed to prohibit entrance by any person other than a peace officer conducting an investigation of the death.

(b) Rent, utility charges, taxes, and all other reasonable expenses accruing against the property of the deceased during the time the premises of the deceased are locked and sealed under this article may be charged against the estate of the deceased.

(c) A person other than a peace officer commits an offense if the person tampers with or removes a lock or seal placed on premises under this article.

(d) An offense under this article is a Class B misdemeanor.

History of CCP art. 49.22: Acts 1965, 59th Leg., vol. 2, ch. 722. Amended by Acts 1987, 70th Leg., ch. 529, §1, eff. Sept. 1, 1987; Acts 1997, 75th Leg., ch. 656, §5, eff. Sept. 1, 1997; Acts 2003, 78th Leg., ch. 1295, §5, eff. Sept. 1, 2003; Acts 2003, 78th Leg., ch. 826, §5, eff. Sept. 1, 2003.

ART. 49.23. OFFICE OF DEATH INVESTIGATOR

(a) The commissioners court of a county may establish an office of death investigator and employ one or more death investigators to provide assistance to those persons in the county who conduct inquests. A death investigator employed under this article is entitled to receive compensation from the county in an amount set by the commissioners court. A death investigator serves at the will of the commissioners court and on terms and conditions set by the commissioners court.

(b) To be eligible for employment as a death investigator, a person must have experience or training in investigative procedures concerning the circumstances, manner, and cause of the death of a deceased person.

(c) At the request of and under the supervision of a justice of the peace or other person conducting an inquest, a death investigator may assist the person conducting the inquest to investigate the time, place, and manner of death and lock and seal the premises of the deceased. A death investigator who assists in an inquest under this subsection shall make a complete report of the death investigator's activities, findings, and conclusions to the justice of the peace or other person conducting the inquest not later than eight hours after the death investigator completes the investigation.

History of CCP art. 49.23: Acts 1965, 59th Leg., vol. 2, ch. 722. Amended by Acts 1987, 70th Leg., ch. 529, §1, eff. Sept. 1, 1987.

ART. 49.24. NOTIFICATION & REPORT OF DEATH OF RESIDENT OF INSTITUTION

(a) A superintendent or general manager of an institution who is required by Article 49.04 to report to a justice of the peace the death of an individual under the care, custody, or control of or residing in the institution shall:

(1) notify the office of the attorney general of the individual's death within 24 hours of the death; and

(2) prepare and submit to the office of the attorney general a report containing all facts relevant to the individual's death within 72 hours of the death.

(b) The superintendent or general manager of the institution shall make a good faith effort to obtain all facts relevant to an individual's death and to include those facts in the report submitted under Subsection (a)(2).

(c) The office of the attorney general may investigate each death reported to the office by an institution that receives payments through the medical assistance program under Chapter 32, Human Resources Code.

(d) Except as provided by Subsection (e), the office of the attorney general shall make a report submitted under Subsection (a)(2) available to any interested person who submits a written request for access to the report.

(e) The office of the attorney general may deny a person access to a report or a portion of a report filed under Subsection (a)(2) if the office determines that the report or a portion of the report is:

(1) privileged from discovery; or

(2) exempt from required public disclosure under Chapter 552, Government Code.

(f) This article does not relieve a superintendent or general manager of an institution of the duty of making any other notification or report of an individual's death as required by law.

(g) For the purposes of this article, the definition of "institution" excludes hospitals.

History of CCP art. 49.24: Acts 2003, 78th Leg., ch. 894, §2, eff. Sept. 1, 2003. Amended by Acts 2005, 79th Leg., ch. 392, §1, eff. June 17, 2005.

History of Former CCP art. 49.24: Repealed by Acts 1987, 70th Leg., ch. 529, §2, eff. Sept. 1, 1987.

SUBCHAPTER B. DUTIES PERFORMED BY MEDICAL EXAMINERS

ART. 49.25. MEDICAL EXAMINERS

§1. Office Authorized

Subject to the provisions of this Act, the Commissioners Court of any county having a population of more than one million and not having a reputable medical school as defined in Articles 4501 and 4503, Revised Civil Statutes of Texas, shall establish and maintain the office of medical examiner, and the Commissioners Court of any county may establish and provide for the maintenance of the office of medical examiner. Population shall be according to the last preceding federal census.

§1-a. Multi-County District; Joint Office

(a) The commissioners courts of two or more counties may enter into an agreement to create a medical examiners district and to jointly operate and maintain the office of medical examiner of the district. The district must include the entire area of all counties involved. The counties within the district must, when taken together, form a continuous area.

(b) There may be only one medical examiner in a medical examiners district, although he may employ, within the district, necessary staff personnel. When a county becomes a part of a medical examiners district, the effect is the same within the county as if the office of medical examiner had been established in that county alone. The district medical examiner has all the powers and duties within the district that a medical examiner who serves in a single county has within that county.

(c) The commissioners court of any county which has become a part of a medical examiners district may withdraw the county from the district, but twelve months' notice of withdrawal must be given to the commissioners courts of all other counties in the district.

§2. Appointments & Qualifications

The commissioners court shall appoint the medical examiner, who shall serve at the pleasure of the commissioners court. No person shall be appointed medical examiner unless he is a physician licensed by the State Board of Medical Examiners. To the greatest extent possible, the medical examiner shall be appointed from persons having training and experience in pathology, toxicology, histology and other medico-legal sciences.

The medical examiner shall devote so much of his time and energy as is necessary in the performance of the duties conferred by this Article.

§3. Assistants

The medical examiner may, subject to the approval of the commissioners court, employ such deputy examiners, scientific experts, trained technicians, officers and employees as may be necessary to the proper performance of the duties imposed by this Article upon the medical examiner.

§4. Salaries

The commissioners court shall establish and pay the salaries and compensations of the medical examiner and his staff.

§5. Offices

The commissioners court shall provide the medical examiner and his staff with adequate office space and shall provide laboratory facilities or make arrangements for the use of existing laboratory facilities in the county, if so requested by the medical examiner.

§6. Death Investigations

(a) Any medical examiner, or his duly authorized deputy, shall be authorized, and it shall be his duty, to hold inquests with or without a jury within his county, in the following cases:

1. When a person shall die within twenty-four hours after admission to a hospital or institution or in prison or in jail;

2. When any person is killed; or from any cause dies an unnatural death, except under sentence of the law; or dies in the absence of one or more good witnesses;

3. When the body or a body part of a person is found, the cause or circumstances of death are unknown, and:

(A) the person is identified; or

(B) the person is unidentified;

4. When the circumstances of the death of any person are such as to lead to suspicion that he came to his death by unlawful means;

5. When any person commits suicide, or the circumstances of his death are such as to lead to suspicion that he committed suicide;

6. When a person dies without having been attended by a duly licensed and practicing physician, and

the local health officer or registrar required to report the cause of death under Section 193.005, Health and Safety Code, does not know the cause of death. When the local health officer or registrar of vital statistics whose duty it is to certify the cause of death does not know the cause of death, he shall so notify the medical examiner of the county in which the death occurred and request an inquest;

7. When the person is a child who is younger than six years of age and the death is reported under Chapter 264, Family Code; and

8. When a person dies who has been attended immediately preceding his death by a duly licensed and practicing physician or physicians, and such physician or physicians are not certain as to the cause of death and are unable to certify with certainty the cause of death as required by Section 193.004, Health and Safety Code. In case of such uncertainty the attending physician or physicians, or the superintendent or general manager of the hospital or institution in which the deceased shall have died, shall so report to the medical examiner of the county in which the death occurred, and request an inquest.

(b) The inquests authorized and required by this Article shall be held by the medical examiner of the county in which the death occurred.

(c) In making such investigations and holding such inquests, the medical examiner or an authorized deputy may administer oaths and take affidavits. In the absence of next of kin or legal representatives of the deceased, the medical examiner or authorized deputy shall take charge of the body and all property found with it.

§6a. Organ Transplant Donors; Notice; Inquests

(a) When death occurs to an individual designated a prospective organ donor for transplantation by a licensed physician under circumstances requiring the medical examiner of the county in which death occurred, or the medical examiner's authorized deputy, to hold an inquest, the medical examiner, or a member of his staff will be so notified by the administrative head of the facility in which the transplantation is to be performed.

(b) When notified pursuant to Subsection (a) of this Section, the medical examiner or the medical examiner's deputy shall perform an inquest on the deceased prospective organ donor.

§7. Reports of Death

(a) Any police officer, superintendent or general manager of an institution, physician, or private citizen who shall become aware of a death under any of the circumstances set out in Section 6(a) of this Article, shall immediately report such death to the office of the medical examiner or to the city or county police departments; any such report to a city or county police department shall be immediately transmitted to the office of the medical examiner.

(b) A person investigating a death described by Subdivision 3(B) of Section 6(a) shall report the death to the missing children and missing persons information clearinghouse of the Department of Public Safety and the national crime information center not later than the 10th working day after the date the investigation began.

(c) A superintendent or general manager of an institution who reports a death under Subsection (a) must comply with the notice and reporting requirements of Article 49.24. The office of the attorney general has the same powers and duties provided the office under that article regarding the dissemination and investigation of the report.

§8. Removal of Bodies

When any death under circumstances set out in Section 6 shall have occurred, the body shall not be disturbed or removed from the position in which it is found by any person without authorization from the medical examiner or authorized deputy, except for the purpose of preserving such body from loss or destruction or maintaining the flow of traffic on a highway, railroad or airport.

§9. Autopsy

(a) If the cause of death shall be determined beyond a reasonable doubt as a result of the investigation, the medical examiner shall file a report thereof setting forth specifically the cause of death with the district attorney or criminal district attorney, or in a county in which there is no district attorney or criminal district attorney with the county attorney, of the county in which the death occurred. If in the opinion of the medical examiner an autopsy is necessary, or if such is requested by the district attorney or criminal district attorney, or county attorney where there is no district attorney or criminal district attorney, the autopsy shall be immediately performed by the medical examiner or

a duly authorized deputy. In those cases where a complete autopsy is deemed unnecessary by the medical examiner to ascertain the cause of death, the medical examiner may perform a limited autopsy involving the taking of blood samples or any other samples of body fluids, tissues or organs, in order to ascertain the cause of death or whether a crime has been committed. In the case of a body of a human being whose identity is unknown, the medical examiner may authorize such investigative and laboratory tests and processes as are required to determine its identity as well as the cause of death. In performing an autopsy the medical examiner or authorized deputy may use the facilities of any city or county hospital within the county or such other facilities as are made available. Upon completion of the autopsy, the medical examiner shall file a report setting forth the findings in detail with the office of the district attorney or criminal district attorney of the county, or if there is no district attorney or criminal district attorney, with the county attorney of the county.

(b) A medical examination on an unidentified person shall include the following information to enable a timely and accurate identification of the person:

(1) all available fingerprints and palm prints;

(2) dental charts and radiographs (X-rays) of the person's teeth;

(3) frontal and lateral facial photographs with scale indicated;

(4) notation and photographs, with scale indicated, of a significant scar, mark, tattoo, or item of clothing or other personal effect found with or near the body;

(5) notation of antemortem medical conditions;

(6) notation of observations pertinent to the estimation of time of death; and

(7) precise documentation of the location of burial of the remains.

(c) A medical examination on an unidentified person may include the following information to enable a timely and accurate identification of the person:

(1) full body radiographs (X-rays); and

(2) hair specimens with roots.

§10. Disinterments & Cremations

When a body upon which an inquest ought to have been held has been interred, the medical examiner may cause it to be disinterred for the purpose of holding such inquest.

Before any body, upon which an inquest is authorized by the provisions of this Article, can be lawfully cremated, an autopsy shall be performed thereon as provided in this Article, or a certificate that no autopsy was necessary shall be furnished by the medical examiner. Before any dead body can be lawfully cremated, the owner or operator of the crematory shall demand and be furnished with a certificate, signed by the medical examiner of the county in which the death occurred showing that an autopsy was performed on said body or that no autopsy thereon was necessary. It shall be the duty of the medical examiner to determine whether or not, from all the circumstances surrounding the death, an autopsy is necessary prior to issuing a certificate under the provisions of this section. No autopsy shall be required by the medical examiner as a prerequisite to cremation in case death is caused by the pestilential diseases of Asiatic cholera, bubonic plague, typhus fever, or smallpox. All certificates furnished to the owner or operator of a crematory by any medical examiner, under the terms of this Article, shall be preserved by such owner or operator of such crematory for a period of two years from the date of the cremation of said body. A medical examiner is not required to perform an autopsy on the body of a deceased person whose death was caused by a communicable disease during a public health disaster.

§10a. Waiting Period Between Death & Cremation

The body of a deceased person shall not be cremated within 48 hours after the time of death as indicated on the regular death certificate, unless the death certificate indicates death was caused by the pestilential diseases of Asiatic cholera, bubonic plague, typhus fever, or smallpox, or unless the time requirement is waived in writing by the county medical examiner or, in counties not having a county medical examiner, a justice of the peace. In a public health disaster, the commissioner of public health may designate other communicable diseases for which cremation within 48 hours of the time of death is authorized.

§10b. Disposal of Unidentified Body

If the body of a deceased person is unidentified, a person may not cremate or direct the cremation of the body under this article. If the body is buried, the investigating agency responsible for the burial shall record and maintain for not less than 10 years all information pertaining to the body and the location of burial.

§11. Records

The medical examiner shall keep full and complete records properly indexed, giving the name if known of every person whose death is investigated, the place where the body was found, the date, the cause and manner of death, and shall issue a death certificate. The full report and detailed findings of the autopsy, if any, shall be a part of the record. Copies of all records shall promptly be delivered to the proper district, county, or criminal district attorney in any case where further investigation is advisable. The records are subject to required public disclosure in accordance with Chapter 552, Government Code, except that a photograph or x-ray of a body taken during an autopsy is excepted from required public disclosure in accordance with Chapter 552, Government Code, but is subject to disclosure:

(1) under a subpoena or authority of other law; or

(2) if the photograph or x-ray is of the body of a person who died while in the custody of law enforcement.

§12. Transfer of Duties of Justice of Peace

When the commissioners court of any county shall establish the office of medical examiner, all powers and duties of justices of the peace in such county relating to the investigation of deaths and inquests shall vest in the office of the medical examiner. Any subsequent General Law pertaining to the duties of justices of the peace in death investigations and inquests shall apply to the medical examiner in such counties as to the extent not inconsistent with this Article, and all laws or parts of laws otherwise in conflict herewith are hereby declared to be inapplicable to this Article.

§13. Use of Forensic Anthropologist

On discovering the body or a body part of a deceased person in the circumstances described by Subdivision 3(B) of Section 6(a), the medical examiner may request the aid of a forensic anthropologist in the examination of the body or body part. The forensic anthropologist must hold a doctoral degree in anthropology with an emphasis in physical anthropology. The forensic anthropologist shall attempt to establish whether the body or body part is of a human or animal, whether evidence of childbirth, injury, or disease exists, and the sex, race, age, stature, and physical anomalies of the body or body part. The forensic anthropologist may also attempt to establish the cause, manner, and time of death.

§14. Penalty

(a) A person commits an offense if the person knowingly violates this article.

(b) An offense under this section is a Class B misdemeanor.

History of CCP art. 49.25: Acts 1965, 59th Leg., vol. 2, ch. 722. Amended by Acts 1969, 61st Leg., ch. 336, §1 (eff. May 27, 1969), ch. 500, §1 (eff. June 10, 1969); Acts 1971, 62nd Leg., ch. 270, §1, eff. Aug. 30, 1971; Acts 1975, 64th Leg., ch. 562, §1, eff. Sept. 1, 1975; Acts 1989, 71st Leg., ch. 1205, §1, eff. June 16, 1989; Acts 1991, 72nd Leg., ch. 14, §284(66), (67), (69) (eff. Sept. 1, 1991), ch. 597, §58 (eff. Sept. 1, 1991); Acts 1995, 74th Leg., ch. 255, §5 (eff. Sept. 1, 1995), ch. 878, §4 (eff. Sept. 1, 1995); Acts 1997, 75th Leg., ch. 656, §6, eff. Sept. 1, 1997; Acts 1999, 76th Leg., ch. 607, §2, eff. Sept. 1, 1999; Acts 2003, 78th Leg., ch. 198, §2.191 (eff. Sept. 1, 2003), ch. 826, §§6, 7 (eff. Sept. 1, 2003), ch. 894, §3 (eff. Sept. 1, 2003), ch. 1295, §§6, 7 (eff. Sept. 1, 2003).

ANNOTATIONS

Garcia v. State, 868 S.W.2d 337, 340 (Tex.Crim. App.1993). "[T]he medical examiner's office is a public office or agency established by statute. [T]he medical examiner has a duty ... to prepare and file a report, including autopsy reports, stating a cause of death and those reports are public records. *At 341-42:* Autopsy reports are *not* necessarily prepared in contemplation of litigation. [T]hey are generally prepared by officials with no motive to fabricate the results of the reports. [¶] [T]he medical examiner's report is not filed until the cause of death has been determined and the report has been completed. [T]he prosecution is not necessarily involved in the medical examiner's investigation or the preparation of the report. [A] medical examiner's office is not ... such a uniquely litigious and prosecution-oriented environment as to create an adversarial context. *At 341 n.9:* [T]he primary responsibility of the medical examiner is the determination of a cause of death in cases where the cause of death is unknown."

CHAPTER 50. FIRE INQUESTS

ART. 50.01. INVESTIGATIONS

When an affidavit is made by a credible person before any justice of the peace that there is ground to believe that any building has been unlawfully set or attempted to be set on fire, such justice shall cause the truth of such complaint to be investigated.

History of CCP art. 50.01: Acts 1965, 59th Leg., vol. 2, ch. 722.

ART. 50.02. PROCEEDINGS

The proceedings in such case shall be governed by the laws relating to inquests upon dead bodies. The officer conducting such investigations shall have the same powers as are conferred upon justices of the peace in the preceding Articles of this Chapter.

History of CCP art. 50.02: Acts 1965, 59th Leg., vol. 2, ch. 722.

ART. 50.03. VERDICT IN FIRE INQUEST

The jury after inspecting the place in question and after hearing the testimony, shall deliver to the justice holding such inquest its written signed verdict in which it shall find and certify how and in what manner such fire happened or was attempted, and all the circumstances attending the same, and who are guilty thereof, and in what manner. If such a jury is unable to so ascertain, it shall find and certify accordingly.

History of CCP art. 50.03: Acts 1965, 59th Leg., vol. 2, ch. 722. Amended by Acts 1973, 63rd Leg., ch. 399, §2(A), eff. Jan. 1, 1974.

ART. 50.04. WITNESSES BOUND OVER

If the jury finds that any building has been unlawfully set on fire or has been attempted so to be, the justice holding such inquest shall bind over the witnesses to appear and testify before the next grand jury of the county in which such offense was committed.

History of CCP art. 50.04: Acts 1965, 59th Leg., vol. 2, ch. 722.

ART. 50.05. WARRANT FOR ACCUSED

If the person charged with the offense, if any, be not in custody, the justice of the peace shall issue a warrant for his arrest, and when arrested, such person shall be dealt with as in other like cases.

History of CCP art. 50.05: Acts 1965, 59th Leg., vol. 2, ch. 722.

ART. 50.06. TESTIMONY WRITTEN DOWN

In all such investigations, the testimony of all witnesses examined before the jury shall be reduced to writing by or under the direction of the justice and signed by each witness. Such testimony together with the verdict and all bail bonds taken in the case shall be certified to and returned by the justice to the next district or criminal district court of his county.

History of CCP art. 50.06: Acts 1965, 59th Leg., vol. 2, ch. 722.

ART. 50.07. COMPENSATION

The pay of the officers and jury making such investigation shall be the same as that allowed for the holding of an inquest upon a dead body, so far as applicable, and shall be paid in like manner.

History of CCP art. 50.07: Acts 1965, 59th Leg., vol. 2, ch. 722.

CHAPTER 51. FUGITIVES FROM JUSTICE

ART. 51.01. DELIVERED UP

A person in any other State of the United States charged with treason or any felony who shall flee from justice and be found in this State, shall on demand of the executive authority of the State from which he fled, be delivered up, to be removed to the State having jurisdiction of the crime.

History of CCP art. 51.01: Acts 1965, 59th Leg., vol. 2, ch. 722.

ART. 51.02. TO AID IN ARREST

All peace officers of the State shall give aid in the arrest and detention of a fugitive from any other State that he may be held subject to a requisition by the Governor of the State from which he fled.

History of CCP art. 51.02: Acts 1965, 59th Leg., vol. 2, ch. 722.

ART. 51.03. MAGISTRATE'S WARRANT

When a complaint is made to a magistrate that any person within his jurisdiction is a fugitive from justice from another State, he shall issue a warrant of arrest directing a peace officer to apprehend and bring the accused before him.

History of CCP art. 51.03: Acts 1965, 59th Leg., vol. 2, ch. 722.

ART. 51.04. COMPLAINT

The complaint shall be sufficient if it recites:

1. The name of the person accused;

2. The State from which he has fled;

3. The offense committed by the accused;

4. That he has fled to this State from the State where the offense was committed; and

5. That the act alleged to have been committed by the accused is a violation of the penal law of the State from which he fled.

History of CCP art. 51.04: Acts 1965, 59th Leg., vol. 2, ch. 722.

ANNOTATIONS

Myer v. State, 686 S.W.2d 735, 738 (Tex.App.—San Antonio 1985, pet. ref'd). "Unless the accusation against the appellant is clearly void, the question of its validity is for the demanding state."

ART. 51.05. BAIL OR COMMITMENT

When the accused is brought before the magistrate, he shall hear proof, and if satisfied that the accused is charged in another State with the offense named in the complaint, he shall require of him bail with sufficient security, in such amount as the magistrate deems reasonable, to appear before such magistrate at a specified time. In default of such bail, he may commit the defendant to jail to await a requisition from the Governor of the State from which he fled. A properly certified transcript of an indictment against the accused is sufficient to show that he is charged with the crime alleged. One arrested under the provisions of this title shall not be committed or held to bail for a longer time than ninety days.

History of CCP art. 51.05: Acts 1965, 59th Leg., vol. 2, ch. 722.

ART. 51.06. NOTICE OF ARREST

The magistrate who held or committed such fugitive shall immediately notify the Secretary of State and the district or county attorney of his county of such fact and the date thereof, stating the name of such fugitive, the State from which he fled, and the crime with which he is charged; and such officers so notified shall in turn notify the Governor of the proper State.

History of CCP art. 51.06: Acts 1965, 59th Leg., vol. 2, ch. 722.

ART. 51.07. DISCHARGE

A fugitive not arrested under a warrant from the Governor of this State before the expiration of ninety days from the day of his commitment or the date of the bail shall be discharged.

History of CCP art. 51.07: Acts 1965, 59th Leg., vol. 2, ch. 722.

ART. 51.08. SECOND ARREST

A person who has once been arrested under the provisions of this title and discharged under the provisions of the preceding Article or by habeas corpus shall not be again arrested upon a charge of the same offense, except by a warrant from the Governor of this State.

History of CCP art. 51.08: Acts 1965, 59th Leg., vol. 2, ch. 722.

ART. 51.09. GOVERNOR MAY DEMAND FUGITIVE

When the Governor deems it proper to demand a person who has committed an offense in this State and has fled to another State, he may commission any suitable person to take such requisition. The accused, if brought back to the State, shall be delivered up to the sheriff of the county in which it is alleged he has committed the offense.

History of CCP art. 51.09: Acts 1965, 59th Leg., vol. 2, ch. 722.

ART. 51.10. PAY OF AGENT; TRAVELING EXPENSES

Sec. 1. The officer or person so commissioned shall receive as compensation the actual and necessary traveling expenses upon requisition of the Governor to be allowed by such Governor and to be paid out of the State Treasury upon a certificate of the Governor reciting the services rendered and the allowance therefor.

Sec. 2. The commissioners court of the county where an offense is committed may in its discretion, on the request of the sheriff and the recommendation of the district attorney, pay the actual and necessary traveling expenses of the officer or person so commissioned out of any fund or funds not otherwise pledged.

History of CCP art. 51.10: Acts 1965, 59th Leg., vol. 2, ch. 722.

ART. 51.11. REWARD

The Governor may offer a reward for the apprehension of one accused of a felony in this State who is evading arrest, by causing such offer to be published in such manner as he deems most likely to effect the arrest. The reward shall be paid out of the State Treasury to the person who becomes entitled to it upon a certificate of the Governor reciting the facts which entitle such person to receive it.

History of CCP art. 51.11: Acts 1965, 59th Leg., vol. 2, ch. 722.

ART. 51.12. SHERIFF TO REPORT

Each sheriff upon the close of any regular term of the district or criminal district court in his county, or within thirty days thereafter, shall make out and mail to the Director of the Department of Public Safety a certified list of all persons, who, after indictment for a felony, have fled from said county. Such lists shall contain the full name of each such fugitive, the offense with which he is charged, and a description giving his age, height, weight, color and occupation, the complexion of the skin and the color of eyes and hair, and any peculiarity in person, speech, manner or gait that may serve to identify such person so far as the sheriff may be able to give them. The Director of the Department of Public Safety shall prescribe and forward to all sheriffs the necessary blanks upon which are to be made the lists herein required.

History of CCP art. 51.12: Acts 1965, 59th Leg., vol. 2, ch. 722.

ART. 51.13. UNIFORM CRIMINAL EXTRADITION ACT

§1. Definitions

Where appearing in this Article, the term "Governor" includes any person performing the functions of Governor by authority of the laws of this State. The term "Executive Authority" includes the Governor, and any person performing the functions of Governor in a State other than this State, and the term "State", referring to a State other than this State, includes any other State organized or unorganized of the United States of America.

§2. Fugitives from Justice; Duty of Governor

Subject to the provisions of this Article, the provisions of the Constitution of the United States controlling, and any and all Acts of Congress enacted in pursuance thereof, it is the duty of the Governor of this State to have arrested and delivered up to the Executive Authority of any other State of the United States any person charged in that State with treason, felony, or other crime, who has fled from justice and is found in this State.

§3. Form of Demand

No demand for the extradition of a person charged with crime in another State shall be recognized by the Governor unless in writing, alleging, except in cases arising under Section 6, that the accused was present in the demanding State at the time of the commission of the alleged crime, and that thereafter he fled from the State, and accompanied by a copy of an indictment found or by information supported by affidavit in the State having jurisdiction of the crime, or by a copy of an affidavit before a magistrate there, together with a copy of any warrant which issued thereupon; or by a copy of a judgment of conviction or of a sentence imposed in execution thereof, together with a statement by the Executive Authority of the demanding State that the person claimed has escaped from confinement or has broken the terms of his bail, probation or parole. The indictment, information, or affidavit made before the magistrate must substantially charge the person demanded with having committed a crime under the law of that State; and the copy of indictment, information, affidavit, judgment of conviction or sentence must be authenticated by the Executive Authority making the demand; provided, however, that all such copies of the aforesaid instruments shall be in duplicate, one complete set of such instruments to be delivered to the defendant or to his attorney.

§4. Governor May Investigate Case

When a demand shall be made upon the Governor of this State by the Executive Authority of another State for the surrender of a person so charged with crime, the Governor may call upon the Secretary of State, Attorney General or any prosecuting officer in this State to investigate or assist in investigating the demand, and to report to him the situation and circumstances of the person so demanded, and whether he ought to be surrendered.

§5. Extradition of Persons Imprisoned or Awaiting Trial in Another State or Who Have Left the Demanding State Under Compulsion

When it is desired to have returned to this State a person charged in this State with a crime, and such person is imprisoned or is held under criminal proceedings then pending against him in another State, the Governor of this State may agree with the Executive Authority of such other State for the extradition of such person before the conclusion of such proceedings or his term of sentence in such other State, upon condition that such person be returned to such other State at the expense of this State as soon as the prosecution in this State is terminated.

The Governor of this State may also surrender on demand of the Executive Authority of any other State any person in this State who is charged in the manner provided in Section 23 of this Act with having violated the laws of the State whose Executive Authority is making the demand, even though such person left the demanding State involuntarily.

§6. Extradition of Persons Not Present in Demanding State at Time of Commission of Crime

The Governor of this State may also surrender, on demand of the Executive Authority of any other State, any person in this State charged in such other State in the manner provided in Section 3 with committing an act in this State, or in a third State, intentionally resulting in a crime in the State whose Executive Authority is making the demand, and the provisions of this Article not otherwise inconsistent, shall apply to such cases, even though the accused was not in that State at the time of the commission of the crime, and has not fled therefrom.

§7. Issue of Governor's Warrant of Arrest; Its Recitals

If the Governor decides that the demand should be complied with, he shall sign a warrant of arrest, which shall be sealed with the state seal and be directed to any peace officer or other person whom he may think fit to entrust with the execution thereof. The warrant must substantially recite the facts necessary to the validity of its issuance.

§8. Manner & Place of Execution

Such warrant shall authorize the peace officer or other person to whom directed to arrest the accused at any time and any place where he may be found within the State and to command the aid of all peace officers and other persons in the execution of the warrant, and to deliver the accused, subject to the provisions of this Article to the duly authorized agent of the demanding State.

§9. Authority of Arresting Officer

Every such peace officer or other person empowered to make the arrest, shall have the same authority, in arresting the accused, to command assistance therein, as peace officers have by law in the execution of any criminal process directed to them, with like penalties against those who refuse their assistance.

§10. Rights of Accused Person; Application for Writ of Habeas Corpus

No person arrested upon such warrant shall be delivered over to the agent whom the Executive Authority demanding him shall have appointed to receive him unless he shall first be taken forthwith before a judge of a court of record in this State, who shall inform him of the demand made for his surrender and of the crime with which he is charged, and that he has the right to demand and procure legal counsel; and if the prisoner or his counsel shall state that he or they desire to test the legality of his arrest, the judge of such court of record shall fix a reasonable time to be allowed him within which to apply for a writ of habeas corpus. When such a writ is applied for, notice thereof, and of the time and place of hearing thereon, shall be given to the prosecuting officer of the county in which the arrest is made and in which the accused is in custody, and to the said agent of the demanding State.

§11. Penalty for Non-Compliance with Preceding Section

Any officer who shall deliver to the agent for extradition of the demanding State a person in his custody under the Governor's warrant, in wilful disobedience to Section 10 of this Act, shall be guilty of a misdemeanor and, on conviction, shall be fined not more than one thousand dollars or be imprisoned not more than six months, or both.

§12. Confinement in Jail, When Necessary

The officer or persons executing the Governor's warrant of arrest, or the agent of the demanding State to whom the prisoner may have been delivered may, when necessary, confine the prisoner in the jail of any county or city through which he may pass; and the keeper of such jail must receive and safely keep the prisoner until the officer or person having charge of him is ready to proceed on his route, such officer or person being chargeable with the expense of keeping.

The officer or agent of a demanding State to whom a prisoner may have been delivered following extradition proceedings in another State, or to whom a prisoner may have been delivered after waiving extradition in such other State, and who is passing through this State with such a prisoner for the purpose of immediately returning such prisoner to the demanding State may, when necessary, confine the prisoner in the jail of any county or city through which he may pass; and the keeper of such jail must receive and safely keep the prisoner until the officer or agent having charge of him is ready to proceed on his route, such officer or agent, however, being chargeable with the expense of keeping; provided, however, that such officer or agent shall produce and show to the keeper of such jail satisfactory written evidence of the fact that he is actually transporting such prisoner to the demanding State after a requisition by the Executive Authority of such demanding State. Such prisoner shall not be entitled to demand a new requisition while in this State.

§13. Arrest Prior to Requisition

Whenever any person within this State shall be charged on the oath of any credible person before any judge or magistrate of this State with the commission of any crime in any other State and except in cases arising under Section 6, with having fled from justice, or with having been convicted of a crime in that State and having escaped from confinement, or having broken the terms of his bail, probation or parole, or whenever complaint shall have been made before any judge or magistrate in this State setting forth on the affidavit of any credible person in another State that a crime has been committed in such other State and that the accused has been charged in such State with the commission of the crime, and except in cases arising under Section 6, has fled from justice, or with having been convicted of a crime in that State and having escaped from confinement, or having broken the terms of his bail, probation or parole and is believed to be in this State, the judge or magistrate shall issue a warrant directed to any peace officer commanding him to apprehend the person named therein, wherever he may be found in this State, and to bring him before the same or any other judge, magistrate or court who or which may be available in or convenient of access to the place where the arrest may be made, to answer the charge or complaint and affidavit, and a certified copy of the sworn charge or complaint and affidavit upon which the warrant is issued shall be attached to the warrant.

§14. Arrest Without a Warrant

The arrest of a person may be lawfully made also by any peace officer or private person, without a warrant upon reasonable information that the accused stands charged in the courts of a State with a crime punishable by death or imprisonment for a term exceeding one year, but when so arrested the accused must be taken before a judge or magistrate with all practicable speed and complaint must be made against him under oath setting forth the ground for the arrest as in the preceding section; and thereafter his answer shall be heard as if he had been arrested on a warrant.

§15. Commitment to Await Requisition; Bail

If from the examination before the judge or magistrate it appears that the person held is the person charged with having committed the crime alleged and except in cases arising under Section 6, that he has fled from justice, the judge or magistrate must, by warrant reciting the accusation, commit him to the county jail for such time not exceeding thirty days and specified in the warrant, as will enable the arrest of the accused to be made under a warrant of the Governor on a requisition of the Executive Authority of the State having jurisdiction of the offense, unless the accused give bail as provided in the next section, or until he shall be legally discharged.

§16. Bail; In What Cases; Conditions of Bond

Unless the offense with which the prisoner is charged is shown to be an offense punishable by death or life imprisonment under the laws of the State in which it was committed, a judge or magistrate in this State may admit the person arrested to bail by bond, with sufficient sureties and in such sum as he deems proper, conditioned for his appearance before him at a time specified in such bond, and for his surrender, to be arrested upon the warrant of the Governor in this State.

§17. Extension of Time of Commitment; Adjournment

If the accused is not arrested under warrant of the Governor by the expiration of the time specified in the warrant or bond, a judge or magistrate may discharge him or may recommit him for a further period not to exceed sixty days, or a judge or magistrate may again take bail for his appearance and surrender, as provided in Section 16, but within a period not to exceed sixty days after the date of such new bond.

§18. Forfeiture of Bail

If the prisoner is admitted to bail and fails to appear and surrender himself according to the conditions of his bond, the judge, or magistrate by proper order, shall declare the bond forfeited and order his immediate arrest without warrant if he be within this State. Recovery may be had on such bond in the name of the State as in the case of other bonds given by the accused in criminal proceedings within this State.

§19. Persons Under Criminal Prosecution in This State at the Time of Requisition

If a criminal prosecution has been instituted against such person under the laws of this State and is still pending, the Governor, in his discretion, either may surrender him on demand of the Executive Authority of another State or hold him until he has been tried and discharged or convicted and punished in this State.

§20. Guilt or Innocence of Accused, When Inquired Into

The guilt or innocence of the accused as to the crime of which he is charged may not be inquired into by the Governor or in any proceeding after the demand for extradition accompanied by a charge of crime in legal form as above provided shall have been presented to the Governor, except as it may be involved in identifying the person held as the person charged with the crime.

§21. Governor May Recall Warrant or Issue Alias

The governor may recall his warrant of the arrest or may issue another warrant whenever he deems proper. Each warrant issued by the Governor shall expire and be of no force and effect when not executed within one year from the date thereof.

§22. Fugitives from This State; Duty of Governor

Whenever the Governor of this State shall demand a person charged with crime or with escaping from confinement or breaking the terms of his bail, probation or parole in this State, from the Executive Authority of any other State, or from the Chief Justice or an Associate Justice of the Supreme Court of the District of Columbia authorized to receive such demand under the laws of the United States, he shall issue a warrant under the state seal, to some agent, commanding him to receive the person so charged if delivered to him and convey him to the proper officer of the county in this State in which the offense was committed, or in which the prosecution for such offense is then pending.

§23. Application for Issuance of Requisition; by Whom Made; Contents

1. When the return to this State of a person charged with crime in this State is required, the State's attorney shall present to the Governor his written motion for a requisition for the return of the person charged, in which motion shall be stated the name of the person so charged, the crime charged against him, the approximate time, place and circumstances of its commission, the State in which he is believed to be, including the location of the accused therein at the time the motion is made and certifying that, in the opinion of the said State's attorney the ends of justice require the arrest and return of the accused to this State for trial and that the proceeding is not instituted to enforce a private claim.

2. When the return to this State is required of a person who has been convicted of a crime in this State

and has escaped from confinement, or broken the terms of his bail, probation or parole, the prosecuting attorney of the county in which the offense was committed, the parole board, or the warden of the institution or sheriff of the county, from which escape was made, shall present to the Governor a written application for a requisition for the return of such person, in which application shall be stated the name of the person, the crime of which he was convicted, the circumstances of his escape from confinement, or the circumstances of the breach of the terms of his bail, probation or parole, the State in which he is believed to be, including the location of the person therein at the time application is made.

3. The application shall be verified by affidavit, shall be executed in duplicate and shall be accompanied by two certified copies of the indictment returned, or information and affidavit filed, or of the complaint made to the judge or magistrate, stating the offense with which the accused is charged, or of the judgment of conviction or of the sentence. The prosecuting officer, parole board, warden or sheriff may also attach such further affidavits and other documents in duplicate as he shall deem proper to be submitted with such application. One copy of the application, with the action of the Governor indicated by endorsement thereon, and one of the certified copies of the indictment, complaint, information, and affidavits, or of the judgment of conviction or of the sentence shall be filed in the office of the Governor. The other copies of all papers shall be forwarded with the Governor's requisition.

§24. Costs & Expenses

In all cases of extradition, the commissioners court of the county where an offense is alleged to have been committed, or in which the prosecution is then pending may in its discretion, on request of the sheriff and the recommendation of the prosecuting attorney, pay the actual and necessary expenses of the officer or person commissioned to receive the person charged, out of any county fund or funds not otherwise pledged.

§25. Immunity from Service of Process in Certain Civil Cases

A person brought into this State by, or after waiver of, extradition based on a criminal charge shall not be subject to service of personal process in civil actions arising out of the same facts as the criminal proceeding to answer which he is being or has been returned, until he has been convicted in the criminal proceeding, or if acquitted, until he has had reasonable opportunity to return to the State from which he was extradited.

§25a. Written Waiver of Extradition Proceedings

Any person arrested in this State charged with having committed any crime in another State or alleged to have escaped from confinement, or broken the terms of his bail, probation, or parole may waive the issuance and service of the warrant provided for in Sections 7 and 8 and all other procedure incidental to extradition proceedings, by executing or subscribing in the presence of a judge or any court of record within this State a writing which states that he consents to return to the demanding State; provided, however, that before such waiver shall be executed or subscribed by such person it shall be the duty of such judge to inform such person of his rights to the issuance and service of a warrant of extradition and to obtain a writ of habeas corpus as provided for in Section 10.

If and when such consent has been duly executed it shall forthwith be forwarded to the office of the Governor of this State and filed therein. The judge shall direct the officer having such person in custody to deliver forthwith such person to the duly accredited agent or agents of the demanding State, and shall deliver or cause to be delivered to such agent or agents a copy of such consent; provided, however, that nothing in this section shall be deemed to limit the rights of the accused person to return voluntarily and without formality to the demanding State, nor shall this waiver procedure be deemed to be an exclusive procedure or to limit the powers, rights or duties of the officers of the demanding State or of this State.

§25b. Non-waiver by This State

Nothing in this Act contained shall be deemed to constitute a waiver by this State of its right, power or privilege to try such demanded person for crime committed within this State, or of its right, power or privilege to regain custody of such person by extradition proceedings or otherwise for the purpose of trial, sentence or punishment for any crime committed within this State, nor shall any proceedings had under this Article which result, or fail to result in, extradition to be deemed a waiver by this State of any of its rights, privileges or jurisdiction in any way whatsoever.

§26. No Right of Asylum, No Immunity from Other Criminal Prosecutions While in This State

After a person has been brought back to this State by, or after waiver of extradition proceedings, he may be tried in this State for other crimes which he may be charged with having committed here as well as that specified in the requisition for his extradition.

§27. Interpretation

The provisions of this Article shall be interpreted and construed as to effectuate its general purposes to make uniform the law of those States which enact it.

History of CCP art. 51.13: Acts 1965, 59th Leg., vol. 2, ch. 722. Amended by Acts 1993, 73rd Leg., ch. 300, §27, eff. Aug. 30, 1993; Acts 1997, 75th Leg., ch. 701, §1, eff. Sept. 1, 1997.

ANNOTATIONS

Generally

Ex parte Stacey, 709 S.W.2d 185, 188 n.2 (Tex. Crim.App.1986). "The only vehicle for testing legality of an arrest and detainment pursuant to a Governor's warrant is filing of an application for writ of habeas corpus."

Art. 51.13, §3

Ex parte Mason, 656 S.W.2d 470, 471 (Tex.Crim. App.1983). "Although a prima facie case may be established by the introduction of the Governor's Warrant regular on its face, such prima facie case may be defeated by the supporting papers. [¶] Because the statutory requirements for the supporting papers are disjunctive, it is not necessary all the instruments listed in Art. 51.13, §3 accompany the demand for extradition. The letter of the statute is satisfied if at least one of the listed instruments accompany the demand."

Ex parte Sanchez, 642 S.W.2d 809, 811 (Tex.Crim. App.1982). A "person whose extradition is sought may cause a judicial inquiry into the legality of his detention under the governor's warrant."

Ex parte Cain, 592 S.W.2d 359, 362 (Tex.Crim.App. 1980). A "defendant or his attorney is entitled to duplicate copies of the papers supporting extradition. A failure to furnish such papers upon request is reversible error."

Art. 51.13, §4

Ex parte Wammack, 482 S.W.2d 859, 860 (Tex. Crim.App.1972). "[T]he failure to notify the accused of an executive hearing on an extradition demand is not a ground upon which the discharge of the accused may be predicated."

Art. 51.13, §7

Ex parte Harrison, 568 S.W.2d 339, 344 (Tex.Crim. App.1978). "The fact that the warrant [of the Governor of Texas] refers to appellant as a 'fugitive' after clearly setting forth that the acts complained of occurred in Texas does not render the warrant void. We will treat and disregard such description as surplusage and find that such error, if any, in referring to appellant as a fugitive is harmless."

Art. 51.13, §10

Ex parte Potter, 21 S.W.3d 290, 294 (Tex.Crim.App. 2000). "[I]ndigents are entitled to appointed counsel in [an extradition proceeding], despite the absence of an express provision in the Extradition Act providing for such appointment. *At 296:* [T]o give effect to a petitioner's right to counsel and his right to test the legality of his arrest in the extradition context, he must be sufficiently competent to consult with his counsel. *At 297:* [I]n the context of extradition proceedings, due process requires that the alleged fugitive has sufficient mental competency to consult with and assist his attorney on the issues of identity and presence."

Wray v. State, 624 S.W.2d 573, 575 (Tex.Crim.App. 1981). "'Once the governor has granted extradition, a court considering release on habeas corpus can do no more than decide (a) whether the extradition documents on their face are in order; (b) whether the petitioner has been charged with a crime in the demanding state; (c) whether the petitioner is the person named in the request for extradition; and (d) whether the petitioner is a fugitive.'"

Ex parte Chapman, 601 S.W.2d 380, 383 (Tex. Crim.App.1980). "The judge makes no judicial determination whatsoever in [a §10] proceeding. ... 'It matters not what positions the litigants took at the hearing, the fact remains that the law guarantees that a citizen shall not be sent to a foreign State for trial until the following steps have been taken...: (1) The Governor of this State shall issue a warrant which orders him delivered to the agent of the demanding State, (2) *He shall be given an opportunity to apply for a writ of habeas corpus*, and (3) He shall be given an opportunity to appeal to this Court from an adverse ruling in the trial court.'"

Ex parte Sullivan, 534 S.W.2d 140, 141 (Tex.Crim. App.1976). "[T]he county court does not have jurisdiction to hold a habeas corpus hearing on extradition in a felony case."

Art. 51.13, §14

Morales v. State, 513 S.W.2d 869, 870 (Tex.Crim. App.1974). "[I]t is not necessary that a requisition from the demanding state be issued prior to the arrest."

Art. 51.13, §25a

Ex parte Medieros, 552 S.W.2d 156, 158 (Tex.Crim. App.1977). "[A]ppellant contends that the waiver is ineffective unless he receives the advice of counsel prior to the waiver. We do not agree with this contention. [¶] [T]he judge, not counsel, is to advise the individual of the rights afforded him before accepting or allowing a waiver of such rights."

ART. 51.14. INTERSTATE AGREEMENT ON DETAINERS

This article may be cited as the "Interstate Agreement on Detainers Act." This agreement on detainers is hereby enacted into law and entered into by this state with all other jurisdictions legally joined therein in the form substantially as follows:

The contracting states solemnly agree that:

Art. I.

The party states find that charges outstanding against a prisoner, detainers based on untried indictments, informations, or complaints, and difficulties in securing speedy trial of persons already incarcerated in other jurisdictions, produce uncertainties which obstruct programs of prisoner treatment and rehabilitation. Accordingly, it is the policy of the party states and the purpose of this agreement to encourage the expeditious and orderly disposition of such charges and determination of the proper status of any and all detainers based on untried indictments, informations, or complaints. The party states also find that proceedings with reference to such charges and detainers, when emanating from another jurisdiction, cannot properly be had in the absence of cooperative procedures. It is the further purpose of this agreement to provide such cooperative procedures.

Art. II.

As used is this agreement:

(a) "State" shall mean a state of the United States; the United States of America; a territory or possession of the United States; the District of Columbia; the Commonwealth of Puerto Rico.

(b) "Sending state" shall mean a state in which a prisoner is incarcerated at the time that he initiates a request for final disposition pursuant to Article III hereof or at the time that a request for custody or availability is initiated pursuant to Article IV hereof.

Art. III.

(a) Whenever a person has entered upon a term of imprisonment in a penal or correctional institution of a party state, and whenever during the continuance of the term of imprisonment there is pending in any other party state any untried indictment, information, or complaint on the basis of which a detainer has been lodged against the prisoner, he shall be brought to trial within 180 days after he shall have caused to be delivered to the prosecuting officer and the appropriate court of the prosecuting officer's jurisdiction written notice of the place of his imprisonment and his request for a final disposition to be made of the indictment, information, or complaint; provided that for good cause shown in open court, the prisoner or his counsel being present, the court having jurisdiction of the matter may grant any necessary or reasonable continuance. The request of the prisoner shall be accompanied by a certificate of the appropriate official having custody of the prisoner, stating the term of commitment under which the prisoner is being held, the time already served, the time remaining to be served on the sentence, the amount of good time earned, the time of parole eligibility of the prisoner, and any decision of the state parole agency relating to the prisoner.

(b) The written notice and request for final disposition referred to in Paragraph (a) hereof shall be given or sent by the prisoner to the warden, commissioner of corrections, or other official having custody of him, who shall promptly forward it together with the certificate to the appropriate prosecuting official and court by registered or certified mail, return receipt requested.

(c) The warden, commissioner of corrections, or other official having custody of the prisoner shall promptly inform him of the source and contents of any detainer lodged against him and shall also inform him of his right to make a request for final disposition of the indictment, information, or complaint on which the detainer is based.

(d) Any request for final disposition made by a prisoner pursuant to Paragraph (a) hereof shall operate as a request for final disposition of all untried indictments, informations, or complaints on the basis of which detainers have been lodged against the prisoner from the state to whose prosecuting official the request for final disposition is specifically directed. The warden, commissioner of corrections, or other official having custody of the prisoner shall forthwith notify all appropriate prosecuting officers and courts in the several jurisdictions within the state to which the prisoner's request for final disposition is being sent of the proceeding being initiated by the prisoner. Any notification sent pursuant to this paragraph shall be accompanied by copies of the prisoner's written notice, request, and the certificate. If trial is not had on any indictment, information, or complaint contemplated hereby prior to the return of the prisoner to the original place of imprisonment, such indictment, information, or complaint shall not be of any further force or effect, and the court shall enter an order dismissing the same with prejudice.

(e) Any request for final disposition made by a prisoner pursuant to Paragraph (a) hereof shall also be deemed to be a waiver of extradition with respect to any charge or proceeding contemplated thereby or included therein by reason of Paragraph (d) hereof, and a waiver of extradition to the receiving state to serve any sentence there imposed upon him after completion of his term of imprisonment in the sending state. The request for final disposition shall also constitute a consent by the prisoner to the production of his body in any court where his presence may be required in order to effectuate the purposes of this agreement and a further consent voluntarily to be returned to the original place of imprisonment in accordance with the provisions of this agreement. Nothing in this paragraph shall prevent the imposition of a concurrent sentence if otherwise permitted by law.

(f) Escape from custody by the prisoner subsequent to his execution of the request for final disposition referred to in Paragraph (a) hereof shall void the request.

Art. IV.

(a) The appropriate officer of the jurisdiction in which an untried indictment, information, or complaint is pending shall be entitled to have a prisoner against whom he has lodged a detainer and who is serving a term of imprisonment in any party state made available in accordance with Paragraph (a) of Article V hereof upon presentation of a written request for temporary custody or availability to the appropriate authorities of the state in which the prisoner is incarcerated; provided that the court having jurisdiction of such indictment, information, or complaint shall have duly approved, recorded, and transmitted the request; and provided further that there shall be a period of 30 days after receipt by the appropriate authorities before the request be honored, within which period the governor of the sending state may disapprove the request for temporary custody or availability, either upon his own motion or upon motion of the prisoner.

(b) Upon receipt of the officer's written request as provided in Paragraph (a) hereof, the appropriate authorities having the prisoner in custody shall furnish the officer with a certificate stating the term of commitment under which the prisoner is being held, the time already served, the time remaining to be served on the sentence, the amount of good time earned, the time of parole eligibility of the prisoner, and any decisions of the state parole agency relating to the prisoner. Said authorities simultaneously shall furnish all other officers and appropriate courts in the receiving state who have lodged detainers against the prisoner with similar certificates and with notices informing them of the request for custody or availability and of the reasons therefor.

(c) In respect of any proceeding made possible by this article, trial shall be commenced within 120 days of the arrival of the prisoner in the receiving state, but for good cause shown in open court, the prisoner or his counsel being present, the court having jurisdiction of the matter may grant any necessary or reasonable continuance.

(d) Nothing contained in this article shall be construed to deprive any prisoner of any right which he may have to contest the legality of his delivery as provided in Paragraph (a) hereof, but such delivery may not be opposed or denied on the ground that the executing authority of the sending state has not affirmatively consented to or ordered such delivery.

(e) If trial is not had on any indictment, information, or complaint contemplated hereby prior to the prisoner's being returned to the original place of imprisonment pursuant to Paragraph (e) of Article V hereof, such indictment, information, or complaint shall not be of any further force or effect, and the court shall enter an order dismissing the same with prejudice.

Art. V.

(a) In response to a request made under Article III or Article IV hereof, the appropriate authority in a sending state shall offer to deliver temporary custody of such prisoner to the appropriate authority in the state where such indictment, information, or complaint is pending against such person in order that speedy and efficient prosecution may be had. If the request for final disposition is made by the prisoner, the offer of temporary custody shall accompany the written notice provided for in Article III of this agreement. In the case of a federal prisoner, the appropriate authority in the receiving state shall be entitled to temporary custody as provided by this agreement or to the prisoner's presence in federal custody at the place of trial, whichever custodial arrangement may be approved by the custodian.

(b) The officer or other representative of a state accepting an offer of temporary custody shall present the following upon demand:

(1) proper identification and evidence of his authority to act for the state into whose temporary custody this prisoner is to be given;

(2) a duly certified copy of the indictment, information, or complaint on the basis of which the detainer has been lodged and on the basis of which the request for temporary custody of the prisoner has been made.

(c) If the appropriate authority shall refuse or fail to accept temporary custody of said person, or in the event that an action on the indictment, information, or complaint on the basis of which the detainer has been lodged is not brought to trial within the period provided in Article III or Article IV hereof, the appropriate court of the jurisdiction where the indictment, information, or complaint has been pending shall enter an order dismissing the same with prejudice, and any detainer based thereon shall cease to be of any force or effect.

(d) The temporary custody referred to in this agreement shall be only for the purpose of permitting prosecution on the charge or charges contained in one or more untried indictments, informations, or complaints which form the basis of the detainer or detainers or for prosecution on any other charge or charges arising out of the same transaction. Except for his attendance at court and while being transported to or from any place at which his presence may be required, the prisoner shall be held in a suitable jail or other facility regularly used for persons awaiting prosecution.

(e) At the earliest practicable time consonant with the purposes of this agreement, the prisoner shall be returned to the sending state.

(f) During the continuance of temporary custody or while the prisoner is otherwise being made available for trial as required by this agreement, time being served on the sentence shall continue to run but good time shall be earned by the prisoner only if, and to the extent that, the law and practice of the jurisdiction which imposed the sentence may allow.

(g) For all purposes other than that for which temporary custody as provided in this agreement is exercised, the prisoner shall be deemed to remain in the custody of and subject to the jurisdiction of the sending state and any escape from temporary custody may be dealt with in the same manner as an escape from the original place of imprisonment or in any other manner permitted by law.

(h) From the time that a party state receives custody of a prisoner pursuant to this agreement until such prisoner is returned to the territory and custody of the sending state, the state in which the one or more untried indictments, informations, or complaints are pending or in which trial is being had shall be responsible for the prisoner and shall also pay all costs of transporting, caring for, keeping, and returning the prisoner. The provisions of this paragraph shall govern unless the states concerned shall have entered into a supplementary agreement providing for a different allocation of costs and responsibilities as between or among themselves. Nothing herein contained shall be construed to alter or affect any internal relationship among the departments, agencies, and officers of and in the government of a party state, or between a party state and its subdivisions, as to the payment of costs, or responsibilities therefor.

Art. VI.

(a) In determining the duration and expiration dates of the time periods provided in Articles III and IV of this agreement, the running of said time periods shall be tolled whenever and for as long as the prisoner is unable to stand trial, as determined by the court having jurisdiction of the matter.

(b) No provision of this agreement, and no remedy made available by this agreement shall apply to any person who is adjudged to be mentally ill.

Art. VII.

Each state party to this agreement shall designate an officer who, acting jointly with like officers of other party states, shall promulgate rules and regulations to carry out more effectively the terms and provisions of this agreement, and who shall provide, within and without the state, information necessary to the effective operation of this agreement.

Art. VIII.

This agreement shall enter into full force and effect as to a party state when such state has enacted the same into law. A state party to this agreement may withdraw herefrom by enacting a statute repealing the same. However, the withdrawal of any state shall not affect the status of any proceedings already initiated by inmates or by state officers at the time such withdrawal takes effect, nor shall it affect their rights in respect thereof.

Art. IX.

(a) This agreement shall be liberally construed so as to effectuate its purposes. The provisions of this agreement shall be severable and if any phrase, clause, sentence, or provision of this agreement is declared to be contrary to the constitution of any party state or of the United States or the applicability thereof to any government, agency, person, or circumstance is held invalid, the validity of the remainder of this agreement and the applicability thereof to any government, agency, person, or circumstance shall not be affected thereby. If this agreement shall be held contrary to the constitution of any state party hereto, the agreement shall remain in full force and effect as to the remaining states and in full force and effect as to the state affected as to all severable matters.

(b) As used in this article, "appropriate court" means a court of record with criminal jurisdiction.

(c) All courts, departments, agencies, officers, and employees of this state and its political subdivisions are hereby directed to enforce this article and to cooperate with one another and with other party states in enforcing the agreement and effectuating its purpose.

(d) Any prisoner escapes from lawful custody while in another state as a result of the application of this article shall be punished as though such escape had occurred within this state.

(e) The governor is empowered to designate the officer who will serve as central administrator of and information agent for the agreement on detainers pursuant to the provisions of Article VII hereof.

(f) Copies of this article, upon its enactment, shall be transmitted to the governor of each state, the Attorney General and the Secretary of State of the United States, and the council of state governments.

History of CCP art. 51.14: Acts 1975, 64th Leg., ch. 343, §1, eff. June 19, 1975.

ANNOTATIONS

Art. 51.14: I

Giles v. State, 908 S.W.2d 303, 305 (Tex.App.—El Paso 1995), *pet. ref'd*, 921 S.W.2d 235 (Tex.Crim.App. 1996). "The IADA establishes a uniform set of procedures for temporarily transferring a prisoner incarcerated in one jurisdiction to the custody of another jurisdiction so that criminal charges pending in the receiving jurisdiction may be resolved."

Art. 51.14: III

Walker v. State, 201 S.W.3d 841, 846 (Tex.App.—Waco 2006, pet. ref'd). "The prisoner bears the burden of demonstrating compliance with the procedural requirements of article III. The prisoner may comply by either: (1) delivering his IAD transfer request to the warden where he is imprisoned to be forwarded to the court and prosecuting attorney of the state which lodged the detainer against him; or (2) delivering his transfer request directly to the court and prosecuting attorney of that state. [¶] If the prisoner delivers the transfer request to the warden where he is incarcerated for forwarding, then the prisoner's 'only obligation [i]s to show that he notified the appropriate [prison] officials of his desire to [be transferred].' Conversely, if the prisoner decides to deliver his transfer request directly to the court and prosecuting attorney of the other state, he is personally responsible to see that the notice is sent by registered or certified mail, return receipt requested, to those authorities."

State v. Miles, 101 S.W.3d 180, 183 (Tex.App.—Dallas 2003, no pet.). "The provisions of article III apply only when a 'detainer' has first been 'lodged against the prisoner' with the custodial jurisdiction. [A] 'detainer' [is] 'a request filed by a criminal justice agency with the institution in which a prisoner is incarcerated, asking that the prisoner be held for the agency, or that the agency be advised when the prisoner's release is imminent.' *At 184:* [A] detainer cannot be lodged against a prisoner ... when the prisoner was not actually in the custody of the criminal justice agency to which the detainer notice was directed."

State v. Powell, 971 S.W.2d 577, 580 (Tex.App.—Dallas 1998, no pet.). "The IADA provides two forms of protection for defendants. Under article III, a prisoner may make a request for final disposition of the pending case in the other jurisdiction. If the defendant properly makes the request for final disposition, he must be tried for the offense within 180 days or the charge must be dismissed with prejudice. Article IV permits a state to request that a defendant imprisoned in another jurisdiction be delivered to it for trial on charges pending in the state; however, the defendant must be tried within 120 days of being brought into the state or the charge must be dismissed with prejudice. [¶] The defendant may ... send the request [for final disposition] to the court and prosecutor of the other jurisdiction himself. If he does so, he is responsible for seeing that the notice is sent in the form required by the IADA, i.e., the notice must be sent by registered mail. The 180-day period does not begin until the request for final disposition of charges is actually received by the court and the prosecutor of the jurisdiction where the charges are pending."

Morganfield v. State, 919 S.W.2d 731, 735 (Tex.App.—San Antonio 1996, no pet.). "[T]he consequences for failure to comply with [the Act's] provisions [are that] the indictment 'shall not be of any further force or effect, and the court shall enter an order dismissing the same with prejudice.'"

Johnson v. State, 900 S.W.2d 475, 485 (Tex.App.—Beaumont 1995), *aff'd*, 930 S.W.2d 589 (Tex.Crim.App. 1996). "*[T]he dismissal* [of the indictment] *comes about when there is no timely action on the untried indictment which was the basis on which the detainer has been activated. At 486:* [A] detainer based on probation violation charges is not governed by or determined by the [IADA]. [A]rticle III ... awards to a prisoner incarcerated in one state the right to demand the speedy disposition of an untried indictment that is the basis of a detainer lodged against him by another state. [¶] The correct interpretation of the adjective 'untried' refers to matters that can be brought to full trial."

Art. 51.14: IV

State v. Williams, 938 S.W.2d 456, 459 (Tex.Crim.App.1997). "[T]he speedy trial/dismissal provisions contained in the IADA do not infringe upon constitutional powers of the trial court."

State v. Sephus, 32 S.W.3d 369, 373 (Tex.App.—Waco 2000, pet. ref'd). "Dismissal [of an indictment] does not depend upon a motion by the prisoner; the right to a dismissal with prejudice flows from the statute. [¶] Applying the literal text of the statute to the facts: '[B]ecause trial [was] not had on [the Leon County] indictment [but the Harris County indictment], ... prior to [Sephus's] being returned to [Pennsylvania] pursuant to Paragraph (e) of Article V hereof, [the Leon County] indictment, [is of no] further force or effect, and the court shall enter an order dismissing the same with prejudice.'" Held: The trial judge correctly analyzed the facts and applied the Detainers Act to them.

Art. 51.14: V

Bokemeyer v. State, 624 S.W.2d 909, 912 (Tex.Crim.App.1981). "We refuse to interpret Article 51.14, Article V(d), as prohibiting a re-indictment for the same offense made the basis for the request for temporary custody whether the re-indictment occurs during pendency of the procedure for temporary custody, ... or occurs after the defendant has been returned to the state where the first untried indictment was pending. It would be the height of absurdity to say that under such circumstances the defendant would have to be returned to the sending state and the procedure for temporary custody renewed successfully before prosecution could be had in the second indictment."

CHAPTER 52. COURT OF INQUIRY

ART. 52.01. COURTS OF INQUIRY CONDUCTED BY DISTRICT JUDGES

(a) When a judge of any district court of this state, acting in his capacity as magistrate, has probable cause to believe that an offense has been committed against the laws of this state, he may request that the presiding judge of the administrative judicial district appoint a district judge to commence a Court of Inquiry. The judge, who shall be appointed in accordance with Subsection (b), may summon and examine any witness in relation to the offense in accordance with the rules hereinafter provided, which procedure is defined as a "Court of Inquiry."

(b)(1) Before requesting the presiding judge to appoint a district judge to commence a Court of Inquiry, a judge must enter into the minutes of his court a sworn affidavit stating the substantial facts establishing probable cause that a specific offense has been committed against the laws of this state.

(2) After the affidavit has been entered into the minutes of his court and a copy filed with the district clerk, the judge shall request the presiding judge of the administrative judicial district in which the affidavit is filed to appoint a judge to commence the Court of Inquiry. The judge appointed to commence the Court of Inquiry shall issue a written order commencing the Court of Inquiry and stating its scope. The presiding judge shall not name the judge who requests the Court of Inquiry to preside over the Court of Inquiry.

(c) The district or county attorney of the district or county in which the Court of Inquiry is held shall assist the district judge in conducting the Court of Inquiry. The attorney shall examine witnesses and evidence admitted before the court to determine if an offense has been committed and shall render other assistance to the judge as is necessary in the proceeding.

(d) If the Court of Inquiry pertains to the activities of the district or county attorney or to the attorney's office, deputies, or employees, or if the attorney is otherwise disqualified in the proceeding, the judge shall appoint one attorney pro tem to assist in the proceeding. In any other circumstance, the judge may appoint an attorney pro tem to assist in the proceeding.

(e) If more than one Court of Inquiry is commenced which pertains to the activities of a state governmental entity or public servant thereof, then, upon motion of the state governmental entity or public servant, made to the presiding judge or judges of the administrative judicial region or regions where the Courts of Inquiry have been commenced, the presiding judge or judges shall transfer the Courts of Inquiry to the presiding administrative judge of Travis County. The presiding administrative judge of Travis County shall consolidate the Courts of Inquiry for further proceedings and shall assign a district judge to preside over the consolidated Courts of Inquiry.

History of CCP art. 52.01: Acts 1965, 59th Leg., vol. 2, ch. 722. Amended by Acts 1967, 60th Leg., ch. 659, §34, eff. Aug. 28, 1967; Acts 1987, 70th Leg., ch. 534, §1, eff. Sept. 1, 1987; Acts 1995, 74th Leg., ch. 318, §65, eff. Sept. 1, 1995.

ART. 52.02. EVIDENCE; DEPOSITION; AFFIDAVITS

At the hearing at a Court of Inquiry, evidence may be taken orally or by deposition, or, in the discretion of the judge, by affidavit. If affidavits are admitted, any witness against whom they may bear has the right to propound written interrogatories to the affiants or to file answering affidavits. The judge in hearing such evidence, at his discretion, may conclude not to sustain objections to all or to any portion of the evidence taken nor exclude same; but any of the witnesses or attorneys engaged in taking the testimony may have any objections they make recorded with the testimony and reserved for the action of any court in which such evidence is thereafter sought to be admitted, but such court is not confined to objections made at the taking of the testimony at the Court of Inquiry. Without restricting the foregoing, the judge may allow the introduction of any documentary or real evidence which he deems reliable, and the testimony adduced before any grand jury.

History of CCP art. 52.02: Acts 1965, 59th Leg., vol. 2, ch. 722. Amended by Acts 1967, 60th Leg., ch. 659, §35, eff. Aug. 28, 1967.

ART. 52.03. SUBPOENAS

The judge or his clerk has power to issue subpoenas which may be served within the same territorial limits as subpoenas issued in felony prosecutions or to summon witnesses before grand juries in this state.

History of CCP art. 52.03: Acts 1965, 59th Leg., vol. 2, ch. 722. Amended by Acts 1967, 60th Leg., ch. 659, §36, eff. Aug. 28, 1967.

ART. 52.04. RIGHTS OF WITNESSES

(a) All witnesses testifying in any Court of Inquiry have the same rights as to testifying as do defendants in felony prosecutions in this state. Before any witness is sworn to testify in any Court of Inquiry, he shall be instructed by the judge that he is entitled to counsel; that he cannot be forced to testify against himself; and that such testimony may be taken down and used against him in a later trial or trials ensuing from the instant Court of Inquiry. Any witness or his counsel has the right to fully cross-examine any of the witnesses whose testimony bears in any manner against him.

(b) If the Court of Inquiry pertains to the activities of a state governmental entity or its officers or employees, the officers and employees of that state governmental entity shall be indemnified for attorney's fees incurred as a result of exercising the employees' or officers' right to counsel under Subsection (a) if:

(1) the officer or employee is found not guilty after a trial or appeal or the complaint, information, or indictment is dismissed without a plea of guilty or nolo contendere being entered; and

(2) the judge commencing the Court of Inquiry, or the judge to whom the Court of Inquiry was transferred pursuant to Article 52.01(e), determines that the complaint, information, or indictment presented against the person was dismissed because:

(A) the presentment was made on mistake, false information, or other similar basis, indicating absence of probable cause to believe, at the time of dismissal, the person committed the offense; or

(B) the complaint, information, or indictment was void.

(c) The county in which the affidavit under Article 52.01 was filed shall be responsible for any attorney's fees awarded under Subsection (b).

History of CCP art. 52.04: Acts 1965, 59th Leg., vol. 2, ch. 722. Amended by Acts 1967, 60th Leg., ch. 659, §37, eff. Aug. 28, 1967; Acts 1995, 74th Leg., ch. 318, §66, eff. Sept. 1, 1995.

ART. 52.05. WITNESS MUST TESTIFY

A person may be compelled to give testimony or produce evidence when legally called upon to do so at any Court of Inquiry; however, if any person refuses or declines to testify or produce evidence on the ground that it may incriminate him under laws of this state, then the judge may, in his discretion, compel such person to testify or produce evidence but the person shall not be prosecuted or subjected to any penalty or forfeiture for, or on account of, any transaction, matter or thing concerning which he may be compelled to testify or produce evidence at such Court of Inquiry.

History of CCP art. 52.05: Acts 1965, 59th Leg., vol. 2, ch. 722. Amended by Acts 1967, 60th Leg., ch. 659, §38, eff. Aug. 28, 1967.

ART. 52.06. CONTEMPT

Contempt of court in a Court of Inquiry may be punished by a fine not exceeding One Hundred Dollars ($100.00) and any witness refusing to testify may be attached and imprisoned until he does testify.

History of CCP art. 52.06: Acts 1965, 59th Leg., vol. 2, ch. 722.

ART. 52.07. STENOGRAPHIC RECORD; PUBLIC HEARING

All evidence taken at a Court of Inquiry shall be transcribed by the court reporter and all proceedings shall be open to the public.

History of CCP art. 52.07: Acts 1965, 59th Leg., vol. 2, ch. 722.

ANNOTATIONS

Eagle Printing Co. v. Delaney, 671 S.W.2d 883, 887 (Tex.Crim.App.1984). "[A]llowing the press unfettered access to proceedings of a Court of Inquiry and to the record made by it was expressly legislated."

ART. 52.08. CRIMINAL PROSECUTIONS

If it appear from a Court of Inquiry or any testimony adduced therein, that an offense has been committed, the Judge shall issue a warrant for the arrest of the offender as if complaint had been made and filed.

History of CCP art. 52.08: Acts 1965, 59th Leg., vol. 2, ch. 722.

ART. 52.09. COSTS & ATTORNEY'S FEES

(a) All costs incurred in conducting a Court of Inquiry, including compensation of an attorney pro tem, shall be borne by the county in which said Court of Inquiry is conducted; provided, however, that where the Attorney General of Texas has submitted a request in writing to the judge for the holding of such Court of Inquiry, then and in that event the costs shall be borne by the State of Texas and shall be taxed to the attorney general and paid in the same manner and from the same funds as other court costs.

(b) Assistance by a county or district attorney to a Court of Inquiry is a duty of the attorney's office, and the attorney may not receive a fee for the service. A county is not liable for attorney's fees claimed for assistance in a Court of Inquiry by any attorney other than an attorney pro tem appointed under Article 52.01(d) of this code.

(c) An attorney pro tem appointed under Article 52.01(d) of this code is entitled to compensation in the same manner as an attorney pro tem appointed under Article 2.07 of this code. The district judge shall set the compensation of the attorney pro tem based on the sworn testimony of the attorney or other evidence that is given in open court.

History of CCP art. 52.09: Acts 1965, 59th Leg., vol. 2, ch. 722. Amended by Acts 1967, 60th Leg., ch. 659, §39, eff. Aug. 28, 1967; Acts 1987, 70th Leg., ch. 534, §1, eff. Sept. 1, 1987.

CHAPTER 53. COSTS & FEES

ART. 53.01. REPEALED

Repealed by Acts 1987, 70th Leg., ch. 167, §4.01(b), eff. Sept. 1, 1987.

ART. 53.02. REPEALED

Repealed by Acts 1985, 69th Leg., ch. 269, §5(1), eff. Sept. 1, 1985.

ARTS. 53.03 TO 53.06. REPEALED

Repealed by Acts 1987, 70th Leg., ch. 167, §4.01(b), eff. Sept. 1, 1987.

ART. 53.07. REPEALED

Repealed by Acts 1985, 69th Leg., ch. 269, §5(1), eff. Sept. 1, 1985.

ARTS. 53.08, 53.09. REPEALED

Repealed by Acts 1987, 70th Leg., ch. 167, §4.01(b), eff. Sept. 1, 1987.

Article 53.10 blank

ART. 53.11. REPEALED

Repealed by Acts 1987, 70th Leg., ch. 167, §4.01(b), eff. Sept. 1, 1987.

CHAPTER 54. MISCELLANEOUS PROVISIONS

ART. 54.01. SEVERABILITY CLAUSE

If any provision, section or clause of this Act or application thereof to any person or circumstances is held invalid, such invalidity shall not affect other provisions or applications hereof which can be given effect without the invalid provision, section or clause, and to this end the provisions of this Act are declared to be severable.

History of CCP art. 54.01: Acts 1965, 59th Leg., vol. 2, ch. 722.

ANNOTATIONS

Jones v. State, 803 S.W.2d 712, 714 (Tex.Crim.App. 1991). "'Invalidity of a part [of a legislative enactment] does not necessarily destroy the entire act, unless the valid part is so intermingled with all parts of the act so as to make it impossible to separate them, and so as to preclude the presumption that the legislature would have passed the act anyhow.'"

ART. 54.02. REPEALING CLAUSE

Sec. 1. (a) Except as otherwise provided in this Article 54.02, all laws relating to criminal procedure in this State that are not embraced, incorporated, or included in this Act and that have not been enacted during the Regular Session of the 59th Legislature are repealed.

(b) None of the following articles of the Code of Criminal Procedure of Texas, 1925, in force on the effective date of this Act, is repealed: 52; 52-1 through 52-161, both inclusive; 367D through 367K, both inclusive; 781B-1, 781B-2; 944 through 951, both inclusive; 1009 through 1035, both inclusive; 1037 through 1056, both inclusive; 1058 through 1064, both inclusive; and 1075 through 1082, both inclusive.

Sec. 2. (a) All laws and parts of laws relating to criminal procedure omitted from this Act have been intentionally omitted, and all additions to and changes in such procedure have been intentionally made. This Act shall be construed to be an independent Act of the Legislature, enacted under its caption, and the articles contained in this Act, as revised, rewritten, changed, combined, and codified, may not be construed as a continuation of former laws except as otherwise provided in this Act. The existing statutes of the Revised Civil Statutes of Texas, 1925, as amended, and of the Penal Code of Texas, 1925, as amended, which contain special or specific provisions of criminal procedure covering specific instances are not repealed by this Act.

(b) A person under recognizance or bond on the effective date of this Act continues under such recognizance or bond pending final disposition of any action pending against him.

History of CCP art. 54.02: Acts 1965, 59th Leg., vol. 2, ch. 722.

ART. 54.03. EMERGENCY CLAUSE

The fact that the laws relating to criminal procedure in this State have not been completely revised and recodified in more than a century past and the further fact that the administration of justice, in the field of criminal law, has undergone changes, through judicial construction and interpretation of constitutional provisions, which have been, in certain instances, modified or nullified, as the case may be, necessitates important changes requiring the revision or modernization of the laws relating to criminal procedure, and the further fact that it is desirous and desirable to strengthen, and to conform, various provisions in such laws to current interpretation and application, emphasizes the importance of this legislation and all of which, together with the crowded condition of the calendar in both Houses, create an emergency and an imperative public necessity that the Constitutional Rule requiring bills to be read on three several days be suspended, and said Rule is hereby suspended, and that this Act shall take effect and be in force and effect from and after 12 o'clock Meridian on the 1st day of January, Anno Domini, 1966, and it is so enacted.

History of CCP art. 54.03: Acts 1965, 59th Leg., vol. 2, ch. 722.

CHAPTER 55. EXPUNCTION OF CRIMINAL RECORDS

ART. 55.01. RIGHT TO EXPUNCTION

(a) A person who has been placed under a custodial or noncustodial arrest for commission of either a felony or misdemeanor is entitled to have all records and files relating to the arrest expunged if:

(1) the person is tried for the offense for which the person was arrested and is:

(A) acquitted by the trial court, except as provided by Subsection (c) of this section; or

(B) convicted and subsequently pardoned; or

(2) each of the following conditions exist:

(A) an indictment or information charging the person with commission of a felony has not been presented against the person for an offense arising out of the transaction for which the person was arrested or, if an indictment or information charging the person with commission of a felony was presented, the indictment or information has been dismissed or quashed, and:

(i) the limitations period expired before the date on which a petition for expunction was filed under Article 55.02; or

(ii) the court finds that the indictment or information was dismissed or quashed because the presentment had been made because of mistake, false information, or other similar reason indicating absence of probable cause at the time of the dismissal to believe the person committed the offense or because it was void;

(B) the person has been released and the charge, if any, has not resulted in a final conviction and is no longer pending and there was no court ordered community supervision under Article 42.12 for any offense other than a Class C misdemeanor; and

(C) the person has not been convicted of a felony in the five years preceding the date of the arrest.

(a-1) Notwithstanding Subsection (a)(2)(C), a person's conviction of a felony in the five years preceding the date of the arrest does not affect the person's entitlement to expunction for purposes of an ex parte petition filed on behalf of the person by the director of the Department of Public Safety under Section 2(e), Article 55.02.

(b) Except as provided by Subsection (c) of this section, a district court may expunge all records and files relating to the arrest of a person who has been arrested for commission of a felony or misdemeanor under the procedure established under Article 55.02 of this code if the person is:

(1) tried for the offense for which the person was arrested;

(2) convicted of the offense; and

(3) acquitted by the court of criminal appeals.

(c) A court may not order the expunction of records and files relating to an arrest for an offense for which a person is subsequently acquitted, whether by the trial court or the court of criminal appeals, if the offense for which the person was acquitted arose out of a criminal episode, as defined by Section 3.01, Penal Code, and the person was convicted of or remains subject to prosecution for at least one other offense occurring during the criminal episode.

(d) A person is entitled to have any information that identifies the person, including the person's name, address, date of birth, driver's license number, and social security number, contained in records and files relating to the arrest of another person expunged if:

(1) the information identifying the person asserting the entitlement to expunction was falsely given by the person arrested as the arrested person's identifying information without the consent of the person asserting the entitlement; and

(2) the only reason for the information identifying the person asserting the entitlement being contained in the arrest records and files of the person arrested is that the information was falsely given by the person arrested as the arrested person's identifying information.

History of CCP art. 55.01: Acts 1977, 65th Leg., ch. 747, §1, eff. Aug. 29, 1977. Amended by Acts 1979, 66th Leg., ch. 604, §1, eff. Aug. 27, 1979; Acts 1989, 71st Leg., ch. 803, §1, eff. Sept. 1, 1989; Acts 1991, 72nd Leg., ch. 14, §284(53), eff. Sept. 1, 1991; Acts 1993, 73rd Leg., ch. 900, §7.02(a), eff. Sept. 1, 1993; Acts 1999, 76th Leg., ch. 1236, §1, eff. Aug. 30, 1999; Acts 2001, 77th Leg., ch. 945, §1 (eff. June 14, 2001), ch. 1021, §1 (eff. Sept. 1, 2001); Acts 2003, 78th Leg., ch. 1236, §1, eff. Sept. 1, 2003; Acts 2005, 79th Leg., ch. 1309, §1, Sept. 1, 2005.

See also *O'Connor's Crimes & Consequences* (2008-09), chart 13-D, "Expunction."

ANNOTATIONS

State v. Beam, 226 S.W.3d 392, 395 (Tex.2007). "Beam was arrested and charged with a misdemeanor offense, but the charge was dismissed pursuant to a plea agreement and she was granted deferred adjudication on a lesser charge. Beam sought expunction pursuant to paragraph (a)(2). No felony indictment or information has yet been presented against Beam, but the limitations period for the underlying offense has not expired. Therefore, Beam does not satisfy the requirements for filing an expunction petition under paragraph (a)(2). Even though Beam was arrested for a misdemeanor offense, she must wait until the two-year limitations period expires on June 20, 2007 before she may seek expunction—assuming she meets article 55.01's remaining requirements, a question we do not reach."

In re A.R., 225 S.W.3d 643, 646 (Tex.App.—El Paso 2006, no pet.). "The right to expunction is a statutory privilege. In a statutory cause of action, all provisions are mandatory and exclusive and a person is entitled to expunction only when all of the conditions have been met. An expunction proceeding is civil rather than criminal in nature, and the burden of proving compliance with the statute rests with the petitioner."

In re C.V., 214 S.W.3d 43, 45 (Tex.App.—El Paso 2006, no pet.). "Insufficient evidence cannot be the basis of an expunction. In order for expunction to lie, the evidence must show that the decision to indict was based on erroneous facts. The lack of cooperation by a complainant or the unwillingness to prosecute goes to the insufficiency of the evidence to convict, and not to whether the presentment of the indictment was based upon mistake, false information, or other reason indicating lack of probable cause." *See also Barker v. State*, 84 S.W.3d 409, 412 (Tex.App.—Fort Worth 2002, no pet.) (inability to locate complainant).

Specialized Waste Sys. v. State, 126 S.W.3d 530, 530 (Tex.App.—Houston [1st Dist.] 2003, pet. denied). "SWS contends that the trial court erred in holding that a corporation may not petition for expunction and in denying its petition. *At 531:* Because corporations cannot be arrested, and because the Legislature has not provided a mechanism for corporations to petition for expunction of criminal records, we hold that the trial court did not err in denying SWS's petition for expunction."

Heine v. Texas DPS, 92 S.W.3d 642, 649 (Tex. App.—Austin 2002, pet. denied). "[W]e hold that [CPRC] §16.051 ... does not act as a bar [through limitations] to the statutory remedy of expunction."

Carson v. State, 65 S.W.3d 774, 783 (Tex.App.—Fort Worth 2001, no pet.). "[W]e hold that 'arrest' as used in article 55.01 includes the submission to the assertion of authority demonstrated by a defendant's appearance in court at the time and place set forth in a Class C misdemeanor citation mailed to him. *At 784:* The only elements Carson was required to prove to establish his entitlement to expunction under article 55.01(a)(1) are that he was: arrested for commission of a misdemeanor; was tried for the offense; and was acquitted."

Travis Cty. Atty. v. J.S.H., 37 S.W.3d 163, 167 (Tex. App.—Austin 2001, no pet.). "We hold that 'final conviction' as that term is used in article 55.01(a)(2)(B) ..., requires that there have been an adjudication of guilt of the offense charged. Therefore, the admitted unadjudicated offenses considered by the trial courts in assessing appellants' punishments for adjudicated offenses in the proceedings conducted pursuant to [Pen. Code] §12.45 ... may be expunged."

Harris Cty. Dist. Atty. v. Small, 920 S.W.2d 740, 744 (Tex.App.—Houston [1st Dist.] 1996, no writ). "The fact that a determination, subsequent to a grand jury's presentment of an indictment, reveals that some or all of the evidence considered by the grand jury would be inadmissible at trial, does not entitle the defendant to an expunction under Article 55.01."

Thomas v. State, 916 S.W.2d 540, 544 (Tex.App.—Waco 1995, no writ). "The petitioner must show: (1) the indictment was presented due to mistake, false information, or other similar reason indicating a lack of probable cause; and (2) that the prosecution dismissed the cause because of this mistake, false information, or other reason indicating a lack of probable cause." *See also Perryman v. State*, 920 S.W.2d 413, 414 (Tex. App.—Dallas 1996, no pet.).

Ex parte Current, 877 S.W.2d 833, 839 (Tex.App.—Waco 1994, no writ). "[W]e conclude that the legislature intended to allow for the expunction of criminal records when the defendant is acquitted by an appellate court and did not intend to limit that eligibility to defendants acquitted only by the Court of Criminal Appeals." *But see* **Harris Cty. v. E.B.H.**, 95 S.W.3d 719, 722 (Tex. App.—Houston [1st Dist.] 2003, pet. denied) (expunction is not available if acquittal comes from appellate court).

Ex parte E.E.H., 869 S.W.2d 496, 498 (Tex.App.—Houston [1st Dist.] 1993, writ denied). "[T]he statute permits expunction of less than all charges arising from a single arrest."

Harris Cty. Dist. Attorney's Office v. D.W.B., 860 S.W.2d 719, 721 (Tex.App.—Houston [1st Dist.] 1993, no writ). The statute "was not 'intended to allow a person who is arrested, pleads guilty to an offense, and receives probation pursuant to a guilty plea to expunge arrest and court records concerning that offense.' [¶] Merely completing the terms of deferred adjudication and obtaining a dismissal does not entitle a petitioner to expunction of criminal records."

ART. 55.02. PROCEDURE FOR EXPUNCTION

Sec. 1. At the request of the defendant and after notice to the state, the trial court presiding over the case in which the defendant was acquitted, if the trial court is a district court, or a district court in the county in which the trial court is located shall enter an order of expunction for a person entitled to expunction under Article 55.01(a)(1)(A) not later than the 30th day after the date of the acquittal. Upon acquittal, the trial court shall advise the defendant of the right to expunction. The defendant shall provide to the district court all of the information required in a petition for expunction under Section 2(b). The attorney for the defendant in the case in which the defendant was acquitted, if the defendant was represented by counsel, or the attorney for the state, if the defendant was not represented by counsel, shall prepare the order for the court's signature.

Sec. 2. (a) A person who is entitled to expunction of records and files under Article 55.01(a) or a person who is eligible for expunction of records and files under Article 55.01(b) may file an ex parte petition for expunction in a district court for the county in which:

(1) the petitioner was arrested; or

(2) the offense was alleged to have occurred.

(b) The petition must be verified and shall include the following or an explanation for why one or more of the following is not included:

(1) the petitioner's:

(A) full name;

(B) sex;

(C) race;

(D) date of birth;

(E) driver's license number;

(F) social security number; and

(G) address at the time of the arrest;

(2) the offense charged against the petitioner;

(3) the date the offense charged against the petitioner was alleged to have been committed;

(4) the date the petitioner was arrested;

(5) the name of the county where the petitioner was arrested and if the arrest occurred in a municipality, the name of the municipality;

(6) the name of the agency that arrested the petitioner;

(7) the case number and court of offense; and

(8) a list of all:

(A) law enforcement agencies, jails or other detention facilities, magistrates, courts, prosecuting attorneys, correctional facilities, central state depositories of criminal records, and other officials or agencies or other entities of this state or of any political subdivision of this state;

(B) central federal depositories of criminal records that the petitioner has reason to believe have records or files that are subject to expunction; and

(C) private entities that compile and disseminate for compensation criminal history record information that the petitioner has reason to believe have information related to records or files that are subject to expunction.

(c) The court shall set a hearing on the matter no sooner than thirty days from the filing of the petition and shall give to each official or agency or other governmental entity named in the petition reasonable notice of the hearing by:

(1) certified mail, return receipt requested; or

(2) secure electronic mail, electronic transmission, or facsimile transmission.

(c-1) An entity described by Subsection (c) may be represented by the attorney responsible for providing the entity with legal representation in other matters.

(d) If the court finds that the petitioner, or a person for whom an ex parte petition is filed under Subsection (e), is entitled to expunction of any records and files that are the subject of the petition, it shall enter an order directing expunction.

(e) The director of the Department of Public Safety or the director's authorized representative may file on behalf of a person described by Subsection (a) of this section or by Section 2a an ex parte petition for expunction in a district court for the county in which:

(1) the person was arrested; or

(2) the offense was alleged to have occurred.

(f) An ex parte petition filed under Subsection (e) must be verified and must include the following or an explanation for why one or more of the following is not included:

(1) the person's:

(A) full name;

(B) sex;

(C) race;

(D) date of birth;

(E) driver's license number;

(F) social security number; and

(G) address at the time of the arrest;

(2) the offense charged against the person;

(3) the date the offense charged against the person was alleged to have been committed;

(4) the date the person was arrested;

(5) the name of the county where the person was arrested and if the arrest occurred in a municipality, the name of the municipality;

(6) the name of the agency that arrested the person;

(7) the case number and court of offense; and

 (8) a list of all:

(A) law enforcement agencies, jails or other detention facilities, magistrates, courts, prosecuting attorneys, correctional facilities, central state depositories of criminal records, and other officials or agencies or other entities of this state or of any political subdivision of this state;

(B) central federal depositories of criminal records that the person has reason to believe have records or files that are subject to expunction; and

(C) private entities that compile and disseminate for compensation criminal history record information

that the person has reason to believe have information relating to records or files that are subject to expunction.

Sec. 2a. (a) A person who is entitled to expunction of information contained in records and files under Article 55.01(d) may file an application for expunction with the attorney representing the state in the prosecution of felonies in the county in which the person resides.

(b) The application must be verified, include authenticated fingerprint records of the applicant, and include the following or an explanation for why one or more of the following is not included:

(1) the applicant's full name, sex, race, date of birth, driver's license number, social security number, and address at the time the person who falsely identified himself or herself as the applicant was arrested;

(2) the following information regarding the arrest:

(A) the date of arrest;

(B) the offense charged against the person arrested;

(C) the name of the county or municipality in which the arrest occurred; and

(D) the name of the arresting agency; and

(3) a statement that:

(A) the applicant is not the person arrested and for whom the arrest records and files were created; and

(B) the applicant did not give the person arrested consent to falsely identify himself or herself as the applicant.

(c) After verifying the allegations in an application received under Subsection (a), the attorney representing the state shall:

(1) include on the application information regarding the arrest that was requested of the applicant but was unknown by the applicant;

(2) forward a copy of the application to the district court for the county;

(3) attach to the copy a list of all:

(A) law enforcement agencies, jails or other detention facilities, magistrates, courts, prosecuting attorneys, correctional facilities, central state depositories of criminal records, and other officials or agencies or other entities of this state or of any political subdivision of this state;

(B) central federal depositories of criminal records that are reasonably likely to have records or files containing information that is subject to expunction; and

(C) private entities that compile and disseminate for compensation criminal history record information that are reasonably likely to have records or files containing information that is subject to expunction; and

(4) request the court to enter an order directing expunction based on an entitlement to expunction under Article 55.01(d).

(d) On receipt of a request under Subsection (c), the court shall, without holding a hearing on the matter, enter a final order directing expunction.

Sec. 3. (a) In an order of expunction issued under this article, the court shall require any state agency that sent information concerning the arrest to a central federal depository to request the depository to return all records and files subject to the order of expunction. The person who is the subject of the expunction order or an agency protesting the expunction may appeal the court's decision in the same manner as in other civil cases.

(b) The order of expunction entered by the court shall have attached and incorporate by reference a copy of the judgment of acquittal and shall include:

(1) the following information on the person who is the subject of the expunction order:

(A) full name;

(B) sex;

(C) race;

(D) date of birth;

(E) driver's license number; and

(F) social security number;

(2) the offense charged against the person who is the subject of the expunction order;

(3) the date the person who is the subject of the expunction order was arrested;

(4) the case number and court of offense; and

(5) the tracking incident number (TRN) assigned to the individual incident of arrest under Article 60.07(b)(1) by the Department of Public Safety.

(c) When the order of expunction is final, the clerk of the court shall send a certified copy of the order to the Crime Records Service of the Department of Public Safety and to each official or agency or other governmental entity of this state or of any political subdivision of this state designated by the person who is the subject of the order. The certified copy of the order must be sent by secure electronic mail, electronic transmission, or facsimile transmission or otherwise by certified mail, return receipt requested. In sending the order to a governmental entity designated by the person, the clerk may elect to substitute hand delivery for certified mail under this subsection, but the clerk must receive a receipt for that hand-delivered order.

(c-1) The Department of Public Safety shall notify any central federal depository of criminal records by any means, including secure electronic mail, electronic transmission, or facsimile transmission, of the order with an explanation of the effect of the order and a request that the depository, as appropriate, either:

(1) destroy or return to the court the records in possession of the depository that are subject to the order, including any information with respect to the order; or

(2) comply with Section 5(f) pertaining to information contained in records and files of a person entitled to expunction under Article 55.01(d).

(c-2) The Department of Public Safety shall also provide, by secure electronic mail, electronic transmission, or facsimile transmission, notice of the order to any private entity that is named in the order or that purchases criminal history record information from the department. The notice must include an explanation of the effect of the order and a request that the entity destroy any information in the possession of the entity that is subject to the order. The department may charge to a private entity that purchases criminal history record information from the department a fee in an amount sufficient to recover costs incurred by the department in providing notice under this subsection to the entity.

(d) Any returned receipts received by the clerk from notices of the hearing and copies of the order shall be maintained in the file on the proceedings under this chapter.

Sec. 4. (a) If the state establishes that the person who is the subject of an expunction order is still subject to conviction for an offense arising out of the transaction for which the person was arrested because the statute of limitations has not run and there is reasonable cause to believe that the state may proceed against the person for the offense, the court may provide in its order that the law enforcement agency and the prosecuting attorney responsible for investigating the offense may retain any records and files that are necessary to the investigation. In the case of a person who is the subject of an expunction order on the basis of an acquittal, the court may provide in the expunction order that the law enforcement agency and the prosecuting attorney retain records and files if:

(1) the records and files are necessary to conduct a subsequent investigation and prosecution of a person other than the person who is the subject of the expunction order; or

(2) the state establishes that the records and files are necessary for use in:

(A) another criminal case, including a prosecution, motion to adjudicate or revoke community supervision, parole revocation hearing, mandatory supervision revocation hearing, punishment hearing, or bond hearing; or

(B) a civil case, including a civil suit or suit for possession of or access to a child.

(b) Unless the person who is the subject of the expunction order is again arrested for or charged with an offense arising out of the transaction for which the person was arrested or unless the court provides for the retention of records and files under Subsection (a) of this section, the provisions of Articles 55.03 and 55.04 of this code apply to files and records retained under this section.

Ⓐ Sec. 5. (a) Except as provided by Subsections (f) and (g), on receipt of the order, each official or agency or other governmental entity named in the order shall:

(1) return all records and files that are subject to the expunction order to the court or, if removal is impracticable, obliterate all portions of the record or file that identify the person who is the subject of the order and notify the court of its action; and

(2) delete from its public records all index references to the records and files that are subject to the expunction order.

(b) Except in the case of a person who is the subject of an expunction order on the basis of an acquittal or an expunction order based on an entitlement under Article 55.01(d), the court may give the person who is the subject of the order all records and files returned to it pursuant to its order.

Ⓐ (c) Except in the case of a person who is the subject of an expunction order based on an entitlement under Article 55.01(d) and except as provided by Subsection (g), if an order of expunction is issued under this article, the court records concerning expunction proceedings are not open for inspection by anyone except the person who is the subject of the order unless the order permits retention of a record under Section 4 of this article and the person is again arrested for or charged with an offense arising out of the transaction for which the person was arrested or unless the court provides for the retention of records and files under Section 4(a) of this article. The clerk of the court issuing the order shall obliterate all public references to the proceeding and maintain the files or other records in an area not open to inspection.

Ⓐ (d) Except in the case of a person who is the subject of an expunction order on the basis of an acquittal or an expunction order based on an entitlement under Article 55.01(d) and except as provided by Subsection (g), the clerk of the court shall destroy all the files or other records maintained under Subsection (c) not earlier than the 60th day after the date the order of expunction is issued or later than the first anniversary of that date unless the records or files were released under Subsection (b).

(d-1) Not later than the 30th day before the date on which the clerk destroys files or other records under Subsection (d), the clerk shall provide notice by mail, electronic mail, or facsimile transmission to the attorney representing the state in the expunction proceeding. If the attorney representing the state in the expunction proceeding objects to the destruction not later than the 20th day after receiving notice under this subsection, the clerk may not destroy the files or other records until the first anniversary of the date the order of expunction is issued or the first business day after that date.

(e) The clerk shall certify to the court the destruction of files or other records under Subsection (d) of this section.

Ⓐ (f) On receipt of an order granting expunction to a person entitled to expunction under Article 55.01(d), each official, agency, or other governmental entity named in the order:

(1) shall:

(A) obliterate all portions of the record or file that identify the petitioner; and

(B) substitute for all obliterated portions of the record or file any available information that identifies the person arrested; and

(2) may not return the record or file or delete index references to the record or file.

E *Subsection (g) below is effective for expunction orders received on or after Sept. 1, 2007.*

(g) Notwithstanding any other provision in this section, an official, agency, court, or other entity may retain receipts, invoices, vouchers, or similar records of financial transactions that arose from the expunction proceeding or prosecution of the underlying criminal cause in accordance with internal financial control procedures. An official, agency, court, or other entity that retains records under this subsection shall obliterate all portions of the record or the file that identify the person who is the subject of the expunction order.

History of CCP art. 55.02: Acts 1977, 65th Leg., ch. 747, §1, eff. Aug. 29, 1977. Amended by Acts 1979, 66th Leg., ch. 604, §1, eff. Aug. 27, 1979; Acts 1989, 71st Leg., ch. 803, §2 (eff. Sept. 1, 1989), ch. 803, §3 (eff. Sept. 1, 1989), ch. 803, §4 (eff. Sept. 1, 1989); Acts 1991, 72nd Leg., ch. 380, §1, eff. Aug. 26, 1991; Acts 1999, 76th Leg., ch. 1236, §2, eff. Aug. 30, 1999; Acts 2001, 77th Leg., ch. 945, §§2, 3 (eff. June 14, 2001), ch. 1021, §2 (eff. Sept. 1, 2001); Acts 2003, 78th Leg., ch. 339, §§2-4, 7 (eff. Sept. 1, 2003), ch. 404, §§1, 2 (eff. Sept. 1, 2003), ch. 1126, §1 (eff. June 20, 2003), ch. 1236, §2 (eff. Sept. 1, 2003); Acts 2005, 79th Leg., ch. 177, §§1, 2 (eff. Sept. 1, 2005), ch. 728, §4.006 (eff. Sept. 1, 2005), ch. 1309, §2 (eff. Sept. 1, 2005); Acts 2007, 80th Leg., ch. 120, §1 (eff. Sept. 1, 2007), ch. 1017, §§1-4 (eff. Sept. 1, 2007).

ANNOTATIONS

Pitts v. State, 113 S.W.3d 393, 397 (Tex.App.—Houston [1st Dist.] 2003, no pet.). "[E]xpunction proceedings are not 'exceptional cases' requiring trial courts to appoint counsel for indigent litigants...."

Heine v. Texas DPS, 92 S.W.3d 642, 649 (Tex. App.—Austin 2002, pet. denied). "The trial court is required to set a hearing on a petition for expunction. Individuals who are incarcerated do not automatically lose their access to the courts as a result of their incarcerated status. Inmates do not, however, have an absolute right to personally appear. In considering whether a personal appearance is warranted, the trial court must balance the government's interest in protecting the integrity of the correctional system against the prisoner's right of access to the courts."

Texas DPS v. Deck, 954 S.W.2d 108, 112 (Tex. App.—San Antonio 1997, no pet.). "The procedures listed in article 55.02 are mandatory and must be complied with in an expunction proceeding. If the record does not indicate that the agency was notified in accordance with the statute, then the record reflects a proceeding in violation of the statute and the expunction order must be set aside."

Texas DPS v. Katopodis, 886 S.W.2d 455, 458 (Tex. App.—Houston [1st Dist.] 1994, no writ). "[I]n an expunction hearing ..., each law enforcement agency cited is entitled to represent itself."

ART. 55.03. EFFECT OF EXPUNCTION

When the order of expunction is final:

(1) the release, maintenance, dissemination, or use of the expunged records and files for any purpose is prohibited;

(2) except as provided in Subdivision (3) of this article, the person arrested may deny the occurrence of the arrest and the existence of the expunction order; and

(3) the person arrested or any other person, when questioned under oath in a criminal proceeding about an arrest for which the records have been expunged, may state only that the matter in question has been expunged.

History of CCP art. 55.03: Acts 1977, 65th Leg., ch. 747, §1, eff. Aug. 29, 1977. Amended by Acts 1979, 66th Leg., ch. 604, §1, eff. Aug. 27, 1979; Acts 1999, 76th Leg., ch. 1236, §3, eff. Aug. 30, 1999; Acts 2001, 77th Leg., ch. 1021, §3, eff. Sept. 1, 2001; Acts 2003, 78th Leg., ch. 1236, §3, eff. Sept. 1, 2003; Acts 2005, 79th Leg., ch. 790, §1 (eff. June 17, 2005), ch. 919, §1 (eff. June 18, 2005).

ART. 55.04. VIOLATION OF EXPUNCTION ORDER

Sec. 1. A person who acquires knowledge of an arrest while an officer or employee of the state or of any agency or other entity of the state or any political subdivision of the state and who knows of an order expunging the records and files relating to that arrest commits an offense if he knowingly releases, disseminates, or otherwise uses the records or files.

Sec. 2. A person who knowingly fails to return or to obliterate identifying portions of a record or file ordered expunged under this chapter commits an offense.

Sec. 3. An offense under this article is a Class B misdemeanor.

History of CCP art. 55.04: Acts 1977, 65th Leg., ch. 747, §1, eff. Aug. 29, 1977. Amended by Acts 1979, 66th Leg., ch. 604, §1, eff. Aug. 27, 1979.

ART. 55.05. NOTICE OF RIGHT TO EXPUNCTION

On release or discharge of an arrested person, the person responsible for the release or discharge shall give him a written explanation of his rights under this chapter and a copy of the provisions of this chapter.

History of CCP art. 55.05: Acts 1977, 65th Leg., ch. 747, §1, eff. Aug. 29, 1977. Amended by Acts 1979, 66th Leg., ch. 604, §1, eff. Aug. 27, 1979.

ART. 55.06. LICENSE SUSPENSIONS & REVOCATIONS

Records relating to the suspension or revocation of a driver's license, permit, or privilege to operate a motor vehicle may not be expunged under this chapter except as provided in Section 524.015, Transportation Code, or Section 724.048 of that code.

History of CCP art. 55.06: Acts 1993, 73rd Leg., ch. 886, §16, eff. Jan. 1, 1995. Amended by Acts 1999, 76th Leg., ch. 1236, §4, eff. Aug. 30, 1999; Acts 1999, 76th Leg., ch. 62, §3.08, eff. Sept. 1, 1999.

CHAPTER 56. RIGHTS OF CRIME VICTIMS

SUBCHAPTER A. CRIME VICTIMS' RIGHTS

ART. 56.01. DEFINITIONS

In this chapter:

(1) "Close relative of a deceased victim" means a person who was the spouse of a deceased victim at the time of the victim's death or who is a parent or adult brother, sister, or child of the deceased victim.

(2) "Guardian of a victim" means a person who is the legal guardian of the victim, whether or not the legal relationship between the guardian and victim exists because of the age of the victim or the physical or mental incompetency of the victim.

E *Subsection (2-a) below is effective for offenses committed on or after Sept. 1, 2007.*

(2-a) "Sexual assault" includes an offense under Section 21.02, Penal Code.

(3) "Victim" means a person who is the victim of the offense of sexual assault, kidnapping, aggravated robbery, or injury to a child, elderly individual, or disabled individual or who has suffered personal injury or death as a result of the criminal conduct of another.

History of CCP art. 56.01: Acts 1985, 69th Leg., ch. 588, §1, eff. Sept. 1, 1985. Amended by Acts 2005, 79th Leg., ch. 66, §1 (eff. Sept. 1, 2005), ch. 268, §1.126 (eff. Sept. 1, 2005); Acts 2007, 80th Leg., ch. 593, §3.20, eff. Sept. 1, 2007.

ART. 56.02. CRIME VICTIMS' RIGHTS

(a) A victim, guardian of a victim, or close relative of a deceased victim is entitled to the following rights within the criminal justice system:

(1) the right to receive from law enforcement agencies adequate protection from harm and threats of harm arising from cooperation with prosecution efforts;

(2) the right to have the magistrate take the safety of the victim or his family into consideration as an element in fixing the amount of bail for the accused;

(3) the right, if requested, to be informed:

(A) by the attorney representing the state of relevant court proceedings, including appellate proceedings, and to be informed if those proceedings have been canceled or rescheduled prior to the event; and

(B) by an appellate court of decisions of the court, after the decisions are entered but before the decisions are made public;

(4) the right to be informed, when requested, by a peace officer concerning the defendant's right to bail and the procedures in criminal investigations and by the district attorney's office concerning the general procedures in the criminal justice system, including general procedures in guilty plea negotiations and arrangements, restitution, and the appeals and parole process;

(5) the right to provide pertinent information to a probation department conducting a presentencing investigation concerning the impact of the offense on the victim and his family by testimony, written statement, or any other manner prior to any sentencing of the offender;

(6) the right to receive information regarding compensation to victims of crime as provided by Subchapter B, including information related to the costs that may be compensated under that subchapter and the amount of compensation, eligibility for compensation, and procedures for application for compensation under that subchapter, the payment for a medical examination under Article 56.06 for a victim of a sexual assault, and when requested, to referral to available social service agencies that may offer additional assistance;

(7) the right to be informed, upon request, of parole procedures, to participate in the parole process, to be notified, if requested, of parole proceedings concerning a defendant in the victim's case, to provide to the Board of Pardons and Paroles for inclusion in the defendant's file information to be considered by the board prior to the parole of any defendant convicted of any crime subject to this subchapter, and to be notified, if requested, of the defendant's release;

(8) the right to be provided with a waiting area, separate or secure from other witnesses, including the offender and relatives of the offender, before testifying in any proceeding concerning the offender; if a separate waiting area is not available, other safeguards should be taken to minimize the victim's contact with the offender and the offender's relatives and witnesses, before and during court proceedings;

(9) the right to prompt return of any property of the victim that is held by a law enforcement agency or the attorney for the state as evidence when the property is no longer required for that purpose;

(10) the right to have the attorney for the state notify the employer of the victim, if requested, of the necessity of the victim's cooperation and testimony in a proceeding that may necessitate the absence of the victim from work for good cause;

A *Subsection (11) below is effective for offenses committed on or after Sept. 1, 2007.*

(11) the right to counseling, on request, regarding acquired immune deficiency syndrome (AIDS) and human immunodeficiency virus (HIV) infection and testing for acquired immune deficiency syndrome (AIDS), human immunodeficiency virus (HIV) infection, antibodies to HIV, or infection with any other probable causative agent of AIDS, if the offense is an offense under Section 21.02, 21.11(a)(1), 22.011, or 22.021, Penal Code;

★

Subsection (11) below is effective for offenses in which any element of the offense was committed before Sept. 1, 2007.

(11) the right to counseling, on request, regarding acquired immune deficiency syndrome (AIDS) and human immunodeficiency virus (HIV) infection and testing for acquired immune deficiency syndrome (AIDS), human immunodeficiency virus (HIV) infection, antibodies to HIV, or infection with any other probable causative agent of AIDS, if the offense is an offense under Section 21.11(a)(1), 22.011, or 22.021, Penal Code;

(12) the right to request victim-offender mediation coordinated by the victim services division of the Texas Department of Criminal Justice;

(13) the right to be informed of the uses of a victim impact statement and the statement's purpose in the criminal justice system, to complete the victim impact statement, and to have the victim impact statement considered:

(A) by the attorney representing the state and the judge before sentencing or before a plea bargain agreement is accepted; and

(B) by the Board of Pardons and Paroles before an inmate is released on parole; and

(14) except as provided by Article 56.06(a), for a victim of a sexual assault, the right to a forensic medical examination if the sexual assault is reported to a law enforcement agency within 96 hours of the assault.

(b) A victim, guardian of a victim, or close relative of a deceased victim is entitled to the right to be present at all public court proceedings related to the offense, subject to the approval of the judge in the case.

(c) The office of the attorney representing the state, and the sheriff, police, and other law enforcement agencies shall ensure to the extent practicable that a victim, guardian of a victim, or close relative of a deceased victim is afforded the rights granted by Subsection (a) of this article and, on request, an explanation of those rights.

(d) A judge, attorney for the state, peace officer, or law enforcement agency is not liable for a failure or inability to provide a right enumerated in this article. The failure or inability of any person to provide a right or service enumerated in this article may not be used by a defendant in a criminal case as a ground for appeal, a ground to set aside the conviction or sentence, or a ground in a habeas corpus petition. A victim, guardian

of a victim, or close relative of a deceased victim does not have standing to participate as a party in a criminal proceeding or to contest the disposition of any charge.

History of CCP art. 56.02: Acts 1985, 69th Leg., ch. 588, §1, eff. Sept. 1, 1985. Amended by Acts 1987, 70th Leg., ch. 433, §1 (eff. Aug. 31, 1987), ch. 929, §1 (eff. Sept. 1, 1987); Acts 1989, 71st Leg., ch. 996, §1, eff. Sept. 1, 1989; Acts 1991, 72nd Leg., ch. 202, §3, eff. Sept. 1, 1991; Acts 1993, 73rd Leg., ch. 811, §3, eff. Sept. 1, 1993; Acts 1995, 74th Leg., ch. 76, §5.95(108), eff. Sept. 1, 1995; Acts 2001, 77th Leg., ch. 1034, §3, eff. Sept. 1, 2001; Acts 2005, 79th Leg., ch. 498, §1, eff. Sept. 1, 2005; Acts 2007, 80th Leg., ch. 593, §3.21, eff. Sept. 1, 2007.

See also Tex. Const. art. 1, §30.

ANNOTATIONS

Ladd v. State, 3 S.W.3d 547, 566 (Tex.Crim.App. 1999). CCP art. 56.02(b) "by its explicit terms, applies only to victims, not to the parents of victims. Thus, the trial court erred in granting [witnesses an exemption from TRE 613]." The Court holds, however, that the error was harmless.

Stahl v. State, 749 S.W.2d 826, 830 n.4 (Tex.Crim. App.1988). "This 'Victim's Bill of Rights' cannot be read to create a right to testify."

ART. 56.03. VICTIM IMPACT STATEMENT

(a) The Texas Crime Victim Clearinghouse, with the participation of the Texas Adult Probation Commission and the Board of Pardons and Paroles, shall develop a form to be used by law enforcement agencies, prosecutors, and other participants in the criminal justice system to record the impact of an offense on a victim of the offense, guardian of a victim, or a close relative of a deceased victim and to provide the agencies, prosecutors, and participants with information needed to contact the victim, guardian, or relative if needed at any stage of a prosecution of a person charged with the offense. The Texas Crime Victim Clearinghouse, with the participation of the Texas Adult Probation Commission and the Board of Pardons and Paroles, shall also develop a victims' information booklet that provides a general explanation of the criminal justice system to victims of an offense, guardians of victims, and relatives of deceased victims.

(b) The victim impact statement must be in a form designed to inform a victim, guardian of a victim, or a close relative of a deceased victim with a clear statement of rights provided by Article 56.02 of this code and to collect the following information:

(1) the name of the victim of the offense or, if the victim has a legal guardian or is deceased, the name of a guardian or close relative of the victim;

(2) the address and telephone number of the victim, guardian, or relative through which the victim, guardian of a victim, or a close relative of a deceased victim, may be contacted;

(3) a statement of economic loss suffered by the victim, guardian, or relative as a result of the offense;

(4) a statement of any physical or psychological injury suffered by the victim, guardian, or relative as a result of the offense, as described by the victim, guardian, relative, or by a physician or counselor;

(5) a statement of any psychological services requested as a result of the offense;

(6) a statement of any change in the victim's, guardian's, or relative's personal welfare or familial relationship as a result of the offense;

(7) a statement as to whether or not the victim, guardian, or relative wishes to be notified in the future of any parole hearing for the defendant and an explanation as to the procedures by which the victim, guardian, or relative may obtain information concerning the release of the defendant from the Texas Department of Corrections; and

(8) any other information, other than facts related to the commission of the offense, related to the impact of the offense on the victim, guardian, or relative.

(c) The victim assistance coordinator, designated in Article 56.04(a) of this code, shall send to a victim, guardian of a victim, or close relative of a deceased victim a victim impact statement, a victims' information booklet, and an application for compensation under Subchapter B, Chapter 56, along with an offer to assist in completing those forms on request. The victim assistance coordinator, on request, shall explain the possible use and consideration of the victim impact statement at sentencing and future parole hearing of the offender.

(d) If a victim, guardian of a victim, or close relative of a deceased victim states on the victim impact statement that he wishes to be notified of parole proceedings, the victim, guardian, or relative is responsible for notifying the Board of Pardons and Paroles of any change of address.

(e) Prior to the imposition of a sentence by the court in a criminal case, the court, if it has received a victim impact statement, shall consider the information provided in the statement. Before sentencing the defendant, the court shall permit the defendant or his counsel a reasonable time to read the statement, excluding the victim's name, address, and telephone number, comment on the statement, and, with the approval of the court, introduce testimony or other information alleging a factual inaccuracy in the statement. If the court sentences the defendant to a term of community supervision, the court shall forward any victim's impact statement received in the case to the community supervision and corrections department supervising the defendant, along with the papers in the case.

(f) The court may not inspect a victim impact statement until after a finding of guilt or until deferred adjudication is ordered and the contents of the statement may not be disclosed to any person unless:

(1) the defendant pleads guilty or nolo contendere or is convicted of the offense; or

(2) the defendant in writing authorizes the court to inspect the statement.

(g) A victim impact statement is subject to discovery under Article 39.14 of this code before the testimony of the victim is taken only if the court determines that the statement contains exculpatory material.

(h) Not later than December 1 of each odd-numbered year, the Texas Crime Victim Clearinghouse, with the participation of the Texas Adult Probation Commission and the Board of Pardons and Paroles, shall update the victim impact statement form and any other information provided by the commission to victims, guardians of victims, and relatives of deceased victims, if necessary, to reflect changes in law relating to criminal justice and the rights of victims and guardians and relatives of victims.

(i) In addition to the information described by Subsections (b)(1)-(8), the victim impact statement must be in a form designed to collect information on whether, if the victim is a child, there is an existing court order granting to the defendant possession of or access to the victim. If information collected under this subsection indicates the defendant is granted access or possession under court order and the defendant is subsequently confined by the Texas Department of Criminal Justice as a result of the commission of the offense, the victim services office of the department shall contact the court issuing the order before the defendant is released from the department on parole or mandatory supervision.

History of CCP art. 56.03: Acts 1985, 69th Leg., ch. 588, §1, eff. Sept. 1, 1985. Amended by Acts 1987, 70th Leg., ch. 929, §2 (eff. Sept. 1, 1987), ch. 433, §2 (eff. Aug. 31, 1987), ch. 929, §3 (eff. Sept. 1, 1987); Acts 1989, 71st Leg., ch. 996, §2, eff. Sept. 1, 1989; Acts 1995, 74th Leg., ch. 76, §5.95(108), eff. Sept. 1, 1995; Acts 1997, 75th Leg., ch. 670, §5, eff. Sept. 1, 1997; Acts 2001, 77th Leg., ch. 1034, §4, eff. Sept. 1, 2001.

See also TRE 615.

Enos v. State, 889 S.W.2d 303, 305 (Tex.Crim.App. 1994). "[A]rticle 56.03(g) does *not* abrogate the *Gaskin* rule with respect to victim impact statements. Article 56.03(g), by its plain language, concerns only the discoverability of victim impact statements *before* a victim testifies, whereas the *Gaskin* rule concerns the discoverability of [written] statements *after* a witness testifies on direct examination. We see no express or implied abrogation of *Gaskin* with respect to victim impact statements."

Brooks v. State, 961 S.W.2d 396, 400 (Tex.App.— Houston [1st Dist.] 1997, no pet.). "[B]efore sentencing the defendant, the court shall permit the defendant a reasonable time to read the [victim impact] statement, comment on it, and with court approval, introduce testimony and evidence alleging a factual inaccuracy in the statement. We consider this to be a legislative determination that such evidence is 'relevant' when judges assess punishment in non-capital offenses. Before deciding punishment, judges 'shall consider' such information, if it is in a 'victim impact statement.' If the jury assesses punishment, the judge obviously has discretion to exclude such evidence, under [TRE 403]."

Johnson v. State, 919 S.W.2d 473, 479 (Tex.App.— Fort Worth 1996, pet. ref'd). "As soon as the victim has testified at trial, the accused is entitled to inspect the victim's impact statement, even though it does not contain exculpatory material."

Truehitt v. State, 916 S.W.2d 721, 723 (Tex.App.— Beaumont 1996, no pet.). "[A]rticle 56.03(e) gives appellant the right of confrontation and cross-examination if he so chooses."

ART. 56.04. VICTIM ASSISTANCE COORDINATOR; CRIME VICTIM LIAISON

(a) The district attorney, criminal district attorney, or county attorney who prosecutes criminal cases shall designate a person to serve as victim assistance coordinator in that jurisdiction.

(b) The duty of the victim assistance coordinator is to ensure that a victim, guardian of a victim, or close relative of a deceased victim is afforded the rights granted victims, guardians, and relatives by Article 56.02 of this code. The victim assistance coordinator shall work closely with appropriate law enforcement agencies, prosecuting attorneys, the Board of Pardons and Paroles, and the judiciary in carrying out that duty.

(c) Each local law enforcement agency shall designate one person to serve as the agency's crime victim liaison. Each agency shall consult with the victim assistance coordinator in the office of the attorney representing the state to determine the most effective manner in which the crime victim liaison can perform the duties imposed on the crime victim liaison under this article.

(d) The duty of the crime victim liaison is to ensure that a victim, guardian of a victim, or close relative of a deceased victim is afforded the rights granted victims, guardians, or close relatives of deceased victims by Subdivisions (4), (6), and (9) of Article 56.02(a) of this code.

(e) The victim assistance coordinator shall send a copy of a victim impact statement to the court sentencing the defendant. If the court sentences the defendant to imprisonment in the Texas Department of Corrections, it shall attach the copy of the victim impact statement to the commitment papers.

E *Subsection (f) below is effective for counseling for a juror or alternate juror in a criminal trial that begins on or after Sept. 1, 2007.*

(f) The commissioners court may approve a program in which the crime victim liaison or victim assistance coordinator may offer not more than 10 hours of posttrial psychological counseling for a person who serves as a juror or an alternate juror in the trial of an offense under Section 19.02, 19.03, 21.11, 22.011, 22.021, 43.05, 43.25, or 43.251, Penal Code, involving graphic evidence or testimony and who requests the posttrial psychological counseling not later than the 180th day after the date on which the jury in the trial is dismissed. The crime victim liaison or victim assistance coordinator may provide the counseling using a provider that assists local criminal justice agencies in providing similar services to victims.

History of CCP art. 56.04: Acts 1985, 69th Leg., ch. 588, §1, eff. Sept. 1, 1985. Amended by Acts 1989, 71st Leg., ch. 996, §3, eff. Sept. 1, 1989; Acts 1991, 72nd Leg., ch. 202, §4, eff. Sept. 1, 1991; Acts 2007, 80th Leg., ch. 1378, §6, eff. Sept. 1, 2007.

ART. 56.045. PRESENCE OF ADVOCATE OR REPRESENTATIVE DURING FORENSIC MEDICAL EXAMINATION

(a) Before conducting a forensic medical examination of a person who consents to such an examination for the collection of evidence for an alleged sexual assault, the physician or other medical services personnel conducting the examination shall offer the person the opportunity to have an advocate from a sexual assault program as defined by Section 420.003, Government Code, who has completed a sexual assault training program described by Section 420.011(b), Government Code, present with the person during the examination, if the advocate is available at the time of the examination.

(b) The advocate may only provide the injured person with:

(1) counseling and other support services; and

(2) information regarding the rights of crime victims under Article 56.02.

(c) Notwithstanding Subsection (a), the advocate and the sexual assault program providing the advocate may not delay or otherwise impede the screening or stabilization of an emergency medical condition.

(d) The sexual assault program providing the advocate shall pay all costs associated with providing the advocate.

(e) Any individual or entity, including a health care facility, that provides an advocate with access to a person consenting to an examination under Subsection (a) is not subject to civil or criminal liability for providing that access. In this subsection, "health care facility" includes a hospital licensed under Chapter 241, Health and Safety Code.

(f) If a person alleging to have sustained injuries as the victim of a sexual assault was confined in a penal institution, as defined by Section 1.07, Penal Code, at the time of the alleged assault, the penal institution shall provide, at the person's request, a representative to be present with the person at any forensic medical examination conducted for the purpose of collecting and preserving evidence related to the investigation or prosecution of the alleged assault. The representative may only provide the injured person with counseling and other support services and with information regarding the rights of crime victims under Article 56.02 and may not delay or otherwise impede the screening or stabilization of an emergency medical condition. The representative must be approved by the penal institution and must be a:

(1) psychologist;

(2) sociologist;

(3) chaplain;

(4) social worker;

(5) case manager; or

(6) volunteer who has completed a sexual assault training program described by Section 420.011(b), Government Code.

History of CCP art. 56.045: Acts 2001, 77th Leg., ch. 1019, §1, eff. Sept. 1, 2001.

ART. 56.05. REPORTS REQUIRED

(a) The Board of Pardons and Paroles, the Texas Adult Probation Commission, and the Texas Crime Victim Clearinghouse, designated as the planning body for the purposes of this article, shall develop a survey plan to maintain statistics on the numbers and types of persons to whom state and local agencies provide victim impact statements during each year.

(b) At intervals specified in the plan, the planning body may require any state or local agency to submit, in a form prescribed for the reporting of the information, statistical data on the numbers and types of persons to whom the agency provides victim impact statements and any other information required by the planning body. The form must be designed to protect the privacy of persons afforded rights under this chapter and to determine whether the selected agency or office is making a good faith effort to protect the rights of the persons served.

(c) The Texas Crime Victim Clearinghouse shall develop crime victim assistance standards and distribute those standards to law enforcement officers and attorneys representing the state to aid those officers and prosecutors in performing duties imposed by this chapter.

History of CCP art. 56.05: Acts 1985, 69th Leg., ch. 588, §1, eff. Sept. 1, 1985. Amended by Acts 1989, 71st Leg., ch. 996, §4, eff. Sept. 1, 1989.

ART. 56.06. MEDICAL EXAMINATION FOR SEXUAL ASSAULT VICTIM; COSTS

(a) If a sexual assault is reported to a law enforcement agency within 96 hours of the assault, the law enforcement agency, with the consent of the victim, a person authorized to act on behalf of the victim, or an employee of the Department of Family and Protective Services, shall request a medical examination of the victim of the alleged assault for use in the investigation or prosecution of the offense. A law enforcement agency may decline to request a medical examination under this subsection only if the person reporting the sexual assault has made one or more false reports of sexual assault to any law enforcement agency and if there is no other evidence to corroborate the current allegations of sexual assault.

(b) If a sexual assault is not reported within the period described by Subsection (a), on receiving the consent described by that subsection the law enforcement agency may request a medical examination of a victim of an alleged sexual assault as considered appropriate by the agency.

(c) A law enforcement agency that requests a medical examination of a victim of an alleged sexual assault for use in the investigation or prosecution of the offense shall pay all costs of the examination. On application to the attorney general, the law enforcement agency is entitled to be reimbursed for the reasonable costs of that examination if the examination was performed by a physician or by a sexual assault examiner or sexual assault nurse examiner, as defined by Section 420.003, Government Code.

(d) A law enforcement agency or prosecuting attorney's office may pay all costs related to the testimony of a licensed health care professional in a criminal proceeding regarding the results of the medical examination or manner in which it was performed.

(e) This article does not require a law enforcement agency to pay any costs of treatment for injuries.

History of CCP art. 56.06: Acts 1989, 71st Leg., ch. 2, §5.05(a), eff. Aug. 28, 1989. Amended by Acts 1991, 72nd Leg., ch. 75, §1, eff. Sept. 1, 1991; Acts 2001, 77th Leg., ch. 1507, §1, eff. June 17, 2001; Acts 2005, 79th Leg., ch. 498, §2, eff. Sept. 1, 2005.

ART. 56.07. NOTIFICATION

(a) At the initial contact or at the earliest possible time after the initial contact between the victim of a reported crime and the law enforcement agency having the responsibility for investigating that crime, that agency shall provide the victim a written notice containing:

(1) information about the availability of emergency and medical services, if applicable;

(2) notice that the victim has the right to receive information regarding compensation to victims of crime as provided by Subchapter B, Chapter 56, including information about:

(A) the costs that may be compensated under that Act and the amount of compensation, eligibility for compensation, and procedures for application for compensation under that Act;

(B) the payment for a medical examination for a victim of a sexual assault under Article 56.06 of this code; and

(C) referral to available social service agencies that may offer additional assistance;

(3) the name, address, and phone number of the law enforcement agency's victim assistance liaison;

(4) the address, phone number, and name of the crime victim assistance coordinator of the office of the attorney representing the state;

(5) the following statement:

"You may call the law enforcement agency's telephone number for the status of the case and information about victims' rights"; and

(6) the rights of crime victims under Article 56.02 of this code.

(b) At the same time a law enforcement agency provides notice under Subsection (a), the agency shall provide, if the agency possesses the relevant information, a referral to a sexual assault program as defined by Section 420.003, Government Code, and a written description of the services provided by that program. A sexual assault program may provide a written description of its services to a law enforcement agency.

History of CCP art. 56.07: Acts 1991, 72nd Leg., ch. 202, §5, eff. Sept. 1, 1991. Amended by Acts 1995, 74th Leg., ch. 76, §5.95(108), eff. Sept. 1, 1995; Acts 2003, 78th Leg., ch. 788, §1, eff. June 20, 2003.

ART. 56.08. NOTIFICATION OF RIGHTS BY ATTORNEY REPRESENTING THE STATE

(a) Not later than the 10th day after the date that an indictment or information is returned against a defendant for an offense, the attorney representing the state shall give to each victim of the offense a written notice containing:

(1) a brief general statement of each procedural stage in the processing of a criminal case, including bail, plea bargaining, parole restitution, and appeal;

(2) notification of the rights and procedures under this chapter;

(3) suggested steps the victim may take if the victim is subjected to threats or intimidation;

(4) notification of the right to receive information regarding compensation to victims of crime as provided by Subchapter B of this chapter, including information about:

(A) the costs that may be compensated under Subchapter B of this chapter, eligibility for compensation, and procedures for application for compensation under Subchapter B of this chapter;

(B) the payment for a medical examination for a victim of a sexual assault under Article 56.06 of this code; and

(C) referral to available social service agencies that may offer additional assistance;

(5) the name, address, and phone number of the local victim assistance coordinator;

(6) the case number and assigned court for the case;

(7) the right to file a victim impact statement with the office of the attorney representing the state and the pardons and paroles division of the Texas Department of Criminal Justice; and

(8) notification of the right of a victim, guardian of a victim, or close relative of a deceased victim, as defined by Section 508.117, Government Code, to appear in person before a member of the Board of Pardons and Paroles as provided by Section 508.153, Government Code.

(b) If requested by the victim, the attorney representing the state, as far as reasonably practical, shall give to the victim notice of any scheduled court proceedings, changes in that schedule, the filing of a request for continuance of a trial setting, and any plea agreements to be presented to the court.

(c) A victim who receives a notice under Subsection (a) of this article and who chooses to receive other notice under law about the same case must keep the following persons informed of the victim's current address and phone number:

(1) the attorney representing the state; and

(2) the pardons and paroles division of the Texas Department of Criminal Justice if after sentencing the defendant is confined in the institutional division.

(d) An attorney representing the state who receives information concerning a victim's current address and phone number shall immediately provide that information to the community supervision and corrections department supervising the defendant, if the defendant is placed on community supervision.

(e) The brief general statement describing the plea bargaining stage in a criminal trial required by Subsection (a)(1) shall include a statement that:

(1) the victim impact statement provided by the victim, guardian of a victim, or close relative of a deceased victim will be considered by the attorney representing the state in entering into the plea bargain agreement; and

(2) the judge before accepting the plea bargain is required under Section 26.13(e) to ask:

(A) whether a victim impact statement has been returned to the attorney; and

(B) if a statement has been returned, for a copy of the statement.

History of CCP art. 56.08: Acts 1991, 72nd Leg., ch. 202, §5, eff. Sept. 1, 1991. Amended by Acts 1995, 74th Leg., ch. 76, §5.95(108) (eff. Sept. 1, 1995), ch. 253, §2 (eff. Sept. 1, 1995); Acts 1997, 75th Leg., ch. 165, §12.04, eff. Sept. 1, 1997; Acts 2001, 77th Leg., ch. 1034, §5, eff. Sept. 1, 2001.

ART. 56.09. VICTIM'S RIGHT TO PRIVACY

As far as reasonably practical, the address of the victim may not be a part of the court file except as necessary to identify the place of the crime. The phone number of the victim may not be a part of the court file.

History of CCP art. 56.09: Acts 1991, 72nd Leg., ch. 202, §5, eff. Sept. 1, 1991.

ART. 56.10. VICTIM'S DISCOVERY ATTENDANCE

Unless absolutely necessary, victims or witnesses who are not incarcerated may not be required to attend depositions in a correctional facility.

History of CCP art. 56.10: Acts 1991, 72nd Leg., ch. 202, §5, eff. Sept. 1, 1991.

ART. 56.11. NOTIFICATION TO VICTIM OR WITNESS OF RELEASE OR ESCAPE OF DEFENDANT

Ⓐ *Article 56.11 below is effective for defendants who are released or escape on or after Sept. 1, 2007.*

(a) The Texas Department of Criminal Justice or the sheriff, whichever has custody of the defendant in the case of a felony, or the sheriff in the case of a misdemeanor, shall notify the victim of the offense or a witness who testified against the defendant at the trial for the offense, other than a witness who testified in the course and scope of the witness's official or professional duties, whenever a defendant convicted of an offense described by Subsection (c):

(1) completes the defendant's sentence and is released; or

(2) escapes from a correctional facility.

(b) If the Texas Department of Criminal Justice is required by Subsection (a) to give notice to a victim or witness, the department shall also give notice to local law enforcement officials in the county in which the victim or witness resides.

(c) This article applies to a defendant convicted of:

(1) an offense under Title 5, Penal Code, that is punishable as a felony;

(2) an offense described by Section 508.187(a), Government Code, other than an offense described by Subdivision (1); or

(3) an offense involving family violence, stalking, or violation of a protective order or magistrate's order.

(d) It is the responsibility of a victim or witness desiring notification of the defendant's release to provide the Texas Department of Criminal Justice or the sheriff, as appropriate, with the e-mail address, mailing address, and telephone number of the victim, witness, or other person through whom the victim or witness may be contacted and to notify the department or the sheriff of any change of address or telephone number of the victim, witness, or other person. Information obtained and maintained by the Texas Department of Criminal Justice or a sheriff under this subsection is privileged and confidential.

(e) The Texas Department of Criminal Justice or the sheriff, as appropriate:

(1) shall make a reasonable attempt to give any notice required by Subsection (a):

(A) not later than the 30th day before the date the defendant completes the sentence and is released; or

(B) immediately if the defendant escapes from the correctional facility; and

(2) may give any notice required by Subsection (a) by e-mail, if possible.

(f) An attempt by the Texas Department of Criminal Justice or the sheriff to give notice to a victim or witness at the victim's or witness's last known mailing address or, if notice via e-mail is possible, last known e-mail address, as shown on the records of the department or agency, constitutes a reasonable attempt to give notice under this article.

(g) Not later than immediately following the conviction of a defendant described by Subsection (c), the attorney who represented the state in the prosecution of the case shall notify in writing a victim or witness described by Subsection (a) of the victim's or witness's right to receive notice under this article.

(h) In this article:

(1) "Correctional facility" has the meaning assigned by Section 1.07, Penal Code.

(2) "Family violence" has the meaning assigned by Section 71.004, Family Code.

History of CCP art. 56.11: Acts 1993, 73rd Leg., ch. 10, §6, eff. March 19, 1993. Amended by Acts 1995, 74th Leg., ch. 657, §6, eff. June 14, 1995; Acts 1997, 75th Leg., ch. 1, §8 (eff. Jan. 28, 1997), ch. 670, §6 (eff. Oct. 1, 1997); Acts 2001, 77th Leg., ch. 978, §3, eff. Sept. 1, 2001; Acts 2003, 78th Leg., ch. 1276, §7.002(k), eff. Sept. 1, 2003; Acts 2007, 80th Leg., ch. 458, §1, eff. Sept. 1, 2007.

ART. 56.11. NOTIFICATION TO VICTIM OF RELEASE OR ESCAPE OF DEFENDANT

Article 56.11 below is effective for defendants who are released or escape before Sept. 1, 2007.

(a) The Texas Department of Criminal Justice or the sheriff, whichever has custody of the defendant in the case of a felony, or the sheriff in the case of a misdemeanor, shall notify the victim of the offense whenever a person convicted of an offense described by Subsection (c):

(1) completes the person's sentence and is released; or

(2) escapes from a correctional facility.

(b) If the Texas Department of Criminal Justice is required by Subsection (a) to give notice to the victim of an offense, the department shall also give notice to local law enforcement officials in the county in which the victim resides.

(c) This article applies to a person convicted of an offense described by Section 508.187(a), Government Code, or an offense involving family violence, stalking, or violation of a protective order or magistrate's order.

(d) It is the responsibility of a victim desiring notification of the offender's release to provide the Texas Department of Criminal Justice or the sheriff, as appropriate, with the address and telephone number of the victim or other person through whom the victim may be contacted and to notify the department or the sheriff of any change of address or telephone number of the victim or other person. Information obtained and maintained by the Texas Department of Criminal Justice or a sheriff under this subsection is privileged and confidential.

(e) The Texas Department of Criminal Justice or the sheriff, as appropriate, shall make a reasonable attempt to give the notice required by Subsection (a):

(1) not later than the 30th day before the person completes the sentence and is released; or

(2) immediately if the person escapes from the correctional facility.

(f) An attempt by the Texas Department of Criminal Justice or the sheriff to give notice to the victim at the victim's last known address, as shown on the records of the department or agency, constitutes a reasonable attempt to give notice under this article.

(g) In this article:

(1) "Correctional facility" has the meaning assigned by Section 1.07, Penal Code.

(2) "Family violence" has the meaning assigned by Section 71.004, Family Code.

ART. 56.12. NOTIFICATION OF ESCAPE OR TRANSFER

🅐 *Article 56.12 below is effective for defendants who are released or escape on or after Sept. 1, 2007.*

(a) The Texas Department of Criminal Justice shall immediately notify the victim of an offense, the victim's guardian, or the victim's close relative, if the victim is deceased, if the victim, victim's guardian, or victim's close relative has notified the institutional division as provided by Subsection (b) of this article, whenever the defendant:

(1) escapes from a facility operated by the institutional division; or

(2) is transferred from the custody of the institutional division to the custody of a peace officer under a writ of attachment or a bench warrant.

🅔 **(a-1)** The Texas Department of Criminal Justice shall immediately notify a witness who testified against a defendant at the trial for the offense for which the defendant is incarcerated, the witness's guardian, or the witness's close relative, if the witness is deceased, if the witness, witness's guardian, or witness's close relative has notified the institutional division as provided by Subsection (b), whenever the defendant:

(1) escapes from a facility operated by the institutional division; or

(2) is transferred from the custody of the institutional division to the custody of a peace officer under a writ of attachment or a bench warrant.

(b) It is the responsibility of the victim, witness, guardian, or close relative desiring notification of a defendant's escape or transfer from custody under a writ

of attachment or bench warrant to notify the Texas Department of Criminal Justice of the desire for notification and any change of address.

(c) In providing notice under Subsection (a)(2) or (a-1)(2), the institutional division shall include the name, address, and telephone number of the peace officer receiving the defendant into custody. On returning the defendant to the custody of the institutional division, the victim services division of the Texas Department of Criminal Justice shall notify the victim, witness, guardian, or close relative, as applicable, of that fact.

🅔 **(d)** In this article, "witness's close relative" means a person who was the spouse of the deceased witness at the time of the witness's death or who is a parent or adult brother, sister, or child of the deceased witness.

History of CCP art. 56.12: Acts 1995, 74th Leg., ch. 251, §1, eff. May 29, 1995. Amended by Acts 2001, 77th Leg., ch. 1034, §6, eff. Sept. 1, 2001; Acts 2007, 80th Leg., ch. 458, §2, eff. Sept. 1, 2007.

ART. 56.12. NOTIFICATION OF ESCAPE OR TRANSFER

Article 56.12 below is effective for defendants who are released or escape before Sept. 1, 2007.

(a) The Texas Department of Criminal Justice shall immediately notify the victim of an offense, the victim's guardian, or the victim's close relative, if the victim is deceased, if the victim, victim's guardian, or victim's close relative has notified the institutional division as provided by Subsection (b) of this article, whenever the offender:

(1) escapes from a facility operated by the institutional division; or

(2) is transferred from the custody of the institutional division to the custody of a peace officer under a writ of attachment or a bench warrant.

(b) It is the responsibility of the victim, guardian, or close relative desiring notification of an offender's escape or transfer from custody under a writ of attachment or bench warrant to notify the Texas Department of Criminal Justice of the desire for notification and any change of address.

(c) In providing notice under Subsection (a)(2), the institutional division shall include the name, address, and telephone number of the peace officer receiving the inmate into custody. On returning the inmate to the custody of the institutional division, the victim services division of the Texas Department of

Criminal Justice shall notify the victim, the victim's guardian, or the victim's close relative if the victim is deceased, of that fact.

ART. 56.13. VICTIM-OFFENDER MEDIATION

The victim services division of the Texas Department of Criminal Justice shall:

(1) train volunteers to act as mediators between victims, guardians of victims, and close relatives of deceased victims and offenders whose criminal conduct caused bodily injury or death to victims; and

(2) provide mediation services through referral of a trained volunteer, if requested by a victim, guardian of a victim, or close relative of a deceased victim.

History of CCP art. 56.13: Acts 2001, 77th Leg., ch. 1034, §7, eff. Sept. 1, 2001.

ART. 56.14. CLEARINGHOUSE ANNUAL CONFERENCE

(a) The Texas Crime Victim Clearinghouse may conduct an annual conference to provide to participants in the criminal justice system training containing information on crime victims' rights.

(b) The clearinghouse may charge fees to persons attending the conference described by Subsection (a).

History of CCP art. 56.14: Acts 2001, 77th Leg., ch. 1034, §7, eff. Sept. 1, 2001.

Ⓔ ART. 56.15. COMPUTERIZED DATABASE; DEFENDANT RELEASE INFORMATION

The Texas Department of Criminal Justice shall:

(1) create and maintain a computerized database containing the release information and release date of a defendant described by Article 56.11(c); and

(2) allow a victim or witness entitled to notice under Article 56.11 or 56.12 to access via the Internet the computerized database maintained under Subdivision (1).

History of art 56.15: Acts 2007, 80th Leg., ch. 458, §3, eff. Sept. 1, 2007.

SUBCHAPTER B. CRIME VICTIMS' COMPENSATION

ART. 56.31. SHORT TITLE

This subchapter may be cited as the Crime Victims' Compensation Act.

History of CCP art. 56.31: Acts 1993, 73rd Leg., ch. 268, §6, eff. Sept. 1, 1993. Amended by Acts 1995, 74th Leg., ch. 76, §5.84(a) (eff. Sept. 1, 1995), ch. 779, §1 (eff. Sept. 1, 1995).

ART. 56.311. LEGISLATIVE FINDINGS & INTENT

The legislature recognizes that many innocent individuals suffer personal injury or death as a result of criminal acts. Crime victims and persons who intervene to prevent criminal acts often suffer disabilities, incur financial burdens, or become dependent on public assistance. The legislature finds that there is a need for the compensation of victims of crime and those who suffer personal injury or death in the prevention of crime or in the apprehension of criminals. It is the legislature's intent that the compensation of innocent victims of violent crime encourage greater public cooperation in the successful apprehension and prosecution of criminals.

History of CCP art. 56.311: Acts 1995, 74th Leg., ch. 779, §1, eff. Sept. 1, 1995.

ART. 56.32. DEFINITIONS

(a) In this subchapter:

(1) "Child" means an individual younger than 18 years of age who:

(A) is not married; or

(B) has not had the disabilities of minority removed for general purposes under Chapter 31, Family Code.

(2) "Claimant" means, except as provided by Subsection (b), any of the following individuals who is entitled to file or has filed a claim for compensation under this subchapter:

(A) an authorized individual acting on behalf of a victim;

(B) an individual who legally assumes the obligation or who voluntarily pays medical or burial expenses of a victim incurred as a result of the criminally injurious conduct of another;

(C) a dependent of a victim who died as a result of criminally injurious conduct;

(D) an immediate family member or household member of a victim who:

(i) requires psychiatric care or counseling as a result of the criminally injurious conduct; or

(ii) as a result of the criminally injurious conduct, incurs with respect to a deceased victim expenses for traveling to and attending the victim's funeral or suffers wage loss from bereavement leave taken in connection with the death of that victim; or

(E) an authorized individual acting on behalf of an individual who is described by Subdivision (C) or (D) and who is a child.

(3) "Collateral source" means any of the following sources of benefits or advantages for pecuniary loss that a claimant or victim has received or that is readily available to the claimant or victim from:

(A) the offender under an order of restitution to the claimant or victim imposed by a court as a condition of community supervision;

(B) the United States, a federal agency, a state or any of its political subdivisions, or an instrumentality of two or more states, unless the law providing for the benefits or advantages makes them in excess of or secondary to benefits under this subchapter;

(C) social security, Medicare, or Medicaid;

(D) another state's or another country's crime victims' compensation program;

(E) workers' compensation;

(F) an employer's wage continuation program, not including vacation and sick leave benefits;

(G) proceeds of an insurance contract payable to or on behalf of the claimant or victim for loss that the claimant or victim sustained because of the criminally injurious conduct;

(H) a contract or self-funded program providing hospital and other health care services or benefits; or

(I) proceeds awarded to the claimant or victim as a result of third-party litigation.

(4) "Criminally injurious conduct" means conduct that:

(A) occurs or is attempted;

(B) poses a substantial threat of personal injury or death;

(C) is punishable by fine, imprisonment, or death, or would be punishable by fine, imprisonment, or death if the person engaging in the conduct possessed capacity to commit the conduct; and

Ⓐ *Subsection (D) below is effective for compensation for criminally injurious conduct occurring on or after Sept. 1, 2007.*

(D) does not arise out of the ownership, maintenance, or use of a motor vehicle, aircraft, or water vehicle, unless the conduct is intended to cause personal injury or death or the conduct is in violation of Section 545.157 or 545.401, Transportation Code, and results in

bodily injury or death, or is in violation of Section 550.021, Transportation Code, or one or more of the following sections of the Penal Code:

(i) Section 19.04 (manslaughter);

(ii) Section 19.05 (criminally negligent homicide);

(iii) Section 22.02 (aggravated assault);

Ⓔ **(iv)** Section 22.05 (deadly conduct);

(v) Section 49.04 (driving while intoxicated);

(vi) Section 49.05 (flying while intoxicated);

(vii) Section 49.06 (boating while intoxicated);

(viii) Section 49.07 (intoxication assault); or

(ix) Section 49.08 (intoxication manslaughter).

Subsection (D) below is effective for criminally injurious conduct in which any element of the offense underlying the conduct occurred before Sept. 1, 2007.

(D) does not arise out of the ownership, maintenance, or use of a motor vehicle, aircraft, or water vehicle, unless the conduct is intended to cause personal injury or death or the conduct is in violation of Section 550.021, Transportation Code, or one or more of the following sections of the Penal Code:

(i) Section 19.04 (manslaughter);

(ii) Section 19.05 (criminally negligent homicide);

(iii) Section 22.02 (aggravated assault);

(iv) Section 49.04 (driving while intoxicated);

(v) Section 49.05 (flying while intoxicated);

(vi) Section 49.06 (boating while intoxicated);

(vii) Section 49.07 (intoxication assault); or

(viii) Section 49.08 (intoxication manslaughter).

(5) "Dependent" means:

(A) a surviving spouse;

(B) a person who is a dependent, within the meaning of the Internal Revenue Code, of a victim; and

(C) a posthumous child of a deceased victim.

(6) "Household member" means an individual who resided in the same permanent household as the victim at the time that the criminally injurious conduct occurred and who is related by consanguinity or affinity to the victim.

(7) "Immediate family member" means an individual who is related to a victim within the second degree by affinity or consanguinity.

(8) "Intervenor" means an individual who goes to the aid of another and is killed or injured in the good faith effort to prevent criminally injurious conduct, to apprehend a person reasonably suspected of having engaged in criminally injurious conduct, or to aid a peace officer.

(9) "Pecuniary loss" means the amount of expense reasonably and necessarily incurred as a result of personal injury or death for:

(A) medical, hospital, nursing, or psychiatric care or counseling, or physical therapy;

(B) actual loss of past earnings and anticipated loss of future earnings and necessary travel expenses because of:

(i) a disability resulting from the personal injury;

(ii) the receipt of medically indicated services related to the disability resulting from the personal injury; or

(iii) participation in or attendance at investigative, prosecutorial, or judicial processes related to the criminally injurious conduct and participation in or attendance at any postconviction or postadjudication proceeding relating to criminally injurious conduct;

(C) care of a child or dependent;

(D) funeral and burial expenses, including, for an immediate family member or household member of the victim, the necessary expenses of traveling to and attending the funeral;

(E) loss of support to a dependent, consistent with Article 56.41(b)(5);

(F) reasonable and necessary costs of cleaning the crime scene;

(G) reasonable replacement costs for clothing, bedding, or property of the victim seized as evidence or rendered unusable as a result of the criminal investigation;

(H) reasonable and necessary costs, as provided by Article 56.42(d), incurred by a victim of family violence or a victim of sexual assault who is assaulted in the victim's place of residence for relocation and housing rental assistance payments;

(I) for an immediate family member or household member of a deceased victim, bereavement leave of not more than 10 work days; and

(J) reasonable and necessary costs of traveling to and from a place of execution for the purpose of witnessing the execution, including one night's lodging near the place at which the execution is conducted.

(10) "Personal injury" means physical or mental harm.

(11) "Victim" means, except as provided by Subsection (c):

(A) an individual who:

(i) suffers personal injury or death as a result of criminally injurious conduct or as a result of actions taken by the individual as an intervenor, if the conduct or actions occurred in this state; and

(ii) is a resident of this state, another state of the United States, the District of Columbia, the Commonwealth of Puerto Rico, or a possession or territory of the United States;

(B) an individual who:

(i) suffers personal injury or death as a result of criminally injurious conduct or as a result of actions taken by the individual as an intervenor, if the conduct or actions occurred in a state or country that does not have a crime victims' compensation program that meets the requirements of Section 1403(b), Crime Victims Compensation Act of 1984 (42 U.S.C. Section 10602(b));

(ii) is a resident of this state; and

(iii) would be entitled to compensation under this subchapter if the criminally injurious conduct or actions had occurred in this state; or

(C) an individual who:

(i) suffers personal injury or death as a result of criminally injurious conduct caused by an act of international terrorism as defined by 18 U.S.C. Section 2331 committed outside of the United States; and

(ii) is a resident of this state.

(12) "Family violence" has the meaning assigned by Section 71.004(1), Family Code.

(13) "Victim-related services or assistance" means compensation, services, or assistance provided directly to a victim or claimant for the purpose of supporting or assisting the recovery of the victim or claimant from the consequences of criminally injurious conduct.

(b) In this subchapter "claimant" does not include a service provider.

History of CCP art. 56.32: Acts 1993, 73rd Leg., ch. 268, §6, eff. Sept. 1, 1993. Amended by Acts 1993, 73rd Leg., ch. 805, §§3, 4, eff. Aug. 30, 1993; Acts 1995, 74th Leg., ch. 76, §§5.84(a), 9.55, 14.27 (eff. Sept. 1, 1995), ch. 779, §1 (eff. Sept. 1, 1995); Acts 1997, 75th Leg., ch. 1434, §1, eff. Sept. 1, 1997; Acts 1999, 76th Leg., ch. 1470, §1, eff. June 19, 1999; Acts 2001, 77th Leg., ch. 11, §§1, 2, eff. Sept. 1, 2001; Acts 2003, 78th Leg., ch. 1286, §1 (eff. Sept. 1, 2003), ch. 1303, §2 (eff. June 21, 2003); Acts 2005, 79th Leg., ch. 66, §2 (eff. Sept. 1, 2005), ch. 728, §4.007 (eff. Sept. 1, 2005); Acts 2007, 80th Leg., ch. 1374, §1, eff. Sept. 1, 2007.

ART. 56.33. ADMINISTRATION; RULES

(a) The attorney general shall adopt rules consistent with this subchapter governing its administration, including rules relating to the method of filing claims and the proof of entitlement to compensation and the review of health care services subject to compensation under this chapter. Subchapters A and B, Chapter 2001, Government Code, except Sections 2001.004(3) and 2001.005, apply to the attorney general.

(b) The attorney general may delegate a power, duty, or responsibility given to the attorney general under this subchapter to a person in the attorney general's office.

History of CCP art. 56.33: Acts 1993, 73rd Leg., ch. 268, §6, eff. Sept. 1, 1993. Amended by Acts 1995, 74th Leg., ch. 76, §5.84(a) (eff. Sept. 1, 1995), ch. 779, §1, eff. Sept. 1, 1995.

ART. 56.34. COMPENSATION

(a) The attorney general shall award compensation for pecuniary loss arising from criminally injurious conduct if the attorney general is satisfied by a preponderance of the evidence that the requirements of this subchapter are met.

(b) The attorney general, shall establish whether, as a direct result of criminally injurious conduct, a claimant or victim suffered personal injury or death that resulted in a pecuniary loss for which the claimant or victim is not compensated from a collateral source.

(c) The attorney general shall award compensation for health care services according to the medical fee guidelines prescribed by Subtitle A, Title 5, Labor Code.

(d) The attorney general, a claimant, or a victim is not liable for health care service charges in excess of the medical fee guidelines. A health care provider shall accept compensation from the attorney general as payment in full for the charges unless an investigation of the charges by the attorney general determines that there is a reasonable health care justification for the deviation from the guidelines.

(e) A claimant or victim is not liable for the balance of service charges left as a result of an adjustment of payment for the charges under Article 56.58.

(f) The compensation to victims of crime fund and the compensation to victims of crime auxiliary fund are the payers of last resort.

History of CCP art. 56.34: Acts 1993, 73rd Leg., ch. 268, §6, eff. Sept. 1, 1993. Amended by Acts 1995, 74th Leg., ch. 76, §5.84(a) (eff. Sept. 1, 1995), ch. 779, §1 (eff. Sept. 1, 1995); Acts 1997, 75th Leg., ch. 1434, §1, eff. Sept. 1, 1997.

ART. 56.35. TYPES OF ASSISTANCE

If the attorney general approves an application for compensation under Article 56.41, the attorney general shall determine what type of state assistance will best aid the claimant or victim. The attorney general may do one or more of the following:

(1) authorize cash payment or payments to or on behalf of a claimant or victim for pecuniary loss;

(2) refer a claimant or victim to a state agency for vocational or other rehabilitative services; or

(3) provide counseling services for a claimant or victim or contract with a private entity to provide counseling services.

History of CCP art. 56.35: Acts 1993, 73rd Leg., ch. 268, §6, eff. Sept. 1, 1993. Amended by Acts 1995, 74th Leg., ch. 76, §5.84(a) (eff. Sept. 1, 1995), ch. 779, §1 (eff. Sept. 1, 1995).

ART. 56.36. APPLICATION

(a) An applicant for compensation under this subchapter must apply in writing on a form prescribed by the attorney general.

(b) An application must be verified and must contain:

(1) the date on which the criminally injurious conduct occurred;

(2) a description of the nature and circumstances of the criminally injurious conduct;

(3) a complete financial statement, including:

(A) the cost of medical care or burial expenses and the loss of wages or support the claimant or victim has incurred or will incur; and

(B) the extent to which the claimant or victim has been indemnified for those expenses from a collateral source;

(4) if appropriate, a statement indicating the extent of a disability resulting from the injury incurred;

(5) an authorization permitting the attorney general to verify the contents of the application; and

(6) other information the attorney general requires.

History of CCP art. 56.36: Acts 1993, 73rd Leg., ch. 268, §6, eff. Sept. 1, 1993. Amended by Acts 1995, 74th Leg., ch. 76, §5.84(a) (eff. Sept. 1, 1995), ch. 779, §1 (eff. Sept. 1, 1995); Acts 1997, 75th Leg., ch. 1434, §1, eff. Sept. 1, 1997.

ART. 56.37. TIME FOR FILING

(a) Except as otherwise provided by this article, a claimant or victim must file an application not later than three years from the date of the criminally injurious conduct.

(b) The attorney general may extend the time for filing for good cause shown by the claimant or victim.

(c) If the victim is a child, the application must be filed within three years from the date the claimant or victim is made aware of the crime but not after the child is 21 years of age.

(d) If a claimant or victim presents medically documented evidence of a physical or mental incapacity that was incurred by the claimant or victim as a result of the criminally injurious conduct and that reasonably prevented the claimant or victim from filing the application within the limitations period under Subsection (a), the period of the incapacity is not included.

History of CCP art. 56.37: Acts 1993, 73rd Leg., ch. 268, §6, eff. Sept. 1, 1993. Amended by Acts 1993, 73rd Leg., ch. 805, §10, eff. Aug. 30, 1993; Acts 1995, 74th Leg., ch. 76, §5.84(a) (eff. Sept. 1, 1995), ch. 779, §1 (eff. Sept. 1, 1995); Acts 1997, 75th Leg., ch. 1434, §1, eff. Sept. 1, 1997.

ART. 56.38. REVIEW; VERIFICATION

(a) The attorney general shall appoint a clerk to review each application for compensation under Article 56.36 to ensure the application is complete. If an application is not complete, the clerk shall return it to the claimant or victim and give a brief statement showing the additional information required. Not later than the 30th day after receiving a returned application, a claimant or victim may:

(1) supply the additional information; or

(2) appeal the action to the attorney general, who shall review the application to determine whether it is complete.

(b) The attorney general may investigate an application.

(c) Incident to the attorney general's review, verification, and hearing duties under this subchapter, the attorney general may:

(1) subpoena witnesses and administer oaths to determine whether and the extent to which a claimant or victim qualifies for an award; and

(2) order a claimant or victim to submit to a mental or physical examination by a physician or psychologist or order an autopsy of a deceased victim as provided by Article 56.39, if the mental, physical, or emotional condition of a claimant or victim is material to a claim.

(d) On request by the attorney general and not later than the 14th business day after the date of the request, a law enforcement agency shall release to the attorney general all reports, including witness statements and criminal history record information, for the purpose of allowing the attorney general to determine whether a claimant or victim qualifies for an award and the extent of the qualification.

History of CCP art. 56.38: Acts 1993, 73rd Leg., ch. 268, §6, eff. Sept. 1, 1993. Amended by Acts 1995, 74th Leg., ch. 76, §5.84(a) (eff. Sept. 1, 1995), ch. 779, §1 (eff. Sept. 1, 1995).

ART. 56.385. REVIEW OF HEALTH CARE SERVICES

(a) The attorney general may review the actual or proposed health care services for which a claimant or victim seeks compensation in an application filed under Article 56.36.

(b) The attorney general may not compensate a claimant or victim for health care services that the attorney general determines are not medically necessary.

(c) The attorney general, a claimant, or a victim is not liable for a charge that is not medically necessary.

History of CCP art. 56.385: Acts 1995, 74th Leg., ch. 76, §5.85(a) (eff. Sept. 1, 1995), ch. 779, §1 (eff. Sept. 1, 1995).

ART. 56.39. MENTAL OR PHYSICAL EXAMINATION; AUTOPSY

(a) An order for a mental or physical examination or an autopsy as provided by Article 56.38(c)(3) may be made for good cause shown on notice to the individual to be examined and to all persons who have appeared.

(b) An order shall:

(1) specify the time, place, manner, conditions, and scope of the examination or autopsy;

(2) specify the person by whom the examination or autopsy is to be made; and

(3) require the person making the examination or autopsy to file with the attorney general a detailed written report of the examination or autopsy.

(c) A report shall set out the findings of the person making the examination or autopsy, including:

(1) the results of any tests made; and

(2) diagnoses, prognoses, and other conclusions and reports of earlier examinations of the same conditions.

(d) On request of the individual examined, the attorney general shall furnish the individual with a copy of the report. If the victim is deceased, the attorney general on request shall furnish the claimant with a copy of the report.

(e) A physician or psychologist making an examination or autopsy under this article shall be compensated from funds appropriated for the administration of this subchapter.

History of CCP art. 56.39: Acts 1993, 73rd Leg., ch. 268, §6, eff. Sept. 1, 1993. Amended by Acts 1995, 74th Leg., ch. 76, §5.84(a) (eff. Sept. 1, 1995), ch. 779, §1 (eff. Sept. 1, 1995).

ART. 56.40. HEARINGS

(a) The attorney general shall determine whether a hearing on an application for compensation under this subchapter is necessary.

(b) If the attorney general determines that a hearing is not necessary, the attorney general may approve the application in accordance with the provisions of Article 56.41.

(c) If the attorney general determines that a hearing is necessary or if the claimant or victim requests a hearing, the attorney general shall consider the application at a hearing at a time and place of the attorney general's choosing. The attorney general shall notify all interested persons not less than 10 days before the date of the hearing.

(d) At the hearing the attorney general shall:

(1) review the application for assistance and the report prepared under Article 56.39 and any other evidence obtained as a result of the attorney general's investigation; and

(2) receive other evidence that the attorney general finds necessary or desirable to evaluate the application properly.

(e) The attorney general may appoint hearing officers to conduct hearings or prehearing conferences under this subchapter.

(f) A hearing or prehearing conference is open to the public unless in a particular case the hearing officer or attorney general determines that the hearing or prehearing conference or a part of it should be held in private because a criminal suspect has not been apprehended or because it is in the interest of the claimant or victim.

(g) The attorney general may suspend the proceedings pending disposition of a criminal prosecution that has been commenced or is imminent, but may make an emergency award under Article 56.50.

(h) Subchapters C through H, Chapter 2001, Government Code, do not apply to the attorney general or the attorney general's orders and decisions.

History of CCP art. 56.40: Acts 1993, 73rd Leg., ch. 268, §6, eff. Sept. 1, 1993. Amended by Acts 1995, 74th Leg., ch. 76, §5.84(a) (eff. Sept. 1, 1995), ch. 779, §1 (eff. Sept. 1, 1995).

ART. 56.41. APPROVAL OF CLAIM

(a) The attorney general shall approve an application for compensation under this subchapter if the attorney general finds by a preponderance of the evidence that grounds for compensation under this subchapter exist.

(b) The attorney general shall deny an application for compensation under this subchapter if:

(1) the criminally injurious conduct is not reported as provided by Article 56.46;

(2) the application is not made in the manner provided by Articles 56.36 and 56.37;

(3) the claimant or victim knowingly and willingly participated in the criminally injurious conduct;

(4) the claimant or victim is the offender or an accomplice of the offender;

(5) an award of compensation to the claimant or victim would benefit the offender or an accomplice of the offender;

(6) the claimant or victim was incarcerated in a penal institution, as defined by Section 1.07, Penal Code, at the time the offense was committed; or

(7) the claimant or victim knowingly or intentionally submits false or forged information to the attorney general.

(c) Except as provided by rules adopted by the attorney general to prevent the unjust enrichment of an offender, the attorney general may not deny an award otherwise payable to a claimant or victim because the claimant or victim:

(1) is an immediate family member of the offender; or

(2) resides in the same household as the offender.

History of CCP art. 56.41: Acts 1993, 73rd Leg., ch. 268, §6, eff. Sept. 1, 1993. Amended by Acts 1995, 74th Leg., ch. 76, §5.84(a) (eff. Sept. 1, 1995), ch. 76, §14.28 (eff. Sept. 1, 1995), ch. 779, §1 (eff. Sept. 1, 1995); Acts 1997, 75th Leg., ch. 1434, §1, eff. Sept. 1, 1997.

ART. 56.42. LIMITS ON COMPENSATION

(a) Except as otherwise provided by this article, awards payable to a victim and all other claimants sustaining pecuniary loss because of injury or death of that victim may not exceed $50,000 in the aggregate.

(b) In addition to an award payable under Subsection (a), the attorney general may award an additional $75,000 for extraordinary pecuniary losses, if the personal injury to a victim is catastrophic and results in a total and permanent disability to the victim, for lost wages and reasonable and necessary costs of:

(1) making a home or automobile accessible;

(2) obtaining job training and vocational rehabilitation;

(3) training in the use of special appliances;

(4) receiving home health care;

(5) durable medical equipment;

(6) rehabilitation technology; and

(7) long-term medical expenses incurred as a result of medically indicated treatment for the personal injury.

(c) The attorney general may by rule establish limitations on any other pecuniary loss compensated for under this subchapter, including limitations on pecuniary loss incurred as a result of a claimant's travel to and attendance of a deceased victim's funeral.

(d) A victim who is a victim of family violence or a victim of sexual assault who is assaulted in the victim's place of residence may receive a onetime-only assistance payment in an amount not to exceed:

(1) $2,000 to be used for relocation expenses, including expenses for rental deposit, utility connections, expenses relating to the moving of belongings, motor vehicle mileage expenses, and for out-of-state moves, transportation, lodging, and meals; and

(2) $1,800 to be used for housing rental expenses.

(e) An immediate family member or household member of a deceased victim may not receive more than $1,000 in lost wages as a result of bereavement leave taken by the family or household member.

History of CCP art. 56.42: Acts 1993, 73rd Leg., ch. 268, §6, eff. Sept. 1, 1993. Amended by Acts 1995, 74th Leg., ch. 76, §5.84(a) (eff. Sept. 1, 1995), ch. 779, §1 (eff. Sept. 1, 1995); Acts 1997, 75th Leg., ch. 1434, §1, eff. Sept. 1, 1997; Acts 1999, 76th Leg., ch. 1301, §1 (eff. June 19, 1999), ch. 1470, §2 (eff. June 19, 1999); Acts 2001, 77th Leg., ch. 11, §3 (eff. Sept. 1, 2001), ch. 274, §1 (eff. Sept. 1, 2001); Acts 2003, 78th Leg., ch. 1286, §2, eff. Sept. 1, 2003.

ART. 56.43. ATTORNEY FEES

(a) As part of an order, the attorney general shall determine and award reasonable attorney's fees, commensurate with legal services rendered, to be paid by the state to the attorney representing the claimant or victim. Attorney fees shall not exceed 25 percent of the amount the attorney assisted the claimant or victim in obtaining. Where there is no dispute of the attorney general's determination of the amount of the award due to the claimant or victim and where no hearing is held, the attorney fee shall be the lesser of either 25 percent of the amount the attorney assisted the claimant or victim in obtaining or $300.

(b) Attorney fees may be denied on a finding that the claim or appeal is frivolous.

(c) An award of attorney fees is in addition to an award of compensation.

(d) An attorney may not contract for or receive an amount larger than that allowed under this article.

(e) Attorney fees may not be paid to an attorney of a claimant or victim unless an award is made to the claimant or victim.

History of CCP art. 56.43: Acts 1993, 73rd Leg., ch. 268, §6, eff. Sept. 1, 1993. Amended by Acts 1993, 73rd Leg., ch. 805, §9, eff. Aug. 30, 1993; Acts 1995, 74th Leg., ch. 76, §5.84(a) (eff. Sept. 1, 1995), ch. 779, §1 (eff. Sept. 1, 1995).

ART. 56.44. PAYMENTS

(a) The attorney general may provide for the payment of an award in a lump sum or in installments. The attorney general shall provide that the part of an award equal to the amount of pecuniary loss accrued to the date of the award be paid in a lump sum. Except as provided in Subsection (b), the attorney general shall pay the part of an award for allowable expense that accrues after the award is made in installments.

(b) At the request of the claimant or victim, the attorney general may provide that an award for future pecuniary loss be paid in a lump sum if the attorney general finds that:

(1) paying the award in a lump sum will promote the interests of the claimant or victim; or

(2) the present value of all future pecuniary loss does not exceed $1,000.

(c) The attorney general may not provide for an award for future pecuniary loss payable in installments for a period for which the attorney general cannot reasonably determine the future pecuniary loss.

(d) The attorney general may make payments only to an individual who is a claimant or a victim or to a provider on the individual's behalf.

History of CCP art. 56.44: Acts 1993, 73rd Leg., ch. 268, §6, eff. Sept. 1, 1993. Amended by Acts 1995, 74th Leg., ch. 76, §5.84(a) (eff. Sept. 1, 1995), ch. 779, §1 (eff. Sept. 1, 1995); Acts 1997, 75th Leg., ch. 1434, §1, eff. Sept. 1, 1997.

ART. 56.45. DENIAL OR REDUCTION OF AWARD

The attorney general may deny or reduce an award otherwise payable:

(1) if the claimant or victim has not substantially cooperated with an appropriate law enforcement agency;

(2) if the claimant or victim bears a share of the responsibility for the act or omission giving rise to the claim because of the claimant's or victim's behavior;

(3) to the extent that pecuniary loss is recouped from a collateral source; or

(4) if the claimant or victim was engaging in an activity that at the time of the criminally injurious conduct was prohibited by law or a rule made under law.

History of CCP art. 56.45: Acts 1993, 73rd Leg., ch. 268, §6, eff. Sept. 1, 1993. Amended by Acts 1995, 74th Leg., ch. 76, §5.84(a) (eff. Sept. 1, 1995), ch. 779, §1 (eff. Sept. 1, 1995); Acts 1997, 75th Leg., ch. 1434, §1, eff. Sept. 1, 1997.

ART. 56.46. REPORTING OF CRIME

(a) Except as otherwise provided by this article, a claimant or victim may not file an application unless the victim reports the criminally injurious conduct to the appropriate state or local public safety or law enforcement agency within a reasonable period of time, but not so late as to interfere with or hamper the investigation and prosecution of the crime after the criminally injurious conduct is committed.

(b) The attorney general may extend the time for reporting the criminally injurious conduct if the attorney general determines that the extension is justified by extraordinary circumstances.

(c) Subsection (a) does not apply if the victim is a child.

History of CCP art. 56.46: Acts 1993, 73rd Leg., ch. 268, §6, eff. Sept. 1, 1993. Amended by Acts 1995, 74th Leg., ch. 76, §5.84(a) (eff. Sept. 1, 1995), ch. 779, §1 (eff. Sept. 1, 1995); Acts 1997, 75th Leg., ch. 1434, §1, eff. Sept. 1, 1997.

ART. 56.47. RECONSIDERATION

(a) The attorney general, on the attorney general's own motion or on request of a claimant or victim, may reconsider:

(1) a decision to make or deny an award; or

(2) the amount of an award.

(b) At least annually, the attorney general shall reconsider each award being paid in installments.

(c) An order on reconsideration may require a refund of an award if:

(1) the award was obtained by fraud or mistake; or

(2) newly discovered evidence shows the claimant or victim to be ineligible for the award under Article 56.41 or 56.45.

History of CCP art. 56.47: Acts 1993, 73rd Leg., ch. 268, §6, eff. Sept. 1, 1993. Amended by Acts 1993, 73rd Leg., ch. 805, §6, eff. Aug. 30, 1993; Acts 1995, 74th Leg., ch. 76, §5.84(a), (b) (eff. Sept. 1, 1995), ch. 779, §1 (eff. Sept. 1, 1995); Acts 1997, 75th Leg., ch. 1434, §1, eff. Sept. 1, 1997.

ART. 56.48. JUDICIAL REVIEW

(a) Not later than the 40th day after the attorney general renders a final decision, a claimant or victim may file with the attorney general a notice of dissatisfaction with the decision. Not later than the 40th day after the claimant or victim gives notice, the claimant or victim shall bring suit in the district court having jurisdiction in the county in which:

(1) the injury or death occurred;

(2) the victim resided at the time the injury or death occurred; or

(3) if the victim resided out of state at the time of the injury or death, in the county where the injury or death occurred or in a district court of Travis County.

(b) While judicial review of a decision by the attorney general is pending, the attorney general:

(1) shall suspend payments to the claimant or victim; and

(2) may not reconsider the award.

(c) The court shall determine the issues by trial de novo. The burden of proof is on the party who filed the notice of dissatisfaction.

(d) A court may award not more than 25 percent of the total recovery by the claimant or victim for attorney fees in the event of review.

(e) In computing a period under this article, if the last day is a legal holiday or Sunday, the last day is not counted, and the time is extended to include the next business day.

History of CCP art. 56.48: Acts 1993, 73rd Leg., ch. 268, §6, eff. Sept. 1, 1993. Amended by Acts 1995, 74th Leg., ch. 76, §5.84(a) (eff. Sept. 1, 1995), ch. 779, §1 (eff. Sept. 1, 1995); Acts 1997, 75th Leg., ch. 1434, §1, eff. Sept. 1, 1997.

ART. 56.49. EXEMPTION; ASSIGNABILITY

(a) An award is not subject to execution, attachment, garnishment, or other process, except that an award is not exempt from a claim of a creditor to the extent that the creditor provided products, services, or accommodations, the costs of which are included in the award.

(b) An assignment or agreement to assign a right to benefits for loss accruing in the future is unenforceable except:

(1) an assignment of a right to benefits for loss of earnings is enforceable to secure payment of alimony, maintenance, or child support; and

(2) an assignment of a right to benefits is enforceable to the extent that the benefits are for the cost of products, services, or accommodations:

(A) made necessary by the injury or death on which the claim is based; and

(B) provided or to be provided by the assignee.

History of CCP art. 56.49: Acts 1993, 73rd Leg., ch. 268, §6, eff. Sept. 1, 1993. Amended by Acts 1995, 74th Leg., ch. 76, §5.84(a) (eff. Sept. 1, 1995), ch. 779, §1 (eff. Sept. 1, 1995).

ART. 56.50. EMERGENCY AWARD

(a) The attorney general may make an emergency award if, before acting on an application for compensation under this subchapter, it appears likely that:

(1) a final award will be made; and

(2) the claimant or victim will suffer undue hardship if immediate economic relief is not obtained.

(b) An emergency award may not exceed $1,500.

(c) The amount of an emergency award shall be:

(1) deducted from the final award; or

(2) repaid by and recoverable from the claimant or victim to the extent the emergency award exceeds the final award.

History of CCP art. 56.50: Acts 1993, 73rd Leg., ch. 268, §6, eff. Sept. 1, 1993. Amended by Acts 1995, 74th Leg., ch. 76, §5.84(a) (eff. Sept. 1, 1995), ch. 779, §1 (eff. Sept. 1, 1995).

ART. 56.51. SUBROGATION

If compensation is awarded under this subchapter, the state is subrogated to all the claimant's or victim's rights to receive or recover benefits for pecuniary loss to the extent compensation is awarded from a collateral source.

History of CCP art. 56.51: Acts 1993, 73rd Leg., ch. 268, §6, eff. Sept. 1, 1993. Amended by Acts 1995, 74th Leg., ch. 76, §5.84(a) (eff. Sept. 1, 1995), ch. 779, §1 (eff. Sept. 1, 1995).

ART. 56.52. NOTICE OF PRIVATE ACTION

(a) Before a claimant or victim may bring an action to recover damages related to criminally injurious conduct for which compensation under this subchapter is claimed or awarded, the claimant or victim must give the attorney general written notice of the proposed action. After receiving the notice, the attorney general shall promptly:

(1) join in the action as a party plaintiff to recover benefits awarded;

(2) require the claimant or victim to bring the action in the claimant's or victim's name as a trustee on behalf of the state to recover benefits awarded; or

(3) reserve the attorney general's rights and do neither in the proposed action.

(b) If the claimant or victim brings the action as trustee and recovers compensation awarded by the attorney general, the claimant or victim may deduct from the benefits recovered on behalf of the state the reasonable expenses of the suit, including attorney fees, expended in pursuing the recovery for the state. The claimant or victim must justify this deduction in writing to the attorney general on a form provided by the attorney general.

(c) A claimant or victim shall not settle or resolve any such action without written authorization to do so from the attorney general. No third party or agents, insurers, or attorneys for third parties shall participate in the settlement or resolution of such an action if they actually know, or should know, that the claimant or victim has received moneys from the fund and is subject to the subrogation provisions of this article. Any attempt by such third party, or agents, insurers, or attorneys of third parties to settle an action is void and shall result in no release from liability to the fund for any rights subrogated pursuant to this article. All such agents, insurers, and attorneys are personally liable to the fund for any moneys paid to a claimant or victim in violation of this subsection, up to the full amount of the fund's right to reimbursement. A claimant, victim, third party, or any agents, attorneys, or insurers of third parties who knowingly or intentionally fail to comply with the requirements of this chapter commits a Class B misdemeanor.

(d) A person adjudged guilty of a Class B misdemeanor shall be punished by:

(1) a fine not to exceed $500;

(2) confinement in jail for a term not to exceed 180 days; or

(3) both such fine and imprisonment.

History of CCP art. 56.52: Acts 1993, 73rd Leg., ch. 268, §6, eff. Sept. 1, 1993. Amended by Acts 1993, 73rd Leg., ch. 805, §11, eff. Aug. 30, 1993; Acts 1995, 74th Leg., ch. 76, §5.84(a) (eff. Sept. 1, 1995), ch. 779, §1 (eff. Sept. 1, 1995).

ART. 56.53. ANNUAL REPORT

Annually, the attorney general shall report to the governor and the legislature on the attorney general's activities, including a statistical summary of claims and awards made and denied. The reporting period is the state fiscal year. The attorney general shall file the report not later than the 100th day after the end of the fiscal year.

History of CCP art. 56.53: Acts 1993, 73rd Leg., ch. 268, §6, eff. Sept. 1, 1993. Amended by Acts 1995, 74th Leg., ch. 76, §5.84(a) (eff. Sept. 1, 1995), ch. 779, §1 (eff. Sept. 1, 1995).

ART. 56.54. FUNDS

(a) The compensation to victims of crime fund and the compensation to victims of crime auxiliary fund are in the state treasury.

(b) Except as provided by Subsections (h), (i), (j), and (k) and Article 56.541, the compensation to victims of crime fund may be used only by the attorney general for the payment of compensation to claimants or victims under this subchapter. For purposes of this subsection, compensation to claimants or victims includes money allocated from the fund to the Crime Victims' Institute created by Section 96.65, Education Code, for the operation of the institute and for other expenses in administering this subchapter. The institute shall use money allocated from the fund only for the purposes of Sections 96.65, 96.651, and 96.652, Education Code.

(c) Except as provided by Subsections (h), (i), and (*l*), the compensation to victims of crime auxiliary fund may be used by the attorney general only for the payment of compensation to claimants or victims under this subchapter.

(d) The attorney general may not make compensation payments in excess of the amount of money available from the combined funds.

(e) General revenues may not be used for payments under this subchapter.

(f) The office of the attorney general is authorized to accept gifts, grants, and donations to be credited to the compensation to victims of crime fund and compensation to victims of crime auxiliary fund and shall file annually with the governor and the presiding officer of each house of the legislature a complete and detailed written report accounting for all gifts, grants, and donations received and disbursed, used, or maintained by the office for the attorney general that are credited to these funds.

(g) Money in the compensation to victims of crime fund or in the compensation to victims of crime auxiliary fund may be used only as provided by this subchapter and is not available for any other purpose. Section 403.095, Government Code, does not apply to the fund.

(h) An amount of money deposited to the credit of the compensation to victims of crime fund not to exceed one-quarter of the amount disbursed from that fund in the form of compensation payments during a fiscal year shall be carried forward into the next succeeding fiscal year and applied toward the amount listed in the next succeeding fiscal year's method of financing.

(i) If the sums available in the compensation to victims of crime fund are sufficient in a fiscal year to make all compensation payments, the attorney general may retain any portion of the fund that was deposited during the fiscal year that was in excess of compensation payments made during that fiscal year as an emergency reserve for the next fiscal year. Such emergency reserve may not exceed $10,000,000. The emergency reserve fund may be used only to make compensation awards in claims and for providing emergency relief and assistance, including crisis intervention, emergency housing, travel, food, or expenses and technical assistance expenses incurred in the implementation of this subsection in incidents resulting from an act of mass violence or from an act of international terrorism as defined by 18 U.S.C. Section 2331, occurring in the state or for Texas residents injured or killed in an act of terrorism outside of the United States.

(j) The legislature may appropriate money in the compensation to victims of crime fund to administer the associate judge program under Subchapter C, Chapter 201, Family Code.

(k) The attorney general may use the compensation to victims of crime fund to reimburse a law enforcement agency for the reasonable costs of a medical examination that are incurred by the agency under Article 56.06.

(*l*) The attorney general may use the compensation to victims of crime auxiliary fund to cover costs incurred by the attorney general in administering the address confidentiality program established under Subchapter C.

History of CCP art. 56.54: Acts 1993, 73rd Leg., ch. 268, §6, eff. Sept. 1, 1993. Amended by Acts 1993, 73rd Leg., ch. 805, §1, eff. Aug. 30, 1993; Acts 1995, 74th Leg., ch. 76, §5.84(a) (eff. Sept. 1, 1995), ch. 779, §1 (eff. Sept. 1, 1995); Acts 1997, 75th Leg., ch. 1042, §1 (eff. June 19, 1997), ch. 1042, §2 (eff. Sept. 1,

1997), ch. 1434, §1 (eff. Sept. 1, 1997); Acts 1999, 76th Leg., ch. 1302, §13, eff. Sept. 1, 1999; Acts 2001, 77th Leg., ch. 1507, §§2, 3, eff. June 17, 2001; Acts 2003, 78th Leg., ch. 927, §2, eff. Sept. 1, 2003; Acts 2007, 80th Leg., ch. 1295, §2, eff. June 15, 2007.

ART. 56.541. APPROPRIATION OF EXCESS MONEY FOR OTHER CRIME VICTIM ASSISTANCE

(a) Not later than December 15 of each even-numbered year, the attorney general, after consulting with the comptroller, shall prepare forecasts and certify estimates of:

(1) the amount of money that the attorney general anticipates will be received from deposits made to the credit of the compensation to victims of crime fund during the next state fiscal biennium, other than deposits of:

(A) gifts, grants, and donations; and

(B) money received from the United States;

(2) the amount of money from the fund that the attorney general anticipates will be obligated during the next state fiscal biennium to comply with this chapter; and

(3) the amount of money in the fund that the attorney general anticipates will remain unexpended at the end of the current state fiscal year and that is available for appropriation in the next state fiscal biennium.

(b) At the time the attorney general certifies the estimates made under Subsection (a), the attorney general shall also certify for the next state fiscal biennium the amount of excess money in the compensation to victims of crime fund for purposes of Subsection (c), calculated by subtracting the amount estimated under Subsection (a)(2) from the sum of the amounts estimated under Subsections (a)(1) and (a)(3).

(c) For a state fiscal biennium, the legislature may appropriate from the compensation to victims of crime fund the amount of excess money in the fund certified for the biennium under Subsection (b) to state agencies that deliver or fund victim-related services or assistance.

(d) The attorney general and the comptroller shall cooperate in determining the proper allocation of the various sources of revenue deposited to the credit of the compensation to victims of crime fund for purposes of this article.

(e) The attorney general may use money appropriated from the compensation to victims of crime fund for grants or contracts supporting victim-related services or assistance, including support for private Texas nonprofit corporations that provide victim-related civil legal services directly to victims, immediate family members of victims, or claimants. A grant supporting victim-related services or assistance is governed by Chapter 783, Government Code.

(f) The attorney general shall adopt rules necessary to carry out this article.

History of CCP art. 56.541: Acts 1997, 75th Leg., ch. 1042, §3, eff. Sept. 1, 1997. Amended by Acts 1999, 76th Leg., ch. 1077, §1, eff. Aug. 30, 1999; Acts 2005, 79th Leg., ch. 66, §3, eff. Sept. 1, 2005.

ART. 56.542. PAYMENTS FOR CERTAIN DISABLED PEACE OFFICERS

(a) In this article, "peace officer":

(1) means an individual elected, appointed, or employed to serve as a peace officer for a governmental entity under Article 2.12 or other law; and

(2) includes a former peace officer who because of an injury suffered while performing duties as a peace officer is entitled to receive payments under this article.

(b) If a peace officer employed by the state or a local governmental entity in this state sustains an injury as a result of criminally injurious conduct on or after September 1, 1989, in the performance of the officer's duties as a peace officer and presents evidence satisfactory to the attorney general that the officer's condition is a total disability resulting in permanent incapacity for work and that the total disability has persisted for more than 12 months, the officer is entitled to an annual payment equal to the difference between:

(1) any amounts received by the officer on account of the injury or disability from other sources of income, including settlements related to the injury or disability, insurance benefits, federal disability benefits, workers' compensation benefits, and benefits from another governmental entity, if those amounts do not exceed the amount described by Subdivision (2); and

(2) an amount equal to the officer's average annual salary during the officer's final three years as a peace officer.

(c) The amount of the payment under Subsection (b) is subject to an annual cost-of-living adjustment computed by the attorney general. The attorney general shall compute the amount of the cost-of-living adjustment by multiplying the amount of the annual payment received by the peace officer under this section during the previous year times the percentage by which the Consumer Price Index for All Urban Consumers published by the Bureau of Labor Statistics of the United States Department of Labor, or its successor index, increased during the previous calendar year.

(d) The attorney general shall compute the amount of an initial payment based on an injury suffered after September 1, 1989, by:

(1) computing the amount to which the officer is entitled under Subsection (b); and

(2) adding to that amount the cumulative successive cost-of-living adjustments for the intervening years computed from the date of the injury.

(e) To receive a payment under this section, a peace officer must furnish to the attorney general:

(1) proof that the injury was sustained in the performance of the applicant's duties as a peace officer and is a total disability resulting in permanent incapacity for work; and

(2) other information or evidence the attorney general requires.

(f) The attorney general may approve the application without a hearing or may conduct a hearing under Article 56.40. The decision of the attorney general is subject to judicial review under Article 56.48.

(g) The attorney general may appoint a panel of physicians to periodically review each application for assistance under this article to ensure the validity of the application and the necessity of continued assistance to the peace officer.

(h) The attorney general shall notify the comptroller of the attorney general's determination that a claim under this section is valid and justifies payment. On receipt of the notice, the comptroller shall issue a warrant to or in behalf of the claimant in the proper amount from amounts in the compensation to victims of crime fund. A payment under this section to or in behalf of a peace officer is payable as soon as possible after the attorney general notifies the comptroller.

(i) The attorney general and the comptroller by rule shall adopt a memorandum of understanding to establish procedures under which annual payments continue to a peace officer until continued assistance is no longer necessary.

(j) Article 56.37 does not apply to the filing of an application under this article. Other provisions of this chapter apply to this article to the extent applicable and consistent with this article.

(k) The limits on compensation imposed by Article 56.42 do not apply to payments made under this article, but the total aggregate amount of all annual payments made to an individual peace officer under this section may not exceed $200,000.

(*l*) A peace officer who is entitled to an annual payment under Subsection (b) may elect to receive the payment in:

(1) a single payment paid each year; or

(2) equal monthly installments.

History of CCP art. 56.542: Acts 2001, 77th Leg., ch. 1512, §2, eff. Sept. 1, 2001. Amended by Acts 2005, 79th Leg., ch. 751, §1, eff. June 17, 2005.

ART. 56.55. REPEALED

Repealed by Acts 2003, 78th Leg., ch. 209, §85(a)(1), eff. Jan. 1, 2004.

ART. 56.56. REPEALED

Repealed by Acts 2003, 78th Leg., ch. 209, §85(a)(2), eff. Jan. 1, 2004.

ART. 56.57. REPEALED

Repealed by Acts 2003, 78th Leg., ch. 209, §85(a)(3), eff. Jan. 1, 2004.

ART. 56.58. ADJUSTMENT OF AWARDS & PAYMENTS

(a) The attorney general shall establish a policy to adjust awards and payments so that the total amount of awards granted in each calendar year does not exceed the amount of money credited to the fund during that year.

(b) If the attorney general establishes a policy to adjust awards under Subsection (a), the attorney general, the claimant, or the victim is not liable for the amount of charges incurred in excess of the adjusted amount for the service on which the adjusted payment is determined.

(c) A service provider who accepts a payment that has been adjusted by a policy established under Subsection (a) agrees to accept the adjusted payment as payment in full for the service and is barred from legal action against the claimant or victim for collection.

History of CCP art. 56.58: Acts 1993, 73rd Leg., ch. 268, §6, eff. Sept. 1, 1993. Amended by Acts 1995, 74th Leg., ch. 76, §5.84(a) (eff. Sept. 1, 1995), ch. 779, §1 (eff. Sept. 1, 1995).

ART. 56.59. REPEALED

Repealed by Acts 2003, 78th Leg., ch. 209, §85(a)(4), eff. Jan. 1, 2004.

ART. 56.60. PUBLIC NOTICE

(a) A hospital licensed under the laws of this state shall display prominently in its emergency room posters giving notification of the existence and general provisions of this subchapter. The attorney general shall

★

set standards for the location of the display and shall provide posters, application forms, and general information regarding this subchapter to each hospital and physician licensed to practice in this state.

(b) Each local law enforcement agency shall inform a claimant or victim of criminally injurious conduct of the provisions of this subchapter and make application forms available. The attorney general shall provide application forms and all other documents that local law enforcement agencies may require to comply with this article. The attorney general shall set standards to be followed by local law enforcement agencies for this purpose and may require them to file with the attorney general a description of the procedures adopted by each agency to comply.

History of CCP art. 56.60: Acts 1993, 73rd Leg., ch. 268, §6, eff. Sept. 1, 1993. Amended by Acts 1995, 74th Leg., ch. 76, §5.84(a) (eff. Sept. 1, 1995), ch. 779, §1 (eff. Sept. 1, 1995).

ART. 56.61. COMPENSATION FOR CERTAIN CRIMINALLY INJURIOUS CONDUCT PROHIBITED

The attorney general may not award compensation for economic loss arising from criminally injurious conduct that occurred before January 1, 1980.

History of CCP art. 56.61: Acts 1993, 73rd Leg., ch. 268, §6, eff. Sept. 1, 1993. Amended by Acts 1995, 74th Leg., ch. 76, §5.84(a) (eff. Sept. 1, 1995), ch. 779, §1 (eff. Sept. 1, 1995).

ART. 56.62. PUBLIC LETTER OF REPRIMAND

(a) The attorney general may issue a letter of reprimand against an individual if the attorney general finds that the person has filed or has caused to be filed under this subchapter an application for benefits or claim for pecuniary loss that contains a statement or representation that the person knows to be false.

(b) The attorney general must give the person notice of the proposed action before issuing the letter.

(c) A person may challenge the denial of compensation and the issuance of a letter of reprimand in a contested case hearing under Chapter 2001, Government Code (Administrative Procedure Act).

(d) A letter of reprimand issued under this article is public information.

History of CCP art. 56.62: Acts 1995, 74th Leg., ch. 779, §1, eff. Sept. 1, 1995.

ART. 56.63. CIVIL PENALTY

(a) A person is subject to a civil penalty of not less than $2,500 or more than $25,000 for each application for compensation that:

(1) is filed under this subchapter by the person or is filed under this subchapter as a result of conduct of the person; and

(2) contains a material statement or representation that the person knows to be false.

(b) The attorney general shall institute and conduct the suit to collect the civil penalty authorized by this article on behalf of the state.

(c) A civil penalty recovered under this article shall be deposited to the credit of the compensation to victims of crime fund.

(d) The civil penalty authorized by this article is in addition to any other civil, administrative, or criminal penalty provided by law.

(e) In addition to the civil penalty authorized by this article, the attorney general may recover expenses incurred by the attorney general in the investigation, institution, and prosecution of the suit, including investigative costs, witness fees, attorney's fees, and deposition expenses.

History of CCP art. 56.63: Acts 1995, 74th Leg., ch. 779, §1, eff. Sept. 1, 1995.

ART. 56.64. ADMINISTRATIVE PENALTY

(a) A person who presents to the attorney general under this subchapter, or engages in conduct that results in the presentation to the attorney general under this subchapter of, an application for compensation under this subchapter that contains a statement or representation the person knows to be false is liable to the attorney general for:

(1) the amount paid in reliance on the application and interest on that amount determined at the rate provided by law for legal judgments and accruing from the date on which the payment was made;

(2) payment of an administrative penalty not to exceed twice the amount paid because of the false application for benefits or claim for pecuniary loss; and

(3) payment of an administrative penalty of not more than $10,000 for each item or service for which payment was claimed.

(b) In determining the amount of the penalty to be assessed under Subsection(a)(3), the attorney general shall consider:

(1) the seriousness of the violation;

(2) whether the person has previously submitted a false application for benefits or a claim for pecuniary loss; and

(3) the amount necessary to deter the person from submitting future false applications for benefits or claims for pecuniary loss.

(c) If the attorney general determines that a violation has occurred, the attorney general may issue a report that states the facts on which the determination is made and the attorney general's recommendation on the imposition of a penalty, including a recommendation on the amount of the penalty.

(d) The attorney general shall give written notice of the report to the person. Notice under this subsection may be given by certified mail and must:

(1) include a brief summary of the alleged violation;

(2) include a statement of the amount of the recommended penalty; and

(3) inform the person of the right to a hearing on:

(A) the occurrence of the violation;

(B) the amount of the penalty; or

(C) both the occurrence of the violation and the amount of the penalty.

(e) Not later than the 20th day after the date the person receives the notice, the person, in writing, may:

(1) accept the attorney general's determination and recommended penalty; or

(2) request in writing a hearing on:

(A) the occurrence of the violation;

(B) the amount of the penalty; or

(C) both the occurrence of the violation and the amount of the penalty.

(f) If the person accepts the determination and recommended penalty of the attorney general, the attorney general by order shall approve the determination and impose the recommended penalty.

(g) If the person requests a hearing as provided by Subsection(e) or fails to respond to the notice in a timely manner, the attorney general shall set a contested case hearing under Chapter 2001, Government Code (Administrative Procedure Act), and notify the person of the hearing. The administrative law judge shall make findings of facts and conclusions of law and promptly issue to the attorney general a proposal for a decision regarding the occurrence of the violation and the amount of a proposed penalty. Based on the findings of fact, conclusions of law, and proposal for a decision, the attorney general by order may:

(1) find that a violation has occurred and impose a penalty; or

(2) find that a violation has not occurred.

(h) Notice of the attorney general's order given to the person under Chapter 2001, Government Code, must include a statement of the right of the person to judicial review of the order.

(i) Not later than the 30th day after the date that the attorney general's order is final under Section 2001.144, Government Code, the person shall:

(1) pay the amount of the penalty;

(2) pay the amount of the penalty and file a petition for judicial review contesting:

(A) the occurrence of the violation;

(B) the amount of the penalty; or

(C) the occurrence of the violation and the amount of the penalty; or

(3) without paying the amount of the penalty, file a petition for judicial review contesting:

(A) the occurrence of the violation;

(B) the amount of the penalty; or

(C) the occurrence of the violation and the amount of the penalty.

(j) Within the 30-day period, a person who acts under Subsection(i)(3) may:

(1) stay enforcement of the penalty by:

(A) paying the amount of the penalty to the court for placement in an escrow account; or

(B) giving to the court a supersedeas bond that is approved by the court for the amount of the penalty and that is effective until all judicial review of the attorney general's order is final; or

(2) request the court to stay enforcement of the penalty by:

(A) filing with the court a sworn affidavit of the person stating that the person is financially unable to pay the amount of the penalty or to give the supersedeas bond; and

(B) delivering a copy of the affidavit to the attorney general by certified mail.

(k) On receipt by the attorney general of a copy of an affidavit under Subsection(j)(2), the attorney general may file with the court, not later than the fifth day after the date the copy is received, a contest to the affidavit. The court shall hold a hearing on the facts alleged in the affidavit as soon as practicable and shall stay the enforcement of the penalty on finding that the alleged facts are true. A person who files an affidavit under Subsection(j)(2) has the burden of proving that the person is financially unable to pay the amount of the penalty or to give a supersedeas bond.

(*l*) If the person does not pay the amount of the penalty and the enforcement of the penalty is not stayed, the attorney general may file suit for collection of the amount of the penalty.

(m) Judicial review of the order of the attorney general:

(1) is instituted by filing a petition as provided by Section 2001.176, Government Code; and

(2) is governed by the substantial evidence rule.

(n) If the court upholds the finding that a violation occurred, the court may order the person to pay the full or reduced amount of the penalty. If the court does not uphold the finding, the court shall order that no penalty is owed.

(o) If the person paid the amount of the penalty and if that amount is reduced or is not upheld by the court, the court shall order that the appropriate amount plus accrued interest be remitted to the person. The rate of the interest is the rate charged on loans to depository institutions by the New York Federal Reserve Bank, and the interest shall be paid for the period beginning on the date the penalty was paid and ending on the date the penalty is remitted. If the person gave a supersedeas bond and if the amount of the penalty is not upheld by the court, the court shall order the release of the bond. If the person gave a supersedeas bond and if the amount of the penalty is reduced, the court shall order the release of the bond after the person pays the amount.

(p) A penalty collected under this article shall be sent to the comptroller and deposited to the credit of the compensation to victims of crime fund.

(q) All proceedings under this article are subject to Chapter 2001, Government Code.

(r) In addition to the administrative penalty authorized by this article, the attorney general may recover all expenses incurred by the attorney general in the investigation, institution, and prosecution of the suit, including investigative costs, witness fees, attorney's fees, and deposition expenses.

History of CCP art. 56.64: Acts 1995, 74th Leg., ch. 779, §1, eff. Sept. 1, 1995.

SUBCHAPTER C. ADDRESS CONFIDENTIALITY PROGRAM FOR VICTIMS OF FAMILY VIOLENCE, SEXUAL ASSAULT, OR STALKING

ART. 56.81. DEFINITIONS

In this subchapter:

(1) "Applicant" means a person who applies to participate in the program.

(2) "Family violence" has the meaning assigned by Section 71.004, Family Code.

(3) "Family violence shelter center" has the meaning assigned by Section 51.002, Human Resources Code.

(4) "Mail" means first class mail and any mail sent by a government agency. The term does not include a package, regardless of size or type of mailing.

(5) "Participant" means an applicant who is certified for participation in the program.

(6) "Program" means the address confidentiality program created under this subchapter.

History of CCP art. 56.81: Acts 2007, 80th Leg., ch. 1295, §1, eff. June 15, 2007.

ART. 56.82. ADDRESS CONFIDENTIALITY PROGRAM

(a) The attorney general shall establish an address confidentiality program, as provided by this subchapter, to assist a victim of family violence or an offense under Section 22.011, 22.021, 25.02, or 42.072, Penal Code, in maintaining a confidential address.

(b) The attorney general shall:

(1) designate a substitute post office box address that a participant may use in place of the participant's true residential, business, or school address;

(2) act as agent to receive service of process and mail on behalf of the participant; and

(3) forward to the participant mail received by the office of the attorney general on behalf of the participant.

(c) A summons, writ, notice, demand, or process may be served on the attorney general on behalf of the participant by delivery of two copies of the document to the office of the attorney general. The attorney general shall retain a copy of the summons, writ, notice, demand, or process and forward the original to the participant not later than the third day after the date of service on the attorney general.

(d) The attorney general shall make and retain a copy of the envelope in which certified mail is received on behalf of the participant.

History of CCP art. 56.82: Acts 2007, 80th Leg., ch. 1295, §1, eff. June 15, 2007.

ART. 56.83. ELIGIBILITY TO PARTICIPATE IN PROGRAM

(a) To be eligible to participate in the program, an applicant must:

(1) meet with a victim's assistance counselor from a state or local agency or other entity, whether for-profit or nonprofit that is identified by the attorney general as an entity that provides counseling and shelter services to victims of family violence;

(2) file an application for participation with the attorney general or a state or local agency or other entity identified by the attorney general under Subdivision (1);

(3) designate the attorney general as agent to receive service of process and mail on behalf of the applicant; and

(4) live at a residential address, or relocate to a residential address, that is unknown to the person who committed or is alleged to have committed the family violence or an offense under Section 22.011, 22.021, 25.02, or 42.072, Penal Code.

(b) An application under Subsection (a)(2) must contain:

(1) a signed, sworn statement by the applicant stating that the applicant fears for the safety of the applicant, the applicant's child, or another person in the applicant's household because of a threat of immediate or future harm caused by the person who committed or is alleged to have committed the family violence or an offense under Section 22.011, 22.021, 25.02, or 42.072, Penal Code;

(2) the applicant's true residential address and, if applicable, the applicant's business and school addresses; and

(3) a statement by the applicant of whether there is an existing court order or a pending court case for child support or child custody or visitation that involves the applicant and, if so, the name and address of:

(A) the legal counsel of record; and

(B) each parent involved in the court order or pending case.

(c) An application under Subsection (a)(2) must be completed by the applicant in person at the state or local agency or other entity with which the application is filed. An applicant who knowingly or intentionally makes a false statement in an application under Subsection (a)(2) is subject to prosecution under Chapter 37, Penal Code.

(d) A state or local agency or other entity with which an application is filed under Subsection (a)(2) shall forward the application to the office of the attorney general.

(e) The attorney general by rule may establish additional eligibility requirements for participation in the program that are consistent with the purpose of the program as stated in Article 56.82(a). The attorney general may establish procedures for requiring an applicant, in appropriate circumstances, to submit with the application under Subsection (a)(2) independent documentary evidence of family violence or an offense under Section 22.011, 22.021, 25.02, or 42.072, Penal Code, in the form of:

(1) an active or recently issued protective order;

(2) an incident report or other record maintained by a law enforcement agency or official;

(3) a statement of a physician or other health care provider regarding the applicant's medical condition as a result of the family violence or offense; or

(4) a statement of a mental health professional, a member of the clergy, an attorney or other legal advocate, a trained staff member of a family violence center, or another professional who has assisted the applicant in addressing the effects of the family violence or offense.

(f) Any assistance or counseling provided by the attorney general or an employee or agent of the attorney general to an applicant does not constitute legal advice.

History of CCP art. 56.83: Acts 2007, 80th Leg., ch. 1295, §1, eff. June 15, 2007.

ART. 56.84. CERTIFICATION; EXPIRATION

(a) The attorney general shall certify for participation in the program an applicant who satisfies the eligibility requirements under Article 56.83.

(b) A certification under this article expires on the third anniversary of the date of certification.

History of CCP art. 56.84: Acts 2007, 80th Leg., ch. 1295, §1, eff. June 15, 2007.

ART. 56.85. RENEWAL

To renew a certification under Article 56.84, a participant must satisfy the eligibility requirements under Article 56.83 as if the participant were originally applying for participation in the program.

History of CCP art. 56.85: Acts 2007, 80th Leg., ch. 1295, §1, eff. June 15, 2007.

ART. 56.86. INELIGIBILITY & CANCELLATION

(a) An applicant is ineligible for, and a participant may be excluded from, participation in the program if the applicant or participant knowingly makes a false statement on an application filed under Article 56.83(a)(2).

(b) A participant may be excluded from participation in the program if:

(1) mail forwarded to the participant by the attorney general is returned undeliverable on at least four occasions;

(2) the participant changes the participant's true residential address as provided in the application filed under Article 56.83(a)(2) and does not notify the attorney general of the change at least 10 days before the date of the change; or

(3) the participant changes the participant's name.

History of CCP art. 56.86: Acts 2007, 80th Leg., ch. 1295, §1, eff. June 15, 2007.

ART. 56.87. WITHDRAWAL

A participant may withdraw from the program by notifying the attorney general in writing of the withdrawal.

History of CCP art. 56.87: Acts 2007, 80th Leg., ch. 1295, §1, eff. June 15, 2007.

ART. 56.88. CONFIDENTIALITY; DESTRUCTION OF INFORMATION

(a) Information relating to a participant:

(1) is confidential, except as provided by Article 56.90; and

(2) may not be disclosed under Chapter 552, Government Code.

(b) Except as provided by Article 56.82(d), the attorney general may not make a copy of any mail received by the office of the attorney general on behalf of the participant.

(c) The attorney general shall destroy all information relating to a participant on the third anniversary of the date participation in the program ends.

History of CCP art. 56.88: Acts 2007, 80th Leg., ch. 1295, §1, eff. June 15, 2007.

ART. 56.89. ACCEPTANCE OF SUBSTITUTE ADDRESS; EXEMPTIONS

(a) Except as provided by Subsection (b), a state or local agency must accept the substitute post office box address designated by the attorney general if the substitute address is presented to the agency by a participant in place of the participant's true residential, business, or school address.

(b) The attorney general by rule may permit an agency to require a participant to provide the participant's true residential, business, or school address, if necessary for the agency to perform a duty or function that is imposed by law or administrative requirement.

History of CCP art. 56.89: Acts 2007, 80th Leg., ch. 1295, §1, eff. June 15, 2007.

ART. 56.90. EXCEPTIONS

(a) The attorney general:

(1) shall disclose a participant's true residential, business, or school address if:

(A) requested by:

(i) a law enforcement agency;

(ii) the Department of Family and Protective Services for the purpose of conducting a child protective services investigation under Chapter 261, Family Code; or

(iii) the Department of State Health Services or a local health authority for the purpose of making a notification described by Article 21.31, Section 54.033, Family Code, or Section 81.051, Health and Safety Code; or

(B) required by court order; and

(2) may disclose a participant's true residential, business, or school address if:

(A) the participant consents to the disclosure; and

(B) the disclosure is necessary to administer the program.

(b) A person to whom a participant's true residential, business, or school address is disclosed under this section shall maintain the requested information in a manner that protects the confidentiality of the participant's true residential, business, or school address.

History of CCP art. 56.90: Acts 2007, 80th Leg., ch. 1295, §1, eff. June 15, 2007.

ⓔ ART. 56.91. LIABILITY

(a) The attorney general or an agent or employee of the attorney general is immune from liability for any act or omission by the agent or employee in administering the program if the agent or employee was acting in good faith and in the course and scope of assigned responsibilities and duties.

(b) An agent or employee of the attorney general who does not act in good faith and in the course and scope of assigned responsibilities and duties in disclosing a participant's true residential, business, or school address is subject to prosecution under Chapter 39, Penal Code.

History of CCP art. 56.91: Acts 2007, 80th Leg., ch. 1295, §1, eff. June 15, 2007.

ⓔ ART. 56.92. PROGRAM INFORMATION & APPLICATION MATERIALS

The attorney general shall make program information and application materials available online.

History of CCP art. 56.92: Acts 2007, 80th Leg., ch. 1295, §1, eff. June 15, 2007.

ⓔ ART. 56.93. RULES

The attorney general shall adopt rules to administer the program.

History of CCP art. 56.93: Acts 2007, 80th Leg., ch. 1295, §1, eff. June 15, 2007.

CHAPTER 57. CONFIDENTIALITY OF IDENTIFYING INFORMATION OF SEX OFFENSE VICTIMS

ART. 57.01. DEFINITIONS

In this chapter:

(1) "Name" means the legal name of a person.

(2) "Pseudonym" means a set of initials or a fictitious name chosen by a victim to designate the victim in all public files and records concerning the offense, including police summary reports, press releases, and records of judicial proceedings.

(3) "Public servant" has the meaning assigned by Subsection (a), Section 1.07, Penal Code.

(4) "Victim" means a person who was the subject of:

(A) an offense the commission of which leads to a reportable conviction or adjudication under Chapter 62; or

(B) an offense that is part of the same criminal episode, as defined by Section 3.01, Penal Code, as an offense described by Paragraph (A).

History of CCP art. 57.01: Acts 1987, 70th Leg., ch. 571, §1, eff. Sept. 1, 1987. Amended by Acts 1997, 75th Leg., ch. 680, §1, eff. Sept. 1, 1997; Acts 2003, 78th Leg., ch. 451, §1 (eff. Sept. 1, 2003), ch. 1276, §5.0025 (eff. Sept. 1, 2003).

ART. 57.02. CONFIDENTIALITY OF FILES & RECORDS

(a) The Sexual Assault Prevention and Crisis Services Program of the office of the attorney general shall develop and distribute to all law enforcement agencies of the state a pseudonym form to record the name, address, telephone number, and pseudonym of a victim.

(b) A victim may choose a pseudonym to be used instead of the victim's name to designate the victim in all public files and records concerning the offense, including police summary reports, press releases, and records of judicial proceedings. A victim who elects to use a pseudonym as provided by this article must complete a pseudonym form developed under this article and return the form to the law enforcement agency investigating the offense.

(c) A victim who completes and returns a pseudonym form to the law enforcement agency investigating the offense may not be required to disclose the victim's name, address, and telephone number in connection with the investigation or prosecution of the offense.

(d) A completed and returned pseudonym form is confidential and may not be disclosed to any person other than a defendant in the case or the defendant's attorney, except on an order of a court of competent jurisdiction. The court finding required by Subsection (g) of this article is not required to disclose the confidential pseudonym form to the defendant in the case or to the defendant's attorney.

(e) If a victim completes and returns a pseudonym form to a law enforcement agency under this article, the law enforcement agency receiving the form shall:

(1) remove the victim's name and substitute the pseudonym for the name on all reports, files, and records in the agency's possession;

(2) notify the attorney for the state of the pseudonym and that the victim has elected to be designated by the pseudonym; and

(3) maintain the form in a manner that protects the confidentiality of the information contained on the form.

(f) An attorney for the state who receives notice that a victim has elected to be designated by a pseudonym shall ensure that the victim is designated by the pseudonym in all legal proceedings concerning the offense.

(g) A court of competent jurisdiction may order the disclosure of a victim's name, address, and telephone number only if the court finds that the information is essential in the trial of the defendant for the offense or the identity of the victim is in issue.

(h) Except as required or permitted by other law or by court order, a public servant or other person who has access to or obtains the name, address, telephone number, or other identifying information of a victim younger than 17 years of age may not release or disclose the identifying information to any person who is not assisting in the investigation, prosecution, or defense of the case. This subsection does not apply to the release or disclosure of a victim's identifying information by:

(1) the victim; or

(2) the victim's parent, conservator, or guardian, unless the parent, conservator, or guardian is a defendant in the case.

☠ **ⓔ** *Subsection (i) below was enacted by Acts 2007, 80th Leg., ch. 619, §1, effective Sept. 1, 2007, without reference to the conflicting enactment made by Acts 2007, 80th Leg., ch. 1217, §1, effective June 15, 2007.*

(i) This article does not prohibit the inspector general of the Texas Department of Criminal Justice from disclosing a victim's identifying information to an employee of the department if the victim is an inmate or state jail defendant confined in a facility operated by or under contract with the department.

☠ **ⓔ** *Subsection (i) below was enacted by Acts 2007, 80th Leg., ch. 1217, §1, effective June 15, 2007, without reference to the conflicting enactment made by Acts 2007, 80th Leg., ch. 619, §1, effective Sept. 1, 2007.*

(i) This article does not prohibit the inspector general of the Texas Department of Criminal Justice from disclosing a victim's identifying information to the department's ombudsperson if the victim is an inmate or state jail defendant confined in a facility operated by or under contract with the department.

History of CCP art. 57.02: Acts 1987, 70th Leg., ch. 571, §1, eff. Sept. 1, 1987. Amended by Acts 2001, 77th Leg., ch. 1057, §3, eff. Sept. 1, 2001; Acts 2005, 79th Leg., ch. 93, §1, eff. Sept. 1, 2005; Acts 2007, 80th Leg., ch. 619, §1 (eff. Sept. 1, 2007), ch. 1217, §1 (eff. June 15, 2007).

See also CCP art. 21.07.

ANNOTATIONS

Stevens v. State, 891 S.W.2d 649, 651 (Tex.Crim. App.1995). "By enacting art. 57.02, the Legislature changed the manner in which the victim may be alleged in an indictment. In doing so the Legislature sought to address and satisfy two competing interests: the defendant's due process right to notice of the offense for which he was indicted; and, the victim's interest in avoiding the embarrassment associated with a public pronouncement of the details of the alleged offense. The pseudonym is used to protect the victim— *not* to deprive the defendant of notice. [W]e hold the fatal variance doctrine is inapplicable to pseudonym cases so long as the defendant's due process right to notice is satisfied."

ART. 57.03. OFFENSE

(a) A public servant with access to the name, address, or telephone number of a victim 17 years of age or older who has chosen a pseudonym under this chapter commits an offense if the public servant knowingly discloses the name, address, or telephone number of the victim to any person who is not assisting in the investigation or prosecution of the offense or to any person other than the defendant, the defendant's attorney, or the person specified in the order of a court of competent jurisdiction.

(b) Unless the disclosure is required or permitted by other law, a public servant or other person commits an offense if the person:

(1) has access to or obtains the name, address, or telephone number of a victim younger than 17 years of age; and

(2) knowingly discloses the name, address, or telephone number of the victim to any person who is not assisting in the investigation or prosecution of the offense or to any person other than the defendant, the defendant's attorney, or a person specified in an order of a court of competent jurisdiction.

(c) It is an affirmative defense to prosecution under Subsection (b) that the actor is:

(1) the victim; or

(2) the victim's parent, conservator, or guardian, unless the actor is a defendant in the case.

☠ **ⓔ** *Subsection (c-1) below was enacted by Acts 2007, 80th Leg., ch. 619, §2, effective Sept. 1, 2007, without reference to the conflicting enactment made by Acts*

2007, 80th Leg., ch. 1217, §2, effective June 15, 2007. Subsection (c-1) below is effective for offenses committed on or after Sept. 1, 2007.

(c-1) It is an exception to the application of this article that:

(1) the person who discloses the name, address, or telephone number of a victim is the inspector general of the Texas Department of Criminal Justice;

(2) the victim is an inmate or state jail defendant confined in a facility operated by or under contract with the Texas Department of Criminal Justice; and

(3) the person to whom the disclosure is made is an employee of the department.

☠ 📧 *Subsection (c-1) below was enacted by Acts 2007, 80th Leg., ch. 1217, §2, effective June 15, 2007, without reference to the conflicting enactment made by Acts 2007, 80th Leg., ch. 619, §2, effective Sept. 1, 2007. Subsection (c-1) below is effective for offenses committed on or after June 15, 2007.*

(c-1) It is an exception to the application of this article that:

(1) the person who discloses the name, address, or telephone number of a victim is the inspector general of the Texas Department of Criminal Justice;

(2) the victim is an inmate or state jail defendant confined in a facility operated by or under contract with the department; and

(3) the person to whom the disclosure is made is the department's ombudsperson.

(d) An offense under this article is a Class C misdemeanor.

History of CCP art. 57.03: Acts 1987, 70th Leg., ch. 571, §1, eff. Sept. 1, 1987. Amended by Acts 2001, 77th Leg., ch. 1057, §4, eff. Sept. 1, 2001; Acts 2007, 80th Leg., ch. 619, §2 (eff. Sept. 1, 2007), ch. 1217, §2 (eff. June 15, 2007).

📧 **CHAPTER 57B. CONFIDENTIALITY OF IDENTIFYING INFORMATION OF FAMILY VIOLENCE VICTIMS**

📧 **ART. 57B.01. DEFINITIONS**

In this chapter:

(1) "Name" means the legal name of a person.

(2) "Pseudonym" means a set of initials or a fictitious name chosen by a victim to designate the victim in all public files and records concerning the offense, including police summary reports, press releases, and records of judicial proceedings.

(3) "Public servant" has the meaning assigned by Subsection (a), Section 1.07, Penal Code.

(4) "Victim" means a person who is the subject of:

(A) an offense that allegedly constitutes family violence, as defined by Section 71.004, Family Code; or

(B) an offense that is part of the same criminal episode, as defined by Section 3.01, Penal Code, as an offense described by Paragraph (A).

History of CCP art. 57B.01: Acts 2007, 80th Leg., ch. 1295, §3, eff. June 15, 2007.

📧 **ART. 57B.02. CONFIDENTIALITY OF FILES & RECORDS**

(a) The office of the attorney general shall develop and distribute to all law enforcement agencies of the state a pseudonym form to record the name, address, telephone number, and pseudonym of a victim.

(b) A victim may choose a pseudonym to be used instead of the victim's name to designate the victim in all public files and records concerning the offense, including police summary reports, press releases, and records of judicial proceedings. A victim who elects to use a pseudonym as provided by this article must complete a pseudonym form developed under this article and return the form to the law enforcement agency investigating the offense.

(c) A victim who completes and returns a pseudonym form to the law enforcement agency investigating the offense may not be required to disclose the victim's name, address, and telephone number in connection with the investigation or prosecution of the offense.

(d) A completed and returned pseudonym form is confidential and may not be disclosed to any person other than a defendant in the case or the defendant's attorney, except on an order of a court of competent jurisdiction. The court finding required by Subsection (g) is not required to disclose the confidential pseudonym form to the defendant in the case or to the defendant's attorney.

(e) If a victim completes and returns a pseudonym form to a law enforcement agency under this article, the law enforcement agency receiving the form shall:

(1) remove the victim's name and substitute the pseudonym for the name on all reports, files, and records in the agency's possession;

(2) notify the attorney for the state of the pseudonym and that the victim has elected to be designated by the pseudonym; and

(3) maintain the form in a manner that protects the confidentiality of the information contained on the form.

(f) An attorney for the state who receives notice that a victim has elected to be designated by a pseudonym shall ensure that the victim is designated by the pseudonym in all legal proceedings concerning the offense.

(g) A court of competent jurisdiction may order the disclosure of a victim's name, address, and telephone number only if the court finds that the information is essential in the trial of the defendant for the offense or the identity of the victim is in issue.

(h) Except as required or permitted by other law or by court order, a public servant or other person who has access to or obtains the name, address, telephone number, or other identifying information of a victim younger than 17 years of age may not release or disclose the identifying information to any person who is not assisting in the investigation, prosecution, or defense of the case. This subsection does not apply to the release or disclosure of a victim's identifying information by:

(1) the victim; or

(2) the victim's parent, conservator, or guardian, unless the victim's parent, conservator, or guardian allegedly committed the offense described by Article 57B.01(4).

History of CCP art. 57B.02: Acts 2007, 80th Leg., ch. 1295, §3, eff. June 15, 2007.

⑤ ART. 57B.03. OFFENSE

(a) A public servant with access to the name, address, or telephone number of a victim 17 years of age or older who has chosen a pseudonym under this chapter commits an offense if the public servant knowingly discloses the name, address, or telephone number of the victim to any person who is not assisting in the investigation or prosecution of the offense or to any person other than the defendant, the defendant's attorney, or the person specified in the order of a court of competent jurisdiction.

(b) Unless the disclosure is required or permitted by other law, a public servant or other person commits an offense if the person:

(1) has access to or obtains the name, address, or telephone number of a victim younger than 17 years of age; and

(2) knowingly discloses the name, address, or telephone number of the victim to any person who is not assisting in the investigation or prosecution of the offense or to any person other than the defendant, the defendant's attorney, or a person specified in an order of a court of competent jurisdiction.

(c) It is an affirmative defense to prosecution under Subsection (b) that the actor is:

(1) the victim; or

(2) the victim's parent, conservator, or guardian, unless the victim's parent, conservator, or guardian allegedly committed the offense described by Article 57B.01(4).

(d) An offense under this article is a Class C misdemeanor.

History of CCP art. 57B.03: Acts 2007, 80th Leg., ch. 1295, §3, eff. June 15, 2007.

⑤ ART. 57B.04. APPLICABILITY OF CHAPTER TO DEPARTMENT OF FAMILY & PROTECTIVE SERVICES

Nothing in this chapter requires the Department of Family and Protective Services to use a pseudonym in a department report, file, or record relating to the abuse, neglect, or exploitation of a child or adult who may also be the subject of an offense described by Article 57B.01(4). To the extent permitted by law, the Department of Family and Protective Services and a department employee, as necessary in performing department duties, may disclose the name of a victim who elects to use a pseudonym under this chapter.

History of CCP art. 57B.04: Acts 2007, 80th Leg., ch. 1295, §3, eff. June 15, 2007.

⑤ ART. 57B.05. APPLICABILITY OF CHAPTER TO POLITICAL SUBDIVISIONS

Nothing in this chapter requires a political subdivision to use a pseudonym in a report, file, or record that is not:

(1) intended for distribution to the public; or

(2) the subject of an open records request under Chapter 552, Government Code.

History of CCP art. 57B.05: Acts 2007, 80th Leg., ch. 1295, §3, eff. June 15, 2007.

CHAPTER 58. SEALING FILES & RECORDS OF CHILDREN

ART. 58.01. REPEALED

Repealed by Acts 2001, 77th Leg., ch. 1297, §71(3), eff. Sept. 1, 2001.

CHAPTER 59. FORFEITURE OF CONTRABAND

ART. 59.01. DEFINITIONS

In this chapter:

(1) "Attorney representing the state" means the prosecutor with felony jurisdiction in the county in which a forfeiture proceeding is held under this chapter or, in a proceeding for forfeiture of contraband as defined under Subdivision (2)(B)(v) of this article, the city attorney of a municipality if the property is seized in that municipality by a peace officer employed by that municipality and the governing body of the municipality has approved procedures for the city attorney acting in a forfeiture proceeding. In a proceeding for forfeiture of contraband as defined under Subdivision (2)(B)(vii) of this article, the term includes the attorney general.

(2) "Contraband" means property of any nature, including real, personal, tangible, or intangible, that is:

(A) used in the commission of:

(i) any first or second degree felony under the Penal Code;

(ii) any felony under Section 15.031(b), 20.05, 21.11, 38.04, Subchapter B of Chapter 43, or Chapter 29, 30, 31, 32, 33, 33A, or 35, Penal Code;

(iii) any felony under The Securities Act (Article 581-1 et seq., Vernon's Texas Civil Statutes); or

(iv) any offense under Chapter 49, Penal Code, that is punishable as a felony of the third degree or state jail felony, if the defendant has been previously convicted three times of an offense under that chapter;

(B) used or intended to be used in the commission of:

(i) any felony under Chapter 481, Health and Safety Code (Texas Controlled Substances Act);

(ii) any felony under Chapter 483, Health and Safety Code;

(iii) a felony under Chapter 153, Finance Code;

(iv) any felony under Chapter 34, Penal Code;

(v) a Class A misdemeanor under Subchapter B, Chapter 365, Health and Safety Code, if the defendant has been previously convicted twice of an offense under that subchapter;

(vi) any felony under Chapter 152, Finance Code;

Ⓐ *Subsection (vii) below is effective for offenses or violations committed on or after Sept. 1, 2007.*

(vii) any felony under Chapter 32, Human Resources Code, or Chapter 31, 32, 35A, or 37, Penal Code, that involves the state Medicaid program; or

Subsection (vii) below is effective for offenses or violations in which any element of the offense or violation was committed before Sept. 1, 2007.

(vii) any felony under Chapter 31, 32, or 37, Penal Code, that involves the state Medicaid program; or any felony under Chapter 36, Human Resources Code; or

Ⓐ *Subsection (viii) below is effective on or after April 1, 2009.*

(viii) a Class B misdemeanor under Chapter 522, Business & Commerce Code;

Ⓐ *Subsection (viii) below is effective until April 1, 2009.*

(viii) a Class B misdemeanor under Section 35.60, Business & Commerce Code; or

Ⓔ **(ix)** a Class A misdemeanor under Section 35.153, Business & Commerce Code;

(C) the proceeds gained from the commission of a felony listed in Paragraph (A) or (B) of this subdivision, a misdemeanor listed in Paragraph (B)(viii) of this subdivision, or a crime of violence;

(D) acquired with proceeds gained from the commission of a felony listed in Paragraph (A) or (B) of this subdivision, a misdemeanor listed in Paragraph (B)(viii) of this subdivision, or a crime of violence; or

(E) used to facilitate or intended to be used to facilitate the commission of a felony under Section 15.031 or 43.25, Penal Code.

(3) "Crime of violence" means:

(A) any criminal offense defined in the Penal Code or in a federal criminal law that results in a personal injury to a victim; or

(B) an act that is not an offense under the Penal Code involving the operation of a motor vehicle, aircraft, or water vehicle that results in injury or death sustained in an accident caused by a driver in violation of Section 550.021, Transportation Code.

(4) "Interest holder" means the bona fide holder of a perfected lien or a perfected security interest in property.

(5) "Law enforcement agency" means an agency of the state or an agency of a political subdivision of the state authorized by law to employ peace officers.

(6) "Owner" means a person who claims an equitable or legal ownership interest in property.

(7) "Proceeds" includes income a person accused or convicted of a crime or the person's representative or assignee receives from:

(A) a movie, book, magazine article, tape recording, phonographic record, radio or television presentation, telephone service, electronic media format, including an Internet website, or live entertainment in which the crime was reenacted; or

(B) the sale of tangible property the value of which is increased by the notoriety gained from the conviction of an offense by the person accused or convicted of the crime.

(8) "Seizure" means the restraint of property by a peace officer under Article 59.03(a) or (b) of this code, whether the officer restrains the property by physical force or by a display of the officer's authority, and includes the collection of property or the act of taking possession of property.

(9) "Depository account" means the obligation of a regulated financial institution to pay the account owner under a written agreement, including a checking account, savings account, money market account, time deposit, NOW account, or certificate of deposit.

(10) "Primary state or federal financial institution regulator" means the state or federal regulatory agency that chartered and comprehensively regulates a regulated financial institution.

(11) "Regulated financial institution" means a depository institution chartered by a state or federal government, the deposits of which are insured by the Federal Deposit Insurance Corporation or the National Credit Union Administration.

History of CCP art. 59.01: Acts 1989, 71st Leg., 1st C.S., ch. 12, §1, eff. Oct. 18, 1989. Amended by Acts 1991, 72nd Leg., ch. 102, §2, eff. Sept. 1, 1991; Acts 1993, 73rd Leg., ch. 761, §5 (eff. Sept. 1, 1993), ch. 780, §1 (eff. Sept. 1, 1993), ch. 828, §1 (eff. Sept. 1, 1993); Acts 1995, 74th Leg., ch. 76, §§5.91, 5.95(112) (eff. Sept. 1, 1995), ch. 621, §3 (eff. Sept. 1, 1995), ch. 708, §2 (eff. Sept. 1, 1995); Acts 1997, 75th Leg., ch. 306, §6, eff. Sept. 1, 1997; Acts 1999, 76th Leg., ch. 62, §§3.09, 7.48, eff. Sept. 1, 1999; Acts 2001, 77th Leg., ch. 124, §1 (eff. Sept. 1, 2001), ch. 438, §1 (eff. Sept. 1, 2001), ch. 467, §1 (eff. Sept. 1, 2001); Acts 2003, 78th Leg., ch. 198, §2.141 (eff. Sept. 1, 2003), ch. 257, §17 (eff. Sept. 1, 2003), ch. 428, §1 (eff. Sept. 1, 2003), ch. 649, §3 (eff. Sept. 1, 2003), ch. 1005, §7 (eff. Sept. 1, 2003); Acts 2005, 79th Leg., ch. 617, §1, (eff. Sept. 1, 2005), ch. 728, §4.008 (eff. Sept. 1, 2005), ch. 944, §§1, 2 (eff. Sept. 1, 2005), ch. 1026, §§3, 4 (eff. Sept. 1, 2005); Acts 2007, 80th Leg., ch. 127, §6 (eff. Sept. 1, 2007), ch. 822, §2 (eff. Sept. 1, 2007), ch. 885, §2.14 (eff. Apr. 1, 2009).

ANNOTATIONS

1991 Nissan Pickup v. State, 896 S.W.2d 344, 345 (Tex.App.—Eastland 1995, no writ). "In forfeiture proceedings, probable cause is 'a reasonable belief that a substantial connection exists between the property to be forfeited and the criminal activity defined by the statute.' Article 59.02 provides that property that is contraband is subject to seizure and forfeiture. ... In order to be 'used in the commission' of a crime, the property must be used 'before or during' the completion of the offense, unless it is a continuing offense."

ART. 59.02. FORFEITURE OF CONTRABAND

(a) Property that is contraband is subject to seizure and forfeiture under this chapter.

(b) Any property that is contraband other than property held as evidence in a criminal investigation or a pending criminal case, money, a negotiable instrument, or a security that is seized under this chapter may be replevied by the owner or interest holder of the property, on execution of a good and valid bond with sufficient surety in a sum equal to the appraised value of the property replevied. The bond may be approved as to form and substance by the court after the court gives notice of the bond to the authority holding the seized property. The bond must be conditioned:

(1) on return of the property to the custody of the state on the day of hearing of the forfeiture proceedings; and

(2) that the interest holder or owner of the property will abide by the decision that may be made in the cause.

(c) An owner or interest holder's interest in property may not be forfeited under this chapter if the owner or interest holder proves by a preponderance of the evidence that the owner or interest holder acquired and perfected the interest:

(1) before or during the act or omission giving rise to forfeiture or, if the property is real property, he acquired an ownership interest, security interest, or lien interest before a lis pendens notice was filed under Article 59.04(g) of this code and did not know or should not reasonably have known of the act or omission giving rise to the forfeiture or that it was likely to occur at or before the time of acquiring and perfecting the interest or, if the property is real property, at or before the time of acquiring the ownership interest, security interest, or lien interest; or

(2) after the act or omission giving rise to the forfeiture, but before the seizure of the property, and only if the owner or interest holder:

(A) was, at the time that the interest in the property was acquired, an owner or interest holder for value; and

(B) was without reasonable cause to believe that the property was contraband and did not purposefully avoid learning that the property was contraband.

(d) Notwithstanding any other law, if property is seized from the possession of an owner or interest holder who asserts an ownership interest, security interest, or lien interest in the property under applicable law, the owner or interest holder's rights remain in effect during the pendency of proceedings under this chapter as if possession of the property had remained with the owner or interest holder.

(e) On motion by any party or on the motion of the court, after notice in the manner provided by Article 59.04 of this code to all known owners and interest holders of property subject to forfeiture under this chapter, and after a hearing on the matter, the court may make appropriate orders to preserve and maintain the value of the property until a final disposition of the property is made under this chapter, including the sale of the property if that is the only method by which the value of the property may be preserved until final disposition.

(f) Any property that is contraband and has been seized by the institutional division of the Texas Department of Criminal Justice shall be forfeited to the institutional division under the same rules and conditions as for other forfeitures.

(g) An individual, firm, corporation, or other entity insured under a policy of title insurance may not assert a claim or cause of action on or because of the policy if the claim or cause of action is based on forfeiture under this chapter and, at or before the time of acquiring the ownership of real property, security interest in real property, or lien interest against real property, the insured knew or reasonably should have known of the act or omission giving rise to the forfeiture or that the act or omission was likely to occur.

(h)(1) An owner or interest holder's interest in property may not be forfeited under this chapter if at the forfeiture hearing the owner or interest holder proves by a preponderance of the evidence that the owner or interest holder was not a party to the offense giving rise to the forfeiture and that the contraband:

(A) was stolen from the owner or interest holder before being used in the commission of the offense giving rise to the forfeiture;

(B) was purchased with:

(i) money stolen from the owner or interest holder; or

(ii) proceeds from the sale of property stolen from the owner or interest holder; or

(C) was used or intended to be used without the effective consent of the owner or interest holder in the commission of the offense giving rise to the forfeiture.

(2) An attorney representing the state who has a reasonable belief that property subject to forfeiture is described by Subdivision (1) and who has a reasonable belief as to the identity of the rightful owner or interest holder of the property shall notify the owner or interest holder as provided by Article 59.04.

(3) An attorney representing the state is not liable in an action for damages resulting from an act or omission in the performance of the duties imposed by Subdivision (2).

(4) The exclusive remedy for failure by the attorney representing the state to provide the notice required under Subdivision (2) is submission of that failure as a ground for new trial in a motion for new trial or bill of review.

(i) The forfeiture provisions of this chapter apply to contraband as defined by Article 59.01(2)(B)(v) of this code only in a municipality with a population of 250,000 or more.

History of CCP art. 59.02: Acts 1989, 71st Leg., 1st C.S., ch. 12, §1, eff. Oct. 18, 1989. Amended by Acts 1993, 73rd Leg., ch. 828, §2, eff. Sept. 1, 1993; Acts 2001, 77th Leg., ch. 438, §2 (eff. Sept. 1, 2001), ch. 929, §1 (eff. Sept. 1, 2001); Acts 2003, 78th Leg., ch. 1275, §2(9), eff. Sept. 1, 2003.

See also U.S. Const. amend. 4; Tex. Const. art. 1, §9.

ANNOTATIONS

Fant v. State, 931 S.W.2d 299, 307 (Tex.Crim.App. 1996). "[T]he jurisdiction of a forfeiture proceeding, as with other proceedings in rem, is dependent upon seizure of the physical object. [¶] [CCP ch. 59] proceedings ... are to be governed at all times by the rules set out to govern civil proceedings. [¶] It is evident that the property, and not an individual, is the target of forfeiture when the statutes provide that a forfeiture can even take place in the absence of an owner, interest holder or possessor. [T]here is no requirement in the Texas statute that 'the State demonstrate scienter in order to establish that the property is subject to forfeiture.' [P]roperty could be forfeited if no owner or interest holder files a claim to it and the State fails to demonstrate a connection between the property and a particular person. [¶] [I]t is not necessary that the owner or interest holder be the person charged with the commission of an underlying criminal offense, so long as the property is shown to be contraband under the statutory definitions. The property, its uses, intended uses, or point of origin as proceeds, is the target of the Texas forfeiture provisions. The fact that the State may, at the civil in rem proceeding, proffer the offenses committed by the holder of the property does not make the forfeiture a punishment for those offenses." *See also Johnson v. State*, 931 S.W.2d 314, 315 (Tex.Crim.App. 1996).

One Car v. State, 122 S.W.3d 422, 427-28 (Tex. App.—Beaumont 2003, no pet.). "[T]he facts in this case do not allow the state to forfeit a truck valued in excess of $10,000. The amount of controlled substance involved was an extremely small amount, too small to be weighed or valued. There was no evidence that the truck in this case was used to distribute or sell controlled substances, or that it was repeatedly used to facilitate ... illegal use of controlled substances. ... The forfeiture [is] grossly disproportional to the offense under [*U.S. v.*] *Bajakajian*, 524 U.S. 321, 118 S.Ct. 2028 (1998)], and we hold that the forfeiture in this case violates the Excessive Fines Clause of the 8th Amendment."

$18,800 v. State, 961 S.W.2d 257, 260 (Tex.App.—Houston [1st Dist.] 1997, no writ). "There is an 'innocent owner' defense which provides an owner's interest in property may not be forfeited under chapter 59 if the owner: (1) acquired and perfected her interest before or during the act giving rise to the forfeiture; and (2) did not know or should not reasonably have known of the act giving rise to the forfeiture or that it was likely to occur at or before the time of acquiring and perfecting the interest. The claimant making the innocent owner defense has the burden to prove it."

ART. 59.03. SEIZURE OF CONTRABAND

(a) Property subject to forfeiture under this chapter, other than property described by Article 59.12, may be seized by any peace officer under authority of a search warrant.

(b) Seizure of property subject to forfeiture may be made without warrant if:

(1) the owner, operator, or agent in charge of the property knowingly consents;

(2) the seizure is incident to a search to which the owner, operator, or agent in charge of the property knowingly consents;

(3) the property subject to seizure has been the subject of a prior judgment in favor of the state in a forfeiture proceeding under this chapter; or

(4) the seizure was incident to a lawful arrest, lawful search, or lawful search incident to arrest.

(c) A peace officer who seizes property under this chapter has custody of the property, subject only to replevy under Article 59.02 of this code or an order of a court. A peace officer who has custody of property shall provide the attorney representing the state with a sworn statement that contains a schedule of the property seized, an acknowledgment that the officer has seized the property, and a list of the officer's reasons for the seizure. Not later than 72 hours after the seizure, the peace officer shall:

(1) place the property under seal;

(2) remove the property to a place ordered by the court; or

(3) require a law enforcement agency of the state or a political subdivision to take custody of the property and move it to a proper location.

(d) A person in the possession of property at the time a peace officer seizes the property under this chapter may at the time of seizure assert the person's interest in or right to the property. A peace officer who seizes property under this chapter may not at the time of seizure request, require, or in any manner induce any person, including a person who asserts an interest in or right to the property seized, to execute a document purporting to waive the person's interest in or rights to the property.

History of CCP art. 59.03: Acts 1989, 71st Leg., 1st C.S., ch. 12, §1, eff. Oct. 18, 1989. Amended by Acts 2001, 77th Leg., ch. 438, §3 (eff. Sept. 1, 2001), ch. 929, §2 (eff. Sept. 1, 2001).

See also Tex. Const. art. 1, §9.

State v. $30,660, 136 S.W.3d 392, 407-08 (Tex. App.—Corpus Christi 2004, pet. denied). "[T]o succeed in a forfeiture action, the State must prove by a preponderance of the evidence that the property is subject to forfeiture. The State does this by establishing that the property is contraband as defined by article 59.01(2). Although chapter 59 specifies no additional evidentiary requirements for forfeiture beyond proof that the property is contraband, the supreme court has held that the State must also show probable cause for seizing a person's property. ... Probable cause in the context of forfeiture statutes is a reasonable belief that a substantial connection exists between the property to be forfeited and the criminal activity defined by the statute. Thus, probable cause to seize is not the same as the probable cause necessary for the lawful search, lawful arrest, or lawful search incident to arrest required by article 59.03(b)(4)." (Internal quotes omitted.)

ART. 59.04. NOTIFICATION OF FORFEITURE PROCEEDING

(a) If a peace officer seizes property under this chapter, the attorney representing the state shall commence proceedings under this section not later than the 30th day after the date of the seizure.

(b) A forfeiture proceeding commences under this chapter when the attorney representing the state files a notice of the seizure and intended forfeiture in the name of the state with the clerk of the district court in the county in which the seizure is made. The attorney representing the state must attach to the notice the peace officer's sworn statement under Article 59.03 of this code or, if the property has been seized under Article 59.12(b), the statement of the terms and amount of the depository account or inventory of assets provided by the regulated financial institution to the peace officer executing the warrant in the manner described by Article 59.12(b). Except as provided by Subsection (c) of this article, the attorney representing the state shall cause certified copies of the notice to be served on the following persons in the same manner as provided for the service of process by citation in civil cases:

(1) the owner of the property; and

(2) any interest holder in the property.

(c) If the property is a motor vehicle, and if there is reasonable cause to believe that the vehicle has been registered under the laws of this state, the attorney representing the state shall ask the Texas Department of Transportation to identify from its records the record owner of the vehicle and any interest holder. If the addresses of the owner and interest holder are not otherwise known, the attorney representing the state shall request citation be served on such persons at the address listed with the Texas Department of Transportation. If the citation issued to such address is returned unserved, the attorney representing the state shall cause a copy of the notice of the seizure and intended forfeiture to be posted at the courthouse door, to remain there for a period of not less than 30 days. If the owner or interest holder does not answer or appear after the notice has been so posted, the court shall enter a judgment by default as to the owner or interest holder, provided that the attorney representing the state files a written motion supported by affidavit setting forth the attempted service. An owner or interest holder whose interest is forfeited in this manner shall not be liable for court costs. If the person in possession of the vehicle at the time of the seizure is not the owner or the interest holder of the vehicle, notification shall be provided to the possessor in the same manner specified for notification to an owner or interest holder.

(d) If the property is a motor vehicle and is not registered in this state, the attorney representing the state shall attempt to ascertain the name and address of the person in whose name the vehicle is licensed in another state. If the vehicle is licensed in a state that has a certificate of title law, the attorney representing the state shall request the appropriate agency of that state to identify the record owner of the vehicle and any interest holder.

(e) If a financing statement is required by law to be filed to perfect a security interest affecting the property, and if there is reasonable cause to believe that a financing statement has been filed, the attorney representing the state who commences the proceedings shall ask the appropriate official designated by Chapter 9, Business & Commerce Code, to identify the record owner of the property and the person who is an interest holder.

(f) If the property is an aircraft or a part of an aircraft, and if there is reasonable cause to believe that a perfected security instrument affects the property, the attorney representing the state shall request an administrator of the Federal Aviation Administration to identify from the records of that agency the record owner of the property and the holder of the perfected security instrument. The attorney representing the state shall also notify the Department of Public Safety in writing of the fact that an aircraft has been seized and shall provide the department with a description of the aircraft.

(g) If the property is real property, the attorney representing the state, not later than the third day after the date proceedings are commenced, shall file a lis pendens notice describing the property with the county clerk of each county in which the property is located.

(h) For all other property subject to forfeiture, if there is reasonable cause to believe that a perfected security instrument affects the property, the attorney representing the state shall make a good faith inquiry to identify the holder of the perfected security instrument.

(i) Except as provided by Section (c) of this article, the attorney representing the state who commences the proceedings shall cause the owner and any interest holder to be named as a party and to be served with citation as provided by the Texas Rules of Civil Procedure.

(j) A person who was in possession of the property at the time it was seized shall be made a party to the proceeding.

(k) If no person was in possession of the property at the time it was seized, and if the owner of the property is unknown, the attorney representing the state shall file with the clerk of the court in which the proceedings are pending an affidavit stating that no person was in possession of the property at the time it was

seized and that the owner of the property is unknown. The clerk of the court shall issue a citation for service by publication addressed to "The Unknown Owner of _____," filling in the blank space with a reasonably detailed description of the property subject to forfeiture. The citation must contain the other requisites prescribed by and be served as provided by Rules 114, 115, and 116, Texas Rules of Civil Procedure.

(*l*) Proceedings commenced under this chapter may not proceed to hearing unless the judge who is to conduct the hearing is satisfied that this article has been complied with and that the attorney representing the state will introduce into evidence at the hearing any answer received from an inquiry required by Subsections (c)-(h) of this article.

History of CCP art. 59.04: Acts 1989, 71st Leg., 1st C.S., ch. 12, §1, eff. Oct. 18, 1989. Amended by Acts 1991, 72nd Leg., ch. 14, §282, eff. Sept. 1, 1991; Acts 1995, 74th Leg., ch. 165, §22(25) (eff. Sept. 1, 1995), ch. 533, §1 (eff. Sept. 1, 1995); Acts 2001, 77th Leg., ch. 438, §4, eff. Sept. 1, 2001.

See also Tex. Const. art. 1, §9.

ANNOTATIONS

State v. Silver Chevrolet Pickup, 140 S.W.3d 691, 692 (Tex.2004). "The [CCP] provides that when the State seeks forfeiture of property used in a criminal enterprise, it 'shall file a lis pendens notice' [under art. 59.04(g)] no later than three days after civil forfeiture proceedings are commenced. In this case, we must decide whether the State's failure to timely file a lis pendens notice deprives the court of jurisdiction. We hold that it does not."

$3,639 v. State, 133 S.W.3d 698, 701 (Tex.App.—Corpus Christi 2003, no pet.). "The State exercised diligence when it issued a citation for service the same day the notice of forfeiture was filed, when it twice attempted personal service, and when it filed a properly supported motion for substituted service. However, by requesting the district clerk to post the citation at the courthouse and pursuing service through a less preferred method, the State failed to comply with the trial court's order granting substituted service under [TRCP] 106(b)."

Ortiz v. State, 24 S.W.3d 603, 605 (Tex.App.—Corpus Christi 2000, no pet.). "Appellant ... points out that service of citation was not completed until 167 days after the filing of the suit for forfeiture. *At 606:* [T]he 167-day delay in service of process upon appellant herein requires a dismissal of the notice of seizure and intent to forfeit."

$217,590 v. State, 970 S.W.2d 660, 663 (Tex. App.—Corpus Christi 1998), *rev'd on other grounds*, 18 S.W.3d 631 (Tex.2000). "The statute does not mandate or suggest that a forfeiture action must be dismissed if the officer's affidavit is not attached. One court of appeals has held that this specific error can be cured beyond the 30th day. Furthermore, we have held that the purpose of the notice is to inform the opposing party, and all that is required to be filed within the 30 days is a pleading sufficient to put a defendant on notice of the State's cause of action. By citing and tracking the applicable statute in the petition, the State gave notice of its basic theory of recovery, and [appellant] suffered no unfair surprise by the State's amended petition beyond the 30th day."

ART. 59.05. FORFEITURE HEARING

(a) All parties must comply with the rules of pleading as required in civil suits.

(b) All cases under this chapter shall proceed to trial in the same manner as in other civil cases. The state has the burden of proving by a preponderance of the evidence that property is subject to forfeiture.

(c) It is an affirmative defense to forfeiture under this chapter of property belonging to the spouse of a person whose acts gave rise to the seizure of community property that, because of an act of family violence, as defined by Section 71.004, Family Code, the spouse was unable to prevent the act giving rise to the seizure.

(d) A final conviction for an underlying offense is not a requirement for forfeiture under this chapter. An owner or interest holder may present evidence of a dismissal or acquittal of an underlying offense in a forfeiture proceeding, and evidence of an acquittal raises a presumption that the property or interest that is the subject of the hearing is nonforfeitable. This presumption can be rebutted by evidence that the owner or interest holder knew or should have known that the property was contraband.

(e) It is the intention of the legislature that asset forfeiture is remedial in nature and not a form of punishment. If the court finds that all or any part of the property is subject to forfeiture, the judge shall forfeit the property to the state, with the attorney representing the state as the agent for the state, except that if the court finds that the nonforfeitable interest of an interest holder in the property is valued in an amount greater than or substantially equal to the present value of the property, the court shall order the property released to the interest holder. If the court finds that the nonforfeitable interest of an interest holder is valued in an amount substantially less than the present value of the property and that the property is subject to forfeiture, the court shall order the property forfeited to the state with the attorney representing the state acting as the agent of the state, and making necessary orders to protect the nonforfeitable interest of the interest holder. On final judgment of forfeiture, the attorney representing the state shall dispose of the property in the manner required by Article 59.06 of this code.

(f) On forfeiture to the state of an amount greater than $2,500, the clerk of the court in which the forfeiture proceeding was held is entitled to court costs in that proceeding as in other civil proceedings unless the forfeiture violates federal requirements for multijurisdictional task force cases authorized under Chapter 362, Local Government Code. The procedure for collecting the costs is the procedure established under Subsections (a) and (c), Article 59.06.

(g) If property is seized at a federal checkpoint, the notice of seizure and intended forfeiture may be filed in and the proceeding may be held in:

(1) the county in which the seizure occurred; or

(2) with the consent of the owner, operator, or agent in charge of the property, a county that is adjacent to the county in which the seizure occurred, if both counties are in the same judicial district.

History of CCP art. 59.05: Acts 1989, 71st Leg., 1st C.S., ch. 12, §1, eff. Oct. 18, 1989. Amended by Acts 1993, 73rd Leg., ch. 780, §2, eff. Sept. 1, 1993; Acts 1995, 74th Leg., ch. 533, §2, eff. Sept. 1, 1995; Acts 1999, 76th Leg., ch. 582, §1, eff. Sept. 1, 1999; Acts 2003, 78th Leg., ch. 1153, §1, eff. Sept. 1, 2003; Acts 2003, 78th Leg., ch. 1276, §7.002(*I*), eff. Sept. 1, 2003.

ANNOTATIONS

Fant v. State, 931 S.W.2d 299, 306-07 (Tex.Crim. App.1996). "[T]he Legislature intended Art. 59 forfeitures to be remedial. [¶] [T]he property, and not an individual, is the target of forfeiture.... [I]t is conceivable that the property could be forfeited if no owner or interest holder files a claim to it and the State fails to demonstrate a connection between the property and a particular person. *At 308:* [T]he *in rem* civil forfeitures prescribed by Chapter 59 are neither 'punishment' nor criminal for purposes of the Double Jeopardy clause of the Fifth Amendment."

$162,950 v. State, 911 S.W.2d 528, 529 (Tex. App.—Eastland 1995, writ denied). Where "findings of fact and conclusions of law are neither filed nor requested, the appellate court must presume that the trial court made all the necessary findings to support the judgment. We must affirm the judgment if it can be upheld on any legal theory that finds support in the evidence. [¶] Where … there is no direct evidence linking the seized property to illegal activity, the State must present sufficient circumstantial evidence. The State does not have to prove that a specific crime was committed."

State v. $20,480, 865 S.W.2d 175, 175 (Tex.App.—Corpus Christi 1993, writ denied). "[O]nce the trial court determined that the currency was contraband, it had no discretion to forfeit the contraband to any entity or person other than the attorney representing the State."

ART. 59.06. DISPOSITION OF FORFEITED PROPERTY

(a) Except as provided by Subsection (k), all forfeited property shall be administered by the attorney representing the state, acting as the agent of the state, in accordance with accepted accounting practices and with the provisions of any local agreement entered into between the attorney representing the state and law enforcement agencies. If a local agreement has not been executed, the property shall be sold on the 75th day after the date of the final judgment of forfeiture at public auction under the direction of the county sheriff, after notice of public auction as provided by law for other sheriff's sales. The proceeds of the sale shall be distributed as follows:

(1) to any interest holder to the extent of the interest holder's nonforfeitable interest; and

(2) the balance, if any, after the deduction of court costs to which a district court clerk is entitled under Article 59.05(f) and, after that deduction, the deduction of storage and disposal costs, to be deposited not later than the 30th day after the date of the sale in the state treasury to the credit of the general revenue fund.

A *Subsection (b) below is effective for personal property seized or taken into custody on or after Sept. 1, 2007.*

(b) If a local agreement exists between the attorney representing the state and law enforcement agencies, the attorney representing the state may transfer the property to law enforcement agencies to maintain, repair, use, and operate the property for official purposes if the property is free of any interest of an interest holder. The agency receiving the forfeited property may purchase the interest of an interest holder so that the property can be released for use by the agency. The agency receiving the forfeited property may maintain, repair, use, and operate the property with money appropriated for current operations. If the property is a motor vehicle subject to registration under the motor vehicle registration laws of this state, the agency receiving the forfeited vehicle is considered to be the purchaser and the certificate of title shall issue to the agency. A law enforcement agency to which property is transferred under this subsection at any time may transfer or loan the property to any other municipal or county agency or to a school district for the use of that agency or district. A municipal or county agency or school district to which a law enforcement agency loans a motor vehicle under this subsection shall maintain any automobile insurance coverage for the vehicle that is required by law.

Subsection (b) below is effective for personal property seized or taken into custody before Sept. 1, 2007.

(b) If a local agreement exists between the attorney representing the state and law enforcement agencies, the attorney representing the state may transfer the property to law enforcement agencies to maintain, repair, use, and operate the property for official purposes if the property is free of any interest of an interest holder. The agency receiving the forfeited property may purchase the interest of an interest holder so that the property can be released for use by the agency. The agency receiving the forfeited property may maintain, repair, use, and operate the property with money appropriated for current operations. If the property is a motor vehicle subject to registration under the motor vehicle registration laws of this state, the agency receiving the forfeited vehicle is considered to be the purchaser and the certificate of title shall issue to the agency. The agency at any time may transfer the property to a municipal or county law enforcement agency for the use of that agency.

E *Subsections (b-1) & (b-2) below are effective for personal property seized or taken into custody on or after Sept. 1, 2007.*

(b-1) If a loan is made by a sheriff's office or by a municipal police department, the commissioners court of the county in which the sheriff has jurisdiction or the governing body of the municipality in which the department has jurisdiction, as applicable, may revoke the loan at any time by notifying the receiving agency or district, by mail, that the receiving agency or district must return the loaned vehicle to the loaning agency before the seventh day after the date the receiving agency or district receives the notice.

(b-2) An agency that loans property under this article shall:

(1) keep a record of the loan, including the name of the agency to which the vehicle was loaned, the fair market value of the vehicle, and where the receiving agency will use the vehicle; and

(2) update the record when the information relating to the vehicle changes.

(c) If a local agreement exists between the attorney representing the state and law enforcement agencies, all money, securities, negotiable instruments, stocks or bonds, or things of value, or proceeds from the sale of those items, shall be deposited, after the deduction of court costs to which a district court clerk is entitled under Article 59.05(f), according to the terms of the agreement into one or more of the following funds:

(1) a special fund in the county treasury for the benefit of the office of the attorney representing the state, to be used by the attorney solely for the official purposes of his office;

(2) a special fund in the municipal treasury if distributed to a municipal law enforcement agency, to be used solely for law enforcement purposes, such as salaries and overtime pay for officers, officer training, specialized investigative equipment and supplies, and items used by officers in direct law enforcement duties;

(3) a special fund in the county treasury if distributed to a county law enforcement agency, to be used solely for law enforcement purposes; or

(4) a special fund in the state law enforcement agency if distributed to a state law enforcement agency, to be used solely for law enforcement purposes.

(d) Proceeds awarded under this chapter to a law enforcement agency or to the attorney representing the state may be spent by the agency or the attorney after a budget for the expenditure of the proceeds has been submitted to the commissioners court or governing body of the municipality. The budget must be detailed and clearly list and define the categories of expenditures, but may not list details that would endanger the

security of an investigation or prosecution. Expenditures are subject to audit provisions established under this article. A commissioners court or governing body of a municipality may not use the existence of an award to offset or decrease total salaries, expenses, and allowances that the agency or the attorney receives from the commissioners court or governing body at or after the time the proceeds are awarded. The head of the agency or attorney representing the state may not use the existence of an award to increase a salary, expense, or allowance for an employee of the attorney or agency who is budgeted by the commissioners court or governing body unless the commissioners court or governing body first approves the expenditure.

(e) On the sale of contraband under this article, the appropriate state agency shall issue a certificate of title to the recipient if a certificate of title is required for the property by other law.

(f) A final judgment of forfeiture under this chapter perfects the title of the state to the property as of the date that the contraband was seized or the date the forfeiture action was filed, whichever occurred first, except that if the property forfeited is real property, the title is perfected as of the date a notice of lis pendens is filed on the property.

 (g)(1) All law enforcement agencies and attorneys representing the state who receive proceeds or property under this chapter shall account for the seizure, forfeiture, receipt, and specific expenditure of all such proceeds and property in an audit, which is to be performed annually by the commissioners court or governing body of a municipality, as appropriate. The annual period of the audit for a law enforcement agency is the fiscal year of the appropriate county or municipality and the annual period for an attorney representing the state is the state fiscal year. The audit shall be completed on a form provided by the attorney general. Certified copies of the audit shall be delivered by the law enforcement agency or attorney representing the state to the comptroller's office and the attorney general not later than the 60th day after the date on which the annual period that is the subject of the audit ends.

(2) If a copy of the audit is not delivered to the attorney general within the period required by Subdivision (1), within five days after the end of the period the attorney general shall notify the law enforcement agency or the attorney representing the state of that fact. On a showing of good cause, the attorney general may grant an extension permitting the agency or attorney to deliver a copy of the audit after the period required by Subdivision (1) and before the 76th day after the date on which the annual period that is the subject of the audit ends. If the law enforcement agency or the attorney representing the state fails to establish good cause for not delivering the copy of the audit within the period required by Subdivision (1) or fails to deliver a copy of an audit within the extension period, the attorney general shall notify the comptroller of that fact. On notice under this subdivision, the comptroller shall perform the audit otherwise required by Subdivision (1). At the conclusion of the audit, the comptroller shall forward a copy of the audit to the attorney general. The law enforcement agency or attorney representing the state is liable to the comptroller for the costs of the comptroller in performing the audit.

(h) As a specific exception to the requirement of Subdivisions (1)-(3) of Subsection (c) of this article that the funds described by those subdivisions be used only for the official purposes of the attorney representing the state or for law enforcement purposes, on agreement between the attorney representing the state or the head of a law enforcement agency and the governing body of a political subdivision, the attorney representing the state or the head of the law enforcement agency shall comply with the request of the governing body to deposit not more than a total of 10 percent of the gross amount credited to the attorney's or agency's fund into the treasury of the political subdivision. The governing body of the political subdivision shall, by ordinance, order, or resolution, use funds received under this subsection for:

(1) nonprofit programs for the prevention of drug abuse;

(2) nonprofit chemical dependency treatment facilities licensed under Chapter 464, Health and Safety Code;

(3) nonprofit drug and alcohol rehabilitation or prevention programs administered or staffed by professionals designated as qualified and credentialed by the Texas Commission on Alcohol and Drug Abuse; or

(4) financial assistance as described by Subsection (o).

(i) The governing body of a political subdivision may not use funds received under this subchapter for

programs or facilities listed under Subsections (h)(1)-(3) if an officer of or member of the Board of Directors of the entity providing the program or facility is related to a member of the governing body, the attorney representing the state, or the head of the law enforcement agency within the third degree by consanguinity or the second degree by affinity.

(j) As a specific exception to Subdivision (4) of Subsection (c) of this article, the director of a state law enforcement agency may use not more than 10 percent of the amount credited to the special fund of the agency under that subdivision for the prevention of drug abuse and the treatment of persons with drug-related problems.

(k)(1) The attorney for the state shall transfer all forfeited property that is income from, or acquired with the income from, a movie, book, magazine article, tape recording, phonographic record, radio or television presentation, telephone service, electronic media format, including an Internet website, or live entertainment in which a crime is reenacted to the attorney general.

(2) The attorney for the state shall transfer to the attorney general all income from the sale of tangible property the value of which is increased by the notoriety gained from the conviction of an offense by the person accused or convicted of the crime, minus the deduction authorized by this subdivision. The attorney for the state shall determine the fair market value of property that is substantially similar to the property that was sold but that has not been increased in value by notoriety and deduct that amount from the proceeds of the sale. After transferring income to the attorney general, the attorney for the state shall transfer the remainder of the proceeds of the sale to the owner of the property. The attorney for the state, the attorney general, or a person who may be entitled to claim money from the escrow account described by Subdivision (3) in satisfaction of a claim may at any time bring an action to enjoin the waste of income described by this subdivision.

(3) The attorney general shall deposit the money or proceeds from the sale of the property into an escrow account. The money in the account is available to satisfy a judgment against the person who committed the crime in favor of a victim of the crime if the judgment is for damages incurred by the victim caused by the commission of the crime. The attorney general shall transfer the money in the account that has not been ordered paid to a victim in satisfaction of a judgment to the compensation to victims of crime fund on the fifth anniversary of the date the account was established. In this subsection, "victim" has the meaning assigned by Article 56.32.

(*l*) A law enforcement agency that, or an attorney representing the state who, does not receive proceeds or property under this chapter during an annual period as described by Subsection (g) shall, not later than the 30th day after the date on which the annual period ends, report to the attorney general that the agency or attorney, as appropriate, did not receive proceeds or property under this chapter during the annual period.

(m) As a specific exception to Subdivisions (1)-(3) of Subsection (c), a law enforcement agency or attorney representing the state may use proceeds received under this chapter to contract with a person or entity to prepare an audit as required by Subsection (g).

(n) As a specific exception to Subsection (c)(2) or (3), a local law enforcement agency may transfer not more than a total of 10 percent of the gross amount credited to the agency's fund to a separate special fund in the treasury of the political subdivision. The agency shall administer the separate special fund, and expenditures from the fund are at the sole discretion of the agency and may be used only for financial assistance as described by Subsection (o).

(o) The governing body of a political subdivision or a local law enforcement agency may provide financial assistance under Subsection (h)(4) or (n) only to a person who is a Texas resident, who plans to enroll or is enrolled at an institution of higher education in an undergraduate degree or certificate program in a field related to law enforcement, and who plans to return to that locality to work for the political subdivision or the agency in a field related to law enforcement. To ensure the promotion of a law enforcement purpose of the political subdivision or the agency, the governing body of the political subdivision or the agency shall impose other reasonable criteria related to the provision of this financial assistance, including a requirement that a recipient of the financial assistance work for a certain period of time for the political subdivision or the agency in a field related to law enforcement and including a requirement that the recipient sign an agreement to perform that work for that period of time. In this subsection, "institution of higher education" has the meaning assigned by Section 61.003, Education Code.

(p) Notwithstanding Subsection (a), and to the extent necessary to protect the commission's ability to recover amounts wrongfully obtained by the owner of the property and associated damages and penalties to which the commission may otherwise be entitled by law, the attorney representing the state shall transfer to the Health and Human Services Commission all forfeited property defined as contraband under Article 59.01(2)(B)(vii). If the forfeited property consists of property other than money or negotiable instruments, the attorney representing the state may, if approved by the commission, sell the property and deliver to the commission the proceeds from the sale, minus costs attributable to the sale. The sale must be conducted in a manner that is reasonably expected to result in receiving the fair market value for the property.

(q)(1) Notwithstanding any other provision of this article, a multicounty drug task force, or a county or municipality participating in the task force, that is not established in accordance with Section 362.004, Local Government Code, or that fails to comply with the policies and procedures established by the Department of Public Safety under that section, and that participates in the seizure of contraband shall forward to the comptroller all proceeds received by the task force from the forfeiture of the contraband. The comptroller shall deposit the proceeds in the state treasury to the credit of the general revenue fund.

(2) The attorney general shall ensure the enforcement of Subdivision (1) by filing any necessary legal proceedings in the county in which the contraband is forfeited or in Travis County.

History of CCP art. 59.06: Acts 1989, 71st Leg., 1st C.S., ch. 12, §1, eff. Oct. 18, 1989. Amended by Acts 1991, 72nd Leg., ch. 312, §§1, 2, eff. Sept. 1, 1991; Acts 1993, 73rd Leg., ch. 780, §§3, 4 (eff. Sept. 1, 1993), ch. 814, §1 (eff. Aug. 30, 1993), ch. 780, §4 (eff. Sept. 1, 1993); Acts 1995, 74th Leg., ch. 76, §5.95(112), eff. Sept. 1, 1995; Acts 1997, 75th Leg., ch. 975, §1, eff. Sept. 1, 1997; Acts 1999, 76th Leg., ch. 481, §§1, 2 (eff. Sept. 1, 1999), ch. 582, §2 (eff. Sept. 1, 1999), ch. 707, §1 (eff. Sept. 1, 1999); Acts 2001, 77th Leg., ch. 124, §2 (eff. Sept. 1, 2001), ch. 929, §3 (eff. Sept. 1, 2001); Acts 2003, 78th Leg., ch. 198, §2.142 (eff. Sept. 1, 2003), ch. 257, §18 (eff. Sept. 1, 2003), ch. 428, §2 (eff. Sept. 1, 2003); Acts 2005, 79th Leg., ch. 556, §4, eff. Sept. 1, 2005; Acts 2007, 80th Leg., ch. 120, §2 (eff. Sept. 1, 2007), ch. 446, §1 (eff. Sept. 1, 2007).

ART. 59.07. IMMUNITY

This chapter does not impose any additional liability on any authorized state, county, or municipal officer engaged in the lawful performance of the officer's duties.

History of CCP art. 59.07: Acts 1989, 71st Leg., 1st C.S., ch. 12, §1, eff. Oct. 18, 1989.

ART. 59.08. DEPOSIT OF MONEY PENDING DISPOSITION

(a) If money that is contraband is seized, the attorney representing the state may deposit the money in an interest-bearing bank account in the jurisdiction of the attorney representing the state until a final judgment is rendered concerning the contraband.

(b) If a final judgment is rendered concerning contraband, money that has been placed in an interest-bearing bank account under Subsection (a) of this article shall be distributed in the same manner as proceeds are distributed under Article 59.06 of this code, with any interest being distributed in the same manner and used for the same purpose as the principal.

History of CCP art. 59.08: Acts 1989, 71st Leg., 1st C.S., ch. 12, §1, eff. Oct. 18, 1989.

ART. 59.09. RIGHT TO ATTORNEY NOT TO BE ABRIDGED

This chapter is not intended to abridge an accused person's right to counsel in a criminal case.

History of CCP art. 59.09: Acts 1989, 71st Leg., 1st C.S., ch. 12, §1, eff. Oct. 18, 1989.

ART. 59.10. ELECTION OF LAWS

If property is subject to forfeiture under this chapter and under any other law of this state, the attorney representing the state may bring forfeiture proceedings under either law.

History of CCP art. 59.10: Acts 1989, 71st Leg., 1st C.S., ch. 12, §1, eff. Oct. 18, 1989.

ART. 59.11. REPORT OF SEIZED & FORFEITED AIRCRAFT

Not later than the 10th day after the last day of each quarter of the fiscal year, the Department of Public Safety shall report to the State Aircraft Pooling Board:

(1) a description of each aircraft that the department has received by forfeiture under this chapter during the preceding quarter and the purposes for which the department intends to use the aircraft; and

(2) a description of each aircraft the department knows to have been seized under this chapter during the preceding quarter and the purposes for which the department would use the aircraft if it were forfeited to the department.

History of CCP art. 59.11: Acts 1991, 72nd Leg., ch. 14, §283, eff. Sept. 1, 1991.

See also Tex. Const. art. 1, §9.

ART. 59.12. SEIZURE OF ACCOUNTS & ASSETS AT REGULATED FINANCIAL INSTITUTION

(a) This article applies to property consisting of a depository account or assets in a regulated financial institution.

(b) A regulated financial institution, at the time a seizure warrant issued under Chapter 18 is served on the institution, may either:

(1) pay an account or tender assets held as security for an obligation owed to the institution at the time of the service of the seizure warrant; or

(2) transfer the depository account or assets to a segregated interest-bearing account in the name of the attorney representing the state as trustee, to remain in the account until the time has expired for an appeal from a decision of the court relating to the forfeiture of accounts or assets under Article 59.05.

(c) Immediately on service of the seizure warrant, the regulated financial institution shall take action as necessary to segregate the account or assets and shall provide evidence, certified by an officer of the institution, of the terms and amount of the account or a detailed inventory of the assets to the peace officer serving the warrant. Except as otherwise provided by this article, a transaction involving an account or assets, other than the deposit or reinvestment of interest, dividends, or other normally recurring payments on the account or assets that do not involve distribution of proceeds to the owner, is not authorized unless approved by the court that issued the seizure warrant or, if a forfeiture action has been instituted, the court in which that action is pending.

(d) Any accrual to the value of the account or assets during the pendency of the forfeiture proceedings is subject to the procedures for the disbursement of interest under Article 59.08.

(e) If the regulated financial institution fails to release the depository account or assets to a peace officer pursuant to a seizure warrant or transfer the account or assets as required by Subsection (b), and as a result cannot comply with the court's forfeiture order, the court:

(1) shall order the regulated financial institution and its culpable officers, agents, or employees to pay actual damages, attorney's fees, and court costs incurred as a result of the institution's failure to comply; and

(2) may find the regulated financial institution and its culpable officers, agents, or employees in contempt.

(f) A regulated financial institution that complies with this article is not liable in damages because of the compliance.

(g) This article does not:

(1) impair the right of the state to obtain possession of physical evidence or to seize a depository account or other assets for purposes other than forfeiture under this chapter; or

(2) waive criminal or civil remedies available under other law.

History of CCP art. 59.12: Acts 2001, 77th Leg., ch. 438, §5, eff. Sept. 1, 2001.

See also Tex. Const. art. 1, §9.

ART. 59.13. DISCLOSURE OF INFORMATION RELATING TO ACCOUNTS & ASSETS AT REGULATED FINANCIAL INSTITUTION

(a) The attorney representing the state may disclose information to the primary state or federal financial institution regulator, including grand jury information or otherwise confidential information, relating to any action contemplated or brought under this chapter that involves property consisting of a depository account in a regulated financial institution or assets held by a regulated financial institution as security for an obligation owed to a regulated financial institution. An attorney representing the state who discloses information as permitted by this subsection is not subject to contempt under Article 20.02 for that disclosure.

(b) A primary state or federal financial institution regulator shall keep confidential any information provided by the attorney representing the state under Subsection (a). The sharing of information under Subsection (a) by a representative of the state is not considered a waiver by the state of any privilege or claim of confidentiality.

(c) A regulator described by Subsection (b) commits an offense if the regulator knowingly discloses information in violation of this article. An offense under this subsection is punishable by confinement in jail for a period not to exceed 30 days, a fine not to exceed $500, or both such confinement and fine.

History of CCP art. 59.13: Acts 2001, 77th Leg., ch. 438, §5, eff. Sept. 1, 2001.

ART. 59.14. NOTICE TO PRIMARY STATE & FEDERAL FINANCIAL INSTITUTION REGULATORS

(a) Before taking any action under this chapter that implicates a potentially culpable officer or director of a regulated financial institution, the attorney representing the state shall notify the banking commissioner, who shall notify the appropriate state or federal financial institution regulator.

(b) A state or federal financial institution regulator shall keep confidential any information provided by the attorney representing the state under Subsection (a).

(c) A regulator described by Subsection (b) commits an offense if the regulator knowingly discloses information in violation of this article. An offense under this subsection is punishable by confinement in jail for a period not to exceed 30 days, a fine not to exceed $500, or both such confinement and fine.

(d) The provision of notice under Subsection (a) is not considered a waiver by the state of any privilege or claim of confidentiality.

History of CCP art. 59.14: Acts 2001, 77th Leg., ch. 438, §5, eff. Sept. 1, 2001.

CHAPTER 60. CRIMINAL HISTORY RECORD SYSTEM

ART. 60.01. DEFINITIONS

In this chapter:

(1) "Administration of criminal justice" means the performance of any of the following activities: detection, apprehension, detention, pretrial release, posttrial release, prosecution, adjudication, correctional supervision, or rehabilitation of an offender. The term includes criminal identification activities and the collection, storage, and dissemination of criminal history record information.

(2) "Appeal" means the review of a decision of a lower court by a superior court other than by collateral attack.

(3) "Computerized criminal history system" means the data base containing arrest, disposition, and other criminal history maintained by the Department of Public Safety.

(4) "Corrections tracking system" means the data base maintained by the Texas Department of Criminal Justice on all offenders under its supervision.

(5) "Council" means the Criminal Justice Policy Council.

(6) "Criminal justice agency" means a federal or state agency that is engaged in the administration of criminal justice under a statute or executive order and allocates a substantial part of its annual budget to the administration of criminal justice.

(7) "Criminal justice information system" means the computerized criminal history system and the corrections tracking system.

(8) "Disposition" means an action that results in the termination, transfer to another jurisdiction, or indeterminate suspension of the prosecution of a criminal charge.

(9) "Incident number" means a unique number assigned to a specific person during a specific arrest.

(10) "Offender" means any person who is assigned an incident number.

(11) "Offense code" means a numeric code for each offense category.

(12) "Rejected case" means:

(A) a charge that, after the arrest of the offender, the prosecutor declines to include in an information or present to a grand jury; or

(B) an information or indictment that, after the arrest of the offender, the prosecutor refuses to prosecute.

(13) "Release" means the termination of jurisdiction over an individual by the criminal justice system.

(14) "State identification number" means a unique number assigned by the Department of Public Safety to each person whose name appears in the criminal justice information system.

(15) "Uniform incident fingerprint card" means a multiple part form containing a unique incident number with space for information relating to the charge or charges for which a person is being arrested, the person's fingerprints, and other information relevant to the arrest.

(16) "Electronic means" means the transmission of data between word processors, data processors, or similar automated information equipment over dedicated cables, commercial lines, or other similar methods of transmission.

History of CCP art. 60.01: Acts 1989, 71st Leg., ch. 785, §6.01, eff. Sept. 1, 1989. Amended by Acts 1990, 71st Leg., 6th C.S., ch. 25, §28, eff. June 18, 1990; Acts 1993, 73rd Leg., ch. 790, §37 (eff. Sept. 1, 1993), ch. 1025, §1 (eff. Sept. 1, 1993).

ART. 60.02. INFORMATION SYSTEMS

(a) The Texas Department of Criminal Justice is responsible for recording data and establishing and maintaining a data base for a corrections tracking system.

(b) The Department of Public Safety is responsible for recording data and maintaining a data base for a computerized criminal history system that serves as the record creation point for criminal history information maintained by the state.

(c) The criminal justice information system shall be established and maintained to supply the state with a system:

(1) that provides law enforcement officers with an accurate criminal history record depository;

(2) that provides criminal justice agencies with an accurate criminal history record depository for operational decision making;

(3) from which accurate criminal justice system modeling can be conducted;

(4) that improves the quality of data used to conduct impact analyses of proposed legislative changes in the criminal justice system; and

(5) that improves the ability of interested parties to analyze the functioning of the criminal justice system.

(d) The data bases must contain the information required by this chapter.

(e) The Department of Public Safety shall designate the offense codes and has the sole responsibility for designating the state identification number for each person whose name appears in the criminal justice information system.

(f) The Department of Public Safety and the Texas Department of Criminal Justice shall implement a system to link the computerized criminal history system and the corrections tracking system. Data received by the Texas Department of Criminal Justice that is required by the Department of Public Safety for the preparation of a criminal history record shall be made available to the computerized criminal history system not later than the seventh day after the date on which the Texas Department of Criminal Justice receives the request for the data from the Department of Public Safety.

(g) The Department of Public Safety is responsible for the operation of the computerized criminal history system and shall develop the necessary interfaces in the system to accommodate inquiries from a statewide automated fingerprint identification system, if such a system is implemented by the department.

(h) Whenever possible, the reporting of information relating to dispositions and subsequent offender processing data shall be conducted electronically.

(i) The Department of Public Safety and the Texas Department of Criminal Justice, with advice from the council and the Department of Information Resources, shall develop biennial plans to improve the reporting and accuracy of the criminal justice information system and to develop and maintain monitoring systems capable of identifying missing information.

(j) At least once during each five-year period the council shall coordinate an examination of the records and operations of the criminal justice information system to ensure the accuracy and completeness of information in the system and to ensure the promptness of information reporting. The state auditor, or other appropriate entity selected by the council, shall conduct the examination with the cooperation of the council, the Department of Public Safety, and the Texas Department of Criminal Justice. The Department of Public Safety, the council, and the Texas Department of Criminal Justice may examine the records of the agencies required to report information to the Department of Public Safety or the Texas Department of Criminal Justice. The examining entity shall submit to the legislature and the council a report that summarizes the findings of each examination and contains recommendations for improving the system. Not later than the first anniversary after the date the examining entity submits its report, the Department of Public Safety shall report to the Legislative Budget Board, the governor, the state auditor, and the council on the department's progress in implementing the examining entity's recommendations, including for each recommendation not implemented the reason for not implementing the recommendation. The Department of Public Safety shall submit a similar report each year following the submission of the first report until each of the examining entity's recommendations is implemented.

(k) The council, the Department of Public Safety, the criminal justice division of the governor's office, and the Department of Information Resources cooperatively shall develop and adopt a grant program, to be implemented by the criminal justice division at a time and in a manner determined by the division, to aid local law enforcement agencies, prosecutors, and court personnel in obtaining equipment and training necessary to operate a telecommunications network capable of:

(1) making inquiries to and receiving responses from the statewide automated fingerprint identification system and from the computerized criminal history system; and

(2) transmitting information to those systems.

(l) Blank.

(m) Notwithstanding Subsection (j), work performed under this section by the state auditor is subject to approval by the legislative audit committee for inclusion in the audit plan under Section 321.013(c), Government Code.

History of CCP art. 60.02: Acts 1989, 71st Leg., ch. 785, §6.01, eff. Sept. 1, 1989. Amended by Acts 1990, 71st Leg., 6th C.S., ch. 25, §28, eff. June 18, 1990; Acts 1991, 72nd Leg., ch. 362, §1, eff. Aug. 26, 1991; Acts 2001, 77th Leg., ch. 1491, §1, eff. Sept. 1, 2001; Acts 2003, 78th Leg., ch. 785, §72, eff. Sept. 1, 2003.

ART. 60.03. INTERAGENCY COOPERATION; CONFIDENTIALITY

(a) Criminal justice agencies, the Legislative Budget Board, and the council are entitled to access to the data bases of the Department of Public Safety, the Texas Juvenile Probation Commission, the Texas Youth Commission, and the Texas Department of Criminal Justice in accordance with applicable state or federal law or regulations. The access granted by this subsection does not grant an agency, the Legislative Budget Board, or the council the right to add, delete, or alter data maintained by another agency.

(b) The council or the Legislative Budget Board may submit to the Department of Public Safety, the Texas Juvenile Probation Commission, the Texas Youth Commission, and the Texas Department of Criminal Justice an annual request for a data file containing data elements from the departments' systems. The Department of Public Safety, the Texas Juvenile Probation Commission, the Texas Youth Commission, and the Texas Department of Criminal Justice shall provide the council and the Legislative Budget Board with that data file for the period requested, in accordance with state and federal law and regulations. If the council submits data file requests other than the annual data file request, the director of the agency maintaining the requested records must approve the request. The Legislative Budget Board may submit data file requests other than the annual data file request without the approval of the director of the agency maintaining the requested records.

(c) Neither a criminal justice agency, the council, nor the Legislative Budget Board may disclose to the public information in an individual's criminal history record if the record is protected by state or federal law or regulation.

History of CCP art. 60.03: Acts 1989, 71st Leg., ch. 785, §6.01, eff. Sept. 1, 1989. Amended by Acts 1990, 71st Leg., 6th C.S., ch. 25, §28, eff. June 18, 1990; Acts 2005, 79th Leg., ch. 741, §1, eff. June 17, 2005.

ART. 60.04. COMPATIBILITY OF DATA

(a) Data supplied to the criminal justice information system must be compatible with the system and must contain both incident numbers and state identification numbers.

(b) A discrete submission of information under any article of this chapter must contain, in conjunction with information required, the defendant's name and state identification number.

History of CCP art. 60.04: Acts 1989, 71st Leg., ch. 785, §6.01, eff. Sept. 1, 1989. Amended by Acts 1990, 71st Leg., 6th C.S., ch. 25, §28, eff. June 18, 1990.

ART. 60.05. TYPES OF INFORMATION COLLECTED

The criminal justice information system must contain but is not limited to the following types of information for each arrest for a felony or a misdemeanor not punishable by fine only:

(1) information relating to offenders;

(2) information relating to arrests;

(3) information relating to prosecutions;

(4) information relating to the disposition of cases by courts;

(5) information relating to sentencing; and

(6) information relating to the handling of offenders received by a correctional agency, facility, or other institution.

History of CCP art. 60.05: Acts 1989, 71st Leg., ch. 785, §6.01, eff. Sept. 1, 1989. Amended by Acts 1990, 71st Leg., 6th C.S., ch. 25, §28, eff. June 18, 1990.

ART. 60.051. INFORMATION IN COMPUTERIZED CRIMINAL HISTORY SYSTEM

(a) Information in the computerized criminal history system relating to an offender must include:

(1) the offender's name, including other names by which the offender is known;

(2) the offender's date of birth;

(3) the offender's physical description, including sex, weight, height, race, ethnicity, eye color, hair color, scars, marks, and tattoos; and

(4) the offender's state identification number.

(b) Information in the computerized criminal history system relating to an arrest must include:

(1) the name of the offender;

(2) the offender's state identification number;

(3) the arresting agency;

(4) the arrest charge by offense code and incident number;

(5) whether the arrest charge is a misdemeanor or felony;

(6) the date of the arrest;

(7) the exact disposition of the case by a law enforcement agency following the arrest; and

(8) the date of disposition of the case by the law enforcement agency.

(c) Information in the computerized criminal history system relating to a prosecution must include:

(1) each charged offense by offense code and incident number;

(2) the level of the offense charged or the degree of the offense charged for each offense in Subdivision (1) of this subsection; and

(3) for a rejected case, the date of rejection, offense code, and incident number, and whether the rejection is a result of a successful pretrial diversion program.

(d) Information in the computerized criminal history system relating to the disposition of a case that was not rejected must include:

(1) the final pleading to each charged offense and the level of the offense;

(2) a listing of each charged offense disposed of by the court and:

(A) the date of disposition;

(B) the offense code for the disposed charge and incident number; and

(C) the type of disposition; and

(3) for a conviction that is appealed the final court decision and the final disposition of the offender on appeal.

(e) Information in the computerized criminal history system relating to sentencing must include for each sentence:

(1) the sentencing date;

(2) the sentence for each offense by offense code and incident number;

(3) if the offender was sentenced to confinement:

(A) the agency that receives custody of the offender;

(B) the length of sentence for each offense; and

(C) if multiple sentences were ordered, whether they were ordered to be served consecutively or concurrently;

(4) if the offender was sentenced to a fine, the amount of the fine;

(5) if a sentence to confinement or fine was ordered but was deferred, probated, suspended, or otherwise not imposed:

(A) the length of sentence or the amount of the fine that was deferred, probated, suspended, or otherwise not imposed; and

(B) the offender's name, offense code, and incident number; and

(6) if a sentence other than fine or confinement was ordered, a description of the sentence ordered.

(f) The department shall maintain in the computerized criminal history system any information the department maintains in the central database under Article 62.005.

Ⓔ *Subsection (g) below is effective for offenses committed on or after Sept. 1, 2007.*

(g) In addition to the information described by Subsections (a)-(f), information in the computerized criminal history system must include the age of the victim of the offense if the defendant was arrested for or charged with an offense under:

(1) Section 21.02 (Continuous sexual abuse of young child or children), Penal Code;

(2) Section 21.11 (Indecency with a child), Penal Code;

(3) Section 22.011 (Sexual assault) or 22.021 (Aggravated sexual assault), Penal Code;

(4) Section 43.25 (Sexual performance by a child), Penal Code;

(5) Section 20.04(a)(4) (Aggravated kidnapping), Penal Code, if the defendant committed the offense with intent to violate or abuse the victim sexually; or

(6) Section 30.02 (Burglary), Penal Code, if the offense is punishable under Subsection (d) of that section and the defendant committed the offense with intent to commit an offense described by Subdivision (2), (3), or (5).

History of CCP art. 60.051: Renumbered from art. 60.05(b) to (f) and amended by Acts 1990, 71st Leg., 6th C.S., ch. 25, §28, eff. June 18, 1990. Amended by Acts 1993, 73rd Leg., ch. 1025, §9, eff. Sept. 1, 1993; Acts 1995, 74th Leg., ch. 258, §14, eff. Sept. 1, 1995; Acts 1997, 75th Leg., ch. 668, §8, eff. Sept. 1, 1997; Acts 2005, 79th Leg., ch. 1008, §2.03, eff. Sept. 1, 2005; Acts 2007, 80th Leg., ch. 593, §1.08, eff. Sept. 1, 2007.

ART. 60.052. INFORMATION IN CORRECTIONS TRACKING SYSTEM

(a) Information in the corrections tracking system relating to a sentence to be served under the jurisdiction of the Texas Department of Criminal Justice must include:

(1) the offender's name;

(2) the offender's state identification number;

(3) the sentencing date;

(4) the sentence for each offense by offense code and incident number;

(5) if the offender was sentenced to imprisonment:

(A) the unit of imprisonment;

(B) the length of sentence for each offense; and

(C) if multiple sentences were ordered, whether they were ordered to be served consecutively or concurrently; and

(6) if a sentence other than a fine or imprisonment was ordered, a description of the sentence ordered.

(b) Sentencing information in the corrections tracking system must also include the following information about each deferred adjudication, probation, or other alternative to imprisonment ordered:

(1) each conviction for which sentence was ordered but was deferred, probated, suspended, or otherwise not imposed, by offense code and incident number; and

(2) if a sentence or portion of a sentence of imprisonment was deferred, probated, suspended, or otherwise not imposed:

(A) the offense, the sentence, and the amount of the sentence deferred, probated, suspended, or otherwise not imposed;

(B) a statement of whether a return to confinement or other imprisonment was a condition of probation or an alternative sentence;

(C) the community supervision and corrections department exercising jurisdiction over the offender;

(D) the date the offender was received by a community supervision and corrections department;

(E) any program in which an offender is placed or has previously been placed and the level of supervision the offender is placed on while under the jurisdiction of a community supervision and corrections department;

(F) the date a program described by Paragraph (E) of this subdivision begins, the date the program ends, and whether the program was completed successfully;

(G) the date a level of supervision described by Paragraph (E) of this subdivision begins and the date the level of supervision ends;

(H) if the offender's probation is revoked:

(i) the reason for the revocation and the date of revocation by offense code and incident number; and

(ii) other current sentences of probation or other alternatives to confinement that have not been revoked, by offense code and incident number; and

(I) the date of the offender's release from the community supervision and corrections department.

(c) Information in the corrections tracking system relating to the handling of offenders must include the following information about each imprisonment, confinement, or execution of an offender:

(1) the date of the imprisonment or confinement;

(2) if the offender was sentenced to death:

(A) the date of execution; and

(B) if the death sentence was commuted, the sentence to which the sentence of death was commuted and the date of commutation;

(3) the date the offender was released from imprisonment or confinement and whether the release was a discharge or a release on parole or mandatory supervision;

(4) if the offender is released on parole or mandatory supervision:

(A) the offense for which the offender was convicted by offense code and incident number;

(B) the date the offender was received by an office of the Board of Pardons and Paroles division;

(C) the county in which the offender resides while under supervision;

(D) any program in which an offender is placed or has previously been placed and the level of supervision the offender is placed on while under the jurisdiction of the Board of Pardons and Paroles division;

(E) the date a program described by Paragraph (D) of this subdivision begins, the date the program ends, and whether the program was completed successfully;

(F) the date a level of supervision described by Paragraph (D) of this subdivision begins and the date the level of supervision ends;

(G) if the offender's release status is revoked, the reason for the revocation and the date of revocation;

(H) the expiration date of the sentence; and

(I) the date of the offender's release from Board of Pardons and Paroles division or the date on which the offender is granted clemency; and

(5) if the offender is released under Section 6(a), Article 42.12, of this code, the date of the offender's release.

History of CCP art. 60.052: Renumbered from art. 60.05(g) to (i) and amended by Acts 1990, 71st Leg., 6th C.S., ch. 25, §28, eff. June 18, 1990.

ART. 60.06. DUTIES OF AGENCIES

(a) Each criminal justice agency shall:

(1) compile and maintain records needed for reporting data required by the Texas Department of Criminal Justice and the Department of Public Safety;

(2) transmit to the Texas Department of Criminal Justice and the Department of Public Safety, when and

CCP ART. 60.052

in the manner the Texas Department of Criminal Justice and the Department of Public Safety direct, all data required by the Texas Department of Criminal Justice and the Department of Public Safety;

(3) give the Department of Public Safety and the Texas Department of Criminal Justice or their accredited agents access to the agency for the purpose of inspection to determine the completeness and accuracy of data reported;

(4) cooperate with the Department of Public Safety and the Texas Department of Criminal Justice so that the Department of Public Safety and the Texas Department of Criminal Justice may properly and efficiently perform their duties under this chapter; and

(5) cooperate with the Department of Public Safety and the Texas Department of Criminal Justice to identify and eliminate redundant reporting of information to the criminal justice information system.

(b) Information on an individual that consists of an identifiable description and notation of an arrest, detention, indictment, information, or other formal criminal charge and a disposition of the charge, including sentencing, correctional supervision, and release that is collected and compiled by the Department of Public Safety and the Texas Department of Criminal Justice from criminal justice agencies and maintained in a central location is not subject to public disclosure except as authorized by federal or state law or regulation.

(c) Subsection (b) of this section does not apply to a document maintained by a criminal justice agency that is the source of information collected by the Department of Public Safety or the Texas Department of Criminal Justice. Each criminal justice agency shall retain documents described by this subsection.

(d) An optical disk or other technology may be used instead of microfilm as a medium to store information if allowed by the applicable state laws or regulations relating to the archiving of state agency information.

(e) An official of an agency may not intentionally conceal or destroy any record with intent to violate this section.

(f) The duties imposed on a criminal justice agency under this article are also imposed on district court and county court clerks.

History of CCP art. 60.06: Acts 1989, 71st Leg., ch. 785, §6.01, eff. Sept. 1, 1989. Amended by Acts 1990, 71st Leg., 6th C.S., ch. 25, §28, eff. June 18, 1990; Acts 1995, 74th Leg., ch. 750, §1, eff. Aug. 28, 1995.

ART. 60.061. INFORMATION ON PERSONS LICENSED BY CERTAIN AGENCIES

(a) The Texas State Board of Medical Examiners, the Texas State Board of Podiatric Medical Examiners, the State Board of Dental Examiners, the Texas State Board of Pharmacy, the Texas State Board of Examiners of Psychologists, and the State Board of Veterinary Medical Examiners shall provide to the Department of Public Safety through electronic means, magnetic tape, or disk, as specified by the department, a list including the name, date of birth, and any other personal descriptive information required by the department for each person licensed by the respective agency. Each agency shall update this information and submit to the Department of Public Safety the updated information quarterly.

(b) The Department of Public Safety shall perform at least quarterly a computer match of the licensing list against the convictions maintained in the computerized criminal history system. The Department of Public Safety shall report to the appropriate licensing agency for verification and administrative action, as considered appropriate by the licensing agency, the name of any person found to have a record of conviction, except a defendant whose prosecution is deferred during a period of community supervision without an adjudication or plea of guilt. The Department of Public Safety may charge the licensing agency a fee not to exceed the actual direct cost incurred by the department in performing a computer match and reporting to the agency.

(c) The transmission of information by electronic means under Subsection (a) of this article does not affect whether the information is subject to disclosure under Chapter 552, Government Code.

History of CCP art. 60.061: Acts 1993, 73rd Leg., ch. 790, §38 (eff. Sept. 1, 1993), ch. 1025, §2 (eff. Sept. 1, 1993). Amended by Acts 1995, 74th Leg., ch. 76, §§3.21, 5.95(88) (eff. Sept. 1, 1995), ch. 965, §78 (eff. Sept. 1, 1995); Acts 1999, 76th Leg., ch. 1189, §43, eff. Sept. 1, 1999; Acts 2005, 79th Leg., ch. 143, §23, eff. Sept. 1, 2005.

ART. 60.07. UNIFORM INCIDENT FINGERPRINT CARD

(a) The Department of Public Safety, in consultation with the council, shall design, print, and distribute to each law enforcement agency in the state a uniform incident fingerprint card.

(b) The incident card must:

(1) be serially numbered with an incident number in such a manner that the individual incident of arrest may be readily ascertained; and

(2) be a multiple part form that can be transmitted with the offender through the criminal justice process and that allows each agency to report required data to the Department of Public Safety or the Texas Department of Criminal Justice.

(c) Subject to available telecommunications capacity, the Department of Public Safety shall develop the capability to receive by electronic means from a law enforcement agency the information on the uniform incident fingerprint card. The information must be in a form that is compatible to the form required of data supplied to the criminal justice information system.

History of CCP art. 60.07: Acts 1989, 71st Leg., ch. 785, §6.01, eff. Sept. 1, 1989. Amended by Acts 1990, 71st Leg., 6th C.S., ch. 25, §28, eff. June 18, 1990; Acts 1993, 73rd Leg., ch. 790, §39 (eff. Sept. 1, 1993), ch. 1025, §3 (eff. Sept. 1, 1993).

ART. 60.08. REPORTING

(a) The Department of Public Safety and the Texas Department of Criminal Justice shall, by rule, develop reporting procedures that:

(1) ensure that the offender processing data is reported from the time an offender is arrested until the time an offender is released; and

(2) provide measures and policies designed to identify and eliminate redundant reporting of information to the criminal justice information system.

(b) The arresting agency shall prepare a uniform incident fingerprint card and initiate the reporting process for each offender charged with a felony or a misdemeanor not punishable by fine only.

(c) The clerk of the court exercising jurisdiction over a case shall report the disposition of the case to the Department of Public Safety.

(d) Except as otherwise required by applicable state laws or regulations, information or data required by this chapter to be reported to the Texas Department of Criminal Justice or the Department of Public Safety shall be reported promptly but not later than the 30th day after the date on which the information or data is received by the agency responsible for reporting it except in the case of an arrest. An offender's arrest shall be reported to the Department of Public Safety not later than the seventh day after the date of the arrest.

(e) A court that orders the release of an offender under Section 6(a), Article 42.12, of this code at a time when the offender is under a bench warrant and not physically imprisoned in the institutional division shall report the release to the institutional division of the Texas Department of Criminal Justice not later than the seventh day after the date of the release.

History of CCP art. 60.08: Acts 1989, 71st Leg., ch. 785, §6.01, eff. Sept. 1, 1989. Amended by Acts 1990, 71st Leg., 6th C.S., ch. 25, §28, eff. June 18, 1990; Acts 1995, 74th Leg., ch. 750, §2, eff. Aug. 28, 1995.

ART. 60.09. LOCAL DATA ADVISORY BOARDS

(a) The commissioners court of each county may create local data advisory boards to, among other duties:

(1) analyze the structure of local automated and manual data systems to identify redundant data entry and data storage;

(2) develop recommendations for the commissioners to improve the local data systems;

(3) develop recommendations, when appropriate, for the effective electronic transfer of required data from local agencies to state agencies; and

(4) perform any related duties to be determined by the commissioners court.

(b) Local officials responsible for collecting, storing, reporting, and using data may be appointed to the local data advisory board.

(c) The council and the Department of Public Safety shall, to the extent that resources allow, provide technical assistance and advice on the request of the local data advisory board.

History of CCP art. 60.09: Acts 1989, 71st Leg., ch. 785, §6.01, eff. Sept. 1, 1989. Amended by Acts 1990, 71st Leg., 6th C.S., ch. 25, §28, eff. June 18, 1990.

ARTS. 60.10, 60.11. REPEALED
Repealed by Acts 2005, 79th Leg., ch. 1218, §6, eff. Sept. 1, 2005.

ART. 60.12. FINGERPRINT & ARREST INFORMATION IN COMPUTERIZED SYSTEM

(a) The Department of Public Safety shall, when a jurisdiction transmits fingerprints and arrest information by a remote terminal accessing the statewide automated fingerprint identification system, use that transmission either to create a permanent record in the criminal justice information system or to create a temporary arrest record in the criminal justice information system to be maintained by the department until the department receives and processes the physical copy of the arrest information.

(b) The Department of Public Safety shall make available to a criminal justice agency making a background criminal inquiry any information contained in a temporary arrest record maintained by the department, including a statement that a physical copy of the arrest information was not available at the time the information was entered in the system.

History of CCP art. 60.12: Acts 1991, 72nd Leg., 2nd C.S., ch. 10, §7.05, eff. Dec. 1, 1991. Amended by Acts 1993, 73rd Leg., ch. 790, §40 (eff. Sept. 1, 1993), ch. 1025, §4 (eff. Sept. 1, 1993).

ART. 60.13. REPEALED

Repealed by Acts 2005, 79th Leg., ch. 1218, §6, eff. Sept. 1, 2005.

ART. 60.14. ALLOCATION OF GRANT PROGRAM MONEY FOR CRIMINAL JUSTICE PROGRAMS

An agency of the state, before allocating money to a county from any federal or state grant program for the enhancement of criminal justice programs, shall certify that the county has taken or will take, using all or part of the allocated funds, all action necessary to provide the Texas Department of Criminal Justice and the Department of Public Safety any criminal history records maintained by the county in the manner specified for purposes of those departments.

History of CCP art. 60.14: Acts 1991, 72nd Leg., 2nd C.S., ch. 10, §7.05, eff. Dec. 1, 1991.

ARTS. 60.15 TO 60.17. REPEALED

Repealed by Acts 2005, 79th Leg., ch. 1218, §6, eff. Sept. 1, 2005.

ART. 60.18. INFORMATION ON SUBSEQUENT ARREST OF CERTAIN INDIVIDUALS

The Texas Department of Criminal Justice and the Department of Public Safety shall develop the capability to send by electronic means information about the subsequent arrest of a person under supervision to, as applicable:

(1) the community supervision and corrections department serving the court of original jurisdiction; or

(2) the district parole office supervising the person.

History of CCP art. 60.18: Acts 1993, 73rd Leg., ch. 790, §41 (eff. Sept. 1, 1993), ch. 1025, §5 (eff. Sept. 1, 1993). Amended by Acts 2005, 79th Leg., ch. 1218, §2, eff. Sept. 1, 2005.

ART. 60.19. INFORMATION RELATED TO MISUSED IDENTITY

(a) On receipt of information from a local law enforcement agency under Article 2.28, the department shall:

(1) provide the notice described by Subdivision (1) of that article to the person whose identity was misused, if the local law enforcement agency was unable to notify the person under that subdivision;

(2) take action to ensure that the information maintained in the computerized criminal history system reflects the use of the person's identity as a stolen alias; and

(3) notify the Texas Department of Criminal Justice that the person's identifying information may have been falsely used by an inmate in the custody of the department.

(b) On receipt of a declaration under Section 411.0421, Government Code, or on receipt of information similar to that contained in a declaration, the department shall separate information maintained in the computerized criminal history system regarding an individual whose identity has been misused from information maintained in that system regarding the person who misused the identity.

History of CCP art. 60.19: Acts 1999, 76th Leg., ch. 1334, §2, eff. Sept. 1, 1999. Amended by Acts 2003, 78th Leg., ch. 339, §5, eff. Sept. 1, 2003.

History of Former CCP art. 60.19: Acts 1995, 74th Leg., ch. 750, §3, eff. Aug. 28, 1995. Former art. 60.19 expired by its own terms Sept. 1, 1997.

ART. 60.20. INFORMATION RELATED TO NON-FINGERPRINT SUPPORTED ACTIONS

On receipt of a report of prosecution or court disposition information from a jurisdiction for which corresponding arrest data does not exist in the computerized criminal history system, the Department of Public Safety shall enter the report into a non-fingerprint supported file that is separate from the computerized criminal history system. The department shall grant access to records in the non-fingerprint supported file that include the subject's name or other identifier in the same manner as the department is required to grant access to criminal history record information under Subchapter F, Chapter 411, Government Code. On receipt of a report of arrest information that corresponds to a record in the non-fingerprint supported file, the department shall transfer the record from the non-fingerprint supported file to the computerized criminal history system.

History of CCP art. 60.20: Acts 2001, 77th Leg., ch. 1491, §2, eff. Sept. 1, 2001.

ART. 60.21. MONITORING TRACKING; INFORMATION SUBMISSION

(a) The Department of Information Resources shall monitor the development of the corrections tracking system by the Texas Department of Criminal Justice to ensure implementation of the system not later than June 1, 2005.

CODE OF CRIMINAL PROCEDURE
CHAPTER 61. INFORMATION PERTAINING TO CRIMINAL COMBINATIONS & STREET GANGS
ARTS. 60.21 - 61.02

CCP ART. 60.21

(b) The Department of Public Safety shall:

(1) monitor the submission of arrest and disposition information by local jurisdictions;

(2) annually submit to the Legislative Budget Board, the governor, the state auditor, and the council a report regarding the level of reporting by local jurisdictions;

(3) identify local jurisdictions that do not report arrest or disposition information or that partially report information; and

(4) for use in determining the status of outstanding dispositions, publish monthly on the Department of Public Safety's Internet website or on another electronic publication a report listing each arrest by local jurisdiction for which there is no corresponding final court disposition.

History of CCP art. 60.21: Acts 2001, 77th Leg., ch. 1491, §2, eff. Sept. 1, 2001. Amended by Acts 2005, 79th Leg., ch. 1218, §3, eff. Sept. 1, 2005.

CHAPTER 61. COMPILATION OF INFORMATION PERTAINING TO CRIMINAL COMBINATIONS & CRIMINAL STREET GANGS

ART. 61.01. DEFINITIONS

In this chapter:

(1) "Combination" and "criminal street gang" have the meanings assigned by Section 71.01, Penal Code.

(2) "Child" has the meaning assigned by Section 51.02, Family Code.

(3) "Criminal information" means facts, material, photograph, or data reasonably related to the investigation or prosecution of criminal activity.

(4) "Criminal activity" means conduct that is subject to prosecution.

(5) "Criminal justice agency" has the meaning assigned by Article 60.01 and also means a municipal or county agency, or school district law enforcement agency, that is engaged in the administration of criminal justice under a statute or executive order.

(6) "Administration of criminal justice" has the meaning assigned by Article 60.01.

(7) "Department" means the Department of Public Safety of the State of Texas.

(8) "Intelligence database" means a collection or compilation of data organized for search and retrieval to evaluate, analyze, disseminate, or use intelligence information relating to a criminal combination or a criminal street gang for the purpose of investigating or prosecuting criminal offenses.

(9) "Law enforcement agency" does not include the Texas Department of Criminal Justice or the Texas Youth Commission.

History of CCP art. 61.01: Acts 1995, 74th Leg., ch. 671, §1, eff. Aug. 28, 1995. Amended by Acts 1999, 76th Leg., ch. 1154, §§1, 2, eff. Sept. 1, 1999.

ART. 61.02. CRIMINAL COMBINATION & CRIMINAL STREET GANG INTELLIGENCE DATABASE; SUBMISSION CRITERIA

(a) Subject to Subsection (b), a criminal justice agency may compile criminal information into an intelligence database for the purpose of investigating or prosecuting the criminal activities of criminal combinations or criminal street gangs. The information may be compiled on paper, by computer, or in any other useful manner.

(b) A law enforcement agency may compile and maintain criminal information relating to a criminal street gang as provided by Subsection (a) in a local or regional intelligence database only if the agency compiles and maintains the information in accordance with the criminal intelligence systems operating policies established under 28 C.F.R. Section 23.1 et seq. and the submission criteria established under Subsection (c).

🅐 **(c)** Criminal information collected under this chapter relating to a criminal street gang must:

(1) be relevant to the identification of an organization that is reasonably suspected of involvement in criminal activity; and

CODE OF CRIMINAL PROCEDURE
CHAPTER 61. INFORMATION PERTAINING TO CRIMINAL COMBINATIONS & STREET GANGS
ARTS. 61.02 - 61.04

★

CCP ART. 61.04

(2) consist of:

(A) a judgment under any law that includes, as a finding or as an element of a criminal offense, participation in a criminal street gang;

(B) a self-admission by the individual of criminal street gang membership that is made during a judicial proceeding; or

(C) any two of the following:

(i) a self-admission by the individual of criminal street gang membership that is not made during a judicial proceeding;

(ii) an identification of the individual as a criminal street gang member by a reliable informant or other individual;

(iii) a corroborated identification of the individual as a criminal street gang member by an informant or other individual of unknown reliability;

(iv) evidence that the individual frequents a documented area of a criminal street gang and associates with known criminal street gang members;

(v) evidence that the individual uses, in more than an incidental manner, criminal street gang dress, hand signals, tattoos, or symbols, including expressions of letters, numbers, words, or marks, regardless of the format or medium in which the symbols are displayed, that are associated with a criminal street gang that operates in an area frequented by the individual and described by Subparagraph (iv); or

(vi) evidence that the individual has been arrested or taken into custody with known criminal street gang members for an offense or conduct consistent with criminal street gang activity.

History of CCP art. 61.02: Acts 1995, 74th Leg., ch. 671, §1, eff. Aug. 28, 1995. Amended by Acts 1999, 76th Leg., ch. 1154, §3, eff. Sept. 1, 1999; Acts 2007, 80th Leg., ch. 258, §18.05, eff. Sept. 1, 2007.

ART. 61.03. RELEASE OF INFORMATION

(a) A criminal justice agency that maintains criminal information under this chapter may release the information on request to:

(1) another criminal justice agency;

(2) a court; or

(3) a defendant in a criminal proceeding who is entitled to the discovery of the information under Chapter 39.

(b) A criminal justice agency or court may use information received under this article only for the administration of criminal justice. A defendant may use information received under this article only for a defense in a criminal proceeding.

(c) If a local law enforcement agency compiles and maintains information under this chapter relating to a criminal street gang, the agency shall send the information to the department.

(d) The department shall establish an intelligence database and shall maintain information received from an agency under Subsection (c) in the database in accordance with the policies established under 28 C.F.R. Section 23.1 et seq. and the submission criteria under Article 61.02(c).

(e) The department shall designate a code to distinguish criminal information contained in the intelligence database relating to a child from criminal information contained in the database relating to an adult offender.

History of CCP art. 61.03: Acts 1995, 74th Leg., ch. 671, §1, eff. Aug. 28, 1995. Amended by Acts 1997, 75th Leg., ch. 898, §1, eff. Sept. 1, 1997; Acts 1999, 76th Leg., ch. 1154, §4, eff. Sept. 1, 1999.

ART. 61.04. CRIMINAL INFORMATION RELATING TO CHILD

(a) Notwithstanding Chapter 58, Family Code, criminal information relating to a child associated with a combination or a criminal street gang may be compiled and released under this chapter regardless of the age of the child.

(b) A criminal justice agency that maintains information under this chapter may release the information to an attorney representing a child who is a party to a proceeding under Title 3, Family Code, if the juvenile court determines the information:

(1) is material to the proceeding; and

(2) is not privileged under law.

(c) An attorney may use information received under this article only for a child's defense in a proceeding under Title 3, Family Code.

(d) If a local law enforcement agency collects criminal information under this chapter relating to a criminal street gang, the governing body of the county or municipality served by the law enforcement agency may adopt a policy to notify the parent or guardian of a child of the agency's observations relating to the child's association with a criminal street gang.

History of CCP art. 61.04: Acts 1995, 74th Leg., ch. 671, §1, eff. Aug. 28, 1995. Amended by Acts 1997, 75th Leg., ch. 165, §7.05 (eff. Sept. 1, 1997), ch. 898, §2 (eff. Sept. 1, 1997); Acts 1999, 76th Leg., ch. 1154, §5, eff. Sept. 1, 1999.

ART. 61.05. UNAUTHORIZED USE OR RELEASE OF CRIMINAL INFORMATION

(a) A person commits an offense if the person knowingly:

(1) uses criminal information obtained under this chapter for an unauthorized purpose; or

(2) releases the information to a person who is not entitled to the information.

(b) An offense under this article is a Class A misdemeanor.

History of CCP art. 61.05: Acts 1995, 74th Leg., ch. 671, §1, eff. Aug. 28, 1995.

ART. 61.06. REMOVAL OF RECORDS RELATING TO AN INDIVIDUAL OTHER THAN A CHILD

(a) This article does not apply to information collected under this chapter by the Texas Department of Criminal Justice or the Texas Youth Commission.

(b) Subject to Subsection (c), information collected under this chapter relating to a criminal street gang must be removed from an intelligence database established under Article 61.02 and the intelligence database maintained by the department under Article 61.03 after three years if:

(1) the information relates to the investigation or prosecution of criminal activity engaged in by an individual other than a child; and

(2) the individual who is the subject of the information has not been arrested for criminal activity reported to the department under Chapter 60.

🅰 **(c)** In determining whether information is required to be removed from an intelligence database under Subsection (b), the three-year period does not include any period during which the individual who is the subject of the information is:

(1) confined in a correctional facility operated by or under contract with the Texas Department of Criminal Justice; or

☠ 🄴 *Subsection (2) below was enacted by Acts 2007, 80th Leg., ch. 1308, §10, effective June 15, 2007, without reference to the conflicting enactment made by Acts 2007, 80th Leg., ch. 258, §18.06, effective Sept. 1, 2007, and ch. 263, §2, effective June 8, 2007.*

(2) confined in a county jail in lieu of being confined in a correctional facility operated by or under contract with the Texas Department of Criminal Justice.

☠ 🄴 *Subsections (2) & (3) below were enacted by Acts 2007, 80th Leg., ch. 258, §18.06, effective Sept. 1, 2007, without reference to the conflicting enactment made by Acts 2007, 80th Leg., ch. 1308, §10, effective June 15, 2007, and ch. 263, §2, effective June 8, 2007.*

(2) committed to a secure correctional facility operated by or under contract with the Texas Youth Commission, as defined by Section 51.02, Family Code; or

(3) confined in a county jail or a facility operated by a juvenile board in lieu of being confined in a correctional facility operated by or under contract with the Texas Department of Criminal Justice or being committed to a secure correctional facility operated by or under contract with the Texas Youth Commission.

☠ 🄴 *Subsections (2) & (3) below were enacted by Acts 2007, 80th Leg., ch. 263, §2, effective June 8, 2007, without reference to the conflicting enactment made by Acts 2007, 80th Leg., ch. 258, §18.06, effective Sept. 1, 2007, and ch. 1308, §10, effective June 15, 2007.*

(2) committed to a secure correctional facility operated by or under contract with the Texas Youth Commission, as defined by Section 51.02, Family Code; or

(3) committed to a facility operated by a juvenile board in lieu of being committed to a secure correctional facility operated by or under contract with the Texas Youth Commission.

History of CCP art. 61.06: Acts 1995, 74th Leg., ch. 671, §1, eff. Aug. 28, 1995. Amended by Acts 1997, 75th Leg., ch. 898, §3, eff. Sept. 1, 1997; Acts 1999, 76th Leg., ch. 1154, §6, eff. Sept. 1, 1999; Acts 2007, 80th Leg., ch. 258, §18.06 (eff. Sept. 1, 2007), ch. 263, §2 (eff. June 8, 2007), ch. 1308, §10 (eff. June 15, 2007).

ART. 61.07. REMOVAL OF RECORDS RELATING TO A CHILD

(a) This article does not apply to information collected under this chapter by the Texas Department of Criminal Justice or the Texas Youth Commission.

(b) Subject to Subsection (c), information collected under this chapter relating to a criminal street gang must be removed from an intelligence database established under Article 61.02 and the intelligence database maintained by the department under Article 61.03 after two years if:

(1) the information relates to the investigation or prosecution of criminal activity engaged in by a child; and

(2) the child who is the subject of the information has not been:

(A) arrested for criminal activity reported to the department under Chapter 60; or

(B) taken into custody for delinquent conduct reported to the department under Chapter 58, Family Code.

(c) In determining whether information is required to be removed from an intelligence database under Subsection (b), the two-year period does not include any period during which the child who is the subject of the information is:

(1) committed to the Texas Youth Commission for conduct that violates a penal law of the grade of felony; or

(2) confined in the institutional division or the state jail division of the Texas Department of Criminal Justice.

History of CCP art. 61.07: Acts 1999, 76th Leg., ch. 1154, §7, eff. Sept. 1, 1999.

ART. 61.075. RIGHT TO REQUEST EXISTENCE OF CRIMINAL INFORMATION

(a) A person or the parent or guardian of a child may request a law enforcement agency to determine whether the agency has collected or is maintaining, under criteria established under Article 61.02(c), criminal information relating solely to the person or child. The law enforcement agency shall respond to the request not later than the 10th business day after the date the agency receives the request.

(b) Before responding to a request under Subsection (a), a law enforcement agency may require reasonable written verification of the identity of the person making the request and the relationship between the parent or guardian and the child, if applicable, including written verification of an address, date of birth, driver's license number, state identification card number, or social security number.

History of CCP art. 61.075: Acts 2007, 80th Leg., ch. 258, §18.07, eff. Sept. 1, 2007.

ART. 61.08. RIGHT TO REQUEST REVIEW OF CRIMINAL INFORMATION

(a) On receipt of a written request of a person or the parent or guardian of a child that includes a showing by the person or the parent or guardian that a law enforcement agency may have collected criminal information under this chapter relating to the person or child

that is inaccurate or that does not comply with the submission criteria under Article 61.02(c), the head of the agency or the designee of the agency head shall review criminal information collected by the agency under this chapter relating to the person or child to determine if:

(1) reasonable suspicion exists to believe that the information is accurate; and

(2) the information complies with the submission criteria established under Article 61.02(c).

(b) If, after conducting a review of criminal information under Subsection (a), the agency head or designee determines that:

(1) reasonable suspicion does not exist to believe that the information is accurate or the information does not comply with the submission criteria, the agency shall:

(A) destroy all records containing the information; and

(B) notify the department and the person who requested the review of the agency's determination and the destruction of the records; or

(2) reasonable suspicion does exist to believe that the information is accurate and the information complies with the submission criteria, the agency shall notify the person who requested the review of the agency's determination and that the person is entitled to seek judicial review of the agency's determination under Article 61.09.

(c) On receipt of notice under Subsection (b), the department shall immediately destroy all records containing the information that is the subject of the notice in the intelligence database maintained by the department under Article 61.03.

(d) A person who is committed to the Texas Youth Commission or confined in the institutional division or the state jail division of the Texas Department of Criminal Justice does not while committed or confined have the right to request review of criminal information under this article.

History of CCP art. 61.08: Acts 1999, 76th Leg., ch. 1154, §7, eff. Sept. 1, 1999.

ART. 61.09. JUDICIAL REVIEW

(a) A person who is entitled to seek judicial review of a determination made under Article 61.08(b)(2) may file a petition for review in district court in the county in which the person resides.

(b) On the filing of a petition for review under Subsection (a), the district court shall conduct an in camera review of the criminal information that is the subject of the determination to determine if:

(1) reasonable suspicion exists to believe that the information is accurate; and

(2) the information complies with the submission criteria under Article 61.02(c).

(c) If, after conducting an in camera review of criminal information under Subsection (b), the court finds that reasonable suspicion does not exist to believe that the information is accurate or that the information does not comply with the submission criteria, the court shall:

(1) order the law enforcement agency that collected the information to destroy all records containing the information; and

(2) notify the department of the court's determination and the destruction of the records.

(d) A petitioner may appeal a final judgment of a district court conducting an in camera review under this article.

(e) Information that is the subject of an in camera review under this article is confidential and may not be disclosed.

History of CCP art. 61.09: Acts 1999, 76th Leg., ch. 1154, §7, eff. Sept. 1, 1999.

ART. 61.10. TEXAS VIOLENT GANG TASK FORCE

(a) In this article, "task force" means the Texas Violent Gang Task Force.

(b) The purpose of the task force is to form a strategic partnership between state, federal, and local law enforcement agencies to better enable law enforcement and correctional agencies to take a proactive stance towards tracking gang activity and the growth and spread of gangs statewide.

(c) The task force shall focus its efforts on:

(1) developing a statewide networking system that will provide timely access to gang information;

(2) establishing communication between different law enforcement agencies, combining independent agency resources, and joining agencies together in a cooperative effort to focus on gang membership, gang activity, and gang migration trends; and

(3) forming a working group of law enforcement and correctional representatives from throughout the state to discuss specific cases and investigations involving gangs and other related gang activities.

(d) The task force may take any other actions as necessary to accomplish the purposes of this article.

(e) The Department of Public Safety shall support the task force to assist in coordinating statewide anti-gang initiatives.

(f) The task force shall consist of:

(1) a representative of the Department of Public Safety designated by the director of that agency;

(2) a representative of the Texas Department of Criminal Justice designated by the executive director of that agency;

(3) a representative of the Texas Youth Commission designated by the executive director of that agency;

(4) a representative of the Texas Juvenile Probation Commission designated by the executive director of that agency;

(5) a representative of the Criminal Justice Policy Council designated by the executive director of that agency;

(6) a representative of the office of the attorney general designated by the attorney general; and

(7) three local law enforcement or adult or juvenile community supervision personnel and a prosecuting attorney designated by the governor.

History of CCP art. 61.10: Acts 1999, 76th Leg., ch. 492, §1, eff. June 18, 1999. Renumbered from art. 61.07 by Acts 2001, 77th Leg., ch. 1420, §21.001(14), eff. Sept. 1, 2001.

ART. 61.11. GANG RESOURCE SYSTEM

(a) The office of the attorney general shall establish an electronic gang resource system to provide criminal justice agencies and juvenile justice agencies with information about criminal street gangs in the state. The system may include the following information with regard to any gang:

(1) gang name;

(2) gang identifiers, such as colors used, tattoos, and clothing preferences;

(3) criminal activities;

(4) migration trends;

(5) recruitment activities; and

(6) a local law enforcement contact.

(b) Upon request by the office of the attorney general, criminal justice agencies and juvenile justice agencies shall make a reasonable attempt to provide gang information to the office of the attorney general for the purpose of maintaining an updated, comprehensive gang resource system.

(c) The office of the attorney general shall cooperate with criminal justice agencies and juvenile justice agencies in collecting and maintaining the accuracy of the information included in the gang resource system.

(d) Information relating to the identity of a specific offender or alleged offender may not be maintained in the gang resource system.

(e) Information in the gang resource system may be used in investigating gang-related crimes but may be included in affidavits or subpoenas or used in connection with any other legal or judicial proceeding only if the information from the system is corroborated by information not provided or maintained in the system.

(f) Access to the gang resource system shall be limited to criminal justice agency personnel and juvenile justice agency personnel.

(g) Information in the gang resource system shall be accessible by:

(1) municipality or county; and

(2) gang name.

(h) The office of the attorney general may coordinate with the Texas Department of Criminal Justice to include information in the gang resource system regarding groups which have been identified by the Security Threat Group Management Office of the Texas Department of Criminal Justice.

History of CCP art. 61.11: Acts 1999, 76th Leg., ch. 491, §1, eff. Aug. 30, 1999. Renumbered from art. 61.08 by Acts 2001, 77th Leg., ch. 1420, §21.001(15), eff. Sept. 1, 2001.

CHAPTER 62. SEX OFFENDER REGISTRATION PROGRAM

SUBCHAPTER A. GENERAL PROVISIONS

ART. 62.001. DEFINITIONS

In this chapter:

(1) "Department" means the Department of Public Safety.

(2) "Local law enforcement authority" means the chief of police of a municipality or the sheriff of a county in this state.

(3) "Penal institution" means a confinement facility operated by or under a contract with any division of the Texas Department of Criminal Justice, a confinement facility operated by or under contract with the Texas Youth Commission, or a juvenile secure preadjudication or post-adjudication facility operated by or under a local juvenile probation department, or a county jail.

(4) "Released" means discharged, paroled, placed in a nonsecure community program for juvenile offenders, or placed on juvenile probation, community supervision, or mandatory supervision.

A (5) "Reportable conviction or adjudication" means a conviction or adjudication, including an adjudication of delinquent conduct or a deferred adjudication, that, regardless of the pendency of an appeal, is a conviction for or an adjudication for or based on:

A *Subsection (A) below is effective for offenses committed on or after Sept. 1, 2007.*

(A) a violation of Section 21.02 (Continuous sexual abuse of young child or children), 21.11 (Indecency with a child), 22.011 (Sexual assault), 22.021 (Aggravated sexual assault), or 25.02 (Prohibited sexual conduct), Penal Code;

Subsection (A) below is effective for offenses in which any element of the offense was committed before Sept. 1, 2007.

(A) a violation of Section 21.11 (Indecency with a child), 22.011 (Sexual assault), 22.021 (Aggravated sexual assault), or 25.02 (Prohibited sexual conduct), Penal Code;

(B) a violation of Section 43.05 (Compelling prostitution), 43.25 (Sexual performance by a child), or 43.26 (Possession or promotion of child pornography), Penal Code;

(C) a violation of Section 20.04(a)(4) (Aggravated kidnapping), Penal Code, if the actor committed the offense or engaged in the conduct with intent to violate or abuse the victim sexually;

(D) a violation of Section 30.02 (Burglary), Penal Code, if the offense or conduct is punishable under Subsection (d) of that section and the actor committed the offense or engaged in the conduct with intent to commit a felony listed in Paragraph (A) or (C);

(E) a violation of Section 20.02 (Unlawful restraint), 20.03 (Kidnapping), or 20.04 (Aggravated kidnapping), Penal Code, if, as applicable:

(i) the judgment in the case contains an affirmative finding under Article 42.015; or

(ii) the order in the hearing or the papers in the case contain an affirmative finding that the victim or intended victim was younger than 17 years of age;

(F) the second violation of Section 21.08 (Indecent exposure), Penal Code, but not if the second violation results in a deferred adjudication;

(G) an attempt, conspiracy, or solicitation, as defined by Chapter 15, Penal Code, to commit an offense or engage in conduct listed in Paragraph (A), (B), (C), (D), or (E);

A *Subsection (H) below is effective for offenses committed on or after Sept. 1, 2007.*

(H) a violation of the laws of another state, federal law, the laws of a foreign country, or the Uniform Code of Military Justice for or based on the violation of an offense containing elements that are substantially similar to the elements of an offense listed under Paragraph (A), (B), (C), (D), (E), (G), or (J), but not if the violation results in a deferred adjudication;

Subsection (H) below is effective for offenses in which any element of the offense was committed before Sept. 1, 2007.

(H) a violation of the laws of another state, federal law, the laws of a foreign country, or the Uniform Code of Military Justice for or based on the violation of an offense containing elements that are substantially similar to the elements of an offense listed under Paragraph (A), (B), (C), (D), (E), (G), or (N), but not if the violation results in deferred adjudication; or

(I) the second violation of the laws of another state, federal law, the laws of a foreign country, or the Uniform Code of Military Justice for or based on the violation of an offense containing elements that are substantially similar to the elements of the offense of indecent exposure, but not if the second violation results in a deferred adjudication; or

E *Subsection (J) below is effective for offenses committed on or after Sept. 1, 2007.*

(J) a violation of Section 33.021 (Online solicitation of a minor), Penal Code.

(6) "Sexually violent offense" means any of the following offenses committed by a person 17 years of age or older:

A *Subsection (A) below is effective for offenses committed on or after Sept. 1, 2007.*

(A) an offense under Section 21.02 (Continuous sexual abuse of young child or children), 21.11(a)(1) (Indecency with a child), 22.011 (Sexual assault), or 22.021 (Aggravated sexual assault), Penal Code;

Subsection (A) below is effective for offenses in which any element of the offense was committed before Sept. 1, 2007.

(A) an offense under Section 21.11(a)(1) (Indecency with a child), 22.011 (Sexual assault), or 22.021 (Aggravated sexual assault), Penal Code;

(B) an offense under Section 43.25 (Sexual performance by a child), Penal Code;

(C) an offense under Section 20.04(a)(4) (Aggravated kidnapping), Penal Code, if the defendant committed the offense with intent to violate or abuse the victim sexually;

(D) an offense under Section 30.02 (Burglary), Penal Code, if the offense is punishable under Subsection (d) of that section and the defendant committed the offense with intent to commit a felony listed in Paragraph (A) or (C) of Subdivision (5); or

(E) an offense under the laws of another state, federal law, the laws of a foreign country, or the Uniform Code of Military Justice if the offense contains elements that are substantially similar to the elements of an offense listed under Paragraph (A), (B), (C), or (D).

(7) "Residence" includes a residence established in this state by a person described by Article 62.152(e).

(8) "Public or private institution of higher education" includes a college, university, community college, or technical or trade institute.

(9) "Authority for campus security" means the authority with primary law enforcement jurisdiction over property under the control of a public or private institution of higher education, other than a local law enforcement authority.

(10) "Extrajurisdictional registrant" means a person who:

(A) is required to register as a sex offender under:

(i) the laws of another state with which the department has entered into a reciprocal registration agreement;

(ii) federal law or the Uniform Code of Military Justice; or

(iii) the laws of a foreign country; and

(B) is not otherwise required to register under this chapter because:

(i) the person does not have a reportable conviction for an offense under the laws of the other state, federal law, the laws of the foreign country, or the Uniform Code of Military Justice containing elements that are substantially similar to the elements of an offense requiring registration under this chapter; or

(ii) the person does not have a reportable adjudication of delinquent conduct based on a violation of an offense under the laws of the other state, federal law, or the laws of the foreign country containing elements that are substantially similar to the elements of an offense requiring registration under this chapter.

History of CCP art. 62.001: Acts 1997, 75th Leg., ch. 668, §1, eff. Sept. 1, 1997. Amended by Acts 1999, 76th Leg., ch. 1193, §4 (eff. Sept. 1, 1999), ch. 1415, §§7, 8 (eff. Sept. 1, 1999); Acts 2003, 78th Leg., ch. 1005, §8, eff. Sept. 1, 2003; Acts 2003, 78th Leg., ch. 347, §1 (eff. Sept. 1, 2003), ch. 1275, §3(4) (eff. Sept. 1, 2003). Renumbered from art. 62.01 and amended by Acts 2005, 79th Leg., ch. 1008, §1.01 (eff. Sept. 1, 2005), ch. 1273, §2 (eff. June 18, 2005). Amended by Acts 2007, 80th Leg., ch. 593, §§3.22, 3.23 (eff. Sept. 1, 2007), ch. 921, §3.002 (eff. Sept. 1, 2007). Source: TRCS art. 6252-13c.1, §1.

See also *O'Connor's Crimes & Consequences* (2008-09), chart 10-A, "Offenses Requiring Registration."

ANNOTATIONS

Fuller v. State, 194 S.W.3d 52, 53-54 (Tex.App.—Fort Worth 2006, pet. ref'd). "Nothing in [art. 62.001(5)(F)] requires that when two or more convictions occur on the same day, as did the convictions at issue, they must occur in sequential order for one of the convictions to qualify as the second conviction. The fact that the legislature chose not to include language in [art. 62.001(5)(F)] that would require convictions to occur in a specified order demonstrates a clear legislative intent not to require the State to prove that the convictions occurred in sequential order or that they arose from separate transactions."

Lutz v. State, 184 S.W.3d 366, 369 (Tex.App.—Austin 2006, no pet.). "[A]rticle 62.001(5) and (6) should be read to include the statutory predecessors of the enumerated offenses."

Turner v. State, 101 S.W.3d 750, 758 (Tex.App.—Houston [1st Dist.] 2003, pet. ref'd). "To the extent that a person was convicted under the sodomy statute for conduct that is now decriminalized or that constitutes conduct currently criminalized under Penal Code §21.06, sodomy *may* not be a 'sexually violent offense' as defined in subarticle 62.01(6) [now art. 62.001(6)]."

ART. 62.002. APPLICABILITY OF CHAPTER

(a) This chapter applies only to a reportable conviction or adjudication occurring on or after September 1, 1970.

(b) Except as provided by Subsection (c), the duties imposed on a person required to register under this chapter on the basis of a reportable conviction or adjudication, and the corresponding duties and powers of other entities in relation to the person required to register on the basis of that conviction or adjudication, are not affected by:

(1) an appeal of the conviction or adjudication; or

(2) a pardon of the conviction or adjudication.

(c) If a conviction or adjudication that is the basis of a duty to register under this chapter is set aside on appeal by a court or if the person required to register under this chapter on the basis of a conviction or adjudication receives a pardon on the basis of subsequent proof of innocence, the duties imposed on the person by this chapter and the corresponding duties and powers of other entities in relation to the person are terminated.

History of CCP art. 62.002: Acts 2005, 79th Leg., ch. 1008, §1.01, eff. Sept. 1, 2005.

See also *O'Connor's Crimes & Consequences* (2008-09), chart 10-A, "Offenses Requiring Registration."

ART. 62.003. DETERMINATION REGARDING SUBSTANTIALLY SIMILAR ELEMENTS OF OFFENSE

(a) For the purposes of this chapter, the department is responsible for determining whether an offense under the laws of another state, federal law, the laws of a foreign country, or the Uniform Code of Military Justice contains elements that are substantially similar to the elements of an offense under the laws of this state.

(b) The department annually shall provide or make available to each prosecuting attorney's office in this state:

(1) the criteria used in making a determination under Subsection (a); and

(2) any existing record or compilation of offenses under the laws of another state, federal law, the laws of a foreign country, and the Uniform Code of Military Justice that the department has already determined to contain elements that are substantially similar to the elements of offenses under the laws of this state.

(c) An appeal of a determination made under this article shall be brought in a district court in Travis County.

History of CCP art. 62.003: Acts 2001, 77th Leg., ch. 211, §2, eff. Sept. 1, 2001. Amended by Acts 2003, 78th Leg., ch. 1005, §9, eff. Sept. 1, 2003. Renumbered from art. 62.0101 and amended by Acts 2005, 79th Leg., ch. 1008, §1.01, eff. Sept. 1, 2005.

ART. 62.004. DETERMINATION REGARDING PRIMARY REGISTRATION AUTHORITY

(a) For each person subject to registration under this chapter, the department shall determine which local law enforcement authority serves as the person's primary registration authority based on the municipality or county in which the person resides or, as provided by Article 62.152, the municipality or county in which the person works or attends school.

(b) The department shall notify each person subject to registration under this chapter of the person's primary registration authority in a timely manner.

History of CCP art. 62.004: Acts 2003, 78th Leg., ch. 347, §2, eff. Sept. 1, 2003. Renumbered from art. 62.0102 and amended by Acts 2005, 79th Leg., ch. 1008, §1.01, eff. Sept. 1, 2005.

ART. 62.005. CENTRAL DATABASE; PUBLIC INFORMATION

(a) The department shall maintain a computerized central database containing the information required for registration under this chapter. The department may include in the computerized central database the numeric risk level assigned to a person under this chapter.

(b) The information contained in the database, including the numeric risk level assigned to a person under this chapter, is public information, with the exception of any information:

(1) regarding the person's social security number, driver's license number, or telephone number;

(2) that is required by the department under Article 62.051(c)(7); or

(3) that would identify the victim of the offense for which the person is subject to registration.

(c) Notwithstanding Chapter 730, Transportation Code, the department shall maintain in the database, and shall post on any department website related to the database, any photograph of the person that is available through the process for obtaining or renewing a personal identification certificate or driver's license under Section 521.103 or 521.272, Transportation Code. The department shall update the photograph in the database and on the website annually or as the photograph otherwise becomes available through the renewal process for the certificate or license.

(d) A local law enforcement authority shall release public information described under Subsection (b) to any person who requests the information from the authority. The authority may charge the person a fee not to exceed the amount reasonably necessary to cover the administrative costs associated with the authority's release of information to the person under this subsection.

(e) The department shall provide a licensing authority with notice of any person required to register under this chapter who holds or seeks a license that is issued by the authority. The department shall provide the notice required by this subsection as the applicable licensing information becomes available through the person's registration or verification of registration.

(f) On the written request of a licensing authority that identifies an individual and states that the individual is an applicant for or a holder of a license issued by the authority, the department shall release any information described by Subsection (a) to the licensing authority.

(g) For the purposes of Subsections (e) and (f):

(1) "License" means a license, certificate, registration, permit, or other authorization that:

(A) is issued by a licensing authority; and

(B) a person must obtain to practice or engage in a particular business, occupation, or profession.

(2) "Licensing authority" means a department, commission, board, office, or other agency of the state or a political subdivision of the state that issues a license.

(h) Not later than the third day after the date on which the applicable information becomes available through the person's registration or verification of registration or under Article 62.058, the department shall send notice of any person required to register under this chapter who is or will be employed, carrying on a vocation, or a student at a public or private institution of higher education in this state to:

(1) for an institution in this state:

(A) the authority for campus security for that institution; or

(B) if an authority for campus security for that institution does not exist, the local law enforcement authority of:

(i) the municipality in which the institution is located; or

(ii) the county in which the institution is located, if the institution is not located in a municipality; or

(2) for an institution in another state, any existing authority for campus security at that institution.

(i) On the written request of an institution of higher education described by Subsection (h) that identifies an individual and states that the individual has applied to work or study at the institution, the department shall release any information described by Subsection (a) to the institution.

History of CCP art. 62.005: Acts 2005, 79th Leg., ch. 1008, §1.01, eff. Sept. 1, 2005.

ART. 62.006. INFORMATION PROVIDED TO PEACE OFFICER ON REQUEST

The department shall establish a procedure by which a peace officer or employee of a law enforcement agency who provides the department with a driver's license number, personal identification certificate number, or license plate number is automatically provided information as to whether the person to whom the driver's license or personal identification certificate is issued is required to register under this chapter or whether the license plate number is entered in the computerized central database under Article 62.005 as assigned to a vehicle owned or driven by a person required to register under this chapter.

History of CCP art. 62.006: Acts 2005, 79th Leg., ch. 1008, §1.01, eff. Sept. 1, 2005.

ART. 62.007. RISK ASSESSMENT REVIEW COMMITTEE; SEX OFFENDER SCREENING TOOL

(a) The Texas Department of Criminal Justice shall establish a risk assessment review committee composed of at least seven members, each of whom serves on the review committee in addition to the member's other employment-related duties. The review committee, to the extent feasible, must include at least:

(1) one member having experience in law enforcement;

(2) one member having experience working with juvenile sex offenders;

(3) one member having experience as a sex offender treatment provider;

(4) one member having experience working with victims of sex offenses;

(5) the executive director of the Council on Sex Offender Treatment; and

(6) one sex offender treatment provider registered under Chapter 110, Occupations Code, and selected by the executive director of the Council on Sex Offender Treatment to serve on the review committee.

(b) The risk assessment review committee functions in an oversight capacity. The committee shall:

(1) develop or select, from among existing tools or from any tool recommended by the Council on Sex Offender Treatment, a sex offender screening tool to be used in determining the level of risk of a person subject to registration under this chapter;

(2) ensure that staff is trained on the use of the screening tool;

(3) monitor the use of the screening tool in the state; and

(4) analyze other screening tools as they become available and revise or replace the existing screening tool if warranted.

(c) The sex offender screening tool must use an objective point system under which a person is assigned a designated number of points for each of various factors. In developing or selecting the sex offender screening tool, the risk assessment review committee shall use or shall select a screening tool that may be adapted to use the following general guidelines:

(1) level one (low): a designated range of points on the sex offender screening tool indicating that the person poses a low danger to the community and will not likely engage in criminal sexual conduct;

(2) level two (moderate): a designated range of points on the sex offender screening tool indicating that the person poses a moderate danger to the community and might continue to engage in criminal sexual conduct; and

(3) level three (high): a designated range of points on the sex offender screening tool indicating that the person poses a serious danger to the community and will continue to engage in criminal sexual conduct.

(d) The risk assessment review committee, the Texas Department of Criminal Justice, the Texas Youth Commission, or a court may override a risk level only if the entity:

(1) believes that the risk level assessed is not an accurate prediction of the risk the offender poses to the community; and

(2) documents the reason for the override in the offender's case file.

(e) Notwithstanding Chapter 58, Family Code, records and files, including records that have been sealed under Section 58.003 of that code, relating to a person for whom a court, the Texas Department of Criminal Justice, or the Texas Youth Commission is required under this article to determine a level of risk shall be released to the court, department, or commission, as appropriate, for the purpose of determining the person's risk level.

(f) Chapter 551, Government Code, does not apply to a meeting of the risk assessment review committee.

(g) The numeric risk level assigned to a person using the sex offender screening tool described by this article is not confidential and is subject to disclosure under Chapter 552, Government Code.

History of CCP art. 62.007: Acts 2005, 79th Leg., ch. 1008, §1.01, eff. Sept. 1, 2005.

ART. 62.008. GENERAL IMMUNITY

The following persons are immune from liability for good faith conduct under this chapter:

(1) an employee or officer of the Texas Department of Criminal Justice, the Texas Youth Commission, the Texas Juvenile Probation Commission, the Department of Public Safety, the Board of Pardons and Paroles, or a local law enforcement authority;

(2) an employee or officer of a community supervision and corrections department or a juvenile probation department;

(3) a member of the judiciary; and

(4) a member of the risk assessment review committee established under Article 62.007.

History of CCP art. 62.008: Acts 2005, 79th Leg., ch. 1008, §1.01, eff. Sept. 1, 2005.

ART. 62.009. IMMUNITY FOR RELEASE OF PUBLIC INFORMATION

(a) The department, a penal institution, a local law enforcement authority, or an authority for campus security may release to the public information regarding a person required to register under this chapter only if the information is public information under this chapter.

(b) An individual, agency, entity, or authority is not liable under Chapter 101, Civil Practice and Remedies Code, or any other law for damages arising from conduct authorized by Subsection (a).

(c) For purposes of determining liability, the release or withholding of information by an appointed or elected officer of an agency, entity, or authority is a discretionary act.

(d) A private primary or secondary school, public or private institution of higher education, or administrator of a private primary or secondary school or public or private institution of higher education may release to the public information regarding a person required to register under this chapter only if the information is public information under this chapter and is released to the administrator under Article 62.005, 62.053, 62.054,

62.055, or 62.153. A private primary or secondary school, public or private institution of higher education, or administrator of a private primary or secondary school or public or private institution of higher education is not liable under any law for damages arising from conduct authorized by this subsection.

History of CCP art. 62.009: Acts 2005, 79th Leg., ch. 1008, §1.01, eff. Sept. 1, 2005.

ART. 62.010. RULEMAKING AUTHORITY

The Texas Department of Criminal Justice, the Texas Youth Commission, the Texas Juvenile Probation Commission, and the department may adopt any rule necessary to implement this chapter.

History of CCP art. 62.010: Acts 2005, 79th Leg., ch. 1008, §1.01, eff. Sept. 1, 2005.

ART. 62.01. RENUMBERED

Renumbered as art. 62.001 by Acts 2005, 79th Leg., ch. 1008, §1.01, eff. Sept. 1, 2005.

ARTS. 62.0101, 62.0102. RENUMBERED

Renumbered as arts. 62.003, 62.004 by Acts 2005, 79th Leg., ch. 1008, §1.01, eff. Sept. 1, 2005.

ARTS. 62.0105, 62.011. DELETED

Deleted by Acts 2005, 79th Leg., ch. 1008, §1.01, eff. Sept. 1, 2005.

ARTS. 62.02, 62.021, 62.03. RENUMBERED

Renumbered as arts. 62.051, 62.052, 62.053 by Acts 2005, 79th Leg., ch. 1008, §1.01, eff. Sept. 1, 2005.

ART. 62.031. DELETED

Deleted by Acts 2005, 79th Leg., ch. 1008, §1.01, eff. Sept. 1, 2005.

ART. 62.032. RENUMBERED

Renumbered as art. 62.054 by Acts 2005, 79th Leg., ch. 1008, §1.01, eff. Sept. 1, 2005.

ART. 62.035. DELETED

Deleted by Acts 2005, 79th Leg., ch. 1008, §1.01, eff. Sept. 1, 2005.

ART. 62.04. RENUMBERED

Renumbered as art. 62.055 by Acts 2005, 79th Leg., ch. 1008, §1.01, eff. Sept. 1, 2005.

ART. 62.041. DELETED

Deleted by Acts 2005, 79th Leg., ch. 1008, §1.01, eff. Sept. 1, 2005.

ART. 62.045. RENUMBERED

Renumbered as art. 62.056 by Acts 2005, 79th Leg., ch. 1008, §1.01, eff. Sept. 1, 2005.

ART. 62.0451. DELETED

Deleted by Acts 2005, 79th Leg., ch. 1008, §1.01, eff. Sept. 1, 2005.

ART. 62.05. RENUMBERED

Renumbered as art. 62.057 by Acts 2005, 79th Leg., ch. 1008, §1.01, eff. Sept. 1, 2005.

SUBCHAPTER B. REGISTRATION & VERIFICATION REQUIREMENTS; RELATED NOTICE

ART. 62.051. REGISTRATION: GENERAL

(a) A person who has a reportable conviction or adjudication or who is required to register as a condition of parole, release to mandatory supervision, or community supervision shall register or, if the person is a person for whom registration is completed under this chapter, verify registration as provided by Subsection (f), with the local law enforcement authority in any municipality where the person resides or intends to reside for more than seven days. If the person does not reside or intend to reside in a municipality, the person shall register or verify registration in any county where the person resides or intends to reside for more than seven days. The person shall satisfy the requirements of this subsection not later than the later of:

(1) the seventh day after the person's arrival in the municipality or county; or

(2) the first date the local law enforcement authority of the municipality or county by policy allows the person to register or verify registration, as applicable.

(b) The department shall provide the Texas Department of Criminal Justice, the Texas Youth Commission, the Texas Juvenile Probation Commission, and each local law enforcement authority, authority for campus security, county jail, and court with a form for registering persons required by this chapter to register.

(c) The registration form shall require:

(1) the person's full name, each alias, date of birth, sex, race, height, weight, eye color, hair color, social security number, driver's license number, shoe size, and home address;

(2) a recent color photograph or, if possible, an electronic digital image of the person and a complete set of the person's fingerprints;

(3) the type of offense the person was convicted of, the age of the victim, the date of conviction, and the punishment received;

(4) an indication as to whether the person is discharged, paroled, or released on juvenile probation, community supervision, or mandatory supervision;

(5) an indication of each license, as defined by Article 62.005(g), that is held or sought by the person;

(6) an indication as to whether the person is or will be employed, carrying on a vocation, or a student at a particular public or private institution of higher education in this state or another state, and the name and address of that institution; and

(7) any other information required by the department.

(d) The registration form must contain a statement and description of any registration duties the person has or may have under this chapter.

(e) Not later than the third day after a person's registering, the local law enforcement authority with whom the person registered shall send a copy of the registration form to the department and, if the person resides on the campus of a public or private institution of higher education, to any authority for campus security for that institution.

(f) A person for whom registration is completed under this chapter shall report to the applicable local law enforcement authority to verify the information in the registration form received by the authority under this chapter. The authority shall require the person to produce proof of the person's identity and residence before the authority gives the registration form to the person for verification. If the information in the registration form is complete and accurate, the person shall verify registration by signing the form. If the information is not complete or not accurate, the person shall make any necessary additions or corrections before signing the form.

(g) A person who is required to register or verify registration under this chapter shall ensure that the person's registration form is complete and accurate with respect to each item of information required by the form in accordance with Subsection (c).

(h) If a person subject to registration under this chapter does not move to an intended residence by the end of the seventh day after the date on which the person is released or the date on which the person leaves a previous residence, the person shall:

(1) report to the juvenile probation officer, community supervision and corrections department officer, or parole officer supervising the person by not later than the seventh day after the date on which the person is released or the date on which the person leaves a previous residence, as applicable, and provide the officer with the address of the person's temporary residence; and

(2) continue to report to the person's supervising officer not less than weekly during any period of time in which the person has not moved to an intended residence and provide the officer with the address of the person's temporary residence.

(i) If the other state has a registration requirement for sex offenders, a person who has a reportable conviction or adjudication, who resides in this state, and who is employed, carries on a vocation, or is a student in another state shall, not later than the 10th day after the date on which the person begins to work or attend school in the other state, register with the law enforcement authority that is identified by the department as the authority designated by that state to receive registration information. If the person is employed, carries on a vocation, or is a student at a public or private institution of higher education in the other state and if an authority for campus security exists at the institution, the person shall also register with that authority not later than the 10th day after the date on which the person begins to work or attend school.

History of CCP art. 62.051: Acts 1997, 75th Leg., ch. 668, §1, eff. Sept. 1, 1997. Amended by Acts 1999, 76th Leg., ch. 444, §1 (eff. Sept. 1, 1999), ch. 1193, §5 (eff. Sept. 1, 1999), ch. 1415, §10 (eff. Sept. 1, 1999); Acts 2001, 77th Leg., ch. 353, §1, eff. Sept. 1, 2001; Acts 2003, 78th Leg., ch. 347, §4 (eff. Sept. 1, 2003), ch. 1276, §5.003(b) (eff. Sept. 1, 2003). Renumbered from art. 62.02 and amended by Acts 2005, 79th Leg., ch. 1008, §1.01, eff. Sept. 1, 2005. Source: TRCS art. 6252-13c.1, §2.

ANNOTATIONS

Ex parte Burr, 185 S.W.3d 451, 452 (Tex.Crim.App. 2006). "The appellant has petitioned this court for discretionary review of an appeal of a motion under the Sex Offender Registration Program. His petition requires us to decide whether we have jurisdiction to review a decision of a court of appeals on such a motion. We hold that we do."

Ex parte Robinson, 116 S.W.3d 794, 796 (Tex.Crim. App.2003). Held: A convicted sex offender does not have a procedural due-process right to a hearing to establish nondangerousness because all sex offenders, regardless of dangerousness, must register. *See also Connecticut DPS v. Doe*, 538 U.S. 1, 7, 123 S.Ct. 1160, 1164 (2003).

ART. 62.052. REGISTRATION: EXTRAJURISDICTIONAL REGISTRANTS

(a) An extrajurisdictional registrant is required to comply with the annual verification requirements of Article 62.058 in the same manner as a person who is required to verify registration on the basis of a reportable conviction or adjudication.

(b) The duty to register for an extrajurisdictional registrant expires on the date the person's duty to register would expire under the laws of the other state or foreign country had the person remained in that state or foreign country, under federal law, or under the Uniform Code of Military Justice, as applicable.

(c) The department may negotiate and enter into a reciprocal registration agreement with any other state to prevent residents of this state and residents of the other state from frustrating the public purpose of the registration of sex offenders by moving from one state to the other.

History of CCP art. 62.052: Acts 1999, 76th Leg., ch. 444, §2 (eff. Sept. 1, 1999), ch. 1415, §11 (eff. Sept. 1, 1999). Amended by Acts 2001, 77th Leg., ch. 211, §3, eff. Sept. 1, 2001; Acts 2003, 78th Leg., ch. 1005, §10, eff. Sept. 1, 2003. Renumbered from art. 62.021 and amended by Acts 2005, 79th Leg., ch. 1008, §1.01, eff. Sept. 1, 2005.

ART. 62.053. PRERELEASE NOTIFICATION

(a) Before a person who will be subject to registration under this chapter is due to be released from a penal institution, the Texas Department of Criminal Justice or the Texas Youth Commission shall determine the person's level of risk to the community using the sex offender screening tool developed or selected under Article 62.007 and assign to the person a numeric risk level of one, two, or three. Before releasing the person, an official of the penal institution shall:

(1) inform the person that:

(A) not later than the later of the seventh day after the date on which the person is released or after the date on which the person moves from a previous residence to a new residence in this state or not later than the later of the first date the applicable local law enforcement authority by policy allows the person to register or verify registration, the person must register or verify registration with the local law enforcement authority in the municipality or county in which the person intends to reside;

(B) not later than the seventh day after the date on which the person is released or the date on which the person moves from a previous residence to a new residence in this state, the person must, if the person has not moved to an intended residence, report to the juvenile probation officer, community supervision and corrections department officer, or parole officer supervising the person;

(C) not later than the seventh day before the date on which the person moves to a new residence in this state or another state, the person must report in person to the local law enforcement authority designated as the person's primary registration authority by the department and to the juvenile probation officer, community supervision and corrections department officer, or parole officer supervising the person;

(D) not later than the 10th day after the date on which the person arrives in another state in which the person intends to reside, the person must register with the law enforcement agency that is identified by the department as the agency designated by that state to receive registration information, if the other state has a registration requirement for sex offenders;

(E) not later than the 30th day after the date on which the person is released, the person must apply to the department in person for the issuance of an original or renewal driver's license or personal identification certificate and a failure to apply to the department as required by this paragraph results in the automatic revocation of any driver's license or personal identification certificate issued by the department to the person; and

(F) the person must notify appropriate entities of any change in status as described by Article 62.057;

(2) require the person to sign a written statement that the person was informed of the person's duties as described by Subdivision (1) or Subsection (g) or, if the person refuses to sign the statement, certify that the person was so informed;

(3) obtain the address where the person expects to reside on the person's release and other registration information, including a photograph and complete set of fingerprints; and

(4) complete the registration form for the person.

(b) On the seventh day before the date on which a person who will be subject to registration under this chapter is due to be released from a penal institution, or on receipt of notice by a penal institution that a person who will be subject to registration under this chapter is due to be released in less than seven days, an official of the penal institution shall send the person's completed registration form and numeric risk level to the department and to:

(1) the applicable local law enforcement authority in the municipality or county in which the person expects to reside, if the person expects to reside in this state; or

(2) the law enforcement agency that is identified by the department as the agency designated by another state to receive registration information, if the person expects to reside in that other state and that other state has a registration requirement for sex offenders.

(c) If a person who is subject to registration under this chapter receives an order deferring adjudication, placing the person on community supervision or juvenile probation, or imposing only a fine, the court pronouncing the order or sentence shall make a determination of the person's numeric risk level using the sex offender screening tool developed or selected under Article 62.007, assign to the person a numeric risk level of one, two, or three, and ensure that the prerelease notification and registration requirements specified in this article are conducted on the day of entering the order or sentencing. If a community supervision and corrections department representative is available in court at the time a court pronounces a sentence of deferred adjudication or community supervision, the representative shall immediately obtain the person's numeric risk level from the court and conduct the prerelease notification and registration requirements specified in this article. In any other case in which the court pronounces a sentence under this subsection, the court shall designate another appropriate individual to obtain the person's numeric risk level from the court and conduct the prerelease notification and registration requirements specified in this article.

(d) If a person who has a reportable conviction described by Article 62.001(5)(H) or (I) is placed under the supervision of the pardons and paroles division of the Texas Department of Criminal Justice or a community supervision and corrections department under Article 42.11, the division or community supervision and corrections department shall conduct the prerelease notification and registration requirements specified in this article on the date the person is placed under the supervision of the division or community supervision and corrections department. If a person who has a reportable adjudication of delinquent conduct described by Article 62.001(5)(H)1 or (I)1 is, as permitted by Section 60.002, Family Code, placed under the supervision of the Texas Youth Commission, a public or private vendor operating under contract with the Texas Youth Commission, a local juvenile probation department, or a juvenile secure pre-adjudication or post-adjudication facility, the commission, vendor, probation department, or facility shall conduct the prerelease notification and registration requirements specified in this article on the date the person is placed under the supervision of the commission, vendor, probation department, or facility.

(e) Not later than the eighth day after receiving a registration form under Subsection (b), (c), or (d), the local law enforcement authority shall verify the age of the victim, the basis on which the person is subject to registration under this chapter, and the person's numeric risk level. The local law enforcement authority shall immediately provide notice to the superintendent of the public school district and to the administrator of any private primary or secondary school located in the public school district in which the person subject to registration intends to reside by mail to the office of the superintendent or administrator, as appropriate, in accordance with Article 62.054. On receipt of a notice under this subsection, the superintendent shall release the information contained in the notice to appropriate school district personnel, including peace officers and security personnel, principals, nurses, and counselors.

(f) The local law enforcement authority shall include in the notice to the superintendent of the public school district and to the administrator of any private primary or secondary school located in the public school district any information the authority determines is necessary to protect the public, except:

(1) the person's social security number, driver's license number, or telephone number; and

(2) any information that would identify the victim of the offense for which the person is subject to registration.

(g) Before a person who will be subject to registration under this chapter is due to be released from a penal institution in this state, an official of the penal institution shall inform the person that:

(1) if the person intends to reside in another state and to work or attend school in this state, the person must, not later than the later of the seventh day after the date on which the person begins to work or attend school or the first date the applicable local law enforcement authority by policy allows the person to register or verify registration, register or verify registration with

the local law enforcement authority in the municipality or county in which the person intends to work or attend school;

(2) if the person intends to reside in this state and to work or attend school in another state and if the other state has a registration requirement for sex offenders, the person must:

(A) not later than the 10th day after the date on which the person begins to work or attend school in the other state, register with the law enforcement authority that is identified by the department as the authority designated by that state to receive registration information; and

(B) if the person intends to be employed, carry on a vocation, or be a student at a public or private institution of higher education in the other state and if an authority for campus security exists at the institution, register with that authority not later than the 10th day after the date on which the person begins to work or attend school; and

(3) regardless of the state in which the person intends to reside, if the person intends to be employed, carry on a vocation, or be a student at a public or private institution of higher education in this state, the person must:

(A) not later than the later of the seventh day after the date on which the person begins to work or attend school or the first date the applicable authority by policy allows the person to register, register with:

(i) the authority for campus security for that institution; or

(ii) except as provided by Article 62.153(e), if an authority for campus security for that institution does not exist, the local law enforcement authority of:

(a) the municipality in which the institution is located; or

(b) the county in which the institution is located, if the institution is not located in a municipality; and

(B) not later than the seventh day after the date the person stops working or attending school, notify the appropriate authority for campus security or local law enforcement authority of the termination of the person's status as a worker or student.

History of CCP art. 62.053: Acts 1997, 75th Leg., ch. 668, §1, eff. Sept. 1, 1997. Amended by Acts 1997, 75th Leg., ch. 667, §5; ch. 1430, §8, eff. Sept. 1, 1997; Acts 1999, 76th Leg., ch. 444, §3 (eff. Sept. 1, 1999), ch. 1193, §§6, 7 (eff. Sept. 1, 1999), ch. 1401, §2 (eff. Sept. 1, 2000), ch. 1557, §1 (eff. Aug. 30, 1999); Acts 2001, 77th Leg., ch. 177, §1 (eff. Sept. 1, 2001), ch. 211, §4 (eff. Sept. 1,

2001), ch. 1420, §3.003 (eff. Sept. 1, 2001); Acts 2003, 78th Leg., ch. 347, §5, eff. Sept. 1, 2003. Renumbered from art. 62.03 and amended by Acts 2005, 79th Leg., ch. 1008, §1.01, eff. Sept. 1, 2005. Source: TRCS art. 6252-13c.1, §3.

ART. 62.054. CIRCUMSTANCES REQUIRING NOTICE TO SUPERINTENDENT OR SCHOOL ADMINISTRATOR

(a) A local law enforcement authority shall provide notice to the superintendent and each administrator under Article 62.053(e) or 62.055(f) only if:

(1) the victim was at the time of the offense a child younger than 17 years of age or a student enrolled in a public or private secondary school;

(2) the person subject to registration is a student enrolled in a public or private secondary school; or

(3) the basis on which the person is subject to registration is a conviction, a deferred adjudication, or an adjudication of delinquent conduct for an offense under Section 43.25 or 43.26, Penal Code, or an offense under the laws of another state, federal law, or the Uniform Code of Military Justice that contains elements substantially similar to the elements of an offense under either of those sections.

(b) A local law enforcement authority may not provide notice to the superintendent or any administrator under Article 62.053(e) or 62.055(f) if the basis on which the person is subject to registration is a conviction, a deferred adjudication, or an adjudication of delinquent conduct for an offense under Section 25.02, Penal Code, or an offense under the laws of another state, federal law, or the Uniform Code of Military Justice that contains elements substantially similar to the elements of an offense under that section.

History of CCP art. 62.054: Acts 2003, 78th Leg., ch. 347, §6, eff. Sept. 1, 2003. Renumbered from art. 62.032 and amended by Acts 2005, 79th Leg., ch. 1008, §1.01, eff. Sept. 1, 2005.

ART. 62.055. CHANGE OF ADDRESS

(a) If a person required to register under this chapter intends to change address, regardless of whether the person intends to move to another state, the person shall, not later than the seventh day before the intended change, report in person to the local law enforcement authority designated as the person's primary registration authority by the department and to the juvenile probation officer, community supervision and corrections department officer, or parole officer supervising the person and provide the authority and the officer with the person's anticipated move date and

new address. If a person required to register changes address, the person shall, not later than the later of the seventh day after changing the address or the first date the applicable local law enforcement authority by policy allows the person to report, report in person to the local law enforcement authority in the municipality or county in which the person's new residence is located and provide the authority with proof of identity and proof of residence.

(b) Not later than the third day after receipt of notice under Subsection (a), the person's juvenile probation officer, community supervision and corrections department officer, or parole officer shall forward the information provided under Subsection (a) to the local law enforcement authority designated as the person's primary registration authority by the department and, if the person intends to move to another municipality or county in this state, to the applicable local law enforcement authority in that municipality or county.

(c) If the person moves to another state that has a registration requirement for sex offenders, the person shall, not later than the 10th day after the date on which the person arrives in the other state, register with the law enforcement agency that is identified by the department as the agency designated by that state to receive registration information.

(d) Not later than the third day after receipt of information under Subsection (a) or (b), whichever is earlier, the local law enforcement authority shall forward this information to the department and, if the person intends to move to another municipality or county in this state, to the applicable local law enforcement authority in that municipality or county.

(e) If a person who reports to a local law enforcement authority under Subsection (a) does not move on or before the anticipated move date or does not move to the new address provided to the authority, the person shall:

(1) not later than the seventh day after the anticipated move date, and not less than weekly after that seventh day, report to the local law enforcement authority designated as the person's primary registration authority by the department and provide an explanation to the authority regarding any changes in the anticipated move date and intended residence; and

(2) report to the juvenile probation officer, community supervision and corrections department officer, or parole officer supervising the person not less than

weekly during any period in which the person has not moved to an intended residence.

(f) If the person moves to another municipality or county in this state, the department shall inform the applicable local law enforcement authority in the new area of the person's residence not later than the third day after the date on which the department receives information under Subsection (a). Not later than the eighth day after the date on which the local law enforcement authority is informed under Subsection (a) or under this subsection, the authority shall verify the age of the victim, the basis on which the person is subject to registration under this chapter, and the person's numeric risk level. The local law enforcement authority shall immediately provide notice to the superintendent of the public school district and to the administrator of any private primary or secondary school located in the public school district in which the person subject to registration intends to reside by mail to the office of the superintendent or administrator, as appropriate, in accordance with Article 62.054. On receipt of a notice under this subsection, the superintendent shall release the information contained in the notice to appropriate school district personnel, including peace officers and security personnel, principals, nurses, and counselors.

(g) The local law enforcement authority shall include in the notice to the superintendent of the public school district and the administrator of any private primary or secondary school located in the public school district any information the authority determines is necessary to protect the public, except:

(1) the person's social security number, driver's license number, or telephone number; and

(2) any information that would identify the victim of the offense for which the person is subject to registration.

(h) If the person moves to another state, the department shall, immediately on receiving information under Subsection (d):

(1) inform the agency that is designated by the other state to receive registration information, if that state has a registration requirement for sex offenders; and

(2) send to the Federal Bureau of Investigation a copy of the person's registration form, including the record of conviction and a complete set of fingerprints.

History of CCP art. 62.055: Acts 1997, 75th Leg., ch. 668, §1, eff. Sept. 1, 1997. Amended by Acts 1997, 75th Leg., ch. 667, §6, ch. 1430, §9, eff. Sept. 1, 1997; Acts 1999, 76th Leg., ch. 762, §4 (eff. Sept. 1, 1999), ch. 1415, §13 (eff.

Sept. 1, 1999), ch. 1557, §3 (eff. Aug. 30, 1999); Acts 2001, 77th Leg., ch. 177, §3 (eff. Sept. 1, 2001), ch. 211, §5 (eff. Sept. 1, 2001), ch. 1420, §3.004 (eff. Sept. 1, 2001); Acts 2003, 78th Leg., ch. 347, §7, eff. Sept. 1, 2003. Renumbered from art. 62.04 and amended by Acts 2005, 79th Leg., ch. 1008, §1.01, eff. Sept. 1, 2005. Source: TRCS art. 6252-13c.1, §4.

ART. 62.056. ADDITIONAL PUBLIC NOTICE FOR CERTAIN OFFENDERS

(a) On receipt of notice under this chapter that a person subject to registration is due to be released from a penal institution, has been placed on community supervision or juvenile probation, or intends to move to a new residence in this state, the department shall verify the person's numeric risk level assigned under this chapter. If the person is assigned a numeric risk level of three, the department shall, not later than the seventh day after the date on which the person is released or the 10th day after the date on which the person moves, provide written notice mailed or delivered to at least each address, other than a post office box, within a one-mile radius, in an area that has not been subdivided, or a three-block area, in an area that has been subdivided, of the place where the person intends to reside. In providing written notice under this subsection, the department shall use employees of the department whose duties in providing the notice are in addition to the employees' regular duties.

(b) The department shall provide the notice in English and Spanish and shall include in the notice any information that is public information under this chapter. The department may not include any information that is not public information under this chapter.

(c) The department shall establish procedures for a person with respect to whom notice is provided under Subsection (a), other than a person subject to registration on the basis of an adjudication of delinquent conduct, to pay to the department all costs incurred by the department in providing the notice. The person shall pay those costs in accordance with the procedures established under this subsection.

(d) On receipt of notice under this chapter that a person subject to registration under this chapter is required to register or verify registration with a local law enforcement authority and has been assigned a numeric risk level of three, the local law enforcement authority may provide notice to the public in any manner determined appropriate by the local law enforcement authority, including publishing notice in a newspaper or other periodical or circular in circulation in the area where the person intends to reside, holding a neighborhood meeting, posting notices in the area where the person intends to reside, distributing printed notices to area residents, or establishing a specialized local website. The local law enforcement authority may include in the notice only information that is public information under this chapter.

(e) An owner, builder, seller, or lessor of a single-family residential real property or any improvement to residential real property or that person's broker, salesperson, or other agent or representative in a residential real estate transaction does not have a duty to make a disclosure to a prospective buyer or lessee about registrants under this chapter. To the extent of any conflict between this subsection and another law imposing a duty to disclose information about registered sex offenders, this subsection controls.

History of CCP art. 62.056: Acts 1999, 76th Leg., ch. 1557, §4, eff. Jan. 1, 2000. Amended by Acts 2001, 77th Leg., ch. 177, §4 (eff. Sept. 1, 2001), ch. 211, §§6, 7 (eff. Sept. 1, 2001). Renumbered from art. 62.045 and amended by Acts 2005, 79th Leg., ch. 1008, §1.01, eff. Sept. 1, 2005.

ART. 62.057. STATUS REPORT BY SUPERVISING OFFICER OR LOCAL LAW ENFORCEMENT AUTHORITY

(a) If the juvenile probation officer, community supervision and corrections department officer, or parole officer supervising a person subject to registration under this chapter receives information to the effect that the person's status has changed in any manner that affects proper supervision of the person, including a change in the person's name, physical health, job or educational status, including higher educational status, incarceration, or terms of release, the supervising officer shall promptly notify the appropriate local law enforcement authority or authorities of that change. If the person required to register intends to change address, the supervising officer shall notify the local law enforcement authorities designated by Article 62.055(b). Not later than the seventh day after the date the supervising officer receives the relevant information, the supervising officer shall notify the local law enforcement authority of any change in the person's job or educational status in which the person:

(1) becomes employed, begins to carry on a vocation, or becomes a student at a particular public or private institution of higher education; or

(2) terminates the person's status in that capacity.

(b) Not later than the seventh day after the date of the change, a person subject to registration under this chapter shall report to the local law enforcement authority designated as the person's primary registration authority by the department any change in the person's name, physical health, or job or educational status, including higher educational status.

(c) For purposes of Subsection (b):

(1) a person's job status changes if the person leaves employment for any reason, remains employed by an employer but changes the location at which the person works, or begins employment with a new employer;

(2) a person's health status changes if the person is hospitalized as a result of an illness;

(3) a change in a person's educational status includes the person's transfer from one educational facility to another; and

(4) regarding a change of name, notice of the proposed name provided to a local law enforcement authority as described by Sections 45.004 and 45.103, Family Code, is sufficient, except that the person shall promptly notify the authority of any denial of the person's petition for a change of name.

(d) Not later than the seventh day after the date the local law enforcement authority receives the relevant information, the local law enforcement authority shall notify the department of any change in the person's job or educational status in which the person:

(1) becomes employed, begins to carry on a vocation, or becomes a student at a particular public or private institution of higher education; or

(2) terminates the person's status in that capacity.

History of CCP art. 62.057: Acts 1997, 75th Leg., ch. 668, §1, eff. Sept. 1, 1997. Amended by Acts 1999, 76th Leg., ch. 762, §6 (eff. Sept. 1, 1999), ch. 1415, §14 (eff. Sept. 1, 1999); Acts 2001, 77th Leg., ch. 19, §1, eff. Sept. 1, 2001; Acts 2003, 78th Leg., ch. 347, §8 (eff. Sept. 1, 2003), ch. 1300, §4 (eff. Sept. 1, 2003). Renumbered from art. 62.05 and amended by Acts 2005, 79th Leg., ch. 1008, §1.01, eff. Sept. 1, 2005.

ART. 62.058. LAW ENFORCEMENT VERIFICATION OF REGISTRATION INFORMATION

(a) A person subject to registration under this chapter who has for a sexually violent offense been convicted two or more times, received an order of deferred adjudication two or more times, or been convicted and received an order of deferred adjudication shall report to the local law enforcement authority designated as the person's primary registration authority by the department not less than once in each 90-day period following the date the person first registered under this chapter to verify the information in the registration form maintained by the authority for that person. A person subject to registration under this chapter who is not subject to the 90-day reporting requirement described by this subsection shall report to the local law enforcement authority designated as the person's primary registration authority by the department once each year not earlier than the 30th day before and not later than the 30th day after the anniversary of the person's date of birth to verify the information in the registration form maintained by the authority for that person. For purposes of this subsection, a person complies with a requirement that the person register within a 90-day period following a date if the person registers at any time on or after the 83rd day following that date but before the 98th day after that date.

(b) A local law enforcement authority designated as a person's primary registration authority by the department may direct the person to report to the authority to verify the information in the registration form maintained by the authority for that person. The authority may direct the person to report under this subsection once in each 90-day period following the date the person first registered under this chapter, if the person is required to report not less than once in each 90-day period under Subsection (a) or once in each year not earlier than the 30th day before and not later than the 30th day after the anniversary of the person's date of birth, if the person is required to report once each year under Subsection (a). A local law enforcement authority may not direct a person to report to the authority under this subsection if the person is required to report under Subsection (a) and is in compliance with the reporting requirements of that subsection.

(c) A local law enforcement authority with whom a person reports under this article shall require the person to produce proof of the person's identity and residence before the authority gives the registration form to the person for verification. If the information in the registration form is complete and accurate, the person shall verify registration by signing the form. If the information is not complete or not accurate, the person shall make any necessary additions or corrections before signing the form.

(d) A local law enforcement authority designated as a person's primary registration authority by the department may at any time mail a nonforwardable verification form to the last reported address of the person.

Not later than the 21st day after receipt of a verification form under this subsection, the person shall:

(1) indicate on the form whether the person still resides at the last reported address and, if not, provide on the form the person's new address;

(2) complete any other information required by the form;

(3) sign the form; and

(4) return the form to the authority.

(e) For purposes of this article, a person receives multiple convictions or orders of deferred adjudication regardless of whether:

(1) the judgments or orders are entered on different dates; or

(2) the offenses for which the person was convicted or placed on deferred adjudication arose out of different criminal transactions.

History of CCP art. 62.058: Acts 1997, 75th Leg., ch. 668, §1, eff. Sept. 1, 1997. Amended by Acts 1999, 76th Leg., ch. 762, §7 (eff. Sept. 1, 1999), ch. 1415, §15 (eff. Sept. 1, 1999); Acts 2001, 77th Leg., ch. 211, §9, eff. Sept. 1, 2001; Acts 2003, 78th Leg., ch. 347, §9, eff. Sept. 1, 2003. Renumbered from art. 62.06 by Acts 2005, 79th Leg., ch. 1008, §1.01, eff. Sept. 1, 2005.

ART. 62.059. REGISTRATION OF PERSONS REGULARLY VISITING LOCATION

(a) A person subject to this chapter who on at least three occasions during any month spends more than 48 consecutive hours in a municipality or county in this state, other than the municipality or county in which the person is registered under this chapter, before the last day of that month shall report that fact to:

(1) the local law enforcement authority of the municipality in which the person is a visitor; or

(2) if the person is a visitor in a location that is not a municipality, the local law enforcement authority of the county in which the person is a visitor.

(b) A person described by Subsection (a) shall provide the local law enforcement authority with:

(1) all information the person is required to provide under Article 62.051(c);

(2) the address of any location in the municipality or county, as appropriate, at which the person was lodged during the month; and

(3) a statement as to whether the person intends to return to the municipality or county during the succeeding month.

(c) This article does not impose on a local law enforcement authority requirements of public notification or notification to schools relating to a person about whom the authority is not otherwise required by this chapter to make notifications.

History of CCP art. 62.059: Acts 1999, 76th Leg., ch. 762, §8 (eff. Sept. 1, 1999), ch. 1415, §16 (eff. Sept. 1, 1999). Renumbered from art. 62.062 and amended by Acts 2005, 79th Leg., ch. 1008, §1.01, eff. Sept. 1, 2005.

ART. 62.06. RENUMBERED

Renumbered as art. 62.058 by Acts 2005, 79th Leg., ch. 1008, §1.01, eff. Sept. 1, 2005.

ART. 62.060. REQUIREMENTS RELATING TO DRIVER'S LICENSE OR PERSONAL IDENTIFICATION CERTIFICATE

(a) A person subject to registration under this chapter shall apply to the department in person for the issuance of, as applicable, an original or renewal driver's license under Section 521.272, Transportation Code, an original or renewal personal identification certificate under Section 521.103, Transportation Code, or an original or renewal commercial driver's license or commercial driver learner's permit under Section 522.033, Transportation Code, not later than the 30th day after the date:

(1) the person is released from a penal institution or is released by a court on community supervision or juvenile probation; or

(2) the department sends written notice to the person of the requirements of this article.

(b) The person shall annually renew in person each driver's license or personal identification certificate issued by the department to the person, including each renewal, duplicate, or corrected license or certificate, until the person's duty to register under this chapter expires.

History of CCP art. 62.060: Acts 1999, 76th Leg., ch. 1401, §3, eff. Sept. 1, 2000. Amended by Acts 2001, 77th Leg., ch. 546, §1, eff. Sept. 1, 2001. Renumbered from art. 62.065 and amended by Acts 2005, 79th Leg., ch. 1008, §1.01, eff. Sept. 1, 2005.

ART. 62.061. DNA SPECIMEN

A person required to register under this chapter shall comply with a request for a DNA specimen made by a law enforcement agency under Section 411.1473, Government Code.

History of CCP art. 62.061: Acts 2005, 79th Leg., ch. 1008, §1.01, eff. Sept. 1, 2005.

History of Former CCP art. 62.061: Deleted by Acts 2005, 79th Leg., ch. 1008, §1.01, eff. Sept. 1, 2005.

ART. 62.062. LIMITATION ON NEWSPAPER PUBLICATION

(a) Except as provided by Subsection (b), a local law enforcement authority may not publish notice in a newspaper or other periodical or circular concerning a person's registration under this chapter if the only basis on which the person is subject to registration is one or more adjudications of delinquent conduct.

(b) This article does not apply to a publication of notice under Article 62.056.

History of CCP art. 62.062: Acts 2005, 79th Leg., ch. 1008, §1.01, eff. Sept. 1, 2005.

History of Former CCP art. 62.062: Renumbered as art. 62.059 by Acts 2005, 79th Leg., ch. 1008, §1.01, eff. Sept. 1, 2005.

ARTS. 62.063, 62.064. DELETED

Deleted by Acts 2005, 79th Leg., ch. 1008, §1.01, eff. Sept. 1, 2005.

ART. 62.065. RENUMBERED

Renumbered as art. 62.060 by Acts 2005, 79th Leg., ch. 1008, §1.01, eff. Sept. 1, 2005.

ARTS. 62.07, 62.08, 62.085, 62.09, 62.091. DELETED

Deleted by Acts 2005, 79th Leg., ch. 1008, §1.01, eff. Sept. 1, 2005.

ART. 62.10. RENUMBERED

Renumbered as art. 62.102 by Acts 2005, 79th Leg., ch. 1008, §1.01, eff. Sept. 1, 2005.

SUBCHAPTER C. EXPIRATION OF DUTY TO REGISTER; GENERAL PENALTIES FOR NONCOMPLIANCE

ART. 62.101. EXPIRATION OF DUTY TO REGISTER

(a) Except as provided by Subsection (b) and Subchapter I, the duty to register for a person ends when the person dies if the person has a reportable conviction or adjudication, other than an adjudication of delinquent conduct, for:

(1) a sexually violent offense;

(2) an offense under Section 25.02, 43.05(a)(2), or 43.26, Penal Code;

(3) an offense under Section 21.11(a)(2), Penal Code, if before or after the person is convicted or adjudicated for the offense under Section 21.11(a)(2), Penal Code, the person receives or has received another reportable conviction or adjudication, other than an adjudication of delinquent conduct, for an offense or conduct that requires registration under this chapter;

(4) an offense under Section 20.02, 20.03, or 20.04, Penal Code, if:

(A) the judgment in the case contains an affirmative finding under Article 42.015 or, for a deferred adjudication, the papers in the case contain an affirmative finding that the victim or intended victim was younger than 17 years of age; and

(B) before or after the person is convicted or adjudicated for the offense under Section 20.02, 20.03, or 20.04, Penal Code, the person receives or has received another reportable conviction or adjudication, other than an adjudication of delinquent conduct, for an offense or conduct that requires registration under this chapter; or

(5) an offense under Section 43.23, Penal Code, that is punishable under Subsection (h) of that section.

(b) Except as provided by Subchapter I, the duty to register for a person otherwise subject to Subsection (a) ends on the 10th anniversary of the date on which the person is released from a penal institution or discharges community supervision or the court dismisses the criminal proceedings against the person and discharges the person, whichever date is later, if the person's duty to register is based on a conviction or an order of deferred adjudication in a cause that was transferred to a district court or criminal district court under Section 54.02, Family Code.

(c) Except as provided by Subchapter I, the duty to register for a person with a reportable conviction or adjudication for an offense other than an offense described by Subsection (a) ends:

(1) if the person's duty to register is based on an adjudication of delinquent conduct, on the 10th anniversary of the date on which the disposition is made or the person completes the terms of the disposition, whichever date is later; or

(2) if the person's duty to register is based on a conviction or on an order of deferred adjudication, on the 10th anniversary of the date on which the court dismisses the criminal proceedings against the person and discharges the person, the person is released from a penal institution, or the person discharges community supervision, whichever date is later.

History of CCP art. 62.101: Acts 2005, 79th Leg., ch. 1008, §1.01, eff. Sept. 1 2005.

History of Former CCP art. 62.101: Acts 1999, 76th Leg., ch. 444, §5(c), eff. Jan. 1, 2000. Renumbered as art. 62.203 and amended by Acts 2005, 79th Leg., ch. 1008, §1.01, eff. Sept. 1, 2005.

See also *O'Connor's Crimes & Consequences* (2008-09), chart 10-A, "Offenses Requiring Registration."

ART. 62.102. FAILURE TO COMPLY WITH REGISTRATION REQUIREMENTS

(a) A person commits an offense if the person is required to register and fails to comply with any requirement of this chapter.

(b) An offense under this article is:

(1) a state jail felony if the actor is a person whose duty to register expires under Article 62.101(b) or (c);

(2) a felony of the third degree if the actor is a person whose duty to register expires under Article 62.101(a) and who is required to verify registration once each year under Article 62.058; and

(3) a felony of the second degree if the actor is a person whose duty to register expires under Article 62.101(a) and who is required to verify registration once each 90-day period under Article 62.058.

(c) If it is shown at the trial of a person for an offense or an attempt to commit an offense under this article that the person has previously been convicted of an offense or an attempt to commit an offense under this article, the punishment for the offense or the attempt to commit the offense is increased to the punishment for the next highest degree of felony.

History of CCP art. 62.102: Acts 1997, 75th Leg., ch. 668, §1, eff. Sept. 1, 1997. Amended by Acts 1999, 76th Leg., ch. 444, §9 (eff. Sept. 1, 1999), ch. 1415, §18 (eff. Sept. 1, 1999). Renumbered from art. 62.10 and amended by Acts 2005, 79th Leg., ch. 1008, §1.01, eff. Sept. 1, 2005. Source: TRCS art. 6252-13c.1, §7.

ANNOTATIONS

Juarez v. State, 198 S.W.3d 790, 794 (Tex.Crim. App.2006). "We hold that the subsections of [CCP] art. 62.10(b) [now CCP art. 62.102(b)] describe separate offenses and are not enhancement provisions."

White v. State, 988 S.W.2d 277, 279 (Tex.App.— Texarkana 1999, no pet.). A "duty to register imposed pursuant to a criminal registration statute is a collateral consequence of a guilty plea because it is remedial rather than punitive in nature, and a trial court therefore does not have a duty to inform the accused of the duty to register prior to acceptance of the plea. [T]he registration requirement is not punishment and [the] *ex post facto* analysis does not apply to its application."

ART. 62.11. DELETED
Deleted by Acts 2005, 79th Leg., ch. 1008, §1.01, eff. Sept. 1, 2005.

ART. 62.12. DELETED
Deleted by Acts 2005, 79th Leg., ch. 1008, §1.01, eff. Sept. 1, 2005.

ART. 62.13. DELETED

Deleted by Acts 2005, 79th Leg., ch. 1008, §1.01, eff. Sept. 1, 2005.

ART. 62.14. RENUMBERED

Renumbered as art. 62.251 by Acts 2005, 79th Leg., ch. 1008, §1.01, eff. Sept. 1, 2005.

SUBCHAPTER D. PROVISIONS APPLICABLE TO CERTAIN WORKERS & STUDENTS

ART. 62.151. DEFINITIONS

For purposes of this subchapter, a person:

(1) is employed or carries on a vocation if the person works or volunteers on a full-time or part-time basis for a consecutive period exceeding 14 days or for an aggregate period exceeding 30 days in a calendar year;

(2) works regardless of whether the person works for compensation or for governmental or educational benefit; and

(3) is a student if the person enrolls on a full-time or part-time basis in any educational facility, including:

(A) a public or private primary or secondary school, including a high school or alternative learning center; or

(B) a public or private institution of higher education.

History of CCP art. 62.151: Acts 2005, 79th Leg., ch. 1008, §1.01, eff. Sept. 1, 2005.

ART. 62.152. REGISTRATION OF CERTAIN WORKERS OR STUDENTS

(a) A person is subject to this subchapter and, except as otherwise provided by this article, to the other subchapters of this chapter if the person:

(1) has a reportable conviction or adjudication;

(2) resides in another state; and

(3) is employed, carries on a vocation, or is a student in this state.

(b) A person described by Subsection (a) is subject to the registration and verification requirements of Articles 62.051 and 62.058 and to the change of address requirements of Article 62.055, except that the registration and verification and the reporting of a change of address are based on the municipality or county in which the person works or attends school. The person is subject to the school notification requirements of Articles 62.053-62.055, except that notice provided to the superintendent and any administrator is based on the public school district in which the person works or attends school.

(c) A person described by Subsection (a) is not subject to Article 62.101.

(d) The duty to register for a person described by Subsection (a) ends when the person no longer works or studies in this state, provides notice of that fact to the local law enforcement authority in the municipality or county in which the person works or attends school, and receives notice of verification of that fact from the authority. The authority must verify that the person no longer works or studies in this state and must provide to the person notice of that verification within a reasonable time.

(e) Notwithstanding Subsection (a), this article does not apply to a person who has a reportable conviction or adjudication, who resides in another state, and who is employed, carries on a vocation, or is a student in this state if the person establishes another residence in this state to work or attend school in this state. However, that person remains subject to the other articles of this chapter based on that person's residence in this state.

History of CCP art. 62.152: Acts 2005, 79th Leg., ch. 1008, §1.01, eff. Sept. 1, 2005.

ART. 62.153. REGISTRATION OF WORKERS OR STUDENTS AT INSTITUTIONS OF HIGHER EDUCATION

(a) Not later than the later of the seventh day after the date on which the person begins to work or attend school or the first date the applicable authority by policy allows the person to register, a person required to register under Article 62.152 or any other provision of this chapter who is employed, carries on a vocation, or is a student at a public or private institution of higher education in this state shall report that fact to:

(1) the authority for campus security for that institution; or

(2) if an authority for campus security for that institution does not exist, the local law enforcement authority of:

(A) the municipality in which the institution is located; or

(B) the county in which the institution is located, if the institution is not located in a municipality.

(b) A person described by Subsection (a) shall provide the authority for campus security or the local law enforcement authority with all information the person is required to provide under Article 62.051(c).

(c) A person described by Subsection (a) shall notify the authority for campus security or the local law enforcement authority not later than the seventh day after the date of termination of the person's status as a worker or student at the institution.

(d) The authority for campus security or the local law enforcement authority shall promptly forward to the administrative office of the institution any information received from the person under this article and any information received from the department under Article 62.005.

(e) Subsection (a)(2) does not require a person to register with a local law enforcement authority if the person is otherwise required by this chapter to register with that authority.

(f) This article does not impose the requirements of public notification or notification to public or private primary or secondary schools on:

(1) an authority for campus security; or

(2) a local law enforcement authority, if those requirements relate to a person about whom the authority is not otherwise required by this chapter to make notifications.

(g) Notwithstanding Article 62.059, the requirements of this article supersede those of Article 62.059 for a person required to register under both this article and Article 62.059.

History of CCP art. 62.153: Acts 2005, 79th Leg., ch. 1008, §1.01, eff. Sept. 1, 2005.

SUBCHAPTER E. PROVISIONS APPLICABLE TO PERSONS SUBJECT TO CIVIL COMMITMENT

ART. 62.201. ADDITIONAL PUBLIC NOTICE FOR INDIVIDUALS SUBJECT TO CIVIL COMMITMENT

(a) On receipt of notice under this chapter that a person subject to registration who is civilly committed as a sexually violent predator is due to be released from a penal institution or intends to move to a new residence in this state, the department shall, not later than the seventh day after the date on which the person is released or the seventh day after the date on which the person moves, provide written notice mailed or delivered to at least each address, other than a post office box, within a one-mile radius, in an area that has not been subdivided, or a three-block area, in an area that has been subdivided, of the place where the person intends to reside.

(b) The department shall provide the notice in English and Spanish and shall include in the notice any information that is public information under this chapter. The department may not include any information that is not public information under this chapter.

(c) The department shall establish procedures for a person with respect to whom notice is provided under this article to pay to the department all costs incurred by the department in providing the notice. The person shall pay those costs in accordance with the procedures established under this subsection.

(d) The department's duty to provide notice under this article in regard to a particular person ends on the date on which a court releases the person from all requirements of the civil commitment process.

History of CCP art. 62.201: Acts 2005, 79th Leg., ch. 1008, §1.01, eff. Sept. 1, 2005.

ART. 62.202. VERIFICATION OF INDIVIDUALS SUBJECT TO COMMITMENT

(a) Notwithstanding Article 62.058, if an individual subject to registration under this chapter is civilly committed as a sexually violent predator, the person shall report to the local law enforcement authority designated as the person's primary registration authority by the department not less than once in each 30-day period following the date the person first registered under this chapter to verify the information in the registration form maintained by the authority for that person. For purposes of this subsection, a person complies with a requirement that the person register within a 30-day period following a date if the person registers at any time on or after the 27th day following that date but before the 33rd day after that date.

(b) On the date a court releases a person described by Subsection (a) from all requirements of the civil commitment process:

(1) the person's duty to verify registration as a sex offender is no longer imposed by this article; and

(2) the person is required to verify registration as provided by Article 62.058.

History of CCP art. 62.202: Acts 2005, 79th Leg., ch. 1008, §1.01, eff. Sept. 1, 2005.

ART. 62.203. FAILURE TO COMPLY: INDIVIDUALS SUBJECT TO COMMITMENT

(a) A person commits an offense if the person, after commitment as a sexually violent predator but before the person is released from all requirements of the civil commitment process, fails to comply with any requirement of this chapter.

(b) An offense under this article is a felony of the second degree.

History of CCP art. 62.203: Acts 1999, 76th Leg., ch. 444, §5(c), eff. Jan. 1, 2000. Renumbered from art. 62.101 and amended by Acts 2005, 79th Leg., ch. 1008, §1.01, eff. Sept. 1, 2005.

SUBCHAPTER F. REMOVAL OF REGISTRATION INFORMATION

ART. 62.251. REMOVING REGISTRATION INFORMATION WHEN DUTY TO REGISTER EXPIRES

(a) When a person is no longer required to register as a sex offender under this chapter, the department shall remove all information about the person from the sex offender registry.

(b) The duty to remove information under Subsection (a) arises if:

(1) the department has received notice from a local law enforcement authority under Subsection (c) or (d) that the person is no longer required to register or will no longer be required to renew registration and the department verifies the correctness of that information;

(2) the court having jurisdiction over the case for which registration is required requests removal and the department determines that the duty to register has expired; or

(3) the person or the person's representative requests removal and the department determines that the duty to register has expired.

(c) When a person required to register under this chapter appears before a local law enforcement authority to renew or modify registration information, the authority shall determine whether the duty to register has expired. If the authority determines that the duty to register has expired, the authority shall remove all information about the person from the sex offender registry and notify the department that the person's duty to register has expired.

(d) When a person required to register under this chapter appears before a local law enforcement authority to renew registration information, the authority shall determine whether the renewal is the final annual renewal of registration required by law. If the authority determines that the person's duty to register will expire

before the next annual renewal is scheduled, the authority shall automatically remove all information about the person from the sex offender registry on expiration of the duty to register and notify the department that the information about the person has been removed from the registry.

(e) When the department has removed information under Subsection (a), the department shall notify all local law enforcement authorities that have provided registration information to the department about the person of the removal. A local law enforcement authority that receives notice from the department under this subsection shall remove all registration information about the person from its registry.

(f) When the department has removed information under Subsection (a), the department shall notify all public and private agencies or organizations to which it has provided registration information about the person of the removal. On receiving notice, the public or private agency or organization shall remove all registration information about the person from any registry the agency or organization maintains that is accessible to the public with or without charge.

History of CCP art. 62.251: Acts 2003, 78th Leg., ch. 283, §37, eff. Sept. 1, 2003. Renumbered from art. 62.14 and amended by Acts 2005, 79th Leg., ch. 1008, §1.01, eff. Sept. 1, 2005.

SUBCHAPTER G. EXEMPTION FROM REGISTRATION FOR CERTAIN YOUNG ADULT SEX OFFENDERS

ART. 62.301. EXEMPTION FROM REGISTRATION FOR CERTAIN YOUNG ADULT SEX OFFENDERS

(a) If eligible under Subsection (b) or (c), a person required to register under this chapter may petition the court having jurisdiction over the case for an order exempting the person from registration under this chapter at any time after the person's sentencing or after the person is placed on deferred adjudication community supervision.

(b) A person is eligible to petition the court as described by Subsection (a) if:

(1) the person is required to register only as a result of a single reportable conviction or adjudication, other than an adjudication of delinquent conduct; and

(2) the court has entered in the appropriate judgment or has filed with the appropriate papers a statement of an affirmative finding described by Article 42.017 or Section 5(g), Article 42.12.

(c) A defendant who before September 1, 2001, is convicted of or placed on deferred adjudication community supervision for an offense under Section 21.11, 22.011, 22.021, or 43.25, Penal Code, is eligible to petition the court as described by Subsection (a). The court may consider the petition only if the petition states and the court finds that the defendant would have been entitled to the entry of an affirmative finding under Article 42.017 or Section 5(g), Article 42.12, as appropriate, had the conviction or placement on deferred adjudication community supervision occurred after September 1, 2001.

(d) After a hearing on the petition described by Subsection (a), the court may issue an order exempting the person from registration under this chapter if it appears by a preponderance of the evidence:

(1) as presented by a registered sex offender treatment provider, that the exemption does not threaten public safety; and

(2) that the person's conduct did not occur without the consent of the victim or intended victim as described by Section 22.011(b), Penal Code.

(e) An order exempting the person from registration under this chapter does not expire, but the court shall withdraw the order if after the order is issued the person receives a reportable conviction or adjudication under this chapter.

History of CCP art. 62.301: Acts 2005, 79th Leg., ch. 1008, §1.01, eff. Sept. 1, 2005.

SUBCHAPTER H. EXEMPTIONS FROM REGISTRATION FOR CERTAIN JUVENILES

ART. 62.351. MOTION & HEARING GENERALLY

(a) During or after disposition of a case under Section 54.04, Family Code, for adjudication of an offense for which registration is required under this chapter, the juvenile court on motion of the respondent shall conduct a hearing to determine whether the interests of the public require registration under this chapter. The motion may be filed and the hearing held regardless of whether the respondent is under 18 years of age. Notice of the motion and hearing shall be provided to the prosecuting attorney.

(b) The hearing is without a jury and the burden of persuasion is on the respondent to show by a preponderance of evidence that the criteria of Article 62.352(a) have been met. The court at the hearing may make its determination based on:

(1) the receipt of exhibits;

(2) the testimony of witnesses;

(3) representations of counsel for the parties; or

(4) the contents of a social history report prepared by the juvenile probation department that may include the results of testing and examination of the respondent by a psychologist, psychiatrist, or counselor.

(c) All written matter considered by the court shall be disclosed to all parties as provided by Section 54.04(b), Family Code.

(d) If a respondent, as part of a plea agreement, promises not to file a motion seeking an order exempting the respondent from registration under this chapter, the court may not recognize a motion filed by a respondent under this article.

History of Art 62.351: Acts 2005, 79th Leg., ch. 1008, §1.01, eff. Sept. 1, 2005.

ART. 62.352. ORDER GENERALLY

(a) The court shall enter an order exempting a respondent from registration under this chapter if the court determines:

(1) that the protection of the public would not be increased by registration of the respondent under this chapter; or

(2) that any potential increase in protection of the public resulting from registration of the respondent is clearly outweighed by the anticipated substantial harm to the respondent and the respondent's family that would result from registration under this chapter.

(b) After a hearing under Article 62.351 or under a plea agreement described by Article 62.355(b), the juvenile court may enter an order:

(1) deferring decision on requiring registration under this chapter until the respondent has completed treatment for the respondent's sexual offense as a condition of probation or while committed to the Texas Youth Commission; or

(2) requiring the respondent to register as a sex offender but providing that the registration information is not public information and is restricted to use by law enforcement and criminal justice agencies, the Council on Sex Offender Treatment, and public or private institutions of higher education.

(c) If the court enters an order described by Subsection (b)(1), the court retains discretion and jurisdiction to require, or exempt the respondent from, registration under this chapter at any time during the treatment or on the successful or unsuccessful completion of treatment, except that during the period of deferral, registration may not be required. Following successful completion of treatment, the respondent is exempted from registration under this chapter unless a hearing under this subchapter is held on motion of the state, regardless of whether the respondent is 18 years of age or older, and the court determines the interests of the public require registration. Not later than the 10th day after the date of the respondent's successful completion of treatment, the treatment provider shall notify the juvenile court and prosecuting attorney of the completion.

(d) Information that is the subject of an order described by Subsection (b)(2) may not be posted on the Internet or released to the public.

History of Art 62.352: Acts 2005, 79th Leg., ch. 1008, §1.01, eff. Sept. 1, 2005.

ART. 62.353. MOTION, HEARING, & ORDER CONCERNING PERSON ALREADY REGISTERED

(a) A person who has registered as a sex offender for an adjudication of delinquent conduct, regardless of when the delinquent conduct or the adjudication for the conduct occurred, may file a motion in the adjudicating juvenile court for a hearing seeking:

(1) exemption from registration under this chapter as provided by Article 62.351; or

(2) an order under Article 62.352(b)(2) that the registration become nonpublic.

(b) The person may file a motion under Subsection (a) in the original juvenile case regardless of whether the person, at the time of filing the motion, is 18 years of age or older. Notice of the motion shall be provided to the prosecuting attorney. A hearing on the motion shall be provided as in other cases under this subchapter.

(c) Only one subsequent motion may be filed under Subsection (a) if a previous motion under this article has been filed concerning the case.

(d) To the extent feasible, the motion under Subsection (a) shall identify those public and private agencies and organizations, including public or private institutions of higher education, that possess sex offender registration information about the case.

(e) The juvenile court, after a hearing, may:

(1) deny a motion filed under Subsection (a);

(2) grant a motion described by Subsection (a)(1); or

(3) grant a motion described by Subsection (a)(2).

(f) If the court grants a motion filed under Subsection (a), the clerk of the court shall by certified mail, return receipt requested, send a copy of the order to the department, to each local law enforcement authority that the person has proved to the juvenile court has registration information about the person, and to each public or private agency or organization that the person has proved to the juvenile court has information about the person that is currently available to the public with or without payment of a fee. The clerk of the court shall by certified mail, return receipt requested, send a copy of the order to any other agency or organization designated by the person. The person shall identify the agency or organization and its address and pay a fee of $20 to the court for each agency or organization the person designates.

(g) In addition to disseminating the order under Subsection (f), at the request of the person, the clerk of the court shall by certified mail, return receipt requested, send a copy of the order to each public or private agency or organization that at any time following the initial dissemination of the order under Subsection (f) gains possession of sex offender registration information pertaining to that person, if the agency or organization did not otherwise receive a copy of the order under Subsection (f).

(h) An order under Subsection (f) must require the recipient to conform its records to the court's order either by deleting the sex offender registration information or changing its status to nonpublic, as applicable. A public or private institution of higher education may not be required to delete the sex offender registration information under this subsection.

(i) A private agency or organization that possesses sex offender registration information the agency or organization obtained from a state, county, or local governmental entity is required to conform the agency's or organization's records to the court's order on or before the 30th day after the date of the entry of the order. Unless the agency or organization is a public or private institution of higher education, failure to comply in that period automatically bars the agency or organization from obtaining sex offender registration information from any state, county, or local governmental entity in this state in the future.

History of Art 62.353: Acts 2005, 79th Leg., ch. 1008, §1.01, eff. Sept. 1, 2005.

ART. 62.354. MOTION, HEARING, & ORDER CONCERNING PERSON REQUIRED TO REGISTER BECAUSE OF OUT-OF-STATE ADJUDICATION

(a) A person required to register as a sex offender in this state because of an out-of-state adjudication of delinquent conduct may file in the juvenile court of the person's county of residence a petition under Article 62.351 for an order exempting the person from registration under this chapter.

(b) If the person is already registered as a sex offender in this state because of an out-of-state adjudication of delinquent conduct, the person may file in the juvenile court of the person's county of residence a petition under Article 62.353 for an order removing the person from sex offender registries in this state.

(c) On receipt of a petition under this article, the juvenile court shall conduct a hearing and make rulings as in other cases under this subchapter.

(d) An order entered under this article requiring removal of registration information applies only to registration information derived from registration in this state.

History of Art 62.354: Acts 2005, 79th Leg., ch. 1008, §1.01, eff. Sept. 1, 2005.

ART. 62.355. WAIVER OF HEARING

(a) The prosecuting attorney may waive the state's right to a hearing under this subchapter and agree that registration under this chapter is not required. A waiver under this subsection must state whether the waiver is entered under a plea agreement.

(b) If the waiver is entered under a plea agreement, the court, without a hearing, shall:

(1) enter an order exempting the respondent from registration under this chapter; or

(2) under Section 54.03(j), Family Code, inform the respondent that the court believes a hearing under this article is required and give the respondent the opportunity to:

(A) withdraw the respondent's plea of guilty, nolo contendere, or true; or

(B) affirm the respondent's plea and participate in the hearing.

(c) If the waiver is entered other than under a plea agreement, the court, without a hearing, shall enter an order exempting the respondent from registration under this chapter.

History of Art 62.355: Acts 2005, 79th Leg., ch. 1008, §1.01, eff. Sept. 1, 2005.

ART. 62.356. EFFECT OF CERTAIN ORDERS

(a) A person who has an adjudication of delinquent conduct that would otherwise be reportable under Article 62.001(5) does not have a reportable adjudication of delinquent conduct for purposes of this chapter if the juvenile court enters an order under this subchapter exempting the person from the registration requirements of this chapter.

(b) If the juvenile court enters an order exempting a person from registration under this chapter, the respondent may not be required to register in this or any other state for the offense for which registration was exempted.

History of Art 62.356: Acts 2005, 79th Leg., ch. 1008, §1.01, eff. Sept. 1, 2005.

ART. 62.357. APPEAL OF CERTAIN ORDERS

(a) Notwithstanding Section 56.01, Family Code, on entry by a juvenile court of an order under Article 62.352(a) exempting a respondent from registration under this chapter, the prosecuting attorney may appeal that order by giving notice of appeal within the time required under Rule 26.2(b), Texas Rules of Appellate Procedure. The appeal is civil and the standard of review in the appellate court is whether the juvenile court committed procedural error or abused its discretion in exempting the respondent from registration under this chapter. The appeal is limited to review of the order exempting the respondent from registration under this chapter and may not include any other issues in the case.

(b) A respondent may under Section 56.01, Family Code, appeal a juvenile court's order under Article 62.352(a) requiring registration in the same manner as the appeal of any other legal issue in the case. The standard of review in the appellate court is whether the juvenile court committed procedural error or abused its discretion in requiring registration.

History of Art 62.357: Acts 2005, 79th Leg., ch. 1008, §1.01, eff. Sept. 1, 2005.

SUBCHAPTER I. EARLY TERMINATION OF CERTAIN PERSONS' OBLIGATION TO REGISTER

ART. 62.401. DEFINITION

In this subchapter, "council" means the Council on Sex Offender Treatment.

History of CCP art. 62.401: Acts 2005, 79th Leg., ch. 1008, §1.01, eff. Sept. 1, 2005.

ART. 62.402. DETERMINATION OF MINIMUM REQUIRED REGISTRATION PERIOD

(a) The council by rule shall determine the minimum required registration period under 42 U.S.C. Section 14071 (Jacob Wetterling Crimes Against Children and Sexually Violent Offender Registration Program) for each reportable conviction or adjudication under this chapter, if this state is to receive the maximum amount of federal money available to a state as described by that law.

(b) After determining the minimum required registration period for each reportable conviction or adjudication under Subsection (a), the council shall compile and publish a list of reportable convictions or adjudications for which a person must register under this chapter for a period that exceeds the minimum required registration period under federal law.

(c) To the extent possible, the council shall periodically verify with the Bureau of Justice Assistance or another appropriate federal agency the accuracy of the list of reportable convictions or adjudications described by Subsection (b).

History of CCP art. 62.402: Acts 2005, 79th Leg., ch. 1008, §1.01, eff. Sept. 1, 2005.

ART. 62.403. INDIVIDUAL RISK ASSESSMENT

(a) The council by rule shall establish, develop, or adopt an individual risk assessment tool or a group of individual risk assessment tools that:

(1) evaluates the criminal history of a person required to register under this chapter; and

(2) seeks to predict:

(A) the likelihood that the person will engage in criminal activity that may result in the person receiving a second or subsequent reportable adjudication or conviction; and

(B) the continuing danger, if any, that the person poses to the community.

(b) On the written request of a person with a single reportable adjudication or conviction that appears on the list published under Article 62.402(b), the council shall:

(1) evaluate the person using the individual risk assessment tool or group of individual risk assessment tools established, developed, or adopted under Subsection (a); and

(2) provide to the person a written report detailing the outcome of an evaluation conducted under Subdivision (1).

(c) An individual risk assessment provided to a person under this subchapter is confidential and is not subject to disclosure under Chapter 552, Government Code.

History of CCP art. 62.403: Acts 2005, 79th Leg., ch. 1008, §1.01, eff. Sept. 1, 2005.

ART. 62.404. MOTION FOR EARLY TERMINATION

(a) A person required to register under this chapter who has requested and received an individual risk assessment under Article 62.403 may file with the trial court that sentenced the person for the reportable conviction or adjudication a motion for early termination of the person's obligation to register under this chapter.

(b) A motion filed under this article must be accompanied by:

(1) a written explanation of how the reportable conviction or adjudication giving rise to the movant's registration under this chapter qualifies as a reportable conviction or adjudication that appears on the list published under Article 62.402(b); and

(2) a certified copy of a written report detailing the outcome of an individual risk assessment evaluation conducted under Article 62.403(b)(1).

History of CCP art. 62.404: Acts 2005, 79th Leg., ch. 1008, §1.01, eff. Sept. 1, 2005.

See also *O'Connor's Crimes & Consequences* (2008-09), chart 10-G, "Early Termination."

ART. 62.405. HEARING ON PETITION

(a) After reviewing a motion filed with the court under Article 62.404, the court may:

(1) deny without a hearing the movant's request for early termination; or

(2) hold a hearing on the motion to determine whether to grant or deny the motion.

(b) The court may not grant a motion filed under Article 62.404 if:

(1) the motion is not accompanied by the documents required under Article 62.404(b); or

(2) the court determines that the reportable conviction or adjudication for which the movant is required to register under this chapter is not a reportable conviction or adjudication for which the movant is required to

CCP ART. 62.402

register for a period that exceeds the minimum required registration period under federal law.

History of CCP art. 62.405: Acts 2005, 79th Leg., ch. 1008, §1.01, eff. Sept. 1, 2005.

See also *O'Connor's Crimes & Consequences* (2008-09), chart 10-G, "Early Termination."

ART. 62.406. COSTS OF INDIVIDUAL RISK ASSESSMENT & OF COURT

A person required to register under this chapter who files a motion for early termination of the person's registration obligation under this chapter is responsible for and shall remit to the council and to the court, as applicable, all costs associated with and incurred by the council in providing the individual risk assessment or by the court in holding a hearing under this subchapter.

History of CCP art. 62.406: Acts 2005, 79th Leg., ch. 1008, §1.01, eff. Sept. 1, 2005.

See also *O'Connor's Crimes & Consequences* (2008-09), chart 10-G, "Early Termination."

ART. 62.407. EFFECT OF ORDER GRANTING EARLY TERMINATION

(a) If, after notice to the person and to the prosecuting attorney and a hearing, the court grants a motion filed under Article 62.404 for the early termination of a person's obligation to register under this chapter, notwithstanding Article 62.101, the person's obligation to register under this chapter ends on the later of:

(1) the date the court enters the order of early termination; or

(2) the date the person has paid each cost described by Section 62.406.

(b) If the court grants a motion filed under Article 62.404 for the early termination of a person's obligation to register under this chapter, all conditions of the person's parole, release to mandatory supervision, or community supervision shall be modified in accordance with the court's order.

History of CCP art. 62.407: Acts 2005, 79th Leg., ch. 1008, §1.01, eff. Sept. 1, 2005.

See also *O'Connor's Crimes & Consequences* (2008-09), chart 10-G, "Early Termination."

ART. 62.408. NONAPPLICABILITY

This subchapter does not apply to a person without a reportable conviction or adjudication who is required to register as a condition of parole, release to mandatory supervision, or community supervision.

History of CCP art. 62.408: Acts 2005, 79th Leg., ch. 1008, §1.01, eff. Sept. 1, 2005.

CHAPTER 63. MISSING CHILDREN & MISSING PERSONS

SUBCHAPTER A. GENERAL PROVISIONS

ART. 63.001. DEFINITIONS

In this chapter:

(1) "Child" means a person under 18 years of age.

(2) "Missing person" means a person 18 years old or older whose disappearance is possibly not voluntary.

(3) "Missing child" means a child whose whereabouts are unknown to the child's legal custodian, the circumstances of whose absence indicate that:

(A) the child did not voluntarily leave the care and control of the custodian, and the taking of the child was not authorized by law;

(B) the child voluntarily left the care and control of his legal custodian without the custodian's consent and without intent to return; or

(C) the child was taken or retained in violation of the terms of a court order for possession of or access to the child.

(4) "Missing child" or "missing person" also includes a person of any age who is missing and:

(A) is under proven physical or mental disability or is senile, and because of one or more of these conditions is subject to immediate danger or is a danger to others;

(B) is in the company of another person or is in a situation the circumstances of which indicate that the missing child's or missing person's safety is in doubt; or

(C) is unemancipated as defined by the law of this state.

(5) "Missing child or missing person report" or "report" means information that is:

(A) given to a law enforcement agency on a form used for sending information to the national crime information center; and

(B) about a child or missing person whose whereabouts are unknown to the reporter and who is alleged in the form by the reporter to be missing.

(6) "Legal custodian of a child" means a parent of a child if no managing conservator or guardian of the person of the child has been appointed, the managing conservator of a child or a guardian of a child if a managing conservator or guardian has been appointed for the child, a possessory conservator of a child if the child is absent from the possessory conservator of the child at a time when the possessory conservator is entitled to possession of the child and the child is not believed to be with the managing conservator, or any other person who has assumed temporary care and control of a child if at the time of disappearance the child was not living with his parent, guardian, managing conservator, or possessory conservator.

(7) "Clearinghouse" means the missing children and missing persons information clearinghouse.

(8) "Law enforcement agency" means a police department of a city in this state, a sheriff of a county in this state, or the Department of Public Safety.

(9) "Possible match" occurs if the similarities between an unidentified body and a missing child or person would lead one to believe they are the same person.

(10) "City or state agency" means an employment commission, the Texas Department of Human Services, the Texas Department of Transportation, and any other agency that is funded or supported by the state or a city government.

(11) "Birth certificate agency" means a municipal or county official that records and maintains birth certificates and the bureau of vital statistics.

(12) "Bureau of vital statistics" means the bureau of vital statistics of the Texas Department of Health.

(13) "School" means a public primary school or private primary school that charges a fee for tuition and has more than 25 students enrolled and attending courses at a single location.

History of CCP art. 63.001: Acts 1997, 75th Leg., ch. 1427, §1, eff. Sept. 1, 1997. Amended by Acts 1997, 75th Leg., ch. 51, §1 (eff. May 7, 1997), ch. 1084, §1 (eff. Sept. 1, 1997). Renumbered from art. 62.001 and amended by Acts 1999, 76th Leg., ch. 62, §§3.10, 19.01(8)(A), eff. Sept. 1, 1999. Amended by Acts 2005, 79th Leg., ch. 319, §1, eff. June 17, 2005. Source: Hum. Res. Code §79.001.

ART. 63.0015. PRESUMPTION REGARDING PARENTAGE

For purposes of this chapter, a person named as a child's mother or father in the child's birth certificate is presumed to be the child's parent.

History of CCP art. 63.0015: Acts 1999, 76th Leg., ch. 685, §2, eff. Sept. 1, 1999.

ART. 63.002. MISSING CHILDREN & MISSING PERSONS INFORMATION CLEARINGHOUSE

(a) The missing children and missing persons information clearinghouse is established within the Department of Public Safety.

(b) The clearinghouse is under the administrative direction of the director of the department.

(c) The clearinghouse shall be used by all law enforcement agencies of the state.

History of CCP art. 63.002: Acts 1997, 75th Leg., ch. 1427, §1, eff. Sept. 1, 1997. Renumbered from art. 62.002 by Acts 1999, 76th Leg., ch. 62, §19.01(8)(A), eff. Sept. 1, 1999. Source: Hum. Res. Code §79.002.

ART. 63.003. FUNCTION OF CLEARINGHOUSE

(a) The clearinghouse is a central repository of information on missing children and missing persons.

(b) The clearinghouse shall:

(1) establish a system of intrastate communication of information relating to missing children and missing persons;

(2) provide a centralized file for the exchange of information on missing children, missing persons, and unidentified dead bodies within the state;

(3) communicate with the national crime information center for the exchange of information on missing children and missing persons suspected of interstate travel;

(4) collect, process, maintain, and disseminate accurate and complete information on missing children and missing persons;

(5) provide a statewide toll-free telephone line for the reporting of missing children and missing persons and for receiving information on missing children and missing persons; and

(6) provide and disseminate to legal custodians, law enforcement agencies, and the Texas Education Agency information that explains how to prevent child abduction and what to do if a child becomes missing.

History of CCP art. 63.003: Acts 1997, 75th Leg., ch. 1427, §1, eff. Sept. 1, 1997. Amended by Acts 1997, 75th Leg., ch. 165, §6.59, eff. Sept. 1, 1997. Renumbered from art. 62.003 by Acts 1999, 76th Leg., ch. 62, §19.01(8)(A), eff. Sept. 1, 1999. Source: Hum. Res. Code §79.003.

ART. 63.004. REPORT FORMS

(a) The Department of Public Safety shall distribute missing children and missing person report forms.

(b) A missing child or missing person report may be made to a law enforcement officer authorized by that department to receive reports in person or by telephone or other indirect method of communication and the officer may enter the information on the form for the reporting person. A report form may also be completed by the reporting person and delivered to a law enforcement officer.

History of CCP art. 63.004: Acts 1997, 75th Leg., ch. 1427, §1, eff. Sept. 1, 1997. Renumbered from art. 62.004 by Acts 1999, 76th Leg., ch. 62, §19.01(8)(A), eff. Sept. 1, 1999. Source: Hum. Res. Code §79.004.

ART. 63.005. DISTRIBUTION OF INFORMATION

(a) The clearinghouse shall print and distribute posters, flyers, and other forms of information containing descriptions of missing children.

(b) The clearinghouse shall also provide to the Texas Education Agency information about missing children who may be located in the school systems.

(c) The clearinghouse may also receive information about missing children from the Public Education Information Management System of the Texas Education Agency and from school districts.

History of CCP art. 63.005: Acts 1997, 75th Leg., ch. 1427, §1, eff. Sept. 1, 1997. Amended by Acts 1997, 75th Leg., ch. 165, §6.60, eff. Sept. 1, 1997. Renumbered from art. 62.005 by Acts 1999, 76th Leg., ch. 62, §19.01(8)(A), eff. Sept. 1, 1999. Source: Hum. Res. Code §79.005.

ART. 63.006. RELEASE OF DENTAL RECORDS

(a) At the time a report is made for a missing child, the person to whom the report is given shall give or mail to the reporter a dental record release form. The officer receiving the report shall endorse the form with the notation that a missing child report has been made in compliance with this chapter. When the form is properly completed by the reporter, and contains the endorsement, the form is sufficient to permit any dentist or physician in this state to release dental records relating to the child reported missing.

(b) At any time a report is made for a missing person the law enforcement officer taking the report shall complete a dental release form that states that the person is missing and that there is reason to believe that the person has not voluntarily relocated or removed himself from communications with others and that authorizes the bearer of the release to obtain dental information records from any dentist or physician in this state.

(c) Any person who obtains dental records through the use of the form authorized by this article shall send the records to the clearinghouse.

(d) The judge of any court of record of this state may for good cause shown authorize the release of dental records of a missing child or missing person.

(e) A dentist or physician who releases dental records to a person presenting a proper release executed or ordered under this article is immune from civil liability or criminal prosecution for the release of those records.

History of CCP art. 63.006: Acts 1997, 75th Leg., ch. 1427, §1, eff. Sept. 1, 1997. Renumbered from art. 62.006 by Acts 1999, 76th Leg., ch. 62, §19.01(8)(A), eff. Sept. 1, 1999. Amended by Acts 1999, 76th Leg., ch. 685, §3, eff. Sept. 1, 1999. Source: Hum. Res. Code §79.006.

ART. 63.007. RELEASE OF MEDICAL RECORDS

(a) At the time a report is made for a missing child or adult, the law enforcement officer taking the report shall give a medical record release form to the parent, spouse, adult child, or legal guardian who is making the report. The officer receiving the report shall endorse the form with the notation that a missing child or missing adult report has been made in compliance with this chapter. When the form is properly completed by the parent, spouse, adult child, or legal guardian, and contains the endorsement, the form is sufficient to permit any physician, health care facility, or other licensed health care provider in this state to release to the law enforcement officer presenting the release dental records, blood type, height, weight, X rays, and information regarding scars, allergies, or any unusual illnesses suffered by the person who is reported missing. Except as provided by Subsection (d), a medical record of a missing child may be released only if the medical record release form is signed by a parent or legal guardian.

(b) At any time a report is made for an adult missing person, the law enforcement officer taking the report shall complete a medical release form that states that the person is missing and that there is reason to believe that the person has not voluntarily relocated or removed himself or herself from communications with others. A release under this subsection is not valid unless it is signed by the adult missing person's:

(1) spouse;

(2) adult child who is reasonably available;

(3) parent; or

(4) legal guardian.

(c) A law enforcement officer who obtains medical records under this article shall send a copy of the records to the clearinghouse. A law enforcement officer who obtains records under this article, a law enforcement agency using the records, and the clearinghouse are prohibited from disclosing the information contained in or obtained through the medical records unless permitted by law. Information contained in or obtained through medical records may be used only for purposes directly related to locating the missing person.

(d) The judge of any court of record of this state may for good cause shown authorize the release of pertinent medical records of a missing child or missing adult.

(e) A physician, health care facility, or other licensed health care provider releasing a medical record to a person presenting a proper release executed or ordered under this article is immune from civil liability or criminal prosecution for the release of the record.

History of CCP art. 63.007: Acts 1997, 75th Leg., ch. 1427, §1, eff. Sept. 1, 1997. Renumbered from art. 62.007 by Acts 1999, 76th Leg., ch. 62, §19.01(8)(A), eff. Sept. 1, 1999. Source: Hum. Res. Code §79.0065.

ART. 63.008. MISSING CHILDREN PROGRAM

(a) The Texas Education Agency shall develop and administer a program for the location of missing children who may be enrolled within the Texas school system, including nonpublic schools, and for the reporting of children who may be missing or who may be unlawfully removed from schools.

(b) The program shall include the use of information received from the missing children and missing persons information clearinghouse and shall be coordinated with the operations of that information clearinghouse.

(c) The State Board of Education may adopt rules for the operation of the program and shall require the participation of all school districts and accredited private schools in this state.

History of CCP art. 63.008: Acts 1997, 75th Leg., ch. 1427, §1, eff. Sept. 1, 1997. Amended by Acts 1997, 75th Leg., ch. 165, §6.61, eff. Sept. 1, 1997. Renumbered from art. 62.008 by Acts 1999, 76th Leg., ch. 62, §19.01(8)(A), eff. Sept. 1, 1999. Source: Hum. Res. Code §79.007.

ART. 63.009. LAW ENFORCEMENT REQUIREMENTS

(a) Local law enforcement agencies, on receiving a report of a missing child or a missing person, shall:

(1) if the subject of the report is a child and the well-being of the child is in danger or if the subject of the report is a person who is known by the agency to have or is reported to have chronic dementia, including Alzheimer's dementia, whether caused by illness, brain defect, or brain injury, immediately start an investigation in order to determine the present location of the child or person;

(2) if the subject of the report is a child or person other than a child or person described by Subdivision

(1), start an investigation with due diligence in order to determine the present location of the child or person;

(3) immediately enter the name of the child or person into the clearinghouse, the national crime information center missing person file if the child or person meets the center's criteria, and the Alzheimer's Association Safe Return crisis number, if applicable, with all available identifying features such as dental records, fingerprints, other physical characteristics, and a description of the clothing worn when last seen, and all available information describing any person reasonably believed to have taken or retained the missing child or missing person; and

(4) inform the person who filed the report of the missing child or missing person that the information will be entered into the clearinghouse, the national crime information center missing person file, and the Alzheimer's Association Safe Return crisis number, if applicable.

(b) Information not immediately available shall be obtained by the agency and entered into the clearinghouse and the national crime information center file as a supplement to the original entry as soon as possible.

(c) All Texas law enforcement agencies are required to enter information about all unidentified bodies into the clearinghouse and the national crime information center unidentified person file. A law enforcement agency shall, not later than the 10th working day after the date the death is reported to the agency, enter all available identifying features of the unidentified body (fingerprints, dental records, any unusual physical characteristics, and a description of the clothing found on the body) into the clearinghouse and the national crime information center file. If an information entry into the national crime information center file results in an automatic entry of the information into the clearinghouse, the law enforcement agency is not required to make a direct entry of that information into the clearinghouse.

(d) If a local law enforcement agency investigating a report of a missing child or missing person obtains a warrant for the arrest of a person for taking or retaining the missing child or missing person, the local law enforcement agency shall immediately enter the name and other descriptive information of the person into the national crime information center wanted person file if

the person meets the center's criteria. The local law enforcement agency shall also enter all available identifying features, including dental records, fingerprints, and other physical characteristics of the missing child or missing person. The information shall be cross-referenced with the information in the national crime information center missing person file.

(e) A local law enforcement agency that has access to the national crime information center database shall cooperate with other law enforcement agencies in entering or retrieving information from the national crime information center database.

(f) Immediately after the return of a missing child or missing person or the identification of an unidentified body, the local law enforcement agency having jurisdiction of the investigation shall cancel the entry in the national crime information center database.

(g) On determining the location of a child under Subsection (a)(1) or (2), other than a child who is subject to the continuing jurisdiction of a district court, an officer shall take possession of the child and shall deliver or arrange for the delivery of the child to a person entitled to possession of the child. If the person entitled to possession of the child is not immediately available, the law enforcement officer shall deliver the child to the Department of Protective and Regulatory Services.

History of CCP art. 63.009: Acts 1997, 75th Leg., ch. 1427, §1, eff. Sept. 1, 1997. Amended by Acts 1997, 75th Leg., ch. 51, §2 (eff. May 7, 1997), ch. 771, §1 (eff. Sept. 1, 1997). Renumbered from art. 62.009 and amended by Acts 1999, 76th Leg., ch. 62, §§3.11, 3.12, 19.01(8)(A), eff. Sept. 1, 1999. Amended by Acts 1999, 76th Leg., ch. 200, §§1, 2 (eff. Sept. 1, 1999), ch. 685, §§4, 5 (eff. Sept. 1, 1999); Acts 2001, 77th Leg., ch. 1420, §3.005, eff. Sept. 1, 2001. Source: Hum. Res. Code §79.008.

ART. 63.010. ATTORNEY GENERAL TO REQUIRE COMPLIANCE

The attorney general shall require each law enforcement agency to comply with this chapter and may seek writs of mandamus or other appropriate remedies to enforce this chapter.

History of CCP art. 63.010: Acts 1997, 75th Leg., ch. 1427, §1, eff. Sept. 1, 1997. Renumbered from art. 62.010 by Acts 1999, 76th Leg., ch. 62, §19.01(8)(A), eff. Sept. 1, 1999. Source: Hum. Res. Code §79.009.

ART. 63.011. MISSING CHILDREN INVESTIGATIONS

On the written request made to a law enforcement agency by a parent, foster parent, managing or possessory conservator, guardian of the person or the estate, or other court-appointed custodian of a child whose whereabouts are unknown, the law enforcement agency shall request from the missing children and missing persons information clearinghouse information concerning the child that may aid the person making the request in the identification or location of the child.

History of CCP art. 63.011: Acts 1997, 75th Leg., ch. 1427, §1, eff. Sept. 1, 1997. Renumbered from art. 62.011 by Acts 1999, 76th Leg., ch. 62, §19.01(8)(A), eff. Sept. 1, 1999. Source: Hum. Res. Code §79.010.

ART. 63.012. REPORT OF INQUIRY

A law enforcement agency to which a request has been made under Article 63.011 of this code shall report to the parent on the results of its inquiry within 14 days after the day that the written request is filed with the law enforcement agency.

History of CCP art. 63.012: Acts 1997, 75th Leg., ch. 1427, §1, eff. Sept. 1, 1997. Renumbered from art. 62.012 and amended by Acts 1999, 76th Leg., ch. 62, §§19.01(8)(A), 19.02(1), eff. Sept. 1, 1999. Source: Hum. Res. Code §79.011.

ART. 63.013. INFORMATION TO CLEARINGHOUSE

Each law enforcement agency shall provide to the missing children and missing persons information clearinghouse any information that would assist in the location or identification of any missing child who has been reported to the agency as missing.

History of CCP art. 63.013: Acts 1997, 75th Leg., ch. 1427, §1, eff. Sept. 1, 1997. Renumbered from art. 62.013 by Acts 1999, 76th Leg., ch. 62, §19.01(8)(A), eff. Sept. 1, 1999. Source: Hum. Res. Code §79.012.

ART. 63.014. CROSS-CHECKING & MATCHING

(a) The clearinghouse shall cross-check and attempt to match unidentified bodies with missing children or missing persons. When the clearinghouse discovers a possible match between an unidentified body and a missing child or missing person, the Department of Public Safety shall notify the appropriate law enforcement agencies.

(b) Those law enforcement agencies that receive notice of a possible match shall make arrangements for positive identification and complete and close out the investigation with notification to the clearinghouse.

History of CCP art. 63.014: Acts 1997, 75th Leg., ch. 1427, §1, eff. Sept. 1, 1997. Renumbered from art. 62.014 by Acts 1999, 76th Leg., ch. 62, §19.01(8)(A), eff. Sept. 1, 1999. Source: Hum. Res. Code §79.013.

ART. 63.015. AVAILABILITY OF INFORMATION THROUGH OTHER AGENCIES

(a) On the request of any law enforcement agency, a city or state agency shall furnish the law enforcement agency with any information about a missing child or missing person that will assist in completing the investigation.

(b) The information given under Subsection (a) of this article is confidential and may not be released to any other person outside of the law enforcement agency.

History of CCP art. 63.015: Acts 1997, 75th Leg., ch. 1427, §1, eff. Sept. 1, 1997. Renumbered from art. 62.015 by Acts 1999, 76th Leg., ch. 62, §19.01(8)(A), eff. Sept. 1, 1999. Source: Hum. Res. Code §79.014.

ART. 63.016. DONATIONS

The Department of Public Safety may accept money donated from any source to assist in financing the activities and purposes of the missing children and missing persons information clearinghouse.

History of CCP art. 63.016: Acts 1997, 75th Leg., ch. 1427, §1, eff. Sept. 1, 1997. Renumbered from art. 62.016 by Acts 1999, 76th Leg., ch. 62, §19.01(8)(A), eff. Sept. 1, 1999. Source: Hum. Res. Code §79.015.

ART. 63.017. CONFIDENTIALITY OF CERTAIN RECORDS

Clearinghouse records that relate to the investigation by a law enforcement agency of a missing child, a missing person, or an unidentified body and records or notations that the clearinghouse maintains for internal use in matters relating to missing children, missing persons, or unidentified bodies are confidential.

History of CCP art. 63.017: Acts 1997, 75th Leg., ch. 1427, §1, eff. Sept. 1, 1997. Renumbered from art. 62.017 by Acts 1999, 76th Leg., ch. 62, §19.01(8)(A), eff. Sept. 1, 1999. Source: Hum. Res. Code §79.016.

ART. 63.018. DEATH CERTIFICATES

A physician who performs a postmortem examination on the body of an unidentified person shall complete and file a death certificate in accordance with Chapter 193, Health and Safety Code. The physician shall note on the certificate the name of the law enforcement agency that submitted the body for examination and shall send a copy of the certificate to the clearinghouse not later than the 10th working day after the date the physician files the certificate.

History of CCP art. 63.018: Acts 1997, 75th Leg., ch. 1427, §1, eff. Sept. 1, 1997. Renumbered from art. 62.018 by Acts 1999, 76th Leg., ch. 62, §19.01(8)(A), eff. Sept. 1, 1999.

ART. 63.019. SCHOOL RECORDS SYSTEM

(a) On enrollment of a child under 11 years of age in a school for the first time at the school, the school shall:

(1) request from the person enrolling the child the name of each previous school attended by the child;

(2) request from each school identified in Subdivision (1), the school records for the child and, if the person enrolling the child provides copies of previous school records, request verification from the school of the child's name, address, birth date, and grades and dates attended; and

(3) notify the person enrolling the student that not later than the 30th day after enrollment, or the 90th day if the child was not born in the United States, the person must provide:

(A) a certified copy of the child's birth certificate; or

(B) other reliable proof of the child's identity and age and a signed statement explaining the person's inability to produce a copy of the child's birth certificate.

(b) If a person enrolls a child under 11 years of age in school and does not provide the valid prior school information or documentation required by this section, the school shall notify the appropriate law enforcement agency before the 31st day after the person fails to comply with this section. On receipt of notification, the law enforcement agency shall immediately check the clearinghouse to determine if the child has been reported missing. If the child has been reported missing, the law enforcement agency shall immediately notify other appropriate law enforcement agencies that the missing child has been located.

History of CCP art. 63.019: Acts 1999, 76th Leg., ch. 62, §19.01(8)(B), eff. Sept. 1, 1999. Source: Hum. Res. Code §79.017.

ART. 63.020. DUTY OF SCHOOLS & OTHER ENTITIES TO FLAG MISSING CHILDREN'S RECORDS

(a) When a report that a child under 11 years of age is missing is received by a law enforcement agency, the agency shall immediately notify each school and day care facility that the child attended or in which the child was enrolled as well as the bureau of vital statistics, if the child was born in the state, that the child is missing.

(b) On receipt of notice that a child under 11 years of age is missing, the bureau of vital statistics shall notify the appropriate municipal or county birth certificate agency that the child is missing.

(c) A school, day care facility, or birth certificate agency that receives notice concerning a child under this section shall flag the child's records that are maintained by the school, facility, or agency.

(d) The law enforcement agency shall notify the clearinghouse that the notification required under this

section has been made. The clearinghouse shall provide the notice required under this section if the clearinghouse determines that the notification has not been made by the law enforcement agency.

(e) If a missing child under 11 years of age, who was the subject of a missing child report made in this state, was born in or attended a school or licensed day care facility in another state, the law enforcement agency shall notify law enforcement or the missing and exploited children clearinghouse in each appropriate state regarding the missing child and request the law enforcement agency or clearinghouse to contact the state birth certificate agency and each school or licensed day care facility the missing child attended to flag the missing child's records.

History of CCP art. 63.020: Acts 1999, 76th Leg., ch. 62, §19.01(8)(B), eff. Sept. 1, 1999. Source: Hum. Res. Code §79.018.

ART. 63.021. SYSTEM FOR FLAGGING RECORDS

(a) On receipt of notification by a law enforcement agency or the clearinghouse regarding a missing child under 11 years of age, the school, day care facility, or birth certificate agency shall maintain the child's records in its possession so that on receipt of a request regarding the child, the school, day care facility, or agency will be able to notify law enforcement or the clearinghouse that a request for a flagged record has been made.

(b) When a request concerning a flagged record is made in person, the school, day care facility, or agency may not advise the requesting party that the request concerns a missing child and shall:

(1) require the person requesting the flagged record to complete a form stating the person's name, address, telephone number, and relationship to the child for whom a request is made and the name, address, and birth date of the child;

(2) obtain a copy of the requesting party's driver's license or other photographic identification, if possible;

(3) if the request is for a birth certificate, inform the requesting party that a copy of a certificate will be sent by mail; and

(4) immediately notify the appropriate law enforcement agency that a request has been made concerning a flagged record and include a physical description of the requesting party, the identity and address of the requesting party, and a copy of the requesting party's driver's license or other photographic identification.

(c) After providing the notification required under Subsection (a)(4), the school, day care facility, or agency shall mail a copy of the requested record to the requesting party on or after the 21st day after the date of the request.

(d) When a request concerning a flagged record is made in writing, the school, day care facility, or agency may not advise the party that the request concerns a missing child and shall immediately notify the appropriate law enforcement agency that a request has been made concerning a flagged record and provide to the law enforcement agency a copy of the written request. After providing the notification under this subsection, the school, day care facility, or agency shall mail a copy of the requested record to the requesting party on or after the 21st day after the date of the request.

History of CCP art. 63.021: Acts 1999, 76th Leg., ch. 62, §19.01(8)(B), eff. Sept. 1, 1999. Source: Hum. Res. Code §79.019.

ART. 63.022. REMOVAL OF FLAG FROM RECORDS

(a) On the return of a missing child under 11 years of age, the law enforcement agency shall notify each school or day care facility that has maintained flagged records for the child and the bureau of vital statistics that the child is no longer missing. The law enforcement agency shall notify the clearinghouse that notification under this section has been made. The bureau of vital statistics shall notify the appropriate municipal or county birth certificate agency. The clearinghouse shall notify the school, day care facility, or bureau of vital statistics that the missing child is no longer missing if the clearinghouse determines that the notification was not provided by the law enforcement agency.

(b) On notification by the law enforcement agency or the clearinghouse that a missing child has been recovered, the school, day care facility, or birth certificate agency that maintained flagged records shall remove the flag from the records.

(c) A school, day care facility, or birth certificate agency that has reason to believe a missing child has been recovered may request confirmation that the missing child has been recovered from the appropriate law enforcement agency or the clearinghouse. If a response is not received after the 45th day after the date

of the request for confirmation, the school, day care facility, or birth certificate agency may remove the flag from the record and shall inform the law enforcement agency or the clearinghouse that the flag has been removed.

History of CCP art. 63.022: Acts 1999, 76th Leg., ch. 62, §19.01(8)(B), eff. Sept. 1, 1999. Source: Hum. Res. Code §79.020.

SUBCHAPTER B. UNIVERSITY OF NORTH TEXAS HEALTH SCIENCE CENTER AT FORT WORTH MISSING PERSONS DNA DATABASE

ART. 63.051. DEFINITIONS

In this subchapter:

(1) "Board" means the board of regents of the University of North Texas System.

(2) "Center" means the University of North Texas Health Science Center at Fort Worth.

(3) "DNA" means deoxyribonucleic acid.

(4) "DNA database" means the database containing forensic DNA analysis results, including any known name of the person who is the subject of the forensic DNA analysis, that is maintained by the center.

(5) "High-risk missing person" means:

(A) a person missing as a result of an abduction by a stranger;

(B) a person missing under suspicious or unknown circumstances; or

(C) a person who has been missing more than 30 days, or less than 30 days at the discretion of the investigating agency, if there is reason to believe that the person is in danger or deceased.

(6) "Law enforcement agency" means the law enforcement agency primarily responsible for investigating a report of a high-risk missing person.

History of CCP art. 63.051: Codified by Acts 2005, 79th Leg., ch. 319, §2, eff. June 17, 2005. Source: Educ. Code §105.451.

ART. 63.052. ESTABLISHMENT OF DNA DATABASE FOR MISSING OR UNIDENTIFIED PERSONS

(a) The board shall develop at the University of North Texas Health Science Center at Fort Worth a DNA database for any case based on the report of unidentified human remains or a report of a high-risk missing person.

(b) The sole purpose of the database is to identify unidentified human remains and high-risk missing persons.

(c) The database is separate from the database established by the Department of Public Safety under Subchapter G, Chapter 411, Government Code.

History of CCP art. 63.052: Codified by Acts 2005, 79th Leg., ch. 319, §2, eff. June 17, 2005. Source: Educ. Code §105.452.

ART. 63.053. INFORMATION STORED IN DATABASE

(a) The database required in Article 63.052 may contain only DNA genetic markers that are commonly recognized as appropriate for human identification. Except to the extent that those markers are appropriate for human identification, the database may not contain DNA genetic markers that predict biological function. The center shall select the DNA genetic markers for inclusion in the DNA database based on existing technology for forensic DNA analysis.

(b) The results of the forensic DNA analysis must be compatible with the CODIS DNA database established by the Federal Bureau of Investigation and the center must make the results available for inclusion in that database.

History of CCP art. 63.053: Codified by Acts 2005, 79th Leg., ch. 319, §2, eff. June 17, 2005. Source: Educ. Code §105.453.

ART. 63.054. COMPARISON OF SAMPLES

The center shall compare DNA samples taken from unidentified human remains with DNA samples taken from personal articles belonging to high-risk missing persons or from parents of high-risk missing persons or other appropriate persons.

History of CCP art. 63.054: Codified by Acts 2005, 79th Leg., ch. 319, §2, eff. June 17, 2005. Source: Educ. Code §105.454.

ART. 63.055. STANDARDS COLLECTION; STORAGE

In consultation with the center, the board by rule shall develop standards and guidelines for the collection of DNA samples submitted to the center and the center's storage of DNA samples.

History of CCP art. 63.055: Codified by Acts 2005, 79th Leg., ch. 319, §2, eff. June 17, 2005. Source: Educ. Code §105.455.

ART. 63.056. COLLECTION OF SAMPLES FROM UNIDENTIFIED HUMAN REMAINS

(a) A physician acting on the request of a justice of the peace under Subchapter A, Chapter 49, a county coroner, a county medical examiner, or other law enforcement entity, as appropriate, shall collect samples

from unidentified human remains. The justice of the peace, coroner, medical examiner, or other law enforcement entity shall submit those samples to the center for forensic DNA analysis and inclusion of the results in the DNA database.

(b) After the center has performed the forensic DNA analysis, the center shall return the remaining sample to the entity that submitted the sample under Subsection (a).

History of CCP art. 63.056: Codified and amended by Acts 2005, 79th Leg., ch. 319, §2, eff. June 17, 2005. Source: Educ. Code §105.456.

ART. 63.057. DUTY OF LAW ENFORCEMENT AGENCY TO NOTIFY APPROPRIATE PERSONS REGARDING PROVISION OF VOLUNTARY SAMPLE

Not later than the 30th day after the date a report of a high-risk missing person is filed, the law enforcement agency shall inform a parent or any other person considered appropriate by the agency that the person may provide:

(1) a DNA sample for forensic DNA analysis; or

(2) for purposes of DNA sampling, a personal article belonging to the high-risk missing person.

History of CCP art. 63.057: Codified by Acts 2005, 79th Leg., ch. 319, §2, eff. June 17, 2005. Source: Educ. Code §105.457.

ART. 63.058. RELEASE FORM

(a) The center shall develop a standard release form that authorizes a parent or other appropriate person to voluntarily provide under Article 63.057 a DNA sample or a personal article for purposes of DNA sampling. The release must explain that the DNA sample is to be used only to identify the high-risk missing person.

(b) A law enforcement agency may not use any form of incentive or coercion to compel the parent or other appropriate person to provide a sample or article under this subchapter.

History of CCP art. 63.058: Codified by Acts 2005, 79th Leg., ch. 319, §2, eff. June 17, 2005. Source: Educ. Code §105.458.

ART. 63.059. PROTOCOL FOR OBTAINING SAMPLES RELATING TO HIGH-RISK MISSING PERSONS

(a) The law enforcement agency shall take DNA samples from parents or other appropriate persons under Article 63.057 in any manner prescribed by the center.

(b) The center shall develop a model kit to be used by a law enforcement agency to take DNA samples from parents or other appropriate persons.

History of CCP art. 63.059: Codified by Acts 2005, 79th Leg., ch. 319, §2, eff. June 17, 2005. Source: Educ. Code §105.459.

ART. 63.060. SUBMISSION OF SAMPLE TO CENTER

(a) Before submitting to the center a DNA sample obtained under Article 63.057, the law enforcement agency shall reverify the status of a high-risk missing person.

(b) As soon as practicable after a DNA sample is obtained, the law enforcement agency shall submit the DNA sample, a copy of the missing person's report, and any supplemental information to the center.

History of CCP art. 63.060: Codified by Acts 2005, 79th Leg., ch. 319, §2, eff. June 17, 2005. Source: Educ. Code §105.460.

ART. 63.061. DESTRUCTION OF SAMPLES

All DNA samples extracted from a living person shall be destroyed after a positive identification is made and a report is issued.

History of CCP art. 63.061: Codified by Acts 2005, 79th Leg., ch. 319, §2, eff. June 17, 2005. Source: Educ. Code §105.461.

ART. 63.062. CONFIDENTIALITY

(a) Except as provided by Subsection (b), the results of a forensic DNA analysis performed by the center are confidential.

(b) The center may disclose the results of a forensic DNA analysis only to:

(1) personnel of the center;

(2) law enforcement agencies;

(3) justices of the peace, coroners, medical examiners, or other law enforcement entities submitting a sample to the center under Article 63.056;

(4) attorneys representing the state; and

(5) a parent or other appropriate person voluntarily providing a DNA sample or an article under Article 63.057.

History of CCP art. 63.062: Codified and amended by Acts 2005, 79th Leg., ch. 319, §2, eff. June 17, 2005. Source: Educ. Code §105.462.

ART. 63.063. CRIMINAL PENALTY

(a) A person who collects, processes, or stores a DNA sample from a living person for forensic DNA analysis under this subchapter commits an offense if the person intentionally violates Article 63.061 or 63.062.

(b) An offense under this section is a Class B misdemeanor.

History of CCP art. 63.063: Codified by Acts 2005, 79th Leg., ch. 319, §2, eff. June 17, 2005. Source: Educ. Code §105.463.

ART. 63.064. CIVIL PENALTY

A person who collects, processes, or stores a DNA sample from a living person for forensic DNA analysis under this subchapter and who intentionally violates Article 63.061 or 63.062 is liable in civil damages to the donor of the DNA in the amount of $5,000 for each violation, plus reasonable attorney's fees and court costs.

History of CCP art. 63.064: Codified by Acts 2005, 79th Leg., ch. 319, §2, eff. June 17, 2005. Source: Educ. Code §105.464.

ART. 63.065. MISSING PERSONS DNA DATABASE FUND

(a) The missing persons DNA database fund is a separate account in the general revenue fund.

(b) Notwithstanding Article 56.54(g), the legislature may appropriate money in the compensation to victims of crime fund and the compensation to victims of crime auxiliary fund to fund the University of North Texas Health Science Center at Fort Worth missing persons DNA database. Legislative appropriations under this subsection shall be deposited to the credit of the account created under Subsection (a).

(c) Money in the account may be used only for purposes of developing and maintaining the DNA database as described by this section.

(d) The center may use money in the account only to:

(1) establish and maintain center infrastructure;

(2) pay the costs of DNA sample storage, forensic DNA analysis, and labor costs for cases of high-risk missing persons and unidentified human remains;

(3) reimburse counties for the purposes of pathology and exhumation as considered necessary by the center;

(4) publicize the DNA database for the purpose of contacting parents and other appropriate persons so that they may provide a DNA sample or a personal article for DNA sampling;

(5) educate law enforcement officers about the DNA database and DNA sampling; and

(6) provide outreach programs related to the purposes of this chapter.

(e) Section 403.095(b), Government Code, does not apply to the account established under Subsection (a).

History of CCP art. 63.065: Codified by Acts 2005, 79th Leg., ch. 319, §2, eff. June 17, 2005. Source: Educ. Code §105.465.

ART. 63.066. BACKLOG OF UNIDENTIFIED HUMAN REMAINS: ADVISORY COMMITTEE & OUTSOURCING

(a) The center shall create an advisory committee, consisting of medical examiners, law enforcement officials, and other interested persons as determined appropriate by the center, to impose priorities regarding the identification of the backlog of high-risk missing person cases and unidentified human remains.

(b) The center shall use any available federal funding to assist in reducing the backlog of high-risk missing person cases and unidentified human remains.

(c) The reduction of the backlog may be outsourced to other appropriate laboratories at the center's discretion.

History of CCP art. 63.066: Codified by Acts 2005, 79th Leg., ch. 319, §2, eff. June 17, 2005. Source: Educ. Code §105.466.

ART. 63.067. EXPIRED

CHAPTER 64. MOTION FOR FORENSIC DNA TESTING

ART. 64.01. MOTION

(a) A convicted person may submit to the convicting court a motion for forensic DNA testing of evidence containing biological material. The motion must be accompanied by an affidavit, sworn to by the convicted person, containing statements of fact in support of the motion.

(b) The motion may request forensic DNA testing only of evidence described by Subsection (a) that was secured in relation to the offense that is the basis of the challenged conviction and was in the possession of the state during the trial of the offense, but:

(1) was not previously subjected to DNA testing:

(A) because DNA testing was:

(i) not available; or

(ii) available, but not technologically capable of providing probative results; or

(B) through no fault of the convicted person, for reasons that are of a nature such that the interests of justice require DNA testing; or

(2) although previously subjected to DNA testing, can be subjected to testing with newer testing techniques that provide a reasonable likelihood of results that are more accurate and probative than the results of the previous test.

 Subsection (c) below is effective for motions for forensic DNA testing filed on or after Sept. 1, 2007.

(c) A convicted person is entitled to counsel during a proceeding under this chapter. The convicting court shall appoint counsel for the convicted person if the person informs the court that the person wishes to submit a motion under this chapter, the court finds reasonable grounds for a motion to be filed, and the court determines that the person is indigent. Counsel must be appointed under this subsection not later than the 45th day after the date the court finds reasonable grounds or the date the court determines that the person is indigent, whichever is later. Compensation of counsel is provided in the same manner as is required by:

(1) Article 11.071 for the representation of a petitioner convicted of a capital felony; and

(2) Chapter 26 for the representation in a habeas corpus hearing of an indigent defendant convicted of a felony other than a capital felony.

Subsection (c) below is effective for motions for forensic DNA testing filed before Sept. 1, 2007.

(c) A convicted person is entitled to counsel during a proceeding under this chapter. The convicting court shall appoint counsel for the convicted person if the person informs the court that the person wishes to submit a motion under this chapter, the court finds reasonable grounds for a motion to be filed, and the court determines that the person is indigent. Compensation of counsel is provided in the same manner as is required by:

(1) Article 11.071 for the representation of a petitioner convicted of a capital felony; and

(2) Chapter 26 for the representation in a habeas corpus hearing of an indigent defendant convicted of a felony other than a capital felony.

History of CCP art. 64.01: Acts 2001, 77th Leg., ch. 2, §2, eff. April 5, 2001. Amended by Acts 2003, 78th Leg., ch. 13, §1, eff. Sept. 1, 2003; Acts 2007, 80th Leg., ch. 1006, §2, eff. Sept. 1, 2007.

See also Gov't Code §§411.141-411.154.

ANNOTATIONS

Routier v. State, ___ S.W.3d ___ (Tex.Crim.App. 2008) (No. AP-75,617; 6-18-08). "As long as it would have been apparent to the appellant at the time of trial that the other individual blood stains on the [evidence] would (or even might) have discrete and independent probative value, the overall import of the statute mandates that she seek such testing at that time, or forego testing later. Accordingly, we construe 'evidence containing biological material' [in subsection (a)] to mean individual samples of biological material, even if taken from the same physical object or source, that have (or may conceivably have) discrete and independent probative value for purposes of the particular issues at trial."

Ex parte Suhre, 185 S.W.3d 898, 899 (Tex.Crim. App.2006). "In *Ex parte Baker*, 185 S.W.3d 894, 898 (Tex.Crim.App.2006), ... we held ... that 'the post-conviction writ of habeas corpus is not available for ... claims of ineffective assistance of counsel in [CCP ch. 64 DNA] proceedings.' However, ... we noted that 'Chapter 64 does not prohibit a second, or successive, motion for forensic DNA testing, and ... a convicting court may order testing of material that was not previously tested through no fault of the convicted person [if] the interests of justice require DNA testing.' Therefore, it is conceivable that a convicted person who receives ineffective assistance of counsel in a DNA proceeding may be entitled to relief by way of a second DNA proceeding." *See also Ex parte Baker*, 185 S.W.3d 894, 894 (Tex.Crim.App.2006).

State v. Young, 242 S.W.3d 926, 929 (Tex.App.— Dallas 2008, no pet.). "Young filed a motion requesting post-conviction forensic DNA testing under [CCP ch.] 64. Young, however, has not been convicted of a crime. Rather, his finding of guilt was deferred, and he successfully completed his deferred adjudication probation. Because chapter 64 specifically provides that a convicted person may seek post-conviction DNA testing, it follows that a person who has not been convicted is not entitled to seek relief under chapter 64."

Welsh v. State, 108 S.W.3d 921, 922-23 (Tex.App.— Dallas 2003, no pet.). "As in the case of deferred adjudication, an order disposing of a motion for DNA testing under chapter 64 ... does not involve a finding of guilt or imposition or suspension of a sentence. Therefore,

we hold a motion for new trial is a nullity and is ineffective to extend the time for filing a notice of appeal."

ART. 64.011. GUARDIANS & OTHER REPRESENTATIVES

(a) In this chapter, "guardian of a convicted person" means a person who is the legal guardian of the convicted person, whether the legal relationship between the guardian and convicted person exists because of the age of the convicted person or because of the physical or mental incompetency of the convicted person.

(b) A guardian of a convicted person may submit motions for the convicted person under this chapter and is entitled to counsel otherwise provided to a convicted person under this chapter.

History of art. 64.011: Acts 2003, 78th Leg., ch. 13, §2, eff. Sept. 1, 2003.

ART. 64.02. NOTICE TO STATE; RESPONSE

Ⓐ *Article 64.02 below is effective for motions for forensic DNA testing filed on or after Sept. 1, 2007.*

(a) On receipt of the motion, the convicting court shall:

(1) provide the attorney representing the state with a copy of the motion; and

(2) require the attorney representing the state to take one of the following actions in response to the motion not later than the 60th day after the date the motion is served on the attorney representing the state:

(A) deliver the evidence to the court, along with a description of the condition of the evidence; or

(B) explain in writing to the court why the state cannot deliver the evidence to the court.

Ⓔ (b) The convicting court may proceed under Article 64.03 after the response period described by Subsection (a)(2) has expired, regardless of whether the attorney representing the state submitted a response under that subsection.

History of CCP art. 64.02: Acts 2001, 77th Leg., ch. 2, §2, eff. April 5, 2001. Amended by Acts 2007, 80th Leg., ch. 1006, §3, eff. Sept. 1, 2007.
See also Gov't Code §§411.141-411.154.

ART. 64.02. NOTICE TO STATE; RESPONSE

Article 64.02 below is effective for motions for forensic DNA testing filed before Sept. 1, 2007.

On receipt of the motion, the convicting court shall:

(1) provide the attorney representing the state with a copy of the motion; and

(2) require the attorney representing the state to:

(A) deliver the evidence to the court, along with a description of the condition of the evidence; or

(B) explain in writing to the court why the state cannot deliver the evidence to the court.

ART. 64.03. REQUIREMENTS; TESTING

(a) A convicting court may order forensic DNA testing under this chapter only if:

(1) the court finds that:

(A) the evidence:

(i) still exists and is in a condition making DNA testing possible; and

(ii) has been subjected to a chain of custody sufficient to establish that it has not been substituted, tampered with, replaced, or altered in any material respect; and

(B) identity was or is an issue in the case; and

(2) the convicted person establishes by a preponderance of the evidence that:

(A) the person would not have been convicted if exculpatory results had been obtained through DNA testing; and

(B) the request for the proposed DNA testing is not made to unreasonably delay the execution of sentence or administration of justice.

 Subsections (b)-(d) below are effective for motions for forensic DNA testing filed on or after Sept. 1, 2007.

(b) A convicted person who pleaded guilty or nolo contendere or, whether before or after conviction, made a confession or similar admission in the case may submit a motion under this chapter, and the convicting court is prohibited from finding that identity was not an issue in the case solely on the basis of that plea, confession, or admission, as applicable.

(c) If the convicting court finds in the affirmative the issues listed in Subsection (a)(1) and the convicted person meets the requirements of Subsection (a)(2), the court shall order that the requested forensic DNA testing be conducted. The court may order the test to be conducted by:

(1) the Department of Public Safety;

(2) a laboratory operating under a contract with the department; or

(3) on the request of the convicted person, another laboratory if that laboratory is accredited under Section 411.0205, Government Code.

(d) If the convicting court orders that the forensic DNA testing be conducted by a laboratory other than a Department of Public Safety laboratory or a laboratory under contract with the department, the State of Texas is not liable for the cost of testing under this subsection unless good cause for payment of that cost has been shown. A political subdivision of the state is not liable for the cost of testing under this subsection, regardless of whether good cause for payment of that cost has been shown. If the court orders that the testing be conducted by a laboratory described by this subsection, the court shall include in the order requirements that:

(1) the DNA testing be conducted in a timely and efficient manner under reasonable conditions designed to protect the integrity of the evidence and the testing process;

(2) the DNA testing employ a scientific method sufficiently reliable and relevant to be admissible under Rule 702, Texas Rules of Evidence; and

(3) on completion of the DNA testing, the results of the testing and all data related to the testing required for an evaluation of the test results be immediately filed with the court and copies of the results and data be served on the convicted person and the attorney representing the state.

Subsections (b)-(d) below are effective for motions for forensic DNA testing filed before Sept. 1, 2007.

(b) A convicted person who pleaded guilty or nolo contendere in the case may submit a motion under this chapter, and the convicting court is prohibited from finding that identity was not an issue in the case solely on the basis of that plea.

(c) If the convicting court finds in the affirmative the issues listed in Subsection (a)(1) and the convicted person meets the requirements of Subsection (a)(2), the court shall order that the requested forensic DNA testing be conducted. The court may order the test to be conducted by the Department of Public Safety, by a laboratory operating under a contract with the department, or, on agreement of the parties, by another laboratory.

(d) If the convicting court orders that the forensic DNA testing be conducted by a laboratory other than a

Department of Public Safety laboratory or a laboratory under contract with the department, the State of Texas is not liable for the cost of testing. If the court orders that the testing be conducted by a laboratory described by this subsection, the court shall include in the order requirements that:

(1) the DNA testing be conducted under reasonable conditions designed to protect the integrity of the evidence and the testing process;

(2) the DNA testing employ a scientific method sufficiently reliable and relevant to be admissible under Rule 702, Texas Rules of Evidence; and

(3) on completion of the DNA testing, the results of the testing and all data related to the testing required for an evaluation of the test results be immediately filed with the court and copies of the results and data be served on the convicted person and the attorney representing the state.

(e) The convicting court, not later than the 30th day after the conclusion of a proceeding under this chapter, shall forward the results to the Department of Public Safety.

History of CCP art. 64.03: Acts 2001, 77th Leg., ch. 2, §2, eff. April 5, 2001. Amended by Acts 2003, 78th Leg., ch. 13, §3, eff. Sept. 1, 2003; Acts 2007, 80th Leg., ch. 1006, §4, eff. Sept. 1, 2007.

See also Gov't Code §§411.141-411.154.

ANNOTATIONS

Blacklock v. State, 235 S.W.3d 231, 233 (Tex.Crim. App.2007). "That the victim testified that she knew appellant and identified him as her attacker is irrelevant to whether appellant's motion for DNA testing makes his identity an issue and whether it shows that exculpatory DNA tests would prove his innocence. The language and legislative history of Article 64.03(a)(1)(B) make it very clear that a defendant, who requests DNA testing, can make identity an issue by showing that exculpatory DNA tests would prove his innocence. This applies even when a defendant has pled guilty, thereby conceding the issue of identity at trial."

Thacker v. State, 177 S.W.3d 926, 927 (Tex.Crim. App.2005). "Appellant claims that his failure to file the motion [for DNA testing] was excused by the pendency of his federal application for writ of habeas corpus.... He asserts that 'habeas counsel was clearly of the view that the two-forum rule would not permit a dual filing in state and federal court.' But nothing legally prevented appellant from filing a motion for DNA testing during the pendency of his federal habeas proceedings. Unlike a state application for writ of habeas corpus, a motion for DNA testing cannot, by itself, result in relief from a conviction or sentence. It is simply a vehicle for obtaining a certain type of evidence, which might then be used in a state or federal habeas proceeding. Moreover, appellant does not assert that he made any attempt to ascertain whether a dual filing would be permitted—such as seeking leave from federal court to file a Chapter 64 motion, and appellant does not allege that he attempted to procure an abatement of federal proceedings to file a Chapter 64 motion, despite the fact that he now contends that DNA testing would provide him with crucial exculpating evidence."

Smith v. State, 165 S.W.3d 361, 365 (Tex.Crim.App. 2005). "Because the trial court took judicial notice of the trial record when he ruled on the motion, and the facts were included in the record, the trial court had enough evidence to determine by a preponderance of the evidence that favorable DNA results would have prevented Smith's conviction. The cause is remanded to the trial court to order DNA testing under Article 64.03(c)."

Bell v. State, 90 S.W.3d 301, 306 (Tex.Crim.App. 2002). Appellant "has not argued, or presented, affirmative evidence of how the presence of a third party's DNA would exonerate appellant. The presence of another person's DNA at the crime scene will not, without more, constitute affirmative evidence of appellant's innocence."

Rivera v. State, 89 S.W.3d 55, 58-59 (Tex.Crim.App. 2002). "Nothing in Article 64.03 requires a hearing of any sort concerning the trial court's determination of whether a defendant is entitled to DNA testing."

Dinkins v. State, 84 S.W.3d 639, 642 (Tex.Crim. App.2002). "Because appellant has failed to provide facts in support of his motion, we cannot say that the convicting court erroneously determined that appellant failed to show the existence of evidence containing biological material that should be subjected to DNA testing."

Flores v. State, 150 S.W.3d 750, 753 (Tex. App.—San Antonio 2004, no pet.). "Although the existence of [victim's] DNA sample for comparison [to DNA on murder weapon] purposes is not an express requirement of Article 64.03, a trial court is not precluded from considering the absence of a comparison sample when conducting its analysis under Article 64.03(a)(2)(A)."

Griggs v. State, 99 S.W.3d 718, 721 (Tex.App.—Houston [1st Dist.] 2003, pet. ref'd). A "convicted person has no constitutional right to be present at a postconviction DNA hearing, nor does he have a right to cross-examine witnesses." *See also Rose v. State*, 198 S.W.3d 271, 272 (Tex.App.—San Antonio 2006, pet. ref'd) (memo op.).

ART. 64.04. FINDING

After examining the results of testing under Article 64.03, the convicting court shall hold a hearing and make a finding as to whether, had the results been available during the trial of the offense, it is reasonably probable that the person would not have been convicted.

History of CCP art. 64.04: Acts 2001, 77th Leg., ch. 2, §2, eff. April 5, 2001. Amended by Acts 2003, 78th Leg., ch. 13, §4, eff. Sept. 1, 2003.

See also Gov't Code §§411.141-411.154.

ART. 64.05. APPEALS

An appeal under this chapter is to a court of appeals in the same manner as an appeal of any other criminal matter, except that if the convicted person was convicted in a capital case and was sentenced to death, the appeal is a direct appeal to the court of criminal appeals.

History of CCP art. 64.05: Acts 2001, 77th Leg., ch. 2, §2, eff. April 5, 2001. Amended by Acts 2003, 78th Leg., ch. 13, §5, eff. Sept. 1, 2003.

ANNOTATIONS

Swearingen v. State, 189 S.W.3d 779, 781 (Tex. Crim.App.2006). "[A] DNA movant must meet applicable filing and time requirements found in the [TRAP]. [¶] These requirements include filing a notice of appeal and filing that notice within thirty days after the appealable order is entered. The 'appealable order' in this case was the order denying DNA testing, entered on April 7, 2005. [¶] Although the trial court later denied other motions that may have been ancillary to the [CCP ch.] 64 proceeding, the outcome of the proceeding was decided on April 7th, and the appellate timetable ran from that date. ... Certainly, the trial court's orders denying the motions for extension of time, for an evidentiary hearing, and for discovery cannot be construed as some sort of modification or recision of the trial court's order denying testing. And although appellant's 'motion for entry of order' suggested that he was entitled to DNA testing, and the trial court denied that motion on May 10th, that order of denial was not tantamount to a new or 'modified' order denying DNA testing from which an appeal could lie."

Wolfe v. State, 120 S.W.3d 368, 372 (Tex.Crim.App. 2003). "[B]ecause the legislature has not specifically provided for appeals of issues unless they are within [CCP art.] 64.03 or 64.04, the trial court's refusal to appoint an expert [for an indigent defendant's CCP ch. 64 hearing] is not appealable under Chapter 64."

Rivera v. State, 89 S.W.3d 55, 59 (Tex.Crim.App. 2002). "In reviewing the trial court's decision, we employ the familiar bifurcated standard of review...: we afford almost total deference to a trial court's determination of issues of historical fact and application-of-law-to-fact issues that turn on credibility and demeanor, while we review *de novo* other application-of-law-to-fact issues." *See also Flores v. State*, 150 S.W.3d 750, 752 (Tex.App.—San Antonio 2004, no pet.).

Kutzner v. State, 75 S.W.3d 427, 431 (Tex.Crim. App.2002). "We hold that a Chapter 64 DNA proceeding is a 'criminal case' for [Tex. Const. art. 5,] §5 purposes."

In re Johnston, 79 S.W.3d 195, 198 (Tex.App.—Texarkana 2002, orig. proceeding). "When no written order is made, the movant's right to appeal is negated. [¶] We conclude the trial court is required to enter a written order in resolving a motion seeking DNA testing of evidence."

TITLE 2

CHAPTER 101. GENERAL PROVISIONS

ART. 101.001. PURPOSE OF TITLE

(a) This title is enacted as a part of the state's continuing statutory revision program, begun by the Texas Legislative Council in 1963 as directed by the legislature in Chapter 448, Acts of the 58th Legislature, Regular Session, 1963 (Article 5429b-1, Vernon's Texas Civil Statutes). The program contemplates a topic-by-topic revision of the state's general and permanent statute law without substantive change.

(b) Consistent with the objectives of the statutory revision program, the purpose of this title is to make the law encompassed by this title more accessible and understandable by:

(1) rearranging the statutes into a more logical order;

(2) employing a format and numbering system designed to facilitate citation of the law and to accommodate future expansion of the law;

(3) eliminating repealed, duplicative, unconstitutional, expired, executed, and other ineffective provisions; and

(4) restating the law in modern American English to the greatest extent possible.

History of CCP art. 101.001: Acts 1985, 69th Leg., ch. 269, §1, eff. Sept. 1, 1985.

ART. 101.002. CONSTRUCTION OF TITLE

The Code Construction Act (Article 5429b-2, Vernon's Texas Civil Statutes[1]) applies to the construction of each provision in this title, except as otherwise expressly provided by this title.

1. **Editor's note:** Repealed. Now Gov't Code §311.001 et seq.

History of CCP art. 101.002: Acts 1985, 69th Leg., ch. 269, §1, eff. Sept. 1, 1985.

See also Gov't Code ch. 311.

ART. 101.003. INTERNAL REFERENCES

In this title:

(1) a reference to a chapter or article without further identification is a reference to a chapter or article of this title; and

(2) a reference to a subchapter, article, subsection, subdivision, paragraph, or other numbered or lettered unit without further identification is a reference to a unit of the next larger unit of this title in which the reference appears.

History of CCP art. 101.003: Acts 1985, 69th Leg., ch. 269, §1, eff. Sept. 1, 1985.

CHAPTER 102. COSTS PAID BY DEFENDANTS

SUBCHAPTER A. GENERAL COSTS

ART. 102.001. FEES FOR SERVICES OF PEACE OFFICERS

(a) Repealed by Acts 1989, 71st Leg., ch. 826, §2, eff. Sept. 1, 1989.

Subsection (b) below was amended by Acts 1989, 71st Leg., ch. 347, §1, enacted May 31, 1989, effective Oct. 1, 1989, without reference to the conflicting repeal of art. 102.001 made by Acts 1989, 71st Leg., ch. 826, §2, enacted May 31, 1989, effective Sept. 1, 1989. For resolving conflicts, see p. V.

(b) In addition to fees provided by Subsection (a), a defendant required to pay fees under this article shall also pay 15 cents per mile for mileage required of an officer to perform a service listed in this subsection and to return from performing that service. If the service provided is the execution of a writ and the writ is directed to two or more persons or the officer executes more than one writ in a case, the defendant is required to pay only mileage actually and necessarily traveled. In calculating mileage, the officer must use the railroad or the most practical route by private conveyance. This subsection applies to:

(1) conveying a prisoner after conviction to the county jail;

(2) conveying a prisoner arrested on a warrant or capias issued in another county to the court or jail of the county in which the warrant or capias was issued; and

(3) traveling to execute criminal process, to summon or attach a witness, and to execute process not otherwise described by this article.

(c) to (e) Repealed by Acts 1989, 71st Leg., ch. 826, §2, eff. Sept. 1, 1989.

☠ *Subsection (f) below was amended by Acts 1989, 71st Leg., ch. 347, §1, enacted May 31, 1989, effective Oct. 1, 1989, without reference to the conflicting repeal of art. 102.001 made by Acts 1989, 71st Leg., ch. 826, §2, enacted May 31, 1989, effective Sept. 1, 1989. For resolving conflicts, see p. V.*

(f) An officer who receives fees imposed under Subsection (a)(1) of this section in a municipal court shall keep separate records of the funds collected and shall deposit the funds in the municipal treasury. The officer collecting the fees under Subsection (a)(1) or (a)(2) of this article in a justice, county, or district court shall keep separate records of the funds collected and shall deposit the funds in the county treasury.

(g) Relettered from (e) by Acts 1989, 71st Leg., ch. 2, §16.01(12), eff. Aug. 28, 1989, and repealed by Acts 1989, 71st Leg., ch. 826, §2, eff. Sept. 1, 1989.

☠ *Subsection (h) below was added by Acts 1989, 71st Leg., ch. 347, §1, enacted May 31, 1989, effective Oct. 1, 1989, without reference to the conflicting repeal of art. 102.001 made by Acts 1989, 71st Leg., ch. 826, §2, enacted May 31, 1989, effective Sept. 1, 1989. For resolving conflicts, see p. V.*

(h) The custodian of a municipal or county treasury who receives fees under Subsection (a)(1) of this article for services performed by peace officers employed by the state shall remit all fees to the comptroller of public accounts in the manner directed by the comptroller. The custodian of a county treasury who receives fees under Subsection (a)(2) of this article for services performed by peace officers employed by the state may retain $2 of the fee for the county and shall forward the remainder to the comptroller in the manner directed by the comptroller. All custodians of municipal and county treasuries who receive fees under Subsection (a)(1) or (a)(2) of this article shall keep records of the amount of funds collected that are on deposit with them and,

not later than the last day of the month following each calendar quarter, shall remit to the comptroller funds collected under Subsection (a)(1) or (a)(2) of this article during the preceding quarter in a manner directed by the comptroller. The municipality or county may retain all interest earned on those funds. The comptroller shall credit funds received under this subsection to the General Revenue Fund.

History of CCP art. 102.001: Acts 1985, 69th Leg., ch. 269, §1, eff. Sept. 1, 1985. Amended by Acts 1987, 70th Leg., ch. 167, §4.01(a) (eff. Sept. 1, 1987), ch. 821, §1 (eff. Sept. 1, 1987); Acts 1989, 71st Leg., ch. 2, §16.01(12) (eff. Aug. 28, 1989), ch. 347, §1 (eff. Oct. 1, 1989), ch. 826, §2 (eff. Sept. 1, 1989).

ART. 102.002. WITNESS FEES

(a) Repealed by Acts 1999, 76th Leg., ch. 580, §11(a), eff. Sept. 1, 1999.

☠ *Subsections (b) & (c) below were amended by Acts 1999, 76th Leg., ch. 1545, §63, enacted May 30, 1999, effective Sept. 1, 1999, without reference to the conflicting repeal of art. 102.002 made by Acts 1999, 76th Leg., ch. 580, §11(a), enacted May 22, 1999, effective Sept. 1, 1999. For resolving conflicts, see p. V.*

(b) The justices of the peace and municipal courts shall maintain a record of and the clerks of district and county courts and county courts at law shall keep a book and record in the book:

(1) the number and style of each criminal action before the court;

(2) the name of each witness subpoenaed, attached, or recognized to testify in the action; and

(3) whether the witness was a witness for the state or for the defendant.

(c) Except as otherwise provided by this subsection, a defendant is liable on conviction for the fees provided by this article for witnesses in the defendant's case. If a defendant convicted of a misdemeanor does not pay the defendant's fines and costs, the county or municipality, as appropriate, is liable for the fees provided by this article for witnesses in the defendant's case.

(d) If a person is subpoenaed as a witness in a criminal case and fails to appear, the person is liable for the costs of an attachment, unless he shows good cause to the court why he did not appear.

History of CCP art. 102.002: Acts 1985, 69th Leg., ch. 269, §1, eff. Sept. 1, 1985. Amended by Acts 1999, 76th Leg., ch. 580, §11(a) (eff. Sept. 1, 1999), ch. 1545, §63 (eff. Sept. 1, 1999).

ART. 102.003. REPEALED

Repealed by Acts 1995, 74th Leg., ch. 122, §4, eff. Sept. 1, 1995.

ART. 102.004. JURY FEE

(a) A defendant convicted by a jury in a trial before a justice or municipal court shall pay a jury fee of $3. A defendant in a justice or municipal court who requests a trial by jury and who withdraws the request not earlier than 24 hours before the time of trial shall pay a jury fee of $3, if the defendant is convicted of the offense or final disposition of the defendant's case is deferred. A defendant convicted by a jury in a county court, a county court at law, or a district court shall pay a jury fee of $20.

(b) If two or more defendants are tried jointly in a justice or municipal court, only one jury fee of $3 may be imposed under this article. If the defendants sever and are tried separately, each defendant convicted shall pay a jury fee.

(c) In this article, "conviction" has the meaning assigned by Section 133.101, Local Government Code.

History of CCP art. 102.004: Acts 1985, 69th Leg., ch. 269, §1, eff. Sept. 1, 1985. Amended by Acts 1989, 71st Leg., ch. 1080, §3, eff. Sept. 1, 1989; Acts 1995, 74th Leg., ch. 122, §2, eff. Sept. 1, 1995; Acts 1999, 76th Leg., ch. 1545, §64, eff. Sept. 1, 1999; Acts 2003, 78th Leg., ch. 209, §67(a), eff. Jan. 1, 2004.

ART. 102.0045. FEE FOR JURY REIMBURSEMENT TO COUNTIES

(a) A person convicted of any offense, other than an offense relating to a pedestrian or the parking of a motor vehicle, shall pay as a court cost, in addition to all other costs, a fee of $4 to be used to reimburse counties for the cost of juror services as provided by Section 61.0015, Government Code.

(b) The clerk of the court shall remit the fees collected under this article to the comptroller in the manner provided by Subchapter B, Chapter 133, Local Government Code. The comptroller shall deposit the fees in the jury service fund.

(c) The jury service fund is created in the state treasury. If, at any time, the unexpended balance of the jury service fund exceeds $10 million, the comptroller shall transfer the amount in excess of $10 million to the fair defense account.

(d) Fees deposited in the jury service fund under this section are exempt from the application of Section 403.095, Government Code.

History of CCP art. 102.0045: Acts 2005, 79th Leg., ch. 1360, §5, eff. Sept. 1, 2005.

ART. 102.005. FEES TO CLERKS

(a) A defendant convicted of an offense in a county court, a county court at law, or a district court shall pay for the services of the clerk of the court a fee of $40.

(b) In this article, a person is considered convicted if:

(1) a sentence is imposed on the person;

(2) the person receives community supervision, including deferred adjudication; or

(3) the court defers final disposition of the person's case.

(c) Except as provided by Subsection (d), the fee imposed under Subsection (a) is for all clerical duties performed by the clerk, including:

(1) filing a complaint or information;

(2) docketing the case;

(3) taxing costs against the defendant;

(4) issuing original writs and subpoenas;

(5) swearing in and impaneling a jury;

(6) receiving and recording the verdict;

(7) filing each paper entered in the case; and

(8) swearing in witnesses in the case.

(d) The fee imposed by law for issuing a certified or noncertified copy is in addition to the fee imposed by Subsection (a). The clerk may issue a copy only if a person requests the copy and pays the appropriate fee as required by Sections 118.011, 118.014, 118.0145, 118.052, 118.060, and 118.0605, Local Government Code, and Sections 51.318 and 51.319, Government Code.

(e) Repealed by Acts 1999, 76th Leg., ch. 580, §11(b), eff. Sept. 1, 1999.

(f) A defendant convicted of an offense in a county court, a county court at law, or a district court shall pay a fee of $25 for records management and preservation services performed by the county as required by Chapter 203, Local Government Code. The fee shall be collected and distributed by the clerk of the court to the county treasurer, or to an official who discharges the duties commonly delegated to the county treasurer, for deposit as follows:

(1) $22.50 to the county records management and preservation fund for records management and preservation, including automation, in various county offices; and

(2) $2.50 to the records management and preservation fund of the clerk of the court for records management and preservation services performed by the clerk of the court.

(g) A fee deposited in accordance with Subsection (f) may be used only to provide funds for specific records management and preservation, including for automation purposes, on approval by the commissioners court of a budget as provided by Chapter 111, Local Government Code.

(h) An expenditure from a records management and preservation fund must comply with Subchapter C, Chapter 262, Local Government Code.

History of CCP art. 102.005: Acts 1985, 69th Leg., ch. 269, §1, eff. Sept. 1, 1985. Amended by Acts 1989, 71st Leg., ch. 1080, §4, eff. Sept. 1, 1989; Acts 1993, 73rd Leg., ch. 675, §6, eff. Sept. 1, 1993; Acts 1995, 74th Leg., ch. 764, §1, eff. Aug. 28, 1995; Acts 1999, 76th Leg., ch. 580, §11(b) (eff. Sept. 1, 1999), ch. 1031, §1 (eff. Sept. 1, 1999); Acts 2005, 79th Leg., ch. 804, §2, eff. June 17, 2005.

ART. 102.006. FEES IN EXPUNCTION PROCEEDINGS

In addition to any other fees required by other law, a petitioner seeking expunction of a criminal record shall pay the following fees:

(1) the fee charged for filing an ex parte petition in a civil action in district court;

(2) $1 plus postage for each certified mailing of notice of the hearing date; and

(3) $2 plus postage for each certified mailing of certified copies of an order of expunction.

History of CCP art. 102.006: Acts 1985, 69th Leg., ch. 269, §1, eff. Sept. 1, 1985. Amended by Acts 2005, 79th Leg., ch. 886, §4, eff. Sept. 1, 2005.

ART. 102.007. FEE FOR COLLECTING & PROCESSING SIGHT ORDER

(a) A county attorney, district attorney, or criminal district attorney may collect a fee if his office collects and processes a check or similar sight order if the check or similar sight order:

(1) has been issued or passed in a manner that makes the issuance or passing an offense under:

(A) Section 31.03, Penal Code;

(B) Section 31.04, Penal Code; or

(C) Section 32.41, Penal Code; or

(2) has been forged, as defined by Section 32.21, Penal Code.

(b) The county attorney, district attorney, or criminal district attorney may collect the fee from any person who is a party to the offense described in Subsection (a).

(c) The amount of the fee may not exceed:

(1) $10 if the face amount of the check or sight order does not exceed $10;

(2) $15 if the face amount of the check or sight order is greater than $10 but does not exceed $100;

(3) $30 if the face amount of the check or sight order is greater than $100 but does not exceed $300;

(4) $50 if the face amount of the check or sight order is greater than $300 but does not exceed $500; and

(5) $75 if the face amount of the check or sight order is greater than $500.

(d) If the person from whom the fee is collected was a party to the offense of forgery, as defined by Section 32.21, Penal Code, committed by altering the face amount of the check or sight order, the face amount as altered governs for the purposes of determining the amount of the fee.

(e) In addition to the collection fee specified in Subsection (c) of this article, the county attorney, district attorney, or criminal district attorney may collect the fee authorized by Section 3.506, Business & Commerce Code, for the benefit of the holder of a check or its assignee, agent, representative, or any other person retained by the holder to seek collection of the check.

(f) Fees collected under Subsection (c) of this article shall be deposited in the county treasury in a special fund to be administered by the county attorney, district attorney, or criminal district attorney. Expenditures from this fund shall be at the sole discretion of the attorney and may be used only to defray the salaries and expenses of the prosecutor's office, but in no event may the county attorney, district attorney, or criminal district attorney supplement his or her own salary from this fund.

E *Subsection (g) below is effective for offenses committed on or after Sept. 1, 2007.*

(g) In addition to the collection fee specified in Subsections (b) and (c), the issuer of a check or similar sight order that has been issued or passed as described by Subsection (a)(1) is liable for a fee in an amount equal to the costs of delivering notification by registered or certified mail with return receipt requested. The fee under this subsection must be collected in all cases described by Subsection (a)(1), and on receipt of proof of the actual costs expended, the fee shall be remitted to the holder of the check or similar sight order.

History of CCP art. 102.007: Acts 1985, 69th Leg., ch. 269, §1, eff. Sept. 1, 1985. Amended by Acts 1991, 72nd Leg., ch. 396, §2, eff. Sept. 1, 1991; Acts 1997, 75th Leg., ch. 256, §1, eff. Sept. 1, 1997; Acts 1999, 76th Leg., ch. 49, §1, eff. Sept. 1, 1999; Acts 2001, 77th Leg., ch. 1420, §2.001(b), eff. Sept. 1, 2001; Acts 2007, 80th Leg., ch. 976, §3, eff. Sept. 1, 2007.

ART. 102.0071. JUSTICE COURT DISHONORED CHECK

On conviction in justice court of an offense under Section 32.41, Penal Code, or an offense under Section 31.03 or 31.04, Penal Code, in which it is shown that the defendant committed the offense by issuing or passing a check that was subsequently dishonored, the court may collect from the defendant and pay to the holder of the check the fee permitted by Section 3.506, Business & Commerce Code.

History of CCP art. 102.0071: Acts 1991, 72nd Leg., ch. 396, §2, eff. Sept. 1, 1991. Amended by Acts 2001, 77th Leg., ch. 1420, §2.001(c), eff. Sept. 1, 2001.

ART. 102.008. FEES FOR SERVICES OF PROSECUTORS

(a) Except as provided by Subsection (b), a defendant convicted of a misdemeanor or a gambling offense shall pay a fee of $25 for the trying of the case by the district or county attorney. If the court appoints an attorney to represent the state in the absence of the district or county attorney, the appointed attorney is entitled to the fee otherwise due.

(b) No fee for the trying of a case may be charged against a defendant prosecuted in a justice court for violation of a penal statute or of the Uniform Act Regulating Traffic on Highways.

(c) If two or more defendants are tried jointly, only one fee may be charged under this article. If the defendants sever and are tried separately, each defendant shall pay the fee.

(d) A defendant is liable for fees imposed by Subsection (a) if the defendant is convicted of an offense and:

(1) the defendant does not appeal the conviction; or

(2) the conviction is affirmed on appeal.

History of CCP art. 102.008: Acts 1985, 69th Leg., ch. 269, §1, eff. Sept. 1, 1985. Amended by Acts 1989, 71st Leg., ch. 1080, §5, eff. Sept. 1, 1989.

ART. 102.009. COURT COSTS IN CERTAIN COUNTIES

In counties with a population of 3.3 million or more, the commissioners court may set court costs for persons convicted of a Class C misdemeanor in the justice courts. Court costs set as provided by this article may not exceed $7 for each conviction.

History of CCP art. 102.009: Acts 1985, 69th Leg., ch. 269, §1, eff. Sept. 1, 1985. Amended by Acts 2001, 77th Leg., ch. 669, §9, eff. Sept. 1, 2001.

Article 102.010 reserved for expansion

ART. 102.011. FEES FOR SERVICES OF PEACE OFFICERS

(a) A defendant convicted of a felony or a misdemeanor shall pay the following fees for services performed in the case by a peace officer:

(1) $5 for issuing a written notice to appear in court following the defendant's violation of a traffic law, municipal ordinance, or penal law of this state, or for making an arrest without a warrant;

Subsection (2) below is effective for fees imposed for the execution or processing of a warrant or capias issued for offenses committed on or after Sept. 1, 2007.

(2) $50 for executing or processing an issued arrest warrant, capias, or capias pro fine with the fee imposed for the services of:

(A) the law enforcement agency that executed the arrest warrant or capias, if the agency requests of the court, not later than the 15th day after the date of the execution of the arrest warrant or capias, the imposition of the fee on conviction; or

(B) the law enforcement agency that processed the arrest warrant or capias, if:

(i) the arrest warrant or capias was not executed; or

(ii) the executing law enforcement agency failed to request the fee within the period required by Paragraph (A) of this subdivision;

Subsection (2) below is effective for fees imposed for the execution or processing of a warrant or capias issued for offenses in which any element of the offense was committed before Sept. 1, 2007.

(2) $50 for executing or processing an issued arrest warrant or capias, with the fee imposed for the services of:

(A) the law enforcement agency that executed the arrest warrant or capias, if the agency requests of the court, not later than the 15th day after the date of the execution of the arrest warrant or capias, the imposition of the fee on conviction; or

(B) the law enforcement agency that processed the arrest warrant or capias, if the executing law enforcement agency failed to request the fee within the period required by Paragraph (A) of this subdivision;

(3) $5 for summoning a witness;

(4) $35 for serving a writ not otherwise listed in this article;

(5) $10 for taking and approving a bond and, if necessary, returning the bond to the courthouse;

(6) $5 for commitment or release;

(7) $5 for summoning a jury, if a jury is summoned; and

(8) $8 for each day's attendance of a prisoner in a habeas corpus case if the prisoner has been remanded to custody or held to bail.

(b) In addition to fees provided by Subsection (a) of this article, a defendant required to pay fees under this article shall also pay 29 cents per mile for mileage required of an officer to perform a service listed in this subsection and to return from performing that service. If the service provided is the execution of a writ and the writ is directed to two or more persons or the officer executes more than one writ in a case, the defendant is required to pay only mileage actually and necessarily traveled. In calculating mileage, the officer must use the railroad or the most practical route by private conveyance. The defendant shall also pay all necessary and reasonable expenses for meals and lodging incurred by the officer in the performance of services under this subsection, to the extent such expenses meet the requirements of Section 611.001, Government Code. This subsection applies to:

(1) conveying a prisoner after conviction to the county jail;

(2) conveying a prisoner arrested on a warrant or capias issued in another county to the court or jail of the county; and

(3) traveling to execute criminal process, to summon or attach a witness, and to execute process not otherwise described by this article.

(c) If an officer attaches a witness on the order of a court outside the county, the defendant shall pay $10 per day or part of a day spent by the officer conveying the witness and actual necessary expenses for travel by the most practical public conveyance. In order to receive expenses under this subsection, the officer must make a sworn statement of the expenses and the judge issuing the attachment must approve the statement.

(d) A defendant shall pay for the services of a sheriff or constable who serves process and attends an examining trial in a felony or a misdemeanor case the same fees allowed for those services in the trial of a felony or a misdemeanor, not to exceed $5.

(e) A fee under Subsection (a)(1) or (a)(2) of this article shall be assessed on conviction, regardless of whether the defendant was also arrested at the same time for another offense, and shall be assessed for each arrest made of a defendant arising out of the offense for which the defendant has been convicted.

(f) to **(h)** Repealed by Acts 2003, 78th Leg., ch. 209, §85(a)(5), eff. Jan. 1, 2004.

(i) In addition to fees provided by Subsections (a) through (g) of this article, a defendant required to pay fees under this article shall also pay the costs of overtime paid to a peace officer for time spent testifying in the trial of the case or for traveling to or from testifying in the trial of the case.

(j) In this article, "conviction" has the meaning assigned by Section 133.101, Local Government Code.

History of CCP art. 102.011: Acts 1987, 70th Leg., ch. 821, §2, eff. Sept. 1, 1987. Amended by Acts 1989, 71st Leg., ch. 826, §1, eff. Sept. 1, 1989; Acts 1991, 72nd Leg., ch. 575, §1, eff. Sept. 1, 1991; Acts 1993, 73rd Leg., ch. 988, §2.04(a), eff. Sept. 1, 1993; Acts 1995, 74th Leg., ch. 267, §1 (eff. Sept. 1, 1995), ch. 560, §1 (eff. Sept. 1, 1995); Acts 1999, 76th Leg., ch. 44, §1, eff. Sept. 1, 1999; Acts 2003, 78th Leg., ch. 209, §§68(a), 85(a)(5), eff. Jan. 1, 2004; Acts 2007, 80th Leg., ch. 1263, §§20, 21, eff. Sept. 1, 2007.

ART. 102.012. FEES FOR PRETRIAL INTERVENTION PROGRAMS

(a) A court that authorizes a defendant to participate in a pretrial intervention program established under Section 76.011, Government Code, may order the defendant to pay to the court a supervision fee in an amount not more than $60 per month as a condition of participating in the program.

 Subsection (b) below is effective for participation in a pretrial intervention program that begins on or after Sept. 1, 2007.

(b) In addition to or in lieu of the supervision fee authorized by Subsection (a), the court may order the defendant to pay or reimburse a community supervision and corrections department for any other expense that is:

(1) incurred as a result of the defendant's participation in the pretrial intervention program, other than an expense described by Article 102.0121; or

(2) necessary to the defendant's successful completion of the program.

Subsection (b) below is effective for participation in a pretrial intervention program that begins before Sept. 1, 2007.

(b) In addition to or in lieu of the supervision fee authorized by Subsection (a), the court may order the defendant to pay or reimburse a community supervision and corrections department for any other expense incurred as a result of the defendant's participation in the pretrial intervention program or that is necessary to the defendant's successful completion of the program.

History of CCP art. 102.012: Acts 1990, 71st Leg., 6th C.S., ch. 25, §20, eff. June 18, 1990. Amended by Acts 1995, 74th Leg., ch. 76, §7.16, eff. Sept. 1, 1995; Acts 2005, 79th Leg., ch. 91, §2, eff. Sept. 1, 2005; Acts 2007, 80th Leg., ch. 1226, §1, eff. Sept. 1, 2007.

ART. 102.0121. FEES FOR CERTAIN EXPENSES RELATED TO PRETRIAL INTERVENTION PROGRAMS

Article 102.0121 below is effective for participation in a pretrial intervention program that begins on or after Sept. 1, 2007.

(a) A district attorney, criminal district attorney, or county attorney may collect a fee in an amount not to exceed $500 to be used to reimburse a county for expenses, including expenses of the district attorney's, criminal district attorney's, or county attorney's office, related to a defendant's participation in a pretrial intervention program offered in that county.

(b) The district attorney, criminal district attorney, or county attorney may collect the fee from any defendant who participates in a pretrial intervention program administered in any part by the attorney's office.

(c) Fees collected under this article shall be deposited in the county treasury in a special fund to be used solely to administer the pretrial intervention program. An expenditure from the fund may be made only in accordance with a budget approved by the commissioners court.

History of CCP art. 102.0121: Acts 2007, 80th Leg., ch. 1226, §2, eff. Sept. 1, 2007.

ART. 102.013. COURT COSTS; CRIME STOPPERS ASSISTANCE ACCOUNT

(a) The legislature shall appropriate funds from the crime stoppers assistance account to the Criminal Justice Division of the Governor's Office. The Criminal Justice Division may use 10 percent of the funds for the operation of the toll-free telephone service under Section 414.012, Government Code, and shall distribute the remainder of the funds only to crime stoppers organizations. The Criminal Justice Division may adopt a budget and rules to implement the distribution of these funds.

(b) All funds distributed by the Criminal Justice Division under Subsection (a) of this article are subject to audit by the state auditor. All funds collected or distributed are subject to audit by the Governor's Division of Planning Coordination.

(c) In this article, "crime stoppers organization" has the meaning assigned by Section 414.001, Government Code.

History of CCP art. 102.013: Acts 1990, 71st Leg., 6th C.S., ch. 28, §1, eff. Sept. 6, 1990. Renumbered from art. 102.012 by Acts 1991, 72nd Leg., ch. 16, §19.01(7), eff. Aug. 26, 1991. Amended by Acts 1991, 72nd Leg., ch. 727, §2, eff. Sept. 1, 1991; Acts 1993, 73rd Leg., ch. 807, §2, eff. Aug. 30, 1993; Acts 1997, 75th Leg., ch. 700, §13 (eff. Sept. 1, 1997), ch. 1100, §1 (eff. Sept. 1, 1997).

ART. 102.014. COURT COSTS FOR CHILD SAFETY FUND IN MUNICIPALITIES

(a) The governing body of a municipality with a population greater than 850,000 according to the most recent federal decennial census that has adopted an ordinance, regulation, or order regulating the stopping, standing, or parking of vehicles as allowed by Section 542.202, Transportation Code, or Chapter 682, Transportation Code, shall by order assess a court cost on each parking violation not less than $2 and not to exceed $5. The court costs under this subsection shall be collected in the same manner that other fines in the case are collected.

(b) The governing body of a municipality with a population less than 850,000 according to the most recent federal decennial census that has adopted an ordinance, regulation, or order regulating the stopping, standing, or parking of vehicles as allowed by Section 542.202, Transportation Code, or Chapter 682, Transportation Code, may by order assess a court cost on each parking violation not to exceed $5. The additional court cost under this subsection shall be collected in the same manner that other fines in the case are collected.

(c) A person convicted of an offense under Subtitle C, Title 7, Transportation Code, when the offense occurs within a school crossing zone as defined by Section 541.302 of that code, shall pay as court costs $25 in addition to other taxable court costs. A person convicted of an offense under Section 545.066, Transportation Code, shall pay as court costs $25 in addition to other taxable court costs. The additional court costs under this subsection shall be collected in the same manner that other fines and taxable court costs in the case are collected and shall be assessed only in a municipality.

(d) A person convicted of an offense under Section 25.093 or 25.094, Education Code, shall pay as taxable court costs $20 in addition to other taxable court costs. The additional court costs under this subsection shall be collected in the same manner that other fines and taxable court costs in the case are collected.

(e) In this article, a person is considered to have been convicted in a case if the person would be considered to have been convicted under Section 133.101, Local Government Code.

(f) In a municipality with a population greater than 850,000 according to the most recent federal decennial census, the officer collecting the costs in a municipal court case shall deposit money collected under this article in the municipal child safety trust fund established as required by Chapter 106, Local Government Code.

(g) In a municipality with a population less than 850,000 according to the most recent federal decennial census, the money collected under this article in a municipal court case must be used for a school crossing guard program if the municipality operates one. If the municipality does not operate a school crossing guard program or if the money received from court costs from municipal court cases exceeds the amount necessary to fund the school crossing guard program, the municipality may either deposit the additional money in an interest-bearing account or expend it for programs designed to enhance child safety, health, or nutrition, including child abuse prevention and intervention and drug and alcohol abuse prevention.

(h) Money collected under this article in a justice, county, or district court shall be used to fund school crossing guard programs in the county where they are collected. If the county does not operate a school crossing guard program, the county may:

(1) remit fee revenues to school districts in its jurisdiction for the purpose of providing school crossing guard services;

(2) fund programs the county is authorized by law to provide which are designed to enhance child safety, health, or nutrition, including child abuse prevention and intervention and drug and alcohol abuse prevention;

(3) provide funding to the sheriff's department for school-related activities;

(4) provide funding to the county juvenile probation department; or

(5) deposit the money in the general fund of the county.

(i) Each collecting officer shall keep separate records of money collected under this article.

History of CCP art. 102.014: Acts 1991, 72nd Leg., ch. 830, §2, eff. July 1, 1991. Amended by Acts 1995, 74th Leg., ch. 76, §10.03, eff. Sept. 1, 1995; Acts 1997, 75th Leg., ch. 50, §1 (eff. Sept. 1, 1997), ch. 1384, §1 (eff. Sept. 1, 1997), ch. 165, §6.05 (eff. Sept. 1, 1997); Acts 2001, 77th Leg., ch. 983, §1 (eff. Sept. 1, 2001); ch. 1514, §10 (eff. Sept. 1, 2001), Acts 2003, 78th Leg., ch. 209, §69(a), eff. Jan. 1, 2004.

ART. 102.015. REPEALED
Repealed by Acts 1997, 75th Leg., ch. 1100, §6(2), eff. Sept. 1, 1997.

ART. 102.016. COSTS FOR BREATH ALCOHOL TESTING PROGRAM

(a) The custodians of municipal and county treasuries may deposit funds collected under this article in interest-bearing accounts and retain for the municipality or county interest earned on the funds. The custodians shall keep records of funds received and disbursed under this article and shall provide a yearly report of all funds received and disbursed under this article to the comptroller, the Department of Public Safety, and to each agency in the county served by the court that participates in or maintains a certified breath alcohol testing program. The comptroller shall approve the form of the report.

(b) The custodian of a municipal or county treasury in a county that maintains a certified breath alcohol testing program but does not use the services of a certified technical supervisor employed by the department may, to defray the costs of maintaining and supporting a certified alcohol breath testing program, retain $22.50 of each court cost collected under Article 102.075 on conviction of an offense under Chapter 49, Penal Code, other than an offense that is a Class C misdemeanor.

(c) The legislature may appropriate money deposited to the credit of the breath alcohol testing account in the general revenue fund under this subsection to the Department of Public Safety for use by the department in the implementation, administration, and maintenance of the statewide certified breath alcohol testing program.

(d) The Department of Public Safety shall maintain a list of counties that do not use the services of a certified technical supervisor employed by the department.

History of CCP art. 102.016: Acts 1991, 72nd Leg., 1st C.S., ch. 5, §5.03(a), eff. Sept. 1, 1991. Amended by Acts 1993, 73rd Leg., ch. 900, §3.03, eff. Sept. 1, 1994; Acts 1997, 75th Leg., ch. 1100, §2, eff. Sept. 1, 1997.

ART. 102.017. COURT COSTS; COURTHOUSE SECURITY FUND; MUNICIPAL COURT BUILDING SECURITY FUND; JUSTICE COURT BUILDING SECURITY FUND

(a) A defendant convicted of a felony offense in a district court shall pay a $5 security fee as a cost of court.

(b) A defendant convicted of a misdemeanor offense in a county court, county court at law, or district court shall pay a $3 security fee as a cost of court. A defendant convicted of a misdemeanor offense in a justice court shall pay a $4 security fee as a cost of court. The governing body of a municipality by ordinance may create a municipal court building security fund and may require a defendant convicted of a misdemeanor offense in a municipal court to pay a $3 security fee as a cost of court.

(c) In this article, a person is considered convicted if:

(1) a sentence is imposed on the person;

(2) the person receives community supervision, including deferred adjudication; or

(3) the court defers final disposition of the person's case.

Ⓐ (d) Except as provided by Subsection (d-2), the clerks of the respective courts shall collect the costs and pay them to the county or municipal treasurer, as appropriate, or to any other official who discharges the duties commonly delegated to the county or municipal treasurer, as appropriate, for deposit in a fund to be known as the courthouse security fund or a fund to be known as the municipal court building security fund, as appropriate. Money deposited in a courthouse security fund may be used only for security personnel, services, and items related to buildings that house the operations of district, county, or justice courts, and money deposited in a municipal court building security fund may be used only for security personnel, services, and items related to buildings that house the operations of municipal courts. For purposes of this subsection, operations of a district, county, or justice court include the activities of associate judges, masters, magistrates, referees, hearing officers, criminal law magistrate court judges, and masters in chancery appointed under:

(1) Section 61.311, Alcoholic Beverage Code;

(2) Section 51.04(g) or Chapter 201, Family Code;

(3) Section 574.0085, Health and Safety Code;

(4) Section 33.71, Tax Code;

(5) Chapter 54, Government Code; or

(6) Rule 171, Texas Rules of Civil Procedure.

Ⓐ (d-1) For purposes of this article, the term "security personnel, services, and items" includes:

(1) the purchase or repair of X-ray machines and conveying systems;

(2) handheld metal detectors;

(3) walkthrough metal detectors;

(4) identification cards and systems;

(5) electronic locking and surveillance equipment;

(6) bailiffs, deputy sheriffs, deputy constables, or contract security personnel during times when they are providing appropriate security services;

(7) signage;

(8) confiscated weapon inventory and tracking systems;

(9) locks, chains, alarms, or similar security devices;

(10) the purchase or repair of bullet-proof glass; and

(11) continuing education on security issues for court personnel and security personnel.

Ⓐ (d-2)(1) This subsection applies only to a justice court located in a county in which one or more justice courts are located in a building that is not the county courthouse.

(2) The county treasurer shall deposit one-fourth of the cost of court collected under Subsection (b) in a justice court described by Subdivision (1) into a fund to be known as the justice court building security fund. A fund designated by this subsection may be used only for the purpose of providing security personnel, services, and items for a justice court located in a building that is not the county courthouse.

(e) The courthouse security fund and the justice court building security fund shall be administered by or under the direction of the commissioners court. The municipal court building fund shall be administered by or under the direction of the governing body of the municipality.

Ⓔ (f) A local administrative judge shall provide to the Office of Court Administration of the Texas Judicial System a written report regarding any security incident involving court security that occurs in or around a building housing a court for which the judge serves as local administrative judge not later than the third business day after the date the incident occurred.

History of CCP art. 102.017: Acts 1993, 73rd Leg., ch. 818, §1, eff. Sept. 1, 1993. Amended by Acts 1995, 74th Leg., ch. 764, §2, eff. Aug. 28, 1995; Acts 1997, 75th Leg., ch. 12, §1, eff. Sept. 1, 1997; Acts 1999, 76th Leg., ch. 110, §1, eff. May 17, 1999; Acts 2005, 79th Leg., ch. 83, §2 (eff. Sept. 1, 2005), ch. 1087, §§1, 2 (eff. Sept. 1, 2005); Acts 2007, 80th Leg., ch. 221, §1, eff. Sept. 1, 2007.

ART. 102.0171. COURT COSTS: JUVENILE DELINQUENCY PREVENTION FUNDS

 Subsection (a) below is effective for offenses committed or conduct engaged in on or after Sept. 1, 2007.

(a) A defendant convicted of an offense under Section 28.08, Penal Code, in a county court, county court at law, or district court shall pay a $50 juvenile delinquency prevention and graffiti eradication fee as a cost of court.

Subsection (a) below is effective for offenses or conduct in which any element of the offense or conduct was committed or engaged in before Sept. 1, 2007.

(a) A defendant convicted of an offense under Section 28.08, Penal Code, in a county court, county court at law, or district court shall pay a $5 graffiti eradication fee as a cost of court.

(b) In this article, a person is considered convicted if:

(1) a sentence is imposed on the person;

(2) the person receives community supervision, including deferred adjudication; or

(3) the court defers final disposition of the person's case.

(c) The clerks of the respective courts shall collect the costs and pay them to the county treasurer or to any other official who discharges the duties commonly delegated to the county treasurer for deposit in a fund to be known as the county juvenile delinquency prevention fund. A fund designated by this subsection may be used only to:

(1) repair damage caused by the commission of offenses under Section 28.08, Penal Code;

 Subsection (2) below is effective for offenses committed or conduct engaged in on or after Sept. 1, 2007.

(2) provide educational and intervention programs and materials, including printed educational materials for distribution to primary and secondary school students, designed to prevent individuals from committing offenses under Section 28.08, Penal Code;

Subsection (2) below is effective for offenses or conduct in which any element of the offense or conduct was committed or engaged in before Sept. 1, 2007.

(2) provide educational and intervention programs designed to prevent individuals from committing offenses under Section 28.08, Penal Code;

(3) provide to the public rewards for identifying and aiding in the apprehension and prosecution of offenders who commit offenses under Section 28.08, Penal Code;

(4) provide funding for teen recognition and teen recreation programs;

(5) provide funding for local teen court programs;

(6) provide funding for the local juvenile probation department; and

(7) provide educational and intervention programs designed to prevent juveniles from engaging in delinquent conduct.

(d) The county juvenile delinquency prevention fund shall be administered by or under the direction of the commissioners court.

History of CCP art. 102.0171: Acts 1997, 75th Leg., ch. 593, §2, eff. Sept. 1, 1997. Amended by Acts 2003, 78th Leg., ch. 601, §§1, 2, eff. Sept. 1, 2003; Acts 2007, 80th Leg., ch. 1053, §3, eff. Sept. 1, 2007.

ART. 102.0172. COURT COSTS; MUNICIPAL COURT TECHNOLOGY FUND

(a) The governing body of a municipality by ordinance may create a municipal court technology fund and may require a defendant convicted of a misdemeanor offense in a municipal court or municipal court of record to pay a technology fee not to exceed $4 as a cost of court.

(b) In this article, a person is considered convicted if:

(1) a sentence is imposed on the person;

(2) the person is placed on community supervision, including deferred adjudication community supervision; or

(3) the court defers final disposition of the person's case.

(c) The municipal court clerk shall collect the costs and pay the funds to the municipal treasurer, or to any other official who discharges the duties commonly delegated to the municipal treasurer, for deposit in a fund to be known as the municipal court technology fund.

(d) A fund designated by this article may be used only to finance the purchase of or to maintain technological enhancements for a municipal court or municipal court of record, including:

(1) computer systems;

(2) computer networks;

(3) computer hardware;

(4) computer software;

(5) imaging systems;

(6) electronic kiosks;

(7) electronic ticket writers; and

(8) docket management systems.

(e) The municipal court technology fund shall be administered by or under the direction of the governing body of the municipality.

(f) Repealed by Acts 2003, 78th Leg., ch. 502, §2, eff. Sept. 1, 2003.

History of CCP art. 102.0172: Acts 1999, 76th Leg., ch. 285, §1, eff. Sept. 1, 1999. Amended by Acts 2003, 78th Leg., ch. 502, §§1, 2, eff. Sept. 1, 2003.

ART. 102.0173. COURT COSTS; JUSTICE COURT TECHNOLOGY FUND

(a) The commissioners court of a county by order shall create a justice court technology fund. A defendant convicted of a misdemeanor offense in justice court shall pay a $4 justice court technology fee as a cost of court for deposit in the fund.

(b) In this article, a person is considered convicted if:

(1) a sentence is imposed on the person; or

(2) the court defers final disposition of the person's case.

(c) The justice court clerk shall collect the costs and pay the funds to the county treasurer, or to any other official who discharges the duties commonly delegated to the county treasurer, for deposit in a fund to be known as the justice court technology fund.

(d) A fund designated by this article may be used only to finance:

(1) the cost of continuing education and training for justice court judges and clerks regarding technological enhancements for justice courts; and

(2) the purchase and maintenance of technological enhancements for a justice court, including:

(A) computer systems;

(B) computer networks;

(C) computer hardware;

(D) computer software;

(E) imaging systems;

(F) electronic kiosks;

(G) electronic ticket writers; and

(H) docket management systems.

(e) The justice court technology fund shall be administered by or under the direction of the commissioners court of the county.

(f) Repealed by Acts 2005, 79th Leg., ch. 240, §3, eff. Sept. 1, 2005.

History of CCP art. 102.0173: Acts 2001, 77th Leg., ch. 977, §1, eff. Sept. 1, 2001. Amended by Acts 2005, 79th Leg., ch. 240, §§1, 3, eff. Sept. 1, 2005.

ART. 102.0174. COURT COSTS; JUVENILE CASE MANAGER FUND

(a) In this article, "fund" means a juvenile case manager fund.

(b) The governing body of a municipality by ordinance may create a juvenile case manager fund and may require a defendant convicted of a fine-only misdemeanor offense in a municipal court to pay a juvenile case manager fee not to exceed $5 as a cost of court.

(c) The commissioners court of a county by order may create a juvenile case manager fund and may require a defendant convicted of a fine-only misdemeanor offense in a justice court, county court, or county court at law to pay a juvenile case manager fee not to exceed $5 as a cost of court.

(d) The ordinance or order must authorize the judge or justice to waive the fee required by Subsection (b) or (c) in a case of financial hardship.

(e) In this article, a defendant is considered convicted if:

(1) a sentence is imposed on the defendant;

(2) the defendant receives deferred disposition, including deferred proceedings under Article 45.052 or 45.053; or

(3) the defendant receives deferred adjudication in county court.

(f) The clerks of the respective courts shall collect the costs and pay them to the county or municipal treasurer, as applicable, or to any other official who discharges the duties commonly delegated to the county or municipal treasurer for deposit in the fund.

(g) A fund created under this section may be used only to finance the salary and benefits of a juvenile case manager employed under Article 45.056.

(h) A fund must be administered by or under the direction of the commissioners court or under the direction of the governing body of the municipality.

History of CCP art. 102.0174: Acts 2005, 79th Leg., ch. 949, §35, eff. Sept. 1, 2005.

ART. 102.0178. COSTS ATTENDANT TO CERTAIN INTOXICATION & DRUG CONVICTIONS

 Article 102.0178 below is effective for offenses committed on or after June 15, 2007.

(a) In addition to other costs on conviction imposed by this chapter, a person shall pay $50 as a court cost on conviction of an offense punishable as a Class B misdemeanor or any higher category of offense under:

(1) Chapter 49, Penal Code; or

(2) Chapter 481, Health and Safety Code.

(b) For purposes of this article, a person is considered to have been convicted if:

(1) a sentence is imposed; or

(2) the defendant receives community supervision or deferred adjudication.

(c) Court costs under this article are collected in the same manner as other fines or costs. An officer collecting the costs shall keep separate records of the funds collected as costs under this article and shall deposit the funds in the county treasury, as appropriate.

(d) The custodian of a county treasury shall:

(1) keep records of the amount of funds on deposit collected under this article; and

(2) except as provided by Subsection (e), send to the comptroller before the last day of the first month following each calendar quarter the funds collected under this article during the preceding quarter.

(e) A county is entitled to:

(1) if the custodian of the county treasury complies with Subsection (d), retain 10 percent of the funds collected under this article by an officer of the county during the calendar quarter as a service fee; and

(2) if the county has established a drug court program or establishes a drug court program before the expiration of the calendar quarter, retain in addition to the 10 percent authorized by Subdivision (1) another 50 percent of the funds collected under this article by an officer of the county during the calendar quarter to be used exclusively for the development and maintenance of drug court programs operated within the county.

(f) If no funds due as costs under this article are deposited in a county treasury in a calendar quarter, the custodian of the treasury shall file the report required for the quarter in the regular manner and must state that no funds were collected.

(g) The comptroller shall deposit the funds received under this article to the credit of the drug court account in the general revenue fund to help fund drug court programs established under Chapter 469, Health and Safety Code. The legislature shall appropriate money from the account solely to the criminal justice division of the governor's office for distribution to drug court programs that apply for the money.

(h) Funds collected under this article are subject to audit by the comptroller.

History of CCP art. 102.0178: Acts 2007, 80th Leg., ch. 625, §8, eff. June 15, 2007.

ART. 102.018. COSTS ATTENDANT TO INTOXICATION CONVICTIONS

(a) Except as provided by Subsection (d) of this article, on conviction of an offense relating to the driving or operating of a motor vehicle under Section 49.04, Penal Code, the court shall impose a cost of $15 on a defendant if, subsequent to the arrest of the defendant, a law enforcement agency visually recorded the defendant with an electronic device. Costs imposed under this subsection are in addition to other court costs and are due whether or not the defendant is granted probation in the case. The court shall collect the costs in the same manner as other costs are collected in the case.

(b) Except as provided by Subsection (d) of this article, on conviction of an offense relating to the driving or operating of a motor vehicle punishable under Section 49.04(b), Penal Code, the court shall impose as a cost of court on the defendant an amount that is equal to the cost of an evaluation of the defendant performed under Section 13(a), Article 42.12, of this code. Costs imposed under this subsection are in addition to other court costs and are due whether or not the defendant is granted probation in the case, except that if the court determines that the defendant is indigent and unable to pay the cost, the court may waive the imposition of the cost.

(c)(1) Except as provided by Subsection (d) of this article, if a person commits an offense under Chapter 49, Penal Code, and as a direct result of the offense the person causes an incident resulting in an accident response by a public agency, the person is liable on conviction for the offense for the reasonable expense to the agency of the accident response. In this article, a person is considered to have been convicted in a case if:

(A) sentence is imposed;

(B) the defendant receives probation or deferred adjudication; or

(C) the court defers final disposition of the case.

(2) The liability authorized by this subsection may be established by civil suit; however, if a determination is made during a criminal trial that a person committed an offense under Chapter 49, Penal Code, and as a direct result of the offense the person caused an incident resulting in an accident response by a public agency, the court may include the obligation for the liability as part of the judgment. A judgment that includes such an obligation is enforceable as any other judgment.

(3) The liability is a debt of the person to the public agency, and the public agency may collect the debt in the same manner as the public agency collects an express or implied contractual obligation to the agency.

(4) A person's liability under this subsection for the reasonable expense of an accident response may not exceed $1,000 for a particular incident. For the purposes of this subdivision, a reasonable expense for an accident response includes only those costs to the public agency arising directly from an accident response to a particular incident, such as the cost of providing police, fire-fighting, rescue, ambulance, and emergency medical services at the scene of the incident and the salaries of the personnel of the public agency responding to the incident.

(5) A bill for the expense of an accident response sent to a person by a public agency under this subsection must contain an itemized accounting of the components of the total charge. A bill that complies with this subdivision is prima facie evidence of the reasonableness of the costs incurred in the accident response to which the bill applies.

(6) A policy of motor vehicle insurance delivered, issued for delivery, or renewed in this state may not cover payment of expenses charged to a person under this subsection.

(7) In this subsection, "public agency" means the state, a county, a municipality district, or a public authority located in whole or in part in this state that provides police, fire-fighting, rescue, ambulance, or emergency medical services.

(d) Subsections (a), (b), and (c) of this article do not apply to an offense under Section 49.02 or 49.03, Penal Code.

History of CCP art. 102.018: Acts 1993, 73rd Leg., ch. 900, §1.07, eff. Sept. 1, 1994. Renumbered from art. 102.017 by Acts 1995, 74th Leg., ch. 76, §17.01(4), eff. Sept. 1, 1995.

ART. 102.0185. ADDITIONAL COSTS ATTENDANT TO INTOXICATION CONVICTIONS: EMERGENCY MEDICAL SERVICES, TRAUMA FACILITIES, & TRAUMA CARE SYSTEMS

(a) In addition to the costs on conviction imposed by Articles 102.016 and 102.018, a person convicted of an offense under Chapter 49, Penal Code, except for Sections 49.02 and 49.031, shall pay $100 on conviction of the offense.

(b) Costs imposed under this article are imposed without regard to whether the defendant is placed on community supervision after being convicted of the offense or receives deferred disposition or deferred adjudication for the offense.

(c) Costs imposed under this article are collected in the same manner as other costs collected under Article 102.075.

(d) The officer collecting the costs under this article shall keep separate records of the money collected and shall pay the money to the custodian of the municipal or county treasury.

(e) The custodian of the municipal or county treasury shall:

(1) keep records of the amount of money collected under this article that is deposited with the treasury under this article; and

(2) not later than the last day of the first month following each calendar quarter:

(A) pay the money collected under this article during the preceding calendar quarter to the comptroller; or

(B) if, in the calendar quarter, the custodian of the municipal or county treasury did not receive any money attributable to costs paid under this article, file a report with the comptroller stating that fact.

(f) The comptroller shall deposit the funds received under this article to the credit of the account established under Section 773.006, Health and Safety Code.

History of CCP art. 102.0185: Acts 2003, 78th Leg., ch. 1213, §4, eff. Sept. 1, 2003.

ART. 102.0186. ADDITIONAL COSTS ATTENDANT TO CERTAIN CHILD SEXUAL ASSAULT & RELATED CONVICTIONS

 Subsection (a) below is effective for offenses committed on or after Sept. 1, 2007.

(a) A person convicted of an offense under Section 21.02, 21.11, 22.011(a)(2), 22.021(a)(1)(B), 43.25, 43.251, or 43.26, Penal Code, shall pay $100 on conviction of the offense.

Subsection (a) below is effective for offenses in which any element of the offense was committed before Sept. 1, 2007.

(a) A person convicted of an offense under Section 21.11, 22.011(a)(2), 22.021(a)(1)(B), 43.25, 43.251, or 43.26, Penal Code, shall pay $100 on conviction of the offense.

(b) Costs imposed under this article are imposed without regard to whether the defendant is placed on community supervision after being convicted of the offense or receives deferred adjudication for the offense.

(c) The clerks of the respective courts shall collect the costs and pay them to the county treasurer or to any other official who discharges the duties commonly delegated to the county treasurer for deposit in a fund to be known as the county child abuse prevention fund. A fund designated by this subsection may be used only to fund child abuse prevention programs in the county where the court is located.

(d) The county child abuse prevention fund shall be administered by or under the direction of the commissioners court.

History of CCP art. 102.0186: Acts 2005, 79th Leg., ch. 268, §1.127(a), eff. Sept. 1, 2005. Amended by Acts 2007, 80th Leg., ch. 593, §3.24, eff. Sept. 1, 2007.

ART. 102.019. REPEALED

Repealed by Acts 2003, 78th Leg., ch. 209, §85(a)(6), eff. Jan. 1, 2004.

ART. 102.020. COSTS ON CONVICTION FOR OFFENSES REQUIRING DNA TESTING

(a) A person shall pay $250 as a court cost on conviction of an offense listed in Section 411.1471(a)(1), Government Code, and $50 as a court cost on conviction of an offense listed in Section 411.1471(a)(3) of that code.

(b) The court shall assess and make a reasonable effort to collect the cost due under this article whether or not any other court cost is assessed or collected.

(c) For purposes of this article, a person is considered to have been convicted if:

(1) a sentence is imposed; or

(2) the defendant receives community supervision or deferred adjudication.

(d) Court costs under this article are collected in the same manner as other fines or costs. An officer collecting the costs shall keep separate records of the funds collected as costs under this article and shall deposit the funds in the county treasury.

(e) The custodian of a county treasury shall:

(1) keep records of the amount of funds on deposit collected under this article; and

(2) send to the comptroller before the last day of the first month following each calendar quarter the funds collected under this article during the preceding quarter.

(f) A county may retain 10 percent of the funds collected under this article by an officer of the county as a collection fee if the custodian of the county treasury complies with Subsection (e).

(g) If no funds due as costs under this article are deposited in a county treasury in a calendar quarter, the custodian of the treasury shall file the report required for the quarter in the regular manner and must state that no funds were collected.

(h) The comptroller shall deposit 35 percent of the funds received under this article in the state treasury to the credit of the state highway fund and 65 percent of the funds received under this article to the credit of the criminal justice planning account in the general revenue fund.

(i) Funds collected under this article are subject to audit by the comptroller.

History of CCP art. 102.020: Acts 2001, 77th Leg., ch. 1490, §6, eff. Sept. 1, 2001.

SUBCHAPTER B. CRIMINAL JUSTICE PLANNING FUND

ARTS. 102.051 TO 102.055. REPEALED

Repealed by Acts 1997, 75th Leg., ch. 1100, §6(3), eff. Sept. 1, 1997.

ART. 102.056. DISTRIBUTION OF FUNDS

(a) The legislature shall determine and appropriate the necessary amount from the criminal justice planning fund to the criminal justice division of the governor's office for expenditure for state and local criminal justice projects and for costs of administering the funds for the projects. The criminal justice division shall allocate not less than 20 percent of these funds to juvenile justice programs. The distribution of the funds to local units of government shall be in an amount equal at least to the same percentage as local expenditures for criminal justice activities are to total state and local expenditures for criminal justice activities for the preceding state fiscal year. Funds shall be allocated among combinations of local units of government taking into consideration the population of the combination of local units of government as compared to the population of the state and the incidence of crime in the jurisdiction of the combination of local units of government as compared to the incidence of crime in the state. All funds collected are subject to audit by the comptroller of public accounts. All funds expended are subject to audit by the State Auditor. All funds collected or expended are subject to audit by the governor's division of planning coordination.

(b) The legislature may appropriate any unobligated balance of the criminal justice planning fund for any court-related purpose.

(c) Notwithstanding any other provision of this section, the criminal justice division shall allocate to a local unit of government or combination of local units of government located in an impacted region occurring as the result of the establishment of a significant new naval military facility an amount that exceeds by 10 percent the amount it would otherwise receive under this section.

(d) In this section "significant new naval military facility" and "impacted region" have the meanings assigned by Section 4, Article 1, National Defense Impacted Region Assistance Act of 1985.

(e) The legislature shall determine and appropriate the necessary amount from the criminal justice planning account to the criminal justice division of the governor's office for reimbursement in the form of grants to local law enforcement agencies for expenses incurred in performing duties imposed on those agencies under Sections 411.1471 and 411.1472, Government Code. On the first day after the end of a calendar quarter, a law enforcement agency incurring expenses described by this subsection in the previous calendar quarter shall send a certified statement of the costs incurred to the criminal justice division. The criminal justice division through a grant shall reimburse the law enforcement agency for the costs not later than the 30th day after the date the certified statement is received. If the criminal justice division does not reimburse the law enforcement agency before the 90th day after the date the certified statement is received, the agency is not required to perform duties imposed under Sections 411.1471 and 411.1472, Government Code, until the agency has been compensated for all costs for which the local law enforcement agency has submitted a certified statement under this subsection.

History of CCP art. 102.056: Acts 1985, 69th Leg., ch. 269, §1, eff. Sept. 1, 1985. Amended by Acts 1986, 69th Leg., 2nd C.S., ch. 11, §8, eff. Sept. 22, 1986; Acts 1991, 72nd Leg., ch. 16, §4.07(a), eff. Aug. 26, 1991; Acts 2001, 77th Leg., ch. 1490, §7, eff. Sept. 1, 2001.

SUBCHAPTER C. COURT COSTS & FEES

ART. 102.071. COLLECTION, ALLOCATION, & ADMINISTRATION

The comptroller of public accounts may require state court costs and fees in criminal cases to be reported in lump-sum amounts. The comptroller shall allocate the amounts received to the appropriate fund, with each fund receiving the same amount of money the fund would have received if the costs and fees had been reported individually.

History of CCP art. 102.071: Acts 1989, 71st Leg., ch. 347, §4, eff. Oct. 1, 1989.

ART. 102.072. ADMINISTRATIVE FEE

An officer listed in Article 103.003 or a community supervision and corrections department may assess an administrative fee for each transaction made by the officer or department relating to the collection of fines, fees, restitution, or other costs imposed by a court. The fee may not exceed $2 for each transaction. This article does not apply to a transaction relating to the collection of child support.

History of CCP art. 102.072: Acts 1995, 74th Leg., ch. 217, §2, eff. May 23, 1995. Amended by Acts 1999, 76th Leg., ch. 1345, §1, eff. Sept. 1, 1999.

ART. 102.075. REPEALED

Repealed by Acts 2003, 78th Leg., ch. 209, §85(a)(7), eff. Jan. 1, 2004.

SUBCHAPTER D. REPEALED

ARTS. 102.081 TO 102.085. REPEALED

Repealed by Acts 1997, 75th Leg., ch. 1100, §6, eff. Sept. 1, 1997.

CHAPTER 103. COLLECTION & RECORDKEEPING

ART. 103.001. COSTS PAYABLE

A cost is not payable by the person charged with the cost until a written bill is produced or is ready to be produced, containing the items of cost, signed by the officer who charged the cost or the officer who is entitled to receive payment for the cost.

History of CCP art. 103.001: Acts 1985, 69th Leg., ch. 269, §1, eff. Sept. 1, 1985.

ART. 103.002. CERTAIN COSTS BARRED

An officer may not impose a cost for a service not performed or for a service for which a cost is not expressly provided by law.

History of CCP art. 103.002: Acts 1985, 69th Leg., ch. 269, §1, eff. Sept. 1, 1985.

ART. 103.003. COLLECTION

(a) District and county attorneys, clerks of district and county courts, sheriffs, constables, and justices of the peace may collect money payable under this title.

(b) A community supervision and corrections department may collect money payable under this title with the written approval of the clerk of the court or fee officer, and may collect money payable as otherwise provided by law.

(c) This article does not limit the authority of a commissioners court to contract with a private vendor or private attorney for the provision of collection services under Article 103.0031.

History of CCP art. 103.003: Acts 1985, 69th Leg., ch. 269, §1, eff. Sept. 1, 1985. Amended by Acts 1995, 74th Leg., ch. 217, §3, eff. May 23, 1995; Acts 2001, 77th Leg., ch. 1279, §1, eff. June 15, 2001; Acts 2005, 79th Leg., ch. 1064, §1, eff. June 18, 2005.

ART. 103.0031. COLLECTION CONTRACTS

(a) The commissioners court of a county or the governing body of a municipality may enter into a contract with a private attorney or a public or private vendor for the provision of collection services for one or more of the following items:

(1) debts and accounts receivable such as unpaid fines, fees, court costs, forfeited bonds, and restitution ordered paid by:

(A) a court serving the county or a court serving the municipality, as applicable; or

(B) a hearing officer serving the municipality under Chapter 682, Transportation Code;

(2) amounts in cases in which the accused has failed to appear:

(A) as promised under Subchapter A, Chapter 543, Transportation Code, or other law;

(B) in compliance with a lawful written notice to appear issued under Article 14.06(b) or other law;

(C) in compliance with a lawful summons issued under Article 15.03(b) or other law;

(D) in compliance with a lawful order of a court serving the county or municipality; or

(E) as specified in a citation, summons, or other notice authorized by Section 682.002, Transportation Code, that charges the accused with a parking or stopping offense; and

(3) false alarm penalties or fees imposed by a county under Chapter 118 or 233, Local Government Code, or by a municipality under a municipal ordinance.

(b) A commissioners court or governing body of a municipality that enters into a contract with a private attorney or private vendor under this article may authorize the addition of a collection fee in the amount of 30 percent on each item described in Subsection (a) that is more than 60 days past due and has been referred to the attorney or vendor for collection. The collection fee does not apply to a case that has been dismissed by a court of competent jurisdiction or to any amount that has been satisfied through time-served credit or community service. The collection fee may be applied to any balance remaining after a partial credit for time served or community service if the balance is more than 60 days past due. Unless the contract provides otherwise, the court shall calculate the amount of any collection fee due to the governmental entity or to the private attorney or private vendor performing the collection services and shall receive all fees, including the collection fee. With respect to cases described by Subsection (a)(2), the amount to which the 30 percent collection fee applies is:

(1) the amount to be paid that is communicated to the accused as acceptable to the court under its standard policy for resolution of the case, if the accused voluntarily agrees to pay that amount; or

(2) the amount ordered paid by the court after plea or trial.

(c) The governing body of a municipality with a population of more than 1.9 million may authorize the addition of collection fees under Subsection (b) for a collection program performed by employees of the governing body.

(d) A defendant is not liable for the collection fees authorized under Subsection (b) if the court of original jurisdiction has determined the defendant is indigent, or has insufficient resources or income, or is otherwise unable to pay all or part of the underlying fine or costs.

(e) If a county or municipality has entered into a contract under Subsection (a) and a person pays an amount that is less than the aggregate total to be collected under Subsections (a) and (b), the allocation to the comptroller, the county or municipality, and the private attorney or vendor shall be reduced proportionately.

(f) An item subject to collection services under Subsection (a) and to the additional collection fee authorized by Subsection (b) is considered more than 60 days past due under Subsection (b) if it remains unpaid on the 61st day after the following appropriate date:

(1) with respect to an item described by Subsection (a)(1), the date on which the debt, fine, fee, forfeited bond, or court cost must be paid in full as determined by the court or hearing officer;

(2) with respect to an item described by Subsection (a)(2), the date by which the accused promised to appear or was notified, summoned, or ordered to appear; or

(3) with respect to an item described by Subsection (a)(3), the date on which a penalty or fee is due under a rule or order adopted under Chapter 233, Local Government Code, or an ordinance, policy, procedure, or rule of a municipality.

(g) A county or municipality that enters into a contract under Subsection (a) may not use the additional 30 percent collection fee authorized by Subsection (b) for any purpose other than compensating the private attorney or private vendor who earns the fee.

(h) This section does not apply to the collection of commercial bail bonds.

(i) The commissioners court of a county or the governing body of a municipality may enter into a contract as described in this article to collect a debt incurred as a result of the commission of a criminal or civil offense committed before the effective date of this subsection. The collection fee does not apply to a debt collected pursuant to a contract entered into under this subsection.

(j) A communication to the accused person regarding the amount of payment that is acceptable to the court under the court's standard policy for resolution of a case must include a notice of the person's right to enter a plea or go to trial on any offense charged.

History of CCP art. 103.0031: Acts 1993, 73rd Leg., ch. 809, §3, eff. Aug. 30, 1993. Amended by Acts 2001, 77th Leg., ch. 1279, §2, eff. June 15, 2001; Acts 2003, 78th Leg., ch. 346, §1, eff. June 18, 2003; Acts 2005, 79th Leg., ch. 1296, §4, eff. June 18, 2005.

ART. 103.0032. COLLECTION IMPROVEMENT PLANS

Not later than January 1 of each even-numbered year, the Office of Court Administration of the Texas Judicial System may award grants to counties and municipalities to prepare a collection plan. The grants shall reimburse the county or municipality for the cost of preparing the plan. The plan shall provide methods to improve the collection of court costs, fees, and fines imposed in criminal cases. The Office of Court Administration of the Texas Judicial System may require that the county or municipality reimburse the state from the additional collections as a condition of the grant.

History of CCP art. 103.0032: Acts 2001, 77th Leg., ch. 1469, §1, eff. Sept. 1, 2001.

ART. 103.0033. COLLECTION IMPROVEMENT PROGRAM

(a) In this article:

(1) "Office" means the Office of Court Administration of the Texas Judicial System.

(2) "Program" means the program to improve the collection of court costs, fees, and fines imposed in criminal cases, as developed and implemented under this article.

(b) This article applies only to:

(1) a county with a population of 50,000 or greater; and

(2) a municipality with a population of 100,000 or greater.

(c) Unless granted a waiver under Subsection (h), each county and municipality shall develop and implement a program that complies with the prioritized implementation schedule under Subsection (h). A county program must include district, county, and justice courts.

(d) The program must consist of:

(1) a component that conforms with a model developed by the office and designed to improve in-house collections through application of best practices; and

(2) a component designed to improve collection of balances more than 60 days past due, which may be implemented by entering into a contract with a private attorney or public or private vendor in accordance with Article 103.0031.

(e) Not later than June 1 of each year, the office shall identify those counties and municipalities that:

(1) have not implemented a program; and

(2) are able to implement a program before April 1 of the following year.

(f) The comptroller, in cooperation with the office, shall develop a methodology for determining the collection rate of counties and municipalities described by Subsection (e) before implementation of a program. The comptroller shall determine the rate for each county and municipality not later than the first anniversary of the county's or municipality's adoption of a program.

(g) The office shall:

(1) make available on the office's Internet website requirements for a program; and

(2) assist counties and municipalities in implementing a program by providing training and consultation, except that the office may not provide employees for implementation of a program.

(h) The office, in consultation with the comptroller, may:

(1) use case dispositions, population, revenue data, or other appropriate measures to develop a prioritized implementation schedule for programs; and

(2) determine whether it is not cost-effective to implement a program in a county or municipality and grant a waiver to the county or municipality.

(i) Each county and municipality shall at least annually submit to the office and the comptroller a written report that includes updated information regarding the program, as determined by the office in cooperation with the comptroller. The report must be in a form approved by the office in cooperation with the comptroller.

(j) The comptroller shall periodically audit counties and municipalities to verify information reported under Subsection (i) and confirm that the county or municipality is conforming with requirements relating to the program. The comptroller shall consult with the office in determining how frequently to conduct audits under this section.

History of CCP art. 103.0033: Acts 2005, 79th Leg., ch. 899, §10.01, eff. Aug. 29, 2005.

ART. 103.004. DISPOSITION OF COLLECTED MONEY

(a) Except as provided by Subsections (b) and (c), an officer who collects recognizances, bail bonds, fines, forfeitures, judgments, jury fees, and other obligations recovered in the name of the state under any provision of this title shall deposit the money in the county treasury not later than the next regular business day after the date that the money is collected. If it is not possible for the officer to deposit the money in the county treasury by that date, the officer shall deposit the money in the county treasury as soon as possible, but not later than the third regular business day after the date that the money is collected.

(b) The commissioners court of a county may authorize an officer who is required to deposit money under Subsection (a) to deposit the money in the county treasury not later than the seventh regular business day after the date that the money is collected.

(c) The commissioners court of a county with a population of less than 50,000 may authorize an officer who is required to deposit money under Subsection (a) to deposit the money in the county treasury not later than the 30th day after the date that the money is collected.

(d) The custodian of the county treasury shall deposit money received from fees imposed under Article 102.012 in the special fund of the county treasury for the community supervision and corrections department serving the county.

History of CCP art. 103.004: Acts 1985, 69th Leg., ch. 269, §1, eff. Sept. 1, 1985. Amended by Acts 1990, 71st Leg., 6th C.S., ch. 25, §21, eff. June 18, 1990; Acts 1999, 76th Leg., ch. 1462, §1, eff. Sept. 1, 1999.

ART. 103.005. REPORT REQUIRED

(a) An officer listed in Article 103.003 who collects money other than taxes for a county shall report to the commissioners court of the county for which the money was collected during each term of the court.

(b) An officer listed in Article 103.003 who collects money other than taxes for the state shall report to the district court having jurisdiction in the county the officer serves on the first day of each term of the court.

(c) The report must state for the reporting period:

(1) the amount of money collected by the officer;

(2) when and from whom the money was collected;

(3) the process by which the money was collected; and

(4) the disposition of the money.

(d) The report must be in writing and under the oath of the officer.

(e) If an officer has not collected money since the last report required to be filed with the court or the commissioners court, the officer shall report that fact to the court or commissioners court.

History of CCP art. 103.005: Acts 1985, 69th Leg., ch. 269, §1, eff. Sept. 1, 1985.

ART. 103.006. TRANSFER OF BILL OF COSTS

If a criminal action or proceeding is transferred from one court to another or is appealed, an officer of the court shall certify and sign a bill of costs stating the costs that have accrued and send the bill of costs to the court to which the action or proceeding is transferred or appealed.

History of CCP art. 103.006: Acts 1985, 69th Leg., ch. 269, §1, eff. Sept. 1, 1985.

ART. 103.007. ADDITIONAL COSTS AFTER PAYMENT

After a defendant has paid costs, no more costs may be charged against the defendant unless the court rules on a motion presented to the court that additional costs are due.

History of CCP art. 103.007: Acts 1985, 69th Leg., ch. 269, §1, eff. Sept. 1, 1985.

ART. 103.008. CORRECTION OF COSTS

(a) On the filing of a motion by a defendant not later than one year after the date of the final disposition of a case in which costs were imposed, the court in which the case is pending or was last pending shall correct any error in the costs.

(b) The defendant must notify each person affected by the correction of costs in the same manner as notice of a similar motion is given in a civil action.

History of CCP art. 103.008: Acts 1985, 69th Leg., ch. 269, §1, eff. Sept. 1, 1985.

ART. 103.009. FEE RECORDS

(a) Each clerk of a court, county judge, justice of the peace, sheriff, constable, and marshal shall keep a fee record. The record must contain:

(1) a statement of each fee or item of cost charged for a service rendered in a criminal action or proceeding;

(2) the number and style of the action or proceeding; and

(3) the name of the officer or person who is entitled to receive the fee.

(b) Any person may inspect a fee record described by Subsection (a).

(c) A statement of an item of cost in a fee record is prima facie evidence of the correctness of the statement.

(d) The county shall provide to officers required to keep a fee record by this article equipment and supplies necessary to keep the record.

History of CCP art. 103.009: Acts 1985, 69th Leg., ch. 269, §1, eff. Sept. 1, 1985. Amended by Acts 1993, 73rd Leg., ch. 988, §2.05, eff. Sept. 1, 1993.

ART. 103.010. RECEIPT BOOK

(a) Each county shall provide a receipt book to each officer collecting fines and fees in criminal cases for the county. The book must contain duplicate official receipts. Each receipt must bear a distinct number and a facsimile of the official seal of the county.

(b) An officer who collects fines or fees in a criminal case shall give the person paying the money a receipt from the receipt book. The receipt must show:

(1) the amount of money paid;

(2) the date the money was paid;

(3) the style and number of the case in which costs were accrued;

(4) the item of costs;

(5) the name of the person paying the money; and

(6) the official signature of the officer receiving the money.

(c) Instead of a receipt book, each officer collecting fines or fees in criminal cases for the county may maintain the information listed in Subsections (b)(1)-(5) in a computer database. The officer shall provide a receipt to each person paying a fine or fee.

History of CCP art. 103.010: Acts 1985, 69th Leg., ch. 269, §1, eff. Sept. 1, 1985. Amended by Acts 1999, 76th Leg., ch. 412, §1, eff. June 18, 1999.

ART. 103.011. AUDIT

An officer shall deliver the receipt book or a copy of any receipt records contained in a computer database to the county auditor at the end of each month's business or at the end of each month shall allow the county auditor electronic access to receipt records contained in the computer database. The county auditor shall examine the receipt book or computer records and determine whether the money collected has been properly disposed of. If each receipt in a receipt book has been used, the county auditor shall keep the book. If any receipt in the book has not been used, the auditor shall return the book to the officer. The county auditor may keep a copy of computer generated receipt records delivered to the county auditor. Any person may inspect a receipt book or a computer generated receipt record kept by the county auditor.

History of CCP art. 103.011: Acts 1985, 69th Leg., ch. 269, §1, eff. Sept. 1, 1985. Amended by Acts 1999, 76th Leg., ch. 412, §2, eff. June 18, 1999.

ART. 103.012. PENALTY

(a) An officer commits an offense if the officer violates a provision of Article 103.010 or Article 103.011.

(b) An offense under this article is a Class C misdemeanor.

(c) An officer who violates a provision of Article 103.010 or Article 103.011 or whose deputy violates a provision of those articles may be removed from office on the petition of the county or district attorney.

History of CCP art. 103.012: Acts 1985, 69th Leg., ch. 269, §1, eff. Sept. 1, 1985.

ART. 103.013. REPEALED

Repealed by Acts 2003, 78th Leg., ch. 1276, §5.004, eff. Sept. 1, 2003.

CHAPTER 104. CERTAIN EXPENSES PAID BY STATE OR COUNTY

ART. 104.001. JURY PAY & EXPENSES FOR JURORS

(a) The sheriff of a county shall, with the approval of the commissioners court, provide food and lodging for jurors impaneled in a felony case tried in the county. A juror may pay his own expenses and draw his script.

(b) A juror in a felony case is entitled to receive as jury pay the amount authorized by Article 2122, Revised Statutes.

(c) The county treasurer shall pay a juror the amount due the juror for expenses under this article after receiving a certificate from a clerk of a court or justice of the peace stating the amount due the juror.

(d) A draft or certificate issued under this article may be transferred by delivery and, without further action of any authority except registration by the county treasurer, may be used at par to pay county taxes owed by the holder of the draft or certificate.

(e) If a defendant is indicted in one county and tried in another county after a change of venue, the county in which the defendant was indicted is liable for jury pay and expenses paid to jurors by the county trying the case.

(f) At each regular meeting of the commissioners court of a county, the court shall determine whether, since the last regular meeting of the court, a defendant described by Subsection (e) has been tried in the county. The commissioners court shall prepare an account against another county liable for jury pay and expenses under this article. The account must show the number of days the jury was impaneled in the case and the jury pay and expenses incurred by the county in the case.

(g) The county judge of the county in which the defendant was tried shall certify the correctness of the account and send the account to the county judge of the county in which the defendant was indicted. The county in which the defendant was indicted shall pay the account in the same manner required for payment of the expenses of transferred prisoners under Article 104.002.

History of CCP art. 104.001: Acts 1985, 69th Leg., ch. 269, §1, eff. Sept. 1, 1985.

ART. 104.002. EXPENSES FOR PRISONERS

(a) Except as otherwise provided by this article, a county is liable for all expenses incurred in the safekeeping of prisoners confined in the county jail or kept under guard by the county. If a prisoner is transferred to a county from another county on a change of venue, for safekeeping, or for a habeas corpus hearing, the county transferring the prisoner is liable for the expenses described by this article.

(b) If a county incurs expenses for the safekeeping of a prisoner from another county, the sheriff shall submit to the county judge an account of expenses incurred by the county for the prisoner. The county judge shall approve the amount he determines is a correct statement of the expenses and sign and date the account.

(c) The county judge shall submit to the commissioners court of the county for which the prisoner was kept, at a regular term of the court, his signed statement of the account described by Subsection (b). If the commissioners court determines that the account is in accordance with the law, it shall order the county treasurer to issue to the sheriff of the county submitting the statement a draft in an amount approved by the court.

(d) A person who is or was a prisoner in a county jail and received medical, dental, or health related services from a county or a hospital district shall be required to pay for such services when they are rendered. If such prisoner is an eligible county resident as defined in Section 61.002, Health and Safety Code, the county or hospital district providing the services has a right of subrogation to the prisoner's right of recovery from any source, limited to the cost of services provided. A prisoner, unless the prisoner fully pays for the cost of services received, shall remain obligated to reimburse the county or hospital district for any medical, dental, or health services provided, and the county or hospital district may apply for reimbursement in the manner provided by Chapter 61, Health and Safety Code. A county or hospital district shall have authority to recover the amount expended in a civil action.

History of CCP art. 104.002: Acts 1985, 69th Leg., ch. 269, §1, eff. Sept. 1, 1985. Amended by Acts 1987, 70th Leg., ch. 1010, §1, eff. June 19, 1987; Acts 1991, 72nd Leg., ch. 14, §284(19) (eff. Sept. 1, 1991), ch. 434, §1 (eff. Aug. 26, 1991); Acts 1995, 74th Leg., ch. 76, §3.22, eff. Sept. 1, 1995.

ART. 104.003. STATE PAYMENT OF CERTAIN PROSECUTION COSTS

 (a) In a prosecution of a criminal offense or delinquent conduct committed on property owned or operated by or under contract with the Texas Department of Criminal Justice or the Texas Youth Commission, or committed by or against a person in the custody of the department or commission while the person is performing a duty away from department or commission

property, the state shall reimburse the county for expenses incurred by the county, in an amount that the court determines to be reasonable, for payment of:

(1) salaries and expenses of foreign language interpreters and interpreters for deaf persons whose services are necessary to the prosecution;

(2) consultation fees of experts whose assistance is directly related to the prosecution;

(3) travel expenses for witnesses;

(4) expenses for the food, lodging, and compensation of jurors;

(5) compensation of witnesses;

(6) the cost of preparation of a statement of facts and a transcript of the trial for purposes of appeal;

(7) if the death of a person is an element of the offense, expenses of an inquest relating to the death;

(8) food, lodging, and travel expenses incurred by the prosecutor's staff during travel essential to the prosecution of the offense;

(9) court reporter's fees; and

(10) the cost of special security officers.

(b) If there is a change of venue, the court may, in its discretion, determine that a special prosecutor should be hired for the prosecution of an offense described in Section (a), and the state shall reimburse the county for the salary and expenses of the special prosecutor if the court determines that the hiring of the special prosecutor was reasonable and necessary for effective prosecution. The amount of reimbursement may not exceed an amount that the court determines to be reasonable.

(c) The court shall certify the amount of reimbursement for expenses under Sections (a) and (b) on presentation by the county of an itemized and verified receipt for those expenses.

(d) The state shall reimburse the county for expenses incurred by the county for the investigation of an offense described in Section (a), whether or not the investigation results in the prosecution of an offense, and shall reimburse the county for reasonable operational expenses of the special prison prosecution unit, including educational activities for the staff and general expenses relating to its investigative and prosecutorial duties.

(e) The court shall certify the amount of reimbursement for expenses under Sections (a) and (b) to the comptroller. The comptroller shall issue a warrant in that amount to the commissioners court of the county or, if the comptroller determines that the amount certified by the court is unreasonable, in an amount that the comptroller determines to be reasonable.

(f) The commissioners court of the county shall certify the amount of reimbursement for expenses under Section (d) to the comptroller. The comptroller shall issue a warrant in that amount to the commissioners court or, if the comptroller determines that the amount certified by the commissioners court is unreasonable, in an amount that the comptroller determines to be reasonable.

(g) Notwithstanding any other provision of this article, the expenses submitted by the county for reimbursement may not exceed the amount the county would pay for the same activity or service, if that activity or service was not reimbursed by the state. The county judge shall certify compliance with this section on request by the comptroller.

History of CCP art. 104.003: Acts 1989, 71st Leg., ch. 2, §5.06(a), eff. Aug. 28, 1989. Amended by Acts 1989, 71st Leg., ch. 461, §1, eff. June 14, 1989; Acts 1991, 72nd Leg., ch. 14, §284(60), eff. Sept. 1, 1991; Acts 2007, 80th Leg., ch. 263, §3, eff. June 8, 2007.

ART. 104.004. EXTRAORDINARY COSTS OF PROSECUTION

(a) The criminal justice division of the governor's office may distribute money appropriated by the legislature for the purposes of this article to a county for the reimbursement of expenses incurred by the county during the fiscal year during which application is made or the fiscal year preceding the year during which application is made for the investigation or prosecution of an offense under Section 19.03, Penal Code, or an offense under the Penal Code alleged by the attorney representing the state to have been committed for a purpose or reason described by Article 42.014.

(b) For each fiscal year, the division shall distribute at least 50 percent of the money distributed under this article during that year to counties with a population of less than 50,000, except that if the total distributions applied for by those counties is less than 50 percent of the money distributed during that year, the division is only required to distribute to those counties the amount of money for which applications have been made.

(c) The division may adopt a budget and rules for the distribution of money under this article.

(d) All money distributed to a county under this article and its expenditure by the county are subject to audit by the state auditor.

History of CCP art. 104.004: Acts 1999, 76th Leg., ch. 664, §1, eff. Sept. 1, 1999; Acts 2001, 77th Leg., ch. 85, §2.01, eff. Sept. 1, 2001.

U.N.T.S. No. 8638

Done at Vienna, on 24 April 1963

CHAPTER II

FACILITIES, PRIVILEGES & IMMUNITIES RELATING TO CONSULAR POSTS, CAREER CONSULAR OFFICERS & OTHER MEMBERS OF A CONSULAR POST

SECTION I

FACILITIES, PRIVILEGES & IMMUNITIES RELATING TO A CONSULAR POST

ARTICLE 36

COMMUNICATION & CONTACT WITH NATIONALS OF THE SENDING STATE

1. With a view to facilitating the exercise of consular functions relating to nationals of the sending State:

(a) consular officers shall be free to communicate with nationals of the sending State and to have access to them. Nationals of the sending State shall have the same freedom with respect to communication with and access to consular officers of the sending State;

(b) if he so requests, the competent authorities of the receiving State shall, without delay, inform the consular post of the sending State if, within its consular district, a national of that State is arrested or committed to prison or to custody pending trial or is detained in any other manner. Any communication addressed to the consular post by the person arrested, in prison, custody or detention shall also be forwarded by the said authorities without delay. The said authorities shall inform the person concerned without delay of his rights under this sub-paragraph;

(c) consular officers shall have the right to visit a national of the sending State who is in prison, custody or detention, to converse and correspond with him and to arrange for his legal representation. They shall also have the right to visit any national of the sending State who is in prison, custody or detention in their district in pursuance of a judgment. Nevertheless, consular officers shall refrain from taking action on behalf of a national who is in prison, custody or detention if he expressly opposes such action.

2. The rights referred to in paragraph 1 of this Article shall be exercised in conformity with the laws and regulations of the receiving State, subject to the proviso, however, that the said laws and regulations must enable full effect to be given to the purposes for which the rights accorded under this Article are intended.

ANNOTATIONS

Sanchez-Llamas v. Oregon, 126 S.Ct. 2669, 2681 (2006). "The failure to inform a defendant of his Article 36 rights is unlikely, with any frequency, to produce unreliable confessions. And unlike the search-and-seizure context—where the need to obtain valuable evidence may tempt authorities to transgress Fourth Amendment limitations—police win little, if any, practical advantage from violating Article 36. Suppression would be a vastly disproportionate remedy for an Article 36 violation. *At 2687:* [C]laims under Article 36 ... may be subjected to the same procedural default rules that apply generally to other federal-law claims."

Sierra v. State, 218 S.W.3d 85, 87 (Tex.Crim.App. 2007). "[T]he exclusionary rule in [CCP art.] 38.23 does not apply to treaty violations. *At 88:* Our decision does not leave detained foreign nationals without any means of vindicating Vienna Convention rights. ... '[A] defendant can raise [a Vienna Convention] Article 36 claim as part of a broader challenge to the voluntariness of his statements to police.' And further, if a defendant 'raises an Article 36 violation at trial, a court can make the appropriate accommodations to ensure the defendant secures, to the extent possible, the benefits of consular assistance.'"

ADVISORY OPINION OF THE INTER-AMERICAN COURT OF HUMAN RIGHTS

The Right to Information on Consular Assistance in the Framework of the Guarantees of the Due Process of Law, Advisory Opinion OC-16/99, October 1, 1999, Inter-Am. Ct. H.R. (Ser A) No. 16 (1999).

IT IS OF THE OPINION

Unanimously,

1. That Article 36 of the Vienna Convention on Consular Relations confers rights upon detained foreign nationals, among them the right to information on consular assistance, and that said rights carry with them correlative obligations for the host State.

Unanimously,

2. That Article 36 of the Vienna Convention on Consular Relations *concerns* the protection of the rights of a national of the sending State and is part of the body of international human rights law.

Unanimously,

3. That the expression "without delay" in Article 36(1)(b) of the Vienna Convention on Consular Relations means that the State must comply with its duty to inform the detainee of the rights that article confers upon him, at the time of his arrest or at least before he makes his first statement before the authorities.

Unanimously,

4. That the enforceability of the rights that Article 36 of the Vienna Convention on Consular Relations confers upon the individual is not subject to the protests of the sending State.

Unanimously,

5. That articles 2, 6, 14 and 50 of the International Covenant on Civil and Political Rights *concern* the protection of human rights *in the American States*.

Unanimously,

6. That the individual's right to information established in Article 36(1)(b) of the Vienna Convention on Consular Relations allows the right to the due process of law recognized in Article 14 of the International Covenant on Civil and Political Rights to have practical effects in concrete cases; Article 14 establishes minimum guarantees that can be amplified in the light of other international instruments such as the Vienna Convention on Consular Relations, which expand the scope of the protection afforded to the accused.

By six votes to one,

7. That failure to observe a detained foreign national's right to information, recognized in Article 36(1)(b) of the Vienna Convention on Consular Relations, is prejudicial to the due process of law and, in such circumstances, imposition of the death penalty is a violation of the right not to be deprived of life "arbitrarily," as stipulated in the relevant provisions of the human rights treaties (*e.g.* American Convention on Human Rights, Article 4; International Covenant on Civil and Political Rights, Article 6), with the juridical consequences that a violation of this nature carries, in other words, those pertaining to the State's international responsibility and the duty to make reparation.

Judge Jackman dissenting.

Unanimously,

8. That the international provisions that concern the protection of human rights in the American States, including the right recognized in Article 36(1)(b) of the Vienna Convention on Consular Relations, must be respected by the American States Party to the respective conventions, regardless of whether theirs is a federal or unitary structure.

CHARTS

TABLE OF CONTENTS

CHARTS

CHARTS

CRIMINAL JURISDICTION OF TEXAS COURTS

This chart has been modified from the Office of Court Administration, *Annual Report of the Texas Judicial System* (1999).

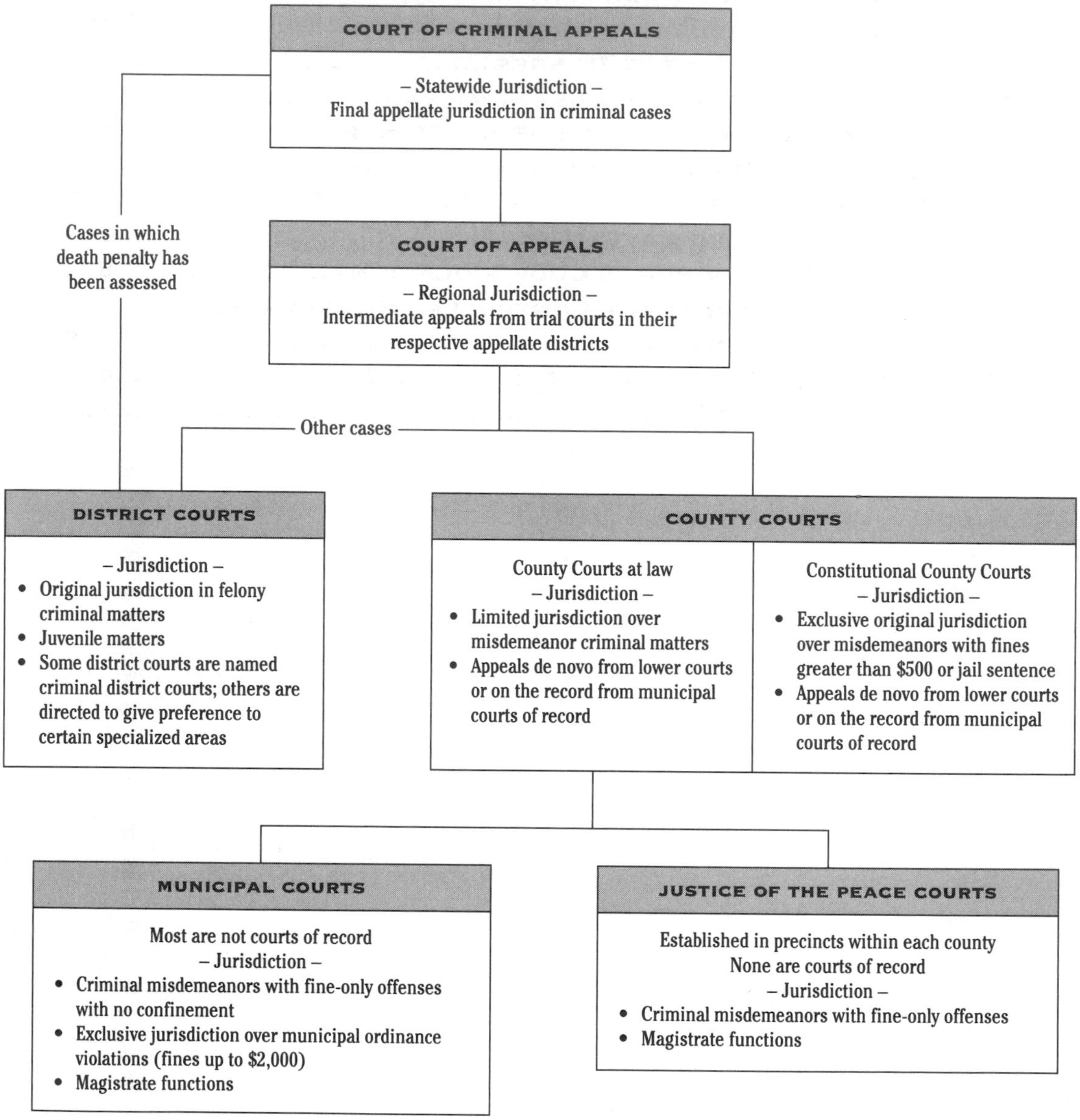

COURT OF CRIMINAL APPEALS

– Statewide Jurisdiction –
Final appellate jurisdiction in criminal cases

Cases in which death penalty has been assessed

COURT OF APPEALS

– Regional Jurisdiction –
Intermediate appeals from trial courts in their respective appellate districts

Other cases

DISTRICT COURTS

– Jurisdiction –
- Original jurisdiction in felony criminal matters
- Juvenile matters
- Some district courts are named criminal district courts; others are directed to give preference to certain specialized areas

COUNTY COURTS

County Courts at law
– Jurisdiction –
- Limited jurisdiction over misdemeanor criminal matters
- Appeals de novo from lower courts or on the record from municipal courts of record

Constitutional County Courts
– Jurisdiction –
- Exclusive original jurisdiction over misdemeanors with fines greater than $500 or jail sentence
- Appeals de novo from lower courts or on the record from municipal courts of record

MUNICIPAL COURTS

Most are not courts of record
– Jurisdiction –
- Criminal misdemeanors with fine-only offenses with no confinement
- Exclusive jurisdiction over municipal ordinance violations (fines up to $2,000)
- Magistrate functions

JUSTICE OF THE PEACE COURTS

Established in precincts within each county
None are courts of record
– Jurisdiction –
- Criminal misdemeanors with fine-only offenses
- Magistrate functions

CHARTS

MISDEMEANOR PUNISHMENT RANGES

From *Texas Sentencing, Fifth Edition* (2007) by Ken Anderson and John Bradley. Lexis Law Publishing, (800) 542-0957. All rights reserved.

CLASS	PENAL CODE	CONFINEMENT	OPTIONAL FINE
Class A misdemeanor	§12.21	Up to 1 year in county jail	$4,000 maximum
Class B misdemeanor	§12.22	Up to 180 days in county jail	$2,000 maximum
Class C misdemeanor	§12.23	None	$500 maximum

ENHANCED MISDEMEANOR PUNISHMENT RANGES

From *Texas Sentencing, Fifth Edition* (2007) by Ken Anderson and John Bradley. Lexis Law Publishing, (800) 542-0957. All rights reserved.

CLASS	PENAL CODE	ENHANCEMENT	ENHANCED PUNISHMENT RANGE
Class A misdemeanor	§12.43(a)	Prior Class A misdemeanor or any felony	(1) $4,000 maximum; (2) 90 days to 1 year in county jail; or (3) Both
Class B misdemeanor	§12.43(b)	Prior Class A or Class B misdemeanor or any felony	(1) $2,000 maximum; (2) 30 to 180 days in county jail; or (3) Both
Class C misdemeanor §42.01, disorderly conduct; §49.02, public intoxication only	§12.43(c)	Any combination of 3 prior convictions under §42.01 or §49.02 within 24 months before commission of current offense	(1) $2,000 maximum; (2) Up to 180 days in county jail; or (3) Both
CAVEAT:	§12.43(d)	If an offense contains a specific enhancement provision increasing punishment, the specific provision controls over this section	

FELONY PUNISHMENT RANGES

From *Texas Sentencing, Fifth Edition* (2007) by Ken Anderson and John Bradley. Lexis Law Publishing, (800) 542-0957. All rights reserved.

	DEGREE	PENAL CODE	CONFINEMENT	OPTIONAL FINE
1	Capital felony	§12.31	Life in prison or death	None
2	1st degree felony	§12.32	Life or 5 to 99 years in prison	$10,000 maximum
3	2d degree felony	§12.33	2 to 20 years in prison	$10,000 maximum
4	3d degree felony	§12.34	2 to 10 years in prison	$10,000 maximum
5	State jail felony	§12.35	180 days to 2 years in state jail	$10,000 maximum
6	State jail felony committed while using or exhibiting a deadly weapon	§12.35(c)(1)	2 to 10 years in prison	$10,000 maximum

---

ENHANCED FELONY PUNISHMENT RANGES FOR
OFFENSES COMMITTED ON OR AFTER SEPT. 1, 2007

From *Texas Sentencing, Fifth Edition* (2007) by Ken Anderson and John Bradley. Lexis Law Publishing, (800) 542-0957. All rights reserved.

	FELONY DEGREE & ENHANCEMENT LEVEL	PENAL CODE	PLEADING & PROOF REQUIRED	ENHANCED PUNISHMENT RANGE
1	1st degree repeat aggravated sexual assault of child offender (Person convicted of offense against victim (1) younger than 6 or (2) younger than 14 if offense committed violently or victim drugged (Pen §22.021(f))	§12.42(c)(3) ❶	State must plead and prove prior conviction under Pen §22.021(f) or under law of another state with elements substantially similar to Pen §22.021(f)	Capital felony ❷
2	1st degree repeat continuous child sex abuser (Pen §21.02)	§12.42(c)(4)	State must plead and prove prior conviction under Pen §21.02 or under law of another state with elements substantially similar to Pen §21.02	Mandatory life without parole
3	1st degree repeat sex offender or repeat sexual assault (Person convicted of (1) indecency with a child—sexual contact (Pen §21.11(a)(1)), (2) sexual assault (Pen §22.011), (3) aggravated sexual assault (Pen §22.021), (4) aggravated kidnapping with intent to sexually abuse (Pen §20.04(a)(4)), or (5) burglary of a habitation with intent to commit either sexual assault, aggravated sexual assault, aggravated kidnapping with intent to sexually abuse, or indecency with a child (Pen §30.02(d))	§12.42(c)(2)	State must plead and prove prior conviction for (1), (2), (3), (4), or (5) on the left, or for continuous sexual abuse of a child (Pen §21.02), sexual performance by a child (Pen §43.25), promotion/possession of child pornography (Pen §43.26), obscenity or an offense punishable under subsection (h) (Pen §43.23), indecency with a child (Pen §21.11), prohibited sexual conduct (Pen §25.02), or burglary of a habitation with intent to commit prohibited sexual conduct (Pen §30.02(d)), or an offense in another state with elements substantially similar to any of the felonies above	Mandatory life
4	1st degree habitual offender	§12.42(d) ❶	State must plead and prove two prior final felony convictions, and second felony committed after first conviction became final	25 to 99 years or life in prison
5	1st degree repeat offender	§12.42(c)(1) ❶	State must plead and prove prior felony conviction	15 to 99 years or life in prison, and up to $10,000 fine
6	2d degree habitual offender	§12.42(d) ❶	State must plead and prove two prior final felony convictions, and second felony committed after first conviction became final	25 to 99 years or life in prison
7	2d degree repeat offender	§12.42(b) ❶	State must plead and prove prior felony conviction	1st degree felony
8	3d degree habitual offender	§12.42(d) ❶	State must plead and prove two prior final felony convictions, and second felony committed after first conviction became final	25 to 99 years or life in prison

❶ A prior conviction for a state jail felony punishable under Pen §12.35(a) cannot be used for enhancement purposes for this subsection. Pen §12.42(e).

❷ Execution for rape of a child was held unconstitutional by the U.S. Supreme Court in *Kennedy v. Louisiana*, ___ U.S. ___ (2008) (No. 07-343; 6-25-08).

	FELONY DEGREE & ENHANCEMENT LEVEL	PENAL CODE	PLEADING & PROOF REQUIRED	ENHANCED PUNISHMENT RANGE
9	3d degree repeat offender	§12.42(a)(3)	State must plead and prove prior felony conviction	2d degree felony
10	State jail violent habitual offender (if the state jail felony is punishable under §12.35(c)) ❸	§12.42(d) ❶	State must plead and prove two prior final felony convictions, and second felony committed after first conviction became final	25 to 99 years or life in prison
11	State jail violent repeat offender (if the state jail felony is punishable under §12.35(c)) ❸	§12.42(a)(3)	State must plead and prove prior felony conviction	2d degree felony
12	State jail habitual offender (if the state jail felony is punishable under §12.35(a))	§12.42(a)(2)	State must plead and prove two prior final felony convictions, and second felony committed after first conviction became final (both prior convictions must be non-state-jail felonies) ❹	2d degree felony
13	State jail violent offender	§12.35(c) ❺	State must plead and prove (1) prior final felony conviction of continuous sex abuse of child (Pen §21.02) or an offense listed in CCP art. 42.12, §3g(a)(1); (2) prior final felony conviction with deadly weapon finding (CCP art. 42.12, §3g(a)(2)); or (3) that a deadly weapon was used or exhibited in offense or during flight from offense for which defendant is being prosecuted	3d degree felony
14	State jail habitual offender (if the state jail felony is punishable under §12.35(a) and the defendant has committed two state jail felonies) ❹	§12.42(a)(1)	State must plead and prove final convictions of two state jail felonies	3d degree felony

❶ A prior conviction for a state jail felony punishable under Pen §12.35(a) cannot be used for enhancement purposes for this subsection. Pen §12.42(e).

❸ The State cannot use a prior felony conviction more than once for enhancement purposes in the same prosecution. Thus, the State cannot use a prior felony conviction to make a state jail felony punishable under Pen §12.35(c) and then use the same prior felony conviction to further enhance the punishment under Pen §12.42. *Hernandez v. State*, 929 S.W.2d 11, 13 (Tex.Crim.App.1996).

❹ *Campbell v. State*, 49 S.W.3d 874, 878 (Tex.Crim.App.2001).

❺ Section (c) can be used to enhance the punishment of a first-time offender. *See* Pen §12.35(c)(1).

ENHANCED FELONY PUNISHMENT RANGES FOR
OFFENSES COMMITTED BEFORE SEPT. 1, 2007

From *Texas Sentencing, Fifth Edition* (2007) by Ken Anderson and John Bradley. Lexis Law Publishing, (800) 542-0957. All rights reserved.

	FELONY DEGREE & ENHANCEMENT LEVEL	PENAL CODE	PLEADING & PROOF REQUIRED	ENHANCED PUNISHMENT RANGE
1	1st degree habitual offender	§12.42(d) ❶	State must plead and prove two prior final felony convictions, and second felony committed after first conviction became final	25 to 99 years or life in prison ❷
2	1st degree repeat offender	§12.42(c)(1) ❶	State must plead and prove prior felony conviction	15 to 99 years or life in prison, and up to $10,000 fine ❷
3	2d degree habitual offender	§12.42(d) ❶	State must plead and prove two prior final felony convictions, and second felony committed after first conviction became final	25 to 99 years or life in prison
4	2d degree repeat offender	§12.42(b) ❶	State must plead and prove prior felony conviction	1st degree felony
5	3d degree habitual offender	§12.42(d) ❶	State must plead and prove two prior final felony convictions, and second felony committed after first conviction became final	25 to 99 years or life in prison
6	3d degree repeat offender	§12.42(a)(3)	State must plead and prove prior felony conviction	2d degree felony
7	State jail violent habitual offender (if the state jail felony is punishable under §12.35(c)) ❸	§12.42(d) ❶	State must plead and prove two prior final felony convictions, and second felony committed after first conviction became final	25 to 99 years or life in prison ❹
8	State jail violent repeat offender (if the state jail felony is punishable under §12.35(c)) ❸	§12.42(a)(3)	State must plead and prove prior felony conviction	2d degree felony
9	State jail habitual offender (if the state jail felony is punishable under §12.35(a))	§12.42(a)(2)	State must plead and prove two prior final felony convictions, and second felony committed after first conviction became final (both prior convictions must be non-state-jail felonies ❺)	2d degree felony

❶ A prior conviction for a state jail felony punishable under Pen §12.35(a) cannot be used for enhancement purposes for this subsection. Pen §12.42(e).

❷ If the defendant is convicted of (1) sexual assault (Pen §22.011), (2) aggravated sexual assault (Pen §22.021), (3) aggravated kidnapping with intent to sexually abuse (Pen §20.04(a)(4)), or (4) burglary of a habitation with intent to commit either sexual assault, aggravated sexual assault, aggravated kidnapping with intent to sexually abuse, or indecency with a child (Pen §30.02(d)), then life is mandatory if the defendant has been previously convicted of (1), (2), (3), or (4) above or of sexual performance by a child (Pen §43.25), promotion/possession of child pornography (Pen §43.26), obscenity or an offense punishable under subsection (h) (Pen §43.23), indecency with a child (Pen §21.11), prohibited sexual conduct (Pen §25.02), or burglary of a habitation with intent to commit prohibited sexual conduct (Pen §30.02(d)), or an offense in another state with elements substantially similar to any of the felonies above. Pen §12.42(c)(2).

❸ The State cannot use a prior felony conviction more than once for enhancement purposes in the same prosecution. Thus, the State cannot use a prior felony conviction to make a state jail felony punishable under Pen §12.35(c) and then use the same prior felony conviction to further enhance the punishment under Pen §12.42. *Hernandez v. State*, 929 S.W.2d 11, 13 (Tex.Crim.App.1996).

❹ *Smith v. State*, 960 S.W.2d 372, 373 n.2 (Tex.App.—Houston [1st Dist.] 1998, pet. ref'd).

❺ *Campbell v. State*, 49 S.W.3d 874, 878 (Tex.Crim.App.2001).

	FELONY DEGREE & ENHANCEMENT LEVEL	PENAL CODE	PLEADING & PROOF REQUIRED	ENHANCED PUNISHMENT RANGE
10	State jail violent offender	§12.35(c) ❻	State must plead and prove (1) prior final felony conviction of offense listed in CCP art. 42.12, §3g(a)(1); (2) prior final felony conviction with deadly weapon finding (CCP art. 42.12, §3g(a)(2)); or (3) that a deadly weapon was used or exhibited in offense or during flight from offense for which defendant is being prosecuted	3d degree felony
11	State jail habitual offender (if the state jail felony is punishable under §12.35(a) and the defendant has committed two state jail felonies)	§12.42(a)(1)	State must plead and prove final convictions of two state jail felonies	3d degree felony

❻ Section (c) can be used to enhance the punishment of a first-time offender. *See* Pen §12.35(c)(1).

2007 STANDARD VALUE LADDER*

AMOUNT OF PECUNIARY LOSS	PUNISHMENT RANGE
$200,000 or more	First degree felony
$100,000 or more but less than $200,000	Second degree felony
$20,000 or more but less than $100,000	Third degree felony
$1,500 or more but less than $20,000	State jail felony
$500 or more but less than $1,500	Class A misdemeanor
$20 or more but less than $500	Class B misdemeanor
Less than $20	Class C misdemeanor

* See Pen §31.04.

PENALTIES FOR PENAL CODE VIOLATIONS

From *Texas Sentencing, Fifth Edition* (2007) by Ken Anderson and John Bradley. Lexis Law Publishing, (800) 542-0957. All rights reserved.

PENAL CODE		OFFENSE	PUNISHMENT
1	§16.01	Unlawful use of criminal instrument	State jail or one category lower than the offense intended
2	§16.02	Unlawful interception, use, or disclosure of wire, oral, or electronic communications	• 2d degree • State jail for manufacture, assembly, possession, or sale of device for nonconsensual interception of communication, or advertisement of same • State jail for interfering with authorized governmental interception of communication
3	§16.03	Unlawful use of pen register or trap & trace device	State jail
4	§16.04	Unlawful access to stored communications	• State jail if to obtain benefit or harm another • Class A
5	§16.05	Illegal divulgence of public communications	• State jail if involving a scrambled or encrypted radio communication • Class A if for tortious or illegal purpose or to gain benefit involving an unscrambled radio communication if the communication is not a public land mobile radio service communication or a paging service communication • Class C if for tortious or illegal purpose or to gain benefit involving an unscrambled radio communication if the communication is a public land mobile radio service communication or a paging service communication
6	§16.06	Unlawful installation of tracking device	Class A
7	§19.02	Murder	• 1st degree • 2d degree if under immediate influence of sudden passion
8	§19.03	Capital murder	Capital felony
9	§19.04	Manslaughter	2d degree
10	§19.05	Criminally negligent homicide	State jail
11	§20.02	Unlawful restraint	• 3d degree if exposure to substantial risk of bodily injury • 3d degree if actor knowingly restrains a public servant who is lawfully discharging an official duty or in retaliation for an exercise of official power • 3d degree if actor, while in custody, restrains any other person • State jail if victim is younger than 17 • Class A
12	§20.03	Kidnapping	3d degree
13	§20.04	Aggravated kidnapping	• 1st degree • 2d degree if victim released voluntarily and in safe place
14	§20.05	Unlawful transport	State jail
15	§20A.02	Trafficking of persons	• 1st degree if person younger than 18 and offense violates a public indecency law (Pen ch. 43) • 1st degree if person who is trafficked dies • 2d degree
16	§21.02	Continuous sexual abuse of young child or children	1st degree with minimum of 25 years imprisonment

PENAL CODE		OFFENSE	PUNISHMENT
17	§21.06	Homosexual conduct	Class C (statute ruled unconstitutional by *Lawrence*, 539 U.S. 558, 123 S.Ct. 2472 (2003))
18	§21.07	Public lewdness	Class A
19	§21.08	Indecent exposure	Class B
20	§21.11	Indecency with a child	• 2d degree if by sexual contact • 3d degree if by exposure
21	§21.12	Improper relationship between educator and student	2d degree
22	§21.15	Improper photography or visual recording	State jail
23	§22.01	Assault	• 3d degree if committed against public servant • 3d degree if committed against someone in dating relationship (Fam §71.0021(b)), family relationship (Fam §71.003), or household relationship (Fam §71.005), with prior conviction of assault, homicide (Pen ch. 19), kidnapping (Pen §20.03), aggravated kidnapping (Pen §20.04), or indecency with a child (Pen §21.11) against someone whose relationship to defendant is described by Fam §§71.0021(b), 71.003, or 71.005 • 3d degree if committed against a person the defendant knows contracts with government to perform a service and committed while person performing that service in the scope of the contract • 3d degree if committed in retaliation for person's performance of a service within scope of contract • 3d degree if committed against a person the defendant knows is a security officer while the officer is performing duties • Class A if bodily injury occurs • Class A if offensive touch to an elderly or disabled person • Class B if committed by a person who is not a sports participant against a person the actor knows is a sports participant either while participant is performing duties in that capacity or in retaliation for participant's performance in that capacity • Class C if offensive or provocative physical contact or threat to cause imminent bodily injury
24	§22.011	Sexual assault	• 1st degree if victim was someone actor was prohibited from marrying under Pen §25.01 (bigamy) • 2d degree
25	§22.015	Coercing, soliciting, or inducing gang membership	• 3d degree if causes bodily injury to a child • State jail if threatens imminent bodily injury to a child
26	§22.02	Aggravated assault	• 1st degree if deadly weapon used against person in dating relationship (Fam §71.0021(b)), family relationship (Fam §71.003), or household relationship (Fam §71.005) causing serious bodily injury • 1st degree if against or by public servant, against a witness or informant, or against a person the defendant knows is a security officer while performing a duty • 2d degree
27	§22.021	Aggravated sexual assault	• 1st degree with minimum of 25 years imprisonment if (1) victim younger than 6 or (2) victim younger than 14 and violence used • 1st degree

CHARTS

PENAL CODE		OFFENSE	PUNISHMENT

28	§22.04	Injury to a child, elderly individual, or disabled individual	• Serious bodily injury, mental deficiency, impairment, or injury:
			  o 1st degree: Intentionally or knowingly
			  o 2d degree: Recklessly
			• Bodily injury or exploitation by owner, operator, or employee of group home, nursing home, or institutional care facility:
			  o 3d degree: Intentionally or knowingly
			  o State jail: Recklessly
			• Any type of injury above:
			  o State jail: Criminal negligence

29	§22.041	Abandoning or endangering child	• 2d degree if abandoned under circumstances that a reasonable person would believe would place the child in imminent danger • 3d degree if abandoned without intent to return • State jail if abandoned with intent to return or endangerment
30	§22.05	Deadly conduct	• 3d degree if knowingly discharging firearm at people or at building if reckless as to whether building is occupied • Class A
31	§22.07	Terroristic threat	• 3d degree if with intent to influence the conduct or activities of a branch or agency of federal or state government • 3d degree if with intent to place the public in fear of serious bodily injury • 3d degree if with intent to cause impairment of public utilities, communications, transport, etc. • State jail if actor causes loss of $1,500 or more to owner of building, room, place, or conveyance • Class A if with intent to prevent occupation of public building, vehicle, etc. • Class A if with intent to place member of household or public servant in fear of imminent serious bodily injury • Class B if with intent to cause reaction by emergency agency or intent to place fear of imminent bodily injury
32	§22.08	Aiding suicide	• State jail if resulting in death or serious bodily injury • Class C
33	§22.09	Tampering with consumer product	• 1st degree if actual tampering and serious bodily injury • 2d degree if actual tampering • 3d degree if threat to tamper
34	§22.10	Leaving a child in a vehicle	Class C
35	§22.11	Harassment by persons in certain correctional facilities; harassment of public servant	3d degree
36	§25.01	Bigamy	• 1st degree if younger than 16 • 2d degree if 16 or older • 3d degree
37	§25.02	Prohibited sexual conduct	• 2d degree if with first cousin • 3d degree
38	§25.03	Interference with child custody	State jail
39	§25.031	Agreement to abduct from custody	State jail
40	§25.04	Enticing a child	• 3d degree if intended to commit felony against child • Class B
41	§25.05	Criminal nonsupport	State jail
42	§25.06	Harboring runaway child	Class A

PENAL CODE		OFFENSE	PUNISHMENT
43	§25.07	Violation of court orders or conditions of bond in a family violence case	• 3d degree if two prior convictions under this section or commits an assault or stalking in violation of order • Class A
44	§25.071	Violation of protective order preventing offense caused by bias or prejudice	• 3d degree if two prior convictions or violates protective order with assault • Class A
45	§25.08	Sale or purchase of child	• 2d degree if defendant commits offense with intent to commit offense under Pen §43.25 • 3d degree
46	§25.09	Advertising for placement of child	• 3d degree if prior conviction under this section • Class A
47	§25.10	Interference with rights of guardian	State jail

48	§28.02	Arson	• 1st degree if causes death or bodily injury, or damages or destroys a habitation or place of worship
			• 2d degree if damages any vegetation, fence, building, habitation, or vehicle
			• 3d degree if defendant intends to damage or destroy building or injure someone and recklessly damages building, habitation, or vehicle
			• If manufacturing or attempting to manufacture controlled substance:
			  o 3d degree if fire or explosion causes death or bodily injury
			  o State jail if fire or explosion damages any building, habitation, or vehicle

49	§28.03	Criminal mischief	• 1st degree if property is livestock and the damage is caused by introducing mad cow disease or a disease under Agric §161.041 • 3d degree if property is transportation communications equipment or device and pecuniary loss less than $100,000 • Standard Value Ladder for damage of $500 or more • State jail if less than $20,000 damage done to place of worship or human burial, public monument, or community center; if less than $1,500 damage done to habitation by firearm or explosive; or damage done to fence used to contain cattle or game • Class A if $500 or more but less than $1,500 or causes impairment or diversion of public utilities or services • Class B if $50 or more but less than $500 • Class C if less than $50 or causes substantial inconvenience
50	§28.04	Reckless damage or destruction	Class C
51	§28.07	Interference with railroad property	• Standard Value Ladder if pecuniary damage results • 3d degree if bodily injury caused by throwing object or discharging firearm at train • Class B if throws object or discharges firearm at train • Class C if by trespass, tampering, obstruction, or derailment, unless causes pecuniary loss
52	§28.08	Graffiti	• Standard Value Ladder if $500 or more • State jail if marking on school, place of worship, etc., and loss less than $20,000 • Class B if less than $500
53	§29.02	Robbery	2d degree
54	§29.03	Aggravated robbery	1st degree

PENAL CODE		OFFENSE	PUNISHMENT
55	§30.02	Burglary	• 1st degree if habitation with intent to commit felony or actual commission of felony other than theft • 2d degree if habitation • State jail if building other than habitation
56	§30.03	Burglary of coin-operated or coin collection machines	Class A
57	§30.04	Burglary of vehicles	• State jail if railcar or if two or more prior convictions under §30.04 • Class A
58	§30.05	Criminal trespass	• Class A if committed in habitation or shelter center, on Superfund site, or on or in a critical infrastructure facility, or if deadly weapon carried • Class B • Class C if agricultural land
59	§30.06	Trespass by holder of license to carry concealed handgun	Class A

60	§31.03	Theft	• Standard Value Ladder with modifications:
			  o 3d degree if 10 or more head of livestock or 100 or more head of sheep or swine valued under $100,000
			  o State jail if less than 10 head of cattle or horses or 100 head of sheep or swine valued under $20,000; or stolen from the person of another or from a corpse or grave; or a firearm; or less than $1,500 with two prior convictions; or an official ballot or official carrier envelope for an election
			  o Class B if at least $50 but less than $500; or at least $20 but less than $500 and obtained by passing check; or less than $50 with a prior theft conviction; or less than $20 with a prior theft conviction and obtained by passing check
			  o Class C if less than $50; or less than $20 and obtained by passing check
			  o Next higher punishment if public servant or under government contract, if at time of offense property owner was an elderly individual, or caused an alarm to sound or otherwise become activated during the commission of the offense. Pen. Code §31.16(e)

61	§31.04	Theft of service	Standard Value Ladder
62	§31.05	Theft of trade secrets	3d degree
63	§31.07	Unauthorized use of a vehicle	State jail
64	§31.11	Tampering with identification numbers	Class A
65	§31.12	Theft of or tampering with multichannel video or information services	• Class A if for remuneration or if had two or more prior convictions for this offense • Class B if one prior conviction for this offense • Class C
66	§31.13	Manufacture, distribution, or advertisement of multichannel video or information services device	Class A
67	§31.14	Sale or lease of multichannel video or information services device	Class A
68	§31.15	Possession, manufacture, or distribution of certain instruments used to commit retail theft	Class A

PENAL CODE		OFFENSE	PUNISHMENT
69	§31.16	Organized retail theft	• Standard Value Ladder • Next higher punishment if organized, supervised, financed, or managed, or caused an alarm to sound during commission of offense
70	§32.21	Forgery	• 3d degree if money, securities, stamps, government record, stocks, bonds • State jail if will, deed, security, credit card, check, contract, authorization to debit an account at a financial institution, etc. • Class A
71	§32.22	Criminal simulation	Class A
72	§32.23	Trademark counterfeiting	Standard Value Ladder
73	§32.24	Stealing or receiving stolen check or similar sight order	Class A
74	§32.31	Credit card or debit card abuse	State jail

75	§32.32	False statement to obtain property or credit	• Standard Value Ladder with modifications:
			  o Class B if $50 or more but less than $500
			  o Class C if less than $50

76	§32.33	Hindering secured creditors	Standard Value Ladder with respect to value of property destroyed, removed, concealed, encumbered, harmed, or reduced in value
77	§32.34	Fraudulent transfer of a motor vehicle	• 3d degree if vehicle valued at $20,000 or more • State jail if vehicle valued at less than $20,000 • Class A if conduct involves failure to disclose to owner location of vehicle
78	§32.35	Credit card transaction record laundering	Standard Value Ladder with respect to amount of the record of sale
79	§32.41	Issuance of bad check	• Class B if for child support • Class C
80	§32.42	Deceptive business practices	• Class A for subdivisions (b)(7)-(12), or if offense committed intentionally, knowingly, or recklessly, or if prior conviction for Class B or Class C misdemeanor under this section • Class C for subdivisions (b)(1)-(6) if offense is result of criminal negligence
81	§32.43	Commercial bribery	• State jail • In some circumstances, court may increase the fine
82	§32.44	Rigging publicly exhibited contest	Class A
83	§32.441	Illegal recruitment of an athlete	Standard Value Ladder with respect to the value of the benefit conferred
84	§32.45	Misapplication of fiduciary property or property of financial institution	• Standard Value Ladder with respect to value of property misapplied • Increased to next higher category of offense if offense committed against an elderly individual
85	§32.46	Securing execution of document by deception	• Standard Value Ladder with respect to value of the property, service, or pecuniary interest • State jail if causes public servant to file purported judgment • Increased to next higher category if against elderly individual or involves state Medicaid program

PENAL CODE		OFFENSE	PUNISHMENT
86	§32.47	Fraudulent destruction, removal, or concealment of writing	• State jail if a will, deed, or other document required to be recorded publicly • Class A
87	§32.48	Simulating legal process	• State jail if prior conviction under this section • Class A
88	§32.49	Refusal to execute release of fraudulent lien or claim	Class A
89	§32.50	Deceptive preparation & marketing of academic product	Class C
90	§32.51	Fraudulent use or possession of identifying information	• 1st degree if number of items 50 or more • 2d degree if number of items 10 or more but fewer than 50 • 3d degree if number of items five or more but fewer than 10 • State jail if number of items less than five
91	§32.52	Fraudulent, substandard, or fictitious degree	Class B
92	§33.02	Breach of computer security	• Standard Value Ladder with respect to benefit or harm for amounts over $1,500 • State jail if less than $1,500 and two or more prior convictions under this chapter • Class A if aggregate benefit or harm is less than $1,500 • Class B, unless actor knowingly benefits or causes harm
93	§33.021	Online solicitation of a minor	• 2d degree if minor is or is believed to be younger than 14 • 2d degree if minor solicited to meet for sex • 3d degree if communicate in sexually explicit manner or distribute sexually explicit material
94	§33.05	Tampering with direct recording electronic voting machine	• 1st degree • 3d degree for attempted tampering
95	§33A.02	Unauthorized use of telecommunications service	• Standard Value Ladder with respect to value of the telecommunication service used or diverted of $500 or more • State jail if less than $1,500 and two prior convictions under this chapter • Class A if less than $500 and prior conviction under this chapter • Class B for value of telecommunication service used or diverted of less than $500
96	§33A.03	Manufacture, possession, or delivery of unlawful telecommunications device	3d degree
97	§33A.04	Theft of telecommunications service	• Standard Value Ladder with respect to value of the service of $500 or more • State jail if value of service is less than $1,500 and two previous convictions under this chapter • Class A if value of service is less than $500 and previous conviction under this chapter • Class B if value of service less than $500
98	§33A.05	Publication of telecommunications access device	• 3d degree if previous conviction under this chapter • Class A
99	§34.02	Money laundering	Standard Value Ladder with respect to value of funds laundered that are $1,500 or greater

PENAL CODE		OFFENSE	PUNISHMENT
100	§35.02	Insurance fraud	• Standard Value Ladder with respect to value of claim of $500 or more • 1st degree if act committed in connection with offense placed person at risk of death or serious bodily injury • State jail if prepared or presented statement known to be false or misleading to defraud insurer • Class B if $50 or more but less than $500 • Class C if less than $50
101	§35A.02	Medicaid fraud	• Standard Value Ladder with respect to amount of payment, value of benefit provided, or claim for payment of $500 or more • State jail if knowingly obstruct attorney general investigation or if amount or value cannot be readily ascertained • Class B if $50 or more but less than $500 • Class C if less than $50
102	§36.02	Bribery	2d degree
103	§36.03	Coercion of public servant or voter	• 3d degree if coercion is threat to commit felony • Class A
104	§36.04	Improper influence	Class A
105	§36.05	Tampering with a witness	State jail
106	§36.06	Obstruction or retaliation	• 2d degree if threat or harm to a juror • 3d degree
107	§36.07	Acceptance of honorarium	Class A
108	§36.08	Gift to public servant by person subject to his jurisdiction	Class A
109	§36.09	Offering gift to public servant	Class A
110	§37.02	Perjury	Class A
111	§37.03	Aggravated perjury	3d degree
112	§37.08	False report to police officer or law enforcement employee	Class B
113	§37.081	False report regarding missing child or missing person	Class C
114	§37.09	Tampering with or fabricating physical evidence	• 2d degree if thing altered, destroyed, or concealed is a human corpse • 3d degree • Class A if person observes human remains under circumstances that would lead a reasonable person to believe offense was committed and person fails to report location of remains

PENAL CODE		OFFENSE	PUNISHMENT
115	§37.10	Tampering with governmental record	• 2d degree if record was public school record, license, permit, etc., and intent to defraud or harm • 2d degree if document is governmental record and intent to defraud • 3d degree if record was public school record, license, permit, seal, title, etc. • 3d degree if document is governmental record and false entry, impairment, or sale of government record • State jail if intent to defraud or harm • Class A • Class B if document is tax appraisal filed by person with contingency interest in appraisal hearing • Class B if document is governmental record and knowledge of falsity • Class C if governmental record used to establish school district residency
116	§37.101	Fraudulent filing of financing statement	• 2d degree if forged and defendant previously convicted under this section two or more times • 3d degree if forged • State jail if groundless or contains material false information and done with intent to harm or defraud • Class A if groundless or contains material false information
117	§37.11	Impersonating public servant	3d degree
118	§37.12	False identification as peace officer; misrepresentation of property	Class B
119	§37.13	Record of a fraudulent court	• 3d degree if defendant has two prior convictions under this section • Class A
120	§38.02	Failure to identify	• Class A if fugitive and gives false information • Class B if fugitive and refuses to give information • Class B if intentionally gives false information • Class C if intentionally refuses to give information
121	§38.03	Resisting arrest, search, or transportation	• 3d degree if deadly weapon used • Class A
122	§38.04	Evading arrest or detention	• 2d degree if another suffers death • 3d degree if another suffers serious bodily injury or if vehicle used and previously convicted • State jail if vehicle used • Class B
123	§38.05	Hindering apprehension or prosecution	• 3d degree if hindering apprehension of a known felon, including offense under CCP art. 62.102 • Class A
124	§38.06	Escape	• 1st degree if serious bodily injury caused or used or threatened to use deadly weapon • 2d degree if bodily injury caused • 3d degree if felon, including felon under CCP art. 62.102, or if escapes from secure correctional facility • Class A
125	§38.07	Permitting or facilitating escape	• 2d degree if used or threatened to use deadly weapon, or felon confined in secure correctional facility • 3d degree if felon or incarcerated felon, other than in secure correctional facility • Class A
126	§38.09	Implements for escape	• 2d degree if deadly weapon provided • 3d degree

PENAL CODE		OFFENSE	PUNISHMENT
127	§38.10	Bail jumping and failure to appear	• 3d degree if offense was felony • Class A • Class C if offense was punishable by fine only
128	§38.11	Prohibited substances and items in correctional or detention facilities or on property of TDCJ or TYC	3d degree
129	§38.111	Improper contact with victim	• 3d degree if committed in correctional facility after conviction for a reportable sex offense listed in CCP art. 62.001(5) • Class A
130	§38.112	Violation of protective order issued on basis of sexual assault	Class A
131	§38.113	Unauthorized absence from community corrections facility, county correctional center, or assignment site	State jail
132	§38.114	Contraband in correctional facility	• Class B if committed by employee or volunteer of correctional facility • Class C
133	§38.12	Barratry and solicitation of professional employment	• 3d degree if committed under subsection (a) or (b), or if committed under subsection (d) with prior conviction under subsection (d) • Class A if under subsection (d)
134	§38.122	Falsely holding oneself out as a lawyer	3d degree
135	§38.123	Unauthorized practice of law	• 3d degree if repeat offense • Class A
136	§38.13	Hindering proceedings by disorderly conduct	Class A
137	§38.14	Taking or attempting to take weapon from peace officer, parole officer, etc.	• 3d degree if weapon is taken • State jail
138	§38.15	Interference with public duties	Class B
139	§38.151	Interference with police service animals	• 2d degree if animal killed or conduct is likely to kill animal • 2d degree if one injures or engages in conduct likely to injure police service animal in a manner that materially and permanently affects its ability to function as such • State jail if injured or conduct is likely to injure animal • Class A if interference with animal or handler, or release of animal, or entering areas of control of animal without consent • Class B if something thrown at animal • Class C if animal taunted, struck, or tormented
140	§38.16	Preventing execution of civil process	Class C
141	§38.17	Failure to stop or report aggravated sexual assault of child	Class A
142	§38.171	Failure to report felony	Class A
143	§38.18	Use of accident report information and other information for pecuniary gain	Class B
144	§38.19	Failure to provide notice and report of death of resident of institution	Class B

PENAL CODE		OFFENSE	PUNISHMENT
145	§39.02	Abuse of official capacity	• Standard Value Ladder with respect to value of use of thing misused • Class A if violation of law relating to public servant's office or employment
146	§39.03	Official oppression	Class A
147	§39.04	Violations of the civil rights of person in custody; improper sexual activity with person in custody	• 2d degree if sexual contact offense committed against a juvenile in custody of a correctional facility financed primarily with state funds or in custody of Texas Youth Commission • State jail if sexual contact • Class A
148	§39.05	Failure to report death of prisoner	Class B
149	§39.06	Misuse of official information	• 3d degree • Class C if public servant offender coerces another not to report
150	§42.01	Disorderly conduct	• Class B if displays firearm in public place to cause alarm or discharges firearm in public place, except public road • Class C
151	§42.02	Riot	• Class B • Same grade of offense as an offense committed by anyone engaged in the riot
152	§42.03	Obstructing highway or other passageway	Class B
153	§42.05	Disrupting meeting or procession	Class B
154	§42.055	Funeral service disruptions	Class B
155	§42.06	False alarm or report	• State jail if involving public schools, utilities, communications, etc. • Class A
156	§42.061	Silent or abusive calls to 911 service	Class B
157	§42.062	Interference with emergency telephone call	• State jail if previous conviction • Class A
158	§42.07	Harassment	• Class A if prior conviction • Class B
159	§42.072	Stalking	• 2d degree if prior conviction • 3d degree
160	§42.08	Abuse of corpse	Class A
161	§42.09	Cruelty to livestock animals	• 3d degree if violation of (a)(1), (5), (6), (7), or (8) and two prior convictions under §42.09, §42.092, or one prior conviction under both sections • State jail if o violation of (a)(1), (5), (6), (7), or (8), or o violation of (a)(2), (3), (4), or (9) and two prior convictions under §42.09, §42.092, or one prior conviction under both sections • Class A if violation of (a)(2), (3), (4), or (9)
162	§42.091	Attack on assistance animal	• 3d degree if assistance animal is killed • State jail if assistance animal is injured • Class A if assistance animal is attacked

PENAL CODE		OFFENSE	PUNISHMENT
163	§42.092	Cruelty to nonlivestock animals	• 3d degree if violation of (b)(1), (2), (7), or (8) and two prior convictions under §42.09, §42.092, or one prior conviction under both sections • State jail if • violation of (b)(1), (2), (7), or (8), or • violation of (b)(3), (4), (5), (6), or (9) and two prior convictions under §42.09, §42.092, or one prior conviction under both sections • Class A if violation of (b)(3), (4), (5), (6), or (9)
164	§42.10	Dog fighting	• State jail if causes dog to fight or participates in earnings of or either operates or permits another to use one's property to operate dog fighting outfit • Class A if trains a fighting dog or attends as spectator a dog fighting exhibition
165	§42.11	Destruction of flag	Class A
166	§42.12	Discharge of firearm in certain municipalities	Class A
167	§42.13	Use of laser pointers	Class C
168	§42.14	Illumination of aircraft by intense light	• Class A if light impairs operator • Class C
169	§43.02	Prostitution	• State jail if three or more previous convictions • Class A if one or two previous convictions • Class B
170	§43.03	Promotion of prostitution	Class A
171	§43.04	Aggravated promotion of prostitution	3d degree
172	§43.05	Compelling prostitution	2d degree
173	§43.22	Obscene display or distribution	Class C
174	§43.23	Obscenity	• State jail if wholesale promotes • Class A • Increased to 3d degree for subsection (a) and state jail under (c) if obscene material depicts activities by a child under 18
175	§43.24	Sale, distribution, or display of harmful material to minor	• 3d degree if hiring minor to assist in offense • Class A
176	§43.25	Sexual performance by a child	• 1st degree if employing or inducing child younger than 14 • 2d degree if employing or inducing • 2d degree if producing or promoting child younger than 14 • 3d degree if producing or promoting
177	§43.251	Employment harmful to children	Class A
178	§43.26	Possession or promotion of child pornography	• 2d degree for promotion • 3d degree
179	§46.02	Unlawful carrying weapons	• 3d degree if on premises allowed to sell alcohol • Class A
180	§46.03	Places weapons prohibited	3d degree
181	§46.035	Unlawful carrying of handgun by license holder	• 3d degree if on premises of business that derives 51% or more of its income from sale or service of alcohol, or a correctional facility • Class A
182	§46.04	Unlawful possession of firearm	• 3d degree if a felon • Class A

PENAL CODE		OFFENSE	PUNISHMENT
183	§46.041	Unlawful possession of metal or body armor by felon	3d degree
184	§46.05	Prohibited weapons	• 3d degree • Class A if switchblade or knuckles
185	§46.06	Unlawful transfer of certain weapons	• State jail if handgun is provided to a person under 18 • Class A
186	§46.08	Hoax bombs	Class A
187	§46.09	Components of explosives	3d degree
188	§46.10	Deadly weapon in penal institution	3d degree
189	§46.11	Penalty if offense committed within weapon-free school zone	Offense under Chapter 46 increased to next highest category if committed within school zone
190	§46.13	Making a firearm accessible to a child	• Class A if child causes death or serious bodily injury • Class C
191	§47.02	Gambling	Class C
192	§47.03	Gambling promotion	Class A
193	§47.04	Keeping a gambling place	Class A
194	§47.05	Communicating gambling information	Class A
195	§47.06	Possession of gambling device, equipment, or paraphernalia	Class A
196	§48.01	Smoking tobacco	Class C
197	§48.015	Prohibitions relating to certain cigarettes	Class A
198	§48.02	Prohibition of the purchase and sale of human organs	Class A
199	§49.02	Public intoxication	Class C
200	§49.031	Possession of alcoholic beverage in motor vehicle	Class C
201	§49.04	Driving while intoxicated	• Class B, minimum 72 hours • Class B, minimum 6 days if with open container • See also §49.09 for subsequent offenses
202	§49.045	DWI with child passenger	State jail
203	§49.05	Flying while intoxicated	• Class B, minimum 72 hours • See also §49.09 for subsequent offenses
204	§49.06	Boating while intoxicated	• Class B, minimum 72 hours • See also §49.09 for subsequent offenses
205	§49.065	Assembling or operating an amusement ride while intoxicated	• Class B, minimum 72 hours • Class B, minimum 6 days if with open container • See also §49.09 for subsequent offenses
206	§49.07	Intoxication assault	• 2d degree if serious bodily injury to peace officer, firefighter, or emergency medical services personnel (§49.09(b-1)) • 3d degree
207	§49.08	Intoxication manslaughter	• 1st degree if caused death of peace officer, firefighter, or emergency services personnel • 2d degree

PENAL CODE		OFFENSE	PUNISHMENT
208	§49.09	Enhanced offenses and penalties	• 3d degree if two or more priors or one prior under §49.08 • Class A, minimum 30 days for second conviction
209	§71.02	Engaging in organized criminal activity	• One category higher than most serious offense committed • Conspiracy – same category as most serious offense conspired to commit
210	§71.021	Violation of court order enjoining organized criminal activity	Class A
211	§71.022	Soliciting membership in a criminal street gang	• 2d degree with prior conviction of this offense • 3d degree

CHARTS

PENALTIES FOR TEXAS CONTROLLED SUBSTANCES ACT VIOLATIONS

From *Texas Sentencing, Fifth Edition* (2007) by Ken Anderson and John Bradley. Lexis Law Publishing, (800) 542-0957. All rights reserved.

	HEALTH & SAFETY CODE	OFFENSE	PUNISHMENT
1	§481.003	Misuse of federal drug enforcement administration number	Class C
2	§481.112	Manufacture or delivery – penalty group 1	• Life or 15 to 99 years and up to $250,000 if 400 g or more • Life or 10 to 99 years and up to $100,000 if 200 g or more but less than 400 g • 1st degree if 4 g or more but less than 200 g • 2d degree if 1 g or more but less than 4 g • State jail if less than 1 g If a child is present during manufacture, the punishments are enchanced (H&SC §481.1122)
3	§481.1121	Manufacture or delivery – penalty group 1-A	• Life or 15 to 99 years and up to $250,000 if 4,000 units or more • 1st degree if 80 units or more but less than 4,000 units • 2d degree if 20 units or more but less than 80 units • State jail if less than 20 units
4	§481.113	Manufacture or delivery – penalty group 2	• Life or 10 to 99 years and up to $100,000 if 400 g or more • 1st degree if 4 g or more but less than 400 g • 2d degree if 1 g or more but less than 4 g • State jail if less than 1 g
5	§481.114	Manufacture or delivery – penalty group 3 or 4	• Life or 10 to 99 years and up to $100,000 if 400 g or more • 1st degree if 200 g or more but less than 400 g • 2d degree if 28 g or more but less than 200 g • State jail if less than 28 g
6	§481.115	Possession – penalty group 1	• Life or 10 to 99 years and up to $100,000 if 400 g or more • 1st degree if 200 g or more but less than 400 g • 2d degree if 4 g or more but less than 200 g • 3d degree if 1 g or more but less than 4 g • State jail if less than 1 g
7	§481.1151	Possession – penalty group 1-A	• Life or 15 to 99 years and up to $250,000 if 8,000 units or more • 1st degree if 4,000 units or more but less than 8,000 units • 2d degree if 80 units or more but less than 4,000 units • 3d degree if 20 units or more but less than 80 units • State jail if less than 20 units
8	§481.116	Possession – penalty group 2	• Life or 5 to 99 years and up to $50,000 if 400 g or more • 2d degree if 4 g or more but less than 400 g • 3d degree if 1 g or more but less than 4 g • State jail if less than 1 g
9	§481.117	Possession – penalty group 3	• Life or 5 to 99 years and up to $50,000 if 400 g or more • 2d degree if 200 g or more but less than 400 g • 3d degree if 28 g or more but less than 200 g • Class A if less than 28 g
10	§481.118	Possession – penalty group 4	• Life or 5 to 99 years and up to $50,000 if 400 g or more • 2d degree if 200 g or more but less than 400 g • 3d degree if 28 g or more but less than 200 g • Class B if less than 28 g
11	§481.119	Manufacture, delivery, or possession – miscellaneous substances	• Class A for manufacture, delivery, or possession with intent to deliver • Class B if possession

HEALTH & SAFETY CODE		OFFENSE	PUNISHMENT
12	§481.120	Delivery of marijuana	• Life or 10 to 99 years and up to $100,000 if more than 2,000 lbs. • 1st degree if more than 50 lbs. and up to 2,000 lbs. • 2d degree if more than 5 lbs. and up to 50 lbs. • State jail if more than ¼ oz. and up to 5 lbs. • Class A if ¼ oz. or less and remuneration • Class B if ¼ oz. or less and no remuneration
13	§481.121	Possession of marijuana	• Life or 5 to 99 years and up to $50,000 if more than 2,000 lbs. • 2d degree if more than 50 lbs. but 2,000 lbs. or less • 3d degree if more than 5 lbs. but 50 lbs. or less • State jail if more than 4 oz. but 5 lbs. or less • Class A if more than 2 oz. but 4 oz. or less • Class B if 2 oz. or less
14	§481.122	Delivery to a minor	2d degree
15	§481.124	Possession or transport of certain chemicals with intent to manufacture controlled substance	• 2d degree if penalty group 1 or 1-A • 3d degree if penalty group 2 • State jail if penalty group 3 or 4 • Class A if listed in schedule of controlled substances but not in penalty group
16	§481.1245	Possession or transport of anhydrous ammonia; use of or tampering with equipment	3d degree
17	§481.125	Possession or delivery of drug paraphernalia	• State jail for delivery to a minor • 90 days to 1 year for delivery if a prior conviction for delivery or delivery to minor • Class A for delivery • Class C for possession
18	§481.126	Illegal barter, expenditure, or investment	• 1st degree if barters property or expends or finances or invests funds defendant knows or believes are derived from commission of an offense or are intended to further commission of the offense • 2d degree if barters property or expends funds or finances or invests in 2d degree felony amount of marijuana
19	§481.127	Unauthorized disclosure of information	State jail
20	§481.128	Commercial matters	State jail

21	§481.129	Fraud	• Subsection (a):
			  o 2d degree for schedule 1 or 2
			  o 3d degree for schedule 3 or 4
			  o Class A for schedule 5
			• Subsection (b):
			  o Class A
			• Subsection (c)(1):
			• 2d degree for schedule 2
			• 3d degree for schedule 3, 4, or 5
			• Subsection (c)(2):
			• State jail for schedule 2 or 3
			• Class B for schedule 4 or 5

22	§481.131	Diversion of controlled substance property or plant	State jail
23	§481.133	Falsification of drug test results	• Class A for manufacture or delivery • Class B for use or possession of falsification device
24	§481.134	Drug-free zones	Enhancement for violations of Controlled Substances Act

HEALTH & SAFETY CODE		OFFENSE	PUNISHMENT
25	§481.136	Unlawful transfer or receipt of chemical precursor	• 3d degree if with prior §481.136 or §481.137 conviction • State jail
26	§481.137	Transfer of precursor substance for unlawful manufacture	3d degree
27	§481.138	Unlawful transfer or receipt of chemical laboratory apparatus	• 3d degree if with prior §481.138 conviction • State jail
28	§481.139	Transfer of chemical laboratory apparatus for unlawful manufacture	3d degree
29	§481.140	Use of child in commission of offense	Enhancement for felonies under §§481.112-481.114, 481.120, and 481.122
30	§481.141	Manufacture or delivery of controlled substance causing death or serious bodily injury	Enhancement for any felony under §§481.112-481.114 and 481.122
31	§482.002	Unlawful delivery or manufacture with intent to deliver	State jail
32	§483.041	Possession of dangerous drug	Class A
33	§483.042	Delivery or offer of delivery of dangerous drug	State jail
34	§483.043	Manufacture of dangerous drug	State jail
35	§483.045	Forging or altering prescription	• Class A with prior Chapter 483 conviction • Class B
36	§483.046	Failure to retain prescription	• Class A with prior Chapter 483 conviction • Class B
37	§483.047	Refilling prescription without authorization	• Class A with prior Chapter 483 conviction • Class B
38	§483.048	Unauthorized communication of prescription	• Class A with prior Chapter 483 conviction • Class B
39	§483.049	Failure to maintain records	• Class A with prior Chapter 483 conviction • Class B
40	§483.050	Refusal to permit inspection	• Class A with prior Chapter 483 conviction • Class B
41	§483.051	Using or revealing trade secret	• Class A with prior Chapter 483 conviction • Class B
42	§483.052	Violation of other provision	• Class A with prior Chapter 483 conviction • Class B
43	§485.031	Possession and use (abusable volatile chemical)	Class B
44	§485.032	Delivery to a minor (abusable volatile chemical)	• State jail • Class A without volatile chemical permit but with sales tax permit and no prior §485.032 conviction after Jan. 1, 1998 • Class B with volatile chemical permit
45	§485.033	Inhalant paraphernalia	• Class A for sale or delivery • Class B for use or possession
46	§485.034	Failure to post sign	Class C
47	§485.035	Sale without permit	Class B

LESSER INCLUDED OFFENSES

This chart was created by Elisa Vasquez and Brian Abbington. Brian Abbington is now a public defender in Pennsylvania. Elisa Vasquez is a shareholder in Monks and Vasquez, P.C., 613 19th Street, Galveston, TX 77550. Her phone number is (409) 763-2131, and her fax number is (409) 763-4104.

	OFFENSE	LESSER INCLUDED	AUTHORITY
1	Attempted murder (Pen §§15.01 & 19.02)	Deadly conduct (Pen §22.05)	*Guzman*, 188 S.W.3d 185, 188-89 (Tex.Crim.App.2006)
		Aggravated assault (Pen §22.02)	*Rocha*, 648 S.W.2d 298, 299 (Tex.Crim.App.1982)
2	Capital murder (Pen §19.03)	First degree murder (Pen §19.02)	*Feldman*, 71 S.W.3d 738, 750 (Tex.Crim.App.2002) (first degree murder); Travis, 921 S.W.2d 559, 564 (Beau. 1996, no pet.) (second degree murder); *Cardenas*, 30 S.W.3d 384, 392 (Tex.Crim.App.2000) (aggravated assault); *Martinez*, 131 S.W.3d 22, 39 (S.A. 2003, no pet.) (aggravated robbery); *Cardenas*, 30 S.W.3d at 392 (criminally negligent homicide); *Ortiz*, 144 S.W.3d 225, 233-34 (Hou. [14th] 2004, ref'd) (deadly conduct); *In re L.M.*, 993 S.W.2d 276, 283 (Aus. 1999, denied) (injury to child); *Bradford*, 178 S.W.3d 875, 877 (F.W. 2005, ref'd) (robbery)
		Second degree murder ❶ (Pen §19.02(d))	
		Manslaughter ❷ (Pen §19.04)	
		Aggravated assault (Pen §22.02)	
		Aggravated robbery (Pen §29.03)	
		Criminally negligent homicide (Pen §19.05)	
		Deadly conduct (Pen §22.05)	
		Injury to a child (Pen §22.04)	
		Robbery (Pen §29.02)	
3	Murder (Pen §19.02)	Second degree murder ❶ • sudden passion from adequate cause • defendants burden by preponderance at punishment (Pen §19.02(d))	*Moore*, 969 S.W.2d 4, 8-11 (Tex.Crim.App.1998) (second degree murder); *Cardenas*, 30 S.W.3d at 392 (manslaughter, criminally negligent homicide, aggravated assault). Aggravated assault by threat is not a lesser included offense of murder. *Hall*, 225 S.W.3d 524, 536 (Tex.Crim.App.2007)
		Manslaughter ❷ (Pen §19.04)	
		Aggravated assault (Pen §22.02)	
		Criminally negligent homicide (Pen §19.05)	
		Deadly conduct (Pen §22.05)	*Ortiz*, 144 S.W.3d at 233-34
4	Manslaughter ❷ (reckless causation) (Pen §19.04)	Aggravated assault • reckless serious bodily injury • use or exhibition of deadly weapon (Pen §22.02)	Compare Penal Code §§19.04, 22.01, with §22.02. Intentional and knowing aggravated assault is not a lesser included offense of manslaughter. *Lawson*, 64 S.W.3d 396, 397 (Tex.Crim.App.2001)

❶ Previously known as voluntary manslaughter.

❷ Previously known as involuntary manslaughter.

	OFFENSE	LESSER INCLUDED	AUTHORITY
5	Criminally negligent homicide (Pen §19.05)		Assault is not a lesser included offense because it requires a higher culpable mental state. **Bayona**, 544 S.W.2d 155, 156 (Tex.Crim.App.1976)
6	Intoxication manslaughter (Pen §49.08)	Driving while intoxicated (Pen §49.04)	**Martin**, 84 S.W.3d 267, 269 (Beau. 2002, ref'd)
7	Aggravated kidnapping (1st degree) (Pen §20.04)	Aggravated kidnapping (2d degree) • safe release of victim • defendants burden by preponderance at punishment (Pen §20.04(d))	**Schweinle**, 915 S.W.2d 17, 19 (Tex.Crim.App.1996) (unlawful restraint); **Ex parte Gutierrez**, 600 S.W.2d 933, 935 (Tex.Crim. App.1980) (unlawful restraint); **Lavarry**, 936 S.W.2d 690, 694 (Dal. 1996, dism'd) (kidnapping); see, e.g., **Thornburg**, 699 S.W.2d 918, 921 (Hou. [1st] 1985, no pet.) (second degree aggravated kidnapping); **Girdy**, 213 S.W.3d 315, 318-19 (Tex.Crim.App.2006)
		Aggravated assault (2d degree) (Pen §22.02)	
		Kidnapping (3d degree) • abduct (Pen §20.03)	
		Unlawful restraint (3d degree) • restrain & recklessly expose to risk of serious bodily injury (Pen §20.02(c)(2))	
		Misdemeanor unlawful restraint (Pen §20.02)	
8	Aggravated sexual assault (Pen §22.021)	Sexual assault (Pen §22.011)	**Hampton**, 109 S.W.3d 437, 440 (Tex.Crim.App.2003) (sexual assault); **Curtis**, 205 S.W.3d 656, 662 (F.W. 2006, ref'd) (aggravated assault); **Braughton**, 749 S.W.2d 528, 530-31 (C.C. 1988, denied) (indecency with a child). But see **Patterson**, 152 S.W.3d 88, 89 (Tex.Crim.App.2004) (indecency by exposure barred by double jeopardy in some cases)
		Aggravated assault (Pen §22.02)	
		Indecency with a child (Pen §21.11)	
		Assault (Pen §22.01)	**Valdez**, 993 S.W.2d 346, 350 (E.P. 1999, ref'd)
9	Indecency with a child (Pen §21.11)	Indecent exposure (Pen §21.08)	**Briceno**, 580 S.W.2d 842, 844 (Tex.Crim.App.1979)
10	Aggravated assault (Pen §22.02)	Assault (Pen §22.01)	**Guzman**, 188 S.W.3d 185, 190 (Tex.Crim.App.2006) (deadly conduct); **Bell**, 693 S.W.2d 434, 439 (Tex.Crim.App.1985) (reckless conduct); **Benge**, 94 S.W.3d 31, 35 (Hou. [14th] 2002, ref'd) (reckless driving); see **Burkholder**, 660 S.W.2d 540, 541 (Tex.Crim.App.1983) (assault)
		Deadly conduct (Pen §22.05)	
		Reckless driving (TransC §545.401)	Resisting arrest is not always a lesser included offense of assault of a public servant (Pen §22.01(b)(1)). **Gilmore**, 44 S.W.3d 92, 96 (Beau. 2001, ref'd)
11	Aggravated assault on a police officer (Pen §22.02(b)(2)(A), (B))	Resisting arrest (Pen §38.03)	**Miller**, 86 S.W.2d 663, 665 (Amar. 2002, ref'd)
12	Any completed offense	Criminal attempt (Pen §15.01)	**Hill**, 521 S.W.2d 253, 255 (Tex.Crim.App.1975)
13	Arson (1st degree) • bodily injury or death (Pen §28.02(d)(1))	Arson (2d degree) (Pen §28.02)	Bodily injury must result from arson and not from some independent action of arsonist. See **Wilson**, 541 S.W.2d 174, 176 (Tex.Crim.App.1976) Criminal mischief (Pen §28.03) is not a lesser included offense of arson. **Prejean**, 704 S.W.2d 119, 122-23 (Hou. [1st] 1986, no pet.)

CHARTS

	OFFENSE	LESSER INCLUDED	AUTHORITY
14	Aggravated robbery (Pen §29.03)	Robbery (Pen §29.02)	*Little*, 659 S.W.2d 425, 425-26 (Tex.Crim.App.1983) (robbery); *Watson*, 605 S.W.2d 877, 884 (Tex.Crim. App.1979) (aggravated assault); *McElhaney*, 899 S.W.2d 15, 17 (Tyler 1995, ref'd) (robbery, assault); *Jones*, ___ S.W.3d ___ (Amar. 2007, n.p.h.) (No. 07-06-0297-CR; 10-8-07) (theft); *Roy*, 76 S.W.2d 87, 96 (Hou. [14th] 2002, no pet.) (unauthorized use of a motor vehicle)
		Aggravated assault (Pen §22.02)	
		Assault (Pen §22.01)	
		Theft (Pen §31.03)	
		Unauthorized use of a vehicle (Pen §31.07)	
15	Robbery (Pen §29.02)	Theft (Pen §31.03)	*Parr*, 658 S.W.2d 620, 622 (Tex.Crim.App.1983) (theft); *Earls*, 707 S.W.2d 82, 84-85 (Tex.Crim.App.1986) (theft from a person); *see McElhaney*, 899 S.W.2d 15, 17 (Tyler 1995, ref'd) (assault)
		Theft from person (Pen §31.03(e)(4)(B))	
		Assault (Pen §22.01)	
		Unauthorized use of a vehicle (Pen §31.07)	*Griffin*, 614 S.W.2d 155, 158 n.4 (Tex.Crim.App.1981)
16	Burglary (intent to commit felony) (Pen §30.02(a)(1), (2))		Aggravated assault is not a lesser included offense of burglary with intent to commit aggravated assault. *Jacob*, 892 S.W.2d 905, 908-09 (Tex.Crim.App.1995)
17	Burglary (attempt or commission of felony) (Pen §30.02(a)(3))	Aggravated assault (Pen §22.02)	*Mitchell*, 137 S.W.3d 842, 845-47 (Hou.[1st] 2004, ref'd)
18	Burglary of a habitation (Pen §30.02(c)(2))	Burglary of a building (Pen §30.02(c)(1))	*Blankenship*, 780 S.W.2d 198, 202 (Tex.Crim.App.1988) (burglary of a building); *DeVaughn*, 239 S.W.3d 351, 356 (S.A. 2007, ref'd) (criminal trespass)
		Criminal trespass (Pen §30.05)	
19	Burglary of a building (Pen §30.02(c)(1))	Criminal trespass (Pen §30.05)	*Aguilar*, 682 S.W.2d 556, 558 (Tex.Crim.App.1985) (criminal trespass). *But see Black*, 183 S.W.3d 925, 928 (Hou. [14th] 2006, ref'd) (trespass of property surrounding a building is not a lesser included offense of burglary of a building)
20	Forgery (felony) (Pen §32.21(d), (e))	Forgery (misdemeanor) (Pen §32.21(c))	*Ramos*, ___ S.W.3d ___ (Hou. [1st] 2008, n.p.h.) (No. 01-06-00521-CR; 5-16-08)
21	Retaliation (Pen §36.06(a)(1))		Terroristic threat (Pen §22.07) is not a lesser included offense of retaliation. *In re D.D.*, 101 S.W.3d 695, 697 (Aus. 2003, no pet.)
22	Taking weapon from peace officer (Pen §38.14)		Resisting arrest is not a lesser included offense of taking a weapon from a peace officer. *Jackson*, 993 S.W.2d 162, 165-66 (East. 1999, no pet.)
23	Delivery of controlled substance (H&SC §§481.112-481.114)	Possession of controlled substance (H&SC §§481.115-481.118)	*Berger*, 104 S.W.3d 199, 204-05 (Aus. 2003, no pet.)
24	Theft (Pen §31.03)	Unauthorized use of a vehicle (Pen §31.07)	*Griffin*, 614 S.W.2d 155, 158 n.4 (Tex.Crim.App.1981)

AFFIRMATIVE LINKS

When a defendant is not in exclusive possession of the place where a controlled substance is found, the State must prove additional independent facts and circumstances that affirmatively link the defendant to the contraband in such a way that it can be concluded that the defendant had knowledge of the contraband and exercised control over it. An affirmative link generates a reasonable inference that the defendant knew of the contrabands existence and exercised control over it. Courts have identified a nonexhaustive list of factors that may help to show an affirmative link to controlled substances. Each case is examined on its own facts, and a factor that contributes to the sufficiency of the evidence in one case may be of little or no value in another case. "It is not the number of affirmative links present that is important, but rather the 'logical force' that they create to prove that the defendant committed the crime." *Nhem v. State*, 129 S.W.3d 696, 699-700 (Tex.App.—Houston [1st Dist.] 2004, no pet.).

	AFFIRMATIVE LINK	AUTHORITY
1	Accused driver or owner of automobile where contraband found	*Mohmed*, 977 S.W.2d 624, 627 (F.W. 1998, ref'd)
2	Accused found with a large amount of cash	*Lassaint*, 79 S.W.3d 736, 745 (C.C. 2002, no pet.) (although recovered cocaine worth $25,000, there was no testimony that accused possessed a large amount of cash)
3	Accused observed in suspicious area under suspicious circumstances	*See, e.g.,* *Trejo*, 766 S.W.2d 381, 385 (Aus. 1989, no pet.) (sitting in car off the street with windows down in cold, rainy weather constitutes suspicious behavior)
4	Accused owned or resided in place where contraband found	*Poindexter*, 153 S.W.3d 402, 411 (Tex.Crim.App.2005)
5	Accused possessed other contraband at time of arrest	*See Rogers*, 853 S.W.2d 29, 32-33 (Tex.Crim.App.1993)
6	Accused present at time of search	*Villegas*, 871 S.W.2d 894, 896-97 (Hou. [1st] 1994, ref'd)
7	Accused's physical condition indicated recent consumption of contraband	*McGaskey*, 451 S.W.2d 486, 487 (Tex.Crim.App.1970)
8	Accused attempted to escape or flee	*See Rhyne*, 620 S.W.2d 599, 601 (Tex.Crim.App.1981)
9	Accused's conduct indicated consciousness of guilt	*Leyva*, 840 S.W.2d 757, 760-61 (E.P. 1992, ref'd)
10	Conflicting statements by vehicle occupants	*Duff*, 546 S.W.2d 283, 288 (Tex.Crim.App.1977)
11	Contraband found in a closet containing men's clothing, if accused is male	*Villegas*, 871 S.W.2d at 896-97
12	Contraband found in close proximity and accessible to accused	*Mohmed*, 977 S.W.2d at 627
13	Contraband found on accused same as contraband found in accused's room	*Nhem*, 129 S.W.3d 696, 700 (Hou. [1st] 2004, no pet.)
14	Contraband in plain view or recovered from enclosed space	*Poindexter*, 153 S.W.3d at 409-10
15	Accused made furtive gestures	*See, e.g.,* *Thomas*, 762 S.W.2d 721, 723 (Hou. [1st] 1988, no pet.) (accused may have been reaching down to adjust the radio or thermostat)
16	Accused made incriminating statements connecting himself to the contraband	*Sandoval*, 946 S.W.2d 472, 476 (C.C. 1997, ref'd)
17	Others present at time of search	*Villegas*, 871 S.W.2d at 896
18	Paraphernalia to use contraband found on or near accused	*Joseph*, 897 S.W.2d 374, 376 (Tex.Crim.App.1995) (accused holding syringe with cocaine in it and sitting among drug paraphernalia); *see Stokes*, 853 S.W.2d 227, 240 (Tyler 1993, no pet.)

	AFFIRMATIVE LINK	AUTHORITY
19	Presence of evidence establishing accused's occupancy of premises	*Classe*, 840 S.W.2d 10, 12 (Hou. [1st] 1992, ref'd); *Nhem*, 129 S.W.3d at 700 (billing statements and drivers license found in same room as contraband)
20	Quantity of contraband	*Poindexter*, 153 S.W.3d at 412
21	Accused had relationship with others who have access to place where contraband found	*Frierson*, 839 S.W.2d 841, 849 (Dallas 1992, ref'd)
22	Accused had special connection to contraband	*Lassaint*, 79 S.W.3d at 740-46 (evidence insufficient to establish special connection)
23	Strong residual odor of contraband present	*Chavez*, 769 S.W.2d 284, 290 (Hou. [1st] 1989, ref'd)
24	Accused knew of existence of place where narcotics were secreted	*Vargas*, 883 S.W.2d 256, 262-63 (C.C. 1994, ref'd)

PENAL CODE

TABLE OF CONTENTS

PENAL CODE

PENAL CODE

TITLE 1. INTRODUCTORY PROVISIONS

CHAPTER 1. GENERAL PROVISIONS

PEN §1.01. SHORT TITLE

This code shall be known and may be cited as the Penal Code.

History of Pen §1.01: Acts 1973, 63rd Leg., ch. 399, §1, eff. Jan. 1, 1974.

PEN §1.02. OBJECTIVES OF CODE

The general purposes of this code are to establish a system of prohibitions, penalties, and correctional measures to deal with conduct that unjustifiably and inexcusably causes or threatens harm to those individual or public interests for which state protection is appropriate. To this end, the provisions of this code are intended, and shall be construed, to achieve the following objectives:

(1) to insure the public safety through:

(A) the deterrent influence of the penalties hereinafter provided;

(B) the rehabilitation of those convicted of violations of this code; and

(C) such punishment as may be necessary to prevent likely recurrence of criminal behavior;

(2) by definition and grading of offenses to give fair warning of what is prohibited and of the consequences of violation;

(3) to prescribe penalties that are proportionate to the seriousness of offenses and that permit recognition of differences in rehabilitation possibilities among individual offenders;

(4) to safeguard conduct that is without guilt from condemnation as criminal;

(5) to guide and limit the exercise of official discretion in law enforcement to prevent arbitrary or oppressive treatment of persons suspected, accused, or convicted of offenses; and

(6) to define the scope of state interest in law enforcement against specific offenses and to systematize the exercise of state criminal jurisdiction.

History of Pen §1.02: Acts 1973, 63rd Leg., ch. 399, §1, eff. Jan. 1, 1974. Amended by Acts 1993, 73rd Leg., ch. 900, §1.01, eff. Sept. 1, 1994.

ANNOTATIONS

Cane v. State, 698 S.W.2d 138, 140 (Tex.Crim.App. 1985). "The objectives of the Penal Code embodied in §1.02 ... are the clear statements of the legislature as to its objectives in formulating a set of laws governing criminal conduct. [T]hose objectives arguably could be considered relevant to the disposition of any criminal case. [A jury] instruction on those objectives ... would be discretionary because it does not involve the law applicable to the facts of the case. The instruction is simply informational that the judge may ... find to be helpful to the jury. [There is] no logic in the proposition that such an instruction would constitute a comment on the weight of the evidence or invite the jury to speculate on matters outside of the evidence."

PEN §1.03. EFFECT OF CODE

(a) Conduct does not constitute an offense unless it is defined as an offense by statute, municipal ordinance, order of a county commissioners court, or rule authorized by and lawfully adopted under a statute.

(b) The provisions of Titles 1, 2, and 3 apply to offenses defined by other laws, unless the statute defining the offense provides otherwise; however, the punishment affixed to an offense defined outside this code shall be applicable unless the punishment is classified in accordance with this code.

(c) This code does not bar, suspend, or otherwise affect a right or liability to damages, penalty, forfeiture, or other remedy authorized by law to be recovered or enforced in a civil suit for conduct this code defines as an offense, and the civil injury is not merged in the offense.

History of Pen §1.03: Acts 1973, 63rd Leg., ch. 399, §1, eff. Jan. 1, 1974. Amended by Acts 1993, 73rd Leg., ch. 900, §1.01, eff. Sept. 1, 1994.

ANNOTATIONS

State v. Colyandro, 233 S.W.3d 870, 884-85 (Tex. Crim.App.2007). "[W]e hold that §1.03(b) controls the application of Penal Code provisions to criminal offenses defined outside the Penal Code. It directs the export of the provisions contained only in Titles 1, 2, and 3 of the Penal Code to criminal offenses defined outside the Penal Code and contemporaneously bars the import of extra-Penal Code offenses to offenses defined in

Titles 4 through 11 of the Penal Code. The offenses defined in Title 4 of the Penal Code[, such as the conspiracy statute, §15.02,] apply to offenses defined outside the Penal Code only where the Legislature has designated that Title 4 is applicable via legislative action like the amendments made to the Controlled Substances Act, the Simulated Controlled Substances Act, the Dangerous Drugs Act, the Abusable and Volatile Chemicals Act, and the Election Code."

Morton v. State, 935 S.W.2d 904, 906 (Tex. App.—San Antonio 1996, no pet.). "There is no requirement that a penal offense be codified within the penal code. Therefore, the fact that the statute is codified somewhere other than the Texas Penal Code is not a dispositive indication of whether the statute may be prosecuted as a criminal offense."

PEN §1.04. TERRITORIAL JURISDICTION

(a) This state has jurisdiction over an offense that a person commits by his own conduct or the conduct of another for which he is criminally responsible if:

(1) either the conduct or a result that is an element of the offense occurs inside this state;

(2) the conduct outside this state constitutes an attempt to commit an offense inside this state;

(3) the conduct outside this state constitutes a conspiracy to commit an offense inside this state, and an act in furtherance of the conspiracy occurs inside this state; or

(4) the conduct inside this state constitutes an attempt, solicitation, or conspiracy to commit, or establishes criminal responsibility for the commission of, an offense in another jurisdiction that is also an offense under the laws of this state.

(b) If the offense is criminal homicide, a "result" is either the physical impact causing death or the death itself. If the body of a criminal homicide victim is found in this state, it is presumed that the death occurred in this state. If death alone is the basis for jurisdiction, it is a defense to the exercise of jurisdiction by this state that the conduct that constitutes the offense is not made criminal in the jurisdiction where the conduct occurred.

(c) An offense based on an omission to perform a duty imposed on an actor by a statute of this state is committed inside this state regardless of the location of the actor at the time of the offense.

(d) This state includes the land and water and the air space above the land and water over which this state has power to define offenses.

History of Pen §1.04: Acts 1973, 63rd Leg., ch. 399, §1, eff. Jan. 1, 1974. Amended by Acts 1993, 73rd Leg., ch. 900, §1.01, eff. Sept. 1, 1994.

ANNOTATIONS

Rodriguez v. State, 146 S.W.3d 674, 676-77 (Tex. Crim.App.2004). "[W]e hold that the phrase 'that is an element of the offense' [in §1.04(a)(1)] applies to both 'conduct' and 'result.' [¶] The kidnapping was the required aggravating 'nature of conduct' element that elevated the offense from murder to capital murder. The kidnapping occurred in Texas, thus Texas has territorial jurisdiction over the offense...."

McGowan v. State, 938 S.W.2d 732, 735 (Tex. App.—Houston [14th Dist.] 1996), *aff'd sub nom. Weightman v. State*, 975 S.W.2d 621 (Tex.Crim. App.1998). "[C]ommercial bribery is a conduct oriented offense, as opposed to a result oriented offense. ... For Texas to have jurisdiction, McGowan must have solicited, accepted or agreed to accept a benefit in Texas. Although money was wired to McGowan from Texas and, presumably in exchange, documents were sent to Texas, these acts are not elements of the offense of commercial bribery. There is no circumstantial or direct evidence indicating that a benefit was solicited, accepted or agreed to in Texas. Thus, jurisdiction may exist in Washington, but not in Texas."

PEN §1.05. CONSTRUCTION OF CODE

(a) The rule that a penal statute is to be strictly construed does not apply to this code. The provisions of this code shall be construed according to the fair import of their terms, to promote justice and effect the objectives of the code.

(b) Unless a different construction is required by the context, Sections 311.011, 311.012, 311.014, 311.015, and 311.021 through 311.032 of Chapter 311, Government Code (Code Construction Act), apply to the construction of this code.

(c) In this code:

(1) a reference to a title, chapter, or section without further identification is a reference to a title, chapter, or section of this code; and

(2) a reference to a subchapter, subsection, subdivision, paragraph, or other numbered or lettered unit

For a quick reference of penalties, see the Chart of Penalties on p. 675.

O'CONNOR'S CRIMINAL CODES 703

PEN §1.05

without further identification is a reference to a unit of the next-larger unit of this code in which the reference appears.

History of Pen §1.05: Acts 1973, 63rd Leg., ch. 399, §1, eff. Jan. 1, 1974. Amended by Acts 1985, 69th Leg., ch. 479, §69, eff. Sept. 1, 1985; Acts 1993, 73rd Leg., ch. 900, §1.01, eff. Sept. 1, 1994.

PEN §1.06. COMPUTATION OF AGE

A person attains a specified age on the day of the anniversary of his birthdate.

History of Pen §1.06: Acts 1973, 63rd Leg., ch. 399, §1, eff. Jan. 1, 1974.

PEN §1.07. DEFINITIONS

(a) In this code:

(1) "Act" means a bodily movement, whether voluntary or involuntary, and includes speech.

(2) "Actor" means a person whose criminal responsibility is in issue in a criminal action. Whenever the term "suspect" is used in this code, it means "actor."

(3) "Agency" includes authority, board, bureau, commission, committee, council, department, district, division, and office.

(4) "Alcoholic beverage" has the meaning assigned by Section 1.04, Alcoholic Beverage Code.

(5) "Another" means a person other than the actor.

(6) "Association" means a government or governmental subdivision or agency, trust, partnership, or two or more persons having a joint or common economic interest.

(7) "Benefit" means anything reasonably regarded as economic gain or advantage, including benefit to any other person in whose welfare the beneficiary is interested.

(8) "Bodily injury" means physical pain, illness, or any impairment of physical condition.

(9) "Coercion" means a threat, however communicated:

(A) to commit an offense;

(B) to inflict bodily injury in the future on the person threatened or another;

(C) to accuse a person of any offense;

(D) to expose a person to hatred, contempt, or ridicule;

(E) to harm the credit or business repute of any person; or

(F) to take or withhold action as a public servant, or to cause a public servant to take or withhold action.

(10) "Conduct" means an act or omission and its accompanying mental state.

(11) "Consent" means assent in fact, whether express or apparent.

(12) "Controlled substance" has the meaning assigned by Section 481.002, Health and Safety Code.

(13) "Corporation" includes nonprofit corporations, professional associations created pursuant to statute, and joint stock companies.

(14) "Correctional facility" means a place designated by law for the confinement of a person arrested for, charged with, or convicted of a criminal offense. The term includes:

(A) a municipal or county jail;

(B) a confinement facility operated by the Texas Department of Criminal Justice;

(C) a confinement facility operated under contract with any division of the Texas Department of Criminal Justice; and

(D) a community corrections facility operated by a community supervision and corrections department.

(15) "Criminal negligence" is defined in Section 6.03 (Culpable Mental States).

(16) "Dangerous drug" has the meaning assigned by Section 483.001, Health and Safety Code.

(17) "Deadly weapon" means:

(A) a firearm or anything manifestly designed, made, or adapted for the purpose of inflicting death or serious bodily injury; or

(B) anything that in the manner of its use or intended use is capable of causing death or serious bodily injury.

(18) "Drug" has the meaning assigned by Section 481.002, Health and Safety Code.

(19) "Effective consent" includes consent by a person legally authorized to act for the owner. Consent is not effective if:

(A) induced by force, threat, or fraud;

(B) given by a person the actor knows is not legally authorized to act for the owner;

(C) given by a person who by reason of youth, mental disease or defect, or intoxication is known by the actor to be unable to make reasonable decisions; or

(D) given solely to detect the commission of an offense.

(20) "Electric generating plant" means a facility that generates electric energy for distribution to the public.

(21) "Electric utility substation" means a facility used to switch or change voltage in connection with the transmission of electric energy for distribution to the public.

(22) "Element of offense" means:

(A) the forbidden conduct;

(B) the required culpability;

(C) any required result; and

(D) the negation of any exception to the offense.

(23) "Felony" means an offense so designated by law or punishable by death or confinement in a penitentiary.

(24) "Government" means:

(A) the state;

(B) a county, municipality, or political subdivision of the state; or

(C) any branch or agency of the state, a county, municipality, or political subdivision.

(25) "Harm" means anything reasonably regarded as loss, disadvantage, or injury, including harm to another person in whose welfare the person affected is interested.

(26) "Individual" means a human being who is alive, including an unborn child at every stage of gestation from fertilization until birth.

(27) "Institutional division" means the institutional division of the Texas Department of Criminal Justice.

(28) "Intentional" is defined in Section 6.03 (Culpable Mental States).

(29) "Knowing" is defined in Section 6.03 (Culpable Mental States).

(30) "Law" means the constitution or a statute of this state or of the United States, a written opinion of a court of record, a municipal ordinance, an order of a county commissioners court, or a rule authorized by and lawfully adopted under a statute.

(31) "Misdemeanor" means an offense so designated by law or punishable by fine, by confinement in jail, or by both fine and confinement in jail.

(32) "Oath" includes affirmation.

(33) "Official proceeding" means any type of administrative, executive, legislative, or judicial proceeding that may be conducted before a public servant.

(34) "Omission" means failure to act.

(35) "Owner" means a person who:

(A) has title to the property, possession of the property, whether lawful or not, or a greater right to possession of the property than the actor; or

(B) is a holder in due course of a negotiable instrument.

(36) "Peace officer" means a person elected, employed, or appointed as a peace officer under Article 2.12, Code of Criminal Procedure, Section 51.212 or 51.214, Education Code, or other law.

(37) "Penal institution" means a place designated by law for confinement of persons arrested for, charged with, or convicted of an offense.

(38) "Person" means an individual, corporation, or association.

(39) "Possession" means actual care, custody, control, or management.

(40) "Public place" means any place to which the public or a substantial group of the public has access and includes, but is not limited to, streets, highways, and the common areas of schools, hospitals, apartment houses, office buildings, transport facilities, and shops.

(41) "Public servant" means a person elected, selected, appointed, employed, or otherwise designated as one of the following, even if he has not yet qualified for office or assumed his duties:

(A) an officer, employee, or agent of government;

(B) a juror or grand juror; or

(C) an arbitrator, referee, or other person who is authorized by law or private written agreement to hear or determine a cause or controversy; or

(D) an attorney at law or notary public when participating in the performance of a governmental function; or

(E) a candidate for nomination or election to public office; or

(F) a person who is performing a governmental function under a claim of right although he is not legally qualified to do so.

(42) "Reasonable belief" means a belief that would be held by an ordinary and prudent man in the same circumstances as the actor.

(43) "Reckless" is defined in Section 6.03 (Culpable Mental States).

(44) "Rule" includes regulation.

For a quick reference of penalties, see the Chart of Penalties on p. 675.

O'CONNOR'S CRIMINAL CODES   705

(45) "Secure correctional facility" means:

(A) a municipal or county jail; or

(B) a confinement facility operated by or under a contract with any division of the Texas Department of Criminal Justice.

(46) "Serious bodily injury" means bodily injury that creates a substantial risk of death or that causes death, serious permanent disfigurement, or protracted loss or impairment of the function of any bodily member or organ.

(47) "Swear" includes affirm.

(48) "Unlawful" means criminal or tortious or both and includes what would be criminal or tortious but for a defense not amounting to justification or privilege.

(49) "Death" includes, for an individual who is an unborn child, the failure to be born alive.

(b) The definition of a term in this code applies to each grammatical variation of the term.

History of Pen §1.07: Acts 1973, 63rd Leg., ch. 399, §1, eff. Jan. 1, 1974. Amended by Acts 1975, 64th Leg., ch. 342, §1, eff. Sept. 1, 1975; Acts 1977, 65th Leg., ch. 848, §1, eff. Aug. 29, 1977; Acts 1979, 66th Leg., ch. 530, §1 (eff. Aug. 27, 1979), ch. 655, §1 (eff. Sept. 1, 1979); Acts 1987, 70th Leg., ch. 167, §5.01(a)(43), eff. Sept. 1, 1987; Acts 1989, 71st Leg., ch. 997, §1, eff. Aug. 28, 1989; Acts 1991, 72nd Leg., ch. 543, §1, eff. Sept. 1, 1991; Acts 1993, 73rd Leg., ch. 900, §1.01, eff. Sept. 1, 1994; Acts 2003, 78th Leg., ch. 822, §2.01, eff. Sept. 1, 2003.

ANNOTATIONS

Generally

Hines v. State, 906 S.W.2d 518, 520 (Tex.Crim.App. 1995). "[W]e are bound to construe Penal Code provisions in light of definitions in the Penal Code itself."

§1.07(a)(8)

Lane v. State, 763 S.W.2d 785, 786 (Tex.Crim.App. 1989). The definition of "bodily injury" is "purposely broad and seems to encompass even relatively minor physical contacts so long as they constitute more than mere offensive touching."

§1.07(a)(9)

Evans v. State, 220 S.W.3d 54, 56-57 (Tex. App.—San Antonio 2006, pet. ref'd). "Each statutory definition of coercion … requires that the defendant threaten to take some affirmative act: commit, accuse, inflict, expose, or harm. Here, there is no evidence Evans threatened to take any affirmative act; rather, as the State recognizes, she threatened to not act and thus 'allow' the harm she purported to foretell to run its course. As the State argues '[t]he threat was simple:

Come up with the money that I demand or I won't say the special prayers and your loved one will die.' [¶] Because there is no evidence that Evans's actions fall within a statutory definition of coercion, we must reverse the trial court's judgment and render a judgment of acquittal."

§1.07(a)(10)

Nejnaoui v. State, 44 S.W.3d 111, 120 (Tex.App.— Houston [14th Dist.] 2001, pet. ref'd). Held: When the statutory definition of conduct is not included in the charge, it is assumed the jury will consider the commonly understood meaning in its deliberations.

§1.07(a)(17)

Flenteroy v. State, 105 S.W.3d 702, 708 n.6 (Tex. App.—Austin 2003), *rev'd on other grounds*, 187 S.W.3d 406 (Tex.Crim.App.2005). "Weapons included in §1.07(a)(17)(A) are sometimes referred to as deadly weapons by 'design' and those included in §1.07(a)(17)(B) are referred to as deadly weapons by 'use.'"

§1.07(a)(17)(A)

Robertson v. State, 163 S.W.3d 730, 732 (Tex.Crim. App.2005). Under the definition in §1.07(a)(17)(A), "an object's physical characteristics determine whether a weapon is deadly by design. Moreover, an object can be a deadly weapon by 'design' only if it has no 'obvious purpose apart from causing death or serious bodily injury.' For this reason, describing an object generically as a knife does not by itself establish the object as a deadly weapon by design because many types of knives have an obvious other purpose (e.g. butcher knives, kitchen knives, utility knives, straight razors, and eating utensils). However, a particular variety of knife may be a deadly weapon by design. Bayonets, scimitars, and various kinds of swords are examples of knives that are deadly by design, because they are designed to cause death. [¶] The question is whether a switchblade knife can qualify as a deadly weapon by 'design,' and if so, under what circumstances. *At 733:* [A] switchblade knife *can* be a deadly weapon by design, and the switchblade knife before us is indeed such a weapon."

Sellers v. State, 961 S.W.2d 351, 353 (Tex.App.— Houston [1st Dist.] 1997, pet. ref'd). "[F]ire is … capable of causing death or serious bodily injury. [A]ppellant's use of fire caused the deaths of four people and injured a fifth. We hold that … fire did constitute a deadly weapon."

Batro v. State, 635 S.W.2d 156, 158 (Tex.App.—Houston [1st Dist.] 1982, no pet.). "There are several factors which a court may consider in determining whether a particular knife is a deadly weapon. They include, 1) injuries; 2) the manner in which the knife was used; 3) the length of the blade; 4) threats. [¶] When ... serious bodily injury has not been shown, the court must discern the manner of the knife's use or its intended use, its size and shape, and its capacity to produce death or serious bodily injury in determining whether a knife was a deadly weapon. [T]he absence of injuries does not preclude a finding that a particular knife is a deadly weapon." *See also Brown v. State*, 716 S.W.2d 939, 946 (Tex.Crim.App.1986); *In re J.A.W.*, 108 S.W.3d 573, 576 (Tex.App.—Amarillo 2003, no pet.); *Blanson v. State*, 107 S.W.3d 103, 105 (Tex.App.—Texarkana 2003, no pet.).

§1.07(a)(17)(B)

Lane v. State, 151 S.W.3d 188, 191 (Tex.Crim.App. 2004). "[A] hand or a foot may be a deadly weapon within the meaning of §1.07(a)(17) 'depending upon the evidence shown.' [T]he injuries, if any, inflicted on the victim are factors to be considered in determining whether a hand or a foot was used as a deadly weapon."

Adame v. State, 69 S.W.3d 581, 582 (Tex.Crim.App. 2002). "With testimony that a BB gun is capable of causing serious bodily injury, it is reasonable for a jury to make a deadly weapon finding. Further, ... where during a convenience store robbery a defendant threatens serious bodily injury to the convenience store clerk by pointing a BB gun at her, a jury may rationally infer that the BB gun is loaded. ... It is not necessary ... to place an additional evidentiary burden on the State to affirmatively prove that a BB gun, which is not a deadly weapon per se, was loaded at the time of the commission of the offense. Rather, in proving use of a deadly weapon other than a deadly weapon per se, the State need show only that the weapon used was capable of causing serious bodily injury or death in its use or intended use."

McCain v. State, 22 S.W.3d 497, 503 (Tex.Crim.App. 2000). "The provision's plain language does not require that the actor actually intend death or serious bodily injury; an object is a deadly weapon if the actor intends a use of the object in which it would be capable of causing death or serious bodily injury. The placement of the word 'capable' in the provision enables the statute to cover conduct that threatens deadly force, even if the actor has no intention of actually using deadly force."

McDowell v. State, 235 S.W.3d 294, 297 (Tex. App.—Texarkana 2007, no pet.). "Gasoline is not a deadly weapon per se, but in the manner of its use or intended use, it can be capable of causing death or serious bodily injury, and therefore can constitute a deadly weapon...."

Moya v. State, 204 S.W.3d 509, 510 (Tex.App.—Amarillo 2006, no pet.). "[M]otor vehicles may fall within [§1.07(a)(17)(B)] depending on their manner of use."

Mathonican v. State, 194 S.W.3d 59, 69 (Tex. App.—Texarkana 2006, no pet.). Seminal fluid "may become a deadly weapon that is used or exhibited, if the man producing it is HIV-positive and engages in unprotected sexual contact."

Johnston v. State, 115 S.W.3d 761, 764 (Tex. App.—Austin 2003), *aff'd*, 145 S.W.3d 215 (Tex.Crim. App. 2004). "While a deadly weapon finding does not require that the object actually cause death or serious bodily injury, it does require that the object have more than a hypothetical capability of causing death or serious bodily injury. A deadly weapon finding must be supported by evidence relating directly to the circumstances of the criminal episode. We hold that the evidence is legally insufficient to support the finding that a single lit cigarette was a deadly weapon in the manner of its use or intended use by appellant...."

§1.07(a)(26)

Cuellar v. State, 957 S.W.2d 134, 136 (Tex.App.—Corpus Christi 1997, pet. ref'd). Appellant argues that "the trial court erred in failing to quash the indictment because the victim of the offense was a fetus at the time of appellant's conduct and, therefore, was not an 'individual' within the legal meaning of that term. *At 137:* In this case, it is undisputed that the victim died as a result of injuries received during the auto collision caused by appellant's drunk driving. It is also undisputed that the victim had not been born at the time of appellant's conduct, and it is undisputed that the victim later was born and later did meet the statutory definition of an individual. *At 140:* We see no reason why the criminal law should not mirror the civil law, and afford protection to children who are born and alive for a period of time before dying as a result of prenatal injuries." *See also Lawrence v. State*, 240 S.W.3d 912,

For a quick reference of penalties, see the Chart of Penalties on p. 675.

O'CONNOR'S CRIMINAL CODES **707**

915-16 (Tex.Crim.App.2007) (holding that "individual" as defined in §1.07(a)(26) is not void for vagueness and that charging a defendant with intentionally or knowingly killing an embryo did not violate substantive due process).

§1.07(a)(35)

Freeman v. State, 707 S.W.2d 597, 603 (Tex.Crim. App.1986). "To eliminate the distinctions between general and special owners, and to give anyone with a conceivable connection to the property ownership status, the Legislature ... gave the word ['owner'] an expansive meaning: anyone having a possessory interest in the property through title, possession, whether lawful or not, or a greater right to possession to the property is an owner of the property. [¶] The issue of 'ownership' goes to the scope of the property interest protected by the law and is intended to protect all ownership interests in property from criminal behavior. When there are equal competing possessory interests in property allegedly stolen, we believe that the key to answering the question of which person has the greater right to possession of the property is who, *at the time of the commission of the offense*, had the greater right to possession of the property." *See also* **House v. State**, 105 S.W.3d 182, 184 (Tex.App.—Houston [14th Dist.] 2003, pet. ref'd).

§1.07(a)(40)

Kirtley v. State, 585 S.W.2d 724, 725 (Tex.Crim. App.1979). "[T]he status of the roadway as public does not extend to a vehicle traveling on that road. Whether or not a vehicle is a 'public place' as it travels on a roadway is a fact question for the trier of fact. *At 726 n.6:* Supportive facts [of whether a motor vehicle is a public place] include but are not limited to (1) the speed of the vehicle, (2) traffic and road conditions, (3) obstructions, (4) lighting conditions, and (5) intended use of the vehicle by the operator; all of which should be aimed at proving 'public place' as defined by statute." *See also* **Longoria v. State**, 624 S.W.2d 582, 583-84 (Tex.Crim.App.1981).

Shaub v. State, 99 S.W.3d 253, 256 (Tex.App.—Fort Worth 2003, pet. ref'd). "The penal code's list of specific areas that are public places is nonexclusive. In determining whether an area is a public place, the relevant inquiry is whether the public has access to it. Although the penal code does not define access, the term is commonly defined as freedom of approach or communication; or the means, power, or opportunity of approaching, communicating, or passing to and from." (Internal quotes omitted.) *See also* **State v. Gerstenkorn**, 239 S.W.3d 357, 359 (Tex.App.—San Antonio 2007, no pet.) (a gated community is a public place); **Woodruff v. State**, 899 S.W.2d 443, 444-45 (Tex. App.—Austin 1995, pet. ref'd) (a U.S. Air Force base is a public place).

§1.07(a)(41)

Carriere v. State, 84 S.W.3d 753, 757 (Tex.App.—Houston [1st Dist.] 2002, pet. ref'd). "'[P]ublic servant' [includes] a police officer."

PEN §1.08. PREEMPTION

No governmental subdivision or agency may enact or enforce a law that makes any conduct covered by this code an offense subject to a criminal penalty. This section shall apply only as long as the law governing the conduct proscribed by this code is legally enforceable.

History of Pen §1.08: Acts 1973, 63rd Leg., ch. 399, §1, eff. Jan. 1, 1974.

ANNOTATIONS

City of Richardson v. Responsible Dog Owners, 794 S.W.2d 17, 19 (Tex.1990). "[T]he mere fact that the legislature has enacted a law addressing a subject does not mean that the subject matter is completely preempted. ... 'A general law and a city ordinance will not be held repugnant to each other if any other reasonable construction leaving both in effect can be reached.'"

PEN §1.09. CONCURRENT JURISDICTION UNDER THIS CODE TO PROSECUTE OFFENSES THAT INVOLVE STATE PROPERTY

With the consent of the appropriate local county or district attorney, the attorney general has concurrent jurisdiction with that consenting local prosecutor to prosecute under this code any offense an element of which occurs on state property or any offense that involves the use, unlawful appropriation, or misapplication of state property, including state funds.

History of Pen §1.09: Acts 2007, 80th Leg., ch. 378, §1, eff. June 15, 2007.

CHAPTER 2. BURDEN OF PROOF

PEN §1.07

★

PEN §2.01. PROOF BEYOND A REASONABLE DOUBT

All persons are presumed to be innocent and no person may be convicted of an offense unless each element of the offense is proved beyond a reasonable doubt. The fact that he has been arrested, confined, or indicted for, or otherwise charged with, the offense gives rise to no inference of guilt at his trial.

History of Pen §2.01: Acts 1973, 63rd Leg., ch. 399, §1, eff. Jan. 1, 1974.

ANNOTATIONS

Goff v. State, 931 S.W.2d 537, 550 (Tex.Crim.App. 1996). "Individual jurors may require different levels of proof in order to be convinced beyond a reasonable doubt, but counsel may not *suggest* to the venire that they *should require* more proof in some cases over others merely due to the seriousness of the charges or the possible punishment."

Lowry v. State, 692 S.W.2d 86, 87 (Tex.Crim.App. 1985). "The U.S. Supreme Court has ... held that it is a violation of the due process clause of the 14th Amendment to shift the burden of proof in a criminal case to the defendant."

Johnson v. State, 673 S.W.2d 190, 194 (Tex.Crim. App.1984). "[I]t is incumbent on the State to prove every element of the offense beyond a reasonable doubt. [T]his is true whether the State is relying upon circumstantial or direct evidence." *See also Peddicord v. State*, 942 S.W.2d 100, 103 (Tex.App.—Amarillo 1997, no pet.).

Rodriguez v. State, 96 S.W.3d 398, 405 (Tex. App.—Austin 2002, pet. ref'd). "Although the complained-of [reasonable doubt] instruction ... does not appear to be too intrusive upon the 'better practice' [of not defining 'reasonable doubt,'] we conclude that it should not have been given over objection." *See also O'Canas v. State*, 140 S.W.3d 695, 701-02 (Tex.App.— Dallas 2003, pet. ref'd).

Garcia v. State, 634 S.W.2d 888, 893 (Tex. App.—San Antonio 1982, no pet.). "[I]t is reversible error for the trial court, over the objection of the defendant, to fail to charge upon the presumption of innocence...."

PEN §2.02. EXCEPTION

(a) An exception to an offense in this code is so labeled by the phrase: "It is an exception to the application of...."

(b) The prosecuting attorney must negate the existence of an exception in the accusation charging commission of the offense and prove beyond a reasonable doubt that the defendant or defendant's conduct does not fall within the exception.

(c) This section does not affect exceptions applicable to offenses enacted prior to the effective date of this code.

History of Pen §2.02: Acts 1973, 63rd Leg., ch. 399, §1, eff. Jan. 1, 1974.

ANNOTATIONS

LaBelle v. State, 692 S.W.2d 102, 105 (Tex.Crim. App.1985). "The negation of an exception to an offense is defined to be an element of the offense. [I]f an indictment fails to negate an exception to the offense, then the indictment has not alleged all of the elements of the offense and the court does not have jurisdiction of the case."

Lopez v. State, 846 S.W.2d 90, 93 (Tex.App.— Corpus Christi 1992, pet. ref'd). "The general rule is that where a penal statute embraces an exception which is part of the statute itself, the State must negate the exception in the indictment. Failing to negate an exception is the same as failing to allege an essential element of the offense—it renders the indictment void. *At 94:* Only those exceptions so labeled must be negated."

PEN §2.03. DEFENSE

(a) A defense to prosecution for an offense in this code is so labeled by the phrase: "It is a defense to prosecution...."

(b) The prosecuting attorney is not required to negate the existence of a defense in the accusation charging commission of the offense.

(c) The issue of the existence of a defense is not submitted to the jury unless evidence is admitted supporting the defense.

(d) If the issue of the existence of a defense is submitted to the jury, the court shall charge that a reasonable doubt on the issue requires that the defendant be acquitted.

(e) A ground of defense in a penal law that is not plainly labeled in accordance with this chapter has the procedural and evidentiary consequences of a defense.

History of Pen §2.03: Acts 1973, 63rd Leg., ch. 399, §1, eff. Jan. 1, 1974.

For a quick reference of penalties, see the Chart of Penalties on p. 675.

O'CONNOR'S CRIMINAL CODES 709

Shaw v. State, 243 S.W.3d 647, 657-58 (Tex.Crim. App.2007). "[U]nder §2.03(c), a defense is supported (or raised) by the evidence if there is some evidence, from any source, on each element of the defense that, if believed by the jury, would support a rational inference that that element is true. In determining whether a defense is thus supported, a court must rely on its own judgment, formed in the light of its own common sense and experience, as to the limits of rational inference from the facts proven. If a defense is supported by the evidence, then the defendant is entitled to an instruction on that defense, even if the evidence supporting the defense is weak or contradicted, and even if the trial court is of the opinion that the evidence is not credible. But the evidence must be such that it will support a rational jury finding as to each element of the defense."

Saxton v. State, 804 S.W.2d 910, 913 (Tex.Crim. App.1991). "[T]he State has the burden of *persuasion* in disproving the evidence of self-defense. That is not a burden of *production*, i.e., one which requires the State to affirmatively produce evidence refuting the self-defense claim, but rather a burden requiring the State to prove its case beyond a reasonable doubt."

Bush v. State, 611 S.W.2d 428, 430 (Tex.Crim.App. 1980), *overruled on other grounds*, *England v. State*, 887 S.W.2d 902 (Tex.Crim.App.1994). "[W]e hold that the provisions of ... §2.03(c) and (d) shall be followed by the trial court in determining a pre-trial claim of entrapment. The effect of this holding is to require the State, at a pre-trial hearing, to disprove the defense of entrapment beyond a reasonable doubt after the issue has been properly raised by the evidence. *At 431:* Entrapment is unique in that it is the only defense that also may be tested at a pre-trial hearing."

PEN §2.04. AFFIRMATIVE DEFENSE

(a) An affirmative defense in this code is so labeled by the phrase: "It is an affirmative defense to prosecution...."

(b) The prosecuting attorney is not required to negate the existence of an affirmative defense in the accusation charging commission of the offense.

(c) The issue of the existence of an affirmative defense is not submitted to the jury unless evidence is admitted supporting the defense.

(d) If the issue of the existence of an affirmative defense is submitted to the jury, the court shall charge that the defendant must prove the affirmative defense by a preponderance of evidence.

History of Pen §2.04: Acts 1973, 63rd Leg., ch. 399, §1, eff. Jan. 1, 1974.

Floyd v. State, 983 S.W.2d 273, 274 (Tex.Crim.App. 1998). "In *Proctor* [*v. State*, 967 S.W.2d 840 (Tex. Crim.App.1998)], we held that a statute of limitations claim is a defense and that the defendant will forfeit this defense if it is not asserted at or before guilt/innocence stage of trial. In this case, appellant failed to raise the statute of limitations defense before trial or during the presentation of evidence on his pleas of nolo contendere. Therefore, appellant forfeited this defense under *Proctor*."

Charles v. State, 636 S.W.2d 5, 6 (Tex.App.— Dallas 1982, pet. ref'd). "[T]he State must be required to prove beyond a reasonable doubt every element necessary to constitute the crime as charged. Only after the State has carried its burden may a burden be placed on a defendant to prove by a preponderance of the credible evidence some fact relieving him of criminal liability."

PEN §2.05. PRESUMPTION

(a) Except as provided by Subsection (b), when this code or another penal law establishes a presumption with respect to any fact, it has the following consequences:

(1) if there is sufficient evidence of the facts that give rise to the presumption, the issue of the existence of the presumed fact must be submitted to the jury, unless the court is satisfied that the evidence as a whole clearly precludes a finding beyond a reasonable doubt of the presumed fact; and

(2) if the existence of the presumed fact is submitted to the jury, the court shall charge the jury, in terms of the presumption and the specific element to which it applies, as follows:

(A) that the facts giving rise to the presumption must be proven beyond a reasonable doubt;

(B) that if such facts are proven beyond a reasonable doubt the jury may find that the element of the offense sought to be presumed exists, but it is not bound to so find;

PEN §2.03

(C) that even though the jury may find the existence of such element, the state must prove beyond a reasonable doubt each of the other elements of the offense charged; and

(D) if the jury has a reasonable doubt as to the existence of a fact or facts giving rise to the presumption, the presumption fails and the jury shall not consider the presumption for any purpose.

(b) When this code or another penal law establishes a presumption in favor of the defendant with respect to any fact, it has the following consequences:

(1) if there is sufficient evidence of the facts that give rise to the presumption, the issue of the existence of the presumed fact must be submitted to the jury unless the court is satisfied that the evidence as a whole clearly precludes a finding beyond a reasonable doubt of the presumed fact; and

(2) if the existence of the presumed fact is submitted to the jury, the court shall charge the jury, in terms of the presumption, that:

(A) the presumption applies unless the state proves beyond a reasonable doubt that the facts giving rise to the presumption do not exist;

(B) if the state fails to prove beyond a reasonable doubt that the facts giving rise to the presumption do not exist, the jury must find that the presumed fact exists;

(C) even though the jury may find that the presumed fact does not exist, the state must prove beyond a reasonable doubt each of the elements of the offense charged; and

(D) if the jury has a reasonable doubt as to whether the presumed fact exists, the presumption applies and the jury must consider the presumed fact to exist.

History of Pen §2.05: Acts 1973, 63rd Leg., ch. 399, §1, eff. Jan. 1, 1974. Amended by Acts 1975, 64th Leg., ch. 342, §2, eff. Sept. 1, 1975; Acts 2005, 79th Leg., ch. 288, §2, eff. Sept. 1, 2005.

ANNOTATIONS

Hooper v. State, 214 S.W.3d 9, 15-16 (Tex.Crim. App.2007). "Under the ***Jackson*** [***v. Virginia***, 443 U.S. 307, 318-19 (1979)] test, we permit juries to draw multiple reasonable inferences as long as each inference is supported by the evidence presented at trial. However, juries are not permitted to come to conclusions based on mere speculation or factually unsupported inferences or presumptions. To correctly apply the ***Jackson*** standard, it is vital that courts of appeal understand the difference between a reasonable inference supported by the evidence at trial, speculation, and a presumption. A presumption is a legal inference that a fact exists if the facts giving rise to the presumption are proven beyond a reasonable doubt. ... A jury may find that the element of the offense sought to be presumed exists, but it is not bound to find so. In contrast, an inference is a conclusion reached by considering other facts and deducing a logical consequence from them. Speculation is mere theorizing or guessing about the possible meaning of facts and evidence presented. A conclusion reached by speculation may not be completely unreasonable, but it is not sufficiently based on facts or evidence to support a finding beyond a reasonable doubt."

Guzman v. State, 188 S.W.3d 185, 193 (Tex.Crim. App.2006). "[A] statutory presumption, such as the one upon which appellant relies, is not an element of an offense because it is not part of the statutory definition of the crime. *At 193 n.17:* All presumptions in criminal cases must be permissive; mandatory presumptions are unconstitutional in criminal cases." *See also **Regalado v. State***, 872 S.W.2d 7, 10-11 (Tex.App.—Houston [14th Dist.] 1994, pet. ref'd).

Browning v. State, 720 S.W.2d 504, 507 (Tex.Crim. App.1986). "[W]hen the trial court ... picks out only one ... inference and instructs the jury that that one, though rebuttable, is a presumption provided by law, the court gives the force of law to that one possible inference. [E]rror lies in *instructing* the jury that they may apply [the] inference."

PEN §2.06. REPEALED

Repealed by Acts 1975, 64th Leg., ch. 342, §12, eff. Sept. 1, 1975.

PEN §3.01. DEFINITION

In this chapter, "criminal episode" means the commission of two or more offenses, regardless of whether the harm is directed toward or inflicted upon more than one person or item of property, under the following circumstances:

For a quick reference of penalties, see the Chart of Penalties on p. 675.

O'CONNOR'S CRIMINAL CODES   711

(1) the offenses are committed pursuant to the same transaction or pursuant to two or more transactions that are connected or constitute a common scheme or plan; or

(2) the offenses are the repeated commission of the same or similar offenses.

History of Pen §3.01: Acts 1973, 63rd Leg., ch. 399, §1, eff. Jan. 1, 1974. Amended by Acts 1987, 70th Leg., ch. 387, §1, eff. Sept. 1, 1987.

ANNOTATIONS

LaPorte v. State, 840 S.W.2d 412, 414 (Tex.Crim. App.1992). "[I]t is clear the Legislature intended 'a single criminal action' to refer to a single trial or plea proceeding. This notice provision of [Pen. Code] §3.02(b) does not change the nature of the proceeding as a single criminal action involving Chapter 3 when the offenses arise out of the same criminal episode. The language of Chapter 3 and the history of joinder and consolidation in light of the 1973 Penal Code mandate this interpretation. These provisions provide a trade-off; a prosecutor is encouraged to clear case dockets by trying more than one case in a single trial whenever multiple offenses arising from a single criminal episode are alleged against a single defendant, and a defendant benefits by not being burdened with the possibility of consecutive sentences and a string of trials for offenses arising out of a single criminal episode."

Baker v. State, 107 S.W.3d 671, 673 (Tex. App.—San Antonio 2003, no pet.). "[A] defendant is prosecuted in a 'single criminal action' when allegations and evidence of more than one offense arising out of the same criminal episode are presented in a single trial or plea proceeding. [¶] The issue here is whether two or all three of these offenses constitute the 'same criminal episode' as defined in Penal Code §3.01. [¶] Each offense was directed at a woman living on or near Hope's Ferry, occurred in or near her home while she was alone, and took place in the early morning hours. This evidence establishes that the three offenses were a continuing course of sexual assault of women living near Hope's Ferry.... In the alternative, because all three offenses entailed sexual assault or attempted sexual assault, they are similar offenses. [¶] Because the State chose to try the cases together, the trial court's stacking order was improper."

Guidry v. State, 909 S.W.2d 584, 585 (Tex.App.— Corpus Christi 1995, pet. ref'd). "Section 3.01(2) does not impose a time differential between the commission of the same or similar offenses."

PEN §3.02. CONSOLIDATION & JOINDER OF PROSECUTIONS

(a) A defendant may be prosecuted in a single criminal action for all offenses arising out of the same criminal episode.

(b) When a single criminal action is based on more than one charging instrument within the jurisdiction of the trial court, the state shall file written notice of the action not less than 30 days prior to the trial.

(c) If a judgment of guilt is reversed, set aside, or vacated, and a new trial ordered, the state may not prosecute in a single criminal action in the new trial any offense not joined in the former prosecution unless evidence to establish probable guilt for that offense was not known to the appropriate prosecuting official at the time the first prosecution commenced.

History of Pen §3.02: Acts 1973, 63rd Leg., ch. 399, §1, eff. Jan. 1, 1974. See also CCP art. 21.24.

ANNOTATIONS

Puente v. State, 71 S.W.3d 340, 341 (Tex.Crim.App. 2002). D entered pleas of guilty to a three-count indictment alleging a felony and two misdemeanors; he was placed on deferred adjudication, which was later adjudicated. "We hold that [D] is entitled to relief only on the misjoined misdemeanor charges because the district court judge did not have jurisdiction to accept a plea on them. *At 343:* A district court has jurisdiction over felony offenses. It does not have original jurisdiction over misdemeanor charges, except those involving official misconduct. [¶] Appellant originally pled guilty to the entire indictment. The original deferred adjudication order was valid for the felony. To the extent that appellant was also placed on deferred adjudication for the two misdemeanor charges, that order contained a jurisdictional defect. A jurisdictional defect may be raised at any time. ... But this general principle does not entitle appellant to greater relief than a correction of the jurisdictional defect."

Llamas v. State, 12 S.W.3d 469, 470 (Tex.Crim.App. 2000). "The Seventh Court of Appeals concluded that the trial court erred in overruling appellant's mandatory right to a severance. It held under ***Cain v. State***, 947 S.W.2d 262 (Tex.Crim.App.1997), the severance error in this case was not proven harmless. *At 471:* [I]f concrete data necessary to conduct a harm analysis is absent, a harmless error test must nevertheless be conducted, and the absence of data is simply taken into account in

★

determining whether or not the harmless error test is passed or failed. When we stated in *Cain* that some errors may 'defy' harm analysis we did not mean that a harm analysis need not be conducted. We meant simply that some errors will not be proven harmless because harm can never be determined due to the lack of data needed for analysis. This is precisely the conclusion that the Seventh Court of Appeals reached in the instant case."

LaPorte v. State, 840 S.W.2d 412, 414 (Tex.Crim. App.1992). "[N]oncompliance with the notice provision [of §3.02(b)] does not take the proceeding out of Chapter 3 and somehow change it from a single criminal action involving consolidation of 'same criminal episode' offenses into a non-Chapter 3 joinder trial. Section 3.02(b) is 'merely' a procedural requirement which can be waived if a defendant so chooses either affirmatively or by inaction. [¶] [T]he Legislature intended 'a single criminal action' to refer to a single trial or plea proceeding. *At 415:* [A] defendant is prosecuted in 'a single criminal action' whenever allegations and evidence of more than one offense arising out of the same criminal episode ... are presented in a single trial or plea proceeding, whether pursuant to one charging instrument or several...."

PEN §3.03. SENTENCES FOR OFFENSES ARISING OUT OF SAME CRIMINAL EPISODE

(a) When the accused is found guilty of more than one offense arising out of the same criminal episode prosecuted in a single criminal action, a sentence for each offense for which he has been found guilty shall be pronounced. Except as provided by Subsection (b), the sentences shall run concurrently.

(b) If the accused is found guilty of more than one offense arising out of the same criminal episode, the sentences may run concurrently or consecutively if each sentence is for a conviction of:

(1) an offense:

(A) under Section 49.07 or 49.08, regardless of whether the accused is convicted of violations of the same section more than once or is convicted of violations of both sections; or

(B) for which a plea agreement was reached in a case in which the accused was charged with more than one offense listed in Paragraph (A), regardless of

whether the accused is charged with violations of the same section more than once or is charged with violations of both sections;

(2) an offense:

 Subsection (A) below is effective for offenses committed on or after Sept. 1, 2007.

(A) under Section 33.021 or an offense under Section 21.02, 21.11, 22.011, 22.021, 25.02, or 43.25 committed against a victim younger than 17 years of age at the time of the commission of the offense regardless of whether the accused is convicted of violations of the same section more than once or is convicted of violations of more than one section; or

Subsection (A) below is effective for offenses in which any element of the offense was committed before Sept. 1, 2007.

(A) under Section 21.11, 22.011, 22.021, 25.02, or 43.25 committed against a victim younger than 17 years of age at the time of the commission of the offense regardless of whether the accused is convicted of violations of the same section more than once or is convicted of violations of more than one section; or

(B) for which a plea agreement was reached in a case in which the accused was charged with more than one offense listed in Paragraph (A) committed against a victim younger than 17 years of age at the time of the commission of the offense regardless of whether the accused is charged with violations of the same section more than once or is charged with violations of more than one section; or

(3) an offense:

(A) under Section 21.15 or 43.26, regardless of whether the accused is convicted of violations of the same section more than once or is convicted of violations of both sections; or

(B) for which a plea agreement was reached in a case in which the accused was charged with more than one offense listed in Paragraph (A), regardless of whether the accused is charged with violations of the same section more than once or is charged with violations of both sections.

History of Pen §3.03: Acts 1973, 63rd Leg., ch. 399, §1, eff. Jan. 1, 1974. Amended by Acts 1995, 74th Leg., ch. 596, §1, eff. Sept. 1, 1995; Acts 1997, 75th Leg., ch. 667, §2, eff. Sept. 1, 1997; Acts 2005, 79th Leg., ch. 527, §1, eff. Sept. 1, 2005; Acts 2007, 80th Leg., ch. 593, §3.47 (eff. Sept. 1, 2007), ch. 1291, §6 (eff. Sept. 1, 2007).

See also CCP art. 42.08.

For a quick reference of penalties, see the Chart of Penalties on p. 675.

O'CONNOR'S CRIMINAL CODES 713

PEN §3.03

Beedy v. State, 250 S.W.3d 107, 109 (Tex.Crim.App. 2008). "[T]he trial judge abused his discretion by stacking [a] ten-year deferred adjudication community supervision term onto [D's] twelve-year prison sentence. [T]he cumulation order was improper because deferred adjudication community supervision is not a 'conviction' for purposes of the statutes authorizing cumulation [Pen. Code §3.03(c) and CCP art. 42.08(a)]. *At 113:* [A]n unlawful cumulation order is remedied by reforming the judgment to set aside the order. Because the trial judge in this case did not have the authority to stack Beedy's deferred adjudication community supervision term onto his prison sentence, the court of appeals was correct when it deleted the cumulation order."

State v. Crook, 248 S.W.3d 172, 177 (Tex.Crim.App. 2008). "Nothing in the legislative history of §3.03(a) indicates that the Legislature intended for the concurrent sentences provision of §3.03(a) to apply to anything but the entire sentence, including fines. This would be consistent with the language that the Legislature used in §3.03(a) that 'the sentences shall run concurrently.' We decide that the concurrent sentences provision of §3.03(a) applies to the entire sentence, including fines."

Barrow v. State, 207 S.W.3d 377, 379 (Tex.Crim.App.2006). "[T]he *Apprendi* line of cases requires that, in any case in which the defendant has elected to exercise his Sixth Amendment right to a jury trial, any discrete finding of fact that has the effect of increasing the maximum punishment that can be assessed must be made by the jury, even if that fact-finding occurs as part of the punishment determination. [¶] These decisions do not ... speak to a trial court's authority to cumulate sentences when that authority is provided by statute and is not based upon discrete fact-finding, but is wholly discretionary. *At 380:* We hold that placing the decision whether to run multiple sentences concurrently or consecutively with the trial court instead of the jury does not violate the Sixth Amendment right a jury trial."

Patterson v. State, 152 S.W.3d 88, 92 (Tex.Crim.App.2004). "Just as a conviction for a completed offense bars prosecution for an attempt to commit the same offense, a conviction for an offense set out in 3.03 bars conviction for conduct that, on the facts of the case, is demonstrably part of the commission of the greater offense. For example, indecency by genital exposure of oneself in the course of manual penetration of another are separate offenses, while penile contact with mouth, genitals, or anus in the course of penile penetration will be subsumed. Thus, indecency by exposure may or may not be a part of sexual assault or indecency by contact, depending on the facts of the case." *See also **Parfait v. State***, 120 S.W.3d 348, 351 (Tex.Crim.App.2003).

Ex parte McJunkins, 954 S.W.2d 39, 40-41 (Tex. Crim.App.1997). "[T]he mandatory concurrent-sentence provision of Penal Code §3.03 is altogether dependent on the choices of the parties. The State has the choice to lay the predicate for mandatory concurrent sentencing by choosing whether to join (or consolidate) them in a single criminal action. If, and only if, the State chooses joinder or consolidation, the defendant has the choice whether to demand a severance. If, and only if, the defendant chooses not to demand a severance will §3.03 come into effect through the trial in a single criminal action of multiple offenses arising from a single criminal episode. [¶] The statement in *LaPorte* that a trial court may not order consecutive sentences when charges arising out of the same criminal episode are tried in a single criminal proceeding [840 S.W.2d at 415] is correct in the context of that case, in which no waiver was made."

Robbins v. State, 914 S.W.2d 582, 583-84 (Tex. Crim.App.1996). "Although Appellant entered separate pleas of guilty to each indictment, the trial court held a consolidated punishment hearing. A plea proceeding is not complete until punishment has been assessed. Had the trial court accepted the plea and rendered sentence in one cause prior to hearing the plea and rendering sentence in the other, we would agree with the Court of Appeals that the trial court 'fully completed one plea proceeding before starting the other.' However, the consolidated punishment hearing defeated the State's and trial court's attempts to comply with the provisions of §3.03, of the Penal Code. Therefore, the cumulation order is void. [¶] The proper remedy is to reform the judgment ... to delete the cumulation order." *See also **Ex parte Pharr***, 897 S.W.2d 795, 796 (Tex.Crim.App. 1995).

Rollins v. State, 994 S.W.2d 429, 430 (Tex.App.— Beaumont 1999, no pet.). "[A]ppellant was separately indicted for two offenses of delivery of marijuana.... Each of the two indictments alleged the delivery was made to a different person.... In September of 1994, the trial court deferred adjudication of Rollins's guilt.... Later the State filed a motion to adjudicate his guilt. In a single proceeding..., the trial court found Rollins guilty in both offenses and ... placed Rollins on probation. A year later, ... the trial court revoked Rollins' probation and imposed his sentence. Punishment was assessed at seven years for each offense, the sentences to run consecutively. *At 432-33:* [W]e are again faced with the issue of what constitutes a 'single criminal action.' ... We conclude that the adjudication of guilt and pronouncement of sentence in the two cases 'are so intertwined that we are left only to conclude they are a single criminal action.' [¶] Having found that the offenses were prosecuted in a single criminal action and that they arose out of the same criminal episode, we conclude that the trial court erred in ordering the sentences to run consecutively...." *See also Frank v. State*, 992 S.W.2d 756, 758 (Tex.App.—Houston [1st Dist.] 1999, pet. ref'd).

PEN §3.04. SEVERANCE

(a) Whenever two or more offenses have been consolidated or joined for trial under Section 3.02, the defendant shall have a right to a severance of the offenses.

(b) In the event of severance under this section, the provisions of Section 3.03 do not apply, and the court in its discretion may order the sentences to run either concurrently or consecutively.

(c) The right to severance under this section does not apply to a prosecution for offenses described by Section 3.03(b) unless the court determines that the defendant or the state would be unfairly prejudiced by a joinder of offenses, in which event the judge may order the offenses to be tried separately or may order other relief as justice requires.

History of Pen §3.04: Acts 1973, 63rd Leg., ch. 399, §1, eff. Jan. 1, 1974. Amended by Acts 1993, 73rd Leg., ch. 900, §1.01, eff. Sept. 1, 1994; Acts 1997, 75th Leg., ch. 667, §3, eff. Sept. 1, 1997; Acts 2005, 79th Leg., ch. 527, §2, eff. Sept. 1, 2005.

ANNOTATIONS

Scott v. State, 235 S.W.3d 255, 257 (Tex.Crim.App. 2007). "A trial judge's failure to grant a mandatory severance under §3.04 is subject to a harm analysis, and the error is harmless if it did not adversely affect the defendant's substantial rights. 'To judge the likelihood

that harm occurred, appellate courts must consider everything in the record including all the evidence admitted at trial, the closing arguments, and ... the jurors' comments during voir dire.'"

Graham v. State, 19 S.W.3d 851, 853 (Tex.Crim. App.2000). "An indictment may contain as many separate paragraphs charging the same offense as is necessary to meet the contingencies of the evidence. Where an indictment charges different theories under which a defendant may have committed a single capital murder, the provisions of §3.04(a) will not apply. [¶] The facts presented in the instant case [establish that] two of the three paragraphs allege *different murders* as the basis for the capital charge. *At 854:* Thus, unlike *Hathorn* [848 S.W.2d 101 (Tex.Crim.App.1992)] where the indictment alleged multiple theories for committing one capital murder ..., the indictment in the instant case alleged two distinct capital offenses. ... [¶] The Court of Appeals erred in concluding that the indictment alleged only one offense and that §3.04(a) did not apply for that reason."

LaPorte v. State, 840 S.W.2d 412, 414-15 (Tex. Crim.App.1992). Pen. Code §3.04 "provides a defendant the right to have separate trials if he so desires. ... If [30 days' notice required by Pen. Code §3.02 is not] given he may either object to the lack of the notice when he discovers the State intends to prosecute for offenses based upon more than one indictment in a single trial, may request the severance provided by §3.04, or may waive the notice and proceed to trial on any charges presented by the State by not objecting to the lack of notice."

Hayes v. State, 166 S.W.3d 899, 902 (Tex.App.— Amarillo 2005, pet. ref'd). "[T]o the extent that [Pen. Code] §3.04(c) ... obligates the trial court to assess the potential for unfair prejudice, we hold that it may utilize the analytical mechanism applied when facing a [TRE] 403 objection. That is, it need not illustrate, of record, how it undertook the requisite analysis. Nor must it specify the indicia or evidence it considered during its analysis. And, unless the record affirmatively shows otherwise, we may presume that by acting upon the request, it performed the duties imposed by §3.04(c)...." *But see Hulsey v. State*, 211 S.W.3d 853, 858 n.1 (Tex.App.—Waco 2006, no pet.) (no objection needed to preserve review of trial court's §3.04(c) analysis).

For a quick reference of penalties, see the Chart of Penalties on p. 675.

O'CONNOR'S CRIMINAL CODES 715

TITLE 2. GENERAL PRINCIPLES OF CRIMINAL RESPONSIBILITY

CHAPTER 6. CULPABILITY GENERALLY

PEN §6.01. REQUIREMENT OF VOLUNTARY ACT OR OMISSION

(a) A person commits an offense only if he voluntarily engages in conduct, including an act, an omission, or possession.

(b) Possession is a voluntary act if the possessor knowingly obtains or receives the thing possessed or is aware of his control of the thing for a sufficient time to permit him to terminate his control.

(c) A person who omits to perform an act does not commit an offense unless a law as defined by Section 1.07 provides that the omission is an offense or otherwise provides that he has a duty to perform the act.

History of Pen §6.01: Acts 1973, 63rd Leg., ch. 399, §1, eff. Jan. 1, 1974. Amended by Acts 1975, 64th Leg., ch. 342, §3, eff. Sept. 1, 1975; Acts 1993, 73rd Leg., ch. 3, §1 (eff. Feb. 25, 1993), ch. 900, §1.01 (eff. Sept. 1, 1994).

ANNOTATIONS

Alford v. State, 866 S.W.2d 619, 624 n.8 (Tex.Crim. App.1993). "Because 'voluntarily' means the *absence* of accidental act, omission or possession, it is not a fact that the State must prove in every case. [T]he State need not prove voluntariness unless the evidence raises the issue of accident, in which case the State must disprove the theory of accident beyond a reasonable doubt." *See also Avila v. State*, 954 S.W.2d 830, 838 (Tex.App.—El Paso 1997, pet. ref'd).

Billingslea v. State, 780 S.W.2d 271, 274 (Tex.Crim. App.1989). "Since §6.01(c) is stated in the disjunctive, it appears to provide alternative grounds for finding a criminally punishable omission. In reality, however, only the second clause is substantive. The first ground is obscure because it purports to allow a penal statute to make an omission an offense merely by stating that 'an omission is an offense.' [F]or there to be an omission, there must be a corresponding duty to act."

Nelson v. State, 149 S.W.3d 206, 210 (Tex.App.— Fort Worth 2004, no pet.). "Involuntary intoxication is a defense to criminal culpability when it is shown that: (1) the accused has exercised no independent judgment or volition in taking the intoxicant; and (2) as a result of his intoxication, the accused did not know that his conduct was wrong or was incapable of conforming his conduct to the requirement of the law he allegedly violated. Involuntary intoxication by prescription medication occurs only 'if the individual had no knowledge of possible intoxicating side effects of the drug, since independent judgment is exercised in taking the drug as medicine, not as an intoxicant.' The defense of involuntary intoxication does not apply to persons who are unconscious or semi-conscious at the time of the alleged offense. Likewise, the defense does not apply when, as here, the defendant's mental state is not an element of the alleged offense."

Payne v. State, 33 S.W.3d 374, 376 (Tex.App.— Houston [1st Dist.] 2000, pet. ref'd). "Although the evidence clearly raised the issue of voluntariness, the jury was not given the opportunity to reach a finding of accidental or involuntary shooting. [¶] [T]he voluntariness of the appellant's actions in firing the gun was the appellant's primary defense; he was entitled to have the jury rule upon that defense and was harmed in not having the requested instruction submitted to the jury."

Wade v. State, 630 S.W.2d 418, 419 (Tex.App.— Houston [14th Dist.] 1982, no pet.). "Before a person's conduct can be deemed criminal, our penal code requires that the conduct be voluntary. This does not eliminate the requirements of a culpable mental state set out in [Pen. Code] §6.02; rather it is a threshold question. The indictment need not allege voluntariness...."

PEN §6.02. REQUIREMENT OF CULPABILITY

(a) Except as provided in Subsection (b), a person does not commit an offense unless he intentionally, knowingly, recklessly, or with criminal negligence engages in conduct as the definition of the offense requires.

(b) If the definition of an offense does not prescribe a culpable mental state, a culpable mental state is nevertheless required unless the definition plainly dispenses with any mental element.

(c) If the definition of an offense does not prescribe a culpable mental state, but one is nevertheless required under Subsection (b), intent, knowledge, or recklessness suffices to establish criminal responsibility.

(d) Culpable mental states are classified according to relative degrees, from highest to lowest, as follows:

PEN §6.01

(1) intentional;

(2) knowing;

(3) reckless;

(4) criminal negligence.

(e) Proof of a higher degree of culpability than that charged constitutes proof of the culpability charged.

(f) An offense defined by municipal ordinance or by order of a county commissioners court may not dispense with the requirement of a culpable mental state if the offense is punishable by a fine exceeding the amount authorized by Section 12.23.

History of Pen §6.02: Acts 1973, 63rd Leg., ch. 399, §1, eff. Jan. 1, 1974. Amended by Acts 1993, 73rd Leg., ch. 900, §1.01, eff. Sept. 1, 1994; Acts 2005, 79th Leg., ch. 1219, §1, eff. Sept. 1, 2005.

ANNOTATIONS

Aguirre v. State, 22 S.W.3d 463, 472 (Tex.Crim.App. 1999). "[A] court must look for a manifest intent to dispense with the requirement of a culpable mental state, and … the silence of a statute about whether a culpable mental state is an element of the offense leaves a presumption that one is [required]. [¶] In the absence of an express intent to dispense with the requirement of a culpable mental state, [the court asks] whether such an intent is manifested by other features of the statute." *See also Robledo v. State*, 126 S.W.3d 150, 153 (Tex.App.—Houston [1st Dist.] 2003, no pet.).

Chandler v. State, 855 S.W.2d 38, 41 (Tex.App.— Fort Worth 1993, no pet.). "Only each offense is required to have a culpable mental state, not each element of an offense."

PEN §6.03. DEFINITIONS OF CULPABLE MENTAL STATES

(a) A person acts intentionally, or with intent, with respect to the nature of his conduct or to a result of his conduct when it is his conscious objective or desire to engage in the conduct or cause the result.

(b) A person acts knowingly, or with knowledge, with respect to the nature of his conduct or to circumstances surrounding his conduct when he is aware of the nature of his conduct or that the circumstances exist. A person acts knowingly, or with knowledge, with respect to a result of his conduct when he is aware that his conduct is reasonably certain to cause the result.

(c) A person acts recklessly, or is reckless, with respect to circumstances surrounding his conduct or the result of his conduct when he is aware of but consciously disregards a substantial and unjustifiable risk that the circumstances exist or the result will occur. The risk must be of such a nature and degree that its disregard constitutes a gross deviation from the standard of care that an ordinary person would exercise under all the circumstances as viewed from the actor's standpoint.

(d) A person acts with criminal negligence, or is criminally negligent, with respect to circumstances surrounding his conduct or the result of his conduct when he ought to be aware of a substantial and unjustifiable risk that the circumstances exist or the result will occur. The risk must be of such a nature and degree that the failure to perceive it constitutes a gross deviation from the standard of care that an ordinary person would exercise under all the circumstances as viewed from the actor's standpoint.

History of Pen §6.03: Acts 1973, 63rd Leg., ch. 399, §1, eff. Jan. 1, 1974.

ANNOTATIONS

Williams v. State, 235 S.W.3d 742, 753 (Tex.Crim. App.2007). "In addressing the sufficiency of evidence to prove criminal recklessness, it is not enough to provide the jury with a set of legally correct definitions and then simply turn them loose and accept whatever they decide. Instead, there are 'intermediate and progressively more demanding burdens of production that must be met by the State, as a matter of law, before the fact-finding process is even ratcheted up from one to the next higher level of possible culpability[.]' The State cannot be permitted to submit its case to the jury unless it has offered a *prima facie* case of a defendant's actual, subjective 'disregard of the risk of a resulting [injury] which … rise[s] to the level of a 'gross deviation' from an ordinary standard of conduct.' The incremental risk and *mens rea* that may transform mere civil negligence into criminal negligence and then possibly into criminal recklessness are, although elusive, substantive elements with unique burdens of production that must be satisfied as a matter of law."

Koah v. State, 604 S.W.2d 156, 160 n.1 (Tex.Crim. App.1980). "The formulated distinction between intentional and knowing, as to results, is thus between desiring the result and being reasonably certain that it will occur."

For a quick reference of penalties, see the Chart of Penalties on p. 675.

O'CONNOR'S CRIMINAL CODES   717

Tello v. State, 180 S.W.3d 150, 158-59 (Tex.Crim. App.2005) (Cochran, J., concurring). "Civil or 'simple' negligence 'means failure to use ordinary care, that is, failing to do that which a person of ordinary prudence would have done under the same or similar circumstances or doing that which a person of ordinary prudence would not have done under the same or similar circumstances.' And 'ordinary care' means 'that degree of care that would be used by a person of ordinary prudence under the same or similar circumstances.' [¶] Criminal negligence, however, requires a significantly greater degree of deviation from this standard of ordinary care before a person may be held criminally liable. It must be a 'gross' or extreme deviation from that standard. And it is measured solely by the degree of negligence, not any element of actual awareness. Conduct that constitutes criminal negligence involves a greater risk of harm to others, without any compensating social utility, than does simple negligence. A person may be found criminally negligent when he inadvertently creates a substantial and unjustifiable risk of which he ought to be (but is not) aware. And a jury must evaluate the defendant's failure of perception and determine whether, under all the circumstances, it was serious enough to be condemned under the criminal law."

Baldwin v. State, ___ S.W.3d ___ (Tex.App.— Houston [1st Dist.] 2008, pet. filed 5-13-08) (No. 01-06-00859-CR; 2-07-08). "The fact finder may infer intent from the accused's acts and words as well as the surrounding circumstances. A jury may reasonably infer that the defendant intentionally, not accidentally, inflicted the injury when the defendant fails to render aid known to be needed. A reasonable inference also arises in the presence of proof that the defendant tried to conceal the conditions that led to the victim's injuries."

State v. Vasquez, 34 S.W.3d 332, 334 (Tex. App.—San Antonio 2000, no pet.). "When the State charges a defendant with acting recklessly in the commission of an offense, the indictment must allege with reasonable certainty the act or acts relied upon to constitute recklessness. The indictment is not sufficient if it merely alleges that the accused acted recklessly in committing the offense."

Fields v. State, 966 S.W.2d 736, 739 (Tex. App.—San Antonio 1998), *rev'd on other grounds*, 1 S.W.3d 687 (Tex.Crim.App.1999). "A 'conduct element' is basically that element of the offense that makes the defendant's conduct proscribable. The Texas

Penal Code identifies three 'conduct elements' that may be implicated in a given crime: (1) the nature of the conduct; (2) the result of the conduct; and (3) the circumstances surrounding the conduct. Texas courts require that, in the judge's charge to the jury, the 'intentional' and 'knowing' requirements be confined to the specific conduct element required to prove the alleged offense. [¶] [W]here all three conduct elements are implicated, the trial judge must still limit the definitions in the jury charge to the conduct element or elements of the offense to which they apply."

PEN §6.04. CAUSATION: CONDUCT & RESULTS

(a) A person is criminally responsible if the result would not have occurred but for his conduct, operating either alone or concurrently with another cause, unless the concurrent cause was clearly sufficient to produce the result and the conduct of the actor clearly insufficient.

(b) A person is nevertheless criminally responsible for causing a result if the only difference between what actually occurred and what he desired, contemplated, or risked is that:

(1) a different offense was committed; or

(2) a different person or property was injured, harmed, or otherwise affected.

History of Pen §6.04: Acts 1973, 63rd Leg., ch. 399, §1, eff. Jan. 1, 1974.

ANNOTATIONS

Thompson v. State, 236 S.W.3d 787, 800 (Tex.Crim. App.2007). "[W]e conclude that §6.04(b)(1) does indeed authorize the transfer of a culpable mental state between offenses contained in the same statute and also between greater and lesser included offenses. That authorization may be overridden by language defining a particular offense, as in the offense of capital murder, but no such impediment arises with respect to the injury-to-a-child offense. Where §6.04(b)(1) permits the transfer of a culpable mental state, mistake of fact may be raised as a defense. The mistake must be reasonable for it to constitute a circumstance that exculpates the defendant of the offense charged, and of course, the defendant would still be guilty of any lesser included offense that would be applicable if the facts were as the defendant believed."

PEN §6.03

Umoja v. State, 965 S.W.2d 3, 9 (Tex.App.—Fort Worth 1997, no pet.). "Under [§6.04], two combinations may exist to satisfy the requisite causal connection between appellant's conduct and the harm that followed: (1) the [defendant's] conduct may be sufficient by itself to have caused the harm, regardless of the existence of a concurrent cause; or (2) the [defendant's] conduct and the other cause *together* may be sufficient to have caused the harm. Section 6.04(a) further defines and limits the 'but for' causality for concurrent causes by the last phrase, 'unless the concurrent cause was clearly sufficient to produce the result and the conduct of the actor clearly insufficient.' If the additional cause, other than the defendant's conduct, is clearly sufficient by itself, to produce the result and the defendant's conduct, by itself, clearly insufficient, then the defendant cannot be convicted." *See also* **Hale v. State**, 194 S.W.3d 39, 42 (Tex.App.—Texarkana 2006, no pet.).

CHAPTER 7. CRIMINAL RESPONSIBILITY FOR CONDUCT OF ANOTHER

Subchapter A. Complicity

§7.01   Parties to offenses
§7.02   Criminal responsibility for conduct of another
§7.03   Defenses excluded

Subchapter B. Corporations & Associations

§7.21   Definitions
§7.22   Criminal responsibility of corporation or association
§7.23   Criminal responsibility of person for conduct in behalf of corporation or association
§7.24   Defense to criminal responsibility of corporation or association

SUBCHAPTER A. COMPLICITY

PEN §7.01. PARTIES TO OFFENSES

(a) A person is criminally responsible as a party to an offense if the offense is committed by his own conduct, by the conduct of another for which he is criminally responsible, or by both.

(b) Each party to an offense may be charged with commission of the offense.

(c) All traditional distinctions between accomplices and principals are abolished by this section, and each party to an offense may be charged and convicted without alleging that he acted as a principal or accomplice.

History of Pen §7.01: Acts 1973, 63rd Leg., ch. 399, §1, eff. Jan. 1, 1974.

Powell v. State, 194 S.W.3d 503, 506 (Tex.Crim. App.2006). "[A] person can be convicted as a party even if the indictment does not explicitly charge him as a party." *See also* **Childress v. State**, 917 S.W.2d 489, 492 (Tex.App.—Houston [14th Dist.] 1996, no pet.).

Goff v. State, 931 S.W.2d 537, 544 (Tex.Crim.App. 1996). "[U]nder the law of parties, the State is able to enlarge a defendant's criminal responsibility to acts in which he may not be the principal actor. Because our penal code generally criminalizes conduct of individuals, the State is required to properly instruct the jury if it proceeds upon a parties theory. Where there is no charge on the law of parties a defendant may only be convicted on the basis of his own conduct."

PEN §7.02. CRIMINAL RESPONSIBILITY FOR CONDUCT OF ANOTHER

(a) A person is criminally responsible for an offense committed by the conduct of another if:

(1) acting with the kind of culpability required for the offense, he causes or aids an innocent or nonresponsible person to engage in conduct prohibited by the definition of the offense;

(2) acting with intent to promote or assist the commission of the offense, he solicits, encourages, directs, aids, or attempts to aid the other person to commit the offense; or

(3) having a legal duty to prevent commission of the offense and acting with intent to promote or assist its commission, he fails to make a reasonable effort to prevent commission of the offense.

(b) If, in the attempt to carry out a conspiracy to commit one felony, another felony is committed by one of the conspirators, all conspirators are guilty of the felony actually committed, though having no intent to commit it, if the offense was committed in furtherance of the unlawful purpose and was one that should have been anticipated as a result of the carrying out of the conspiracy.

History of Pen §7.02: Acts 1973, 63rd Leg., ch. 399, §1, eff. Jan. 1, 1974.

Ex parte Thompson, 179 S.W.3d 549, 553-54 (Tex. Crim.App.2005). "[O]ne accomplice may be found guilty of a different, more serious offense than other

PEN §7.02

For a quick reference of penalties, see the Chart of Penalties on p. 675.

O'CONNOR'S CRIMINAL CODES   719

accomplices. Indeed, the acquittal of the principal does not prevent conviction of his accomplice. And it does not matter whether the acquittal of the principal occurs before or after the accomplice's trial. What matters under §7.02(a) is the criminal *mens rea* of each accomplice; each may be convicted only of those crimes for which he had the requisite mental state." *See also Cienfuegos v. State*, 113 S.W.3d 481, 493-94 (Tex. App.—Houston [1st Dist.] 2003, pet. ref'd).

Solomon v. State, 49 S.W.3d 356, 368 (Tex.Crim. App.2001). "[T]here is no enumerated defense of 'independent impulse' in the Penal Code.... All that is required [for a proper jury charge on conspiracy liability] is for the appropriate portions of the jury charge to track the language of §7.02(b)."

Brown v. State, 716 S.W.2d 939, 944 (Tex.Crim. App.1986). "[T]he test for ascertaining whether a person is a party to an offense by virtue of his own conduct or by the conduct of another for which he is criminally responsible [is]: '[T]he trial court should first remove from consideration the acts and conduct of the non-defendant [or codefendant] actor[s]. Then, if the evidence of the conduct of the defendant then on trial would be sufficient, in and of itself, to sustain the conviction, no submission of the law of principals [parties] is required.... On the other hand, if the evidence introduced upon the trial of the cause shows, or raises an issue, that the conduct of the defendant then upon trial is not sufficient, in and of itself, to sustain a conviction, the State's case rests upon the law of principals [parties] and is dependent, at least in part, upon the conduct of another. In such a case, the law of principals [parties] must be submitted and made applicable to the facts of the case.'"

Wooden v. State, 101 S.W.3d 542, 546 (Tex.App.— Fort Worth 2003, pet. ref'd). "Standing alone, proof that an accused was present at the scene of the crime or assisted the primary actor in making his getaway is insufficient [to hold the accused criminally responsible for the conduct of another]. The evidence must show that at the time of the offense the parties were acting together, each contributing some part towards the execution of their common purpose. Evidence is legally sufficient to convict under the law of parties when the defendant is physically present at the commission of the offense and encourages its commission by acts, words, or other agreement. Whether an accused participated as a party to an offense may be determined by examining the events occurring before, during, and after the commission of the offense and by the actions of the accused which show an understanding and common design to commit the offense. *At 547-48:* In order to convict a defendant as a party to an aggravated offense, the State must prove that the defendant was criminally responsible for the aggravating element."

Hill v. State, 883 S.W.2d 765, 771 (Tex.App.— Amarillo 1994, pet. ref'd). "[A]ppellant is criminally responsible for the offense committed by [other D] only if the evidence shows that she *knew [D's] unlawful intent* when she acted to promote or assist in his conduct."

PEN §7.03. DEFENSES EXCLUDED

In a prosecution in which an actor's criminal responsibility is based on the conduct of another, the actor may be convicted on proof of commission of the offense and that he was a party to its commission, and it is no defense:

(1) that the actor belongs to a class of persons that by definition of the offense is legally incapable of committing the offense in an individual capacity; or

(2) that the person for whose conduct the actor is criminally responsible has been acquitted, has not been prosecuted or convicted, has been convicted of a different offense or of a different type or class of offense, or is immune from prosecution.

History of Pen §7.03: Acts 1973, 63rd Leg., ch. 399, §1, eff. Jan. 1, 1974.

ANNOTATIONS

Ex parte Thompson, 179 S.W.3d 549, 555-56 (Tex. Crim.App.2005). "Applicant argues that [accomplice's] subsequent acquittal of capital murder proves that, under §7.03, no capital murder was ever committed. Applicant misreads §7.03. That provision applies to the proof offered at applicant's trial, not the evidence offered in some other trial. It was in applicant's trial that the State bore the burden of offering 'proof of commission of the offense' of capital murder. And indeed it did. There is evidence aplenty that [accomplice], as well as applicant, intended to cause [victim's] death...."

SUBCHAPTER B. CORPORATIONS & ASSOCIATIONS

PEN §7.21. DEFINITIONS

In this subchapter:

(1) "Agent" means a director, officer, employee, or other person authorized to act in behalf of a corporation or association.

(2) "High managerial agent" means:

(A) a partner in a partnership;

(B) an officer of a corporation or association;

(C) an agent of a corporation or association who has duties of such responsibility that his conduct reasonably may be assumed to represent the policy of the corporation or association.

History of Pen §7.21: Acts 1973, 63rd Leg., ch. 399, §1, eff. Jan. 1, 1974.

PEN §7.22. CRIMINAL RESPONSIBILITY OF CORPORATION OR ASSOCIATION

(a) If conduct constituting an offense is performed by an agent acting in behalf of a corporation or association and within the scope of his office or employment, the corporation or association is criminally responsible for an offense defined:

(1) in this code where corporations and associations are made subject thereto;

(2) by law other than this code in which a legislative purpose to impose criminal responsibility on corporations or associations plainly appears; or

(3) by law other than this code for which strict liability is imposed, unless a legislative purpose not to impose criminal responsibility on corporations or associations plainly appears.

(b) A corporation or association is criminally responsible for a felony offense only if its commission was authorized, requested, commanded, performed, or recklessly tolerated by:

(1) a majority of the governing board acting in behalf of the corporation or association; or

(2) a high managerial agent acting in behalf of the corporation or association and within the scope of his office or employment.

History of Pen §7.22: Acts 1973, 63rd Leg., ch. 399, §1, eff. Jan. 1, 1974. Amended by Acts 1975, 64th Leg., ch. 342, §4, eff. Sept. 1, 1975.

ANNOTATIONS

Vaughan & Sons, Inc. v. State, 737 S.W.2d 805, 806 (Tex.Crim.App.1987). "[T]he general rule is that a corporation may be held liable for criminal acts performed by its agents acting on its behalf."

PEN §7.23. CRIMINAL RESPONSIBILITY OF PERSON FOR CONDUCT IN BEHALF OF CORPORATION OR ASSOCIATION

(a) An individual is criminally responsible for conduct that he performs in the name of or in behalf of a corporation or association to the same extent as if the conduct were performed in his own name or behalf.

(b) An agent having primary responsibility for the discharge of a duty to act imposed by law on a corporation or association is criminally responsible for omission to discharge the duty to the same extent as if the duty were imposed by law directly on him.

(c) If an individual is convicted of conduct constituting an offense performed in the name of or on behalf of a corporation or association, he is subject to the sentence authorized by law for an individual convicted of the offense.

History of Pen §7.23: Acts 1973, 63rd Leg., ch. 399, §1, eff. Jan. 1, 1974.

PEN §7.24. DEFENSE TO CRIMINAL RESPONSIBILITY OF CORPORATION OR ASSOCIATION

It is an affirmative defense to prosecution of a corporation or association under Section 7.22(a)(1) or (a)(2) that the high managerial agent having supervisory responsibility over the subject matter of the offense employed due diligence to prevent its commission.

History of Pen §7.24: Acts 1973, 63rd Leg., ch. 399, §1, eff. Jan. 1, 1974. Amended by Acts 1975, 64th Leg., ch. 342, §5, eff. Sept. 1, 1975; Acts 1993, 73rd Leg., ch. 900, §1.01, eff. Sept. 1, 1994.

CHAPTER 8. GENERAL DEFENSES TO CRIMINAL RESPONSIBILITY

PEN §8.01. INSANITY

(a) It is an affirmative defense to prosecution that, at the time of the conduct charged, the actor, as a result of severe mental disease or defect, did not know that his conduct was wrong.

(b) The term "mental disease or defect" does not include an abnormality manifested only by repeated criminal or otherwise antisocial conduct.

History of Pen §8.01: Acts 1973, 63rd Leg., ch. 399, §1, eff. Jan. 1, 1974. Amended by Acts 1983, 68th Leg., ch. 454, §1, eff. Aug. 29, 1983.
See also CCP ch. 46C.

ANNOTATIONS

Mendenhall v. State, 77 S.W.3d 815, 818 (Tex. Crim.App.2002). "We have carefully reviewed the legislative history of [Pen. Code] §8.01(a), and nothing in it

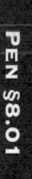

PEN §8.01

For a quick reference of penalties, see the Chart of Penalties on p. 675.

O'CONNOR'S CRIMINAL CODES 721

suggests that any legislators intended for the insanity defense [based on involuntary intoxication] to apply to persons who were unconscious or semi-conscious at the time of the alleged offense. [P]ersons who were unconscious or semi-conscious at the time of the alleged offense may argue either that they lacked the *mens rea* necessary for criminal liability, *see* [Pen. Code] §6.02(a), or that they did not engage in a voluntary act, *see* [Pen. Code] §6.01(a)." *See also Nelson v. State*, 149 S.W.3d 206, 211 (Tex.App.—Fort Worth 2004, no pet.).

Riley v. State, 830 S.W.2d 584, 585 (Tex.Crim.App. 1992). "Insanity is an affirmative defense, which means the defendant has the burden of proving his insanity by a preponderance of the evidence. As a general rule the State has no obligation to bring forward evidence which establishes the defendant was sane at the time of the commission of the alleged offense. However, an exception to that general rule exists whenever the defendant has previously been adjudicated insane and such adjudication has not been vacated. In that situation, there is a presumption that the insanity continues and the burden is upon the State to prove, beyond a reasonable doubt, that the defendant was *sane* at the time of the alleged offense."

Pacheco v. State, 757 S.W.2d 729, 733 (Tex.Crim. App.1988). "Properly admitted opinion testimony of lay witnesses is sufficient to support a finding of insanity. Therefore, when medical experts testify that accused is afflicted with a specific disease of mind that produced insanity, a charge restricting the defense to that particular form of insanity is incorrect; it would detract from testimony of nonexpert witnesses who express an opinion on the question of general insanity or sanity, for the latter could not know or testify that accused was so laboring under a named disease of mind."

Schuessler v. State, 719 S.W.2d 320, 329 (Tex. Crim.App.1986), *overruled on other grounds*, *Meraz v. State*, 785 S.W.2d 146 (Tex.Crim.App.1990). "[I]f a defendant's evidence is undisputed as to the presence of a mental disease or defect, even if it established *medical* insanity, it would not necessarily establish *legal* insanity."

Graham v. State, 566 S.W.2d 941, 949 (Tex.Crim. App.1978). "The [insanity] issue is not strictly medical, and expert witnesses, although capable of giving testimony that may aid the jury in its determination of the

ultimate issue, are not capable of dictating determination of that issue. Only the jury can join the non-medical components that must also be considered in deciding the ultimate issue. That ultimate issue of criminal responsibility is beyond the province of expert witnesses. Were it otherwise, the issue would be tried in hospitals rather than the courts."

Aschbacher v. State, 61 S.W.3d 532, 539 (Tex. App.—San Antonio 2001, pet. ref'd). "'When words are not specially defined by the Legislature, they are to be understood as ordinary usage allows, and jurors may freely read the statutory language to have any meaning which is acceptable in common speech.' The term 'wrong' is not defined in the Penal Code. The jury, therefore, was to interpret the word according to its common meaning."

PEN §8.02. MISTAKE OF FACT

(a) It is a defense to prosecution that the actor through mistake formed a reasonable belief about a matter of fact if his mistaken belief negated the kind of culpability required for commission of the offense.

(b) Although an actor's mistake of fact may constitute a defense to the offense charged, he may nevertheless be convicted of any lesser included offense of which he would be guilty if the fact were as he believed.

History of Pen §8.02: Acts 1973, 63rd Leg., ch. 399, §1, eff. Jan. 1, 1974.

ANNOTATIONS

Granger v. State, 3 S.W.3d 36, 38-39 (Tex.Crim. App.1999). "The question … is whether the reasonableness requirement [of §8.02] is a preliminary issue for the judge to decide in determining whether each element of the defense was 'raised' by the evidence, or whether it is a fact issue that should be left to the jury. [¶] [W]hether appellant's mistaken belief was 'reasonable' … should have been left for the jury to decide as trier of fact."

Willis v. State, 790 S.W.2d 307, 314 (Tex.Crim.App. 1990). "In [certain] circumstances, the defendant would be entitled to a defensive instruction of 'mistake of fact,' and should not be required to admit the other elements of the crime."

Johnson v. State, 734 S.W.2d 199, 203-04 (Tex. App.—Houston [1st Dist.] 1987, pet. ref'd). "The defense [of mistake of fact] impliedly looks to the conduct of others only to the extent that such conduct

PEN §8.01

contributes to the actor's mistaken belief, and does not look at all to the belief or state of mind of any other person."

PEN §8.03. MISTAKE OF LAW

(a) It is no defense to prosecution that the actor was ignorant of the provisions of any law after the law has taken effect.

(b) It is an affirmative defense to prosecution that the actor reasonably believed the conduct charged did not constitute a crime and that he acted in reasonable reliance upon:

(1) an official statement of the law contained in a written order or grant of permission by an administrative agency charged by law with responsibility for interpreting the law in question; or

(2) a written interpretation of the law contained in an opinion of a court of record or made by a public official charged by law with responsibility for interpreting the law in question.

(c) Although an actor's mistake of law may constitute a defense to the offense charged, he may nevertheless be convicted of a lesser included offense of which he would be guilty if the law were as he believed.

History of Pen §8.03: Acts 1973, 63rd Leg., ch. 399, §1, eff. Jan. 1, 1974.

PEN §8.04. INTOXICATION

(a) Voluntary intoxication does not constitute a defense to the commission of crime.

(b) Evidence of temporary insanity caused by intoxication may be introduced by the actor in mitigation of the penalty attached to the offense for which he is being tried.

(c) When temporary insanity is relied upon as a defense and the evidence tends to show that such insanity was caused by intoxication, the court shall charge the jury in accordance with the provisions of this section.

(d) For purposes of this section "intoxication" means disturbance of mental or physical capacity resulting from the introduction of any substance into the body.

History of Pen §8.04: Acts 1973, 63rd Leg., ch. 399, §1, eff. Jan. 1, 1974.

ANNOTATIONS

Morrow v. State, 910 S.W.2d 471, 473 n.5 (Tex. Crim.App.1995). "Section 8.04 does *not* provide that evidence of voluntary intoxication is mitigating as a matter of law."

Tucker v. State, 771 S.W.2d 523, 534 (Tex.Crim. App.1988). "Appellant [who was convicted of capital murder and assessed the death penalty] argues the ... charge [under §8.04] allowed the jury to consider her drug use and intoxication on the date of the killings as mitigation of punishment *only* if they first found her voluntary intoxication rose to the level of temporary insanity. This limitation impermissibly limited the mitigating significance the jury could have given it. [¶] Although appellant was not prevented from introducing mitigating evidence, the above instruction required the jury to find her intoxication at the time of the killings rendered her temporarily insane before they could consider her drug use in mitigation of her punishment. The charge on its face instructed the jury to consider the mitigating evidence only in this light, thereby implying that it may not have been considered for any other purpose. Appellant maintains she is entitled to whatever mitigating significance the jury might choose to give the fact of her intoxication, irrespective of whether it rose to the level of temporary insanity. However, we need not reach the merits of her contention. [¶] The record reflects that appellant insisted upon the charge on §8.04, and the court submitted her instruction exactly as she had requested it. ... Because appellant's charge on voluntary intoxication was submitted precisely as she had requested, any error was invited. Appellant's ... point of error is overruled."

Nethery v. State, 692 S.W.2d 686, 711 (Tex.Crim. App.1985). The court's charge should "include[ ] a definition of 'insanity' as it applies to [Pen. Code] §8.04. ... If such a charge is necessary, the jury should be given definitions of 'intoxication' under §8.04, and 'insanity' under the applicable part of [Pen. Code] §8.01.... Without both definitions, [the jury] cannot adequately evaluate the evidence and apply the law."

Taylor v. State, 856 S.W.2d 459, 472 (Tex.App.— Houston [1st Dist.] 1993), *aff'd*, 885 S.W.2d 154 (Tex. Crim.App.1994). "A charge on voluntary intoxication generally belongs in the court's charge at the punishment stage, not at the guilt-innocence stage. This is because [Pen. Code] §8.04(b) provides that evidence of temporary insanity caused by intoxication may be introduced in mitigation of the penalty for an offense."

PEN §8.05. DURESS

(a) It is an affirmative defense to prosecution that the actor engaged in the proscribed conduct because he

For a quick reference of penalties, see the Chart of Penalties on p. 675.

O'CONNOR'S CRIMINAL CODES   723

PEN §8.05

★

was compelled to do so by threat of imminent death or serious bodily injury to himself or another.

(b) In a prosecution for an offense that does not constitute a felony, it is an affirmative defense to prosecution that the actor engaged in the proscribed conduct because he was compelled to do so by force or threat of force.

(c) Compulsion within the meaning of this section exists only if the force or threat of force would render a person of reasonable firmness incapable of resisting the pressure.

(d) The defense provided by this section is unavailable if the actor intentionally, knowingly, or recklessly placed himself in a situation in which it was probable that he would be subjected to compulsion.

(e) It is no defense that a person acted at the command or persuasion of his spouse, unless he acted under compulsion that would establish a defense under this section.

History of Pen §8.05: Acts 1973, 63rd Leg., ch. 399, §1, eff. Jan. 1, 1974.

ANNOTATIONS

Miller v. State, 36 S.W.3d 503, 508 (Tex.Crim.App. 2001). "[A]ppellant testified that [drug dealer] threatened her, forcing her to make the delivery to the undercover officer. ... When [drug dealer] caught up to her a few hours after the delivery and discovered the deal had not gone down the way he wanted and that he would not receive the money from the delivery which he expected, he then carried out the threat he made before the delivery and assaulted appellant. A rational jury could find that this evidence helps to prove that appellant was under a constant state of duress from [drug dealer] when she delivered the cocaine, that this duress caused her to fear for her safety, and that her fear was reasonable."

Maestas v. State, 963 S.W.2d 151, 156 (Tex.App.— Corpus Christi 1998), *aff'd*, 987 S.W.2d 59 (Tex.Crim. App.1999). "To be successful with the duress defense, appellant's claim had to have an objective, reasonable basis. *At 157:* The duress defense is based on compulsion by threat and focuses on the conduct of the person making the threats."

PEN §8.06. ENTRAPMENT

(a) It is a defense to prosecution that the actor engaged in the conduct charged because he was induced to do so by a law enforcement agent using persuasion or other means likely to cause persons to commit the offense. Conduct merely affording a person an opportunity to commit an offense does not constitute entrapment.

(b) In this section "law enforcement agent" includes personnel of the state and local law enforcement agencies as well as of the United States and any person acting in accordance with instructions from such agents.

History of Pen §8.06: Acts 1973, 63rd Leg., ch. 399, §1, eff. Jan. 1, 1974.

ANNOTATIONS

Hernandez v. State, 161 S.W.3d 491, 494 (Tex. Crim.App.2005). "We granted review to decide whether a trial judge could rationally deny an 'entrapment as a matter of law' motion by concluding that the defendant's testimony was not credible. Or, put conversely, is the defendant necessarily entitled to prevail in his 'entrapment as a matter of law' motion if the State does not offer affirmative evidence that directly contradicts a defendant's testimony? We conclude that, under *State v. Ross* [, 32 S.W.3d 853 (Tex.Crim.App.2000)], a trial judge is not required to believe a defendant's version of events supporting entrapment defense, even if it is largely uncontradicted. *At 499:* Although the wording in some of our prior cases has been inconsistent, a defendant is entitled to dismissal of the charges under §8.06 in the pretrial hearing context only when he can establish entrapment as a matter of law with *conflict-free, uncontradicted, uncontested* or *undisputed* evidence. If the facts concerning entrapment are in dispute, there cannot be entrapment 'as a matter of law' determined at the pretrial stage. It is the defendant, not the State, who must 'establish beyond a reasonable doubt that he was entrapped' at the pretrial stage. At that stage, the State has no burden of proof; it need only raise a fact issue that a jury would be required to resolve. It is only at the trial stage that the State has the burden to disprove the factual defense of entrapment beyond a reasonable doubt."

England v. State, 887 S.W.2d 902, 908 (Tex.Crim. App.1994). "[W]ith §8.06 the Legislature adopted an 'objective' test for entrapment. [O]nce it is determined that the accused was 'induced,' the only issue left to be resolved is 'the nature of the police activity involved, without reference to the predisposition of the particular defendant.' ... Once the defendant can show he has been the target of persuasive police conduct, regardless

PEN §8.05

of whether he was in fact persuaded to commit an offense, the focus is directed to the police conduct itself. The question becomes whether the persuasion used by the law enforcement agent was such as to cause ... an ordinarily lawabiding person of average resistance ... to commit the offense, *not* whether it was such as to cause the accused himself, given his proclivities, to commit it." *See also Lopez v. State*, 824 S.W.2d 298, 303 (Tex.App.—Houston [1st Dist.] 1992, no pet.).

Taylor v. State, 886 S.W.2d 262, 265 (Tex.Crim.App. 1994). "The entrapment defense is unique in that the Legislature deliberately provided it may be tested and determined at a pretrial hearing. [¶] When the entrapment issue is determined favorably to accused, the only question remaining is the proper remedy."

Ivatury v. State, 792 S.W.2d 845, 848 (Tex.App.—Dallas 1990, pet. ref'd). "The entrapment defense becomes available if the officer specifically instructed his agent or informant to use an improper procedure to 'make a case' against a particular defendant."

Evans v. State, 690 S.W.2d 112, 113 (Tex.App.—El Paso 1985, pet. ref'd). A "concession to the elements of the offense is a necessary predicate to the defense of entrapment. An express admission from the stand is not necessary, but denial of the elements is a bar to assertion of the defense. Hence, the defendant who pleads guilty and either does not testify or does not testify inconsistently with the offense may still be entitled to offer the defense."

PEN §8.07. AGE AFFECTING CRIMINAL RESPONSIBILITY

(a) A person may not be prosecuted for or convicted of any offense that the person committed when younger than 15 years of age except:

(1) perjury and aggravated perjury when it appears by proof that the person had sufficient discretion to understand the nature and obligation of an oath;

(2) a violation of a penal statute cognizable under Chapter 729, Transportation Code, except for conduct for which the person convicted may be sentenced to imprisonment or confinement in jail;

(3) a violation of a motor vehicle traffic ordinance of an incorporated city or town in this state;

(4) a misdemeanor punishable by fine only other than public intoxication;

(5) a violation of a penal ordinance of a political subdivision;

(6) a violation of a penal statute that is, or is a lesser included offense of, a capital felony, an aggravated controlled substance felony, or a felony of the first degree for which the person is transferred to the court under Section 54.02, Family Code, for prosecution if the person committed the offense when 14 years of age or older; or

(7) a capital felony or an offense under Section 19.02 for which the person is transferred to the court under Section 54.02(j)(2)(A), Family Code.

(b) Unless the juvenile court waives jurisdiction under Section 54.02, Family Code, and certifies the individual for criminal prosecution or the juvenile court has previously waived jurisdiction under that section and certified the individual for criminal prosecution, a person may not be prosecuted for or convicted of any offense committed before reaching 17 years of age except an offense described by Subsections (a)(1)-(5).

(c) No person may, in any case, be punished by death for an offense committed while the person was younger than 18 years.

History of Pen §8.07: Acts 1973, 63rd Leg., ch. 399, §1, eff. Jan. 1, 1974. Amended by Acts 1975, 64th Leg., ch. 693, §24, eff. Sept. 1, 1975; Acts 1987, 70th Leg., ch. 1040, §26, eff. Sept. 1, 1987; Acts 1989, 71st Leg., ch. 1245, §3, eff. Sept. 1, 1989; Acts 1991, 72nd Leg., ch. 169, §3, eff. Sept. 1, 1991; Acts 1993, 73rd Leg., ch. 900, §1.01, eff. Sept. 1, 1994; Acts 1995, 74th Leg., ch. 262, §77, eff. Jan. 1, 1996; Acts 1997, 75th Leg., ch. 165, §30.236 (eff. Sept. 1, 1997), ch. 822, §4 (eff. Sept. 1, 1997), ch. 1086, §42 (eff. Sept. 1, 1997); Acts 2001, 77th Leg., ch. 1297, §68, eff. Sept. 1, 2001; Acts 2003, 78th Leg., ch. 283, §52, eff. Sept. 1, 2003; Acts 2005, 79th Leg., ch. 787, §2 (eff. Sept. 1, 2005), ch. 949, §45 (eff. Sept. 1, 2005).

ANNOTATIONS

Gonzales v. State, 681 S.W.2d 270, 274 (Tex. App.—San Antonio 1984, no pet.). A "child who is too young to be prosecuted cannot be an accomplice witness as a matter of law or fact."

CHAPTER 9. JUSTIFICATION EXCLUDING CRIMINAL RESPONSIBILITY

PEN §8.07

For a quick reference of penalties, see the Chart of Penalties on p. 675.

O'CONNOR'S CRIMINAL CODES   725

SUBCHAPTER A. GENERAL PROVISIONS

PEN §9.01. DEFINITIONS

In this chapter:

(1) "Custody" has the meaning assigned by Section 38.01.

(2) "Escape" has the meaning assigned by Section 38.01.

(3) "Deadly force" means force that is intended or known by the actor to cause, or in the manner of its use or intended use is capable of causing, death or serious bodily injury.

Ⓔ (4) "Habitation" has the meaning assigned by Section 30.01.

Ⓔ (5) "Vehicle" has the meaning assigned by Section 30.01.

History of Pen §9.01: Acts 1973, 63rd Leg., ch. 399, §1, eff. Jan. 1, 1974. Amended by Acts 1993, 73rd Leg., ch. 900, §1.01, eff. Sept. 1, 1994; Acts 1997, 75th Leg., ch. 293, §1, eff. Sept. 1, 1997; Acts 2007, 80th Leg., ch. 1, §1, eff. Sept. 1, 2007.

PEN §9.02. JUSTIFICATION AS A DEFENSE

It is a defense to prosecution that the conduct in question is justified under this chapter.

History of Pen §9.02: Acts 1973, 63rd Leg., ch. 399, §1, eff. Jan. 1, 1974.

PEN §9.03. CONFINEMENT AS JUSTIFIABLE FORCE

Confinement is justified when force is justified by this chapter if the actor takes reasonable measures to terminate the confinement as soon as he knows he safely can unless the person confined has been arrested for an offense.

History of Pen §9.03: Acts 1973, 63rd Leg., ch. 399, §1, eff. Jan. 1, 1974.

ANNOTATIONS

Adelman v. State, 828 S.W.2d 418, 423 (Tex.Crim. App.1992). "[T]he requirements of §9.03 are not met when the actor 'releases' her captive into another form of captivity."

PEN §9.04. THREATS AS JUSTIFIABLE FORCE

The threat of force is justified when the use of force is justified by this chapter. For purposes of this section, a threat to cause death or serious bodily injury by the production of a weapon or otherwise, as long as the actor's purpose is limited to creating an apprehension that he will use deadly force if necessary, does not constitute the use of deadly force.

History of Pen §9.04: Acts 1973, 63rd Leg., ch. 399, §1, eff. Jan. 1, 1974.

PEN §9.05. RECKLESS INJURY OF INNOCENT THIRD PERSON

Even though an actor is justified under this chapter in threatening or using force or deadly force against another, if in doing so he also recklessly injures or kills an innocent third person, the justification afforded by this chapter is unavailable in a prosecution for the reckless injury or killing of the innocent third person.

History of Pen §9.05: Acts 1973, 63rd Leg., ch. 399, §1, eff. Jan. 1, 1974.

ANNOTATIONS

Brunson v. State, 764 S.W.2d 888, 891 (Tex.App.— Austin 1989, pet. ref'd). "Section 9.05 … measur[es] the actor's culpability independently as to each of his victims, whether intended or unintended."

PEN §9.06. CIVIL REMEDIES UNAFFECTED

The fact that conduct is justified under this chapter does not abolish or impair any remedy for the conduct that is available in a civil suit.

History of Pen §9.06: Acts 1973, 63rd Leg., ch. 399, §1, eff. Jan. 1, 1974.

SUBCHAPTER B. JUSTIFICATION GENERALLY

PEN §9.21. PUBLIC DUTY

(a) Except as qualified by Subsections (b) and (c), conduct is justified if the actor reasonably believes the conduct is required or authorized by law, by the judgment or order of a competent court or other governmental tribunal, or in the execution of legal process.

(b) The other sections of this chapter control when force is used against a person to protect persons (Subchapter C), to protect property (Subchapter D), for law enforcement (Subchapter E), or by virtue of a special relationship (Subchapter F).

(c) The use of deadly force is not justified under this section unless the actor reasonably believes the deadly force is specifically required by statute or unless it occurs in the lawful conduct of war. If deadly force is so justified, there is no duty to retreat before using it.

(d) The justification afforded by this section is available if the actor reasonably believes:

(1) the court or governmental tribunal has jurisdiction or the process is lawful, even though the court or governmental tribunal lacks jurisdiction or the process is unlawful; or

(2) his conduct is required or authorized to assist a public servant in the performance of his official duty, even though the servant exceeds his lawful authority.

History of Pen §9.21: Acts 1973, 63rd Leg., ch. 399, §1, eff. Jan. 1, 1974. Amended by Acts 1993, 73rd Leg., ch. 900, §1.01, eff. Sept. 1, 1994.

ANNOTATIONS

Rosalez v. State, 875 S.W.2d 705, 717 (Tex.App.—Dallas 1993, pet. ref'd). Peace officers "reasonably believed their entry onto appellant's property was required to carry out their statutory duty to suppress crime and prevent offenses against the property of another. As such, their conduct was justified under §9.21...."

Wilson v. State, 777 S.W.2d 823, 825 (Tex.App.—Austin 1989), *aff'd*, 853 S.W.2d 547 (Tex.Crim.App. 1993). "Appellant contends that international law authorized his [seizing the office of a president of a state university] because apartheid violates international law. *At 826:* [E]ven assuming that [there is] an international law violation, it [does] not follow that illegal action [is] justified when lawful means [are] available."

PEN §9.22. NECESSITY

Conduct is justified if:

(1) the actor reasonably believes the conduct is immediately necessary to avoid imminent harm;

(2) the desirability and urgency of avoiding the harm clearly outweigh, according to ordinary standards of reasonableness, the harm sought to be prevented by the law proscribing the conduct; and

(3) a legislative purpose to exclude the justification claimed for the conduct does not otherwise plainly appear.

History of Pen §9.22: Acts 1973, 63rd Leg., ch. 399, §1, eff. Jan. 1, 1974. Amended by Acts 1993, 73rd Leg., ch. 900, §1.01, eff. Sept. 1, 1994.

ANNOTATIONS

Spakes v. State, 913 S.W.2d 597, 598 (Tex.Crim. App.1996). "The plain language codifying the necessity defense evinces a legislative intent that the defense apply to all offenses unless the legislature has specifically excluded it from them."

Fitzgerald v. State, 782 S.W.2d 876, 885 (Tex.Crim. App.1990). "[T]he factfinder is ... called on to evaluate a given perception of the situation as it appeared to be just before [the conduct]."

Hubbard v. State, 133 S.W.3d 797, 801-02 (Tex. App.—Texarkana 2004, pet. ref'd). "We agree with the general rule that a defendant must admit the conduct charged in the indictment and then offer evidence justifying the conduct. 'Admitting the conduct, however, does not necessarily mean admitting the commission of every statutory element of the offense.' That is, even if a defendant denies the specific allegations in the indictment, he or she is not necessarily precluded from raising defensive issues as long as he or she sufficiently admits conduct underlying the offense and provides evidence justifying a defensive instruction. [A]lthough Hubbard did not admit intentionally, knowingly, or recklessly causing [cellmate's] death, he did admit the conduct underlying the offense, that is, striking [cellmate]. We hold this admission sufficient to satisfy the admission element required to raise the issue of necessity." *See also* **Maldonado v. State**, 902 S.W.2d 708, 712 (Tex.App.—El Paso 1995, no pet.).

Pennington v. State, 54 S.W.3d 852, 859 (Tex. App.—Fort Worth 2001, pet. ref'd). "While the availability of legal alternatives may be relevant to the reasonableness of an actor's conduct, the unavailability of alternative legal courses of conduct is not a requirement of the defense of necessity."

Darty v. State, 994 S.W.2d 215, 219 (Tex. App.—San Antonio 1999, pet. ref'd). "If the defendant offers more than one defense, and there is evidence to support those defenses, then the defendant's denial of some element of the offense does not necessarily preclude a necessity charge, since the defendant is entitled to submission of every defensive issue raised by the evidence, even if inconsistent with other defenses."

For a quick reference of penalties, see the Chart of Penalties on p. 675.

O'CONNOR'S CRIMINAL CODES 727

PEN §9.22

★

Brazelton v. State, 947 S.W.2d 644, 648 (Tex. App.—Fort Worth 1997, no pet.). "The first prong of the necessity defense requires affirmative evidence of imminent harm. Evidence of a generalized fear of harm is not sufficient to raise the issue of imminent harm."

Shafer v. State, 919 S.W.2d 885, 887 (Tex.App.—Fort Worth 1996, pet. ref'd). A "person who is responsible for having placed himself in the position from which he attempts to extricate himself by committing a criminal offense is not entitled to a charge authorizing his acquittal of that offense based upon necessity."

Rosalez v. State, 875 S.W.2d 705, 717 n.17 (Tex. App.—Dallas 1993, pet. ref'd). "[T]he legislative history indicates §9.22 ... may also provide a defense to prosecution for peace officers."

Egger v. State, 817 S.W.2d 183, 185-86 (Tex. App.—El Paso 1991, pet. ref'd). "[T]he accused's belief can be unreasonable as a matter of law. Unreasonableness as a matter of law is derived not from a balancing of harms in the necessity defense's second prong. [I]t arises in the absence of material and relevant evidence to support the first prong."

SUBCHAPTER C. PROTECTION OF PERSONS

PEN §9.31. SELF-DEFENSE

Ⓐ *Subsection (a) below is effective for offenses committed on or after Sept. 1, 2007.*

(a) Except as provided in Subsection (b), a person is justified in using force against another when and to the degree the actor reasonably believes the force is immediately necessary to protect the actor against the other's use or attempted use of unlawful force. The actor's belief that the force was immediately necessary as described by this subsection is presumed to be reasonable if the actor:

(1) knew or had reason to believe that the person against whom the force was used:

(A) unlawfully and with force entered, or was attempting to enter unlawfully and with force, the actor's occupied habitation, vehicle, or place of business or employment;

(B) unlawfully and with force removed, or was attempting to remove unlawfully and with force, the actor from the actor's habitation, vehicle, or place of business or employment; or

(C) was committing or attempting to commit aggravated kidnapping, murder, sexual assault, aggravated sexual assault, robbery, or aggravated robbery;

(2) did not provoke the person against whom the force was used; and

(3) was not otherwise engaged in criminal activity, other than a Class C misdemeanor that is a violation of a law or ordinance regulating traffic at the time the force was used.

Subsection (a) below is effective for offenses in which any element of the offense was committed before Sept. 1, 2007.

(a) Except as provided in Subsection (b), a person is justified in using force against another when and to the degree he reasonably believes the force is immediately necessary to protect himself against the other's use or attempted use of unlawful force.

(b) The use of force against another is not justified:

(1) in response to verbal provocation alone;

(2) to resist an arrest or search that the actor knows is being made by a peace officer, or by a person acting in a peace officer's presence and at his direction, even though the arrest or search is unlawful, unless the resistance is justified under Subsection (c);

(3) if the actor consented to the exact force used or attempted by the other;

(4) if the actor provoked the other's use or attempted use of unlawful force, unless:

(A) the actor abandons the encounter, or clearly communicates to the other his intent to do so reasonably believing he cannot safely abandon the encounter; and

(B) the other nevertheless continues or attempts to use unlawful force against the actor; or

(5) if the actor sought an explanation from or discussion with the other person concerning the actor's differences with the other person while the actor was:

(A) carrying a weapon in violation of Section 46.02; or

(B) possessing or transporting a weapon in violation of Section 46.05.

(c) The use of force to resist an arrest or search is justified:

(1) if, before the actor offers any resistance, the peace officer (or person acting at his direction) uses or attempts to use greater force than necessary to make the arrest or search; and

(2) when and to the degree the actor reasonably believes the force is immediately necessary to protect himself against the peace officer's (or other person's) use or attempted use of greater force than necessary.

(d) The use of deadly force is not justified under this subchapter except as provided in Sections 9.32, 9.33, and 9.34.

E *Subsections (e) & (f) below are effective for offenses committed on or after Sept. 1, 2007.*

(e) A person who has a right to be present at the location where the force is used, who has not provoked the person against whom the force is used, and who is not engaged in criminal activity at the time the force is used is not required to retreat before using force as described by this section.

(f) For purposes of Subsection (a), in determining whether an actor described by Subsection (e) reasonably believed that the use of force was necessary, a finder of fact may not consider whether the actor failed to retreat.

History of Pen §9.31: Acts 1973, 63rd Leg., ch. 399, §1, eff. Jan. 1, 1974. Amended by Acts 1993, 73rd Leg., ch. 900, §1.01, eff. Sept. 1, 1994; Acts 1995, 74th Leg., ch. 190, §1, eff. Sept. 1, 1995; Acts 2007, 80th Leg., ch. 1, §2, eff. Sept. 1, 2007.

ANNOTATIONS

Walters v. State, 247 S.W.3d 204, 212 (Tex.Crim. App.2007). "[W]e hold that, generally speaking, neither the defendant nor the State is entitled to a special jury instruction relating to a statutory offense or defense if that instruction (1) is not grounded in the Penal Code, (2) is covered by the general charge to the jury, and (3) focuses the jury's attention on a specific type of evidence that may support an element of an offense or a defense. In such a case, the non-statutory instruction would constitute a prohibited comment on the weight of the evidence. *At 214:* [T]hough the parties may offer any evidence that would support or refute a finding of self-defense, the parties are not entitled to special, non-statutory jury instructions on how to consider or evaluate specific types of evidence introduced to prove or disprove that defense. Normally, if the instruction is not derived from the code, it is not 'applicable law.'"

Bowen v. State, 162 S.W.3d 226, 226 (Tex.Crim. App.2005). "[T]he Court of Appeals held that [Pen. Code §9.31 demonstrated a legislative purpose to exclude the necessity defense under [Pen. Code] §9.22(3). We disagree."

Torres v. State, 117 S.W.3d 891, 894-95 (Tex.Crim. App.2003). "When a defendant in a homicide prosecution raises the issue of self-defense, he may introduce evidence of the deceased's violent character. Specific acts of violence may be introduced to demonstrate the reasonableness of the defendant's fear of danger or to demonstrate that the deceased was the first aggressor. However, such specific acts of violence are admissible only to the extent that they are relevant apart from showing character conformity. [S]pecific, violent acts are relevant apart from showing character conformity in the context of proving that the deceased was the first aggressor by demonstrating the deceased's intent, motive, or state of mind. Because the specific act is probative of the deceased's state of mind or intent, the witness must know, but the defendant need not know of the act. [¶] There must be some evidence of aggression by the deceased during the events that gave rise to the criminal charges in the case before the defendant may introduce evidence of a prior specific violent act that tends to explain the deceased's later conduct."

Boget v. State, 74 S.W.3d 23, 31 (Tex.Crim.App. 2002). "[W]e conclude that §9.31 is available in a prosecution for criminal mischief where the mischief arises out of the accused's use of force against another. ... Therefore, we overrule that portion of ***Johnson*** [*v. State*, 650 S.W.2d 414 (Tex.Crim.App.1983)] which holds self-defense is a justification only where the defendant is charged with an offense involving the use of force against another."

Smith v. State, 965 S.W.2d 509, 513 (Tex.Crim.App. 1998). "A charge on provocation is required when there is sufficient evidence (1) that the defendant did some act or used some words which provoked the attack on him, (2) that such act or words were reasonably calculated to provoke the attack, and (3) that the act was done or the words were used for the purpose and with the intent that the defendant would have a pretext for inflicting harm upon the other. *At 514:* An instruction on provocation should only be given when there is evidence from which a rational jury could find every element of provocation beyond a reasonable doubt. Under such an analysis the appellate court asks if there was

For a quick reference of penalties, see the Chart of Penalties on p. 675.

O'CONNOR'S CRIMINAL CODES **729**

PEN §9.31

sufficient evidence from which a rational jury could have found provocation beyond a reasonable doubt, viewing the evidence in the light most favorable to giving the instruction."

Porteous v. State, ___ S.W.3d ___ (Tex.App.—Houston [1st Dist.] 2007, pet. filed 5-30-07) (No. 01-06-00419-CR; 3-29-07), *pet. dism'd*, ___ S.W.3d ___ (Tex.Crim.App.2008) (No. PD-0684-07; 5-7-08). "Under [§9.31(c)], a defendant must show greater force than necessary on the part of the police officer before the justification of self-defense is applicable. Thus, to be entitled to an instruction on self-defense when resisting an arrest or search that a defendant knows is being made by a peace officer, there must be some evidence in the record to raise the issue of whether the peace officer used or attempted to use greater force than necessary in attempting to arrest or search the defendant."

Jones v. State, 241 S.W.3d 666, 669 (Tex.App.—Texarkana 2007, no pet.). "[W]hen an accused claims self-defense, the State, in order to show the accused's intent, may introduce rebuttal evidence of prior violent acts by the accused in order to show the intent of the person claiming self-defense."

Kemph v. State, 12 S.W.3d 530, 531 (Tex. App.—San Antonio 1999, pet. ref'd). "'A defendant is entitled to a charge on the right of self-defense against multiple assailants if there is evidence, viewed from the accused's standpoint, that he was in danger of an unlawful attack or a threatened attack at the hands of more than one assailant.'"

Torres v. State, 7 S.W.3d 712, 714 (Tex.App.—Houston [14th Dist.] 1999, pet. ref'd). "Throughout his trial, it was clear that Torres wished to assert self-defense due to apparent danger. He testified about his wife's previous violent conduct and its impact on him at the time of this offense. This is an established method of proof in raising self-defense to an apparent danger. *At 716:* Torres admitted to grabbing his wife by her hair, possibly hitting her in the face when he grabbed the hair at her forehead, struggling with her, and pushing her away. He denied intentionally and knowingly causing bodily injury to her. ... Torres sufficiently admitted his conduct to allow him to raise the issues of self-defense and apparent danger." *See also* ***Courtney v. State***, 908 S.W.2d 48, 52 (Tex.App.—Houston [1st Dist.] 1995, pet. ref'd).

Tidmore v. State, 976 S.W.2d 724, 729 (Tex.App.—Tyler 1998, pet. ref'd). "The defendant has the initial burden of producing some evidence to justify submission of a self-defense instruction. The State must then persuade the jury beyond a reasonable doubt that the defendant did not act in self-defense. Although the State has the burden of persuasion, it does not have the burden of producing evidence to affirmatively refute self-defense."

Halbert v. State, 881 S.W.2d 121, 125 (Tex.App.—Houston [1st Dist.] 1994, pet. ref'd). "The mere fact that she believed he would attack her is insufficient to give rise to a right to a self-defense instruction."

PEN §9.32. DEADLY FORCE IN DEFENSE OF PERSON

 Section 9.32 below is effective for offenses committed on or after Sept. 1, 2007.

(a) A person is justified in using deadly force against another:

(1) if the actor would be justified in using force against the other under Section 9.31; and

(2) when and to the degree the actor reasonably believes the deadly force is immediately necessary:

(A) to protect the actor against the other's use or attempted use of unlawful deadly force; or

(B) to prevent the other's imminent commission of aggravated kidnapping, murder, sexual assault, aggravated sexual assault, robbery, or aggravated robbery.

(b) The actor's belief under Subsection (a)(2) that the deadly force was immediately necessary as described by that subdivision is presumed to be reasonable if the actor:

(1) knew or had reason to believe that the person against whom the deadly force was used:

(A) unlawfully and with force entered, or was attempting to enter unlawfully and with force, the actor's occupied habitation, vehicle, or place of business or employment;

(B) unlawfully and with force removed, or was attempting to remove unlawfully and with force, the actor from the actor's habitation, vehicle, or place of business or employment; or

(C) was committing or attempting to commit an offense described by Subsection (a)(2)(B);

(2) did not provoke the person against whom the force was used; and

(3) was not otherwise engaged in criminal activity, other than a Class C misdemeanor that is a violation of a law or ordinance regulating traffic at the time the force was used.

(c) A person who has a right to be present at the location where the deadly force is used, who has not provoked the person against whom the deadly force is used, and who is not engaged in criminal activity at the time the deadly force is used is not required to retreat before using deadly force as described by this section.

(d) For purposes of Subsection (a)(2), in determining whether an actor described by Subsection (c) reasonably believed that the use of deadly force was necessary, a finder of fact may not consider whether the actor failed to retreat.

History of Pen §9.32: Acts 1973, 63rd Leg., ch. 399, §1, eff. Jan. 1, 1974. Amended by Acts 1983, 68th Leg., ch. 977, §5, eff. Sept. 1, 1983; Acts 1993, 73rd Leg., ch. 900, §1.01, eff. Sept. 1, 1994; Acts 1995, 74th Leg., ch. 235, §1, eff. Sept. 1, 1995; Acts 2007, 80th Leg., ch. 1, §3, eff. Sept. 1, 2007.

ANNOTATIONS

Tidmore v. State, 976 S.W.2d 724, 729 (Tex.App.—Tyler 1998, pet. ref'd). "The defendant has the initial burden of producing some evidence to justify submission of a self-defense instruction. The State must then persuade the jury beyond a reasonable doubt that the defendant did not act in self-defense. Although the State has the burden of persuasion, it does not have the burden of producing evidence to affirmatively refute self-defense."

Fry v. State, 915 S.W.2d 554, 559 (Tex.App.—Houston [14th Dist.] 1995, no pet.). "[I]t is possible for an actor to employ deadly force in self-defense while under the grip of terror so great as to render his mind incapable of cool reflection...."

Halbert v. State, 881 S.W.2d 121, 125-26 (Tex. App.—Houston [1st Dist.] 1994, pet. ref'd). "[P]rovocation has a narrow meaning for the purposes of §9.32. '[T]he elements of provoking the difficulty [are] intent to provoke and act or words or both, calculated to provoke, and that did provoke.' This requires a specific intent to goad the victim into attacking the defendant so that the defendant can then kill or injure the victim. [T]he defendant, in order to have a pretext for killing or injuring the victim, must have done some act or used some words intended and calculated to bring on the attack."

PEN §9.32. DEADLY FORCE IN DEFENSE OF PERSON

Section 9.32 below is effective for offenses in which any element of the offense was committed before Sept. 1, 2007.

(a) A person is justified in using deadly force against another:

(1) if he would be justified in using force against the other under Section 9.31;

(2) if a reasonable person in the actor's situation would not have retreated; and

(3) when and to the degree he reasonably believes the deadly force is immediately necessary:

(A) to protect himself against the other's use or attempted use of unlawful deadly force; or

(B) to prevent the other's imminent commission of aggravated kidnapping, murder, sexual assault, aggravated sexual assault, robbery, or aggravated robbery.

(b) The requirement imposed by Subsection (a)(2) does not apply to an actor who uses force against a person who is at the time of the use of force committing an offense of unlawful entry in the habitation of the actor.

PEN §9.33. DEFENSE OF THIRD PERSON

A person is justified in using force or deadly force against another to protect a third person if:

(1) under the circumstances as the actor reasonably believes them to be, the actor would be justified under Section 9.31 or 9.32 in using force or deadly force to protect himself against the unlawful force or unlawful deadly force he reasonably believes to be threatening the third person he seeks to protect; and

(2) the actor reasonably believes that his intervention is immediately necessary to protect the third person.

History of Pen §9.33: Acts 1973, 63rd Leg., ch. 399, §1, eff. Jan. 1, 1974. Amended by Acts 1993, 73rd Leg., ch. 900, §1.01, eff. Sept. 1, 1994.

ANNOTATIONS

Bennett v. State, 235 S.W.3d 241, 242 (Tex.Crim. App.2007). "Does a request for a jury instruction on self-defense preserve a complaint on appeal regarding the trial judge's failure to submit a jury instruction on defense of a third person? The answer is 'no.'"

For a quick reference of penalties, see the Chart of Penalties on p. 675.

O'CONNOR'S CRIMINAL CODES   731

Hughes v. State, 719 S.W.2d 560, 564 (Tex.Crim. App.1986). "Because ... an accused must reasonably believe that his intervention is '*immediately* necessary to protect the third person,' it would be paradoxical ... to suggest that the Legislature intended that he first be required to retreat. [T]he Legislature was merely placing the accused, who is the 'actor' under §9.33 ... in the shoes of the third person. So long as the accused reasonably believes that the third person would be justified in using deadly force to protect himself, the accused may step in and exercise deadly force on behalf of that person." *See also* ***Hamel v. State***, 916 S.W.2d 491, 493 (Tex.Crim.App.1996).

Boushey v. State, 804 S.W.2d 148, 150 (Tex.App.— Corpus Christi 1990, pet. ref'd). "No Texas court has held that the defense of 'third person defense' includes the defense of the unborn. ... An unborn fetus is not a 'person' for purposes of the defense."

PEN §9.34. PROTECTION OF LIFE OR HEALTH

(a) A person is justified in using force, but not deadly force, against another when and to the degree he reasonably believes the force is immediately necessary to prevent the other from committing suicide or inflicting serious bodily injury to himself.

(b) A person is justified in using both force and deadly force against another when and to the degree he reasonably believes the force or deadly force is immediately necessary to preserve the other's life in an emergency.

History of Pen §9.34: Acts 1973, 63rd Leg., ch. 399, §1, eff. Jan. 1, 1974.

SUBCHAPTER D. PROTECTION OF PROPERTY

PEN §9.41. PROTECTION OF ONE'S OWN PROPERTY

(a) A person in lawful possession of land or tangible, movable property is justified in using force against another when and to the degree the actor reasonably believes the force is immediately necessary to prevent or terminate the other's trespass on the land or unlawful interference with the property.

(b) A person unlawfully dispossessed of land or tangible, movable property by another is justified in using force against the other when and to the degree the actor reasonably believes the force is immediately necessary to reenter the land or recover the property if the actor uses the force immediately or in fresh pursuit after the dispossession and:

(1) the actor reasonably believes the other had no claim of right when he dispossessed the actor; or

(2) the other accomplished the dispossession by using force, threat, or fraud against the actor.

History of Pen §9.41: Acts 1973, 63rd Leg., ch. 399, §1, eff. Jan. 1, 1974.

PEN §9.42. DEADLY FORCE TO PROTECT PROPERTY

A person is justified in using deadly force against another to protect land or tangible, movable property:

(1) if he would be justified in using force against the other under Section 9.41; and

(2) when and to the degree he reasonably believes the deadly force is immediately necessary:

(A) to prevent the other's imminent commission of arson, burglary, robbery, aggravated robbery, theft during the nighttime, or criminal mischief during the nighttime; or

(B) to prevent the other who is fleeing immediately after committing burglary, robbery, aggravated robbery, or theft during the nighttime from escaping with the property; and

(3) he reasonably believes that:

(A) the land or property cannot be protected or recovered by any other means; or

(B) the use of force other than deadly force to protect or recover the land or property would expose the actor or another to a substantial risk of death or serious bodily injury.

History of Pen §9.42: Acts 1973, 63rd Leg., ch. 399, §1, eff. Jan. 1, 1974. Amended by Acts 1993, 73rd Leg., ch. 900, §1.01, eff. Sept. 1, 1994.

ANNOTATIONS

Hernandez v. State, 914 S.W.2d 218, 224 (Tex. App.—El Paso 1996, pet. ref'd). "[D] argues that the issue of defense of property was raised by evidence that his house had been the target of a drive-by shooting and his testimony that he was concerned that the perpetrators might return and harm his family. This evidence is insufficient, however, to entitle him to an instruction on defense of property because there is no evidence of *imminent* criminal mischief; the drive-by

PEN §9.33

★

shooting of [D's] home had already been completed prior to [D's] use of deadly force."

Fry v. State, 915 S.W.2d 554, 559 (Tex.App.— Houston [14th Dist.] 1995, no pet.). "Appellant's speculation that the victim *might* have intended to come back and rob him falls well short of satisfying the elements of defense of property. [Victim] had left appellant's home, and deadly force was not immediately necessary to prevent the victim's imminent commission of robbery or theft."

PEN §9.43. PROTECTION OF THIRD PERSON'S PROPERTY

A person is justified in using force or deadly force against another to protect land or tangible, movable property of a third person if, under the circumstances as he reasonably believes them to be, the actor would be justified under Section 9.41 or 9.42 in using force or deadly force to protect his own land or property and:

(1) the actor reasonably believes the unlawful interference constitutes attempted or consummated theft of or criminal mischief to the tangible, movable property; or

(2) the actor reasonably believes that:

(A) the third person has requested his protection of the land or property;

(B) he has a legal duty to protect the third person's land or property; or

(C) the third person whose land or property he uses force or deadly force to protect is the actor's spouse, parent, or child, resides with the actor, or is under the actor's care.

History of Pen §9.43: Acts 1973, 63rd Leg., ch. 399, §1, eff. Jan. 1, 1974. Amended by Acts 1993, 73rd Leg., ch. 900, §1.01, eff. Sept. 1, 1994.

PEN §9.44. USE OF DEVICE TO PROTECT PROPERTY

The justification afforded by Sections 9.41 and 9.43 applies to the use of a device to protect land or tangible, movable property if:

(1) the device is not designed to cause, or known by the actor to create a substantial risk of causing, death or serious bodily injury; and

(2) use of the device is reasonable under all the circumstances as the actor reasonably believes them to be when he installs the device.

History of Pen §9.44: Acts 1973, 63rd Leg., ch. 399, §1, eff. Jan. 1, 1974. Amended by Acts 1975, 64th Leg., ch. 342, §6, eff. Sept. 1, 1975; Acts 1993, 73rd Leg., ch. 900, §1.01, eff. Sept. 1, 1994.

SUBCHAPTER E. LAW ENFORCEMENT

PEN §9.51. ARREST & SEARCH

(a) A peace officer, or a person acting in a peace officer's presence and at his direction, is justified in using force against another when and to the degree the actor reasonably believes the force is immediately necessary to make or assist in making an arrest or search, or to prevent or assist in preventing escape after arrest, if:

(1) the actor reasonably believes the arrest or search is lawful or, if the arrest or search is made under a warrant, he reasonably believes the warrant is valid; and

(2) before using force, the actor manifests his purpose to arrest or search and identifies himself as a peace officer or as one acting at a peace officer's direction, unless he reasonably believes his purpose and identity are already known by or cannot reasonably be made known to the person to be arrested.

(b) A person other than a peace officer (or one acting at his direction) is justified in using force against another when and to the degree the actor reasonably believes the force is immediately necessary to make or assist in making a lawful arrest, or to prevent or assist in preventing escape after lawful arrest if, before using force, the actor manifests his purpose to and the reason for the arrest or reasonably believes his purpose and the reason are already known by or cannot reasonably be made known to the person to be arrested.

(c) A peace officer is justified in using deadly force against another when and to the degree the peace officer reasonably believes the deadly force is immediately necessary to make an arrest, or to prevent escape after arrest, if the use of force would have been justified under Subsection (a) and:

(1) the actor reasonably believes the conduct for which arrest is authorized included the use or attempted use of deadly force; or

(2) the actor reasonably believes there is a substantial risk that the person to be arrested will cause death or serious bodily injury to the actor or another if the arrest is delayed.

(d) A person other than a peace officer acting in a peace officer's presence and at his direction is justified in using deadly force against another when and to the degree the person reasonably believes the deadly force

For a quick reference of penalties, see the Chart of Penalties on p. 675.

O'CONNOR'S CRIMINAL CODES   **733**

is immediately necessary to make a lawful arrest, or to prevent escape after a lawful arrest, if the use of force would have been justified under Subsection (b) and:

(1) the actor reasonably believes the felony or offense against the public peace for which arrest is authorized included the use or attempted use of deadly force; or

(2) the actor reasonably believes there is a substantial risk that the person to be arrested will cause death or serious bodily injury to another if the arrest is delayed.

(e) There is no duty to retreat before using deadly force justified by Subsection (c) or (d).

(f) Nothing in this section relating to the actor's manifestation of purpose or identity shall be construed as conflicting with any other law relating to the issuance, service, and execution of an arrest or search warrant either under the laws of this state or the United States.

(g) Deadly force may only be used under the circumstances enumerated in Subsections (c) and (d).

History of Pen §9.51: Acts 1973, 63rd Leg., ch. 399, §1, eff. Jan. 1, 1974. Amended by Acts 1993, 73rd Leg., ch. 900, §1.01, eff. Sept. 1, 1994.

ANNOTATIONS

Vasquez v. Hernandez, 844 S.W.2d 802, 805 (Tex. App.—San Antonio 1992, writ dism'd). "When the suspect refused to stop and to 'drop the gun' as ordered and continued to advance upon the officer, under the authority of §9.51 …, the [force used] by the officer was in good faith in his discretionary capacity within the scope of his authority."

PEN §9.52. PREVENTION OF ESCAPE FROM CUSTODY

The use of force to prevent the escape of an arrested person from custody is justifiable when the force could have been employed to effect the arrest under which the person is in custody, except that a guard employed by a correctional facility or a peace officer is justified in using any force, including deadly force, that he reasonably believes to be immediately necessary to prevent the escape of a person from the correctional facility.

History of Pen §9.52: Acts 1973, 63rd Leg., ch. 399, §1, eff. Jan. 1, 1974. Amended by Acts 1993, 73rd Leg., ch. 900, §1.01, eff. Sept. 1, 1994.

PEN §9.53. MAINTAINING SECURITY IN CORRECTIONAL FACILITY

An officer or employee of a correctional facility is justified in using force against a person in custody when and to the degree the officer or employee reasonably believes the force is necessary to maintain the security of the correctional facility, the safety or security of other persons in custody or employed by the correctional facility, or his own safety or security.

History of Pen §9.53: Acts 1987, 70th Leg., ch. 512, §1, eff. Sept. 1, 1987. Amended by Acts 1993, 73rd Leg., ch. 900, §1.01, eff. Sept. 1, 1994.

SUBCHAPTER F. SPECIAL RELATIONSHIPS

PEN §9.61. PARENT-CHILD

(a) The use of force, but not deadly force, against a child younger than 18 years is justified:

(1) if the actor is the child's parent or stepparent or is acting in loco parentis to the child; and

(2) when and to the degree the actor reasonably believes the force is necessary to discipline the child or to safeguard or promote his welfare.

(b) For purposes of this section, "in loco parentis" includes grandparent and guardian, any person acting by, through, or under the direction of a court with jurisdiction over the child, and anyone who has express or implied consent of the parent or parents.

History of Pen §9.61: Acts 1973, 63rd Leg., ch. 399, §1, eff. Jan. 1, 1974.

PEN §9.62. EDUCATOR-STUDENT

The use of force, but not deadly force, against a person is justified:

(1) if the actor is entrusted with the care, supervision, or administration of the person for a special purpose; and

(2) when and to the degree the actor reasonably believes the force is necessary to further the special purpose or to maintain discipline in a group.

History of Pen §9.62: Acts 1973, 63rd Leg., ch. 399, §1, eff. Jan. 1, 1974.

ANNOTATIONS

Smith v. State, 133 S.W.3d 665, 667 (Tex.App.— Corpus Christi 2003, no pet.). "Similar to self-defense, a defendant cannot establish that his conduct was justified by the 'educator-student' relationship without first admitting that the conduct occurred."

Spacek v. Charles, 928 S.W.2d 88, 95 (Tex.App.— Houston [14th Dist.] 1996, writ dism'd). "Section 9.62 is generally expressive of the … rule that public school

PEN §9.51

teachers standing in *loco parentis* may use reasonable force to discipline their charges. [¶] [A] teacher may not use physical violence against a child merely because the child is unable or fails to perform, either academically or athletically, at a desired level of ability, even though the teacher considers such violence to be instruction and encouragement." (Internal quotes omitted.)

PEN §9.63. GUARDIAN-INCOMPETENT

The use of force, but not deadly force, against a mental incompetent is justified:

(1) if the actor is the incompetent's guardian or someone similarly responsible for the general care and supervision of the incompetent; and

(2) when and to the degree the actor reasonably believes the force is necessary:

(A) to safeguard and promote the incompetent's welfare; or

(B) if the incompetent is in an institution for his care and custody, to maintain discipline in the institution.

History of Pen §9.63: Acts 1973, 63rd Leg., ch. 399, §1, eff. Jan. 1, 1974.

TITLE 3. PUNISHMENTS

CHAPTER 12. PUNISHMENTS

SUBCHAPTER A. GENERAL PROVISIONS

PEN §12.01. PUNISHMENT IN ACCORDANCE WITH CODE

(a) A person adjudged guilty of an offense under this code shall be punished in accordance with this chapter and the Code of Criminal Procedure.

(b) Penal laws enacted after the effective date of this code shall be classified for punishment purposes in accordance with this chapter.

(c) This chapter does not deprive a court of authority conferred by law to forfeit property, dissolve a corporation, suspend or cancel a license or permit, remove a person from office, cite for contempt, or impose any other civil penalty. The civil penalty may be included in the sentence.

History of Pen §12.01: Acts 1973, 63rd Leg., ch. 399, §1, eff. Jan. 1, 1974. Amended by Acts 1993, 73rd Leg., ch. 900, §1.01, eff. Sept. 1, 1994.

See also Tex. Const. art. 1, §13.

PEN §12.02. CLASSIFICATION OF OFFENSES

Offenses are designated as felonies or misdemeanors.

History of Pen §12.02: Acts 1973, 63rd Leg., ch. 399, §1, eff. Jan. 1, 1974.

> **ANNOTATIONS**

Schmidt v. State, 778 S.W.2d 549, 551 (Tex.App.—Houston [1st Dist.] 1989, pet. ref'd). "The Penal Code provisions affecting punishment apply to offenses defined by other laws, unless the specific statute provides otherwise."

PEN §12.03. CLASSIFICATION OF MISDEMEANORS

(a) Misdemeanors are classified according to the relative seriousness of the offense into three categories:

(1) Class A misdemeanors;

(2) Class B misdemeanors;

(3) Class C misdemeanors.

For a quick reference of penalties, see the Chart of Penalties on p. 675.

O'CONNOR'S CRIMINAL CODES   735

(b) An offense designated a misdemeanor in this code without specification as to punishment or category is a Class C misdemeanor.

(c) Conviction of a Class C misdemeanor does not impose any legal disability or disadvantage.

History of Pen §12.03: Acts 1973, 63rd Leg., ch. 399, §1, eff. Jan. 1, 1974.

PEN §12.04. CLASSIFICATION OF FELONIES

(a) Felonies are classified according to the relative seriousness of the offense into five categories:

(1) capital felonies;

(2) felonies of the first degree;

(3) felonies of the second degree;

(4) felonies of the third degree; and

(5) state jail felonies.

(b) An offense designated a felony in this code without specification as to category is a state jail felony.

History of Pen §12.04: Acts 1973, 63rd Leg., ch. 399, §1, eff. Jan. 1, 1974. Amended by Acts 1973, 63rd Leg., ch. 426, art. 2, §3, eff. Jan. 1, 1974; Acts 1993, 73rd Leg., ch. 900, §1.01, eff. Sept. 1, 1994.

SUBCHAPTER B. ORDINARY MISDEMEANOR PUNISHMENTS

For a quick reference of misdemeanor punishments, see the Misdemeanor Punishment Ranges Chart on p. 669.

PEN §12.21. CLASS A MISDEMEANOR

An individual adjudged guilty of a Class A misdemeanor shall be punished by:

(1) a fine not to exceed $4,000;

(2) confinement in jail for a term not to exceed one year; or

(3) both such fine and confinement.

History of Pen §12.21: Acts 1973, 63rd Leg., ch. 399, §1, eff. Jan. 1, 1974. Amended by Acts 1991, 72nd Leg., ch. 108, §1, eff. Sept. 1, 1991; Acts 1993, 73rd Leg., ch. 900, §1.01, eff. Sept. 1, 1994.

PEN §12.22. CLASS B MISDEMEANOR

An individual adjudged guilty of a Class B misdemeanor shall be punished by:

(1) a fine not to exceed $2,000;

(2) confinement in jail for a term not to exceed 180 days; or

(3) both such fine and confinement.

History of Pen §12.22: Acts 1973, 63rd Leg., ch. 399, §1, eff. Jan. 1, 1974. Amended by Acts 1991, 72nd Leg., ch. 108, §1, eff. Sept. 1, 1991.

PEN §12.23. CLASS C MISDEMEANOR

An individual adjudged guilty of a Class C misdemeanor shall be punished by a fine not to exceed $500.

History of Pen §12.23: Acts 1973, 63rd Leg., ch. 399, §1, eff. Jan. 1, 1974. Amended by Acts 1991, 72nd Leg., ch. 108, §1, eff. Sept. 1, 1991.

SUBCHAPTER C. ORDINARY FELONY PUNISHMENTS

For a quick reference of felony punishments, see the Felony Punishment Ranges Chart on p. 670.

PEN §12.31. CAPITAL FELONY

(a) An individual adjudged guilty of a capital felony in a case in which the state seeks the death penalty shall be punished by imprisonment in the institutional division for life without parole or by death. An individual adjudged guilty of a capital felony in a case in which the state does not seek the death penalty shall be punished by imprisonment in the institutional division for life without parole.

(b) In a capital felony trial in which the state seeks the death penalty, prospective jurors shall be informed that a sentence of life imprisonment without parole or death is mandatory on conviction of a capital felony. In a capital felony trial in which the state does not seek the death penalty, prospective jurors shall be informed that the state is not seeking the death penalty and that a sentence of life imprisonment without parole is mandatory on conviction of the capital felony.

History of Pen §12.31: Acts 1973, 63rd Leg., ch. 426, art. 2, §2, eff. Jan. 1, 1974. Amended by Acts 1991, 72nd Leg., ch. 652, §12 (eff. Sept. 1, 1991), ch. 838, §4 (eff. Sept. 1, 1991); Acts 1993, 73rd Leg., ch. 900, §1.01, eff. Sept. 1, 1994; Acts 2005, 79th Leg., ch. 787, §1, eff. Sept. 1, 2005.

PEN §12.32. FIRST DEGREE FELONY PUNISHMENT

(a) An individual adjudged guilty of a felony of the first degree shall be punished by imprisonment in the institutional division for life or for any term of not more than 99 years or less than 5 years.

(b) In addition to imprisonment, an individual adjudged guilty of a felony of the first degree may be punished by a fine not to exceed $10,000.

History of Pen §12.32: Acts 1973, 63rd Leg., ch. 399, §1, eff. Jan. 1, 1974. Renumbered from §12.31 by Acts 1973, 63rd Leg., ch. 426, art. 2, §2, eff. Jan. 1, 1974. Amended by Acts 1979, 66th Leg., ch. 488, §1, eff. Sept. 1, 1979; Acts 1993, 73rd Leg., ch. 900, §1.01, eff. Sept. 1, 1994.

PEN §12.33. SECOND DEGREE FELONY PUNISHMENT

(a) An individual adjudged guilty of a felony of the second degree shall be punished by imprisonment in the institutional division for any term of not more than 20 years or less than 2 years.

(b) In addition to imprisonment, an individual adjudged guilty of a felony of the second degree may be punished by a fine not to exceed $10,000.

History of Pen §12.33: Acts 1973, 63rd Leg., ch. 399, §1, eff. Jan. 1, 1974. Renumbered from §12.32 by Acts 1973, 63rd Leg., ch. 426, art. 2, §2, eff. Jan. 1, 1974. Amended by Acts 1993, 73rd Leg., ch. 900, §1.01, eff. Sept. 1, 1994.

Mendez v. State, 212 S.W.3d 382, 388 (Tex.App.—Austin 2006, pet. ref'd). "[T]he reading of the enhancement allegations and the entry of the defendant's plea thereon are mandatory, and ... no issue is joined between the State and the defendant with respect to the defendant's prior criminal record if this is not done. [¶] The only evidence that Mendez had been previously convicted was introduced before he entered his plea to the enhancement allegations. This evidence was not properly before the jury, and it is clear that the jury's consideration of this evidence for the purpose of enhancement harmed Mendez. Because there was no properly admitted evidence to support the enhancement allegations, the jury should have limited its deliberations to the range of punishment applicable to an unenhanced second degree felony."

PEN §12.34. THIRD DEGREE FELONY PUNISHMENT

(a) An individual adjudged guilty of a felony of the third degree shall be punished by imprisonment in the institutional division for any term of not more than 10 years or less than 2 years.

(b) In addition to imprisonment, an individual adjudged guilty of a felony of the third degree may be punished by a fine not to exceed $10,000.

History of Pen §12.34: Acts 1973, 63rd Leg., ch. 399, §1, eff. Jan. 1, 1974. Amended by Acts 1973, 63rd Leg., ch. 426, art. 2, §2, eff. Jan. 1, 1974; Acts 1989, 71st Leg., ch. 785, §4.01, eff. Sept. 1, 1989; Acts 1990, 71st Leg., 6th C.S., ch. 25, §7, eff. June 18, 1990; Acts 1993, 73rd Leg., ch. 900, §1.01, eff. Sept. 1, 1994.

PEN §12.35. STATE JAIL FELONY PUNISHMENT

(a) Except as provided by Subsection (c), an individual adjudged guilty of a state jail felony shall be punished by confinement in a state jail for any term of not more than two years or less than 180 days.

(b) In addition to confinement, an individual adjudged guilty of a state jail felony may be punished by a fine not to exceed $10,000.

(c) An individual adjudged guilty of a state jail felony shall be punished for a third degree felony if it is shown on the trial of the offense that:

(1) a deadly weapon as defined by Section 1.07 was used or exhibited during the commission of the offense or during immediate flight following the commission of the offense, and that the individual used or exhibited the deadly weapon or was a party to the offense and knew that a deadly weapon would be used or exhibited; or

(2) the individual has previously been finally convicted of any felony:

 Subsection (A) below is effective for offenses committed on or after Sept. 1, 2007.

(A) under Section 21.02 or listed in Section 3g(a)(1), Article 42.12, Code of Criminal Procedure; or

Subsection (A) below is effective for offenses in which any element of the offense was committed before Sept. 1, 2007.

(A) listed in Section 3g(a)(1), Article 42.12, Code of Criminal Procedure; or

(B) for which the judgment contains an affirmative finding under Section 3g(a)(2), Article 42.12, Code of Criminal Procedure.

History of Pen §12.35: Acts 1993, 73rd Leg., ch. 900, §1.01, eff. Sept. 1, 1994. Amended by Acts 2007, 80th Leg., ch. 593, §3.48, eff. Sept. 1, 2007.

Hernandez v. State, 929 S.W.2d 11, 13 (Tex.Crim. App.1996). The state jail felony "was properly enhanced to a third degree felony because the judgment for appellant's robbery conviction contains an affirmative finding [under Pen. Code §12.35(c)]. However, the Court of Appeals erred in holding the same robbery conviction could be used again to enhance appellant's punishment under [Pen. Code] §12.42(d). The State is not permitted to use the same prior conviction more than once in the same prosecution."

State v. Webb, 980 S.W.2d 924, 927 (Tex.App.—Fort Worth 1998), *aff'd*, 12 S.W.3d 808 (Tex.Crim. App.2000). "[T]he issue ... is whether an *enhanced* state jail felony is subject to further enhancement under the habitual offender provision.... [D] was not convicted of an *aggravated* state jail felony under [Pen. Code] §12.35(c), but of a *nonaggravated* state jail felony under §12.35(a), which was then *enhanced* under [Pen. Code] §12.42(a)(2) to the punishment range

For a quick reference of penalties, see the Chart of Penalties on p. 675.

O'CONNOR'S CRIMINAL CODES 737

for second degree felonies. ... We ... conclude that the trial court was correct to find that [D's] enhanced state jail felony conviction was not subject to further enhancement."

Smith v. State, 960 S.W.2d 372, 374-75 (Tex.App.— Houston [1st Dist.] 1998, pet. ref'd). The legislature treats "aggravated state jail felonies as equivalent to third-degree felonies, which may be enhanced to habitual offender status, in [Pen. Code] §§12.35(c) and 12.42(a), (b), (c), and (e)."

SUBCHAPTER D. EXCEPTIONAL SENTENCES

For a quick reference of enhancements, see the Enhanced Misdemeanor Punishment Ranges Chart on p. 669 and the Enhanced Felony Punishment Ranges Charts beginning on p. 671.

PEN §12.41. CLASSIFICATION OF OFFENSES OUTSIDE THIS CODE

For purposes of this subchapter, any conviction not obtained from a prosecution under this code shall be classified as follows:

(1) "felony of the third degree" if imprisonment in a penitentiary is affixed to the offense as a possible punishment;

(2) "Class B misdemeanor" if the offense is not a felony and confinement in a jail is affixed to the offense as a possible punishment;

(3) "Class C misdemeanor" if the offense is punishable by fine only.

History of Pen §12.41: Acts 1973, 63rd Leg., ch. 399, §1, eff. Jan. 1, 1974. Amended by Acts 1993, 73rd Leg., ch. 900, §1.01, eff. Sept. 1, 1994.

ANNOTATIONS

Childress v. State, 784 S.W.2d 361, 365 (Tex.Crim. App.1990). "[W]hether a conviction was obtained from a prosecution under the [Pen. Code] depends on whether the 'outside' statute defining the offense affixes punishment as *classified* in the [Pen. Code]. That is, 'conviction' must be read to include possible punishment attached to the primary offense. [¶] [W]e hold that §12.41 applies to determine classification of an offense *to be* enhanced under [Pen. Code] subchapter D of chapter 12 ..., when that offense is defined outside the Penal Code and not classified in accordance with its provisions."

Tucker v. State, 136 S.W.3d 699, 701 (Tex.App.— Texarkana 2004, no pet.). It is "appropriate to determine whether the [out-of-state] crime involved was a felony [for Texas enhancement purposes] based on the intent of the legislature of the sister state to make the crime a felony even though the same conduct may not have been a felony in Texas."

PEN §12.42. PENALTIES FOR REPEAT & HABITUAL FELONY OFFENDERS

(a)(1) If it is shown on the trial of a state jail felony punishable under Section 12.35(a) that the defendant has previously been finally convicted of two state jail felonies, on conviction the defendant shall be punished for a third-degree felony.

(2) If it is shown on the trial of a state jail felony punishable under Section 12.35(a) that the defendant has previously been finally convicted of two felonies, and the second previous felony conviction is for an offense that occurred subsequent to the first previous conviction having become final, on conviction the defendant shall be punished for a second-degree felony.

🅐 *Subsection (3) below is effective for offenses committed on or after Sept. 1, 2007.*

(3) Except as provided by Subsection (c)(2), if it is shown on the trial of a state jail felony punishable under Section 12.35(c) or on the trial of a third-degree felony that the defendant has been once before convicted of a felony, on conviction he shall be punished for a second-degree felony.

Subsection (3) below is effective for offenses in which any element of the offense was committed before Sept. 1, 2007.

(3) If it is shown on the trial of a state jail felony punishable under Section 12.35(c) or on the trial of a third-degree felony that the defendant has been once before convicted of a felony, on conviction he shall be punished for a second-degree felony.

🅐 *Subsection (b) below is effective for offenses committed on or after Sept. 1, 2007.*

(b) Except as provided by Subsection (c)(2), if it is shown on the trial of a second-degree felony that the defendant has been once before convicted of a felony, on conviction he shall be punished for a first-degree felony.

Subsection (b) below is effective for offenses in which any element of the offense was committed before Sept. 1, 2007.

(b) If it is shown on the trial of a second-degree felony that the defendant has been once before convicted of a felony, on conviction he shall be punished for a first-degree felony.

Ⓐ *Subsection (c) below is effective for offenses committed on or after Sept. 1, 2007.*

(c)(1) If it is shown on the trial of a first-degree felony that the defendant has been once before convicted of a felony, on conviction he shall be punished by imprisonment in the Texas Department of Criminal Justice for life, or for any term of not more than 99 years or less than 15 years. In addition to imprisonment, an individual may be punished by a fine not to exceed $10,000.

(2) Notwithstanding Subdivision (1), a defendant shall be punished by imprisonment in the Texas Department of Criminal Justice for life if:

(A) the defendant is convicted of an offense:

(i) under Section 21.11(a)(1), 22.021, or 22.011, Penal Code;

(ii) under Section 20.04(a)(4), Penal Code, if the defendant committed the offense with the intent to violate or abuse the victim sexually; or

(iii) under Section 30.02, Penal Code, punishable under Subsection (d) of that section, if the defendant committed the offense with the intent to commit a felony described by Subparagraph (i) or (ii) or a felony under Section 21.11, Penal Code; and

(B) the defendant has been previously convicted of an offense:

(i) under Section 43.25 or 43.26, Penal Code, or an offense under Section 43.23, Penal Code, punishable under Subsection (h) of that section;

(ii) under Section 21.02, 21.11, 22.011, 22.021, or 25.02, Penal Code;

(iii) under Section 20.04(a)(4), Penal Code, if the defendant committed the offense with the intent to violate or abuse the victim sexually;

(iv) under Section 30.02, Penal Code, punishable under Subsection (d) of that section, if the defendant committed the offense with the intent to commit a felony described by Subparagraph (ii) or (iii); or

(v) under the laws of another state containing elements that are substantially similar to the elements of an offense listed in Subparagraph (i), (ii), (iii), or (iv).

*In **Kennedy v. Louisiana**, ___ U.S. ___ (2008) (No. 07-343; 6-25-08), the U.S. Supreme Court held that execution of a person who committed sexual assault that did not result in the death of the child was unconstitutional.*

(3) Notwithstanding Subdivision (1) or (2), a defendant shall be punished for a capital felony if it is shown on the trial of an offense under Section 22.021 otherwise punishable under Subsection (f) of that section that the defendant has previously been finally convicted of:

(A) an offense under Section 22.021 that was committed against a victim described by Section 22.021(f)(1) or was committed against a victim described by Section 22.021(f)(2) and in a manner described by Section 22.021(a)(2)(A); or

(B) an offense that was committed under the laws of another state that:

(i) contains elements that are substantially similar to the elements of an offense under Section 22.021; and

(ii) was committed against a victim described by Section 22.021(f)(1) or was committed against a victim described by Section 22.021(f)(2) and in a manner substantially similar to a manner described by Section 22.021(a)(2)(A).

Ⓔ **(4)** Notwithstanding Subdivision (1) or (2), a defendant shall be punished by imprisonment in the Texas Department of Criminal Justice for life without parole if it is shown on the trial of an offense under Section 21.02 that the defendant has previously been finally convicted of:

(A) an offense under Section 21.02; or

(B) an offense that was committed under the laws of another state and that contains elements that are substantially similar to the elements of an offense under Section 21.02.

Subsection (c) below is effective for offenses in which any element of the offense was committed before Sept. 1, 2007.

(c)(1) Except as provided by Subdivision (2), if it is shown on the trial of a first-degree felony that the defendant has been once before convicted of a felony, on conviction he shall be punished by imprisonment in the institutional division of the Texas Department of Criminal Justice for life, or for any term of not more than 99 years or less than 15 years. In addition to imprisonment, an individual may be punished by a fine not to exceed $10,000.

(2) A defendant shall be punished by imprisonment in the institutional division for life if:

(A) the defendant is convicted of an offense:

(i) under Section 22.021 or 22.011, Penal Code;

For a quick reference of penalties, see the Chart of Penalties on p. 675.

O'CONNOR'S CRIMINAL CODES   739

(ii) under Section 20.04(a)(4), Penal Code, if the defendant committed the offense with the intent to violate or abuse the victim sexually; or

(iii) under Section 30.02, Penal Code, punishable under Subsection (d) of that section, if the defendant committed the offense with the intent to commit a felony described by Subparagraph (i) or (ii) or a felony under Section 21.11 or 22.011, Penal Code; and

(B) the defendant has been previously convicted of an offense:

(i) under Section 43.25 or 43.26, Penal Code, or an offense under Section 43.23, Penal Code, punishable under Subsection (h) of that section;

(ii) under Section 21.11, 22.011, 22.021, or 25.02, Penal Code;

(iii) under Section 20.04(a)(4), Penal Code, if the defendant committed the offense with the intent to violate or abuse the victim sexually;

(iv) under Section 30.02, Penal Code, punishable under Subsection (d) of that section, if the defendant committed the offense with the intent to commit a felony described by Subparagraph (ii) or (iii); or

(v) under the laws of another state containing elements that are substantially similar to the elements of an offense listed in Subparagraph (i), (ii), (iii), or (iv).

Ⓐ *Subsection (d) below is effective for offenses committed on or after Sept. 1, 2007.*

(d) Except as provided by Subsection (c)(2), if it is shown on the trial of a felony offense other than a state jail felony punishable under Section 12.35(a) that the defendant has previously been finally convicted of two felony offenses, and the second previous felony conviction is for an offense that occurred subsequent to the first previous conviction having become final, on conviction he shall be punished by imprisonment in the institutional division of the Texas Department of Criminal Justice for life, or for any term of not more than 99 years or less than 25 years.

Subsection (d) below is effective for offenses in which any element of the offense was committed before Sept. 1, 2007.

(d) If it is shown on the trial of a felony offense other than a state jail felony punishable under Section 12.35(a) that the defendant has previously been finally convicted of two felony offenses, and the second previous felony conviction is for an offense that occurred

subsequent to the first previous conviction having become final, on conviction he shall be punished by imprisonment in the institutional division of the Texas Department of Criminal Justice for life, or for any term of not more than 99 years or less than 25 years.

(e) A previous conviction for a state jail felony punished under Section 12.35(a) may not be used for enhancement purposes under Subsection (b), (c), or (d).

(f) For the purposes of Subsections (a), (b), (c)(1), and (e), an adjudication by a juvenile court under Section 54.03, Family Code, that a child engaged in delinquent conduct on or after January 1, 1996, constituting a felony offense for which the child is committed to the Texas Youth Commission under Section 54.04(d)(2), (d)(3), or (m), Family Code, or Section 54.05(f), Family Code, is a final felony conviction.

(g) For the purposes of Subsection (c)(2):

(1) a defendant has been previously convicted of an offense listed under Subsection (c)(2)(B) if the defendant was adjudged guilty of the offense or entered a plea of guilty or nolo contendere in return for a grant of deferred adjudication, regardless of whether the sentence for the offense was ever imposed or whether the sentence was probated and the defendant was subsequently discharged from community supervision; and

(2) a conviction under the laws of another state for an offense containing elements that are substantially similar to the elements of an offense listed under Subsection (c)(2)(B) is a conviction of an offense listed under Subsection (c)(2)(B).

History of Pen §12.42: Acts 1973, 63rd Leg., ch. 399, §1, eff. Jan. 1, 1974. Amended by Acts 1983, 68th Leg., ch. 339, §1, eff. Sept. 1, 1983; Acts 1985, 69th Leg., ch. 582, §1, eff. Sept. 1, 1985; Acts 1993, 73rd Leg., ch. 900, §1.01, eff. Sept. 1, 1994; Acts 1995, 74th Leg., ch. 250, §1 (eff. Sept. 1, 1995), ch. 262, §78 (eff. Jan. 1, 1996), ch. 318, §1 (eff. Jan. 1, 1996); Acts 1997, 75th Leg., ch. 665, §2 (eff. Sept. 1, 1997), ch. 667, §4 (eff. Sept. 1, 1997); Acts 1999, 76th Leg., ch. 62, §15.01, eff. Sept. 1, 1999; Acts 2003, 78th Leg., ch. 283, §53 (eff. Sept. 1, 2003), ch. 1005, §2 (eff. Sept. 1, 2003); Acts 2007, 80th Leg., ch. 340, §§1-4 (eff. Sept. 1, 2007), ch. 593, §§1.14-1.16 (eff. Sept. 1, 2007).

ANNOTATIONS

Generally

McNatt v. State, 188 S.W.3d 198, 204 (Tex.Crim. App.2006). "As long as the enhancement is not barred by other considerations (e.g. prosecutorial vindictiveness), the State is free to use a prior conviction for enhancement if proper notice of its intent to do so is conveyed with respect to the new punishment hearing."

Brooks v. State, 957 S.W.2d 30, 33 (Tex.Crim.App. 1997). "[A] defendant is entitled to notice of prior convictions to be used for enhancement. But alleging an

Side tab: PEN §12.42

enhancement in an indictment is not the only reasonable method of conveying such notice. *At 34:* As with deadly weapon findings, prior convictions used as enhancements must be pled in some form, but they need not be pled in the indictment—although it is permissible and perhaps preferable to do so. In this case, the requisite notice was conveyed by the State's motion and the trial court's order."

Ex parte Langley, 833 S.W.2d 141, 143 (Tex.Crim. App.1992). "[A] probated sentence is not a final conviction for enhancement purposes unless it is revoked. ... A successfully served probation is not available for enhancement purposes. In the case of 'shock' probation, the defendant is also convicted, and punishment is assessed. However, sentence is imposed, but later the further execution of the sentence is suspended. ... In 'shock' probation, when further execution of the sentence is suspended, the conviction becomes non-final for purposes of enhancement, and will not become final for such purposes unless revoked."

Ex parte Blume, 618 S.W.2d 373, 376 (Tex.Crim. App.1981). "[T]he Legislature intended to make convictions for felonies in federal courts as well as courts of other states available for enhancement purposes."

Mikel v. State, 167 S.W.3d 556, 559 (Tex.App.— Houston [14th Dist.] 2005, no pet.). "[W]hen a defendant pleads true to an enhancement paragraph, the State is relieved of the burden of proving the enhancements, and the defendant cannot complain on appeal that the evidence is insufficient to support the enhancements. However, there is a narrow exception to this rule. If the record 'affirmatively reflects' that a prior conviction was not final, then the conviction cannot be used to enhance punishment, even though the defendant pled 'true' to the enhancement paragraph. [¶] The First Court of Appeals has extended [this] exception, applying it not only to cases in which a non-final conviction was improperly used to enhance punishment, but to any case in which a 'defendant pleads true to an enhancement paragraph allegation, [and] the record affirmatively reflect[s] that the prior conviction' should not have been used for enhancement purposes.'"

Sims v. State, 84 S.W.3d 768, 779-80 (Tex.App.— Dallas 2002, pet. ref'd). "[A]s a matter of law, appellant's November 1995 juvenile felony adjudication cannot be considered a prior conviction for purposes of

enhancement. An order of adjudication is not a conviction of crime except as provided in [Fam. Code] §51.13(d).... Under [that section], only a felony adjudication in which a child engaged in conduct that occurred on or after January 1, 1996 can be a final felony conviction for enhancement purposes."

Dominque v. State, 787 S.W.2d 107, 108 (Tex. App.—Houston [14th Dist.] 1990, pet. ref'd). "Under Texas law, when probation is granted, no sentence is imposed. Therefore, a prior probated sentence entered by a Texas court would not be available to enhance punishment for a subsequent offense unless the probation had been revoked. [¶] However, when probation is granted under Louisiana law, it does constitute a final conviction for purposes of enhancement. *At 109:* We are satisfied that the State met its burden of proving that the conviction was considered 'final' under Louisiana law."

§12.42(a)

Campbell v. State, 49 S.W.3d 874, 878 (Tex.Crim. App.2001). "[A]s used in [Pen. Code] 12.42(a), the terms 'felony' and 'state jail felony' are mutually exclusive; a defendant charged under [Pen. Code] 12.35(a) who has previously acquired only state-jail felony convictions, whether sequential or non-sequential, must be punished for a third-degree felony under subsection 12.42(a)(1), rather than a second-degree felony under subsection 12.42(a)(2)." *See also Ex parte Beck*, 922 S.W.2d 181, 182 (Tex.Crim.App.1996); *State v. White*, 959 S.W.2d 375, 377-378 (Tex.App.—Fort Worth 1998, pet. ref'd).

Brown v. State, 14 S.W.3d 832, 832-33 (Tex.App.— Austin 2000, pet. ref'd). Pen. Code §31.03(e)(4)(D) "provides that theft of property having a value of less than $1500 is a state jail felony if the defendant 'has been previously convicted *two or more* times of any grade of theft.' Under this subsection, a defendant's history of theft convictions, regardless of their number or degree, cannot elevate a subsequent theft of property worth less than $1500 beyond the status of a state jail felony. For this reason, the punishment for third offense theft under §31.03(e)(4)(D) cannot be enhanced pursuant to [Pen. Code] §12.42(a) by proof of additional felony theft convictions."

§12.42(b)

Dickson v. State, 986 S.W.2d 799, 804 (Tex.App.— Waco 1999, pet. ref'd). "[P]unishment for a non-aggravated state jail felony offense enhanced under §12.42(a)(2) cannot be further enhanced under the provisions of §12.42(b)."

For a quick reference of penalties, see the Chart of Penalties on p. 675.

O'CONNOR'S CRIMINAL CODES   741

PEN §12.42

§12.42(c)

Kennedy v. Louisiana, ___ U.S. ___ (2008) (No. 07-343; 6-25-08). "This case presents the question whether the Constitution bars [State] from imposing the death penalty for the rape of a child where the crime did not result, and was not intended to result, in death of the victim. We hold the Eighth Amendment prohibits the death penalty for this offense."

Ex parte White, 211 S.W.3d 316, 319-20 (Tex.Crim. App.2007). "[W]e hold that a prior foreign conviction for an offense containing elements that are substantially similar to the elements of an offense listed under subsection 12.42(c)(2)(B) may be used to enhance punishment in Texas under subsection 12.42(c)(2), even if the sentence for that conviction was probated and the probation was not revoked. In this case, the probated Delaware conviction was properly used to enhance the punishment range for the charged offenses."

Griffith v. State, 116 S.W.3d 782, 784 (Tex.Crim. App.2003). "[W]e are called upon [to] decide whether [Pen. Code] §12.42(c)(2)(B) includes the statutory predecessors to the offenses enumerated therein. We conclude that they do."

§12.42(d)

Jordan v. State, ___ S.W.3d ___ (Tex.Crim.App. 2008) (No. PD-973-06; 6-18-08). "[W]e have never considered the application of, or conducted, a harm analysis after concluding that the State failed to present sufficient evidence to prove the proper sequence of the defendant's prior felony convictions for enhancement purposes under §12.42(d). Similarly, we have never applied a harm analysis where the State failed to establish that an enhancement conviction was final before the defendant committed the primary offense. In fact, we have explicitly disavowed the application of a harm analysis where the State failed to meet its burden of showing finality. In doing so, we said: 'A harmless error analysis should not be undertaken when the State fails to meet its burden of proof.' [¶] [W]e ... conclude that the court of appeals was correct in refusing to conduct a harm analysis in this case."

Rhodes v. State, 240 S.W.3d 882, 884 (Tex.Crim. App.2007). "We must determine whether a defendant may collaterally attack a prior judgment of conviction used to enhance a new offense, in the trial of that new offense, on the ground that the prior judgment was too lenient. We hold that he cannot."

Valdez v. State, 218 S.W.3d 82, 84 (Tex.Crim.App. 2007). "Appellant argues that the jury was permitted to assess an enhanced punishment under §12.42(d) 'without reaching a consensus as to which enhancement convictions, paragraphs and attendant cause numbers that the State was required to prove beyond a reasonable doubt.' Appellant further argues that the jury should have been 'required to reach a unanimous decision as to which convictions, if any, could be used to enhance punishment.' *At 85:* In cases like this, when a combination of more than two felonies is charged for enhancement purposes, jury unanimity is not required on any two specific felonies out of this combination."

State v. Webb, 12 S.W.3d 808, 811 (Tex.Crim.App. 2000). Pen. Code §12.42(d) "refers specifically to '*the trial of a felony offense other than a state jail felony* punishable under [Pen. Code] §12.35(a).' (Emphasis added.) Thus, the enhancement is applied with reference *to the offense tried*. In the instant case, appellee was tried for a non-aggravated state jail felony, i.e., a state jail felony punishable under §12.35(a). Following his conviction, his punishment was then enhanced, pursuant to §12.42(a)(2), to the equivalent of a second degree felony. Regardless of the enhancement, appellee was tried for a state jail felony punishable under §12.35(a); that his punishment, as opposed to the offense itself, was then subject to enhancement does not change that fact. As such, §12.42(d) is not applicable to appellee."

§12.42(e)

Fortier v. State, 105 S.W.3d 697, 700 (Tex.App.— Amarillo 2003, pet. ref'd). Held: Although D's punishment given after a motion for adjudication of a second degree felony fell within the permissible punishment range, the trial court stated that punishment was for a second degree felony *enhanced* to a first degree felony. However, the trial court impermissibly enhanced the second degree felony with a state jail felony. Because nothing in the record indicated what D's sentence would have been before deferred adjudication, the appellate court remanded to the trial court for a new punishment hearing.

PEN §12.422. DELETED
Deleted by Acts 1993, 73rd Leg., ch. 900, §1.01, eff. Sept. 1, 1993.

PEN §12.43. PENALTIES FOR REPEAT & HABITUAL MISDEMEANOR OFFENDERS

(a) If it is shown on the trial of a Class A misdemeanor that the defendant has been before convicted of a Class A misdemeanor or any degree of felony, on conviction he shall be punished by:

(1) a fine not to exceed $4,000;

(2) confinement in jail for any term of not more than one year or less than 90 days; or

(3) both such fine and confinement.

(b) If it is shown on the trial of a Class B misdemeanor that the defendant has been before convicted of a Class A or Class B misdemeanor or any degree of felony, on conviction he shall be punished by:

(1) a fine not to exceed $2,000;

(2) confinement in jail for any term of not more than 180 days or less than 30 days; or

(3) both such fine and confinement.

(c) If it is shown on the trial of an offense punishable as a Class C misdemeanor under Section 42.01 or 49.02 that the defendant has been before convicted under either of those sections three times or three times for any combination of those offenses and each prior offense was committed in the 24 months preceding the date of commission of the instant offense, the defendant shall be punished by:

(1) a fine not to exceed $2,000;

(2) confinement in jail for a term not to exceed 180 days; or

(3) both such fine and confinement.

(d) If the punishment scheme for an offense contains a specific enhancement provision increasing punishment for a defendant who has previously been convicted of the offense, the specific enhancement provision controls over this section.

History of Pen §12.43: Acts 1973, 63rd Leg., ch. 399, §1, eff. Jan. 1, 1974. Amended by Acts 1993, 73rd Leg., ch. 900, §1.01, eff. Sept. 1, 1994; Acts 1995, 74th Leg., ch. 318, §2, eff. Sept. 1, 1995; Acts 1999, 76th Leg., ch. 564, §1, eff. Sept. 1, 1999.

ANNOTATIONS

Beal v. State, 91 S.W.3d 794, 794-95 (Tex.Crim.App. 2002). "Today we settle the question of which date should be used in determining the finality of a prior conviction alleged in an indictment for enhancement purposes. We hold that it becomes final when the appellate court issues its mandate affirming the conviction."

Hudson v. State, 145 S.W.3d 323, 326 (Tex.App.—Fort Worth 2004, pet. ref'd). "[T]he State's notice, which included evidence of three prior felony convictions, each specified by cause number, classification of offense, county of conviction, and date of conviction,

was a sufficient pleading that gave notice of the prior convictions that would be used for enhancement of punishment. [¶] Here, although notice was given to Hudson's counsel six days before the punishment phase of the trial, no notice was given before guilt-innocence began. Therefore ... we hold that notice in this case was untimely."

PEN §12.44. REDUCTION OF STATE JAIL FELONY PUNISHMENT TO MISDEMEANOR PUNISHMENT

(a) A court may punish a defendant who is convicted of a state jail felony by imposing the confinement permissible as punishment for a Class A misdemeanor if, after considering the gravity and circumstances of the felony committed and the history, character, and rehabilitative needs of the defendant, the court finds that such punishment would best serve the ends of justice.

(b) At the request of the prosecuting attorney, the court may authorize the prosecuting attorney to prosecute a state jail felony as a Class A misdemeanor.

History of Pen §12.44: Acts 1973, 63rd Leg., ch. 399, §1, eff. Jan. 1, 1974. Amended by Acts 1989, 71st Leg., ch. 785, §4.02, eff. Sept. 1, 1989; Acts 1993, 73rd Leg., ch. 900, §1.01, eff. Sept. 1, 1994; Acts 1995, 74th Leg., ch. 318, §3, eff. Sept. 1, 1995; Acts 2005, 79th Leg., ch. 1276, §1, eff. Sept. 1, 2005.

PEN §12.45. ADMISSION OF UNADJUDICATED OFFENSE

(a) A person may, with the consent of the attorney for the state, admit during the sentencing hearing his guilt of one or more unadjudicated offenses and request the court to take each into account in determining sentence for the offense or offenses of which he stands adjudged guilty.

(b) Before a court may take into account an admitted offense over which exclusive venue lies in another county or district, the court must obtain permission from the prosecuting attorney with jurisdiction over the offense.

(c) If a court lawfully takes into account an admitted offense, prosecution is barred for that offense.

History of Pen §12.45: Acts 1973, 63rd Leg., ch. 399, §1, eff. Jan. 1, 1974. Amended by Acts 1983, 68th Leg., ch. 649, §1, eff. Aug. 29, 1983; Acts 1993, 73rd Leg., ch. 900, §1.01, eff. Sept. 1, 1994.

ANNOTATIONS

Lopez v. State, ___ S.W.3d ___ (Tex.Crim.App. 2008) (No. PD-1124-07; 5-14-08). Pen. Code §12.45 "permits a defendant (with the prosecutor's consent) to admit guilt of an unadjudicated extraneous offense,

For a quick reference of penalties, see the Chart of Penalties on p. 675.

O'CONNOR'S CRIMINAL CODES 743

have that offense taken into account by the trial court in sentencing on the primary offense, and thereafter bar any future prosecution for that extraneous offense. In a prior prosecution, appellant and the State followed this procedure, and the trial court took into account two extraneous drug offenses. In the present case, the State sought to introduce evidence of those drug offenses as 'prior convictions' to impeach appellant as a witness under [TRE] 609. Two issues are presented: First, did appellant forfeit error by failing to object when the State cross-examined him about the prior offenses? Second, do extraneous offenses considered under §12.45 constitute prior convictions available for impeachment under Rule 609? We answer both questions 'no' and affirm the judgment of the court of appeals."

PEN §12.46. USE OF PRIOR CONVICTIONS

The use of a conviction for enhancement purposes shall not preclude the subsequent use of such conviction for enhancement purposes.

History of Pen §12.46: Acts 1979, 66th Leg., p. 1027, ch. 459, §1, eff. June 7, 1979. Amended by Acts 1993, 73rd Leg., ch. 900, §1.01, eff. Sept. 1, 1994.

ANNOTATIONS

Beal v. State, 91 S.W.3d 794, 794-95 (Tex.Crim.App. 2002). "Today we settle the question of which date should be used in determining the finality of a prior conviction alleged in an indictment for enhancement purposes. We hold that it becomes final when the appellate court issues its mandate affirming the conviction."

Wisdom v. State, 708 S.W.2d 840, 845 (Tex.Crim. App.1986). "This Court must decide if §12.46 permits the State to use a prior conviction within one indictment for the dual purpose of proving an essential element of an offense and enhancing that same offense. We hold it does not. [¶] In the instant case, the State was barred from using the appellant's rape conviction to enhance the offense, after the conviction had been used to allege an essential element of that offense. The use of a prior conviction to prove an essential element of an offense bars the subsequent use of that prior conviction in the same indictment for enhancement purposes."

PEN §12.47. PENALTY IF OFFENSE COMMITTED BECAUSE OF BIAS OR PREJUDICE

(a) If an affirmative finding under Article 42.014, Code of Criminal Procedure, is made in the trial of an offense other than a first degree felony or a Class A misdemeanor, the punishment for the offense is increased to the punishment prescribed for the next highest category of offense. If the offense is a Class A misdemeanor, the minimum term of confinement for the offense is increased to 180 days. This section does not apply to the trial of an offense of injury to a disabled individual under Section 22.04, if the affirmative finding in the case under Article 42.014, Code of Criminal Procedure, shows that the defendant intentionally selected the victim because the victim was disabled.

(b) The attorney general, if requested to do so by a prosecuting attorney, may assist the prosecuting attorney in the investigation or prosecution of an offense committed because of bias or prejudice. The attorney general shall designate one individual in the division of the attorney general's office that assists in the prosecution of criminal cases to coordinate responses to requests made under this subsection.

History of Pen §12.47: Acts 1993, 73rd Leg., ch. 987, §1, eff. Sept. 1, 1993. Amended by Acts 1997, 75th Leg., ch. 751, §1, eff. Sept. 1, 1997; Acts 2001, 77th Leg., ch. 85, §1.01, eff. Sept. 1, 2001.

History of Former Pen §12.47: Repealed by Acts 1993, 73rd Leg., ch. 900, §1.01, eff. Sept. 1, 1994.

ANNOTATIONS

Jaynes v. State, 216 S.W.3d 839, 846 (Tex.App.—Corpus Christi 2006, no pet.). "[E]nhancement under the Texas Hate Crimes Act may be based on circumstantial evidence of the defendant's bias or prejudicial motive, including previous racial epithets directed at the victim, provided, however, the circumstantial evidence must be relevant and reliable to prevent enhancement of punishment for crimes committed by a person who entertains a bias or prejudice, but whose bias was not the primary motivation for the criminal conduct. [¶] [T]he State must prove a causal link between the crime and the proven bias or prejudice."

PEN §12.48. CERTAIN OFFENSES RESULTING IN LOSS TO NURSING & CONVALESCENT HOMES

If it is shown on the trial of an offense under Chapter 31 or 32 that, as a result of a loss incurred because of the conduct charged, a trustee was appointed and emergency assistance funds, other than funds used to pay the expenses of the trustee, were used for a nursing or convalescent home under Subchapter D, Chapter

PEN §12.45

242, Health and Safety Code, the punishment for the offense is increased to the punishment prescribed for the next higher category of offense except that a felony of the first degree is punished as a felony of the first degree.

History of Pen §12.48: Acts 1999, 76th Leg., ch. 439, §4, eff. Sept. 1, 1999.

PEN §12.49. PENALTY IF CONTROLLED SUBSTANCE USED TO COMMIT OFFENSE

If the court makes an affirmative finding under Article 42.012, Code of Criminal Procedure, in the punishment phase of the trial of an offense under Chapter 29, Chapter 31, or Title 5, other than a first degree felony or a Class A misdemeanor, the punishment for the offense is increased to the punishment prescribed for the next highest category of offense. If the offense is a Class A misdemeanor, the minimum term of confinement for the offense is increased to 180 days.

History of Pen §12.49: Acts 1999, 76th Leg., ch. 417, §2(a), eff. Sept. 1, 1999. Renumbered from §12.48 and amended by Acts 2001, 77th Leg., ch. 1420, §§21.001(93), 21.002(15), eff. Sept. 1, 2001.

SUBCHAPTER E. CORPORATIONS & ASSOCIATIONS

PEN §12.51. AUTHORIZED PUNISHMENTS FOR CORPORATIONS & ASSOCIATIONS

(a) If a corporation or association is adjudged guilty of an offense that provides a penalty consisting of a fine only, a court may sentence the corporation or association to pay a fine in an amount fixed by the court, not to exceed the fine provided by the offense.

(b) If a corporation or association is adjudged guilty of an offense that provides a penalty including imprisonment, or that provides no specific penalty, a court may sentence the corporation or association to pay a fine in an amount fixed by the court, not to exceed:

(1) $20,000 if the offense is a felony of any category;

(2) $10,000 if the offense is a Class A or Class B misdemeanor;

(3) $2,000 if the offense is a Class C misdemeanor; or

(4) $50,000 if, as a result of an offense classified as a felony or Class A misdemeanor, an individual suffers serious bodily injury or death.

(c) In lieu of the fines authorized by Subsections (a), (b)(1), (b)(2), and (b)(4), if a court finds that the corporation or association gained money or property or caused personal injury or death, property damage, or other loss through the commission of a felony or Class A or Class B misdemeanor, the court may sentence the corporation or association to pay a fine in an amount fixed by the court, not to exceed double the amount gained or caused by the corporation or association to be lost or damaged, whichever is greater.

(d) In addition to any sentence that may be imposed by this section, a corporation or association that has been adjudged guilty of an offense may be ordered by the court to give notice of the conviction to any person the court deems appropriate.

(e) On conviction of a corporation or association, the court shall notify the attorney general of that fact.

History of Pen §12.51: Acts 1973, 63rd Leg., ch. 399, §1, eff. Jan. 1, 1974. Amended by Acts 1977, 65th Leg., ch. 768, §1, eff. June 16, 1977; Acts 1987, 70th Leg., ch. 1085, §1, eff. Sept. 1, 1987; Acts 1993, 73rd Leg., ch. 900, §1.01, eff. Sept. 1, 1994.

TITLE 4. INCHOATE OFFENSES

CHAPTER 15. PREPARATORY OFFENSES

PEN §15.01. CRIMINAL ATTEMPT

(a) A person commits an offense if, with specific intent to commit an offense, he does an act amounting to more than mere preparation that tends but fails to effect the commission of the offense intended.

(b) If a person attempts an offense that may be aggravated, his conduct constitutes an attempt to commit the aggravated offense if an element that aggravates the offense accompanies the attempt.

(c) It is no defense to prosecution for criminal attempt that the offense attempted was actually committed.

(d) An offense under this section is one category lower than the offense attempted, and if the offense attempted is a state jail felony, the offense is a Class A misdemeanor.

History of Pen §15.01: Acts 1973, 63rd Leg., ch. 399, §1, eff. Jan. 1, 1974. Amended by Acts 1975, 64th Leg., ch. 203, §4, eff. Sept. 1, 1975; Acts 1993, 73rd Leg., ch. 900, §1.01, eff. Sept. 1, 1994.

For a quick reference of penalties, see the Chart of Penalties on p. 675.

Chen v. State, 42 S.W.3d 926, 930 (Tex.Crim.App. 2001). "Appellant's goal was to commit the offense of sexual performance by a child. Because that goal is a crime by law, the doctrine of legal impossibility is not at issue in this case. Rather, this case presents a factual impossibility scenario. Due to a factual condition unknown to appellant (that Julie Cirello did not actually exist), the offense of sexual performance by a child could not be completed. It is true that ... the actual offense of sexual performance by a child would have been impossible for appellant to *complete*; the complainant, Julie Cirello, did not physically exist. But completion of the crime was apparently possible to appellant. He had *specific intent* to commit the offense of sexual performance by a child, and he committed an act amounting to more than mere preparation that tended but failed to effect the commission of the offense. The State presented evidence for each of the necessary elements of attempted sexual performance by a child."

Mims v. State, 3 S.W.3d 923, 923 (Tex.Crim.App. 1999). The question is "whether a defendant in an attempted murder prosecution is entitled to an instruction on ... sudden passion ... when the instruction is raised by the evidence." *At 924:* The plain language of both the murder and attempt statutes support the conclusion that the attempt statute and the sudden passion issue should, in an appropriate case, combine to create a third degree felony. *At 928:* "[I]f raised by the evidence, the sudden passion issue should be submitted in the punishment phase of an attempted murder prosecution."

Yalch v. State, 743 S.W.2d 231, 233 (Tex.Crim.App. 1988). "[H]arm, or lack of it, to the victim is not an element of the offense of attempted murder and, therefore, need not be proven at trial. [¶] The elements of a criminal attempt are: (1) a person (2) with specific intent to commit an offense (3) does an act amounting to more than mere preparation (4) that tends but fails to effect the commission of the offense intended."

Ex parte Bartmess, 739 S.W.2d 51, 53 (Tex.Crim. App.1987). "[T]he allegation of attempt satisfies the need for a culpable mental state as to the attempted felony. Use of the word 'attempt' rather than 'intent' does not render an indictment fundamentally defective on the ground that it fails to allege specific intent."

In re J.B.M., 157 S.W.3d 823, 826 (Tex.App.—Fort Worth 2005, no pet.). "In a case where the charge is attempted sexual assault, intent may be inferred from the accused's actions, words, and conduct."

Strong v. State, 87 S.W.3d 206, 217 (Tex.App.—Dallas 2002, pet. ref'd). "The attempt statute does not apply when the culpable mental state for the offense attempted is less than knowing.... DWI has no culpable mental state; thus, the attempt statute cannot apply to the offense of DWI."

Lindsey v. State, 764 S.W.2d 376, 378 (Tex.App.—Texarkana 1989, no pet.). "Convictions for attempted offenses under §15.01 ... must necessarily be considered on a case-by-case basis. [¶] The criminal attempt statute, §15.01 ..., does not require that every act short of actual commission be accomplished in order for one to be convicted of an attempted offense."

PEN §15.02. CRIMINAL CONSPIRACY

(a) A person commits criminal conspiracy if, with intent that a felony be committed:

(1) he agrees with one or more persons that they or one or more of them engage in conduct that would constitute the offense; and

(2) he or one or more of them performs an overt act in pursuance of the agreement.

(b) An agreement constituting a conspiracy may be inferred from acts of the parties.

(c) It is no defense to prosecution for criminal conspiracy that:

(1) one or more of the coconspirators is not criminally responsible for the object offense;

(2) one or more of the coconspirators has been acquitted, so long as two or more coconspirators have not been acquitted;

(3) one or more of the coconspirators has not been prosecuted or convicted, has been convicted of a different offense, or is immune from prosecution;

(4) the actor belongs to a class of persons that by definition of the object offense is legally incapable of committing the object offense in an individual capacity; or

(5) the object offense was actually committed.

(d) An offense under this section is one category lower than the most serious felony that is the object of the conspiracy, and if the most serious felony that is the object of the conspiracy is a state jail felony, the offense is a Class A misdemeanor.

History of Pen §15.02: Acts 1973, 63rd Leg., ch. 399, §1, eff. Jan. 1, 1974. Amended by Acts 1993, 73rd Leg., ch. 900, §1.01, eff. Sept. 1, 1994.

ANNOTATIONS

Barber v. State, 764 S.W.2d 232, 234 (Tex.Crim. App.1988). "One person acting alone cannot commit conspiracy. The rule has evolved that, 'inasmuch as two persons are necessary to a conspiracy, if two are tried and one is acquitted, the other must also be acquitted.'"

Woods v. State, 801 S.W.2d 932, 943 (Tex.App.— Austin 1990, pet. ref'd). "The overt act element is included to require proof beyond the bare agreement that a socially dangerous combination exists. Although the overt act ... might be sufficient to constitute the act under [Pen. Code] §15.01 in criminal attempt, it does not necessarily have to be so since the concept of criminal conspiracy reaches further back into preparatory conduct constituting inchoate offenses than does criminal attempt. [¶] Usually, an indictment which tracks the language of the statute is legally sufficient, and the State need not allege facts which are merely evidentiary in nature." (Internal quotes omitted.)

PEN §15.03. CRIMINAL SOLICITATION

(a) A person commits an offense if, with intent that a capital felony or felony of the first degree be committed, he requests, commands, or attempts to induce another to engage in specific conduct that, under the circumstances surrounding his conduct as the actor believes them to be, would constitute the felony or make the other a party to its commission.

(b) A person may not be convicted under this section on the uncorroborated testimony of the person allegedly solicited and unless the solicitation is made under circumstances strongly corroborative of both the solicitation itself and the actor's intent that the other person act on the solicitation.

(c) It is no defense to prosecution under this section that:

(1) the person solicited is not criminally responsible for the felony solicited;

(2) the person solicited has been acquitted, has not been prosecuted or convicted, has been convicted of a different offense or of a different type or class of offense, or is immune from prosecution;

(3) the actor belongs to a class of persons that by definition of the felony solicited is legally incapable of committing the offense in an individual capacity; or

(4) the felony solicited was actually committed.

(d) An offense under this section is:

(1) a felony of the first degree if the offense solicited is a capital offense; or

(2) a felony of the second degree if the offense solicited is a felony of the first degree.

History of Pen §15.03: Acts 1973, 63rd Leg., ch. 399, §1, eff. Jan. 1, 1974. Amended by Acts 1993, 73rd Leg., ch. 462, §1 (eff. Sept. 1, 1993), ch. 900, §1.01 (eff. Sept. 1, 1994).

See also CCP art. 38.14.

ANNOTATIONS

Schwenk v. State, 733 S.W.2d 142, 144 (Tex.Crim. App.1981). "[I]t is because criminal solicitation *'reaches so far back into preparatory conduct,'* that it applies only to the most serious offenses. *At 145:* '[T]he acts prohibited by [§15.03(a)] are *of an active, positive nature*, and the culpable mental state required is specific intent. Moreover, *the solicitation must be of specific conduct....'"*

Guthrie v. State, 149 S.W.2d 829, 832 (Tex.App.— Waco 2004, pet. ref'd). "[A] §15.03(b) instruction is required in a criminal solicitation case. For criminal solicitation, corroboration is required regardless of whether the person allegedly solicited to commit the crime is an accomplice witness."

Claxton v. State, 124 S.W.3d 761, 765 (Tex.App.— Houston [1st Dist.] 2003, pet. ref'd). "We read [Pen. Code] §15.03(b) in conjunction with [CCP art. 38.14], which addresses accomplice-witness corroboration in non-solicitation cases. The word 'strongly' in §15.03(b) emphasizes the need for an additional safeguard, but does not indicate a different standard. Rather, it mandates corroboration of both the solicitation itself and the defendant's intent that the solicitation be acted on."

Ganesan v. State, 45 S.W.3d 197, 201 (Tex.App.— Austin 2001, pet. ref'd). Pen. Code §15.03(b) "is analogous to the accomplice witness statute [CCP art. 38.37], and the same test for evaluating the sufficiency of the corroboration is used. *At 203:* '[B]ootstrapping' cannot be used to corroborate an accomplice, and by extension cannot be used to corroborate a solicitee."

State v. Brinkley, 764 S.W.2d 913, 915 (Tex.App.— Tyler 1989, no pet.). "The offense of criminal solicitation is completed when the culpable request or inducement to commit a capital felony or a first degree felony is unilaterally presented. Proof that the felony is

For a quick reference of penalties, see the Chart of Penalties on p. 675.

O'CONNOR'S CRIMINAL CODES **747**

actually committed is not required to establish the offense of solicitation. Guilt of solicitation may be established solely by proving the communication and the culpable intent."

PEN §15.031. CRIMINAL SOLICITATION OF A MINOR

(a) A person commits an offense if, with intent that an offense listed by Section 3g(a)(1), Article 42.12, Code of Criminal Procedure, be committed, the person requests, commands, or attempts to induce a minor to engage in specific conduct that, under the circumstances surrounding the actor's conduct as the actor believes them to be, would constitute an offense listed by Section 3g(a)(1), Article 42.12, or make the minor a party to the commission of an offense listed by Section 3g(a)(1), Article 42.12.

 Subsection (b) below is effective for offenses committed on or after Sept. 1, 2007.

(b) A person commits an offense if, with intent that an offense under Section 21.02, 21.11, 22.011, 22.021, or 43.25 be committed, the person by any means requests, commands, or attempts to induce a minor or another whom the person believes to be a minor to engage in specific conduct that, under the circumstances surrounding the actor's conduct as the actor believes them to be, would constitute an offense under one of those sections or would make the minor or other believed by the person to be a minor a party to the commission of an offense under one of those sections.

Subsection (b) below is effective for offenses in which any element of the offense was committed before Sept. 1, 2007.

(b) A person commits an offense if, with intent that an offense under Section 21.11, 22.011, 22.021, or 43.25 be committed, the person by any means requests, commands, or attempts to induce a minor or another whom the person believes to be a minor to engage in specific conduct that, under the circumstances surrounding the actor's conduct as the actor believes them to be, would constitute an offense under one of those sections or would make the minor or other believed by the person to be a minor a party to the commission of an offense under one of those sections.

(c) A person may not be convicted under this section on the uncorroborated testimony of the minor allegedly solicited unless the solicitation is made under circumstances strongly corroborative of both the solicitation itself and the actor's intent that the minor act on the solicitation.

(d) It is no defense to prosecution under this section that:

(1) the minor solicited is not criminally responsible for the offense solicited;

(2) the minor solicited has been acquitted, has not been prosecuted or convicted, has been convicted of a different offense or of a different type or class of offense, or is immune from prosecution;

(3) the actor belongs to a class of persons that by definition of the offense solicited is legally incapable of committing the offense in an individual capacity; or

(4) the offense solicited was actually committed.

(e) An offense under this section is one category lower than the solicited offense.

(f) In this section, "minor" means an individual younger than 17 years of age.

History of Pen §15.031: Acts 1995, 74th Leg., ch. 262, §79, eff. Jan. 1, 1996. Amended by Acts 1999, 76th Leg., ch. 1415, §22(a), eff. Sept. 1, 1999; Acts 2007, 80th Leg., ch. 593, §3.49, eff. Sept. 1, 2007.

ANNOTATIONS

Lankford v. State, ____ S.W.3d ____ (Tex.App.—Waco 2008, n.p.h.) (No. 10-06-00363-CR; 3-26-08). "The corroboration required under the criminal solicitation statute is analogous to the corroboration requirement found in the accomplice-witness statute [CCP art. 38.14]. Due to the similarities between these two statutes, the test for evaluating the sufficiency of the corroboration evidence is the same under each. In assessing the sufficiency of the evidence corroborating the victim's testimony, the test requires that we eliminate the minor victim's testimony from consideration and then determine whether there is other incriminating evidence tending to connect the accused with the crime. It is not necessary that the corroboration evidence directly link the accused with the crime or that it be sufficient in itself to establish guilt."

PEN §15.04. RENUNCIATION DEFENSE

(a) It is an affirmative defense to prosecution under Section 15.01 that under circumstances manifesting a voluntary and complete renunciation of his criminal objective the actor avoided commission of the offense attempted by abandoning his criminal conduct

★

or, if abandonment was insufficient to avoid commission of the offense, by taking further affirmative action that prevented the commission.

(b) It is an affirmative defense to prosecution under Section 15.02 or 15.03 that under circumstances manifesting a voluntary and complete renunciation of his criminal objective the actor countermanded his solicitation or withdrew from the conspiracy before commission of the object offense and took further affirmative action that prevented the commission of the object offense.

(c) Renunciation is not voluntary if it is motivated in whole or in part:

(1) by circumstances not present or apparent at the inception of the actor's course of conduct that increase the probability of detection or apprehension or that make more difficult the accomplishment of the objective; or

(2) by a decision to postpone the criminal conduct until another time or to transfer the criminal act to another but similar objective or victim.

(d) Evidence that the defendant renounced his criminal objective by abandoning his criminal conduct, countermanding his solicitation, or withdrawing from the conspiracy before the criminal offense was committed and made substantial effort to prevent the commission of the object offense shall be admissible as mitigation at the hearing on punishment if he has been found guilty of criminal attempt, criminal solicitation, or criminal conspiracy; and in the event of a finding of renunciation under this subsection, the punishment shall be one grade lower than that provided for the offense committed.

History of Pen §15.04: Acts 1973, 63rd Leg., ch. 399, §1, eff. Jan. 1, 1974. Amended by Acts 1993, 73rd Leg., ch. 900, §1.01, eff. Sept. 1, 1994.

ANNOTATIONS

Thomas v. State, 708 S.W.2d 861, 862-63 (Tex. Crim.App.1986). There is a "twofold purpose for permitting the defense of renunciation. First, the defense tends to negative dangerousness; second, it provides actors with motive for desisting in criminal objective, thus, diminishing the risk that the substantive crime will be committed. [¶] [W]e interpret §15.04(a) to mean that if a person avoids committing the *object offense* and circumstances show voluntary and complete renunciation of the *attempt to commit the object offense*, he has established the defense of renunciation."

PEN §15.05. NO OFFENSE

Attempt or conspiracy to commit, or solicitation of, a preparatory offense defined in this chapter is not an offense.

History of Pen §15.05: Acts 1973, 63rd Leg., ch. 399, §1, eff. Jan. 1, 1974.

CHAPTER 16. CRIMINAL INSTRUMENTS, INTERCEPTION OF WIRE OR ORAL COMMUNICATION, & INSTALLATION OF TRACKING DEVICE

PEN §16.01. UNLAWFUL USE OF CRIMINAL INSTRUMENT

(a) A person commits an offense if:

(1) he possesses a criminal instrument with intent to use it in the commission of an offense; or

(2) with knowledge of its character and with intent to use or aid or permit another to use in the commission of an offense, he manufactures, adapts, sells, installs, or sets up a criminal instrument.

(b) For the purpose of this section, "criminal instrument" means anything, the possession, manufacture, or sale of which is not otherwise an offense, that is specially designed, made, or adapted for use in the commission of an offense.

(c) An offense under Subsection (a)(1) is one category lower than the offense intended. An offense under Subsection (a)(2) is a state jail felony.

History of Pen §16.01: Acts 1973, 63rd Leg., ch. 399, §1, eff. Jan. 1, 1974. Amended by Acts 1975, 64th Leg., ch. 342, §7, eff. Sept. 1, 1975; Acts 1993, 73rd Leg., ch. 900, §1.01, eff. Sept. 1, 1994; Acts 1999, 76th Leg., ch. 728, §2, eff. Sept. 1, 1999.

ANNOTATIONS

Danzi v. State, 101 S.W.3d 786, 793 (Tex.App.—El Paso 2003, pet. ref'd). Held: A "slim jim" is not a criminal instrument proscribed by §16.01(b).

Janjua v. State, 991 S.W.2d 419, 426 (Tex.App.— Houston [14th Dist.] 1999, no pet.). "No device, sitting passively on the shelf, is a criminal instrument. [A] criminal instrument under §16.01 must be determined by both (1) its design or adaptation and (2) the facts and circumstances establishing its intended use."

PEN §16.01

For a quick reference of penalties, see the Chart of Penalties on p. 675.

O'CONNOR'S CRIMINAL CODES   749

★

Ex parte Andrews, 814 S.W.2d 839, 841 (Tex. App.—Houston [1st Dist.] 1991), *pet. dism'd sub nom. Ex parte Chunn*, 831 S.W.2d 326 (Tex.Crim.App.1992). "[T]he gravamen of the offense intended by the language used by the legislature is the physical adaptation of the alleged instrument for a specific criminal intent. [A]ny illegality to be proved is in the inherent characteristics of the object itself as adapted, and not in the conduct of defendants in using the object within a particular criminal episode. An object does not become a criminal instrument by the context of its use, but by the limited nature and specialized criminal use of its own distinctive properties." *Contra Janjua v. State*, above.

PEN §16.02. UNLAWFUL INTERCEPTION, USE, OR DISCLOSURE OF WIRE, ORAL, OR ELECTRONIC COMMUNICATIONS

(a) In this section, "computer trespasser," "covert entry," "communication common carrier," "contents," "electronic communication," "electronic, mechanical, or other device," "immediate life-threatening situation," "intercept," "investigative or law enforcement officer," "member of a law enforcement unit specially trained to respond to and deal with life-threatening situations," "oral communication," "protected computer," "readily accessible to the general public," and "wire communication" have the meanings given those terms in Article 18.20, Code of Criminal Procedure.

(b) A person commits an offense if the person:

(1) intentionally intercepts, endeavors to intercept, or procures another person to intercept or endeavor to intercept a wire, oral, or electronic communication;

(2) intentionally discloses or endeavors to disclose to another person the contents of a wire, oral, or electronic communication if the person knows or has reason to know the information was obtained through the interception of a wire, oral, or electronic communication in violation of this subsection;

(3) intentionally uses or endeavors to use the contents of a wire, oral, or electronic communication if the person knows or is reckless about whether the information was obtained through the interception of a wire, oral, or electronic communication in violation of this subsection;

(4) knowingly or intentionally effects a covert entry for the purpose of intercepting wire, oral, or electronic communications without court order or authorization; or

(5) intentionally uses, endeavors to use, or procures any other person to use or endeavor to use any electronic, mechanical, or other device to intercept any oral communication when the device:

(A) is affixed to, or otherwise transmits a signal through a wire, cable, or other connection used in wire communications; or

(B) transmits communications by radio or interferes with the transmission of communications by radio.

(c) It is an affirmative defense to prosecution under Subsection (b) that:

(1) an operator of a switchboard or an officer, employee, or agent of a communication common carrier whose facilities are used in the transmission of a wire or electronic communication intercepts a communication or discloses or uses an intercepted communication in the normal course of employment while engaged in an activity that is a necessary incident to the rendition of service or to the protection of the rights or property of the carrier of the communication, unless the interception results from the communication common carrier's use of service observing or random monitoring for purposes other than mechanical or service quality control checks;

(2) an officer, employee, or agent of a communication common carrier provides information, facilities, or technical assistance to an investigative or law enforcement officer who is authorized as provided by this section to intercept a wire, oral, or electronic communication;

(3) a person acting under color of law intercepts:

(A) a wire, oral, or electronic communication, if the person is a party to the communication or if one of the parties to the communication has given prior consent to the interception;

(B) a wire, oral, or electronic communication, if the person is acting under the authority of Article 18.20, Code of Criminal Procedure; or

(C) a wire or electronic communication made by a computer trespasser and transmitted to, through, or from a protected computer, if:

(i) the interception did not acquire a communication other than one transmitted to or from the computer trespasser;

(ii) the owner of the protected computer consented to the interception of the computer trespasser's communications on the protected computer; and

(iii) actor was lawfully engaged in an ongoing criminal investigation and the actor had reasonable suspicion to believe that the contents of the computer trespasser's communications likely to be obtained would be material to the investigation;

(4) a person not acting under color of law intercepts a wire, oral, or electronic communication, if:

(A) the person is a party to the communication; or

(B) one of the parties to the communication has given prior consent to the interception, unless the communication is intercepted for the purpose of committing an unlawful act;

(5) a person acting under color of law intercepts a wire, oral, or electronic communication if:

(A) oral or written consent for the interception is given by a magistrate before the interception;

(B) an immediate life-threatening situation exists;

(C) the person is a member of a law enforcement unit specially trained to:

(i) respond to and deal with life-threatening situations; or

(ii) install electronic, mechanical, or other devices; and

(D) the interception ceases immediately on termination of the life-threatening situation;

(6) an officer, employee, or agent of the Federal Communications Commission intercepts a communication transmitted by radio or discloses or uses an intercepted communication in the normal course of employment and in the discharge of the monitoring responsibilities exercised by the Federal Communications Commission in the enforcement of Chapter 5, Title 47, United States Code;

(7) a person intercepts or obtains access to an electronic communication that was made through an electronic communication system that is configured to permit the communication to be readily accessible to the general public;

(8) a person intercepts radio communication, other than a cordless telephone communication that is transmitted between a cordless telephone handset and a base unit, that is transmitted:

(A) by a station for the use of the general public;

(B) to ships, aircraft, vehicles, or persons in distress;

(C) by a governmental, law enforcement, civil defense, private land mobile, or public safety communications system that is readily accessible to the general public, unless the radio communication is transmitted by a law enforcement representative to or from a mobile data terminal;

(D) by a station operating on an authorized frequency within the bands allocated to the amateur, citizens band, or general mobile radio services; or

(E) by a marine or aeronautical communications system;

(9) a person intercepts a wire or electronic communication the transmission of which causes harmful interference to a lawfully operating station or consumer electronic equipment, to the extent necessary to identify the source of the interference;

(10) a user of the same frequency intercepts a radio communication made through a system that uses frequencies monitored by individuals engaged in the provision or the use of the system, if the communication is not scrambled or encrypted; or

(11) a provider of electronic communications service records the fact that a wire or electronic communication was initiated or completed in order to protect the provider, another provider furnishing service towards the completion of the communication, or a user of that service from fraudulent, unlawful, or abusive use of the service.

(d) A person commits an offense if the person:

(1) intentionally manufactures, assembles, possesses, or sells an electronic, mechanical, or other device knowing or having reason to know that the device is designed primarily for nonconsensual interception of wire, electronic, or oral communications and that the device or a component of the device has been or will be used for an unlawful purpose; or

(2) places in a newspaper, magazine, handbill, or other publication an advertisement of an electronic, mechanical, or other device:

(A) knowing or having reason to know that the device is designed primarily for nonconsensual interception of wire, electronic, or oral communications;

For a quick reference of penalties, see the Chart of Penalties on p. 675.

O'CONNOR'S CRIMINAL CODES 751

(B) promoting the use of the device for the purpose of nonconsensual interception of wire, electronic, or oral communications; or

(C) knowing or having reason to know that the advertisement will promote the use of the device for the purpose of nonconsensual interception of wire, electronic, or oral communications.

(e) It is an affirmative defense to prosecution under Subsection (d) that the manufacture, assembly, possession, or sale of an electronic, mechanical, or other device that is designed primarily for the purpose of nonconsensual interception of wire, electronic, or oral communication is by:

(1) a communication common carrier or a provider of wire or electronic communications service or an officer, agent, or employee of or a person under contract with a communication common carrier or provider acting in the normal course of the provider's or communication carrier's business;

(2) an officer, agent, or employee of a person under contract with, bidding on contracts with, or doing business with the United States or this state acting in the normal course of the activities of the United States or this state;

(3) a member of the Department of Public Safety who is specifically trained to install wire, oral, or electronic communications intercept equipment; or

(4) a member of a local law enforcement agency that has an established unit specifically designated to respond to and deal with life-threatening situations.

(f) An offense under this section is a felony of the second degree, unless the offense is committed under Subsection (d) or (g), in which event the offense is a state jail felony.

(g) A person commits an offense if, knowing that a government attorney or an investigative or law enforcement officer has been authorized or has applied for authorization to intercept wire, electronic, or oral communications, the person obstructs, impedes, prevents, gives notice to another of, or attempts to give notice to another of the interception.

(h) Repealed by Acts 2005, 79th Leg., ch. 889, §1, eff. June 17, 2005.

History of Pen §16.02: Acts 1981, 67th Leg., ch. 275, §2, eff. Aug. 31, 1981. Amended by Acts 1983, 68th Leg., ch. 864, §§1 to 3, eff. June 19, 1983; Acts 1989, 71st Leg., ch. 1166, §16, eff. Sept. 1, 1989; Acts 1993, 73rd Leg., ch. 790, §16 (eff. Sept. 1, 1993), ch. 900, §1.01 (eff. Sept. 1, 1994); Acts 1997, 75th Leg., ch. 1051, §9, eff. Sept. 1, 1997; Acts 2001, 77th Leg., ch. 1270, §11, eff. Sept. 1, 2001; Acts 2003, 78th Leg., ch. 678, §1, eff. Sept. 1, 2003; Acts 2005, 79th Leg., ch. 889, §1, eff. June 17, 2005.

ANNOTATIONS

Alameda v. State, 181 S.W.3d 772, 778 (Tex.App.—Fort Worth 2005), *aff'd*, 235 S.W.3d 218 (Tex.Crim.App.2007). "We agree with the federal and state courts that have adopted the vicarious consent doctrine. [A]s long as a parent has a good faith, objectively reasonable basis for believing that the taping of telephone conversations is in the best interest of the parent's minor child, the parent may vicariously consent to the recording on behalf of the child."

Collins v. Collins, 904 S.W.2d 792, 797 (Tex.App.—Houston [1st Dist.] 1995), *writ denied*, 923 S.W.2d 569 (Tex.1996). "Neither the state nor the federal wiretap statutes contain any exception for wiretaps between spouses." *Contra Duffy v. State*, 33 S.W.3d 17, 24-25 (Tex.App.—El Paso 2000, no pet.).

PEN §16.021. DELETED
Deleted by Acts 1993, 73rd Leg., ch. 900, §1.01, eff. Sept. 1, 1994.

PEN §16.03. UNLAWFUL USE OF PEN REGISTER OR TRAP & TRACE DEVICE

(a) A person commits an offense if the person knowingly installs or uses a pen register or trap and trace device to record or decode electronic or other impulses for the purpose of identifying telephone numbers dialed or otherwise transmitted on a telephone line.

(b) In this section, "authorized peace officer," "communications common carrier," "pen register," and "trap and trace device" have the meanings assigned by Article 18.21, Code of Criminal Procedure.

(c) It is an affirmative defense to prosecution under Subsection (a) that the actor is:

(1) an officer, employee, or agent of a communications common carrier and the actor installs or uses a device or equipment to record a number dialed from or to a telephone instrument in the normal course of business of the carrier for purposes of:

(A) protecting property or services provided by the carrier; or

(B) assisting another who the actor reasonably believes to be a peace officer authorized to install or use a pen register or trap and trace device under Article 18.21, Code of Criminal Procedure;

PEN §16.02

⎯⎯⎯⎯⎯⎯⎯⎯⎯⎯ ✭ ⎯⎯⎯⎯⎯⎯⎯⎯⎯⎯

(2) an officer, employee, or agent of a lawful enterprise and the actor installs or uses a device or equipment while engaged in an activity that:

(A) is a necessary incident to the rendition of service or to the protection of property of or services provided by the enterprise; and

(B) is not made for the purpose of gathering information for a law enforcement agency or private investigative agency, other than information related to the theft of communication or information services provided by the enterprise; or

(3) a person authorized to install or use a pen register or trap and trace device under Article 18.21, Code of Criminal Procedure.

(d) An offense under this section is a state jail felony.

History of Pen §16.03: Acts 1985, 69th Leg., ch. 587, §6, eff. Aug. 26, 1985. Amended by Acts 1989, 71st Leg., ch. 958, §2, eff. Sept. 1, 1989; Acts 1993, 73rd Leg., ch. 900, §1.01, eff. Sept. 1, 1994; Acts 1997, 75th Leg., ch. 1051, §10, eff. Sept. 1, 1997.

PEN §16.04. UNLAWFUL ACCESS TO STORED COMMUNICATIONS

(a) In this section, "electronic communication," "electronic storage," "user," and "wire communication" have the meanings assigned to those terms in Article 18.21, Code of Criminal Procedure.

(b) A person commits an offense if the person obtains, alters, or prevents authorized access to a wire or electronic communication while the communication is in electronic storage by:

(1) intentionally obtaining access without authorization to a facility through which a wire or electronic communications service is provided; or

(2) intentionally exceeding an authorization for access to a facility through which a wire or electronic communications service is provided.

(c) Except as provided by Subsection (d), an offense under Subsection (b) is a Class A misdemeanor.

(d) If committed to obtain a benefit or to harm another, an offense is a state jail felony.

(e) It is an affirmative defense to prosecution under Subsection (b) that the conduct was authorized by:

(1) the provider of the wire or electronic communications service;

(2) the user of the wire or electronic communications service;

(3) the addressee or intended recipient of the wire or electronic communication; or

(4) Article 18.21, Code of Criminal Procedure.

History of Pen §16.04: Acts 1989, 71st Leg., ch. 958, §3, eff. Sept. 1, 1989. Amended by Acts 1993, 73rd Leg., ch. 900, §1.01, eff. Sept. 1, 1994; Acts 1997, 75th Leg., ch. 1051, §11, eff. Sept. 1, 1997.

PEN §16.05. ILLEGAL DIVULGENCE OF PUBLIC COMMUNICATIONS

(a) In this section, "electronic communication," "electronic communications service," and "electronic communications system" have the meanings given those terms in Article 18.20, Code of Criminal Procedure.

(b) A person who provides electronic communications service to the public commits an offense if the person knowingly divulges the contents of a communication to another who is not the intended recipient of the communication.

(c) It is an affirmative defense to prosecution under Subsection (b) that the actor divulged the contents of the communication:

(1) as authorized by federal or state law;

(2) to a person employed, authorized, or whose facilities are used to forward the communication to the communication's destination; or

(3) to a law enforcement agency if the contents reasonably appear to pertain to the commission of a crime.

(d) Except as provided by Subsection (e), an offense under Subsection (b) that involves a scrambled or encrypted radio communication is a state jail felony.

(e) If committed for a tortious or illegal purpose or to gain a benefit, an offense under Subsection (b) that involves a radio communication that is not scrambled or encrypted:

(1) is a Class A misdemeanor if the communication is not a public land mobile radio service communication or a paging service communication; or

(2) is a Class C misdemeanor if the communication is a public land mobile radio service communication or a paging service communication.

(f) Repealed by Acts 1997, 75th Leg., ch. 1051, §13, eff. Sept. 1, 1997.

History of Pen §16.05: Acts 1989, 71st Leg., ch. 1166, §17, eff. Sept. 1, 1989. Renumbered from §16.04 by Acts 1990, 71st Leg., 6th C.S., ch. 12, §2(24), eff. Sept. 6, 1990. Amended by Acts 1993, 73rd Leg., ch. 900, §1.01, eff. Sept. 1, 1994; Acts 1997, 75th Leg., ch. 1051, §§12, 13, eff. Sept. 1, 1997.

For a quick reference of penalties, see the Chart of Penalties on p. 675.

O'CONNOR'S CRIMINAL CODES   753

PEN §16.06. UNLAWFUL INSTALLATION OF TRACKING DEVICE

(a) In this section:

(1) "Electronic or mechanical tracking device" means a device capable of emitting an electronic frequency or other signal that may be used by a person to identify, monitor, or record the location of another person or object.

(2) "Motor vehicle" has the meaning assigned by Section 501.002, Transportation Code.

(b) A person commits an offense if the person knowingly installs an electronic or mechanical tracking device on a motor vehicle owned or leased by another person.

(c) An offense under this section is a Class A misdemeanor.

(d) It is an affirmative defense to prosecution under this section that the person:

(1) obtained the effective consent of the owner or lessee of the motor vehicle before the electronic or mechanical tracking device was installed;

(2) was a peace officer who installed the device in the course of a criminal investigation or pursuant to an order of a court to gather information for a law enforcement agency;

(3) assisted another whom the person reasonably believed to be a peace officer authorized to install the device in the course of a criminal investigation or pursuant to an order of a court to gather information for a law enforcement agency; or

(4) was a private investigator licensed under Chapter 1702, Occupations Code, who installed the device:

(A) with written consent:

(i) to install the device given by the owner or lessee of the motor vehicle; and

(ii) to enter private residential property, if that entry was necessary to install the device, given by the owner or lessee of the property; or

(B) pursuant to an order of or other authorization from a court to gather information.

History of Pen §16.06: Acts 1999, 76th Leg., ch. 728, §1, eff. Sept. 1, 1999. Amended by Acts 2001, 77th Leg., ch. 1420, §14.828, eff. Sept. 1, 2001.

TITLE 5. OFFENSES AGAINST THE PERSON

CHAPTER 19. CRIMINAL HOMICIDE

PEN §19.01. TYPES OF CRIMINAL HOMICIDE

(a) A person commits criminal homicide if he intentionally, knowingly, recklessly, or with criminal negligence causes the death of an individual.

(b) Criminal homicide is murder, capital murder, manslaughter, or criminally negligent homicide.

History of Pen §19.01: Acts 1973, 63rd Leg., ch. 399, §1, eff. Jan. 1, 1974. Amended by Acts 1973, 63rd Leg., ch. 426, art. 2, §1, eff. Jan. 1, 1974; Acts 1993, 73rd Leg., ch. 900, §1.01, eff. Sept. 1, 1994.

ANNOTATIONS

Womble v. State, 618 S.W.2d 59, 64 (Tex.Crim.App. 1981). "The distinction to be drawn in determining if the homicide is criminal is not whether the act is intentional or unintentional, but whether the act is voluntary or involuntary. A person may act unintentionally and still commit a criminal offense, provided he acts with knowledge, recklessness or negligence. In order for the homicide to be punishable, the evidence must show that the appellant committed a voluntary act with the requisite culpable mental state."

Grotti v. State, 209 S.W.3d 747, 761 (Tex.App.—Fort Worth 2006), aff'd, ___ S.W.3d ___ (Tex.Crim. App.2008) (No. PD-134-07; 6-25-08). "[W]e ... use [H&SC] §671.001(a)'s cardiopulmonary definition of 'death' in conducting our sufficiency review [in a physician's alleged criminally negligent homicide of an ER patient]."

PEN §19.02. MURDER

(a) In this section:

(1) "Adequate cause" means cause that would commonly produce a degree of anger, rage, resentment, or terror in a person of ordinary temper, sufficient to render the mind incapable of cool reflection.

(2) "Sudden passion" means passion directly caused by and arising out of provocation by the individual killed or another acting with the person killed

PEN §16.06

which passion arises at the time of the offense and is not solely the result of former provocation.

(b) A person commits an offense if he:

(1) intentionally or knowingly causes the death of an individual;

(2) intends to cause serious bodily injury and commits an act clearly dangerous to human life that causes the death of an individual; or

(3) commits or attempts to commit a felony, other than manslaughter, and in the course of and in furtherance of the commission or attempt, or in immediate flight from the commission or attempt, he commits or attempts to commit an act clearly dangerous to human life that causes the death of an individual.

(c) Except as provided by Subsection (d), an offense under this section is a felony of the first degree.

(d) At the punishment stage of a trial, the defendant may raise the issue as to whether he caused the death under the immediate influence of sudden passion arising from an adequate cause. If the defendant proves the issue in the affirmative by a preponderance of the evidence, the offense is a felony of the second degree.

History of Pen §19.02: Acts 1973, 63rd Leg., ch. 399, §1, eff. Jan. 1, 1974. Amended by Acts 1973, 63rd Leg., ch. 426, art. 2, §1, eff. Jan. 1, 1974; Acts 1993, 73rd Leg., ch. 900, §1.01, eff. Sept. 1, 1994.

ANNOTATIONS

Generally

Lomax v. State, 233 S.W.3d 302, 303 (Tex.Crim. App.2007). "[F]elony driving while intoxicated (felony DWI) can be the underlying felony in a 'felony-murder' prosecution under §19.02(b)(3)....'" *See also **Hollin v. State***, 227 S.W.3d 117, 120 (Tex.App.—Houston [1st Dist.] 2006, pet. ref'd).

White v. State, 208 S.W.3d 467, 469 (Tex.Crim.App. 2006). "We ... decide that, when an indictment alleges multiple felonies in a prosecution under §19.02(b)(3), these specifically named felonies are not elements about which a jury must be unanimous. These felonies constitute the manner or means that make up the 'felony' element of §19.02(b)(3). We further decide that dispensing with jury unanimity on the felonies alleged in this case does not violate due process because these felonies are 'basically morally and conceptually equivalent.'"

Cook v. State, 884 S.W.2d 485, 491 (Tex.Crim.App. 1994). "Intentional murder ... is a 'result of conduct' offense.... It is error for a trial judge to not limit the

definitions of the culpable mental states as they relate to the conduct elements involved in the particular offense."

Martin v. State, 246 S.W.3d 246, 263 (Tex.App.— Houston [14th Dist.] 2007, no pet.). "Proof of a culpable mental state almost invariably depends upon circumstantial evidence. Intent can be inferred from the extent of the injuries to the victim, the method used to produce the injuries, and the relative size and strength of the parties. In a murder case, evidence of a particularly brutal or ferocious mechanism of death, inflicted upon a helpless victim, can be controlling upon the issue of intent or knowledge. Additionally, culpable mental state can be inferred from the acts, words, and conduct of the accused."

Cleveland v. State, 177 S.W.3d 374, 385-86 (Tex. App.—Houston [1st Dist.] 2005, pet. ref'd). "The State contends that we lack jurisdiction to conduct a legal sufficiency review of a jury's negative finding on the sudden passion issue. *At 387:* [W]e conclude that the proper standard in criminal cases for review of legal sufficiency challenges to a jury's negative finding on an issue that the defendant had to prove is the same standard applied in civil cases. Under that standard, a criminal defendant who attacks the legal sufficiency of the evidence to support a negative finding on an issue that he had to prove must overcome two hurdles. First, the court of appeals must examine the record for evidence that supports the finding while ignoring all evidence to the contrary. Second, if no evidence supports the negative finding, the appellate court examines the entire record to determine whether it establishes the contrary proposition as a matter of law."

Adequate Cause

McCartney v. State, 542 S.W.2d 156, 160 (Tex. Crim.App.1976). "The definition of adequate cause ... is both objective and subjective. It is objective because it views the alleged provocation through the eyes of the ordinary man; it is subjective because the fact-finder must view from the actor's standpoint in order to determine the condition of the mind of the accused at the time of the offense, which is necessitated by the mens rea requirement...." (Internal quotes omitted.)

Lesser Included Offenses

Hall v. State, 225 S.W.3d 524, 536-37 (Tex.Crim. App.2007). "Applying the first step of the lesser included-offense analysis in the instant case ... we consider only the statutory elements of murder as they

For a quick reference of penalties, see the Chart of Penalties on p. 675.

O'CONNOR'S CRIMINAL CODES 755

were modified by the particular allegations in the indictment.... We then compare them with the elements of the lesser offense of aggravated assault by threat that could be included in that offense.... We then ask the question that Article 37.09(a) poses: are the elements of the lesser offense 'established by proof of the same or less than all the facts required to established the commission of the offense charged'? [¶] The answer is that they are not. The facts required to prove the lesser offense include two that are not the same as, or less than, those required to establish the offense charged: threatening and display. [¶] It is true that the evidence may show threatening or display. The evidence may show a number of other lesser offenses as well.... But those offenses likewise are not established by the same or less than the proof required to prove the allegations in the indictment for murder. Aggravated assault by threat ... requires proof of additional facts."

Hayward v. State, 158 S.W.3d 476, 477 (Tex.Crim. App.2005). "[A]n assault using fists is not a lesser-included offense of murder by stabbing."

Schroeder v. State, 123 S.W.3d 398, 398-99 (Tex. Crim.App.2003). "[I]n a prosecution for murder, is a defendant's inability to remember engaging in the charged conduct alone sufficient evidence of recklessness to raise the lesser-included offense of manslaughter? [B]ecause the culpable mental states for both murder (intent) and manslaughter (recklessness) relate to the result of the conduct—the causing of the death—evidence that a defendant does not remember engaging in that conduct does not raise the lesser-included offense."

Lawson v. State, 64 S.W.3d 396, 397 (Tex.Crim. App.2001). "[A] 'conviction for felony murder under §19.02(b)(3)[] will not lie when the underlying felony is manslaughter or a lesser included offense of manslaughter.' [¶] An 'intentional and knowing' aggravated assault is not a lesser included offense of manslaughter, nor is it statutorily includable in manslaughter."

Fry v. State, 915 S.W.2d 554, 559 (Tex.App.—Houston [14th Dist.] 1995, no pet.). "'Self-defense' and 'cool reflection' are not mutually exclusive concepts. An actor who fears for his life may coolly and deliberately dispatch his assailant without panic or hysteria. An instruction on self-defense does not automatically obligate the trial court to give a concomitant charge on voluntary manslaughter."

Sudden Passion

McKinney v. State, 179 S.W.3d 565, 569 (Tex.Crim. App.2005). "[B]efore a defendant is allowed a jury instruction on sudden passion, he must prove that there was an adequate provocation, that a passion or an emotion such as fear, terror, anger, rage, or resentment existed, that the homicide occurred while the passion still existed and before there was reasonable opportunity for the passion to cool; and that there was a causal connection between the provocation, the passion, and the homicide. [¶] A jury should receive a sudden passion charge if it is raised by the evidence, even if that evidence is weak, impeached, contradicted, or unbelievable. However, the evidence cannot be so weak, contested, or incredible that it could not support such a finding by a rational jury."

Sanchez v. State, 23 S.W.3d 30, 33 (Tex.Crim.App. 2000). CCP art. 37.07 "requires the jury to 'agree' on punishment. To 'agree' on punishment means a unanimous vote. The special issue on sudden passion determines the applicable punishment range. We discern no significant distinction between 'punishment' and 'punishment range.' Thus, we conclude that if the jury's answer is not unanimous on the issue of sudden passion, the jury has not 'agreed' on punishment."

Escobedo v. State, 202 S.W.3d 844, 846 (Tex. App.—Waco 2006, pet. ref'd). "Various circumstances may establish a lack of sudden passion: (1) absence of 'provocative conduct, or at least none occurring at the time of the offense,' thus negating adequate cause; (2) provocation *sufficient* to 'render a man of ordinary temper incapable of cool reflection,' but defendant still acted 'coolly and deliberately;' or (3) provocation *insufficient* to 'render a man of ordinary temper incapable of cool reflection,' but that provoked defendant. Where sudden passion is raised by the evidence and the jury renders a murder conviction, the defendant may challenge the sufficiency of the evidence in two distinct ways: 1. Whether the evidence was sufficient to establish the offense of murder; and 2. Whether the evidence was sufficient to disprove the issue of [sudden passion]."

Trevino v. State, 60 S.W.3d 188, 195 (Tex.App.—Fort Worth 2001), *aff'd*, 100 S.W.3d 232 (Tex.Crim.App. 2003). "[I]t has been observed that '[w]hen the defendant raises issues of self-defense during the guilt/innocence phase of trial, the issue of sudden passion is typically also raised.... Accordingly, trial courts should give both instructions when requested.'"

PEN §19.03. CAPITAL MURDER

(a) A person commits an offense if the person commits murder as defined under Section 19.02(b)(1) and:

(1) the person murders a peace officer or fireman who is acting in the lawful discharge of an official duty and who the person knows is a peace officer or fireman;

(2) the person intentionally commits the murder in the course of committing or attempting to commit kidnapping, burglary, robbery, aggravated sexual assault, arson, obstruction or retaliation, or terroristic threat under Section 22.07(a)(1), (3), (4), (5), or (6);

(3) the person commits the murder for remuneration or the promise of remuneration or employs another to commit the murder for remuneration or the promise of remuneration;

(4) the person commits the murder while escaping or attempting to escape from a penal institution;

(5) the person, while incarcerated in a penal institution, murders another:

(A) who is employed in the operation of the penal institution; or

(B) with the intent to establish, maintain, or participate in a combination or in the profits of a combination;

(6) the person:

(A) while incarcerated for an offense under this section or Section 19.02, murders another; or

(B) while serving a sentence of life imprisonment or a term of 99 years for an offense under Section 20.04, 22.021, or 29.03, murders another;

(7) the person murders more than one person:

(A) during the same criminal transaction; or

(B) during different criminal transactions but the murders are committed pursuant to the same scheme or course of conduct;

(8) the person murders an individual under six years of age; or

(9) the person murders another person in retaliation for or on account of the service or status of the other person as a judge or justice of the supreme court, the court of criminal appeals, a court of appeals, a district court, a criminal district court, a constitutional county court, a statutory county court, a justice court, or a municipal court.

(b) An offense under this section is a capital felony.

(c) If the jury or, when authorized by law, the judge does not find beyond a reasonable doubt that the defendant is guilty of an offense under this section, he may be convicted of murder or of any other lesser included offense.

History of Pen §19.03: Acts 1973, 63rd Leg., ch. 426, art. 2, §1, eff. Jan. 1, 1974. Amended by Acts 1983, 68th Leg., ch. 977, §6, eff. Sept. 1, 1983; Acts 1985, 69th Leg., ch. 44, §1, eff. Sept. 1, 1985; Acts 1991, 72nd Leg., ch. 652, §13, eff. Sept. 1, 1991; Acts 1993, 73rd Leg., ch. 715, §1 (eff. Sept. 1, 1993), ch. 887, §1 (eff. Sept. 1, 1993), ch. 900, §1.01 (eff. Sept. 1, 1994); Acts 2003, 78th Leg., ch. 388, §1, eff. Sept. 1, 2003; Acts 2005, 79th Leg., ch. 428, §1, eff. Sept. 1, 2005.

ANNOTATIONS

Saenz v. State, 166 S.W.3d 270, 272 (Tex.Crim.App. 2005). "Unlike other violent offenses, for which the allowable unit of prosecution is each individual victim, the capital murder statute under [§19.03(a)(7)(A)] requires, at minimum, two victims. Thus, an accused may not be charged under the capital murder statute absent 'more than one' homicide. *At 273:* Thus, we conclude the statute reflects that the killing of at least two persons allows the State to charge a single count of capital murder under §19.03(a)(7)(A). *At 274:* [W]e hold that the Double Jeopardy Clause of the Fifth Amendment was violated when the State charged [Saenz] with three separate counts of capital murder under §19.03(a)(7)(A) because the charges rely on the same three murders for each charge."

Hall v. State, 160 S.W.3d 24, 39 (Tex.Crim.App. 2004). "[M]ental retardation is the type of issue that must be proven by the defendant by a preponderance of the evidence—regardless of when the claim is presented."

Rodriguez v. State, 146 S.W.3d 674, 676-77 (Tex. Crim.App.2004). "After reviewing the aggravating factors set out in [Pen. Code] §19.03(a)(1-8), we are persuaded that the legislature's inclusion of the elements of [Pen. Code] §19.02(b)(1) in the capital-murder statute by reference only was not intended to require that the murder be committed in Texas, but was an expression of the legislature's desire to limit capital murder to intentional and knowing murders that are committed in circumstances that the legislature found particularly egregious. [¶] The kidnapping was the required aggravating 'nature of conduct' element that elevated the offense from murder to capital murder. The kidnapping occurred in Texas, thus Texas has territorial jurisdiction over the offense...."

For a quick reference of penalties, see the Chart of Penalties on p. 675.

O'CONNOR'S CRIMINAL CODES 757

Threadgill v. State, 146 S.W.3d 654, 665 (Tex.Crim. App.2004). "The element distinguishing capital murder from felony murder is the intent to kill. Felony murder is an unintentional murder committed in the course of committing a felony while capital murder includes an intentional murder committed in the course of robbery. To be entitled to an instruction on felony murder there must be some evidence that would permit a jury rationally to find the defendant had the intent to commit robbery but not to cause the death of the victim."

Martinez v. State, 129 S.W.3d 101, 103 (Tex.Crim. App.2004). "When an indictment alleges differing methods of committing capital murder [under §19.03(a)(2)] in the conjunctive, the jury may properly be charged in the disjunctive."

Canales v. State, 98 S.W.3d 690, 694 (Tex.Crim. App.2003). "The State argues that it did not have to prove that three or more persons who meet the definition of 'combination' in [Pen. Code] §71.01(a) were involved in the victim's death. The State argues that appellant could have acted alone in murdering the victim and still be guilty of capital murder under §19.03(a)(5)(B) so long as appellant murdered the victim with the intent to participate in a combination as defined by §71.01(a). [¶] We agree."

Black v. State, 26 S.W.3d 895, 897 (Tex.Crim.App. 2000). "We hold that there is no requirement in §19.03(a)(8) that an offender know or intend that his victim be a child under six." *See also* **Ramos v. State**, 961 S.W.2d 637, 638 (Tex.App.—San Antonio 1998, no pet.).

Robertson v. State, 871 S.W.2d 701, 705 (Tex.Crim. App.1993). "This Court has defined 'in the course of committing' an offense ... as conduct occurring in an attempt to commit, during the commission, or in the immediate flight after the attempt or commission of the offense. In order for the murder to qualify as capital murder ... the intent to [commit the offense] must be formed prior to or concurrent with the murder."

Corwin v. State, 870 S.W.2d 23, 28 n.5 (Tex.Crim. App.1993). During the same criminal transaction "was meant to cover 'mass' murders, such as terrorist bombings or the killing of a number of people in a bar at the same time, while [during different criminal transactions but under the same scheme or course of conduct]

was meant to embrace 'serial' murders." *See also* **Heiselbetz v. State**, 906 S.W.2d 500, 506 (Tex.Crim. App.1995).

Turner v. State, 805 S.W.2d 423, 430 (Tex.Crim. App.1991). "Capital murder is defined in terms of one's intent to produce a specified result. Not only must the accused be found to have intended to engage in the act that caused the death, he also must have specifically intended that death result from that conduct; the mere intent to pull the trigger of a firearm will not satisfy the statute." *See also* **Hughes v. State**, 897 S.W.2d 285, 295 (Tex.Crim.App.1994).

Ibanez v. State, 749 S.W.2d 804, 807 (Tex.Crim. App.1986). "The State, in order to obtain a conviction, was bound to prove, beyond a reasonable doubt, that appellant committed the murder during the commission of a robbery. Since the State alleged the same assaultive conduct for both the murder and the robbery, it had to prove that the appellant intentionally strangled the deceased *with the intent to obtain control of the deceased's property*. A killing and unrelated taking of property do not constitute capital murder under 19.03(a)(2): the State must prove a nexus between the murder and the theft, i.e. that the murder occurred in order to facilitate the taking of the property." *See also* **Herrin v. State**, 125 S.W.3d 436, 441 (Tex.Crim.App. 2002).

PEN §19.04. MANSLAUGHTER

(a) A person commits an offense if he recklessly causes the death of an individual.

(b) An offense under this section is a felony of the second degree.

History of Pen §19.04: Acts 1973, 63rd Leg., ch. 399, §1, eff. Jan. 1, 1974. Renumbered from §19.04 by Acts 1973, 63rd Leg., ch. 426, art. 2, §1, eff. Jan. 1, 1974. Amended by Acts 1987, 70th Leg., ch. 307, §1, eff. Sept. 1, 1987. Renumbered from §19.05 and amended by Acts 1993, 73rd Leg., ch. 900, §1.01, eff. Sept. 1, 1994.

ANNOTATIONS

Lawson v. State, 64 S.W.3d 396, 397 (Tex.Crim. App.2001). A "'conviction for felony murder under [Pen. Code] §19.02(b)(3)[] will not lie when the underlying felony is manslaughter or a lesser included offense of manslaughter.' [¶] [T]he issue here is whether an 'intentional and knowing' aggravated assault is a lesser included offense of manslaughter. Manslaughter is defined as recklessly causing an individual's death. The statutory underlying felony with which appellant was charged is an 'intentional and knowing' aggravated assault. An 'intentional and knowing' aggravated assault is not a lesser included offense of manslaughter, nor is it statutorily includable in manslaughter."

Rubio v. State, 203 S.W.3d 448, 452 (Tex.App.—El Paso 2006, pet. ref'd). "Appellant contends that driving while under the influence of alcohol is a separate criminal act of intoxication manslaughter. We disagree. 'Driving under the influence of alcohol' is not the same as 'driving while intoxicated.' The latter suggests a person who was driving in a public place had lost normal use of either mental or physical faculties or had a blood alcohol concentration of .08 or more [under Pen. Code §49.08]. The former suggests a person was driving after having consumed alcohol without requiring any determination as to the illegality of situation. The fact that one may legally drive after consuming alcohol does not prevent the State from alleging the driver was reckless in doing so. Thus, the actions of driving under the influence of alcohol can be used to show a conscious disregard of a substantial risk [under Pen. Code §19.04]."

PEN §19.05. CRIMINALLY NEGLIGENT HOMICIDE

(a) A person commits an offense if he causes the death of an individual by criminal negligence.

(b) An offense under this section is a state jail felony.

History of Pen §19.05: Acts 1973, 63rd Leg., ch. 399, §1, eff. Jan. 1, 1974. Renumbered from §19.06 by Acts 1973, 63rd Leg., ch. 426, art. 2, §1, eff. Jan. 1, 1974. Renumbered from §19.07 and amended by Acts 1993, 73rd Leg., ch. 900, §1.01, eff. Sept. 1, 1994.

ANNOTATIONS

Tello v. State, 180 S.W.3d 150, 158 (Tex.Crim.App. 2005). "[C]riminally negligent homicide requires not only a failure to perceive a risk of death, but also some serious blameworthiness in the conduct that caused it. The risk involved must have been substantial and unjustifiable, and the failure to perceive that risk must have been a gross deviation from reasonable care." (Internal quotes omitted.)

Torres v. State, 52 S.W.3d 285, 287 (Tex.App.—Corpus Christi 2001, no pet.). "[W]ith the modification of the offense of involuntary manslaughter and its placement in chapter 49 … as an intoxication offense, the legislature has clearly dispensed with any mental

state requirement for conviction of intoxication manslaughter. [¶] We hold the trial court did not err in failing to charge the jury on the offense of criminally negligent homicide."

PEN §19.06. APPLICABILITY TO CERTAIN CONDUCT

This chapter does not apply to the death of an unborn child if the conduct charged is:

(1) conduct committed by the mother of the unborn child;

(2) a lawful medical procedure performed by a physician or other licensed health care provider with the requisite consent, if the death of the unborn child was the intended result of the procedure;

(3) a lawful medical procedure performed by a physician or other licensed health care provider with the requisite consent as part of an assisted reproduction as defined by Section 160.102, Family Code; or

(4) the dispensation of a drug in accordance with law or administration of a drug prescribed in accordance with law.

History of Pen §19.06: Acts 2003, 78th Leg., ch. 822, §2.02, eff. Sept. 1, 2003.

History of Former Pen §19.06: Deleted by Acts 1993, 73rd Leg., ch. 900, §1.01, eff. Sept. 1, 1994.

PEN §19.07. RENUMBERED

Renumbered as §19.05 by Acts 1993, 73rd Leg., ch. 900, §1.01, eff. Sept. 1, 1994.

CHAPTER 20. KIDNAPPING & UNLAWFUL RESTRAINT

PEN §20.01. DEFINITIONS

In this chapter:

(1) "Restrain" means to restrict a person's movements without consent, so as to interfere substantially with the person's liberty, by moving the person from one place to another or by confining the person. Restraint is "without consent" if it is accomplished by:

(A) force, intimidation, or deception; or

(B) any means, including acquiescence of the victim, if:

(i) the victim is a child who is less than 14 years of age or an incompetent person and the parent, guardian,

For a quick reference of penalties, see the Chart of Penalties on p. 675.

O'CONNOR'S CRIMINAL CODES 759

or person or institution acting in loco parentis has not acquiesced in the movement or confinement; or

(ii) the victim is a child who is 14 years of age or older and younger than 17 years of age, the victim is taken outside of the state and outside a 120-mile radius from the victim's residence, and the parent, guardian, or person or institution acting in loco parentis has not acquiesced in the movement.

(2) "Abduct" means to restrain a person with intent to prevent his liberation by:

(A) secreting or holding him in a place where he is not likely to be found; or

(B) using or threatening to use deadly force.

(3) "Relative" means a parent or stepparent, ancestor, sibling, or uncle or aunt, including an adoptive relative of the same degree through marriage or adoption.

(4) "Person" means an individual, corporation, or association.

(5) Notwithstanding Section 1.07, "individual" means a human being who has been born and is alive.

History of Pen §20.01: Acts 1973, 63rd Leg., ch. 399, §1, eff. Jan. 1, 1974. Amended by Acts 1999, 76th Leg., ch. 790, §1, eff. Sept. 1, 1999; Acts 2003, 78th Leg., ch. 822, §2.03, eff. Sept. 1, 2003.

ANNOTATIONS

Brimage v. State, 918 S.W.2d 466, 475-76 (Tex. Crim.App.1994). "The State had the burden of proving 1) a restraint made 2) with a specific intent to prevent liberation by either of two particular means. [S]ecretion and the use or threatened use of deadly force are merely two alternative components of the specific intent element. It is therefore not necessary ... that the State prove a restraint accomplished by either secretion or deadly force. Instead, the State must prove that a restraint was completed and that the actor evidenced a specific intent to prevent liberation by either secretion or deadly force."

Miller v. State, 815 S.W.2d 582, 585 (Tex.Crim.App. 1991). "[A]ppellant [is] entitled to an instruction on the defense of mistake of fact if there [is] evidence that through mistake she formed a reasonable belief about a matter of fact and her mistaken belief would negate a conscious objective or desire to abduct the child by restraining the child without parental consent."

Rodriguez v. State, 646 S.W.2d 524, 526 (Tex. App.—Houston [1st Dist.] 1982, no pet.). "The word 'substantial' does not require any minimum length of time for which the victim must be restrained."

PEN §20.02. UNLAWFUL RESTRAINT

(a) A person commits an offense if he intentionally or knowingly restrains another person.

(b) It is an affirmative defense to prosecution under this section that:

(1) the person restrained was a child younger than 14 years of age;

(2) the actor was a relative of the child; and

(3) the actor's sole intent was to assume lawful control of the child.

(c) An offense under this section is a Class A misdemeanor, except that the offense is:

(1) a state jail felony if the person restrained was a child younger than 17 years of age; or

(2) a felony of the third degree if:

(A) the actor recklessly exposes the victim to a substantial risk of serious bodily injury;

(B) the actor restrains an individual the actor knows is a public servant while the public servant is lawfully discharging an official duty or in retaliation or on account of an exercise of official power or performance of an official duty as a public servant; or

(C) the actor while in custody restrains any other person.

(d) It is no offense to detain or move another under this section when it is for the purpose of effecting a lawful arrest or detaining an individual lawfully arrested.

(e) It is an affirmative defense to prosecution under this section that:

(1) the person restrained was a child who is 14 years of age or older and younger than 17 years of age;

(2) the actor does not restrain the child by force, intimidation, or deception; and

(3) the actor is not more than three years older than the child.

History of Pen §20.02: Acts 1973, 63rd Leg., ch. 399, §1, eff. Jan. 1, 1974. Amended by Acts 1993, 73rd Leg., ch. 900, §1.01, eff. Sept. 1, 1994; Acts 1997, 75th Leg., ch. 707, §§1(b), 2, eff. Sept. 1, 1997; Acts 1999, 76th Leg., ch. 790, §2, eff. Sept. 1, 1999; Acts 2001, 77th Leg., ch. 524, §1, eff. Sept. 1, 2001.

PEN §20.01

Ex parte Gutierrez, 600 S.W.2d 933, 935 (Tex. Crim.App.1980). "Both the felony and misdemeanor offenses of false imprisonment are lesser included offenses of kidnapping and aggravated kidnapping."

PEN §20.03. KIDNAPPING

(a) A person commits an offense if he intentionally or knowingly abducts another person.

(b) It is an affirmative defense to prosecution under this section that:

(1) the abduction was not coupled with intent to use or to threaten to use deadly force;

(2) the actor was a relative of the person abducted; and

(3) the actor's sole intent was to assume lawful control of the victim.

(c) An offense under this section is a felony of the third degree.

History of Pen §20.03: Acts 1973, 63rd Leg., ch. 399, §1, eff. Jan. 1, 1974.

Hines v. State, 75 S.W.3d 444, 447 (Tex.Crim.App. 2002). "[N]othing in the Texas [kidnapping] statute ... even *suggests* that it is necessary for the State to prove that a defendant moved his victim a certain distance, or that he held him a specific length of time before he can be found guilty of kidnapping."

Mason v. State, 905 S.W.2d 570, 575 (Tex.Crim. App.1995). "Secretion and the use of deadly force are part of the *mens rea* of kidnapping, not the *actus reus*.... A kidnapping becomes a completed offense when a restraint is accomplished, and there is evidence that the actor intended to prevent liberation and that he intended to do so by either secretion or the use or threatened use of deadly force. Therefore, the State had the burden to prove that a restraint was completed and that the appellant evidenced a specific intent to prevent liberation by either secretion or deadly force."

PEN §20.04. AGGRAVATED KIDNAPPING

(a) A person commits an offense if he intentionally or knowingly abducts another person with the intent to:

(1) hold him for ransom or reward;

(2) use him as a shield or hostage;

(3) facilitate the commission of a felony or the flight after the attempt or commission of a felony;

(4) inflict bodily injury on him or violate or abuse him sexually;

(5) terrorize him or a third person; or

(6) interfere with the performance of any governmental or political function.

(b) A person commits an offense if the person intentionally or knowingly abducts another person and uses or exhibits a deadly weapon during the commission of the offense.

(c) Except as provided by Subsection (d), an offense under this section is a felony of the first degree.

(d) At the punishment stage of a trial, the defendant may raise the issue as to whether he voluntarily released the victim in a safe place. If the defendant proves the issue in the affirmative by a preponderance of the evidence, the offense is a felony of the second degree.

History of Pen §20.04: Acts 1973, 63rd Leg., ch. 399, §1, eff. Jan. 1, 1974. Amended by Acts 1993, 73rd Leg., ch. 900, §1.01, eff. Sept. 1, 1994; Acts 1995, 74th Leg., ch. 318, §4, eff. Sept. 1, 1995.

Brown v. State, 98 S.W.3d 180, 188 (Tex.Crim.App. 2003). "We reject a broad interpretation in favor of a narrow interpretation of 'voluntarily' in §20.04(d) such as the absence 'of rescue by the police [or others] or escape by the [kidnap] victim.' A narrow rather than a broad interpretation of 'voluntarily' in §20.04(d) is likely to effectuate the legislative purpose of §20.04(d) of encouraging kidnappers to release their kidnap victims."

Nolan v. State, 102 S.W.3d 231, 238 (Tex.App.— Houston [14th Dist.] 2003, pet. ref'd). "In assessing whether appellant released his victim in a safe place, we consider the following factors: (1) the remoteness of the location; (2) the proximity of authorities or persons who could aid or assist; (3) the time of day; (4) climatic conditions; (5) the condition of the victim; (6) the character of the location or surrounding neighborhood; and (7) the victim's familiarity with the location or surrounding neighborhood." *See also Rodriguez v. State*, 766 S.W.2d 360, 361 (Tex.App.— Texarkana 1989, pet. ref'd).

For a quick reference of penalties, see the Chart of Penalties on p. 675.

O'CONNOR'S CRIMINAL CODES 761

PEN §20.04

PEN §20.05. UNLAWFUL TRANSPORT

(a) A person commits an offense if the person for pecuniary benefit transports an individual in a manner that:

(1) is designed to conceal the individual from local, state, or federal law enforcement authorities; and

(2) creates a substantial likelihood that the individual will suffer serious bodily injury or death.

(b) An offense under this section is a state jail felony.

History of Pen §20.05: Acts 1999, 76th Leg., ch. 1014, §1, eff. Sept. 1, 1999.

CHAPTER 20A. TRAFFICKING OF PERSONS

§20A.01   Definitions
§20A.02   Trafficking of persons

PEN §20A.01. DEFINITIONS

A *Section 20A.01 below is effective for offenses committed on or after June 15, 2007.*

In this chapter:

(1) "Forced labor or services" means labor or services, including conduct that constitutes an offense under Section 43.02, that are performed or provided by another person and obtained through an actor's:

(A) causing or threatening to cause bodily injury to the person or another person or otherwise causing the person performing or providing labor or services to believe that the person or another person will suffer bodily injury;

(B) restraining or threatening to restrain the person or another person in a manner described by Section 20.01(1) or causing the person performing or providing labor or services to believe that the person or another person will be restrained;

(C) knowingly destroying, concealing, removing, confiscating, or withholding from the person or another person, or threatening to destroy, conceal, remove, confiscate, or withhold from the person or another person, the person's actual or purported:

(i) government records;

(ii) identifying information; or

(iii) personal property;

E (D) threatening the person with abuse of the law or the legal process in relation to the person or another person;

E (E) threatening to report the person or another person to immigration officials or other law enforcement officials or otherwise blackmailing or extorting the person or another person;

E (F) exerting financial control over the person or another person by placing the person or another person under the actor's control as security for a debt to the extent that:

(i) the value of the services provided by the person or another person as reasonably assessed is not applied toward the liquidation of the debt;

(ii) the duration of the services provided by the person or another person is not limited and the nature of the services provided by the person or another person is not defined; or

(iii) the principal amount of the debt does not reasonably reflect the value of the items or services for which the debt was incurred; or

E (G) using any scheme, plan, or pattern intended to cause the person to believe that the person or another person will be subjected to serious harm or restraint if the person does not perform or provide the labor or services.

(2) "Traffic" means to transport, entice, recruit, harbor, provide, or otherwise obtain another person by any means.

History of Pen §20A.01: Acts 2003, 78th Leg., ch. 641, §2, eff. Sept. 1, 2003. Amended by Acts 2007, 80th Leg., ch. 258, §16.01 (eff. Sept. 1, 2007), ch. 849, §4 (eff. June. 15, 2007).

PEN §20A.01. DEFINITIONS

Section 20A.01 below is effective for offenses in which any element of the offense was committed before June 15, 2007.

In this chapter:

(1) "Forced labor or services" means labor or services that are performed or provided by another person and obtained through an actor's:

(A) threatening to cause bodily injury to another;

(B) restraining another in a manner described by Section 20.01(1); or

(C) withholding from another the person's:

(i) government records;

(ii) identifying information; or

(iii) personal property.

(2) "Traffic" means to transport another person or to entice, recruit, harbor, provide, or otherwise obtain another person for transport by deception, coercion, or force.

PEN §20A.02. TRAFFICKING OF PERSONS

A *Subsections (a) & (b) below are effective for offenses committed on or after June 15, 2007.*

(a) A person commits an offense if the person:

(1) knowingly traffics another person with the intent or knowledge that the trafficked person will engage in forced labor or services; or

(2) intentionally or knowingly benefits from participating in a venture that involves an activity described by Subdivision (1), including by receiving labor or services the person knows are forced labor or services.

(b) Except as otherwise provided by this subsection, an offense under this section is a felony of the second degree. An offense under this section is a felony of the first degree if:

(1) the applicable conduct constitutes an offense under Section 43.02 and the person who is trafficked is younger than 18 years of age at the time of the offense; or

(2) the commission of the offense results in the death of the person who is trafficked.

Subsections (a) & (b) below are effective for offenses in which any element of the offense was committed before June 15, 2007.

(a) A person commits an offense if the person knowingly traffics another person with the intent that the trafficked person engage in:

(1) forced labor or services; or

(2) conduct that constitutes an offense under Chapter 43.

(b) Except as otherwise provided by this subsection, an offense under this section is a felony of the second degree. An offense under this section is a felony of the first degree if:

(1) the offense is committed under Subsection (a)(2) and the person who is trafficked is younger than 14 years of age at the time of the offense; or

(2) the commission of the offense results in the death of the person who is trafficked.

(c) If conduct constituting an offense under this section also constitutes an offense under another section of this code, the actor may be prosecuted under either section or under both sections.

History of Pen §20A.02: Acts 2003, 78th Leg., ch. 641, §2, eff. Sept. 1, 2003; Acts 2007, 80th Leg., ch. 258, §16.02 (eff. Sept. 1, 2007), ch. 849, §5 (eff. June 15, 2007).

CHAPTER 21. SEXUAL OFFENSES

For the admissibility of evidence of extraneous acts or offenses, see CCP art. 38.37.

PEN §21.01. DEFINITIONS

In this chapter:

(1) "Deviate sexual intercourse" means:

(A) any contact between any part of the genitals of one person and the mouth or anus of another person; or

(B) the penetration of the genitals or the anus of another person with an object.

(2) "Sexual contact" means, except as provided by Section 21.11, any touching of the anus, breast, or any part of the genitals of another person with intent to arouse or gratify the sexual desire of any person.

(3) "Sexual intercourse" means any penetration of the female sex organ by the male sex organ.

(4) "Spouse" means a person to whom a person is legally married under Subtitle A, Title 1, Family Code, or a comparable law of another jurisdiction.

History of Pen §21.01: Acts 1973, 63rd Leg., ch. 399, §1, eff. Jan. 1, 1974. Amended by Acts 1979, 66th Leg., ch. 168, §1, eff. Aug. 27, 1979; Acts 1981, 67th Leg., p. 203, ch. 96, §3, eff. Sept. 1, 1981; Acts 2001, 77th Leg., ch. 739, §1, eff. Sept. 1, 2001; Acts 2005, 79th Leg., ch. 268, §1.124, eff. Sept. 1, 2005.

ANNOTATIONS

Deviate Sexual Intercourse
Donoho v. State, 643 S.W.2d 698, 700 (Tex.Crim. App.1982). Under the definition of deviate sexual intercourse, "we hold that 'any contact between' a part of the genitals of one person and the mouth of another person contemplates ... either penetration of the mouth by bared genitalia or placing the mouth directly *on* genitalia of another human being. [T]he conduct of appellant [whose contact with genitalia was through a layer of

For a quick reference of penalties, see the Chart of Penalties on p. 675.

O'CONNOR'S CRIMINAL CODES   763

PEN §21.01

clothing] did not constitute an act of deviate sexual intercourse within the meaning of … §21.01(1)."

Coachman v. State, 692 S.W.2d 940, 942 (Tex. App.—Houston [1st Dist.] 1985, pet. ref'd). "Appellant asserts that a finger is not an 'object' and therefore the indictment fails to state [the] offense [of deviate sexual intercourse]. [¶] [D]eviate sexual intercourse … means 'the penetration of the genitals or the anus of another person with any object, animate or inanimate, other than the male sex organ.'" Held: Finger is an object.

Sexual Contact

Carmell v. State, 963 S.W.2d 833, 837 (Tex.App.—Fort Worth 1998, pet. ref'd), *rev'd on other grounds*, 529 U.S. 513, 120 S.Ct. 1620 (2000). "Indecency with a child requires 'sexual contact' between the victim and the defendant. … The external genital organs include the mons pubis, which is 'the rounded eminence in front of the pubic symphysis [that] is formed by a collection of fatty tissue beneath the integument. It becomes covered with hair at the time of puberty.' Thus, by touching K.M.'s pubic hair, appellant touched a part of her genitals."

Williams v. State, 911 S.W.2d 788, 790 (Tex. App.—San Antonio 1995, no pet.). "'Where the child has sufficiently communicated to the trier of fact that the touching occurred to a part of the body within the definition of §21.01, the evidence will be sufficient to support a conviction regardless of the unsophisticated language that the child uses.' [¶] [C]omplainant children testified about the sexual contacts by [D] using terms like 'dick,' 'penis,' and 'private part.' [C]omplainant children 'sufficiently communicated to the trier of fact that the touching occurred to a part of the body within the definition of §21.01'.…"

Pierce v. State, 733 S.W.2d 314, 318 (Tex.App.—Tyler 1987, no pet.). "[I]t is clear that the definition of 'Sexual Contact' set forth in §21.01 is limited to the sexual offenses defined in Chapter 21 of Title 5 of the [Pen. Code]."

Wright v. State, 693 S.W.2d 734, 735 (Tex.App.—Dallas 1985, pet. ref'd). In the definition of sexual contact, "[n]owhere does the [Pen. Code] criminalize the touching of the buttocks. Instead, the touching of the 'anus' is specified. [T]he two words are [not] analogous. The practice commentary to §21.01 notes: 'Anus'

… is intended in its strict anatomical sense—the posterior opening of the alimentary canal—thus excluding the buttocks."

Hilliard v. State, 652 S.W.2d 602, 605 (Tex.App.—Austin 1983, pet. ref'd). "[A]ppellant's motion to quash [the indictment] challenges the sufficiency of the notice afforded by the word 'touching' which is found within the definition of 'sexual contact.' The method by which appellant 'touched' the complainant, is essentially evidentiary. '[I]n [any] manner employed, the defendant must use his body directly or indirectly to commit the offense.'"

PEN §21.02. CONTINUOUS SEXUAL ABUSE OF YOUNG CHILD OR CHILDREN

 Section 21.02 below is effective for offenses committed on or after Sept. 1, 2007.

(a) In this section, "child" has the meaning assigned by Section 22.011(c).

(b) A person commits an offense if:

(1) during a period that is 30 or more days in duration, the person commits two or more acts of sexual abuse, regardless of whether the acts of sexual abuse are committed against one or more victims; and

(2) at the time of the commission of each of the acts of sexual abuse, the actor is 17 years of age or older and the victim is a child younger than 14 years of age.

(c) For purposes of this section, "act of sexual abuse" means any act that is a violation of one or more of the following penal laws:

(1) aggravated kidnapping under Section 20.04(a)(4), if the actor committed the offense with the intent to violate or abuse the victim sexually;

(2) indecency with a child under Section 21.11(a)(1), if the actor committed the offense in a manner other than by touching, including touching through clothing, the breast of a child;

(3) sexual assault under Section 22.011;

(4) aggravated sexual assault under Section 22.021;

(5) burglary under Section 30.02, if the offense is punishable under Subsection (d) of that section and the actor committed the offense with the intent to commit an offense listed in Subdivisions (1)-(4); and

(6) sexual performance by a child under Section 43.25.

(d) If a jury is the trier of fact, members of the jury are not required to agree unanimously on which specific acts of sexual abuse were committed by the defendant or the exact date when those acts were committed. The jury must agree unanimously that the defendant, during a period that is 30 or more days in duration, committed two or more acts of sexual abuse.

(e) A defendant may not be convicted in the same criminal action of an offense listed under Subsection (c) the victim of which is the same victim as a victim of the offense alleged under Subsection (b) unless the offense listed in Subsection (c):

(1) is charged in the alternative;

(2) occurred outside the period in which the offense alleged under Subsection (b) was committed; or

(3) is considered by the trier of fact to be a lesser included offense of the offense alleged under Subsection (b).

(f) A defendant may not be charged with more than one count under Subsection (b) if all of the specific acts of sexual abuse that are alleged to have been committed are alleged to have been committed against a single victim.

(g) It is an affirmative defense to prosecution under this section that the actor:

(1) was not more than five years older than:

(A) the victim of the offense, if the offense is alleged to have been committed against only one victim; or

(B) the youngest victim of the offense, if the offense is alleged to have been committed against more than one victim;

(2) did not use duress, force, or a threat against a victim at the time of the commission of any of the acts of sexual abuse alleged as an element of the offense; and

(3) at the time of the commission of any of the acts of sexual abuse alleged as an element of the offense:

(A) was not required under Chapter 62, Code of Criminal Procedure, to register for life as a sex offender; or

(B) was not a person who under Chapter 62 had a reportable conviction or adjudication for an offense under this section or an act of sexual abuse as described by Subsection (c).

(h) An offense under this section is a felony of the first degree, punishable by imprisonment in the Texas Department of Criminal Justice for life, or for any term of not more than 99 years or less than 25 years.

History of Pen §21.02: Acts 2007, 80th Leg., ch. 593, §1.17, eff. Sept. 1, 2007.

PEN §§21.03 TO 21.05. REPEALED

Repealed by Acts 1983, 68th Leg., ch. 997, §12, eff. Sept. 1, 1983.

PEN §21.06. HOMOSEXUAL CONDUCT

*Section 21.06 below was declared unconstitutional by the U.S. Supreme Court on grounds of violation of due process in **Lawrence v. Texas**, 539 U.S. 558, 123 S.Ct. 2472 (2003), below.*

(a) A person commits an offense if he engages in deviate sexual intercourse with another individual of the same sex.

(b) An offense under this section is a Class C misdemeanor.

History of Pen §21.06: Acts 1973, 63rd Leg., ch. 399, §1, eff. Jan. 1, 1974.

ANNOTATIONS

Lawrence v. Texas, 539 U.S. 558, 578, 123 S.Ct. 2472, 2484 (2003). "The Texas statute furthers no legitimate state interest which can justify its intrusion into the personal and private life of the individual."

PEN §21.07. PUBLIC LEWDNESS

(a) A person commits an offense if he knowingly engages in any of the following acts in a public place or, if not in a public place, he is reckless about whether another is present who will be offended or alarmed by his:

(1) act of sexual intercourse;

(2) act of deviate sexual intercourse;

(3) act of sexual contact; or

(4) act involving contact between the person's mouth or genitals and the anus or genitals of an animal or fowl.

(b) An offense under this section is a Class A misdemeanor.

History of Pen §21.07: Acts 1973, 63rd Leg., ch. 399, §1, eff. Jan. 1, 1974. Amended by Acts 1993, 73rd Leg., ch. 900, §1.01, eff. Sept. 1, 1994.

See also CCP arts. 38.072, 38.37.

ANNOTATIONS

Hines v. State, 906 S.W.2d 518, 522 (Tex.Crim.App. 1995). "[J]udging by the structure and language of the statute as a whole, it is almost certain that the Legislature contemplated that the 'person other than the actor'

For a quick reference of penalties, see the Chart of Penalties on p. 675.

O'CONNOR'S CRIMINAL CODES **765**

PEN §21.07

... would be someone other than both the actor *and* the person with whom the actor engages in one of the enumerated sexual acts."

Cammack v. State, 641 S.W.2d 906, 908 (Tex.Crim. App.1982). "The question is whether [a viewing booth in a bookstore, adult book shop, or newsstand containing a movie section with individual booths showing peep shows] was a public place within the meaning of [Pen. Code] §21.07. [¶] The public nature of the booth [cannot] be changed by the appellant, acting alone, closing and locking the door, closeting himself with a stranger."

Smykay v. State, 898 S.W.2d 350, 351 (Tex. App.—San Antonio 1995, pet. ref'd). "The court knows of no cases where a person has been successfully convicted of public lewdness and the act occurred in a private place with no one present except the actor and the victim. ... If every unwanted sexual overture that took place in a private place made the actor guilty of public lewdness, the State would be gripped in a giant crime wave. The government intrusion on private lives would be intolerable because it would reach into the parlor of every home."

Balash v. State, 720 S.W.2d 878, 879 (Tex.App.— Houston [14th Dist.] 1986, pet. ref'd). "Intent to arouse or gratify sexual desire may be inferred from the surrounding circumstances."

Honeycutt v. State, 690 S.W.2d 64, 65 (Tex.App.— Houston [14th Dist.] 1985, pet. ref'd). "[T]he determination of whether the interior of a car is a public place [under the Pen. Code] must be made on a case-by-case basis."

Westbrook v. State, 624 S.W.2d 294, 295-96 (Tex. App.—Dallas 1981, no pet.). "The culpable mental state of 'knowingly' as prescribed by the statute applies to the sexual contact and not to the place where such act was committed."

PEN §21.08. INDECENT EXPOSURE

(a) A person commits an offense if he exposes his anus or any part of his genitals with intent to arouse or gratify the sexual desire of any person, and he is reckless about whether another is present who will be offended or alarmed by his act.

(b) An offense under this section is a Class B misdemeanor.

History of Pen §21.08: Acts 1973, 63rd Leg., ch. 399, §1, eff. Jan. 1, 1974. Amended by Acts 1983, 68th Leg., p. 509, ch. 924, §1, eff. Sept. 1, 1983.

See also CCP arts. 38.072, 38.37.

Hankins v. State, 85 S.W.3d 433, 436-37 (Tex. App.—Corpus Christi 2002, no pet.). "A charge of indecent exposure requires the State to allege circumstances which indicate the appellant was aware of the risk that another person was present who would be offended by the exposure and that the appellant acted in conscious disregard of that risk."

Hefner v. State, 934 S.W.2d 855, 857 (Tex.App.— Houston [1st Dist.] 1996, pet. ref'd). "The statute does not require ... that appellant offend [the arresting officer]. [T]he person 'to whom the offense is directed is not an essential element.' The issue ... is whether appellant was reckless about whether another was present who would be offended, not whether [the arresting officer] was offended. [¶] This objective standard is viewed through the eyes of the ordinary person standing in appellant's shoes."

Beasley v. State, 906 S.W.2d 270, 272 (Tex.App.— Beaumont 1995, no pet.). "Since appellant effectively hid his genitals from view ... there was no exposure within the meaning of the statute." *But see Metts v. State*, 22 S.W.3d 544, 547 (Tex.App.—Fort Worth 2000, pet. ref'd).

Baggett v. State, 860 S.W.2d 207, 209 (Tex.App.— Houston [1st Dist.] 1993, no pet.). "[A]ppellant committed a single act of exposure to four different people. [¶] The State would have been justified in indicting, prosecuting, and punishing him for four acts of indecent exposure or two acts of indecent exposure and two acts of indecency with a child. The essence of this multiple prosecution is that each offense required proof of a fact that the others did not: the identity of the victim."

PEN §§21.09 TO 21.10. REPEALED

Repealed by Acts 1983, 68th Leg., ch. 997, §12, eff. Sept. 1, 1983.

PEN §21.11. INDECENCY WITH A CHILD

(a) A person commits an offense if, with a child younger than 17 years and not the person's spouse, whether the child is of the same or opposite sex, the person:

(1) engages in sexual contact with the child or causes the child to engage in sexual contact; or

(2) with intent to arouse or gratify the sexual desire of any person:

(A) exposes the person's anus or any part of the person's genitals, knowing the child is present; or

(B) causes the child to expose the child's anus or any part of the child's genitals.

(b) It is an affirmative defense to prosecution under this section that the actor:

(1) was not more than three years older than the victim and of the opposite sex;

(2) did not use duress, force, or a threat against the victim at the time of the offense; and

(3) at the time of the offense:

(A) was not required under Chapter 62, Code of Criminal Procedure, to register for life as a sex offender; or

(B) was not a person who under Chapter 62 had a reportable conviction or adjudication for an offense under this section.

(c) In this section, "sexual contact" means the following acts, if committed with the intent to arouse or gratify the sexual desire of any person:

(1) any touching by a person, including touching through clothing, of the anus, breast, or any part of the genitals of a child; or

(2) any touching of any part of the body of a child, including touching through clothing, with the anus, breast, or any part of the genitals of a person.

(d) An offense under Subsection (a)(1) is a felony of the second degree and an offense under Subsection (a)(2) is a felony of the third degree.

History of Pen §21.11: Acts 1973, 63rd Leg., ch. 399, §1, eff. Jan. 1, 1974. Amended by Acts 1981, 67th Leg., ch. 202, §3, eff. Sept. 1, 1981; Acts 1987, 70th Leg., ch. 1028, §1, eff. Sept. 1, 1987; Acts 1993, 73rd Leg., ch. 900, §1.01, eff. Sept. 1, 1994; Acts 1999, 76th Leg., ch. 1415, §23, eff. Sept. 1, 1999; Acts 2001, 77th Leg., ch. 739, §2, eff. Sept. 1, 2001.

See also CCP arts. 38.072, 38.37; Pen §3.03.

ANNOTATIONS

Pizzo v. State, 235 S.W.3d 711, 719 (Tex.Crim.App. 2007). "[T]he offense of indecency with a child by contact in [§21.11(a)(1)] is a conduct-oriented offense. 'Sexual contact,' as defined in [§21.01(2)], criminalizes three separate types of conduct—touching the anus, touching the breast, and touching the genitals with the requisite mental state. Therefore, each act constitutes a different criminal offense and juror unanimity is required as to the commission of any one of these acts."

Patterson v. State, 152 S.W.3d 88, 89 (Tex.Crim. App.2004). "'Where a defendant is convicted of the offense of indecency with a child by exposure and also of the offense of aggravated sexual assault of a child, is the indecency conviction barred by double jeopardy if that exposure occurred prior to the aggravated sexual assault and during the defendant's unsuccessful attempt to commit a third offense that, if completed, would not have been jeopardy barred?'" Held: Yes, the charge of indecency with a child by exposure is barred.

Johnson v. State, 967 S.W.2d 848, 850 (Tex.Crim. App.1998). "[T]he State is not required to show that appellant knew the victim to be under the age of 17."

Scott v. State, 202 S.W.3d 405, 407 (Tex.App.— Texarkana 2006, pet. ref'd). "The offense of indecency with a child requires proof of the accused's intent to engage in the proscribed contact, rather than intent to bring about a particular result. *At 408:* [T]he fact-finder can infer the requisite intent to arouse or gratify the sexual desire from conduct, remarks, or all the surrounding circumstances. The intent to arouse or gratify may be inferred from conduct alone. No oral expression of intent or visible evidence of sexual arousal is necessary. *At 410:* [W]e conclude [child's] use of the term 'private areas' and her failure to use the technical term 'genitals' does not render the evidence legally or factually insufficient."

Means v. State, 955 S.W.2d 686, 691 (Tex.App.— Amarillo 1997, pet. ref'd). "It cannot be said that ... touching ['with intent to arouse or gratify the sexual desire of any person'] occurs if the touching is accidental. Simply put, one cannot intentionally do something accidentally or accidentally do something intentionally. So, the acts of accidental touching constitute no evidence that appellant touched [alleged victim] with the intent to arouse or gratify sexual desire."

Castillo v. State, 771 S.W.2d 239, 240-41 (Tex. App.—San Antonio 1989, no pet.). "[I]ndecency with a child pursuant to §21.11(a)(2) requires the defendant to know that a child is present. In addition, it must be established that the defendant had the intent to arouse or gratify the sexual desire of any person."

Guia v. State, 723 S.W.2d 763, 766 (Tex.App.— Dallas 1986, pet. ref'd). "Appellant ... argues that he did not engage in sexual contact because at the time of the touching the complainant was fully clothed. [T]he mere interposition of a layer of fabric between a person's hand and the genitals of another did not prevent

For a quick reference of penalties, see the Chart of Penalties on p. 675.

O'CONNOR'S CRIMINAL CODES 767

the occurrence of sexual contact because the touching will still engender the sense of feeling perceived by the person touched. [¶] If the mere interposition of a layer of fabric does not prevent the occurrence of sexual contact for the offense of public lewdness, it should not prevent the occurrence of sexual contact for the offense of indecency with a child."

PEN §21.12. IMPROPER RELATIONSHIP BETWEEN EDUCATOR & STUDENT

(a) An employee of a public or private primary or secondary school commits an offense if the employee engages in:

(1) sexual contact, sexual intercourse, or deviate sexual intercourse with a person who is enrolled in a public or private primary or secondary school at which the employee works and who is not the employee's spouse; or

E *Subsection (2) below is effective for offenses committed on or after Sept. 1, 2007.*

(2) conduct described by Section 33.021, with a person described by Subdivision (1), regardless of the age of that person.

(b) An offense under this section is a felony of the second degree.

(c) If conduct constituting an offense under this section also constitutes an offense under another section of this code, the actor may be prosecuted under either section or both sections.

E (d) The name of a person who is enrolled in a public or private primary or secondary school and involved in an improper relationship with an educator as provided by Subsection (a) may not be released to the public and is not public information under Chapter 552, Government Code.

History of Pen §21.12: Acts 2003, 78th Leg., ch. 224, §1, eff. Sept. 1, 2003. Amended by Acts 2007, 80th Leg., ch. 610, §1 (eff. Sept. 1, 2007), ch. 772, §1 (eff. Sept. 1, 2007).

History of Former Pen §21.12: Repealed by Acts 1983, 68th Leg., ch. 997, §12, eff. Sept. 1, 1983.

See also CCP arts. 38.072, 38.37.

PEN §21.13. RENUMBERED

Renumbered as §22.065 by Acts 1983, 68th Leg., ch. 997, §4, eff. Sept. 1, 1983.

PEN §21.14. DELETED

Deleted by Acts 1993, 73rd Leg., ch. 900, §1.01, eff. Sept. 1, 1994.

PEN §21.15. IMPROPER PHOTOGRAPHY OR VISUAL RECORDING

(a) In this section, "promote" has the meaning assigned by Section 43.21.

 Subsection (b) below is effective for offenses committed on or after Sept. 1, 2007.

(b) A person commits an offense if the person:

(1) photographs or by videotape or other electronic means records, broadcasts, or transmits a visual image of another at a location that is not a bathroom or private dressing room:

(A) without the other person's consent; and

(B) with intent to arouse or gratify the sexual desire of any person;

E (2) photographs or by videotape or other electronic means records, broadcasts, or transmits a visual image of another at a location that is a bathroom or private dressing room:

(A) without the other person's consent; and

(B) with intent to:

(i) invade the privacy of the other person; or

(ii) arouse or gratify the sexual desire of any person; or

(3) knowing the character and content of the photograph, recording, broadcast, or transmission, promotes a photograph, recording, broadcast, or transmission described by Subdivision (1) or (2).

Subsection (b) below is effective for offenses in which any element of the offense was committed before Sept. 1, 2007.

(b) A person commits an offense if the person:

(1) photographs or by videotape or other electronic means visually records another:

(A) without the other person's consent; and

(B) with intent to arouse or gratify the sexual desire of any person; or

(2) knowing the character and content of the photograph or recording, promotes a photograph or visual recording described by Subdivision (1).

(c) An offense under this section is a state jail felony.

(d) If conduct that constitutes an offense under this section also constitutes an offense under any other law, the actor may be prosecuted under this section or the other law.

———————— ★ ————————

 Subsection (e) below is effective for offenses committed on or after Sept. 1, 2007.

(e) For purposes of Subsection (b)(2), a sign or signs posted indicating that the person is being photographed or that a visual image of the person is being recorded, broadcast, or transmitted is not sufficient to establish the person's consent under that subdivision.

History of Pen §21.15: Acts 2001, 77th Leg., ch. 458, §1, eff. Sept. 1, 2001. Amended by Acts 2003, 78th Leg., ch. 500, §1, eff. Sept. 1, 2003; Acts 2007, 80th Leg., ch. 306, §1, eff. Sept. 1, 2007.

See also CCP arts. 38.072, 38.37.

CHAPTER 22. ASSAULTIVE OFFENSES

For the admissibility of evidence of extraneous acts or offenses, see CCP art. 38.37.

PEN §22.01. ASSAULT

(a) A person commits an offense if the person:

(1) intentionally, knowingly, or recklessly causes bodily injury to another, including the person's spouse;

(2) intentionally or knowingly threatens another with imminent bodily injury, including the person's spouse; or

(3) intentionally or knowingly causes physical contact with another when the person knows or should reasonably believe that the other will regard the contact as offensive or provocative.

(b) An offense under Subsection (a)(1) is a Class A misdemeanor, except that the offense is a felony of the third degree if the offense is committed against:

(1) a person the actor knows is a public servant while the public servant is lawfully discharging an official duty, or in retaliation or on account of an exercise of official power or performance of an official duty as a public servant;

(2) a person whose relationship to or association with the defendant is described by Section 71.0021(b), 71.003, or 71.005, Family Code, if it is shown on the trial of the offense that the defendant has been previously convicted of an offense under this chapter, Chapter 19, or Section 20.03, 20.04, or 21.11 against a person whose relationship to or association with the defendant is described by Section 71.0021(b), 71.003, or 71.005, Family Code;

(3) a person who contracts with government to perform a service in a facility as defined by Section 1.07(a)(14), Penal Code, or Section 51.02(13) or (14), Family Code, or an employee of that person:

(A) while the person or employee is engaged in performing a service within the scope of the contract, if the actor knows the person or employee is authorized by government to provide the service; or

(B) in retaliation for or on account of the person's or employee's performance of a service within the scope of the contract;

(4) a person the actor knows is a security officer while the officer is performing a duty as a security officer; or

 Subsection (5) below is effective for offenses committed on or after Sept. 1, 2007.

(5) a person the actor knows is emergency services personnel while the person is providing emergency services.

(c) An offense under Subsection (a)(2) or (3) is a Class C misdemeanor, except that the offense is:

(1) a Class A misdemeanor if the offense is committed under Subsection (a)(3) against an elderly individual or disabled individual, as those terms are defined by Section 22.04; or

(2) a Class B misdemeanor if the offense is committed by a person who is not a sports participant against a person the actor knows is a sports participant either:

(A) while the participant is performing duties or responsibilities in the participant's capacity as a sports participant; or

(B) in retaliation for or on account of the participant's performance of a duty or responsibility within the participant's capacity as a sports participant.

 Subsection (d) below is effective for offenses committed on or after Sept. 1, 2007.

(d) For purposes of Subsection (b), the actor is presumed to have known the person assaulted was a public

For a quick reference of penalties, see the Chart of Penalties on p. 675.

O'CONNOR'S CRIMINAL CODES   769

PEN §22.01

servant, a security officer, or emergency services personnel if the person was wearing a distinctive uniform or badge indicating the person's employment as a public servant or status as a security officer or emergency services personnel.

Subsection (d) below is effective for offenses in which any element of the offense was committed before Sept. 1, 2007.

(d) For purposes of Subsection (b), the actor is presumed to have known the person assaulted was a public servant or a security officer if the person was wearing a distinctive uniform or badge indicating the person's employment as a public servant or status as a security officer.

(e) In this section:

E *Subsection (1) below is effective for offenses committed on or after Sept. 1, 2007.*

(1) "Emergency services personnel" includes firefighters, emergency medical services personnel as defined by Section 773.003, Health and Safety Code, and other individuals who, in the course and scope of employment or as a volunteer, provide services for the benefit of the general public during emergency situations.

(2) Repealed by Acts 2005, 79th Leg., ch. 788, §6, eff. Sept. 1, 2005.

(3) "Security officer" means a commissioned security officer as defined by Section 1702.002, Occupations Code, or a noncommissioned security officer registered under Section 1702.221, Occupations Code.

(4) "Sports participant" means a person who participates in any official capacity with respect to an interscholastic, intercollegiate, or other organized amateur or professional athletic competition and includes an athlete, referee, umpire, linesman, coach, instructor, administrator, or staff member.

(f) For the purposes of Subsection (b)(2):

(1) a defendant has been previously convicted of an offense listed in Subsection (b)(2) committed against a person whose relationship to or association with the defendant is described by Section 71.0021(b), 71.003, or 71.005, Family Code, if the defendant was adjudged guilty of the offense or entered a plea of guilty or nolo contendere in return for a grant of deferred adjudication, regardless of whether the sentence for the offense was ever imposed or whether the sentence was probated and the defendant was subsequently discharged from community supervision; and

(2) a conviction under the laws of another state for an offense containing elements that are substantially similar to the elements of an offense listed in Subsection (b)(2) is a conviction of an offense listed in Subsection (b)(2).

History of Pen §22.01: Acts 1973, 63rd Leg., ch. 399, §1, eff. Jan. 1, 1974. Amended by Acts 1977, 65th Leg., 1st C.S., ch. 2, §§12, 13, eff. July 22, 1977; Acts 1979, 66th Leg., ch. 135, §§1, 2 (eff. Aug. 27, 1979), ch. 164, §2 (eff. Sept. 1, 1979); Acts 1983, 68th Leg., ch. 977, §1, eff. Sept. 1, 1983; Acts 1987, 70th Leg., ch. 1052, §2.08, eff. Sept. 1, 1987; Acts 1989, 71st Leg., ch. 739, §§1-3, eff. Sept. 1, 1989; Acts 1991, 72nd Leg., ch. 14, §284(23)-(26) (eff. Sept. 1, 1991), ch. 334, §1 (eff. Sept. 1, 1991), ch. 366, §1 (eff. Sept. 1, 1991); Acts 1993, 73rd Leg., ch. 900, §1.01, eff. Sept. 1, 1994; Acts 1995, 74th Leg., ch. 318, §5 (eff. Sept. 1, 1995), ch. 659, §1 (eff. Sept. 1, 1995); Acts 1997, 75th Leg., ch. 165, §§27.01, 31.01(68), eff. Sept. 1, 1997; Acts 1999, 76th Leg., ch. 62, §15.02(a) (eff. Sept. 1, 1999), ch. 1158, §1 (eff. Sept. 1, 1999); Acts 2003, 78th Leg., ch. 294, §1 (eff. Sept. 1, 2003), ch. 1019, §§1, 2 (eff. Sept. 1, 2003), ch. 1028, §1 (eff. Sept. 1, 2003); Acts 2005, 79th Leg., ch. 728, §§16.001, 16.00 (eff. Sept. 1, 2005), ch. 788, §§1, 2, 6 (eff. Sept. 1, 2005); Acts 2007, 80th Leg., ch. 623, §§1, 2, eff. Sept. 1, 2007.

See also CCP arts. 38.072, 38.37.

ANNOTATIONS

Olivas v. State, 203 S.W.3d 341, 345 (Tex.Crim.App. 2006). Section 22.01(a)(2) "does not explicitly indicate whether the intended victim must perceive or receive the threat. The question turns on the meaning of the term 'threaten' as used in the Penal Code. Does it mean an act that must be perceived by the intended victim? Or must the actor only act with the intent that the victim perceive his threat? *At 347:* In our view the better position holds that although the question whether the defendant's conduct produced fear in the victim is relevant, the crucial inquiry remains whether the assailant acted in such a manner as would under the circumstances portend an immediate threat of danger to a person of reasonable sensibility."

Hall v. State, 158 S.W.3d 470, 471 (Tex.Crim.App. 2005). "[I]f there is record evidence that demonstrates a public officer is *unlawfully* discharging his official duties at the time a person assaults him, the defendant is entitled to a lesser-included charge. But because appellant did not offer evidence that [officer] acted 'unlawfully,' we affirm the judgment of the court of appeals."

Edison v. State, 235 S.W.3d 305, ___ (Tex.App.— Beaumont 2008, no pet.). "State may use the defendant's judicial confession to show that the defendant was previously convicted of an offense against a member of the family or household [under §22.01(b)(2)]. The previous conviction for assault against a family or household member must be shown at trial to elevate the offense from a Class A misdemeanor to a third degree felony. We do not agree that the prior conviction simply results in a punishment enhancement for a misdemeanor offense." *But see* ***State v. Cagle***, 77 S.W.3d 344, 346 n.1-2 (Tex.App.—Houston [14th Dist.] 2002, pet. ref'd) (a prior assault is a sentence enhancement, rather than an element of the offense).

Haynes v. State, ___ S.W.3d ___ (Tex.App.—Houston [1st Dist.] 2007) (No. 01-05-00803-CR; 2-20-07), *aff'd*, ___ S.W.3d ___ (Tex.Crim.App.2008) (No. PD-1923-06; 4-30-08). "We hold that [Pen. Code] §22.01, which expressly refers to [Fam. Code] §71.005, does not authorize the State to use [Fam. Code] §71.006 to define who constitutes a household member for the purposes of committing felony assault. The State, therefore, must prove as an element of the offense of felony assault on a household member that the defendant and the complainant were living together in the same dwelling when the offense was committed."

Dolkart v. State, 197 S.W.3d 887, 893 (Tex.App.—Dallas 2006, pet. ref'd). "[A]ssault by threat and assault by injury differ in the conduct element, the culpability element, and the required result. Therefore, we cannot conclude that assault by threat and assault by injury are merely underlying 'brute facts' or means that make up a particular element of a single assault. Rather, we conclude that the legislature created separate offenses."

Mitchell v. State, 102 S.W.3d 772, 775 (Tex.App.—Austin 2003, pet. ref'd). "We reject appellant's argument that proof of a previous conviction for assault against a family or household member necessarily requires [a CCP art.] 42.013 finding in the earlier assault judgment."

In re S.D.W., 811 S.W.2d 739, 752 (Tex.App.—Houston [1st Dist.] 1991, no pet.). "Assault is a lesser included offense of aggravated robbery."

Redfearn v. State, 738 S.W.2d 28, 29-30 (Tex.App.—Texarkana 1987, pet. ref'd). "[A]n assault may be accomplished through the use of an animate or inanimate object, and … an assault may be had through the use of a dog … which was not alleged to be dangerous. [A] threat to release snakes into a person's residence, whether or not the snakes are stated to be poisonous, is calculated to raise a reasonable apprehension of bodily harm on the part of the person threatened. [¶] Acts which have been held to constitute threats include the burning of a cross on a victim's property, … shooting a gun at a police officer, … and a statement that a bomb *had* been placed in the victim's place of business. The test is what is reasonably communicated to the victim."

PEN §22.011. SEXUAL ASSAULT

(a) A person commits an offense if the person:

(1) intentionally or knowingly:

(A) causes the penetration of the anus or sexual organ of another person by any means, without that person's consent;

(B) causes the penetration of the mouth of another person by the sexual organ of the actor, without that person's consent; or

(C) causes the sexual organ of another person, without that person's consent, to contact or penetrate the mouth, anus, or sexual organ of another person, including the actor; or

(2) intentionally or knowingly:

(A) causes the penetration of the anus or sexual organ of a child by any means;

(B) causes the penetration of the mouth of a child by the sexual organ of the actor;

(C) causes the sexual organ of a child to contact or penetrate the mouth, anus, or sexual organ of another person, including the actor;

(D) causes the anus of a child to contact the mouth, anus, or sexual organ of another person, including the actor; or

(E) causes the mouth of a child to contact the anus or sexual organ of another person, including the actor.

(b) A sexual assault under Subsection (a)(1) is without the consent of the other person if:

(1) the actor compels the other person to submit or participate by the use of physical force or violence;

(2) the actor compels the other person to submit or participate by threatening to use force or violence against the other person, and the other person believes that the actor has the present ability to execute the threat;

(3) the other person has not consented and the actor knows the other person is unconscious or physically unable to resist;

(4) the actor knows that as a result of mental disease or defect the other person is at the time of the sexual assault incapable either of appraising the nature of the act or of resisting it;

For a quick reference of penalties, see the Chart of Penalties on p. 675.

O'CONNOR'S CRIMINAL CODES 771

(5) the other person has not consented and the actor knows the other person is unaware that the sexual assault is occurring;

(6) the actor has intentionally impaired the other person's power to appraise or control the other person's conduct by administering any substance without the other person's knowledge;

(7) the actor compels the other person to submit or participate by threatening to use force or violence against any person, and the other person believes that the actor has the ability to execute the threat;

(8) the actor is a public servant who coerces the other person to submit or participate;

(9) the actor is a mental health services provider or a health care services provider who causes the other person, who is a patient or former patient of the actor, to submit or participate by exploiting the other person's emotional dependency on the actor;

(10) the actor is a clergyman who causes the other person to submit or participate by exploiting the other person's emotional dependency on the clergyman in the clergyman's professional character as spiritual adviser; or

(11) the actor is an employee of a facility where the other person is a resident, unless the employee and resident are formally or informally married to each other under Chapter 2, Family Code.

(c) In this section:

(1) "Child" means a person younger than 17 years of age who is not the spouse of the actor.

(2) "Spouse" means a person who is legally married to another.

(3) "Health care services provider" means:

(A) a physician licensed under Subtitle B, Title 3, Occupations Code;

(B) a chiropractor licensed under Chapter 201, Occupations Code;

(C) a physical therapist licensed under Chapter 453, Occupations Code;

(D) a physician assistant licensed under Chapter 204, Occupations Code; or

(E) a registered nurse, a vocational nurse, or an advanced practice nurse licensed under Chapter 301, Occupations Code.

(4) "Mental health services provider" means an individual, licensed or unlicensed, who performs or purports to perform mental health services, including a:

(A) licensed social worker as defined by Section 505.002, Occupations Code;

(B) chemical dependency counselor as defined by Section 504.001, Occupations Code;

(C) licensed professional counselor as defined by Section 503.002, Occupations Code;

(D) licensed marriage and family therapist as defined by Section 502.002, Occupations Code;

(E) member of the clergy;

(F) psychologist offering psychological services as defined by Section 501.003, Occupations Code; or

(G) special officer for mental health assignment certified under Section 1701.404, Occupations Code.

(5) "Employee of a facility" means a person who is an employee of a facility defined by Section 250.001, Health and Safety Code, or any other person who provides services for a facility for compensation, including a contract laborer.

(d) It is a defense to prosecution under Subsection (a)(2) that the conduct consisted of medical care for the child and did not include any contact between the anus or sexual organ of the child and the mouth, anus, or sexual organ of the actor or a third party.

(e) It is an affirmative defense to prosecution under Subsection (a)(2) that:

(1) the actor was not more than three years older than the victim and at the time of the offense:

(A) was not required under Chapter 62, Code of Criminal Procedure, to register for life as a sex offender; or

(B) was not a person who under Chapter 62, Code of Criminal Procedure, had a reportable conviction or adjudication for an offense under this section; and

(2) the victim:

(A) was a child of 14 years of age or older; and

(B) was not a person whom the actor was prohibited from marrying or purporting to marry or with whom the actor was prohibited from living under the appearance of being married under Section 25.01.

(f) An offense under this section is a felony of the second degree, except that an offense under this section is a felony of the first degree if the victim was a person whom the actor was prohibited from marrying or purporting to marry or with whom the actor was prohibited from living under the appearance of being married under Section 25.01.

History of Pen §22.011: Acts 1983, 68th Leg., ch. 977, §3, eff. Sept. 1, 1983. Amended by Acts 1985, 69th Leg., ch. 557, §1, eff. Sept. 1, 1985; Acts 1987, 70th Leg., ch. 1029, §1, eff. Sept. 1, 1987; Acts 1991, 72nd Leg., ch. 662, §1, eff. Sept. 1, 1991; Acts 1993, 73rd Leg., ch. 900, §1.01, eff. Sept. 1, 1994; Acts 1995, 74th Leg., ch. 273, §1 (eff. Sept. 1, 1995), ch. 318, §6 (eff. Sept. 1, 1995); Acts 1997, 75th Leg., ch. 1031, §§1, 2 (eff. Sept. 1, 1997), ch. 1286, §1 (eff. Sept. 1, 1997); Acts 1999, 76th Leg., ch. 1102, §3 (eff. Sept. 1, 1999), ch. 1415, §24 (eff. Sept. 1, 1999); Acts 2001, 77th Leg., ch. 1420, §14.829, eff. Sept. 1, 2001; Acts 2003, 78th Leg., ch. 155, §§1, 2 (eff. Sept. 1, 2003), ch. 528, §1 (eff. Sept. 1, 2003), ch. 553, §2.017 (eff. Feb. 1, 2004); Acts 2005, 79th Leg., ch. 268, §4.02, eff. Sept. 1, 2005.

See also CCP arts. 38.072, 38.37; Pen §3.03.

ANNOTATIONS

Hernandez v. State, 861 S.W.2d 908, 909 (Tex. Crim.App.1993). "The plain language of §22.011 provides for two general methods of committing sexual assault: (1) involving specified contacts made upon a complainant without the complainant's consent ... and (2) involving specified contacts made upon a complainant who is a child.... The second method ... makes no mention whatsoever of consent; thus consent (or nonconsent) is not an element in proving the second method. [¶] It is quite possible to prosecute and convict someone of sexually assaulting a promiscuous 14 through 16-year-old child. The method of doing so is ... by alleging and proving lack of consent. If that method is alleged, obviously consent (or nonconsent) is an issue, while promiscuity, which statutorily only applies to method two, is not a defense."

Elliott v. State, 858 S.W.2d 478, 485 (Tex.Crim.App. 1993). "[W]here assent in fact has not been given, and the actor knows that the victim's physical impairment is such that resistance is not reasonably to be expected, sexual intercourse is 'without consent' under the sexual assault statute."

Mathonican v. State, 194 S.W.3d 59, 66 (Tex. App.—Texarkana 2006, no pet.). "Section 22.011 ... is a conduct-oriented statute that prohibits distinct, yet very specific acts, with each act therein proscribed constituting an independent unit of prosecution."

Ex parte Pruitt, 187 S.W.3d 635, 640 (Tex.App.— Austin 2006), *aff'd*, 233 S.W.3d 338 (Tex.Crim. App.2007). "[S]exual assault by genital-to-genital contact as defined in penal code §22.011(a)(2)(C) is a separate statutory offense from sexual assault by genital penetration as defined in §22.011(a)(2)(A). [¶] Genital-to-genital contact that occurs in the course of an act of penile penetration is subsumed in the completed act. A conviction for both the completed act of penetration and the contact incident to the penetration constitutes double jeopardy. Similarly, the State may not in this cause prosecute Pruitt for sexual assault based on genital-to-genital contact that was incident to and subsumed within the alleged sexual assaults by genital penetration for which he was placed in jeopardy and acquitted...."

Burns v. State, 728 S.W.2d 114, 116 (Tex.App.— Houston [14th Dist.] 1987, pet. ref'd). "[F]or purposes of [Pen. Code] §§22.011 and 22.021, the 'criminal episode' commences when the attacker in any way restricts the victim's freedom of movement and it ends with the final release or escape of the victim from the attacker's control."

PEN §22.012. DELETED

Deleted by Acts 1993, 73rd Leg., ch. 900, §1.01, eff. Sept. 1, 1994.

PEN §22.015. COERCING, SOLICITING, OR INDUCING GANG MEMBERSHIP

(a) In this section:

(1) "Child" means an individual younger than 17 years of age.

(2) "Criminal street gang" has the meaning assigned by Section 71.01.

(b) A person commits an offense if, with intent to coerce, induce, or solicit a child to actively participate in the activities of a criminal street gang, the person:

(1) threatens the child with imminent bodily injury; or

(2) causes bodily injury to the child.

(c) An offense under Subsection (b)(1) is a state jail felony. An offense under Subsection (b)(2) is a felony of the third degree.

History of Pen §22.015: Acts 1999, 76th Leg., ch. 708, §1, eff. Sept. 1, 1999.

PEN §22.02. AGGRAVATED ASSAULT

(a) A person commits an offense if the person commits assault as defined in Section 22.01 and the person:

(1) causes serious bodily injury to another, including the person's spouse; or

(2) uses or exhibits a deadly weapon during the commission of the assault.

(b) An offense under this section is a felony of the second degree, except that the offense is a felony of the first degree if:

(1) the actor uses a deadly weapon during the commission of the assault and causes serious bodily injury

For a quick reference of penalties, see the Chart of Penalties on p. 675.

O'CONNOR'S CRIMINAL CODES   773

to a person whose relationship to or association with the defendant is described by Section 71.0021(b), 71.003, or 71.005, Family Code; or

(2) regardless of whether the offense is committed under Subsection (a)(1) or (a)(2), the offense is committed:

(A) by a public servant acting under color of the servant's office or employment;

(B) against a person the actor knows is a public servant while the public servant is lawfully discharging an official duty, or in retaliation or on account of an exercise of official power or performance of an official duty as a public servant;

(C) in retaliation against or on account of the service of another as a witness, prospective witness, informant, or person who has reported the occurrence of a crime; or

(D) against a person the actor knows is a security officer while the officer is performing a duty as a security officer.

(c) The actor is presumed to have known the person assaulted was a public servant or a security officer if the person was wearing a distinctive uniform or badge indicating the person's employment as a public servant or status as a security officer.

(d) In this section, "security officer" means a commissioned security officer as defined by Section 1702.002, Occupations Code, or a noncommissioned security officer registered under Section 1702.221, Occupations Code.

History of Pen §22.02: Acts 1973, 63rd Leg., ch. 399, §1, eff. Jan. 1, 1974. Amended by Acts 1979, 66th Leg., ch. 164, §2 (eff. Sept. 1, 1979), ch. 655, §2 (eff. Sept. 1, 1979); Acts 1983, 68th Leg., ch. 79, §1 (eff. Sept. 1, 1983), ch. 977, §2 (eff. Sept. 1, 1983); Acts 1985, 69th Leg., ch. 223, §1, eff. Sept. 1, 1985; Acts 1987, 70th Leg., ch. 18, §3 (eff. Apr. 14, 1987), ch. 1101, §12 (eff. Sept. 1, 1987); Acts 1989, 71st Leg., ch. 939, §§1-3, eff. Sept. 1, 1989; Acts 1991, 72nd Leg., ch. 334, §2 (eff. Sept. 1, 1991), ch. 903, §1 (eff. Sept. 1, 1991); Acts 1993, 73rd Leg., ch. 900, §1.01, eff. Sept. 1, 1994; Acts 2003, 78th Leg., ch. 1019, §3, eff. Sept. 1, 2003; Acts 2005, 79th Leg., ch. 788, §3, eff. Sept. 1, 2005.

See also CCP arts. 38.072, 38.37.

ANNOTATIONS

Irving v. State, 176 S.W.3d 842, 846 (Tex.Crim.App. 2005). "Because the conduct [grabbing and falling on victim] constituting the offense of assault for which the Appellant wanted an instruction is not the same as the conduct [striking victim with baseball bat] charged in the indictment for aggravated assault, assault by grabbing the victim and eventually falling on top of her is not a lesser-included offense of aggravated assault by

striking the victim with a bat. This offense fails to meet the requirements of [CCP] Art. 37.09 because the same facts or less than the same facts required to prove the greater aggravated assault offense are not required to prove the assault offense."

Phillips v. State, 787 S.W.2d 391, 395 (Tex.Crim. App.1990). "[A]n actor commits a distinct offense against any person he injures and each of those injured constitutes a separate 'allowable unit of prosecution.' The Double Jeopardy Clause has no application to a multiple victim offense when ... it is the legislative intent to prohibit serious bodily injury to persons and, accordingly, to enforce this intent by proscribing the appropriate punishment for each such offense."

Ethridge v. State, 648 S.W.2d 306, 306 (Tex.Crim. App.1983). "[A]ggravated assault [is] a lesser-included offense of an attempted murder."

Benge v. State, 94 S.W.3d 31, 35 (Tex.App.— Houston [14th Dist.] 2002, pet. ref'd). "[T]he elements of reckless driving are included within the facts required to establish aggravated assault [with a motor vehicle]."

Ford v. State, 38 S.W.3d 836, 846 (Tex.App.— Houston [14th Dist.] 2001, pet. ref'd). "[D]eadly conduct under ... §22.05(a) is a lesser included offense of aggravated assault under ... §22.02(a)(2)." *See also Isaac v. State*, 167 S.W.3d 469, 473-74 (Tex.App.— Houston [14th Dist.] 2005, pet. ref'd).

Lane v. State, 805 S.W.2d 576, 578 (Tex.App.— Dallas 1991, no pet.). "Violence has been described as proof of an assault and putting in fear. ... The term 'violence' includes *all* application of force, whether or not bodily injury results. It appears that the term 'bodily injury' is, for purposes of §22.02..., a subset of the broader term 'violence.' [B]odily injury, or a threat of imminent bodily injury, in the context of an aggravated assault charge, is synonymous with violence or placing in fear of violence."

Gaston v. State, 672 S.W.2d 819, 821 (Tex.App.— Dallas 1983, no pet.). "When a defendant points an automatic pistol at another person, pulls the trigger, but the gun fails to discharge, aggravated assault is committed. The weapon need not be functioning during the assault. What is necessary is that the defendant be using a deadly weapon to 'intentionally or knowingly threaten another with imminent bodily injury.'"

PEN §22.02

PEN §22.021. AGGRAVATED SEXUAL ASSAULT

(a) A person commits an offense:

(1) if the person:

(A) intentionally or knowingly:

(i) causes the penetration of the anus or sexual organ of another person by any means, without that person's consent;

(ii) causes the penetration of the mouth of another person by the sexual organ of the actor, without that person's consent; or

(iii) causes the sexual organ of another person, without that person's consent, to contact or penetrate the mouth, anus, or sexual organ of another person, including the actor; or

(B) intentionally or knowingly:

(i) causes the penetration of the anus or sexual organ of a child by any means;

(ii) causes the penetration of the mouth of a child by the sexual organ of the actor;

(iii) causes the sexual organ of a child to contact or penetrate the mouth, anus, or sexual organ of another person, including the actor;

(iv) causes the anus of a child to contact the mouth, anus, or sexual organ of another person, including the actor; or

(v) causes the mouth of a child to contact the anus or sexual organ of another person, including the actor; and

(2) if:

(A) the person:

(i) causes serious bodily injury or attempts to cause the death of the victim or another person in the course of the same criminal episode;

(ii) by acts or words places the victim in fear that death, serious bodily injury, or kidnapping will be imminently inflicted on any person;

(iii) by acts or words occurring in the presence of the victim threatens to cause the death, serious bodily injury, or kidnapping of any person;

(iv) uses or exhibits a deadly weapon in the course of the same criminal episode;

(v) acts in concert with another who engages in conduct described by Subdivision (1) directed toward the same victim and occurring during the course of the same criminal episode; or

(vi) administers or provides flunitrazepam, otherwise known as rohypnol, gamma hydroxybutyrate, or ketamine to the victim of the offense with the intent of facilitating the commission of the offense;

(B) the victim is younger than 14 years of age; or

(C) the victim is an elderly individual or a disabled individual.

(b) In this section:

(1) "Child" has the meaning assigned by Section 22.011(c).

(2) "Elderly individual" and "disabled individual" have the meanings assigned by Section 22.04(c).

(c) An aggravated sexual assault under this section is without the consent of the other person if the aggravated sexual assault occurs under the same circumstances listed in Section 22.011(b).

(d) The defense provided by Section 22.011(d) applies to this section.

(e) An offense under this section is a felony of the first degree.

E *Subsection (f) below is effective for offenses committed on or after Sept. 1, 2007.*

(f) The minimum term of imprisonment for an offense under this section is increased to 25 years if:

(1) the victim of the offense is younger than six years of age at the time the offense is committed; or

(2) the victim of the offense is younger than 14 years of age at the time the offense is committed and the actor commits the offense in a manner described by Subsection (a)(2)(A).

History of Pen §22.021: Acts 1983, 68th Leg., ch. 977, §3, eff. Sept. 1, 1983. Amended by Acts 1987, 70th Leg., ch. 573, §1 (eff. Sept. 1, 1987), 2nd C.S., ch. 16, §1 (eff. Sept. 1, 1987); Acts 1993, 73rd Leg., ch. 900, §1.01, eff. Sept. 1, 1994; Acts 1995, 74th Leg., ch. 318, §7, eff. Sept. 1, 1995; Acts 1997, 75th Leg., ch. 1286, §2, eff. Sept. 1, 1997; Acts 1999, 76th Leg., ch. 417, §1, eff. Sept. 1, 1999; Acts 2001, 77th Leg., ch. 459, §5, eff. Sept. 1, 2001; Acts 2003, 78th Leg., ch. 528, §2 (eff. Sept. 1, 2003), ch. 896, §1 (eff. Sept. 1, 2003); Acts 2007, 80th Leg., ch. 593, §1.18, eff. Sept. 1, 2007.

See also CCP arts. 38.072, 38.37; Pen. Code §3.03.

ANNOTATIONS

Vick v. State, 991 S.W.2d 830, 833 (Tex.Crim.App. 1999). "In sum, §22.021 is a conduct-oriented statute; it uses the conjunctive 'or' to distinguish and separate different conduct; and its various sections specifically define sexual conduct in ways that usually require different and distinct acts to commit. These considerations lead us to conclude that the Legislature intended

For a quick reference of penalties, see the Chart of Penalties on p. 675.

O'CONNOR'S CRIMINAL CODES 775

that each separately described conduct constitutes a separate statutory offense."

Johnson v. State, 227 S.W.3d 180, 183 (Tex.App.—Houston [1st Dist.] 2007, pet. ref'd). "The definitions of consent that are more specific to the offense of aggravated sexual assault are those found in [Pen. Code] §22.011(b), which is incorporated by reference into the aggravated-sexual-assault statute. In contrast, [Pen. Code] §1.07(a)(11)'s definition of consent is not specific to any offense."

Cruz v. State, 238 S.W.3d 389, 398 (Tex.App.—Houston [1st Dist.] 2006, pet. ref'd). "[W]e must decide whether a deadly weapon finding in a sexual assault case [under CCP art. 42.12, §3g(a)(2)] is ..., a *de facto* conviction for aggravated sexual assault [under Pen. Code §22.021]. [¶] Because a deadly weapon finding under article 42.12, §3g(a)(2) is not necessarily the same as using or exhibiting a deadly weapon under the aggravated assault statute, the trial court erred by charging the jury that it could assess [D's] punishment as an aggravated sexual assault."

Valdez v. State, 211 S.W.3d 395, 400-01 (Tex.App.—Eastland 2006, no pet.). "Lower courts have ... identified two exceptions to the general rule that each allegation under §22.021 constitutes a separate offense. The first involves subsumed conduct. ... Section 22.021 identifies different types of conduct which constitute separate offenses—even if they occur in the same transaction—except in cases in which one of the acts would necessarily be subsumed by another, such as contact and penetration. [¶] The allegation that Valdez caused [child's] anus to contact his sexual organ is subsumed with the allegation that he penetrated [child's] anus with his sexual organ. [¶] The second exception arises when the allegations involve a single incident—as opposed to a single transaction. [A]llegations that the defendant penetrated the minor's sexual organ with his finger or with an unknown object alleged two different means or manners of committing a single offense rather than two separate offenses. [B]oth acts implicated the same statutory subsection, 22.021(a)(1)(B)(iii), and that the state's case was based upon only one incident of penetration."

Tinker v. State, 148 S.W.3d 666, 670-71 (Tex. App.—Houston [14th Dist.] 2004, no pet.). Held: A separated shoulder was serious bodily injury.

Pitre v. State, 44 S.W.3d 616, 620 (Tex.App.—Eastland 2001, pet. ref'd). "It is when [the result elements, causing penetration of the victim's vagina or anus,] are combined with the element of 'without the consent of the victim' that the overall conduct [is] criminal.... The first two elements become 'culpable mental states' ... because of their combination with the third element of 'without the consent of the victim.' The trial court did not err in giving the full definition of 'intentionally' or 'with intent' in its charge to the jury."

Lewis v. State, 984 S.W.2d 732, 735 (Tex.App.—Fort Worth 1998, pet. ref'd). "[T]he defendant's conduct is examined to determine whether that conduct was the producing cause of the victim's fear and whether the subjective state of fear was reasonable in light of such conduct. [T]he subjective fear of the victim alone is not sufficient to establish the aggravating factor required in §22.021(a)(2)(A)(ii). The State must show that the fear of the victim was the proximate result of objective conduct employed by the defendant."

Jiminez v. State, 953 S.W.2d 293, 297 (Tex.App.—Austin 1997, pet. ref'd). "[C]ommon sense and usage, as well as the purpose of the statute, lead to the conclusion that 'mouth,' as used in §22.021(a)(1)(B)(iii), includes both the oral cavity and its constituent parts, including the lips, teeth, and tongue."

Karnes v. State, 873 S.W.2d 92, 96 (Tex.App.—Dallas 1994, no pet.). "Penetration, within the meaning of §22.021 ..., occurs so long as contact with the female sexual organ could reasonably be regarded by ordinary English speakers as more intrusive than contact with outer vaginal lips. Penetration of the vaginal canal is not required to prove penetration. 'Female sexual organ' is a more general term than 'vagina' and refers to the entire female genitalia, including both vagina and the vulva. Touching beneath the fold of the external genitalia amounts to penetration within the meaning of the aggravated sexual assault statute."

Hellums v. State, 831 S.W.2d 545, 547 (Tex.App.—Austin 1992, no pet.). "[E]ven in the absence of an outcry statement, the victim's uncorroborated testimony supports a conviction under [Pen.] Code §22.021 if the victim was younger than fourteen years old at the time of the offense. [T]he testimony of a sexual assault victim alone is sufficient evidence of penetration to support a conviction, even if the victim is a child."

PEN §22.03. DELETED

Deleted by Acts 1993, 73rd Leg., ch. 900, §1.01, eff. Sept. 1, 1994.

PEN §22.021

PEN §22.04. INJURY TO A CHILD, ELDERLY INDIVIDUAL, OR DISABLED INDIVIDUAL

(a) A person commits an offense if he intentionally, knowingly, recklessly, or with criminal negligence, by act or intentionally, knowingly, or recklessly by omission, causes to a child, elderly individual, or disabled individual:

(1) serious bodily injury;

(2) serious mental deficiency, impairment, or injury; or

(3) bodily injury.

(a-1) A person commits an offense if the person is an owner, operator, or employee of a group home, nursing facility, assisted living facility, intermediate care facility for persons with mental retardation, or other institutional care facility and the person intentionally, knowingly, recklessly, or with criminal negligence by omission causes to a child, elderly individual, or disabled individual who is a resident of that group home or facility:

(1) serious bodily injury;

(2) serious mental deficiency, impairment, or injury;

(3) bodily injury; or

(4) exploitation.

(b) An omission that causes a condition described by Subsection (a)(1), (2), or (3) or (a-1)(1), (2), (3), or (4) is conduct constituting an offense under this section if:

(1) the actor has a legal or statutory duty to act; or

(2) the actor has assumed care, custody, or control of a child, elderly individual, or disabled individual.

(c) In this section:

(1) "Child" means a person 14 years of age or younger.

(2) "Elderly individual" means a person 65 years of age or older.

(3) "Disabled individual" means a person older than 14 years of age who by reason of age or physical or mental disease, defect, or injury is substantially unable to protect himself from harm or to provide food, shelter, or medical care for himself.

(4) "Exploitation" means the illegal or improper use of an individual or of the resources of the individual for monetary or personal benefit, profit, or gain.

(d) For purposes of an omission that causes a condition described by Subsection (a)(1), (2), or (3), the actor has assumed care, custody, or control if he has by act, words, or course of conduct acted so as to cause a reasonable person to conclude that he has accepted responsibility for protection, food, shelter, and medical care for a child, elderly individual, or disabled individual. For purposes of an omission that causes a condition described by Subsection (a-1)(1), (2), (3), or (4), the actor acting during the actor's capacity as owner, operator, or employee of a group home or facility described by Subsection (a-1) is considered to have accepted responsibility for protection, food, shelter, and medical care for the child, elderly individual, or disabled individual who is a resident of the group home or facility.

(e) An offense under Subsection (a)(1) or (2) or (a-1)(1) or (2) is a felony of the first degree when the conduct is committed intentionally or knowingly. When the conduct is engaged in recklessly, the offense is a felony of the second degree.

(f) An offense under Subsection (a)(3) or (a-1)(3) or (4) is a felony of the third degree when the conduct is committed intentionally or knowingly. When the conduct is engaged in recklessly, the offense is a state jail felony.

(g) An offense under Subsection (a) is a state jail felony when the person acts with criminal negligence. An offense under Subsection (a-1) is a state jail felony when the person, with criminal negligence and by omission, causes a condition described by Subsection (a-1)(1), (2), (3), or (4).

(h) A person who is subject to prosecution under both this section and another section of this code may be prosecuted under either or both sections. Section 3.04 does not apply to criminal episodes prosecuted under both this section and another section of this code. If a criminal episode is prosecuted under both this section and another section of this code and sentences are assessed for convictions under both sections, the sentences shall run concurrently.

(i) It is an affirmative defense to prosecution under Subsection (b)(2) that before the offense the actor:

(1) notified in person the child, elderly individual, or disabled individual that he would no longer provide any of the care described by Subsection (d); and

(2) notified in writing the parents or person other than himself acting in loco parentis to the child, elderly

For a quick reference of penalties, see the Chart of Penalties on p. 675.

O'CONNOR'S CRIMINAL CODES   777

individual, or disabled individual that he would no longer provide any of the care described by Subsection (d); or

(3) notified in writing the Department of Protective and Regulatory Services that he would no longer provide any of the care set forth in Subsection (d).

(j) Written notification under Subsection (i)(2) or (i)(3) is not effective unless it contains the name and address of the actor, the name and address of the child, elderly individual, or disabled individual, the type of care provided by the actor, and the date the care was discontinued.

(k) It is a defense to prosecution under this section that the act or omission consisted of:

(1) reasonable medical care occurring under the direction of or by a licensed physician; or

(2) emergency medical care administered in good faith and with reasonable care by a person not licensed in the healing arts.

(*l*) It is an affirmative defense to prosecution under this section:

(1) that the act or omission was based on treatment in accordance with the tenets and practices of a recognized religious method of healing with a generally accepted record of efficacy;

(2) for a person charged with an act of omission causing to a child, elderly individual, or disabled individual a condition described by Subsection (a)(1), (2), or (3) that:

(A) there is no evidence that, on the date prior to the offense charged, the defendant was aware of an incident of injury to the child, elderly individual, or disabled individual and failed to report the incident; and

(B) the person:

(i) was a victim of family violence, as that term is defined by Section 71.004, Family Code, committed by a person who is also charged with an offense against the child, elderly individual, or disabled individual under this section or any other section of this title;

(ii) did not cause a condition described by Subsection (a)(1), (2), or (3); and

(iii) did not reasonably believe at the time of the omission that an effort to prevent the person also charged with an offense against the child, elderly individual, or disabled individual from committing the offense would have an effect; or

(3) that:

(A) the actor was not more than three years older than the victim at the time of the offense; and

(B) the victim was a child at the time of the offense.

History of Pen §22.04: Acts 1973, 63rd Leg., ch. 399, §1, eff. Jan. 1, 1974. Amended by Acts 1977, 65th Leg., p. 2067, ch. 819, §1, eff. Aug. 29, 1977; Acts 1979, 66th Leg., ch. 162, §1, eff. Aug. 27, 1979; Acts 1981, 67th Leg., ch. 202, §4 (eff. Sept. 1, 1981), ch. 604, §1 (eff. Sept. 1, 1981); Acts 1989, 71st Leg., ch. 357, §1, eff. Sept. 1, 1989; Acts 1991, 72nd Leg., ch. 497, §1, eff. Sept. 1, 1991; Acts 1993, 73rd Leg., ch. 900, §1.01, eff. Sept. 1, 1994; Acts 1995, 74th Leg., ch. 76, §8.139, eff. Sept. 1, 1995; Acts 1999, 76th Leg., ch. 62, §15.02(b), eff. Sept. 1, 1999; Acts 2005, 79th Leg., ch. 268, §1.125(a) (eff. Sept. 1, 2005), ch. 949, §46 (eff. Sept. 1, 2005).

See also CCP arts. 38.072, 38.37.

ANNOTATIONS

Shaw v. State, 243 S.W.3d 647, 649 (Tex.Crim.App. 2007). "We ... hold that, in order to obtain an instruction on the 'Good Samaritan' defense embodied in §22.04(k) ... the appellant must show that the record contains evidence sufficient to support a rational finding, not that she lacked the requisite mental state necessary to commit the offense, but that she in fact harbored the requisite mental state, but nevertheless engaged in the conduct under emergency circumstances, in good faith, and with reasonable care."

Hicks v. State, 241 S.W.3d 543, 546 (Tex.Crim.App. 2007). "The Legislature has clearly provided the standard for establishing when an actor has assumed 'care, custody, or control' of a disabled individual under subsection (b)(2). This standard is clearly and unambiguously set out in subsection (d). Although 'possession' in [Pen. Code] §1.07(a)(39) is defined as 'care, custody, or control,' the court of appeals incorrectly assumed that 'care, custody, or control' under [Pen. Code] §22.04(b)(2) means 'possession.' ... Because the language of §22.04(d) is clear, the court of appeals should have applied the plain language of subsection (d) and refrained from looking beyond the text of the statute in interpreting it. By looking outside subsection (d) to the definition of 'possession,' the court of appeals ignored established principles of statutory construction by modifying the standard provided in subsection (d)."

Jefferson v. State, 189 S.W.3d 305, 312 (Tex.Crim. App.2006). "The first question we address ... is whether the Legislature intended to make 'act or omission' in §22.04(a) separate elements of the offense or underlying 'brute facts [or means that] make up a particular element.' We believe it clear that the Legislature intended the latter—that 'act or omission' constitute the means of committing the course of conduct element of injury to a child. [¶] We, therefore, decide that 'act or omission' are not elements of an injury to a child offense about which a jury must be unanimous." Held: The jury must be unanimous only about the fact that D caused injury to the child. Unanimity is not required about the means of causing injury. *See also Villanueva v. State*, 227 S.W.3d 774, 748 (Tex.Crim.App.2007) (double jeopardy).

Zubia v. State, 998 S.W.2d 226, 227 (Tex.Crim.App. 1999). Section 22.04 "does not require the State to prove (a defendant) had intent or knowledge *in connection with the victim's age*."

Hawkins v. State, 891 S.W.2d 257, 259 (Tex.Crim. App.1994). "[N]o 'familial relationship' is necessary to show a legal duty to act. [T]he plain meaning of §22.04(b)(2) does not require that the actor possess a duty under the Texas Family Code to protect the child victim."

Beggs v. State, 597 S.W.2d 375, 377 (Tex.Crim.App. 1980). "The significance of §22.04 is that it adds a stiffer penalty if the victim of an assault is a child. [N]otwithstanding the phrase 'engages in conduct that,' §22.04 is focused on the result of the suspect's conduct. This is important because it determines the definitions of the culpable mental states, which in turn affect the defense of mistake of fact." *See also Morales v. State*, 853 S.W.2d 583, 585 (Tex.Crim.App.1993); *Maupin v. State*, 930 S.W.2d 267, 268 (Tex.App.—Fort Worth 1996, pet. ref'd).

Baldwin v. State, ___ S.W.3d ___ (Tex.App.— Houston [1st Dist.] 2008, pet. filed 5-13-08) (No. 01-06-00859-CR; 2-07-08). "Injury to a child is a result-oriented offense requiring a mental state that relates not to the charged conduct but to the result of the conduct. It is not enough for the State to prove that the defendant engaged in the alleged conduct with the requisite criminal intent; the State must also prove that the defendant caused the result with the requisite criminal intent." *See also Payton v. State*, 106 S.W.3d 326, 331 (Tex.App.—Fort Worth 2003, pet. ref'd) (omission); *Millslagle v. State*, 81 S.W.3d 895, 898 (Tex.App.— Austin 2002, pet. ref'd); *Whitmire v. State*, 913 S.W.2d 738, 740 (Tex.App.—Eastland 1996), *pet. dism'd*, 943 S.W.2d 894 (Tex.Crim.App.1997) (drunk driving). *But see Cleburn v. State*, 138 S.W.3d 542, 544 (Tex.App.— Houston [14th Dist.] 2004, pet. ref'd).

Jimenez v. State, 240 S.W.3d 384, 417-18 (Tex. App.—Austin 2007, pet. dism'd). "When a legislature specifically authorizes multiple punishments under two statutes, even if those two statutes proscribe the 'same' conduct, 'a court's task of statutory construction is at an end and the prosecutor may seek and the trial court or jury may impose cumulative punishment … in a single trial.' [¶] '[T]his statute plainly authorizes multiple punishments when a defendant's conduct violates both §22.04 and another penal code section.'"

Hilton v. State, 659 S.W.2d 154, 158 (Tex.App.— Fort Worth 1983, pet. ref'd). "[P]roof that the defendant acted intentionally, knowingly, recklessly, *or* with criminal negligence is sufficient to establish the scienter element of the offense. Therefore, it is not error for the trial court to charge the jury in the disjunctive substituting the word, 'or', for the conjunctive, 'and', in the indictment."

PEN §22.041. ABANDONING OR ENDANGERING CHILD

(a) In this section, "abandon" means to leave a child in any place without providing reasonable and necessary care for the child, under circumstances under which no reasonable, similarly situated adult would leave a child of that age and ability.

(b) A person commits an offense if, having custody, care, or control of a child younger than 15 years, he intentionally abandons the child in any place under circumstances that expose the child to an unreasonable risk of harm.

(c) A person commits an offense if he intentionally, knowingly, recklessly, or with criminal negligence, by act or omission, engages in conduct that places a child younger than 15 years in imminent danger of death, bodily injury, or physical or mental impairment.

 Subsection (c-1) below is effective for offenses committed on or after Sept. 1, 2007.

(c-1) For purposes of Subsection (c), it is presumed that a person engaged in conduct that places a child in imminent danger of death, bodily injury, or physical or mental impairment if:

(1) the person manufactured, possessed, or in any way introduced into the body of any person the controlled substance methamphetamine in the presence of the child;

For a quick reference of penalties, see the Chart of Penalties on p. 675.

O'CONNOR'S CRIMINAL CODES   779

(2) the person's conduct related to the proximity or accessibility of the controlled substance methamphetamine to the child and an analysis of a specimen of the child's blood, urine, or other bodily substance indicates the presence of methamphetamine in the child's body; or

(3) the person injected, ingested, inhaled, or otherwise introduced a controlled substance listed in Penalty Group 1, Section 481.102, Health and Safety Code, into the human body when the person was not in lawful possession of the substance as defined by Section 481.002(24) of that code.

Subsection (c-1) below is effective for offenses in which any element of the offense was committed before Sept. 1, 2007.

(c-1) For purposes of Subsection (c), it is presumed that a person engaged in conduct that places a child in imminent danger of death, bodily injury, or physical or mental impairment if the person manufactured the controlled substance methamphetamine in the presence of the child.

(d) Except as provided by Subsection (e), an offense under Subsection (b) is:

(1) a state jail felony if the actor abandoned the child with intent to return for the child; or

(2) a felony of the third degree if the actor abandoned the child without intent to return for the child.

(e) An offense under Subsection (b) is a felony of the second degree if the actor abandons the child under circumstances that a reasonable person would believe would place the child in imminent danger of death, bodily injury, or physical or mental impairment.

(f) An offense under Subsection (c) is a state jail felony.

(g) It is a defense to prosecution under Subsection (c) that the act or omission enables the child to practice for or participate in an organized athletic event and that appropriate safety equipment and procedures are employed in the event.

(h) It is an exception to the application of this section that the actor voluntarily delivered the child to a designated emergency infant care provider under Section 262.302, Family Code.

History of Pen §22.041: Acts 1985, 69th Leg., ch. 791, §1, eff. Sept. 1, 1985. Amended by Acts 1989, 71st Leg., ch. 904, §1, eff. Sept. 1, 1989; Acts 1993, 73rd Leg., ch. 900, §1.01, eff. Sept. 1, 1994; Acts 1997, 75th Leg., ch. 687, §1, eff. Sept. 1, 1997; Acts 1999, 76th Leg., ch. 1087, §3, eff. Sept. 1, 1999; Acts 2001, 77th Leg., ch. 807, §7, eff. Sept. 1, 2001; Acts 2005, 79th Leg., ch. 282, §10, eff. Aug. 1, 2005; Acts 2007, 80th Leg., ch. 840, §2, eff. Sept. 1, 2007.

See also CCP arts. 38.072, 38.37.

Schultz v. State, 923 S.W.2d 1, 2 (Tex.Crim.App. 1996). "[A]ccording to the plain language of §22.041, the fact that 'intentionally' immediately precedes 'abandons' means that the prescribed mental state is connected with the act of abandonment itself. Had the Legislature intended to require that the actor be aware of the risk of harm, it would have been a simple matter to have included language to that effect."

Rey v. State, 238 S.W.3d 840, 842 (Tex.App.—Amarillo 2007, pet. granted 2-6-08). "[T]he record is bereft of any evidence illustrating that [stepparent-D] accepted the responsibility to protect, shelter, feed and care for the three-year-old. This is of import because the status of stepparent alone does not obligate the stepparent to care for his stepchild [under §22.041(b)]. Rather, the stepparent must 'receive' the child into the family or accept the child as a family member before such obligations arise. When that occurs, the parent stands *in loco parentis* towards the child, and the relationship with its accompanying duties continues as long as the child remains part of the family."

Elder v. State, 993 S.W.2d 229, 230 (Tex.App.—San Antonio 1999, no pet.). "[T]he State urges us to hold that, as a matter of law, a parent cannot live with a 'known child molester' without putting her child in imminent danger. We decline the State's invitation."

PEN §22.05. DEADLY CONDUCT

(a) A person commits an offense if he recklessly engages in conduct that places another in imminent danger of serious bodily injury.

(b) A person commits an offense if he knowingly discharges a firearm at or in the direction of:

(1) one or more individuals; or

(2) a habitation, building, or vehicle and is reckless as to whether the habitation, building, or vehicle is occupied.

(c) Recklessness and danger are presumed if the actor knowingly pointed a firearm at or in the direction of another whether or not the actor believed the firearm to be loaded.

(d) For purposes of this section, "building," "habitation," and "vehicle" have the meanings assigned those terms by Section 30.01.

⭐

(e) An offense under Subsection (a) is a Class A misdemeanor. An offense under Subsection (b) is a felony of the third degree.

History of Pen §22.05: Acts 1973, 63rd Leg., ch. 399, §1, eff. Jan. 1, 1974. Amended by Acts 1993, 73rd Leg., ch. 900, §1.01, eff. Sept. 1, 1994.

See also CCP arts. 38.072, 38.37.

Guzman v. State, 188 S.W.3d 185, 192 (Tex.Crim. App.2006). "[D]eadly conduct [as defined in subsection (a)] is a lesser-included offense of both attempted murder as alleged in the indictment and aggravated assault as contained in the jury charge."

Reed v. State, 214 S.W.3d 626, 628 (Tex.App.— Waco 2006, pet. granted 8-22-07). "[C]onsidering common usage of the term and reading it in context, 'discharging a firearm at or in the direction of a habitation' assumes that the actor is outside the habitation."

Webber v. State, 29 S.W.3d 226, 231 (Tex.App.— Houston [14th Dist.] 2000, pet. ref'd). "[T]he trial court instructed the jury on the presumptions in [Pen. Code] §22.05(c) but did not instruct the jury on the effect of the presumption as mandated by [Pen. Code] §2.05(2). ... Because [the] charge created a mandatory presumption, the trial court committed both statutory and constitutional error by omitting a §2.05(2) instruction."

Scott v. State, 861 S.W.2d 440, 448 (Tex.App.— Austin 1993, no pet.). "'Section 22.05 applies to those acts that fall short of injuring another.'"

Beebe v. State, 756 S.W.2d 759, 761 (Tex.App.— Corpus Christi 1988), *aff'd*, 811 S.W.2d 604 (Tex.Crim. App.1991). "Terroristic threat ... requires a threat to commit an offense including violence with intent to *place another in fear*; whereas, reckless conduct requires engaging in conduct that *places another in imminent danger*. [R]eckless conduct is not a lesser included offense of a terroristic threat as alleged under [Pen. Code] 22.07(a)(2)."

PEN §22.06. CONSENT AS DEFENSE TO ASSAULTIVE CONDUCT

(a) The victim's effective consent or the actor's reasonable belief that the victim consented to the actor's conduct is a defense to prosecution under Section 22.01 (Assault), 22.02 (Aggravated Assault), or 22.05 (Deadly Conduct) if:

(1) the conduct did not threaten or inflict serious bodily injury; or

(2) the victim knew the conduct was a risk of:

(A) his occupation;

(B) recognized medical treatment; or

(C) a scientific experiment conducted by recognized methods.

 Subsection (b) below is effective for offenses committed on or after Sept. 1, 2007.

(b) The defense to prosecution provided by Subsection (a) is not available to a defendant who commits an offense described by Subsection (a) as a condition of the defendant's or the victim's initiation or continued membership in a criminal street gang, as defined by Section 71.01.

History of Pen §22.06: Acts 1973, 63rd Leg., ch. 399, §1, eff. Jan. 1, 1974. Amended by Acts 1993, 73rd Leg., ch. 900, §1.01, eff. Sept. 1, 1994; Acts 2007, 80th Leg., ch. 273, §1, eff. Sept. 1, 2007.

Bufkin v. State, 207 S.W.3d 779, 781 (Tex.Crim. App.2006). "With regard to the bite allegation, [D's girlfriend] denied that she was bitten on August 9th and claimed that the bite marks on her body were actually the result of 'love bites' that were a part of consensual sexual activity occurring on the prior evening (August 8th). *At 784-85:* [B]ecause the jury charge included the standard 'on or about' language in its application paragraph—giving the State leeway (as it should) in proving when the offense occurred—conduct consisting of 'consensual biting on August 8th' was encompassed by the application paragraph's allegations. The consent instruction is what would have given the jury a vehicle to effectuate any belief in [D's] claim that the biting incident, and the bite marks that resulted, were a product of consensual conduct that was not against the law. [¶] It is true that the State also prosecuted appellant for striking [his girlfriend] with his hand. But the jury charge submitted the biting and striking allegations in the disjunctive, so [D's] proposed instruction was needed to rebut a theory of liability upon which the jury could have decided to solely rely. We conclude that the court of appeals was correct in holding that the trial court erred in denying [D's] requested instruction."

Tanksley v. State, 656 S.W.2d 194, 197 (Tex.App.— Austin 1983, no pet.). "The provisions of §22.06 ... do not *define* effective consent to mean engaging in an occupation having a risk of assault.... Rather, the victim's express or apparent assent to an accused's conduct is effective as a defense *if* the victim knew that such conduct was a risk of his occupation."

For a quick reference of penalties, see the Chart of Penalties on p. 675.

O'CONNOR'S CRIMINAL CODES 781

PEN §22.065. REPEALED

Repealed by Dec. 18, 1985, order of the Texas Court of Criminal Appeals under the authority of Acts 1985, 69th Leg., ch. 685, §9. 701 S.W.2d xxix, lxvi- lxvii.

PEN §22.07. TERRORISTIC THREAT

(a) A person commits an offense if he threatens to commit any offense involving violence to any person or property with intent to:

(1) cause a reaction of any type to his threat by an official or volunteer agency organized to deal with emergencies;

(2) place any person in fear of imminent serious bodily injury;

(3) prevent or interrupt the occupation or use of a building, room, place of assembly, place to which the public has access, place of employment or occupation, aircraft, automobile, or other form of conveyance, or other public place;

(4) cause impairment or interruption of public communications, public transportation, public water, gas, or power supply or other public service;

(5) place the public or a substantial group of the public in fear of serious bodily injury; or

(6) influence the conduct or activities of a branch or agency of the federal government, the state, or a political subdivision of the state.

(b) An offense under Subsection (a)(1) is a Class B misdemeanor.

(c) An offense under Subsection (a)(2) is a Class B misdemeanor, except that the offense is a Class A misdemeanor if the offense:

(1) is committed against a member of the person's family or household or otherwise constitutes family violence; or

(2) is committed against a public servant.

(d) An offense under Subsection (a)(3) is a Class A misdemeanor, unless the actor causes pecuniary loss of $1,500 or more to the owner of the building, room, place, or conveyance, in which event the offense is a state jail felony.

(e) An offense under Subsection (a)(4), (a)(5), or (a)(6) is a felony of the third degree.

(f) In this section:

(1) "Family" has the meaning assigned by Section 71.003, Family Code.

(2) "Family violence" has the meaning assigned by Section 71.004, Family Code.

(3) "Household" has the meaning assigned by Section 71.005, Family Code.

(g) For purposes of Subsection (d), the amount of pecuniary loss is the amount of economic loss suffered by the owner of the building, room, place, or conveyance as a result of the prevention or interruption of the occupation or use of the building, room, place, or conveyance.

History of Pen §22.07: Acts 1973, 63rd Leg., ch. 399, §1, eff. Jan. 1, 1974. Amended by Acts 1979, 66th Leg., ch. 530, §2, eff. Aug. 27, 1979; Acts 1993, 73rd Leg., ch. 900, §1.01, eff. Sept. 1, 1994; Acts 2003, 78th Leg., ch. 139, §1 (eff. Sept. 1, 2003), ch. 388, §2 (eff. Sept. 1, 2003), ch. 446, §1 (eff. Sept. 1, 2003); Acts 2005, 79th Leg., ch. 728, §16.003, eff. Sept. 1, 2005.

ANNOTATIONS

Williams v. State, 194 S.W.3d 568, 574-75 (Tex. App.—Houston [14th Dist.] 2006), *aff'd*, 252 S.W.3d 353 (Tex.2008). "Imminent means '[n]ear at hand; mediate rather than immediate; close rather than touching; impending; on the point of happening; threatening; menacing; perilous.' The accused's threat of violence, made with the intent to place the victim in fear of imminent serious bodily injury, is what constitutes the offense. It is not necessary for the victim to actually be placed in fear of imminent serious bodily injury or for the accused to have the capability or the intention to actually carry out the threat. The offense is completed if the accused, by his threat, sought as a desired reaction, to place a person in fear of imminent serious bodily injury. [¶] [C]onditioning a threat of harm on the occurrence of a future event does not necessarily mean that the harmful consequences are not imminent. Thus, in gauging imminence, we must look to the proximity of the threatened harm to the condition. The focus of the inquiry should be whether the victim was afraid of imminent serious bodily injury at the time of the offense. The desired and sought after reaction of the victim, regardless of whether the threat was real or was carried out, is some evidence of the defendant's intent to place the victim in fear of imminent serious injury. The requisite intent can be inferred from the acts, words, and conduct of the accused." *See also Hadnot v. State*, 884 S.W.2d 922, 925-26 (Tex. App.—Beaumont 1994, no pet.).

George v. State, 841 S.W.2d 544, 546 (Tex.App.—Houston [1st Dist.] 1992), *aff'd*, 890 S.W.2d 73 (Tex. Crim.App.1994). Section 22.07 "'is broad enough to cover threats to commit any crime of violence if the actor's intent is to cause fear, emergency action, or substantial inconvenience.'"

PEN §22.08. AIDING SUICIDE

(a) A person commits an offense if, with intent to promote or assist the commission of suicide by another, he aids or attempts to aid the other to commit or attempt to commit suicide.

(b) An offense under this section is a Class C misdemeanor unless the actor's conduct causes suicide or attempted suicide that results in serious bodily injury, in which event the offense is a state jail felony.

History of Pen §22.08: Acts 1973, 63rd Leg., ch. 399, §1, eff. Jan. 1, 1974. Amended by Acts 1993, 73rd Leg., ch. 900, §1.01, eff. Sept. 1, 1994.

ANNOTATIONS

Chanslor v. State, 697 S.W.2d 393, 395 (Tex.Crim. App.1985), *disapproved on other grounds*, *Hall v. State*, 225 S.W.3d 524 (Tex.Crim.App.2007). "[A]iding a suicide is a separate offense which is statutorily defined in our Penal Code. It is not a defense to the crime of solicitation to commit murder or any other offense in the Penal Code. ... Merely being guilty of aiding suicide without more does not negate one's culpability as to anything."

PEN §22.09. TAMPERING WITH CONSUMER PRODUCT

(a) In this section:

(1) "Consumer Product" means any product offered for sale to or for consumption by the public and includes "food" and "drugs" as those terms are defined in Section 431.002, Health and Safety Code.

(2) "Tamper" means to alter or add a foreign substance to a consumer product to make it probable that the consumer product will cause serious bodily injury.

(b) A person commits an offense if he knowingly or intentionally tampers with a consumer product knowing that the consumer product will be offered for sale to the public or as a gift to another.

(c) A person commits an offense if he knowingly or intentionally threatens to tamper with a consumer product with the intent to cause fear, to affect the sale of the consumer product, or to cause bodily injury to any person.

(d) An offense under Subsection (b) is a felony of the second degree unless a person suffers serious bodily injury, in which event it is a felony of the first degree. An offense under Subsection (c) is a felony of the third degree.

History of Pen §22.09: Acts 1983, 68th Leg., ch. 481, §1, eff. Sept. 1, 1983. Amended by Acts 1989, 71st Leg., ch. 1008, §1, eff. Sept. 1, 1989; Acts 1991, 72nd Leg., ch. 14, §284(32), eff. Sept. 1, 1991; Acts 1993, 73rd Leg., ch. 900, §1.01, eff. Sept. 1, 1994.

PEN §22.10. LEAVING A CHILD IN A VEHICLE

(a) A person commits an offense if he intentionally or knowingly leaves a child in a motor vehicle for longer than five minutes, knowing that the child is:

(1) younger than seven years of age; and

(2) not attended by an individual in the vehicle who is 14 years of age or older.

(b) An offense under this section is a Class C misdemeanor.

History of Pen §22.10: Acts 1984, 68th Leg., 2nd C.S., ch. 24, §1, eff. Oct. 2, 1984.

PEN §22.11. HARASSMENT BY PERSONS IN CERTAIN CORRECTIONAL FACILITIES; HARASSMENT OF PUBLIC SERVANT

(a) A person commits an offense if, with the intent to assault, harass, or alarm, the person:

(1) while imprisoned or confined in a correctional or detention facility, causes another person to contact the blood, seminal fluid, vaginal fluid, saliva, urine, or feces of the actor, any other person, or an animal; or

(2) causes another person the actor knows to be a public servant to contact the blood, seminal fluid, vaginal fluid, saliva, urine, or feces of the actor, any other person, or an animal while the public servant is lawfully discharging an official duty or in retaliation or on account of an exercise of the public servant's official power or performance of an official duty.

(b) An offense under this section is a felony of the third degree.

(c) If conduct constituting an offense under this section also constitutes an offense under another section of this code, the actor may be prosecuted under either section.

(d) In this section, "correctional or detention facility" means:

(1) a secure correctional facility; or

(2) a "secure correctional facility" or a "secure detention facility" as defined by Section 51.02, Family Code, operated by or under contract with a juvenile board or the Texas Youth Commission or any other facility operated by or under contract with that commission.

For a quick reference of penalties, see the Chart of Penalties on p. 675.

PEN §22.11

(e) For purposes of Subsection (a)(2), the actor is presumed to have known the person was a public servant if the person was wearing a distinctive uniform or badge indicating the person's employment as a public servant.

History of Pen §22.11: Acts 1999, 76th Leg., ch. 335, §1, eff. Sept. 1, 1999; Acts 2003, 78th Leg., ch. 878, §1 (eff. Sept. 1, 2003), ch. 1006, §1 (eff. Sept. 1, 2003); Acts 2005, 79th Leg., ch. 543, §§1, 2, eff. Sept. 1, 2005.

PEN §22.12. APPLICABILITY TO CERTAIN CONDUCT

This chapter does not apply to conduct charged as having been committed against an individual who is an unborn child if the conduct is:

(1) committed by the mother of the unborn child;

(2) a lawful medical procedure performed by a physician or other health care provider with the requisite consent;

(3) a lawful medical procedure performed by a physician or other licensed health care provider with the requisite consent as part of an assisted reproduction as defined by Section 160.102, Family Code; or

(4) the dispensation of a drug in accordance with law or administration of a drug prescribed in accordance with law.

History of Pen §22.12: Acts 2003, 78th Leg., ch. 822, §2.04, eff. Sept. 1, 2003.

TITLE 6. OFFENSES AGAINST THE FAMILY

CHAPTER 25. OFFENSES AGAINST THE FAMILY

PEN §25.01. BIGAMY

(a) An individual commits an offense if:

(1) he is legally married and he:

(A) purports to marry or does marry a person other than his spouse in this state, or any other state or foreign country, under circumstances that would, but for the actor's prior marriage, constitute a marriage; or

(B) lives with a person other than his spouse in this state under the appearance of being married; or

(2) he knows that a married person other than his spouse is married and he:

(A) purports to marry or does marry that person in this state, or any other state or foreign country, under circumstances that would, but for the person's prior marriage, constitute a marriage; or

(B) lives with that person in this state under the appearance of being married.

(b) For purposes of this section, "under the appearance of being married" means holding out that the parties are married with cohabitation and an intent to be married by either party.

(c) It is a defense to prosecution under Subsection (a)(1) that the actor reasonably believed at the time of the commission of the offense that the actor and the person whom the actor married or purported to marry or with whom the actor lived under the appearance of being married were legally eligible to be married because the actor's prior marriage was void or had been dissolved by death, divorce, or annulment. For purposes of this subsection, an actor's belief is reasonable if the belief is substantiated by a certified copy of a death certificate or other signed document issued by a court.

(d) For the purposes of this section, the lawful wife or husband of the actor may testify both for or against the actor concerning proof of the original marriage.

(e) An offense under this section is a felony of the third degree, except that if at the time of the commission of the offense, the person whom the actor marries or purports to marry or with whom the actor lives under the appearance of being married is:

(1) 16 years of age or older, the offense is a felony of the second degree; or

(2) younger than 16 years of age, the offense is a felony of the first degree.

History of Pen §25.01: Acts 1973, 63rd Leg., ch. 399, §1, eff. Jan. 1, 1974. Amended by Acts 1993, 73rd Leg., ch. 900, §1.01, eff. Sept. 1, 1994; Acts 2005, 79th Leg., ch. 268, §4.03, eff. Sept. 1, 2005.

See also *O'Connor's Family Law Handbook*, "Bigamy," ch. 3-C, §3.2, p. 237.

PEN §25.02. PROHIBITED SEXUAL CONDUCT

(a) A person commits an offense if the person engages in sexual intercourse or deviate sexual intercourse with another person the actor knows to be, without regard to legitimacy:

(1) the actor's ancestor or descendant by blood or adoption;

(2) the actor's current or former stepchild or stepparent;

(3) the actor's parent's brother or sister of the whole or half blood;

(4) the actor's brother or sister of the whole or half blood or by adoption;

(5) the children of the actor's brother or sister of the whole or half blood or by adoption; or

(6) the son or daughter of the actor's aunt or uncle of the whole or half blood or by adoption.

(b) For purposes of this section:

(1) "Deviate sexual intercourse" means any contact between the genitals of one person and the mouth or anus of another person with intent to arouse or gratify the sexual desire of any person.

(2) "Sexual intercourse" means any penetration of the female sex organ by the male sex organ.

(c) An offense under this section is a felony of the third degree, unless the offense is committed under Subsection (a)(6), in which event the offense is a felony of the second degree.

History of Pen §25.02: Acts 1973, 63rd Leg., ch. 399, §1, eff. Jan. 1, 1974. Amended by Acts 1993, 73rd Leg., ch. 900, §1.01, eff. Sept. 1, 1994; Acts 2005, 79th Leg., ch. 268, §4.04, eff. Sept. 1, 2005.

See also CCP arts. 38.072, 38.37; Pen. Code §3.03; *O'Connor's Family Law Handbook*, "Parent engages in criminal conduct," ch. 4-H, §11.1.4, p. 495.

ANNOTATIONS

Martinez v. State, 662 S.W.2d 393, 395 (Tex. App.—Corpus Christi 1983, pet. ref'd). Section §25.02 "requires proof of a relationship between the accused and the complainant."

PEN §25.03. INTERFERENCE WITH CHILD CUSTODY

(a) A person commits an offense if the person takes or retains a child younger than 18 years when the person:

A *Subsection (1) below is effective for offenses committed on or after Sept. 1, 2007.*

(1) knows that the person's taking or retention violates the express terms of a judgment or order, including a temporary order, of a court disposing of the child's custody; or

Subsection (1) below is effective for offenses in which any element of the offense was committed before Sept. 1, 2007.

(1) knows that the person's taking or retention violates the express terms of a judgment or order of a court disposing of the child's custody; or

(2) has not been awarded custody of the child by a court of competent jurisdiction, knows that a suit for divorce or a civil suit or application for habeas corpus to dispose of the child's custody has been filed, and takes the child out of the geographic area of the counties composing the judicial district if the court is a district court or the county if the court is a statutory county court, without the permission of the court and with the intent to deprive the court of authority over the child.

(b) A noncustodial parent commits an offense if, with the intent to interfere with the lawful custody of a child younger than 18 years, the noncustodial parent knowingly entices or persuades the child to leave the custody of the custodial parent, guardian, or person standing in the stead of the custodial parent or guardian of the child.

(c) It is a defense to prosecution under Subsection (a)(2) that the actor returned the child to the geographic area of the counties composing the judicial district if the court is a district court or the county if the court is a statutory county court, within three days after the date of the commission of the offense.

(d) An offense under this section is a state jail felony.

History of Pen §25.03: Acts 1973, 63rd Leg., ch. 399, §1, eff. Jan. 1, 1974. Amended by Acts 1979, 66th Leg., ch. 527, §1, eff. Aug. 27, 1979; Acts 1987, 70th Leg., ch. 444, §1, eff. Sept. 1, 1987; Acts 1989, 71st Leg., ch. 830, §1, eff. Sept. 1, 1989; Acts 1993, 73rd Leg., ch. 900, §1.01, eff. Sept. 1, 1994; Acts 2001, 77th Leg., ch. 332, §1, eff. May 24, 2001; Acts 2007, 80th Leg., ch. 272, §1, eff. Sept. 1, 2007.

ANNOTATIONS

Roberts v. State, 619 S.W.2d 161, 164 (Tex.Crim. App.1981). "In cases prosecuted under [Pen. Code] §25.03, the act of retaining the child outside the state, in violation of a valid Texas court order, has the necessary consequence and detrimental effect and result of frustrating the power of the Texas judiciary and of

For a quick reference of penalties, see the Chart of Penalties on p. 675.

O'CONNOR'S CRIMINAL CODES 785

denying a Texas resident the possession of a child to which he has been awarded the legal custody. This interest in protecting the viability of its judgments and the rights of possession of its residents gives the State of Texas jurisdiction to punish the acts of a person committed wholly outside the territorial boundaries of Texas when those acts thwart this valid interest."

Garcia v. State, 172 S.W.3d 270, 273 (Tex.App.—El Paso 2005, no pet.). "We find that the plain meaning of the word 'custody' in [subsection (a)(1)] encompasses both the conduct of the managing conservator and the possessory conservator who was awarded visitation rights." *See also Perry v. State*, 727 S.W.2d 781, 783 (Tex.App.—Austin 1987, pet. ref'd).

Ex parte Jones, 36 S.W.3d 139, 141 (Tex.App.— Houston [1st Dist.] 2000, pet. ref'd). The trial court "concluded that double jeopardy barred prosecution of the interference with child custody charge [holding] that the family court's 1998 contempt order was a constructive criminal contempt conviction. *At 142:* We disagree with the [trial court's] ruling.... The 1998 contempt order attempted to coerce the *future* actions of Mother in returning Brittany to Father. The order contained no provision punishing Mother for past action. [¶] Accordingly, the 5th Amendment protection against successive prosecutions for the same offense is not implicated in this case." (Emphasis added.)

PEN §25.031. AGREEMENT TO ABDUCT FROM CUSTODY

Ⓐ *Subsection (a) below is effective for offenses committed on or after Sept. 1, 2007.*

(a) A person commits an offense if the person agrees, for remuneration or the promise of remuneration, to abduct a child younger than 18 years of age by force, threat of force, misrepresentation, stealth, or unlawful entry, knowing that the child is under the care and control of a person having custody or physical possession of the child under a court order, including a temporary order, or under the care and control of another person who is exercising care and control with the consent of a person having custody or physical possession under a court order, including a temporary order.

Subsection (a) below is effective for offenses in which any element of the offense was committed before Sept. 1, 2007.

(a) A person commits an offense if the person agrees, for remuneration or the promise of remuneration, to abduct a child younger than 18 years of age by force, threat of force, misrepresentation, stealth, or unlawful entry, knowing that the child is under the care and control of a person having custody or physical possession of the child under a court order or under the care and control of another person who is exercising care and control with the consent of a person having custody or physical possession under a court order.

(b) An offense under this section is a state jail felony.

History of Pen §25.031: Acts 1987, 70th Leg., ch. 444, §3, eff. Sept. 1, 1987. Amended by Acts 1993, 73rd Leg., ch. 900, §1.01, eff. Sept. 1, 1994; Acts 2007, 80th Leg., ch. 272, §2, eff. Sept. 1, 2007.

PEN §25.04. ENTICING A CHILD

(a) A person commits an offense if, with the intent to interfere with the lawful custody of a child younger than 18 years, he knowingly entices, persuades, or takes the child from the custody of the parent or guardian or person standing in the stead of the parent or guardian of such child.

(b) An offense under this section is a Class B misdemeanor, unless it is shown on the trial of the offense that the actor intended to commit a felony against the child, in which event an offense under this section is a felony of the third degree.

History of Pen §25.04: Acts 1973, 63rd Leg., ch. 399, §1, eff. Jan. 1, 1974. Amended by Acts 1999, 76th Leg., ch. 685, §7, eff. Sept. 1, 1999.

ANNOTATIONS

Cunyus v. State, 727 S.W.2d 561, 565 (Tex.Crim. App.1987). "[T]he mere offer of an activity to a child which would remove the child from where the parents or legal guardians have permitted the child to be will not alone constitute an offense."

Sanchez v. State, 712 S.W.2d 170, 171 (Tex.App.— Austin 1986, no pet.). Under §25.04 "the consent of the minor is irrelevant and it is of no legal effect that her actions in leaving are in fact voluntary."

PEN §25.05. CRIMINAL NONSUPPORT

(a) An individual commits an offense if the individual intentionally or knowingly fails to provide support for the individual's child younger than 18 years of age, or for the individual's child who is the subject of a court order requiring the individual to support the child.

(b) For purposes of this section, "child" includes a child born out of wedlock whose paternity has either been acknowledged by the actor or has been established in a civil suit under the Family Code or the law of another state.

(c) Under this section, a conviction may be had on the uncorroborated testimony of a party to the offense.

(d) It is an affirmative defense to prosecution under this section that the actor could not provide support for the actor's child.

(e) The pendency of a prosecution under this section does not affect the power of a court to enter an order for child support under the Family Code.

(f) An offense under this section is a state jail felony.

History of Pen §25.05: Acts 1973, 63rd Leg., ch. 399, §1, eff. Jan. 1, 1974. Amended by Acts 1987, 70th Leg., 2nd C.S., ch. 73, §13, eff. Nov. 1, 1987; Acts 1993, 73rd Leg., ch. 900, §1.01, eff. Sept. 1, 1994; Acts 2001, 77th Leg., ch. 375, §1, eff. May 25, 2001.

See also Fam. Code ch. 157, "Enforcement," ch. 232, "Suspension of License"; Gov't Code §21.002; 42 U.S.C. §651 et seq.

ANNOTATIONS

Lyons v. State, 835 S.W.2d 715, 718 (Tex.App.—Texarkana 1992, pet. ref'd). "Section 25.05 does not define 'support,' and the term is not defined elsewhere in the Penal Code. [¶] What constitutes 'support' is evidentiary, and it is therefore not essential for notice to the accused that the definition be included in the information. [¶] The ability to pay child support is no longer an element of the offense under §25.05(a)...."

PEN §25.06. HARBORING RUNAWAY CHILD

(a) A person commits an offense if he knowingly harbors a child and he is criminally negligent about whether the child:

(1) is younger than 18 years; and

(2) has escaped from the custody of a peace officer, a probation officer, the Texas Youth Council, or a detention facility for children, or is voluntarily absent from the child's home without the consent of the child's parent or guardian for a substantial length of time or without the intent to return.

(b) It is a defense to prosecution under this section that the actor was related to the child within the second degree by consanguinity or affinity, as determined under Chapter 573, Government Code.

(c) It is a defense to prosecution under this section that the actor notified:

(1) the person or agency from which the child escaped or a law enforcement agency of the presence of the child within 24 hours after discovering that the child had escaped from custody; or

(2) a law enforcement agency or a person at the child's home of the presence of the child within 24 hours after discovering that the child was voluntarily absent from home without the consent of the child's parent or guardian.

(d) An offense under this section is a Class A misdemeanor.

(e) On the receipt of a report from a peace officer, probation officer, the Texas Youth Council, a foster home, or a detention facility for children that a child has escaped its custody or upon receipt of a report from a parent, guardian, conservator, or legal custodian that a child is missing, a law enforcement agency shall immediately enter a record of the child into the National Crime Information Center.

History of Pen §25.06: Acts 1979, 66th Leg., ch. 558, §1, eff. Sept. 1, 1979. Amended by Acts 1983, 68th Leg., ch. 831, §1, eff. Sept. 1, 1983; Acts 1991, 72nd Leg., ch. 561, §40, eff. Aug. 26, 1991. Renumbered from §36.07 by Acts 1993, 73rd Leg., ch. 900, §1.01, eff. Sept. 1, 1994; Acts 1995, 74th Leg., ch. 76, §5.95(27), eff. Sept. 1, 1995.

ⓐ PEN §25.07. VIOLATION OF CERTAIN COURT ORDERS OR CONDITIONS OF BOND IN A FAMILY VIOLENCE CASE

Section 25.07 below is effective for offenses committed on or after Jan. 1, 2008.

(a) A person commits an offense if, in violation of a condition of bond set in a family violence case and related to the safety of the victim or the safety of the community, an order issued under Article 17.292, Code of Criminal Procedure, an order issued under Section 6.504, Family Code, Chapter 83, Family Code, if the temporary ex parte order has been served on the person, or Chapter 85, Family Code, or an order issued by another jurisdiction as provided by Chapter 88, Family Code, the person knowingly or intentionally:

ⓐ *Subsection (1) below is effective for defendants arrested on or after May 11, 2007.*

(1) commits family violence or an act in furtherance of an offense under Section 22.011, 22.021, or 42.072;

Subsection (1) below is effective for defendants arrested before May 11, 2007.

(1) commits family violence or an act in furtherance of an offense under Section 42.072;

For a quick reference of penalties, see the Chart of Penalties on p. 675.

O'CONNOR'S CRIMINAL CODES 787

(2) communicates:

(A) directly with a protected individual or a member of the family or household in a threatening or harassing manner;

(B) a threat through any person to a protected individual or a member of the family or household; or

(C) in any manner with the protected individual or a member of the family or household except through the person's attorney or a person appointed by the court, if the violation is of an order described by this subsection and the order prohibits any communication with a protected individual or a member of the family or household;

(3) goes to or near any of the following places as specifically described in the order or condition of bond:

(A) the residence or place of employment or business of a protected individual or a member of the family or household; or

(B) any child care facility, residence, or school where a child protected by the order or condition of bond normally resides or attends; or

(4) possesses a firearm.

(b) For the purposes of this section:

(1) "Family violence," "family," "household," and "member of a household" have the meanings assigned by Chapter 71, Family Code.

(2) "Firearm" has the meaning assigned by Chapter 46.

(c) If conduct constituting an offense under this section also constitutes an offense under another section of this code, the actor may be prosecuted under either section or under both sections.

(d) Reconciliatory actions or agreements made by persons affected by an order do not affect the validity of the order or the duty of a peace officer to enforce this section.

(e) A peace officer investigating conduct that may constitute an offense under this section for a violation of an order may not arrest a person protected by that order for a violation of that order.

(f) It is not a defense to prosecution under this section that certain information has been excluded, as provided by Section 85.007, Family Code, or Article 17.292, Code of Criminal Procedure, from an order to which this section applies.

(g) An offense under this section is a Class A misdemeanor unless it is shown on the trial of the offense that the defendant has previously been convicted under this section two or more times or has violated the order or condition of bond by committing an assault or the offense of stalking, in which event the offense is a third degree felony.

History of Pen §25.07: Acts 1983, 68th Leg., ch. 631, §3, eff. Sept. 1, 1983. Amended by Acts 1985, 69th Leg., ch. 583, §3, eff. Sept. 1, 1985; Acts 1987, 70th Leg., ch. 170, §1 (eff. Sept. 1, 1987), ch. 677, §8 (eff. Sept. 1, 1987); Acts 1989, 71st Leg., ch. 614, §§23-26 (eff. Sept. 1, 1989), ch. 739, §§4-7 (eff. Sept. 1, 1989); Acts 1991, 72nd Leg., ch. 366, §2, eff. Sept. 1, 1991. Renumbered from §25.08 and amended by Acts 1993, 73rd Leg., ch. 900, §1.01, eff. Sept. 1, 1994. Amended by Acts 1995, 74th Leg., ch. 658, §§2, 3 (eff. June 14, 1995), ch. 660, §§1, 2 (eff. Sept. 1, 1995), ch. 1024, §23 (eff. Sept. 1, 1995); Acts 1997, 75th Leg., ch. 1, §2 (eff. Jan. 28, 1997), ch. 1193, §21 (eff. Sept. 1, 1997); Acts 1999, 76th Leg., ch. 62, §15.02(e), eff. Sept. 1, 1999; Acts 2001, 77th Leg., ch. 23, §1, eff. Sept. 1, 2001; Acts 2003, 78th Leg., ch. 134, §1, eff. Sept. 1, 2003; Acts 2007, 80th Leg., ch. 66, §2 (eff. May 11, 2007), ch. 1113, §§1, 2 (eff. Jan. 1, 2008).

ANNOTATIONS

Harvey v. State, 78 S.W.3d 368, 368-69 (Tex.Crim. App.2002). "Does [Pen. Code §25.07(a)] require a culpable mental state as to the element of 'in violation of an order'? *At 373:* The term 'in violation of an order issued under [Fam. Code] §6.504 or chapter 85 [or] under [CCP art.] 17.292, ...' means 'in violation of an order that was ... issued under one of those statutes at a proceeding that the defendant attended or at a hearing held after the defendant received service of the application for a protective order and notice of the hearing.' [¶] [T]he statute requires some knowledge of the protective order." *See also **Small v. State**,* 809 S.W.2d 253, 256 (Tex.App.—San Antonio 1991, pet. ref'd).

Lee v. State, 799 S.W.2d 750, 752 (Tex.Crim.App. 1990). "[T]o sentence an individual to confinement for *contempt of a prior court order*, the order must be 'unequivocal to be sufficient.' *At 753:* Unlike a civil contempt judgment, [Pen. Code] §25.08 [now §25.07] is directed toward the *misconduct* proscribed rather than the court's authority to enforce its own order. ... The public policy consideration forming the basis of the enactment is to remove the perpetrator from the scene and into custody.... *At 754:* A fair reading of §25.08 [now §25.07] does not indicate that a successful citation is a prerequisite for a successful prosecution.... To hold otherwise would be to frustrate the intent of the Legislature...."

Patton v. State, 835 S.W.2d 684, 689 (Tex.App.— Dallas 1992, no pet.). "Exclusion of information from a protective order pursuant to [Fam. Code §85.007] is not a defense to prosecution for violation of that order.

[T]he protective order is not invalid and Husband cannot use exclusion of [Wife's work] address as a defense to prosecution for violating the order."

PEN §25.07. VIOLATION OF PROTECTIVE ORDER OR MAGISTRATE'S ORDER

Section 25.07 below is effective for offenses in which any element of the offense was committed before Jan. 1, 2008.

(a) A person commits an offense if, in violation of an order issued under Section 6.504 or Chapter 85, Family Code, under Article 17.292, Code of Criminal Procedure, or by another jurisdiction as provided by Chapter 88, Family Code, the person knowingly or intentionally:

Ⓐ *Subsection (1) below is effective for defendants arrested on or after May 11, 2007.*

(1) commits family violence or an act in furtherance of an offense under Section 22.011, 22.021, or 42.072;

Subsection (1) below is effective for defendants arrested before May 11, 2007.

(1) commits family violence or an act in furtherance of an offense under Section 42.072;

(2) communicates:

(A) directly with a protected individual or a member of the family or household in a threatening or harassing manner;

(B) a threat through any person to a protected individual or a member of the family or household; or

(C) in any manner with the protected individual or a member of the family or household except through the person's attorney or a person appointed by the court, if the order prohibits any communication with a protected individual or a member of the family or household;

(3) goes to or near any of the following places as specifically described in the order:

(A) the residence or place of employment or business of a protected individual or a member of the family or household; or

(B) any child care facility, residence, or school where a child protected by the order normally resides or attends; or

(4) possesses a firearm.

(b) For the purposes of this section:

(1) "Family violence," "family," "household," and "member of a household" have the meanings assigned by Chapter 71, Family Code.

(2) "Firearm" has the meaning assigned by Chapter 46.

(c) If conduct constituting an offense under this section also constitutes an offense under another section of this code, the actor may be prosecuted under either section or under both sections.

(d) Reconciliatory actions or agreements made by persons affected by an order do not affect the validity of the order or the duty of a peace officer to enforce this section.

(e) A peace officer investigating conduct that may constitute an offense under this section for a violation of an order may not arrest a person protected by that order for a violation of that order.

(f) It is not a defense to prosecution under this section that certain information has been excluded, as provided by Section 85.007, Family Code, or Article 17.292, Code of Criminal Procedure, from an order to which this section applies.

(g) An offense under this section is a Class A misdemeanor unless it is shown on the trial of the offense that the defendant has previously been convicted under this section two or more times or has violated the protective order by committing an assault or the offense of stalking, in which event the offense is a third degree felony.

PEN §25.071. VIOLATION OF PROTECTIVE ORDER PREVENTING OFFENSE CAUSED BY BIAS OR PREJUDICE

(a) A person commits an offense if, in violation of an order issued under Article 6.08, Code of Criminal Procedure, the person knowingly or intentionally:

(1) commits an offense under Title 5 or Section 28.02, 28.03, or 28.08 and commits the offense because of bias or prejudice as described by Article 42.014, Code of Criminal Procedure;

(2) communicates:

(A) directly with a protected individual in a threatening or harassing manner;

(B) a threat through any person to a protected individual; or

For a quick reference of penalties, see the Chart of Penalties on p. 675.

O'CONNOR'S CRIMINAL CODES   789

(C) in any manner with the protected individual, if the order prohibits any communication with a protected individual; or

(3) goes to or near the residence or place of employment or business of a protected individual.

(b) If conduct constituting an offense under this section also constitutes an offense under another section of this code, the actor may be prosecuted under either section or under both sections.

(c) A peace officer investigating conduct that may constitute an offense under this section for a violation of an order may not arrest a person protected by that order for a violation of that order.

(d) An offense under this section is a Class A misdemeanor unless it is shown on the trial of the offense that the defendant has previously been convicted under this section two or more times or has violated the protective order by committing an assault, in which event the offense is a third degree felony.

History of Pen §25.071: Acts 2001, 77th Leg., ch. 85, §3.02, eff. Sept. 1, 2001.

PEN §25.08. SALE OR PURCHASE OF CHILD

(a) A person commits an offense if he:

(1) possesses a child younger than 18 years of age or has the custody, conservatorship, or guardianship of a child younger than 18 years of age, whether or not he has actual possession of the child, and he offers to accept, agrees to accept, or accepts a thing of value for the delivery of the child to another or for the possession of the child by another for purposes of adoption; or

(2) offers to give, agrees to give, or gives a thing of value to another for acquiring or maintaining the possession of a child for the purpose of adoption.

(b) It is an exception to the application of this section that the thing of value is:

(1) a fee or reimbursement paid to a child-placing agency as authorized by law;

(2) a fee paid to an attorney, social worker, mental health professional, or physician for services rendered in the usual course of legal or medical practice or in providing adoption counseling;

(3) a reimbursement of legal or medical expenses incurred by a person for the benefit of the child; or

(4) a necessary pregnancy-related expense paid by a child-placing agency for the benefit of the child's parent during the pregnancy or after the birth of the child

as permitted by the minimum standards for child-placing agencies and Department of Protective and Regulatory Services rules.

(c) An offense under this section is a felony of the third degree, except that the offense is a felony of the second degree if the actor commits the offense with intent to commit an offense under Section 43.25.

History of Pen §25.08: Acts 1977, 65th Leg., ch. 38, §1, eff. Mar. 30, 1977. Amended by Acts 1981, 67th Leg., ch. 514, §1, eff. Sept. 1, 1981. Renumbered from §25.06 by Acts 1987, 70th Leg., ch. 167, §5.01(a)(44). Renumbered from §25.11 and amended by Acts 1993, 73rd Leg., ch. 900, §1.01, eff. Sept. 1, 1994. Amended by Acts 2001, 77th Leg., ch. 134, §1, eff. Sept. 1, 2001; Acts 2003, 78th Leg., ch. 1005, §3, eff. Sept. 1, 2003.

ANNOTATIONS

Thacker v. State, 889 S.W.2d 380, 386 (Tex.App.—Houston [14th Dist.] 1994, pet. ref'd). Pen. Code §25.11, now §25.08 "'was adopted to deter the potentially coercive effect of payments to expectant mothers at a time when the best interests of the child, and ... the mother and father, are most likely to be subordinated by greed or other ulterior motives....' *At 399:* Section 25.11 [now §25.08] contains only three exceptions to its prohibitions.... The statute contains no exceptions relating to payments intended for housing costs, food, utilities, clothing, personal hygiene products, or transportation."

PEN §25.09. ADVERTISING FOR PLACEMENT OF CHILD

(a) A person commits an offense if the person advertises in the public media that the person will place a child for adoption or will provide or obtain a child for adoption.

(b) This section does not apply to a licensed child-placing agency that is identified in the advertisement as a licensed child-placing agency.

(c) An offense under this section is a Class A misdemeanor unless the person has been convicted previously under this section, in which event the offense is a felony of the third degree.

(d) In this section:

(1) "Child" has the meaning assigned by Section 101.003, Family Code.

(2) "Public media" has the meaning assigned by Section 38.01. The term also includes communications through the use of the Internet or another public computer network.

History of Pen §25.09: Acts 1997, 75th Leg., ch. 561, §31, eff. Sept. 1, 1997.

PEN §25.10. INTERFERENCE WITH RIGHTS OF GUARDIAN OF THE PERSON

(a) In this section:

(1) "Possessory right" means the right of a guardian of the person to have physical possession of a ward and to establish the ward's legal domicile, as provided by Section 767(1), Texas Probate Code.

(2) "Ward" has the meaning assigned by Section 601, Texas Probate Code.

(b) A person commits an offense if the person takes, retains, or conceals a ward when the person knows that the person's taking, retention, or concealment interferes with a possessory right with respect to the ward.

(c) An offense under this section is a state jail felony.

(d) This section does not apply to a governmental entity where the taking, retention, or concealment of the ward was authorized by Subtitle E, Title 5, Family Code, or Chapter 48, Human Resources Code.

History of Pen §25.10: Acts 2003, 78th Leg., ch. 549, §32, eff. Sept. 1, 2003.

PEN §25.11. RENUMBERED

Renumbered as §25.08 by Acts 1993, 73rd Leg., ch. 900, §1.01, eff. Sept. 1, 1994.

TITLE 7. OFFENSES AGAINST PROPERTY

CHAPTER 28. ARSON, CRIMINAL MISCHIEF, & OTHER PROPERTY DAMAGE OR DESTRUCTION

PEN §28.01. DEFINITIONS

In this chapter:

(1) "Habitation" means a structure or vehicle that is adapted for the overnight accommodation of persons and includes:

(A) each separately secured or occupied portion of the structure or vehicle; and

(B) each structure appurtenant to or connected with the structure or vehicle.

(2) "Building" means any structure or enclosure intended for use or occupation as a habitation or for some purpose of trade, manufacture, ornament, or use.

(3) "Property" means:

(A) real property;

(B) tangible or intangible personal property, including anything severed from land; or

(C) a document, including money, that represents or embodies anything of value.

(4) "Vehicle" includes any device in, on, or by which any person or property is or may be propelled, moved, or drawn in the normal course of commerce or transportation.

(5) "Open-space land" means real property that is undeveloped for the purpose of human habitation.

(6) "Controlled burning" means the burning of unwanted vegetation with the consent of the owner of the property on which the vegetation is located and in such a manner that the fire is controlled and limited to a designated area.

History of Pen §28.01: Acts 1973, 63rd Leg., ch. 399, §1, eff. Jan. 1, 1974. Amended by Acts 1979, 66th Leg., ch. 588, §1, eff. Sept. 1, 1979; Acts 1989, 71st Leg., ch. 31, §1, eff. Sept. 1, 1989.

PEN §28.02. ARSON

(a) A person commits an offense if the person starts a fire, regardless of whether the fire continues after ignition, or causes an explosion with intent to destroy or damage:

(1) any vegetation, fence, or structure on open-space land; or

(2) any building, habitation, or vehicle:

(A) knowing that it is within the limits of an incorporated city or town;

(B) knowing that it is insured against damage or destruction;

(C) knowing that it is subject to a mortgage or other security interest;

(D) knowing that it is located on property belonging to another;

(E) knowing that it has located within it property belonging to another; or

(F) when the person is reckless about whether the burning or explosion will endanger the life of some individual or the safety of the property of another.

(a-1) A person commits an offense if the person recklessly starts a fire or causes an explosion while

For a quick reference of penalties, see the Chart of Penalties on p. 675.

O'CONNOR'S CRIMINAL CODES 791

PEN §28.02

manufacturing or attempting to manufacture a controlled substance and the fire or explosion damages any building, habitation, or vehicle.

(b) It is an exception to the application of Subsection (a)(1) that the fire or explosion was a part of the controlled burning of open-space land.

(c) It is a defense to prosecution under Subsection (a)(2)(A) that prior to starting the fire or causing the explosion, the actor obtained a permit or other written authorization granted in accordance with a city ordinance, if any, regulating fires and explosions.

(d) An offense under Subsection (a) is a felony of the second degree, except that the offense is a felony of the first degree if it is shown on the trial of the offense that:

(1) bodily injury or death was suffered by any person by reason of the commission of the offense; or

(2) the property intended to be damaged or destroyed by the actor was a habitation or a place of assembly or worship.

(e) An offense under Subsection (a-1) is a state jail felony, except that the offense is a felony of the third degree if it is shown on the trial of the offense that bodily injury or death was suffered by any person by reason of the commission of the offense.

(f) It is a felony of the third degree if a person commits an offense under Subsection (a)(2) of this section and the person intentionally starts a fire in or on a building, habitation, or vehicle, with intent to damage or destroy property belonging to another, or with intent to injure any person, and in so doing, recklessly causes damage to the building, habitation, or vehicle.

(g) If conduct that constitutes an offense under Subsection (a-1) or that constitutes an offense under Subsection (f) also constitutes an offense under another subsection of this section or another section of this code, the actor may be prosecuted under Subsection (a-1) or Subsection (f), under the other subsection of this section, or under the other section of this code.

History of Pen §28.02: Acts 1973, 63rd Leg., ch. 399, §1, eff. Jan. 1, 1974. Amended by Acts 1979, 66th Leg., ch. 588, §2, eff. Sept. 1, 1979; Acts 1981, 67th Leg., ch. 425, §1, eff. Sept. 1, 1981; Acts 1989, 71st Leg., ch. 31, §2, eff. Sept. 1, 1989; Acts 1993, 73rd Leg., ch. 900, §1.01, eff. Sept. 1, 1994; Acts 1997, 75th Leg., ch. 1006, §1, eff. Sept. 1, 1997; Acts 2001, 77th Leg., ch. 976, §1, eff. Sept. 1, 2001; Acts 2005, 79th Leg., ch. 960, §1, eff. Sept. 1, 2005.

ANNOTATIONS

Sellers v. State, 961 S.W.2d 351, 352 (Tex.App.—Houston [1st Dist.] 1997, pet. ref'd). "In this case, it is undisputed that [arson victims] both died in one fire occurring on April 13th. Appellant was twice indicted for arson in connection with that fire—once related to the death of [each of two victims of fire]. In each of the indictments, the State alleged appellant 'intentionally and knowingly start[ed] a fire in a building … with intent to destroy and damage the said building [and knew] the said building … was within the limits of an incorporated city.' He was, therefore, twice indicted—and convicted and punished—for the same offense. [¶] [W]e sustain appellant's [double-jeopardy argument]."

Mosher v. State, 901 S.W.2d 547, 549 (Tex. App.—El Paso 1995, no pet.). "[T]he offense of arson is complete whenever the actor starts a fire with the requisite culpable mental state, whether or not damage of any kind actually occurs."

Taylor v. State, 735 S.W.2d 930, 941 (Tex.App.—Dallas 1987), *aff'd*, 786 S.W.2d 295 (Tex.Crim.App. 1990). "Motive and opportunity alone are not sufficient to establish that an accused set fire to a building. There must be some testimony showing that … someone intentionally burned the building. *At 943:* Allegation of manner and means of 'starting a fire' under §28.02 is not a fundamental requisite of charging the offense for purposes of invoking the trial court's jurisdiction."

PEN §28.03. CRIMINAL MISCHIEF

(a) A person commits an offense if, without the effective consent of the owner:

(1) he intentionally or knowingly damages or destroys the tangible property of the owner;

(2) he intentionally or knowingly tampers with the tangible property of the owner and causes pecuniary loss or substantial inconvenience to the owner or a third person; or

(3) he intentionally or knowingly makes markings, including inscriptions, slogans, drawings, or paintings, on the tangible property of the owner.

(b) Except as provided by Subsections (f) and (h), an offense under this section is:

(1) a Class C misdemeanor if:

(A) the amount of pecuniary loss is less than $50; or

--- ⭐ ---

(B) except as provided in Subdivision (3)(A) or (3)(B), it causes substantial inconvenience to others;

(2) a Class B misdemeanor if the amount of pecuniary loss is $50 or more but less than $500;

(3) a Class A misdemeanor if:

(A) the amount of pecuniary loss is:

(i) $500 or more but less than $1,500; or

(ii) less than $1,500 and the actor causes in whole or in part impairment or interruption of public communications, public transportation, public gas or power supply, or other public service, or causes to be diverted in whole, in part, or in any manner, including installation or removal of any device for any such purpose, any public communications or public gas or power supply; or

(B) the actor causes in whole or in part impairment or interruption of any public water supply, or causes to be diverted in whole, in part, or in any manner, including installation or removal of any device for any such purpose, any public water supply, regardless of the amount of the pecuniary loss;

(4) a state jail felony if the amount of pecuniary loss is:

(A) $1,500 or more but less than $20,000;

(B) less than $1,500, if the property damaged or destroyed is a habitation and if the damage or destruction is caused by a firearm or explosive weapon; or

(C) less than $1,500, if the property was a fence used for the production or containment of:

(i) cattle, bison, horses, sheep, swine, goats, exotic livestock, or exotic poultry; or

(ii) game animals as that term is defined by Section 63.001, Parks and Wildlife Code;

(5) a felony of the third degree if the amount of the pecuniary loss is $20,000 or more but less than $100,000;

(6) a felony of the second degree if the amount of pecuniary loss is $100,000 or more but less than $200,000; or

(7) a felony of the first degree if the amount of pecuniary loss is $200,000 or more.

(c) For the purposes of this section, it shall be presumed that a person who is receiving the economic benefit of public communications, public water, gas, or power supply, has knowingly tampered with the tangible property of the owner if the communication or supply has been:

(1) diverted from passing through a metering device; or

(2) prevented from being correctly registered by a metering device; or

(3) activated by any device installed to obtain public communications, public water, gas, or power supply without a metering device.

(d) The terms "public communication, public transportation, public gas or power supply, or other public service" and "public water supply" shall mean, refer to, and include any such services subject to regulation by the Public Utility Commission of Texas, the Railroad Commission of Texas, or the Texas Natural Resource Conservation Commission or any such services enfranchised by the State of Texas or any political subdivision thereof.

(e) When more than one item of tangible property, belonging to one or more owners, is damaged, destroyed, or tampered with in violation of this section pursuant to one scheme or continuing course of conduct, the conduct may be considered as one offense, and the amounts of pecuniary loss to property resulting from the damage to, destruction of, or tampering with the property may be aggregated in determining the grade of the offense.

(f) An offense under this section is a state jail felony if the damage or destruction is inflicted on a place of worship or human burial, a public monument, or a community center that provides medical, social, or educational programs and the amount of the pecuniary loss to real property or to tangible personal property is less than $20,000.

(g) In this section:

(1) "Explosive weapon" means any explosive or incendiary device that is designed, made, or adapted for the purpose of inflicting serious bodily injury, death, or substantial property damage, or for the principal purpose of causing such a loud report as to cause undue public alarm or terror, and includes:

(A) an explosive or incendiary bomb, grenade, rocket, and mine;

(B) a device designed, made, or adapted for delivering or shooting an explosive weapon; and

(C) a device designed, made, or adapted to start a fire in a time-delayed manner.

(2) "Firearm" has the meaning assigned by Section 46.01.

For a quick reference of penalties, see the Chart of Penalties on p. 675.

O'CONNOR'S CRIMINAL CODES   793

(3) "Institution of higher education" has the meaning assigned by Section 61.003, Education Code.

 Subsections (4)-(8) below are effective for offenses committed on or after Sept. 1, 2007.

(4) "Aluminum wiring" means insulated or noninsulated wire or cable that consists of at least 50 percent aluminum, including any tubing or conduit attached to the wire or cable.

(5) "Bronze wiring" means insulated or noninsulated wire or cable that consists of at least 50 percent bronze, including any tubing or conduit attached to the wire or cable.

(6) "Copper wiring" means insulated or noninsulated wire or cable that consists of at least 50 percent copper, including any tubing or conduit attached to the wire or cable.

(7) "Transportation communications equipment" means:

(A) an official traffic-control device, railroad sign or signal, or traffic-control signal, as those terms are defined by Section 541.304, Transportation Code; or

(B) a sign, signal, or device erected by a railroad, public body, or public officer to direct the movement of a railroad train, as defined by Section 541.202, Transportation Code.

(8) "Transportation communications device" means any item attached to transportation communications equipment, including aluminum wiring, bronze wiring, and copper wiring.

(h) An offense under this section is a state jail felony if the amount of the pecuniary loss to real property or to tangible personal property is $1,500 or more but less than $20,000 and the damage or destruction is inflicted on a public or private elementary school, secondary school, or institution of higher education.

(i) Notwithstanding Subsection (b), an offense under this section is a felony of the first degree if the property is livestock and the damage is caused by introducing bovine spongiform encephalopathy, commonly known as mad cow disease, or a disease described by Section 161.041(a), Agriculture Code. In this subsection, "livestock" has the meaning assigned by Section 161.001, Agriculture Code.

 Subsection (j) below is effective for offenses committed on or after Sept. 1, 2007.

(j) Notwithstanding Subsection (b), an offense under this section is a felony of the third degree if:

(1) the tangible property damaged, destroyed, or tampered with is transportation communications equipment or a transportation communications device; and

(2) the amount of the pecuniary loss to the tangible property is less than $100,000.

History of Pen §28.03: Acts 1973, 63rd Leg., ch. 399, §1, eff. Jan. 1, 1974. Amended by Acts 1981, 67th Leg., ch. 29, §1, eff. Aug. 31, 1981; Acts 1983, 68th Leg., ch. 497, §1, eff. Sept. 1, 1983; Acts 1985, 69th Leg., ch. 352, §1, eff. Sept. 1, 1985; Acts 1989, 71st Leg., ch. 559, §1 (eff. June 14, 1989), ch. 1253, §1 (eff. Sept. 1, 1989), 1st C.S., ch. 42, §1 (eff. Sept. 1, 1989); Acts 1993, 73rd Leg., ch. 900, §1.01, eff. Sept. 1, 1994; Acts 1995, 74th Leg., ch. 76, §11.280, eff. Sept. 1, 1995; Acts 1997, 75th Leg., ch. 1083, §1, eff. Sept. 1, 1997; Acts 1999, 76th Leg., ch. 686, §1, eff. Sept. 1, 1999; Acts 2001, 77th Leg., ch. 976, §2 (eff. Sept. 1, 2001), ch. 747, §1 (eff. Sept. 1, 2001); Acts 2003, 78th Leg., ch. 1280, §1, eff. Sept. 1, 2003; Acts 2007, 80th Leg., ch. 690, §§1, 2, eff. Sept. 1, 2007.

ANNOTATIONS

Santana v. State, 59 S.W.3d 187, 192 (Tex.Crim. App.2001). "[T]he language of subsection (b)(3) allows a conviction for Class 'A' misdemeanor criminal mischief upon a showing of pecuniary loss (more than $500 or less than $1,500), *or*, if the pecuniary loss is less than $1,500, there is substantial inconvenience of the type described in subsection (b)(3)(B)."

Athey v. State, 697 S.W.2d 818, 820 (Tex.App.— Dallas 1985, no pet.). "This statute does not require an intent to hurt or damage the owner, but only to damage or destroy the property without the owner's consent. Thus, any intent appellant may have had to repair the damage and then restore whatever loss he may have caused the owner is immaterial."

Sebree v. State, 695 S.W.2d 303, 305 (Tex.App.— Houston [1st Dist.] 1985, no pet.). "[T]he statute does not require that property be repaired to establish the cost of repair.... [A]n estimate of damage or an opinion on the amount of damage without further evidence is insufficient to prove the cost of repair...."

PEN §28.04. RECKLESS DAMAGE OR DESTRUCTION

(a) A person commits an offense if, without the effective consent of the owner, he recklessly damages or destroys property of the owner.

(b) An offense under this section is a Class C misdemeanor.

History of Pen §28.04: Acts 1973, 63rd Leg., ch. 399, §1, eff. Jan. 1, 1974.

PEN §28.05. ACTOR'S INTEREST IN PROPERTY

It is no defense to prosecution under this chapter that the actor has an interest in the property damaged or destroyed if another person also has an interest that the actor is not entitled to infringe.

History of Pen §28.05: Acts 1973, 63rd Leg., ch. 399, §1, eff. Jan. 1, 1974.

ANNOTATIONS

Krupa v. State, 750 S.W.2d 258, 262 (Tex.App.—Dallas 1988), *pet. ref'd*, 775 S.W.2d 644 (Tex.Crim.App. 1989). Appellant "is not arguing that his interest in the property excused or justified actions that, in the absence of such an interest, would establish criminal mischief. Clearly, §28.05 forecloses that defense. Instead, we understand [appellant] to argue that the element of 'ownership' is an essential element of the State's case and, because the State alleged in the indictment that the complainant's ownership was 'by virtue of [her] having a greater right of possession,' those facts were 'descriptive of that which is legally essential' to charge an offense of criminal mischief; therefore, the State must prove those facts. We agree."

PEN §28.06. AMOUNT OF PECUNIARY LOSS

(a) The amount of pecuniary loss under this chapter, if the property is destroyed, is:

(1) the fair market value of the property at the time and place of the destruction; or

(2) if the fair market value of the property cannot be ascertained, the cost of replacing the property within a reasonable time after the destruction.

(b) The amount of pecuniary loss under this chapter, if the property is damaged, is the cost of repairing or restoring the damaged property within a reasonable time after the damage occurred.

(c) The amount of pecuniary loss under this chapter for documents, other than those having a readily ascertainable market value, is:

(1) the amount due and collectible at maturity less any part that has been satisfied, if the document constitutes evidence of a debt; or

(2) the greatest amount of economic loss that the owner might reasonably suffer by virtue of the destruction or damage if the document is other than evidence of a debt.

(d) If the amount of pecuniary loss cannot be ascertained by the criteria set forth in Subsections (a) through (c), the amount of loss is deemed to be greater than $500 but less than $1,500.

(e) If the actor proves by a preponderance of the evidence that he gave consideration for or had a legal interest in the property involved, the value of the interest so proven shall be deducted from:

(1) the amount of pecuniary loss if the property is destroyed; or

(2) the amount of pecuniary loss to the extent of an amount equal to the ratio the value of the interest bears to the total value of the property, if the property is damaged.

History of Pen §28.06: Acts 1973, 63rd Leg., ch. 399, §1, eff. Jan. 1, 1974. Amended by Acts 1983, 68th Leg., ch. 497, §2, eff. Sept. 1, 1983; Acts 1993, 73rd Leg., ch. 900, §1.01, eff. Sept. 1, 1994.

ANNOTATIONS

Elomary v. State, 796 S.W.2d 191, 193 (Tex.Crim.App.1990). "[T]he criminal mischief statute does not require that damaged property that can be repaired be actually repaired in order to establish the cost of the repair work as set forth in §28.06(b). [W]e [agree] that 'an estimate of damage or an opinion on the amount of damage *without further evidence* is insufficient to prove the cost of repairs as required by §28.06(b).'"

Deas v. State, 752 S.W.2d 573, 575 (Tex.Crim.App. 1988). "To consider replacement cost in determining pecuniary loss requires the property to have been destroyed. [¶] Before replacement value can be used to determine the pecuniary loss, the evidence must demonstrate that the fair market value cannot be ascertained."

Espinoza v. State, 955 S.W.2d 108, 112 (Tex. App.—Waco 1997, pet. ref'd). "If property is merely damaged, not destroyed, then the amount of pecuniary loss is 'the cost of repairing or restoring the damaged property within a reasonable time after the damage occurred.' If the property is destroyed and the fair market value of the property is ascertainable, then the measure of pecuniary damage is 'the fair market value of the property at the time and place of the destruction.' Under 28.06 there is no requirement that repairs to the damaged property actually be made, only the fair market value of the cost of repairs is necessary to formulate the amount of pecuniary loss."

For a quick reference of penalties, see the Chart of Penalties on p. 675.

O'CONNOR'S CRIMINAL CODES   795

PEN §28.07. INTERFERENCE WITH RAILROAD PROPERTY

(a) In this section:

(1) "Railroad property" means:

(A) a train, locomotive, railroad car, caboose, work equipment, rolling stock, safety device, switch, or connection that is owned, leased, operated, or possessed by a railroad; or

(B) a railroad track, rail, bridge, trestle, or right-of-way owned or used by a railroad.

(2) "Tamper" means to move, alter, or interfere with railroad property.

(b) A person commits an offense if the person:

(1) throws an object or discharges a firearm or weapon at a train or rail-mounted work equipment; or

(2) without the effective consent of the owner:

(A) enters or remains on railroad property, knowing that it is railroad property;

(B) tampers with railroad property;

(C) places an obstruction on a railroad track or right-of-way; or

(D) causes in any manner the derailment of a train, railroad car, or other railroad property that moves on tracks.

(c) An offense under Subsection (b)(1) is a Class B misdemeanor unless the person causes bodily injury to another, in which event the offense is a felony of the third degree.

(d) An offense under Subsection (b)(2)(A) is a Class C misdemeanor.

(e) An offense under Subsection (b)(2)(B), (b)(2)(C), or (b)(2)(D) is a Class C misdemeanor unless the person causes pecuniary loss, in which event the offense is:

(1) a Class B misdemeanor if the amount of pecuniary loss is $20 or more but less than $500;

(2) a Class A misdemeanor if the amount of pecuniary loss is $500 or more but less than $1,500;

(3) a state jail felony if the amount of pecuniary loss is $1,500 or more but less than $20,000;

(4) a felony of the third degree if the amount of the pecuniary loss is $20,000 or more but less than $100,000;

(5) a felony of the second degree if the amount of pecuniary loss is $100,000 or more but less than $200,000; or

(6) a felony of the first degree if the amount of the pecuniary loss is $200,000 or more.

(f) The conduct described in Subsection (b)(2)(A) is not an offense under this section if it is undertaken by an employee of the railroad or by a representative of a labor organization which represents or is seeking to represent the employees of the railroad as long as the employee or representative has a right to engage in such conduct under the Railway Labor Act (45 U.S.C. Section 151 et seq.).

History of Pen §28.07: Acts 1989, 71st Leg., ch. 908, §1, eff. Sept. 1, 1989. Amended by Acts 1993, 73rd Leg., ch. 900, §1.01, eff. Sept. 1, 1994.

PEN §28.08. GRAFFITI

(a) A person commits an offense if, without the effective consent of the owner, the person intentionally or knowingly makes markings, including inscriptions, slogans, drawings, or paintings, on the tangible property of the owner with:

(1) aerosol paint;

(2) an indelible marker; or

(3) an etching or engraving device.

(b) Except as provided by Subsection (d), an offense under this section is:

(1) a Class B misdemeanor if the amount of pecuniary loss is less than $500;

(2) a Class A misdemeanor if the amount of pecuniary loss is $500 or more but less than $1,500;

(3) a state jail felony if the amount of pecuniary loss is $1,500 or more but less than $20,000;

(4) a felony of the third degree if the amount of pecuniary loss is $20,000 or more but less than $100,000;

(5) a felony of the second degree if the amount of pecuniary loss is $100,000 or more but less than $200,000; or

(6) a felony of the first degree if the amount of pecuniary loss is $200,000 or more.

(c) When more than one item of tangible property, belonging to one or more owners, is marked in violation of this section pursuant to one scheme or continuing course of conduct, the conduct may be considered as one offense, and the amounts of pecuniary loss to property resulting from the marking of the property may be aggregated in determining the grade of the offense.

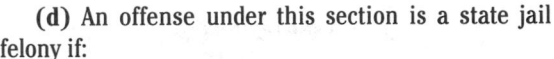

(d) An offense under this section is a state jail felony if:

(1) the marking is made on a school, an institution of higher education, a place of worship or human burial, a public monument, or a community center that provides medical, social, or educational programs; and

(2) the amount of the pecuniary loss to real property or to tangible personal property is less than $20,000.

(e) In this section:

(1) "Aerosol paint" means an aerosolized paint product.

(2) "Etching or engraving device" means a device that makes a delineation or impression on tangible property, regardless of the manufacturer's intended use for that device.

(3) "Indelible marker" means a device that makes a mark with a paint or ink product that is specifically formulated to be more difficult to erase, wash out, or remove than ordinary paint or ink products.

(4) "Institution of higher education" has the meaning assigned by Section 481.134, Health and Safety Code.

(5) "School" means a private or public elementary or secondary school.

History of Pen §28.08: Acts 1997, 75th Leg., ch. 593, §1, eff. Sept. 1, 1997. Amended by Acts 1999, 76th Leg., ch. 166, §§1-2 (eff. Sept. 1, 1999), ch. 695, §1 (eff. Sept. 1, 1999); Acts 2001, 77th Leg., ch. 1420, §16.001, eff. Sept. 1, 2001.

History of Former Pen §28.08: Deleted by Acts 1993, 73rd Leg., ch. 900, §1.01, eff. Sept. 1, 1994.

CHAPTER 29. ROBBERY

§29.01   Definitions
§29.02   Robbery
§29.03   Aggravated robbery

PEN §29.01. DEFINITIONS

In this chapter:

(1) "In the course of committing theft" means conduct that occurs in an attempt to commit, during the commission, or in immediate flight after the attempt or commission of theft.

(2) "Property" means:

(A) tangible or intangible personal property including anything severed from land; or

(B) a document, including money, that represents or embodies anything of value.

History of Pen §29.01: Acts 1973, 63rd Leg., ch. 399, §1, eff. Jan. 1, 1974. Amended by Acts 1993, 73rd Leg., ch. 900, §1.01, eff. Sept. 1, 1994.

PEN §29.02. ROBBERY

(a) A person commits an offense if, in the course of committing theft as defined in Chapter 31 and with intent to obtain or maintain control of the property, he:

(1) intentionally, knowingly, or recklessly causes bodily injury to another; or

(2) intentionally or knowingly threatens or places another in fear of imminent bodily injury or death.

(b) An offense under this section is a felony of the second degree.

History of Pen §29.02: Acts 1973, 63rd Leg., ch. 399, §1, eff. Jan. 1, 1974.

ANNOTATIONS

Cooper v. State, 67 S.W.3d 221, 224 (Tex.Crim.App. 2002). "[A] theft occurring immediately after an assault will support an inference that the assault was intended to facilitate the theft." *See also Taylor v. State*, 859 S.W.2d 466, 468 (Tex.App.—Dallas 1993, no pet.).

Ex Parte Hawkins, 6 S.W.3d 554, 560 (Tex.Crim. App.1999). "Since robbery is a form of assault, the allowable unit of prosecution for robbery should be the same as that for an assault. And in Texas the allowable unit of prosecution for an assaultive offense is each victim. *At 561:* Prosecuting the applicant twice for robbery did not violate the Double Jeopardy Clause of the 5th Amendment because the allowable unit of prosecution for robbery is each victim, and [D] assaulted two victims in the course of committing a theft."

White v. State, 671 S.W.2d 40, 41-42 (Tex.Crim.App. 1984). "No completed theft is required in order for the proscribed conduct to constitute the offense of robbery…. Nor is it necessary that the victim of the theft or attempted theft and the victim of the robbery be the same."

Pierce v. State, 218 S.W.3d 211, 215-16 (Tex. App.—Texarkana 2007, pet. ref'd). Held: A creditor who uses force to collect from a debtor commits robbery.

Pitte v. State, 102 S.W.3d 786, 792 (Tex.App.— Texarkana 2003, no pet.). "When examining a conditional threat to determine whether it involves future harm or imminent harm, the courts will consider the remoteness of the occurrence of the condition and the present capability of the accused to carry out the threat. [¶] The accused need not expressly threaten another or display a weapon to commit robbery. It is sufficient to constitute robbery if the accused places the complainant in fear of bodily injury or death to the degree that

For a quick reference of penalties, see the Chart of Penalties on p. 675.

O'CONNOR'S CRIMINAL CODES   797

'reason and common experience' will likely induce the complainant to part with his property against his will."

Williams v. State, 827 S.W.2d 614, 616 (Tex.App.—Houston [1st Dist.] 1992, pet. ref'd). "We note that an element of the crime of robbery, '*places* another in fear of imminent bodily injury,' differs from an often compared, but vastly dissimilar element for the crime of assault, '*threatens* another with imminent bodily injury.' The general, passive requirement that another be 'placed in fear' cannot be equated with the specific, active requirement that the actor 'threaten another with imminent bodily injury.' Under the 'placed in fear' language in §29.02 ..., the factfinder may conclude that an individual perceived fear or was 'placed in fear,' in circumstances where no actual threats were conveyed by the accused."

Banks v. State, 638 S.W.2d 532, 534 (Tex.App.—Houston [1st Dist.] 1982, pet. ref'd). "When a party, during immediate flight from the scene of a theft, places another in fear of immediate bodily injury or death in order to assure his escape, the violent conduct aggravates the act of theft, notwithstanding that control over the stolen property is relinquished in the process of escaping. The relinquishment of the property does not lessen the danger of the situation, since the motive is still escape."

PEN §29.03. AGGRAVATED ROBBERY

(a) A person commits an offense if he commits robbery as defined in Section 29.02, and he:

(1) causes serious bodily injury to another;

(2) uses or exhibits a deadly weapon; or

(3) causes bodily injury to another person or threatens or places another person in fear of imminent bodily injury or death, if the other person is:

(A) 65 years of age or older; or

(B) a disabled person.

(b) An offense under this section is a felony of the first degree.

(c) In this section, "disabled person" means an individual with a mental, physical, or developmental disability who is substantially unable to protect himself from harm.

History of Pen §29.03: Acts 1973, 63rd Leg., ch. 399, §1, eff. Jan. 1, 1974. Amended by Acts 1989, 71st Leg., ch. 357, §2, eff. Sept. 1, 1989; Acts 1993, 73rd Leg., ch. 900, §1.01, eff. Sept. 1, 1994.

ANNOTATIONS

Herring v. State, 202 S.W.3d 764, 766 (Tex.Crim.App.2006). "The only issue before us is whether or not Herring used or exhibited the knife in question. [¶] We have said that '*any* employment of a deadly weapon, even its simple possession, if such possession facilitates the associated felony' constitutes use. Herring's admission that he possessed the knife, coupled with his threat to kill and his taking of the money, is legally sufficient evidence of use." *See also McCain v. State*, 22 S.W.3d 497, 503 (Tex.Crim.App.2000).

Flenteroy v. State, 187 S.W.3d 406, 411 (Tex.Crim.App.2005). "Appellant's defense did not depend on whether any particular type of weapon was used. On the contrary, appellant denied that any weapon was used. The variance between the indictment's allegation of a 'screwdriver' and the State's proof at trial of 'a hard metal-like object' was, therefore, immaterial."

Adame v. State, 69 S.W.3d 581, 582 (Tex.Crim.App.2002). "With testimony that a BB gun is capable of causing serious bodily injury, it is reasonable for a jury to make a deadly weapon finding. Further, ... where during a convenience store robbery a defendant threatens serious bodily injury to the convenience store clerk by pointing a BB gun at her, a jury may rationally infer that the BB gun is loaded. ... It is not necessary ... to place an additional evidentiary burden on the State to affirmatively prove that a BB gun, which is not a deadly weapon per se, was loaded at the time of the commission of the offense. Rather, in proving use of a deadly weapon other than a deadly weapon per se, the State need show only that the weapon used was capable of causing serious bodily injury or death in its use or intended use."

Bignall v. State, 887 S.W.2d 21, 23 (Tex.Crim.App.1994). "[I]f any evidence exists in the record that would permit a rational jury to find that a deadly weapon was not used or exhibited, Appellant is entitled to an instruction on theft."

Posey v. State, 763 S.W.2d 872, 876 (Tex.App.—Houston [14th Dist.] 1988, pet. ref'd). "The intent element is directed to the state of mind in threatening or placing the victim in fear, the assaultive component of the offense of aggravated robbery. Knowledge and intent can be inferred from the conduct of, remarks by, and circumstances surrounding the acts engaged in by the accused."

Stevens v. State, 636 S.W.2d 857, 859 (Tex.App.—Waco 1982, pet. ref'd). "[A] description of the property taken is not required under [the] aggravated robbery statute...."

CHAPTER 30. BURGLARY & CRIMINAL TRESPASS

§30.01   Definitions
§30.02   Burglary
§30.03   Burglary of coin-operated or coin collection machines
§30.04   Burglary of vehicles
§30.05   Criminal trespass
§30.06   Trespass by holder of license to carry concealed handgun

PEN §30.01. DEFINITIONS

In this chapter:

(1) "Habitation" means a structure or vehicle that is adapted for the overnight accommodation of persons, and includes:

(A) each separately secured or occupied portion of the structure or vehicle; and

(B) each structure appurtenant to or connected with the structure or vehicle.

(2) "Building" means any enclosed structure intended for use or occupation as a habitation or for some purpose of trade, manufacture, ornament, or use.

(3) "Vehicle" includes any device in, on, or by which any person or property is or may be propelled, moved, or drawn in the normal course of commerce or transportation, except such devices as are classified as "habitation."

History of Pen §30.01: Acts 1973, 63rd Leg., ch. 399, §1, eff. Jan. 1, 1974.

ANNOTATIONS

Habitation

In re E.P., 963 S.W.2d 191, 193 (Tex.App.—Austin 1998, no pet.). "[D]etermining whether a structure is or is not suitable for the overnight accommodation of persons is a 'complex, subjective factual question fit for a jury's determination.' Factors to be considered include whether the structure was being used as a residence at the time of the trespass; whether the structure 'contained bedding, furniture, utilities, or other belongings common to a residential structure'; and whether the structure was of such character that it was likely intended to accommodate persons overnight. '[A]ll of these factors are relevant; none are essential or necessarily dispositive.'"

Johnson v. State, 844 S.W.2d 872, 874 (Tex.App.—Amarillo 1992, no pet.). "[A] garage [can be] a 'habitation.' [A]n unattached garage may be considered to be a 'structure appurtenant to' a residence and thus, within the statutory definition of a 'habitation.'"

Olaniyi-Oke v. State, 827 S.W.2d 537, 538 (Tex. App.—Houston [1st Dist.] 1992, pet. ref'd). "[T]he ... jail is a habitation as defined by §30.01(1)."

Frazier v. State, 760 S.W.2d 334, 336 (Tex.App.—Texarkana 1988, pet. ref'd). "The place burglarized was a motel, and even though the particular rooms were not rented on the evening of the burglary, they were adapted for overnight or monthly accommodations. [A] motel is a habitation within the [Pen. Code] definition."

Building

Gilliam v. State, 746 S.W.2d 323, 325 (Tex.App.—Eastland 1988, no pet.). "The boathouse was designed as an 'enclosed structure' to secure the owner's boat and property. The fact that the boathouse floats on the surface of the lake does not prevent the structure from being a building as defined in §30.01(2)."

Vehicle

Van Dalen v. State, 789 S.W.2d 334, 336 (Tex. App.—Houston [14th Dist.] 1990, no pet.). "The fact that the truck was without a motor or rear wheels did not destroy its character as a 'vehicle.' It is the design and construction of the vehicle and not its temporary condition that is controlling."

PEN §30.02. BURGLARY

(a) A person commits an offense if, without the effective consent of the owner, the person:

(1) enters a habitation, or a building (or any portion of a building) not then open to the public, with intent to commit a felony, theft, or an assault; or

(2) remains concealed, with intent to commit a felony, theft, or an assault, in a building or habitation; or

(3) enters a building or habitation and commits or attempts to commit a felony, theft, or an assault.

(b) For purposes of this section, "enter" means to intrude:

(1) any part of the body; or

(2) any physical object connected with the body.

(c) Except as provided in Subsection (d), an offense under this section is a:

For a quick reference of penalties, see the Chart of Penalties on p. 675.

O'CONNOR'S CRIMINAL CODES   799

(1) state jail felony if committed in a building other than a habitation; or

(2) felony of the second degree if committed in a habitation.

(d) An offense under this section is a felony of the first degree if:

(1) the premises are a habitation; and

(2) any party to the offense entered the habitation with intent to commit a felony other than felony theft or committed or attempted to commit a felony other than felony theft.

History of Pen §30.02: Acts 1973, 63rd Leg., ch. 399, §1, eff. Jan. 1, 1974. Amended by Acts 1993, 73rd Leg., ch. 900, §1.01, eff. Sept. 1, 1994; Acts 1995, 74th Leg., ch. 318, §8, eff. Sept. 1, 1995; Acts 1999, 76th Leg., ch. 727, §1, eff. Sept. 1, 1999.

ANNOTATIONS

Ex parte Cavazos, 203 S.W.3d 333, 335 (Tex.Crim. App.2006). "The issue before us is whether convicting applicant of two counts of burglary of a habitation, each with a different complainant but arising from a single unlawful entry, violates the Double Jeopardy Clause of the U.S. Constitution. *At 337:* [T]he complainant is not the appropriate allowable unit of prosecution in a burglary, rather, the allowable unit of prosecution in a burglary is the unlawful entry. Applicant's convictions violate double jeopardy because he was punished multiple times for a single unlawful entry."

Powell v. State, 194 S.W.3d 503, 506-07 (Tex.Crim. App.2006). "[A]n individual may be guilty of burglary of a habitation even though he does not personally enter the burglarized premises if he is acting together with another in the commission of the offense."

Langs v. State, 183 S.W.3d 680, 686 (Tex.Crim.App. 2006). "[A] defendant may not be punished for both the underlying felony and burglary if the burglary allegation is that the defendant entered a home without the consent of the owner and *then* committed the underlying felony within the home as defined in §30.02(a)(3). Thus, the State may obtain either a burglary or the underlying felony (or theft or assault) conviction if it alleges a burglary under §30.02(a)(3) …, but not both." *See also* ***Mitchell v. State***, 137 S.W.3d 842, 846-47 (Tex.App.—Houston [1st Dist.] 2004, pet. ref'd).

Gonzales v. State, 931 S.W.2d 574, 575 (Tex.Crim. App.1996). "Consent is not effective 'if given by a person the actor knows is not legally authorized to act for the owner.' [D] could not reasonably have believed that [murder victims' daughter] was 'legally authorized to act' for her parents in consenting to appellant's entry for the purpose of killing them. As such, [daughter's] participation in the offense rendered her consent ineffective." *See also* ***Ashcraft v. State***, 900 S.W.2d 817, 833 (Tex.App.—Corpus Christi 1995, pet. ref'd).

Richardson v. State, 888 S.W.2d 822, 823-24 (Tex. Crim.App.1994). "[T]he 'entry' requirement in the statutes is intended to protect 'the interior or enclosed part of the described object, be it a house, a building or a vehicle.' In contrast, these statutes do not criminalize the theft of an external part of a structure or a vehicle when accomplished without any physical entry into the protected area. … 'Stealing a mailbox or a window shutter attached to the side of a house would not be entry so as to constitute burglary.'" *But see* ***Alexander v. State***, 873 S.W.2d 793, 795 (Tex.App.—Beaumont 1994, pet. ref'd) (removal of window-unit air conditioner was burglary).

Tabor v. State, 88 S.W.3d 783, 786 (Tex.App.— Tyler 2002, no pet.). "In cases where there is independent evidence of a burglary, the unexplained personal possession of recently stolen property may constitute sufficient evidence to support a conviction. Mere possession of stolen property does not give rise to a presumption of guilt, but rather it will support an inference of guilt of the offense in which the property was stolen. To warrant an inference of guilt based solely on the possession of stolen property, it must be established that the possession was personal, recent, and unexplained. Also, the possession must involve a distinct and conscious assertion of right to the property by the defendant. If the defendant offers an explanation for his possession of the stolen property, the record must demonstrate the account is false or unreasonable. Whether a defendant's explanation for possession of recently stolen property is true or reasonable is a question of fact to be resolved by the trier of fact." *See also* ***Poncio v. State***, 185 S.W.3d 904, 904-05 (Tex.Crim.App. 2006).

Villarreal v. State, 79 S.W.3d 806, 811 (Tex.App.— Corpus Christi 2002, pet. ref'd). "Generally, fingerprint evidence alone will be sufficient to sustain a conviction if the evidence shows that the prints were necessarily made at the time of the burglary. One important factor in determining the sufficiency of fingerprint evidence is the extent to which the fingerprinted object was accessible to the defendant."

Espinoza v. State, 955 S.W.2d 108, 111 (Tex. App.—Waco 1997, pet. ref'd). "If a defendant is charged with burglary under subsections (a)(1) or (a)(2), the State is required to prove the defendant's intent to commit a felony or theft at the time the defendant entered or remained concealed in a habitation or building. However, when a defendant is charged under subsection (a)(3), the State is not required to prove that the defendant intended to commit the felony or theft at the time of entry. The State must simply prove that the defendant intentionally or knowingly entered the building or habitation without the owner's consent and while inside committed or attempted to commit a felony or theft. *At 114:* The text of the burglary statute unambiguously states that an attempt to commit a felony is sufficient for the jury to convict a defendant of burglary. The statute does not require that the defendant have actually committed a felony, only that he attempted to commit one."

Mack v. State, 928 S.W.2d 219, 222 (Tex.App.—Austin 1996, pet. ref'd). "[U]nder the burglary statute, anyone with a greater right to the actual care, custody, or control of the building than the defendant may be alleged as the 'owner'. This 'greater right of possession' doctrine applies to any prosecution for burglary. [¶] [There is] a clear trend to classify any person with a colorable possessory interest in the building as an owner under the greater right of possession doctrine."

PEN §30.03. BURGLARY OF COIN-OPERATED OR COIN COLLECTION MACHINES

(a) A person commits an offense if, without the effective consent of the owner, he breaks or enters into any coin-operated machine, coin collection machine, or other coin-operated or coin collection receptacle, contrivance, apparatus, or equipment used for the purpose of providing lawful amusement, sales of goods, services, or other valuable things, or telecommunications with intent to obtain property or services.

(b) For purposes of this section, "entry" includes every kind of entry except one made with the effective consent of the owner.

(c) An offense under this section is a Class A misdemeanor.

History of Pen §30.03: Acts 1973, 63rd Leg., ch. 399, §1, eff. Jan. 1, 1974. Amended by Acts 1987, 70th Leg., ch. 62, §1, eff. Sept. 1, 1987.

PEN §30.04. BURGLARY OF VEHICLES

(a) A person commits an offense if, without the effective consent of the owner, he breaks into or enters a vehicle or any part of a vehicle with intent to commit any felony or theft.

(b) For purposes of this section, "enter" means to intrude:

(1) any part of the body; or

(2) any physical object connected with the body.

(c) For purposes of this section, a container or trailer carried on a rail car is a part of the rail car.

A *Subsection (d) below is effective for offenses committed on or after Sept. 1, 2007.*

(d) An offense under this section is a Class A misdemeanor, except that:

(1) the offense is a Class A misdemeanor with a minimum term of confinement of six months if it is shown on the trial of the offense that the defendant has been previously convicted of an offense under this section; and

(2) the offense is a state jail felony if:

(A) it is shown on the trial of the offense that the defendant has been previously convicted two or more times of an offense under this section; or

(B) the vehicle or part of the vehicle broken into or entered is a rail car.

Subsection (d) below is effective for offenses in which any element of the offense was committed before Sept. 1, 2007.

(d) An offense under this section is a Class A misdemeanor unless the vehicle or part of the vehicle broken into or entered is a rail car, in which event the offense is a state jail felony.

E *Subsection (d-1) below is effective for offenses committed on or after Sept. 1, 2007.*

(d-1) For the purposes of Subsection (d), a defendant has been previously convicted under this section if the defendant was adjudged guilty of the offense or entered a plea of guilty or nolo contendere in return for a grant of deferred adjudication, regardless of whether the sentence for the offense was ever imposed or

For a quick reference of penalties, see the Chart of Penalties on p. 675.

O'CONNOR'S CRIMINAL CODES 801

whether the sentence was probated and the defendant was subsequently discharged from community supervision.

(e) It is a defense to prosecution under this section that the actor entered a rail car or any part of a rail car and was at that time an employee or a representative of employees exercising a right under the Railway Labor Act (45 U.S.C. Section 151 et seq.).

History of Pen §30.04: Acts 1973, 63rd Leg., ch. 399, §1, eff. Jan. 1, 1974. Amended by Acts 1993, 73rd Leg., ch. 900, §1.01, eff. Sept. 1, 1994; Acts 1999, 76th Leg., ch. 916, §1, eff. Sept. 1, 1999; Acts 2007, 80th Leg., ch. 308, §1, eff. Sept. 1, 2007.

ANNOTATIONS

Richardson v. State, 888 S.W.2d 822, 824 (Tex. Crim.App.1994). "[A]n individual who reaches into the open bed of a pickup truck with the intent to remove property does break the close of the vehicle and … enters part of the vehicle for purposes of §30.04."

Griffin v. State, 815 S.W.2d 576, 579 (Tex.Crim. App.1991). "[T]aking the hubcaps or tires that are attached to the outside of the car, when no entry into any enclosed portion of the car is made to effectuate the taking, is not burglary of a vehicle."

PEN §30.05. CRIMINAL TRESPASS

(a) A person commits an offense if he enters or remains on or in property, including an aircraft or other vehicle, of another without effective consent or he enters or remains in a building of another without effective consent and he:

(1) had notice that the entry was forbidden; or

(2) received notice to depart but failed to do so.

(b) For purposes of this section:

(1) "Entry" means the intrusion of the entire body.

(2) "Notice" means:

(A) oral or written communication by the owner or someone with apparent authority to act for the owner;

(B) fencing or other enclosure obviously designed to exclude intruders or to contain livestock;

(C) a sign or signs posted on the property or at the entrance to the building, reasonably likely to come to the attention of intruders, indicating that entry is forbidden;

(D) the placement of identifying purple paint marks on trees or posts on the property, provided that the marks are:

(i) vertical lines of not less than eight inches in length and not less than one inch in width;

(ii) placed so that the bottom of the mark is not less than three feet from the ground or more than five feet from the ground; and

(iii) placed at locations that are readily visible to any person approaching the property and no more than:

(a) 100 feet apart on forest land; or

(b) 1,000 feet apart on land other than forest land; or

(E) the visible presence on the property of a crop grown for human consumption that is under cultivation, in the process of being harvested, or marketable if harvested at the time of entry.

(3) "Shelter center" has the meaning assigned by Section 51.002, Human Resources Code.

(4) "Forest land" means land on which the trees are potentially valuable for timber products.

(5) "Agricultural land" has the meaning assigned by Section 75.001, Civil Practice and Remedies Code.

(6) "Superfund site" means a facility that:

(A) is on the National Priorities List established under Section 105 of the federal Comprehensive Environmental Response, Compensation, and Liability Act of 1980 (42 U.S.C. Section 9605); or

(B) is listed on the state registry established under Section 361.181, Health and Safety Code.

(7) "Critical infrastructure facility" means one of the following, if completely enclosed by a fence or other physical barrier that is obviously designed to exclude intruders:

(A) a chemical manufacturing facility;

(B) a refinery;

(C) an electrical power generating facility, substation, switching station, electrical control center, or electrical transmission or distribution facility;

(D) a water intake structure, water treatment facility, wastewater treatment plant, or pump station;

(E) a natural gas transmission compressor station;

(F) a liquid natural gas terminal or storage facility;

(G) a telecommunications central switching office;

(H) a port, railroad switching yard, trucking terminal, or other freight transportation facility;

(I) a gas processing plant, including a plant used in the processing, treatment, or fractionation of natural gas; or

(J) a transmission facility used by a federally licensed radio or television station.

(c) It is a defense to prosecution under this section that the actor at the time of the offense was a fire fighter or emergency medical services personnel, as that term is defined by Section 773.003, Health and Safety Code, acting in the lawful discharge of an official duty under exigent circumstances.

(d) An offense under Subsection (e) is a Class C misdemeanor unless it is committed in a habitation or unless the actor carries a deadly weapon on or about the actor's person during the commission of the offense, in which event it is a Class A misdemeanor. An offense under Subsection (a) is a Class B misdemeanor, except that the offense is a Class A misdemeanor if:

(1) the offense is committed:

(A) in a habitation or a shelter center;

(B) on a Superfund site; or

(C) on or in a critical infrastructure facility; or

(2) the actor carries a deadly weapon on or about his person during the commission of the offense.

(e) A person commits an offense if without express consent or if without authorization provided by any law, whether in writing or other form, the person:

(1) enters or remains on agricultural land of another;

(2) is on the agricultural land and within 100 feet of the boundary of the land when apprehended; and

(3) had notice that the entry was forbidden or received notice to depart but failed to do so.

(f) It is a defense to prosecution under this section that:

(1) the basis on which entry on the property or land or in the building was forbidden is that entry with a handgun was forbidden; and

(2) the person was carrying a concealed handgun and a license issued under Subchapter H, Chapter 411, Government Code, to carry a concealed handgun of the same category the person was carrying.

(g) It is a defense to prosecution under this section that the actor entered a railroad switching yard or any part of a railroad switching yard and was at that time an employee or a representative of employees exercising a right under the Railway Labor Act (45 U.S.C. Section 151 et seq.).

(h) At the punishment stage of a trial in which the attorney representing the state seeks the increase in punishment provided by Subsection (d)(1)(C), the defendant may raise the issue as to whether the defendant entered or remained on or in a critical infrastructure facility as part of a peaceful or lawful assembly, including an attempt to exercise rights guaranteed by state or federal labor laws. If the defendant proves the issue in the affirmative by a preponderance of the evidence, the increase in punishment provided by Subsection (d)(1)(C) does not apply.

Ⓐ **(i)** This section does not apply if:

(1) the basis on which entry on the property or land or in the building was forbidden is that entry with a handgun or other weapon was forbidden; and

(2) the actor at the time of the offense was a peace officer, including a commissioned peace officer of a recognized state, or a special investigator under Article 2.122, Code of Criminal Procedure, regardless of whether the peace officer or special investigator was engaged in the actual discharge of an official duty while carrying the weapon.

Ⓐ **(j)** For purposes of Subsection (i), "recognized state" means another state with which the attorney general of this state, with the approval of the governor of this state, negotiated an agreement after determining that the other state:

(1) has firearm proficiency requirements for peace officers; and

(2) fully recognizes the right of peace officers commissioned in this state to carry weapons in the other state.

History of Pen §30.05: Acts 1973, 63rd Leg., ch. 399, §1, eff. Jan. 1, 1974. Amended by Acts 1979, 66th Leg., ch. 530, §3, eff. Aug. 27, 1979; Acts 1981, 67th Leg., ch. 596, §1, eff. Sept. 1, 1981; Acts 1989, 71st Leg., ch. 139, §1, eff. Sept. 1, 1989; Acts 1991, 72nd Leg., ch. 308, §1, eff. Sept. 1, 1991; Acts 1993, 73rd Leg., ch. 24, §1 (eff. Sept. 1, 1993), ch. 900, §1.01 (eff. Sept. 1, 1994); Acts 1997, 75th Leg., ch. 1229, §§1, 2, eff. Sept. 1, 1997; Acts 1999, 76th Leg., ch. 161, §1 (eff. Sept. 1, 1999), ch. 169, §§1, 2 (eff. Sept. 1, 1999), ch. 765, §§1, 2 (eff. Sept. 1, 1999); Acts 2001, 77th Leg., ch. 1420, §§16.002, 21.001(94), eff. Sept. 1, 2001; Acts 2003, 78th Leg., ch. 1078, §1, eff. Sept. 1, 2003; Acts 2003, 78th Leg., ch. 1276, §14B.001, eff. Sept. 1, 2003; Acts 2003, 78th Leg., ch. 1178, §1, eff. Sept. 1, 2003; Acts 2005, 79th Leg., ch. 1093, §3 (eff. Sept. 1, 2005), ch. 1337, §§20, 21 (eff. June 18, 2005); Acts 2007, 80th Leg., ch. 921, §§17.001(61), 17.002(13), eff. Sept. 1, 2007.

ANNOTATIONS

Arnold v. State, 867 S.W.2d 378, 379 (Tex.Crim. App.1993). Section 30.05 "requires only that the defendant enter or remain on property of *another*. However, if the State unnecessarily alleges ownership of the

For a quick reference of penalties, see the Chart of Penalties on p. 675.

O'CONNOR'S CRIMINAL CODES 803

property, the State assumes the burden of proving that allegation. [¶] [I]n criminal trespass cases where the State alleges ownership, ... the State may establish ownership by proving, beyond a reasonable doubt, that the complainant had a greater right to possession of the property than the defendant." *See also Anthony v. State*, 209 S.W.3d 296, 309-10 (Tex.App.—Texarkana 2006, no pet.).

Gollinger v. State, 834 S.W.2d 553, 556 (Tex. App.—Houston [14th Dist.] 1992, no pet.). "Section 30.05 ... 'may be constitutionally applied, even to those who trespass to communicate, so long as it is applied without discrimination and is not used to purposefully suppress speech.'"

Moses v. State, 814 S.W.2d 437, 442 (Tex.App.— Austin 1991, pet. ref'd). "No culpable mental state is required under the criminal trespass statute, other than a volitional refusal to leave when requested."

Reed v. State, 762 S.W.2d 640, 645 (Tex.App.— Texarkana 1988, pet. ref'd). "Trespass is an offense against the owner's possession and control of property, rather than an offense *against the property itself....*"

PEN §30.06. TRESPASS BY HOLDER OF LICENSE TO CARRY CONCEALED HANDGUN

(a) A license holder commits an offense if the license holder:

(1) carries a handgun under the authority of Subchapter H, Chapter 411, Government Code, on property of another without effective consent; and

(2) received notice that:

(A) entry on the property by a license holder with a concealed handgun was forbidden; or

(B) remaining on the property with a concealed handgun was forbidden and failed to depart.

(b) For purposes of this section, a person receives notice if the owner of the property or someone with apparent authority to act for the owner provides notice to the person by oral or written communication.

(c) In this section:

(1) "Entry" has the meaning assigned by Section 30.05(b).

(2) "License holder" has the meaning assigned by Section 46.035(f).

(3) "Written communication" means:

(A) a card or other document on which is written language identical to the following: "Pursuant to Section 30.06, Penal Code (trespass by holder of license to carry a concealed handgun), a person licensed under Subchapter H, Chapter 411, Government Code (concealed handgun law), may not enter this property with a concealed handgun"; or

(B) a sign posted on the property that:

(i) includes the language described by Paragraph (A) in both English and Spanish;

(ii) appears in contrasting colors with block letters at least one inch in height; and

(iii) is displayed in a conspicuous manner clearly visible to the public.

(d) An offense under this section is a Class A misdemeanor.

(e) It is an exception to the application of this section that the property on which the license holder carries a handgun is owned or leased by a governmental entity and is not a premises or other place on which the license holder is prohibited from carrying the handgun under Section 46.03 or 46.035.

History of Pen §30.06: Acts 1997, 75th Leg., ch. 1261, §23, eff. Sept. 1, 1997. Amended by Acts 1999, 76th Leg., ch. 62, §9.24, eff. Sept. 1, 1999; Acts 2003, 78th Leg., ch. 1178, §2, eff. Sept. 1, 2003.

CHAPTER 31. THEFT

PEN §31.01. DEFINITIONS

In this chapter:

(1) "Deception" means:

PEN §30.05

(A) creating or confirming by words or conduct a false impression of law or fact that is likely to affect the judgment of another in the transaction, and that the actor does not believe to be true;

(B) failing to correct a false impression of law or fact that is likely to affect the judgment of another in the transaction, that the actor previously created or confirmed by words or conduct, and that the actor does not now believe to be true;

(C) preventing another from acquiring information likely to affect his judgment in the transaction;

(D) selling or otherwise transferring or encumbering property without disclosing a lien, security interest, adverse claim, or other legal impediment to the enjoyment of the property, whether the lien, security interest, claim, or impediment is or is not valid, or is or is not a matter of official record; or

(E) promising performance that is likely to affect the judgment of another in the transaction and that the actor does not intend to perform or knows will not be performed, except that failure to perform the promise in issue without other evidence of intent or knowledge is not sufficient proof that the actor did not intend to perform or knew the promise would not be performed.

(2) "Deprive" means:

(A) to withhold property from the owner permanently or for so extended a period of time that a major portion of the value or enjoyment of the property is lost to the owner;

(B) to restore property only upon payment of reward or other compensation; or

(C) to dispose of property in a manner that makes recovery of the property by the owner unlikely.

(3) "Effective consent" includes consent by a person legally authorized to act for the owner. Consent is not effective if:

(A) induced by deception or coercion;

(B) given by a person the actor knows is not legally authorized to act for the owner;

(C) given by a person who by reason of youth, mental disease or defect, or intoxication is known by the actor to be unable to make reasonable property dispositions;

(D) given solely to detect the commission of an offense; or

(E) given by a person who by reason of advanced age is known by the actor to have a diminished capacity to make informed and rational decisions about the reasonable disposition of property.

(4) "Appropriate" means:

(A) to bring about a transfer or purported transfer of title to or other nonpossessory interest in property, whether to the actor or another; or

(B) to acquire or otherwise exercise control over property other than real property.

(5) "Property" means:

(A) real property;

(B) tangible or intangible personal property including anything severed from land; or

(C) a document, including money, that represents or embodies anything of value.

(6) "Service" includes:

(A) labor and professional service;

(B) telecommunication, public utility, or transportation service;

(C) lodging, restaurant service, and entertainment; and

(D) the supply of a motor vehicle or other property for use.

(7) "Steal" means to acquire property or service by theft.

(8) "Certificate of title" has the meaning assigned by Section 501.002, Transportation Code.

(9) "Used or secondhand motor vehicle" means a used motor vehicle, as that term is defined by Section 501.002, Transportation Code.

(10) "Elderly individual" has the meaning assigned by Section 22.04(c).

History of Pen §31.01: Acts 1973, 63rd Leg., ch. 399, §1, eff. Jan. 1, 1974. Amended by Acts 1975, 64th Leg., ch. 342, §9, eff. Sept. 1, 1975; Acts 1985, 69th Leg., ch. 901, §2, eff. Sept. 1, 1985; Acts 1993, 73rd Leg., ch. 900, §1.01, eff. Sept. 1, 1994; Acts 1997, 75th Leg., ch. 165, §30.237, eff. Sept. 1, 1997; Acts 2003, 78th Leg., ch. 432, §1, eff. Sept. 1, 2003.

ANNOTATIONS

Newman v. State, 115 S.W.3d 118, 121 (Tex.App.—Texarkana 2003, no pet.). "In the employer-employee context, an unlawful appropriation occurs when an employee exercises unauthorized control over property belonging to the employee's employer. Theft does not occur until a fiduciary acts in some way inconsistent with his or her lawful authority. But when the employee decides ... to unlawfully deprive the lawful owner of the

For a quick reference of penalties, see the Chart of Penalties on p. 675.

O'CONNOR'S CRIMINAL CODES 805

property, such employee acts in an unauthorized capacity. In short, unlawful appropriation occurs at that moment in time when the employee breaches the trust that employee's employer placed in her or him. The line between lawful and unlawful activity by an employee, therefore, is a question of the employee's scope of authority."

State v. Bartee, 894 S.W.2d 34, 40 (Tex.App.—San Antonio 1994, no pet.). "The property subject to theft … includes 'anything capable of being possessed or owned, whether tangible or intangible, and whether inherently valuable or merely representative of something of value.' [I]n dealing with property subject to theft, we are dealing with a broad general definition without exclusions."

PEN §31.02. CONSOLIDATION OF THEFT OFFENSES

Theft as defined in Section 31.03 constitutes a single offense superseding the separate offenses previously known as theft, theft by false pretext, conversion by a bailee, theft from the person, shoplifting, acquisition of property by threat, swindling, swindling by worthless check, embezzlement, extortion, receiving or concealing embezzled property, and receiving or concealing stolen property.

History of Pen §31.02: Acts 1973, 63rd Leg., ch. 399, §1, eff. Jan. 1, 1974. Amended by Acts 1993, 73rd Leg., ch. 900, §1.01, eff. Sept. 1, 1994.

ANNOTATIONS

Noel v. State, 769 S.W.2d 366, 368 (Tex.App.—San Antonio 1989, no pet.). "Although any of the [offenses listed in §31.02] constitute theft…, upon proper motion, an accused, to prepare his defense, is entitled to know how he had allegedly taken the property.…"

PEN §31.03. THEFT

(a) A person commits an offense if he unlawfully appropriates property with intent to deprive the owner of property.

(b) Appropriation of property is unlawful if:

(1) it is without the owner's effective consent;

(2) the property is stolen and the actor appropriates the property knowing it was stolen by another; or

(3) property in the custody of any law enforcement agency was explicitly represented by any law enforcement agent to the actor as being stolen and the actor appropriates the property believing it was stolen by another.

(c) For purposes of Subsection (b):

(1) evidence that the actor has previously participated in recent transactions other than, but similar to, that which the prosecution is based is admissible for the purpose of showing knowledge or intent and the issues of knowledge or intent are raised by the actor's plea of not guilty;

(2) the testimony of an accomplice shall be corroborated by proof that tends to connect the actor to the crime, but the actor's knowledge or intent may be established by the uncorroborated testimony of the accomplice;

(3) an actor engaged in the business of buying and selling used or secondhand personal property, or lending money on the security of personal property deposited with the actor, is presumed to know upon receipt by the actor of stolen property (other than a motor vehicle subject to Chapter 501, Transportation Code) that the property has been previously stolen from another if the actor pays for or loans against the property $25 or more (or consideration of equivalent value) and the actor knowingly or recklessly:

(A) fails to record the name, address, and physical description or identification number of the seller or pledgor;

(B) fails to record a complete description of the property, including the serial number, if reasonably available, or other identifying characteristics; or

(C) fails to obtain a signed warranty from the seller or pledgor that the seller or pledgor has the right to possess the property. It is the express intent of this provision that the presumption arises unless the actor complies with each of the numbered requirements;

(4) for the purposes of Subdivision (3)(A), "identification number" means driver's license number, military identification number, identification certificate, or other official number capable of identifying an individual;

(5) stolen property does not lose its character as stolen when recovered by any law enforcement agency;

(6) an actor engaged in the business of obtaining abandoned or wrecked motor vehicles or parts of an abandoned or wrecked motor vehicle for resale, disposal, scrap, repair, rebuilding, demolition, or other form of salvage is presumed to know on receipt by the actor of stolen property that the property has been previously stolen from another if the actor knowingly or recklessly:

(A) fails to maintain an accurate and legible inventory of each motor vehicle component part purchased by or delivered to the actor, including the date of purchase or delivery, the name, age, address, sex, and driver's license number of the seller or person making the delivery, the license plate number of the motor vehicle in which the part was delivered, a complete description of the part, and the vehicle identification number of the motor vehicle from which the part was removed, or in lieu of maintaining an inventory, fails to record the name and certificate of inventory number of the person who dismantled the motor vehicle from which the part was obtained;

(B) fails on receipt of a motor vehicle to obtain a certificate of authority, sales receipt, or transfer document as required by Chapter 683, Transportation Code, or a certificate of title showing that the motor vehicle is not subject to a lien or that all recorded liens on the motor vehicle have been released; or

(C) fails on receipt of a motor vehicle to immediately remove an unexpired license plate from the motor vehicle, to keep the plate in a secure and locked place, or to maintain an inventory, on forms provided by the Texas Department of Transportation, of license plates kept under this paragraph, including for each plate or set of plates the license plate number and the make, motor number, and vehicle identification number of the motor vehicle from which the plate was removed;

(7) an actor who purchases or receives a used or secondhand motor vehicle is presumed to know on receipt by the actor of the motor vehicle that the motor vehicle has been previously stolen from another if the actor knowingly or recklessly:

(A) fails to report to the Texas Department of Transportation the failure of the person who sold or delivered the motor vehicle to the actor to deliver to the actor a properly executed certificate of title to the motor vehicle at the time the motor vehicle was delivered; or

(B) fails to file with the county tax assessor-collector of the county in which the actor received the motor vehicle, not later than the 20th day after the date the actor received the motor vehicle, the registration license receipt and certificate of title or evidence of title delivered to the actor in accordance with Subchapter D, Chapter 520, Transportation Code, at the time the motor vehicle was delivered;

(8) an actor who purchases or receives from any source other than a licensed retailer or distributor of pesticides a restricted-use pesticide or a state-limited-use pesticide or a compound, mixture, or preparation containing a restricted-use or state-limited-use pesticide is presumed to know on receipt by the actor of the pesticide or compound, mixture, or preparation that the pesticide or compound, mixture, or preparation has been previously stolen from another if the actor:

(A) fails to record the name, address, and physical description of the seller or pledgor;

(B) fails to record a complete description of the amount and type of pesticide or compound, mixture, or preparation purchased or received; and

(C) fails to obtain a signed warranty from the seller or pledgor that the seller or pledgor has the right to possess the property; and

(9) an actor who is subject to Section 409, Packers and Stockyards Act (7 U.S.C. Section 228b), that obtains livestock from a commission merchant by representing that the actor will make prompt payment is presumed to have induced the commission merchant's consent by deception if the actor fails to make full payment in accordance with Section 409, Packers and Stockyards Act (7 U.S.C. Section 228b).

(d) It is not a defense to prosecution under this section that:

(1) the offense occurred as a result of a deception or strategy on the part of a law enforcement agency, including the use of an undercover operative or peace officer;

(2) the actor was provided by a law enforcement agency with a facility in which to commit the offense or an opportunity to engage in conduct constituting the offense; or

(3) the actor was solicited to commit the offense by a peace officer, and the solicitation was of a type that would encourage a person predisposed to commit the offense to actually commit the offense, but would not encourage a person not predisposed to commit the offense to actually commit the offense.

(e) Except as provided by Subsection (f), an offense under this section is:

(1) a Class C misdemeanor if the value of the property stolen is less than:

(A) $50; or

(B) $20 and the defendant obtained the property by issuing or passing a check or similar sight order in a manner described by Section 31.06;

For a quick reference of penalties, see the Chart of Penalties on p. 675.

O'CONNOR'S CRIMINAL CODES 807

PEN §31.03

(2) a Class B misdemeanor if:

(A) the value of the property stolen is:

(i) $50 or more but less than $500; or

(ii) $20 or more but less than $500 and the defendant obtained the property by issuing or passing a check or similar sight order in a manner described by Section 31.06; or

(B) the value of the property stolen is less than:

(i) $50 and the defendant has previously been convicted of any grade of theft; or

(ii) $20, the defendant has previously been convicted of any grade of theft, and the defendant obtained the property by issuing or passing a check or similar sight order in a manner described by Section 31.06;

(3) a Class A misdemeanor if the value of the property stolen is $500 or more but less than $1,500;

(4) a state jail felony if:

(A) the value of the property stolen is $1,500 or more but less than $20,000, or the property is less than 10 head of cattle, horses, or exotic livestock or exotic fowl as defined by Section 142.001, Agriculture Code, or any part thereof under the value of $20,000, or less than 100 head of sheep, swine, or goats or any part thereof under the value of $20,000;

(B) regardless of value, the property is stolen from the person of another or from a human corpse or grave;

(C) the property stolen is a firearm, as defined by Section 46.01;

(D) the value of the property stolen is less than $1,500 and the defendant has been previously convicted two or more times of any grade of theft;

(E) the property stolen is an official ballot or official carrier envelope for an election; or

 Subsection (F) below is effective for offenses committed on or after Sept. 1, 2007.

(F) the value of the property stolen is less than $20,000 and the property stolen is insulated or noninsulated wire or cable that consists of at least 50 percent:

(i) aluminum;

(ii) bronze; or

(iii) copper;

(5) a felony of the third degree if the value of the property stolen is $20,000 or more but less than $100,000, or the property is:

(A) 10 or more head of cattle, horses, or exotic livestock or exotic fowl as defined by Section 142.001, Agriculture Code, stolen during a single transaction and having an aggregate value of less than $100,000; or

(B) 100 or more head of sheep, swine, or goats stolen during a single transaction and having an aggregate value of less than $100,000;

(6) a felony of the second degree if the value of the property stolen is $100,000 or more but less than $200,000; or

(7) a felony of the first degree if the value of the property stolen is $200,000 or more.

(f) An offense described for purposes of punishment by Subsections (e)(1)-(6) is increased to the next higher category of offense if it is shown on the trial of the offense that:

(1) the actor was a public servant at the time of the offense and the property appropriated came into the actor's custody, possession, or control by virtue of his status as a public servant;

(2) the actor was in a contractual relationship with government at the time of the offense and the property appropriated came into the actor's custody, possession, or control by virtue of the contractual relationship; or

(3) the owner of the property appropriated was at the time of the offense an elderly individual.

(g) For the purposes of Subsection (a), a person is the owner of exotic livestock or exotic fowl as defined by Section 142.001, Agriculture Code, only if the person qualifies to claim the animal under Section 142.0021, Agriculture Code, if the animal is an estray.

(h) In this section:

(1) "Restricted-use pesticide" means a pesticide classified as a restricted-use pesticide by the administrator of the Environmental Protection Agency under 7 U.S.C. Section 136a, as that law existed on January 1, 1995, and containing an active ingredient listed in the federal regulations adopted under that law (40 C.F.R. Section 152.175) and in effect on that date.

(2) "State-limited-use pesticide" means a pesticide classified as a state-limited-use pesticide by the Department of Agriculture under Section 76.003, Agriculture Code, as that section existed on January 1, 1995, and containing an active ingredient listed in the rules adopted under that section (4 TAC Section 7.24) as that section existed on that date.

PEN §31.03

(i) For purposes of Subsection (c)(9), "livestock" and "commission merchant" have the meanings assigned by Section 147.001, Agriculture Code.

(j) With the consent of the appropriate local county or district attorney, the attorney general has concurrent jurisdiction with that consenting local prosecutor to prosecute an offense under this section that involves the state Medicaid program.

History of Pen §31.03: Acts 1973, 63rd Leg., ch. 399, §1, eff. Jan. 1, 1974. Amended by Acts 1975, 64th Leg., ch. 342, §10, eff. Sept. 1, 1975; Acts 1977, 65th Leg., ch. 349, §1, eff. Aug. 29, 1977; Acts 1981, 67th Leg., ch. 298, §1 (eff. Sept. 1, 1981), ch. 455, §1 (eff. June 11, 1981); Acts 1983, 68th Leg., ch. 497, §3 (eff. Sept. 1, 1983), ch. 558, §11 (eff. Sept. 1, 1983), ch. 741, §1 (eff. Sept. 1, 1983); Acts 1985, 69th Leg., ch. 599, §1 (eff. Sept. 1, 1985), ch. 901, §1 (eff. Sept. 1, 1985); Acts 1987, 70th Leg., ch. 167, §5.01(a)(45), eff. Sept. 1, 1987; Acts 1989, 71st Leg., ch. 245, §1 (eff. Sept. 1, 1989), ch. 724, §§2, 3 (eff. Sept. 1, 1989); Acts 1991, 72nd Leg., ch. 14, §284(80) (eff. Sept. 1, 1991), ch. 565, §1 (eff. Sept. 1, 1991); Acts 1993, 73rd Leg., ch. 203, §§4, 5 (eff. Sept. 1, 1993), ch. 900, §1.01 (eff. Sept. 1, 1994); Acts 1995, 74th Leg., ch. 318, §9 (eff. Sept. 1, 1995), ch. 734, §1 (eff. Sept. 1, 1995), ch. 843, §1 (eff. Sept. 1, 1995); Acts 1997, 75th Leg., ch. 165, §§30.238, 31.01(69) (eff. Sept. 1, 1997), ch. 1153, §7.01 (eff. Sept. 1, 1997); Acts 2001, 77th Leg., ch. 1276, §1, eff. Sept. 1, 2001; Acts 2003, 78th Leg., ch. 198, §2.136 (eff. Sept. 1, 2003), ch. 257, §13 (eff. Sept. 1, 2003), ch. 393, §20 (eff. Sept. 1, 2003), ch. 432, §2 (eff. Sept. 1, 2003); Acts 2007, 80th Leg., ch. 304, §1, eff. Sept. 1, 2007.

ANNOTATIONS

Generally

Stewart v. State, 44 S.W.3d 582, 589 (Tex.Crim. App.2001). "We hold that the crucial element of theft is the deprivation of property from the rightful owner, without the owner's consent, regardless of whether the defendant at that moment has taken possession of the property."

Warren v. State, 810 S.W.2d 202, 203 (Tex.Crim. App.1991). "[T]he indictment alleged that appellant appropriated the property in the conjunctive—watch, chain, money, *and* pants. The charge could have properly alleged the items in the disjunctive—watch, chain, money, *or* pants. ... However, the jury was instructed to find appellant guilty if they found appellant appropriated 'one watch, one necklace, cash money, *and* one pair of pants.' *At 204:* Our law provides that when the court's charge to the jury is otherwise correct but places a higher burden on the State, failure to object constitutes an acceptance of that higher burden by the State."

Lehman v. State, 792 S.W.2d 82, 84-85 (Tex.Crim. App.1990). "[A] theft conviction can never rest in whole or in part upon theft of property not alleged in the indictment as stolen. ... However, once the defendant has been given proper notice that he must prepare to defend himself against a charge that he has stolen a certain 'bundle' of property, there is no reason that he should be acquitted if the evidence shows him guilty of stealing enough of the 'bundle' to make him guilty of the offense charged. [T]he State should be allowed to plead all property which the evidence may ultimately prove stolen without thereby being required to prove theft of any larger quantum of property than the statute at issue requires."

§31.03(a)

Rice v. State, 861 S.W.2d 925, 925-26 (Tex.Crim. App.1993). A defendant's "conviction on [a] burglary charge following his conviction on [a] theft charge is not barred under [the] **Blockburger** [double jeopardy test] because the burglary and the theft offenses contain an element the other does not contain. The theft charge requires the State to prove appropriation of property without the owner's effective consent; the burglary charge does not. The burglary charge requires the State to prove entry into a building not open to the public without effective consent of the owner; the theft charge does not."

Barnes v. State, 824 S.W.2d 560, 562-63 (Tex.Crim. App.1991), *overruled on other grounds*, **Proctor v. State**, 967 S.W.2d 840 (Tex.Crim.App.1998). "[T]heft by exercising control is committed and the statute of limitations commences once possession of the property becomes unlawful."

Rowland v. State, 744 S.W.2d 610, 612 (Tex.Crim. App.1988). "Deprivation is not an element of intent to deprive; therefore, the State need not prove actual deprivation in order to prove intent to deprive. While evidence of actual deprivation may be evidence of intent to deprive, other evidence may also indicate whether intent to deprive exists." *See also* **Hawkins v. State**, 214 S.W.3d 668, 670 (Tex.App.—Waco 2007, no pet.) (asportation).

Christensen v. State, 240 S.W.3d 25, 32 (Tex. App.—Houston [1st Dist.] 2007, pet. ref'd). "In determining whether the defendant had criminal intent to commit theft, we may consider whether the defendant experienced personal gain from the property obtained from the complainants. *At 33:* The evidence may be legally insufficient to show criminal intent when the evidence shows partial performance of the matter for which funds were tendered. *At 34:* The critical distinction between conduct that is criminal versus civil in nature is whether the record shows deception and not merely a failure to perform. *At 35:* The State points to appellant's 'deception' after the search warrant was run

For a quick reference of penalties, see the Chart of Penalties on p. 675.

O'CONNOR'S CRIMINAL CODES **809**

on [subcontractor's] business to show deception by appellant. Deception after an alleged crime is a circumstance that may permit an inference of guilt. However, evidence that only shows deception after the fact is legally insufficient to establish criminal intent at the time of the [alleged criminal act]."

Bokor v. State, 114 S.W.3d 558, 560 (Tex.App.—Fort Worth 2002, no pet.). "If a bona fide dispute exists as to the ownership of the property, then the evidence is legally insufficient to sustain a theft conviction."

§31.03(b)

Flowers v. State, 843 S.W.2d 38, 39 (Tex.Crim.App. 1992). Chenault, a Texas Ranger, "testified he told [D] the equipment was 'ripped-off' from Texaco. Chenault stated 'ripped-off' meant stolen. However, testimony elicited by the defense during trial indicated 'ripped-off' could also mean obtained at a very low price. Because of this dual meaning ..., the Court of Appeals held no explicit representation that the property was stolen was made by Chenault to [D]. *At 40-41:* When conflicting evidence is introduced as to the meaning of slang terminology, the factfinder is free to decide which definition to accept. Apparently the jury accepted Chenault's definition. ... Therefore, the Court of Appeals erred in holding the evidence insufficient to support the conviction."

§31.03(c)

Willis v. State, 790 S.W.2d 307, 311 (Tex.Crim.App. 1990). "[T]he §31.03(c)(3) presumption in the jury charge before us, introduces the presumption with: '[a] person is presumed to know,' and then continues to follow the statutory language. [T]he charge in this case unequivocally informs the jurors that 'if [the facts giving rise to the presumption] are proven beyond a reasonable doubt, you may find that [D] knew that the property in question ... had been stolen, if it had been, *but you are not bound to so find*.' ... We can conclude that ..., a reasonable juror would understand that he or she was free to accept or reject the presumption making it a permissive presumption."

Naranjo v. State, 217 S.W.3d 560, 568 (Tex. App.—San Antonio 2006, no pet.). "[A] defendant's status as an employee of an automobile body repair shop—standing alone—is an insufficient basis upon which to submit the §31.03(c)(6)(B) presumption."

Ballard v. State, 945 S.W.2d 902, 905 (Tex.App.—Beaumont 1997, no pet.). "The admission of extraneous acts under Section 31.03(c)(1) requires a 'recent'

transaction. [W]e conclude that the 6 year time span between the charged offense and the extraneous transaction in the instant case is not recent."

§31.03(e)

Simmons v. State, 109 S.W.3d 469, 477-78 (Tex. Crim.App.2003). "[A] check is a 'document that represents or embodies value' and checks embody, in the all but the exceptional cases, a value equivalent to what is written on their faces. Accordingly, we hold that the face amount of the instrument is presumptive evidence of its value. Assuming that no evidence is produced to rebut the logical inference that the payee was entitled to receive the face amount of the check, it is sufficient evidence of value to show the face amount of the check."

Barnes v. State, 103 S.W.3d 494, 497 (Tex. App.—San Antonio 2003, no pet.). "When a misdemeanor theft is elevated to a felony theft, the prior theft convictions create a new offense and vest jurisdiction in the district court. The prior theft convictions become jurisdictional elements of the theft charge and cannot be waived. The State must prove the underlying theft and the two prior theft convictions. Accordingly, if the State fails to prove the prior felony convictions, but proves the underlying theft, then the case must be transferred to a court with misdemeanor jurisdiction."

Bruns v. State, 22 S.W.3d 540, 543-44 (Tex. App.—El Paso 2000, no pet.). "Section 31.03(e)(4)(D) requires that the offenses utilized to upgrade a misdemeanor offense to a felony must be theft offenses. ... It was clear that the [prior] offenses were actually forgeries and, accordingly, the trial court never obtained jurisdiction over the case."

§31.03(f)

Ex parte Balderrama, 214 S.W.3d 530, 535 (Tex. App.—Austin 2006, pet. ref'd). "[U]nder §31.03(a) and (f)(1), the offense of theft by a public servant is established by evidence that (1) the accused unlawfully appropriated property with the requisite intent, (2) the accused was a public servant at the time of the theft, and (3) the property came into the accused's custody, possession, or control by virtue of the accused's status as a public servant."

PEN §31.04. THEFT OF SERVICE

(a) A person commits theft of service if, with intent to avoid payment for service that he knows is provided only for compensation:

(1) he intentionally or knowingly secures performance of the service by deception, threat, or false token;

(2) having control over the disposition of services of another to which he is not entitled, he intentionally or knowingly diverts the other's services to his own benefit or to the benefit of another not entitled to them;

(3) having control of personal property under a written rental agreement, he holds the property beyond the expiration of the rental period without the effective consent of the owner of the property, thereby depriving the owner of the property of its use in further rentals; or

(4) he intentionally or knowingly secures the performance of the service by agreeing to provide compensation and, after the service is rendered, fails to make payment after receiving notice demanding payment.

(b) For purposes of this section, intent to avoid payment is presumed if:

(1) the actor absconded without paying for the service or expressly refused to pay for the service in circumstances where payment is ordinarily made immediately upon rendering of the service, as in hotels, campgrounds, recreational vehicle parks, restaurants, and comparable establishments;

(2) the actor failed to make payment under a service agreement within 10 days after receiving notice demanding payment;

(3) the actor returns property held under a rental agreement after the expiration of the rental agreement and fails to pay the applicable rental charge for the property within 10 days after the date on which the actor received notice demanding payment; or

(4) the actor failed to return the property held under a rental agreement:

(A) within five days after receiving notice demanding return, if the property is valued at less than $1,500; or

(B) within three days after receiving notice demanding return, if the property is valued at $1,500 or more.

(c) For purposes of Subsections (a)(4), (b)(2), and (b)(4), notice shall be notice in writing, sent by registered or certified mail with return receipt requested or by telegram with report of delivery requested, and addressed to the actor at his address shown on the rental agreement or service agreement.

(d) If written notice is given in accordance with Subsection (c), it is presumed that the notice was received no later than five days after it was sent.

(e) An offense under this section is:

(1) a Class C misdemeanor if the value of the service stolen is less than $20;

(2) a Class B misdemeanor if the value of the service stolen is $20 or more but less than $500;

(3) a Class A misdemeanor if the value of the service stolen is $500 or more but less than $1,500;

(4) a state jail felony if the value of the service stolen is $1,500 or more but less than $20,000;

(5) a felony of the third degree if the value of the service stolen is $20,000 or more but less than $100,000;

(6) a felony of the second degree if the value of the service stolen is $100,000 or more but less than $200,000; or

(7) a felony of the first degree if the value of the service stolen is $200,000 or more.

(f) Notwithstanding any other provision of this code, any police or other report of stolen vehicles by a political subdivision of this state shall include on the report any rental vehicles whose renters have been shown to such reporting agency to be in violation of Subsection (b)(2) and shall indicate that the renting agency has complied with the notice requirements demanding return as provided in this section.

(g) It is a defense to prosecution under this section that:

(1) the defendant secured the performance of the service by giving a post-dated check or similar sight order to the person performing the service; and

(2) the person performing the service or any other person presented the check or sight order for payment before the date on the check or sight order.

History of Pen §31.04: Acts 1973, 63rd Leg., ch. 399, §1, eff. Jan. 1, 1974. Amended by Acts 1977, 65th Leg., ch. 429, §1, eff. Aug. 29, 1977; Acts 1983, 68th Leg., ch. 497, §4, eff. Sept. 1, 1983; Acts 1991, 72nd Leg., ch. 565, §15, eff. Sept. 1, 1991; Acts 1993, 73rd Leg., ch. 900, §1.01, eff. Sept. 1, 1994; Acts 1995, 74th Leg., ch. 479, §1, eff. Aug. 28, 1995; Acts 1999, 76th Leg., ch. 843, §1, eff. Sept. 1, 1999; Acts 2001, 77th Leg., ch. 1245, §§1, 2, eff. Sept. 1, 2001; Acts 2003, 78th Leg., ch. 419, §1, eff. Sept. 1, 2003.

ANNOTATIONS

Huse v. State, 180 S.W.3d 847, 850 (Tex.App.—Eastland 2005, pet. ref'd). "[I]f one simply pays for a completed transaction with an insufficient-funds check, no violation [of §31.04] is shown. On the other

PEN §31.04

For a quick reference of penalties, see the Chart of Penalties on p. 675.

O'CONNOR'S CRIMINAL CODES   811

hand, if one prepays for services with that same check, the statute is implicated. The distinction is the vendor's reliance. The statute requires proof that appellant *secured* services with a deceptive act. In the first instance, because the services were provided before the check was tendered, it cannot be said that the vendor relied upon it or that appellant secured anything with it. In the latter, assuming no services would have been provided without the prepayment, it can be safely said that the vendor relied upon the check and that appellant successfully secured services with it."

Raney v. State, 769 S.W.2d 698, 700 (Tex.App.—Corpus Christi 1989, no pet.). "Section 31.04(a)(3) proscribes the theft of services, not property. Property is involved in §31.04(a)(3) only to the extent that withholding it, with the intent to avoid payment for services, deprives the owner of further rentals on the property."

PEN §31.05. THEFT OF TRADE SECRETS

(a) For purposes of this section:

(1) "Article" means any object, material, device, or substance or any copy thereof, including a writing, recording, drawing, sample, specimen, prototype, model, photograph, microorganism, blueprint, or map.

(2) "Copy" means a facsimile, replica, photograph, or other reproduction of an article or a note, drawing, or sketch made of or from an article.

(3) "Representing" means describing, depicting, containing, constituting, reflecting, or recording.

(4) "Trade secret" means the whole or any part of any scientific or technical information, design, process, procedure, formula, or improvement that has value and that the owner has taken measures to prevent from becoming available to persons other than those selected by the owner to have access for limited purposes.

(b) A person commits an offense if, without the owner's effective consent, he knowingly:

(1) steals a trade secret;

(2) makes a copy of an article representing a trade secret; or

(3) communicates or transmits a trade secret.

(c) An offense under this section is a felony of the third degree.

History of Pen §31.05: Acts 1973, 63rd Leg., ch. 399, §1, eff. Jan. 1, 1974.

ANNOTATIONS

Schalk v. State, 823 S.W.2d 633, 644 (Tex.Crim. App.1991). "[T]he combination of employment agreements, strict plant security, restricted computer access, the non-authorization of disclosure of the subject programs and the general non-disclosure of those programs by TI and its employees served to support trade secret status of the computer programs that are the subject of the instant indictments. Appellants neither requested nor received permission to copy the files containing these programs. The unauthorized copying of an article representing a trade secret constitutes an offense under Penal Code §31.05(b)(2). [T]he subject programs are trade secrets."

McGowan v. State, 938 S.W.2d 732, 737 (Tex. App.—Houston [14th Dist.] 1996), *aff'd sub nom.* *Weightman v. State*, 975 S.W.2d 621 (Tex.Crim. App.1998). "The core element of a trade secret is that it must remain a secret, although absolute secrecy is not required. There must be a substantial element of secrecy and the owner must have taken measures to prevent the trade secret from becoming available to persons other than those selected by the owner to have access for limited purposes. To determine whether the measures taken were effective to maintain substantial secrecy of the drawings, the following factors are relevant: (1) non-disclosure agreements, (2) plant security, (3) access to information, and (4) other measures. *At 738:* Although the record reflects that many [of appellant's employer's] drawings were available in the secondary market, [another employee's] testimony regarding the selection of these particular drawings, the security measures implemented during this time frame, and appellant's actions in retrieving these particular drawings from a secured facility support the jury's finding that the documents appellant transmitted or communicated were, in fact, trade secrets."

PEN §31.06. PRESUMPTION FOR THEFT BY CHECK

(a) If the actor obtained property or secured performance of service by issuing or passing a check or similar sight order for the payment of money, when the issuer did not have sufficient funds in or on deposit with the bank or other drawee for the payment in full of the check or order as well as all other checks or orders then outstanding, it is prima facie evidence of his intent to

---

deprive the owner of property under Section 31.03 (Theft) including a drawee or third-party holder in due course who negotiated the check or to avoid payment for service under Section 31.04 (Theft of Service) (except in the case of a postdated check or order) if:

(1) he had no account with the bank or other drawee at the time he issued the check or order; or

(2) payment was refused by the bank or other drawee for lack of funds or insufficient funds, on presentation within 30 days after issue, and the issuer failed to pay the holder in full within 10 days after receiving notice of that refusal.

(b) For purposes of Subsection (a)(2) or (f)(3), notice may be actual notice or notice in writing that:

 Subsection (1) below is effective for offenses committed on or after Sept. 1, 2007.

(1) is sent by:

(A) first class mail, evidenced by an affidavit of service; or

(B) registered or certified mail with return receipt requested;

Subsection (1) below is effective for offenses in which any element of the offense was committed before Sept. 1, 2007.

(1) is sent by registered or certified mail with return receipt requested or by telegram with report of delivery requested;

(2) is addressed to the issuer at the issuer's address shown on:

(A) the check or order;

(B) the records of the bank or other drawee; or

(C) the records of the person to whom the check or order has been issued or passed; and

(3) contains the following statement:

"This is a demand for payment in full for a check or order not paid because of a lack of funds or insufficient funds. If you fail to make payment in full within 10 days after the date of receipt of this notice, the failure to pay creates a presumption for committing an offense, and this matter may be referred for criminal prosecution."

(c) If written notice is given in accordance with Subsection (b), it is presumed that the notice was received no later than five days after it was sent.

(d) Nothing in this section prevents the prosecution from establishing the requisite intent by direct evidence.

(e) Partial restitution does not preclude the presumption of the requisite intent under this section.

(f) If the actor obtained property by issuing or passing a check or similar sight order for the payment of money, the actor's intent to deprive the owner of the property under Section 31.03 (Theft) is presumed, except in the case of a postdated check or order, if:

(1) the actor ordered the bank or other drawee to stop payment on the check or order;

(2) the bank or drawee refused payment to the holder on presentation of the check or order within 30 days after issue;

(3) the owner gave the actor notice of the refusal of payment and made a demand to the actor for payment or return of the property; and

(4) the actor failed to:

(A) pay the holder within 10 days after receiving the demand for payment; or

(B) return the property to the owner within 10 days after receiving the demand for return of the property.

History of Pen §31.06: Acts 1973, 63rd Leg., ch. 399, §1, eff. Jan. 1, 1974. Amended by Acts 1991, 72nd Leg., ch. 543, §2, eff. Sept. 1, 1991; Acts 1993, 73rd Leg., ch. 900, §1.01, eff. Sept. 1, 1994; Acts 1995, 74th Leg., ch. 753, §1, eff. Sept. 1, 1995; Acts 2007, 80th Leg., ch. 976, §1, eff. Sept. 1, 2007.

ANNOTATIONS

Bagsby v. State, 721 S.W.2d 567, 571 (Tex.App.— Fort Worth 1986, no pet.). "The presumption, not being an element of an offense, need not be pled."

Richie v. State, 721 S.W.2d 560, 562 (Tex.App.— Beaumont 1986, no pet.). "*Section 31.06* does not separately create a specific offense. It merely provides an evidentiary presumption of intent to deprive which is ancillary to the general theft statute, and codifies a presumption which the state may rely upon in appropriate cases. Many times there will be evidence to demonstrate a defendant's intent without exclusive reliance on the presumption. *Section 31.06(d)* specifically allows direct evidence of intent independent of the presumption it creates."

PEN §31.07. UNAUTHORIZED USE OF A VEHICLE

(a) A person commits an offense if he intentionally or knowingly operates another's boat, airplane, or motor-propelled vehicle without the effective consent of the owner.

(b) An offense under this section is a state jail felony.

For a quick reference of penalties, see the Chart of Penalties on p. 675.

O'CONNOR'S CRIMINAL CODES 813

History of Pen §31.07: Acts 1973, 63rd Leg., ch. 399, §1, eff. Jan. 1, 1974. Amended by Acts 1993, 73rd Leg., ch. 900, §1.01, eff. Sept. 1, 1994.

Denton v. State, 911 S.W.2d 388, 389 (Tex.Crim. App.1995). "[T]he term 'operate' is not defined in the Penal Code.... [¶] [W]hile driving does involve operation, operation does not necessarily involve driving. *At 390:* To find operation ..., the totality of the circumstances must demonstrate that the defendant took action to affect the functioning of his vehicle in a manner that would enable the vehicle's use."

McQueen v. State, 781 S.W.2d 600, 603 (Tex.Crim. App.1989). "[I]n an unauthorized use of a motor vehicle case, a culpable mental state applies to whether the defendant knew his use of the motor vehicle was without the effective consent of the owner."

Medina v. State, 962 S.W.2d 83, 86 (Tex.App.— Houston [1st Dist.] 1997, pet. ref'd). "[U]nauthorized use of a motor vehicle can be a continuing offense."

Spencer v. State, 867 S.W.2d 81, 84 (Tex.App.— Texarkana 1993, pet. ref'd). "The license plate number [in the indictment] describes with unnecessary particularity a thing (motor-propelled vehicle) necessary to be mentioned in the indictment. [¶] The State did not necessarily have to plead and prove the truck's license plate number. Indeed, had the indictment simply charged that Spencer had operated Vaughn's pickup truck without authorization, it would have been sufficient to allege the charged offense. Having included such an identifying description in the indictment and in the charge, the State undertook the burden of proving these specific allegations."

Walker v. State, 846 S.W.2d 379, 381 (Tex.App.— Houston [14th Dist.] 1992, pet. ref'd). "[T]he requisite culpable mental states apply both to operation of the vehicle, and to the phrase 'without the effective consent of the owner.'"

McLemore v. State, 669 S.W.2d 856, 858 (Tex. App.—Austin 1984, no pet.). "A 'vehicle' is 'any device or contrivance for carrying or conveying persons or objects, including land conveyances, vessels, aircraft, and spacecraft.' [A] 'motor-propelled vehicle' is any device or contrivance for carrying or conveying persons or objects that is motor-propelled, including motor-propelled boats and aircraft. [¶] Even if 'boat' and 'airplane' did not appear in §31.07(a) ... proof the accused operated

a motorboat or motor-powered aircraft would nevertheless support a conviction for unauthorized use of a 'motor-propelled vehicle.' ... The inclusion of 'boat' and 'airplane' in §31.07 has been explained as the expression of a legislative intent to include within the scope of the statute boats and aircraft that are not motor-propelled. [P]roof the accused operated an airplane constitutes a fatal variance from the allegation he operated a 'motor-propelled vehicle' only if the airplane was motorless."

PEN §31.08. VALUE

(a) Subject to the additional criteria of Subsections (b) and (c), value under this chapter is:

(1) the fair market value of the property or service at the time and place of the offense; or

(2) if the fair market value of the property cannot be ascertained, the cost of replacing the property within a reasonable time after the theft.

(b) The value of documents, other than those having a readily ascertainable market value, is:

(1) the amount due and collectible at maturity less that part which has been satisfied, if the document constitutes evidence of a debt; or

(2) the greatest amount of economic loss that the owner might reasonably suffer by virtue of loss of the document, if the document is other than evidence of a debt.

(c) If property or service has value that cannot be reasonably ascertained by the criteria set forth in Subsections (a) and (b), the property or service is deemed to have a value of $500 or more but less than $1,500.

(d) If the actor proves by a preponderance of the evidence that he gave consideration for or had a legal interest in the property or service stolen, the amount of the consideration or the value of the interest so proven shall be deducted from the value of the property or service ascertained under Subsection (a), (b), or (c) to determine value for purposes of this chapter.

History of Pen §31.08: Acts 1973, 63rd Leg., ch. 399, §1, eff. Jan. 1, 1974. Amended by Acts 1983, 68th Leg., ch. 497, §5, eff. Sept. 1, 1983; Acts 1993, 73rd Leg., ch. 900, §1.01, eff. Sept. 1, 1994.

Simmons v. State, 109 S.W.3d 469, 473 (Tex.Crim. App.2003). "Do signed checks which are made payable to a specific person have a readily ascertainable market value? Common sense and case law from other jurisdictions suggest that the answer is 'no.' While 'market

PEN §31.07

value' is not statutorily defined in the Texas Penal Code, this Court has defined the phrase 'fair market value' as the dollar amount the property would sell for in cash, given a reasonable time for selling it. Put otherwise, fair market value is 'the price the property will bring when offered for sale by one who desires to sell, but is not obliged to sell, and is bought by one who desires to buy, but is under no necessity of buying.' An unendorsed check made out to a specific person does not have a readily ascertainable market value because there is not much of a commercial market for unendorsed checks. *At 475:* [W]e hold that the face amount of a check is presumptive evidence of its value. [A] *prima facie* showing of value by proof of the face amount of a signed check may be rebutted with other evidence."

Sullivan v. State, 701 S.W.2d 905, 909 (Tex.Crim. App.1986). "[T]here seems to be two corollaries to the rule regarding proof of value. When the proof of value is given by a non-owner, the non-owner must be qualified as to his knowledge of the value of the property and must give testimony explicitly as to the fair market value or replacement value of the property. [¶] However, when the owner of the property is testifying as to the value of the property, he or she may testify as to his or her opinion or estimate of the value of the property in general and commonly understood terms. Testimony of this nature is an offer of the witness' best knowledge of the value of his property. ... This is true even in the absence of a specific statement as to 'market value' or 'replacement value.'"

Ray v. State, 106 S.W.3d 299, 301 (Tex.App.— Houston [1st Dist.] 2003, no pet.). "[F]air market value is ... the amount the property would sell for in cash, given a reasonable time for selling it. Fair market value can be proven by evidence of the retail price or sale price, by testimony of an owner's opinion of value, or an expert opinion of value. No one method has been held to be exclusive. ... A person may testify as the 'special owner' of property if it is shown that he has care, custody, or control of the property by virtue of his employment relationship with the corporation that owns the property."

Drost v. State, 47 S.W.3d 41, 44 (Tex.App.—El Paso 2001, pet. ref'd). The "evidence is legally insufficient to prove value if there was no evidence presented from which a reasonable fact finder could find fair market value beyond a reasonable doubt; or if it is shown that

fair market value cannot be ascertained, if there was no evidence from which the fact finder could find replacement value beyond a reasonable doubt."

Jones v. State, 821 S.W.2d 234, 237 (Tex.App.— Houston [14th Dist.] 1991, pet. ref'd). "[I]n a prosecution for felony theft, proof of value of the property by hearsay is permissible."

Jones v. State, 814 S.W.2d 801, 803 (Tex.App.— Houston [14th Dist.] 1991, no pet.). "If appellant wishes to rebut the owner's opinion evidence he must do more than merely impeach the witness' credibility during cross-examination; he must offer controverting evidence as to the value of the property."

PEN §31.09. AGGREGATION OF AMOUNTS INVOLVED IN THEFT

When amounts are obtained in violation of this chapter pursuant to one scheme or continuing course of conduct, whether from the same or several sources, the conduct may be considered as one offense and the amounts aggregated in determining the grade of the offense.

History of Pen §31.09: Acts 1973, 63rd Leg., ch. 399, §1, eff. Jan. 1, 1974.

ANNOTATIONS

Kellar v. State, 108 S.W.3d 311, 312 (Tex.Crim.App. 2003). "[U]nder Penal Code §31.09, the indictment must allege only aggregation, not the specific acts of theft. *At 313:* While the statute does not require the level of specificity in an indictment urged by the appellant, a defendant does have a constitutional right to sufficient notice so as to enable him to prepare a defense. However, this due process requirement may be satisfied by means other than the language in the charging instrument." *See also **Whitehead v. State***, 745 S.W.2d 374, 377 (Tex.Crim.App.1988).

Graves v. State, 795 S.W.2d 185, 187 (Tex.Crim. App.1990). "[S]ection 31.09 adequately creates a separate offense and defines conduct for purposes of jurisdiction, punishment and period of limitation from prosecution." *See also **Skillern v. State***, 890 S.W.2d 849, 873 (Tex.App.—Austin 1994, pet. ref'd).

Cupit v. State, 122 S.W.3d 243, 246 (Tex.App.— Houston [1st Dist.] 2003, pet. ref'd). "Theft is a single offense, not a continuing offense. *At 247:* When a defendant has committed multiple thefts over a period of time, the State may choose to aggregate the thefts pursuant to §31.09.... If the State chooses to indict a defendant based on §31.09, the indictment must include

For a quick reference of penalties, see the Chart of Penalties on p. 675.

O'CONNOR'S CRIMINAL CODES **815**

language to the effect that the State is aggregating the amounts pursuant to a continuing scheme or course of conduct. This language is considered an element of the offense. When it is omitted, it is reversible error. Thus, if appellant were correct in classifying the offense as two thefts that should have been aggregated, we would sustain her sufficiency challenge because the indictment here did not include the required language. Instead, we reject her argument because we conclude the offense was a single theft. [¶] In those cases in which Texas courts have addressed indictments for aggregated theft, the continuing course of conduct has occurred over prolonged periods of time—weeks, months, even years—and often involve multiple complainants. Here, the scheme took approximately three hours to complete and involved only one complainant. [¶] [W]e conclude that appellant committed a series of steps, all of which were the result of her original impulse to swindle money from the complainant, that constituted a single offense."

Vitiello v. State, 848 S.W.2d 885, 887-88 (Tex. App.—Houston [14th Dist.] 1993, pet. ref'd). "[T]he State aggregated seven third degree felonies into one second degree felony. One of the incidents of theft occurred outside the five year limitations period. Nonetheless, §31.09 allows the State to aggregate the separate incidents of theft into a single offense. ... Since the offense, comprised of the separate incidents of theft, was [completed within the statute of limitations period], the prosecution was not barred by the statute of limitations."

PEN §31.10. ACTOR'S INTEREST IN PROPERTY

It is no defense to prosecution under this chapter that the actor has an interest in the property or service stolen if another person has the right of exclusive possession of the property.

History of Pen §31.10: Acts 1973, 63rd Leg., ch. 399, §1, eff. Jan. 1, 1974.

PEN §31.11. TAMPERING WITH IDENTIFICATION NUMBERS

(a) A person commits an offense if the person:

(1) knowingly or intentionally removes, alters, or obliterates the serial number or other permanent identification marking on tangible personal property; or

(2) possesses, sells, or offers for sale tangible personal property and:

(A) the actor knows that the serial number or other permanent identification marking has been removed, altered, or obliterated; or

(B) a reasonable person in the position of the actor would have known that the serial number or other permanent identification marking has been removed, altered, or obliterated.

(b) It is an affirmative defense to prosecution under this section that the person was:

(1) the owner or acting with the effective consent of the owner of the property involved;

(2) a peace officer acting in the actual discharge of official duties; or

(3) acting with respect to a number assigned to a vehicle by the Texas Department of Transportation and the person was:

(A) in the actual discharge of official duties as an employee or agent of the department; or

(B) in full compliance with the rules of the department as an applicant for an assigned number approved by the department.

(c) Property involved in a violation of this section may be treated as stolen for purposes of custody and disposition of the property.

(d) An offense under this section is a Class A misdemeanor.

(e) In this section, "vehicle" has the meaning given by Section 541.201, Transportation Code.

History of Pen §31.11: Acts 1979, 66th Leg., ch. 191, §1, eff. Sept. 1, 1979. Amended by Acts 1983, 68th Leg., ch. 741, §2, eff. Sept. 1, 1983; Acts 1991, 72nd Leg., ch. 113, §1, eff. Sept. 1, 1991; Acts 1993, 73rd Leg., ch. 900, §1.01, eff. Sept. 1, 1994; Acts 1997, 75th Leg., ch. 165, §30.239, eff. Sept. 1, 1997.

ANNOTATIONS

Dill v. State, 697 S.W.2d 702, 707 (Tex.App.—Corpus Christi 1985, pet. ref'd). "Probable cause to arrest for §31.11 must be based on a reasonable belief the actor tampered with the serial number or possessed the property knowing the serial number had been tampered with *without the effective consent of the owner*."

PEN §31.12. THEFT OF OR TAMPERING WITH MULTICHANNEL VIDEO OR INFORMATION SERVICES

(a) A person commits an offense if, without the authorization of the multichannel video or information services provider, the person intentionally or knowingly:

(1) makes or maintains a connection, whether physically, electrically, electronically, or inductively, to:

(A) a cable, wire, or other component of or media attached to a multichannel video or information services system; or

(B) a television set, videotape recorder, or other receiver attached to a multichannel video or information system;

(2) attaches, causes to be attached, or maintains the attachment of a device to:

(A) a cable, wire, or other component of or media attached to a multichannel video or information services system; or

(B) a television set, videotape recorder, or other receiver attached to a multichannel video or information services system;

(3) tampers with, modifies, or maintains a modification to a device installed by a multichannel video or information services provider; or

(4) tampers with, modifies, or maintains a modification to an access device or uses that access device or any unauthorized access device to obtain services from a multichannel video or information services provider.

(b) In this section:

(1) "Access device," "connection," and "device" mean an access device, connection, or device wholly or partly designed to make intelligible an encrypted, encoded, scrambled, or other nonstandard signal carried by a multichannel video or information services provider.

(2) "Encrypted, encoded, scrambled, or other nonstandard signal" means any type of signal or transmission not intended to produce an intelligible program or service without the use of a device, signal, or information provided by a multichannel video or information services provider.

(3) "Multichannel video or information services provider" means a licensed cable television system, video dialtone system, multichannel multipoint distribution services system, direct broadcast satellite system, or other system providing video or information services that are distributed by cable, wire, radio frequency, or other media.

(c) This section does not prohibit the manufacture, distribution, sale, or use of satellite receiving antennas that are otherwise permitted by state or federal law.

(d) An offense under this section is a Class C misdemeanor unless it is shown on the trial of the offense that the actor:

(1) has been previously convicted one time of an offense under this section, in which event the offense is a Class B misdemeanor, or convicted two or more times of an offense under this section, in which event the offense is a Class A misdemeanor; or

(2) committed the offense for remuneration, in which event the offense is a Class A misdemeanor, unless it is also shown on the trial of the offense that the actor has been previously convicted two or more times of an offense under this section, in which event the offense is a Class A misdemeanor with a minimum fine of $2,000 and a minimum term of confinement of 180 days.

(e) For the purposes of this section, each connection, attachment, modification, or act of tampering is a separate offense.

History of Pen §31.12: Acts 1995, 74th Leg., ch. 318, §10, eff. Sept. 1, 1995. Amended by Acts 1999, 76th Leg., ch. 858, §1, eff. Sept. 1, 1999.

History of Former Pen §31.12: Deleted by Acts 1993, 73rd Leg., ch. 900, §1.04, eff. Sept. 1, 1994.

PEN §31.13. MANUFACTURE, DISTRIBUTION, OR ADVERTISEMENT OF MULTICHANNEL VIDEO OR INFORMATION SERVICES DEVICE

(a) A person commits an offense if the person for remuneration intentionally or knowingly manufactures, assembles, modifies, imports into the state, exports out of the state, distributes, advertises, or offers for sale, with an intent to aid in the commission of an offense under Section 31.12, a device, a kit or part for a device, or a plan for a system of components wholly or partly designed to make intelligible an encrypted, encoded, scrambled, or other nonstandard signal carried or caused by a multichannel video or information services provider.

(b) In this section, "device," "encrypted, encoded, scrambled, or other nonstandard signal," and "multichannel video or information services provider" have the meanings assigned by Section 31.12.

(c) This section does not prohibit the manufacture, distribution, advertisement, offer for sale, or use of satellite receiving antennas that are otherwise permitted by state or federal law.

(d) An offense under this section is a Class A misdemeanor.

For a quick reference of penalties, see the Chart of Penalties on p. 675.

O'CONNOR'S CRIMINAL CODES 817

✦

History of Pen §31.13: Acts 1995, 74th Leg., ch. 318, §10, eff. Sept. 1, 1995. Amended by Acts 1999, 76th Leg., ch. 858, §2, eff. Sept. 1, 1999.

History of Former Pen §31.13: Deleted by Acts 1993, 73rd Leg., ch. 900, §1.01, eff. Sept. 1, 1994.

PEN §31.14. SALE OR LEASE OF MULTICHANNEL VIDEO OR INFORMATION SERVICES DEVICE

(a) A person commits an offense if the person intentionally or knowingly sells or leases, with an intent to aid in the commission of an offense under Section 31.12, a device, a kit or part for a device, or a plan for a system of components wholly or partly designed to make intelligible an encrypted, encoded, scrambled, or other nonstandard signal carried or caused by a multichannel video or information services provider.

(b) In this section, "device," "encrypted, encoded, scrambled, or other nonstandard signal," and "multichannel video or information services provider" have the meanings assigned by Section 31.12.

(c) This section does not prohibit the sale or lease of satellite receiving antennas that are otherwise permitted by state or federal law without providing notice to the comptroller.

(d) An offense under this section is a Class A misdemeanor.

History of Pen §31.14: Acts 1999, 76th Leg., ch. 858, §3, eff. Sept. 1, 1999.

PEN §31.15. POSSESSION, MANUFACTURE, OR DISTRIBUTION OF CERTAIN INSTRUMENTS USED TO COMMIT RETAIL THEFT

(a) In this section:

(1) "Retail theft detector" means an electrical, mechanical, electronic, or magnetic device used to prevent or detect shoplifting and includes any article or component part essential to the proper operation of the device.

(2) "Shielding or deactivation instrument" means any item or tool designed, made, or adapted for the purpose of preventing the detection of stolen merchandise by a retail theft detector. The term includes a metal-lined or foil-lined shopping bag and any item used to remove a security tag affixed to retail merchandise.

(b) A person commits an offense if, with the intent to use the instrument to commit theft, the person:

(1) possesses a shielding or deactivation instrument; or

(2) knowingly manufactures, sells, offers for sale, or otherwise distributes a shielding or deactivation instrument.

(c) An offense under this section is a Class A misdemeanor.

History of Pen §31.15: Acts 2001, 77th Leg., ch. 109, §1, eff. Sept. 1, 2001.

 ## PEN §31.16. ORGANIZED RETAIL THEFT

(a) In this section, "retail merchandise" means one or more items of tangible personal property displayed, held, stored, or offered for sale in a retail establishment.

(b) A person commits an offense if the person intentionally conducts, promotes, or facilitates an activity in which the person receives, possesses, conceals, stores, barters, sells, or disposes of a total value of not less than $1,500 of:

(1) stolen retail merchandise; or

(2) merchandise explicitly represented to the person as being stolen retail merchandise.

(c) An offense under this section is:

(1) a state jail felony if the total value of the merchandise involved in the activity is $1,500 or more but less than $20,000;

(2) a felony of the third degree if the total value of the merchandise involved in the activity is $20,000 or more but less than $100,000;

(3) a felony of the second degree if the total value of the merchandise involved in the activity is $100,000 or more but less than $200,000; or

(4) a felony of the first degree if the total value of the merchandise involved in the activity is $200,000 or more.

(d) An offense described for purposes of punishment by Subsections (c)(1)-(3) is increased to the next higher category of offense if it is shown on the trial of the offense that the person organized, supervised, financed, or managed one or more other persons engaged in an activity described by Subsection (b).

Subsection (e) below is effective for offenses committed on or after Sept. 1, 2007.

(e) For the purposes of punishment, an offense under this section or an offense described by Section 31.03(e)(1) or (2) is increased to the next highest category of offense if it is shown at the trial of the offense that the defendant, with the intent that a distraction from the commission of the offense be created, intentionally, knowingly, or recklessly caused an alarm to sound or otherwise become activated during the commission of the offense.

History of Pen §31.16: Acts 2007, 80th Leg., ch. 1274, §1, eff. Sept. 1, 2007.

PEN §31.13

CHAPTER 32. FRAUD

SUBCHAPTER A. GENERAL PROVISIONS

PEN §32.01. DEFINITIONS

In this chapter:

(1) "Financial institution" means a bank, trust company, insurance company, credit union, building and loan association, savings and loan association, investment trust, investment company, or any other organization held out to the public as a place for deposit of funds or medium of savings or collective investment.

(2) "Property" means:

(A) real property;

(B) tangible or intangible personal property including anything severed from land; or

(C) a document, including money, that represents or embodies anything of value.

(3) "Service" includes:

(A) labor and professional service;

(B) telecommunication, public utility, and transportation service;

(C) lodging, restaurant service, and entertainment; and

(D) the supply of a motor vehicle or other property for use.

(4) "Steal" means to acquire property or service by theft.

History of Pen §32.01: Acts 1973, 63rd Leg., ch. 399, §1, eff. Jan. 1, 1974. Amended by Acts 1993, 73rd Leg., ch. 900, §1.01, eff. Sept. 1, 1994.

PEN §32.02. VALUE

(a) Subject to the additional criteria of Subsections (b) and (c), value under this chapter is:

(1) the fair market value of the property or service at the time and place of the offense; or

(2) if the fair market value of the property cannot be ascertained, the cost of replacing the property within a reasonable time after the offense.

(b) The value of documents, other than those having a readily ascertainable market value, is:

(1) the amount due and collectible at maturity less any part that has been satisfied, if the document constitutes evidence of a debt; or

(2) the greatest amount of economic loss that the owner might reasonably suffer by virtue of loss of the document, if the document is other than evidence of a debt.

(c) If property or service has value that cannot be reasonably ascertained by the criteria set forth in Subsections (a) and (b), the property or service is deemed to have a value of $500 or more but less than $1,500.

(d) If the actor proves by a preponderance of the evidence that he gave consideration for or had a legal interest in the property or service stolen, the amount of the consideration or the value of the interest so proven shall be deducted from the value of the property or service ascertained under Subsection (a), (b), or (c) to determine value for purposes of this chapter.

History of Pen §32.02: Acts 1973, 63rd Leg., ch. 399, §1, eff. Jan. 1, 1974. Amended by Acts 1993, 73rd Leg., ch. 900, §1.01, eff. Sept. 1, 1994.

For a quick reference of penalties, see the Chart of Penalties on p. 675.

O'CONNOR'S CRIMINAL CODES   819

PEN §32.03. AGGREGATION OF AMOUNTS INVOLVED IN FRAUD

When amounts are obtained in violation of this chapter pursuant to one scheme or continuing course of conduct, whether from the same or several sources, the conduct may be considered as one offense and the amounts aggregated in determining the grade of offense.

History of Pen §32.03: Acts 1973, 63rd Leg., ch. 399, §1, eff. Jan. 1, 1974. Amended by Acts 1993, 73rd Leg., ch. 900, §1.01, eff. Sept. 1, 1994.

ANNOTATIONS

Drake v. State, 686 S.W.2d 935, 943 (Tex.Crim.App. 1985), *overruled on other grounds*, ***Fortune v. State***, 745 S.W.2d 364 (Tex.Crim.App.1988). "Aggregation of amounts to determine the grade of what is considered a single offense is a matter entirely different from joinder of two or more offenses in a single charging instrument."

State v. McFall, 961 S.W.2d 588, 589 (Tex. App.—San Antonio 1997, pet. ref'd). "Since fraud is often committed in small amounts as part of a continuing course of conduct, §32.03 permits the State to aggregate amounts involved in classifying the offense. *At 590:* Rather than an offense, §32.03 is an aggregation provision that permits the State to punish a continuing course of conduct or conduct pursuant to a common scheme."

SUBCHAPTER B. FORGERY

PEN §32.21. FORGERY

(a) For purposes of this section:

(1) "Forge" means:

(A) to alter, make, complete, execute, or authenticate any writing so that it purports:

(i) to be the act of another who did not authorize that act;

(ii) to have been executed at a time or place or in a numbered sequence other than was in fact the case; or

(iii) to be a copy of an original when no such original existed;

(B) to issue, transfer, register the transfer of, pass, publish, or otherwise utter a writing that is forged within the meaning of Paragraph (A); or

(C) to possess a writing that is forged within the meaning of Paragraph (A) with intent to utter it in a manner specified in Paragraph (B).

(2) "Writing" includes:

(A) printing or any other method of recording information;

(B) money, coins, tokens, stamps, seals, credit cards, badges, and trademarks; and

(C) symbols of value, right, privilege, or identification.

(b) A person commits an offense if he forges a writing with intent to defraud or harm another.

(c) Except as provided in Subsections (d) and (e) an offense under this section is a Class A misdemeanor.

(d) An offense under this section is a state jail felony if the writing is or purports to be a will, codicil, deed, deed of trust, mortgage, security instrument, security agreement, credit card, check, authorization to debit an account at a financial institution, or similar sight order for payment of money, contract, release, or other commercial instrument.

(e) An offense under this section is a felony of the third degree if the writing is or purports to be:

(1) part of an issue of money, securities, postage or revenue stamps;

(2) a government record listed in Section 37.01(2)(C); or

(3) other instruments issued by a state or national government or by a subdivision of either, or part of an issue of stock, bonds, or other instruments representing interests in or claims against another person.

(f) A person is presumed to intend to defraud or harm another if the person acts with respect to two or more writings of the same type and if each writing is a government record listed in Section 37.01(2)(C).

History of Pen §32.21: Acts 1973, 63rd Leg., ch. 399, §1, eff. Jan. 1, 1974. Amended by Acts 1991, 72nd Leg., ch. 113, §2, eff. Sept. 1, 1991; Acts 1993, 73rd Leg., ch. 900, §1.01, eff. Sept. 1, 1994; Acts 1997, 75th Leg., ch. 189, §1, eff. May 21, 1997; Acts 2003, 78th Leg., ch. 1104, §1, eff. Sept. 1, 2003.

ANNOTATIONS

Parker v. State, 985 S.W.2d 460, 464 (Tex.Crim. App.1999). "[A]n instrument is passed within the meaning of the forgery statute if it is delivered or circulated ... 'where a person presents a forged instrument to one individual, and allows the instrument to be given to a second individual with the intention that the second individual will accept and give value for the instrument, he has passed that instrument to the second individual.' [¶] In this case, the evidence shows that appellant first presented the forged instrument to Followill, who in turn took the check to Baker for approval. Either Followill or Baker could be named in the indictment as the individual to whom the instrument was passed."

Griffin v. State, 908 S.W.2d 624, 627 (Tex.App.—Beaumont 1995, no pet.). "The intent to defraud or harm may be established by circumstantial evidence. … If the State proves that an actor has knowledge that a particular check is forged, proof of intent to defraud is inferred. [I]f there is sufficient evidence to establish an actor's theft of the instrument ultimately forged, the evidence is deemed sufficient to show knowledge of the forgery, and therefore sufficient to show an intent to defraud or harm."

Choice v. State, 883 S.W.2d 325, 329 (Tex.App.—Tyler 1994, pet. ref'd). "The State must prove the element of intent by showing that Appellant falsely represented to others that he was the maker of the check, or that he was in possession of the stolen check without a reasonable explanation."

Edwards v. State, 835 S.W.2d 660, 664 (Tex.App.—Dallas 1992, no pet.). A "person may commit forgery by signing his own name to a check where he does so to create confusion with another depositor."

Smith v. State, 762 S.W.2d 303, 304 (Tex.App.—Houston [1st Dist.] 1988, no pet.). "[T]he term 'utter' … is sufficiently explained by the word 'pass'.…"

PEN §32.22. CRIMINAL SIMULATION

(a) A person commits an offense if, with intent to defraud or harm another:

(1) he makes or alters an object, in whole or in part, so that it appears to have value because of age, antiquity, rarity, source, or authorship that it does not have;

(2) he possesses an object so made or altered, with intent to sell, pass, or otherwise utter it; or

(3) he authenticates or certifies an object so made or altered as genuine or as different from what it is.

(b) An offense under this section is a Class A misdemeanor.

History of Pen §32.22: Acts 1973, 63rd Leg., ch. 399, §1, eff. Jan. 1, 1974. Amended by Acts 1993, 73rd Leg., ch. 900, §1.01, eff. Sept. 1, 1994.

ANNOTATIONS

Steptoe v. State, 783 S.W.2d 9, 10 (Tex.App.—Houston [14th Dist.] 1989, no pet.). "Although the criminal simulation prohibition proscribes the *sale* of

objects altered under its terms, … this does not mean its 'forbidden conduct' is acquisitive, as is the conduct which the theft statute prohibits. '[I]t is the guarantee of authenticity implicit in the act of selling that completes the offense, not the fact that something is obtained in return.'"

PEN §32.23. TRADEMARK COUNTERFEITING

(a) In this section:

(1) "Counterfeit mark" means a mark that is identical to or substantially indistinguishable from a protected mark the use or production of which is not authorized by the owner of the protected mark.

(2) "Identification mark" means a data plate, serial number, or part identification number.

(3) "Protected mark" means a trademark or service mark or an identification mark that is:

(A) registered with the secretary of state;

(B) registered on the principal register of the United States Patent and Trademark Office;

(C) registered under the laws of another state; or

(D) protected by Section 16.30, Business & Commerce Code, or by 36 U.S.C. Section 371 et seq.

(4) "Retail value" means the actor's regular selling price for a counterfeit mark or an item or service that bears or is identified by a counterfeit mark, except that if an item bearing a counterfeit mark is a component of a finished product, the retail value means the actor's regular selling price of the finished product on or in which the component is used, distributed, or sold.

(5) "Service mark" has the meaning assigned by Section 16.01, Business & Commerce Code.

(6) "Trademark" has the meaning assigned by Section 16.01, Business & Commerce Code.

(b) A person commits an offense if the person intentionally manufactures, displays, advertises, distributes, offers for sale, sells, or possesses with intent to sell or distribute a counterfeit mark or an item or service that:

(1) bears or is identified by a counterfeit mark; or

(2) the person knows or should have known bears or is identified by a counterfeit mark.

(c) A state or federal certificate of registration of intellectual property is prima facie evidence of the facts stated in the certificate.

For a quick reference of penalties, see the Chart of Penalties on p. 675.

O'CONNOR'S CRIMINAL CODES 821

(d) For the purposes of Subsection (e), when items or services are the subject of counterfeiting in violation of this section pursuant to one scheme or continuing course of conduct, the conduct may be considered as one offense and the retail value of the items or services aggregated in determining the grade of offense.

(e) An offense under this section is a:

(1) Class C misdemeanor if the retail value of the item or service is less than $20;

(2) Class B misdemeanor if the retail value of the item or service is $20 or more but less than $500;

(3) Class A misdemeanor if the retail value of the item or service is $500 or more but less than $1,500;

(4) state jail felony if the retail value of the item or service is $1,500 or more but less than $20,000;

(5) felony of the third degree if the retail value of the item or service is $20,000 or more but less than $100,000;

(6) felony of the second degree if the retail value of the item or service is $100,000 or more but less than $200,000; or

(7) felony of the first degree if the retail value of the item or service is $200,000 or more.

History of Pen §32.23: Acts 1997, 75th Leg., ch. 1161, §2, eff. Sept. 1, 1997.

PEN §32.24. STEALING OR RECEIVING STOLEN CHECK OR SIMILAR SIGHT ORDER

(a) A person commits an offense if the person steals an unsigned check or similar sight order or, with knowledge that an unsigned check or similar sight order has been stolen, receives the check or sight order with intent to use it, to sell it, or to transfer it to a person other than the person from whom the check or sight order was stolen.

(b) An offense under this section is a Class A misdemeanor.

History of Pen §32.24: Acts 1999, 76th Leg., ch. 1413, §1, eff. Sept. 1, 1999.

SUBCHAPTER C. CREDIT

PEN §32.31. CREDIT CARD OR DEBIT CARD ABUSE

(a) For purposes of this section:

(1) "Cardholder" means the person named on the face of a credit card or debit card to whom or for whose benefit the card is issued.

(2) "Credit card" means an identification card, plate, coupon, book, number, or any other device authorizing a designated person or bearer to obtain property or services on credit. The term includes the number or description of the device if the device itself is not produced at the time of ordering or obtaining the property or service.

(3) "Expired credit card" means a credit card bearing an expiration date after that date has passed.

(4) "Debit card" means an identification card, plate, coupon, book, number, or any other device authorizing a designated person or bearer to communicate a request to an unmanned teller machine or a customer convenience terminal or obtain property or services by debit to an account at a financial institution. The term includes the number or description of the device if the device itself is not produced at the time of ordering or obtaining the benefit.

(5) "Expired debit card" means a debit card bearing as its expiration date a date that has passed.

(6) "Unmanned teller machine" means a machine, other than a telephone, capable of being operated by a customer, by which a customer may communicate to a financial institution a request to withdraw a benefit for himself or for another directly from the customer's account or from the customer's account under a line of credit previously authorized by the institution for the customer.

(7) "Customer convenience terminal" means an unmanned teller machine the use of which does not involve personnel of a financial institution.

(b) A person commits an offense if:

(1) with intent to obtain a benefit fraudulently, he presents or uses a credit card or debit card with knowledge that:

(A) the card, whether or not expired, has not been issued to him and is not used with the effective consent of the cardholder; or

(B) the card has expired or has been revoked or cancelled;

(2) with intent to obtain a benefit, he uses a fictitious credit card or debit card or the pretended number or description of a fictitious card;

(3) he receives a benefit that he knows has been obtained in violation of this section;

(4) he steals a credit card or debit card or, with knowledge that it has been stolen, receives a credit

PEN §32.23

card or debit card with intent to use it, to sell it, or to transfer it to a person other than the issuer or the cardholder;

(5) he buys a credit card or debit card from a person who he knows is not the issuer;

(6) not being the issuer, he sells a credit card or debit card;

(7) he uses or induces the cardholder to use the cardholder's credit card or debit card to obtain property or service for the actor's benefit for which the cardholder is financially unable to pay;

(8) not being the cardholder, and without the effective consent of the cardholder, he possesses a credit card or debit card with intent to use it;

(9) he possesses two or more incomplete credit cards or debit cards that have not been issued to him with intent to complete them without the effective consent of the issuer. For purposes of this subdivision, a card is incomplete if part of the matter that an issuer requires to appear on the card before it can be used, other than the signature of the cardholder, has not yet been stamped, embossed, imprinted, or written on it;

(10) being authorized by an issuer to furnish goods or services on presentation of a credit card or debit card, he, with intent to defraud the issuer or the cardholder, furnishes goods or services on presentation of a credit card or debit card obtained or retained in violation of this section or a credit card or debit card that is forged, expired, or revoked; or

(11) being authorized by an issuer to furnish goods or services on presentation of a credit card or debit card, he, with intent to defraud the issuer or a cardholder, fails to furnish goods or services that he represents in writing to the issuer that he has furnished.

(c) It is presumed that a person who used a revoked, cancelled, or expired credit card or debit card had knowledge that the card had been revoked, cancelled, or expired if he had received notice of revocation, cancellation, or expiration from the issuer. For purposes of this section, notice may be either notice given orally in person or by telephone, or in writing by mail or by telegram. If written notice was sent by registered or certified mail with return receipt requested, or by telegram with report of delivery requested, addressed to the cardholder at the last address shown by the records of the issuer, it is presumed that the notice was received by the cardholder no later than five days after sent.

(d) An offense under this section is a state jail felony.

History of Pen §32.31: Acts 1973, 63rd Leg., ch. 399, §1, eff. Jan. 1, 1974. Amended by Acts 1993, 73rd Leg., ch. 900, §1.01, eff. Sept. 1, 1994; Acts 2003, 78th Leg., ch. 1104, §§2, 3, eff. Sept. 1, 2003; Acts 2005, 79th Leg., ch. 1054, §1, eff. Sept. 1, 2005.

ANNOTATIONS

Olurebi v. State, 870 S.W.2d 58, 61 (Tex.Crim.App. 1994). "[A] 'fictitious credit card' ... is either a credit card not issued by the purported owner or a credit card with an actual owner but issued to a nonexistent cardholder."

Hayden v. State, 818 S.W.2d 194, 198 (Tex.App.—Corpus Christi 1991, no pet.). "[O]wnership is not an element of the crime of credit card abuse. [T]he State must allege lack of consent of the *cardholder* whose name appears on the face of the card."

Rabb v. State, 681 S.W.2d 152, 155 (Tex.App.—Houston [14th Dist.] 1984, pet. ref'd). "[A]n attempt to obtain merchandise with a stolen credit card, and by inference, with no intention of ever paying the charge, can constitute theft as well as credit card abuse."

PEN §32.32. FALSE STATEMENT TO OBTAIN PROPERTY OR CREDIT

(a) For purposes of this section, "credit" includes:

(1) a loan of money;

(2) furnishing property or service on credit;

(3) extending the due date of an obligation;

(4) comaking, endorsing, or guaranteeing a note or other instrument for obtaining credit;

(5) a line or letter of credit;

(6) a credit card, as defined in Section 32.31 (Credit Card or Debit Card Abuse); and

E (7) a mortgage loan.

A (b) A person commits an offense if he intentionally or knowingly makes a materially false or misleading written statement to obtain property or credit, including a mortgage loan.

(c) An offense under this section is:

(1) a Class C misdemeanor if the value of the property or the amount of credit is less than $50;

For a quick reference of penalties, see the Chart of Penalties on p. 675.

O'CONNOR'S CRIMINAL CODES   823

(2) a Class B misdemeanor if the value of the property or the amount of credit is $50 or more but less than $500;

(3) a Class A misdemeanor if the value of the property or the amount of credit is $500 or more but less than $1,500;

(4) a state jail felony if the value of the property or the amount of credit is $1,500 or more but less than $20,000;

(5) a felony of the third degree if the value of the property or the amount of credit is $20,000 or more but less than $100,000;

(6) a felony of the second degree if the value of the property or the amount of credit is $100,000 or more but less than $200,000; or

(7) a felony of the first degree if the value of the property or the amount of credit is $200,000 or more.

E (d) The following agencies shall assist a prosecuting attorney of the United States or of a county or judicial district of this state, a county or state law enforcement agency of this state, or a federal law enforcement agency in the investigation of an offense under this section involving a mortgage loan:

(1) the office of the attorney general;

(2) the Department of Public Safety;

(3) the Texas Department of Insurance;

(4) the Office of Consumer Credit Commissioner;

(5) the Texas Department of Banking;

(6) the credit union department;

(7) the Department of Savings and Mortgage Lending;

(8) the Texas Real Estate Commission; and

(9) the Texas Appraiser Licensing and Certification Board.

E (e) With the consent of the appropriate local county or district attorney, the attorney general has concurrent jurisdiction with that consenting local prosecutor to prosecute an offense under this section that involves a mortgage loan.

History of Pen §32.32: Acts 1973, 63rd Leg., ch. 399, §1, eff. Jan. 1, 1974. Amended by Acts 1993, 73rd Leg., ch. 900, §1.01, eff. Sept. 1, 1994; Acts 1995, 74th Leg., ch. 76, §14.50, eff. Sept. 1, 1995; Acts 2001, 77th Leg., ch. 1245, §3, eff. Sept. 1, 2001; Acts 2007, 80th Leg., ch. 285, §5, eff. Sept. 1, 2007.

ANNOTATIONS

Cheney v. State, 755 S.W.2d 123, 129 (Tex.Crim. App.1988). "[T]he 'forbidden conduct' in §32.32 is the intentional or knowing *making* of a materially false or misleading statement to obtain property or credit. The offense is complete once the written, deceptive statement relevant to obtaining property or credit is made, even if the perpetrator is not successful in obtaining the property or credit as a result of his written deception. *At 130:* [S]ection 32.32 may under some circumstances be a lesser included offense of theft when the State fails to prove that a defendant obtained property or fails to prove the value of such property."

PEN §32.33. HINDERING SECURED CREDITORS

(a) For purposes of this section:

(1) "Remove" means transport, without the effective consent of the secured party, from the state in which the property was located when the security interest or lien attached.

(2) "Security interest" means an interest in personal property or fixtures that secures payment or performance of an obligation.

(b) A person who has signed a security agreement creating a security interest in property or a mortgage or deed of trust creating a lien on property commits an offense if, with intent to hinder enforcement of that interest or lien, he destroys, removes, conceals, encumbers, or otherwise harms or reduces the value of the property.

(c) For purposes of this section, a person is presumed to have intended to hinder enforcement of the security interest or lien if, when any part of the debt secured by the security interest or lien was due, he failed:

(1) to pay the part then due; and

(2) if the secured party had made demand, to deliver possession of the secured property to the secured party.

(d) An offense under Subsection (b) is a:

(1) Class C misdemeanor if the value of the property destroyed, removed, concealed, encumbered, or otherwise harmed or reduced in value is less than $20;

(2) Class B misdemeanor if the value of the property destroyed, removed, concealed, encumbered, or otherwise harmed or reduced in value is $20 or more but less than $500;

(3) Class A misdemeanor if the value of the property destroyed, removed, concealed, encumbered, or otherwise harmed or reduced in value is $500 or more but less than $1,500;

PEN §32.32

(4) state jail felony if the value of the property destroyed, removed, concealed, encumbered, or otherwise harmed or reduced in value is $1,500 or more but less than $20,000;

(5) felony of the third degree if the value of the property destroyed, removed, concealed, encumbered, or otherwise harmed or reduced in value is $20,000 or more but less than $100,000;

(6) felony of the second degree if the value of the property destroyed, removed, concealed, encumbered, or otherwise harmed or reduced in value is $100,000 or more but less than $200,000; or

(7) felony of the first degree if the value of the property destroyed, removed, concealed, encumbered, or otherwise harmed or reduced in value is $200,000 or more.

(e) A person who is a debtor under a security agreement, and who does not have a right to sell or dispose of the secured property or is required to account to the secured party for the proceeds of a permitted sale or disposition, commits an offense if the person sells or otherwise disposes of the secured property, or does not account to the secured party for the proceeds of a sale or other disposition as required, with intent to appropriate (as defined in Chapter 31) the proceeds or value of the secured property. A person is presumed to have intended to appropriate proceeds if the person does not deliver the proceeds to the secured party or account to the secured party for the proceeds before the 11th day after the day that the secured party makes a lawful demand for the proceeds or account. An offense under this subsection is:

(1) a Class C misdemeanor if the proceeds obtained from the sale or other disposition are money or goods having a value of less than $20;

(2) a Class B misdemeanor if the proceeds obtained from the sale or other disposition are money or goods having a value of $20 or more but less than $500;

(3) a Class A misdemeanor if the proceeds obtained from the sale or other disposition are money or goods having a value of $500 or more but less than $1,500;

(4) a state jail felony if the proceeds obtained from the sale or other disposition are money or goods having a value of $1,500 or more but less than $20,000;

(5) a felony of the third degree if the proceeds obtained from the sale or other disposition are money or goods having a value of $20,000 or more but less than $100,000;

(6) a felony of the second degree if the proceeds obtained from the sale or other disposition are money or goods having a value of $100,000 or more but less than $200,000; or

(7) a felony of the first degree if the proceeds obtained from the sale or other disposition are money or goods having a value of $200,000 or more.

History of Pen §32.33: Acts 1973, 63rd Leg., ch. 399, §1, eff. Jan. 1, 1974. Amended by Acts 1979, 66th Leg., p. 501, ch. 232, §1, eff. Sept. 1, 1979; Acts 1985, 69th Leg., ch. 914, §5, eff. Sept. 1, 1985; Acts 1993, 73rd Leg., ch. 900, §1.01, eff. Sept. 1, 1994.

ANNOTATIONS

Williams v. State, 641 S.W.2d 236, 238 (Tex.Crim. App.1982). "Nothing on the face of the statute makes a distinction between secured creditors who are owners of secured property and secured creditors who are not."

Montgomery v. State, 91 S.W.3d 426, 430 (Tex. App.—Eastland 2002, pet. ref'd). "The permissive language in §32.03 provides evidence that the legislature intended to allow the State to prosecute an individual for a separate offense of hindering a secured creditor for each item of secured property that the defendant destroys, removes, conceals, encumbers, or otherwise harms or reduces the value of in violation of §32.33(b)."

PEN §32.34. FRAUDULENT TRANSFER OF A MOTOR VEHICLE

(a) In this section:

(1) "Lease" means the grant of use and possession of a motor vehicle for consideration, whether or not the grant includes an option to buy the vehicle.

(2) "Motor vehicle" means a device in, on, or by which a person or property is or may be transported or drawn on a highway, except a device used exclusively on stationary rails or tracks.

(3) "Security interest" means an interest in personal property or fixtures that secures payment or performance of an obligation.

(4) "Third party" means a person other than the actor or the owner of the vehicle.

For a quick reference of penalties, see the Chart of Penalties on p. 675.

O'CONNOR'S CRIMINAL CODES 825

PEN §32.34

(5) "Transfer" means to transfer possession, whether or not another right is also transferred, by means of a sale, lease, sublease, lease assignment, or other property transfer.

(b) A person commits an offense if the person acquires, accepts possession of, or exercises control over the motor vehicle of another under a written or oral agreement to arrange for the transfer of the vehicle to a third party and:

(1) knowing the vehicle is subject to a security interest, lease, or lien, the person transfers the vehicle to a third party without first obtaining written authorization from the vehicle's secured creditor, lessor, or lienholder;

(2) intending to defraud or harm the vehicle's owner, the person transfers the vehicle to a third party;

(3) intending to defraud or harm the vehicle's owner, the person disposes of the vehicle in a manner other than by transfer to a third party; or

(4) the person does not disclose the location of the vehicle on the request of the vehicle's owner, secured creditor, lessor, or lienholder.

(c) For the purposes of Subsection (b)(2), the actor is presumed to have intended to defraud or harm the motor vehicle's owner if the actor does not take reasonable steps to determine whether or not the third party is financially able to pay for the vehicle.

(d) It is a defense to prosecution under Subsection (b)(1) that the entire indebtedness secured by or owed under the security interest, lease, or lien is paid or satisfied in full not later than the 30th day after the date that the transfer was made.

(e) It is not a defense to prosecution under Subsection (b)(1) that the motor vehicle's owner has violated a contract creating a security interest, lease, or lien in the motor vehicle.

(f) An offense under Subsection (b)(1), (b)(2), or (b)(3) is:

(1) a state jail felony if the value of the motor vehicle is less than $20,000; or

(2) a felony of the third degree if the value of the motor vehicle is $20,000 or more.

(g) An offense under Subsection (b)(4) is a Class A misdemeanor.

History of Pen §32.34: Acts 1989, 71st Leg., ch. 954, §1, eff. Sept. 1, 1989. Renumbered from §32.36 and amended by Acts 1993, 73rd Leg., ch. 900, §1.01, eff. Sept. 1, 1994.

PEN §32.35. CREDIT CARD TRANSACTION RECORD LAUNDERING

(a) In this section:

(1) "Agent" means a person authorized to act on behalf of another and includes an employee.

(2) "Authorized vendor" means a person authorized by a creditor to furnish property, service, or anything else of value upon presentation of a credit card by a cardholder.

(3) "Cardholder" means the person named on the face of a credit card to whom or for whose benefit the credit card is issued, and includes the named person's agents.

(4) "Credit card" means an identification card, plate, coupon, book, number, or any other device authorizing a designated person or bearer to obtain property or services on credit. It includes the number or description on the device if the device itself is not produced at the time of ordering or obtaining the property or service.

(5) "Creditor" means a person licensed under Chapter 342, Finance Code, a bank, savings and loan association, credit union, or other regulated financial institution that lends money or otherwise extends credit to a cardholder through a credit card and that authorizes other persons to honor the credit card.

(b) A person commits an offense if the person is an authorized vendor who, with intent to defraud the creditor or cardholder, presents to a creditor, for payment, a credit card transaction record of a sale that was not made by the authorized vendor or the vendor's agent.

(c) A person commits an offense if, without the creditor's authorization, the person employs, solicits, or otherwise causes an authorized vendor or the vendor's agent to present to a creditor, for payment, a credit card transaction record of a sale that was not made by the authorized vendor or the vendor's agent.

(d) It is presumed that a person is not the agent of an authorized vendor if a fee is paid or offered to be paid by the person to the authorized vendor in connection with the vendor's presentment to a creditor of a credit card transaction record.

(e) An offense under this section is a:

(1) Class C misdemeanor if the amount of the record of a sale is less than $20;

---

(2) Class B misdemeanor if the amount of the record of a sale is $20 or more but less than $500;

(3) Class A misdemeanor if the amount of the record of a sale is $500 or more but less than $1,500;

(4) state jail felony if the amount of the record of a sale is $1,500 or more but less than $20,000;

(5) felony of the third degree if the amount of the record of a sale is $20,000 or more but less than $100,000;

(6) felony of the second degree if the amount of the record of a sale is $100,000 or more but less than $200,000; or

(7) felony of the first degree if the amount of the record of a sale is $200,000 or more.

History of Pen §32.35: Acts 1991, 72nd Leg., ch. 792, §1, eff. Aug. 26, 1991. Renumbered from §32.37 and amended by Acts 1993, 73rd Leg., ch. 900, §1.01, eff. Sept. 1, 1994; Acts 1997, 75th Leg., ch. 1396, §38, eff. Sept. 1, 1997; Acts 1999, 76th Leg., ch. 62, §7.83, eff. Sept. 1, 1999.

SUBCHAPTER D. OTHER DECEPTIVE PRACTICES

PEN §32.41. ISSUANCE OF BAD CHECK

(a) A person commits an offense if he issues or passes a check or similar sight order for the payment of money knowing that the issuer does not have sufficient funds in or on deposit with the bank or other drawee for the payment in full of the check or order as well as all other checks or orders outstanding at the time of issuance.

(b) This section does not prevent the prosecution from establishing the required knowledge by direct evidence; however, for purposes of this section, the issuer's knowledge of insufficient funds is presumed (except in the case of a postdated check or order) if:

(1) he had no account with the bank or other drawee at the time he issued the check or order; or

(2) payment was refused by the bank or other drawee for lack of funds or insufficient funds on presentation within 30 days after issue and the issuer failed to pay the holder in full within 10 days after receiving notice of that refusal.

(c) Notice for purposes of Subsection (b)(2) may be actual notice or notice in writing that:

 Subsection (1) below is effective for offenses committed on or after Sept. 1, 2007.

(1) is sent by:

(A) first class mail, evidenced by an affidavit of service; or

(B) registered or certified mail with return receipt requested;

Subsection (1) below is effective for offenses in which any element of the offense was committed before Sept. 1, 2007.

(1) is sent by registered or certified mail with return receipt requested, by telegram with report of delivery requested, or by first class mail if the letter was returned unopened with markings indicating that the address is incorrect and that there is no current forwarding order;

(2) is addressed to the issuer at the issuer's address shown on:

(A) the check or order;

(B) the records of the bank or other drawee; or

(C) the records of the person to whom the check or order has been issued or passed; and

(3) contains the following statement:

"This is a demand for payment in full for a check or order not paid because of a lack of funds or insufficient funds. If you fail to make payment in full within 10 days after the date of receipt of this notice, the failure to pay creates a presumption for committing an offense, and this matter may be referred for criminal prosecution."

(d) If notice is given in accordance with Subsection (c), it is presumed that the notice was received no later than five days after it was sent.

(e) A person charged with an offense under this section may make restitution for the bad checks. Restitution shall be made through the prosecutor's office if collection and processing were initiated through that office. In other cases restitution may be, with the approval of the court in which the offense is filed:

(1) made through the court; or

Subsection (2) below is effective for warrants executed by a peace officer on or after Sept. 1, 2007.

(2) collected by a law enforcement agency if a peace officer of that agency executes a warrant against the person charged with the offense.

(f) Except as otherwise provided by this subsection, an offense under this section is a Class C misdemeanor. If the check or similar sight order that was issued or passed was for a child support payment the

For a quick reference of penalties, see the Chart of Penalties on p. 675.

O'CONNOR'S CRIMINAL CODES   827

obligation for which is established under a court order, the offense is a Class B misdemeanor.

(g) An offense under this section is not a lesser included offense of an offense under Section 31.03 or 31.04.

History of Pen §32.41: Acts 1973, 63rd Leg., ch. 399, §1, eff. Jan. 1, 1974. Amended by Acts 1983, 68th Leg., p. 5050, ch. 911, §1, eff. Aug. 29, 1983; Acts 1987, 70th Leg., ch. 687, §2, eff. June 18, 1987; Acts 1989, 71st Leg., ch. 1038, §1, eff. June 16, 1989; Acts 1993, 73rd Leg., ch. 900, §1.01, eff. Sept. 1, 1994; Acts 1995, 74th Leg., ch. 753, §2, eff. Sept. 1, 1995; Acts 1997, 75th Leg., ch. 702, §14, eff. Sept. 1, 1997; Acts 2007, 80th Leg., ch. 976, §2 (eff. Sept. 1, 2007), ch. 1393, §1 (eff. Sept. 1, 2007).

ANNOTATIONS

Esquivel v. Watson, 823 S.W.2d 589, 590 (Tex. 1992). "The term 'issuance' as used in the context of Penal Code §32.41 ... requires *delivery* of a check with the knowledge that there are insufficient funds to cover it." (Civil case.)

PEN §32.42. DECEPTIVE BUSINESS PRACTICES

(a) For purposes of this section:

(1) "Adulterated" means varying from the standard of composition or quality prescribed by law or set by established commercial usage.

(2) "Business" includes trade and commerce and advertising, selling, and buying service or property.

(3) "Commodity" means any tangible or intangible personal property.

(4) "Contest" includes sweepstake, puzzle, and game of chance.

(5) "Deceptive sales contest" means a sales contest:

(A) that misrepresents the participant's chance of winning a prize;

(B) that fails to disclose to participants on a conspicuously displayed permanent poster (if the contest is conducted by or through a retail outlet) or on each card game piece, entry blank, or other paraphernalia required for participation in the contest (if the contest is not conducted by or through a retail outlet):

(i) the geographical area or number of outlets in which the contest is to be conducted;

(ii) an accurate description of each type of prize;

(iii) the minimum number and minimum amount of cash prizes; and

(iv) the minimum number of each other type of prize; or

(C) that is manipulated or rigged so that prizes are given to predetermined persons or retail establishments. A sales contest is not deceptive if the total value of prizes to each retail outlet is in a uniform ratio to the number of game pieces distributed to that outlet.

(6) "Mislabeled" means varying from the standard of truth or disclosure in labeling prescribed by law or set by established commercial usage.

(7) "Prize" includes gift, discount, coupon, certificate, gratuity, and any other thing of value awarded in a sales contest.

(8) "Sales contest" means a contest in connection with the sale of a commodity or service by which a person may, as determined by drawing, guessing, matching, or chance, receive a prize and which is not regulated by the rules of a federal regulatory agency.

(9) "Sell" and "sale" include offer for sale, advertise for sale, expose for sale, keep for the purpose of sale, deliver for or after sale, solicit and offer to buy, and every disposition for value.

(b) A person commits an offense if in the course of business he intentionally, knowingly, recklessly, or with criminal negligence commits one or more of the following deceptive business practices:

(1) using, selling, or possessing for use or sale a false weight or measure, or any other device for falsely determining or recording any quality or quantity;

(2) selling less than the represented quantity of a property or service;

(3) taking more than the represented quantity of property or service when as a buyer the actor furnishes the weight or measure;

(4) selling an adulterated or mislabeled commodity;

(5) passing off property or service as that of another;

(6) representing that a commodity is original or new if it is deteriorated, altered, rebuilt, reconditioned, reclaimed, used, or secondhand;

(7) representing that a commodity or service is of a particular style, grade, or model if it is of another;

(8) advertising property or service with intent:

(A) not to sell it as advertised, or

(B) not to supply reasonably expectable public demand, unless the advertising adequately discloses a time or quantity limit;

PEN §32.41

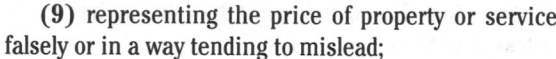

(9) representing the price of property or service falsely or in a way tending to mislead;

(10) making a materially false or misleading statement of fact concerning the reason for, existence of, or amount of a price or price reduction;

(11) conducting a deceptive sales contest; or

(12) making a materially false or misleading statement:

(A) in an advertisement for the purchase or sale of property or service; or

(B) otherwise in connection with the purchase or sale of property or service.

(c) An offense under Subsections (b)(1), (b)(2), (b)(3), (b)(4), (b)(5), and (b)(6) is:

(1) a Class C misdemeanor if the actor commits an offense with criminal negligence and if he has not previously been convicted of a deceptive business practice; or

(2) a Class A misdemeanor if the actor commits an offense intentionally, knowingly, recklessly or if he has been previously convicted of a Class B or C misdemeanor under this section.

(d) An offense under Subsections (b)(7), (b)(8), (b)(9), (b)(10), (b)(11), and (b)(12) is a Class A misdemeanor.

History of Pen §32.42: Acts 1973, 63rd Leg., ch. 399, §1, eff. Jan. 1, 1974. Amended by Acts 1975, 64th Leg., ch. 508, §§1, 2, eff. Sept. 1, 1975; Acts 1993, 73rd Leg., ch. 900, §1.01, eff. Sept. 1, 1994.

Guerra v. Datapoint Corp., 956 S.W.2d 653, 658 (Tex.App.—San Antonio 1997, no pet.). "[T]he culpable mental state must attach to the materially false or misleading statement at the time of the purchase or sale of the property or service."

PEN §32.43. COMMERCIAL BRIBERY

(a) For purposes of this section:

(1) "Beneficiary" means a person for whom a fiduciary is acting.

(2) "Fiduciary" means:

(A) an agent or employee;

(B) a trustee, guardian, custodian, administrator, executor, conservator, receiver, or similar fiduciary;

(C) a lawyer, physician, accountant, appraiser, or other professional advisor; or

(D) an officer, director, partner, manager, or other participant in the direction of the affairs of a corporation or association.

(b) A person who is a fiduciary commits an offense if, without the consent of his beneficiary, he intentionally or knowingly solicits, accepts, or agrees to accept any benefit from another person on agreement or understanding that the benefit will influence the conduct of the fiduciary in relation to the affairs of his beneficiary.

(c) A person commits an offense if he offers, confers, or agrees to confer any benefit the acceptance of which is an offense under Subsection (b).

(d) An offense under this section is a state jail felony.

(e) In lieu of a fine that is authorized by Subsection (d), and in addition to the imprisonment that is authorized by that subsection, if the court finds that an individual who is a fiduciary gained a benefit through the commission of an offense under Subsection (b), the court may sentence the individual to pay a fine in an amount fixed by the court, not to exceed double the value of the benefit gained. This subsection does not affect the application of Section 12.51(c) to an offense under this section committed by a corporation or association.

History of Pen §32.43: Acts 1973, 63rd Leg., ch. 399, §1, eff. Jan. 1, 1974. Amended by Acts 1983, 68th Leg., ch. 357, §1, eff. Sept. 1, 1983; Acts 1993, 73rd Leg., ch. 900, §1.01, eff. Sept. 1, 1994.

McGowan v. State, 938 S.W.2d 732, 735 (Tex. App.—Houston [14th Dist.] 1996), *aff'd sub nom.* ***Weightman v. State***, 975 S.W.2d 621 (Tex.Crim. App.1998). "[C]ommercial bribery is a conduct oriented offense, as opposed to a result oriented offense. In other words, the crime is defined to cover the conscious act of the wrongdoer, rather than the consequences of the act."

Ex parte Mattox, 683 S.W.2d 93, 97 (Tex.App.— Austin 1984), *pet. ref'd*, 685 S.W.2d 53 (Tex.Crim. App.1985). "[O]ne can offer a benefit in consideration for a breach of a fiduciary duty only if one knows the offeree is a fiduciary, and that he would violate a duty owed to his beneficiary or otherwise cause harm to his beneficiary by accepting the offered benefit. [T]he State must prove such knowledge in a prosecution pursuant to §32.43(c)."

For a quick reference of penalties, see the Chart of Penalties on p. 675.

O'CONNOR'S CRIMINAL CODES 829

PEN §32.43

PEN §32.44. RIGGING PUBLICLY EXHIBITED CONTEST

(a) A person commits an offense if, with intent to affect the outcome (including the score) of a publicly exhibited contest:

(1) he offers, confers, or agrees to confer any benefit on, or threatens harm to:

(A) a participant in the contest to induce him not to use his best efforts; or

(B) an official or other person associated with the contest; or

(2) he tampers with a person, animal, or thing in a manner contrary to the rules of the contest.

(b) A person commits an offense if he intentionally or knowingly solicits, accepts, or agrees to accept any benefit the conferring of which is an offense under Subsection (a).

(c) An offense under this section is a Class A misdemeanor.

History of Pen §32.44: Acts 1973, 63rd Leg., ch. 399, §1, eff. Jan. 1, 1974. Amended by Acts 1993, 73rd Leg., ch. 900, §1.01, eff. Sept. 1, 1994.

PEN §32.441. ILLEGAL RECRUITMENT OF AN ATHLETE

(a) A person commits an offense if, without the consent of the governing body or a designee of the governing body of an institution of higher education, the person intentionally or knowingly solicits, accepts, or agrees to accept any benefit from another on an agreement or understanding that the benefit will influence the conduct of the person in enrolling in the institution and participating in intercollegiate athletics.

(b) A person commits an offense if he offers, confers, or agrees to confer any benefit the acceptance of which is an offense under Subsection (a).

(c) It is an exception to prosecution under this section that the person offering, conferring, or agreeing to confer a benefit and the person soliciting, accepting, or agreeing to accept a benefit are related within the second degree of consanguinity or affinity, as determined under Chapter 573, Government Code.

(d) It is an exception to prosecution under Subsection (a) that, not later than the 60th day after the date the person accepted or agreed to accept a benefit, the person contacted a law enforcement agency and furnished testimony or evidence about the offense.

(e) An offense under this section is a:

(1) Class C misdemeanor if the value of the benefit is less than $20;

(2) Class B misdemeanor if the value of the benefit is $20 or more but less than $500;

(3) Class A misdemeanor if the value of the benefit is $500 or more but less than $1,500;

(4) state jail felony if the value of the benefit is $1,500 or more but less than $20,000;

(5) felony of the third degree if the value of the benefit is $20,000 or more but less than $100,000;

(6) felony of the second degree if the value of the benefit is $100,000 or more but less than $200,000; or

(7) felony of the first degree if the value of the benefit is $200,000 or more.

History of Pen §32.441: Acts 1989, 71st Leg., ch. 125, §1, eff. Sept. 1, 1989. Amended by Acts 1991, 72nd Leg., ch. 561, §41, eff. Aug. 26, 1991; Acts 1993, 73rd Leg., ch. 900, §1.01, eff. Sept. 1, 1994; Acts 1995, 74th Leg., ch. 76, §5.95(27), eff. Sept. 1, 1995.

PEN §32.45. MISAPPLICATION OF FIDUCIARY PROPERTY OR PROPERTY OF FINANCIAL INSTITUTION

(a) For purposes of this section:

(1) "Fiduciary" includes:

(A) a trustee, guardian, administrator, executor, conservator, and receiver;

(B) an attorney in fact or agent appointed under a durable power of attorney as provided by Chapter XII, Texas Probate Code;

(C) any other person acting in a fiduciary capacity, but not a commercial bailee unless the commercial bailee is a party in a motor fuel sales agreement with a distributor or supplier, as those terms are defined by Section 153.001, Tax Code; and

(D) an officer, manager, employee, or agent carrying on fiduciary functions on behalf of a fiduciary.

(2) "Misapply" means deal with property contrary to:

(A) an agreement under which the fiduciary holds the property; or

(B) a law prescribing the custody or disposition of the property.

(b) A person commits an offense if he intentionally, knowingly, or recklessly misapplies property he holds as a fiduciary or property of a financial institution in a manner that involves substantial risk of loss to the owner of the property or to a person for whose benefit the property is held.

PEN §32.44

(c) An offense under this section is:

(1) a Class C misdemeanor if the value of the property misapplied is less than $20;

(2) a Class B misdemeanor if the value of the property misapplied is $20 or more but less than $500;

(3) a Class A misdemeanor if the value of the property misapplied is $500 or more but less than $1,500;

(4) a state jail felony if the value of the property misapplied is $1,500 or more but less than $20,000;

(5) a felony of the third degree if the value of the property misapplied is $20,000 or more but less than $100,000;

(6) a felony of the second degree if the value of the property misapplied is $100,000 or more but less than $200,000; or

(7) a felony of the first degree if the value of the property misapplied is $200,000 or more.

(d) An offense described for purposes of punishment by Subsections (c)(1)-(6) is increased to the next higher category of offense if it is shown on the trial of the offense that the offense was committed against an elderly individual as defined by Section 22.04.

(e) With the consent of the appropriate local county or district attorney, the attorney general has concurrent jurisdiction with that consenting local prosecutor to prosecute an offense under this section that involves the state Medicaid program.

History of Pen §32.45: Acts 1973, 63rd Leg., ch. 399, §1, eff. Jan. 1, 1974. Amended by Acts 1991, 72nd Leg., ch. 565, §2, eff. Sept. 1, 1991; Acts 1993, 73rd Leg., ch. 900, §1.01, eff. Sept. 1, 1994; Acts 1997, 75th Leg., ch. 1036, §14, eff. Sept. 1, 1997; Acts 2001, 77th Leg., ch. 1047, §1, eff. Sept. 1, 2001; Acts 2003, 78th Leg., ch. 198, §2.137 (eff. Sept. 1, 2003), ch. 257, §14 (eff. Sept. 1, 2003), ch. 432, §3 (eff. Sept. 1, 2003); Acts 2005, 79th Leg., ch. 728, §23.001(77), eff. Sept. 1, 2005.

ANNOTATIONS

State v. Moff, 154 S.W.3d 599, 603 (Tex.Crim.App. 2004). "The indictment in the case before us alleges that the illegal purchases occurred 'on or about and between January 1, 1993 and December 31, 1999.' [I]n his capacity as Chief Appraiser of the Nueces County Appraisal District, Moff used money and credit cards to make numerous purchases of equipment and supplies during the time period alleged in the indictment. Although the indictment correctly tracks the language of the statute, in this type of case, that alone is not sufficient to fulfill the constitutional and statutory requirements of specificity. It is unreasonable to require the defendant to gather evidence and prepare a defense for each of the credit card and cash transactions he made during the seven-year time frame in the indictment. Thus, additional information that is reasonably necessary for the defense to prepare its case must be provided."

Bynum v. State, 767 S.W.2d 769, 775 (Tex.Crim. App.1989). "An individual charged with the responsibilities of a fiduciary with regards to specific property may not misapply the property. The property may be deemed misapplied only if it is handled in a manner giving rise to a substantial risk of loss and in contravention of an established duty to do otherwise."

Coplin v. State, 585 S.W.2d 734, 735 (Tex.Crim.App. 1979). "We hold that 'any other person acting in a fiduciary capacity' embraces any fiduciary, including a joint adventurer or partner, not enumerated in §32.45(a)(1)(A)."

Talamantez v. State, 790 S.W.2d 33, 37 (Tex. App.—San Antonio 1990, pet. ref'd). "'It is not an element of the offense that the actor or anyone else receive a benefit from the misapplication. If he does receive a benefit, there may also be a violation of [Pen. Code ch.] 31 (theft).'"

Little v. State, 699 S.W.2d 316, 318 (Tex.App.—San Antonio 1985, no pet.). Section 32.45 "requires the State to identify the parties to an agreement, the property pledged, the duty owed, and the breach of that duty. [¶] Misapplication ... can be an omission, or failure to act where a duty to act exists. [¶] If an agreement requires a person to hold funds in trust and to promptly pay the funds to the beneficiary, failure to pay the funds to the beneficiary is a breach of the agreement and when added to the other elements, constitutes an offense. The actual disposition of the money is immaterial—whether he kept it or donated it to charity. [T]he State is not required ... to prove how the fiduciary applied the funds, if the State has proved that the fiduciary failed to apply the funds according to the terms of the agreement."

PEN §32.46. SECURING EXECUTION OF DOCUMENT BY DECEPTION

(a) A person commits an offense if, with intent to defraud or harm any person, he, by deception:

(1) causes another to sign or execute any document affecting property or service or the pecuniary interest of any person; or

For a quick reference of penalties, see the Chart of Penalties on p. 675.

O'CONNOR'S CRIMINAL CODES 831

(2) causes or induces a public servant to file or record any purported judgment or other document purporting to memorialize or evidence an act, an order, a directive, or process of:

(A) a purported court that is not expressly created or established under the constitution or the laws of this state or of the United States;

(B) a purported judicial entity that is not expressly created or established under the constitution or laws of this state or of the United States; or

(C) a purported judicial officer of a purported court or purported judicial entity described by Paragraph (A) or (B).

(b) An offense under Subsection (a)(1) is a:

(1) Class C misdemeanor if the value of the property, service, or pecuniary interest is less than $20;

(2) Class B misdemeanor if the value of the property, service, or pecuniary interest is $20 or more but less than $500;

(3) Class A misdemeanor if the value of the property, service, or pecuniary interest is $500 or more but less than $1,500;

(4) state jail felony if the value of the property, service, or pecuniary interest is $1,500 or more but less than $20,000;

(5) felony of the third degree if the value of the property, service, or pecuniary interest is $20,000 or more but less than $100,000;

(6) felony of the second degree if the value of the property, service, or pecuniary interest is $100,000 or more but less than $200,000; or

(7) felony of the first degree if the value of the property, service, or pecuniary interest is $200,000 or more.

(c) An offense under Subsection (a)(2) is a state jail felony.

 Subsection (c-1) below is effective for offenses committed on or after Sept. 1, 2007.

(c-1) An offense described for purposes of punishment by Subsections (b)(1)-(6) and (c) is increased to the next higher category of offense if it is shown on the trial of the offense that the offense was committed against an elderly individual as defined by Section 22.04 or involves the state Medicaid program.

Subsection (c-1) below is effective for offenses in which any element of the offense was committed before Sept. 1, 2007.

(c-1) An offense described for purposes of punishment by Subsections (b)(1)-(6) and (c) is increased to the next higher category of offense if it is shown on the trial of the offense that the offense was committed against an elderly individual as defined by Section 22.04.

(d) In this section, "deception" has the meaning assigned by Section 31.01.

(e) With the consent of the appropriate local county or district attorney, the attorney general has concurrent jurisdiction with that consenting local prosecutor to prosecute an offense under this section that involves the state Medicaid program.

History of Pen §32.46: Acts 1973, 63rd Leg., ch. 399, §1, eff. Jan. 1, 1974. Amended by Acts 1993, 73rd Leg., ch. 900, §1.01, eff. Sept. 1, 1994; Acts 1997, 75th Leg., ch. 189, §2, eff. May 21, 1997; Acts 2003, 78th Leg., ch. 432, §4 (eff. Sept. 1, 2003), ch. 257, §15 (eff. Sept. 1, 2003), ch. 198, §2.138 (eff. Sept. 1, 2003); Acts 2007, 80th Leg., ch. 127, §4, eff. Sept. 1, 2007.

ANNOTATIONS

Mills v. State, 722 S.W.2d 411, 416 (Tex.Crim.App. 1986). Section 32.46 "was intended to proscribe conduct that is deceptive, not acquisitive."

Goldstein v. State, 803 S.W.2d 777, 789 (Tex. App.—Dallas 1991, pet. ref'd). Section 32.46 "has the purpose of discouraging loss that might result to a party signing a document brought on by deception. [T]he victim to be protected is the party with whom the accused deals directly, *i.e.*, the person deceived."

PEN §32.47. FRAUDULENT DESTRUCTION, REMOVAL, OR CONCEALMENT OF WRITING

(a) A person commits an offense if, with intent to defraud or harm another, he destroys, removes, conceals, alters, substitutes, or otherwise impairs the verity, legibility, or availability of a writing, other than a governmental record.

(b) For purposes of this section, "writing" includes:

(1) printing or any other method of recording information;

(2) money, coins, tokens, stamps, seals, credit cards, badges, trademarks;

(3) symbols of value, right, privilege, or identification; and

(4) universal product codes, labels, price tags, or markings on goods.

(c) Except as provided in Subsection (d), an offense under this section is a Class A misdemeanor.

(d) An offense under this section is a state jail felony if the writing:

(1) is a will or codicil of another, whether or not the maker is alive or dead and whether or not it has been admitted to probate; or

(2) is a deed, mortgage, deed of trust, security instrument, security agreement, or other writing for which the law provides public recording or filing, whether or not the writing has been acknowledged.

History of Pen §32.47: Acts 1973, 63rd Leg., ch. 399, §1, eff. Jan. 1, 1974. Amended by Acts 1993, 73rd Leg., ch. 900, §1.01, eff. Sept. 1, 1994; Acts 2001, 77th Leg., ch. 21, §1, eff. Sept. 1, 2001.

PEN §32.48. SIMULATING LEGAL PROCESS

(a) A person commits an offense if the person recklessly causes to be delivered to another any document that simulates a summons, complaint, judgment, or other court process with the intent to:

(1) induce payment of a claim from another person; or

(2) cause another to:

(A) submit to the putative authority of the document; or

(B) take any action or refrain from taking any action in response to the document, in compliance with the document, or on the basis of the document.

(b) Proof that the document was mailed to any person with the intent that it be forwarded to the intended recipient is a sufficient showing that the document was delivered.

(c) It is not a defense to prosecution under this section that the simulating document:

(1) states that it is not legal process; or

(2) purports to have been issued or authorized by a person or entity who did not have lawful authority to issue or authorize the document.

(d) If it is shown on the trial of an offense under this section that the simulating document was filed with, presented to, or delivered to a clerk of a court or an employee of a clerk of a court created or established under the constitution or laws of this state, there is a rebuttable presumption that the document was delivered with the intent described by Subsection (a).

(e) Except as provided by Subsection (f), an offense under this section is a Class A misdemeanor.

(f) If it is shown on the trial of an offense under this section that the defendant has previously been convicted of a violation of this section, the offense is a state jail felony.

History of Pen §32.48: Acts 1997, 75th Leg., ch. 189, §3, eff. May 21, 1997.
History of Former Pen §32.48: Repealed by Acts 1995, 74th Leg., ch. 463, §3, eff. Sept. 1, 1995.

ANNOTATIONS

Saldana v. State, 109 S.W.3d 4, 9 (Tex.App.—El Paso 2002, no pet.). "The phrase 'or other court process' in the statute leads us to the conclusion that the statute contemplates that the '… summons, complaint, judgment' is necessarily couched in terms of a judicial process. *At 10:* [W]e do not perceive that the 'Notice to Appear' constitutes an abuse of the statute. This phrase references the fact that the citation itself is a notice to appear and does not call upon the recipient of the papers to appear."

PEN §32.49. REFUSAL TO EXECUTE RELEASE OF FRAUDULENT LIEN OR CLAIM

(a) A person commits an offense if, with intent to defraud or harm another, the person:

(1) owns, holds, or is the beneficiary of a purported lien or claim asserted against real or personal property or an interest in real or personal property that is fraudulent, as described by Section 51.901(c), Government Code; and

(2) not later than the 21st day after the date of receipt of actual or written notice sent by either certified or registered mail, return receipt requested, to the person's last known address, or by telephonic document transfer to the recipient's current telecopier number, requesting the execution of a release of the fraudulent lien or claim, refuses to execute the release on the request of:

(A) the obligor or debtor; or

(B) any person who owns any interest in the real or personal property described in the document or instrument that is the basis for the lien or claim.

(b) A person who fails to execute a release of the purported lien or claim within the period prescribed by Subsection (a)(2) is presumed to have had the intent to harm or defraud another.

For a quick reference of penalties, see the Chart of Penalties on p. 675.

O'CONNOR'S CRIMINAL CODES 833

PEN §32.49

(c) An offense under this section is a Class A misdemeanor.

History of Pen §32.49: Acts 1997, 75th Leg., ch. 189, §4, eff. May 21, 1997.

History of Former Pen §32.49: Deleted by Acts 1993, 73rd Leg., ch. 900, §1.01 eff. Sept. 1, 1994.

PEN §32.50. DECEPTIVE PREPARATION & MARKETING OF ACADEMIC PRODUCT

(a) For purposes of this section:

(1) "Academic product" means a term paper, thesis, dissertation, essay, report, recording, work of art, or other written, recorded, pictorial, or artistic product or material submitted or intended to be submitted by a person to satisfy an academic requirement of the person.

(2) "Academic requirement" means a requirement or prerequisite to receive course credit or to complete a course of study or degree, diploma, or certificate program at an institution of higher education.

(3) "Institution of higher education" means an institution of higher education or private or independent institution of higher education as those terms are defined by Section 61.003, Education Code, or a private postsecondary educational institution as that term is defined by Section 61.302, Education Code.

(b) A person commits an offense if, with intent to make a profit, the person prepares, sells, offers or advertises for sale, or delivers to another person an academic product when the person knows, or should reasonably have known, that a person intends to submit or use the academic product to satisfy an academic requirement of a person other than the person who prepared the product.

(c) A person commits an offense if, with intent to induce another person to enter into an agreement or obligation to obtain or have prepared an academic product, the person knowingly makes or disseminates a written or oral statement that the person will prepare or cause to be prepared an academic product to be sold for use in satisfying an academic requirement of a person other than the person who prepared the product.

(d) It is a defense to prosecution under this section that the actor's conduct consisted solely of action taken as an employee of an institution of higher education in providing instruction, counseling, or tutoring in research or writing to students of the institution.

(e) It is a defense to prosecution under this section that the actor's conduct consisted solely of offering or providing tutorial or editing assistance to another person in connection with the other person's preparation of an academic product to satisfy the other person's academic requirement, and the actor does not offer or provide substantial preparation, writing, or research in the production of the academic product.

(f) It is a defense to prosecution under this section that the actor's conduct consisted solely of typing, transcribing, or reproducing a manuscript for a fee, or of offering to do so.

(g) An offense under this section is a Class C misdemeanor.

History of Pen §32.50: Acts 1997, 75th Leg., ch. 730, §1, eff. Sept. 1, 1997. Renumbered from §32.49 by Acts 1999, 76th Leg., ch. 62, §19.01(88), eff. Sept. 1, 1999.

History of Former Pen §32.50: Deleted by Acts 1993, 73rd Leg., ch. 900, §1.01, eff. Sept. 1, 1994.

PEN §32.51. FRAUDULENT USE OR POSSESSION OF IDENTIFYING INFORMATION

(a) In this section:

Subsection (1) below is effective for offenses committed on or after Sept. 1, 2007.

(1) "Identifying information" means information that alone or in conjunction with other information identifies a person, including a person's:

(A) name and social security number, date of birth, or government-issued identification number;

(B) unique biometric data, including the person's fingerprint, voice print, or retina or iris image;

(C) unique electronic identification number, address, routing code, or financial institution account number; and

(D) telecommunication identifying information or access device.

Subsection (1) below is effective for offenses in which any element of the offense was committed before Sept. 1, 2007.

(1) "Identifying information" means information that alone or in conjunction with other information identifies an individual, including an individual's:

(A) name, social security number, date of birth, or government-issued identification number;

(B) unique biometric data, including the individual's fingerprint, voice print, and retina or iris image;

(C) unique electronic identification number, address, and routing code, financial institution account number; and

PEN §32.49

(D) telecommunication identifying information or access device.

(2) "Telecommunication access device" means a card, plate, code, account number, personal identification number, electronic serial number, mobile identification number, or other telecommunications service, equipment, or instrument identifier or means of account access that alone or in conjunction with another telecommunication access device may be used to:

(A) obtain money, goods, services, or other thing of value; or

(B) initiate a transfer of funds other than a transfer originated solely by paper instrument.

Subsection (b) below was amended by Acts 2007, 80th Leg., ch. 631, §1, enacted May 22, 2007, effective Sept. 1, 2007, without reference to the conflicting amendment made by Acts 2007, 80th Leg., ch. 1173, §2, enacted May 25, 2007, effective Sept. 1, 2007, and the conflicting amendment made by Acts 2007, 80th Leg., ch. 1163, §1, enacted May 26, 2007, effective Sept. 1, 2007. For resolving conflicts, see p. V. Subsection (b) below is effective for offenses committed on or after Sept. 1, 2007.

(b) A person commits an offense if the person, with intent to harm or defraud another, obtains, possesses, transfers, or uses identifying information of:

(1) another person without the other person's consent; or

(2) a child younger than 18 years of age.

Subsection (b) below was amended by Acts 2007, 80th Leg., ch. 1173, §2, enacted May 25, 2007, effective Sept. 1, 2007, without reference to the conflicting amendment made by Acts 2007, 80th Leg., ch. 1163, §1, enacted May 26, 2007, effective Sept. 1, 2007, and the conflicting amendment made by Acts 2007, 80th Leg., ch. 631, §1, enacted May 22, 2007, effective Sept. 1, 2007. For resolving conflicts, see p. V. Subsection (b) below is effective for offenses committed on or after Sept. 1, 2007.

(b) A person commits an offense if the person, with the intent to harm or defraud another, obtains, possesses, transfers, or uses an item of identifying information of:

(1) a deceased natural person, including a stillborn infant or fetus, without legal authorization; or

(2) another person without the other person's consent.

Subsection (b) below was amended by Acts 2007, 80th Leg., ch. 1163, §1, enacted May 26, 2007, effective Sept. 1, 2007, without reference to the conflicting amendment made by Acts 2007, 80th Leg., ch. 1173, §2, enacted May 25, 2007, effective Sept. 1, 2007, and the conflicting amendment made by Acts 2007, 80th Leg., ch. 631, §1, enacted May 22, 2007, effective Sept. 1, 2007. For resolving conflicts, see p. V. Subsection (b) below is effective for offenses committed on or after Sept. 1, 2007.

(b) A person commits an offense if the person, with the intent to harm or defraud another, obtains, possesses, transfers, or uses:

(1) identifying information of another person without the other person's consent; or

(2) without legal authorization, information concerning a deceased person that would be identifying information of that person were that person alive.

Subsection (b) below is effective for offenses in which any element of the offense was committed before Sept. 1, 2007.

(b) A person commits an offense if the person obtains, possesses, transfers, or uses identifying information of another person without the other person's consent and with intent to harm or defraud another.

Subsections (b-1) & (b-2) below are effective for offenses committed on or after Sept. 1, 2007.

(b-1) For the purposes of Subsection (b)[1], the actor is presumed to have the intent to harm or defraud another if the actor possesses:

(1) the identifying information of three or more other persons;

(2) information described by Subsection (b)(2) concerning three or more deceased persons; or

(3) information described by Subdivision (1) or (2) concerning three or more persons or deceased persons.

(b-2) The presumption established under Subsection (b-1) does not apply to a business or other commercial entity or a government agency that is engaged in a business activity or governmental function that does not violate a penal law of this state.

Subsection (c) below is effective for offenses committed on or after Sept. 1, 2007.

(c) An offense under this section is:

(1) a state jail felony if the number of items obtained, possessed, transferred, or used is less than five;

For a quick reference of penalties, see the Chart of Penalties on p. 675.

O'CONNOR'S CRIMINAL CODES 835

PEN §32.51

(2) a felony of the third degree if the number of items obtained, possessed, transferred, or used is five or more but less than 10;

(3) a felony of the second degree if the number of items obtained, possessed, transferred, or used is 10 or more but less than 50; or

(4) a felony of the first degree if the number of items obtained, possessed, transferred, or used is 50 or more.

Subsection (c) below is effective for offenses in which any element of the offense was committed before Sept. 1, 2007.

(c) An offense under this section is a state jail felony.

(d) If a court orders a defendant convicted of an offense under this section to make restitution to the victim of the offense, the court may order the defendant to reimburse the victim for lost income or other expenses, other than attorney's fees, incurred as a result of the offense.

Ⓐ *Subsection (e) below is effective for offenses committed on or after Sept. 1, 2007.*

(e) If conduct that constitutes an offense under this section also constitutes an offense under any other law, the actor may be prosecuted under this section, the other law, or both.

Subsection (e) below is effective for offenses in which any element of the offense was committed before Sept. 1, 2007.

(e) If conduct that constitutes an offense under this section also constitutes an offense under any other law, the actor may be prosecuted under this section or the other law.

   1. **Editors note:** Refers to subsection (b) as amended by Acts 2007, 80th Leg., ch. 1163, §1, eff. Sept. 1, 2007.

   History of Pen §32.51: Acts 1999, 76th Leg., ch. 1159, §1, eff. Sept. 1, 1999. Amended by Acts 2003, 78th Leg., ch. 1104, §4, eff. Sept. 1, 2003; Acts 2007, 80th Leg., ch. 631, §1 (eff. Sept. 1, 2007), ch. 1163, §1 (eff. Sept. 1, 2007), ch. 1173, §§1, 2 (eff. Sept. 1, 2007).

   History of Former Pen §32.51: Deleted by Acts 1993, 73rd Leg., ch. 900, §1.01, eff. Sept. 1, 1994.

PEN §32.52. FRAUDULENT, SUBSTANDARD, OR FICTITIOUS DEGREE

(a) In this section, "fraudulent or substandard degree" has the meaning assigned by Section 61.302, Education Code.

(b) A person commits an offense if the person:

(1) uses or claims to hold a postsecondary degree that the person knows:

(A) is a fraudulent or substandard degree;

(B) is fictitious or has otherwise not been granted to the person; or

(C) has been revoked; and

(2) uses or claims to hold that degree:

(A) in a written or oral advertisement or other promotion of a business; or

(B) with the intent to:

(i) obtain employment;

(ii) obtain a license or certificate to practice a trade, profession, or occupation;

(iii) obtain a promotion, a compensation or other benefit, or an increase in compensation or other benefit, in employment or in the practice of a trade, profession, or occupation;

(iv) obtain admission to an educational program in this state; or

(v) gain a position in government with authority over another person, regardless of whether the actor receives compensation for the position.

(c) An offense under this section is a Class B misdemeanor.

(d) If conduct that constitutes an offense under this section also constitutes an offense under any other law, the actor may be prosecuted under this section or the other law.

   History of Pen §32.52: Acts 2005, 79th Leg., ch. 1039, §8, eff. Sept. 1, 2005.

PEN §§32.53 TO 32.54. DELETED
   Deleted by Acts 1993, 73rd Leg., ch. 900, §1.01, eff. Sept. 1, 1994.

PEN §32.55. DELETED
   Deleted by Acts 1993, 73rd Leg., ch. 900, §13.02, eff. Sept. 1, 1994.

SUBCHAPTER E. SAVINGS & LOAN ASSOCIATIONS

PEN §§32.71, 32.72. DELETED
   Deleted by Acts 1993, 73rd Leg., ch. 900, §1.01, eff. Sept. 1, 1994.

CHAPTER 33. COMPUTER CRIMES

PEN §33.01. DEFINITIONS

In this chapter:

(1) "Access" means to approach, instruct, communicate with, store data in, retrieve or intercept data from, alter data or computer software in, or otherwise make use of any resource of a computer, computer network, computer program, or computer system.

(2) "Aggregate amount" means the amount of:

(A) any direct or indirect loss incurred by a victim, including the value of money, property, or service stolen or rendered unrecoverable by the offense; or

(B) any expenditure required by the victim to verify that a computer, computer network, computer program, or computer system was not altered, acquired, damaged, deleted, or disrupted by the offense.

(3) "Communications common carrier" means a person who owns or operates a telephone system in this state that includes equipment or facilities for the conveyance, transmission, or reception of communications and who receives compensation from persons who use that system.

(4) "Computer" means an electronic, magnetic, optical, electrochemical, or other high-speed data processing device that performs logical, arithmetic, or memory functions by the manipulations of electronic or magnetic impulses and includes all input, output, processing, storage, or communication facilities that are connected or related to the device.

(5) "Computer network" means the interconnection of two or more computers or computer systems by satellite, microwave, line, or other communication medium with the capability to transmit information among the computers.

(6) "Computer program" means an ordered set of data representing coded instructions or statements that when executed by a computer cause the computer to process data or perform specific functions.

(7) "Computer services" means the product of the use of a computer, the information stored in the computer, or the personnel supporting the computer, including computer time, data processing, and storage functions.

(8) "Computer system" means any combination of a computer or computer network with the documentation, computer software, or physical facilities supporting the computer or computer network.

(9) "Computer software" means a set of computer programs, procedures, and associated documentation related to the operation of a computer, computer system, or computer network.

(10) "Computer virus" means an unwanted computer program or other set of instructions inserted into a computer's memory, operating system, or program that is specifically constructed with the ability to replicate itself or to affect the other programs or files in the computer by attaching a copy of the unwanted program or other set of instructions to one or more computer programs or files.

(11) "Data" means a representation of information, knowledge, facts, concepts, or instructions that is being prepared or has been prepared in a formalized manner and is intended to be stored or processed, is being stored or processed, or has been stored or processed in a computer. Data may be embodied in any form, including but not limited to computer printouts, magnetic storage media, laser storage media, and punchcards, or may be stored internally in the memory of the computer.

(12) "Effective consent" includes consent by a person legally authorized to act for the owner. Consent is not effective if:

(A) induced by deception, as defined by Section 31.01, or induced by coercion;

(B) given by a person the actor knows is not legally authorized to act for the owner;

(C) given by a person who by reason of youth, mental disease or defect, or intoxication is known by the actor to be unable to make reasonable property dispositions;

(D) given solely to detect the commission of an offense; or

(E) used for a purpose other than that for which the consent was given.

(13) "Electric utility" has the meaning assigned by Section 31.002, Utilities Code.

(14) "Harm" includes partial or total alteration, damage, or erasure of stored data, interruption of computer services, introduction of a computer virus, or any other loss, disadvantage, or injury that might reasonably be suffered as a result of the actor's conduct.

(15) "Owner" means a person who:

(A) has title to the property, possession of the property, whether lawful or not, or a greater right to possession of the property than the actor;

For a quick reference of penalties, see the Chart of Penalties on p. 675.

O'CONNOR'S CRIMINAL CODES 837

(B) has the right to restrict access to the property; or

(C) is the licensee of data or computer software.

(16) "Property" means:

(A) tangible or intangible personal property including a computer, computer system, computer network, computer software, or data; or

(B) the use of a computer, computer system, computer network, computer software, or data.

History of Pen §33.01: Acts 1985, 69th Leg., ch. 600, §1, eff. Sept. 1, 1985. Amended by Acts 1989, 71st Leg., ch. 306, §1, eff. Sept. 1, 1989; Acts 1993, 73rd Leg., ch. 900, §1.01, eff. Sept. 1, 1994; Acts 1997, 75th Leg., ch. 306, §1, eff. Sept. 1, 1997; Acts 1999, 76th Leg., ch. 62, §18.44, eff. Sept. 1, 1999.

ANNOTATIONS

Burleson v. State, 802 S.W.2d 429, 436 (Tex.App.— Fort Worth 1991, pet. ref'd). A "crime involving computer technology [does not require] a hypertechnical indictment. ... The indictment is sufficient if it uses ordinary and concise wording so as to inform a person of common understanding what is meant and, with a degree of certainty, gives the accused notice of the offense with which he is charged. [W]e also find no merit in Burleson's argument that the indictment is deficient because it fails to distinguish between physical and logical deletions of data. Although the distinction between physical and logical deletions may be significant to a programmer, ... such is a distinction without a difference for the purpose of §33.03 [now §33.01(14)]."

PEN §33.02. BREACH OF COMPUTER SECURITY

(a) A person commits an offense if the person knowingly accesses a computer, computer network, or computer system without the effective consent of the owner.

(b) An offense under this section is a Class B misdemeanor unless in committing the offense the actor knowingly obtains a benefit, defrauds or harms another, or alters, damages, or deletes property, in which event the offense is:

(1) a Class A misdemeanor if the aggregate amount involved is less than $1,500;

(2) a state jail felony if:

(A) the aggregate amount involved is $1,500 or more but less than $20,000; or

(B) the aggregate amount involved is less than $1,500 and the defendant has been previously convicted two or more times of an offense under this chapter;

(3) a felony of the third degree if the aggregate amount involved is $20,000 or more but less than $100,000;

(4) a felony of the second degree if the aggregate amount involved is $100,000 or more but less than $200,000; or

(5) a felony of the first degree if the aggregate amount involved is $200,000 or more.

(c) When benefits are obtained, a victim is defrauded or harmed, or property is altered, damaged, or deleted in violation of this section, whether or not in a single incident, the conduct may be considered as one offense and the value of the benefits obtained and of the losses incurred because of the fraud, harm, or alteration, damage, or deletion of property may be aggregated in determining the grade of the offense.

(d) A person who is subject to prosecution under this section and any other section of this code may be prosecuted under either or both sections.

History of Pen §33.02: Acts 1985, 69th Leg., ch. 600, §1, eff. Sept. 1, 1985. Amended by Acts 1989, 71st Leg., ch. 306, §2, eff. Sept. 1, 1989; Acts 1993, 73rd Leg., ch. 900, §1.01, eff. Sept. 1, 1994; Acts 1997, 75th Leg., ch. 306, §2, eff. Sept. 1, 1997; Acts 2001, 77th Leg., ch. 1411, §1, eff. Sept. 1, 2001.

PEN §33.021. ONLINE SOLICITATION OF A MINOR

(a) In this section:

(1) "Minor" means:

(A) an individual who represents himself or herself to be younger than 17 years of age; or

(B) an individual whom the actor believes to be younger than 17 years of age.

(2) "Sexual contact," "sexual intercourse," and "deviate sexual intercourse" have the meanings assigned by Section 21.01.

(3) "Sexually explicit" means any communication, language, or material, including a photographic or video image, that relates to or describes sexual conduct, as defined by Section 43.25.

🅐 *Subsections (b) & (c) below are effective for offenses committed on or after Sept. 1, 2007.*

(b) A person who is 17 years of age or older commits an offense if, with the intent to arouse or gratify

PEN §33.01

the sexual desire of any person, the person, over the Internet, by electronic mail or text message or other electronic message service or system, or through a commercial online service, intentionally:

(1) communicates in a sexually explicit manner with a minor; or

(2) distributes sexually explicit material to a minor.

(c) A person commits an offense if the person, over the Internet, by electronic mail or text message or other electronic message service or system, or through a commercial online service, knowingly solicits a minor to meet another person, including the actor, with the intent that the minor will engage in sexual contact, sexual intercourse, or deviate sexual intercourse with the actor or another person.

Subsections (b) & (c) below are effective for offenses in which any element of the offense was committed before Sept. 1, 2007.

(b) A person who is 17 years of age or older commits an offense if, with the intent to arouse or gratify the sexual desire of any person, the person, over the Internet or by electronic mail or a commercial online service, intentionally:

(1) communicates in a sexually explicit manner with a minor; or

(2) distributes sexually explicit material to a minor.

(c) A person commits an offense if the person, over the Internet or by electronic mail or a commercial online service, knowingly solicits a minor to meet another person, including the actor, with the intent that the minor will engage in sexual contact, sexual intercourse, or deviate sexual intercourse with the actor or another person.

(d) It is not a defense to prosecution under Subsection (c) that:

(1) the meeting did not occur;

(2) the actor did not intend for the meeting to occur; or

(3) the actor was engaged in a fantasy at the time of commission of the offense.

(e) It is a defense to prosecution under this section that at the time conduct described by Subsection (b) or (c) was committed:

(1) the actor was married to the minor; or

(2) the actor was not more than three years older than the minor and the minor consented to the conduct.

 Subsection (f) below is effective for offenses committed on or after Sept. 1, 2007.

(f) An offense under Subsection (b) is a felony of the third degree, except that the offense is a felony of the second degree if the minor is younger than 14 years of age or is an individual whom the actor believes to be younger than 14 years of age at the time of the commission of the offense. An offense under Subsection (c) is a felony of the second degree.

Subsection (f) below is effective for offenses in which any element of the offense was committed before Sept. 1, 2007.

(f) An offense under Subsection (b) is a state jail felony, and an offense under Subsection (c) is a felony of the third degree, except that an offense under Subsection (b) or (c) is a felony of the second degree if the minor is younger than 14 years of age or is an individual whom the actor believes to be younger than 14 years of age.

(g) If conduct that constitutes an offense under this section also constitutes an offense under any other law, the actor may be prosecuted under this section, the other law, or both.

History of Pen §33.021: Acts 2005, 79th Leg., ch. 1273, §1, eff. June 18, 2005. Amended by Acts 2007, 80th Leg., ch. 610, §2 (eff. Sept. 1, 2007), ch. 1291, §7 (eff. Sept. 1, 2007).

PEN §33.03. DEFENSES

It is an affirmative defense to prosecution under Section 33.02 that the actor was an officer, employee, or agent of a communications common carrier or electric utility and committed the proscribed act or acts in the course of employment while engaged in an activity that is a necessary incident to the rendition of service or to the protection of the rights or property of the communications common carrier or electric utility.

History of Pen §33.03: Acts 1985, 69th Leg., ch. 600, §1, eff. Sept. 1, 1985. Renumbered from §33.04 and amended by Acts 1993, 73rd Leg., ch. 900, §1.01, eff. Sept. 1, 1994.

PEN §33.04. ASSISTANCE BY ATTORNEY GENERAL

The attorney general, if requested to do so by a prosecuting attorney, may assist the prosecuting attorney in the investigation or prosecution of an offense under this chapter or of any other offense involving the use of a computer.

For a quick reference of penalties, see the Chart of Penalties on p. 675.

O'CONNOR'S CRIMINAL CODES 839

History of Pen §33.04: Acts 1985, 69th Leg., ch. 600, §1, eff. Sept. 1, 1985. Renumbered from §33.05 by Acts 1993, 73rd Leg., ch. 900, §1.01, eff. Sept. 1, 1994.

PEN §33.05. TAMPERING WITH DIRECT RECORDING ELECTRONIC VOTING MACHINE

(a) In this section:

(1) "Direct recording electronic voting machine" has the meaning assigned by Section 121.003, Election Code.

(2) "Measure" has the meaning assigned by Section 1.005, Election Code.

(b) A person commits an offense if the person knowingly accesses a computer, computer network, computer program, computer software, or computer system that is a part of a voting system that uses direct recording electronic voting machines and by means of that access:

(1) prevents a person from lawfully casting a vote;

(2) changes a lawfully cast vote;

(3) prevents a lawfully cast vote from being counted; or

(4) causes a vote that was not lawfully cast to be counted.

(c) An offense under this section does not require that the votes as affected by the person's actions described by Subsection (b) actually be the votes used in the official determination of the outcome of the election.

(d) An offense under this section is a felony of the first degree.

(e) Notwithstanding Section 15.01(d), an offense under Section 15.01(a) is a felony of the third degree if the offense the actor intends to commit is an offense under this section.

History of Pen §33.05: Acts 2005, 79th Leg., ch. 470, §1, eff. Sept. 1, 2005.

CHAPTER 33A. TELECOMMUNICATIONS CRIMES

PEN §33A.01. DEFINITIONS

In this chapter:

(1) "Counterfeit telecommunications access device" means a telecommunications access device that is false, fraudulent, not issued to a legitimate telecommunications access device subscriber account, or otherwise unlawful or invalid.

(2) "Counterfeit telecommunications device" means a telecommunications device that has been altered or programmed alone or with another telecommunications device to acquire, intercept, receive, or otherwise facilitate the use of a telecommunications service without the authority or consent of the telecommunications service provider and includes a clone telephone, clone microchip, tumbler telephone, tumbler microchip, or wireless scanning device capable of acquiring, intercepting, receiving, or otherwise facilitating the use of a telecommunications service without immediate detection.

(3) "Deliver" means to actually or constructively sell, give, loan, or otherwise transfer a telecommunications device, or a counterfeit telecommunications device or any telecommunications plans, instructions, or materials, to another person.

(4) "Publish" means to communicate information or make information available to another person orally, in writing, or by means of telecommunications and includes communicating information on a computer bulletin board or similar system.

(5) "Telecommunications" means the origination, emission, transmission, or reception of data, images, signals, sounds, or other intelligence or equivalence of intelligence over a communications system by any method, including an electronic, magnetic, optical, digital, or analog method.

(6) "Telecommunications access device" means an instrument, device, card, plate, code, account number, personal identification number, electronic serial number, mobile identification number, counterfeit number, or financial transaction device that alone or with another telecommunications access device can acquire, intercept, provide, receive, use, or otherwise facilitate the use of a telecommunications device, counterfeit telecommunications device, or telecommunications service.

(7) "Telecommunications device" means any instrument, equipment, machine, or device that facilitates telecommunications and includes a computer, computer chip or circuit, telephone, pager, personal communications device, transponder, receiver, radio, modem, or device that enables use of a modem.

(8) "Telecommunications service" means the provision, facilitation, or generation of telecommunications through the use of a telecommunications device or telecommunications access device over a telecommunications system.

(9) "Value of the telecommunications service obtained or attempted to be obtained" includes the value of:

(A) a lawful charge for telecommunications service avoided or attempted to be avoided;

(B) money, property, or telecommunications service lost, stolen, or rendered unrecoverable by an offense; and

(C) an expenditure incurred by a victim to verify that a telecommunications device or telecommunications access device or telecommunications service was not altered, acquired, damaged, or disrupted as a result of an offense.

History of Pen §33A.01: Acts 1997, 75th Leg., ch. 306, §3, eff. Sept. 1, 1997.

PEN §33A.02. UNAUTHORIZED USE OF TELECOMMUNICATIONS SERVICE

(a) A person commits an offense if the person is an officer, shareholder, partner, employee, agent, or independent contractor of a telecommunications service provider and the person knowingly and without authority uses or diverts telecommunications service for the person's own benefit or to the benefit of another.

(b) An offense under this section is:

(1) a Class B misdemeanor if the value of the telecommunications service used or diverted is less than $500;

(2) a Class A misdemeanor if:

(A) the value of the telecommunications service used or diverted is $500 or more but less than $1,500; or

(B) the value of the telecommunications service used or diverted is less than $500 and the defendant has been previously convicted of an offense under this chapter;

(3) a state jail felony if:

(A) the value of the telecommunications service used or diverted is $1,500 or more but less than $20,000; or

(B) the value of the telecommunications service used or diverted is less than $1,500 and the defendant has been previously convicted two or more times of an offense under this chapter;

(4) a felony of the third degree if the value of the telecommunications service used or diverted is $20,000 or more but less than $100,000;

(5) a felony of the second degree if the value of the telecommunications service used or diverted is $100,000 or more but less than $200,000; or

(6) a felony of the first degree if the value of the telecommunications service used or diverted is $200,000 or more.

(c) When telecommunications service is used or diverted in violation of this section pursuant to one scheme or continuing course of conduct, whether or not in a single incident, the conduct may be considered as one offense and the values of the service used or diverted may be aggregated in determining the grade of the offense.

History of Pen §33A.02: Acts 1997, 75th Leg., ch. 306, §3, eff. Sept. 1, 1997.

PEN §33A.03. MANUFACTURE, POSSESSION, OR DELIVERY OF UNLAWFUL TELECOMMUNICATIONS DEVICE

(a) A person commits an offense if the person manufactures, possesses, delivers, offers to deliver, or advertises:

(1) a counterfeit telecommunications device; or

(2) a telecommunications device that is intended to be used to:

(A) commit an offense under Section 33A.04; or

(B) conceal the existence or place of origin or destination of a telecommunications service.

(b) A person commits an offense if the person delivers, offers to deliver, or advertises plans, instructions, or materials for manufacture of:

(1) a counterfeit telecommunications device; or

(2) a telecommunications device that is intended to be used to commit an offense under Subsection (a).

(c) An offense under this section is a felony of the third degree.

(d) It is a defense to prosecution under this section that the person was an officer, agent, or employee of a telecommunications service provider who engaged in the conduct for the purpose of gathering information for a law enforcement investigation related to an offense under this chapter.

History of Pen §33A.03: Acts 1997, 75th Leg., ch. 306, §3, eff. Sept. 1, 1997.

For a quick reference of penalties, see the Chart of Penalties on p. 675.

O'CONNOR'S CRIMINAL CODES **841**

PEN §33A.04. THEFT OF TELECOMMUNICATIONS SERVICE

(a) A person commits an offense if the person knowingly obtains or attempts to obtain telecommunications service to avoid or cause another person to avoid a lawful charge for that service by using:

(1) a telecommunications access device without the authority or consent of the subscriber or lawful holder of the device or pursuant to an agreement for an exchange of value with the subscriber or lawful holder of the device to allow another person to use the device;

(2) a counterfeit telecommunications access device;

(3) a telecommunications device or counterfeit telecommunications device; or

(4) a fraudulent or deceptive scheme, pretense, method, or conspiracy, or other device or means, including a false, altered, or stolen identification.

(b) An offense under this section is:

(1) a Class B misdemeanor if the value of the telecommunications service obtained or attempted to be obtained is less than $500;

(2) a Class A misdemeanor if:

(A) the value of the telecommunications service obtained or attempted to be obtained is $500 or more but less than $1,500; or

(B) the value of the telecommunications service obtained or attempted to be obtained is less than $500 and the defendant has been previously convicted of an offense under this chapter;

(3) a state jail felony if:

(A) the value of the telecommunications service obtained or attempted to be obtained is $1,500 or more but less than $20,000; or

(B) the value of the telecommunications service obtained or attempted to be obtained is less than $1,500 and the defendant has been previously convicted two or more times of an offense under this chapter;

(4) a felony of the third degree if the value of the telecommunications service obtained or attempted to be obtained is $20,000 or more but less than $100,000;

(5) a felony of the second degree if the value of the telecommunications service obtained or attempted to be obtained is $100,000 or more but less than $200,000; or

(6) a felony of the first degree if the value of the telecommunications service obtained or attempted to be obtained is $200,000 or more.

(c) When telecommunications service is obtained or attempted to be obtained in violation of this section pursuant to one scheme or continuing course of conduct, whether or not in a single incident, the conduct may be considered as one offense and the values of the service obtained or attempted to be obtained may be aggregated in determining the grade of the offense.

History of Pen §33A.04: Acts 1997, 75th Leg., ch. 306, §3, eff. Sept. 1, 1997.

PEN §33A.05. PUBLICATION OF TELECOMMUNICATIONS ACCESS DEVICE

(a) A person commits an offense if the person with criminal negligence publishes a telecommunications access device or counterfeit telecommunications access device that is designed to be used to commit an offense under Section 33A.04.

(b) Except as otherwise provided by this subsection, an offense under this section is a Class A misdemeanor. An offense under this section is a felony of the third degree if the person has been previously convicted of an offense under this chapter.

History of Pen §33A.05: Acts 1997, 75th Leg., ch. 306, §3, eff. Sept. 1, 1997.

PEN §33A.06. ASSISTANCE BY ATTORNEY GENERAL

The attorney general, if requested to do so by a prosecuting attorney, may assist the prosecuting attorney in the investigation or prosecution of an offense under this chapter or of any other offense involving the use of telecommunications equipment, services, or devices.

History of Pen §33A.06: Acts 1997, 75th Leg., ch. 306, §3, eff. Sept. 1, 1997.

CHAPTER 34. MONEY LAUNDERING

PEN §34.01. DEFINITIONS

In this chapter:

(1) "Criminal activity" means any offense, including any preparatory offense, that is:

(A) classified as a felony under the laws of this state or the United States; or

(B) punishable by confinement for more than one year under the laws of another state.

(2) "Funds" includes:

(A) coin or paper money of the United States or any other country that is designated as legal tender and that circulates and is customarily used and accepted as a medium of exchange in the country of issue;

(B) United States silver certificates, United States Treasury notes, and Federal Reserve System notes;

(C) an official foreign bank note that is customarily used and accepted as a medium of exchange in a foreign country and a foreign bank draft; and

(D) currency or its equivalent, including an electronic fund, personal check, bank check, traveler's check, money order, bearer negotiable instrument, bearer investment security, bearer security, or certificate of stock in a form that allows title to pass on delivery.

(3) "Financial institution" has the meaning assigned by Section 32.01.

(4) "Proceeds" means funds acquired or derived directly or indirectly from, produced through, or realized through an act.

History of Pen §34.01: Acts 1993, 73rd Leg., ch. 761, §2, eff. Sept. 1, 1993. Amended by Acts 2005, 79th Leg., ch. 1162, §1, eff. Sept. 1, 2005.

PEN §34.02. MONEY LAUNDERING

(a) A person commits an offense if the person knowingly:

(1) acquires or maintains an interest in, conceals, possesses, transfers, or transports the proceeds of criminal activity;

(2) conducts, supervises, or facilitates a transaction involving the proceeds of criminal activity;

(3) invests, expends, or receives, or offers to invest, expend, or receive, the proceeds of criminal activity or funds that the person believes are the proceeds of criminal activity; or

(4) finances or invests or intends to finance or invest funds that the person believes are intended to further the commission of criminal activity.

(a-1) Knowledge of the specific nature of the criminal activity giving rise to the proceeds is not required to establish a culpable mental state under this section.

(b) For purposes of this section, a person is presumed to believe that funds are the proceeds of or are intended to further the commission of criminal activity if a peace officer or a person acting at the direction of a peace officer represents to the person that the funds are proceeds of or are intended to further the commission of criminal activity, as applicable, regardless of whether the peace officer or person acting at the peace officer's direction discloses the person's status as a peace officer or that the person is acting at the direction of a peace officer.

(c) It is a defense to prosecution under this section that the person acted with intent to facilitate the lawful seizure, forfeiture, or disposition of funds or other legitimate law enforcement purpose pursuant to the laws of this state or the United States.

(d) It is a defense to prosecution under this section that the transaction was necessary to preserve a person's right to representation as guaranteed by the Sixth Amendment of the United States Constitution and by Article 1, Section 10, of the Texas Constitution or that the funds were received as bona fide legal fees by a licensed attorney and at the time of their receipt, the attorney did not have actual knowledge that the funds were derived from criminal activity.

(e) An offense under this section is:

(1) a state jail felony if the value of the funds is $1,500 or more but less than $20,000;

(2) a felony of the third degree if the value of the funds is $20,000 or more but less than $100,000;

(3) a felony of the second degree if the value of the funds is $100,000 or more but less than $200,000; or

(4) a felony of the first degree if the value of the funds is $200,000 or more.

(f) For purposes of this section, if proceeds of criminal activity are related to one scheme or continuing course of conduct, whether from the same or several sources, the conduct may be considered as one offense and the value of the proceeds aggregated in determining the classification of the offense.

(g) For purposes of this section, funds on deposit at a branch of a financial institution are considered the property of that branch and any other branch of the financial institution.

(h) If conduct that constitutes an offense under this section also constitutes an offense under any other law, the actor may be prosecuted under this section, the other law, or both.

History of Pen §34.02: Acts 1993, 73rd Leg., ch. 761, §2, eff. Sept. 1, 1993. Amended by Acts 2005, 79th Leg., ch. 1162, §2, eff. Sept. 1, 2005.

PEN §34.021. PROTECTION FROM CIVIL LIABILITY

Notwithstanding Section 1.03(c), a financial institution or an agent of the financial institution acting in a manner described by Section 34.02(c) is not liable for civil damages to a person who:

For a quick reference of penalties, see the Chart of Penalties on p. 675.

O'CONNOR'S CRIMINAL CODES 843

PEN §34.021

(1) claims an ownership interest in funds involved in an offense under Section 34.02; or

(2) conducts with the financial institution or an insurer, as defined by Article 1.02, Insurance Code, a transaction concerning funds involved in an offense under Section 34.02.

History of Pen §34.021: Acts 2005, 79th Leg., ch. 1162, §3, eff. Sept. 1, 2005.

PEN §34.03. ASSISTANCE BY ATTORNEY GENERAL

The attorney general, if requested to do so by a prosecuting attorney, may assist in the prosecution of an offense under this chapter.

History of Pen §34.03: Acts 1993, 73rd Leg., ch. 761, §2, eff. Sept. 1, 1993.

CHAPTER 35. INSURANCE FRAUD

PEN §35.01. DEFINITIONS

In this chapter:

(1) "Insurance policy" means a written instrument in which is provided the terms of any certificate of insurance, binder of coverage, contract of insurance, benefit plan, nonprofit hospital service plan, motor club service plan, surety bond, cash bond, or any other alternative to insurance authorized by Chapter 601, Transportation Code. The term includes any instrument authorized to be regulated by the Texas Department of Insurance.

(2) "Insurer" has the meaning assigned by Article 1.02, Insurance Code.

(3) "Statement" means an oral or written communication or a record or documented representation of fact made to an insurer. The term includes computer-generated information.

(4) "Value of the claim" means the total dollar amount of a claim for payment under an insurance policy or, as applicable, the value of the claim determined under Section 35.025.

History of Pen §35.01: Acts 1995, 74th Leg., ch. 621, §1, eff. Sept. 1, 1995. Amended by Acts 2001, 77th Leg., ch. 1420, §14.830, eff. Sept. 1, 2001; Acts 2003, 78th Leg., ch. 1276, §10A.541, eff. Sept. 1, 2003; Acts 2005, 79th Leg., ch. 1162, §4, eff. Sept. 1, 2005.

PEN §35.015. MATERIALITY

A statement is material for the purposes of this chapter, regardless of the admissibility of the statement at trial, if the statement could have affected:

(1) the eligibility for coverage or amount of the payment on a claim for payment under an insurance policy; or

(2) the decision of an insurer whether to issue an insurance policy.

History of Pen §35.015: Acts 2005, 79th Leg., ch. 1162, §4, eff. Sept. 1, 2005.

PEN §35.02. INSURANCE FRAUD

(a) A person commits an offense if, with intent to defraud or deceive an insurer, the person, in support of a claim for payment under an insurance policy:

(1) prepares or causes to be prepared a statement that:

(A) the person knows contains false or misleading material information; and

(B) is presented to an insurer; or

(2) presents or causes to be presented to an insurer a statement that the person knows contains false or misleading material information.

(a-1) A person commits an offense if the person, with intent to defraud or deceive an insurer and in support of an application for an insurance policy:

(1) prepares or causes to be prepared a statement that:

(A) the person knows contains false or misleading material information; and

(B) is presented to an insurer; or

(2) presents or causes to be presented to an insurer a statement that the person knows contains false or misleading material information.

(b) A person commits an offense if, with intent to defraud or deceive an insurer, the person solicits, offers, pays, or receives a benefit in connection with the furnishing of goods or services for which a claim for payment is submitted under an insurance policy.

(c) An offense under Subsection (a) or (b) is:

(1) a Class C misdemeanor if the value of the claim is less than $50;

(2) a Class B misdemeanor if the value of the claim is $50 or more but less than $500;

(3) a Class A misdemeanor if the value of the claim is $500 or more but less than $1,500;

(4) a state jail felony if the value of the claim is $1,500 or more but less than $20,000;

(5) a felony of the third degree if the value of the claim is $20,000 or more but less than $100,000;

(6) a felony of the second degree if the value of the claim is $100,000 or more but less than $200,000; or

(7) a felony of the first degree if:

(A) the value of the claim is $200,000 or more; or

(B) an act committed in connection with the commission of the offense places a person at risk of death or serious bodily injury.

(d) An offense under Subsection (a-1) is a state jail felony.

(e) The court shall order a defendant convicted of an offense under this section to pay restitution, including court costs and attorney's fees, to an affected insurer.

(f) If conduct that constitutes an offense under this section also constitutes an offense under any other law, the actor may be prosecuted under this section, the other law, or both.

(g) For purposes of this section, if the actor proves by a preponderance of the evidence that a portion of the claim for payment under an insurance policy resulted from a valid loss, injury, expense, or service covered by the policy, the value of the claim is equal to the difference between the total claim amount and the amount of the valid portion of the claim.

(h) If it is shown on the trial of an offense under this section that the actor submitted a bill for goods or services in support of a claim for payment under an insurance policy to the insurer issuing the policy, a rebuttable presumption exists that the actor caused the claim for payment to be prepared or presented.

History of Pen §35.02: Acts 1995, 74th Leg., ch. 621, §1, eff. Sept. 1, 1995. Amended by Acts 2003, 78th Leg., ch. 605, §1, eff. Sept. 1, 2003; Acts 2005, 79th Leg., ch. 1162, §4, eff. Sept. 1, 2005.

ANNOTATIONS

Logan v. State, 89 S.W.3d 619, 630 (Tex.Crim.App. 2002). "[T]he Legislature meant 'value of the claim' in §35.02(d) [now §35.02(c)] to mean the fraudulent portion of the claim."

PEN §35.025. VALUE OF CLAIM

(a) Except as provided by Subsection (b) and subject to Subsection (c), for the purposes of Section 35.02(c), if the value of a claim is not readily ascertainable, the value of the claim is:

(1) the fair market value, at the time and place of the offense, of the goods or services that are the subject of the claim; or

(2) the cost of replacing the goods or services that are the subject of the claim within a reasonable time after the claim.

(b) If goods or services that are the subject of a claim cannot be reasonably ascertained under Subsection (a), the goods or services are considered to have a value of $500 or more but less than $1,500.

(c) If the actor proves by a preponderance of the evidence that a portion of the claim for payment under an insurance policy resulted from a valid loss, injury, expense, or service covered by the policy, the value of the claim is equal to the difference between the total claim amount and the amount of the valid portion of the claim.

History of Pen.: §35.025: Acts 2005, 79th Leg., ch. 1162, §4, eff. Sept. 1, 2005.

PEN §35.03. AGGREGATION & MULTIPLE OFFENSES

(a) When separate claims in violation of this chapter are communicated to an insurer or group of insurers pursuant to one scheme or continuing course of conduct, the conduct may be considered as one offense and the value of the claims aggregated in determining the classification of the offense. If claims are aggregated under this subsection, Subsection (b) shall not apply.

(b) When three or more separate claims in violation of this chapter are communicated to an insurer or group of insurers pursuant to one scheme or continuing course of conduct, the conduct may be considered as one offense, and the classification of the offense shall be one category higher than the most serious single offense proven from the separate claims, except that if the most serious offense is a felony of the first degree, the offense is a felony of the first degree. This subsection shall not be applied if claims are aggregated under Subsection (a).

History of Pen §35.03: Acts 1995, 74th Leg., ch. 621, §1, eff. Sept. 1, 1995.

PEN §35.04. JURISDICTION OF ATTORNEY GENERAL

(a) The attorney general may offer to an attorney representing the state in the prosecution of an offense under Section 35.02 the investigative, technical, and litigation assistance of the attorney general's office.

(b) The attorney general may prosecute or assist in the prosecution of an offense under Section 35.02 on the request of the attorney representing the state described by Subsection (a).

History of Pen §35.04: Acts 1995, 74th Leg., ch. 621, §1, eff. Sept. 1, 1995.

For a quick reference of penalties, see the Chart of Penalties on p. 675.

O'CONNOR'S CRIMINAL CODES 845

PEN §35.04

CHAPTER 35A. MEDICAID FRAUD

§35A.01 Definitions
§35A.02 Medicaid fraud

PEN §35A.01. DEFINITIONS

In this chapter:

(1) "Claim" has the meaning assigned by Section 36.001, Human Resources Code.

(2) "Fiscal agent" has the meaning assigned by Section 36.001, Human Resources Code.

(3) "Health care practitioner" has the meaning assigned by Section 36.001, Human Resources Code.

(4) "Managed care organization" has the meaning assigned by Section 36.001, Human Resources Code.

(5) "Medicaid program" has the meaning assigned by Section 36.001, Human Resources Code.

(6) "Medicaid recipient" has the meaning assigned by Section 36.001, Human Resources Code.

(7) "Physician" has the meaning assigned by Section 36.001, Human Resources Code.

(8) "Provider" has the meaning assigned by Section 36.001, Human Resources Code.

(9) "Service" has the meaning assigned by Section 36.001, Human Resources Code.

History of Pen §35A.01: Acts 2005, 79th Leg., ch. 806, §16, eff. Sept. 1, 2005.

PEN §35A.02. MEDICAID FRAUD

(a) A person commits an offense if the person:

(1) knowingly makes or causes to be made a false statement or misrepresentation of a material fact to permit a person to receive a benefit or payment under the Medicaid program that is not authorized or that is greater than the benefit or payment that is authorized;

(2) knowingly conceals or fails to disclose information that permits a person to receive a benefit or payment under the Medicaid program that is not authorized or that is greater than the benefit or payment that is authorized;

(3) knowingly applies for and receives a benefit or payment on behalf of another person under the Medicaid program and converts any part of the benefit or payment to a use other than for the benefit of the person on whose behalf it was received;

(4) knowingly makes, causes to be made, induces, or seeks to induce the making of a false statement or misrepresentation of material fact concerning:

(A) the conditions or operation of a facility in order that the facility may qualify for certification or recertification required by the Medicaid program, including certification or recertification as:

(i) a hospital;

(ii) a nursing facility or skilled nursing facility;

(iii) a hospice;

(iv) an intermediate care facility for the mentally retarded;

(v) an assisted living facility; or

(vi) a home health agency; or

(B) information required to be provided by a federal or state law, rule, regulation, or provider agreement pertaining to the Medicaid program;

(5) except as authorized under the Medicaid program, knowingly pays, charges, solicits, accepts, or receives, in addition to an amount paid under the Medicaid program, a gift, money, a donation, or other consideration as a condition to the provision of a service or product or the continued provision of a service or product if the cost of the service or product is paid for, in whole or in part, under the Medicaid program;

(6) knowingly presents or causes to be presented a claim for payment under the Medicaid program for a product provided or a service rendered by a person who:

(A) is not licensed to provide the product or render the service, if a license is required; or

(B) is not licensed in the manner claimed;

(7) knowingly makes a claim under the Medicaid program for:

(A) a service or product that has not been approved or acquiesced in by a treating physician or health care practitioner;

(B) a service or product that is substantially inadequate or inappropriate when compared to generally recognized standards within the particular discipline or within the health care industry; or

(C) a product that has been adulterated, debased, mislabeled, or that is otherwise inappropriate;

(8) makes a claim under the Medicaid program and knowingly fails to indicate the type of license and the identification number of the licensed health care provider who actually provided the service;

(9) knowingly enters into an agreement, combination, or conspiracy to defraud the state by obtaining or

PEN §35A.01

aiding another person in obtaining an unauthorized payment or benefit from the Medicaid program or a fiscal agent;

(10) is a managed care organization that contracts with the Health and Human Services Commission or other state agency to provide or arrange to provide health care benefits or services to individuals eligible under the Medicaid program and knowingly:

(A) fails to provide to an individual a health care benefit or service that the organization is required to provide under the contract;

(B) fails to provide to the commission or appropriate state agency information required to be provided by law, commission or agency rule, or contractual provision; or

(C) engages in a fraudulent activity in connection with the enrollment of an individual eligible under the Medicaid program in the organization's managed care plan or in connection with marketing the organization's services to an individual eligible under the Medicaid program;

Ⓐ *Subsection (11) below is effective for offenses committed on or after Sept. 1, 2007.*

(11) knowingly obstructs an investigation by the attorney general of an alleged unlawful act under this section or under Section 32.039, 32.0391, or 36.002, Human Resources Code; or

Subsection (11) below is effective for offenses in which any element of the offense was committed before Sept. 1, 2007.

(11) knowingly obstructs an investigation by the attorney general of an alleged unlawful act under Section 36.002, Human Resources Code; or

(12) knowingly makes, uses, or causes the making or use of a false record or statement to conceal, avoid, or decrease an obligation to pay or transmit money or property to this state under the Medicaid program.

Ⓐ *Subsection (b) below is effective for offenses committed on or after Sept. 1, 2007.*

(b) An offense under this section is:

(1) a Class C misdemeanor if the amount of any payment or the value of any monetary or in-kind benefit provided or claim for payment made under the Medicaid program, directly or indirectly, as a result of the conduct is less than $50;

(2) a Class B misdemeanor if the amount of any payment or the value of any monetary or in-kind benefit provided or claim for payment made under the Medicaid program, directly or indirectly, as a result of the conduct is $50 or more but less than $500;

(3) a Class A misdemeanor if the amount of any payment or the value of any monetary or in-kind benefit provided or claim for payment made under the Medicaid program, directly or indirectly, as a result of the conduct is $500 or more but less than $1,500;

(4) a state jail felony if:

(A) the amount of any payment or the value of any monetary or in-kind benefit provided or claim for payment made under the Medicaid program, directly or indirectly, as a result of the conduct is $1,500 or more but less than $20,000;

Ⓔ **(B)** the offense is committed under Subsection (a)(11); or

Ⓔ **(C)** it is shown on the trial of the offense that the amount of the payment or value of the benefit described by this subsection cannot be reasonably ascertained;

(5) a felony of the third degree if the amount of any payment or the value of any monetary or in-kind benefit provided or claim for payment made under the Medicaid program, directly or indirectly, as a result of the conduct is $20,000 or more but less than $100,000;

(6) a felony of the second degree if the amount of any payment or the value of any monetary or in-kind benefit provided or claim for payment made under the Medicaid program, directly or indirectly, as a result of the conduct is $100,000 or more but less than $200,000; or

(7) a felony of the first degree if the amount of any payment or the value of any monetary or in-kind benefit provided or claim for payment made under the Medicaid program, directly or indirectly, as a result of the conduct is $200,000 or more.

Subsection (b) below is effective for offenses in which any element of the offense was committed before Sept. 1, 2007.

(b) An offense under this section is:

(1) a Class C misdemeanor if the amount of any payment or the value of any monetary or in-kind benefit provided under the Medicaid program, directly or indirectly, as a result of the conduct is less than $50;

For a quick reference of penalties, see the Chart of Penalties on p. 675.

O'CONNOR'S CRIMINAL CODES 847

(2) a Class B misdemeanor if the amount of any payment or the value of any monetary or in-kind benefit provided under the Medicaid program, directly or indirectly, as a result of the conduct is $50 or more but less than $500;

(3) a Class A misdemeanor if the amount of any payment or the value of any monetary or in-kind benefit provided under the Medicaid program, directly or indirectly, as a result of the conduct is $500 or more but less than $1,500;

(4) a state jail felony if the amount of any payment or the value of any monetary or in-kind benefit provided under the Medicaid program, directly or indirectly, as a result of the conduct is $1,500 or more but less than $20,000;

(5) a felony of the third degree if the amount of any payment or the value of any monetary or in-kind benefit provided under the Medicaid program, directly or indirectly, as a result of the conduct is $20,000 or more but less than $100,000;

(6) a felony of the second degree if the amount of any payment or the value of any monetary or in-kind benefit provided under the Medicaid program, directly or indirectly, as a result of the conduct is $100,000 or more but less than $200,000; or

(7) a felony of the first degree if the amount of any payment or the value of any monetary or in-kind benefit provided under the Medicaid program, directly or indirectly, as a result of the conduct is $200,000 or more.

(c) If conduct constituting an offense under this section also constitutes an offense under another section of this code or another provision of law, the actor may be prosecuted under either this section or the other section or provision.

(d) When multiple payments or monetary or in-kind benefits are provided under the Medicaid program as a result of one scheme or continuing course of conduct, the conduct may be considered as one offense and the amounts of the payments or monetary or in-kind benefits aggregated in determining the grade of the offense.

History of Pen §35A.02: Acts 2005, 79th Leg., ch. 806, §16, eff. Sept. 1, 2005. Amended by Acts 2007, 80th Leg., ch. 127, §5, eff. Sept. 1, 2007.

TITLE 8. OFFENSES AGAINST PUBLIC ADMINISTRATION

CHAPTER 36. BRIBERY & CORRUPT INFLUENCE

PEN §36.01. DEFINITIONS

In this chapter:

(1) "Custody" means:

(A) detained or under arrest by a peace officer; or

(B) under restraint by a public servant pursuant to an order of a court.

(2) "Party official" means a person who holds any position or office in a political party, whether by election, appointment, or employment.

(3) "Benefit" means anything reasonably regarded as pecuniary gain or pecuniary advantage, including benefit to any other person in whose welfare the beneficiary has a direct and substantial interest.

(4) "Vote" means to cast a ballot in an election regulated by law.

History of Pen §36.01: Acts 1973, 63rd Leg., ch. 399, §1, eff. Jan. 1, 1974. Amended by Acts 1975, 64th Leg., ch. 342, §11, eff. Sept. 1, 1975; Acts 1983, 68th Leg., ch. 558, §1, eff. Sept. 1, 1983; Acts 1989, 71st Leg., ch. 67, §2, eff. Sept. 1, 1989; Acts 1991, 72nd Leg., ch. 304, §4.01 (eff. Jan. 1, 1992), ch. 565, §3 (eff. Sept. 1, 1991); Acts 1993, 73rd Leg., ch. 900, §1.01, eff. Sept. 1, 1994.

ANNOTATIONS

Kaisner v. State, 772 S.W.2d 528, 529 (Tex.App.—Beaumont 1989), *pet. ref'd*, 780 S.W.2d 226 (Tex.Crim. App.1989). Appellant's political opponent "was clearly a public servant under the Code. The decision to withdraw from the runoff would have been the exercise of discretion as a public servant. Under [Pen. Code] §36.01 [now §36.02(a)(1)], the offer of the job was the offer of a benefit. [¶] Appellant's argument is that the offer of a job to a political opponent falls within the traditional notion of political patronage and is therefore outside the statutory prohibition. We disagree. No such exception, justification or defense was authorized by the legislature."

PEN §36.02. BRIBERY

(a) A person commits an offense if he intentionally or knowingly offers, confers, or agrees to confer on another, or solicits, accepts, or agrees to accept from another:

PEN §35A.02

(1) any benefit as consideration for the recipient's decision, opinion, recommendation, vote, or other exercise of discretion as a public servant, party official, or voter;

(2) any benefit as consideration for the recipient's decision, vote, recommendation, or other exercise of official discretion in a judicial or administrative proceeding;

(3) any benefit as consideration for a violation of a duty imposed by law on a public servant or party official; or

(4) any benefit that is a political contribution as defined by Title 15, Election Code, or that is an expenditure made and reported in accordance with Chapter 305, Government Code, if the benefit was offered, conferred, solicited, accepted, or agreed to pursuant to an express agreement to take or withhold a specific exercise of official discretion if such exercise of official discretion would not have been taken or withheld but for the benefit; notwithstanding any rule of evidence or jury instruction allowing factual inferences in the absence of certain evidence, direct evidence of the express agreement shall be required in any prosecution under this subdivision.

(b) It is no defense to prosecution under this section that a person whom the actor sought to influence was not qualified to act in the desired way whether because he had not yet assumed office or he lacked jurisdiction or for any other reason.

(c) It is no defense to prosecution under this section that the benefit is not offered or conferred or that the benefit is not solicited or accepted until after:

(1) the decision, opinion, recommendation, vote, or other exercise of discretion has occurred; or

(2) the public servant ceases to be a public servant.

(d) It is an exception to the application of Subdivisions (1), (2), and (3) of Subsection (a) that the benefit is a political contribution as defined by Title 15, Election Code, or an expenditure made and reported in accordance with Chapter 305, Government Code.

(e) An offense under this section is a felony of the second degree.

History of Pen §36.02: Acts 1973, 63rd Leg., ch. 399, §1, eff. Jan. 1, 1974. Amended by Acts 1975, 64th Leg., ch. 342, §11, eff. Sept. 1, 1975; Acts 1983, 68th Leg., ch. 558, §2, eff. Sept. 1, 1983; Acts 1991, 72nd Leg., ch. 304, §4.02, eff. Jan. 1, 1992; Acts 1993, 73rd Leg., ch. 900, §1.01, eff. Sept. 1, 1994.

ANNOTATIONS

Cerda v. State, 750 S.W.2d 925, 927 (Tex.App.—Corpus Christi 1988, pet. ref'd). "Section 36.02 focuses on the mental state of the actor, and is complete if a private citizen, by offering, conferring or agreeing to confer; or a public servant, by soliciting, accepting, or agreeing to accept, intends an agreement. [¶] Appellant [municipal court bailiff] committed an offense under §36.02 when he agreed to destroy, conceal, or remove governmental records; i.e., two traffic citations, in exchange for a pecuniary benefit. No actual destruction, concealment, or removal of those governmental records [was] necessary to sustain a conviction."

Tweedy v. State, 722 S.W.2d 30, 31-32 (Tex.App.—Dallas 1986, pet. ref'd). "The indictment in this case alleged that the law imposing the duty [on a public servant] was a resolution adopted by the Mesquite City Council. Appellant argues that the indictment fails to allege the offense of bribery since a resolution, unlike an ordinance, is not a law as contemplated by the Penal Code. We disagree. [¶] Articles 1011, 1015, and 1175 of the [TRCS] supply authorization for the City of Mesquite to make and enforce rules and regulations concerning the construction of sewer and water systems within its municipal limits. [T]he resolution in question was a rule authorized by and lawfully adopted under a statute."

Martinez v. State, 696 S.W.2d 930, 933 (Tex. App.—Austin 1985, pet. ref'd). "[W]here it is alleged the accused offered or solicited a benefit as consideration for an official act, it is not necessary for the State to prove the party to whom the offer or solicitation was made accepted the proposition or even understood the unlawful nature of the proposition; proof that the offer or solicitation was made by the accused with the purpose to promote or facilitate the exchange of the benefit for the official action is all that is required."

PEN §36.03. COERCION OF PUBLIC SERVANT OR VOTER

(a) A person commits an offense if by means of coercion he:

(1) influences or attempts to influence a public servant in a specific exercise of his official power or a specific performance of his official duty or influences or attempts to influence a public servant to violate the public servant's known legal duty; or

For a quick reference of penalties, see the Chart of Penalties on p. 675.

O'CONNOR'S CRIMINAL CODES 849

(2) influences or attempts to influence a voter not to vote or to vote in a particular manner.

(b) An offense under this section is a Class A misdemeanor unless the coercion is a threat to commit a felony, in which event it is a felony of the third degree.

(c) It is an exception to the application of Subsection (a)(1) of this section that the person who influences or attempts to influence the public servant is a member of the governing body of a governmental entity, and that the action that influences or attempts to influence the public servant is an official action taken by the member of the governing body. For the purposes of this subsection, the term "official action" includes deliberations by the governing body of a governmental entity.

History of Pen §36.03: Acts 1973, 63rd Leg., ch. 399, §1, eff. Jan. 1, 1974. Amended by Acts 1989, 71st Leg., ch. 67, §§1, 3, eff. Sept. 1, 1989.

PEN §36.04. IMPROPER INFLUENCE

(a) A person commits an offense if he privately addresses a representation, entreaty, argument, or other communication to any public servant who exercises or will exercise official discretion in an adjudicatory proceeding with an intent to influence the outcome of the proceeding on the basis of considerations other than those authorized by law.

(b) For purposes of this section, "adjudicatory proceeding" means any proceeding before a court or any other agency of government in which the legal rights, powers, duties, or privileges of specified parties are determined.

(c) An offense under this section is a Class A misdemeanor.

History of Pen §36.04: Acts 1973, 63rd Leg., ch. 399, §1, eff. Jan. 1, 1974.

PEN §36.05. TAMPERING WITH WITNESS

(a) A person commits an offense if, with intent to influence the witness, he offers, confers, or agrees to confer any benefit on a witness or prospective witness in an official proceeding or coerces a witness or prospective witness in an official proceeding:

(1) to testify falsely;

(2) to withhold any testimony, information, document, or thing;

(3) to elude legal process summoning him to testify or supply evidence;

(4) to absent himself from an official proceeding to which he has been legally summoned; or

(5) to abstain from, discontinue, or delay the prosecution of another.

(b) A witness or prospective witness in an official proceeding commits an offense if he knowingly solicits, accepts, or agrees to accept any benefit on the representation or understanding that he will do any of the things specified in Subsection (a).

(c) It is a defense to prosecution under Subsection (a)(5) that the benefit received was:

(1) reasonable restitution for damages suffered by the complaining witness as a result of the offense; and

(2) a result of an agreement negotiated with the assistance or acquiescence of an attorney for the state who represented the state in the case.

(d) An offense under this section is a state jail felony.

History of Pen §36.05: Acts 1973, 63rd Leg., ch. 399, §1, eff. Jan. 1, 1974. Amended by Acts 1993, 73rd Leg., ch. 900, §1.01, eff. Sept. 1, 1994; Acts 1997, 75th Leg., ch. 721, §1, eff. Sept. 1, 1997.

ANNOTATIONS

Arnold v. State, 68 S.W.3d 93, 99-100 (Tex.App.—Dallas 2001, pet. ref'd). "[T]he State is not required to prove the existence of a subpoena to satisfy the 'eluding legal process' component of §36.05(a)(3). Nor is the State even required to prove an accused had actual knowledge of the existence of a subpoena or other legal process, if any was extant. As long as the State proves, circumstantially or otherwise, that the accused believed a subpoena or other legal process was extant or imminent, then proof of the requisite mental state is met."

Navarro v. State, 810 S.W.2d 432, 437 (Tex. App.—San Antonio 1991, pet. ref'd). "The ... offense of tampering with a witness was complete when the appellant offered and conferred and agreed to confer a benefit (money) to the witness in a manner calculated to cause false testimony."

PEN §36.06. OBSTRUCTION OR RETALIATION

(a) A person commits an offense if he intentionally or knowingly harms or threatens to harm another by an unlawful act:

(1) in retaliation for or on account of the service or status of another as a:

(A) public servant, witness, prospective witness, or informant; or

(B) person who has reported or who the actor knows intends to report the occurrence of a crime; or

(2) to prevent or delay the service of another as a:

(A) public servant, witness, prospective witness, or informant; or

(B) person who has reported or who the actor knows intends to report the occurrence of a crime.

(b) In this section:

(1) "Honorably retired peace officer" means a peace officer who:

(A) did not retire in lieu of any disciplinary action;

(B) was eligible to retire from a law enforcement agency or was ineligible to retire only as a result of an injury received in the course of the officer's employment with the agency; and

(C) is entitled to receive a pension or annuity for service as a law enforcement officer or is not entitled to receive a pension or annuity only because the law enforcement agency that employed the officer does not offer a pension or annuity to its employees.

(2) "Informant" means a person who has communicated information to the government in connection with any governmental function.

(3) "Public servant" includes an honorably retired peace officer.

(c) An offense under this section is a felony of the third degree unless the victim of the offense was harmed or threatened because of the victim's service or status as a juror, in which event the offense is a felony of the second degree.

History of Pen §36.06: Acts 1973, 63rd Leg., ch. 399, §1, eff. Jan. 1, 1974. Amended by Acts 1983, 68th Leg., ch. 558, §4, eff. Sept. 1, 1983; Acts 1989, 71st Leg., ch. 557, §1, eff. Sept. 1, 1989; Acts 1993, 73rd Leg., ch. 900, §1.01, eff. Sept. 1, 1994; Acts 1997, 75th Leg., ch. 239, §1, eff. Sept. 1, 1997; Acts 2001, 77th Leg., ch. 835, §1, eff. Sept. 1, 2001; Acts 2003, 78th Leg., ch. 246, §1, eff. Sept. 1, 2003.

ANNOTATIONS

Schmidt v. State, 232 S.W.3d 66, 67 (Tex.Crim.App. 2007). "The State's first issue asks whether a threat of harm and actual harm can arise from the same act and occur simultaneously or whether the threat must precede the harm. The court of appeals took too narrow a view of the statutory meaning of 'threaten' when it created a bright-line rule that 'one cannot simultaneously be threatened with harm while the threatened harm is being inflicted' and that the threat must precede the actual harm. Whether a threat has been communicated is a fact-specific inquiry and such a bright-line rule and the court's application of the rule are too restrictive."

Ortiz v. State, 93 S.W.3d 79, 86 (Tex.Crim.App. 2002). "[A] 'prospective witness' is any 'person who may testify in an official proceeding'. Formal proceedings 'need not be initiated.' Any person who is involved in an offense with a defendant, who sees the defendant committing an offense, or who hears the defendant discuss committing an offense is a 'prospective witness' in the prosecution of that defendant because he 'may' testify." *See also Morrow v. State*, 862 S.W.2d 612, 615 (Tex.Crim.App.1993); *Davis v. State*, 890 S.W.2d 489, 491 (Tex.App.—Eastland 1994, no pet.).

In re D.D., 101 S.W.3d 695, 697 (Tex.App.—Austin 2003, no pet.). "Terroristic threat is not a lesser-included offense of retaliation."

Carriere v. State, 84 S.W.3d 753, 757 (Tex.App.—Houston [1st Dist.] 2002, pet. ref'd). "'[P]ublic servant' ... include[s] a police officer."

Webb v. State, 991 S.W.2d 408, 415 (Tex.App.—Houston [14th Dist.] 1999, pet. ref'd). "A threat is not protected speech. ... The statute punishes only threatening speech and does not reach a substantial amount of constitutionally protected conduct." *See also Jacobs v. State*, 903 S.W.2d 848, 851 (Tex.App.—Texarkana 1995, pet. ref'd).

Wright v. State, 979 S.W.2d 868, 869 (Tex.App.—Beaumont 1998, pet. ref'd). Pen. Code §36.06(a) "does not require the threat or harm be in retaliation for past service as a public servant." *Contra Riley*, below.

Riley v. State, 965 S.W.2d 1, 2 (Tex.App.—Houston [1st Dist.] 1997, pet. ref'd). "[T]o support a conviction under [Pen. Code] §36.06(a)(1), it is not enough that the State demonstrate a public servant was harmed while lawfully discharging his official duties. It must prove the harm inflicted resulted from a retributive attack for duties already performed." *Contra Wright*, above.

Coward v. State, 931 S.W.2d 386, 389 (Tex.App.—Houston [14th Dist.] 1996, no pet.). "'Obstruction or Retaliation,' does not require that the threat to harm in retaliation be imminent." *See also Puckett v. State*, 801 S.W.2d 188, 194 (Tex.App.—Houston [14th Dist.] 1990, pet. ref'd).

Herrera v. State, 915 S.W.2d 94, 97-98 (Tex.App.—San Antonio 1996, no pet.). "[O]bstruction is in fact a result oriented offense. ... The mental state necessary to satisfy the elements of the offense are intent

For a quick reference of penalties, see the Chart of Penalties on p. 675.

O'CONNOR'S CRIMINAL CODES 851

PEN §36.06

⭐

---

to cause harm or to threaten to cause harm and intent to prevent or delay the service of another as a public servant. Intent to *engage in conduct* that results in the harm and the prevention or delay of a public servant is not an element of obstruction. [T]he nature of the actor's conduct in committing obstruction is inconsequential to the commission of the crime. The focus is on whether the conduct is done with the intent to effect the result specified in the statute." *See also* **Wilkins v. State**, ___ S.W.3d ___ (Tex.App.—Amarillo 2007, no pet.) (No. 07-05-0396-CR; 3-19-07).

PEN §36.07. ACCEPTANCE OF HONORARIUM

(a) A public servant commits an offense if the public servant solicits, accepts, or agrees to accept an honorarium in consideration for services that the public servant would not have been requested to provide but for the public servant's official position or duties.

(b) This section does not prohibit a public servant from accepting transportation and lodging expenses in connection with a conference or similar event in which the public servant renders services, such as addressing an audience or engaging in a seminar, to the extent that those services are more than merely perfunctory, or from accepting meals in connection with such an event.

(c) An offense under this section is a Class A misdemeanor.

History of Pen §36.07: Acts 1991, 72nd Leg., ch. 304, §4.03, eff. Jan. 1, 1992. Amended by Acts 1993, 73rd Leg., ch. 900, §1.01, eff. Sept. 1, 1994.

PEN §36.08. GIFT TO PUBLIC SERVANT BY PERSON SUBJECT TO HIS JURISDICTION

(a) A public servant in an agency performing regulatory functions or conducting inspections or investigations commits an offense if he solicits, accepts, or agrees to accept any benefit from a person the public servant knows to be subject to regulation, inspection, or investigation by the public servant or his agency.

(b) A public servant in an agency having custody of prisoners commits an offense if he solicits, accepts, or agrees to accept any benefit from a person the public servant knows to be in his custody or the custody of his agency.

(c) A public servant in an agency carrying on civil or criminal litigation on behalf of government commits an offense if he solicits, accepts, or agrees to accept any benefit from a person against whom the public servant knows litigation is pending or contemplated by the public servant or his agency.

(d) A public servant who exercises discretion in connection with contracts, purchases, payments, claims, or other pecuniary transactions of government commits an offense if he solicits, accepts, or agrees to accept any benefit from a person the public servant knows is interested in or likely to become interested in any contract, purchase, payment, claim, or transaction involving the exercise of his discretion.

(e) A public servant who has judicial or administrative authority, who is employed by or in a tribunal having judicial or administrative authority, or who participates in the enforcement of the tribunal's decision, commits an offense if he solicits, accepts, or agrees to accept any benefit from a person the public servant knows is interested in or likely to become interested in any matter before the public servant or tribunal.

(f) A member of the legislature, the governor, the lieutenant governor, or a person employed by a member of the legislature, the governor, the lieutenant governor, or an agency of the legislature commits an offense if he solicits, accepts, or agrees to accept any benefit from any person.

(g) A public servant who is a hearing examiner employed by an agency performing regulatory functions and who conducts hearings in contested cases commits an offense if the public servant solicits, accepts, or agrees to accept any benefit from any person who is appearing before the agency in a contested case, who is doing business with the agency, or who the public servant knows is interested in any matter before the public servant. The exception provided by Section 36.10(b) does not apply to a benefit under this subsection.

(h) An offense under this section is a Class A misdemeanor.

(i) A public servant who receives an unsolicited benefit that the public servant is prohibited from accepting under this section may donate the benefit to a governmental entity that has the authority to accept the gift or may donate the benefit to a recognized tax-exempt charitable organization formed for educational, religious, or scientific purposes.

History of Pen §36.08: Acts 1973, 63rd Leg., ch. 399, §1, eff. Jan. 1, 1974. Amended by Acts 1975, 64th Leg., ch. 342, §11, eff. Sept. 1, 1975; Acts 1983, 68th Leg., ch. 558, §5, eff. Sept. 1, 1983; Acts 1991, 72nd Leg., ch. 304, §4.04, eff. Jan. 1, 1992; Acts 1993, 73rd Leg., ch. 900, §1.01, eff. Sept. 1, 1994.

PEN §36.09. OFFERING GIFT TO PUBLIC SERVANT

(a) A person commits an offense if he offers, confers, or agrees to confer any benefit on a public servant that he knows the public servant is prohibited by law from accepting.

(b) An offense under this section is a Class A misdemeanor.

History of Pen §36.09: Acts 1973, 63rd Leg., ch. 399, §1, eff. Jan. 1, 1974.

PEN §36.10. NON-APPLICABLE

(a) Sections 36.08 (Gift to Public Servant) and 36.09 (Offering Gift to Public Servant) do not apply to:

(1) a fee prescribed by law to be received by a public servant or any other benefit to which the public servant is lawfully entitled or for which he gives legitimate consideration in a capacity other than as a public servant;

(2) a gift or other benefit conferred on account of kinship or a personal, professional, or business relationship independent of the official status of the recipient; or

(3) a benefit to a public servant required to file a statement under Chapter 572, Government Code, or a report under Title 15, Election Code, that is derived from a function in honor or appreciation of the recipient if:

(A) the benefit and the source of any benefit in excess of $50 is reported in the statement; and

(B) the benefit is used solely to defray the expenses that accrue in the performance of duties or activities in connection with the office which are nonreimbursable by the state or political subdivision;

(4) a political contribution as defined by Title 15, Election Code;

(5) a gift, award, or memento to a member of the legislative or executive branch that is required to be reported under Chapter 305, Government Code;

(6) an item with a value of less than $50, excluding cash or a negotiable instrument as described by Section 3.104, Business & Commerce Code; or

(7) an item issued by a governmental entity that allows the use of property or facilities owned, leased, or operated by the governmental entity.

(b) Section 36.08 (Gift to Public Servant) does not apply to food, lodging, transportation, or entertainment accepted as a guest and, if the donee is required by law to report those items, reported by the donee in accordance with that law.

(c) Section 36.09 (Offering Gift to Public Servant) does not apply to food, lodging, transportation, or entertainment accepted as a guest and, if the donor is required by law to report those items, reported by the donor in accordance with that law.

(d) Section 36.08 (Gift to Public Servant) does not apply to a gratuity accepted and reported in accordance with Section 11.0262, Parks and Wildlife Code. Section 36.09 (Offering Gift to Public Servant) does not apply to a gratuity that is offered in accordance with Section 11.0262, Parks and Wildlife Code.

History of Pen §36.10: Acts 1973, 63rd Leg., ch. 399, §1, eff. Jan. 1, 1974. Amended by Acts 1975, 64th Leg., ch. 342, §11, eff. Sept. 1, 1975; Acts 1981, 67th Leg., p. 2707, ch. 738, §1, eff. Jan. 1, 1982; Acts 1983, 68th Leg., ch. 558, §6, eff. Sept. 1, 1983; Acts 1987, 70th Leg., ch. 472, §60, eff. Sept. 1, 1987; Acts 1991, 72nd Leg., ch. 304, §4.05, eff. Jan. 1, 1992; Acts 1993, 73rd Leg., ch. 900, §1.01, eff. Sept. 1, 1994; Acts 1995, 74th Leg., ch. 76, §5.95(38), eff. Sept. 1, 1995; Acts 2005, 79th Leg., ch. 639, §2, eff. Sept. 1, 2005.

CHAPTER 37. PERJURY & OTHER FALSIFICATION

PEN §37.01. DEFINITIONS

In this chapter:

(1) "Court record" means a decree, judgment, order, subpoena, warrant, minutes, or other document issued by a court of:

(A) this state;

(B) another state;

(C) the United States;

(D) a foreign country recognized by an act of congress or a treaty or other international convention to which the United States is a party;

For a quick reference of penalties, see the Chart of Penalties on p. 675.

O'CONNOR'S CRIMINAL CODES 853

PEN §37.01

(E) an Indian tribe recognized by the United States; or

(F) any other jurisdiction, territory, or protectorate entitled to full faith and credit in this state under the United States Constitution.

(2) "Governmental record" means:

(A) anything belonging to, received by, or kept by government for information, including a court record;

(B) anything required by law to be kept by others for information of government;

(C) a license, certificate, permit, seal, title, letter of patent, or similar document issued by government, by another state, or by the United States;

(D) a standard proof of motor vehicle liability insurance form described by Section 601.081, Transportation Code, a certificate of an insurance company described by Section 601.083 of that code, a document purporting to be such a form or certificate that is not issued by an insurer authorized to write motor vehicle liability insurance in this state, an electronic submission in a form described by Section 502.153(i), Transportation Code, or an evidence of financial responsibility described by Section 601.053 of that code;

(E) an official ballot or other election record; or

 (F) the written documentation a mobile food unit is required to obtain under Section 437.0074, Health and Safety Code.

(3) "Statement" means any representation of fact.

History of Pen §37.01: Acts 1973, 63rd Leg., ch. 399, §1, eff. Jan. 1, 1974. Amended by Acts 1991, 72nd Leg., ch. 113, §3, eff. Sept. 1, 1991; Acts 1993, 73rd Leg., ch. 900, §1.01, eff. Sept. 1, 1994; Acts 1997, 75th Leg., ch. 189, §5 (eff. Sept. 1, 1997), ch. 823, §3 (eff. Sept. 1, 1997); Acts 1999, 76th Leg., ch. 659, §1, eff. Sept. 1, 1999; Acts 2003, 78th Leg., ch. 393, §21, eff. Sept. 1, 2003; Acts 2007, 80th Leg., ch. 1276, §2, eff. Sept. 1, 2007.

ANNOTATIONS

Governmental Record

State v. Vasilas, 187 S.W.3d 486, 487 (Tex.Crim. App.2006). "We granted the State's petition for discretionary review to decide whether a petition for expunction qualifies as a 'governmental record' under §37.01…. We will resolve whether pleadings *filed with* but not *issued* by a court fall within the definition of a governmental record pursuant to §37.01(2)(A). *At 491:* We conclude that the legislature's definition of a governmental record is clear and unambiguous and may include a court record, such as the petition for expunction at issue."

PEN §37.02. PERJURY

(a) A person commits an offense if, with intent to deceive and with knowledge of the statement's meaning:

(1) he makes a false statement under oath or swears to the truth of a false statement previously made and the statement is required or authorized by law to be made under oath; or

(2) he makes a false unsworn declaration under Chapter 132, Civil Practice and Remedies Code.

(b) An offense under this section is a Class A misdemeanor.

History of Pen §37.02: Acts 1973, 63rd Leg., ch. 399, §1, eff. Jan. 1, 1974. Amended by Acts 1993, 73rd Leg., ch. 900, §1.01, eff. Sept. 1, 1994.

ANNOTATIONS

State v. Salinas, 982 S.W.2d 9, 11-12 (Tex.App.— Houston [1st Dist.] 1998, pet. ref'd). "[T]he Election Code provides: 'This code supersedes a conflicting statute outside this code unless this code or the outside statute expressly provides otherwise.' Because neither the Election Code nor the perjury statute expressly provides otherwise, the Election Code supersedes the perjury statute." Held: Prosecution for inaccurate contribution and expenditure reports must be conducted under Election Code.

Martin v. State, 896 S.W.2d 336, 339 (Tex.App.— Amarillo 1995, no pet.). "[S]imply pledging to act truthfully and faithfully before someone authorized to administer oaths constitutes a valid oath. For instance, one orally pledging to the truthfulness 'of statements made or to be made' confirms, by oath, the veracity of those statements. *At 340:* After completing her[ ] [affidavit], and knowing portions thereof to be false, [appellant] swore to its accuracy before a notary public. At that instant, the crime became choate."

Brasher v. State, 715 S.W.2d 827, 831 (Tex.App.— Houston [14th Dist.] 1986, no pet.). A "witness cannot be guilty of perjury in giving his opinion as to the legal effect of facts about which he is to testify. [¶] [A] person who swears to facts in an affidavit made on affirmation or belief can be indicted for perjury. … A person who willfully swears falsely to a belief in the existence of a fact which he knows does not exist is as guilty of perjury as if he had sworn directly to the existence of a fact which he knew did not exist."

PEN §37.03. AGGRAVATED PERJURY

(a) A person commits an offense if he commits perjury as defined in Section 37.02, and the false statement:

(1) is made during or in connection with an official proceeding; and

(2) is material.

(b) An offense under this section is a felony of the third degree.

History of Pen §37.03: Acts 1973, 63rd Leg., ch. 399, §1, eff. Jan. 1, 1974. Amended by Acts 1993, 73rd Leg., ch. 900, §1.01, eff. Sept. 1, 1994.

ANNOTATIONS

Pack v. State, 223 S.W.3d 697, 700 (Tex.App.—Texarkana 2007, pet. ref'd). "To establish aggravated perjury, the State must prove that the defendant, (1) with intent to deceive and (2) with knowledge of the statement's meaning, (3) made a false statement under oath, (4) that was required or authorized by law to be made under oath, (5) in connection with an official proceeding, and that (6) the false statement was material."

PEN §37.04. MATERIALITY

(a) A statement is material, regardless of the admissibility of the statement under the rules of evidence, if it could have affected the course or outcome of the official proceeding.

(b) It is no defense to prosecution under Section 37.03 (Aggravated Perjury) that the declarant mistakenly believed the statement to be immaterial.

(c) Whether a statement is material in a given factual situation is a question of law.

History of Pen §37.04: Acts 1973, 63rd Leg., ch. 399, §1, eff. Jan. 1, 1974. Amended by Acts 1993, 73rd Leg., ch. 900, §1.01, eff. Sept. 1, 1994.

ANNOTATIONS

U.S. v. Gaudin, 515 U.S. 506, 522-23, 115 S.Ct. 2310, 2320 (1995). "The [U.S.] Constitution gives a criminal defendant the right to have a jury determine, beyond a reasonable doubt, his guilt of every element of the crime with which he is charged. [A] trial judge's refusal to allow the jury to pass on the 'materiality' of [a defendant's] false statements infringe[s] that right."

Mitchell v. State, 608 S.W.2d 226, 228 (Tex.Crim. App.1980). "'[M]ateriality' refers to 'misstatements having some substantial potential for obstructing justice' and excludes 'utterly trivial falsifications.'"

State v. Rosenbaum, 910 S.W.2d 934, 948 (Tex. Crim.App.1995) (Clinton, J., dissenting), *reh'g adopting dissent as maj. opinion*, 910 S.W.2d 934, 948 (Tex. Crim.App.1995). "[I]n a pretrial setting there is no constitutional or statutory authority for an accused to raise and for a trial court to determine sufficiency of evidence to support or defeat an alleged element of an offense such as 'materiality' in a perjury case."

Ly v. State, 931 S.W.2d 22, 24 (Tex.App.—Houston [1st Dist.] 1996, no pet.). "[S]ection 37.04(a) expressly renders evidentiary materiality moot. The only prerequisite for a false statement to be material for purposes of aggravated perjury is whether it could affect the course or outcome of the proceeding. The extent of additional materiality is not important; perjury may be assigned on false statements as to facts that are collaterally, remotely, or circumstantially material."

PEN §37.05. RETRACTION

It is a defense to prosecution under Section 37.03 (Aggravated Perjury) that the actor retracted his false statement:

(1) before completion of the testimony at the official proceeding; and

(2) before it became manifest that the falsity of the statement would be exposed.

History of Pen §37.05: Acts 1973, 63rd Leg., ch. 399, §1, eff. Jan. 1, 1974. Amended by Acts 1993, 73rd Leg., ch. 900, §1.01, eff. Sept. 1, 1994.

PEN §37.06. INCONSISTENT STATEMENTS

An information or indictment for perjury under Section 37.02 or aggravated perjury under Section 37.03 that alleges that the declarant has made statements under oath, both of which cannot be true, need not allege which statement is false. At the trial the prosecution need not prove which statement is false.

History of Pen §37.06: Acts 1973, 63rd Leg., ch. 399, §1, eff. Jan. 1, 1974. Amended by Acts 1993, 73rd Leg., ch. 900, §1.01, eff. Sept. 1, 1994.

ANNOTATIONS

Ex parte Tamez, 4 S.W.3d 854, 857 (Tex.App.—Houston [1st Dist.] 1999), *aff'd*, 38 S.W.3d 159 (Tex. Crim.App.2001). "[A]ppellant concedes the first statement (barred by statute of limitations) was false but claims the second (not barred by statute of limitations) was true, which bars her prosecution. [¶] [Pen. Code] §37.06 creates an entirely separate offense, and defines conduct for purposes of jurisdiction, punishment,

For a quick reference of penalties, see the Chart of Penalties on p. 675.

O'CONNOR'S CRIMINAL CODES 855

PEN §37.06

and periods of limitations from prosecution. Therefore, appellant's first statement was only one part of her crime, which was not completed for limitations purposes until she made her second, inconsistent statement."

PEN §37.07. IRREGULARITIES NO DEFENSE

(a) It is no defense to prosecution under Section 37.02 (Perjury) or 37.03 (Aggravated Perjury) that the oath was administered or taken in an irregular manner, or that there was some irregularity in the appointment or qualification of the person who administered the oath.

(b) It is no defense to prosecution under Section 37.02 (Perjury) or 37.03 (Aggravated Perjury) that a document was not sworn to if the document contains a recital that it was made under oath, the declarant was aware of the recital when he signed the document, and the document contains the signed jurat of a public servant authorized to administer oaths.

History of Pen §37.07: Acts 1973, 63rd Leg., ch. 399, §1, eff. Jan. 1, 1974. Amended by Acts 1993, 73rd Leg., ch. 900, §1.01, eff. Sept. 1, 1994.

PEN §37.08. FALSE REPORT TO PEACE OFFICER OR LAW ENFORCEMENT EMPLOYEE

(a) A person commits an offense if, with intent to deceive, he knowingly makes a false statement that is material to a criminal investigation and makes the statement to:

(1) a peace officer conducting the investigation; or

(2) any employee of a law enforcement agency that is authorized by the agency to conduct the investigation and that the actor knows is conducting the investigation.

(b) In this section, "law enforcement agency" has the meaning assigned by Article 59.01, Code of Criminal Procedure.

(c) An offense under this section is a Class B misdemeanor.

History of Pen §37.08: Acts 1973, 63rd Leg., ch. 399, §1, eff. Jan. 1, 1974. Amended by Acts 1993, 73rd Leg., ch. 900, §1.01, eff. Sept. 1, 1994; Acts 1997, 75th Leg., ch. 925, §1, eff. Sept. 1, 1997.

PEN §37.081. FALSE REPORT REGARDING MISSING CHILD OR MISSING PERSON

(a) A person commits an offense if, with intent to deceive, the person knowingly:

(1) files a false report of a missing child or missing person with a law enforcement officer or agency; or

(2) makes a false statement to a law enforcement officer or other employee of a law enforcement agency relating to a missing child or missing person.

(b) An offense under this section is a Class C misdemeanor.

History of Pen §37.081: Acts 1999, 76th Leg., ch. 200, §3, eff. Sept. 1, 1999.

PEN §37.09. TAMPERING WITH OR FABRICATING PHYSICAL EVIDENCE

(a) A person commits an offense if, knowing that an investigation or official proceeding is pending or in progress, he:

(1) alters, destroys, or conceals any record, document, or thing with intent to impair its verity, legibility, or availability as evidence in the investigation or official proceeding; or

(2) makes, presents, or uses any record, document, or thing with knowledge of its falsity and with intent to affect the course or outcome of the investigation or official proceeding.

(b) This section shall not apply if the record, document, or thing concealed is privileged or is the work product of the parties to the investigation or official proceeding.

A *Subsections (c) & (d) below are effective for offenses committed on or after Sept. 1, 2007.*

(c) An offense under Subsection (a) or Subsection (d)(1) is a felony of the third degree, unless the thing altered, destroyed, or concealed is a human corpse, in which case the offense is a felony of the second degree. An offense under Subsection (d)(2) is a Class A misdemeanor.

(d) A person commits an offense if the person:

(1) knowing that an offense has been committed, alters, destroys, or conceals any record, document, or thing with intent to impair its verity, legibility, or availability as evidence in any subsequent investigation of or official proceeding related to the offense; or

(2) observes a human corpse under circumstances in which a reasonable person would believe that an offense had been committed, knows or reasonably should know that a law enforcement agency is not aware of the existence of or location of the corpse, and fails to report the existence of and location of the corpse to a law enforcement agency.

Subsections (c) & (d) below are effective for offenses in which any element of the offense was committed before Sept. 1, 2007.

(c) An offense under Subsection (a) or Subsection (d)(1) is a felony of the third degree. An offense under Subsection (d)(2) is a Class A misdemeanor.

(d) A person commits an offense if the person:

(1) knowing that an offense has been committed, alters, destroys, or conceals any record, document, or thing with intent to impair its verity, legibility, or availability as evidence in any subsequent investigation of or official proceeding related to the offense; or

(2) observes human remains under circumstances in which a reasonable person would believe that an offense had been committed, knows or reasonably should know that a law enforcement agency is not aware of the existence of or location of the remains, and fails to report the existence of and location of the remains to a law enforcement agency.

E *Subsection (e) below is effective for offenses committed on or after Sept. 1, 2007.*

(e) In this section, "human corpse" has the meaning assigned by Section 42.08.

History of Pen §37.09: Acts 1973, 63rd Leg., ch. 399, §1, eff. Jan. 1, 1974. Amended by Acts 1991, 72nd Leg., ch. 565, §4, eff. Sept. 1, 1991; Acts 1997, 75th Leg., ch. 1284, §1, eff. Sept. 1, 1997; Acts 2007, 80th Leg., ch. 287, §1, eff. Sept. 1, 2007.

ANNOTATIONS

Stewart v. State, 240 S.W.3d 872, 874 (Tex.Crim. App.2007). "It is not enough that appellant *knew* that his action would impair the availability of the marihuana as evidence. He must have *intended* to impair its availability. That is, impairing the marihuana's availability as evidence must have been appellant's conscious objective or desire. The court of appeals erred in analyzing the sufficiency of the evidence for the culpable mental state of knowledge when the statute proscribes the higher culpable mental state of intent." *See also* **Hollingsworth v. State**, 15 S.W.3d 586, 595 (Tex. App.—Austin 2000, no pet.).

Rotenberry v. State, 245 S.W.3d 583, 586 (Tex. App.—Fort Worth 2007, pet. ref'd). "[T]he State charged Appellant with concealing physical evidence [under §37.09(a)(1)] by telling [officer] that he did not know where [decedent's body] was. [¶] The State's theory of liability is flawed because when Appellant lied to [officer], he concealed *information*, not

physical evidence. Section 37.09 criminalizes the concealment of physical evidence, not the concealment of information."

Waldrop v. State, 219 S.W.3d 531, 535 (Tex.App.—Texarkana 2007, no pet.). Section 37.09(a)(2) "does not require that the actor present the evidence directly to each agency investigating the matter. [¶] To read into the statute that an actor would have to turn over falsified evidence directly to each agency that may have become involved would render the statute unworkable in the reality of complex investigations."

Lumpkin v. State, 129 S.W.3d 659, 663 (Tex.App.—Houston [1st Dist.] 2004, pet. ref'd). "[T]he State alleged only that appellant knew that an investigation was 'in progress,' not that one was 'pending.' The investigation that was in progress was a traffic stop. Appellant had already swallowed the cocaine before the investigation that was in progress became one concerning narcotics. Thus, we have a case in which the State elected to allege the wrong culpable mental state with which the tampering-with-evidence offense was committed. We have no choice but to hold the evidence legally insufficient to support the State's allegation, which was tracked in the jury charge." *See also* **Pannell v. State**, 7 S.W.3d 222, 224 (Tex.App.—Dallas 1999, pet. ref'd) (throwing small amount of marijuana from car legally insufficient).

Carrion v. State, 926 S.W.2d 625, 627 (Tex.App.—Eastland 1996, pet. ref'd). "We find no cases where solely giving a false statement rises to the level of fabricating physical evidence."

Brosky v. State, 915 S.W.2d 120, 144 (Tex.App.—Fort Worth 1996, pet. ref'd). "[F]or a person's actions to fall within ... §37.09, a separate criminal offense must *already* have been committed; otherwise, the actor could not 'kn[ow]' that an investigation ... is pending.'"

Spector v. State, 746 S.W.2d 945, 946 (Tex.App.—Austin 1988, no pet.). "We believe something is destroyed within the meaning of [Pen. Code] §37.09(a)(1) when its evidentiary value is destroyed. Form changes without a loss of evidentiary value are mere *attempts* to destroy or alterations. [¶] [T]he only way evidence can be destroyed when part is recovered is when the part recovered has less evidentiary value than the whole."

For a quick reference of penalties, see the Chart of Penalties on p. 675.

O'CONNOR'S CRIMINAL CODES 857

PEN §37.10. TAMPERING WITH GOVERNMENTAL RECORD

(a) A person commits an offense if he:

(1) knowingly makes a false entry in, or false alteration of, a governmental record;

(2) makes, presents, or uses any record, document, or thing with knowledge of its falsity and with intent that it be taken as a genuine governmental record;

(3) intentionally destroys, conceals, removes, or otherwise impairs the verity, legibility, or availability of a governmental record;

(4) possesses, sells, or offers to sell a governmental record or a blank governmental record form with intent that it be used unlawfully;

(5) makes, presents, or uses a governmental record with knowledge of its falsity; or

(6) possesses, sells, or offers to sell a governmental record or a blank governmental record form with knowledge that it was obtained unlawfully.

(b) It is an exception to the application of Subsection (a)(3) that the governmental record is destroyed pursuant to legal authorization or transferred under Section 441.204, Government Code. With regard to the destruction of a local government record, legal authorization includes compliance with the provisions of Subtitle C, Title 6, Local Government Code.

A *Subsection (c)(1) below is effective for offenses committed on or after Sept. 1, 2007.*

(c)(1) Except as provided by Subdivisions (2), (3), and (4) and by Subsection (d), an offense under this section is a Class A misdemeanor unless the actor's intent is to defraud or harm another, in which event the offense is a state jail felony.

Subsection (1) below is effective for offenses in which any element of the offense was committed before Sept. 1, 2007.

(1) Except as provided by Subdivisions (2) and (3) and by Subsection (d), an offense under this section is a Class A misdemeanor unless the actor's intent is to defraud or harm another, in which event the offense is a state jail felony.

(2) An offense under this section is a felony of the third degree if it is shown on the trial of the offense that the governmental record was a public school record, report, or assessment instrument required under Chapter 39, Education Code, or was a license, certificate, permit, seal, title, letter of patent, or similar document issued by government, by another state, or by the United States, unless the actor's intent is to defraud or harm another, in which event the offense is a felony of the second degree.

(3) An offense under this section is a Class C misdemeanor if it is shown on the trial of the offense that the governmental record is a governmental record that is required for enrollment of a student in a school district and was used by the actor to establish the residency of the student.

E *Subsection (4) below is effective for offenses committed on or after Sept. 1, 2007.*

(4) An offense under this section is a Class B misdemeanor if it is shown on the trial of the offense that the governmental record is a written appraisal filed with an appraisal review board under Section 41.43(a-1), Tax Code, that was performed by a person who had a contingency interest in the outcome of the appraisal review board hearing.

(d) An offense under this section, if it is shown on the trial of the offense that the governmental record is described by Section 37.01(2)(D), is:

(1) a Class B misdemeanor if the offense is committed under Subsection (a)(2) or Subsection (a)(5) and the defendant is convicted of presenting or using the record;

(2) a felony of the third degree if the offense is committed under:

(A) Subsection (a)(1), (3), (4), or (6); or

(B) Subsection (a)(2) or (5) and the defendant is convicted of making the record; and

(3) a felony of the second degree, notwithstanding Subdivisions (1) and (2), if the actor's intent in committing the offense was to defraud or harm another.

(e) It is an affirmative defense to prosecution for possession under Subsection (a)(6) that the possession occurred in the actual discharge of official duties as a public servant.

(f) It is a defense to prosecution under Subsection (a)(1), (a)(2), or (a)(5) that the false entry or false information could have no effect on the government's purpose for requiring the governmental record.

(g) A person is presumed to intend to defraud or harm another if the person acts with respect to two or more of the same type of governmental records or blank governmental record forms and if each governmental record or blank governmental record form is a license, certificate, permit, seal, title, or similar document issued by government.

(h) If conduct that constitutes an offense under this section also constitutes an offense under Section 32.48 or 37.13, the actor may be prosecuted under any of those sections.

(i) With the consent of the appropriate local county or district attorney, the attorney general has concurrent jurisdiction with that consenting local prosecutor to prosecute an offense under this section that involves the state Medicaid program.

History of Pen §37.10: Acts 1973, 63rd Leg., ch. 399, §1, eff. Jan. 1, 1974. Amended by Acts 1989, 71st Leg., ch. 1248, §66, eff. Sept. 1, 1989; Acts 1991, 72nd Leg., ch. 113, §4 (eff. Sept. 1, 1991), ch. 565, §5 (eff. Sept. 1, 1991); Acts 1993, 73rd Leg., ch. 900, §1.01, eff. Sept. 1, 1994; Acts 1997, 75th Leg., ch. 189, §6 (eff. May 21, 1997), ch. 823, §4 (eff. May 21, 1997); Acts 1999, 76th Leg., ch. 659, §2 (eff. Sept. 1, 1999), ch. 718, §1 (eff. Sept. 1, 1999); Acts 2001, 77th Leg., ch. 771, §3, eff. June 13, 2001; Acts 2003, 78th Leg., ch. 198, §2.139 (eff. Sept. 1, 2003), ch. 257, §16 (eff. Sept. 1, 2003); Acts 2005, 79th Leg., ch. 1364, §1, eff. June 18, 2005; Acts 2007, 80th Leg., ch. 1085, §2, eff. Sept. 1, 2007.

ANNOTATIONS

State v. Maitland, 993 S.W.2d 880, 881 (Tex. App.—Fort Worth 1999, no pet.). "[W]e are asked to decide whether in a prosecution for the offense of making a false entry in a governmental record under §37.10(a)(1), the 5th Amendment privilege against self-incrimination bars admission of the statement which forms the basis of the charged offense. We hold that it does not."

Fleming v. State, 958 S.W.2d 846, 847 (Tex.App.—Eastland 1997, no pet.). "Under [Gov't Code] §601.087 ... only one of the 7 types of evidence of financial responsibility listed in §601.053 is a governmental record: the standard proof of liability form. In order to give effect to §601.087, we must presume that the legislature specifically intended for tampering with a standard proof of liability form to be an offense punishable under [Pen. Code §37.10]. Forging any of the 6 other types of evidence of financial responsibility remains an offense under [Gov't Code] §601.196 but is not an offense under §37.10. Reading the statutes to give effect to both §601.087 and §601.196, we find no irreconcilable conflict."

PEN §37.101. FRAUDULENT FILING OF FINANCING STATEMENT

(a) A person commits an offense if the person knowingly presents for filing or causes to be presented for filing a financing statement that the person knows:

(1) is forged;

(2) contains a material false statement; or

(3) is groundless.

(b) An offense under Subsection (a)(1) is a felony of the third degree, unless it is shown on the trial of the offense that the person had previously been convicted under this section on two or more occasions, in which event the offense is a felony of the second degree. An offense under Subsection (a)(2) or (a)(3) is a Class A misdemeanor, unless the person commits the offense with the intent to defraud or harm another, in which event the offense is a state jail felony.

History of Pen §37.101: Acts 1997, 75th Leg., ch. 189, §10, eff. May 21, 1997.

PEN §37.11. IMPERSONATING PUBLIC SERVANT

(a) A person commits an offense if he:

(1) impersonates a public servant with intent to induce another to submit to his pretended official authority or to rely on his pretended official acts; or

(2) knowingly purports to exercise any function of a public servant or of a public office, including that of a judge and court, and the position or office through which he purports to exercise a function of a public servant or public office has no lawful existence under the constitution or laws of this state or of the United States.

(b) An offense under this section is a felony of the third degree.

History of Pen §37.11: Acts 1973, 63rd Leg., ch. 399, §1, eff. Jan. 1, 1974. Amended by Acts 1997, 75th Leg., ch. 189, §7, eff. May 21, 1997.

ANNOTATIONS

Rice v. State, 195 S.W.3d 876, 882 (Tex.App.—Dallas 2006, pet. ref'd). "[S]ection 37.11 is not limited to only those persons impersonating officers, employees, or agents of the State of Texas, but includes persons impersonating officers, employees, or agents of other states."

Tovar v. State, 777 S.W.2d 481, 489 (Tex.App.—Corpus Christi 1989, pet. ref'd). "To violate §37.11(a), there must be a false assumption or pretension by a person that he is a public servant and overt action in this capacity."

For a quick reference of penalties, see the Chart of Penalties on p. 675.

O'CONNOR'S CRIMINAL CODES 859

PEN §37.12. FALSE IDENTIFICATION AS PEACE OFFICER; MISREPRESENTATION OF PROPERTY

(a) A person commits an offense if:

(1) the person makes, provides to another person, or possesses a card, document, badge, insignia, shoulder emblem, or other item bearing an insignia of a law enforcement agency that identifies a person as a peace officer or a reserve law enforcement officer; and

(2) the person who makes, provides, or possesses the item bearing the insignia knows that the person so identified by the item is not commissioned as a peace officer or reserve law enforcement officer as indicated on the item.

(b) It is a defense to prosecution under this section that:

(1) the card, document, badge, insignia, shoulder emblem, or other item bearing an insignia of a law enforcement agency clearly identifies the person as an honorary or junior peace officer or reserve law enforcement officer, or as a member of a junior posse;

(2) the person identified as a peace officer or reserve law enforcement officer by the item bearing the insignia was commissioned in that capacity when the item was made; or

(3) the item was used or intended for use exclusively for decorative purposes or in an artistic or dramatic presentation.

(c) In this section, "reserve law enforcement officer" has the same meaning as is given that term in Section 1701.001, Occupations Code.

(d) A person commits an offense if the person intentionally or knowingly misrepresents an object as property belonging to a law enforcement agency.

(e) An offense under this section is a Class B misdemeanor.

History of Pen §37.12: Acts 1983, 68th Leg., ch. 1075, §1, eff. Sept. 1, 1983. Amended by Acts 1987, 70th Leg., ch. 514, §1, eff. Sept. 1, 1987; Acts 1993, 73rd Leg., ch. 900, §1.01, eff. Sept. 1, 1994; Acts 2001, 77th Leg., ch. 1420, §14.831, eff. Sept. 1, 2001.

ANNOTATIONS

Gatewood v. State, 156 S.W.3d 679, 681 (Tex. App.—Amarillo 2005, pet. ref'd). "[T]he office of 'sheriff' in Texas constitutes an 'official' law enforcement agency. This, coupled with the evidence that the word 'sheriff' appeared on the badge appellant wore, the badge likened to others utilized by official law enforcement agencies in Texas, the badge contained a lone star (our state's emblem), and the word 'Texas' appeared in the star, constitutes sufficient evidence upon which a fact finder could rationally conclude, beyond reasonable doubt, that appellant possessed an insignia of an official law enforcement agency identifying him as a commissioned peace officer. And, that the badge may have also contained language of an entity falling outside the scope of such an agency does not require us to hold otherwise."

Fallin v. State, 93 S.W.3d 394, 396 (Tex.App.—Houston [14th Dist.] 2002, pet. ref'd). "Because an offense under §37.12 requires a finding of conduct satisfying both (a)(1) and (a)(2), we conclude the only reasonable construction of the statute as a whole is that the item possessed, whether or not specifically identified in subsection (a)(1), must bear an insignia of a law enforcement agency. [¶] We find the phrase 'an insignia of a law enforcement agency' ... unambiguously refers to any distinguishing mark that identifies the item as one originating from an official law enforcement agency."

PEN §37.13. RECORD OF A FRAUDULENT COURT

(a) A person commits an offense if the person makes, presents, or uses any document or other record with:

(1) knowledge that the document or other record is not a record of a court created under or established by the constitution or laws of this state or of the United States; and

(2) the intent that the document or other record be given the same legal effect as a record of a court created under or established by the constitution or laws of this state or of the United States.

(b) An offense under this section is a Class A misdemeanor, except that the offense is a felony of the third degree if it is shown on the trial of the offense that the defendant has previously been convicted under this section on two or more occasions.

(c) If conduct that constitutes an offense under this section also constitutes an offense under Section 32.48 or 37.10, the actor may be prosecuted under any of those sections.

History of Pen §37.13: Acts 1997, 75th Leg., ch. 189, §8, eff. May 21, 1997.

PEN §38.01. DEFINITIONS

In this chapter:

(1) "Custody" means:

(A) under arrest by a peace officer or under restraint by a public servant pursuant to an order of a court of this state or another state of the United States; or

(B) under restraint by an agent or employee of a facility that is operated by or under contract with the United States and that confines persons arrested for, charged with, or convicted of criminal offenses.

(2) "Escape" means unauthorized departure from custody or failure to return to custody following temporary leave for a specific purpose or limited period or leave that is part of an intermittent sentence, but does not include a violation of conditions of community supervision or parole other than conditions that impose a period of confinement in a secure correctional facility.

(3) "Economic benefit" means anything reasonably regarded as an economic gain or advantage, including accepting or offering to accept employment for a fee, accepting or offering to accept a fee, entering into a fee contract, or accepting or agreeing to accept money or anything of value.

(4) "Finance" means to provide funds or capital or to furnish with necessary funds.

(5) "Fugitive from justice" means a person for whom a valid arrest warrant has been issued.

(6) "Governmental function" includes any activity that a public servant is lawfully authorized to undertake on behalf of government.

(7) "Invest funds" means to commit money to earn a financial return.

(8) "Member of the family" means anyone related within the third degree of consanguinity or affinity, as determined under Chapter 573, Government Code.

(9) "Qualified nonprofit organization" means a nonprofit organization that meets the following conditions:

(A) the primary purposes of the organization do not include the rendition of legal services or education regarding legal services;

(B) the recommending, furnishing, paying for, or educating persons regarding legal services is incidental and reasonably related to the primary purposes of the organization;

(C) the organization does not derive a financial benefit from the rendition of legal services by a lawyer; and

(D) the person for whom the legal services are rendered, and not the organization, is recognized as the client of a lawyer.

(10) "Public media" means a telephone directory or legal directory, newspaper or other periodical, billboard or other sign, radio or television broadcast, recorded message the public may access by dialing a telephone number, or a written communication not prohibited by Section 38.12(d).

(11) "Solicit employment" means to communicate in person or by telephone with a prospective client or a member of the prospective client's family concerning

For a quick reference of penalties, see the Chart of Penalties on p. 675.

O'CONNOR'S CRIMINAL CODES 861

professional employment within the scope of a professional's license, registration, or certification arising out of a particular occurrence or event, or series of occurrences or events, or concerning an existing problem of the prospective client within the scope of the professional's license, registration, or certification, for the purpose of providing professional services to the prospective client, when neither the person receiving the communication nor anyone acting on that person's behalf has requested the communication. The term does not include a communication initiated by a family member of the person receiving a communication, a communication by a professional who has a prior or existing professional-client relationship with the person receiving the communication, or communication by an attorney for a qualified nonprofit organization with the organization's members for the purpose of educating the organization's members to understand the law, to recognize legal problems, to make intelligent selection of legal counsel, or to use available legal services. The term does not include an advertisement by a professional through public media.

(12) "Professional" means an attorney, chiropractor, physician, surgeon, private investigator, or any other person licensed, certified, or registered by a state agency that regulates a health care profession.

History of Pen §38.01: Acts 1973, 63rd Leg., ch. 399, §1, eff. Jan. 1, 1974. Amended by Acts 1989, 71st Leg., ch. 866, §1, eff. Sept. 1, 1989; Acts 1991, 72nd Leg., ch. 14, §284(14) (eff. Sept. 1, 1991), ch. 561, §42 (eff. Aug. 26, 1991); Acts 1993, 73rd Leg., ch. 723, §1 (eff. Sept. 1, 1993), ch. 900, §1.01 (eff. Sept. 1, 1994); Acts 1995, 74th Leg., ch. 76, §5.95(27) (eff. Sept. 1, 1995), ch. 321, §1.103 (eff. Sept. 1, 1995); Acts 1997, 75th Leg., ch. 293, §2 (eff. Sept. 1, 1997), ch. 750, §1 (eff. Sept. 1, 1997).

ANNOTATIONS

Deltenre v. State, 808 S.W.2d 97, 99 n.5 (Tex.Crim.App.1991). "Escape involves fleeing from the custody of a peace officer or a public servant. The language of this statute envisions two separate theories in which to commit the offense of escape. One may escape from the custody of a peace officer while under detention or arrest, or one may escape from a public servant while under restraint pursuant to an order of a court."

PEN §38.02. FAILURE TO IDENTIFY

(a) A person commits an offense if he intentionally refuses to give his name, residence address, or date of birth to a peace officer who has lawfully arrested the person and requested the information.

(b) A person commits an offense if he intentionally gives a false or fictitious name, residence address, or date of birth to a peace officer who has:

(1) lawfully arrested the person;

(2) lawfully detained the person; or

(3) requested the information from a person that the peace officer has good cause to believe is a witness to a criminal offense.

(c) Except as provided by Subsections (d) and (e), an offense under this section is:

(1) a Class C misdemeanor if the offense is committed under Subsection (a); or

(2) a Class B misdemeanor if the offense is committed under Subsection (b).

(d) If it is shown on the trial of an offense under this section that the defendant was a fugitive from justice at the time of the offense, the offense is:

(1) a Class B misdemeanor if the offense is committed under Subsection (a); or

(2) a Class A misdemeanor if the offense is committed under Subsection (b).

(e) If conduct that constitutes an offense under this section also constitutes an offense under Section 106.07, Alcoholic Beverage Code, the actor may be prosecuted only under Section 106.07.

History of Pen §38.02: Acts 1973, 63rd Leg., ch. 399, §1, eff. Jan. 1, 1974. Amended by Acts 1987, 70th Leg., ch. 869, §1, eff. Sept. 1, 1987; Acts 1991, 72nd Leg., ch. 821, §1, eff. Sept. 1, 1991; Acts 1993, 73rd Leg., ch. 900, §1.01, eff. Sept. 1, 1994; Acts 2003, 78th Leg., ch. 1009, §1, eff. Sept. 1, 2003.

ANNOTATIONS

Ledesma v. State, 677 S.W.2d 529, 531-32 (Tex.Crim.App.1984). "[I]n order to convict a citizen for 'Failure to Identify as Witness', the State must *plead and prove* that the defendant who refused to identify himself knew that the person requesting the information was a peace officer."

Freeman v. State, 45 S.W.3d 655, 656 (Tex.App.—Houston [14th Dist.] 2000, pet. ref'd). "The centerpiece of appellant's appeal is the distinction between 'warrant' and 'capias.' He contends the capias outstanding at the time he gave the allegedly false identification does not satisfy the requirement of a 'valid arrest warrant' which would render him a 'fugitive from justice' as alleged in the information.' *At 657:* We find the intent of the Legislature was to punish those wanted by the law who sought to avoid detection by giving false information. Interpreting the statute to exclude those actors who were wanted only on a capias

Sidebar: PEN §38.01

would be a hypertechnical reading of the law which would thwart the orderly administration of justice and serve no useful purpose."

Quick v. State, 999 S.W.2d 79, 80-81 (Tex.App.—Houston [14th Dist.] 1999, no pet.). "Quick gave the officer a false name after learning the officer's authority and that the officer had a capias warrant to arrest him for a felony; Quick then acknowledged who he was and surrendered himself to the officer. Inasmuch as Quick had not yielded to the officer's show of authority or been physically forced to yield at the time that he gave the officer a false name, Quick had not been detained at that time. He had acknowledged who he was by the time that he yielded to the officer's show of authority. Because Quick was not under arrest or detained at the time that he gave the officer a false name, the evidence was legally insufficient to support his conviction."

PEN §38.03. RESISTING ARREST, SEARCH, OR TRANSPORTATION

(a) A person commits an offense if he intentionally prevents or obstructs a person he knows is a peace officer or a person acting in a peace officer's presence and at his direction from effecting an arrest, search, or transportation of the actor or another by using force against the peace officer or another.

(b) It is no defense to prosecution under this section that the arrest or search was unlawful.

(c) Except as provided in Subsection (d), an offense under this section is a Class A misdemeanor.

(d) An offense under this section is a felony of the third degree if the actor uses a deadly weapon to resist the arrest or search.

History of Pen §38.03: Acts 1973, 63rd Leg., ch. 399, §1, eff. Jan. 1, 1974. Amended by Acts 1991, 72nd Leg., ch. 277, §§1, 2, eff. Sept. 1, 1991; Acts 1993, 73rd Leg., ch. 900, §1.01, eff. Sept. 1, 1994.

ANNOTATIONS

Bowen v. State, 162 S.W.3d 226, 229 (Tex.Crim. App.2005). Pen. Code §38.03 "does not limit the necessity defense's [Pen. Code §9.22] application because a legislative purpose to exclude the defense does not plainly appear in its text. On its face, we cannot glean any clear legislative purpose indicating that the necessity defense is not available."

Clement v. State, 248 S.W.3d 791, 802 (Tex.App.—Fort Worth 2008, no pet.). "Based on the definitions and common usage of ['prevent' and 'obstruct'], we

cannot conclude that they describe different types of conduct. [¶] We adopt the reasoning of the Dallas and Houston Courts of Appeals and join these courts in holding that … §38.03 describes only one offense, but identifies three different means by which it can be committed." *See also* **Finster v. State**, 152 S.W.3d 215, 219 (Tex.App.—Dallas 2004, no pet.). *But see* **Vaughn v. State**, 983 S.W.2d 860, 862 (Tex.App.—Houston [14th Dist.] 1998, no pet.) (3 separate offenses).

Sheehan v. State, 201 S.W.3d 820, 822 (Tex.App.—Waco 2006, no pet.). "The officer testified that, in her opinion, Sheehan had resisted arrest by pulling his arms in to his chest and interlocking them. She also described his conduct as pulling his hands in, holding them tight, refusing to move them, standing up, and moving toward the bunk area [of the jail]. *At 823:* [R]efusing to cooperate with being arrested does not constitute resisting arrest by force. [¶] In this case, there was no evidence of danger of injury to the officers from Sheehan's passive non-cooperation, and thus there was no evidence that Sheehan used force against the officers."

Gary v. State, 195 S.W.3d 339, 341 (Tex.App.—Waco 2006, no pet.). "The activity of releasing a vicious dog to attack an officer goes beyond simply pulling one's arm away or threatening an officer. This action endangered the officer and was sufficient to qualify as 'use of force' within the meaning of the statute."

In re M.C.L., 110 S.W.3d 591, 596 (Tex.App.—Austin 2003, no pet.). "'Effecting an arrest' entails a process or transaction, which has a beginning and an end. A conviction for resisting an arrest requires the obstruction or resistance to occur after the arrest begins but before it ends. *At 597:* The arrest was complete, at the earliest, when M.C.L. was handcuffed and placed on his couch, and at the latest when he was moved to the police car where he remained for at least ten minutes, still handcuffed." Held: D did not resist arrest.

Haliburton v. State, 80 S.W.3d 309, 312-13 (Tex. App.—Fort Worth 2002, no pet.). A "person can forcefully resist an arrest without successfully making physical contact with the one making the arrest. [W]e hold that 'kicking at' does constitute the use of force required under §38.03(a)."

Bryant v. State, 923 S.W.2d 199, 206 (Tex.App.—Waco 1996), *pet. ref'd*, 940 S.W.2d 663 (Tex.Crim. App.1997). "'Striking an arresting officer's arm away constitutes force directed against the officer. This is

For a quick reference of penalties, see the Chart of Penalties on p. 675.

O'CONNOR'S CRIMINAL CODES 863

distinctly different from the direction of force employed in simply pulling one's arm away. There is no danger of injury to the officer in the latter action.' *At 207:* 'Merely trying to flee does not ... involve sufficient force directed at the peace officer to sustain a conviction for resisting arrest.' [¶] Section 38.03 prohibits the use of 'force *against* [a] peace officer or another,' not the use of force *toward* a peace officer." *See also Washington v. State*, 525 S.W.2d 189, 190 (Tex.Crim.App.1975). *But see Pumphrey v. State*, 245 S.W.3d 85, 89 (Tex.App.—Texarkana 2008, pet. filed 3-31-08) (pulling one's arm away is resisting arrest).

Molina v. State, 754 S.W.2d 468, 474 (Tex. App.—San Antonio 1988, no pet.). Pen. Code §38.03 "contemplates resisting an effort to implement traditional arrest and not ... resisting an investigative detention or stop. Clearly the language of §38.03 together with the statutory definition of arrest [CCP art. 15.22] address such an arrest as requires the presence of probable cause or warrant." *See also Vaughn v. State*, 983 S.W.2d 860, 863 (Tex.App.—Houston [14th Dist.] 1998, no pet.).

PEN §38.04. EVADING ARREST OR DETENTION

(a) A person commits an offense if he intentionally flees from a person he knows is a peace officer attempting lawfully to arrest or detain him.

(b) An offense under this section is a Class B misdemeanor, except that the offense is:

(1) a state jail felony if the actor uses a vehicle while the actor is in flight and the actor has not been previously convicted under this section;

(2) a felony of the third degree if:

(A) the actor uses a vehicle while the actor is in flight and the actor has been previously convicted under this section; or

(B) another suffers serious bodily injury as a direct result of an attempt by the officer from whom the actor is fleeing to apprehend the actor while the actor is in flight; or

(3) a felony of the second degree if another suffers death as a direct result of an attempt by the officer from whom the actor is fleeing to apprehend the actor while the actor is in flight.

(c) In this section, "vehicle" has the meaning assigned by Section 541.201, Transportation Code.

(d) A person who is subject to prosecution under both this section and another law may be prosecuted under either or both this section and the other law.

History of Pen §38.04: Acts 1973, 63rd Leg., ch. 399, §1, eff. Jan. 1, 1974. Amended by Acts 1987, 70th Leg., ch. 504, §1, eff. Sept. 1, 1987; Acts 1989, 71st Leg., ch. 126, §1, eff. Sept. 1, 1989; Acts 1993, 73rd Leg., ch. 900, §1.01, eff. Sept. 1, 1994; Acts 1995, 74th Leg., ch. 708, §1, eff. Sept. 1, 1995; Acts 1997, 75th Leg., ch. 165, §30.240, eff. Sept. 1, 1997; Acts 2001, 77th Leg., ch. 1334, §3 (eff. Sept. 1, 2001), ch. 1480, §1 (eff. Sept. 1, 2001).

ANNOTATIONS

Farrakhan v. State, 247 S.W.3d 720, 720 (Tex. Crim.App.2008). "[W]e must determine whether the court of appeals erred in holding that the misdemeanor offense of fleeing [Transp. Code §545.421] is not a lesser-included offense of the felony offense of evading detention with a motor vehicle." Held: The court of appeals did not err.

Calton v. State, 176 S.W.3d 231, 232 (Tex.Crim. App.2005). "Evading arrest is a third-degree felony if the actor uses a vehicle and has previously been convicted of evading arrest. We must decide whether the prior conviction must be proved at the guilt-innocence or punishment stage of trial. We conclude that it must be proved at the guilt stage of trial because the statute presents it as an element of the offense, not as an enhancement provision."

Hobbs v. State, 175 S.W.3d 777, 779 (Tex.Crim.App. 2005). "The grounds upon which we granted discretionary review state: 1) Is felony evading arrest in a motor vehicle a continuing offense after the vehicle is no longer in use? 2) Is it legally possible to enter a habitation with the intent to commit the felony of evading arrest in a motor vehicle when the actor is not in possession of the vehicle?" Held: The answers are "yes" and "yes."

Woods v. State, 153 S.W.3d 413, 415 (Tex.Crim.App. 2005). Is there "constitutional or statutory authority for a defendant to raise, and for a trial court to determine, before trial the legality of a seizure of a defendant in a prosecution for the offense of evading arrest or detention under [Pen. Code] §38.04...? ... We ... conclude that the statutes authorizing pre-trial proceedings [and motions] do not contemplate a 'mini-trial' on the sufficiency of the evidence to support an element of the offense." Held: The issue of the seizure's legality was improperly raised in a pretrial motion to suppress.

Alejos v. State, 555 S.W.2d 444, 449 (Tex.Crim.App. 1977). Section 38.04 "was obviously designed to apply where there has been a non-forceful evasion of arrest

PEN §38.03

under the circumstances to which neither [Pen. Code] §38.03 (resisting arrest) nor [Pen. Code] §38.07 [now 38.06] (escape) is applicable. ... The section's intent is to deter flight from arrest by the threat of an additional penalty, thus discouraging forceful conflicts between the police and suspects. [¶] [Section] 38.04 is general in nature in that it applies to all types of non-forceful evasion of arrest."

PEN §38.05. HINDERING APPREHENSION OR PROSECUTION

(a) A person commits an offense if, with intent to hinder the arrest, prosecution, conviction, or punishment of another for an offense or, with intent to hinder the arrest, detention, adjudication, or disposition of a child for engaging in delinquent conduct that violates a penal law of the state, or with intent to hinder the arrest of another under the authority of a warrant or capias, he:

(1) harbors or conceals the other;

(2) provides or aids in providing the other with any means of avoiding arrest or effecting escape; or

(3) warns the other of impending discovery or apprehension.

(b) It is a defense to prosecution under Subsection (a)(3) that the warning was given in connection with an effort to bring another into compliance with the law.

Ⓐ *Subsection (c) below is effective for offenses committed on or after Sept. 1, 2007.*

(c) Except as provided by Subsection (d), an offense under this section is a Class A misdemeanor.

Subsection (c) below is effective for offenses in which any element of the offense was committed before Sept. 1, 2007.

(c) An offense under this section is a Class A misdemeanor, except that the offense is a felony of the third degree if the person who is harbored, concealed, provided with a means of avoiding arrest or effecting escape, or warned of discovery or apprehension is under arrest for, charged with, or convicted of a felony, or is in custody or detention for, is alleged in a petition to have engaged in, or has been adjudicated as having engaged in delinquent conduct that violates a penal law of the grade of felony, and the person charged under this section knew that the person they harbored, concealed, provided with a means of avoiding arrest or effecting

escape, or warned of discovery or apprehension is under arrest for, charged with, or convicted of a felony, or is in custody or detention for, is alleged in a petition to have engaged in, or has been adjudicated as having engaged in delinquent conduct that violates a penal law of the grade of felony.

Ⓐ *Subsection (d) below is effective for offenses committed on or after Sept. 1, 2007.*

(d) An offense under this section is a felony of the third degree if the person who is harbored, concealed, provided with a means of avoiding arrest or effecting escape, or warned of discovery or apprehension is under arrest for, charged with, or convicted of a felony, including an offense under Section 62.102, Code of Criminal Procedure, or is in custody or detention for, is alleged in a petition to have engaged in, or has been adjudicated as having engaged in delinquent conduct that violates a penal law of the grade of felony, including an offense under Section 62.102, Code of Criminal Procedure, and the person charged under this section knew that the person they harbored, concealed, provided with a means of avoiding arrest or effecting escape, or warned of discovery or apprehension is under arrest for, charged with, or convicted of a felony, or is in custody or detention for, is alleged in a petition to have engaged in, or has been adjudicated as having engaged in delinquent conduct that violates a penal law of the grade of felony.

History of Pen §38.05: Acts 1973, 63rd Leg., ch. 399, §1, eff. Jan. 1, 1974. Amended by Acts 1991, 72nd Leg., ch. 748, §1, eff. Sept. 1, 1991; Acts 1993, 73rd Leg., ch. 900, §1.01, eff. Sept. 1, 1994; Acts 1995, 74th Leg., ch. 318, §11, eff. Sept. 1, 1995; Acts 2005, 79th Leg., ch. 607, §1, eff. Sept. 1, 2005; Acts 2007, 80th Leg., ch. 593, §1.19, eff. Sept. 1, 2007.

PEN §38.06. ESCAPE

(a) A person commits an offense if he escapes from custody when he is:

(1) under arrest for, charged with, or convicted of an offense;

(2) in custody pursuant to a lawful order of a court;

Ⓔ *Subsections (3) & (4) below are effective for conduct occurring on or after Sept. 1, 2007; for orders rendered by a juvenile court on or after Sept. 1, 2007; and for information and documents relating to juvenile cases before, on, or after Sept. 1, 2007. Conduct violating penal law occurs on or after Sept. 1, 2007, if any element of the violation occurs on or after that date. In all other instances, the law is effective on Sept. 1, 2007.*

(3) detained in a secure detention facility, as that term is defined by Section 51.02, Family Code; or

For a quick reference of penalties, see the Chart of Penalties on p. 675.

O'CONNOR'S CRIMINAL CODES 865

PEN §38.06

(4) in the custody of a juvenile probation officer for violating an order imposed by the juvenile court under Section 52.01, Family Code.

(b) Except as provided in Subsections (c), (d), and (e), an offense under this section is a Class A misdemeanor.

(c) An offense under this section is a felony of the third degree if the actor:

(1) is under arrest for, charged with, or convicted of a felony;

(2) is confined in a secure correctional facility; or

(3) is committed to a secure correctional facility, as defined by Section 51.02, Family Code, other than a halfway house, operated by or under contract with the Texas Youth Commission.

(d) An offense under this section is a felony of the second degree if the actor to effect his escape causes bodily injury.

(e) An offense under this section is a felony of the first degree if to effect his escape the actor:

(1) causes serious bodily injury; or

(2) uses or threatens to use a deadly weapon.

History of Pen §38.06: Acts 1973, 63rd Leg., ch. 399, §1, eff. Jan. 1, 1974. Amended by Acts 1985, 69th Leg., ch. 328, §1, eff. Sept. 1, 1985. Renumbered from §38.07 and amended by Acts 1993, 73rd Leg., ch. 900, §1.01, eff. Sept. 1, 1994. Amended by Acts 1999, 76th Leg., ch. 526, §1, eff. Sept. 1, 1999; Acts 2007, 80th Leg., ch. 908, §38, eff. Sept. 1, 2007.

ANNOTATIONS

Medford v. State, 13 S.W.3d 769, 773 (Tex.Crim. App.2000). "For purposes of the escape statute, an 'arrest' is complete when a person's liberty of movement is successfully restricted or restrained, whether this is achieved by an officer's physical force or the suspect's submission to the officer's authority. Furthermore, an arrest is complete only if 'a reasonable person in the suspect's position would have understood the situation to constitute a restraint of freedom of movement of the degree which the law associates with formal arrest.'" *See also Medford v. State*, ___ S.W.3d ___ (Tex.Crim. App.2008) (No. PD-1644-06; 7-2-08).

Lawhorn v. State, 898 S.W.2d 886, 890 (Tex.Crim. App.1995). "It is ... an element of the offense that the defendant depart from custody without permission. [¶] '[F]light is not an essential element of the offense of escape because the offense is complete when an unauthorized departure from custody is made.'"

Harrell v. State, 743 S.W.2d 229, 231 (Tex.Crim. App.1987). "[A]ctual, physical 'hands-on' restraint is not a prerequisite to a showing of custody in the context of the offense of escape. Rather it is appropriate to look at the legal status of the individual at the time of the escape." *See also Russell v. State*, 90 S.W.3d 865 (Tex.App.—San Antonio 2002, pet. ref'd).

PEN §38.07. PERMITTING OR FACILITATING ESCAPE

(a) An official or employee of a correctional facility commits an offense if he knowingly permits or facilitates the escape of a person in custody.

(b) A person commits an offense if he knowingly causes or facilitates the escape of one who is in custody pursuant to:

(1) an allegation or adjudication of delinquency; or

(2) involuntary commitment for mental illness under Subtitle C, Title 7, Health and Safety Code, or for chemical dependency under Chapter 462, Health and Safety Code.

(c) Except as provided in Subsections (d) and (e), an offense under this section is a Class A misdemeanor.

(d) An offense under this section is a felony of the third degree if the person in custody:

(1) was under arrest for, charged with, or convicted of a felony; or

(2) was confined in a correctional facility other than a secure correctional facility after conviction of a felony.

(e) An offense under this section is a felony of the second degree if:

(1) the actor or the person in custody used or threatened to use a deadly weapon to effect the escape; or

(2) the person in custody was confined in a secure correctional facility after conviction of a felony.

E *Subsection (f) below is effective for conduct occurring on or after Sept. 1, 2007; for orders rendered by a juvenile court on or after Sept. 1, 2007; and for information and documents relating to juvenile cases before, on, or after Sept. 1, 2007. Conduct violating penal law occurs on or after Sept. 1, 2007, if any element of the violation occurs on or after that date. In all other instances, the law is effective on Sept. 1, 2007.*

(f) In this section, "correctional facility" means:

(1) any place described by Section 1.07(a)(14); or

PEN §38.06

(2) a "secure correctional facility" or "secure detention facility" as those terms are defined by Section 51.02, Family Code.

History of Pen §38.07: Acts 1973, 63rd Leg., ch. 399, §1, eff. Jan. 1, 1974. Renumbered from §38.08 and amended by Acts 1993, 73rd Leg., ch. 900, §1.01, eff. Sept. 1, 1994. Amended by Acts 2007, 80th Leg., ch. 908, §39, eff. Sept. 1, 2007.

PEN §38.08. EFFECT OF UNLAWFUL CUSTODY

It is no defense to prosecution under Section 38.06 or 38.07 that the custody was unlawful.

History of Pen §38.08: Acts 1973, 63rd Leg., ch. 399, §1, eff. Jan. 1, 1974. Renumbered from §38.09 and amended by Acts 1993, 73rd Leg., ch. 900, §1.01, eff. Sept. 1, 1994.

PEN §38.09. IMPLEMENTS FOR ESCAPE

(a) A person commits an offense if, with intent to facilitate escape, he introduces into a correctional facility, or provides a person in custody or an inmate with, a deadly weapon or anything that may be useful for escape.

(b) An offense under this section is a felony of the third degree unless the actor introduced or provided a deadly weapon, in which event the offense is a felony of the second degree.

E *Subsection (c) below is effective for conduct occurring on or after Sept. 1, 2007; for orders rendered by a juvenile court on or after Sept. 1, 2007; and for information and documents relating to juvenile cases before, on, or after Sept. 1, 2007. Conduct violating penal law occurs on or after Sept. 1, 2007, if any element of the violation occurs on or after that date. In all other instances, the law is effective on Sept. 1, 2007.*

(c) In this section, "correctional facility" means:

(1) any place described by Section 1.07(a)(14); or

(2) a "secure correctional facility" or "secure detention facility" as those terms are defined by Section 51.02, Family Code.

History of Pen §38.09: Acts 1973, 63rd Leg., ch. 399, §1, eff. Jan. 1, 1974. Renumbered from §38.10 and amended by Acts 1993, 73rd Leg., ch. 900, §1.01, eff. Sept. 1, 1994. Amended by Acts 2007, 80th Leg., ch. 908, §40, eff. Sept. 1, 2007.

PEN §38.10. BAIL JUMPING & FAILURE TO APPEAR

(a) A person lawfully released from custody, with or without bail, on condition that he subsequently appear commits an offense if he intentionally or knowingly fails to appear in accordance with the terms of his release.

(b) It is a defense to prosecution under this section that the appearance was incident to community supervision, parole, or an intermittent sentence.

(c) It is a defense to prosecution under this section that the actor had a reasonable excuse for his failure to appear in accordance with the terms of his release.

(d) Except as provided in Subsections (e) and (f), an offense under this section is a Class A misdemeanor.

(e) An offense under this section is a Class C misdemeanor if the offense for which the actor's appearance was required is punishable by fine only.

(f) An offense under this section is a felony of the third degree if the offense for which the actor's appearance was required is classified as a felony.

History of Pen §38.10: Acts 1973, 63rd Leg., ch. 399, §1, eff. Jan. 1, 1974. Renumbered from §38.11 and amended by Acts 1993, 73rd Leg., ch. 900, §1.01, eff. Sept. 1, 1994.

ANNOTATIONS

Azeez v. State, 248 S.W.3d 182, 192-93 (Tex.Crim. App.2008). Pen. Code §38.10(a) "has 'broadly defined' the offense of failure to appear when conditionally released from custody, regardless of the basis for that custody. Because a motorist who has been pulled over for the issuance of a speeding citation *is* 'under arrest' in contemplation of [Pen. Code] §38.01(1)(A)'s definition of 'custody,' then a person in the appellant's position, who signed a promise to appear to answer for a speeding offense but then failed to appear as promised, is subject to prosecution under this broad provision. But [Transp. Code] §543.009(b) ... has more narrowly hewn an offense, complete in itself, to specifically proscribe the failure to appear in court pursuant to a written promise upon being arrested for an offense under Title 7, Subtitle C of the Transportation Code—an offense which would otherwise meet every element of, and hence be punishable under, the Penal Code provision. ... The Legislature has clearly manifested a policy that a failure to appear in court to answer for a traffic infraction should carry a less severe punishment than other failures to appear. Because the appellant was prosecuted under the Penal Code, and assessed a fine in excess of what was allowable for the Transportation Code offense, he suffered a violation of due process."

Luce v. State, 101 S.W.3d 692, 694 (Tex.App.— Texarkana 2003, no pet.). "[A]n excuse that relies on voluntary intoxication cannot be a reasonable excuse under the Texas Penal Code as a matter of law."

For a quick reference of penalties, see the Chart of Penalties on p. 675.

O'CONNOR'S CRIMINAL CODES 867

Gallegos v. State, 828 S.W.2d 577, 579 (Tex.App.— Houston [1st Dist.] 1992, no pet.). "[I]f a jury believes or has a reasonable doubt that an ordinary and prudent person in the same or similar position as appellant would have failed to make a court appearance in reliance on the advice of counsel, and if the jury believes or has a reasonable doubt that appellant actually received such advice, then appellant has a reasonable excuse for his failure to appear under §38.11(c) [now §38.10(c)], and the jury should find him not guilty."

Doucette v. State, 774 S.W.2d 88, 91 (Tex.App.— Beaumont 1989), *pet. dism'd*, 812 S.W.2d 319 (Tex. Crim.App.1990). "The gravamen of the offense of felony bail jumping is the failure to appear. Whether the underlying felony offense is proven is immaterial. The state is merely required to show that the charges for the felony offenses were *then pending against the defendant*."

Richardson v. State, 699 S.W.2d 235, 238 (Tex. App.—Austin 1985, pet. ref'd). "[I]n a prosecution under [Pen. Code] §38.11 [now §38.10], proof the defendant was free pursuant to an instanter bond constitutes a prima facie showing that he had notice of the proceeding at which he failed to appear. This prima facie showing will satisfy the State's burden of proving a culpable mental state in the absence of any evidence to the contrary. But where … there is evidence the defendant did not, in fact, have notice of the proceeding in question, the State must do more than prove the terms of the bond in order to meet its burden of proving an intentional or knowing failure to appear. In such cases, the State must offer evidence that the defendant did have actual notice, or that he engaged in a course of conduct designed to prevent him from receiving notice."

PEN §38.11. PROHIBITED SUBSTANCES & ITEMS IN ADULT OR JUVENILE CORRECTIONAL OR DETENTION FACILITY OR ON PROPERTY OF TEXAS DEPARTMENT OF CRIMINAL JUSTICE OR TEXAS YOUTH COMMISSION

(a) A person commits an offense if the person provides:

(1) an alcoholic beverage, controlled substance, or dangerous drug to an inmate of a correctional facility or to a person in the custody of a secure correctional facility or secure detention facility for juveniles, except on the prescription of a physician or practitioner, as defined in Section 551.003, Occupations Code;

(2) a deadly weapon to an inmate of a correctional facility or to a person in the custody of a secure correctional facility or secure detention facility for juveniles;

(3) a cellular telephone or other wireless communications device or a component of one of those devices, cigarette, tobacco product, or money to an inmate of a correctional facility operated by or under contract with the Texas Department of Criminal Justice or to a person in the custody of a secure correctional facility or secure detention facility for juveniles, except for money that is provided for the benefit of the juvenile in accordance with facility rules;

(4) a cellular telephone or money to a person confined in a local jail regulated by the Commission on Jail Standards; or

(5) a cigarette or tobacco product to a person confined in a local jail regulated by the Commission on Jail Standards and in providing the cigarette or tobacco product the person violates a rule or regulation adopted by the sheriff or jail administrator that:

(A) prohibits the possession of a cigarette or tobacco product by an inmate confined in the jail; or

(B) places restrictions on:

(i) the possession of a cigarette or tobacco product by an inmate confined in the jail; or

(ii) the manner in which a cigarette or tobacco product may be provided to an inmate confined in the jail.

(b) A person commits an offense if the person takes an alcoholic beverage, controlled substance, or dangerous drug into a correctional facility or a secure correctional facility or secure detention facility for juveniles, except for delivery to a facility warehouse, pharmacy, or physician.

(c) A person commits an offense if the person takes a controlled substance or dangerous drug on property owned, used, or controlled by the Texas Department of Criminal Justice, the Texas Youth Commission, or a secure correctional facility or secure detention facility for juveniles, except for delivery to a warehouse, pharmacy, or physician on property owned, used, or controlled by the department, the commission, or the facility.

(d) A person commits an offense if the person:

(1) possesses a controlled substance or dangerous drug while:

(A) on property owned, used, or controlled by the Texas Department of Criminal Justice, the Texas Youth Commission, or a secure correctional facility or secure detention facility for juveniles; or

(B) in a correctional facility or a secure correctional facility or secure detention facility for juveniles; or

(2) possesses a deadly weapon while in a correctional facility or in a secure correctional facility or secure detention facility for juveniles.

(e) It is an affirmative defense to prosecution under Subsection (d)(1) of this section that the person possessed the controlled substance or dangerous drug pursuant to a prescription issued by a practitioner or while delivering the substance or drug to a warehouse, pharmacy, or physician on property owned, used, or controlled by the department, the Texas Youth Commission, or by the operator of a secure correctional facility or secure detention facility for juveniles. It is an affirmative defense to prosecution under Subsection (d)(2) of this section that the person possessing the deadly weapon is a peace officer or is an officer or employee of the correctional facility authorized to possess the deadly weapon while on duty or traveling to or from the person's place of assignment.

(f) In this section:

(1) "Practitioner" has the meaning assigned by Section 481.002, Health and Safety Code.

(2) "Prescription" has the meaning assigned by Section 481.002, Health and Safety Code.

(3) "Cigarette" has the meaning assigned by Section 154.001, Tax Code.

(4) "Tobacco product" has the meaning assigned by Section 155.001, Tax Code.

(5) "Secure correctional facility" and "secure detention facility" have the meanings assigned by Section 51.02, Family Code.

(g) An offense under this section is a felony of the third degree.

(h) Notwithstanding Section 15.01(d), if a person commits the offense of criminal attempt to commit an offense under Subsection (a) or (b), the offense committed under Section 15.01 is a felony of the third degree.

(i) It is an affirmative defense to prosecution under Subsection (b) that the actor:

(1) is a duly authorized member of the clergy with rights and privileges granted by an ordaining authority that includes administration of a religious ritual or ceremony requiring the presence or consumption of an alcoholic beverage; and

(2) takes four ounces or less of an alcoholic beverage into the correctional facility or the secure correctional facility or secure detention facility for juveniles and personally consumes all of the alcoholic beverage or departs from the facility with any portion of the beverage not consumed.

(j) A person commits an offense if the person while an inmate of a correctional facility operated by or under contract with the Texas Department of Criminal Justice or while in the custody of a secure correctional facility or secure detention facility for juveniles possesses a cellular telephone or other wireless communications device or a component of one of those devices.

History of Pen §38.11: Acts 1991, 72nd Leg., 2nd C.S., ch. 10, §5.01, eff. Oct. 1, 1991. Renumbered from §38.112 and amended by Acts 1993, 73rd Leg., ch. 900, §1.01, eff. Sept. 1, 1994. Amended by Acts 1999, 76th Leg., ch. 362, §1 (eff. Sept. 1, 1999), ch. 649, §1 (eff. Sept. 1, 1999); Acts 2003, 78th Leg., ch. 470, §§1-3, eff. Sept. 1, 2003; Acts 2005, 79th Leg., ch. 499, §1, eff. June 17, 2005, ch. 949, §§47, 48 (eff. Sept. 1, 2005), ch. 1092, §1 (eff. Sept. 1, 2005).

ANNOTATIONS

Brown v. State, 89 S.W.3d 630, 633 (Tex.Crim.App. 2002). "Appellant does not dispute that he possessed marihuana in the jail, but rather claims that he did not 'voluntarily' bring it into the jail. [W]e reject[ ] a broad definition of voluntary that would incorporate a concept of free will. [W]e [hold] that voluntarily 'means the absence of an accidental act, omission or possession,' and that voluntariness 'refers only to one's physical bodily movements.' [¶] Appellant makes no claim of involuntary physical bodily movements but asserts only that he, 'in custody, under restraint,' was compelled to enter into the correctional facility." Held: Although under arrest, appellant voluntarily brought the marijuana into jail.

PEN §38.111. IMPROPER CONTACT WITH VICTIM

(a) A person commits an offense if the person, while confined in a correctional facility after being charged with or convicted of an offense listed in Article 62.001(5), Code of Criminal Procedure, contacts by letter, telephone, or any other means, either directly or through a third party, a victim of the offense or a member of the victim's family, if:

(1) the victim was younger than 17 years of age at the time of the commission of the offense for which the person is confined; and

For a quick reference of penalties, see the Chart of Penalties on p. 675.

O'CONNOR'S CRIMINAL CODES 869

PEN §38.111

(2) the director of the correctional facility has not, before the person makes contact with the victim:

(A) received written and dated consent to the contact from:

(i) a parent of the victim;

(ii) a legal guardian of the victim;

(iii) the victim, if the victim is 17 years of age or older at the time of giving the consent; or

(iv) a member of the victim's family who is 17 years of age or older; and

(B) provided the person with a copy of the consent.

(b) The person confined in a correctional facility may not give the written consent required under Subsection (a)(2)(A).

(c) It is an affirmative defense to prosecution under this section that the contact was:

(1) indirect contact made through an attorney representing the person in custody; and

(2) solely for the purpose of representing the person in a criminal proceeding.

(d) An offense under this section is a Class A misdemeanor unless the actor is confined in a correctional facility after being convicted of a felony described by Subsection (a), in which event the offense is a felony of the third degree.

E *Subsection (e) below is effective for conduct occurring on or after Sept. 1, 2007; for orders rendered by a juvenile court on or after Sept. 1, 2007; and for information and documents relating to juvenile cases before, on, or after Sept. 1, 2007. Conduct violating penal law occurs on or after Sept. 1, 2007, if any element of the violation occurs on or after that date. In all other instances, the law is effective on Sept. 1, 2007.*

(e) In this section, "correctional facility" means:

(1) any place described by Section 1.07(a)(14); or

(2) a "secure correctional facility" or "secure detention facility" as those terms are defined by Section 51.02, Family Code.

History of Pen §38.111: Acts 2001, 77th Leg., ch. 1337, §1, eff. Sept. 1, 2001; Amended by Acts 2005, 79th Leg., ch. 1008, §2.11, eff. Sept. 1, 2005; Acts 2007, 80th Leg., ch. 908, §41, eff. Sept. 1, 2007.

PEN §38.112. VIOLATION OF PROTECTIVE ORDER ISSUED ON BASIS OF SEXUAL ASSAULT

(a) A person commits an offense if, in violation of an order issued under Chapter 7A, Code of Criminal Procedure, the person knowingly:

(1) communicates directly or indirectly with the applicant or any member of the applicant's family or household in a threatening or harassing manner;

(2) goes to or near the residence, place of employment or business, or child-care facility or school of the applicant or any member of the applicant's family or household; or

(3) possesses a firearm.

(b) If conduct constituting an offense under this section also constitutes an offense under another section of this code, the actor may be prosecuted under either section or under both sections.

(c) An offense under this section is a Class A misdemeanor.

History of Pen §38.112: Acts 2003, 78th Leg., ch. 836, §3, eff. Sept. 1, 2003.

PEN §38.113. UNAUTHORIZED ABSENCE FROM COMMUNITY CORRECTIONS FACILITY, COUNTY CORRECTIONAL CENTER, OR ASSIGNMENT SITE

(a) A person commits an offense if the person:

(1) is sentenced to or is required as a condition of community supervision or correctional programming to submit to a period of detention or treatment in a community corrections facility or county correctional center;

(2) fails to report to or leaves the facility, the center, or a community service assignment site as directed by the court, community supervision and corrections department supervising the person, or director of the facility or center in which the person is detained or treated, as appropriate; and

(3) in failing to report or leaving acts without the approval of the court, the community supervision and corrections department supervising the person, or the director of the facility or center in which the person is detained or treated.

(b) An offense under this section is a state jail felony.

History of Pen §38.113: Acts 1993, 73rd Leg., ch. 900, §1.01, eff. Sept. 1, 1994. Amended by Acts 1995, 74th Leg., ch. 318, §12, eff. Sept. 1, 1995.

PEN §38.114. CONTRABAND IN CORRECTIONAL FACILITY

(a) A person commits an offense if the person:

(1) provides contraband to an inmate of a correctional facility;

(2) otherwise introduces contraband into a correctional facility; or

(3) possesses contraband while confined in a correctional facility.

(b) In this section, "contraband":

(1) means:

(A) any item not provided by or authorized by the operator of the correctional facility; or

(B) any item provided by or authorized by the operator of the correctional facility that has been altered to accommodate a use other than the originally intended use; and

(2) does not include any item specifically prohibited under Section 38.11.

(c) An offense under this section is a Class C misdemeanor, unless the offense is committed by an employee or a volunteer of the correctional facility, in which event the offense is a Class B misdemeanor.

E *Subsection (d) below is effective for conduct occurring on or after Sept. 1, 2007; for orders rendered by a juvenile court on or after Sept. 1, 2007; and for information and documents relating to juvenile cases before, on, or after Sept. 1, 2007. Conduct violating penal law occurs on or after Sept. 1, 2007, if any element of the violation occurs on or after that date. In all other instances, the law is effective on Sept. 1, 2007.*

(d) In this section, "correctional facility" means:

(1) any place described by Section 1.07(a)(14); or

(2) a "secure correctional facility" or "secure detention facility" as those terms are defined by Section 51.02, Family Code.

History of Pen §38.114: Acts 2005, 79th Leg., ch. 499, §2, eff. June 17, 2005. Amended by Acts 2007, 80th Leg., ch. 908, §42, eff. Sept. 1, 2007.

PEN §38.12. BARRATRY & SOLICITATION OF PROFESSIONAL EMPLOYMENT

(a) A person commits an offense if, with intent to obtain an economic benefit the person:

(1) knowingly institutes a suit or claim that the person has not been authorized to pursue;

(2) solicits employment, either in person or by telephone, for himself or for another;

(3) pays, gives, or advances or offers to pay, give, or advance to a prospective client money or anything of value to obtain employment as a professional from the prospective client;

(4) pays or gives or offers to pay or give a person money or anything of value to solicit employment;

(5) pays or gives or offers to pay or give a family member of a prospective client money or anything of value to solicit employment; or

(6) accepts or agrees to accept money or anything of value to solicit employment.

(b) A person commits an offense if the person:

(1) knowingly finances the commission of an offense under Subsection (a);

(2) invests funds the person knows or believes are intended to further the commission of an offense under Subsection (a); or

(3) is a professional who knowingly accepts employment within the scope of the person's license, registration, or certification that results from the solicitation of employment in violation of Subsection (a).

(c) It is an exception to prosecution under Subsection (a) or (b) that the person's conduct is authorized by the Texas Disciplinary Rules of Professional Conduct or any rule of court.

(d) A person commits an offense if the person:

(1) is an attorney, chiropractor, physician, surgeon, or private investigator licensed to practice in this state or any person licensed, certified, or registered by a health care regulatory agency of this state;

(2) with the intent to obtain professional employment for himself or for another, sends or knowingly permits to be sent to an individual who has not sought the person's employment, legal representation, advice, or care a written communication that:

(A)[1] concerns an action for personal injury or wrongful death or otherwise relates to an accident or disaster involving the person to whom the communication is addressed or a relative of that person and that was mailed before the 31st day after the date on which the accident or disaster occurred;

(B)[1] concerns a specific matter and relates to legal representation and the person knows or reasonably should know that the person to whom the communication is directed is represented by a lawyer in the matter;

(C)[1] concerns an arrest of or issuance of a summons to the person to whom the communication is addressed or a relative of that person and that was mailed before the 31st day after the date on which the arrest or issuance of the summons occurred;

For a quick reference of penalties, see the Chart of Penalties on p. 675.

O'CONNOR'S CRIMINAL CODES 871

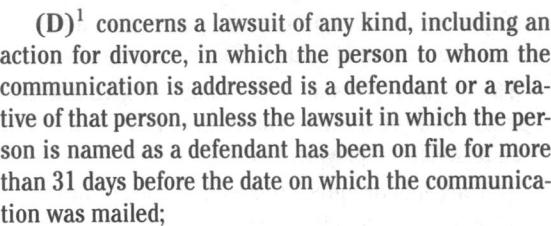

(D)[1] concerns a lawsuit of any kind, including an action for divorce, in which the person to whom the communication is addressed is a defendant or a relative of that person, unless the lawsuit in which the person is named as a defendant has been on file for more than 31 days before the date on which the communication was mailed;

(E) is sent or permitted to be sent by a person who knows or reasonably should know that the injured person or relative of the injured person has indicated a desire not to be contacted by or receive communications concerning employment;

(F) involves coercion, duress, fraud, overreaching, harassment, intimidation, or undue influence; or

(G) contains a false, fraudulent, misleading, deceptive, or unfair statement or claim.

(e) For purposes of Subsection (d)(2)(E), a desire not to be contacted is presumed if an accident report reflects that such an indication has been made by an injured person or that person's relative.

(f) An offense under Subsection (a) or (b) is a felony of the third degree.

(g) Except as provided by Subsection (h), an offense under Subsection (d) is a Class A misdemeanor.

(h) An offense under Subsection (d) is a felony of the third degree if it is shown on the trial of the offense that the defendant has previously been convicted under Subsection (d).

(i) Final conviction of felony barratry is a serious crime for all purposes and acts, specifically including the State Bar Rules and the Texas Rules of Disciplinary Procedure.

1. **Editor's note:** Subsections 38.12(d)(2)(A)-(D) were declared unconstitutional by *Moore v. Morales*, 843 F.Supp. 1124, 1133 (S.D.Tex.1994). Subsection (A) was later ruled constitutional as applied to attorneys. *Moore v. Morales*, 63 F.3d 358, 363 (5th Cir.1995).

History of Pen §38.12: Acts 1973, 63rd Leg., ch. 399, §1, eff. Jan. 1, 1974. Amended by Acts 1989, 71st Leg., ch. 866, §2, eff. Sept. 1, 1989; Acts 1993, 73rd Leg., ch. 723, §2 (eff. Sept. 1, 1993), ch. 900, §1.01 (eff. Sept. 1, 1994); Acts 1997, 75th Leg., ch. 750, §2, eff. Sept. 1, 1997.

ANNOTATIONS

State v. Mays, 967 S.W.2d 404, 409 (Tex.Crim.App. 1998). "'[T]he statute in this case [does not] define 'solicit employment' in such a way as to implicate 'inherently innocent' activities. The statute clearly outlines the activities which constitute barratry, and its parameters fall within historical bounds of barratry by solicitation. The indictment in this case, by carefully tracking the statutory definition of a manner or means of commission of barratry, provided ample notice to appellee and met constitutional and statutory requirements."

State v. Jimenez, 148 S.W.3d 574, 575 (Tex. App.—El Paso 2004, pet. ref'd). "The ... issue in the case is whether the State may maintain a barratry prosecution against a chiropractor who has allegedly solicited business for an attorney where he acted with the intent that the attorney would refer the clients back to the chiropractor for chiropractic treatment." Held: Yes, the chiropractor may be charged with barratry.

PEN §38.122. FALSELY HOLDING ONESELF OUT AS A LAWYER

(a) A person commits an offense if, with intent to obtain an economic benefit for himself or herself, the person holds himself or herself out as a lawyer, unless he or she is currently licensed to practice law in this state, another state, or a foreign country and is in good standing with the State Bar of Texas and the state bar or licensing authority of any and all other states and foreign countries where licensed.

(b) An offense under Subsection (a) of this section is a felony of the third degree.

(c) Final conviction of falsely holding oneself out to be a lawyer is a serious crime for all purposes and acts, specifically including the State Bar Rules.

History of Pen §38.122: Acts 1993, 73rd Leg., ch. 723, §§5, 8, eff. Sept. 1, 1993.

ANNOTATIONS

Satterwhite v. State, 979 S.W.2d 626, 629 (Tex. Crim.App.1998). "The retroactive effect of the payment of past-due State Bar dues has no effect on appellant's conviction for falsely holding himself out as an attorney while not in good standing with the State Bar."

PEN §38.123. UNAUTHORIZED PRACTICE OF LAW

(a) A person commits an offense if, with intent to obtain an economic benefit for himself or herself, the person:

(1) contracts with any person to represent that person with regard to personal causes of action for property damages or personal injury;

(2) advises any person as to the person's rights and the advisability of making claims for personal injuries or property damages;

PEN §38.12

★

(3) advises any person as to whether or not to accept an offered sum of money in settlement of claims for personal injuries or property damages;

(4) enters into any contract with another person to represent that person in personal injury or property damage matters on a contingent fee basis with an attempted assignment of a portion of the person's cause of action; or

(5) enters into any contract with a third person which purports to grant the exclusive right to select and retain legal counsel to represent the individual in any legal proceeding.

(b) This section does not apply to a person currently licensed to practice law in this state, another state, or a foreign country and in good standing with the State Bar of Texas and the state bar or licensing authority of any and all other states and foreign countries where licensed.

(c) Except as provided by Subsection (d) of this section, an offense under Subsection (a) of this section is a Class A misdemeanor.

(d) An offense under Subsection (a) of this section is a felony of the third degree if it is shown on the trial of the offense that the defendant has previously been convicted under Subsection (a) of this section.

History of Pen §38.123: Acts 1993, 73rd Leg., ch. 723, §§5, 8, eff. Sept. 1, 1993.

Unauthorized Practice of Law Cmte. v. American Home Assur. Co., ___ S.W.3d ___ (Tex.2008) (No. 04-0138; 3-28-08). "[A]n issuer may use staff attorneys to defend a claim against an insured if the insurer's interest and the insured's interest are congruent, but not otherwise. Their interests are congruent when they are aligned in defeating the claim and there is no conflict of interest between the insurer and the insured. [A] staff attorney must [also] fully disclose to an insured his or her affiliation with the insurer."

PEN §38.13. HINDERING PROCEEDINGS BY DISORDERLY CONDUCT

(a) A person commits an offense if he intentionally hinders an official proceeding by noise or violent or tumultuous behavior or disturbance.

(b) A person commits an offense if he recklessly hinders an official proceeding by noise or violent or tumultuous behavior or disturbance and continues after explicit official request to desist.

(c) An offense under this section is a Class A misdemeanor.

History of Pen §38.13: Acts 1973, 63rd Leg., ch. 399, §1, eff. Jan. 1, 1974. Amended by Acts 1993, 73rd Leg., ch. 900, §1.01, eff. Sept. 1, 1994.

PEN §38.14. TAKING OR ATTEMPTING TO TAKE WEAPON FROM PEACE OFFICER, PAROLE OFFICER, OR COMMUNITY SUPERVISION & CORRECTIONS DEPARTMENT OFFICER

(a) In this section:

(1) "Firearm" has the meanings assigned by Section 46.01.

(2) "Stun gun" means a device designed to propel darts or other projectiles attached to wires that, on contact, will deliver an electrical pulse capable of incapacitating a person.

(b) A person commits an offense if the person intentionally or knowingly and with force takes or attempts to take from a peace officer, parole officer, or community supervision and corrections department officer the officer's firearm, nightstick, stun gun, or personal protection chemical dispensing device with the intention of harming the officer or a third person.

(c) The actor is presumed to have known that the peace officer, parole officer, or community supervision and corrections department officer was a peace officer, parole officer, or community supervision and corrections department officer if the officer was wearing a distinctive uniform or badge indicating his employment, or if the officer identified himself as a peace officer, parole officer, or community supervision and corrections department officer.

(d) It is a defense to prosecution under this section that the defendant took or attempted to take the weapon from a peace officer, parole officer, or community supervision and corrections department officer who was using force against the defendant or another in excess of the amount of force permitted by law.

(e) An offense under this section is a felony of the third degree if the defendant took a weapon described by Subsection (b) from an officer described by Subsection (b) and is a state jail felony if the defendant attempted to take the weapon from the officer.

History of Pen §38.14: Acts 1989, 71st Leg., ch. 986, §1, eff. Sept. 1, 1989. Renumbered from §38.16 by Acts 1990, 71st Leg., 6th C.S., ch. 12, §2(25), eff. Sept. 6, 1990. Renumbered from §38.17 and amended by Acts 1993, 73rd Leg.,

For a quick reference of penalties, see the Chart of Penalties on p. 675.

O'CONNOR'S CRIMINAL CODES 873

ch. 900, §1.01, eff. Sept. 1, 1994. Amended by Acts 1999, 76th Leg., ch. 714, §1, eff. Sept. 1, 1999; Acts 2001, 77th Leg., ch. 322, §1, eff. Sept. 1, 2001; Acts 2005, 79th Leg., ch. 1201, §1, eff. Sept. 1, 2005.

Jackson v. State, 993 S.W.2d 162, 165 (Tex.App.—Eastland 1999, no pet.). "[R]esisting arrest is not a lesser included offense of taking or attempting to take a weapon from a police officer."

PEN §38.15. INTERFERENCE WITH PUBLIC DUTIES

(a) A person commits an offense if the person with criminal negligence interrupts, disrupts, impedes, or otherwise interferes with:

(1) a peace officer while the peace officer is performing a duty or exercising authority imposed or granted by law;

(2) a person who is employed to provide emergency medical services including the transportation of ill or injured persons while the person is performing that duty;

(3) a fire fighter, while the fire fighter is fighting a fire or investigating the cause of a fire;

(4) an animal under the supervision of a peace officer, corrections officer, or jailer, if the person knows the animal is being used for law enforcement, corrections, prison or jail security, or investigative purposes;

(5) the transmission of a communication over a citizen's band radio channel, the purpose of which communication is to inform or inquire about an emergency;

(6) an officer with responsibility for animal control in a county or municipality, while the officer is performing a duty or exercising authority imposed or granted under Chapter 821 or 822, Health and Safety Code; or

E *Subsection (7) below is effective for offenses committed on or after Sept. 1, 2007.*

(7) a person who:

(A) has responsibility for assessing, enacting, or enforcing public health, environmental, radiation, or safety measures for the state or a county or municipality;

(B) is investigating a particular site as part of the person's responsibilities under Paragraph (A);

(C) is acting in accordance with policies and procedures related to the safety and security of the site described by Paragraph (B); and

(D) is performing a duty or exercising authority imposed or granted under the Agriculture Code, Health and Safety Code, Occupations Code, or Water Code.

(b) An offense under this section is a Class B misdemeanor.

(c) It is a defense to prosecution under Subsection (a)(1) that the conduct engaged in by the defendant was intended to warn a person operating a motor vehicle of the presence of a peace officer who was enforcing Subtitle C, Title 7, Transportation Code.

(d) It is a defense to prosecution under this section that the interruption, disruption, impediment, or interference alleged consisted of speech only.

(e) In this section, "emergency" means a condition or circumstance in which an individual is or is reasonably believed by the person transmitting the communication to be in imminent danger of serious bodily injury or in which property is or is reasonably believed by the person transmitting the communication to be in imminent danger of damage or destruction.

History of Pen §38.15: Acts 1989, 71st Leg., ch. 1162, §1, eff. Sept. 1, 1989. Renumbered from §38.16 by Acts 1990, 71st Leg., 6th C.S., ch. 12, §2(26), eff. Sept. 6, 1990. Renumbered from §38.18 and amended by Acts 1993, 73rd Leg., ch. 900, §1.01, eff. Sept. 1, 1994. Amended by Acts 1997, 75th Leg., ch. 165, §30.241, eff. Sept. 1, 1997; Acts 2005, 79th Leg., ch. 1212, §1, eff. Sept. 1, 2005; Acts 2007, 80th Leg., ch. 1251, §1, eff. Sept. 1, 2007.

Barnes v. State, 206 S.W.3d 601, 605-06 (Tex.Crim. App.2006). "Each of the three acts [D] was charged with [during a traffic stop]—moving her vehicle forward, disregarding officer safety commands by removing her hands from view, and shouting to her child to 'run'—consists of more than simply refusing to make a written promise to appear, and it is for those acts that she was prosecuted. [¶] [W]e disagree with the court's conclusion that appellant's shout to her son to 'run' was 'speech only.' Appellant's shout to her seven-year-old son was a command to act. In the First Amendment context, from which the 'speech only' defense was apparently derived, words that are specifically designed to prompt an associate to action are not simply speech, but are conduct that may be treated accordingly."

Stitt v. State, 102 S.W.3d 845, 849 (Tex.App.—Texarkana 2003, pet. ref'd). "The character trait of truthfulness is not a pertinent trait to [a] charge [under §38.15]."

Carney v. State, 31 S.W.3d 392, 398 (Tex.App.—Austin 2000, no pet.). "Under §38.15, arguing with the officers does not constitute an actionable offense.

PEN §38.14

Speech is a statutory defense to the offense charge even if the end result is 'stalling.' The culpable mental state under the statute is criminal negligence."

PEN §38.151. INTERFERENCE WITH POLICE SERVICE ANIMALS

(a) In this section:

(1) "Area of control" includes a vehicle, trailer, kennel, pen, or yard.

(2) "Handler or rider" means a peace officer, corrections officer, or jailer who is specially trained to use a police service animal for law enforcement, corrections, prison or jail security, or investigative purposes.

(3) "Police service animal" means a dog, horse, or other domesticated animal that is specially trained for use by a handler or rider.

(b) A person commits an offense if the person recklessly:

(1) taunts, torments, or strikes a police service animal;

(2) throws an object or substance at a police service animal;

(3) interferes with or obstructs a police service animal or interferes with or obstructs the handler or rider of a police service animal in a manner that:

(A) inhibits or restricts the handler's or rider's control of the animal; or

(B) deprives the handler or rider of control of the animal;

(4) releases a police service animal from its area of control;

(5) enters the area of control of a police service animal without the effective consent of the handler or rider, including placing food or any other object or substance into that area;

(6) injures or kills a police service animal; or

(7) engages in conduct likely to injure or kill a police service animal, including administering or setting a poison, trap, or any other object or substance.

(c) An offense under this section is:

(1) a Class C misdemeanor if the person commits an offense under Subsection (b)(1);

(2) a Class B misdemeanor if the person commits an offense under Subsection (b)(2);

(3) a Class A misdemeanor if the person commits an offense under Subsection (b)(3), (4), or (5);

Subsections (4) & (5) below are effective for offenses committed on or after Sept. 1, 2007.

(4) except as provided by Subdivision (5), a state jail felony if the person commits an offense under Subsection (b)(6) or (7) by injuring a police service animal or by engaging in conduct likely to injure the animal; or

(5) a felony of the second degree if the person commits an offense under Subsection (b)(6) or (7) by:

(A) killing a police service animal or engaging in conduct likely to kill the animal;

(B) injuring a police service animal in a manner that materially and permanently affects the ability of the animal to perform as a police service animal; or

(C) engaging in conduct likely to injure a police service animal in a manner that would materially and permanently affect the ability of the animal to perform as a police service animal.

Subsections (4) & (5) below are effective for offenses in which any element of the offense was committed before Sept. 1, 2007.

(4) a state jail felony if the person commits an offense under Subsection (b)(6) or (7) by injuring a police service animal or by engaging in conduct likely to injure the animal; or

(5) a felony of the third degree if the person commits an offense under Subsection (b)(6) or (7) by killing a police service animal or by engaging in conduct likely to kill the animal.

History of Pen §38.151: Acts 2001, 77th Leg., ch. 979, §1, eff. Sept. 1, 2001. Amended by Acts 2007, 80th Leg., ch. 1331, §5, eff. Sept. 1, 2007.

PEN §38.16. PREVENTING EXECUTION OF CIVIL PROCESS

(a) A person commits an offense if he intentionally or knowingly by words or physical action prevents the execution of any process in a civil cause.

(b) It is an exception to the application of this section that the actor evaded service of process by avoiding detection.

(c) An offense under this section is a Class C misdemeanor.

History of Pen §38.16: Acts 1995, 74th Leg., ch. 318, §13, eff. Sept. 1, 1995.

PEN §38.17. FAILURE TO STOP OR REPORT AGGRAVATED SEXUAL ASSAULT OF CHILD

(a) A person, other than a person who has a relationship with a child described by Section 22.04(b), commits an offense if:

For a quick reference of penalties, see the Chart of Penalties on p. 675.

O'CONNOR'S CRIMINAL CODES 875

A *Subsection (1) below is effective for offenses committed on or after Sept. 1, 2007.*

(1) the actor observes the commission or attempted commission of an offense prohibited by Section 21.02 or 22.021(a)(2)(B) under circumstances in which a reasonable person would believe that an offense of a sexual or assaultive nature was being committed or was about to be committed against the child;

Subsection (1) below is effective for offenses in which any element of the offense was committed before Sept. 1, 2007.

(1) the actor observes the commission or attempted commission of an offense prohibited by Section 22.021(a)(2)(B) under circumstances in which a reasonable person would believe that an offense of a sexual or assaultive nature was being committed or was about to be committed against the child;

(2) the actor fails to assist the child or immediately report the commission of the offense to a peace officer or law enforcement agency; and

(3) the actor could assist the child or immediately report the commission of the offense without placing the actor in danger of suffering serious bodily injury or death.

(b) An offense under this section is a Class A misdemeanor.

History of Pen §38.17: Acts 1999, 76th Leg., ch. 1344, §1, eff. Sept. 1, 1999. Amended by Acts 2007, 80th Leg., ch. 593, §3.50, eff. Sept. 1, 2007.

History of Former Pen §38.17: Renumbered as §38.14 by Acts 1993, 73rd Leg., ch. 900, §1.01, eff. Sept. 1, 1994.

PEN §38.171. FAILURE TO REPORT FELONY

(a) A person commits an offense if the person:

(1) observes the commission of a felony under circumstances in which a reasonable person would believe that an offense had been committed in which serious bodily injury or death may have resulted; and

(2) fails to immediately report the commission of the offense to a peace officer or law enforcement agency under circumstances in which:

(A) a reasonable person would believe that the commission of the offense had not been reported; and

(B) the person could immediately report the commission of the offense without placing himself or herself in danger of suffering serious bodily injury or death.

(b) An offense under this section is a Class A misdemeanor.

History of Pen §38.171: Acts 2003, 78th Leg., ch. 1009, §2, eff. Sept. 1, 2003.

PEN §38.18. USE OF ACCIDENT REPORT INFORMATION & OTHER INFORMATION FOR PECUNIARY GAIN

(a) This section applies to:

(1) information described by Section 550.065(a), Transportation Code;

(2) information reported under Chapter 772, Health and Safety Code, other than information that is confidential under that chapter; and

(3) information contained in a dispatch log, a towing record, or a record of a 9-1-1 service provider, other than information that is confidential under Chapter 772, Health and Safety Code.

(b) A person commits an offense if:

(1) the person obtains information described by Subsection (a) from the Department of Public Safety of the State of Texas or other governmental entity; and

(2) the information is subsequently used for the direct solicitation of business or employment for pecuniary gain by:

(A) the person;

(B) an agent or employee of the person; or

(C) the person on whose behalf the information was requested.

(c) A person who employs or engages another to obtain information described by Subsection (a) from the Department of Public Safety or other governmental entity commits an offense if the person subsequently uses the information for direct solicitation of business or employment for pecuniary gain.

(d) An offense under this section is a Class B misdemeanor.

History of Pen §38.18: Acts 2001, 77th Leg., ch. 1032, §1, eff. Sept. 1, 2001.

ANNOTATIONS

Anderson Courier Serv. v. State, 104 S.W.3d 121, 126 (Tex.App.—Austin 2003, pet. denied). "H.B. 1544 [which enacted §38.18] unconstitutionally regulates commercial free speech."

PEN §38.19. FAILURE TO PROVIDE NOTICE & REPORT OF DEATH OF RESIDENT OF INSTITUTION

(a) A superintendent or general manager of an institution commits an offense if, as required by Article 49.24 or 49.25, Code of Criminal Procedure, the person fails to:

(1) provide notice of the death of an individual under the care, custody, or control of or residing in the institution;

(2) submit a report on the death of the individual; or

(3) include in the report material facts known or discovered by the person at the time the report was filed.

(b) An offense under this section is a Class B misdemeanor.

History of Pen §38.19: Acts 2003, 78th Leg., ch. 894, §4., eff. Sept. 1, 2003.

CHAPTER 39. ABUSE OF OFFICE

PEN §39.01. DEFINITIONS

In this chapter:

(1) "Law relating to a public servant's office or employment" means a law that specifically applies to a person acting in the capacity of a public servant and that directly or indirectly:

(A) imposes a duty on the public servant; or

(B) governs the conduct of the public servant.

(2) "Misuse" means to deal with property contrary to:

(A) an agreement under which the public servant holds the property;

(B) a contract of employment or oath of office of a public servant;

(C) a law, including provisions of the General Appropriations Act specifically relating to government property, that prescribes the manner of custody or disposition of the property; or

(D) a limited purpose for which the property is delivered or received.

History of Pen §39.01: Acts 1993, 73rd Leg., ch. 900, §1.01, eff. Sept. 1, 1994.

Ⓔ PEN §39.015. CONCURRENT JURISDICTION TO PROSECUTE OFFENSES UNDER THIS CHAPTER

With the consent of the appropriate local county or district attorney, the attorney general has concurrent jurisdiction with that consenting local prosecutor to prosecute an offense under this chapter.

History of Pen §39.015: Acts 2007, 80th Leg., ch. 378, §2, eff. June 15, 2007.

PEN §39.02. ABUSE OF OFFICIAL CAPACITY

(a) A public servant commits an offense if, with intent to obtain a benefit or with intent to harm or defraud another, he intentionally or knowingly:

(1) violates a law relating to the public servant's office or employment; or

(2) misuses government property, services, personnel, or any other thing of value belonging to the government that has come into the public servant's custody or possession by virtue of the public servant's office or employment.

(b) An offense under Subsection (a)(1) is a Class A misdemeanor.

(c) An offense under Subsection (a)(2) is:

(1) a Class C misdemeanor if the value of the use of the thing misused is less than $20;

(2) a Class B misdemeanor if the value of the use of the thing misused is $20 or more but less than $500;

(3) a Class A misdemeanor if the value of the use of the thing misused is $500 or more but less than $1,500;

(4) a state jail felony if the value of the use of the thing misused is $1,500 or more but less than $20,000;

(5) a felony of the third degree if the value of the use of the thing misused is $20,000 or more but less than $100,000;

(6) a felony of the second degree if the value of the use of the thing misused is $100,000 or more but less than $200,000; or

(7) a felony of the first degree if the value of the use of the thing misused is $200,000 or more.

(d) A discount or award given for travel, such as frequent flyer miles, rental car or hotel discounts, or

For a quick reference of penalties, see the Chart of Penalties on p. 675.

O'CONNOR'S CRIMINAL CODES   877

food coupons, are not things of value belonging to the government for purposes of this section due to the administrative difficulty and cost involved in recapturing the discount or award for a governmental entity.

History of Pen §39.02: Acts 1973, 63rd Leg., ch. 399, §1, eff. Jan. 1, 1974. Amended by Acts 1983, 68th Leg., ch. 558, §7, eff. Sept. 1, 1983. Renumbered from §39.01 and amended by Acts 1993, 73rd Leg., ch. 900, §1.01, eff. Sept. 1, 1994.

ANNOTATIONS

Margraves v. State, 34 S.W.3d 912, 921 (Tex.Crim. App.2000). "We do not find the statute to be unconstitutionally vague. The statute requires that a public servant use government property only in ways that are authorized. Using that property for personal benefit is an unauthorized misapplication...."

Talamantez v. State, 829 S.W.2d 174, 183 (Tex. Crim.App.1992). "[A]n indictment may properly allege 'official misconduct,' *in gross*, ... consisting of misapplication of any thing of value over a period of time with intent to benefit others for as long as the 'thing' is being thus used."

Knorpp v. State, 645 S.W.2d 892, 904 (Tex. App.—El Paso 1983, no pet.). "Appellant's status as a payee-holder of the check is not determinative of guilt or innocence. The indictment charged misapplication of the funds themselves, not the check. Even if Appellant had a greater right to possession of the check because of his payee status, this would not exonerate him from subsequent unlawful retention of the money represented by the check."

PEN §§39.021, 39.022. RENUMBERED

Renumbered as §§39.04, 39.05 by Acts 1993, 73rd Leg., ch. 900, §1.01, eff. Sept. 1, 1994.

PEN §39.03. OFFICIAL OPPRESSION

(a) A public servant acting under color of his office or employment commits an offense if he:

(1) intentionally subjects another to mistreatment or to arrest, detention, search, seizure, dispossession, assessment, or lien that he knows is unlawful;

(2) intentionally denies or impedes another in the exercise or enjoyment of any right, privilege, power, or immunity, knowing his conduct is unlawful; or

(3) intentionally subjects another to sexual harassment.

(b) For purposes of this section, a public servant acts under color of his office or employment if he acts or purports to act in an official capacity or takes advantage of such actual or purported capacity.

(c) In this section, "sexual harassment" means unwelcome sexual advances, requests for sexual favors, or other verbal or physical conduct of a sexual nature, submission to which is made a term or condition of a person's exercise or enjoyment of any right, privilege, power, or immunity, either explicitly or implicitly.

(d) An offense under this section is a Class A misdemeanor.

History of Pen §39.03: Acts 1973, 63rd Leg., ch. 399, §1, eff. Jan. 1, 1974. Amended by Acts 1989, 71st Leg., ch. 1217, §1, eff. Sept. 1, 1989; Acts 1991, 72nd Leg., ch. 16, §19.01(34), eff. Aug. 26, 1991. Renumbered from §39.02 by Acts 1993, 73rd Leg., ch. 900, §1.01, eff. Sept. 1, 1994.

ANNOTATIONS

Haight v. State, 137 S.W.3d 48, 50-51 (Tex.Crim. App.2004). "[T]he statute's various phrases and subsections are separated by the disjunctive 'or,' which is at least some indication that any one of the prohibited types of conduct would constitute a separate offense. [W]e conclude that the Legislature intended each of the prohibited types of conduct to be a separate statutory offense, even though such criminal acts might be in close temporal proximity."

Sanchez v. State, 995 S.W.2d 677, 685 (Tex.Crim. App.1999). "[T]he statute does not impose a reasonable person requirement. ... The statute specifies *both* the perpetrator's and the victim's sensitivities. The phrase 'intentionally subjects another to sexual harassment' indicates that (1) someone is subjected to sexual harassment, *i.e.*, the victim's sensitivities are affected, and (2) the perpetrator intends that someone be subjected to sexual harassment, *i.e.*, the perpetrator's own sensitivities are involved. [¶] Moreover, the statute requires intent on the part of the perpetrator that the conduct be of a sexual nature, not merely that the recipient perceive the conduct as sexual. To intentionally subject someone to a sexual advance, for example, the actor must be *intending a sexual* advance.... [¶] Further, by making 'sexual harassment' the object of 'intentionally subjects' and then defining sexual harassment separately, the statute makes clear that the perpetrator's intent relates to the entire definition of sexual harassment. The statute requires that the perpetrator not only intentionally subject a victim to the specified unwelcome sexual conduct (sexual advances, request for sexual favors, etc.), the perpetrator must also intend that submission to the conduct is made a term or condition of a person's exercise of any right, privilege, power, or immunity. In other words, the culpable mental state applies to both (1) sexual conduct, and (2) the *quid pro quo*."

State v. Edmond, 933 S.W.2d 120, 126-27 (Tex. Crim.App.1996). "[W]e decline to adopt the State's contention that intentional mistreatment is, by itself, criminal. Rather, we adopt the ... interpretation of §39.02(a)(1) [now 39.03(a)(1)] that 'knowledge of illegality' modifies 'mistreatment.' ... 'Unlawful' both clarifies the meaning of 'mistreatment' and provides law enforcement authorities with an objective standard by which to determine whether 'mistreatment' is criminal. [¶] [A] defendant charged under §39.02(a)(1) must mistreat another and must also know that his conduct is criminal or tortious. This interpretation avoids constitutional difficulties because potential defendants are not subject to the arbitrary predilection of law enforcement regarding the meaning of 'mistreatment'; only 'mistreatment' which is criminal or tortious is condemned."

PEN §39.04. VIOLATIONS OF THE CIVIL RIGHTS OF PERSON IN CUSTODY; IMPROPER SEXUAL ACTIVITY WITH PERSON IN CUSTODY

(a) An official of a correctional facility, an employee of a correctional facility, a person other than an employee who works for compensation at a correctional facility, a volunteer at a correctional facility, or a peace officer commits an offense if the person intentionally:

(1) denies or impedes a person in custody in the exercise or enjoyment of any right, privilege, or immunity knowing his conduct is unlawful; or

 Subsection (2) below is effective for offenses committed on or after June 8, 2007.

(2) engages in sexual contact, sexual intercourse, or deviate sexual intercourse with an individual in custody or, in the case of an individual in the custody of the Texas Youth Commission, employs, authorizes, or induces the individual to engage in sexual conduct or a sexual performance.

Subsection (2) below is effective for offenses in which any element of the offense was committed before June 8, 2007.

(2) engages in sexual contact, sexual intercourse, or deviate sexual intercourse with an individual in custody.

☠ **A** *Subsection (b) below was amended by Acts 2007, 80th Leg., ch. 378, §3, enacted May 18, 2007, effective June 15, 2007, without reference to the conflicting amendment made by Acts 2007, 80th Leg., ch. 263, §62, enacted May 25, 2007, effective June 8, 2007. For resolving conflicts, see p. V. Subsection (b) below is effective for offenses committed on or after June 15, 2007.*

(b) An offense under Subsection (a)(1) is a Class A misdemeanor. An offense under Subsection (a)(2) is a state jail felony, except that the offense is a felony of the second degree if the offense is committed against a juvenile offender detained in or committed to a correctional facility the operation of which is financed primarily with state funds.

☠ **A** *Subsection (b) below was amended by Acts 2007, 80th Leg., ch. 263, §62, enacted May 25, 2007, effective June 8, 2007, without reference to the conflicting amendment made by Acts 2007, 80th Leg., ch. 378, §3, enacted May 18, 2007, effective June 15, 2007. For resolving conflicts, see p. V. Subsection (b) below is effective for offenses committed on or after June 8, 2007.*

(b) An offense under Subsection (a)(1) is a Class A misdemeanor. An offense under Subsection (a)(2) is a state jail felony, except that an offense under Subsection (a)(2) is a felony of the second degree if the individual is in the custody of the Texas Youth Commission.

Subsection (b) below is effective for offenses in which any element of the offense was committed before June 8, 2007.

(b) An offense under Subsection (a)(1) is a Class A misdemeanor. An offense under Subsection (a)(2) is a state jail felony.

(c) This section shall not preclude prosecution for any other offense set out in this code.

(d) The Attorney General of Texas shall have concurrent jurisdiction with law enforcement agencies to investigate violations of this statute involving serious bodily injury or death.

(e) In this section:

(1) "Correctional facility" means:

(A) any place described by Section 1.07(a)(14); or

(B) a "secure correctional facility" or "secure detention facility" as defined by Section 51.02, Family Code.

(2) "Custody" means the detention, arrest, or confinement of an adult offender or the detention or the commitment of a juvenile offender to a facility operated

For a quick reference of penalties, see the Chart of Penalties on p. 675.

O'CONNOR'S CRIMINAL CODES   879

by or under a contract with the Texas Youth Commission or a facility operated by or under contract with a juvenile board.

(3) "Sexual contact," "sexual intercourse," and "deviate sexual intercourse" have the meanings assigned by Section 21.01.

E *Subsections (4) & (5) below are effective for offenses committed on or after June 8, 2007.*

(4) "Sexual conduct" and "performance" have the meanings assigned by Section 43.25.

(5) "Sexual performance" means any performance or part thereof that includes sexual conduct by an individual.

A *Subsection (f) below is effective for conduct occurring on or after Sept. 1, 2007; for orders rendered by a juvenile court on or after Sept. 1, 2007; and for information and documents relating to juvenile cases before, on, or after Sept. 1, 2007. Conduct violating penal law occurs on or after Sept. 1, 2007, if any element of the violation occurs on or after that date. In all other instances, the law is effective on Sept. 1, 2007.*

(f) An employee of the Texas Department of Criminal Justice, the Texas Youth Commission, or a local juvenile probation department commits an offense if the employee engages in sexual contact, sexual intercourse, or deviate sexual intercourse with an individual who is not the employee's spouse and who the employee knows is under the supervision of the department, commission, or probation department but not in the custody of the department, commission, or probation department.

> *Subsection (f) below is effective for conduct occurring and appeals of juvenile orders rendered before Sept. 1, 2007. In all other instances, the former law is effective until Sept. 1, 2007.*
>
> (f) An employee of the Texas Department of Criminal Justice commits an offense if the employee engages in sexual contact, sexual intercourse, or deviate sexual intercourse with an individual who is not the employee's spouse and who the employee knows is under the supervision of the department but not in the custody of the department.

(g) An offense under Subsection (f) is a state jail felony.

History of Pen §39.04: Acts 1979, 66th Leg., ch. 618, §1, eff. Sept. 1, 1979. Amended by Acts 1983, 68th Leg., ch. 558, §8, eff. Sept. 1, 1983; Acts 1987, 70th Leg., ch. 18, §5, eff. Apr. 15, 1987. Renumbered from §39.021 and amended by

Acts 1993, 73rd Leg., ch. 900, §1.01, eff. Sept. 1, 1994; Acts 1997, 75th Leg., ch. 1406, §1, eff. Sept. 1, 1997. Amended by Acts 1999, 76th Leg., ch. 158, §§1-3, eff. Sept. 1, 1999; Acts 2001, 77th Leg., ch. 1070, §1 (eff. Sept. 1, 2001), ch. 1297, §69 (eff. Sept. 1, 2001); Acts 2007, 80th Leg., ch. 263, §§62, 63 (eff. June 8, 2007), ch. 378, §3 (eff. June 15, 2007), ch. 908, §43 (eff. Sept. 1, 2007).

ANNOTATIONS

Pastrano v. State, 250 S.W.3d 128, 132-33 (Tex. App.—Austin 2008, pet. filed 6-11-08). "[T]he legislature used ['offender' in the definition of 'custody'] because the conduct with which §39.04 is concerned most often (but not always) takes place in a correctional facility and involves individuals who are, in fact, convicted offenders. However, there is nothing in the history of §39.04 or in the plain language of subsection (e)(2) to suggest that the legislature intended the terms 'adult offender' and 'juvenile offender' to define or limit the meaning of 'individual' in subsection (a)(2). [¶] [W]e are convinced that the legislature intended to prohibit a peace officer from engaging in sexual contact with any individual in the officer's custody, adult or juvenile, guilty or innocent, and that the legislature did not intend to excuse such conduct if the individual is thereafter released from custody without being accused of a crime."

Edwards v. State, 97 S.W.3d 279, 289 (Tex.App.—Houston [14th Dist.] 2003, pet. ref'd). "The test ... for whether appellant was an 'employee' of the Harris County Jail is whether he was subject to the Jail's control." Held: Driver of prisoner transportation van was agent, and therefore "employee," of jail.

PEN §39.05. FAILURE TO REPORT DEATH OF PRISONER

(a) A person commits an offense if the person is required to conduct an investigation and file a report by Article 49.18, Code of Criminal Procedure, and the person fails to investigate the death, fails to file the report as required, or fails to include in a filed report facts known or discovered in the investigation.

(b) A person commits an offense if the person is required by Section 501.055, Government Code, to:

(1) give notice of the death of an inmate and the person fails to give the notice; or

(2) conduct an investigation and file a report and the person:

(A) fails to conduct the investigation or file the report; or

(B) fails to include in the report facts known to the person or discovered by the person in the investigation.

(c) An offense under this section is a Class B misdemeanor.

History of Pen §39.05: Acts 1983, 68th Leg., ch. 441, §2, eff. Sept. 1, 1983. Renumbered from §39.022 and amended by Acts 1993, 73rd Leg., ch. 900, §1.01, eff. Sept. 1, 1994. Amended by Acts 1995, 74th Leg., ch. 321, §1.104, eff. Sept. 1, 1995.

PEN §39.06. MISUSE OF OFFICIAL INFORMATION

(a) A public servant commits an offense if, in reliance on information to which he has access by virtue of his office or employment and that has not been made public, he:

(1) acquires or aids another to acquire a pecuniary interest in any property, transaction, or enterprise that may be affected by the information;

(2) speculates or aids another to speculate on the basis of the information; or

(3) as a public servant, including as a principal of a school, coerces another into suppressing or failing to report that information to a law enforcement agency.

(b) A public servant commits an offense if with intent to obtain a benefit or with intent to harm or defraud another, he discloses or uses information for a nongovernmental purpose that:

(1) he has access to by means of his office or employment; and

(2) has not been made public.

(c) A person commits an offense if, with intent to obtain a benefit or with intent to harm or defraud another, he solicits or receives from a public servant information that:

(1) the public servant has access to by means of his office or employment; and

(2) has not been made public.

(d) In this section, "information that has not been made public" means any information to which the public does not generally have access, and that is prohibited from disclosure under Chapter 552, Government Code.

(e) Except as provided by Subsection (f), an offense under this section is a felony of the third degree.

(f) An offense under Subsection (a)(3) is a Class C misdemeanor.

History of Pen §39.06: Acts 1973, 63rd Leg., ch. 399, §1, eff. Jan. 1, 1974. Amended by Acts 1983, 68th Leg., ch. 558, §9, eff. Sept. 1, 1983; Acts 1987, 70th Leg., ch. 30, §1 (eff. Sept. 1, 1987), 2nd C.S., ch. 43, §3 (eff. Oct. 20, 1987); Acts 1989, 71st Leg., ch. 927, §1, eff. Aug. 28, 1989. Renumbered from §39.03 and amended by Acts 1993, 73rd Leg., ch. 900, §1.01, eff. Sept. 1, 1994; Acts 1995, 74th Leg., ch. 76, §5.95(90) (eff. Sept. 1, 1995), ch. 76, §14.52 (eff. Sept. 1, 1995).

State v. Ford, 179 S.W.3d 117, 125 (Tex.App.—San Antonio 2005, pet. dism'd). "We conclude that because the grand jury is an extension of the judiciary, and judicial information is not 'public information' within the meaning of the Open Records Act, grand jury information is not subject to the Open Records Act. Because the Open Records Act is simply *not applicable* to information presented to a grand jury, the information that [attorneys] allegedly solicited or received from the grand jurors did not fall within the Act's scope, and thus could not be 'prohibited from disclosure under Chapter 552,' as required by §39.06(d) of the Penal Code."

TITLE 9. OFFENSES AGAINST PUBLIC ORDER & DECENCY

CHAPTER 42. DISORDERLY CONDUCT & RELATED OFFENSES

PEN §42.01. DISORDERLY CONDUCT

(a) A person commits an offense if he intentionally or knowingly:

(1) uses abusive, indecent, profane, or vulgar language in a public place, and the language by its very utterance tends to incite an immediate breach of the peace;

(2) makes an offensive gesture or display in a public place, and the gesture or display tends to incite an immediate breach of the peace;

For a quick reference of penalties, see the Chart of Penalties on p. 675.

O'CONNOR'S CRIMINAL CODES   881

PEN §42.01

(3) creates, by chemical means, a noxious and unreasonable odor in a public place;

(4) abuses or threatens a person in a public place in an obviously offensive manner;

(5) makes unreasonable noise in a public place other than a sport shooting range, as defined by Section 250.001, Local Government Code, or in or near a private residence that he has no right to occupy;

(6) fights with another in a public place;

(7) discharges a firearm in a public place other than a public road or a sport shooting range, as defined by Section 250.001, Local Government Code;

(8) displays a firearm or other deadly weapon in a public place in a manner calculated to alarm;

(9) discharges a firearm on or across a public road;

(10) exposes his anus or genitals in a public place and is reckless about whether another may be present who will be offended or alarmed by his act; or

(11) for a lewd or unlawful purpose:

(A) enters on the property of another and looks into a dwelling on the property through any window or other opening in the dwelling;

(B) while on the premises of a hotel or comparable establishment, looks into a guest room not the person's own through a window or other opening in the room; or

(C) while on the premises of a public place, looks into an area such as a restroom or shower stall or changing or dressing room that is designed to provide privacy to a person using the area.

(b) It is a defense to prosecution under Subsection (a)(4) that the actor had significant provocation for his abusive or threatening conduct.

(c) For purposes of this section:

(1) an act is deemed to occur in a public place or near a private residence if it produces its offensive or proscribed consequences in the public place or near a private residence; and

(2) a noise is presumed to be unreasonable if the noise exceeds a decibel level of 85 after the person making the noise receives notice from a magistrate or peace officer that the noise is a public nuisance.

(d) An offense under this section is a Class C misdemeanor unless committed under Subsection (a)(7) or (a)(8), in which event it is a Class B misdemeanor.

(e) It is a defense to prosecution for an offense under Subsection (a)(7) or (9) that the person who discharged the firearm had a reasonable fear of bodily injury to the person or to another by a dangerous wild animal as defined by Section 822.101, Health and Safety Code.

History of Pen §42.01: Acts 1973, 63rd Leg., ch. 399, §1, eff. Jan. 1, 1974. Amended by Acts 1977, 65th Leg., ch. 89, §§1, 2, eff. Aug. 29, 1977; Acts 1983, 68th Leg., ch. 800, §1, eff. Sept. 1, 1983; Acts 1991, 72nd Leg., ch. 145, §2, eff. Aug. 26, 1991; Acts 1993, 73rd Leg., ch. 900, §1.01, eff. Sept. 1, 1994; Acts 1995, 74th Leg., ch. 318, §14, eff. Sept. 1, 1995; Acts 2001, 77th Leg., ch. 54, §4, eff. Sept. 1, 2001; Acts 2003, 78th Leg., ch. 389, §1, eff. Sept. 1, 2003.

ANNOTATIONS

Lacour v. State, 8 S.W.3d 670, 671 (Tex.Crim.App. 2000). "Section 42.01(a)(12) [now §42.01(a)(10)] makes no exceptions for public places that are 'remote' or 'secluded' or for when others are 'regularly engaged in the same conduct.' [¶] A rational jury could have inferred the ultimate fact of appellant's recklessness from the basic fact of his nakedness on a public beach. ... This holding does not dispense with the State's obligation to prove recklessness...."

Coggin v. State, 123 S.W.3d 82, 86 (Tex.App.—Austin 2003, pet. ref'd). "Appellant was charged solely with disorderly conduct by the gesture of extending his middle finger. *At 92:* But given the circumstances—the brief exposure to the gesture as one car passed the other, made stranger to stranger, causing momentary hostility on [victim's] part—we cannot conclude that appellant's conduct tends to incite an immediate breach of the peace. There was no actual or threatened violence, 'which is an essential element of a breach of the peace.'"

Ste-Marie v. State, 32 S.W.3d 446, 449 (Tex.App.—Houston [14th Dist.] 2000, no pet.). Breach of the peace means "an act that disturbs or threatens to disturb the tranquility enjoyed by the citizens. [F]ighting words are those that inflict injury or tend to incite an immediate breach of the peace by their very utterance. We can find no law ... that differentiates between fighting words spoken to an adult versus a child. Therefore, we hold the statute applies to minors as much as adults. ... Appellant's utterance of the profanity provides sufficient articulable facts on which [officer] could reasonably believe that appellant engaged in disorderly conduct. Accordingly, his detention of appellant was not illegal...."

Blanco v. State, 761 S.W.2d 38, 42 (Tex.App.—Houston [14th Dist.] 1988, no pet.). "Noise commonly means a loud, confused, or senseless outcry, or a sound noticeably loud, harsh, or discordant."

PEN §42.015. DELETED

Deleted by Acts 1993, 73rd Leg., ch. 900, §13.02, eff. Sept. 1, 1994.

PEN §42.02. RIOT

(a) For the purpose of this section, "riot" means the assemblage of seven or more persons resulting in conduct which:

(1) creates an immediate danger of damage to property or injury to persons;

(2) substantially obstructs law enforcement or other governmental functions or services; or

(3) by force, threat of force, or physical action deprives any person of a legal right or disturbs any person in the enjoyment of a legal right.

(b) A person commits an offense if he knowingly participates in a riot.

(c) It is a defense to prosecution under this section that the assembly was at first lawful and when one of those assembled manifested an intent to engage in conduct enumerated in Subsection (a), the actor retired from the assembly.

(d) It is no defense to prosecution under this section that another who was a party to the riot has been acquitted, has not been arrested, prosecuted, or convicted, has been convicted of a different offense or of a different type or class of offense, or is immune from prosecution.

(e) Except as provided in Subsection (f), an offense under this section is a Class B misdemeanor.

(f) An offense under this section is an offense of the same classification as any offense of a higher grade committed by anyone engaged in the riot if the offense was:

(1) in the furtherance of the purpose of the assembly; or

(2) an offense which should have been anticipated as a result of the assembly.

History of Pen §42.02: Acts 1973, 63rd Leg., ch. 399, §1, eff. Jan. 1, 1974. Amended by Acts 1993, 73rd Leg., ch. 900, §1.01, eff. Sept. 1, 1994.

PEN §42.03. OBSTRUCTING HIGHWAY OR OTHER PASSAGEWAY

(a) A person commits an offense if, without legal privilege or authority, he intentionally, knowingly, or recklessly:

(1) obstructs a highway, street, sidewalk, railway, waterway, elevator, aisle, hallway, entrance, or exit to which the public or a substantial group of the public has access, or any other place used for the passage of persons, vehicles, or conveyances, regardless of the means of creating the obstruction and whether the obstruction arises from his acts alone or from his acts and the acts of others; or

(2) disobeys a reasonable request or order to move issued by a person the actor knows to be or is informed is a peace officer, a fireman, or a person with authority to control the use of the premises:

(A) to prevent obstruction of a highway or any of those areas mentioned in Subdivision (1); or

(B) to maintain public safety by dispersing those gathered in dangerous proximity to a fire, riot, or other hazard.

(b) For purposes of this section, "obstruct" means to render impassable or to render passage unreasonably inconvenient or hazardous.

(c) An offense under this section is a Class B misdemeanor.

History of Pen §42.03: Acts 1973, 63rd Leg., ch. 399, §1, eff. Jan. 1, 1974. Amended by Acts 1993, 73rd Leg., ch. 900, §1.01, eff. Sept. 1, 1994.

ANNOTATIONS

Lauderback v. State, 789 S.W.2d 343, 345 (Tex. App.—Fort Worth 1990, pet. ref'd). The word "'privilege' refers to the right to obstruct a passageway, not to whether a person may use a passageway if they do not create an obstruction. [W]hile a person may generally stand on a sidewalk, he may be arrested if doing so creates an obstruction. A pedestrian or a wheelchair user's right to use a highway is similarly limited by the law regarding obstructions. *At 346:* The fact that only one person has to go around someone and walk in the mud has been found sufficient to prove that the passage was rendered unreasonably inconvenient and the defendant therefore created an obstruction."

Breeding v. State, 762 S.W.2d 737, 740 (Tex.App.—Amarillo 1988, pet. ref'd). "The object or purpose of §42.03 is to promote public order by outlawing the unprivileged obstruction of any place used for the passage of persons or vehicles."

PEN §42.04. DEFENSE WHEN CONDUCT CONSISTS OF SPEECH OR OTHER EXPRESSION

(a) If conduct that would otherwise violate Section 42.01(a)(5) (Unreasonable Noise), 42.03 (Obstructing

PEN §42.04

For a quick reference of penalties, see the Chart of Penalties on p. 675.

O'CONNOR'S CRIMINAL CODES   883

Passageway), or 42.055 (Funeral Service Disruptions) consists of speech or other communication, of gathering with others to hear or observe such speech or communication, or of gathering with others to picket or otherwise express in a nonviolent manner a position on social, economic, political, or religious questions, the actor must be ordered to move, disperse, or otherwise remedy the violation prior to his arrest if he has not yet intentionally harmed the interests of others which those sections seek to protect.

(b) The order required by this section may be given by a peace officer, a fireman, a person with authority to control the use of the premises, or any person directly affected by the violation.

(c) It is a defense to prosecution under Section 42.01(a)(5), 42.03, or 42.055:

(1) that in circumstances in which this section requires an order no order was given;

(2) that an order, if given, was manifestly unreasonable in scope; or

(3) that an order, if given, was promptly obeyed.

History of Pen §42.04: Acts 1973, 63rd Leg., ch. 399, §1, eff. Jan. 1, 1974. Amended by Acts 1993, 73rd Leg., ch. 900, §1.01, eff. Sept. 1, 1994; Acts 2006, 79th Leg., ch. 2, §2, 3d C.S., eff. May 19, 2006.

PEN §42.05. DISRUPTING MEETING OR PROCESSION

(a) A person commits an offense if, with intent to prevent or disrupt a lawful meeting, procession, or gathering, he obstructs or interferes with the meeting, procession, or gathering by physical action or verbal utterance.

(b) An offense under this section is a Class B misdemeanor.

History of Pen §42.05: Acts 1973, 63rd Leg., ch. 399, §1, eff. Jan. 1, 1974.

ANNOTATIONS

State v. Markovich, 77 S.W.3d 274, 277 (Tex.Crim. App.2002). "[W]e have never considered curtailment of others' First Amendment rights to be an element of §42.05. *At 280:* [W]e hold that §42.05 is not unconstitutionally vague on its face." *See also* **Morehead v. State**, 807 S.W.2d 577, 581 (Tex.Crim.App.1991).

PEN §42.055. FUNERAL SERVICE DISRUPTIONS

(a) In this section:

(1) "Facility" means a building at which any portion of a funeral service takes place, including a funeral parlor, mortuary, private home, or established place of worship.

(2) "Funeral service" means a ceremony, procession, or memorial service, including a wake or viewing, held in connection with the burial or cremation of the dead.

(3) "Picketing" means:

(A) standing, sitting, or repeated walking, riding, driving, or other similar action by a person displaying or carrying a banner, placard, or sign;

(B) engaging in loud singing, chanting, whistling, or yelling, with or without noise amplification through a device such as a bullhorn or microphone; or

(C) blocking access to a facility or cemetery being used for a funeral service.

 Subsection (b) below is effective for offenses committed on or after June 4, 2007.

(b) A person commits an offense if, during the period beginning one hour before the service begins and ending one hour after the service is completed, the person engages in picketing within 1,000 feet of a facility or cemetery being used for a funeral service.

Subsection (b) below is effective for offenses in which any element of the offense was committed before June 4, 2007.

(b) A person commits an offense if, during the period beginning one hour before the service begins and ending one hour after the service is completed, the person engages in picketing within 500 feet of a facility or cemetery being used for a funeral service.

(c) An offense under this section is a Class B misdemeanor.

History of Pen §42.055: Acts 2006, 79th Leg., 3d C.S., ch. 2, §1, May 19, 2006; Acts 2007, 80th Leg., ch. 256, §1, eff. June 4, 2007.

PEN §42.06. FALSE ALARM OR REPORT

(a) A person commits an offense if he knowingly initiates, communicates or circulates a report of a present, past, or future bombing, fire, offense, or other emergency that he knows is false or baseless and that would ordinarily:

(1) cause action by an official or volunteer agency organized to deal with emergencies;

(2) place a person in fear of imminent serious bodily injury; or

(3) prevent or interrupt the occupation of a building, room, place of assembly, place to which the public has access, or aircraft, automobile, or other mode of conveyance.

(b) An offense under this section is a Class A misdemeanor unless the false report is of an emergency involving a public primary or secondary school, public communications, public transportation, public water, gas, or power supply or other public service, in which event the offense is a state jail felony.

History of Pen §42.06: Acts 1973, 63rd Leg., ch. 399, §1, eff. Jan. 1, 1974. Amended by Acts 1979, 66th Leg., ch. 530, §4, eff. Aug. 27, 1979; Acts 1993, 73rd Leg., ch. 900, §1.01, eff. Sept. 1, 1994.

PEN §42.061. SILENT OR ABUSIVE CALLS TO 9-1-1 SERVICE

(a) In this section "9-1-1 service" and "public safety answering point" or "PSAP" have the meanings assigned by Section 772.001, Health and Safety Code.

(b) A person commits an offense if the person makes a telephone call to 9-1-1 when there is not an emergency and knowingly or intentionally:

(1) remains silent; or

(2) makes abusive or harassing statements to a PSAP employee.

(c) A person commits an offense if the person knowingly permits a telephone under the person's control to be used by another person in a manner described in Subsection (b).

(d) An offense under this section is a Class B misdemeanor.

History of Pen §42.061: Acts 1989, 71st Leg., ch. 582, §1, eff. Sept. 1, 1989. Amended by Acts 1991, 72nd Leg., ch. 14, §284(2), eff. Sept. 1, 1991; Acts 1993, 73rd Leg., ch. 900, §1.01, eff. Sept. 1, 1994.

PEN §42.062. INTERFERENCE WITH EMERGENCY TELEPHONE CALL

(a) An individual commits an offense if the individual knowingly prevents or interferes with another individual's ability to place an emergency telephone call or to request assistance in an emergency from a law enforcement agency, medical facility, or other agency or entity the primary purpose of which is to provide for the safety of individuals.

(b) An individual commits an offense if the individual recklessly renders unusable a telephone that would otherwise be used by another individual to place an emergency telephone call or to request assistance in an emergency from a law enforcement agency, medical facility, or other agency or entity the primary purpose of which is to provide for the safety of individuals.

(c) An offense under this section is a Class A misdemeanor, except that the offense is a state jail felony if the actor has previously been convicted under this section.

(d) In this section, "emergency" means a condition or circumstance in which any individual is or is reasonably believed by the individual making a telephone call to be in fear of imminent assault or in which property is or is reasonably believed by the individual making the telephone call to be in imminent danger of damage or destruction.

History of Pen §42.062: Acts 2001, 77th Leg., ch. 690, §1, eff. Sept. 1, 2001. Amended by Acts 2003, 78th Leg., ch. 460, §1 (eff. Sept. 1, 2003), ch. 1164, §1 (eff. Sept. 1, 2003).

PEN §42.07. HARASSMENT

(a) A person commits an offense if, with intent to harass, annoy, alarm, abuse, torment, or embarrass another, he:

(1) initiates communication by telephone, in writing, or by electronic communication and in the course of the communication makes a comment, request, suggestion, or proposal that is obscene;

(2) threatens, by telephone, in writing, or by electronic communication, in a manner reasonably likely to alarm the person receiving the threat, to inflict bodily injury on the person or to commit a felony against the person, a member of his family or household, or his property;

(3) conveys, in a manner reasonably likely to alarm the person receiving the report, a false report, which is known by the conveyor to be false, that another person has suffered death or serious bodily injury;

(4) causes the telephone of another to ring repeatedly or makes repeated telephone communications anonymously or in a manner reasonably likely to harass, annoy, alarm, abuse, torment, embarrass, or offend another;

(5) makes a telephone call and intentionally fails to hang up or disengage the connection;

(6) knowingly permits a telephone under the person's control to be used by another to commit an offense under this section; or

(7) sends repeated electronic communications in a manner reasonably likely to harass, annoy, alarm, abuse, torment, embarrass, or offend another.

(b) In this section:

(1) "Electronic communication" means a transfer of signs, signals, writing, images, sounds, data, or intelligence of any nature transmitted in whole or in part by a wire, radio, electromagnetic, photoelectronic, or photo-optical system. The term includes:

For a quick reference of penalties, see the Chart of Penalties on p. 675.

O'CONNOR'S CRIMINAL CODES   885

(A) a communication initiated by electronic mail, instant message, network call, or facsimile machine; and

(B) a communication made to a pager.

(2) "Family" and "household" have the meaning assigned by Chapter 71, Family Code.

(3) "Obscene" means containing a patently offensive description of or a solicitation to commit an ultimate sex act, including sexual intercourse, masturbation, cunnilingus, fellatio, or anilingus, or a description of an excretory function.

(c) An offense under this section is a Class B misdemeanor, except that the offense is a Class A misdemeanor if the actor has previously been convicted under this section.

History of Pen §42.07: Acts 1973, 63rd Leg., ch. 399, §1, eff. Jan. 1, 1974. Amended by Acts 1983, 68th Leg., p. 2204, ch. 411, §1, eff. Sept. 1, 1983; Acts 1993, 73rd Leg., ch. 10, §1 (eff. Mar. 19, 1993), ch. 900, §1.01 (eff. Sept. 1, 1994); Acts 1995, 74th Leg., ch. 657, §1, eff. June 14, 1995; Acts 1999, 76th Leg., ch. 62, §15.02(d), eff. Sept. 1, 1999; Acts 2001, 77th Leg., ch. 1222, §1, eff. Sept. 1, 2001.

ANNOTATIONS

Lefevers v. State, 20 S.W.3d 707, 712 (Tex.Crim. App.2000). "As used in §42.07, the phrase 'ultimate sex act' includes 'sexual intercourse, masturbation, cunnilingus, fellatio, or anilingus, or a description of an excretory function.' Each of the enumerated actions involves genital contact, anal contact, or an excretory function. In the instant case, appellant stated, 'I want to feel your breasts.' This statement refers to an action which is encompassed by none of those three categories. Consequently, it cannot be said that appellant described an 'ultimate sex act,' as defined in §42.07(b). This interpretation also gives 'ultimate sex act' a meaning readily comprehended by the average person." *See also Pettijohn v. State*, 782 S.W.2d 866, 868 (Tex.Crim. App.1989); *Campbell v. State*, 653 S.W.2d 23, 26 (Tex. Crim.App.1983).

Karenev v. State, ___ S.W.3d ___ (Tex.App.—Fort Worth 2008, pet. filed 6-17-08) (No. 2-05-425-CR; 4-03-08). "Because we hold that §42.07(a)(7) is unconstitutionally vague, we also hold that it is void."

Segura v. State, 100 S.W.3d 652, 656 (Tex.App.—Dallas 2003, no pet.). "The elements of harassment … may be satisfied with only one offense and without actions directed at one specific person. *At 657:* Although the offenses of stalking and harassment partially overlap in subject matter, they address different conduct

and do not share a common purpose or object. [S]talking and harassment are not *in pari materia*. It follows that one statute could not be considered controlling as to the other. It was therefore in the State's discretion to prosecute appellant for stalking rather than for harassment."

Blount v. State, 961 S.W.2d 282, 284 (Tex.App.—Houston [1st Dist.] 1997, pet. ref'd). "The legislature clearly intended for a defendant to be criminally responsible for the crime of telephone harassment *only* when he intended, that is, consciously desired, the result of his actions. The intent of the accused may be inferred from circumstantial evidence."

Salisbury v. State, 867 S.W.2d 894, 898 (Tex. App.—Houston [14th Dist.] 1993, pet. ref'd). Under §42.07 "venue may lie in any county where the communication was initiated as well as any county where the communication was received."

PEN §42.071. REPEALED
Repealed by Acts 1997, 75th Leg., ch. 1, §1, eff. Jan. 28, 1997.

PEN §42.072. STALKING

(a) A person commits an offense if the person, on more than one occasion and pursuant to the same scheme or course of conduct that is directed specifically at another person, knowingly engages in conduct, including following the other person, that:

(1) the actor knows or reasonably believes the other person will regard as threatening:

(A) bodily injury or death for the other person;

(B) bodily injury or death for a member of the other person's family or household; or

(C) that an offense will be committed against the other person's property;

(2) causes the other person or a member of the other person's family or household to be placed in fear of bodily injury or death or fear that an offense will be committed against the other person's property; and

(3) would cause a reasonable person to fear:

(A) bodily injury or death for himself or herself;

(B) bodily injury or death for a member of the person's family or household; or

(C) that an offense will be committed against the person's property.

(b) An offense under this section is a felony of the third degree, except that the offense is a felony of the second degree if the actor has previously been convicted under this section.

(c) In this section, "family," "household," and "member of a household" have the meanings assigned by Chapter 71, Family Code.

History of Pen §42.072: Acts 1997, 75th Leg., ch. 1, §1, eff. Jan. 28, 1997. Amended by Acts 1999, 76th Leg., ch. 62, §15.02(e), eff. Sept. 1, 1999; Acts 2001, 77th Leg., ch. 1222, §2, eff. Sept. 1, 2001.

Ploeger v. State, 189 S.W.3d 799, 805 (Tex.App.—Houston [1st Dist.] 2006, no pet.). "We agree with the parties' position on appeal that sub-paragraphs (1), (2), and (3) of §42.072(a) are each elements of a single offense. *At 807:* We hold that the trial court erred in charging the statutory elements disjunctively, so that the charge allowed the jury to find appellant guilty upon finding fewer than all of the elements of the offense of stalking."

State v. Newsom, 64 S.W.3d 478, 481 (Tex. App.—El Paso 2001, no pet.). "It is undisputed that [appellee's] prior conviction [for stalking] is a probated sentence which had not been revoked at the time he allegedly committed the new stalking offense. Because the prior conviction is not a final conviction, the trial court properly granted the motion to quash and dismissed the enhancement allegation."

PEN §42.08. ABUSE OF CORPSE

(a) A person commits an offense if the person, without legal authority, knowingly:

(1) disinters, disturbs, damages, dissects, in whole or in part, carries away, or treats in an offensive manner a human corpse;

(2) conceals a human corpse knowing it to be illegally disinterred;

(3) sells or buys a human corpse or in any way traffics in a human corpse;

(4) transmits or conveys, or procures to be transmitted or conveyed, a human corpse to a place outside the state; or

(5) vandalizes, damages, or treats in an offensive manner the space in which a human corpse has been interred or otherwise permanently laid to rest.

(b) An offense under this section is a Class A misdemeanor.

(c) In this section, "human corpse" includes:

(1) any portion of a human corpse;

(2) the cremated remains of a human corpse; or

(3) any portion of the cremated remains of a human corpse.

(d) If conduct constituting an offense under this section also constitutes an offense under another section of this code, the actor may be prosecuted under either section or both sections.

(e) It is a defense to prosecution under this section that the actor:

(1) as a member or agent of a cemetery organization, removed or damaged anything that had been placed in or on any portion of the organization's cemetery in violation of the rules of the organization; or

(2) removed anything:

(A) placed in the cemetery in violation of the rules of the cemetery organization; or

(B) placed in the cemetery by or with the cemetery organization's consent but that, in the organization's judgment, had become wrecked, unsightly, or dilapidated.

(f) In this section, "cemetery" and "cemetery organization" have the meanings assigned by Section 711.001, Health and Safety Code.

History of Pen §42.08: Acts 1973, 63rd Leg., ch. 399, §1, eff. Jan. 1, 1974. Renumbered from §42.10 by Acts 1993, 73rd Leg., ch. 900, §1.01, eff. Sept. 1, 1994; Amended by Acts 2005, 79th Leg., ch. 1025, §1, eff. June 18, 2005.

PEN §42.09. CRUELTY TO LIVESTOCK ANIMALS

🅐 *Section 42.09 below is effective for offenses committed on or after Sept. 1, 2007.*

(a) A person commits an offense if the person intentionally or knowingly:

(1) tortures a livestock animal;

(2) fails unreasonably to provide necessary food, water, or care for a livestock animal in the person's custody;

(3) abandons unreasonably a livestock animal in the person's custody;

(4) transports or confines a livestock animal in a cruel and unusual manner;

(5) administers poison to a livestock animal, other than cattle, horses, sheep, swine, or goats, belonging to another without legal authority or the owner's effective consent;

(6) causes one livestock animal to fight with another livestock animal or with an animal as defined by Section 42.092;

For a quick reference of penalties, see the Chart of Penalties on p. 675.

O'CONNOR'S CRIMINAL CODES 887

(7) uses a live livestock animal as a lure in dog race training or in dog coursing on a racetrack;

(8) trips a horse; or

(9) seriously overworks a livestock animal.

(b) In this section:

(1) "Abandon" includes abandoning a livestock animal in the person's custody without making reasonable arrangements for assumption of custody by another person.

(2) "Cruel manner" includes a manner that causes or permits unjustified or unwarranted pain or suffering.

(3) "Custody" includes responsibility for the health, safety, and welfare of a livestock animal subject to the person's care and control, regardless of ownership of the livestock animal.

(4) "Depredation" has the meaning assigned by Section 71.001, Parks and Wildlife Code.

(5) "Livestock animal" means:

(A) cattle, sheep, swine, goats, ratites, or poultry commonly raised for human consumption;

(B) a horse, pony, mule, donkey, or hinny;

(C) native or nonnative hoofstock raised under agriculture practices; or

(D) native or nonnative fowl commonly raised under agricultural practices.

(6) "Necessary food, water, or care" includes food, water, or care provided to the extent required to maintain the livestock animal in a state of good health.

(7) "Torture" includes any act that causes unjustifiable pain or suffering.

(8) "Trip" means to use an object to cause a horse to fall or lose its balance.

(c) An offense under Subsection (a)(2), (3), (4), or (9) is a Class A misdemeanor, except that the offense is a state jail felony if the person has previously been convicted two times under this section, two times under Section 42.092, or one time under this section and one time under Section 42.092. An offense under Subsection (a)(1), (5), (6), (7), or (8) is a state jail felony, except that the offense is a felony of the third degree if the person has previously been convicted two times under this section, two times under Section 42.092, or one time under this section and one time under Section 42.092.

(d) It is a defense to prosecution under Subsection (a)(8) that the actor tripped the horse for the purpose of identifying the ownership of the horse or giving veterinary care to the horse.

(e) It is a defense to prosecution for an offense under this section that the actor was engaged in bona fide experimentation for scientific research.

(f) It is an exception to the application of this section that the conduct engaged in by the actor is a generally accepted and otherwise lawful:

(1) form of conduct occurring solely for the purpose of or in support of:

(A) fishing, hunting, or trapping; or

(B) wildlife management, wildlife or depredation control, or shooting preserve practices as regulated by state and federal law; or

(2) animal husbandry or agriculture practice involving livestock animals.

(g) This section does not create a civil cause of action for damages or enforcement of this section.

History of Pen §42.09: Acts 1973, 63rd Leg., ch. 399, §1, eff. Jan. 1, 1974. Amended by Acts 1975, 64th Leg., ch. 342, §12, eff. Sept. 1, 1975; Acts 1985, 69th Leg., ch. 549, §1, eff. Sept. 1, 1985; Acts 1991, 72nd Leg., ch. 78, §1, eff. Aug. 26, 1991. Renumbered from §42.11 and amended by Acts 1993, 73rd Leg., ch. 900, §1.01, eff. Sept. 1, 1994. Amended by Acts 1995, 74th Leg., ch. 318, §15, eff. Sept. 1, 1995; Acts 1997, 75th Leg., ch. 1283, §1, eff. Sept. 1, 1997; Acts 2001, 77th Leg., ch. 54, §3 (eff. Sept. 1, 2001), ch. 450, §1 (eff. Sept. 1, 2001); Acts 2003, 78th Leg., ch. 1275, §2(116), eff. Sept. 1, 2003; Acts 2007, 80th Leg., ch. 886, §1, eff. Sept. 1, 2007.

PEN §42.09. CRUELTY TO ANIMALS

Section 42.09 below is effective for offenses in which any element of the offense was committed before Sept. 1, 2007.

(a) A person commits an offense if the person intentionally or knowingly:

(1) tortures an animal;

(2) fails unreasonably to provide necessary food, care, or shelter for an animal in the person's custody;

(3) abandons unreasonably an animal in the person's custody;

(4) transports or confines an animal in a cruel manner;

(5) kills, seriously injures, or administers poison to an animal, other than cattle, horses, sheep, swine, or goats, belonging to another without legal authority or the owner's effective consent;

(6) causes one animal to fight with another;

(7) uses a live animal as a lure in dog race training or in dog coursing on a racetrack;

(8) trips a horse;

(9) injures an animal, other than cattle, horses, sheep, swine, or goats, belonging to another without legal authority or the owner's effective consent; or

(10) seriously overworks an animal.

(b) It is a defense to prosecution under this section that the actor was engaged in bona fide experimentation for scientific research.

(c) For purposes of this section:

(1) "Abandon" includes abandoning an animal in the person's custody without making reasonable arrangements for assumption of custody by another person.

(2) "Animal" means a domesticated living creature and wild living creature previously captured. "Animal" does not include an uncaptured wild creature or a wild creature whose capture was accomplished by conduct at issue under this section.

(3) "Cruel manner" includes a manner that causes or permits unjustified or unwarranted pain or suffering.

(4) "Custody" includes responsibility for the health, safety, and welfare of an animal subject to the person's care and control, regardless of ownership of the animal.

(5) "Necessary food, care, or shelter" includes food, care, or shelter provided to the extent required to maintain the animal in a state of good health.

(6) "Trip" means to use an object to cause a horse to fall or lose its balance.

(d) An offense under Subsection (a)(2), (3), (4), (9), or (10) is a Class A misdemeanor, except that the offense is a state jail felony if the person has previously been convicted two times under this section.

(e) It is a defense to prosecution under Subsection (a)(5) that the animal was discovered on the person's property in the act of or immediately after injuring or killing the person's goats, sheep, cattle, horses, swine, or poultry and that the person killed or injured the animal at the time of this discovery.

(f) It is a defense to prosecution under Subsection (a)(8) that the actor tripped the horse for the purpose of identifying the ownership of the horse or giving veterinary care to the horse.

(g) It is a defense to prosecution for an offense under this section that the person had a reasonable fear of bodily injury to the person or to another by a dangerous wild animal as defined by Section 822.101, Health and Safety Code.

(h) It is an exception to the application of this section that the conduct engaged in by the actor is a generally accepted and otherwise lawful:

(1) use of an animal if that use occurs solely for the purpose of:

(A) fishing, hunting, or trapping; or

(B) wildlife control as regulated by state and federal law; or

(2) animal husbandry or farming practice involving livestock.

(i) An offense under Subsection (a)(1), (5), (6), (7), or (8) is a state jail felony, except that the offense is a felony of the third degree if the person has previously been convicted two times under this section.

PEN §42.091. ATTACK ON ASSISTANCE ANIMAL

(a) A person commits an offense if the person intentionally, knowingly, or recklessly attacks, injures, or kills an assistance animal.

(b) A person commits an offense if the person intentionally, knowingly, or recklessly incites or permits an animal owned by or otherwise in the custody of the actor to attack, injure, or kill an assistance animal and, as a result of the person's conduct, the assistance animal is attacked, injured, or killed.

(c) An offense under this section is a:

(1) Class A misdemeanor if the actor or an animal owned by or otherwise in the custody of the actor attacks an assistance animal;

(2) state jail felony if the actor or an animal owned by or otherwise in the custody of the actor injures an assistance animal; or

(3) felony of the third degree if the actor or an animal owned by or otherwise in the custody of the actor kills an assistance animal.

(d) A court shall order a defendant convicted of an offense under Subsection (a) to make restitution to the owner of the assistance animal for:

(1) related veterinary or medical bills;

(2) the cost of:

(A) replacing the assistance animal; or

For a quick reference of penalties, see the Chart of Penalties on p. 675.

O'CONNOR'S CRIMINAL CODES   889

(B) retraining an injured assistance animal by an organization generally recognized by agencies involved in the rehabilitation of persons with disabilities as reputable and competent to provide special equipment for or special training to an animal to help a person with a disability; and

(3) any other expense reasonably incurred as a result of the offense.

(e) In this section:

(1) "Assistance animal" has the meaning assigned by Section 121.002, Human Resources Code.

(2) "Custody" has the meaning assigned by Section 42.09.

History of Pen §42.091: Acts 2003, 78th Leg., ch. 710, §2, eff. Sept. 1, 2003.

PEN §42.092. CRUELTY TO NONLIVESTOCK ANIMALS

 Section 42.092 below is effective for offenses committed on or after Sept. 1, 2007.

(a) In this section:

(1) "Abandon" includes abandoning an animal in the person's custody without making reasonable arrangements for assumption of custody by another person.

(2) "Animal" means a domesticated living creature, including any stray or feral cat or dog, and a wild living creature previously captured. The term does not include an uncaptured wild living creature or a livestock animal.

(3) "Cruel manner" includes a manner that causes or permits unjustified or unwarranted pain or suffering.

(4) "Custody" includes responsibility for the health, safety, and welfare of an animal subject to the person's care and control, regardless of ownership of the animal.

(5) "Depredation" has the meaning assigned by Section 71.001, Parks and Wildlife Code.

(6) "Livestock animal" has the meaning assigned by Section 42.09.

(7) "Necessary food, water, care, or shelter" includes food, water, care, or shelter provided to the extent required to maintain the animal in a state of good health.

(8) "Torture" includes any act that causes unjustifiable pain or suffering.

(b) A person commits an offense if the person intentionally, knowingly, or recklessly:

(1) tortures an animal or in a cruel manner kills or causes serious bodily injury to an animal;

(2) without the owner's effective consent, kills, administers poison to, or causes serious bodily injury to an animal;

(3) fails unreasonably to provide necessary food, water, care, or shelter for an animal in the person's custody;

(4) abandons unreasonably an animal in the person's custody;

(5) transports or confines an animal in a cruel manner;

(6) without the owner's effective consent, causes bodily injury to an animal;

(7) causes one animal to fight with another animal, if either animal is not a dog;

(8) uses a live animal as a lure in dog race training or in dog coursing on a racetrack; or

(9) seriously overworks an animal.

(c) An offense under Subsection (b)(3), (4), (5), (6), or (9) is a Class A misdemeanor, except that the offense is a state jail felony if the person has previously been convicted two times under this section, two times under Section 42.09, or one time under this section and one time under Section 42.09. An offense under Subsection (b)(1), (2), (7), or (8) is a state jail felony, except that the offense is a felony of the third degree if the person has previously been convicted two times under this section, two times under Section 42.09, or one time under this section and one time under Section 42.09.

(d) It is a defense to prosecution under this section that:

(1) the actor had a reasonable fear of bodily injury to the actor or to another person by a dangerous wild animal as defined by Section 822.101, Health and Safety Code; or

(2) the actor was engaged in bona fide experimentation for scientific research.

(e) It is a defense to prosecution under Subsection (b)(2) or (6) that:

(1) the animal was discovered on the person's property in the act of or after injuring or killing the person's livestock animals or damaging the person's crops and that the person killed or injured the animal at the time of this discovery; or

PEN §42.091

(2) the person killed or injured the animal within the scope of the person's employment as a public servant or in furtherance of activities or operations associated with electricity transmission or distribution, electricity generation or operations associated with the generation of electricity, or natural gas delivery.

(f) It is an exception to the application of this section that the conduct engaged in by the actor is a generally accepted and otherwise lawful:

(1) form of conduct occurring solely for the purpose of or in support of:

(A) fishing, hunting, or trapping; or

(B) wildlife management, wildlife or depredation control, or shooting preserve practices as regulated by state and federal law; or

(2) animal husbandry or agriculture practice involving livestock animals.

(g) This section does not create a civil cause of action for damages or enforcement of the section.

History of Pen §42.092: Acts 2007, 80th Leg., ch. 886, §2, eff. Sept. 1, 2007.

ANNOTATIONS

State v. Kingsbury, 129 S.W.3d 202, 207 (Tex. App.—Corpus Christi 2004, no pet.). "[W]e find the criminal act of failing to provide necessary food, care, or shelter for an animal does not constitute the felony offense of torture. The two criminal acts are separate and distinct from one another. Therefore, the indictment, by alleging torture by failing to provide food and water, did not sufficiently allege a felony under [§42.092(b)(1)]. Instead, the indictment charged appellees with a misdemeanor under [§42.092(b)(3)]."

Granger v. Folk, 931 S.W.2d 390, 392 (Tex.App.—Beaumont 1996, no pet.). "[T]wo avenues exist for the State in protecting animals from cruel treatment, i.e., criminal prosecution under [Pen. Code §42.092] and the civil remedy provided under [H&SC §821.023]. [¶] [I]n the criminal proceeding, a defendant may face loss of freedom or fine or both, whereas, a proceeding under §821.023 may subject the defendant to a loss, forfeiture and confiscation of property rights and interests."

PEN §42.10. DOG FIGHTING

 (a) A person commits an offense if he intentionally or knowingly:

(1) causes a dog to fight with another dog;

(2) participates in the earnings of or operates a facility used for dog fighting;

Subsection (2) below is effective for offenses in which any element of the offense was committed before Sept. 1, 2007.

(2) for a pecuniary benefit causes a dog to fight with another dog;

(3) uses or permits another to use any real estate, building, room, tent, arena, or other property for dog fighting;

(4) owns or trains a dog with the intent that the dog be used in an exhibition of dog fighting; or

(5) attends as a spectator an exhibition of dog fighting.

(b) In this section, "dog fighting" means any situation in which one dog attacks or fights with another dog.

 Subsections (c)-(e) below are effective for offenses committed on or after Sept. 1, 2007.

(c) A conviction under Subsection (a)(2) or (3) may be had upon the uncorroborated testimony of a party to the offense.

(d) It is a defense to prosecution under Subsection (a)(1) that the actor caused a dog to fight with another dog to protect livestock, other property, or a person from the other dog, and for no other purpose.

(e) An offense under Subsection (a)(4) or (5) is a Class A misdemeanor. An offense under Subsection (a)(1), (2), or (3) is a state jail felony.

Subsections (c)-(e) below are effective for offenses in which any element of the offense was committed before Sept. 1, 2007.

(c) A conviction under Subdivision (2), (3), or (4) of Subsection (a) may be had upon the uncorroborated testimony of a party to the offense.

(d) It is a defense to prosecution under Subdivision (1) or (2) of Subsection (a) that the actor caused a dog to fight with another dog to protect livestock, other property, or a person from the other dog, and for no other purpose.

(e) An offense under Subdivision (1) or (5) of Subsection (a) is a Class A misdemeanor. An offense under Subdivision (2), (3), or (4) of Subsection (a) is a state jail felony. An offense under Subdivision (6) of Subsection (a) is a Class C misdemeanor.

History of Pen §42.10: Acts 1983, 68th Leg., ch. 305, §1, eff. Sept. 1, 1983. Renumbered from §42.111 and amended by Acts 1993, 73rd Leg., ch. 900, §1.01, eff. Sept. 1, 1994. Amended by Acts 2007, 80th Leg., ch. 644, §1, eff. Sept. 1, 2007.

For a quick reference of penalties, see the Chart of Penalties on p. 675.

O'CONNOR'S CRIMINAL CODES 891

PEN §42.10

PEN §42.11. DESTRUCTION OF FLAG

(a) A person commits an offense if the person intentionally or knowingly damages, defaces, mutilates, or burns the flag of the United States or the State of Texas.

(b) In this section, "flag" means an emblem, banner, or other standard or a copy of an emblem, standard, or banner that is an official or commonly recognized depiction of the flag of the United States or of this state and is capable of being flown from a staff of any character or size. The term does not include a representation of a flag on a written or printed document, a periodical, stationery, a painting or photograph, or an article of clothing or jewelry.

(c) It is an exception to the application of this section that the act that would otherwise constitute an offense is done in conformity with statutes of the United States or of this state relating to the proper disposal of damaged flags.

(d) An offense under this section is a Class A misdemeanor.

Editor's note: Former §42.09, "Desecration of Venerated Object," was repealed after the U.S. Supreme Court declared it unconstitutional as applied to a protester. *Texas v. Johnson*, 491 U.S. 397, 109 S.Ct. 2533 (1989). As a response, the Texas Legislature passed §42.11 above.

History of Pen §42.11: Acts 1989, 71st Leg., 1st C.S., ch. 27, §1, eff. Sept. 1, 1989. Renumbered from §42.14 by Acts 1993, 73rd Leg., ch. 900, §1.01, eff. Sept. 1, 1994.

PEN §42.111. RENUMBERED

Renumbered as §42.10 by Acts 1993, 73rd Leg., ch. 900, §1.01, eff. Sept. 1, 1994.

PEN §42.12. DISCHARGE OF FIREARM IN CERTAIN MUNICIPALITIES

(a) A person commits an offense if the person recklessly discharges a firearm inside the corporate limits of a municipality having a population of 100,000 or more.

(b) An offense under this section is a Class A misdemeanor.

(c) If conduct constituting an offense under this section also constitutes an offense under another section of this code, the person may be prosecuted under either section.

(d) Subsection (a) does not affect the authority of a municipality to enact an ordinance which prohibits the discharge of a firearm.

History of Pen §42.12: Acts 1995, 74th Leg., ch. 663, §1, eff. Sept. 1, 1995.

State v. Vasquez, 34 S.W.3d 332, 334 (Tex. App.—San Antonio 2000, no pet.). It is "a misdemeanor offense to 'recklessly discharge a firearm inside the corporate limits of a municipality having a population of 100,000 or more.' When the State charges a defendant with acting recklessly in the commission of an offense, the indictment must allege with reasonable certainty the act or acts relied upon to constitute recklessness. The indictment is not sufficient if it merely alleges that the accused acted recklessly in committing the offense."

PEN §42.13. USE OF LASER POINTERS

(a) A person commits an offense if the person knowingly directs a light from a laser pointer at a uniformed safety officer, including a peace officer, security guard, firefighter, emergency medical service worker, or other uniformed municipal, state, or federal officer.

(b) In this section, "laser pointer" means a device that emits a visible light amplified by the stimulated emission of radiation.

(c) An offense under this section is a Class C misdemeanor.

History of Pen §42.13: Acts 2003, 78th Leg., ch. 467, §1, eff. Sept. 1, 2003.
History of Former Pen §42.13: Deleted by Acts 1993, 73rd Leg., ch. 900, §1.01, eff. Sept. 1, 1994.

E ## PEN §42.14. ILLUMINATION OF AIRCRAFT BY INTENSE LIGHT

(a) A person commits an offense if:

(1) the person intentionally directs a light from a laser pointer or other light source at an aircraft; and

(2) the light has an intensity sufficient to impair the operator's ability to control the aircraft.

(b) It is an affirmative defense to prosecution under this section that the actor was using the light to send an emergency distress signal.

(c) An offense under this section is a Class C misdemeanor unless the intensity of the light impairs the operator's ability to control the aircraft, in which event the offense is a Class A misdemeanor.

(d) If conduct that constitutes an offense under this section also constitutes an offense under any other law, the actor may be prosecuted under this section or the other law.

(e) In this section, "laser pointer" has the meaning assigned by Section 42.13.

History of Pen §42.14: Acts 2007, 80th Leg., ch. 680, §1, eff. Sept. 1, 2007.

CHAPTER 43. PUBLIC INDECENCY

SUBCHAPTER A. PROSTITUTION

PEN §43.01. DEFINITIONS

In this subchapter:

(1) "Deviate sexual intercourse" means any contact between the genitals of one person and the mouth or anus of another person.

(2) "Prostitution" means the offense defined in Section 43.02.

(3) "Sexual contact" means any touching of the anus, breast, or any part of the genitals of another person with intent to arouse or gratify the sexual desire of any person.

(4) "Sexual conduct" includes deviate sexual intercourse, sexual contact, and sexual intercourse.

(5) "Sexual intercourse" means any penetration of the female sex organ by the male sex organ.

History of Pen §43.01: Acts 1973, 63rd Leg., ch. 399, §1, eff. Jan. 1, 1974. Amended by Acts 1979, 66th Leg., ch. 168, §2, eff. Aug. 27, 1979; Acts 1993, 73rd Leg., ch. 900, §1.01, eff. Sept. 1, 1994.

PEN §43.02. PROSTITUTION

(a) A person commits an offense if he knowingly:

(1) offers to engage, agrees to engage, or engages in sexual conduct for a fee; or

(2) solicits another in a public place to engage with him in sexual conduct for hire.

(b) An offense is established under Subsection (a)(1) whether the actor is to receive or pay a fee. An offense is established under Subsection (a)(2) whether the actor solicits a person to hire him or offers to hire the person solicited.

(c) An offense under this section is a Class B misdemeanor, unless the actor has previously been convicted one or two times of an offense under this section, in which event it is a Class A misdemeanor. If the actor has previously been convicted three or more times of an offense under this section, the offense is a state jail felony.

History of Pen §43.02: Acts 1973, 63rd Leg., ch. 399, §1, eff. Jan. 1, 1974. Amended by Acts 1977, 65th Leg., ch. 286, §1, eff. May 27, 1977; Acts 1993, 73rd Leg., ch. 900, §1.01, eff. Sept. 1, 1994; Acts 2001, 77th Leg., ch. 987, §1, eff. Sept. 1, 2001.

ANNOTATIONS

Mattias v. State, 731 S.W.2d 936, 937 (Tex.Crim. App.1987). "A person may knowingly offer to engage in or agree to engage in sexual conduct for a fee and commit an offense under §43.02(a)(1) ... without having the intent to actually consummate the sexual conduct. [I]ntent to consummate an offer or agreement to engage in sexual conduct is not an element of the offense of prostitution under §43.02(a)(1)."

Robinson v. State, 643 S.W.2d 141, 143 (Tex.Crim. App.1982). Appellant "challenges the sufficiency of the evidence in that no 'fee certain' was ever agreed to between the parties, and appellant withdrew from all negotiations and left the officer's car before a final agreement had been made. [W]e have been ... unable to find any requirement that a definite 'sum certain' be ascertained or a requirement that any type of final agreement be entered into in a prosecution for the offense of 'offering to engage in sexual conduct.'"

PEN §43.03. PROMOTION OF PROSTITUTION

(a) A person commits an offense if, acting other than as a prostitute receiving compensation for personally rendered prostitution services, he or she knowingly:

(1) receives money or other property pursuant to an agreement to participate in the proceeds of prostitution; or

(2) solicits another to engage in sexual conduct with another person for compensation.

For a quick reference of penalties, see the Chart of Penalties on p. 675.

O'CONNOR'S CRIMINAL CODES   893

(b) An offense under this section is a Class A misdemeanor.

History of Pen §43.03: Acts 1973, 63rd Leg., ch. 399, §1, eff. Jan. 1, 1974. Amended by Acts 1977, 65th Leg., ch. 287, §1, eff. May 27, 1977.

PEN §43.04. AGGRAVATED PROMOTION OF PROSTITUTION

(a) A person commits an offense if he knowingly owns, invests in, finances, controls, supervises, or manages a prostitution enterprise that uses two or more prostitutes.

(b) An offense under this section is a felony of the third degree.

History of Pen §43.04: Acts 1973, 63rd Leg., ch. 399, §1, eff. Jan. 1, 1974.

ANNOTATIONS

Armentrout v. State, 645 S.W.2d 298, 302 (Tex. Crim.App.1983). "Though not defined by our penal code, 'prostitution enterprise,' as used in §43.04 ... has been construed by the Court to mean 'a plan or design for a venture or undertaking in which two or more persons offer to, agree to, or engage in sexual conduct in return for a fee payable to them.'"

Smithwick v. State, 762 S.W.2d 232, 234 (Tex. App.—Austin 1988, pet. ref'd). "[W]ithin the context of §43.04, the term prostitute is capable of only one meaning—a person who engages in prostitution."

PEN §43.05. COMPELLING PROSTITUTION

(a) A person commits an offense if he knowingly:

(1) causes another by force, threat, or fraud to commit prostitution; or

(2) causes by any means a person younger than 17 years to commit prostitution.

(b) An offense under this section is a felony of the second degree.

History of Pen §43.05: Acts 1973, 63rd Leg., ch. 399, §1, eff. Jan. 1, 1974.

ANNOTATIONS

Davis v. State, 635 S.W.2d 737, 739 (Tex.Crim.App. 1982). "The actual commission of the offense of prostitution is not a prerequisite to the commission of the offense of compelling prostitution."

Tubbs v. State, 670 S.W.2d 407, 408 (Tex.App.—Dallas 1984, no pet.). "We interpret ... §43.05(a)(2) as stating that a person commits an offense if he knowingly causes a person younger than 17 years to commit

prostitution *regardless of the means used*. Thus, because an offense occurs if a defendant compels prostitution regardless of the means used to compel the prostitution, it logically follows that an indictment is not fundamentally defective for failing to describe the specific means used."

PEN §43.06. ACCOMPLICE WITNESS; TESTIMONY & IMMUNITY

(a) A party to an offense under this subchapter may be required to furnish evidence or testify about the offense.

(b) A party to an offense under this subchapter may not be prosecuted for any offense about which he is required to furnish evidence or testify, and the evidence and testimony may not be used against the party in any adjudicatory proceeding except a prosecution for aggravated perjury.

(c) For purposes of this section, "adjudicatory proceeding" means a proceeding before a court or any other agency of government in which the legal rights, powers, duties, or privileges of specified parties are determined.

(d) A conviction under this subchapter may be had upon the uncorroborated testimony of a party to the offense.

History of Pen §43.06: Acts 1973, 63rd Leg., ch. 399, §1, eff. Jan. 1, 1974. See also CCP art. 38.14.

ANNOTATIONS

J.A.F.R. v. State, 752 S.W.2d 216, 216-17 (Tex. App.—El Paso 1988, no pet.). "Section 43.06 allows conviction [for prostitution] on uncorroborated testimony of a party to the offense."

SUBCHAPTER B. OBSCENITY

PEN §43.21. DEFINITIONS

(a) In this subchapter:

(1) "Obscene" means material or a performance that:

(A) the average person, applying contemporary community standards, would find that taken as a whole appeals to the prurient interest in sex;

(B) depicts or describes:

(i) patently offensive representations or descriptions of ultimate sexual acts, normal or perverted, actual or simulated, including sexual intercourse, sodomy, and sexual bestiality; or

(ii) patently offensive representations or descriptions of masturbation, excretory functions, sadism, masochism, lewd exhibition of the genitals, the male or female genitals in a state of sexual stimulation or arousal, covered male genitals in a discernibly turgid state or a device designed and marketed as useful primarily for stimulation of the human genital organs; and

(C) taken as a whole, lacks serious literary, artistic, political, and scientific value.

(2) "Material" means anything tangible that is capable of being used or adapted to arouse interest, whether through the medium of reading, observation, sound, or in any other manner, but does not include an actual three dimensional obscene device.

(3) "Performance" means a play, motion picture, dance, or other exhibition performed before an audience.

(4) "Patently offensive" means so offensive on its face as to affront current community standards of decency.

(5) "Promote" means to manufacture, issue, sell, give, provide, lend, mail, deliver, transfer, transmit, publish, distribute, circulate, disseminate, present, exhibit, or advertise, or to offer or agree to do the same.

(6) "Wholesale promote" means to manufacture, issue, sell, provide, mail, deliver, transfer, transmit, publish, distribute, circulate, disseminate, or to offer or agree to do the same for purpose of resale.

(7) "Obscene device" means a device including a dildo or artificial vagina, designed or marketed as useful primarily for the stimulation of human genital organs.

(b) If any of the depictions or descriptions of sexual conduct described in this section are declared by a court of competent jurisdiction to be unlawfully included herein, this declaration shall not invalidate this section as to other patently offensive sexual conduct included herein.

History of Pen §43.21: Acts 1973, 63rd Leg., ch. 399, §1, eff. Jan. 1, 1974. Amended by Acts 1975, 64th Leg., ch. 163, §1, eff. Sept. 1, 1975; Acts 1979, 66th Leg., ch. 778, §1, eff. Sept. 1, 1979.

ANNOTATIONS

Larue v. State, 637 S.W.2d 934, 935 (Tex.Crim.App. 1982). "[T]he proper community scope for determination of the obscenity issue is not limited to one county. [I]t [is] error for the court to charge on a county-wide standard over the objection made by the defendant."

Varkonyi v. State, ___ S.W.3d ___ (Tex.App.—El Paso 2008, n.p.h.) (No. 08-06-00255-CR; 5-8-08). "Section 43.21(a)'s definition of obscene comports with the test set forth in *Miller v. California*, 413 U.S. 15, 24 ... (1973)."

State v. Stone, 137 S.W.3d 167, 181 (Tex.App.— Houston [1st Dist.] 2004, pet. ref'd). "[A]n accused's knowledge of the content and character of obscene material may be shown by either direct or circumstantial evidence."

Porter v. State, 638 S.W.2d 249, 251 (Tex.App.— Fort Worth 1982), *overruled on other grounds*, *Davis v. State*, 658 S.W.2d 572 (Tex.Crim.App.1983). "So long as the fact finder does not employ personal subjective reactions and uses as one factor what is tolerated by the average person in determining a contemporary community standard of decency the Texas [obscenity] statute is not overly broad."

PEN §43.22. OBSCENE DISPLAY OR DISTRIBUTION

(a) A person commits an offense if he intentionally or knowingly displays or distributes an obscene photograph, drawing, or similar visual representation or other obscene material and is reckless about whether a person is present who will be offended or alarmed by the display or distribution.

(b) An offense under this section is a Class C misdemeanor.

History of Pen §43.22: Acts 1973, 63rd Leg., ch. 399, §1, eff. Jan. 1, 1974.

PEN §43.23. OBSCENITY

(a) A person commits an offense if, knowing its content and character, he wholesale promotes or possesses with intent to wholesale promote any obscene material or obscene device.

(b) Except as provided by Subsection (h), an offense under Subsection (a) is a state jail felony.

(c) A person commits an offense if, knowing its content and character, he:

(1) promotes or possesses with intent to promote any obscene material or obscene device; or

(2) produces, presents, or directs an obscene performance or participates in a portion thereof that is obscene or that contributes to its obscenity.

(d) Except as provided by Subsection (h), an offense under Subsection (c) is a Class A misdemeanor.

For a quick reference of penalties, see the Chart of Penalties on p. 675.

O'CONNOR'S CRIMINAL CODES   895

(e) A person who promotes or wholesale promotes obscene material or an obscene device or possesses the same with intent to promote or wholesale promote it in the course of his business is presumed to do so with knowledge of its content and character.

(f) A person who possesses six or more obscene devices or identical or similar obscene articles is presumed to possess them with intent to promote the same.

(g) It is an affirmative defense to prosecution under this section that the person who possesses or promotes material or a device proscribed by this section does so for a bona fide medical, psychiatric, judicial, legislative, or law enforcement purpose.

(h) The punishment for an offense under Subsection (a) is increased to the punishment for a felony of the third degree and the punishment for an offense under Subsection (c) is increased to the punishment for a state jail felony if it is shown on the trial of the offense that obscene material that is the subject of the offense visually depicts activities described by Section 43.21(a)(1)(B) engaged in by:

(1) a child younger than 18 years of age at the time the image of the child was made;

(2) an image that to a reasonable person would be virtually indistinguishable from the image of a child younger than 18 years of age; or

(3) an image created, adapted, or modified to be the image of an identifiable child.

(i) In this section, "identifiable child" means a person, recognizable as an actual person by the person's face, likeness, or other distinguishing characteristic, such as a unique birthmark or other recognizable feature:

(1) who was younger than 18 years of age at the time the visual depiction was created, adapted, or modified; or

(2) whose image as a person younger than 18 years of age was used in creating, adapting, or modifying the visual depiction.

(j) An attorney representing the state who seeks an increase in punishment under Subsection (h)(3) is not required to prove the actual identity of an identifiable child.

History of Pen §43.23: Acts 1973, 63rd Leg., ch. 399, §1, eff. Jan. 1, 1974. Amended by Acts 1979, 66th Leg., ch. 778, §2, eff. Sept. 1, 1979; Acts 1993, 73rd Leg., ch. 900, §1.01, eff. Sept. 1, 1994; Acts 2003, 78th Leg., ch. 1005, §1, eff. Sept. 1, 2003.

ANNOTATIONS

Burden v. State, 55 S.W.3d 608, 613 (Tex.Crim.App. 2001). "We see nothing in the language of §43.23(c)(1) that requires a defendant to have knowledge that what he promotes is legally obscene. All §43.23(c)(1) requires is that a defendant have knowledge of the material's sexually explicit character and content."

Shealy v. State, 675 S.W.2d 215, 217 (Tex.Crim. App.1984). "[W]hen the promoted [obscene] material is protected by the provisions of the 1st Amendment to the Federal Constitution, or by the provisions of [Tex. Const. art.] 1, §8, ... and the trial court errs by instructing the jury that the prosecution may establish through the use of the statutory presumption [in Pen. Code §43.23(e)] that the accused had knowledge of the content and character of the promoted material, such cannot ever be harmless error."

Video News, Inc. v. State, 781 S.W.2d 411, 412 (Tex.App.—Houston [1st Dist.] 1989), *pet. ref'd*, 786 S.W.2d 356 (Tex.Crim.App.1990). Pen. Code §43.23 is "a statute denouncing the possession of [obscene] material for sale and utilizing the prurient interest test. [T]he statute is constitutional under [Tex. Const. art.] 1, §8...." *See also Ex parte Dave*, 220 S.W.3d 154, 160 (Tex.App.—Fort Worth 2007, pet. ref'd) (affirming the constitutionality of §43.23 under the 1st and 14th Amendments to the U.S. Constitution).

Burch v. State, 695 S.W.2d 264, 265-66 (Tex.App.—Houston [1st Dist.] 1985), *pet. ref'd*, 712 S.W.2d 163 (Tex.Crim.App.1986). Both the appellate court "and the trial court are obligated to evaluate the obscene material in question to determine whether it [is] factually and constitutionally obscene. The stipulation of evidence [by the parties] does not eliminate this need for independent review."

Gholson v. State, 667 S.W.2d 168, 177 (Tex.App.—Houston [14th Dist.] 1983, pet. ref'd). A "person who sells refreshments [at an adult movie theater] may not be prosecuted under the obscenity statutes because he is engaged in conduct 'merely incidental to the *exhibition* of obscenity.'"

PEN §43.24. SALE, DISTRIBUTION, OR DISPLAY OF HARMFUL MATERIAL TO MINOR

(a) For purposes of this section:

(1) "Minor" means an individual younger than 18 years.

(2) "Harmful material" means material whose dominant theme taken as a whole:

(A) appeals to the prurient interest of a minor, in sex, nudity, or excretion;

(B) is patently offensive to prevailing standards in the adult community as a whole with respect to what is suitable for minors; and

(C) is utterly without redeeming social value for minors.

(b) A person commits an offense if, knowing that the material is harmful:

(1) and knowing the person is a minor, he sells, distributes, exhibits, or possesses for sale, distribution, or exhibition to a minor harmful material;

(2) he displays harmful material and is reckless about whether a minor is present who will be offended or alarmed by the display; or

(3) he hires, employs, or uses a minor to do or accomplish or assist in doing or accomplishing any of the acts prohibited in Subsection (b)(1) or (b)(2).

(c) It is a defense to prosecution under this section that:

(1) the sale, distribution, or exhibition was by a person having scientific, educational, governmental, or other similar justification; or

(2) the sale, distribution, or exhibition was to a minor who was accompanied by a consenting parent, guardian, or spouse.

(d) An offense under this section is a Class A misdemeanor unless it is committed under Subsection (b)(3) in which event it is a felony of the third degree.

History of Pen §43.24: Acts 1973, 63rd Leg., ch. 399, §1, eff. Jan. 1, 1974. Amended by Acts 1993, 73rd Leg., ch. 900, §1.01, eff. Sept. 1, 1994.

ANNOTATIONS

State v. Stone, 137 S.W.3d 167, 176 (Tex.App.— Houston [1st Dist.] 2004, pet. ref'd). "[I]nternet e-mails, pictures, or communications fall within the Penal Code's definition of 'material,' as these communications are capable of being used or adapted to arouse interest through the medium of internet transmission. Thus, it is legally possible to violate [Pen. Code] §43.24 by displaying harmful materials in cyberspace. *At 183:* Due to a factual condition unknown to Stone, namely that [imaginary 13-year old] was actually [a 50-year old detective], the offense of distribution of harmful material to a minor could not be completed. However, Stone

was not charged with an actual violation of §43.24(b)(1), but with an attempted violation of the statute, which made the offense factually impossible but not legally impossible. [I]t is immaterial that the crime of display of harmful material to a minor was factually impossible to complete."

PEN §43.25. SEXUAL PERFORMANCE BY A CHILD

(a) In this section:

(1) "Sexual performance" means any performance or part thereof that includes sexual conduct by a child younger than 18 years of age.

(2) "Sexual conduct" means sexual contact, actual or simulated sexual intercourse, deviate sexual intercourse, sexual bestiality, masturbation, sado-masochistic abuse, or lewd exhibition of the genitals, the anus, or any portion of the female breast below the top of the areola.

(3) "Performance" means any play, motion picture, photograph, dance, or other visual representation that can be exhibited before an audience of one or more persons.

(4) "Produce" with respect to a sexual performance includes any conduct that directly contributes to the creation or manufacture of the sexual performance.

(5) "Promote" means to procure, manufacture, issue, sell, give, provide, lend, mail, deliver, transfer, transmit, publish, distribute, circulate, disseminate, present, exhibit, or advertise or to offer or agree to do any of the above.

(6) "Simulated" means the explicit depiction of sexual conduct that creates the appearance of actual sexual conduct and during which a person engaging in the conduct exhibits any uncovered portion of the breasts, genitals, or buttocks.

(7) "Deviate sexual intercourse" and "sexual contact" have the meanings assigned by Section 43.01.

(b) A person commits an offense if, knowing the character and content thereof, he employs, authorizes, or induces a child younger than 18 years of age to engage in sexual conduct or a sexual performance. A parent or legal guardian or custodian of a child younger than 18 years of age commits an offense if he consents to the participation by the child in a sexual performance.

For a quick reference of penalties, see the Chart of Penalties on p. 675.

O'CONNOR'S CRIMINAL CODES **897**

Subsection (c) below is effective for offenses committed on or after Sept. 1, 2007.

(c) An offense under Subsection (b) is a felony of the second degree, except that the offense is a felony of the first degree if the victim is younger than 14 years of age at the time the offense is committed.

Subsection (c) below is effective for offenses in which any element of the offense was committed before Sept. 1, 2007.

(c) An offense under Subsection (b) is a felony of the second degree.

(d) A person commits an offense if, knowing the character and content of the material, he produces, directs, or promotes a performance that includes sexual conduct by a child younger than 18 years of age.

 Subsection (e) below is effective for offenses committed on or after Sept. 1, 2007.

(e) An offense under Subsection (d) is a felony of the third degree, except that the offense is a felony of the second degree if the victim is younger than 14 years of age at the time the offense is committed.

Subsection (e) below is effective for offenses in which any element of the offense was committed before Sept. 1, 2007.

(e) An offense under Subsection (d) is a felony of the third degree.

(f) It is an affirmative defense to a prosecution under this section that:

(1) the defendant was the spouse of the child at the time of the offense;

(2) the conduct was for a bona fide educational, medical, psychological, psychiatric, judicial, law enforcement, or legislative purpose; or

(3) the defendant is not more than two years older than the child.

(g) When it becomes necessary for the purposes of this section or Section 43.26 to determine whether a child who participated in sexual conduct was younger than 18 years of age, the court or jury may make this determination by any of the following methods:

(1) personal inspection of the child;

(2) inspection of the photograph or motion picture that shows the child engaging in the sexual performance;

(3) oral testimony by a witness to the sexual performance as to the age of the child based on the child's appearance at the time;

(4) expert medical testimony based on the appearance of the child engaging in the sexual performance; or

(5) any other method authorized by law or by the rules of evidence at common law.

History of Pen §43.25: Acts 1977, 65th Leg., ch. 381, §1, eff. June 10, 1977. Amended by Acts 1979, 66th Leg., ch. 779, §1, eff. Sept. 1, 1979; Acts 1985, 69th Leg., ch. 530, §1, eff. Sept. 1, 1985; Acts 1993, 73rd Leg., ch. 900, §1.01, eff. Sept. 1, 1994; Acts 1999, 76th Leg., ch. 1415, §22(b), eff. Sept. 1, 1999; Acts 2003, 78th Leg., ch. 1005, §§4, 5, eff. Sept. 1, 2003; Acts 2007, 80th Leg., ch. 593, §1.20, eff. Sept. 1, 2007.

See also CCP arts. 38.072, 38.37; Pen §3.03.

ANNOTATIONS

Franklin v. State, 193 S.W.3d 616, 620 (Tex.App.—Fort Worth 2006, no pet.). "The term 'authorized' [in §43.25(b)] is not defined by statute. Therefore it must be given its common, ordinary, or usual meaning. 'Authorize' is defined as: 1) to give official approval to or permission for; 2) to give power or authority to; 3) to empower or commission; or 4) to give justification for or warrant."

Scott v. State, 173 S.W.3d 856, 863 (Tex.App.—Texarkana 2005), *rev'd on other grounds*, 235 S.W.3d 255 (Tex.Crim.App.2007). "[I]nducing the boys to take a shower does not violate the statute. Indeed, it is the masturbation [in the shower] that satisfies the sexual conduct element of the offense. It is this specific conduct which must be induced in order to violate the statute. *At 864:* [D] did induce the boys to take a shower and then capitalized on the boys' tendencies to masturbate by recording them for his own gratification. [O]n these facts, the offense was not one of inducement of a sexual performance or sexual conduct as contemplated by §43.25(b)."

Tovar v. State, 165 S.W.3d 785, 790 (Tex.App.—San Antonio 2005, no pet.). "Because the term 'lewd' is not statutorily defined and because 'lewd' has a common meaning that jurors can be fairly presumed to know and apply, the trial court was not required to define 'lewd' in the jury charge." *See also **Garay v. State***, 954 S.W.2d 59, 63 (Tex.App.—San Antonio 1997, pet. ref'd).

Alexander v. State, 906 S.W.2d 107, 110 (Tex.App.—Dallas 1995, no pet.). "[W]hen a child is the subject of a photograph, lewdness is not to be considered as a characteristic of the child, but rather as a

PEN §43.25

✦

---

characteristic of the photograph itself. [W]hether the content of a photograph constitutes a lewd or lascivious exhibition of a child's genitals depends on the intent of the photographer."

Ex parte Anderson, 902 S.W.2d 695, 699 (Tex. App.—Austin 1995, pet. ref'd). "Whether the legislature intended to define 'sado-masochistic abuse' and did not, or whether there was a mistake, omission or oversight in legislative draftsmanship, the term itself is neither vague nor indefinite."

PEN §43.251. EMPLOYMENT HARMFUL TO CHILDREN

(a) In this section:

(1) "Child" means a person younger than 18 years of age.

(2) "Massage" has the meaning assigned to the term "massage therapy" by Section 455.001, Occupations Code.

(3) "Massage establishment" has the meaning assigned by Section 455.001, Occupations Code.

(4) "Nude" means a child who is:

(A) entirely unclothed; or

(B) clothed in a manner that leaves uncovered or visible through less than fully opaque clothing any portion of the breasts below the top of the areola of the breasts, if the child is female, or any portion of the genitals or buttocks.

(5) "Sexually oriented commercial activity" means a massage establishment, nude studio, modeling studio, love parlor, or other similar commercial enterprise the primary business of which is the offering of a service that is intended to provide sexual stimulation or sexual gratification to the customer.

(6) "Topless" means a female child clothed in a manner that leaves uncovered or visible through less than fully opaque clothing any portion of her breasts below the top of the areola.

(b) A person commits an offense if the person employs, authorizes, or induces a child to work:

(1) in a sexually oriented commercial activity; or

(2) in any place of business permitting, requesting, or requiring a child to work nude or topless.

(c) An offense under this section is a Class A misdemeanor.

History of Pen §43.251: Acts 1987, 70th Leg., ch. 783, §1, eff. Aug. 31, 1987. Amended by Acts 1993, 73rd Leg., ch. 900, §1.01, eff. Sept. 1, 1994; Acts 2001, 77th Leg., ch. 1420, §14.832, eff. Sept. 1, 2001.

PEN §43.26. POSSESSION OR PROMOTION OF CHILD PORNOGRAPHY

(a) A person commits an offense if:

(1) the person knowingly or intentionally possesses visual material that visually depicts a child younger than 18 years of age at the time the image of the child was made who is engaging in sexual conduct; and

(2) the person knows that the material depicts the child as described by Subdivision (1).

(b) In this section:

(1) "Promote" has the meaning assigned by Section 43.25.

(2) "Sexual conduct" has the meaning assigned by Section 43.25.

(3) "Visual material" means:

(A) any film, photograph, videotape, negative, or slide or any photographic reproduction that contains or incorporates in any manner any film, photograph, videotape, negative, or slide; or

(B) any disk, diskette, or other physical medium that allows an image to be displayed on a computer or other video screen and any image transmitted to a computer or other video screen by telephone line, cable, satellite transmission, or other method.

(c) The affirmative defenses provided by Section 43.25(f) also apply to a prosecution under this section.

(d) An offense under Subsection (a) is a felony of the third degree.

(e) A person commits an offense if:

(1) the person knowingly or intentionally promotes or possesses with intent to promote material described by Subsection (a)(1); and

(2) the person knows that the material depicts the child as described by Subsection (a)(1).

(f) A person who possesses visual material that contains six or more identical visual depictions of a child as described by Subsection (a)(1) is presumed to possess the material with the intent to promote the material.

(g) An offense under Subsection (e) is a felony of the second degree.

History of Pen §43.26: Acts 1985, 69th Leg., ch. 530, §2, eff. Sept. 1, 1985. Amended by Acts 1989, 71st Leg., ch. 361, §1 (eff. Sept. 1, 1989), ch. 968, §1 (eff. Sept. 1, 1989); Acts 1993, 73rd Leg., ch. 900, §1.01, eff. Sept. 1, 1994; Acts 1995, 74th Leg., ch. 76, §14.51, eff. Sept. 1, 1995; Acts 1997, 75th Leg., ch. 933, §1, eff. Sept. 1, 1997; Acts 1999, 76th Leg., ch. 1415, §22(c), eff. Sept. 1, 1999.

For a quick reference of penalties, see the Chart of Penalties on p. 675.

O'CONNOR'S CRIMINAL CODES 899

ANNOTATIONS

Vineyard v. State, 958 S.W.2d 834, 838 (Tex.Crim. App.1998). "[W]e hold the Legislature intended ... to make possession of each item of child pornography an 'allowable unit of prosecution.'"

Roise v. State, 7 S.W.3d 225, 237-38 (Tex.App.— Austin 1999, pet. ref'd). "[T]he purpose of [Pen. Code §43.26(a)] is the protection of the individual child from exploitation, but that purpose does not authorize the 'harm to children' testimony presented in this case. The 'purpose' is not an essential element of the offense of possession of child pornography. The evidence, in addition to being unreliable as presented, was not relevant. The trial court abused its discretion in admitting [expert witness's] testimony as to the sexual arousal analysis and the 'harm to the particular children and to society' testimony."

PEN §43.27. DUTY TO REPORT

(a) For purposes of this section, "visual material" has the meaning assigned by Section 43.26.

(b) A business that develops or processes visual material and determines that the material may be evidence of a criminal offense under this subchapter shall report the existence of the visual material to a local law enforcement agency.

History of Pen §43.27: Acts 2003, 78th Leg., ch. 1005, §6, eff. Sept. 1, 2003.

TITLE 10. OFFENSES AGAINST PUBLIC HEALTH, SAFETY, & MORALS

CHAPTER 46. WEAPONS

PEN §46.01. DEFINITIONS

In this chapter:

(1) "Club" means an instrument that is specially designed, made, or adapted for the purpose of inflicting serious bodily injury or death by striking a person with the instrument, and includes but is not limited to the following:

(A) blackjack;

(B) nightstick;

(C) mace;

(D) tomahawk.

(2) "Explosive weapon" means any explosive or incendiary bomb, grenade, rocket, or mine, that is designed, made, or adapted for the purpose of inflicting serious bodily injury, death, or substantial property damage, or for the principal purpose of causing such a loud report as to cause undue public alarm or terror, and includes a device designed, made, or adapted for delivery or shooting an explosive weapon.

(3) "Firearm" means any device designed, made, or adapted to expel a projectile through a barrel by using the energy generated by an explosion or burning substance or any device readily convertible to that use. Firearm does not include a firearm that may have, as an integral part, a folding knife blade or other characteristics of weapons made illegal by this chapter and that is:

(A) an antique or curio firearm manufactured before 1899; or

(B) a replica of an antique or curio firearm manufactured before 1899, but only if the replica does not use rim fire or center fire ammunition.

(4) "Firearm silencer" means any device designed, made, or adapted to muffle the report of a firearm.

(5) "Handgun" means any firearm that is designed, made, or adapted to be fired with one hand.

(6) "Illegal knife" means a:

(A) knife with a blade over five and one-half inches;

(B) hand instrument designed to cut or stab another by being thrown;

 (C) dagger, including but not limited to a dirk, stiletto, and poniard;

(D) bowie knife;

(E) sword; or

(F) spear.

(7) "Knife" means any bladed hand instrument that is capable of inflicting serious bodily injury or death by cutting or stabbing a person with the instrument.

(8) "Knuckles" means any instrument that consists of finger rings or guards made of a hard substance and that is designed, made, or adapted for the purpose of inflicting serious bodily injury or death by striking a person with a fist enclosed in the knuckles.

(9) "Machine gun" means any firearm that is capable of shooting more than two shots automatically, without manual reloading, by a single function of the trigger.

(10) "Short-barrel firearm" means a rifle with a barrel length of less than 16 inches or a shotgun with a barrel length of less than 18 inches, or any weapon made from a shotgun or rifle if, as altered, it has an overall length of less than 26 inches.

(11) "Switchblade knife" means any knife that has a blade that folds, closes, or retracts into the handle or sheath, and that:

(A) opens automatically by pressure applied to a button or other device located on the handle; or

(B) opens or releases a blade from the handle or sheath by the force of gravity or by the application of centrifugal force.

(12) "Armor-piercing ammunition" means handgun ammunition that is designed primarily for the purpose of penetrating metal or body armor and to be used principally in pistols and revolvers.

(13) "Hoax bomb" means a device that:

(A) reasonably appears to be an explosive or incendiary device; or

(B) by its design causes alarm or reaction of any type by an official of a public safety agency or a volunteer agency organized to deal with emergencies.

(14) "Chemical dispensing device" means a device, other than a small chemical dispenser sold commercially for personal protection, that is designed, made, or adapted for the purpose of dispensing a substance capable of causing an adverse psychological or physiological effect on a human being.

(15) "Racetrack" has the meaning assigned that term by the Texas Racing Act (Article 179e, Vernon's Texas Civil Statutes).

(16) "Zip gun" means a device or combination of devices that was not originally a firearm and is adapted to expel a projectile through a smooth-bore or rifled-bore barrel by using the energy generated by an explosion or burning substance.

History of Pen §46.01: Acts 1973, 63rd Leg., ch. 399, §1, eff. Jan. 1, 1974. Amended by Acts 1975, 64th Leg., ch. 342, §13, eff. Sept. 1, 1975; Acts 1983, 68th Leg., ch. 457, §1 (eff. Sept. 1, 1983), ch. 852, §1 (eff. Sept. 1, 1983); Acts 1987, 70th Leg., ch. 167, §5.01(a)(46), eff. Sept. 1, 1987; Acts 1989, 71st Leg., ch. 749, §1, eff. Sept. 1, 1989; Acts 1991, 72nd Leg., ch. 229, §1, eff. Sept. 1, 1991; Acts 1993, 73rd Leg., ch. 900, §1.01, eff. Sept. 1, 1994; Acts 1999, 76th Leg., ch. 1445, §1, eff. Sept. 1, 1999; Acts 2007, 80th Leg., ch. 921, §12A.001, eff. Sept. 1, 2007.

ANNOTATIONS

Meza v. State, 652 S.W.2d 399, 400-01 (Tex.Crim. App.1983). "We cannot infer that an instrument merely described as a 'club' is an instrument specifically designed, made, or adapted for the purpose of inflicting serious bodily injury or death."

Lee v. State, 866 S.W.2d 298, 300 (Tex.App.—Fort Worth 1993, pet. ref'd). "[T]he definitions in §46.01 can be used as an aid to determine whether a particular weapon is a 'deadly weapon' within the context of an affirmative finding."

PEN §46.02. UNLAWFUL CARRYING WEAPONS

Ⓐ *Subsection (a) below is effective for offenses committed on or after Sept. 1, 2007.*

(a) A person commits an offense if the person intentionally, knowingly, or recklessly carries on or about his or her person a handgun, illegal knife, or club if the person is not:

(1) on the person's own premises or premises under the person's control; or

(2) inside of or directly en route to a motor vehicle that is owned by the person or under the person's control.

Subsection (a) below is effective for offenses in which any element of the offense was committed before Sept. 1, 2007.

(a) A person commits an offense if he intentionally, knowingly, or recklessly carries on or about his person a handgun, illegal knife, or club.

Ⓔ *Subsections (a-1) & (a-2) below are effective for offenses committed on or after Sept. 1, 2007.*

(a-1) A person commits an offense if the person intentionally, knowingly, or recklessly carries on or about his or her person a handgun in a motor vehicle that is owned by the person or under the person's control at any time in which:

For a quick reference of penalties, see the Chart of Penalties on p. 675.

O'CONNOR'S CRIMINAL CODES **901**

(1) the handgun is in plain view; or

(2) the person is:

(A) engaged in criminal activity, other than a Class C misdemeanor that is a violation of a law or ordinance regulating traffic;

(B) prohibited by law from possessing a firearm; or

(C) a member of a criminal street gang, as defined by Section 71.01.

(a-2) For purposes of this section, "premises" includes real property and a recreational vehicle that is being used as living quarters, regardless of whether that use is temporary or permanent. In this subsection, "recreational vehicle" means a motor vehicle primarily designed as temporary living quarters or a vehicle that contains temporary living quarters and is designed to be towed by a motor vehicle. The term includes a travel trailer, camping trailer, truck camper, motor home, and horse trailer with living quarters.

(b) Except as provided by Subsection (c), an offense under this section is a Class A misdemeanor.

(c) An offense under this section is a felony of the third degree if the offense is committed on any premises licensed or issued a permit by this state for the sale of alcoholic beverages.

History of Pen §46.02: Acts 1973, 63rd Leg., ch. 399, §1, eff. Jan. 1, 1974. Amended by Acts 1975, 64th Leg., ch. 49, §1 (eff. Apr. 15, 1975), ch. 342, §14 (eff. Sept. 1, 1975), ch. 494, §2 (eff. June 19, 1975); Acts 1977, 65th Leg., ch. 746, §26, eff. Aug. 29, 1977; Acts 1981, 67th Leg., ch. 552, §1, eff. Aug. 31, 1981; Acts 1983, 68th Leg., ch. 931, §1, eff. Aug. 29, 1983; Acts 1987, 70th Leg., ch. 262, §21 (eff. Sept. 1, 1987), ch. 873, §25 (eff. Sept. 1, 1987); Acts 1991, 72nd Leg., ch. 168, §1, eff. Sept. 1, 1991; Acts 1993, 73rd Leg., ch. 900, §1.01, eff. Sept. 1, 1994; Acts 1995, 74th Leg., ch. 229, §2 (eff. Sept. 1, 1995), ch. 318, §16 (eff. Sept. 1, 1995), ch. 754, §15 (eff. Sept. 1, 1995), ch. 790, §16 (eff. Sept. 1, 1995), ch. 998, §3 (eff. Sept. 1, 1995); Acts 1997, 75th Leg., ch. 165, §10.02 (eff. Sept. 1, 1997), ch. 1221, §1 (eff. June 20, 1997), ch. 1261, §24 (eff. Sept. 1, 1997); Acts 2007, 80th Leg., ch. 693, §1, eff. Sept. 1, 2007.

See also Pen. Code §46.15.

ANNOTATIONS

Johnson v. State, 650 S.W.2d 414, 416 (Tex.Crim. App.1983), *overruled on other grounds*, *Boget v. State*, 74 S.W.3d 23 (Tex.Crim.App.2002). "[T]he defense of necessity is not unavailable in a prosecution under §46.02 ... as a matter of law."

Ex parte Gonzalez, 147 S.W.3d 474, 479 (Tex. App.—San Antonio 2004, pet. ref'd). "We hold that the allowable unit of prosecution under §46.02 is the weapon. Therefore, the unlawful carrying of a knife and the unlawful carrying of a gun are two separate and distinct offenses for which [D] may be prosecuted."

Bergman v. State, 90 S.W.3d 855, 857-58 (Tex. App.—San Antonio 2002, no pet.). "[A] defense [to unlawfully carrying a weapon] permits a person to carry a handgun from his place of business to his home or from his home to his place of business provided that: (1) the weapon is not habitually carried between those places; (2) the purpose for carrying the weapon is legitimate; (3) the route taken is a practical one; and (4) the journey proceeds without undue delay or unnecessary or unreasonable deviation."

Contreras v. State, 853 S.W.2d 694, 696 (Tex. App.—Houston [1st Dist.] 1993, no pet.). "When applied to persons occupying vehicles, the phrase 'on or about the person' has been expanded to include the area near by, close at hand, convenient of access, and within such distance of the party so that, without materially changing his position, the party could get his hand on it."

PEN §46.03. PLACES WEAPONS PROHIBITED

(a) A person commits an offense if the person intentionally, knowingly, or recklessly possesses or goes with a firearm, illegal knife, club, or prohibited weapon listed in Section 46.05(a):

(1) on the physical premises of a school or educational institution, any grounds or building on which an activity sponsored by a school or educational institution is being conducted, or a passenger transportation vehicle of a school or educational institution, whether the school or educational institution is public or private, unless pursuant to written regulations or written authorization of the institution;

(2) on the premises of a polling place on the day of an election or while early voting is in progress;

(3) on the premises of any government court or offices utilized by the court, unless pursuant to written regulations or written authorization of the court;

(4) on the premises of a racetrack;

(5) in or into a secured area of an airport; or

(6) within 1,000 feet of premises the location of which is designated by the Texas Department of Criminal Justice as a place of execution under Article 43.19, Code of Criminal Procedure, on a day that a sentence of death is set to be imposed on the designated premises and the person received notice that:

(A) going within 1,000 feet of the premises with a weapon listed under this subsection was prohibited; or

(B) possessing a weapon listed under this subsection within 1,000 feet of the premises was prohibited.

(b) It is a defense to prosecution under Subsections (a)(1)-(4) that the actor possessed a firearm while in the actual discharge of his official duties as a member of the armed forces or national guard or a guard employed by a penal institution, or an officer of the court.

(c) In this section:

(1) "Premises" has the meaning assigned by Section 46.035.

(2) "Secured area" means an area of an airport terminal building to which access is controlled by the inspection of persons and property under federal law.

(d) It is a defense to prosecution under Subsection (a)(5) that the actor possessed a firearm or club while traveling to or from the actor's place of assignment or in the actual discharge of duties as:

(1) a member of the armed forces or national guard;

(2) a guard employed by a penal institution; or

(3) a security officer commissioned by the Texas Board of Private Investigators and Private Security Agencies if:

(A) the actor is wearing a distinctive uniform; and

(B) the firearm or club is in plain view; or

(4) Deleted by Acts 1995, 74th Leg., ch. 318, §17, eff. Sept. 1, 1995.

(5) a security officer who holds a personal protection authorization under the Private Investigators and Private Security Agencies Act (Article 4413(29bb), Vernon's Texas Civil Statutes).

(e) It is a defense to prosecution under Subsection (a)(5) that the actor checked all firearms as baggage in accordance with federal or state law or regulations before entering a secured area.

(f) It is not a defense to prosecution under this section that the actor possessed a handgun and was licensed to carry a concealed handgun under Subchapter H, Chapter 411, Government Code.

(g) An offense under this section is a third degree felony.

(h) It is a defense to prosecution under Subsection (a)(4) that the actor possessed a firearm or club while traveling to or from the actor's place of assignment or in the actual discharge of duties as a security officer

commissioned by the Texas Board of Private Investigators and Private Security Agencies, if:

(1) the actor is wearing a distinctive uniform; and

(2) the firearm or club is in plain view.

(i) It is an exception to the application of Subsection (a)(6) that the actor possessed a firearm or club:

(1) while in a vehicle being driven on a public road; or

(2) at the actor's residence or place of employment.

History of Pen §46.03: Acts 1973, 63rd Leg., ch. 399, §1, eff. Jan. 1, 1974. Amended by Acts 1983, 68th Leg., ch. 508, §1, eff. Aug. 29, 1983; Acts 1989, 71st Leg., ch. 749, §2, eff. Sept. 1, 1989; Acts 1991, 72nd Leg., ch. 203, §2.79 (eff. Sept. 1, 1991), ch. 386, §71 (eff. Aug. 26, 1991), ch. 433, §1 (eff. Sept. 1, 1991), ch. 554, §50 (eff. Sept. 1, 1991). Renumbered from §46.04 and amended by Acts 1993, 73rd Leg., ch. 900, §1.01, eff. Sept. 1, 1994; Acts 1995, 74th Leg., ch. 229, §3 (eff. Sept. 1, 1995), ch. 260, §42 (eff. May 30, 1995), ch. 318, §17 (eff. Sept. 1, 1995), ch. 790, §17 (eff. Sept. 1, 1995); Acts 1997, 75th Leg., ch. 165, §§10.02, 31.01(70) (eff. Sept. 1, 1997), ch. 1043, §1 (eff. Sept. 1, 1997), ch. 1221, §§2, 3 (eff. June 20, 1997), ch. 1261, §25 (eff. Sept. 1, 1997); Acts 2001, 77th Leg., ch. 1060, §§1, 2, eff. Sept. 1, 2001; Acts 2003, 78th Leg., ch. 1178, §3, eff. Sept. 1, 2003.

See also Pen. Code §46.15.

PEN §46.035. UNLAWFUL CARRYING OF HANDGUN BY LICENSE HOLDER

(a) A license holder commits an offense if the license holder carries a handgun on or about the license holder's person under the authority of Subchapter H, Chapter 411, Government Code, and intentionally fails to conceal the handgun.

(b) A license holder commits an offense if the license holder intentionally, knowingly, or recklessly carries a handgun under the authority of Subchapter H, Chapter 411, Government Code, regardless of whether the handgun is concealed, on or about the license holder's person:

(1) on the premises of a business that has a permit or license issued under Chapter 25, 28, 32, 69, or 74, Alcoholic Beverage Code, if the business derives 51 percent or more of its income from the sale or service of alcoholic beverages for on-premises consumption, as determined by the Texas Alcoholic Beverage Commission under Section 104.06, Alcoholic Beverage Code;

(2) on the premises where a high school, collegiate, or professional sporting event or interscholastic event is taking place, unless the license holder is a participant in the event and a handgun is used in the event;

(3) on the premises of a correctional facility;

(4) on the premises of a hospital licensed under Chapter 241, Health and Safety Code, or on the premises of a nursing home licensed under Chapter 242,

For a quick reference of penalties, see the Chart of Penalties on p. 675.

O'CONNOR'S CRIMINAL CODES   903

PEN §46.035

Health and Safety Code, unless the license holder has written authorization of the hospital or nursing home administration, as appropriate;

(5) in an amusement park; or

(6) on the premises of a church, synagogue, or other established place of religious worship.

(c) A license holder commits an offense if the license holder intentionally, knowingly, or recklessly carries a handgun under the authority of Subchapter H, Chapter 411, Government Code, regardless of whether the handgun is concealed, at any meeting of a governmental entity.

(d) A license holder commits an offense if, while intoxicated, the license holder carries a handgun under the authority of Subchapter H, Chapter 411, Government Code, regardless of whether the handgun is concealed.

(e) A license holder who is licensed as a security officer under Chapter 1702, Occupations Code, and employed as a security officer commits an offense if, while in the course and scope of the security officer's employment, the security officer violates a provision of Subchapter H, Chapter 411, Government Code.

(f) In this section:

(1) "Amusement park" means a permanent indoor or outdoor facility or park where amusement rides are available for use by the public that is located in a county with a population of more than one million, encompasses at least 75 acres in surface area, is enclosed with access only through controlled entries, is open for operation more than 120 days in each calendar year, and has security guards on the premises at all times. The term does not include any public or private driveway, street, sidewalk or walkway, parking lot, parking garage, or other parking area.

(2) "License holder" means a person licensed to carry a handgun under Subchapter H, Chapter 411, Government Code.

(3) "Premises" means a building or a portion of a building. The term does not include any public or private driveway, street, sidewalk or walkway, parking lot, parking garage, or other parking area.

(g) An offense under Subsection (a), (b), (c), (d), or (e) is a Class A misdemeanor, unless the offense is committed under Subsection (b)(1) or (b)(3), in which event the offense is a felony of the third degree.

(h) It is a defense to prosecution under Subsection (a) that the actor, at the time of the commission of the

offense, displayed the handgun under circumstances in which the actor would have been justified in the use of deadly force under Chapter 9.

✠ 🅔 *Subsection (h-1) below was enacted by Acts 2007, 80th Leg., ch. 1222, §5, effective June 15, 2007, without reference to the conflicting enactment made by Acts 2007, 80th Leg., ch. 1214, §2, effective June 15, 2007. Subsection (h-1) below is effective for offenses committed on or after June 15, 2007.*

(h-1) It is a defense to prosecution under Subsections (b)(1), (2), and (4)-(6), and (c) that at the time of the commission of the offense, the actor was:

(1) a judge or justice of a federal court;

(2) an active judicial officer, as defined by Section 411.201, Government Code; or

(3) a district attorney, assistant district attorney, criminal district attorney, assistant criminal district attorney, county attorney, or assistant county attorney.

✠ 🅔 *Subsection (h-1) below was enacted by Acts 2007, 80th Leg., ch. 1214, §2, effective June 15, 2007, without reference to the conflicting enactment made by Acts 2007, 80th Leg., ch. 1222, §5, effective June 15, 2007. Subsection (h-1) below is effective for offenses committed on or after June 15, 2007.*

(h-1) It is a defense to prosecution under Subsections (b) and (c) that the actor, at the time of the commission of the offense, was:

(1) an active judicial officer, as defined by Section 411.201, Government Code; or

(2) a bailiff designated by the active judicial officer and engaged in escorting the officer.

(i) Subsections (b)(4), (b)(5), (b)(6), and (c) do not apply if the actor was not given effective notice under Section 30.06.

(j) Subsections (a) and (b)(1) do not apply to a historical reenactment performed in compliance with the rules of the Texas Alcoholic Beverage Commission.

History of Pen §46.035: Acts 1995, 74th Leg., ch. 229, §4, eff. Sept. 1, 1995. Amended by Acts 1997, 75th Leg., ch. 165, §10.04 (eff. Sept. 1, 1997), ch. 1261, §26 (eff. Oct. 1, 1998), §27 (eff. Sept. 1, 1997); Acts 2001, 77th Leg., ch. 1420, §14.833, eff. Sept. 1, 2001; Acts 2005, 79th Leg., ch. 976, §3, eff. Sept. 1, 2005; Acts 2007, 80th Leg., ch. 1214, §2 (eff. June 15, 2007), ch. 1222, §5 (eff. June 15, 2007).

PEN §46.04. UNLAWFUL POSSESSION OF FIREARM

(a) A person who has been convicted of a felony commits an offense if he possesses a firearm:

(1) after conviction and before the fifth anniversary of the person's release from confinement following conviction of the felony or the person's release from supervision under community supervision, parole, or mandatory supervision, whichever date is later; or

(2) after the period described by Subdivision (1), at any location other than the premises at which the person lives.

(b) A person who has been convicted of an offense under Section 22.01, punishable as a Class A misdemeanor and involving a member of the person's family or household, commits an offense if the person possesses a firearm before the fifth anniversary of the later of:

(1) the date of the person's release from confinement following conviction of the misdemeanor; or

(2) the date of the person's release from community supervision following conviction of the misdemeanor.

(c) A person, other than a peace officer, as defined by Section 1.07, actively engaged in employment as a sworn, full-time paid employee of a state agency or political subdivision, who is subject to an order issued under Section 6.504 or Chapter 85, Family Code, under Article 17.292 or Chapter 7A, Code of Criminal Procedure, or by another jurisdiction as provided by Chapter 88, Family Code, commits an offense if the person possesses a firearm after receiving notice of the order and before expiration of the order.

(d) In this section, "family," "household," and "member of a household" have the meanings assigned by Chapter 71, Family Code.

(e) An offense under Subsection (a) is a felony of the third degree. An offense under Subsection (b) or (c) is a Class A misdemeanor.

History of Pen §46.04: Acts 1973, 63rd Leg., ch. 399, §1, eff. Jan. 1, 1974. Renumbered from §46.05 and amended by Acts 1993, 73rd Leg., ch. 900, §1.01, eff. Sept. 1, 1994. Amended by Acts 2001, 77th Leg., ch. 23, §2, eff. Sept. 1, 2001; Acts 2003, 78th Leg., ch. 836, §4, eff. Sept. 1, 2003.

See also chart, "Affirmative Links," p. 695.

ANNOTATIONS

Cuellar v. State, 70 S.W.3d 815, 820 (Tex.Crim.App. 2002). "Penal Code §46.04(a) requires a felony conviction as an element of the offense. Here, appellant's prior felony conviction was set aside pursuant to [a CCP art.] 42.12, §20, order. Accordingly, there was no predicate felony conviction to support a conviction under §46.04(a)."

Vasquez v. State, 830 S.W.2d 948, 950 (Tex.Crim. App.1992). "The legislature has not excluded the justification of necessity as a defense to the offense of possession of a firearm by a felon. Nor has it legislatively been excluded as a defense when an offense is enhanced. [N]ecessity is a defense available to a defendant charged with the lesser included offense of unlawfully carrying a weapon."

Bollinger v. State, 224 S.W.3d 768, 774 (Tex. App.—Eastland 2007, pet. ref'd). "The State does not have to prove that the accused had exclusive possession of the firearm; joint possession is sufficient to sustain a conviction. The State can meet its burden with direct or circumstantial evidence, but it must establish that the defendant's connection with the firearm was more than fortuitous."

McIlroy v. State, 188 S.W.3d 789, 791 (Tex.App.—Fort Worth 2006, no pet.). "We hold that when a defendant charged with possession of a firearm by a felon stipulates to her status as a felon and to the prior felony offense and when she objects to the reading of the portion of the indictment describing the type of prior felony offense committed, it is error to permit the State to read those facts to the jury as they have no probative value and can serve only to prove the defendant's bad character or to provide a prejudicial conformity inference."

Davis v. State, 93 S.W.3d 664, 667 (Tex.App.—Texarkana 2002, pet. ref'd). "To support a conviction for possession of a firearm, the state must show (1) that the accused exercised actual care, control, or custody of the firearm, (2) that the accused was conscious of his or her connection with it, and (3) that he or she possessed the firearm knowingly or intentionally."

State v. Hoffman, 999 S.W.2d 573, 575 (Tex.App.—Austin 1999, no pet.). "Because supervision will always be 'later' than confinement (or in lieu thereof), the phrase 'whichever date is later' conveys the meaning that a convicted felon is prohibited from possessing a firearm until five years until after his release from confinement unless he serves community supervision, parole, or mandatory supervision after or in lieu of confinement, in which case the prohibition continues until five years after his release from supervision."

PEN §46.041. UNLAWFUL POSSESSION OF METAL OR BODY ARMOR BY FELON

(a) In this section, "metal or body armor" means any body covering manifestly designed, made, or adapted for the purpose of protecting a person against gunfire.

For a quick reference of penalties, see the Chart of Penalties on p. 675.

O'CONNOR'S CRIMINAL CODES   905

(b) A person who has been convicted of a felony commits an offense if after the conviction the person possesses metal or body armor.

(c) An offense under this section is a felony of the third degree.

History of Pen §46.041: Acts 2001, 77th Leg., ch. 452, §1, eff. Sept. 1, 2001.

PEN §46.05. PROHIBITED WEAPONS

(a) A person commits an offense if he intentionally or knowingly possesses, manufactures, transports, repairs, or sells:

(1) an explosive weapon;

(2) a machine gun;

(3) a short-barrel firearm;

(4) a firearm silencer;

(5) a switchblade knife;

(6) knuckles;

(7) armor-piercing ammunition;

(8) a chemical dispensing device; or

(9) a zip gun.

(b) It is a defense to prosecution under this section that the actor's conduct was incidental to the performance of official duty by the armed forces or national guard, a governmental law enforcement agency, or a correctional facility.

(c) It is a defense to prosecution under this section that the actor's possession was pursuant to registration pursuant to the National Firearms Act,[1] as amended.

(d) It is an affirmative defense to prosecution under this section that the actor's conduct:

(1) was incidental to dealing with a switchblade knife, springblade knife, or short-barrel firearm solely as an antique or curio; or

(2) was incidental to dealing with armor-piercing ammunition solely for the purpose of making the ammunition available to an organization, agency, or institution listed in Subsection (b).

(e) An offense under this section is a felony of the third degree unless it is committed under Subsection (a)(5) or (a)(6), in which event, it is a Class A misdemeanor.

(f) It is a defense to prosecution under this section for the possession of a chemical dispensing device that the actor is a security officer and has received training on the use of the chemical dispensing device by a training program that is:

(1) provided by the Commission on Law Enforcement Officer Standards and Education; or

(2) approved for the purposes described by this subsection by the Texas Private Security Board of the Department of Public Safety.

(g) In Subsection (f), "security officer" means a commissioned security officer as defined by Section 1702.002, Occupations Code, or a noncommissioned security officer registered under Section 1702.221, Occupations Code.

1. **Editor's note:** 26 U.S.C. §5801 et seq.

History of Pen §46.05: Acts 1973, 63rd Leg., ch. 399, §1, eff. Jan. 1, 1974. Amended by Acts 1975, 64th Leg., ch. 342, §15, eff. Sept. 1, 1975; Acts 1983, 68th Leg., ch. 457, §2 (eff. Sept. 1, 1983), ch. 852, §2 (eff. Sept. 1, 1983); Acts 1987, 70th Leg., ch. 167, §5.01(a)(47), eff. Sept. 1, 1987; Acts 1991, 72nd Leg., ch. 229, §2, eff. Sept. 1, 1991; Acts 1993, 73rd Leg., ch. 900, §1.01, eff. Sept. 1, 1994; Acts 2003, 78th Leg., ch. 1071, §1, eff. Sept. 1, 2003; Acts 2005, 79th Leg., ch. 1035, §2.01 (eff. Sept. 1, 2005), ch. 1278, §7 (eff. Sept. 1, 2005).

ANNOTATIONS

Jennings v. State, 107 S.W.3d 85, 88 (Tex. App.—San Antonio 2003, no pet.). "In the context of a prohibited weapon, th[e] non-exclusive list of [affirmative links to its possession] includes whether: (1) the weapon was in a place owned by the accused; (2) the weapon was in a vehicle driven by the accused; (3) the weapon was conveniently accessible to the accused; (4) the weapon was in plain view; (5) the weapon was found in an enclosed space; (6) the weapon was found on the same side of the vehicle as the accused; (7) the conduct of the accused indicated a consciousness of guilt; (8) the accused had a special relationship to the weapon; and (9) affirmative statements connect the accused to the weapon."

PEN §46.06. UNLAWFUL TRANSFER OF CERTAIN WEAPONS

(a) A person commits an offense if the person:

(1) sells, rents, leases, loans, or gives a handgun to any person knowing that the person to whom the handgun is to be delivered intends to use it unlawfully or in the commission of an unlawful act;

(2) intentionally or knowingly sells, rents, leases, or gives or offers to sell, rent, lease, or give to any child younger than 18 years any firearm, club, or illegal knife;

(3) intentionally, knowingly, or recklessly sells a firearm or ammunition for a firearm to any person who is intoxicated;

(4) knowingly sells a firearm or ammunition for a firearm to any person who has been convicted of a felony before the fifth anniversary of the later of the following dates:

(A) the person's release from confinement following conviction of the felony; or

(B) the person's release from supervision under community supervision, parole, or mandatory supervision following conviction of the felony;

(5) sells, rents, leases, loans, or gives a handgun to any person knowing that an active protective order is directed to the person to whom the handgun is to be delivered; or

(6) knowingly purchases, rents, leases, or receives as a loan or gift from another a handgun while an active protective order is directed to the actor.

(b) In this section:

(1) "Intoxicated" means substantial impairment of mental or physical capacity resulting from introduction of any substance into the body.

(2) "Active protective order" means a protective order issued under Title 4, Family Code, that is in effect. The term does not include a temporary protective order issued before the court holds a hearing on the matter.

(c) It is an affirmative defense to prosecution under Subsection (a)(2) that the transfer was to a minor whose parent or the person having legal custody of the minor had given written permission for the sale or, if the transfer was other than a sale, the parent or person having legal custody had given effective consent.

(d) An offense under this section is a Class A misdemeanor, except that an offense under Subsection (a)(2) is a state jail felony if the weapon that is the subject of the offense is a handgun.

History of Pen §46.06: Acts 1973, 63rd Leg., ch. 399, §1, eff. Jan. 1, 1974. Amended by Acts 1985, 69th Leg., ch. 686, §1, eff. Sept. 1, 1985. Renumbered from §46.07 and amended by Acts 1993, 73rd Leg., ch. 900, §1.01, eff. Sept. 1, 1994; Acts 1995, 74th Leg., ch. 324, §1, eff. Jan. 1, 1996; Acts 1997, 75th Leg., ch. 1193, §22 (eff. Sept. 1, 1997), ch. 1304, §1 (eff. Sept. 1, 1997); Acts 1999, 76th Leg., ch. 62, §15.02(f), eff. Sept. 1, 1999.

PEN §46.07. INTERSTATE PURCHASE

A resident of this state may, if not otherwise precluded by law, purchase firearms, ammunition, reloading components, or firearm accessories in contiguous states. This authorization is enacted in conformance with Section 922(b)(3)(A), Public Law 90-618, 90th Congress.

History of Pen §46.07: Acts 1973, 63rd Leg., ch. 399, §1, eff. Jan. 1, 1974. Renumbered from §46.08 by Acts 1993, 73rd Leg., ch. 900, §1.01, eff. Sept. 1, 1994.

Ex parte Mulchahey, 621 S.W.2d 602, 605 (Tex. Crim.App.1981). "[S]ection 46.08 [now §46.07] constitutes a grant of authority and is not an attempt to define as punishable, conduct which would be a criminal offense."

PEN §46.08. HOAX BOMBS

(a) A person commits an offense if the person knowingly manufactures, sells, purchases, transports, or possesses a hoax bomb with intent to use the hoax bomb to:

(1) make another believe that the hoax bomb is an explosive or incendiary device; or

(2) cause alarm or reaction of any type by an official of a public safety agency or volunteer agency organized to deal with emergencies.

(b) An offense under this section is a Class A misdemeanor.

History of Pen §46.08: Acts 1983, 68th Leg., ch. 852, §3, eff. Sept. 1, 1983. Renumbered from §46.09 by Acts 1993, 73rd Leg., ch. 900, §1.01, eff. Sept. 1, 1994.

PEN §46.09. COMPONENTS OF EXPLOSIVES

(a) A person commits an offense if the person knowingly possesses components of an explosive weapon with the intent to combine the components into an explosive weapon for use in a criminal endeavor.

(b) An offense under this section is a felony of the third degree.

History of Pen §46.09: Acts 1983, 68th Leg., ch. 852, §4, eff. Sept. 1, 1983. Renumbered from §46.10 by Acts 1993, 73rd Leg., ch. 900, §1.01, eff. Sept. 1, 1994.

PEN §46.10. DEADLY WEAPON IN PENAL INSTITUTION

(a) A person commits an offense if, while confined in a penal institution, he intentionally, knowingly, or recklessly:

(1) carries on or about his person a deadly weapon; or

(2) possesses or conceals a deadly weapon in the penal institution.

(b) It is an affirmative defense to prosecution under this section that at the time of the offense the actor was engaged in conduct authorized by an employee of the penal institution.

For a quick reference of penalties, see the Chart of Penalties on p. 675.

O'CONNOR'S CRIMINAL CODES 907

(c) A person who is subject to prosecution under both this section and another section under this chapter may be prosecuted under either section.

(d) An offense under this section is a felony of the third degree.

History of Pen §46.10: Acts 1985, 69th Leg., ch. 46, §1, eff. Sept. 1, 1985. Amended by Acts 1987, 70th Leg., ch. 714, §1, eff. Sept. 1, 1987. Renumbered from §46.11 by Acts 1993, 73rd Leg., ch. 900, §1.01, eff. Sept. 1, 1994.

PEN §46.11. PENALTY IF OFFENSE COMMITTED WITHIN WEAPON-FREE SCHOOL ZONE

(a) Except as provided by Subsection (b), the punishment prescribed for an offense under this chapter is increased to the punishment prescribed for the next highest category of offense if it is shown beyond a reasonable doubt on the trial of the offense that the actor committed the offense in a place that the actor knew was:

(1) within 300 feet of the premises of a school; or

(2) on premises where:

(A) an official school function is taking place; or

(B) an event sponsored or sanctioned by the University Interscholastic League is taking place.

(b) This section does not apply to an offense under Section 46.03(a)(1).

(c) In this section:

(1) "Institution of higher education" and "premises" have the meanings assigned by Section 481.134, Health and Safety Code.

(2) "School" means a private or public elementary or secondary school.

History of Pen §46.11: Acts 1995, 74th Leg., ch. 320, §1, eff. Sept. 1, 1995. Amended by Acts 1997, 75th Leg., ch. 1063, §10, eff. Sept. 1, 1997.

PEN §46.12. MAPS AS EVIDENCE OF LOCATION OR AREA

(a) In a prosecution of an offense for which punishment is increased under Section 46.11, a map produced or reproduced by a municipal or county engineer for the purpose of showing the location and boundaries of weapon-free zones is admissible in evidence and is prima facie evidence of the location or boundaries of those areas if the governing body of the municipality or county adopts a resolution or ordinance approving the map as an official finding and record of the location or boundaries of those areas.

(b) A municipal or county engineer may, on request of the governing body of the municipality or county, revise a map that has been approved by the governing body of the municipality or county as provided by Subsection (a).

(c) A municipal or county engineer shall file the original or a copy of every approved or revised map approved as provided by Subsection (a) with the county clerk of each county in which the area is located.

(d) This section does not prevent the prosecution from:

(1) introducing or relying on any other evidence or testimony to establish any element of an offense for which punishment is increased under Section 46.11; or

(2) using or introducing any other map or diagram otherwise admissible under the Texas Rules of Evidence.

History of Pen §46.12: Acts 1995, 74th Leg., ch. 320, §2, eff. Sept. 1, 1995. Amended by Acts 2005, 79th Leg., ch. 728, §16.004, eff. Sept. 1, 2005.

History of Former Pen §46.12: Repealed by Acts 1994, 73rd Leg., ch. 900, §1.01, eff. Sept. 1, 1994

PEN §46.13. MAKING A FIREARM ACCESSIBLE TO A CHILD

(a) In this section:

(1) "Child" means a person younger than 17 years of age.

(2) "Readily dischargeable firearm" means a firearm that is loaded with ammunition, whether or not a round is in the chamber.

(3) "Secure" means to take steps that a reasonable person would take to prevent the access to a readily dischargeable firearm by a child, including but not limited to placing a firearm in a locked container or temporarily rendering the firearm inoperable by a trigger lock or other means.

(b) A person commits an offense if a child gains access to a readily dischargeable firearm and the person with criminal negligence:

(1) failed to secure the firearm; or

(2) left the firearm in a place to which the person knew or should have known the child would gain access.

(c) It is an affirmative defense to prosecution under this section that the child's access to the firearm:

(1) was supervised by a person older than 18 years of age and was for hunting, sporting, or other lawful purposes;

(2) consisted of lawful defense by the child of people or property;

(3) was gained by entering property in violation of this code; or

(4) occurred during a time when the actor was engaged in an agricultural enterprise.

(d) Except as provided by Subsection (e), an offense under this section is a Class C misdemeanor.

(e) An offense under this section is a Class A misdemeanor if the child discharges the firearm and causes death or serious bodily injury to himself or another person.

(f) A peace officer or other person may not arrest the actor before the seventh day after the date on which the offense is committed if:

(1) the actor is a member of the family, as defined by Section 71.003, Family Code, of the child who discharged the firearm; and

(2) the child in discharging the firearm caused the death of or serious injury to the child.

(g) A dealer of firearms shall post in a conspicuous position on the premises where the dealer conducts business a sign that contains the following warning in block letters not less than one inch in height:

"IT IS UNLAWFUL TO STORE, TRANSPORT, OR ABANDON AN UNSECURED FIREARM IN A PLACE WHERE CHILDREN ARE LIKELY TO BE AND CAN OBTAIN ACCESS TO THE FIREARM."

History of Pen §46.13: Acts 1995, 74th Leg., ch. 83, §1, eff. Sept. 1, 1995. Amended by Acts 1999, 76th Leg., ch. 62, §15.02(g), eff. Sept. 1, 1999.

Section 46.14 blank

PEN §46.15. NONAPPLICABILITY

(a) Sections 46.02 and 46.03 do not apply to:

(1) peace officers or special investigators under Article 2.122, Code of Criminal Procedure, and neither section prohibits a peace officer or special investigator from carrying a weapon in this state, including in an establishment in this state serving the public, regardless of whether the peace officer or special investigator is engaged in the actual discharge of the officer's or investigator's duties while carrying the weapon;

(2) parole officers and neither section prohibits an officer from carrying a weapon in this state if the officer is:

(A) engaged in the actual discharge of the officer's duties while carrying the weapon; and

(B) in compliance with policies and procedures adopted by the Texas Department of Criminal Justice regarding the possession of a weapon by an officer while on duty;

(3) community supervision and corrections department officers appointed or employed under Section 76.004, Government Code, and neither section prohibits an officer from carrying a weapon in this state if the officer is:

(A) engaged in the actual discharge of the officer's duties while carrying the weapon; and

(B) authorized to carry a weapon under Section 76.0051, Government Code;

(4) a judge or justice of a federal court, the supreme court, the court of criminal appeals, a court of appeals, a district court, a criminal district court, a constitutional county court, a statutory county court, a justice court, or a municipal court who is licensed to carry a concealed handgun under Subchapter H, Chapter 411, Government Code;

(5) an honorably retired peace officer or federal criminal investigator who holds a certificate of proficiency issued under Section 1701.357, Occupations Code, and is carrying a photo identification that:

(A) verifies that the officer honorably retired after not less than 15 years of service as a commissioned officer; and

(B) is issued by a state or local law enforcement agency;

A *Subsection (6) below is effective for offenses committed on or after June 15, 2007.*

(6) a district attorney, criminal district attorney, municipal attorney, or county attorney who is licensed to carry a concealed handgun under Subchapter H, Chapter 411, Government Code; or

Subsection (6) below is effective for offenses in which any element of the offense was committed before June 15, 2007.

(6) a district attorney, criminal district attorney, or county attorney who is licensed to carry a concealed handgun under Subchapter H, Chapter 411, Government Code.

E *Subsection (7) below was enacted by Acts 2007, 80th Leg., ch. 1214, §1, effective June 15, 2007, without reference to the conflicting enactment made by Acts*

For a quick reference of penalties, see the Chart of Penalties on p. 675.

O'CONNOR'S CRIMINAL CODES   909

2007, 80th Leg., ch. 1222, §6, effective June 15, 2007. Subsection (7) below is effective for offenses committed on or after June 15, 2007.

(7) a bailiff designated by an active judicial officer as defined by Section 411.201, Government Code, who is:

(A) licensed to carry a concealed handgun under Chapter 411, Government Code; and

(B) engaged in escorting the judicial officer.

Subsection (7) below was enacted by Acts 2007, 80th Leg., ch. 1222, §6, effective June 15, 2007, without reference to the conflicting enactment made by Acts 2007, 80th Leg., ch. 1214, §1, effective June 15, 2007. Subsection (7) below is effective for offenses committed on or after June 15, 2007.

(7) an assistant district attorney, assistant criminal district attorney, or assistant county attorney who is licensed to carry a concealed handgun under Subchapter H, Chapter 411, Government Code.

Subsection (b) below was amended by Acts 2007, 80th Leg., ch. 647, §1, enacted May 23, 2007, effective Sept. 1, 2007, without reference to the conflicting amendment made by Acts 2007, 80th Leg., ch. 1048, §3, enacted May 23, 2007, effective Sept. 1, 2007, and the conflicting amendment made by Acts 2007, 80th Leg., ch. 693, §2, enacted May 23, 2007, effective Sept. 1, 2007. For resolving conflicts, see p. V. Subsection (b) below is effective for offenses committed on or after Sept. 1, 2007.

(b) Section 46.02 does not apply to a person who:

(1) is in the actual discharge of official duties as a member of the armed forces or state military forces as defined by Section 431.001, Government Code, or as a guard employed by a penal institution;

(2) is on the person's own premises or premises under the person's control unless the person is an employee or agent of the owner of the premises and the person's primary responsibility is to act in the capacity of a security guard to protect persons or property, in which event the person must comply with Subdivision (5);

(3) is traveling;

(4) is engaging in lawful hunting, fishing, or other sporting activity on the immediate premises where the activity is conducted, or is en route between the premises and the actor's residence, if the weapon is a type commonly used in the activity;

(5) holds a security officer commission issued by the Texas Private Security Board, if:

(A) the person is engaged in the performance of the person's duties as a security officer or traveling to and from the person's place of assignment;

(B) the person is wearing a distinctive uniform; and

(C) the weapon is in plain view;

(6) is carrying a concealed handgun and a valid license issued under Subchapter H, Chapter 411, Government Code, to carry a concealed handgun of the same category as the handgun the person is carrying;

(7) holds a security officer commission and a personal protection officer authorization issued by the Texas Private Security Board and is providing personal protection under Chapter 1702, Occupations Code;

(8) holds an alcoholic beverage permit or license or is an employee of a holder of an alcoholic beverage permit or license if the person is supervising the operation of the permitted or licensed premises; or

(9) is a student in a law enforcement class engaging in an activity required as part of the class, if the weapon is a type commonly used in the activity and the person is:

(A) on the immediate premises where the activity is conducted; or

(B) en route between those premises and the person's residence and is carrying the weapon unloaded.

Subsection (b) below was amended by Acts 2007, 80th Leg., ch. 1048, §3, enacted May 23, 2007, effective Sept. 1, 2007, without reference to the conflicting amendment made by Acts 2007, 80th Leg., ch. 647, §1, enacted May 23, 2007, effective Sept. 1, 2007, and the conflicting amendment made by Acts 2007, 80th Leg., ch. 693, §2, enacted May 23, 2007, effective Sept. 1, 2007. For resolving conflicts, see p. V. Subsection (b) below is effective for offenses committed on or after Sept. 1, 2007.

(b) Section 46.02 does not apply to a person who:

(1) is in the actual discharge of official duties as a member of the armed forces or state military forces as defined by Section 431.001, Government Code, or as a guard employed by a penal institution;

(2) is on the person's own premises or premises under the person's control unless the person is an employee or agent of the owner of the premises and the person's primary responsibility is to act in the capacity of a

PEN §46.15

security guard to protect persons or property, in which event the person must comply with Subdivision (5);

(3) is traveling;

(4) is engaging in lawful hunting, fishing, or other sporting activity on the immediate premises where the activity is conducted, or is en route between the premises and the actor's residence, if the weapon is a type commonly used in the activity;

(5) holds a security officer commission issued by the Texas Private Security Board, if the person:

(A) is engaged in the performance of the person's duties as an officer commissioned under Chapter 1702, Occupations Code, or is traveling to or from the person's place of assignment; and

(B) is either:

(i) wearing the officer's uniform and carrying the officer's weapon in plain view; or

(ii) acting as a personal protection officer and carrying the person's security officer commission and personal protection officer authorization;

(6) is carrying a concealed handgun and a valid license issued under Subchapter H, Chapter 411, Government Code, to carry a concealed handgun of the same category as the handgun the person is carrying; or

(7) holds an alcoholic beverage permit or license or is an employee of a holder of an alcoholic beverage permit or license if the person is supervising the operation of the permitted or licensed premises.

☠ **Ⓐ** *Subsection (b) below was amended by Acts 2007, 80th Leg., ch. 693, §2, enacted May 23, 2007, effective Sept. 1, 2007, without reference to the conflicting amendment made by Acts 2007, 80th Leg., ch. 1048, §3, enacted May 23, 2007, effective Sept. 1, 2007, and the conflicting enactment made by Acts 2007, 80th Leg., ch. 647, §1, enacted May 23, 2007, effective Sept. 1, 2007. For resolving conflicts, see p. V. Subsection (b) below is effective for offenses committed on or after Sept. 1, 2007.*

(b) Section 46.02 does not apply to a person who:

(1) is in the actual discharge of official duties as a member of the armed forces or state military forces as defined by Section 431.001, Government Code, or as a guard employed by a penal institution;

(2) is traveling;

(3) is engaging in lawful hunting, fishing, or other sporting activity on the immediate premises where the

activity is conducted, or is en route between the premises and the actor's residence or motor vehicle, if the weapon is a type commonly used in the activity;

(4) holds a security officer commission issued by the Texas Private Security Board, if:

(A) the person is engaged in the performance of the person's duties as a security officer or traveling to and from the person's place of assignment;

(B) the person is wearing a distinctive uniform; and

(C) the weapon is in plain view;

(5) is carrying a concealed handgun and a valid license issued under Subchapter H, Chapter 411, Government Code, to carry a concealed handgun of the same category as the handgun the person is carrying;

(6) holds a security officer commission and a personal protection officer authorization issued by the Texas Private Security Board and is providing personal protection under Chapter 1702, Occupations Code; or

(7) holds an alcoholic beverage permit or license or is an employee of a holder of an alcoholic beverage permit or license if the person is supervising the operation of the permitted or licensed premises.

Subsection (b) below is effective for offenses in which any element of the offense was committed before Sept. 1, 2007.

(b) Section 46.02 does not apply to a person who:

☠ *Subsection (1) below was added by Acts 1997, 75th Leg., ch. 1221, §4, effective June 20, 1997, without reference to the conflicting enactment made by Acts 1997, 75th Leg., ch. 1261, §28, effective Sept. 1, 1997.*

(1) is in the actual discharge of official duties as a member of the armed forces or state military forces as defined by Section 431.001, Government Code, or as an employee of a penal institution who is performing a security function;

☠ *Subsection (1) below was added by Acts 1997, 75th Leg., ch. 1261, §28, effective Sept. 1, 1997, without reference to the conflicting enactment made by Acts 1997, 75th Leg., ch. 1221, §4, effective June 20, 1997.*

(1) is in the actual discharge of official duties as a member of the armed forces or state military forces as defined by Section 431.001, Government Code, or as a guard employed by a penal institution;

(2) is on the person's own premises or premises under the person's control unless the person is an employee or agent of the owner of the premises and the person's primary responsibility is to act in the capacity of a

For a quick reference of penalties, see the Chart of Penalties on p. 675.

O'CONNOR'S CRIMINAL CODES 911

PEN §46.15

security guard to protect persons or property, in which event the person must comply with Subdivision (5);

(3) is traveling;

(4) is engaging in lawful hunting, fishing, or other sporting activity on the immediate premises where the activity is conducted, or is directly[1] en route between the premises and the actor's residence, if the weapon is a type commonly used in the activity;

(5) holds a security officer commission issued by the Texas Board of Private Investigators and Private Security Agencies, if:

(A) the person is engaged in the performance of the person's duties as a security officer or traveling to and from the person's place of assignment;

(B) the person is wearing a distinctive uniform; and

(C) the weapon is in plain view;

(6) is carrying a concealed handgun and a valid license issued under Article 4413(29ee), Revised Statutes, to carry a concealed handgun of the same category as the handgun the person is carrying;

(7) holds a security officer commission and a personal protection authorization issued by the Texas Board of Private Investigators and Private Security Agencies and who is providing personal protection under the Private Investigators and Private Security Agencies Act (Article 4413(29bb), Vernon's Texas Civil Statutes); or

(8) holds an alcoholic beverage permit or license or is an employee of a holder of an alcoholic beverage permit or license if the person is supervising the operation of the permitted or licensed premises.

(c) The provision of Section 46.02 prohibiting the carrying of a club does not apply to a noncommissioned security guard at an institution of higher education who carries a nightstick or similar club, and who has undergone 15 hours of training in the proper use of the club, including at least seven hours of training in the use of the club for nonviolent restraint. For the purposes of this subsection, "nonviolent restraint" means the use of reasonable force, not intended and not likely to inflict bodily injury.

(d) The provisions of Section 46.02 prohibiting the carrying of a firearm or carrying of a club do not apply to a public security officer employed by the adjutant general under Section 431.029, Government Code, in performance of official duties or while traveling to or from a place of duty.

(e) The provisions of Section 46.02 prohibiting the carrying of an illegal knife do not apply to an individual carrying a bowie knife or a sword used in a historical demonstration or in a ceremony in which the knife or sword is significant to the performance of the ceremony.

(f) Section 46.03(a)(6) does not apply to a person who possesses a firearm or club while in the actual discharge of official duties as:

(1) a member of the armed forces or state military forces, as defined by Section 431.001, Government Code; or

(2) an employee of a penal institution.

(g) Repealed by Acts 2005, 79th Leg., ch. 1179, §3, eff. Sept. 1, 2005 and Acts 2005, 79th Leg., ch. 1093, §4, eff. Sept. 1, 2005.

(h) Repealed by Acts 2007, 80th Leg., ch. 693, §3(1), eff. Sept. 1, 2007.

Subsection (h) below is effective for offenses in which any element of the offense was committed before Sept. 1, 2007.

(h) For the purpose of Subsection (b)(2), "premises" includes a recreational vehicle that is being used by the person carrying the handgun, illegal knife, or club as living quarters, regardless of whether that use is temporary or permanent. In this subsection, "recreational vehicle" means a motor vehicle primarily designed as temporary living quarters or a vehicle that contains temporary living quarters and is designed to be towed by a motor vehicle. The term includes a travel trailer, camping trailer, truck camper, motor home, and horse trailer with living quarters.

(i) Repealed by Acts 2007, 80th Leg., ch. 693, §3(2), eff. Sept. 1, 2007.

Subsection (i) below is effective for offenses in which any element of the offense was committed before Sept. 1, 2007.

(i) For purposes of Subsection (b)(3), a person is presumed to be traveling if the person is:

(1) in a private motor vehicle;

(2) not otherwise engaged in criminal activity, other than a Class C misdemeanor that is a violation of a law or ordinance regulating traffic;

(3) not otherwise prohibited by law from possessing a firearm;

(4) not a member of a criminal street gang, as defined by Section 71.01; and

(5) not carrying a handgun in plain view.

 (j) The provisions of Section 46.02 prohibiting the carrying of a handgun do not apply to an individual who carries a handgun as a participant in a historical reenactment performed in accordance with the rules of the Texas Alcoholic Beverage Commission.

1. **Editor's note:** The amendment by Acts 1997, 75th Leg., ch. 1221, §4, does not contain the word "directly."

History of Pen §46.15: Acts 1995, 74th Leg., ch. 318, §18, eff. Sept. 1, 1995. Amended by Acts 1997, 75th Leg., ch. 1221, §4 (eff. June 20, 1997), ch. 1261, §28 (eff. Sept. 1, 1997); Acts 1999, 76th Leg., ch. 62, §9.25 (eff. Sept. 1, 1999), ch. 1445, §2 (eff. Sept. 1, 1999); Acts 2001, 77th Leg., ch. 1060, §3, eff. Sept. 1, 2001; Acts 2003, 78th Leg., ch. 421, §1 (eff. Sept. 1, 2003), §1 (eff. June 20, 2003), ch. 325, §2 (eff. Sept. 1, 2003); Acts 2005, 79th Leg., ch. 288, §1 (eff. Sept. 1, 2005), ch. 976, §4 (eff. Sept. 1, 2005), ch. 728, §23.001(78) (eff. Sept. 1, 2005), ch. 1093, §§1, 4 (eff. Sept. 1, 2005), ch. 1200, §§2, 3 (eff. Sept. 1, 2005); Acts 2007, 80th Leg., ch. 647, §1 (eff. Sept. 1, 2007), ch. 693, §2, 3 (eff. Sept. 1, 2007), ch. 921, §17.001(62) (eff. Sept. 1, 2007), ch. 1048, §3 (eff. Sept. 1, 2007), ch. 1214, §1 (eff. June 15, 2007), ch. 1222, §6 (eff. June 15, 2007).

ANNOTATIONS

Heins v. State, 157 S.W.3d 457, 460 (Tex.App.—Houston [14th Dist.] 2004, no pet.). "[T]he jury was instructed as follows: ... It is not an offense for a person to carry a handgun [if the person] is on the person's own premises under the person's control. ... [T]he charge should have read: [It is not an offense for a person to carry a handgun if the person] is on the person's own premises *or premises* under the person's control. *At 461:* By omitting the [words 'or premises'], the charge as issued required that appellant both own the premises and have them under her control. Whether the premises were under her control is arguable; whether she owned them is not. ... Had a proper charge been given, a jury could have determined that appellant qualified for the third exemption to the law against unlawfully carrying a handgun. [¶] We believe that the omission of these words constituted egregious error by both going to the basis of the case and vitally affecting appellant's defensive theory."

Soderman v. State, 915 S.W.2d 605, 609 (Tex. App.—Houston [14th Dist.] 1996, pet. ref'd). "[T]raveling status ceases when a traveler has returned from his journey. [¶] [I]f a traveler loiters along the way or unnecessarily deviates from the course of travel, the travel exemption does not apply. [I]nterruption of the journey for legitimate incidental purposes does not forfeit the traveler's right to carry a pistol."

Dixon v. State, 908 S.W.2d 616, 619 (Tex.App.—Amarillo 1995, pet. ref'd). "In addition to the statutory exceptions, [another] provides that 'a person may lawfully carry a pistol from his place of business to his home or from his home to his place of business, provided that the weapon is not habitually carried between those places and the purpose is a legitimate one.' The court ... qualified the exception by quoting with approval a statement that 'the route taken for the transportation must be a practical one, though not necessarily the shortest or most practical. It is essential also that the journey should proceed without undue delay or unnecessary or unreasonable deviation.'"

Ayesh v. State, 734 S.W.2d 106, 108 (Tex.App.—Austin 1987, no pet.). "[T]he 'traveling' exception to the prohibition on carrying weapons applies to persons on a journey which takes them some distance from their home in excess of 35 miles, or 40 miles, and the trip must typically be overnight. The exception has also been applied to those in the process of moving from one home to another. Deviation from the business of the journey will, however, terminate traveler status."

CHAPTER 47. GAMBLING

PEN §47.01. DEFINITIONS

In this chapter:

(1) "Bet" means an agreement to win or lose something of value solely or partially by chance. A bet does not include:

(A) contracts of indemnity or guaranty, or life, health, property, or accident insurance;

(B) an offer of a prize, award, or compensation to the actual contestants in a bona fide contest for the determination of skill, speed, strength, or endurance or to the owners of animals, vehicles, watercraft, or aircraft entered in a contest; or

(C) an offer of merchandise, with a value not greater than $25, made by the proprietor of a bona fide

For a quick reference of penalties, see the Chart of Penalties on p. 675.

O'CONNOR'S CRIMINAL CODES   913

PEN §47.01

carnival contest conducted at a carnival sponsored by a nonprofit religious, fraternal, school, law enforcement, youth, agricultural, or civic group, including any nonprofit agricultural or civic group incorporated by the state before 1955, if the person to receive the merchandise from the proprietor is the person who performs the carnival contest.

(2) "Bookmaking" means:

(A) to receive and record or to forward more than five bets or offers to bet in a period of 24 hours;

(B) to receive and record or to forward bets or offers to bet totaling more than $1,000 in a period of 24 hours; or

(C) a scheme by three or more persons to receive, record, or forward a bet or an offer to bet.

(3) "Gambling place" means any real estate, building, room, tent, vehicle, boat, or other property whatsoever, one of the uses of which is the making or settling of bets, bookmaking, or the conducting of a lottery or the playing of gambling devices.

(4) "Gambling device" means any electronic, electromechanical, or mechanical contrivance not excluded under Paragraph (B) that for a consideration affords the player an opportunity to obtain anything of value, the award of which is determined solely or partially by chance, even though accompanied by some skill, whether or not the prize is automatically paid by the contrivance. The term:

(A) includes, but is not limited to, gambling device versions of bingo, keno, blackjack, lottery, roulette, video poker, or similar electronic, electromechanical, or mechanical games, or facsimiles thereof, that operate by chance or partially so, that as a result of the play or operation of the game award credits or free games, and that record the number of free games or credits so awarded and the cancellation or removal of the free games or credits; and

(B) does not include any electronic, electromechanical, or mechanical contrivance designed, made, and adapted solely for bona fide amusement purposes if the contrivance rewards the player exclusively with noncash merchandise prizes, toys, or novelties, or a representation of value redeemable for those items, that have a wholesale value available from a single play of the game or device of not more than 10 times the amount charged to play the game or device once or $5, whichever is less.

(5) "Altered gambling equipment" means any contrivance that has been altered in some manner, including, but not limited to, shaved dice, loaded dice, magnetic dice, mirror rings, electronic sensors, shaved cards, marked cards, and any other equipment altered or designed to enhance the actor's chances of winning.

(6) "Gambling paraphernalia" means any book, instrument, or apparatus by means of which bets have been or may be recorded or registered; any record, ticket, certificate, bill, slip, token, writing, scratch sheet, or other means of carrying on bookmaking, wagering pools, lotteries, numbers, policy, or similar games.

(7) "Lottery" means any scheme or procedure whereby one or more prizes are distributed by chance among persons who have paid or promised consideration for a chance to win anything of value, whether such scheme or procedure is called a pool, lottery, raffle, gift, gift enterprise, sale, policy game, or some other name.

(8) "Private place" means a place to which the public does not have access, and excludes, among other places, streets, highways, restaurants, taverns, nightclubs, schools, hospitals, and the common areas of apartment houses, hotels, motels, office buildings, transportation facilities, and shops.

(9) "Thing of value" means any benefit, but does not include an unrecorded and immediate right of replay not exchangeable for value.

History of Pen §47.01: Acts 1973, 63rd Leg., ch. 399, §1, eff. Jan. 1, 1974. Amended by Acts 1987, 70th Leg., ch. 313, §§1, 2, eff. Sept. 1, 1987; Acts 1989, 71st Leg., ch. 396, §1, eff. June 14, 1989; Acts 1993, 73rd Leg., ch. 774, §1 (eff. Aug. 30, 1993), ch. 900, §1.01 (eff. Sept. 1, 1994); Acts 1995, 74th Leg., ch. 318, §19, eff. Sept. 1, 1995.

ANNOTATIONS

Hardy v. State, 102 S.W.3d 123, 125 (Tex.2003). "[G]ift certificates ... are equivalent to the monetary amount on the face thereof in cash, and that gaming machines that dispense tickets that may be exchanged for such certificates do not come within the exclusion to the definition of a gambling device in 47.01(4)(B). Finally, we hold that an eight-liner that rewards the player with cash, even if that cash is used only to play another machine, fails to satisfy the §47.01(4)(B) exclusion."

State v. Mendel, 871 S.W.2d 906, 909 (Tex.App.—Houston [14th Dist.] 1994, no pet.). "[An] essential element of a gambling device is that the operation of the device requires the payment of consideration. The legislature intended [§47.01(4)] to reach devices such as slot machines and roulette wheels."

PEN §47.02. GAMBLING

(a) A person commits an offense if he:

(1) makes a bet on the partial or final result of a game or contest or on the performance of a participant in a game or contest;

(2) makes a bet on the result of any political nomination, appointment, or election or on the degree of success of any nominee, appointee, or candidate; or

(3) plays and bets for money or other thing of value at any game played with cards, dice, balls, or any other gambling device.

(b) It is a defense to prosecution under this section that:

(1) the actor engaged in gambling in a private place;

(2) no person received any economic benefit other than personal winnings; and

(3) except for the advantage of skill or luck, the risks of losing and the chances of winning were the same for all participants.

(c) It is a defense to prosecution under this section that the actor reasonably believed that the conduct:

(1) was permitted under Chapter 2001, Occupations Code;

(2) was permitted under Chapter 2002, Occupations Code;

(3) consisted entirely of participation in the state lottery authorized by the State Lottery Act (Chapter 466, Government Code);

(4) was permitted under the Texas Racing Act (Article 179e, Vernon's Texas Civil Statutes); or

(5) consisted entirely of participation in a drawing for the opportunity to participate in a hunting, fishing, or other recreational event conducted by the Parks and Wildlife Department.

(d) An offense under this section is a Class C misdemeanor.

(e) It is a defense to prosecution under this section that a person played for something of value other than money using an electronic, electromechanical, or mechanical contrivance excluded from the definition of "gambling device" under Section 47.01(4)(B).

History of Pen §47.02: Acts 1973, 63rd Leg., ch. 399, §1, eff. Jan. 1, 1974. Amended by Acts 1981, 67th Leg., 1st C.S., ch. 11, §43, eff. Nov. 10, 1981; Acts 1989, 71st Leg., ch. 957, §2, eff. Jan. 1, 1990; Acts 1991, 72nd Leg., 1st C.S., ch. 6, §3 (eff. Nov. 5, 1991); Acts 1993, 73rd Leg., ch. 107, §4.04 (eff. Aug. 30, 1993), ch. 774, §2 (eff. Aug. 30, 1993), ch. 900, §1.01 (eff. Sept. 1, 1994); Acts 1995, 74th Leg., ch. 76, §14.53 (eff. Sept. 1, 1995), ch. 318, §20 (eff. Sept. 1, 1995), ch. 931, §79 (eff. June 16, 1995); Acts 1997, 75th Leg., ch. 1256, §124, eff. Sept. 1, 1997; Acts 2001, 77th Leg., ch. 1420, §14.834, eff. Sept. 1, 2001.

ANNOTATIONS

Miller v. State, 874 S.W.2d 908, 912 (Tex.App.—Houston [1st Dist.] 1994, pet. ref'd). "If the odds of the game are stacked in favor of one party, Subsection (b)(3) excludes the defense. However, the equal risks and chances requirement of Subsection *(b)(3) refers only to the rules of the game*, not to the advantages that accrue to a skilled player. Therefore, a game that ensures a percentage to the house or banker, regardless of the luck or skill involved, is not a friendly game to which the defense applies; but the presence of a superior, even professional player, who relies on skill and luck, does not vitiate the defense." (Internal quotes omitted.)

State v. Gambling Device, 859 S.W.2d 519, 523 (Tex.App.—Houston [1st Dist.] 1993, writ denied). "Even a contrivance that is predominantly a game of skill may be determined by chance. … A player's level of skill may influence the *degree* of chance involved, but it does not eliminate the element of chance altogether. … [I]t is the incorporation of chance that is the essential element of a gambling device, not the incorporation of a particular proportion of chance and skill. *At 524:* Gambling activities are, traditionally, those activities that involve the elements of consideration, chance, and profit."

PEN §47.03. GAMBLING PROMOTION

(a) A person commits an offense if he intentionally or knowingly does any of the following acts:

(1) operates or participates in the earnings of a gambling place;

(2) engages in bookmaking;

(3) for gain, becomes a custodian of anything of value bet or offered to be bet;

(4) sells chances on the partial or final result of or on the margin of victory in any game or contest or on the performance of any participant in any game or contest or on the result of any political nomination, appointment, or election or on the degree of success of any nominee, appointee, or candidate; or

For a quick reference of penalties, see the Chart of Penalties on p. 675.

O'CONNOR'S CRIMINAL CODES 915

(5) for gain, sets up or promotes any lottery or sells or offers to sell or knowingly possesses for transfer, or transfers any card, stub, ticket, check, or other device designed to serve as evidence of participation in any lottery.

(b) An offense under this section is a Class A misdemeanor.

History of Pen §47.03: Acts 1973, 63rd Leg., ch. 399, §1, eff. Jan. 1, 1974. Amended by Acts 1987, 70th Leg., ch. 313, §3, eff. Sept. 1, 1987; Acts 1993, 73rd Leg., ch. 900, §1.01, eff. Sept. 1, 1994.

ANNOTATIONS

Ex parte Elliott, 746 S.W.2d 762, 764 (Tex.Crim. App.1988). "The bet or offer to bet is an essential element of the offense of gambling promotion and therefore must be pled and proved."

PEN §47.04. KEEPING A GAMBLING PLACE

(a) A person commits an offense if he knowingly uses or permits another to use as a gambling place any real estate, building, room, tent, vehicle, boat, or other property whatsoever owned by him or under his control, or rents or lets any such property with a view or expectation that it be so used.

(b) It is an affirmative defense to prosecution under this section that:

(1) the gambling occurred in a private place;

(2) no person received any economic benefit other than personal winnings; and

(3) except for the advantage of skill or luck, the risks of losing and the chances of winning were the same for all participants.

(c) An offense under this section is a Class A misdemeanor.

History of Pen §47.04: Acts 1973, 63rd Leg., ch. 399, §1, eff. Jan. 1, 1974. Amended by Acts 1977, 65th Leg., ch. 251, §1, eff. Aug. 29, 1977; Acts 1989, 71st Leg., ch. 1030, §1, eff. Sept. 1, 1989; Acts 1993, 73rd Leg., ch. 900, §1.01, eff. Sept. 1, 1994.

ANNOTATIONS

State v. Taylor, 805 S.W.2d 440, 442 (Tex.Crim.App. 1991). "'This section defines a special variety of *gambling promotion*—furnishing a location—that analytically is a form of complicity responsibility. ... It covers not only the owner-operator, whose conduct at the location will no doubt violate the general promotion section, but the true facilitator as well, one who has no

connection with the actual gambling but rents the premises with knowledge that they will be used for that purpose.' [¶] [T]he legislature intended to punish the party responsible for either *using or permitting another to use a location* for the purposes of promoting gambling more harshly than the party engaged in mere gambling."

PEN §47.05. COMMUNICATING GAMBLING INFORMATION

(a) A person commits an offense if, with the intent to further gambling, he knowingly communicates information as to bets, betting odds, or changes in betting odds or he knowingly provides, installs, or maintains equipment for the transmission or receipt of such information.

(b) It is an exception to the application of Subsection (a) that the information communicated is intended for use in placing a lawful wager under Article 11, Texas Racing Act (Article 179e, Vernon's Texas Civil Statutes), and is not communicated in violation of Section 14.01 of that Act.

(c) An offense under this section is a Class A misdemeanor.

History of Pen §47.05: Acts 1973, 63rd Leg., ch. 399, §1, eff. Jan. 1, 1974. Amended by Acts 1993, 73rd Leg., ch. 900, §1.01, eff. Sept. 1, 1994.

PEN §47.06. POSSESSION OF GAMBLING DEVICE, EQUIPMENT, OR PARAPHERNALIA

(a) A person commits an offense if, with the intent to further gambling, he knowingly owns, manufactures, transfers, or possesses any gambling device that he knows is designed for gambling purposes or any equipment that he knows is designed as a subassembly or essential part of a gambling device.

(b) A person commits an offense if, with the intent to further gambling, he knowingly owns, manufactures, transfers commercially, or possesses any altered gambling equipment that he knows is designed for gambling purposes or any equipment that he knows is designed as a subassembly or essential part of such device.

(c) A person commits an offense if, with the intent to further gambling, the person knowingly owns, manufactures, transfers commercially, or possesses gambling paraphernalia.

(d) It is a defense to prosecution under Subsections (a) and (c) that:

(1) the device, equipment, or paraphernalia is used for or is intended for use in gambling that is to occur entirely in a private place;

(2) a person involved in the gambling does not receive any economic benefit other than personal winnings; and

(3) except for the advantage of skill or luck, the chance of winning is the same for all participants.

(e) An offense under this section is a Class A misdemeanor.

(f) It is a defense to prosecution under Subsection (a) or (c) that the person owned, manufactured, transferred, or possessed the gambling device, equipment, or paraphernalia for the sole purpose of shipping it to another jurisdiction where the possession or use of the device, equipment, or paraphernalia was legal.

(g) A district or county attorney is not required to have a search warrant or subpoena to inspect a gambling device or gambling equipment or paraphernalia on an ocean-going vessel that enters the territorial waters of this state to call at a port in this state.

History of Pen §47.06: Acts 1973, 63rd Leg., ch. 399, §1, eff. Jan. 1, 1974. Amended by Acts 1977, 65th Leg., ch. 251, §2 (eff. Aug. 29, 1977), ch. 741, §1 (eff. Aug. 29, 1977); Acts 1987, 70th Leg., ch. 167, §5.01(a)(48) (eff. Sept. 1, 1987), ch. 458, §1 (eff. Sept. 1, 1987); Acts 1989, 71st Leg., ch. 1030, §2, eff. Sept. 1, 1989; Acts 1991, 72nd Leg., ch. 44, §1 (eff. Aug. 26, 1991), ch. 315, §1 (eff. Sept. 1, 1991), 1st C.S., ch. 6, §4 (eff. Nov. 5, 1991); Acts 1993, 73rd Leg., ch. 107, §4.05 (eff. Aug. 30, 1993), ch. 284, §30 (eff. Sept. 1, 1993), ch. 900, §1.01 (eff. Sept. 1, 1994).

ANNOTATIONS

State v. Gambling Device, 859 S.W.2d 519, 524 (Tex.App.—Houston [1st Dist.] 1993, writ denied). "Gambling activities are, traditionally, those activities that involve the elements of consideration, chance, and profit. By analogy, gambling devices are devices used in a fashion so as to incorporate these elements, even if the devices also incorporate the element of skill."

PEN §47.07. EVIDENCE

In any prosecution under this chapter in which it is relevant to prove the occurrence of a sporting event, a published report of its occurrence in a daily newspaper, magazine, or other periodically printed publication of general circulation shall be admissible in evidence and is prima facie evidence that the event occurred.

History of Pen §47.07: Acts 1973, 63rd Leg., ch. 399, §1, eff. Jan. 1, 1974. Renumbered from §47.08 and amended by Acts 1993, 73rd Leg., ch. 900, §1.01, eff. Sept. 1, 1994.

PEN §47.08. TESTIMONIAL IMMUNITY

(a) A party to an offense under this chapter may be required to furnish evidence or testify about the offense.

(b) A party to an offense under this chapter may not be prosecuted for any offense about which he is required to furnish evidence or testify, and the evidence and testimony may not be used against the party in any adjudicatory proceeding except a prosecution for aggravated perjury.

(c) For purposes of this section, "adjudicatory proceeding" means a proceeding before a court or any other agency of government in which the legal rights, powers, duties, or privileges of specified parties are determined.

(d) A conviction under this chapter may be had upon the uncorroborated testimony of a party to the offense.

History of Pen §47.08: Acts 1973, 63rd Leg., ch. 399, §1, eff. Jan. 1, 1974. Renumbered from §47.09 by Acts 1993, 73rd Leg., ch. 900, §1.01, eff. Sept. 1, 1994.

PEN §47.09. OTHER DEFENSES

(a) It is a defense to prosecution under this chapter that the conduct:

(1) was authorized under:

(A) Chapter 2001, Occupations Code;

(B) Chapter 2002, Occupations Code; or

(C) the Texas Racing Act (Article 179e, Vernon's Texas Civil Statutes);

(2) consisted entirely of participation in the state lottery authorized by Chapter 466, Government Code; or

(3) was a necessary incident to the operation of the state lottery and was directly or indirectly authorized by:

(A) Chapter 466, Government Code;

(B) the lottery division of the Texas Lottery Commission;

(C) the Texas Lottery Commission; or

(D) the director of the lottery division of the Texas Lottery Commission.

(b) It is an affirmative defense to prosecution under Sections 47.04, 47.06(a), and 47.06(c) that the gambling device, equipment, or paraphernalia is aboard an ocean-going vessel that enters the territorial waters of this state to call at a port in this state if:

For a quick reference of penalties, see the Chart of Penalties on p. 675.

O'CONNOR'S CRIMINAL CODES 917

(1) before the vessel enters the territorial waters of this state, the district attorney or, if there is no district attorney, the county attorney for the county in which the port is located receives notice of the existence of the device, equipment, or paraphernalia on board the vessel and of the anticipated dates on which the vessel will enter and leave the territorial waters of this state;

(2) at all times while the vessel is in the territorial waters of this state all devices, equipment, or paraphernalia are disabled, electronically or by another method, from a remote and secured area of the vessel in a manner that allows only the master or crew of the vessel to remove any disabling device;

(3) at all times while the vessel is in the territorial waters of this state any disabling device is not removed except for the purposes of inspecting or repairing the device, equipment, or paraphernalia; and

(4) the device, equipment, or paraphernalia is not used for gambling or other gaming purposes while the vessel is in the territorial waters of this state.

History of Pen §47.09: Acts 1993, 73rd Leg., ch. 900, §1.01, eff. Sept. 1, 1994. Amended by Acts 1995, 74th Leg., ch. 76, §14.54, eff. Sept. 1, 1995; Acts 1997, 75th Leg., ch. 111, §1 (eff. May 16, 1997), ch. 1035, §55 (eff. June 19, 1997); Acts 1999, 76th Leg., ch. 844, §1, eff. Sept. 1, 1999; Acts 2001, 77th Leg., ch. 1420, §14.835, eff. Sept. 1, 2001.

PEN §47.10. AMERICAN DOCUMENTATION OF VESSEL REQUIRED

If 18 U.S.C. Section 1082 is repealed, the affirmative defenses provided by Section 47.09(b) apply only if the vessel is documented under the laws of the United States.

History of Pen §47.10: Acts 1989, 71st Leg., ch. 1030, §4, eff. Sept. 1, 1989. Renumbered from §47.12 by Acts 1990, 71st Leg., 6th C.S., ch. 12, §2(27), eff. Sept. 6, 1990. Renumbered from §47.13 and amended by Acts 1993, 73rd Leg., ch. 900, §1.01, eff. Sept. 1, 1994.

PEN §47.11. DELETED

Deleted by Acts 1993, 73rd Leg., ch. 900, §1.01, eff. Sept. 1, 1994.

PEN §47.111. DELETED

Deleted by Acts 1993, 73rd Leg., ch. 900, §13.02, eff. Sept. 1, 1994.

PEN §47.12. DELETED

Deleted by Acts 1993, 73rd Leg., ch. 900, §1.01, eff. Sept. 1, 1994.

PEN §47.13. RENUMBERED

Renumbered as §47.10 by Acts 1993, 73rd Leg., ch. 900, §1.01, eff. Sept. 1, 1994.

PEN §47.14. DELETED

Deleted by Acts 1993, 73rd Leg., ch. 900, §1.01, eff. Sept. 1, 1994.

CHAPTER 48. CONDUCT AFFECTING PUBLIC HEALTH

PEN §48.01. SMOKING TOBACCO

(a) A person commits an offense if he is in possession of a burning tobacco product or smokes tobacco in a facility of a public primary or secondary school or an elevator, enclosed theater or movie house, library, museum, hospital, transit system bus, or intrastate bus, as defined by Section 541.201, Transportation Code, plane, or train which is a public place.

(b) It is a defense to prosecution under this section that the conveyance or public place in which the offense takes place does not have prominently displayed a reasonably sized notice that smoking is prohibited by state law in such conveyance or public place and that an offense is punishable by a fine not to exceed $500.

(c) All conveyances and public places set out in Subsection (a) of Section 48.01 shall be equipped with facilities for extinguishment of smoking materials and it shall be a defense to prosecution under this section if the conveyance or public place within which the offense takes place is not so equipped.

(d) It is an exception to the application of Subsection (a) if the person is in possession of the burning tobacco product or smokes tobacco exclusively within an area designated for smoking tobacco or as a participant in an authorized theatrical performance.

(e) An area designated for smoking tobacco on a transit system bus or intrastate plane or train must also include the area occupied by the operator of the transit system bus, plane, or train.

(f) An offense under this section is punishable as a Class C misdemeanor.

History of Pen §48.01: Acts 1975, 64th Leg., ch. 290, §1, eff. Sept. 1, 1975. Amended by Acts 1991, 72nd Leg., ch. 108, §2, eff. Sept. 1, 1991; 75th Leg., ch. 165, §30.242, eff. Sept. 1, 1997.

PEN §48.015. PROHIBITIONS RELATING TO CERTAIN CIGARETTES

(a) A person may not acquire, hold, own, possess, or transport for sale or distribution in this state or import or cause to be imported into this state for sale or distribution in this state:

(1) cigarettes that do not comply with all applicable requirements imposed by or under federal law and implementing regulations; or

(2) cigarettes to which stamps may not be affixed under Section 154.0415, Tax Code, other than cigarettes lawfully imported or brought into the state for personal use and cigarettes lawfully sold or intended to be sold as duty-free merchandise by a duty-free sales enterprise in accordance with 19 U.S.C. Section 1555(b), as amended.

(b) A person who commits an act prohibited by Subsection (a), knowing or having reason to know that the person is doing so, is guilty of a Class A misdemeanor.

History of Pen §48.015: Acts 2001, 77th Leg., ch. 1104, §6, eff. Sept. 1, 2001.

PEN §48.02. PROHIBITION OF THE PURCHASE & SALE OF HUMAN ORGANS

(a) "Human organ" means the human kidney, liver, heart, lung, pancreas, eye, bone, skin, fetal tissue, or any other human organ or tissue, but does not include hair or blood, blood components (including plasma), blood derivatives, or blood reagents.

(b) A person commits an offense if he or she knowingly or intentionally offers to buy, offers to sell, acquires, receives, sells, or otherwise transfers any human organ for valuable consideration.

(c) It is an exception to the application of this section that the valuable consideration is: (1) a fee paid to a physician or to other medical personnel for services rendered in the usual course of medical practice or a fee paid for hospital or other clinical services; (2) reimbursement of legal or medical expenses incurred for the benefit of the ultimate receiver of the organ; or (3) reimbursement of expenses of travel, housing, and lost wages incurred by the donor of a human organ in connection with the donation of the organ.

(d) A violation of this section is a Class A misdemeanor.

History of Pen §48.02: Acts 1985, 69th Leg., ch. 40, §1, eff. Aug. 26, 1985. Amended by Acts 1993, 73rd Leg., ch. 900, §1.01, eff. Sept. 1, 1994.

CHAPTER 49. INTOXICATION & ALCOHOLIC BEVERAGE OFFENSES

PEN §49.01. DEFINITIONS

In this chapter:

(1) "Alcohol concentration" means the number of grams of alcohol per:

(A) 210 liters of breath;

(B) 100 milliliters of blood; or

(C) 67 milliliters of urine.

(2) "Intoxicated" means:

(A) not having the normal use of mental or physical faculties by reason of the introduction of alcohol, a controlled substance, a drug, a dangerous drug, a combination of two or more of those substances, or any other substance into the body; or

(B) having an alcohol concentration of 0.08 or more.

(3) "Motor vehicle" has the meaning assigned by Section 32.34(a).

(4) "Watercraft" means a vessel, one or more water skis, an aquaplane, or another device used for transporting or carrying a person on water, other than a device propelled only by the current of water.

(5) "Amusement ride" has the meaning assigned by Section 2151.002, Occupations Code.

(6) "Mobile amusement ride" has the meaning assigned by Section 2151.002, Occupations Code.

History of Pen §49.01: Acts 1993, 73rd Leg., ch. 900, §1.01, eff. Sept. 1, 1994. Amended by Acts 1999, 76th Leg., ch. 234, §1 (eff. Sept. 1, 1999), ch. 1364, §8 (eff. Jan. 1, 2000); Acts 2001, 77th Leg., ch. 1420, §14.707, eff. Sept. 1, 2001.

ANNOTATIONS

Bagheri v. State, 119 S.W.3d 755, 762 (Tex.Crim. App.2003). "[T]he definitions contained in §49.01 set forth alternate means by which the State may prove intoxication, rather than alternate means of committing the offense. The conduct proscribed by the Penal Code is the act of driving while in a state of intoxication. That does not change whether the State uses the per se definition or the impairment definition to prove the offense."

For a quick reference of penalties, see the Chart of Penalties on p. 675.

O'CONNOR'S CRIMINAL CODES 919

Bradford v. State, 230 S.W.3d 719, 723 (Tex. App.—Houston [14th Dist.] 2007, no pet.). "Because there was only a single criminal act of [DWI] alleged in this case, there were no separate criminal acts on which the jurors could disagree to produce a lack of unanimity. Similarly, because the per se [§49.01(2)(B)] and impairment [§49.01(2)(A)] theories are not themselves separate elements of a DWI offense on which unanimity is required, the loss of physical verses mental ability, as a component of the impairment theory, is also not a separate element of the offense."

Harris v. State, 204 S.W.3d 19, 25 (Tex.App.—Houston [14th Dist.] 2006, pet. ref'd). "Evidence of intoxication may include (1) slurred speech, (2) bloodshot eyes, (3) the odor of alcohol on the person, (4) the odor of alcohol on the breath, (5) unsteady balance, or (6) a staggered gait."

State v. Marrs, 104 S.W.3d 914, 918 (Tex.App.—Corpus Christi 2003, no pet.). "Since the definition of 'intoxicated' includes not having the normal use of mental or physical faculties, any sign of impairment in an accused's ability to perform a breathalyzer test is circumstantially relevant to whether the person was legally intoxicated while driving."

Morris v. State, 89 S.W.3d 146, 149-50 (Tex.App.—Corpus Christi 2002, no pet.). "'Type of intoxicant' refers to those substances listed in §49.01(2)(A)...; *i.e.*, alcohol, a controlled substance, a drug, a dangerous drug, or a combination of two or more of these substances. [T]o give adequate notice, an information charging a person with DWI need not specify which specific drug or controlled substance caused the intoxication, as long as the type of intoxicant listed in §49.01(2)(A) is alleged."

Atkins v. State, 990 S.W.2d 763, 767 (Tex.App.—Austin 1999, pet. ref'd). The Penal Code "specifically ties the intoxication standard under §49.01(2)(A) to the listed individual substances, or the synergistic effect caused by the combination of two or more of these substances; fatigue, or any other purely natural deterioration of the body, is not listed. *At 768:* We conclude that the trial court erred in charging the jury with the instruction as given on the synergistic effect of fatigue and alcohol on intoxication."

Owen v. State, 905 S.W.2d 434, 439 (Tex.App.—Waco 1995, pet. ref'd). "In a given case, as the time-gap increases between the offense and the test, the proba-

tive value of the intoxilyzer test as evidence of the defendant's alcohol concentration at the time of the offense diminishes, increasing the possibility that it will be substantially outweighed by the danger of unfair prejudice, confusion of the issues, or misleading the jury. The task of balancing those factors to determine admissibility is for the trial judge, subject to review for abuse of discretion."

PEN §49.02. PUBLIC INTOXICATION

(a) A person commits an offense if the person appears in a public place while intoxicated to the degree that the person may endanger the person or another.

ⓔ *Subsection (a-1) below is effective for offenses committed on or after Sept. 1, 2007.*

(a-1) For the purposes of this section, a premises licensed or permitted under the Alcoholic Beverage Code is a public place.

(b) It is a defense to prosecution under this section that the alcohol or other substance was administered for therapeutic purposes and as a part of the person's professional medical treatment by a licensed physician.

(c) Except as provided by Subsection (e), an offense under this section is a Class C misdemeanor.

(d) An offense under this section is not a lesser included offense under Section 49.04.

(e) An offense under this section committed by a person younger than 21 years of age is punishable in the same manner as if the minor committed an offense to which Section 106.071, Alcoholic Beverage Code, applies.

History of Pen §49.02: Acts 1993, 73rd Leg., ch. 900, §1.01, eff. Sept. 1, 1994; Acts 1997, 75th Leg., ch. 1013, §12, eff. Sept. 1, 1997. Amended by Acts 2007, 80th Leg., ch. 68, §25, eff. Sept. 1, 2007.

ANNOTATIONS

Kirtley v. State, 585 S.W.2d 724, 725 (Tex.Crim. App.1979). "[T]he status of the roadway as public does not extend to a vehicle traveling on that road. Whether or not a vehicle is a 'public place' as it travels on a roadway is a fact question for the trier of fact. *At 726 n.6:* Supportive facts [of whether a motor vehicle is a public place] include but are not limited to (1) the speed of the vehicle, (2) traffic and road conditions, (3) obstructions, (4) lighting conditions, and (5) intended use of the vehicle by the operator; all of which should be

(sidebar) PEN §49.01

aimed at proving 'public place' as defined by statute." *See also* **Longoria v. State**, 624 S.W.2d 582, 583-84 (Tex.Crim.App.1981).

PEN §49.03. REPEALED

Repealed by Acts 2001, 77th Leg., ch. 969, §10, eff. Sept. 1, 2001.

PEN §49.031. POSSESSION OF ALCOHOLIC BEVERAGE IN MOTOR VEHICLE

(a) In this section:

(1) "Open container" means a bottle, can, or other receptacle that contains any amount of alcoholic beverage and that is open, that has been opened, that has a broken seal, or the contents of which are partially removed.

(2) "Passenger area of a motor vehicle" means the area of a motor vehicle designed for the seating of the operator and passengers of the vehicle. The term does not include:

(A) a glove compartment or similar storage container that is locked;

(B) the trunk of a vehicle; or

(C) the area behind the last upright seat of the vehicle, if the vehicle does not have a trunk.

(3) "Public highway" means the entire width between and immediately adjacent to the boundary lines of any public road, street, highway, interstate, or other publicly maintained way if any part is open for public use for the purpose of motor vehicle travel. The term includes the right-of-way of a public highway.

(b) A person commits an offense if the person knowingly possesses an open container in a passenger area of a motor vehicle that is located on a public highway, regardless of whether the vehicle is being operated or is stopped or parked. Possession by a person of one or more open containers in a single criminal episode is a single offense.

(c) It is an exception to the application of Subsection (b) that at the time of the offense the defendant was a passenger in:

(1) the passenger area of a motor vehicle designed, maintained, or used primarily for the transportation of persons for compensation, including a bus, taxicab, or limousine; or

(2) the living quarters of a motorized house coach or motorized house trailer, including a self-contained camper, a motor home, or a recreational vehicle.

(d) An offense under this section is a Class C misdemeanor.

(e) A peace officer charging a person with an offense under this section, instead of taking the person before a magistrate, shall issue to the person a written citation and notice to appear that contains the time and place the person must appear before a magistrate, the name and address of the person charged, and the offense charged. If the person makes a written promise to appear before the magistrate by signing in duplicate the citation and notice to appear issued by the officer, the officer shall release the person.

History of Pen §49.031: Acts 2001, 77th Leg., ch. 969, §2, eff. Sept. 1, 2001.

PEN §49.04. DRIVING WHILE INTOXICATED

(a) A person commits an offense if the person is intoxicated while operating a motor vehicle in a public place.

(b) Except as provided by Subsection (c) and Section 49.09, an offense under this section is a Class B misdemeanor, with a minimum term of confinement of 72 hours.

(c) If it is shown on the trial of an offense under this section that at the time of the offense the person operating the motor vehicle had an open container of alcohol in the person's immediate possession, the offense is a Class B misdemeanor, with a minimum term of confinement of six days.

History of Pen §49.04: Acts 1993, 73rd Leg., ch. 900, §1.01, eff. Sept. 1, 1994. Amended by Acts 1995, 74th Leg., ch. 76, §14.55, eff. Sept. 1, 1995.

ANNOTATIONS

State v. Barbernell, ___ S.W.3d ___ (Tex.Crim. App.2008) (No. PD-0867-07; 7-2-08). "With the understanding that 'intoxicated' is an element of DWI and that §49.01(2) sets out two definitions for 'intoxicated,' we ask whether the definitions of 'intoxicated' concern an act or omission and create two different manners and means of committing DWI. [T]he answer to this question is 'no.' [T]he definitions of 'intoxicated' are purely evidentiary matters; therefore, they do not need to be alleged in a charging instrument to provide a defendant with sufficient notice. ... A charging instrument that pleads the offense of DWI provides adequate notice when it sets out the elements of the offense as provided in §49.04."

For a quick reference of penalties, see the Chart of Penalties on p. 675.

O'CONNOR'S CRIMINAL CODES 921

Otto v. State, ___ S.W.3d ___ (Tex.Crim.App.2008) (No. PD-1311-06; 2-06-08). "The issue presented in this case is whether a concurrent-causation jury instruction, that defines intoxication as the 'introduction of alcohol, operating either alone or concurrently with an unknown drug,' is substantively different from a jury instruction, that defines intoxication as the 'introduction of a combination of alcohol and an unknown drug.' We decide that there is no substantive or legally significant difference between these two charges and that the concurrent-causation jury charge in this case improperly expanded on the allegations in the indictment. [¶] The indictment alleged that appellant was intoxicated by 'not having the normal use of his (sic) mental and physical faculties by the reason of the introduction of alcohol into his (sic) body.'" *See also* **Rodriguez v. State**, 18 S.W.3d 228, 231-32 (Tex.Crim.App.2000).

Gray v. State, 152 S.W.3d 125, 132 (Tex.Crim.App. 2004). "[T]he substance that causes intoxication is not an element of the offense. It is not the forbidden conduct, the required culpability, any required result, or the negation of any exception to the offense. Instead, it is an evidentiary matter."

Lorenz v. State, 176 S.W.3d 492, 496-97 (Tex. App.—Houston [1st Dist.] 2004, pet. ref'd). "A peace officer may not correlate a defendant's blood alcohol content (BAC) with the defendant's performance on field-sobriety tests. In short, a peace officer may give qualitative, but not quantitative, results from field-sobriety tests. [¶] The question before this court is whether testimony that field-sobriety tests are 91 to 95 percent accurate impermissibly correlates to a defendant's quantitative BAC. Under the circumstances presented here, we conclude that it does not."

Zavala v. State, 89 S.W.3d 134, 139 (Tex.App.—Corpus Christi 2002, no pet.). "Proof of the precise time of an accident or of driving is not the *sine qua non* of [DWI]. [T]he critical issue is that there must be proof from which the fact finder can conclude that at the time of the driving in question, whenever that might be, the defendant was intoxicated, in other words, a 'link' between the driving and the intoxication."

Murphy v. State, 44 S.W.3d 656, 662 (Tex.App.—Austin 2001, no pet.). "The trial court … added [to the definition of 'intoxication'] a special definition of 'normal use,' a term that has not been administratively or legislatively defined. Moreover, the term is included within the statutory definition of 'intoxicated,' which related to an essential element of the offense charged. *At 664:* The trial court was beyond its power in independently and separately defining 'normal use' in the instant jury instructions."

Doneburg v. State, 44 S.W.3d 651, 655 (Tex.App.—Fort Worth 2001, pet. ref'd). "We agree with Appellant that the prosecutor's reading of the open container allegation during guilt/innocence was improper because it is not an essential element of the offense of [DWI]. The allegation is merely an enhancement provision, and as such is properly reserved for the punishment phase of the trial."

State v. Magee, 29 S.W.3d 639, 640 (Tex.App.—Houston [1st Dist.] 2000, pet. ref'd). "[T]he specific provision of [Pen. Code] §49.04(b), which requires a 72-hour minimum confinement in jail, controls over the general provision of [Pen. Code] §12.22, which allows a trial court to sentence a defendant convicted of a Class B misdemeanor to a fine only. [T]he trial court was required to sentence appellee to a minimum of 72-hours confinement in jail."

Milam v. State, 976 S.W.2d 788, 789 (Tex.App.—Houston [1st Dist.] 1998, pet. ref'd). "Appellant argues that because he was asleep, he was not 'operating' his car. [¶] Appellant was sitting alone in a parked car. The engine was running, the car was in gear, and appellant's foot was on the brake. The car had been in its location for less than five minutes. When awakened, appellant put the car in reverse. From these facts, a rational fact finder could conclude that appellant had 'operated' his car."

Ex parte Gee, 926 S.W.2d 615, 616 (Tex.App.—Houston [1st Dist.] 1996, pet. ref'd). "[T]he administrative suspension of a driver's license of a person who refuses to take a breath test after being arrested for DWI does not constitute a bar to prosecution for DWI on the basis of double jeopardy."

Walton v. State, 831 S.W.2d 488, 490 (Tex.App.—Houston [14th Dist.] 1992, no writ). "[C]ollateral estoppel is inapplicable [to a prosecution for drunk driving after an administrative judge found there was insufficient proof of DWI] because a hearing to suspend a person's license is not a traditional adversarial hearing, but is administrative and civil in nature." *But see* **State v. Aguilar**, 947 S.W.2d 257 (Tex.Crim.App. 1997).

PEN §49.045. DRIVING WHILE INTOXICATED WITH CHILD PASSENGER

(a) A person commits an offense if:

(1) the person is intoxicated while operating a motor vehicle in a public place; and

(2) the vehicle being operated by the person is occupied by a passenger who is younger than 15 years of age.

(b) An offense under this section is a state jail felony.

History of Pen §49.045: Acts 2003, 78th Leg., ch. 787, §1, eff. Sept. 1, 2003.

PEN §49.05. FLYING WHILE INTOXICATED

(a) A person commits an offense if the person is intoxicated while operating an aircraft.

(b) Except as provided by Section 49.09, an offense under this section is a Class B misdemeanor, with a minimum term of confinement of 72 hours.

History of Pen §49.05: Acts 1993, 73rd Leg., ch. 900, §1.01, eff. Sept. 1, 1994.

PEN §49.06. BOATING WHILE INTOXICATED

(a) A person commits an offense if the person is intoxicated while operating a watercraft.

(b) Except as provided by Section 49.09, an offense under this section is a Class B misdemeanor, with a minimum term of confinement of 72 hours.

History of Pen §49.06: Acts 1993, 73rd Leg., ch. 900, §1.01, eff. Sept. 1, 1994.

PEN §49.065. ASSEMBLING OR OPERATING AN AMUSEMENT RIDE WHILE INTOXICATED

(a) A person commits an offense if the person is intoxicated while operating an amusement ride or while assembling a mobile amusement ride.

(b) Except as provided by Subsection (c) and Section 49.09, an offense under this section is a Class B misdemeanor with a minimum term of confinement of 72 hours.

(c) If it is shown on the trial of an offense under this section that at the time of the offense the person operating the amusement ride or assembling the mobile amusement ride had an open container of alcohol in the person's immediate possession, the offense is a Class B misdemeanor with a minimum term of confinement of six days.

History of Pen §49.065: Acts 1999, 76th Leg., ch. 1364, §9, eff. Jan. 1, 2000.

PEN §49.07. INTOXICATION ASSAULT

(a) A person commits an offense if the person, by accident or mistake:

(1) while operating an aircraft, watercraft, or amusement ride while intoxicated, or while operating a motor vehicle in a public place while intoxicated, by reason of that intoxication causes serious bodily injury to another; or

(2) as a result of assembling a mobile amusement ride while intoxicated causes serious bodily injury to another.

(b) In this section, "serious bodily injury" means injury that creates a substantial risk of death or that causes serious permanent disfigurement or protracted loss or impairment of the function of any bodily member or organ.

 Subsection (c) below is effective for offenses committed on or after Sept. 1, 2007.

(c) Except as provided by Section 49.09, an offense under this section is a felony of the third degree.

Subsection (c) below is effective for offenses in which any element of the offense was committed before Sept. 1, 2007.

(c) An offense under this section is a felony of the third degree.

History of Pen §49.07: Acts 1993, 73rd Leg., ch. 900, §1.01, eff. Sept. 1, 1994. Amended by Acts 1999, 76th Leg., ch. 1364, §10, eff. Jan. 1, 2000; Acts 2007, 80th Leg., ch. 662, §2, eff. Sept. 1, 2007.

See also Pen. Code §3.03.

PEN §49.08. INTOXICATION MANSLAUGHTER

(a) A person commits an offense if the person:

(1) operates a motor vehicle in a public place, operates an aircraft, a watercraft, or an amusement ride, or assembles a mobile amusement ride; and

(2) is intoxicated and by reason of that intoxication causes the death of another by accident or mistake.

 Subsection (b) below is effective for offenses committed on or after Sept. 1, 2007.

(b) Except as provided by Section 49.09, an offense under this section is a felony of the second degree.

Subsection (b) below is effective for offenses in which any element of the offense was committed before Sept. 1, 2007.

(b) An offense under this section is a felony of the second degree.

For a quick reference of penalties, see the Chart of Penalties on p. 675.

O'CONNOR'S CRIMINAL CODES   923

History of Pen §49.08: Acts 1993, 73rd Leg., ch. 900, §1.01, eff. Sept. 1, 1994. Amended by Acts 1999, 76th Leg., ch. 1364, §11, eff. Jan. 1, 2000; Acts 2007, 80th Leg., ch. 662, §3, eff. Sept. 1, 2007.

See also Pen. Code §3.03.

ANNOTATIONS

Lomax v. State, 233 S.W.3d 302, 311 (Tex.Crim. App.2007). "We … decide that felony DWI is not a lesser included offense of intoxication manslaughter."

Ex parte Taylor, 101 S.W.3d 434, 436 (Tex.Crim. App.2002). "We must determine whether the appellant's acquittal in the first trial, of intoxication manslaughter, prevents the State from attempting to prove, in another criminal proceeding, an alternate theory of intoxication [by alcohol and marijuana or marijuana alone versus alcohol alone] for causing the death of his second passenger. The [court of appeals] held that collateral estoppel barred the State from relitigating the ultimate issue—intoxication—regardless of whether the State alleged a different *type* of intoxicant. We agree."

Cuellar v. State, 957 S.W.2d 134, 137 (Tex.App.— Corpus Christi 1997, pet. ref'd). "[T]his case presents the question of whether the Penal Code authorizes a conviction only when a victim meets the definition of an individual at the time of the alleged misconduct, or whether a conviction may also be authorized if a victim attains the status of an individual after the alleged misconduct. *At 140:* It is undisputed that [victim] died by reason of [D's] intoxication. It is also undisputed that [victim] was born and was alive for a period of time. Therefore, in applying the statutory definition 'has been born and is alive' to the facts of this case, we hold that [victim] was an 'individual' under the criminal law of this state."

PEN §49.09. ENHANCED OFFENSES & PENALTIES

(a) Except as provided by Subsection (b), an offense under Section 49.04, 49.05, 49.06, or 49.065 is a Class A misdemeanor, with a minimum term of confinement of 30 days, if it is shown on the trial of the offense that the person has previously been convicted one time of an offense relating to the operating of a motor vehicle while intoxicated, an offense of operating an aircraft while intoxicated, an offense of operating a watercraft while intoxicated, or an offense of operating or assembling an amusement ride while intoxicated.

(b) An offense under Section 49.04, 49.05, 49.06, or 49.065 is a felony of the third degree if it is shown on the trial of the offense that the person has previously been convicted:

(1) one time of an offense under Section 49.08 or an offense under the laws of another state if the offense contains elements that are substantially similar to the elements of an offense under Section 49.08; or

(2) two times of any other offense relating to the operating of a motor vehicle while intoxicated, operating an aircraft while intoxicated, operating a watercraft while intoxicated, or operating or assembling an amusement ride while intoxicated.

 Subsections (b-1)-(b-3) below are effective for offenses committed on or after Sept. 1, 2007.

(b-1) An offense under Section 49.07 is a felony of the second degree if it is shown on the trial of the offense that the person caused serious bodily injury to a peace officer, a firefighter, or emergency medical services personnel while in the actual discharge of an official duty.

(b-2) An offense under Section 49.08 is a felony of the first degree if it is shown on the trial of the offense that the person caused the death of a person described by Subsection (b-1).

(b-3) For the purposes of Subsection (b-1):

(1) "Emergency medical services personnel" has the meaning assigned by Section 773.003, Health and Safety Code.

(2) "Firefighter" means:

(A) an individual employed by this state or by a political or legal subdivision of this state who is subject to certification by the Texas Commission on Fire Protection; or

(B) a member of an organized volunteer fire-fighting unit that:

(i) renders fire-fighting services without remuneration; and

(ii) conducts a minimum of two drills each month, each at least two hours long.

(c) For the purposes of this section:

(1) "Offense relating to the operating of a motor vehicle while intoxicated" means:

(A) an offense under Section 49.04 or 49.045;

(B) an offense under Section 49.07 or 49.08, if the vehicle operated was a motor vehicle;

(C) an offense under Article 6701l-1, Revised Statutes, as that law existed before September 1, 1994;

(D) an offense under Article 6701l-2, Revised Statutes, as that law existed before January 1, 1984;

(E) an offense under Section 19.05(a)(2), as that law existed before September 1, 1994, if the vehicle operated was a motor vehicle; or

(F) an offense under the laws of another state that prohibit the operation of a motor vehicle while intoxicated.

(2) "Offense of operating an aircraft while intoxicated" means:

(A) an offense under Section 49.05;

(B) an offense under Section 49.07 or 49.08, if the vehicle operated was an aircraft;

(C) an offense under Section 1, Chapter 46, Acts of the 58th Legislature, Regular Session, 1963 (Article 46f-3, Vernon's Texas Civil Statutes), as that law existed before September 1, 1994;

(D) an offense under Section 19.05(a)(2), as that law existed before September 1, 1994, if the vehicle operated was an aircraft; or

(E) an offense under the laws of another state that prohibit the operation of an aircraft while intoxicated.

(3) "Offense of operating a watercraft while intoxicated" means:

(A) an offense under Section 49.06;

(B) an offense under Section 49.07 or 49.08, if the vehicle operated was a watercraft;

(C) an offense under Section 31.097, Parks and Wildlife Code, as that law existed before September 1, 1994;

(D) an offense under Section 19.05(a)(2), as that law existed before September 1, 1994, if the vehicle operated was a watercraft; or

(E) an offense under the laws of another state that prohibit the operation of a watercraft while intoxicated.

(4) "Offense of operating or assembling an amusement ride while intoxicated" means:

(A) an offense under Section 49.065;

(B) an offense under Section 49.07 or 49.08, if the offense involved the operation or assembly of an amusement ride; or

(C) an offense under the law of another state that prohibits the operation of an amusement ride while intoxicated or the assembly of a mobile amusement ride while intoxicated.

(d) For the purposes of this section, a conviction for an offense under Section 49.04, 49.045, 49.05, 49.06, 49.065, 49.07, or 49.08 that occurs on or after September 1, 1994, is a final conviction, whether the sentence for the conviction is imposed or probated.

(e), (f) Repealed by Acts 2005, 79th Leg., ch. 996, §3, eff. Sept. 1, 2005.

(g) A conviction may be used for purposes of enhancement under this section or enhancement under Subchapter D, Chapter 12, but not under both this section and Subchapter D.

(h) This subsection applies only to a person convicted of a second or subsequent offense relating to the operating of a motor vehicle while intoxicated committed within five years of the date on which the most recent preceding offense was committed. The court shall enter an order that requires the defendant to have a device installed, on each motor vehicle owned or operated by the defendant, that uses a deep-lung breath analysis mechanism to make impractical the operation of the motor vehicle if ethyl alcohol is detected in the breath of the operator, and that requires that before the first anniversary of the ending date of the period of license suspension under Section 521.344, Transportation Code, the defendant not operate any motor vehicle that is not equipped with that device. The court shall require the defendant to obtain the device at the defendant's own cost on or before that ending date, require the defendant to provide evidence to the court on or before that ending date that the device has been installed on each appropriate vehicle, and order the device to remain installed on each vehicle until the first anniversary of that ending date. If the court determines the offender is unable to pay for the device, the court may impose a reasonable payment schedule not to extend beyond the first anniversary of the date of installation. The Department of Public Safety shall approve devices for use under this subsection. Section 521.247, Transportation Code, applies to the approval of a device under this subsection and the consequences of that approval. Failure to comply with an order entered under this subsection is punishable by contempt. For the purpose of enforcing this subsection, the court that enters an order under this subsection retains jurisdiction over the defendant until the date on which the device is no longer required to remain installed. To the extent of a conflict between this subsection and Section 13(i), Article 42.12, Code of Criminal Procedure, this subsection controls.

For a quick reference of penalties, see the Chart of Penalties on p. 675.

O'CONNOR'S CRIMINAL CODES 925

PEN §49.09

History of Pen §49.09: Acts 1993, 73rd Leg., ch. 900, §1.01, eff. Sept. 1, 1994. Amended by Acts 1995, 74th Leg., ch. 76, §14.56 (eff. Sept. 1, 1995), ch. 318, §21 (eff. Sept. 1, 1995); Acts 1999, 76th Leg., ch. 1364, §§12, 13, eff. Jan. 1, 2000; Acts 2001, 77th Leg., ch. 648, §§1, 2 (eff. Sept. 1, 2001), ch. 969, §3 (eff. Sept. 1, 2001); Acts 2003, 78th Leg., ch. 787, §2 (eff. Sept. 1, 2003), ch. 1275, §2(117) (eff. Sept. 1, 2003); Acts 2005, ch. 996, §§1, 3, eff. Sept 1, 2005; Acts 2007, 80th Leg., ch. 662, §4, eff. Sept. 1, 2007.

ANNOTATIONS

Bell v. State, 201 S.W.3d 708, 711 (Tex.Crim.App. 2006). "We hold that federal [Assimilative Crimes Act, 18 U.S.C. §3,] convictions assimilating a state-law offense contained in [Pen. Code] §49.04 may be used for enhancement purposes under [Pen. Code] §49.09(b)(2)."

Martin v. State, 200 S.W.3d 635, 640-41 (Tex.Crim. App.2006). "We briefly summarize the current status of the law when a defendant offers to stipulate to the two jurisdictional prior DWI convictions in a felony DWI trial: 1) The State must plead two jurisdictional prior DWI convictions in a felony DWI indictment; it is the indictment that confers jurisdiction in the district court; The State may (but is not required to) read the entire indictment, including the two jurisdictional allegations (but only those two), in arraigning the defendant in the presence of the jury; 3) Both the State and the defense may voir dire the jury concerning the range of punishment for both a felony and misdemeanor DWI; 4) Nothing in the law *requires* that the jury be informed of the particulars of the prior convictions in reading the indictment, voir dire, opening or closing arguments or in the jury charge itself; 5) A defendant's stipulation to the two prior DWIs, being in the nature of a judicial admission, has the legal effect of removing the jurisdictional element from contention; a defendant may not offer evidence or argument in opposition to his stipulation; 6) During the trial, the jury may be informed of the stipulation and any written stipulation may be offered into evidence before the jury, but the evidence is sufficient to support a defendant's conviction even if the stipulation is not given or read to the jury; In a bench trial, the guilt and punishment stages are not bifurcated, so the State is not required to offer the stipulation during the initial portion of the hearing, even if the proceeding is improperly bifurcated. To that list, we now add: 8) The jury charge must include some reference to the jurisdictional element of two prior DWI convictions in a felony DWI trial; 9) The jury charge must include some reference to the defendant's stipulation and its legal effect of establishing the jurisdictional element. 10) Any error in failing to include, in the jury charge, some reference to the jurisdictional element and the stipulation is analyzed under *Almanza. At 640 n.12:* It is the defendant's responsibility to draft an acceptable written stipulation, signed by the defendant. The trial judge need not accept a stipulation that is not dispositive of the jurisdictional element." *See also Hollen v. State*, 117 S.W.3d 798, 802 (Tex.Crim.App.2003); *Robles v. State*, 85 S.W.3d 211, 213-14 (Tex.Crim.App. 2002); *Tamez v. State*, 11 S.W.3d 198, 202-03 (Tex. Crim.App.2000).

Gibson v. State, 995 S.W.2d 693, 696 (Tex.Crim. App.1999). "[P]rior intoxication-related convictions serve the purpose of enhancing the offense in [Pen. Code] §49.09(b) whereas the prior convictions used in [Pen. Code] §12.42(d) serve the purpose of enhancing punishment. Section 49.09(b) is distinguishable from §12.42(d) on this basis. *At 697:* Section 49.09(b) does not require the State to prove the prior convictions occurred sequentially. Instead, the State must show a defendant was twice previously convicted for offenses related to operating a motor vehicle, aircraft, or watercraft while intoxicated. [T]he State did not err in relying on appellant's two previous convictions for involuntary manslaughter based on two deaths arising out of a single illegal act in order to prove the instant offense was a third degree felony." *See also Rodriguez v. State*, 31 S.W.3d 359, 364 (Tex.App.—San Antonio 2000, pet. ref'd).

State v. Pieper, 231 S.W.3d 9, 15 (Tex.App.— Houston [14th Dist.] 2007, no pet.). "[T]he 2005 changes to the DWI enhancement statute, by removing all time limitations on the use of prior DWI convictions to enhance current DWI charges, did not increase appellee's punishment for his prior convictions and is therefore not an *ex post facto* law."

Haskins v. State, 960 S.W.2d 207, 209 (Tex.App.— Corpus Christi 1997, no pet.). "During the punishment phase of the trial, the State elicited testimony from appellant that he had been convicted of DWI in Wyoming. When appellant attempted to inform the jury the difference between a DWI conviction in Wyoming versus a DWI conviction in the State of Texas, the trial court sustained the State's objection. *At 210:* [W]hile the jury may have been informed appellant was not driving, they were still left with the knowledge that appellant had a prior conviction for driving while intoxicated, an irreconcilable dichotomy under Texas law. We thus conclude the trial court erred in prohibiting appellant from informing the jury that Wyoming permits a conviction for DWI without the defendant actually being the driver of the motor vehicle."

PEN §49.10. NO DEFENSE

In a prosecution under Section 49.03, 49.04, 49.045, 49.05, 49.06, 49.065, 49.07, or 49.08, the fact that the defendant is or has been entitled to use the alcohol, controlled substance, drug, dangerous drug, or other substance is not a defense.

History of Pen §49.10: Acts 1993, 73rd Leg., ch. 900, §1.01, eff. Sept. 1, 1994. Amended by Acts 1999, 76th Leg., ch. 1364, §14, eff. Jan. 1, 2000; Acts 2003, 78th Leg., ch. 787, §3, eff. Sept. 1, 2003.

PEN §49.11. PROOF OF MENTAL STATE UNNECESSARY

(a) Notwithstanding Section 6.02(b), proof of a culpable mental state is not required for conviction of an offense under this chapter.

(b) Subsection (a) does not apply to an offense under Section 49.031.

History of Pen §49.11: Acts 1995, 74th Leg., ch. 318, §22, eff. Sept. 1, 1995. Amended by Acts 2001, 77th Leg., ch. 969, §4, eff. Sept. 1, 2001.

ANNOTATIONS

Strong v. State, 87 S.W.3d 206, 217 (Tex.App.—Dallas 2002, pet. ref'd). "The attempt statute [Pen. Code §15.01] does not apply when the culpable mental state for the offense attempted is less than knowing.... DWI has no culpable mental state; thus, the attempt statute cannot apply to the offense of DWI."

PEN §49.12. APPLICABILITY TO CERTAIN CONDUCT

Sections 49.07 and 49.08 do not apply to injury to or the death of an unborn child if the conduct charged is conduct committed by the mother of the unborn child.

History of Pen §49.12: Acts 2003, 78th Leg., ch. 822, §2.05, eff. Sept. 1, 2003.

TITLE 11. ORGANIZED CRIME

CHAPTER 71. ORGANIZED CRIME

PEN §71.01. DEFINITIONS

In this chapter,

(a) "Combination" means three or more persons who collaborate in carrying on criminal activities, although:

(1) participants may not know each other's identity;

(2) membership in the combination may change from time to time; and

(3) participants may stand in a wholesaler-retailer or other arm's-length relationship in illicit distribution operations.

(b) "Conspires to commit" means that a person agrees with one or more persons that they or one or more of them engage in conduct that would constitute the offense and that person and one or more of them perform an overt act in pursuance of the agreement. An agreement constituting conspiring to commit may be inferred from the acts of the parties.

(c) "Profits" means property constituting or derived from any proceeds obtained, directly or indirectly, from an offense listed in Section 71.02.

(d) "Criminal street gang" means three or more persons having a common identifying sign or symbol or an identifiable leadership who continuously or regularly associate in the commission of criminal activities.

History of Pen §71.01: Acts 1977, 65th Leg., ch. 346, §1, eff. June 10, 1977. Amended by Acts 1989, 71st Leg., ch. 782, §1, eff. Sept. 1, 1989; Acts 1991, 72nd Leg., ch. 555, §1, eff. Sept. 1, 1991; Acts 1993, 73rd Leg., ch. 900, §1.01, eff. Sept. 1, 1994; Acts 1995, 74th Leg., ch. 318, §23, eff. Sept. 1, 1995.

ANNOTATIONS

Shears v. State, 895 S.W.2d 456, 459 (Tex.App.—Tyler 1995, no pet.). "Evidence of the [D's] conduct, systematic methods of operation, together with evidence of group participation in joint activities, supports a conviction. [D's] intent can be determined from his words, acts, and conduct. An agreement may be inferred from the acts of the parties. [¶] Because of the nature of the offense of working within a conspiracy, direct evidence is rarely available, and the State must rely on circumstantial evidence to prove the essential elements of the offense. In a circumstantial evidence case, it is not necessary that every fact point directly and independently to the guilt of the accused."

For a quick reference of penalties, see the Chart of Penalties on p. 675.

O'CONNOR'S CRIMINAL CODES 927

PEN §71.01

PEN §71.02. ENGAGING IN ORGANIZED CRIMINAL ACTIVITY

(a) A person commits an offense if, with the intent to establish, maintain, or participate in a combination or in the profits of a combination or as a member of a criminal street gang, he commits or conspires to commit one or more of the following:

(1) murder, capital murder, arson, aggravated robbery, robbery, burglary, theft, aggravated kidnapping, kidnapping, aggravated assault, aggravated sexual assault, sexual assault, forgery, deadly conduct, assault punishable as a Class A misdemeanor, burglary of a motor vehicle, or unauthorized use of a motor vehicle;

(2) any gambling offense punishable as a Class A misdemeanor;

(3) promotion of prostitution, aggravated promotion of prostitution, or compelling prostitution;

(4) unlawful manufacture, transportation, repair, or sale of firearms or prohibited weapons;

(5) unlawful manufacture, delivery, dispensation, or distribution of a controlled substance or dangerous drug, or unlawful possession of a controlled substance or dangerous drug through forgery, fraud, misrepresentation, or deception;

(6) any unlawful wholesale promotion or possession of any obscene material or obscene device with the intent to wholesale promote the same;

(7) any offense under Subchapter B, Chapter 43, depicting or involving conduct by or directed toward a child younger than 18 years of age;

(8) any felony offense under Chapter 32;

(9) any offense under Chapter 36;

(10) any offense under Chapter 34 or 35;

(11) any offense under Section 37.11(a);

(12) any offense under Chapter 20A; or

E *Subsection (13) below is effective for offenses committed on or after Sept. 1, 2007.*

(13) any offense under Section 37.10.

☠ *Subsection (b) below was amended by Acts 1993, 73rd Leg., ch. 761, §3, enacted May 28, 1993, effective Sept. 1, 1993, without reference to the conflicting amendment made by Acts 1993, 73rd Leg., ch. 900, §1.01, enacted May 31, 1993, effective Sept. 1, 1994. For resolving conflicts, see p. V.*

(b) Except as provided in Subsection (c) of this section, an offense under this section is one category

higher than the most serious offense listed in Subdivisions (1) through (10) of Subsection (a) of this section that was committed, and if the most serious offense is a Class A misdemeanor, the offense is a felony of the third degree, except that if the most serious offense is a felony of the first degree, the offense is a felony of the first degree.

☠ *Subsection (b) below was amended by Acts 1993, 73rd Leg., ch. 900, §1.01, enacted May 31, 1993, effective Sept. 1, 1994, without reference to the conflicting amendment made by Acts 1993, 73rd Leg., ch. 761, §3, enacted May 28, 1993, effective Sept. 1, 1993. For resolving conflicts, see p. V.*

(b) Except as provided in Subsections (c) and (d), an offense under this section is one category higher than the most serious offense listed in Subsection (a) that was committed, and if the most serious offense is a Class A misdemeanor, the offense is a state jail felony, except that if the most serious offense is a felony of the first degree, the offense is a felony of the first degree.

☠ *Subsection (c) below was amended by Acts 1993, 73rd Leg., ch. 761, §3, enacted May 28, 1993, effective Sept. 1, 1993, without reference to the conflicting amendment made by Acts 1993, 73rd Leg., ch. 900, §1.01, enacted May 31, 1993, effective Sept. 1, 1994. For resolving conflicts, see p. V.*

(c) Conspiring to commit an offense under this section is of the same degree as the most serious offense listed in Subdivisions (1) through (10) of Subsection (a) of this section that the person conspired to commit.

☠ *Subsection (c) below was amended by Acts 1993, 73rd Leg., ch. 900, §1.01, enacted May 31, 1993, effective Sept. 1, 1994, without reference to the conflicting amendment made by Acts 1993, 73rd Leg., ch. 761, §3, enacted May 28, 1993, effective Sept. 1, 1993. For resolving conflicts, see p. V.*

(c) Conspiring to commit an offense under this section is of the same degree as the most serious offense listed in Subsection (a) that the person conspired to commit.

(d) At the punishment stage of a trial, the defendant may raise the issue as to whether in voluntary and complete renunciation of the offense he withdrew from the combination before commission of an offense listed in Subsection (a) and made substantial effort to prevent the commission of the offense. If the defendant proves the issue in the affirmative by a preponderance of the evidence the offense is the same category of offense as the most serious offense listed in Subsection (a) that is committed, unless the defendant is convicted of conspiring to commit the offense, in which event the offense is one category lower than the most serious offense that the defendant conspired to commit.

History of Pen §71.02: Acts 1977, 65th Leg., ch. 346, §1, eff. June 10, 1977. Amended by Acts 1981, 67th Leg., ch. 587, §§1-3, eff. Sept. 1, 1981; Acts 1989, 71st Leg., ch. 782, §2, eff. Sept. 1, 1989; Acts 1991, 72nd Leg., ch. 555, §1, eff. Sept. 1, 1991; Acts 1993, 73rd Leg., ch. 761, §3 (eff. Sept. 1, 1993), ch. 900, §1.01 (eff. Sept. 1, 1994); Acts 1995, 74th Leg., ch. 318, §24, eff. Sept. 1, 1995; Acts 1997, 75th Leg., ch. 189, §9, eff. May 21, 1997; Acts 1999, 76th Leg., ch. 685, §8, eff. Sept. 1, 1999; Acts 2003, 78th Leg., ch. 641 §3, eff. Sept. 1, 2003; Acts 2005, 79th Leg., ch. 1162, §5, eff. Sept. 1, 2005; Acts 2007, 80th Leg., ch. 1163, §2, eff. Sept. 1, 2007.

ANNOTATIONS

Garza v. State, 213 S.W.3d 338, 348 (Tex.Crim.App. 2007). "[D]oes §71.02 define organized criminal activity as an offense susceptible to capital punishment when the 'offense' that the accused 'commits' 'as a member of a criminal street gang' is capital murder, which is one of the offenses enumerated in Subsection [(a)(1)]? [I]f so, does it violate the multiple-punishment prohibition of the Double Jeopardy Clause of the Fifth Amendment to assess the death penalty against him *both* for the capital murder itself *and* for committing capital murder as a member of a criminal street gang? After careful consideration, we hold that capital punishment *is not* available under these circumstances. However, we also conclude that it does *not* violate double jeopardy to try and to punish the appellant in a single proceeding for both the capital murder offense and the organized criminal activity offense." *See also **Lam v. State***, 17 S.W.3d 381, 385 (Tex.App.—Houston [1st Dist.] 2000, pet. ref'd).

Hart v. State, 89 S.W.3d 61, 63-64 (Tex.Crim.App. 2002). "[A] person need not be a member of a combination to be guilty of engaging in organized criminal activity. [¶] There are two parts to the mental state requirement in engaging in organized criminal activity. One mental state requirement is included in the commission of one of the enumerated offenses. [¶] The other mental state requirement in §71.02(a) is that the defendant intend to establish, maintain, participate in, or participate in the profits of a combination. This second requirement must be more than the intent to commit the enumerated offense because otherwise the statutory element would be superfluous. The proof must consist of more than evidence that a combination existed and that the defendant committed one of the enumerated offenses; the evidence must support a finding that the defendant intended to establish, maintain, participate in, or participate in the profits of a combination." *See also **Renteria v. State***, 199 S.W.3d 499, 504-05 (Tex.App.—Houston [1st Dist.] 2006, pet. ref'd).

McIntosh v. State, 52 S.W.3d 196, 201 (Tex.Crim. App.2001). "[N]o inconsistency exists in requiring that an accused personally commit an overt act to support conviction of engaging in organized criminal activity by conspiring to commit the object offense and in using party liability to support conviction under the same statute for the commission of the object offense."

Nguyen v. State, 1 S.W.3d 694, 696 (Tex.Crim.App. 1999). "The State argues that the phrase 'collaborate in carrying on criminal activities,' given its broadest possible meaning, can be understood to include an agreement to jointly commit a single crime. We hold that it cannot. *At 697:* [T]he State must prove that the appellant intended to 'establish, maintain, or participate in' a group of three or more, in which the members intend to work together in a continuing course of criminal activities." The Court notes that the acts which prove this element of the offense do not necessarily have to be criminal offenses. [¶] "'[O]ne may engage in organized crime by committing one or more of the proscribed acts with the intent to *establish* a combination; accordingly, the proscribed action may be the first actual crime committed by a member of the combination.' The holding of the Court of Appeals that something more than proof of the commission of the enumerated offense is required, which we have approved today, is not a requirement that more than one criminal offense must be proved to establish the offense."

Fee v. State, 841 S.W.2d 392, 395 (Tex.Crim.App. 1992). Pen. Code §71.02 "requires no more than proof of the existence of a combination, and that appellant either committed one of the enumerated offenses in order to facilitate the combination, or that he conspired with at least one other to commit such an offense and he *and* at least one other performed an overt act pursuant to the conspiracy, with intent to facilitate the combination." *See also **Bolden v. State***, 923 S.W.2d 730, 732 (Tex.App.—Tyler 1996, no pet.).

For a quick reference of penalties, see the Chart of Penalties on p. 675.

O'CONNOR'S CRIMINAL CODES 929

PEN §71.02

Garcia v. State, 46 S.W.3d 323, 327 (Tex.App.—Austin 2001, pet. ref'd). "[T]he identities of the persons with whom [Ds] conspired, and the overt acts actually committed pursuant to the agreements, were preliminary fact issues as to which jury unanimity need not be required."

Garcia v. State, 32 S.W.3d 328, 333 (Tex. App.—San Antonio 2000, no pet.). "Although the jury charge properly set forth the allegations of a combination, the charge fails to allege all of the elements of the offense as set forth in the controlling penal provision. Because the instruction fails to set out the listed offense of unlawful possession of a controlled substance 'through forgery, fraud, misrepresentation, or deception,' the charge contains error."

Ross v. State, 9 S.W.3d 878, 882 (Tex.App.—Austin 2000, pet. ref'd). "A case-specific inquiry is required to determine whether a series of offenses committed by the same group indicates that a combination existed. In appropriate circumstances, the commission by the same group of more than one criminal act can, by itself, give rise to a reasonable inference of an intent to engage in a continuing course of criminal activities. If, for example, several people join together to commit a burglary one night, then commit another burglary a week later, an inference of continuity might be raised. [¶] In the present case, however, the evidence does not show that appellant intended to participate in a group that would work together in a continuing course of criminal activities. Rather, ... the case presents a spontaneous, retaliatory series of actions that were all part of the same criminal episode."

PEN §71.021. VIOLATION OF COURT ORDER ENJOINING ORGANIZED CRIMINAL ACTIVITY

(a) A person commits an offense if the person knowingly violates a temporary or permanent order issued under Section 125.065(a) or (b), Civil Practice and Remedies Code.

(b) If conduct constituting an offense under this section also constitutes an offense under another section of this code, the actor may be prosecuted under either section or under both sections.

(c) An offense under this section is a Class A misdemeanor.

History of Pen §71.021: Acts 1995, 74th Leg., ch. 584, §1, eff. Sept. 1, 1995.

PEN §71.022. SOLICITING MEMBERSHIP IN A CRIMINAL STREET GANG

(a) A person commits an offense if the person knowingly causes, enables, encourages, recruits, or solicits another person to become a member of a criminal street gang which, as a condition of initiation, admission, membership, or continued membership, requires the commission of any conduct which constitutes an offense punishable as a Class A misdemeanor or a felony.

(b) Except as provided by Subsection (c), an offense under this section is a felony of the third degree.

(c) A second or subsequent offense under this section is a felony of the second degree.

History of Pen §71.022: Acts 1999, 76th Leg., ch. 1555, §1, eff. Sept. 1, 1999.

PEN §71.03. DEFENSES EXCLUDED

It is no defense to prosecution under Section 71.02 that:

(1) one or more members of the combination are not criminally responsible for the object offense;

(2) one or more members of the combination have been acquitted, have not been prosecuted or convicted, have been convicted of a different offense, or are immune from prosecution;

(3) a person has been charged with, acquitted, or convicted of any offense listed in Subsection (a) of Section 71.02; or

(4) once the initial combination of three or more persons is formed there is a change in the number or identity of persons in the combination as long as two or more persons remain in the combination and are involved in a continuing course of conduct constituting an offense under this chapter.

History of Pen §71.03: Acts 1977, 65th Leg., ch. 346, §1, eff. June 10, 1977. Amended by Acts 1993, 73rd Leg., ch. 900, §1.01, eff. Sept. 1, 1994.

PEN §71.04. TESTIMONIAL IMMUNITY

(a) A party to an offense under this chapter may be required to furnish evidence or testify about the offense.

(b) No evidence or testimony required to be furnished under the provisions of this section nor any information directly or indirectly derived from such evidence or testimony may be used against the witness in any criminal case, except a prosecution for aggravated perjury or contempt.

History of Pen §71.04: Acts 1977, 65th Leg., ch. 346, §1, eff. June 10, 1977.

PEN §71.05. RENUNCIATION DEFENSE

☠ *Subsection (a) below was amended by Acts 1993, 73rd Leg., ch. 761, §3, enacted May 28, 1993, effective Sept. 1, 1993, without reference to the conflicting amendment made by Acts 1993, 73rd Leg., ch. 900, §1.01, enacted May 31, 1993, effective Sept. 1, 1994. For resolving conflicts, see p. V.*

(a) It is an affirmative defense to prosecution under Section 71.02 of this code that under circumstances manifesting a voluntary and complete renunciation of his criminal objective the actor withdrew from the combination before commission of an offense listed in Subdivisions (1) through (7) or Subdivision (10) of Subsection (a) of Section 71.02 of this code and took further affirmative action that prevented the commission of the offense.

☠ *Subsection (a) below was amended by Acts 1993, 73rd Leg., ch. 900, §1.01, enacted May 31, 1993, effective Sept. 1, 1994, without reference to the conflicting amendment made by Acts 1993, 73rd Leg., ch. 761, §3, enacted May 28, 1993, effective Sept. 1, 1993. For resolving conflicts, see p. V.*

(a) It is an affirmative defense to prosecution under Section 71.02 that under circumstances manifesting a voluntary and complete renunciation of his criminal objective the actor withdrew from the combination before commission of an offense listed in Subsection (a) of Section 71.02 and took further affirmative action that prevented the commission of the offense.

(b) For the purposes of this section and Subsection (d) of Section 71.02, renunciation is not voluntary if it is motivated in whole or in part:

(1) by circumstances not present or apparent at the inception of the actor's course of conduct that increase the probability of detection or apprehension or that make more difficult the accomplishment of the objective; or

(2) by a decision to postpone the criminal conduct until another time or to transfer the criminal act to another but similar objective or victim.

☠ *Subsection (c) below was amended by Acts 1993, 73rd Leg., ch. 761, §3, enacted May 28, 1993, effective Sept. 1, 1993, without reference to the deletion of subsection (c) made by Acts 1993, 73rd Leg., ch. 900, §1.01, enacted May 31, 1993, effective Sept. 1, 1994. For resolving conflicts, see p. V.*

(c) Evidence that the defendant withdrew from the combination before commission of an offense listed in Subdivisions (1) through (7) or Subdivision (10) of Subsection (a) of Section 71.02 of this code and made substantial effort to prevent the commission of an offense listed in Subdivisions (1) through (7) or Subdivision (10) of Subsection (a) of Section 71.02 of this code shall be admissible as mitigation at the hearing on punishment if he has been found guilty under Section 71.02 of this code, and in the event of a finding of renunciation under this subsection, the punishment shall be one grade lower than that provided under Section 71.02 of this code.

History of Pen §71.05: Acts 1977, 65th Leg., ch. 346, §1, eff. June 10, 1977. Amended by Acts 1981, 67th Leg., ch. 587, §§4, 5, eff. Sept. 1, 1981; Acts 1993, 73rd Leg., ch. 761, §4 (eff. Sept. 1, 1993), ch. 900, §1.01 (eff. Sept. 1, 1994).

For a quick reference of penalties, see the Chart of Penalties on p. 675.

PEN §71.05

TCSA

─────────────── ★ ───────────────

TCSA

TITLE 6. FOOD, DRUGS, ALCOHOL, & HAZARDOUS SUBSTANCES

SUBTITLE C. SUBSTANCE ABUSE REGULATION & CRIMES

CHAPTER 481. TEXAS CONTROLLED SUBSTANCES ACT

SUBCHAPTER A. GENERAL PROVISIONS

H&SC §481.001. SHORT TITLE

This chapter may be cited as the Texas Controlled Substances Act.

History of H&SC §481.001: Acts 1989, 71st Leg., ch. 678, §1, eff. Sept. 1, 1989.

ANNOTATIONS

$162,950 v. State, 911 S.W.2d 528, 529-30 (Tex. App.—Eastland 1995, writ denied). "In its original Notice of Seizure and Intended Forfeiture, the State alleged that the $162,950 was contraband and claimed that the money was used in the commission of money laundering. [T]he State [also] asserted that the money was the proceeds of criminal activity under the [TCSA]. Property that is contraband is subject to seizure and forfeiture. Money is subject to forfeiture if it is derived from or intended for use in manufacturing, delivering, selling, or possessing a controlled substance."

$22,922 v. State, 853 S.W.2d 99, 101 (Tex.App.— Houston [14th Dist.] 1993, writ denied). "A forfeiture proceeding under the forfeiture of contraband statute is a civil proceeding. The State has the burden to prove by a preponderance of the evidence that the property is subject to forfeiture. The State must prove that, considering all the evidence, it was more reasonably probable than not that the seized money was either intended for use in, or derived from, a violation of one of the offenses enumerated in the forfeiture statute. One category of offenses included in the forfeiture statute are violations of the [TCSA]."

Frierson v. State, 839 S.W.2d 841, 847 (Tex.App.— Dallas 1992, pet. ref'd). "The [TCSA] does not define controlled substances by their chemical activity. Rather, it prohibits the possession of particular chemical compounds such as MDMA. Under the Act, adulterants [or] diluents are substances intended for use in cutting a controlled substance. [W]e conclude that, in order for the State to use the remainder [of the substance other than the MDMA] to aggravate a possession offense, the State must prove that the remainder was added to the controlled substance with the intent to increase its quantity or bulk, and not with the intent of reacting the controlled substance and the remainder to form another chemical compound such as in intermediate stages of manufacturing."

H&SC §481.002. DEFINITIONS

In this chapter:

(1) "Administer" means to directly apply a controlled substance by injection, inhalation, ingestion, or other means to the body of a patient or research subject by:

(A) a practitioner or an agent of the practitioner in the presence of the practitioner; or

(B) the patient or research subject at the direction and in the presence of a practitioner.

(2) "Agent" means an authorized person who acts on behalf of or at the direction of a manufacturer, distributor, or dispenser. The term does not include a common or contract carrier, public warehouseman, or employee of a carrier or warehouseman acting in the usual and lawful course of employment.

(3) "Commissioner" means the commissioner of public health or the commissioner's designee.

(4) "Controlled premises" means:

(A) a place where original or other records or documents required under this chapter are kept or are required to be kept; or

(B) a place, including a factory, warehouse, other establishment, or conveyance, where a person registered under this chapter may lawfully hold, manufacture, distribute, dispense, administer, possess, or otherwise dispose of a controlled substance or other item governed by this chapter, including a chemical precursor and a chemical laboratory apparatus.

(5) "Controlled substance" means a substance, including a drug, an adulterant, and a dilutant, listed in Schedules I through V or Penalty Groups 1, 1-A, or 2 through 4. The term includes the aggregate weight of any mixture, solution, or other substance containing a controlled substance.

(6) "Controlled substance analogue" means:

(A) a substance with a chemical structure substantially similar to the chemical structure of a controlled substance in Schedule I or II or Penalty Group 1, 1-A, or 2; or

TCSA §481.001

(B) a substance specifically designed to produce an effect substantially similar to, or greater than, the effect of a controlled substance in Schedule I or II or Penalty Group 1, 1-A, or 2.

(7) "Counterfeit substance" means a controlled substance that, without authorization, bears or is in a container or has a label that bears an actual or simulated trademark, trade name, or other identifying mark, imprint, number, or device of a manufacturer, distributor, or dispenser other than the person who in fact manufactured, distributed, or dispensed the substance.

(8) "Deliver" means to transfer, actually or constructively, to another a controlled substance, counterfeit substance, or drug paraphernalia, regardless of whether there is an agency relationship. The term includes offering to sell a controlled substance, counterfeit substance, or drug paraphernalia.

(9) "Delivery" or "drug transaction" means the act of delivering.

(10) "Designated agent" means an individual designated under Section 481.073 to communicate a practitioner's instructions to a pharmacist.

(11) "Director" means the director of the Department of Public Safety or an employee of the department designated by the director.

(12) "Dispense" means the delivery of a controlled substance in the course of professional practice or research, by a practitioner or person acting under the lawful order of a practitioner, to an ultimate user or research subject. The term includes the prescribing, administering, packaging, labeling, or compounding necessary to prepare the substance for delivery.

(13) "Dispenser" means a practitioner, institutional practitioner, pharmacist, or pharmacy that dispenses a controlled substance.

(14) "Distribute" means to deliver a controlled substance other than by administering or dispensing the substance.

(15) "Distributor" means a person who distributes.

(16) "Drug" means a substance, other than a device or a component, part, or accessory of a device, that is:

(A) recognized as a drug in the official United States Pharmacopoeia, official Homeopathic Pharmacopoeia of the United States, official National Formulary, or a supplement to either pharmacopoeia or the formulary;

(B) intended for use in the diagnosis, cure, mitigation, treatment, or prevention of disease in man or animals;

(C) intended to affect the structure or function of the body of man or animals but is not food; or

(D) intended for use as a component of a substance described by Paragraph (A), (B), or (C).

(17) "Drug paraphernalia" means equipment, a product, or material that is used or intended for use in planting, propagating, cultivating, growing, harvesting, manufacturing, compounding, converting, producing, processing, preparing, testing, analyzing, packaging, repackaging, storing, containing, or concealing a controlled substance in violation of this chapter or in injecting, ingesting, inhaling, or otherwise introducing into the human body a controlled substance in violation of this chapter. The term includes:

(A) a kit used or intended for use in planting, propagating, cultivating, growing, or harvesting a species of plant that is a controlled substance or from which a controlled substance may be derived;

(B) a material, compound, mixture, preparation, or kit used or intended for use in manufacturing, compounding, converting, producing, processing, or preparing a controlled substance;

(C) an isomerization device used or intended for use in increasing the potency of a species of plant that is a controlled substance;

(D) testing equipment used or intended for use in identifying or in analyzing the strength, effectiveness, or purity of a controlled substance;

(E) a scale or balance used or intended for use in weighing or measuring a controlled substance;

(F) a dilutant or adulterant, such as quinine hydrochloride, mannitol, inositol, nicotinamide, dextrose, lactose, or absorbent, blotter-type material, that is used or intended to be used to increase the amount or weight of or to transfer a controlled substance regardless of whether the dilutant or adulterant diminishes the efficacy of the controlled substance;

(G) a separation gin or sifter used or intended for use in removing twigs and seeds from or in otherwise cleaning or refining marihuana;

(H) a blender, bowl, container, spoon, or mixing device used or intended for use in compounding a controlled substance;

TCSA §481.002

(I) a capsule, balloon, envelope, or other container used or intended for use in packaging small quantities of a controlled substance;

(J) a container or other object used or intended for use in storing or concealing a controlled substance;

(K) a hypodermic syringe, needle, or other object used or intended for use in parenterally injecting a controlled substance into the human body; and

(L) an object used or intended for use in ingesting, inhaling, or otherwise introducing marihuana, cocaine, hashish, or hashish oil into the human body, including:

(i) a metal, wooden, acrylic, glass, stone, plastic, or ceramic pipe with or without a screen, permanent screen, hashish head, or punctured metal bowl;

(ii) a water pipe;

(iii) a carburetion tube or device;

(iv) a smoking or carburetion mask;

(v) a chamber pipe;

(vi) a carburetor pipe;

(vii) an electric pipe;

(viii) an air-driven pipe;

(ix) a chillum;

(x) a bong; or

(xi) an ice pipe or chiller.

(18) "Federal Controlled Substances Act" means the Federal Comprehensive Drug Abuse Prevention and Control Act of 1970 (21 U.S.C. Section 801 et seq.) or its successor statute.

(19) "Federal Drug Enforcement Administration" means the Drug Enforcement Administration of the United States Department of Justice or its successor agency.

(20) "Hospital" means:

(A) a general or special hospital as defined by Section 241.003 (Texas Hospital Licensing Law); or

(B) an ambulatory surgical center licensed by the Texas Department of Health and approved by the federal government to perform surgery paid by Medicaid on patients admitted for a period of not more than 24 hours.

(21) "Human consumption" means the injection, inhalation, ingestion, or application of a substance to or into a human body.

(22) "Immediate precursor" means a substance the director finds to be and by rule designates as being:

(A) a principal compound commonly used or produced primarily for use in the manufacture of a controlled substance;

(B) a substance that is an immediate chemical intermediary used or likely to be used in the manufacture of a controlled substance; and

(C) a substance the control of which is necessary to prevent, curtail, or limit the manufacture of a controlled substance.

(23) "Institutional practitioner" means an intern, resident physician, fellow, or person in an equivalent professional position who:

(A) is not licensed by the appropriate state professional licensing board;

(B) is enrolled in a bona fide professional training program in a base hospital or institutional training facility registered by the Federal Drug Enforcement Administration; and

(C) is authorized by the base hospital or institutional training facility to administer, dispense, or prescribe controlled substances.

(24) "Lawful possession" means the possession of a controlled substance that has been obtained in accordance with state or federal law.

(25) "Manufacture" means the production, preparation, propagation, compounding, conversion, or processing of a controlled substance other than marihuana, directly or indirectly by extraction from substances of natural origin, independently by means of chemical synthesis, or by a combination of extraction and chemical synthesis, and includes the packaging or repackaging of the substance or labeling or relabeling of its container. However, the term does not include the preparation, compounding, packaging, or labeling of a controlled substance:

(A) by a practitioner as an incident to the practitioner's administering or dispensing a controlled substance in the course of professional practice; or

(B) by a practitioner, or by an authorized agent under the supervision of the practitioner, for or as an incident to research, teaching, or chemical analysis and not for delivery.

(26) "Marihuana" means the plant Cannabis sativa L., whether growing or not, the seeds of that plant, and every compound, manufacture, salt, derivative, mixture, or preparation of that plant or its seeds. The term does not include:

(A) the resin extracted from a part of the plant or a compound, manufacture, salt, derivative, mixture, or preparation of the resin;

(B) the mature stalks of the plant or fiber produced from the stalks;

(C) oil or cake made from the seeds of the plant;

(D) a compound, manufacture, salt, derivative, mixture, or preparation of the mature stalks, fiber, oil, or cake; or

(E) the sterilized seeds of the plant that are incapable of beginning germination.

(27) "Medical purpose" means the use of a controlled substance for relieving or curing a mental or physical disease or infirmity.

(28) "Medication order" means an order from a practitioner to dispense a drug to a patient in a hospital for immediate administration while the patient is in the hospital or for emergency use on the patient's release from the hospital.

(29) "Narcotic drug" means any of the following, produced directly or indirectly by extraction from substances of vegetable origin, independently by means of chemical synthesis, or by a combination of extraction and chemical synthesis:

(A) opium and opiates, and a salt, compound, derivative, or preparation of opium or opiates;

(B) a salt, compound, isomer, derivative, or preparation of a salt, compound, isomer, or derivative that is chemically equivalent or identical to a substance listed in Paragraph (A) other than the isoquinoline alkaloids of opium;

(C) opium poppy and poppy straw; or

(D) cocaine, including:

(i) its salts, its optical, position, or geometric isomers, and the salts of those isomers;

(ii) coca leaves and a salt, compound, derivative, or preparation of coca leaves; and

(iii) a salt, compound, derivative, or preparation of a salt, compound, or derivative that is chemically equivalent or identical to a substance described by Subparagraph (i) or (ii), other than decocainized coca leaves or extractions of coca leaves that do not contain cocaine or ecgonine.

(30) "Opiate" means a substance that has an addiction-forming or addiction-sustaining liability similar to morphine or is capable of conversion into a drug having addiction-forming or addiction-sustaining liability. The term includes its racemic and levorotatory forms. The term does not include, unless specifically designated as controlled under Subchapter B, the dextrorotatory isomer of 3-methoxy-n-methylmorphinan and its salts (dextromethorphan).

(31) "Opium poppy" means the plant of the species Papaver somniferum L., other than its seeds.

(32) "Patient" means a human for whom or an animal for which a drug is administered, dispensed, delivered, or prescribed by a practitioner.

(33) "Person" means an individual, corporation, government, business trust, estate, trust, partnership, association, or any other legal entity.

(34) "Pharmacist" means a person licensed by the Texas State Board of Pharmacy to practice pharmacy and who acts as an agent for a pharmacy.

(35) "Pharmacist-in-charge" means the pharmacist designated on a pharmacy license as the pharmacist who has the authority or responsibility for the pharmacy's compliance with this chapter and other laws relating to pharmacy.

(36) "Pharmacy" means a facility licensed by the Texas State Board of Pharmacy where a prescription for a controlled substance is received or processed in accordance with state or federal law.

(37) "Poppy straw" means all parts, other than the seeds, of the opium poppy, after mowing.

(38) "Possession" means actual care, custody, control, or management.

(39) "Practitioner" means:

(A) a physician, dentist, veterinarian, podiatrist, scientific investigator, or other person licensed, registered, or otherwise permitted to distribute, dispense, analyze, conduct research with respect to, or administer a controlled substance in the course of professional practice or research in this state;

(B) a pharmacy, hospital, or other institution licensed, registered, or otherwise permitted to distribute, dispense, conduct research with respect to, or administer a controlled substance in the course of professional practice or research in this state;

(C) a person practicing in and licensed by another state as a physician, dentist, veterinarian, or podiatrist, having a current Federal Drug Enforcement Administration registration number, who may legally prescribe Schedule II, III, IV, or V controlled substances in that state; or

(D) an advanced practice nurse or physician assistant to whom a physician has delegated the authority to carry out or sign prescription drug orders under Section 157.0511, 157.052, 157.053, 157.054, 157.0541, or 157.0542, Occupations Code.

(40) "Prescribe" means the act of a practitioner to authorize a controlled substance to be dispensed to an ultimate user.

(41) "Prescription" means an order by a practitioner to a pharmacist for a controlled substance for a particular patient that specifies:

(A) the date of issue;

(B) the name and address of the patient or, if the controlled substance is prescribed for an animal, the species of the animal and the name and address of its owner;

(C) the name and quantity of the controlled substance prescribed with the quantity shown numerically followed by the number written as a word if the order is written or, if the order is communicated orally or telephonically, with the quantity given by the practitioner and transcribed by the pharmacist numerically;

(D) directions for the use of the drug;

(E) the intended use of the drug unless the practitioner determines the furnishing of this information is not in the best interest of the patient; and

(F) the legibly printed or stamped name, address, Federal Drug Enforcement Administration registration number, and telephone number of the practitioner at the practitioner's usual place of business.

(42) "Principal place of business" means a location where a person manufactures, distributes, dispenses, analyzes, or possesses a controlled substance. The term does not include a location where a practitioner dispenses a controlled substance on an outpatient basis unless the controlled substance is stored at that location.

(43) "Production" includes the manufacturing, planting, cultivating, growing, or harvesting of a controlled substance.

(44) "Raw material" means a compound, material, substance, or equipment used or intended for use, alone or in any combination, in manufacturing a controlled substance.

(45) "Registrant" means a person who is registered under Section 481.063.

(46) "Substitution" means the dispensing of a drug or a brand of drug other than that which is ordered or prescribed.

(47) "Official prescription form" means a prescription form that contains the prescription information required by Section 481.075.

(48) "Ultimate user" means a person who has lawfully obtained and possesses a controlled substance for the person's own use, for the use of a member of the person's household, or for administering to an animal owned by the person or by a member of the person's household.

(49) "Adulterant or dilutant" means any material that increases the bulk or quantity of a controlled substance, regardless of its effect on the chemical activity of the controlled substance.

(50) "Abuse unit" means:

(A) except as provided by Paragraph (B):

(i) a single unit on or in any adulterant, dilutant, or similar carrier medium, including marked or perforated blotter paper, a tablet, gelatin wafer, sugar cube, or stamp, or other medium that contains any amount of a controlled substance listed in Penalty Group 1-A, if the unit is commonly used in abuse of that substance; or

(ii) each quarter-inch square section of paper, if the adulterant, dilutant, or carrier medium is paper not marked or perforated into individual abuse units; or

(B) if the controlled substance is in liquid form, 40 micrograms of the controlled substance including any adulterant or dilutant.

(51) "Chemical precursor" means:

(A) Methylamine;

(B) Ethylamine;

(C) D-lysergic acid;

(D) Ergotamine tartrate;

(E) Diethyl malonate;

(F) Malonic acid;

(G) Ethyl malonate;

(H) Barbituric acid;

(I) Piperidine;

(J) N-acetylanthranilic acid;

(K) Pyrrolidine;

(L) Phenylacetic acid;

(M) Anthranilic acid;

(N) Ephedrine;

(O) Pseudoephedrine;

(P) Norpseudoephedrine; or

(Q) Phenylpropanolamine.

(52) "Department" means the Department of Public Safety.

(53) "Chemical laboratory apparatus" means any item of equipment designed, made, or adapted to manufacture a controlled substance or a controlled substance analogue, including:

(A) a condenser;

(B) a distilling apparatus;

(C) a vacuum drier;

(D) a three-neck or distilling flask;

(E) a tableting machine;

(F) an encapsulating machine;

(G) a filter, Buchner, or separatory funnel;

(H) an Erlenmeyer, two-neck, or single-neck flask;

(I) a round-bottom, Florence, thermometer, or filtering flask;

(J) a Soxhlet extractor;

(K) a transformer;

(L) a flask heater;

(M) a heating mantel; or

(N) an adaptor tube.

(54) to **(55)** Repealed by Acts 1999, 76th Leg., ch. 145, §5(1), eff. Sept. 1, 1999.

History of H&SC §481.002: Acts 1989, 71st Leg., ch. 678, §1 (eff. Sept. 1, 1989), ch. 1100, §5.02(b) (eff. Sept. 1, 1989). Amended by Acts 1993, 73rd Leg., ch. 351, §27 (eff. Sept. 1, 1993), ch. 789, §15 (eff. Sept. 1, 1993), ch. 900, §2.01 (eff. Sept. 1, 1994); Acts 1997, 75th Leg., ch. 745, §§1, 2, eff. Sept. 1, 1997; Acts 1999, 76th Leg., ch. 145, §§1, 5(1), eff. Sept. 1, 1999; Acts 2001, 77th Leg., ch. 251, §1 (eff. Sept. 1, 2001), ch. 1188, §1 (eff. Sept. 1, 2001); Acts 2003, 78th Leg., ch. 88, §9 (eff. May 20, 2003), ch. 1099, §4 (eff. Sept. 1, 2003).

ANNOTATIONS

§481.002(5)

Ex parte Kopecky, 821 S.W.2d 957, 959 (Tex.Crim. App.1992). Tax Code ch. 159 "provides for a tax upon 'taxable substances' and the issuance by the comptroller of a certificate, to be affixed to the 'taxable substance'.... Subchapter A of Chapter 159 defines 'taxable substance' to include ... a 'controlled substance' as that term is defined in the Controlled Substances Act. The Controlled Substances Act in turn defines a 'controlled substance' as a 'substance ... listed in Schedules I through V or Penalty Groups 1 through 4.' Because phenylacetone is listed in Penalty Group 2 ... it is indeed a 'controlled substance' within the meaning of [Tax Code ch.] 159.... Subchapter C of Chapter 159

contains a penal provision outlawing possession of a 'taxable substance' for which the requisite tax has not been paid." *See also* ***Courtney v. State***, 904 S.W.2d 907, 910 (Tex.App.—Houston [1st Dist.] 1995, pet. ref'd).

Jackson v. State, 94 S.W.3d 46, 49 (Tex.App.—Tyler 2002, pet. ref'd). "[T]he clear, logical intent of the legislature was to permit prosecution for possession of a controlled substance based on the total weight, without regard for the proportion of enumerated substance or the amount of adulterants or dilutants."

Ex parte Luster, 846 S.W.2d 928, 930 (Tex.App.—Fort Worth 1993, pet. ref'd). "As used in the Act, 'controlled substance' means a substance, including a drug and an immediate precursor, listed in Schedules I through V or Penalty Groups 1 through 4. Amphetamine is a drug listed in Penalty Group 2 ... and phenylacetic acid is a main precursor used to make amphetamine. Thus, [D] had fair notice that his transaction involving phenylacetic acid was forbidden by §481.126(a)(2)."

§481.002(8)

Sims v. State, 117 S.W.3d 267, 277-78 (Tex.Crim. App.2003). "[O]ne method of constructive transfer is for the transferor to instruct the recipient on the location of the contraband. If the contraband is already in place, the constructive transfer is complete at the time the transferor gives the instruction. When the recipient retrieves the contraband, there is then a completed actual transfer." Held: Actual and constructive transfers can occur in the same transaction.

Heberling v. State, 834 S.W.2d 350, 354 (Tex.Crim. App.1992). "Because the term actual transfer is not defined in the [TCSA], it must be given its plain meaning. [F]or our purposes, actual delivery consists in completely transferring the real possession and control of a controlled substance from one person to another person. ... Actual delivery consists of the giving real possession to the vendee *or his servants or special agents who are identified with him in law and represent him.* We believe this to be an accurate observation, and we now hold that an actual transfer or delivery, as commonly understood, contemplates the manual transfer of property from the transferor to the transferee *or to the transferee's agents or to someone identified in law with the transferee.*" (Internal quotes omitted.)

Jackson v. State, 84 S.W.3d 742, 745 (Tex.App.—Houston [1st Dist.] 2002, no pet.). "[T]he following rules are applicable to a constructive delivery: (1) prior to an alleged delivery, the transferor must have either direct or indirect control of the substance transferred and (2) the transferor must know of the existence of the transferee."

Verduzco v. State, 24 S.W.3d 384, 386 (Tex.App.—Houston [1st Dist.] 2000, no pet.). Undercover officer "established that appellant offered to sell the cocaine for the stated price of $8,000 when appellant showed [undercover officer] the cocaine and [alleged accomplice] told [undercover officer] in appellant's presence to 'go get the money.' There is no evidence that [undercover officer] ever touched the cocaine, and the State at trial abandoned the theory of delivery of cocaine by an offer to sell. There is also no evidence of a constructive transfer.... [T]he evidence is legally insufficient to support appellant's conviction."

Schneider v. State, 951 S.W.2d 856, 861 (Tex. App.—Texarkana 1997, pet. ref'd). "Because [H&SC] §§481.002(8) and 481.112 clearly place men of reasonable intelligence on notice that they cannot promote an exchange of a controlled substance to another person for value either by words or deed, the word 'offer' is not unconstitutionally vague. [¶] [D] asserts that the culpable conduct is identical under [§§482.002 and 481.112] and the disparate sentences violate his right to due process. However, the culpable conduct is not identical. The culpable conduct penalized under §481.112 is the offering to sell a controlled substance, regardless of whether the controlled substance is sold, and therefore, the focus is on the transaction at the time that the offer is made. The culpable conduct penalized under §482.002 is the offering to sell a *simulated* controlled substance, and therefore, the focus is on the item sold. Because of the substance's simulated nature and lesser range of punishment, we can presume the legislature determined that this behavior constitutes a lesser harm to society than delivery of an actual controlled substance."

§481.002(9)

Becker v. State, 840 S.W.2d 743, 745 (Tex.App.—Houston [1st Dist.] 1992, no pet.). "Actual transfer, constructive transfer, and offer to sell are mutually exclusive ways in which 'delivery' might occur. However, 'delivery' may be accomplished by nothing more than making the drug available to another by placing it within his reach, even though there is no actual handing of the thing from one person to another."

§481.002(17)

Nichols v. State, 886 S.W.2d 324, 326 (Tex.App.—Houston [1st Dist.] 1994, pet. ref'd). "A metal pipe is drug paraphernalia when it is intended for use or is used to contain, ingest, or inhale a controlled substance. The term 'drug paraphernalia' includes by specific statutory designation 'an object used ... in ... inhaling marijuana, ... including a metal ... pipe with ... a screen....' A person commits the offense of possession of drug paraphernalia if the person knowingly uses or possesses with intent to use drug paraphernalia to contain a controlled substance or to inhale into the human body a controlled substance."

Frierson v. State, 839 S.W.2d 841, 846 n.2 (Tex. App.—Dallas 1992, pet. ref'd). The TCSA "uses the word 'dilutant' except in §481.002(17)(F) which refers to 'diluent.' Both experts used the word 'diluent.' The Court of Criminal Appeals considers the terms to be synonymous."

Sims v. State, 833 S.W.2d 281, 284 n.1 (Tex.App.—Houston [14th Dist.] 1992, pet. ref'd). "A matchbox, unlike a metal crack pipe, is not necessarily drug paraphernalia."

§481.002(25)

Green v. State, 930 S.W.2d 655, 657 (Tex.App.—Fort Worth 1996, pet. ref'd). "The form in which a controlled substance is recovered is not determinative of whether the accused has committed the offense of manufacturing the drug. Evidence that shows any of the procedures listed in §481.002(25) is sufficient to support a conviction of the manufacture of a controlled substance. [¶] Although an accused's mere presence at the scene of a drug laboratory is insufficient to support a conviction for drug manufacture, it is a circumstance tending to prove guilt that, when combined with other facts, shows that the accused was a participant in the manufacture." *See also* ***Goforth v. State***, 883 S.W.2d 251, 253 (Tex.App.—Eastland 1994, no pet.).

§481.002(26)

Williams v. State, 524 S.W.2d 705, 710 (Tex.Crim. App.1975). "We cannot conclude that the Legislature ... intended to limit offenses relating to marihuana to those cases in which it was shown that the species involved was sativa L. and exempt other species [such as cannabis indica and cannabis ruderalis].... We are persuaded by the soundness of the numerous federal appeals court opinions in rejecting identical arguments advanced under a similar statute."

TCSA §481.002

Nowling v. State, 801 S.W.2d 182, 184 (Tex.App.—Houston [14th Dist.] 1990, pet. ref'd). "The Court of Criminal Appeals has held that §481.002(26)(A)-(E) which excludes certain material from the definition of marihuana are in the nature of exceptions and that the burden of going forward with the evidence pertaining thereto rests upon the person claiming their benefit. The accused has the burden to show any exception he claims. This requires the accused to produce evidence to establish a defensive plea concerning the weight of the marihuana. Therefore, [D] has the burden to present evidence as to what the proper weight of the marihuana is excluding stalks or other excludable material when he disputes the state's contention as to weight."

§481.002(38)

Joseph v. State, 897 S.W.2d 374, 376 (Tex.Crim. App.1995). "To prove unlawful possession of a controlled substance, the State must prove that: (1) the accused exercised control, management, and care over the substance; and (2) the accused knew the matter possessed was contraband. There is no requirement that one must possess a usable amount of a controlled substance in order to be convicted of unlawful possession of a controlled substance. There is also no requirement that the substance be visible to the naked eye."

Caballero v. State, 881 S.W.2d 745, 748 (Tex. App.—Houston [14th Dist.] 1994, no pet.). "Visibility and measurability are sufficient evidence of knowing possession. [¶] We note that visibility and measurability are *sufficient*, not *necessary*, conditions to establish knowing possession. [Section §481.002(38)] contains no visibility or minimum measurability requirements. … The fact that the cocaine was found in an item of drug paraphernalia or an item closely associated with drug use is evidence of knowing possession."

Fonseca v. State, 881 S.W.2d 144, 151 (Tex.App.—Corpus Christi 1994, no pet.). "[A]n indictment does not have to specifically define the term 'possession' since the term is defined by statute. '[P]ossession' [is] 'not an act, nor is it an omission, but is defined as something distinct from both act and omission.' Since the term does not go to an act or omission of the defendant, no more precise definition is required. [¶] We hold that the indictments were sufficient to give [defendants] notice of the offense charged and that they were not fatally defective for failing to allege which type of 'possession' the State intended to prove."

Freeman v. State, 864 S.W.2d 757, 759 (Tex.App.—Houston [1st Dist.] 1993, pet. ref'd). "The Court of Criminal Appeals has declined to equate the element of 'carrying on or about [the] person' in [Pen. Code] §46.02(a) with the element of unlawful possession as set forth in the [TCSA] and other possessory offenses found in the [Pen. Code]."

§481.002(49)

Seals v. State, 187 S.W.3d 417, 420 (Tex.Crim.App. 2005). "The literal meaning of the legislature's adulterant and dilutant definition is that any substance that is added to or mixed with a controlled substance, regardless of when, how, or why that substance was added, may be added to the aggregate weight of the controlled substance as an adulterant or dilutant." Held: The blood mixed with the methamphetamine could properly be considered an adulterant or dilutant. *See also Wright v. State*, 201 S.W.3d 765, 770 (Tex.Crim.App.2006) (including unusable material from manufacture of controlled substance in aggregate weight of controlled substance does not lead to an absurd result).

H&SC §481.003. RULES

(a) The director may adopt rules to administer and enforce this chapter.

(b) The director by rule shall prohibit a person in this state, including a person regulated by the Texas Department of Insurance under the Insurance Code or the other insurance laws of this state, from using a practitioner's Federal Drug Enforcement Administration number for a purpose other than a purpose described by federal law or by this chapter. A person who violates a rule adopted under this subsection commits a Class C misdemeanor.

History of H&SC §481.003: Acts 1997, 75th Leg., ch. 745, §3, eff. Sept. 1, 1997. Amended by Acts 1999, 76th Leg., ch. 1266, §1, eff. Sept. 1, 1999.

Sections 481.004-481.030 reserved for expansion

SUBCHAPTER B. SCHEDULES

H&SC §481.031. NOMENCLATURE

Controlled substances listed in Schedules I through V and Penalty Groups 1 through 4 are included by whatever official, common, usual, chemical, or trade name they may be designated.

History of H&SC §481.031: Acts 1989, 71st Leg., ch. 678, §1, eff. Sept. 1, 1989.

H&SC §481.032. SCHEDULES

(a) The commissioner shall establish and modify the following schedules of controlled substances under this subchapter: Schedule I, Schedule II, Schedule III, Schedule IV, and Schedule V.

(b) A reference to a schedule in this chapter means the most current version of the schedule established or altered by the commissioner under this subchapter and published in the Texas Register on or after January 1, 1998.

History of H&SC §481.032: Acts 1989, 71st Leg., ch. 678, §1, ch. 1100, §5.02(c) (eff. Sept. 1, 1989). Amended by Acts 1997, 75th Leg., ch. 745, §4, eff. Sept. 1, 1997; Acts 2001, 77th Leg., ch. 251, §2, eff. Sept. 1, 2001.

H&SC §481.033. EXCLUSION FROM SCHEDULES & APPLICATION OF ACT

(a) A nonnarcotic substance is excluded from Schedules I through V if the substance may lawfully be sold over the counter without a prescription, under the Federal Food, Drug, and Cosmetic Act (21 U.S.C. Section 301 et seq.).

(b) The commissioner may not include in the schedules:

(1) a substance described by Subsection (a); or

(2) distilled spirits, wine, malt beverages, or tobacco.

(c) A compound, mixture, or preparation containing a stimulant substance listed in Schedule II and having a potential for abuse associated with a stimulant effect on the central nervous system is excepted from the application of this chapter if the compound, mixture, or preparation contains one or more active medicinal ingredients not having a stimulant effect on the central nervous system and if the admixtures are included in combinations, quantity, proportions, or concentrations that vitiate the potential for abuse of the substance having a stimulant effect on the central nervous system.

(d) A compound, mixture, or preparation containing a depressant substance listed in Schedule III or IV and having a potential for abuse associated with a depressant effect on the central nervous system is excepted from the application of this chapter if the compound, mixture, or preparation contains one or more active medicinal ingredients not having a depressant effect on the central nervous system and if the admixtures are included in combinations, quantity, proportions, or concentrations that vitiate the potential for abuse of the substance having a depressant effect on the central nervous system.

(e) A nonnarcotic prescription substance is exempted from Schedules I through V and the application of this chapter to the same extent that the substance has been exempted from the application of the Federal Controlled Substances Act, if the substance is listed as an exempt prescription product under 21 C.F.R. Section 1308.32 and its subsequent amendments.

(f) A chemical substance that is intended for laboratory, industrial, educational, or special research purposes and not for general administration to a human being or other animal is exempted from Schedules I through V and the application of this chapter to the same extent that the substance has been exempted from the application of the Federal Controlled Substances Act, if the substance is listed as an exempt chemical preparation under 21 C.F.R. Section 1308.24 and its subsequent amendments.

(g) An anabolic steroid product, which has no significant potential for abuse due to concentration, preparation, mixture, or delivery system, is exempted from Schedules I through V and the application of this chapter to the same extent that the substance has been exempted from the application of the Federal Controlled Substances Act, if the substance is listed as an exempt anabolic steroid product under 21 C.F.R. Section 1308.34 and its subsequent amendments.

History of H&SC §481.033: Acts 1989, 71st Leg., ch. 678, §1, eff. Sept. 1, 1989. Amended by Acts 1993, 73rd Leg., ch. 532, §1, eff. Sept. 1, 1993. Renumbered from §481.037 and amended by Acts 1997, 75th Leg., ch. 745, §4, eff. Sept. 1, 1997.

H&SC §481.034. ESTABLISHMENT & MODIFICATION OF SCHEDULES BY COMMISSIONER

(a) The commissioner shall annually establish the schedules of controlled substances. These annual schedules shall include the complete list of all controlled substances from the previous schedules and modifications in the federal schedules of controlled substances as required by Subsection (g). Any further additions to and deletions from these schedules, any rescheduling of substances and any other modifications made by the commissioner to these schedules of controlled substances shall be made:

(1) in accordance with Section 481.035;

(2) in a manner consistent with this subchapter; and

(3) with approval of the Texas Board of Health.

(b) Except for alterations in schedules required by Subsection (g), the commissioner may not make an alteration in a schedule unless the commissioner holds a public hearing on the matter in Austin and obtains approval from the Texas Board of Health.

(c) The commissioner may not:

(1) add a substance to the schedules if the substance has been deleted from the schedules by the legislature;

(2) delete a substance from the schedules if the substance has been added to the schedules by the legislature; or

(3) reschedule a substance if the substance has been placed in a schedule by the legislature.

(d) In making a determination regarding a substance, the commissioner shall consider:

(1) the actual or relative potential for its abuse;

(2) the scientific evidence of its pharmacological effect, if known;

(3) the state of current scientific knowledge regarding the substance;

(4) the history and current pattern of its abuse;

(5) the scope, duration, and significance of its abuse;

(6) the risk to the public health;

(7) the potential of the substance to produce psychological or physiological dependence liability; and

(8) whether the substance is a controlled substance analogue, chemical precursor, or an immediate precursor of a substance controlled under this chapter.

(e) After considering the factors listed in Subsection (d), the commissioner shall make findings with respect to those factors and adopt a rule controlling the substance if the commissioner finds the substance has a potential for abuse.

(f) Repealed by Acts 2003, 78th Leg., ch. 1099, §17, eff. Sept. 1, 2003.

(g) Except as otherwise provided by this subsection, if a substance is designated, rescheduled, or deleted as a controlled substance under federal law and notice of that fact is given to the commissioner, the commissioner similarly shall control the substance under this chapter. After the expiration of a 30-day period beginning on the day after the date of publication in the Federal Register of a final order designating a substance as a controlled substance or rescheduling or deleting a substance, the commissioner similarly shall designate, reschedule, or delete the substance, unless the commissioner objects during the period. If the commissioner objects, the commissioner shall publish the reasons for the objection and give all interested parties an opportunity to be heard. At the conclusion of the hearing, the commissioner shall publish a decision, which is final unless altered by statute. On publication of an objection by the commissioner, control as to that particular substance under this chapter is stayed until the commissioner publishes the commissioner's decision.

(h) Not later than the 10th day after the date on which the commissioner designates, deletes, or reschedules a substance under Subsection (a), the commissioner shall give written notice of that action to the director and to each state licensing agency having jurisdiction over practitioners.

History of H&SC §481.034: Acts 1989, 71st Leg., ch. 678, §1, eff. Sept. 1, 1989. Renumbered from §481.038 and amended by Acts 1997, 75th Leg., ch. 745, §4, eff. Sept. 1, 1997. Amended by Acts 2003, 78th Leg., ch. 1099, §§5, 17, eff. Sept. 1, 2003.

H&SC §481.035. FINDINGS

(a) The commissioner shall place a substance in Schedule I if the commissioner finds that the substance:

(1) has a high potential for abuse; and

(2) has no accepted medical use in treatment in the United States or lacks accepted safety for use in treatment under medical supervision.

(b) The commissioner shall place a substance in Schedule II if the commissioner finds that:

(1) the substance has a high potential for abuse;

(2) the substance has currently accepted medical use in treatment in the United States; and

(3) abuse of the substance may lead to severe psychological or physical dependence.

(c) The commissioner shall place a substance in Schedule III if the commissioner finds that:

(1) the substance has a potential for abuse less than that of the substances listed in Schedules I and II;

(2) the substance has currently accepted medical use in treatment in the United States; and

(3) abuse of the substance may lead to moderate or low physical dependence or high psychological dependence.

TCSA §481.035

(d) The commissioner shall place a substance in Schedule IV if the commissioner finds that:

(1) the substance has a lower potential for abuse than that of the substances listed in Schedule III;

(2) the substance has currently accepted medical use in treatment in the United States; and

(3) abuse of the substance may lead to a more limited physical or psychological dependence than that of the substances listed in Schedule III.

(e) The commissioner shall place a substance in Schedule V if the commissioner finds that the substance:

(1) has a lower potential for abuse than that of the substances listed in Schedule IV;

(2) has currently accepted medical use in treatment in the United States; and

(3) may lead to a more limited physical or psychological dependence liability than that of the substances listed in Schedule IV.

History of H&SC §481.035: Acts 1989, 71st Leg., ch. 678, §1, eff. Sept. 1, 1989. Renumbered from §481.039 and amended by Acts 1997, 75th Leg., ch. 745, §4, eff. Sept. 1, 1997.

Martinez v. State, 883 S.W.2d 771, 774 (Tex. App.—Fort Worth 1994, pet. ref'd). "In ***Chalin***, the court ... held that where an isomer of methamphetamine was specifically named in Schedule IV of the [TCSA], it could not be considered to be included in the general class of isomers of methamphetamine contained in Schedule II of the Act."

H&SC §481.036. PUBLICATION OF SCHEDULES

(a) The commissioner shall publish the schedules by filing a certified copy of the schedules with the secretary of state for publication in the Texas Register not later than the fifth working day after the date the commissioner takes action under this subchapter.

(b) Each published schedule must show changes, if any, made in the schedule since its latest publication.

(c) An action by the commissioner that establishes or modifies a schedule under this subchapter may take effect not earlier than the 21st day after the date on which the schedule or modification is published in the Texas Register unless an emergency exists that necessitates earlier action to avoid an imminent hazard to the public safety.

History of H&SC §481.036: Acts 1989, 71st Leg., ch. 678, §1, eff. Sept. 1, 1989. Renumbered from §481.040 and amended by Acts 1997, 75th Leg., ch. 745, §4, eff. Sept. 1, 1997.

H&SC §§481.037 TO 481.040. RENUMBERED

Renumbered by Acts 1997, 75th Leg., ch. 745, §4, eff. Jan. 1, 1998.

Sections 481.0041-481.060 reserved for expansion

SUBCHAPTER C. REGULATION OF MANUFACTURE, DISTRIBUTION, & DISPENSATION OF CONTROLLED SUBSTANCES, CHEMICAL PRECURSORS, & CHEMICAL LABORATORY APPARATUS

H&SC §481.061. REGISTRATION REQUIRED

(a) Except as otherwise provided by this chapter, a person who is not a registrant may not manufacture, distribute, prescribe, possess, analyze, or dispense a controlled substance in this state.

(b) A person who is registered by the director to manufacture, distribute, analyze, dispense, or conduct research with a controlled substance may possess, manufacture, distribute, analyze, dispense, or conduct research with that substance to the extent authorized by the person's registration and in conformity with this chapter.

(c) A separate registration is required at each principal place of business or professional practice where the applicant manufactures, distributes, analyzes, dispenses, or possesses a controlled substance. However, the director may not require separate registration for a practitioner engaged in research with a nonnarcotic controlled substance listed in Schedules II through V if the registrant is already registered under this subchapter in another capacity.

History of H&SC §481.061: Acts 1989, 71st Leg., ch. 678, §1, eff. Sept. 1, 1989. Amended by Acts 1997, 75th Leg., ch. 745, §4, eff. Sept. 1, 1997.

H&SC §481.062. EXEMPTIONS

(a) The following persons are not required to register and may possess a controlled substance under this chapter:

(1) an agent or employee of a registered manufacturer, distributor, analyzer, or dispenser of the controlled substance acting in the usual course of business or employment;

(2) a common or contract carrier, a warehouseman, or an employee of a carrier or warehouseman whose possession of the controlled substance is in the usual course of business or employment;

(3) an ultimate user or a person in possession of the controlled substance under a lawful order of a practitioner or in lawful possession of the controlled substance if it is listed in Schedule V;

(4) an officer or employee of this state, another state, a political subdivision of this state or another state, or the United States who is lawfully engaged in the enforcement of a law relating to a controlled substance or drug or to a customs law and authorized to possess the controlled substance in the discharge of the person's official duties; or

(5) if the substance is tetrahydrocannabinol or one of its derivatives:

(A) a Texas Department of Health official, a medical school researcher, or a research program participant possessing the substance as authorized under Subchapter G; or

(B) a practitioner or an ultimate user possessing the substance as a participant in a federally approved therapeutic research program that the commissioner has reviewed and found, in writing, to contain a medically responsible research protocol.

(b) The director by rule may waive the requirement for registration of certain manufacturers, distributors, or dispensers if the director finds it consistent with the public health and safety and if the attorney general of the United States has issued a similar waiver under the Federal Controlled Substances Act.[1]

1. **Editor's note:** 21 U.S.C. §801 et seq.

History of H&SC §481.062: Acts 1989, 71st Leg., ch. 678, §1, eff. Sept. 1, 1989. Amended by Acts 1997, 75th Leg., ch. 745, §6, eff. Sept. 1, 1997. Renumbered from §461.062 by Acts 2001, 77th Leg., ch. 1420, §21.001(79), eff. Sept. 1, 2001. Amended by Acts 2001, 77th Leg., ch. 251, §3, eff. Sept. 1, 2001.

H&SC §481.0621. EXCEPTIONS

(a) This subchapter does not apply to an educational or research program of a school district or a public or private institution of higher education. This subchapter does not apply to a manufacturer, wholesaler, retailer, or other person who sells, transfers, or furnishes materials covered by this subchapter to those educational or research programs.

(b) The department and the Texas Higher Education Coordinating Board shall adopt a memorandum of understanding that establishes the responsibilities of the board, the department, and the public or private institutions of higher education in implementing and maintaining a program for reporting information concerning controlled substances, controlled substance analogues, chemical precursors, and chemical laboratory apparatus used in educational or research activities of institutions of higher education.

(c) The department and the Texas Education Agency shall adopt a memorandum of understanding that establishes the responsibilities of the agency, the department, and school districts in implementing and maintaining a program for reporting information concerning controlled substances, controlled substance analogues, chemical precursors, and chemical laboratory apparatus used in educational or research activities of those schools and school districts.

History of H&SC §481.0621: Acts 1989, 71st Leg., ch. 1100, §5.02(e), eff. Sept. 1, 1989. Amended by Acts 1997, 75th Leg., ch. 745, §7 (eff. Sept. 1, 1997), ch. 165, §6.45 (eff. Sept. 1, 1997).

ANNOTATIONS

Lopez v. State, 837 S.W.2d 863, 865-66 (Tex.App.—Houston [1st Dist.] 1992, no pet.). Defendant's "argument centers around his perceived conflict between the tax and the classification of marihuana as a controlled substance. [D] wants this Court to hold that if the State chooses to tax a substance, it must declare it legal no matter who possesses the substance. This argument is without merit. There are situations in which one can legally possess a controlled substance. There are also situations in which the possession of marihuana does not require the tax stamp."

H&SC §481.063. REGISTRATION APPLICATION; ISSUANCE OR DENIAL

(a) The director may refuse to issue a registration to a person to manufacture, distribute, analyze, or conduct research with a controlled substance if the person fails or refuses to provide to the director a consent form signed by the person granting the director the right to inspect the person's controlled premises and any record, controlled substance, or other item covered by this chapter.

(b) The director may not issue a registration to a person to dispense a controlled substance unless the director receives a consent form signed by the person granting the director the right to inspect records as required by this chapter.

(c) The director shall register a person to manufacture, distribute, or analyze a controlled substance listed in Schedules II through V if:

(1) the person furnishes the director evidence that the person is registered for that purpose under the Federal Controlled Substances Act;[1]

(2) the person has made proper application and paid the applicable fee; and

(3) the person has not been found by the director to have violated a provision of Subsection (e).

(d) The director shall register a person to dispense or conduct research with a controlled substance listed in Schedules II through V if the person:

(1) is a practitioner licensed under the laws of this state;

(2) has made proper application and paid the applicable fee; and

(3) has not been found by the director to have violated a provision of Subsection (e).

(e) An application for registration to manufacture, distribute, analyze, dispense, or conduct research with a controlled substance may be denied on a finding that the applicant:

(1) has furnished material information in an application filed under this chapter that the applicant knows is false or fraudulent;

(2) has been convicted of or placed on community supervision or other probation for:

(A) a felony;

(B) a violation of this chapter or of Chapters 482-485; or

(C) an offense reasonably related to the registration sought;

(3) has voluntarily surrendered or has had suspended, denied, or revoked a registration or application for registration to manufacture, distribute, analyze, or dispense controlled substances under the Federal Controlled Substances Act;[1]

(4) has had suspended, probated, or revoked a registration or a practitioner's license under the laws of this state or another state;

(5) has intentionally or knowingly failed to establish and maintain effective security controls against diversion of controlled substances into other than legitimate medical, scientific, or industrial channels as provided by federal regulations or laws, this chapter, or a rule adopted under this chapter;

(6) has intentionally or knowingly failed to maintain records required to be kept by this chapter or a rule adopted under this chapter;

(7) has refused to allow an inspection authorized by this chapter or a rule adopted under this chapter;

(8) has intentionally or knowingly violated this chapter or a rule adopted under this chapter; or

(9) has voluntarily surrendered a registration that has not been reinstated.

(f) The director may inspect the premises or establishment of an applicant for registration in accordance with this chapter.

(g) A registration is valid until the first anniversary of the date of issuance and may be renewed annually under rules adopted by the director, unless a rule provides for a longer period of validity or renewal.

(h) Chapter 2001, Government Code, does not apply to a denial of a registration under Subsection (e)(2)(A) or (B), (e)(3), (e)(4), or (e)(9).

(i) For good cause shown, the director may probate the denial of an application for registration. If a denial of an application is probated, the director may require the person to report regularly to the department on matters that are the basis of the probation or may limit activities of the person to those prescribed by the director, or both.

1. **Editor's note:** 21 U.S.C. §801 et seq.

History of H&SC §481.063: Acts 1989, 71st Leg., ch. 678, §1, ch. 1100, §5.02(f) (eff. Sept. 1, 1989). Amended by Acts 1993, 73rd Leg., ch. 76, §5.95(49) (eff. Sept. 1, 1995), ch. 790, §19 (eff. Sept. 1, 1995); Acts 1997, 75th Leg., ch. 745, §8, eff. Sept. 1, 1997; Acts 2001, 77th Leg., ch. 251, §4, eff. Sept. 1, 2001.

H&SC §481.064. REGISTRATION FEES

A **(a)** The director may charge a nonrefundable fee of not more than $25 before processing an application for annual registration and may charge a late fee of not more than $50 for each application for renewal the department receives after the date the registration expires. The director by rule shall set the amounts of the fees at the amounts that are necessary to cover the cost of administering and enforcing this subchapter. Except as provided by Subsection (b), registrants shall pay the fees to the director. Not later than 60 days before the date the registration expires, the director shall send a renewal notice to the registrant at the last known address of the registrant according to department records.

(b) The director may authorize a contract between the department and an appropriate state agency for the collection and remittance of the fees. The director by rule may provide for remittance of the fees collected by state agencies for the department.

(c) The director shall deposit the collected fees to the credit of the operator's and chauffeur's license account in the general revenue fund. The fees may be used only by the department in the administration or enforcement of this subchapter.

History of H&SC §481.064: Acts 1989, 71st Leg., ch. 678, §1, eff. Sept. 1, 1989. Amended by Acts 1997, 75th Leg., ch. 745, §9, eff. Sept. 1, 1997; Acts 2001, 77th Leg., ch. 251, §5, eff. Sept. 1, 2001; Acts 2007, 80th Leg., ch. 1391, §1, eff. Sept. 1, 2007.

H&SC §481.065. AUTHORIZATION FOR CERTAIN ACTIVITIES

(a) The director may authorize the possession, distribution, planting, and cultivation of controlled substances by a person engaged in research, training animals to detect controlled substances, or designing or calibrating devices to detect controlled substances. A person who obtains an authorization under this subsection does not commit an offense involving the possession or distribution of controlled substances to the extent that the possession or distribution is authorized.

(b) A person may conduct research with or analyze substances listed in Schedule I in this state only if the person is a practitioner registered under federal law to conduct research with or analyze those substances and the person provides the director with evidence of federal registration.

History of H&SC §481.065: Acts 1989, 71st Leg., ch. 678, §1, eff. Sept. 1, 1989.

H&SC §481.066. VOLUNTARY SURRENDER, CANCELLATION, SUSPENSION, PROBATION, OR REVOCATION OF REGISTRATION

(a) The director may accept a voluntary surrender of a registration.

(b) The director may cancel, suspend, or revoke a registration, place on probation a person whose license has been suspended, or reprimand a registrant for a cause described by Section 481.063(e).

(c) The director may cancel a registration that was issued in error.

(d) The director may limit the cancellation, suspension, probation, or revocation to the particular schedule or controlled substance within a schedule for which grounds for cancellation, suspension, probation, or revocation exist.

(e) After accepting the voluntary surrender of a registration or ordering the cancellation, suspension, probation, or revocation of a registration, the director may seize or place under seal all controlled substances owned or possessed by the registrant under the authority of that registration. If the director orders the cancellation, suspension, probation, or revocation of a registration, a disposition may not be made of the seized or sealed substances until the time for administrative appeal of the order has elapsed or until all appeals have been concluded, except that the director may order the sale of perishable substances and deposit of the proceeds of the sale in a special interest-bearing account in the general revenue fund. When a surrender or cancellation, suspension, probation, or revocation order becomes final, all controlled substances may be forfeited to the state as provided under Subchapter E.

(f) The operation of a registrant in violation of this section is a public nuisance, and the director may apply to any court of competent jurisdiction for an injunction suspending the registration of the registrant.

(g) Chapter 2001, Government Code, applies to a proceeding under this section to the extent that that chapter does not conflict with this subchapter. Chapter 2001, Government Code, does not apply to a cancellation, suspension, probation, or revocation of a registration for a cause described by Section 481.063(e)(2)(A) or (B), (e)(3), (e)(4), or (e)(9).

(h) The director shall promptly notify appropriate state agencies of an order accepting a voluntary surrender or canceling, suspending, probating, or revoking a registration and the forfeiture of controlled substances.

(i) The director shall give written notice to the applicant or registrant of the acceptance of a voluntary surrender of a registration, or of the cancellation, suspension, probation, revocation, or denial of a registration. The notice shall be sent by certified mail, return receipt requested, to the most current address of the applicant or registrant contained in department files.

(j) After a voluntary surrender, cancellation, suspension, probation, revocation, or denial of a registration, on petition of the applicant or former registrant, the director may issue or reinstate the registration for good cause shown by the petitioner.

History of H&SC §481.066: Acts 1989, 71st Leg., ch. 678, §1, eff. Sept. 1, 1989. Amended by Acts 1997, 75th Leg., ch. 745, §10, eff. Sept. 1, 1997; Acts 2001, 77th Leg., ch. 251, §6, eff. Sept. 1, 2001.

H&SC §481.067. RECORDS

(a) A person who is registered to manufacture, distribute, analyze, or dispense a controlled substance shall keep records and maintain inventories in compliance with recordkeeping and inventory requirements of federal law and with additional rules the director adopts.

(b) The pharmacist-in-charge of a pharmacy shall maintain the records and inventories required by this section.

(c) A record required by this section must be made at the time of the transaction that is the basis of the record. A record or inventory required by this section must be kept or maintained for at least two years after the date the record or inventory is made.

History of H&SC §481.067: Acts 1989, 71st Leg., ch. 678, §1, eff. Sept. 1, 1989. Amended by Acts 2001, 77th Leg., ch. 251, §7, eff. Sept. 1, 2001.

H&SC §481.068. CONFIDENTIALITY

(a) The director may authorize a person engaged in research on the use and effects of a controlled substance to withhold the names and other identifying characteristics of individuals who are the subjects of the research. A person who obtains the authorization may not be compelled in a civil, criminal, administrative, legislative, or other proceeding to identify the individuals who are the subjects of the research for which the authorization is obtained.

(b) Except as provided by Sections 481.074 and 481.075, a practitioner engaged in authorized medical practice or research may not be required to furnish the name or identity of a patient or research subject to the department, the director of the Texas Commission on Alcohol and Drug Abuse, or any other agency, public official, or law enforcement officer. A practitioner may not be compelled in a state or local civil, criminal, administrative, legislative, or other proceeding to furnish the name or identity of an individual that the practitioner is obligated to keep confidential.

(c) The director may not provide to a federal, state, or local law enforcement agency the name or identity of a patient or research subject whose identity could not be obtained under Subsection (b).

History of H&SC §481.068: Acts 1989, 71st Leg., ch. 678, §1, eff. Sept. 1, 1989. Amended by Acts 2001, 77th Leg., ch. 251, §8, eff. Sept. 1, 2001.

H&SC §481.069. ORDER FORMS

A registrant may not distribute or order a controlled substance listed in Schedule I or II to or from another registrant except under an order form. A registrant complying with the federal law concerning order forms is in compliance with this section.

History of H&SC §481.069: Acts 1989, 71st Leg., ch. 678, §1 (eff. Sept. 1, 1989), ch. 1100, §5.02(g) (eff. Sept. 1, 1989).

H&SC §481.070. ADMINISTERING OR DISPENSING SCHEDULE I CONTROLLED SUBSTANCE

Except as permitted by this chapter, a person may not administer or dispense a controlled substance listed in Schedule I.

History of H&SC §481.070: Acts 1989, 71st Leg., ch. 678, §1, eff. Sept. 1, 1989.

H&SC §481.071. MEDICAL PURPOSE REQUIRED BEFORE PRESCRIBING, DISPENSING, DELIVERING, OR ADMINISTERING CONTROLLED SUBSTANCE

(a) A practitioner defined by Section 481.002(39)(A) may not prescribe, dispense, deliver, or administer a controlled substance or cause a controlled substance to be administered under the practitioner's direction and supervision except for a valid medical purpose and in the course of medical practice.

(b) An anabolic steroid or human growth hormone listed in Schedule III may only be:

(1) dispensed, prescribed, delivered, or administered by a practitioner, as defined by Section 481.002(39)(A), for a valid medical purpose and in the course of professional practice; or

(2) dispensed or delivered by a pharmacist according to a prescription issued by a practitioner, as defined by Section 481.002(39)(A) or (C), for a valid medical purpose and in the course of professional practice.

(c) For the purposes of Subsection (b), bodybuilding, muscle enhancement, or increasing muscle bulk or strength through the use of an anabolic steroid or human growth hormone listed in Schedule III by a person who is in good health is not a valid medical purpose.

History of H&SC §481.071: Acts 1989, 71st Leg., ch. 678, §1 (eff. Sept. 1, 1989), ch. 1100, §5.03(b) (eff. Sept. 1, 1989). Amended by Acts 1997, 75th Leg., ch. 745, §11, eff. Sept. 1, 1997.

H&SC §481.072. MEDICAL PURPOSE REQUIRED BEFORE DISTRIBUTING OR DISPENSING SCHEDULE V CONTROLLED SUBSTANCE

A person may not distribute or dispense a controlled substance listed in Schedule V except for a valid medical purpose.

History of H&SC §481.072: Acts 1989, 71st Leg., ch. 678, §1, eff. Sept. 1, 1989.

TCSA §481.067

H&SC §481.073. COMMUNICATION OF PRESCRIPTIONS BY AGENT

(a) Only a practitioner defined by Section 481.002(39)(A) and an agent designated in writing by the practitioner in accordance with rules adopted by the department may communicate a prescription by telephone. A pharmacy that receives a telephonically communicated prescription shall promptly write the prescription and file and retain the prescription in the manner required by this subchapter. A practitioner who designates an agent to communicate prescriptions shall maintain the written designation of the agent in the practitioner's usual place of business and shall make the designation available for inspection by investigators for the Texas State Board of Medical Examiners, the State Board of Dental Examiners, the State Board of Veterinary Medical Examiners, and the department. A practitioner who designates a different agent shall designate that agent in writing and maintain the designation in the same manner in which the practitioner initially designated an agent under this section.

(b) On the request of a pharmacist, a practitioner shall furnish a copy of the written designation authorized under Subsection (a).

(c) This section does not relieve a practitioner or the practitioner's designated agent from the requirement of Subchapter A, Chapter 562, Occupations Code. A practitioner is personally responsible for the actions of the designated agent in communicating a prescription to a pharmacist.

History of H&SC §481.073: Acts 1989, 71st Leg., ch. 678, §1, eff. Sept. 1, 1989. Amended by Acts 2001, 77th Leg., ch. 251, §9 (eff. Sept. 1, 2001), ch. 1420, §14.794 (eff. Sept. 1, 2001).

H&SC §481.074. PRESCRIPTIONS

(a) A pharmacist may not:

(1) dispense or deliver a controlled substance or cause a controlled substance to be dispensed or delivered under the pharmacist's direction or supervision except under a valid prescription and in the course of professional practice;

(2) dispense a controlled substance if the pharmacist knows or should have known that the prescription was issued without a valid patient-practitioner relationship;

(3) fill a prescription that is not prepared or issued as prescribed by this chapter;

(4) permit or allow a person who is not a licensed pharmacist or pharmacist intern to dispense, distribute, or in any other manner deliver a controlled substance even if under the supervision of a pharmacist, except that after the pharmacist or pharmacist intern has fulfilled his professional and legal responsibilities, a nonpharmacist may complete the actual cash or credit transaction and delivery; or

(5) permit the delivery of a controlled substance to any person not known to the pharmacist, the pharmacist intern, or the person authorized by the pharmacist to deliver the controlled substance without first requiring identification of the person taking possession of the controlled substance, except as provided by Subsection (n).

(b) Except in an emergency as defined by rule of the director or as provided by Subsection (o) or Section 481.075(j) or (m), a person may not dispense or administer a controlled substance listed in Schedule II without the written prescription of a practitioner on an official prescription form that meets the requirements of and is completed by the practitioner in accordance with Section 481.075. In an emergency, a person may dispense or administer a controlled substance listed in Schedule II on the oral or telephonically communicated prescription of a practitioner. The person who administers or dispenses the substance shall:

(1) if the person is a prescribing practitioner or a pharmacist, promptly comply with Subsection (c); or

(2) if the person is not a prescribing practitioner or a pharmacist, promptly write the oral or telephonically communicated prescription and include in the written record of the prescription the name, address, department registration number, and Federal Drug Enforcement Administration number of the prescribing practitioner, all information required to be provided by a practitioner under Section 481.075(e)(1), and all information required to be provided by a dispensing pharmacist under Section 481.075(e)(2).

(c) Not later than the seventh day after the date a prescribing practitioner authorizes an emergency oral or telephonically communicated prescription, the prescribing practitioner shall cause a written prescription, completed in the manner required by Section 481.075, to be delivered in person or mailed to the dispensing pharmacist at the pharmacy where the prescription was dispensed. The envelope of a prescription delivered by mail must be postmarked not later than the seventh day after the date the prescription was authorized. On receipt of the prescription, the dispensing pharmacy shall file the transcription of the telephonically communicated prescription and the pharmacy copy and shall send information to the director as required by Section 481.075.

🄰 (d) Except as specified in Subsections (e) and (f), the director, by rule and in consultation with the Texas Medical Board and the Texas State Board of Pharmacy, shall establish the period after the date on which the prescription is issued that a person may fill a prescription for a controlled substance listed in Schedule II. A person may not refill a prescription for a substance listed in Schedule II.

(e) The partial filling of a prescription for a controlled substance listed in Schedule II is permissible, if the pharmacist is unable to supply the full quantity called for in a written or emergency oral prescription and the pharmacist makes a notation of the quantity supplied on the face of the written prescription or written record of the emergency oral prescription. The remaining portion of the prescription may be filled within 72 hours of the first partial filling; however, if the remaining portion is not or cannot be filled within the 72-hour period, the pharmacist shall so notify the prescribing individual practitioner. No further quantity may be supplied beyond 72 hours without a new prescription.

(f) A prescription for a Schedule II controlled substance written for a patient in a long-term care facility (LTCF) or for a patient with a medical diagnosis documenting a terminal illness may be filled in partial quantities to include individual dosage units. If there is any question about whether a patient may be classified as having a terminal illness, the pharmacist must contact the practitioner before partially filling the prescription. Both the pharmacist and the practitioner have a corresponding responsibility to assure that the controlled substance is for a terminally ill patient. The pharmacist must record the prescription on an official prescription form and must indicate on the form whether the patient is "terminally ill" or an "LTCF patient." A prescription that is partially filled and does not contain the notation "terminally ill" or "LTCF patient" is considered to have been filled in violation of this chapter. For each partial filling, the dispensing pharmacist shall record on the back of the official prescription form the date of the partial filling, the quantity dispensed, the remaining quantity authorized to be dispensed, and the identification of the dispensing pharmacist. Before any subsequent partial filling, the pharmacist must determine

that the additional partial filling is necessary. The total quantity of Schedule II controlled substances dispensed in all partial fillings may not exceed the total quantity prescribed. Schedule II prescriptions for patients in a long-term care facility or patients with a medical diagnosis documenting a terminal illness are valid for a period not to exceed 60 days following the issue date unless sooner terminated by discontinuance of the medication.

🄰 *Subsections (g) & (h) below are effective for conduct occurring on or after Sept. 1, 2007.*

(g) A person may not dispense a controlled substance in Schedule III or IV that is a prescription drug under the Federal Food, Drug, and Cosmetic Act (21 U.S.C. Section 301 et seq.) without a written, oral, or telephonically or electronically communicated prescription of a practitioner defined by Section 481.002(39)(A) or (D), except that the practitioner may dispense the substance directly to an ultimate user. A prescription for a controlled substance listed in Schedule III or IV may not be filled or refilled later than six months after the date on which the prescription is issued and may not be refilled more than five times, unless the prescription is renewed by the practitioner. A prescription under this subsection must comply with other applicable state and federal laws.

(h) A pharmacist may dispense a controlled substance listed in Schedule III, IV, or V under a written, oral, or telephonically or electronically communicated prescription issued by a practitioner defined by Section 481.002(39)(C) and only if the pharmacist determines that the prescription was issued for a valid medical purpose and in the course of professional practice. A prescription issued under this subsection may not be filled or refilled later than six months after the date the prescription is issued and may not be refilled more than five times, unless the prescription is renewed by the practitioner.

Subsections (g) & (h) below are effective for conduct occurring before Sept. 1, 2007.

(g) A person may not dispense a controlled substance in Schedule III or IV that is a prescription drug under the Federal Food, Drug, and Cosmetic Act (21 U.S.C. Section 301 et seq.) without a written, oral, or telephonically communicated prescription of a practitioner defined by Section 481.002(39)(A), except that the practitioner may dispense the substance directly to an ultimate user. A prescription for a controlled substance listed in Schedule III or IV may not be filled or refilled later than six months after the date on which the prescription is issued and may not be refilled more than five times, unless the prescription is renewed by the practitioner.

(h) A pharmacist may dispense a controlled substance listed in Schedule III, IV, or V under an original written prescription issued by a practitioner defined by Section 481.002(39)(C) and only if the pharmacist determines that the prescription was issued for a valid medical purpose and in the course of professional practice. A prescription issued under this subsection may not be filled or refilled later than six months after the date the prescription is issued, and a prescription authorized to be refilled on the original prescription may not be refilled more than five times.

(i) A person may not dispense a controlled substance listed in Schedule V and containing 200 milligrams or less of codeine, or any of its salts, per 100 milliliters or per 100 grams, or containing 100 milligrams or less of dihydrocodeine, or any of its salts, per 100 milliliters or per 100 grams, without the prescription of a practitioner defined by Section 481.002(39)(A), except that a practitioner may dispense the substance directly to an ultimate user. A prescription issued under this subsection may not be filled or refilled later than six months after the date the prescription is issued and may not be refilled more than five times, unless the prescription is renewed by the practitioner.

(j) A practitioner or institutional practitioner may not allow a patient, on the patient's release from the hospital, to possess a controlled substance prescribed by the practitioner unless:

(1) the substance was dispensed under a medication order while the patient was admitted to the hospital;

(2) the substance is in a properly labeled container; and

(3) the patient possesses not more than a seven-day supply of the substance.

(k) A prescription for a controlled substance must show:

(1) the quantity of the substance prescribed:

(A) numerically, followed by the number written as a word, if the prescription is written; or

(B) if the prescription is communicated orally or telephonically, as transcribed by the receiving pharmacist;

(2) the date of issue;

🅐 (3) the name, address, and date of birth or age of the patient or, if the controlled substance is prescribed for an animal, the species of the animal and the name and address of its owner;

(4) the name and strength of the controlled substance prescribed;

(5) the directions for use of the controlled substance;

(6) the intended use of the substance prescribed unless the practitioner determines the furnishing of this information is not in the best interest of the patient;

(7) the legibly printed or stamped name, address, Federal Drug Enforcement Administration registration number, and telephone number of the practitioner at the practitioner's usual place of business;

🅔 *Subsections (8) & (9) below are effective when the Department of Public Safety establishes a means for pharmacies to electronically access and verify registration numbers.*

(8) if the prescription is handwritten, the signature of the prescribing practitioner; and

(9) if the prescribing practitioner is licensed in this state, the practitioner's department registration number.

(*l*) A pharmacist may exercise his professional judgment in refilling a prescription for a controlled substance in Schedule III, IV, or V without the authorization of the prescribing practitioner provided:

(1) failure to refill the prescription might result in an interruption of a therapeutic regimen or create patient suffering;

(2) either:

(A) a natural or manmade disaster has occurred which prohibits the pharmacist from being able to contact the practitioner; or

(B) the pharmacist is unable to contact the practitioner after reasonable effort;

(3) the quantity of prescription drug dispensed does not exceed a 72-hour supply;

(4) the pharmacist informs the patient or the patient's agent at the time of dispensing that the refill is

being provided without such authorization and that authorization of the practitioner is required for future refills; and

(5) the pharmacist informs the practitioner of the emergency refill at the earliest reasonable time.

 (*l*-1) Notwithstanding Subsection (*l*), in the event of a natural or manmade disaster, a pharmacist may dispense not more than a 30-day supply of a prescription drug, other than a controlled substance listed in Schedule II, without the authorization of the prescribing practitioner if:

(1) failure to refill the prescription might result in an interruption of a therapeutic regimen or create patient suffering;

(2) the natural or manmade disaster prohibits the pharmacist from being able to contact the practitioner;

(3) the governor has declared a state of disaster under Chapter 418, Government Code; and

(4) the Texas State Board of Pharmacy, through its executive director, has notified pharmacies in this state that pharmacists may dispense up to a 30-day supply of a prescription drug.

 (*l*-2) The prescribing practitioner is not liable for an act or omission by a pharmacist in dispensing a prescription drug under Subsection (*l*-1).

(m) A pharmacist may permit the delivery of a controlled substance by an authorized delivery person, by a person known to the pharmacist, a pharmacist intern, or the authorized delivery person, or by mail to the person or address of the person authorized by the prescription to receive the controlled substance. If a pharmacist permits delivery of a controlled substance under this subsection, the pharmacist shall retain in the records of the pharmacy for a period of not less than two years:

(1) the name of the authorized delivery person, if delivery is made by that person;

(2) the name of the person known to the pharmacist, a pharmacist intern, or the authorized delivery person if delivery is made by that person; or

(3) the mailing address to which delivery is made, if delivery is made by mail.

(n) A pharmacist may permit the delivery of a controlled substance to a person not known to the pharmacist, a pharmacist intern, or the authorized delivery person without first requiring the identification of the person to whom the controlled substance is delivered if the pharmacist determines that an emergency exists

and that the controlled substance is needed for the immediate well-being of the patient for whom the controlled substance is prescribed. If a pharmacist permits delivery of a controlled substance under this subsection, the pharmacist shall retain in the records of the pharmacy for a period of not less than two years all information relevant to the delivery known to the pharmacist, including the name, address, and date of birth or age of the person to whom the controlled substance is delivered.

(o) A pharmacist may dispense a Schedule II controlled substance pursuant to a facsimile copy of an official prescription completed in the manner required by Section 481.075 and transmitted by the practitioner or the practitioner's agent to the pharmacy if:

(1) the prescription is written for:

(A) a Schedule II narcotic or nonnarcotic substance for a patient in a long-term care facility (LTCF), and the practitioner notes on the prescription "LTCF patient";

(B) a Schedule II narcotic product to be compounded for the direct administration to a patient by parenteral, intravenous, intramuscular, subcutaneous, or intraspinal infusion; or

(C) a Schedule II narcotic substance for a patient with a medical diagnosis documenting a terminal illness or a patient enrolled in a hospice care program certified or paid for by Medicare under Title XVIII, Social Security Act (42 U.S.C. Section 1395 et seq.), as amended, by Medicaid, or by a hospice program that is licensed under Chapter 142, and the practitioner or the practitioner's agent notes on the prescription "terminally ill" or "hospice patient"; and

(2) after transmitting the prescription, the prescribing practitioner or the practitioner's agent:

(A) writes across the face of the official prescription "VOID—sent by fax to (name and telephone number of receiving pharmacy)"; and

(B) files the official prescription in the patient's medical records instead of delivering it to the patient.

(p) On receipt of the prescription, the dispensing pharmacy shall file the facsimile copy of the prescription and shall send information to the director as required by Section 481.075.

 (q) Each dispensing pharmacist shall send all information required by the director, including any information required to complete the Schedule III through V prescription forms, to the director by electronic transfer or another form approved by the director not later than the 15th day after the last day of the month in which the prescription is completely filled.

History of H&SC §481.074: Acts 1989, 71st Leg., ch. 678, §1 (eff. Sept. 1, 1989), ch. 1100, §5.02(h) (eff. Sept. 1, 1989). Amended by Acts 1991, 72nd Leg., ch. 615, §10 (eff. Sept. 1, 1991), ch. 761, §6 (eff. Sept. 1, 1991); Acts 1993, 73rd Leg., ch. 351, §28 (eff. Sept. 1, 1993), ch. 789, §16 (eff. Sept. 1, 1993); Acts 1997, 75th Leg., ch. 745, §§12, 13, eff. Sept. 1, 1997; Acts 1999, 76th Leg., ch. 145, §2, eff. Sept. 1, 1999; Acts 2001, 77th Leg., ch. 251, §10 (eff. Sept. 1, 2001), ch. 1254, §10 (eff. Sept. 1, 2001); Acts 2005, 79th Leg., ch. 349, §21(a) (eff. Sept. 1, 2005), ch. 1345, §44(a) (eff. June 18, 2005); Acts 2007, 80th Leg., ch. 535, §1 (eff. Sept. 1, 2007), ch. 567, §2 (eff. Sept. 1, 2007), ch. 1391, §2 (eff. Sept. 1, 2008, or when Department of Public Safety satisfies certain conditions).

H&SC §481.075. OFFICIAL PRESCRIPTION PROGRAM

(a) A practitioner who prescribes a controlled substance listed in Schedule II shall, except as provided by rule adopted under Section 481.0761, record the prescription on an official prescription form that includes the information required by this section.

(b) Each official prescription form must be sequentially numbered.

(c) The director shall issue official prescription forms to practitioners for a fee covering the actual cost of printing, processing, and mailing the forms at 100 a package. Before mailing or otherwise delivering prescription forms to a practitioner, the director shall print on each form the number of the form and any other information the director determines is necessary.

(d) A person may not obtain an official prescription form unless the person is a practitioner as defined by Section 481.002(39)(A) or an institutional practitioner.

(e) Each official prescription form used to prescribe a Schedule II controlled substance must contain:

(1) information provided by the prescribing practitioner, including:

(A) the date the prescription is written;

(B) the controlled substance prescribed;

(C) the quantity of controlled substance prescribed, shown numerically followed by the number written as a word;

(D) the intended use of the controlled substance or the diagnosis for which it is prescribed and the instructions for use of the substance;

(E) the practitioner's name, address, department registration number, and Federal Drug Enforcement Administration number; and

(F) the name, address, and date of birth or age of the person for whom the controlled substance is prescribed;

(2) information provided by the dispensing pharmacist, including the date the prescription is filled; and

(3) the signatures of the prescribing practitioner and the dispensing pharmacist.

(f) Not more than one prescription may be recorded on an official prescription form, except as provided by rule adopted under Section 481.0761.

(g) Except for an oral prescription prescribed under Section 481.074(b), the prescribing practitioner shall:

(1) legibly fill in, or direct a designated agent to legibly fill in, on the official prescription form, each item of information required to be provided by the prescribing practitioner under Subsection (e)(1), unless the practitioner determines that:

(A) under rule adopted by the director for this purpose, it is unnecessary for the practitioner or the practitioner's agent to provide the patient identification number; or

(B) it is not in the best interest of the patient for the practitioner or practitioner's agent to provide information regarding the intended use of the controlled substance or the diagnosis for which it is prescribed; and

(2) sign the official prescription form and give the form to the person authorized to receive the prescription.

(h) In the case of an oral prescription prescribed under Section 481.074(b), the prescribing practitioner shall give the dispensing pharmacy the information needed to complete the form.

(i) Each dispensing pharmacist shall:

(1) fill in on the official prescription form each item of information given orally to the dispensing pharmacy under Subsection (h), the date the prescription is filled, and the dispensing pharmacist's signature;

(2) retain with the records of the pharmacy for at least two years:

(A) the official prescription form; and

(B) the name or other patient identification required by Section 481.074(m) or (n); and

(3) send all information required by the director, including any information required to complete an official prescription form, to the director by electronic transfer or another form approved by the director not later than the 15th day after the last day of the month in which the prescription is completely filled.

(j) A medication order written for a patient who is admitted to a hospital at the time the medication order is written and filled is not required to be on a form that meets the requirements of this section.

(k) Not later than the 30th day after the date a practitioner's department registration number, Federal Drug Enforcement Administration number, or license to practice has been denied, suspended, canceled, surrendered, or revoked, the practitioner shall return to the department all official prescription forms in the practitioner's possession that have not been used for prescriptions.

(*l*) Each prescribing practitioner:

(1) may use an official prescription form only to prescribe a controlled substance;

(2) shall date or sign an official prescription form only on the date the prescription is issued; and

(3) shall take reasonable precautionary measures to ensure that an official prescription form issued to the practitioner is not used by another person to violate this subchapter or a rule adopted under this subchapter.

(m) A pharmacy in this state may fill a prescription for a controlled substance listed in Schedule II issued by a practitioner in another state if:

(1) a share of the pharmacy's business involves the dispensing and delivery or mailing of controlled substances;

(2) the prescription is issued by a prescribing practitioner in the other state in the ordinary course of practice; and

(3) the prescription is filled in compliance with a written plan providing the manner in which the pharmacy may fill a Schedule II prescription issued by a practitioner in another state that:

(A) is submitted by the pharmacy to the director; and

(B) is approved by the director in consultation with the Texas State Board of Pharmacy.

(n) Repealed by Acts 1999, 76th Leg., ch. 145, §5(2), eff. Sept. 1, 1999.

History of H&SC §481.075: Acts 1989, 71st Leg., ch. 678, §1 (eff. Sept. 1, 1989), ch. 1100, §5.02(i) (eff. Sept. 1, 1989). Amended by Acts 1993, 73rd Leg., ch. 789, §17, eff. Sept. 1, 1993; Acts 1997, 75th Leg., ch. 745, §14, eff. Sept. 1, 1999; Acts 1999, 76th Leg., ch. 145, §§3, 5(2), eff. Sept. 1, 1999; Acts 2001, 77th Leg., ch. 251, §11, eff. Sept. 1, 2001.

H&SC §481.076. OFFICIAL PRESCRIPTION INFORMATION

(a) The director may not permit any person to have access to information submitted to the director under Section 481.074(q) or 481.075 except:

(1) an investigator for the Texas Medical Board, the Texas State Board of Podiatric Medical Examiners, the State Board of Dental Examiners, the State Board of Veterinary Medical Examiners, or the Texas State Board of Pharmacy;

(2) an authorized officer or member of the department engaged in the administration, investigation, or enforcement of this chapter or another law governing illicit drugs in this state or another state; or

(3) if the director finds that proper need has been shown to the director:

(A) a law enforcement or prosecutorial official engaged in the administration, investigation, or enforcement of this chapter or another law governing illicit drugs in this state or another state;

(B) a pharmacist or practitioner who is a physician, dentist, veterinarian, podiatrist, or advanced practice nurse or physician assistant described by Section 481.002(39)(D) and is inquiring about a recent Schedule II, III, IV, or V prescription history of a particular patient of the practitioner; or

(C) a pharmacist or practitioner who is inquiring about the person's own dispensing or prescribing activity.

(b) This section does not prohibit the director from creating, using, or disclosing statistical data about information received by the director under this section if the director removes any information reasonably likely to reveal the identity of each patient, practitioner, or other person who is a subject of the information.

(c) The director by rule shall design and implement a system for submission of information to the director by electronic or other means and for retrieval of information submitted to the director under this section and Sections 481.074 and 481.075. The director shall use automated information security techniques and devices to preclude improper access to the information. The director shall submit the system design to the Texas State Board of Pharmacy and the Texas Medical Board for review and approval or comment a reasonable time before implementation of the system and shall comply with the comments of those agencies unless it is unreasonable to do so.

TCSA §481.075

(d) Information submitted to the director under this section may be used only for:

(1) the administration, investigation, or enforcement of this chapter or another law governing illicit drugs in this state or another state;

(2) investigatory or evidentiary purposes in connection with the functions of an agency listed in Subsection (a)(1); or

(3) dissemination by the director to the public in the form of a statistical tabulation or report if all information reasonably likely to reveal the identity of each patient, practitioner, or other person who is a subject of the information has been removed.

(e) The director shall remove from the information retrieval system, destroy, and make irretrievable the record of the identity of a patient submitted under this section to the director not later than the end of the 12th calendar month after the month in which the identity is entered into the system. However, the director may retain a patient identity that is necessary for use in a specific ongoing investigation conducted in accordance with this section until the 30th day after the end of the month in which the necessity for retention of the identity ends.

(f) If the director permits access to information under Subsection (a)(2) relating to a person licensed or regulated by an agency listed in Subsection (a)(1), the director shall notify and cooperate with that agency regarding the disposition of the matter before taking action against the person, unless the director determines that notification is reasonably likely to interfere with an administrative or criminal investigation or prosecution.

(g) If the director permits access to information under Subsection (a)(3)(A) relating to a person licensed or regulated by an agency listed in Subsection (a)(1), the director shall notify that agency of the disclosure of the information not later than the 10th working day after the date the information is disclosed.

(h) If the director withholds notification to an agency under Subsection (f), the director shall notify the agency of the disclosure of the information and the reason for withholding notification when the director determines that notification is no longer likely to interfere with an administrative or criminal investigation or prosecution.

(i) Information submitted to the director under Section 481.075 is confidential and remains confidential regardless of whether the director permits access to the information under this section.

(j) Repealed by Acts 1999, 76th Leg., ch. 145, §5(3), eff. Sept. 1, 1999.

History of H&SC §481.076: Acts 1989, 71st Leg., ch. 678, §1, eff. Sept. 1, 1989. Amended by Acts 1995, 74th Leg., ch. 965, §81, eff. June 16, 1995; Acts 1997, 75th Leg., ch. 745, §15, eff. Sept. 1, 1999; Acts 1999, 76th Leg., ch. 145, §§4, 5(3), eff. Sept. 1, 1999; Acts 2007, 80th Leg., ch. 1391, §3, eff. Sept. 1, 2008.

H&SC §481.0761. RULES; AUTHORITY TO CONTRACT

(a) The director shall consult with the Texas State Board of Pharmacy and by rule establish and revise as necessary a standardized database format that may be used by a pharmacy to transmit the information required by Sections 481.074(q) and 481.075(i) to the director electronically or to deliver the information on storage media, including disks, tapes, and cassettes.

(b) The director shall consult with the Department of State Health Services, the Texas State Board of Pharmacy, and the Texas Medical Board and by rule may:

(1) remove a controlled substance listed in Schedules II through V from the official prescription program, if the director determines that the burden imposed by the program substantially outweighs the risk of diversion of the particular controlled substance; or

(2) return a substance previously removed from Schedules II through V to the official prescription program, if the director determines that the risk of diversion substantially outweighs the burden imposed by the program on the particular controlled substance.

(c) The director by rule may:

(1) permit more than one prescription to be administered or dispensed and recorded on one prescription form for a Schedule III through V controlled substance;

(2) remove from or return to the official prescription program any aspect of a practitioner's or pharmacist's hospital practice, including administering or dispensing;

(3) waive or delay any requirement relating to the time or manner of reporting;

(4) establish compatibility protocols for electronic data transfer hardware, software, or format;

(5) establish a procedure to control the release of information under Sections 481.074, 481.075, and 481.076; and

TCSA §481.0761

(6) establish a minimum level of prescription activity below which a reporting activity may be modified or deleted.

(d) The director by rule shall authorize a practitioner to determine whether it is necessary to obtain a particular patient identification number and to provide that number on the official prescription form.

(e) In adopting a rule relating to the electronic transfer of information under this subchapter, the director shall consider the economic impact of the rule on practitioners and pharmacists and, to the extent permitted by law, act to minimize any negative economic impact, including the imposition of costs related to computer hardware or software or to the transfer of information. The director may not adopt a rule relating to the electronic transfer of information under this subchapter that imposes a fee in addition to the fees authorized by Section 481.064.

(f) The director may authorize a contract between the department and another agency of this state or a private vendor as necessary to ensure the effective operation of the official prescription program.

(g) Repealed by Acts 1999, 76th Leg., ch. 145, §5(4), eff. Sept. 1, 1999.

History of H&SC §481.0761: Acts 1997, 75th Leg., ch. 745, §16, eff. Sept. 1, 1997. Amended by Acts 1999, 76th Leg., ch. 145, §5(4), eff. Sept. 1, 1999; Acts 2007, 80th Leg., ch. 1391, §4, eff. Sept. 1, 2007.

H&SC §481.077. CHEMICAL PRECURSOR RECORDS & REPORTS

(a) Except as provided by Subsection (*l*), a person who sells, transfers, or otherwise furnishes a chemical precursor to another person shall make an accurate and legible record of the transaction and maintain the record for at least two years after the date of the transaction.

(b) The director by rule may:

(1) name an additional chemical substance as a chemical precursor for purposes of Subsection (a) if the director determines that public health and welfare are jeopardized by evidenced proliferation or use of the chemical substance in the illicit manufacture of a controlled substance or controlled substance analogue; or

(2) exempt a chemical precursor from the requirements of Subsection (a) if the director determines that the chemical precursor does not jeopardize public health and welfare or is not used in the illicit manufacture of a controlled substance or a controlled substance analogue.

(b-1) If the director names a chemical substance as a chemical precursor for purposes of Subsection (a) or designates a substance as an immediate precursor, a substance that is a precursor of the chemical precursor or the immediate precursor is not subject to control solely because it is a precursor of the chemical precursor or the immediate precursor.

(c) This section and Section 481.078 do not apply to a person to whom a registration has been issued under Section 481.063.

(d) Before selling, transferring, or otherwise furnishing to a person in this state a chemical precursor subject to Subsection (a), a manufacturer, wholesaler, retailer, or other person shall:

(1) if the recipient does not represent a business, obtain from the recipient:

(A) the recipient's driver's license number or other personal identification certificate number, date of birth, and residential or mailing address, other than a post office box number, from a driver's license or personal identification certificate issued by the department that contains a photograph of the recipient;

(B) the year, state, and number of the motor vehicle license of the motor vehicle owned or operated by the recipient;

(C) a complete description of how the chemical precursor is to be used; and

(D) the recipient's signature; or

(2) if the recipient represents a business, obtain from the recipient:

(A) a letter of authorization from the business that includes the business license or comptroller tax identification number, address, area code, and telephone number and a complete description of how the chemical precursor is to be used; and

(B) the recipient's signature; and

(3) for any recipient, sign as a witness to the signature and identification of the recipient.

(e) If the recipient does not represent a business, the recipient shall present to the manufacturer, wholesaler, retailer, or other person a permit issued in the name of the recipient by the department under Section 481.078.

(f) Except as provided by Subsection (h), a manufacturer, wholesaler, retailer, or other person who sells, transfers, or otherwise furnishes to a person in this state a chemical precursor subject to Subsection (a)

TCSA §481.0761

shall submit, at least 21 days before the delivery of the chemical precursor, a report of the transaction on a form obtained from the director that includes the information required by Subsection (d).

(**g**) The director shall supply to a manufacturer, wholesaler, retailer, or other person who sells, transfers, or otherwise furnishes a chemical precursor subject to Subsection (a) a form for the submission of:

(**1**) the report required by Subsection (f);

(**2**) the name and measured amount of the chemical precursor delivered; and

(**3**) any other information required by the director.

(**h**) The director may authorize a manufacturer, wholesaler, retailer, or other person to submit a comprehensive monthly report instead of the report required by Subsection (f) if the director determines that:

(**1**) there is a pattern of regular supply and purchase of the chemical precursor between the furnisher and the recipient; or

(**2**) the recipient has established a record of use of the chemical precursor solely for a lawful purpose.

(**i**) A manufacturer, wholesaler, retailer, or other person who receives from a source outside this state a chemical precursor subject to Subsection (a) or who discovers a loss or theft of a chemical precursor subject to Subsection (a) shall:

(**1**) submit a report of the transaction to the director in accordance with department rule; and

(**2**) include in the report:

(**A**) any difference between the amount of the chemical precursor actually received and the amount of the chemical precursor shipped according to the shipping statement or invoice; or

(**B**) the amount of the loss or theft.

(**j**) A report under Subsection (i) must:

(**1**) be made not later than the third day after the date that the manufacturer, wholesaler, retailer, or other person learns of the discrepancy, loss, or theft; and

(**2**) if the discrepancy, loss, or theft occurred during a shipment of the chemical precursor, include the name of the common carrier or person who transported the chemical precursor and the date that the chemical precursor was shipped.

(**k**) Unless the person is the holder of only a permit issued under Section 481.078(b)(1), a manufacturer, wholesaler, retailer, or other person who sells, transfers, or otherwise furnishes any chemical precursor

subject to Subsection (a) or a permit holder, commercial purchaser, or other person who receives a chemical precursor subject to Subsection (a):

(**1**) shall maintain records and inventories in accordance with rules established by the director;

(**2**) shall allow a member of the department or a peace officer to conduct audits and inspect records of purchases and sales and all other records made in accordance with this section at any reasonable time; and

(**3**) may not interfere with the audit or with the full and complete inspection or copying of those records.

(**l**) This section does not apply to the sale or transfer of any compound, mixture, or preparation containing ephedrine, pseudoephedrine, or norpseudoephedrine that is in liquid, liquid capsule, or liquid gel capsule form.

History of H&SC §481.077: Acts 1989, 71st Leg., ch. 678, §1 (eff. Sept. 1, 1989), ch. 1100, §5.02(k) (eff. Sept. 1, 1989). Amended by Acts 1997, 75th Leg., ch. 745, §17, eff. Sept. 1, 1997; Acts 2001, 77th Leg., ch. 251, §12, eff. Sept. 1, 2001; Acts 2003, 78th Leg., ch. 570, §1 (eff. Sept. 1, 2003), ch. 1099, §6 (eff. Sept. 1, 2003); Acts 2005, 79th Leg., ch. 282, §4, eff. Aug. 1, 2005.

H&SC §481.0771. RECORDS & REPORTS ON PSEUDOEPHEDRINE

(**a**) A wholesaler who sells, transfers, or otherwise furnishes a product containing ephedrine, pseudoephedrine, or norpseudoephedrine to a retailer shall:

(**1**) before delivering the product, obtain from the retailer the retailer's address, area code, and telephone number; and

(**2**) make an accurate and legible record of the transaction and maintain the record for at least two years after the date of the transaction.

(**b**) The wholesaler shall make all records available to the director in accordance with department rule, including:

(**1**) the information required by Subsection (a)(1);

(**2**) the amount of the product containing ephedrine, pseudoephedrine, or norpseudoephedrine delivered; and

(**3**) any other information required by the director.

(**c**) Not later than 10 business days after receipt of an order for a product containing ephedrine, pseudoephedrine, or norpseudoephedrine that requests delivery of a suspicious quantity of the product as determined by department rule, a wholesaler shall submit to the director a report of the order in accordance with department rule.

TCSA §481.0771

(d) A wholesaler who, with reckless disregard for the duty to report, fails to report as required by Subsection (c) may be subject to disciplinary action in accordance with department rule.

History of H&SC §481.0771: Acts 2005, 79th Leg., ch. 282, §5, eff. Aug. 1, 2005.

H&SC §481.078. CHEMICAL PRECURSOR TRANSFER PERMIT

(a) A person must obtain a chemical precursor transfer permit from the department to be eligible:

(1) to sell, transfer, or otherwise furnish a chemical precursor subject to Section 481.077(a) to a person in this state;

(2) to receive a chemical precursor subject to Section 481.077(a) from a source outside this state; or

(3) to receive a chemical precursor subject to Section 481.077(a) if the person, in receiving the chemical precursor, does not represent a business.

(b) The director by rule shall adopt procedures and standards for the issuance and renewal or the voluntary surrender, cancellation, suspension, probation, or revocation of:

(1) a permit for one sale, transfer, receipt, or otherwise furnishing of a chemical precursor; or

(2) a permit for more than one sale, transfer, receipt, or otherwise furnishing of a chemical precursor.

(c) A permit issued or renewed under Subsection (b)(1) is valid only for the transaction indicated on the permit. A permit issued or renewed under Subsection (b)(2) is valid for one year after the date of issuance or renewal.

(d) A permit holder must report in writing or by telephone to the director a change in the holder's business name, address, area code, and telephone number not later than the seventh day after the date of the change.

(e) The director may not issue a permit under this section unless the person applying for the permit delivers to the director a written consent to inspect signed by the person that grants to the director the right to inspect any controlled premises, record, chemical precursor, or other item governed by this chapter in the care, custody, or control of the person. After the director receives the consent, the director may inspect any controlled premises, record, chemical precursor, or other item to which the consent applies.

(f) The director may adopt rules to establish security controls and provide for the inspection of a place, entity, or item to which a chemical precursor transfer permit applies.

History of H&SC §481.078: Acts 1989, 71st Leg., ch. 1100, §5.02(*l*), eff. Sept. 1, 1989. Amended by Acts 1997, 75th Leg., ch. 745, §18, eff. Sept. 1, 1997; Acts 2001, 77th Leg., ch. 251, §13, eff. Sept. 1, 2001.

H&SC §481.079. REPEALED

Repealed by Acts 1997, 75th Leg., ch. 745, §37, eff. Sept. 1, 1997.

H&SC §481.080. CHEMICAL LABORATORY APPARATUS RECORD-KEEPING REQUIREMENTS & PENALTIES

(a) A manufacturer, wholesaler, retailer, or other person who sells, transfers, or otherwise furnishes a chemical laboratory apparatus shall make an accurate and legible record of the transaction and maintain the record for at least two years after the date of the transaction.

(b) The director may adopt rules to implement this section.

(c) The director by rule may:

(1) name an additional item of equipment as a chemical laboratory apparatus for purposes of Subsection (a) if the director determines that public health and welfare are jeopardized by evidenced proliferation or use of the item of equipment in the illicit manufacture of a controlled substance or controlled substance analogue; or

(2) exempt a chemical laboratory apparatus from the requirement of Subsection (a) if the director determines that the apparatus does not jeopardize public health and welfare or is not used in the illicit manufacture of a controlled substance or a controlled substance analogue.

(d) This section and Section 481.081 do not apply to a person to whom a registration has been issued under Section 481.063.

(e) Before selling, transferring, or otherwise furnishing to a person in this state a chemical laboratory apparatus subject to Subsection (a), a manufacturer, wholesaler, retailer, or other person shall:

(1) if the recipient does not represent a business, obtain from the recipient:

(A) the recipient's driver's license number or other personal identification certificate number, date of birth, and residential or mailing address, other than a

TCSA §481.0771

post office box number, from a driver's license or personal identification certificate issued by the department that contains a photograph of the recipient;

(B) the year, state, and number of the motor vehicle license of the motor vehicle owned or operated by the recipient;

(C) a complete description of how the apparatus is to be used; and

(D) the recipient's signature; or

(2) if the recipient represents a business, obtain from the recipient:

(A) a letter of authorization from the business that includes the business license or comptroller tax identification number, address, area code, and telephone number and a complete description of how the apparatus is to be used; and

(B) the recipient's signature; and

(3) for any recipient, sign as a witness to the signature and identification of the recipient.

(f) If the recipient docs not represent a business, the recipient shall present to the manufacturer, wholesaler, retailer, or other person a permit issued in the name of the recipient by the department under Section 481.081.

(g) Except as provided by Subsection (i), a manufacturer, wholesaler, retailer, or other person who sells, transfers, or otherwise furnishes to a person in this state a chemical laboratory apparatus subject to Subsection (a) shall, at least 21 days before the delivery of the apparatus, submit a report of the transaction on a form obtained from the director that includes the information required by Subsection (e).

(h) The director shall supply to a manufacturer, wholesaler, retailer, or other person who sells, transfers, or otherwise furnishes a chemical laboratory apparatus subject to Subsection (a) a form for the submission of:

(1) the report required by Subsection (g);

(2) the name and number of apparatus delivered; and

(3) any other information required by the director.

(i) The director may authorize a manufacturer, wholesaler, retailer, or other person to submit a comprehensive monthly report instead of the report required by Subsection (g) if the director determines that:

(1) there is a pattern of regular supply and purchase of the apparatus between the furnisher and the recipient; or

(2) the recipient has established a record of use of the apparatus solely for a lawful purpose.

(j) A manufacturer, wholesaler, retailer, or other person who receives from a source outside this state a chemical laboratory apparatus subject to Subsection (a) or who discovers a loss or theft of such an apparatus shall:

(1) submit a report of the transaction to the director in accordance with department rule; and

(2) include in the report:

(A) any difference between the number of the apparatus actually received and the number of the apparatus shipped according to the shipping statement or invoice; or

(B) the number of the loss or theft.

(k) A report under Subsection (j) must:

(1) be made not later than the third day after the date that the manufacturer, wholesaler, retailer, or other person learns of the discrepancy, loss, or theft; and

(2) if the discrepancy, loss, or theft occurred during a shipment of the apparatus, include the name of the common carrier or person who transported the apparatus and the date that the apparatus was shipped.

(*l*) This subsection applies to a manufacturer, wholesaler, retailer, or other person who sells, transfers, or otherwise furnishes any chemical laboratory apparatus subject to Subsection (a) and to a permit holder, commercial purchaser, or other person who receives such an apparatus unless the person is the holder of only a permit issued under Section 481.081(b)(1). A person covered by this subsection:

(1) shall maintain records and inventories in accordance with rules established by the director;

(2) shall allow a member of the department or a peace officer to conduct audits and inspect records of purchases and sales and all other records made in accordance with this section at any reasonable time; and

(3) may not interfere with the audit or with the full and complete inspection or copying of those records.

History of H&SC §481.080; Acts 1989, 71st Leg., ch. 1100, §5.02(*l*), eff. Sept. 1, 1989. Amended by Acts 1997, 75th Leg., ch. 745, §19, eff. Sept. 1, 1997; Acts 2001, 77th Leg., ch. 251, §14, eff. Sept. 1, 2001.

TCSA §481.080

H&SC §481.081. CHEMICAL LABORATORY APPARATUS TRANSFER PERMIT

(a) A person must obtain a chemical laboratory apparatus transfer permit from the department to be eligible:

(1) to sell, transfer, or otherwise furnish an apparatus subject to Section 481.080(a) to a person in this state;

(2) to receive an apparatus subject to Section 481.080(a) from a source outside this state; or

(3) to receive an apparatus subject to Section 481.080(a) if the person, in receiving the apparatus, does not represent a business.

(b) The director by rule shall adopt procedures and standards for the issuance and renewal or the voluntary surrender, cancellation, suspension, probation, or revocation of:

(1) a permit for one sale, transfer, receipt, or otherwise furnishing of a chemical laboratory apparatus; or

(2) a permit for more than one sale, transfer, receipt, or otherwise furnishing of a chemical laboratory apparatus.

(c) A permit issued or renewed under Subsection (b)(1) is valid only for the transaction indicated on the permit. A permit issued or renewed under Subsection (b)(2) is valid for one year after the date of issuance or renewal.

(d) A permit holder must report in writing or by telephone to the director a change in the holder's business name, address, area code, and telephone number not later than the seventh day after the date of the change.

(e) The director may not issue a permit under this section unless the person applying for the permit delivers to the director a written consent to inspect signed by the person that grants to the director the right to inspect any controlled premises, record, chemical laboratory apparatus, or other item governed by this chapter in the care, custody, or control of the person. After the director receives the consent, the director may inspect any controlled premises, record, chemical laboratory apparatus, or other item to which the consent applies.

(f) The director may by rule establish security controls and provide for the inspection of a place, entity, or item to which a chemical laboratory apparatus transfer permit applies.

History of H&SC §481.081: Acts 1989, 71st Leg., ch. 1100, §5.02(*l*), eff. Sept. 1, 1989. Amended by Acts 1997, 75th Leg., ch. 745, §20, eff. Sept. 1, 1997; Acts 2001, 77th Leg., ch. 251, §15, eff. Sept. 1, 2001.

H&SC §481.082. REPEALED

Repealed by Acts 1997, 75th Leg., ch. 745, §37, eff. Sept. 1, 1997.

Sections 481.083-481.100 reserved for expansion

SUBCHAPTER D. OFFENSES & PENALTIES

For a quick reference of penalties, see the Chart of Penalties on p. 689.

H&SC §481.101. CRIMINAL CLASSIFICATION

For the purpose of establishing criminal penalties for violations of this chapter, controlled substances, including a material, compound, mixture, or preparation containing the controlled substance, are divided into Penalty Groups 1 through 4.

History of H&SC §481.101: Acts 1989, 71st Leg., ch. 678, §1 (eff. Sept. 1, 1989), ch. 1100, §5.02(n) (eff. Sept. 1, 1989).

ANNOTATIONS

Watson v. State, 900 S.W.2d 60, 62 (Tex.Crim.App. 1995). "The [H&SC] classifies heroin and cocaine as Penalty Group 1 substances for the purpose of establishing criminal penalties for violations of the [TCSA]. [¶] The Legislature ... classified controlled substances into four penalty groups for the purpose of establishing criminal penalties for possession, manufacture, or sale of various controlled substances.... We hold that the Legislature intended to make possession of *each* individual substance within the same penalty group a separate or distinct offense. [¶] [D] was convicted of *two* distinct possession offenses, not one. [¶] Thus, [D's] multiple punishments do not violate the Fifth Amendment's protection against double jeopardy because each punishment is for a separate and distinct offense."

H&SC §481.102. PENALTY GROUP 1

Penalty Group 1 consists of:

(1) the following opiates, including their isomers, esters, ethers, salts, and salts of isomers, esters, and ethers, unless specifically excepted, if the existence of these isomers, esters, ethers, and salts is possible within the specific chemical designation:

Alfentanil;

Allylprodine;

Alphacetylmethadol;

Benzethidine;

Betaprodine;

Clonitazene;

Diampromide;

Diethylthiambutene;

Difenoxin not listed in Penalty Group 3 or 4;

Dimenoxadol;

Dimethylthiambutene;

Dioxaphetyl butyrate;

Dipipanone;

Ethylmethylthiambutene;

Etonitazene;

Etoxeridine;

Furethidine;

Hydroxypethidine;

Ketobemidone;

Levophenacylmorphan;

Meprodine;

Methadol;

Moramide;

Morpheridine;

Noracymethadol;

Norlevorphanol;

Normethadone;

Norpipanone;

Phenadoxone;

Phenampromide;

Phenomorphan;

Phenoperidine;

Piritramide;

Proheptazine;

Properidine;

Propiram;

Sufentanil;

Tilidine; and

Trimeperidine;

(2) the following opium derivatives, their salts, isomers, and salts of isomers, unless specifically excepted, if the existence of these salts, isomers, and salts of isomers is possible within the specific chemical designation:

Acetorphine;

Acetyldihydrocodeine;

Benzylmorphine;

Codeine methylbromide;

Codeine-N-Oxide;

Cyprenorphine;

Desomorphine;

Dihydromorphine;

Drotebanol;

Etorphine, except hydrochloride salt;

Heroin;

Hydromorphinol;

Methyldesorphine;

Methyldihydromorphine;

Monoacetylmorphine;

Morphine methylbromide;

Morphine methylsulfonate;

Morphine-N-Oxide;

Myrophine;

Nicocodeine;

Nicomorphine;

Normorphine;

Pholcodine; and

Thebacon;

(3) the following substances, however produced, except those narcotic drugs listed in another group:

(A) Opium and opiate not listed in Penalty Group 3 or 4, and a salt, compound, derivative, or preparation of opium or opiate, other than thebaine derived butorphanol, nalmefene and its salts, naloxone and its salts, and naltrexone and its salts, but including:

Codeine not listed in Penalty Group 3 or 4;

Dihydroetorphine;

Ethylmorphine not listed in Penalty Group 3 or 4;

Granulated opium;

Hydrocodone not listed in Penalty Group 3;

Hydromorphone;

Metopon;

Morphine not listed in Penalty Group 3;

Opium extracts;

Opium fluid extracts;

Oxycodone;

Oxymorphone;

Powdered opium;

Raw opium;

Thebaine; and

Tincture of opium;

(B) a salt, compound, isomer, derivative, or preparation of a substance that is chemically equivalent or identical to a substance described by Paragraph (A), other than the isoquinoline alkaloids of opium;

(C) Opium poppy and poppy straw;

(D) Cocaine, including:

(i) its salts, its optical, position, and geometric isomers, and the salts of those isomers;

(ii) coca leaves and a salt, compound, derivative, or preparation of coca leaves;

(iii) a salt, compound, derivative, or preparation of a salt, compound, or derivative that is chemically equivalent or identical to a substance described by Subparagraph (i) or (ii), other than decocainized coca leaves or extractions of coca leaves that do not contain cocaine or ecgonine; and

(E) concentrate of poppy straw, meaning the crude extract of poppy straw in liquid, solid, or powder form that contains the phenanthrine alkaloids of the opium poppy;

(4) the following opiates, including their isomers, esters, ethers, salts, and salts of isomers, if the existence of these isomers, esters, ethers, and salts is possible within the specific chemical designation:

Acetyl-alpha-methylfentanyl (N-[1-(1-methyl-2-phenethyl)-4-piperidinyl]-N-phenylacetamide);

Alpha-methylthiofentanyl (N-[1-methyl-2-(2-thienyl)ethyl-4-piperidinyl]-N-phenylpropanamide);

Alphaprodine;

Anileridine;

Beta-hydroxyfentanyl (N-[1-(2-hydroxy-2-phenethyl)-4-piperidinyl]-N-phenylpropanamide);

Beta-hydroxy-3-methylfentanyl;

Bezitramide;

Carfentanil;

Dihydrocodeine not listed in Penalty Group 3 or 4;

Diphenoxylate not listed in Penalty Group 3 or 4;

Fentanyl or alpha-methylfentanyl, or any other derivative of Fentanyl;

Isomethadone;

Levomethorphan;

Levorphanol;

Metazocine;

Methadone;

Methadone-Intermediate, 4-cyano-2-dimethylamino-4, 4-diphenyl butane;

3-methylfentanyl (N-[3-methyl-1-(2-phenylethyl)-4-piperidyl]-N-phenylpropanamide);

3-methylthiofentanyl (N-[3-methyl-1-(2-thienyl)ethyl-4-piperidinyl]-N-phenylpropanamide);

Moramide-Intermediate, 2-methyl-3-morpholino-1, 1-diphenyl-propane-carboxylic acid;

Para-fluorofentanyl (N-(4-fluorophenyl)-N-1-(2-phenylethyl)-4-piperidinylpropanamide);

PEPAP (1-(2-phenethyl)-4-phenyl-4-acetoxypiperidine);

Pethidine (Meperidine);

Pethidine-Intermediate-A, 4-cyano-1-methyl-4-phenylpiperidine;

Pethidine-Intermediate-B, ethyl-4-phenylpiperidine-4 carboxylate;

Pethidine-Intermediate-C, 1-methyl-4-phenylpiperidine-4-carboxylic acid;

Phenazocine;

Piminodine;

Racemethorphan;

Racemorphan;

Remifentanil; and

Thiofentanyl (N-phenyl-N-[1-(2-thienyl)ethyl-4-piperidinyl]-propanamide);

(5) Flunitrazepam (trade or other name: Rohypnol);

(6) Methamphetamine, including its salts, optical isomers, and salts of optical isomers;

(7) Phenylacetone and methylamine, if possessed together with intent to manufacture methamphetamine;

(8) Phencyclidine, including its salts;

(9) Gamma hydroxybutyric acid (some trade or other names: gamma hydroxybutyrate, GHB), including its salts; and

(10) Ketamine.

History of H&SC §481.102: Acts 1989, 71st Leg., ch. 678, §1, ch. 1100, §5.02(n) (eff. Sept. 1, 1989). Amended by Acts 1991, 72nd Leg., ch. 761, §1, eff. Sept. 1, 1991; Acts 1997, 75th Leg., ch. 745, §21, eff. Sept. 1, 1997; Acts 2001, 77th Leg., ch. 459, §1 (eff. Sept. 1, 2001), ch. 251, §16 (eff. Sept. 1, 2001); Acts 2003, 78th Leg., ch. 1099, §7, eff. Sept. 1, 2003.

ANNOTATIONS

Watson v. State, 900 S.W.2d 60, 62 (Tex.Crim.App. 1995). D argues "that the Legislature intended to make the penalty group, rather than the individual controlled substance, an essential element of the offense. This interpretation would mean an individual could possess ten different substances described in Penalty Group 1 and be chargeable with only one offense, yet he could be charged with two offenses if he possessed one Penalty Group 1 substance and one Penalty Group 2 substance. ... We hold that the Legislature intended to make possession of *each* individual substance within the same penalty group a separate and distinct offense."

Employee Ret. Sys. v. Cash, 906 S.W.2d 204, 208 (Tex.App.—Austin 1995, writ denied). "[P]ossession of either cocaine or methadone without a valid prescription is a felony offense. [D] did not argue or present any evidence that her husband held a valid prescription for methadone, as was her burden. The combined amount of these drugs was measurable and hence sufficient to uphold a possession offense."

H&SC §481.1021. PENALTY GROUP 1-A

Penalty Group 1-A consists of lysergic acid diethylamide (LSD), including its salts, isomers, and salts of isomers.

History of H&SC §481.1021: Enacted by 75th Leg., ch. 745, §22, eff. Sept. 1, 1997.

H&SC §481.103. PENALTY GROUP 2

(a) Penalty Group 2 consists of:

(1) any quantity of the following hallucinogenic substances, their salts, isomers, and salts of isomers, unless specifically excepted, if the existence of these salts, isomers, and salts of isomers is possible within the specific chemical designation:

alpha-ethyltryptamine;

4-bromo-2, 5-dimethoxyamphetamine (some trade or other names: 4-bromo- 2, 5-dimethoxy-alpha-methylphenethylamine; 4-bromo-2, 5-DMA);

4-bromo-2, 5-dimethoxyphenethylamine;

Bufotenine (some trade and other names: 3-(beta-Dimethylaminoethyl)-5-hydroxyindole; 3-(2-dimethylaminoethyl)-5- indolol; N, N-dimethylserotonin; 5-hydroxy-N, N-dimethyltryptamine; mappine);

Diethyltryptamine (some trade and other names: N, N-Diethyltryptamine, DET);

2, 5-dimethoxyamphetamine (some trade or other names: 2, 5-dimethoxy- alpha-methylphenethylamine; 2, 5-DMA);

2, 5-dimethoxy-4-ethylamphetamine (trade or other name: DOET);

2,5-dimethoxy-4-(n)-propylthiophenethylamine (trade or other name: 2C-T-7);

Dimethyltryptamine (trade or other name: DMT);

Dronabinol (synthetic) in sesame oil and encapsulated in a soft gelatin capsule in a U.S. Food and Drug Administration approved drug product (some trade or other names for Dronabinol: (a6aR-trans)-6a,7,8,10a-tetrahydro- 6,6, 9-trimethyl-3-pentyl-6H-dibenzo [b,d] pyran-1-ol or (-)-delta-9-(trans)- tetrahydrocannabinol);

Ethylamine Analog of Phencyclidine (some trade or other names: N-ethyl-1-phenylcyclohexylamine, (1-phenylcyclohexyl) ethylamine, N-(1- phenylcyclohexyl) ethylamine, cyclohexamine, PCE);

Ibogaine (some trade or other names: 7-Ethyl-6, 6, beta 7, 8, 9, 10, 12, 13-octahydro-2-methoxy-6, 9-methano-5H-pyrido [1', 2':1, 2] azepino [5, 4-b] indole; tabernanthe iboga.);

Mescaline;

5-methoxy-3, 4-methylenedioxy amphetamine;

4-methoxyamphetamine (some trade or other names: 4-methoxy-alpha-methylphenethylamine; paramethoxyamphetamine; PMA);

1-methyl-4-phenyl-4-propionoxypiperidine (MPPP, PPMP);

4-methyl-2, 5-dimethoxyamphetamine (some trade and other names: 4- methyl-2, 5-dimethoxy-alpha-methylphenethylamine; "DOM"; "STP");

3,4-methylenedioxy methamphetamine (MDMA, MDM);

3,4-methylenedioxy amphetamine;

3,4-methylenedioxy N-ethylamphetamine (Also known as N-ethyl MDA);

Nabilone (Another name for nabilone: (+)-trans-3-(1,1-dimethylheptyl)- 6,6a,7,8,10,10a-hexahydro-1- hydroxy-6,6- dimethyl-9H-dibenzo[b,d] pyran-9-one;

N-benzylpiperazine (some trade or other names: BZP; 1-benzylpiperazine);

N-ethyl-3-piperidyl benzilate;

N-hydroxy-3,4-methylenedioxyamphetamine (Also known as N-hydroxy MDA);

4-methylaminorex;

N-methyl-3-piperidyl benzilate;

Parahexyl (some trade or other names: 3-Hexyl-1-hydroxy-7, 8, 9, 10- tetrahydro-6, 6, 9-trimethyl-6H-dibenzo [b,d] pyran; Synhexyl);

1-Phenylcyclohexylamine;

1-Piperidinocyclohexanecarbonitrile (PCC);

Psilocin;

Psilocybin;

Pyrrolidine Analog of Phencyclidine (some trade or other names: 1-(1-phenylcyclohexyl)-pyrrolidine, PCPy, PHP);

Tetrahydrocannabinols, other than marihuana, and synthetic equivalents of the substances contained in the plant, or in the resinous extractives of Cannabis, or synthetic substances, derivatives, and their isomers with similar chemical structure and pharmacological activity such as:

delta-1 cis or trans tetrahydrocannabinol, and their optical isomers;

delta-6 cis or trans tetrahydrocannabinol, and their optical isomers;

delta-3, 4 cis or trans tetrahydrocannabinol, and its optical isomers;

compounds of these structures, regardless of numerical designation of atomic positions, since nomenclature of these substances is not internationally standardized;

Thiophene Analog of Phencyclidine (some trade or other names: 1-[1-(2-thienyl) cyclohexyl] piperidine; 2-Thienyl Analog of Phencyclidine; TPCP, TCP);

1-[1-(2-thienyl)cyclohexyl]pyrrolidine (some trade or other name: TCPy);

1-(3-trifluoromethylphenyl)piperazine (trade or other name: TFMPP); and

3,4,5-trimethoxy amphetamine;

(2) Phenylacetone (some trade or other names: Phenyl-2-propanone; P2P, Benzymethyl ketone, methyl benzyl ketone); and

(3) unless specifically excepted or unless listed in another Penalty Group, a material, compound, mixture, or preparation that contains any quantity of the following substances having a potential for abuse associated with a depressant or stimulant effect on the central nervous system:

Aminorex (some trade or other names: aminoxaphen; 2-amino-5-phenyl-2-oxazoline; 4,5-dihydro-5-phenyl-2-oxazolamine);

Amphetamine, its salts, optical isomers, and salts of optical isomers;

Cathinone (some trade or other names: 2-amino-1-phenyl-1-propanone, alpha-aminopropiophenone, 2-aminopropiophenone);

Etorphine Hydrochloride;

Fenethylline and its salts;

Mecloqualone and its salts;

Methaqualone and its salts;

Methcathinone (some trade or other names: 2-methylamino-propiophenone; alpha-(methylamino) propriophenone; 2-(methylamino)-1-phenylpropan-1-one; alpha-N-methylaminopropriophenone; monomethylpropion; ephedrone, N-methylcathinone; methylcathinone; AL-464; AL-422; AL-463; and UR 1431);

N-Ethylamphetamine, its salts, optical isomers, and salts of optical isomers; and

N,N-dimethylamphetamine (some trade or other names: N,N,alpha-trimethylbenzeneethaneamine; N, N,-alpha-trimethylphenethylamine), its salts, optical isomers, and salts of optical isomers.

(b) For the purposes of Subsection (a)(1) only, the term "isomer" includes an optical, position, or geometric isomer.

History of H&SC §481.103: Acts 1989, 71st Leg., ch. 678, §1 (eff. Sept. 1, 1989), ch. 1100, §5.02(n) (eff. Sept. 1, 1989). Amended by Acts 1991, 72nd Leg., ch. 761, §2, eff. Sept. 1, 1991; Acts 1997, 75th Leg., ch. 745, §23, eff. Sept. 1, 1997; Acts 2001, 77th Leg., ch. 251, §17, eff. Sept. 1, 2001; Acts 2003, 78th Leg., ch. 1099, §8, eff. Sept. 1, 2003.

ANNOTATIONS

Ex parte Kopecky, 821 S.W.2d 957, 959 (Tex.Crim. App.1992). Tax Code ch. 159 "provides for a tax upon 'taxable substances' ... and the issuance by the comptroller of a certificate, to be affixed to the 'taxable substance'.... Because phenylacetone is listed in Penalty Group 2 ... it is indeed a 'controlled substance' within the meaning of [Tax Code ch.] 159.... Subchapter C of Chapter 159 contains a penal provision outlawing possession of a 'taxable substance' for which the requisite tax has not been paid."

Ex parte Luster, 846 S.W.2d 928, 930 (Tex.App.—Fort Worth 1993, pet. ref'd). D argues "that he did not have fair notice that financing or investing funds for a transaction involving phenylacetic acid was forbidden under [H&SC] §481.126(a)(2) because that substance is not listed in Penalty Group 2. [¶] '[C]ontrolled substance' means a substance, including a drug and an immediate precursor, listed in Schedules I through V or

Penalty Groups 1 through 4. Amphetamine is a drug listed in Penalty Group 2 ... and phenylacetic acid is a main precursor used to make amphetamine. Thus, [D] had fair notice that his transaction involving phenylacetic acid was forbidden by §481.126(a)(2)."

H&SC §481.104. PENALTY GROUP 3

(a) Penalty Group 3 consists of:

(1) a material, compound, mixture, or preparation that contains any quantity of the following substances having a potential for abuse associated with a stimulant effect on the central nervous system:

Methylphenidate and its salts; and

Phenmetrazine and its salts;

(2) a material, compound, mixture, or preparation that contains any quantity of the following substances having a potential for abuse associated with a depressant effect on the central nervous system:

a substance that contains any quantity of a derivative of barbituric acid, or any salt of a derivative of barbituric acid not otherwise described by this subsection;

a compound, mixture, or preparation containing amobarbital, secobarbital, pentobarbital, or any salt of any of these, and one or more active medicinal ingredients that are not listed in any penalty group;

a suppository dosage form containing amobarbital, secobarbital, pentobarbital, or any salt of any of these drugs, and approved by the United States Food and Drug Administration for marketing only as a suppository;

Alprazolam;

Amobarbital;

Bromazepam;

Camazepam;

Chlordiazepoxide;

Chlorhexadol;

Clobazam;

Clonazepam;

Clorazepate;

Clotiazepam;

Cloxazolam;

Delorazepam;

Diazepam;

Estazolam;

Ethyl loflazepate;

Fludiazepam;

Flurazepam;

Glutethimide;

Halazepam;

Haloxzolam;

Ketazolam;

Loprazolam;

Lorazepam;

Lormetazepam;

Lysergic acid, including its salts, isomers, and salts of isomers;

Lysergic acid amide, including its salts, isomers, and salts of isomers;

Mebutamate;

Medazepam;

Methyprylon;

Midazolam;

Nimetazepam;

Nitrazepam;

Nordiazepam;

Oxazepam;

Oxazolam;

Pentazocine, its salts, derivatives, or compounds or mixtures thereof;

Pentobarbital;

Pinazepam;

Prazepam;

Quazepam;

Secobarbital;

Sulfondiethylmethane;

Sulfonethylmethane;

Sulfonmethane;

Temazepam;

Tetrazepam;

Tiletamine and zolazepam in combination, and its salts. (some trade or other names for a tiletamine-zolazepam combination product: Telazol, for tiletamine: 2-(ethylamino)-2-(2-thienyl)-cyclohexanone, and for zolazepam: 4-(2-fluorophenyl)-6,8-dihydro-1,3,8,-trimethylpyrazolo-[3,4-e](1,4)-d diazepin-7(1H)-one, flupyrazapon);

Triazolam;

Zaleplon; and

Zolpidem;

(3) Nalorphine;

(4) a material, compound, mixture, or preparation containing limited quantities of the following narcotic drugs, or any of their salts:

not more than 1.8 grams of codeine, or any of its salts, per 100 milliliters or not more than 90 milligrams per dosage unit, with an equal or greater quantity of an isoquinoline alkaloid of opium;

not more than 1.8 grams of codeine, or any of its salts, per 100 milliliters or not more than 90 milligrams per dosage unit, with one or more active, nonnarcotic ingredients in recognized therapeutic amounts;

not more than 300 milligrams of dihydrocodeinone (hydrocodone), or any of its salts, per 100 milliliters or not more than 15 milligrams per dosage unit, with a fourfold or greater quantity of an isoquinoline alkaloid of opium;

not more than 300 milligrams of dihydrocodeinone (hydrocodone), or any of its salts, per 100 milliliters or not more than 15 milligrams per dosage unit, with one or more active, nonnarcotic ingredients in recognized therapeutic amounts;

not more than 1.8 grams of dihydrocodeine, or any of its salts, per 100 milliliters or not more than 90 milligrams per dosage unit, with one or more active, nonnarcotic ingredients in recognized therapeutic amounts;

not more than 300 milligrams of ethylmorphine, or any of its salts, per 100 milliliters or not more than 15 milligrams per dosage unit, with one or more active, nonnarcotic ingredients in recognized therapeutic amounts;

not more than 500 milligrams of opium per 100 milliliters or per 100 grams, or not more than 25 milligrams per dosage unit, with one or more active, nonnarcotic ingredients in recognized therapeutic amounts;

not more than 50 milligrams of morphine, or any of its salts, per 100 milliliters or per 100 grams with one or more active, nonnarcotic ingredients in recognized therapeutic amounts; and

not more than 1 milligram of difenoxin and not less than 25 micrograms of atropine sulfate per dosage unit;

(5) a material, compound, mixture, or preparation that contains any quantity of the following substances:

Barbital;

Chloral betaine;

Chloral hydrate;

Ethchlorvynol;

Ethinamate;

Meprobamate;

Methohexital;

Methylphenobarbital (Mephobarbital);

Paraldehyde;

Petrichloral; and

Phenobarbital;

(6) Peyote, unless unharvested and growing in its natural state, meaning all parts of the plant classified botanically as Lophophora, whether growing or not, the seeds of the plant, an extract from a part of the plant, and every compound, manufacture, salt, derivative, mixture, or preparation of the plant, its seeds, or extracts;

(7) unless listed in another penalty group, a material, compound, mixture, or preparation that contains any quantity of the following substances having a stimulant effect on the central nervous system, including the substance's salts, optical, position, or geometric isomers, and salts of the substance's isomers, if the existence of the salts, isomers, and salts of isomers is possible within the specific chemical designation:

Benzphetamine;

Cathine [(+)-norpseudoephedrine];

Chlorphentermine;

Clortermine;

Diethylpropion;

Fencamfamin;

Fenfluramine;

Fenproporex;

Mazindol;

Mefenorex;

Modafinil;

Pemoline (including organometallic complexes and their chelates);

Phendimetrazine;

Phentermine;

Pipradrol;

Sibutramine; and

SPA [(-)-1-dimethylamino-1,2-diphenylethane];

(8) unless specifically excepted or unless listed in another penalty group, a material, compound, mixture, or preparation that contains any quantity of the following substance, including its salts:

Dextropropoxyphene (Alpha-(+)-4-dimethylamino-1, 2-diphenyl-3-methyl-2-propionoxybutane); and

(9) an anabolic steroid or any substance that is chemically or pharmacologically related to testosterone, other than an estrogen, progestin, or corticosteroid, and promotes muscle growth, including:

Boldenone;

Chlorotestosterone (4-chlortestosterone);

Clostebol;

Dehydrochlormethyltestosterone;

Dihydrotestosterone (4-dihydrotestosterone);

Drostanolone;

Ethylestrenol;

Fluoxymesterone;

Formebulone;

Mesterolone;

Methandienone;

Methandranone;

Methandriol;

Methandrostenolone;

Methenolone;

Methyltestosterone;

Mibolerone;

Nandrolone;

Norethandrolone;

Oxandrolone;

Oxymesterone;

Oxymetholone;

Stanolone;

Stanozolol;

Testolactone;

Testosterone; and

Trenbolone.

(b) Penalty Group 3 does not include a compound, mixture, or preparation containing a stimulant substance listed in Subsection (a)(1) if the compound, mixture, or preparation contains one or more active medicinal ingredients not having a stimulant effect on the central nervous system and if the admixtures are included in combinations, quantity, proportion, or concentration that vitiate the potential for abuse of the substances that have a stimulant effect on the central nervous system.

(c) Penalty Group 3 does not include a compound, mixture, or preparation containing a depressant substance listed in Subsection (a)(2) or (a)(5) if the compound, mixture, or preparation contains one or more active medicinal ingredients not having a depressant effect on the central nervous system and if the admixtures are included in combinations, quantity, proportion, or concentration that vitiate the potential for abuse of the substances that have a depressant effect on the central nervous system.

History of H&SC §481.104: Acts 1989, 71st Leg., ch. 678, §1 (eff. Sept. 1, 1989), ch. 1100, §5.02(n) (eff. Sept. 1, 1989). Amended by Acts 1991, 72nd Leg., ch. 761, §3, eff. Sept. 1, 1991; Acts 1997, 75th Leg., ch. 745, §24, eff. Sept. 1, 1997; Acts 2001, 77th Leg., ch. 251, §18, eff. Sept. 1, 2001.

H&SC §481.105. PENALTY GROUP 4

Penalty Group 4 consists of:

(1) a compound, mixture, or preparation containing limited quantities of any of the following narcotic drugs that includes one or more nonnarcotic active medicinal ingredients in sufficient proportion to confer on the compound, mixture, or preparation valuable medicinal qualities other than those possessed by the narcotic drug alone:

not more than 200 milligrams of codeine per 100 milliliters or per 100 grams;

not more than 100 milligrams of dihydrocodeine per 100 milliliters or per 100 grams;

not more than 100 milligrams of ethylmorphine per 100 milliliters or per 100 grams;

not more than 2.5 milligrams of diphenoxylate and not less than 25 micrograms of atropine sulfate per dosage unit;

not more than 15 milligrams of opium per 29.5729 milliliters or per 28.35 grams; and

not more than 0.5 milligram of difenoxin and not less than 25 micrograms of atropine sulfate per dosage unit;

(2) unless specifically excepted or unless listed in another penalty group, a material, compound, mixture, or preparation containing any quantity of the narcotic drug Buprenorphine or Butorphanol or a salt of either; and

(3) unless specifically exempted or excluded or unless listed in another penalty group, any material, compound, mixture, or preparation that contains any quantity of pyrovalerone, a substance having a stimulant effect on the central nervous system, including its salts, isomers, and salts of isomers.

History of H&SC §481.105: Acts 1989, 71st Leg., ch. 678, §1 (eff. Sept. 1, 1989), ch. 1100, §5.04(a) (eff. Sept. 1, 1989). Amended by Acts 1991, 72nd Leg., ch. 761, §4, eff. Sept. 1, 1991; Acts 1997, 75th Leg., ch. 745, §25, eff. Sept. 1, 1997; Acts 2001, 77th Leg., ch. 251, §19, eff. Sept. 1, 2001.

TCSA §481.105

H&SC §481.106. CLASSIFICATION OF CONTROLLED SUBSTANCE ANALOGUE

For the purposes of the prosecution of an offense under this subchapter involving the manufacture, delivery, or possession of a controlled substance, Penalty Groups 1, 1-A, and 2 include a controlled substance analogue that:

(1) has a chemical structure substantially similar to the chemical structure of a controlled substance listed in the applicable penalty group; or

(2) is specifically designed to produce an effect substantially similar to, or greater than, a controlled substance listed in the applicable penalty group.

History of H&SC §481.106: Acts 2003, 78th Leg., ch. 1099, §9, eff. Sept. 1, 2003.

H&SC §481.107. REPEALED

Repealed by Acts 1993, 73rd Leg., ch. 900, §2.07, eff. Sept. 1, 1994.

H&SC §481.108. PREPARATORY OFFENSES

Title 4, Penal Code, applies to an offense under this chapter.

History of H&SC §481.108: Acts 1989, 71st Leg., ch. 678, §1, eff. Sept. 1, 1989. Amended by Acts 1993, 73rd Leg., ch. 900, §2.02, eff. Sept. 1, 1994; Acts 1995, 74th Leg., ch. 318, §36, eff. Sept. 1, 1995.

ANNOTATIONS

Hudson v. State, 794 S.W.2d 883, 886 (Tex.App.—Tyler 1990, no pet.). "[C]riminal conspiracy has to be an aggravated offense when it involves a controlled substance. Yet under the organized crime statute no specific amount of delivery of cocaine had to be proved."

H&SC §§481.109, 481.110. REPEALED

Repealed by Acts 1991, 72nd Leg., ch. 141, §6, eff. Sept. 1, 1991.

H&SC §481.111. EXEMPTIONS

(a) The provisions of this chapter relating to the possession and distribution of peyote do not apply to the use of peyote by a member of the Native American Church in bona fide religious ceremonies of the church. However, a person who supplies the substance to the church must register and maintain appropriate records of receipts and disbursements in accordance with rules adopted by the director. An exemption granted to a member of the Native American Church under this section does not apply to a member with less than 25 percent Indian blood.

(b) The provisions of this chapter relating to the possession of denatured sodium pentobarbital do not apply to possession by personnel of a humane society or an animal control agency for the purpose of destroying injured, sick, homeless, or unwanted animals if the humane society or animal control agency is registered with the Federal Drug Enforcement Administration. The provisions of this chapter relating to the distribution of denatured sodium pentobarbital do not apply to a person registered as required by Subchapter C, who is distributing the substance for that purpose to a humane society or an animal control agency registered with the Federal Drug Enforcement Administration.

(c) A person does not violate Section 481.113, 481.116, 481.121, or 481.125 if the person possesses or delivers tetrahydrocannabinols or their derivatives, or drug paraphernalia to be used to introduce tetrahydrocannabinols or their derivatives into the human body, for use in a federally approved therapeutic research program.

(d) The provisions of this chapter relating to the possession and distribution of anabolic steroids do not apply to the use of anabolic steroids that are administered to livestock or poultry.

History of H&SC §481.111: Acts 1989, 71st Leg., ch. 678, §1 (eff. Sept. 1, 1989), ch. 1100, §5.03(d) (eff. Sept. 1, 1989).

H&SC §481.112. OFFENSE: MANUFACTURE OR DELIVERY OF SUBSTANCE IN PENALTY GROUP 1

(a) Except as authorized by this chapter, a person commits an offense if the person knowingly manufactures, delivers, or possesses with intent to deliver a controlled substance listed in Penalty Group 1.

(b) An offense under Subsection (a) is a state jail felony if the amount of the controlled substance to which the offense applies is, by aggregate weight, including adulterants or dilutants, less than one gram.

(c) An offense under Subsection (a) is a felony of the second degree if the amount of the controlled substance to which the offense applies is, by aggregate weight, including adulterants or dilutants, one gram or more but less than four grams.

(d) An offense under Subsection (a) is a felony of the first degree if the amount of the controlled substance to which the offense applies is, by aggregate weight, including adulterants or dilutants, four grams or more but less than 200 grams.

(e) An offense under Subsection (a) is punishable by imprisonment in the institutional division of the Texas Department of Criminal Justice for life or for a term of not more than 99 years or less than 10 years, and a fine not to exceed $100,000, if the amount of the controlled substance to which the offense applies is, by aggregate weight, including adulterants or dilutants, 200 grams or more but less than 400 grams.

(f) An offense under Subsection (a) is punishable by imprisonment in the institutional division of the Texas Department of Criminal Justice for life or for a term of not more than 99 years or less than 15 years, and a fine not to exceed $250,000, if the amount of the controlled substance to which the offense applies is, by aggregate weight, including adulterants or dilutants, 400 grams or more.

History of H&SC §481.112: Acts 1989, 71st Leg., ch. 678, §1, eff. Sept. 1, 1989. Amended by Acts 1993, 73rd Leg., ch. 900, §2.02, eff. Sept. 1, 1994; Acts 2001, 77th Leg., ch. 1188, §2, eff. Sept. 1, 2001.

ANNOTATIONS

Lopez v. State, 108 S.W.3d 293, 297 (Tex.Crim.App. 2003). "[T]here are at least five ways to commit an offense under [H&SC] §481.112: through knowing 1) manufacture; 2) an offer to sell; or 3) possession with intent to deliver; or through knowing delivery by 4) actual transfer; or 5) constructive transfer. *At 298:* Courts of appeals have also recognized that two delivery offenses may be joined under [H&SC] §481.132(b) when, for instance, there are two separate quantities of the same drug involved…. *At 300:* Under §481.112, the fact that a transfer is thwarted will not negate conviction for delivery of that drug. Similarly, if an actor possesses a quantity of drugs sufficient to permit the jury to conclude that he possessed them with the intent to distribute them, the statute does not require any existing offer to sell or prospective buyer before he may be held liable under §481.112. [¶] The statute, however, cannot be turned on its head to allow several 'delivery' convictions where there is only one single sale of one drug. Therefore, we hold that the offer to sell and the possession of drugs to complete that specific sale is one single offense. Although the State may charge the offense as being committed in either of these modes, it cannot obtain two convictions for the same sale under §481.112(a)."

Watson v. State, 900 S.W.2d 60, 62 (Tex.Crim.App. 1995). H&SC §§482.112(a)-481.118 "make[] it clear that it is an offense to possess, manufacture or deliver a controlled substance listed in the particular penalty group. This language cannot reasonably be construed … to make possession, sale or delivery of two or more controlled substances within the same penalty group one offense. [T]he Legislature intended to make possession of *each* individual substance within the same penalty group a separate and distinct offense."

Utomi v. State, 243 S.W.3d 75, 82 (Tex.App.— Houston [1st Dist.] 2007, pet. ref'd). "Intent to deliver a controlled substance can be proved by circumstantial evidence, including evidence regarding an accused's possession of the contraband. An oral expression of intent is not required. Additional factors that courts have considered in determining whether the accused had the intent to deliver include (1) the nature of the location at which the accused was arrested; (2) the quantity of contraband in the accused's possession; (3) the manner of packaging; (4) the presence, or lack thereof, of drug paraphernalia for either use or sale; (5) the accused's possession of large amounts of cash; and (6) the accused's status as a drug user. Expert testimony by experienced law enforcement officers may also be used to establish an accused's intent to deliver." *See also Brown v. State*, 243 S.W.3d 141, 149–50 (Tex. App.—Eastland 2007, no pet.); *Taylor v. State*, 106 S.W.3d 827, 831 (Tex.App.—Dallas 2003, no pet.).

Nhem v. State, 129 S.W.3d 696, 699 (Tex.App.— Houston [1st Dist.] 2004, no pet.). "In a possession with intent to deliver case, the State must prove that the defendant: (1) exercised care, custody, control, or management over the controlled substance; (2) intended to deliver the controlled substance to another; and (3) knew that the substance in his possession was a controlled substance." *See also Hernandez v. State*, 956 S.W.2d 699, 703 (Tex.App.—Texarkana 1997, no pet.).

Berger v. State, 104 S.W.3d 199, 204 (Tex.App.— Austin 2003, no pet.). "[P]ossession of a controlled substance is a lesser-included offense of possession with intent to deliver."

Scott v. State, 988 S.W.2d 947, 948 (Tex.App.— Houston [1st Dist.] 1999, no pet.). "[A]ppellant contends a new punishment hearing is required because the trial judge did not assess the fine mandated by

TCSA §481.112

★

[H&SC] §481.112(f). [¶] We cannot reform the judgment by adding punishment of any amount, as the State suggests. Nor has appellant waived his complaint by not raising it below. A void sentence cannot be waived. Thus, the sole remedy is a new punishment hearing."

Schneider v. State, 951 S.W.2d 856, 861 (Tex. App.—Texarkana 1997, pet. ref'd). "Because [H&SC] §§481.002(8) and 481.112 clearly place men of reasonable intelligence on notice that they cannot promote an exchange of a controlled substance to another person for value either by words or deed, the word 'offer' is not unconstitutionally vague. [¶] [D] asserts that the culpable conduct is identical under [§§482.002 and 481.112] and the disparate sentences violate his right to due process. However, the culpable conduct is not identical. The culpable conduct penalized under §481.112 is the offering to sell a controlled substance, regardless of whether the controlled substance is sold, and therefore, the focus is on the transaction at the time that the offer is made. The culpable conduct penalized under §482.002 is the offering to sell a *simulated* controlled substance, and therefore, the focus is on the item sold. Because of the substance's simulated nature and lesser range of punishment, we can presume the legislature determined that this behavior constitutes a lesser harm to society than delivery of an actual controlled substance."

H&SC §481.1121. OFFENSE: MANUFACTURE OR DELIVERY OF SUBSTANCE IN PENALTY GROUP 1-A

(a) Except as provided by this chapter, a person commits an offense if the person knowingly manufactures, delivers, or possesses with intent to deliver a controlled substance listed in Penalty Group 1-A.

(b) An offense under this section is:

(1) a state jail felony if the number of abuse units of the controlled substance is fewer than 20;

(2) a felony of the second degree if the number of abuse units of the controlled substance is 20 or more but fewer than 80;

(3) a felony of the first degree if the number of abuse units of the controlled substance is 80 or more but fewer than 4,000; and

(4) punishable by imprisonment in the institutional division of the Texas Department of Criminal

Justice for life or for a term of not more than 99 years or less than 15 years and a fine not to exceed $250,000, if the number of abuse units of the controlled substance is 4,000 or more.

History of H&SC §481.1121: Acts 1997, 75th Leg., ch. 745, §26, eff. Sept. 1, 1997. Amended by Acts 2001, 77th Leg., ch. 1188, §3, eff. Sept. 1, 2001.

H&SC §481.1122. MANUFACTURE OF SUBSTANCE IN PENALTY GROUP 1: PRESENCE OF CHILD

 Section 481.1122 below is effective for offenses committed on or after Sept. 1, 2007.

If it is shown at the punishment phase of a trial for the manufacture of a controlled substance listed in Penalty Group 1 that when the offense was committed a child younger than 18 years of age was present on the premises where the offense was committed:

(1) the punishments specified by Sections 481.112(b) and (c) are increased by one degree;

(2) the minimum term of imprisonment specified by Section 481.112(e) is increased to 15 years and the maximum fine specified by that section is increased to $150,000; and

(3) the minimum term of imprisonment specified by Section 481.112(f) is increased to 20 years and the maximum fine specified by that section is increased to $300,000.

History of H&SC §481.1122: Acts 2007, 80th Leg., ch. 840, §1, eff. Sept. 1, 2007.

H&SC §481.113. OFFENSE: MANUFACTURE OR DELIVERY OF SUBSTANCE IN PENALTY GROUP 2

(a) Except as authorized by this chapter, a person commits an offense if the person knowingly manufactures, delivers, or possesses with intent to deliver a controlled substance listed in Penalty Group 2.

(b) An offense under Subsection (a) is a state jail felony if the amount of the controlled substance to which the offense applies is, by aggregate weight, including adulterants or dilutants, less than one gram.

(c) An offense under Subsection (a) is a felony of the second degree if the amount of the controlled substance to which the offense applies is, by aggregate weight, including adulterants or dilutants, one gram or more but less than four grams.

(d) An offense under Subsection (a) is a felony of the first degree if the amount of the controlled substance to which the offense applies is, by aggregate weight, including adulterants or dilutants, four grams or more but less than 400 grams.

(e) An offense under Subsection (a) is punishable by imprisonment in the institutional division of the Texas Department of Criminal Justice for life or for a term of not more than 99 years or less than 10 years, and a fine not to exceed $100,000, if the amount of the controlled substance to which the offense applies is, by aggregate weight, including adulterants or dilutants, 400 grams or more.

History of H&SC §481.113: Acts 1989, 71st Leg., ch. 678, §1, eff. Sept. 1, 1989. Amended by Acts 1993, 73rd Leg., ch. 900, §2.02, eff. Sept. 1, 1994; Acts 2001, 77th Leg., ch. 1188, §4, eff. Sept. 1, 2001.

H&SC §481.114. OFFENSE: MANUFACTURE OR DELIVERY OF SUBSTANCE IN PENALTY GROUP 3 OR 4

(a) Except as authorized by this chapter, a person commits an offense if the person knowingly manufactures, delivers, or possesses with intent to deliver a controlled substance listed in Penalty Group 3 or 4.

(b) An offense under Subsection (a) is a state jail felony if the amount of the controlled substance to which the offense applies is, by aggregate weight, including adulterants or dilutants, less than 28 grams.

(c) An offense under Subsection (a) is a felony of the second degree if the amount of the controlled substance to which the offense applies is, by aggregate weight, including adulterants or dilutants, 28 grams or more but less than 200 grams.

(d) An offense under Subsection (a) is a felony of the first degree, if the amount of the controlled substance to which the offense applies is, by aggregate weight, including adulterants or dilutants, 200 grams or more but less than 400 grams.

(e) An offense under Subsection (a) is punishable by imprisonment in the institutional division of the Texas Department of Criminal Justice for life or for a term of not more than 99 years or less than 10 years, and a fine not to exceed $100,000, if the amount of the controlled substance to which the offense applies is, by aggregate weight, including any adulterants or dilutants, 400 grams or more.

History of H&SC §481.114: Acts 1989, 71st Leg., ch. 678, §1, eff. Sept. 1, 1989. Amended by Acts 1993, 73rd Leg., ch. 900, §2.02, eff. Sept. 1, 1994; Acts 2001, 77th Leg., ch. 1188, §5, eff. Sept. 1, 2001.

H&SC §481.115. OFFENSE: POSSESSION OF SUBSTANCE IN PENALTY GROUP 1

(a) Except as authorized by this chapter, a person commits an offense if the person knowingly or intentionally possesses a controlled substance listed in Penalty Group 1, unless the person obtained the substance directly from or under a valid prescription or order of a practitioner acting in the course of professional practice.

(b) An offense under Subsection (a) is a state jail felony if the amount of the controlled substance possessed is, by aggregate weight, including adulterants or dilutants, less than one gram.

(c) An offense under Subsection (a) is a felony of the third degree if the amount of the controlled substance possessed is, by aggregate weight, including adulterants or dilutants, one gram or more but less than four grams.

(d) An offense under Subsection (a) is a felony of the second degree if the amount of the controlled substance possessed is, by aggregate weight, including adulterants or dilutants, four grams or more but less than 200 grams.

(e) An offense under Subsection (a) is a felony of the first degree if the amount of the controlled substance possessed is, by aggregate weight, including adulterants or dilutants, 200 grams or more but less than 400 grams.

(f) An offense under Subsection (a) is punishable by imprisonment in the institutional division of the Texas Department of Criminal Justice for life or for a term of not more than 99 years or less than 10 years, and a fine not to exceed $100,000, if the amount of the controlled substance possessed is, by aggregate weight, including adulterants or dilutants, 400 grams or more.

History of H&SC §481.115: Acts 1989, 71st Leg., ch. 678, §1, eff. Sept. 1, 1989. Amended by Acts 1993, 73rd Leg., ch. 900, §2.02, eff. Sept. 1, 1994.

See also chart, "Affirmative Links," p. 695; *O'Connor's Crimes & Consequences* (2008-09), chart 4-C, "Mandatory Community Supervision."

ANNOTATIONS

Poindexter v. State, 153 S.W.3d 402, 405 (Tex. Crim.App.2005). "To prove unlawful possession of a controlled substance, the State must prove that: (1) the accused exercised control, management, or care over the substance; and (2) the accused knew the matter possessed was contraband."

TCSA §481.115

Melton v. State, 120 S.W.3d 339, 344 (Tex.Crim. App.2003). "[T]he State is no longer required to determine the amount of controlled substance and the amount of adulterant and dilutant that constitute the mixture. The State has to prove only that the aggregate weight of the controlled substance mixture, including adulterants and dilutants, equals the alleged minimum weight."

H&SC §481.1151. OFFENSE: POSSESSION OF SUBSTANCE IN PENALTY GROUP 1-A

(a) Except as provided by this chapter, a person commits an offense if the person knowingly possesses a controlled substance listed in Penalty Group 1-A.

(b) An offense under this section is:

(1) a state jail felony if the number of abuse units of the controlled substance is fewer than 20;

(2) a felony of the third degree if the number of abuse units of the controlled substance is 20 or more but fewer than 80;

(3) a felony of the second degree if the number of abuse units of the controlled substance is 80 or more but fewer than 4,000;

(4) a felony of the first degree if the number of abuse units of the controlled substance is 4,000 or more but fewer than 8,000; and

(5) punishable by imprisonment in the institutional division of the Texas Department of Criminal Justice for life or for a term of not more than 99 years or less than 15 years and a fine not to exceed $250,000, if the number of abuse units of the controlled substance is 8,000 or more.

History of H&SC §481.1151: Acts 1997, 75th Leg., ch. 745, §26, eff. Sept. 1, 1997.

See also chart, "Affirmative Links," p. 695; *O'Connor's Crimes & Consequences* (2008-09), chart 4-C, "Mandatory Community Supervision."

H&SC §481.116. OFFENSE: POSSESSION OF SUBSTANCE IN PENALTY GROUP 2

(a) Except as authorized by this chapter, a person commits an offense if the person knowingly or intentionally possesses a controlled substance listed in Penalty Group 2, unless the person obtained the substance directly from or under a valid prescription or order of a practitioner acting in the course of professional practice.

(b) An offense under Subsection (a) is a state jail felony if the amount of the controlled substance possessed is, by aggregate weight, including adulterants or dilutants, less than one gram.

(c) An offense under Subsection (a) is a felony of the third degree if the amount of the controlled substance possessed is, by aggregate weight, including adulterants or dilutants, one gram or more but less than four grams.

(d) An offense under Subsection (a) is a felony of the second degree if the amount of the controlled substance possessed is, by aggregate weight, including adulterants or dilutants, four grams or more but less than 400 grams.

(e) An offense under Subsection (a) is punishable by imprisonment in the institutional division of the Texas Department of Criminal Justice for life or for a term of not more than 99 years or less than five years, and a fine not to exceed $50,000, if the amount of the controlled substance possessed is, by aggregate weight, including adulterants or dilutants, 400 grams or more.

History of H&SC §481.116: Acts 1989, 71st Leg., ch. 678, §1, eff. Sept. 1, 1989. Amended by Acts 1993, 73rd Leg., ch. 900, §2.02, eff. Sept. 1, 1994.

See also chart, "Affirmative Links," p. 695; *O'Connor's Crimes & Consequences* (2008-09), chart 4-C, "Mandatory Community Supervision."

ANNOTATIONS

Muckleroy v. State, 206 S.W.3d 746, 748 (Tex. App.—Texarkana 2006, pet. ref'd). "The statutes authorize conviction for possession of any amount below the statutory level. There is no minimum limitation. Thus, if any amount of contraband can be found by any level of scientific analysis, no matter how minuscule the amount might be, conviction is authorized under the statute."

H&SC §481.117. OFFENSE: POSSESSION OF SUBSTANCE IN PENALTY GROUP 3

(a) Except as authorized by this chapter, a person commits an offense if the person knowingly or intentionally possesses a controlled substance listed in Penalty Group 3, unless the person obtains the substance directly from or under a valid prescription or order of a practitioner acting in the course of professional practice.

(b) An offense under Subsection (a) is a Class A misdemeanor if the amount of the controlled substance

TCSA §481.115

possessed is, by aggregate weight, including adulterants or dilutants, less than 28 grams.

(c) An offense under Subsection (a) is a felony of the third degree if the amount of the controlled substance possessed is, by aggregate weight, including adulterants or dilutants, 28 grams or more but less than 200 grams.

(d) An offense under Subsection (a) is a felony of the second degree, if the amount of the controlled substance possessed is, by aggregate weight, including adulterants or dilutants, 200 grams or more but less than 400 grams.

(e) An offense under Subsection (a) is punishable by imprisonment in the institutional division of the Texas Department of Criminal Justice for life or for a term of not more than 99 years or less than five years, and a fine not to exceed $50,000, if the amount of the controlled substance possessed is, by aggregate weight, including adulterants or dilutants, 400 grams or more.

History of H&SC §481.117: Acts 1989, 71st Leg., ch. 678, §1, eff. Sept. 1, 1989. Amended by Acts 1993, 73rd Leg., ch. 900, §2.02, eff. Sept. 1, 1994.

See also chart, "Affirmative Links," p. 695.

ANNOTATIONS

Wright v. State, 981 S.W.2d 197, 201 (Tex.Crim. App.1998). It "is a defense to prosecution under [H&SC] §481.117(a) for possession of a controlled substance that (1) the substance was obtained abroad for personal medical use directly from, or pursuant to a valid prescription from, a physician permitted in his jurisdiction to dispense controlled substances and (2) the substance was brought into the United States in accordance with 21 C.F.R. §1301.26."

H&SC §481.118. OFFENSE: POSSESSION OF SUBSTANCE IN PENALTY GROUP 4

(a) Except as authorized by this chapter, a person commits an offense if the person knowingly or intentionally possesses a controlled substance listed in Penalty Group 4, unless the person obtained the substance directly from or under a valid prescription or order of a practitioner acting in the course of practice.

(b) An offense under Subsection (a) is a Class B misdemeanor if the amount of the controlled substance possessed is, by aggregate weight, including adulterants or dilutants, less than 28 grams.

(c) An offense under Subsection (a) is a felony of the third degree if the amount of the controlled substance possessed is, by aggregate weight, including adulterants or dilutants, 28 grams or more but less than 200 grams.

(d) An offense under Subsection (a) is a felony of the second degree, if the amount of the controlled substance possessed is, by aggregate weight, including adulterants or dilutants, 200 grams or more but less than 400 grams.

(e) An offense under Subsection (a) is punishable by imprisonment in the institutional division of the Texas Department of Criminal Justice for life or for a term of not more than 99 years or less than five years, and a fine not to exceed $50,000, if the amount of the controlled substance possessed is, by aggregate weight, including adulterants or dilutants, 400 grams or more.

History of H&SC §481.118: Acts 1989, 71st Leg., ch. 678, §1, eff. Sept. 1, 1989. Amended by Acts 1993, 73rd Leg., ch. 900, §2.02, eff. Sept. 1, 1994.

H&SC §481.119. OFFENSE: MANUFACTURE, DELIVERY, OR POSSESSION OF MISCELLANEOUS SUBSTANCES

(a) A person commits an offense if the person knowingly manufactures, delivers, or possesses with intent to deliver a controlled substance listed in a schedule by an action of the commissioner under this chapter but not listed in a penalty group. An offense under this subsection is a Class A misdemeanor.

(b) A person commits an offense if the person knowingly or intentionally possesses a controlled substance listed in a schedule by an action of the commissioner under this chapter but not listed in a penalty group. An offense under this subsection is a Class B misdemeanor.

History of H&SC §481.119: Acts 1989, 71st Leg., ch. 678, §1, eff. Sept. 1, 1989. Amended by Acts 2001, 77th Leg., ch. 1188, §6, eff. Sept. 1, 2001.

See also chart, "Affirmative Links," p. 695.

H&SC §481.120. OFFENSE: DELIVERY OF MARIHUANA

(a) Except as authorized by this chapter, a person commits an offense if the person knowingly or intentionally delivers marihuana.

(b) An offense under Subsection (a) is:

(1) a Class B misdemeanor if the amount of marihuana delivered is one-fourth ounce or less and the person committing the offense does not receive remuneration for the marihuana;

(2) a Class A misdemeanor if the amount of marihuana delivered is one-fourth ounce or less and the person committing the offense receives remuneration for the marihuana;

(3) a state jail felony if the amount of marihuana delivered is five pounds or less but more than one-fourth ounce;

(4) a felony of the second degree if the amount of marihuana delivered is 50 pounds or less but more than five pounds;

(5) a felony of the first degree if the amount of marihuana delivered is 2,000 pounds or less but more than 50 pounds; and

(6) punishable by imprisonment in the institutional division of the Texas Department of Criminal Justice for life or for a term of not more than 99 years or less than 10 years, and a fine not to exceed $100,000, if the amount of marihuana delivered is more than 2,000 pounds.

History of H&SC §481.120: Acts 1989, 71st Leg., ch. 678, §1, eff. Sept. 1, 1989. Amended by Acts 1993, 73rd Leg., ch. 900, §2.02, eff. Sept. 1, 1994.

See also chart, "Affirmative Links," p. 695.

$24,180 v. State, 865 S.W.2d 181, 186 (Tex.App.—Corpus Christi 1993, writ denied). "The question ... is whether the amount of money seized, or the amount of marihuana which [was to be purchased], determines whether the offense of delivery of marihuana is aggravated. We believe that it is the amount of the marihuana which [would have been] purchased, and not the amount of money actually seized, that determines whether the offense was aggravated within the meaning of the [TCSA]."

H&SC §481.121. OFFENSE: POSSESSION OF MARIHUANA

(a) Except as authorized by this chapter, a person commits an offense if the person knowingly or intentionally possesses a usable quantity of marihuana.

(b) An offense under Subsection (a) is:

(1) a Class B misdemeanor if the amount of marihuana possessed is two ounces or less;

(2) a Class A misdemeanor if the amount of marihuana possessed is four ounces or less but more than two ounces;

(3) a state jail felony if the amount of marihuana possessed is five pounds or less but more than four ounces;

(4) a felony of the third degree if the amount of marihuana possessed is 50 pounds or less but more than 5 pounds;

(5) a felony of the second degree if the amount of marihuana possessed is 2,000 pounds or less but more than 50 pounds; and

(6) punishable by imprisonment in the institutional division of the Texas Department of Criminal Justice for life or for a term of not more than 99 years or less than 5 years, and a fine not to exceed $50,000, if the amount of marihuana possessed is more than 2,000 pounds.

History of H&SC §481.121: Acts 1989, 71st Leg., ch. 678, §1, eff. Sept. 1, 1989. Amended by Acts 1993, 73rd Leg., ch. 900, §2.02, eff. Sept. 1, 1994.

See also chart, "Affirmative Links," p. 695; *O'Connor's Crimes & Consequences* (2008-09), chart 4-C, "Mandatory Community Supervision."

Young v. State, 922 S.W.2d 676, 677 (Tex.App.—Beaumont 1996, pet. ref'd). It is "the defendant's burden at trial to present evidence of the weight of any materials excluded from the statutory definition of marijuana so as to show the weight alleged and/or proven by the State was incorrect. [¶] With regard to any other non-marijuana material, the record in the instant case reflects that said material would be limited to the plastic wrappings in which the green leafy material was bundled. *At 678:* We believe that any rational trier of fact could have found that the State proved, beyond a reasonable doubt, that the amount of marijuana possessed by appellant was in excess of 50 pounds, but under 200 pounds."

Lopez v. State, 837 S.W.2d 863, 865-66 (Tex.App.—Houston [1st Dist.] 1992, no pet.). D's "argument centers around his perceived conflict between the tax and the classification of marihuana as a controlled substance. [D] wants this Court to hold that if the State chooses to tax a substance, it must declare it legal no matter who possesses the substance. This argument is without merit. There are situations in which one can legally possess a controlled substance. There are also situations in which the possession of marihuana does not require the tax stamp."

H&SC §481.122. OFFENSE: DELIVERY OF CONTROLLED SUBSTANCE OR MARIHUANA TO CHILD

(a) A person commits an offense if the person knowingly delivers a controlled substance listed in

Penalty Group 1, 1-A, 2, or 3 or knowingly delivers marihuana and the person delivers the controlled substance or marihuana to a person:

(1) who is a child;

(2) who is enrolled in a public or private primary or secondary school; or

(3) who the actor knows or believes intends to deliver the controlled substance or marihuana to a person described by Subdivision (1) or (2).

(b) It is an affirmative defense to prosecution under this section that:

(1) the actor was a child when the offense was committed; or

(2) the actor:

(A) was younger than 21 years of age when the offense was committed;

(B) delivered only marihuana in an amount equal to or less than one-fourth ounce; and

(C) did not receive remuneration for the delivery.

(c) An offense under this section is a felony of the second degree.

(d) In this section, "child" means a person younger than 18 years of age.

(e) If conduct that is an offense under this section is also an offense under another section of this chapter, the actor may be prosecuted under either section or both.

History of H&SC §481.122: Acts 1989, 71st Leg., ch. 678, §1, eff. Sept. 1, 1989. Amended by Acts 1993, 73rd Leg., ch. 900, §2.02, eff. Sept. 1, 1994; Acts 1997, 75th Leg., ch. 745, §27, eff. Sept. 1, 1997; Acts 2001, 77th Leg., ch. 251, §20, eff. Sept. 1, 2001.

ANNOTATIONS

Ex parte Perales, 215 S.W.3d 418, 420 (Tex.Crim. App.2007). "[A]n allegation of delivery of a controlled substance by actual transfer to an unborn child cannot constitute delivery, which we have held 'contemplates the manual transfer of property from the transferor to the transferee or to the transferee's agents or to someone identified in law with the transferee.' We have also held that such a transfer occurs when the defendant transfers or surrenders actual possession and control of a controlled substance to another. Since such an actual transfer delivery from a mother to her unborn child is not possible, we conclude that, as a matter of law, delivery by actual transfer as alleged did not occur."

H&SC §481.123. DEFENSE TO PROSECUTION FOR OFFENSE INVOLVING CONTROLLED SUBSTANCE ANALOGUE

(a) It is an affirmative defense to the prosecution of an offense under this subchapter involving the manufacture, delivery, or possession of a controlled substance analogue that the analogue:

(1) was not in any part intended for human consumption;

(2) was a substance for which there is an approved new drug application under Section 505 of the Federal Food, Drug, and Cosmetic Act (21 U.S.C. Section 355); or

(3) was a substance for which an exemption for investigational use has been granted under Section 505 of the Federal Food, Drug, and Cosmetic Act (21 U.S.C. Section 355), if the actor's conduct with respect to the substance is in accord with the exemption.

(b) For the purposes of this section, Section 505 of the Federal Food, Drug, and Cosmetic Act (21 U.S.C. Section 355) applies to the introduction or delivery for introduction of any new drug into intrastate, interstate, or foreign commerce.

History of H&SC §481.123: Acts 1989, 71st Leg., ch. 678, §1, eff. Sept. 1, 1989. Amended by Acts 1997, 75th Leg., ch. 745, §28, eff. Sept. 1, 1997; Acts 2003, 78th Leg., ch. 1099, §10, eff. Sept. 1, 2003.

H&SC §481.124. OFFENSE: POSSESSION OR TRANSPORT OF CERTAIN CHEMICALS WITH INTENT TO MANUFACTURE CONTROLLED SUBSTANCE

(a) A person commits an offense if, with intent to unlawfully manufacture a controlled substance, the person possesses or transports:

(1) anhydrous ammonia;

(2) an immediate precursor; or

(3) a chemical precursor or an additional chemical substance named as a precursor by the director under Section 481.077(b)(1).

(b) For purposes of this section, an intent to unlawfully manufacture the controlled substance methamphetamine is presumed if the actor possesses or transports:

(1) anhydrous ammonia in a container or receptacle that is not designed and manufactured to lawfully hold or transport anhydrous ammonia;

(2) lithium metal removed from a battery and immersed in kerosene, mineral spirits, or similar liquid that prevents or retards hydration; or

TCSA §481.124

(3) in one container, vehicle, or building, phenylacetic acid, or more than nine grams, three containers packaged for retail sale, or 300 tablets or capsules of a product containing ephedrine or pseudoephedrine, and:

(A) anhydrous ammonia;

(B) at least three of the following categories of substances commonly used in the manufacture of methamphetamine:

(i) lithium or sodium metal or red phosphorus, iodine, or iodine crystals;

(ii) lye, sulfuric acid, hydrochloric acid, or muriatic acid;

(iii) an organic solvent, including ethyl ether, alcohol, or acetone;

(iv) a petroleum distillate, including naphtha, paint thinner, or charcoal lighter fluid; or

(v) aquarium, rock, or table salt; or

(C) at least three of the following items:

(i) an item of equipment subject to regulation under Section 481.080, if the person is not registered under Section 481.063; or

(ii) glassware, a plastic or metal container, tubing, a hose, or other item specially designed, assembled, or adapted for use in the manufacture, processing, analyzing, storing, or concealing of methamphetamine.

(c) For purposes of this section, a substance is presumed to be anhydrous ammonia if the substance is in a container or receptacle that is:

(1) designed and manufactured to lawfully hold or transport anhydrous ammonia; or

(2) not designed and manufactured to lawfully hold or transport anhydrous ammonia, if:

(A) a properly administered field test of the substance using a testing device or instrument designed and manufactured for that purpose produces a positive result for anhydrous ammonia; or

(B) a laboratory test of a water solution of the substance produces a positive result for ammonia.

(d) An offense under this section is:

(1) a felony of the second degree if the controlled substance is listed in Penalty Group 1 or 1-A;

(2) a felony of the third degree if the controlled substance is listed in Penalty Group 2;

(3) a state jail felony if the controlled substance is listed in Penalty Group 3 or 4; or

(4) a Class A misdemeanor if the controlled substance is listed in a schedule by an action of the commissioner under this chapter but not listed in a penalty group.

(e) If conduct constituting an offense under this section also constitutes an offense under another section of this code, the actor may be prosecuted under either section or under both sections.

(f) This section does not apply to a chemical precursor exempted by the director under Section 481.077(b)(2) from the requirements of that section.

History of H&SC §481.124: Acts 2001, 77th Leg., ch. 1188, §7, eff. Sept. 1, 2001. Amended by Acts 2003, 78th Leg., ch. 570, §2, eff. Sept. 1, 2003; Acts 2005, 79th Leg., ch. 282, §6, eff. Aug. 1, 2005.

History of Former H&SC §481.124: Repealed by Acts 1989, 71st Leg., ch. 1100, §5.02(j), eff. Sept. 1, 1989.

ANNOTATIONS

Shaffer v. State, 184 S.W.3d 353, 361 (Tex.App.—Fort Worth 2006, pet. ref'd). "[T]he cold medicine Appellant possessed was contained in sealed packages. Additionally, … the labeling on the packages reliably established that the cold medicine contained pseudoephedrine. We hold that this evidence is legally and factually sufficient to prove that Appellant was in possession of the chemical precursor pseudoephedrine."

H&SC §481.1245. OFFENSE: POSSESSION OR TRANSPORT OF ANHYDROUS AMMONIA; USE OF OR TAMPERING WITH EQUIPMENT

(a) A person commits an offense if the person:

(1) possesses or transports anhydrous ammonia in a container or receptacle that is not designed or manufactured to hold or transport anhydrous ammonia;

(2) uses, transfers, or sells a container or receptacle that is designed or manufactured to hold anhydrous ammonia without the express consent of the owner of the container or receptacle; or

(3) tampers with equipment that is manufactured or used to hold, apply, or transport anhydrous ammonia without the express consent of the owner of the equipment.

(b) An offense under this section is a felony of the third degree.

History of H&SC §481.1245: Acts 2005, 79th Leg., ch. 282, §7, eff. Aug. 1, 2005.

H&SC §481.125. OFFENSE: POSSESSION OR DELIVERY OF DRUG PARAPHERNALIA

(a) A person commits an offense if the person knowingly or intentionally uses or possesses with intent to use drug paraphernalia to plant, propagate, cultivate, grow, harvest, manufacture, compound, convert, produce, process, prepare, test, analyze, pack, repack, store, contain, or conceal a controlled substance in violation of this chapter or to inject, ingest, inhale, or otherwise introduce into the human body a controlled substance in violation of this chapter.

(b) A person commits an offense if the person knowingly or intentionally delivers, possesses with intent to deliver, or manufactures with intent to deliver drug paraphernalia knowing that the person who receives or who is intended to receive the drug paraphernalia intends that it be used to plant, propagate, cultivate, grow, harvest, manufacture, compound, convert, produce, process, prepare, test, analyze, pack, repack, store, contain, or conceal a controlled substance in violation of this chapter or to inject, ingest, inhale, or otherwise introduce into the human body a controlled substance in violation of this chapter.

(c) A person commits an offense if the person commits an offense under Subsection (b), is 18 years of age or older, and the person who receives or who is intended to receive the drug paraphernalia is younger than 18 years of age and at least three years younger than the actor.

(d) An offense under Subsection (a) is a Class C misdemeanor.

(e) An offense under Subsection (b) is a Class A misdemeanor, unless it is shown on the trial of a defendant that the defendant has previously been convicted under Subsection (b) or (c), in which event the offense is punishable by confinement in jail for a term of not more than one year or less than 90 days.

(f) An offense under Subsection (c) is a state jail felony.

History of H&SC §481.125: Acts 1989, 71st Leg., ch. 678, §1, eff. Sept. 1, 1989. Amended by Acts 1993, 73rd Leg., ch. 900, §2.02, eff. Sept. 1, 1994.

ANNOTATIONS

State v. Holguin, 861 S.W.2d 919, 920 (Tex.Crim. App.1993). "To convict appellee of possession of drug paraphernalia, the State must establish (1) appellee

(2) intentionally or knowingly (3) possessed with intent to use (4) drug paraphernalia (5) in order to store, contain, or conceal a controlled substance or to ingest, inject, inhale, or otherwise introduce into the human body a controlled substance."

Nichols v. State, 886 S.W.2d 324, 326 (Tex.App.— Houston [1st Dist.] 1994, pet. ref'd). Officer "was not required to *know* that the pipe was contraband before seizing it; his reasonable belief that it was contraband was sufficient."

H&SC §481.126. OFFENSE: ILLEGAL BARTER, EXPENDITURE, OR INVESTMENT

(a) A person commits an offense if the person:

(1) barters property or expends funds the person knows are derived from the commission of an offense under this chapter punishable by imprisonment in the institutional division of the Texas Department of Criminal Justice for life;

(2) barters property or expends funds the person knows are derived from the commission of an offense under Section 481.121(a) that is punishable under Section 481.121(b)(5);

(3) barters property or finances or invests funds the person knows or believes are intended to further the commission of an offense for which the punishment is described by Subdivision (1); or

(4) barters property or finances or invests funds the person knows or believes are intended to further the commission of an offense under Section 481.121(a) that is punishable under Section 481.121(b)(5).

(b) An offense under Subsection (a)(1) or (3) is a felony of the first degree. An offense under Subsection (a)(2) or (4) is a felony of the second degree.

History of H&SC §481.126: Acts 1989, 71st Leg., ch. 678, §1, eff. Sept. 1, 1989. Amended by Acts 1993, 73rd Leg., ch. 900, §2.02, eff. Sept. 1, 1994; Acts 1995, 74th Leg., ch. 318, §37, eff. Sept. 1, 1995; Acts 2001, 77th Leg., ch. 251, §21, eff. Sept. 1, 2001; Acts 2003, 78th Leg., ch. 712, §1, eff. Sept. 1, 2003.

ANNOTATIONS

Diaz v. State, 902 S.W.2d 149, 151 (Tex.App.— Houston [1st Dist.] 1995, no pet.). "The terms 'finance' and 'invest' include 'to raise' or 'to commit money by agreement in order to earn a financial return.' [S]ection 481.126 is not limited to an accused's investment of personal funds. [T]he terms 'finance' and 'invest' [are] broad enough to encompass the defendant's personal conduct. [There can be] sufficient evidence … to affirm [a defendant's] conviction as a party for illegal investment, even though [the defendant] himself had no money to expend or invest."

Howard v. State, 890 S.W.2d 514, 517 (Tex.App.— Beaumont 1994, no pet.). "[T]he *actual* transfer of funds need not be proven in an Illegal Expenditure or Investment prosecution. [T]he language of the applicable statute does not speak in terms of transferring funds; the offense merely requires that there be an intent to 'finance' or 'invest.' [¶] [A] conviction for Illegal Expenditure or Investment under of §481.126(a)(2) may be sustained without either the funds or the contraband changing hands. [W]ith the gravamen of the offense being the 'intent to finance or invest' funds, there is apparently no need to prove that any contraband actually existed during the course of the undercover operation so long as there is proof that the accused either knew or believed that the funds in question were intended to further the commission of any of the enumerated drug offenses."

$24,180 v. State, 865 S.W.2d 181, 186 (Tex.App.— Corpus Christi 1993, writ denied). "[T]he illegal investment statute only requires that the investment be intended to *further* the commission of aggravated delivery of marihuana. *At 187:* [There is] no language in H&SC §481.126 which supports the inference that a 'final agreement' must be reached before the offense of illegal investment is complete."

H&SC §481.127. OFFENSE: UNAUTHORIZED DISCLOSURE OF INFORMATION

(a) A person commits an offense if the person knowingly gives, permits, or obtains unauthorized access to information submitted to the director under Section 481.075.

(b) An offense under this section is a state jail felony.

History of H&SC §481.127: Acts 1989, 71st Leg., ch. 678, §1, eff. Sept. 1, 1989. Amended by Acts 1993, 73rd Leg., ch. 900, §2.02, eff. Sept. 1, 1994; Acts 1997, 75th Leg., ch. 745, §29, eff. Sept. 1, 1999.

H&SC §481.128. OFFENSE & CIVIL PENALTY: COMMERCIAL MATTERS

(a) A registrant or dispenser commits an offense if the registrant or dispenser knowingly:

(1) distributes, delivers, administers, or dispenses a controlled substance in violation of Sections 481.070-481.075;

(2) manufactures a controlled substance not authorized by the person's registration or distributes or dispenses a controlled substance not authorized by the person's registration to another registrant or other person;

(3) refuses or fails to make, keep, or furnish a record, report, notification, order form, statement, invoice, or information required by this chapter;

(4) prints, manufactures, possesses, or produces an official prescription form without the approval of the director;

(5) delivers or possesses a counterfeit official prescription form;

(6) refuses an entry into a premise for an inspection authorized by this chapter;

(7) refuses or fails to return an official prescription form as required by Section 481.075(k);

(8) refuses or fails to make, keep, or furnish a record, report, notification, order form, statement, invoice, or information required by a rule adopted by the director; or

(9) refuses or fails to maintain security required by this chapter or a rule adopted under this chapter.

(b) If the registrant or dispenser knowingly refuses or fails to make, keep, or furnish a record, report, notification, order form, statement, invoice, or information or maintain security required by a rule adopted by the director, the registrant or dispenser is liable to the state for a civil penalty of not more than $5,000 for each act.

(c) An offense under Subsection (a) is a state jail felony.

(d) If a person commits an act that would otherwise be an offense under Subsection (a) except that it was committed without the requisite culpable mental state, the person is liable to the state for a civil penalty of not more than $1,000 for each act.

(e) A district attorney of the county where the act occurred may file suit in district court in that county to collect a civil penalty under this section, or the district attorney of Travis County or the attorney general may file suit in district court in Travis County to collect the penalty.

History of H&SC §481.128: Acts 1989, 71st Leg., ch. 678, §1, eff. Sept. 1, 1989. Amended by Acts 1991, 72nd Leg., ch. 761, §5, eff. June 16, 1991; Acts 1993, 73rd Leg., ch. 900, §2.02, eff. Sept. 1, 1994; Acts 1997, 75th Leg., ch. 745, §30, eff. Sept. 1, 1997 & Sept. 1, 1999; Acts 2001, 77th Leg., ch. 251, §22, eff. Sept. 1, 2001.

H&SC §481.129. OFFENSE: FRAUD

(a) A person commits an offense if the person knowingly:

(1) distributes as a registrant or dispenser a controlled substance listed in Schedule I or II, unless the person distributes the controlled substance under an order form as required by Section 481.069;

(2) uses in the course of manufacturing, prescribing, or distributing a controlled substance a registration number that is fictitious, revoked, suspended, or issued to another person;

(3) issues a prescription bearing a forged or fictitious signature;

(4) uses a prescription issued to another person to prescribe a Schedule II controlled substance;

(5) possesses, obtains, or attempts to possess or obtain a controlled substance or an increased quantity of a controlled substance:

(A) by misrepresentation, fraud, forgery, deception, or subterfuge;

(B) through use of a fraudulent prescription form; or

(C) through use of a fraudulent oral or telephonically communicated prescription; or

(6) furnishes false or fraudulent material information in or omits material information from an application, report, record, or other document required to be kept or filed under this chapter.

(b) A person commits an offense if the person knowingly or intentionally:

(1) makes, distributes, or possesses a punch, die, plate, stone, or other thing designed to print, imprint, or reproduce an actual or simulated trademark, trade name, or other identifying mark, imprint, or device of another on a controlled substance or the container or label of a container for a controlled substance, so as to make the controlled substance a counterfeit substance; or

(2) manufactures, delivers, or possesses with intent to deliver a counterfeit substance.

(c) A person commits an offense if the person knowingly or intentionally:

(1) delivers a prescription or a prescription form for other than a valid medical purpose in the course of professional practice; or

(2) possesses a prescription for a controlled substance or a prescription form unless the prescription or prescription form is possessed:

(A) during the manufacturing or distribution process;

(B) by a practitioner, practitioner's agent, or an institutional practitioner for a valid medical purpose during the course of professional practice;

(C) by a pharmacist or agent of a pharmacy during the professional practice of pharmacy;

(D) under a practitioner's order made by the practitioner for a valid medical purpose in the course of professional practice; or

(E) by an officer or investigator authorized to enforce this chapter within the scope of the officer's or investigator's official duties.

(d) An offense under Subsection (a) is:

(1) a felony of the second degree if the controlled substance that is the subject of the offense is listed in Schedule I or II;

(2) a felony of the third degree if the controlled substance that is the subject of the offense is listed in Schedule III or IV; and

(3) a Class A misdemeanor if the controlled substance that is the subject of the offense is listed in Schedule V.

(e) An offense under Subsection (b) is a Class A misdemeanor.

(f) An offense under Subsection (c)(1) is:

(1) a felony of the second degree if the defendant delivers:

(A) a prescription form; or

(B) a prescription for a controlled substance listed in Schedule II; and

(2) a felony of the third degree if the defendant delivers a prescription for a controlled substance listed in Schedule III, IV, or V.

(g) An offense under Subsection (c)(2) is:

(1) a state jail felony if the defendant possesses:

(A) a prescription form; or

(B) a prescription for a controlled substance listed in Schedule II or III; and

(2) a Class B misdemeanor if the defendant possesses a prescription for a controlled substance listed in Schedule IV or V.

TCSA §481.129

History of H&SC §481.129: Acts 1989, 71st Leg., ch. 678, §1, eff. Sept. 1, 1989. Amended by Acts 1989, 71st Leg., ch. 1100, §5.02(p), eff. Sept. 1, 1989; Acts 1993, 73rd Leg., ch. 900, §2.02, eff. Sept. 1, 1994; Acts 1997, 75th Leg., ch. 745, §31, eff. Sept. 1, 1997, except for subsection (a), which is eff. Sept. 1, 1999; Acts 2001, 77th Leg., ch. 251, §23, eff. Sept. 1, 2001.

See also *O'Connor's Crimes & Consequences* (2008-09), chart 4-C, "Mandatory Community Supervision."

ANNOTATIONS

Krumboltz v. State, 945 S.W.2d 176, 178 (Tex. App.—San Antonio 1997, no pet.). "Obtaining a controlled substance by a forged instrument carries a range of punishment of two to twenty years imprisonment; possession of a forged check carries a range of punishment of two to ten years imprisonment; and possession of a controlled substance under 28 grams is punishable by two to ten years imprisonment. … In light of the nature of [D's] multiple offenses, the punishment range available for each offense, and the imposition of concurrent sentences, we are unable to find that his punishment violates the 8th Amendment of the U.S. Constitution or [Tex. Const. art.] I, §13."

Ryan v. State, 937 S.W.2d 93, 100 (Tex.App.— Beaumont 1996, pet. ref'd). "Intent is … an essential element of the offense of possession of a controlled substance by fraud. '[W]here intent or guilty knowledge is an essential element of the offense which the State must prove to obtain a conviction, its materiality goes without saying.' Evidence of extraneous acts is admissible '[t]o prove scienter, where intent or guilty knowledge is an essential element of the State's case and *cannot be inferred from the act itself.*'"

H&SC §481.130. PENALTIES UNDER OTHER LAW

A penalty imposed for an offense under this chapter is in addition to any civil or administrative penalty or other sanction imposed by law.

History of H&SC §481.130: Acts 1989, 71st Leg., ch. 678, §1, eff. Sept. 1, 1989.

H&SC §481.131. OFFENSE: DIVERSION OF CONTROLLED SUBSTANCE PROPERTY OR PLANT

(a) A person commits an offense if the person intentionally or knowingly:

(1) converts to the person's own use or benefit a controlled substance property or plant seized under Section 481.152 or 481.153; or

(2) diverts to the unlawful use or benefit of another person a controlled substance property or plant seized under Section 481.152 or 481.153.

(b) An offense under this section is a state jail felony.

History of H&SC §481.131: Acts 1991, 72nd Leg., ch. 141, §2, eff. Sept. 1, 1991; Acts 1993, 73rd Leg., ch. 900, §2.02, eff. Sept. 1, 1994.

H&SC §481.132. MULTIPLE PROSECUTIONS

(a) In this section, "criminal episode" means the commission of two or more offenses under this chapter under the following circumstances:

(1) the offenses are committed pursuant to the same transaction or pursuant to two or more transactions that are connected or constitute a common scheme, plan, or continuing course of conduct; or

(2) the offenses are the repeated commission of the same or similar offenses.

(b) A defendant may be prosecuted in a single criminal action for all offenses arising out of the same criminal episode. If a single criminal action is based on more than one charging instrument within the jurisdiction of the trial court, not later than the 30th day before the date of the trial, the state shall file written notice of the action.

(c) If a judgment of guilt is reversed, set aside, or vacated and a new trial is ordered, the state may not prosecute in a single criminal action in the new trial any offense not joined in the former prosecution unless evidence to establish probable guilt for that offense was not known to the appropriate prosecution official at the time the first prosecution began.

(d) If the accused is found guilty of more than one offense arising out of the same criminal episode prosecuted in a single criminal action, sentence for each offense for which the accused has been found guilty shall be pronounced, and those sentences run concurrently.

(e) If it appears that a defendant or the state is prejudiced by a joinder of offenses, the court may order separate trials of the offenses or provide other relief as justice requires.

(f) This section provides the exclusive method for consolidation and joinder of prosecutions for offenses under this chapter. This section is not a limitation of Article 36.09 or 36.10, Code of Criminal Procedure.

History of H&SC §481.132: Acts 1991, 72nd Leg., ch. 193, §1, eff. Sept. 1, 1991. Renumbered from §481.131 by Acts 1991, 72nd Leg., 1st C.S., ch. 14, §8.01(17a), eff. Nov. 12, 1991.

See also Pen. Code §§3.02, 3.03.

Williams v. State, ___ S.W.3d ___ (Tex.Crim.App. 2008) (No. PD-1948-06; 5-14-08). "In three separate indictments, Appellant was charged with the delivery of one gram or more, but less than four grams, of cocaine, a controlled substance in Penalty Group 1. One of the indictments contained a paragraph alleging that the offense occurred within 1,000 feet of a school—a drug-free-zone [under H&SC §481.134(c)]. Prior to trial, the court granted the State's motion to consolidate the three causes for one trial under [Pen. Code] §3.03. [¶] Appellant was convicted of all three offenses and sentenced by the trial judge. ... The trial judge then ordered the sentence for the drug-free zone offense to be served consecutively to the other two sentences, which would be served concurrently. [¶] Because §481.134(h) did not apply to Appellant's sentencing, [H&SC] §481.132 controls in this situation. We reverse the decision of the court of appeals and reform the judgment to reflect that all three sentences run concurrently."

Watson v. State, 900 S.W.2d 60, 63 (Tex.Crim.App. 1995). "In the present case, [D] was observed by the police doing acts consistent with dealing drugs. When they arrested him, they seized a plastic bag containing capsules, some of which tested positive for heroin and others of which tested positive for cocaine. Given these facts, both of the charged offenses arose out of the same 'criminal episode' as defined in §481.132(a). Therefore, joinder of the two offenses in a single indictment was proper under [H&SC] §481.132(b)."

Rollins v. State, 994 S.W.2d 429, 430 (Tex.App.—Beaumont 1999, no pet.). "[A]ppellant was separately indicted for two offenses of delivery of marihuana.... Each of the two indictments alleged the delivery was made to a different person.... In September of 1994, the trial court deferred adjudication of Rollins's guilt.... Later the State filed a motion to adjudicate his guilt. In a single proceeding ... the trial court found Rollins guilty in both offenses and ... placed Rollins on probation. *At 432-33:* [W]e are again faced with the issue of what constitutes a 'single criminal action.' ... Since the trial court treated the charged offenses at the adjudication of guilt proceeding as a single criminal action, we find the other requirement of §481.132(d) was satisfied. We conclude that the adjudication of guilt and

pronouncement of sentence in the two cases 'are so intertwined that we are left only to conclude they are a single criminal action.' [¶] Having found that the offenses were prosecuted in a single criminal action and that they arose out of the same criminal episode, we conclude that the trial court erred in ordering the sentences to run consecutively...."

Gongora v. State, 916 S.W.2d 570, 575 (Tex.App.—Houston [1st Dist.] 1996, pet. ref'd). "[D] asserts that [H&SC] §481.132 'specifically bars the State from multiple prosecutions.' We disagree. Section 481.132 is, by its terms, permissive. It neither requires the consolidation of offenses committed in the same criminal episode, nor precludes multiple prosecutions. [¶] Chapter three of the [Pen. Code] deals with multiple prosecutions. The language of [Pen. Code] §3.02 is the equivalent of portions of [H&SC] §481.132. [S]ection 3.02(a) is permissive, and ... a defendant does not have a right to consolidate offenses committed in the same criminal episode. We see no reason why §481.132 should be interpreted differently."

H&SC §481.133. OFFENSE: FALSIFICATION OF DRUG TEST RESULTS

(a) A person commits an offense if the person knowingly or intentionally uses or possesses with intent to use any substance or device designed to falsify drug test results.

(b) A person commits an offense if the person knowingly or intentionally delivers, possesses with intent to deliver, or manufactures with intent to deliver a substance or device designed to falsify drug test results.

(c) In this section, "drug test" means a lawfully administered test designed to detect the presence of a controlled substance or marihuana.

(d) An offense under Subsection (a) is a Class B misdemeanor.

(e) An offense under Subsection (b) is a Class A misdemeanor.

History of H&SC §481.133: Acts 1991, 72nd Leg., ch. 274, §1, eff. Sept. 1, 1991. Renumbered from §481.131 by Acts 1991, 72nd Leg., 1st C.S., ch. 14, §8.01(17b), eff. Nov. 12, 1991.

H&SC §481.134. DRUG-FREE ZONES

(a) In this section:

(1) "Minor" means a person who is younger than 18 years of age.

(2) "Institution of higher education" means any public or private technical institute, junior college, senior college or university, medical or dental unit, or other agency of higher education as defined by Section 61.003, Education Code.

(3) "Playground" means any outdoor facility that is not on the premises of a school and that:

(A) is intended for recreation;

(B) is open to the public; and

(C) contains three or more separate apparatus intended for the recreation of children, such as slides, swing sets, and teeterboards.

(4) "Premises" means real property and all buildings and appurtenances pertaining to the real property.

(5) "School" means a private or public elementary or secondary school or a day-care center, as defined by Section 42.002, Human Resources Code.

(6) "Video arcade facility" means any facility that:

(A) is open to the public, including persons who are 17 years of age or younger;

(B) is intended primarily for the use of pinball or video machines; and

(C) contains at least three pinball or video machines.

(7) "Youth center" means any recreational facility or gymnasium that:

(A) is intended primarily for use by persons who are 17 years of age or younger; and

(B) regularly provides athletic, civic, or cultural activities.

(b) An offense otherwise punishable as a state jail felony under Section 481.112, 481.113, 481.114, or 481.120 is punishable as a felony of the third degree, and an offense otherwise punishable as a felony of the second degree under any of those sections is punishable as a felony of the first degree, if it is shown at the punishment phase of the trial of the offense that the offense was committed:

(1) in, on, or within 1,000 feet of premises owned, rented, or leased by an institution of higher learning, the premises of a public or private youth center, or a playground; or

(2) in, on, or within 300 feet of the premises of a public swimming pool or video arcade facility.

(c) The minimum term of confinement or imprisonment for an offense otherwise punishable under Section 481.112(c), (d), (e), or (f), 481.113(c), (d), or (e),

481.114(c), (d), or (e), 481.115(c)-(f), 481.116(c), (d), or (e), 481.117(c), (d), or (e), 481.118(c), (d), or (e), 481.120(b)(4), (5), or (6), or 481.121(b)(4), (5), or (6) is increased by five years and the maximum fine for the offense is doubled if it is shown on the trial of the offense that the offense was committed:

(1) in, on, or within 1,000 feet of premises of a school or a public or private youth center; or

(2) on a school bus.

(d) An offense otherwise punishable under Section 481.112(b), 481.113(b), 481.114(b), 481.115(b), 481.116(b), 481.120(b)(3), or 481.121(b)(3) is a felony of the third degree if it is shown on the trial of the offense that the offense was committed:

(1) in, on, or within 1,000 feet of any real property that is owned, rented, or leased to a school or school board or the premises of a public or private youth center; or

(2) on a school bus.

(e) An offense otherwise punishable under Section 481.117(b), 481.119(a), 481.120(b)(2), or 481.121(b)(2) is a state jail felony if it is shown on the trial of the offense that the offense was committed:

(1) in, on, or within 1,000 feet of any real property that is owned, rented, or leased to a school or school board or the premises of a public or private youth center; or

(2) on a school bus.

(f) An offense otherwise punishable under Section 481.118(b), 481.119(b), 481.120(b)(1), or 481.121(b)(1) is a Class A misdemeanor if it is shown on the trial of the offense that the offense was committed:

(1) in, on, or within 1,000 feet of any real property that is owned, rented, or leased to a school or school board or the premises of a public or private youth center; or

(2) on a school bus.

(g) Subsection (f) does not apply to an offense if:

(1) the offense was committed inside a private residence; and

(2) no minor was present in the private residence at the time the offense was committed.

(h) Punishment that is increased for a conviction for an offense listed under this section may not run concurrently with punishment for a conviction under any other criminal statute.

History of H&SC §481.134: Acts 1993, 73rd Leg., ch. 888, §1, eff. Sept. 1, 1993. Amended by Acts 1995, 74th Leg., ch. 260, §39 (eff. May 30, 1995), ch. 318, §38 (eff. Sept. 1, 1995); Acts 1997, 75th Leg., ch. 1063, §9, eff. Sept. 1, 1997; Acts 2003, 78th Leg., ch. 570, §3, eff. Sept. 1, 2003.

ANNOTATIONS

Young v. State, 14 S.W.3d 748, 750-51 (Tex.Crim. App.2000). The Court held "in *Malik v. State*[, 953 S.W.2d 234 (Tex.Crim.App.1997)] that 'sufficiency of the evidence should be measured by the elements of the offense as defined by the hypothetically correct jury charge for the case.' While this formula, as written, applies only to the elements of the offense necessary to sustain a conviction, *Malik*'s principles apply equally to the affirmative findings necessary to sustain the imposition of an enhanced punishment. Thus the sufficiency of the evidence in this context should be measured by the elements of the hypothetically correct jury charge for the enhancement, as defined by statute. [¶] The statute which defines the hypothetically correct jury charge for appellant's drug-free zone enhancement is [H&SC] §481.134 ...."

Merritt v. State, 252 S.W.3d 751, 759 (Tex.App.— Texarkana 2008, no pet.). "All three prosecutions involved possession in a drug-free zone of controlled substances [and arose from the same criminal episode]. [¶] The dilemma and the question is, thus, this: does the trial court impose the sentence for this conviction to run concurrently with the other two convictions under [Pen. Code §3.03] and/or [H&SC §481.132(d)], or must the court order the sentences to run consecutively under [H&SC §481.134(h)]?" Held: The sentences must run concurrently.

Harris v. State, 125 S.W.3d 45, 53 (Tex.App.— Austin 2003, pet. dism'd). "[T]he trial court was correct in permitting evidence of the occurrence of the offense [within 1,000 feet of school property] to be presented at the guilt/innocence stage of the trial and submitting the offenses to the jury in the court's charge at that stage of the proceedings."

H&SC §481.135. MAPS AS EVIDENCE OF LOCATION OR AREA

(a) In a prosecution under Section 481.134, a map produced or reproduced by a municipal or county engineer for the purpose of showing the location and boundaries of drug-free zones is admissible in evidence and is prima facie evidence of the location or boundaries of those areas if the governing body of the municipality or county adopts a resolution or ordinance approving the map as an official finding and record of the location or boundaries of those areas.

(b) A municipal or county engineer may, on request of the governing body of the municipality or county, revise a map that has been approved by the governing body of the municipality or county as provided by Subsection (a).

(c) A municipal or county engineer shall file the original or a copy of every approved or revised map approved as provided by Subsection (a) with the county clerk of each county in which the area is located.

(d) This section does not prevent the prosecution from:

(1) introducing or relying on any other evidence or testimony to establish any element of an offense for which punishment is increased under Section 481.134; or

(2) using or introducing any other map or diagram otherwise admissible under the Texas Rules of Evidence.

History of H&SC §481.135: Acts 1993, 73rd Leg., ch. 888, §3, eff. Sept. 1, 1993. Amended by Acts 2005, 79th Leg., ch. 728, §9.004, eff. Sept. 1, 2005.

H&SC §481.136. OFFENSE: UNLAWFUL TRANSFER OR RECEIPT OF CHEMICAL PRECURSOR

(a) A person commits an offense if the person sells, transfers, furnishes, or receives a chemical precursor subject to Section 481.077(a) and the person:

(1) does not hold a chemical precursor transfer permit as required by Section 481.078 at the time of the transaction;

(2) does not comply with Section 481.077 or 481.0771;

(3) knowingly makes a false statement in a report or record required by Section 481.077, 481.0771, or 481.078; or

(4) knowingly violates a rule adopted under Section 481.077, 481.0771, or 481.078.

(b) An offense under this section is a state jail felony, unless it is shown on the trial of the offense that the defendant has been previously convicted of an offense under this section or Section 481.137, in which event the offense is a felony of the third degree.

History of H&SC §481.136: Acts 1997, 75th Leg., ch. 745, §32, eff. Sept. 1, 1997. Amended by Acts 2001, 77th Leg., ch. 251, §24, eff. Sept. 1, 2001; Acts 2005, 79th Leg., ch. 282, §8, eff. Aug. 1, 2005.

TCSA §481.136

H&SC §481.137. OFFENSE: TRANSFER OF PRECURSOR SUBSTANCE FOR UNLAWFUL MANUFACTURE

(a) A person commits an offense if the person sells, transfers, or otherwise furnishes a chemical precursor subject to Section 481.077(a) with the knowledge or intent that the recipient will use the chemical precursor to unlawfully manufacture a controlled substance or controlled substance analogue.

(b) An offense under this section is a felony of the third degree.

History of H&SC §481.137: Acts 1997, 75th Leg., ch. 745, §32, eff. Sept. 1, 1997. Amended by Acts 2001, 77th Leg., ch. 251, §25, eff. Sept. 1, 2001.

H&SC §481.138. OFFENSE: UNLAWFUL TRANSFER OR RECEIPT OF CHEMICAL LABORATORY APPARATUS

(a) A person commits an offense if the person sells, transfers, furnishes, or receives a chemical laboratory apparatus subject to Section 481.080(a) and the person:

(1) does not have a chemical laboratory apparatus transfer permit as required by Section 481.081 at the time of the transaction;

(2) does not comply with Section 481.080;

(3) knowingly makes a false statement in a report or record required by Section 481.080 or 481.081; or

(4) knowingly violates a rule adopted under Section 481.080 or 481.081.

(b) An offense under this section is a state jail felony, unless it is shown on the trial of the offense that the defendant has been previously convicted of an offense under this section, in which event the offense is a felony of the third degree.

History of H&SC §481.138: Acts 1997, 75th Leg., ch. 745, §32, eff. Sept. 1, 1997. Amended by Acts 2001, 77th Leg., ch. 251, §26, eff. Sept. 1, 2001.

H&SC §481.139. OFFENSE: TRANSFER OF CHEMICAL LABORATORY APPARATUS FOR UNLAWFUL MANUFACTURE

(a) A person commits an offense if the person sells, transfers, or otherwise furnishes a chemical laboratory apparatus with the knowledge or intent that the recipient will use the apparatus to unlawfully manufacture a controlled substance or controlled substance analogue.

(b) An offense under Subsection (a) is a felony of the third degree.

History of H&SC §481.139: Acts 1997, 75th Leg., ch. 745, §32, eff. Sept. 1, 1997. Amended by Acts 2001, 77th Leg., ch. 251, §27, eff. Sept. 1, 2001.

H&SC §481.140. USE OF CHILD IN COMMISSION OF OFFENSE

(a) If it is shown at the punishment phase of the trial of an offense otherwise punishable as a state jail felony, felony of the third degree, or felony of the second degree under Section 481.112, 481.1121, 481.113, 481.114, 481.120, or 481.122 that the defendant used or attempted to use a child younger than 18 years of age to commit or assist in the commission of the offense, the punishment is increased by one degree, unless the defendant used or threatened to use force against the child or another to gain the child's assistance, in which event the punishment for the offense is a felony of the first degree.

(b) Notwithstanding Article 42.08, Code of Criminal Procedure, if punishment for a defendant is increased under this section, the court may not order the sentence for the offense to run concurrently with any other sentence the court imposes on the defendant.

History of H&SC §481.140: Acts 2001, 77th Leg., ch. 786, §1, eff. June 14, 2001.

H&SC §481.141. MANUFACTURE OR DELIVERY OF CONTROLLED SUBSTANCE CAUSING DEATH OR SERIOUS BODILY INJURY

(a) If at the guilt or innocence phase of the trial of an offense described by Subsection (b), the judge or jury, whichever is the trier of fact, determines beyond a reasonable doubt that a person died or suffered serious bodily injury as a result of injecting, ingesting, inhaling, or introducing into the person's body any amount of the controlled substance manufactured or delivered by the defendant, regardless of whether the controlled substance was used by itself or with another substance, including a drug, adulterant, or dilutant, the punishment for the offense is increased by one degree.

(b) This section applies to an offense otherwise punishable as a state jail felony, felony of the third degree, or felony of the second degree under Section 481.112, 481.1121, 481.113, 481.114, or 481.122.

(c) Notwithstanding Article 42.08, Code of Criminal Procedure, if punishment for a defendant is increased under this section, the court may not order the

───────── ✦ ─────────

sentence for the offense to run concurrently with any other sentence the court imposes on the defendant.

History of H&SC §481.141: Acts 2003, 78th Leg., ch. 712, §2, eff. Sept. 1, 2003.

Sections 481.142-481.150 reserved for expansion

SUBCHAPTER E. FORFEITURE

H&SC §481.151. DEFINITIONS

In this subchapter:

(1) "Controlled substance property" means a controlled substance, mixture containing a controlled substance, controlled substance analogue, counterfeit controlled substance, drug paraphernalia, chemical precursor, chemical laboratory apparatus, or raw material.

(2) "Controlled substance plant" means a species of plant from which a controlled substance listed in Schedule I or II may be derived.

(3) "Summary destruction" or "summarily destroy" means destruction without the necessity of any court action, a court order, or further proceedings.

(4) "Summary forfeiture" or "summarily forfeit" means forfeiture without the necessity of any court action, a court order, or further proceedings.

History of H&SC §481.151: Acts 1991, 72nd Leg., ch. 141, §1, eff. Sept. 1, 1991. Amended by Acts 2001, 77th Leg., ch. 251, §28, eff. Sept. 1, 2001; Acts 2007, 80th Leg., ch. 152, §1, eff. May 21, 2007.

History of Former H&SC §481.151: Repealed by Acts 1989, 71st Leg., 1st C.S., ch. 12, §6, eff. Oct. 18, 1989.

H&SC §481.152. SEIZURE, SUMMARY FORFEITURE, & SUMMARY DESTRUCTION OF CONTROLLED SUBSTANCE PLANTS

(a) Controlled substance plants are subject to seizure and summary forfeiture to the state if:

(1) the plants have been planted, cultivated, or harvested in violation of this chapter;

(2) the plants are wild growths; or

(3) the owners or cultivators of the plants are unknown.

(b) Subsection (a) does not apply to unharvested peyote growing in its natural state.

(c) If a person who occupies or controls land or premises on which the plants are growing fails on the demand of a peace officer to produce an appropriate registration or proof that the person is the holder of the registration, the officer may seize and summarily forfeit the plants.

(d) If a controlled substance plant is seized and forfeited under this section, a court may order the disposition of the plant under Section 481.159, or the department or a peace officer may summarily destroy the property under the rules of the department.

History of H&SC §481.152: Acts 1989, 71st Leg., ch. 678, §1, eff. Sept. 1, 1989. Amended by Acts 1991, 72nd Leg., ch. 141, §1, eff. Sept. 1, 1991; Acts 2007, 80th Leg., ch. 152, §§2, 3, eff. May 21, 2007.

H&SC §481.153. SEIZURE, SUMMARY FORFEITURE, & SUMMARY DESTRUCTION OF CONTROLLED SUBSTANCE PROPERTY

(a) Controlled substance property that is manufactured, delivered, or possessed in violation of this chapter is subject to seizure and summary forfeiture to the state.

(b) If an item of controlled substance property is seized and forfeited under this section, a court may order the disposition of the property under Section 481.159, or the department or a peace officer may summarily destroy the property under the rules of the department.

History of H&SC §481.153: Acts 1991, 72nd Leg., ch. 141, §1, eff. Sept. 1, 1991. Amended by Acts 2007, 80th Leg., ch. 152, §§4, 5, eff. May 21, 2007.

History of Former H&SC §481.153: Repealed by Acts 1989, 71st Leg., 1st C.S., ch. 12, §6, eff. Oct. 18, 1989.

ANNOTATIONS

Fisher v. State, 839 S.W.2d 463, 468 (Tex.App.—Dallas 1992, pet. ref'd). "If a law enforcement agency or officer wants to use controlled substances, which the agency or officer has obtained through seizure and forfeiture proceedings, in a future sting operation, the agency or officer must obtain a district court order. A law enforcement agency or officer is not required to obtain a court order if the agency or the officer obtained the controlled substance in some manner other than by seizure and forfeiture."

H&SC §481.154. RULES

(a) The director may adopt reasonable rules and procedures, not inconsistent with the provisions of this chapter, concerning:

(1) summary forfeiture and summary destruction of controlled substance property or plants;

(2) establishment and operation of a secure storage area;

(3) delegation by a law enforcement agency head of the authority to access a secure storage area; and

(4) minimum tolerance for and the circumstances of loss or destruction during an investigation.

(b) The rules for the destruction of controlled substance property or plants must require:

(1) more than one person to witness the destruction of the property or plants;

(2) the preparation of an inventory of the property or plants destroyed; and

(3) the preparation of a statement that contains the names of the persons who witness the destruction and the details of the destruction.

(c) A document prepared under a rule adopted under this section must be completed, retained, and made available for inspection by the director.

History of H&SC §481.154: Acts 1991, 72nd Leg., ch. 141, §1, eff. Sept. 1, 1991. Amended by Acts 2007, 80th Leg., ch. 152, §6, eff. May 21, 2007.

History of Former H&SC §481.154: Repealed by Acts 1989, 71st Leg., 1st C.S., ch. 12, §6, eff. Oct. 18, 1989.

H&SC §§481.155 TO 481.158. REPEALED

Repealed by Acts 1989, 71st Leg., 1st C.S., ch. 12, §6, eff. Oct. 18, 1989.

H&SC §481.159. DISPOSITION OF CONTROLLED SUBSTANCE PROPERTY OR PLANT

(a) If a district court orders the forfeiture of a controlled substance property or plant under Chapter 59, Code of Criminal Procedure, or under this code, the court shall also order a law enforcement agency to:

(1) retain the property or plant for its official purposes, including use in the investigation of offenses under this code;

(2) deliver the property or plant to a government agency for official purposes;

(3) deliver the property or plant to a person authorized by the court to receive it;

(4) deliver the property or plant to a person authorized by the director to receive it for a purpose described by Section 481.065(a); or

(5) destroy the property or plant that is not otherwise disposed of in the manner prescribed by this subchapter.

(b) The district court may not require the department to receive, analyze, or retain a controlled substance property or plant forfeited to a law enforcement agency other than the department.

(c) In order to ensure that a controlled substance property or plant is not diluted, substituted, diverted, or tampered with while being used in the investigation of offenses under this code, law enforcement agencies using the property or plant for this purpose shall:

(1) employ a qualified individual to conduct qualitative and quantitative analyses of the property or plant before and after their use in an investigation;

(2) maintain the property or plant in a secure storage area accessible only to the law enforcement agency head and the individual responsible for analyzing, preserving, and maintaining security over the property or plant; and

(3) maintain a log documenting:

(A) the date of issue, date of return, type, amount, and concentration of property or plant used in an investigation; and

(B) the signature and the printed or typed name of the peace officer to whom the property or plant was issued and the signature and the printed or typed name of the individual issuing the property or plant.

(d) A law enforcement agency may contract with another law enforcement agency to provide security that complies with Subsection (c) for controlled substance property or plants.

(e) A law enforcement agency may adopt a written policy with more stringent requirements than those required by Subsection (c). The director may enter and inspect, in accordance with Section 481.181, a location at which an agency maintains records or controlled substance property or plants as required by this section.

(f) If a law enforcement agency uses a controlled substance property or plant in the investigation of an offense under this code and the property or plant has been transported across state lines before the forfeiture, the agency shall cooperate with a federal agency in the investigation if requested to do so by the federal agency.

(g) Under the rules of the department, a law enforcement agency head may grant to another person access to a secure storage facility under Subsection (c)(2).

(h) A county, justice, or municipal court may order forfeiture of a controlled substance property or plant, unless the lawful possession of and title to the property or plant can be ascertained. If the court determines that a person had lawful possession of and title to the controlled substance property or plant before it was seized, the court shall order the controlled substance property

TCSA §481.154

or plant returned to the person, if the person so desires. The court may only order the destruction of a controlled substance property or plant that is not otherwise disposed of in the manner prescribed by Section 481.160.

(i) If a controlled substance property or plant seized under this chapter was forfeited to an agency for the purpose of destruction or for any purpose other than investigation, the property or plant may not be used in an investigation unless a district court orders disposition under this section and permits the use of the property or plant in the investigation.

History of H&SC §481.159: Acts 1989, 71st Leg., ch. 678, §1 (eff. Sept. 1, 1989), 1st C.S., ch. 12, §5(a) (eff. Oct. 18, 1989). Amended by Acts 1991, 72nd Leg., ch. 141, §1, eff. Sept. 1, 1991.

ANNOTATIONS

Lopez v. State, 817 S.W.2d 150, 153 (Tex.App.—El Paso 1991, no pet.). "The stated purpose of the provisions contained in [H&SC] §481.159(c) are 'to ensure that controlled substances or raw materials are not diluted, substituted, or tampered with while being used in the investigation of offenses under this chapter....' Thus, §481.159 is clearly related to the security of controlled substances which have been retained by the law enforcement agency for official purposes and particularly to prevent dilution, substitution or tampering with the substances while they are being used in the investigation of offenses. On the other hand, [CCP art.] 38.23 relates to *illegally obtained* evidence, such as that obtained as a result of an improper search or a coerced confession, not to evidence that although legally obtained, was perhaps improperly handled under §481.159.... [T]here is no showing that the marihuana was illegally obtained. Moreover, the marihuana used in this investigation did not play a direct part in the apprehension of the [D] and the other parties."

H&SC §481.160. DESTRUCTION OF EXCESS QUANTITIES

(a) If a controlled substance property or plant is forfeited under this code or under Chapter 59, Code of Criminal Procedure, the law enforcement agency that seized the property or plant or to which the property or plant is forfeited may summarily destroy the property or plant without a court order before the disposition of a case arising out of the forfeiture if the agency ensures that:

(1) at least five random and representative samples are taken from the total amount of the property or plant and a sufficient quantity is preserved to provide for discovery by parties entitled to discovery;

(2) photographs are taken that reasonably depict the total amount of the property or plant; and

(3) the gross weight or liquid measure of the property or plant is determined, either by actually weighing or measuring the property or plant or by estimating its weight or measurement after making dimensional measurements of the total amount seized.

(b) If the property consists of a single container of liquid, taking and preserving one representative sample complies with Subsection (a)(1).

(c) A representative sample, photograph, or record made under this section is admissible in civil or criminal proceedings in the same manner and to the same extent as if the total quantity of the suspected controlled substance property or plant was offered in evidence, regardless of whether the remainder of the property or plant has been destroyed. An inference or presumption of spoliation does not apply to a property or plant destroyed under this section.

(d) If hazardous waste, residuals, contaminated glassware, associated equipment, or by-products from illicit chemical laboratories or similar operations that create a health or environmental hazard or are not capable of being safely stored are forfeited, those items may be disposed of under Subsection (a) or may be seized and summarily forfeited and destroyed by a law enforcement agency without a court order before the disposition of a case arising out of the forfeiture if current environmental protection standards are followed.

(e) A law enforcement agency seizing and destroying or disposing of materials described in Subsection (d) shall ensure that photographs are taken that reasonably depict the total amount of the materials seized and the manner in which the materials were physically arranged or positioned before seizure.

(f) Repealed by Acts 2005, 79th Leg., ch. 1224, §19(2), eff. Sept. 1, 2005.

History of H&SC §481.160: Acts 1989, 71st Leg., ch. 678, §1 (eff. Sept. 1, 1989), ch. 1100, §5.02(r) (eff. Sept. 1, 1989). Amended by Acts 1991, 72nd Leg., ch. 14, §199 (eff. Sept. 1, 1991), ch. 141, §1 (eff. Sept. 1, 1991), ch. 285, §2 (eff. Sept. 1, 1991); Acts 1997, 75th Leg., ch. 745, §33, eff. Jan. 1, 1998. Reenacted and amended by Acts 2001, 77th Leg., ch. 251, §29, eff. Sept. 1, 2001. Amended by Acts 2005, 79th Leg., ch. 1224 §19(2), eff. Sept. 1, 2005.

Sections 481.161-481.180 reserved for expansion

SUBCHAPTER F. INSPECTIONS, EVIDENCE, & MISCELLANEOUS LAW ENFORCEMENT PROVISIONS

H&SC §481.181. INSPECTIONS

(a) The director may enter controlled premises at any reasonable time and inspect the premises and items described by Subsection (b) in order to inspect, copy, and verify the correctness of a record, report, or other document required to be made or kept under this chapter and to perform other functions under this chapter. For purposes of this subsection, "reasonable time" means any time during the normal business hours of the person or activity regulated under this chapter or any time an activity regulated under this chapter is occurring on the premises. The director shall:

(1) state the purpose of the entry;

(2) display to the owner, operator, or agent in charge of the premises appropriate credentials; and

(3) deliver to the owner, operator, or agent in charge of the premises a written notice of inspection authority.

(b) The director may:

(1) inspect and copy a record, report, or other document required to be made or kept under this chapter;

(2) inspect, within reasonable limits and in a reasonable manner, the controlled premises and all pertinent equipment, finished and unfinished drugs, other substances, and materials, containers, labels, records, files, papers, processes, controls, and facilities as appropriate to verify a record, report, or document required to be kept under this chapter or to administer this chapter;

(3) examine and inventory stock of a controlled substance and obtain samples of the controlled substance;

(4) examine a hypodermic syringe, needle, pipe, or other instrument, device, contrivance, equipment, control, container, label, or facility relating to a possible violation of this chapter; and

(5) examine a material used, intended to be used, or capable of being used to dilute or adulterate a controlled substance.

(c) Unless the owner, operator, or agent in charge of the controlled premises consents in writing, the director may not inspect:

(1) financial data;

(2) sales data other than shipment data; or

(3) pricing data.

History of H&SC §481.181: Acts 1989, 71st Leg., ch. 678, §1, eff. Sept. 1, 1989. Amended by Acts 2003, 78th Leg., ch. 1099, §11, eff. Sept. 1, 2003.

H&SC §481.182. EVIDENTIARY RULES RELATING TO OFFER OF DELIVERY

For the purpose of establishing a delivery under this chapter, proof of an offer to sell must be corroborated by:

(1) a person other than the person to whom the offer is made; or

(2) evidence other than a statement of the person to whom the offer is made.

History of H&SC §481.182: Acts 2003, 78th Leg., ch. 1099, §12, eff. Sept. 1, 2003.

History of Former H&SC §481.182: Acts 1989, 71st Leg., ch. 678, §1, eff. Sept. 1, 1989. Deleted by Acts 2003, 78th Leg., ch. 1099, §12, eff. Sept. 1, 2003.

ANNOTATIONS

Iniguez v. State, 835 S.W.2d 167, 170 (Tex.App.—Houston [1st Dist.] 1992, pet. ref'd). "Proof of an offer to sell must be corroborated by a person other than the offeree or by evidence other than a statement of the offeree. Therefore, the jury had to find that [witnesses'] testimony concerning [D's] offer to sell her three and one-half kilograms of cocaine was corroborated by testimony of another person or by the evidence in order to find [D] guilty of delivery by offer to sell of at least 400 grams of cocaine."

Vivanco v. State, 825 S.W.2d 187, 191 (Tex.App.—Houston [14th Dist.] 1992, pet. ref'd). "[T]he stringent corroboration requirements applicable in accomplice witness settings are not applicable in delivery by offer to sell cases. *At 192:* This court must determine if based on the evidence presented a rational trier of fact could have found that the offer was corroborated beyond a reasonable doubt. We hold that there was sufficient evidence for the jury to find that the offer was actually made. The testimony of [officers] taken together with the four different meetings where [D] was the contact man provides sufficient corroborating evidence of the offer. The delivery of some drugs also serves to corroborate the offer to sell."

H&SC §481.183. EVIDENTIARY RULES RELATING TO DRUG PARAPHERNALIA

(a) In considering whether an item is drug paraphernalia under this chapter, a court or other authority shall consider, in addition to all other logically relevant factors, and subject to rules of evidence:

(1) statements by an owner or person in control of the object concerning its use;

(2) the existence of any residue of a controlled substance on the object;

(3) direct or circumstantial evidence of the intent of an owner or other person in control of the object to deliver it to a person whom the person knows or should reasonably know intends to use the object to facilitate a violation of this chapter;

(4) oral or written instructions provided with the object concerning its use;

(5) descriptive material accompanying the object that explains or depicts its use;

(6) the manner in which the object is displayed for sale;

(7) whether the owner or person in control of the object is a supplier of similar or related items to the community, such as a licensed distributor or dealer of tobacco products;

(8) direct or circumstantial evidence of the ratio of sales of the object to the total sales of the business enterprise;

(9) the existence and scope of uses for the object in the community;

(10) the physical design characteristics of the item; and

(11) expert testimony concerning the item's use.

(b) The innocence of an owner or other person in charge of an object as to a direct violation of this chapter does not prevent a finding that the object is intended or designed for use as drug paraphernalia.

History of H&SC §481.183: Acts 1989, 71st Leg., ch. 678, §1, eff. Sept. 1, 1989. Amended by Acts 2003, 78th Leg., ch. 1099, §13, eff. Sept. 1, 2003.

H&SC §481.184. BURDEN OF PROOF; LIABILITIES

(a) The state is not required to negate an exemption or exception provided by this chapter in a complaint, information, indictment, or other pleading or in any trial, hearing, or other proceeding under this chapter. A person claiming the benefit of an exemption or exception has the burden of going forward with the evidence with respect to the exemption or exception.

(b) In the absence of proof that a person is the duly authorized holder of an appropriate registration or order form issued under this chapter, the person is presumed not to be the holder of the registration or form. The presumption is subject to rebuttal by a person charged with an offense under this chapter.

(c) This chapter does not impose a liability on an authorized state, county, or municipal officer engaged in the lawful performance of official duties.

History of H&SC §481.184: Acts 1989, 71st Leg., ch. 678, §1, eff. Sept. 1, 1989. Amended by Acts 2003, 78th Leg., ch. 1099, §14, eff. Sept. 1, 2003.

ANNOTATIONS

Employee Retirement Sys. v. Cash, 906 S.W.2d 204, 208 (Tex.App.—Austin 1995, writ denied). "It is undisputed that possession of either cocaine or methadone without a valid prescription is a felony offense. [D] did not argue or present any evidence that her husband held a valid prescription for methadone, as was her burden. ... The combined amount of these drugs was measurable and hence sufficient to uphold a possession offense."

Armendarez v. State, 822 S.W.2d 321, 323 (Tex. App.—Fort Worth 1992, pet. ref'd). "[D] asserts that [§481.184(c)] applies only to the possession of controlled substances by police officers, and does not permit the delivery or sale of controlled substances by police officers. [¶] We find [D's] logic faulty. [T]he statute does not ... promote violations of state and federal law because the activity is limited to the 'lawful performance of the officer's duties.' Therefore, we find that the police conduct of posing as a seller of narcotics in its undercover operations was not unlawful."

Nowling v. State, 801 S.W.2d 182, 185 (Tex.App.— Houston [14th Dist.] 1990, pet. ref'd). H&SC §481.184(a) "squarely placed the burden on the [D] to establish any exceptions under [H&SC] §481.002(26) that he wished to raise. The denial of his motion for a quantitative analysis and the lack of evidence as to the weight of the marihuana excluding the mature stalks and non-germinable seeds creates a reasonable doubt that did not otherwise exist. We find that the trial court abused its discretion in denying appellant's motion."

TCSA §481.184

H&SC §481.185. ARREST REPORTS

(a) Each law enforcement agency in this state shall file monthly with the director a report of all arrests made for drug offenses and quantities of controlled substances seized during the preceding month. The agency shall make the report on a form provided by the director and shall provide the information required by the form.

(b) The director shall publish an annual summary of all drug arrests and controlled substances seized in the state.

History of H&SC §481.185: Acts 1989, 71st Leg., ch. 678, §1, eff. Sept. 1, 1989.

H&SC §481.186. COOPERATIVE ARRANGEMENTS

(a) The director shall cooperate with federal and state agencies in discharging the director's responsibilities concerning traffic in controlled substances and in suppressing the abuse of controlled substances. The director may:

(1) arrange for the exchange of information among government officials concerning the use and abuse of controlled substances;

(2) cooperate in and coordinate training programs concerning controlled substances law enforcement at local and state levels;

(3) cooperate with the Federal Drug Enforcement Administration and state agencies by establishing a centralized unit to accept, catalog, file, and collect statistics, including records on drug-dependent persons and other controlled substance law offenders in this state and, except as provided by Section 481.068, make the information available for federal, state, and local law enforcement purposes; and

(4) conduct programs of eradication aimed at destroying wild or illegal growth of plant species from which controlled substances may be extracted.

(b) In the exercise of regulatory functions under this chapter, the director may rely on results, information, and evidence relating to the regulatory functions of this chapter received from the Federal Drug Enforcement Administration or a state agency.

History of H&SC §481.186: Acts 1989, 71st Leg., ch. 678, §1, eff. Sept. 1, 1989. Amended by Acts 2003, 78th Leg., ch. 1099, §15, eff. Sept. 1, 2003.

Sections 481.187-481.200 reserved for expansion

SUBCHAPTER G. THERAPEUTIC RESEARCH PROGRAM

H&SC §481.201. RESEARCH PROGRAM; REVIEW BOARD

(a) The Texas Board of Health may establish a controlled substance therapeutic research program for the supervised use of tetrahydrocannabinols for medical and research purposes to be conducted in accordance with this chapter.

(b) If the Texas Board of Health establishes the program, the board shall create a research program review board. The review board members are appointed by the Texas Board of Health and serve at the will of the board.

(c) The review board shall be composed of:

(1) a licensed physician certified by the American Board of Ophthalmology;

(2) a licensed physician certified by the American Board of Internal Medicine and certified in the subspecialty of medical oncology;

(3) a licensed physician certified by the American Board of Psychiatry;

(4) a licensed physician certified by the American Board of Surgery;

(5) a licensed physician certified by the American Board of Radiology; and

(6) a licensed attorney with experience in law pertaining to the practice of medicine.

(d) Members serve without compensation but are entitled to reimbursement for actual and necessary expenses incurred in performing official duties.

History of H&SC §481.201: Acts 1989, 71st Leg., ch. 678, §1, eff. Sept. 1, 1989.

H&SC §481.202. REVIEW BOARD POWERS & DUTIES

(a) The review board shall review research proposals submitted and medical case histories of persons recommended for participation in a research program and determine which research programs and persons are most suitable for the therapy and research purposes of the program. The review board shall approve the research programs, certify program participants, and conduct periodic reviews of the research and participants.

(b) The review board, after approval of the Texas Board of Health, may seek authorization to expand the research program to include diseases not covered by this subchapter.

(c) The review board shall maintain a record of all persons in charge of approved research programs and of all persons who participate in the program as researchers or as patients.

(d) The Texas Board of Health may terminate the distribution of tetrahydrocannabinols and their derivatives to a research program as it determines necessary.

History of H&SC §481.202: Acts 1989, 71st Leg., ch. 678, §1, eff. Sept. 1, 1989.

H&SC §481.203. PATIENT PARTICIPATION

(a) A person may not be considered for participation as a recipient of tetrahydrocannabinols and their derivatives through a research program unless the person is recommended to a person in charge of an approved research program and the review board by a physician who is licensed by the Texas State Board of Medical Examiners and is attending the person.

(b) A physician may not recommend a person for the research program unless the person:

(1) has glaucoma or cancer;

(2) is not responding to conventional treatment for glaucoma or cancer or is experiencing severe side effects from treatment; and

(3) has symptoms or side effects from treatment that may be alleviated by medical use of tetrahydrocannabinols or their derivatives.

History of H&SC §481.203: Acts 1989, 71st Leg., ch. 678, §1, eff. Sept. 1, 1989.

H&SC §481.204. ACQUISITION & DISTRIBUTION OF CONTROLLED SUBSTANCES

(a) The Texas Board of Health shall acquire the tetrahydrocannabinols and their derivatives for use in the research program by contracting with the National Institute on Drug Abuse to receive tetrahydrocannabinols and their derivatives that are safe for human consumption according to the regulations adopted by the institute, the Food and Drug Administration, and the Federal Drug Enforcement Administration.

(b) The Texas Board of Health shall supervise the distribution of the tetrahydrocannabinols and their derivatives to program participants. The tetrahydrocannabinols and derivatives of tetrahydrocannabinols may be distributed only by the person in charge of the research program to physicians caring for program participant patients, under rules adopted by the Texas

Board of Health in such a manner as to prevent unauthorized diversion of the substances and in compliance with all requirements of the Federal Drug Enforcement Administration. The physician is responsible for dispensing the substances to patients.

History of H&SC §481.204: Acts 1989, 71st Leg., ch. 678, §1, eff. Sept. 1, 1989.

H&SC §481.205. RULES; REPORTS

(a) The Texas Board of Health shall adopt rules necessary for implementing the research program.

(b) If the Texas Board of Health establishes a program under this subchapter, the commissioner shall publish a report not later than January 1 of each odd-numbered year on the medical effectiveness of the use of tetrahydrocannabinols and their derivatives and any other medical findings of the research program.

History of H&SC §481.205: Acts 1989, 71st Leg., ch. 678, §1, eff. Sept. 1, 1989.

● SUBCHAPTER H. ADMINISTRATIVE PENALTY

● H&SC §481.301. IMPOSITION OF PENALTY

The department may impose an administrative penalty on a person who violates Section 481.061, 481.066, 481.067, 481.069, 481.074, 481.075, 481.077, 481.0771, 481.078, 481.080, or 481.081 or a rule or order adopted under any of those sections.

History of H&SC §481.301: Acts 2007, 80th Leg., ch. 1391, §5, eff. Sept. 1, 2007.

● H&SC §481.302. AMOUNT OF PENALTY

(a) The amount of the penalty may not exceed $1,000 for each violation, and each day a violation continues or occurs is a separate violation for purposes of imposing a penalty. The total amount of the penalty assessed for a violation continuing or occurring on separate days under this subsection may not exceed $20,000.

(b) The amount shall be based on:

(1) the seriousness of the violation, including the nature, circumstances, extent, and gravity of the violation;

(2) the threat to health or safety caused by the violation;

(3) the history of previous violations;

TCSA §481.302

(4) the amount necessary to deter a future violation;

(5) whether the violator demonstrated good faith, including when applicable whether the violator made good faith efforts to correct the violation; and

(6) any other matter that justice may require.

History of H&SC §481.302: Acts 2007, 80th Leg., ch. 1391, §5, eff. Sept. 1, 2007.

H&SC §481.303. REPORT & NOTICE OF VIOLATION & PENALTY

(a) If the department initially determines that a violation occurred, the department shall give written notice of the report to the person by certified mail, registered mail, personal delivery, or another manner of delivery that records the person's receipt of the notice.

(b) The notice must:

(1) include a brief summary of the alleged violation;

(2) state the amount of the recommended penalty; and

(3) inform the person of the person's right to a hearing on the occurrence of the violation, the amount of the penalty, or both.

History of H&SC 481.303: Acts 2007, 80th Leg., ch. 1391, §5, eff. Sept. 1, 2007.

H&SC §481.304. PENALTY TO BE PAID OR INFORMAL HEARING REQUESTED

(a) Before the 21st day after the date the person receives notice under Section 481.303, the person in writing may:

(1) accept the determination and recommended penalty; or

(2) make a request for an informal hearing held by the department on the occurrence of the violation, the amount of the penalty, or both.

(b) At the conclusion of an informal hearing requested under Subsection (a), the department may modify the amount of the recommended penalty.

(c) If the person accepts the determination and recommended penalty, including any modification of the amount, or if the person fails to timely respond to the notice, the director by order shall approve the determination and impose the recommended penalty.

History of H&SC §481.304: Acts 2007, 80th Leg., ch. 1391, §5, eff. Sept. 1, 2007.

H&SC §481.305. FORMAL HEARING

(a) The person may request a formal hearing only after participating in an informal hearing.

(b) The request must be submitted in writing and received by the department before the 21st day after the date the person is notified of the decision from the informal hearing.

(c) If a timely request for a formal hearing is not received, the director by order shall approve the determination from the informal hearing and impose the recommended penalty.

(d) If the person timely requests a formal hearing, the director shall refer the matter to the State Office of Administrative Hearings, which shall promptly set a hearing date and give written notice of the time and place of the hearing to the director and to the person. An administrative law judge of the State Office of Administrative Hearings shall conduct the hearing.

(e) The administrative law judge shall make findings of fact and conclusions of law and promptly issue to the director a proposal for a decision about the occurrence of the violation and the amount of any proposed penalty.

(f) If a penalty is proposed under Subsection (e), the administrative law judge shall include in the proposal for a decision a finding setting out costs, fees, expenses, and reasonable and necessary attorney's fees incurred by the state in bringing the proceeding. The director may adopt the finding and impose the costs, fees, and expenses on the person as part of the final order entered in the proceeding.

History of H&SC §481.305: Acts 2007, 80th Leg., ch. 1391, §5, eff. Sept. 1, 2007.

H&SC §481.306. DECISION

(a) Based on the findings of fact, conclusions of law, and proposal for a decision, the director by order may:

(1) find that a violation occurred and impose a penalty; or

(2) find that a violation did not occur.

(b) The notice of the director's order under Subsection (a) that is sent to the person in the manner provided by Chapter 2001, Government Code, must include a statement of the right of the person to judicial review of the order.

History of H&SC §481.306: Acts 2007, 80th Leg., ch. 1391, §5, eff. Sept. 1, 2007.

TCSA §481.302

H&SC §481.307. OPTIONS FOLLOWING DECISION: PAY OR APPEAL

Before the 31st day after the date the order under Section 481.306 that imposes an administrative penalty becomes final, the person shall:

(1) pay the penalty; or

(2) file a petition for judicial review of the order contesting the occurrence of the violation, the amount of the penalty, or both.

History of H&SC §481.307: Acts 2007, 80th Leg., ch. 1391, §5, eff. Sept. 1, 2007.

H&SC §481.308. STAY OF ENFORCEMENT OF PENALTY

(a) Within the period prescribed by Section 481.307, a person who files a petition for judicial review may:

(1) stay enforcement of the penalty by:

(A) paying the penalty to the court for placement in an escrow account; or

(B) giving the court a supersedeas bond approved by the court that:

(i) is for the amount of the penalty; and

(ii) is effective until all judicial review of the order is final; or

(2) request the court to stay enforcement of the penalty by:

(A) filing with the court a sworn affidavit of the person stating that the person is financially unable to pay the penalty and is financially unable to give the supersedeas bond; and

(B) sending a copy of the affidavit to the director by certified mail.

(b) Following receipt of a copy of an affidavit under Subsection (a)(2), the director may file with the court, before the sixth day after the date of receipt, a contest to the affidavit. The court shall hold a hearing on the facts alleged in the affidavit as soon as practicable and shall stay the enforcement of the penalty on finding that the alleged facts are true. The person who files an affidavit has the burden of proving that the person is financially unable to pay the penalty or to give a supersedeas bond.

History of H&SC §481.308: Acts 2007, 80th Leg., ch. 1391, §5, eff. Sept. 1, 2007.

H&SC §481.309. COLLECTION OF PENALTY

(a) If the person does not pay the penalty and the enforcement of the penalty is not stayed, the penalty may be collected.

(b) The attorney general may sue to collect the penalty.

History of H&SC, §481.309: Acts 2007, 80th Leg., ch. 1391, §5, eff. Sept. 1, 2007.

H&SC §481.310. DECISION BY COURT

(a) If the court sustains the finding that a violation occurred, the court may uphold or reduce the amount of the penalty and order the person to pay the full or reduced amount of the penalty.

(b) If the court does not sustain the finding that a violation occurred, the court shall order that a penalty is not owed.

History of H&SC §481.310: Acts 2007, 80th Leg., ch. 1391, §5, eff. Sept. 1, 2007.

H&SC §481.311. REMITTANCE OF PENALTY & INTEREST

(a) If the person paid the penalty and if the amount of the penalty is reduced or the penalty is not upheld by the court, the court shall order, when the court's judgment becomes final, that the appropriate amount plus accrued interest be remitted to the person before the 31st day after the date that the judgment of the court becomes final.

(b) The interest accrues at the rate charged on loans to depository institutions by the New York Federal Reserve Bank.

(c) The interest shall be paid for the period beginning on the date the penalty is paid and ending on the date the penalty is remitted.

History of H&SC §481.311: Acts 2007, 80th Leg., ch. 1391, §5, eff. Sept. 1, 2007.

H&SC §481.312. RELEASE OF BOND

(a) If the person gave a supersedeas bond and the penalty is not upheld by the court, the court shall order, when the court's judgment becomes final, the release of the bond.

(b) If the person gave a supersedeas bond and the amount of the penalty is reduced, the court shall order the release of the bond after the person pays the reduced amount.

History of H&SC §481.312: Acts 2007, 80th Leg., ch. 1391, §5, eff. Sept. 1, 2007.

TCSA §481.312

H&SC §481.313. ADMINISTRATIVE PROCEDURE

A proceeding to impose the penalty is considered to be a contested case under Chapter 2001, Government Code.

History of H&SC §481.313: Acts 2007, 80th Leg., ch. 1391, §5, eff. Sept. 1, 2007.

H&SC §481.314. DISPOSITION OF PENALTY

The department shall send any amount collected as a penalty under this subchapter to the comptroller for deposit to the credit of the general revenue fund.

History of H&SC §481.314: Acts 2007, 80th Leg., ch. 1391, §5, eff. Sept. 1, 2007.

CHAPTER 482. SIMULATED CONTROLLED SUBSTANCES

For a quick reference of penalties, see the Chart of Penalties on p. 689.

H&SC §482.001. DEFINITIONS

In this chapter:

(1) "Controlled substance" has the meaning assigned by Section 481.002 (Texas Controlled Substances Act).

(2) "Deliver" means to transfer, actually or constructively, from one person to another a simulated controlled substance, regardless of whether there is an agency relationship. The term includes offering to sell a simulated controlled substance.

(3) "Manufacture" means to make a simulated controlled substance and includes the preparation of the substance in dosage form by mixing, compounding, encapsulating, tableting, or any other process.

(4) "Simulated controlled substance" means a substance that is purported to be a controlled substance, but is chemically different from the controlled substance it is purported to be.

History of H&SC §482.001: Acts 1989, 71st Leg., ch. 678, §1, eff. Sept. 1, 1989.

ANNOTATIONS

Evans v. State, 945 S.W.2d 259, 261 (Tex.App.— Houston [1st Dist.] 1997, pet. ref'd). "[T]he definitive chemical difference of §482.001 is quantitative rather than exclusive and a simulated controlled substance can be chemically different from the controlled substance it is purported to be even though some unsubstantial amount of the controlled substance is present.

To state it differently, a controlled substance can be simulated by adding some of that substance to something else in order to give a false appearance there is a substantial amount of the controlled substance present. Accordingly, something other than cocaine, with cocaine sprinkled on it to create the false appearance the entire concoction contained a substantial amount of cocaine, could be a simulated controlled substance."

Reid v. State, 834 S.W.2d 125, 126 (Tex.App.— Houston [1st Dist.] 1992, no pet.). "[A] simulated controlled substance, by definition, cannot be the controlled substance it is purported to be. [¶] [T]he evidence shows that [D] delivered to [police officer] a substance that [D] claimed was ecstacy. Tests on that substance revealed that it was not ecstacy.... Therefore, the evidence shows that [D] delivered a substance that he represented to be a controlled substance, but was chemically different from the controlled substance it was purported to be."

H&SC §482.002. UNLAWFUL DELIVERY OR MANUFACTURE WITH INTENT TO DELIVER; CRIMINAL PENALTY

(a) A person commits an offense if the person knowingly or intentionally manufactures with the intent to deliver or delivers a simulated controlled substance and the person:

(1) expressly represents the substance to be a controlled substance;

(2) represents the substance to be a controlled substance in a manner that would lead a reasonable person to believe that the substance is a controlled substance; or

(3) states to the person receiving or intended to receive the simulated controlled substance that the person may successfully represent the substance to be a controlled substance to a third party.

(b) It is a defense to prosecution under this section that the person manufacturing with the intent to deliver or delivering the simulated controlled substance was:

(1) acting in the discharge of the person's official duties as a peace officer;

(2) manufacturing the substance for or delivering the substance to a licensed medical practitioner for use as a placebo in the course of the practitioner's research or practice; or

(3) a licensed medical practitioner, pharmacist, or other person authorized to dispense or administer a controlled substance, and the person was acting in the legitimate performance of the person's professional duties.

(c) It is not a defense to prosecution under this section that the person manufacturing with the intent to deliver or delivering the simulated controlled substance believed the substance to be a controlled substance.

(d) An offense under this section is a state jail felony.

History of H&SC §482.002: Acts 1989, 71st Leg., ch. 678, §1, eff. Sept. 1, 1989. Amended by Acts 1993, 73rd Leg., ch. 900, §2.03, eff. Sept. 1, 1994.

ANNOTATIONS

Flowers v. State, 843 S.W.2d 38, 40 (Tex.Crim.App. 1992). By "including the word 'express,' the legislature meant that only terms which are unmistakable in meaning could support a conviction under §482.002(a)(1). Slang terms, on the other hand, are not unmistakable because their meanings can change. Thus, in construing §482.002(a)(1), ... only representations employing the statutory controlled substances terms [are] appropriate because they are always unmistakable." *See also Grant v. State*, 822 S.W.2d 639, 640 (Tex.Crim.App.1992); *Boykin v. State*, 818 S.W.2d 782, 786 (Tex.Crim.App.1991).

Schneider v. State, 951 S.W.2d 856, 861 (Tex. App.—Texarkana 1997, pet. ref'd). "[D] asserts that the culpable conduct is identical under [H&SC §§482.002 and 481.112] and the disparate sentences violate his right to due process. However, the culpable conduct is not identical. The culpable conduct penalized under §481.112 is the offering to sell a controlled substance, regardless of whether the controlled substance is sold, and therefore, the focus is on the transaction at the time that the offer is made. The culpable conduct penalized under §482.002 is the offering to sell a *simulated* controlled substance, and therefore, the focus is on the item sold."

Rodriguez v. State, 879 S.W.2d 283, 285 (Tex. App.—Houston [14th Dist.] 1994, pet. ref'd). "Section 482.002 applies to delivery of a simulated controlled substance.... 'Delivery' under §482.002 also includes offering to sell a simulated controlled substance. [D] was also subject to conviction under §482.002. We find

... that §482.002 more specifically describes [D's] conduct, because his actions ... *precisely* conform with the description of the offense proscribed by §482.002."

H&SC §482.003. EVIDENTIARY RULES

(a) In determining whether a person has represented a simulated controlled substance to be a controlled substance in a manner that would lead a reasonable person to believe the substance was a controlled substance, a court may consider, in addition to all other logically relevant factors, whether:

(1) the simulated controlled substance was packaged in a manner normally used for the delivery of a controlled substance;

(2) the delivery or intended delivery included an exchange of or demand for property as consideration for delivery of the substance and the amount of the consideration was substantially in excess of the reasonable value of the simulated controlled substance; and

(3) the physical appearance of the finished product containing the substance was substantially identical to a controlled substance.

(b) Proof of an offer to sell a simulated controlled substance must be corroborated by a person other than the offeree or by evidence other than a statement of the offeree.

History of H&SC §482.003: Acts 1989, 71st Leg., ch. 678, §1, eff. Sept. 1, 1989.

ANNOTATIONS

Evans v. State, 945 S.W.2d 259, 261 (Tex.App.—Houston [1st Dist.] 1997, pet. ref'd). "We hold the evidence, which includes the chemist's testimony she sliced open each of the four packages, removed a sample, tested each, and determined none contained cocaine, was sufficient proof to allow the jury to rationally conclude the packages contained a simulated controlled substance."

Bruns v. State, 924 S.W.2d 176, 178 (Tex. App.—San Antonio 1996, no pet.). "[D's] indictment charged that he knowingly and intentionally delivered a simulated controlled substance representing it to be cocaine in a manner that would lead a reasonable person to believe the substance was cocaine. *At 179:* In the instant case, the substance was packaged in a cellophane cigarette wrapper which the informant testified is a common way to package rock cocaine. The substance was exchanged for $20.00, which was substantially in excess of its actual value. The substance was a white rock-like substance, and appellant told the informant it was 'dope.' Therefore, each of the factors in §482.003(a) was met."

Anderson v. State, 895 S.W.2d 756, 758 (Tex. App.—Texarkana 1994, no pet.). "[D] contends that the rock or pebble that he delivered is not substantially identical to a rock of cocaine. Substantial identity is one of the evidentiary factors to be considered [for the offense of delivering a simulated controlled substance], but it is not necessarily dispositive."

Owens v. State, 820 S.W.2d 912, 913 (Tex.App.—Houston [1st Dist.] 1991, pet. ref'd). "These three acts [§482.003(a)(1)-(3)]are ways of falsely 'representing' the simulated controlled substance without engaging in speech."

H&SC §482.004. SUMMARY FORFEITURE

A simulated controlled substance seized as a result of an offense under this chapter is subject to summary forfeiture and to destruction or disposition in the same manner as is a controlled substance property under Subchapter E, Chapter 481.

History of H&SC §482.004: Acts 1989, 71st Leg., ch. 678, §1, eff. Sept. 1, 1989. Amended by Acts 1991, 72nd Leg., ch. 141, §3, eff. Sept. 1, 1991.

H&SC §482.005. PREPARATORY OFFENSES

Title 4, Penal Code, applies to an offense under this chapter.

History of H&SC §482.005: Acts 1995, 74th Leg., ch. 318, §39, eff. Sept. 1, 1995.

CHAPTER 483. DANGEROUS DRUGS

SUBCHAPTER A. GENERAL PROVISIONS

H&SC §483.0001. SHORT TITLE

This Act may be cited as the Texas Dangerous Drug Act.

History of H&SC §483.0001: Acts 1993, 73rd Leg., ch. 789, §18, eff. Sept. 1, 1993.

H&SC §483.001. DEFINITIONS

In this chapter:

(1) "Board" means the Texas State Board of Pharmacy.

(2) "Dangerous drug" means a device or a drug that is unsafe for self-medication and that is not included in Schedules I through V or Penalty Groups 1 through 4 of Chapter 481 (Texas Controlled Substances Act). The term includes a device or a drug that bears or is required to bear the legend:

(A) "Caution: federal law prohibits dispensing without prescription" or "Rx only" or another legend that complies with federal law; or

(B) "Caution: federal law restricts this drug to use by or on the order of a licensed veterinarian."

(3) "Deliver" means to sell, dispense, give away, or supply in any other manner.

(4) "Designated agent" means:

(A) a licensed nurse, physician assistant, pharmacist, or other individual designated by a practitioner to communicate prescription drug orders to a pharmacist;

(B) a licensed nurse, physician assistant, or pharmacist employed in a health care facility to whom the practitioner communicates a prescription drug order; or

(C) a registered nurse or physician assistant authorized by a practitioner to carry out a prescription drug order for dangerous drugs under Subchapter B, Chapter 157, Occupations Code.

(5) "Dispense" means to prepare, package, compound, or label a dangerous drug in the course of professional practice for delivery under the lawful order of a practitioner to an ultimate user or the user's agent.

(6) "Manufacturer" means a person, other than a pharmacist, who manufactures dangerous drugs. The term includes a person who prepares dangerous drugs in dosage form by mixing, compounding, encapsulating, entableting, or any other process.

(7) "Patient" means:

(A) an individual for whom a dangerous drug is prescribed or to whom a dangerous drug is administered; or

(B) an owner or the agent of an owner of an animal for which a dangerous drug is prescribed or to which a dangerous drug is administered.

(8) "Person" includes an individual, corporation, partnership, and association.

(9) "Pharmacist" means a person licensed by the Texas State Board of Pharmacy to practice pharmacy.

(10) "Pharmacy" means a facility where prescription drug or medication orders are received, processed, dispensed, or distributed under this chapter, Chapter 481 of this code, and Subtitle J, Title 3, Occupations Code. The term does not include a narcotic drug treatment program that is regulated by Chapter 466, Health and Safety Code.

(11) "Practice of pharmacy" means:

(A) provision of those acts or services necessary to provide pharmaceutical care;

(B) interpretation and evaluation of prescription drug orders or medication orders;

(C) participation in drug and device selection as authorized by law, drug administration, drug regimen review, or drug or drug-related research;

(D) provision of patient counseling;

(E) responsibility for:

(i) dispensing of prescription drug orders or distribution of medication orders in the patient's best interest;

(ii) compounding and labeling of drugs and devices, except labeling by a manufacturer, repackager, or distributor of nonprescription drugs and commercially packaged prescription drugs and devices;

(iii) proper and safe storage of drugs and devices; or

(iv) maintenance of proper records for drugs and devices. In this subdivision, "device" has the meaning assigned by Subtitle J, Title 3, Occupations Code; or

(F) performance of a specific act of drug therapy management for a patient delegated to a pharmacist by a written protocol from a physician licensed by the state under Subtitle B, Title 3, Occupations Code.

(12) "Practitioner" means a person licensed:

(A) by the Texas State Board of Medical Examiners, State Board of Dental Examiners, Texas State Board of Podiatric Medical Examiners, Texas Optometry Board, or State Board of Veterinary Medical Examiners to prescribe and administer dangerous drugs;

(B) by another state in a health field in which, under the laws of this state, a licensee may legally prescribe dangerous drugs;

(C) in Canada or Mexico in a health field in which, under the laws of this state, a licensee may legally prescribe dangerous drugs; or

(D) an advanced practice nurse or physician assistant to whom a physician has delegated the authority to carry out or sign prescription drug orders under Section 157.0511, 157.052, 157.053, 157.054, 157.0541, or 157.0542, Occupations Code.

(13) "Prescription" means an order from a practitioner, or an agent of the practitioner designated in writing as authorized to communicate prescriptions, or

an order made in accordance with Subchapter B, Chapter 157, Occupations Code, or Section 203.353, Occupations Code, to a pharmacist for a dangerous drug to be dispensed that states:

(A) the date of the order's issue;

(B) the name and address of the patient;

(C) if the drug is prescribed for an animal, the species of the animal;

(D) the name and quantity of the drug prescribed;

(E) the directions for the use of the drug;

(F) the intended use of the drug unless the practitioner determines the furnishing of this information is not in the best interest of the patient;

(G) the name, address, and telephone number of the practitioner at the practitioner's usual place of business, legibly printed or stamped; and

(H) the name, address, and telephone number of the licensed midwife, registered nurse, or physician assistant, legibly printed or stamped, if signed by a licensed midwife, registered nurse, or physician assistant.

(14) "Warehouseman" means a person who stores dangerous drugs for others and who has no control over the disposition of the drugs except for the purpose of storage.

(15) "Wholesaler" means a person engaged in the business of distributing dangerous drugs to a person listed in Sections 483.041(c)(1)-(6).

History of H&SC §483.001: Acts 1989, 71st Leg., ch. 678, §1 (eff. Sept. 1, 1989), ch. 1100, §§5.03(h), 5.04(b) (eff. Sept. 1, 1989). Amended by Acts 1991, 72nd Leg., ch. 14, §200 (eff. Sept. 1, 1991), ch. 237, §10 (eff. Sept. 1, 1991), ch. 588, §26 (eff. Sept. 1, 1991); Acts 1993, 73rd Leg., ch. 351, §29 (eff. Sept. 1, 1993), ch. 789, §18 (eff. Sept. 1, 1993); Acts 1995, 74th Leg., ch. 965, §§6, 82, eff. June 16, 1995; Acts 1997, 75th Leg., ch. 1095, §18 (eff. Sept. 1, 1997), ch. 1180, §22 (eff. Sept 1, 1997); Acts 2001, 77th Leg., ch. 112, §6 (eff. May 11, 2001), ch. 1254, §11 (eff. Sept. 1, 2001), ch. 1420, §14.795 (eff. Sept. 1, 2001); Acts 2003, 78th Leg., ch. 88, §10, eff. May 20, 2003; Acts 2005, 79th Leg., ch. 1240, §54, eff. Sept. 1, 2005.

H&SC §483.002. RULES

The board may adopt rules for the proper administration and enforcement of this chapter.

History of H&SC §483.002: Acts 1989, 71st Leg., ch. 678, §1, eff. Sept. 1, 1989.

H&SC §483.003. BOARD OF HEALTH HEARINGS REGARDING CERTAIN DANGEROUS DRUGS

(a) The Texas Board of Health may hold public hearings in accordance with Chapter 2001, Government Code to determine whether there is compelling

TCSA §483.003

evidence that a dangerous drug has been abused, either by being prescribed for nontherapeutic purposes or by the ultimate user.

(b) On making that finding, the Texas Board of Health may limit the availability of the abused drug by permitting its dispensing only on the prescription of a practitioner described by Section 483.001(12)(A), (B), or (D).

History of H&SC §483.003: Acts 1989, 71st Leg., ch. 678, §1, eff. Sept. 1, 1989. Amended by Acts 1995, 74th Leg., ch. 76, §5.95(49), eff. Sept. 1, 1995; Acts 1997, 75th Leg., ch. 1180, §23, eff. Sept. 1, 1997; Acts 2001, 77th Leg., ch. 112, §7, eff. May 11, 2001.

H&SC §483.004. COMMISSIONER OF HEALTH EMERGENCY AUTHORITY RELATING TO DANGEROUS DRUGS

If the commissioner of health has compelling evidence that an immediate danger to the public health exists as a result of the prescription of a dangerous drug by practitioners described by Section 483.001(12)(C), the commissioner may use the commissioner's existing emergency authority to limit the availability of the drug by permitting its prescription only by practitioners described by Section 483.001(12)(A), (B), or (D).

History of H&SC §483.004: Acts 1989, 71st Leg., ch. 678, §1, eff. Sept. 1, 1989. Amended by Acts 2001, 77th Leg., ch. 112, §8, eff. May 11, 2001.

Sections 483.005-483.020 reserved for expansion

SUBCHAPTER B. DUTIES OF PHARMACISTS, PRACTITIONERS, & OTHER PERSONS

H&SC §483.021. DETERMINATION BY PHARMACIST ON REQUEST TO DISPENSE DRUG

(a) A pharmacist who is requested to dispense a dangerous drug under a prescription issued by a practitioner shall determine, in the exercise of the pharmacist's professional judgment, that the prescription is a valid prescription. A pharmacist may not dispense a dangerous drug if the pharmacist knows or should have known that the prescription was issued without a valid patient-practitioner relationship.

(b) A pharmacist who is requested to dispense a dangerous drug under a prescription issued by a therapeutic optometrist shall determine, in the exercise of the pharmacist's professional judgment, whether the prescription is for a dangerous drug that a therapeutic optometrist is authorized to prescribe under Section 351.358, Occupations Code.

History of H&SC §483.021: Acts 1989, 71st Leg., ch. 678, §1, eff. Sept. 1, 1989. Amended by Acts 1991, 72nd Leg., ch. 588, §27, eff. Sept. 1, 1991; Acts 2001, 77th Leg., ch. 1254, §12 (eff. Sept. 1, 2001), ch. 1420, §14.796 (eff. Sept. 1, 2001).

H&SC §483.022. PRACTITIONER'S DESIGNATED AGENT; PRACTITIONER'S RESPONSIBILITIES

(a) A practitioner shall provide in writing the name of each designated agent as defined by Section 483.001(4)(A) and (C), and the name of each healthcare facility which employs persons defined by Section 483.001(4)(B).

(b) The practitioner shall maintain at the practitioner's usual place of business a list of the designated agents or healthcare facilities as defined by Section 483.001(4).

(c) The practitioner shall provide a pharmacist with a copy of the practitioner's written authorization for a designated agent as defined by Section 483.001(4) on the pharmacist's request.

(d) This section does not relieve a practitioner or the practitioner's designated agent from the requirements of Subchapter A, Chapter 562, Occupations Code.

(e) A practitioner remains personally responsible for the actions of a designated agent who communicates a prescription to a pharmacist.

(f) A practitioner may designate a person who is a licensed vocational nurse or has an education equivalent to or greater than that required for a licensed vocational nurse to communicate prescriptions of an advanced practice nurse or physician assistant authorized by the practitioner to sign prescription drug orders under Subchapter B, Chapter 157, Occupations Code.

History of H&SC §483.022: Acts 1989, 71st Leg., ch. 678, §1, eff. Sept. 1, 1989. Amended by Acts 1991, 72nd Leg., ch. 14, §201 (eff. Sept. 1, 1991), ch. 237, §11 (eff. Sept. 1, 1991); Acts 1993, 73rd Leg., ch. 789, §19, eff. Sept. 1, 1993; Acts 1999, 76th Leg., ch. 428, §4, eff. Sept. 1, 1999; Acts 2001, 77th Leg., ch. 1420, §14.797, eff. Sept. 1, 2001.

H&SC §483.023. RETENTION OF PRESCRIPTIONS

A pharmacy shall retain a prescription for a dangerous drug dispensed by the pharmacy for two years after the date of the initial dispensing or the last refilling of the prescription, whichever date is later.

History of H&SC §483.023: Acts 1989, 71st Leg., ch. 678, §1, eff. Sept. 1, 1989.

TCSA §483.003

H&SC §483.024. RECORDS OF ACQUISITION OR DISPOSAL

The following persons shall maintain a record of each acquisition and each disposal of a dangerous drug for two years after the date of the acquisition or disposal:

(1) a pharmacy;

(2) a practitioner;

(3) a person who obtains a dangerous drug for lawful research, teaching, or testing purposes, but not for resale;

(4) a hospital that obtains a dangerous drug for lawful administration by a practitioner; and

(5) a manufacturer or wholesaler registered with the commissioner of health under Chapter 431 (Texas Food, Drug, and Cosmetic Act).

History of H&SC §483.024: Acts 1989, 71st Leg., ch. 678, §1, eff. Sept. 1, 1989.

H&SC §483.025. INSPECTIONS; INVENTORIES

A person required to keep records relating to dangerous drugs shall:

(1) make the records available for inspection and copying at all reasonable hours by any public official or employee engaged in enforcing this chapter; and

(2) allow the official or employee to inventory all stocks of dangerous drugs on hand.

History of H&SC §483.025: Acts 1989, 71st Leg., ch. 678, §1, eff. Sept. 1, 1989.

H&SC §483.026. REPEALED

Repealed by Acts 1989, 71st Leg., ch. 1100, §5.03(h), eff. Sept. 1, 1989.

Sections 483.027-483.040 reserved for expansion

SUBCHAPTER C. CRIMINAL PENALTIES

For a quick reference of penalties, see the Chart of Penalties on p. 689.

H&SC §483.041. POSSESSION OF DANGEROUS DRUG

(a) A person commits an offense if the person possesses a dangerous drug unless the person obtains the drug from a pharmacist acting in the manner described by Section 483.042(a)(1) or a practitioner acting in the manner described by Section 483.042(a)(2).

(b) Except as permitted by this chapter, a person commits an offense if the person possesses a dangerous drug for the purpose of selling the drug.

(c) Subsection (a) does not apply to the possession of a dangerous drug in the usual course of business or practice or in the performance of official duties by the following persons or an agent or employee of the person:

(1) a pharmacy licensed by the board;

(2) a practitioner;

(3) a person who obtains a dangerous drug for lawful research, teaching, or testing, but not for resale;

(4) a hospital that obtains a dangerous drug for lawful administration by a practitioner;

(5) an officer or employee of the federal, state, or local government;

(6) a manufacturer or wholesaler licensed by the Department of State Health Services under Chapter 431 (Texas Food, Drug, and Cosmetic Act);

(7) a carrier or warehouseman;

(8) a home and community support services agency licensed under and acting in accordance with Chapter 142;

(9) a licensed midwife who obtains oxygen for administration to a mother or newborn or who obtains a dangerous drug for the administration of prophylaxis to a newborn for the prevention of ophthalmia neonatorum in accordance with Section 203.353, Occupations Code; or

(10) a salvage broker or salvage operator licensed under Chapter 432.

(d) An offense under this section is a Class A misdemeanor.

History of H&SC §483.041: Acts 1989, 71st Leg., ch. 678, §1 (eff. Sept. 1, 1989), ch. 1100, §5.03(f) (eff. Sept. 1, 1989). Amended by Acts 1993, 73rd Leg., ch. 16, §2 (eff. April 2, 1993), ch. 789, §20 (eff. Sept. 1, 1993); Acts 1995, 74th Leg., ch. 307, §2 (eff. Sept. 1, 1995), ch. 318, §41 (eff. Sept. 1, 1995); Acts 1997, 75th Leg., ch. 1095, §19 (eff. Sept. 1, 1997), ch. 1129, §2 (eff. Sept. 1, 1997); Acts 2001, 77th Leg., ch. 265, §9 (eff. May 23, 2001), ch. 1420, §14.798 (eff. Sept. 1, 2001); Acts 2005, 79th Leg., ch. 1240, §55, eff. Sept. 1, 2005.

ANNOTATIONS

Drennan v. Community Health Inv., 905 S.W.2d 811, 825 (Tex.App.—Amarillo 1995, writ denied). "The purpose behind the statutes governing the distribution of dangerous drugs is to protect the public from abuses in the sale of prescription drugs to users, not to control the administration of drugs by those qualified to prescribe and administer them as medically indicated."

TCSA §483.041

H&SC §483.042. DELIVERY OR OFFER OF DELIVERY OF DANGEROUS DRUG

(a) A person commits an offense if the person delivers or offers to deliver a dangerous drug:

(1) unless:

(A) the dangerous drug is delivered or offered for delivery by a pharmacist under:

(i) a prescription issued by a practitioner described by Section 483.001(12)(A) or (B);

(ii) a prescription signed by a registered nurse or physician assistant in accordance with Subchapter B, Chapter 157, Occupations Code; or

(iii) an original written prescription issued by a practitioner described by Section 483.001(12)(C); and

(B) a label is attached to the immediate container in which the drug is delivered or offered to be delivered and the label contains the following information:

(i) the name and address of the pharmacy from which the drug is delivered or offered for delivery;

(ii) the date the prescription for the drug is dispensed;

(iii) the number of the prescription as filed in the prescription files of the pharmacy from which the prescription is dispensed;

(iv) the name of the practitioner who prescribed the drug and, if applicable, the name of the registered nurse or physician assistant who signed the prescription;

(v) the name of the patient and, if the drug is prescribed for an animal, a statement of the species of the animal; and

(vi) directions for the use of the drug as contained in the prescription; or

(2) unless:

(A) the dangerous drug is delivered or offered for delivery by:

(i) a practitioner in the course of practice; or

(ii) a registered nurse or physician assistant in the course of practice in accordance with Subchapter B, Chapter 157, Occupations Code; and

(B) a label is attached to the immediate container in which the drug is delivered or offered to be delivered and the label contains the following information:

(i) the name and address of the practitioner who prescribed the drug, and if applicable, the name and address of the registered nurse or physician assistant;

(ii) the date the drug is delivered;

(iii) the name of the patient and, if the drug is prescribed for an animal, a statement of the species of the animal; and

(iv) the name of the drug, the strength of the drug, and directions for the use of the drug.

(b) Subsection (a) does not apply to the delivery or offer for delivery of a dangerous drug to a person listed in Section 483.041(c) for use in the usual course of business or practice or in the performance of official duties by the person.

(c) Proof of an offer to sell a dangerous drug must be corroborated by a person other than the offeree or by evidence other than a statement by the offeree.

(d) An offense under this section is a state jail felony.

(e) The labeling provisions of Subsection (a) do not apply to a dangerous drug prescribed or dispensed for administration to a patient who is institutionalized. The board shall adopt rules for the labeling of such a drug.

(f) Provided all federal requirements are met, the labeling provisions of Subsection (a) do not apply to a dangerous drug prescribed or dispensed for administration to food production animals in an agricultural operation under a written medical directive or treatment guideline from a veterinarian licensed under Chapter 801, Occupations Code.

History of H&SC §483.042: Acts 1989, 71st Leg., ch. 678, §1 (eff. Sept. 1, 1989), ch. 1100, §5.03(g) (eff. Sept. 1, 1989). Amended by Acts 1993, 73rd Leg., ch. 287, §34 (eff. Sept. 1, 1994), ch. 789, §21 (eff. Sept. 1, 1994), ch. 900, §2.04 (eff. Sept. 1, 1994); Acts 1995, 74th Leg., ch. 965, §7, eff. June 16, 1995; Acts 1997, 75th Leg., ch. 1180, §24, eff. Sept. 1, 1997; Acts 1999, 76th Leg., ch. 1404, §1, eff. Sept. 1, 1999; Acts 2001, 77th Leg., ch. 1420, §14.799, eff. Sept. 1, 2001.

ANNOTATIONS

Drennan v. Community Health Inv. Corp., 905 S.W.2d 811, 825 (Tex.App.—Amarillo 1995, writ denied). "Section 483.042 is not applicable to pharmacies...."

Soto v. State, 810 S.W.2d 861, 864 (Tex.App.—Fort Worth 1991, pet. ref'd). "Section 483.042(a)(2) describes the delivery of the dangerous drug by a practitioner with a label attached containing the name and address of the practitioner, the date the drug is delivered, the name of the patient, and other information, including the name and strength of the drug and instructions for its use. [D's drug] did not include such a label. Consequently, [police officer] had probable

TCSA §483.042

cause to arrest [D] for the possession of a dangerous drug…. [D's] arrest was … valid, even though [officer] mistakenly believed Pamelor was a controlled substance."

H&SC §483.043. MANUFACTURE OF DANGEROUS DRUG

(a) A person commits an offense if the person manufactures a dangerous drug and the person is not authorized by law to manufacture the drug.

(b) An offense under this section is a state jail felony.

History of H&SC §483.043: Acts 1989, 71st Leg., ch. 678, §1, eff. Sept. 1, 1989. Amended by Acts 1993, 73rd Leg., ch. 900, §2.05, eff. Sept. 1, 1994.

H&SC §483.044. REPEALED

Repealed by Acts 1989, 71st Leg., ch. 1100, §5.03(h), eff. Sept. 1, 1989.

H&SC §483.045. FORGING OR ALTERING PRESCRIPTION

(a) A person commits an offense if the person:

(1) forges a prescription or increases the prescribed quantity of a dangerous drug in a prescription;

(2) issues a prescription bearing a forged or fictitious signature;

(3) obtains or attempts to obtain a dangerous drug by using a forged, fictitious, or altered prescription;

(4) obtains or attempts to obtain a dangerous drug by means of a fictitious or fraudulent telephone call; or

(5) possesses a dangerous drug obtained by a forged, fictitious, or altered prescription or by means of a fictitious or fraudulent telephone call.

(b) An offense under this section is a Class B misdemeanor unless it is shown on the trial of the defendant that the defendant has previously been convicted of an offense under this chapter, in which event the offense is a Class A misdemeanor.

History of H&SC §483.045: Acts 1989, 71st Leg., ch. 678, §1, eff. Sept. 1, 1989.

H&SC §483.046. FAILURE TO RETAIN PRESCRIPTION

(a) A pharmacist commits an offense if the pharmacist:

(1) delivers a dangerous drug under a prescription; and

(2) fails to retain the prescription as required by Section 483.023.

(b) An offense under this section is a Class B misdemeanor unless it is shown on the trial of the defendant that the defendant has previously been convicted of an offense under this chapter, in which event the offense is a Class A misdemeanor.

History of H&SC §483.046: Acts 1989, 71st Leg., ch. 678, §1, eff. Sept. 1, 1989.

H&SC §483.047. REFILLING PRESCRIPTION WITHOUT AUTHORIZATION

(a) Except as authorized by Subsection (b), a pharmacist commits an offense if the pharmacist refills a prescription unless:

(1) the prescription contains an authorization by the practitioner for the refilling of the prescription, and the pharmacist refills the prescription in the manner provided by the authorization; or

(2) at the time of refilling the prescription, the pharmacist is authorized to do so by the practitioner who issued the prescription.

(b) A pharmacist may exercise his professional judgment in refilling a prescription for a dangerous drug without the authorization of the prescribing practitioner provided:

(1) failure to refill the prescription might result in an interruption of a therapeutic regimen or create patient suffering;

(2) either:

(A) a natural or manmade disaster has occurred which prohibits the pharmacist from being able to contact the practitioner; or

(B) the pharmacist is unable to contact the practitioner after reasonable effort;

(3) the quantity of drug dispensed does not exceed a 72-hour supply;

(4) the pharmacist informs the patient or the patient's agent at the time of dispensing that the refill is being provided without such authorization and that authorization of the practitioner is required for future refills; and

(5) the pharmacist informs the practitioner of the emergency refill at the earliest reasonable time.

(c) An offense under this section is a Class B misdemeanor unless it is shown on the trial of the defendant that the defendant has previously been convicted under this chapter, in which event the offense is a Class A misdemeanor.

TCSA §483.047

History of H&SC §483.047: Acts 1989, 71st Leg., ch. 678, §1, eff. Sept. 1, 1989. Amended by Acts 1993, 73rd Leg., ch. 789, §22, eff. Sept. 1, 1993.

H&SC §483.048. UNAUTHORIZED COMMUNICATION OF PRESCRIPTION

(a) An agent of a practitioner commits an offense if the agent communicates by telephone a prescription unless the agent is designated in writing under Section 483.022 as authorized by the practitioner to communicate prescriptions by telephone.

(b) An offense under this section is a Class B misdemeanor unless it is shown on the trial of the defendant that the defendant has previously been convicted of an offense under this chapter, in which event the offense is a Class A misdemeanor.

History of H&SC §483.048: Acts 1989, 71st Leg., ch. 678, §1, eff. Sept. 1, 1989.

H&SC §483.049. FAILURE TO MAINTAIN RECORDS

(a) A person commits an offense if the person is required to maintain a record under Section 483.023 or 483.024 and the person fails to maintain the record in the manner required by those sections.

(b) An offense under this section is a Class B misdemeanor unless it is shown on the trial of the defendant that the defendant has previously been convicted of an offense under this chapter, in which event the offense is a Class A misdemeanor.

History of H&SC §483.049: Acts 1989, 71st Leg., ch. 678, §1, eff. Sept. 1, 1989.

H&SC §483.050. REFUSAL TO PERMIT INSPECTION

(a) A person commits an offense if the person is required to permit an inspection authorized by Section 483.025 and fails to permit the inspection in the manner required by that section.

(b) An offense under this section is a Class B misdemeanor unless it is shown on the trial of the defendant that the defendant has previously been convicted of an offense under this chapter, in which event the offense is a Class A misdemeanor.

History of H&SC §483.050: Acts 1989, 71st Leg., ch. 678, §1, eff. Sept. 1, 1989.

H&SC §483.051. USING OR REVEALING TRADE SECRET

(a) A person commits an offense if the person uses for the person's advantage or reveals to another person, other than to an officer or employee of the board or to a court in a judicial proceeding relevant to this chapter, information relating to dangerous drugs required to be kept under this chapter, if that information concerns a method or process subject to protection as a trade secret.

(b) An offense under this section is a Class B misdemeanor unless it is shown on the trial of the defendant that the defendant has previously been convicted of an offense under this chapter, in which event the offense is a Class A misdemeanor.

History of H&SC §483.051: Acts 1989, 71st Leg., ch. 678, §1, eff. Sept. 1, 1989.

H&SC §483.052. VIOLATION OF OTHER PROVISION

(a) A person commits an offense if the person violates a provision of this chapter other than a provision for which a specific offense is otherwise described by this chapter.

(b) An offense under this section is a Class B misdemeanor, unless it is shown on the trial of the defendant that the defendant has previously been convicted of an offense under this chapter, in which event the offense is a Class A misdemeanor.

History of H&SC §483.052: Acts 1989, 71st Leg., ch. 678, §1, eff. Sept. 1, 1989.

H&SC §483.053. PREPARATORY OFFENSES

Title 4, Penal Code, applies to an offense under this subchapter.

History of H&SC §483.053: Acts 1995, 74th Leg., ch. 318, §40, eff. Sept. 1, 1995.

Sections 483.054-483.070 reserved for expansion

SUBCHAPTER D. CRIMINAL & CIVIL PROCEDURE

H&SC §483.071. EXCEPTIONS; BURDEN OF PROOF

(a) In a complaint, information, indictment, or other action or proceeding brought for the enforcement of this chapter, the state is not required to negate an exception, excuse, proviso, or exemption contained in this chapter.

(b) The defendant has the burden of proving the exception, excuse, proviso, or exemption.

History of H&SC §483.071: Acts 1989, 71st Leg., ch. 678, §1, eff. Sept. 1, 1989.

H&SC §483.072. UNCORROBORATED TESTIMONY

A conviction under this chapter may be obtained on the uncorroborated testimony of a party to the offense.

History of H&SC §483.072: Acts 1989, 71st Leg., ch. 678, §1, eff. Sept. 1, 1989.

H&SC §483.073. SEARCH WARRANT

A peace officer may apply for a search warrant to search for dangerous drugs possessed in violation of this chapter. The peace officer must apply for and execute the search warrant in the manner prescribed by the Code of Criminal Procedure.

History of H&SC §483.073: Acts 1989, 71st Leg., ch. 678, §1, eff. Sept. 1, 1989.

H&SC §483.074. SEIZURE & DESTRUCTION

(a) A dangerous drug that is manufactured, sold, or possessed in violation of this chapter is contraband and may be seized by an employee of the board or by a peace officer authorized to enforce this chapter and charged with that duty.

(b) If a dangerous drug is seized under Subsection (a), the board may direct an employee of the board or an authorized peace officer to destroy the drug. The employee or authorized peace officer directed to destroy the drug must act in the presence of another employee of the board or authorized peace officer and shall destroy the drug in any manner designated as appropriate by the board.

(c) Before the dangerous drug is destroyed, an inventory of the drug must be prepared. The inventory must be accompanied by a statement that the dangerous drug is being destroyed at the direction of the board, by an employee of the board or an authorized peace officer, and in the presence of another employee of the board or authorized peace officer. The statement must also contain the names of the persons in attendance at the time of destruction, state the capacity in which each of those persons acts, be signed by those persons, and be sworn to by those persons that the statement is correct. The statement shall be filed with the board.

History of H&SC §483.074: Acts 1989, 71st Leg., ch. 678, §1, eff. Sept. 1, 1989. Amended by Acts 1991, 72nd Leg., ch. 237, §12, eff. Sept. 1, 1991.

H&SC §483.075. INJUNCTION

The board may institute an action in its own name to enjoin a violation of this chapter.

History of H&SC §483.075: Acts 1989, 71st Leg., ch. 678, §1, eff. Sept. 1, 1989.

H&SC §483.076. LEGAL REPRESENTATION OF BOARD

(a) If the board institutes a legal proceeding under this chapter, the board may be represented only by a county attorney, a district attorney, or the attorney general.

(b) The board may not employ private counsel in any legal proceeding instituted by or against the board under this chapter.

History of H&SC §483.076: Acts 1989, 71st Leg., ch. 678, §1, eff. Sept. 1, 1989.

CHAPTER 484. REPEALED

Repealed by Acts 2001, 77th Leg., ch. 1463, §4, eff. Sept. 1, 2001.

CHAPTER 485. ABUSABLE VOLATILE CHEMICALS

SUBCHAPTER A. GENERAL PROVISIONS

H&SC §485.001. DEFINITIONS

In this chapter:

(1) "Abusable volatile chemical" means:

(A) a chemical, including aerosol paint, that:

(i) is packaged in a container subject to the labeling requirements concerning precautions against inhalation established under the Federal Hazardous Substances Act (15 U.S.C. Section 1261 et seq.), as amended, and regulations adopted under that Act and is labeled with the statement of principal hazard on the principal display panel "VAPOR HARMFUL" or other labeling requirement subsequently established under that Act or those regulations;

(ii) when inhaled, ingested, or otherwise introduced into a person's body, may:

(a) affect the person's central nervous system;

(b) create or induce in the person a condition of intoxication, hallucination, or elation; or

(c) change, distort, or disturb the person's eyesight, thinking process, balance, or coordination; and

(iii) is not:

(a) a pesticide subject to Chapter 76, Agriculture Code, or to the Federal Environmental Pesticide Control Act of 1972 (7 U.S.C. Section 136 et seq.), as amended;

(b) a food, drug, or cosmetic subject to Chapter 431 or to the Federal Food, Drug, and Cosmetic Act (21 U.S.C. Section 301 et seq.), as amended; or

(c) a beverage subject to the Federal Alcohol Administration Act (27 U.S.C. Section 201 et seq.), as amended; or

(B) nitrous oxide that is not:

(i) a pesticide subject to Chapter 76, Agriculture Code, or to the Federal Environmental Pesticide Control Act of 1972 (7 U.S.C. Section 136 et seq.), as amended;

(ii) a food, drug, or cosmetic subject to Chapter 431 or to the Federal Food, Drug, and Cosmetic Act (21 U.S.C. Section 301 et seq.), as amended; or

(iii) a beverage subject to the Federal Alcohol Administration Act (27 U.S.C. Section 201 et seq.), as amended.

(2) "Aerosol paint" means an aerosolized paint product, including a clear or pigmented lacquer or finish.

(3) "Board" means the Texas Board of Health.

(4) "Commissioner" means the commissioner of health.

(5) "Deliver" means to make the actual or constructive transfer from one person to another of an abusable volatile chemical, regardless of whether there is an agency relationship. The term includes an offer to sell an abusable volatile chemical.

(6) "Delivery" means the act of delivering.

(7) "Department" means the Texas Department of Health.

(8) "Inhalant paraphernalia" means equipment or materials of any kind that are intended for use in inhaling, ingesting, or otherwise introducing into the human body an abusable volatile chemical. The term includes a tube, balloon, bag, fabric, bottle, or other container used to concentrate or hold in suspension an abusable volatile chemical or vapors of the chemical.

(9) "Sell" includes a conveyance, exchange, barter, or trade.

History of H&SC §485.001: Acts 1989, 71st Leg., ch. 678, §1, eff. Sept. 1, 1989. Amended by Acts 2001, 77th Leg., ch. 1463, §§1, 2, eff. Sept. 1, 2001.

H&SC §485.002. RULES

The board may adopt rules necessary to comply with any labeling requirements concerning precautions against inhalation of an abusable volatile chemical established under the Federal Hazardous Substances Act (15 U.S.C. Section 1261 et seq.), as amended, or under regulations adopted under that Act.

History of H&SC §485.002: Acts 2001, 77th Leg., ch. 1463, §2, eff. Sept. 1, 2001.

Sections 485.003-485.010 reserved for expansion

SUBCHAPTER B. SALES PERMITS & SIGNS

H&SC §485.011. PERMIT REQUIRED

A person may not sell an abusable volatile chemical at retail unless the person or the person's employer holds, at the time of the sale, a volatile chemical sales permit for the location of the sale.

History of H&SC §485.011: Acts 1989, 71st Leg., ch. 678, §1, eff. Sept. 1, 1989. Amended and renumbered from §485.012 by Acts 2001, 77th Leg., ch. 1463, §2, eff. Sept. 1, 2001.

History of Former H&SC §485.011: Acts 1989, 71st Leg., ch. 678, §1, eff. Sept. 1, 1989. Deleted by Acts 2001, 77th Leg., ch. 1463, §2, eff. Sept. 1, 2001.

H&SC §485.012. ISSUANCE & RENEWAL OF PERMIT

(a) To be eligible for the issuance or renewal of a volatile chemical sales permit, a person must:

(1) hold a sales tax permit that has been issued to the person;

(2) complete and return to the department an application as required by the department; and

(3) pay to the department the application fee established under Section 485.013 for each location at which an abusable volatile chemical may be sold by the person holding a volatile chemical sales permit.

(b) The board shall adopt rules as necessary to administer this chapter, including application procedures and procedures by which the department shall give each permit holder reasonable notice of permit expiration and renewal requirements.

(c) The department shall issue or deny a permit and notify the applicant of the department's action not later than the 60th day after the date on which the department receives the complete application and appropriate fee. If the department denies an application, the department shall include in the notice the reasons for the denial.

(d) A permit issued or renewed under this chapter is valid for one year from the date of issuance or renewal.

(e) A permit is not valid if the permit holder has been convicted more than once in the preceding year of an offense committed:

(1) at a location for which the permit is issued; and

(2) under Section 485.031, 485.032, or 485.033.

(f) A permit issued by the department is the property of the department and must be surrendered on demand by the department.

(g) The department shall prepare an annual roster of permit holders.

(h) The department shall monitor and enforce compliance with this chapter.

History of H&SC §485.012: Acts 1989, 71st Leg., ch. 678, §1, eff. Sept. 1, 1989. Amended by Acts 1991, 72nd Leg., ch. 14, §203, eff. Sept. 1, 1991. Amended and renumbered from §485.013 by Acts 2001, 77th Leg., ch. 1463, §2, eff. Sept. 1, 2001.

H&SC §485.013. FEE

The board by rule may establish fees in amounts not to exceed $25 for the issuance of a permit under this chapter.

History of H&SC §485.013: Acts 2001, 77th Leg., ch. 1463, §2, eff. Sept. 1, 2001.

H&SC §485.014. PERMIT AVAILABLE FOR INSPECTION

A permit holder must have the volatile chemical sales permit or a copy of the permit available for inspection by the public at each location where the permit holder sells an abusable volatile chemical.

History of H&SC §485.014: Acts 1989, 71st Leg., ch. 678, §1, eff. Sept. 1, 1989. Amended by Acts 2001, 77th Leg., ch. 1463, §2, eff. Sept. 1, 2001.

H&SC §485.015. REFUSAL TO ISSUE OR RENEW PERMIT

A proceeding for the failure to issue or renew a volatile chemical sales permit under Section 485.012 or for an appeal from that proceeding is governed by the contested case provisions of Chapter 2001, Government Code.

History of H&SC §485.015: Acts 1989, 71st Leg., ch. 678, §1, eff. Sept. 1, 1989. Amended by Acts 1995, 74th Leg., ch. 76, §5.95(49), eff. Sept. 1, 1995; Acts 2001, 77th Leg., ch. 1463, §2, eff. Sept. 1, 2001.

H&SC §485.016. DISPOSITION OF FUNDS; EDUCATION & PREVENTION PROGRAMS

(a) The department shall account for all amounts received under Section 485.013 and send those amounts to the comptroller.

(b) The comptroller shall deposit the amounts received under Subsection (a) in the state treasury to the credit of the general revenue fund to be used only by the department to:

(1) administer, monitor, and enforce this chapter; and

(2) finance statewide education projects concerning the hazards of abusable volatile chemicals and the prevention of inhalant abuse.

History of H&SC §485.016: Acts 1989, 71st Leg., ch. 678, §1, eff. Sept. 1, 1989. Amended by Acts 1991, 72nd Leg., ch. 14, §204, eff. Sept. 1, 1991; Acts 2001, 77th Leg., ch. 1463, §2, eff. Sept. 1, 2001.

H&SC §485.017. SIGNS

A business establishment that sells an abusable volatile chemical at retail shall display a conspicuous sign, in English and Spanish, that states the following:

It is unlawful for a person to sell or deliver an abusable volatile chemical to a person under 18 years of age. Except in limited situations, such an offense is a state jail felony.

It is also unlawful for a person to abuse a volatile chemical by inhaling, ingesting, applying, using, or possessing with intent to inhale, ingest, apply, or use a volatile chemical in a manner designed to affect the central nervous system. Such an offense is a Class B misdemeanor.

History of H&SC §485.017: Acts 1989, 71st Leg., ch. 678, §1, eff. Sept. 1, 1989. Amended by Acts 2001, 77th Leg., ch. 1463, §2, eff. Sept. 1, 2001.

H&SC §485.018. PROHIBITED ORDINANCE & RULE

(a) A political subdivision or an agency of this state may not enact an ordinance or rule that requires a business establishment to display an abusable volatile chemical in a manner that makes the chemical accessible to patrons of the business only with the assistance of personnel of the business.

(b) This section does not apply to an ordinance or rule that was enacted before September 1, 1989.

History of H&SC §485.018: Acts 1991, 72nd Leg., ch. 14, §205, eff. Sept. 1, 1991. Amended by Acts 2001, 77th Leg., ch. 1463, §2, eff. Sept. 1, 2001.

H&SC §485.019. RESTRICTION OF ACCESS TO AEROSOL PAINT

(a) A business establishment that holds a permit under Section 485.012 and that displays aerosol paint shall display the paint:

(1) in a place that is in the line of sight of a cashier or in the line of sight from a workstation normally continuously occupied during business hours;

(2) in a manner that makes the paint accessible to a patron of the business establishment only with the assistance of an employee of the establishment; or

(3) in an area electronically protected, or viewed by surveillance equipment that is monitored, during business hours.

(b) This section does not apply to a business establishment that has in place a computerized checkout system at the point of sale for merchandise that alerts the cashier that a person purchasing aerosol paint must be over 18 years of age.

(c) A court may issue a warning to a business establishment or impose a civil penalty of $50 on the business establishment for a first violation of this section. After receiving a warning or penalty for the first violation, the business establishment is liable to the state for a civil penalty of $100 for each subsequent violation.

(d) For the third violation of this section in a calendar year, a court may issue an injunction prohibiting the business establishment from selling aerosol paint for a period of not more than two years. A business establishment that violates the injunction is liable to the state for a civil penalty of $100, in addition to any other penalty authorized by law, for each day the violation continues.

(e) If a business establishment fails to pay a civil penalty under this section, the court may issue an injunction prohibiting the establishment from selling aerosol paint until the establishment pays the penalty, attorney's fees, and court costs.

(f) The district or county attorney for the county in which a violation of this section is alleged to have occurred, or the attorney general, if requested by the district or county attorney for that county, may file suit for the issuance of a warning, the collection of a penalty, or the issuance of an injunction.

(g) A penalty collected under this section shall be sent to the comptroller for deposit in the state treasury to the credit of the general revenue fund.

(h) This section applies only to a business establishment that is located in a county with a population of 75,000 or more.

History of H&SC §485.019: Acts 1997, 75th Leg., ch. 593, §4, eff. Sept. 1, 1997.

Sections 485.020-485.030 reserved for expansion

SUBCHAPTER C. CRIMINAL PENALTIES

For a quick reference of penalties, see the Chart of Penalties on p. 689.

H&SC §485.031. POSSESSION & USE

(a) A person commits an offense if the person inhales, ingests, applies, uses, or possesses an abusable volatile chemical with intent to inhale, ingest, apply, or use the chemical in a manner:

(1) contrary to directions for use, cautions, or warnings appearing on a label of a container of the chemical; and

(2) designed to:

(A) affect the person's central nervous system;

(B) create or induce a condition of intoxication, hallucination, or elation; or

(C) change, distort, or disturb the person's eyesight, thinking process, balance, or coordination.

(b) An offense under this section is a Class B misdemeanor.

History of H&SC §485.031: Acts 1989, 71st Leg., ch. 678, §1, eff. Sept. 1, 1989. Amended by Acts 2001, 77th Leg., ch. 1463, §2, eff. Sept. 1, 2001.

ANNOTATIONS

State v. Garcia, 859 S.W.2d 125, 126 (Tex.App.—Fort Worth 1993, pet. ref'd). CCP art. 14.01 "provides that a peace officer may arrest an offender without a warrant for any offense committed in his presence or within his view. [H&SC] §485.031 provides that a person commits an offense if he possesses an aerosol paint with intent to inhale it in a manner contrary to certain provisions on its label and in a manner designed to affect the central nervous system, create a condition of intoxication, hallucination, or elation, or change, distort, or disturb the person's eyesight, thinking process, balance, or coordination." Held: Officer's arrest of defendant was legal.

H&SC §485.032. DELIVERY TO A MINOR

(a) A person commits an offense if the person knowingly delivers an abusable volatile chemical to a person who is younger than 18 years of age.

(b) It is a defense to prosecution under this section that:

(1) the abusable volatile chemical that was delivered contains additive material that effectively discourages intentional abuse by inhalation; or

(2) the person making the delivery is not the manufacturer of the chemical and the manufacturer of the chemical failed to label the chemical with the statement of principal hazard on the principal display panel "VAPOR HARMFUL" or other labeling requirement subsequently established under the Federal Hazardous Substances Act (15 U.S.C. Section 1261 et seq.), as amended, or regulations subsequently adopted under that Act.

(c) It is an affirmative defense to prosecution under this section that:

(1) the person making the delivery is an adult having supervisory responsibility over the person younger than 18 years of age and:

(A) the adult permits the use of the abusable volatile chemical only under the adult's direct supervision and in the adult's presence and only for its intended purpose; and

(B) the adult removes the chemical from the person younger than 18 years of age on completion of that use; or

(2) the person to whom the abusable volatile chemical was delivered presented to the defendant an apparently valid Texas driver's license or an identification certificate, issued by the Department of Public Safety of the State of Texas and containing a physical description consistent with the person's appearance, that purported to establish that the person was 18 years of age or older.

(d) Except as provided by Subsections (c) and (f), an offense under this section is a state jail felony.

(e) An offense under this section is a Class B misdemeanor if it is shown on the trial of the defendant that at the time of the delivery the defendant or the defendant's employer held a volatile chemical sales permit for the location of the sale.

(f) An offense under this section is a Class A misdemeanor if it is shown on the trial of the defendant that at the time of the delivery the defendant or the defendant's employer:

(1) did not hold a volatile chemical sales permit but did hold a sales tax permit for the location of the sale; and

(2) had not been convicted previously under this section for an offense committed after January 1, 1988.

History of H&SC §485.032: Acts 1989, 71st Leg., ch. 678, §1, eff. Sept. 1, 1989. Amended by Acts 1993, 73rd Leg., ch. 900, §2.06, eff. Sept. 1, 1994. Amended and renumbered from §485.033 by Acts 2001, 77th Leg., ch. 1463, §2, eff. Sept. 1, 2001.

History of Former H&SC §485.032: Acts 1989, 71st Leg., ch. 678, §1, eff. Sept. 1, 1989. Deleted by Acts 2001, 77th Leg., ch. 1463, §2, eff. Sept. 1, 2001.

H&SC §485.033. INHALANT PARAPHERNALIA

(a) A person commits an offense if the person knowingly uses or possesses with intent to use inhalant paraphernalia to inhale, ingest, or otherwise introduce into the human body an abusable volatile chemical in violation of Section 485.031.

(b) A person commits an offense if the person:

(1) knowingly:

(A) delivers or sells inhalant paraphernalia;

(B) possesses, with intent to deliver or sell, inhalant paraphernalia; or

(C) manufactures, with intent to deliver or sell, inhalant paraphernalia; and

(2) at the time of the act described by Subdivision (1), knows that the person who receives or is intended to receive the paraphernalia intends that it be used to inhale, ingest, apply, use, or otherwise introduce into the human body a volatile chemical in violation of Section 485.031.

(c) An offense under Subsection (a) is a Class B misdemeanor, and an offense under Subsection (b) is a Class A misdemeanor.

History of H&SC §485.033: Acts 1989, 71st Leg., ch. 678, §1, eff. Sept. 1, 1989. Amended by Acts 1991, 72nd Leg., ch. 14, §206, eff. Sept. 1, 1991. Amended and renumbered from §485.034 by Acts 2001, 77th Leg., ch. 1463, §2, eff. Sept. 1, 2001.

History of Former H&SC §485.034: Deleted by Acts 2001, 77th Leg., ch. 1463, §4, eff. Sept. 1, 2001.

H&SC §485.034. FAILURE TO POST SIGN

(a) A person commits an offense if the person sells an abusable volatile chemical in a business establishment and the person does not display the sign required by Section 485.017.

(b) An offense under this section is a Class C misdemeanor.

History of H&SC §485.034: Acts 1989, 71st Leg., ch. 678, §1, eff. Sept. 1, 1989. Amended and renumbered from §485.035 by Acts 2001, 77th Leg., ch. 1463, §2, eff. Sept. 1, 2001.

H&SC §485.035. SALE WITHOUT PERMIT

(a) A person commits an offense if the person sells an abusable volatile chemical in violation of Section 485.011 and the purchaser is 18 years of age or older.

(b) An offense under this section is a Class B misdemeanor.

H&SC §485.036. PROOF OF OFFER TO SELL

Proof of an offer to sell an abusable volatile chemical must be corroborated by a person other than the offeree or by evidence other than a statement of the offeree.

H&SC §485.037. SUMMARY FORFEITURE

An abusable volatile chemical or inhalant paraphernalia seized as a result of an offense under this chapter is subject to summary forfeiture and to destruction or disposition in the same manner as controlled substance property under Subchapter E, Chapter 481.

H&SC §485.038. PREPARATORY OFFENSES

Title 4, Penal Code, applies to an offense under this subchapter.

Sections 485.039-485.100 blank

SUBCHAPTER D. ADMINISTRATIVE PENALTY

H&SC §485.101. IMPOSITION OF PENALTY

(a) The department may impose an administrative penalty on a person who sells abusable glue or aerosol paint at retail who violates this chapter or a rule or order adopted under this chapter.

(b) A penalty collected under this subchapter shall be deposited in the state treasury in the general revenue fund.

H&SC §485.102. AMOUNT OF PENALTY

(a) The amount of the penalty may not exceed $1,000 for each violation, and each day a violation continues or occurs is a separate violation for purposes of imposing a penalty. The total amount of the penalty assessed for a violation continuing or occurring on separate days under this subsection may not exceed $5,000.

(b) The amount shall be based on:

(1) the seriousness of the violation, including the nature, circumstances, extent, and gravity of the violation;

(2) the threat to health or safety caused by the violation;

(3) the history of previous violations;

(4) the amount necessary to deter a future violation;

(5) whether the violator demonstrated good faith, including when applicable whether the violator made good faith efforts to correct the violation; and

(6) any other matter that justice may require.

H&SC §485.103. REPORT & NOTICE OF VIOLATION & PENALTY

(a) If the department initially determines that a violation occurred, the department shall give written notice of the report by certified mail to the person.

(b) The notice must:

(1) include a brief summary of the alleged violation;

(2) state the amount of the recommended penalty; and

(3) inform the person of the person's right to a hearing on the occurrence of the violation, the amount of the penalty, or both.

H&SC §485.104. PENALTY TO BE PAID OR HEARING REQUESTED

(a) Within 20 days after the date the person receives the notice sent under Section 485.103, the person in writing may:

(1) accept the determination and recommended penalty of the department; or

(2) make a request for a hearing on the occurrence of the violation, the amount of the penalty, or both.

(b) If the person accepts the determination and recommended penalty or if the person fails to respond to the notice, the commissioner by order shall approve the determination and impose the recommended penalty.

History of H&SC §485.104: Acts 1999, 76th Leg., ch. 1411, §6.01, eff. Sept. 1, 1999.

H&SC §485.105. HEARING

(a) If the person requests a hearing, the commissioner shall refer the matter to the State Office of Administrative Hearings, which shall promptly set a hearing date and give written notice of the time and place of the hearing to the person. An administrative law judge of the State Office of Administrative Hearings shall conduct the hearing.

(b) The administrative law judge shall make findings of fact and conclusions of law and promptly issue to the commissioner a proposal for a decision about the occurrence of the violation and the amount of a proposed penalty.

History of H&SC §485.105: Acts 1999, 76th Leg., ch. 1411, §6.01, eff. Sept. 1, 1999.

H&SC §485.106. DECISION BY COMMISSIONER

(a) Based on the findings of fact, conclusions of law, and proposal for a decision, the commissioner by order may:

(1) find that a violation occurred and impose a penalty; or

(2) find that a violation did not occur.

(b) The notice of the commissioner's order under Subsection (a) that is sent to the person in accordance with Chapter 2001, Government Code, must include a statement of the right of the person to judicial review of the order.

History of H&SC §485.106: Acts 1999, 76th Leg., ch. 1411, §6.01, eff. Sept. 1, 1999.

H&SC §485.107. OPTIONS FOLLOWING DECISION: PAY OR APPEAL

Within 30 days after the date the order of the commissioner under Section 485.106 that imposes an administrative penalty becomes final, the person shall:

(1) pay the penalty; or

(2) file a petition for judicial review of the commissioner's order contesting the occurrence of the violation, the amount of the penalty, or both.

History of H&SC §485.107: Acts 1999, 76th Leg., ch. 1411, §6.01, eff. Sept. 1, 1999.

H&SC §485.108. STAY OF ENFORCEMENT OF PENALTY

(a) Within the 30-day period prescribed by Section 485.107, a person who files a petition for judicial review may:

(1) stay enforcement of the penalty by:

(A) paying the penalty to the court for placement in an escrow account; or

(B) giving the court a supersedeas bond approved by the court that:

(i) is for the amount of the penalty; and

(ii) is effective until all judicial review of the commissioner's order is final; or

(2) request the court to stay enforcement of the penalty by:

(A) filing with the court a sworn affidavit of the person stating that the person is financially unable to pay the penalty and is financially unable to give the supersedeas bond; and

(B) sending a copy of the affidavit to the commissioner by certified mail.

(b) If the commissioner receives a copy of an affidavit under Subsection (a)(2), the commissioner may file with the court, within five days after the date the copy is received, a contest to the affidavit. The court shall hold a hearing on the facts alleged in the affidavit as soon as practicable and shall stay the enforcement of the penalty on finding that the alleged facts are true. The person who files an affidavit has the burden of proving that the person is financially unable to pay the penalty or to give a supersedeas bond.

History of H&SC §485.108: Acts 1999, 76th Leg., ch. 1411, §6.01, eff. Sept. 1, 1999.

H&SC §485.109. COLLECTION OF PENALTY

(a) If the person does not pay the penalty and the enforcement of the penalty is not stayed, the penalty may be collected.

(b) The attorney general may sue to collect the penalty.

History of H&SC §485.109: Acts 1999, 76th Leg., ch. 1411, §6.01, eff. Sept. 1, 1999.

H&SC §485.110. DECISION BY COURT

(a) If the court sustains the finding that a violation occurred, the court may uphold or reduce the amount of

✫

the penalty and order the person to pay the full or reduced amount of the penalty.

(b) If the court does not sustain the finding that a violation occurred, the court shall order that a penalty is not owed.

History of H&SC §485.110: Acts 1999, 76th Leg., ch. 1411, §6.01, eff. Sept. 1, 1999.

H&SC §485.111. REMITTANCE OF PENALTY & INTEREST

(a) If the person paid the penalty and if the amount of the penalty is reduced or the penalty is not upheld by the court, the court shall order, when the court's judgment becomes final, that the appropriate amount plus accrued interest be remitted to the person within 30 days after the date that the judgment of the court becomes final.

(b) The interest accrues at the rate charged on loans to depository institutions by the New York Federal Reserve Bank.

(c) The interest shall be paid for the period beginning on the date the penalty is paid and ending on the date the penalty is remitted.

History of H&SC §485.111: Acts 1999, 76th Leg., ch. 1411, §6.01, eff. Sept. 1, 1999.

H&SC §485.112. RELEASE OF BOND

(a) If the person gave a supersedeas bond and the penalty is not upheld by the court, the court shall order, when the court's judgment becomes final, the release of the bond.

(b) If the person gave a supersedeas bond and the amount of the penalty is reduced, the court shall order the release of the bond after the person pays the reduced amount.

History of H&SC §485.112: Acts 1999, 76th Leg., ch. 1411, §6.01, eff. Sept. 1, 1999.

H&SC §485.113. ADMINISTRATIVE PROCEDURE

A proceeding to impose the penalty is considered to be a contested case under Chapter 2001, Government Code.

History of H&SC §485.113: Acts 1999, 76th Leg., ch. 1411, §6.01, eff. Sept. 1, 1999.

TCSA §485.110

SCHEDULES OF CONTROLLED SUBSTANCES

PURSUANT TO THE TEXAS CONTROLLED SUBSTANCES ACT, HEALTH AND SAFETY CODE, CHAPTER 481, THESE SCHEDULES SUPERCEDE PREVIOUS SCHEDULES AND CONTAIN THE MOST CURRENT VERSION OF THE SCHEDULES OF ALL CONTROLLED SUBSTANCES FROM THE PREVIOUS SCHEDULES AND MODIFICATIONS.

This annual publication of the Texas Controlled Substances was signed by David L. Lakey, Commissioner of Health, and will take effect 21 days following publication of this notice in the Texas Register. [Eff. Feb. 8, 2008.]

Changes to the schedules are designated by an asterisk (*). Additional information can be obtained by contacting the Department of Health Services, Drugs and Medical Devices Group, 1100 West 49th Street, Austin, Texas 78756. The telephone number is (512) 834-6755, and the website is www.dshs.state.tx.us/dmd.

SCHEDULES

Nomenclature: Controlled substances listed in these schedules are included by whatever official, common, usual, chemical, or trade name they may be designated.

SCHEDULE ONE

Schedule I consists of:

SCHEDULE I OPIATES

the following opiates, including their isomers, esters, ethers, salts, and salts of isomers, esters, and ethers, unless specifically excepted, if the existence of these isomers, esters, ethers, and salts is possible within the specific chemical designation:

(1) Acetyl-alpha-methylfentanyl (N-[1-(1-methyl-2-phenethyl)-4-piperidinyl]-N- phenylacetamide);

(2) Allylprodine;

(3) Alphacetylmethadol (except levo-alphacetyl-methadol, also known as levo-alpha-acetylmethadol, levomethadyl acetate, or LAAM);

(4) Alpha-methylfentanyl or any other derivative of Fentanyl;

(5) Alpha-methylthiofentanyl (N-[1-methyl-2-(2-thienyl) ethyl-4-piperidinyl]-N- phenylpropanamide);

(6) Benzethidine;

(7) Beta-hydroxyfentanyl (N-[1-(2-hydroxy-2-phenethyl)-4-piperidinyl]-N-phenyl-propanamide);

(8) Beta-hydroxy-3-methylfentanyl (N-[1-(2-hydroxy-2-phenethyl)-3-methyl-4-piperidinyl]-N-phenyl-propanamide);

(9) Betaprodine;

(10) Clonitazene;

(11) Diampromide;

(12) Diethylthiambutene;

(13) Difenoxin;

(14) Dimenoxadol;

(15) Dimethylthiambutene;

(16) Dioxaphetyl butyrate;

(17) Dipipanone;

(18) Ethylmethylthiambutene;

(19) Etonitazene;

(20) Etoxeridine;

(21) Furethidine;

(22) Hydroxypethidine;

(23) Ketobemidone;

(24) Levophenacylmorphan;

(25) Meprodine;

(26) Methadol;

(27) 3-methylfentanyl (N-[3-methyl-1-(2-phenyl-ethyl)-4-piperidyl]-N-phenylpropanamide), its optical and geometric isomers;

(28) 3-methylthiofentanyl (N-[3-methyl-1-(2-thienyl) ethyl-4-piperidinyl]-N-phenylpropanamide);

(29) Moramide;

(30) Morpheridine;

(31) MPPP (1-methyl-4-phenyl-4-propionoxypiperidine);

(32) Noracymethadol;

(33) Norlevorphanol;

(34) Normethadone;

(35) Norpipanone;

(36) Para-fluorofentanyl (N-(4-fluorophenyl)-N-[1-(2-phenethyl)-4-piperidinyl]-propanamide);

(37) PEPAP (1-(2-phenethyl)-4-phenyl-4-acetoxypiperidine);

(38) Phenadoxone;

(39) Phenampromide;

(40) Phencyclidine;

(41) Phenomorphan;

(42) Phenoperidine;

(43) Piritramide;

(44) Proheptazine;

(45) Properidine;

(46) Propiram;

(47) Thiofentanyl   (N-phenyl-N-[1-(2-thienyl)ethyl-4-piperidinyl]-propanamide);

(48) Tilidine; and

(49) Trimeperidine;

SCHEDULE I OPIUM DERIVATIVES

the following opium derivatives, their salts, isomers, and salts of isomers, unless specifically excepted, if the existence of these salts, isomers, and salts of isomers is possible within the specific chemical designation:

(1) Acetorphine;

(2) Acetyldihydrocodeine;

(3) Benzylmorphine;

(4) Codeine methylbromide;

(5) Codeine-N-Oxide;

(6) Cyprenorphine;

(7) Desomorphine;

(8) Dihydromorphine;

(9) Drotebanol;

(10) Etorphine (except hydrochloride salt);

(11) Heroin;

(12) Hydromorphinol;

(13) Methyldesorphine;

(14) Methyldihydromorphine;

(15) Monoacetylmorphine;

(16) Morphine methylbromide;

(17) Morphine methylsulfonate;

(18) Morphine-N-Oxide;

(19) Myrophine;

(20) Nicocodeine;

(21) Nicomorphine;

(22) Normorphine;

(23) Pholcodine; and

(24) Thebacon;

SCHEDULE I HALLUCINOGENIC SUBSTANCES

unless specifically excepted or unless listed in another schedule, a material, compound, mixture, or preparation that contains any quantity of the following hallucinogenic substances or that contains any of the substance's salts, isomers, and salts of isomers if the existence of the salts, isomers, and salts of isomers is possible within the specific chemical designation (for the purposes of this Schedule I hallucinogenic substances section only, the term "isomer" includes optical, position, and geometric isomers):

(1) Alpha-ethyltryptamine (some trade or other names: etryptamine; Monase; alpha-ethyl-1H-indole-3-ethanamine; 3-(2-aminobutyl) indole; alpha-ET; AET);

*(2) alpha-methyltriptamine (AMT), its isomers, salts, and salts of isomers;

(3) 4-bromo-2,5-dimethoxyamphetamine (some trade or other names: 4-bromo-2,5- dimethoxy-alpha-methylphenethylamine; 4-bromo-2,5-DMA);

(4) 4-bromo-2,5-dimethoxyphenethylamine (some trade or other names: Nexus; 2C-B; 2-(4-bromo-2,5-dimethoxyphenyl)-1-aminoethane;   alpha-desmethyl DOB);

(5) 2,5-dimethoxyamphetamine (some trade or other names: 2,5-dimethoxy-alpha-methylphen- ethylamine; 2,5-DMA);

(6) 2,5-dimethoxy-4-ethylamphetamine   (some trade or other names: DOET);

(7) 2,5-dimethoxy-4-(n)-propylthiophenethylamine (2C-T-7), its optical isomers, salts and salts of isomers;

*(8) 5-methoxy-N, N-diisopropyltryptamine (5-MeO-DIPT), its isomers, salts, and salts of isomers;

(9) 5-methoxy-3,4-methylenedioxy-amphetamine;

(10) 4-methoxyamphetamine (some trade or other names: 4-methoxy-alpha-methyl-phenethylamine; paramethoxyamphetamine; PMA);

(11) 1-methyl-4-phenyl-1,2,5,6-tetrahydro-pyridine (MPTP);

(12) 4-methyl-2,5-dimethoxyamphetamine (some trade and other names: 4-methyl- 2,5-dimethoxy-alpha-methyl-phenethylamine; "DOM"; and "STP");

(13) 3,4-methylenedioxy-amphetamine;

(14) 3,4-methylenedioxy-methamphetamine (MDMA, MDM);

(15) 3,4-methylenedioxy-N-ethylamphetamine (some trade or other names: N-ethyl-alpha-methyl-3,4(methylenedioxy)phenethylamine; N-ethyl MDA; MDE; MDEA);

(16) 3,4,5-trimethoxy amphetamine;

(17) N-hydroxy-3,4-methylenedioxyamphetamine (Also known as N-hydroxy MDA);

(18) Bufotenine (some trade and other names: 3-(beta-Dimethylaminoethyl)-5-hydroxyindole; 3-(2-dimethylaminoethyl)-5-indolol; N,N-dimethylserotonin; 5-hydroxy-N,N-dimethyltryptamine; mappine);

(19) Diethyltryptamine (some trade and other names: N,N-Diethyltryptamine; DET);

(20) Dimethyltryptamine (some trade and other names: DMT);

(21) Ethylamine Analog of Phencyclidine (some trade or other names: N-ethyl-1-phenylcyclohexyl-amine; (1-phenylcyclohexyl) ethylamine; N-(1-phenyl-cyclohexyl)-ethylamine; cyclohexamine; PCE);

(22) Ibogaine (some trade or other names: 7-Ethyl-6,6-beta,7,8,9,10,12,13-octa-hydro-2-methoxy-6,9-methano-5H-pyrido[1',2':1,2] azepino [5,4-b] in-dole; taber- nanthe iboga);

(23) Lysergic acid diethylamide;

(24) Marihuana;

(25) Mescaline;

(26) N-ethyl-3-piperidyl benzilate;

(27) N-methyl-3-piperidyl benzilate;

(28) Parahexyl (some trade or other names: 3-Hexyl-1-hydroxy-7,8,9,10-tetrahydro-6,6,9-trimethyl-6H-dibenzo [b,d] pyran; Synhexyl);

(29) Peyote, unless unharvested and growing in its natural state, meaning all parts of the plant classi-fied botanically as *Lophophora*, whether growing or not, the seeds of the plant, an extract from a part of the plant, and every compound, manufacture, salt, deriva-tive, mixture, or preparation of the plant, its seeds, or extracts;

(30) Psilocybin;

(31) Psilocin;

(32) Pyrrolidine analog of phencyclidine (some trade or other names: 1-(1-phenyl-cyclohexyl)-pyrroli-dine, PCPy, PHP);

*__(33)__ Tetrahydrocannabinols

Meaning tetrahydrocannabinols naturally con-tained in a plant of the genus Cannabis (cannabis plant), as well as synthetic equivalents of the sub-stances contained in the cannabis plant, or in the res-inous extractives of such plant, and/or synthetic sub-stances, derivatives, and their isomers with similar chemical structure and pharmacological activity to those substances contained in the plant, such as the following:

1 cis or trans tetrahydrocannabinol, and their opti-cal isomers

6 cis or trans tetrahydrocannabinol, and their opti-cal isomers

3,4 cis or trans tetrahydrocannabinol, and its optical isomers;

(34) Thiophene analog of phencyclidine (some trade or other names: 1-[1-(2-thienyl)cyclohexyl] pip-eridine; 2-thienyl analog of phencyclidine; TPCP); and,

(35) 1-[1-(2-thienyl)cyclohexyl]pyrrolidine (some trade or other names: TCPy).

SCHEDULE I STIMULANTS

unless specifically excepted or unless listed in another schedule, a material, compound, mixture, or prepara-tion that contains any quantity of the following sub-stances having a stimulant effect on the central ner-vous system, including the substance's salts, isomers, and salts of isomers if the existence of the salts, iso-mers, and salts of isomers is possible within the spe-cific chemical designation:

(1) Aminorex (some other names: aminoxaphen; 2-amino-5-phenyl-2-oxazoline; 4,5-dihydro-5-phenyl-2-oxazolamine);

(2) Cathinone (some trade or other names: 2-amino-1-phenyl-1-propanone; alpha-aminopropiophe-none; 2-aminopropiophenone and norephedrone);

(3) Fenethylline;

(4) Methcathinone (some other names: 2-(methy-lamino)-propiophenone; alpha-(methylamino) pro-piophenone; 2-(methylamino)-1-phenylpropan-1-one; alpha-N-methylaminopropiophenone; monomethylpro-pion; ephedrone; N-methylcathinone; methylcathinone; AL-464; AL-422; AL-463; and UR1432);

(5) 4-methylaminorex;

(6) N-ethylamphetamine; and

(7) N,N-dimethylamphetamine (some other names: N,N-alpha-trimethylbenzene-ethaneamine; N,N-alpha-trimethylphenethylamine).

SCHEDULE I DEPRESSANTS

unless specifically excepted or unless listed in another schedule, a material, compound, mixture, or prepara-tion that contains any quantity of the following sub-stances having a depressant on the central nervous sys-tem, including the substance's salts, isomers, and salts of isomers if the existence of the salts, isomers, and salts of isomers is possible within the specific chemical designation:

(1) Gamma-hydroxybutyric acid (some other names include GHB; gamma-hydroxybutyrate; 4-hydroxybutyrate; 4-hydroxybutanoic acid; sodium oxybate; sodium oxybutyrate);

(2) Mecloqualone; and

(3) Methaqualone.

SCHEDULE II

Schedule II consists of:

SCHEDULE II SUBSTANCES, VEGETABLE ORIGIN OR CHEMICAL SYNTHESIS

the following substances, however produced, except those narcotic drugs listed in other schedules:

(1) Opium and opiate, and a salt, compound, derivative, or preparation of opium or opiate, other than thebaine-derived butorphanol, naloxone and its salts, naltrexone and its salts, and nalmefene and its salts, but including:

(1-1) Codeine;

(1-2) Dihydroetorphine;

(1-3) Ethylmorphine;

(1-4) Etorphine hydrochloride;

(1-5) Granulated opium;

(1-6) Hydrocodone;

(1-7) Hydromorphone;

(1-8) Metopon;

(1-9) Morphine;

(1-10) Opium extracts;

(1-11) Opium fluid extracts;

(1-12) Oripavine

(1-13) Oxycodone;

(1-14) Oxymorphone;

(1-15) Powdered opium;

(1-16) Raw opium;

(1-17) Thebaine; and

(1-18) Tincture of opium;

(2) a salt, compound, isomer, derivative, or preparation of a substance that is chemically equivalent or identical to a substance described by Paragraph (1) of Schedule II substances, vegetable origin or chemical synthesis, other than the isoquinoline alkaloids of opium;

(3) Opium poppy and poppy straw;

(4) Cocaine, including:

(4-1) its salts, its optical, position, and geometric isomers, and the salts of those isomers; and,

(4-2) coca leaves and a salt, compound, derivative, or preparation of coca leaves that is chemically equivalent or identical to a substance described by this paragraph, other than decocainized coca leaves or extractions of coca leaves that do not contain cocaine or ecgonine; and,

(5) Concentrate of poppy straw, meaning the crude extract of poppy straw in liquid, solid, or powder form that contains the phenanthrene alkaloids of the opium poppy;

OPIATES

the following opiates, including their isomers, esters, ethers, salts, and salts of isomers, if the existence of these isomers, esters, ethers, and salts is possible within the specific chemical designation:

(1) Alfentanil;

(2) Alphaprodine;

(3) Anileridine;

(4) Bezitramide;

(5) Carfentanil;

(6) Dextropropoxyphene, bulk (nondosage form);

(7) Dihydrocodeine;

(8) Diphenoxylate;

(9) Fentanyl;

(10) Isomethadone;

(11) Levo-alphacetylmethadol (some trade or other names: levo-alpha-acetylmethadol, levomethadyl acetate, LAAM);

(12) Levomethorphan;

(13) Levorphanol;

(14) Metazocine;

(15) Methadone;

(16) Methadone-Intermediate, 4-cyano-2-di- methylamino-4,4-diphenyl butane;

(17) Moramide-Intermediate, 2-methyl-3-morpholino-1,1-diphenyl-propane-carboxylic acid;

(18) Pethidine (meperidine);

(19) Pethidine-Intermediate-A, 4-cyano-1-methyl-4-phenylpiperidine;

(20) Pethidine-Intermediate-B, ethyl-4-phenylpiperidine-4-carboxylate;

(21) Pethidine-Intermediate-C, 1-methyl-4- phenylpiperidine-4-carboxylic acid;

(22) Phenazocine;

(23) Piminodine;

(24) Racemethorphan;

(25) Racemorphan;

(26) Remifentanil; and

(27) Sufentanil;

SCHEDULE II STIMULANTS

unless listed in another schedule and except as provided by the Texas Controlled Substances Act, Health and Safety Code, Section 481.033, a material, compound, mixture, or preparation that contains any quantity of the following substances having a potential for abuse associated with a stimulant effect on the central nervous system:

(1) Amphetamine, its salts, optical isomers, and salts of its optical isomers;

(2) Methamphetamine, including its salts, optical isomers, and salts of optical isomers;

(3) Methylphenidate and its salts; and

(4) Phenmetrazine and its salts;

***(5)** Lisdexamfetamine, including its salts, isomers, and salts of its isomers.

SCHEDULE II DEPRESSANTS

unless listed in another schedule, a material, compound, mixture or preparation that contains any quantity of the following substances having a depressant effect on the central nervous system, including the substance's salts, isomers, and salts of isomers if the existence of the salts, isomers, and salts of isomers is possible within the specific chemical designation:

(1) Amobarbital;

(2) Glutethimide;

(3) Pentobarbital; and

(4) Secobarbital;

SCHEDULE II HALLUCINOGENIC SUBSTANCES

(1) Nabilone (Another name for nabilone: (±)-trans-3-(1,1-dimethylheptyl)-6,6a,7,8,10,10a-hexahydro-1-hydroxy-6,6-dimethyl-9H-dibenzo[b,d]pyran-9-one);

SCHEDULE II PRECURSORS

unless specifically excepted or listed in another schedule, a material, compound, mixture, or preparation that contains any quantity of the following substances:

(1) Immediate precursor to methamphetamine:

(2) Phenylacetone and methylamine if possessed together with intent to manufacture methamphetamine;

(3) Immediate precursor to amphetamine and methamphetamine:

(4) Phenylacetone (some trade or other names: phenyl-2-propanone; P2P; benzyl methyl ketone; methyl benzyl ketone); and

(5) Immediate precursors to phencyclidine (PCP):

(6) 1-phenylcyclohexylamine; and

(7) 1-piperidinocyclohexanecarbonitrile (PCC).

SCHEDULE III

Schedule III consists of:

SCHEDULE III DEPRESSANTS

unless listed in another schedule and except as provided by the Texas Controlled Substances Act, Health and Safety Code, Section 481.033, a material, compound, mixture, or preparation that contains any quantity of the following substances having a potential for abuse associated with a depressant effect on the central nervous system:

(1) a compound, mixture, or preparation containing amobarbital, secobarbital, pentobarbital, or any of their salts and one or more active medicinal ingredients that are not listed in a schedule;

(2) a suppository dosage form containing amobarbital, secobarbital, pentobarbital, or any of their salts and approved by the Food and Drug Administration for marketing only as a suppository;

(3) a substance that contains any quantity of a derivative of barbituric acid, or any salt of a derivative of barbituric acid, except those substances that are specifically listed in other schedules;

(4) Chlorhexadol;

(5) Any drug product containing gamma hydroxybutyric acid, including its salts, isomers, and salts of isomers, for which an application is approved under section 505 of the Federal Food Drug and Cosmetic Act:

(6) Ketamine, its salts, isomers, and salts of isomers. Some other names for ketamine: (±)-2-(2-chlorophenyl)-2-(methylamino)-cyclohexanone;

(7) Lysergic acid;

(8) Lysergic acid amide;

(9) Methyprylon;

(10) Sulfondiethylmethane;

(11) Sulfonethylmethane;

(12) Sulfonmethane; and

(13) Tiletamine and zolazepam or any salt thereof. Some trade or other names for a tiletamine-zolazepam combination product: Telazol. Some trade or other names for tiletamine: 2-(ethylamino)-2-(2-thienyl)-cyclohexanone. Some trade or other names for zolazepam: 4-(2-fluorophenyl)-6,8-dihydro-1,3,8-trimethyl-pyrazolo-[3,4-e][1,4]-diazepin-7(1H)-one, flupyrazapon.

NALORPHINE

SCHEDULE III NARCOTICS

(1) a material, compound, mixture, or preparation containing limited quantities of any of the following narcotic drugs, or any of their salts:

(1-1) not more than 1.8 grams of codeine, or any of its salts, per 100 milliliters or not more than 90 milligrams per dosage unit, with an equal or greater quantity of an isoquinoline alkaloid of opium;

(1-2) not more than 1.8 grams of codeine, or any of its salts, per 100 milliliters or not more than 90 milligrams per dosage unit, with one or more active, nonnarcotic ingredients in recognized therapeutic amounts;

(1-3) not more than 300 milligrams of dihydrocodeinone (hydrocodone), or any of its salts, per 100 milliliters or not more than 15 milligrams per dosage unit, with a fourfold or greater quantity of an isoquinoline alkaloid of opium;

(1-4) not more than 300 milligrams of dihydrocodeinone (hydrocodone), or any of its salts, per 100 milliliters or not more than 15 milligrams per dosage unit, with one or more active, nonnarcotic ingredients in recognized therapeutic amounts;

(1-5) not more than 1.8 grams of dihydrocodeine, or any of its salts, per 100 milliliters or not more than 90 milligrams per dosage unit, with one or more active, nonnarcotic ingredients in recognized therapeutic amounts;

(1-6) not more than 300 milligrams of ethylmorphine, or any of its salts, per 100 milliliters or not more than 15 milligrams per dosage unit, with one or more active, non- narcotic ingredients in recognized therapeutic amounts;

(1-7) not more than 500 milligrams of opium per 100 milliliters or per 100 grams, or not more than 25 milligrams per dosage unit, with one or more active, nonnarcotic ingredients in recognized therapeutic amounts; and

(1-8) not more than 50 milligrams of morphine, or any of its salts, per 100 milliliters or per 100 grams with one or more active, nonnarcotic ingredients in recognized therapeutic amounts;

(2) any material, compound, mixture, or preparation containing any of the following narcotic drugs or their salts:

(2-1) Buprenorphine

SCHEDULE III STIMULANTS

unless listed in another schedule, a material, compound, mixture or preparation that contains any quantity of the following substances having a stimulant effect on the central nervous system, including the substance's salts, optical, position, or geometric isomers, and salts of the substance's isomers, if the existence of the salts, isomers, and salts of isomers is possible within the specific chemical designation:

(1) Benzphetamine;

(2) Chlorphentermine;

(3) Clortermine; and

(4) Phendimetrazine;

SCHEDULE III ANABOLIC STEROIDS & HORMONES

anabolic steroids, including any drug or hormonal substance, chemically and pharmacologically related to testosterone (other than estrogens, progestins, corticosteroids, and dehydroepiandrosterone), and include the following:

(1) androstanediol—

(1-1) 3 beta,17 beta-dihydroxy-5 alpha-androstane; and

(1-2) 3 alpha,17 beta -dihydroxy-5 alpha-androstane;

(2) androstanedione (5 alpha-androstan-3,17-dione);

(3) androstenediol—

(3-1) 1-androstenediol (3 beta,17 beta-dihydroxy-5 alpha-androst-1-ene);

(3-2) 1-androstenediol (3 alpha,17 beta-dihydroxy-5 alpha-androst-1-ene);

(3-3) 4-androstenediol (3 beta,17 beta-dihydroxy-androst-4-ene); and,

(3-4) 5-androstenediol (3 beta,17 beta-dihydroxy-androst-5-ene);

(4) androstenedione—

(4-1) 1-androstenedione ([5 alpha]-androst-1-en-3,17-dione);

(4-2) 4-androstenedione (androst-4-en-3,17-dione); and

(4-3) 5-androstenedione (androst-5-en-3,17-dione);

(5) bolasterone (7 alpha,17 alpha-dimethyl-17 beta-hydroxyandrost-4-en-3-one);

(6) boldenone (17 beta-hydroxyandrost-1,4,-diene-3-one);

(7) calusterone (7 beta,17 alpha-dimethyl-17 beta-hydroxyandrost-4-en-3-one);

(8) clostebol (4-chloro-17 beta-hydroxyandrost-4-en-3-one);

(9) dehydrochloromethyltestosterone (4-chloro-17 beta-hydroxy-17alpha-methyl-androst-1,4-dien-3-one);

(10) delta-1-dihydrotestosterone (a.k.a. '1-testosterone') (17 beta-hydroxy-5 alpha-androst-1-en-3-one);

(11) 4-dihydrotestosterone (17 beta-hydroxy-androstan-3-one);

(12) drostanolone (17 beta-hydroxy-2 alpha-methyl-5 alpha-androstan-3-one);

(13) ethylestrenol (17 alpha-ethyl-17 beta-hydroxyestr-4-ene);

(14) fluoxymesterone (9-fluoro-17 alpha-methyl-11 beta,17 beta-dihydroxyandrost-4-en-3-one);

(15) formebolone (2-formyl-17 alpha-methyl-11 alpha,17 beta-dihydroxyandrost-1,4-dien-3-one);

(16) furazabol (17 alpha-methyl-17 beta-hydroxyandrostano[2,3-c]-furazan);

***(17)** 13 beta-ethyl-17 beta-hydroxygon-4-en-3-one;

(18) 4-hydroxytestosterone (4,17 beta-dihydroxy-androst-4-en-3-one);

(19) 4-hydroxy-19-nortestosterone (4,17 beta-dihydroxy-estr-4-en-3-one);

(20) mestanolone (17 alpha-methyl-17 beta-hydroxy-5 alpha-androstan-3-one);

(21) mesterolone (1 alpha-methyl-17 beta-hydroxy-[5 alpha]-androstan-3-one);

(22) methandienone (17 alpha-methyl-17 beta-hydroxyandrost-1,4-dien-3-one);

(23) methandriol (17 alpha-methyl-3 beta,17 beta-dihydroxyandrost-5-ene);

(24) methenolone (1-methyl-17 beta-hydroxy-5 alpha-androst-1-en-3-one);

(25) 17 alpha-methyl-3 beta, 17 beta-dihydroxy-5 alpha-androstane;

(26) 17alpha-methyl-3 alpha,17 beta-dihydroxy-5 alpha-androstane;

(27) 17 alpha-methyl-3 beta,17 beta-dihydroxyandrost-4-ene.

(28) 17 alpha-methyl-4-hydroxynandrolone (17 alpha-methyl-4-hydroxy-17 beta-hydroxyestr-4-en-3-one);

(29) methyldienolone (17 alpha-methyl-17 beta-hydroxyestra-4,9(10)-dien-3-one);

(30) methyltrienolone (17 alpha-methyl-17 beta-hydroxyestra-4,9-11-trien-3-one);

(31) methyltestosterone (17 alpha-methyl-17 beta-hydroxyandrost-4-en-3-one);

(32) mibolerone (7 alpha,17 alpha-dimethyl-17 beta-hydroxyestr-4-en-3-one);

(33) 17 alpha-methyl-delta-1-dihydrotestosterone (17 beta-hydroxy-17 alpha-methyl-5 alpha-androst-1-en-3-one) (a.k.a. '17-alpha-methyl-1-testosterone');

(34) nandrolone (17 beta-hydroxyestr-4-en-3-one);

(35) norandrostenediol—

(35-1) 19-nor-4-androstenediol (3 beta, 17 beta-dihydroxyestr-4-ene);

(35-2) 19-nor-4-androstenediol (3 alpha, 17 beta-dihydroxyestr-4-ene);

(35-3) 19-nor-5-androstenediol (3 beta, 17 beta-dihydroxyestr-5-ene); and

(35-4) 19-nor-5-androstenediol (3 alpha, 17 beta-dihydroxyestr-5-ene);

(36) norandrostenedione—

(36-1) 19-nor-4-androstenedione (estr-4-en-3,17-dione); and

(36-2) 19-nor-5-androstenedione (estr-5-en-3,17-dione;

(37) norbolethone (13 beta,17alpha-diethyl-17 beta-hydroxygon-4-en-3-one);

(38) norclostebol (4-chloro-17 beta-hydroxyestr-4-en-3-one);

(39) norethandrolone (17 alpha-ethyl-17 beta-hydroxyestr-4-en-3-one);

(40) normethandrolone (17 alpha-methyl-17 beta-hydroxyestr-4-en-3-one);

(41) oxandrolone (17 alpha-methyl-17 beta-hydroxy-2-oxa-[5 alpha]-androstan-3-one);

(42) oxymesterone (17 alpha-methyl-4,17 beta-dihydroxyandrost-4-en-3-one);

(43) oxymetholone (17 alpha-methyl-2-hydroxymethylene-17 beta-hydroxy-[5 alpha]-androstan-3-one);

*****(44)** stanozolol (17 alpha-methyl-17 beta-hydroxy-[5 alpha]-androst-2-eno[3,2-c]-pyrazole);

(45) stenbolone (17 beta-hydroxy-2-methyl-[5 alpha]-androst-1-en-3-one);

(46) testolactone (13-hydroxy-3-oxo-13,17-secoandrosta-1,4-dien-17-oic acid lactone);

(47) testosterone (17 beta-hydroxyandrost-4-en-3-one);

(48) tetrahydrogestrinone (13 beta,17 alpha-diethyl-17 beta-hydroxygon-4,9,11-trien-3-one);

(49) trenbolone (17 beta-hydroxyestr-4,9,11-trien-3-one); and

(50) any salt, ester, or ether of a drug or substance described in this paragraph.

SCHEDULE III HALLUCINOGENIC SUBSTANCES

(1) Dronabinol (synthetic) in sesame oil and encapsulated in a soft gelatin capsule in a U.S. Food and Drug Administration approved drug product. (Some other names for dronabinol: (6aR-trans)-6a,7,8,10a-tetrahydro-6,6,9-tri-methyl-3-pentyl-6H-dibenzo[b,d]pyran-1-ol, or (-)-delta-9-(trans)-tetrahydrocannabinol).

SCHEDULE IV
Schedule IV consists of:

SCHEDULE IV DEPRESSANTS
except as provided by the Texas Controlled Substances Act, Health and Safety Code, Section 481.033, a material, compound, mixture, or preparation that contains any quantity of the following substances having a potential for abuse associated with a depressant effect on the central nervous system:

(1) Alprazolam;

(2) Barbital;

(3) Bromazepam;

(4) Camazepam;

(5) Chloral betaine;

(6) Chloral hydrate;

(7) Chlordiazepoxide;

(8) Clobazam;

(9) Clonazepam;

(10) Clorazepate;

(11) Clotiazepam;

(12) Cloxazolam;

(13) Delorazepam;

(14) Diazepam;

(15) Dichloralphenazone;

(16) Estazolam;

(17) Ethchlorvynol;

(18) Ethinamate;

(19) Ethyl loflazepate;

(20) Fludiazepam;

(21) Flunitrazepam;

(22) Flurazepam;

(23) Halazepam;

(24) Haloxazolam;

(25) Ketazolam;

(26) Loprazolam;

(27) Lorazepam;

(28) Lormetazepam;

(29) Mebutamate;

(30) Medazepam;

(31) Meprobamate;

(32) Methohexital;

(33) Methylphenobarbital (mephobarbital);

(34) Midazolam;

(35) Nimetazepam;

(36) Nitrazepam;

(37) Nordiazepam;

(38) Oxazepam;

(39) Oxazolam;

(40) Paraldehyde;

(41) Petrichloral;

(42) Phenobarbital;

(43) Pinazepam;

(44) Prazepam;

(45) Quazepam;

(46) Temazepam;

(47) Tetrazepam;

(48) Triazolam;

(49) Zaleplon;

(50) Zolpidem; and

(51) Zopiclone, its salts, isomers, and salts of isomers

SCHEDULE IV STIMULANTS

unless listed in another schedule, a material, compound, mixture, or preparation that contains any quantity of the following substances having a stimulant effect on the central nervous system, including the substance's salts, optical, position, or geometric isomers, and salts of those isomers if the existence of the salts, isomers, and salts of isomers is possible within the specific chemical designation:

(1) Cathine [(+)-norpseudoephedrine];

(2) Diethylpropion;

(3) Fencamfamin;

(4) Fenfluramine;

(5) Fenproporex;

(6) Mazindol;

(7) Mefenorex;

(8) Modafinil;

(9) Pemoline (including organometallic complexes and their chelates);

(10) Phentermine;

(11) Pipradrol;

(12) SPA [(-)-1-dimethylamino-1,2-diphenylethane]; and

(13) Sibutramine

SCHEDULE IV NARCOTICS

unless specifically excepted or unless listed in another schedule, a material, compound, mixture, or preparation containing limited quantities of the following narcotic drugs or their salts:

(1) Not more than 1 milligram of difenoxin and not less than 25 micrograms of atropine sulfate per dosage unit; and

(2) Dextropropoxyphene (Alpha-(+)-4-dimethylamino-1,2-diphenyl-3-methyl-2-propionoxybutane).

SCHEDULE IV OTHER SUBSTANCES

unless specifically excepted or unless listed in another schedule, a material, compound, mixture, or preparation that contains any quantity of the following substances, including the substance's salts:

(1) Butorphanol, including its optical isomers; and

(2) Pentazocine, its salts, derivatives, compounds, or mixtures.

SCHEDULE V

Schedule V consists of:

SCHEDULE V NARCOTICS

unless specifically excepted or unless listed in another schedule, a material, compound, mixture, or preparation containing any of the following narcotic drugs and their salts:

(1) Buprenorphine;

SCHEDULE V NARCOTICS CONTAINING NON-NARCOTIC ACTIVE MEDICINAL INGREDIENTS

a compound, mixture, or preparation containing limited quantities of any of the following narcotic drugs that also contain one or more nonnarcotic active medicinal ingredients in sufficient proportion to confer on the compound, mixture or preparation valuable medicinal qualities other than those possessed by the narcotic drug alone:

(1) Not more than 200 milligrams of codeine, or any of its salts, per 100 milliliters or per 100 grams;

(2) Not more than 100 milligrams of dihydrocodeine, or any of its salts, per 100 milliliters or per 100 grams;

(3) Not more than 100 milligrams of ethylmorphine, or any of its salts, per 100 milliliters or per 100 grams;

(4) Not more than 2.5 milligrams of diphenoxylate and not less than 25 micrograms of atropine sulfate per dosage unit;

(5) Not more than 15 milligrams of opium per 29.5729 milliliters or per 28.35 grams; and,

(6) Not more than 0.5 milligram of difenoxin and not less than 25 micrograms of atropine sulfate per dosage unit;

SCHEDULE V STIMULANTS

unless specifically exempted or excluded or unless listed in another schedule, a compound, mixture, or preparation which contains any quantity of the following substances having a stimulant effect on the central nervous system, including its salts, isomers and salts of isomers:

(1) Pyrovalerone.

SCHEDULE V DEPRESSANTS*

unless specifically exempted or excluded or unless listed in another schedule, any material, compound, mixture, or preparation, which contains any quantity of the following substances having a depressant effect on the central nervous system, including its salts.

(1) Pregabalin   [(S)-3-(aminomethyl)-5-methyl-hexanoic acid].

---- ★ ----

GOVERNMENT CODE

SELECTED PROVISIONS
TABLE OF CONTENTS

---⭐---

TITLE 2. JUDICIAL BRANCH

SUBTITLE A. COURTS

CHAPTER 21. GENERAL PROVISIONS

GOVT §21.005. DISQUALIFICATION

A judge or a justice of the peace may not sit in a case if either of the parties is related to him by affinity or consanguinity within the third degree, as determined under Chapter 573.

History of Govt §21.005: Acts 1987, 70th Leg., ch. 148, §2.01(a), eff. Sept. 1, 1987. Amended by Acts 1991, 72nd Leg., ch. 561, §21, eff. Aug. 26, 1991; Acts 1995, 74th Leg., ch. 76, §5.95(28), eff. Sept. 1, 1995.

SUBTITLE E. JURIES

CHAPTER 62. PETIT JURIES

SUBCHAPTER B. JUROR QUALIFICATIONS

GOVT §62.110. JUDICIAL EXCUSE OF JURORS

(a) Except as provided by this section, a court may hear any reasonable sworn excuse of a prospective juror, including any claim of an exemption or a lack of qualification, and if the excuse is considered sufficient shall release him from jury service entirely or until another day of the term, as appropriate.

(b) Pursuant to a plan approved by the commissioners court of the county in the same manner as a plan is approved for jury selection under Section 62.011, the court's designee may:

(1) hear any reasonable excuse of a prospective juror, including any claim of an exemption or a lack of qualification; and

(2) discharge the juror or release him from jury service until a specified day of the term, as appropriate, if:

(A) the excuse is considered sufficient; and

(B) the juror submits to the court's designee a statement of the ground of the exemption or lack of qualification or other excuse.

(c) The court or the court's designee as provided by this section may not excuse a prospective juror for an economic reason unless each party of record is present and approves the release of the juror for that reason.

History of Govt §62.110: Acts 1985, 69th Leg., ch. 480, §1, eff. Sept. 1, 1985. Amended by Acts 1987, 70th Leg., ch. 589, §3, eff. Aug. 31, 1987; Acts 1987, 70th Leg., 2nd C.S., ch. 43, §4, eff. Oct. 20, 1987; Acts 2005, 79th Leg., ch. 905, §2, eff. Sept. 1, 2005.

Gray v. State, 159 S.W.3d 95, 95-96 (Tex.Crim.App. 2005). "When a trial court erroneously excuses a prospective juror for economic reasons in violation of … §62.110(c), is the error 'structural,' requiring reversal without a harm analysis? The answer is 'no.'"

TITLE 3. LEGISLATIVE BRANCH

SUBTITLE B. LEGISLATION

CHAPTER 311. CODE CONSTRUCTION ACT

SUBCHAPTER A. GENERAL PROVISIONS

GOVT §311.001. SHORT TITLE

This chapter may be cited as the Code Construction Act.

History of Govt §311.001: Acts 1985, 69th Leg., ch. 479, §1, eff. Sept. 1, 1985.

GOVT §311.002. APPLICATION

This chapter applies to:

(1) each code enacted by the 60th or a subsequent legislature as part of the state's continuing statutory revision program;

(2) each amendment, repeal, revision, and reenactment of a code or code provision by the 60th or a subsequent legislature;

(3) each repeal of a statute by a code; and

(4) each rule adopted under a code.

History of Govt §311.002: Acts 1985, 69th Leg., ch. 479, §1, eff. Sept. 1, 1985.

GOVT §311.003. RULES NOT EXCLUSIVE

The rules provided in this chapter are not exclusive but are meant to describe and clarify common situations in order to guide the preparation and construction of codes.

History of Govt §311.003: Acts 1985, 69th Leg., ch. 479, §1, eff. Sept. 1, 1985.

GOVT §311.004. CITATION OF CODES

A code may be cited by its name preceded by the specific part concerned. Examples of citations are:

(1) Title 1, Business & Commerce Code;

(2) Chapter 5, Business & Commerce Code;

(3) Section 9.304, Business & Commerce Code;

GOVT §21.005

(4) Section 15.06(a), Business & Commerce Code; and

(5) Section 17.18(b)(1)(B)(ii), Business & Commerce Code.

History of Govt §311.004: Acts 1985, 69th Leg., ch. 479, §1, eff. Sept. 1, 1985. Amended by Acts 1985, 69th Leg., ch. 117, §13(b), eff. Sept. 1, 1985.

GOVT §311.005. GENERAL DEFINITIONS

The following definitions apply unless the statute or context in which the word or phrase is used requires a different definition:

(1) "Oath" includes affirmation.

(2) "Person" includes corporation, organization, government or governmental subdivision or agency, business trust, estate, trust, partnership, association, and any other legal entity.

(3) "Population" means the population shown by the most recent federal decennial census.

(4) "Property" means real and personal property.

(5) "Rule" includes regulation.

(6) "Signed" includes any symbol executed or adopted by a person with present intention to authenticate a writing.

(7) "State," when referring to a part of the United States, includes any state, district, commonwealth, territory, and insular possession of the United States and any area subject to the legislative authority of the United States of America.

(8) "Swear" includes affirm.

(9) "United States" includes a department, bureau, or other agency of the United States of America.

(10) "Week" means seven consecutive days.

(11) "Written" includes any representation of words, letters, symbols, or figures.

(12) "Year" means 12 consecutive months.

(13) "Includes" and "including" are terms of enlargement and not of limitation or exclusive enumeration, and use of the terms does not create a presumption that components not expressed are excluded.

History of Govt §311.005: Acts 1985, 69th Leg., ch. 479, §1, eff. Sept. 1, 1985. Amended by Acts 1989, 71st Leg., ch. 340, §1, eff. Aug. 28, 1989.

GOVT §311.006. INTERNAL REFERENCES

In a code:

(1) a reference to a title, chapter, or section without further identification is a reference to a title, chapter, or section of the code; and

(2) a reference to a subtitle, subchapter, subsection, subdivision, paragraph, or other numbered or lettered unit without further identification is a reference to a unit of the next larger unit of the code in which the reference appears.

History of Govt §311.006: Acts 1993, 73rd Leg., ch. 131, §1, eff. May 11, 1993.

SUBCHAPTER B. CONSTRUCTION OF WORDS & PHRASES

GOVT §311.011. COMMON & TECHNICAL USAGE OF WORDS

(a) Words and phrases shall be read in context and construed according to the rules of grammar and common usage.

(b) Words and phrases that have acquired a technical or particular meaning, whether by legislative definition or otherwise, shall be construed accordingly.

History of Govt §311.011: Acts 1985, 69th Leg., ch. 479, §1, eff. Sept. 1, 1985.

GOVT §311.012. TENSE, NUMBER, & GENDER

(a) Words in the present tense include the future tense.

(b) The singular includes the plural and the plural includes the singular.

(c) Words of one gender include the other genders.

History of Govt §311.012: Acts 1985, 69th Leg., ch. 479, §1, eff. Sept. 1, 1985.

GOVT §311.013. AUTHORITY & QUORUM OF PUBLIC BODY

(a) A grant of authority to three or more persons as a public body confers the authority on a majority of the number of members fixed by statute.

(b) A quorum of a public body is a majority of the number of members fixed by statute.

History of Govt §311.013: Acts 1985, 69th Leg., ch. 479, §1, eff. Sept. 1, 1985.

GOVT §311.014. COMPUTATION OF TIME

(a) In computing a period of days, the first day is excluded and the last day is included.

(b) If the last day of any period is a Saturday, Sunday, or legal holiday, the period is extended to include the next day that is not a Saturday, Sunday, or legal holiday.

(c) If a number of months is to be computed by counting the months from a particular day, the period ends on the same numerical day in the concluding month as the day of the month from which the computation is begun, unless there are not that many days in the concluding month, in which case the period ends on the last day of that month.

History of Govt §311.014: Acts 1985, 69th Leg., ch. 479, §1, eff. Sept. 1, 1985.

GOVT §311.015. REFERENCE TO A SERIES

If a statute refers to a series of numbers or letters, the first and last numbers or letters are included.

History of Govt §311.015: Acts 1985, 69th Leg., ch. 479, §1, eff. Sept. 1, 1985.

GOVT §311.016. "MAY," "SHALL," "MUST," ETC.

The following constructions apply unless the context in which the word or phrase appears necessarily requires a different construction or unless a different construction is expressly provided by statute:

(1) "May" creates discretionary authority or grants permission or a power.

(2) "Shall" imposes a duty.

(3) "Must" creates or recognizes a condition precedent.

(4) "Is entitled to" creates or recognizes a right.

(5) "May not" imposes a prohibition and is synonymous with "shall not."

(6) "Is not entitled to" negates a right.

(7) "Is not required to" negates a duty or condition precedent.

History of Govt §311.016: Acts 1997, 75th Leg., ch. 220, §1, eff. May 23, 1997.

SUBCHAPTER C. CONSTRUCTION OF STATUTES

GOVT §311.021. INTENTION IN ENACTMENT OF STATUTES

In enacting a statute, it is presumed that:

(1) compliance with the constitutions of this state and the United States is intended;

(2) the entire statute is intended to be effective;

(3) a just and reasonable result is intended;

(4) a result feasible of execution is intended; and

(5) public interest is favored over any private interest.

History of Govt §311.021: Acts 1985, 69th Leg., ch. 479, §1, eff. Sept. 1, 1985.

GOVT §311.022. PROSPECTIVE OPERATION OF STATUTES

A statute is presumed to be prospective in its operation unless expressly made retrospective.

History of Govt §311.022: Acts 1985, 69th Leg., ch. 479, §1, eff. Sept. 1, 1985.

GOVT §311.023. STATUTE CONSTRUCTION AIDS

In construing a statute, whether or not the statute is considered ambiguous on its face, a court may consider among other matters the:

(1) object sought to be attained;

(2) circumstances under which the statute was enacted;

(3) legislative history;

(4) common law or former statutory provisions, including laws on the same or similar subjects;

(5) consequences of a particular construction;

(6) administrative construction of the statute; and

(7) title (caption), preamble, and emergency provision.

History of Govt §311.023: Acts 1985, 69th Leg., ch. 479, §1, eff. Sept. 1, 1985.

GOVT §311.024. HEADINGS

The heading of a title, subtitle, chapter, subchapter, or section does not limit or expand the meaning of a statute.

History of Govt §311.024: Acts 1985, 69th Leg., ch. 479, §1, eff. Sept. 1, 1985.

GOVT §311.025. IRRECONCILABLE STATUTES & AMENDMENTS

(a) Except as provided by Section 311.031(d), if statutes enacted at the same or different sessions of the legislature are irreconcilable, the statute latest in date of enactment prevails.

(b) Except as provided by Section 311.031(d), if amendments to the same statute are enacted at the same session of the legislature, one amendment without reference to another, the amendments shall be harmonized, if possible, so that effect may be given to each. If the amendments are irreconcilable, the latest in date of enactment prevails.

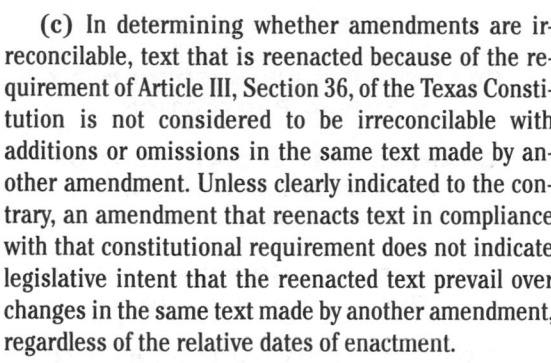

(c) In determining whether amendments are irreconcilable, text that is reenacted because of the requirement of Article III, Section 36, of the Texas Constitution is not considered to be irreconcilable with additions or omissions in the same text made by another amendment. Unless clearly indicated to the contrary, an amendment that reenacts text in compliance with that constitutional requirement does not indicate legislative intent that the reenacted text prevail over changes in the same text made by another amendment, regardless of the relative dates of enactment.

(d) In this section, the date of enactment is the date on which the last legislative vote is taken on the bill enacting the statute.

(e) If the journals or other legislative records fail to disclose which of two or more bills in conflict is latest in date of enactment, the date of enactment of the respective bills is considered to be, in order of priority:

(1) the date on which the last presiding officer signed the bill;

(2) the date on which the governor signed the bill; or

(3) the date on which the bill became law by operation of law.

History of Govt §311.025: Acts 1985, 69th Leg., ch. 479, §1, eff. Sept. 1, 1985. Amended by Acts 1989, 71st Leg., ch. 340, §2, eff. Aug. 28, 1989; Acts 1997, 75th Leg., ch. 220, §2, eff. May 23, 1997.

GOVT §311.026. SPECIAL OR LOCAL PROVISION PREVAILS OVER GENERAL

(a) If a general provision conflicts with a special or local provision, the provisions shall be construed, if possible, so that effect is given to both.

(b) If the conflict between the general provision and the special or local provision is irreconcilable, the special or local provision prevails as an exception to the general provision, unless the general provision is the later enactment and the manifest intent is that the general provision prevail.

History of Govt §311.026: Acts 1985, 69th Leg., ch. 479, §1, eff. Sept. 1, 1985.

GOVT §311.027. STATUTORY REFERENCES

Unless expressly provided otherwise, a reference to any portion of a statute or rule applies to all reenactments, revisions, or amendments of the statute or rule.

History of Govt §311.027: Acts 1985, 69th Leg., ch. 479, §1, eff. Sept. 1, 1985. Amended by Acts 1993, 73rd Leg., ch. 131, §2, eff. May 11, 1993.

GOVT §311.028. UNIFORM CONSTRUCTION OF UNIFORM ACTS

A uniform act included in a code shall be construed to effect its general purpose to make uniform the law of those states that enact it.

History of Govt §311.028: Acts 1985, 69th Leg., ch. 479, §1, eff. Sept. 1, 1985.

GOVT §311.029. ENROLLED BILL CONTROLS

If the language of the enrolled bill version of a statute conflicts with the language of any subsequent printing or reprinting of the statute, the language of the enrolled bill version controls.

History of Govt §311.029: Acts 1985, 69th Leg., ch. 479, §1, eff. Sept. 1, 1985.

GOVT §311.030. REPEAL OF REPEALING STATUTE

The repeal of a repealing statute does not revive the statute originally repealed nor impair the effect of any saving provision in it.

History of Govt §311.030: Acts 1985, 69th Leg., ch. 479, §1, eff. Sept. 1, 1985.

GOVT §311.031. SAVING PROVISIONS

(a) Except as provided by Subsection (b), the reenactment, revision, amendment, or repeal of a statute does not affect:

(1) the prior operation of the statute or any prior action taken under it;

(2) any validation, cure, right, privilege, obligation, or liability previously acquired, accrued, accorded, or incurred under it;

(3) any violation of the statute or any penalty, forfeiture, or punishment incurred under the statute before its amendment or repeal; or

(4) any investigation, proceeding, or remedy concerning any privilege, obligation, liability, penalty, forfeiture, or punishment; and the investigation, proceeding, or remedy may be instituted, continued, or enforced, and the penalty, forfeiture, or punishment imposed, as if the statute had not been repealed or amended.

(b) If the penalty, forfeiture, or punishment for any offense is reduced by a reenactment, revision, or amendment of a statute, the penalty, forfeiture, or punishment, if not already imposed, shall be imposed according to the statute as amended.

(c) The repeal of a statute by a code does not affect an amendment, revision, or reenactment of the statute by the same legislature that enacted the code. The amendment, revision, or reenactment is preserved and given effect as part of the code provision that revised the statute so amended, revised, or reenacted.

(d) If any provision of a code conflicts with a statute enacted by the same legislature that enacted the code, the statute controls.

History of Govt §311.031: Acts 1985, 69th Leg., ch. 479, §1, eff. Sept. 1, 1985.

GOVT §311.032. SEVERABILITY OF STATUTES

(a) If any statute contains a provision for severability, that provision prevails in interpreting that statute.

(b) If any statute contains a provision for nonseverability, that provision prevails in interpreting that statute.

(c) In a statute that does not contain a provision for severability or nonseverability, if any provision of the statute or its application to any person or circumstance is held invalid, the invalidity does not affect other provisions or applications of the statute that can be given effect without the invalid provision or application, and to this end the provisions of the statute are severable.

History of Govt §311.032: Acts 1985, 69th Leg., ch. 479, §1, eff. Sept. 1, 1985.

Section 311.033 blank

GOVT §311.034. WAIVER OF SOVEREIGN IMMUNITY

In order to preserve the legislature's interest in managing state fiscal matters through the appropriations process, a statute shall not be construed as a waiver of sovereign immunity unless the waiver is effected by clear and unambiguous language. In a statute, the use of "person," as defined by Section 311.005 to include governmental entities, does not indicate legislative intent to waive sovereign immunity unless the context of the statute indicates no other reasonable construction. Statutory prerequisites to a suit, including the provision of notice, are jurisdictional requirements in all suits against a governmental entity.

History of Govt §311.034: Acts 2001, 77th Leg., ch. 1158, §8, eff. June 15, 2001. Amended by Acts 2005, 79th Leg., ch. 1150, §1, eff. Sept. 1, 2005.

TITLE 4. EXECUTIVE BRANCH

SUBTITLE B. LAW ENFORCEMENT & PUBLIC PROTECTION

CHAPTER 411. DEPARTMENT OF PUBLIC SAFETY OF THE STATE OF TEXAS

SUBCHAPTER F. CRIMINAL HISTORY RECORD INFORMATION

GOVT §411.081. APPLICATION OF SUBCHAPTER

(a) This subchapter does not apply to criminal history record information that is contained in:

(1) posters, announcements, or lists for identifying or apprehending fugitives or wanted persons;

(2) original records of entry, including police blotters maintained by a criminal justice agency that are compiled chronologically and required by law or longstanding practice to be available to the public;

(3) public judicial, administrative, or legislative proceedings;

(4) court records of public judicial proceedings;

(5) published judicial or administrative opinions; or

(6) announcements of executive clemency.

(b) This subchapter does not prohibit a criminal justice agency from disclosing to the public criminal history record information that is related to the offense for which a person is involved in the criminal justice system.

(c) This subchapter does not prohibit a criminal justice agency from confirming previous criminal history record information to any person on specific inquiry about whether a named person was arrested, detained, indicted, or formally charged on a specified date, if the information disclosed is based on data excluded by Subsection (b).

(d) Notwithstanding any other provision of this subchapter, if a person is placed on deferred adjudication community supervision under Section 5, Article 42.12, Code of Criminal Procedure, subsequently receives a discharge and dismissal under Section 5(c), Article 42.12, and satisfies the requirements of Subsection (e), the person may petition the court that placed the defendant on deferred adjudication for an order of nondisclosure under this subsection. Except as provided by Subsection (e), a person may petition the court under this subsection regardless of whether the person has been previously placed on deferred adjudication community supervision for another offense. After notice to the state and a hearing on whether the person is entitled to file the petition and issuance of the order is in the best interest of justice, the court shall issue an order prohibiting criminal justice agencies from disclosing to the public criminal history record information related to the offense giving rise to the deferred adjudication. A criminal justice agency may disclose criminal history record information that is the subject of the order only to other criminal justice agencies, for criminal justice or regulatory licensing purposes, an agency or entity listed in Subsection (i), or the person who is the subject of the order. A person may petition the court that placed the person on deferred adjudication for an order of nondisclosure on payment of a $28 fee to the clerk of the court in addition to any other fee that generally applies to the filing of a civil petition. The payment may be made only on or after:

(1) the discharge and dismissal, if the offense for which the person was placed on deferred adjudication was a misdemeanor other than a misdemeanor described by Subdivision (2);

(2) the second anniversary of the discharge and dismissal, if the offense for which the person was placed on deferred adjudication was a misdemeanor under Chapter 20, 21, 22, 25, 42, or 46, Penal Code; or

(3) the fifth anniversary of the discharge and dismissal, if the offense for which the person was placed on deferred adjudication was a felony.

(e) A person is entitled to petition the court under Subsection (d) only if during the period of the deferred adjudication community supervision for which the order of nondisclosure is requested and during the applicable period described by Subsection (d)(1), (2), or (3), as appropriate, the person is not convicted of or placed on deferred adjudication community supervision under Section 5, Article 42.12, Code of Criminal Procedure, for any offense other than an offense under the Transportation Code punishable by fine only. A person is not entitled to petition the court under Subsection (d) if the person was placed on the deferred adjudication community supervision for or has been previously convicted or placed on any other deferred adjudication for:

(1) an offense requiring registration as a sex offender under Chapter 62, Code of Criminal Procedure;

(2) an offense under Section 20.04, Penal Code, regardless of whether the offense is a reportable conviction or adjudication for purposes of Chapter 62, Code of Criminal Procedure;

(3) an offense under Section 19.02, 19.03, 22.04, 22.041, 25.07, or 42.072, Penal Code; or

(4) any other offense involving family violence, as defined by Section 71.004, Family Code.

(f) For purposes of Subsection (d), a person is considered to have been placed on deferred adjudication community supervision if, regardless of the statutory authorization:

(1) the person entered a plea of guilty or nolo contendere;

(2) the judge deferred further proceedings without entering an adjudication of guilt and placed the person under the supervision of the court or an officer under the supervision of the court; and

(3) at the end of the period of supervision the judge dismissed the proceedings and discharged the person.

(g) Not later than the 15th business day after the date an order of nondisclosure is issued under this section, the clerk of the court shall send all relevant criminal history record information contained in the order or a copy of the order by certified mail, return receipt requested, or secure electronic mail, electronic transmission, or facsimile transmission to the Crime Records Service of the Department of Public Safety.

(g-1) Not later than 10 business days after receipt of relevant criminal history record information contained in an order or a copy of an order under Subsection (g), the Department of Public Safety shall seal any criminal history record information maintained by the department that is the subject of the order. The department shall also send all relevant criminal history record information contained in the order or a copy of the order by certified mail, return receipt requested, or secure electronic mail, electronic transmission, or facsimile transmission to all:

(1) law enforcement agencies, jails or other detention facilities, magistrates, courts, prosecuting attorneys, correctional facilities, central state depositories of criminal records, and other officials or agencies or other entities of this state or of any political subdivision of this state;

(2) central federal depositories of criminal records that there is reason to believe have criminal history record information that is the subject of the order; and

(3) private entities that purchase criminal history record information from the department or that otherwise are likely to have criminal history record information that is subject to the order.

E (g-1a) The director shall adopt rules regarding minimum standards for the security of secure electronic mail, electronic transmissions, and facsimile transmissions under Subsections (g) and (g-1). In adopting rules under this subsection, the director shall consult with the Office of Court Administration of the Texas Judicial System.

A (g-1b) Not later than 30 business days after receipt of relevant criminal history record information contained in an order or a copy of an order from the Department of Public Safety under Subsection (g-1), an individual or entity described by Subsection (g-1)(1) shall seal any criminal history record information maintained by the individual or entity that is the subject of the order.

E (g-1c) The department may charge to a private entity that purchases criminal history record information from the department a fee in an amount sufficient to recover costs incurred by the department in providing relevant criminal history record information contained in an order or a copy of an order under Subsection (g-1)(3) to the entity.

(g-2) A person whose criminal history record information has been sealed under this section is not required in any application for employment, information, or licensing to state that the person has been the subject of any criminal proceeding related to the information that is the subject of an order issued under this section.

(h) The clerk of a court that collects a fee under Subsection (d) shall remit the fee to the comptroller not later than the last day of the month following the end of the calendar quarter in which the fee is collected, and the comptroller shall deposit the fee in the general revenue fund. The Department of Public Safety shall submit a report to the legislature not later than December 1 of each even-numbered year that includes information on:

(1) the number of petitions for nondisclosure and orders of nondisclosure received by the department in each of the previous two years;

(2) the actions taken by the department with respect to the petitions and orders received;

(3) the costs incurred by the department in taking those actions; and

(4) the number of persons who are the subject of an order of nondisclosure and who became the subject of criminal charges for an offense committed after the order was issued.

(i) A criminal justice agency may disclose criminal history record information that is the subject of an order of nondisclosure to the following noncriminal justice agencies or entities only:

(1) the State Board for Educator Certification;

(2) a school district, charter school, private school, regional education service center, commercial transportation company, or education shared service arrangement;

A (3) the Texas Medical Board;

(4) the Texas School for the Blind and Visually Impaired;

(5) the Board of Law Examiners;

(6) the State Bar of Texas;

(7) a district court regarding a petition for name change under Subchapter B, Chapter 45, Family Code;

(8) the Texas School for the Deaf;

(9) the Department of Family and Protective Services;

(10) the Texas Youth Commission;

(11) the Department of Assistive and Rehabilitative Services;

(12) the Department of State Health Services, a local mental health service, a local mental retardation authority, or a community center providing services to persons with mental illness or retardation;

(13) the Texas Private Security Board;

(14) a municipal or volunteer fire department;

A (15) the Texas Board of Nursing;

(16) a safe house providing shelter to children in harmful situations;

(17) a public or nonprofit hospital or hospital district;

(18) the Texas Juvenile Probation Commission;

A (19) the securities commissioner, the banking commissioner, the savings and mortgage lending commissioner, or the credit union commissioner;

(20) the Texas State Board of Public Accountancy;

(21) the Texas Department of Licensing and Regulation;

(22) the Health and Human Services Commission;

(23) the Department of Aging and Disability Services; and

(E) **(24)** the Texas Education Agency.

(j) Repealed by Acts 2007, 80th Leg., ch. 1017, §11, eff. Sept. 1, 2007.

History of Govt §411.081: Acts 1993, 73rd Leg., ch. 790, §35, eff. Sept. 1, 1993. Amended by Acts 2003, 78th Leg., ch. 1236, §4, eff. Sept. 1, 2003; Acts 2005, 79th Leg., ch. 177, §3 (eff. Sept. 1, 2005), ch. 1309, §3 (eff. Sept. 1, 2005); Acts 2007, 80th Leg., ch. 889, §54 (eff. Sept. 1, 2007), ch. 921, §6.061 (eff. Sept. 1, 2007), ch. 1017, §§5, 6, 11 (eff. Sept. 1, 2007), ch. 1372, §16 (eff. June 15, 2007).

See also *O'Connor's Crimes & Consequences* (2008-09), chart 13-A, "Eligible for Nondisclosure," 13-B, "Not Eligible for Nondisclosure."

ANNOTATIONS

Huth v. State, 241 S.W.3d 206, 208 (Tex.App.—Amarillo 2007, pet. denied). "Because §411.081 does not expressly create a right of appeal and because nothing in the record shows an amount in controversy in the case exceeding $100, exclusive of interests and costs, we are without jurisdiction."

SUBCHAPTER G. DNA DATABASE SYSTEM

GOVT §411.141. DEFINITIONS

In this subchapter:

(1) "CODIS" means the FBI's Combined DNA Index System. The term includes the national DNA index system sponsored by the FBI.

(2) "Conviction" includes conviction by a jury or a court, a guilty plea, a plea of nolo contendere, or a finding of not guilty by reason of insanity.

(3) "Criminal justice agency" has the meaning assigned by Article 60.01, Code of Criminal Procedure.

(4) "DNA" means deoxyribonucleic acid.

(5) "DNA database" means one or more databases that contain forensic DNA records maintained by the director.

(6) "DNA laboratory" means a laboratory that performs forensic DNA analysis on samples or specimens derived from a human body, physical evidence, or a crime scene. The term includes a department crime laboratory facility that conducts forensic DNA analysis.

(7) "DNA record" means the results of a forensic DNA analysis performed by a DNA laboratory. The term includes a DNA profile and related records, which may include a code or other identifying number referenced to a separate database to locate:

(A) the originating entity; and

(B) if known, the name and other personally identifying information concerning the individual who is the subject of the analysis.

(8) "DNA sample" means a blood sample or other biological sample or specimen provided by an individual under this subchapter or submitted to the director under this subchapter for DNA analysis or storage.

(9) "FBI" means the Federal Bureau of Investigation.

(10) "Forensic analysis" has the meaning assigned by Article 38.35, Code of Criminal Procedure.

(11) "Institution of higher education" has the meaning assigned by Section 61.003, Education Code.

(12) "Penal institution" has the meaning assigned by Section 1.07, Penal Code.

History of Govt §411.141: Acts 1995, 74th Leg., ch. 595, §1, eff. Sept. 1, 1995. Amended by Acts 2005, 79th Leg., ch. 1224, §4, eff. Sept. 1, 2005.

GOVT §411.142. DNA DATABASE

(a) The director shall record DNA data and establish and maintain a computerized database that serves as the central depository in the state for DNA records.

(b) The director may maintain the DNA database in the department's crime laboratory in Austin or another suitable location.

(c) The director may receive, analyze, store, and destroy a record or DNA sample for the purposes described by Section 411.143.

(d) The DNA database must be capable of classifying, matching, and storing the results of analyses of DNA.

(e) The director, with advice from the Department of Information Resources, shall develop biennial plans to:

(1) improve the reporting and accuracy of the DNA database; and

(2) develop and maintain a monitoring system capable of identifying inaccurate or incomplete information.

(f) The DNA database must be compatible with the national DNA identification index system (CODIS) used by the FBI to the extent required by the FBI to permit the useful exchange and storage of DNA records or information derived from those records.

(g) The DNA database may contain DNA records for the following:

 (1) an individual described by this subchapter, including Section 411.1471, 411.148, or 411.154;

(2) a biological specimen of a deceased victim of a crime;

(3) a biological specimen that is legally obtained in the investigation of a crime, regardless of origin;

(4) results of testing ordered by a court under this subchapter, Article 64.03, Code of Criminal Procedure, or other law permitting or requiring the creation of a DNA record;

(5) an unidentified missing person, or unidentified skeletal remains or body parts;

(6) a close biological relative of a person who has been reported missing to a law enforcement agency;

(7) a person at risk of becoming lost, such as a child or a person declared by a court to be mentally incapacitated, if the record is required by court order or a parent, conservator, or guardian of the person consents to the record; or

(8) an unidentified person, if the record does not contain personal identifying information.

(h) The director shall establish standards for DNA analysis by the DNA laboratory that meet or exceed the current standards for quality assurance and proficiency testing for forensic DNA analysis issued by the FBI. The DNA database may contain only DNA records of DNA analyses performed according to the standards adopted by the director.

History of Govt §411.142: Acts 1995, 74th Leg., ch. 595, §1, eff. Sept. 1, 1995. Amended by Acts 2001, 77th Leg., ch. 2, §4, eff. May 5, 2001; Acts 2005, 79th Leg., ch. 1224, §5, eff. Sept. 1, 2005; Acts 2007, 80th Leg., ch. 760, §1, eff. June 15, 2007.

GOVT §411.143. PURPOSES

(a) The principal purpose of the DNA database is to assist a federal, state, or local criminal justice agency in the investigation or prosecution of sex-related offenses or other offenses in which biological evidence is recovered.

(b) In criminal cases, the purposes of the DNA database are only for use in the investigation of an offense, the exclusion or identification of suspects or offenders, and the prosecution or defense of the case.

(c) Other purposes of the database include:

(1) assisting in the recovery or identification of human remains from a disaster or for humanitarian purposes;

(2) assisting in the identification of living or deceased missing persons;

(3) if personal identifying information is removed:

(A) establishing a population statistics database; and

(B) assisting in identification research, forensic validation studies, or forensic protocol development; and

(4) retesting to validate or update the original analysis or assisting in database or DNA laboratory quality control.

(d) The information contained in the DNA database may not be collected, analyzed, or stored to obtain information about human physical traits or predisposition for disease unless the purpose for obtaining the information is related to a purpose described by this section.

(e) The director may not store a name or other personal identifying information in the CODIS database. A file or reference number to another information system may be included in the CODIS database only if the director determines the information is necessary to:

(1) generate an investigative lead or exclusion;

(2) support the statistical interpretation of a test result; or

(3) allow for the successful implementation of the DNA database.

(f) Except as provided by this subchapter, the DNA database may not include criminal history record information.

(g) A party contracting to carry out a function of another entity under this subchapter shall comply with:

(1) a requirement imposed by this subchapter on the other entity, unless the party or other entity is exempted by the director; and

(2) any additional requirement imposed by the director on the party.

History of Govt §411.143: Acts 1995, 74th Leg., ch. 595, §1, eff. Sept. 1, 1995. Amended by Acts 2005, 79th Leg., ch. 1224, §6, eff. Sept. 1, 2005.

GOVT §411.144. REGULATION OF DNA LABORATORIES; PENALTIES

(a) The director by rule shall establish procedures for a DNA laboratory or criminal justice agency in the collection, preservation, shipment, analysis, and use of a DNA sample for forensic DNA analysis in a manner that permits the exchange of DNA evidence between DNA laboratories and the use of the evidence in a criminal case.

(b) A DNA laboratory or criminal justice agency shall follow the procedures:

(1) established by the director under this section; and

(2) specified by the FBI, including use of comparable test procedures, laboratory equipment, supplies, and computer software.

(c) The director may at any reasonable time enter and inspect the premises or audit the records, reports, procedures, or other quality assurance matters of any DNA laboratory that:

(1) provides DNA records to the director under this subchapter; or

(2) conducts forensic analysis.

(d) A DNA laboratory conducting a forensic DNA analysis under this subchapter shall:

(1) forward the DNA record of the analysis to the director at the department's crime laboratory or another location as required by the director; and

(2) comply with this subchapter and rules adopted under this subchapter.

(e) The director is the Texas liaison for DNA data, records, evidence, and other related matters between:

(1) the FBI; and

(2) a DNA laboratory or a criminal justice agency.

(f) The director may:

(1) conduct DNA analyses; or

(2) contract with a laboratory, state agency, private entity, or institution of higher education for services to perform DNA analyses for the director.

History of Govt §411.144: Acts 1995, 74th Leg., ch. 595, §1, eff. Sept. 1, 1995. Amended by Acts 2005, 79th Leg., ch. 1224, §7, eff. Sept. 1, 2005.

GOVT §411.145. FEES

(a) The director may collect a reasonable fee under this subchapter for:

(1) the DNA analysis of a DNA sample submitted voluntarily to the director; or

(2) providing population statistics data or other appropriate research data.

(b) If the director provides a copy of an audit or other report made under this subchapter, the director may charge $6 for the copy, in addition to any other cost permitted under Chapter 552 or a rule adopted under that chapter.

(c) A fee collected under this section shall be deposited in the state treasury to the credit of the state highway fund, and money deposited to the state highway fund under this section and under Articles 42.12 and 102.020(h), Code of Criminal Procedure, may be used only to defray the cost of administering this subchapter and Section 411.0205.

History of Govt §411.145: Acts 1995, 74th Leg., ch. 595, §1, eff. Sept. 1, 1995. Amended by Acts 2001, 77th Leg., ch. 1490, §1, eff. Sept. 1, 2001; Acts 2005, 79th Leg., ch. 1224, §8, eff. Sept. 1, 2005.

GOVT §411.146. DNA SAMPLES

(a) The director may not accept a DNA record or DNA sample collected from an individual who at the time of collection is alive, unless the director reasonably believes the sample was submitted voluntarily or as required by this subchapter and is:

(1) a blood sample collected in a medically approved manner by:

(A) a physician, registered nurse, licensed vocational nurse, licensed clinical laboratory technologist; or

(B) an individual who is trained to properly collect blood samples under this subchapter; or

(2) a specimen other than a blood sample collected:

(A) in a manner approved by the director by rule adopted under this section; and

(B) by an individual who is trained to properly collect the specimen under this subchapter.

(b) The director shall provide at no cost to a person collecting a DNA sample as described by Subsection (a) the collection kits, labels, report forms, instructions, and training for collection of DNA samples under this section.

(c)(1) The director shall adopt rules regarding the collection, preservation, shipment, and analysis of a DNA database sample under this subchapter, including the type of sample or specimen taken.

(2) A criminal justice agency permitted or required to collect a DNA sample for forensic DNA analysis under this subchapter:

(A) may collect the sample or contract with a phlebotomist, laboratory, state agency, private entity, or institution of higher education for services to collect the sample at the time determined by the agency; and

(B) shall:

(i) preserve each sample collected until it is forwarded to the director under Subsection (d); and

(ii) maintain a record of the collection of the sample.

(d) A criminal justice agency that collects a DNA sample under this section shall send the sample to:

(1) the director at the department's crime laboratory; or

(2) another location as required by the director by rule.

(e) A DNA laboratory may analyze a DNA sample collected under this section only:

(1) to type the genetic markers contained in the sample;

(2) for criminal justice or law enforcement purposes; or

(3) for other purposes described by this subchapter.

(f) If possible, a second DNA sample must be collected from an individual in a criminal investigation if forensic DNA evidence is necessary for use as substantive evidence in the investigation, prosecution, or defense of a case.

History of Govt §411.146: Acts 1995, 74th Leg., ch. 595, §1, eff. Sept. 1, 1995. Amended by Acts 2005, 79th Leg., ch. 1224, §9, eff. Sept. 1, 2005.

GOVT §411.147. ACCESS TO DNA DATABASE INFORMATION

(a) The director by rule shall establish procedures:

(1) to prevent unauthorized access to the DNA database; and

(2) to release from the DNA database a DNA sample, analysis, record, or other information maintained under this subchapter.

(b) The director may adopt rules relating to the internal disclosure, access, or use of a sample or DNA record in a DNA laboratory.

(c) The director may release a DNA sample, analysis, or record only:

(1) to a criminal justice agency for criminal justice or law enforcement identification purposes;

(2) for a judicial proceeding, if otherwise admissible under law;

(3) for criminal defense purposes to a defendant, if related to the case in which the defendant is charged or

released from custody under Article 17.47, Code of Criminal Procedure, or other court order; or

(4) for another purpose:

(A) described in Section 411.143; or

(B) required under federal law as a condition for obtaining federal funding.

(d) The director may release a record of the number of requests made for a defendant's individual DNA record and the name of the requesting person.

(e) A criminal justice agency may have access to a DNA sample for a law enforcement purpose through:

(1) the agency's laboratory; or

(2) a laboratory used by the agency.

(f) The director shall maintain a record of requests made under this section.

History of Govt §411.147: Acts 1995, 74th Leg., ch. 595, §1, eff. Sept. 1, 1995. Amended by Acts 2005, 79th Leg., ch. 1224, §10, eff. Sept. 1, 2005.

GOVT §411.1471. DNA RECORDS OF PERSONS CHARGED WITH OR CONVICTED OF CERTAIN FELONIES

(a) This section applies to a defendant who is:

(1) indicted or waives indictment for a felony prohibited or punishable under any of the following Penal Code sections:

(A) Section 20.04(a)(4);

(B) Section 21.11;

(C) Section 22.011;

(D) Section 22.021;

(E) Section 25.02;

(F) Section 30.02(d);

(G) Section 43.05;

(H) Section 43.25;

(I) Section 43.26; or

ⓔ *Subsection (J) below is effective for offenses committed on or after Sept. 1, 2007.*

(J) Section 21.02;

(2) arrested for a felony described by Subdivision (1) after having been previously convicted of or placed on deferred adjudication for an offense described by Subdivision (1) or an offense punishable under Section 30.02(c)(2), Penal Code; or

(3) convicted of an offense under Section 21.07 or 21.08, Penal Code.

(b) After a defendant described by Subsection (a)(1) is indicted or waives indictment, the court in

★

which the case is pending shall require the defendant to provide to a law enforcement agency one or more specimens for the purpose of creating a DNA record. A law enforcement agency arresting a defendant described by Subsection (a)(2), immediately after fingerprinting the defendant and at the same location as the fingerprinting occurs, shall require the defendant to provide one or more specimens for the purpose of creating a DNA record. After a defendant described by Subsection (a)(3) is convicted or placed on deferred adjudication, the court shall require the defendant to provide to a law enforcement agency one or more specimens for the purpose of creating a DNA record.

(c) A defendant described by Subsection (a)(1) or (3) may at any time voluntarily provide a specimen for the purposes described by Subsection (b).

(d) The director by rule shall require law enforcement agencies taking a specimen under this section to preserve the specimen and maintain a record of the collection of the specimen. A law enforcement agency taking a specimen under this section may use any method to take the specimen approved by the director in the rule adopted under this subsection. The rule adopted by the director must prohibit a law enforcement agency from taking a blood sample for the purpose of creating a DNA record under this section. The agency may either send the specimen to the director or send to the director an analysis of the sample performed at a laboratory chosen by the agency and approved by the director.

(e) Notwithstanding Subsection (d), on acquittal of a defendant described by Subsection (a)(1) or (2) or dismissal of the case against the defendant, the court shall order the law enforcement agency taking the specimen to immediately destroy the record of the collection of the specimen and require the department to destroy the specimen and the record of its receipt.

(A) **(f)** A defendant who provides a DNA sample under this section is not required to provide a DNA sample under Section 411.148 unless an attorney representing the state in the prosecution of felony offenses establishes to the satisfaction of the director that the interests of justice or public safety require that the defendant provide additional samples.

History of Govt §411.1471: Acts 2001, 77th Leg., ch. 1490, §2, eff. Sept. 1, 2001. Amended by Acts 2007, 80th Leg., ch. 593, §3.34 (eff. Sept. 1, 2007), ch. 760, §2 (eff. June 15, 2007).

See also *O'Connor's Crimes & Consequences* (2008-09), chart 2-K, "DNA Records of Persons Charged or Convicted of Certain Felony Offenses."

GOVT §411.1472. REPEALED

Repealed by Acts 2005, 79th Leg., ch. 1224, §19(1), eff. Sept. 1, 2005.

GOVT §411.1473. DNA RECORDS OF CERTAIN REGISTERED SEX OFFENDERS

(a) This section applies only to a person who is required to register under Chapter 62, Code of Criminal Procedure.

(b) The department by rule shall require a law enforcement agency serving as a person's primary registration authority under Chapter 62, Code of Criminal Procedure, to:

(1) take one or more specimens from a person described by Subsection (a) for the purpose of creating a DNA record; and

(2) preserve the specimen and maintain a record of the collection of the specimen.

(c) A law enforcement agency taking a specimen under this section may either send the specimen to the director or send to the director an analysis of the specimen performed by a laboratory chosen by the agency and approved by the director.

(d) A law enforcement agency is not required to take and a person is not required to provide a specimen under this section if the person is required to and has provided a specimen under this chapter or other law.

History of Govt §411.1473: Acts 2005, 79th Leg., ch. 1008, §1.05, eff. Sept. 1, 2005.

History of Govt §411.148: Acts 1995, 74th Leg., ch. 595, §1, eff. Sept. 1, 1995. Amended by Acts 1999, 76th Leg., ch. 1063, §1 (eff. Sept. 1, 1999); ch. 1368, §1 (eff. Sept. 1, 1999); Acts 2001, 77th Leg., ch. 211, §14 (eff. Sept. 1, 2001), ch. 1509, §§1, 2 (eff. pending federal funding); Acts 2005, 79th Leg., ch. 1224, §11 (eff. Sept. 1, 2005), ch. 1245, §1 (eff. Sept. 1, 2005).

GOVT §411.148. MANDATORY DNA RECORD

(a) This section applies to:

(1) an individual who is:

(A) ordered by a magistrate or court to provide a sample under Section 411.154 or other law; or

(B) confined in a penal institution operated by or under contract with the Texas Department of Criminal Justice; or

(2) a juvenile who is, after an adjudication for conduct constituting a felony, confined in a facility operated by or under contract with the Texas Youth Commission.

(b) An individual described by Subsection (a) shall provide one or more DNA samples for the purpose of creating a DNA record.

(c) A criminal justice agency shall collect a sample ordered by a magistrate or court in compliance with the order.

(d) If an individual described by Subsection (a)(1)(B) is received into custody by the Texas Department of Criminal Justice, that department shall collect the sample from the individual during the diagnostic process or at another time determined by the Texas Department of Criminal Justice.

(e) If an individual described by Subsection (a)(2) is received into custody by the Texas Youth Commission, the youth commission shall collect the sample from the individual during the initial examination or at another time determined by the youth commission.

Ⓐ (f) The Texas Department of Criminal Justice shall notify the director that an individual described by Subsection (a)(1)(B) is to be released from custody not earlier than the 120th day before the individual's statutory release date and not later than the 90th day before the individual's statutory release date. An individual described by Subsection (a)(1)(B) may not be held past the individual's statutory release date if the individual fails or refuses to provide a DNA sample under this section. The Texas Department of Criminal Justice may take lawful administrative action, including disciplinary action resulting in the loss of good conduct time, against an individual described by Subsection (a)(1)(B) who refuses to provide a sample under this section. In this subsection, "statutory release date" means the date on which an individual is discharged from the individual's controlling sentence.

Ⓐ (f-1) The Texas Youth Commission shall notify the director that an individual described by Subsection (a)(2) is to be released from custody not earlier than the 120th day before the individual's release date.

Ⓐ (f-2) The Texas Department of Criminal Justice and the Texas Youth Commission, in consultation with the director, shall determine the form of the notification described by Subsections (f) and (f-1).

(g) A medical staff employee of a criminal justice agency may collect a voluntary sample from an individual at any time.

(h) An employee of a criminal justice agency may use force against an individual required to provide a DNA sample under this section when and to the degree the employee reasonably believes the force is immediately necessary to collect the sample.

(i)(1) The Texas Department of Criminal Justice as soon as practicable shall cause a sample to be collected from an individual described by Subsection (a)(1)(B) if:

(A) the individual is confined in another penal institution after sentencing and before admission to the department; and

(B) the department determines that the individual is likely to be released before being admitted to the department.

(2) The administrator of the other penal institution shall cooperate with the Texas Department of Criminal Justice as necessary to allow the Texas Department of Criminal Justice to perform its duties under this subsection.

(j)(1) The Texas Youth Commission as soon as practicable shall cause a sample to be collected from an individual described by Subsection (a)(2) if:

(A) the individual is detained in another juvenile detention facility after adjudication and before admission to the youth commission; and

(B) the youth commission determines the individual is likely to be released before being admitted to the youth commission.

(2) The administrator of the other juvenile detention facility shall cooperate with the Texas Youth Commission as necessary to allow the youth commission to perform its duties under this subsection.

(k) When a criminal justice agency of this state agrees to accept custody of an individual from another state or jurisdiction under an interstate compact or a reciprocal agreement with a local, county, state, or federal agency, the acceptance is conditional on the individual providing a DNA sample under this subchapter if the individual was convicted of a felony.

(*l*) If, in consultation with the director, it is determined that an acceptable sample has already been received from an individual, additional samples are not required unless requested by the director.

History of Govt §411.148: Acts 1995, 74th Leg., ch. 595, §1, eff. Sept. 1, 1995. Amended by Acts 1999, 76th Leg., ch. 1063, §1 (eff. Sept. 1, 1999), ch. 1368, §1 (eff. Sept. 1, 1999); Acts 2001, 77th Leg., ch. 211, §14 (eff. Sept. 1, 2001), ch. 1509, §§1, 2 (eff. pending federal funding); Acts 2005, 79th Leg., ch. 1224, §11 (eff. Sept. 1, 2005), ch. 1245, §1 (eff. Sept. 1, 2005); Acts 2007, 80th Leg., ch. 760, §3, eff. June 15, 2007.

GOVT §411.1481. REPEALED

Repealed by Acts 2005, 79th Leg., ch. 1224, §19(1), eff. Sept. 1, 2005.

GOVT §411.149. VOLUNTARY DNA RECORD

An individual, including an individual required to provide a DNA sample under this subchapter, may at any time voluntarily provide or cause to be provided to a criminal justice agency a sample to be forwarded to the director for the purpose of creating a DNA record under this subchapter.

History of Govt §411.149: Acts 1995, 74th Leg., ch. 595, §1, eff. Sept. 1, 1995. Amended by Acts 2005, 79th Leg., ch. 1224, §12, eff. Sept. 1, 2005.

GOVT §411.150. REPEALED

Repealed by Acts 2007, 80th Leg., ch. 760, §5, eff. June 15, 2007.

GOVT §411.151. EXPUNCTION OR REMOVAL OF DNA RECORDS

(a) The director shall expunge a DNA record of an individual from a DNA database if the person:

(1) notifies the director in writing that the DNA record has been ordered to be expunged under this section or Chapter 55, Code of Criminal Procedure, and provides the director with a certified copy of the court order that expunges the DNA record; or

(2) provides the director with a certified copy of a court order issued under Section 58.003, Family Code, that seals the juvenile record of the adjudication that resulted in the DNA record.

(b) A person may petition for the expunction of a DNA record under the procedures established under Article 55.02, Code of Criminal Procedure, if the person is entitled to the expunction of records relating to the offense to which the DNA record is related under Article 55.01, Code of Criminal Procedure.

(c) This section does not require the director to expunge a record or destroy a sample if the director determines that the individual is otherwise required to submit a DNA sample under this subchapter.

(d) The director by rule may permit administrative removal of a record, sample, or other information erroneously included in a database.

History of Govt §411.151: Acts 1995, 74th Leg., ch. 595, §1, eff. Sept. 1, 1995. Amended by Acts 2003, 78th Leg., ch. 283, §44, eff. Sept. 1, 2003; Acts 2005, 79th Leg., ch. 1224, §13, eff. Sept. 1, 2005.

GOVT §411.152. RULES

(a) The director may adopt rules permitted by this subchapter that are necessary to administer or enforce this subchapter but shall adopt a rule expressly required by this subchapter.

(b) The director by rule may release or permit access to information to confirm or deny whether an individual has a preexisting record under this subchapter. After receiving a request regarding an individual whose DNA record has been expunged or removed under Section 411.151, the director shall deny the preexisting record.

(c) The director by rule may exempt:

(1) a laboratory conducting non-human forensic DNA analysis from a rule adopted under this subchapter; and

(2) certain categories of individuals from a requirement to provide an additional sample after an acceptable DNA record exists for the individual.

(d) The director by rule may determine whether a DNA sample complies with a collection provision of this subchapter.

History of Govt §411.152: Acts 1995, 74th Leg., ch. 595, §1, eff. Sept. 1, 1995. Amended by Acts 2005, 79th Leg., ch. 1224, §14, eff. Sept. 1, 2005.

GOVT §411.153. CONFIDENTIALITY OF DNA RECORDS

(a) A DNA record stored in the DNA database is confidential and is not subject to disclosure under the public information law, Chapter 552.

🅐 (b) A person commits an offense if the person knowingly discloses to an unauthorized recipient information in a DNA record or information related to a DNA analysis of a sample collected under this subchapter.

(c) An offense under this section is a state jail felony.

(d) A violation under this section constitutes official misconduct.

History of Govt §411.153: Acts 1995, 74th Leg., ch. 595, §1, eff. Sept. 1, 1995. Amended by Acts 2001, 77th Leg., ch. 1490, §3 (eff. Sept. 1, 2001), ch. 1509, §3 (eff. pending federal funding); Acts 2005, 79th Leg., ch. 1224, §15, eff. Sept. 1, 2005; Acts 2007, 80th Leg., ch. 760, §4, eff. June 15, 2007.

GOVT §§411.1531, 411.1532. REPEALED

Repealed by Acts 2005, 79th Leg., ch. 1224, §19(1), eff. Sept. 1, 2005.

GOVT §411.154. ENFORCEMENT BY COURT ORDER

(a) On the request of the director, a district or county attorney or the attorney general may petition a district court for an order requiring a person to:

(1) comply with this subchapter or a rule adopted under this subchapter; or

(2) refrain from acting in violation of this subchapter or a rule adopted under this subchapter.

(b) The court may issue an order requiring a person:

(1) to act in compliance with this subchapter or a rule adopted under this subchapter;

(2) to refrain from acting in violation of this subchapter or a rule adopted under this subchapter;

(3) to provide a DNA sample; or

(4) if the person has already provided a DNA sample, to provide another sample if good cause is shown.

(c) An order issued under this section is appealable as a criminal matter and if appealed is to be reviewed under an abuse of discretion standard.

History of Govt §411.154: Acts 1995, 74th Leg., ch. 595, §1, eff. Sept. 1, 1995. Amended by Acts 2005, 79th Leg., ch. 1224, §16, eff. Sept. 1, 2005.

SUBCHAPTER H. LICENSE TO CARRY A CONCEALED HANDGUN

GOVT §411.171. DEFINITIONS

In this subchapter:

(1) "Action" means single action, revolver, or semi-automatic action.

(2) "Chemically dependent person" means a person who frequently or repeatedly becomes intoxicated by excessive indulgence in alcohol or uses controlled substances or dangerous drugs so as to acquire a fixed habit and an involuntary tendency to become intoxicated or use those substances as often as the opportunity is presented.

(3) "Concealed handgun" means a handgun, the presence of which is not openly discernible to the ordinary observation of a reasonable person.

(4) "Convicted" means an adjudication of guilt or, except as provided in Section 411.1711, an order of deferred adjudication entered against a person by a court of competent jurisdiction whether or not the imposition of the sentence is subsequently probated and the person is discharged from community supervision. The term does not include an adjudication of guilt or an order of deferred adjudication that has been subsequently:

(A) expunged; or

(B) pardoned under the authority of a state or federal official.

 Subsections (4-a) & (4-b) below are effective for causes of action accruing or offenses committed on or after Sept. 1, 2007.

(4-a) "Federal judge" means:

(A) a judge of a United States court of appeals;

(B) a judge of a United States district court;

(C) a judge of a United States bankruptcy court; or

(D) a magistrate judge of a United States district court.

(4-b) "State judge" means:

(A) the judge of an appellate court, a district court, or a county court at law of this state; or

(B) an associate judge appointed under Chapter 201, Family Code.

(5) "Handgun" has the meaning assigned by Section 46.01, Penal Code.

(6) "Intoxicated" has the meaning assigned by Section 49.01, Penal Code.

(7) "Qualified handgun instructor" means a person who is certified to instruct in the use of handguns by the department.

(8) Repealed by Acts 1999, 76th Leg., ch. 62, §9.02(a), eff. Sept. 1, 1999.

History of Govt §411.171: Codified by Acts 1997, 75th Leg., ch. 165, §10.01(a), eff. Sept. 1, 1997. Amended by Acts 1999, 76th Leg., ch. 62, §§9.01(a), 9.02(a), eff. Sept. 1, 1999; Acts 2005, 79th Leg., ch. 1084, §1, eff. Sept. 1, 2005; Acts 2007, 80th Leg., ch. 594, §8, eff. Sept. 1, 2007. Source: TRCS art. 4413(29ee), §1.

ANNOTATIONS

Tune v. Texas DPS, 23 S.W.3d 358, 360 (Tex.2000). "[W]e must consider the meaning of the term 'convicted' as it is used in the Concealed Handgun Act.... We conclude that petitioner, who entered a felony guilty plea and completed a probation period, and as a result had his conviction set aside and the indictment dismissed, remains 'convicted' for purposes of the Handgun Act." *See also **Texas DPS v. Loeb**,* 149 S.W.3d 741, 744 (Tex.App.—Austin 2004, no pet.) ("convicted" includes set-aside conviction under Federal Youth Corrections Act).

GOVT §411.1711. CERTAIN EXEMPTIONS FROM CONVICTIONS

A person is not convicted, as that term is defined by Section 411.171, if an order of deferred adjudication was entered against the person on a date not less than

GOVT §411.154

10 years preceding the date of the person's application for a license under this subchapter unless the order of deferred adjudication was entered against the person for an offense under Title 5, Penal Code, or Chapter 29, Penal Code.

History of Govt §411.1711: Acts 2005, 79th Leg., ch. 1084, §2, eff. Sept. 1, 2005.

GOVT §411.172. ELIGIBILITY

(a) A person is eligible for a license to carry a concealed handgun if the person:

(1) is a legal resident of this state for the six-month period preceding the date of application under this subchapter or is otherwise eligible for a license under Section 411.173(a);

(2) is at least 21 years of age;

(3) has not been convicted of a felony;

(4) is not charged with the commission of a Class A or Class B misdemeanor or an offense under Section 42.01, Penal Code, or of a felony under an information or indictment;

(5) is not a fugitive from justice for a felony or a Class A or Class B misdemeanor;

(6) is not a chemically dependent person;

(7) is not incapable of exercising sound judgment with respect to the proper use and storage of a handgun;

(8) has not, in the five years preceding the date of application, been convicted of a Class A or Class B misdemeanor or an offense under Section 42.01, Penal Code;

(9) is fully qualified under applicable federal and state law to purchase a handgun;

(10) has not been finally determined to be delinquent in making a child support payment administered or collected by the attorney general;

(11) has not been finally determined to be delinquent in the payment of a tax or other money collected by the comptroller, the tax collector of a political subdivision of the state, or any agency or subdivision of the state;

(12) has not been finally determined to be in default on a loan made under Chapter 57, Education Code;

(13) is not currently restricted under a court protective order or subject to a restraining order affecting the spousal relationship, other than a restraining order solely affecting property interests;

(14) has not, in the 10 years preceding the date of application, been adjudicated as having engaged in delinquent conduct violating a penal law of the grade of felony; and

(15) has not made any material misrepresentation, or failed to disclose any material fact, in an application submitted pursuant to Section 411.174 or in a request for application submitted pursuant to Section 411.175.

(b) For the purposes of this section, an offense under the laws of this state, another state, or the United States is:

(1) a felony if the offense, at the time of a person's application for a license to carry a concealed handgun:

(A) is designated by a law of this state as a felony;

(B) contains all the elements of an offense designated by a law of this state as a felony; or

(C) is punishable by confinement for one year or more in a penitentiary; and

(2) a Class A misdemeanor if the offense is not a felony and confinement in a jail other than a state jail felony facility is affixed as a possible punishment.

(c) An individual who has been convicted two times within the 10-year period preceding the date on which the person applies for a license of an offense of the grade of Class B misdemeanor or greater that involves the use of alcohol or a controlled substance as a statutory element of the offense is a chemically dependent person for purposes of this section and is not qualified to receive a license under this subchapter. This subsection does not preclude the disqualification of an individual for being a chemically dependent person if other evidence exists to show that the person is a chemically dependent person.

(d) For purposes of Subsection (a)(7), a person is incapable of exercising sound judgment with respect to the proper use and storage of a handgun if the person:

(1) has been diagnosed by a licensed physician as suffering from a psychiatric disorder or condition that causes or is likely to cause substantial impairment in judgment, mood, perception, impulse control, or intellectual ability;

(2) suffers from a psychiatric disorder or condition described by Subdivision (1) that:

(A) is in remission but is reasonably likely to redevelop at a future time; or

GOVT §411.172

(B) requires continuous medical treatment to avoid redevelopment;

(3) has been diagnosed by a licensed physician or declared by a court to be incompetent to manage the person's own affairs; or

(4) has entered in a criminal proceeding a plea of not guilty by reason of insanity.

(e) The following constitutes evidence that a person has a psychiatric disorder or condition described by Subsection (d)(1):

(1) involuntary psychiatric hospitalization in the preceding five-year period;

(2) psychiatric hospitalization in the preceding two-year period;

(3) inpatient or residential substance abuse treatment in the preceding five-year period;

(4) diagnosis in the preceding five-year period by a licensed physician that the person is dependent on alcohol, a controlled substance, or a similar substance; or

(5) diagnosis at any time by a licensed physician that the person suffers or has suffered from a psychiatric disorder or condition consisting of or relating to:

(A) schizophrenia or delusional disorder;

(B) bipolar disorder;

(C) chronic dementia, whether caused by illness, brain defect, or brain injury;

(D) dissociative identity disorder;

(E) intermittent explosive disorder; or

(F) antisocial personality disorder.

(f) Notwithstanding Subsection (d), a person who has previously been diagnosed as suffering from a psychiatric disorder or condition described by Subsection (d) or listed in Subsection (e) is not because of that disorder or condition incapable of exercising sound judgment with respect to the proper use and storage of a handgun if the person provides the department with a certificate from a licensed physician whose primary practice is in the field of psychiatry stating that the psychiatric disorder or condition is in remission and is not reasonably likely to develop at a future time.

(g) Notwithstanding Subsection (a)(2), a person who is at least 18 years of age but not yet 21 years of age is eligible for a license to carry a concealed handgun if the person:

(1) is a member or veteran of the United States armed forces, including a member or veteran of the reserves or national guard;

(2) was discharged under honorable conditions, if discharged from the United States armed forces, reserves, or national guard; and

(3) meets the other eligibility requirements of Subsection (a) except for the minimum age required by federal law to purchase a handgun.

(h) The issuance of a license to carry a concealed handgun to a person eligible under Subsection (g) does not affect the person's ability to purchase a handgun or ammunition under federal law.

History of Govt §411.172: Codified by Acts 1997, 75th Leg., ch. 165, §10.01(a), eff. Sept. 1, 1997. Amended by Acts 1999, 76th Leg., ch. 62, §§9.03(a), 9.04(a), eff. Sept. 1, 1999; Acts 2003, 78th Leg., ch. 255, §1, eff. Sept. 1, 2003; Acts 2005, 79th Leg., ch. 486, §1, eff. Sept. 1, 2005. Source: TRCS art. 4413(29ee), §2.

ANNOTATIONS

Satterfield v. Texas DPS, 221 S.W.3d 909, 913-14 (Tex.App.—Beaumont 2007, no pet.). "When §411.172(b) speaks of 'offense,' the term encompasses the offense elements and the conduct for which the person was charged and convicted. The question here is whether the offense, [an aggravated assault punished as a misdemeanor] in 1962, would have constituted a felony at the time Satterfield applied for the license. ... Without information on the applicable aggravating factor for the 1962 misdemeanor conviction, it is not possible to determine whether, at the time of Satterfield's 2005 renewal application, the offense under which he was charged and convicted would be 'designated by the law of this state as a felony.'" Held: The court remanded for a new evidentiary hearing.

GOVT §411.173. NONRESIDENT LICENSE

(a) The department by rule shall establish a procedure for a person who meets the eligibility requirements of this subchapter other than the residency requirement established by Section 411.172(a)(1) to obtain a license under this subchapter if the person is a legal resident of another state or if the person relocates to this state with the intent to establish residency in this state. The procedure must include payment of a fee in an amount sufficient to recover the average cost to the department of obtaining a criminal history record check and investigation on a nonresident applicant. A license issued in accordance with the procedure established under this subsection:

(1) remains in effect until the license expires under Section 411.183; and

(2) may be renewed under Section 411.185.

(a-1) Repealed by Acts 2005, 79th Leg., ch. 915, §4, eff. Sept. 1, 2005.

(b) The governor shall negotiate an agreement with any other state that provides for the issuance of a license to carry a concealed handgun under which a license issued by the other state is recognized in this state or shall issue a proclamation that a license issued by the other state is recognized in this state if the attorney general of the State of Texas determines that a background check of each applicant for a license issued by that state is initiated by state or local authorities or an agent of the state or local authorities before the license is issued. For purposes of this subsection, "background check" means a search of the National Crime Information Center database and the Interstate Identification Index maintained by the Federal Bureau of Investigation.

(c) The attorney general of the State of Texas shall annually:

(1) submit a report to the governor, lieutenant governor, and speaker of the house of representatives listing the states the attorney general has determined qualify for recognition under Subsection (b); and

(2) review the statutes of states that the attorney general has determined do not qualify for recognition under Subsection (b) to determine the changes to their statutes that are necessary to qualify for recognition under that subsection.

(d) The attorney general of the State of Texas shall submit the report required by Subsection (c)(1) not later than January 1 of each calendar year.

History of Govt §411.173: Codified by Acts 1997, 75th Leg., ch. 165, §10.01(a), eff. Sept. 1, 1997. Amended by Acts 1999, 76th Leg., ch. 62, §9.05(a), eff. Sept. 1, 1999; Acts 2003, 78th Leg., ch. 255, §2, eff. Sept. 1, 2003; Acts 2003, 78th Leg., ch. 752, §1, eff. Sept. 1, 2003; Acts 2005, 79th Leg., ch. 915, §§1, 2, 4, eff. Sept. 1, 2005. Source: TRCS art. 4413(29ee), §35.

GOVT §411.174. APPLICATION

(a) An applicant for a license to carry a concealed handgun must submit to the director's designee described by Section 411.176:

(1) a completed application on a form provided by the department that requires only the information listed in Subsection (b);

(2) two recent color passport photographs of the applicant, except that an applicant who is younger than 21 years of age must submit two recent color passport photographs in profile of the applicant;

(3) a certified copy of the applicant's birth certificate or certified proof of age;

(4) proof of residency in this state;

(5) two complete sets of legible and classifiable fingerprints of the applicant taken by a person appropriately trained in recording fingerprints who is employed by a law enforcement agency or by a private entity designated by a law enforcement agency as an entity qualified to take fingerprints of an applicant for a license under this subchapter;

(6) a nonrefundable application and license fee of $140 paid to the department;

(7) a handgun proficiency certificate described by Section 411.189;

(8) an affidavit signed by the applicant stating that the applicant:

(A) has read and understands each provision of this subchapter that creates an offense under the laws of this state and each provision of the laws of this state related to use of deadly force; and

(B) fulfills all the eligibility requirements listed under Section 411.172; and

(9) a form executed by the applicant that authorizes the director to make an inquiry into any noncriminal history records that are necessary to determine the applicant's eligibility for a license under Section 411.172(a).

(b) An applicant must provide on the application a statement of the applicant's:

(1) full name and place and date of birth;

(2) race and sex;

(3) residence and business addresses for the preceding five years;

(4) hair and eye color;

(5) height and weight;

(6) driver's license number or identification certificate number issued by the department;

(7) criminal history record information of the type maintained by the department under this chapter, including a list of offenses for which the applicant was arrested, charged, or under an information or indictment and the disposition of the offenses; and

(8) history during the preceding five years, if any, of treatment received by, commitment to, or residence in:

GOVT §411.174

(A) a drug or alcohol treatment center licensed to provide drug or alcohol treatment under the laws of this state or another state; or

(B) a psychiatric hospital.

(c) The department shall distribute on request a copy of this subchapter and application materials.

History of Govt §411.174: Codified by Acts 1997, 75th Leg., ch. 165, §10.01(a), eff. Sept. 1, 1997. Amended by Acts 1999, 76th Leg., ch. 62, §9.06(a), eff. Sept. 1, 1999; Acts 2005, 79th Leg., ch. 486, §2, eff. Sept. 1, 2005. Source: TRCS art. 4413(29ee), §3.

GOVT §411.175. REQUEST FOR APPLICATION MATERIALS

(a) A person applying for a license to carry a concealed handgun must apply by obtaining a request for application materials from a handgun dealer, the department, or any other person or entity approved by the department. The request for application materials must include the applicant's full name, address, race, sex, height, date of birth, and driver's license number and such other identifying information as required by department rule. The department shall prescribe the form of the request and make the form available to interested parties. An individual who desires to receive application materials must complete the request for application materials and forward it to the department at its Austin address. The department shall review all requests for application materials and make a preliminary determination as to whether or not the individual is qualified to receive a handgun license. If an individual is not disqualified to receive a handgun license, the department shall forward to the individual the appropriate application materials. The applicant must complete the application materials and forward the completed materials to the department at its Austin address.

(b) If a preliminary review indicates that an individual will not be qualified to receive a handgun license, the department shall send written notification to that individual. The notice shall provide the reason that the preliminary review indicates that the individual is not entitled to receive a handgun license. The department shall give the individual an opportunity to correct whatever defect may exist.

History of Govt §411.175: Codified by Acts 1997, 75th Leg., ch. 165, §10.01(a), eff. Sept. 1, 1997. Source: TRCS art. 4413(29ee), §4.

GOVT §411.176. REVIEW OF APPLICATION MATERIALS

(a) On receipt of the application materials by the department at its Austin headquarters, the department shall conduct the appropriate criminal history record check of the applicant through its computerized criminal history system. Not later than the 30th day after the date the department receives the application materials, the department shall forward the materials to the director's designee in the geographical area of the applicant's residence so that the designee may conduct the investigation described by Subsection (b).

(b) The director's designee as needed shall conduct an additional criminal history record check of the applicant and an investigation of the applicant's local official records to verify the accuracy of the application materials. The scope of the record check and the investigation are at the sole discretion of the department, except that the director's designee shall complete the record check and investigation not later than the 60th day after the date the department receives the application materials. The department shall send a fingerprint card to the Federal Bureau of Investigation for a national criminal history check of the applicant. On completion of the investigation, the director's designee shall return all materials and the result of the investigation to the appropriate division of the department at its Austin headquarters. The director's designee may submit to the appropriate division of the department, at the department's Austin headquarters, along with the application materials a written recommendation for disapproval of the application, accompanied by an affidavit stating personal knowledge or naming persons with personal knowledge of a ground for denial under Section 411.172. The director's designee in the appropriate geographical area may also submit the application and the recommendation that the license be issued. On receipt at the department's Austin headquarters of the application materials and the result of the investigation by the director's designee, the department shall conduct any further record check or investigation the department determines is necessary if a question exists with respect to the accuracy of the application materials or the eligibility of the applicant, except that the department shall complete the record check and investigation not later than the 180th day after the date the department receives the application materials from the applicant.

History of Govt §411.176: Codified by Acts 1997, 75th Leg., ch. 165, §10.01(a), eff. Sept. 1, 1997. Amended by Acts 1999, 76th Leg., ch. 62, §9.07(a), eff. Sept. 1, 1999. Source: TRCS art. 4413(29ee), §5.

GOVERNMENT CODE
CHAPTER 411. DEPARTMENT OF PUBLIC SAFETY OF THE STATE OF TEXAS
SUBCHAPTER H. LICENSE TO CARRY A CONCEALED HANDGUN

GOVT §411.177. ISSUANCE OR DENIAL OF LICENSE

(a) The department shall issue a license to carry a concealed handgun to an applicant if the applicant meets all the eligibility requirements and submits all the application materials. The department may issue a license to carry handguns only of the categories indicated on the applicant's certificate of proficiency issued under Section 411.189. The department shall administer the licensing procedures in good faith so that any applicant who meets all the eligibility requirements and submits all the application materials shall receive a license. The department may not deny an application on the basis of a capricious or arbitrary decision by the department.

(b) The department shall, not later than the 60th day after the date of the receipt by the director's designee of the completed application materials:

(1) issue the license;

(2) notify the applicant in writing that the application was denied:

(A) on the grounds that the applicant failed to qualify under the criteria listed in Section 411.172;

(B) based on the affidavit of the director's designee submitted to the department under Section 411.176(b); or

(C) based on the affidavit of the qualified handgun instructor submitted to the department under Section 411.189(c); or

(3) notify the applicant in writing that the department is unable to make a determination regarding the issuance or denial of a license to the applicant within the 60-day period prescribed by this subsection and include in that notification an explanation of the reason for the inability and an estimation of the amount of time the department will need to make the determination.

(c) Failure of the department to issue or deny a license for a period of more than 30 days after the department is required to act under Subsection (b) constitutes denial.

(d) A license issued under this subchapter is effective from the date of issuance.

History of Govt §411.177: Codified by Acts 1997, 75th Leg., ch. 165, §10.01(a), eff. Sept. 1, 1997. Amended by Acts 1999, 76th Leg., ch. 62, §9.08(a), eff. Sept. 1, 1999. Source: TRCS art. 4413(29ee), §6.

GOVT §411.178. NOTICE TO LOCAL LAW ENFORCEMENT

On request of a local law enforcement agency, the department shall notify the agency of the licenses that have been issued to license holders who reside in the county in which the agency is located.

History of Govt §411.178: Codified by Acts 1997, 75th Leg., ch. 165, §10.01(a), eff. Sept. 1, 1997. Amended by Acts 1999, 76th Leg., ch. 1189, §14, eff. Sept. 1, 1999. Source: TRCS art. 4413(29ee), §6(c).

GOVT §411.179. FORM OF LICENSE

(a) The department by rule shall adopt the form of the license. A license must include:

(1) a number assigned to the license holder by the department;

(2) a statement of the period for which the license is effective;

(3) a statement of the category or categories of handguns the license holder may carry as provided by Subsection (b);

(4) a color photograph of the license holder;

Ⓐ *Subsection (5) below is effective for causes of action accruing or offenses committed on or after Sept. 1, 2007.*

(5) the license holder's full name, date of birth, hair and eye color, height, weight, and signature;

Subsection (5) below is effective for causes of action accruing or offenses committed before Sept. 1, 2007.

(5) the license holder's full name, date of birth, residence address, hair and eye color, height, weight, signature, and the number of a driver's license or an identification certificate issued to the license holder by the department.

Ⓔ *Subsection (6) below is effective for causes of action accruing or offenses committed on or after Sept. 1, 2007.*

(6) the license holder's residence address or, as provided by Subsection (c), the street address of the courthouse in which the license holder or license holder's spouse serves as a federal judge or the license holder serves as a state judge; and

(7) the number of a driver's license or an identification certificate issued to the license holder by the department.

(b) A category of handguns contains handguns that are not prohibited by law and are of certain actions. The categories of handguns are:

(1) SA: any handguns, whether semi-automatic or not; and

(2) NSA: handguns that are not semi-automatic.

--- ★ ---

 Subsection (c) below was enacted by Acts 2007, 80th Leg., ch. 594, §9, effective Sept. 1, 2007, without reference to the conflicting enactment made by Acts 2007, 80th Leg., ch. 1222, §1, effective June 15, 2007. Subsection (c) below is effective for causes of action accruing or offenses committed on or after Sept. 1, 2007.

(c) In adopting the form of the license under Subsection (a), the department shall establish a procedure for the license of a federal judge, a state judge, or the spouse of a federal judge or state judge to omit the license holder's residence address and to include, in lieu of that address, the street address of the courthouse in which the license holder or license holder's spouse serves as a federal judge or state judge. In establishing the procedure, the department shall require sufficient documentary evidence to establish the license holder's status as a federal judge, a state judge, or the spouse of a federal judge or state judge.

 Subsection (c) below was enacted by Acts 2007, 80th Leg., ch. 1222, §1, effective June 15, 2007, without reference to the conflicting enactment made by Acts 2007, 80th Leg., ch. 594, §9, effective Sept. 1, 2007. Subsection (c) below is effective for offenses committed on or after Sept. 1, 2007.

(c) In adopting the form of the license under Subsection (a), the department shall establish a procedure for the license of a judge, justice, prosecuting attorney, or assistant prosecuting attorney, as described by Section 46.15(a)(4) or (6), Penal Code, to indicate on the license the license holder's status as a judge, justice, district attorney, criminal district attorney, or county attorney. In establishing the procedure, the department shall require sufficient documentary evidence to establish the license holder's status under this subsection.

History of Govt §411.179: Codified by Acts 1997, 75th Leg., ch. 165, §10.01(a), eff. Sept. 1, 1997; Amended by Acts 2007, 80th Leg., ch. 594, §9 (eff. Sept. 1, 2007), ch. 1222, §1 (eff. June 15, 2007). Source: TRCS art. 4413(29ee), §6(e).

GOVT §411.180. NOTIFICATION OF DENIAL, REVOCATION, OR SUSPENSION OF LICENSE; REVIEW

(a) The department shall give written notice to each applicant for a handgun license of any denial, revocation, or suspension of that license. Not later than the 30th day after the notice is received by the applicant, according to the records of the department, the applicant or license holder may request a hearing on the denial, revocation, or suspension. The applicant must make a written request for a hearing addressed to the department at its Austin address. The request for hearing must reach the department in Austin prior to the 30th day after the date of receipt of the written notice. On receipt of a request for hearing from a license holder or applicant, the department shall promptly schedule a hearing in the appropriate justice court in the county of residence of the applicant or license holder. The justice court shall conduct a hearing to review the denial, revocation, or suspension of the license. In a proceeding under this section, a justice of the peace shall act as an administrative hearing officer. A hearing under this section is not subject to Chapter 2001 (Administrative Procedure Act). A district attorney or county attorney, the attorney general, or a designated member of the department may represent the department.

(b) The department, on receipt of a request for hearing, shall file the appropriate petition in the justice court selected for the hearing and send a copy of that petition to the applicant or license holder at the address contained in departmental records. A hearing under this section must be scheduled within 30 days of receipt of the request for a hearing. The hearing shall be held expeditiously but in no event more than 60 days after the date that the applicant or license holder requested the hearing. The date of the hearing may be reset on the motion of either party, by agreement of the parties, or by the court as necessary to accommodate the court's docket.

(c) The justice court shall determine if the denial, revocation, or suspension is supported by a preponderance of the evidence. Both the applicant or license holder and the department may present evidence. The court shall affirm the denial, revocation, or suspension if the court determines that denial, revocation, or suspension is supported by a preponderance of the evidence. If the court determines that the denial, revocation, or suspension is not supported by a preponderance of the evidence, the court shall order the department to immediately issue or return the license to the applicant or license holder.

(d) A proceeding under this section is subject to Chapter 105, Civil Practice and Remedies Code, relating to fees, expenses, and attorney's fees.

(e) A party adversely affected by the court's ruling following a hearing under this section may appeal the ruling by filing within 30 days after the ruling a petition in a county court at law in the county in which the applicant or license holder resides or, if there is no county court at law in the county, in the county court of the county. A person who appeals under this section must send by certified mail a copy of the person's petition, certified by the clerk of the court in which the petition is filed, to the appropriate division of the department at its Austin headquarters. The trial on appeal shall be a trial de novo without a jury. A district or county attorney or the attorney general may represent the department.

(f) A suspension of a license may not be probated.

(g) If an applicant or a license holder does not petition the justice court, a denial becomes final and a revocation or suspension takes effect on the 30th day after receipt of written notice.

(h) The department may use and introduce into evidence certified copies of governmental records to establish the existence of certain events that could result in the denial, revocation, or suspension of a license under this subchapter, including records regarding convictions, judicial findings regarding mental competency, judicial findings regarding chemical dependency, or other matters that may be established by governmental records that have been properly authenticated.

(i) This section does not apply to a suspension of a license under Section 85.022, Family Code, or Article 17.292, Code of Criminal Procedure.

History of Govt §411.180: Codified by Acts 1997, 75th Leg., ch. 165, §10.01(a), eff. Sept. 1, 1997. Amended by Acts 1999, 76th Leg., ch. 1412, §5, eff. Sept. 1, 1999. Source: TRCS art. 4413(29ee), §7.

ANNOTATIONS

Tune v. Texas DPS, 23 S.W.3d 358, 360 (Tex.2000). "[W]e must determine whether the courts of appeals have jurisdiction over appeals involving the grant or denial of a concealed-handgun license. We conclude that they do, because the amount in controversy in a license-denial case exceeds the statutory jurisdictional requirement of $100."

State v. Jones, 220 S.W.3d 604, 606-07 (Tex.App.—Texarkana 2007, no pet.). "The 'may' (which indicates a choice) as used in [subsection (e)] applies to the word 'appeal,' not to the term 'within 30 days.' In other words, if the person whose license has been suspended elects to do so, he has the option of appealing the justice court ruling. If he does so, he must evidence the choice to appeal by filing his appeal within thirty days; upon the expiration of thirty days, the ruling becomes final."

Texas DPS v. Forsgard, 108 S.W.3d 344, 347 (Tex. App.—Tyler 2003, no pet.). Held: Applicant cannot receive a license just because DPS did not schedule a §411.180(b) hearing within 30 days after hearing request.

GOVT §411.181. NOTICE OF CHANGE OF ADDRESS OR NAME

 Subsections (a) & (b) below were amended by Acts 2007, 80th Leg., ch. 594, §10, enacted May 21, 2007, effective Sept. 1, 2007, without reference to the conflicting amendment made by Acts 2007, 80th Leg., ch. 1222, §2, enacted May 25, 2007, effective June 15, 2007. For resolving conflicts, see p. V. Subsections (a) & (b) below are effective for causes of action accruing or offenses committed on or after Sept. 1, 2007.

(a) If a person who is a current license holder moves to a new residence address, if the name of the person is changed by marriage or otherwise, or if the person's status as a federal judge, a state judge, or the spouse of a federal judge or state judge, becomes inapplicable, the person shall, not later than the 30th day after the date of the address, name, or status change, notify the department and provide the department with the number of the person's license and, as applicable, the person's:

(1) former and new addresses; or

(2) former and new names.

(b) If the name of the license holder is changed by marriage or otherwise, or if the person's status as a federal judge or state judge, or the spouse of a federal judge or state judge becomes inapplicable, the person shall apply for a duplicate license. The duplicate license must include the person's current residence address.

 Subsections (a) & (b) below were amended by Acts 2007, 80th Leg., ch. 1222, §2, enacted May 25, 2007, effective June 15, 2007, without reference to the conflicting amendment made by Acts 2007, 80th Leg., ch. 594, §10, enacted May 21, 2007, effective Sept. 1, 2007. For resolving conflicts, see p. V. Subsections (a) & (b) below are effective for offenses committed on or after June 15, 2007.

(a) If a person who is a current license holder moves from the address stated on the license, if the name of the person is changed by marriage or otherwise, or if the person's status as a judge, justice, district attorney, prosecuting attorney, or assistant prosecuting attorney becomes inapplicable for purposes of Section 411.179(c), the person shall, not later than the 30th day after the date of the address, name, or status change, notify the department and provide the department with the number of the person's license and, as applicable, the person's:

(1) former and new addresses; or

(2) former and new names.

(b) If the name of the license holder is changed by marriage or otherwise, or if the person's status becomes inapplicable as described by Subsection (a), the person shall apply for a duplicate license. The duplicate license must reflect the person's current name and status.

Subsections (a) & (b) below are effective for offenses in which any element of the offense was committed before June 15, 2007 and for causes of action that accrue before Sept. 1, 2007.

(a) If a person who is a current license holder moves from the address stated on the license or if the name of the person is changed by marriage or otherwise, the person shall, not later than the 30th day after the date of the address or name change, notify the department and provide the department with the number of the person's license and the person's:

(1) former and new addresses; or

(2) former and new names.

(b) If the name of the license holder is changed by marriage or otherwise, the person shall apply for a duplicate license.

(c) If a license holder moves from the address stated on the license, the person shall apply for a duplicate license.

(d) The department shall charge a license holder a fee of $25 for a duplicate license.

(e) The department shall make the forms available on request.

(f) On request of a local law enforcement agency, the department shall notify the agency of changes made under Subsection (a) by license holders who reside in the county in which the agency is located.

(g) If a license is lost, stolen, or destroyed, the license holder shall apply for a duplicate license not later than the 30th day after the date of the loss, theft, or destruction of the license.

(h) If a license holder is required under this section to apply for a duplicate license and the license expires not later than the 60th day after the date of the loss, theft, or destruction of the license, the applicant may renew the license with the modified information included on the new license. The applicant must pay only the nonrefundable renewal fee.

(i) A license holder whose application fee for a duplicate license under this section is dishonored or reversed may reapply for a duplicate license at any time, provided the application fee and a dishonored payment charge of $25 is paid by cashier's check or money order made payable to the "Texas Department of Public Safety."

History of Govt §411.181: Codified by Acts 1997, 75th Leg., ch. 165, §10.01(a), eff. Sept. 1, 1997. Amended by Acts 1999, 76th Leg., ch. 1189, §15, eff. Sept. 1, 1999; Acts 2005, 79th Leg., ch. 1065, §3, eff. Sept. 1, 2005; Acts 2007, 80th Leg., ch. 594, §10 (eff. Sept. 1, 2007), ch. 1222, §2 (eff. June 15, 2007). Source: TRCS art. 4413(29ee), §8.

GOVT §411.182. NOTICE

(a) For the purpose of a notice required by this subchapter, the department may assume that the address currently reported to the department by the applicant or license holder is the correct address.

(b) A written notice meets the requirements under this subchapter if the notice is sent by certified mail to the current address reported by the applicant or license holder to the department.

(c) If a notice is returned to the department because the notice is not deliverable, the department may give notice by publication once in a newspaper of general interest in the county of the applicant's or license holder's last reported address. On the 31st day after the date the notice is published, the department may take the action proposed in the notice.

History of Govt §411.182: Codified by Acts 1997, 75th Leg., ch. 165, §10.01(a), eff. Sept. 1, 1997. Source: TRCS art. 4413(29ee), §24.

GOVT §411.183. EXPIRATION

(a) A license issued under this subchapter expires on the first birthday of the license holder occurring after the fourth anniversary of the date of issuance.

(b) A renewed license expires on the license holder's birthdate, five years after the date of the expiration of the previous license.

(c) A duplicate license expires on the date the license that was duplicated would have expired.

(d) A modified license expires on the date the license that was modified would have expired.

(e) Expired.

History of Govt §411.183: Codified by Acts 1997, 75th Leg., ch. 165, §10.01(a), eff. Sept. 1, 1997. Acts 2005, 79th Leg., ch. 915, §3, eff. Sept. 1, 2005. Source: TRCS art. 4413(29ee), §9.

GOVT §411.184. MODIFICATION

(a) To modify a license to allow a license holder to carry a handgun of a different category than the license indicates, the license holder must:

(1) complete a proficiency examination as provided by Section 411.188(e);

(2) obtain a handgun proficiency certificate under Section 411.189 not more than six months before the date of application for a modified license; and

(3) submit to the department:

(A) an application for a modified license on a form provided by the department;

(B) a copy of the handgun proficiency certificate;

(C) payment of a modified license fee of $25; and

(D) two recent color passport photographs of the license holder, except that an applicant who is younger than 21 years of age must submit two recent color passport photographs in profile of the applicant.

(b) The director by rule shall adopt a modified license application form requiring an update of the information on the original completed application.

(c) The department may modify the license of a license holder who meets all the eligibility requirements and submits all the modification materials. Not later than the 45th day after receipt of the modification materials, the department shall issue the modified license or notify the license holder in writing that the modified license application was denied.

(d) On receipt of a modified license, the license holder shall return the previously issued license to the department.

(e) A license holder whose application fee for a modified license under this section is dishonored or reversed may reapply for a modified license at any time, provided the application fee and a dishonored payment charge of $25 is paid by cashier's check or money order made payable to the "Texas Department of Public Safety."

History of Govt §411.184: Codified by Acts 1997, 75th Leg., ch. 165, §10.01(a), eff. Sept. 1, 1997; Acts 2005, 79th Leg., ch. 486, §3 (eff. Sept. 1, 2005), ch. 1065, §4 (eff. Sept. 1, 2005). Source: TRCS art. 4413(29ee), §10.

GOVT §411.185. RENEWAL

Ⓐ **(a)** To renew a license, a license holder must:

(1) complete a continuing education course in handgun proficiency under Section 411.188(c) within the six-month period preceding:

(A) the date of application for renewal, for a first or second renewal; and

Ⓔ *Subsection (B) below is effective for licenses renewed on or after Sept. 1, 2007.*

(B) the date of application for renewal or the date of application for the preceding renewal, for a third or subsequent renewal, to ensure that the license holder is not required to complete the course more than once in any 10-year period;

(2) obtain a handgun proficiency certificate under Section 411.189 within the six-month period preceding:

(A) the date of application for renewal, for a first or second renewal; and

Ⓔ *Subsection (B) below is effective for licenses renewed on or after Sept. 1, 2007.*

(B) the date of application for renewal or the date of application for the preceding renewal, for a third or subsequent renewal, to ensure that the license holder is not required to obtain the certificate more than once in any 10-year period; and

(3) submit to the department:

(A) an application for renewal on a form provided by the department;

(B) a copy of the handgun proficiency certificate;

(C) payment of a nonrefundable renewal fee as set by the department; and

(D) two recent color passport photographs of the applicant.

(b) The director by rule shall adopt a renewal application form requiring an update of the information on the original completed application. The director by rule shall set the renewal fee in an amount that is sufficient to cover the actual cost to the department to renew a license. Not later than the 60th day before the expiration date of the license, the department shall mail to each license holder a written notice of the expiration of the license and a renewal form.

(c) The department shall renew the license of a license holder who meets all the eligibility requirements and submits all the renewal materials. Not later than the 45th day after receipt of the renewal materials, the department shall issue the renewal or notify the license holder in writing that the renewal application was denied.

(d) The director by rule shall adopt a procedure by which a license holder who satisfies the eligibility criteria may renew a license by mail. The materials for renewal by mail must include a form to be signed and returned to the department by the applicant that describes state law regarding:

(1) the use of deadly force; and

(2) the places where it is unlawful for the holder of a license issued under this subchapter to carry a concealed handgun.

History of Govt §411.185: Codified by Acts 1997, 75th Leg., ch. 165, §10.01(a), eff. Sept. 1, 1997. Amended by Acts 2007, 80th Leg., ch. 694, §1, eff. Sept. 1, 2007. Source: TRCS art. 4413(29ee), §11.

GOVT §411.186. REVOCATION

(a) A license may be revoked under this section if the license holder:

(1) was not entitled to the license at the time it was issued;

(2) gave false information on the application;

(3) subsequently becomes ineligible for a license under Section 411.172, unless the sole basis for the ineligibility is that the license holder is charged with the commission of a Class A or Class B misdemeanor or an offense under Section 42.01, Penal Code, or of a felony under an information or indictment;

(4) is convicted of an offense under Section 46.035, Penal Code;

(5) is determined by the department to have engaged in conduct constituting a reason to suspend a license listed in Section 411.187(a) after the person's license has been previously suspended twice for the same reason; or

(6) submits an application fee that is dishonored or reversed.

(b) If a peace officer believes a reason listed in Subsection (a) to revoke a license exists, the officer shall prepare an affidavit on a form provided by the department stating the reason for the revocation of the license and giving the department all of the information available to the officer at the time of the preparation of the form. The officer shall attach the officer's reports relating to the license holder to the form and send the form and attachments to the appropriate division of the department at its Austin headquarters not later than the fifth working day after the date the form is prepared. The officer shall send a copy of the form and the attachments to the license holder. If the license holder has not surrendered the license or the license was not seized as evidence, the license holder shall surrender the license to the appropriate division of the department not later than the 10th day after the date the license holder receives the notice of revocation from the department, unless the license holder requests a hearing from the department. The license holder may request that the justice court in the justice court precinct in which the license holder resides review the revocation as provided by Section 411.180. If a request is made for the justice court to review the revocation and hold a hearing, the license holder shall surrender the license on the date an order of revocation is entered by the justice court.

(c) A license holder whose license is revoked for a reason listed in Subsections (a)(1)-(5) may reapply as a new applicant for the issuance of a license under this subchapter after the second anniversary of the date of the revocation if the cause for revocation does not exist on the date of the second anniversary. If the cause for revocation exists on the date of the second anniversary after the date of revocation, the license holder may not apply for a new license until the cause for revocation no longer exists and has not existed for a period of two years.

(d) A license holder whose license is revoked under Subsection (a)(6) may reapply for an original or renewed license at any time, provided the application fee and a dishonored payment charge of $25 is paid by cashier's check or money order made payable to the "Texas Department of Public Safety."

History of Govt §411.186: Codified by Acts 1997, 75th Leg., ch. 165, §10.01(a), eff. Sept. 1, 1997. Amended by Acts 1999, 76th Leg., ch. 62, §9.09(a), eff. Sept. 1, 1999; Acts 2005, 79th Leg., ch. 1065, §2, eff. Sept. 1, 2005. Source: TRCS art. 4413(29ee), §12.

GOVT §411.187. SUSPENSION OF LICENSE

(a) A license may be suspended under this section if the license holder:

(1) is charged with the commission of a Class A or Class B misdemeanor or an offense under Section 42.01, Penal Code, or of a felony under an information or indictment;

(2) fails to display a license as required by Section 411.205;

(3) fails to notify the department of a change of address or name as required by Section 411.181;

(4) carries a concealed handgun under the authority of this subchapter of a different category than the license holder is licensed to carry;

(5) fails to return a previously issued license after a license is modified as required by Section 411.184(d);

(6) commits an act of family violence and is the subject of an active protective order rendered under Title 4, Family Code; or

(7) is arrested for an offense involving family violence or an offense under Section 42.072, Penal Code, and is the subject of an order for emergency protection issued under Article 17.292, Code of Criminal Procedure.

(b) If a peace officer believes a reason listed in Subsection (a) to suspend a license exists, the officer shall prepare an affidavit on a form provided by the department stating the reason for the suspension of the license and giving the department all of the information available to the officer at the time of the preparation of the form. The officer shall attach the officer's reports relating to the license holder to the form and send the form and the attachments to the appropriate division of the department at its Austin headquarters not later than the fifth working day after the date the form is prepared. The officer shall send a copy of the form and the attachments to the license holder. If the license holder has not surrendered the license or the license was not seized as evidence, the license holder shall surrender the license to the appropriate division of the department not later than the 10th day after the date the license holder receives the notice of suspension from the department unless the license holder requests a hearing from the department. The license holder may request that the justice court in the justice court precinct in which the license holder resides review the suspension as provided by Section 411.180. If a request is made for the justice court to review the suspension and hold a hearing, the license holder shall surrender the license on the date an order of suspension is entered by the justice court.

(c) A license may be suspended under this section:

(1) for 30 days, if the person's license is subject to suspension for a reason listed in Subsection (a)(3), (4), or (5), except as provided by Subdivision (3);

(2) for 90 days, if the person's license is subject to suspension for a reason listed in Subsection (a)(2), except as provided by Subdivision (3);

(3) for not less than one year and not more than three years if the person's license is subject to suspension for a reason listed in Subsection (a), other than the reason listed in Subsection (a)(1), and the person's license has been previously suspended for the same reason;

(4) until dismissal of the charges if the person's license is subject to suspension for the reason listed in Subsection (a)(1); or

(5) for the duration of or the period specified by:

(A) the protective order issued under Title 4, Family Code, if the person's license is subject to suspension for the reason listed in Subsection (a)(6); or

(B) the order for emergency protection issued under Article 17.292, Code of Criminal Procedure, if the person's license is subject to suspension for the reason listed in Subsection (a)(7).

History of Govt §411.187: Codified by Acts 1997, 75th Leg., ch. 165, §10.01(a), eff. Sept. 1, 1997. Amended by Acts 1999, 76th Leg., ch. 62, §9.10(a) (eff. Sept. 1, 1999), ch. 1412, §6 (eff. Sept. 1, 1999). Source: TRCS art. 4413(29ee), §13.

GOVT §411.188. HANDGUN PROFICIENCY REQUIREMENT

(a) The director by rule shall establish minimum standards for handgun proficiency and shall develop a course to teach handgun proficiency and examinations to measure handgun proficiency. The course to teach handgun proficiency must contain training sessions divided into two parts. One part of the course must be classroom instruction and the other part must be range instruction and an actual demonstration by the applicant of the applicant's ability to safely and proficiently use the category of handgun for which the applicant seeks certification. An applicant may not be certified unless the applicant demonstrates, at a minimum, the degree of proficiency that is required to effectively operate a handgun of .32 caliber or above. The department shall distribute the standards, course requirements, and examinations on request to any qualified handgun instructor.

(b) Only a qualified handgun instructor may administer a handgun proficiency course. The handgun proficiency course must include at least 10 hours and not more than 15 hours of instruction on:

(1) the laws that relate to weapons and to the use of deadly force;

(2) handgun use, proficiency, and safety;

(3) nonviolent dispute resolution; and

(4) proper storage practices for handguns with an emphasis on storage practices that eliminate the possibility of accidental injury to a child.

(c) The department by rule shall develop a continuing education course in handgun proficiency for a license holder who wishes to renew a license. Only a qualified handgun instructor may administer the continuing education course. The course must include:

(1) at least four hours of instruction on one or more of the subjects listed in Subsection (b); and

(2) other information the director determines is appropriate.

(d) Only a qualified handgun instructor may administer the proficiency examination to obtain or to renew a license. The proficiency examination must include:

(1) a written section on the subjects listed in Subsection (b); and

(2) a physical demonstration of proficiency in the use of one or more handguns of specific categories and in handgun safety procedures.

(e) Only a qualified handgun instructor may administer the proficiency examination to modify a license. The proficiency examination must include a physical demonstration of the proficiency in the use of one or more handguns of specific categories and in handgun safety procedures.

(f) The department shall develop and distribute directions and materials for course instruction, test administration, and recordkeeping. All test results shall be sent to the department, and the department shall maintain a record of the results.

(g) A person who wishes to obtain or renew a license to carry a concealed handgun must apply in person to a qualified handgun instructor to take the appropriate course in handgun proficiency, demonstrate handgun proficiency, and obtain a handgun proficiency certificate as described by Section 411.189.

(h) A license holder who wishes to modify a license to allow the license holder to carry a handgun of a different category than the license indicates must apply in person to a qualified handgun instructor to demonstrate the required knowledge and proficiency to obtain a handgun proficiency certificate in that category as described by Section 411.189.

(i) A certified firearms instructor of the department may monitor any class or training presented by a qualified handgun instructor. A qualified handgun instructor shall cooperate with the department in the department's efforts to monitor the presentation of training by the qualified handgun instructor. A qualified handgun instructor shall make available for inspection to the department any and all records maintained by a qualified handgun instructor under this subchapter. The qualified handgun instructor shall keep a record of all certificates of handgun proficiency issued by the qualified handgun instructor and other information required by department rule.

History of Govt §411.188: Codified by Acts 1997, 75th Leg., ch. 165, §10.01(a), eff. Sept. 1, 1997. Amended by Acts 1999, 76th Leg., ch. 62, §9.11(a), eff. Sept. 1, 1999. Source: TRCS art. 4413(29ee), §16.

GOVT §411.1881. EXEMPTION FROM INSTRUCTION FOR CERTAIN PERSONS

(a) Notwithstanding any other provision of this subchapter, a person may not be required to complete the range instruction portion of a handgun proficiency course to obtain or renew a concealed handgun license issued under this subchapter if the person:

(1) is currently serving in or is honorably discharged from:

(A) the army, navy, air force, coast guard, or marine corps of the United States or an auxiliary service or reserve unit of one of those branches of the armed forces; or

(B) the state military forces, as defined by Section 431.001; and

(2) has, within the five years preceding the date of the person's application for an original or renewed license, as applicable, completed a course of training in handgun proficiency or familiarization as part of the person's service with the armed forces or state military forces.

(b) The director by rule shall adopt a procedure by which a license holder who is exempt under Subsection (a) from the range instruction portion of the handgun proficiency requirement may submit a form demonstrating the license holder's qualification for an exemption under that subsection. The form must provide sufficient information to allow the department to verify whether the license holder qualifies for the exemption.

History of Govt §411.1881: Acts 2005, 79th Leg., ch. 132, §1, eff. Sept. 1, 2005.

GOVT §411.1882. EXEMPTION FROM HANDGUN PROFICIENCY CERTIFICATE REQUIREMENT FOR CERTAIN PERSONS

 Section 411.1882 below is effective for offenses committed on or after June 15, 2007.

(a) Notwithstanding any other provision of this subchapter, a person may not be required to submit to the department a handgun proficiency certificate to obtain or renew a concealed handgun license issued under this subchapter if:

(1) the person is currently serving in this state as:

(A) a judge or justice of a federal court;

(B) an active judicial officer, as defined by Section 411.201, Government Code; or

(C) a district attorney, assistant district attorney, criminal district attorney, assistant criminal district attorney, county attorney, or assistant county attorney; and

(2) a handgun proficiency instructor approved by the Commission on Law Enforcement Officer Standards and Education for purposes of Section 1702.1675, Occupations Code, makes a sworn statement indicating that the person demonstrated proficiency to the instructor in the use of handguns during the 12-month period preceding the date of the person's application to the department and designating the types of handguns with which the person demonstrated proficiency.

(b) The director by rule shall adopt a procedure by which a person who is exempt under Subsection (a) from the handgun proficiency certificate requirement may submit a form demonstrating the person's qualification for an exemption under that subsection. The form must provide sufficient information to allow the department to verify whether the person qualifies for the exemption.

(c) A license issued under this section automatically expires on the six-month anniversary of the date the person's status under Subsection (a) becomes inapplicable. A license that expires under this subsection may be renewed under Section 411.185.

History of Govt §411.1882: Acts 2007, 80th Leg., ch. 1222, §3, eff. June 15, 2007.

GOVT §411.189. HANDGUN PROFICIENCY CERTIFICATE

(a) The department shall develop a sequentially numbered handgun proficiency certificate and distribute the certificate to qualified handgun instructors who administer the handgun proficiency examination described in Section 411.188. The department by rule may set a fee not to exceed $5 to cover the cost of the certificates.

(b) If a person successfully completes the proficiency requirements as described in Section 411.188, the instructor shall endorse a certificate of handgun proficiency provided by the department. An applicant must successfully complete both classroom and range instruction to receive a certificate. The certificate must indicate the category of any handgun for which the applicant demonstrated proficiency during the examination.

(c) A qualified handgun instructor may submit to the department a written recommendation for disapproval of the application for a license, renewal, or modification of a license, accompanied by an affidavit stating personal knowledge or naming persons with personal knowledge of facts that lead the instructor to believe that an applicant is not qualified for handgun proficiency certification. The department may use a written recommendation submitted under this subsection as the basis for denial of a license only if the department determines that the recommendation is made in good faith and is supported by a preponderance of the evidence. The department shall make a determination under this subsection not later than the 45th day after the date the department receives the written recommendation. The 60-day period in which the department must take action under Section 411.177(b) is extended one day for each day a determination is pending under this subsection.

History of Govt §411.189: Codified by Acts 1997, 75th Leg., ch. 165, §10.01(a), eff. Sept. 1, 1997. Amended by Acts 1999, 76th Leg., ch. 62, §9.12(a), eff. Sept. 1, 1999. Source: TRCS art. 4413(29ee), §17.

GOVT §411.190. QUALIFIED HANDGUN INSTRUCTORS

(a) The director may certify as a qualified handgun instructor a person who:

(1) is certified by the Commission on Law Enforcement Officer Standards and Education or under Chapter 1702, Occupations Code, to instruct others in the use of handguns;

(2) regularly instructs others in the use of handguns and has graduated from a handgun instructor school that uses a nationally accepted course designed to train persons as handgun instructors; or

(3) is certified by the National Rifle Association of America as a handgun instructor.

(b) In addition to the qualifications described by Subsection (a), a qualified handgun instructor must be qualified to instruct persons in:

(1) the laws that relate to weapons and to the use of deadly force;

(2) handgun use, proficiency, and safety;

(3) nonviolent dispute resolution; and

(4) proper storage practices for handguns, including storage practices that eliminate the possibility of accidental injury to a child.

(c) In the manner applicable to a person who applies for a license to carry a concealed handgun, the department shall conduct a background check of a person who applies for certification as a qualified handgun instructor. If the background check indicates that the applicant for certification would not qualify to receive a handgun license, the department may not certify the applicant as a qualified handgun instructor. If the background check indicates that the applicant for certification would qualify to receive a handgun license, the department shall provide handgun instructor training to the applicant. The applicant shall pay a fee of $100 to the department for the training. The applicant must take and successfully complete the training offered by the department and pay the training fee before the department may certify the applicant as a qualified handgun instructor. The department shall issue a license to carry a concealed handgun under the authority of this subchapter to any person who is certified as a qualified handgun instructor and who pays to the department a fee of $100 in addition to the training fee. The department by rule may prorate or waive the training fee for an employee of another governmental entity.

(d) The certification of a qualified handgun instructor expires on the second anniversary after the date of certification. To renew a certification, the qualified handgun instructor must pay a fee of $100 and take and successfully complete the retraining courses required by department rule.

(e) After certification, a qualified handgun instructor may conduct training for applicants for a license under this subchapter.

(f) If the department determines that a reason exists to revoke, suspend, or deny a license to carry a concealed handgun with respect to a person who is a qualified handgun instructor or an applicant for certification as a qualified handgun instructor, the department shall take that action against the person's:

(1) license to carry a concealed handgun if the person is an applicant for or the holder of a license issued under this subchapter; and

(2) certification as a qualified handgun instructor.

History of Govt §411.190: Codified by Acts 1997, 75th Leg., ch. 165, §10.01(a), eff. Sept. 1, 1997. Amended by Acts 1999, 76th Leg., ch. 62, §9.13(a) (eff. Sept. 1, 1999), ch. 199, §1 (eff. Sept. 1, 1999); Acts 2001, 77th Leg., ch. 1420, §14.758, eff. Sept. 1, 2001. Source: TRCS art. 4413(29ee), §18.

GOVT §411.191. REVIEW OF DENIAL, REVOCATION, OR SUSPENSION OF CERTIFICATION AS QUALIFIED HANDGUN INSTRUCTOR

The procedures for the review of a denial, revocation, or suspension of a license under Section 411.180 apply to the review of a denial, revocation, or suspension of certification as a qualified handgun instructor. The notice provisions of this subchapter relating to denial, revocation, or suspension of handgun licenses apply to the proposed denial, revocation, or suspension of a certification of a qualified handgun instructor or an applicant for certification as a qualified handgun instructor.

History of Govt §411.191: Codified by Acts 1997, 75th Leg., ch. 165, §10.01(a), eff. Sept. 1, 1997. Source: TRCS art. 4413(29ee), §19.

GOVT §411.192. CONFIDENTIALITY OF RECORDS

(a) The department shall disclose to a criminal justice agency information contained in its files and records regarding whether a named individual or any individual named in a specified list is licensed under this subchapter. Information on an individual subject to disclosure under this section includes the individual's name, date of birth, gender, race, and zip code. Except as otherwise provided by this section and by Section 411.193, all other records maintained under this subchapter are confidential and are not subject to mandatory disclosure under the open records law, Chapter 552.

(b) An applicant or license holder may be furnished a copy of disclosable records regarding the applicant or license holder on request and the payment of a reasonable fee.

(c) The department shall notify a license holder of any request that is made for information relating to the license holder under this section and provide the name of the agency making the request.

(d) This section does not prohibit the department from making public and distributing to the public at no cost lists of individuals who are certified as qualified handgun instructors by the department.

History of Govt §411.192: Codified by Acts 1997, 75th Leg., ch. 165, §10.01(a), eff. Sept. 1, 1997. Amended by Acts 2007, 80th Leg., ch. 172, §1, eff. May 23, 2007. Source: TRCS art. 4413(29ee), §20.

GOVT §411.193. STATISTICAL REPORT

The department shall make available, on request and payment of a reasonable fee to cover costs of copying, a statistical report that includes the number of licenses issued, denied, revoked, or suspended by the department during the preceding month, listed by age, gender, race, and zip code of the applicant or license holder.

History of Govt §411.193: Codified by Acts 1997, 75th Leg., ch. 165, §10.01(a), eff. Sept. 1, 1997. Source: TRCS art. 4413(29ee), §21.

GOVT §411.194. REDUCTION OF FEES DUE TO INDIGENCY

(a) Notwithstanding any other provision of this subchapter, the department shall reduce by 50 percent any fee required for the issuance of an original, duplicate, modified, or renewed license under this subchapter if the department determines that the applicant is indigent.

(b) The department shall require an applicant requesting a reduction of a fee to submit proof of indigency with the application materials.

(c) For purposes of this section, an applicant is indigent if the applicant's income is not more than 100 percent of the applicable income level established by the federal poverty guidelines.

History of Govt §411.194: Codified by Acts 1997, 75th Leg., ch. 165, §10.01(a), eff. Sept. 1, 1997. Source: TRCS art. 4413(29ee), §33.

GOVT §411.195. REDUCTION OF FEES FOR SENIOR CITIZENS

Notwithstanding any other provision of this subchapter, the department shall reduce by 50 percent any fee required for the issuance of an original, duplicate, modified, or renewed license under this subchapter if the applicant for the license is 60 years of age or older.

History of Govt §411.195: Codified by Acts 1997, 75th Leg., ch. 165, §10.01(a), eff. Sept. 1, 1997. Amended by Acts 2005, 79th Leg., ch. 289, §1, eff. Sept. 1, 2005. Source: TRCS art. 4413(29ee), §34.

Ⓐ GOVT §411.1951. WAIVER OR REDUCTION OF FEES FOR MEMBERS OR VETERANS OF UNITED STATES ARMED FORCES

Ⓔ (a) In this section, "veteran" means a person who:

(1) has served in:

(A) the army, navy, air force, coast guard, or marine corps of the United States;

(B) the state military forces as defined by Section 431.001; or

(C) an auxiliary service of one of those branches of the armed forces; and

(2) has been honorably discharged from the branch of the service in which the person served.

(b) Notwithstanding any other provision of this subchapter, the department shall waive any fee required for the issuance of an original, duplicate, modified, or renewed license under this subchapter if the applicant for the license is:

(1) a member of the United States armed forces, including a member of the reserves, national guard, or state guard; or

(2) a veteran who, within 365 days preceding the date of the application, was honorably discharged from the branch of service in which the person served.

Ⓔ (c) Notwithstanding any other provision of this subchapter, the department shall reduce by 50 percent any fee required for the issuance of an original, duplicate, modified, or renewed license under this subchapter if the applicant for the license is a veteran who, more than 365 days preceding the date of the application, was honorably discharged from the branch of the service in which the person served.

History of Govt §411.1951: Acts 2005, 79th Leg., ch. 486, §4, eff. Sept. 1, 2005. Amended by Acts 2007, 80th Leg., ch. 200, §1, eff. Sept. 1, 2007.

GOVT §411.196. METHOD OF PAYMENT

A person may pay a fee required by this subchapter by cash, credit card, personal check, cashier's check, or money order. A person who pays a fee required by this subchapter by cash must pay the fee in person. Checks or money orders must be made payable to the "Texas Department of Public Safety." A person whose payment for a fee required by this subchapter is dishonored or reversed must pay any future fees required by this subchapter by cashier's check or money order made payable to the "Texas Department of Public Safety." A fee received by the department under this subchapter is nonrefundable.

History of Govt §411.196: Codified by Acts 1997, 75th Leg., ch. 165, §10.01(a), eff. Sept. 1, 1997. Amended by Acts 2005, 79th Leg., ch. 1065, §1, eff. Sept. 1, 2005. Source: TRCS art. 4413(29ee), §25.

GOVT §411.197. RULES

The director shall adopt rules to administer this subchapter.

History of Govt §411.197: Codified by Acts 1997, 75th Leg., ch. 165, §10.01(a), eff. Sept. 1, 1997. Source: TRCS art. 4413(29ee), §22.

GOVT §411.198. LAW ENFORCEMENT OFFICER ALIAS HANDGUN LICENSE

(a) On written approval of the director, the department may issue to a law enforcement officer an alias license to carry a concealed handgun to be used in supervised activities involving criminal investigations.

(b) It is a defense to prosecution under Section 46.035, Penal Code, that the actor, at the time of the commission of the offense, was the holder of an alias license issued under this section.

History of Govt §411.198: Codified by Acts 1997, 75th Leg., ch. 165, §10.01(a), eff. Sept. 1, 1997. Source: TRCS art. 4413(29ee), §27.

GOVT §411.199. HONORABLY RETIRED PEACE OFFICERS

(a) A person who is licensed as a peace officer under Chapter 415 and who has been employed full-time as a peace officer by a law enforcement agency may apply for a license under this subchapter at any time after retirement.

(b) The person shall submit two complete sets of legible and classifiable fingerprints and a sworn statement from the head of the law enforcement agency employing the applicant. A head of a law enforcement agency may not refuse to issue a statement under this subsection. If the applicant alleges that the statement is untrue, the department shall investigate the validity of the statement. The statement must include:

(1) the name and rank of the applicant;

(2) the status of the applicant before retirement;

(3) whether or not the applicant was accused of misconduct at the time of the retirement;

(4) the physical and mental condition of the applicant;

(5) the type of weapons the applicant had demonstrated proficiency with during the last year of employment;

(6) whether the applicant would be eligible for re-employment with the agency, and if not, the reasons the applicant is not eligible; and

(7) a recommendation from the agency head regarding the issuance of a license under this subchapter.

(c) The department may issue a license under this subchapter to an applicant under this section if the applicant is honorably retired and physically and emotionally fit to possess a handgun. In this subsection, "honorably retired" means the applicant:

(1) did not retire in lieu of any disciplinary action;

(2) was eligible to retire from the law enforcement agency or was ineligible to retire only as a result of an injury received in the course of the applicant's employment with the agency; and

(3) is entitled to receive a pension or annuity for service as a law enforcement officer or is not entitled to receive a pension or annuity only because the law enforcement agency that employed the applicant does not offer a pension or annuity to its employees.

(d) An applicant under this section must pay a fee of $25 for a license issued under this subchapter.

(e) A retired peace officer who obtains a license under this subchapter must maintain, for the category of weapon licensed, the proficiency required for a peace officer under Section 415.035. The department or a local law enforcement agency shall allow a retired peace officer of the department or agency an opportunity to annually demonstrate the required proficiency. The proficiency shall be reported to the department on application and renewal.

(f) A license issued under this section expires as provided by Section 411.183.

(g) A retired officer of the United States who was eligible to carry a firearm in the discharge of the officer's official duties is eligible for a license under this section. An applicant described by this subsection may submit the application at any time after retirement. The applicant shall submit with the application proper proof of retired status by presenting the following documents prepared by the agency from which the applicant retired:

(1) retirement credentials; and

(2) a letter from the agency head stating the applicant retired in good standing.

History of Govt §411.199: Codified by Acts 1997, 75th Leg., ch. 165, §10.01(a), eff. Sept. 1, 1997. Amended by Acts 1999, 76th Leg., ch. 25, §1 (eff. May 3, 1999), ch. 62, §9.14 (eff. Sept. 1, 1999); Acts 2001, 77th Leg., ch. 196, §1, eff. Sept. 1, 2001. Source: TRCS art. 4413(29ee), §28.

GOVT §411.1991. ACTIVE PEACE OFFICERS

(a) A person who is licensed as a peace officer under Chapter 415 and is employed full-time as a peace officer by a law enforcement agency may apply for a license under this subchapter. The person shall submit to the department two complete sets of legible and classifiable fingerprints and a sworn statement of the head of the law enforcement agency employing the applicant. A head of a law enforcement agency may not refuse to issue a statement under this subsection. If the applicant alleges that the statement is untrue, the department shall investigate the validity of the statement. The statement must include:

(1) the name and rank of the applicant;

(2) whether the applicant has been accused of misconduct at any time during the applicant's period of employment with the agency and the disposition of that accusation;

(3) a description of the physical and mental condition of the applicant;

(4) a list of the types of weapons the applicant has demonstrated proficiency with during the preceding year; and

(5) a recommendation from the agency head that a license be issued to the person under this subchapter.

(b) The department may issue a license under this subchapter to an applicant under this section if the statement from the head of the law enforcement agency employing the applicant complies with Subsection (a) and indicates that the applicant is qualified and physically and mentally fit to carry a handgun.

(c) An applicant under this section shall pay a fee of $25 for a license issued under this subchapter.

(d) A license issued under this section expires as provided by Section 411.183.

History of Govt §411.1991: Acts 1999, 76th Leg., ch. 62, §9.15(a), eff. Sept. 1, 1999.

GOVT §411.200. APPLICATION TO LICENSED SECURITY OFFICERS

This subchapter does not exempt a license holder who is also employed as a security officer and licensed under Chapter 1702, Occupations Code, from the duty to comply with Chapter 1702, Occupations Code, or Section 46.02, Penal Code.

History of Govt §411.200: Codified by Acts 1997, 75th Leg., ch. 165, §10.01(a), eff. Sept. 1, 1997. Amended by Acts 2001, 77th Leg., ch. 1420, §14.759, eff. Sept. 1, 2001. Source: TRCS art. 4413(29ee), §29.

GOVT §411.201. ACTIVE & RETIRED JUDICIAL OFFICERS

(a) In this section:

(1) "Active judicial officer" means:

(A) a person serving as a judge or justice of the supreme court, the court of criminal appeals, a court of appeals, a district court, a criminal district court, a constitutional county court, a statutory county court, a justice court, or a municipal court; or

 Subsection (B) below is effective for offenses committed on or after June 15, 2007.

(B) a federal judge who is a resident of this state.

(2) "Retired judicial officer" means:

(A) a special judge appointed under Section 26.023 or 26.024; or

(B) a senior judge designated under Section 75.001 or a judicial officer as designated or defined by Section 75.001, 831.001, or 836.001.

(b) Notwithstanding any other provision of this subchapter, the department shall issue a license under this subchapter to an active or retired judicial officer who meets the requirements of this section.

(c) An active judicial officer is eligible for a license to carry a concealed handgun under the authority of this subchapter. A retired judicial officer is eligible for a license to carry a concealed handgun under the authority of this subchapter if the officer:

(1) has not been convicted of a felony;

(2) has not, in the five years preceding the date of application, been convicted of a Class A or Class B misdemeanor;

(3) is not charged with the commission of a Class A or Class B misdemeanor or of a felony under an information or indictment;

(4) is not a chemically dependent person; and

(5) is not a person of unsound mind.

(d) An applicant for a license who is an active or retired judicial officer must submit to the department:

(1) a completed application on a form prescribed by the department;

(2) two recent color passport photographs of the applicant;

(3) a handgun proficiency certificate issued to the applicant as evidence that the applicant successfully completed the proficiency requirements of this subchapter;

(4) a nonrefundable application and license fee set by the department in an amount reasonably designed to cover the administrative costs associated with issuance of a license to carry a concealed handgun under this subchapter; and

GOVT §411.201

(5) if the applicant is a retired judicial officer:

(A) two complete sets of legible and classifiable fingerprints of the applicant taken by a person employed by a law enforcement agency who is appropriately trained in recording fingerprints; and

(B) a form executed by the applicant that authorizes the department to make an inquiry into any noncriminal history records that are necessary to determine the applicant's eligibility for a license under this subchapter.

(e) On receipt of all the application materials required by this section, the department shall:

(1) if the applicant is an active judicial officer, issue a license to carry a concealed handgun under the authority of this subchapter; or

(2) if the applicant is a retired judicial officer, conduct an appropriate background investigation to determine the applicant's eligibility for the license and, if the applicant is eligible, issue a license to carry a concealed handgun under the authority of this subchapter.

(f) Except as otherwise provided by this subsection, an applicant for a license under this section must satisfy the handgun proficiency requirements of Section 411.188. The classroom instruction part of the proficiency course for an active judicial officer is not subject to a minimum hour requirement. The instruction must include instruction only on:

(1) handgun use, proficiency, and safety; and

(2) proper storage practices for handguns with an emphasis on storage practices that eliminate the possibility of accidental injury to a child.

(g) A license issued under this section expires as provided by Section 411.183 and, except as otherwise provided by this subsection, may be renewed in accordance with Section 411.185 of this subchapter. An active judicial officer is not required to attend the classroom instruction part of the continuing education proficiency course to renew a license.

(h) The department shall issue a license to carry a concealed handgun under the authority of this subchapter to an elected attorney representing the state in the prosecution of felony cases who meets the requirements of this section for an active judicial officer. The department shall waive any fee required for the issuance of an original, duplicate, or renewed license under this subchapter for an applicant who is an attorney elected or employed to represent the state in the prosecution of felony cases.

History of Govt §411.201: Codified by Acts 1997, 75th Leg., ch. 165, §10.01(a), eff. Sept. 1, 1997. Amended by Acts 2007, 80th Leg., ch. 1222, §4 (eff. June 15, 2007), ch. 402, §1 (eff. June 15, 2007). Source: TRCS art. 4413(29ee), §30.

GOVT §411.202. LICENSE A BENEFIT

The issuance of a license under this subchapter is a benefit to the license holder for purposes of those sections of the Penal Code to which the definition of "benefit" under Section 1.07, Penal Code, applies.

History of Govt §411.202: Codified by Acts 1997, 75th Leg., ch. 165, §10.01(a), eff. Sept. 1, 1997. Source: TRCS art. 4413(29ee), §26.

GOVT §411.203. RIGHTS OF EMPLOYERS

This subchapter does not prevent or otherwise limit the right of a public or private employer to prohibit persons who are licensed under this subchapter from carrying a concealed handgun on the premises of the business.

History of Govt §411.203: Codified by Acts 1997, 75th Leg., ch. 165, §10.01(a), eff. Sept. 1, 1997. Source: TRCS art. 4413(29ee), §32.

GOVT §411.204. NOTICE REQUIRED ON CERTAIN PREMISES

(a) A business that has a permit or license issued under Chapter 25, 28, 32, 69, or 74, Alcoholic Beverage Code, and that derives 51 percent or more of its income from the sale of alcoholic beverages for on-premises consumption as determined by the Texas Alcoholic Beverage Commission under Section 104.06, Alcoholic Beverage Code, shall prominently display at each entrance to the business premises a sign that complies with the requirements of Subsection (c).

(b) A hospital licensed under Chapter 241, Health and Safety Code, or a nursing home licensed under Chapter 242, Health and Safety Code, shall prominently display at each entrance to the hospital or nursing home, as appropriate, a sign that complies with the requirements of Subsection (c) other than the requirement that the sign include on its face the number "51".

(c) The sign required under Subsections (a) and (b) must give notice in both English and Spanish that it is unlawful for a person licensed under this subchapter to carry a handgun on the premises. The sign must appear in contrasting colors with block letters at least one inch in height and must include on its face the number "51" printed in solid red at least five inches in height. The sign shall be displayed in a conspicuous manner clearly visible to the public.

(d) A business that has a permit or license issued under the Alcoholic Beverage Code and that is not required to display a sign under this section may be required to display a sign under Section 11.041 or 61.11, Alcoholic Beverage Code.

(e) This section does not apply to a business that has a food and beverage certificate issued under the Alcoholic Beverage Code.

History of Govt §411.204: Codified by Acts 1997, 75th Leg., ch. 165, §10.01(a), eff. Sept. 1, 1997. Amended by Acts 1999, 76th Leg., ch. 62, §9.16(a) (eff. Sept. 1, 1999), ch. 523, §1 (eff. June 18, 1999). Source: TRCS art. 4413(29ee), §31.

GOVT §411.205. DISPLAYING LICENSE; PENALTY

(a) If a license holder is carrying a handgun on or about the license holder's person when a magistrate or a peace officer demands that the license holder display identification, the license holder shall display both the license holder's driver's license or identification certificate issued by the department and the license holder's handgun license. A person who fails or refuses to display the license and identification as required by this subsection is subject to suspension of the person's license as provided by Section 411.187.

(b) A person commits an offense if the person fails or refuses to display the license and identification as required by Subsection (a) after previously having had the person's license suspended for a violation of that subsection. An offense under this subsection is a Class B misdemeanor.

History of Govt §411.205: Codified by Acts 1997, 75th Leg., ch. 165, §10.01(a), eff. Sept. 1, 1997. Amended by Acts 1999, 76th Leg., ch. 62, §9.17(a), eff. Sept. 1, 1999. Source: TRCS art. 4413(29ee), §§6(g), (h), (i).

GOVT §411.206. SEIZURE OF HANDGUN & LICENSE

(a) If a peace officer arrests and takes into custody a license holder who is carrying a handgun under the authority of this subchapter, the officer shall seize the license holder's handgun and license as evidence.

(b) The provisions of Article 18.19, Code of Criminal Procedure, relating to the disposition of weapons seized in connection with criminal offenses, apply to a handgun seized under this subsection.

(c) Any judgment of conviction entered by any court for an offense under Section 46.035, Penal Code, must contain the handgun license number of the convicted license holder. A certified copy of the judgment is conclusive and sufficient evidence to justify revocation of a license under Section 411.186(a)(4).

History of Govt §411.206: Codified by Acts 1997, 75th Leg., ch. 165, §10.01(a), eff. Sept. 1, 1997. Source: TRCS art. 4413(29ee), §14.

GOVT §411.207. AUTHORITY OF PEACE OFFICER TO DISARM

(a) A peace officer who is acting in the lawful discharge of the officer's official duties may disarm a license holder at any time the officer reasonably believes it is necessary for the protection of the license holder, officer, or another individual. The peace officer shall return the handgun to the license holder before discharging the license holder from the scene if the officer determines that the license holder is not a threat to the officer, license holder, or another individual and if the license holder has not violated any provision of this subchapter or committed any other violation that results in the arrest of the license holder.

🄴 **(b)** A peace officer who is acting in the lawful discharge of the officer's official duties may temporarily disarm a license holder when a license holder enters a nonpublic, secure portion of a law enforcement facility, if the law enforcement agency provides a gun locker where the peace officer can secure the license holder's handgun. The peace officer shall secure the handgun in the locker and shall return the handgun to the license holder immediately after the license holder leaves the nonpublic, secure portion of the law enforcement facility.

🄴 **(c)** A law enforcement facility shall prominently display at each entrance to a nonpublic, secure portion of the facility a sign that gives notice in both English and Spanish that, under this section, a peace officer may temporarily disarm a license holder when the license holder enters the nonpublic, secure portion of the facility. The sign must appear in contrasting colors with block letters at least one inch in height. The sign shall be displayed in a clearly visible and conspicuous manner.

🄴 **(d)** In this section:

(1) "Law enforcement facility" means a building or a portion of a building used exclusively by a law enforcement agency that employs peace officers as described by Articles 2.12(1) and (3), Code of Criminal Procedure, and support personnel to conduct the official business of the agency. The term does not include:

(A) any portion of a building not actively used exclusively to conduct the official business of the agency; or

(B) any public or private driveway, street, sidewalk, walkway, parking lot, parking garage, or other parking area.

(2) "Nonpublic, secure portion of a law enforcement facility" means that portion of a law enforcement facility to which the general public is denied access without express permission and to which access is granted solely to conduct the official business of the law enforcement agency.

History of Govt §411.207: Codified by Acts 1997, 75th Leg., ch. 165, §10.01(a), eff. Sept. 1, 1997. Amended by Acts 2007, 80th Leg., ch. 572, §1, eff. Sept. 1, 2007. Source: TRCS art. 4413(29ee), §36.

GOVT §411.208. LIMITATION OF LIABILITY

(a) A court may not hold the state, an agency or subdivision of the state, an officer or employee of the state, a peace officer, or a qualified handgun instructor liable for damages caused by:

(1) an action authorized under this subchapter or a failure to perform a duty imposed by this subchapter; or

(2) the actions of an applicant or license holder that occur after the applicant has received a license or been denied a license under this subchapter.

(b) A cause of action in damages may not be brought against the state, an agency or subdivision of the state, an officer or employee of the state, a peace officer, or a qualified handgun instructor for any damage caused by the actions of an applicant or license holder under this subchapter.

(c) The department is not responsible for any injury or damage inflicted on any person by an applicant or license holder arising or alleged to have arisen from an action taken by the department under this subchapter.

(d) The immunities granted under Subsections (a), (b), and (c) do not apply to an act or a failure to act by the state, an agency or subdivision of the state, an officer of the state, or a peace officer if the act or failure to act was capricious or arbitrary.

History of Govt §411.208: Codified by Acts 1997, 75th Leg., ch. 165, §10.01(a), eff. Sept. 1, 1997. Source: TRCS art. 4413(29ee), §15.

SUBTITLE G. CORRECTIONS

CHAPTER 508. PAROLE & MANDATORY SUPERVISION

SUBCHAPTER A. GENERAL PROVISIONS

GOVT §508.001. DEFINITIONS

In this chapter:

(1) "Board" means the Board of Pardons and Paroles.

(2) "Community supervision and corrections department" means a department established under Chapter 76.

(3) "Director" means the director of the pardons and paroles division.

(4) "Division" means the pardons and paroles division.

(5) "Mandatory supervision" means the release of an eligible inmate sentenced to the institutional division so that the inmate may serve the remainder of the inmate's sentence not on parole but under the supervision of the pardons and paroles division.

(6) "Parole" means the discretionary and conditional release of an eligible inmate sentenced to the institutional division so that the inmate may serve the remainder of the inmate's sentence under the supervision of the pardons and paroles division.

(7) "Parole officer" means a person appointed by the director and assigned the duties of assessment of risks and needs, investigation, case management, and supervision of releasees to ensure that releasees are complying with the conditions of parole or mandatory supervision.

(8) "Parole commissioner" means a person employed by the board to perform the duties described by Section 508.0441.

(9) "Releasee" means a person released on parole or to mandatory supervision.

(10) "Presiding officer" means the presiding officer of the Board of Pardons and Paroles.

History of Govt §508.001: Codified by Acts 1997, 75th Leg., ch. 165, §12.01, eff. Sept. 1, 1997. Amended by Acts 1999, 76th Leg., ch. 62, §10.01, eff. Sept. 1, 1999; Acts 2003, 78th Leg., 3d C.S., ch. 3, §11.02, eff. Jan. 11, 2004. Source: CCP art. 42.18, §2

GOVT §508.002. CLEMENCY, COMMUTATION DISTINGUISHED

Neither parole nor mandatory supervision is a commutation of sentence or any other form of clemency.

History of Govt §508.002: Codified by Acts 1997, 75th Leg., ch. 165, §12.01, eff. Sept. 1, 1997. Source: CCP art. 42.18, §2.

GOVT §508.003. INAPPLICABLE TO JUVENILES & CERTAIN INMATES

(a) This chapter does not apply to an emergency absence under escort granted to an inmate by the institutional division under Section 501.006.

(b) Except as provided by Subsection (c), this chapter does not apply to release on parole from an institution for juveniles.

(c) The provisions of this chapter not in conflict with Section 508.156 apply to parole of a person from the Texas Youth Commission under that section.

History of Govt §508.003: Codified by Acts 1997, 75th Leg., ch. 165, §12.01, eff. Sept. 1, 1997. Source: CCP art. 42.18, §20(a), (b).

Sections 508.004-508.030 reserved for expansion

SUBCHAPTER B. [OMITTED BY EDITOR]

SUBCHAPTER C. REPRESENTATION OF INMATES

GOVT §508.081. DEFINITIONS

In this subchapter:

(1) "Compensation" has the meaning assigned by Section 305.002.

(2) "Inmate" includes:

(A) an administrative releasee;

(B) an inmate imprisoned in the institutional division; and

(C) a person confined in a transfer facility or county jail awaiting:

(i) transfer to the institutional division; or

(ii) a revocation hearing.

(3) "Represent" means to directly or indirectly contact in person or by telephone, facsimile transmission, or correspondence a member or employee of the board or an employee of the department on behalf of an inmate.

History of Govt §508.081: Codified by Acts 1997, 75th Leg., ch. 165, §12.01, eff. Sept. 1, 1997. Source: CCP art. 42.18, §11(M)(1)-(3).

GOVT §508.082. RULES

The board shall adopt rules relating to:

(1) the submission and presentation of information and arguments to the board, a parole panel, and the department for and in behalf of an inmate; and

(2) the time, place, and manner of contact between a person representing an inmate and:

(A) a member of the board or a parole commissioner;

(B) an employee of the board; or

(C) an employee of the department.

History of Govt §508.082: Codified by Acts 1997, 75th Leg., ch. 165, §12.01, eff. Sept. 1, 1997. Amended by Acts 1999, 76th Leg., ch. 62, §10.18, eff. Sept. 1, 1999; Acts 2003, 78th Leg., 3d C.S., ch. 3, §11.16, eff. Jan. 11, 2004. Source: CCP art. 42.18, §11(a)(1)-(2).

GOVT §508.083. ELIGIBILITY TO REPRESENT INMATES

(a) A person who represents an inmate for compensation must:

(1) be an attorney licensed in this state; and

(2) register with the division.

(b) A person serving as a member or employee of the board or the Texas Board of Criminal Justice may not, before the second anniversary of the date the person ceases to be a board member or employee:

(1) represent any person in a matter before the board or a parole panel; or

(2) receive compensation for services rendered on behalf of any person regarding a matter pending before the board or a parole panel.

(c) A person, other than a person subject to Subsection (b), who is employed by the department may not, before the second anniversary of the date the person terminates service with the department:

(1) represent an inmate in a matter before the board or a parole panel; or

(2) receive compensation for services rendered on behalf of any person regarding a matter pending before the board or a parole panel.

(d) Repealed by Acts 2003, 78th Leg., ch. 1007, §2, eff. Sept. 1, 2003.

History of Govt §508.083: Codified by Acts 1997, 75th Leg., ch. 165, §12.01, eff. Sept. 1, 1997. Amended by Acts 2003, 78th Leg., ch. 1007, 301, §§1, 2, eff. Sept. 1, 2003. Source: CCP art. 42.18, §§4A(b)-(d), 11(b).

GOVT §508.084. FEE AFFIDAVIT

(a) A person required to register under Section 508.083, before the person first contacts a member of the board, an employee of the board, or an employee of the department on behalf of an inmate, shall file a fee affidavit with the department in a form prescribed by the department for each inmate the person represents for compensation.

(b) The fee affidavit must be written and verified and contain a statement of:

(1) the registrant's full name and address;

(2) the registrant's normal business, business phone number, and business address;

(3) the full name of any former member or employee of the board or the Texas Board of Criminal Justice or any former employee of the department with whom the registrant:

(A) is associated;

(B) has a relationship as an employer or employee; or

(C) maintains a contractual relationship to provide services;

(4) the full name and institutional identification number of the inmate the registrant represents;

(5) the amount of compensation the registrant has received or expects to receive in exchange for the representation; and

(6) the name of the person providing the compensation.

(c) If a registrant receives compensation in excess of the amount reported on the fee affidavit, the registrant shall file with the department, not later than the fifth day after the date the registrant receives compensation in excess of the reported amount, a supplemental fee affidavit in a form prescribed by the department indicating the total amount of compensation received for representing the inmate.

(d) For each fee affidavit and supplemental fee affidavit received, the department shall:

(1) keep a copy of the affidavit in a central location; and

(2) not later than the third day after the date the affidavit is filed, place a copy of the affidavit in the inmate's file that is reviewed by a parole panel or the board.

History of Govt §508.084: Codified by Acts 1997, 75th Leg., ch. 165, §12.01, eff. Sept. 1, 1997. Source: CCP art. 42.18, §11(c)-(f).

GOVT §508.085. REPRESENTATION SUMMARY FORM

(a) A person required to register under Section 508.083 shall, for each calendar year in which the person represents an inmate, file a representation summary form with the division on a form prescribed by the division.

(b) The form must be filed not later than January 31 of the year succeeding the year for which the report is filed and must include a statement of:

(1) the registrant's full name and address;

(2) the registrant's normal business, business phone number, and business address;

(3) the full name of any former member or employee of the board or the Texas Board of Criminal Justice or any former employee of the department with whom the registrant:

(A) is associated;

(B) has a relationship as an employer or employee; or

(C) maintains a contractual relationship to provide services;

(4) the full name and institutional identification number of each inmate the registrant represented in the previous calendar year; and

(5) the amount of compensation the registrant has received for representing each inmate in the previous calendar year.

(c) A person who files a form under this section and for whom the information required for the form has changed shall, not later than the 10th day after the date the information changes, file a supplemental statement with the division indicating the change.

History of Govt §508.085: Codified by Acts 1997, 75th Leg., ch. 165, §12.01, eff. Sept. 1, 1997. Source: CCP art. 42.18, §11(g), (h).

GOVT §508.086. CRIMINAL PENALTIES

(a) A former member or employee of the board or the Texas Board of Criminal Justice or a former employee of the department commits an offense if the former member or employee violates Section 508.083(b), (c), or (d).

(b) A person who represents an inmate for compensation commits an offense if the person is not an attorney licensed in this state.

(c) A person who is required to file an affidavit under Section 508.084(a) or (c) or a form or statement under Section 508.085 commits an offense if the person fails to file the affidavit, form, or statement.

(d) An offense under Subsection (a) is a Class A misdemeanor. An offense under Subsection (b) or (c) is a Class C misdemeanor.

History of Govt §508.086: Codified by Acts 1997, 75th Leg., ch. 165, §12.01, eff. Sept. 1, 1997. Source: CCP art. 42.18, §11(j), (k).

Sections 508.087-508.110 reserved for expansion

SUBCHAPTER D. PARDONS & PAROLES DIVISION

GOVT §508.111. DIRECTOR

(a) The executive director shall hire the director of the division.

(b) The director is responsible for the administration of the division.

History of Govt §508.111: Codified by Acts 1997, 75th Leg., ch. 165, §12.01, eff. Sept. 1, 1997. Source: CCP art. 42.18, §6(b).

GOVT §508.112. DUTY OF DIVISION

The division is responsible for the investigation and supervision of all releasees.

History of Govt §508.112: Codified by Acts 1997, 75th Leg., ch. 165, §12.01, eff. Sept. 1, 1997. Source: CCP art. 42.18, §17(a).

GOVT §508.113. PAROLE OFFICERS, SUPERVISORS: QUALIFICATIONS

(a) This subsection and Subsection (b) apply only to a person employed as a parole officer or supervisor on or before September 1, 1990. A person may not be employed as a parole officer or supervisor, or be responsible for investigating or supervising a releasee, unless the person has:

(1) four years of successfully completed education in an accredited college or university;

(2) two years of full-time paid employment in responsible correctional work with adults or juveniles or in a related field; and

(3) any other qualifications that may be specified by the director.

(b) Additional experience in a category described by Subsection (a)(2) may be substituted year for year for the required college education, with a maximum substitution of two years.

(c) The director shall establish qualifications for parole officers and supervisors that are the same as qualifications for community supervision and corrections department officers imposed by Section 76.005. A person may not begin employment as a parole officer or supervisor after September 1, 1990, unless the person meets the qualifications established by the director.

(d) A person who is serving as a peace officer or as a prosecuting attorney may not act as a parole officer or be responsible for supervising a releasee.

History of Govt §508.113: Codified by Acts 1997, 75th Leg., ch. 165, §12.01, eff. Sept. 1, 1997. Source: CCP art. 42.18, §19(a), (c), (e).

ⓔ GOVT §508.1131. SALARY CAREER LADDER FOR PAROLE OFFICERS

(a) The executive director shall adopt a salary career ladder for parole officers. The salary career ladder must base a parole officer's salary on the officer's classification and years of service with the department.

(b) For purposes of the salary schedule, the department shall classify all parole officer positions as Parole Officer I, Parole Officer II, Parole Officer III, Parole Officer IV, or Parole Officer V.

(c) Under the salary career ladder adopted under Subsection (a), a parole officer to whom the schedule applies and who received an overall evaluation of at least satisfactory in the officer's most recent annual evaluation is entitled to an annual salary increase, during each of the officer's first 10 years of service in a designated parole officer classification as described by Subsection (b), equal to one-tenth of the difference between:

(1) the officer's current annual salary; and

(2) the minimum annual salary of a parole officer in the next highest classification.

History of Govt §508.1131: Acts 2007, 80th Leg., ch. 1308, §37, eff. June 15, 2007.

GOVT §508.114. PAROLE OFFICERS, SUPERVISORS: ADDITIONAL DUTIES

(a) The judge of a court having original jurisdiction of criminal actions may, with the approval of the director, designate a parole officer or supervisor as a community supervision and corrections department officer. The director must give prior written approval for the payment of a proportional part of the salary paid to the parole officer or supervisor in compensation for service as a community supervision and corrections department officer. The director shall periodically report to the governor and the legislature the proportional salary payments.

(b) A parole officer or supervisor, on request of the governor or on order of the director, shall be responsible for supervising an inmate placed on conditional pardon or granted an emergency absence under escort.

History of Govt §508.114: Codified by Acts 1997, 75th Leg., ch. 165, §12.01, eff. Sept. 1, 1997. Source: CCP art. 42.18, §19.

GOVT §508.1141. SPECIALIZED TRAINING: GANG MEMBERS

The department shall develop and provide specialized training for parole officers supervising releasees previously identified by the department as being members of prison gangs, criminal street gangs, or security threat groups.

History of Govt §508.1141: Acts 1999, 76th Leg., ch. 490, §1, eff. Sept. 1, 1999.

ⓔ GOVT §508.1142. PAROLE OFFICER MAXIMUM CASELOADS

(a) The department shall adopt a policy that establishes guidelines for a maximum caseload for each parole officer of:

(1) 60 active releasees, if the releasees are not in a specialized program described by Subdivisions (2)-(6);

(2) 35 active releasees, if the releasees are in the special needs offender program;

(3) 35 active releasees, if the releasees are in the therapeutic community substance abuse aftercare treatment program;

(4) 24 active releasees, if the releasees are in the sex offender program;

(5) 20 active releasees, if the releasees are electronically monitored; and

(6) 11 active releasees, if the releasees are in the super-intensive supervision program.

(b) If the department is unable to meet the maximum caseload guidelines, the department shall submit a report to the Legislative Budget Board, at the end of each fiscal year in which the department fails to meet the guidelines, stating the amount of money needed by the department to meet the guidelines.

History of Govt §508.1142: Acts 2007, 80th Leg., ch. 1421, §1, eff. June 15, 2007.

GOVT §508.115. NOTIFICATION OF RELEASE OF INMATE

(a) Not later than the 11th day before the date a parole panel orders the release on parole of an inmate or not later than the 11th day after the date the board recommends that the governor grant executive clemency, the division shall notify the sheriffs, each chief of police, the prosecuting attorneys, and the district judges in the county in which the inmate was convicted and the county to which the inmate is released that a parole panel is considering release on parole or the governor is considering clemency.

(b) In a case in which there was a change of venue, the division shall notify the sheriff, the prosecuting attorney, and the district judge in the county in which the prosecution was originated if, not later than the 30th day after the date the inmate was sentenced, those officials request in writing that the division give the officials notice under this section of a release of the inmate.

(c) Not later than the 10th day after the date a parole panel orders the transfer of an inmate to a halfway house under this chapter, the division shall give notice in accordance with Subsection (d) to:

(1) the sheriff of the county in which the inmate was convicted;

(2) the sheriff of the county in which the halfway house is located and each chief of police in the county; and

(3) the attorney who represents the state in the prosecution of felonies in the county in which the halfway house is located.

(d) The notice must state:

(1) the inmate's name;

(2) the county in which the inmate was convicted; and

(3) the offense for which the inmate was convicted.

History of Govt §508.115: Codified by Acts 1997, 75th Leg., ch. 165, §12.01, eff. Sept. 1, 1997. Amended by Acts 1999, 76th Leg., ch. 62, §10.19, eff. Sept. 1, 1999; Acts 2001, 77th Leg., ch. 856, §5, eff. Sept. 1, 2001. Source: CCP art. 42.18, §8(h).

GOVT §508.116. PAROLE INFORMATION PROGRAM

(a) The division shall develop and implement a comprehensive program to inform inmates, the inmates' families, and other interested parties about the parole process.

(b) The division shall update the program annually.

History of Govt §508.116: Codified by Acts 1997, 75th Leg., ch. 165, §12.01, eff. Sept. 1, 1997. Source: CCP art. 42.18, §8(o) (Acts 1993, 73rd Leg., ch. 988, §11.03).

GOVT §508.117. VICTIM NOTIFICATION

(a) Before a parole panel considers for release on parole an inmate who is serving a sentence for an offense in which a person was a victim, the division, using the name and address provided on the victim impact statement, shall make a reasonable effort to notify:

(1) the victim;

(2) if the victim has a guardian, the guardian; or

(3) if the victim is deceased, a close relative of the deceased victim.

(b) A victim, guardian of a victim, or close relative of a deceased victim who would have been entitled to notification of parole consideration by the division but failed to provide a victim impact statement containing the person's name and address may file with the division a written request for notification. After receiving the written request, the division shall grant to the person all privileges, including notification under this section, to which the person would have been entitled had the person submitted a completed victim impact statement.

(c) If the notice is sent to a guardian or close relative of a deceased victim, the notice must contain a

✦

request by the division that the guardian or relative inform other persons having an interest in the matter that the inmate is being considered for release on parole.

(d) The failure of the division to comply with notice requirements of this section is not a ground for revocation of parole.

(e) Before an inmate is released from the institutional division on parole or to mandatory supervision, the pardons and paroles division shall give notice of the release to a person entitled to notification of parole consideration for the inmate under Subsection (a) or (b).

(f) Except as necessary to comply with this section, the board or the department may not disclose to any person the name or address of a person entitled to notice under this section unless:

(1) the person approves the disclosure; or

(2) a court determines that there is good cause for disclosure and orders the board or the department to disclose the information.

(g) In this section:

(1) "Close relative of a deceased victim" means a person who was:

(A) the spouse of the victim at the time of the victim's death;

(B) a parent of the deceased victim;

(C) an adult brother, sister, or child of the deceased victim; or

Ⓔ **(D)** the nearest relative of the deceased victim by consanguinity, if the persons described by Paragraphs (A) through (C) are deceased or are incapacitated due to physical or mental illness or infirmity.

(2) "Guardian of a victim" means a person who is the legal guardian of a victim, whether or not the legal relationship between the guardian and the victim exists because of the age of the victim or the physical or mental incompetency of the victim.

Ⓔ *Subsection (2-a) below is effective for offenses committed on or after Sept. 1, 2007.*

(2-a) "Sexual assault" includes an offense under Section 21.02, Penal Code.

(3) "Victim" means a person who:

(A) is a victim of sexual assault, kidnapping, aggravated robbery, or felony stalking; or

(B) has suffered bodily injury or death as the result of the criminal conduct of another.

History of Govt §508.117: Codified by Acts 1997, 75th Leg., ch. 165, §12.01, eff. Sept. 1, 1997. Amended by Acts 2007, 80th Leg., ch. 593, §3.39 (eff. Sept. 1, 2007), ch. 826, §1 (eff. June 15, 2007), ch. 1308, §38 (eff. June 15, 2007). Source: CCP art. 42.18, §8(f).

GOVT §508.118. HALFWAY HOUSES

(a) The division, in conjunction with the institutional division, shall use halfway houses to divert from housing in regular units of the institutional division suitable low-risk inmates and other inmates who would benefit from a smoother transition from incarceration to supervised release.

(b) Before transferring an inmate to a halfway house, the division shall send to the director of the halfway house all information relating to the inmate that the division determines will aid the halfway house in helping the inmate make a transition from the institutional division to supervised release.

(c) The division is responsible for supervising an inmate:

(1) for whom a presumptive parole date has been established; and

(2) who is transferred into a preparole residence in a halfway house under Subchapter A, Chapter 499.

History of Govt §508.118: Codified by Acts 1997, 75th Leg., ch. 165, §12.01, eff. Sept. 1, 1997. Source: CCP art. 42.18, §8(i).

GOVT §508.119. COMMUNITY RESIDENTIAL FACILITIES

(a) The purpose of a community residential facility is to provide housing, supervision, counseling, personal, social, and work adjustment training, and other programs to:

(1) releasees who are required by a parole panel as a condition of release on parole or to mandatory supervision to serve a period in a community residential facility; and

(2) releasees whose parole or mandatory supervision has been continued or modified under Section 508.283 and on whom sanctions have been imposed under that section.

(b) The division may establish and operate, or contract for the operation of, community residential facilities.

(c) The division may contract with a public or private vendor for the financing, construction, operation, or management of a community residential facility using a lease-purchase or installment sale contract to provide or supplement housing, board, or supervision for releasees placed in a community residential facility. A releasee housed or supervised in a facility operated by a vendor under a contract is subject to the same laws as if the housing or supervision were provided directly by the division.

(d) Unless the division or a vendor proposing to operate a community residential facility provides notice of a following proposed action and a hearing on the issues in the same manner as required under Section 509.010, the division may not:

(1) establish or contract for a community residential facility;

(2) change the use of a community residential facility;

(3) significantly increase the capacity of a community residential facility; or

(4) increase the capacity of a community residential facility to more than 500 residents, regardless of whether the increase is significant.

(e) Subsection (d) applies to any residential facility that the division establishes or contracts for under:

(1) this chapter;

(2) Subchapter C, Chapter 497; or

(3) Subchapter A, Chapter 499.

(f) The Texas Board of Criminal Justice shall adopt rules necessary for the management of a community residential facility.

(g) The division may charge to a releasee housed in a community residential facility a reasonable fee for the cost of housing, board, and the part of the administrative costs of the facility that is properly allocable to the releasee. The fee may not exceed the actual costs to the division for services to that releasee. The division may not deny placement in a community residential facility to a releasee because the releasee is unable to pay the fee.

(h) A parole panel or a designated agent of the division may grant a limited release to a releasee placed in a community residential facility to maintain or seek employment or participation in an education or training course or to seek housing after release from the facility.

(i) The notice required by Subsection (d) must clearly state that the proposed action concerns a facility in which persons who have been released from prison on parole or to mandatory supervision are to be housed.

History of Govt §508.119: Codified by Acts 1997, 75th Leg., ch. 165, §12.01, eff. Sept. 1, 1997. Amended by Acts 1999, 76th Leg., ch. 62, §10.20, eff. Sept. 1, 1999. Source: CCP art. 42.18, §25.

Sections 508.120-508.140 reserved for expansion

SUBCHAPTER E. PAROLE & MANDATORY SUPERVISION; RELEASE PROCEDURES

GOVT §508.141. AUTHORITY TO CONSIDER & ORDER RELEASE ON PAROLE

(a) A parole panel may consider for release and release on parole an inmate who:

(1) has been sentenced to a term of imprisonment in the institutional division;

(2) is confined in a penal or correctional institution, including a jail in this state, a federal correctional institution, or a jail or a correctional institution in another state; and

(3) is eligible for release on parole.

(b) A parole is issued only on the order of a parole panel.

(c) Before releasing an inmate on parole, a parole panel may have the inmate appear before the panel and interview the inmate.

(d) A parole panel may release an inmate on parole during the parole month established for the inmate if the panel determines that the inmate's release will not increase the likelihood of harm to the public.

(e) A parole panel may release an inmate on parole only when:

(1) arrangements have been made for the inmate's employment or for the inmate's maintenance and care; and

(2) the parole panel believes that the inmate is able and willing to fulfill the obligations of a law-abiding citizen.

(f) A parole panel may order a parole only for the best interest of society and not as an award of clemency.

(g) The board shall adopt a policy establishing the date on which the board may reconsider for release an inmate who has previously been denied release. The policy must require the board to reconsider for release an inmate serving a sentence for an offense listed in Section 508.149(a) during a month designated by the parole panel that denied release. The designated month must begin after the first anniversary of the date of the denial and end before the fifth anniversary of the date of the denial. The policy must require the board to reconsider for release an inmate other than an inmate serving a sentence for an offense listed in Section 508.149(a) as soon as practicable after the first anniversary of the date of the denial.

History of Govt §508.141: Codified by Acts 1997, 75th Leg., ch. 165, §12.01, eff. Sept. 1, 1997. Amended by Acts 2003, 78th Leg., ch. 349, §1 (eff. June 18, 2003); 3d C.S., ch. 3, §11.17 (eff. Jan. 11, 2004). Source: CCP art. 42.18, §8(a), (f)(5).

GOVT §508.142. PERIOD OF PAROLE

(a) The institutional division shall provide the board with sentence time credit information for each inmate who is eligible for release on parole.

(b) Good conduct time credit is computed for an inmate as if the inmate were confined in the institutional division during the entire time the inmate was actually confined.

(c) The period of parole is computed by subtracting from the term for which the inmate was sentenced the calendar time served on the sentence.

History of Govt §508.142: Codified by Acts 1997, 75th Leg., ch. 165, §12.01, eff. Sept. 1, 1997. Source: CCP art. 42.18, §8(a).

GOVT §508.143. LEGAL CUSTODY OF RELEASEE

(a) A releasee while on parole is in the legal custody of the division.

(b) A releasee while on mandatory supervision is in the legal custody of the state.

History of Govt §508.143: Codified by Acts 1997, 75th Leg., ch. 165, §12.01, eff. Sept. 1, 1997. Source: CCP art. 42.18, §8(a), (c).

GOVT §508.144. PAROLE GUIDELINES

(a) The board shall:

(1) develop according to an acceptable research method the parole guidelines that are the basic criteria on which a parole decision is made;

(2) base the guidelines on the seriousness of the offense and the likelihood of a favorable parole outcome;

(3) ensure that the guidelines require consideration of an inmate's progress in any programs in which the inmate participated during the inmate's term of confinement; and

(4) implement the guidelines.

Subsection (b) below is effective for parole decisions made on or after June 15, 2007.

(b) If a board member or parole commissioner deviates from the parole guidelines in voting on a parole decision, the member or parole commissioner shall:

(1) produce a written statement describing in detail the specific circumstances regarding the departure from the guidelines;

(2) place a copy of the statement in the file of the inmate for whom the parole decision was made; and

(3) provide a copy of the statement to the inmate.

Subsection (b) below is effective for parole decisions made before June 15, 2007.

(b) If a board member or parole commissioner deviates from the parole guidelines in voting on a parole decision, the member or parole commissioner shall:

(1) produce a brief written statement describing the circumstances regarding the departure from the guidelines; and

(2) place a copy of the statement in the file of the inmate for whom the parole decision was made.

(c) The board shall keep a copy of a statement made under Subsection (b) in a central location.

(d) The board shall meet annually to review and discuss the parole guidelines developed under Subsection (a). The board may consult outside experts to assist with the review. The board must consider:

(1) how the parole guidelines serve the needs of parole decision-making;

(2) how well the parole guidelines reflect parole panel decisions; and

(3) how well parole guidelines predict successful parole outcomes.

(e) Based on the board's review of the parole guidelines under Subsection (d), the board may:

(1) update the guidelines by:

(A) including new risk factors; or

(B) changing the values of offense severity or risk factor scores; or

(2) modify the recommended parole approval rates under the guidelines, if parole approval rates differ significantly from the recommended rates.

(f) The board is not required to hold an open meeting to review the guidelines as required by Subsection (d), but any modifications or updates to the guidelines made by the board under Subsection (e) must occur in an open meeting.

History of Govt §508.144: Codified by Acts 1997, 75th Leg., ch. 165, §12.01, eff. Sept. 1, 1997; Acts 2003, 78th Leg., 3d C.S., ch. 3, §11.18, eff. Jan. 11, 2004. Amended by Acts 2007, 80th Leg., ch. 1308, §39, eff. June 15, 2007. Source: CCP art. 42.18, §8(f), (5).

E GOVT §508.1445. ANNUAL REPORT ON GUIDELINES REQUIRED

(a) The board annually shall submit a report to the Criminal Justice Legislative Oversight Committee, the lieutenant governor, the speaker of the house of representatives, and the presiding officers of the standing committees in the senate and house of representatives primarily responsible for criminal justice regarding the board's application of the parole guidelines adopted under Section 508.144.

(b) The report must include:

(1) a brief explanation of the parole guidelines, including how the board:

(A) defines the risk factors and offense severity levels; and

(B) determines the recommended parole approval rates for each guideline score;

(2) a comparison of the recommended approval rates under the parole guidelines to the actual approval rates for individual parole panel members, regional offices, and the state as a whole; and

(3) a description of instances in which the actual parole approval rates do not meet the recommended approval rates under the parole guidelines, an explanation of the variations, and a list of actions that the board has taken or will take to meet the guidelines.

History of Govt §508.1145: Acts 2007, 80th Leg., ch. 1308, §40, eff. June 15, 2007.

GOVT §508.145. ELIGIBILITY FOR RELEASE ON PAROLE; COMPUTATION OF PAROLE ELIGIBILITY DATE

A *Subsection (a) below is effective for offenses committed on or after Sept. 1, 2007.*

(a) An inmate under sentence of death, serving a sentence of life imprisonment without parole, serving a sentence for an offense under Section 21.02, Penal Code, or serving a sentence for an offense under Section 22.021, Penal Code, that is punishable under Subsection (f) of that section is not eligible for release on parole.

Subsection (a) below is effective for offenses in which any element of the offense was committed before Sept. 1, 2007.

(a) An inmate under sentence of death or serving a sentence of life imprisonment without parole is not eligible for release on parole.

(b) Repealed by Acts 2005, 79th Leg., ch. 787, §12, eff. Sept. 1, 2005.

(c) An inmate serving a sentence under Section 12.42(c)(2), Penal Code, is not eligible for release on parole until the actual calendar time the inmate has served, without consideration of good conduct time, equals 35 calendar years.

A *Subsection (d) below is effective for offenses committed on or after Sept. 1, 2007.*

(d) An inmate serving a sentence for an offense described by Section 3g(a)(1)(A), (C), (D), (E), (F), (G), (H), or (I), Article 42.12, Code of Criminal Procedure, or for an offense for which the judgment contains an affirmative finding under Section 3g(a)(2) of that article, is not eligible for release on parole until the inmate's actual calendar time served, without consideration of good conduct time, equals one-half of the sentence or 30 calendar years, whichever is less, but in no event is the inmate eligible for release on parole in less than two calendar years.

Subsection (d) below is effective for offenses in which any element of the offense was committed before Sept. 1, 2007.

(d) An inmate serving a sentence for an offense described by Section 3g(a)(1)(A), (C), (D), (E), (F), (G), or (H), Article 42.12, Code of Criminal Procedure, or for an offense for which the judgment contains an affirmative finding under Section 3g(a)(2) of that article, is not eligible for release on parole until the inmate's actual calendar time served, without consideration of good conduct time, equals one-half of the sentence or 30 calendar years, whichever is less, but in no event is the inmate eligible for release on parole in less than two calendar years.

(e) An inmate serving a sentence for which the punishment is increased under Section 481.134, Health and Safety Code, is not eligible for release on parole until the inmate's actual calendar time served, without consideration of good conduct time, equals five years or the term to which the inmate was sentenced, whichever is less.

GOVT §508.144

(f) Except as provided by Section 508.146, any other inmate is eligible for release on parole when the inmate's actual calendar time served plus good conduct time equals one-fourth of the sentence imposed or 15 years, whichever is less.

History of Govt §508.145: Codified by Acts 1997, 75th Leg., ch. 165, §12.01, eff. Sept. 1, 1997. Amended by Acts 1999, 76th Leg., ch. 62, §10.21, eff. Sept. 1, 1999; Acts 2005, 79th Leg., ch. 787, §§4, 12, eff. Sept. 1, 2005; Acts 2007, 80th Leg., ch. 405, §2 (eff. Sept. 1, 2007), ch. 593, §1.10 (eff. Sept. 1, 2007). Source: CCP art. 42.18, §8(b).

See *O'Connor's Crimes & Consequences* (2008-09), chart 12, "Parole Eligibility."

ANNOTATIONS

Cain v. Board of Pardons & Paroles, 104 S.W.3d 215, 218 (Tex.App.—Austin 2003, no pet.). "Section 508.145(f) ... provides that an inmate serving a single sentence generally is eligible for parole after accruing credit for one-quarter of his sentence. This does not mean that the inmate is automatically entitled to be released on parole; instead, he is entitled to a review to determine whether he will in fact be released. In other words, §508.145(f) does not mandate *when* an inmate is to be released on parole, it merely states the earliest date on which he *may* be released."

GOVT §508.146. MEDICALLY RECOMMENDED INTENSIVE SUPERVISION

🅐 **(a)** An inmate other than an inmate who is serving a sentence of death or life without parole may be released on medically recommended intensive supervision on a date designated by a parole panel described by Subsection (e), except that an inmate with an instant offense that is an offense described in Section 3g, Article 42.12, Code of Criminal Procedure, or an inmate who has a reportable conviction or adjudication under Chapter 62, Code of Criminal Procedure, may only be considered if a medical condition of terminal illness or long-term care has been diagnosed by a physician, if:

(1) the Texas Correctional Office on Offenders with Medical or Mental Impairments, in cooperation with the Correctional Managed Health Care Committee, identifies the inmate as being:

(A) elderly, physically disabled, mentally ill, terminally ill, or mentally retarded or having a condition requiring long-term care, if the inmate is an inmate with an instant offense that is described in Section 3g, Article 42.12, Code of Criminal Procedure; or

🅔 **(B)** in a persistent vegetative state or being a person with an organic brain syndrome with significant to total mobility impairment, if the inmate is an inmate who has a reportable conviction or adjudication under Chapter 62, Code of Criminal Procedure;

(2) the parole panel determines that, based on the inmate's condition and a medical evaluation, the inmate does not constitute a threat to public safety; and

(3) the Texas Correctional Office on Offenders with Medical or Mental Impairments, in cooperation with the pardons and paroles division, has prepared for the inmate a medically recommended intensive supervision plan that requires the inmate to submit to electronic monitoring, places the inmate on super-intensive supervision, or otherwise ensures appropriate supervision of the inmate.

(b) An inmate may be released on medically recommended intensive supervision only if the inmate's medically recommended intensive supervision plan under Subsection (a)(3) is approved by the Texas Correctional Office on Offenders with Medical or Mental Impairments.

(c) The parole panel shall require as a condition of release under Subsection (a) that the releasee remain under the care of a physician and in a medically suitable placement. At least once each calendar quarter, the Texas Correctional Office on Offenders with Medical or Mental Impairments shall report to the parole panel on the releasee's medical and placement status. On the basis of the report, the parole panel may modify conditions of release and impose any condition on the releasee that a panel could impose on a releasee released under Section 508.145, including a condition that the releasee reside in a halfway house or community residential facility.

(d) The Texas Correctional Office on Offenders with Medical or Mental Impairments and the Texas Department of Human Services shall jointly request proposals from public or private vendors to provide under contract services for inmates released on medically recommended intensive supervision. A request for proposals under this subsection may require that the services be provided in a medical care facility located in an urban area. For the purposes of this subsection, "urban area" means the area in this state within a metropolitan statistical area, according to the standards of the United States Bureau of the Census.

(e) Only parole panels composed of the presiding officer of the board and two members appointed to the panel by the presiding officer may make determinations regarding the release of inmates on medically recommended intensive supervision under Subsection (a) or of inmates released pending deportation. If the Texas Council on Offenders with Mental Impairments identifies an inmate as a candidate for release under the guidelines established by Subsection (a)(1), the council shall present to a parole panel described by this subsection relevant information concerning the inmate and the inmate's potential for release under this section.

(f) An inmate who is not a citizen of the United States, as defined by federal law, who is not under a sentence of death or life without parole, and who does not have a reportable conviction or adjudication under Chapter 62, Code of Criminal Procedure, or an instant offense described in Section 3g, Article 42.12, Code of Criminal Procedure, may be released to immigration authorities pending deportation on a date designated by a parole panel described by Subsection (e) if the parole panel determines that on release the inmate would be deported to another country and that the inmate does not constitute a threat to public safety in the other country or this country and is unlikely to reenter this country illegally.

History of Govt §508.146: Codified by Acts 1997, 75th Leg., ch. 165, §12.01, eff. Sept. 1, 1997. Amended by Acts 2001, 77th Leg., ch. 1435, §1, eff. Sept. 1, 2001; Acts 2003, 78th Leg., ch. 252, §1, (eff. Sept. 1, 2003), ch. 856, §21, (eff. Sept. 1, 2003); Acts 2005, 79th Leg., ch. 787, §5, eff. Sept. 1, 2005; Acts 2007, 80th Leg., ch. 1247, §1, eff. Sept. 1, 2007. Source: CCP art. 42.18, §8(m), (n).

GOVT §508.147. RELEASE TO MANDATORY SUPERVISION

(a) Except as provided by Section 508.149, a parole panel shall order the release of an inmate who is not on parole to mandatory supervision when the actual calendar time the inmate has served plus any accrued good conduct time equals the term to which the inmate was sentenced.

(b) An inmate released to mandatory supervision is considered to be released on parole.

(c) To the extent practicable, arrangements for the inmate's proper employment, maintenance, and care must be made before the inmate's release to mandatory supervision.

History of Govt §508.147: Codified by Acts 1997, 75th Leg., ch. 165, §12.01, eff. Sept. 1, 1997. Source: CCP art. 42.18, §8(c).

GOVT §508.148. PERIOD OF MANDATORY SUPERVISION

(a) The period of mandatory supervision is computed by subtracting from the term for which the inmate was sentenced the calendar time served on the sentence.

(b) The time served on mandatory supervision is computed as calendar time.

History of Govt §508.148: Codified by Acts 1997, 75th Leg., ch. 165, §12.01, eff. Sept. 1, 1997. Source: CCP art. 42.18, §8(c).

GOVT §508.149. INMATES INELIGIBLE FOR MANDATORY SUPERVISION

(a) An inmate may not be released to mandatory supervision if the inmate is serving a sentence for or has been previously convicted of:

(1) an offense for which the judgment contains an affirmative finding under Section 3g(a)(2), Article 42.12, Code of Criminal Procedure;

(2) a first degree felony or a second degree felony under Section 19.02, Penal Code;

(3) a capital felony under Section 19.03, Penal Code;

(4) a first degree felony or a second degree felony under Section 20.04, Penal Code;

 Subsections (5) & (6) below are effective for offenses committed on or after Sept. 1, 2007.

(5) an offense under Section 21.11, Penal Code;

(6) a felony under Section 22.011, Penal Code;

Subsections (5) & (6) below are effective for offenses in which any element of the offense was committed before Sept. 1, 2007.

(5) a second degree felony or a third degree felony under Section 21.11, Penal Code;

(6) a second degree felony under Section 22.011, Penal Code;

(7) a first degree felony or a second degree felony under Section 22.02, Penal Code;

(8) a first degree felony under Section 22.021, Penal Code;

(9) a first degree felony under Section 22.04, Penal Code;

(10) a first degree felony under Section 28.02, Penal Code;

(11) a second degree felony under Section 29.02, Penal Code;

(12) a first degree felony under Section 29.03, Penal Code;

(13) a first degree felony under Section 30.02, Penal Code;

GOVT §508.146

⸻ ★ ⸻

(14) a felony for which the punishment is increased under Section 481.134 or Section 481.140, Health and Safety Code;

Ⓔ *Subsections (15) & (16) below are effective for offenses committed on or after Sept. 1, 2007.*

(15) an offense under Section 43.25, Penal Code; or

(16) an offense under Section 21.02, Penal Code.

(b) An inmate may not be released to mandatory supervision if a parole panel determines that:

(1) the inmate's accrued good conduct time is not an accurate reflection of the inmate's potential for rehabilitation; and

(2) the inmate's release would endanger the public.

(c) A parole panel that makes a determination under Subsection (b) shall specify in writing the reasons for the determination.

(d) A determination under Subsection (b) is not subject to administrative or judicial review, except that the parole panel making the determination shall reconsider the inmate for release to mandatory supervision at least twice during the two years after the date of the determination.

History of Govt §508.149: Codified by Acts 1997, 75th Leg., ch. 165, §12.01, eff. Sept. 1, 1997. Amended by Acts 1999, 76th Leg., ch. 62, §10.22, eff. Sept. 1, 1999; Acts 2001, 77th Leg., ch. 786, §3, eff. June 14, 2001; Acts 2007, 80th Leg., ch. 593, §1.11, eff. Sept. 1, 2007. Source: CCP art. 42.18, §8(c), (c-1).

ANNOTATIONS

Ex parte Ervin, 187 S.W.3d 386, 389 (Tex.Crim.App. 2005). "We hold that §508.149(c) includes the predecessors to the enumerated offenses that currently make an inmate ineligible for mandatory supervision release. Inmates who have been convicted of a predecessor to one of the enumerated offenses are ineligible for mandatory supervision release." *See also Ex parte Byrd*, 162 S.W.3d 250, 252-53 (Tex.Crim.App.2005).

Ex parte Retzlaff, 135 S.W.3d 45, 49 (Tex.Crim. App.2004). "The two statutory findings [under §508.149(b)] that justify non-release are predictive judgments based upon discrete factual conclusions and subjective appraisals. [T]hey are highly contingent upon accurate, up-to-date information and explanation. *At 50:* [W]ritten notice that an inmate will be reviewed at some unspecified time in the future, coupled with a request that he submit relevant materials 'as soon as possible,' is constitutionally deficient notice. [¶] [A]n inmate is entitled to notice of the specific month and year in which he will be reviewed for release on mandatory supervision. We also hold that he must be given at least thirty days advance notice that he will be reviewed in the specified month so that he has a sufficient opportunity to submit materials on his behalf."

GOVT §508.150. CONSECUTIVE FELONY SENTENCES

(a) If an inmate is sentenced to consecutive felony sentences under Article 42.08, Code of Criminal Procedure, a parole panel shall designate during each sentence the date, if any, the inmate would have been eligible for release on parole if the inmate had been sentenced to serve a single sentence.

(b) For the purposes of Article 42.08, Code of Criminal Procedure, the judgment and sentence of an inmate sentenced for a felony, other than the last sentence in a series of consecutive sentences, cease to operate:

(1) when the actual calendar time served by the inmate equals the sentence imposed by the court; or

(2) on the date a parole panel designates as the date the inmate would have been eligible for release on parole if the inmate had been sentenced to serve a single sentence.

(c) A parole panel may not:

(1) consider consecutive sentences as a single sentence for purposes of parole; or

(2) release on parole an inmate sentenced to serve consecutive felony sentences before the date the inmate becomes eligible for release on parole from the last sentence imposed on the inmate.

(d) A parole panel may not use calendar time served and good conduct time accrued by an inmate that are used by the panel in determining when a judgment and sentence cease to operate:

(1) for the same purpose in determining that date in a subsequent sentence in the same series of consecutive sentences; or

(2) for determining the date an inmate becomes eligible for release on parole from the last sentence in a series of consecutive sentences.

History of Govt §508.150: Codified by Acts 1997, 75th Leg., ch. 165, §12.01, eff. Sept. 1, 1997. Source: CCP art. 42.18, §8(d).

ANNOTATIONS

Ex parte Cowan, 171 S.W.3d 890, 894 (Tex.Crim. App.2005). "[A] sentence ceases to operate when it is served out in full day-for-day or on the date a parole

---

★

---

panel designates as the date an inmate would have been eligible for release on parole if the inmate had been sentenced to serve a single sentence."

Cain v. Board of Pardons & Paroles, 104 S.W.3d 215, 218-19 (Tex.App.—Austin 2003, no pet.). "Only after the inmate has served or earned the right to parole on each of his sentences, including his final sentence, is he eligible for *actual release* on parole. [W]hen an inmate is serving a non-final consecutive sentence, he may be reviewed for parole consideration and, if the Board determines that he would have been a candidate for release had he been serving only one sentence, the Board should set the date on which he would have become eligible; if the Board finds he would not have been released even if he had been serving a single sentence, it may decline to determine an eligibility date and set the case for further review in the future."

GOVT §508.151. PRESUMPTIVE PAROLE DATE

(a) For the purpose of diverting inmates to halfway houses under Section 508.118, a parole panel, after reviewing all available pertinent information, may designate a presumptive parole date for an inmate who:

 Subsection (1) below is effective for offenses committed on or after Sept. 1, 2007.

(1) has never been convicted of an offense listed under Section 3g(a)(1), Article 42.12, Code of Criminal Procedure, or an offense under Section 21.02, Penal Code; and

Subsection (1) below is effective for offenses in which any element of the offense was committed before Sept. 1, 2007.

(1) has never been convicted of an offense listed under Section 3g(a)(1), Article 42.12, Code of Criminal Procedure; and

(2) has never had a conviction with a judgment that contains an affirmative finding under Section 3g(a)(2), Article 42.12, Code of Criminal Procedure.

(b) The presumptive parole date may not be a date that is earlier than the inmate's initial parole eligibility date computed under Section 508.145.

(c) A parole panel may rescind or postpone a previously established presumptive parole date on the basis of a report from an agent of the division responsible for supervision or an agent of the institutional division acting in the case.

(d) If an inmate transferred to preparole status has satisfactorily served the inmate's sentence in the halfway house to which the inmate is assigned from the date of transfer to the presumptive parole date, without rescission or postponement of the date, the parole panel shall order the inmate's release on parole and issue an appropriate certificate of release. The releasee is subject to the provisions of this chapter governing release on parole.

History of Govt §508.151: Codified by Acts 1997, 75th Leg., ch. 165, §12.01, eff. Sept. 1, 1997. Amended by Acts 2007, 80th Leg., ch. 593, §3.40, eff. Sept. 1, 2007. Source: CCP art. 42.18, §8(i).

GOVT §508.152. PROPOSED PROGRAM OF INSTITUTIONAL PROGRESS

(a) Not later than the 120th day after the date an inmate is admitted to the institutional division, the department shall obtain all pertinent information relating to the inmate, including:

(1) the court judgment;

(2) any sentencing report;

(3) the circumstances of the inmate's offense;

(4) the inmate's previous social history and criminal record;

(5) the inmate's physical and mental health record;

(6) a record of the inmate's conduct, employment history, and attitude in the institutional division; and

(7) any written comments or information provided by local trial officials or victims of the offense.

(b) The department shall:

(1) establish for the inmate a proposed program of measurable institutional progress; and

(2) submit the proposed program to the board at the time of the board's consideration of the inmate's case for release.

(c) The board shall conduct an initial review of an eligible inmate not later than the 180th day after the date of the inmate's admission to the institutional division.

(d) Before the inmate is approved for release on parole, the inmate must agree to participate in the programs and activities described by the proposed program of measurable institutional progress.

(e) The institutional division shall:

(1) work closely with the board to monitor the progress of the inmate in the institutional division; and

(2) report the progress to the board before the inmate's release.

(f) An attorney representing the state in the prosecution of an inmate serving a sentence for an offense described by Section 508.187(a) shall provide written comments to the department on the circumstances related to the commission of the offense and other information determined by the attorney to be relevant to any subsequent parole decisions regarding the inmate.

History of Govt §508.152: Codified by Acts 1997, 75th Leg., ch. 165, §12.01, eff. Sept. 1, 1997. Amended by Acts 2001, 77th Leg., ch. 978, §1, eff. Sept. 1, 2001. Source: CCP art. 42.18, §8(e).

GOVT §508.153. STATEMENTS OF VICTIM

(a) A parole panel considering for release on parole or mandatory supervision an inmate who is serving a sentence for an offense in which a person was a victim shall allow:

(1) the victim, a guardian of the victim, a close relative of the deceased victim, or a representative of the victim, the victim's guardian, or the victim's close relative to provide a written statement to the panel; and

(2) the victim, guardian of the victim, or close relative of the deceased victim to appear in person before the board members to present a statement of the person's views about:

(A) the offense;

(B) the inmate; and

(C) the effect of the offense on the victim.

(b) If more than one person is entitled to appear in person before the board members or parole commissioners, only the person chosen by all persons entitled to appear as the persons' sole representative may appear.

(c) The panel shall consider the statements and the information provided in a victim impact statement in determining whether to recommend an inmate for release on parole.

(d) This section does not limit the number of persons who may provide written statements for or against the release of the inmate on parole.

(e) In this section, "close relative of a deceased victim," "guardian of a victim," and "victim" have the meanings assigned by Section 508.117.

History of Govt §508.153: Codified by Acts 1997, 75th Leg., ch. 165, §12.01, eff. Sept. 1, 1997. Amended by Acts 2001, 77th Leg., ch. 856, §6, eff. Sept. 1, 2001; Acts 2003, 78th Leg., 3d C.S., ch. 3, §11.19, eff. Jan. 11, 2004. Source: CCP art. 42.18, §8(f)(1), (2).

GOVT §508.154. CONTRACT ON RELEASE

(a) An inmate to be released on parole shall be furnished a contract stating in clear and intelligible language the conditions and rules of parole.

(b) Acceptance, signing, and execution of the contract by the inmate to be paroled is a precondition to release on parole.

(c) An inmate released to mandatory supervision shall be furnished a written statement stating in clear and intelligible language the conditions and rules of mandatory supervision.

(d) A releasee while on parole or mandatory supervision must be amenable to the conditions of supervision ordered by a parole panel.

History of Govt §508.154: Codified by Acts 1997, 75th Leg., ch. 165, §12.01, eff. Sept. 1, 1997. Source: CCP art. 42.18, §8(g).

GOVT §508.155. COMPLETION OF PAROLE PERIOD

(a) To complete a parole period, a releasee must serve the entire period of parole.

(b) The time on parole is computed as calendar time.

(c) The division may allow a releasee to serve the remainder of the releasee's sentence without supervision and without being required to report if a parole supervisor at the regional level has approved the releasee's early release from supervision under Section 508.1555.

(d) The division may require a person released from supervision and reporting under Subsection (c) to resubmit to supervision and resume reporting at any time and for any reason.

History of Govt §508.155: Codified by Acts 1997, 75th Leg., ch. 165, §12.01, eff. Sept. 1, 1997. Amended by Acts 2007, 80th Leg., ch. 1308, §41, eff. June 15, 2007. Source: CCP art. 42.18, §15.

GOVT §508.1555. PROCEDURE FOR THE EARLY RELEASE FROM SUPERVISION OF CERTAIN RELEASEES

(a) A parole officer annually shall identify the releasees under the parole officer's supervision who are eligible for early release from supervision under Section 508.155(c). A releasee is eligible for early release if:

(1) the releasee has been under supervision for at least one-half of the time that remained on the releasee's sentence when the releasee was released from imprisonment;

(2) during the preceding two-year period, the releasee has not committed any violation of the rules or conditions of release;

(3) during the period of supervision the releasee's parole or release to mandatory supervision has not been revoked; and

(4) the division determines:

(A) that the releasee has made a good faith effort to comply with any restitution order imposed on the releasee by a court; and

(B) that allowing the releasee to serve the remainder of the releasee's sentence without supervision and reporting is in the best interest of society.

(b) After identifying any releasees who are eligible for early release under Subsection (a), the parole officer shall review the eligible releasees, including any releasees the parole officer has previously declined to recommend for early release, to determine if a recommendation for early release from supervision is appropriate. In conducting the review and determining recommendations, the parole officer shall consider whether the releasee:

(1) has a low risk of recidivism as determined by an assessment developed by the department; and

(2) has made a good faith effort to comply with the conditions of release.

(c) A parole officer shall forward to the parole supervisor at the regional level any recommendations for early release the parole officer makes under Subsection (b). If the parole supervisor approves the recommendation, the division shall allow a releasee to serve the remainder of the releasee's sentence without supervision and without being required to report as authorized by Section 508.155.

History of Govt §508.1555: Acts 2007, 80th Leg., ch. 1308, §42, eff. June 15, 2007.

GOVT §508.156. DETERMINATE SENTENCE PAROLE

A **(a)** Before the release of a person who is transferred under Section 61.081(f) or 61.084(g), Human Resources Code, to the division for release on parole, a parole panel shall review the person's records and may interview the person or any other person the panel considers necessary to determine the conditions of parole. The panel may impose any reasonable condition of parole on the person that the panel may impose on an adult inmate under this chapter.

(b) The panel shall furnish the person with a written statement clearly describing the conditions and rules of parole. The person must accept and sign the statement as a precondition to release on parole.

(c) While on parole, the person remains in the legal custody of the state and shall comply with the conditions of parole ordered by a panel under this section.

(d) The period of parole for a person released on parole under this section is the term for which the person was sentenced less calendar time served at the Texas Youth Commission and in a juvenile detention facility in connection with the conduct for which the person was adjudicated.

(e) If a parole panel revokes the person's parole, the panel may require the person to serve the remaining portion of the person's sentence in the institutional division. The remaining portion of the person's sentence is computed without credit for the time from the date of the person's release to the date of revocation. The panel may not recommit the person to the Texas Youth Commission.

(f) For purposes of this chapter, a person released from the Texas Youth Commission on parole under this section is considered to have been convicted of the offense for which the person has been adjudicated.

History of Govt §508.156: Codified by Acts 1997, 75th Leg., ch. 165, §12.01, eff. Sept. 1, 1997. Amended by Acts 2007, 80th Leg., ch. 263, §19, eff. June 8, 2007. Source: CCP art. 42.18, §29.

Sections 508.157-508.180 reserved for expansion

SUBCHAPTER F. MANDATORY CONDITIONS OF PAROLE OR MANDATORY SUPERVISION

GOVT §508.181. RESIDENCE DURING RELEASE

(a) Except as provided by Subsections (b) and (c), a parole panel shall require as a condition of parole or mandatory supervision that the releasee reside in the county in which:

(1) the releasee resided at the time of committing the offense for which the releasee was sentenced to the institutional division; or

(2) the releasee committed the offense for which the releasee was sentenced to the institutional division, if the releasee was not a resident of this state at the time of committing the offense.

(b) A parole panel may require a releasee to reside in a county other than the county required under Subsection (a) to:

(1) protect the life or safety of:

(A) a victim of the releasee's offense;

(B) the releasee;

(C) a witness in the case; or

(D) any other person; or

(2) increase the likelihood of the releasee's successful completion of parole or mandatory supervision, because of:

(A) written expressions of significant public concern in the county in which the releasee would otherwise be required to reside;

(B) the presence of family members or friends in the other county who have expressed a willingness to assist the releasee in successfully completing the conditions of the releasee's parole or mandatory supervision;

(C) the verified existence of a job offer in the other county; or

(D) the availability of a treatment program, educational program, or other social service program in the other county that is not available in the county in which the releasee is otherwise required to reside under Subsection (a).

(c) At any time after a releasee is released on parole or to mandatory supervision, a parole panel may modify the conditions of parole or mandatory supervision to require the releasee to reside in a county other than the county required by the original conditions. In making a decision under this subsection, a parole panel must consider the factors listed under Subsection (b).

(d) If a parole panel initially requires the releasee to reside in a county other than the county required under Subsection (a), the parole panel shall subsequently require the releasee to reside in the county described under Subsection (a) if the requirement that the releasee reside in the other county was based on:

(1) the verified existence of a job offer under Subsection (b)(2)(C) and the releasee is no longer employed or actively seeking employment; or

(2) the availability of a treatment program, educational program, or other social service program under Subsection (b)(2)(D) and the releasee:

(A) no longer regularly participates in the program as required by a condition of parole or mandatory supervision; or

(B) has successfully completed the program but has violated another condition of the releasee's parole or mandatory supervision.

(e) If a parole panel requires the releasee to reside in a county other than the county required under Subsection (a), the panel shall:

(1) state in writing the reason for the panel's decision; and

(2) place the statement in the releasee's permanent record.

(f) This section does not apply to a decision by a parole panel to require a releasee to serve the period of parole or mandatory supervision in another state.

(g) The division shall, on the first working day of each month, notify the sheriff of any county in which the total number of sex offenders under the supervision and control of the division residing in the county exceeds 10 percent of the total number of sex offenders in the state under the supervision and control of the division. If the total number of sex offenders under the supervision and control of the division residing in a county exceeds 22 percent of the total number of sex offenders in the state under the supervision and control of the division, a parole panel may require a sex offender to reside in that county only as required by Subsection (a) or for the reason stated in Subsection (b)(2)(B). In this subsection, "sex offender" means a person who is released on parole or to mandatory supervision after serving a sentence for an offense described by Section 508.187(a).

(h) If a parole panel requires a releasee to reside in a county other than the county required under Subsection (a), the division shall include the reason for residency exemption in the required notification to the sheriff of the county in which the defendant is to reside, the chief of police of the municipality in which the halfway house is located, and the attorney who represents the state in the prosecution of felonies in that county.

History of Govt §508.181: Codified by Acts 1997, 75th Leg., ch. 165, §12.01, eff. Sept. 1, 1997. Amended by Acts 1999, 76th Leg., ch. 62, §§10.23, 10.24, eff. Sept. 1, 1999. Source: CCP art. 42.18, §8A.

GOVT §508.182. PAROLE SUPERVISION FEE; ADMINISTRATIVE FEE

(a) A parole panel shall require as a condition of parole or mandatory supervision that a releasee pay to the division for each month during which the releasee is under parole supervision:

(1) a parole supervision fee of $10; and

(2) an administrative fee of $8.

GOVERNMENT CODE

CHAPTER 508. PAROLE & MANDATORY SUPERVISION
SUBCHAPTER F. MANDATORY CONDITIONS OF PAROLE OR MANDATORY SUPERVISION

(b) A fee under this section applies to an inmate released in another state who is required as a condition of the inmate's release to report to a parole officer or supervisor in this state for parole supervision.

(c) On the request of the releasee, a parole panel may allow the releasee to defer one or more payments under this section. The releasee remains responsible for payment of the fee and shall pay the amount of the deferred payment not later than the second anniversary of the date the payment becomes due.

(d) The Texas Board of Criminal Justice shall adopt rules relating to the method of payment required of the releasee.

(e) The division shall remit fees collected under this section to the comptroller. The comptroller shall deposit the fees collected under:

(1) Subsection (a)(1) in the general revenue fund; and

(2) Subsection (a)(2) in the compensation to victims of crime fund.

(f) In a parole or mandatory supervision revocation hearing under Section 508.281 at which it is alleged only that the releasee failed to make a payment under this section, it is an affirmative defense to revocation that the releasee is unable to pay the amount as ordered by a parole panel. The releasee must prove the affirmative defense by a preponderance of the evidence.

History of Govt §508.182: Codified by Acts 1997, 75th Leg., ch. 165, §12.01, eff. Sept. 1, 1997. Source: CCP art. 42.18, §8(j), (o) (Acts 1993, 73rd Leg., ch. 805, §8).

GOVT §508.183. EDUCATIONAL SKILL LEVEL

(a) A parole panel shall require as a condition of release on parole or release to mandatory supervision that an inmate demonstrate to the parole panel whether the inmate has an educational skill level that is equal to or greater than the average skill level of students who have completed the sixth grade in a public school in this state.

(b) If the parole panel determines that the inmate has not attained that skill level, the parole panel shall require as a condition of parole or mandatory supervision that the inmate as a releasee attain that level of educational skill, unless the parole panel determines that the inmate lacks the intellectual capacity or the learning ability to ever achieve that level of skill.

History of Govt §508.183: Codified by Acts 1997, 75th Leg., ch. 165, §12.01, eff. Sept. 1, 1997. Source: CCP art. 42.18, §8(k).

GOVT §508.184. CONTROLLED SUBSTANCE TESTING

(a) A parole panel shall require as a condition of parole or mandatory supervision that a releasee submit to testing for controlled substances on evidence that:

(1) a controlled substance is present in the releasee's body;

(2) the releasee has used a controlled substance; or

(3) the use of a controlled substance is related to the offense for which the releasee was convicted.

(b) The Texas Board of Criminal Justice by rule shall adopt procedures for the administration of a test required under this section.

History of Govt §508.184: Codified by Acts 1997, 75th Leg., ch. 165, §12.01, eff. Sept. 1, 1997. Source: CCP art. 42.18, §8(*l*).

GOVT §508.185. SUBSTANCE ABUSE TREATMENT

(a) A parole panel shall require as a condition of release on parole or release to mandatory supervision that an inmate who immediately before release is a participant in the program established under Section 501.0931 participate as a releasee in a drug or alcohol abuse continuum of care treatment program.

(b) The Texas Commission on Alcohol and Drug Abuse shall develop the continuum of care treatment program.

History of Govt §508.185: Codified by Acts 1997, 75th Leg., ch. 165, §12.01, eff. Sept. 1, 1997. Source: CCP art. 42.18, §8(g) (Acts 1993, 73rd Leg., ch. 398, §3.03).

GOVT §508.186. SEX OFFENDER REGISTRATION

A parole panel shall require as a condition of parole or mandatory supervision that a releasee required to register as a sex offender under Chapter 62, Code of Criminal Procedure:

(1) register under that chapter; and

(2) submit a blood sample or other specimen to the Department of Public Safety under Subchapter G, Chapter 411, for the purpose of creating a DNA record of the releasee, unless the releasee has already submitted the required specimen under other state law.

History of Govt §508.186: Codified by Acts 1997, 75th Leg., ch. 165, §12.01, eff. Sept. 1, 1997. Amended by Acts 1999, 76th Leg., ch. 62, §10.25, eff. Sept. 1, 1999; Acts 2001, 77th Leg., ch. 211, §16, eff. Sept. 1, 2001; Acts 2003, 78th Leg., ch. 1300, §9, eff. Sept. 1, 2003; Acts 2005, 79th Leg., ch. 1008, §1.06, eff. Sept. 1, 2005. Source: CCP art. 42.18, §8(r).

★

GOVT §508.187. CHILD SAFETY ZONE

(a) This section applies only to a releasee serving a sentence for an offense under:

(1) Section 43.25 or 43.26, Penal Code;

 Subsection (2) below is effective for offenses committed on or after Sept. 1, 2007.

(2) Section 21.02, 21.11, 22.011, 22.021, or 25.02, Penal Code;

Subsection (2) below is effective for offenses in which any element of the offense was committed before Sept. 1, 2007.

(2) Section 21.11, 22.011, 22.021, or 25.02, Penal Code;

(3) Section 20.04(a)(4), Penal Code, if the releasee committed the offense with the intent to violate or abuse the victim sexually; or

(4) Section 30.02, Penal Code, punishable under Subsection (d) of that section, if the releasee committed the offense with the intent to commit a felony listed in Subdivision (2) or (3).

(b) A parole panel shall establish a child safety zone applicable to a releasee if the panel determines that a child as defined by Section 22.011(c), Penal Code, was the victim of the offense, by requiring as a condition of parole or mandatory supervision that the releasee:

(1) not:

(A) supervise or participate in any program that includes as participants or recipients persons who are 17 years of age or younger and that regularly provides athletic, civic, or cultural activities; or

(B) go in, on, or within a distance specified by the panel of premises where children commonly gather, including a school, day-care facility, playground, public or private youth center, public swimming pool, or video arcade facility; and

(2) attend for a period of time determined necessary by the panel psychological counseling sessions for sex offenders with an individual or organization that provides sex offender treatment or counseling as specified by the parole officer supervising the releasee after release.

(c) A parole officer who under Subsection (b)(2) specifies a sex offender treatment provider to provide counseling to a releasee shall:

(1) contact the provider before the releasee is released;

(2) establish the date, time, and place of the first session between the releasee and the provider; and

(3) request the provider to immediately notify the officer if the releasee fails to attend the first session or any subsequent scheduled session.

(d) At any time after the imposition of a condition under Subsection (b)(1), the releasee may request the parole panel to modify the child safety zone applicable to the releasee because the zone as created by the panel:

(1) interferes with the releasee's ability to attend school or hold a job and consequently constitutes an undue hardship for the releasee; or

(2) is broader than necessary to protect the public, given the nature and circumstances of the offense.

(e) A parole officer supervising a releasee may permit the releasee to enter on an event-by-event basis into the child safety zone that the releasee is otherwise prohibited from entering if:

(1) the releasee has served at least two years of the period of supervision imposed on release;

(2) the releasee enters the zone as part of a program to reunite with the releasee's family;

(3) the releasee presents to the parole officer a written proposal specifying:

(A) where the releasee intends to go within the zone;

(B) why and with whom the releasee is going; and

(C) how the releasee intends to cope with any stressful situations that occur;

(4) the sex offender treatment provider treating the releasee agrees with the officer that the releasee should be allowed to attend the event; and

(5) the officer and the treatment provider agree on a chaperon to accompany the releasee, and the chaperon agrees to perform that duty.

(f) In this section, "playground," "premises," "school," "video arcade facility," and "youth center" have the meanings assigned by Section 481.134, Health and Safety Code.

History of Govt §508.187: Codified by Acts 1997, 75th Leg., ch. 165, §12.01, eff. Sept. 1, 1997. Amended by Acts 2001, 77th Leg., ch. 978, §2, eff. Sept. 1, 2001; Acts 2007, 80th Leg., ch. 593, §3.41, eff. Sept. 1, 2007. Source: CCP art. 42.18, §8(u).

GOVT §508.188. COMMUNITY SERVICE FOR CERTAIN RELEASEES

A parole panel shall require as a condition of parole or mandatory supervision that a releasee for whom the court has made an affirmative finding under Article 42.014, Code of Criminal Procedure, perform not less than 300 hours of community service at a project designated by the parole panel that primarily serves the person or group that was the target of the releasee.

History of Govt §508.188: Codified by Acts 1997, 75th Leg., ch. 165, §12.01, eff. Sept. 1, 1997. Source: CCP art. 42.18, §8(o) (Acts 1993, 73rd Leg., ch. 987, §6).

GOVT §508.189. PAROLE FEE FOR CERTAIN RELEASEES

 Subsection (a) below is effective for offenses committed on or after Sept. 1, 2007.

(a) A parole panel shall require as a condition of parole or mandatory supervision that a releasee convicted of an offense under Section 21.02, 21.08, 21.11, 22.011, 22.021, 25.02, 43.25, or 43.26, Penal Code, pay to the division a parole supervision fee of $5 each month during the period of parole supervision.

Subsection (a) below is effective for offenses in which any element of the offense was committed before Sept. 1, 2007.

(a) A parole panel shall require as a condition of parole or mandatory supervision that a releasee convicted of an offense under Section 21.08, 21.11, 22.011, 22.021, 25.02, 43.25, or 43.26, Penal Code, pay to the division a parole supervision fee of $5 each month during the period of parole supervision.

(b) The division shall send fees collected under this section to the comptroller. The comptroller shall deposit the fees in the general revenue fund to the credit of the sexual assault program fund established under Section 44.0061, Health and Safety Code.

History of Govt §508.189: Codified by Acts 1997, 75th Leg., ch. 165, §12.01, eff. Sept. 1, 1997. Amended by Acts 2007, 80th Leg., ch. 593, §3.42, eff. Sept. 1, 2007. Source: CCP art. 42.18, §8(p), (q).

GOVT §508.190. AVOIDING VICTIM OF STALKING OFFENSE

(a) A parole panel shall require as a condition of parole or mandatory supervision that a releasee serving a sentence for an offense under Section 42.072, Penal Code, not:

(1) communicate directly or indirectly with the victim;

(2) go to or near the residence, place of employment, or business of the victim; or

(3) go to or near a school, day-care facility, or similar facility where a dependent child of the victim is in attendance.

(b) If a parole panel requires the prohibition contained in Subsection (a)(2) or (3) as a condition of parole or mandatory supervision, the parole panel shall specifically describe the prohibited locations and the minimum distances, if any, that the releasee must maintain from the locations.

History of Govt §508.190: Acts 1999, 76th Leg., ch. 62, §10.26, eff. Sept. 1, 1999.

GOVT §508.191. NO CONTACT WITH VICTIM

(a) If a parole panel releases a defendant on parole or to mandatory supervision, the panel shall require as a condition of parole or mandatory supervision that the defendant not intentionally or knowingly communicate directly or indirectly with a victim of the offense or intentionally or knowingly go near a residence, school, place of employment, or business of a victim. At any time after the defendant is released on parole or to mandatory supervision, a victim of the offense may petition the panel for a modification of the conditions of the defendant's parole or mandatory supervision allowing the defendant contact with the victim subject to reasonable restrictions.

(b) Notwithstanding Subsection (a), a defendant may participate in victim-offender mediation authorized by Section 508.324 on the request of the victim or a guardian of the victim or a close relative of a deceased victim.

(c) In this section, "victim" has the meaning assigned by Article 56.01(3), Code of Criminal Procedure.

History of Govt §508.191: Acts 1999, 76th Leg., ch. 62, §10.27, eff. Sept. 1, 1999.

Sections 508.192-508.220 reserved for expansion

SUBCHAPTER G. DISCRETIONARY CONDITIONS OF PAROLE OR MANDATORY SUPERVISION

GOVT §508.221. CONDITIONS PERMITTED GENERALLY

A parole panel may impose as a condition of parole or mandatory supervision any condition that a court may impose on a defendant placed on community supervision under Article 42.12, Code of Criminal Procedure, including the condition that a releasee submit to testing for controlled substances or submit to electronic monitoring if the parole panel determines that without testing for controlled substances or participation in an electronic monitoring program the inmate would not be released on parole.

History of Govt §508.221: Codified by Acts 1997, 75th Leg., ch. 165, §12.01, eff. Sept. 1, 1997. Source: CCP art. 42.18, §8(g).

GOVT §508.222. PAYMENT OF CERTAIN DAMAGES

A parole panel may require as a condition of parole or mandatory supervision that a releasee make payments in satisfaction of damages for which the releasee is liable under Section 500.002.

History of Govt §508.222: Codified by Acts 1997, 75th Leg., ch. 165, §12.01, eff. Sept. 1, 1997. Source: CCP art. 42.18, §8(g).

GOVT §508.223. PSYCHOLOGICAL COUNSELING

A parole panel may require as a condition of parole or mandatory supervision that a releasee serving a sentence for an offense under Section 42.072, Penal Code, attend psychological counseling sessions of a type and for a duration as specified by the parole panel, if the parole panel determines in consultation with a local mental health services provider that appropriate mental health services are available through the Texas Department of Mental Health and Mental Retardation in accordance with Section 534.053, Health and Safety Code, or through another mental health services provider.

History of Govt §508.223: Codified by Acts 1997, 75th Leg., ch. 165, §12.01, eff. Sept. 1, 1997. Amended by Acts 1999, 76th Leg., ch. 62, §10.28, eff. Sept. 1, 1999. Source: CCP art. 42.18, §8(o) (Acts 1993, 73rd Leg., ch. 10, §5, ch. 657, §5).

GOVT §508.224. SUBSTANCE ABUSE COUNSELING

A parole panel may require as a condition of parole or mandatory supervision that the releasee attend counseling sessions for substance abusers or participate in substance abuse treatment services in a program or facility approved or licensed by the Texas Commission on Alcohol and Drug Abuse if:

(1) the releasee was sentenced for an offense involving a controlled substance; or

(2) the panel determines that the releasee's substance abuse was related to the commission of the offense.

History of Govt §508.224: Codified by Acts 1997, 75th Leg., ch. 165, §12.01, eff. Sept. 1, 1997. Source: CCP art. 42.18, §8(g) (Acts 1993, 73rd Leg., ch. 397, §1).

GOVT §508.225. CHILD SAFETY ZONE

(a) If the nature of the offense for which an inmate is serving a sentence warrants the establishment of a child safety zone, a parole panel may establish a child safety zone applicable to an inmate serving a sentence for an offense listed in Section 3g(a)(1), Article 42.12, Code of Criminal Procedure, or for which the judgment contains an affirmative finding under Section 3g(a)(2), Article 42.12, Code of Criminal Procedure, by requiring as a condition of parole or release to mandatory supervision that the inmate not:

(1) supervise or participate in any program that includes as participants or recipients persons who are 17 years of age or younger and that regularly provides athletic, civic, or cultural activities; or

(2) go in or on, or within a distance specified by the panel of, a premises where children commonly gather, including a school, day-care facility, playground, public or private youth center, public swimming pool, or video arcade facility.

(b) At any time after the imposition of a condition under Subsection (a), the inmate may request the parole panel to modify the child safety zone applicable to the inmate because the zone as created by the panel:

(1) interferes with the ability of the inmate to attend school or hold a job and consequently constitutes an undue hardship for the inmate; or

(2) is broader than is necessary to protect the public, given the nature and circumstances of the offense.

(c) This section does not apply to an inmate described by Section 508.187.

(d) In this section, "playground," "premises," "school," "video arcade facility," and "youth center" have the meanings assigned by Section 481.134, Health and Safety Code.

History of Govt §508.225: Acts 1999, 76th Leg., ch. 56, §2, eff. Sept. 1, 1999.

GOVT §508.226. ORCHIECTOMY AS CONDITION PROHIBITED

A parole panel may not require an inmate to undergo an orchiectomy as a condition of release on parole or to mandatory supervision.

History of Govt §508.226: Acts 1999, 76th Leg., ch. 62, §10.29, eff. Sept. 1, 1999. Renumbered from §508.225 by Acts 2001, 77th Leg., ch. 1420, §21.001(45), eff. Sept. 1, 2001.

Sections 508.227-508.250 reserved for expansion

SUBCHAPTER H. WARRANTS

GOVT §508.251. ISSUANCE OF WARRANT OR SUMMONS

(a) In a case of parole or mandatory supervision, the director or a designated agent of the director or, in another case, the board on order by the governor, may issue a warrant as provided by Section 508.252 for the return of:

(1) a releasee;

(2) an inmate released although not eligible for release;

(3) a resident released to a preparole or work program;

(4) an inmate released on emergency reprieve or on emergency absence under escort; or

(5) a person released on a conditional pardon.

(b) A warrant issued under Subsection (a) must require the return of the person to the institution from which the person was paroled or released.

(c) Instead of the issuance of a warrant under this section, the division may issue to the person a summons requiring the person to appear for a hearing under Section 508.281 unless the person is a releasee who is on intensive supervision or superintensive supervision, who is an absconder, or who is determined by the division to be a threat to public safety. The summons must state the time, date, place, and purpose of the hearing.

(d) A designated agent of the director acts independently from a parole officer and must receive specialized training as determined by the director.

History of Govt §508.251: Codified by Acts 1997, 75th Leg., ch. 165, §12.01, eff. Sept. 1, 1997. Amended by Acts 2003, 78th Leg., ch. 264, §1, eff. Sept. 1, 2003. Source: CCP art. 42.18, §13(a).

GOVT §508.252. GROUNDS FOR ISSUANCE OF WARRANT OR SUMMONS

A warrant or summons may be issued under Section 508.251 if:

(1) there is reason to believe that the person has been released although not eligible for release;

(2) the person has been arrested for an offense;

(3) there is a document that is self-authenticating as provided by Rule 902, Texas Rules of Evidence, stating that the person violated a rule or condition of release; or

(4) there is reliable evidence that the person has exhibited behavior during the person's release that indicates to a reasonable person that the person poses a danger to society that warrants the person's immediate return to custody.

History of Govt §508.252: Codified by Acts 1997, 75th Leg., ch. 165, §12.01, eff. Sept. 1, 1997. Amended by Acts 1999, 76th Leg., ch. 62, §10.30, eff. Sept. 1, 1999; Acts 2003, 78th Leg., ch. 264, §2, eff. Sept. 1, 2003. Source: CCP art. 42.18, §13(a).

GOVT §508.253. EFFECT ON SENTENCE AFTER ISSUANCE OF WARRANT

If it appears a releasee has violated a condition or provision of the releasee's parole or mandatory supervision, the date of the issuance of the warrant to the date of the releasee's arrest is not counted as a part of the time served under the releasee's sentence.

History of Govt §508.253: Codified by Acts 1997, 75th Leg., ch. 165, §12.01, eff. Sept. 1, 1997. Source: CCP art. 42.18, §13(b).

GOVT §508.254. DETENTION UNDER WARRANT

(a) A person who is the subject of a warrant may be held in custody pending a determination of all facts surrounding the alleged offense, violation of a rule or condition of release, or dangerous behavior.

(b) A warrant authorizes any officer named by the warrant to take custody of the person and detain the person until a parole panel orders the return of the person to the institution from which the person was released.

(c) Pending a hearing on a charge of parole violation, ineligible release, or violation of a condition of mandatory supervision, a person returned to custody shall remain confined.

History of Govt §508.254: Codified by Acts 1997, 75th Leg., ch. 165, §12.01, eff. Sept. 1, 1997. Source: CCP art. 42.18, §13(a).

GOVT §508.255. STATUS AS FUGITIVE FROM JUSTICE

(a) After the issuance of a warrant, a person for whose return a warrant was issued is a fugitive from justice.

(b) The law relating to the right of the state to extradite a person and return a fugitive from justice and Article 42.11, Code of Criminal Procedure, relating to the waiver of all legal requirements to obtain extradition of a fugitive from justice from another state to this state, are not impaired by this chapter and remain in full force and effect.

History of Govt §508.255: Codified by Acts 1997, 75th Leg., ch. 165, §12.01, eff. Sept. 1, 1997. Source: CCP art. 42.18, §13(b).

GOVT §508.256. WITHDRAWAL OF WARRANT

At any time before setting a revocation hearing date under Section 508.282, the division may withdraw a warrant and continue supervision of a releasee.

History of Govt §508.256: Codified by Acts 1997, 75th Leg., ch. 165, §12.01, eff. Sept. 1, 1997. Source: CCP art. 42.18, §17(c).

Sections 508.257-508.280 reserved for expansion

SUBCHAPTER I. HEARINGS & SANCTIONS

GOVT §508.281. HEARING

(a) A releasee, a person released although ineligible for release, or a person granted a conditional pardon is entitled to a hearing before a parole panel or a designated agent of the board under the rules adopted by the board and within a period that permits a parole panel, a designee of the board, or the department to dispose of the charges within the periods established by Sections 508.282(a) and (b) if the releasee or person:

(1) is accused of a violation of the releasee's parole or mandatory supervision or the person's conditional pardon, on information and complaint by a peace officer or parole officer; or

(2) is arrested after an ineligible release.

(b) If a parole panel or designated agent of the board determines that a releasee or person granted a conditional pardon has been convicted of a felony offense committed while an administrative releasee and has been sentenced to a term of confinement in a penal institution, the determination is considered to be a sufficient hearing to revoke the parole or mandatory supervision or recommend to the governor revocation of a conditional pardon without further hearing, except that the parole panel or designated agent shall conduct a hearing to consider mitigating circumstances if requested by the releasee or person granted a conditional pardon.

(c) If a hearing before a designated agent of the board is held under this section for a releasee who appears in compliance with a summons, the sheriff of the county in which the releasee is required to appear shall provide the designated agent with a place at the county jail to hold the hearing. Immediately on conclusion of a hearing in which the designated agent determines that a releasee has violated a condition of release, a warrant may be issued requiring the releasee to be held in the county jail pending:

(1) the action of a parole panel on any recommendations made by the designated agent; and

(2) if subsequently ordered by the parole panel, the return of the releasee to the institution from which the releasee was released.

History of Govt §508.281: Codified by Acts 1997, 75th Leg., ch. 165, §12.01, eff. Sept. 1, 1997. Amended by Acts 1999, 76th Leg., ch. 62, §10.31, eff. Sept. 1, 1999; Acts 2003, 78th Leg., ch. 246 §3 (eff. Sept. 1, 2003); 3d C.S., ch. 3, §11.20, eff. Jan. 11, 2004. Source: CCP art. 42.18, §14(a).

ANNOTATIONS

Ex parte Taylor, 957 S.W.2d 43, 45 (Tex.Crim.App. 1997). "Parole revocation proceedings are a much lesser protected arena and start with the premise, contrary to that in criminal trials, that the right to confrontation may be limited if good cause is shown. *At 46:* Good cause is shown to deny confrontation rights when (1) after looking at the witness and the State's interest, there is a need for the particular witness to testify out of the parolee's presence and (2) the procedures used adequately ensure the reliability of the evidence."

GOVT §508.2811. PRELIMINARY HEARING

A parole panel or a designee of the board shall provide within a reasonable time to an inmate or person described by Section 508.281(a) a preliminary hearing to determine whether probable cause or reasonable grounds exist to believe that the inmate or person has committed an act that would constitute a violation of a condition of release, unless the inmate or person:

(1) waives the preliminary hearing; or

(2) after release:

(A) has been charged only with an administrative violation of a condition of release; or

(B) has been adjudicated guilty of or has pleaded guilty or nolo contendere to an offense committed after release, other than an offense punishable by fine only involving the operation of a motor vehicle, regardless of whether the court has deferred disposition of the case, imposed a sentence in the case, or placed the inmate or person on community supervision.

History of Govt §508.2811: Acts 1999, 76th Leg., ch. 62, §10.32, eff. Sept. 1, 1999.

GOVT §508.282. DEADLINES

(a) Except as provided by Subsection (b), a parole panel, a designee of the board, or the department shall dispose of the charges against an inmate or person described by Section 508.281(a):

(1) before the 41st day after the date on which:

(A) a warrant issued as provided by Section 508.251 is executed, if the inmate or person is arrested only on a charge that the inmate or person has committed an administrative violation of a condition of release, and the inmate or person is not charged before the 41st day with the commission of an offense described by Section 508.2811(2)(B); or

(B) the sheriff having custody of an inmate or person alleged to have committed an offense after release notifies the department that:

(i) the inmate or person has discharged the sentence for the offense; or

(ii) the prosecution of the alleged offense has been dismissed by the attorney representing the state in the manner provided by Article 32.02, Code of Criminal Procedure; or

(2) within a reasonable time after the date on which the inmate or person is returned to the custody of the department, if:

(A) immediately before the return the inmate or person was in custody in another state or in a federal correctional system; or

(B) the inmate or person is transferred to the custody of the department under Section 508.284.

(b) A parole panel, a designee of the board, or the department is not required to dispose of the charges against an inmate or person within the period required by Subsection (a) if:

(1) the inmate or person is in custody in another state or a federal correctional institution;

(2) the parole panel or a designee of the board is not provided a place by the sheriff to hold the hearing, in which event the department, parole panel, or designee is not required to dispose of the charges against the inmate or person until the 30th day after the date on which the sheriff provides a place to hold the hearing; or

(3) the inmate or person is granted a continuance by a parole panel or a designee of the board in the inmate's or person's hearing under Section 508.281(a), but in no event may a parole panel, a designee of the

board, or the department dispose of the charges against the person later than the 15th day after the date on which the parole panel, designee, or department would otherwise be required to dispose of the charges under this section, unless the inmate or person is released from custody and a summons is issued under Section 508.251 requiring the inmate or person to appear for a hearing under Section 508.281.

(c) In Subsections (a), (b), and (f), charges against an inmate or person are disposed of when:

(1) the inmate's or person's conditional pardon, parole, or release to mandatory supervision is:

(A) revoked; or

(B) continued or modified and the inmate or person is released from the county jail;

(2) the warrant for the inmate or person issued under Section 508.251 is withdrawn; or

(3) the inmate or person is transferred to a facility described by Section 508.284 for further proceedings.

(d) A sheriff, not later than the 10th day before the date on which the sheriff intends to release from custody an inmate or person described by Section 508.281(a) or transfer the inmate or person to the custody of an entity other than the department, shall notify the department of the intended release or transfer.

(e) If a warrant for an inmate or person issued under Section 508.251 is withdrawn, a summons may be issued requiring the inmate or person to appear for a hearing under Section 508.281.

(f) A parole panel, a designee of the board, or the department shall dispose of the charges against a releasee for whom a warrant is issued under Section 508.281(c) not later than the 31st day after the date on which the warrant is issued.

History of Govt §508.282: Codified by Acts 1997, 75th Leg., ch. 165, §12.01, eff. Sept. 1, 1997. Amended by Acts 1999, 76th Leg., ch. 62, §10.33, eff. Sept. 1, 1999; Acts 2003, 78th Leg., ch. 264, §4, eff. Sept. 1, 2003; Acts 2003, 78th Leg., ch. 1194, §1, eff. Sept. 1, 2003. Source: CCP art. 42.18, §14(a), (c).

GOVT §508.283. SANCTIONS

(a) After a parole panel or designated agent of the board has held a hearing under Section 508.281, in any manner warranted by the evidence:

(1) the board may recommend to the governor to continue, revoke, or modify the conditional pardon; and

(2) a parole panel may continue, revoke, or modify the parole or mandatory supervision.

(b) If the parole, mandatory supervision, or conditional pardon of a person described by Section 508.149(a) is revoked, the person may be required to serve the remaining portion of the sentence on which the person was released. The remaining portion is computed without credit for the time from the date of the person's release to the date of revocation.

(c) If the parole, mandatory supervision, or conditional pardon of a person other than a person described by Section 508.149(a) is revoked, the person may be required to serve the remaining portion of the sentence on which the person was released. For a person who on the date of issuance of a warrant or summons initiating the revocation process is subject to a sentence the remaining portion of which is greater than the amount of time from the date of the person's release to the date of issuance of the warrant or summons, the remaining portion is to be served without credit for the time from the date of the person's release to the date of revocation. For a person who on the date of issuance of the warrant or summons is subject to a sentence the remaining portion of which is less than the amount of time from the date of the person's release to the date of issuance of the warrant or summons, the remaining portion is to be served without credit for an amount of time equal to the remaining portion of the sentence on the date of issuance of the warrant or citation.

(d) If a warrant is issued charging a violation of a release condition or a summons is issued for a hearing under Section 508.281, the sentence time credit may be suspended until a determination is made in the case. The suspended time credit may be reinstated if the parole, mandatory supervision, or conditional pardon is continued.

(e) If a person's parole or mandatory supervision is modified after it is established that the person violated conditions of release, the board may require the releasee to remain under custodial supervision in a county jail for a period of not less than 60 days or more than 180 days. A sheriff is required to accept an inmate sanctioned under this subsection only if the commissioners court of the county in which the sheriff serves and the Texas Department of Criminal Justice have entered into a contract providing for the housing of persons sanctioned under this subsection.

History of Govt §508.283: Codified by Acts 1997, 75th Leg., ch. 165, §12.01, eff. Sept. 1, 1997. Amended by Acts 1999, 76th Leg., ch. 62, §10.34, eff. Sept. 1, 1999; Acts 2001, 77th Leg., ch. 856, §7 (eff. Sept. 1, 2001), ch. 1197, §1 (eff. Sept. 1, 2001); Acts 2003, 78th Leg., ch. 1275, §2(62), eff. Sept. 1, 2003. Source: CCP art. 42.18, §14(a).

ANNOTATIONS

Ex parte Spann, 132 S.W.3d 390, 392-93 (Tex.Crim. App.2004). "[S]ection 508.283(c) says that certain parole violators will receive street-time credit if the 'remaining portion' of their sentence is less than the amount of time they have spent out on parole. [S]ection 508.283(c) … can be simplified into the following 2-pronged test for the purpose of determining whether Applicant receives street-time credit: 1. If, on the SUMMONS date, the 'remaining portion' of Applicant's sentence is greater than the time spent on parole, Applicant receives no street-time credit for the time spent on parole. 2. If, however, on the SUMMONS date, the 'remaining portion' of Applicant's sentence is less than the time spent on parole, Applicant receives street-time credit for the amount of time spent on parole. *At 392 n.2:* Street-time credit refers to calendar time a person receives towards his sentence for days spent on parole or mandatory supervision. *At 396:* 'Remaining portion' in §508.283(c) refers to that part of the sentence remaining at the RELEASE date, less time spent on parole."

GOVT §508.284. TRANSFER PENDING REVOCATION HEARING

The department, as provided by Section 508.282(c), may authorize a facility that is otherwise required to detain and house an inmate or person to transfer the inmate or person to a correctional facility operated by the department or under contract with the department if:

(1) the department determines that adequate space is available in the facility to which the inmate or person is to be transferred; and

(2) the facility to which the inmate or person is to be transferred is located not more than 150 miles from the facility from which the inmate or person is to be transferred.

History of Govt §508.284: Acts 1999, 76th Leg., ch. 62, §10.35, eff. Sept. 1, 1999.

Sections 508.285-508.310 reserved for expansion

SUBCHAPTER J. MISCELLANEOUS

GOVT §508.311. DUTY TO PROVIDE INFORMATION

On request of a member of the board or employee of the board or department, a public official of the state, including a judge, district attorney, county attorney, or

---

✦

---

police officer, who has information relating to an inmate eligible for parole shall send to the department in writing the information in the official's possession or under the official's control.

History of Govt §508.311: Codified by Acts 1997, 75th Leg., ch. 165, §12.01, eff. Sept. 1, 1997. Source: CCP art. 42.18, §9(a).

GOVT §508.312. INFORMATION ON RECIDIVISM OF RELEASEES

The Texas Board of Criminal Justice shall collect information on recidivism of releasees under the supervision of the division and shall use the information to evaluate operations.

History of Govt §508.312: Codified by Acts 1997, 75th Leg., ch. 165, §12.01, eff. Sept. 1, 1997. Source: CCP art. 42.18, §17(b).

GOVT §508.313. CONFIDENTIAL INFORMATION

(a) All information obtained and maintained, including a victim protest letter or other correspondence, a victim impact statement, a list of inmates eligible for release on parole, and an arrest record of an inmate, is confidential and privileged if the information relates to:

(1) an inmate of the institutional division subject to release on parole, release to mandatory supervision, or executive clemency;

(2) a releasee; or

(3) a person directly identified in any proposed plan of release for an inmate.

(b) Statistical and general information relating to the parole and mandatory supervision system, including the names of releasees and data recorded relating to parole and mandatory supervision services, is not confidential or privileged and must be made available for public inspection at any reasonable time.

(c) The department, on request or in the normal course of official business, shall provide information that is confidential and privileged under Subsection (a) to:

(1) the governor;

(2) a member of the board or a parole commissioner;

(3) the Criminal Justice Policy Council in performing duties of the council under Section 413.017; or

(4) an eligible entity requesting information for a law enforcement, prosecutorial, correctional, clemency, or treatment purpose.

(d) In this section, "eligible entity" means:

(1) a government agency, including the office of a prosecuting attorney;

(2) an organization with which the department contracts or an organization to which the department provides a grant; or

(3) an organization to which inmates are referred for services by the department.

(e) This section does not apply to information relating to a sex offender that is authorized for release under Chapter 62, Code of Criminal Procedure.

(f) This section does not apply to information that is subject to required public disclosure under Section 552.029.

History of Govt §508.313: Codified by Acts 1997, 75th Leg., ch. 165, §12.01, eff. Sept. 1, 1997. Amended by Acts 1999, 76th Leg., ch. 62, §10.36 (eff. Sept. 1, 1999), ch. 783, §3 (eff. Aug. 30, 1999); Acts 2001, 77th Leg., ch. 856, §8, eff. Sept. 1, 2001; Acts 2003, 78th Leg., ch. 6, §3 (eff. April 10, 2003); 3d C.S., ch. 3, §11.21, eff. Jan. 11, 2004. Source: CCP art. 42.18, §18.

GOVT §508.314. ACCESS TO INMATES

The department shall:

(1) grant to a member or employee of the board access at all reasonable times to any inmate;

(2) provide for the member or employee or a representative of the member or employee facilities for communicating with or observing an inmate; and

(3) furnish to the member or employee:

(A) any report the member or employee requires relating to the conduct or character of an inmate; or

(B) other facts a parole panel considers pertinent in determining whether an inmate will be released on parole.

History of Govt §508.314: Codified by Acts 1997, 75th Leg., ch. 165, §12.01, eff. Sept. 1, 1997. Source: CCP art. 42.18, §10.

GOVT §508.315. ELECTRONIC MONITORING PROGRAMS

(a) To establish and maintain an electronic monitoring program under this chapter, the department may:

(1) fund an electronic monitoring program in a parole office;

(2) develop standards for the operation of an electronic monitoring program in a parole office; and

(3) fund the purchase, lease, or maintenance of electronic monitoring equipment.

(b) In determining whether electronic monitoring equipment should be leased or purchased, the department shall consider the rate at which technological change makes electronic monitoring equipment obsolete.

History of Govt §508.315: Codified by Acts 1997, 75th Leg., ch. 165, §12.01, eff. Sept. 1, 1997. Source: CCP art. 42.18, §22.

GOVT §508.316. SPECIAL PROGRAMS

(a) The department may contract for services for releasees if funds are appropriated to the department for the services, including services for releasees who have a history of:

(1) mental impairment or mental retardation;

(2) substance abuse; or

(3) sexual offenses.

(b) The department shall seek funding for a contract under this section as a priority item.

History of Govt §508.316: Codified by Acts 1997, 75th Leg., ch. 165, §12.01, eff. Sept. 1, 1997. Source: CCP art. 42.18, §23.

GOVT §508.317. INTENSIVE SUPERVISION PROGRAM; SUPER-INTENSIVE SUPERVISION PROGRAM

(a) The department shall establish a program to provide intensive supervision to inmates released under Subchapter B, Chapter 499, and other inmates determined by a parole panel or the department to require intensive supervision.

(b) The Texas Board of Criminal Justice shall adopt rules that establish standards for determining which inmates require intensive supervision.

(c) The program must provide the level of supervision the department provides that is higher than any level of supervision other than the level of supervision described by Subsection (d).

(d) The department shall establish a program to provide super-intensive supervision to inmates released on parole or mandatory supervision and determined by parole panels to require super-intensive supervision. The program must provide the highest level of supervision provided by the department.

History of Govt §508.317: Codified by Acts 1997, 75th Leg., ch. 165, §12.01, eff. Sept. 1, 1997. Amended by Acts 1999, 76th Leg., ch. 62, §10.37, eff. Sept. 1, 1999. Source: CCP art. 42.18, §24.

GOVT §508.318. CONTINUING EDUCATION PROGRAM

(a) The Texas Board of Criminal Justice and the Texas Education Agency shall adopt a memorandum of understanding that establishes the respective responsibilities of the board and the agency in implementing a continuing education program to increase the literacy of releasees.

(b) The Texas Board of Criminal Justice and the agency shall coordinate the development of the memorandum of understanding and each by rule shall adopt the memorandum.

History of Govt §508.318: Codified by Acts 1997, 75th Leg., ch. 165, §12.01, eff. Sept. 1, 1997. Source: CCP art. 42.18, §21.

GOVT §508.319. PROGRAM TO ASSESS & ENHANCE EDUCATIONAL & VOCATIONAL SKILLS

(a) The department, with the assistance of public school districts, community and public junior colleges, public and private institutions of higher education, and other appropriate public and private entities, may establish a developmental program based on information obtained under Section 508.183 for an inmate to be released to the supervision of the division.

(b) The developmental program may provide the inmate with the educational and vocational training necessary to:

(1) meet the average skill level required under Section 508.183; and

(2) acquire employment while in the custody of the division to lessen the likelihood that the inmate will return to the institutional division.

(c) To decrease state expense for a program established under this section, the Texas Workforce Commission shall provide to the department and the other entities described by Subsection (a) information relating to obtaining financial assistance under applicable programs of public or private entities.

(d) The department may establish a developmental program similar to the program described by Subsection (a) for inmates released from the institutional division who will not be supervised by the department.

History of Govt §508.319: Codified by Acts 1997, 75th Leg., ch. 165, §12.01, eff. Sept. 1, 1997. Source: CCP art. 42.18, §27.

GOVT §508.320. CONTRACTS FOR LEASE OF FEDERAL FACILITIES

(a) The department may contract with the federal government for the lease of a military base or other federal facility that is not being used by the federal government.

(b) The department may use a facility leased under this section to house releasees in the custody of the division.

(c) The department may not enter into a contract under this section unless funds have been appropriated specifically to make payments on a contract under this section.

(d) The department shall attempt to enter into contracts that will provide the department with facilities located in various parts of the state.

History of Govt §508.320: Codified by Acts 1997, 75th Leg., ch. 165, §12.01, eff. Sept. 1, 1997. Source: CCP art. 42.18, §26.

GOVT §508.321. REPORTING, MANAGEMENT, & COLLECTION SERVICES

The department, with the approval of the Texas Board of Criminal Justice, may contract with a public or private vendor to provide telephone reporting, automated caseload management, or collection services for:

(1) fines, fees, restitution, or other costs ordered to be paid by a court; or

(2) fees collected by the division.

History of Govt §508.321: Codified by Acts 1997, 75th Leg., ch. 165, §12.01, eff. Sept. 1, 1997. Source: CCP art. 42.18, §28.

GOVT §508.322. RELEASEE RESTITUTION FUND

(a) The releasee restitution fund is a fund outside the treasury and consists of restitution payments made by releasees. Money in the fund may be used only to pay restitution as required by a condition of parole or mandatory supervision to victims of criminal offenses.

(b) The comptroller is the trustee of the releasee restitution fund as provided by Section 404.073.

(c) When a parole panel orders the payment of restitution from a releasee as provided by Article 42.037(h), Code of Criminal Procedure, the department shall:

(1) collect the payment for disbursement to the victim;

(2) deposit the payment in the releasee restitution fund; and

(3) transmit the payment to the victim as soon as practicable.

(d) If a victim who is entitled to restitution cannot be located, immediately after receiving a final payment in satisfaction of an order of restitution for the victim, the department shall attempt to notify the victim of that fact by certified mail, mailed to the last known address of the victim. If a victim then makes a claim for payment, the department promptly shall remit the payment to the victim.

(e) Money that remains unclaimed shall be transferred to the compensation to victims of crime auxiliary fund on the fifth anniversary of the date the money was deposited to the credit of the releasee restitution fund.

History of Govt §508.322: Codified by Acts 1997, 75th Leg., ch. 165, §12.01, eff. Sept. 1, 1997. Amended by Acts 2001, 77th Leg., ch. 856, §9, eff. Sept. 1, 2001. Source: CCP art. 42.18, §8B.

GOVT §508.323. AUDIT

The financial transactions of the division and the board are subject to audit by the state auditor in accordance with Chapter 321.

History of Govt §508.323: Codified by Acts 1997, 75th Leg., ch. 165, §12.01, eff. Sept. 1, 1997. Source: CCP art. 42.18, §4(h).

GOVT §508.324. VICTIM-OFFENDER MEDIATION

If the pardons and paroles division receives notice from the victim services office of the department that a victim of the defendant, or the victim's guardian or close relative, wishes to participate in victim-offender mediation with a person released on parole or to mandatory supervision, the division shall cooperate and assist the person if the person chooses to participate in the mediation program provided by the office. The pardons and paroles division may not require the defendant to participate and may not reward the person for participation by modifying conditions of release or the person's level of supervision or by granting any other benefit to the person.

History of Govt §508.324: Acts 1999, 76th Leg., ch. 62, §10.38, eff. Sept. 1, 1999.

TITLE 5. OPEN GOVERNMENT; ETHICS

SUBTITLE A. OPEN GOVERNMENT

CHAPTER 552. PUBLIC INFORMATION

SUBCHAPTER B. RIGHT OF ACCESS TO PUBLIC INFORMATION

GOVT §552.021. AVAILABILITY OF PUBLIC INFORMATION

Public information is available to the public at a minimum during the normal business hours of the governmental body.

History of Govt §552.021: Acts 1993, 73rd Leg., ch. 268, §1, eff. Sept. 1, 1993. Amended by Acts 1995, 74th Leg., ch. 1035, §2, eff. Sept. 1, 1995.

SUBCHAPTER C. INFORMATION EXCEPTED FROM REQUIRED DISCLOSURE

GOVT §552.108. EXCEPTION: CERTAIN LAW ENFORCEMENT, CORRECTIONS, & PROSECUTORIAL INFORMATION

(a) Information held by a law enforcement agency or prosecutor that deals with the detection, investigation, or prosecution of crime is excepted from the requirements of Section 552.021 if:

(1) release of the information would interfere with the detection, investigation, or prosecution of crime;

(2) it is information that deals with the detection, investigation, or prosecution of crime only in relation to an investigation that did not result in conviction or deferred adjudication;

(3) it is information relating to a threat against a peace officer or detention officer collected or disseminated under Section 411.048; or

(4) it is information that:

(A) is prepared by an attorney representing the state in anticipation of or in the course of preparing for criminal litigation; or

(B) reflects the mental impressions or legal reasoning of an attorney representing the state.

(b) An internal record or notation of a law enforcement agency or prosecutor that is maintained for internal use in matters relating to law enforcement or prosecution is excepted from the requirements of Section 552.021 if:

(1) release of the internal record or notation would interfere with law enforcement or prosecution;

(2) the internal record or notation relates to law enforcement only in relation to an investigation that did not result in conviction or deferred adjudication; or

(3) the internal record or notation:

(A) is prepared by an attorney representing the state in anticipation of or in the course of preparing for criminal litigation; or

(B) reflects the mental impressions or legal reasoning of an attorney representing the state.

(c) This section does not except from the requirements of Section 552.021 information that is basic information about an arrested person, an arrest, or a crime.

History of Govt §552.108: Acts 1993, 73rd Leg., ch. 268, §1, eff. Sept. 1, 1993. Amended by Acts 1995, 74th Leg., ch. 1035, §7, eff. Sept. 1, 1995; Acts 1997, 75th Leg., ch. 1231, §1, eff. Sept. 1, 1997; Acts 2001, 77th Leg., ch. 474, §6, eff. Sept. 1, 2001; Acts 2005, 79th Leg., ch. 557, §§3, 4, eff. Sept. 1, 2005.

SUBTITLE B. ETHICS

CHAPTER 573. DEGREES OF RELATIONSHIP; NEPOTISM PROHIBITIONS

SUBCHAPTER B. RELATIONSHIPS BY CONSANGUINITY OR BY AFFINITY

GOVT §573.021. METHOD OF COMPUTING DEGREE OF RELATIONSHIP

The degree of a relationship is computed by the civil law method.

History of Govt §573.021: Acts 1993, 73rd Leg., ch. 268, §1, eff. Sept. 1, 1993.

See also chart, "Relatives by Degrees," p. 261.

GOVT §573.022. DETERMINATION OF CONSANGUINITY

(a) Two individuals are related to each other by consanguinity if:

(1) one is a descendant of the other; or

(2) they share a common ancestor.

(b) An adopted child is considered to be a child of the adoptive parent for this purpose.

History of Govt §573.022: Acts 1993, 73rd Leg., ch. 268, §1, eff. Sept. 1, 1993.

See also chart, "Relatives by Degrees," p. 261.

GOVT §573.023. COMPUTATION OF DEGREE OF CONSANGUINITY

(a) The degree of relationship by consanguinity between an individual and the individual's descendant is determined by the number of generations that separate them. A parent and child are related in the first degree, a grandparent and grandchild in the second degree, a great-grandparent and great-grandchild in the third degree and so on.

(b) If an individual and the individual's relative are related by consanguinity, but neither is descended from the other, the degree of relationship is determined by adding:

(1) the number of generations between the individual and the nearest common ancestor of the individual and the individual's relative; and

(2) the number of generations between the relative and the nearest common ancestor.

(c) An individual's relatives within the third degree by consanguinity are the individual's:

(1) parent or child (relatives in the first degree);

(2) brother, sister, grandparent, or grandchild (relatives in the second degree); and

(3) great-grandparent, great-grandchild, aunt who is a sister of a parent of the individual, uncle who is a brother of a parent of the individual, nephew who is a child of a brother or sister of the individual, or niece who is a child of a brother or sister of the individual (relatives in the third degree).

History of Govt §573.023: Acts 1993, 73rd Leg., ch. 268, §1, eff. Sept. 1, 1993.

See also chart, "Relatives by Degrees," p. 261.

GOVT §573.024. DETERMINATION OF AFFINITY

(a) Two individuals are related to each other by affinity if:

(1) they are married to each other; or

(2) the spouse of one of the individuals is related by consanguinity to the other individual.

(b) The ending of a marriage by divorce or the death of a spouse ends relationships by affinity created by that marriage unless a child of that marriage is living, in which case the marriage is considered to continue as long as a child of that marriage lives.

(c) Subsection (b) applies to a member of the board of trustees of or an officer of a school district only until the youngest child of the marriage reaches the age of 21 years.

History of Govt §573.024: Acts 1993, 73rd Leg., ch. 268, §1, eff. Sept. 1, 1993. Amended by Acts 1995, 74th Leg., ch. 260, §32, eff. May 30, 1995.

See also chart, "Relatives by Degrees," p. 261.

GOVT §573.025. COMPUTATION OF DEGREE OF AFFINITY

(a) A husband and wife are related to each other in the first degree by affinity. For other relationships by affinity, the degree of relationship is the same as the degree of the underlying relationship by consanguinity. For example: if two individuals are related to each other in the second degree by consanguinity, the spouse of one of the individuals is related to the other individual in the second degree by affinity.

(b) An individual's relatives within the third degree by affinity are:

(1) anyone related by consanguinity to the individual's spouse in one of the ways named in Section 573.023(c); and

(2) the spouse of anyone related to the individual by consanguinity in one of the ways named in Section 573.023(c).

History of Govt §573.025: Acts 1993, 73rd Leg., ch. 268, §1, eff. Sept. 1, 1993.

See also chart, "Relatives by Degrees," p. 261.

SUBCHAPTER C. NEPOTISM PROHIBITIONS

GOVT §573.041. PROHIBITION APPLICABLE TO PUBLIC OFFICIAL

A public official may not appoint, confirm the appointment of, or vote for the appointment or confirmation of the appointment of an individual to a position that is to be directly or indirectly compensated from public funds or fees of office if:

(1) the individual is related to the public official within a degree described by Section 573.002; or

(2) the public official holds the appointment or confirmation authority as a member of a state or local board, the legislature, or a court and the individual is related to another member of that board, legislature, or court within a degree described by Section 573.002.

History of Govt §573.041: Acts 1993, 73rd Leg., ch. 268, §1, eff. Sept. 1, 1993.

GOVT §573.042. PROHIBITION APPLICABLE TO CANDIDATE

(a) A candidate may not take an affirmative action to influence the following individuals regarding the appointment, reappointment, confirmation of the appointment or reappointment, employment, reemployment, change in status, compensation, or dismissal of another individual related to the candidate within a degree described by Section 573.002:

(1) an employee of the office to which the candidate seeks election; or

(2) an employee or another officer of the governmental body to which the candidate seeks election, if the office the candidate seeks is one office of a multimember governmental body.

(b) The prohibition imposed by this section does not apply to a candidate's actions taken regarding a bona fide class or category of employees or prospective employees.

History of Govt §573.042: Acts 1993, 73rd Leg., ch. 268, §1, eff. Sept. 1, 1993.

GOVT §573.043. PROHIBITION APPLICABLE TO DISTRICT JUDGE

A district judge may not appoint as official stenographer of the judge's district an individual related to the judge or to the district attorney of the district within the third degree.

History of Govt §573.043: Acts 1993, 73rd Leg., ch. 268, §1, eff. Sept. 1, 1993.

GOVT §573.044. PROHIBITION APPLICABLE TO TRADING

A public official may not appoint, confirm the appointment of, or vote for the appointment or confirmation of the appointment of an individual to a position in which the individual's services are under the public official's direction or control and that is to be compensated directly or indirectly from public funds or fees of office if:

(1) the individual is related to another public official within a degree described by Section 573.002; and

(2) the appointment, confirmation of the appointment, or vote for appointment or confirmation of the appointment would be carried out in whole or partial consideration for the other public official appointing, confirming the appointment, or voting for the appointment or confirmation of the appointment of an individual who is related to the first public official within a degree described by Section 573.002.

History of Govt §573.044: Acts 1993, 73rd Leg., ch. 268, §1, eff. Sept. 1, 1993.

SUBCHAPTER D. EXCEPTIONS

GOVT §573.061. GENERAL EXCEPTIONS

Section 573.041 does not apply to:

(1) an appointment to the office of a notary public or to the confirmation of that appointment;

(2) an appointment of a page, secretary, attendant, or other employee by the legislature for attendance on any member of the legislature who, because of physical infirmities, is required to have a personal attendant;

(3) a confirmation of the appointment of an appointee appointed to a first term on a date when no individual related to the appointee within a degree described by Section 573.002 was a member of or a candidate for the legislature, or confirmation on reappointment of the appointee to any subsequent consecutive term;

(4) an appointment or employment of a bus driver by a school district if:

(A) the district is located wholly in a county with a population of less than 35,000; or

(B) the district is located in more than one county and the county in which the largest part of the district is located has a population of less than 35,000;

(5) an appointment or employment of a personal attendant by an officer of the state or a political subdivision of the state for attendance on the officer who, because of physical infirmities, is required to have a personal attendant;

(6) an appointment or employment of a substitute teacher by a school district; or

(7) an appointment or employment of a person by a municipality that has a population of less than 200.

History of Govt §573.061: Acts 1993, 73rd Leg., ch. 268, §1, eff. Sept. 1, 1993. Amended by Acts 1995, 74th Leg., ch. 76, §5.07(a) (eff. Sept. 1, 1995), ch. 260, §33 (eff. May 30, 1995); Acts 1997, 75th Leg., ch. 165, §31.01(48), eff. Sept. 1, 1997; Acts 1999, 76th Leg., ch. 1026, §1, eff. June 18, 1999.

GOVT §573.062. CONTINUOUS EMPLOYMENT

(a) A nepotism prohibition prescribed by Section 573.041 or by a municipal charter or ordinance does not apply to an appointment, confirmation of an appointment, or vote for an appointment or confirmation of an appointment of an individual to a position if:

(1) the individual is employed in the position immediately before the election or appointment of the public official to whom the individual is related in a prohibited degree; and

(2) that prior employment of the individual is continuous for at least:

(A) 30 days, if the public official is appointed;

(B) six months, if the public official is elected at an election other than the general election for state and county officers; or

(C) one year, if the public official is elected at the general election for state and county officers.

(b) If, under Subsection (a), an individual continues in a position, the public official to whom the individual is related in a prohibited degree may not participate in any deliberation or voting on the appointment, reappointment, confirmation of the appointment or reappointment, employment, reemployment, change in status, compensation, or dismissal of the individual if that action applies only to the individual and is not taken regarding a bona fide class or category of employees.

History of Govt §573.062: Acts 1993, 73rd Leg., ch. 268, §1, eff. Sept. 1, 1993.

TITLE 7. VEHICLES & TRAFFIC

SUBTITLE B. DRIVER'S LICENSES & PERSONAL IDENTIFICATION CARDS

CHAPTER 524. ADMINISTRATIVE SUSPENSION OF DRIVER'S LICENSE FOR FAILURE TO PASS TEST FOR INTOXICATION[1]

SUBCHAPTER A. GENERAL PROVISIONS

TRANSP §524.001. DEFINITIONS

In this chapter:

(1) "Adult" means an individual 21 years of age or older.

(2) "Alcohol concentration" has the meaning assigned by Section 49.01, Penal Code.

(3) "Alcohol-related or drug-related enforcement contact" means a driver's license suspension, disqualification, or prohibition order under the laws of this state or another state resulting from:

(A) a conviction of an offense prohibiting the operation of a motor vehicle while:

(i) intoxicated;

(ii) under the influence of alcohol; or

(iii) under the influence of a controlled substance;

(B) a refusal to submit to the taking of a breath or blood specimen following an arrest for an offense prohibiting the operation of a motor vehicle while:

(i) intoxicated;

(ii) under the influence of alcohol; or

(iii) under the influence of a controlled substance; or

(C) an analysis of a breath or blood specimen showing an alcohol concentration of a level specified by Section 49.01, Penal Code, following an arrest for an offense prohibiting the operation of a motor vehicle while intoxicated.

(4) "Arrest" includes the taking into custody of a child, as defined by Section 51.02, Family Code.

(5) "Conviction" includes an adjudication under Title 3, Family Code.

(6) "Criminal charge" includes a charge that may result in a proceeding under Title 3, Family Code.

(7) "Criminal prosecution" includes a proceeding under Title 3, Family Code.

(8) "Department" means the Department of Public Safety.

(9) "Director" means the public safety director of the department.

(10) "Driver's license" has the meaning assigned by Section 521.001. The term includes a commercial driver's license or a commercial driver learner's permit issued under Chapter 522.

(11) "Minor" means an individual under 21 years of age.

(12) "Public place" has the meaning assigned by Section 1.07(a), Penal Code.

1. **Editor's note:** For an overview of ALR hearing procedures, see Doug Murphy and Gary Trichter, *Administrative License Revocation Hearings: A DWI Specialist's Primer for the General Practitioner*, 65 Tex.B.J. 598 (2002).

History of Transp §524.001: Acts 1995, 74th Leg., ch. 165, §1, eff. Sept. 1, 1995. Amended by Acts 1997, 75th Leg., ch. 1013, §21, eff. Sept. 1, 1997; Acts 2001, 77th Leg., ch. 444, §1, eff. Sept. 1, 2001. Source: TRCS art. 6687b-1, §1.

ANNOTATIONS

Ex parte Tharp, 935 S.W.2d 157, 159 (Tex.Crim. App.1996). "The primary purpose of the administrative license suspension statute is not to deter the licensee or to seek retribution, but is to protect the public from the carnage on the public roads of Texas caused by drunk drivers. This primary purpose is clearly remedial, although it also has a secondary deterrent effect on motorists who realize that an arrest for driving while intoxicated may well result in suspension of their licenses."

Ex parte Campos, 936 S.W.2d 23, 23 (Tex. App.—San Antonio 1996, pet. ref'd). "[D] claims that the federal and state double jeopardy clauses bar his pending DWI prosecution. *At 25:* License suspension under chapter 524 of the Transportation Code is not 'punishment' for purposes of double jeopardy."

TRANSP §524.002. RULES; APPLICATION OF ADMINISTRATIVE PROCEDURE ACT

(a) The department and the State Office of Administrative Hearings shall adopt rules to administer this chapter.

(b) Chapter 2001, Government Code, applies to a proceeding under this chapter to the extent consistent with this chapter.

(c) The State Office of Administrative Hearings may adopt a rule that conflicts with Chapter 2001, Government Code, if a conflict is necessary to expedite the hearings process within the time required by this chapter and applicable federal funding guidelines.

History of Transp §524.002: Acts 1995, 74th Leg., ch. 165, §1, eff. Sept. 1, 1995. Source: TRCS art. 6687b-1, §§7(p), 9.

ANNOTATIONS

Texas DPS v. Watson, 945 S.W.2d 262, 264-65 (Tex.App.—Houston [1st Dist.] 1997, no writ). "[D] appealed the decision of the administrative law judge to the county court at law. In these circumstances, a county court at law may not substitute its judgment for that of the administrative law judge on the weight of the evidence, but it may reverse the case if the substantive rights of the appellant have been prejudiced because the administrative findings are: (1) in violation of a constitutional or statutory provision; (2) in excess of the agency's statutory authority; (3) made through unlawful procedure; (4) affected by other error of law; (5) not reasonably supported by substantial evidence considering the reliable and probative evidence in the record as a whole; or (6) arbitrary or capricious."

Texas DPS v. Lavender, 935 S.W.2d 925, 929-30 (Tex.App.—Waco 1996, writ denied). "Without the record from the agency hearing, we are unable to find that the administrative order is not supported by substantial evidence.... [D] argues that the rules promulgated by the State Office of Administrative Hearings do not require that the agency record be admitted into evidence in an appeal from the administrative hearing. However, the rules cover the methodology for taking an appeal from the administrative hearing to the trial court; they do not control the procedures after the court has acquired jurisdiction over the appeal."

Sections 524.003-524.010 reserved for expansion

SUBCHAPTER B. SUSPENSION DETERMINATION & NOTICE

TRANSP §524.011. OFFICER'S DUTIES FOR DRIVER'S LICENSE SUSPENSION

(a) An officer arresting a person shall comply with Subsection (b) if:

(1) the person is arrested for an offense under Section 49.04, Penal Code, or an offense under Section 49.07 or 49.08 of that code involving the operation of a motor vehicle, submits to the taking of a specimen of breath or blood and an analysis of the specimen shows the person had an alcohol concentration of a level specified by Section 49.01(2)(B), Penal Code; or

(2) the person is a minor arrested for an offense under Section 106.041, Alcoholic Beverage Code, or Section 49.04, Penal Code, or an offense under Section 49.07 or 49.08, Penal Code, involving the operation of a motor vehicle and:

(A) the minor is not requested to submit to the taking of a specimen; or

(B) the minor submits to the taking of a specimen and an analysis of the specimen shows that the minor had an alcohol concentration of greater than .00 but less than the level specified by Section 49.01(2)(B), Penal Code.

(b) A peace officer shall:

(1) serve or, if a specimen is taken and the analysis of the specimen is not returned to the arresting officer before the person is admitted to bail, released from custody, delivered as provided by Title 3, Family Code, or committed to jail, attempt to serve notice of driver's license suspension by delivering the notice to the arrested person;

(2) take possession of any driver's license issued by this state and held by the person arrested;

(3) issue a temporary driving permit to the person unless department records show or the officer otherwise determines that the person does not hold a driver's license to operate a motor vehicle in this state; and

(4) send to the department not later than the fifth business day after the date of the arrest:

(A) a copy of the driver's license suspension notice;

(B) any driver's license taken by the officer under this subsection;

(C) a copy of any temporary driving permit issued under this subsection; and

(D) a sworn report of information relevant to the arrest.

(c) The report required under Subsection (b)(4)(D) must:

(1) identify the arrested person;

(2) state the arresting officer's grounds for believing the person committed the offense;

(3) give the analysis of the specimen if any; and

(4) include a copy of the criminal complaint filed in the case, if any.

(d) A peace officer shall make the report on a form approved by the department and in the manner specified by the department.

(e) The department shall develop forms for the notice of driver's license suspension and temporary driving permits to be used by all state and local law enforcement agencies.

(f) A temporary driving permit issued under this section expires on the 41st day after the date of issuance. If the person was driving a commercial motor vehicle, as defined by Section 522.003, a temporary driving permit that authorizes the person to drive a commercial motor vehicle is not effective until 24 hours after the time of arrest.

History of Transp §524.011: Acts 1995, 74th Leg., ch. 165, §1, eff. Sept. 1, 1995. Amended by Acts 1997, 75th Leg., ch. 609, §1 (eff. Sept. 1, 1997), ch. 1013, §22 (eff. Sept. 1, 1997); Acts 2001, 77th Leg., ch. 444, §2, eff. Sept. 1, 2001; Acts 2005, 79th Leg., ch. 728, §20.0045, eff. Sept. 1, 2005. Source: TRCS art. 6687b-1, §§2, 3.

ANNOTATIONS

Todd v. State, 956 S.W.2d 777, 778 (Tex.App.—Waco 1997, pet. ref'd). "The DPS has the authority to suspend driver's licenses.... [Transp. Code ch. 524] allows the suspension of a driver's license when a person arrested for [DWI] gives a breath or blood sample which shows an alcohol concentration of 0.10 or more [now 0.08 or more]. If the driver requests a hearing after notice of a suspension, an ALJ must find by a preponderance of the evidence that (1) the person was operating a motor vehicle with an alcohol concentration of 0.10 or more [now 0.08 or more], and (2) reasonable suspicion to stop or probable cause to arrest the person existed. [¶] If the ALJ fails to find a required issue ... the DPS must reinstate the person's driver's license."

Dowling v. State, 926 S.W.2d 752, 754 (Tex.App.—Amarillo 1996, pet. ref'd). "At the time of [D's] arrest, the arresting officer requested and received from him a specimen of his breath. Analysis revealed an alcohol concentration of at least .10. This obligated the officer to notify [D] that his driver's license would be suspended in accordance with [Transp. Code] §524.011."

Ex parte Ledbetter, 925 S.W.2d 283, 284 (Tex. App.—Corpus Christi 1996, no pet.). "[D] asserts that she had already been punished for her offense by having her driver's license suspended through an administrative license revocation.... *At 286:* [D's] license was temporarily suspended for sixty days. We cannot say that this sanction is overwhelmingly disproportionate

to the State's primary remedial purpose. Because she does not claim other punitive effects, we conclude that ... ALR is not punishment for double jeopardy purposes."

Ex parte Arnold, 916 S.W.2d 640, 640 (Tex.App.—Austin 1996, pet. ref'd). "[D] was arrested for the offense of driving while intoxicated (DWI) after having failed sobriety tests. A breathalyzer test showed that [D] had an alcohol concentration of .108. The arresting officer gave [D] written notice that his driver's license would be suspended pursuant to Texas law. ... [T]he Texas DPS notified [D] that his driver's license would be suspended for sixty days. [D] did not exercise his statutory right to appeal the suspension to the State Office of Administrative Hearings."

TRANSP §524.012. DEPARTMENT'S DETERMINATION FOR DRIVER'S LICENSE SUSPENSION

(a) On receipt of a report under Section 524.011, if the officer did not serve a notice of suspension of driver's license at the time the results of the analysis of a breath or blood specimen were obtained, the department shall determine from the information in the report whether to suspend the person's driver's license.

(b) The department shall suspend the person's driver's license if the department determines that:

(1) the person had an alcohol concentration of a level specified by Section 49.01(2)(B), Penal Code, while operating a motor vehicle in a public place; or

(2) the person is a minor and had any detectable amount of alcohol in the minor's system while operating a motor vehicle in a public place.

(c) The department may not suspend a person's driver's license if:

(1) the person is an adult and the analysis of the person's breath or blood specimen determined that the person had an alcohol concentration of a level below that specified by Section 49.01(2)(B), Penal Code, at the time the specimen was taken; or

(2) the person is a minor and the department does not determine that the minor had any detectable amount of alcohol in the minor's system when the minor was arrested.

(d) A determination under this section is final unless a hearing is requested under Section 524.031.

(e) A determination under this section:

(1) is a civil matter;

(2) is independent of and is not an estoppel to any matter in issue in an adjudication of a criminal charge arising from the occurrence that is the basis for the suspension; and

(3) does not preclude litigation of the same or similar facts in a criminal prosecution.

History of Transp §524.012: Acts 1995, 74th Leg., ch. 165, §1, eff. Sept. 1, 1995. Amended by Acts 1997, 75th Leg., ch. 165, §30.102 (eff. Sept. 1, 1997), ch. 1013, §23 (eff. Sept. 1, 1997). Source: TRCS art. 6687b-1, §§4(a), 5.

Author's note: It is unclear whether the Legislature's apparent attempt to preclude application of the doctrine of collateral estoppel to criminal prosecutions and cases where DPS has been unsuccessful in its attempt to suspend a driver's license arising from the same operative events can withstand constitutional scrutiny. In *State v. Aguilar*, 947 S.W.2d 257 (Tex.Crim.App.1997), the Court held *on the facts presented* that the doctrine of collateral estoppel did not bar the prosecution of the defendant for DWI after a finding had been made at an administrative hearing where the State did not establish probable cause to stop him. Of particular significance was the fact that the state was not represented by counsel at the administrative hearing. The Court reasoned that the evidence in the record did not establish that the parties had had an opportunity to fairly and thoroughly litigate the probable-cause fact issue below. In addition, the defendant failed to establish that the issues presented in the two proceedings were identical. *See also Reynolds v. State*, 4 S.W.3d 13 (Tex.Crim.App. 1999).

See also *O'Connor's Crimes & Consequences* (2008-09), chart 11-A, "ALR Suspensions (21 Years of Age or Older)," 11-B, "ALR Suspensions (Under 21 Years of Age)."

ANNOTATIONS

Ex parte Pipkin, 935 S.W.2d 213, 216 (Tex.App.— Amarillo 1996, pet. ref'd). "[T]he attempt to administratively suspend [D's] driver's license was a civil matter. [T]he sanction that would have been levied had the State succeeded did, and does, not constitute punishment. Thus, there was no former proceeding 'essentially criminal' in nature upon which [D] could base his claim of estoppel."

TRANSP §524.013. NOTICE OF DEPARTMENT'S DETERMINATION

(a) If the department suspends a person's driver's license, the department shall send a notice of suspension by first class mail to the person's address:

(1) in the records of the department; or

(2) in the peace officer's report if it is different from the address in the department's records.

(b) Notice is considered received on the fifth day after the date the notice is mailed.

(c) If the department determines not to suspend a person's driver's license, the department shall notify the person of that determination and shall rescind any notice of driver's license suspension served on the person.

History of Transp §524.013: Acts 1995, 74th Leg., ch. 165, §1, eff. Sept. 1, 1995. Amended by Acts 1999, 76th Leg., ch. 1409, §4, eff. Sept. 1, 1999. Source: TRCS art. 6687b-1, §4.

TRANSP §524.014. NOTICE OF SUSPENSION

A notice of suspension under Section 524.013 must state:

(1) the reason and statutory grounds for the suspension;

(2) the effective date of the suspension;

(3) the right of the person to a hearing;

(4) how to request a hearing; and

(5) the period in which the person must request a hearing.

History of Transp §524.014: Acts 1995, 74th Leg., ch. 165, §1, eff. Sept. 1, 1995. Source: TRCS art. 6687b-1, §4(c).

TRANSP §524.015. EFFECT OF DISPOSITION OF CRIMINAL CHARGE ON DRIVER'S LICENSE SUSPENSION

(a) Except as provided by Subsection (b), the disposition of a criminal charge does not affect a driver's license suspension under this chapter and does not bar any matter in issue in a driver's license suspension proceeding under this chapter.

(b) A suspension may not be imposed under this chapter on a person who is acquitted of a criminal charge under Section 49.04, 49.07, or 49.08, Penal Code, or Section 106.041, Alcoholic Beverage Code, arising from the occurrence that was the basis for the suspension. If a suspension was imposed before the acquittal, the department shall rescind the suspension and shall remove any reference to the suspension from the person's computerized driving record.

History of Transp §524.015: Acts 1995, 74th Leg., ch. 165, §1, eff. Sept. 1, 1995. Amended by Acts 1997, 75th Leg., ch. 1013, §24, eff. Sept. 1, 1997. Source: TRCS art. 6687b-1, §5(d).

ANNOTATIONS

Ex parte Pipkin, 935 S.W.2d 213, 216 (Tex.App.— Amarillo 1996, pet. ref'd). "[T]he administrative proceeding contemplated by [Transp. Code] §524.001, *et seq.* is not punitive. Rather, it is remedial in nature and does nothing more than limit one's enjoyment of a mere privilege, as opposed to a right. That is, it exists to protect the public from the accused while the State prepares to vindicate the public's right to prosecute and punish him for allegedly committing an illegal act.

[T]he suspension levied, if any, is brief, and dissipates if and when the defendant is acquitted after the actual criminal trial."

Sections 524.016-524.020 reserved for expansion

SUBCHAPTER C. SUSPENSION PROVISIONS

TRANSP §524.021. SUSPENSION EFFECTIVE DATE

(a) A driver's license suspension under this chapter takes effect on the 40th day after the date the person:

(1) receives a notice of suspension under Section 524.011; or

(2) is presumed to have received notice of suspension under Section 524.013.

(b) A suspension under this chapter may not be probated.

History of Transp §524.021: Acts 1995, 74th Leg., ch. 165, §1, eff. Sept. 1, 1995. Source: TRCS art. 6687b-1, §6(a), 7(*l*).

TRANSP §524.022. PERIOD OF SUSPENSION

(a) A period of suspension under this chapter for an adult is:

(1) 90 days if the person's driving record shows no alcohol-related or drug-related enforcement contact during the 10 years preceding the date of the person's arrest; or

(2) one year if the person's driving record shows one or more alcohol-related or drug-related enforcement contacts during the 10 years preceding the date of the person's arrest.

(b) A period of suspension under this chapter for a minor is:

(1) 60 days if the minor has not been previously convicted of an offense under Section 106.041, Alcoholic Beverage Code, or Section 49.04, Penal Code, or an offense under Section 49.07 or 49.08, Penal Code, involving the operation of a motor vehicle;

(2) 120 days if the minor has been previously convicted once of an offense listed by Subdivision (1); or

(3) 180 days if the minor has been previously convicted twice or more of an offense listed by Subdivision (1).

(c) For the purposes of determining whether a minor has been previously convicted of an offense described by Subsection (b)(1):

(1) an adjudication under Title 3, Family Code, that the minor engaged in conduct described by Subsection (b)(1) is considered a conviction under that provision; and

(2) an order of deferred adjudication for an offense alleged under a provision described by Subsection (b)(1) is considered a conviction of an offense under that provision.

(d) A minor whose driver's license is suspended under this chapter is not eligible for an occupational license under Subchapter L, Chapter 521, for:

(1) the first 30 days of a suspension under Subsection (b)(1);

(2) the first 90 days of a suspension under Subsection (b)(2); or

(3) the entire period of a suspension under Subsection (b)(3).

History of Transp §524.022: Acts 1995, 74th Leg., ch. 165, §1, eff. Sept. 1, 1995. Amended by Acts 1997, 75th Leg., ch. 1013, §25, eff. Sept. 1, 1997; Acts 2001, 77th Leg., ch. 444, §3, eff. Sept. 1, 2001. Source: TRCS art. 6687b-1, §6(b).

See also *O'Connor's Crimes & Consequences* (2008-09), chart 11-A, "ALR Suspensions (21 Years of Age or Older)," 11-B, "ALR Suspensions (Under 21 Years of Age)."

ANNOTATIONS

Texas DPS v. Stacy, 933 S.W.2d 746, 747-48 (Tex. App.—San Antonio 1996, no writ). "[D] maintains that his driver's license was suspended for more than sixty days [and therefore] this appeal is moot. [¶] The suspension order of the administrative law judge was stayed pursuant to statute when [D] filed his appeal in the county court.... [A]ny administrative order issued after that date was void. [¶] Because the Department's orders were void, [D] has not served his entire sixty-day suspension. Thus, this appeal is far from moot. Even if [D] had served the full suspension, this appeal would not be moot because the Department has an interest in the actual suspension and its future 'enhancement' effect under [Transp. Code] §524.022."

TRANSP §524.023. APPLICATION OF SUSPENSION UNDER OTHER LAWS

(a) If a person is convicted of an offense under Section 106.041, Alcoholic Beverage Code, or Section 49.04, 49.07, or 49.08, Penal Code, and if any conduct on which that conviction is based is a ground for a driver's license suspension under this chapter and Section 106.041, Alcoholic Beverage Code, Subchapter O, Chapter 521, or Subchapter H, Chapter 522, each of the suspensions shall be imposed.

(b) The court imposing a driver's license suspension under Section 106.041, Alcoholic Beverage Code, or Chapter 521 or 522 as required by Subsection (a) shall credit a period of suspension imposed under this chapter toward the period of suspension required under Section 106.041, Alcoholic Beverage Code, or Subchapter O, Chapter 521, or Subchapter H, Chapter 522, unless the person was convicted of an offense under Article 6701l-1, Revised Statutes, as that law existed before September 1, 1994, Section 19.05(a)(2), Penal Code, as that law existed before September 1, 1994, Section 49.04, 49.07, or 49.08, Penal Code, or Section 106.041, Alcoholic Beverage Code, before the date of the conviction on which the suspension is based, in which event credit may not be given.

History of Transp §524.023: Acts 1995, 74th Leg., ch. 165, §1, eff. Sept. 1, 1995. Amended by Acts 1997, 75th Leg., ch. 1013, §26, eff. Sept. 1, 1997. Source: TRCS art. 6687b-1, §6(c).

Sections 524.024-524.030 reserved for expansion

SUBCHAPTER D. HEARING & APPEAL

TRANSP §524.031. HEARING REQUEST

If, not later than the 15th day after the date on which the person receives notice of suspension under Section 524.011 or is presumed to have received notice under Section 524.013, the department receives at its headquarters in Austin, in writing, including a facsimile transmission, or by another manner prescribed by the department, a request that a hearing be held, a hearing shall be held as provided by this subchapter.

History of Transp §524.031: Acts 1995, 74th Leg., ch. 165, §1, eff. Sept. 1, 1995. Source: TRCS art. 6687b-1, §7(a).

ANNOTATIONS

Ex parte Avilez, 929 S.W.2d 677, 679 (Tex. App.—San Antonio 1996, no pet.). "[T]exas's license forfeiture statute creates a summary administrative procedure for the automatic suspension of a driver's license. Therefore, while the driver may request an administrative hearing, the process is expedited, and the burden of proof is a preponderance of the evidence. We therefore conclude that the Texas legislature intended license suspension to be a civil *in rem* proceeding."

TRANSP §524.032. HEARING DATE; RESCHEDULING

(a) A hearing requested under this subchapter shall be held not earlier than the 11th day after the date

on which the person requesting the hearing is notified of the hearing unless the parties agree to waive this requirement. The hearing shall be held before the effective date of the suspension.

(b) A hearing shall be rescheduled if, before the fifth day before the date scheduled for the hearing, the department receives a request for a continuance from the person who requested the hearing. Unless both parties agree otherwise, the hearing shall be rescheduled for a date not earlier than the fifth day after the date the department receives the request for the continuance.

(c) A person who requests a hearing under this chapter may obtain only one continuance under this section unless the person shows that a medical condition prevents the person from attending the rescheduled hearing, in which event one additional continuance may be granted for a period not to exceed 10 days.

(d) A request for a hearing stays suspension of a person's driver's license until the date of the final decision of the administrative law judge. If the person's driver's license was taken by a peace officer under Section 524.011(b), the department shall notify the person of the effect of the request on the suspension of the person's license before the expiration of any temporary driving permit issued to the person, if the person is otherwise eligible, in a manner that will permit the person to establish to a peace officer that the person's driver's license is not suspended.

History of Transp §524.032: Acts 1995, 74th Leg., ch. 165, §1, eff. Sept. 1, 1995. Amended by Acts 2001, 77th Leg., ch. 444, §4, eff. Sept. 1, 2001. Source: TRCS art. 6687b-1, §7(a), (b), (f).

TRANSP §524.033. STATE OFFICE OF ADMINISTRATIVE HEARINGS

(a) A hearing under this subchapter shall be heard by an administrative law judge employed by the State Office of Administrative Hearings.

(b) The State Office of Administrative Hearings shall provide for the stenographic or electronic recording of the hearing.

History of Transp §524.033: Acts 1995, 74th Leg., ch. 165, §1, eff. Sept. 1, 1995. Source: TRCS art. 6687b-1, §7(a), (b).

TRANSP §524.034. HEARING LOCATION

A hearing under this subchapter shall be held:

(1) at a location designated by the State Office of Administrative Hearings:

(A) in the county of arrest if the arrest occurred in a county with a population of 300,000 or more; or

(B) in the county in which the person is alleged to have committed the offense for which the person was arrested or not more than 75 miles from the county seat of the county in which the person was arrested; or

(2) with the consent of the person and the department, by telephone conference call.

History of Transp §524.034: Acts 1995, 74th Leg., ch. 165, §1, eff. Sept. 1, 1995. Source: TRCS art. 6687b-1, §7(b), (c).

TRANSP §524.035. HEARING

(a) The issues that must be proved at a hearing by a preponderance of the evidence are:

(1) whether:

(A) the person had an alcohol concentration of a level specified by Section 49.01(2)(B), Penal Code, while operating a motor vehicle in a public place; or

(B) the person is a minor and had any detectable amount of alcohol in the minor's system while operating a motor vehicle in a public place; and

(2) whether reasonable suspicion to stop or probable cause to arrest the person existed.

(b) If the administrative law judge finds in the affirmative on each issue in Subsection (a), the suspension is sustained.

(c) If the administrative law judge does not find in the affirmative on each issue in Subsection (a), the department shall:

(1) return the person's driver's license to the person, if the license was taken by a peace officer under Section 524.011(b);

(2) reinstate the person's driver's license; and

(3) rescind an order prohibiting the issuance of a driver's license to the person.

(d) An administrative law judge may not find in the affirmative on the issue in Subsection (a)(1) if:

(1) the person is an adult and the analysis of the person's breath or blood determined that the person had an alcohol concentration of a level below that specified by Section 49.01, Penal Code, at the time the specimen was taken; or

(2) the person is a minor and the administrative law judge does not find that the minor had any detectable amount of alcohol in the minor's system when the minor was arrested.

(e) The decision of the administrative law judge is final when issued and signed.

History of Transp §524.035: Acts 1995, 74th Leg., ch. 165, §1, eff. Sept. 1, 1995. Amended by Acts 1997, 75th Leg., ch. 1013, §27, eff. Sept. 1, 1997; Acts 2001, 77th Leg., ch. 444, §5, eff. Sept. 1, 2001. Source: TRCS art. 6687b-1, §7(b), (d), (p).

Mireles v. Texas DPS, 9 S.W.3d 128, 131 (Tex. 1999). "If unextrapolated breath-test results are sufficient to sustain a criminal conviction for drunk driving, they are certainly sufficient to sustain an administrative license suspension."

Todd v. State, 956 S.W.2d 777, 778 (Tex.App.—Waco 1997, pet. ref'd). "The DPS has the authority to suspend driver's licenses.... [Transp. Code ch. 524] allows the suspension of a driver's license when a person arrested for driving while intoxicated gives a breath or blood sample which shows an alcohol concentration of 0.10 or more [now 0.08 or more]. If the driver requests a hearing after notice of a suspension, an ALJ must find by a preponderance of the evidence that (1) the person was operating a motor vehicle with an alcohol concentration of 0.10 or more, and (2) reasonable suspicion to stop or probable cause to arrest the person existed. [¶] If the ALJ fails to find a required issue ... the DPS must reinstate the person's driver's license."

TRANSP §524.036. FAILURE TO APPEAR

A person who requests a hearing and fails to appear without just cause waives the right to a hearing and the department's determination is final.

History of Transp §524.036: Acts 1995, 74th Leg., ch. 165, §1, eff. Sept. 1, 1995. Source: TRCS art. 6687b-1, §7(e).

TRANSP §524.037. CONTINUANCE

(a) A continuance under Section 524.032 stays the suspension of a driver's license until the date of the final decision of the administrative law judge.

(b) A suspension order may not go into effect pending a final decision of the administrative law judge as a result of a continuance granted under Section 524.039.

(c) If the person's driver's license was taken by a peace officer under Section 524.011(b), the department shall notify the person of the effect of the continuance on the suspension of the person's license before the expiration of any temporary driving permit issued to the person, if the person is otherwise eligible, in a manner that will permit the person to establish to a peace officer that the person's driver's license is not suspended.

History of Transp §524.037: Acts 1995, 74th Leg., ch. 165, §1, eff. Sept. 1, 1995. Amended by Acts 2001, 77th Leg., ch. 444, §6, eff. Sept. 1, 2001. Source: TRCS art. 6687b-1, §7(f), (n).

TRANSP §524.038. INSTRUMENT RELIABILITY & ANALYSIS VALIDITY

(a) The reliability of an instrument used to take or analyze a specimen of a person's breath to determine alcohol concentration and the validity of the results of the analysis may be attested to in a proceeding under this subchapter by affidavit from the certified breath test technical supervisor responsible for maintaining and directing the operation of breath test instruments in compliance with department rule.

(b) An affidavit submitted under Subsection (a) must contain statements on:

(1) the reliability of the instrument and the analytical results; and

(2) compliance with state law in the administration of the program.

(c) An affidavit of an expert witness contesting the reliability of the instrument or the results is admissible.

(d) An affidavit from a person whose presence is timely requested under this section is inadmissible if the person fails to appear at a hearing without a showing of good cause. Otherwise, an affidavit under this section may be submitted in lieu of an appearance at the hearing by the breath test operator, breath test technical supervisor, or expert witness.

History of Transp §524.038: Acts 1995, 74th Leg., ch. 165, §1, eff. Sept. 1, 1995. Source: TRCS art. 6687b-1, §7(m), (n).

ANNOTATIONS

Texas DPS v. Cantu, 944 S.W.2d 493, 496 (Tex. App.—Houston [14th Dist.] 1997, no writ). The DPS "challenges [D's] contention that his substantial rights were prejudiced by the administrative judge's decision to allow inadmissible hearsay in the form of the Breath Test Technical Supervisor's Affidavit. [D] claimed the Affidavit was hearsay.... Section 524.038..., which controls the admissibility of the Affidavit, provides a statutory exception to the hearsay rule, and does not require the presence of the supervisor when the test is administered. [¶] The Breath Test Technical Supervisor's Affidavit submitted to the administrative judge in the present case complied with the statute in all respects. ... We find that the Affidavit was properly entered into evidence...."

TRANSP §524.039. APPEARANCE OF TECHNICIANS AT HEARING

(a) Notwithstanding Section 524.038, if not later than the fifth day before the date of a scheduled hearing the department receives from the person who requested a hearing written notice, including a facsimile transmission, requesting the presence at the hearing of the breath test operator who took the specimen of the person's breath to determine alcohol concentration or the certified breath test technical supervisor responsible for maintaining and directing the operation of the breath test instrument used to analyze the specimen of the person's breath, or both, each requested person must appear at the hearing.

(b) The department may reschedule a hearing once not less than 48 hours before the hearing if the person requested to attend under Subsection (a) is unavailable. The department may also reschedule the hearing on showing good cause that the person requested under Subsection (a) is not available at the time of the hearing.

History of Transp §524.039: Acts 1995, 74th Leg., ch. 165, §1, eff. Sept. 1, 1995. Source: TRCS art. 6687b-1, §7(n).

TRANSP §524.040. NOTICE REQUIREMENTS

(a) Notice required to be provided by the department under this subchapter may be given by telephone or other electronic means. If notice is given by telephone or other electronic means, written notice must also be provided.

(b) Notice by mail is considered received on the fifth day after the date the notice is deposited with the United States Postal Service.

History of Transp §524.040: Acts 1995, 74th Leg., ch. 165, §1, eff. Sept. 1, 1995. Source: TRCS art. 6687b-1, §7(p).

TRANSP §524.041. APPEAL FROM ADMINISTRATIVE HEARING

(a) A person whose driver's license suspension is sustained may appeal the decision by filing a petition not later than the 30th day after the date the administrative law judge's decision is final. The administrative law judge's final decision is immediately appealable without the requirement of a motion for rehearing.

(b) A petition under Subsection (a) must be filed in a county court at law in the county in which the person was arrested or, if there is not a county court at law in the county, in the county court. If the county judge is not a licensed attorney, the county judge shall transfer the case to a district court for the county on the motion of either party or of the judge.

(c) A person who files an appeal under this section shall send a copy of the petition by certified mail to the department and to the State Office of Administrative Hearings at each agency's headquarters in Austin. The copy must be certified by the clerk of the court in which the petition is filed.

(d) The department's right to appeal is limited to issues of law.

(e) A district or county attorney may represent the department in an appeal.

History of Transp §524.041: Acts 1995, 74th Leg., ch. 165, §1, eff. Sept. 1, 1995. Source: TRCS art. 6687b-1, §7(g), (i), (p).

Texas DPS v. Styron, 226 S.W.3d 576, 580 (Tex. App.—Houston [1st Dist.] 2007, no pet.). "Because the legislature has specifically made a driver's license suspension proceeding a civil matter and has specifically limited the subject matter jurisdiction of Harris County criminal courts to criminal cases, it follows that the legislature intended petitions for judicial review of administrative determinations regarding driver's license suspensions to be heard by one of the four civil county courts at law in Harris County. *At 581:* We conclude that county criminal courts in Harris County do not have subject matter jurisdiction to judicially review administrative determinations regarding driver's license suspensions."

TRANSP §524.042. STAY OF SUSPENSION ON APPEAL

(a) A suspension of a driver's license under this chapter is stayed on the filing of an appeal petition only if:

(1) the person's driver's license has not been suspended as a result of an alcohol-related or drug-related enforcement contact during the five years preceding the date of the person's arrest; and

(2) the person has not been convicted during the 10 years preceding the date of the person's arrest of an offense under:

(A) Article 6701l-1, Revised Statutes, as that law existed before September 1, 1994;

(B) Section 19.05(a)(2), Penal Code, as that law existed before September 1, 1994;

(C) Section 49.04, Penal Code;

(D) Section 49.07 or 49.08, Penal Code, if the offense involved the operation of a motor vehicle; or

(E) Section 106.041, Alcoholic Beverage Code.

(b) A stay under this section is effective for not more than 90 days after the date the appeal petition is filed. On the expiration of the stay, the department shall impose the suspension. The department or court may not grant an extension of the stay or an additional stay.

History of Transp §524.042: Acts 1995, 74th Leg., ch. 165, §1, eff. Sept. 1, 1995. Amended by Acts 1997, 75th Leg., ch. 1013, §28, eff. Sept. 1, 1997. Source: TRCS art. 6687b-1, §7(h).

TRANSP §524.043. REVIEW; ADDITIONAL EVIDENCE

(a) Review on appeal is on the record certified by the State Office of Administrative Hearings with no additional testimony.

(b) On appeal, a party may apply to the court to present additional evidence. If the court is satisfied that the additional evidence is material and that there were good reasons for the failure to present it in the proceeding before the administrative law judge, the court may order that the additional evidence be taken before an administrative law judge on conditions determined by the court.

(c) There is no right to a jury trial in an appeal under this section.

(d) An administrative law judge may change a finding or decision as to whether the person had an alcohol concentration of a level specified in Section 49.01, Penal Code, or whether a minor had any detectable amount of alcohol in the minor's system because of the additional evidence and shall file the additional evidence and any changes, new findings, or decisions with the reviewing court.

(e) A remand under this section does not stay the suspension of a driver's license.

History of Transp §524.043: Acts 1995, 74th Leg., ch. 165, §1, eff. Sept. 1, 1995. Amended by Acts 1997, 75th Leg., ch. 1013, §29, eff. Sept. 1, 1997. Source: TRCS art. 6687b-1, §7(h)-(j).

Texas DPS v. Latimer, 939 S.W.2d 240, 242 (Tex. App.—Austin 1997, no writ). "An appeal from the ALJ's decision to sustain the suspension is to the county court at law, if one exists in the county in which the offense occurred and if the county court at law judge is an attorney. The appeal is based on the administrative record certified by SOAH. *At 243:* [T]he administrative record should always be before the reviewing court since [Gov't Code] §2001.175(b) requires the state agency to file the administrative record with the clerk of the reviewing court. [W]ith limited exceptions, the reviewing court can consider *only* the administrative record in arriving at its decision. Therefore, there should be no confusion about the record before the reviewing court."

TRANSP §524.044. TRANSCRIPT OF ADMINISTRATIVE HEARING

(a) To obtain a transcript of an administrative hearing, the party who appeals the administrative law judge's decision must apply to the State Office of Administrative Hearings.

(b) On payment of a fee not to exceed the actual cost of preparing the transcript, the State Office of Administrative Hearings shall promptly furnish both parties with a transcript of the administrative hearing.

History of Transp §524.044: Acts 1995, 74th Leg., ch. 165, §1, eff. Sept. 1, 1995. Source: TRCS art. 6687b-1, §7(k).

Sections 524.045-524.050 reserved for expansion

SUBCHAPTER E. REINSTATEMENT & REISSUANCE OF DRIVER'S LICENSE

TRANSP §524.051. REINSTATEMENT & REISSUANCE

(a) A driver's license suspended under this chapter may not be reinstated or another driver's license issued to the person until the person pays the department a fee of $125 in addition to any other fee required by law.

(b) The payment of a reinstatement fee is not required if a suspension under this chapter is:

(1) rescinded by the department; or

(2) not sustained by an administrative law judge, or a court.

(c) Each fee collected under this section shall be deposited to the credit of the Texas mobility fund.

History of Transp §524.051: Acts 1995, 74th Leg., ch. 165, §1, eff. Sept. 1, 1995. Amended by Acts 2001, 77th Leg., ch. 444, §14(a), eff. Sept. 1, 2001; Acts 2003, 78th Leg., ch. 1325, §11.06, eff. Sept. 1, 2003. Source: TRCS art. 6687b-1, §8(a), (b).

SUBTITLE C. RULES OF THE ROAD

CHAPTER 550. ACCIDENTS & ACCIDENT REPORTS

SUBCHAPTER B. DUTIES FOLLOWING ACCIDENT

TRANSP §550.021. ACCIDENT INVOLVING PERSONAL INJURY OR DEATH

(a) The operator of a vehicle involved in an accident resulting in injury to or death of a person shall:

(1) immediately stop the vehicle at the scene of the accident or as close to the scene as possible;

(2) immediately return to the scene of the accident if the vehicle is not stopped at the scene of the accident; and

(3) remain at the scene of the accident until the operator complies with the requirements of Section 550.023.

(b) An operator of a vehicle required to stop the vehicle by Subsection (a) shall do so without obstructing traffic more than is necessary.

🅐 *Subsection (c) below is effective for offenses committed on or after Sept. 1, 2007.*

(c) A person commits an offense if the person does not stop or does not comply with the requirements of this section. An offense under this section:

🅔 **(1)** involving an accident resulting in death of or serious bodily injury, as defined by Section 1.07, Penal Code, to a person is a felony of the third degree; and

(2) involving an accident resulting in injury to which Subdivision (1) does not apply is punishable by:

(A) imprisonment in the Texas Department of Criminal Justice for not more than five years or confinement in the county jail for not more than one year;

(B) a fine not to exceed $5,000; or

(C) both the fine and the imprisonment or confinement.

Subsection (c) below is effective for offenses in which any element of the offense was committed before Sept. 1, 2007.

(c) A person commits an offense if the person does not stop or does not comply with the requirements of this section. An offense under this section is punishable by:

(1) imprisonment in the institutional division of the Texas Department of Criminal Justice for not more than five years or confinement in the county jail for not more than one year;

(2) a fine not to exceed $5,000; or

(3) both the fine and the imprisonment or confinement.

History of Transp §550.021: Acts 1995, 74th Leg., ch. 165, §1, eff. Sept. 1, 1995. Amended by Acts 2007, 80th Leg., ch. 97, §2, eff. Sept. 1, 2007.

TRANSP §550.023. DUTY TO GIVE INFORMATION & RENDER AID

The operator of a vehicle involved in an accident resulting in the injury or death of a person or damage to a vehicle that is driven or attended by a person shall:

(1) give the operator's name and address, the registration number of the vehicle the operator was driving, and the name of the operator's motor vehicle liability insurer to any person injured or the operator or occupant of or person attending a vehicle involved in the collision;

(2) if requested and available, show the operator's driver's license to a person described by Subdivision (1); and

(3) provide any person injured in the accident reasonable assistance, including transporting or making arrangements for transporting the person to a physician or hospital for medical treatment if it is apparent that treatment is necessary, or if the injured person requests the transportation.

History of Transp §550.023: Acts 1995, 74th Leg., ch. 165, §1, eff. Sept. 1, 1995.

ANNOTATIONS

Aguilar v. State, 202 S.W.3d 833, 839 (Tex.App.—Waco 2006, pet. ref'd). Section 550.023(3) "does not mean that a person involved in a collision which results in personal injury to another must personally transport the injured person to a hospital, particularly when the person's own vehicle has been damaged. However, this requirement at a minimum means that such a driver must remain at the scene until emergency personnel or someone whom the driver knows is capable of providing emergency medical assistance has arrived at the scene."

Ramirez v. State, 90 S.W.3d 884, 886 (Tex. App.—San Antonio 2002, pet. ref'd). "Ramirez asserts that charging him with two offenses of failing to stop

and render aid arising from a single traffic accident violated his rights against double jeopardy. [I]f the accident involves more than one victim, the double jeopardy clause does not apply. Two individuals were in the other car involved in the accident. The court has expressly held, 'The Double Jeopardy Clause has no application to a multiple victim offense when, as here, it is the legislative intent to aid all victims in a hit-and-run offense and, accordingly, to enforce this intent through appropriate punishment for each individual not so aided.'" *See also* **Spradling v. State**, 773 S.W.2d 553, 557 (Tex.Crim.App.1989).

SUBTITLE J. MISCELLANEOUS PROVISIONS

CHAPTER 724. IMPLIED CONSENT

SUBCHAPTER A. GENERAL PROVISIONS

TRANSP §724.001. DEFINITIONS

In this chapter:

(1) "Alcohol concentration" has the meaning assigned by Section 49.01, Penal Code.

(2) "Arrest" includes the taking into custody of a child, as defined by Section 51.02, Family Code.

(3) "Controlled substance" has the meaning assigned by Section 481.002, Health and Safety Code.

(4) "Criminal charge" includes a charge that may result in a proceeding under Title 3, Family Code.

(5) "Criminal proceeding" includes a proceeding under Title 3, Family Code.

(6) "Dangerous drug" has the meaning assigned by Section 483.001, Health and Safety Code.

(7) "Department" means the Department of Public Safety.

(8) "Drug" has the meaning assigned by Section 481.002, Health and Safety Code.

(9) "Intoxicated" has the meaning assigned by Section 49.01, Penal Code.

(10) "License" has the meaning assigned by Section 521.001.

(11) "Operate" means to drive or be in actual control of a motor vehicle or watercraft.

(12) "Public place" has the meaning assigned by Section 1.07, Penal Code.

1. **Editor's note:** For an overview of ALR hearing procedures, see Doug Murphy & Gary Trichter, *Administrative License Revocation Hearings: A DWI Specialist's Primer for the General Practitioner*, 65 Tex.B.J. 598 (2002).

History of Transp §724.001: Acts 1995, 74th Leg., ch. 165, §1, eff. Sept. 1, 1995. Amended by Acts 1997, 75th Leg., ch. 1013, §31, eff. Sept. 1, 1997. Source: TRCS art. 6701*l*-5, §3(j)(1)-(6).

TRANSP §724.002. APPLICABILITY

The provisions of this chapter that apply to suspension of a license for refusal to submit to the taking of a specimen (Sections 724.013, 724.015, and 724.048 and Subchapters C and D) apply only to a person arrested for an offense involving the operation of a motor vehicle or watercraft powered with an engine having a manufacturer's rating of 50 horsepower or above.

History of Transp §724.002: Acts 1995, 74th Leg., ch. 165, §1, eff. Sept. 1, 1995. Amended by Acts 2001, 77th Leg., ch. 444, §7, eff. Sept. 1, 2001. Source: TRCS art. 6701 *l*-5, §2(j).

ANNOTATIONS

Texas DPS v. Watson, 945 S.W.2d 262, 266 (Tex. App.—Houston [1st Dist.] 1997, no writ). "'Implied consent' means that if a person is arrested for an offense arising out of the operation of a motor vehicle in a public place while intoxicated, he is deemed to have consented to the taking of one or more specimens of his breath or blood for analysis to determine alcohol concentration. [¶] However, a person cannot be forced to breathe into a breathalyzer or have a needle with syringe forcibly poked into his arm. Notwithstanding a person's 'implied consent,' a specimen can be taken only if the person agrees to the request of a peace officer for one. If a person refuses a peace officer's request to submit to the taking of a specimen, however, the Department is required to suspend his driver's license. [¶] The provisions of the implied consent law apply *postarrest*. Additionally, 'one or more specimens' may be requested and taken."

TRANSP §724.003. RULEMAKING

The department and the State Office of Administrative Hearings shall adopt rules to administer this chapter.

History of Transp §724.003: Acts 1995, 74th Leg., ch. 165, §1, eff. Sept. 1, 1995. Source: TRCS art. 6701 *l*-5, §4A.

Sections 724.004-724.010 reserved for expansion

SUBCHAPTER B. TAKING & ANALYSIS OF SPECIMEN

TRANSP §724.011. CONSENT TO TAKING OF SPECIMEN

(a) If a person is arrested for an offense arising out of acts alleged to have been committed while the person was operating a motor vehicle in a public place, or a watercraft, while intoxicated, or an offense under Section 106.041, Alcoholic Beverage Code, the person is deemed to have consented, subject to this chapter, to submit to the taking of one or more specimens of the person's breath or blood for analysis to determine the alcohol concentration or the presence in the person's body of a controlled substance, drug, dangerous drug, or other substance.

(b) A person arrested for an offense described by Subsection (a) may consent to submit to the taking of any other type of specimen to determine the person's alcohol concentration.

History of Transp §724.011: Acts 1995, 74th Leg., ch. 165, §1, eff. Sept. 1, 1995. Amended by Acts 1997, 75th Leg., ch. 1013, §32, eff. Sept. 1, 1997. Source: TRCS art. 6701 *l*-5, §1.

ANNOTATIONS

Beeman v. State, 86 S.W.3d 613, 614-15 (Tex.Crim. App.2002). "We must determine whether the implied consent statute prohibits drawing a suspect's blood under a search warrant. We conclude that it does not."

State v. Laird, 38 S.W.3d 707, 713-14 (Tex.App.— Austin 2000, pet. ref'd). Chapter 724 "applies only to persons under arrest when the blood sample is taken. Accordingly, Texas courts apply the probable cause and exigent circumstances test only in cases where a blood sample is taken from someone not under arrest. [¶] On the other hand, Texas courts require full compliance with the provisions of chapter 724 when a blood sample is taken from an arrested suspect even though exigent circumstances exist." Held: Emergency medical technician was not authorized to take D's blood at request of police.

Arnold v. State, 971 S.W.2d 588, 590 (Tex.App.— Dallas 1998, no pet.). "Under the implied consent law, any person who operates a motor vehicle in a public place is deemed to have given consent to submit to a breath or blood test if arrested 'for any offense arising out of acts alleged to have been committed while a person was driving or in actual physical control of a motor vehicle … while intoxicated.' The implied consent law requires any such person be warned upon arrest that a refusal to take the intoxilyzer test may be admissible in a subsequent prosecution and will result in the suspension of his drivers license."

Elliott v. State, 908 S.W.2d 590, 593 (Tex.App.— Austin 1995, pet. ref'd). "It is obvious … that the implied consent law applies to a person arrested for any offense, not just driving while intoxicated, arising out of the operation of a motor vehicle while intoxicated."

TRANSP §724.012. TAKING OF SPECIMEN

(a) One or more specimens of a person's breath or blood may be taken if the person is arrested and at the request of a peace officer having reasonable grounds to believe the person:

(1) while intoxicated was operating a motor vehicle in a public place, or a watercraft; or

(2) was in violation of Section 106.041, Alcoholic Beverage Code.

(b) A peace officer shall require the taking of a specimen of the person's breath or blood if:

(1) the officer arrests the person for an offense under Chapter 49, Penal Code, involving the operation of a motor vehicle or a watercraft;

(2) the person was the operator of a motor vehicle or a watercraft involved in an accident that the officer reasonably believes occurred as a result of the offense;

(3) at the time of the arrest the officer reasonably believes that as a direct result of the accident:

(A) any individual has died or will die; or

(B) an individual other than the person has suffered serious bodily injury; and

(4) the person refuses the officer's request to submit to the taking of a specimen voluntarily.

(c) The peace officer shall designate the type of specimen to be taken.

(d) In this section, "serious bodily injury" has the meaning assigned by Section 1.07, Penal Code.

History of Transp §724.012: Acts 1995, 74th Leg., ch. 165, §1, eff. Sept. 1, 1995. Amended by Acts 1997, 75th Leg., ch. 1013, §33, eff. Sept. 1, 1997; Acts 2003, 78th Leg., ch. 422, §1, eff. Sept. 1, 2003. Source: TRCS art. 6701*l*-5, §§1, 3(i).

ANNOTATIONS

State v. Neesley, 239 S.W.3d 780, 781 (Tex.Crim. App.2007). "This case addresses the questions of how the term 'specimen' should be interpreted in the context of §724.012(b) ... and how many specimens the statute permits to be taken. We hold that specimen should be construed to mean a usable sample, and that one and only one specimen (as so defined) may be taken."

Badgett v. State, 42 S.W.3d 136, 139 (Tex.Crim.App. 2001). "By making the 'reasonable belief' requirement separate from the requirements that there be a life-threatening accident and that there be an arrest for an intoxication offense, the plain language of the statute indicates that the officer's 'reasonable belief' that the accident occurred as the result of the offense must be based on something more than the mere fact of the accident and the officer's arrest of the defendant for an intoxication offense. [S]uch a belief must be based upon specific and articulable facts of causation. Articulable belief can result from any number of factors, including but not limited to, witness interviews, conclusions drawn from experience in combination with observation of the accident scene, or determinations made by an accident reconstruction team."

McBride v. State, 946 S.W.2d 100, 101 (Tex.App.— Texarkana 1997, pet. ref'd). "[D] contends that [§724.012] requires that the specimen may be taken only if requested by the same individual who observed the person operating a vehicle (who therefore had reasonable grounds) to believe that the person was intoxicated. [¶] [D] notes that [§724.012(b)] provides that a peace officer shall require the sample if 'the officer' arrests, and if 'the officer believes,' and if the person refuses 'the officer's request.' She contends that this language means that only a single officer may be involved and that multiple officers may not rely on each other's actions or knowledge in reaching the multiple conclusions required by the statute in order to require the taking of a specimen. [¶] Section 724.012(b) is written in the conjunctive, and this case does not meet its requirements. Three essential elements are missing: (1) there was no accident, (2) there was no death or danger of death as a result of her acts, and (3) [D] did not refuse a request to submit a specimen. Thus, §724.012(b) is not applicable to this case."

Texas DPS v. Watson, 945 S.W.2d 262, 266 (Tex. App.—Houston [1st Dist.] 1997, no writ). A "person cannot be forced to breathe into a breathalyzer or have a needle with syringe forcibly poked into his arm. [A] specimen can be taken only if the person agrees to the request of a peace officer for one. If a person refuses a peace officer's request to submit to the taking of a specimen, however, the Department is required to suspend his driver's license. [¶] The provisions of the implied consent law apply *postarrest*. Additionally, 'one or more specimens' may be requested and taken. *At 267:*

[Peace officer] used the PBT as an indicator of intoxication. [D] refused to provide a specimen when one was requested by a peace officer in accordance with the provisions of Transp. Code chapter 724 and after receiving the requisite statutory warnings. Even if the PBT constituted the giving of a specimen under chapter 724, [D] did not have the luxury of refusing a second specimen under chapter 724 without the attendant risk of license suspension. *At 266 n.5:* Despite the general prohibition on taking a specimen, if the person refuses a request for one, there are specific instances where a specimen must be taken."

TRANSP §724.013. PROHIBITION ON TAKING SPECIMEN IF PERSON REFUSES; EXCEPTION

Except as provided by Section 724.012(b), a specimen may not be taken if a person refuses to submit to the taking of a specimen designated by a peace officer.

History of Transp §724.013: Acts 1995, 74th Leg., ch. 165, §1, eff. Sept. 1, 1995. Source: TRCS art. 6701 *l*-5, §2(a).

ANNOTATIONS

Texas DPS v. Watson, 945 S.W.2d 262, 266 (Tex. App.—Houston [1st Dist.] 1997, no writ). "Notwithstanding a person's 'implied consent,' a specimen can be taken only if the person agrees to the request of a peace officer for one. If a person refuses a peace officer's request to submit to the taking of a specimen, however, the Department is required to suspend his driver's license. [¶] The provisions of the implied consent law apply *postarrest*."

Serrano v. State, 936 S.W.2d 387, 389 (Tex.App.—Houston [14th Dist.] 1996, pet. ref'd). Transp. Code §724.013 "provides that a blood sample may be taken at the request of the State when a person is under arrest for an alcohol-related driving offense, but only if the arrestee does not withdraw consent to the test. [¶] This case falls outside the parameters of Article 6701l-5(2)(a) [now Transp. Code §724.013]. [D] was unable to sign a consent for medical treatment at the time of his admittance to the hospital. [T]o provide medical assistance, hospital staff collected a sample of [D's] blood, apparently without his consent. [T]he investigating officer [did not] request[] the hospital to collect the blood sample or to test it for alcohol content. [T]here is no evidence that [D] was under arrest either at the accident scene or at the hospital. ... Therefore, [D's] consent to a blood test was not required."

TRANSP §724.014. PERSON INCAPABLE OF REFUSAL

(a) A person who is dead, unconscious, or otherwise incapable of refusal is considered not to have withdrawn the consent provided by Section 724.011.

(b) If the person is dead, a specimen may be taken by:

(1) the county medical examiner or the examiner's designated agent; or

(2) a licensed mortician or a person authorized under Section 724.016 or 724.017 if there is not a county medical examiner for the county.

(c) If the person is alive but is incapable of refusal, a specimen may be taken by a person authorized under Section 724.016 or 724.017.

History of Transp §724.014: Acts 1995, 74th Leg., ch. 165, §1, eff. Sept. 1, 1995. Source: TRCS art. 6701 *l*-5, §3(h).

TRANSP §724.015. INFORMATION PROVIDED BY OFFICER BEFORE REQUESTING SPECIMEN

Before requesting a person to submit to the taking of a specimen, the officer shall inform the person orally and in writing that:

(1) if the person refuses to submit to the taking of the specimen, that refusal may be admissible in a subsequent prosecution;

(2) if the person refuses to submit to the taking of the specimen, the person's license to operate a motor vehicle will be automatically suspended, whether or not the person is subsequently prosecuted as a result of the arrest, for not less than 180 days;

(3) if the person is 21 years of age or older and submits to the taking of a specimen designated by the officer and an analysis of the specimen shows the person had an alcohol concentration of a level specified by Chapter 49, Penal Code, the person's license to operate a motor vehicle will be automatically suspended for not less than 90 days, whether or not the person is subsequently prosecuted as a result of the arrest;

(4) if the person is younger than 21 years of age and has any detectable amount of alcohol in the person's system, the person's license to operate a motor vehicle will be automatically suspended for not less than 60 days even if the person submits to the taking of the specimen, but that if the person submits to the taking of the specimen and an analysis of the specimen shows that the person had an alcohol concentration

less than the level specified by Chapter 49, Penal Code, the person may be subject to criminal penalties less severe than those provided under that chapter;

(5) if the officer determines that the person is a resident without a license to operate a motor vehicle in this state, the department will deny to the person the issuance of a license, whether or not the person is subsequently prosecuted as a result of the arrest, under the same conditions and for the same periods that would have applied to a revocation of the person's driver's license if the person had held a driver's license issued by this state; and

(6) the person has a right to a hearing on the suspension or denial if, not later than the 15th day after the date on which the person receives the notice of suspension or denial or on which the person is considered to have received the notice by mail as provided by law, the department receives, at its headquarters in Austin, a written demand, including a facsimile transmission, or a request in another form prescribed by the department for the hearing.

History of Transp §724.015: Acts 1995, 74th Leg., ch. 165, §1, eff. Sept. 1, 1995. Amended by Acts 1997, 75th Leg., ch. 1013, §34, eff. Sept. 1, 1997; Acts 2001, 77th Leg., ch. 444, §8, eff. Sept. 1, 2001. Source: TRCS art. 6701*l*-5, §2(b), (c).

ANNOTATIONS

Harrison v. State, 205 S.W.3d 549, 553-54 (Tex. Crim.App.2006). "Texas statutes did not require that [D] be given any statutory warnings before she was asked for her consent to provide a urine specimen. And the officers were not required to inform [D] that she could refuse to provide a urine sample without losing her driver's license simply because they first sought breath and blood specimens after giving her the required statutory warnings. ... Our conclusion is that the request for breath and blood specimens, to which the statutory warnings were applicable, is entirely distinct from the request for a urine specimen. The request for a urine specimen, which followed the request for breath and blood specimens, did not need to be paired with a statement that the previously given statutory warnings were inapplicable."

Gette v. State, 209 S.W.3d 139, 145 (Tex.App.— Houston [1st Dist.] 2006, no pet.). "A suspect's consent to a breath test must be voluntary. For consent to a breath test to be deemed 'voluntary,' a suspect's decision must not be the result of physical pressure or psychological pressure brought to bear by law enforcement

officials. A suspect's decision to submit to a breath test must be his own, made freely, and with a correct understanding of the statutory consequences of refusal. [¶] [S]tatements about the consequences of passing or failing the breath test 'are not of the same coercive nature' as statements about the consequences of refusing to take a breath test."

State v. Woehst, 175 S.W.3d 329, 332 (Tex.App.— Houston [1st Dist.] 2004, no pet.). "[D] was warned that if she refused to give a specimen, her license would be suspended for not fewer than 90 days. This warning is admittedly factually inaccurate. In reality, her refusal would result in her license's being suspended for not less than 180 days, and the Transportation Code requires that this exact warning be given to a suspect. The failure to warn [D] of the accurate statutory consequences of her refusal thus violated the Transportation Code. [¶] [I]n order for [D's] refusal to be excluded, there must be a causal connection between her refusal and the State's violation of §724.015(2).... *At 333:* [D] established a causal connection, by showing that the officer's misinformation and failure to provide a proper warning had caused her to refuse to consent to the breath test, and the trial court implicitly found her to be credible."

Texas DPS v. Struve, 79 S.W.3d 796, 801 (Tex. App.—Corpus Christi 2002, pet. denied). "[T]he warning under §724.015 encompasses all motor vehicles, including a commercial motor vehicle. Therefore, because Struve was given the warning under §724.015, he had notice that his license to operate a motor vehicle, either commercial or personal, would be suspended for at least 90 days."

Martin v. DPS, 964 S.W.2d 772, 774-75 (Tex.App.— Austin 1998, no pet.). "The legislature's use of the word 'had,' as opposed to 'have,' in §724.015(3) is somewhat ambiguous. That is, we agree that in isolation the statutory warning does not make clear whether the suspension will be imposed as a consequence of the licensee's state of intoxication at the time he or she was driving or at the time he or she takes the breath test. [¶] Several ... statutory provisions pertaining to administrative license suspensions for failure to pass a test for intoxication shed light on this issue. We first note the language of §724.015(3) itself: a license suspension is *automatic* after a failed breath test, 'whether or not the person is subsequently prosecuted as a result of the arrest.' Second, upon failure of a breath test, an arresting officer must serve a 'notice of driver's license suspension' on the licensee if the licensee is still in custody. The suspension automatically becomes effective 40 days after such service, unless the licensee timely requests a hearing on the suspension. In that event, the request for the hearing 'stays' the suspension until the date of the ALJ's final decision. Furthermore, the purpose of the administrative hearing is to determine whether a previously imposed suspension will be 'sustained' or 'rescinded.' Only at this review hearing does the issue of the licensee's level of intoxication *while driving* come into play. The ALJ must rescind the suspension at the hearing if the ALJ does not find from a preponderance of the evidence that the person had an alcohol concentration of at least 0.10 [now 0.08] *while driving.* That does not mean, however, that the suspension was not authorized in the first instance upon failure of a breath test. These provisions reveal that the failure of a breath test after an arrest for driving while intoxicated triggers a license suspension, regardless of whether the suspension will ultimately be sustained in an administrative hearing."

Texas DPS v. Latimer, 939 S.W.2d 240, 245 (Tex. App.—Austin 1997, no writ). "Neither party disputes that the officer orally requested [D] to submit a blood specimen. However, [D] argues that he was not given the written notice required by §724.015. We disagree. [Officer] testified that he made the written notice available to [D] in the hospital room but did not leave it there because [D] did not have control over his possessions. Instead, [officer] returned the next day and left the written notice with a nurse to give to [D]. Tendering the written notice is all that is required under §724.015."

TRANSP §724.016. BREATH SPECIMEN

(a) A breath specimen taken at the request or order of a peace officer must be taken and analyzed under rules of the department by an individual possessing a certificate issued by the department certifying that the individual is qualified to perform the analysis.

(b) The department may:

(1) adopt rules approving satisfactory analytical methods; and

(2) ascertain the qualifications of an individual to perform the analysis.

(c) The department may revoke a certificate for cause.

History of Transp §724.016: Acts 1995, 74th Leg., ch. 165, §1, eff. Sept. 1, 1995. Source: TRCS art. 6701 *l*-5, §3(b), (c).

TRANSP §724.017. BLOOD SPECIMEN

(a) Only a physician, qualified technician, chemist, registered professional nurse, or licensed vocational nurse may take a blood specimen at the request or order of a peace officer under this chapter. The blood specimen must be taken in a sanitary place.

(b) The person who takes the blood specimen under this chapter, or the hospital where the blood specimen is taken, is not liable for damages arising from the request or order of the peace officer to take the blood specimen as provided by this chapter if the blood specimen was taken according to recognized medical procedures. This subsection does not relieve a person from liability for negligence in the taking of a blood specimen.

(c) In this section, "qualified technician" does not include emergency medical services personnel.

History of Transp §724.017: Acts 1995, 74th Leg., ch. 165, §1, eff. Sept. 1, 1995. Source: TRCS art. 6701 *l*-5, §3(c).

ANNOTATIONS

Serrano v. State, 936 S.W.2d 387, 390 (Tex.App.— Houston [14th Dist.] 1996, pet. ref'd). "The record reflects that an individual identified only by the initials BB collected [D's] blood. [¶] [D] contends the admission of the blood test…, without evidence of who conducted the blood test, deprived him of the right to confront witnesses…. [¶] In this case, [D] failed to object on the grounds that the admission of the blood test deprived him of his constitutional right of confrontation. Consequently, once the State established the proper predicate…, the trial court properly admitted the record." *See also* **Texas DPS v. Hutcheson**, 235 S.W.3d 312, 316 (Tex.App.—Corpus Christi 2007, pet. denied).

TRANSP §724.018. FURNISHING INFORMATION CONCERNING TEST RESULTS

On the request of a person who has given a specimen at the request of a peace officer, full information concerning the analysis of the specimen shall be made available to the person or the person's attorney.

History of Transp §724.018: Acts 1995, 74th Leg., ch. 165, §1, eff. Sept. 1, 1995. Source: TRCS art. 6701 *l*-5, §3(e).

TRANSP §724.019. ADDITIONAL ANALYSIS BY REQUEST

(a) A person who submits to the taking of a specimen of breath, blood, urine, or another bodily substance at the request or order of a peace officer may, on request and within a reasonable time not to exceed two hours after the arrest, have a physician, qualified technician, chemist, or registered professional nurse selected by the person take for analysis an additional specimen of the person's blood.

(b) The person shall be allowed a reasonable opportunity to contact a person specified by Subsection (a).

(c) A peace officer or law enforcement agency is not required to transport for testing a person who requests that a blood specimen be taken under this section.

(d) The failure or inability to obtain an additional specimen or analysis under this section does not preclude the admission of evidence relating to the analysis of the specimen taken at the request or order of the peace officer.

(e) A peace officer, another person acting for or on behalf of the state, or a law enforcement agency is not liable for damages arising from a person's request to have a blood specimen taken.

History of Transp §724.019: Acts 1995, 74th Leg., ch. 165, §1, eff. Sept. 1, 1995. Source: TRCS art. 6701 *l*-5, §3(d).

Sections 724.020-724.030 reserved for expansion

SUBCHAPTER C. SUSPENSION OR DENIAL OF LICENSE ON REFUSAL OF SPECIMEN

TRANSP §724.031. STATEMENT REQUESTED ON REFUSAL

If a person refuses the request of a peace officer to submit to the taking of a specimen, the peace officer shall request the person to sign a statement that:

(1) the officer requested that the person submit to the taking of a specimen;

(2) the person was informed of the consequences of not submitting to the taking of a specimen; and

(3) the person refused to submit to the taking of a specimen.

History of Transp §724.031: Acts 1995, 74th Leg., ch. 165, §1, eff. Sept. 1, 1995. Source: TRCS art. 6701 *l*-5, §2(c).

TRANSP §724.032. OFFICER'S DUTIES FOR LICENSE SUSPENSION; WRITTEN REFUSAL REPORT

(a) If a person refuses to submit to the taking of a specimen, whether expressly or because of an intentional failure of the person to give the specimen, the peace officer shall:

(1) serve notice of license suspension or denial on the person;

(2) take possession of any license issued by this state and held by the person arrested;

(3) issue a temporary driving permit to the person unless department records show or the officer otherwise determines that the person does not hold a license to operate a motor vehicle in this state; and

(4) make a written report of the refusal to the director of the department.

(b) The director must approve the form of the refusal report. The report must:

(1) show the grounds for the officer's belief that the person had been operating a motor vehicle or watercraft powered with an engine having a manufacturer's rating of 50 horsepower or above while intoxicated; and

(2) contain a copy of:

(A) the refusal statement requested under Section 724.031; or

(B) a statement signed by the officer that the person refused to:

(i) submit to the taking of the requested specimen; and

(ii) sign the requested statement under Section 724.031.

(c) The officer shall forward to the department not later than the fifth business day after the date of the arrest:

(1) a copy of the notice of suspension or denial;

(2) any license taken by the officer under Subsection (a);

(3) a copy of any temporary driving permit issued under Subsection (a); and

(4) a copy of the refusal report.

(d) The department shall develop forms for notices of suspension or denial and temporary driving permits to be used by all state and local law enforcement agencies.

(e) A temporary driving permit issued under this section expires on the 41st day after the date of issuance. If the person was driving a commercial motor vehicle, as defined by Section 522.003, a temporary driving permit that authorizes the person to drive a commercial motor vehicle is not effective until 24 hours after the time of arrest.

History of Transp §724.032: Acts 1995, 74th Leg., ch. 165, §1, eff. Sept. 1, 1995. Amended by Acts 2001, 77th Leg., ch. 444, §9, eff. Sept. 1, 2001. Source: TRCS art. 6701 *l*-5, §2(d)-(g).

Texas DPS v. Kimbrough, 106 S.W.3d 747, 750 (Tex.App.—Fort Worth 2003, no pet.). "[T]he five-day forwarding requirement is mandatory. [¶] [However], we hold that the failure of an officer to comply with the statute does not render [an exhibit] inadmissible at an administrative hearing."

TRANSP §724.033. ISSUANCE BY DEPARTMENT OF NOTICE OF SUSPENSION OR DENIAL OF LICENSE

(a) On receipt of a report of a peace officer under Section 724.032, if the officer did not serve notice of suspension or denial of a license at the time of refusal to submit to the taking of a specimen, the department shall mail notice of suspension or denial, by first class mail, to the address of the person shown by the records of the department or to the address given in the peace officer's report, if different.

(b) Notice is considered received on the fifth day after the date it is mailed.

History of Transp §724.033: Acts 1995, 74th Leg., ch. 165, §1, eff. Sept. 1, 1995. Amended by Acts 1999, 76th Leg., ch. 1409, §5, eff. Sept. 1, 1999. Source: TRCS art. 6701 *l*-5, §2(h).

TRANSP §724.034. CONTENTS OF NOTICE OF SUSPENSION OR DENIAL OF LICENSE

A notice of suspension or denial of a license must state:

(1) the reason and statutory grounds for the action;

(2) the effective date of the suspension or denial;

(3) the right of the person to a hearing;

(4) how to request a hearing; and

(5) the period in which a request for a hearing must be received by the department.

History of Transp §724.034: Acts 1995, 74th Leg., ch. 165, §1, eff. Sept. 1, 1995. Source: TRCS art. 6701 *l*-5, §2(b).

TRANSP §724.035. SUSPENSION OR DENIAL OF LICENSE

(a) If a person refuses the request of a peace officer to submit to the taking of a specimen, the department shall:

(1) suspend the person's license to operate a motor vehicle on a public highway for 180 days; or

(2) if the person is a resident without a license, issue an order denying the issuance of a license to the person for 180 days.

(b) The period of suspension or denial is two years if the person's driving record shows one or more alcohol-related or drug-related enforcement contacts, as defined by Section 524.001(3), during the 10 years preceding the date of the person's arrest.

(c) A suspension or denial takes effect on the 40th day after the date on which the person:

(1) receives notice of suspension or denial under Section 724.032(a); or

(2) is considered to have received notice of suspension or denial under Section 724.033.

History of Transp §724.035: Acts 1995, 74th Leg., ch. 165, §1, eff. Sept. 1, 1995. Amended by Acts 1997, 75th Leg., ch. 165, §30.163 (eff. Sept. 1, 1997), ch. 1013, §35 (eff. Sept. 1, 1997); Acts 2001, 77th Leg., ch. 444, §10, eff. Sept. 1, 2001. Source: TRCS art. 6701*l*-5, §2(i).

See also *O'Connor's Crimes & Consequences* (2008-09), chart 11-A, "ALR Suspensions (21 Years of Age or Older)," 11-B, "ALR Suspensions (Under 21 Years of Age)."

Todd v. State, 956 S.W.2d 777, 778 (Tex.App.—Waco 1997, pet. ref'd). "The DPS has the authority to suspend driver's licenses.... [¶] [Transp. Code ch. 724], 'Implied Consent,' provides for the suspension of a driver's license when a person arrested for an intoxication offense involving a motor vehicle refuses to give a breath or blood specimen. If the driver requests a hearing on this type of suspension, the ALJ must find by a preponderance of the evidence that (1) reasonable suspicion or probable cause existed to stop or arrest the person; (2) probable cause existed to believe that the person was operating a motor vehicle in a public place while intoxicated; (3) the person was placed under arrest by the officer and was requested to submit to the taking of a specimen; and (4) the person refused to submit to the taking of a specimen on request of the officer. [¶] If the ALJ fails to find a required issue..., the DPS must reinstate the person's driver's license."

Texas DPS v. Watson, 945 S.W.2d 262, 266 (Tex. App.—Houston [1st Dist.] 1997, no writ). "If a person refuses a peace officer's request to submit to the taking of a specimen ... the Department is required to suspend his driver's license."

Sections 724.036-724.040 reserved for expansion

SUBCHAPTER D. HEARING

TRANSP §724.041. HEARING ON SUSPENSION OR DENIAL

(a) If, not later than the 15th day after the date on which the person receives notice of suspension or denial under Section 724.032(a) or is considered to have received notice under Section 724.033, the department receives at its headquarters in Austin, in writing, including a facsimile transmission, or by another manner prescribed by the department, a request that a hearing be held, the State Office of Administrative Hearings shall hold a hearing.

(b) A hearing shall be held not earlier than the 11th day after the date the person is notified, unless the parties agree to waive this requirement, but before the effective date of the notice of suspension or denial.

(c) A request for a hearing stays the suspension or denial until the date of the final decision of the administrative law judge. If the person's license was taken by a peace officer under Section 724.032(a), the department shall notify the person of the effect of the request on the suspension of the person's license before the expiration of any temporary driving permit issued to the person, if the person is otherwise eligible, in a manner that will permit the person to establish to a peace officer that the person's license is not suspended.

(d) A hearing shall be held by an administrative law judge employed by the State Office of Administrative Hearings.

(e) A hearing shall be held:

(1) at a location designated by the State Office of Administrative Hearings:

(A) in the county of arrest if the county has a population of 300,000 or more; or

(B) in the county in which the person was alleged to have committed the offense for which the person was

arrested or not more than 75 miles from the county seat of the county of arrest if the population of the county of arrest is less than 300,000; or

(2) with the consent of the person requesting the hearing and the department, by telephone conference call.

(f) The State Office of Administrative Hearings shall provide for the stenographic or electronic recording of a hearing under this subchapter.

(g) An administrative hearing under this section is governed by Sections 524.032(b) and (c), 524.035(e), 524.037(a), and 524.040.

History of Transp §724.041: Acts 1995, 74th Leg., ch. 165, §1, eff. Sept. 1, 1995. Amended by Acts 1997, 75th Leg., ch. 165, §30.164, eff. Sept. 1, 1997; Acts 2001, 77th Leg., ch. 444, §11, eff. Sept. 1, 2001. Source: TRCS art. 6701*l*-5, §2(j), (k), (s).

Texas DPS v. Latimer, 939 S.W.2d 240, 242 (Tex. App.—Austin 1997, no writ). "Unless successfully challenged, a person's driver's license is automatically suspended if that person refuses an officer's request that he or she give a blood or breath sample. A person challenging the automatic suspension of his or her driver's license is entitled to a hearing before an administrative law judge ('ALJ') of the State Office of Administrative Hearings ('SOAH')."

TRANSP §724.042. ISSUES AT HEARING

The issues at a hearing under this subchapter are whether:

(1) reasonable suspicion or probable cause existed to stop or arrest the person;

(2) probable cause existed to believe that the person was:

(A) operating a motor vehicle in a public place while intoxicated; or

(B) operating a watercraft powered with an engine having a manufacturer's rating of 50 horsepower or above while intoxicated;

(3) the person was placed under arrest by the officer and was requested to submit to the taking of a specimen; and

(4) the person refused to submit to the taking of a specimen on request of the officer.

History of Transp §724.042: Acts 1995, 74th Leg., ch. 165, §1, eff. Sept. 1, 1995. Amended by Acts 2001, 77th Leg., ch. 444, §12, eff. Sept. 1, 2001. Source: TRCS art. 6701 *l*-5, §2(*l*).

Texas DPS v. Rodriguez, 953 S.W.2d 362, 364 (Tex. App.—Austin 1997, no writ). Section 724.042 "requires evidence of probable cause to initially stop the motorist as well as probable cause to detain the motorist further in order to investigate whether the motorist was driving while intoxicated. [¶] The evidence in the record is completely silent on any causal connection between the initial stop and the subsequent field sobriety tests. [W]hile the first stop was justified because [D] was speeding, the second 'stop' (detaining [D] to perform the field sobriety tests) was not. [¶] In the present case, [there is] no evidence indicating that [o]fficer … had probable cause to administer field sobriety tests to [D]."

Texas DPS v. Ray, 943 S.W.2d 87, 88 (Tex.App.— Fort Worth 1997, no writ). "In order to uphold an automatic driver's license suspension under article 6701*l*-5 [now Transp. Code §724.042], an ALJ must consider [four] issues. *At 89:* If the ALJ finds that all four issues are answered in the affirmative, the ALJ shall sustain the suspension." *See also Texas DPS v. Latimer*, 939 S.W.2d 240, 242 (Tex.App.—Austin 1997, no writ).

Church v. State, 942 S.W.2d 139, 140 (Tex.App.— Houston [1st Dist.] 1997, pet. ref'd). "In an ALR hearing, the ALJ is to decide 'whether probable cause existed to believe [defendant] was operating a motor vehicle in a public place while intoxicated.' The statute authorizing the suspension hearing neither requires nor empowers the ALJ to decide the ultimate issue of whether [defendant] was actually operating a motor vehicle while intoxicated. In short, the 'fact' forming the basis of [D's] collateral estoppel argument was beyond the authority of the ALJ to find. As such, any finding of fact on that issue by the ALJ is of no import. The administrative judge's finding, therefore, cannot operate as a collateral estoppel bar to the DWI prosecution of [D]." *But see State v. Aguilar*, 947 S.W.2d 257 (Tex. Crim.App.1997), discussed at §524.012.

TRANSP §724.043. FINDINGS OF ADMINISTRATIVE LAW JUDGE

(a) If the administrative law judge finds in the affirmative on each issue under Section 724.042, the suspension order is sustained. If the person is a resident without a license, the department shall continue to deny to the person the issuance of a license for the applicable period provided by Section 724.035.

(b) If the administrative law judge does not find in the affirmative on each issue under Section 724.042, the department shall return the person's license to the person, if the license was taken by a peace officer under Section 724.032(a), and reinstate the person's license or rescind any order denying the issuance of a license because of the person's refusal to submit to the taking of a specimen under Section 724.032(a).

History of Transp §724.043: Acts 1995, 74th Leg., ch. 165, §1, eff. Sept. 1, 1995. Amended by Acts 2001, 77th Leg., ch. 444, §13, eff. Sept. 1, 2001. Source: TRCS art. 6701*l*-5, §2(n).

Texas DPS v. Ray, 943 S.W.2d 87, 89 (Tex.App.— Fort Worth 1997, no writ). "If the ALJ finds that all four issues [in Transp. Code §724.042] are answered in the affirmative, the ALJ shall sustain the suspension."

TRANSP §724.044. WAIVER OF RIGHT TO HEARING

A person waives the right to a hearing under this subchapter and the department's suspension or denial is final and may not be appealed if the person:

(1) fails to request a hearing under Section 724.041; or

(2) requests a hearing and fails to appear, without good cause.

History of Transp §724.044: Acts 1995, 74th Leg., ch. 165, §1, eff. Sept. 1, 1995. Source: TRCS art. 6701 *l*-5, §2(o), (q).

TRANSP §724.045. PROHIBITION ON PROBATION OF SUSPENSION

A suspension under this chapter may not be probated.

History of Transp §724.045: Acts 1995, 74th Leg., ch. 165, §1, eff. Sept. 1, 1995. Source: TRCS art. 6701 *l*-5, §2(k), (n).

TRANSP §724.046. REINSTATEMENT OF LICENSE OR ISSUANCE OF NEW LICENSE

(a) A license suspended under this chapter may not be reinstated or a new license issued until the person whose license has been suspended pays to the department a fee of $125 in addition to any other fee required by law. A person subject to a denial order issued under this chapter may not obtain a license after the period of denial has ended until the person pays to the department a fee of $125 in addition to any other fee required by law.

(b) If a suspension or denial under this chapter is rescinded by the department, an administrative law judge, or a court, payment of the fee under this section is not required for reinstatement or issuance of a license.

(c) Each fee collected under this section shall be deposited to the credit of the Texas mobility fund.

History of Transp §724.046: Acts 1995, 74th Leg., ch. 165, §1, eff. Sept. 1, 1995. Amended by Acts 2001, 77th Leg., ch. 444, §14(b), eff. Sept. 1, 2001; Acts 2003, 78th Leg., ch. 1325, §11.09, eff. Sept. 1, 2003. Source: TRCS art. 6701 *l*-5, §2(v)(1), (2).

ANNOTATIONS

Allen v. State, 48 S.W.3d 775, 777 (Tex.Crim.App. 2001). "We read the plain language of the text of §724.046(a) … to require the procurement of a new license once the 90 day suspension period has expired and the $100 fee is not paid. Requiring a reinstatement fee to be paid before ending a suspension would otherwise create suspensions of indefinite length. The statute under which the appellant's license was suspended prescribed a *definite period* of suspension (90 days)."

TRANSP §724.047. APPEAL

Chapter 524 governs an appeal from an action of the department, following an administrative hearing under this chapter, in suspending or denying the issuance of a license.

History of Transp §724.047: Acts 1995, 74th Leg., ch. 165, §1, eff. Sept. 1, 1995. Source: TRCS art. 6701 *l*-5, §4.

ANNOTATIONS

Texas DPS v. Watson, 945 S.W.2d 262, 264-65 (Tex.App.—Houston [1st Dist.] 1997, no writ). "[D] appealed the decision of the administrative law judge to the county court at law. In these circumstances, a county court at law may not substitute its judgment for that of the administrative law judge on the weight of the evidence, but it may reverse the case if the substantive rights of the appellant have been prejudiced because the administrative findings are: (1) in violation of a constitutional or statutory provision; (2) in excess of the agency's statutory authority; (3) made through unlawful procedure; (4) affected by other error of law; (5) not reasonably supported by substantial evidence considering the reliable and probative evidence in the record as a whole; or (6) arbitrary or capricious."

TRANSP §724.048. RELATIONSHIP OF ADMINISTRATIVE PROCEEDING TO CRIMINAL PROCEEDING

(a) The determination of the department or administrative law judge:

(1) is a civil matter;

(2) is independent of and is not an estoppel as to any matter in issue in an adjudication of a criminal charge arising from the occurrence that is the basis for the suspension or denial; and

(3) does not preclude litigation of the same or similar facts in a criminal prosecution.

(b) Except as provided by Subsection (c), the disposition of a criminal charge does not affect a license suspension or denial under this chapter and is not an estoppel as to any matter in issue in a suspension or denial proceeding under this chapter.

(c) If a criminal charge arising from the same arrest as a suspension under this chapter results in an acquittal, the suspension under this chapter may not be imposed. If a suspension under this chapter has already been imposed, the department shall rescind the suspension and remove references to the suspension from the computerized driving record of the individual.

History of Transp §724.048: Acts 1995, 74th Leg., ch. 165, §1, eff. Sept. 1, 1995. Amended by Acts 1997, 75th Leg., ch. 1013, §36, eff. Sept. 1, 1997. Source: TRCS art. 6701 *l*-5, §2(r).

But see State v. Aguilar, 947 S.W.2d 257 (Tex.Crim.App.1997), discussed in note at §524.012.

ANNOTATIONS

Texas DPS v. Nielson, 102 S.W.3d 313, 316 (Tex. App.—Beaumont 2003, no pet.). "[A] pre-trial order of dismissal where jeopardy has not attached shall not be regarded as an acquittal. [¶] An acquittal is an 'official factfinding' 'that the accused is not guilty of the criminal offense with which he is charged.' For a dismissal or abandonment of a criminal accusation to be the equivalent of an acquittal, jeopardy must have attached. Jeopardy attaches when both sides have announced ready and the defendant has pled to the charging instrument."

State v. Montgomery, 957 S.W.2d 581, 584 (Tex. App.—Houston [14th Dist.] 1997, pet. ref'd). "By enacting §724.048, the Legislature did not redefine collateral estoppel in contravention of constitutional double jeopardy protection but explicitly expressed its intent that administrative collateral estoppel not bar the relitigation of findings made by the DPS or an administrative law judge following a license revocation hearing under [Transp. Code ch. 724]."

Todd v. State, 956 S.W.2d 777, 780 (Tex.App.—Waco 1997, pet. ref'd). "The Court [of Criminal Appeals] has determined that an administrative driver's license suspension is a remedial, civil matter which does not constitute 'punishment' for double jeopardy purposes."

Church v. State, 942 S.W.2d 139, 139 (Tex.App.—Houston [1st Dist.] 1997, pet. ref'd). Transp. Code §724.048 "provides that the administrative findings shall not constitute a bar to any criminal proceedings. This reflects the Legislature's intent that the ALJ limit herself to the issues set out in [Transp. Code] §724.042 rather than—as this judge did—attempting to rule on issues of ultimate fact to be presented at the DWI prosecution."

Sections 724.049-724.060 reserved for expansion

SUBCHAPTER E. ADMISSIBILITY OF EVIDENCE

TRANSP §724.061. ADMISSIBILITY OF REFUSAL OF PERSON TO SUBMIT TO TAKING OF SPECIMEN

A person's refusal of a request by an officer to submit to the taking of a specimen of breath or blood, whether the refusal was express or the result of an intentional failure to give the specimen, may be introduced into evidence at the person's trial.

History of Transp §724.061: Acts 1995, 74th Leg., ch. 165, §1, eff. Sept. 1, 1995. Source: TRCS art. 6701 *l*-5, §3(g).

TRANSP §724.062. ADMISSIBILITY OF REFUSAL OF REQUEST FOR ADDITIONAL TEST

The fact that a person's request to have an additional analysis under Section 724.019 is refused by the officer or another person acting for or on behalf of the state, that the person was not provided a reasonable opportunity to contact a person specified by Section 724.019(a) to take the specimen, or that reasonable access was not allowed to the arrested person may be introduced into evidence at the person's trial.

History of Transp §724.062: Acts 1995, 74th Leg., ch. 165, §1, eff. Sept. 1, 1995. Source: TRCS art. 6701 *l*-5, §3(f).

Vester v. State, 916 S.W.2d 708, 711 (Tex.App.—Texarkana 1996, no pet.). "[D's] complaint in this case … is that he was misled by the officer when he consented to the breath test because he did so on the basis that he would also then be able to get a blood test administered by a person of his choosing. The remedy for the failure to provide a reasonable opportunity for a blood test is set out in [H&SC §724.062].… [¶] Thus, by statute, the only relief for the failure to make a blood test accessible upon request is the right to bring this fact before the fact finder."

TRANSP §724.063. ADMISSIBILITY OF ALCOHOL CONCENTRATION OR PRESENCE OF SUBSTANCE

Evidence of alcohol concentration or the presence of a controlled substance, drug, dangerous drug, or other substance obtained by an analysis authorized by Section 724.014 is admissible in a civil or criminal action.

History of Transp §724.063: Acts 1995, 74th Leg., ch. 165, §1, eff. Sept. 1, 1995. Amended by Acts 1997, 75th Leg., ch. 165, §30.165, eff. Sept. 1, 1997. Source: TRCS art. 6701 *l*-5, §3(h).

TRANSP §724.064. ADMISSIBILITY IN CRIMINAL PROCEEDING OF SPECIMEN ANALYSIS

On the trial of a criminal proceeding arising out of an offense under Chapter 49, Penal Code, involving the operation of a motor vehicle or a watercraft, or an offense under Section 106.041, Alcoholic Beverage Code, evidence of the alcohol concentration or presence of a controlled substance, drug, dangerous drug, or other substance as shown by analysis of a specimen of the person's blood, breath, or urine or any other bodily substance taken at the request or order of a peace officer is admissible.

History of Transp §724.064: Acts 1995, 74th Leg., ch. 165, §1, eff. Sept. 1, 1995. Amended by Acts 1997, 75th Leg., ch. 1013, §37, eff. Sept. 1, 1997. Source: TRCS art. 6701 *l*-5, §3(a).

Bagheri v. State, 119 S.W.3d 755, 760 (Tex.Crim. App.2003). "[W]e do not interpret §724.064 … as a legislative mandate requiring juries to engage in retrograde extrapolation. The determination that breath test results should be admissible in DWI prosecutions without the necessity of establishing the scientific basis for such tests under *Daubert* and *Kelly* does not ... relieve the State of the burden of showing that those test results in any given case are relevant, in the sense that they accurately reflect the subject's alcohol concentration at the time of the offense."

Woodall v. State, 216 S.W.3d 530, 536 (Tex.App.—Texarkana 2007, pet. granted 6-6-07). "The statute provides that the Legislature found the type of scientific tests, when performed with proper procedures on an approved machine, are sufficiently reliable to be admissible as evidence. The statute, however, does not provide that the tests are conclusive or that the efficacy of a particular machine to properly analyze the breath for blood-alcohol content is unassailable. The mere fact that it has not yet been attacked effectively in a reported case in Texas does not mean that it is of such undeniable reliability that counsel should not be able to cross-examine a State's witness to attempt to search out and expose the weaknesses (if any actually exist) which the machine may possess."

TITLE 2. WATER ADMINISTRATION

SUBTITLE A. EXECUTIVE AGENCIES

CHAPTER 7. ENFORCEMENT

SUBCHAPTER E. CRIMINAL OFFENSES & PENALTIES

WATER §7.141. DEFINITIONS

In this subchapter:

(1) "Appropriate regulatory agency" means the commission, the Texas Department of Health, or any other agency authorized to regulate the handling and disposal of medical waste.

(2) "Corporation" and "association" have the meanings assigned by Section 1.07, Penal Code, except that the terms do not include a government.

(3) "Large quantity generator" means a person who generates more than 50 pounds of medical waste each month.

(4) "Medical waste" includes animal waste, bulk blood and blood products, microbiological waste, pathological waste, sharps, and special waste from health care-related facilities as those terms are defined in 25 T.A.C. Section 1.132 (Texas Department of Health, Definition, Treatment, and Disposition of Special Waste from Health Care-Related Facilities). The term does not include medical waste produced on farmland and ranchland as defined by Section 252.001(6), Agriculture Code.

(5) "Serious bodily injury" has the meaning assigned by Section 1.07, Penal Code.

(6) "Small quantity generator" means a person who generates 50 pounds or less of medical waste each month.

History of Water §7.141: Acts 1997, 75th Leg., ch. 1072, §2, eff. Sept. 1, 1997.

WATER §7.142. VIOLATIONS RELATING TO UNLAWFUL USE OF STATE WATER

(a) A person commits an offense if the person violates:

(1) Section 11.081;

(2) Section 11.083;

(3) Section 11.084;

(4) Section 11.087;

(5) Section 11.088;

(6) Section 11.089;

(7) Section 11.090;

(8) Section 11.091;

(9) Section 11.092;

(10) Section 11.093;

(11) Section 11.094;

(12) Section 11.096;

(13) Section 11.203; or

(14) Section 11.205.

(b) An offense under Subsection (a)(9), (a)(10), or (a)(14) is punishable under Section 7.187(1)(A) or Section 7.187(2)(B) or both.

(c) An offense under Subsection (a)(1), (a)(2), (a)(4), (a)(6), (a)(7), or (a)(8) is punishable under Section 7.187(1)(A) or Section 7.187(2)(C) or both.

(d) An offense under Subsection (a)(3) or (a)(11) is punishable under Section 7.187(1)(A) or Section 7.187(2)(D) or both.

(e) An offense under Subsection (a)(5) is punishable under Section 7.187(1)(A) or Section 7.187(2)(E) or both.

(f) Possession of state water when the right to its use has not been acquired according to Chapter 11 is prima facie evidence of a violation of Section 11.081.

(g) Possession or use of water on a person's land by a person not entitled to the water under this code is prima facie evidence of a violation of Section 11.083.

History of Water §7.142: Acts 1997, 75th Leg., ch. 1072, §2, eff. Sept. 1, 1997.

WATER §7.143. VIOLATION OF MINIMUM STATE STANDARDS OR MODEL POLITICAL SUBDIVISION RULES

(a) A person commits an offense if the person knowingly or intentionally violates a rule adopted under Subchapter J, Chapter 16.

(b) An offense under this section is a Class A misdemeanor.

History of Water §7.143: Acts 1997, 75th Leg., ch. 1072, §2, eff. Sept. 1, 1997.

WATER §7.144. REPEALED

Repealed by Acts 2001, 77th Leg., ch. 376, §3.06, eff. Sept. 1, 2001.

WATER §7.145. INTENTIONAL OR KNOWING UNAUTHORIZED DISCHARGE

(a) A person commits an offense if the person, acting intentionally or knowingly with respect to the person's conduct, discharges or allows the discharge of a waste or pollutant:

(1) into or adjacent to water in the state that causes or threatens to cause water pollution unless the waste or pollutant is discharged in strict compliance with all required permits or with an order issued or a rule adopted by the appropriate regulatory agency; or

(2) from a point source in violation of Chapter 26 or of a rule, permit, or order of the appropriate regulatory agency.

(b) An offense under this section is punishable for an individual under Section 7.187(1)(C) or Section 7.187(2)(F) or both.

(c) An offense under this section is punishable for a person other than an individual under Section 7.187(1)(D).

History of Water §7.145: Acts 1997, 75th Leg., ch. 1072, §2, eff. Sept. 1, 1997. Amended by Acts 2001, 77th Leg., ch. 934, §1, eff. June 14, 2001.

ANNOTATIONS

Landry v. State, 60 S.W.3d 263, 266-67 (Tex.App.—Houston [14th Dist.] 2001, pet. ref'd). Water Code §7.146, now §7.145(a)(2), "requires the State to show the defendant (1) intentionally or knowingly (2) discharged or allowed a discharge (3) of waste or a pollutant (4) from a point source (5) in violation of Chapter 26 or of a rule, permit, or order of the appropriate regulatory agency. [Water Code] §7.147, on the other hand, requires no *mens rea*, providing liability where (1) the discharge of waste (2) causes or threatens to cause pollution (3) unless the discharge occurs in strict compliance with all required permits or a valid and effective order issued or rule adopted by the appropriate regulatory agency. A conflict would occur where it would be impossible to comply with both laws.... Here, nothing prevents appellant from complying with both. Likewise, §7.146 [now §7.145(a)(2)] does not authorize something which §7.147 prohibits or *vice versa*."

WATER §7.146. REPEALED

Repealed by Acts 2001, 77th Leg., ch. 934, §2, eff. June 14, 2001.

WATER §7.147. UNAUTHORIZED DISCHARGE

(a) A person commits an offense if the person discharges or allows the discharge of any waste or pollutant into any water in the state that causes or threatens to cause water pollution unless the waste or pollutant:

(1) is discharged in strict compliance with all required permits or with a valid and currently effective order issued or rule adopted by the appropriate regulatory agency; or

(2) consists of used oil and the concentration of used oil in the waste stream resulting from the discharge as it enters water in the state is less than 15 parts per million following the discharge and the person is authorized to discharge storm water under a general permit issued under Section 26.040.

(b) An offense under this section may be prosecuted without alleging or proving any culpable mental state.

(c) An offense under this section is punishable for an individual under Section 7.187(1)(B) or Section 7.187(2)(D) or both.

(d) An offense under this section is punishable for a person other than an individual under Section 7.187(1)(C).

History of Water §7.147: Acts 1997, 75th Leg., ch. 1072, §2, eff. Sept. 1, 1997. Amended by Acts 2005, 79th Leg., ch. 366, §1, eff. Sept. 1, 2005.

ANNOTATIONS

Valero Ref., L.P. v. State, 203 S.W.3d 556, 560 (Tex.App.—Houston [14th Dist.] 2006, no pet.). "Appellant ... claims that the State failed to allege an offense in its information. Appellant argues that the State charged appellant with an omission under [§]7.147 ... when there was no concomitant statutory duty to act. Therefore, appellant contends the State omitted an element necessary to constitute the offense. [W]e conclude the legislature, by employing the word 'allow,' created a positive duty on persons standing in a responsible relation to the prohibited act of unauthorized discharge to act to prevent a violation of §7.147.... Therefore, the State sufficiently alleged a statutory duty to act by tracking the language of §7.147."

WATER §7.148. FAILURE TO PROPERLY USE POLLUTION CONTROL MEASURES

(a) A person commits an offense if the person intentionally or knowingly tampers with, modifies, disables, or fails to use pollution control or monitoring devices, systems, methods, or practices required by

Chapter 26 or a rule adopted or a permit or an order issued under Chapter 26 by the commission or one of its predecessor agencies unless done in strict compliance with the rule, permit, or order.

(b) An offense under this section is punishable for an individual under Section 7.187(1)(C) or Section 7.187(2)(D) or both.

(c) An offense under this section is punishable for a person other than an individual under Section 7.187(1)(D).

History of Water §7.148: Acts 1997, 75th Leg., ch. 1072, §2, eff. Sept. 1, 1997.

WATER §7.149. FALSE STATEMENT

(a) A person commits an offense if the person intentionally or knowingly makes or causes to be made a false material statement, representation, or certification in, or omits or causes to be omitted material information from, an application, notice, record, report, plan, or other document, including monitoring device data, filed or required to be maintained by Chapter 26 or by a rule adopted or a permit or an order issued by the appropriate regulatory agency under Chapter 26.

(b) An offense under this section is punishable for an individual under Section 7.187(1)(C) or Section 7.187(2)(D) or both.

(c) An offense under this section is punishable for a person other than an individual under Section 7.187(1)(D).

History of Water §7.149: Acts 1997, 75th Leg., ch. 1072, §2, eff. Sept. 1, 1997.

WATER §7.150. FAILURE TO NOTIFY OR REPORT

(a) A person commits an offense if the person intentionally or knowingly fails to notify or report to the commission as required under Chapter 26 or by a rule adopted or a permit or an order issued by the appropriate regulatory agency under Chapter 26.

(b) An offense under this section is punishable for an individual under Section 7.187(1)(C) or Section 7.187(2)(D) or both.

(c) An offense under this section is punishable for a person other than an individual under Section 7.187(1)(D).

History of Water §7.150: Acts 1997, 75th Leg., ch. 1072, §2, eff. Sept. 1, 1997.

WATER §7.151. FAILURE TO PAY FEE

(a) A person commits an offense if the person intentionally or knowingly fails to pay a fee required by Chapter 26 or by a rule adopted or a permit or an order issued by the appropriate regulatory agency under Chapter 26.

(b) An offense under this section is punishable for an individual under Section 7.187(1)(H) or Section 7.187(2)(B) or both.

(c) An offense under this section is punishable for a person other than an individual under Section 7.187(1)(H).

History of Water §7.151: Acts 1997, 75th Leg., ch. 1072, §2, eff. Sept. 1, 1997.

WATER §7.152. INTENTIONAL OR KNOWING UNAUTHORIZED DISCHARGE & KNOWING ENDANGERMENT

(a) A person commits an offense if the person, acting intentionally or knowingly, discharges or allows the discharge of a waste or pollutant into or adjacent to water in the state and by that action knowingly places another person in imminent danger of death or serious bodily injury, unless the discharge is made in strict compliance with all required permits or with an order issued or rule adopted by the appropriate regulatory agency.

(b) For purposes of Subsection (a), in determining whether a defendant who is an individual knew that the violation placed another person in imminent danger of death or serious bodily injury, the defendant is responsible only for the defendant's actual awareness or actual belief possessed. Knowledge possessed by a person other than the defendant may not be attributed to the defendant. To prove a defendant's actual knowledge, circumstantial evidence may be used, including evidence that the defendant took affirmative steps to be shielded from relevant information.

(c) An offense under this section is punishable for an individual under Section 7.187(1)(D) or Section 7.187(2)(G) or both. If an offense committed by an individual under this section results in death or serious bodily injury to another person, the individual may be punished under Section 7.187(1)(E) or Section 7.187(2)(I) or both.

(d) An offense under this section is punishable for a person other than an individual under Section 7.187(1)(E). If an offense committed by a person other than an individual under this section results in death

WATER §7.148 (side tab)

or serious bodily injury to another person, the person may be punished under Section 7.187(1)(F).

History of Water §7.152: Acts 1997, 75th Leg., ch. 1072, §2, eff. Sept. 1, 1997.

WATER §7.153. INTENTIONAL OR KNOWING UNAUTHORIZED DISCHARGE & ENDANGERMENT

(a) A person commits an offense if the person, acting intentionally or knowingly with respect to the person's conduct, discharges or allows the discharge of a waste or pollutant into or adjacent to water in the state and by that action places another person in imminent danger of death or serious bodily injury, unless the discharge is made in strict compliance with all required permits or with a valid and currently effective order issued or rule adopted by the appropriate regulatory agency.

(b) An offense under this section is punishable for an individual under Section 7.187(1)(D) or Section 7.187(2)(F) or both. If an offense committed by an individual under this section results in death or serious bodily injury to another person, the individual may be punished under Section 7.187(1)(E) or Section 7.187(2)(G) or both.

(c) An offense under this section is punishable for a person other than an individual under Section 7.187(1)(E). If an offense committed by a person other than an individual under this section results in death or serious bodily injury to another person, the person may be punished under Section 7.187(1)(F).

History of Water §7.153: Acts 1997, 75th Leg., ch. 1072, §2, eff. Sept. 1, 1997.

WATER §7.154. RECKLESS UNAUTHORIZED DISCHARGE & ENDANGERMENT

(a) A person commits an offense if the person, acting recklessly with respect to the person's conduct, discharges or allows the discharge of a waste or pollutant into or adjacent to water in the state and by that action places another person in imminent danger of death or serious bodily injury, unless the discharge is made in strict compliance with all required permits or with a valid and currently effective order issued or rule adopted by the appropriate regulatory agency.

(b) An offense under this section is punishable for an individual under Section 7.187(1)(C) or Section 7.187(2)(D) or both. If an offense committed by an individual under this section results in death or serious

bodily injury to another person, the individual may be punished under Section 7.187(1)(D) or Section 7.187(2)(F) or both.

(c) An offense under this section is punishable for a person other than an individual under Section 7.187(1)(D). If an offense committed by a person other than an individual under this section results in death or serious bodily injury to another person, the person may be punished under Section 7.187(1)(E).

History of Water §7.154: Acts 1997, 75th Leg., ch. 1072, §2, eff. Sept. 1, 1997.

WATER §7.155. VIOLATION RELATING TO DISCHARGE OR SPILL

(a) A person commits an offense if the person:

(1) operates, is in charge of, or is responsible for a facility or vessel that causes a discharge or spill as defined by Section 26.263 and does not report the spill or discharge on discovery; or

(2) knowingly falsifies a record or report concerning the prevention or cleanup of a discharge or spill.

(b) An offense under Subsection (a)(1) is a Class A misdemeanor.

(c) An offense under Subsection (a)(2) is a felony of the third degree.

History of Water §7.155: Acts 1997, 75th Leg., ch. 1072, §2, eff. Sept. 1, 1997.

WATER §7.156. VIOLATION RELATING TO UNDERGROUND STORAGE TANK

(a) A person or business entity commits an offense if:

(1) the person or business entity engages in the installation, repair, or removal of an underground storage tank and the person or business entity:

(A) does not hold a registration under Section 26.452; and

(B) is not under the substantial control of a person or business entity who holds a registration under Section 26.452;

(2) the person or business entity:

(A) authorizes or allows the installation, repair, or removal of an underground storage tank to be conducted by a person or business entity who does not hold a registration under Section 26.452; or

WATER §7.156

(B) authorizes or allows the installation, repair, or removal of an underground storage tank to be performed or supervised by a person or business entity who does not hold a license under Section 26.456; or

(3) the conduct of the person or business entity makes the person or business entity responsible for a violation of Subchapter K, Chapter 26, or of a rule adopted or order issued under that subchapter.

(b) A person commits an offense if the person performs or supervises the installation, repair, or removal of an underground storage tank unless:

(1) the person holds a license under Section 26.456; or

(2) another person who holds a license under Section 26.456 is substantially responsible for the performance or supervision of the installation, repair, or removal.

(c) A person commits an offense if the person is an owner or operator of an underground storage tank regulated under Chapter 26 into which any regulated substance is delivered unless the underground storage tank has been issued a valid, current underground storage tank registration and certificate of compliance under Section 26.346.

(d) An offense under this section is a Class A misdemeanor.

History of Water §7.156: Acts 1997, 75th Leg., ch. 1072, §2, eff. Sept. 1, 1997. Amended by Acts 1999, 76th Leg., ch. 1441, §4, eff. Sept. 1, 1999; Acts 2001, 77th Leg., ch. 880, §4, eff. Sept. 1, 2001; Acts 2005, 79th Leg., ch. 722, §1 (eff. Sept. 1, 2005), ch. 1256, §1 (eff. Sept. 1, 2005).

WATER §7.1565. PRESUMPTION

If in the exercise of good faith a person depositing or causing to be deposited a regulated substance into an underground storage tank regulated under Chapter 26 receives a certificate of compliance for that underground storage tank under Section 26.346, the receipt of the certificate of compliance shall be considered prima facie evidence of compliance with this section.

History of Water §7.1565: Acts 1999, 76th Leg., ch. 1441, §5, eff. Sept. 1, 1999.

WATER §7.157. VIOLATION RELATING TO INJECTION WELLS

(a) A person commits an offense if the person knowingly or intentionally violates Chapter 27 or a rule adopted or an order or a permit issued under Chapter 27.

(b) An offense under this section is punishable under Section 7.187(1)(B).

History of Water §7.157: Acts 1997, 75th Leg., ch. 1072, §2, eff. Sept. 1, 1997.

WATER §7.158. VIOLATION RELATING TO PLUGGING WELLS

(a) A person commits an offense if the person is the owner of a well that is required to be cased or plugged by Chapter 28 and the person:

(1) fails or refuses to case or plug the well within the 30-day period following the date of the commission's order to do so; or

(2) fails to comply with any other order issued by the commission under Chapter 28 within the 30-day period following the date of the order.

(b) An offense under this section is a misdemeanor and is punishable under Section 7.187(1)(A).

History of Water §7.158: Acts 1997, 75th Leg., ch. 1072, §2, eff. Sept. 1, 1997.

WATER §7.159. VIOLATION RELATING TO WATER WELLS OR DRILLED OR MINED SHAFTS

(a) A person commits an offense if the person knowingly or intentionally violates Chapter 28 or a commission rule adopted or an order or a permit issued under that chapter.

(b) An offense under this section is punishable under Section 7.187(1)(B).

History of Water §7.159: Acts 1997, 75th Leg., ch. 1072, §2, eff. Sept. 1, 1997.

WATER §7.160. VIOLATION RELATING TO CERTAIN SUBSURFACE EXCAVATIONS

(a) A person commits an offense if the person knowingly or intentionally violates Chapter 31 or a commission rule adopted or an order or a permit issued under that chapter.

(b) An offense under this section is punishable under Section 7.187(1)(B).

History of Water §7.160: Acts 1997, 75th Leg., ch. 1072, §2, eff. Sept. 1, 1997.

WATER §7.161. VIOLATION RELATING TO SOLID WASTE IN ENCLOSED CONTAINERS OR VEHICLES

(a) An operator of a solid waste facility or a solid waste hauler commits an offense if the operator or hauler disposes of solid waste in a completely enclosed container or vehicle at a solid waste site or operation permitted as a Type IV landfill:

(1) without having in possession the special permit required by Section 361.091, Health and Safety Code;

(2) on a date or time not authorized by the commission; or

(3) without a commission inspector present to verify that the solid waste is free of putrescible, hazardous, and infectious waste.

(b) An offense under this section is a Class B misdemeanor.

(c) This section does not apply to:

(1) a stationary compactor that is at a specific location and that has an annual permit under Section 361.091, Health and Safety Code, issued by the commission, on certification to the commission by the generator that the contents of the compactor are free of putrescible, hazardous, or infectious waste; or

(2) an enclosed vehicle of a municipality if the vehicle has a permit issued by the commission to transport brush or construction-demolition waste and rubbish on designated dates, on certification by the municipality to the commission that the contents of the vehicle are free of putrescible, hazardous, or infectious waste.

(d) In this section, "putrescible waste" means organic waste, such as garbage, wastewater treatment plant sludge, and grease trap waste, that may:

(1) be decomposed by microorganisms with sufficient rapidity as to cause odors or gases; or

(2) provide food for or attract birds, animals, or disease vectors.

History of Water §7.161: Acts 1997, 75th Leg., ch. 1072, §2, eff. Sept. 1, 1997.

WATER §7.162. VIOLATIONS RELATING TO HAZARDOUS WASTE

(a) A person commits an offense if the person, acting intentionally or knowingly with respect to the person's conduct:

(1) transports, or causes or allows to be transported, for storage, processing, or disposal, any hazardous waste to any location that does not have all required permits;

(2) stores, processes, exports, or disposes of, or causes to be stored, processed, exported, or disposed of, any hazardous waste without all permits required by the appropriate regulatory agency or in knowing violation of any material condition or requirement of a permit or of an applicable interim status rule or standard;

(3) omits or causes to be omitted material information or makes or causes to be made any false material statement or representation in any application, label, manifest, record, report, permit, plan, or other document filed, maintained, or used to comply with any requirement of Chapter 361, Health and Safety Code, applicable to hazardous waste;

(4) generates, transports, stores, processes, or disposes of, or otherwise handles, or causes to be generated, transported, stored, processed, disposed of, or otherwise handled, hazardous waste, whether the activity took place before or after September 1, 1981, and who knowingly destroys, alters, conceals, or does not file, or causes to be destroyed, altered, concealed, or not filed, any record, application, manifest, report, or other document required to be maintained or filed to comply with the rules of the appropriate regulatory agency adopted under Chapter 361, Health and Safety Code;

(5) transports without a manifest, or causes or allows to be transported without a manifest, any hazardous waste required by rules adopted under Chapter 361, Health and Safety Code, to be accompanied by a manifest;

(6) tampers with, modifies, disables, or fails to use required pollution control or monitoring devices, systems, methods, or practices, unless done in strict compliance with Chapter 361, Health and Safety Code, or with an order, rule, or permit of the appropriate regulatory agency;

(7) releases, causes, or allows the release of a hazardous waste that causes or threatens to cause pollution, unless the release is made in strict compliance with all required permits or an order, rule, or permit of the appropriate regulatory agency; or

(8) does not notify or report to the appropriate regulatory agency as required by Chapter 361, Health and Safety Code, or by a rule adopted or an order or a permit issued by the appropriate regulatory agency under that chapter.

(b) An offense under Subsection (a)(1) or (a)(2) is punishable for an individual under Section 7.187(1)(B) or Section 7.187(2)(G) or both. An offense under Subsection (a)(3), (a)(4), or (a)(5) is punishable for an individual under Section 7.187(1)(B) or Section 7.187(2)(E) or both. An offense under Subsection (a)(6), (a)(7), or (a)(8) is punishable for an individual under Section 7.187(1)(C) or Section 7.187(2)(D) or both.

WATER §7.162

(c) If it is shown on the trial of an individual that the individual has been previously convicted of an offense under this section, an offense under Subsection (a)(1) or (a)(2) is punishable for an individual under Section 7.187(1)(C) or Section 7.187(2)(G) or both, and an offense under Subsection (a)(3), (a)(4), or (a)(5) is punishable for an individual under Section 7.187(1)(C) or Section 7.187(2)(F) or both.

(d) An offense under Subsection (a)(1), (a)(2), (a)(3), (a)(4), or (a)(5) is punishable for a person other than an individual under Section 7.187(1)(D). If it is shown on the trial of a person other than an individual that the person previously has been convicted of an offense under Subsection (a)(1), (a)(2), (a)(3), (a)(4), or (a)(5), the offense is punishable under Section 7.187(1)(E). An offense under Subsection (a)(6), (a)(7), or (a)(8) is punishable for a person other than an individual under Section 7.187(1)(D).

History of Water §7.162: Acts 1997, 75th Leg., ch. 1072, §2, eff. Sept. 1, 1997.

ANNOTATIONS

L.B. Foster Co. v. State, 106 S.W.3d 194, 200 (Tex. App.—Houston [1st Dist.] 2003, pet. ref'd). "As a felony offense, a three-year statute of limitations applies to a charge under subsection 7.162(a)(2). *At 207:* We conclude that, for purposes of criminal prosecutions under … 7.162(a)(2), the term 'disposal' does not include the passive disposal of hazardous wastes. In other words, a 'disposal' of hazardous waste under §7.162 requires more than the passive migration of waste through the soil unaided by affirmative human conduct. Some form of affirmative human conduct must accompany a disposal for it to rise to the level of criminal culpability." *See also* ***Slott v. State***, 148 S.W.3d 624, 629 (Tex.App.—Houston [14th Dist.] 2004, pet. ref'd); ***Ex parte Canady***, 140 S.W.3d 845, 849 (Tex.App.—Houston [14th Dist.] 2004, no pet.).

WATER §7.163. VIOLATIONS RELATING TO HAZARDOUS WASTE & ENDANGERMENT

(a) A person commits an offense if:

(1) acting intentionally or knowingly, the person transports, processes, stores, exports, or disposes of, or causes to be transported, processed, stored, exported, or disposed of, hazardous waste in violation of Chapter 361, Health and Safety Code, and by that action knowingly places another person in imminent danger of death or serious bodily injury;

(2) acting intentionally or knowingly with respect to the person's conduct, transports, processes, stores, exports, or disposes of, or causes to be transported, processed, stored, exported, or disposed of, hazardous waste in violation of Chapter 361, Health and Safety Code, and by that action places another person in imminent danger of death or serious bodily injury, unless the conduct charged is done in strict compliance with all required permits or with an order issued or a rule adopted by the appropriate regulatory agency;

(3) acting intentionally or knowingly with respect to the person's conduct, releases or causes or allows the release of a hazardous waste into the environment and by that action places another person in imminent danger of death or serious bodily injury, unless the release is made in strict compliance with all required permits or an order issued or a rule adopted by the appropriate regulatory agency; or

(4) acting recklessly with respect to the person's conduct, releases or causes or allows the release of a hazardous waste into the environment and by that action places another person in imminent danger of death or serious bodily injury, unless the release is made in strict compliance with all required permits or an order issued or a rule adopted by the appropriate regulatory agency.

(b) An offense under Subsection (a)(1) is punishable for an individual under Section 7.187(1)(E) or Section 7.187(2)(H) or both. An offense under Subsection (a)(1) is punishable for a person other than an individual under Section 7.187(1)(F). If an offense committed by an individual under Subsection (a)(1) results in death or serious bodily injury to another person, the individual may be punished under Section 7.187(1)(F) or Section 7.187(2)(J) or both. If an offense committed by a person other than an individual under Subsection (a)(1) results in death or serious bodily injury to another person, the person may be punished under Section 7.187(1)(G). For purposes of Subsection (a)(1), in determining whether a defendant who is an individual knew that the violation placed another person in imminent danger of death or serious bodily injury, the defendant is responsible only for the defendant's actual awareness or actual belief possessed. Knowledge possessed by a person other than the defendant may not be

———————— ————————

attributed to the defendant. To prove a defendant's actual knowledge, circumstantial evidence may be used, including evidence that the defendant took affirmative steps to be shielded from relevant information.

(c) An offense under Subsection (a)(2) is punishable for an individual under Section 7.187(1)(D) or Section 7.187(2)(F) or both. An offense under Subsection (a)(2) is punishable for a person other than an individual under Section 7.187(1)(E). If an offense committed under Subsection (a)(2) results in death or serious bodily injury to another person, an individual may be punished under Section 7.187(1)(E) or Section 7.187(2)(G) or both. If an offense committed by a person other than an individual under Subsection (a)(2) results in death or serious bodily injury to another person, the person may be punished under Section 7.187(1)(F).

(d) An offense under Subsection (a)(3) is punishable for an individual under Section 7.187(1)(D) or Section 7.187(2)(F) or both. An offense under Subsection (a)(3) is punishable for a person other than an individual under Section 7.187(1)(E). If an offense committed by an individual under Subsection (a)(3) results in death or serious bodily injury to another person, the individual may be punished under Section 7.187(1)(E) or Section 7.187(2)(G) or both. If an offense committed by a person other than an individual under Subsection (a)(3) results in death or serious bodily injury to another person, the person may be punished under Section 7.187(1)(F).

(e) An offense under Subsection (a)(4) is punishable for an individual under Section 7.187(1)(C) or Section 7.187(2)(D) or both. An offense under Subsection (a)(4) is punishable for a person other than an individual under Section 7.187(1)(E). If an offense committed by an individual under Subsection (a)(4) results in death or serious bodily injury to another person, the individual may be punished under Section 7.187(1)(E) or Section 7.187(2)(E) or both. If an offense committed by a person other than an individual under Subsection (a)(4) results in death or serious bodily injury to another person, the person may be punished under Section 7.187(1)(F).

History of Water §7.163: Acts 1997, 75th Leg., ch. 1072, §2, eff. Sept. 1, 1997.

WATER §7.164. VIOLATIONS RELATING TO MEDICAL WASTE: LARGE GENERATOR

(a) A person commits an offense if the person is a large quantity generator and the person, acting intentionally or knowingly with respect to the person's conduct:

(1) generates, collects, stores, processes, exports, or disposes of, or causes or allows to be generated, collected, stored, processed, exported, or disposed of, any medical waste without all permits required by the appropriate regulatory agency or in knowing violation of a material condition or requirement of a permit or of an applicable interim status rule or standard; or

(2) generates, collects, stores, treats, transports, or disposes of, or causes or allows to be generated, collected, stored, treated, transported, or disposed of, or otherwise handles any medical waste, and knowingly destroys, alters, conceals, or does not file a record, report, manifest, or other document required to be maintained or filed under rules adopted by the appropriate regulatory agency.

(b) An offense under this section is punishable for an individual under Section 7.187(1)(B) or Section 7.187(2)(G) or both. If it is shown on the trial of an individual that the individual has been previously convicted of an offense under this section, the offense is punishable for an individual under Section 7.187(1)(C) or Section 7.187(2)(I) or both.

(c) An offense under this section is punishable for a person other than an individual under Section 7.187(1)(B). If it is shown on the trial of a person other than an individual that the person has been previously convicted of an offense under this section, the offense is punishable by Section 7.187(1)(C).

History of Water §7.164: Acts 1997, 75th Leg., ch. 1072, §2, eff. Sept. 1, 1997.

WATER §7.165. VIOLATIONS RELATING TO MEDICAL WASTE: SMALL GENERATOR

(a) A person commits an offense if the person is a small quantity generator and the person, acting intentionally or knowingly with respect to the person's conduct:

(1) generates, collects, stores, processes, exports, or disposes of, or causes or allows to be generated, collected, stored, processed, exported, or disposed of, any medical waste without all permits required by the appropriate regulatory agency or in knowing violation of any material condition or requirement of a permit or of an applicable interim status rule or standard; or

(2) generates, collects, stores, treats, transports, or disposes of, or causes or allows to be generated, collected, stored, treated, transported, or disposed of, or otherwise handles any medical waste, and knowingly destroys, alters, conceals, or does not file a record, report, manifest, or other document required to be maintained or filed under rules adopted by the appropriate regulatory agency.

(b) An offense under this section is punishable for an individual under Section 7.187(1)(A). If it is shown on the trial of an individual that the individual has been previously convicted of an offense under this section, the offense is punishable for an individual under Section 7.187(1)(B) or Section 7.187(2)(C) or both.

(c) An offense under this section is punishable for a person other than an individual under Section 7.187(1)(B). If it is shown on the trial of a person other than an individual that the person has been previously convicted of an offense under this section, the offense is punishable under Section 7.187(1)(C).

History of Water §7.165: Acts 1997, 75th Leg., ch. 1072, §2, eff. Sept. 1, 1997.

WATER §7.166. VIOLATIONS RELATING TO TRANSPORTATION OF MEDICAL WASTE

(a) A person commits an offense if the person, acting intentionally or knowingly with respect to the person's conduct:

(1) transports, or causes or allows to be transported, for storage, processing, or disposal, any medical waste to a location that does not have all required permits;

(2) transports without a manifest, or causes or allows to be transported without a manifest, any medical waste required to be accompanied by a manifest under rules adopted by the appropriate regulatory agency; or

(3) operates a vehicle that is transporting medical waste, or that is authorized to transport medical waste, in violation of a rule adopted by the appropriate regulatory agency, including cleaning and safety regulations, that specifically relates to the transportation of medical waste.

(b) An offense under this section is punishable for an individual under Section 7.187(1)(B) or Section 7.187(2)(D) or both. If it is shown on the trial of an individual that the individual has been previously convicted of an offense under this section, the offense is punishable for an individual under Section 7.187(1)(C) or Section 7.187(2)(E) or both.

(c) An offense under this section is punishable for a person other than an individual under Section

7.187(1)(E). If it is shown on the trial of a person other than an individual that the person has been previously convicted of an offense under this section, the offense is punishable under Section 7.187(1)(F).

History of Water §7.166: Acts 1997, 75th Leg., ch. 1072, §2, eff. Sept. 1, 1997.

WATER §7.167. FALSE STATEMENTS RELATING TO MEDICAL WASTE

(a) A person commits an offense if the person knowingly:

(1) makes a false material statement, or knowingly causes or knowingly allows to be made a false material statement, to a person who prepares a regulated medical waste label, manifest, application, permit, plan, registration, record, report, or other document required by an order or a rule of the appropriate regulatory agency; or

(2) omits material information, or causes or allows material information to be omitted, from a regulated medical waste label, manifest, application, permit, plan, registration, record, report, or other document required by an order or a rule of the appropriate regulatory agency.

(b) An offense under this section is punishable for an individual under Section 7.187(1)(B) or Section 7.187(2)(D) or both. If it is shown on the trial of an individual that the individual has been previously convicted of an offense under this section, the offense is punishable for an individual under Section 7.187(1)(C) or Section 7.187(2)(E) or both.

(c) An offense under this section is punishable for a person other than an individual under Section 7.187(1)(B). If it is shown on the trial of a person other than an individual that the person has been previously convicted of an offense under this section, the offense is punishable under Section 7.187(1)(C).

History of Water §7.167: Acts 1997, 75th Leg., ch. 1072, §2, eff. Sept. 1, 1997.

WATER §7.168. INTENTIONAL OR KNOWING VIOLATION RELATING TO MEDICAL WASTE & KNOWING ENDANGERMENT

(a) A person commits an offense if the person, acting intentionally or knowingly, transports, processes, stores, exports, or disposes of, or causes to be transported, processed, stored, exported, or disposed of, medical waste in violation of Chapter 361, Health and

Safety Code, and by that action knowingly places another person in imminent danger of death or serious bodily injury.

(b) An offense under this section is punishable for an individual under Section 7.187(1)(E) or Section 7.187(2)(H) or both. If an offense committed by an individual under this section results in death or serious bodily injury to another person, the offense is punishable for an individual under Section 7.187(1)(F) or Section 7.187(2)(J) or both.

(c) An offense under this section is punishable for a person other than an individual under Section 7.187(1)(F). If an offense committed by a person other than an individual under this section results in death or serious bodily injury to another person, the offense is punishable under Section 7.187(1)(G).

History of Water §7.168: Acts 1997, 75th Leg., ch. 1072, §2, eff. Sept. 1, 1997.

WATER §7.169. INTENTIONAL OR KNOWING VIOLATION RELATING TO MEDICAL WASTE & ENDANGERMENT

(a) A person commits an offense if the person, acting intentionally or knowingly with respect to the person's conduct, transports, processes, stores, exports, or disposes of medical waste in violation of Chapter 361, Health and Safety Code, and by that action places another person in imminent danger of death or serious bodily injury, unless the conduct charged is done in strict compliance with all required permits or with an order issued or rule adopted by the appropriate regulatory agency.

(b) An offense under this section is punishable for an individual under Section 7.187(1)(D) or Section 7.187(2)(F) or both. If an offense committed by an individual under this section results in death or serious bodily injury to another person, the offense is punishable for an individual under Section 7.187(1)(E) or Section 7.187(2)(G) or both.

(c) An offense under this section is punishable for a person other than an individual under Section 7.187(1)(E). If an offense committed by a person other than an individual under this section results in death or serious bodily injury to another person, the offense is punishable under Section 7.187(1)(F).

History of Water §7.169: Acts 1997, 75th Leg., ch. 1072, §2, eff. Sept. 1, 1997.

WATER §7.170. INTENTIONAL OR KNOWING RELEASE OF MEDICAL WASTE INTO ENVIRONMENT & ENDANGERMENT

(a) A person commits an offense if the person, acting intentionally or knowingly with respect to the person's conduct, releases or causes or allows the release of a medical waste into the environment and by that action places another person in imminent danger of death or serious bodily injury, unless the release is done in strict compliance with all required permits or an order issued or rule adopted by the appropriate regulatory agency.

(b) An offense under this section is punishable for an individual under Section 7.187(1)(D) or Section 7.187(2)(G) or both. If an offense committed by an individual under this section results in death or serious bodily injury to another person, the offense is punishable for an individual under Section 7.187(1)(E) or Section 7.187(2)(G) or both.

(c) An offense under this section is punishable for a person other than an individual under Section 7.187(1)(E). If an offense committed by a person other than an individual under this section results in death or serious bodily injury to another person, the offense is punishable under Section 7.187(1)(F).

History of Water §7.170: Acts 1997, 75th Leg., ch. 1072, §2, eff. Sept. 1, 1997.

WATER §7.171. RECKLESS RELEASE OF MEDICAL WASTE INTO ENVIRONMENT & ENDANGERMENT

(a) A person commits an offense if the person, acting recklessly with respect to a person's conduct, releases or causes or allows the release of a medical waste into the environment and by that action places another person in imminent danger of death or serious bodily injury, unless the release is made in strict compliance with all required permits or an order issued or rule adopted by the appropriate regulatory agency.

(b) An offense under this section is punishable for an individual under Section 7.187(1)(D) or Section 7.187(2)(D) or both. If an offense committed by an individual under this section results in death or serious bodily injury to another person, the offense is punishable for an individual under Section 7.187(1)(E) or Section 7.187(2)(E) or both.

(c) An offense under this section is punishable for a person other than an individual under Section

7.187(1)(E). If an offense committed by a person other than an individual under this section results in death or serious bodily injury to another person, the offense is punishable under Section 7.187(1)(F).

History of Water §7.171: Acts 1997, 75th Leg., ch. 1072, §2, eff. Sept. 1, 1997.

WATER §7.172. FAILURE OF SEWAGE SYSTEM INSTALLER TO REGISTER

(a) A person commits an offense if the person violates Section 366.071, Health and Safety Code.

(b) Except as provided by this subsection, an offense under this section is a Class C misdemeanor. If it is shown on the trial of the defendant that the defendant has been previously convicted of an offense under this section, the offense is punishable under Section 7.187(1)(A) or Section 7.187(2)(A) or both.

History of Water §7.172: Acts 1997, 75th Leg., ch. 1072, §2, eff. Sept. 1, 1997.

WATER §7.173. VIOLATION RELATING TO SEWAGE DISPOSAL

(a) A person commits an offense if the person violates a rule adopted by the commission under Chapter 366, Health and Safety Code, or an order or resolution adopted by an authorized agent under Subchapter C, Chapter 366, Health and Safety Code.

(b) Except as provided by this subsection, an offense under this section is a Class C misdemeanor. If it is shown on the trial of the defendant that the defendant has been previously convicted of an offense under this section, the offense is punishable under Section 7.187(1)(A) or Section 7.187(2)(A) or both.

History of Water §7.173: Acts 1997, 75th Leg., ch. 1072, §2, eff. Sept. 1, 1997. Amended by Acts 1999, 76th Leg., ch. 824, §1, eff. Sept. 1, 1999.

WATER §7.1735. VIOLATION RELATING TO MAINTENANCE OF SEWAGE DISPOSAL SYSTEM

(a) A person commits an offense if the person knowingly violates an order or resolution adopted by an authorized agent under Section 366.0515, Health and Safety Code.

(b) An offense under this section is a Class C misdemeanor.

History of Water §7.1735: Acts 2005, 79th Leg., ch. 1129, §3, eff. Sept. 1, 2005.

WATER §7.174. VIOLATION OF SEWAGE DISPOSAL SYSTEM PERMIT PROVISION

(a) A person commits an offense if the person begins to construct, alter, repair, or extend an on-site sewage disposal system owned by another person before the owner of the system obtains a permit to construct, alter, repair, or extend the on-site sewage disposal system as required by Subchapter D, Chapter 366, Health and Safety Code.

(b) Except as provided by this subsection, an offense under this section is a Class C misdemeanor. If it is shown on the trial of the defendant that the defendant has previously been convicted of an offense under this section, the offense is punishable under Section 7.187(1)(A) or Section 7.187(2)(A) or both.

History of Water §7.174: Acts 1997, 75th Leg., ch. 1072, §2, eff. Sept. 1, 1997.

WATER §7.175. EMERGENCY REPAIR NOT AN OFFENSE

An emergency repair to an on-site sewage disposal system without a permit in accordance with the rules adopted under Section 366.012(a)(1)(C), Health and Safety Code, is not an offense under Section 7.172, 7.173, or 7.174 if a written statement describing the need for the repair is provided to the commission or its authorized agent not later than 72 hours after the repair is begun.

History of Water §7.175: Acts 1997, 75th Leg., ch. 1072, §2, eff. Sept. 1, 1997.

WATER §7.176. VIOLATIONS RELATING TO HANDLING OF USED OIL

(a) A person commits an offense if the person:

(1) intentionally discharges used oil into:

(A) a sewer or septic tank; or

(B) a drainage system, surface water or groundwater, a watercourse, or marine water unless the concentration of used oil in the waste stream resulting from the discharge as it enters water in the state is less than 15 parts per million following the discharge and the person is authorized to discharge storm water under a general permit issued under Section 26.040;

(2) knowingly mixes or commingles used oil with solid waste that is to be disposed of in landfills or directly disposes of used oil on land or in landfills, unless the mixing or commingling of used oil with solid waste

that is to be disposed of in landfills is incident to and the unavoidable result of the dismantling or mechanical shredding of motor vehicles, appliances, or other items of scrap, used, or obsolete metals;

(3) knowingly transports, treats, stores, disposes of, recycles, causes to be transported, or otherwise handles any used oil within the state:

(A) in violation of standards or rules for the management of used oil; or

(B) without first complying with the registration requirements of Chapter 371, Health and Safety Code, and rules adopted under that chapter;

(4) intentionally applies used oil to roads or land for dust suppression, weed abatement, or other similar uses that introduce used oil into the environment;

(5) violates an order of the commission to cease and desist an activity prohibited by this section or a rule applicable to a prohibited activity; or

(6) intentionally makes a false statement or representation in an application, label, manifest, record, report, permit, or other document filed, maintained, or used for purposes of program compliance.

(b) It is an exception to the application of this section that a person unknowingly disposes into the environment any used oil that has not been properly segregated or separated by the generator from other solid wastes.

(c) It is an exception to the application of Subsection (a)(2) that the mixing or commingling of used oil with solid waste that is to be disposed of in landfills is incident to and the unavoidable result of the dismantling or mechanical shredding of motor vehicles, appliances, or other items of scrap, used, or obsolete metals.

(d) Except as provided by this subsection, an offense under this section is punishable under Section 7.187(1)(B) or Section 7.187(2)(F), or both. If it is shown on the trial of the defendant that the defendant has been previously convicted of an offense under this section, the offense is punishable under Section 7.187(1)(C) or Section 7.187(2)(H) or both.

History of Water §7.176: Acts 1997, 75th Leg., ch. 1072, §2, eff. Sept. 1, 1997. Amended by Acts 2005, 79th Leg., ch. 38, §1 (eff. Sept. 1, 2005), ch. 366, §2 (eff. Sept. 1, 2005).

ANNOTATIONS

L.B. Foster Co. v. State, 106 S.W.3d 194, 208 (Tex. App.—Houston [1st Dist.] 2003, pet. ref'd). "'[P]erson' [includes] corporations for purposes of prosecuting violations under … 7.176(a)(2). *At 209:* [T]he term

'directly' [in §7.176(a)(2)] signals to the reader that a distinction exists between the two offenses. From the context of the statutory provision, it is clear that the distinction is as follows: one offense involves mixing or commingling used oil with solid waste before disposing of it, while the other offense does not. *At 210:* We conclude that evidence supporting a conviction under subsection 7.176(a)(2) will not be deemed insufficient merely because the State fails to show that the defendant 'directly,' *i.e.*, without an intervening agent, poured or dumped used oil on the ground."

Tarlton v. State, 93 S.W.3d 168, 173 (Tex.App.—Houston [14th Dist.] 2002, pet. ref'd). "[A]ppellant contends that the trial court erred in denying his motion to set aside the indictment because it fails to negate the two exceptions set forth in the statute. The State must negate the existence of any exception to an offense in the indictment. The negation of an exception to an offense constitutes an element of the offense. However, the State need not expressly negate an exception in the indictment; it may do so implicitly. [¶] Here, we find the indictment implicitly negated both exceptions set forth in §7.176. By alleging in the indictment that appellant acted 'knowingly,' the State negated the first exception, which states the statute does not apply to one who '*unknowingly* disposes' of certain products into the environment. The indictment also alleged that appellant disposed of used oil 'on land.' Thus, the State implicitly negated the second exception, which provides that §7.176(a)(2) does not apply [to used oil mixed with solid waste that is to be disposed of *in landfills*]."

WATER §7.177. VIOLATIONS OF CLEAN AIR ACT

(a) A person commits an offense if the person intentionally or knowingly, with respect to the person's conduct, violates:

(1) Section 382.0518(a), Health and Safety Code;

(2) Section 382.054, Health and Safety Code;

(3) Section 382.056(a), Health and Safety Code;

(4) Section 382.058(a), Health and Safety Code; or

(5) an order, permit, or exemption issued or a rule adopted under Chapter 382, Health and Safety Code.

(b) An offense under this section is punishable for an individual under Section 7.187(1)(B) or Section 7.187(2)(C) or both.

(c) An offense under this section is punishable for a person other than an individual under Section 7.187(1)(C).

History of Water §7.177: Acts 1997, 75th Leg., ch. 1072, §2, eff. Sept. 1, 1997.

WATER §7.178. FAILURE TO PAY FEES UNDER CLEAN AIR ACT

(a) A person commits an offense if the person intentionally or knowingly does not pay a fee required by Chapter 382, Health and Safety Code, or by a rule adopted or an order issued under that chapter.

(b) An offense under this section is punishable for an individual under Section 7.187(1)(H) or Section 7.187(2)(B) or both.

(c) An offense under this section is punishable for a person other than an individual under Section 7.187(1)(H).

History of Water §7.178: Acts 1997, 75th Leg., ch. 1072, §2, eff. Sept. 1, 1997.

WATER §7.179. FALSE REPRESENTATIONS UNDER CLEAN AIR ACT

(a) A person commits an offense if the person intentionally or knowingly makes or causes to be made a false material statement, representation, or certification in, or omits material information from, or knowingly alters, conceals, or does not file or maintain a notice, application, record, report, plan, or other document required to be filed or maintained by Chapter 382, Health and Safety Code, or by a rule adopted or a permit or order issued under that chapter.

(b) An offense under this section is punishable for an individual under Section 7.187(1)(C) or Section 7.187(2)(D) or both.

(c) An offense under this section is punishable for a person other than an individual under Section 7.187(1)(D).

History of Water §7.179: Acts 1997, 75th Leg., ch. 1072, §2, eff. Sept. 1, 1997.

WATER §7.180. FAILURE TO NOTIFY UNDER CLEAN AIR ACT

(a) A person commits an offense if the person intentionally or knowingly does not notify or report to the commission as required by Chapter 382, Health and Safety Code, or by a rule adopted or a permit or order issued under that chapter.

(b) An offense under this section is punishable for an individual under Section 7.187(1)(C) or Section 7.187(2)(D) or both.

(c) An offense under this section is punishable for a person other than an individual under Section 7.187(1)(D).

History of Water §7.180: Acts 1997, 75th Leg., ch. 1072, §2, eff. Sept. 1, 1997.

WATER §7.181. IMPROPER USE OF MONITORING DEVICE

(a) A person commits an offense if the person intentionally or knowingly tampers with, modifies, disables, or fails to use a required monitoring device; tampers with, modifies, or disables a monitoring device; or falsifies, fabricates, or omits data from a monitoring device, unless the act is done in strict compliance with Chapter 382, Health and Safety Code, or a permit, variance, or order issued or a rule adopted by the commission.

(b) An offense under this section is punishable for an individual under Section 7.187(1)(C) or Section 7.187(2)(D) or both.

(c) An offense under this section is punishable for a person other than an individual under Section 7.187(1)(D).

History of Water §7.181: Acts 1997, 75th Leg., ch. 1072, §2, eff. Sept. 1, 1997.

WATER §7.182. RECKLESS EMISSION OF AIR CONTAMINANT & ENDANGERMENT

(a) A person commits an offense if the person recklessly, with respect to the person's conduct, emits an air contaminant that places another person in imminent danger of death or serious bodily injury, unless the emission is made in strict compliance with Chapter 382, Health and Safety Code, or a permit, variance, or order issued or a rule adopted by the commission.

(b) An offense under this section is punishable for an individual under Section 7.187(1)(D) or Section 7.187(2)(F) or both.

(c) An offense under this section is punishable for a person other than an individual under Section 7.187(1)(E).

History of Water §7.182: Acts 1997, 75th Leg., ch. 1072, §2, eff. Sept. 1, 1997.

WATER §7.183. INTENTIONAL OR KNOWING EMISSION OF AIR CONTAMINANT & KNOWING ENDANGERMENT

(a) A person commits an offense if the person intentionally or knowingly, with respect to the person's conduct, emits an air contaminant with the knowledge that the person is placing another person in imminent danger of death or serious bodily injury unless the emission is made in strict compliance with Chapter 382, Health and Safety Code, or a permit, variance, or order issued or a rule adopted by the commission.

(b) An offense under this section is punishable for an individual under Section 7.187(1)(E) or Section 7.187(2)(F) or both.

(c) An offense under this section is punishable for a person other than an individual under Section 7.187(1)(F).

History of Water §7.183: Acts 1997, 75th Leg., ch. 1072, §2, eff. Sept. 1, 1997.

WATER §7.184. VIOLATIONS RELATING TO LOW-LEVEL RADIOACTIVE WASTE

(a) A person commits an offense if the person:

(1) intentionally or knowingly violates a provision of Chapter 401, Health and Safety Code, other than the offense described by Subdivision (2); or

(2) intentionally or knowingly receives, processes, concentrates, stores, transports, or disposes of low-level radioactive waste without a license issued under Chapter 401, Health and Safety Code.

(b) Except as provided by this subsection, an offense under Subsection (a)(1) is a Class B misdemeanor. If it is shown on the trial of the person that the person has previously been convicted of an offense under Subsection (a)(1), the offense is a Class A misdemeanor.

(c) Except as provided by this subsection, an offense under Subsection (a)(2) is a Class A misdemeanor. If it is shown on the trial of the person that the person has previously been convicted of an offense under Subsection (a)(2), the offense is punishable under Section 7.187(1)(D) or Section 7.187(2)(D) or both.

History of Water §7.184: Acts 1997, 75th Leg., ch. 1072, §2, eff. Sept. 1, 1997. Amended by Acts 1999, 76th Leg., ch. 1367, §38, eff. Sept. 1, 1999.

WATER §7.185. KNOWING OR INTENTIONAL UNAUTHORIZED DISPOSAL OF LEAD-ACID BATTERIES

(a) A person commits an offense if the person knowingly or intentionally disposes of a lead-acid battery other than as provided by Section 361.451, Health and Safety Code.

(b) An offense under this section is a Class A misdemeanor.

History of Water §7.185: Acts 1997, 75th Leg., ch. 1072, §2, eff. Sept. 1, 1997.

WATER §7.186. SEPARATE OFFENSES

Each day a person engages in conduct proscribed by this subchapter constitutes a separate offense.

History of Water §7.186: Acts 1997, 75th Leg., ch. 1072, §2, eff. Sept. 1, 1997.

WATER §7.187. PENALTIES

A person convicted of an offense under this subchapter is punishable by:

(1) a fine, as imposed under the section creating the offense, of:

(A) not more than $1,000;

(B) not less than $1,000 or more than $50,000;

(C) not less than $1,000 or more than $100,000;

(D) not less than $1,000 or more than $250,000;

(E) not less than $2,000 or more than $500,000;

(F) not less than $5,000 or more than $1,000,000;

(G) not less than $10,000 or more than $1,500,000; or

(H) not more than twice the amount of the required fee;

(2) confinement for a period, as imposed by the section creating the offense, not to exceed:

(A) 30 days;

(B) 90 days;

(C) 180 days;

(D) one year;

(E) two years;

(F) five years;

(G) 10 years;

(H) 15 years;

(I) 20 years; or

(J) 30 years; or

(3) both fine and confinement, as imposed by the section creating the offense.

History of Water §7.187: Acts 1997, 75th Leg., ch. 1072, §2, eff. Sept. 1, 1997.

WATER §7.188. REPEAT OFFENSES

If it is shown at the trial of the defendant that the defendant has previously been convicted of the same offense under this subchapter, the maximum punishment is doubled with respect to both the fine and confinement, unless the section creating the offense specifies otherwise.

History of Water §7.188: Acts 1997, 75th Leg., ch. 1072, §2, eff. Sept. 1, 1997.

WATER §7.189. VENUE

Venue for prosecution of an alleged violation under this subchapter is in:

(1) the county in which the violation is alleged to have occurred;

(2) the county where the defendant resides;

(3) if the alleged violation involves the transportation of a discharge, waste, or pollutant, any county to which or through which the discharge, waste, or pollutant was transported; or

(4) Travis County.

History of Water §7.189: Acts 1997, 75th Leg., ch. 1072, §2, eff. Sept. 1, 1997.

WATER §7.190. DISPOSITION OF FINES

A fine recovered through a prosecution brought under this subchapter shall be divided equally between the state and any local government significantly involved in prosecuting the case, except that if the court determines that the state or the local government bore significantly more of the burden of prosecuting the case, the court may apportion up to 75 percent of the fine to the government that predominantly prosecuted the case.

History of Water §7.190: Acts 1997, 75th Leg., ch. 1072, §2, eff. Sept. 1, 1997.

WATER §7.191. NOTICE OF CONVICTION

In addition to a sentence that may be imposed under this subchapter, a person other than an individual that has been adjudged guilty of an offense may be ordered by the court to give notice of the conviction to any person the court considers appropriate.

History of Water §7.191: Acts 1997, 75th Leg., ch. 1072, §2, eff. Sept. 1, 1997.

WATER §7.192. JUDGMENT OF CONVICTION

On conviction under this subchapter, the clerk of the court in which the conviction is returned shall send a copy of the judgment to the commission.

History of Water §7.192: Acts 1997, 75th Leg., ch. 1072, §2, eff. Sept. 1, 1997.

WATER §7.193. PEACE OFFICERS

For purposes of this subchapter, the authorized agents and employees of the Parks and Wildlife Department are peace officers. Those agents and employees are empowered to enforce this subchapter the same as any other peace officer and for that purpose have the powers and duties of peace officers assigned by Chapter 2, Code of Criminal Procedure.

History of Water §7.193: Acts 1997, 75th Leg., ch. 1072, §2, eff. Sept. 1, 1997.

WATER §7.194. ALLEGATIONS

In alleging the name of a defendant private corporation, it is sufficient to state in the complaint, indictment, or information the corporate name or to state any name or designation by which the corporation is known or may be identified. It is not necessary to allege that the defendant was lawfully incorporated.

History of Water §7.194: Acts 1997, 75th Leg., ch. 1072, §2, eff. Sept. 1, 1997.

WATER §7.195. SUMMONS & ARREST

(a) After a complaint is filed or an indictment or information presented against a private corporation under this subchapter, the court or clerk shall issue a summons to the corporation. The summons shall be in the same form as a capias except that:

(1) it shall summon the corporation to appear before the court named at the place stated in the summons;

(2) it shall be accompanied by a certified copy of the complaint, indictment, or information; and

(3) it shall provide that the corporation appear before the court named at or before 10 a.m. of the Monday next after the expiration of 20 days after it is served with summons, except when service is made on the secretary of state, in which instance the summons shall provide that the corporation appear before the court named at or before 10 a.m. of the Monday next after the expiration of 30 days after the secretary of state is served with summons.

(b) No individual may be arrested upon a complaint, indictment, or information against a private corporation.

History of Water §7.195: Acts 1997, 75th Leg., ch. 1072, §2, eff. Sept. 1, 1997.

WATER §7.196. SERVICE OF SUMMONS

(a) A peace officer shall serve a summons on a private corporation by personally delivering a copy of it to the corporation's registered agent for service. If a registered agent has not been designated or cannot with reasonable diligence be found at the registered office, the peace officer shall serve the summons by personally delivering a copy of it to the president or a vice president of the corporation.

(b) If the peace officer certifies on the return that the peace officer diligently but unsuccessfully attempted to effect service under Subsection (a) or if the corporation is a foreign corporation that has no certificate of authority, the peace officer shall serve the summons on the secretary of state. On receipt of the summons copy, the secretary of state shall immediately forward it by certified or registered mail, return receipt requested, addressed to the defendant corporation at its registered office or, if it is a foreign corporation, at its principal office in the state or country under whose law it was incorporated.

(c) The secretary of state shall keep a permanent record of the date and time of receipt and the disposition of each summons served under Subsection (b) together with the return receipt.

History of Water §7.196: Acts 1997, 75th Leg., ch. 1072, §2, eff. Sept. 1, 1997.

WATER §7.197. ARRAIGNMENT & PLEADINGS

In any criminal action instituted against a private corporation under this subchapter:

(1) appearance is for the purpose of arraignment; and

(2) the corporation has 10 full days after the day the arraignment takes place and before the day the trial begins to file written pleadings.

History of Water §7.197: Acts 1997, 75th Leg., ch. 1072, §2, eff. Sept. 1, 1997.

WATER §7.198. APPEARANCE

(a) A defendant private corporation appears through counsel or its representative.

(b) If a private corporation does not appear in response to summons or appears but does not plead, the corporation is considered to be present in person for all purposes, and the court shall enter a plea of not guilty on the corporation's behalf and may proceed with trial, judgment, and sentencing.

(c) After appearing and entering a plea in response to summons, if a private corporation is absent without good cause at any time during later proceedings, the corporation is considered to be present in person for all purposes, and the court may proceed with trial, judgment, or sentencing.

History of Water §7.198: Acts 1997, 75th Leg., ch. 1072, §2, eff. Sept. 1, 1997.

WATER §7.199. FINE TREATED AS JUDGMENT IN CIVIL ACTION

If a person other than an individual is found guilty of a violation of this subchapter and a fine is imposed, the fine shall be entered and docketed by the clerk of the court as a judgment against the person, and the fine shall be of the same force and effect and be enforced against the person in the same manner as if the judgment were recovered in a civil action.

History of Water §7.199: Acts 1997, 75th Leg., ch. 1072, §2, eff. Sept. 1, 1997.

WATER §7.200. EFFECT ON CERTAIN OTHER LAWS

Conduct punishable as an offense under this subchapter that is also punishable under another law may be prosecuted under either law.

History of Water §7.200: Acts 1997, 75th Leg., ch. 1072, §2, eff. Sept. 1, 1997.

WATER §7.201. DEFENSE EXCLUDED

It is not a defense to prosecution under this subchapter that the person did not know of or was not aware of a rule, order, or statute.

History of Water §7.201: Acts 1997, 75th Leg., ch. 1072, §2, eff. Sept. 1, 1997.

WATER §7.202. PROOF OF KNOWLEDGE

In determining whether a defendant who is an individual knew that the violation placed another person in imminent danger of death or serious bodily injury under Section 7.168, 7.169, 7.170, or 7.171, the defendant is responsible only for the defendant's actual awareness or actual belief possessed. Knowledge possessed by a person other than the defendant may not be attributed to the defendant. To prove a defendant's actual knowledge, however, circumstantial evidence may be used, including evidence that the defendant took affirmative steps to be shielded from relevant information.

History of Water §7.202: Acts 1997, 75th Leg., ch. 1072, §2, eff. Sept. 1, 1997.

WATER §7.203. CRIMINAL ENFORCEMENT REVIEW

(a) This section is applicable to criminal prosecution of alleged environmental violations of this code, of the Health and Safety Code, or of any other statute, rule, order, permit, or other decision of the commission that is within the commission's jurisdiction committed by a defendant holding a permit issued by the commission or a defendant employed by a person holding such a permit and that is related to the activity for which the permit was issued. This section does not apply to an alleged environmental violation that clearly involves imminent danger of death or bodily injury under an endangerment offense specified in Section 7.252. Nothing in this section limits the power of a peace officer to arrest a person for an alleged offense.

(b) Before a peace officer, as that term is defined in Section 7.193 or Chapter 2, Code of Criminal Procedure, may refer any alleged criminal environmental violation by a person holding a permit issued by the commission or an employee of that person of this code, of the Health and Safety Code, or of any other statute, rule, order, permit, or other decision of the commission that is within the commission's jurisdiction to a prosecuting attorney for criminal prosecution, the peace officer shall notify the commission in writing of the alleged criminal environmental violation and include with the notification a report describing the facts and circumstances of the alleged criminal environmental violation. This section does not prohibit a peace officer from issuing a citation or making an arrest.

(c) As soon as practicable and in no event later than the 45th day after receiving a notice and report under Subsection (b), the commission shall evaluate the report and determine whether an alleged environmental violation exists and whether administrative or civil remedies would adequately and appropriately address the alleged environmental violation. In making its evaluation and determination, the commission shall consider the factors prescribed in Section 7.053. If the commission does not make a determination within the 45-day period required by this subsection:

(1) the appropriate prosecuting attorney may bring an action for criminal prosecution; and

(2) notwithstanding Subsection (e), the commission or the state is not entitled to receive any part of an amount recovered through a prosecution brought by that prosecuting attorney.

(d) If the commission determines that an alleged environmental violation exists and that administrative or civil remedies are inadequate or inappropriate to address the violation, the commission shall notify the peace officer in writing of the reasons why administrative or civil remedies are inadequate or inappropriate and recommending criminal prosecution, and the prosecuting attorney may proceed with the criminal prosecution of the alleged violation. In all other cases, the commission shall issue written notification to the peace officer that the alleged environmental violation is to be resolved through administrative or civil means by the appropriate authorities and the reasons why administrative or civil remedies are adequate or appropriate. A prosecuting attorney may not prosecute an alleged violation if the commission determines that administrative or civil remedies are adequate and appropriate.

(e) Any fine, penalty, or settlement recovered through a prosecution subject to this section and brought in the name and by authority of the State of Texas, whether recovered through any form of pretrial resolution, plea agreement, or sentencing after trial, shall be apportioned 70 percent to the state to cover the costs of instituting the procedures and requirements of Subsections (a)-(d) and 30 percent to any local government significantly involved in prosecuting the case. In a case where the procedures described in this section do not apply, the provisions of Section 7.190 apply.

History of Water §7.203: Acts 2003, 78th Leg., ch. 937, §1, eff. Sept. 1, 2003.

SUBCHAPTER F. DEFENSES

WATER §7.251. ACT OF GOD

If a person can establish that an event that would otherwise be a violation of a statute within the commission's jurisdiction or a rule adopted or an order or a permit issued under such a statute was caused solely by an act of God, war, strike, riot, or other catastrophe, the event is not a violation of that statute, rule, order, or permit.

History of Water §7.251: Acts 1997, 75th Leg., ch. 1072, §2, eff. Sept. 1, 1997.

WATER §7.252. DEFENSES TO ENDANGERMENT OFFENSES

It is an affirmative defense to prosecution under Section 7.152, 7.153, 7.154, 7.163, 7.168, 7.169, 7.170, 7.171, 7.182, or 7.183 that:

(1) the conduct charged was freely consented to by the person endangered and that the danger and conduct charged were reasonably foreseeable hazards of the person's occupation, business, or profession or a medical treatment or medical or scientific experimentation conducted by professionally approved methods and the person endangered had been made aware of the risks involved before giving consent; or

(2) the person charged was an employee who was carrying out the person's normal activities and was acting under orders from the person's employer, unless the person charged engaged in knowing and wilful violations.

History of Water §7.252: Acts 1997, 75th Leg., ch. 1072, §2, eff. Sept. 1, 1997.

WATER §7.253. DEFENSES AVAILABLE TO PERSON RESPONSIBLE FOR SOLID WASTE VIOLATIONS

(a) For purposes of an enforcement action initiated under this chapter, a person responsible for solid waste under Section 361.271, Health and Safety Code, is liable for a violation of a statutory or regulatory prohibition against releasing or creating an imminent threat of releasing solid waste unless the person can establish by a preponderance of the evidence that the release or threatened release was caused solely by an act or omission of a third person and that the defendant:

(1) exercised due care concerning the solid waste, considering the characteristics of the solid waste, in light of all relevant facts and circumstances; and

(2) took precautions against foreseeable acts or omissions of the third person and the consequences that could foreseeably result from those acts or omissions.

(b) The defense under Subsection (a) does not apply if the third person:

(1) is an employee or agent of the defendant; or

(2) has a direct or indirect contractual relationship with the defendant and the act or omission of the third person occurred in connection with the contractual relationship. The term "contractual relationship" includes land contracts, deeds, or other instruments transferring title or possession of real property.

(c) A defendant who enters into a contractual relationship as provided by Subsection (b)(2) is not liable under a statute or rule within the commission's jurisdiction if:

(1) the sole contractual relationship is acceptance for rail carriage by a common carrier under a published tariff; or

(2) the defendant acquired the real property on which the facility requiring the remedial action is located after the disposal or placement of the hazardous substance on, in, or at the facility, and the defendant establishes by a preponderance of the evidence that:

(A) the defendant exercised due care concerning the solid waste, considering the characteristics of the solid waste, in light of all relevant facts and circumstances; and

(B) the defendant took precautions against foreseeable acts or omissions of the third person and the consequences that could foreseeably result from those acts or omissions; or

(C) at the time the defendant acquired the facility the defendant did not know and had no reason to know that a hazardous substance that is the subject of the release or threatened release was disposed of on, in, or at the facility;

(D) the defendant is a governmental entity that acquired the facility by escheat, by other involuntary transfer or acquisition, or by the exercise of the power of eminent domain; or

(E) the defendant acquired the facility by inheritance or bequest.

(d) To demonstrate the condition under Subsection (c)(2)(C), the defendant must have made, at the time of acquisition, appropriate inquiry into the previous ownership and uses of the property consistent with good commercial or customary practice in an effort to minimize liability. In deciding whether the defendant meets this condition, the court shall consider:

(1) any specialized knowledge or experience of the defendant;

(2) the relationship of the purchase price to the value of the property if the property were uncontaminated;

(3) commonly known or reasonably ascertainable information about the property;

(4) the obvious presence or likely presence of contamination of the property; and

(5) the defendant's ability to detect the contamination by appropriate inspection.

(e) This section does not decrease the liability of a previous owner or operator of a facility who is liable under a statute or rule within the commission's jurisdiction. If the defendant obtained actual knowledge of the release or threatened release of a hazardous substance at a facility at the time the defendant owned the real property on which the facility is located and subsequently transferred ownership of the property to another person without disclosing that knowledge, the defendant is liable and a defense under this section is not available to the defendant.

(f) Subsections (c), (d), and (e) do not affect the liability, under a statute or rule within the commission's jurisdiction, of a defendant who, by an act or omission, caused or contributed to the release or threatened release of a hazardous substance that is the subject of the action concerning the facility.

History of Water §7.253: Acts 1997, 75th Leg., ch. 1072, §2, eff. Sept. 1, 1997.

WATER §7.254. DEFENSE TO USED OIL OFFENSES

It is an affirmative defense to prosecution under Section 7.176 that the person unknowingly disposed of used oil into the environment because the used oil had not been properly segregated or separated by the generator from other solid wastes.

History of Water §7.254: Acts 1997, 75th Leg., ch. 1072, §2, eff. Sept. 1, 1997.

WATER §7.255. DEFENSE EXCLUDED

Unless otherwise provided by this chapter, the fact that a person holds a permit issued by the commission does not relieve that person from liability for the violation of a statute within the commission's jurisdiction or a rule adopted or an order or a permit issued under such a statute.

History of Water §7.255: Acts 1997, 75th Leg., ch. 1072, §2, eff. Sept. 1, 1997.

TEXAS RULES OF EVIDENCE

TABLE OF CONTENTS

★

TEXAS RULES OF EVIDENCE

ARTICLE I. GENERAL PROVISIONS

TRE 101. TITLE & SCOPE

(a) **Title.** These rules shall be known and cited as the Texas Rules of Evidence.

(b) **Scope.** Except as otherwise provided by statute, these rules govern civil and criminal proceedings (including examining trials before magistrates) in all courts of Texas, except small claims courts.

(c) **Hierarchical Governance in Criminal Proceedings.** Hierarchical governance shall be in the following order: the Constitution of the United States, those federal statutes that control states under the supremacy clause, the Constitution of Texas, the Code of Criminal Procedure and the Penal Code, civil statutes, these rules, and the common law. Where possible, inconsistency is to be removed by reasonable construction.

(d) **Special Rules of Applicability in Criminal Proceedings.**

(1) *Rules not applicable in certain proceedings.* These rules, except with respect to privileges, do not apply in the following situations:

(A) the determination of questions of fact preliminary to admissibility of evidence when the issue is to be determined by the court under Rule 104;

(B) proceedings before grand juries;

(C) proceedings in an application for habeas corpus in extradition, rendition, or interstate detainer;

(D) a hearing under Code of Criminal Procedure article 46.02, by the court out of the presence of a jury, to determine whether there is sufficient evidence of incompetency to require a jury determination of the question of incompetency;

(E) proceedings regarding bail except hearings to deny, revoke or increase bail;

(F) a hearing on justification for pretrial detention not involving bail;

(G) proceedings for the issuance of a search or arrest warrant; or

(H) proceedings in a direct contempt determination.

(2) *Applicability of privileges.* These rules with respect to privileges apply at all stages of all actions, cases, and proceedings.

(3) *Military justice hearings.* Evidence in hearings under the Texas Code of Military Justice, Tex. Gov't Code §432.001-432.195, shall be governed by that Code.

Smith v. State, 5 S.W.3d 673, 679 (Tex.Crim.App. 1999). TREs 404(b) and 403 can be "congruously" applied with CCP art. 38.36(a). Therefore, art. 38.36(a) does not conflict with TREs 404(b) and 403.

TRE 102. PURPOSE & CONSTRUCTION

These rules shall be construed to secure fairness in administration, elimination of unjustifiable expense and delay, and promotion of growth and development of the law of evidence to the end that the truth may be ascertained and proceedings justly determined.

TRE 103. RULINGS ON EVIDENCE

(a) **Effect of Erroneous Ruling.** Error may not be predicated upon a ruling which admits or excludes evidence unless a substantial right of the party is affected, and

(1) *Objection.* In case the ruling is one admitting evidence, a timely objection or motion to strike appears of record, stating the specific ground of objection, if the specific ground was not apparent from the context. When the court hears objections to offered evidence out of the presence of the jury and rules that such evidence be admitted, such objections shall be deemed to apply to such evidence when it is admitted before the jury without the necessity of repeating those objections.

(2) *Offer of proof.* In case the ruling is one excluding evidence, the substance of the evidence was made known to the court by offer, or was apparent from the context within which questions were asked.

(b) **Record of Offer and Ruling.** The offering party shall, as soon as practicable, but before the court's charge is read to the jury, be allowed to make, in the absence of the jury, its offer of proof. The court may add any other or further statement which shows the character of the evidence, the form in which it was offered, the objection made, and the ruling thereon. The court may, or at the request of a party shall, direct the making of an offer in question and answer form.

(c) **Hearing of Jury.** In jury cases, proceedings shall be conducted, to the extent practicable, so as to prevent inadmissible evidence from being suggested to the jury by any means, such as making statements or offers of proof or asking questions in the hearing of the jury.

(d) Fundamental Error in Criminal Cases. In a criminal case, nothing in these rules precludes taking notice of fundamental errors affecting substantial rights although they were not brought to the attention of the court.

Haley v. State, 173 S.W.3d 510, 517 (Tex.Crim.App. 2005). "While it is clear from the record that Haley's counsel did not obtain a running objection, we find that the bench conference was a hearing outside the presence of the jury and satisfied [TRE] 103(a). ... Therefore, we find Haley properly preserved this alleged error in the trial court and the Court of Appeals was correct in addressing whether the trial court erred in admitting this testimony."

Warner v. State, 969 S.W.2d 1, 2 (Tex.Crim.App. 1998). "An offer of proof may be in question-and-answer form, or it may be in the form of a concise statement by counsel. An offer of proof to be accomplished by counsel's concise statement must include a reasonably specific summary of the evidence offered and must state the relevance of the evidence unless the relevance is apparent, so that the court can determine whether the evidence is relevant and admissible. [¶] [A] State's motion in limine that excludes defense evidence is subject to reconsideration throughout trial and that to preserve error an offer of the evidence must be made at trial."

Hess v. State, 953 S.W.2d 837, 841 (Tex.App.—Fort Worth 1997, pet. ref'd). "[A]ny error in admission of evidence is cured by admission of the same evidence elsewhere without objection."

Higgins v. State, 924 S.W.2d 739, 745 (Tex.App.— Texarkana 1996, pet. ref'd). "A timely objection is one that is made at the earliest possible opportunity, or as soon as the grounds for the objection become apparent."

Mack v. State, 872 S.W.2d 36, 38 (Tex.App.—Fort Worth 1994, no pet.). "Defense counsel must continue to object each time the evidence is offered. ... There are two exceptions to the contemporaneous objection rule. Error may be preserved with the continuing or running objection. Defense counsel may also lodge a valid objection to all the offered testimony it deems objectionable on a given subject at one time out of the jury's presence. If the trial court admits the evidence, any error in its admission is preserved."

TRE 104. PRELIMINARY QUESTIONS

(a) Questions of Admissibility Generally. Preliminary questions concerning the qualification of a person to be a witness, the existence of a privilege, or the admissibility of evidence shall be determined by the court, subject to the provisions of subdivision (b). In making its determination the court is not bound by the rules of evidence except those with respect to privileges.

(b) Relevancy Conditioned on Fact. When the relevancy of evidence depends upon the fulfillment of a condition of fact, the court shall admit it upon, or subject to, the introduction of evidence sufficient to support a finding of the fulfillment of the condition.

(c) Hearing of Jury. In a criminal case, a hearing on the admissibility of a confession shall be conducted out of the hearing of the jury. All other civil or criminal hearings on preliminary matters shall be conducted out of the hearing of the jury when the interests of justice so require or in a criminal case when an accused is a witness and so requests.

(d) Testimony by Accused Out of the Hearing of the Jury. The accused in a criminal case does not, by testifying upon a preliminary matter out of the hearing of the jury, become subject to cross-examination as to other issues in the case.

(e) Weight and Credibility. This rule does not limit the right of a party to introduce before the jury evidence relevant to weight or credibility.

Granados v. State, 85 S.W.3d 217, 227 (Tex.Crim. App.2002). "Because suppression hearings involve the determination of preliminary questions concerning the admissibility of evidence, the language of the current rules indicates that the rules of evidence (except privileges) no longer apply to suppression hearings. This conclusion is consistent with the U.S. Supreme Court's interpretation of the [FRE], which has a counterpart to [TRE] 104(a)...."

Fischer v. State, 235 S.W.3d 470, 473 (Tex. App.—San Antonio 2007, pet. granted 2-06-08). "Rule 104(b) governs the admissibility of evidence that is not relevant unless other connecting facts are proven. '[I]n deciding whether to admit extraneous offense evidence … the trial court must, under Rule 104(b), make an initial determination at the proffer of the evidence, that a jury could reasonably find beyond a reasonable doubt that the defendant committed the extraneous offense.' Proof of a culpable connection between the accused and the extraneous offense is an essential precondition to establishing the relevance of the extraneous offense." *See also Harrell v. State*, 884 S.W.2d 154, 159-60 (Tex. Crim.App.1994).

Harty v. State, 229 S.W.3d 849, 853 (Tex.App.— Texarkana 2007, pet. ref'd). "[G]enerally, a defendant may not testify for a limited purpose at a trial on the merits. [¶] There are exceptions, though, to the general rule. A defendant may testify at a pretrial hearing on the issue of voluntariness and limit the scope of cross-examination. If a defendant testifies pretrial, the scope of cross-examination is limited to the issue of voluntariness, and the fact that the defendant testifies pretrial does not compel him to take the stand at the trial on the merits." (Internal quotes omitted.)

Lookingbill v. State, 855 S.W.2d 66, 70 (Tex. App.—Corpus Christi 1993, pet. ref'd). "The party objecting to the evidence, not the trial court, has the duty to notice whether the conditions of admissibility are subsequently met."

TRE 105. LIMITED ADMISSIBILITY

(a) **Limiting Instruction.** When evidence which is admissible as to one party or for one purpose but not admissible as to another party or for another purpose is admitted, the court, upon request, shall restrict the evidence to its proper scope and instruct the jury accordingly; but, in the absence of such request the court's action in admitting such evidence without limitation shall not be a ground for complaint on appeal.

(b) **Offering Evidence for Limited Purpose.** When evidence referred to in paragraph (a) is excluded, such exclusion shall not be a ground for complaint on appeal unless the proponent expressly offers the evidence for its limited, admissible purpose or limits its offer to the party against whom it is admissible.

ANNOTATIONS

Hammock v. State, 46 S.W.3d 889, 892 (Tex.Crim. App.2001). "[T]he 'party opposing evidence has the burden of objecting and requesting the limiting in-struction at the [time of the] introduction of the evidence.' Once evidence is received without a limiting instruction, it becomes part of the general evidence and may be used for all purposes. *At 893:* [TRE] 105(a) does not require an objection to the admission of evidence before requesting a limiting instruction on that evidence. Rule 105(a) requires only a defendant to 'request' that the trial court 'restrict the evidence to its proper scope and instruct the jury accordingly.'"

Rankin v. State, 974 S.W.2d 707, 712 (Tex.Crim. App.1996). "The language of [TRCE] 105(a) [now TRE 105(a)] does not address … when limiting instructions should be given, but, rather, sets out the circumstances under which an instruction must be given. … [L]ogic demands that the instruction be given at the first opportunity. [¶] Limiting instructions given for the first time during the jury charge thus do not constitute an efficacious application of [TRCE] 105(a) [now TRE 105(a)] since it allows for the possibility that evidence will be used improperly in clear contravention to the purpose of the rule. [L]imiting instructions operate most effectively when given simultaneously with the relevant evidence.…"

Payton v. State, 830 S.W.2d 722, 730 (Tex.App.— Houston [14th Dist.] 1992, no pet.). "No limiting instruction is required when an extraneous offense is offered to directly prove one of the main issues in the indicted case such as motive, *intent* or malice."

TRE 106. REMAINDER OF OR RELATED WRITINGS OR RECORDED STATEMENTS

When a writing or recorded statement or part thereof is introduced by a party, an adverse party may at that time introduce any other part or any other writing or recorded statement which ought in fairness to be considered contemporaneously with it. "Writing or recorded statement" includes depositions.

ANNOTATIONS

Reece v. State, 772 S.W.2d 198, 203 (Tex.App.— Houston [14th Dist.] 1989, no pet.). "Under [TRCE] 106 [now TRE 106], a party whose opponent introduces part of a writing or recorded statement may *at that time* introduce 'any other part.' Not only may the adverse party immediately offer the remainder, he may interrupt his opponent's case to do so, subject only to [TRCE] 610(a) [now TRE 611(a)]. But the rule is truly *optional* ... and does not require the adverse party who seeks to introduce the remainder to present it during his opponent's case; he can rely instead on [TRCE] 107 [now TRE 107]."

TRE 107. RULE OF OPTIONAL COMPLETENESS

When part of an act, declaration, conversation, writing or recorded statement is given in evidence by one party, the whole on the same subject may be inquired into by the other, and any other act, declaration, writing or recorded statement which is necessary to make it fully understood or to explain the same may also be given in evidence, as when a letter is read, all letters on the same subject between the same parties may be given. "Writing or recorded statement" includes depositions.

ANNOTATIONS

Walters v. State, 247 S.W.3d 204, 205 (Tex.Crim. App.2007). "Appellant ... asserted that the trial judge violated the rule of optional completeness under [TRE] 107 when he allowed a 911 operator to testify that he asked appellant if he wanted to talk about what had happened, but excluded appellant's response. *At 217-18:* Hearsay statements are generally not admissible unless the statement falls within a recognized exception to the hearsay rule. Rule 107, the rule of optional completeness, is one such rule. This rule is one of admissibility and permits the introduction of otherwise inadmissible evidence when that evidence is necessary to fully and fairly explain a matter 'opened up' by the adverse party. It is designed to reduce the possibility of the jury receiving a false impression from hearing only a part of some act, conversation, or writing. Rule 107 does not permit the introduction of other similar, but inadmissible, evidence unless it is necessary to explain properly admitted evidence. Further, the rule is not invoked by the mere reference to a document, statement, or act. And it is limited by [TRE] 403, which permits a trial judge to exclude otherwise relevant evidence if its unfair prejudicial effect or its likelihood of confusing the issues substantially outweighs its probative value. *At 220:* We agree that the trial court's ruling excluding the evidence of the second 911 conversation was an abuse of discretion."

Tovar v. State, 221 S.W.3d 185, 190-91 (Tex.App.— Houston [1st Dist.] 2006, no pet.). "A party who opens a door to an issue 'cannot complain when the opposing party desires to go into the details of that subject.' More specifically, under rule 107, the State is entitled to admission of a complainant's videotaped statement when (1) the defense attorney asks questions concerning some of the complainant's statements on the videotape, (2) the defense attorney's questions leave the possibility of the jury's receiving a false impression from hearing only a part of the conversation, with statements taken out of context, and (3) the videotape is necessary for the conversation to be fully understood. Although the defense attorney's questions pertain to the complainant's statements on the videotape, rule 107 does not permit the introduction of the videotape by the State when (1) the videotape is unnecessary to show the context of the statement, such as the absence of a statement by the complainant rather than the existence of any directly contradictory statement, and (2) the admission of the videotape would likely create confusion, such as through references to extraneous offense evidence."

ARTICLE II. JUDICIAL NOTICE

TRE 201. JUDICIAL NOTICE OF ADJUDICATIVE FACTS

(a) Scope of Rule. This rule governs only judicial notice of adjudicative facts.

(b) Kinds of Facts. A judicially noticed fact must be one not subject to reasonable dispute in that it is either (1) generally known within the territorial jurisdiction of the trial court or (2) capable of accurate and ready determination by resort to sources whose accuracy cannot reasonably be questioned.

(c) When Discretionary. A court may take judicial notice, whether requested or not.

(d) When Mandatory. A court shall take judicial notice if requested by a party and supplied with the necessary information.

(e) Opportunity to Be Heard. A party is entitled upon timely request to an opportunity to be heard as to the propriety of taking judicial notice and the tenor of the matter noticed. In the absence of prior notification, the request may be made after judicial notice has been taken.

(f) Time of Taking Notice. Judicial notice may be taken at any stage of the proceeding.

(g) Instructing Jury. In civil cases, the court shall instruct the jury to accept as conclusive any fact judicially noticed. In criminal cases, the court shall instruct the jury that it may, but is not required to, accept as conclusive any fact judicially noticed.

See also CCP art. 21.18.

ANNOTATIONS

Watts v. State, 99 S.W.3d 604, 606-07 (Tex.Crim. App.2003). "Because we find that the trial judge did not judicially notice an adjudicative fact, but rather directly addressed the jury on the application of a point of law, immediately before the parties rested and before she read the charge to the jury, we hold that the trial judge committed error by commenting on the weight of the evidence. Although we find that the trial judge's interpretation of our holding in ***American Plant Food*** was essentially correct, it was for the jury to decide if the drainage ditch water in *this* case constituted 'water in the State.'"

Mata v. State, 46 S.W.3d 902, 910 (Tex.Crim.App. 2001). "We may take judicial notice of scientific literature not presented by either party at trial or on appeal."

Perkins v. State, 905 S.W.2d 452, 453 (Tex. App.—El Paso 1995, pet. ref'd). "While a court has discretion to take judicial notice of legislative facts, it is not required to do so in the absence of a request."

Elwell v. State, 872 S.W.2d 797, 799 (Tex.App.— Dallas 1994, no pet.). "[W]e cannot take judicial notice of the records of any court not properly admitted into evidence before the trial court, even though the records might be attached to a defendant's brief."

Granados v. State, 843 S.W.2d 736, 738 (Tex. App.—Corpus Christi 1992, no pet.). "An appellate court may take judicial notice for the first time on appeal."

Jubert v. State, 753 S.W.2d 458, 459 (Tex.App.— Texarkana 1988, no pet.). "The court is permitted to take judicial notice of its own orders, records and judgments."

Stowe v. State, 745 S.W.2d 568, 570 (Tex.App.— Houston [1st Dist.] 1988, no pet.). "Because statements by an individual outside a judicial proceeding may be subject to varying interpretations, we hold that they are not the kind of 'adjudicative facts' covered by [TRCE] 201 [now TRE 201], and are not subject to judicial [notice]."

TRE 202. DETERMINATION OF LAW OF OTHER STATES

A court upon its own motion may, or upon the motion of a party shall, take judicial notice of the constitutions, public statutes, rules, regulations, ordinances, court decisions, and common law of every other state, territory, or jurisdiction of the United States. A party requesting that judicial notice be taken of such matter shall furnish the court sufficient information to enable it properly to comply with the request, and shall give all parties such notice, if any, as the court may deem necessary, to enable all parties fairly to prepare to meet the request. A party is entitled upon timely request to an opportunity to be heard as to the propriety of taking judicial notice and the tenor of the matter noticed. In the absence of prior notification, the request may be made after judicial notice has been taken. Judicial notice of such matters may be taken at any stage of the proceeding. The court's determination shall be subject to review as a ruling on a question of law.

ANNOTATIONS

Lewis v. State, 737 S.W.2d 857, 860 (Tex.App.— Houston [1st Dist.] 1987, pet. ref'd). "This Court may take judicial notice on its own motion of the judicial decisions of other states."

TRE 203. DETERMINATION OF THE LAWS OF FOREIGN COUNTRIES

A party who intends to raise an issue concerning the law of a foreign country shall give notice in the pleadings or other reasonable written notice, and at least 30 days prior to the date of trial such party shall furnish all parties copies of any written materials or sources that the party intends to use as proof of the foreign law. If the materials or sources were originally written in a language other than English, the party intending to rely upon them shall furnish all parties both a copy of the foreign language text and an English translation. The court, in determining the law of a foreign nation, may consider any material or source, whether or not submitted by a party or admissible under the rules of evidence, including but not limited to affidavits, testimony, briefs, and treatises. If the court considers sources other than those submitted by a party, it shall give all parties notice and a reasonable opportunity to comment on the sources and to submit further materials for review by the court. The court, and not a jury, shall determine the laws of foreign countries. The court's determination shall be subject to review as a ruling on a question of law.

ANNOTATIONS

Alvarado v. State, 804 S.W.2d 669, 670 (Tex. App.—El Paso 1991), *aff'd*, 853 S.W.2d 17 (Tex.Crim. App. 1993). "We note Appellant's objection in the trial court to the manner of proof concerning the laws of the Republic of Mexico.... Only the explanatory testimony of Secretary Medina was offered. ... While the more formal procedure of [TRCE] 203 [now TRE 203] was not followed, that rule does permit the trial judge to consider 'any material or source, whether or not submitted by a party or admissible under the rules of evidence, including but not limited to affidavits, testimony, briefs and treatises.' ... We consider Medina's explanation a proper basis for consideration of the Mexican rules by the trial judge."

TRE 204. DETERMINATION OF TEXAS CITY & COUNTY ORDINANCES, THE CONTENTS OF THE TEXAS REGISTER, & THE RULES OF AGENCIES PUBLISHED IN THE ADMINISTRATIVE CODE

A court upon its own motion may, or upon the motion of a party shall, take judicial notice of the ordinances of municipalities and counties of Texas, of the contents of the Texas Register, and of the codified rules of the agencies published in the Administrative Code. Any party requesting that judicial notice be taken of such matter shall furnish the court sufficient information to enable it properly to comply with the request, and shall give all parties such notice, if any, as the court may deem necessary, to enable all parties fairly to prepare to meet the request. A party is entitled upon timely request to an opportunity to be heard as to the propriety of taking judicial notice and the tenor of the matter noticed. In the absence of prior notification, the request may be made after judicial notice has been taken. The court's determination shall be subject to review as a ruling on a question of law.

ANNOTATIONS

Gette v. State, 209 S.W.3d 139, 144 (Tex.App.— Houston [1st Dist.] 2006, no pet.). "[W]e hold that an appellate court as well as a trial court may take judicial notice of an ordinance as long as a party or parties comply with the provisions of Rule 204. [¶] In order for a court to take judicial notice of an ordinance, it must be authenticated." *See also* *Volosen v. State*, 227 S.W.3d 77, 81 (Tex.Crim.App.2007).

ARTICLE III. PRESUMPTIONS

[No rules adopted at this time.]

ARTICLE IV. RELEVANCY & ITS LIMITS

TRE 401. DEFINITION OF "RELEVANT EVIDENCE"

"Relevant evidence" means evidence having any tendency to make the existence of any fact that is of consequence to the determination of the action more probable or less probable than it would be without the evidence.

ANNOTATIONS

Haley v. State, 173 S.W.3d 510, 518 (Tex.Crim.App. 2005). "The Court of Appeals correctly noted that Haley faced an indictment that did not identify a victim and charged only the offense of possession of cocaine with the intent to deliver. [Witness's] testimony in the form of victim-impact and victim-character testimony regarding an extraneous offense or bad act was irrelevant under Rule 401 to the determination of the appropriate sentence Haley should receive on the facts of this case. We agree with the lower court's holding that the trial court erred in admitting victim-impact evidence relating to the extraneous offense of murder in the punishment phase of Haley's cocaine possession trial."

Bigby v. State, 892 S.W.2d 864, 883 (Tex.Crim.App. 1994). "Evidence of flight or escape is admissible as a circumstance from which an inference of guilt may be drawn. To support the admission of evidence of escape from custody or flight it must appear that the escape or flight have some legal relevance to the offense under prosecution. To have such evidence excluded under relevancy challenges, the burden shifts to the defendant to show affirmatively the escape and flight directly connected to some other transaction and further that it was not connected with the offense at trial."

Fuller v. State, 829 S.W.2d 191, 198 (Tex.Crim.App. 1992). "[E]vidence not excludable on policy grounds may properly be received over a relevancy objection if it has any tendency at all, even potentially, to make a fact

TRE 401

of consequence more or less likely than it would be without the evidence. [¶] But if, after all proof on the question has been received, the evidence does not in the aggregate support a rational finding that such matter of consequence is true, the factfinder should not be allowed to pass upon it." *See also Levario v. State*, 964 S.W.2d 290, 297 (Tex.App.—El Paso 1997, no pet.).

Mayes v. State, 816 S.W.2d 79, 85 (Tex.Crim.App. 1991). "'Evidence which is essentially background in nature ... is universally offered and admitted as an aid to understanding.' ... It therefore appears that background evidence was meant to be included within the definition of relevancy, not necessarily because it influences a consequential fact, but because it illuminates a circumstance otherwise dimly perceived by the factfinder."

Montgomery v. State, 810 S.W.2d 372, 376 (Tex. Crim.App.1990). "In deciding whether a particular piece of evidence is relevant, a trial court judge should ask 'would a reasonable person, with some experience in the real world believe that the particular piece of evidence is helpful in determining the truth or falsity of any fact that is of consequence to the lawsuit.'"

Arzaga v. State, 86 S.W.3d 767, 776 (Tex.App.—El Paso 2002, no pet.). "Bolstering occurs when evidence is admitted for the sole purpose of convincing the fact finder that a particular witness or source of evidence is worthy of credit, without substantively contributing to make the existence of a fact that is of consequence to the determination of the action more or less probable than it would be without the evidence. Accordingly, if the evidence makes any substantive contribution, even if it only incrementally tends to further establish a fact of consequence, it is not bolstering."

Peters v. State, 31 S.W.3d 704, 706 (Tex.App.—Houston [1st Dist.] 2000, pet. ref'd). "Like all other relevant evidence, the admission of relevant expert testimony is favored, and one opposing it has the burden to show that its probative value is 'substantially' outweighed by other factors."

TRE 402. RELEVANT EVIDENCE GENERALLY ADMISSIBLE; IRRELEVANT EVIDENCE INADMISSIBLE

All relevant evidence is admissible, except as otherwise provided by Constitution, by statute, by these rules, or by other rules prescribed pursuant to statutory authority. Evidence which is not relevant is inadmissible.

TRE 403. EXCLUSION OF RELEVANT EVIDENCE ON SPECIAL GROUNDS

Although relevant, evidence may be excluded if its probative value is substantially outweighed by the danger of unfair prejudice, confusion of the issues, or misleading the jury, or by considerations of undue delay, or needless presentation of cumulative evidence.

ANNOTATIONS

Gigliobianco v. State, 210 S.W.3d 637, 641-42 (Tex. Crim.App.2006). "[A] trial court, when undertaking a Rule 403 analysis, must balance (1) the inherent probative force of the proffered item of evidence along with (2) the proponent's need for that evidence against (3) any tendency of the evidence to suggest decision on an improper basis, (4) any tendency of the evidence to confuse or distract the jury from the main issues, (5) any tendency of the evidence to be given undue weight by a jury that has not been equipped to evaluate the probative force of the evidence, and (6) the likelihood that presentation of the evidence will consume an inordinate amount of time or merely repeat evidence already admitted. Of course, these factors may well blend together in practice." *See also Wiley v. State*, 74 S.W.3d 399, 407 n.21 (Tex.Crim.App.2002); *Wheeler v. State*, 67 S.W.3d 879, 888 (Tex.Crim.App.2002).

Rodriguez v. State, 203 S.W.3d 837, 839 (Tex.Crim. App.2006). "We granted review to determine whether evidence of crimes committed by others is relevant to a defendant's sentence, and if relevant, whether such evidence is admissible under [TRE] 403. Finally, we ... address whether Appellant's due process rights were denied when he himself did not commit the other crimes introduced at the sentencing phase of his trial. [¶] We hold that the trial court did not err in admitting evidence of the crimes committed by persons other than [D, who was charged as a party to the offense] at [D's] sentencing...."

Powell v. State, 189 S.W.3d 285, 288 (Tex.Crim. App.2006). "Rule 403's use of the word 'may' reflects the draftsman's intent that the trial judge be given a very substantial discretion in balancing probative value on the one hand and unfair prejudice on the other, and that he should not be reversed simply because an appellate court believes that it would have decided the matter otherwise." (Internal quotes omitted.)

TRE 401

Hayes v. State, 85 S.W.3d 809, 815 (Tex.Crim.App. 2002). "A court may consider many factors in determining whether the probative value of photographs is substantially outweighed by the danger of unfair prejudice. These factors include: the number of exhibits offered, their gruesomeness, their detail, their size, whether they are in color or in black and white, whether they are close-up and whether the body depicted is clothed or naked. A court, however, should not be limited to this list. The availability of other means of proof and the circumstances unique to each individual case should also be noted. *At 816:* [A]utopsy photographs are generally admissible unless they depict mutilation of the victim caused by the autopsy itself. Changes rendered by the autopsy process are of minor significance if the disturbing nature of the photograph is primarily due to the injuries caused by the appellant." *See also Erazo v. State*, 144 S.W.3d 487, 488 (Tex.Crim.App.2004).

Mozon v. State, 991 S.W.2d 841, 846 n.6 (Tex.Crim. App.1999). "The trial court need not engage in [a] balancing test unless the opponent of the evidence further objects based upon Rule 403, that the probative value of the evidence is substantially outweighed by the danger of unfair prejudice, confusion of the issues, or misleading the jury, or by considerations of undue delay, or needless presentation of cumulative evidence. Once a Rule 403 objection is raised, however, the trial court has no discretion as to whether or not to engage in the balancing process."

TRE 404. CHARACTER EVIDENCE NOT ADMISSIBLE TO PROVE CONDUCT; EXCEPTIONS; OTHER CRIMES

(a) **Character Evidence Generally.** Evidence of a person's character or character trait is not admissible for the purpose of proving action in conformity therewith on a particular occasion, except:

(1) *Character of accused.* Evidence of a pertinent character trait offered:

(A) by an accused in a criminal case, or by the prosecution to rebut the same, or

(B) by a party accused in a civil case of conduct involving moral turpitude, or by the accusing party to rebut the same;

(2) *Character of victim.* In a criminal case and subject to Rule 412, evidence of a pertinent character trait of the victim of the crime offered by an accused, or by the prosecution to rebut the same, or evidence of peaceable character of the victim offered by the prosecution in a homicide case to rebut evidence that the victim was the first aggressor; or in a civil case, evidence of character for violence of the alleged victim of assaultive conduct offered on the issue of self-defense by a party accused of the assaultive conduct, or evidence of peaceable character to rebut the same;

(3) *Character of witness.* Evidence of the character of a witness, as provided in rules 607, 608 and 609.

(b) **Other Crimes, Wrongs or Acts.** Evidence of other crimes, wrongs or acts is not admissible to prove the character of a person in order to show action in conformity therewith. It may, however, be admissible for other purposes, such as proof of motive, opportunity, intent, preparation, plan, knowledge, identity, or absence of mistake or accident, provided that upon timely request by the accused in a criminal case, reasonable notice is given in advance of trial of intent to introduce in the State's case-in-chief such evidence other than that arising in the same transaction.

See also CCP arts. 38.36, 38.37.

ANNOTATIONS

TRE 404(a)

Torres v. State, 117 S.W.3d 891, 894-95 (Tex.Crim. App.2003). "When a defendant in a homicide prosecution raises the issue of self-defense, he may introduce evidence of the deceased's violent character. Specific acts of violence may be introduced to demonstrate the reasonableness of the defendant's fear of danger or to demonstrate that the deceased was the first aggressor. However, such specific acts of violence are admissible only to the extent that they are relevant apart from showing character conformity. [S]pecific, violent acts are relevant apart from showing character conformity in the context of proving that the deceased was the first aggressor by demonstrating the deceased's intent, motive, or state of mind. Because the specific act is probative of the deceased's state of mind or intent, the witness must know, but the defendant need not know of the act. [¶] There must be some evidence of aggression by the deceased during the events that gave rise to the criminal charges in the case before the defendant may introduce evidence of a prior specific violent act that tends to explain the deceased's later conduct."

Melgar v. State, 236 S.W.3d 302, 306-07 (Tex. App.—Houston [1st Dist.] 2007, pet. ref'd). "Generally, character evidence is not admissible to show that a person acted in conformity with a character trait on a particular occasion. However, an accused in a criminal case is permitted to introduce evidence of a specific good-character trait to show that it is improbable that he committed the charged offense, when that character trait is relevant to the offense. *At 308:* If evidence of a person's character or character trait is admissible [under rule 404(a)(1)(A)], proof may be made through *reputation or opinion* testimony. Therefore, the character witnesses' testimony was not inadmissible simply because it was in the form of an opinion rather than reputation. Under the [TRE], the rigid common-law distinction between opinion and reputation evidence has been relaxed." *See also* **Kirby v. State**, 208 S.W.3d 568, 573 (Tex.App.—Austin 2006, no pet.) (sexual abuse).

Stitt v. State, 102 S.W.3d 845, 849 (Tex.App.— Texarkana 2003, pet. ref'd). "A pertinent character trait is 'one that relates to a trait involved in the offense charged or a defense raised.'" *See also* **Santellan v. State**, 939 S.W.2d 155, 167 (Tex.Crim.App.1997); **Brazelton v. State**, 947 S.W.2d 644, 650 (Tex.App.—Fort Worth 1997, no pet.).

TRE 404(b)—Generally

Casey v. State, 215 S.W.3d 870, 879 (Tex.Crim.App. 2007). "Extraneous-offense evidence is not inadmissible under Rule 404(b) when it is offered to rebut an affirmative defense or a defensive issue that negates one of the elements of the crime. [¶] Once a trial court rules that uncharged misconduct evidence is not barred under Rule 404(b), the opponent of the evidence may further object under Rule 403."

Daggett v. State, 187 S.W.3d 444, 451-52 (Tex.Crim. App.2005). "If a defendant testifies to a blanket statement of good conduct or character—*e.g.*, 'I would never have sex with a minor'—he may 'open the door' by leaving a false impression with the jury about a relevant act or character trait. Evidence of an extraneous act that tends to rebut such testimony may be admissible to impeach the defendant. When such evidence is admitted, however, the jury may not consider it as substantive evidence of the charged offense, but only as evidence that the defendant misrepresented himself.

Thus, upon request, a judge must provide a limiting instruction informing the jury that they may use the evidence only to gauge the defendant's credibility, not as any proof that he is guilty of the charged offense. *At 454:* [If] extraneous offense evidence is improperly introduced during the State's case-in-chief, any error may be cured by the defendant's subsequent testimony which 'opens the door' to rebuttal." *See also* **Clay v. State**, 102 S.W.3d 794, 797 (Tex.App.—Texarkana 2003, no pet.).

Johnston v. State, 145 S.W.3d 215, 219 (Tex.Crim. App.2004). TRE 404(b) "prohibits only that evidence which is offered to prove a person's character, from which the trier of fact is then to infer that the person acted in conformity with that character trait on the occasion in question. [¶] Extraneous offense evidence may, however, be admissible if [it] is logically relevant to prove some other fact. [The] list [of other purposes in 404(b)] is illustrative, not exhaustive." *See also* **Rodriguez v. State**, 104 S.W.3d 87, 88 (Tex.Crim.App. 2003).

Castaldo v. State, 78 S.W.3d 345, 346 (Tex.Crim. App.2002). "In this case we address whether Rule 404(b) prohibits the admission of extraneous bad acts committed by a third party and whether same transaction contextual evidence ever requires a limiting instruction." Held: The answer to both questions is no.

Ex parte Varelas, 45 S.W.3d 627, 631 (Tex.Crim. App.2001). "[A] jury should be instructed that they are not to consider extraneous act evidence unless they believe beyond a reasonable doubt that the defendant committed that act. 'If a defendant, during the guilt/innocence phase, asks for an instruction to the jury on the standard of proof required for admitting extraneous offenses, the defendant is entitled to that instruction.'"

Pollard v. State, ___ S.W.3d ___ (Tex.App.—San Antonio 2008, pet. granted 6-11-08) (No. 04-06-00844-CR; 1-30-2008). There are "two types of contextual evidence: (1) 'same transaction contextual evidence' and (2) 'background' contextual evidence. When several crimes are intermixed or connected and testimony regarding one crime cannot be given without showing the other crimes, or it would be impracticable to do so, the evidence may be deemed admissible as 'same transaction contextual evidence.' On the other hand, character evidence offered simply because it is background evidence offered to help the jury understand the offense, but which otherwise conflicts with the proscription of Rule 404(b), is not admissible." *See also England v. State*, 887 S.W.2d 902, 915 (Tex.Crim. App.1994).

Castillo v. State, 59 S.W.3d 357, 361 (Tex.App.— Dallas 2001, pet. ref'd). "'To constitute an extraneous offense, the evidence must show a crime or bad act and that the defendant was connected to it.' The evidence must include some sort of extraneous *conduct* on behalf of the defendant which forms part of the alleged extraneous offense. Statements concerning a defendant's thoughts of wrongdoing are merely inchoate thoughts. Absent any actual conduct involved which alone or in combination with such thoughts could constitute a bad act, wrong, or crime, a defendant's comments about a desire or intent to commit an offense do not constitute prior misconduct and, therefore, do not implicate rule 404(b)."

Peoples v. State, 874 S.W.2d 804, 809 (Tex.App.— Fort Worth 1994, pet. ref'd). "[E]vidence that a witness has been threatened or that someone has attempted to coerce her testimony is admissible to show the accused's 'consciousness of guilt.' Threats or other attempts at coercion are 'hardly the actions of an innocent accused,' and evidence of such is every bit as probative of guilt as would be flight by the accused."

TRE 404(b)—Absence of Mistake

Johnston v. State, 145 S.W.3d 215, 222 (Tex.Crim. App.2004). "A second proper theory of admissibility under Rule 404(b) is evidence of uncharged misconduct to show the absence of mistake or accident. Sometimes a defendant admits the conduct, but raises a defense of 'it was an accident,' or 'it was inadvertent.' ... In such a case, the State may rebut the defense of 'accident' or 'mistake' with evidence of other conduct by the defendant which tends to show that his actions on those occasions, and hence on this occasion as well, were not mistaken, inadvertent, or accidental."

TRE 404(b)—Identity

Page v. State, 213 S.W.3d 332, 336 (Tex.Crim.App. 2006). "An extraneous offense may be admissible to show identity only when identity is at issue in the case. [T]he issue of identity may be raised by a defendant during cross-examination of the state's witnesses and ... in this case, appellant's identity was at issue after defense counsel cross-examined the complainant about appellant's weight. [¶] When the extraneous offense is introduced to prove identity by comparing common characteristics, it must be so similar to the

charged offense that the offenses illustrate the defendant's 'distinctive and idiosyncratic manner of committing criminal acts.' Such extraneous-offense evidence is admissible to prove identity when the common characteristics of each offense are so unusual as to act as the defendant's 'signature.' The signature must be apparent from a comparison of the circumstances in both cases."

Johnston v. State, 145 S.W.3d 215, 221 (Tex.Crim. App.2004). "[B]efore admitting evidence of another act of misconduct to show the identity of the assailant under this particular theory, the State must first show that the defendant is, in fact, the person who committed the other act."

Galvez v. State, 962 S.W.2d 203, 205 (Tex.App.— Austin 1998, pet. ref'd). "The State [argues] that 'gang' evidence is not subject to the restrictions of signature or *modus operandi* crimes because the proffered evidence was not an extraneous offense or bad act but rather was a status or trait tending to prove Galvez's identity. But Rule 404 bars use of such 'status' evidence to prove that the accused acted in conformity with the character trait presented." *See also Lane v. State*, 933 S.W.2d 504, 519 (Tex.Crim.App.1996).

TRE 404(b)—Intent

Robbins v. State, 88 S.W.3d 256, 261 (Tex.Crim. App.2002). Held: A defendant who goes beyond a simple plea of not guilty and puts his intent at issue for 404(b) purposes through vigorous cross-examination or other means (such as the presentation of various defensive theories) allows the trial court to decide that evidence of the defendant's other acts is relevant to a non-character-conformity purpose of establishing the defendant's intent.

Tate v. State, 981 S.W.2d 189, 191 (Tex.Crim.App. 1998). "[T]he issue ... is whether an uncommunicated threat is admissible under Rule 404(b) for purposes other than to show the victim's character and his conformity therewith. *At 193:* Appellant's purpose in offering [his aunt's] testimony was not to prove [victim's] character, but rather to prove [victim's] intent or motive to cause him harm on the night in question. Thus, the evidence of this uncommunicated threat by [victim], allegedly made only a month or two before [victim's] death, had relevance beyond its tendency to demonstrate [victim's] character. A reasonable jury could have believed this evidence shed light upon [victim's] state of mind when he arrived at appellant's house on the night in question, and, as long as it was otherwise admissible, appellant possessed the right to present it for the jury's consideration."

Brown v. State, 96 S.W.3d 508, 512-13 (Tex.App.—Austin 2002, no pet.). "When the defendant's intent to commit the offense charged is at issue, the relevance of an extraneous offense derives from the doctrine of chances—the instinctive recognition of that logical process which eliminates the element of innocent intent by multiplying instances of the same result until it is perceived that this element cannot explain them all. An unusual or abnormal element might be present in one instance, but the more often it occurs the less likely it is to be the true explanation. For the doctrine to apply, there must be a similarity between the charged and extraneous offenses, since it is the improbability of a like result being repeated by mere chance that gives the extraneous offense probative weight. The degree of similarity required, however, is not as great when intent is the material issue as when identity is the material issue and the extraneous offense is offered to prove *modus operandi*."

TRE 404(b)—Motive

Torres v. State, 71 S.W.3d 758, 761-62 (Tex.Crim.App.2002). "When a defendant claims that the deceased was the first aggressor, prior specific acts of violence relevant to the ultimate confrontation may be offered to show a deceased's state of mind, intent, or motive. We have not required that the specific, violent acts be directed against the defendant to be admissible. In fact, we have found error in excluding such acts where they were directed towards *third parties*." (Emphasis added.) *See also* **Hayes v. State**, 161 S.W.3d 507, 509 (Tex.Crim.App.2005).

TRE 404(b)—Notice

McDonald v. State, 179 S.W.3d 571, 577 (Tex.Crim.App.2005). "An exception to the notice requirement [of TRE 404(b)] is when the evidence arises from the same transaction. Under Rule 404(b), however, same transaction contextual evidence is admissible 'only to the extent that it is necessary to the jury's understanding of the offense.' It is admissible 'only when the offense would make little or no sense without also bringing in the same transaction evidence.' That is, it is admissible when several offenses are 'so intermixed or connected as to form a single, indivisible criminal transaction, such that in narrating the one, it is impracticable to avoid describing the other.' *At 578:* When

the facts of the primary offense can be understood on their own, notice is needed for evidence of uncharged misconduct. In this case, the primary offense was understandable on its own facts. We therefore conclude that the trial court abused its discretion in admitting the uncharged offense without notice because the appellant was entitled to notice upon request under Rule 404(b)."

Hernandez v. State, 176 S.W.3d 821, 823-24 (Tex.Crim.App.2005). "We understand the State to argue that a trial court may admit Rule 404(b) evidence notwithstanding the State's noncompliance with the notice provision of Rule 404(b) if the trial court determines that admitting the evidence would not frustrate the purpose of this notice provision of preventing surprise. The State, therefore, argues that the Rule 404(b) notice provision is not a rule of evidence admissibility. [¶] We disagree. Rule 404(b) literally conditions the admissibility of other-crimes evidence on the State's compliance with the notice provision of Rule 404(b). This is not to say that a trial court is without discretion to utilize its powers (such as granting continuances to reduce surprise) to permit the State to bring itself in compliance with the notice provision of Rule 404(b). But, a trial court must use these powers to ensure compliance and not to excuse noncompliance."

Hayden v. State, 66 S.W.3d 269, 272 (Tex.Crim.App. 2001). "[D]elivery to the defense of witness statements detailing extraneous offenses may ... satisfy the notice requirements of Rule 404(b). ... Whether the delivery of witness statements constitutes reasonable notice depends in part on the timing of that delivery. If the State gave the statements to the defense shortly after receiving the request for notice, the implicit statement is: 'These are the extraneous offenses that we intend to offer in the case-in-chief.' The longer the time lapse between the receipt of the notice and the delivery of the witness statements, the less likely that the recipient will conclude, 'This is the evidence that responds to my request.' Because a reasonable conclusion to be drawn when delivery of witness statements follows upon the heels of a timely request for notice, is that the State intends to use the evidence, 'reasonable' notice is implicit in the delivery." *See also* **Mozon v. State**, 991 S.W.2d 841, 845-46 (Tex.Crim.App.1999).

Buchanan v. State, 911 S.W.2d 11, 15 (Tex.Crim.App.1995). "We cannot conclude that the mere opening of [the State's] file containing an offense report detailing extraneous evidence satisfies the requirement of giving notice 'of intent to introduce' such evidence. The mere presence of an offense report indicating the State's awareness of the existence of such evidence does not indicate an 'intent to introduce' such evidence in its case in chief."

Espinosa v. State, 853 S.W.2d 36, 39 (Tex.Crim. App.1993). "[W]hen a defendant relies on a motion for discovery to request notice pursuant to [TRE] 404(b), it is incumbent upon him to secure a ruling on his motion in order to trigger the notice requirements of that rule."

Webb v. State, 36 S.W.3d 164, 177 (Tex.App.— Houston [14th Dist.] 2000, pet. ref'd). "Unlike a motion, any request for notice under rule 404(b) the appellant files while representing himself is effective for all purposes and remains in effect even if the appellant subsequently retains counsel. Therefore, we reject the notion that the State is not required to respond to a *pro se* request for notice under rule 404(b) because the accused's counsel did not later adopt it. [¶] To be effective, a request under rule 404(b) 'should be in writing and served on the prosecution.' A certificate of service creates a presumption that a document properly sent is received by the addressee. This presumption may be rebutted by an offer of proof of non-receipt, but absent any such proof, the presumption has the force of a rule of law."

TRE 404(b)—Plan

Daggett v. State, 187 S.W.3d 444, 451-52 (Tex.Crim. App.2005). An exception "under Rule 404(b) is proof of the defendant's 'plan,' frequently, but misleadingly, termed 'common scheme or plan.' [¶] When used properly, the 'plan' exception allows admission of evidence to show steps taken by the defendant in preparation for the charged offense. [¶] Unfortunately, courts frequently admit evidence of extraneous acts under this exception not to show acts the defendant took in preparation for the ultimate charged offense, but to show repeated acts that are similar to the charged offense. Repetition of the same act or same crime does not equal a 'plan.' It equals the repeated commission of the same criminal offense offered obliquely to show bad character and conduct in conformity with that bad character—'once a thief, always a thief.' This bad-character-conformity purpose, whether express or not, is precisely what is barred by Rule 404(b). Thus, if the

proponent is unable to articulate exactly how an extraneous act tends to prove a step toward an ultimate goal or overarching plan, the evidence is not admissible to prove part of a 'plan.'"

TRE 405. METHODS OF PROVING CHARACTER

(a) Reputation or Opinion. In all cases in which evidence of a person's character or character trait is admissible, proof may be made by testimony as to reputation or by testimony in the form of an opinion. In a criminal case, to be qualified to testify at the guilt stage of trial concerning the character or character trait of an accused, a witness must have been familiar with the reputation, or with the underlying facts or information upon which the opinion is based, prior to the day of the offense. In all cases where testimony is admitted under this rule, on cross-examination inquiry is allowable into relevant specific instances of conduct.

(b) Specific Instances of Conduct. In cases in which a person's character or character trait is an essential element of a charge, claim or defense, proof may also be made of specific instances of that person's conduct.

See also CCP art. 38.37.

ANNOTATIONS

Harrison v. State, 241 S.W.3d 23, 27-28 (Tex.Crim. App.2007). "Under [TREs] 404 and 405, if the defendant offers evidence of his good character, the prosecution can introduce its own character evidence to rebut the implications of the defendant's character evidence. There is no nonresponsiveness exception to this right. [Witness] offered evidence of Appellant's character through her statement that Appellant was a 'good' and 'sweet' boy. Although Appellant did not intentionally elicit [witness's] character testimony, the nonresponsiveness of [witness's] statement does not change the fact that it was character evidence offered by a defense witness. The trial court correctly permitted the State to rebut the character evidence introduced by [witness] with the evidence of Appellant's prior assault convictions and citations."

Turner v. State, 805 S.W.2d 423, 429 (Tex.Crim. App.1991). "A reputation witness's testimony must be based on discussion with others concerning the defendant, or on hearing others discuss the defendant's reputation, and not just on personal knowledge. Discussions with other police officers are sufficient to qualify a witness on reputation. General reputation testimony is admissible even though it is partially based on discussions concerning the offense for which the defendant is being tried, if it is also based on a discussion of matters other than the instant offense." *See also Hernandez v. State*, 800 S.W.2d 523, 525 (Tex.Crim.App. 1990).

Lopez v. State, 860 S.W.2d 938, 944 (Tex. App.—San Antonio 1993, no pet.). "The procedure to be followed when admitting reputation testimony is to permit the opposing party to test the qualification of the witness outside the presence of the jury before he testifies as to the defendant's reputation. [¶] [TRCE] 405 [now TRE 405] requires substantial familiarity with the reputation of the accused. Substantial familiarity with specific acts is not substantial familiarity with reputation."

Reynolds v. State, 848 S.W.2d 785, 788 (Tex. App.—Houston [14th Dist.] 1993, pet. ref'd). "[W]hile reputation witnesses are asked 'have you heard' questions, opinion witnesses are asked 'do you know' questions. The exception to this rule is where a witness 'converts himself from a reputation witness to an opinion witness and vice versa.' The rationale is that reputation witnesses may be asked 'have you heard' questions in order to test the weight of their testimony. Opinion witnesses are asked 'do you know' questions to test the basis of their personal opinions. [¶] [T]he 'right to cross-examine a character witness on specific instances of a defendant's conduct is subject to two limitations: first, there must be some factual basis for the incidents inquired about; and second, those incidents must be relevant to character traits at issue in the trial.' The foundation for inquiring into the specific instances of conduct must be laid outside the jury's presence."

Gonzales v. State, 838 S.W.2d 848, 861 (Tex. App.—Houston [1st Dist.] 1992), *pet. dism'd*, 864 S.W.2d 522 (Tex.Crim.App.1993). "[E]vidence admissible under [TRCE] 404(a)(2) [now TRE 404(a)(2)] and 405 [now TRE 405] is not excludable because of remoteness." *See also DeLeon v. State*, 758 S.W.2d 621, 627 (Tex.App.—Houston [14th Dist.] 1988, no pet.).

Davis v. State, 831 S.W.2d 839, 844 (Tex.App.—Dallas 1992, pet. ref'd). "It is improper to permit a witness to testify that a defendant's general reputation for being a peaceable, law-abiding citizen is bad based

upon the offense for which he is on trial. It also is improper to test the knowledge of a witness who has testified to the good reputation of a defendant for being a peaceable law-abiding citizen by asking 'have you heard' questions about the offense for which he is being tried."

Turner v. State, 762 S.W.2d 705, 706 (Tex.App.—Houston [14th Dist.] 1988, pet. ref'd). TRCE 405, now TRE 405, "does not mandate a final conviction be obtained before the witness can be questioned about [the specific instance]."

TRE 406. HABIT; ROUTINE PRACTICE

Evidence of the habit of a person or of the routine practice of an organization, whether corroborated or not and regardless of the presence of eyewitnesses, is relevant to prove that the conduct of the person or organization on a particular occasion was in conformity with the habit or routine practice.

TRE 407. SUBSEQUENT REMEDIAL MEASURES; NOTIFICATION OF DEFECT

(a) Subsequent Remedial Measures. When, after an injury or harm allegedly caused by an event, measures are taken that, if taken previously, would have made the injury or harm less likely to occur, evidence of the subsequent remedial measures is not admissible to prove negligence, culpable conduct, a defect in a product, a defect in a product's design, or a need for a warning or instruction. This rule does not require the exclusion of evidence of subsequent remedial measures when offered for another purpose, such as proving ownership, control, or feasibility of precautionary measures, if controverted, or impeachment.

(b) Notification of Defect. A written notification by a manufacturer of any defect in a product produced by such manufacturer to purchasers thereof is admissible against the manufacturer on the issue of existence of the defect to the extent that it is relevant.

TRE 408. COMPROMISE & OFFERS TO COMPROMISE

Evidence of (1) furnishing or offering or promising to furnish or (2) accepting or offering or promising to accept, a valuable consideration in compromising or attempting to compromise a claim which was disputed as to either validity or amount is not admissible to prove liability for or invalidity of the claim or its amount. Evidence of conduct or statements made in compromise negotiations is likewise not admissible. This rule does not require the exclusion of any evidence otherwise discoverable merely because it is presented in the course of compromise negotiations. This rule also does not require exclusion when the evidence is offered for another purpose, such as proving bias or prejudice or interest of a witness or a party, negativing a contention of undue delay, or proving an effort to obstruct a criminal investigation or prosecution.

ANNOTATIONS

Pichon v. State, 756 S.W.2d 16, 21 (Tex.App.—Houston [14th Dist.] 1988, pet. ref'd). "[D] maintains that because the prosecutor had agreed to dismiss the indictment if he passed the polygraph test, the statements made to [person administering the polygraph test] constitute evidence in furtherance of a negotiated settlement of the case. [D] submits his statement was therefore inadmissible pursuant to [TRCE] 408 [now TRE 408]. We disagree."

TRE 409. PAYMENT OF MEDICAL & SIMILAR EXPENSES

Evidence of furnishing or offering or promising to pay medical, hospital, or similar expenses occasioned by an injury is not admissible to prove liability for the injury.

TRE 410. INADMISSIBILITY OF PLEAS, PLEA DISCUSSIONS & RELATED STATEMENTS

Except as otherwise provided in this rule, evidence of the following is not admissible against the defendant who made the plea or was a participant in the plea discussions:

(1) a plea of guilty that was later withdrawn;

(2) in civil cases, a plea of *nolo contendere*, and in criminal cases, a plea of *nolo contendere* that was later withdrawn;

(3) any statement made in the course of any proceedings under Rule 11 of the Federal Rules of Criminal Procedure or comparable state procedure regarding, in a civil case, either a plea of guilty that was later withdrawn or a plea of *nolo contendere*, or in a criminal case,

either a plea of guilty that was later withdrawn or a plea of *nolo contendere* that was later withdrawn; or

(4) any statement made in the course of plea discussions with an attorney for the prosecuting authority, in a civil case, that do not result in a plea of guilty or that result in a plea of guilty later withdrawn, or in a criminal case, that do not result in a plea of guilty or a plea of *nolo contendere* or that results in a plea, later withdrawn, of guilty or *nolo contendere*.

However, such a statement is admissible in any proceeding wherein another statement made in the course of the same plea or plea discussions has been introduced and the statement ought in fairness be considered contemporaneously with it.

ANNOTATIONS

Bowie v. State, 135 S.W.3d 55, 57 (Tex.Crim.App. 2004). "The question ... is whether punishment testimony by a defendant offered in the course of a 'timely pass for plea' proceeding [in which the defendant enters a guilty plea, the court hears evidence supporting the plea and evidence and argument on the issue of punishment, and the judge announces the sentence, but the D has the option of withdrawing his plea and receiving a jury trial if he does not like the proposed sentence] is protected by [TRE] 410. We hold that it is."

Childs v. State, 837 S.W.2d 822, 824-25 (Tex. App.—San Antonio 1992, pet. ref'd). "[I]t is reversible error for the trial court to allow the introduction of evidence of a prior plea of guilty by a defendant at his new trial on the same charge when he has timely changed his plea to one of not guilty."

TRE 411. LIABILITY INSURANCE

Evidence that a person was or was not insured against liability is not admissible upon the issue whether the person acted negligently or otherwise wrongfully. This rule does not require the exclusion of evidence of insurance against liability when offered for another issue, such as proof of agency, ownership, or control, if disputed, or bias or prejudice of a witness.

TRE 412. EVIDENCE OF PREVIOUS SEXUAL CONDUCT IN CRIMINAL CASES

(a) Reputation or Opinion Evidence. In a prosecution for sexual assault or aggravated sexual assault, or attempt to commit sexual assault or aggravated sexual assault, reputation or opinion evidence of the past sexual behavior of an alleged victim of such crime is not admissible.

(b) Evidence of Specific Instances. In a prosecution for sexual assault or aggravated sexual assault, or attempt to commit sexual assault or aggravated sexual assault, evidence of specific instances of an alleged victim's past sexual behavior is also not admissible, unless:

(1) such evidence is admitted in accordance with paragraphs (c) and (d) of this rule;

(2) it is evidence:

(A) that is necessary to rebut or explain scientific or medical evidence offered by the State;

(B) of past sexual behavior with the accused and is offered by the accused upon the issue of whether the alleged victim consented to the sexual behavior which is the basis of the offense charged;

(C) that relates to the motive or bias of the alleged victim;

(D) is admissible under Rule 609; or

(E) that is constitutionally required to be admitted; and

(3) its probative value outweighs the danger of unfair prejudice.

(c) Procedure for Offering Evidence. If the defendant proposes to introduce any documentary evidence or to ask any question, either by direct examination or cross-examination of any witness, concerning specific instances of the alleged victim's past sexual behavior, the defendant must inform the court out of the hearing of the jury prior to introducing any such evidence or asking any such question. After this notice, the court shall conduct an in camera hearing, recorded by the court reporter, to determine whether the proposed evidence is admissible under paragraph (b) of this rule. The court shall determine what evidence is admissible and shall accordingly limit the questioning. The defendant shall not go outside these limits or refer to any evidence ruled inadmissible in camera without prior approval of the court without the presence of the jury.

(d) Record Sealed. The court shall seal the record of the in camera hearing required in paragraph (c) of this rule for delivery to the appellate court in the event of an appeal.

Lapointe v. State, 225 S.W.3d 513, 520 (Tex.Crim. App.2007). "We conclude that the *in camera* proceeding contemplated by Rule 412 is an adversarial hearing at which the parties are present and the attorneys are permitted to question witnesses. *At 524:* We further hold that the remedy for a trial court's failure to follow this requirement is to abate the appeal and remand the case to the trial court to conduct (retrospectively) a proper hearing."

Boyle v. State, 820 S.W.2d 122, 149 (Tex.Crim.App. 1989), *overruled on other grounds*, *Gordon v. State*, 801 S.W.2d 899 (Tex.Crim.App.1990). "While evidence of previous sexual relations with others is ordinarily not probative on the issue of consent, this category recognizes that such behavior between the complainant and the defendant is of greater relevance. The probative value of the evidence ... rests ... on the nature of the specific relationship between the complainant and the defendant. Whether its probative value will outweigh the danger of unfair prejudice will depend on a variety of factors, such as the similarity in circumstances and the proximity in time of the previous sexual relations to the alleged assault."

Miles v. State, 61 S.W.3d 682, 686 (Tex.App.— Houston [1st Dist.] 2001, pet. ref'd). "The defense attempted to offer ... that [victim] had sex with [friend of victim's uncle]. This evidence was offered to explain or rebut the only medical evidence presented at trial ... which stated that [victim] had sexual intercourse sometime prior to the examination. *At 687:* The trial court abused its discretion by not allowing [D] to cross-examine [victim] or introduce other evidence of prior sexual history."

Kesterson v. State, 959 S.W.2d 247, 249 (Tex. App.—Dallas 1997, no pet.). "[W]e conclude an appellant is not entitled to review the sealed record from an in camera hearing conducted pursuant to [TRCE] 412 [now TRE 412] to determine what complaints to raise on appeal. Accordingly, we deny appellant's February 2, 1997 motion to allow counsel to review sealed portions of the record."

Draheim v. State, 916 S.W.2d 593, 599 (Tex. App.—San Antonio 1996, pet. ref'd). TRCE 412, now TRE 412, "is commonly referred to as the Texas rape shield law. [¶] [TRE 412] restrict[s] the introduction of evidence regarding the complainant's prior *consensual* sexual behavior to situations in which the evidence is both relevant to a defendant's defense and not unduly prejudicial or inflammatory."

Wofford v. State, 903 S.W.2d 796, 798 (Tex.App.—Dallas 1995, pet. ref'd). "A sealed record of the in camera hearing preserves any excluded testimony for appellate purposes. [¶] The in camera hearing should exclude not only the presence of the jury, but also the presence of any unnecessary spectators. *At 799:* The trial court does not err in excluding evidence of a complainant's promiscuity with third parties unless those particular sexual activities are material to an issue in the case, *and* appellant raises consent as a defense."

Cuyler v. State, 841 S.W.2d 933, 936 (Tex.App.—Austin 1992, no pet.), *abrogated on other grounds*, *Halstead v. State*, 891 S.W.2d 11 (Tex.App.—Austin 1994, no pet.). "We believe that the point of reference of [TRCE] 412 [now TRE 412] is the date of trial, and that 'past sexual behavior' means sexual behavior that occurs before trial. We hold that in a prosecution for sexual assault or other offense to which it applies, [TRE 412] governs the admission of *all* evidence of extraneous sexual behavior of the complaining witness, including sexual behavior that occurs after the alleged offense."

ARTICLE V. PRIVILEGES

TRE 501. PRIVILEGES RECOGNIZED ONLY AS PROVIDED

Except as otherwise provided by Constitution, by statute, by these rules, or by other rules prescribed pursuant to statutory authority, no person has a privilege to:

(1) refuse to be a witness;

(2) refuse to disclose any matter;

(3) refuse to produce any object or writing; or

(4) prevent another from being a witness or disclosing any matter or producing any object or writing.

ANNOTATIONS

State ex rel. Healey v. McMeans, 884 S.W.2d 772, 775 (Tex.Crim.App.1994). "Although [TRCE] art. V [now TRE art. V] contains a variety of evidentiary privileges, it does not contain a privilege for newsmen."

TRE 502. REQUIRED REPORTS PRIVILEGED BY STATUTE

A person, corporation, association, or other organization or entity, either public or private, making a return or report required by law to be made has a privilege to refuse to disclose and to prevent any other person from disclosing the return or report, if the law requiring it to be made so provides. A public officer or agency to whom a return or report is required by law to be made has a privilege to refuse to disclose the return or report if the law requiring it to be made so provides. No privilege exists under this rule in actions involving perjury, false statements, fraud in the return or report, or other failure to comply with the law in question.

TRE 503. LAWYER-CLIENT PRIVILEGE

(a) **Definitions.** As used in this rule:

(1) A "client" is a person, public officer, or corporation, association, or other organization or entity, either public or private, who is rendered professional legal services by a lawyer, or who consults a lawyer with a view to obtaining professional legal services from that lawyer.

(2) A "representative of the client" is:

(A) a person having authority to obtain professional legal services, or to act on advice thereby rendered, on behalf of the client, or

(B) any other person who, for the purpose of effectuating legal representation for the client, makes or receives a confidential communication while acting in the scope of employment for the client.

(3) A "lawyer" is a person authorized, or reasonably believed by the client to be authorized, to engage in the practice of law in any state or nation.

(4) A "representative of the lawyer" is:

(A) one employed by the lawyer to assist the lawyer in the rendition of professional legal services; or

(B) an accountant who is reasonably necessary for the lawyer's rendition of professional legal services.

(5) A communication is "confidential" if not intended to be disclosed to third persons other than those to whom disclosure is made in furtherance of the rendition of professional legal services to the client or those reasonably necessary for the transmission of the communication.

(b) Rules of Privilege.

(1) *General rule of privilege.* A client has a privilege to refuse to disclose and to prevent any other person from disclosing confidential communications made for the purpose of facilitating the rendition of professional legal services to the client:

(A) between the client or a representative of the client and the client's lawyer or a representative of the lawyer;

(B) between the lawyer and the lawyer's representative;

(C) by the client or a representative of the client, or the client's lawyer or a representative of the lawyer, to a lawyer or a representative of a lawyer representing another party in a pending action and concerning a matter of common interest therein;

(D) between representatives of the client or between the client and a representative of the client; or

(E) among lawyers and their representatives representing the same client.

(2) *Special rule of privilege in criminal cases.* In criminal cases, a client has a privilege to prevent the lawyer or lawyer's representative from disclosing any other fact which came to the knowledge of the lawyer or the lawyer's representative by reason of the attorney-client relationship.

(c) Who May Claim the Privilege. The privilege may be claimed by the client, the client's guardian or conservator, the personal representative of a deceased client, or the successor, trustee, or similar representative of a corporation, association, or other organization, whether or not in existence. The person who was the lawyer or the lawyer's representative at the time of the communication is presumed to have authority to claim the privilege but only on behalf of the client.

(d) Exceptions. There is no privilege under this rule:

(1) *Furtherance of crime or fraud.* If the services of the lawyer were sought or obtained to enable or aid anyone to commit or plan to commit what the client knew or reasonably should have known to be a crime or fraud;

(2) *Claimants through same deceased client.* As to a communication relevant to an issue between parties who claim through the same deceased client, regardless of whether the claims are by testate or intestate succession or by inter vivos transactions;

(3) *Breach of duty by a lawyer or client.* As to a communication relevant to an issue of breach of duty by a lawyer to the client or by a client to the lawyer;

(4) *Document attested by a lawyer.* As to a communication relevant to an issue concerning an attested document to which the lawyer is an attesting witness; or

(5) *Joint clients.* As to a communication relevant to a matter of common interest between or among two or more clients if the communication was made by any of them to a lawyer retained or consulted in common, when offered in an action between or among any of the clients.

ANNOTATIONS

Generally

Mixon v. State, 224 S.W.3d 206, 206 (Tex.Crim.App. 2007). "[W]e are asked to determine whether, under [TRE] 503, an attorney-client privilege is established when a person consults with a lawyer with a view to obtaining professional legal services from him, even if the lawyer declines to represent that person at the end of the consultation. We hold that it does."

Pope v. State, 207 S.W.3d 352, 357-59 (Tex.Crim. App.2006). "The scope of the attorney work-product doctrine is sometimes confused with that of the attorney-client privilege. The attorney-client privilege is an evidentiary privilege and protects against the compelled disclosure of confidential communications. This privilege belongs to and protects the client. The attorney work-product doctrine, while not a true evidentiary privilege, belongs to and protects the attorney. Its purpose is to stimulate the production of information for trials, and it rewards an attorney's creative efforts by giving his work product a qualified privilege from being shared with others. It is premised on the notion that an attorney should not be compelled to disclose the fruits of his labor to his adversary. Under Texas civil rules, material that reflects the attorney's personal thought processes is 'core work product' and receives absolute protection, while other materials, such as documents, reports, or memoranda compiled by the attorney or his agents and communications made in anticipation of litigation or trial are 'other work product' and receive qualified protection. While the work-product doctrine protects the communications of parties, attorneys, and agents, the underlying factual information is not protected. For example, descriptions of potential witnesses and statements that would reveal whether the party had spoken to potential witnesses are not work product and are discoverable. [F]acts that are divulged by or exist independent of the attorney or his agents are not protected, but statements or documents that set out their thoughts concerning the significance of these facts or the strategic conclusions that the attorney or his agents draw from them may well be protected. Thus, material prepared by a consulting expert appointed by the trial court to assist the defense in developing strategies and theories is protected by the work-product doctrine when that material reflects the expert's thoughts regarding the strength and weaknesses of a defense theory. *At 361:* But what happens when the party who has designated a particular person as an expert later decides that the expert's opinions and testimony could do its side more harm than good?" Held: The opposing party may mention the expert, his qualifications, and whether or not the expert called for testing. *See also Skinner v. State*, 956 S.W.2d 532, 538 (Tex.Crim.App. 1997).

Carmona v. State, 941 S.W.2d 949, 953 (Tex.Crim. App.1997). "[A]n objection based on the attorney-client privilege does not preserve for appeal a claim based on the work-product doctrine. [¶] [T]he party seeking to benefit by a finding of waiver has the burden of going forward with evidence that supports a finding of waiver, and the mere fact privileged materials have been disclosed does not establish a 'presumptive' or 'automatic waiver.' *At 954:* [T]he totality of the circumstances and reasonable inferences therefrom may support a finding of waiver."

TRE 503(b)

Austin v. State, 934 S.W.2d 672, 673 (Tex.Crim.App. 1996). "[A]ttorneys may testify regarding information they possess about a client so long as no communication is revealed. *At 674:* The client bears the burden of establishing the existence of the privilege. *At 675:* [When the attorney] is a 'mere conduit' for the trial judge passing on a routine message, ... such communication is not confidential because it does not involve the subject matter of the client's legal problems."

Strong v. State, 773 S.W.2d 543, 550-01 (Tex.Crim. App.1989). "Courts in several cases have found a confidential relationship to exist despite the fact that the communication in question was made to counsel for the co-defendant(s). [¶] [W]e must first examine the purpose of the communication made by the appellant to attorney [for co-defendant]: was it made in confidence

for the purpose of facilitating the rendition of professional legal services? *At 552:* Next, we must determine whether there was some common interest or defense between [co-defendant] and appellant.... The burden of establishing the privilege is on the party asserting it. Unilaterally asserting a joint defense based on a common interest does not give rise to the lawyer-client privilege. ... Absent facts in the record showing any shared defenses between [co-defendant] and appellant, we hold the lawyer-client privilege inapplicable under the 'common interest' provision in [TRCE] 503(b)(3) [now TRE 503(b)(1)(C)]."

Sanford v. State, 21 S.W.3d 337, 344 (Tex.App.—El Paso 2000, no pet.). "Whether the State may introduce into evidence the fact that counsel is the source of the evidence is an issue of first impression in Texas. However, several other jurisdictions hold that the State may not, when introducing the evidence received from counsel, reveal the source of the evidence in the presence of the jury because it would violate the attorney-client privilege. By allowing the State to recover the evidence, the public interest is served, and by refusing the State an opportunity to disclose the source of the evidence, the attorney-client privilege is preserved. We are persuaded that this balancing of interests is the correct approach."

Neugebauer v. State, 974 S.W.2d 374, 376 (Tex. App.—Amarillo 1998, pet. ref'd). "[I]t is clear that the question [propounded by prosecutor during cross-examination of D] was an attempt to address a privileged communication between appellant and his attorney concerning the potential outcome of the case. *At 377:* [W]hile the State is entitled to considerable latitude conducting cross-examination, in doing so, it may not intrude into the sacrosanct attorney-client privilege long recognized and zealously protected in our Anglo-American jurisprudence." *See also Womack v. State*, 834 S.W.2d 545, 547 (Tex.App.—Houston [14th Dist.] 1992, no pet.).

TRE 503(c)

Carmona v. State, 947 S.W.2d 661, 663 (Tex. App.—Austin 1997, no pet.). "A communication is confidential if it is not intended to be disclosed to persons other than those to whom disclosure is made to further rendition of professional legal services to the client. The privilege belongs to the client. The client can waive the privilege by voluntarily disclosing or consenting to the disclosure of a significant part of the privileged matter. Disclosure by the attorney does not waive the privilege absent the client's consent."

TRE 503(d)

Henderson v. State, 962 S.W.2d 544, 553 (Tex. Crim.App.1997). "[T]he crime-fraud exception can [not] be satisfied by the mere pendency of ongoing criminal activity or the mere threat of future activity. The attorney's services must be sought or used to further the activity in question. *At 556:* The client cannot use [TRCE] 503 [now TRE 503] to prevent an attorney's disclosure, in accordance with the disciplinary rules, of ongoing or future criminal activity. The next question ... is whether an attorney may be *compelled* to disclose such information. Because the ethical rules do not themselves modify the attorney-client privilege, but merely reflect strong policy considerations to which the attorney-client privilege might yield, the assertion of strong policy interests is not limited to the situation in which the client's attorney is the party seeking disclosure. But, for a third party to intrude upon the attorney-client relationship, the policy justification must be strong enough that it imposes a duty upon the attorney to disclose. Hence, a third party can compel information only if needed to prevent or terminate a crime or fraud that is likely to result in death or serious bodily injury."

TRE 504. HUSBAND-WIFE PRIVILEGES

(a) Confidential Communication Privilege.

(1) *Definition.* A communication is confidential if it is made privately by any person to the person's spouse and it is not intended for disclosure to any other person.

(2) *Rule of privilege.* A person, whether or not a party, or the guardian or representative of an incompetent or deceased person, has a privilege during marriage and afterwards to refuse to disclose and to prevent another from disclosing a confidential communication made to the person's spouse while they were married.

(3) *Who may claim the privilege.* The confidential communication privilege may be claimed by the person or the person's guardian or representative, or by the spouse on the person's behalf. The authority of the spouse to do so is presumed.

(4) *Exceptions.* There is no confidential communication privilege:

(A) *Furtherance of crime or fraud.* If the communication was made, in whole or in part, to enable or aid anyone to commit or plan to commit a crime or fraud.

(B) *Proceeding between spouses in civil cases.* In (A)[1] a proceeding brought by or on behalf of one spouse against the other spouse, or (B)[2] a proceeding between a surviving spouse and a person who claims through the deceased spouse, regardless of whether the claim is by testate or intestate succession or by inter vivos transaction.

(C) *Crime against spouse or minor child.* In a proceeding in which the party is accused of conduct which, if proved, is a crime against the person of the spouse, any minor child, or any member of the household of either spouse, or, in a criminal proceeding, when the offense charged is under Section 25.01, Penal Code (Bigamy).

(D) *Commitment or similar proceeding.* In a proceeding to commit either spouse or otherwise to place that person or that person's property, or both, under the control of another because of an alleged mental or physical condition.

(E) *Proceeding to establish competence.* In a proceeding brought by or on behalf of either spouse to establish competence.

(b) Privilege Not to Testify in Criminal Case.

(1) *Rule of privilege.* In a criminal case, the spouse of the accused has a privilege not to be called as a witness for the state. This rule does not prohibit the spouse from testifying voluntarily for the state, even over objection by the accused. A spouse who testifies on behalf of an accused is subject to cross-examination as provided in rule 611(b).

(2) *Failure to call as witness.* Failure by an accused to call the accused's spouse as a witness, where other evidence indicates that the spouse could testify to relevant matters, is a proper subject of comment by counsel.

(3) *Who may claim the privilege.* The privilege not to testify may be claimed by the person or the person's guardian or representative but not by that person's spouse.

(4) *Exceptions.* The privilege of a person's spouse not to be called as a witness for the state does not apply:

(A) *Certain criminal proceedings.* In any proceeding in which the person is charged with a crime against the person's spouse, a member of the household of either spouse, or any minor, or in an offense charged under Section 25.01, Penal Code (Bigamy).

(B) *Matters occurring prior to marriage.* As to matters occurring prior to the marriage.

> 1. **Editor's note:** This should probably read "(i)."
> 2. **Editor's note:** This should probably read "(ii)."
> See also CCP art. 38.10.

ANNOTATIONS

Generally

Weaver v. State, 855 S.W.2d 116, 119-20 (Tex. App.—Houston [14th Dist.] 1993, no pet.). "[T]he spousal privilege rule has two parts, one dealing with those communications to the spouse which were intended to be kept private, and the privilege for the spouse of the accused not to be called as a witness at all."

Riley v. State, 849 S.W.2d 901, 903 (Tex.App.—Austin 1993, pet. ref'd). "[T]he legislature defined the term 'member of the household' in the Family Code.... The Family Code defines household as 'a unit composed of persons living together in the same dwelling, whether or not they are related to each other.' ... Using this definition to determine the scope of the privilege is appropriate...."

TRE 504(a)

Colburn v. State, 966 S.W.2d 511, 514 (Tex.Crim. App.1998). "Under [TRCE] 504 [now TRE 504], the spouse of an accused has a privilege not to be called as a witness for the state. This privilege does not extend to matters occurring prior to the marriage. Appellant and [witness] were never ceremonially married; therefore, appellant had to prove that a common-law marriage existed at the time of the events to which [woman] testified. [¶] A properly recorded declaration of informal marriage constitutes prima facie proof of the informal marriage. Thus, the trial court may find the common law marriage proven based upon the declaration alone, but evidence may be offered rebutting the existence of the marriage as sworn to or stated in the declaration. *At 515:* Common law marriage requires that there be some agreement presently to be married, not to marry some time in the future." *See also* ***Weaver v. State***, 855 S.W.2d 116, 121 (Tex.App.—Houston [14th Dist.] 1993, no pet.) (privilege not to testify against one's spouse does not extend to putative marriages).

TRE 504(b)

Boyle v. State, 820 S.W.2d 122, 145 (Tex.Crim.App. 1989), *overruled on other grounds*, ***Gordon v. State***, 801 S.W.2d 899 (Tex.Crim.App.1990). The spousal "privilege may be asserted only by the defendant's spouse, and the defendant has no power to prevent his or her spouse from testifying for the State. [A] spouse may testify even over the defendant spouse's objection." *See also* ***Anderson v. State***, 880 S.W.2d 35, 37 (Tex.App.—Tyler 1994, pet. ref'd).

Huddleston v. State, 997 S.W.2d 319, 321 (Tex. App.—Houston [1st Dist.] 1999, no pet.). "The language of amended rule 504(b)(4)(A) makes it clear that the exception [to the spousal privilege] applies when the spouse is charged with a crime against *any* minor."

Tejeda v. State, 905 S.W.2d 313, 316 (Tex. App.—San Antonio 1995, pet. ref'd). "[T]he spousal privilege does not prohibit evidence of out-of-court statements made by the witness spouse. ... In other words, the privilege prevents compelled speech, it does not compel the capture of words already spoken. *At 317:* [W]e find that requiring a witness spouse to stand and be identified is outside the protection of the spousal privilege."

McDuffie v. State, 854 S.W.2d 195, 217 (Tex. App.—Beaumont 1993, pet. ref'd). TRCE 504(2)(a), now TRE 504(b)(2), "allows the State to comment on the failure of the defendant to call his or her spouse, when 'other evidence indicates that the spouse could testify to relevant matters.'"

TRE 505. COMMUNICATIONS TO MEMBERS OF THE CLERGY

(a) Definitions. As used in this rule:

(1) A "member of the clergy" is a minister, priest, rabbi, accredited Christian Science Practitioner, or other similar functionary of a religious organization or an individual reasonably believed so to be by the person consulting with such individual.

(2) A communication is "confidential" if made privately and not intended for further disclosure except to other persons present in furtherance of the purpose of the communication.

(b) General Rule of Privilege. A person has a privilege to refuse to disclose and to prevent another from disclosing a confidential communication by the person to a member of the clergy in the member's professional character as spiritual adviser.

(c) Who May Claim the Privilege. The privilege may be claimed by the person, by the person's guardian or conservator, or by the personal representative of the person if the person is deceased. The member of the clergy to whom the communication was made is presumed to have authority to claim the privilege but only on behalf of the communicant.

ANNOTATIONS

Gonzalez v. State, 45 S.W.3d 101, 104-05 (Tex. Crim.App.2001). "[W]ith respect to choice-of-law questions involving privileged communications, the Texas Supreme Court applies the 'most significant relationship' test as set forth in the Restatement (2d) provision pertaining to privileged communications. We agree with our sister court that the choice-of-laws rule for privileged communications set out in the [Restatement] is a reasonable one. *At 106:* [T]he state where the communication took place is generally the state with the most significant relationship. *At 107:* [W]e hold that the Court of Appeals did not err in its application of the 'most significant relationship' test to the conflict of laws question [penitent-clergyman privilege]."

Almendarez v. State, 153 S.W.3d 727, 728 (Tex. App.—Dallas 2005, no pet.). "[I]n a proceeding regarding the abuse or neglect of a child, evidence may not be excluded on the ground of privileged communication except in the case of communications between an attorney and client."

Maldonado v. State, 59 S.W.3d 251, 253 (Tex. App.—Corpus Christi 2001, pet. ref'd). "Under the express language of [TRE 505(b)], the privilege only extends to communications addressed to a clergyman in his professional capacity as a spiritual advisor, not to every private communication made to a clergy member. Thus, statements made during a disciplinary/administrative meeting are not communications made for the purpose of obtaining spiritual guidance or consolation and do not fall under the privilege."

TRE 506. POLITICAL VOTE

Every person has a privilege to refuse to disclose the tenor of the person's vote at a political election conducted by secret ballot unless the vote was cast illegally.

TRE 507. TRADE SECRETS

A person has a privilege, which may be claimed by the person or the person's agent or employee, to refuse to disclose and to prevent other persons from disclosing a trade secret owned by the person, if the allowance of the privilege will not tend to conceal fraud or otherwise work injustice. When disclosure is directed, the judge shall take such protective measure as the interests of the holder of the privilege and of the parties and the furtherance of justice may require.

TRE 508. IDENTITY OF INFORMER

(a) Rule of Privilege. The United States or a state or subdivision thereof has a privilege to refuse to disclose the identity of a person who has furnished information relating to or assisting in an investigation of a possible violation of a law to a law enforcement officer or member of a legislative committee or its staff conducting an investigation.

(b) Who May Claim. The privilege may be claimed by an appropriate representative of the public entity to which the information was furnished, except the privilege shall not be allowed in criminal cases if the state objects.

(c) Exceptions.

(1) *Voluntary disclosure; informer a witness.* No privilege exists under this rule if the identity of the informer or the informer's interest in the subject matter of the communication has been disclosed to those who would have cause to resent the communication by a holder of the privilege or by the informer's own action, or if the informer appears as a witness for the public entity.

(2) *Testimony on merits.* If it appears from the evidence in the case or from other showing by a party that an informer may be able to give testimony necessary to a fair determination of a material issue on the merits in a civil case to which the public entity is a party, or on guilt or innocence in a criminal case, and the public entity invokes the privilege, the court shall give the public entity an opportunity to show in camera facts relevant to determining whether the informer can, in fact, supply that testimony. The showing will ordinarily be in the form of affidavits, but the court may direct that testimony be taken if it finds that the matter cannot be resolved satisfactorily upon affidavit. If the court finds that there is a reasonable probability that the informer can give the testimony, and the public entity elects not to disclose the informer's identity, the court in a civil case may make any order that justice requires, and in a criminal case shall, on motion of the defendant, and may, on the court's own motion, dismiss the charges as to which the testimony would relate. Evidence submitted to the court shall be sealed and preserved to be made available to the appellate court in the event of an appeal, and the contents shall not otherwise be revealed without consent of the public entity. All counsel and parties shall be permitted to be present at every stage of proceedings under this subdivision except a showing in camera, at which no counsel or party shall be permitted to be present.

(3) *Legality of obtaining evidence.* If information from an informer is relied upon to establish the legality of the means by which evidence was obtained and the court is not satisfied that the information was received from an informer reasonably believed to be reliable or credible, it may require the identity of the informer to be disclosed. The court shall, on request of the public entity, direct that the disclosure be made in camera. All counsel and parties concerned with the issue of legality shall be permitted to be present at every stage of proceedings under this subdivision except a disclosure in camera, at which no counsel or party shall be permitted to be present. If disclosure of the identity of the informer is made in camera, the record thereof shall be sealed and preserved to be made available to the appellate court in the event of an appeal, and the contents shall not otherwise be revealed without consent of the public entity.

Bodin v. State, 807 S.W.2d 313, 318 (Tex.Crim.App. 1991). "Since the defendant may not actually know the nature of the informer's testimony ... he or she should only be required to make a plausible showing of how the informer's information may be important. [¶] The mere *filing* of a [TRCE] 508 [now TRE 508] motion is insufficient to obtain a hearing, much less compel disclosure. *At 319:* We ... reject the Court of Appeals' holding that under [TRCE] 508(c)(2) [now TRE 508(c)(2)], only the public entity may request the in camera hearing. ... While the State causes the in camera hearing by invoking the privilege, there is no indication in the rule that only the State may request such a hearing."

Southwell v. State, 80 S.W.3d 648, 649-50 (Tex. App.—Houston [1st Dist.] 2002, no pet.). TRE 508 "does not allow us to give an appellant access to the sealed material from the in camera hearing. [¶] The privilege [not to disclose an informant's identity] does not apply in a criminal case (1) if the informer's identity has been voluntarily disclosed, (2) if the informer may be able to give testimony necessary to a fair determination of guilt or innocence, or (3) if the court is not satisfied that information was obtained from an informer reasonably believed to be reliable. [¶] The informant's potential testimony must significantly aid the defendant and mere conjecture or supposition about possible relevancy is insufficient. A defendant has the threshold burden of demonstrating that identity must be disclosed. However, because the defendant may not actually know the nature of the informant's testimony, he or she is only required to make a plausible showing of how the informer's information may be important. [¶] Once a plausible showing is made, the court should conduct an in camera hearing to determine whether there is a reasonable probability the informant could give testimony necessary to a fair determination of guilt or innocence."

Lary v. State, 15 S.W.3d 581, 584 (Tex.App.—Amarillo 2000, pet. ref'd). "The evidence establishes that the informant was an eyewitness to the offense [meeting TRE 508's first step of applicability]. The second step was satisfied when the prosecution invoked privilege against disclosing information about the informant. The State did not seek an in camera review to present additional facts whether the informant could give relevant testimony. Moreover, the trial court was not requested to, and did not, make a determination of whether there was a reasonable probability that the informer could give relevant testimony. *At 585:* [T]he withholding of the name of the informant and the failure of the trial court to make a determination that the informant's testimony was not necessary for a fair determination of the identity issue deprived appellant of the opportunity to hear the informant's testimony and deprived him of the opportunity to cross-examine the witness." *See also* **Sanchez v. State**, 98 S.W.3d 349, 355-56 (Tex.App.—Houston [1st Dist.] 2003, pet. ref'd).

Heard v. State, 995 S.W.2d 317, 321 (Tex.App.—Corpus Christi 1999, pet. ref'd). "While disclosure is indeed required when a confidential informer is 'present at the scene' or 'a material witness to the transaction itself,' there may be many circumstances other than those two where the informer 'can give testimony necessary to a fair determination of guilt or innocence.' [¶] The [open court hearing on disclosure of the informer] employed by the trial court precluded any meaningful verification of the investigator's testimony. … We hold that the trial court erred in overruling appellant's motion without conducting an proper inquiry as directed by rule 508."

Menefee v. State, 928 S.W.2d 274, 279 (Tex.App.—Tyler 1996, no pet.). "'Evidence from any source, but not mere conjecture or speculation, must be presented to make the required showing that the informer's identity must be disclosed. The mere filing of a [TRCE] 508 [now TRE 508] motion is insufficient to obtain a hearing, much less compel disclosure.' To determine whether the trial court erred by not requiring the State to disclose its informer's identity, an appellate court must consider all of the circumstances of the case."

ANNOTATIONS

Hackleman v. State, 919 S.W.2d 440, 450 (Tex. App.—Austin 1996, pet. ref'd). "[W]e do not interpret [TRCE] 508(c)(3) [now TRE 508(c)(3)] to preclude a trial court from conducting an in camera hearing sua sponte in proper circumstances."

TRE 509. PHYSICIAN-PATIENT PRIVILEGE

(a) Definitions. As used in this rule:

(1) A "patient" means any person who consults or is seen by a physician to receive medical care.

(2) A "physician" means a person licensed to practice medicine in any state or nation, or reasonably believed by the patient so to be.

(3) A communication is "confidential" if not intended to be disclosed to third persons other than those present to further the interest of the patient in the consultation, examination, or interview, or those reasonably necessary for the transmission of the communication, or those who are participating in the diagnosis and treatment under the direction of the physician, including members of the patient's family.

(b) Limited Privilege in Criminal Proceedings. There is no physician-patient privilege in criminal proceedings. However, a communication to any person involved in the treatment or examination of alcohol or drug abuse by a person being treated voluntarily or being examined for admission to treatment for alcohol or drug abuse is not admissible in a criminal proceeding.

(c) General Rule of Privilege in Civil Proceedings. In a civil proceeding:

(1) Confidential communications between a physician and a patient, relative to or in connection with any professional services rendered by a physician to the patient are privileged and may not be disclosed.

(2) Records of the identity, diagnosis, evaluation, or treatment of a patient by a physician that are created or maintained by a physician are confidential and privileged and may not be disclosed.

(3) The provisions of this rule apply even if the patient received the services of a physician prior to the enactment of the Medical Liability and Insurance Improvement Act, Tex. Rev. Civ. Stat. art. 4590i.[1]

(d) Who May Claim the Privilege in a Civil Proceeding. In a civil proceeding:

(1) The privilege of confidentiality may be claimed by the patient or by a representative of the patient acting on the patient's behalf.

(2) The physician may claim the privilege of confidentiality, but only on behalf of the patient. The authority to do so is presumed in the absence of evidence to the contrary.

(e) Exceptions in a Civil Proceeding. Exceptions to confidentiality or privilege in administrative proceedings or in civil proceedings in court exist:

(1) when the proceedings are brought by the patient against a physician, including but not limited to malpractice proceedings, and in any license revocation proceeding in which the patient is a complaining witness and in which disclosure is relevant to the claims or defense of a physician;

(2) when the patient or someone authorized to act on the patient's behalf submits a written consent to the release of any privileged information, as provided in paragraph (f);

(3) when the purpose of the proceedings is to substantiate and collect on a claim for medical services rendered to the patient;

(4) as to a communication or record relevant to an issue of the physical, mental or emotional condition of a patient in any proceeding in which any party relies upon the condition as a part of the party's claim or defense;

(5) in any disciplinary investigation or proceeding of a physician conducted under or pursuant to the Medical Practice Act, Tex. Rev. Civ. Stat. art. 4495b[2], or of a registered nurse under or pursuant to Tex. Rev. Civ. Stat. arts. 4525, 4527a, 4527b, and 4527c, provided that the board shall protect the identity of any patient whose medical records are examined, except for those patients covered under subparagraph (e)(1) or those patients who have submitted written consent to the release of their medical records as provided by paragraph (f);

(6) in an involuntary civil commitment proceeding, proceeding for court-ordered treatment, or probable cause hearing under Tex. Health & Safety Code ch. 462; tit. 7, subtit. C; and tit. 7, subtit. D;

(7) in any proceeding regarding the abuse or neglect, or the cause of any abuse or neglect, of the resident of an "institution" as defined in Tex. Health & Safety Code §242.002.

(f) Consent.

(1) Consent for the release of privileged information must be in writing and signed by the patient, or a parent or legal guardian if the patient is a minor, or a legal guardian if the patient has been adjudicated incompetent to manage personal affairs, or an attorney ad litem appointed for the patient, as authorized by Tex. Health & Safety Code tit. 7, subtits. C and D; Tex. Prob. Code ch. V; and Tex. Fam. Code §107.011; or a personal representative if the patient is deceased, provided that the written consent specifies the following:

(A) the information or medical records to be covered by the release;

(B) the reasons or purposes for the release; and

(C) the person to whom the information is to be released.

(2) The patient, or other person authorized to consent, has the right to withdraw consent to the release of any information. Withdrawal of consent does not affect any information disclosed prior to the written notice of the withdrawal.

(3) Any person who received information made privileged by this rule may disclose the information to others only to the extent consistent with the authorized purposes for which consent to release the information was obtained.

1. **Editor's note:** Now CPRC ch. 74.
2. **Editor's note:** Now Occ. Code chs. 151-165.

State v. Hardy, 963 S.W.2d 516, 521 (Tex.Crim.App. 1997). "The Medical Practices Act created a physician-client privilege but excepted criminal cases from that privilege. There are three textual differences between the criminal exception to the privilege in [TRCS art. 4495b,] §5.08 [now Occ. Code §159.003] and [TRE 509]: (1) the §5.08 exception applied to criminal 'prosecutions' while [TRE 509] applies to criminal 'proceedings,' (2) the §5.08 exception applied only to instances in which the patient is a victim, witness, or defendant while [TRE 509] contains no such apparent limitation, and (3) §5.08 contained an in camera inspection requirement before records were discoverable while [TRE 509] contains no such requirement. *At 523:* [TRE 509] expressly abrogates the physician-patient privilege. If the Legislature had intended to overturn [TRE 509], it could have mentioned the rule in its legislation."

TRE 510. CONFIDENTIALITY OF MENTAL HEALTH INFORMATION IN CIVIL CASES

(a) Definitions. As used in this rule:

(1) "Professional" means any person:

(A) authorized to practice medicine in any state or nation;

(B) licensed or certified by the State of Texas in the diagnosis, evaluation or treatment of any mental or emotional disorder;

(C) involved in the treatment or examination of drug abusers; or

(D) reasonably believed by the patient to be included in any of the preceding categories.

(2) "Patient" means any person who:

(A) consults, or is interviewed by, a professional for purposes of diagnosis, evaluation, or treatment of any mental or emotional condition or disorder, including alcoholism and drug addiction; or

(B) is being treated voluntarily or being examined for admission to voluntary treatment for drug abuse.

(3) A representative of the patient is:

(A) any person bearing the written consent of the patient;

(B) a parent if the patient is a minor;

(C) a guardian if the patient has been adjudicated incompetent to manage the patient's personal affairs; or

(D) the patient's personal representative if the patient is deceased.

(4) A communication is "confidential" if not intended to be disclosed to third persons other than those present to further the interest of the patient in the diagnosis, examination, evaluation, or treatment, or those reasonably necessary for the transmission of the communication, or those who are participating in the diagnosis, examination, evaluation, or treatment under the direction of the professional, including members of the patient's family.

(b) General Rule of Privilege.

(1) Communication between a patient and a professional is confidential and shall not be disclosed in civil cases.

(2) Records of the identity, diagnosis, evaluation, or treatment of a patient which are created or maintained by a professional are confidential and shall not be disclosed in civil cases.

(3) Any person who received information from confidential communications or records as defined herein, other than a representative of the patient acting on the patient's behalf, shall not disclose in civil cases the information except to the extent that disclosure is consistent with the authorized purposes for which the information was first obtained.

(4) The provisions of this rule apply even if the patient received the services of a professional prior to the enactment of Tex. Rev. Civ. Stat. art. 5561h (Vernon Supp. 1984) (now codified as Tex. Health & Safety Code §§611.001-611.008).

(c) Who May Claim the Privilege.

(1) The privilege of confidentiality may be claimed by the patient or by a representative of the patient acting on the patient's behalf.

(2) The professional may claim the privilege of confidentiality but only on behalf of the patient. The authority to do so is presumed in the absence of evidence to the contrary.

(d) Exceptions. Exceptions to the privilege in court or administrative proceedings exist:

(1) when the proceedings are brought by the patient against a professional, including but not limited to malpractice proceedings, and in any license revocation proceedings in which the patient is a complaining witness and in which disclosure is relevant to the claim or defense of a professional;

(2) when the patient waives the right in writing to the privilege of confidentiality of any information, or when a representative of the patient acting on the patient's behalf submits a written waiver to the confidentiality privilege;

(3) when the purpose of the proceeding is to substantiate and collect on a claim for mental or emotional health services rendered to the patient;

(4) when the judge finds that the patient after having been previously informed that communications would not be privileged, has made communications to a professional in the course of a court-ordered examination relating to the patient's mental or emotional condition or disorder, providing that such communications shall not be privileged only with respect to issues involving the patient's mental or emotional health. On granting of the order, the court, in determining the extent to which any disclosure of all or any part of any communication is necessary, shall impose appropriate safeguards against unauthorized disclosure;

(5) as to a communication or record relevant to an issue of the physical, mental or emotional condition of a patient in any proceeding in which any party relies upon the condition as a part of the party's claim or defense;

(6) in any proceeding regarding the abuse or neglect, or the cause of any abuse or neglect, of the resident of an institution as defined in Tex. Health and Safety Code §242.002.

See also CCP art. 38.101.

TRE 511. WAIVER OF PRIVILEGE BY VOLUNTARY DISCLOSURE

A person upon whom these rules confer a privilege against disclosure waives the privilege if:

(1) the person or a predecessor of the person while holder of the privilege voluntarily discloses or consents to disclosure of any significant part of the privileged matter unless such disclosure itself is privileged; or

(2) the person or a representative of the person calls a person to whom privileged communications have been made to testify as to the person's character or character trait insofar as such communications are relevant to such character or character trait.

Carmona v. State, 941 S.W.2d 949, 953 (Tex.Crim. App.1997). "[T]he party seeking to benefit by a finding of waiver has the burden of going forward with evidence that supports a finding of waiver, and the mere fact privileged materials already have been disclosed does not establish a 'presumptive' or 'automatic' waiver.'"

TRE 512. PRIVILEGED MATTER DISCLOSED UNDER COMPULSION OR WITHOUT OPPORTUNITY TO CLAIM PRIVILEGE

A claim of privilege is not defeated by a disclosure which was (1) compelled erroneously or (2) made without opportunity to claim the privilege.

TRE 513. COMMENT UPON OR INFERENCE FROM CLAIM OF PRIVILEGE; INSTRUCTION

(a) Comment or Inference Not Permitted. Except as permitted in Rule 504(b)(2), the claim of a privilege, whether in the present proceeding or upon a prior occasion, is not a proper subject of comment by judge or counsel, and no inference may be drawn therefrom.

(b) Claiming Privilege Without Knowledge of Jury. In jury cases, proceedings shall be conducted, to the extent practicable, so as to facilitate the making of claims of privilege without the knowledge of the jury.

(c) Claim of Privilege Against Self-Incrimination in Civil Cases. Paragraphs (a) and (b) shall not apply with respect to a party's claim, in the present civil proceeding, of the privilege against self-incrimination.

(d) Jury Instruction. Except as provided in Rule 504(b)(2) and in paragraph (c) of this Rule, upon request any party against whom the jury might draw an adverse inference from a claim of privilege is entitled to an instruction that no inference may be drawn therefrom.

TRE 513(d)

Torres v. State, 137 S.W.3d 191, 197-98 (Tex. App.—Houston [1st Dist.] 2004, no pet.). "[A]ppellant contends the trial court erred by refusing to include an instruction in the jury charge that it could not draw any inference from [co-defendant's] refusal to testify based on his assertion of his Fifth Amendment privilege against self-incrimination. [¶] [T]he State argues that, in this case, rule 513(d) does not require an instruction because the jury could not have drawn any 'adverse inference' against appellant because of [co-defendant's] claim of privilege. We disagree. [¶] Because appellant was charged as a party to [co-defendant's] offense, such an inference could also tend to incriminate appellant.... In other words, by creating an inference that [co-defendant] was guilty, the State needed only then to prove that appellant 'solicited, encouraged, directed, aided or attempted to aid' [co-defendant]. Any inference that [co-defendant] was guilty could implicate appellant, who was charged as a party with [co-defendant]. Therefore, we conclude that after appellant requested the instruction, the trial court erred by refusing to include the instruction in the charge."

ARTICLE VI. WITNESSES

TRE 601. COMPETENCY & INCOMPETENCY OF WITNESSES

(a) General Rule. Every person is competent to be a witness except as otherwise provided in these rules. The following witnesses shall be incompetent to testify in any proceeding subject to these rules:

(1) *Insane persons.* Insane persons who, in the opinion of the court, are in an insane condition of mind at the time when they are offered as a witness, or who, in the opinion of the court, were in that condition when the events happened of which they are called to testify.

(2) *Children.* Children or other persons who, after being examined by the court, appear not to possess sufficient intellect to relate transactions with respect to which they are interrogated.

(b) "Dead Man's Rule" in Civil Actions. In civil actions by or against executors, administrators, or guardians, in which judgment may be rendered for or against them as such, neither party shall be allowed to testify against the others as to any oral statement by the testator, intestate or ward, unless that testimony to the oral statement is corroborated or unless the witness is called at the trial to testify thereto by the opposite party; and, the provisions of this article shall extend to and include all actions by or against the heirs or legal representatives of a decedent based in whole or in part

TRE 601

on such oral statement. Except for the foregoing, a witness is not precluded from giving evidence of or concerning any transaction with, any conversations with, any admissions of, or statement by, a deceased or insane party or person merely because the witness is a party to the action or a person interested in the event thereof. The trial court shall, in a proper case, where this rule prohibits an interested party or witness from testifying, instruct the jury that such person is not permitted by the law to give evidence relating to any oral statement by the deceased or ward unless the oral statement is corroborated or unless the party or witness is called at the trial by the opposite party.

See also Tex. Const. art. 1, §5.

ANNOTATIONS

McGinn v. State, 961 S.W.2d 161, 165 (Tex.Crim. App.1998). TRCE 601, now TRE 601, "does not expressly require that a party request an examination by the court. However, unlike the incompetency to stand trial statute, [TRE 601] does not expressly impose upon the trial court the duty to conduct an inquiry on its own motion. Where the rule specifies the right to a hearing upon request, an objection to the substance of the testimony that would be the subject of such a hearing does not preserve error regarding the trial court's failure to conduct the hearing."

Broussard v. State, 910 S.W.2d 952, 960 (Tex.Crim. App.1995). TRCE 601(a)(2), now TRE 601(a)(2), "places the power to determine a witness' competency into the hands of the trial judge. [TRCE] 601 [now TRE 601] does not require, nor does it empower a judge to force a witness to undergo psychiatric evaluation for the purpose of a competency determination."

Fields v. State, 500 S.W.2d 500, 502 (Tex.Crim.App. 1973). "[E]ven though a child states he does not know the meaning of an oath or what it means to swear, he may nevertheless be a competent witness if he knows it is wrong to lie...."

Hollinger v. State, 911 S.W.2d 35, 38-39 (Tex. App.—Tyler 1995, pet. ref'd). TRCE 601, now TRE 601, "creates a presumption that a person is competent to testify. The testimony of a witness will only be excluded when questioning convinces the court that the witness does not possess sufficient intellect to accurately relate transactions about which the witness is being interrogated. The three elements to be considered by the court in making a determination of competency to testify are:

(1) the competence of the witness to observe intelligently the events in question at the time of the occurrence; (2) the capacity of the witness to recollect the events, and; (3) the capacity of the witness to narrate the facts. The third element requires the witness to be able to understand the questions that are asked, to be able to frame intelligent answers to those questions, and to be able to understand the moral responsibility to tell the truth."

Contreras v. State, 745 S.W.2d 59, 62 (Tex. App.—San Antonio 1987, no pet.). "The burden of raising and proving the incompetency of a witness is on the party alleging it."

TRE 602. LACK OF PERSONAL KNOWLEDGE

A witness may not testify to a matter unless evidence is introduced sufficient to support a finding that the witness has personal knowledge of the matter. Evidence to prove personal knowledge may, but need not, consist of the testimony of the witness. This rule is subject to the provisions of Rule 703, relating to opinion testimony by expert witnesses.

ANNOTATIONS

Turro v. State, 950 S.W.2d 390, 403 (Tex.App.— Fort Worth 1997, pet. ref'd). TRCE 701's, now TRE 701's, "requirement that the testimony be based on the witness's perception presumes the witness observed or experienced the underlying facts, thus meeting the personal-knowledge requirement of [TRCE] 602 [now TRE 602]."

TRE 603. OATH OR AFFIRMATION

Before testifying, every witness shall be required to declare that the witness will testify truthfully, by oath or affirmation administered in a form calculated to awaken the witness' conscience and impress the witness' mind with the duty to do so.

TRE 604. INTERPRETERS

An interpreter is subject to the provisions of these rules relating to qualification as an expert and the administration of an oath or affirmation to make a true translation.

TRE 605. COMPETENCY OF JUDGE AS A WITNESS

The judge presiding at the trial may not testify in that trial as a witness. No objection need be made in order to preserve the point.

Hensarling v. State, 829 S.W.2d 168, 170 (Tex. Crim.App.1992). "The phrase 'the judge presiding at *the* trial may not testify in *that* trial' means that the judge who is presiding over a proceeding may not 'step down from the bench' and become a witness in the very same proceeding over which he is currently presiding. [TRCE] 605 [now TRE 605] addresses only that specific situation; the rule does not encompass any future proceedings in which the judge is participating but not over which the judge is presiding. *At 171:* [T]his narrow interpretation of [TRE 605] accomplishes the objective of this rule [which is] to preserve [the judge's] posture of impartiality before the parties and particularly in the eyes of the jury." *See also Janecka v. State*, 937 S.W.2d 456, 472-73 (Tex.Crim.App.1996).

State v. Krueger, 179 S.W.3d 663, 668 (Tex.App.— Beaumont 2005, no pet.). "[W]e observe without deciding that an attempt to tender a trial judge's affidavit or testimony at a new trial hearing could result in the State raising any number of objections, *e.g.*, 'violation of Rule 606(b),' 'hearsay,' and 'violation of [TRE] 605.'"

Franks v. State, 90 S.W.3d 771, 781 (Tex.App.— Fort Worth 2002, no pet.). "When requested to testify, [trial judge] refused and explained that he could not testify in the case. Appellant then introduced [trial judge's] testimony from the recusal hearing without any objection by the State, and [trial judge] admitted it into evidence. [¶] Appellant can not now complain on appeal that the trial court violated rule 605 based on evidence Appellant introduced. We understand that rule 605 specifically provides that a party need not object to the violation of the rule; however, application of the rule in a situation where the party not only failed to object to the trial court's testimony, but also requested it not once but twice is unjustifiable."

TRE 606. COMPETENCY OF JUROR AS A WITNESS

(a) At the Trial. A member of the jury may not testify as a witness before that jury in the trial of the case in which the juror is sitting as a juror. If the juror is called so to testify, the opposing party shall be afforded an opportunity to object out of the presence of the jury.

(b) Inquiry Into Validity of Verdict or Indictment. Upon an inquiry into the validity of a verdict or indictment, a juror may not testify as to any matter or statement occurring during the jury's deliberations, or to the effect of anything on any juror's mind or emotions or mental processes, as influencing any juror's assent to or dissent from the verdict or indictment. Nor may a juror's affidavit or any statement by a juror concerning any matter about which the juror would be precluded from testifying be admitted in evidence for any of these purposes. However, a juror may testify: (1) whether any outside influence was improperly brought to bear upon any juror; or (2) to rebut a claim that the juror was not qualified to serve.

White v. State, 225 S.W.3d 571, 574-75 (Tex.Crim. App.2007). "The plain language of the [TRE] 606(b) indicates that an outside influence is something outside of both the jury room and the juror. [¶] We are ... unconvinced by appellant's contention that the challenged jurors' mere presence was 'significant harm' and that holding otherwise, coupled with the prohibitions in [TRE] 606(b), would preclude any possible avenue for discovering whether these jurors caused substantial harm.... The U.S. Supreme Court has held that, while juror testimony is barred under [FRE] 606(b), 'a party may seek to impeach the verdict by non-juror evidence of misconduct.' Likewise, [TRE] 606(b) does not prevent appellant from demonstrating such 'significant harm' by use of non-juror evidence."

Gahagan v. State, 242 S.W.3d 80, 89-90 (Tex. App.—Houston [1st Dist.] 2007, pet. filed 5-15-08). "[A] new trial is warranted only when 'other evidence' involved in the alleged jury misconduct is an influence external to both the jury and the deliberations brought to bear on a juror."

Pena v. State, 102 S.W.3d 450, 455 (Tex.App.— Eastland 2003, no pet.). "When appellant's attorney asked to examine [juror] before her discharge, the trial court told him that he could do that later by affidavit. ... The trial court was correct. ... Rule 606(b) does not permit a juror to impeach the verdict by testimony or affidavit about any matter or statement 'during the jury's deliberations'; however, the record shows that the jury had not begun its deliberations at the time [juror] was excused." *See also Golden Eagle Archery, Inc. v. Jackson*, 24 S.W.3d 362, 371-72 (Tex.2000).

TRE 607. WHO MAY IMPEACH
The credibility of a witness may be attacked by any party, including the party calling the witness.

Michael v. State, 235 S.W.3d 723, 725-26 (Tex. Crim.App.2007). "There are five major forms of impeachment: two are specific, and three are nonspecific. The two specific forms of impeachment are impeachment by prior inconsistent statements (also known as self-contradiction) and impeachment by another witness. The three non-specific forms of impeachment are impeachment through bias or motive or interest, impeachment by highlighting testimonial defects, and impeachment by general credibility or lack of truthfulness. Specific impeachment is an attack on the accuracy of the specific testimony (*i.e.*, the witness may normally be a truthteller, but she is wrong about X), while non-specific impeachment is an attack on the witness generally (the witness is a liar, therefore she is wrong about X). [¶] When a witness's credibility has been attacked by any one of the five forms of impeachment, the sponsoring party may rehabilitate the witness only in *direct* response to the attack."

Hughes v. State, 4 S.W.3d 1, 5 (Tex.Crim.App. 1999). "[W]e conclude the State's knowledge that its own witness will testify unfavorably is a factor that the trial court must consider when determining whether the evidence is admissible under [TRE] 403. Analyzing lack of surprise or injury in terms of Rule 403 is preferable not only because it comports with the plain language of Rule 607, but because it will lead to the conclusion that a trial court abuses its discretion under Rule 403 when it allows the State to admit impeachment evidence for the primary use of placing evidence before the jury that was otherwise inadmissible. The impeachment evidence must be excluded under Rule 403's balancing test because the State profits from the witness' testimony only if the jury misuses the evidence by considering it for its truth. Consequently, any probative value the impeachment testimony may have is substantially outweighed by its prejudicial effect."

TRE 608. EVIDENCE OF CHARACTER & CONDUCT OF A WITNESS

(a) Opinion and Reputation Evidence of Character. The credibility of a witness may be attacked or supported by evidence in the form of opinion or reputation, but subject to these limitations:

(1) the evidence may refer only to character for truthfulness or untruthfulness; and

(2) evidence of truthful character is admissible only after the character of the witness for truthfulness has been attacked by opinion or reputation evidence or otherwise.

(b) Specific Instances of Conduct. Specific instances of the conduct of a witness, for the purpose of attacking or supporting the witness' credibility, other than conviction of crime as provided in Rule 609, may not be inquired into on cross-examination of the witness nor proved by extrinsic evidence.

Michael v. State, 235 S.W.3d 723, 725 (Tex.Crim. App.2007). "Impeaching a witness with a prior inconsistent statement is not necessarily an attack on credibility that would allow rehabilitative evidence of character for truthfulness under [TRE] 608(a). Although rehabilitation may be permitted under 608(a), it is not automatic. *At 726:* Impeachment by a prior inconsistent statement (or 'self-contradiction') is normally just an attack on the witness's accuracy, not his character for truthfulness. *At 728:* [W]e hold that the question for the trial judge [under TRE 608(a)(2) in allowing rehabilitative evidence of a witness's truthfulness after the witness's prior inconsistent statements are introduced] is whether a reasonable juror would believe that a witness's character for truthfulness has been attacked by cross-examination, evidence from other witnesses, or statements of counsel (*e.g.*, during voir dire or opening statements)."

Lopez v. State, 18 S.W.3d 220, 223 (Tex.Crim.App. 2000). "The issue we face is whether, in a case involving a sexual offense, the Confrontation Clause demands that evidence of the complainant's prior false allegations of abuse against a person other than the defendant be admissible, despite Rule 608(b)'s proscription against admitting specific instances of conduct. We must decide whether the Confrontation Clause requires us to carve out a special exception to the [TRE] for sexual offenses." Held: There is no exception on the facts of this case.

Schutz v. State, 957 S.W.2d 52, 69-70 (Tex.Crim. App.1997). "Under [TRCE] 608(a) [now TRE 608(a)], a party may attack a witness' or other declarant's *general* capacity or disposition to tell the truth. The other party may respond to such an attack with evidence supporting that person's *general* capacity or disposition for truthfulness. An attack or response concerning a person's general capacity for truthfulness may be related to a particular time period. General capacity evidence includes whether a person can distinguish between reality and fantasy and/or whether the person's physical or mental condition adversely affects a person's ability to accurately perceive and/or relate events. Where mental capacity and moral disposition can be clearly distinguished, a party may respond with evidence supporting mental capacity only when mental capacity has been attacked and likewise for moral disposition. Where the distinction is blurred or unclear, the trial court has discretion on whether to admit certain evidence supporting truthfulness and should be reversed only for an abuse of discretion. [¶] Likewise, a party may attack the credibility of a witness or other declarant by offering the following kinds of manipulation evidence: (a) evidence that the person is, in general, the kind of person who is easily manipulated, (b) common signs or symptoms of manipulation and evidence that the person displays some or all of these signs or symptoms, and (c) evidence of third person acts or words designed to manipulate. The other party may respond to such attacks with (a) evidence that the person is *not,* in general, the kind of person who is easily manipulated, (b) common signs or symptoms of manipulation and evidence that the person does *not* display these signs or symptoms, and (c) evidence rebutting the existence of third person acts or words of manipulation. A party may respond to any of the first three categories with evidence from any of the second three categories provided that the latter evidence is logically relevant to rebut the former. *At 72:* In determining whether the door is opened to the introduction of certain testimony, it important to distinguish proper rebuttal testimony under [TRE 608(a)] and comments on credibility that fall outside of that provision. Although some minimal relevance is required, general evidence supporting truthful character as outlined by [TRE 608(a)] may be liberally employed to respond to attacks on truthful character: there need only be a 'loose fit' between the rebuttal evidence and the predicate attacks on character. Moreover, such predicate attacks on character may include not only the introduction of evidence but also the use of questions designed to call a witness' character for truthfulness into doubt. But, evidence that falls outside of the recognized rebuttal category in [TRE 608(a)] is illegitimate and a much more specific showing of relevance to character attacks must be shown:

there must be a 'tight fit' between the rebuttal evidence and the predicate attacks on character. [M]erely asking questions designed to cast doubt upon a witness' character for truthfulness should not ordinarily be sufficient to open the door to evidence supporting the truthfulness of specific allegations; favorable answers to such questions must ordinarily be obtained in order to justify the introduction of such specific testimony."

Pavlacka v. State, 892 S.W.2d 897, 902-03 (Tex. Crim.App.1994). "A complainant's testimony regarding the charged offense may be undermined in any number of ways, including: 1) by prior inconsistent statement, [TRE 613(a)]; 2) evidence of bad character for truthfulness, [TRE] 608(a); or 3) simply by a denial by the accused that what the complainant testified to ever took place. The State may counter with evidence that logically rehabilitates that complainant. Such rehabilitation may take the form of: 1) prior consistent statements, [TREs 613(c)] and 801(e)(1)(B), or expert testimony explaining why child complainants may seem to prevaricate; 2) evidence of good character for truthfulness, [TRE] 608(a)(2); or 3) any evidence that logically corroborates the complainant's account of the charged offense. Moreover, we have suggested that evidence from some source other than the impeached complainant that an accused standing *in loco parentis* to the complainant molested him on another occasion may be admissible to the extent that it logically serves to rehabilitate the complainant."

Perry v. State, 236 S.W.3d 859, 865 (Tex.App.—Texarkana 2007, no pet.). "[T]he jury is entitled to hear evidence as to the mental status of the witness and the extent of his or her mental impairment. '[T]he mental capacity of the witness is the proper subject of consideration and impeachment as bearing upon his credibility.' Therefore, the right to cross-examination includes the right to impeach the witness with evidence that might go to any impairment or disability affecting the witness' credibility. [¶] Cross-examination of a testifying State's witness to show that the witness has suffered a recent mental illness or disturbance is proper, provided that such mental illness or disturbance is such that it might tend to reflect on the witness' credibility."

Palmer v. State, 222 S.W.3d 92, 95 (Tex.App.—Houston [14th Dist.] 2006, pet. ref'd). "A defendant seeking to impeach a witness with evidence of a previous false accusation against a third party must, as a

TRE 608

threshold evidentiary matter, produce evidence showing the prior accusation is actually false."

Gonzales v. State, 929 S.W.2d 546, 549 (Tex. App.—Austin 1996, pet. ref'd). "The rules of evidence grant a party greater latitude to prove a witness's bias than to prove a witness's untruthful character. For the purpose of impeaching his credibility, a witness's character may be attacked by opinion or reputation evidence and by proof of certain criminal convictions. Other than conviction of a crime, a witness's character for truthfulness may not be impeached by proof of specific instances of conduct. [TRCE] 608(b) [now TRE 608(b)] is very restrictive and allows for no exceptions."

Norrid v. State, 925 S.W.2d 342, 347 (Tex.App.—Fort Worth 1996, no pet.). "The general rule is that a party is not entitled to impeach a witness on a collateral matter. 'The test as to whether a matter is collateral is whether the cross-examining party would be entitled to prove it as a part of his case tending to establish his plea.'"

Cunningham v. State, 815 S.W.2d 313, 319 (Tex. App.—Dallas 1991, no pet.). "[W]hen the accused testifies gratuitously about some matter that is irrelevant or collateral to the proceeding, as with any other witness, the State may impeach him by a showing that he has lied or is in error regarding that matter. The permissible inference from such exposure is that, if the accused lied or was in error about a collateral matter, he is likely to have lied or been in error in the balance of testimony—those aspects of his testimony that are relevant to material issues in the case."

TRE 609. IMPEACHMENT BY EVIDENCE OF CONVICTION OF CRIME

(a) General Rule. For the purpose of attacking the credibility of a witness, evidence that the witness has been convicted of a crime shall be admitted if elicited from the witness or established by public record but only if the crime was a felony or involved moral turpitude, regardless of punishment, and the court determines that the probative value of admitting this evidence outweighs its prejudicial effect to a party.

(b) Time Limit. Evidence of a conviction under this rule is not admissible if a period of more than ten years has elapsed since the date of the conviction or of the release of the witness from the confinement imposed for that conviction, whichever is the later date,

unless the court determines, in the interests of justice, that the probative value of the conviction supported by specific facts and circumstances substantially outweighs its prejudicial effect.

(c) Effect of Pardon, Annulment, or Certificate of Rehabilitation. Evidence of a conviction is not admissible under this rule if:

(1) based on the finding of the rehabilitation of the person convicted, the conviction has been the subject of a pardon, annulment, certificate of rehabilitation, or other equivalent procedure, and that person has not been convicted of a subsequent crime which was classified as a felony or involved moral turpitude, regardless of punishment;

(2) probation has been satisfactorily completed for the crime for which the person was convicted, and that person has not been convicted of a subsequent crime which was classified as a felony or involved moral turpitude, regardless of punishment; or

(3) based on a finding of innocence, the conviction has been the subject of a pardon, annulment, or other equivalent procedure.

(d) Juvenile Adjudications. Evidence of juvenile adjudications is not admissible, except for proceedings conducted pursuant to Title III, Family Code, in which the witness is a party, under this rule unless required to be admitted by the Constitution of the United States or Texas.

(e) Pendency of Appeal. Pendency of an appeal renders evidence of a conviction inadmissible.

(f) Notice. Evidence of a conviction is not admissible if after timely written request by the adverse party specifying the witness or witnesses, the proponent fails to give to the adverse party sufficient advance written notice of intent to use such evidence to provide the adverse party with a fair opportunity to contest the use of such evidence.

See also *O'Connor's Crimes & Consequences* (2008-09), ch. 18, "Crimes of Moral Turpitude."

ANNOTATIONS

Lopez v. State, ___ S.W.3d ___ (Tex.Crim.App. 2008) (No. PD-1124-07; 5-14-08). Pen. Code §12.45 "permits a defendant (with the prosecutor's consent) to admit guilt of an unadjudicated extraneous offense, have that offense taken into account by the trial court in sentencing on the primary offense, and thereafter bar any future prosecution for that extraneous offense.

In a prior prosecution, appellant and the State followed this procedure, and the trial court took into account two extraneous drug offenses. In the present case, the State sought to introduce evidence of those drug offenses as 'prior convictions' to impeach appellant as a witness under [TRE] 609. Two issues are presented: First, did appellant forfeit error by failing to object when the State cross-examined him about the prior offenses? Second, do extraneous offenses considered under [Pen. Code] §12.45 constitute prior convictions available for impeachment under Rule 609? We answer both questions 'no' and affirm the judgment of the court of appeals."

Winegarner v. State, 235 S.W.3d 787, 790-91 (Tex. Crim.App.2007). "We have recognized before that when a witness, on direct examination, makes a blanket assertion of fact and thereby leaves a false impression with respect to his prior behavior or the extent of his prior troubles with the law, he opens the door on his otherwise irrelevant past criminal history and opposing counsel may [impeach him by] expos[ing] the falsehood. We have also recognized that when a witness's blanket assertion of exemplary conduct is directly relevant to the offense charged, the opponent may both cross-examine the [witness] and offer extrinsic evidence rebutting the statement. On the other hand, [under TRE 403] a trial court may exclude any relevant evidence if its probative value is substantially outweighed by any or all of the countervailing factors specified in Rule 403." (Internal quotes omitted.)

Escobedo v. State, 202 S.W.3d 844, 848 (Tex. App.—Waco 2006, pet. ref'd). "Moral turpitude encompasses crimes involving: (1) 'dishonesty, fraud, deceit, misrepresentation, or deliberate violence;' (2) matters of 'personal morality;' (3) conduct committed 'knowingly contrary to justice, honesty, principle, or good morals;' (4) 'baseness, vileness, or depravity;' (5) conduct 'immoral in itself, regardless of whether it is punishable by law,' in that the 'doing of the act itself, and not its prohibition by statute, fixes the moral turpitude;' or (6) 'immoral conduct' that is 'willful, flagrant, or shameless, and which shows a moral indifference to the opinion of the good and respectable members of the community.' *At 849:* [W]e hold that public lewdness, as defined by the Penal Code [§21.07], constitutes a crime of moral turpitude and may be used to impeach a witness' credibility." *See also In re Thacker*, 881 S.W.2d 307, 309 (Tex.1994); *Arnold v. State*, 36 S.W.3d

542, 547 (Tex.App.—Tyler 2000, pet. ref'd) (criminally negligent homicide does not involve moral turpitude); *Polk v. State*, 865 S.W.2d 627, 630 (Tex.App.—Fort Worth 1993, pet. ref'd) (indecent exposure involves moral turpitude); *Robertson v. State*, 685 S.W.2d 488, 492 (Tex.App.—Fort Worth 1985, no pet.) (lying to a police officer involves moral turpitude).

Dale v. State, 90 S.W.3d 826, 830 (Tex.App.—San Antonio 2002, pet. ref'd). "When determining whether the probative value of a defendant's previous conviction outweighs its prejudicial effect, the court examines: (1) the impeachment value of the prior crime; (2) the temporal proximity of the past crime relative to the charged offense and the witness's subsequent history; (3) the similarity between the past crime and the offense being prosecuted; (4) the importance of the defendant's testimony; and (5) the importance of the credibility issue." *See also DeLeon v. State*, 126 S.W.3d 210, 215-16 (Tex.App.—Houston [1st Dist.] 2003, pet. dism'd).

Dallas Cty. Bail Bond Bd. v. Mason, 773 S.W.2d 586, 589 (Tex.App.—Dallas 1989, no writ). "[T]he offense of issuance of a bad check does not involve moral turpitude unless it can be shown that the offense contained the element of intent to defraud."

TRE 610. RELIGIOUS BELIEFS OR OPINIONS

Evidence of the beliefs or opinions of a witness on matters of religion is not admissible for the purpose of showing that by reason of their nature the witness' credibility is impaired or enhanced.

TRE 611. MODE & ORDER OF INTERROGATION & PRESENTATION

(a) Control by Court. The court shall exercise reasonable control over the mode and order of interrogating witnesses and presenting evidence so as to (1) make the interrogation and presentation effective for the ascertainment of the truth, (2) avoid needless consumption of time, and (3) protect witnesses from harassment or undue embarrassment.

(b) Scope of Cross-Examination. A witness may be cross-examined on any matter relevant to any issue in the case, including credibility.

(c) Leading Questions. Leading questions should not be used on the direct examination of a witness except as may be necessary to develop the testimony of the witness. Ordinarily leading questions should be permitted on cross-examination. When a party calls a hostile witness, an adverse party, or a witness identified with an adverse party, interrogation may be by leading questions.

TRE 612. WRITING USED TO REFRESH MEMORY

If a witness uses a writing to refresh memory for the purpose of testifying either

(1) while testifying;

(2) before testifying, in civil cases, if the court in its discretion determines it is necessary in the interests of justice; or

(3) before testifying, in criminal cases;

an adverse party is entitled to have the writing produced at the hearing, to inspect it, to cross-examine the witness thereon, and to introduce in evidence those portions which relate to the testimony of the witness. If it is claimed that the writing contains matters not related to the subject matter of the testimony the court shall examine the writing in camera, excise any portion not so related, and order delivery of the remainder to the party entitled thereto. Any portion withheld over objections shall be preserved and made available to the appellate court in the event of an appeal. If a writing is not produced or delivered pursuant to order under this rule, the court shall make any order justice requires, except that in criminal cases when the prosecution elects not to comply, the order shall be one striking the testimony or, if the court in its discretion determines that the interests of justice so require, declaring a mistrial.

ANNOTATIONS

Pondexter v. State, 942 S.W.2d 577, 582 (Tex.Crim. App.1996). "[D] contends that the trial court erred in failing to require the prosecution to deliver its notes taken during jury selection to him for use in cross-examination concerning the credibility of the prosecution's explanation for his peremptory challenges. [¶] The State asserts that the prosecutor was never called as a witness at this hearing, but we can not agree with this. Although the prosecutor was not actually sworn as a witness, he did give testimony to the court regarding the reasons for his peremptory strikes. However, appellant is only entitled to the notes if they were actually used by the prosecutor to refresh his memory."

Davis v. State, 93 S.W.3d 664, 669 (Tex.App.—Texarkana 2002, pet. ref'd). TRE 612 "requires production of material used to refresh the witness' memory during *any* hearing [including pretrial suppression hearings], not merely during a trial in front of a jury."

De La Rosa v. State, 961 S.W.2d 495, 498 (Tex. App.—San Antonio 1997, no pet.). "Whether [TRCE] 611's [now TRE 612's] entitlement to have impeaching memoranda admitted guarantees a 'substantial right' is a more difficult question, but one that the new [appellate] rules forces this court to answer. We hold that the right is substantial. [TRE 612] gives a jury the opportunity to compare documents used to refresh a witness's testimony with the statements that witness made at trial. Such comparisons may yield inconsistencies or discrepancies in the witness's testimony that would test the witness's credibility. The evaluation of witness credibility is one of the foremost functions of a jury. Thus, [TRE 612] facilitates the ability of both parties in a criminal case to present a complete version of the events and all the testimony relevant to those events."

TRE 613. PRIOR STATEMENTS OF WITNESSES: IMPEACHMENT & SUPPORT

(a) Examining Witness Concerning Prior Inconsistent Statement. In examining a witness concerning a prior inconsistent statement made by the witness, whether oral or written, and before further cross-examination concerning, or extrinsic evidence of, such statement may be allowed, the witness must be told the contents of such statement and the time and place and the person to whom it was made, and must be afforded an opportunity to explain or deny such statement. If written, the writing need not be shown to the witness at that time, but on request the same shall be shown to opposing counsel. If the witness unequivocally admits having made such statement, extrinsic evidence of same shall not be admitted. This provision does not apply to admissions of a party-opponent as defined in Rule 801(e)(2).

(b) Examining Witness Concerning Bias or Interest. In impeaching a witness by proof of circumstances or statements showing bias or interest on the part of such witness, and before further cross-examination concerning, or extrinsic evidence of, such bias or interest may be allowed, the circumstances supporting

TRE 611

such claim or the details of such statement, including the contents and where, when and to whom made, must be made known to the witness, and the witness must be given an opportunity to explain or to deny such circumstances or statement. If written, the writing need not be shown to the witness at that time, but on request the same shall be shown to opposing counsel. If the witness unequivocally admits such bias or interest, extrinsic evidence of same shall not be admitted. A party shall be permitted to present evidence rebutting any evidence impeaching one of said party's witnesses on grounds of bias or interest.

(c) Prior Consistent Statements of Witnesses. A prior statement of a witness which is consistent with the testimony of the witness is inadmissible except as provided in Rule 801(e)(1)(B).

ANNOTATIONS

Maxwell v. State, 48 S.W.3d 196, 200 (Tex.Crim. App.2001). "[A] defendant is permitted to cross-examine a State's witness on the status of his deferred adjudication probation in order to show a potential motive, bias or interest to testify for the State...."

Dixon v. State, 2 S.W.3d 263, 271 (Tex.Crim.App. 1999). "Unlike [TRE] 608(b), Rule [613(b)] does not expressly bar the use of specific instances of conduct to show bias or interest."

Bigby v. State, 892 S.W.2d 864, 886 (Tex.Crim.App. 1994). "Appellant's trial objections were based upon [TRE 613]. Section (a) provides for the examination of a witness concerning a prior inconsistent statement. However, the statement must be made by her. In this instance the pleadings were not signed by [wife of murder victim], but rather by her attorney, and therefore, they are not her prior inconsistent statements within the meaning of [TRE 613(a)]."

Cohn v. State, 849 S.W.2d 817, 820 (Tex.Crim.App. 1993). TRCE 612(c), now TRE 613(c), "is also a 'bolstering' rule to the extent it prevents the use of prior consistent statements of a witness for the sole purpose of enhancing his credibility. But ..., [TRE 613(c)] says nothing about the admissibility of substantive evidence that happens to corroborate a witness. Nor do we know of any other provision in the Rules of Criminal Evidence that mandates exclusion of relevant evidence simply because it corroborates testimony of an earlier witness."

Fields v. State, 966 S.W.2d 736, 741 (Tex. App.—San Antonio 1998), *rev'd on other grounds*, 1 S.W.3d 687 (Tex.Crim.App.1999). "To lay ... a predicate [for admission of extrinsic evidence of prior inconsistent statements], an attorney must ask the witness if he made the contradictory statement at a certain place and time and to a certain person. If the witness denies making the statement, extrinsic proof may be admitted to prove the statement. If he admits the statement, no extrinsic evidence is allowed. Because this rule is designed to give the witness an opportunity to explain prior inconsistencies, the opposing party must provide the witness enough information to explain the prior statement or to admit or deny it."

Staley v. State, 888 S.W.2d 45, 49 (Tex.App.—Tyler 1994, no pet.). "The rule of admissibility of prior inconsistent statements should be liberally construed and the trial judge has the discretion to receive any evidence that gives promise of exposing a falsehood. ... If a witness only qualifiedly or partially admits to making a prior inconsistent statement, the statement may be used to impeach him."

TRE 614. EXCLUSION OF WITNESSES

At the request of a party the court shall order witnesses excluded so that they cannot hear the testimony of other witnesses, and it may make the order of its own motion. This rule does not authorize exclusion of:

(1) a party who is a natural person or in civil cases the spouse of such natural person;

(2) an officer or employee of a party in a civil case or a defendant in a criminal case that is not a natural person designated as its representative by its attorney;

(3) a person whose presence is shown by a party to be essential to the presentation of the party's cause; or

(4) the victim in a criminal case, unless the victim is to testify and the court determines that the victim's testimony would be materially affected if the victim hears other testimony at the trial.

See also CCP arts. 36.03-36.06.

ANNOTATIONS

Russell v. State, 155 S.W.3d 176, 181 (Tex.Crim. App.2005). "The State's designating a witness as a 'case agent' does not make a witness one whom the court may not exclude from the courtroom under Rule 614. [T]he government's designation of a 'case agent'

in the trial of a criminal case is permitted in federal courts by the federal counterpart of Rule 614, but it is not permitted in the courts of this state. [¶] Because the State did not meet its burden to show that [officer] was a witness whose exclusion from the courtroom was not authorized by Rule 614, the trial court erred in permitting [officer] to remain in the courtroom during the trial." Held: The error was harmless.

Bell v. State, 938 S.W.2d 35, 50 (Tex.Crim.App. 1996). TRE 614 "does not mention what, if any, sanctions a trial court should impose for violations of the rule. Two possible sanctions a trial court may use are holding a witness who violates the exclusion order in contempt, and the more remedial sanction of refusing to allow the witness to testify. Unlike the trial court's obligation to order witnesses excluded during other witnesses' testimony, the court's decision to allow testimony from a witness who has violated the rule is a discretionary matter. ... In reviewing the trial court's decision to allow the testimony, we look at whether or not the defendant was harmed or prejudiced by the witness's violation; that is, whether or not the witness's *presence* during other testimony resulted in injury to the defendant."

Moore v. State, 882 S.W.2d 844, 848 (Tex.Crim.App. 1994). "The party seeking an exception under [TRCE] 613 [now TRE 614] has the burden of showing that one of the enumerated sections is met. No such showing in this cause was made. ... Therefore, the trial court abused its discretion in permitting the State's expert witness to remain in the courtroom during a portion of the trial. [¶] Recognizing such an error, we must determine if the error requires reversal." Held: Point of error overruled. *But see Martinez*, below.

Martinez v. State, 867 S.W.2d 30, 40 (Tex.Crim. App.1993). "'The trial court is vested with discretion and may permit expert witnesses to be exempt from the rule in order that they may hear other witnesses testify and then base their opinion on such testimony.' [¶] [witness] was to give his expert opinion whether appellant would constitute a continuing threat to society. Therefore, we cannot say that the trial judge abused his discretion in allowing [witness] to observe the testimony of appellant's brother and sister." *But see Moore*, above.

Minor v. State, 91 S.W.3d 824, 829 (Tex.App.—Fort Worth 2002, pet. ref'd). "We perform a two-step analysis in determining whether a trial court has abused its discretion in allowing a violation of the [TRE 614]. First,

we ascertain what kind of witness was involved. Violations of the Rule involve two main categories of witnesses: (1) witnesses who have been sworn or listed as witnesses in the case and either hear testimony or discuss another's testimony; and (2) persons who were not intended to be witnesses and are not connected with the case-in-chief but who have, due to events during trial, become necessary witnesses. If the witness was one who had no connection with either the State's case-in-chief or the defendant's case-in-chief and who, because of a lack of personal knowledge regarding the offense, was not likely to be called as a witness, *then no abuse of discretion can be shown*. [¶] Under the second step of the analysis, we must determine: (1) whether the witness actually conferred with or heard the testimony of another witness without court permission; and (2) whether 'the witness's testimony contradict[ed] the testimony of a witness he actually heard from the opposing side or corroborate[d] the testimony of another witness he actually heard from the same side on an issue of fact bearing upon the issue of guilt or innocence.' If both of the above criteria are met, then the trial court abused its discretion." *See also White v. State*, 958 S.W.2d 460, 463-65 (Tex.App.—Waco 1997, no pet.).

Jordan v. State, 1 S.W.3d 153, 159 (Tex.App.—Waco 1999, pet. ref'd). CCP art. 38.30(a) "provides ... that interpreters are governed by 'the same rules and penalties as are provided for witnesses.' Thus, the Rule applies to interpreters in the same manner as it applies to witnesses. [¶] [W]e conclude the court abused its discretion in failing to exclude the interpreter from the courtroom during the officers' testimony."

Lopez v. State, 960 S.W.2d 948, 953 (Tex.App.—Houston [1st Dist.] 1998, pet. ref'd). "[T]he test for determining if a court properly exercised its discretion in excluding testimony [is]: (1) whether the 'particular and extraordinary circumstances' show the defendant or his counsel consented, procured, connived, or had knowledge of a witness or potential witness who is in violation of the sequestration rule, and (2) if no particular circumstances exist to justify disqualification, was the testimony of the witness crucial to the defense. Appellant has the burden of establishing both prongs."

TRE 615. PRODUCTION OF STATEMENTS OF WITNESSES IN CRIMINAL CASES

(a) Motion for Production. After a witness other than the defendant has testified on direct examination,

TRE 614

the court, on motion of a party who did not call the witness, shall order the attorney for the state or the defendant and defendant's attorney, as the case may be, to produce, for the examination and use of the moving party, any statement of the witness that is in their possession and that relates to the subject matter concerning which the witness has testified.

(b) Production of Entire Statement. If the entire contents of the statement relate to the subject matter concerning which the witness has testified, the court shall order that the statement be delivered to the moving party.

(c) Production of Excised Statement. If the other party claims that the statement contains matter that does not relate to the subject matter concerning which the witness has testified, the court shall order that it be delivered to the court in camera. Upon inspection, the court shall excise the portions of the statement that do not relate to the subject matter concerning which the witness has testified, and shall order that the statement, with such material excised, be delivered to the moving party. Any portion withheld over objection shall be preserved and made available to the appellate court in the event of appeal.

(d) Recess for Examination of Statement. Upon delivery of the statement to the moving party, the court, upon application of that party, shall recess proceedings in the trial for a reasonable examination of such statement and for preparation for its use in the trial.

(e) Sanction for Failure to Produce Statement. If the other party elects not to comply with an order to deliver a statement to the moving party, the court shall order that the testimony of the witness be stricken from the record and that the trial proceed, or, if it is the attorney for the state who elects not to comply, shall declare a mistrial if required by the interest of justice.

(f) Definition. As used in this rule, a "statement" of a witness means:

(1) a written statement made by the witness that is signed or otherwise adopted or approved by the witness;

(2) a substantially verbatim recital of an oral statement made by the witness that is recorded contemporaneously with the making of the oral statement and that is contained in a stenographic, mechanical, electrical, or other recording or a transcription thereof; or

(3) a statement, however taken or recorded, or a transcription thereof, made by the witness to a grand jury.

See also CCP art. 56.03.

ARTICLE VII. OPINIONS & EXPERT TESTIMONY

TRE 701. OPINION TESTIMONY BY LAY WITNESSES

If the witness is not testifying as an expert, the witness' testimony in the form of opinions or inferences is limited to those opinions or inferences which are (a) rationally based on the perception of the witness and (b) helpful to a clear understanding of the witness' testimony or the determination of a fact in issue.

ANNOTATIONS

Osbourn v. State, 92 S.W.3d 531, 538 (Tex.Crim. App.2002). "Unlike other drugs that may require chemical analysis, marihuana has a distinct appearance and odor that are familiar and easily recognizable to anyone who has encountered it. So [officer's] opinion that appellant possessed marihuana, based on the odor she smelled and the green, leafy substance she saw, was one that a reasonable person could draw from the circumstances. Her testimony regarding the identification of the marihuana was admissible as a lay opinion...."

Fairow v. State, 943 S.W.2d 895, 899 (Tex.Crim. App.1997). "It is impossible for a witness to possess personal knowledge of what someone else is thinking. [I]f the trial court determines that a proffered lay-witness opinion is an attempt to communicate the actual subjective mental state of the actor, the court should exclude the opinion because it could never be based on personal knowledge. [¶] [W]hile a witness cannot possess personal knowledge of another's mental state, he may possess personal knowledge of facts from which an opinion regarding mental state may be drawn."

Plouff v. State, 192 S.W.3d 213, 224 (Tex.App.—Houston [14th Dist.] 2006, no pet.). "[T]estimony by the arresting officer concerning the one-leg stand and walk-and-turn tests [for intoxication] is lay witness testimony governed by Rule 701."

Singleton v. State, 91 S.W.3d 342, 351 (Tex.App.—Texarkana 2002, no pet.). "Any lay witness may give an opinion as to intoxication."

Turro v. State, 950 S.W.2d 390, 403 (Tex.App.— Fort Worth 1997, pet. ref'd). TRCE 701's, now TRE 701's, "requirement that the testimony be based on the witness's perception presumes the witness observed or experienced the underlying facts, thus meeting the personal-knowledge requirement of [TRCE] 602 [now TRE 602]."

Rodriguez v. State, 903 S.W.2d 405, 410 (Tex. App.—Texarkana 1995, pet. ref'd). "[T]he opinion of a witness is not admissible to interpret the meaning of the acts, conduct, or language of another."

TRE 702. TESTIMONY BY EXPERTS

If scientific, technical, or other specialized knowledge will assist the trier of fact to understand the evidence or to determine a fact in issue, a witness qualified as an expert by knowledge, skill, experience, training, or education may testify thereto in the form of an opinion or otherwise.

ANNOTATIONS

Vela v. State, 209 S.W.3d 128, 130 (Tex.Crim.App. 2006). "The [TREs] set out three separate conditions regarding admissibility of expert testimony. [The conditions are in TREs 104(a), 401, 402, and 702.] *At 131:* These rules require a trial judge to make three separate inquiries, which must all be met before admitting expert testimony: (1) the witness qualifies as an expert by reason of his knowledge, skill, experience, training, or education; (2) the subject matter of the testimony is an appropriate one for expert testimony; and (3) admitting the expert testimony will actually assist the factfinder in deciding the case. These conditions are commonly referred to as (1) qualification, (2) reliability, and (3) relevance. [¶] [A]n appellate court should consider three criteria when determining whether a trial court abused its discretion in evaluating a witness's qualifications as an expert: (1) is the field of expertise complex?; (2) how conclusive is the expert's opinion?; and (3) how central is the area of expertise to the resolution of the lawsuit? [¶] Qualification is distinct from reliability and relevance and … should be evaluated independently. *At 133-34:* While qualification deals with the witness's background and experience, reliability focuses on the subject matter of the witness's testimony. [¶] [TRE] 705(c) governs the reliability of expert testimony…. Reliability depends upon whether the evidence has its basis in sound scientific methodology. This demands a certain technical showing that … gives a trial judge the opportunity to weed out testimony pertaining to so-called junk science. [¶] [S]cientific evidence must meet three criteria to be reliable: (a) the underlying scientific theory must be valid; (b) the technique applying the theory must be valid; and (c) the technique must have been properly applied on the occasion in question. [A] list of non-exclusive factors that could affect a trial judge's decision on reliability [includes]: (1) the extent to which the underlying scientific theory and technique are accepted as valid by the relevant scientific community, if such a community can be ascertained; (2) the qualifications of the experts testifying; (3) the existence of literature supporting or rejecting the underlying scientific theory and technique; (4) the potential rate of error of the technique; (5) the availability of other experts to test and evaluate the technique; (6) the clarity with which the underlying scientific theory and technique can be explained to the court; and (7) the experience and skill of the person(s) who applied the technique on the occasion in question. [¶] And even if the traditional *Kelly* reliability factors do not perfectly apply to particular testimony, the proponent is not excused from proving its reliability. … The reliability inquiry is, thus, a flexible one. In some cases, the reliability of scientific knowledge will be at issue; in others, the relevant reliability concerns may focus upon personal knowledge or experience. But the proponent must establish some foundation for the reliability of an expert's opinion. Experience alone may provide a sufficient basis for an expert's testimony in some cases, but it cannot do so in every case." (Internal quotes omitted.) *See also Acevedo v. State*, ___ S.W.3d ___ (Tex. App.—San Antonio 2008, pet. filed 5-5-08) (No. 04-06-00098-CR; 1-30-08) (holding expert's testimony unreliable).

Rodgers v. State, 205 S.W.3d 525, 526 (Tex.Crim. App.2006). "[W]e hold that a motion to strike an expert witness's testimony based on his lack of qualifications, which is made after the witness has testified, can serve as a renewed objection to the trial court's earlier ruling that the witness was qualified. In these circumstances, an appellate court reviews the trial court's ruling based upon all of the evidence before the court at the time of the motion to strike."

Reynolds v. State, 204 S.W.3d 386, 390-91 (Tex. Crim.App.2006). "[W]e hold that, when evidence of alcohol concentration as shown by the results of analysis of breath specimens taken at the request or order of a peace officer is offered in the trial of a DWI offense, (1) the underlying scientific theory has been determined by the legislature to be valid; (2) the technique applying the theory has been determined by the legislature to be valid when the specimen was taken and analyzed by individuals who are certified by, and were using methods approved by the rules of, DPS; and (3) the trial court must determine whether the technique was properly applied in accordance with the department's rules, on the occasion in question."

State v. Medrano, 127 S.W.3d 781, 783 (Tex.Crim. App.2004). "Under the **Zani** [**v. State**, 758 S.W.2d 233 (Tex.Crim.App.1988)] standard, the Court instituted procedural safeguards to protect against 'the four-prong dangers of hypnosis: hypersuggestibility, loss of critical judgment, confabulation, and memory cementing.' ... The **Zani** standard permits admission of hypnotically enhanced testimony '[i]f, after consideration of the totality of the circumstances, the trial court should find by clear and convincing evidence that hypnosis neither rendered the witness's posthypnotic memory untrustworthy nor substantially impaired the ability of the opponent fairly to test the witness's recall by cross[-]examination.' At 787: **Zani** remains the standard to be applied by Texas trial courts in assessing the reliability and determining the admissibility of hypnotically enhanced testimony."

Hernandez v. State, 116 S.W.3d 26, 29 (Tex.Crim. App.2003). "Once a scientific principle is generally accepted in the pertinent professional community and has been accepted in a sufficient number of trial courts through adversarial **Daubert/Kelly** hearings, subsequent courts may take judicial notice of the scientific validity (or invalidity) of that scientific theory based upon the process, materials, and evidence produced in those prior hearings. [¶] Similarly, once some courts have, through a **Daubert/Kelly** 'gatekeeping' hearing, determined the scientific reliability and validity of a specific methodology to implement or test the particular scientific theory, other courts may take judicial notice of the reliability (or unreliability) of that particular methodology."

Sexton v. State, 93 S.W.3d 96, 101 (Tex.Crim.App. 2002). "We conclude ... that the underlying theory of toolmark examination could be reliable in a given case, but that the State failed to produce evidence of the reliability of the technique used in this case."

Mata v. State, 46 S.W.3d 902, 916 (Tex.Crim.App. 2001). "We believe that the science of retrograde extrapolation can be reliable in a given case. The expert's ability to apply the science and explain it with clarity to the court is a paramount consideration. In addition, the expert must demonstrate some understanding of the difficulties associated with a retrograde extrapolation. He must demonstrate an awareness of the subtleties of the science and the risks inherent in any extrapolation. Finally, he must be able to clearly and consistently apply the science. [¶] The court evaluating the reliability of a retrograde extrapolation should also consider (a) the length of time between the offense and the test(s) administered; (b) the number of tests given and the length of time between each test; and (c) whether, and if so, to what extent, any individual characteristics of the defendant were known to the expert in providing his extrapolation. These characteristics and behaviors might include, but are not limited to, the person's weight and gender, the person's typical drinking pattern and tolerance for alcohol, how much the person had to drink on the day or night in question, what the person drank, the duration of the drinking spree, the time of the last drink, and how much and what the person had to eat either before, during, or after the drinking." See also **Ellis v. State**, 86 S.W.3d 759, 760 (Tex. App.—Waco 2002, pet. ref'd) (DWI horizontal gaze nystagmus test); **Quinney v. State**, 99 S.W.3d 853, 856-58 (Tex.App.—Houston [14th Dist.] 2003, no pet.).

Morales v. State, 32 S.W.3d 862, 865 (Tex.Crim. App.2000). "When examining the Rule 702 issue, the trial court must determine whether the expert make[s] an effort to tie pertinent facts of the case to the scientific principles which are the subject of his testimony. Restated, the testimony must be sufficiently tied to the facts to meet the simple requirement that it be helpful to the jury." (Internal quotes omitted.) See also **$18,000 v. State**, 961 S.W.2d 257, 265 (Tex.App.—Houston [1st Dist.] 1997, no pet.).

Weatherred v. State, 15 S.W.3d 540, 542 (Tex. Crim.App.2000). "Under Rule 702, the proponent of scientific evidence must show, by clear and convincing proof, that the evidence he is proffering is sufficiently relevant and reliable to assist the jury in accurately understanding other evidence or in determining a fact in issue. The reliability of 'soft' scientific evidence ... may be established by showing that (1) the field of expertise involved is a legitimate one, (2) the subject matter of the expert's testimony is within the scope of that field, and (3) the expert's testimony properly relies upon or utilizes the principles involved in that field." *See also Campbell v. State*, 910 S.W.2d 475, 478 (Tex.Crim.App. 1995).

Schutz v. State, 957 S.W.2d 52, 59 (Tex.Crim.App. 1997). "Expert testimony does not assist the jury if it constitutes 'a direct opinion on the truthfulness' of a child complainant's allegations. [¶] The question we must resolve here is whether testimony concerning 'manipulation' or 'fantasy' is equivalent to testimony about 'truthfulness,' or if different, whether such testimony nevertheless merits similar treatment under the rules of evidence. An important aspect of this question is whether the concept of 'truthfulness' encompasses nonmoral as well as moral considerations. For instance, a child who 'fantasizes' could be doing one of two things: (1) ... making up events that he or she knows never occurred ... (moral considerations), or (2) ... relating events that he or she truly believes occurred but did not in fact occur ... (nonmoral considerations). ... [W]here 'fantasizing' is used as a synonym for 'lying' the two should be treated the same. *At 70:* [W]hen evidence relating to capacity, fantasy, or manipulation is presented in the form of expert testimony, such evidence must also assist the trier of fact under [TRCE] 702 [now TRE 702]. To do so, the testimony must meet the proper tests for scientific reliability, and the testimony must reflect information outside the general knowledge of lay persons. [E]xpert rebuttal testimony supporting truthfulness is ordinarily admissible even if the predicate attacks on truthfulness comes from lay rather than expert witnesses, so long as the above conditions are met. *At 72:* [W]e reject the idea that lay opinion testimony on the truthfulness of allegations can open the door to expert testimony, but we do not foreclose the possibility that in some instances this might be the case, such as where a lay opinion witness' testimony takes on 'expert-like' qualities or perhaps where there is no available lay rehabilitation testimony."

Yount v. State, 872 S.W.2d 706, 712 (Tex.Crim.App. 1993). TRCE 702, now TRE 702, "does not permit an expert to give an opinion that the complainant or class of persons to which the complainant belongs is truthful." *See also Wilson v. State*, 90 S.W.3d 391, 392-93 (Tex. App.—Dallas 2002, no pet.).

Stovall v. State, 140 S.W.3d 712, 718 (Tex.App.— Tyler 2004, no pet.). "No Texas court has assessed the reliability of [vertical gaze nystagmus] tests. Therefore, the trial court's admission of the challenged testimony without making such an assessment is outside the zone of reasonable disagreement and constitutes an abuse of discretion."

DeLarue v. State, 102 S.W.3d 388, 396 (Tex.App.— Houston [14th Dist.] 2003, pet. ref'd). "As a general rule, police officers are not qualified to render expert opinions regarding accidents based on their position as police officers alone. However, police officers are qualified to testify regarding accident reconstruction if they are trained in the science about which they will testify and possess the high degree of knowledge sufficient to qualify as an expert."

Gregory v. State, 56 S.W.3d 164, 179-80 (Tex. App.—Houston [14th Dist.] 2001, pet. dism'd). "A medical license or degree is not the litmus test for qualification as an expert witness. [*E*]xperience alone can provide a sufficient basis to qualify a witness as an expert. [¶] [A] nurse with extensive experience in the identification and treatment of child sexual abuse victims could be *more* qualified to determine whether a child has been sexually abused than a medical doctor whose field of specialization does not touch on that subject. *At 181:* While [a nurse] is precluded from making a medical diagnosis or otherwise practicing medicine, she is not precluded from *testifying* about her mandatory duties to perform assessments, make nursing diagnoses, document a patient's symptoms, administer medications and treatments, and implement other measures to make the patient safe. [W]e find that [nurse] was qualified to testify as an expert under Rule 702." *See also Duran v. State*, 163 S.W.3d 253, 258 (Tex.App.—Fort Worth 2005, no pet.).

Perez v. State, 25 S.W.3d 830, 838 (Tex.App.— Houston [1st Dist.] 2000, no pet.). "[T]he trial court abused its discretion by allowing [witness] to testify concerning the 'child abuse accommodation syndrome' theory of [published psychiatrist]. Although [witness] has substantial experience in the field of child sexual abuse investigation, she is not an expert in the field of psychology, psychiatry, medicine, or science. Furthermore, the record is weak regarding the acceptance of [published psychiatrist's] writings in the relevant scientific community and the existence of literature supporting [published psychiatrist's] findings. [¶] [Witness] testified about the behavior of sexually abused children based partly on [published psychiatrist's] articles and partly on her own personal experience. The testimony about [published psychiatrist's] theory was error because it allowed [witness] to increase the credibility of her own expert testimony by adding to it the veneer of [published psychiatrist's] psychiatric expertise." *See also* **Hernandez v. State**, 53 S.W.3d 742, 746-51 (Tex.App.—Houston [1st Dist.] 2001, pet. ref'd).

Daubert v. Merrell Dow Pharm., Inc., 509 U.S. 579, 592-93, 113 S.Ct. 2786, 2796 (1993). "Faced with a proffer of expert scientific testimony, ... the trial judge must determine at the outset, pursuant to [FRE] 104(a), whether the expert is proposing to testify to (1) scientific knowledge that (2) will assist the trier of fact to understand or determine a fact in issue. This entails a preliminary assessment of whether the reasoning or methodology underlying the testimony is scientifically valid and of whether that reasoning or methodology properly can be applied to the facts in issue. [¶] [A] key question to be answered in determining whether a theory or technique is scientific knowledge that will assist the trier of fact will be whether it can be (and has been) tested. *At 2797:* Another ... consideration is whether the theory or technique has been subjected to peer review and publication. *At 594:* Additionally, in the case of a particular scientific technique, the court ordinarily should consider the known or potential rate of error ... and the existence and maintenance of standards controlling the technique's operation. Finally, 'general acceptance' can yet have a bearing on the inquiry. A 'reliability assessment does not require, although it does permit, explicit identification of a relevant scientific community and an express determination of a particular degree of acceptance within that community.' Widespread acceptance can be an important factor in ruling particular evidence admissible, and 'a known technique that has been able to attract only minimal support within the community,' may properly be viewed with skepticism. *At 595:* [A] judge assessing a proffer of expert scientific testimony under [FRE] 702 should also be mindful of other applicable rules. *At 2798:* [FRE] 706 allows the court at its discretion to procure the assistance of an expert of its own choosing. 'Expert evidence can be both powerful and quite misleading because of the difficulty in evaluating it. Because of this risk, the judge in weighing possible prejudice against probative force under [FRE] 403

of the present rules exercises more control over experts than over lay witnesses.'" *See also* **Emerson v. State**, 880 S.W.2d 759, 763 (Tex.Crim.App.1994).

TRE 703. BASES OF OPINION TESTIMONY BY EXPERTS

The facts or data in the particular case upon which an expert bases an opinion or inference may be those perceived by, reviewed by, or made known to the expert at or before the hearing. If of a type reasonably relied upon by experts in the particular field in forming opinions or inferences upon the subject, the facts or data need not be admissible in evidence.

ANNOTATIONS

Joiner v. State, 825 S.W.2d 701, 707-08 (Tex.Crim. App.1992). "If the trial court finds that a particular witness has specialized skill, training or education on a fact that is at issue before the court, and that the testimony of such witness will assist the jury, then such testimony is admissible. It does not matter if the testimony is based upon facts or data learned prior to trial, if it is of a type reasonably relied upon by experts within the field. The expert can further base his opinion partially on facts or data which is inadmissible, if such information is commonly relied upon by experts within his field."

Duckett v. State, 797 S.W.2d 906, 920 n.17 (Tex. Crim.App.1990), *overruled on other grounds*, **Cohn v. State**, 849 S.W.2d 817 (Tex.Crim.App.1993). "The rule foresees the witness' presence in the courtroom and does not prohibit his testimony simply because he did not examine the particular person at issue. Examination, or lack thereof, would go to the weight of the testimony, not its admissibility."

TRE 704. OPINION ON ULTIMATE ISSUE

Testimony in the form of an opinion or inference otherwise admissible is not objectionable because it embraces an ultimate issue to be decided by the trier of fact.

ANNOTATIONS

Duckett v. State, 797 S.W.2d 906, 920 (Tex.Crim. App.1990), *overruled on other grounds*, **Cohn v. State**, 849 S.W.2d 817 (Tex.Crim.App.1993). "Under our interpretation of the rules, ... testimony which merely *embraces* an ultimate issue is clearly admissible under

[TRCE] 704 [now TRE 704]. *At 915 n.13:* [A]n expert's testimony which in effect 'matches' general or 'classic' behavioral characteristics with a complainant's behavior patterns, but does not directly comment on the credibility of the victim, is admissible under [TRCEs] 702 and 704 [now TREs 702 and 704] as relevant and probative of the ultimate issue of guilt before the trier of fact."

TRE 705. DISCLOSURE OF FACTS OR DATA UNDERLYING EXPERT OPINION

(a) Disclosure of Facts or Data. The expert may testify in terms of opinion or inference and give the expert's reasons therefor without prior disclosure of the underlying facts or data, unless the court requires otherwise. The expert may in any event disclose on direct examination, or be required to disclose on cross-examination, the underlying facts or data.

(b) Voir Dire. Prior to the expert giving the expert's opinion or disclosing the underlying facts or data, a party against whom the opinion is offered upon request in a criminal case shall, or in a civil case may, be permitted to conduct a *voir dire* examination directed to the underlying facts or data upon which the opinion is based. This examination shall be conducted out of the hearing of the jury.

(c) Admissibility of Opinion. If the court determines that the underlying facts or data do not provide a sufficient basis for the expert's opinion under Rule 702 or 703, the opinion is inadmissible.

(d) Balancing Test; Limiting Instructions. When the underlying facts or data would be inadmissible in evidence, the court shall exclude the underlying facts or data if the danger that they will be used for a purpose other than as explanation or support for the expert's opinion outweighs their value as explanation or support or are unfairly prejudicial. If otherwise inadmissible facts or data are disclosed before the jury, a limiting instruction by the court shall be given upon request.

ANNOTATIONS

Skinner v. State, 956 S.W.2d 532, 540 (Tex.Crim. App.1997). The exhibit "reflects [expert witness's] mental processes upon his initial review of the case— his thoughts about the strengths and weaknesses of the defense theory and questions he wanted to discuss with defense counsel. While these mental impressions may have been *based upon* facts and data ..., subjective impressions, questions, and comments do not amount to an 'actual occurrence,' 'information presented as having objective reality,' or 'factual information.' [TRCE] 705 [now TRE 705] does not apply...."

Alba v. State, 905 S.W.2d 581, 588 (Tex.Crim.App. 1995). "Affording a defendant the chance to voir dire the State's expert witnesses gives defense counsel the opportunity to determine the foundation of the expert's opinion without fear of eliciting damaging hearsay or other inadmissible evidence in the jury's presence. A [TRCE] 705(b) [now TRE 705(b)] hearing may also supply defense counsel with sufficient ammunition to make a timely objection to the expert's testimony on the ground that it lacks a sufficient basis for admissibility."

Wheeler v. State, 79 S.W.3d 78, 82 (Tex.App.— Beaumont 2002, no pet.). "The general rule that an expert may be cross-examined on the basis of his or her opinion with the purpose, *inter alia*, of impeachment with out-of-court statements is now applicable to circumstances in which the expert did not rely on said out-of-court statements in formulating his or her ultimate opinion."

Vasquez v. State, 819 S.W.2d 932, 935 (Tex.App.— Corpus Christi 1991, pet. ref'd). TRCE 705, now TRE 705, "addresses the situation when the expert is testifying as to an opinion that is directly related to an issue at trial. '[T]his rule does not preclude a party from conducting a voir dire examination into the qualifications of an expert.' When an expert gives only general opinions not based on an analysis of the specific facts at issue, the voir dire allowed by [TRE 705(b)] is not implicated."

TRE 706. AUDIT IN CIVIL CASES

Despite any other evidence rule to the contrary, verified reports of auditors prepared pursuant to Rule of Civil Procedure 172, whether in the form of summaries, opinions, or otherwise, shall be admitted in evidence when offered by any party whether or not the facts or data in the reports are otherwise admissible and whether or not the reports embrace the ultimate issues to be decided by the trier of fact. Where exceptions to the reports have been filed, a party may contradict the reports by evidence supporting the exceptions.

ARTICLE VIII. HEARSAY

TRE 801. DEFINITIONS

The following definitions apply under this article:

(a) Statement. A "statement" is (1) an oral or written verbal expression or (2) nonverbal conduct of a person, if it is intended by the person as a substitute for verbal expression.

(b) Declarant. A "declarant" is a person who makes a statement.

(c) Matter Asserted. "Matter asserted" includes any matter explicitly asserted, and any matter implied by a statement, if the probative value of the statement as offered flows from declarant's belief as to the matter.

(d) Hearsay. "Hearsay" is a statement, other than one made by the declarant while testifying at the trial or hearing, offered in evidence to prove the truth of the matter asserted.

(e) Statements Which Are Not Hearsay. A statement is not hearsay if:

(1) *Prior statement by witness.* The declarant testifies at the trial or hearing and is subject to cross-examination concerning the statement, and the statement is:

(A) inconsistent with the declarant's testimony, and was given under oath subject to the penalty of perjury at a trial, hearing, or other proceeding except a grand jury proceeding in a criminal case, or in a deposition;

(B) consistent with the declarant's testimony and is offered to rebut an express or implied charge against the declarant of recent fabrication or improper influence or motive;

(C) one of identification of a person made after perceiving the person; or

(D) taken and offered in a criminal case in accordance with Code of Criminal Procedure article 38.071.

(2) *Admission by party-opponent.* The statement is offered against a party and is:

(A) the party's own statement in either an individual or representative capacity;

(B) a statement of which the party has manifested an adoption or belief in its truth;

(C) a statement by a person authorized by the party to make a statement concerning the subject;

(D) a statement by the party's agent or servant concerning a matter within the scope of the agency or employment, made during the existence of the relationship; or

(E) a statement by a co-conspirator of a party during the course and in furtherance of the conspiracy.

(3) *Depositions.* In a civil case, it is a deposition taken in the same proceeding, as same proceeding is defined in Rule of Civil Procedure 203.6(b). Unavailability of deponent is not a requirement for admissibility.

ANNOTATIONS

Generally

Jones v. State, 843 S.W.2d 487, 492-93 (Tex.Crim. App.1992), *overruled on other grounds,* **Maxwell v. State**, 48 S.W.3d 196 (Tex.Crim.App.2001). "Inadmissible hearsay testimony does not become admissible simply because it is contained within an admissible document or transcript. The trial court need never sort through challenged evidence in order to segregate the admissible from the excludable, nor is the trial court required to admit only the former part or exclude only the latter part. If evidence is offered and challenged which contains some of each, the trial court may safely admit it all or exclude it all, and the losing party ... will be made to suffer on appeal the consequences of his insufficiently specific offer or objection. ... When evidence which is partially admissible and partially inadmissible is excluded, a party may not complain upon appeal unless the admissible evidence was specifically offered."

TRE 801(d)

Dinkins v. State, 894 S.W.2d 330, 347 (Tex.Crim. App.1995). "An extrajudicial statement or writing which is offered for the purpose of showing *what* was said rather than for the *truth* of the matter stated therein does not constitute hearsay."

Johnson v. State, 987 S.W.2d 79, 90 (Tex.App.— Houston [14th Dist.] 1998, pet. ref'd). "[C]onduct which is not intended as a substitute for verbal expression is not hearsay."

Hammons v. State, 239 S.W.3d 798, 804-05 (Tex. Crim.App.2007). "Rule 801(e)(1)(B) gives substantive, non-hearsay status to prior consistent statements of a witness 'offered to rebut an express or implied charge against the declarant of recent fabrication or improper influence or motive.' [There are four requirements that must be met:] (1) the declarant must testify at trial and be subject to cross-examination; (2) there must be an express or implied charge of recent fabrication or improper influence or motive of the declarant's testimony by the opponent; (3) the proponent must offer a prior statement that is consistent with the declarant's challenged in-court testimony; and, (4) the prior consistent statement must be made prior to the time that the supposed motive to falsify arose. The rule sets forth a minimal foundation requirement of an implied or express charge of fabrication or improper motive. [E]ven an attack upon the accuracy of the witness's memory might suffice to permit the introduction of a prior consistent statement. In any event, 'there need be only a suggestion that the witness consciously altered his testimony in order to permit the use of earlier statements that are generally consistent with the testimony at trial.' The fact that 'there need be only a suggestion' of conscious alteration or fabrication gives the trial court substantial discretion to admit prior consistent statements under the rule. However, the rule cannot be construed to permit the admission of what would otherwise be hearsay any time a witness's credibility or memory is challenged. Were that true, mere cross-examination would always turn the prior consistent statement into non-hearsay. There is no bright line between a general challenge to memory or credibility and a suggestion of conscious fabrication, but the trial court should determine whether the cross-examiner's questions or the tenor of that questioning would reasonably imply an intent by the witness to fabricate."

Haughton v. State, 805 S.W.2d 405, 408 (Tex. Crim.App.1990). TRCE 801(e)(1)(B), now TRE 801(e)(1)(B), "requires that a prior consistent statement be made before the alleged improper influence or motive arose."

Miranda v. State, 813 S.W.2d 724, 735 (Tex. App.—San Antonio 1991, pet. ref'd). "Prior inconsistent statements that have been made under oath and subject to the penalty of perjury at a trial, hearing, other proceeding (except before a grand jury), or in a deposition, have … a non-hearsay status. These statements may be used as substantive evidence as well as for impeachment purposes. [¶] A party should not, however, be permitted to use a straw-man ploy to get impeachment evidence before the jury as substantive evidence."

Byrd v. State, 187 S.W.3d 436, 441-43 (Tex.Crim. App.2005). "*Krulewitch* [*v. U.S.*, 336 U.S. 440 (1949)] provides no support for appellant's claim that [appellant's brother's] out-of-court statement is inadmissible under TRE 801(e)(2)(E) simply because it was a statement about events [the victim's murder] that allegedly transpired before the beginning of the alleged conspiracy.' The State is not claiming here that a conspiracy to conceal the victim's murder was part of a charged conspiracy (to murder the victim). [¶] In this case, the Court of Appeals decided that the conspiracy was much broader than just a conspiracy to conceal the victim's murder. The Court of Appeals decided that there was a conspiracy 'to hinder appellant's apprehension.' This conspiracy was still ongoing at the time of the conversation between [appellant's brother and his girlfriend] very soon after the victim's murder. And, [appellant's brother's] out-of-court statements to [his girlfriend] about taking responsibility for the murder and protecting [his girlfriend] advanced the objectives of this conspiracy."

Paredes v. State, 129 S.W.3d 530, 534 (Tex.Crim. App.2004). "When appellant stood by and listened to [codefendant's] description of the murders and the surrounding events without disputing them, pointing out that [witness] 'should have been there' because he 'would have had some fun,' he manifested his agreement with the statements. Thus, the complained-of testimony was admissible as an adoptive admission and was not hearsay. *At 536:* [W]hether or not appellant would have been afraid to disagree with [codefendant's] narrative is a factor that bears on the credibility and weight of the statement, not its admissibility as an adoptive admission. By his silence and later embellishments, appellant indicated his adoption of the statements."

Carrasco v. State, 154 S.W.3d 127, 131-32 (Tex. Crim.App.2005). Cochran, J., concurring. "After the first trial ended in a mistrial, the trial court had the judicial discretion to allow [D] to withdraw the stipulation of evidence (which contained both appellant's admission of specific facts and his agreement to the admissibility of certain evidence). [¶] However, appellant's admission of facts remains an evidentiary admission under Rule 801(e)(2) forever. Unlike a guilty plea and statements made during plea negotiations which, under certain circumstances, may be withdrawn before a person is convicted and sentenced, an admission by a party-opponent will never disappear. It cannot be erased."

King v. State, 189 S.W.3d 347, 360 (Tex.App.—Fort Worth 2006, no pet.). "The out-of-court statement by a co-conspirator must be more than merely related to the conspiracy; it must further the conspiracy. A statement only furthers a conspiracy if it advances the cause of the conspiracy or serves to facilitate it. [¶] Statements that are made in furtherance of a conspiracy include those made (1) with intent to induce another to deal with co-conspirators or in any other way to cooperate with or assist co-conspirators, (2) with intent to induce another to join the conspiracy; (3) in formulating future strategies of concealment to benefit the conspiracy, (4) with intent to induce continued involvement in the conspiracy, or (5) for the purpose of identifying the role of one conspirator to another. Conversely, statements that are not made in furtherance of a conspiracy, and thus remain hearsay, include those that are (1) casual admissions of culpability to someone the declarant had individually decided to trust; (2) mere narrative descriptions; (3) mere conversations between conspirators; or (4) 'puffing' or 'boasting' by co-conspirators." *See also Guidry v. State*, 9 S.W.3d 133, 148 (Tex.Crim.App.1999); *Meador v. State*, 812 S.W.2d 330, 333 (Tex.Crim.App.1991).

Logan v. State, 71 S.W.3d 865, 869 (Tex.App.—Fort Worth 2002, pet. ref'd). "The defendant and the State, not the complaining witness or witnesses, are party opponents. ... We hold that a statement by a victim or complainant in a criminal case is not admissible under rule 801(e)(2) as an admission by a party opponent."

TRE 802. HEARSAY RULE

Hearsay is not admissible except as provided by statute or these rules or by other rules prescribed pursuant to statutory authority. Inadmissible hearsay admitted without objection shall not be denied probative value merely because it is hearsay.

ANNOTATIONS

Morin v. State, 960 S.W.2d 132, 138 (Tex.App.—Corpus Christi 1997, no pet.). "Appellant contends that the State elicited 'back door' hearsay consisting of [an] out-of-court statement that the appellant was involved in the murder. The State implicitly acknowledges that the testimony ... conveys [witness's] out-of-court statement, but counters that the testimony was not being used to prove that appellant was involved in the murder, but rather to show only how investigator ... came to suspect [witness] was a party to the murder. [¶] We believe the testimony ... was inadmissible hearsay. [¶] Courts are to discriminate between cases where some hearsay is allowed to explain the officers actions from those cases where such hearsay is inadmissible based on the degree to which the actions of the police officer have been challenged by the defendant."

Jefferson v. State, 900 S.W.2d 97, 100 (Tex.App.—Houston [14th Dist.] 1995, no pet.). "[A] party does not have the right to have inadmissible hearsay admitted simply because the State fails to specifically object on hearsay grounds. ... The [second sentence] of [TRCE] 802 [now TRE 802] ... applies only to hearsay which is inadvertently admitted despite its defined inadmissibility. It does not serve to eviscerate hearsay's presumptively inadmissible nature."

Benford v. State, 895 S.W.2d 716, 718 (Tex.App.—Houston [14th Dist.] 1994, pet. ref'd). "Statements made by a third party to an officer, who uses these statements to determine probable cause, are not hearsay under [TRCE] 802 [now TRE 802]. ... In a hearing to determine the admissibility of certain extraneous evidence where probable cause is questioned, trial judges are not looking at the statements to determine the truth of the matter, but rather, only to see what knowledge the officer actually had, and whether it was reasonably trustworthy.... However, an officer who testifies to why another officer believed he had probable cause to search or arrest a particular defendant offers the testimony for the truth of the matter asserted."

TRE 803. HEARSAY EXCEPTIONS; AVAILABILITY OF DECLARANT IMMATERIAL

The following are not excluded by the hearsay rule, even though the declarant is available as a witness:

(1) Present Sense Impression. A statement describing or explaining an event or condition made while the declarant was perceiving the event or condition, or immediately thereafter.

(2) Excited Utterance. A statement relating to a startling event or condition made while the declarant was under the stress of excitement caused by the event or condition.

(3) Then Existing Mental, Emotional, or Physical Condition. A statement of the declarant's then existing state of mind, emotion, sensation, or physical condition (such as intent, plan, motive, design, mental feeling, pain, or bodily health), but not including a statement of memory or belief to prove the fact remembered or believed unless it relates to the execution, revocation, identification, or terms of declarant's will.

(4) Statements for Purposes of Medical Diagnosis or Treatment. Statements made for purposes of medical diagnosis or treatment and describing medical history, or past or present symptoms, pain, or sensations, or the inception or general character of the cause or external source thereof insofar as reasonably pertinent to diagnosis or treatment.

(5) Recorded Recollection. A memorandum or record concerning a matter about which a witness once had personal knowledge but now has insufficient recollection to enable the witness to testify fully and accurately, shown to have been made or adopted by the witness when the matter was fresh in the witness' memory and to reflect that knowledge correctly, unless the circumstances of preparation cast doubt on the document's trustworthiness. If admitted, the memorandum or record may be read into evidence but may not itself be received as an exhibit unless offered by an adverse party.

(6) Records of Regularly Conducted Activity. A memorandum, report, record, or data compilation, in any form, of acts, events, conditions, opinions, or diagnoses, made at or near the time by, or from information transmitted by, a person with knowledge, if kept in the course of a regularly conducted business activity, and if it was the regular practice of that business activity to make the memorandum, report, record, or data compilation, all as shown by the testimony of the custodian or other qualified witness, or by affidavit that complies with Rule 902(10), unless the source of information or the method or circumstances of preparation indicate lack of trustworthiness. "Business" as used in this paragraph includes any and every kind of regular organized activity whether conducted for profit or not.

(7) Absence of Entry in Records Kept in Accordance With the Provisions of Paragraph (6). Evidence that a matter is not included in the memoranda, reports, records, or data compilations, in any form, kept in accordance with the provisions of paragraph (6), to prove the nonoccurrence or nonexistence of the matter, if the matter was of a kind of which a memorandum, report, record, or data compilation was regularly made and preserved, unless the sources of information or other circumstances indicate lack of trustworthiness.

(8) Public Records and Reports. Records, reports, statements, or data compilations, in any form, of public offices or agencies setting forth:

(A) the activities of the office or agency;

(B) matters observed pursuant to duty imposed by law as to which matters there was a duty to report, excluding in criminal cases matters observed by police officers and other law enforcement personnel; or

(C) in civil cases as to any party and in criminal cases as against the state, factual findings resulting from an investigation made pursuant to authority granted by law;

unless the sources of information or other circumstances indicate lack of trustworthiness.

(9) Records of Vital Statistics. Records or data compilations, in any form, of births, fetal deaths, deaths, or marriages, if the report thereof was made to a public office pursuant to requirements of law.

(10) Absence of Public Record or Entry. To prove the absence of a record, report, statement, or data compilation, in any form, or the nonoccurrence or nonexistence of a matter of which a record, report, statement, or data compilation, in any form, was regularly made and preserved by a public office or agency, evidence in the form of a certification in accordance with Rule 902, or testimony, that diligent search failed to disclose the record, report statement, or data compilation, or entry.

(11) Records of Religious Organizations. Statements of births, marriages, divorces, deaths, legitimacy, ancestry, relationship by blood or marriage, or other similar facts of personal or family history, contained in a regularly kept record of a religious organization.

(12) Marriage, Baptismal, and Similar Certificates. Statements of fact contained in a certificate that the maker performed a marriage or other ceremony or administered a sacrament, made by a member of the clergy, public official, or other person authorized by the rules or practices of a religious organization or by law to perform the act certified, and purporting to have been issued at the time of the act or within a reasonable time thereafter.

(13) Family Records. Statements of fact concerning personal or family history contained in family Bibles, genealogies, charts, engravings on rings, inscriptions on family portraits, engravings on urns, crypts, or tombstones, or the like.

(14) Records of Documents Affecting an Interest in Property. The record of a document purporting to establish or affect an interest in property, as proof of the content of the original recorded document and its execution and delivery by each person by whom it purports to have been executed, if the record is a record of a public office and an applicable statute authorizes the recording of documents of that kind in that office.

(15) Statements in Documents Affecting an Interest in Property. A statement contained in a document purporting to establish or affect an interest in property if the matter stated was relevant to the purpose of the document, unless dealings with the property since the document was made have been inconsistent with the truth of the statement or the purport of the document.

(16) Statements in Ancient Documents. Statements in a document in existence twenty years or more the authenticity of which is established.

(17) Market Reports, Commercial Publications. Market quotations, tabulations, lists, directories, or other published compilations, generally used and relied upon by the public or by persons in particular occupations.

(18) Learned Treatises. To the extent called to the attention of an expert witness upon cross-examination or relied upon by the expert in direct examination, statements contained in published treatises, periodicals, or pamphlets on a subject of history, medicine, or other science or art established as a reliable authority by the testimony or admission of the witness or by other expert testimony or by judicial notice. If admitted, the statements may be read into evidence but may not be received as exhibits.

(19) Reputation Concerning Personal or Family History. Reputation among members of a person's family by blood, adoption, or marriage, or among a person's associates, or in the community, concerning a person's birth, adoption, marriage, divorce, death, legitimacy, relationship by blood, adoption, or marriage, ancestry, or other similar fact of personal or family history.

(20) Reputation Concerning Boundaries or General History. Reputation in a community, arising before the controversy, as to boundaries of or customs affecting lands in the community, and reputation as to events of general history important to the community or state or nation in which located.

(21) Reputation as to Character. Reputation of a person's character among associates or in the community.

(22) Judgment of Previous Conviction. In civil cases, evidence of a judgment, entered after a trial or upon a plea of guilty (but not upon a plea of *nolo contendere*), judging a person guilty of a felony, to prove any fact essential to sustain the judgment of conviction. In criminal cases, evidence of a judgment, entered after a trial or upon a plea of guilty or nolo contendere, adjudging a person guilty of a criminal offense, to prove any fact essential to sustain the judgment of conviction, but not including, when offered by the state for purposes other than impeachment, judgments against persons other than the accused. In all cases, the pendency of an appeal renders such evidence inadmissible.

(23) Judgment as to Personal, Family, or General History, or Boundaries. Judgments as proof of matters of personal, family or general history, or boundaries, essential to the judgment, if the same would be provable by evidence of reputation.

(24) Statement Against Interest. A statement which was at the time of its making so far contrary to the declarant's pecuniary or proprietary interest, or so far tended to subject the declarant to civil or criminal liability, or to render invalid a claim by the declarant against another, or to make the declarant an object of hatred, ridicule, or disgrace, that a reasonable person in declarant's position would not have made the statement unless believing it to be true. In criminal cases, a statement tending to expose the declarant to criminal liability is not admissible unless corroborating circumstances clearly indicate the trustworthiness of the statement.

ANNOTATIONS

TRE 803(1)

Fischer v. State, 252 S.W.3d 375, 376 (Tex.Crim. App.2008). "This case presents a novel question in Texas evidentiary law: Are a law enforcement officer's factual observations of a DWI suspect, contemporaneously dictated on his patrol-car videotape, admissible as a present sense impression exception to the hearsay rule under [TRE] 803(1)? They are not. An officer may testify in the courtroom to what he saw, did, heard, smelled, and felt at the scene, but he cannot substitute or augment his in-court testimony with an out-of-court oral narrative. This calculated narrative in an adversarial setting was a 'speaking offense report.' It was not the type of unreflective, street-corner statement that the present sense impression exception to the hearsay rule is designed to allow."

Beauchamp v. State, 870 S.W.2d 649, 653 (Tex. App.—El Paso 1994, pet. ref'd). "[T]here is no *per se* rule for determining whether too much time has passed between the making of the statement and the occurrence of the events or conditions which precipitated the comment. [A] functional test should be applied, namely, whether the proximity in time is sufficient to reduce the hearsay dangers of faulty memory and insincerity. [W]here the declarant has had time to reflect not only upon the events and conditions previously observed but also upon those facts that he has subsequently learned about the events and conditions, ... then the statement is no longer sufficiently contemporaneous so as to be reliable."

TRE 803(2)

McCarty v. State, ___ S.W.3d ___ (Tex.Crim.App. 2008) (No. PD-1139-07; 6-25-08). "[W]e must determine whether, under [TRE] 803(2), the event about which an excited utterance is made has to be the same event that caused the declarant's excitement. We hold that it does not...."

Wall v. State, 184 S.W.3d 730, 742 (Tex.Crim.App. 2006). "'[T]he excited utterance and testimonial hearsay inquiries are separate, but related. While both inquiries look to the surrounding circumstances to make determinations about the declarant's mindset at the time of the statement, their focal points are different. The excited utterance inquiry focuses on whether the declarant was under the stress of a startling event. The testimonial hearsay inquiry focuses on whether a reasonable declarant, similarly situated (that is, excited by the stress of a startling event), would have had the capacity to appreciate the legal ramifications of her statement. [¶] These parallel inquiries require an ad hoc, case-by-case approach. An inquiring court first should determine whether a particular hearsay statement qualifies as an excited utterance. If not, the inquiry ends. If, however, the statement so qualifies, the court

then must look to the attendant circumstances and assess the likelihood that a reasonable person would have either retained or regained the capacity to make a testimonial statement at the time of the utterance.' [¶] [G]enerally statements made to police while the declarant (or another person) is still in personal danger are not made with consideration of their legal ramifications because the declarant usually speaks out of urgency and a desire to obtain a prompt response; thus, those statements will not normally be deemed testimonial. But after the immediate danger has dissipated, a person who speaks while still under the stress of a startling event is more likely to comprehend the larger significance of his words: 'If the record fairly supports a finding of comprehension, the fact that the statement also qualifies as an excited utterance will not alter its testimonial nature.'" *See also* **King v. State**, 953 S.W.2d 266, 269 n.5 (Tex.Crim.App.1997).

Apolinar v. State, 155 S.W.3d 184, 186-87 (Tex. Crim.App.2005). "To determine whether a statement is an excited utterance, trial courts should determine 'whether the declarant was still dominated by the emotions, excitement, fear, or pain of the event or condition' when the statement is made. Factors that the trial court may consider include the length of time between the occurrence and the statement, the nature of the declarant, whether the statement is made in response to a question, and whether the statement is self-serving. *At 189-90:* A useful rule of thumb is that where the time interval between the event and the statement is long enough to permit reflective thought, the statement will be excluded in the absence of some proof that the declarant did not in fact engage in a reflective thought process. Testimony that the declarant still appeared 'nervous' or 'distraught' and that there was a reasonable basis for continuing emotional upset will often suffice. [¶] [W]e conclude that the declarant need not necessarily have been unconscious for the entire period between the startling event and the statement, so long as the record supports the reasonable conclusion that the declarant did not have a meaningful opportunity to reflect." *See also* **Penry v. State**, 691 S.W.2d 636, 647 (Tex.Crim.App.1985), *rev'd on other grounds sub nom.* **Penry v. Lynaugh**, 492 U.S. 302 (1989); **Mosely v. State**, 960 S.W.2d 200, 203-04 (Tex.App.—Corpus Christi 1997, no pet.).

TRE 803(3)

Dorsey v. State, 24 S.W.3d 921, 928-29 (Tex.App.— Beaumont 2000, no pet.). "[T]estimony recounting [appellant's wife's] statement that if anything strange happened to her, like a car crash, it meant that Dorsey had killed her ... represents a belief held by [her], [so] we conclude it does not fall under the exception in Rule 803(3). [¶] Likewise, inadmissible are [wife's] out-of-court statements that Dorsey had once held her down on the bed with a knife to her throat, that he held a gun to her head and throat and had put a gun into her mouth, and that he followed her every day to work to make certain she was there. Such statements are not reflective of her state of mind or a belief, but simply recount her memory of events."

Green v. State, 839 S.W.2d 935, 942 (Tex.App.—Waco 1992, pet. ref'd). "Texas precedent allows state-of-mind declarations to be admitted to prove the joint conduct of the declarant and another. [TRCE] 803(3) [now TRE 803(3)] should ... be interpreted as permitting this practice."

TRE 803(4)

Jones v. State, 92 S.W.3d 619, 623 (Tex.App.—Austin 2002, no pet.). "The two-part test for admitting [statements under TRE 803(4)] is: (1) the declarant must make the statements for the purpose of receiving medical treatment, and (2) 'the content of the statement must be such as is reasonably relied on by a physician in treatment or diagnosis.' Thus, the declarant must first have a motive consistent with obtaining medical care, knowing that proper diagnosis or treatment depends upon the veracity of such statements. Further, the statement must concern facts that are 'reasonably pertinent to diagnosis or treatment': medical history, symptoms, or the cause or general character of the cause or external source. [¶] 'Rule 803(4) is premised on the patient's selfish motive in receiving appropriate treatment.' This motive is no longer present once a diagnosis has been made and treatment has begun." Held: Counselor's testimony about victim's statements made during counseling sessions was inadmissible.

Puderbaugh v. State, 31 S.W.3d 683, 685 (Tex. App.—Beaumont 2000, pet. ref'd). "[T]he medical treatment exception to the hearsay rule is based on the assumption that the patient appreciates that the effectiveness of the treatment may depend upon the accuracy of the information provided.... [Social worker] acknowledged that in the course of treatment in counseling [complainant], it had been conveyed to [complainant] that the reason for seeing him was to help her with her emotional problems. [Social worker

and complainant] discussed the importance of telling the truth to him, and [complainant] understood the difference between telling the truth and telling a lie. Thus, the State established both the medical care component of [social worker's] sessions with [complainant] and [complainant's] awareness of the purpose of the treatment. The trial court did not err in admitting the evidence under Rule 803(4)." *See also Moore v. State*, 82 S.W.3d 399, 404 (Tex.App.—Austin 2002, pet. ref'd).

Gohring v. State, 967 S.W.2d 459, 462 (Tex.App.—Beaumont 1998, no pet.). "Without the child appreciating that any statement made to the [CPS worker] was for the purpose of medical treatment, there is no basis for the statement having the trustworthiness upon which this exception is based. Consequently, the trial court erred in admitting the testimony because it does not fall within the exception set forth in Rule 803(4)." *See also Wright v. State*, 154 S.W.3d 235, 240-41 (Tex. App.—Texarkana 2005, pet. ref'd); *Perez v. State*, 113 S.W.3d 819, 827 (Tex.App.—Austin 2003, pet. ref'd); *Powell v. State*, 88 S.W.3d 794, 800-01 (Tex.App.—El Paso 2002, no pet.).

TRE 803(5)

Johnson v. State, 967 S.W.2d 410, 416 (Tex.Crim. App.1998). "The predicate for past recollection recorded is set forth in [TRCE] 803(5) [now TRE 803(5)] and requires that four elements be met: (1) the witness must have had first-hand knowledge of the event, (2) the written statement must be an original memorandum made at or near the time of the event while the witness had a clear and accurate memory of it, (3) the witness must lack a present recollection of the event, and (4) the witness must vouch for the accuracy of the written memorandum. In particular, to meet the fourth element, the witness may testify that she presently remembers recording the fact correctly or remembers recognizing the writing as accurate when she read it at an earlier time. But if her present memory is less effective, it is sufficient if the witness testifies that she knows the memorandum is correct because of a habit or practice to record matters accurately or to check them for accuracy. At the extreme, it is even sufficient if the individual testifies to recognizing her signature on the statement and believes the statement is correct because she would not have signed it if she had not believed it true at the time. However, the witness must acknowledge at trial the accuracy of the statement. An assertion of the statement's accuracy in the acknowledgment line of a written memoranda or such an acknowledgment made previously under oath will not be sufficient. No statement should be allowed to verify itself, especially by boilerplate language routinely added by police, lawyers, or others experienced in litigation."

Phea v. State, 767 S.W.2d 263, 267 (Tex.App.—Amarillo 1989, pet. ref'd). "The language 'unless the circumstances of preparation cast doubt on the document's trustworthiness' found in [TRCE] 803(5) [now TRE 803(5)] does not require any 'indicia of reliability' over and above the other provisions of the rule. The admissibility of hearsay under the past recollection recorded exception remains within the sound discretion of the trial court, and the trial court's ruling will not be disturbed absent an abuse of that discretion."

TRE 803(6)

Russeau v. State, 171 S.W.3d 871, 880-81 (Tex. Crim.App.2005). "[A]ppellant argues that the trial court violated his Sixth Amendment right to confront the witnesses against him when the court admitted in evidence, at the punishment phase, ... Smith County Jail 'incident reports,' and ... TDCJ 'disciplinary reports.' The trial court admitted these reports under the business records exception to the hearsay rule. The reports contained statements which appeared to have been written by corrections officers and which purported to document, in the most detailed and graphic of terms, numerous and repeated disciplinary offenses on the part of appellant while he was incarcerated. It further appeared that, in writing the statements, the corrections officers relied upon their own observations or, in several instances, the observations of others. [¶] [The Confrontation Clause] is applicable in both federal and state prosecutions, and bars the admission of testimonial statements of a witness who does not appear at trial unless he is unavailable to testify *and* the defendant had a prior opportunity to cross-examine him. Generally speaking, a statement is 'testimonial' if it is a solemn declaration made for the purpose of establishing some fact. [¶] The reports in question contained testimonial statements which were inadmissible under the Confrontation Clause, because the State did not show that the declarants were unavailable to testify and appellant never had an opportunity to cross-examine any of them. ... The trial court erred in admitting those portions of the reports that contained the testimonial statements."

Garcia v. State, 126 S.W.3d 921, 926-27 (Tex.Crim. App.2004). "When a business receives information from a person who is outside the business and who has no business duty to report or to report accurately, those statements are not covered by the business records exception. Those statements must independently qualify for admission under their own hearsay exception—such as statements made for medical diagnosis or treatment, statements concerning a present sense impression, an excited utterance, or an admission by a party opponent."

West v. State, 124 S.W.3d 732, 736 (Tex.App.—Houston [1st Dist.] 2003, pet. ref'd). "The definition of 'business' found in Rule 803(6) must be considered within the context of the rule itself. Within the context of Rule 803(6), the term acts as one of two restrictive modifiers, limiting the records to which the exception applies to those of 'regularly conducted business activities.' Because Rule 803(6) expressly provides that an activity to which records pertain must not only be a business activity but also a 'regularly conducted' activity, 'business' cannot connote a regularity in the activity recorded. Otherwise, the phrase 'regularly conducted' would become superfluous. ... For the same reason, it would be improper to conclude that the term 'business' connotes a regularity in keeping the records, as such a connotation would render unnecessary the rule's language requiring that the regular practice of a business activity be to keep the records at issue. [¶] We conclude testimony reflecting that records are maintained as part of a business does not relieve a party from otherwise showing that the records were kept in the course of a regularly conducted business activity and that it was the regular practice of that business activity to make the records."

Adams v. State, 985 S.W.2d 582, 583 (Tex.App.—Eastland 1998, pet. ref'd). "During its case in chief, the State offered medical records .... A separate business records affidavit accompanied each set of medical records for self-authentication purposes. Appellant objected to the admission of the records on the ground that the affidavits were defective, making them unreliable. Both affidavits misstated the number of pages in each exhibit.... [¶] Rule 803(6) authorizes the trial court to exclude a business record if the source of the information or the method or circumstances of its preparation indicate an absence of trustworthiness. *At 584:* There is no evidence showing that the source of the information or the method or circumstances of the medical records' preparation was not trustworthy. The affidavits before us are not patently false although it is not clear whether the affidavits misstated the number of pages contained in the medical records or whether there are pages missing from the medical records. Whether the affidavits are inaccurate or whether there are pages missing from the medical records should affect the weight to be given the evidence not the admissibility. Appellant has not shown that the trial court abused its discretion."

Perry v. State, 957 S.W.2d 894, 899 (Tex.App.— Texarkana 1997, pet. ref'd). "There must ... be no indication that the source of information or the method of preparation lacks trustworthiness. There is no requirement that the testifying witness must have created the records, or even have personal knowledge of the contents of the records. The testifying witness only must have personal knowledge of the mode of preparation of the records." *See also* **Huff v. State**, 897 S.W.2d 829, 839 (Tex.App.—Dallas 1995, pet. ref'd); *Venable v. State*, 113 S.W.3d 797, 800 (Tex.App.—Beaumont 2003, pet. ref'd).

TRE 803(8)

Martinez v. State, 22 S.W.3d 504, 508 (Tex.Crim. App.2000). Expert "testified at trial as to his present opinion of the test results. While [expert] relied on [a] report to form the opinion he testified to, the report itself was never offered into evidence. The underlying data and facts were never elicited before the jury. [¶] Since the trial court implicitly found [witness] qualified as an expert, the State had no burden to invoke an exception to the hearsay rule. [Expert] was free to offer his opinion based on [the] report. And since Martinez never challenged [expert's] qualifications, his present opinion regarding the test results was properly admitted over Martinez's hearsay objections."

Pondexter v. State, 942 S.W.2d 577, 585 (Tex.Crim. App.1996). "[T]he reason for [FRE] 803(8)(b), after which the Texas rule was modeled, was the presumed unreliability of observations that are made by officers at the scene of a crime. The reasons for the possible impairment of judgment are not implicated in situations where officers are conducting routine business matters, such as the recording of 'objective observations.' Since this is a situation where the police officer was performing his ordinary, routine, duties of recording

the [seized] property that was taken in and out of the [police] property room, his observations, and notation should be presumed reliable."

Garcia v. State, 868 S.W.2d 337, 341 (Tex.Crim. App.1993). "[M]edical examiners, as a general rule, are disinterested third parties who do not have an *inherent* motive to distort the results of their reports. ... Autopsy reports are *not* necessarily prepared in contemplation of litigation. *At 342:* [E]ven though autopsy reports are partially subjective, they are generally prepared by officials with no motive to fabricate the results of the reports. [¶] [A] medical examiner's office is not, as a general rule, such a uniquely litigious and prosecution-oriented environment as to create an adversarial context. [¶] [M]edical examiners are not considered 'other law enforcement personnel' under [TRCE] 803(8)(B) [now TRE 803(8)(B)] as far as their duties relate to the preparation of autopsy reports."

Cole v. State, 839 S.W.2d 798, 803 (Tex.Crim.App. 1990). "[F]ull-time chemists of the Texas Department of Public Safety are 'law enforcement personnel' within the meaning of [TRE 803(8)(B)]. [T]he role of the chemists in this instance did not terminate with the completion of the chemical analyses and submission of any resulting report, but participation continued until one chemist had testified as a crucial prosecution witness at trial. *At 805:* [T]he reports were not prepared for purposes independent of specific litigation, nor were they ministerial, objective observations of an unambiguous factual nature. [T]he letter reports in the present case fail to satisfy the requirements of [TRE 803(8)(B)], since they constitute 'matters observed' by 'other law enforcement personnel,' and are therefore inadmissible. *At 806:* [I]t would be inconsistent with the intended effect of that rule to ... allow such evidence to be admitted under TRCE 803(6) [now TRE 803(6)] as a business record. [¶] [TRE 803(6)] should not [serve] as an alternative route for admissibility of these particular records otherwise barred by [TRE 803(8)]."

Johnston v. State, 959 S.W.2d 230, 240-241 (Tex. App.—Dallas 1997, no pet.). "A jail nurse is not a police officer or other type of law enforcement personnel within the scope of [TRCE] 803(8)(B) [now TRE 803(8)(B)]. A jail nurse does not perform law enforcement duties comparable to those of a police officer."

Perry v. State, 957 S.W.2d 894, 899 (Tex.App.—Texarkana 1997, pet. ref'd). Held: Child-support-enforcement officers for the Attorney General were not law-enforcement personnel within meaning of this section, and their reports do not contain matters observed by law-enforcement personnel. Summary report created by the child-support-enforcement officer was "an objective, routine, determination of unambiguous facts prepared by an official with no inherent motivation to distort the results."

Durham v. State, 956 S.W.2d 62, 65 (Tex.App.—Tyler 1997, pet. ref'd). "There is no evidence to suggest that the BCFSC (Bexar County Forensic Science Center) is an 'inherently adversarial, litigious, and prosecution-oriented' entity. [C]hemists and toxicologists of the BCFSC were not 'law enforcement personnel' in this case and [a copy of the results of a blood test administered in an involuntary manslaughter investigation] was admissible without the testimony of the conducting chemist under [TRCE] 803(6) or 803(8) [now TRE 803(6) or 803(8)]."

TRE 803(15)

Guidry v. State, 9 S.W.3d 133, 147 (Tex.Crim.App. 1999). "Appellant correctly views State's Exhibit No. 1 as hearsay. It is an out-of-court statement offered for the truth of the matter asserted (that Fratta had a property interest in a Jeep). The document falls within the parameters of the hearsay exception provided in Rule 803(15).... State's Exhibit No. 1 does not 'establish' or 'affect' an interest in property in the sense of a deed or mortgage, but reflects Fratta's interest in the property listed there and it 'bears more than an adequate indicia of reliability.'"

TRE 803(18)

Loven v. State, 831 S.W.2d 387, 397 (Tex.App.—Amarillo 1992, no pet.). TRCE 803(18), now TRE 803(18), "does not extend to videotapes by virtue of its express language. However, we believe that [TRE 803(18)] should be read contextually in order to promote the growth and development of the law of evidence. Videotapes are nothing more than a contemporary variant of a published treatise, periodical or pamphlet. [V]ideotapes may qualify as learned treatises for purposes of the learned treatise exception to the hearsay rule."

TRE 803(24)

Simpson v. State, 119 S.W.3d 262, 269 (Tex.Crim. App.2003). TRE 803(24) "does not provide an exception for a declarant's statements against someone else's interest, such as a third party, co-actor, or co-defendant, unless the statement against the other person's interest is also sufficiently against the declarant's interest to be considered reliable. [¶] Even if a hearsay statement meets the requirements for an exception to the general prohibition, it must also bear sufficient 'indicia of reliability' for it to be admissible under the Confrontation Clause. A statement is *per se* reliable if it falls within a 'firmly rooted' exception to the hearsay rule. Even if a statement does not fall within a firmly rooted exception to the hearsay rule, it may still be sufficiently reliable for Confrontation Clause purposes if it has 'particularized guarantees of trustworthiness.'" *See also Zarychta v. State*, 961 S.W.2d 455, 458-59 (Tex. App.—Houston [1st Dist.] 1997, pet. ref'd).

Dewberry v. State, 4 S.W.3d 735, 751 (Tex.Crim. App.1999). "In order for a declaration against interest to be admissible under Rule 803(24) [now TRE 803(24)], the statement must be self-inculpatory with corroborating circumstances to indicate the trustworthiness of the statements. It is not necessary for the declarant to be unavailable as a witness. A statement which is self-inculpatory can be admissible against a defendant who is not the declarant of the statement. [¶] A trial court should consider [the following factors for corroboration of a statement against interest] are: (1) whether guilt of declarant is inconsistent with guilt of defendant, (2) whether declarant was so situated that he might have committed the crime, (3) the timing of the declaration, (4) the spontaneity of the declaration, (5) the relationship between the declarant and the party to whom the statement was made, and (6) the existence of independent corroborative facts." *See also Woods v. State*, 152 S.W.3d 105, 112-13 (Tex.Crim.App. 2004).

Bingham v. State, 987 S.W.2d 54, 56 (Tex.Crim. App.1999). "The Court of Appeals was clearly in error in holding that a declarant's hearsay statements against interest are admissible in the criminal trial of that declarant only. ... '[A] trial court does not always abuse its discretion in admitting a hearsay statement which inculpates not only the declarant but the defendant as well, because ... factors need to be considered in determining the existence of corroborating facts so as to avoid admitting a fabrication, i.e., a false statement.' [¶] The reason for this exception to the general exclusion of hearsay is that statements against interest are considered particularly trustworthy, since '... people generally do not lightly make statements that are damaging to their interests.' Thus, such statements are considered reliable, regardless of whether or not the criminal defendant is the declarant of the statement. *At 57:* Any determination regarding the admissibility of a statement in accordance with rule 803(24) requires a two-step inquiry. First, the trial court must determine whether the statement in question tends to expose the declarant to criminal liability. Second, the trial court must determine if there are corroborating circumstances that clearly indicate the trustworthiness of the statement. If both these criteria are met, then rule 803(24) is satisfied." *Author's note:* **Bingham**'s sweeping proclamations are very much in doubt in light of *Lilly v. Virginia*, p. 1187.

Jahanian v. State, 145 S.W.3d 346, 350 (Tex. App.—Houston [14th Dist.] 2004, no pet.). "While the Rules of Evidence permit exceptions to the normal prohibition against hearsay evidence, these exceptions do not apply to evidence that is testimonial in nature. The [U.S.] Constitution [6th Am.] simply does not permit the admission of a testimonial statement of a witness who did not appear at trial unless he was unavailable to testify and the defendant had a prior opportunity for cross-examination. ... Accordingly, the trial court erred in permitting [witness's] statement into evidence."

Owens v. State, 916 S.W.2d 713, 718 (Tex.App.—Waco 1996, no pet.). "To be admissible, a statement against interest that makes the declarant the object of hatred, ridicule, or disgrace must be in the context of the declarant's social interests. Although [victim's] account of the assault may have been embarrassing for her to give, we cannot say that it made her an object of disgrace at the time she made it. To do so would label all victims 'disgraceful' and declare that it is against one's social interest to admit they were a victim of a crime."

Jefferson v. State, 909 S.W.2d 247, 251 (Tex. App.—Texarkana 1995, pet. ref'd). "The trial court may consider evidence which undermines the reliability of the statement as well as evidence corroborating its trustworthiness. The burden is on the party seeking admission of the statement to establish corroborating circumstances clearly indicating trustworthiness."

Lilly v. Virginia, 527 U.S. 116, 133-34, 119 S.Ct. 1887, 1898-99 (1999). "It is clear that our cases consistently have viewed an accomplice's statements that shift or spread the blame to a criminal defendant as falling outside the realm of those hearsay exception[s] [that are] so trustworthy that adversarial testing can be expected to add little to [the statements'] reliability. ... The decisive fact ... is that accomplices' confessions that inculpate a criminal defendant are not within a firmly rooted exception to the hearsay rule as that concept has been defined in our Confrontation Clause jurisprudence. *At 137-39, 1900-01:* For these reasons, when deciding whether the admission of a declarant's out-of-court statement violates the Confrontation Clause, courts should independently review whether the government's proffered guarantees of trustworthiness satisfy the demands of the Clause. It is highly unlikely that the presumptive unreliability that attaches to accomplices' confessions that shift or spread blame can be effectively rebutted when the statements are given under conditions that implicate the core concerns of the old *ex parte* affidavit practice—that is, when the government is involved in the statements' production, and when the statements describe past events and have not been subjected to adversarial testing. [¶] That other evidence at trial corroborated portions of Mark's [accomplice confession] is irrelevant. We have squarely rejected the notion that evidence corroborating the truth of a hearsay statement may properly support a finding that the statement bears particularized guarantees of trustworthiness. ... To be admissible under the Confrontation Clause ... hearsay evidence used to convict a defendant must possess indicia of reliability by virtue of its inherent trustworthiness, not by reference to other evidence at trial. [¶] Nor did the police's informing Mark of his *Miranda* rights render the circumstances surrounding his statements significantly more trustworthy. [W]e believe that a suspect's consciousness of his *Miranda* rights has little, if any, bearing on the likelihood of truthfulness of his statements. When a suspect is in custody for his obvious involvement in serious crimes, his knowledge that anything he says may be used against him militates against depending on his veracity. [¶] [T]hat Mark knew he was exposing himself to criminal liability—merely restates the fact that portions of his statements were technically against penal interest. And, as we have explained, such statements are suspect insofar as they inculpate other persons. [T]hat a person is making a broadly self-inculpatory confession does not make more credible the confession's non-self-inculpatory parts. The admission of the untested confession of Mark Lilly violated petitioner's Confrontation Clause rights." (Internal quotes omitted.)

TRE 804. HEARSAY EXCEPTIONS; DECLARANT UNAVAILABLE

(a) Definition of Unavailability. "Unavailability as a witness" includes situations in which the declarant:

(1) is exempted by ruling of the court on the ground of privilege from testifying concerning the subject matter of the declarant's statement;

(2) persists in refusing to testify concerning the subject matter of the declarant's statement despite an order of the court to do so;

(3) testifies to a lack of memory of the subject matter of the declarant's statement;

(4) is unable to be present or to testify at the hearing because of death or then existing physical or mental illness or infirmity; or

(5) is absent from the hearing and the proponent of the declarant's statement has been unable to procure the declarant's attendance or testimony by process or other reasonable means.

A declarant is not unavailable as a witness if the declarant's exemption, refusal, claim of lack of memory, inability, or absence is due to the procurement or wrong-doing of the proponent of the declarant's statement for the purpose of preventing the witness from attending or testifying.

(b) Hearsay Exceptions. The following are not excluded if the declarant is unavailable as a witness:

(1) *Former testimony.* In civil cases, testimony given as a witness at another hearing of the same or a different proceeding, or in a deposition taken in the course of another proceeding, if the party against whom the testimony is now offered, or a person with a similar interest, had an opportunity and similar motive to develop the testimony by direct, cross, or redirect examination. In criminal cases, testimony given as a witness at another hearing of the same or a different proceeding, if the party against whom the testimony is now offered had an opportunity and similar motive to develop the testimony by direct, cross, or redirect examination. In criminal cases the use of depositions is controlled by Chapter 39 of the Code of Criminal Procedure.

(2) *Dying declarations.* A statement made by a declarant while believing that the declarant's death was imminent, concerning the cause or circumstances of what the declarant believed to be impending death.

(3) *Statement of personal or family history.*

(A) A statement concerning the declarant's own birth, adoption, marriage, divorce, legitimacy, relationship by blood, adoption, or marriage, ancestry, or other similar fact of personal or family history even though declarant had no means of acquiring personal knowledge of the matter stated; or

(B) A statement concerning the foregoing matters, and death also, of another person, if the declarant was related to the other by blood, adoption, or marriage or was so intimately associated with the other's family as to be likely to have accurate information concerning the matter declared.

ANNOTATIONS

Gonzalez v. State, 195 S.W.3d 114, 119 (Tex.Crim. App.2006). "[A] party forfeits the right to object, on hearsay grounds, to the admission of a declarant's prior statement when that party's deliberate wrongdoing procured the unavailability of the declarant as a witness."

Wall v. State, 184 S.W.3d 730, 734-35 (Tex.Crim. App.2006). "The [U.S.] Supreme Court held that the admission of a hearsay statement made by a non-testifying declarant violates the Sixth Amendment if the statement was testimonial, and the defendant lacked a prior opportunity for cross-examination. Thus, a testimonial statement is inadmissible absent a showing that the declarant is presently unavailable and the defendant had a prior opportunity for cross-examination, even if the statement falls under a firmly rooted hearsay exception or bears particularized guarantees of trustworthiness. The Court stressed that if testimonial evidence is at issue, the Sixth Amendment demands what the common law required: unavailability and a prior opportunity for cross-examination. [¶] The Court identified three kinds of statements that could be regarded as testimonial: (1) ex parte in-court testimony or its functional equivalent—that is, material such as affidavits, custodial examinations, prior testimony that the defendant was unable to cross-examine, or similar pretrial statements that declarants would reasonably expect to be used prosecutorially; (2) extra-judicial statements ... contained in formalized testimonial materials, such as affidavits, depositions, prior testimony, or confessions; and (3) statements that were made under circumstances which would lead an objective witness reasonably to believe that the statement would be available for use at a later trial. *At 736:* The Supreme Court noted that some statements qualify as testimonial under any definition—for example, *ex parte* testimony at a preliminary hearing and [s]tatements taken by police officers in the course of interrogations. The Court continued: even if the Sixth Amendment is not solely concerned with testimonial hearsay, that is its primary object, and interrogations by law enforcement officers fall squarely within that class." (Internal quotes omitted.) *See also* **Crawford v. Washington**, 124 S.Ct. 1354, 1374 (2004); **Davis v. State**, 203 S.W.3d 845, 849 (Tex.Crim.App.2006).

Davis v. State, 961 S.W.2d 156, 157 (Tex.Crim.App. 1998). A "defendant who invokes his Fifth Amendment privilege does not become unavailable under [TRCE] 804 [now TRE 804] when he seeks to offer his own prior testimony. [¶] The exception to unavailability found in [TRE 804(a)] did not apply because the State was the proponent of the evidence, and the State did not procure [D's] invocation of [his] Fifth Amendment privilege. *At 157 n.1:* The procurement provision of [TRE 804(a)] is inapplicable to the State here simply because it is the opposite party—not because it is the 'State.' If the State were to procure the absence of a witness, then the State would be barred from using that witness's former testimony by the hearsay rule, even though the defendant could utilize the witness's former testimony under [TRE 804]." *See also* **Castro v. State**, 914 S.W.2d 159, 163 (Tex.App.—San Antonio 1995, pet. ref'd).

Coffin v. State, 885 S.W.2d 140, 147 (Tex.Crim.App. 1994). TRCE 804(b)(1), now TRE 804(b)(1), "does not require that in order for prior testimony to be admitted ... the opponent of the evidence have had an *identical* motive to challenge the testimony at the prior proceeding as he now has at trial. It requires only that he have had a 'similar' motive. ... As with opportunity, similar motive *vel non* must be determined on a case-by-case basis, according to the particular facts and circumstances. *At 149:* By its terms, applicability of the

exception does not turn on whether the opponent actually availed himself of that opportunity. To be sure, that he did not take the opportunity may be one indicator that he lacked a similar motive. We do not consider it, however, to be a conclusive one."

Wilks v. State, 983 S.W.2d 863, 866 (Tex.App.— Corpus Christi 1998, no pet.). Appellant "complains that the trial court erred in allowing testimony concerning another statement that [victim] made to a witness at the hospital that 'I always figured he would kill me, but I figured he would use a gun.' [¶] [Appellant] argues that the present statement says nothing about the circumstances of [victim's] death, but does improperly suggest that there must have been an abusive relationship in the past that caused [victim] to think that [appellant] would kill her. [¶] Had [victim] related her fears to someone else before the fire, it would not have been admissible to show that [appellant] acted in conformity with those fears. [¶] However, taken in the context of [victim's] injuries and her impending death, her statement clearly implied that [appellant] did in fact kill her as she had earlier suspected that he would. Accordingly, [victim's] statement concerned the cause of her death and was properly admissible as a dying declaration to yet another witness that [appellant] killed her."

Bisby v. State, 907 S.W.2d 949, 956 (Tex.App.— Fort Worth 1995, pet. ref'd). "While the declaration must be made under a sense of approaching death, it is not necessary that the declarant state in specific terms that he is conscious of his impending death. The requirement that the declarant believed his death was imminent may be inferred from the circumstances of the case such as the nature of the injury, medical opinions stated to the declarant, and the declarant's conduct at the time."

Reyes v. State, 845 S.W.2d 328, 331 (Tex.App.—El Paso 1992, no pet.). "The determination of whether the efforts to secure the presence of the witness were sufficient to meet the test of [TRCE] 804(a) [now TRE 804(a)] is within the sound discretion of the trial judge. The test has been described as 'good faith efforts undertaken prior to trial to locate and present that witness.'" *But see* **Ledbetter v. State**, 49 S.W.3d 588, 593-94 (Tex.App.—Amarillo 2001, pet. ref'd) ("good-faith efforts" to locate witness are not the same as "due diligence" to obtain continuance).

TRE 804

TRE 805. HEARSAY WITHIN HEARSAY

Hearsay included within hearsay is not excluded under the hearsay rule if each part of the combined statements conforms with an exception to the hearsay rule provided in these rules.

TRE 806. ATTACKING & SUPPORTING CREDIBILITY OF DECLARANT

When a hearsay statement, or a statement defined in Rule 801(e)(2)(C), (D), or (E), or in civil cases a statement defined in Rule 801(e)(3), has been admitted in evidence, the credibility of the declarant may be attacked, and if attacked may be supported by any evidence which would be admissible for those purposes if declarant had testified as a witness. Evidence of a statement or conduct by the declarant at any time, offered to impeach the declarant, is not subject to any requirement that the declarant may have been afforded an opportunity to deny or explain. If the party against whom a hearsay statement has been admitted calls the declarant as a witness, the party is entitled to examine the declarant on the statement as if under cross-examination.

ANNOTATIONS

Sohail v. State, ___ S.W.3d ___ (Tex.App.—Houston [1st Dist.] 2008, pet. filed 5-9-08) (No. 01-06-00682-CR; 2-21-2008). "[T]he State cannot try a case based largely on complainant's hearsay statements, without calling complainant as a witness, and then legitimately object when appellant seeks to admit complainant's other inconsistent hearsay statements to impeach complainant. Evidence that a complainant later disavows his or her prior statements reflects on the credibility of that complainant, and such evidence pertaining to credibility would be admissible if complainant had testified as a witness. Although impeachment evidence is admissible under Rule 806, the evidence offered can be utilized only for that single purpose. If the evidence is submitted primarily to prove the truth of the matter asserted, and not wholly for purposes of impeachment, the trial court should exclude it."

Enriquez v. State, 56 S.W.3d 596, 600-01 (Tex. App.—Corpus Christi 2001, pet. ref'd). "[D]efense counsel asked [officer] (1) why he returned to the impoundment yard and took more pictures of the vehicle,

and (2) if appellant had told him that he was hit from behind. [C]ounsel was trying to find out why [officer] returned to the impound yard in order to take photos of the back of appellant's vehicle. [Officer's] answer contained out-of-court statements told to him by appellant about how the accident allegedly occurred. There is no indication that the statements were offered to prove the truth of the matter asserted. Rather, they were offered as an explanation of the officer's return to reinspect the car. [¶] Because the statements were not offered to prove the truth of the matter asserted they were not hearsay. The State's attack on the credibility of the appellant was wholly predicated on the statements being hearsay under Rule 806. Accordingly we hold that the trial court abused its discretion in admitting appellant's three prior convictions into evidence in order to impeach appellant's credibility."

ARTICLE IX. AUTHENTICATION & IDENTIFICATION

TRE 901. REQUIREMENT OF AUTHENTICATION OR IDENTIFICATION

(a) General Provision. The requirement of authentication or identification as a condition precedent to admissibility is satisfied by evidence sufficient to support a finding that the matter in question is what its proponent claims.

(b) Illustrations. By way of illustration only, and not by way of limitation, the following are examples of authentication or identification conforming with the requirements of this rule:

(1) *Testimony of witness with knowledge.* Testimony that a matter is what it is claimed to be.

(2) *Nonexpert opinion on handwriting.* Nonexpert opinion as to the genuineness of handwriting, based upon familiarity not acquired for purposes of the litigation.

(3) *Comparison by trier or expert witness.* Comparison by the trier of fact or by expert witness with specimens which have been found by the court to be genuine.

(4) *Distinctive characteristics and the like.* Appearance, contents, substance, internal patterns, or other distinctive characteristics, taken in conjunction with circumstances.

(5) *Voice identification.* Identification of a voice, whether heard firsthand or through mechanical or electronic transmission or recording, by opinion based upon hearing the voice at anytime under circumstances connecting it with the alleged speaker.

(6) *Telephone conversations.* Telephone conversations, by evidence that a call was made to the number assigned at the time by the telephone company to a particular person or business, if:

(A) in the case of a person, circumstances, including self-identification, show the person answering to be the one called; or

(B) in the case of a business, the call was made to a place of business and the conversation related to business reasonably transacted over the telephone.

(7) *Public records or reports.* Evidence that a writing authorized by law to be recorded or filed and in fact recorded or filed in a public office, or a purported public record, report, statement, or data compilation, in any form, is from the public office where items of this nature are kept.

(8) *Ancient documents or data compilation.* Evidence that a document or data compilation, in any form, (A) is in such condition as to create no suspicion concerning its authenticity, (B) was in a place where it, if authentic, would likely be, and (C) has been in existence twenty years or more at the time it is offered.

(9) *Process or system.* Evidence describing a process or system used to produce a result and showing that the process or system produces an accurate result.

(10) *Methods provided by statute or rule.* Any method of authentication or identification provided by statute or by other rule prescribed pursuant to statutory authority.

ANNOTATIONS

Maldonado v. State, 998 S.W.2d 239, 244 (Tex. Crim.App.1999). TRE 901 "cannot allow a proponent of evidence to bypass the requirements of [CCP art.] 38.22...."

Varkonyi v. State, ___ S.W.3d ___ (Tex.App.—El Paso 2008, n.p.h.) (No. 08-06-00255-CR; 5-8-08). "Under [the reply-letter] doctrine [TRE 901(b)(4)], a letter received in the due course of mail purportedly in answer to another letter is *prima facie* genuine and admissible without further proof of authenticity. A reply letter needs no further authentication because it is unlikely that anyone other than the purported writer would know of and respond to the contents of the earlier letter addressed to him. Because the reply-letter

doctrine has been applied to telegrams, ... it logically would apply to e-mail communications."

Hartsfield v. State, 200 S.W.3d 813, 817-18 (Tex. App.—Texarkana 2006, pet. ref'd). "In providing the proof necessary to comply with Rule 901, the proponent of the item of evidence must present differing types of evidence depending on the nature of the item. Articles that are easily identifiable and are substantially unchanged normally do not require the introduction of a chain of custody. If the item has distinct or unique characteristics, a witness may authenticate it by testifying that he or she has previously seen the item at the relevant time and place and that the witness recognizes it by its distinctive characteristics. However, if the article of evidence has no distinctive features or is fungible, the item must be proven by showing a chain of custody, typically from the scene of the crime to the courtroom. Authentication of such an article may be accomplished by marking the item and identifying it at trial as the same, so long as there is no evidence of tampering or alteration. The chain of custody is conclusively proven if the officer is able to identify that he or she seized the item of physical evidence, put an identification mark on it, placed it in the property room, and then retrieved the item being offered on the day of trial. Generally, when the evidence sought to be admitted may be distinguished only via scientific testing, then a chain of custody must be demonstrated. Any gaps in the chain of custody go to the weight of the evidence, not admissibility; however, proof should be shown as to the beginning and end of the chain."

Massimo v. State, 144 S.W.3d 210, 215 (Tex.App.—Fort Worth 2004, no pet.). "There is a paucity of case law applying [TRE 901] to e-mails, but one federal court, applying identical [FRE] 901(a) and (b)(4), found that a district court had not abused its discretion in admitting e-mail evidence by applying [FRE] 901(b)(4), utilizing characteristic evidence such as: (1) consistency with the e-mail address on another e-mail sent by the defendant; (2) the author's awareness through the e-mail of the details of defendant's conduct; (3) the e-mail's inclusion of similar requests that the defendant had made by phone during the time period; and (4) the e-mail's reference to the author by the defendant's nickname."

Spaulding v. State, 896 S.W.2d 587, 590 (Tex. App.—Houston [1st Dist.] 1995, no pet.). "A document may be authenticated under either [TRCE] 901 or 902 [now TRE 901 or 902], and it need not be authenticated under both."

Levi v. State, 809 S.W.2d 668, 671 (Tex.App.—Beaumont 1991, no pet.). "[W]hile an actual item of controlled substance may be a relevant piece of evidence, the trial court must be satisfied ... that the item tested and proved to be a controlled substance was properly identified as the same item delivered by the accused. This is normally done by a witness with knowledge of the transaction. Most often it is the undercover police person who made the purchase of the item."

TRE 902. SELF-AUTHENTICATION

Extrinsic evidence of authenticity as a condition precedent to admissibility is not required with respect to the following:

(1) Domestic Public Documents Under Seal. A document bearing a seal purporting to be that of the United States, or of any State, district, Commonwealth, territory, or insular possession thereof, or the Panama Canal Zone, or the Trust Territory of the Pacific Islands, or of a political subdivision, department, officer, or agency thereof, and a signature purporting to be an attestation or execution.

(2) Domestic Public Documents Not Under Seal. A document purporting to bear the signature in the official capacity of an officer or employee of any entity included in paragraph (1) hereof, having no seal, if a public officer having a seal and having official duties in the district or political subdivision of the officer or employee certifies under seal that the signer has the official capacity and that the signature is genuine.

(3) Foreign Public Documents. A document purporting to be executed or attested in an official capacity by a person, authorized by the laws of a foreign country to make the execution or attestation, and accompanied by a final certification as to the genuineness of the signature and official position (A) of the executing or attesting person, or (B) of any foreign official whose certificate of genuineness of signature and official position relates to the execution or attestation or is in a chain of certificates of genuineness of signature and official position relating to the execution or attestation. A final certification may be made by a secretary of embassy or legation, consul general, consul, vice consul, or consular agent of the United States, or a diplomatic or consular official of the foreign country assigned or accredited to the United States. If reasonable opportunity

has been given to all parties to investigate the authenticity and accuracy of official documents, the court may, for good cause shown, order that they be treated as presumptively authentic without final certification or permit them to be evidenced by an attested summary with or without final certification. The final certification shall be dispensed with whenever both the United States and the foreign country in which the official record is located are parties to a treaty or convention that abolishes or displaces such requirement, in which case the record and the attestation shall be certified by the means provided in the treaty or convention.

(4) Certified Copies of Public Records. A copy of an official record or report or entry therein, or of a document authorized by law to be recorded or filed and actually recorded or filed in a public office, including data compilations in any form certified as correct by the custodian or other person authorized to make the certification, by certificate complying with paragraph (1), (2) or (3) of this rule or complying with any statute or other rule prescribed pursuant to statutory authority.

(5) Official Publications. Books, pamphlets, or other publications purporting to be issued by public authority.

(6) Newspapers and Periodicals. Printed materials purporting to be newspapers or periodicals.

(7) Trade Inscriptions and the Like. Inscriptions, signs, tags, or labels purporting to have been affixed in the course of business and indicating ownership, control, or origin.

(8) Acknowledged Documents. Documents accompanied by a certificate of acknowledgment executed in the manner provided by law by a notary public or other officer authorized by law to take acknowledgments.

(9) Commercial Paper and Related Documents. Commercial paper, signatures thereon, and documents relating thereto to the extent provided by general commercial law.

(10) Business Records Accompanied by Affidavit.

(a) *Records or photocopies; admissibility; affidavit; filing.* Any record or set of records or photographically reproduced copies of such records, which would be admissible under Rule 803(6) or (7) shall be admissible in evidence in any court in this state upon the affidavit of the person who would otherwise provide the prerequisites of Rule 803(6) or (7), that such records attached to such affidavit were in fact so kept as required by Rule 803(6) or (7), provided further, that such record or records along with such affidavit are filed with the clerk of the court for inclusion with the papers in the cause in which the record or records are sought to be used as evidence at least fourteen days prior to the day upon which trial of said cause commences, and provided the other parties to said cause are given prompt notice by the party filing same of the filing of such record or records and affidavit, which notice shall identify the name and employer, if any, of the person making the affidavit and such records shall be made available to the counsel for other parties to the action or litigation for inspection and copying. The expense for copying shall be borne by the party, parties or persons who desire copies and not by the party or parties who file the records and serve notice of said filing, in compliance with this rule. Notice shall be deemed to have been promptly given if it is served in the manner contemplated by Rule of Civil Procedure 21a fourteen days prior to commencement of trial in said cause.

(b) *Form of affidavit.* A form for the affidavit of such person as shall make such affidavit as is permitted in paragraph (a) above shall be sufficient if it follows this form though this form shall not be exclusive, and an affidavit which substantially complies with the provisions of this rule shall suffice, to-wit:

No. _____

John Doe (Name of Plaintiff)	§ §	IN THE
		COURT IN AND FOR
v.	§	
John Roe (Name of Defendant)	§ §	COUNTY, TEXAS

AFFIDAVIT

Before me, the undersigned authority, personally appeared _____, who, being by me duly sworn, deposed as follows:

My name is _____, I am of sound mind, capable of making this affidavit, and personally acquainted with the facts herein stated:

I am the custodian of the records of _____. Attached hereto are _____ pages of records from

_____. These said _____ pages of records are kept by _____ in the regular course of business, and it was the regular course of business of _____ for an employee or representative of _____, with knowledge of the act, event, condition, opinion, or diagnosis, recorded to make the record or to transmit information thereof to be included in such record; and the record was made at or near the time or reasonably soon thereafter. The records attached hereto are the original or exact duplicates of the original.

Affiant

SWORN TO AND SUBSCRIBED before me on the _____ day of _____, 19 ____.

Notary Public, State of Texas
Notary's printed name:

My commission expires:

(11) Presumptions Under Statutes or Other Rules. Any signature, document, or other matter declared by statute or by other rules prescribed pursuant to statutory authority to be presumptively or prima facie genuine or authentic.

ANNOTATIONS

Flowers v. State, 220 S.W.3d 919, 922-23 (Tex. Crim.App.2007). "A computer-generated compilation of information setting out the specifics of a criminal conviction that is certified as correct by the county or district clerk of the court in which the conviction was obtained is admissible under Rule 902."

State v. Handsbur, 816 S.W.2d 749, 750 (Tex.Crim. App.1991). "[A] proper certification by the custodian of records at a State correctional institution is sufficient authentication under both [TRCEs] 901 and 902(4) [now TREs 901 and 902(4)] for the admission of a copy of a prior conviction contained in that institution's files." *See also* **Reed v. State**, 811 S.W.2d 582, 585-87 (Tex.Crim.App.1991).

Banks v. State, 158 S.W.3d 649, 653 (Tex.App.— Houston [14th Dist.] 2005, pet. ref'd). "Appellant's Illinois penitentiary packet contains three single-page documents.... Because the packet lacks certification and a seal, appellant's penitentiary packet was not self-authenticating under [TRE] 902."

Landrum v. State, 153 S.W.3d 635, 638 (Tex. App.—Amarillo 2004, no pet.). Held: TRCP 4's method of computing time does not apply to TRE 902(10)'s filing deadlines. An instrument is deemed filed when it is placed in the custody or control of the clerk.

TRE 903. SUBSCRIBING WITNESS' TESTIMONY UNNECESSARY

The testimony of a subscribing witness is not necessary to authenticate a writing unless required by the laws of the jurisdiction whose laws govern the validity of the writing.

ARTICLE X. CONTENTS OF WRITINGS, RECORDINGS, & PHOTOGRAPHS

TRE 1001. DEFINITIONS

For purposes of this article the following definitions are applicable:

(a) Writings and Recordings. "Writings" and "recordings" consist of letters, words, or numbers or their equivalent, set down by handwriting, typewriting, printing, photostating, photographing, magnetic impulse, mechanical or electronic recording, or other form of data compilation.

(b) Photographs. "Photographs" include still photographs, X-ray films, video tapes, and motion pictures.

(c) Original. An "original" of a writing or recording is the writing or recording itself or any counterpart intended to have the same effect by a person executing or issuing it. An "original" of a photograph includes the negative or any print therefrom. If data are stored in a computer or similar device, any printout or other output readable by sight, shown to reflect the data accurately, is an "original."

(d) Duplicate. A "duplicate" is a counterpart produced by the same impression as the original, or from the same matrix, or by means of photography, including enlargements and miniatures, or by mechanical or electronic re-recording, or by chemical reproduction, or by other equivalent techniques which accurately reproduce the original.

TRE 1002. REQUIREMENT OF ORIGINALS

To prove the content of a writing, recording, or photograph, the original writing, recording, or photograph is required except as otherwise provided in these rules or by law.

Menefee v. State, 928 S.W.2d 274, 278 (Tex.App.—Tyler 1996, no pet.). "An objection that evidence is not the 'best evidence' asserts that a copy or reproduction of a writing, recording, or photograph is inadequate and should be replaced by the original."

Washington v. State, 905 S.W.2d 665, 668 (Tex. App.—Houston [14th Dist.] 1995, pet. ref'd). "[A] pen packet certified by the record clerk of the Institutional Division of the Texas Department of Criminal Justice is admissible evidence[, and] these packets are admissible under the 'best evidence' rule."

TRE 1003. ADMISSIBILITY OF DUPLICATES

A duplicate is admissible to the same extent as an original unless (1) a question is raised as to the authenticity of the original or (2) in the circumstances it would be unfair to admit the duplicate in lieu of the original.

Englund v. State, 946 S.W.2d 64, 67 (Tex.Crim.App. 1997). "The question is whether a fax of the certified copy was admissible in lieu of the certified copy that was the source document for the facsimile transmission. *At 71:* [County clerk's] office sent the exhibit to [district attorney's] office via a facsimile telecopier.... The Rules are flexible enough to [allow] for an interpretation leading to the conclusion that the exhibit was admissible under [TRCEs] 1005 and 1003 [now TREs 1005 and 1003]. *At n.13:* [A] copy of a certified copy of a public record obtained by facsimile transmission will [not] always be admissible. If a party raises an objection the trial court must exercise discretion under [TRE 1003] in determining whether a question is raised as to the authenticity of the original or whether in the circumstances it would be unfair to admit the duplicate in lieu of the original. [A] party may [not] manipulate [TRCEs] 1003, 1004, and 1005 [now TREs 1003, 1004, and 1005] and offer other evidence of the contents of a public record, other than a duplicate of a certified copy, without first showing that a certified or compared copy could not be obtained by the exercise of reasonable diligence."

TRE 902

Hood v. State, 944 S.W.2d 743, 747 (Tex.App.— Amarillo 1997, no pet.). "[W]hen the only concern is with getting the words or contents of the document before the fact finder, then duplicate of the original serves as well as the original."

TRE 1004. ADMISSIBILITY OF OTHER EVIDENCE OF CONTENTS

The original is not required, and other evidence of the contents of a writing, recording, or photograph is admissible if:

(a) Originals Lost or Destroyed. All originals are lost or have been destroyed, unless the proponent lost or destroyed them in bad faith;

(b) Original Not Obtainable. No original can be obtained by any available judicial process or procedure;

(c) Original Outside the State. No original is located in Texas;

(d) Original in Possession of Opponent. At a time when an original was under the control of the party against whom offered, that party was put on notice, by the pleadings or otherwise, that the content would be a subject of proof at the hearing, and that party does not produce the original at the hearing; or

(e) Collateral Matters. The writing, recording or photograph is not closely related to a controlling issue.

TRE 1005. PUBLIC RECORDS

The contents of an official record or of a document authorized to be recorded or filed and actually recorded or filed, including data compilations in any form, if otherwise admissible, may be proved by copy, certified as correct in accordance with Rule 902 or testified to be correct by a witness who has compared it with the original. If a copy which complies with the foregoing cannot be obtained by the exercise of reasonable diligence, then other evidence of the contents may be given.

TRE 1006. SUMMARIES

The contents of voluminous writings, recordings, or photographs, otherwise admissible, which cannot conveniently be examined in court may be presented in the form of a chart, summary, or calculation. The originals, or duplicates, shall be made available for examination or copying, or both, by other parties at a reasonable time and place. The court may order that they be produced in court.

Callahan v. State, 937 S.W.2d 553, 559 (Tex. App.—Texarkana 1996, no pet.). "Summaries are permitted under [TRCE] 1006 [now TRE 1006]. This rule, however, applies to summary of the contents of voluminous writings, recordings, photographs, or such matters that cannot be conveniently examined in court, but may be better understood by a jury or judge in the form of a chart, summary, or calculation. This rule is not applicable to a medical opinion testified to by an expert witness in open court."

TRE 1007. TESTIMONY OR WRITTEN ADMISSION OF PARTY

Contents of writings, recordings, or photographs may be proved by the testimony or deposition of the party against whom offered or by that party's written admission, without accounting for the nonproduction of the original.

TRE 1008. FUNCTIONS OF COURT & JURY

When the admissibility of other evidence of contents of writings, recordings, or photographs under these rules depends upon the fulfillment of a condition of fact, the question whether the condition has been fulfilled is ordinarily for the court to determine in accordance with the provisions of Rule 104. However, when an issue is raised (a) whether the asserted writing ever existed, or (b) whether another writing, recording, or photograph produced at the trial is the original, or (c) whether other evidence of contents correctly reflects the contents, the issue is for the trier of fact to determine as in the case of other issues of fact.

TRE 1009. TRANSLATION OF FOREIGN LANGUAGE DOCUMENTS

(a) Translations. A translation of foreign language documents shall be admissible upon the affidavit of a qualified translator setting forth the qualifications of the translator and certifying that the translation is fair and accurate. Such affidavit, along with the translation and the underlying foreign language documents, shall be served upon all parties at least 45 days prior to the date of trial.

(b) Objections. Any party may object to the accuracy of another party's translation by pointing out the

TRE 1009

specific inaccuracies of the translation and by stating with specificity what the objecting party contends is a fair and accurate translation. Such objection shall be served upon all parties at least 15 days prior to the date of trial.

(c) Effect of Failure to Object or Offer Conflicting Translation. If no conflicting translation or objection is timely served, the court shall admit a translation submitted under paragraph (a) without need of proof, provided however that the underlying foreign language documents are otherwise admissible under the Texas Rules of Evidence. Failure to serve a conflicting translation under paragraph (a) or failure to timely and properly object to the accuracy of a translation under paragraph (b) shall preclude a party from attacking or offering evidence contradicting the accuracy of such translation at trial.

(d) Effect of Objections or Conflicting Translations. In the event of conflicting translations under paragraph (a) or if objections to another party's translation are served under paragraph (b), the court shall determine whether there is a genuine issue as to the accuracy of a material part of the translation to be resolved by the trier of fact.

(e) Expert Testimony of Translator. Except as provided in paragraph (c), this Rule does not preclude the admission of a translation of foreign language documents at trial either by live testimony or by deposition testimony of a qualified expert translator.

(f) Varying of Time Limits. The court, upon motion of any party and for good cause shown, may enlarge or shorten the time limits set forth in this Rule.

(g) Court Appointment. The court, if necessary, may appoint a qualified translator, the reasonable value of whose services shall be taxed as court costs.

TEXAS RULES OF APPELLATE PROCEDURE

TABLE OF CONTENTS

★

TRAP

TEXAS RULES OF APPELLATE PROCEDURE

SECTION ONE: GENERAL PROVISIONS

TRAP 1. SCOPE OF RULES; LOCAL RULES OF COURTS OF APPEALS

1.1 **Scope.** These rules govern procedure in appellate courts and before appellate judges and post-trial procedure in trial courts in criminal cases.

1.2 **Local Rules.**

(a) *Promulgation.* A court of appeals may promulgate rules governing its practice that are not inconsistent with these rules. Local rules governing civil cases must first be approved by the Supreme Court. Local rules governing criminal cases must first be approved by the Court of Criminal Appeals.

(b) *Copies.* The clerk must provide a copy of the court's local rules to anyone who requests it.

(c) *Party's noncompliance.* A court must not dismiss an appeal for noncompliance with a local rule without giving the noncomplying party notice and a reasonable opportunity to cure the noncompliance.

TRAP 2. SUSPENSION OF RULES

On a party's motion or on its own initiative an appellate court may—to expedite a decision or for other good cause—suspend a rule's operation in a particular case and order a different procedure; but a court must not construe this rule to suspend any provision in the Code of Criminal Procedure or to alter the time for perfecting an appeal in a civil case.

ANNOTATIONS

Sossamon v. State, 110 S.W.3d 57, 59 (Tex.App.—Waco 2002, pet. ref'd). "Rule 2 may not be used by an appellate court to extend the time limits provided by the appellate rules for the filing of a motion for new trial."

TRAP 3. DEFINITIONS; UNIFORM TERMINOLOGY

3.1 **Definitions.**

(a) *Appellant* means a party taking an appeal to an appellate court.

(b) *Appellate court* means the courts of appeals, the Court of Criminal Appeals, and the Supreme Court.

(c) *Appellee* means a party adverse to an appellant.

(d) *Applicant* means a person seeking relief by a habeas corpus in a criminal case.

(e) *Petitioner* means a party petitioning the Supreme Court or the Court of Criminal Appeals for review.

(f) *Relator* means a person seeking relief in an original proceeding in an appellate court other than by habeas corpus in a criminal case.

(g) *Reporter* or *court reporter* means the court reporter or court recorder.

(h) *Respondent* means:

(1) a party adverse to a petitioner in the Supreme Court or the Court of Criminal Appeals; or

(2) a party against whom relief is sought in an original proceeding in an appellate court.

3.2 **Uniform Terminology in Criminal Cases.** In documents filed in criminal appeals, the parties are the *State* and the *appellant*. But if the State has appealed under Article 44.01 of the Code of Criminal Procedure, the defendant is the *appellee*. Otherwise, papers should use real names for parties, and such labels as *appellee, petitioner, respondent,* and *movant* should be avoided unless necessary for clarity. In habeas corpus proceedings, the person for whose relief the writ is requested is the *applicant*; Code of Criminal Procedure article 11.13.

TRAP 4. TIME & NOTICE PROVISIONS

4.1 **Computing Time.**

(a) *In general.* The day of an act, event, or default after which a designated period begins to run is not included when computing a period prescribed or allowed by these rules, by court order, or by statute. The last day of the period is included, but if that day is a Saturday, Sunday, or legal holiday, the period extends to the end of the next day that is not a Saturday, Sunday, or legal holiday.

(b) *Clerk's office closed or inaccessible.* If the act to be done is filing a document, and if the clerk's office where the document is to be filed is closed or inaccessible during regular hours on the last day for filing the document, the period for filing the document extends to the end of the next day when the clerk's office is open and accessible. The closing or inaccessibility of the clerk's office may be proved by a certificate of the clerk or counsel, by a party's affidavit, or by other satisfactory proof, and may be controverted in the same manner.

TRAP 1

4.2 No Notice of Trial Court's Judgment in Civil Case.

(a) *Additional time to file documents.*

(1) *In general.* If a party affected by a judgment or other appealable order has not—within 20 days after the judgment or order was signed—either received the notice required by Texas Rule of Civil Procedure 306a.3 or acquired actual knowledge of the signing, then a period that, under these rules, runs from the signing will begin for that party on the earlier of the date when the party receives notice or acquires actual knowledge of the signing. But in no event may the period begin more than 90 days after the judgment or order was signed.

(2) *Exception for restricted appeal.* Subparagraph (1) does not extend the time for perfecting a restricted appeal.

(b) *Procedure to gain additional time.* The procedure to gain additional time is governed by Texas Rule of Civil Procedure 306a.5.

(c) *The court's order.* After hearing the motion, the trial court must sign a written order that finds the date when the party or the party's attorney first either received notice or acquired actual knowledge that the judgment or order was signed.

4.3 Periods Affected by Modified Judgment in Civil Case.

(a) *During plenary-power period.* If a judgment is modified in any respect while the trial court retains plenary power, a period that, under these rules, runs from the date when the judgment is signed will run from the date when the modified judgment is signed.

(b) *After plenary power expires.* If the trial court corrects or reforms the judgment under Texas Rule of Civil Procedure 316 after expiration of the trial court's plenary power, all periods provided in these rules that run from the date the judgment is signed run from the date the corrected judgment is signed for complaints that would not apply to the original judgment.

4.4 Periods Affected When Process Served by Publication. If process was served by publication and if a motion for new trial was filed under Texas Rule of Civil Procedure 329 more than 30 days after the judgment was signed, a period that, under these rules, runs from the date when the judgment is signed will be computed as if the judgment were signed on the date when the motion for new trial was filed.

 4.5 No Notice of Judgment or Order of Appellate Court; Effect on Time to File Certain Documents.

(a) *Additional time to file documents.* A party may move for additional time to file a motion for rehearing or en banc reconsideration in the court of appeals, a petition for review, or a petition for discretionary review, if the party did not—until after the time expired for filing the document—either receive notice of the judgment or order from the clerk or acquire actual knowledge of the rendition of the judgment or order.

(b) *Procedure to gain additional time.* The motion must state the earliest date when the party or the party's attorney received notice or acquired actual knowledge that the judgment or order had been rendered. The motion must be filed within 15 days of that date but in no event more than 90 days after the date of the judgment or order.

(c) *Where to file.*

(1) A motion for additional time to file a motion for rehearing or en banc reconsideration in the court of appeals must be filed in and ruled on by the court of appeals in which the case is pending.

(2) A motion for additional time to file a petition for review must be filed in and ruled on by the Supreme Court.

(3) A motion for additional time to file a petition for discretionary review must be filed in and ruled on by the Court of Criminal Appeals.

(d) *Order of the court.* If the court finds that the motion for additional time was timely filed and the party did not—within the time for filing the motion for rehearing or en banc reconsideration, petition for review, or petition for discretionary review, as the case may be—receive the notice or have actual knowledge of the judgment or order, the court must grant the motion. The time for filing the document will begin to run on the date when the court grants the motion.

TRAP 5. FEES IN CIVIL CASES

A party who is not excused by statute or these rules from paying costs must pay—at the time an item is presented for filing—whatever fees are required by statute or Supreme Court order. The appellate court may enforce this rule by any order that is just.

TRAP 6. REPRESENTATION BY COUNSEL

6.1 Lead Counsel.

(a) *For appellant.* Unless another attorney is designated, lead counsel for an appellant is the attorney whose signature first appears on the notice of appeal.

(b) *For a party other than appellant.* Unless another attorney is designated, lead counsel for a party other than an appellant is the attorney whose signature first appears on the first document filed in the appellate court on that party's behalf.

(c) *How to designate.* The original or a new lead counsel may be designated by filing a notice stating that attorney's name, mailing address, telephone number, fax number, if any, and State Bar of Texas identification number. If a new lead counsel is being designated, both the new attorney and either the party or the former lead counsel must sign the notice.

6.2 Appearance of Other Attorneys. An attorney other than lead counsel may file a notice stating that the attorney represents a specified party to the proceeding and giving that attorney's name, mailing address, telephone number, fax number, if any, and State Bar of Texas identification number. The clerk will note on the docket the attorney's appearance. When a brief or motion is filed, the clerk will note on the docket the name of each attorney, if not already noted, who appears on the document.

6.3 To Whom Communications Sent. Any notice, copies of documents filed in an appellate court, or other communications must be sent to:

(a) each party's lead counsel on appeal;

(b) a party's lead counsel in the trial court if:

(1) that party was represented by counsel in the trial court;

(2) lead counsel on appeal has not yet been designated for that party; and

(3) lead counsel in the trial court has not filed a nonrepresentation notice or been allowed to withdraw;

(c) a party if the party is not represented by counsel.

6.4 Nonrepresentation Notice.

(a) *In general.* If, in accordance with paragraph 6.3(b), the lead counsel in the trial court is being sent notices, copies of documents, or other communications, that attorney may file a nonrepresentation notice in the appellate court. The notice must:

(1) state that the attorney is not representing the party on appeal;

(2) state that the court and other counsel should communicate directly with the party in the future;

(3) give the party's name and last known address and telephone number; and

(4) be signed by the party.

(b) *Appointed counsel.* In a criminal case, an attorney appointed by the trial court to represent an indigent party cannot file a nonrepresentation notice.

6.5 Withdrawal. An appellate court may, on appropriate terms and conditions, permit an attorney to withdraw from representing a party in the appellate court.

(a) *Contents of motion.* A motion for leave to withdraw must contain the following:

(1) a list of current deadlines and settings in the case;

(2) the party's name and last known address and telephone number;

(3) a statement that a copy of the motion was delivered to the party; and

(4) a statement that the party was notified in writing of the right to object to the motion.

(b) *Delivery to party.* The motion must be delivered to the party in person or mailed—both by certified and by first-class mail—to the party at the party's last known address.

(c) *If motion granted.* If the court grants the motion, the withdrawing attorney must immediately notify the party, in writing, of any deadlines or settings that the attorney knows about at the time of withdrawal but that were not previously disclosed to the party. The withdrawing attorney must file a copy of that notice with the court clerk.

(d) *Exception for substitution of counsel.* If an attorney substitutes for a withdrawing attorney, the motion to withdraw need not comply with (a) but must state only the substitute attorney's name, mailing address, telephone number, fax number, if any, and State Bar of Texas identification number. The withdrawing attorney must comply with (b) but not (c).

6.6 Agreements of Parties or Counsel. To be enforceable, an agreement of parties or their counsel concerning an appellate court proceeding must be in writing and signed by the parties or their counsel. Such an agreement is subject to any appellate court order necessary to ensure that the case is properly presented.

Generally

Cormier v. State, 85 S.W.3d 496, 497 (Tex.App.—Houston [1st Dist.] 2002, pet. ref'd). "We ... consider whether a criminal appellant has a right to appellate self-representation. We conclude that there is no such right." *But see Fewins v. State*, 170 S.W.3d 293, 294-95 (Tex.App.—Waco 2005, order) (CCP art. 1.051 allows self-representation).

TRAP 6.1

Bonner v. State, 29 S.W.3d 360, 361 (Tex.App.—Waco 2000, pet. ref'd). "The motion [for substitution of attorney] contains all of the required information [from Rule 6.2]. Thus, the retained attorney has made an appropriate appearance before us on this case.... However, the appointed attorney remains the 'lead attorney' because the motion does not comply with the requirements of Rule 6.1(c), which sets out the procedure for changing the lead attorney for a party."

TRAP 7. SUBSTITUTING PARTIES

7.1 **Parties Who Are Not Public Officers.**

(a) *Death of a party.*

(1) *Civil cases.* If a party to a civil case dies after the trial court renders judgment but before the case has been finally disposed of on appeal, the appeal may be perfected, and the appellate court will proceed to adjudicate the appeal as if all parties were alive. The appellate court's judgment will have the same force and effect as if rendered when all parties were living. The decedent party's name may be used on all papers.

(2) *Criminal cases.* If the appellant in a criminal case dies after an appeal is perfected but before the appellate court issues the mandate, the appeal will be permanently abated.

(b) *Substitution for other reasons.* If substitution of a party in the appellate court is necessary for a reason other than death, the appellate court may order substitution on any party's motion at any time.

7.2 **Public Officers.**

(a) *Automatic substitution of officer.* When a public officer is a party in an official capacity to an appeal or original proceeding, and if that person ceases to hold office before the appeal or original proceeding is

finally disposed of, the public officer's successor is automatically substituted as a party if appropriate. Proceedings following substitution are to be in the name of the substituted party, but any misnomer that does not affect the substantial rights of the parties may be disregarded. Substitution may be ordered at any time, but failure to order substitution of the successor does not affect the substitution.

(b) *Abatement.* If the case is an original proceeding under Rule 52, the court must abate the proceeding to allow the successor to reconsider the original party's decision. In all other cases, the suit will not abate, and the successor will be bound by the appellate court's judgment or order as if the successor were the original party.

TRAP 7.1

McCaffrey v. State, 76 S.W.3d 392, 393 (Tex.Crim. App.2002). "[T]he proper disposition is dismissal of the appeal rather than permanent abatement [when State is appealing party in a criminal case and appellee dies while appeal is pending]."

TRAP 7.2

In re Guerra, 235 S.W.3d 392, 403 (Tex.App.—Corpus Christi 2007, orig. proceeding). "A 'successor' in the context of rule 7.2 ... is an individual who succeeds a public officer who has *ceased to hold office.*"

TRAP 8. BANKRUPTCY IN CIVIL CASES

08 **8.1** **Notice of Bankruptcy.** Any party may file a notice that a party is in bankruptcy. The notice must contain:

(a) the bankrupt party's name;

(b) the court in which the bankruptcy proceeding is pending;

(c) the bankruptcy proceeding's style and case number; and

(d) the date when the bankruptcy petition was filed.

8.2 **Effect of Bankruptcy.** A bankruptcy suspends the appeal and all periods in these rules from the date when the bankruptcy petition is filed until the appellate court reinstates or severs the appeal in accordance with federal law. A period that began to run and had not expired at the time the proceeding was suspended begins anew when the proceeding is reinstated or severed under 8.3. A document filed by a party while the proceeding is suspended will be deemed filed on the same day, but after, the court reinstates or severs the appeal and will not be considered ineffective because it was filed while the proceeding was suspended.

8.3 **Motion to Reinstate or Sever Appeal Suspended by Bankruptcy.**

(a) *Motion to reinstate.* If a case has been suspended by a bankruptcy filing, a party may move that the appellate court reinstate the appeal if permitted by federal law or the bankruptcy court. If the bankruptcy court has lifted or terminated the stay, a certified copy of the order must be attached to the motion.

(b) *Motion to sever.* A party may move to sever the appeal with respect to the bankrupt party and to reinstate the appeal with respect to the other parties. The motion must show that the case is severable and must comply with applicable federal law regarding severance of a bankrupt party. The court may proceed under this paragraph on its own initiative.

TRAP 9. PAPERS GENERALLY

9.1 **Signing.**

(a) *Represented parties.* If a party is represented by counsel, a document filed on that party's behalf must be signed by at least one of the party's attorneys. For each attorney whose name appears on a document as representing that party, the document must contain that attorney's State Bar of Texas identification number, mailing address, telephone number, and fax number, if any.

(b) *Unrepresented parties.* A party not represented by counsel must sign any document that the party files and give the party's mailing address, telephone number, and fax number, if any.

9.2 **Filing.**

(a) *With whom.* A document is filed in an appellate court by delivering it to:

(1) the clerk of the court in which the document is to be filed; or

(2) a justice or judge of that court who is willing to accept delivery. A justice or judge who accepts delivery must note on the document the date and time of delivery, which will be considered the time of filing, and must promptly send it to the clerk.

(b) *Filing by mail.*

(1) *Timely filing.* A document received within ten days after the filing deadline is considered timely filed if:

(A) it was sent to the proper clerk by United States Postal Service first-class, express, registered, or certified mail;

(B) it was placed in an envelope or wrapper properly addressed and stamped; and

(C) it was deposited in the mail on or before the last day for filing.

(2) *Proof of mailing.* Though it may consider other proof, the appellate court will accept the following as conclusive proof of the date of mailing:

(A) a legible postmark affixed by the United States Postal Service;

(B) a receipt for registered or certified mail if the receipt is endorsed by the United States Postal Service; or

(C) a certificate of mailing by the United States Postal Service.

(c) *Electronic filing.* A court of appeals may by local rule permit documents to be filed, signed, or verified by electronic means that are consistent with technological standards, if any, that the Supreme Court establishes.

9.3 **Number of Copies.**

(a) *Courts of appeals.*

(1) A party must file:

(A) the original and three copies of all documents in an original proceeding;

(B) the original and two copies of all motions in an appellate proceeding; and

(C) the original and five copies of all other documents.

(2) A court of appeals may by local rule require the filing of more or fewer copies of any document other than a petition for discretionary review.

 (b) *Supreme Court and Court of Criminal Appeals.* A party must file the original and 11 copies of any document addressed to either the Supreme Court or the Court of Criminal Appeals, except that in the Supreme Court, only an original and two copies must be filed of a motion for extension of time or a response to the motion, and in the Court of Criminal Appeals, only the original must be filed of a motion for extension of time or a response to the motion, or a pleading under Code of Criminal Procedure article 11.07.

(c) *Exception for record.* Only the original record need be filed in any proceeding.

9.4 Form. Except for the record, a document filed with an appellate court must—unless the court accepts another form in the interest of justice—be in the following form:

(a) *Printing.* A document may be produced by standard typographic printing or by any duplicating process that produces a distinct black image. Printing may be on both sides of the paper.

(b) *Paper type and size.* The paper on which the document is produced must be white or nearly white, and opaque. Paper must be 8 1/2 by 11 inches.

(c) *Margins.* Papers must have at least one-inch margins on both sides and at the top and bottom.

(d) *Spacing.* Text must be double-spaced, but footnotes, block quotations, short lists, and issues or points of error may be single-spaced.

(e) *Typeface.* A document must be printed in standard 10-character-per-inch (cpi) nonproportionally spaced Courier typeface or in 13-point or larger proportionally spaced typeface. But if the document is printed in a proportionally spaced typeface, footnotes may be printed in typeface no smaller than 10-point.

(f) *Binding and covering.* A document must be bound so as to ensure that it will not lose its cover or fall apart in regular use. A document should be stapled once in the top left-hand corner or be bound so that it will lie flat when open. A petition or brief should have durable front and back covers which must not be plastic or be red, black, or dark blue.

(g) *Contents of cover.* A document's front cover, if any, must contain the case style, the case number, the title of the document being filed, the name of the party filing the document, and the name, mailing address, telephone number, fax number, if any, and State Bar of Texas identification number of the lead counsel for the filing party. If a party requests oral argument in the court of appeals, the request must appear on the front cover of that party's first brief.

(h) *Appendix.* An appendix may be bound either with the document to which it is related or separately. If separately bound, the appendix must comply with paragraph (f). An appendix should be tabbed and indexed.

(i) *Nonconforming documents.* Unless every copy of a document conforms to these rules, the court may strike the document and return all nonconforming copies to the filing party. The court must identify the error to be corrected and state a deadline for the party to resubmit the document in a conforming format. If another nonconforming document is filed, the court may strike the document and prohibit the party from filing further documents of the same kind. The use of footnotes, smaller or condensed typeface, or compacted or compressed printing features to avoid the limits of these rules are grounds for the court to strike a document.

9.5 Service.

(a) *Service of all documents required.* At or before the time of a document's filing, the filing party must serve a copy on all parties to the proceeding. But a party need not serve a copy of the record.

(b) *Manner of service.* Service on a party represented by counsel must be made on that party's lead counsel. Service may be personal, by mail, by commercial delivery service, or by fax. Personal service includes delivery to any responsible person at the office of the lead counsel for the party served.

(c) *When complete.*

(1) Service by mail is complete on mailing.

(2) Service by commercial delivery service is complete when the document is placed in the control of the delivery service.

(3) Service by fax is complete on receipt.

(d) *Proof of service.* A document presented for filing must contain a proof of service in the form of either an acknowledgment of service by the person served or a certificate of service. Proof of service may appear on or be affixed to the filed document. The clerk may permit a document to be filed without proof of service, but will require the proof to be filed promptly.

(e) *Certificate requirements.* A certificate of service must be signed by the person who made the service and must state:

(1) the date and manner of service;

(2) the name and address of each person served; and

(3) if the person served is a party's attorney, the name of the party represented by that attorney.

★

9.6 **Communications with the Court.** Parties and counsel may communicate with the appellate court about a case only through the clerk.

9.7 **Adoption by Reference.** Any party may join in or adopt by reference all or any part of a brief, petition, response, motion, or other document filed in an appellate court by another party in the same case.

 9.8 **Protection of Minor's Identity in Parental-Rights Termination Cases and Juvenile Court Cases.**

(a) *Alias defined.* For purposes of this rule, an alias means one or more of a person's initials or a fictitious name, used to refer to the person.

(b) *Parental-rights termination cases.* In an appeal or an original proceeding in an appellate court, arising out of a case in which the termination of parental rights was at issue:

(1) except for a docketing statement, in all papers submitted to the court, including all appendix items submitted with a brief, petition, or motion:

(A) a minor must be identified only by an alias unless the court orders otherwise;

(B) the court may order that a minor's parent or other family member be identified only by an alias if necessary to protect a minor's identity; and

(C) all documents must be redacted accordingly;

(2) the court must, in its opinion, use an alias to refer to a minor, and if necessary to protect the minor's identity, to the minor's parent or other family member.

(c) *Juvenile court cases.* In an appeal or an original proceeding in an appellate court, arising out of a case under Title 3 of the Family Code:

(1) except for a docketing statement, in all papers submitted to the court, including all appendix items submitted with a brief, petition, or motion:

(A) a minor must be identified only by an alias;

(B) a minor's parent or other family member must be identified only by an alias; and

(C) all documents must be redacted accordingly;

(2) the court must, in its opinion, use an alias to refer to a minor and to the minor's parent or other family member.

(d) *No alteration of appellate record.* Nothing in this rule permits alteration of the original appellate record except as specifically authorized by court order.

TRAP 10. MOTIONS IN THE APPELLATE COURTS

10.1 **Contents of Motions; Response.**

(a) *Motion.* Unless these rules prescribe another form, a party must apply by motion for an order or other relief. The motion must:

(1) contain or be accompanied by any matter specifically required by a rule governing such a motion;

(2) state with particularity the grounds on which it is based;

(3) set forth the order or relief sought;

(4) be served and filed with any brief, affidavit, or other paper filed in support of the motion; and

(5) in civil cases, except for motions for rehearing and en banc reconsideration, contain or be accompanied by a certificate stating that the filing party conferred, or made a reasonable attempt to confer, with all other parties about the merits of the motion and whether those parties oppose the motion.

(b) *Response.* A party may file a response to a motion at any time before the court rules on the motion or by any deadline set by the court. The court may determine a motion before a response is filed.

10.2 **Evidence on Motions.** A motion need not be verified unless it depends on the following types of facts, in which case the motion must be supported by affidavit or other satisfactory evidence. The types of facts requiring proof are those that are:

(a) not in the record;

(b) not within the court's knowledge in its official capacity; and

(c) not within the personal knowledge of the attorney signing the motion.

10.3 **Determining Motions.**

(a) *Time for determination.* A court should not hear or determine a motion until 10 days after the motion was filed, unless:

(1) the motion is to extend time to file a brief, a petition for review, or a petition for discretionary review;

(2) the motion states that the parties have conferred and that no party opposes the motion; or

(3) the motion is an emergency.

(b) *Reconsideration.* If a motion is determined prematurely, any party adversely affected may request the court to reconsider its order.

TRAP 9

10.4 Power of Panel or Single Justice or Judge to Entertain Motions.

(a) *Single justice.* In addition to the authority expressly conferred by these rules or by law, a single justice or judge of an appellate court may grant or deny a request for relief that these rules allow to be sought by motion. But in a civil case, a single justice should not do the following:

(1) act on a petition for an extraordinary writ; or

(2) dismiss or otherwise determine an appeal or a motion for rehearing.

(b) *Panel.* An appellate court may provide, by order or rule, that a panel or the full court must act on any motion or class of motions.

10.5 Particular Motions.

(a) *Motions relating to informalities in the record.* A motion relating to informalities in the manner of bringing a case into court must be filed within 30 days after the record is filed in the court of appeals. The objection, if waivable, will otherwise be deemed waived.

(b) *Motions to extend time.*

(1) *Contents of motion in general.* All motions to extend time, except a motion to extend time for filing a notice of appeal, must state:

(A) the deadline for filing the item in question;

(B) the length of the extension sought;

(C) the facts relied on to reasonably explain the need for an extension; and

(D) the number of previous extensions granted regarding the item in question.

(2) *Contents of motion to extend time to file notice of appeal.* A motion to extend the time for filing a notice of appeal must:

(A) comply with (1)(A) and (C);

(B) identify the trial court;

(C) state the date of the trial court's judgment or appealable order; and

(D) state the case number and style of the case in the trial court.

(3) *Contents of motion to extend time to file petition for review or petition for discretionary review.* A motion to extend time to file a petition for review or petition for discretionary review must also specify:

(A) the court of appeals;

(B) the date of the court of appeals' judgment; and

(C) the case number and style of the case in the court of appeals; and

 (D) the date every motion for rehearing or en banc reconsideration was filed, and either the date and nature of the court of appeals' ruling on the motion, or that it remains pending.

(c) *Motions to postpone argument.* Unless all parties agree, or unless sufficient cause is apparent to the court, a motion to postpone argument of a case must be supported by sufficient cause.

TRAP 10.2

State v. Pilkinton, 7 S.W.3d 291, 293 (Tex.App.—Beaumont 1999, pet. ref'd). "The requirement of an affidavit or verification as a prerequisite for an evidentiary hearing has been judicially imposed. There is further support for the affidavit requirement in the [TRAPs], which require verification of motions requiring proof of facts not in the record. If a defendant's motion for new trial and supporting affidavit are sufficient, a hearing on the motion is mandatory if the motion raises matters that cannot be determined from the record. On the other hand, it is well-settled that a defendant is not entitled to an evidentiary hearing on an unsupported motion for new trial."

TRAP 11. AMICUS CURIAE BRIEFS

An appellate clerk may receive, but not file, an amicus curiae brief. But the court for good cause may refuse to consider the brief and order that it be returned. An amicus curiae brief must:

(a) comply with the briefing rules for parties;

(b) identify the person or entity on whose behalf the brief is tendered;

(c) disclose the source of any fee paid or to be paid for preparing the brief; and

(d) certify that copies have been served on all parties.

TRAP 12. DUTIES OF APPELLATE CLERK

12.1 Docketing the Case. On receiving a copy of the notice of appeal, the petition for review, the petition for discretionary review, the petition in an original proceeding, or a certified question, the appellate clerk must:

(a) endorse on the document the date of receipt;

(b) collect any filing fee;

(c) docket the case;

(d) notify all parties of the receipt of the document; and

(e) if the document filed is a petition for review filed in the Supreme Court, notify the court of appeals clerk of the filing of the petition.

12.2 Docket Numbers. The clerk must put the case's docket number on each item received in connection with the case and must put the docket number on the envelope in which the record is stored.

(a) *Numbering system.* Each case filed in a court of appeals must be assigned a docket number consisting of the following four parts, separated by hyphens:

(1) the number of the court of appeals district;

(2) the last two digits of the year in which the case is filed;

(3) the number assigned to the case; and

(4) the designation "CV" for a civil case or "CR" for a criminal case.

(b) *Numbering order.* Each case must be docketed in the order of its filing.

(c) *Multiple notices of appeal.* All notices of appeal filed in the same case must be given the same docket number.

(d) *Appeals not yet filed.* A motion relating to an appeal that has been perfected but not yet filed must be docketed and assigned a docket number that will also be assigned to the appeal when it is filed.

12.3 Custody of Papers. The clerk must safeguard the record and every other item filed in a case. If the record or any part of it or any other item is missing, the court will make an order for the replacement of the record or item that is just under the circumstances.

12.4 Withdrawing Papers. The clerk may permit the record or other filed item to be taken from the clerk's office at any time, on the following conditions:

(a) the clerk must have a receipt for the record or item;

(b) the clerk should make reasonable conditions to ensure that the withdrawn record or item is preserved and returned;

(c) the clerk may demand the return of the record or item at any time;

(d) after the case is submitted to the court and before the court's decision, the record cannot be withdrawn;

(e) after the court's decision, the losing party must be given priority in withdrawing the record;

(f) the clerk may not allow original documents filed under Rule 34.5(f) or original exhibits filed under Rule 34.6(g) to be taken from the clerk's office;

(g) if the court allows an original document or exhibit to be taken by a party and it is not returned, the court may accept the opposing party's statement concerning the document's or exhibit's nature and contents;

(h) withdrawn material must not be removed from the court's jurisdiction; and

(i) the court may, on the motion of any party or its own initiative, modify any of these conditions.

12.5 Clerk's Duty to Account. The clerk of an appellate court who receives money due another court must promptly pay the money to the court to whom it is due. This rule is enforceable by the Supreme Court.

12.6 Notices of Court's Judgments and Orders. In any proceeding, the clerk of an appellate court must promptly send a notice of any judgment, mandate, or other court order to all parties to the proceeding.

TRAP 13. COURT REPORTERS & COURT RECORDERS

13.1 Duties of Court Reporters and Recorders. The official court reporter or court recorder must:

(a) unless excused by agreement of the parties, attend court sessions and make a full record of the proceedings;

(b) take all exhibits offered in evidence during a proceeding and ensure that they are marked;

(c) file all exhibits with the trial court clerk after a proceeding ends;

(d) perform the duties prescribed by Rules 34.6 and 35; and

(e) perform other acts relating to the reporter's or recorder's official duties, as the trial court directs.

13.2 Additional Duties of Court Recorder. The official court recorder must also:

(a) ensure that the recording system functions properly throughout the proceeding and that a complete, clear, and transcribable recording is made;

TRAP 12

(b) make a detailed, legible log of all proceedings being recorded, showing:

(1) the number and style of the case before the court;

(2) the name of each person speaking;

(3) the event being recorded such as the voir dire, the opening statement, direct and cross-examinations, and bench conferences;

(4) each exhibit offered, admitted, or excluded;

(5) the time of day of each event; and

(6) the index number on the recording device showing where each event is recorded;

(c) after a proceeding ends, file with the clerk the original log;

(d) have the original recording stored to ensure that it is preserved and is accessible; and

(e) ensure that no one gains access to the original recording without the court's written order.

13.3 **Priorities of Reporters.** The trial court must help ensure that the court reporter's work is timely accomplished by setting work priorities. The reporter's duties relating to proceedings before the court take preference over other work.

13.4 **Report of Reporters.** To aid the trial court in setting priorities under 13.3, each court reporter must give the trial court a monthly written report showing the amount and nature of the business pending in the reporter's office. A copy of this report must be filed with the appellate clerk of each district in which the court sits.

13.5 **Appointing Deputy Reporter.** When the official court reporter is unable to perform the duties in 13.1 or 13.2 because of illness, press of official work, or unavoidable absence or disability, the trial court may designate a deputy reporter. If the court appoints a deputy reporter, that person must file with the trial court clerk a document stating:

(a) the date the deputy worked;

(b) the court in which the deputy worked; and

(c) the number and style of the case on which the deputy worked.

13.6 **Filing of Notes in a Criminal Case.** When a defendant is convicted and sentenced, or is granted deferred adjudication for a felony other than a state jail felony, and does not appeal, the court reporter must—within 20 days after the time to perfect the appeal has expired—file the untranscribed notes or the original recording of the proceeding with the trial court clerk. The trial court clerk need not retain the notes beyond 15 years of their filing date.

ANNOTATIONS

TRAP 13.1

Garza v. State, 212 S.W.3d 503, 505-06 (Tex.App.—Austin 2006, no pet.). "Some appellate courts have concluded that the failure of a court reporter to record portions of trial proceedings constitutes error because [TRAP] 13.1(a) requires the court reporter to make a record unless the parties agree otherwise. [¶] However, this Court has previously disagreed with this conclusion. [T]his Court noted that the requirement in rule 13.1(a) that a court reporter attend all court sessions unless the parties agree otherwise conflicts with the requirements of [Gov't Code §52.046]. [¶] Other courts have also concluded that rule 13.1(a) conflicts with §52.046(a) ... and, therefore, rule 13.1(a) yields to the requirements of §52.046. These courts further concluded that if a party wants to have a court reporter record the proceedings, the party must make that request under §52.046." *But see **Brossette**, below.*

Brossette v. State, 99 S.W.3d 277, 285-86 (Tex. App.—Texarkana 2003, pet. dism'd). The "failure of the court reporter to record the trial court's reading of the charge to the jury was error because it violated Rule 13.1.... However, this was not a constitutional violation, and there is no evidence that this influenced the jury's decision. None of Brossette's substantial rights have been affected. We must, therefore, disregard this error." *But see **Garza**, above.*

TRAP 13.2

In re G.M.S., 991 S.W.2d 923, 925 (Tex.App.—Fort Worth 1999, pet. denied). "[T]he State [argues] that because appellant acquiesced to having the trial taped and failed to ensure that the tape was working properly, his lack of due diligence negates his right to a new trial. However, rule 13.2 clearly states that it is the court recorder's duty.... Thus, it was not appellant's duty to make sure the recording was audible."

TRAP 14. RECORDING & BROADCASTING COURT PROCEEDINGS

14.1 **Recording and Broadcasting Permitted.** An appellate court may permit courtroom proceedings to be broadcast, televised, recorded, or photographed in accordance with this rule.

TRAP 14

14.2 Procedure.

(a) *Request to cover court proceeding.*

(1) A person wishing to broadcast, televise, record, or photograph a court proceeding must file with the court clerk a request to cover the proceeding. The request must state:

(A) the case style and number;

(B) the date and time when the proceeding is to begin;

(C) the name of the requesting person or organization;

(D) the type of coverage requested (for example, televising or photographing); and

(E) the type and extent of equipment to be used.

(2) A request to cover argument of a case must be filed no later than five days before the date the case is set for argument and must be served on all parties to the case. A request to cover any other proceeding must be filed no later than two days before the date when the proceeding is to begin.

(b) *Response.* Any party may file a response to the request. If the request is to cover argument, the response must be filed no later than two days before the date set for argument. If a party objects to coverage of the argument, the response should state the injury that will allegedly result from coverage.

(c) *Court may shorten time.* The court may, in the interest of justice, shorten the time for filing a document under this rule if no party or interested person would be unduly prejudiced.

(d) *Decision of court.* In deciding whether to allow coverage, the court may consider information known *ex parte* to the court. The court may allow, deny, limit, or terminate coverage for any reason the court considers necessary or appropriate, such as protecting the parties' rights or the dignity of the court and ensuring the orderly conduct of the proceedings.

14.3 Equipment and Personnel. The court may, among other things:

(a) require that a person seeking to cover a proceeding demonstrate or display the equipment that will be used;

(b) prohibit equipment that produces distracting sound or light;

(c) prohibit signal lights or devices showing when equipment is operating, or require their concealment;

(d) prohibit moving lights, flash attachments, or sudden lighting changes;

(e) require the use of the courtroom's existing video, audio, and lighting systems, if any;

(f) specify the placement of personnel and equipment;

(g) determine the number of cameras to be allowed in the courtroom; and

(h) require pooling of equipment if more than one person wishes to cover a proceeding.

14.4 Enforcement. The court may sanction a violation of this rule by measures that include barring a person or organization from access to future coverage of proceedings in that court for a defined period.

TRAP 15. ISSUANCE OF WRIT OR PROCESS BY APPELLATE COURT

15.1 In General.

(a) *Signature under seal.* A writ or process issuing from an appellate court must bear the court's seal and be signed by the clerk.

(b) *To whom directed; by whom served.* Unless a rule or statute provides otherwise, the writ or process must be directed to the person or court to be served. The writ or process may be served by the sheriff, constable, or other peace officer whose jurisdiction includes the county in which the person or court to be served may be found.

(c) *Return; lack of execution; simultaneous writs.* The writ or process must be returned to the issuing court according to the writ's direction. If the writ or process is not executed, the clerk may issue another writ or process if requested by the party who requested the former writ or process. At a party's request, the clerk may issue two or more writs simultaneously.

15.2 Appearance Without Service; Actual Knowledge. A party who appears in person or by attorney in an appellate court proceeding—or who has actual knowledge of the court's opinion, judgment, or order related to a writ or process—is bound by the opinion, judgment, or order to the same extent as if personally served under 15.1.

TRAP 16. DISQUALIFICATION OR RECUSAL OF APPELLATE JUDGES

16.1 Grounds for Disqualification. The grounds for disqualification of an appellate court justice or judge are determined by the Constitution and laws of Texas.

16.2 Grounds for Recusal. The grounds for recusal of an appellate court justice or judge are the same as those provided in the Rules of Civil Procedure. In addition, a justice or judge must recuse in a proceeding if it presents a material issue which the justice or judge participated in deciding while serving on another court in which the proceeding was pending.

16.3 Procedure for Recusal.

(a) *Motion.* A party may file a motion to recuse a justice or judge before whom the case is pending. The motion must be filed promptly after the party has reason to believe that the justice or judge should not participate in deciding the case.

(b) *Decision.* Before any further proceeding in the case, the challenged justice or judge must either remove himself or herself from all participation in the case or certify the matter to the entire court, which will decide the motion by a majority of the remaining judges sitting en banc. The challenged justice or judge must not sit with the remainder of the court to consider the motion as to him or her.

(c) *Appeal.* An order of recusal is not reviewable, but denial of a recusal motion is reviewable.

TRAP 17. COURT OF APPEALS UNABLE TO TAKE IMMEDIATE ACTION

17.1 Inability to Act. A court of appeals is unable to take immediate action if it cannot—within the time when action must be taken—assemble a panel because members of the court are ill, absent, or unavailable. A justice who is disqualified or recused is unavailable. A court of appeals' inability to act immediately may be established by certificate of the clerk, a member of the court, or a party's counsel, or by affidavit of a party.

17.2 Nearest Available Court of Appeals. If a court of appeals is unable to take immediate action, the nearest court of appeals that is able to take immediate action may do so with the same effect as the other court. The nearest court of appeals is the one whose courthouse is nearest—measured by a straight line—the courthouse of the trial court.

17.3 Further Proceedings. After acting or refusing to act, the nearest court of appeals must promptly send a copy of its order, and the original or a copy of any document presented to it, to the other court, which will conduct any further proceedings in the matter.

TRAP 18. MANDATE

18.1 Issuance. The clerk of the appellate court that rendered the judgment must issue a mandate in accordance with the judgment and send it to the clerk of the court to which it is directed and to all parties to the proceeding when one of the following periods expires:

(a) *In the court of appeals.*

(1) Ten days after the time has expired for filing a motion to extend time to file a petition for review or a petition for discretionary review if:

(A) no timely petition for review or petition for discretionary review has been filed;

(B) no timely filed motion to extend time to file a petition for review or petition for discretionary review is pending; and

(C) in a criminal case, the Court of Criminal Appeals has not granted review on its own initiative.

(2) Ten days after the time has expired for filing a motion to extend time to file a motion for rehearing of a denial, refusal, or dismissal of a petition for review, or a refusal or dismissal of a petition for discretionary review, if no timely filed motion for rehearing or motion to extend time is pending.

(b) *In the Supreme Court and the Court of Criminal Appeals.* Ten days after the time has expired for filing a motion to extend time to file a motion for rehearing if no timely filed motion for rehearing or motion to extend time is pending.

(c) *Agreement to issue.* The mandate may be issued earlier if the parties so agree, or for good cause on the motion of a party.

18.2 Stay of Mandate. A party may move to stay issuance of the mandate pending the United States Supreme Court's disposition of a petition for writ of certiorari. The motion must state the grounds for the petition and the circumstances requiring the stay. The appellate court authorized to issue the mandate may grant a stay if it finds that the grounds are substantial and that the petitioner or others would incur serious hardship from the mandate's issuance if the United States Supreme Court were later to reverse the judgment. In a criminal case, the stay will last for no more than 90 days, to permit the timely filing of a petition for writ of certiorari. After that period and others mentioned in this rule expire, the mandate will issue.

18.3 Trial Court Case Number. The mandate must state the trial court case number.

18.4 **Filing of Mandate.** The clerk receiving the mandate will file it with the case's other papers and note it on the docket.

18.5 **Costs.** The mandate will be issued without waiting for costs to be paid. If the Supreme Court declines to grant review, Supreme Court costs must be included in the court of appeals' mandate.

18.6 **Mandate in Accelerated Appeals.** The appellate court's judgment on an appeal from an interlocutory order takes effect when the mandate is issued. The court may issue the mandate with its judgment or delay the mandate until the appeal is finally disposed of. If the mandate is issued, any further proceeding in the trial court must conform to the mandate.

18.7 **Recall of Mandate.** If an appellate court vacates or modifies its judgment or order after issuing its mandate, the appellate clerk must promptly notify the clerk of the court to which the mandate was directed and all parties. The mandate will have no effect and a new mandate may be issued.

TRAP 19. PLENARY POWER OF THE COURTS OF APPEALS & EXPIRATION OF TERM

08 **19.1** **Plenary Power of Courts of Appeals.** A court of appeals' plenary power over its judgment expires:

(a) 60 days after judgment if no timely filed motion for rehearing or en banc reconsideration, or timely filed motion to extend time to file such a motion, is then pending; or

(b) 30 days after the court overrules all timely filed motions for rehearing or en banc reconsideration, and all timely filed motions to extend time to file such a motion.

19.2 **Plenary Power Continues After Petition Filed.** In a civil case, the court of appeals retains plenary power to vacate or modify its judgment during the periods prescribed in 19.1 even if a party has filed a petition for review in the Supreme Court.

19.3 **Proceedings After Plenary Power Expires.** After its plenary power expires, the court cannot vacate or modify its judgment. But the court may:

(a) correct a clerical error in its judgment or opinion;

(b) issue and recall its mandate as these rules provide;

(c) enforce or suspend enforcement of its judgment as these rules or applicable law provide;

(d) order or modify the amount and type of security required to suspend a judgment, and decide the sufficiency of the sureties, under Rule 24; and

(e) order its opinion published in accordance with Rule 47.

19.4 **Expiration of Term.** The expiration of the appellate court's term does not affect the court's plenary power or its jurisdiction over a case that is pending when the court's term expires.

TRAP 20. WHEN PARTY IS INDIGENT

08 **20.1** **Civil Cases.**

(a) *Establishing indigence.*

(1) *By certificate.* If the appellant proceeded in the trial court without advance payment of costs pursuant to a certificate under Texas Rule of Civil Procedure 145(c) confirming that the appellant was screened for eligibility to receive free legal services under income guidelines used by a program funded by Interest on Lawyers Trust Accounts or the Texas Access to Justice Foundation, an additional certificate may be filed in the appellate court confirming that the appellant was re-screened after rendition of the trial court's judgment and again found eligible under program guidelines. A party's affidavit of inability accompanied by the certificate may not be contested.

(2) *By affidavit.* A party who cannot pay the costs in an appellate court may proceed without advance payment of costs if:

(A) the party files an affidavit of indigence in compliance with this rule;

(B) the claim of indigence is not contestable, is not contested, or, if contested, the contest is not sustained by written order; and

(C) the party timely files a notice of appeal.

(b) *Contents of affidavit.* The affidavit of indigence must identify the party filing the affidavit and must state what amount of costs, if any, the party can pay. The affidavit must also contain complete information about:

(1) the nature and amount of the party's current employment income, government-entitlement income, and other income;

(2) the income of the party's spouse and whether that income is available to the party;

(3) real and personal property the party owns;

(4) cash the party holds and amounts on deposit that the party may withdraw;

(5) the party's other assets;

(6) the number and relationship to the party of any dependents;

(7) the nature and amount of the party's debts;

(8) the nature and amount of the party's monthly expenses;

(9) the party's ability to obtain a loan for court costs;

(10) whether an attorney is providing free legal services to the party without a contingent fee;

(11) whether an attorney has agreed to pay or advance court costs; and

(12) if applicable, the party's lack of the skill and access to equipment necessary to prepare the appendix, as required by Rule 38.5(d).

(c) *When and where affidavit filed.*

(1) *Appeals.* An appellant must file the affidavit of indigence in the trial court with or before the notice of appeal. The prior filing of an affidavit of indigence in the trial court pursuant to Texas Rule of Civil Procedure 145 does not meet the requirements of this rule, which requires a separate affidavit and proof of current indigence. An appellee who is required to pay part of the cost of preparation of the record under Rule 34.5(b)(3) or 34.6(c)(3) must file an affidavit of indigence in the trial court within 15 days after the date when the appellee becomes responsible for paying that cost.

(2) *Other proceedings.* In any other appellate court proceeding, a petitioner must file the affidavit of indigence in the court in which the proceeding is filed, with or before the document seeking relief. A respondent who requests preparation of a record in connection with an appellate court proceeding must file an affidavit of indigence in the appellate court within 15 days after the date when the respondent requests preparation of the record.

(3) *Extension of time.* The appellate court may extend the time to file an affidavit of indigence if, within 15 days after the deadline for filing the affidavit, the party files in the appellate court a motion complying with Rule 10.5(b). But the court may not dismiss the appeal or affirm the trial court's judgment on the ground that the appellant has failed to file an affidavit or a sufficient affidavit of indigence unless the court has first provided the appellant notice of the deficiency and a reasonable time to remedy it.

(d) *Duty of clerk.*

(1) *Trial court clerk.* If the affidavit of indigence is filed with the trial court clerk under (c)(1), the clerk must promptly send a copy of the affidavit to the appropriate court reporter.

(2) *Appellate court clerk.* If the affidavit of indigence is filed with the appellate court clerk and if the filing party is requesting the preparation of a record, the appellate court clerk must:

(A) send a copy of the affidavit to the trial court clerk and the appropriate court reporter; and

(B) send to the trial court clerk, the court reporter, and all parties, a notice stating the deadline for filing a contest to the affidavit of indigence.

(e) *Contest to affidavit.* The clerk, the court reporter, the court recorder, or any party may challenge an affidavit that is not accompanied by a TAJF certificate by filing—in the court in which the affidavit was filed—a contest to the affidavit. The contest must be filed on or before the date set by the clerk if the affidavit was filed in the appellate court, or within 10 days after the date when the affidavit was filed if the affidavit was filed in the trial court. The contest need not be sworn.

(f) *No contest filed.* Unless a contest is timely filed, no hearing will be conducted, the affidavit's allegations will be deemed true, and the party will be allowed to proceed without advance payment of costs.

(g) *Burden of proof.* If a contest is filed, the party who filed the affidavit of indigence must prove the affidavit's allegations. If the indigent party is incarcerated at the time the hearing on a contest is held, the affidavit must be considered as evidence and is sufficient to meet the indigent party's burden to present evidence without the indigent party's attending the hearing.

(h) *Decision in appellate court.* If the affidavit of indigence is filed in an appellate court and a contest is filed, the court may:

(1) conduct a hearing and decide the contest;

(2) decide the contest based on the affidavit and any other timely filed documents;

(3) request the written submission of additional evidence and, without conducting a hearing, decide the contest based on the evidence; or

(4) refer the matter to the trial court with instructions to hear evidence and grant the appropriate relief.

(i) *Hearing and decision in the trial court.*

(1) *Notice required.* If the affidavit of indigence is filed in the trial court and a contest is filed, or if the appellate court refers a contest to the trial court, the trial court must set a hearing and notify the parties and the appropriate court reporter of the setting.

(2) *Time for hearing.* The trial court must either conduct a hearing or sign an order extending the time to conduct a hearing:

(A) within 10 days after the contest was filed, if initially filed in the trial court; or

(B) within 10 days after the trial court received a contest referred from the appellate court.

(3) *Extension of time for hearing.* The time for conducting a hearing on the contest must not be extended for more than 20 days from the date the order is signed.

(4) *Time for written decision; effect.* Unless—within the period set for the hearing—the trial court signs an order sustaining the contest, the affidavit's allegations will be deemed true, and the party will be allowed to proceed without advance payment of costs.

(j) *Record to be prepared without prepayment.* If a party establishes indigence, the trial court clerk and the court reporter must prepare the appellate record without prepayment.

(k) *Partial payment of costs.* If the party can pay or give security for some of the costs, the court must order the party, in writing, to pay or give security, or both, to the extent of the party's ability. The court will allocate the payment among the officials to whom payment is due.

(l) *Later ability to pay.* If a party who has proceeded in the appellate court without having to pay all the costs is later able to pay some or all of the costs, the appellate court may order the party to pay costs to the extent of the party's ability.

(m) *Costs defined.* As used in this rule, *costs* means:

(1) a filing fee relating to the case in which the affidavit of inability is filed; and

(2) the charges for preparing the appellate record in that case.

20.2 Criminal Cases. Within the time for perfecting the appeal, an appellant who is unable to pay for the appellate record may, by motion and affidavit, ask the trial court to have the appellate record furnished without charge. If after hearing the motion the court finds that the appellant cannot pay or give security for the appellate record, the court must order the reporter to transcribe the proceedings. When the court certifies that the appellate record has been furnished to the appellant, the reporter must be paid from the general funds of the county in which the offense was committed, in the amount set by the trial court.

ANNOTATIONS

TRAP 20.2

Tuck v. State, 215 S.W.3d 411, 416 (Tex.Crim.App. 2007). "We hold that an inquiry into the reasonableness of a defendant's expenses is appropriate in order to adequately determine whether a defendant can pay or give security for an appellate record. ... If a defendant's own evidence proffered in support of a showing of indigence demonstrates unreasonable expenses, or expenses that are manifestly unreasonably high, that may serve as a basis in the record to support a trial court's conclusion that he is not indigent. [¶] However, the reasonableness of a defendant's expenses and financial obligations must be viewed in light of the totality of his financial situation and not in isolation. The fact that a defendant's income is less than his expenses does not create an automatic presumption that his expenses are unreasonable. ... A court cannot presume unreasonableness; some aspect of the record must support such a determination."

Whitehead v. State, 130 S.W.3d 866, 873-74 (Tex. Crim.App.2004). "The appellate rule authorizing a free appellate record also contains an oath requirement. Rule 20.2 provides that a defendant, within the time for perfecting an appeal, may request a free record by 'motion and affidavit.' As with appointment of counsel statute, the free record rule does not offer the option of ruling upon the motion itself. We conclude ... that only sworn allegations are to be considered in determining whether a defendant is entitled to a free record. We also hold that allegations in the motion to appoint counsel are not evidence for the purpose of appointing counsel or for obtaining a free record."

Ramadan v. State, 89 S.W.3d 744, 746 (Tex.App.— Houston [1st Dist.] 2002, no pet.). "Indigency determinations are made on a case-by-case basis, and it is clear that any attempt by a court to set rigid standards will not be accepted. The trial court must determine appellant's financial status at the time of appeal, not at the time of trial. Unless legally bound to pay, outside sources such as parents or relatives may not be considered by the trial court in the determination of indigency. [A]n appellant may not be deprived of a free record simply because the appellant was represented by retained counsel at trial."

SECTION TWO: APPEALS FROM TRIAL COURT JUDGMENTS & ORDERS

TRAP 21. NEW TRIALS IN CRIMINAL CASES

21.1 **Definitions.**

(a) *New trial* means the rehearing of a criminal action after the trial court has, on the defendant's motion, set aside a finding or verdict of guilt.

(b) *New trial on punishment* means a new hearing of the punishment stage of a criminal action after the trial court has, on the defendant's motion, set aside an assessment of punishment without setting aside a finding or verdict of guilt.

21.2 **When Motion for New Trial Required.** A motion for new trial is a prerequisite to presenting a point of error on appeal only when necessary to adduce facts not in the record.

21.3 **Grounds.** The defendant must be granted a new trial, or a new trial on punishment, for any of the following reasons:

(a) except in a misdemeanor case in which the maximum possible punishment is a fine, when the defendant has been unlawfully tried in absentia or has been denied counsel;

(b) when the court has misdirected the jury about the law or has committed some other material error likely to injure the defendant's rights;

(c) when the verdict has been decided by lot or in any manner other than a fair expression of the jurors' opinion;

(d) when a juror has been bribed to convict or has been guilty of any other corrupt conduct;

(e) when a material defense witness has been kept from court by force, threats, or fraud, or when evidence tending to establish the defendant's innocence has been intentionally destroyed or withheld, thus preventing its production at trial;

(f) when, after retiring to deliberate, the jury has received other evidence; when a juror has talked with anyone about the case; or when a juror became so intoxicated that his or her vote was probably influenced as a result;

(g) when the jury has engaged in such misconduct that the defendant did not receive a fair and impartial trial; or

(h) when the verdict is contrary to the law and the evidence.

21.4 **Time to File and Amend Motion.**

(a) *To file.* The defendant may file a motion for new trial before, but no later than 30 days after, the date when the trial court imposes or suspends sentence in open court.

(b) *To amend.* Within 30 days after the date when the trial court imposes or suspends sentence in open court but before the court overrules any preceding motion for new trial, a defendant may, without leave of court, file one or more amended motions for new trial.

21.5 **State May Controvert; Effect.** The State may oppose in writing any reason the defendant sets forth in the motion for new trial. The State's having opposed a motion for new trial does not affect a defendant's responsibilities under 21.6.

21.6 **Time to Present.** The defendant must present the motion for new trial to the trial court within 10 days of filing it, unless the trial court in its discretion permits it to be presented and heard within 75 days from the date when the court imposes or suspends sentence in open court.

21.7 **Types of Evidence Allowed at Hearing.** The court may receive evidence by affidavit or otherwise.

21.8 **Court's Ruling.**

(a) *Time to rule.* The court must rule on a motion for new trial within 75 days after imposing or suspending sentence in open court.

(b) *Ruling.* In ruling on a motion for new trial, the court may make oral or written findings of fact. The granting of a motion for new trial must be accomplished by written order. A docket entry does not constitute a written order.

(c) *Failure to rule.* A motion not timely ruled on by written order will be deemed denied when the period prescribed in (a) expires.

21.9 **Granting a New Trial.**

(a) A court must grant a new trial when it has found a meritorious ground for new trial, but a court must grant only a new trial on punishment when it has found a ground that affected only the assessment of punishment.

(b) Granting a new trial restores the case to its position before the former trial, including, at any party's option, arraignment or pretrial proceedings initiated by that party.

(c) Granting a new trial on punishment restores the case to its position after the defendant was found guilty. Unless the defendant, State, and trial court all agree to a change, punishment in a new trial shall be assessed in accordance with the defendant's original election under article 37.07, §2(b) of the Code of Criminal Procedure.

(d) A finding or verdict of guilt in the former trial must not be regarded as a presumption of guilt, nor may it be alluded to in the presence of the jury that hears the case on retrial of guilt. A finding of fact or an assessment of punishment in the former trial may not be alluded to in the presence of the jury that hears the case on retrial of punishment.

ANNOTATIONS

Generally

Murphy v. State, 223 S.W.3d 427, 429 (Tex.App.—Amarillo 2006, no pet.). "Given that 1) the trial court accepted the plea agreement and pronounced sentence upon appellant based on what it understood the terms to be and 2) defendant did not move for new trial or otherwise attempt to withdraw his plea, the trial court erred in *sua sponte* retracting its sentence and granting new trial."

TRAP 21.1

Garcia v. State, 29 S.W.3d 899, 900 (Tex.App.—Houston [14th Dist.] 2000, no pet.). "There can be no judgment in a deferred adjudication proceeding because there is no conviction. Similarly, there can be no imposition or suspension of sentence because no punishment is assessed. Because there is no finding or verdict of guilt, and no imposition or suspension of sentence, Rules 21.1 and 21.4 do not apply to a deferred adjudication proceeding."

TRAP 21.3

State v. Herndon, 215 S.W.3d 901, 909 (Tex.Crim. App.2007). "[A] trial court would not generally abuse its discretion in granting a motion for new trial if the defendant: (1) articulated a valid legal claim in his motion for new trial; (2) produced evidence or pointed to evidence in the trial record that substantiated his legal claim; and (3) showed prejudice to his substantial rights under the standards in [TRAP] 44.2…. The defendant need not establish reversible error as a matter of law before the trial court may exercise its discretion in granting a motion for new trial. On the other hand, trial courts do not have the discretion to grant a new trial unless the defendant demonstrates that his first trial was seriously flawed and that the flaws adversely affected his substantial rights to a fair trial."

Igo v. State, 210 S.W.3d 645, 646 (Tex.Crim.App. 2006). "When a defendant complains on appeal that the trial court erroneously denied a motion for new trial that alleged a claim of jury-charge error, is he entitled to have the underlying jury-charge error reviewed under a different harm standard than would have applied to that error absent the motion for new trial? We answer that question 'no.'"

Taylor v. State, 163 S.W.3d 277, 282 (Tex.App.—Austin 2005, pet. dism'd). "For over one hundred and thirty years, our trial courts have had the discretion to grant new trials in the interest of justice. Rule 21.3 … does not provide an exclusive list of the grounds for granting a new trial. The granting or denying of a motion for a new trial is within the sound discretion of the trial court."

Jennings v. State, 107 S.W.3d 85, 90 (Tex. App.—San Antonio 2003, no pet.). "To demonstrate jury misconduct, the defendant must show that (1) the misconduct occurred and (2) the misconduct resulted in harm to the movant. [¶] [Juror] recounts how she changed her vote of 'not guilty' to a vote of 'guilty' because of the jurors' agreement to be bound to vote in accordance with the longer of the two lists [of facts that tended to prove that defendant was either guilty or not guilty] and even though she still had reasonable doubts about Jennings' guilt. [¶] Because the uncontroverted evidence establishes juror misconduct under Rule 21.3(c), we hold the trial court abused its discretion in denying Jennings' motion for new trial."

TRAP 21.4

Cooks v. State, 240 S.W.3d 906, 907-08 (Tex.Crim. App.2007). "A defendant has 30 days to file a motion for new trial after the date that the trial court imposes or suspends sentence in open court. This case presents the question of whether this 30-day period of time is a 'critical stage' during which a defendant is constitutionally entitled to effective assistance of counsel in filing a motion for new trial. We decide that this period is a critical stage of a criminal proceeding, but that the deprivation of effective assistance of counsel is subject to an analysis for prejudice or harm."

State v. Moore, 225 S.W.3d 556, 558 (Tex.Crim.App. 2007). "We hold that Rule 21.4(b) does prohibit a defendant from filing an amended motion for new trial after the 30-day period prescribed, even *with* leave of court. We also hold, however, that this prohibition does not deprive the trial court of jurisdiction; nor does it deprive the trial court of the authority to rule on a tardy amendment to a timely motion for new trial, at least absent an objection from the State, at any time within the 75 days for ruling on a motion for new trial."

Bitterman v. State, 195 S.W.3d 777, 779 (Tex. App.—Waco 2006, pet. ref'd). "Bitterman timely filed his motion for new trial. [¶] Although [he] did not verify the motion or provide affidavits to support it, the court nevertheless heard the motion. Because the allegations of the motion could be determined from the trial record and did not require any additional evidence, the fact that [his] motion for new trial is not verified or supported by affidavit has no bearing on this issue."

Mercier v. State, 96 S.W.3d 560, 562 (Tex.App.— Fort Worth 2002, no pet.). "The fact that the new trial is based on newly discovered evidence has no impact on the appellate time table."

TRAP 21.6

Rozell v. State, 176 S.W.3d 228, 230 (Tex.Crim.App. 2005). "[A]ppellant argues that his motion [for new trial] was timely filed and presented to the trial court, was supported by affidavits, and raised matters that were not determinable from the record. He claims that all of the procedural requirements were met and that a hearing on the motion was mandatory. He believes that the court of appeals erred by creating a new requirement to obtain a hearing on a motion for new trial. [¶] The State argues that the appellant did not request a hearing, and therefore, he cannot complain now that

the trial court did not hold one. *At 231:* On the record before us in this case, we cannot conclude that the appellant's desire for a hearing was brought to the attention of the trial court. Nowhere in the motion did the appellant request a hearing. [¶] The record does not support the conclusion that the appellant presented a motion with a request for a hearing. Therefore, we hold that the error in failing to hold a hearing, if any, was not preserved for review."

Carranza v. State, 960 S.W.2d 76, 79 (Tex.Crim. App.1998). "'[P]resent' as used in [TRAP] 31(c)(1) [now 21.6] means the record must show the movant for a new trial sustained the burden of actually delivering the motion for new trial to the trial court or otherwise bringing the motion to the attention or actual notice of the trial court. This may be accomplished in several ways such as, for example, obtaining the trial court's ruling on a motion for new trial." *See also* **Musgrove v. State**, 960 S.W.2d 74, 75 (Tex.Crim.App.1998).

Butler v. State, 6 S.W.3d 636, 641 (Tex.App.— Houston [1st Dist.] 1999, pet. ref'd). "[I]t is clear that presentation [of the motion for new trial] to the court coordinator satisfies the presentment requirement of giving actual notice to the trial court."

TRAP 21.7

Holden v. State, 201 S.W.3d 761, 762 (Tex.Crim. App.2006). "The issue in this case is whether a trial court always errs by deciding a motion for new trial on the basis of affidavits when a party has requested a hearing. We hold that such a procedure is not always in error. [¶] In this case, the basis of the motion for new trial was ineffective assistance of trial counsel. *At 764:* We do not accept a *per se* rule that a trial court must hear live testimony whenever there is a factual dispute in affidavits and a party asks for testimony."

TRAP 21.8

Charles v. State, 146 S.W.3d 204, 210 (Tex.Crim. App.2004). "[W]e agree with the court of appeals that, in the context of the denial of a motion for new trial, '[a] deferential rather than de novo standard applies to our review of a trial court's determination of historical facts when that determination is based, as here, solely upon affidavits' regardless of whether the affidavits are controverted. We overrule appellant's second ground for review. *At 213:* We hold that, because the trial judge is prohibited from commenting on the evidence in ruling on a motion for new trial, reviewing courts may impute implicit factual findings that support the trial judge's ultimate ruling on that motion when such implicit factual findings are both reasonable and supported in the record."

Awadelkarien v. State, 974 S.W.2d 721, 728 (Tex. Crim.App.1998). "[A]n order granting or denying a motion for new trial may be freely rescinded so long as such action occurs within the 75 days provided by the rules (i.e., current Rule 21.8(a) & (c))…. However, after the 75-day period expires, an order granting or denying a new trial becomes 'final….'"

Stepan v. State, 244 S.W.3d 642, 646 (Tex.App.— Austin 2008, no pet.). "[I]t is apparent from the record that the trial court inadvertently signed the May 9 new trial order believing that it was signing an order granting defense counsel's motion to withdraw. We hold that because the May 9 order was signed as a result of clerical error rather than judicial error, the trial court was authorized to set it aside even after the time for acting on the motion for new trial had expired."

State v. Vinson, 6 S.W.3d 704, 705 (Tex.App.— Waco 1999, no pet.). "Each of the blanks [on order attached to motion for new trial] is appropriately filled in and the judge signed the order, but the word 'grants' is not circled nor is the word 'denies' scratched out. Thus, the order neither grants nor denies the motion for new trial. [¶] Because this cannot be said to be a written order granting the motion for new trial as required by Rule 21.8(b), the motion was overruled by operation of law on the 75th day."

TRAP 21.9

McNatt v. State, 188 S.W.3d 198, 204 (Tex.Crim. App.2006). "We conclude that the Court of Appeals erred in holding that the untimeliness of an enhancement allegation carries over to any retrial of the punishment proceedings. As long as the enhancement is not barred by other considerations (e.g. prosecutorial vindictiveness), the State is free to use a prior conviction for enhancement if proper notice of its intent to do so is conveyed with respect to the new punishment hearing."

TRAP 22. ARREST OF JUDGMENT IN CRIMINAL CASES

22.1 **Definition.** *Motion in arrest of judgment* means a defendant's oral or written suggestion that, for reasons stated in the motion, the judgment rendered against the defendant was contrary to law. Such a motion is made in the trial court.

22.2 **Grounds.** The motion may be based on any of the following grounds:

(a) that the indictment or information is subject to an exception on substantive grounds;

(b) that in relation to the indictment or information a verdict is substantively defective; or

(c) that the judgment is invalid for some other reason.

22.3 **Time to File Motion.** A defendant may file a motion in arrest of judgment before, but no later than 30 days after, the date when the trial court imposes or suspends sentence in open court.

22.4 **Court's Ruling.**

(a) *Time to rule; form of ruling.* The court must rule on a motion in arrest of judgment within 75 days after imposing or suspending sentence in open court. The ruling may be oral or in writing.

(b) *Failure to rule.* A motion not timely ruled on will be deemed denied when the period prescribed in (a) expires.

22.5 **Effect of Denying.** For purposes of the defendant's giving notice of appeal, an order denying a motion in arrest of judgment will be considered an order denying a motion for new trial.

22.6 **Effect of Granting.**

(a) *Defendant restored.* If judgment is arrested, the defendant is restored to the position that he or she had before the indictment or information was presented.

(b) *Defendant discharged or remanded.* If the judgment is arrested, the defendant will be discharged. But the trial court may remand the defendant to custody or fix bail if the court determines, from the evidence adduced at trial, that the defendant may be convicted on a proper indictment or information, or on a proper verdict in relation to the indictment or information.

TRAP 23. NUNC PRO TUNC PROCEEDINGS IN CRIMINAL CASES

23.1 **Judgment and Sentence.** Unless the trial court has granted a new trial or arrested the judgment, or unless the defendant has appealed, a failure to render judgment and pronounce sentence may be corrected at any time by the court's doing so.

23.2 **Credit on Sentence.** When sentence is pronounced, the trial court must give the defendant credit on that sentence for:

(a) all time the defendant has been confined since the time when judgment and sentence should have been entered and pronounced; and

(b) all time between the defendant's arrest and confinement to the time when judgment and sentence should have been entered and pronounced.

TRAP 23.2

Ex parte Ybarra, 149 S.W.3d 147, 148 (Tex.Crim. App.2004). "The trial court is required to grant the Applicant pre-sentence jail time credit when sentence is pronounced. In the event the court fails to award such credit at the time the sentence is imposed, the trial court has the authority to correct the judgment to reflect the appropriate time credit by *nunc pro tunc order* and should do so. [M]atters which may be raised and resolved by *nunc pro tunc* proceedings should not be considered by way of writ of habeas corpus."

TRAP 24. SUSPENSION OF ENFORCEMENT OF JUDGMENT PENDING APPEAL IN CIVIL CASES

24.1 **Suspension of Enforcement.**

(a) *Methods.* Unless the law or these rules provide otherwise, a judgment debtor may supersede the judgment by:

(1) filing with the trial court clerk a written agreement with the judgment creditor for suspending enforcement of the judgment;

(2) filing with the trial court clerk a good and sufficient bond;

(3) making a deposit with the trial court clerk in lieu of a bond; or

(4) providing alternate security ordered by the court.

(b) *Bonds.*

(1) A bond must be:

(A) in the amount required by 24.2;

(B) payable to the judgment creditor;

(C) signed by the judgment debtor or the debtor's agent;

(D) signed by a sufficient surety or sureties as obligors; and

(E) conditioned as required by (d).

(2) To be effective a bond must be approved by the trial court clerk. On motion of any party, the trial court will review the bond.

(c) *Deposit in lieu of bond.*

(1) *Types of deposits.* Instead of filing a surety bond, a party may deposit with the trial court clerk:

(A) cash;

(B) a cashier's check payable to the clerk, drawn on any federally insured and federally or state-chartered bank or savings-and-loan association; or

(C) with leave of court, a negotiable obligation of the federal government or of any federally insured and federally or state-chartered bank or savings-and-loan association.

(2) *Amount of deposit.* The deposit must be in the amount required by 24.2.

(3) *Clerk's duties.* The clerk must promptly deposit any cash or a cashier's check in accordance with law. The clerk must hold the deposit until the conditions of liability in (d) are extinguished. The clerk must then release any remaining funds in the deposit to the judgment debtor.

(d) *Conditions of liability.* The surety or sureties on a bond, any deposit in lieu of a bond, or any alternate security ordered by the court is subject to liability for all damages and costs that may be awarded against the debtor—up to the amount of the bond, deposit, or security—if:

(1) the debtor does not perfect an appeal or the debtor's appeal is dismissed, and the debtor does not perform the trial court's judgment;

(2) the debtor does not perform an adverse judgment final on appeal; or

(3) the judgment is for the recovery of an interest in real or personal property, and the debtor does not pay the creditor the value of the property interest's rent or revenue during the pendency of the appeal.

(e) *Orders of trial court.* The trial court may make any order necessary to adequately protect the judgment creditor against loss or damage that the appeal might cause.

(f) *Effect of supersedeas.* Enforcement of a judgment must be suspended if the judgment is superseded. Enforcement begun before the judgment is superseded must cease when the judgment is superseded. If execution has been issued, the clerk will promptly issue a writ of supersedeas.

24.2 **Amount of Bond, Deposit, or Security.**

(a) *Type of judgment.*

(1) *For recovery of money.* When the judgment is for money, the amount of the bond, deposit, or security must equal the sum of compensatory damages awarded in the judgment, interest for the estimated duration of the appeal, and costs awarded in the judgment. But the amount must not exceed the lesser of:

(A) 50 percent of the judgment debtor's current net worth; or

(B) 25 million dollars.

(2) *For recovery of property.* When the judgment is for the recovery of an interest in real or personal property, the trial court will determine the type of security that the judgment debtor must post. The amount of that security must be at least:

(A) the value of the property interest's rent or revenue, if the property interest is real; or

(B) the value of the property interest on the date when the court rendered judgment, if the property interest is personal.

(3) *Other judgment.* When the judgment is for something other than money or an interest in property, the trial court must set the amount and type of security that the judgment debtor must post. The security must adequately protect the judgment creditor against loss or damage that the appeal might cause. But the trial court may decline to permit the judgment to be superseded if the judgment creditor posts security ordered by the trial court in an amount and type that will secure the judgment debtor against any loss or damage caused by the relief granted the judgment creditor if an appellate court determines, on final disposition, that that relief was improper.

(4) *Conservatorship or custody.* When the judgment involves the conservatorship or custody of a minor or other person under legal disability, enforcement of the judgment will not be suspended, with or without security, unless ordered by the trial court. But upon a proper showing, the appellate court may suspend enforcement of the judgment with or without security.

(5) *For a governmental entity.* When a judgment in favor of a governmental entity in its governmental capacity is one in which the entity has no pecuniary interest, the trial court must determine whether to suspend enforcement, with or without security, taking into account the harm that is likely to result to the judgment debtor if enforcement is not suspended, and the harm that is likely to result to others if enforcement is suspended. The appellate court may review the trial court's determination and suspend enforcement of the judgment, with or without security, or refuse to suspend the judgment. If security is required, recovery is limited to the governmental entity's actual damages resulting from suspension of the judgment.

(b) *Lesser amount.* The trial court must lower the amount of security required by (a) to an amount that will not cause the judgment debtor substantial economic harm if, after notice to all parties and a hearing, the court finds that posting a bond, deposit, or security in the amount required by (a) is likely to cause the judgment debtor substantial economic harm.

 (c) *Determination of net worth.*

(1) *Judgment debtor's affidavit required; contents; prima facie evidence.* A judgment debtor who provides a bond, deposit, or security under (a)(1)(A) in an amount based on the debtor's net worth must simultaneously file with the trial court clerk an affidavit that states the debtor's net worth and states complete, detailed information concerning the debtor's assets and liabilities from which net worth can be ascertained. An affidavit that meets these requirements is prima facie evidence of the debtor's net worth for the purpose of establishing the amount of the bond, deposit, or security required to suspend enforcement of the judgment. A trial court clerk must receive and file a net-worth affidavit tendered for filing by a judgment debtor.

(2) *Contest; discovery.* A judgment creditor may file a contest to the debtor's claimed net worth. The contest need not be sworn. The creditor may conduct reasonable discovery concerning the judgment debtor's net worth.

(3) *Hearing; burden of proof; findings; additional security.* The trial court must hear a judgment creditor's contest of the judgment debtor's claimed net worth promptly after any discovery has been completed. The judgment debtor has the burden of proving net worth. The trial court must issue an order that states the debtor's net worth and states with particularity the factual basis for that determination. If the trial court orders additional or other security to supersede the judgment, the enforcement of the judgment will be suspended for twenty days after the trial court's order. If the judgment debtor does not comply with the order within that period, the judgment may be enforced against the judgment debtor.

(d) *Injunction.* The trial court may enjoin the judgment debtor from dissipating or transferring assets to avoid satisfaction of the judgment, but the trial court may not make any order that interferes with the judgment debtor's use, transfer, conveyance, or dissipation of assets in the normal course of business.

24.3 **Continuing Trial Court Jurisdiction; Duties of Judgment Debtor.**

(a) *Continuing jurisdiction.* Even after the trial court's plenary power expires, the trial court has continuing jurisdiction to do the following:

(1) order the amount and type of security and decide the sufficiency of sureties; and

(2) if circumstances change, modify the amount or type of security required to continue the suspension of a judgment's execution.

(b) *Duties of judgment debtor.* If, after jurisdiction attaches in an appellate court, the trial court orders or modifies the security or decides the sufficiency of sureties, the judgment debtor must notify the appellate court of the trial court's action.

24.4 **Appellate Review.**

 (a) *Motions; review.* A party may seek review of the trial court's ruling by motion filed in the court of appeals with jurisdiction or potential jurisdiction over the appeal from the judgment in the case. A party may seek review of the court of appeals' ruling on the motion by petition for writ of mandamus in the Supreme Court. The appellate court may review:

(1) the sufficiency or excessiveness of the amount of security, but when the judgment is for money, the appellate court must not modify the amount of security to exceed the limits imposed by Rule 24.2(a)(1);

(2) the sureties on any bond;

(3) the type of security;

(4) the determination whether to permit suspension of enforcement; and

(5) the trial court's exercise of discretion under Rule 24.3(a).

(b) *Grounds of review.* Review may be based both on conditions as they existed at the time the trial court signed an order and on changes in those conditions afterward.

(c) *Temporary orders.* The appellate court may issue any temporary orders necessary to preserve the parties' rights.

(d) *Action by appellate court.* The motion must be heard at the earliest practicable time. The appellate court may require that the amount of a bond, deposit, or other security be increased or decreased, and that another bond, deposit, or security be provided and approved by the trial court clerk. The appellate court may require other changes in the trial court order. The appellate court may remand to the trial court for entry of findings of fact or for the taking of evidence.

(e) *Effect of ruling.* If the appellate court orders additional or other security to supersede the judgment, enforcement will be suspended for 20 days after the appellate court's order. If the judgment debtor does not comply with the order within that period, the judgment may be enforced. When any additional bond, deposit, or security has been filed, the trial court clerk must notify the appellate court. The posting of additional security will not release the previously posted security or affect any alternative security arrangements that the judgment debtor previously made unless specifically ordered by the appellate court.

TRAP 25. PERFECTING APPEAL

25.1 Civil Cases.

(a) *Notice of appeal.* An appeal is perfected when a written notice of appeal is filed with the trial court clerk. If a notice of appeal is mistakenly filed with the appellate court, the notice is deemed to have been filed the same day with the trial court clerk, and the appellate clerk must immediately send the trial court clerk a copy of the notice.

(b) *Jurisdiction of appellate court.* The filing of a notice of appeal by any party invokes the appellate court's jurisdiction over all parties to the trial court's judgment or order appealed from. Any party's failure to take any other step required by these rules, including the failure of another party to perfect an appeal under (c), does not deprive the appellate court of jurisdiction but is ground only for the appellate court to act appropriately, including dismissing the appeal.

(c) *Who must file notice.* A party who seeks to alter the trial court's judgment or other appealable order must file a notice of appeal. Parties whose interests are aligned may file a joint notice of appeal. The appellate court may not grant a party who does not file a notice of appeal more favorable relief than did the trial court except for just cause.

(d) *Contents of notice.* The notice of appeal must:

(1) identify the trial court and state the case's trial court number and style;

(2) state the date of the judgment or order appealed from;

(3) state that the party desires to appeal;

(4) state the court to which the appeal is taken unless the appeal is to either the First or Fourteenth Court of Appeals, in which case the notice must state that the appeal is to either of those courts;

(5) state the name of each party filing the notice;

(6) in an accelerated appeal, state that the appeal is accelerated; and

(7) in a restricted appeal:

(A) state that the appellant is a party affected by the trial court's judgment but did not participate—either in person or through counsel—in the hearing that resulted in the judgment complained of;

(B) state that the appellant did not timely file either a postjudgment motion, request for findings of fact and conclusions of law, or notice of appeal; and

(C) be verified by the appellant if the appellant does not have counsel.

(e) *Service of notice; copy filed with appellate court.* The notice of appeal must be served on all parties to the trial court's final judgment or, in an interlocutory appeal, on all parties to the trial court proceeding. A copy of the notice of appeal must be filed with the appellate court clerk.

(f) *Amending the notice.* An amended notice of appeal correcting a defect or omission in an earlier filed notice may be filed in the appellate court at any time before the appellant's brief is filed. The amended notice is subject to being struck for cause on the motion of any party affected by the amended notice. After the appellant's brief is filed, the notice may be amended only on leave of the appellate court and on such terms as the court may prescribe.

(g) *Enforcement of judgment not suspended by appeal.* The filing of a notice of appeal does not suspend enforcement of the judgment. Enforcement of the judgment may proceed unless:

(1) the judgment is superseded in accordance with Rule 24, or

(2) the appellant is entitled to supersede the judgment without security by filing a notice of appeal.

25.2 **Criminal Cases.**

(a) *Rights to appeal.*

(1) *Of the State.* The State is entitled to appeal a court's order in a criminal case as provided by Code of Criminal Procedure article 44.01.

(2) *Of the defendant.* A defendant in a criminal case has the right of appeal under Code of Criminal Procedure article 44.02 and these rules. The trial court shall enter a certification of the defendant's right of appeal each time it enters a judgment of guilt or other appealable order. In a plea bargain case—that is, a case in which a defendant's plea was guilty or nolo contendere and the punishment did not exceed the punishment recommended by the prosecutor and agreed to by the defendant—a defendant may appeal only:

(A) those matters that were raised by written motion filed and ruled on before trial, or

(B) after getting the trial court's permission to appeal.

 (b) *Perfection of appeal.* In a criminal case, appeal is perfected by timely filing a sufficient notice of appeal. In a death-penalty case it is unnecessary to file a notice of appeal, but, in every death-penalty case, the clerk of the trial court shall file a notice of conviction with the Court of Criminal Appeals within thirty days after the defendant is sentenced to death.

(c) *Form and sufficiency of notice.*

(1) Notice must be given in writing and filed with the trial court clerk. If the notice of appeal is received in the court of appeals, the clerk of that court shall immediately record on the notice the date that it was received and send the notice to the trial court clerk.

(2) Notice is sufficient if it shows the party's desire to appeal from the judgment or other appealable order, and, if the State is the appellant, the notice complies with Code of Criminal Procedure article 44.01.

(d) *Certification of defendant's right of appeal.* If the defendant is the appellant, the record must include the trial court's certification of the defendant's right of appeal under Rule 25.2(a)(2). The certification shall include a notice that the defendant has been informed of his rights concerning an appeal, as well as any right to file a *pro se* petition for discretionary review. This notification shall be signed by the defendant, with a copy given to him. The certification should be part of the record when notice is filed, but may be added by timely amendment or supplementation under this rule or Rule 34.5(c)(1) or Rule 37.1 or by order of the appellate court under Rule 34.5(c)(2). The appeal must be dismissed if a certification that shows the defendant has the right of appeal has not been made part of the record under these rules.

(e) *Clerk's duties.* The trial court clerk must note on the copies of the notice of appeal and the trial court's certification of the defendant's right of appeal the case number and the date when each was filed. The clerk must then immediately send one copy of each to the clerk of the appropriate court of appeals and, if the defendant is the appellant, one copy of each to the State's attorney.

(f) *Amending the notice or certification.* An amended notice of appeal or trial court's certification of the defendant's right of appeal correcting a defect or omission in an earlier filed notice or certification, including a defect in the notification of the defendant's appellate rights, may be filed in the appellate court in accordance with Rule 37.1, or at any time before the appealing party's brief is filed if the court of appeals has not used Rule 37.1. The amended notice or certification is subject to being struck for cause on the motion of any party affected by the amended notice or certification. After the appealing party's brief is filed, the notice or certification may be amended only on leave of the appellate court and on such terms as the court may prescribe.

(g) *Effect of appeal.* Once the record has been filed in the appellate court, all further proceedings in the trial court—except as provided otherwise by law or by these rules—will be suspended until the trial court receives the appellate-court mandate.

(h) *Advice of right of appeal.* When a court enters a judgment or other appealable order and the defendant has a right of appeal, the court (orally or in writing) shall advise the defendant of his right of appeal and of the requirements for timely filing a sufficient notice of appeal.

ANNOTATIONS

Generally

Rankin v. State, 46 S.W.3d 899, 901 (Tex.Crim.App. 2001). "[W]hether entered with or without an agreed recommendation of punishment by the State, a valid plea of guilty or nolo contendere waives or forfeits the right to appeal a claim of error only when the judgment of guilt was rendered independent of, and is not supported by, the error." (Internal quotes omitted.)

Delatorre v. State, 957 S.W.2d 145, 149 (Tex. App.—Austin 1997, pet. ref'd). "A criminal defendant may waive many rights he enjoys, including the right to appeal. A written or oral waiver prevents a defendant from appealing as long as the waiver was made knowingly and intelligently *and* with certainty as to what punishment would be assessed. [¶] A waiver may be premature if made at a time when the defendant had no way of knowing with certainty the punishment to be assessed. [D] voluntarily waived his right to appeal with full knowledge of his sentence."

TRAP 25.2(a)

Chavez v. State, 183 S.W.3d 675, 680 (Tex.Crim. App.2006). "Rule 25.2(a)(2) provides that a defendant may appeal only matters that were raised by written motion filed and ruled on before trial or after getting the trial court's permission to appeal. Thus, if a jurisdictional issue were raised by written motion filed and ruled on before trial, or the trial court granted permission to appeal such an issue, a defendant who plea-bargained would have a right to appeal that issue, provided the appeal is properly perfected pursuant to Rule 25.2(b)." *See also* ***Griffin v. State***, 145 S.W.3d 645, 649 (Tex.Crim.App.2004).

Hargesheimer v. State, 182 S.W.3d 906, 913 (Tex. Crim.App.2006). "[I]n a plea-bargain case for deferred adjudication community supervision, the plea bargain is complete at the time the defendant enters his plea of guilty in exchange for deferred adjudication community supervision. Rule 25.2(a)(2) will restrict appeal only when the defendant appeals his placement on deferred adjudication community supervision pursuant to the original plea. Under this circumstance, the trial judge certifying the defendant's right of appeal may designate the case on the certification form as 'a plea-bargain case, and the defendant has NO right of appeal.' It is important to note, however, that if the defendant filed written motions that were ruled on before his placement on deferred adjudication community supervision pursuant to 25.2(a)(2)(A), or obtained the permission of the trial court for the appeal of his placement on deferred adjudication community supervision pursuant to Rule 25.2(a)(2)(B), he still has the right of appeal." *See also* **Kirtley v. State**, 56 S.W.3d 48, 51-52 (Tex.Crim.App.2001); **Vidaurri v. State**, 49 S.W.3d 880, 885 (Tex.Crim.App.2001) (deprivation of separate punishment hearing).

Dears v. State, 154 S.W.3d 610, 613 (Tex.Crim.App. 2005). "The Court of Appeals misapplied Rule 25.2(a)(2). The rule refers only to plea bargains with regard to guilty pleas, not pleas of true on revocation motions. Regardless of whether a court feels that a defendant should be 'bound' by an agreement on a plea of true, the plain language of Rule 25.2(a)(2) does not contemplate that situation."

Willis v. State, 121 S.W.3d 400, 403 (Tex.Crim.App. 2003). "We ... hold that the trial court's subsequent handwritten permission to appeal controls over a defendant's previous waiver of the right to appeal, allowing the defendant to appeal despite the boilerplate waiver."

Shankle v. State, 119 S.W.3d 808, 809 (Tex.Crim. App.2003). "When a defendant pleads guilty to one offense pursuant to a plea-bargain agreement by which the State consented to an unadjudicated offense's being taken into account in assessing punishment, is the sentence for the offense a 'punishment recommended by the prosecutor' for purposes of the rule that limits the right of plea-bargainers to appeal? We hold that it is." Held: D could not appeal the plea bargain.

Cooper v. State, 45 S.W.3d 77, 81 (Tex.Crim.App. 2001). "When we actually consider the issue of whether voluntariness of a guilty plea may be raised on appeal from a plea-bargained, felony conviction, we find that the answer must be that it may not. *At 82:* [M]eritorious claims of involuntary pleas may be raised by other procedures.... These procedures are not only adequate to resolve claims of involuntary pleas, but they are superior to appeal in that the claim may be supported by information from sources broader than the appellate record."

Sankey v. State, 3 S.W.3d 43, 44 (Tex.Crim.App. 1999). TRAP 25.2 limits "a court of appeals' jurisdiction in plea bargain cases. [¶] But this rule has nothing to do with the claim that the appellate record has been lost or destroyed. The lack of an appellate record is something which is not even apparent at the time the notice of appeal was filed. ... The content of the notice of appeal is irrelevant in considering this claim."

Feagin v. State, 967 S.W.2d 417, 419 (Tex.Crim. App.1998). "The restrictions of [TRAP 25.2(a)(2)] apply to appeals attacking the propriety of the defendant's conviction. The restrictions of the rule also apply to a defendant's appeal of an order deferring adjudication of guilt. [TRAP 25.2(a)(2)] is, however, inapplicable to appeals attacking the propriety of orders revoking probation. [¶] In the present case, appellant's appeal was limited to a single issue which was unrelated to her conviction, i.e., whether the trial court erred in denying her motion to dismiss the revocation hearing because the State had failed to use due diligence in apprehending her. The court of appeals properly exercised jurisdiction over appellant's appeal. And appellant properly sought a general appeal from the trial court's order revoking probation." *See also* **Marcum v. State**, 983 S.W.2d 762, 765 (Tex.App.—Houston [14th Dist.] 1998, pet. ref'd).

Rodriguez v. State, 153 S.W.3d 245, 248 (Tex. App.—El Paso 2004, no pet.). "We conclude that the restrictions of Rule 25.2(a)(2) do not apply to an appeal from the denial of post-conviction DNA testing."

State v. Gutierrez, 143 S.W.3d 829, 831 (Tex. App.—Corpus Christi 2004, no pet.). "The filing of a notice of appeal simply invokes appellate jurisdiction. ... The notice of appeal does not divest the trial court of jurisdiction to hear, consider, and rule on a timely filed motion for new trial. The filing of the appellate record, not the notice of appeal, severs the trial court's jurisdiction to adjudicate the case."

TRAP 25.2(b)

Strong v. State, 87 S.W.3d 206 (Tex.App.—Dallas 2002, pet. ref'd). Held: The State must file a TRAP 25.2(a), now 25.2(b), notice of appeal when it appeals under CCP art. 44.01(c). *But see* **Mizell v. State**, 70 S.W.3d 156, 163 (Tex.App.—San Antonio 2001), *aff'd*, 119 S.W.3d 804 (Tex.Crim.App.2003).

TRAP 25.2(c)

Douglas v. State, 987 S.W.2d 605, 605 (Tex.App.— Houston [1st Dist.] 1999, no pet.). "We are without jurisdiction to entertain this appeal. Appellant was sentenced by the trial judge on June 10, 1998. No motion for new trial was filed. The deadline for filing notice of appeal was July 10, 1998. Appellant mailed a pro se notice of appeal, postmarked July 3, 1998, to the Fourteenth Court of Appeals. According to [TRAP] 25.2(b)(1) [now 25.2(c)(1)], notice of appeal must be filed with the trial court clerk. The notice of appeal was not filed in the trial court until July 14, 1998, four days after it was due."

TRAP 25.2(d)

Ex parte Tarango, 116 S.W.3d 201, 203 (Tex. App.—El Paso 2003, no pet.). "Because a misdemeanor post-conviction writ of habeas corpus proceeding is an appealable criminal action within the meaning of [CCP art.] 44.02 and the order denying habeas corpus relief is an appealable order within the meaning of [TRAP] 25.2(a)(2), we conclude that the certification requirement of Rule 25.2(d) applies in the instant appeal."

TRAP 25.2(e)

Stansberry v. State, 239 S.W.3d 260, 264 (Tex. Crim.App.2007). "A timely tendered notice of appeal vests an intermediate appellate court with jurisdiction to consider the merits of an appeal. The appellant timely presented his notice of appeal into the clerk's custody for filing and thereby preserved his right to appeal. The subsequent clerical error did not divest the appellate court of jurisdiction or prejudice the appellant's right to appeal."

In re Swarthout, 982 S.W.2d 92, 92 (Tex.App.— Houston [1st Dist.] 1998, orig. proceeding). Even though the trial court denied D permission to appeal, "the trial court clerk had a ministerial duty to forward the notice of appeal to the appropriate court of appeals. When the trial court clerk failed to do so, and this Court became aware of the failure, we ordered a copy of the notice of appeal. Therefrom, we determined relator had timely filed notice of appeal and he is therefore entitled to appeal."

TRAP 25.2(f)

Few v. State, 230 S.W.3d 184, 187 (Tex.Crim.App. 2007). "The court of appeals concluded that it did not have jurisdiction over this case because appellant had mistakenly written the wrong cause number on his notice of appeal just as the trial court had mistakenly written the wrong cause number on his certification notice. For judges, defendants, and prosecutors, to err is human, but to repair is now possible. The [TRAPs] were amended in 2002 to prevent trivial, repairable mistakes

or defects from divesting appellate courts of the jurisdiction to consider the merits of both State and defense appeals in criminal cases. Defective notices of appeal may now be amended 'at any time before the appealing party's brief is filed[.]'"

TRAP 25.2(g)

Berry v. State, 995 S.W.2d 699, 700-01 (Tex.Crim. App.1999). "In the case at bar, the trial record was received by the court of appeals on June 20, 1997. The trial court made the supplemental findings of fact and conclusions of law on August 19, 1997. Because the supplemental findings of the trial court were made after the trial record was received by the court of appeals, the trial court was without jurisdiction to make the supplemental Findings of Fact and Conclusions of Law. The trial court's findings of fact are thus null and void, and should not have been considered by the court of appeals."

Taylor v. State, 163 S.W.3d 277, 279 (Tex.App.— Austin 2005, pet. dism'd). "On October 20, 2003, appellant filed a notice of appeal followed by a motion for new trial on November 6, 2003, both documents being filed within the thirty-day periods required. The record reflects and the trial court acknowledged that the motion for new trial was timely filed and presented to the court on November 6, 2003, and that a hearing was set on the motion for December 15, 2003, within the seventy-five day period for hearing motions for new trials. [¶] Six days later, on November 12, 2003, the court reporter's record was filed in [the Court of Appeals] followed by the filing ... of the clerk's record on November 21, 2003. [¶] On December 15, 2003, when the trial court called for a hearing on the timely filed and presented motion for new trial within the 75-day period, the State objected on the basis that the trial court had lost jurisdiction as the appellate record had been filed in this Court. The trial court sustained the State's objection. *At 282:* Appellant had a right to have his timely filed motion for new trial heard. The trial court clerk and the court reporter forwarded their records to this Court without regard to or without being aware of the pending motion for a new trial. [¶] Under these circumstances, we do not interpret the jurisdictional bar of Rule 25.2(g) to foreclose the trial court's consideration of a timely filed motion for new trial."

TRAP 26. TIME TO PERFECT APPEAL

26.1 **Civil Cases.** The notice of appeal must be filed within 30 days after the judgment is signed, except as follows:

TRAP 26

(a) the notice of appeal must be filed within 90 days after the judgment is signed if any party timely files:

(1) a motion for new trial;

(2) a motion to modify the judgment;

(3) a motion to reinstate under Texas Rule of Civil Procedure 165a; or

(4) a request for findings of fact and conclusions of law if findings and conclusions either are required by the Rules of Civil Procedure or, if not required, could properly be considered by the appellate court;

(b) in an accelerated appeal, the notice of appeal must be filed within 20 days after the judgment or order is signed;

(c) in a restricted appeal, the notice of appeal must be filed within six months after the judgment or order is signed; and

(d) if any party timely files a notice of appeal, another party may file a notice of appeal within the applicable period stated above or 14 days after the first filed notice of appeal, whichever is later.

26.2 **Criminal Cases.**

(a) *By the defendant.* The notice of appeal must be filed:

(1) within 30 days after the day sentence is imposed or suspended in open court, or after the day the trial court enters an appealable order; or

(2) within 90 days after the day sentence is imposed or suspended in open court if the defendant timely files a motion for new trial.

08 **(b)** *By the State.* The notice of appeal must be filed within 20 days after the day the trial court enters the order, ruling, or sentence to be appealed.

26.3 **Extension of Time.** The appellate court may extend the time to file the notice of appeal if, within 15 days after the deadline for filing the notice of appeal, the party:

(a) files in the trial court the notice of appeal; and

(b) files in the appellate court a motion complying with Rule 10.5(b).

ANNOTATIONS

TRAP 26.2

Bailey v. State, 160 S.W.3d 11, 16 (Tex.Crim.App. 2004). "[A]ppellant was not ordered to make restitution until the March 12 hearing (which was more than 30 days after sentence was originally imposed). Before

that time, he could not have appealed a decision granting restitution because there was no restitution award to appeal. In the unique facts of this case, the parties considered the sentencing to be incomplete until the amount of restitution, if any, was set. Because of these facts, the day the sentence was 'suspended in open court,' within the meaning of Rule 26.2(a)(1), was the day the last condition of probation was decided, and appellant's filing of his appeal was timely."

Slaton v. State, 981 S.W.2d 208, 210 (Tex.Crim.App. 1998). "A notice of appeal which complies with the requirements of [TRAP] 26 is essential to vest the court of appeals with jurisdiction. If an appeal is not timely perfected, a court of appeals does not obtain jurisdiction to address the merits of the appeal. Under those circumstances it can take no action other than to dismiss the appeal."

Ex parte Delgado, 214 S.W.3d 56, 58 (Tex.App.—El Paso 2006, pet. ref'd). "An order denying habeas corpus relief under [CCP art. 11.072, §8] is an appealable order. Such an order does not impose or suspend a sentence. Therefore, a motion for new trial is ineffective to extend the appellate timetable under Rule 26.2(a)(2) and the appellant's notice of appeal must be filed within the thirty-day time period specified in Rule 26.2(a)(1)."

TRAP 26.3

Rodman v. State, 47 S.W.3d 545, 548 (Tex.App.—Amarillo 2000, no pet.). "Facts showing that appellant intentionally or deliberately failed to file a notice of appeal within the time limits prescribed by TRAP 26.2(a), and then later changed his mind, do not 'reasonably explain the need for an extension' within the meaning of TRAP 10.5(b)(1)(C) so that we may grant the motion for extension pursuant to TRAP 26.3."

Moreno v. State, 954 S.W.2d 97, 98 (Tex. App.—San Antonio 1997, no pet.). "By granting Moreno habeas corpus relief [out-of-time appeal], the Court of Criminal Appeals returned him 'to the point at which he *can* give notice of appeal.' Thus, the notice of appeal was due to be filed in the trial court, [TRAP 40(b)(1), now 26.3(a)], while the motion for extension of time was due to be filed in the court of appeals. The trial court in this case, therefore, lacked jurisdiction to grant Moreno's motion for extension of time, even if were timely filed. Because Moreno's notice of appeal was untimely, we dismiss his out-of-time appeal for lack of jurisdiction."

TRAP 27. PREMATURE FILINGS

27.1 Prematurely Filed Notice of Appeal.

(a) *Civil cases.* In a civil case, a prematurely filed notice of appeal is effective and deemed filed on the day of, but after, the event that begins the period for perfecting the appeal.

(b) *Criminal cases.* In a criminal case, a prematurely filed notice of appeal is effective and deemed filed on the same day, but after, sentence is imposed or suspended in open court, or the appealable order is signed by the trial court. But a notice of appeal is not effective if filed before the trial court makes a finding of guilt or receives a jury verdict.

27.2 Other Premature Actions. The appellate court may treat actions taken before an appealable order is signed as relating to an appeal of that order and give them effect as if they had been taken after the order was signed. The appellate court may allow an appealed order that is not final to be modified so as to be made final and may allow the modified order and all proceedings relating to it to be included in a supplemental record.

27.3 If Appealed Order Modified or Vacated. After an order or judgment in a civil case has been appealed, if the trial court modifies the order or judgment, or if the trial court vacates the order or judgment and replaces it with another appealable order or judgment, the appellate court must treat the appeal as from the subsequent order or judgment and may treat actions relating to the appeal of the first order or judgment as relating to the appeal of the subsequent order or judgment. The subsequent order or judgment and actions relating to it may be included in the original or supplemental record. Any party may nonetheless appeal from the subsequent order or judgment.

TRAP 28. ACCELERATED & AGREED INTERLOCUTORY APPEALS IN CIVIL CASES

28.1 Accelerated Appeals.

(a) *Types of accelerated appeals.* Appeals from interlocutory orders (when allowed as of right by statute), appeals in quo warranto proceedings, appeals required by statute to be accelerated or expedited, and appeals required by law to be filed or perfected within less than 30 days after the date of the order or judgment being appealed are accelerated appeals.

(b) *Perfection of accelerated appeal.* Unless otherwise provided by statute, an accelerated appeal is perfected by filing a notice of appeal in compliance with Rule 25.1 within the time allowed by Rule 26.1(b) or as extended by Rule 26.3. Filing a motion for new trial, any other post-trial motion, or a request for findings of fact will not extend the time to perfect an accelerated appeal.

(c) *Appeals of interlocutory orders.* The trial court need not file findings of fact and conclusions of law but may do so within 30 days after the order is signed.

(d) *Quo warranto appeals.* The trial court may grant a motion for new trial timely filed under Texas Rule of Civil Procedure 329b (a)-(b) until 50 days after the trial court's final judgment is signed. If not determined by signed written order within that period, the motion will be deemed overruled by operation of law on expiration of that period.

(e) *Record and briefs.* In lieu of the clerk's record, the appellate court may hear an accelerated appeal on the original papers forwarded by the trial court or on sworn and uncontroverted copies of those papers. The appellate court may allow the case to be submitted without briefs. The deadlines and procedures for filing the record and briefs in an accelerated appeal are provided in Rules 35.1 and 38.6.

28.2 Agreed Interlocutory Appeals in Civil Cases.

(a) *Perfecting appeal.* An agreed appeal of an interlocutory order permitted by statute must be perfected as provided in Rule 25.1. The notice of appeal must be filed no later than the 20th day after the date the trial court signs a written order granting permission to appeal, unless the court of appeals extends the time for filing pursuant to Rule 26.3.

(b) *Other requirements.* In addition to perfecting appeal, the appellant must file with the clerk of the appellate court a docketing statement as provided in Rule 32.1 and pay to the clerk of the appellate court all required fees authorized to be collected by the clerk.

(c) *Contents of notice.* The notice of accelerated appeal must contain, in addition to the items required by Rule 25.1(d), the following:

(1) a list of the names of all parties to the trial court proceeding and the names, addresses, and telefax numbers of all trial and appellate counsel;

TRAP 28

(2) a copy of the trial court's order granting permission to appeal;

(3) a copy of the trial court order appealed from;

(4) a statement that all parties to the trial court proceeding agreed to the trial court's order granting permission to appeal;

(5) a statement that all parties to the trial court proceeding agreed that the order granting permission to appeal involves a controlling question of law as to which there is a substantial ground for difference of opinion;

(6) a brief statement of the issues or points presented; and

(7) a concise explanation of how an immediate appeal may materially advance the ultimate termination of the litigation.

(d) *Determination of jurisdiction.* If the court of appeals determines that a notice of appeal filed under this rule does not demonstrate the court's jurisdiction, it may order the appellant to file an amended notice of appeal. On a party's motion or its own initiative, the court of appeals may also order the appellant or any other party to file briefing addressing whether the appeal meets the statutory requirements, and may direct the parties to file supporting evidence. If, after providing an opportunity to file an amended notice of appeal or briefing addressing potential jurisdictional defects, the court of appeals concludes that a jurisdictional defect exists, it may dismiss the appeal for want of jurisdiction at any stage of the appeal.

(e) *Record; briefs.* The rules governing the filing of the appellate record and briefs in accelerated appeals apply. A party may address in its brief any issues related to the court of appeals' jurisdiction, including whether the appeal meets the statutory requirements.

(f) *No automatic stay of proceedings in trial court.* An agreed appeal of an interlocutory order permitted by statute does not stay proceedings in the trial court except as agreed by the parties and ordered by the trial court or the court of appeals.

TRAP 29. ORDERS PENDING INTERLOCUTORY APPEAL IN CIVIL CASES

29.1 **Effect of Appeal.** Perfecting an appeal from an order granting interlocutory relief does not suspend the order appealed from unless:

(a) the order is superseded in accordance with 29.2; or

(b) the appellant is entitled to supersede the order without security by filing a notice of appeal.

29.2 **Security.** The trial court may permit an order granting interlocutory relief to be superseded pending an appeal from the order, in which event the appellant may supersede the order in accordance with Rule 24. If the trial court refuses to permit the appellant to supersede the order, the appellant may move the appellate court to review that decision for abuse of discretion.

29.3 **Temporary Orders of Appellate Court.** When an appeal from an interlocutory order is perfected, the appellate court may make any temporary orders necessary to preserve the parties' rights until disposition of the appeal and may require appropriate security. But the appellate court must not suspend the trial court's order if the appellant's rights would be adequately protected by supersedeas or another order made under Rule 24.

29.4 **Enforcement of Temporary Orders.** While an appeal from an interlocutory order is pending, only the appellate court in which the appeal is pending may enforce the order. But the appellate court may refer any enforcement proceeding to the trial court with instructions to:

(a) hear evidence and grant appropriate relief; or

(b) make findings and recommendations and report them to the appellate court.

29.5 **Further Proceedings in Trial Court.** While an appeal from an interlocutory order is pending, the trial court retains jurisdiction of the case and unless prohibited by statute may make further orders, including one dissolving the order complained of on appeal. If permitted by law, the trial court may proceed with a trial on the merits. But the court must not make an order that:

(a) is inconsistent with any appellate court temporary order; or

(b) interferes with or impairs the jurisdiction of the appellate court or effectiveness of any relief sought or that may be granted on appeal.

29.6 **Review of Further Orders.**

(a) *Motion to review further orders.* While an appeal from an interlocutory order is pending, on a party's motion or on the appellate court's own initiative, the appellate court may review the following:

(1) a further appealable interlocutory order concerning the same subject matter; and

(2) any interlocutory order that interferes with or impairs the effectiveness of the relief sought or that may be granted on appeal.

(b) *Record.* The party filing the motion may rely on the original record or may file a supplemental record with the motion.

TRAP 30. RESTRICTED APPEAL TO COURT OF APPEALS IN CIVIL CASES

A party who did not participate—either in person or through counsel—in the hearing that resulted in the judgment complained of and who did not timely file a postjudgment motion or request for findings of fact and conclusions of law, or a notice of appeal within the time permitted by Rule 26.1(a), may file a notice of appeal within the time permitted by Rule 26.1(c). Restricted appeals replace writ of error appeals to the court of appeals. Statutes pertaining to writ of error appeals to the court of appeals apply equally to restricted appeals.

TRAP 31. APPEALS IN HABEAS CORPUS, BAIL, & EXTRADITION PROCEEDINGS IN CRIMINAL CASES

31.1 **Filing the Record; Submission.** When written notice of appeal from a judgment or order in a habeas corpus or bail proceeding is filed, the trial court clerk must prepare and certify the clerk's record and, if the appellant requests, the court reporter must prepare and certify a reporter's record. The clerk must send the clerk's record and the court reporter must send the reporter's record to the appellate court within 15 days after the notice of appeal is filed. On reasonable explanation, the appellate court may shorten or extend the time to file the record. When the appellate court receives the record, the court will—if it desires briefs—set the time for filing briefs, and will set the appeal for submission.

31.2 **Hearing.** An appeal in a habeas corpus or bail proceeding will be heard at the earliest practicable time. The applicant need not personally appear, and the appeal will be heard and determined upon the law and the facts shown by the record. The appellate court will not review any incidental question that might have arisen on the hearing of the application before the trial court. The sole purpose of the appeal is to do substantial justice to the parties.

31.3 **Orders on Appeal.** The appellate court will render whatever judgment and make whatever orders the law and the nature of the case require. The court may make an appropriate order relating to costs, whether allowing costs and fixing the amount, or allowing no costs.

31.4 **Stay of Mandate.**

(a) *When motion for stay required.* Despite Rule 18 or any other of these rules, in the following circumstances a party who in good faith intends to seek discretionary review must—within 15 days after the court of appeals renders judgment—file with the court of appeals clerk a motion for stay of mandate, to which is appended the party's petition for discretionary review showing reasons why the Court of Criminal Appeals should review the appellate court judgment:

(1) when a court of appeals affirms the judgment of the trial court in an extradition matter and thereby sanctions a defendant's extradition; or

(2) when a court of appeals reverses the trial court's judgment in a bail matter—including bail pending appeal under Code of Criminal Procedure article 44.04(g)—and thereby grants or reduces the amount of bail.

(b) *Determination of the motion.* The clerk must promptly submit the motion and appendix to the court of appeals, or to one or more judges as the court deems appropriate, for immediate consideration and determination.

(1) If the motion for stay is granted, the clerk will file the petition for discretionary review and process the case in accordance with Rule 68.7.

(2) If the motion is denied, the clerk will issue a mandate in accordance with the court of appeals' judgment.

(c) *Denial of stay.* If the motion for stay is denied under 31.4(b)(2), the losing party may then present the motion and appendix to the clerk of the Court of Criminal Appeals, who will promptly submit them to the Court, or to one or more judges as the Court deems appropriate, for immediate consideration and determination. The Court of Criminal Appeals may deny the motion or stay or recall the mandate. If the mandate is stayed or recalled, the court of appeals clerk will file the petition for discretionary review and process the case in accordance with Rule 68.7.

TRAP 31

31.5 Judgment Conclusive. The court of appeals' judgment is final and conclusive if the Court of Criminal Appeals does not grant discretionary review. If the Court of Criminal Appeals grants discretionary review, that court's judgment is final and conclusive. In either case, no further application in the same case can be made for the writ unless the law provides otherwise.

31.6 Defendant Detained by Other Than Officer. If the defendant is held by a person other than an officer, the sheriff receiving the appellate court mandate so ordering must immediately cause the defendant to be discharged, for which discharge the mandate is sufficient authority.

31.7 Judgment to be Certified. The appellate court clerk will certify the court's judgment to the officer holding the defendant in custody or, if the defendant is held by a person other than an officer, to the appropriate sheriff.

ANNOTATIONS

TRAP 31.1

Vargas v. State, 109 S.W.3d 26, 29 (Tex.App.—Amarillo 2003, no pet.). "The courts of appeals have split over whether appellate jurisdiction exists in regard to direct appeals from pretrial bail rulings such as the one before us. [¶] We lack a statutory grant of jurisdiction over this appeal. And, although TRAP 31 addresses, in part, appeals from bail proceedings, we note that the [TRAPs] do not establish jurisdiction of courts of appeals, and cannot create jurisdiction where none exists. [¶] We lack jurisdiction over this direct appeal from interlocutory pretrial orders refusing to lower bail pursuant to CCP [art.] 17.151." *See also Benford v. State*, 994 S.W.2d 404, 409 (Tex.App.—Waco 1999, no pet.) (no appellate jurisdiction); *Ex parte Shumake*, 953 S.W.2d 842, 846-47 (Tex.App.—Austin 1997, no pet.) (same). *But see Ramos v. State*, 89 S.W.3d 122, 124-26 (Tex.App.—Corpus Christi 2002, no pet.) (TRAP 31.1 contemplates appeals of orders in bail proceedings).

TRAP 32. DOCKETING STATEMENT

32.1 Civil Cases. Upon perfecting the appeal in a civil case, the appellant must file in the appellate court a docketing statement that includes the following information:

(a)(1) if the appellant filing the statement has counsel, the name of that appellant and the name, address, telephone number, fax number, if any, and State Bar of Texas identification number of the appellant's lead counsel; or

(2) if the appellant filing the statement is not represented by an attorney, that party's name, address, telephone number, and fax number, if any;

(b) the date the notice of appeal was filed in the trial court and, if mailed to the trial court clerk, the date of mailing;

(c) the trial court's name and county, the name of the judge who tried the case, and the date the judgment or order appealed from was signed;

(d) the date of filing of any motion for new trial, motion to modify the judgment, request for findings of fact, motion to reinstate, or other filing that affects the time for perfecting the appeal;

(e) the names of all other parties to the trial court's judgment or the order appealed from, and:

(1) if represented by counsel, their lead counsel's names, addresses, telephone numbers, and fax numbers, if any; or

(2) if not represented by counsel, the name, address, and telephone number of the party, or a statement that the appellant diligently inquired but could not discover that information;

(f) the general nature of the case—for example, personal injury, breach of contract, or temporary injunction;

(g) whether the appeal's submission should be given priority or whether the appeal is an accelerated one under Rule 28 or another rule or statute;

(h) whether the appellant has requested or will request a reporter's record, and whether the trial was electronically recorded;

(i) the name of the court reporter;

(j) whether the appellant intends to seek temporary or ancillary relief while the appeal is pending;

(k)(1) the date of filing of any affidavit of indigence;

(2) the date of filing of any contest;

(3) the date of any order on the contest; and

(4) whether the contest was sustained or overruled;

(*l*) whether the appellant has filed or will file a supersedeas bond; and

(m) any other information the appellate court requires.

32.2 Criminal Cases. Upon perfecting the appeal in a criminal case, the appellant must file in the appellate court a docketing statement that includes the following information:

(a)(1) if the appellant has counsel, the name of the appellant and the name, address, telephone number, fax number, if any, and State Bar of Texas identification number of the appellant's counsel, and whether the counsel is appointed or retained; or

(2) if the appellant is not represented by an attorney, that party's name, address, telephone number, and fax number, if any;

(b) the date the notice of appeal was filed in the trial court and, if mailed to the trial court clerk, the date of mailing;

(c) the trial court's name and county, and the name of the judge who tried the case;

(d) the date the trial court imposed or suspended sentence in open court, or the date the judgment or order appealed from was signed;

(e) the date of filing any motion for new trial, motion in arrest of judgment, or any other filing that affects the time for perfecting the appeal;

(f) the offense charged and the date of the offense;

(g) the defendant's plea;

(h) whether the trial was jury or nonjury;

(i) the punishment assessed;

(j) whether the appeal is from a pretrial order;

(k) whether the appeal involves the validity of a statute, ordinance, or rule;

(l) whether a reporter's record has been or will be requested, and whether the trial was electronically recorded;

(m) the name of the court reporter;

(n)(1) the dates of filing of any motion and affidavit of indigence;

(2) the date of any hearing;

(3) the date of any order; and

(4) whether the motion was granted or denied; and

(o) any other information the appellate court requires.

32.3 Supplemental Statements. Any party may file a statement supplementing or correcting the docketing statement.

32.4 Purpose of Statement. The docketing statement is for administrative purposes and does not affect the appellate court's jurisdiction.

TRAP 33. PRESERVATION OF APPELLATE COMPLAINTS

33.1 Preservation; How Shown.

(a) *In general.* As a prerequisite to presenting a complaint for appellate review, the record must show that:

(1) the complaint was made to the trial court by a timely request, objection, or motion that:

(A) stated the grounds for the ruling that the complaining party sought from the trial court with sufficient specificity to make the trial court aware of the complaint, unless the specific grounds were apparent from the context; and

(B) complied with the requirements of the Texas Rules of Civil or Criminal Evidence or the Texas Rules of Civil or Appellate Procedure; and

(2) the trial court:

(A) ruled on the request, objection, or motion, either expressly or implicitly; or

(B) refused to rule on the request, objection, or motion, and the complaining party objected to the refusal.

(b) *Ruling by operation of law.* In a civil case, the overruling by operation of law of a motion for new trial or a motion to modify the judgment preserves for appellate review a complaint properly made in the motion, unless taking evidence was necessary to properly present the complaint in the trial court.

(c) *Formal exception and separate order not required.* Neither a formal exception to a trial court ruling or order nor a signed, separate order is required to preserve a complaint for appeal.

(d) *Sufficiency of evidence complaints in non-jury cases.* In a nonjury case, a complaint regarding the legal or factual insufficiency of the evidence—including a complaint that the damages found by the court are excessive or inadequate, as distinguished from a complaint that the trial court erred in refusing to amend a fact finding or to make an additional finding of fact—may be made for the first time on appeal in the complaining party's brief.

TRAP 33

33.2 **Formal Bills of Exception.** To complain on appeal about a matter that would not otherwise appear in the record, a party must file a formal bill of exception.

(a) *Form.* No particular form of words is required in a bill of exception. But the objection to the court's ruling or action, and the ruling complained of, must be stated with sufficient specificity to make the trial court aware of the complaint.

(b) *Evidence.* When the appellate record contains the evidence needed to explain a bill of exception, the bill itself need not repeat the evidence, and a party may attach and incorporate a transcription of the evidence certified by the court reporter.

(c) *Procedure.*

(1) The complaining party must first present a formal bill of exception to the trial court.

(2) If the parties agree on the contents of the bill of exception, the judge must sign the bill and file it with the trial court clerk. If the parties do not agree on the contents of the bill, the trial judge must—after notice and hearing—do one of the following things:

(A) sign the bill of exception and file it with the trial court clerk if the judge finds that it is correct;

(B) suggest to the complaining party those corrections to the bill that the judge believes are necessary to make it accurately reflect the proceedings in the trial court, and if the party agrees to the corrections, have the corrections made, sign the bill, and file it with the trial court clerk; or

(C) if the complaining party will not agree to the corrections suggested by the judge, return the bill to the complaining party with the judge's refusal written on it, and prepare, sign, and file with the trial court clerk such bill as will, in the judge's opinion, accurately reflect the proceedings in the trial court.

(3) If the complaining party is dissatisfied with the bill of exception filed by the judge under (2)(C), the party may file with the trial court clerk the bill that was rejected by the judge. That party must also file the affidavits of at least three people who observed the matter to which the bill of exception is addressed. The affidavits must attest to the correctness of the bill as presented by the party. The matters contained in that bill of exception may be controverted and maintained by additional affidavits filed by any party within ten days after the filing of that bill. The truth of the bill of exception will be determined by the appellate court.

(d) *Conflict.* If a formal bill of exception conflicts with the reporter's record, the bill controls.

(e) *Time to file.*

(1) *Civil cases.* In a civil case, a formal bill of exception must be filed no later than 30 days after the filing party's notice of appeal is filed.

(2) *Criminal cases.* In a criminal case, a formal bill of exception must be filed:

(A) no later than 60 days after the trial court pronounces or suspends sentence in open court; or

(B) if a motion for new trial has been timely filed, no later than 90 days after the trial court pronounces or suspends sentence in open court.

(3) *Extension of time.* The appellate court may extend the time to file a formal bill of exception if, within 15 days after the deadline for filing the bill, the party files in the appellate court a motion complying with Rule 10.5(b).

(f) *Inclusion in clerk's record.* When filed, a formal bill of exception should be included in the appellate record.

ANNOTATIONS

TRAP 33.1

Cameron v. State, 241 S.W.3d 15, 18 (Tex.Crim. App.2007). "Where a trial court, in excluding evidence from a trial, gives a specific legal reason for its exclusion, and the proponent of the evidence explains why he believes that such reason is not valid, is the proponent of the evidence then required to also explain why other, unmentioned legal objections which might also have been made to the introduction of such evidence are also not valid?" Held: No.

Griggs v. State, 213 S.W.3d 923, 927 (Tex.Crim.App. 2007). "A motion for mistrial is timely only if it is made as soon as the grounds for it become apparent."

Young v. State, 137 S.W.3d 65, 69-70 (Tex.Crim. App.2004). "A defendant's complaint may take three forms: (1) a timely, specific objection, (2) a request for an instruction to disregard, and (3) a motion for a mistrial. [¶] [T]he traditional and preferred procedure for a party to voice its complaint has been to seek them in sequence…. However, this sequence is not essential to preserve complaints for appellate review. The essential requirement is a timely, specific request that the trial court refuses. [¶] [W]hen a party's first action is to move for mistrial, as this appellant's was, the scope of appellate review is limited to the question whether the trial court erred in not taking the most serious action of ending the trial; in other words, an event that could have been prevented by timely objection or cured by instruction to the jury will not lead an appellate court to reverse a judgment on an appeal by the party who did not request these lesser remedies in the trial court."

Garza v. State, 126 S.W.3d 79, 84-85 (Tex.Crim. App.2004). "[W]e do agree with appellant that he preserved error. It is generally accepted that, '[w]hen a court overrules a pretrial motion to suppress evidence, the defendant need not subsequently object to the admission of the same evidence at trial to preserve error.' Here, however, the judge did not rule on the pre-trial motion to suppress; rather, the judge directed it to be carried with trial. [¶] Though the general rule would require appellant to object and obtain a ruling at the earliest opportunity, the specific pre-trial comments made by the judge in this case essentially directed appellant to wait until all the evidence was presented before he obtained any ruling from the judge. ... Appellant was reasonable to interpret those comments as an instruction to seek a ruling at the conclusion of the State's presentation of evidence, and not sooner." *See also **Gillenwaters v. State***, 205 S.W.3d 534, 538 (Tex. Crim.App.2006) (motion for new trial).

Geuder v. State, 115 S.W.3d 11, 13 (Tex.Crim.App. 2003). "[W]ith two exceptions, the law in Texas requires a party to continue to object each time inadmissible evidence is offered. The two exceptions require counsel to either (1) obtain a running objection, or (2) request a hearing outside the presence of the jury.' *At 15:* Because appellant made a timely and sufficiently specific objection which complied with [TRE] 103(a)(1) and the trial court expressly ruled on that objection, appellant preserved his complaint concerning [TRE] 609(f)." *See also **Gutierrez v. State***, 36 S.W.3d 509, 511 (Tex.Crim.App.2001).

Speth v. State, 6 S.W.3d 530, 535 (Tex.Crim.App. 1999). "Appellant did not object at trial to the imposition of the [probation] conditions. The Court of Appeals erred in holding appellant could complain about the community supervision conditions for the first time on appeal."

Richardson v. State, 981 S.W.2d 453, 455 (Tex. App.—El Paso 1998, pet. ref'd). "While the conference itself was not contemporaneously recorded, the trial court's description of what occurred at that conference

and his ruling is adequate to show that Appellant requested a jury shuffle before the State began its voir dire examination. This satisfies Rule 33.1's requirement that the record show the complaining party presented his complaint to the trial court and obtained an adverse ruling."

TRAP 33.2

Franklin v. State, 986 S.W.2d 349, 354 (Tex.App.— Texarkana 1999), *rev'd on other grounds*, 12 S.W.3d 473 (Tex.Crim.App.2000). "A defendant is entitled to a reversal because a juror has withheld information if two criteria are met: (1) the omission is *material*; and (2) the defendant has exercised due diligence in eliciting that information. ... Material information includes information regarding a juror's relationship with any party in a criminal proceeding."

TRAP 34. APPELLATE RECORD

34.1 **Contents.** The appellate record consists of the clerk's record and, if necessary to the appeal, the reporter's record. Even if more than one notice of appeal is filed, there should be only one appellate record in a case.

34.2 **Agreed Record.** By written stipulation filed with the trial court clerk, the parties may agree on the contents of the appellate record. An agreed record will be presumed to contain all evidence and filings relevant to the appeal. To request matter to be included in the agreed record, the parties must comply with the procedures in Rules 34.5 and 34.6.

34.3 **Agreed Statement of the Case.** In lieu of a reporter's record, the parties may agree on a brief statement of the case. The statement must be filed with the trial court clerk and included in the appellate record.

34.4 **Form.** The Supreme Court and Court of Criminal Appeals will prescribe the form of the appellate record.

34.5 **Clerk's Record.**

(a) *Contents.* Unless the parties designate the filings in the appellate record by agreement under Rule 34.2, the record must include copies of the following:

(1) in civil cases, all pleadings on which the trial was held;

(2) in criminal cases, the indictment or information, any special plea or defense motion that was presented to the court and overruled, any written waiver, any written stipulation, and, in cases in which a plea of guilty or nolo contendere has been entered, any documents executed for the plea;

(3) the court's docket sheet;

(4) the court's charge and the jury's verdict, or the court's findings of fact and conclusions of law;

(5) the court's judgment or other order that is being appealed;

(6) any request for findings of fact and conclusions of law, any post-judgment motion, and the court's order on the motion;

(7) the notice of appeal;

(8) any formal bill of exception;

(9) any request for a reporter's record, including any statement of points or issues under Rule 34.6(c);

(10) any request for preparation of the clerk's record;

(11) in civil cases, a certified bill of costs including the cost of preparing the clerk's record, showing credits for payments made;

(12) in criminal cases, the trial court's certification of the defendant's right of appeal under Rule 25.2; and

(13) subject to (b), any filing that a party designates to have included in the record.

(b) *Request for additional items.*

(1) *Time for request.* At any time before the clerk's record is prepared, any party may file with the trial court clerk a written designation specifying items to be included in the record.

(2) *Request must be specific.* A party requesting that an item be included in the clerk's record must specifically describe the item so that the clerk can readily identify it. The clerk will disregard a general designation, such as one for "all papers filed in the case."

(3) *Requesting unnecessary items.* In a civil case, if a party requests that more items than necessary be included in the clerk's record or any supplement, the appellate court may—regardless of the appeal's outcome—require that party to pay the costs for the preparation of the unnecessary portion.

(4) *Failure to timely request.* An appellate court must not refuse to file the clerk's record or a supplemental clerk's record because of a failure to timely request items to be included in the clerk's record.

(c) *Supplementation.*

(1) If a relevant item has been omitted from the clerk's record, the trial court, the appellate court, or any party may by letter direct the trial court clerk to prepare, certify, and file in the appellate court a supplement containing the omitted item.

(2) If the appellate court in a criminal case orders the trial court to prepare and file findings of fact and conclusions of law as required by law or certification of the defendant's right of appeal as required by these rules, the trial court clerk must prepare, certify, and file in the appellate court a supplemental clerk's record containing those findings and conclusions.

(3) Any supplemental clerk's record will be part of the appellate record.

(d) *Defects or inaccuracies.* If the clerk's record is defective or inaccurate, the appellate clerk must inform the trial court clerk of the defect or inaccuracy and instruct the clerk to make the correction.

(e) *Clerk's record lost or destroyed.* If a filing designated for inclusion in the clerk's record has been lost or destroyed, the parties may, by written stipulation, deliver a copy of that item to the trial court clerk for inclusion in the clerk's record or a supplement. If the parties cannot agree, the trial court must—on any party's motion or at the appellate court's request—determine what constitutes an accurate copy of the missing item and order it to be included in the clerk's record or a supplement.

(f) *Original documents.* If the trial court determines that original documents filed with the trial court clerk should be inspected by the appellate court or sent to that court in lieu of copies, the trial court must make an order for the safekeeping, transportation, and return of those original documents. The order must list the original documents and briefly describe them. All the documents must be arranged in their listed sequence and bound firmly together. On any party's motion or its own initiative, the appellate court may direct the trial court clerk to send it any original document.

(g) *Additional copies of clerk's record in criminal cases.* In a criminal case, the clerk's record must be made in duplicate, and in a case in which the death penalty was assessed, in triplicate. The trial court clerk must retain the copy or copies for the parties to use with the court's permission.

(h) *Clerk may consult with parties.* The clerk may consult with the parties concerning the contents of the clerk's record.

34.6 Reporter's Record.

(a) *Contents.*

(1) *Stenographic recording.* If the proceedings were stenographically recorded, the reporter's record consists of the court reporter's transcription of so much of the proceedings, and any of the exhibits, that the parties to the appeal designate.

(2) *Electronic recording.* If the proceedings were electronically recorded, the reporter's record consists of certified copies of all tapes or other audio-storage devices on which the proceedings were recorded, any of the exhibits that the parties to the appeal designate, and certified copies of the logs prepared by the court recorder under Rule 13.2.

(b) *Request for preparation.*

(1) *Request to court reporter.* At or before the time for perfecting the appeal, the appellant must request in writing that the official reporter prepare the reporter's record. The request must designate the exhibits to be included. A request to the court reporter—but not the court recorder—must also designate the portions of the proceedings to be included.

(2) *Filing.* The appellant must file a copy of the request with the trial court clerk.

(3) *Failure to timely request.* An appellate court must not refuse to file a reporter's record or a supplemental reporter's record because of a failure to timely request it.

(c) *Partial reporter's record.*

(1) *Effect on appellate points or issues.* If the appellant requests a partial reporter's record, the appellant must include in the request a statement of the points or issues to be presented on appeal and will then be limited to those points or issues.

(2) *Other parties may designate additions.* Any other party may designate additional exhibits and portions of the testimony to be included in the reporter's record.

(3) *Costs; requesting unnecessary matter.* Additions requested by another party must be included in the reporter's record at the appellant's cost. But if the trial court finds that all or part of the designated additions are unnecessary to the appeal, the trial court may order the other party to pay the costs for the preparation of the unnecessary additions. This paragraph does not affect the appellate court's power to tax costs differently.

(4) *Presumptions.* The appellate court must presume that the partial reporter's record designated by the parties constitutes the entire record for purposes of reviewing the stated points or issues. This presumption applies even if the statement includes a point or issue complaining of the legal or factual insufficiency of the evidence to support a specific factual finding identified in that point or issue.

(5) *Criminal cases.* In a criminal case, if the statement contains a point complaining that the evidence is insufficient to support a finding of guilt, the record must include all the evidence admitted at the trial on the issue of guilt or innocence and punishment.

(d) *Supplementation.* If anything relevant is omitted from the reporter's record, the trial court, the appellate court, or any party may by letter direct the official court reporter to prepare, certify, and file in the appellate court a supplemental reporter's record containing the omitted items. Any supplemental reporter's record is part of the appellate record.

(e) *Inaccuracies in the reporter's record.*

(1) *Correction of inaccuracies by agreement.* The parties may agree to correct an inaccuracy in the reporter's record, including an exhibit, without the court reporter's recertification.

(2) *Correction of inaccuracies by trial court.* If the parties cannot agree on whether or how to correct the reporter's record so that the text accurately discloses what occurred in the trial court and the exhibits are accurate, the trial court must—after notice and hearing—settle the dispute. If the court finds any inaccuracy, it must order the court reporter to conform the reporter's record (including text and any exhibits) to what occurred in the trial court, and to file certified corrections in the appellate court.

(3) *Correction after filing in appellate court.* If the dispute arises after the reporter's record has been filed in the appellate court, that court may submit the dispute to the trial court for resolution. The trial court must then proceed as under subparagraph (e)(2).

(f) *Reporter's record lost or destroyed.* An appellant is entitled to a new trial under the following circumstances:

(1) if the appellant has timely requested a reporter's record;

(2) if, without the appellant's fault, a significant exhibit or a significant portion of the court reporter's

TRAP 34

notes and records has been lost or destroyed or—if the proceedings were electronically recorded—a significant portion of the recording has been lost or destroyed or is inaudible;

(3) if the lost, destroyed, or inaudible portion of the reporter's record, or the lost or destroyed exhibit, is necessary to the appeal's resolution; and

(4) if the lost, destroyed or inaudible portion of the reporter's record cannot be replaced by agreement of the parties, or the lost or destroyed exhibit cannot be replaced either by agreement of the parties or with a copy determined by the trial court to accurately duplicate with reasonable certainty the original exhibit.

(g) *Original exhibits.*

(1) *Reporter may use in preparing reporter's record.* At the court reporter's request, the trial court clerk must give all original exhibits to the reporter for use in preparing the reporter's record. Unless ordered to include original exhibits in the reporter's record, the court reporter must return the original exhibits to the clerk after copying them for inclusion in the reporter's record. If someone other than the trial court clerk possesses an original exhibit, either the trial court or the appellate court may order that person to deliver the exhibit to the trial court clerk.

(2) *Use of original exhibits by appellate court.* If the trial court determines that original exhibits should be inspected by the appellate court or sent to that court in lieu of copies, the trial court must make an order for the safekeeping, transportation, and return of those exhibits. The order must list the exhibits and briefly describe them. To the extent practicable, all the exhibits must be arranged in their listed order and bound firmly together before being sent to the appellate clerk. On any party's motion or its own initiative, the appellate court may direct the trial court clerk to send it any original exhibit.

(h) *Additional copies of reporter's record in criminal cases.* In a criminal case in which a party requests a reporter's record, the court reporter must prepare a duplicate of the reporter's record and file it with the trial court clerk. In a case where the death penalty was assessed, the court reporter must prepare two duplicates of the reporter's record.

(i) *Supreme Court and Court of Criminal Appeals may set fee.* From time to time, the Supreme Court and the Court of Criminal Appeals may set the fee that the court reporters may charge for preparing the reporter's record.

ANNOTATIONS

TRAP 34.5

Osuch v. State, 976 S.W.2d 810, 811 (Tex.App.—Houston [1st Dist.] 1998, no pet.). TRAP 34.5 "includes a requirement that the missing portion of the record or exhibit be necessary to the appeal's resolution. *At 812:* Because appellant timely requested the inclusion of State's exhibit one [DWI videotape] in the appellate record, because it was destroyed without appellant's fault, because it cannot be reproduced and there are no copies of it elsewhere in the record, and because it is necessary for our resolution of this appeal, we [grant appellant a new trial]."

TRAP 34.6

Amador v. State, 221 S.W.3d 666, 676-77 (Tex.Crim.App.2007). "'[T]he record may be supplemented … if something has been omitted, [but] the supplementation rules cannot be used to create new evidence.' … If the record as originally designated by the parties does not fully reflect the evidence considered by the factfinder, then the trial judge, the court of appeals, or any of the parties may direct the court reporter to supplement the appellate record with the missing items. If the parties have a dispute over what items are missing from the appellate record, or they dispute the accuracy or completeness of those items, the trial court will resolve that dispute."

Johnson v. State, 151 S.W.3d 193, 194 (Tex.Crim.App.2004). "When a court reporter fails or refuses to comply with the deadlines for filing the reporter's record, does an appellate court properly conclude that the appellate record is 'lost or destroyed' for the purpose of [TRAP] 34.6(f)? The answer is 'no.' *At 196:* An appellate court can and should exercise its contempt power to compel an errant court reporter to prepare and file the record. The [TRAPs] also give appellate courts the power to take other actions designed to ensure the preparation and filing of the record, including the appointment of a substitute court reporter to prepare and file the record from the original court reporter's notes. A court reporter's notes and records, or portions thereof, can be considered 'lost' only if the missing portions of the appellate record are irretrievable."

TRAP 34

Rowell v. State, 66 S.W.3d 279, 280 (Tex.Crim.App. 2001). "May a court of appeals, without examining a reporter's record of a guilty plea and sentencing, decide that a trial court erred in denying an appellant's motion to suppress evidence? We hold that it may. *At 283:* In light of Rule 34.6 and the State's failure to have the record supplemented, the court of appeals was permitted to decide this appeal on the basis of the record that the parties chose to file."

Kirtley v. State, 56 S.W.3d 48, 52 (Tex.Crim.App. 2001). "There is nothing to prohibit appellant from claiming ineffective assistance of counsel during the punishment hearing on appeal. Because appellant can make that claim, the record is 'necessary to the appeal's resolution' as is required by Rule 34.6(f)(3)."

Issac v. State, 989 S.W.2d 754, 757 (Tex.Crim.App. 1999). "Rule 34.6(f)(3) specifies that a new trial may be granted only if the missing portion of the record 'is necessary to the appeal's resolution.' That provision is itself a harm analysis. If the missing portion of the record is not necessary to the appeal's resolution, then the loss of that portion of the record is harmless under the rule, and a new trial is not required. In enacting that provision of the rule, we necessarily rejected the contention that a missing record could never be found unnecessary to an appeal's resolution. [¶] Although the lack of a record may in some cases deprive an appellate court of the ability to determine whether the absent portions are necessary to the appeal's resolution, an automatic rule of reversal is not justified." *See also* *Daniels v. State*, 30 S.W.3d 407, 408 (Tex.Crim.App. 2000); *Gomez v. State*, 962 S.W.2d 572, 576 (Tex.Crim. App.1998) (lost exhibits).

McDougal v. State, 105 S.W.3d 119, 121 (Tex. App.—Fort Worth 2003, pet. ref'd). "A criminal defendant may not waive the making of a record and then, on appeal, rely on the absence of evidence to support reversal of his conviction. Rather, an appellant in a criminal case must bring forth a complete record of the evidence before the factfinder and bears the burden of demonstrating that the State failed to satisfy the evidentiary requirements of [CCP art.] 1.15. [*Rowell v. State*] does not relieve an appellant of the obligation of including in the appellate record all evidence admitted at trial when the appellant challenges the sufficiency of the evidence. Nor does it remove that burden when an appellant challenges the State's compliance with the evidentiary requirements of article 1.15."

TRAP 35. TIME TO FILE RECORD; RESPONSIBILITY FOR FILING RECORD

35.1 **Civil Cases.** The appellate record must be filed in the appellate court within 60 days after the judgment is signed, except as follows:

(a) if Rule 26.1(a) applies, within 120 days after the judgment is signed;

(b) if Rule 26.1(b) applies, within 10 days after the notice of appeal is filed; or

(c) if Rule 26.1(c) applies, within 30 days after the notice of appeal is filed.

35.2 **Criminal Cases.** The appellate record must be filed in the appellate court:

(a) if a motion for new trial is not filed, within 60 days after the date the sentence is imposed or suspended in open court or the order appealed from is signed;

(b) if a timely motion for new trial is filed and denied, within 120 days after the date the sentence is imposed or suspended in open court; or

(c) if a motion for new trial is granted, within 60 days after the order granting the motion is signed.

35.3 **Responsibility for Filing Record.**

(a) *Clerk's record.* The trial court clerk is responsible for preparing, certifying, and timely filing the clerk's record if:

(1) a notice of appeal has been filed, and in criminal proceedings, the trial court has certified the defendant's right of appeal, as required by Rule 25.2(d); and

(2) the party responsible for paying for the preparation of the clerk's record has paid the clerk's fee, has made satisfactory arrangements with the clerk to pay the fee, or is entitled to appeal without paying the fee.

(b) *Reporter's record.* The official or deputy reporter is responsible for preparing, certifying, and timely filing the reporter's record if:

(1) a notice of appeal has been filed;

(2) the appellant has requested that the reporter's record be prepared; and

(3) the party responsible for paying for the preparation of the reporter's record has paid the reporter's fee, or has made satisfactory arrangements with the reporter to pay the fee, or is entitled to appeal without paying the fee.

TRAP 35

(c) *Courts to ensure record timely filed.* The trial and appellate courts are jointly responsible for ensuring that the appellate record is timely filed. The appellate court must allow the record to be filed late when the delay is not the appellant's fault, and may do so when the delay is the appellant's fault. The appellate court may enter any order necessary to ensure the timely filing of the appellate record.

See *Commentaries*, "Appellate Deadlines," ch. 11-C, p. 18; "Costs of Appeal," ch. 11-H, p. 43; "Motion to Accelerate Appeal," ch. 13-C, p. 75; "Appellate Record," ch. 16-A, p. 185; "Reporter's Record," ch. 16-C, p. 196.

TRAP 36. AGENCY RECORD IN ADMINISTRATIVE APPEALS

36.1 **Scope.** This rule applies only to cases involving judicial review of state agency decisions in contested cases under the Administrative Procedure Act.

36.2 **Inclusion in Appellate Record.** The record of an agency proceeding filed in the trial court may be included in either the clerk's record or the reporter's record.

36.3 **Correcting the Record.**

(a) *Correction by agreement.* At any stage of the proceeding, the parties may agree to correct an agency record filed under Section 2001.175(b) of the Government Code to ensure that the agency record accurately reflects the contested case proceedings before the agency. The court reporter need not recertify the agency record.

(b) *Correction by trial court.* If the parties cannot agree to a correction to the agency record, the appellate court must—on any party's motion or its own incentive—send the question to the trial court. After notice and hearing, the trial court must determine what constitutes an accurate copy of the agency record and order the agency to send an accurate copy to the clerk of the court in which the case is pending.

TRAP 37. DUTIES OF THE APPELLATE CLERK ON RECEIVING THE NOTICE OF APPEAL & RECORD

37.1 **On Receiving the Notice of Appeal.** If the appellate clerk determines that the notice of appeal or certification of defendant's right of appeal in a criminal case is defective, the clerk must notify the parties of the defect so that it can be remedied, if possible. If a proper notice of appeal or certification of a criminal defendant's right of appeal is not filed in the trial court

within 30 days of the date of the clerk's notice, the clerk must refer the matter to the appellate court, which will make an appropriate order under this rule or Rule 34.5(c)(2).

37.2 **On Receiving the Record.** On receiving the clerk's record from the trial court clerk or the reporter's record from the reporter, the appellate clerk must determine whether each complies with the Supreme Court's and Court of Criminal Appeals' order on preparation of the record. If so, the clerk must endorse on each the date of receipt, file it, and notify the parties of the filing and the date. If not, the clerk must endorse on the clerk's record or reporter's record—whichever is defective—the date of receipt and return it to the official responsible for filing it. The appellate court clerk must specify the defects and instruct the official to correct the defects and return the record to the appellate court by a specified date.

37.3 **If No Record Filed.**

(a) *Notice of late record.*

(1) *Civil cases.* If the clerk's record or reporter's record has not been timely filed, the appellate clerk must send notice to the official responsible for filing it, stating that the record is late and requesting that the record be filed within 30 days if an ordinary or restricted appeal, or 10 days if an accelerated appeal. The appellate clerk must send a copy of this notice to the parties and the trial court. If the clerk does not receive the record within the stated period, the clerk must refer the matter to the appellate court. The court must make whatever order is appropriate to avoid further delay and to preserve the parties' rights.

(2) *Criminal cases.* If the clerk's record or reporter's record has not been timely filed, the appellate court clerk must refer the matter to the appellate court. The court must make whatever order is appropriate to avoid further delay and to preserve the parties' rights.

(b) *If no clerk's record filed due to appellant's fault.* If the trial court clerk failed to file the clerk's record because the appellant failed to pay or make arrangements to pay the clerk's fee for preparing the clerk's record, the appellate court may—on a party's motion or its own initiative—dismiss the appeal for want of prosecution unless the appellant was entitled to proceed without payment of costs. The court must give the appellant a reasonable opportunity to cure before dismissal.

(c) *If no reporter's record filed due to appellant's fault.* Under the following circumstances, and if the clerk's record has been filed, the appellate court may—after first giving the appellant notice and a reasonable opportunity to cure—consider and decide those issues or points that do not require a reporter's record for a decision. The court may do this if no reporter's record has been filed because:

(1) the appellant failed to request a reporter's record; or

(2)(A) appellant failed to pay or make arrangements to pay the reporter's fee to prepare the reporter's record; and

(B) the appellant is not entitled to proceed without payment of costs.

ANNOTATIONS

TRAP 37.1

Dears v. State, 154 S.W.3d 610, 614-15 (Tex.Crim. App.2005). "[A] defective certification should include a certification which is correct in form but which, when compared with the record before the court, proves to be inaccurate. That way, a defendant ... has her right to appeal preserved. [¶] We conclude that an appellate court has the ability to examine a certification for defectiveness, and to use [TRAPs] 37.1 and 34.5(c) to obtain another certification, whenever appropriate. Neither of those rules provide any time limitation to their use. If the court chooses to examine a certification before the record is filed, it obviously cannot compare the certification to the record. If the court chooses to examine a certification after the record is filed, it has the ability to compare the certification to the record and, in that instance, a duty to do so."

Daniels v. State, 110 S.W.3d 174, 175 (Tex. App.—San Antonio 2003, pet. ref'd). "[W]e must determine the proper course of action when the trial court's certification under [TRAP] 25.2(a)(2) states the case 'is a plea-bargain case, and the defendant has NO right of appeal'; these statements are supported by the clerk's and reporter's records; but the appellant's brief has not been filed. We hold the proper course of action is to issue the notice provided for in [TRAP 37.1], because the certification, although it conforms to the form mandated by the [Court of Criminal Appeals], is 'defective' within the meaning we ascribe to the word in Rule 37.1 since it does not show the defendant has

the right of appeal." *But see Walker v. State*, 110 S.W.3d 509, 511 (Tex.App.—Waco 2003, no pet.) (certification taken at face value).

TRAP 38. REQUISITES OF BRIEFS

 38.1 Appellant's Brief. The appellant's brief must, under appropriate headings and in the order here indicated, contain the following:

(a) *Identity of parties and counsel.* The brief must give a complete list of all parties to the trial court's judgment or order appealed from, and the names and addresses of all trial and appellate counsel, except as otherwise provided in Rule 9.8.

(b) *Table of contents.* The brief must have a table of contents with references to the pages of the brief. The table of contents must indicate the subject matter of each issue or point, or group of issues or points.

(c) *Index of authorities.* The brief must have an index of authorities arranged alphabetically and indicating the pages of the brief where the authorities are cited.

(d) *Statement of the case.* The brief must state concisely the nature of the case (e.g., whether it is a suit for damages, on a note, or involving a murder prosecution), the course of proceedings, and the trial court's disposition of the case. The statement should be supported by record references, should seldom exceed one-half page, and should not discuss the facts.

(e) *Any statement regarding oral argument.* The brief may include a statement explaining why oral argument should or should not be permitted. Any such statement must not exceed one page and should address how the court's decisional process would, or would not, be aided by oral argument. As required by Rule 39.7, any party requesting oral argument must note that request on the front cover of the party's brief.

(f) *Issues presented.* The brief must state concisely all issues or points presented for review. The statement of an issue or point will be treated as covering every subsidiary question that is fairly included.

(g) *Statement of facts.* The brief must state concisely and without argument the facts pertinent to the issues or points presented. In a civil case, the court will accept as true the facts stated unless another party contradicts them. The statement must be supported by record references.

(h) *Summary of the argument.* The brief must contain a succinct, clear, and accurate statement of the arguments made in the body of the brief. This summary must not merely repeat the issues or points presented for review.

(i) *Argument.* The brief must contain a clear and concise argument for the contentions made, with appropriate citations to authorities and to the record.

(j) *Prayer.* The brief must contain a short conclusion that clearly states the nature of the relief sought.

(k) *Appendix in civil cases.*

(1) *Necessary contents.* Unless voluminous or impracticable, the appendix must contain a copy of:

(A) the trial court's judgment or other appealable order from which relief is sought;

(B) the jury charge and verdict, if any, or the trial court's findings of fact and conclusions of law, if any; and

(C) the text of any rule, regulation, ordinance, statute, constitutional provision, or other law (excluding case law) on which the argument is based, and the text of any contract or other document that is central to the argument.

(2) *Optional contents.* The appendix may contain any other item pertinent to the issues or points presented for review, including copies or excerpts of relevant court opinions, laws, documents on which the suit was based, pleadings, excerpts from the reporter's record, and similar material. Items should not be included in the appendix to attempt to avoid the page limits for the brief.

38.2 **Appellee's Brief.**

(a) *Form of brief.*

(1) An appellee's brief must conform to the requirements of Rule 38.1, except that:

(A) the list of parties and counsel is not required unless necessary to supplement or correct the appellant's list;

(B) the appellee's brief need not include a statement of the case, a statement of the issues presented, or a statement of facts, unless the appellee is dissatisfied with that portion of the appellant's brief; and

(C) the appendix to the appellee's brief need not contain any item already contained in an appendix filed by the appellant.

(2) When practicable, the appellee's brief should respond to the appellant's issues or points in the order the appellant presented those issues or points.

(b) *Cross-points.*

(1) *Judgment notwithstanding the verdict.* When the trial court renders judgment notwithstanding the verdict on one or more questions, the appellee must bring forward by cross-point any issue or point that would have vitiated the verdict or that would have prevented an affirmance of the judgment if the trial court had rendered judgment on the verdict. Failure to bring forward by cross-point an issue or point that would vitiate the verdict or prevent an affirmance of the judgment waives that complaint. Included in this requirement is a point that:

(A) the verdict or one or more jury findings have insufficient evidentiary support or are against the overwhelming preponderance of the evidence as a matter of fact; or

(B) the verdict should be set aside because of improper argument of counsel.

(2) *When evidentiary hearing needed.* The appellate court must remand a case to the trial court to take evidence if:

(A) the appellate court has sustained a point raised by the appellant; and

(B) the appellee raised a cross-point that requires the taking of additional evidence.

38.3 **Reply Brief.** The appellant may file a reply brief addressing any matter in the appellee's brief. However, the appellate court may consider and decide the case before a reply brief is filed.

 38.4 **Length of Briefs.** An appellant's brief or appellee's brief must be no longer than 50 pages, exclusive of the pages containing the identity of parties and counsel, any statement regarding oral argument, the table of contents, the index of authorities, the statement of the case, the issues presented, the signature, the proof of service, and the appendix. A reply brief must be no longer than 25 pages, exclusive of the items stated above. But in a civil case, the aggregate number of pages of all briefs filed by a party must not exceed 90, exclusive of the items stated above. The court may, on motion, permit a longer brief.

38.5 **Appendix for Cases Recorded Electronically.** In cases where the proceedings were electronically recorded, the following rules apply:

(a) *Appendix.*

(1) *In general.* At or before the time a party's brief is due, the party must file one copy of an appendix containing a transcription of all portions of the recording that the party considers relevant to the appellate issues or points. Unless another party objects, the transcription will be presumed accurate.

(2) *Repetition not required.* A party's appendix need not repeat evidence included in any previously filed appendix.

(3) *Form.* The form of the appendix and transcription must conform to any specifications of the Supreme Court and Court of Criminal Appeals concerning the form of the reporter's record except that it need not have the reporter's certificate.

(4) *Notice.* At the time the appendix is filed, the party must give written notice of the filing to all parties to the trial court's judgment or order. The notice must specify, by referring to the index numbers in the court recorder's logs, those parts of the recording that are included in the appendix. The filing party need not serve a copy of the appendix but must make a copy available to all parties for inspection and copying.

(b) *Presumptions.* The same presumptions that apply to a partial reporter's record under Rule 34.6(c)(4) apply to the parties' appendixes. The appellate court need not review any part of the electronic recording.

(c) *Supplemental appendix.* The appellate court may direct or allow a party to file a supplemental appendix containing a transcription of additional portions of the recording.

(d) *Inability to pay.* A party who cannot pay the cost of an appendix must file the affidavit provided for by Rule 20. The party must also state in the affidavit or a supplemental affidavit that the party has neither the access to the equipment necessary nor the skill necessary to prepare the appendix. If a contest to the affidavit is not sustained by written order, the court recorder must transcribe or have transcribed those portions of the recording that the party designates and must file the transcription as that party's appendix, along with all exhibits.

(e) *Inaccuracies.*

(1) *Correction by agreement.* The parties may agree to correct an inaccuracy in the transcription of the recording.

(2) *Correction by appellate or trial court.* If the parties dispute whether an electronic recording or transcription accurately discloses what occurred in the trial court but cannot agree on corrections, the appellate court may:

(A) settle the dispute by reviewing the recording; or

(B) submit the dispute to the trial court, which must—after notice and hearing—settle the dispute and ensure that the recording or transcription is made to conform to what occurred in the trial court.

(f) *Costs.* The actual expense of preparing the appendixes or the amount prescribed for official reporters, whichever is less, is taxed as costs. The appellate court may disallow the cost of any portion of the appendixes that it considers surplusage or that does not conform to any specifications prescribed by the Supreme Court or Court of Criminal Appeals.

38.6 Time to File Briefs.

(a) *Appellant's filing date.* Except in a habeas corpus or bail appeal, which is governed by Rule 31, an appellant must file a brief within 30 days—20 days in an accelerated appeal—after the later of:

(1) the date the clerk's record was filed; or

(2) the date the reporter's record was filed.

(b) *Appellee's filing date.* The appellee's brief must be filed within 30 days—20 days in an accelerated appeal—after the date the appellant's brief was filed. In a civil case, if the appellant has not filed a brief as provided in this rule, an appellee may file a brief within 30 days—20 days in an accelerated appeal—after the date the appellant's brief was due.

(c) *Filing date for reply brief.* A reply brief, if any, must be filed within 20 days after the date the appellee's brief was filed.

(d) *Modifications of filing time.* On motion complying with Rule 10.5(b), the appellate court may extend the time for filing a brief and may postpone submission of the case. A motion to extend the time to file a brief may be filed before or after the date the brief is due. The court may also, in the interests of justice, shorten the time for filing briefs and for submission of the case.

38.7 Amendment or Supplementation. A brief may be amended or supplemented whenever justice requires, on whatever reasonable terms the court may prescribe.

38.8 Failure of Appellant to File Brief.

(a) *Civil cases.* If an appellant fails to timely file a brief, the appellate court may:

(1) dismiss the appeal for want of prosecution, unless the appellant reasonably explains the failure and the appellee is not significantly injured by the appellant's failure to timely file a brief;

(2) decline to dismiss the appeal and give further direction to the case as it considers proper; or

(3) if an appellee's brief is filed, the court may regard that brief as correctly presenting the case and may affirm the trial court's judgment upon that brief without examining the record.

(b) *Criminal cases.*

(1) *Effect.* An appellant's failure to timely file a brief does not authorize either dismissal of the appeal or, except as provided in (4), consideration of the appeal without briefs.

(2) *Notice.* If the appellant's brief is not timely filed, the appellate clerk must notify counsel for the parties and the trial court of that fact. If the appellate court does not receive a satisfactory response within ten days, the court must order the trial court to immediately conduct a hearing to determine whether the appellant desires to prosecute his appeal, whether the appellant is indigent, or, if not indigent, whether retained counsel has abandoned the appeal, and to make appropriate findings and recommendations.

(3) *Hearing.* In accordance with (2), the trial court must conduct any necessary hearings, make appropriate findings and recommendations, and have a record of the proceedings prepared, which record—including any order and findings—must be sent to the appellate court.

(4) *Appellate court action.* Based on the trial court's record, the appellate court may act appropriately to ensure that the appellant's rights are protected, including initiating contempt proceedings against appellant's counsel. If the trial court has found that the appellant no longer desires to prosecute the appeal, or that the appellant is not indigent but has not made the necessary arrangements for filing a brief, the appellate court may consider the appeal without briefs, as justice may require.

38.9 **Briefing Rules to Be Construed Liberally.** Because briefs are meant to acquaint the court with the issues in a case and to present argument that will enable the court to decide the case, substantial compliance with this rule is sufficient, subject to the following.

(a) *Formal defects.* If the court determines that this rule has been flagrantly violated, it may require a brief to be amended, supplemented, or redrawn. If another brief that does not comply with this rule is filed, the court may strike the brief, prohibit the party from filing another, and proceed as if the party had failed to file a brief.

(b) *Substantive defects.* If the court determines, either before or after submission, that the case has not been properly presented in the briefs, or that the law and authorities have not been properly cited in the briefs, the court may postpone submission, require additional briefing, and make any other order necessary for a satisfactory submission of the case.

Generally

Pena v. State, 191 S.W.3d 133, 136 (Tex.Crim.App. 2006). "We have previously held, and reaffirm today, that appellate courts are free to review 'unassigned error'—a claim that was preserved in the trial below but was not raised on appeal. ... We recognize that many, if not most, of the types of error that would prompt *sua sponte* appellate attention need not be assigned because the error involved constitutes an obvious violation of established rules. Novel constitutional issues are a different matter."

TRAP 38.1

Walder v. State, 85 S.W.3d 824, 828 (Tex.App.—Waco 2002, no pet.). "'Appropriate citations to authorities' should include pertinent cases, statutes, rules and constitutional provisions. When citing cases, counsel should identify and cite, at a minimum, pertinent decisions of the Supreme Court of the U.S., the Court of Criminal Appeals, of this Court when available, and if no cases from this Court can be located on the issue presented, of other Texas intermediate courts of appeals. Counsel need not cite more than three cases on settled issues or principles. 'In citing cases, specific page citations should be given to the pages where the relevant holdings or quotations may be found.' Counsel should research the subsequent history of any case cited to be sure that it has not been reversed or modified. When counsel cites a decision of one of the fourteen intermediate courts of appeals, counsel should provide a subsequent history on any petition for discretionary review or indicate that no petition was filed."

TRAP 38.8

Volosen v. State, 227 S.W.3d 77, 80 (Tex.Crim.App. 2007). "Because the State prevailed at trial, it was not required to raise any allegations before the court of appeals. The [TRAPs] require an appellant to file a brief but impose no such requirement on an appellee. Regardless of whether an appellee files a brief, a first-level appellate court has the obligation to conduct a thorough review of an appellant's claims, including any subsidiary issues that might result in upholding the trial court's judgment. An appellee's failure to make a particular argument is a factor that may be considered when this Court decides whether to exercise its discretion to grant review, but it does not bar this Court from granting review to address the issue if the Court, in its discretion, decides that review is warranted."

Reich-Bacot v. State, 952 S.W.2d 542, 543 (Tex. Crim.App.1997). "[I]ndigent appellant is entitled to assistance of counsel in filing a brief on remand from this Court. If no brief is timely filed the Court of Appeals must inquire as to the reason for that omission. [¶] The record does not reflect that notice was sent to Appellant informing him of his right to file a brief, or that the Court of Appeals inquired as to why one was not filed. In the absence of any brief by counsel or inquiry by the appellate court, it must be presumed that Appellant was not represented by counsel."

TRAP 38.9

State v. Bailey, 201 S.W.3d 739, 743 (Tex.Crim.App. 2006). "[I]t violates 'ordinary notions of procedural default' for a court of appeals to reverse a trial court's decision on a legal theory that the complaining party did not present to the trial court. Accordingly, we have established that an appellate court may not reverse a trial court 'on a theory that the trial court did not have the opportunity to rule upon and upon which the non-appealing party did not have an opportunity to develop a complete factual record.'"

Bufkin v. State, 179 S.W.3d 166, 173-74 (Tex. App.—Houston [14th Dist.] 2005), *aff'd*, 207 S.W.3d 779 (Tex.Crim.App.2006). "[T]he State chastens this court for failing to address its contention that appellant has failed to present anything for review by omitting citations to the record regarding this point of error. [I]t is the court's prerogative, not the parties,' to insist on unerring compliance with the briefing rules. Where … the court has had no difficulty locating the pertinent portions of the record relating to appellant's third point of error, it is within the court's discretion to review the point of error."

TRAP 39. ORAL ARGUMENT; DECISION WITHOUT ARGUMENT

39.1 **Right to Oral Argument.** A party who has filed a brief and who has timely requested oral argument may argue the case to the court unless the court, after examining the briefs, decides that oral argument is unnecessary for any of the following reasons:

(a) the appeal is frivolous;

(b) the dispositive issue or issues have been authoritatively decided;

(c) the facts and legal arguments are adequately presented in the briefs and record; or

(d) the decisional process would not be significantly aided by oral argument.

39.2 **Purpose of Argument.** Oral argument should emphasize and clarify the written arguments in the briefs. Counsel should not merely read from prepared text. Counsel should assume that all members of the court have read the briefs before oral argument and counsel should be prepared to respond to questions. A party should not refer to or comment on matters not involved in or pertaining to what is in the record.

39.3 **Time Allowed.** The court will set the time that will be allowed for argument. Counsel must complete argument in the time allotted and may continue after the expiration of the allotted time only with permission of the court. Counsel is not required to use all the allotted time. The appellant must be allowed to conclude the argument.

39.4 **Number of Counsel.** Generally, only one counsel should argue for each side. Except on leave of court, no more than two counsel on each side may argue. Only one counsel may argue in rebuttal.

39.5 **Argument by Amicus.** With leave of court obtained before the argument and with a party's consent, an amicus curiae may share allotted time with that party. Otherwise, counsel for amicus may not argue.

39.6 **When Only One Party Files a Brief.** If counsel for only one party has filed a brief, the court may allow that party to argue.

39.7 Request and Waiver. A party desiring oral argument must note that request on the front cover of the party's brief. A party's failure to request oral argument waives the party's right to argue. But even if a party has waived oral argument, the court may direct the party to appear and argue.

(08) 39.8 Clerk's Notice. The clerk must send to the parties—at least 21 days before the date the case is set for argument or submission without argument—a notice telling the parties:

(a) whether the court will allow oral argument or will submit the case without argument;

(b) the date of argument or submission without argument;

(c) if argument is allowed, the time allotted for argument; and

(d) the names of the members of the panel to which the case will be argued or submitted, subject to change by the court.

A party's failure to receive the notice does not prevent a case's argument or submission on the scheduled date.

TRAP 40. ORDER OF DECISION

40.1 Civil Cases. The court of appeals may determine the order in which civil cases will be decided. But the following types of cases have precedence over all others:

(a) a case given precedence by law;

(b) an accelerated appeal; and

(c) a case that the court determines should be given precedence in the interest of justice.

40.2 Criminal Cases. In cases not otherwise given precedence by law, the court of appeals must hear and determine a criminal appeal at the earliest possible time, having due regard for the parties' rights and for the proper administration of justice.

(08) TRAP 41. PANEL & EN BANC DECISION

41.1 Decision by Panel.

(a) Constitution of panel. Unless a court of appeals with more than three justices votes to decide a case en banc, a case must be assigned for decision to a panel of the court consisting of three justices, although not every member of the panel must be present for argument. If the case is decided without argument, three justices must participate in the decision. A majority of the panel, which constitutes a quorum, must agree on the judgment. Except as otherwise provided in these rules, a panel's opinion constitutes the court's opinion, and the court must render a judgment in accordance with the panel opinion.

(b) When panel cannot agree on judgment. After argument, if for any reason a member of the panel cannot participate in deciding a case, the case may be decided by the two remaining justices. If they cannot agree on a judgment, the chief justice of the court of appeals must:

(1) designate another justice of the court to sit on the panel to consider the case;

(2) request the Chief Justice of the Supreme Court to temporarily assign an eligible justice or judge to sit on the panel to consider the case; or

(3) convene the court en banc to consider the case.

The reconstituted panel or the en banc court may order the case reargued.

(c) When court cannot agree on judgment. After argument, if for any reason a member of a court consisting of only three justices cannot participate in deciding a case, the case may be decided by the two remaining justices. If they cannot agree on a judgment, that fact must be certified to the Chief Justice of the Supreme Court. The Chief Justice may then temporarily assign an eligible justice or judge to sit with the court of appeals to consider the case. The reconstituted court may order the case reargued.

41.2 Decision by En Banc Court.

(a) Constitution of en banc court. An en banc court consists of all members of the court who are not disqualified or recused and—if the case was originally argued before or decided by a panel—any members of the panel who are not members of the court but remain eligible for assignment to the court. A majority of the en banc court constitutes a quorum. A majority of the en banc court must agree on a judgment.

(b) When en banc court cannot agree on judgment. If a majority of an en banc court cannot agree on a judgment, that fact must be certified to the Chief Justice of the Supreme Court. The Chief Justice may then temporarily assign an eligible justice or judge to sit with the court of appeals to consider the case. The reconstituted court may order the case reargued.

TRAP 39

(c) *En banc consideration disfavored.* En banc consideration of a case is not favored and should not be ordered unless necessary to secure or maintain uniformity of the court's decisions or unless extraordinary circumstances require en banc consideration. A vote to determine whether a case will be heard or reheard en banc need not be taken unless a justice of the court requests a vote. If a vote is requested and a majority of the court's members vote to hear or rehear the case en banc, the en banc court will hear or rehear the case. Otherwise, a panel of the court will consider the case.

41.3 **Precedent in Transferred Cases.** In cases transferred by the Supreme Court from one court of appeals to another, the court of appeals to which the case is transferred must decide the case in accordance with the precedent of the transferor court under principles of stare decisis if the transferee court's decision otherwise would have been inconsistent with the precedent of the transferor court. The court's opinion may state whether the outcome would have been different had the transferee court not been required to decide the case in accordance with the transferor court's precedent.

TRAP 42. DISMISSAL; SETTLEMENT

42.1 **Voluntary Dismissal and Settlement in Civil Cases.**

(a) *On motion or by agreement.* The appellate court may dispose of an appeal as follows:

(1) *On motion of appellant.* In accordance with a motion of appellant, the court may dismiss the appeal or affirm the appealed judgment or order unless such disposition would prevent a party from seeking relief to which it would otherwise be entitled.

(2) *By agreement.* In accordance with an agreement signed by the parties or their attorneys and filed with the clerk, the court may:

(A) render judgment effectuating the parties' agreement;

(B) set aside the trial court's judgment without regard to the merits and remand the case to the trial court for rendition of judgment in accordance with the agreement; or

(C) abate the appeal and permit proceedings in the trial court to effectuate the agreement.

(b) *Partial disposition.* A severable portion of the proceeding may be disposed of under (a) if it will not prejudice the remaining parties.

(c) *Effect on court's opinion.* In dismissing a proceeding, the appellate court will determine whether to withdraw any opinion it has already issued. An agreement or motion for dismissal cannot be conditioned on withdrawal of the opinion.

(d) *Costs.* Absent agreement of the parties, the court will tax costs against the appellant.

42.2 **Voluntary Dismissal in Criminal Cases.**

(a) At any time before the appellate court's decision, the appellate court may dismiss the appeal upon the appellant's motion. The appellant and his or her attorney must sign the written motion to dismiss and file it in duplicate with the appellate clerk, who must immediately send the duplicate copy to the trial court clerk.

(b) After the court of appeals hands down its opinion, it may not grant an appellant's motion to dismiss the appeal unless the other parties consent. If the other parties consent and the court of appeals grants the appellant's motion to dismiss the appeal, the appellate opinion must be withdrawn and the appeal dismissed. The appellate clerk must send notice of the dismissal to the trial court clerk.

42.3 **Involuntary Dismissal in Civil Cases.** Under the following circumstances, on any party's motion—or on its own initiative after giving ten days' notice to all parties—the appellate court may dismiss the appeal or affirm the appealed judgment or order. Dismissal or affirmance may occur if the appeal is subject to dismissal:

(a) for want of jurisdiction;

(b) for want of prosecution; or

(c) because the appellant has failed to comply with a requirement of these rules, a court order, or a notice from the clerk requiring a response or other action within a specified time.

42.4 **Involuntary Dismissal in Criminal Cases.** The appellate court must dismiss an appeal on the State's motion, supported by affidavit, showing that the appellant has escaped from custody pending the appeal and that to the affiant's knowledge, the appellant has not, within ten days after escaping, voluntarily returned to lawful custody within the state.

(a) *Timely return to custody; reinstatement.* The appeal may not be dismissed—or, if dismissed, must be reinstated—if an affidavit of an officer or other credible person is filed showing that the appellant, within ten days after escaping, voluntarily returned to lawful custody within the state.

(b) *Life sentence.* The appellate court may overrule the motion to dismiss—or, if the motion was granted, may reinstate the appeal—if:

(1) the appellant received a life sentence; and

(2) the appellant is recaptured or voluntarily surrenders within 30 days after escaping.

ANNOTATIONS

TRAP 42.2

Conners v. State, 966 S.W.2d 108, 111 (Tex.App.—Houston [1st Dist.] 1998, pet. ref'd). "[W]e suspend the requirements of rule 42.2(a) in this case. Despite counsel's refusal to prepare and sign a rule-conforming motion, we dismiss the appeal at appellant's request...."

TRAP 42.4

Ike v. State, 998 S.W.2d 323, 324 (Tex.App.—Houston [1st Dist.] 1999, no pet.). "In determining whether Appellant has escaped for purposes of Rule 42.4, we do not necessarily apply the definition under the Texas Penal Code, but rather, we apply the term's 'commonly-accepted meaning.' [¶] [A]ppellant had been released on bond and remained on bond at the time he disappeared. The fact that appellant's bond had been forfeited shows that the trial court did not approve of his disappearance. Because he was on bond at the time of his disappearance, appellant's liberties were restrained. We conclude that appellant escaped from custody for purposes of Rule 42.4."

TRAP 43. JUDGMENT OF THE COURT OF APPEALS

43.1 **Time.** The court of appeals should render its judgment promptly after submission of a case.

43.2 **Types of Judgment.** The court of appeals may:

(a) affirm the trial court's judgment in whole or in part;

(b) modify the trial court's judgment and affirm it as modified;

(c) reverse the trial court's judgment in whole or in part and render the judgment that the trial court should have rendered;

(d) reverse the trial court's judgment and remand the case for further proceedings;

(e) vacate the trial court's judgment and dismiss the case; or

(f) dismiss the appeal.

43.3 **Rendition Appropriate Unless Remand Necessary.** When reversing a trial court's judgment, the court must render the judgment that the trial court should have rendered, except when:

(a) a remand is necessary for further proceedings; or

(b) the interests of justice require a remand for another trial.

43.4 **Judgment for Costs in Civil Cases.** In a civil case, the court of appeal's judgment should award to the prevailing party the appellate costs—including preparation costs for the clerk's record and the reporter's record—that were incurred by that party. But the court of appeals may tax costs otherwise as required by law or for good cause.

43.5 **Judgment Against Sureties in Civil Cases.** When a court of appeals affirms the trial court judgment, or modifies that judgment and renders judgment against the appellant, the court of appeals must render judgment against the sureties on the appellant's supersedeas bond, if any, for the performance of the judgment and for any costs taxed against the appellant.

43.6 **Other Orders.** The court of appeals may make any other appropriate order that the law and the nature of the case require.

ANNOTATIONS

TRAP 43.2

Collier v. State, 999 S.W.2d 779, 782 (Tex.Crim. App.1999). "[A] court of appeals may reform a judgment of conviction to reflect conviction of a lesser included offense only if (1) the court finds that the evidence is insufficient to support conviction of the charged offense but sufficient to support conviction of the lesser included offense and (2) either the jury was instructed on the lesser included offense (at the request of a party or by the trial court *sua sponte*) or one of the parties asked for but was denied such an instruction. [¶] If the trial court does not instruct the jury on the lesser included offense and neither party seeks such an instruction, then the court of appeals will not be authorized to reform the judgment and thereby give the State the benefit of jury instructions no one at trial requested." *See also* **Haynes v. State**, ___ S.W.3d ___ (Tex.Crim.App.2008) (No. PD-1923-06; 4-30-08).

TRAP 44. REVERSIBLE ERROR

44.1 Reversible Error in Civil Cases.

(a) *Standard for reversible error.* No judgment may be reversed on appeal on the ground that the trial court made an error of law unless the court of appeals concludes that the error complained of:

(1) probably caused the rendition of an improper judgment; or

(2) probably prevented the appellant from properly presenting the case to the court of appeals.

(b) *Error affecting only part of case.* If the error affects part of, but not all, the matter in controversy and that part is separable without unfairness to the parties, the judgment must be reversed and a new trial ordered only as to the part affected by the error. The court may not order a separate trial solely on unliquidated damages if liability is contested.

44.2 Reversible Error in Criminal Cases.

(a) *Constitutional error.* If the appellate record in a criminal case reveals constitutional error that is subject to harmless error review, the court of appeals must reverse a judgment of conviction or punishment unless the court determines beyond a reasonable doubt that the error did not contribute to the conviction or punishment.

(b) *Other errors.* Any other error, defect, irregularity, or variance that does not affect substantial rights must be disregarded.

(c) *Presumptions.* Unless the following matters were disputed in the trial court, or unless the record affirmatively shows the contrary, the court of appeals must presume:

(1) that venue was proved in the trial court;

(2) that the jury was properly impaneled and sworn;

(3) that the defendant was arraigned;

(4) that the defendant pleaded to the indictment or other charging instrument; and

(5) that the court's charge was certified by the trial court and filed by the clerk before it was read to the jury.

44.3 Defects in Procedure. A court of appeals must not affirm or reverse a judgment or dismiss an appeal for formal defects or irregularities in appellate procedure without allowing a reasonable time to correct or amend the defects or irregularities.

44.4 Remediable Error of the Trial Court.

(a) *Generally.* A court of appeals must not affirm or reverse a judgment or dismiss an appeal if:

(1) the trial court's erroneous action or failure or refusal to act prevents the proper presentation of a case to the court of appeals; and

(2) the trial court can correct its action or failure to act.

(b) *Court of appeals direction if error remediable.* If the circumstances described in (a) exist, the court of appeals must direct the trial court to correct the error. The court of appeals will then proceed as if the erroneous action or failure to act had not occurred.

ANNOTATIONS

TRAP 44.2(a)

Scott v. State, 227 S.W.3d 670, 690–91 (Tex.Crim. App.2007). "In determining specifically whether constitutional error under **Crawford** [*v. Washington*, 541 U.S. 36, 124 S.Ct. 1354 (2004)] may be declared harmless beyond a reasonable doubt, ... the following factors are relevant: 1) how important was the out-of-court statement to the State's case; 2) whether the out-of-court statement was cumulative of other evidence; 3) the presence or absence of evidence corroborating or contradicting the out-of-court statement on material points; and 4) the overall strength of the prosecution's case. [T]he emphasis of a harm analysis pursuant to Rule 44.2(a) should not be on 'the propriety of the outcome of the trial.' That is to say, the question for the reviewing court is not whether the jury verdict was supported by the evidence. Instead, the question is the likelihood that the constitutional error was actually a contributing factor in the jury's deliberations in arriving at that verdict-whether, in other words, the error adversely affected 'the integrity of the process leading to the conviction.' In reaching that decision, the reviewing court may also consider, in addition to the factors listed above, ... the source and nature of the error, to what extent, if any, it was emphasized by the State, and how weighty the jury may have found the erroneously admitted evidence to be compared to the balance

TRAP 44

of the evidence with respect to the element or defensive issue to which it is relevant. With these considerations in mind, the reviewing court must ask itself whether there is a reasonable possibility that the *Crawford* error moved the jury from a state of non-persuasion to one of persuasion on a particular issue. Ultimately, after considering these various factors, the reviewing court must be able to declare itself satisfied, to a level of confidence beyond a reasonable doubt, 'that the error did not contribute to the conviction' before it can affirm it."

Olivas v. State, 202 S.W.3d 137, 145 (Tex.Crim.App. 2006). "The court of appeals ... held that, even if the error were not structural [the deadly weapon issue did not explicitly incorporate the required beyond-a-reasonable-doubt burden of proof], it was constitutionally harmful error under [TRAP] 44.2(a). However, Rule 44.2(a) does not apply to jury-charge error. The appropriate standard for all errors in the jury-charge, statutory or constitutional, is that set out in *Almanza* [*v. State*, 686 S.W.2d 157 (Tex.Crim.App.1984)]."

Franklin v. State, 138 S.W.3d 351, 355 (Tex.Crim. App.2004). "We hesitate to hold Franklin to a burden of showing actual bias or prejudice [by juror] when the trial judge denied him the ability to develop evidence of actual bias or prejudice on the record. We believe that all of these factors together—[juror's] failure to reveal her relationship to the victim, the judge's denial of a mistrial, and the trial judge's refusal to allow defense counsel to question [juror] about her relationship to the victim—affected Franklin's right to a trial by an impartial jury. So, we conclude that the Court of Appeals properly applied the constitutional standard of harm under Rule 44.2(a)."

Potier v. State, 68 S.W.3d 657, 665 (Tex.Crim.App. 2002). "We hold that the exclusion of a defendant's evidence will be constitutional error only if the evidence forms such a vital portion of the case that exclusion effectively precludes the defendant from presenting a defense."

Hernandez v. State, 60 S.W.3d 106, 106 (Tex.Crim. App.2001). "In this case, we granted review to determine whether the court of appeals erred in holding that the admission of evidence obtained in violation of the 4th Amendment is non-constitutional error. The Supreme Court has concluded that the 4th Amendment requires exclusion of evidence obtained in violation thereof and has held that requirement applicable to the

states by the 14th Amendment. Therefore, we hold that the proper harm analysis in this case is the constitutional one of [TRAP] 44.2(a)."

TRAP 44.2(b)

Rich v. State, 160 S.W.3d 575, 577-78 (Tex.Crim. App.2005). D was improperly prevented from asking venirepersons what 'reasonable doubt' meant to them. "[A] harm analysis in this instance should [use 44.2(b) to] assess whether the defendant's substantial rights were affected—that is, whether the error had a substantial and injurious effect or influence in determining the jury's verdict. In the case of the erroneous admission of evidence, we have said that the appellate court should consider everything in the record, including any testimony or physical evidence admitted for the jury's consideration, the nature of the evidence supporting the verdict, the character of the alleged error and how it might be considered in connection with other evidence in the case, the jury instructions, the State's theory and any defensive theories, closing arguments, voir dire, and whether the State emphasized the error. We believe these same general factors are relevant considerations in determining the harm from being denied a proper question to the venire."

Guevara v. State, 152 S.W.3d 45, 47 (Tex.Crim.App. 2004). "[W]e hold that the correct standard of review for jury-charge error is [CCP art.] 36.19.... *At 54:* We also hold that the Court of Appeals erred in using [TRAP] 44.2(b) as the standard by which to assess harm for the jury-charge error."

Hawkins v. State, 135 S.W.3d 72, 77 (Tex.Crim.App. 2004). "[T]he question of whether a mistrial should have been granted involves most, if not all, of the same considerations that attend a harm analysis. A mistrial is the trial court's remedy for improper conduct that is 'so prejudicial that expenditure of further time and expense would be wasteful and futile.' In effect, the trial court conducts an appellate function: determining whether improper conduct is so harmful that the case must be redone. Of course, the harm analysis is conducted in light of the trial court's curative instruction. Only in extreme circumstances, where the prejudice is incurable, will a mistrial be required. [¶] [T]he *Mosley* factors should be used to evaluate whether the trial court abused its discretion in denying a mistrial for improper argument, at least in cases like this one, in which constitutional rights are not implicated. [¶] We balance three factors: (1) the severity of the misconduct (prejudicial effect), (2) curative measures, and (3) the certainty of the punishment assessed absent the misconduct (likelihood of the same punishment being assessed)."

Burnett v. State, 88 S.W.3d 633, 637-38 (Tex.Crim.App.2002). "Courts of appeals must conduct the harm analysis of statutory errors, as a species of other errors, under Rule 44.2(b), disregarding the error unless it affect[ed] [appellant's] substantial rights. For claims of non-constitutional error, we ... hold that a conviction should not be overturned unless, after examining the record as a whole, a court concludes that an error may have had substantial influence on the outcome of the proceeding. Put another way, if the reviewing court has a grave doubt that the result was free from the substantial influence of the error, then it must treat the error as if it did. Grave doubt means that in the judge's mind, the matter is so evenly balanced that he feels himself in virtual equipoise as to the harmlessness of the error. Thus, in cases of grave doubt as to harmlessness the petitioner must win. [¶] Neither the appellant nor the State have any formal burden to show harm or harmlessness under Rule 44.2(b)." (Internal quotes omitted.) *See also* **McGowen v. State**, 25 S.W.3d 741, 746 (Tex.App.—Houston [14th Dist.] 2000, pet. ref'd); **King v. State**, 953 S.W.2d 266, 271 (Tex.Crim.App. 1997).

Motilla v. State, 78 S.W.3d 352, 353-54 (Tex.Crim.App.2002). "In a harm analysis under Rule 44.2(b), is an appellate court required to disregard overwhelming evidence of the defendant's guilt? The answer is no. We reaffirm our previous holdings that an appellate court can and should consider overwhelming evidence of guilt in a harm analysis."

Mosley v. State, 983 S.W.2d 249, 259 (Tex.Crim.App.1998). TRAP 44.2(b) "is taken directly from [FRCvP] 52(a) without substantive change. Hence, in construing the impact of Rule 44.2(b), federal case law would appear to provide especially useful guidance."

Daggett v. State, 103 S.W.2d 444, 451 (Tex.App.—San Antonio 2002), *vacated on other grounds*, 187 S.W.3d 444 (Tex.Crim.App.2005). "A trial court's rulings regarding improper jury argument is non-constitutional error reviewed under a substantial rights analysis."

Roberson v. State, 100 S.W.3d 36, 44 (Tex.App.—Waco 2002, pet. ref'd). "Because we are reviewing an error which occurred during the punishment phase, Rule 44.2(a) requires a reversal of the 'judgment of punishment' unless we 'determine[ ] beyond a reasonable doubt that the error did not contribute to the ... punishment.'"

TRAP 44.4(a)

State v. Cullen, 195 S.W.3d 696, 700 (Tex.Crim.App. 2006). "Because an appellate court's review of a trial court's ruling is restricted by an inadequate record of the basis for the trial court's ruling, we find it necessary to require a trial court to express its findings of fact and conclusions of law when requested by the losing party."

TRAP 44.4(b)

Lapointe v. State, 225 S.W.3d 513, 522 (Tex.Crim.App.2007). "When a trial court has erroneously withheld information necessary to evaluate a defendant's claim on appeal (e.g. failure to file required findings of fact) or has prevented the defendant from submitting information necessary to evaluate his claim (e.g. refusing to permit an offer of proof), the appellate court is directed to step in and order the trial court to correct the situation. The key to Rule 44.4 is that there must be an error that the appellate court can correct, And if the error in question is subject to the usual rules of procedural default, then it must have been preserved by objection."

TRAP 45. DAMAGES FOR FRIVOLOUS APPEALS IN CIVIL CASES

If the court of appeals determines that an appeal is frivolous, it may—on motion of any party or on its own initiative, after notice and a reasonable opportunity for response—award each prevailing party just damages. In determining whether to award damages, the court must not consider any matter that does not appear in the record, briefs, or other papers filed in the court of appeals.

TRAP 46. REMITTITUR IN CIVIL CASES

46.1 **Remittitur After Appeal Perfected.** If the trial court suggests a remittitur but the case is appealed before the remittitur is filed, the party who would make the remittitur may do so in the court of appeals in the same manner as in the trial court. The court of appeals must then render the judgment that the trial court should have rendered if the remittitur had been made in the trial court.

46.2 Appeal on Remittitur. If a party makes the remittitur at the trial judge's suggestion and the party benefiting from the remittitur appeals, the remitting party is not barred from contending in the court of appeals that all or part of the remittitur should not have been required, but the remitting party must perfect an appeal to raise that point. If the court of appeals sustains the remitting party's contention that remittitur should not have been required, the court must render the judgment that the trial court should have rendered.

46.3 Suggestion of Remittitur by Court of Appeals. The court of appeals may suggest a remittitur. If the remittitur is timely filed, the court must reform and affirm the trial court's judgment in accordance with the remittitur. If the remittitur is not timely filed, the court must reverse the trial court's judgment.

46.4 Refusal to Remit Must Not Be Mentioned in Later Trial. If the court of appeals suggests a remittitur but no remittitur is filed, evidence of the court's determination regarding remittitur is inadmissible in a later trial of the case.

46.5 Voluntary Remittitur. If a court of appeals reverses the trial court's judgment because of a legal error that affects only part of the damages awarded by the judgment, the affected party may—within 15 days after the court of appeals' judgment—voluntarily remit the amount that the affected party believes will cure the reversible error. A party may include in a motion for rehearing—without waiving any complaint that the court of appeals erred—a conditional request that the court accept the remittitur and affirm the trial court's judgment as reduced. If the court of appeals determines that the voluntary remittitur is not sufficient to cure the reversible error, but that remittitur is appropriate, the court must suggest a remittitur in accordance with Rule 46.3. If the remittitur is timely filed and the court of appeals determines that the voluntary remittitur cures the reversible error, then the court must accept the remittitur and reform and affirm the trial court judgment in accordance with the remittitur.

TRAP 47. OPINIONS, PUBLICATION & CITATION

47.1 Written Opinions. The court of appeals must hand down a written opinion that is as brief as practicable but that addresses every issue raised and necessary to final disposition of the appeal.

 47.2 Designation and Signing of Opinions; Participating Justices.

(a) *Civil and criminal cases.* Each opinion of the court must be designated either an "Opinion" or a "Memorandum Opinion." A majority of the justices who participate in considering the case must determine whether the opinion will be signed by a justice or will be per curiam and whether it will be designated an opinion or memorandum opinion. The names of the participating justices must be noted on all written opinions or orders of the court or a panel of the court.

(b) *Criminal cases.* In addition, each opinion and memorandum opinion in a criminal case must bear the notation "publish" or "do not publish" as determined—before the opinion is handed down—by a majority of the justices who participate in considering the case. Any party may move the appellate court to change the notation, but the court of appeals must not change the notation after the Court of Criminal Appeals has acted on any party's petition for discretionary review or other request for relief. The Court of Criminal Appeals may, at any time, order that a "do not publish" notation be changed to "publish."

(c) *Civil cases.* Opinions and memorandum opinions in civil cases issued on or after January 1, 2003 shall not be designated "do not publish."

47.3 Distribution of Opinions. All opinions of the courts of appeals are open to the public and must be made available to public reporting services, print or electronic.

47.4 Memorandum Opinions. If the issues are settled, the court should write a brief memorandum opinion no longer than necessary to advise the parties of the court's decision and the basic reasons for it. An opinion may not be designated a memorandum opinion if the author of a concurrence or dissent opposes that designation. An opinion must be designated a memorandum opinion unless it does any of the following:

(a) establishes a new rule of law, alters or modifies an existing rule, or applies an existing rule to a novel fact situation likely to recur in future cases;

(b) involves issues of constitutional law or other legal issues important to the jurisprudence of Texas;

(c) criticizes existing law; or

(d) resolves an apparent conflict of authority.

47.5 Concurring and Dissenting Opinions.
Only a justice who participated in the decision of a case may file or join in an opinion concurring in or dissenting from the judgment of the court of appeals. Any justice on the court may file an opinion in connection with a denial of a hearing or rehearing en banc.

47.6 Change in Designation by En Banc Court.
A court en banc may change a panel's designation of an opinion.

08 47.7 Citation of Unpublished Opinions.

(a) *Criminal cases.* Opinions and memorandum opinions not designated for publication by the court of appeals under these or prior rules have no precedential value but may be cited with the notation, "(not designated for publication)."

(b) *Civil cases.* Opinions and memorandum opinions designated "do not publish" under these rules by the courts of appeals prior to January 1, 2003 have no precedential value but may be cited with the notation, "(not designated for publication)." If an opinion or memorandum opinion issued on or after that date is erroneously designated "do not publish," the erroneous designation will not affect the precedential value of the decision.

ANNOTATIONS

TRAP 47.1

Garrett v. State, 220 S.W.3d 926, 928-29 (Tex.Crim. App.2007). "Because the court of appeals' orders ordering briefing on the sufficiency of the evidence did not grant or even impliedly grant a supplemental issue for review, we conclude that [TRAP] 38.1(e) controls the resolution of Garrett's complaint. Rule 38.1 requires that an appellant designate all issues for review in the original brief. Indeed, Rule 38.1 allows an appellant to present whatever issues for review he or she desires, with very few limitations. Thus, an appellant is the master of his or her own destiny with respect to what issues the court of appeals is required to address within its written opinion. Had Garrett raised the sufficiency of the evidence in his original brief, or had the court of appeals explicitly granted the supplemental issue for review when it requested supplemental briefing, the court of appeals, pursuant to Rule 47.1, would have been required to address the issue concerning the factual sufficiency of the evidence in its written opinion."

Kombudo v. State, 171 S.W.3d 888, 889 (Tex.Crim. App.2005). TRAP 47.1 "requires a court of appeals to address an appellee's reply that the appellant's point was not preserved for review. When an opinion fails to address even an alternative argument in an appellee's reply, [Court of Criminal Appeals] may remand the case to the court of appeals."

Light v. State, 15 S.W.3d 104, 105 (Tex.Crim.App. 2000). "The courts of appeals are required to review every argument raised by a party that is necessary to the disposition of that appeal." *See also* TRAP 41.1.(a); *Davis v. State*, 817 S.W.2d 345, 346 (Tex.Crim.App. 1991).

TRAP 47.7

Carrillo v. State, 98 S.W.3d 789, 794 (Tex.App.— Amarillo 2003, pet. ref'd). "By stating that unpublished opinions may be cited but have no precedential value, we perceive the intent of the rule to be that a court has no obligation to follow such opinions. The effect of the rule is to afford parties more flexibility in pointing out such opinions and the reasoning employed in them rather then simply arguing, without reference, that same reasoning."

TRAP 48. COPY OF OPINION & JUDGMENT TO INTERESTED PARTIES & OTHER COURTS

48.1 Mailing Opinion and Judgment in All Cases. On the date when an appellate court's opinion is handed down, the appellate clerk must mail or deliver copies of the opinion and judgment to the following persons:

(a) the trial judge;

(b) the trial court clerk;

(c) the regional administrative judge; and

(d) all parties to the appeal.

48.2 Additional Recipients in Criminal Cases. In criminal cases, copies of the opinion and judgment will also be mailed or delivered to the State Prosecuting Attorney.

48.3 Filing Opinion and Judgment. The trial court clerk must file a copy of the opinion and judgment among the papers of the case in that court.

48.4 Opinion Sent to Criminal Defendant. In criminal cases, the attorney representing the defendant on appeal shall, within five days after the opinion is handed down, send his client a copy of the opinion and judgment, along with notification of the defendant's right to file a *pro se* petition for discretionary review under Rule 68. This notification shall be sent certified mail, return receipt requested, to the defendant at his last known address. The attorney shall also send the court of appeals a letter certifying his compliance with this rule and attaching a copy of the return receipt within the time for filing a motion for rehearing. The court of appeals shall file this letter in its record of the appeal.

TRAP 49. MOTION FOR REHEARING & EN BANC RECONSIDERATION

49.1 **Motion for Rehearing.** A motion for rehearing may be filed within 15 days after the court of appeals' judgment or order is rendered. The motion must clearly state the points relied on for the rehearing.

49.2 **Response.** No response to a motion for rehearing need be filed unless the court so requests. A motion will not be granted unless a response has been filed or requested by the court.

49.3 **Decision on Motion.** A motion for rehearing may be granted by a majority of the justices who participated in the decision of the case. Otherwise, it must be denied. If rehearing is granted, the court or panel may dispose of the case with or without rebriefing and oral argument.

49.4 **Accelerated Appeals.** In an accelerated appeal, the appellate court may deny the right to file a motion for rehearing or shorten the time to file such a motion.

49.5 **Further Motion for Rehearing.** After a motion for rehearing is decided, a further motion for rehearing may be filed within 15 days of the court's action if the court:

(a) modifies its judgment;

(b) vacates its judgment and renders a new judgment; or

08 (c) issues a different opinion.

08 **49.6** **Amendments.** A motion for rehearing or en banc reconsideration may be amended as a matter of right anytime before the 15-day period allowed for filing the motion expires, and with leave of the court, anytime before the court of appeals decides the motion.

 49.7 **En Banc Reconsideration.** A party may file a motion for en banc reconsideration as a separate motion, with or without filing a motion for rehearing. The motion must be filed within 15 days after the court of appeals' judgment or order, or when permitted, within 15 days after the court of appeals' denial of the party's last timely filed motion for rehearing or en banc reconsideration. While the court has plenary power, a majority of the en banc court may, with or without a motion, order en banc reconsideration of a panel's decision. If a majority orders reconsideration, the panel's judgment or order does not become final, and the case will be resubmitted to the court for en banc review and disposition.

08 **49.8** **Extension of Time.** A court of appeals may extend the time for filing a motion for rehearing or en banc reconsideration if a party files a motion complying with Rule 10.5(b) no later than 15 days after the last date for filing the motion.

49.9 **Not Required for Review.** A motion for rehearing is not a prerequisite to filing a petition for review in the Supreme Court or a petition for discretionary review in the Court of Criminal Appeals nor is it required to preserve error.

49.10 **Length of Motion and Response.** A motion or response must be no longer than 15 pages.

08 **49.11** **Relationship to Petition for Review.** A party may not file a motion for rehearing or en banc reconsideration in the court of appeals after that party has filed a petition for review in the Supreme Court unless the court of appeals modifies its opinion or judgment after the petition for review is filed. The filing of a petition for review does not preclude another party from filing a motion for rehearing or en banc reconsideration or preclude the court of appeals from ruling on the motion. If a motion for rehearing or en banc reconsideration is timely filed after a petition for review is filed, the petitioner must immediately notify the Supreme Court clerk of the filing of the motion, and must notify the clerk when the last timely filed motion is overruled by the court of appeals.

08 **49.12** **Certificate of Conference Not Required.** A certificate of conference is not required for a motion for rehearing or en banc reconsideration of a panel's decision.

 TRAP 50. RECONSIDERATION ON PETITION FOR DISCRETIONARY REVIEW

Within 60 days after a petition for discretionary review is filed with the clerk of the court of appeals that delivered the decision, the justices who participated in the decision may, as provided by subsection (a), reconsider and correct or modify the court's opinion or judgment. Within the same period of time, any of the justices who participated in the decision may issue a concurring or dissenting opinion.

(a) If the court's original opinion or judgment is corrected or modified, that opinion or judgment is withdrawn and the modified or corrected opinion or judgment is substituted as the opinion or judgment of the court. No further opinions may be issued by the court of appeals. The original petition for discretionary review is not dismissed by operation of law, unless the filing party files a new petition in the court of appeals. In the alternative, the petitioning party shall submit to the court of appeals copies of the corrected or modified opinion or judgment as an amendment to the original petition.

(b) Any party may then file with the court of appeals a new petition for discretionary review seeking review of the corrected or modified opinion or judgment, including any dissents or concurrences, under Rule 68.2.

ANNOTATIONS

Beller v. State, 191 S.W.3d 718, 718 (Tex.Crim.App. 2005). "The Court of Appeals did not act properly under [TRAP] 50, which requires that the corrected or modified opinion be substituted as the opinion or judgment of the court within 30 days after a petition for discretionary review has been filed with the clerk of the court of appeals. Accordingly, the court had no authority to withdraw its opinion without substituting another within the proper time period. After the 30 day period, the court of appeals had no jurisdiction to act concerning its opinion. Therefore, the Court of Appeals' opinion issued on September 15, 2004, is ordered reinstated."

TRAP 51. ENFORCEMENT OF JUDGMENTS AFTER MANDATE

51.1 Civil Cases.

(a) *Statement of costs.* The appellate clerk must prepare, and send to the trial court clerk with the mandate, a statement of costs showing:

(1) the preparation costs for the appellate record, and any court of appeals filing fees, with a notation of those items that have been paid and those that are owing; and

(2) the party or parties against whom costs have been adjudged.

(b) *Enforcement of judgment.* When the trial court clerk receives the mandate, the appellate court's judgment must be enforced. Appellate court costs must be included with the trial court costs in any process to enforce the judgment. If all or part of the costs are collected, the trial court clerk must immediately remit to the appellate court clerk any amount due to that clerk. The trial court need not make any further order in the case, and the appellate court's judgment may be enforced as in other cases, when the appellate judgment:

(1) affirms the trial court's judgment;

(2) modifies the trial court's judgment and, as so modified, affirms that judgment; or

(3) renders the judgment the trial court should have rendered.

51.2 Criminal Cases. When the trial court clerk receives the mandate, the appellate court's judgment must be enforced as follows:

(a) *Clerk's duties.* The trial court clerk must:

(1) send an acknowledgment to the appellate clerk of the mandate's receipt; and

(2) immediately file the mandate.

(b) *Judgment of affirmance;defendant not in custody.*

(1) *Capias to be issued.* If the judgment contains a sentence of confinement or imprisonment that has not been suspended, the trial court must promptly issue a capias for the defendant's arrest so that the court's sentence can be executed.

(2) *Contents of capias.* The capias may issue to any county of this state and must be executed and returned as in felony cases, except that no bail may be taken. The capias must:

(A) recite the fact of conviction;

(B) set forth the offense and the court's judgment and sentence;

(C) state that the judgment was appealed from and affirmed, and that the mandate has been filed; and

(D) command the sheriff to arrest and take the defendant into his custody, and to place and keep the defendant in custody until delivered to the proper authorities as directed by the sentence.

(3) *Sheriff's duties.* The sheriff must promptly execute the capias as directed. The sheriff must notify the trial court clerk and the appellate clerk when the mandate has been carried out and executed.

(c) *Judgment of reversal.*

(1) *When new trial ordered.* When the appellate court reverses the trial court's judgment and grants the defendant a new trial, the procedure is governed by Code of Criminal Procedure article 44.29. If the defendant is in custody and entitled to bail, the defendant must be released upon giving bail.

(2) *When case dismissed.* When the appellate court reverses the trial court's judgment and orders the case to be dismissed, the defendant—if in custody—must be discharged.

(d) *Judgment of acquittal.* When the appellate court reverses a judgment and orders the defendant's acquittal, the defendant—if in custody—must be discharged, and no further order or judgment of the trial court is necessary.

ANNOTATIONS

TRAP 51.2

In re Guarino, 64 S.W.3d 597, 600 (Tex.App.—Houston [1st Dist.] 2001, no pet.). "Rule 51.2(b)(2)(D) requires that the capias must 'command the sheriff to arrest and take the defendant into his custody, **and to place and keep the defendant in custody until delivered to the proper authorities as directed by the sentence.**' This rule makes no provision for a later 'voluntary surrender,' as [trial judge] ordered in this case. [¶] We hold that [trial judge] erred in not issuing a capias upon receipt of this Court's mandates, as it was her ministerial duty to do. The November 8, 2001 order does not constitute a capias because it does not command a peace officer to [make an] arrest …, as required by Rule 51.2(b)(2)(D). "

SECTION THREE: ORIGINAL PROCEEDINGS IN SUPREME COURT & COURTS OF APPEALS

TRAP 52. ORIGINAL PROCEEDINGS

52.1 **Commencement.** An original appellate proceeding seeking extraordinary relief—such as a writ of habeas corpus, mandamus, prohibition, injunction, or quo warranto—is commenced by filing a petition with the clerk of the appropriate appellate court. The petition must be captioned "*In re* [name of relator]."

52.2 **Designation of Parties.** The party seeking the relief is the relator. In original proceedings other than habeas corpus, the person against whom relief is sought—whether a judge, court, tribunal, officer, or other person—is the respondent. A person whose interest would be directly affected by the relief sought is a real party in interest and a party to the case.

 52.3 **Form and Contents of Petition.** The petition must, under appropriate headings and in the order here indicated, contain the following:

(a) *Identity of parties and counsel.* The petition must give a complete list of all parties, and the names, and addresses of all counsel.

(b) *Table of contents.* The petition must include a table of contents with references to the pages of the petition. The table of contents must indicate the subject matter of each issue or point, or group of issues or points.

(c) *Index of authorities.* The petition must include an index of authorities arranged alphabetically and indicating the pages of the petition where the authorities are cited.

(d) *Statement of the case.* The petition must contain a statement of the case that should seldom exceed one page and should not discuss the facts. The statement must contain the following:

(1) a concise description of the nature of any underlying proceeding (e.g., a suit for damages, a contempt proceeding for failure to pay child support, or the certification of a candidate for inclusion on an election ballot);

(2) if the respondent is a judge, the name of the judge, the designation of the court in which the judge was sitting, and the county in which the court is located; and if the respondent is an official other than a judge, the designation and location of the office held by the respondent;

(3) a concise description of the respondent's action from which the relator seeks relief;

(4) if the relator seeks a writ of habeas corpus, a statement describing how and where the relator is being deprived of liberty;

(5) if the petition is filed in the Supreme Court after a petition requesting the same relief was filed in the court of appeals:

(A) the date the petition was filed in the court of appeals;

(B) the district of the court of appeals and the names of the justices who participated in the decision;

(C) the author of any opinion for the court of appeals and the author of any separate opinion;

(08) (D) the citation of the court's opinion;

(E) the disposition of the case by the court of appeals, and the date of the court of appeals' order.

(e) *Statement of jurisdiction.* The petition must state, without argument, the basis of the court's jurisdiction. If the Supreme Court and the court of appeals have concurrent jurisdiction, the petition must be presented first to the court of appeals unless there is a compelling reason not to do so. If the petition is filed in the Supreme Court without first being presented to the court of appeals, the petition must state the compelling reason why the petition was not first presented to the court of appeals.

(f) *Issues presented.* The petition must state concisely all issues or points presented for relief. The statement of an issue or point will be treated as covering every subsidiary question that is fairly included.

(08) (g) *Statement of facts.* The petition must state concisely and without argument the facts pertinent to the issues or points presented. Every statement of fact in the petition must be supported by citation to competent evidence included in the appendix or record.

(h) *Argument.* The petition must contain a clear and concise argument for the contentions made, with appropriate citations to authorities and to the appendix or record.

(i) *Prayer.* The petition must contain a short conclusion that clearly states the nature of the relief sought.

(08) (j) *Certification.* The person filing the petition must certify that he or she has reviewed the petition and concluded that every factual statement in the petition is supported by competent evidence included in the appendix or record.

(k) *Appendix.*

(1) *Necessary contents.* The appendix must contain:

(A) a certified or sworn copy of any order complained of, or any other document showing the matter complained of;

(B) any order or opinion of the court of appeals, if the petition is filed in the Supreme Court;

(C) unless voluminous or impracticable, the text of any rule, regulation, ordinance, statute, constitutional provision, or other law (excluding case law) on which the argument is based; and

(D) if a writ of habeas corpus is sought, proof that the relator is being restrained.

(2) *Optional contents.* The appendix may contain any other item pertinent to the issues or points presented for review, including copies or excerpts of relevant court opinions, statutes, constitutional provisions, documents on which the suit was based, pleadings, and similar material. Items should not be included in the appendix to attempt to avoid the page limits for the petition. The appendix should not contain any evidence or other item that is not necessary for a decision.

52.4 **Response.** Any party may file a response to the petition, but it is not mandatory. The court must not grant relief—other than temporary relief—before a response has been filed or requested by the court. The response must conform to the requirements of 52.3, except that:

(a) the list of parties and counsel is not required unless necessary to supplement or correct the list contained in the petition;

(b) the response need not include a statement of the case, a statement of the issues presented, or a statement of the facts unless the responding party is dissatisfied with that portion of the petition;

(c) a statement of jurisdiction should be omitted unless the petition fails to assert valid grounds for jurisdiction, in which case the reasons why the court lacks jurisdiction must be concisely stated;

(d) the argument must be confined to the issues or points presented in the petition; and

(e) the appendix to the response need not contain any item already contained in an appendix filed by the relator.

TRAP 52

52.5 Relator's Reply to Response. The relator may file a reply addressing any matter in the response. However, the court may consider and decide the case before a reply brief is filed.

 52.6 Length of Petition, Response, and Reply. Excluding those pages containing the identity of parties and counsel, the table of contents, the index of authorities, the statement of the case, the statement of jurisdiction, the issues presented, the signature, the proof of service, the certification, and the appendix, the petition and response must not exceed 50 pages each if filed in the court of appeals, or 15 pages each if filed in the Supreme Court. A reply may be no longer than 25 pages if filed in the court of appeals or 8 pages if filed in the Supreme Court, exclusive of the items stated above. The court may, on motion, permit a longer petition, response, or reply.

52.7 Record.

(a) *Filing by relator required.* Relator must file with the petition:

(1) a certified or sworn copy of every document that is material to the relator's claim for relief and that was filed in any underlying proceeding; and

(2) a properly authenticated transcript of any relevant testimony from any underlying proceeding, including any exhibits offered in evidence, or a statement that no testimony was adduced in connection with the matter complained.

(b) *Supplementation permitted.* After the record is filed, relator or any other party to the proceeding may file additional materials for inclusion in the record.

(c) *Service of record on all parties.* Relator and any party who files materials for inclusion in the record must—at the same time—serve on each party:

(1) those materials not previously served on that party as part of the record in another original appellate proceeding in the same or another court; and

(2) an index listing the materials filed and describing them in sufficient detail to identify them.

52.8 Action on Petition.

(a) *Relief denied.* If the court determines from the petition and any response and reply that the relator is not entitled to the relief sought, the court must deny the petition. If the relator in a habeas corpus proceeding has been released on bond, the court must remand the relator to custody and issue an order of commitment. If the relator is not returned to custody, the court may declare the bond to be forfeited and render judgment against the surety.

(b) *Interim action.* If the court is of the tentative opinion that relator is entitled to the relief sought or that a serious question concerning the relief requires further consideration:

(1) the court must request a response if one has not been filed;

(2) the Supreme Court may request full briefing under Rule 55;

(3) in a habeas corpus proceeding, the court may order that relator be discharged on execution and filing of a bond in an amount set by the court; and

(4) the court may set the case for oral argument.

(c) *Relief granted.* If the court determines that relator is entitled to relief, it must make an appropriate order. The court may grant relief without hearing oral argument.

(d) *Opinion.* When denying relief, the court may hand down an opinion but is not required to do so. When granting relief, the court must hand down an opinion as in any other case. Rule 47 is applicable to an order or opinion by a court of appeals except that the court of appeals may not order an unpublished opinion published after the Supreme Court or Court of Criminal Appeals has acted on any party's petition for extraordinary relief addressing the same issues.

52.9 Motion for Rehearing. Any party may file a motion for rehearing within 15 days after the final order is rendered. The motion must clearly state the points relied on for the rehearing. No response to a motion for rehearing need be filed unless the court so requests. The court will not grant a motion for rehearing unless a response has been filed or requested. A motion or response must be no longer than 15 pages.

52.10 Temporary Relief.

(a) *Motion for temporary relief; certificate of compliance.* The relator may file a motion to stay any underlying proceedings or for any other temporary relief pending the court's action on the petition. The relator must notify or make a diligent effort to notify all parties by expedited means (such as by telephone or fax) that a motion for temporary relief has been or will be filed and must certify to the court that the relator has complied with this paragraph before temporary relief will be granted.

(b) *Grant of temporary relief.* The court—on motion of any party or on its own initiative—may without notice grant any just relief pending the court's action on the petition. As a condition of granting temporary relief, the court may require a bond to protect the parties who will be affected by the relief. Unless vacated or modified, an order granting temporary relief is effective until the case is finally decided.

(c) *Motion to reconsider.* Any party may move the court at any time to reconsider a grant of temporary relief.

52.11 **Groundless Petition or Misleading Statement or Record.** On motion of any party or on its own initiative, the court may—after notice and a reasonable opportunity to respond—impose just sanctions on a party or attorney who is not acting in good faith as indicated by any of the following:

(a) filing a petition that is clearly groundless;

(b) bringing the petition solely for delay of an underlying proceeding;

(c) grossly misstating or omitting an obviously important and material fact in the petition or response; or

(d) filing an appendix or record that is clearly misleading because of the omission of obviously important and material evidence or documents.

SECTION FOUR: PROCEEDINGS IN THE SUPREME COURT

TRAP 53. PETITION FOR REVIEW

53.1 **Method of Review.** The Supreme Court may review a court of appeals' final judgment on a petition for review addressed to "The Supreme Court of Texas." A party who seeks to alter the court of appeals' judgment must file a petition for review. The petition for review procedure replaces the writ of error procedure. Statutes pertaining to the writ of error in the Supreme Court apply equally to the petition for review.

53.2 **Contents of Petition.** The petition for review must, under appropriate headings and in the order here indicated, contain the following items:

(a) *Identity of parties and counsel.* The petition must give a complete list of all parties to the trial court's final judgment, and the names and addresses of all trial and appellate counsel.

(b) *Table of contents.* The petition must have a table of contents with references to the pages of the petition. The table of contents must indicate the subject matter of each issue or point, or group of issues or points.

(c) *Index of authorities.* The petition must have an index of authorities arranged alphabetically and indicating the pages of the petition where the authorities are cited.

(d) *Statement of the case.* The petition must contain a statement of the case that should seldom exceed one page and should not discuss the facts. The statement must contain the following:

(1) a concise description of the nature of the case (e.g., whether it is a suit for damages, on a note, or in trespass to try title);

(2) the name of the judge who signed the order or judgment appealed from;

(3) the designation of the trial court and the county in which it is located;

(4) the disposition of the case by the trial court;

(5) the parties in the court of appeals;

(6) the district of the court of appeals;

(7) the names of the justices who participated in the decision in the court of appeals, the author of the opinion for the court, and the author of any separate opinion;

(8) the citation for the court of appeals' opinion; and

(9) the disposition of the case by the court of appeals, including the disposition of any motions for rehearing or en banc reconsideration, and whether any motions for rehearing or en banc reconsideration are pending in the court of appeals at the time the petition for review is filed.

(e) *Statement of jurisdiction.* The petition must state, without argument, the basis of the Court's jurisdiction.

(f) *Issues presented.* The petition must state concisely all issues or points presented for review. The statement of an issue or point will be treated as covering every subsidiary question that is fairly included. If the matter complained of originated in the trial court, it should have been preserved for appellate review in the trial court and assigned as error in the court of appeals.

(g) *Statement of facts.* The petition must affirm that the court of appeals correctly stated the nature of the case, except in any particulars pointed out. The petition must state concisely and without argument the facts and procedural background pertinent to the issues or points presented. The statement must be supported by record references.

(h) *Summary of the argument.* The petition must contain a succinct, clear, and accurate statement of the arguments made in the body of the petition. This summary must not merely repeat the issues or points presented for review.

(i) *Argument.* The petition must contain a clear and concise argument for the contentions made, with appropriate citations to authorities and to the record. The argument need not address every issue or point included in the statement of issues or points. Any issue or point not addressed may be addressed in the brief on the merits if one is requested by the Court. The argument should state the reasons why the Supreme Court should exercise jurisdiction to hear the case with specific reference to the factors listed in Rule 56.1(a). The petition need not quote at length from a matter included in the appendix; a reference to the appendix is sufficient. The Court will consider the court of appeals' opinion along with the petition, so statements in that opinion need not be repeated.

(j) *Prayer.* The petition must contain a short conclusion that clearly states the nature of the relief sought.

(k) *Appendix.*

(1) *Necessary contents.* Unless voluminous or impracticable, the appendix must contain a copy of:

(A) the judgment or other appealable order of the trial court from which relief in the court of appeals was sought;

(B) the jury charge and verdict, if any, or the trial court's findings of fact and conclusions of law, if any;

(C) the opinion and judgment of the court of appeals; and

(D) the text of any rule, regulation, ordinance, statute, constitutional provision, or other law on which the argument is based (excluding case law), and the text of any contract or other document that is central to the argument.

(2) *Optional contents.* The appendix may contain any other item pertinent to the issues or points presented for review, including copies or excerpts of relevant court opinions, statutes, constitutional provisions, documents on which the suit was based, pleadings, and similar material. Items should not be included in the appendix to attempt to avoid the page limits for the petition.

53.3 **Response to Petition for Review.** Any other party to the appeal may file a response to the petition for review, but it is not mandatory. If no response is timely filed, or if a party files a waiver of response, the Court will consider the petition without a response. A petition will not be granted before a response has been filed or requested by the Court. The response must conform to the requirements of 53.2, except that:

(a) the list of parties and counsel is not required unless necessary to supplement or correct the list contained in the petition;

(b) a statement of the case and a statement of the facts need not be made unless the respondent is dissatisfied with that portion of the petition;

(c) a statement of the issues presented need not be made unless:

(1) the respondent is dissatisfied with the statement made in the petition;

(2) the respondent is asserting independent grounds for affirmance of the court of appeals' judgment; or

(3) the respondent is asserting grounds that establish the respondent's right to a judgment that is less favorable to the respondent than the judgment rendered by the court of appeals but more favorable to the respondent than the judgment that might be awarded to the petitioner (e.g., a remand for a new trial rather than a rendition of judgment in favor of the petitioner);

(d) a statement of jurisdiction should be omitted unless the petition fails to assert valid grounds for jurisdiction, in which case the reasons why the Supreme Court lacks jurisdiction must be concisely stated;

(e) the respondent's argument must be confined to the issues or points presented in the petition or asserted by the respondent in the respondent's statement of issues; and

(f) the appendix to the response need not contain any item already contained in an appendix filed by the petitioner.

53.4 **Points Not Considered in Court of Appeals.** To obtain a remand to the court of appeals for consideration of issues or points briefed in that court but not decided by that court, or to request that the Supreme Court consider such issues or points, a party may raise those issues or points in the petition, the response, the reply, any brief, or a motion for rehearing.

53.5 **Petitioner's Reply to Response.** The petitioner may file a reply addressing any matter in the response. However, the Court may consider and decide the case before a reply brief is filed.

53.6 **Length of Petition, Response, and Reply.** The petition and any response must be no longer than 15 pages each, exclusive of pages containing the identity of parties and counsel, the table of contents, the index of authorities, the statement of the case, the statement of jurisdiction, the issues presented, the signature, the proof of service, and the appendix. A reply may be no longer than 8 pages, exclusive of the items stated above. The Court may, on motion, permit a longer petition, response, or reply.

53.7 **Time and Place of Filing.**

08 (a) *Petition.* Unless the Supreme Court orders an earlier filing deadline, the petition must be filed with the Supreme Court clerk within 45 days after the following:

(1) the date the court of appeals rendered judgment, if no motion for rehearing or en banc reconsideration is timely filed; or

(2) the date of the court of appeals' last ruling on all timely filed motions for rehearing or en banc reconsideration.

08 (b) *Premature filing.* A petition filed before the last ruling on all timely filed motions for rehearing and en banc reconsideration is treated as having been filed on the date of, but after, the last ruling on any such motion. If a party files a petition for review while a motion for rehearing or en banc reconsideration is pending in the court of appeals, the party must include that information in its petition for review.

(c) *Petitions filed by other parties.* If a party files a petition for review within the time specified in 53.7(a)—or within the time specified by the Supreme Court in an order granting an extension of time to file a petition—any other party required to file a petition may do so within 45 days after the last timely motion for rehearing is overruled or within 30 days after any preceding petition is filed, whichever date is later.

(d) *Response.* Any response must be filed with the Supreme Court clerk within 30 days after the petition is filed.

(e) *Reply.* Any reply must be filed with the Supreme Court clerk within 15 days after the response is filed.

(f) *Extension of time.* The Supreme Court may extend the time to file a petition for review if a party files a motion complying with Rule 10.5(b) no later than 15 days after the last day for filing the petition. The Supreme Court may extend the time to file a response or reply if a party files a motion complying with Rule 10.5(b) either before or after the response or reply is due.

(g) *Petition filed in court of appeals.* If a petition is mistakenly filed in the court of appeals, the petition is deemed to have been filed the same day with the Supreme Court clerk, and the court of appeals clerk must immediately send the petition to the Supreme Court clerk.

53.8 **Amendment.** On motion showing good cause, the Court may allow the petition, response, or reply to be amended on such reasonable terms as the Court may prescribe.

53.9 **Court May Require Revision.** If a petition, response, or reply does not conform with these rules, the Supreme Court may require the document to be revised or may return the document to the party who filed it and consider the case without allowing the document to be revised.

TRAP 54. FILING THE RECORD

54.1 **Request for Record.** With or without granting the petition for review, the Supreme Court may request that the record from the court of appeals be filed with the clerk of the Supreme Court.

54.2 **Duty of Court of Appeals Clerk.**

(a) *Request for record.* The court of appeals clerk must not send the record to the Supreme Court unless it is requested. Upon receiving the Supreme Court clerk's request for the record, the court of appeals clerk must promptly send to the Supreme Court clerk all of the following:

(1) the original record;

(2) any motion filed in the court of appeals;

(3) copies of all orders of the court of appeals; and

(4) copies of all opinions and the judgment of the court of appeals.

(b) *Nondocumentary exhibits.* The clerk should not send any nondocumentary exhibits unless the Supreme Court specifically requests.

54.3 **Expenses.** The petitioner must pay to the court of appeals clerk a sum sufficient to pay the cost of mailing or shipping the record to and from the Supreme Court clerk.

54.4 **Duty of Supreme Court Clerk.** Upon receiving the record, the Supreme Court clerk must file it and enter the filing on the docket. The clerk may refuse the record if the charges for mailing or shipping have not been paid.

TRAP 55. BRIEFS ON THE MERITS

55.1 **Request by Court.** A brief on the merits must not be filed unless requested by the Court. With or without granting the petition for review, the Court may request the parties to file briefs on the merits. In appropriate cases, the Court may realign parties and direct that parties file consolidated briefs.

55.2 **Petitioner's Brief on the Merits.** The petitioner's brief on the merits must be confined to the issues or points stated in the petition for review and must, under appropriate headings and in the order here indicated, contain the following items:

(a) *Identity of parties and counsel.* The brief must give a complete list of all parties to the trial court's final judgment, and the names and addresses of all trial and appellate counsel.

(b) *Table of contents.* The brief must have a table of contents with references to the pages of the brief. The table of contents must indicate the subject matter of each issue or point, or group of issues or points.

(c) *Index of authorities.* The brief must have an index of authorities arranged alphabetically and indicating the pages of the brief where the authorities are cited.

(d) *Statement of the case.* The brief must contain a statement of the case that should seldom exceed one page and should not discuss the facts. The statement must contain the following:

(1) a concise description of the nature of the case (e.g., whether it is a suit for damages, on a note, or in trespass to try title);

(2) the name of the judge who signed the order or judgment appealed from;

(3) the designation of the trial court and the county in which it is located;

(4) the disposition of the case by the trial court;

(5) the parties in the court of appeals;

(6) the district of the court of appeals;

(7) the names of the justices who participated in the decision in the court of appeals, the author of the opinion for the court, and the author of any separate opinion;

(8) the citation for the court of appeals' opinion, if available, or a statement that the opinion was unpublished; and

(9) the disposition of the case by the court of appeals.

(e) *Statement of jurisdiction.* The brief must state, without argument, the basis of the Court's jurisdiction.

(f) *Issues presented.* The brief must state concisely all issues or points presented for review. The statement of an issue or point will be treated as covering every subsidiary question that is fairly included. The phrasing of the issues or points need not be identical to the statement of issues or points in the petition for review, but the brief may not raise additional issues or points or change the substance of the issues or points presented in the petition.

(g) *Statement of facts.* The brief must affirm that the court of appeals correctly stated the nature of the case, except in any particulars pointed out. The brief must state concisely and without argument the facts and procedural background pertinent to the issues or points presented. The statement must be supported by record references.

(h) *Summary of the argument.* The brief must contain a succinct, clear, and accurate statement of the arguments made in the body of the brief. This summary must not merely repeat the issues or points presented for review.

(i) *Argument.* The brief must contain a clear and concise argument for the contentions made, with appropriate citations to authorities and to the record.

(j) *Prayer.* The brief must contain a short conclusion that clearly states the nature of the relief sought.

55.3 **Respondent's Brief.** If the petitioner files a brief on the merits, any other party to the appeal may file a brief in response, which must conform to 55.2, except that:

(a) the list of parties and counsel is not required unless necessary to supplement or correct the list contained in the petitioner's brief;

(b) a statement of the case and a statement of the facts need not be made unless the respondent is dissatisfied with that portion of the petitioner's brief; and

(c) a statement of the issues presented need not be made unless:

(1) the respondent is dissatisfied with the statement made in the petitioner's brief;

(2) the respondent is asserting independent grounds for affirmance of the court of appeals' judgment; or

(3) the respondent is asserting grounds that establish the respondent's right to a judgment that is less favorable to the respondent than the judgment rendered by the court of appeals but more favorable to the respondent than the judgment that might be awarded to the petitioner (e.g., a remand for a new trial rather than a rendition of judgment in favor of the petitioner);

(d) a statement of jurisdiction should be omitted unless the petition fails to assert valid grounds for jurisdiction; and

(e) the respondent's argument must be confined to the issues or points presented in the petitioner's brief or asserted by the respondent in the respondent's statement of issues.

55.4 **Petitioner's Brief in Reply.** The petitioner may file a reply brief addressing any matter in the brief in response. However, the Court may consider and decide the case before a reply brief is filed.

55.5 **Reliance on Prior Brief.** As a brief on the merits or a brief in response, a party may file the brief that the party filed in the court of appeals.

55.6 **Length of Briefs.** A brief on the merits or brief in response must not exceed 50 pages, exclusive of pages containing the identity of parties and counsel, the table of contents, the index of authorities, the statement of the case, the statement of jurisdiction, the issues presented, the signature, and the proof of service. A brief in reply may be no longer than 25 pages, exclusive of the items stated above. The Court may, on motion, permit a longer brief.

55.7 **Time and Place of Filing; Extension of Time.** Briefs must be filed with the Supreme Court clerk in accordance with the schedule stated in the clerk's notice that the Court has requested briefs on the merits. If no schedule is stated in the notice, petitioner must file a brief on the merits within 30 days after the date of the notice, respondent must file a brief in response within 20 days after receiving petitioner's brief, and petitioner must file any reply brief within 15 days after receiving respondent's brief. On motion complying with Rule 10.5(b) either before or after the brief is due, the Supreme Court may extend the time to file a brief.

55.8 **Amendment.** On motion showing good cause, the Court may allow a party to amend a brief on such reasonable terms as the Court may prescribe.

55.9 **Court May Require Revision.** If a brief does not conform with these rules, the Supreme Court may require the brief to be revised or may return it to the party who filed it and consider the case without further briefing by that party.

TRAP 56. ORDERS ON PETITION FOR REVIEW

56.1 **Orders on Petition for Review.**

(a) *Considerations in granting review.* Whether to grant review is a matter of judicial discretion. Among the factors the Supreme Court considers in deciding whether to grant a petition for review are the following:

(1) whether the justices of the court of appeals disagree on an important point of law;

(2) whether there is a conflict between the courts of appeals on an important point of law;

(3) whether a case involves the construction or validity of a statute;

(4) whether a case involves constitutional issues;

(5) whether the court of appeals appears to have committed an error of law of such importance to the state's jurisprudence that it should be corrected; and

(6) whether the court of appeals has decided an important question of state law that should be, but has not been, resolved by the Supreme Court.

(b) *Petition denied or dismissed.* When the petition has been on file in the Supreme Court for 30 days, the Court may deny or dismiss the petition—whether or not a response has been filed—with one of the following notations:

(1) *"Denied."* If the Supreme Court is not satisfied that the opinion of the court of appeals has correctly declared the law in all respects, but determines that the petition presents no error that requires reversal or that is of such importance to the jurisprudence of the state as to require correction, the Court will deny the petition with the notation "Denied."

(2) *"Dismissed w.o.j."* If the Supreme Court lacks jurisdiction, the Court will dismiss the petition with the notation "Dismissed for Want of Jurisdiction."

(c) *Petition refused.* If the Supreme Court determines—after a response has been filed or requested—that the court of appeals' judgment is correct and that the legal principles announced in the opinion are likewise correct, the Court will refuse the petition with the notation "Refused." The court of appeals' opinion in the case has the same precedential value as an opinion of the Supreme Court.

(d) *Improvident grant.* If the Court has granted review but later decides that review should not have been granted, the Court may, without opinion, set aside the order granting review and dismiss the petition or deny or refuse review as though review had never been granted.

56.2 **Moot Cases.** If a case is moot, the Supreme Court may, after notice to the parties, grant the petition and, without hearing argument, dismiss the case or the appealable portion of it without addressing the merits of the appeal.

56.3 **Settled Cases.** If a case is settled by agreement of the parties and the parties so move, the Supreme Court may grant the petition if it has not already been granted and, without hearing argument or considering the merits, render a judgment to effectuate the agreement. The Supreme Court's action may include setting aside the judgment of the court of appeals or the trial court without regard to the merits and remanding the case to the trial court for rendition of a judgment in accordance with the agreement. The Supreme Court may abate the case until the lower court's proceedings to effectuate the agreement are complete. A severable portion of the proceeding may be disposed of if it will not prejudice the remaining parties. In any event, the Supreme Court's order does not vacate the court of appeals' opinion unless the order specifically provides otherwise. An agreement or motion cannot be conditioned on vacating the court of appeals' opinion.

56.4 **Notice to Parties.** When the Supreme Court grants, denies, refuses, or dismisses a petition for review, the Supreme Court clerk must send a written notice of the disposition to the court of appeals, the trial court, and all parties to the appeal.

56.5 **Return of Documents to Court of Appeals.** When the Supreme Court denies, refuses, or dismisses a petition for review, the clerk will retain the petition, together with the record and accompanying papers, for 30 days after the order is rendered. If no motion for rehearing has been filed by the end of that period or when any motion for rehearing of the order has been overruled, the clerk must send a certified copy of its order to the court of appeals and return the record and all papers (except for documents filed in the Supreme Court) to the court of appeals clerk.

TRAP 57. DIRECT APPEALS TO THE SUPREME COURT

57.1 **Application.** This rule governs direct appeals to the Supreme Court that are authorized by the Constitution and by statute. Except when inconsistent with a statute or this rule, the rules governing appeals to courts of appeals also apply to direct appeals to the Supreme Court.

57.2 **Jurisdiction.** The Supreme Court may not take jurisdiction over a direct appeal from the decision of any court other than a district court or county court, or over any question of fact. The Supreme Court may decline to exercise jurisdiction over a direct appeal of an interlocutory order if the record is not adequately developed, or if its decision would be advisory, or if the case is not of such importance to the jurisprudence of the state that a direct appeal should be allowed.

57.3 **Statement of Jurisdiction.** Appellant must file with the record a statement fully but plainly setting out the basis asserted for exercise of the Supreme Court's jurisdiction. Appellee may file a response to appellant's statement of jurisdiction within ten days after the statement is filed.

57.4 **Preliminary Ruling on Jurisdiction.** If the Supreme Court notes probable jurisdiction over a direct appeal, the parties must file briefs under Rule 38 as in any other case. If the Supreme Court does not note probable jurisdiction over a direct appeal, the appeal will be dismissed.

57.5 **Direct Appeal Exclusive While Pending.** If a direct appeal to the Supreme Court is filed, the parties to the appeal must not, while that appeal is pending, pursue an appeal to the court of appeals. But if the direct appeal is dismissed, any party may pursue any

TRAP 56

other appeal available at the time when the direct appeal was filed. The other appeal must be perfected within ten days after dismissal of the direct appeal.

TRAP 58. CERTIFICATION OF QUESTIONS OF LAW BY UNITED STATES COURTS

58.1 **Certification.** The Supreme Court of Texas may answer questions of law certified to it by any federal appellate court if the certifying court is presented with determinative questions of Texas law having no controlling Supreme Court precedent. The Supreme Court may decline to answer the questions certified to it.

58.2 **Contents of the Certification Order.** An order from the certifying court must set forth:

(a) the questions of law to be answered; and

(b) a stipulated statement of all facts relevant to the questions certified, showing fully the nature of the controversy in which the questions arose.

58.3 **Transmission of Certification Order.** The clerk of the certifying court must send to the clerk of the Supreme Court of Texas the following:

(a) the certification order under the certifying court's official seal;

(b) a list of the names of all parties to the pending case, giving the address and telephone number, if known, of any party not represented by counsel; and

(c) a list of the names, addresses, and telephone numbers of counsel for each party.

58.4 **Transmission of Record.** The certifying court should not send the Supreme Court of Texas the record in the pending case with the certification order. The Supreme Court may later require the original or copies of all or part of the record before the certifying court to be filed with the Supreme Court clerk.

58.5 **Fees and Costs.** Unless the certifying court orders otherwise in its certification order, the parties must bear equally the fees under Rule 5.

58.6 **Notice.** If the Supreme Court agrees to answer the questions certified to it, the Court will notify all parties and the certifying court. The Supreme Court clerk must also send a notice to the Attorney General of Texas if:

(a) the constitutionality of a Texas statute is the subject of a certified question that the Supreme Court has agreed to answer; and

(b) the State of Texas or an officer, agency, or employee of the state is not a party to the proceeding in the certifying court.

58.7 **Briefs and Oral Argument.**

(a) *Briefs.* The appealing party in the certifying court must file a brief with the Supreme Court clerk within 30 days after the date of the notice. Opposing parties must file an answering brief within 20 days after receiving the opening brief. Briefs must comply with Rule 55 to the extent its provisions apply. On motion complying with Rule 10.5(b), either before or after the brief is due, the Supreme Court may extend the time to file a brief.

(b) *Oral argument.* Oral argument may be granted either on a party's request or on the Court's own initiative. Argument is governed by Rule 59.

58.8 **Intervention by the State.** If the constitutionality of a Texas statute is the subject of a certified question that the Supreme Court has agreed to answer the State of Texas may intervene at any reasonable time for briefing and oral argument (if argument is allowed), on the question of constitutionality.

58.9 **Opinion on Certified Questions.** If the Supreme Court has agreed to answer a certified question, it will hand down an opinion as in any other case.

58.10 **Answering Certified Questions.** After all motions for rehearing have been overruled, the Supreme Court clerk must send to the certifying court the written opinion on the certified questions. The opinion must be under the Supreme Court's seal.

TRAP 59. SUBMISSION & ARGUMENT

59.1 **Submission Without Argument.** If at least six members of the Court so vote, a petition may be granted and an opinion handed down without oral argument.

59.2 **Submission With Argument.** If the Supreme Court decides that oral argument would aid the Court, the Court will set the case for argument. The clerk will notify all parties of the submission date.

59.3 **Purpose of Argument.** Oral argument should emphasize and clarify the written arguments in the briefs. Counsel should not merely read from a prepared text. Counsel should assume that all Justices have read the briefs before oral argument and should be prepared to respond to the Justices' questions.

TRAP 59

59.4 Time for Argument. Each side is allowed only as much time as the Court orders. Counsel is not required to use all the allotted time. On motion filed before the day of argument, the Court may extend the time for argument. The Court may also align the parties for purposes of presenting argument.

59.5 Number of Counsel. Generally, only one counsel should argue for each side. Except on leave of court, no more than two counsel on each side may argue. Only one counsel may argue in rebuttal.

59.6 Argument by Amicus Curiae. With leave of court obtained before the argument and with a party's consent, an amicus may share allotted time with that party. Otherwise, counsel for amicus curiae may not argue.

TRAP 60. JUDGMENTS IN THE SUPREME COURT

60.1 Announcement of Judgments. The Court's judgments will be announced by the clerk.

60.2 Types of Judgment. The Supreme Court may:

(a) affirm the lower court's judgment in whole or in part;

(b) modify the lower court's judgment and affirm it as modified;

(c) reverse the lower court's judgment in whole or in part and render the judgment that the lower court should have rendered;

(d) reverse the lower court's judgment and remand the case for further proceedings;

(e) vacate the judgments of the lower courts and dismiss the case; or

(f) vacate the lower court's judgment and remand the case for further proceedings in light of changes in the law.

60.3 Remand in the Interest of Justice. When reversing the court of appeals' judgment, the Supreme Court may, in the interest of justice, remand the case to the trial court even if a rendition of judgment is otherwise appropriate.

60.4 Judgment for Costs. The Supreme Court's judgment will award to the prevailing party the costs incurred by that party in the Supreme Court. If appropriate, the judgment may also award the prevailing party the costs—including preparation costs for the

record—incurred by that party in the court of appeals and in the trial court. But the Court may tax costs otherwise as required by law or for good cause.

60.5 Judgment Against Sureties. When affirming, modifying, or rendering a judgment against the party who was the appellant in the court of appeals, the Supreme Court must render judgment against the sureties on that party's supersedeas bond, if any, for the performance of the judgment. If the Supreme Court taxes costs against the party who was the appellant in the court of appeals, the Court must render judgment for those costs against the sureties on that party's supersedeas bond, if any.

60.6 Other Orders. The Supreme Court may make any other appropriate order required by the law and the nature of the case.

TRAP 61. REVERSIBLE ERROR

61.1 Standard for Reversible Error. No judgment may be reversed on appeal on the ground that the trial court made an error of law unless the Supreme Court concludes that the error complained of:

(a) probably caused the rendition of an improper judgment; or

(b) probably prevented the petitioner from properly presenting the case to the appellate courts.

61.2 Error Affecting Only Part of the Case. If the error affects a part, but not all, of the matter in controversy, and that part is separable without unfairness to the parties, the judgment must be reversed and a new trial ordered only as to the part affected by the error. The Court may not order a separate trial solely on unliquidated damages if liability is contested.

61.3 Defects in Procedure. The Supreme Court will not affirm or reverse a judgment or dismiss a petition for review for formal defects or irregularities in appellate procedure without allowing a reasonable time to correct or amend the defects or irregularities.

61.4 Remediable Error of the Trial Court or Court of Appeals.

(a) *Generally.* The Supreme Court will not affirm or reverse a judgment or dismiss a petition for review if:

(1) the trial court's or court of appeals' erroneous action or failure or refusal to act prevents the proper presentation of a case to the Supreme Court; and

TRAP 59

(2) the trial court or court of appeals can correct its action or failure to act.

(b) *Supreme Court direction if error remediable.* If the circumstances described in (a) exist, the Supreme Court will direct the trial court or court of appeals to correct the error. The Supreme Court will then proceed as if the error had not occurred.

TRAP 62. DAMAGES FOR FRIVOLOUS APPEALS

If the Supreme Court determines that a direct appeal or a petition for review is frivolous, it may—on motion of any party or on its own initiative, after notice and a reasonable opportunity for response—award to each prevailing party just damages. In determining whether to award damages, the Court must not consider any matter that does not appear in the record, briefs, or other papers filed in the court of appeals or the Supreme Court.

TRAP 63. OPINIONS; COPY OF OPINION & JUDGMENT TO INTERESTED PARTIES & OTHER COURTS

The Supreme Court will hand down a written opinion in all cases in which it renders a judgment. The clerk will send a copy of the opinion and judgment to the court of appeals clerk, the trial court clerk, the regional administrative judge, and all parties to the appeal.

TRAP 64. MOTION FOR REHEARING

64.1 **Time for Filing.** A motion for rehearing may be filed with the Supreme Court clerk within 15 days from the date when the Court renders judgment or makes an order disposing of a petition for review. In exceptional cases, if justice requires, the Court may shorten the time within which the motion may be filed or even deny the right to file it altogether.

64.2 **Contents.** The motion must specify the points relied on for the rehearing.

64.3 **Response and Decision.** No response to a motion for rehearing need be filed unless the Court so requests. A motion will not be granted unless a response has been filed or requested by the Court. But in exceptional cases, if justice so requires, the Court may deny the right to file a response and act on a motion any time after it is filed.

 64.4 **Second Motion.** The Court will not consider a second motion for rehearing unless the Court modifies its judgment, vacates its judgment and renders a new judgment, or issues a different opinion.

64.5 **Extensions of Time.** The Court may extend the time to file a motion for rehearing in the Supreme Court, if a motion complying with Rule 10.5(b) is filed with the Court no later than 15 days after the last date for filing a motion for rehearing.

64.6 **Length of Motion and Response.** A motion or response must be no longer than 15 pages.

TRAP 65. ENFORCEMENT OF JUDGMENT AFTER MANDATE

65.1 **Statement of Costs.** The Supreme Court clerk will prepare, and send to the clerk to whom the mandate is directed, a statement of costs showing:

(a) the costs that were incurred in the Supreme Court, with a notation of those items that have been paid and those that are owing; and

(b) the party or parties against whom costs have been adjudged.

65.2 **Enforcement of Judgment.** If the Supreme Court renders judgment, the trial court need not make any further order. Upon receiving the Supreme Court's mandate, the trial court clerk must proceed to enforce the judgment of the Supreme Court's as in any other case. Appellate court costs must be included with the trial court costs in any process to enforce the judgment. If all or part of the costs are collected, the trial court clerk must immediately remit to the appellate court clerk any amount due to that clerk.

SECTION FIVE: PROCEEDINGS IN THE COURT OF CRIMINAL APPEALS

TRAP 66. DISCRETIONARY REVIEW IN GENERAL

66.1 **With or Without Petition.** The Court of Criminal Appeals may review a court of appeals' decision in a criminal case on its own initiative under Rule 67 or on the petition of a party under Rule 68.

66.2 **Not a Matter of Right.** Discretionary review by the Court of Criminal Appeals is not a matter of right, but of the Court's discretion.

66.3 **Reasons for Granting Review.** While neither controlling nor fully measuring the Court of Criminal Appeals' discretion, the following will be considered by the Court in deciding whether to grant discretionary review:

(a) whether a court of appeals' decision conflicts with another court of appeals' decision on the same issue;

(b) whether a court of appeals has decided an important question of state or federal law that has not been, but should be, settled by the Court of Criminal Appeals;

(c) whether a court of appeals has decided an important question of state or federal law in a way that conflicts with the applicable decisions of the Court of Criminal Appeals or the Supreme Court of the United States;

(d) whether a court of appeals has declared a statute, rule, regulation, or ordinance unconstitutional, or appears to have misconstrued a statute, rule, regulation, or ordinance;

(e) whether the justices of a court of appeals have disagreed on a material question of law necessary to the court's decision; and

(f) whether a court of appeals has so far departed from the accepted and usual course of judicial proceedings, or so far sanctioned such a departure by a lower court, as to call for an exercise of the Court of Criminal Appeals' power of supervision.

66.4 **Documents to Aid Decision.**

(a) *Acquiring documents.* The Court of Criminal Appeals—or any judge of the Court—may order the court of appeals clerk to promptly send the following items to the Court in order to aid it in deciding whether to grant discretionary review:

(1) the appellate record;

(2) a copy of the opinions of the court of appeals;

(3) a copy of the motions filed in the court of appeals; and

(4) certified copies of any judgment or order of the court of appeals.

(b) *Return of documents.* If discretionary review is not granted, the clerk of the Court of Criminal Appeals will return the appellate record to the court of appeals clerk.

TRAP 67. DISCRETIONARY REVIEW WITHOUT PETITION

67.1 **Four Judges' Vote.** By a vote of at least four judges, the Court of Criminal Appeals may grant review of a court of appeals' decision in a criminal case at any time before the mandate of the court of appeals issues. An order granting review will be filed with the clerk of the Court of Criminal Appeals, who must send a copy to the court of appeals clerk.

67.2 **Order Staying Mandate.** To provide enough time for the Court of Criminal Appeals to decide whether to grant discretionary review under 67.1, the Court—or any judge of the Court—may file with the clerk of the court of appeals an order staying the court of appeals' mandate. The order must be signed by a judge of the Court of Criminal Appeals. The clerk of the Court of Criminal Appeals must immediately send a copy of the order to the court of appeals clerk.

67.3 **Time to Issue Mandate Extended.** Unless otherwise limited in the order itself, an order staying the court of appeals' mandate under 67.2 will extend for an additional 45 days the time before issuance of the court of appeals' mandate. An order granting review prevents the issuance of the court of appeals' mandate pending the further order of the Court of Criminal Appeals. If four judges do not agree to grant review within that time the court of appeals clerk must issue the mandate.

TRAP 68. DISCRETIONARY REVIEW WITH PETITION

68.1 **Generally.** On petition by any party, the Court of Criminal Appeals may review a court of appeals' decision in a criminal case.

68.2 **Time to File Petition.**

(a) *First petition.* The petition must be filed within 30 days after either the day the court of appeals' judgment was rendered or the day the last timely motion for rehearing was overruled by the court of appeals.

(b) *Subsequent petition.* Even if the time specified in (a) has expired, a party who otherwise may file a petition may do so within 10 days after the timely filing of another party's petition.

(c) *Extension of time.* The Court of Criminal Appeals may extend the time to file a petition for discretionary review if a party files a motion complying with

TRAP 66

Rule 10.5(b) no later than 15 days after the last day for filing the petition. The Court of Criminal Appeals may extend the time to file a response or reply if a party files a motion complying with Rule 10.5(b) either before or after the response or reply is due.

68.3 **Where to File Petition.** The petition and all copies of the petition must be filed with the clerk of the court of appeals, but if the State's Prosecuting Attorney files a petition, the State's Prosecuting Attorney may file the copies of the petition—but not the original—with the clerk of the Court of Criminal Appeals instead of with the court of appeals clerk.

68.4 **Contents of Petition.** A petition for discretionary review must be as brief as possible. It must be addressed to the "Court of Criminal Appeals of Texas" and must state the name of the party or parties applying for review. The petition must contain the following items:

(a) *Table of contents.* The petition must include a table of contents with references to the pages of the petition. The table of contents must indicate the subject matter of each ground or question presented for review.

(b) *Index of authorities.* The petition must include an index of authorities arranged alphabetically and indicating the pages of the petition where the authorities are cited.

(c) *Statement regarding oral argument.* The petition must include a short statement of why oral argument would be helpful, or a statement that oral argument is waived. If a reply or cross-petition is filed, it likewise must include a statement of why oral argument should or should not be heard.

(d) *Statement of the case.* The petition must state briefly the nature of the case. This statement should seldom exceed half a page. The details of the case should be reserved and stated with the pertinent grounds or questions.

(e) *Statement of procedural history.* The petition must state:

(1) the date any opinion of the court of appeals was handed down, or the date of any order of the court of appeals disposing of the case without an opinion;

(2) the date any motion for rehearing was filed (or a statement that none was filed); and

(3) the date the motion for rehearing was overruled or otherwise disposed of.

(f) *Grounds for review.* The petition must state briefly, without argument, the grounds on which the petition is based. The grounds must be separately numbered. If the petitioner has access to the record, the petitioner must (after each ground) refer to the page of the record where the matter complained of is found. Instead of listing grounds for review, the petition may contain the questions presented for review, expressed in the terms and circumstances of the case but without unnecessary detail. The statement of questions should be short and concise, not argumentative or repetitious.

(g) *Argument.* The petition must contain a direct and concise argument, with supporting authorities, amplifying the reasons for granting review. See Rule 66.3. The court of appeals' opinions will be considered with the petition, and statements in those opinions need not be repeated if counsel accepts them as correct.

(h) *Prayer for relief.* The petition must state clearly the nature of the relief sought.

(i) *Appendix.* The petition must contain a copy of any opinion of the court of appeals.

68.5 **Length of Petition and Reply.** The petition must be no longer than 15 pages, exclusive of pages containing the table of contents, the index of authorities, the statement regarding oral argument, the statement of the case, the statement of procedural history, and the appendix. A reply may be no longer than 8 pages, exclusive of the items stated above. The Court may, on motion, permit a longer petition or reply.

68.6 **Nonconforming Petition.** The Court may strike, order redrawn, or summarily refuse a petition for discretionary review that is unnecessarily lengthy or that does not conform to these rules.

08 **68.7** **Court of Appeals Clerk's Duties.**

(a) *On filing of the petition.* Upon receiving the petition, the court of appeals clerk must file the original petition and note the filing on the docket.

(b) *Reply.* The opposing party has 30 days after the timely filing of the petition in the court of appeals to file a reply to the petition with the clerk of the court of appeals. Upon receiving a reply to the petition, the clerk for the court of appeals must file the reply and note the filing on the docket.

(c) *Sending petition and reply to Court of Criminal Appeals.* Unless a petition for discretionary review is dismissed under Rule 50, the clerk of the court of appeals must, within 60 days after the petition is filed, send to the clerk of the Court of Criminal Appeals the petition and any copies furnished by counsel, the reply, if any, and any copies furnished by counsel, together with the record, copies of the motions filed in the case, and copies of any judgments, opinions, and orders of the court of appeals. The clerk need not forward any nondocumentary exhibits unless ordered to do so by the Court of Criminal Appeals.

68.8 **Court of Criminal Appeals Clerk's Duties on Receipt of Petition.** The clerk of the Court of Criminal Appeals will receive a petition for discretionary review, file the petition and the accompanying record from the court of appeals, note the filing of the petition and record on the docket, and notify the parties by U.S. Mail of the filing. The Court may dispense with notice and grant or refuse the petition immediately upon its filing.

08 **68.9** [Deleted.]

68.10 **Amendment.** The petition or a reply may be amended or supplemented within 30 days after the original petition was filed in the court of appeals or at any time when justice requires. The record may be amended in the Court of Criminal Appeals under the same circumstances and in the same manner as in the court of appeals.

68.11 **Service on State Prosecuting Attorney.** In addition to the service required by Rule 9.5, service of the petition, the reply, and any amendment or supplementation of a petition or reply must be made on the State Prosecuting Attorney, P.O. Box 12405, Austin, Texas 78711.

TRAP 69. ACTION OF COURT ON PETITION FOR DISCRETIONARY REVIEW & AFTER GRANTING REVIEW

69.1 **Granting or Refusal.** If four judges do not vote to grant a petition for discretionary review, the Court will enter a docket notation that the petition is *refused*. If four judges vote to grant a petition, the Court will enter a docket notation that discretionary review is *granted*.

69.2 **Setting Case for Submission.** If discretionary review is granted, either on the petition of a party or by the Court on its own initiative, the case will be set for submission.

69.3 **Improvident Grant of Review.** If, after granting discretionary review, five judges are of the opinion that discretionary review should not have been granted, the case will be dismissed.

69.4 **Clerk's Duties.**

(a) *On refusal or dismissal.* When the Court refuses or dismisses a petition, the clerk will send to the parties and the State Prosecuting Attorney a notice informing them that the petition was refused or dismissed. The clerk will retain the petition and all other items filed in the case for at least 15 days from the date of the refusal or dismissal. At the end of that time, if no motion for rehearing has been timely filed, or upon the overruling or dismissal of such a motion, the clerk will send to the court of appeals clerk a certified copy of the order refusing or dismissing the petition (as well as any order overruling a motion for rehearing). The clerk of the Court of Criminal Appeals will return the appellate record to the court of appeals clerk but will retain the petition, and other documents filed in the Court of Criminal Appeals.

(b) *On granting review.* If the Court grants discretionary review, the clerk will send to the parties and the State Prosecuting Attorney a notice informing them that discretionary review was granted.

TRAP 70. BRIEF ON THE MERITS

70.1 **Initial Brief.** If review is granted, the petitioner—or, if there was no petition, the party who lost in the court of appeals—must file a brief within 30 days after review is granted.

70.2 **Reply Brief.** The opposing party must file a brief within 30 days after the petitioner's brief is filed.

08 **70.3** **Brief Contents and Form.** Briefs must comply with the requirements of Rule 38, except that they need not contain the appendix (Rule 38.1(k)). Copies must be served as required by Rule 68.11.

70.4 **Other Briefs.** The Court of Criminal Appeals may direct that a party file a brief, or an additional brief, in a particular case.

TRAP 71. DIRECT APPEALS

71.1 **Direct Appeal.** Cases in which the death penalty has been assessed under Code of Criminal

Procedure article 37.071, and cases in which bail has been denied in non-capital cases under Article I, Section 11a of the Constitution, are appealed directly to the Court of Criminal Appeals.

71.2 Record. The appellate record should be prepared and filed in accordance with Rules 31, 32, 34, 35 and 37, except that the record must be filed in the Court of Criminal Appeals. After disposition of the appeal, the Court may discard copies of juror information cards or other portions of the clerk's record that are not relevant to an issue on appeal.

 71.3 Briefs. Briefs in a direct appeal should be prepared and filed in accordance with Rule 38, except that the brief need not contain an appendix (Rule 38.1(k)), and the brief in a case in which the death penalty has been assessed may not exceed 125 pages. All briefs must be filed in the Court of Criminal Appeals. The brief must include a short statement of why oral argument would be helpful, or a statement that oral argument is waived.

TRAP 72. EXTRAORDINARY MATTERS

72.1 Leave to File. A motion for leave to file must accompany an original petition for writ of habeas corpus, mandamus, procedendo, prohibition, certiorari, or other extraordinary writ, or any other motion not otherwise provided for in these rules.

72.2 Disposition. If five judges tentatively believe that the case should be filed and set for submission, the motion for leave will be granted and the case will then be handled and disposed of in accordance with Rule 52.7. If the motion for leave is denied, no motions for rehearing or reconsideration will be entertained. But the Court may, on its own initiative, reconsider a denial of a motion for leave.

ANNOTATIONS

Padilla v. McDaniel, 122 S.W.3d 805, 808 (Tex. Crim.App.2003). "We hold that when a court of appeals and this court have concurrent, original jurisdiction of a petition for a writ of mandamus against the judge of a district or county court, the petition should be presented first to the court of appeals unless there is a compelling reason not to do so."

TRAP 73. POSTCONVICTION APPLICATIONS FOR WRITS OF HABEAS CORPUS

73.1 Form of Application in Felony Case (other than Capital).

(a) *Prescribed Form.* An application for post conviction habeas corpus relief in a felony case without a death penalty, under Code of Criminal Procedure article 11.07, must be made in the form prescribed by the Court of Criminal Appeals in an order entered for that purpose.

(b) *Availability of form.* The clerk of the convicting court will make the forms available to applicants on request, without charge.

(c) *Contents.* The person making the application must provide all information required by the form. The application must specify all grounds for relief, and must set forth in summary fashion the facts supporting each ground. The application must not cite cases or other law. Legal citations and arguments may be made in a separate memorandum. The application must be typewritten or handwritten legibly.

(d) *Verification.* The application must be verified by either:

(1) oath made before a notary public or other officer authorized to administer oaths, or

(2) if the person making the application is an inmate in the Institutional Division of the Department of Criminal Justice or in a county jail, an unsworn declaration in substantially the form required in Civil Practice and Remedies Code chapter 132.

73.2 Noncompliance. The clerk of the convicting court will not file an application that is not on the form prescribed by the Court of Criminal Appeals, and will return the application to the person who filed it, with a copy of the official form. The clerk of the Court of Criminal Appeals may, without filing an application that does not comply with this rule, return it to the clerk of the convicting court, with a notation of the defect, and the clerk of the convicting court will return the application to the person who filed it, with a copy of the official form.

73.3 Summary Sheet. When a district clerk transmits the record in a postconviction application for habeas corpus under Code of Criminal Procedure articles 11.07 or 11.071, the district clerk must prepare and transmit a summary sheet that includes the following information:

(a) the convicting court's name and county, and the name of the judge who tried the case;

(b) the applicant's name, the offense, the plea, the cause number, the sentence, and the date of sentence, as shown in the judgment of conviction;

(c) the cause number of any appeal from the conviction and the citation to any published report;

(d) whether a hearing was held on the application, whether findings of fact were made, any recommendation of the convicting court, and the name of the judge who presided over the application.

The Court of Criminal Appeals may by order adopt a form of summary sheet that the district clerks must use.

73.4 **Action on Application.** The Court may deny relief based upon its own review of the application or may issue such other instructions or orders as may be appropriate.

TRAP 74. REVIEW OF CERTIFIED STATE CRIMINAL-LAW QUESTIONS

74.1 **Certification.** The Court of Criminal Appeals may answer questions of Texas criminal law certified to it by any federal appellate court if the certifying court is presented with determinative questions of Texas criminal law having no controlling Court of Criminal Appeals precedent. The Court may decline to answer the questions certified to it.

74.2 **Contents of the Certification Order.** An order from the certifying court must set forth:

(a) the questions of law to be answered; and

(b) a stipulated statement of all facts relevant to the questions certified, showing fully the nature of the controversy in which the questions arose.

74.3 **Transmission of Certification Order.** The clerk of the certifying court must send to the clerk of the Court of Criminal Appeals the following:

(a) the certification order under the certifying court's official seal;

(b) a list of the names of each party to the pending case, giving the address and telephone number, if known, of any party not represented by counsel; and

(c) a list of the names and addresses of counsel for each party.

74.4 **Transmission of Record.** The certifying court should not send to the Court of Criminal Appeals the record in the pending case with the certification order. The Court of Criminal Appeals may later require the original or copies of all or part of the record before the certifying court to be filed with the Court of Criminal Appeals clerk.

74.5 **Notice.** If the Court of Criminal Appeals agrees to answer the questions certified to it, the Court will notify all parties and the certifying court. The Court of Criminal Appeals clerk must also send a notice to the Attorney General of Texas if:

(a) the constitutionality of a Texas statute is the subject of a certified question that the Court of Criminal Appeals has agreed to answer; and

(b) the State of Texas or an officer, agency, or employee of the State is not a party to the proceeding in the certifying court.

74.6 **Briefs and Oral Argument.**

(a) *Briefs.* The appealing party in the certifying court must file a brief with the clerk of the Court of Criminal Appeals within 30 days after the date of the notice. Opposing parties must file an answering brief within 15 days of receiving the opening brief. Briefs must comply with Rule 38 to the extent that its provisions apply.

(b) *Oral argument.* Oral argument may be granted either on a party's request or on the Court's own initiative. Argument is governed by Rule 39.

74.7 **Intervention by the State.** If the constitutionality of a Texas statute is the subject of a certified question that the Court of Criminal Appeals has agreed to answer, the State of Texas may intervene at any reasonable time for briefing and oral argument (if argument is allowed) on the question of constitutionality.

74.8 **Opinion on Certified Question.** If the Court of Criminal Appeals has agreed to answer a certified question, it will hand down an opinion as in any other case.

74.9 **Motion for Rehearing.** Any party may file a motion for rehearing within 15 days after the opinion is handed down. The motion must clearly state the points relied on for the rehearing. No reply to a motion for rehearing need be filed unless the Court so requests. The

TRAP 73

Court will not grant a motion for rehearing unless a response has been filed or requested.

74.10 **Answering Certified Questions.** After all motions for rehearing have been overruled, the clerk of the Court of Criminal Appeals must send to the certifying court the written opinion on the certified questions. The opinion must be under the Court of Criminal Appeals' seal.

TRAP 75. NOTIFICATION; ORAL ARGUMENT

75.1 **Notification of Argument or Submission.** Oral argument will be permitted only in cases designated by the Court of Criminal Appeals. If the Court permits argument in a case, the clerk will notify the parties of the date set for argument. If a case will be submitted without argument, the clerk will notify the parties of the date of submission. The clerk must use all reasonable diligence to notify counsel of settings, but counsel's failure to receive notice will not necessarily prevent argument or submission of the case on the day it is set.

75.2 **Request for Argument.** If a case is not designated for oral argument but counsel desires oral argument, counsel may—within 30 days of the date of the clerk's notice—petition the Court to allow oral argument. This petition must contain specific reasons why oral argument is desired.

75.3 **Oral Argument.** Unless extended in a special case, the total maximum time for oral argument is 20 minutes per side. Counsel for the appellant or petitioner is entitled to open and conclude the argument. Counsel should not read at length from the briefs, records, or authorities. Counsel may orally correct a brief, but multiple additional citations should not be given orally; instead, these citations should be filed in writing with the clerk.

TRAP 76. SUBMISSIONS EN BANC

The Court will sit en banc to consider the following types of cases:

(a) direct appeals;

(b) cases of discretionary review;

(c) cases in which leave to file was granted under Rule 72;

(d) cases that were docketed under Code of Criminal Procedure articles 11.07 or 11.071;

(e) certified questions; and

(f) rehearings under Rule 79.

TRAP 77. OPINIONS

77.1 **Generally.** In each case that is argued or submitted without argument to the Court of Criminal Appeals, the Court will hand down a written opinion setting forth the reasons for its decision and any germane precedent. Any judge may file an opinion dissenting from or concurring in the Court's judgment.

77.2 **Signing; Publication.** A majority of the judges will determine whether an opinion will be signed by a judge or issued per curiam, and whether the opinion (or a portion of the opinion) will be published.

77.3 **Unpublished Opinions.** Unpublished opinions have no precedential value and must not be cited as authority by counsel or by a court.

77.4 **Copies.** On the date when an opinion is handed down or an order rendered, the clerk of the Court of Criminal Appeals must mail copies of the opinion or order to:

(a) the parties;

(b) the State Prosecuting Attorney;

(c) the trial court clerk; and

(d) if the case is of discretionary review, the court of appeals clerk.

TRAP 78. JUDGMENTS IN THE COURT OF CRIMINAL APPEALS

78.1 **Types of Judgment.** The Court of Criminal Appeals may:

(a) affirm the lower court's judgment in whole or in part;

(b) modify the lower court's judgment and affirm it as modified;

(c) reverse the court's judgment in whole or in part and render the judgment that the lower court should have rendered;

(d) reverse the lower court's judgment and remand the case for further proceedings;

(e) vacate the judgments of the lower courts and dismiss the case;

(f) vacate the lower court's judgment and remand the case for further proceedings in light of changes in the law; or

(g) dismiss the appeal.

78.2 Remand in the Interests of Justice. When reversing the court of appeals' judgment, the Court of Criminal Appeals may, in the interests of justice, remand the case to the trial court even if a rendition of judgment is otherwise appropriate.

78.3 Other Orders. The Court of Criminal Appeals may make any other appropriate order required by the law and the nature of the case.

ANNOTATIONS

TRAP 78.1

Carroll v. State, 101 S.W.3d 454, 455 (Tex.Crim. App.2003). "We granted review to determine whether it is within the court of appeals' scope of review on remand to reconsider a particular point of error and decide it based on grounds not expressly contemplated by this Court's remand order. We find that it is...."

Herrin v. State, 125 S.W.3d 436, 444 (Tex.Crim.App. 2002). "[W]e hold that under Rule 78.1 this Court has the authority in the direct review of a death penalty case, to (among other things) reform the judgment of the trial court below."

TRAP 79. REHEARINGS

79.1 Motion for Rehearing. A motion for rehearing may be filed with the Court of Criminal Appeals clerk within 15 days from the date of the judgment or order. In exceptional cases, if justice requires, the Court may shorten the time within which the motion may be filed or even deny the right to file it altogether.

79.2 Contents.

(a) The motion must briefly and distinctly state the grounds and arguments relied on for rehearing.

(b) A motion for rehearing an order that grants discretionary review may not be filed.

(c) A motion for rehearing an order that refuses or dismisses a petition for discretionary review may be grounded only on substantial intervening circumstances which are specified in the motion. Counsel must certify that the motion is so grounded and that the motion is made in good faith and not for delay.

(d) A motion for rehearing an order that denies habeas corpus relief under Code of Criminal Procedure, articles 11.07 or 11.071, may not be filed. The Court may on its own initiative reconsider the case.

79.3 Amendments. A motion for rehearing may be amended anytime before the period allowed for filing the motion expires, and with leave of the court, anytime before the Court decides the motion.

79.4 Decision. If the Court grants rehearing, the case will be set for submission. Oral argument may, but normally will not, be permitted.

79.5 Further Motion for Rehearing. The Court will not consider a second motion for rehearing after rehearing is denied. If rehearing is granted and the Court delivers an opinion on rehearing, a party may file a further motion for rehearing.

79.6 Extension of Time. The Court may extend the time for filing a motion or a further motion for rehearing if a party files a motion complying with Rule 10.5(b) within the time for filing a motion or further motion for rehearing.

79.7 Service. The requirements of Rule 68.11 apply.

APPENDIX
COURT OF CRIMINAL
APPEALS ORDERS

The following orders of the Court of Criminal Appeals of Texas are effective September 1, 1997.

IN THE COURT OF CRIMINAL APPEALS OF TEXAS

Order Directing the Form of the Appellate Record in Criminal Cases

ORDERED that:

Pursuant to Texas Rule of Appellate Procedure 34.4, the Court of Criminal Appeals of Texas orders that the appellate record in criminal cases be in the form specified below. All references in this Order to a rule are to the Texas Rules of Appellate Procedure unless otherwise stated.

A. Clerk's Record

1. The trial court clerk must prepare and file the clerk's record in accordance with Rules 34.5 and 35. Even if more than one notice of appeal or request for inclusion of items is filed, the clerk should prepare only one record in a case. To prepare the clerk's record, the trial court clerk must:

(a) gather the documents required by Rule 34.5(a) and those requested by a party under Rule 34.5(b);

(b) make a legible copy of the documents on opaque, white, 8½ x 11 inch paper, if practicable;

(c) arrange the documents in ascending chronological order, by date of filing or occurrence;

(d) consecutively number the pages in the bottom right-hand corner;

(e) bind the documents together in one or more groups under a heavy cover;

(f) prepare, label, and certify the clerk's record as required by this Order.

2. The clerk's record should be in the following form:

(a) It is preferred that the clerk's record lie flat when opened.

(b) If the clerk's record will lie flat when opened, two-sided copies may be included in the clerk's record; otherwise, only one-sided copies may be included.

(c) Each individual document must start on a new page.

(d) The first volume should be numbered "1" and each succeeding volume numbered sequentially.

(e) Page numbering should start on the first page of the first volume of the clerk's record and continue to the final page of the clerk's record without regard for the number of volumes in the clerk's record.

(f) It is preferred that the clerk's record be tabbed to show the beginning of each document.

(g) Each document must show the date of filing.

(h) As far as practicable, each order and judgment must show the date of signing by the judge.

(i) The front cover of the first volume of the clerk's record must include the following information and be in substantially the following form:

CLERK'S RECORD
VOLUME _____ of _____

Trial Court Cause No. _____
In the _____ (District or County) Court
of _____ County, Texas,
Honorable _____, Judge, Presiding.

_____, Plaintiff(s)

vs.

_____, Defendant(s)

Appealed to the
(Supreme Court of Texas, at Austin, Texas,
or Court of Criminal Appeals of Texas at Austin, Texas,
or Court of Appeals for the __ District of Texas, at __, Texas).

Attorney for Appellant(s):
Name _____
Address _____
Telephone no. _____
Fax no. _____
SBOT no. _____
Attorney for: _____, Appellant(s)

Delivered to the (Supreme Court of Texas at Austin, Texas,
or Court of Criminal Appeals of Texas at Austin, Texas,
or Court of Appeals for the __ District of Texas, at __, Texas)
on the _____ day of _____, _____.
signature of clerk_____
name of clerk _____
title _____

Appellate Court Cause No. _____

Filed in the (Supreme Court of Texas at Austin, Texas,
or Court of Criminal Appeals of Texas at Austin, Texas,

or Court of Appeals for the ___ District of Texas, at ___, Texas) this _____ day of _____, _____.

_____, Clerk

By _____, Deputy

(j) The front cover of the second and subsequent volumes of the clerk's record must include the same information and be in substantially the same form except that second and subsequent volumes may, but need not, include statements of delivery and filing.

(k) The clerk must prepare and include on the first pages of the clerk's record a detailed index identifying each document included in the clerk's record, the date of filing, and the page where it first appears. The index must be double spaced and conform to the order in which matters appear in the clerk's record, rather than in alphabetical order.

(*l*) After the index, the clerk must include the following:

The State of Texas §

County of _____ §

In the _____ (County Court or Judicial District Court) of _____ County, Texas, the Honorable _____, Judge Presiding, the following proceedings were held and the following instruments and other papers were filed in this cause, to wit:

Trial Court Cause No. _____

_____, Plaintiff(s) § IN THE _____ COURT

§

vs. §

§

_____, Defendant(s) § _____ COUNTY, TEXAS

(m) The clerk's record must conclude with a certificate in substantially the following form:

The State of Texas §

County of _____ §

I, _____, Clerk of the _____ Court of _____County, Texas do hereby certify that the documents contained in this record to which this certification is attached are all of the documents specified by Texas Rule of Appellate Procedure 34.5(a) and all other documents timely requested by a party to this proceeding under Texas Rule of Appellate Procedure 34.5(b).

GIVEN UNDER MY HAND AND SEAL at my office in _____, County, Texas this _____ day of _____, ____.

signature of clerk_____

name of clerk _____

title _____

3. A supplement must be prepared in conformity with this Order.

4. In the event of a flagrant violation of this Order in the preparation of the clerk's record, on motion of a party or on its own initiative, the appellate court may require the clerk to amend the clerk's record or to prepare a new clerk's record in proper form—and provide it to any party who has previously made a copy of the original, defective clerk's record—at the clerk's expense.

B. Reporter's Record

(1) The court reporter must prepare and file the reporter's record in accordance with Rules 34.6 and 35 and the Uniform Format Manual for Texas Court Reporters. Even if more than one notice of appeal or request for preparation of the record is filed, the reporter should prepare only one record in a case.

(2) In the event of a flagrant violation of this Order in the preparation of a reporter's record, on motion of a party or on the court's own initiative, the appellate court may require the court reporter, to amend the reporter's record or to prepare a new reporter's record in proper form—and provide it to any party who has previously made a copy of the original, defective reporter's record—at the reporter's expense. Failure of a reporter to comply with the requirements of the Uniform Format Manual for Texas Court Reporters is also subject to discipline by the Court Reporter's Certification Board.

IN THE COURT OF CRIMINAL APPEALS OF TEXAS

Order Adopting Summary Sheet for Post-conviction Applications for Writ of Habeas Corpus

ORDERED that:

Pursuant to Texas Rule of Appellate Procedure 73, the Court of Criminal Appeals hereby orders that the attached form to be used when a postconviction application for writ of habeas corpus is transmitted to the Court of Criminal Appeals.

Application for writ of Habeas Corpus

Ex Parte _____ from _____ County

(Name of Applicant)   _____

Court

TRIAL COURT WRIT NO. _____

CLERK'S SUMMARY SHEET

APPLICANT'S NAME: _____

(As reflected on the judgment)

★

OFFENSE: _____

(As described on the judgment)

CAUSE NO: _____

(As reflected in the judgment)

SENTENCE: _____

(As described on the judgment)

TRIAL DATE: _____

(Date upon which sentence was imposed)

JUDGE'S NAME: _____

(Judge presiding at trial)

APPEAL NO: _____

(If applicable)

CITATION TO OPINION: _____ S.W.2d _____

(If applicable)

HEARING HELD: _____YES _____ NO

(Pertaining to the application for writ)

FINDINGS AND CONCLUSIONS FILED: _____YES _____ NO

(Pertaining to the application for writ)

RECOMMENDATION: ____ GRANT ____ DENY ____ NONE

(Trial court's recommendation regarding application)

JUDGE'S NAME: _____

(Judge presiding over habeas proceeding)

IN THE COURT OF CRIMINAL APPEALS OF TEXAS

Order Regarding Court of Appeals Clerk Preparing the Record to Send to the Court of Criminal Appeals

ORDERED that:

The court of appeals clerk must gather together the appellate record and the papers filed in the court of appeals and file them with the clerk of the Court of Criminal Appeals in one or more envelopes that conform to the following specifications:

(1) extra-heavyweight stock;

(2) one-piece construction with flaps;

(3) congress-tie, noncollapsing-style construction with closed corners;

(4) dimensions of 11½ inches in width, 9 inches in height, and a thickness of 1, 1½, 2, 3, or 4 inches; and

(5) the front of each envelope must show the trial court style and case number and the court of appeals style and case number.

COURT OF CRIMINAL APPEALS OF TEXAS

Application for a Writ of Habeas Corpus Seeking Relief From Final Felony Conviction Under Code Of Criminal Procedure, Article 11.07

INSTRUCTIONS

1.   You must use the complete form, which begins on the following page, to file an application for a writ of habeas corpus seeking relief from a final felony conviction under Article 11.07 of the Code of Criminal Procedure. (This form is not for death-penalty cases, probated sentences which have not been revoked, or misdemeanors.)

2.   The clerk of the trial court in which you were convicted will make this form available to you, on request, without charge.

3.   You must file the entire writ application form, including those sections that do not apply to you. If any pages are missing from the form, or if the form has been downloaded and the questions have been renumbered or omitted, your entire application will be returned as non-compliant. If your application is returned as non-compliant, the clerk of the trial court will write a note of the defect on your application and return the form to you without filing it.

4.   You must make a separate application on a separate form for each judgment of conviction you seek relief from. Even if the judgments were entered in the same court on the same day, you must make a separate application for each one.

5.   Answer every item that applies to you on the form. You may use additional pages only if you need them for item 17, the facts supporting your ground for relief. Do not attach any additional pages for any other item 17.[1]

6.   You must include all grounds for relief on the application form as provided by the instructions under item 17. You must also briefly summarize the facts of your claim on the application form as provided by the instructions under item 17.

7.   Do not cite cases or other law in this application form. Do not make legal arguments in this form. Legal citations and arguments may be made in a separate memorandum.

8.   You must verify the application by signing either the Oath Before Notary Public or the Inmate's Declaration, which are at the end of this form on pages 11

and 12. You may be prosecuted and convicted for aggravated perjury if you make any false statement of a material fact in this application.

9. When the application is fully completed, mail the original to the clerk of the convicting district court. Keep a copy of the application for your records.

10. You must notify the clerk of the convicting district court of any change in address after you have filed your application.

1. **Editor's note:** This sentence should probably end "any item other than item 17."

Case No. _____

(The Clerk of the convicting court will fill this line in.)

IN THE COURT OF CRIMINAL APPEALS OF TEXAS

Application for a Writ of Habeas Corpus Seeking Relief From Final Felony Conviction Under Code of Criminal Procedure, Article 11.07

NAME: _____

DATE OF BIRTH: _____

PLACE OF CONFINEMENT: _____

TDCJ-CID NUMBER: _____

SID NUMBER: _____

(1) This application concerns (check all that apply):

☐   a conviction

☐   parole

☐   a sentence

☐   mandatory supervision

☐   time credit

☐   out-of-time appeal or petition for discretionary review

(2) What district court entered the judgment of the conviction you want relief from? (Include the court number and county.)

_____

(3) What was the case number in the trial court? _____

_____

(4) What was the name of the trial judge? _____

(5) Were you represented by counsel? If yes, provide the attorney's name: _____

_____

(6) What was the date that the judgment was entered? ____

_____

(7) For what offense were you convicted and what was the sentence? _____

_____

(8) If you were sentenced on more than one count of an indictment in the same court at the same time, what counts were you convicted of and what was the sentence in each count?

_____

_____

(9) What was the plea you entered? (Check one.)

☐   guilty-open plea

☐   guilty-plea bargain

☐   not guilty

☐   nolo contendere/no contest

If you entered different pleas to counts in a multi-count indictment, please explain: _____

_____

_____

(10) What kind of trial did you have?

☐   no jury

☐   jury for guilt and punishment

☐   jury for guilt, judge for punishment

(11) Did you testify at trial? If yes, at what phase of the trial did you testify? _____

_____

(12) Did you appeal from the judgment of conviction? ____

☐   yes

☐   no

If you did appeal, answer the following questions:

(A) What court of appeals did you appeal to? _____

_____

(B) What was the case number? _____

_____

(C) Were you represented by counsel on appeal? If yes, provide the attorney's name: _____

_____

(D) What was the decision and the date of the decision? __

(13) Did you file a petition for discretionary review in the Court of Criminal Appeals? _____

_____

☐   yes

☐   no

If you did file a petition for discretionary review, answer the following questions:

(A) What was the case number? _____

(B) What was the decision and the date of the decision?

_____

(14) Have you previously filed an application for a writ of habeas corpus under Article 11.07 of the Texas Code of Criminal Procedure challenging this conviction?

☐   yes

☐   no

If you answered yes, answer the following questions: _____

(A) What was the Court of Criminal Appeals' writ number?

_____

(B) What was the decision and the date of the decision? __

_____

(C) Please identify the reason that the current claims were not presented and could not have been presented on your previous application. _____

_____

_____

(15) Do you currently have any petition or appeal pending in any other state or federal court?

☐   yes

☐   no

If you answered yes, please provide the name of the court and the case number: _____

(16) If you are presenting a claim for time credit, have you exhausted your administrative remedies by presenting your claim to the time credit resolution system of the Texas Department of Criminal Justice? (This requirement applies to any final felony conviction, including state jail felonies)

☐   yes

☐   no

If you answered yes, answer the following questions:

(A) What date did you present the claim? _____

_____

(B) Did you receive a decision and, if yes, what was the date of the decision? _____

_____

If you answered no, please explain why you have not submitted your claim: _____

_____

_____

_____

(17) Beginning on page 6 [**Editor's note:** "Ground One," below.], state concisely every legal ground for your claim that you are being unlawfully restrained, and then briefly summarize the facts supporting each ground. You must present each ground on the form application and a brief summary of the facts. If your grounds and brief summary of the facts have not been presented on the form application, the Court will not consider your grounds.

If you have more than four grounds, use page 10 [**Editor's note:** "Ground," below.] of the form, which you may copy as many times as needed to give you a separate page for each ground, with each ground numbered in sequence.

You may attach a memorandum of law to the form application if you want to present legal authorities, but the Court will not consider grounds for relief in a memorandum of law that were not stated on the form application. If you are challenging the

validity of your conviction, please include a summary of the facts pertaining to your offense and trial in your memorandum.

GROUND ONE: _____

_____

FACTS SUPPORTING GROUND ONE: _____

_____

_____

_____

_____

GROUND TWO: _____

_____

FACTS SUPPORTING GROUND TWO: _____

_____

_____

_____

_____

_____

_____

GROUND THREE: _____

_____

FACTS SUPPORTING GROUND THREE: _____

_____

_____

_____

_____

_____

_____

_____

GROUND FOUR: _____

_____

FACTS SUPPORTING GROUND FOUR: _____

_____

_____

_____

_____

_____

_____

GROUND: _____

_____

FACTS SUPPORTING GROUND: _____

_____

_____

_____

_____

WHEREFORE, APPLICANT PRAYS THAT THE COURT GRANT APPLICANT RELIEF TO WHICH HE MAY BE ENTITLED IN THIS PROCEEDING.

★

VERIFICATION

(Complete <u>EITHER</u> the "oath before a notary public" OR the "inmate's declaration.")

OATH BEFORE NOTARY PUBLIC

STATE OF TEXAS, COUNTY OF _____.

_____, BEING FIRST DULY SWORN, UNDER OATH, SAYS: THAT HE/SHE IS THE APPLICANT IN THIS ACTION AND KNOWS THE CONTENT OF THE ABOVE APPLICATION AND ACCORDING TO APPLICANT'S BELIEF, THE FACTS STATED IN THE APPLICATION ARE TRUE.

_____
Signature of Applicant

SUBSCRIBED AND SWORN TO BEFORE ME THIS _____ DAY OF _____.

_____
Signature of Notary Public

INMATE'S DECLARATION

I, _____,

BEING PRESENTLY INCARCERATED IN _____ _____, DECLARE UNDER PENALTY OF PERJURY THAT, ACCORDING TO MY BELIEF, THE FACTS STATED IN THE APPLICATION ARE TRUE AND CORRECT.

SIGNED ON _____.

_____
Signature of Applicant

_____
Signature of Attorney

Attorney Name: _____

SBOT Number: _____

Address: _____

_____

_____

Telephone: _____

Trial Court's Certification of Defendant's Right of Appeal*

I, judge of the trial court, certify this criminal case:

☐   is not a plea-bargain case, and the defendant has the right of appeal. [*or*]

☐   is a plea-bargain case, but matters were raised by written motion filed and ruled on before trial and not withdrawn or waived, and the defendant has the right of appeal. [*or*]

☐   is a plea-bargain case, but the trial court has given permission to appeal, and the defendant has the right of appeal. [*or*]

☐   is a plea-bargain case, and the defendant has NO right of appeal. [*or*]

☐   the defendant has waived the right of appeal.

_____   _____
Judge   Date signed

I have received a copy of this certification. I have also been informed of my rights concerning any appeal of this criminal case, including any right to file a *pro se* petition for discretionary review pursuant to Rule 68 of the Texas Rules of Appellate Procedure. I have been admonished that my attorney must mail a copy of the court of appeals's judgment and opinion to my last known address and that I have only 30 days in which to file a *pro se* petition for discretionary review in the court of appeals. Tex. R. App. P. 68.2 I acknowledge that, if I wish to appeal this case and if I am entitled to do so, it is my duty to inform my appellate attorney, by written communication, of any change in the address at which I am currently living or any change in my current prison unit. I understand that, because of appellate deadlines, if I fail to timely inform my appellate attorney of any change in my address, I may lose the opportunity to file a *pro se* petition for discretionary review.

_____   _____
Defendant   Defendant's Counsel
                           State Bar of Texas
                           identification number: _____

Mailing address: _____   Mailing address: _____

Telephone number: _____   Telephone number: _____

Fax number (if any): _____   Fax number (if any): _____

* "A defendant in a criminal case has the right of appeal under these rules. The trial court shall enter a certification of the defendant's right to appeal in every case in which it enters a judgment of guilt or other appealable order. In a plea bargain case—that is, a case in which a defendant's plea was guilty or nolo contendere and the punishment did not exceed the punishment recommended by the prosecutor and agreed to by the defendant—a defendant may appeal only: (A) those matters that were raised by written motion filed and ruled on before trial, or (B) after getting the trial court's permission to appeal." Texas Rule of Appellate Procedure 25.2(a)(2).

TIMETABLES

STEP	ACTION	RULE	DEADLINE	DUE	DONE
1	Trial court signs judgment or order in habeas corpus, bail, or extradition proceeding ❶	CCP 11.05, 11.15, 12.151, 51.13 §15			
2	Appellant perfects the appeal by filing written notice of appeal	TRAP 25.2, 26.2; CCP 1.15, 44.01, 44.02	For defendant – Step 1 + 30 days if no MNT Step 1 + 90 days if MNT For State – Step 1 + 20 days		
3	Clerk of trial court must prepare, certify & file clerk's record with CA	TRAP 31.1	Step 2 + 15 days		
4	If requested, court reporter must prepare, certify & file reporter's record with CA	TRAP 31.1	Step 2 + 15 days		
5	Clerk of CA must notify parties of date the record is filed	TRAP 37.2	At Steps 3 & 4		
6	If CA desires briefs, set time for filing appellant's brief	TRAP 31.1	At Steps 3 & 4		
7	If CA desires briefs, set time for filing appellee's brief	TRAP 31.1	At Steps 3 & 4		
8	If requested by CA, appellant files brief in CA (original & 5 copies) & request for oral argument (on brief cover)	TRAP 9.3(a), 9.4(g), 31.1, 39.7	As set by court		
9	If requested by CA, appellee files brief in CA (original & 5 copies) & request for oral argument (on brief cover)	TRAP 9.3(a), 9.4(g), 31.1, 39.7	As set by court		
10	Date for oral argument or submission in CA	TRAP 31.2	As set by clerk, at earliest practicable time		
11	CA issues judgment & opinion	TRAP 43.1	Promptly		
12	If party intends to file PDR, party must file with CA a motion for stay of mandate & attach copy of PDR	TRAP 31.4(a)	Step 11 + 15 days		
13	CA clerk must submit to one or more justices, as CA deems appropriate, for immediate consideration	TRAP 31.4(b)	Immediately		
14	If stay denied, CA will issue mandate according to CA opinion	TRAP 18, 31.4(b)(2)			

© 2008 McClure F.L.P.

❶ The courts of appeals are split on whether an appellate court has jurisdiction to hear a direct appeal from a pretrial bail ruling. ***Vargas v. State***, 109 S.W.3d 26, 29 (Tex.App.—Amarillo 2003, no pet.).

STEP	ACTION	RULE	DEADLINE	DUE	DONE
15	If stay granted, clerk will file PDR & process case according to TRAP 68.7	TRAP 31.4(b)(1)			
16	State may file PDR (original & 11 copies) with CA	TRAP 9.3(b), 68.2(b)	Step 15 + 10 days		
17	Serve copies of PDR and briefs on state prosecuting attorney	TRAP 68.11	At Step 15, 16, 21, 25 & 26		
18	CA may summarily reconsider opinion & correct or modify it	TRAP 50	Step 15 + 60 days Step 16 + 60 days		
19	Clerk of CA forwards PDR & record to CCA	TRAP 68.7(c)	Step 15 + 60 days Step 16 + 60 days		
20	Clerk of CCA notifies parties of date of filing of PDR with CCA	TRAP 68.8			
21	Respondent files reply to PDR (original & 11 copies) with CCA	TRAP 9.3(b), 68.7(b)	Step 20 + 30 days, unless add'l time allowed		
22	Clerk of CCA notifies parties that PDR denied	TRAP 69.4(a)			
23	Clerk of CCA notifies parties that PDR granted & whether argument ordered	TRAP 69.4(b), 75.1			
24	If PDR granted but case not designated for oral argument, party may file request for oral argument	TRAP 75.2	Step 23 + 30 days		
25	Petitioner files brief on the merits in CCA	TRAP 70.1, 70.3, 68.11, 38	Step 23 + 30 days		
26	Respondent files reply brief on the merits in CCA	TRAP 70.2, 70.3, 68.11, 38	Step 25 + 30 days		
27	Oral argument in CCA	TRAP 75.1, 75.3	As set by court		
28	CCA issues its judgment & opinion	TRAP 77, 78			
29	Dissatisfied party files MReh in CCA	TRAP 79	Step 28 + 15 days ❷		
30	CCA overrules MReh	TRAP 79.4			
31	Mandate issues	TRAP 18.1(b)	10 days after deadline to file motion to extend time to file MReh		

❷ In exceptional cases, CCA may shorten time or deny right to file. TRAP 79.1.

TIMETABLES

Legend:

CA	Court of Appeals
CCA	Court of Criminal Appeals
CCP	Texas Code of Criminal Procedure
MNT	Motion for new trial
MReh	Motion for rehearing
PDR	Petition for discretionary review
TRAP	Texas Rules of Appellate Procedure

STEP	ACTION	RULE	DEADLINE	DUE	DONE
1	Trial court imposes or suspends sentence in open court	CCP 42.01, 42.02			
2	Appellant files MNT or MAJ	TRAP 21.4(a), 22.3	Step 1 + 30 days		
3	Appellant files amended MNT	TRAP 21.4(b)	Step 1 + 30 days but before preceding MNT overruled		
4	Appellant must present MNT to court for ruling	TRAP 21.6	Step 2 + 10 days Step 1 + 75 days with court's permission		
5	Hearing on MNT or MAJ	TRAP 21.8, 22.4	Step 1 + 75 days		
6	MNT or MAJ is granted or overruled	TRAP 21.8, 22.4	Step 1 + 75 days (overruled by operation of law); or earlier by written order		
7	Appellant perfects appeal by filing written notice of appeal with trial court. If appeal is from guilty or nolo plea under CCP 1.15, notice must comply with TRAP 25.2(a)(2)	TRAP 25.2, 26.2; CCP 1.15, 44.01-44.02	For defendant – Step 1 + 30 days if no MNT Step 1 + 90 days if MNT For State – Step 1 + 20 days		
8	Appellant files docketing statement with CA	TRAP 32.2	Step 7		
9	If indigent, appellant files motion & affidavit with trial court for free appellate record	TRAP 20.2	Step 7		
10	If notice of appeal defective, trial court clerk must notify parties so defect can be corrected	TRAP 37.1	Immediately		
11	Trial court clerk notes date & case number on notice of appeal and sends copy to CA & State's attorney	TRAP 25.2(c)	Immediately		
12	Appellant makes arrangements to pay trial court clerk for clerk's record	TRAP 35.3(a)	Before clerk's record is prepared		
13	Either party may send request to trial court clerk to include additional matters in clerk's record	TRAP 34.5(b)	Before clerk's record is prepared		

© 2008 McClure F.L.P.

TIMETABLES

STEP	ACTION	RULE	DEADLINE	DUE	DONE
14	Appellant (a) makes arrangements to pay court reporter for reporter's record, (b) sends written request to court reporter requesting record & list of exhibits, and (c) files copy of request with trial court	TRAP 34.6(b), 35.3(b)	Step 7		
15	Deadline to file formal bill of exceptions	TRAP 33.2(e)(2)	Step 1 + 60 days if no MNT Step 1 + 90 days if MNT		
16	Trial court loses plenary power over judgment ❶	TRAP 21.4, 21.8, 22.3-22.4	Step 1 + 30 days if no MNT Step 6 if MNT or MAJ ❷		
17	Trial clerk must file clerk's record in CA if appellant's right of appeal has been certified by trial court	TRAP 35.2, 35.3(a)	If MNT – not filed, Step 1 + 60 days denied, Step 1 + 120 days granted, Step 6 + 60 days		
18	Court reporter must file reporter's record in CA	TRAP 35.2, 35.3(b)	If MNT – not filed, Step 1 + 60 days denied, Step 1 + 120 days granted, Step 6 + 60 days		
19	CA clerk must notify parties of date the appellate record is filed	TRAP 37.2	Steps 17 & 18		
20	Appellant files brief in CA (50 pages, original & 5 copies) & request for oral argument (on brief cover)	TRAP 9.3(a)(1)(C), 38.4, 38.6(a), 39.7	Whichever is later in a regular appeal – Step 17 + 30 days Step 18 + 30 days; in an accelerated appeal – Step 17 + 20 days Step 18 + 20 days		
21	If appellant does not file brief, clerk must notify counsel for parties & trial court	TRAP 38.8(b)	Step 20		
22	CA must order trial court to conduct hearing to determine whether appellant wants to appeal, make findings, & forward findings & record to CA	TRAP 38.8(b)	Step 21 + 10 days if CA does not receive satisfactory response		
23	Appellee files brief in CA (50 pages, original & 5 copies) & request for oral argument (on brief cover)	TRAP 9.3(a)(1)(C), 38.4, 38.6(b), 39.7	Step 20 + 30 days Step 20 + 20 days if accelerated appeal		

© 2008 McClure F.L.P.

❶ The trial court still maintains jurisdiction relative to bond pending appeal (CCP art. 44.04(d)) and also may consider questions of indigency and right to counsel (CCP art. 26.04).

❷ See *Cobb v. Godfrey*, 739 S.W.2d 47, 49 (Tex.Crim.App.1987).

STEP	ACTION	RULE	DEADLINE	DUE	DONE
24	Optional – appellant files reply brief in CA (25 pages; original & 5 copies)	TRAP 9.3(a)(1)(C), 38.4, 38.6(c)	Step 23 + 20 days		
25	Either party may file motion to extend time to file briefs in CA (original & 2 copies)	TRAP 9.3(a)(1)(B), 38.6(d), 10.5(b)	Before or after date brief is due		
26	CA clerk sends notice to parties regarding oral argument, if requested	TRAP 39.8	21 days before Step 27		
27	Date for oral argument or written submission in CA	TRAP 39.8	As set by CA		
28	CA issues judgment & opinion	TRAP 43.1	Promptly		
29	Optional – dissatisfied party files MReh in CA	TRAP 49.1	Step 28 + 15 days		
30	Optional – dissatisfied party files motion to extend time to file MReh in CA	TRAP 10.5(b), 49.7	Step 29 + 15 days		
31	Optional – dissatisfied party	TRAP 49.6	Step 28 + 15 days Step 29 + 15 days		
32	CA overrules MReh or motion for en banc reconsideration	TRAP 49.3			
33	CA may order en banc rehearing with or without a motion	TRAP 49.7	Before Step 34		
34	CA loses plenary power over judgment	TRAP 19.1	Step 28 + 60 days if no MReh or en banc reconsideration Step 32 + 30 days if MReh or en banc reconsideration		
35	Petitioner files PDR (15 pages; original & 11 copies) with CA	TRAP 9.3(b), 68.1-68.5	Step 28 + 30 days if no MReh or en banc reconsideration Step 32 + 30 days if MReh or en banc reconsideration		
36	Other party may file PDR (15 pages; original & 11 copies) with CA	TRAP 9.3(b), 68.1-68.5	Step 28 + 30 days if no MReh or en banc reconsideration Step 32 + 30 days if MReh or en banc reconsideration Step 35 + 10 days		
37	Parties must serve copies of briefs on state prosecuting attorney, Austin	TRAP 68.11	Whenever the parties file briefs, motions for rehearing, or petitions		
38	CA may summarily reconsider opinion & correct or modify it	TRAP 50	Step 35 + 60 days Step 36 + 60 days		
39	CA clerk forwards PDR & record to CCA	TRAP 68.7(c)	Step 35 + 60 days Step 36 + 60 days		

STEP	ACTION	RULE	DEADLINE	DUE	DONE
40	For deadlines for filing a petition for discretionary review in the Texas Court of Criminal Appeals, see timetable, "Petition for Discretionary Review with Court of Criminal Appeals," p. 1290				
41	Mandate issues	TRAP 18.1(b)	10 days after deadline to file motion to extend time to file MReh		

© 2008 McClure F.L.P.

Legend:

CA	Texas Court of Appeals
CCA	Texas Court of Criminal Appeals
CCP	Texas Code of Criminal Procedure
MAJ	Motion to arrest judgment
MNT	Motion for new trial
MReh	Motion for rehearing
PDR	Petition for discretionary review
TRAP	Texas Rules of Appellate Procedure

───────────── ★ ─────────────

STEP	ACTION	RULE	DEADLINE	DUE	DONE
1	Trial court imposes sentence in open court	CCP 42.01, 42.02			
2	Convicted files application for writ of habeas corpus with clerk of convicting court	CCP 11.07 §3(b); TRAP 73	Anytime after final conviction		
3	Writ of habeas corpus returnable to CCA issues by operation of law	CCP 11.07 §3(b)	Immediately after Step 2		
4	Convicting court clerk assigns file number	CCP 11.07 §3(b)	After Step 2		
5	Convicting court clerk forwards application to attorney representing state	CCP 11.07 §3(b)	Step 4		
6	Attorney representing state receives forwarded application	CCP 11.07 §3(b)			
7	Attorney representing state answers application	CCP 11.07 §3(b)	Step 6 + 15 days		
8	Convicting court decides whether there are controverted, previously unresolved material facts	CCP 11.07 §3(c)	Step 7 + 20 days		
9a	If convicting court decides there are no controverted facts, clerk sends a copy of the application, answers filed, and certificate with date of finding to CCA	CCP 11.07 §3(c); TRAP 73.3	Immediately after Step 8		
9b	If convicting court decides there are controverted, previously unresolved facts, it issues order designating facts to be resolved	CCP 11.07 §3(d)	Step 7 + 20 days		
10	Convicting court appoints attorney for convicted	CCP 1.051(d), 11.07 §3(d), §6, 26.05	7 days before Step 12		
11	Attorney representing State receives notice of hearing	CCP 11.07 §6	7 days before Step 12		
12	Optional – convicting court holds hearing	CCP 11.07 §3(d)	After Step 9b		
13	Court reporter prepares transcript of hearing	CCP 11.07 §3(d)	Step 12 + 15 days		
14	Convicting court makes findings of fact	CCP 11.07 §3(d)	After Step 12		

© 2008 McClure F.L.P.

 If the court does not make a finding within the 20 days, the inaction is deemed a finding of no controverted facts. CCP 11.07 §3(c).

STEP	ACTION	RULE	DEADLINE	DUE	DONE
15	Convicting court clerk sends application, answers, motions, transcripts, affidavits, etc. to CCA	CCP 11.07 §3(d); TRAP 73.3	Immediately after Step 14		
16a	CCA denies relief based on findings of fact without docketing cause (Skip to Step 23)	CCP 11.07 §5; TRAP 73.4	After Step 15		
16b	CCA dockets cause	CCP 11.07 §5; TRAP 73.4	After Step 15		
17	Clerk of CCA notifies parties that cause docketed & whether oral argument ordered	TRAP 69.4(b), 75.1; *see* TRAP 69.2			
18	If cause docketed but not designated for oral argument, either party may file request for oral argument	TRAP 75.2	Step 17 + 30 days		
19	Convicted files brief on the merits in CCA (only original filed)	TRAP 9.3(b), 38, 68.11, 70.1, 70.3	Step 17 + 30 days		
20	Attorney representing State files reply brief on the merits in CCA (only original filed)	TRAP 9.3(b), 38, 68.11, 70.2, 70.3	Step 19 + 30 days		
21	Oral argument in CCA sitting en banc or written submission	TRAP 75.1, 75.3, 76(d)	As set by court		
22	CCA issues its judgment & opinion	TRAP 73.4, 77, 78, 79.2(d)			
23	CCA issues mandate	CCP 11.07 §5; *see* TRAP 18.1(b)	Step 22 + 10 days		

© 2008 McClure F.L.P.

Legend:
CCA   Court of Criminal Appeals
CCP   Texas Code of Criminal Procedure
TRAP   Texas Rules of Appellate Procedure

This timetable also serves for cases under Texas Constitution art. 1, §11a.

STEP	ACTION	RULE	DEADLINE	DUE	DONE
1	Trial court imposes or suspends sentence in open court	CCP 42.01, 42.02, 37.071			
2	Petitioner files MNT or MAJ	TRAP 21.4(a), 22.3	Step 1 + 30 days		
3	Petitioner files amended MNT	TRAP 21.4(b)	Step 1 + 30 days but before preceding MNT overruled		
4	Petitioner must present MNT to court for ruling	TRAP 21.6	Step 2 + 10 days Step 2 + 75 days with permission of trial court		
5	MNT or MAJ is granted	TRAP 21.8, 22.4	Step 1 + 75 days		
6	MNT or MAJ is overruled	TRAP 21.8, 22.4	Step 1 + 75 days by operation of law, or earlier by written order		
7	Plenary power of the trial court expires ❶	TRAP 21.4, 21.8, 22.3-22.4	Step 1 + 30 days Step 6 if MNT or MAJ ❷		
8	Optional – petitioner files written notice of appeal with trial court	TRAP 25.2(c), 26.2(a)	Step 1 + 30 days if no MNT Step 1 + 90 days if MNT		
9	Petitioner files docketing statement with CCA	TRAP 32.2	At Step 8		
10	If indigent, appellant files motion & affidavit with trial court for free appellate record	TRAP 20.2	Step 8		
11	If not indigent, appellant makes arrangements to pay clerk's fee for clerk's record	TRAP 35.3(a), 71.2	Before clerk's record is prepared		
12	Either party sends request to trial court clerk designating additional matters for the clerk's record	TRAP 34.5(b), 71.2	Before clerk's record is prepared		
13	Petitioner (a) makes arrangements to pay court reporter for reporter's record, (b) sends written request to court reporter requesting record, and (c) files copy of request with trial court clerk	TRAP 34.6(b), 35.3(b), 71.2	At or before Step 8		
14	Deadline to file formal bill of exceptions	TRAP 33.2(e)(2)	Step 1 + 60 days Step 1 + 90 days if MNT		

© 2008 McClure F.L.P.

❶ The trial court still maintains jurisdiction relative to bond pending appeal (CCP art. 44.04(d)) and also may consider questions of indigency and right to counsel (CCP art. 26.04).

❷ See *Cobb v. Godfrey*, 739 S.W.2d 47, 49 (Tex.Crim.App.1987).

STEP	ACTION	RULE	DEADLINE	DUE	DONE
15	Clerk must file clerk's record in CCA if appellant's right of appeal has been certified by trial court	TRAP 35.2, 71.2, 35.3(a)	If MNT – not filed, Step 1 + 60 days denied, Step 1 + 120 days granted, Step 5 + 60 days		
16	Court reporter must file reporter's record in CCA	TRAP 35.2, 71.2, 35.3(b)	If MNT – not filed, Step 1 + 60 days denied, Step 1 + 120 days granted, Step 5 + 60 days		
17	CCA clerk must notify parties of date appellate record is filed	TRAP 37.2, 71.2	At Steps 15 & 16		
18	Petitioner files brief with clerk of CCA (death case 125 pages; bail case 50 pages; original & 11 copies) & request for oral argument (on brief cover)	TRAP 9.3(b), 38, 38.4, 38.6, 39.7, 71.3	Whichever is later – Step 15 + 30 days Step 16 + 30 days		
19	Respondent files reply brief with clerk of CCA (death case 125 pages; bail case 50 pages; original & 11 copies) & request for oral argument (on brief cover)	TRAP 9.3(b), 38, 39.7, 71.3	Step 18 + 30 days		
20	Either party may file motion to extend time to file briefs in CCA (1 copy)	TRAP 9.3(b), 10.5(b), 38.6(d)	Before or after date brief is due		
21	Both parties must serve copies of briefs on state prosecuting attorney	TRAP 68.11	Whenever the parties file briefs, motions for rehearing, or PDR		
22	Date for oral argument or written submission in CCA	TRAP 75.1	As set by court		
23	CCA issues its judgment & opinion	TRAP 77, 78			
24	Dissatisfied party files MReh in CCA	TRAP 79.1	Step 23 + 15 days ❸		
25	Dissatisfied party files motion to extend time to file MReh in CCA	TRAP 79.6, 10.5(b)	Step 23 + 15 days		
26	CCA overrules MReh	TRAP 79.4			
27	Mandate issues	TRAP 18.1(b)	10 days after time to file motion to extend time to file MReh has expired		

© 2008 McClure F.L.P.

❸ In exceptional cases, the Court of Criminal Appeals may shorten the time or deny the right to file a motion for rehearing. TRAP 79.1.

Legend:

CCA	Court of Criminal Appeals
CCP	Texas Code of Criminal Procedure
MAJ	Motion to arrest judgment
MNT	Motion for new trial
MReh	Motion for rehearing
TRAP	Texas Rules of Appellate Procedure

STEP	ACTION	RULE	DEADLINE	DUE	DONE
1	Insert date CA overruled last timely filed motion for rehearing				
2	If no timely motions for rehearing were filed, insert date CA rendered its judgment				
3	CA loses plenary power over judgment	TRAP 19.1	Step 1 + 30 days if MReh or en banc reconsideration Step 2 + 60 days if no MReh or en banc reconsideration		
4	Petitioner files PDR (15 pages; original & 11 copies) with CA	TRAP 9.3(b), 68.1-68.5	Step 1 + 30 days Step 2 + 30 days		
5	Petitioner files motion to extend time to file PDR (original) in CCA	TRAP 68.2(c), 10.5(b), 9.3(b)	Step 4 + 15 days		
6	Other party may file PDR (15 pages; original & 11 copies) with CA	TRAP 9.3(b), 68.2(b)	Step 1 + 30 days Step 2 + 30 days Step 4 + 10 days Step 5 + 10 days		
7	Parties must serve copies of briefs on state prosecuting attorney, Austin	TRAP 68.11	Whenever parties file briefs, motions for rehearing, or petitions		
8	CA may summarily reconsider opinion & correct or modify it	TRAP 50	Step 4 + 60 days Step 5 + 60 days Step 6 + 60 days		
9	CA clerk forwards PDR & record to CCA	TRAP 68.7(c)	Step 4 + 60 days Step 5 + 60 days Step 6 + 60 days		
10	Clerk of CCA notifies parties of date of filing of PDR in the CCA	TRAP 68.8	When received from CA clerk		
11	Respondent files reply to PDR (8 pages; original & 11 copies) with the CCA	TRAP 9.3(b), 68.5, 68.7(b)	Step 10 + 30 days, unless add'l time allowed		
12	Either party may amend or supplement petition, reply, or record	TRAP 68.10, 34.5(c), 34.6(d)	Step 10 + 30 days, unless add'l time allowed		
13	Clerk of CCA notifies parties that PDR denied	TRAP 69.4(a)			
14	Clerk of CCA notifies parties that PDR granted & whether case set for oral argument or written submission	TRAP 69.2, 69.4(b)			

© 2008 McClure F.L.P.

STEP	ACTION	RULE	DEADLINE	DUE	DONE
15	If PDR granted but not set for oral argument, either party may file request for oral argument	TRAP 75.2	Step 14 + 30 days		
16	Petitioner files brief on the merits in CCA (50 pages; original & 11 copies)	TRAP 9.3(b), 38.4, 68.11, 70.1	Step 14 + 30 days		
17	Respondent files brief on the merits in CCA (50 pages; original & 11 copies)	TRAP 9.3(b), 38.4, 68.11, 70.2	Step 16 + 30 days		
18	Date for oral or written submission	TRAP 75.1	As set by court		
19	CCA issues its judgment & opinion	TRAP 77, 78			
20	Dissatisfied party files MReh in CCA	TRAP 79.1	Step 19 + 15 days ❶		
21	Dissatisfied party files motion to extend time to file MReh in CCA	TRAP 79.6, 10.5(b)	Step 19 + 15 days		
22	CCA overrules MReh	TRAP 79.4			
23	Mandate issues	TRAP 18.1(b)	10 days after deadline to file motion to extend time to file MReh		

© 2008 McClure F.L.P.

❶ In exceptional cases, the Court of Criminal Appeals may shorten the time or deny the right to file a motion for rehearing. TRAP 79.1.

Legend:

CA	Texas Court of Appeals
CCA	Texas Court of Criminal Appeals
MReh	Motion for rehearing
PDR	Petition for discretionary review
TRAP	Texas Rules of Appellate Procedure

TIMETABLES

STEP	ACTION	RULE	DEADLINE	DUE	DONE
1	FCA sends certification order under seal & list of parties & counsel to clerk of CCA	TRAP 74.3			
2	If CCA agrees to answer certified question, CCA will notify parties & FCA; if constitutionality of Texas statute is at issue & Texas is not a party in FCA, CCA must notify Tex. Atty. Gen.	TRAP 74.5			
3	Appellant in FCA must file brief with CCA (50 pages; original & 11 copies) & request oral argument (on cover of brief)	TRAP 9.3(b), 38, 38.4, 39.7, 74.6(a)	Step 2 + 30 days		
4	Opposing party in FCA must file brief with CCA (50 pages; original & 11 copies) & request oral argument (on cover of brief)	TRAP 9.3(b), 38, 38.4, 39.7, 74.6(a)	Step 3 + 15 days		
5	If constitutionality of Texas statute is at issue, Tex. Atty. Gen. may intervene, file brief, and argue	TRAP 74.7	In reasonable time to brief & argue		
6	Clerk of CCA notifies parties that case is set for oral argument or written submission	TRAP 75.1			
7	If case set for written submission, any party may request oral argument	TRAP 74.6(b), 75.2	Step 6 + 30 days if case is set for written submission		
8	Date case set for oral argument or written submission in CCA	TRAP 75.1	As set by court		
9	CCA issues opinion	TRAP 74.8, 77, 78			
10	Dissatisfied party files MReh in CCA	TRAP 74.9	Step 9 + 15 days		
11	Reply brief to MReh not required unless requested by CCA	TRAP 74.9	As set by court		
12	CCA overrules MReh	TRAP 74.9			
13	CCA sends opinion to FCA	TRAP 74.10	After all MReh are overruled		

TIMETABLES

Legend:

CCA	Court of Criminal Appeals
FCA	Federal Court of Appeals
MReh	Motion for rehearing
TRAP	Texas Rules of Appellate Procedure

INDEX

INDEX

INDEX

INDEX

✦

INDEX

⭐

INDEX

☆

⭐

INDEX

INDEX

INMATES
DNA records, GOVT 411.148

INNOCENCE
Extradition, CCP 51.13
Presumption
Generally, CCP 38.03; PEN 2.01
Not to be impaired, CCP 2.03

INQUESTS
Generally, CCP 49.01 et seq.
Application of law, CCP 49.02
Autopsies, CCP 49.10 et seq.
Blood samples, CCP 49.10
Chemical analysis, CCP 49.11
Commitment of homicide suspect, CCP 21.11
County medical examiners, CCP 49.25
Cremation restrictions, CCP 49.09
Crimes, CCP 49.05 et seq.
Death
Certificates, CCP 49.16
Institution resident, notice, CCP 49.24
Investigator, CCP 49.23
Requiring an inquest, CCP 49.04
Defined, CCP 49.01
Depositions, CCP 39.01
Disinterment of body, CCP 49.25
Evidence, CCP 49.14, 49.17
Fines & penalties, CCP 49.05 et seq.
Fire inquests, CCP 50.01 et seq.
Hearings, CCP 49.14 et seq.
Hindering proceedings, CCP 49.06
Jury, CCP 49.14
Lock & seal premises of deceased, CCP 49.22
Notice, CCP 49.07
Orders, CCP 49.16
Partial autopsies, CCP 49.10, 49.11
Records & recordation, CCP 49.15
Removal of bodies, CCP 49.25
Reopening, CCP 49.041
Subpoenas
Generally, CCP 49.14
Coroner's inquest, CCP 24.01
Sudden-infant-death syndrome, CCP 49.04 et seq.
Suicides, CCP 49.04
Time, CCP 49.05
Transcripts, CCP 49.14
Warrant of arrest, CCP 49.19, 49.20
Witnesses, CCP 49.14

INSANITY DEFENSE
Generally, CCP ch. 46C; PEN 8.01
Acquittal
Generally, CCP 46C.155
Appeals, CCP 46C.270
Continuing jurisdiction, CCP 46C.158
Dangerous person, CCP 46C.157, 46C.251-46C.270
Detention, CCP 46C.160, 46C.202, 46C.267
Nondangerous person, CCP 46C.159, 46C.201, 46C.202
Experts
Appointing, CCP 46C.101
Compensation, CCP 46C.106

INSANITY DEFENSE (continued)
Experts (continued)
Concurrent appointment, CCP 46C.103
Examination of defendant, CCP 46C.104, 46C.107
Qualifications, CCP 46C.102
Report, CCP 46C.105
Inpatient treatment
Generally, CCP 46C.256
Renewal of order, CCP 46C.261
Judge, CCP 46C.152, 46C.153, 46C.255
Judgment, CCP 46C.156
Jury, CCP 46C.151, 46C.153, 46C.154, 46C.255
Maximum commitment, CCP 46C.002
Outpatient treatment
Generally, CCP 46C.257, 46C.262, 46C.263
Modification of order, CCP 46C.266
Renewal of order, CCP 46C.261
Raising
Failure to give notice, CCP 46C.051
Notice of intent to raise, CCP 46C.051

INSPECTION & INSPECTORS
Disposal sites
Chemical-dispensing devices, CCP 18.181
Explosive weapons, CCP 18.181
Photographic evidence, CCP 38.34
Receipt books, CCP 103.011

INSTITUTIONAL DIVISION
Defined
Crimes, PEN 1.07
Indigent inmates, CCP 26.051

INSTRUCTED VERDICT
Acquittal, CCP 38.17

INSTRUCTIONS TO JURY
See Jury, this index

INSURANCE
See also Arson, this index
Admissibility, TRE 411
Fraud
Generally, PEN 35.01 et seq.
Fiduciary property, PEN 32.45
Jurisdiction, PEN 35.04
Material statement, PEN 35.015
Misapplication of property, PEN 32.45
Multiple offenses, PEN 35.03
Notice by clerk, CCP 42.0181
Value of claim, PEN 35.025
Investigators as peace officers, CCP 2.12

INSURRECTION & SEDITION
Powers & duties of peace officers, CCP 2.17
Searches & seizures, CCP 18.02

INTENTIONALLY
Defined, PEN 6.03

INTERCEPTION
See also Electronic Communications, this index
See also Wiretap, this index
Emergency installation of device, CCP 18.20
ESN reader, CCP 18.21

INTERCEPTION (continued)
Pen registers, CCP 18.21
Telecommunications, CCP 18.20, 18.21
Unlawful communications, PEN 16.02
Wire or oral communications, CCP 18.20; PEN 16.02

INTERPRETER
Deaf person, CCP 38.31

INTERROGATORIES
Courts of inquiry, CCP 52.02
Crimes, CCP 39.06

INTOXICATION
See also Alcohol Offenses, this index
See also Alcoholic Beverages, this index
Assault
Generally, PEN 49.07
Unborn child, PEN 49.12
Boating while intoxicated, PEN 49.06
Convictions, costs, CCP 102.0178, 102.018, 102.0185
Defense, PEN 8.04
Definitions, PEN 49.01
DWI
Generally, PEN 49.04
Child passenger, PEN 49.045
Enhanced penalties, PEN 49.09
Flying while intoxicated, PEN 49.05
Manslaughter, PEN 49.08, 49.12
Operating amusement ride, PEN 49.065
Public, PEN 49.02

INTOXILYZER
See Breathalyzer Test, this index

INVENTORIES
Searches & seizures, CCP 18.06, 18.10
Stolen property recovered, CCP 47.03

JAILS
See also Correctional Institutions, this index
See also Escape, this index
Absence & absentees, PEN 38.113
Abusive treatment of prisoners, CCP 1.099, 16.219, 43.24
Arrest, CCP 24.29
Attachment for convict witnesses, CCP 24.13
Certified copy of judgment & sentence, CCP 43.11
Civil rights
Generally, PEN 39.04
Restoration, CCP 48.05
Community service
Generally, CCP 42.036
Privileges & immunities, CCP 42.20, 43.131
Community supervision
Confinement, CCP 42.12
Officers & employees, CCP 42.011
Confinement
Authority, CCP 43.11, 45.015
Reimbursement for expenses, CCP 42.038
Work-release-program participants, CCP 42.031
County expenses, CCP 104.002

INDEX

INDEX

INDEX

★

⭐

WITNESSES
See also Bail, this index
See also Compensation, this index
See also Examining Courts, this index
See also Perjury, this index
Generally, TRE 601 et seq.
Absence, CCP 29.04-29.07
Accomplices & accessories
    Generally, CCP 38.14
    Competency, CCP 38.14
    Prostitution, PEN 43.06
Age
    Children, TRE 601
    Examining trials, CCP 39.01
Appearance, CCP 1.15
Arrest, CCP 24.29
Atheists, CCP 1.17, 38.12
Attachment, CCP 24.11 et seq.
Authentication, TRE 901 et seq.
Bailiffs, CCP 36.24
Bonds, CCP 24.14
Bribery & corruption
    Retaliation, PEN 36.06
    Tampering with witnesses, PEN 36.05
Character & reputation
    Generally, TRE 404, 405, 608
    Subpoenas, CCP 24.16
Children & minors
    Competency, TRE 601
    Subpoenas, CCP 24.011
Comments on failure of defendant to testify,
    CCP 38.08
Competency, TRE 601
Confrontation by accused, CCP 1.05, 1.15,
    1.25
Contempt
    Foreign states, CCP 24.28
    Inquest hearings, CCP 49.14
    Placing under, CCP 36.06
Credibility
    Conviction of crime, TRE 609
    Hearsay, TRE 806
    Impeachment, TRE 607
Crimes
    Children & minors, subpoenas, CCP 24.011
    Obstruction for service, PEN 36.06
    Prisoner rendition, CCP 24.29
    Retaliation for service, PEN 36.06
    Tampering with witness, PEN 36.05
Cross-examination
    Generally, CCP 1.05; TRE 611
    Character & reputation, TRE 405
    Waiver, CCP 1.15
Declarant unavailable, TRE 804
Defendants
    Generally, CCP 38.08
    Liability for fees, CCP 102.002
    Separate indictments, CCP 36.09
Depositions, CCP 39.02
Disclosure, expert witnesses, TRE 705
Exclusion, CCP 36.03; TRE 614
Expert & opinion testimony, CCP 38.35;
    TRE 701 et seq.
Fees, CCP 24.16, 35.27, 102.002

WITNESSES (continued)
Fines & penalties
    Disobedience, CCP 24.08
    Foreign state, securing attendance,
        CCP 24.28
    Refusal to obey subpoena, CCP 24.22
    Tampering with witness, PEN 36.05
Former testimony, TRE 804
Hearsay, TRE 801
Hostile, TRE 611
Identity & identification, TRE 901 et seq.
Impeachment
    Generally, CCP 39.13
    Conviction of crime, TRE 609
    Credibility, TRE 607
    Prior statements, TRE 613
    Statements of accused, CCP 38.22
Insurance, bias or prejudice, TRE 411
Interpreters, CCP 38.30; TRE 604
Interrogation, TRE 611
Invoking the Rule, CCP 36.03; TRE 614
Judges, TRE 605
Justice court, CCP 45.031
Knowledge
    Authentication & identification,
        TRE 901 et seq.
    Personal, TRE 602
Leading questions, TRE 611
Municipal court, CCP 45.031
Nonresident, CCP 35.27
Notice, release or escape of defendant,
    CCP 56.11, 56.15
Obstruction, PEN 36.06
Opinion & expert testimony
    Generally, TRE 701 et seq.
    Authentication or identification,
        TRE 901 et seq.
    Handwriting, CCP 38.27
    Indigent persons, arraignment, CCP 26.05
    Lay witness, TRE 701
Orders, rendition, CCP 24.29
Organized crime, PEN 71.04
Out-of-county, subpoenas, CCP 24.16
Personal knowledge, TRE 602
Preliminary questions, TRE 104
Prior statements, TRE 613, 801
Privileges & immunities, TRE 501
Prostitution, PEN 43.06
Refreshing memory, TRE 612
Religious beliefs & opinions, CCP 1.17, 38.12;
    TRE 610
Rendition, CCP 24.29
Retaliation, PEN 36.06
Rights of accused, CCP 1.05
Secreting witnesses, CCP 2.01
Sexual assault, CCP 56.06
Sexual offenses, CCP 38.07
State witness, CCP 24.28
Statements
    Accused's, CCP 38.22
    Prior statements, TRE 613, 801
    Production, TRE 615
Subscribing, TRE 903
Tampering with, PEN 36.05

WITNESSES (continued)
Testimony
    Inmates, CCP 38.073
    Undercover peace officer, CCP 38.141
Transfer of causes, CCP 21.30
Treason, CCP 38.15
Two witnesses
    Generally, CCP 38.17
    Perjury or false swearing, CCP 38.18
    Treason, CCP 1.20, 38.15
Ultimate issues, TRE 704
Uniform act, secure attendance from witness
    outside state, CCP 24.28
Victims' rights, CCP 56.02
Voir dire, TRE 705
Waiver, plea of guilty, CCP 1.15

WOMEN
Jury & jurors, housing, CCP 35.23
Manual labor, CCP 43.10

WORK RELEASE
Generally, CCP 42.031
Jail program, CCP 42.034
Pretrial detainees, CCP 43.101

WORKHOUSES
Generally, CCP 43.09, 43.10

WORSHIP, PLACE OF
Arson, PEN 28.02
Graffiti, PEN 28.08

WRITS
See also Arrest, this index
See also Attachment, this index
See also Certiorari, this index
See also Court of Criminal Appeals, this index
See also Executions, this index
See also Habeas Corpus, this index
See also Injunctions, this index
See also Subpoenas, this index
See also Warrants, this index
Fees
    Issuance, CCP 102.005
    Service, CCP 103.001
Style, CCP 1.23

WRITS OF ERROR
See Appeal & Error, this index

WRITTEN INSTRUMENTS
Fraudulent destruction, removal, or
    concealment, PEN 32.47
Interrogatories, deposition, CCP 39.06
Stolen property, disposition, CCP 47.08

ZONES
Child safety, CCP 42.12
Drug-free, H&SC 481.134
Weapon-free
    Maps as evidence, PEN 46.12
    Peace officers, nonapplicability, PEN 46.15
    School zone, PEN 46.11

NOTES

NOTES

NOTES

NOTES

NOTES

NOTES

NOTES